AMERICA'S
TEST KITCHEN

AMERICA'S
TEST KITCHEN

AMERICA'S
TEST KITCHEN

AMERICA'S
TEST KITCHEN

AMERICA'S
TEST KITCHEN

AMERICA'S
TEST KITCHEN

THE COMPLETE AMERICA'S TEST KITCHEN TV SHOW COOKBOOK 2001–2018

THE EDITORS AT **AMERICA'S TEST KITCHEN**

PHOTOGRAPHY **CARL TREMBLAY, KELLER + KELLER, STEVE KLISE, AND DANIEL J. VAN ACKERE**

AMERICA'S TEST KITCHEN
21 Drydock Avenue, Suite 210E, Boston, MA 02210

AMERICA'S TEST KITCHEN®

THE COMPLETE AMERICA'S TEST KITCHEN TV SHOW COOKBOOK:
Every recipe from the hit TV show with product ratings and a look behind the scenes

Revised Edition

ISBN: 978-1-945256-01-1
ISSN: 2162-6944

Manufactured in the United States of America

10 9 8 7 6 5 4 3 2 1

Distributed by: Penguin Random House Publisher Services, tel: 800-733-3000

CHIEF CREATIVE OFFICER: Jack Bishop
EDITORIAL DIRECTOR, BOOKS: Elizabeth Carduff
SENIOR MANAGING EDITOR: Debra Hudak
EDITORIAL ASSISTANT: Alyssa Langer
DESIGN DIRECTOR, BOOKS: Carole Goodman
DEPUTY ART DIRECTORS, BOOKS: Jen Kanavos Hoffman and Allison Boales
GRAPHIC DESIGNER: Katie Barranger
PRODUCTION DESIGNER: Reinaldo Cruz
PHOTOGRAPHY DIRECTOR: Julie Bozzo Cote
SENIOR STAFF PHOTOGRAPHER: Daniel J. van Ackere
STAFF PHOTOGRAPHER: Steve Klise
PHOTOGRAPHY PRODUCER: Mary Ball
FOOD STYLING: Catrine Kelty, Marie Piraino, and Mary Jane Sawyer
PRODUCTION DIRECTOR: Guy Rochford
SENIOR PRODUCTION MANAGER: Jessica Lindheimer Quirk
PRODUCTION MANAGER: Christine Walsh
IMAGING MANAGER: Lauren Robbins
PRODUCTION AND IMAGING SPECIALISTS: Heather Dube, Sean MacDonald, Dennis Noble, and Jessica Voas
COPYEDITOR: Cheryl Redmond
PROOFREADERS: Christine Corcoran Cox, Elizabeth Emery, and Jeffrey Schier
INDEXER: Elizabeth Parson

CONTENTS

JULIA AND BRIDGET TALK COOKING AND TV

What inspired your career in cooking?
Bridget: I've always been inspired by my mother, who is still a great cook, but I'd say that it goes back to watching Julia Child on PBS each Saturday morning.

Julia: I grew up cooking alongside my mother (she cooked full meals nearly every night), and I loved the hands-on work of preparing food. In my senior year of college, it dawned on me that culinary school should be my next step—it was the kind of work I naturally gravitated toward. So I enrolled in the Culinary Institute of America in Hyde Park, NY. I barely had enough kitchen experience to qualify for the admissions process, but as soon as I became a student there, I knew I had made the right decision. I loved it.

How did your long career at America's Test Kitchen prepare you to host the TV show?
Bridget: I started as a test cook in 1998, and back then, there were three of us working in the test kitchen, developing recipes, washing dishes, and shopping for all the ingredients ourselves. Over the years I've seen the evolution of the test kitchen: the physical space, the increase in the number of test cooks, the testing process. During this time I've worn many hats at ATK including running the kitchen for *Cook's Country* magazine in its early days, developing content for the online cooking school, and co-hosting *America's Test Kitchen Radio.* Of course I've been on the TV show since its inception. I have a sense of pride for what we do, and after being on the show for all 18 seasons, it's easy for me to be a cheerleader.

Julia: I joined the *Cook's Illustrated* team in 1999 developing recipes for the magazine. When we shot our first half season of the TV show in 2000, I was one of the initial on-screen test cooks; in fact, pretty much everyone who worked in the kitchen was on the show. Eighteen seasons later, I've witnessed the incredible growth of the company, including the start of *Cook's Country* magazine and both TV shows, our cookbook department (where I oversee the recipe development), the radio show, the online cooking school . . . I could go on. In a sense, I grew up here at ATK. And at every turn, I've learned more about food and about what our viewers and readers really want from us: unbiased and well-vetted information about cooking and shopping that will help everyone cook better at home. Not only do I have all of the recipes ATK has developed over the past 15 to 20 years logged in my head, but I also have a clear vision for how we should continue to do this work in the years to come.

What are some of the most interesting recipes this season?
Bridget: I think that some of the most interesting recipes are new takes on very simple foods. Grown-Up Stovetop Macaroni and Cheese, for instance (page 262); who would have thought that there was science behind making mac and cheese? But it turns out that the emulsifying salts in American cheese prevent the cheese sauce from breaking. Turkey Meatloaf (page 269) is another one. The recipe is simple but includes a technique (using oats, cornstarch, and butter) to provide structure and juiciness that ground turkey can often lack. Clever little recipe.

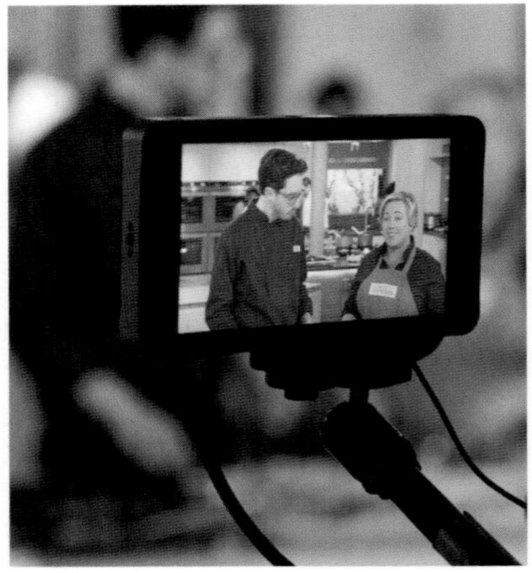

Julia: A few recipes come to mind this year, one of which is Olive Oil Cake (page 744). Though most people associate cake with butter, extra virgin olive oil is a great choice because it provides moisture, tenderness, and richness. And the slightly savory notes of EVOO can lend appealing complexity to a cake. Another recipe I love is for an easy pressure-cooker chicken noodle soup (page 4), which is a great way to get a lot of savory chicken flavor in a short amount of time. I make this recipe at home and can't wait to share it with our viewers.

The tastings and testings are a big part of the show. What's your favorite piece of equipment featured this season?

Julia: The tastings really blow my mind, because they've proven that a recipe can be greatly affected by the products you use. Choose the wrong brand of broth and your soup will taste like dishwater no matter how great the recipe is. My two favorite pieces of equipment we've reviewed are blenders and espresso machines; they can be quite expensive, and choosing the best one will ensure you don't waste your money.

Bridget: The tastings and testings are what set us apart from so many other cooking shows. They are there to provide the viewer with tangible information that they can use to better stock their kitchen. My favorite piece of equipment we've reviewed this season is the manual pasta machine. Making your own pasta from scratch takes a little more effort than using boxed pasta, but the results are out of this world. Having a good machine to use is essential.

What do you hope the audience of the show will learn?

Julia: My number one hope is that viewers will simply think "I could do that. I could make that dish in my own kitchen and it will look and taste just like it does on TV."

Bridget: I always hope that folks will take away at least one piece of useful cooking info per show—something that they can use in a broader sense when they are cooking in their own kitchens.

There are more cast members now. How does that change the show?

Bridget: It's a brilliant move to feature more test cooks! We have so many talented people that work all year long to develop incredible content (recipes, tastings, and testings), and more of them will have a voice on the show, giving viewers a better glimpse into the test kitchen.

Julia: I think that it's great that we will have some fresh faces on camera to show more of the people who do the recipe development work in the kitchen all year round. I'm excited to pull back the curtain to show what our kitchen is really like and to show what it takes to develop one of our recipes start to finish.

What is your favorite ATK recipe?

Bridget: Of all time? The coconut layer cake (page 765) that we made on the show many years ago. Coconut everywhere—in the cake, the frosting, the toasted crunchy coconut topping—so good.

Julia: At the moment, it's Weeknight Roast Chicken (page 114). A whole chicken is roasted in a preheated skillet and the oven is turned off during the second half of the cooking time, ensuring that both the white and dark meat are tender and juicy. The recipe is so easy (both my husband and I have it memorized by now) and turns out perfectly every time. It's the simple recipes, like roast chicken, that get me most excited because they are the hardest to get right; there are no bells and whistles to cover up any mistakes.

WELCOME TO AMERICA'S TEST KITCHEN

This book has been tested, written, and edited by the folks at America's Test Kitchen. Located in Boston's Seaport District in the historic Innovation and Design Building, it features 15,000 square feet of kitchen space including multiple photography and video studios. It is the home of *Cook's Illustrated* magazine and *Cook's Country* magazine and is the workday destination for more than 60 test cooks, editors, and cookware specialists. Our mission is to test recipes over and over again until we understand how and why they work and until we arrive at the "best" version.

Our television show highlights the best recipes developed in the test kitchen during the past year—those recipes that our test kitchen staff makes at home time and time again. These recipes are accompanied by our most exhaustive equipment tests and our most interesting food tastings.

Julia Collin Davison and Bridget Lancaster co-host the show and ask the questions you might ask. It's the job of our chefs, Tim Chin, Keith Dresser, Becky Hays, Erin McMurrer, Elle Simone, and Dan Souza to demonstrate our recipes. The chefs show Julia and Bridget what works and what doesn't, and they explain why. In the process, they discuss (and show you) the best examples from our development process as well as the worst.

Adam Ried, our equipment expert, and Lisa McManus, our gadget guru, share the highlights from our detailed testing process in equipment corner segments. They bring with them our favorite (and least favorite) gadgets and tools. Jack Bishop is our ingredient expert. He has Julia and Bridget taste our favorite (and least favorite) brands of common food products. Julia and Bridget may not always enjoy these exercises (hot sauce isn't exactly as fun to taste as mozzarella or dark chocolate), but they usually learn something as Jack explains what makes one brand superior to another. Dan Souza explains the science behind certain ingredients and recipes.

Although just 11 cooks and editors appear on the television show, another 50 people worked to make the show a reality. Executive Producer Mary Agnes conceived and developed each episode with help from Producer Kaitlin Keleher, Production Manager Heather Prince, and Associate Producer Sara Joyner. Debby Paddock assisted with all the photo research, and Meg Ragland assisted with our historical research. Guy Crosby, our science expert, researched the science behind the recipes. Along with the on-air crew, executive chefs Erin McMurrer and Keith Dresser helped plan and organize the 26 television episodes shot in May 2017 and ran the "back kitchen," where all the food that appeared on camera originated.

Kate Shannon, Lauren Savoie, Miye Bromberg, Emily Phares, and Carolyn Grillo organized the tasting and equipment segments.

During filming, chefs Morgan Bolling, Steve Dunn, Andrea Geary, Andrew Janjigian, Cecelia Jenkins, Nicole Konstantinakos, Timothy McQuinn, Christie Morrison, Stephanie Pixley, Anne Petito, Lan Lam, Joe Gitter, Katherine Perry, and Anne Wolf cooked all the food needed on set. Chefs Leah Colins, Russell Selander, Lawman Johnson, and Eric Haessler, and interns Sarah Ewald, Emily Elliott, and Luciana Lamboy worked on-set developing recipes for our magazines and books. Assistant Test Kitchen Director Alexxa Benson, Test Kitchen Manager Meridith Lippard, and Test Kitchen Facilities Manager Sophie Clingan Darack were charged with making sure all the ingredients and kitchen equipment we needed were on hand. Kitchen assistants Ena Gudiel, Blanca Castanaza, Gladis Campos, and John Mitchell also worked long hours. Chefs Allison Berkey, Afton Cyrus, Katie Callahan, Daniel Cellucci, Mady Nichas, and Jessica Rudolph helped coordinate the efforts of the kitchen with the television set by readying props, equipment, and food. Deva Djaafar and Morgan Mannino led all tours of the test kitchen during filming.

Special thanks to director Herb Sevush and director of photography Dan Anderson.

We also appreciate the hard work of the video production team, including David Cambria, Stephen McCarthy, Craig Beck, Michael Mulvey, Andrew Hobbs, Shawn Gauvain, Eric Goddard, Jason Bowen, Bob Nadrowski, Matt Goddard, Jared Detsikas, Shan Shan Tam, Elizabeth Mindreau, Wilson Chao, Honah Lee Milne, Claudia Moriel, Jennifer Tawa, Scott Brawn, and Caroline Rickert. Thanks also to Nick Dakoulas and Conor Olmstead, the second unit videographers.

We also would like to thank Karen Fritz and Dani Cook at WETA Station Relations, and the team at American Public Television that presents the show: Cynthia Fenneman, Chris Funkhouser, Judy Barlow, and Tom Davison. Thanks also for production support from Zebra Productions, New York.

Bob's Red Mill, Kohler, Holland America, Sub-Zero, and Wolf sponsored the show, and we thank them for their support. We also thank Sara Domville, Christine Anagnostis, Kate Zebrowski, and Claire Gambee for serving our sponsors.

Meat was provided by Kinnealey Meats of Brockton, MA. Fish was supplied by Wulf's Fish. Produce was supplied by Sid Wainer & Son. Aprons were made by Crooked Brook.

CHAPTER 1

SOUP'S ON!

CLASSIC CHICKEN NOODLE SOUP

WHY THIS RECIPE WORKS: Classic chicken noodle soup is one of *the* all-time comfort foods. We eat it to nurse a cold or pair it with a simple sandwich for a satisfying meal. But making chicken noodle soup from scratch can take all day. We wanted a simple recipe but we wanted to make it the old-fashioned way—starting with a whole chicken—rather than cheating with store-bought broth.

We began by cutting the chicken into small pieces that could be browned in batches. To develop additional flavor, we sweated the browned pieces in a covered pot with an onion, then simmered them for less than half an hour. Now we had a stock that just needed some salt and bay leaves to round out its flavor. We reserved some of the skimmed fat from the stock to sauté aromatics and carrots for the soup, and we added in tender chicken breast pieces that had already been poached in our stock. For extra flavor, we cooked the egg noodles right in the soup pot so they could absorb rich, meaty flavor from the stock. With a final sprinkling of chopped parsley, our chicken noodle soup was complete—rich, homemade broth, moist pieces of chicken, tender vegetables, and perfectly cooked noodles.

Classic Chicken Noodle Soup

SERVES 6 TO 8

Make sure to reserve the chicken breast pieces until step 2; they should not be browned. If you use a cleaver, you will be able to cut up the chicken parts quickly. A chef's knife or kitchen shears will also work. Be sure to reserve 2 tablespoons of chicken fat for sautéing the aromatics in step 4; however, if you prefer not to use chicken fat, vegetable oil can be substituted.

STOCK

- 1 tablespoon vegetable oil
- 1 (4-pound) whole chicken, breast removed, split, and reserved; remaining chicken cut into 2-inch pieces (see note)
- 1 medium onion, chopped medium
- 2 quarts boiling water
- 2 teaspoons table salt
- 2 bay leaves

SOUP

- 2 tablespoons chicken fat, reserved from making stock, or vegetable oil (see note)
- 1 medium onion, chopped medium
- 1 large carrot, peeled and sliced ¼ inch thick
- 1 celery rib, sliced ¼ inch thick
- ½ teaspoon dried thyme
- 3 ounces egg noodles (about 2 cups)
- ¼ cup minced fresh parsley leaves
- Table salt and ground black pepper

1. FOR THE STOCK: Heat the oil in a large Dutch oven over medium-high heat until shimmering. Add half of the chicken pieces and cook until lightly browned, about 5 minutes per side. Transfer the cooked chicken to a bowl and repeat with the remaining chicken pieces; transfer to the bowl with the first batch. Add the onion and cook, stirring frequently, until the onion is translucent, 3 to 5 minutes. Return the chicken pieces to the pot. Reduce the heat to low, cover, and cook until the chicken releases its juices, about 20 minutes.

2. Increase the heat to high; add the boiling water, reserved chicken breast pieces, salt, and bay leaves. Reduce the heat to medium-low and simmer until the flavors have blended, about 20 minutes.

3. Remove the breast pieces from the pot. When cool, remove the skin and bones from the breast pieces and discard. Shred the meat with your fingers or two forks and set aside. Strain the stock through a fine-mesh strainer into a container, pressing on the solids to extract as much liquid as possible; discard the solids. Allow the liquid to settle about 5 minutes and skim off the fat; reserve 2 tablespoons, if desired (see note). (The shredded chicken, strained stock, and fat can be refrigerated in separate airtight containers for up to 2 days.)

4. FOR THE SOUP: Heat the reserved chicken fat in a large Dutch oven over medium-high heat. Add the onion, carrot, and celery and cook until softened, about 5 minutes. Add the thyme and reserved stock and simmer until the vegetables are tender, 10 to 15 minutes.

5. Add the noodles and reserved shredded chicken and cook until just tender, 5 to 8 minutes. Stir in the parsley, season with salt and pepper to taste, and serve.

HEARTY CHICKEN NOODLE SOUP

WHY THIS RECIPE WORKS: Sometimes we prefer a simple bowl of chicken soup—a brothy soup modestly enriched with chicken, noodles, and vegetables. Other times, a heartier version of chicken noodle soup is what we crave—one chock-full of chicken, noodles, and vegetables—a true meal in a bowl.

We began by jump-starting the flavor of our soup with a mixture of store-bought chicken broth and water, but the broth-and-water base had a distinctly flat flavor. A few pounds of chicken parts created a rich stock, but browning the parts and then simmering them was just too fussy for what we wanted. Instead, we turned to a somewhat unlikely but more convenient substitute—store-bought ground chicken. Ground chicken offers more surface area and exponentially more flavor, providing a great-tasting stock when sautéed with aromatics and then simmered with the broth and water. All the stock needed was some body and thickening, which we got from a little cornstarch. With our broth down, we were ready to add the chicken (breasts that had been poached in the stock until just cooked through and then shredded), vegetables, and noodles. Along with onion, celery, and carrots, we further enriched the soup with potato and Swiss chard. Our streamlined hearty chicken noodle soup was now rich and satisfying.

Hearty Chicken Noodle Soup

SERVES 4 TO 6

When skimming the fat off the stock, we prefer to leave a little bit on the surface to enhance the soup's flavor.

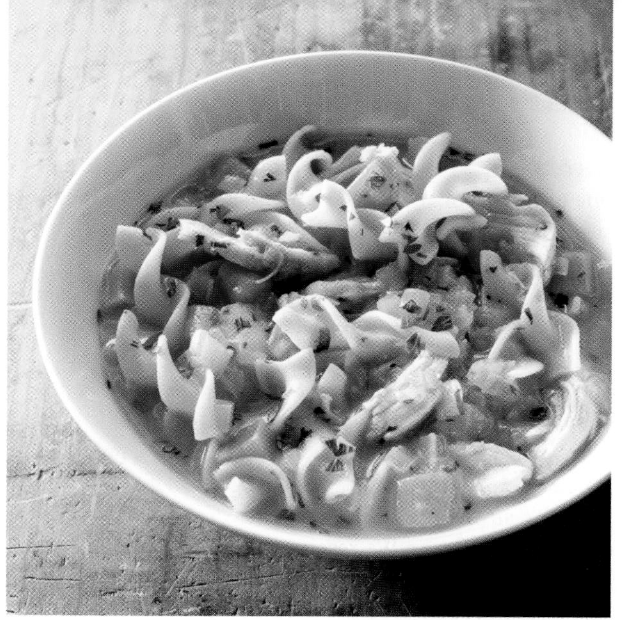

STOCK

- 1 tablespoon vegetable oil
- 1 pound ground chicken
- 1 small onion, chopped medium
- 1 medium carrot, peeled and chopped medium
- 1 celery rib, chopped medium
- 2 quarts low-sodium chicken broth
- 4 cups water
- 2 bay leaves
- 2 teaspoons table salt
- 2 (12-ounce) bone-in, skin-on chicken breast halves, cut in half crosswise

SOUP

- ¼ cup cold water
- 3 tablespoons cornstarch
- 1 small onion, halved and sliced thin
- 2 medium carrots, peeled, halved lengthwise, and cut crosswise into ¾-inch pieces
- 1 medium celery rib, halved lengthwise and cut crosswise into ½-inch pieces
- 1 medium russet potato (about 8 ounces), peeled and cut into ¾-inch cubes
- 1½ ounces egg noodles (about 1 cup)
- 4–6 Swiss chard leaves, ribs removed, torn into 1-inch pieces (about 2 cups; optional)
- 1 tablespoon minced fresh parsley leaves
- Table salt and ground black pepper

1. FOR THE STOCK: Heat the oil in a large Dutch oven over medium-high heat until shimmering. Add the ground chicken, onion, carrot, and celery. Cook, stirring frequently, until the chicken is no longer pink, 5 to 10 minutes (do not brown the chicken).

2. Reduce the heat to medium-low. Add the broth, water, bay leaves, salt, and chicken breasts; cover and cook for 30 minutes. Remove the lid, increase the heat to high, and bring to a boil. (If the liquid is already boiling when the lid is removed, remove the chicken breasts immediately and continue with the recipe.) Transfer the chicken breasts to a large plate and set aside. Continue to cook the stock for 20 minutes, adjusting the heat to maintain a gentle boil. Strain the stock through a fine-mesh strainer into a container, pressing on the solids to extract as much liquid as possible; discard the solids. Allow the liquid to settle about 5 minutes and skim off the fat (see note). (The strained stock can be refrigerated in an airtight container for up to 2 days or frozen for up to 3 months. The chicken breasts can be stored in a zipper-lock bag with the air squeezed out.)

3. FOR THE SOUP: Return the stock to a Dutch oven set over medium-high heat. In a small bowl, combine the water and cornstarch until a smooth slurry forms; stir into the stock and bring to a gentle boil. Add the onion, carrots, celery, and potato and cook until the potato pieces are almost tender, 10 to 15 minutes, adjusting the heat as necessary to maintain a gentle boil. Add the egg noodles and continue to cook until all the vegetables and noodles are tender, about 5 minutes longer.

4. Meanwhile, remove the skin and bones from the reserved cooked chicken and discard. Shred the meat with your fingers or two forks. Add the shredded chicken, Swiss chard (if using), and parsley to the soup and cook until heated through, about 2 minutes. Season with salt and pepper to taste and serve.

OLD-FASHIONED SLOW-COOKER CHICKEN NOODLE SOUP

WHY THIS RECIPE WORKS: Making chicken noodle soup with a deep, satisfying flavor requires a few tricks when using a slow cooker. First, we used a combination of bone-in chicken thighs and breasts; cooked and shredded breast meat was the perfect choice for the final soup, but bone-in thighs were key for giving the broth its deep flavor during the long cooking time. We found browning the chicken thighs before adding them to the slow cooker really maximized the flavor. To prevent the breast meat from overcooking we wrapped the chicken breast inside a foil packet. Since we were already dirtying a skillet to brown the chicken thighs, it was no effort to brown and soften the vegetables and aromatics as well, and this step was well worth the depth of flavor it lent. An unlikely ingredient, tomato paste, gave the soup body and brought out the savory notes of our soup. We cooked the noodles separately to ensure perfect texture and added them in at the end, along with frozen peas that we simply let sit in the soup for 5 minutes to heat through.

Old-Fashioned Slow-Cooker Chicken Noodle Soup

SERVES 6 TO 8

Do not try to cook the noodles in the slow cooker or they will turn out mushy and taste raw.

- 1½ pounds bone-in, skin-on chicken thighs, trimmed
- Table salt and ground black pepper
- 1 tablespoon vegetable oil
- 3 medium carrots, peeled and chopped medium
- 2 celery ribs, chopped medium
- 1 medium onion, minced
- 3 medium garlic cloves, minced or pressed through a garlic press (about 1 tablespoon)
- 1 tablespoon tomato paste
- 2 teaspoons minced fresh thyme or ½ teaspoon dried
- ⅛ teaspoon red pepper flakes
- 8 cups low-sodium chicken broth
- 2 bay leaves
- 1 (12-ounce) bone-in, skin-on split chicken breast, trimmed
- 1½ ounces wide egg noodles (about 1 cup)
- ½ cup frozen peas
- 2 tablespoons minced fresh parsley leaves

1. Dry the chicken thighs with paper towels and season with salt and pepper. Heat the oil in a 12-inch skillet over medium-high heat until just smoking. Brown the chicken thighs well on both sides, 6 to 8 minutes. Transfer to a plate, let cool slightly, and discard the skin.

2. Pour off all but 1 tablespoon fat left in the skillet. Add the carrots, celery, and onion and cook over medium heat until the vegetables are softened, 7 to 10 minutes. Stir in the garlic, tomato paste, thyme, and red pepper flakes and cook until fragrant, about 30 seconds. Stir in 1 cup of the chicken broth, scraping up any browned bits; transfer to the slow cooker.

3. Stir the remaining 7 cups broth and the bay leaves into the slow cooker. Nestle the browned chicken thighs with any accumulated juice into the slow cooker. Season the chicken breast with salt and pepper and place on one side of a large piece of aluminum foil. Fold the foil over the chicken and crimp to seal the edges. Place the foil packet on top of the soup, pressing gently as needed to fit. Cover and cook until the chicken is tender, 4 to 6 hours on low.

4. Remove the foil packet, open it carefully (watch for steam), and transfer the chicken breast to a cutting board. Transfer the chicken thighs to a cutting board. Let all of the chicken cool slightly, then shred it into bite-size pieces with two forks, discarding the skin and bones. Let the soup settle for 5 minutes, then skim the fat from the surface using a large spoon. Discard the bay leaves.

5. Bring 4 quarts water to a boil in a large pot. Add 1 tablespoon salt and the noodles to the boiling water and cook until tender, then drain. Stir the cooked noodles, shredded chicken, and peas into the soup and let sit until heated through, about 5 minutes. Stir in the parsley, season with salt and pepper to taste, and serve.

PRESSURE-COOKER CHICKEN NOODLE SOUP

WHY THIS RECIPE WORKS: With its velvety broth and deep flavor, old-fashioned chicken noodle soup is an ideal pressure-cooker candidate since the pressure cooker can extract flavor from the meat, skin, and bones of a whole chicken in just 20 minutes. We started by putting the chicken into the pot with some aromatics, carrots, celery, and water. Placing the chicken in the pot breast side up allowed the thighs and more delicate breast meat to cook through at the same time since the thighs were in contact with the pot's bottom. After 20 minutes, the meat practically fell off the bones, making it easy to shred and stir back in. Soy sauce gave the broth even deeper, richer meaty flavor. To keep things simple, we cooked the noodles in the broth while we shredded the chicken.

Pressure-Cooker Chicken Noodle Soup

SERVES 8

- 1 tablespoon vegetable oil
- 1 onion, chopped fine
- 3 garlic cloves, minced (about 1 teaspoon)
- 1 minced fresh thyme or ¼ teaspoon dried
- 8 cups water
- 4 carrots, peeled and sliced
- 2 celery ribs, sliced ½ inch thick
- 2 tablespoons soy sauce
- 1 (4-pound) whole chicken, giblets discarded
- Salt and pepper
- 4 ounces (2⅔ cups) wide egg noodles
- ¼ cup minced fresh parsley

1. Heat oil in pressure-cooker pot over medium heat until shimmering. Add onion and cook until softened, about 5 minutes. Stir in garlic and thyme and cook until fragrant, about 30 seconds. Stir in water, carrots, celery, and soy sauce, scraping up any browned bits. Season chicken with salt and pepper and place, breast side up, in pot.

2. Lock pressure-cooker lid in place and bring to high pressure over medium-high heat. As soon as pot reaches high pressure, reduce heat to medium-low and cook for 20 minutes, adjusting heat as needed to maintain high pressure.

3. Remove pot from heat. Quick release pressure, then carefully remove lid, allowing steam to escape away from you.

4. Transfer chicken to cutting board, let cool slightly, then shred meat into bite-size pieces, discarding skin and bones. Meanwhile, using large spoon, skim excess fat from surface of soup. Bring soup to boil, stir in noodles, and cook until tender, about 5 minutes. Stir in shredded chicken and parsley, season with salt and pepper to taste, and serve.

Pressure-Cooker Chicken and Rice Soup

Substitute 1 cup long-grain white rice for egg noodles and cook until tender, 15 to 18 minutes.

BEST BEEF STEW

WHY THIS RECIPE WORKS: The taste of beef stew is rarely as complex as its rich aroma would lead you to believe. We wanted a rich-tasting but approachable beef stew with tender meat, flavorful vegetables, and a rich brown gravy that justified the time it took to prepare. After browning the beef (chuck-eye is our preferred cut for stew), we caramelized the usual choices of onions and carrots, rather than just adding them raw to the broth. To mimic the luxurious, mouth-coating texture of beef stews made with homemade stock (provided by the collagen in bones that is transformed into gelatin when simmered), we included powdered gelatin and flour. We added frozen pearl onions toward the end of cooking along with some frozen peas.

Best Beef Stew

SERVES 6 TO 8

Use a good-quality medium-bodied wine, such as a Côtes du Rhône or Pinot Noir, for this stew. Try to find beef that is well marbled with white veins of fat. Meat that is too lean will come out slightly dry. Four pounds of blade steaks, trimmed of gristle and silver skin, can be substituted for the chuck-eye roast. While the blade steak will yield slightly thinner pieces after trimming, it should still be cut into 1½-inch pieces. Look for salt pork that looks meaty and is roughly 75 percent lean.

- 2 medium garlic cloves, minced or pressed through a garlic press (about 2 teaspoons)
- 4 anchovy fillets, minced fine (about 2 teaspoons)
- 1 tablespoon tomato paste
- 1 (4-pound) boneless chuck-eye roast, trimmed of excess fat and cut into 1½-inch pieces
- 2 tablespoons vegetable oil
- 1 large onion, halved and sliced ⅛ inch thick
- 4 carrots, peeled and cut into 1-inch pieces
- ¼ cup unbleached all-purpose flour
- 2 cups red wine (see note)
- 2 cups low-sodium chicken broth
- 4 ounces salt pork (see note), rinsed of excess salt
- 2 bay leaves
- 4 sprigs fresh thyme
- 1 pound Yukon Gold potatoes, scrubbed and cut into 1-inch pieces
- 1½ cups frozen pearl onions, thawed
- 2 teaspoons (about 1 packet) unflavored powdered gelatin
- ½ cup water
- 1 cup frozen peas, thawed
- Table salt and ground black pepper

1. Adjust an oven rack to the lower-middle position and heat the oven to 300 degrees. Combine the garlic and anchovies in a small bowl and press the mixture with the back of a fork to form a paste. Stir in the tomato paste and set the mixture aside.

2. Pat the meat dry with paper towels (do not season the meat). Heat 1 tablespoon of the vegetable oil in a large Dutch oven over high heat until just starting to smoke. Add half of the beef and cook until well browned on all sides, about 8 minutes total, reducing the heat if the oil begins to smoke or the fond begins to burn. Transfer the beef to a large plate. Repeat with the remaining 1 tablespoon vegetable oil and remaining beef, leaving the second batch of meat in the pot after browning.

3. Reduce the heat to medium and return the first batch of beef to the pot. Add the onion and carrots to the pot and stir to combine with the beef. Cook, scraping the bottom of the pan to loosen any browned bits, until the onion is softened, 1 to 2 minutes. Add the garlic mixture and cook, stirring constantly, until fragrant, about 30 seconds. Add the flour and cook, stirring constantly, until no dry flour remains, about 30 seconds.

4. Slowly add the wine, scraping the bottom of the pan to loosen any browned bits. Increase the heat to high and allow the wine to simmer until thickened and slightly reduced, about 2 minutes. Stir in the broth, salt pork, bay leaves, and thyme. Bring to a simmer, cover, transfer to the oven, and cook for 1½ hours.

5. Remove the pot from the oven. Remove and discard the bay leaves and salt pork. Stir in the potatoes, cover, return the pot to the oven, and cook until the potatoes are almost tender, about 45 minutes.

6. Using a large spoon, skim any excess fat from the surface of the stew. Stir in the pearl onions. Cook over medium heat until the potatoes and onions are cooked through and the meat offers little resistance when poked with a fork (the meat should not be falling apart), about 15 minutes. Meanwhile, sprinkle the gelatin over the water in a small bowl and allow to soften for 5 minutes.

7. Increase the heat to high and stir in the softened gelatin mixture and the peas. Simmer until the gelatin is fully dissolved and the stew is thickened, about 3 minutes. Season with salt and pepper to taste. Serve. (The stew can be cooled, covered tightly, and refrigerated for up to 2 days. Reheat it gently before serving.)

TUSCAN-STYLE BEEF STEW

WHY THIS RECIPE WORKS: Tuscany's rich beef stew, *peposo*, is meant to be a simple dish of slow-cooked beef shin, Chianti, garlic, and peppercorns, but following tradition to the letter yielded bland beef. To give our stew plenty of body, we salted chunks of short ribs and browned half of the meat to kickstart the sauce with flavorful fond. We deglazed the pot with red wine and stirred in the sauce's building blocks: water, shallots, carrots, garlic, rosemary, bay leaves, and peppercorns. Gelatin, tomato paste, and anchovy paste created a smooth texture and rich taste. We added in the uncooked beef chunks and brought the stew to a simmer before transferring it to the oven for a long, slow braise. Before serving, we removed the tender beef, strained and defatted the liquid, and returned the liquid to the pot. Adding more wine reinforced and freshened its impact before we reduced it to a thick, lush sauce. Just before spooning the sauce over the beef, we poured in one more hit of Chianti, this time mixed with a couple teaspoons of cornstarch for a final thickening boost.

Tuscan-Style Beef Stew

SERVES 6 TO 8

We prefer boneless short ribs in this recipe because they require very little trimming. If you cannot find them, substitute a 5-pound chuck roast. Trim the roast of large pieces of fat and sinew, and cut it into 2-inch pieces. If Chianti is unavailable, a medium-bodied wine such as Côtes du Rhône or Pinot Noir makes a nice substitute. Serve with polenta or crusty bread.

- 4 pounds boneless beef short ribs, trimmed and cut into 2-inch pieces
- Salt
- 1 tablespoon vegetable oil
- 1 (750-ml) bottle Chianti
- 1 cup water
- 4 shallots, halved lengthwise
- 2 carrots, peeled and halved lengthwise
- 1 garlic head, cloves separated, unpeeled, and crushed
- 4 sprigs fresh rosemary
- 2 bay leaves
- 1 tablespoon cracked black peppercorns, plus extra for serving
- 1 tablespoon unflavored gelatin
- 1 tablespoon tomato paste
- 1 teaspoon anchovy paste
- 2 teaspoons pepper
- 2 teaspoons cornstarch

1. Toss beef and 1½ teaspoons salt together in bowl and let stand at room temperature for 30 minutes. Adjust oven rack to lower-middle position and heat oven to 300 degrees.

2. Heat oil in large Dutch oven over medium-high heat until just smoking. Pat beef dry with paper towels. Add half of beef in single layer and cook until well browned on all sides, about 8 minutes total, reducing heat if fond begins to burn. Stir in 2 cups wine, water, shallots, carrots, garlic, rosemary, bay leaves, cracked peppercorns, gelatin, tomato paste, anchovy paste, and remaining beef. Bring to simmer and cover tightly with sheet of heavy-duty aluminum foil, then lid. Transfer to oven and cook until beef is tender, 2 to 2¼ hours, stirring halfway through cooking.

3. Using slotted spoon, transfer beef to bowl; cover tightly with foil and set aside. Strain sauce through fine-mesh strainer into fat separator. Wipe out pot with paper towels. Let liquid settle for 5 minutes, then return defatted liquid to pot.

4. Add 1 cup wine and pepper and bring mixture to boil over medium-high heat. Simmer briskly, stirring occasionally, until sauce is thickened to consistency of heavy cream, 12 to 15 minutes.

5. Combine remaining wine and cornstarch in small bowl. Reduce heat to medium-low, return beef to pot, and stir in cornstarch-wine mixture. Cover and simmer until just heated through, 5 to 8 minutes. Season with salt to taste. Serve, passing extra cracked peppercorns separately. (Stew can be refrigerated for up to 3 days.)

PORTUGUESE-STYLE BEEF STEW (ALCATRA)

WHY THIS RECIPE WORKS: *Alcatra*, a simple and meaty Portuguese beef stew, features tender chunks of beef braised with onions, garlic, spices, and wine. Unlike beef stews that require searing the beef to build savory flavor or adding flavor boosters like tomato paste and anchovies, this recipe skips those steps and ingredients, highlighting the warm and bright flavors of the spices and wine as much as the meatiness of the beef. We used beef shank because it is lean (which means the cooking liquid doesn't need to be skimmed) and full of collagen, which broke down into gelatin and gave the sauce full body. Submerging the sliced onions completely in the liquid under the meat caused them to form a meaty-tasting compound that amped up the savory flavor of the broth. Slices of smoky-sweet Spanish chorizo sausage matched up perfectly with the other flavors in the stew.

Portuguese-Style Beef Stew (Alcatra)

SERVES 6

Beef shank is sold both crosscut and long-cut (with and without bones). We prefer long-cut since it has more collagen. You can substitute 4 pounds of bone-in crosscut shank if that's all you can find. Remove the bones before cooking and save them for another use. Crosscut shank cooks more quickly, so check the stew for doneness in step 2 after 3 hours. A 3½- to 4-pound chuck roast, trimmed of fat and cut into 2½-inch pieces, can be substituted for the shank. Serve this dish with crusty bread or boiled potatoes.

- 3 pounds boneless long-cut beef shanks
  Salt and pepper
- 5 garlic cloves, peeled and smashed
- 5 allspice berries
- 4 bay leaves
- 1½ teaspoons peppercorns
- 2 large onions, halved and sliced thin
- 2¼ cups dry white wine
- ¼ teaspoon ground cinnamon
- 8 ounces Spanish-style chorizo sausage, cut into ¼-inch-thick rounds

1. Adjust oven rack to middle position and heat oven to 325 degrees. Trim away any fat or large pieces of connective tissue from exterior of shanks (silverskin can be left on meat). Cut each shank crosswise into 2½-inch pieces. Sprinkle meat with 1 teaspoon salt.

2. Cut 8-inch square of triple-thickness cheesecloth. Place garlic, allspice berries, bay leaves, and peppercorns in center of cheesecloth and tie into bundle with kitchen twine. Arrange onions and spice bundle in Dutch oven in even layer. Add wine and cinnamon. Arrange shank pieces in single layer on top of onions. Cover and cook until beef is tender, about 3½ hours.

3. Remove pot from oven and add chorizo. Using tongs, flip each piece of beef over, making sure that chorizo is submerged. Cover and let stand until chorizo is warmed through, about 20 minutes. Discard spice bundle. Season with salt and pepper to taste. Serve.

OUR FAVORITE CHILI

WHY THIS RECIPE WORKS: Our goal in creating an "ultimate" beef chili was to determine which of the "secret ingredients" recommended by chili experts around the world were spot-on—and which were expendable. We started with the beef. Most recipes call for ground beef, but we preferred meaty blade steaks, which don't require much trimming and stayed in big chunks in our finished chili. For complex chile flavor, we traded in the commercial chili powder in favor of ground dried ancho and de árbol chiles; for a grassy heat, we added fresh jalapeños. Dried beans, brined before cooking, stayed creamy for the duration of cooking. Beer and chicken broth outperformed red wine, coffee, and beef broth as the liquid components. For balancing sweetness, light molasses beat out other offbeat ingredients (including prunes and Coca-Cola). And finally, for the right level of thickness, flour and peanut butter didn't perform as promised; instead, a small amount of ordinary cornmeal sealed the deal, providing just the right consistency in our ultimate beef chili.

Our Favorite Chili

SERVES 6 TO 8

A 4-pound chuck-eye roast, well trimmed of fat, can be substituted for the steak. Because much of the chili flavor is held in the fat of this dish, refrain from skimming fat from the surface. Dried New Mexican or guajillo chiles make a good substitute for the anchos; each dried de árbol may be replaced with ⅛ teaspoon cayenne pepper. If you prefer not to work with any whole dried chiles, the anchos and de árbols can be replaced with ½ cup commercial chili powder and ¼ to ½ teaspoon cayenne pepper, though the texture of the chili will be slightly compromised. Good choices for condiments include diced avocado, finely chopped red onion, chopped cilantro leaves, lime wedges, sour cream, and shredded Monterey Jack or cheddar cheese.

- Table salt
- 8 ounces dried pinto beans (1¼ cups), picked over and rinsed
- 6 dried ancho chiles, stemmed, seeded, and torn into 1-inch pieces
- 2–4 dried de árbol chiles, stemmed, seeded, and split into 2 pieces
- 3 tablespoons cornmeal
- 2 teaspoons dried oregano
- 2 teaspoons ground cumin
- 2 teaspoons cocoa powder
- 2½ cups low-sodium chicken broth
- 2 medium onions, cut into ¾-inch pieces
- 3 small jalapeño chiles, stemmed, seeded, and cut into ½-inch pieces
- 3 tablespoons vegetable oil
- 4 medium garlic cloves, minced or pressed through a garlic press (about 4 teaspoons)
- 1 (14.5-ounce) can diced tomatoes
- 2 teaspoons light molasses
- 3½ pounds blade steak, ¾ inch thick, trimmed and cut into ¾-inch pieces
- 1 (12-ounce) bottle mild lager, such as Budweiser

1. Combine 3 tablespoons salt, 4 quarts water, and the beans in a Dutch oven and bring to a boil over high heat. Remove the pot from the heat, cover, and let sit for 1 hour. Drain and rinse well.

2. Adjust an oven rack to the lower-middle position and heat the oven to 300 degrees. Place the ancho chiles in a 12-inch skillet set over medium-high heat; toast, stirring frequently, until the flesh is fragrant, 4 to 6 minutes, reducing the heat if the chiles begin to smoke. Transfer to a food processor and cool. Do not wash out the skillet.

3. Add the de árbol chiles, cornmeal, oregano, cumin, cocoa, and ½ teaspoon salt to the food processor with the toasted ancho chiles; process until finely ground, about 2 minutes. With the processor running, slowly add ½ cup chicken broth until a smooth paste forms, about 45 seconds, scraping down the sides of the bowl as necessary. Transfer the paste to a small bowl. Place the onions in the now-empty processor and pulse until roughly chopped, about 4 pulses. Add the jalapeños and pulse until the consistency of chunky salsa, about 4 pulses, scraping down the bowl as necessary.

4. Heat 1 tablespoon oil in the Dutch oven over medium-high heat. Add the onion mixture and cook, stirring occasionally, until the moisture has evaporated and the vegetables are softened, 7 to 9 minutes. Add the garlic and cook until fragrant, about 1 minute. Add the chile paste, tomatoes, and molasses; stir until the chile paste is thoroughly combined. Add the remaining 2 cups chicken broth and the drained beans; bring to a boil, then reduce the heat to a simmer.

5. Meanwhile, heat 1 tablespoon more oil in the 12-inch skillet over medium-high heat until shimmering. Pat the beef dry with paper towels and sprinkle with 1 teaspoon salt. Add half of the beef and cook until browned on all sides, about 10 minutes. Transfer the meat to the Dutch oven. Add half of the beer to the skillet, scraping up any browned bits from the bottom of the skillet, and bring to a simmer. Transfer the beer to the Dutch oven. Repeat with the remaining 1 tablespoon oil, the remaining steak, and the remaining beer. Stir to combine and return the mixture to a simmer.

6. Cover the pot and transfer to the oven. Cook until the meat and beans are fully tender, 1½ to 2 hours. Let the chili stand, uncovered, for 10 minutes. Stir well, season with salt to taste, and serve. (The chili can be refrigerated for up to 3 days.)

BEST GROUND BEEF CHILI

WHY THIS RECIPE WORKS: Our ground beef chili can hold its own against the traditional chunky beef kind. We started by using 85 percent lean ground beef for flavor and tenderness. To protect the meat, we treated it with salt and baking soda. Both ingredients helped the meat hold on to moisture; since it didn't shed liquid during cooking the whole 2 pounds of beef could conveniently be browned in one batch. Simmering the meat for 90 minutes gave its collagen enough time to break down. We made a homemade chili powder for potent spicy flavor and used some tortilla chips to bulk it up and to add some corn flavor. Lastly we stirred any orange fat collected on the top back into the chili before serving since it contains much of the flavor from the fat-soluble spices.

Best Ground Beef Chili

SERVES 8 TO 10

Diced avocado, sour cream, and shredded Monterey Jack or cheddar cheese are also good options for garnishing. This chili is intensely flavored and should be served with tortilla chips and/or plenty of steamed white rice.

- 2 pounds 85 percent lean ground beef
- 2 tablespoons plus 2 cups water
- Salt and pepper
- ¾ teaspoon baking soda
- 6 dried ancho chiles, stemmed, seeded, and torn into 1-inch pieces
- 1 ounce tortilla chips, crushed (¼ cup)
- 2 tablespoons ground cumin
- 1 tablespoon paprika
- 1 tablespoon garlic powder
- 1 tablespoon ground coriander
- 2 teaspoons dried oregano
- ½ teaspoon dried thyme
- 1 (14.5-ounce) can whole peeled tomatoes
- 1 tablespoon vegetable oil
- 1 onion, chopped fine
- 3 garlic cloves, minced
- 1–2 teaspoons minced canned chipotle chile in adobo sauce
- 1 (15-ounce) can pinto beans
- 2 teaspoons sugar
- 2 tablespoons cider vinegar
- Lime wedges
- Coarsely chopped cilantro
- Chopped red onion

1. Adjust oven rack to lower-middle position and heat oven to 275 degrees. Toss beef with 2 tablespoons water, 1½ teaspoons salt, and baking soda in bowl until thoroughly combined. Set aside for 20 minutes.

2. Meanwhile, place anchos in Dutch oven set over medium-high heat; toast, stirring frequently, until fragrant, 4 to 6 minutes, reducing heat if anchos begin to smoke. Transfer to food processor and let cool.

3. Add tortilla chips, cumin, paprika, garlic powder, coriander, oregano, thyme, and 2 teaspoons pepper to food processor with anchos and process until finely ground, about 2 minutes. Transfer mixture to bowl. Process tomatoes and their juice in now-empty workbowl until smooth, about 30 seconds.

4. Heat oil in now-empty pot over medium-high heat until shimmering. Add onion and cook, stirring occasionally, until softened, 4 to 6 minutes. Add garlic and cook until fragrant, about 1 minute. Add beef and cook, stirring with wooden spoon to break meat up into ¼-inch pieces, until beef is browned and fond begins to form on pot bottom, 12 to 14 minutes. Add ancho mixture and chipotle; cook, stirring frequently, until fragrant, 1 to 2 minutes.

5. Add remaining 2 cups water, beans and their liquid, sugar, and tomato puree. Bring to boil, scraping bottom of pot to loosen any browned bits. Cover, transfer to oven, and cook until meat is tender and chili is slightly thickened, 1½ to 2 hours, stirring occasionally to prevent sticking.

6. Remove chili from oven and let stand, uncovered, for 10 minutes. Stir in any fat that has risen to top of chili, then add vinegar and season with salt to taste. Serve, passing lime wedges, cilantro, and chopped onion separately. (Chili can be refrigerated for up to 3 days.)

QUICK BEEF AND VEGETABLE SOUP

WHY THIS RECIPE WORKS: Rich and hearty beef and vegetable soup with old-fashioned flavor is a snap to make—if you have a few hours free and several pounds of beef and bones hanging around. We wanted to find another way to develop the same flavors and textures in under an hour.

We knew the key to this recipe would be finding the right cut of meat, one that had great beefy flavor and that would cook up tender in a reasonable amount of time. Tender cuts, like strip steak and rib eye, became tough, livery, and chalky when simmered in soup. Sirloin tip steak was the best choice—when cut into small pieces, the meat was tender and offered the illusion of being cooked for hours, plus its meaty flavor imparted richness to the soup.

In place of labor-intensive homemade beef broth, we doctored store-bought beef broth with aromatics and lightened its flavor profile with chicken broth. To further boost the flavor of the beef, we added cremini mushrooms, tomato paste, soy sauce, and red wine, ingredients that are rich in glutamates, naturally occurring compounds that accentuate the meat's hearty flavor. To mimic the rich body of a homemade meat stock (made rich through the gelatin released by the meat bones' collagen during the long simmering process), we relied on powdered gelatin. Our beef and vegetable soup now had the same richness and flavor as cooked-all-day versions in a whole lot less time.

Quick Beef and Vegetable Soup

SERVES 4 TO 6

Choose whole sirloin tip steaks over ones that have been cut into small pieces for stir-fries. If sirloin tip steaks are unavailable, substitute blade or flank steak, removing any hard gristle or excess fat. Button mushrooms can be used in place of the cremini mushrooms, with some trade-off in flavor. If you like, add 1 cup frozen peas, frozen corn, or frozen cut green beans during the last 5 minutes of cooking. For a heartier soup, add 10 ounces red potatoes, cut into ½-inch pieces (2 cups), during the last 15 minutes of cooking.

- 1 pound sirloin tip steaks, trimmed of excess fat and cut into ½-inch pieces (see note)
- 2 tablespoons soy sauce
- 1 teaspoon vegetable oil
- 1 pound cremini mushrooms, stems trimmed, caps wiped clean, and quartered (see note)
- 1 large onion, chopped medium
- 2 tablespoons tomato paste
- 1 medium garlic clove, minced or pressed through a garlic press (about 1 teaspoon)
- ½ cup red wine
- 4 cups beef broth
- 1¾ cups low-sodium chicken broth
- 4 medium carrots, peeled and cut into ½-inch pieces
- 2 medium celery ribs, cut into ½-inch pieces
- 1 bay leaf
- 1 tablespoon unflavored powdered gelatin
- ½ cup cold water
- 2 tablespoons minced fresh parsley leaves
- Table salt and ground black pepper

1. Combine the beef and soy sauce in a medium bowl; set aside for 15 minutes.

2. Heat the oil in a large Dutch oven over medium-high heat until just smoking. Add the mushrooms and onion; cook, stirring frequently, until the onion is browned and dark bits form on the pan bottom, 8 to 12 minutes. Transfer the vegetables to a bowl.

3. Add the beef and cook, stirring occasionally, until the liquid evaporates and the meat starts to brown, 6 to 10 minutes. Add the tomato paste and garlic; cook, stirring constantly, until fragrant, about 30 seconds. Add the red wine, scraping the bottom of the pot with a wooden spoon to loosen any browned bits, and cook until syrupy, 1 to 2 minutes.

4. Add the beef broth, chicken broth, carrots, celery, bay leaf, and browned mushrooms and onion; bring to a boil. Reduce the heat to low, cover, and simmer until the vegetables and meat are tender, 25 to 30 minutes. While the soup is simmering, sprinkle the gelatin over the cold water and let stand.

5. When the soup is finished, turn off the heat. Remove and discard the bay leaf. Add the gelatin mixture and stir until completely dissolved. Stir in the parsley, season with salt and pepper to taste, and serve.

VIETNAMESE BEEF PHO

WHY THIS RECIPE WORKS: Traditional versions of this Vietnamese beef and noodle soup call for simmering beef bones for hours to make a deeply flavorful broth. We wanted to make this soup suitable for the home cook, which meant that beef bones were out of the question. Instead, we simmered ground beef in spiced store-bought broth, which gave us the complexity and depth we were after in a fraction of the time. To serve the soup, we poured our broth over thinly sliced strip steak and gathered a variety of essential garnishes, such as lime wedges, hoisin and chile sauces, and bean sprouts.

Vietnamese Beef Pho

SERVES 4 TO 6

Our favorite store-bought beef broth is Rachael Ray Stock-in-a-Box All-Natural Beef Flavored Stock. Use a Dutch oven that holds 6 quarts or more. An equal weight of tri-tip steak or blade steak can be substituted for the strip steak; make sure to trim all connective tissue and excess fat. One 14- or 16-ounce package of rice noodles will serve four to six. Look for noodles that are about ⅛ inch wide; these are often labeled "small." Don't use Thai Kitchen Stir-Fry Rice Noodles since they are too thick and don't adequately soak up the broth.

- 1 pound 85 percent lean ground beef
- 2 onions, quartered through root end
- 12 cups beef broth
- ¼ cup fish sauce, plus extra for seasoning
- 1 (4-inch) piece ginger, sliced into thin rounds
- 1 cinnamon stick
- 2 tablespoons sugar, plus extra for seasoning
- 6 star anise pods
- 6 whole cloves
- Salt
- 1 teaspoon black peppercorns
- 1 (1-pound) boneless strip steak, trimmed and halved
- 14–16 ounces (⅛-inch-wide) rice noodles
- ⅓ cup chopped fresh cilantro
- 3 scallions, sliced thin (optional)
- Bean sprouts
- Sprigs fresh Thai or Italian basil
- Lime wedges
- Hoisin sauce
- Sriracha sauce

1. Break ground beef into rough 1-inch chunks and drop in Dutch oven. Add water to cover by 1 inch. Bring mixture to boil over high heat. Boil for 2 minutes, stirring once or twice. Drain ground beef in colander and rinse well under running water. Wash out pot and return ground beef to pot.

2. Place 6 onion quarters in pot with ground beef. Slice remaining 2 onion quarters as thin as possible and set aside for garnish. Add broth, 2 cups water, fish sauce, ginger, cinnamon, sugar, star anise, cloves, 2 teaspoons salt, and peppercorns to pot and bring to boil over high heat. Reduce heat to medium-low and simmer, partially covered, for 45 minutes.

3. Pour broth through colander set in large bowl. Discard solids. Strain broth through fine-mesh strainer lined with triple thickness of cheesecloth; add water as needed to equal 11 cups. Return broth to pot and season with extra sugar and salt (broth should taste overseasoned). Cover and keep warm over low heat.

4. While broth simmers, place steak on large plate and freeze until very firm, 35 to 45 minutes. Once firm, cut against grain into ⅛-inch-thick slices. Return steak to plate and refrigerate until needed.

5. Place noodles in large container and cover with hot tap water. Soak until noodles are pliable, 10 to 15 minutes; drain noodles. Meanwhile, bring 4 quarts water to boil in large pot. Add drained noodles and cook until almost tender, 30 to 60 seconds. Drain immediately and divide noodles among individual bowls.

6. Bring broth to rolling boil over high heat. Divide steak among individual bowls, shingling slices on top of noodles. Pile reserved onion slices on top of steak slices and sprinkle with cilantro and scallions, if using. Ladle hot broth into each bowl. Serve immediately, passing bean sprouts, basil sprigs, lime wedges, hoisin, Sriracha, and extra fish sauce separately.

QUINOA AND VEGETABLE STEW

WHY THIS RECIPE WORKS: Quinoa stews are common in many South American regions. But authentic recipes call for obscure ingredients, such as annatto powder or Peruvian varieties of potatoes and corn. We set out to make a traditional quinoa stew with an easy-to-navigate ingredient list. We found that paprika has a similar flavor profile to annatto powder; we rounded it out with cumin and coriander. Red bell pepper, tomatoes, red potatoes, sweet corn, and frozen peas were a nice mix of vegetables. We added the quinoa after the potatoes had softened and cooked it until it released starch to help give body to the stew. Finally, we added the traditional garnishes: *queso fresco*, avocado, and cilantro.

Quinoa And Vegetable Stew

SERVES 6 TO 8

We like the convenience of prewashed quinoa. If you buy unwashed quinoa (or are unsure whether it's washed), be sure to rinse it before cooking to remove its bitter protective coating (called saponin). This stew tends to thicken as it sits; add additional warm vegetable broth to loosen. Do not omit the garnishes; they are important to the flavor of the stew.

- 2 tablespoons vegetable oil
- 1 onion, chopped
- 1 red bell pepper, stemmed, seeded, and cut into ½-inch pieces
- 5 garlic cloves, minced
- 1 tablespoon paprika
- 2 teaspoons ground coriander
- 1½ teaspoons ground cumin
- 6 cups vegetable broth
- 1 pound red potatoes, unpeeled, cut into ½-inch pieces
- 1 cup prewashed white quinoa
- 1 cup fresh or frozen corn
- 2 tomatoes, cored and chopped coarse
- 1 cup frozen peas
- Salt and pepper
- 8 ounces queso fresco or feta cheese, crumbled (2 cups)
- 1 avocado, halved, pitted, and diced
- ½ cup minced fresh cilantro

1. Heat oil in Dutch oven over medium heat until shimmering. Add onion and bell pepper and cook until softened, 5 to 7 minutes. Stir in garlic, paprika, coriander, and cumin and cook until fragrant, about 30 seconds. Stir in broth and potatoes and bring to boil over high heat. Reduce heat to medium-low and simmer gently for 10 minutes.

2. Stir in quinoa and simmer for 8 minutes. Stir in corn and simmer until potatoes and quinoa are just tender, 5 to 7 minutes. Stir in tomatoes and peas and let heat through, about 2 minutes.

3. Off heat, season with salt and pepper to taste. Sprinkle individual portions with queso fresco, avocado, and cilantro before serving.

Quinoa and Vegetable Stew with Eggs

Serving this stew with a cooked egg on top is a common practice in Peru.

Crack 6 large eggs evenly over top of stew after removing from heat and seasoning with salt and pepper in step 3; cover and let eggs poach off heat until whites have set but yolks are still soft, about 4 minutes. To serve, carefully scoop cooked eggs and stew from pot with large spoon.

CLASSIC CREAM OF TOMATO SOUP

WHY THIS RECIPE WORKS: Canned cream of tomato soup is a childhood favorite. But grown-up tastes deserve something better—and let's face it, the canned soup's overly sweet flavors are just not all that appealing today. We wanted a well-balanced cream of tomato soup, one with rich color, great tomato flavor, and a silky texture.

Right away, we turned to canned tomatoes; fresh tomatoes are at their best just a few months out of the year and we didn't want to restrict our soup-making to just one season. To coax the most flavor from our canned whole tomatoes, it was essential to roast them in the oven. The intense dry heat worked to evaporate surface liquids and concentrate the flavor, and a sprinkling of brown sugar encouraged caramelization. We cooked our roasted tomatoes with shallots, chicken broth, and reserved tomato juice to develop robust flavor, then pureed the tomatoes (with broth) to keep the deep flavor of the tomato broth intact. Finished with heavy cream and a splash of brandy, this cream of tomato soup will satisfy everyone at the table.

Classic Cream of Tomato Soup

SERVES 6

Make sure to use canned whole tomatoes packed in juice. To obtain 3 cups of juice, use the packing juice as well as the liquid that falls from the tomatoes when they are seeded.

- 2 (28-ounce) cans whole tomatoes packed in juice, drained, 3 cups juice reserved (see note)
- 1½ tablespoons dark brown sugar
- 4 tablespoons (½ stick) unsalted butter
- 2 large shallots, minced (about ½ cup)
- 1 tablespoon tomato paste
- Pinch ground allspice
- 2 tablespoons unbleached all-purpose flour
- 1¾ cups low-sodium chicken broth
- ½ cup heavy cream
- 2 tablespoons brandy or dry sherry
- Table salt and cayenne pepper

1. Adjust an oven rack to the upper-middle position and heat the oven to 450 degrees. Line a large rimmed baking sheet with foil. With your fingers, carefully open the whole tomatoes over a fine-mesh strainer set in a bowl and push out the seeds, allowing the juices to fall through the strainer into the bowl; discard the seeds. Spread the seeded tomatoes in a single layer on the foil and sprinkle evenly with the brown sugar. Bake until all the liquid has evaporated and the tomatoes begin to color, about 30 minutes. Cool the tomatoes slightly, then peel them off the foil; transfer to a small bowl and set aside.

2. Melt the butter in a large saucepan over medium heat. Add the shallots, tomato paste, and allspice. Reduce the heat to low, cover, and cook, stirring occasionally, until the shallots are softened, 7 to 10 minutes. Add the flour and cook, stirring constantly, until thoroughly combined, about 30 seconds. Gradually add the chicken broth, whisking constantly to combine; stir in the reserved tomato juice and roasted tomatoes. Cover, increase the heat to medium, and bring to a boil. Reduce the heat to low and simmer, stirring occasionally, for 10 minutes.

3. Pour the mixture through a fine-mesh strainer into a medium bowl; rinse and dry the saucepan. Transfer the tomatoes and solids in the strainer to a blender; add 1 cup of the strained liquid and puree until smooth. Add the pureed mixture and the remaining strained liquid to the saucepan. Add the cream and warm over low heat until hot, about 3 minutes. Off the heat, stir in the brandy, season with salt and cayenne to taste, and serve. (The soup can be refrigerated in an airtight container for up to 2 days. Warm over low heat until hot; do not boil.)

BEHIND THE SCENES

WHY OUR EQUIPMENT RATINGS ARE DIFFERENT

For many viewers, the equipment corner is the most valuable part of the TV show. Why? Besides the fact that we save you big bucks (more often than not the expensive model is beaten by a much cheaper option), viewers know they can trust our ratings. That's because we're independent (we don't accept advertising) and because we put equipment through real-world tests.

On the television show, Adam has Bridget and Julia re-create some of the tests that were used when rating kitchen equipment. For example, to test the heat consistency of six different gas grills, Adam preheated the grills on high for 15 minutes and then mapped the heat distribution by covering the entire grill surface with white sandwich bread. As he and Julia saw, the top grills provided evenly browned toast, while other grills left the bread different shades of black, brown, and white.

Off camera, Adam and his team used thermocouples to check the accuracy of the grills' lid thermometers while grilling and tasting hamburgers and thick strip steaks and smoking 5-pound pork butts. They also tried grilling 12-pound turkeys to find out if they would fit under each grill lid with room to spare. The bottom line: You can rest assured that our winning grill is well-designed, responsive, and durable.

That's just a sample of the work involved in our equipment tests. The testing team often spends hundreds of kitchen hours on each one of our equipment ratings.

CREAMLESS CREAMY TOMATO SOUP

WHY THIS RECIPE WORKS: Creamy tomato soup boasts a bright, sweet tomato flavor when done right, but not everyone is a fan of rich cream soups. We wanted to keep the sharp tomatoey flavor in this classic soup, but ditch the dairy and tame the tartness in other ways.

Our first step was to choose canned tomatoes over fresh tomatoes—canned are simply more consistent in flavor than your average supermarket tomato. We mashed whole tomatoes (preferred over diced or crushed for their concentrated flavor) with a potato masher, then combined them with aromatics sautéed in extra-virgin olive oil, not butter, which guaranteed bright, clean flavor. Stirring in some olive oil before pureeing our soup added back vital flavor that was lost when we cooked the oil. To combat the acid in the tomatoes, we added full-flavored brown sugar. And for an ultra-creamy texture without the cream, we pureed sandwich bread into the soup. For a final touch, we stirred chicken broth into the pot and simmered the soup briefly to give our creamless creamy tomato soup a rich and velvety feel.

Creamless Creamy Tomato Soup

SERVES 6

If half of the soup fills your blender more than halfway, process the soup in three batches, but do not add more olive oil for the third batch. You can also use a hand-held blender to process the soup directly in the pot. Serve this soup topped with Classic Croutons (recipe follows), if desired. For an even smoother soup, strain the pureed mixture through a fine-mesh strainer before stirring in the chicken broth in step 2.

- ¼ cup extra-virgin olive oil, plus extra for drizzling (see note)
- 1 medium onion, chopped medium
- 3 medium garlic cloves, minced or pressed through a garlic press (about 1 tablespoon)
- Pinch red pepper flakes (optional)
- 1 bay leaf
- 2 (28-ounce) cans whole tomatoes
- 3 slices high-quality white sandwich bread, crusts removed, torn into 1-inch pieces
- 1 tablespoon brown sugar
- 2 cups low-sodium chicken broth
- 2 tablespoons brandy (optional)
- Table salt and ground black pepper
- ¼ cup chopped fresh chives

1. Heat 2 tablespoons of the oil in a large Dutch oven over medium-high heat until shimmering. Add the onion, garlic, red pepper flakes (if using), and bay leaf. Cook, stirring frequently, until the onion is translucent, 3 to 5 minutes. Stir in the tomatoes with their juice. Using a potato masher, mash until no pieces bigger than 2 inches remain. Stir in the bread and sugar and bring the soup to a boil. Reduce the heat to medium and cook, stirring occasionally, until the bread is completely saturated and starts to break down, about 5 minutes. Remove and discard the bay leaf.

2. Transfer half of the soup to a blender. Add 1 tablespoon more oil and process until the soup is smooth and creamy, 2 to 3 minutes. Transfer to a large bowl and repeat with the remaining soup and the remaining 1 tablespoon oil. Rinse and dry the Dutch oven and return the soup to the pot. Stir in the chicken broth and brandy (if using). Return the soup to a boil and season with salt and pepper to taste. Ladle the soup into bowls, sprinkle with the chopped chives, drizzle with olive oil, and serve. (The soup, minus the garnish, can be refrigerated in an airtight container for up to 2 days. Warm over low heat until hot; do not boil.)

Classic Croutons

MAKES ABOUT 1½ CUPS

- 3 slices high-quality white sandwich bread, crusts removed, cut into ½-inch cubes (about 1½ cups)
- 1½ tablespoons olive oil
- Table salt and ground black pepper

1. Adjust an oven rack to the upper-middle position and heat the oven to 400 degrees. Combine the bread cubes and oil in a medium bowl and toss to coat. Season with salt and pepper to taste.

2. Spread the bread cubes in an even layer on a rimmed baking sheet and bake, stirring occasionally, until golden, 8 to 10 minutes. Cool on the baking sheet to room temperature. (The croutons can be stored in an airtight container or a plastic bag for up to 3 days.)

CARROT-GINGER SOUP

WHY THIS RECIPE WORKS: The coupling of sweet carrots and pungent ginger has the potential to produce an elegant, flavorful soup. But in most versions, the hapless addition of other vegetables, fruits, or dairy makes it difficult to truly taste the starring flavors. Another common problem is a grainy consistency. We wanted to bring this soup to its full potential and produce a version with a smooth, silken texture and pure, clean flavors.

For unadulterated carrot flavor, we used water in place of vegetable broth, eliminating the blurred vegetable background. Swapping ¾ cup of carrot juice for some of the water and stirring in another ¾ cup right before serving gave us intense carrot flavor. We also used peeled and sliced carrots; the earthy, sweet cooked carrots and the bright, raw carrot juice provided a well-balanced depth of flavor. To amp up ginger flavor, we used a combination of fresh and crystallized ginger, with the former supplying spiciness and the latter delivering the almost citrusy freshness that ginger is prized for. For the silkiest possible consistency, we turned to one of the test kitchen's secret weapons: baking soda. Just ½ teaspoon of baking soda helped to break down the cell walls of the carrots for a soup that was downright velvety—without the need for lengthy cooking or fussy straining. As finishing touches, a sprinkle of fresh chives and a swirl of sour cream provided subtle onion flavor and mild tang. A few crispy, buttery croutons provided textural contrast.

Carrot-Ginger Soup

SERVES 6

In addition to sour cream and chives, serve the soup with Buttery Croutons (recipe follows).

- 2 tablespoons unsalted butter
- 2 onions, chopped fine
- ¼ cup minced crystallized ginger
- 1 tablespoon grated fresh ginger
- 2 garlic cloves, peeled and smashed
- Salt and pepper
- 1 teaspoon sugar
- 2 pounds carrots, peeled and sliced ¼ inch thick
- 4 cups water
- 1½ cups carrot juice
- 2 sprigs fresh thyme
- ½ teaspoon baking soda
- 1 tablespoon cider vinegar
- Chopped chives
- Sour cream

1. Melt butter in large saucepan over medium heat. Add onions, crystallized ginger, fresh ginger, garlic, 2 teaspoons salt, and sugar; cook, stirring frequently, until onions are softened but not browned, 5 to 7 minutes.

2. Increase heat to high; add carrots, water, ¾ cup carrot juice, thyme sprigs, and baking soda and bring to simmer. Reduce heat to medium-low and simmer, covered, until carrots are very tender, 20 to 25 minutes.

3. Discard thyme sprigs. Working in batches, process soup in blender until smooth, 1 to 2 minutes. Return soup to clean pot and stir in vinegar and remaining ¾ cup carrot juice. (Soup can be refrigerated for up to 4 days.) Return to simmer over medium heat and season with salt and pepper to taste. Serve with sprinkle of chives and dollop of sour cream.

Buttery Croutons

MAKES ABOUT 2 CUPS

- 3 tablespoons unsalted butter
- 1 tablespoon olive oil
- 3 large slices high-quality sandwich bread, cut into ½-inch cubes (about 2 cups)
- Table salt

Heat the butter and oil in a 12-inch skillet over medium heat. When the foaming subsides, add the bread cubes and cook, stirring frequently, until golden brown, about 10 minutes. Transfer the croutons to a paper towel–lined plate and season with salt to taste.

CREAMY PEA SOUP

WHY THIS RECIPE WORKS: Sweet pea soup is a labor of love—fresh peas are shelled, blanched, cooked with other vegetables, then passed through a sieve. We were after a fuss-free but still elegant version of this special soup. Our goal was a streamlined approach that would produce a soup with silky texture and real pea flavor.

Both garden and grocery store peas can be disappointing; fresh pods often reveal tough, starchy pellets that require a significant amount of time spent shelling. Instead, we decided to use frozen peas. For maximum pea flavor, we ground the frozen peas in a food processor before adding them to our simple soup base of chicken broth and shallots. Adding some Boston lettuce leaves gave the soup a wonderfully frothy texture. And a small dose of heavy cream added richness.

Creamy Pea Soup

SERVES 4 TO 6

A few Classic Croutons (page 13) are the perfect embellishment to this smooth soup.

- 4 tablespoons (½ stick) unsalted butter
- 4 large shallots, minced (about 1 cup), or 2 medium leeks, white and light green parts chopped fine and rinsed thoroughly (about 1⅓ cups)
- 2 tablespoons unbleached all-purpose flour
- 3½ cups low-sodium chicken broth
- 1½ pounds frozen peas (about 4½ cups), partially thawed at room temperature for 10 minutes
- 12 small leaves Boston lettuce (about 3 ounces), washed and dried
- ½ cup heavy cream
- Table salt and ground black pepper

1. Melt the butter in a large saucepan over low heat. Add the shallots and cook, covered, until softened, 8 to 10 minutes, stirring occasionally. Add the flour and cook, stirring constantly, until thoroughly combined, about 30 seconds. Whisking constantly, gradually add the chicken broth. Increase the heat to high and bring to a boil. Reduce the heat to medium-low and simmer for 3 to 5 minutes.

2. Meanwhile, process the peas in a food processor until coarsely chopped, about 20 seconds. Add the peas and lettuce to the saucepan. Increase the heat to medium-high, cover, and return to a simmer; cook for 3 minutes. Uncover, reduce the heat to medium-low, and continue to simmer 2 minutes longer.

3. Working in batches, puree the soup in a blender until smooth, filling the blender jar only halfway for each batch. Strain the soup through a fine-mesh strainer into a large bowl; discard the solids in the strainer. Rinse and dry the saucepan; return the pureed mixture to the saucepan and stir in the cream. Warm the soup over low heat until hot, about 3 minutes. Season with salt and pepper to taste and serve. (The soup can be refrigerated in an airtight container for up to 2 days. Warm over low heat until hot; do not boil.)

CREAMY CAULIFLOWER SOUP

WHY THIS RECIPE WORKS: For a creamy cauliflower soup that tasted first and foremost of cauliflower, we did away with the distractions—no cream, flour, or overpowering seasonings. Cauliflower, simmered until tender, produced a creamy, velvety smooth puree, without the aid of any cream, due to its low insoluble fiber content. For the purest flavor, we cooked it in salted water (instead of broth), skipped the spice rack entirely, and bolstered it with sautéed onion and leek. We added the cauliflower to the simmering water in two stages so our soup offered the grassy flavor of just-cooked cauliflower and the sweeter, nuttier flavor of long-cooked cauliflower. Finally, we fried a portion of the florets in butter until both the cauliflower and butter were golden brown and used each as a separate, richly flavored garnish.

Creamy Cauliflower Soup

SERVES 4 TO 6

White wine vinegar may be substituted for the sherry vinegar. For best flavor and texture, trim core thoroughly of green leaves and leaf stems, which can be fibrous and contribute to a grainy texture in the soup.

- 1 head cauliflower (2 pounds)
- 8 tablespoons unsalted butter, cut into 8 pieces
- 1 leek, white and light green parts only, halved lengthwise, sliced thin, and washed thoroughly
- 1 small onion, halved and sliced thin
- Salt and pepper
- 4½ cups water
- ½ teaspoon sherry vinegar
- 3 tablespoons minced fresh chives

1. Pull off outer leaves of cauliflower and trim stem. Using paring knife, cut around core to remove; thinly slice core and reserve. Cut heaping 1 cup of ½-inch florets from head of cauliflower; set aside. Cut remaining cauliflower crosswise into ½-inch-thick slices.

2. Melt 3 tablespoons butter in large saucepan over medium-low heat. Add leek, onion, and 1½ teaspoons salt; cook, stirring frequently, until onion is softened but not browned, about 7 minutes.

3. Increase heat to medium-high; add water, sliced core, and half of sliced cauliflower; and bring to simmer. Reduce heat to medium-low and simmer gently for 15 minutes. Add remaining sliced cauliflower, return to simmer, and continue to cook until cauliflower is tender and crumbles easily, 15 to 20 minutes longer.

4. While soup simmers, melt remaining 5 tablespoons butter in 8-inch skillet over medium heat. Add reserved florets and cook, stirring frequently, until florets are golden brown and butter is browned, 6 to 8 minutes. Remove skillet from heat and use slotted spoon to transfer florets to small bowl. Toss florets with vinegar and season with salt to taste. Pour browned butter in skillet into small bowl and reserve for garnishing.

5. Process soup in blender until smooth, about 45 seconds. Rinse out pan. Return pureed soup to pan and return to simmer over medium heat, adjusting consistency with up to ½ cup water as needed (soup should have thick, velvety texture, but should be thin enough to settle with a flat surface after being stirred) and seasoning with salt to taste. Serve, garnishing individual bowls with browned florets, drizzles of browned butter, and chives and seasoning with pepper to taste.

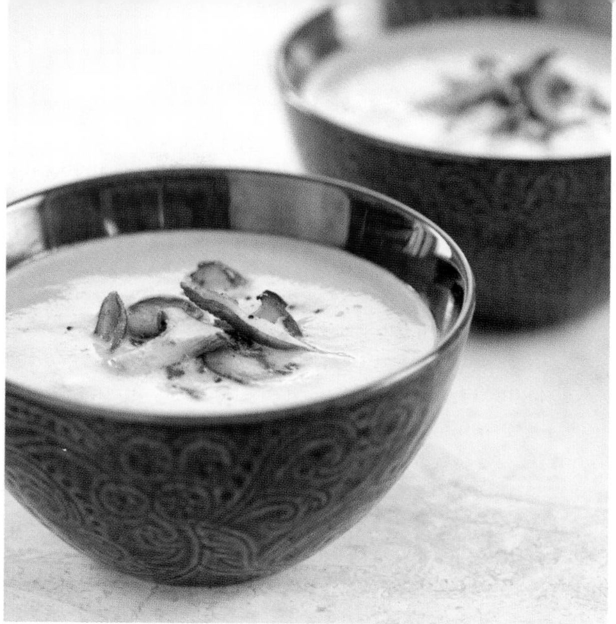

CREAMY MUSHROOM SOUP

WHY THIS RECIPE WORKS: Mushroom soups have great potential, but they often disappoint with their lackluster taste and less-than-stellar texture. We knew this pureed soup could be richly textured, neither too thick nor too thin, and showcase the deep, earthy flavor of mushrooms.

We chose to use readily available white mushrooms, which are often underestimated. To bring out the most flavor from the mushrooms, we had to slice them by hand (processing made for uneven and bruised pieces) and then sweat them in a covered pot with butter and shallots; roasted mushrooms were nixed because the juices released during roasting had browned on the pan and were lost, making for flavorless soup. Chicken broth proved a better addition than water for the liquid base, and dried porcini mushrooms amplified the mushroom flavor. After pureeing the soup, we added cream and a splash of Madeira for body. Our creamy mushroom soup was now texturally light and full of deep, rich flavor.

Creamy Mushroom Soup

SERVES 6 TO 8

The garnish of sautéed mushrooms (recipe follows) adds visual and textural appeal to this creamy soup.

- 6 tablespoons (¾ stick) unsalted butter
- 3 large shallots, minced (about ¾ cup)
- 1 medium garlic clove, minced or pressed through a garlic press (about 1 teaspoon)
- ½ teaspoon freshly grated nutmeg
- 2 pounds white mushrooms, wiped clean and sliced ¼ inch thick
- 4 cups hot water
- 3½ cups low-sodium chicken broth
- ½ ounce dried porcini mushrooms, rinsed well
- ⅓ cup Madeira or dry sherry
- 1 cup heavy cream
- 2 teaspoons juice from 1 lemon
- Table salt and ground black pepper
- 1 recipe Sautéed Wild Mushrooms, for garnish (recipe follows; see note)

1. Melt the butter in a large Dutch oven over medium-low heat. Add the shallots and sauté, stirring frequently, until softened, about 4 minutes. Stir in the garlic and nutmeg and cook until fragrant, about 30 seconds. Increase the heat to medium, add the white mushrooms, and stir to coat with the butter. Cook, stirring occasionally, until the mushrooms release some liquid, about 7 minutes. Reduce the heat to medium-low, cover the pot, and cook, stirring occasionally, until the mushrooms have released all their liquid, about 20 minutes.

2. Add the water, chicken broth, and porcini mushrooms. Cover, bring to a simmer, then reduce the heat to low and simmer until the mushrooms are fully tender, about 20 minutes.

3. Working in batches, puree the soup in a blender until smooth, filling the blender jar only halfway for each batch. Rinse and dry the pot; return the soup to the pot. Stir in the Madeira and cream and bring to a simmer over low heat. Add the lemon juice and season with salt and pepper to taste. Ladle the soup into bowls, garnish with sautéed wild mushrooms, and serve. (The soup, minus the garnish, can be refrigerated in an airtight container for up to 2 days. Warm over low heat until hot; do not boil.)

Sautéed Wild Mushrooms

MAKES ENOUGH TO GARNISH 6 TO 8 BOWLS OF SOUP

- 2 tablespoons unsalted butter
- 8 ounces shiitake, chanterelle, oyster, or cremini mushrooms, stems trimmed and discarded, mushrooms wiped clean and sliced thin
- Table salt and ground black pepper

1. Melt the butter in a medium skillet over low heat. Add the mushrooms and season with salt and pepper to taste. Cover and cook, stirring occasionally, until the mushrooms release their liquid, about 10 minutes for shiitakes and chanterelles, about 5 minutes for oysters, and about 9 minutes for cremini.

2. Uncover and continue to cook, stirring occasionally, until the liquid released by the mushrooms has evaporated and the mushrooms are browned, about 2 minutes for shiitakes, oysters, and cremini and about 3 minutes for chanterelles. Serve immediately as garnish for the soup.

MUSHROOM BISQUE

WHY THIS RECIPE WORKS: Mushroom bisque should be luxuriously creamy but packed with distinct earthy flavor, so we started with the mushrooms. A combination of white, cremini, and shiitake mushrooms promised the perfect balance of buttery and earthy notes, and microwaving them concentrated their intensity by expelling the excess moisture. We saved the flavorful liquid for later and browned the mushrooms in oil in a Dutch oven. Adding a chopped onion, fresh thyme, and pepper boosted the base's flavors and a splash of sherry elevated the mushrooms' meaty profile. Stirring in the reserved mushroom juices at this point reinforced the fungi's impact. After adding water and broth, we brought the pot to a simmer, removed the thyme sprig, and blended the mushroom mixture into a creamy bisque with a blender. Taking a tip from Julia Child's recipe, we whisked together cream and egg yolks to form a classic French thickener called a *liaison*. The yolks contributed the same silkening effect of heavy cream but without dulling or diluting the bisque. A touch of lemon juice at the very end sharpened the flavor to perfection.

Mushroom Bisque

SERVES 6 TO 10

Tying the thyme sprig with twine makes it easier to remove from the pot. For the smoothest result, use a conventional blender rather than an immersion blender. Our Fried Shallots (recipe follows) can replace the garnish of cream and chopped chives.

- 1 pound white mushrooms, trimmed
- 8 ounces cremini mushrooms, trimmed
- 8 ounces shiitake mushrooms, stemmed
- Kosher salt and pepper
- 2 tablespoons vegetable oil
- 1 small onion, chopped fine
- 1 sprig fresh thyme, tied with kitchen twine
- 2 tablespoons dry sherry
- 4 cups water
- 3½ cups chicken broth
- ⅔ cup heavy cream, plus extra for serving
- 2 large egg yolks
- 1 teaspoon lemon juice
- Chopped fresh chives

1. Toss white mushrooms, cremini mushrooms, shiitake mushrooms, and 1 tablespoon salt together in large bowl. Cover with large plate and microwave, stirring every 4 minutes, until mushrooms have released their liquid and reduced to about one-third their original volume, about 12 minutes. Transfer mushrooms to colander set in second large bowl and drain well. Reserve liquid.

2. Heat oil in Dutch oven over medium heat until shimmering. Add mushrooms and cook, stirring occasionally, until mushrooms are browned and fond has formed on bottom of pot, about 8 minutes. Add onion, thyme sprig, and ¼ teaspoon pepper and cook, stirring occasionally, until onion is just softened, about 2 minutes. Add sherry and cook until evaporated. Stir in reserved mushroom liquid and cook, scraping up any browned bits. Stir in water and broth and bring to simmer. Reduce heat to low and simmer for 20 minutes.

3. Discard thyme sprig. Working in batches, process soup in blender until very smooth, 1½ to 2 minutes per batch. Return soup to now-empty pot and bring to simmer over low heat. (Soup can be refrigerated for up to 2 days. Warm to 150 degrees before proceeding with recipe.)

4. Whisk cream and egg yolks together in medium bowl. Stirring slowly and constantly, add 2 cups soup to cream mixture. Stirring constantly, slowly pour cream mixture into simmering soup. Heat gently, stirring constantly, until soup registers 165 degrees (do not overheat). Stir in lemon juice and season with salt and pepper to taste. Serve immediately, garnishing each serving with 1 teaspoon extra cream and sprinkle of chives.

Fried Shallots

MAKES 1 CUP

Once cooled, you can store the shallots in an airtight container at room temperature for up to 3 days. You can strain the oil after cooking the shallots and reserve it for another use.

- ½ cup vegetable oil
- 3 shallots, sliced thin
- Salt

Cook oil and shallots in medium saucepan over high heat, stirring constantly, until shallots are deep golden, 11 to 13 minutes (they will still be soft; do not overcook). Using slotted spoon, transfer shallots to paper towel–lined plate, season with salt, and let drain and turn crisp, about 5 minutes, before serving.

WILD RICE AND MUSHROOM SOUP

WHY THIS RECIPE WORKS: For a rich, earthy, nutty-tasting soup, we had to figure out how to make the wild rice and mushrooms do more than just add bulk. Fresh cremini mushrooms provided a meaty texture, and dried shiitakes, ground into a powder and added to the broth, ensured full-bodied mushroom flavor. Simmering the wild rice with baking soda decreased the cooking time and brought out its complex flavor. Cooking the rice in the oven, instead of on the stovetop, made it tender with a pleasant chew. To infuse the entire soup with wild rice flavor, we replaced some of the water in the soup with the rice's leftover cooking liquid. Including tomato paste and soy sauce amplified the nutty, earthy flavor profile. A final addition of cornstarch helped suspend the rice in the broth to give our soup a velvety texture.

Wild Rice and Mushroom Soup

SERVES 6 TO 8

White mushrooms can be substituted for the cremini mushrooms. We use a spice grinder to process the dried shiitake mushrooms, but a blender also works.

- ¼ ounce dried shiitake mushrooms, rinsed
- 4¼ cups water
- 1 sprig fresh thyme
- 1 bay leaf
- 5 garlic cloves, peeled (1 whole, 4 minced)
- Salt and pepper
- ¼ teaspoon baking soda
- 1 cup wild rice
- 4 tablespoons unsalted butter
- 1 pound cremini mushrooms, trimmed and sliced ¼ inch thick
- 1 onion, chopped fine
- 1 teaspoon tomato paste
- ⅔ cup dry sherry
- 4 cups chicken broth
- 1 tablespoon soy sauce
- ¼ cup cornstarch
- ½ cup heavy cream
- ¼ cup minced fresh chives
- ¼ teaspoon finely grated lemon zest

1. Adjust oven rack to middle position and heat oven to 375 degrees. Grind shiitake mushrooms in spice grinder until finely ground (you should have about 3 tablespoons).

2. Bring 4 cups water, thyme sprig, bay leaf, garlic clove, ¾ teaspoon salt, and baking soda to boil in medium saucepan over high heat. Add rice and return to boil. Cover saucepan, transfer to oven, and bake until rice is tender, 35 to 50 minutes. Strain rice through fine-mesh strainer set in 4-cup liquid measuring cup; discard thyme sprig, bay leaf, and garlic clove. Add enough water to reserved cooking liquid to measure 3 cups.

3. Melt butter in Dutch oven over high heat. Add cremini mushrooms, onion, minced garlic, tomato paste, ¾ teaspoon salt, and 1 teaspoon pepper. Cook, stirring occasionally, until vegetables are browned and dark fond develops on bottom of pot, 15 minutes. Add sherry, scraping up any browned bits, and cook until reduced and pot is almost dry, about 2 minutes. Add ground shiitake mushrooms, reserved rice cooking liquid, broth, and soy sauce and bring to boil. Reduce heat to low and simmer, covered, until onion and mushrooms are tender, about 20 minutes.

4. Whisk cornstarch and remaining ¼ cup water in small bowl. Stir cornstarch slurry into soup, return to simmer, and cook until thickened, about 2 minutes. Remove pot from heat and stir in cooked rice, cream, chives, and lemon zest. Cover and let stand for 20 minutes. Season with salt and pepper to taste and serve.

BUTTERNUT SQUASH SOUP

WHY THIS RECIPE WORKS: Butternut squash soup strikes a perfect balance between nuttiness and sweetness. But getting that balance right depends on selecting just a few key ingredients so the sweet squash flavor can take center stage.

We found our answer to intense squash flavor in the squash's seeds and fibers. We sautéed shallots and butter with the seeds and fibers, simmered them in water, then used the liquid to steam the unpeeled quartered squash (thereby eliminating the pesky task of peeling raw squash). Once cooled, we scooped the flesh from the skin and pureed the squash with the steaming liquid (strained of seeds and fibers) for a soup with a perfectly smooth texture. A little dark brown sugar added to the soup also intensified the sweetness of the squash. Finally, we enriched the soup with a splash of heavy cream and a pinch of nutmeg to round out this velvety soup's rich flavors.

Butternut Squash Soup

SERVES 4 TO 6

Lightly toasted pumpkin seeds, drizzles of balsamic vinegar, or sprinklings of paprika or cracked black pepper make appealing accompaniments to this soup.

- 4 tablespoons (½ stick) unsalted butter
- 1 large shallot, minced (about ¼ cup)
- 3 pounds butternut squash (about 1 large squash), cut in half lengthwise, each half cut in half widthwise; seeds and fibers scraped out and reserved
- 6 cups water
- Table salt
- ½ cup heavy cream
- 1 teaspoon dark brown sugar
- Pinch grated nutmeg

1. Melt the butter in a large Dutch oven over medium-low heat. Add the shallot and cook, stirring frequently, until translucent, about 3 minutes. Add the seeds and fibers from the squash and cook, stirring occasionally, until the butter turns a saffron color, about 4 minutes.

2. Add the water and 1 teaspoon salt to the pot and bring to a boil over high heat. Reduce the heat to medium-low, place the squash, cut side down, in a steamer basket, and lower the basket into the pot. Cover and steam until the squash is completely tender, about 30 minutes. Take the pot off the heat and use tongs to transfer the squash to a rimmed baking sheet. When cool enough to handle, use a large spoon to scrape the flesh from the skin. Reserve the squash flesh in a bowl and discard the skin.

3. Strain the steaming liquid through a fine-mesh strainer into a second bowl; discard the solids in the strainer. (You should have 2½ to 3 cups liquid.) Rinse and dry the pot.

4. Working in batches and filling the blender jar only halfway for each batch, puree the squash, adding enough reserved steaming liquid to obtain a smooth consistency. Transfer the puree to the clean pot and stir in the remaining steaming liquid, the cream, and brown sugar. Warm the soup over medium-low heat until hot, about 3 minutes. Stir in the nutmeg, season with salt to taste, and serve. (The soup can be refrigerated in an airtight container for up to 2 days. Warm over low heat until hot; do not boil.)

SWEET POTATO SOUP

WHY THIS RECIPE WORKS: The secrets to a creamy sweet potato soup are to use the peels and turn off the heat. Most recipes call for so many other ingredients that the sweet potato flavor ends up muted and overpowered. By cutting back to shallot, thyme, and butter and using water instead of broth, we put the focus on the main ingredient. For extra earthiness, we also pureed some of the potato skins into the soup. However, the real key to intensifying the sweet potato flavor was to use only a minimal amount of flavor-diluting water. To do so, we let the sweet potatoes sit in hot water off heat to make use of an enzyme that converts their starch content to sugar. Less starch meant we could create a soup with less water, keeping the sweet potato flavor in the forefront.

Sweet Potato Soup

SERVES 4 TO 6 AS A MAIN DISH OR 8 AS A STARTER

To highlight the earthiness of the sweet potatoes, we incorporate a quarter of the skins into the soup. In addition to the chives, serve the soup with one of our suggested garnishes (recipes follow). The garnish can be prepared during step 1 while the sweet potatoes stand in the water.

- 4 tablespoons unsalted butter
- 1 shallot, sliced thin
- 4 sprigs fresh thyme
- 4¼ cups water, plus extra as needed
- 2 pounds sweet potatoes, peeled, halved lengthwise, and sliced ¼ inch thick, ¼ of peels reserved
- 1 tablespoon packed brown sugar
- ½ teaspoon cider vinegar
- Salt and pepper
- Minced fresh chives

1. Melt butter in large saucepan over medium-low heat. Add shallot and thyme sprigs and cook until shallot is softened but not browned, about 5 minutes. Add water, increase heat to high, and bring to simmer. Remove pot from heat, add sweet potatoes and reserved peels, and let stand uncovered for 20 minutes.

2. Add sugar, vinegar, 1½ teaspoons salt, and ¼ teaspoon pepper. Bring to simmer over high heat. Reduce heat to medium-low, cover, and cook until potatoes are very soft, about 10 minutes.

3. Discard thyme sprigs. Working in batches, process soup in blender until smooth, 45 to 60 seconds. Return soup to clean pot. Bring to simmer over medium heat, adjusting consistency with extra water if desired. Season with salt and pepper to taste. Serve, topping each portion with sprinkle of chives.

NOTES FROM THE TEST KITCHEN

PUTTING PEELS TO WORK

Instead of discarding the sweet potato peels, we blend some of them into our soup to take advantage of an earthy-tasting compound they contain called methoxypyrazine.

Because the compound in the peels is potent—it's detectable in water in levels as low as one part per trillion—we use only one-quarter of the peels in order to avoid overwhelming the soup.

Buttery Rye Croutons

MAKES 1½ CUPS

The croutons can be made ahead and stored in an airtight container for up to 1 week.

- 3 tablespoons unsalted butter
- 1 tablespoon olive oil
- 2 slices light rye bread, cut into ½-inch cubes (about 1½ cups)
- Salt

Heat butter and oil in 10-inch skillet over medium heat. When foaming subsides, add bread cubes and cook, stirring frequently, until golden brown, about 10 minutes. Transfer croutons to paper towel–lined plate and season with salt to taste.

Candied Bacon Bits

MAKES ABOUT ¼ CUP

Break up any large chunks before serving.

- 4 slices bacon, cut into ½-inch pieces
- 2 teaspoons packed dark brown sugar
- ½ teaspoon cider vinegar

Cook bacon in 10-inch nonstick skillet over medium heat until crisp and well rendered, 6 to 8 minutes. Using slotted spoon, remove bacon from skillet and discard fat. Return bacon to skillet and add brown sugar and vinegar. Cook over low heat, stirring constantly, until bacon is evenly coated. Transfer to plate in single layer. Let bacon cool completely.

Maple Sour Cream

MAKES ⅓ CUP

Maple balances the sweet potatoes' earthiness.

- ⅓ cup sour cream
- 1 tablespoon maple syrup

Combine ingredients in bowl.

SUPER GREENS SOUP WITH LEMON-TARRAGON CREAM

WHY THIS RECIPE WORKS: We wanted a deceptively delicious, silky-smooth soup that delivered a big dose of healthy greens. It should be packed with all the essential nutrients of hearty greens and boast a deep, complex flavor brightened with a garnish of lemon and herb cream. First, we built a flavorful foundation of sweet caramelized onions and earthy sautéed mushrooms. We added broth, water, and lots of leafy greens (we liked a mix of chard, kale, arugula, and parsley), and simmered until the greens became tender before blending them smooth. We were happy with the soup's depth of flavor, but it was watery and too thin. Many recipes we found used potatoes as a thickener, but they lent an overwhelmingly earthy flavor. Instead, we tried using Arborio rice. The rice's high starch content thickened the soup to a velvety, lush consistency without clouding its bright, vegetal flavors. For a vibrant finish, we whisked together heavy cream, sour cream, lemon zest, lemon juice, and tarragon and drizzled it over the top.

Super Greens Soup with Lemon-Tarragon Cream

SERVES 4 TO 6

Our favorite brand of Arborio rice is RiceSelect.

- ¼ cup heavy cream
- 3 tablespoons sour cream
- 2 tablespoons plus ½ teaspoon extra-virgin olive oil
- ¼ teaspoon finely grated lemon zest plus ½ teaspoon juice
- ½ teaspoon minced fresh tarragon
- Salt and pepper
- 1 onion, halved through root end and sliced thin
- ¾ teaspoon light brown sugar
- 3 ounces white mushrooms, trimmed and sliced thin
- 2 garlic cloves, minced
- Pinch cayenne pepper
- 3 cups water
- 3 cups vegetable broth
- ⅓ cup Arborio rice
- 12 ounces Swiss chard, stemmed and chopped coarse
- 9 ounces kale, stemmed and chopped coarse
- ¼ cup fresh parsley leaves
- 2 ounces (2 cups) baby arugula

1. Combine cream, sour cream, ½ teaspoon oil, lemon zest and juice, tarragon, and ¼ teaspoon salt in bowl. Cover and refrigerate until ready to serve.

2. Heat remaining 2 tablespoons oil in Dutch oven over medium-high heat until shimmering. Stir in onion, sugar, and 1 teaspoon salt and cook, stirring occasionally, until onion releases some moisture, about 5 minutes. Reduce heat to low and cook, stirring often and scraping up any browned bits, until onion is deeply browned and slightly sticky, about 30 minutes. (If onion is sizzling or scorching, reduce heat. If onion is not browning after 15 to 20 minutes, increase heat.)

3. Stir in mushrooms and cook until they have released their moisture, about 5 minutes. Stir in garlic and cayenne and cook until fragrant, about 30 seconds. Stir in water, broth, and rice, scraping up any browned bits, and bring to boil. Reduce heat to low, cover, and simmer for 15 minutes.

4. Stir in chard, kale, and parsley, 1 handful at a time, until wilted and submerged in liquid. Return to simmer, cover, and cook until greens are tender, about 10 minutes.

5. Off heat, stir in arugula until wilted. Working in batches, process soup in blender until smooth, about 1 minute per batch. Return pureed soup to clean pot and season with salt and pepper to taste. Drizzle individual portions with lemon-tarragon cream and serve.

RUSTIC POTATO-LEEK SOUP

WHY THIS RECIPE WORKS: Rustic potato-leek soup often disappoints with soft, mealy potatoes and dingy, overcooked leeks. We wanted to perfect this soup so both ingredients would be at their best and the dish would retain its textural integrity and bright flavor.

We quickly eliminated potatoes with high or medium starch levels because they broke down too quickly in the chicken broth. Waxy, low-starch red potatoes were perfect—they kept their shape and didn't become waterlogged during cooking. To pump up the flavor of the soup, we used a substantial amount of leeks and sautéed both the white and light green parts in butter. Leeks and potatoes require different cooking times, so we staggered the cooking—leeks first, then potatoes, and then we removed the pot from the stove so the potatoes could gently cook through in the hot broth without becoming overcooked and mushy. We also added a bit of flour with the sautéed leeks to give our broth some body. At last, we had a flavorful, oniony soup, full of perfectly cooked potatoes and sweet, tender leeks.

Rustic Potato-Leek Soup

SERVES 6

Leeks can vary in size; if your leeks have large white and light green parts, use the smaller amount of leeks.

- 6 tablespoons (¾ stick) unsalted butter
- 4–5 pounds leeks, white and light green parts only, halved lengthwise, sliced crosswise 1 inch thick, and rinsed thoroughly (about 11 cups; see note)
- 1 tablespoon unbleached all-purpose flour
- 5¼ cups low-sodium chicken broth
- 1¾ pounds red potatoes (about 5 medium), peeled and cut into ¾-inch chunks
- 1 bay leaf
- Table salt and ground black pepper

1. Melt the butter in a large Dutch oven over medium-low heat. Add the leeks, increase the heat to medium, cover, and cook, stirring occasionally, until the leeks are tender but not mushy, 15 to 20 minutes; do not brown them. Add the flour and cook, stirring constantly, until thoroughly combined, about 2 minutes.

2. Increase the heat to high; whisking constantly, gradually add the broth. Add the potatoes and bay leaf, cover, and bring to a boil. Reduce the heat to medium-low and simmer, covered, until the potatoes are almost tender, 5 to 7 minutes. Remove the pot from the heat and let stand, covered, until the potatoes are tender, 10 to 15 minutes. Discard the bay leaf, season with salt and pepper to taste, and serve. (The soup can be refrigerated in an airtight container for up to 2 days. Warm over low heat until hot; do not boil.)

BROCCOLI-CHEESE SOUP

WHY THIS RECIPE WORKS: We were after a soup with pure broccoli flavor that wasn't hiding behind the cream or the cheese. Overcooked broccoli has a sulfurous flavor, but we discovered when we cooked our broccoli beyond the point of just overcooked—for a full hour—those sulfur-containing compounds broke down, leaving behind intense, nutty broccoli. Its texture was fairly soft, but that was perfect for use in a soup. Adding baking soda to the pot sped up the process, shortening the broccoli's cooking time to a mere 20 minutes. A little spinach lent bright green color to the soup without taking over the flavor. After adding cheddar and Parmesan, we had a soup so full of flavor and richness that it didn't even need the typical cream.

Broccoli-Cheese Soup

SERVES 6 TO 8

To make a vegetarian version of this soup, substitute vegetable broth for the chicken broth.

- 2 tablespoons unsalted butter
- 2 pounds broccoli, florets chopped into 1-inch pieces, stems peeled and sliced ¼ inch thick
- 1 medium onion, chopped coarse
- 2 medium garlic cloves, minced or pressed through a garlic press (about 2 teaspoons)
- 1½ teaspoons dry mustard
- Pinch cayenne pepper
- Table salt and ground black pepper
- 3–4 cups water
- ¼ teaspoon baking soda
- 2 cups low-sodium chicken broth
- 2 ounces baby spinach (about 2 cups)

- 3 ounces sharp cheddar cheese, shredded (about ¾ cup)
- 1½ ounces Parmesan cheese, grated fine (about ¾ cup), plus extra for serving
- 1 recipe Buttery Croutons (page 13)

1. Melt the butter in a Dutch oven over medium-high heat. Add the broccoli, onion, garlic, mustard, cayenne, and 1 teaspoon salt and cook, stirring frequently, until fragrant, about 6 minutes. Add 1 cup water and the baking soda. Bring to a simmer, cover, and cook until the broccoli is very soft, about 20 minutes, stirring once during cooking.

2. Add the broth and 2 cups more water and increase the heat to medium-high. When the mixture begins to simmer, stir in the spinach and cook until wilted, about 1 minute. Transfer half of the soup to a blender, add the cheddar and Parmesan, and process until smooth, about 1 minute. Transfer the soup to a medium bowl and repeat with the remaining soup. Return the soup to the Dutch oven, place over medium heat and bring to a simmer. Adjust the consistency of the soup with up to 1 cup water. Season with salt and pepper to taste. Serve, passing extra Parmesan.

MODERN HAM AND SPLIT PEA SOUP

WHY THIS RECIPE WORKS: We wanted a spoon-coating, richly flavorful broth studded with tender shreds of sweet-smoky meat. To avoid having to bake a ham beforehand, we needed a substitute for the traditional ham bone. Ham hock made the soup greasy and was skimpy on the meat. Ham steak, however, was plenty meaty and infused the soup with a fuller pork flavor—and we could get away with using just 1 pound. Our soup still needed richness and smokiness, and adding a few strips of raw bacon to the pot did the job. Unsoaked peas broke down just as well as soaked and were better at absorbing the flavor of the soup, so we skipped the traditional soaking step. To dress up our recipe, we garnished it with a handful of fresh peas; their sweetness popped against the hearty, smoky broth. Fresh chopped mint leaves and a drizzle of good balsamic vinegar added visual appeal and punched up the flavors even more. Floating gently fried croutons on the surface rounded off our updated version of this classic soup.

Modern Ham and Split Pea Soup

SERVES 6 TO 8

Four ounces of regular sliced bacon can be used, but the thinner slices are a little harder to remove from the soup. Depending on the age and brand of split peas, the consistency of the soup may vary slightly. If the soup is too thin at the end of step 3, increase the heat and simmer, uncovered, until the desired consistency is reached. If it is too thick, thin it with a little water. In addition to sprinkling the soup with Buttery Croutons (page 13), we also like to garnish it with fresh peas, chopped mint, and a drizzle of aged balsamic vinegar.

- 2 tablespoons unsalted butter
- 1 large onion, chopped fine
- Table salt and ground black pepper
- 2 medium garlic cloves, minced or pressed through a garlic press (about 2 teaspoons)
- 7 cups water
- 1 ham steak (about 1 pound), skin removed, cut into quarters
- 3 slices thick-cut bacon
- 1 pound (2 cups) green split peas, picked over and rinsed
- 2 sprigs fresh thyme
- 2 bay leaves
- 2 medium carrots, peeled and cut into ½-inch pieces
- 1 medium celery rib, cut into ½-inch pieces

1. Heat the butter in a Dutch oven over medium-high heat. Add the onion and ½ teaspoon salt and cook, stirring frequently, until the onion is softened, about 3 to 4 minutes. Add the garlic and cook until fragrant, about 30 seconds. Add the water, ham steak, bacon, peas, thyme, and bay leaves. Increase the heat to high and bring to a simmer, stirring frequently to keep the peas from sticking to the bottom. Reduce the heat to low, cover, and simmer until the peas are tender but not falling apart, about 45 minutes.

2. Remove the ham steak, cover with aluminum foil or plastic wrap to prevent drying out, and set aside. Stir in the carrots and celery and continue to simmer, covered, until the vegetables are tender and the peas have almost completely broken down, about 30 minutes longer.

3. When cool enough to handle, shred the ham into small bite-size pieces. Remove and discard the thyme, bay leaves, and bacon slices. Stir the ham back into the soup and return to a simmer. Season with salt and pepper to taste and serve. (The soup can be refrigerated for up to 3 days. If necessary, thin it with water when reheating.)

HEARTY HAM AND SPLIT PEA SOUP WITH POTATOES

WHY THIS RECIPE WORKS: Split pea soup tends to show up on the home cook's menu only when the previous meal (usually a holiday celebration) featured a big ham—and the leftovers are begging to be made into soup. We wanted a recipe for an old-fashioned ham and split pea soup that could be made anytime, with a readily available cut of ham that would also provide enough meat for really hearty soup. We found that we could get good, meaty ham stock with a picnic shoulder, a small, inexpensive cut that adds great flavor and provides plenty of meat for the soup (and some leftovers too). While it was easy enough to cook the peas in the ham stock, our vegetables benefited from a sauté in a separate pan. We found that caramelized vegetables gave this straightforward soup a richness and depth of flavor that had been missing—it was well worth the time spent washing an extra pan. Adding in a few red potatoes with the carrots, celery, and onions turned our soup into a truly satisfying meal.

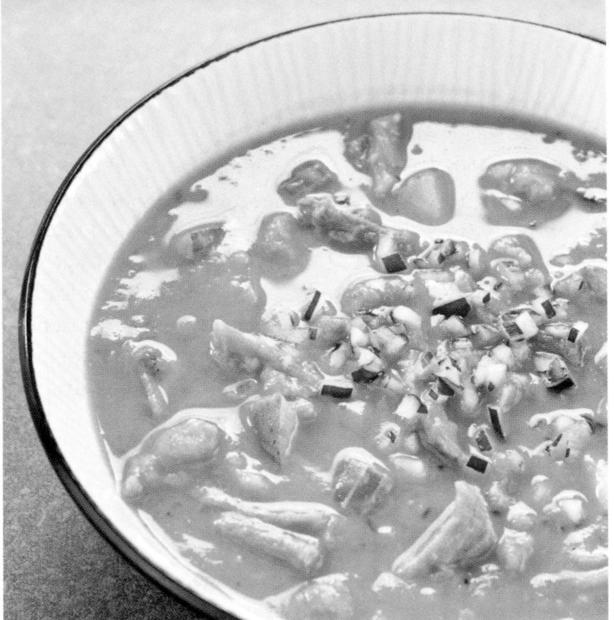

Hearty Ham and Split Pea Soup with Potatoes

SERVES 6

Use an entire small 2½-pound smoked picnic portion ham if you can find one. Otherwise, buy a half-picnic ham and remove some meat, which you can roast and use in sandwiches, salads, or omelets. To remove the meat, loosen the large comma-shaped muscles on top of the ham with your fingers, then use a knife to cut the membrane separating the comma-shaped muscles from the rest of the ham.

- 1 (2½-pound) smoked bone-in picnic ham (see note)
- 4 bay leaves
- 3 quarts water
- 1 pound (2 cups) green split peas, picked over and rinsed
- 1 teaspoon dried thyme
- 2 tablespoons extra-virgin olive oil
- 2 medium onions, chopped medium
- 2 medium carrots, peeled and chopped medium
- 2 celery ribs, chopped medium
- 1 tablespoon unsalted butter
- 2 medium garlic cloves, minced or pressed through a garlic press (about 2 teaspoons)
- Pinch sugar
- 3 small red potatoes (about ½ pound), scrubbed and cut into ½-inch chunks
- Ground black pepper
- Minced red onion (optional)
- Balsamic vinegar

1. Place the ham in a large Dutch oven, add the bay leaves and water, cover, and bring to a boil over medium-high heat. Reduce the heat to low and simmer until the meat is tender and pulls away from the bone, 2 to 2½ hours. Remove the ham meat and bone from the pot and set aside.

2. Add the split peas and thyme to the stock. Bring to a boil, reduce the heat, and simmer, uncovered, until the peas are tender but not dissolved, about 45 minutes. While the vegetables are cooking, shred the meat with your fingers or two forks and set aside. Discard the rind and bone.

3. Meanwhile, heat the oil in a large skillet over medium-high heat until shimmering. Add the onions, carrots, and celery and sauté, stirring frequently, until most of the liquid evaporates and the vegetables begin to brown, 5 to 6 minutes. Reduce the heat to medium-low and add the butter, garlic, and sugar. Cook the vegetables, stirring frequently, until deeply browned, 30 to 35 minutes; set aside.

4. Add the sautéed vegetables, potatoes, and shredded ham to the pot with the split peas. Simmer until the potatoes are tender, the peas dissolve, and the soup thickens to the consistency of light cream, about 20 minutes. Season with pepper to taste. Discard the bay leaves and ladle the soup into bowls. Sprinkle with red onion (if using) and serve, passing balsamic vinegar separately. (The soup, minus the garnishes, can be refrigerated in an airtight container for up to 2 days. Warm over low heat until hot; do not boil.)

HEARTY LENTIL SOUP

WHY THIS RECIPE WORKS: A hot bowl of lentil soup provides warm comfort on a cold day and, when properly prepared, tastes great—maybe even better—the next day. We wanted a hearty lentil soup worthy of a second bowl, not the tasteless variety we have so often encountered.

While *lentilles du Puy* are our top choice for lentil soup, we found that almost any lentil (other than red lentils) can be used. To keep the lentils from losing their shape as they cooked, we sweated them with sautéed aromatic vegetables before adding chicken broth to the soup pot. These lentils stayed intact in our final soup, but their flavor was weak. Revisiting this step, we added canned tomatoes and crisp bacon, which gave our lentils a huge flavor boost. And because we cooked the bacon first, we could then use the rendered fat to sauté our vegetables and aromatics, which brought a nice smoky flavor to the soup. For a texture that was neither too smooth nor too thick, we pureed a few cups of the soup and added it back to the pot to warm through. Lentil soup needs plenty of acidity, so we used white wine as part of the broth and finished the soup with balsamic vinegar.

Hearty Lentil Soup

SERVES 4 TO 6

Lentilles du Puy, sometimes called French green lentils, are our first choice for this recipe, but brown, black, or regular green lentils are fine, too. Note that cooking times will vary depending on the type of lentils used. Be sure to rinse and then carefully sort through the lentils to remove any small stones.

- 3 ounces (3 slices) bacon, cut into ¼-inch pieces
- 1 large onion, minced
- 2 medium carrots, peeled and chopped medium

- 3 medium garlic cloves, minced or pressed through a garlic press (about 1 tablespoon)
- 1 (14.5-ounce) can diced tomatoes, drained
- 1 bay leaf
- 1 teaspoon minced fresh thyme leaves
- 1 cup (7 ounces) lentils, rinsed and picked over (see note)
- 1 teaspoon table salt
- Ground black pepper
- ½ cup dry white wine
- 4½ cups low-sodium chicken broth
- 1½ cups water
- 1½ teaspoons balsamic vinegar
- 3 tablespoons minced fresh parsley leaves

1. Fry the bacon in a large Dutch oven over medium-high heat, stirring occasionally, until the fat is rendered and the bacon is crisp, 3 to 4 minutes. Add the onion and carrots; cook, stirring occasionally, until the vegetables begin to soften, about 2 minutes. Add the garlic and cook until fragrant, about 30 seconds. Stir in the tomatoes, bay leaf, and thyme; cook until fragrant, about 30 seconds. Stir in the lentils, salt, and pepper to taste; cover, reduce the heat to medium-low, and cook until the vegetables are softened and the lentils have darkened, 8 to 10 minutes.

2. Uncover, increase the heat to high, add the wine, and bring to a simmer. Add the chicken broth and water; bring to a boil, cover partially, and reduce the heat to low. Simmer until the lentils are tender but still hold their shape, 30 to 35 minutes; discard the bay leaf.

3. Puree 3 cups of the soup in a blender until smooth, then return to the pot. Stir in the vinegar and heat the soup over medium-low heat until hot, about 5 minutes. Stir in 2 tablespoons of the parsley. Ladle the soup into bowls, garnish with the remaining parsley, and serve. (The soup, minus the garnish, can be refrigerated in an airtight container for up to 2 days. Warm over low heat until hot; do not boil.)

HEARTY SPANISH-STYLE LENTIL AND CHORIZO SOUP

WHY THIS RECIPE WORKS: For our own version of Spain's thick and smoky lentil soup, we started with the lentils. Soaking them in a warm brine for 30 minutes before cooking prevented blowouts and ensured they were well seasoned. Browning links of Spanish chorizo and then simmering them in the soup ensured a juicy texture. Slowly sweating finely chopped aromatics in the chorizo's fat gave our soup incredible depth of flavor. For more intensity, we finished the soup with an Indian preparation called a *tarka*, which is a mixture of spices (smoked paprika ramped up the smoky notes) and finely minced aromatics (we used onion and garlic) bloomed in oil. Adding a little flour helped thicken the soup and some sherry vinegar brightened its flavors.

Hearty Spanish-Style Lentil and Chorizo Soup

SERVES 6 TO 8

We prefer French green lentils, or *lentilles du Puy*, for this recipe, but it will work with any type of lentil except red or yellow. Grate the onion on the large holes of a box grater. If Spanish-style chorizo is not available, kielbasa sausage can be substituted. Red wine vinegar can be substituted for the sherry vinegar. Smoked paprika comes in three varieties: sweet (dulce), bittersweet or medium hot (agridulce), and hot (picante). For this recipe, we prefer the sweet kind.

- 1 pound (2¼ cups) lentils, picked over and rinsed
- Salt and pepper
- 1 large onion
- 5 tablespoons extra-virgin olive oil
- 1½ pounds Spanish-style chorizo sausage, pricked with fork several times
- 3 carrots, peeled and cut into ¼-inch pieces
- 3 tablespoons minced fresh parsley
- 3 tablespoons sherry vinegar, plus extra for seasoning
- 7 cups water, plus extra as needed
- 2 bay leaves
- ⅛ teaspoon ground cloves
- 2 tablespoons sweet smoked paprika
- 3 garlic cloves, minced
- 1 tablespoon all-purpose flour

1. Place lentils and 2 teaspoons salt in heatproof container. Cover with 4 cups boiling water and let soak for 30 minutes. Drain well.

2. Meanwhile, finely chop three-quarters of onion (you should have about 1 cup) and grate remaining quarter (you should have about 3 tablespoons). Heat 2 tablespoons oil in Dutch oven over medium heat until shimmering. Add chorizo and cook until browned on all sides, 6 to 8 minutes. Transfer chorizo to large

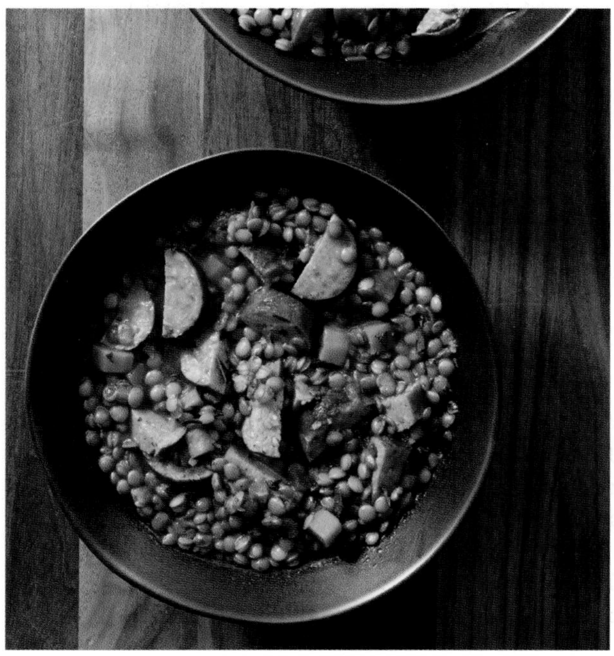

plate. Reduce heat to low and add chopped onion, carrots, 1 tablespoon parsley, and 1 teaspoon salt. Cover and cook, stirring occasionally, until vegetables are very soft but not brown, 25 to 30 minutes. If vegetables begin to brown, add 1 tablespoon water to pot.

3. Add lentils and sherry vinegar to vegetables; increase heat to medium-high; and cook, stirring frequently, until vinegar starts to evaporate, 3 to 4 minutes. Add 7 cups water, chorizo, bay leaves, and cloves; bring to simmer. Reduce heat to low, cover, and cook until lentils are tender, about 30 minutes.

4. Heat remaining 3 tablespoons oil in small saucepan over medium heat until shimmering. Add paprika, grated onion, garlic, and ½ teaspoon pepper; cook, stirring constantly, until fragrant, 2 minutes. Add flour and cook, stirring constantly, 1 minute longer. Remove chorizo and bay leaves from lentils. Stir paprika mixture into lentils and continue to cook until flavors have blended and soup has thickened, 10 to 15 minutes. When chorizo is cool enough to handle, cut in half lengthwise, then cut each half into ¼-inch-thick slices. Return chorizo to soup along with remaining 2 tablespoons parsley and heat through, about 1 minute. Season with salt, pepper, and up to 2 teaspoons sherry vinegar to taste, and serve. (Soup can be made up to 3 days in advance.)

Hearty Spanish-Style Lentil and Chorizo Soup with Kale

Add 12 ounces kale, stemmed and cut into ½-inch pieces, to simmering soup after 15 minutes in step 3. Continue to simmer until lentils and kale are tender, about 15 minutes.

RED LENTIL SOUP WITH NORTH AFRICAN SPICES

WHY THIS RECIPE WORKS: Red lentils are one of our favorite legumes. They cook quickly and don't require any presoaking or brining like other beans. One of their best qualities, however, is that they disintegrate when cooked, forming a creamy, thick puree—perfect for a satisfying soup. Their mild flavor does require a bit of embellishment, so we started by sautéing onions in butter and used the warm mixture to bloom some fragrant North African spices. Tomato paste and garlic completed the base before the addition of the lentils, and a mix of chicken broth and water gave the soup a full, rounded character. After only 15 minutes of cooking, the lentils were soft enough to be pureed with a whisk. A generous dose of lemon juice brought the flavors into focus, and a drizzle of spice-infused butter and a sprinkle of fresh cilantro completed the transformation of commonplace ingredients into an exotic yet comforting soup.

Red Lentil Soup With North African Spices

SERVES 4 TO 6

Pair this soup with a salad and bread for lunch or a light supper.

- 4 tablespoons unsalted butter
- 1 large onion, chopped fine
- Salt and pepper
- ¾ teaspoon ground coriander
- ½ teaspoon ground cumin
- ¼ teaspoon ground ginger
- ⅛ teaspoon ground cinnamon
- Pinch cayenne pepper
- 1 tablespoon tomato paste
- 1 garlic clove, minced
- 4 cups chicken broth
- 2 cups water
- 10½ ounces (1½ cups) red lentils, picked over and rinsed
- 2 tablespoons lemon juice, plus extra for seasoning
- 1½ teaspoons dried mint, crumbled
- 1 teaspoon paprika
- ¼ cup chopped fresh cilantro

1. Melt 2 tablespoons butter in large saucepan over medium heat. Add onion and 1 teaspoon salt and cook, stirring occasionally, until softened but not browned, about 5 minutes. Add coriander, cumin, ginger, cinnamon, cayenne, and ¼ teaspoon pepper and cook until fragrant, about 2 minutes. Stir in tomato paste and garlic and cook for 1 minute. Stir in broth, water, and lentils and bring to simmer. Simmer vigorously, stirring occasionally, until lentils are soft and about half are broken down, about 15 minutes.

2. Whisk soup vigorously until it is coarsely pureed, about 30 seconds. Stir in lemon juice and season with salt and extra lemon juice to taste. Cover and keep warm. (Soup can be refrigerated for up to 3 days. Thin soup with water, if desired, when reheating.)

3. Melt remaining 2 tablespoons butter in small skillet over medium-low heat. Remove from heat and stir in mint and paprika. Ladle soup into individual bowls, drizzle each portion with 1 teaspoon spiced butter, sprinkle with cilantro, and serve.

MULLIGATAWNY SOUP

WHY THIS RECIPE WORKS: As with many other dishes of Indian origin, mulligatawny soup is mildly spicy and richly flavored, with a number of spices in its lineup. We wanted an elegant, but potent, rendition of this classic soup, not the thin, raw-tasting version found in many restaurants.

Chicken broth proved to be the best base for this pureed vegetable-laden soup; beef broth was too strong and vegetable broth gave us an overly vegetal soup. For the spices, good-quality curry powder is a must, and a little cumin and cayenne pepper made for the perfect spice mix. Garlic, ginger, and coconut were a given—essentials in mulligatawny—but the best way to incorporate them wasn't immediately clear. We ended up adopting a technique common in Indian cooking—we pureed the raw garlic and ginger with water so they could

be mixed into the soup for fresh bites of garlic and ginger. The best source for true coconut flavor turned out to be shredded unsweetened coconut.

Finally, to give the finished soup the right amount of body, we made a roux with our aromatics and pureed the soup with a banana, which imparted a rich, sweet flavor to the dish (a potato worked fine, too). A swirl of yogurt and sprinkling of cilantro were the crowning touches on our richly spiced, velvety mulligatawny.

Mulligatawny Soup

SERVES 6 TO 8

Leave the garlic and ginger puree from step 1 in the blender while making the soup; when the finished soup is pureed in the same blender, it will pick up a hit of spicy raw garlic and ginger. For a heartier soup, stir in cooked white rice.

- 4 medium garlic cloves, 2 peeled and 2 minced or pressed through a garlic press (see note)
- 1½ tablespoons minced or grated fresh ginger (see note)
- ¼ cup water
- 3 tablespoons unsalted butter
- 2 medium onions, chopped medium
- 1 teaspoon tomato paste
- ½ cup shredded unsweetened coconut
- ¼ cup unbleached all-purpose flour
- 1½ tablespoons curry powder
- 1 teaspoon ground cumin
- ¼ teaspoon cayenne pepper
- 7 cups low-sodium chicken broth
- 2 medium carrots, peeled and chopped medium
- 1 celery rib, chopped medium
- 1 medium very ripe banana (about 5 ounces), peeled, or 1 medium red potato (about 5 ounces), peeled and cut into 1-inch chunks
- Table salt and ground black pepper
- Plain yogurt
- 2 tablespoons minced fresh cilantro leaves

1. Puree the 2 peeled whole garlic cloves, 2 teaspoons of the ginger, and the water in a blender until smooth; leave the mixture in the blender and set aside.

2. Melt the butter in a large Dutch oven over medium heat. Add the onions and tomato paste and cook, stirring frequently, until the onions are softened and beginning to brown, about 3 minutes. Stir in the coconut and cook until fragrant, about 1 minute. Add the minced garlic, the remaining 2½ teaspoons ginger, the flour, curry powder, cumin, and cayenne; stir until evenly combined, about 1 minute. Whisking constantly, gradually add the chicken broth.

3. Add the carrots, celery, and banana to the pot. Increase the heat to medium-high and bring to a boil. Cover, reduce the heat to low, and simmer until the vegetables are tender, about 20 minutes.

4. Working in batches, puree the soup in the blender with the garlic and ginger until smooth, filling the blender jar only halfway for each batch. Wash and dry the pot. Return the pureed soup to the pot and season with salt and pepper to taste. Warm the soup over medium heat until hot, about 1 minute. Ladle the soup into bowls, spoon a dollop of yogurt into each bowl, sprinkle with the cilantro, and serve. (The soup, minus the garnishes, can be refrigerated in an airtight container for up to 3 days. Warm over low heat until hot; do not boil.)

CHICKEN AND SAUSAGE GUMBO

WHY THIS RECIPE WORKS: Most recipes for the beloved Louisiana soup, gumbo, start with a wet roux, a cooked paste of flour and fat that can take an hour or more to make. We streamlined this process by using a dry roux of oven-toasted flour, which gave the same effect as a wet roux but without the oil. To flavor our gumbo we used easy-to-work-with boneless, skinless chicken thighs and andouille sausage, rounding out the dish with garlic, thyme, bay leaves, and spices. We stirred in white vinegar rather than hot sauce at the end for acidity without adding heat to an already well-seasoned dish.

Chicken and Sausage Gumbo

SERVES 6

This recipe is engineered for efficiency: Get the flour toasting in the oven and then prep the remaining ingredients before you begin cooking. We strongly recommend using andouille, but in a pinch, kielbasa can be substituted. The salt level of the final dish may vary depending on the brand of sausage, so liberal seasoning with additional salt at the end may be necessary. Serve over white rice.

- 1 cup (5 ounces) all-purpose flour
- 1 tablespoon vegetable oil
- 1 onion, chopped fine
- 1 green bell pepper, chopped fine
- 2 celery ribs, chopped fine
- 3 garlic cloves, minced
- 2 bay leaves
- 1 tablespoon minced fresh thyme
- 1 teaspoon paprika
- ½ teaspoon cayenne pepper
- Salt and pepper
- 4 cups chicken broth, room temperature
- 2 pounds boneless, skinless chicken thighs, trimmed
- 8 ounces andouille sausage, sliced into ¼-inch thick half-moons
- 6 scallions, sliced thin
- 1 teaspoon distilled white vinegar
- Hot sauce

1. Adjust oven rack to middle position and heat oven to 425 degrees. Place flour in 12-inch skillet and bake, stirring occasionally, until color of ground cinnamon or dark brown sugar, 40 to 55 minutes. (As flour approaches desired color it will take on very nutty aroma that will smell faintly of burnt popcorn and it will need to be stirred more frequently.) Transfer flour to medium bowl and cool. (Toasted flour can be stored in airtight container for up to 1 week.)

2. Heat oil in Dutch oven over medium heat until shimmering. Add onion, pepper, and celery and cook, stirring frequently, until softened, 5 to 7 minutes. Stir in garlic, bay leaves, thyme, paprika, cayenne, ¼ teaspoon salt, and ¼ teaspoon pepper and cook until fragrant, about 1 minute. Stir in 2 cups broth. Add chicken thighs in single layer (they will not be completely submerged by liquid) and bring to simmer. Reduce heat to medium-low, cover, and simmer until chicken is fork tender, 15 to 17 minutes. Transfer chicken to plate.

3. Slowly whisk remaining 2 cups broth into toasted flour until thick, batter-like paste forms. (Add broth in small increments to prevent clumps from forming.) Return pot to medium heat and slowly whisk flour paste into gumbo, making sure each addition is incorporated before adding next. Stir sausage into gumbo. Simmer, uncovered, until gumbo thickens slightly, 20 to 25 minutes.

4. Once cool enough to handle, shred chicken into bite-size pieces. Stir chicken and scallions into gumbo. Remove pot from heat and stir in vinegar and season with salt to taste. Discard bay leaves. Serve, passing hot sauce at table. (Gumbo can be refrigerated in airtight container for up to 24 hours).

HEARTY MINESTRONE

WHY THIS RECIPE WORKS: Excellent minestrone soup relies on perfectly ripe vegetables. But we're often stuck with lackluster supermarket offerings. We wanted a soup that squeezed every ounce of flavor out of supermarket vegetables and was as satisfying as minestrone served in Italy.

To start, we limited our vegetables to a manageable six: onions, celery, carrots, cabbage, zucchini, and tomato. We began our soup by sautéing some finely diced pancetta in a Dutch oven, then browned the vegetables in the rendered fat, which helped develop sweetness and lent a rich flavor. We decided to use cannellini beans (a favorite for their creamy texture and buttery flavor), which we soaked overnight in salted water to ensure they cooked evenly and turned out well seasoned. We added the soaked beans along with the cooking liquid (and a Parmesan rind) and simmered them together vigorously—this helped the beans release their starch to thicken the soup. Once the beans were tender, we returned the vegetables to the pot and simmered everything together. Rather than using all water, we replaced a portion with chicken broth. But it wasn't until we landed on an unusual addition—V8 juice, rather than canned tomatoes—that our soup boasted consistent tomato flavor in every spoonful.

Hearty Minestrone

SERVES 6 TO 8

If you are pressed for time you can "quick-brine" your beans. In step 1, combine the salt, water, and beans in a large Dutch oven and bring to a boil over high heat. Remove the pot from the heat, cover, and let stand 1 hour. Drain and rinse the beans and proceed with the recipe. We prefer cannellini beans, but navy or great Northern beans can be used. We prefer pancetta, but bacon can be used in its place. A Parmesan rind is added for flavor, but can be replaced with a 2-inch chunk of the cheese. In order for the starch from the beans to thicken the soup, it is important to maintain a vigorous simmer in step 3.

- Table salt
- ½ pound dried cannellini beans (about 1 cup), rinsed and picked over (see note)
- 1 tablespoon extra-virgin olive oil, plus extra for serving
- 3 ounces pancetta, cut into ¼-inch pieces (see note)
- 2 medium celery ribs, cut into ½-inch pieces (about ¾ cup)

- 1 medium carrot, peeled and cut into ½-inch pieces (about ¾ cup)
- 2 small onions, peeled and cut into ½-inch pieces (about 1½ cups)
- 1 medium zucchini, trimmed and cut into ½-inch pieces (about 1 cup)
- ½ small head green cabbage, halved, cored, and cut into ½-inch pieces (about 2 cups)
- 2 medium garlic cloves, minced or pressed through a garlic press (about 2 teaspoons)
- ⅛–¼ teaspoon red pepper flakes
- 8 cups water
- 2 cups low-sodium chicken broth
- 1 piece Parmesan cheese rind, about 5 by 2 inches (see note)
- 1 bay leaf
- 1½ cups V8 juice
- ½ cup chopped fresh basil leaves
- Ground black pepper
- Grated Parmesan cheese, for serving

1. Dissolve 1½ tablespoons salt in 2 quarts cold water in a large bowl or container. Add the beans and soak at room temperature for at least 8 hours and up to 24 hours. Drain the beans and rinse well.

2. Heat the oil and pancetta in a large Dutch oven over medium-high heat. Cook, stirring occasionally, until the pancetta is lightly browned and the fat has rendered, 3 to 5 minutes. Add the celery, carrot, onions, and zucchini; cook, stirring frequently, until the vegetables are softened and lightly browned, 5 to 9 minutes. Stir in the cabbage, garlic, ½ teaspoon salt, and red pepper flakes; continue to cook until the cabbage starts to wilt, 1 to 2 minutes longer. Transfer the vegetables to a rimmed baking sheet and set aside.

3. Add the soaked beans, water, broth, Parmesan rind, and bay leaf to the now-empty Dutch oven and bring to a boil over high heat. Reduce the heat and vigorously simmer, stirring occasionally, until the beans are fully tender and the liquid begins to thicken, 45 to 60 minutes.

4. Add the reserved vegetables and V8 juice to the pot; cook until the vegetables are soft, about 15 minutes. Discard the bay leaf and Parmesan rind, stir in the basil, and season with salt and pepper to taste. Serve with olive oil and grated Parmesan.

FARMHOUSE VEGETABLE AND BARLEY SOUP

WHY THIS RECIPE WORKS: Most recipes for hearty winter vegetable soups, it turns out, are neither quick nor easy. For a satisfying soup that doesn't take the better part of a day to make, we started with canned chicken broth. To this we added soy sauce and ground dried porcini mushrooms. These ingredients added a savory, almost meaty flavor to the soup base. To make the soup more filling, we added barley to the hearty combination of carrots, potatoes, leeks, cabbage, and turnips.

Farmhouse Vegetable and Barley Soup

SERVES 6 TO 8

We prefer an acidic, unoaked white wine such as Sauvignon Blanc for this recipe. We love the richness added by the Lemon-Thyme Butter and the crunch of Herbed Croutons (recipes follow) but the soup can also be garnished with crisp bacon or crumbled cheddar cheese. You will need at least a 6-quart Dutch oven for this recipe.

- ⅛ ounce dried porcini mushrooms, rinsed
- 8 sprigs fresh parsley plus 3 tablespoons minced
- 4 sprigs fresh thyme
- 1 bay leaf
- 2 tablespoons unsalted butter
- 1½ pounds leeks, white and light green parts sliced ½ inch thick and washed thoroughly
- 2 carrots, peeled and cut into ½-inch pieces
- 2 celery ribs, cut into ¼-inch pieces
- ⅓ cup dry white wine
- 2 teaspoons soy sauce
- Salt and pepper
- 6 cups water
- 4 cups low-sodium chicken broth or vegetable broth
- ½ cup pearl barley
- 1 garlic clove, peeled and smashed
- 1½ pounds Yukon Gold potatoes, peeled and cut into ½-inch pieces
- 1 turnip, peeled and cut into ¾-inch pieces
- 1½ cups chopped green cabbage
- 1 cup frozen peas
- 1 teaspoon lemon juice

1. Grind mushrooms with spice grinder until they resemble fine meal, 10 to 30 seconds. Measure out 2 teaspoons porcini powder; reserve remainder for another use. Using kitchen twine, tie together parsley sprigs, thyme sprigs, and bay leaf.

2. Melt butter in large Dutch oven over medium heat. Add leeks, carrots, celery, wine, soy sauce, and 2 teaspoons salt.

Cook, stirring occasionally, until liquid has evaporated and celery is softened, about 10 minutes.

3. Add water, chicken broth, barley, porcini powder, herb bundle, and garlic; increase heat to high and bring to boil. Reduce heat to medium-low and simmer, partially covered, for 25 minutes.

4. Add potatoes, turnip, and cabbage; return to simmer and cook until barley, potatoes, turnip, and cabbage are tender, 18 to 20 minutes.

5. Remove pot from heat and remove herb bundle. Stir in peas, lemon juice, and minced parsley; season with salt and pepper to taste. Serve, passing Lemon-Thyme Butter and Herbed Croutons separately.

Lemon-Thyme Butter

MAKES 6 TABLESPOONS

- 6 tablespoons unsalted butter, softened
- 1 tablespoon minced fresh thyme
- ¾ teaspoon finely grated lemon zest plus ¼ teaspoon juice
- Pinch salt

Combine all ingredients in bowl.

Herbed Croutons

MAKES ABOUT 2½ CUPS

Our favorite brand of sandwich bread is Arnold Country Classic White Bread.

- 1 tablespoon unsalted butter
- 1 teaspoon minced fresh parsley
- ½ teaspoon minced fresh thyme
- 4 slices hearty white sandwich bread, cut into ½-inch pieces
- Salt and pepper

Melt butter in 10-inch skillet over medium heat. Add parsley and thyme; cook, stirring constantly, for 20 seconds. Add bread and cook, stirring frequently, until light golden brown, 5 to 10 minutes. Season with salt and pepper to taste.

CLASSIC GAZPACHO

WHY THIS RECIPE WORKS: Spain's famous chilled soup, gazpacho, boasts bright flavors, distinct pieces of vegetables, and a bracing tomato broth. But all too often, gazpacho is either grainy with the addition of too much bread (a common thickener) or watery from an abundance of macerated vegetables. We were after a chunky gazpacho that was well seasoned with vibrant tomato flavor.

We had to figure out the best method for preparing the vegetables. Although it was a breeze to use, the blender broke down our vegetables beyond recognition. Next, we tried the food processor, but even this machine pulverized some of our tomatoes, and the resulting soup was closer to a slushie than a good gazpacho. For the best texture, we had to chop the vegetables by hand.

Tomatoes are the star player in this dish, and early on we decided that full, ripe beefsteaks were the best option. As for peppers, we preferred red over green for their sweeter flavor. Onion and garlic are usually too overpowering in gazpacho, so we kept to modest levels. A combination of tomato juice and ice cubes—to help chill the soup—provided the right amount of liquid for our broth. And instead of using bread as a thickener, we saved it to make croutons. Now our gazpacho was nice and chunky, and brightly flavored.

Classic Gazpacho

SERVES 8 TO 10

This recipe makes a large quantity, but it can be easily halved if you prefer. Traditionally, the same vegetables used in the soup are also used as garnish. If that appeals to you, cut additional vegetables while you prepare those called for in the recipe. Other garnish possibilities include Garlic Croutons (recipe follows), chopped pitted black olives, chopped Foolproof Hard-Cooked Eggs (page 38), and finely diced avocado.

- 3 medium ripe beefsteak tomatoes (about 1½ pounds), cored and cut into ¼-inch cubes (about 4 cups)
- 2 medium red bell peppers (about 1 pound), stemmed, seeded, and cut into ¼-inch cubes (about 2 cups)
- 2 small cucumbers (about 1 pound), one peeled and the other with skin on, both seeded and cut into ¼-inch cubes (about 2 cups)
- ½ small sweet onion (such as Vidalia, Maui, or Walla Walla) or 2 large shallots, minced (about ½ cup)
- 2 medium garlic cloves, minced or pressed through a garlic press (about 2 teaspoons)
- ⅓ cup sherry vinegar
- Table salt and ground black pepper
- 5 cups tomato juice
- 8 ice cubes
- 1 teaspoon hot pepper sauce (optional)
- Extra-virgin olive oil, for serving

1. Combine the tomatoes, peppers, cucumbers, onion, garlic, vinegar, 2 teaspoons salt, and pepper to taste in a large (at least 4-quart) nonreactive bowl. Let stand until the vegetables just begin to release their juices, about 5 minutes. Stir in the tomato juice, ice cubes, and hot pepper sauce (if using). Cover tightly and refrigerate to blend flavors, at least 4 hours and up to 2 days.

2. Season with salt and pepper to taste and remove and discard any unmelted ice cubes. Serve cold, drizzling each portion with about 1 teaspoon olive oil and topping with the desired garnishes (see note).

Garlic Croutons

MAKES ABOUT 3 CUPS

- 3 tablespoons extra-virgin olive oil
- 3 medium garlic cloves, minced or pressed through a garlic press (about 1 tablespoon)
- ¼ teaspoon table salt
- 6 slices high-quality white sandwich bread, cut into ½-inch cubes (about 3 cups)

1. Adjust an oven rack to the middle position and heat the oven to 350 degrees. Combine the oil, garlic, and salt in a small bowl; let stand 20 minutes, then pour through a fine-mesh strainer into a medium bowl. Discard the garlic. Add the bread cubes to the bowl with the oil and toss to coat.

2. Spread the bread cubes in an even layer on a rimmed baking sheet and bake, stirring occasionally, until golden, about 15 minutes. Cool on the baking sheet to room temperature. (The croutons can be stored in an airtight container or a plastic bag for up to 1 day.)

GAZPACHO ANDALUZ

WHY THIS RECIPE WORKS: In the States, the classic "liquid salsa" style of gazpacho reigns supreme. But in Spain, the birthplace of gazpacho, a variety of styles abound. The most popular type by far comes from Andalusia, the southernmost region of the country. It starts with the same vegetables as its chunky cousin, but is blended with bread to give it some body. The result is a creamy, complex soup. But unless you have fresh, flavorful vegetables, in particular fresh, ripe tomatoes, this soup can be unremarkable and bland.

So how could we ensure a flavorful gazpacho if we had to rely on supermarket tomatoes? In a word, salt. Salting gave our tomatoes—even mid-winter specimens—a deep, full flavor. Figuring the same process could only improve the cucumbers, onions, and bell peppers, we salted them as well. To maximize the flavor of our soup even more, we soaked the bread in a portion of the vegetables' exuded liquid, rather than water. With a garnish of chopped vegetables, fresh herbs, and drizzles of extra-virgin olive oil and sherry vinegar, this Spanish classic can be enjoyed any time of the year.

Creamy Gazpacho Andaluz

SERVES 4 TO 6

For ideal flavor, allow the gazpacho to sit in the refrigerator overnight. Serve the soup with additional extra-virgin olive oil, sherry vinegar, ground black pepper, and the reserved diced vegetables. Red wine vinegar can be substituted for the sherry vinegar. Although we prefer kosher salt in this soup, half the amount of table salt can be used.

- 3 pounds (about 6 medium) ripe tomatoes, cored
- 1 small cucumber, peeled, halved, and seeded
- 1 medium green bell pepper, halved, cored, and seeded
- 1 small red onion, peeled and halved
- 2 medium garlic cloves, peeled and quartered
- 1 small serrano chile, stemmed and halved lengthwise
- Kosher salt (see note)
- 1 slice high-quality white sandwich bread, crust removed, torn into 1-inch pieces
- ½ cup extra-virgin olive oil, plus extra for serving
- 2 tablespoons sherry vinegar, plus extra for serving (see note)
- 2 tablespoons finely minced parsley, chives, or basil leaves
- Ground black pepper

1. Roughly chop 2 pounds of the tomatoes, half of the cucumber, half of the bell pepper, and half of the onion and place in a large bowl. Add the garlic, chile, and 1½ teaspoons salt; toss until well combined. Set aside.

2. Cut the remaining tomatoes, cucumber, and pepper into ¼-inch dice; place the vegetables in a medium bowl. Mince the remaining onion and add to the diced vegetables. Toss with ½ teaspoon salt and transfer to a fine-mesh strainer set over a medium bowl. Set aside for 1 hour.

3. Transfer the drained diced vegetables to a medium bowl and set aside. Add the bread pieces to the exuded liquid (there should be about ¼ cup) and soak for 1 minute. Add the soaked bread and any remaining liquid to the roughly chopped vegetables and toss thoroughly to combine.

4. Transfer half of the vegetable-bread mixture to a blender and process for 30 seconds. With the blender running, slowly drizzle in ¼ cup of the oil and continue to blend until completely smooth, about 2 minutes. Strain the soup through a fine-mesh strainer into a large bowl, using the back of a ladle or rubber spatula to press the soup through the strainer. Repeat with the remaining vegetable-bread mixture and ¼ cup more olive oil.

5. Stir the vinegar, parsley, and half of the diced vegetables into the soup and season with salt and pepper to taste. Cover and refrigerate overnight or for at least 2 hours to chill completely and develop the flavors. Serve, passing the remaining diced vegetables, olive oil, vinegar, and pepper separately.

WHITE GAZPACHO

WHY THIS RECIPE WORKS: Spanish white gazpacho, or *ajo blanco*, predates the familiar red version. It is a silky soup that requires only a handful of ingredients: almonds, garlic, bread, vinegar, and water. It's served ice-cold and garnished with almonds, sliced grapes, or even peppery olive oil. At its best, it is a study in contrasts: Some bites offer a nutty crunch, while others are sharply fruity and floral. But the first batches we whipped up were far from impressive. Some were watery and bland; others were grainy and salad dressing-esque. We wanted to nail down a foolproof way to make this chilled soup.

When it came to technique, we found that the order in which we added ingredients to the blender made all the difference. First, we buzzed the almonds until they were powdery, then added bread (which had been soaked in water), a clove of garlic, a splash of sherry vinegar, and salt and pepper. Once these ingredients were pureed, we drizzled in the olive oil and finally thinned the soup with more water. We liked the fruity, peppery pop that we got from premium olive oil. The sherry vinegar and a pinch of cayenne added brightness and bite. For just a hint of flowery bitter almond flavor, we mixed a tablespoon of the pureed soup with 1/8 teaspoon almond extract, then stirred a teaspoon of the mixture back into the soup. For garnishes, we thinly sliced green grapes and toasted a few almonds in oil to add crunch. An extra drizzle of olive oil made for a rich finish and a beautiful presentation.

Spanish Chilled Almond and Garlic Soup

SERVES 6 TO 8

This rich soup is best when served in small portions (about 6 ounces). Use a good-quality extra-virgin olive oil. Our favorite supermarket brand is California Olive Ranch Everyday Extra Virgin Olive Oil. Too much almond extract can ruin the soup. Hence, the unusual mixing technique in step 4.

- 6 slices hearty white sandwich bread, crusts removed
- 4 cups water
- 2½ cups (8¾ ounces) plus ⅓ cup sliced blanched almonds
- 1 garlic clove, peeled
- 3 tablespoons sherry vinegar
- Kosher salt and pepper
- Pinch cayenne pepper
- ½ cup extra-virgin olive oil, plus extra for drizzling
- ⅛ teaspoon almond extract
- 2 teaspoons vegetable oil
- 6 ounces seedless green grapes, sliced thin (1 cup)

1. Combine bread and water in bowl and let soak for 5 minutes. Process 2½ cups almonds in blender until finely ground, about 30 seconds, scraping down sides of blender jar as needed.

2. Using your hands, remove bread from water, squeeze it lightly, and transfer to blender with almonds. Measure 3 cups soaking water and set aside; transfer remaining soaking water to blender.

3. Add garlic, vinegar, 1¼ teaspoons salt, and cayenne to blender and process until mixture has consistency of cake batter, 30 to 45 seconds. With blender running, add olive oil in thin, steady stream, about 30 seconds. Add reserved soaking water and process for 1 minute. Season with salt and pepper to taste. Strain soup through fine-mesh strainer set in bowl, pressing on solids to extract liquid.

4. Measure 1 tablespoon of soup into second bowl and stir in almond extract. Return 1 teaspoon of extract mixture to soup; discard remainder. Chill for at least 3 hours or up to 24 hours.

5. Heat vegetable oil in 8-inch skillet over medium-high heat until oil begins to shimmer. Add remaining ⅓ cup almonds and cook, stirring constantly, until golden brown, 3 to 4 minutes. Immediately transfer to bowl and stir in ¼ teaspoon salt.

6. Ladle soup into shallow bowls. Mound an equal amount of grapes in center of each bowl. Sprinkle cooled almonds over soup and drizzle with extra-virgin olive oil. Serve immediately.

CALDO VERDE

WHY THIS RECIPE WORKS: This soup of sausage, potatoes, and hearty greens is a staple in many Portuguese households. While the flavors are rich, it's not a heavy soup. Without changing the soup's essentially light character, we wanted to create a slightly heartier result—something that could function as a main course.

To start, we replaced the hard-to-find Portuguese linguiça sausage with widely available Spanish-style chorizo, which boasts a similar garlicky profile. We sautéed the sausage right in the Dutch oven in just 1 tablespoon of olive oil, eliminating the need to dirty an extra skillet. For deeper flavor, we split the water with an equal amount of chicken broth. Collard greens offered a more delicate sweetness and a meatier bite than kale, and chopping the leaves into bite-size pieces made them more spoon-friendly. Finally, we swapped out starchy russet potatoes for sturdy Yukon Golds, which held their shape during cooking. Pureeing some of the potatoes and a few tablespoons of olive oil into our soup base made a creamier, heartier dish. A bit of white wine vinegar brightened the pot.

Caldo Verde

SERVES 6 TO 8

We prefer collard greens, but kale can be substituted. Serve this soup with hearty bread and, for added richness, a final drizzle of extra-virgin olive oil.

- ¼ cup extra-virgin olive oil
- 12 ounces Spanish-style chorizo sausage, cut into ½-inch pieces
- 1 onion, chopped fine
- 4 garlic cloves, minced
- Salt and pepper
- ¼ teaspoon red pepper flakes
- 2 pounds Yukon Gold potatoes, peeled and cut into ¾-inch pieces
- 4 cups chicken broth
- 4 cups water
- 1 pound collard greens, stemmed and cut into 1-inch pieces
- 2 teaspoons white wine vinegar

1. Heat 1 tablespoon oil in Dutch oven over medium-high heat until shimmering. Add chorizo and cook, stirring occasionally, until lightly browned, 4 to 5 minutes. Transfer chorizo to bowl and set aside. Reduce heat to medium and add onion, garlic, 1¼ teaspoons salt, and pepper flakes and season with pepper to taste. Cook, stirring frequently, until onion is translucent, 2 to 3 minutes. Add potatoes, broth, and water; increase heat to high and bring to boil. Reduce heat to medium-low and simmer, uncovered, until potatoes are just tender, 8 to 10 minutes.

2. Transfer ¾ cup solids and ¾ cup broth to blender jar. Add collard greens to pot and simmer for 10 minutes. Stir in chorizo and continue to simmer until greens are tender, 8 to 10 minutes longer.

3. Add remaining 3 tablespoons oil to soup in blender and process until very smooth and homogeneous, about 1 minute. Remove pot from heat and stir pureed soup mixture and vinegar into soup. Season with salt and pepper to taste, and serve. (Soup can be refrigerated for up to 2 days.)

CORN CHOWDER

WHY THIS RECIPE WORKS: We were looking for a corn chowder recipe that would pack lots of corn flavor in every spoonful while still maintaining a satisfying, yet not too thick, chowder texture. Inspired by a recipe we found that juiced corn kernels, a trick that delivered pronounced corn flavor, we strained the scrapings and pulp from several cobs through a kitchen towel to get unadulterated corn juice (when we added the unstrained pulp to the pot, the soup curdled). This delivered the intense corn flavor we were after. We lightened things up by using water as our primary liquid, which allowed the pure corn flavor to shine through, then added just 1 cup of half-and-half to give our chowder the right richness. A sprinkling of basil before serving lent a fresh finish.

Lighter Corn Chowder

SERVES 6

When removing the kernels from the cob make sure to remove only the part of the kernel sticking out of the cob. Cutting deeper will result in too much fibrous material coming off the corn. Yukon Gold potatoes can be substituted for the red potatoes. Minced chives can be used in place of the basil.

- 8 ears corn, husks and silk removed
- 3 tablespoons unsalted butter
- 1 medium onion, chopped fine
- 4 ounces (about 4 slices) bacon, halved lengthwise, then cut crosswise into ¼-inch pieces
- 2 teaspoons minced fresh thyme leaves
- Table salt and ground black pepper
- ¼ cup unbleached all-purpose flour
- 5 cups water
- 12 ounces red potatoes, cut into ½-inch cubes
- 1 cup half-and-half
- Sugar
- 3 tablespoons chopped fresh basil leaves

1. Using a chef's knife, cut the kernels from the ears of corn; transfer to a bowl and set aside (you should have 5 to 6 cups). Holding the cobs over a second bowl, use the back of a butter knife to firmly scrape any pulp remaining on the cobs into the bowl (you should have 2 to 2½ cups of pulp).

Transfer the pulp to the center of a clean kitchen towel set in a medium bowl. Wrap the towel tightly around the pulp and squeeze until dry. Discard the pulp in the towel and set the corn juice aside (you should have about ⅔ cup of juice).

2. Melt the butter in a Dutch oven over medium heat. Add the onion, bacon, thyme, 2 teaspoons salt, and 1 teaspoon pepper and cook, stirring frequently, until the onion is softened and beginning to brown, 8 to 10 minutes. Stir in the flour and cook, stirring constantly, for 2 minutes. Whisking constantly, gradually add the water and then bring to a boil. Add the corn kernels and the potatoes. Return to a simmer, reduce the heat to medium-low, and cook until the potatoes have softened, 15 to 18 minutes.

3. Transfer 2 cups of the chowder to a blender and process until smooth, 1 to 2 minutes. Return the puree to the pot, stir in the half-and-half, and return to a simmer. Remove the pot from the heat and stir in the reserved corn juice. Season with salt, pepper, and up to 1 tablespoon sugar to taste. Sprinkle with the basil and serve.

NEW ENGLAND CLAM CHOWDER

WHY THIS RECIPE WORKS: Good traditional chowder isn't that hard to make, but it can be daunting for the home cook. The biggest hurdle is a finicky ingredient that most people don't know how to work with—clams. We wanted to come up with a clam chowder that was economical, could be prepared quickly, and provided a simple method for working with the star ingredient.

We tested a variety of clams and ultimately found that medium-size hard-shell clams guaranteed the most clam flavor. Rather than shucking the raw clams (which can be tedious and time-consuming) and adding them to the pot, we steamed the clams to open them, then used the steaming liquid as our broth. The steamed clams had to be pulled from the pot when they had just opened; allowing them to open completely meant they would overcook quickly when returned to the soup to heat through. We found waxy red potatoes to be the best choice for our creamy chowder; high-starch potatoes, like russets, broke down too much. Bacon made a nice substitute for the traditional salt pork and gave our chowder great smoky flavor. As for the creaminess factor, using a modest amount of heavy cream instead of milk meant that we could use less dairy for a rich, creamy chowder that tasted distinctly of clams.

New England Clam Chowder

SERVES 6

Don't skip the step of scrubbing the clams; many clams have bits of sand embedded in their shells that can ruin a pot of chowder. To remove the sand, simply scrub them under cold, running water using a soft brush.

- 7 pounds medium-size hard-shell clams, such as cherrystones, washed and scrubbed clean (see note)
- 5 ounces (about 3 slices) thick-cut bacon, cut into ¼-inch pieces
- 1 large onion, chopped medium
- 2 tablespoons unbleached all-purpose flour
- 1½ pounds red potatoes (about 4 medium), cut into ½-inch chunks
- 1 bay leaf
- 1 teaspoon fresh thyme leaves or ¼ teaspoon dried thyme
- 1 cup heavy cream
- 2 tablespoons minced fresh parsley leaves
- Table salt and ground black pepper

1. Bring 3 cups water to a boil in a large Dutch oven. Add the clams and cover with a tight-fitting lid. Cook for 5 minutes, uncover, and stir with a wooden spoon. Quickly cover the pot and steam until the clams just open, 2 to 4 minutes. (Don't let the clams open completely.) Transfer the clams to a large bowl and cool slightly; reserve the broth. Open the clams with a paring knife, holding the clams over a bowl to catch any juices. With the knife, sever the muscle that attaches the clam to the bottom shell and transfer the meat to a cutting board; discard the shells. Mince the clams and set aside. Pour the clam broth into a large bowl, holding back the last few tablespoons of broth in case of sediment; set the clam broth aside. (You should have about 5 cups. If not, add bottled clam juice or water to make this amount.) Rinse and dry the pot, then return the pot to the burner.

2. Fry the bacon in the pot over medium-low heat until the fat renders and the bacon crisps, 5 to 7 minutes. Add the onion and cook, stirring occasionally, until softened, about 5 minutes. Add the flour and stir until lightly colored, about 1 minute. Gradually whisk in the reserved clam broth. Add the potatoes, bay leaf, and thyme and simmer until the potatoes are tender, about 10 minutes. Add the clams, cream, parsley, and salt and pepper to taste; bring to a simmer. Remove from the heat, discard the bay leaf, and serve.

VEGETABLE BROTH BASE

WHY THIS RECIPE WORKS: Homemade broth enlivens any dish, but for vegetarian cooking, an overpowering broth can be ruinous. For our base, we focused on mild but impactful vegetables. Mirepoix, a mix of chopped onions, celery, and carrots, is a classic combination; we started there, swapping in leeks for their mild onion flavor and minimal moisture content. Celery root had a creamier, more complex celery taste. Dried minced onions reinforced the leeks and carrots contributed pleasant sweetness. Tomato paste and soy sauce bolstered the savory qualities and parsley added brightness. Kosher salt seasoned the broth while keeping it convenient: Salt lowers water's freezing point, so the concentrate would remain easy to scoop. Even better, our base had less salt than most store-bought broths. Creating the base was easy: We pulsed the ingredients in a food processor and froze the paste.

Vegetable Broth Base

MAKES ABOUT 1¾ CUPS BASE; ENOUGH FOR 7 QUARTS BROTH

For the best balance of flavors, measure the prepped vegetables by weight. Kosher salt aids in grinding the vegetables. The broth base contains enough salt to keep it from freezing solid, making it easy to remove 1 tablespoon at a time. To make 1 cup of broth, stir 1 tablespoon of fresh or frozen broth base into 1 cup of boiling water. If particle-free broth is desired, let the broth steep for 5 minutes and then strain it through a fine-mesh strainer.

- 2 leeks, white and light green parts only, chopped and washed thoroughly (2½ cups or 5 ounces)
- 2 carrots, peeled and cut into ½-inch pieces (⅔ cup or 3 ounces)
- ½ small celery root, peeled and cut into ½-inch pieces (¾ cup or 3 ounces)
- ½ cup (½ ounce) parsley leaves and thin stems
- 3 tablespoons dried minced onions
- 2 tablespoons kosher salt
- 1½ tablespoons tomato paste
- 3 tablespoons soy sauce

Process leeks, carrots, celery root, parsley, minced onions, and salt in food processor, scraping down sides of bowl frequently, until paste is as fine as possible, 3 to 4 minutes. Add tomato paste and process for 1 minute, scraping down sides of bowl every 20 seconds. Add soy sauce and continue to process 1 minute longer. Transfer mixture to airtight container and tap firmly on counter to remove air bubbles. Press small piece of parchment paper flush against surface of mixture and cover. Freeze for up to 6 months.

BEHIND THE SCENES

MAKING GOOD TV IN THE TEST KITCHEN

The process of creating our show begins several months before filming starts, in all-day script meetings. A group of six editors argues the merits of each recipe developed in the test kitchen for *Cook's Illustrated* magazine during the past year, choosing only the very best recipes to present on television. We're looking for recipes that not only taste great (obviously) but are also visually and editorially interesting. Passions run high, and coming to an agreement isn't always so easy or smooth. One year, for a show on drive-in specials, some editors rooted for pairing frothy chocolate milkshakes with hamburgers. Sounds good, but in the end, the process of making the milkshakes—dump ingredients into a blender and press a button—turned out to be as interesting as watching paint dry. The result? Goodbye milkshakes, hello oven-fried onion rings.

Once the recipe lineup is settled, we then spend several months hammering out scripts. Instead of mapping out dialogue, these scripts detail what the camera is going to see—for example: "Julia chops onions and then sautés them in a 12-inch skillet with pinch of salt until golden, about 5 minutes." So why do we write our scripts this way? Cooking is the heart of the show and it's why, we hope, you tune in. And frankly, Julia and Bridget and the chefs don't need scripts to banter (or argue) with each other. They've had plenty of practice at script meetings.

CHAPTER 2

SALAD DAYS

FOOLPROOF VINAIGRETTES

WHY THIS RECIPE WORKS: Vinaigrettes often seem a little slipshod—harsh and bristling in one bite, dull and oily in the next. We were determined to nail down a formula for the perfect vinaigrette, one that would consistently yield a homogeneous, harmonious blend of bright vinegar and rich oil in every forkful.

For starters, top-notch ingredients are crucial. Balsamic vinegar works best with more assertive greens. Fruity extra-virgin olive oil is preferred as an all-purpose oil option, while walnut oil is best for nuttier vinaigrettes. As for mixing methods, whisking together the ingredients only gets you so far. A key ingredient—mayonnaise—is necessary to emulsify (bind together) the oil and vinegar for a stabilized, smooth dressing.

Foolproof Vinaigrette

MAKES ABOUT ¼ CUP, ENOUGH TO DRESS 8 TO 10 CUPS LIGHTLY PACKED GREENS

Red wine, white wine, or champagne vinegar will work in this recipe; however, it is important to use high-quality ingredients (see pages 926–927 for our top-rated brands of white wine vinegar and red wine vinegar and page 916 for our top-rated brand of extra-virgin olive oil). This vinaigrette works with nearly any type of green (as do the walnut and herb variations). For a hint of garlic flavor, rub the inside of the salad bowl with a cut clove of garlic before adding the lettuce.

- 1 tablespoon wine vinegar (see note)
- 1½ teaspoons very finely minced shallot
- ½ teaspoon regular or light mayonnaise
- ½ teaspoon Dijon mustard
- ⅛ teaspoon table salt
- Ground black pepper
- 3 tablespoons extra-virgin olive oil (see note)

1. Combine the vinegar, shallot, mayonnaise, mustard, salt, and pepper to taste in a small nonreactive bowl. Whisk until the mixture is milky in appearance and no lumps of mayonnaise remain.

2. Place the oil in a small measuring cup so that it is easy to pour. Whisking constantly, very slowly drizzle the oil into the vinegar mixture. If pools of oil are gathering on the surface as you whisk, stop adding the oil and whisk the mixture well to combine, then resume whisking in the oil in a slow stream. The vinaigrette should be glossy and lightly thickened, with no pools of oil on its surface.

Foolproof Lemon Vinaigrette

This vinaigrette is best for dressing mild greens.

Follow the recipe for Foolproof Vinaigrette, substituting lemon juice for the vinegar, omitting the shallot, and adding ¼ teaspoon finely grated lemon zest and a pinch of sugar along with the salt and pepper.

Foolproof Balsamic-Mustard Vinaigrette

This vinaigrette is best for dressing assertive greens. See page 926 for our top-rated brand of balsamic vinegar.

Follow the recipe for Foolproof Vinaigrette, substituting balsamic vinegar for the wine vinegar, increasing the mustard to 2 teaspoons, and adding ½ teaspoon chopped fresh thyme along with the salt and pepper.

Foolproof Walnut Vinaigrette

Follow the recipe for Foolproof Vinaigrette, substituting 1½ tablespoons roasted walnut oil and 1½ tablespoons regular olive oil for the extra-virgin olive oil.

Foolproof Herb Vinaigrette

Follow the recipe for Foolproof Vinaigrette, adding 1 tablespoon minced fresh parsley leaves or chives and ½ teaspoon minced fresh thyme, tarragon, marjoram, or oregano leaves to the vinaigrette just before use.

LEAFY GREEN SALAD WITH RED WINE VINAIGRETTE

WHY THIS RECIPE WORKS: A leafy green salad with red wine vinaigrette is a vital recipe to have in your arsenal. We wanted to develop a recipe for this basic salad—a mix of well-chosen greens tossed with a light vinaigrette that was neither harsh nor oily. We went back to the basics and revisited standard vinaigrette proportions. In most cases, 4 parts oil to 1 part vinegar produces the best balance of flavors in a vinaigrette, so that's where we started. Red wine vinegar was the foundation of our vinaigrette. Before whisking the vinaigrette ingredients together, we added salt and pepper to the vinegar. This step mutes these seasonings a bit and prevents them from becoming too overpowering. With the right mix of salad greens—we like a combination of mild, delicate greens and peppery greens—this leafy salad makes the perfect complement to any main dish.

Leafy Green Salad with Red Wine Vinaigrette

SERVES 4 TO 6

For the best results, use at least two kinds of greens. A blend of mild, delicate greens, such as Boston and leaf lettuces, and peppery greens, such as arugula and watercress, is ideal. Romaine adds crunch and texture. If you like, add mild fresh herbs, such as chives, tarragon, or basil, in small amounts.

- 2¼ teaspoons red wine vinegar
- ⅛ teaspoon table salt
- Pinch ground black pepper
- 3 tablespoons extra-virgin olive oil
- 8 cups mixed salad greens, washed, dried, and torn into bite-sized pieces (see note)

Combine the vinegar, salt, and pepper in a bowl; add the oil and whisk until combined. Place the greens in a large bowl, drizzle the vinaigrette over the greens, and toss to coat evenly. Serve.

LEAFY GREEN SALAD WITH RICH AND CREAMY BLUE CHEESE DRESSING

WHY THIS RECIPE WORKS: Cool and crunchy salad greens coated with creamy blue cheese dressing are simply irresistible. But getting the right proportion of dressing to greens can be tricky. We wanted lettuce lightly napped with a creamy, tangy dressing.

Starting with the dressing, we found that the secret to proper flavor and texture was in using the right creamy components. We determined that three creamy ingredients were essential: mayonnaise to give the dressing body, sour cream to supply tang, and buttermilk to thin out and further reinforce the dressing's bold flavors. A bit of sugar brought some much-needed sweetness, and white wine vinegar gave our dressing some zing. As for the main ingredient, we ruled out really pungent blue cheeses as too overpowering; a mild blue cheese works best. For the right chunky consistency, we mixed the crumbled blue cheese with the buttermilk before adding any other ingredients.

Leafy Green Salad with Rich and Creamy Blue Cheese Dressing

SERVES 4 TO 6

Sturdy romaine and curly leaf lettuce hold up well to this thick dressing. In a pinch, whole milk can be used in place of the buttermilk; the dressing will be a bit lighter and milder in flavor, but will still taste good.

- 2½ ounces blue cheese, crumbled (about ½ cup)
- 3 tablespoons buttermilk (see note)
- 3 tablespoons sour cream
- 2 tablespoons mayonnaise
- 2 teaspoons white wine vinegar
- ¼ teaspoon sugar
- ⅛ teaspoon garlic powder
- Table salt and ground black pepper
- 10 cups loosely packed sturdy salad greens, such as romaine or curly leaf lettuce, washed, dried, and torn into bite size pieces (see note)

1. Mash the blue cheese and buttermilk in a small bowl with a fork until the mixture resembles cottage cheese with small curds. Stir in the sour cream, mayonnaise, vinegar, sugar, and garlic powder and season with salt and pepper to taste. (The dressing can be refrigerated in an airtight container for up to 2 weeks.)

2. Place the greens in a large bowl. Pour the dressing over the greens and toss to coat evenly. Serve.

SPICY SALAD WITH MUSTARD AND BALSAMIC VINAIGRETTE

WHY THIS RECIPE WORKS: Some salads act as humble introductions to the main course, while other salads demand attention and pack a flavor punch all their own. We had a craving for a bold salad, one using spicy and bitter greens dressed in a pungent, mustardy vinaigrette.

We started by focusing on the greens, and chose peppery greens like arugula and watercress. We envisioned this salad as standing up to rich main dishes, like fettuccine Alfredo or a hearty meat stew, so we used both balsamic vinegar and Dijon mustard as the acidic components. Minced shallot provided another strong flavor and added a bit of texture to our vinaigrette. We mixed the greens and vinaigrette together a little at a time to ensure that all the greens were well covered. Boldly flavored, this spicy salad with mustard and balsamic vinaigrette will wake up any dulled palate.

Spicy Salad with Mustard and Balsamic Vinaigrette

SERVES 8 TO 10

This salad makes a perfect partner to rich main dishes, like lasagna, because its bitter greens and zesty vinaigrette help to cut the richness.

- 6 tablespoons extra-virgin olive oil
- 4 teaspoons balsamic vinegar
- 1 tablespoon Dijon mustard
- 1 teaspoon finely minced shallot
- ¼ teaspoon table salt
- ⅛ teaspoon ground black pepper
- 16 cups spicy greens, such as arugula, watercress, mizuna, and baby mustard greens, washed and dried

Whisk the oil, vinegar, mustard, shallot, salt, and pepper together in a bowl until combined. Place the greens in a large bowl, drizzle the dressing over the greens a little at a time, and toss to coat evenly, adding more vinaigrette if the greens seem dry. Serve.

WILTED SPINACH SALAD

WHY THIS RECIPE WORKS: Traditional wilted spinach salad, tossed with warm bacon dressing, makes for an appealing and elegant salad. But too often, this salad is a soggy mess of slimy spinach, bogged down from too much oil and too much heat. We wanted perfectly wilted spinach, a rich, balanced dressing, and crisp pieces of meaty bacon throughout.

Baby spinach was preferred over the mature variety for its tender, sweet qualities. Fried thick-cut bacon provided more textural interest than regular sliced bacon. And using the bacon fat left in the skillet to cook our onion and garlic gave the finished salad a smoky flavor. For the vinaigrette, a generous amount of cider vinegar, enhanced with sugar, cut the richness of the bacon fat. We found that pouring the hot vinaigrette right over the baby spinach provided enough heat to wilt the spinach without saturating it. With wedges of hard-cooked egg for some heartiness, this wilted spinach salad delivers on all fronts.

Wilted Spinach Salad with Warm Bacon Dressing

SERVES 4 TO 6

This salad comes together quickly, so have the ingredients ready before you begin cooking. When adding the vinegar mixture to the skillet, step back from the stovetop—the aroma is quite potent.

- 6 ounces baby spinach (about 6 cups), washed and dried
- 3 tablespoons cider vinegar
- ½ teaspoon sugar
- ¼ teaspoon ground black pepper
- Pinch table salt
- 10 ounces (about 8 slices) thick-cut bacon, cut into ½-inch pieces
- ½ medium red onion, chopped medium
- 1 small garlic clove, minced or pressed through a garlic press (about ½ teaspoon)
- 3 hard-cooked eggs (recipe follows), peeled and quartered

1. Place the spinach in a large bowl. Whisk the vinegar, sugar, pepper, and salt in a small bowl until the sugar dissolves; set aside.

2. Fry the bacon in a medium skillet over medium-high heat, stirring occasionally, until crisp, about 10 minutes. Using a slotted spoon, transfer the bacon to a paper towel–lined plate. Pour off all but 3 tablespoons of the bacon fat left in the pan. Add the onion to the skillet and cook over medium heat, stirring frequently, until softened, about 3 minutes. Stir in the garlic and cook until fragrant, about 15 seconds. Add the vinegar mixture, then remove the skillet from the heat. Working quickly, scrape the bottom of the skillet with a wooden spoon to loosen the browned bits. Pour the hot dressing over the spinach, add the bacon, and toss gently until the spinach is slightly wilted. Divide the salad among individual plates, arrange the egg quarters over each, and serve.

Foolproof Hard-Cooked Eggs

MAKES 3

You can double or triple this recipe as long as you use a pot large enough to hold the eggs in a single layer, covered by an inch of water.

- 3 large eggs

1. Place the eggs in a medium saucepan, cover with 1 inch of water, and bring to a boil over high heat. Remove the pan from the heat, cover, and let sit for 10 minutes. Meanwhile, fill a medium bowl with 1 quart water and one tray of ice cubes.

2. Transfer the eggs to the ice bath with a slotted spoon and let sit for 5 minutes. Peel the eggs.

ARUGULA SALAD

WHY THIS RECIPE WORKS: Unlike everyday iceberg lettuce, spicy arugula is more than just a leafy backdrop for salad garnishes. But arugula's complex, peppery flavor also makes it something of a challenge to pair with other ingredients. We wanted a truly outstanding arugula-based salad with co-starring ingredients that would stand up to these spicy greens.

Salad combinations with harsh, one-dimensional flavor profiles (adding radishes and lemon-buttermilk dressing to arugula, for example) struck out, with too much abrasive flavor. What we did like were the salads containing fruit and cheese, so we decided to pair our arugula with sweet and salty ingredients. Fried prosciutto strips and shaved Parmesan fit the bill when it came to upping the saltiness of our salad. A spoonful of jam added to the vinaigrette helped to emulsify the dressing and provided a sweet contrast to arugula's peppery bite. For additional sweetness, dried figs worked well and toasted walnuts delivered just the right amount of crunch.

BEHIND THE SCENES

STAYING GREEN IN THE TEST KITCHEN

It's not unusual for the test kitchen fridge to be packed with salad greens. And although we try to work with the greens the day they arrive, it's not always a possibility. As a result, we've come up with a couple of storage tips for greens. First, remove any rubber band or tie from the greens. Constriction only encourages rotting. Gently wash the greens and spin them dry in a salad spinner. Then depending on the type of greens, store them one of two ways:

For delicate greens, line an empty salad spinner with paper towels. Layer the dried greens in the bowl, covering each layer with additional towels, and refrigerate. Greens stored in this manner should keep for at least two days.

For sturdier greens, loosely roll the leaves in paper towels, then seal in a zipper-lock bag and refrigerate. Greens stored this way should keep for up to one week.

We applied our storage techniques to basil too, especially because recipes often call for just a few leaves. First, we found that it's essential not to wash the basil before storage. In our tests, washing basil before storage decreased its storage life by half. Instead, gently wrap basil in a damp paper towel. It should keep for up to one week.

Arugula Salad with Figs, Prosciutto, Walnuts, and Parmesan

SERVES 6

Although frying the prosciutto adds crisp texture to the salad, if you prefer, you can simply cut it into ribbons and use it as a garnish. Honey can be substituted for the jam in either of these salads.

- 4 tablespoons extra-virgin olive oil
- 2 ounces thinly sliced prosciutto, cut into ¼-inch strips
- 3 tablespoons balsamic vinegar
- 1 tablespoon raspberry jam
- ½ cup dried figs, stems removed, fruit chopped into ¼-inch pieces
- 1 small shallot, minced (about 1 tablespoon)
- Table salt and ground black pepper
- 5 ounces loosely packed baby arugula (about 5 cups), washed and dried
- ½ cup walnuts, toasted and chopped
- 2 ounces Parmesan cheese, shaved into thin strips with a vegetable peeler

1. Heat 1 tablespoon of the oil in a 10-inch nonstick skillet over medium heat; add the prosciutto and fry until crisp, stirring frequently, about 7 minutes. Using a slotted spoon, transfer to a paper towel–lined plate and set aside to cool.

2. Whisk the vinegar and jam together in a medium microwave-safe bowl until combined; stir in the figs. Cover with plastic wrap, cut several steam vents in the plastic, and microwave on high until the figs are plump, 30 seconds to 1 minute. Whisk in the remaining 3 tablespoons oil, the shallot, ¼ teaspoon salt, and ⅛ teaspoon pepper until combined. Cool to room temperature.

3. Toss the arugula with the vinaigrette in a large bowl; season with salt and pepper to taste. Divide the salad among individual plates; top each with a portion of the prosciutto, walnuts, and Parmesan. Serve.

BAKED GOAT CHEESE SALAD

WHY THIS RECIPE WORKS: Warm goat cheese salad has been a fixture on restaurant menus for years, featuring artisanal cheeses, organic greens, barrel-aged vinegars, and imported oils. But too often what arrives is an unremarkable salad at a price that defies reason. We wanted to bring this restaurant favorite home with creamy cheese rounds infused with the flavor of fresh herbs and surrounded by crisp, golden breading, all cradled by lightly dressed greens.

Ground Melba toasts (those ultra-dry and crispy crackers) made the crispiest crust for the goat cheese. After dipping the cheese rounds in beaten egg and herbs, we coated them with the crumbs, shaped them into attractive disks, and froze them to set the cheese and the crust. With the oven super hot and the cheese very cold, the cheese developed a crispy crust (with no oozing) and kept its shape, and a quick brush of olive oil on the outside of the disks lent flavor to the crumbs without turning them oily. A mix of greens paired well with the tangy flavor of the goat cheese, and a simple, light vinaigrette was all that was needed to finish this elegant salad.

Salad with Herbed Baked Goat Cheese and Vinaigrette

SERVES 6

The baked goat cheese should be served warm. Prepare the salad components while the cheese is in the freezer, then toss the greens and vinaigrette while the cheese cools a bit after baking.

GOAT CHEESE

- 3 ounces white Melba toasts (about 2 cups)
- 1 teaspoon ground black pepper
- 3 large eggs
- 2 tablespoons Dijon mustard
- 1 tablespoon chopped fresh thyme leaves
- 1 tablespoon chopped fresh chives
- 12 ounces goat cheese
- Extra-virgin olive oil

SALAD

- 6 tablespoons extra-virgin olive oil
- 2 tablespoons red wine vinegar
- 1 tablespoon Dijon mustard
- 1 teaspoon minced shallot
- ¼ teaspoon table salt
- Ground black pepper
- 14 cups mixed delicate and spicy salad greens, such as arugula, baby spinach, and frisée, washed and dried

1. FOR THE CHEESE: In a food processor, process the Melba toasts to fine, even crumbs, about 1½ minutes; transfer the crumbs to a medium bowl and stir in the pepper. Whisk the eggs and mustard in a second medium bowl until combined. Combine the thyme and chives in a small bowl.

2. Using dental floss or kitchen twine, divide the cheese into 12 equal pieces by slicing the log lengthwise through the middle and each half into six even pieces. Roll each piece of cheese into a ball; roll each ball in the combined fresh herbs to coat lightly. Transfer 6 pieces to the egg mixture and turn each piece to coat; transfer to the Melba crumbs and turn each piece to coat, pressing the crumbs into the cheese. Flatten each ball gently with your fingertips into a disk about 1½ inches wide and 1 inch thick and set on a baking sheet. Repeat with the remaining 6 pieces of cheese. Transfer the baking sheet to the freezer and freeze the disks until firm, about 30 minutes. Adjust an oven rack to the top position and heat the oven to 475 degrees.

3. FOR THE SALAD: Meanwhile, whisk the oil, vinegar, mustard, shallot, and salt in a small bowl until combined; season with pepper to taste. Set aside.

4. Remove the cheese from the freezer and brush the tops and sides evenly with olive oil. Bake until the crumbs are golden brown and the cheese is slightly soft, 7 to 9 minutes (or 9 to 12 minutes if the cheese is completely frozen). Using a thin metal spatula, transfer the cheese to a paper towel–lined plate and cool for 3 minutes.

5. Place the greens in a large bowl, drizzle the vinaigrette over them, and toss to coat. Divide the greens among individual plates; place two rounds of goat cheese on each salad and serve.

NUT-CRUSTED CHICKEN WITH SPINACH SALAD

WHY THIS RECIPE WORKS: When leafy greens are paired with sautéed chicken, a simple salad becomes a satisfying, one-dish meal. We wanted to create an easy recipe for such a dish, and thought incorporating nuts in the coating of the chicken would make for a heartier, more elegant meal.

We started by pounding store-bought chicken breasts to the same thickness to ensure that they would cook evenly. Ground almonds paired with panko (Japanese-style bread crumbs) created a rich-tasting crust that was both light and crisp. After dipping the chicken breasts in eggs and the nut and panko mixture, we let them sit for a few minutes so the coating could set. Much like regular breaded chicken, the breasts had to be pan-fried in a fair amount of oil. Pan-frying can make a mess in a traditional skillet, so we used a nonstick pan. To make a quick salad with bright flavors, we heated orange slices to create a dressing in the skillet, then used the hot dressing to wilt the spinach.

Almond-Crusted Chicken with Wilted Spinach Salad

SERVES 4

Don't process the nuts longer than directed or they will turn pasty and oily.

CHICKEN

- 4 (5 to 6-ounce) boneless, skinless chicken breasts, trimmed
- Table salt and ground black pepper
- 1 cup sliced almonds
- ½ cup panko (Japanese-style bread crumbs)
- 2 large eggs
- 1 teaspoon Dijon mustard
- 1¼ teaspoons grated zest from 1 orange
- ¾ cup plus 2 tablespoons vegetable oil

SALAD

- 5 ounces baby spinach (about 5 cups)
- 2 medium oranges, peel and pith removed (see page 250), quartered and sliced ¼ inch thick
- 1 small shallot, minced (about 1 tablespoon)

1. FOR THE CHICKEN: Adjust an oven rack to the middle position and heat the oven to 200 degrees. Pound each breast between two sheets of plastic wrap to a uniform ½-inch thickness. Pat the chicken dry with paper towels and season with salt and pepper.

2. Process the almonds in a food processor to fine crumbs, about 10 seconds (do not over process; see note). Toss the nuts with the panko in a shallow dish. Whisk the eggs, mustard, 1 teaspoon of the orange zest, ½ teaspoon salt, and ¼ teaspoon pepper together in another shallow dish. Working with 1 chicken breast at a time, dip the chicken into the egg mixture, turning to coat well and allowing the excess to drip off, then coat with the nut mixture, pressing gently so that the nuts adhere. Place the breaded chicken in a single layer on a wire rack set over a rimmed baking sheet and let sit for 5 minutes.

3. Heat 6 tablespoons of the oil in a 12-inch nonstick skillet over medium heat until shimmering. Add 2 of the chicken breasts and cook until browned on both sides, 4 to 6 minutes total. Drain the chicken briefly on a paper towel–lined plate, then transfer to a clean wire rack set over a rimmed baking sheet and keep warm in the oven. Discard the oil and wipe out the skillet with paper towels. Repeat with 6 tablespoons more oil and the remaining chicken. Discard the oil and wipe out the skillet with paper towels.

4. FOR THE SALAD: Place the spinach in a large bowl. Heat 1 tablespoon more oil in the skillet over high heat until just smoking. Add the orange slices and cook until lightly browned around the edges, 1½ to 2 minutes. Remove the pan from the heat and add the remaining 1 tablespoon oil, the shallot, remaining ¼ teaspoon zest, ¼ teaspoon salt, and ⅛ teaspoon pepper and allow residual heat to soften the shallot, about 30 seconds. Pour the warm dressing with the oranges over the spinach and toss gently. Divide the greens among individual plates. Remove the chicken from the oven, set a cutlet over each portion, and serve.

WARM SPINACH SALAD WITH PAN-SEARED SCALLOPS

WHY THIS RECIPE WORKS: Attempts to make perfectly seared, caramelized sea scallops usually result in overcooking these tender mollusks, rendering them rubbery and tough. We wanted a concentrated, nutty, rich-colored crust encasing an interior of sweet, creamy, perfectly cooked scallop meat. And for a complete meal, we wanted to incorporate our scallops into a main course salad that would be both elegant and satisfying.

We tackled the scallops first: To get scallops with a crusty exterior, using the unprocessed variety is a must. We found it was essential to dry the scallops thoroughly before adding them to the pan, to further guard against the scallops steaming rather than searing. Equally important is to avoid crowding the pan. We cooked the scallops in batches, browning each batch on just one side, then returned them all to the skillet at once to cook through on the other side, so that each salad would have hot, not tepid, scallops.

For the salad, we liked baby spinach and watercress for easy prep and moist, tender greens. A bright dressing with sherry vinegar and fresh orange complemented the rich scallops. For a finishing touch, toasted sliced almonds lent our salad nutty flavor and welcome crunch.

Pan-Seared Scallops with Wilted Spinach, Watercress, and Orange Salad

SERVES 4

Sea scallops can vary dramatically in size from 1 to 1½ ounces each. A dinner portion, therefore, can range from four to six scallops per person. To ensure that the scallops cook at the same rate, be sure to buy scallops of similar size. Note that scallops have a small, rough-textured, crescent-shaped muscle that toughens once cooked. It's easy to remove—simply peel it from the side of each scallop before cooking.

SALAD

- 5 ounces baby spinach (about 5 cups)
- 4 ounces watercress or arugula (about 4 cups)
- ¾ cup sliced almonds, toasted

SCALLOPS

- 1½ pounds large sea scallops (16 to 24 scallops), tendons removed (see note)
- Table salt and ground black pepper
- ¼ cup vegetable oil

DRESSING

- 3 tablespoons extra-virgin olive oil
- ½ medium red onion, sliced thin
- 1 teaspoon minced fresh thyme leaves
- 2 large oranges, peel and pith removed (see page 250), quartered and sliced ¼ inch thick
- 2 tablespoons sherry vinegar

1. FOR THE SALAD: Toss the spinach, watercress, and almonds together in a large bowl; set aside.

2. FOR THE SCALLOPS: Place the scallops on a dish towel–lined plate or baking sheet and season with salt and pepper. Lay a single layer of paper towels over the scallops; set aside.

3. Add 2 tablespoons of the vegetable oil to a 12-inch skillet and heat over high heat until just smoking. Meanwhile, press the paper towel flush to the scallops to dry. Add half of the scallops to the skillet, dry side facing down, and cook until evenly golden, 1 to 2 minutes. Using tongs, transfer the scallops, browned side facing up, to a large plate; set aside. Wipe out the skillet using a wad of paper towels. Repeat with the remaining 2 tablespoons oil and the remaining scallops. Once the first side is golden, turn the heat to medium, turn the scallops over with tongs, and return the first batch of scallops to the pan, golden side facing up. Cook until the sides on all the scallops have firmed up and all but the middle third of each scallop is opaque, 30 to 60 seconds longer. Transfer all the scallops to a clean, large plate; set aside.

4. FOR THE DRESSING: Wipe the skillet clean with a wad of paper towels. Add the olive oil, onion, thyme, and ½ teaspoon salt to the skillet and return to medium-high heat; cook until the onion is slightly softened, about 1 minute. Add the oranges and vinegar to the pan and swirl to incorporate. Remove from the heat.

5. TO FINISH THE SALAD: Pour the warm dressing over the salad mixture and gently toss to wilt. Divide the spinach salad among four plates and arrange the scallops on top. Serve immediately.

KALE CAESAR SALAD

WHY THIS RECIPE WORKS: We weren't willing to sacrifice flavor in order to make a healthier version of classic Caesar salad. It had to include a rich, creamy dressing, but we did want to eliminate some of the usual fat. We tried both mayonnaise-based and egg-based dressings, but found that the heartier kale really needed a thicker mayonnaise base to stand up to it. Using that as a starting point, we cut out half the mayonnaise, replacing it with low-fat yogurt. We found we only needed a half cup of Parmesan to get the satisfying, nutty flavor so essential to Caesar dressing. The addition of anchovy fillets provided rich umami notes. A 10-minute soak in warm water tenderized the kale. We swapped the usual white bread croutons for croutons made from whole-grain bread, as the hearty greens paired well with the more rustic croutons.

Kale Caesar Salad

SERVES 4

- 12 ounces curly kale, stemmed and cut into 1-inch pieces (16 cups)
- 3 ounces rustic whole-grain bread, cut into ½-inch cubes (1½ cups)
- 2 tablespoons extra-virgin olive oil
- Salt and pepper
- 3 tablespoons mayonnaise
- 3 tablespoons plain low-fat yogurt
- 1 ounce Parmesan cheese, grated (½ cup)
- 1 tablespoon lemon juice
- 2 teaspoons white wine vinegar
- 2 teaspoons Worcestershire sauce
- 2 teaspoons Dijon mustard
- 3 anchovy fillets, rinsed and minced
- 1 garlic clove, minced

1. Adjust oven rack to middle position and heat oven to 350 degrees. Place kale in large bowl and cover with warm tap water (110 to 115 degrees). Swish kale around to remove grit. Let kale sit in warm water bath for 10 minutes. Remove kale from water and spin dry in salad spinner in multiple batches. Pat leaves dry with paper towels if still wet.

2. Toss bread, 1 tablespoon oil, ⅛ teaspoon salt, and ⅛ teaspoon pepper together in bowl. Spread on rimmed baking sheet and bake until golden and crisp, about 15 minutes. Let croutons cool completely on sheet. (Cooled croutons can be stored in airtight container at room temperature for up to 24 hours.)

3. In large bowl whisk mayonnaise, yogurt, ¼ cup Parmesan, lemon juice, vinegar, Worcestershire sauce, mustard, anchovies, garlic, ½ teaspoon salt, and ½ teaspoon pepper together until well combined. Whisking constantly, drizzle in remaining 1 tablespoon oil until combined.

4. Toss kale with dressing and refrigerate for at least 20 minutes or up to 6 hours. Toss dressed kale with croutons and remaining ¼ cup Parmesan. Serve.

BETTER CHOPPED SALADS

WHY THIS RECIPE WORKS: Chopped salads are often little better than a random collection of cut-up produce from the crisper drawer exuding moisture that turns the salad watery and bland. We wanted lively, thoughtfully chosen compositions of lettuce, vegetables, and perhaps fruit—cut into bite-size pieces—with supporting players like nuts and cheese contributing hearty flavors and textures. Salting some of the vegetables—cucumbers and tomatoes—to remove excess moisture was an important first step. As for the dressing, most recipes we tried called for a ratio of 3 parts oil to 1 part vinegar, but we found that a more assertive blend of equal parts oil and vinegar was far better at delivering the bright, acidic kick needed in salads boasting hearty flavors and chunky textures. We also found that marinating ingredients such as bell peppers, onions, and fruit in the dressing for 5 minutes before adding cheese and other tender components brought a welcome flavor boost.

Pear and Cranberry Chopped Salad

SERVES 4 TO 6

Chopped dried cherries can be substituted for the cranberries.

- 1 cucumber, peeled, halved lengthwise, seeded, and cut into ½-inch dice (about 1¼ cups; see page 47)
- Table salt
- 3 tablespoons extra-virgin olive oil
- 3 tablespoons sherry vinegar
- 1 red bell pepper, stemmed, seeded, and cut into ¼-inch pieces (about 1 cup)
- 1 ripe but firm pear, cut into ¼-inch pieces (about 1 cup)
- ½ small red onion, minced (about ¼ cup)
- ½ cup dried cranberries
- 1 romaine heart, cut into ½-inch pieces (about 3 cups)
- 4 ounces blue cheese, crumbled (about 1 cup)
- ½ cup pistachios, toasted and chopped coarse
- Ground black pepper

1. Combine the cucumber and ½ teaspoon salt in a colander set over a bowl and drain for 15 minutes.

2. Whisk the oil and vinegar together in a large bowl. Add the drained cucumber, bell pepper, pear, onion, and cranberries. Toss and let stand at room temperature to blend the flavors, 5 minutes.

3. Add the romaine, blue cheese, and pistachios and toss to combine. Season with salt and pepper to taste and serve.

Mediterranean Chopped Salad

SERVES 4 TO 6

For information on our top-rated brand of feta cheese, see page 907.

- 1 cucumber, peeled, halved lengthwise, seeded, and cut into ½-inch dice (about 1¼ cups; see page 47)
- 1 pint grape tomatoes, quartered (about 1½ cups)
- Table salt
- 3 tablespoons extra-virgin olive oil
- 3 tablespoons red wine vinegar
- 1 medium garlic clove, minced or pressed through a garlic press (about 1 teaspoon)
- 1 (15-ounce) can chickpeas, drained and rinsed
- ½ cup pitted kalamata olives, chopped
- ½ small red onion, minced (about ¼ cup)
- ½ cup chopped fresh parsley leaves
- 1 romaine heart, cut into ½-inch pieces (about 3 cups)
- 4 ounces feta cheese, crumbled (about 1 cup)
- Ground black pepper

1. Combine the cucumber, tomatoes, and 1 teaspoon salt in a colander set over a bowl and drain for 15 minutes.

2. Whisk the oil, vinegar, and garlic together in a large bowl. Add the drained cucumber and tomatoes, chickpeas, olives, onion, and parsley. Toss and let stand at room temperature to blend the flavors, 5 minutes.

3. Add the romaine and feta and toss to combine. Season with salt and pepper to taste and serve.

Fennel and Apple Chopped Salad

SERVES 4 TO 6

Braeburn, Jonagold, or Red Delicious apples all work well here. The cheese is sprinkled on the salads after plating because goat cheese tends to clump when tossed.

- 1 cucumber, peeled, halved lengthwise, seeded, and cut into ½-inch dice (about 1¼ cups; see page 47)
- Table salt
- 3 tablespoons extra-virgin olive oil
- 3 tablespoons white wine vinegar
- 1 fennel bulb, halved lengthwise, cored, and cut into ¼-inch dice (about 1½ cups; see photos)
- 2 apples, cored and cut into ¼-inch dice (about 2 cups; see note)
- ½ small red onion, minced (about ¼ cup)
- ¼ cup chopped fresh tarragon leaves
- 1 romaine heart, cut into ½-inch pieces (about 3 cups)
- ½ cup chopped walnuts, toasted
- Ground back pepper
- 4 ounces crumbled goat cheese (about 1 cup)

1. Combine the cucumber and ½ teaspoon salt in a colander set over a bowl and drain for 15 minutes.

2. Whisk the oil and vinegar together in a large bowl. Add the drained cucumber, fennel, apples, onion, and tarragon. Toss and let stand at room temperature to blend the flavors, 5 minutes.

3. Add the romaine and walnuts and toss to combine. Season with salt and pepper to taste. Divide the salad among individual plates; top each with some goat cheese and serve.

NOTES FROM THE TEST KITCHEN

TRIMMING AND CORING FENNEL

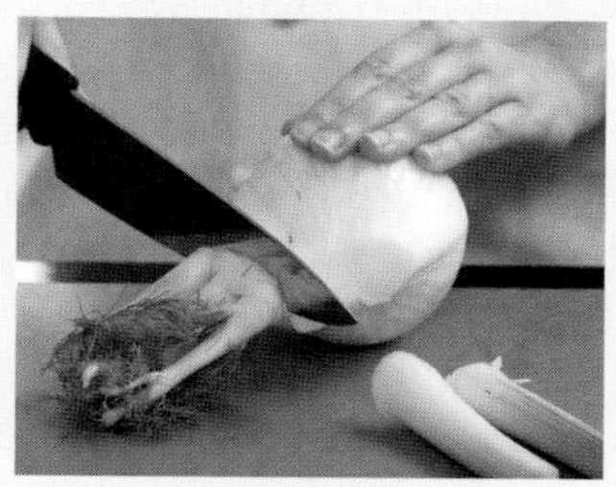

1. Cut off the stems and feathery fronds.

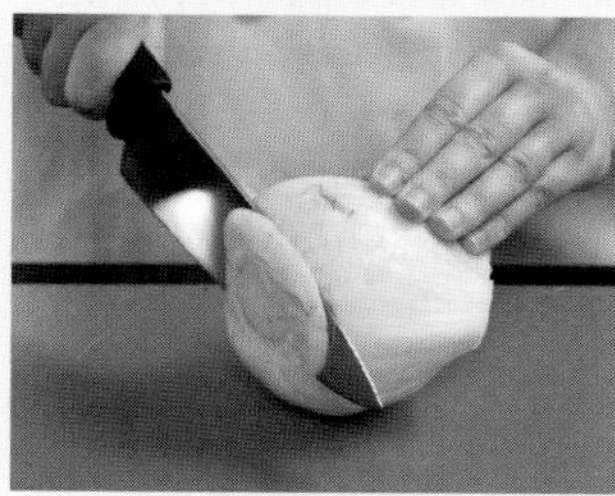

2. Trim a very thin slice from the base of the bulb and remove any tough or blemished outer layers.

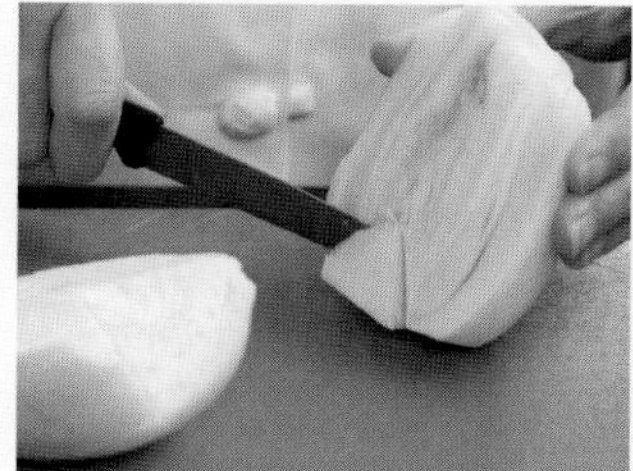

3. After cutting the bulb in half through the base, use a small, sharp knife to remove the pyramid-shaped core. Slice or chop the fennel as directed.

MANGO, ORANGE, AND JÍCAMA SALAD

WHY THIS RECIPE WORKS: When the summer fruit crops are at the peak of ripeness, it doesn't require much forethought to put together a stunning fruit salad. Come winter, however, and the task requires a little more creativity. Working with the abundant citrus and tropical fruits available in colder months, we set our sights on a nuanced salad. A pairing of 1 part citrus fruit to 4 parts tropical fruit produced a juicy—not waterlogged—salad. We started with oranges and mangoes and then we created a simple bright dressing by heating sugar, lime juice, lime zest, red pepper flakes, and a pinch of salt to form a tangy-sweet syrup infused with just a touch of spicy heat. The mild sweetness and supercrisp texture of jícama, softened slightly in the hot syrup, contributed just enough crunch to finish off the salad.

Mango, Orange, and Jícama Salad

SERVES 4 TO 6

Make sure that the syrup has cooled before pouring it over the fruit.

- 3 tablespoons sugar
- ¼ teaspoon grated lime zest plus 3 tablespoons juice (2 limes)
- ¼ teaspoon red pepper flakes
- Pinch salt
- 12 ounces jícama, peeled and cut into ¼-inch dice (1½ cups)
- 2 oranges
- 2 mangos, peeled, pitted, and cut into ½-inch dice

1. Bring sugar, lime zest and juice, pepper flakes, and salt to simmer in small saucepan over medium heat, stirring constantly, until sugar is dissolved, 1 to 2 minutes. Remove pan from heat, stir in jícama, and let syrup cool for 20 minutes.

2. Meanwhile, cut away peel and pith from oranges. Slice into ½-inch-thick rounds, then cut rounds into ½-inch pieces. Place oranges and mangos in large bowl.

3. When syrup is cool, pour over oranges and mangos and toss to combine. Refrigerate for 15 minutes before serving.

Papaya, Clementine, and Chayote Salad

Chayote, also called mirliton, is often sold with other tropical fruits and vegetables. If you can't find chayote, substitute an equal amount of jícama.

Substitute 2 teaspoons grated fresh ginger for red pepper flakes; 1 chayote, peeled, halved, pitted, and cut into ¼-inch dice, for jícama; 3 clementines, peeled and each segment cut into 3 pieces, for oranges; and 2 large papayas, peeled, seeded, and cut into ½-inch dice, for mangos.

Pineapple, Grapefruit, and Cucumber Salad

Substitute ground cardamom for red pepper flakes; 1 cucumber, peeled, halved lengthwise, seeded, and cut into ¼-inch dice, for jícama; 1 grapefruit for oranges; and 1 pineapple, peeled, cored, and cut into ½-inch dice, for mangos.

CHERRY TOMATO SALAD

WHY THIS RECIPE WORKS: Cherry tomatoes are sweet, juicy, and available year-round—and especially tempting during those cold winter months when summer seems eons away. We wanted an easy recipe that would make the most of their sweetness so we could enjoy fresh tomatoes anytime we wanted. Simply slicing cherry tomatoes in half and sprucing them up with vinaigrette resulted in a waterlogged salad

with no flavor at all. To prevent this soggy, watery outcome, we quartered and salted them, and then took them for a spin in a salad spinner to remove as much of the jelly and seeds as possible. Reducing the jelly with red wine vinegar concentrated its flavor, and adding olive oil made for a dressing that brought the tomato flavor to the forefront. Cucumber contributed welcome crunch, while chopped olives and crumbled feta added a briny touch that brought the whole dish together.

Cherry Tomato Salad with Feta and Olives

SERVES 4 TO 6

If in-season cherry tomatoes are unavailable, substitute vine-ripened cherry tomatoes or grape tomatoes from the supermarket. Cut grape tomatoes in half along the equator (rather than quartering them). If you don't have a salad spinner, after the salted tomatoes have stood for 30 minutes, wrap the bowl tightly with plastic wrap and gently shake to remove seeds and excess liquid. Strain the liquid and proceed with the recipe as directed. The amount of liquid given off by the tomatoes will depend on their ripeness. If you have less than ½ cup juice after spinning, proceed with the recipe using the entire amount of juice and reduce it to 3 tablespoons as directed (the cooking time will be shorter).

- 2 pints ripe cherry tomatoes, quartered (about 4 cups; see note)
- ½ teaspoon sugar
- Table salt
- 1 medium shallot, minced (about 3 tablespoons)
- 1 tablespoon red wine vinegar
- 2 medium garlic cloves, minced or pressed through a garlic press (about 2 teaspoons)
- ½ teaspoon dried oregano
- 2 tablespoons extra-virgin olive oil
- Ground black pepper
- 1 small cucumber, peeled, halved lengthwise, seeded, and cut into ½-inch pieces (see page 47)

- ½ cup chopped pitted kalamata olives
- 4 ounces feta cheese, crumbled (about 1 cup)
- 3 tablespoons chopped fresh parsley leaves

1. Toss the tomatoes, sugar, and ¼ teaspoon salt in a medium bowl; let stand for 30 minutes. Transfer the tomatoes to a salad spinner and spin until the seeds and excess liquid have been removed, 45 to 60 seconds, stirring to redistribute the tomatoes several times during spinning. Return the tomatoes to the bowl and set aside. Strain the tomato liquid through a fine-mesh strainer into a liquid measuring cup, pressing on the solids to extract as much liquid as possible.

2. Bring ½ cup of the tomato liquid (discard any extra), the shallot, vinegar, garlic, and oregano to a simmer in a small saucepan over medium heat. Simmer until reduced to 3 tablespoons, 6 to 8 minutes. Transfer the mixture to a small bowl and cool to room temperature, about 5 minutes. Whisk in the oil until combined and season with salt and pepper to taste.

3. Add the cucumber, olives, feta, parsley, and dressing to the bowl with the tomatoes; toss gently and serve.

ITALIAN BREAD SALAD

WHY THIS RECIPE WORKS: When the rustic Italian bread salad panzanella is done well, the sweet juice of the tomatoes mixes with a bright-tasting vinaigrette, moistening chunks of thick-crusted bread until they're soft and just a little chewy—but the line between lightly moistened and unpleasantly soggy is very thin. Toasting fresh bread in the oven, rather than using the traditional day-old bread, was a good start. With this method, the bread lost enough moisture in the oven to absorb the dressing without getting waterlogged. A 10-minute soak in the flavorful dressing yielded perfectly moistened, nutty-tasting bread ready to be tossed with the tomatoes, which we salted to intensify their flavor. A thinly sliced cucumber and shallot for crunch and bite plus a handful of chopped fresh basil perfected our salad.

Italian Bread Salad (Panzanella)

SERVES 4

The success of this recipe depends on high-quality ingredients, including ripe, in-season tomatoes and fruity olive oil. Fresh basil is also a must. Your bread may vary in density, so you may not need the entire loaf for this recipe.

- 1 (1-pound) loaf rustic Italian or French bread, cut or torn into 1-inch pieces (about 6 cups)
- ½ cup extra-virgin olive oil
- Table salt and ground black pepper
- 1½ pounds tomatoes, cored, seeded, and cut into 1-inch pieces
- 3 tablespoons red wine vinegar
- 1 medium cucumber, peeled, halved lengthwise, seeded, and sliced thin (see page 47)
- 1 medium shallot, sliced thin
- ¼ cup chopped fresh basil leaves

1. Adjust an oven rack to the middle position and heat the oven to 400 degrees. Toss the bread pieces with 2 tablespoons of the oil and ¼ teaspoon salt; arrange the bread in a single layer on a rimmed baking sheet. Toast the bread pieces until just starting to turn light golden, 15 to 20 minutes, stirring halfway through baking. Set aside and let cool to room temperature.

2. Gently toss the tomatoes and ½ teaspoon salt in a large bowl. Transfer to a colander set over a bowl; set aside to drain for 15 minutes, tossing occasionally.

3. Whisk the remaining 6 tablespoons oil, the vinegar, and ¼ teaspoon pepper into the tomato juices. Add the bread pieces, toss to coat, and let stand for 10 minutes, tossing occasionally.

4. Add the tomatoes, cucumber, shallot, and basil to the bowl with the bread pieces and toss to coat. Season with salt and pepper to taste and serve immediately.

PITA BREAD SALAD WITH TOMATOES AND CUCUMBER

WHY THIS RECIPE WORKS: This Middle Eastern salad is at its best when it combines fresh, flavorful produce with crisp pita and bright herbs. Many recipes eliminate excess moisture from the salad by taking the time-consuming step of seeding and salting the cucumbers and tomatoes. We skipped that process, favoring the crisp texture of the cucumber (the English variety, which has fewer seeds) and the flavorful seeds and jelly of the tomato. We fended off soggy bread by making the pita moisture-repellent, brushing its craggy sides with plenty of olive oil before baking. The oil soaked into the bread and prevented the pita chips from absorbing the salad's moisture while still allowing them to take on some of its flavor. A fresh, summery blend of mint, cilantro, and peppery arugula comprised the salad's greenery and a vinaigrette of lemon juice, garlic, salt, and olive oil lent it an uncomplicated, bright finish.

Pita Bread Salad with Tomatoes and Cucumber (Fattoush)

SERVES 4

The success of this recipe depends on ripe, in-season tomatoes. A rasp-style grater makes quick work of turning the garlic into a paste.

- 2 (8-inch) pita breads
- 3 tablespoons plus ¼ cup extra-virgin olive oil
- Salt and pepper
- 3 tablespoons lemon juice
- ¼ teaspoon garlic, minced to paste
- 1 pound tomatoes, cored and cut into ¾-inch pieces
- 1 English cucumber, peeled and sliced ⅛-inch thick
- 1 cup arugula, chopped coarse
- ½ cup chopped fresh cilantro
- ½ cup chopped fresh mint
- 4 scallions, sliced thin

1. Adjust oven rack to middle position and heat oven to 375 degrees. Using kitchen shears, cut around perimeter of each pita and separate into 2 thin rounds. Cut each round in half. Place pita bread, smooth side down, on wire rack set in rimmed baking sheet. Brush 3 tablespoons oil over surface of pita. (Pita does not need to be uniformly coated. Oil will absorb and spread as it bakes.) Season with salt and pepper. Bake until pita is crisp and pale golden brown, 10 to 14 minutes.

2. While pita toasts, whisk lemon juice, garlic, and ¼ teaspoon salt together in small bowl. Let stand 10 minutes

3. Place tomatoes, cucumber, arugula, cilantro, mint, and scallions in large bowl. Break pita into ½-inch pieces and place in bowl with vegetables. Add lemon-garlic mixture and remaining ¼ cup oil and toss to coat. Season with salt and pepper to taste. Serve immediately.

GREEK SALAD

WHY THIS RECIPE WORKS: Most versions of Greek salad consist of iceberg lettuce, chunks of green pepper, and a few pale wedges of tomato, sparsely dotted with cubes of feta and garnished with one or two olives. We wanted a salad with crisp ingredients and bold flavors. A combination of lemon juice, red wine vinegar, garlic, and olive oil made a zesty vinaigrette. We marinated onion and cucumber slices in the vinaigrette which helped mute the sting of raw onion in the salad. We swapped in crisp, flavorful romaine for the iceberg. And along with sliced tomatoes, we added jarred roasted red peppers for a bit of sweetness. A handful of kalamata olives and tangy feta cheese lent the traditional touches, and torn mint and parsley leaves gave our salad a fresh finish.

Classic Greek Salad

SERVES 6 TO 8

Marinating the onion and cucumber in the vinaigrette tones down the onion's harshness and flavors the cucumber. For efficiency, prepare the other salad ingredients while the onion and cucumber marinate.

VINAIGRETTE

- 6 tablespoons extra-virgin olive oil
- 3 tablespoons red wine vinegar
- 2 teaspoons minced fresh oregano leaves
- 1½ teaspoons juice from 1 lemon
- 1 medium garlic clove, minced or pressed through a garlic press (about 1 teaspoon)
- ½ teaspoon table salt
- ⅛ teaspoon ground black pepper

SALAD

- ½ medium red onion, sliced thin (about ¾ cup)
- 1 medium cucumber, peeled, halved lengthwise, seeded, and sliced ⅛ inch thick (see page 47)
- 2 romaine hearts, washed, dried, and torn into 1½-inch pieces (about 8 cups)
- 2 medium, firm, ripe tomatoes (6 ounces each), cored, seeded, and each tomato cut into 12 wedges
- 6 ounces jarred roasted red bell peppers, cut into 2 by ½-inch strips (about 1 cup)
- ¼ cup loosely packed fresh parsley leaves, torn
- ¼ cup loosely packed fresh mint leaves, torn
- 20 large pitted kalamata olives, quartered
- 5 ounces feta cheese, crumbled (about 1¼ cups)

1. FOR THE VINAIGRETTE: Whisk the oil, vinegar, oregano, lemon juice, garlic, salt, and pepper in a large bowl until combined.

2. Add the onion and cucumber to the vinaigrette and toss; let stand to blend the flavors, about 20 minutes.

3. FOR THE SALAD: Add the romaine, tomatoes, peppers, parsley, and mint to the bowl with the onions and cucumbers; toss to coat with the vinaigrette.

4. Transfer the salad to a serving bowl or platter; sprinkle the olives and feta over the salad and serve.

CUCUMBER SALAD

WHY THIS RECIPE WORKS: More often than not, cucumbers in cucumber salad turn soft and watery, having lost their crunchy texture and released enough liquid to dilute the dressing. This phenomenon made the primary goal of our cucumber salad easy to identify: Maximize the crunch.

Because water makes cucumbers lose their texture, we had to salt and weight the cucumbers to draw off excess moisture. We also rinsed them and patted them dry before tossing the cucumbers with a rice vinegar, lemon juice, and sesame oil vinaigrette, a flavorful combination. Toasted sesame seeds added even more textural interest.

NOTES FROM THE TEST KITCHEN

SEEDING CUCUMBERS

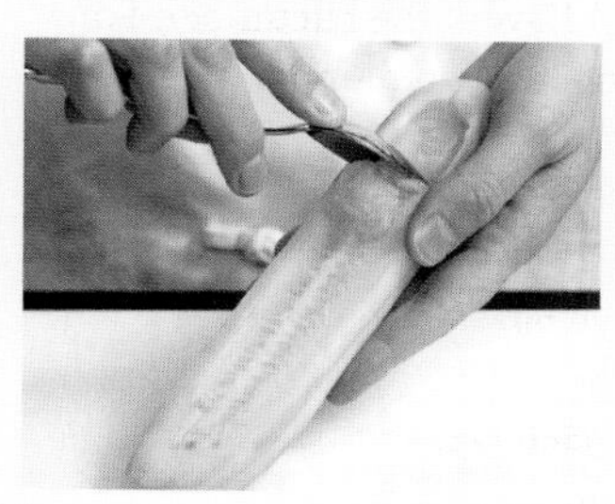

Peel the cucumber, cut it in half lengthwise, and scoop out the seeds with a spoon.

CHOPPING CUCUMBERS

1. Cut each half crosswise into 2 to 3-inch pieces.

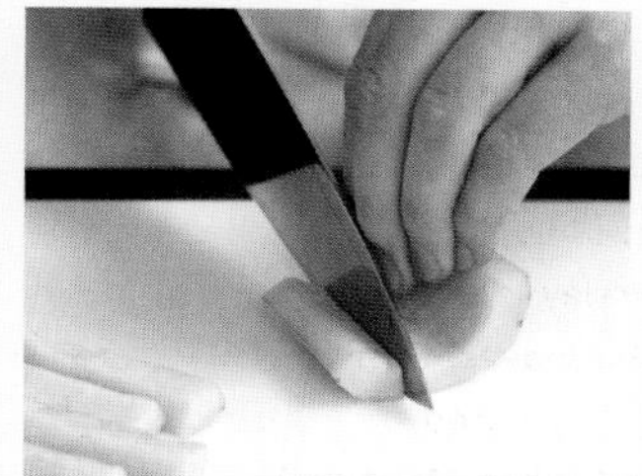

2. Place the pieces cut side up on a cutting board, then slice them lengthwise into even batons.

3. Cut the batons crosswise into an even dice.

Sesame-Lemon Cucumber Salad

SERVES 4

Mild rice vinegar works well in this Asian-inspired dressing.

- 3 medium cucumbers (about 2 pounds), peeled, halved lengthwise, seeded, and sliced ¼ inch thick (see page 47)
- 1 tablespoon table salt
- ¼ cup rice vinegar (see note)
- 2 tablespoons toasted sesame oil
- 1 tablespoon juice from 1 lemon
- 1 tablespoon sesame seeds, toasted
- 2 teaspoons sugar
- ⅛ teaspoon red pepper flakes

1. Toss the cucumbers with the salt in a colander set over a large bowl. Weight the cucumbers with a gallon-sized zipper-lock bag filled with water; drain for 1 to 3 hours. Rinse and pat dry.

2. Whisk the remaining ingredients together in a medium bowl. Add the cucumbers; toss to coat. Serve chilled or at room temperature.

CREAMY COLESLAW

WHY THIS RECIPE WORKS: No other food embodies an outdoor grillfest quite like coleslaw. This summery salad offers a crunch and creaminess that contrasts well with sweet and savory barbecued meats and vegetables. But, despite its simplicity, coleslaw can be tough to get just right. Usually, the coleslaw ends up limp and sitting in a pool of water. We wanted a crisp salad and a creamy dressing that wouldn't be waterlogged. To prevent the salad from getting watery, we salted the cabbage until it wilted, then rinsed and dried it. Removing the excess water helped to keep our dressing thick and creamy, and ensured the cabbage stayed crunchy. For the dressing, we used mayonnaise and rice vinegar; these made a creamy dressing that was flavorful but not too harsh. All our coleslaw needed now was black pepper and some shredded carrot for color, further crunch, and a little sweetness.

Creamy Coleslaw

SERVES 4

If you like caraway or celery seeds, add ¼ teaspoon of either with the mayonnaise and vinegar. If you like a tangier slaw, replace some or all of the mayonnaise with an equal amount of sour cream. To serve the coleslaw immediately, rinse the salted cabbage and carrot in a large bowl of ice water, drain them in a colander, pick out any ice cubes, then pat the vegetables dry before dressing.

- 1 pound red or green cabbage (about ½ medium head), shredded (about 6 cups; see page 49)
- 1 large carrot, peeled and shredded
- 1 teaspoon table salt
- ½ small onion, minced
- ½ cup mayonnaise (see note)
- 2 tablespoons rice vinegar
- Ground black pepper

1. Toss the cabbage and carrot with the salt in a colander set over a medium bowl. Let stand until the cabbage wilts, at least 1 hour or up to 4 hours. Rinse the cabbage and carrot under cold running water (or in a large bowl of ice water if serving immediately). Press, but do not squeeze, to drain; pat dry with paper towels.

2. Combine the cabbage, carrot, onion, mayonnaise, and vinegar in a medium bowl; toss to coat and season with pepper to taste. Serve chilled or at room temperature. (The coleslaw can be refrigerated in an airtight container for up to 2 days.)

BUTTERMILK COLESLAW

WHY THIS RECIPE WORKS: Order barbecue down South, and you won't just get coleslaw on the side, you'll get buttermilk coleslaw. Unlike all-mayonnaise coleslaw, buttermilk coleslaw is coated in a light, creamy, and refreshingly tart dressing. We wanted a recipe that showcased its best attributes: a pickle-crisp texture and a tangy dressing.

To prevent watery coleslaw, we salted, rinsed, and dried our shredded cabbage. This also gave us the texture we wanted—as the salted cabbage sat, moisture was pulled out of it, wilting it to the right crispy texture. For a tangy dressing that clung to the cabbage and didn't pool at the bottom of the bowl, we supplemented the buttermilk with mayonnaise and sour cream. For finishing touches, we added shredded carrot, which contributed both color and sweetness. The mild flavor of shallot was a welcome addition, and sugar, mustard, and cider vinegar amped up the slaw's tanginess.

Creamy Buttermilk Coleslaw

SERVES 4

To serve the coleslaw immediately, rinse the salted cabbage in a large bowl of ice water, drain it in a colander, pick out any ice cubes, then pat the cabbage dry before dressing.

- 1 pound red or green cabbage (about ½ medium head), shredded (about 6 cups; see page 49)
- Table salt
- 1 large carrot, peeled and shredded
- ½ cup buttermilk
- 2 tablespoons mayonnaise
- 2 tablespoons sour cream
- 1 small shallot, minced (about 1 tablespoon)
- 2 tablespoons minced fresh parsley leaves
- ½ teaspoon cider vinegar
- ¼ teaspoon Dijon mustard
- ½ teaspoon sugar
- ⅛ teaspoon ground black pepper

1. Toss the cabbage with 1 teaspoon salt in a colander set over a medium bowl. Let stand until the cabbage wilts, at least 1 hour or up to 4 hours. Rinse the cabbage under cold running water (or in a large bowl of ice water if serving immediately). Press, but do not squeeze, to drain; pat dry with paper towels. Transfer the cabbage to a large bowl; add the carrot.

2. Combine the remaining ingredients with ¼ teaspoon salt in a small bowl. Pour the buttermilk dressing over the cabbage and carrot and toss to coat. Serve chilled or at room temperature. (The coleslaw can be refrigerated in an airtight container for up to 2 days.)

CABBAGE SALAD

WHY THIS RECIPE WORKS: Cabbage makes a great salad—not just as coleslaw but as a crunchy, flavorful, dress-up kind of salad. We aimed to develop an Asian-inspired cabbage salad that incorporated spicy, sweet flavors for a salad side dish that was a refreshing change from the same old slaw.

Salting the cabbage and setting it over a colander helped to extract excess liquid, which otherwise would dilute the potent flavors of the dressing. Shredded carrot gave the salad some sweetness, and radishes brought a peppery crunch. For the dressing, we started with smooth peanut butter for its rich flavor and velvety texture. Rice vinegar and soy sauce provided bright, tangy notes. White sugar would have contributed too much sweetness, but a small amount of honey was just right. Last touches to the dressing came in the form of a spicy jalapeño chile and fresh ginger. Processed to a smooth consistency, our spicy peanut dressing provided the perfect lush coating to the crisp vegetables.

Confetti Cabbage Salad with Spicy Peanut Dressing

SERVES 6

Serve this Asian-inspired cabbage salad with simple pork or chicken dishes. To serve the salad immediately, rinse the salted cabbage and carrot in a large bowl of ice water, drain them in a colander, pick out any ice cubes, then pat the vegetables dry before dressing.

- 1 pound red or green cabbage (about ½ medium head), shredded (about 6 cups)
- 1 large carrot, peeled and shredded
- Table salt
- 2 tablespoons smooth peanut butter
- 2 tablespoons peanut oil
- 2 tablespoons rice vinegar
- 1 tablespoon soy sauce
- 1 teaspoon honey
- 2 medium garlic cloves, minced or pressed through a garlic press (about 2 teaspoons)
- 1½ tablespoons minced or grated fresh ginger
- ½ jalapeño chile, seeds and ribs removed
- 4 medium radishes, halved lengthwise and sliced thin
- 4 scallions, sliced thin

NOTES FROM THE TEST KITCHEN

SHREDDING CABBAGE

1. Cut the cabbage into quarters, then trim and discard the hard core.

2. Separate the cabbage into small stacks of leaves that flatten when pressed.

3. Use a chef's knife to cut each stack of cabbage leaves into thin shreds.

1. Toss the cabbage and carrot with 1 teaspoon salt in a colander set over a medium bowl. Let stand until the cabbage wilts, at least 1 hour or up to 4 hours. Rinse the cabbage and carrot under cold running water (or in a large bowl of ice water if serving immediately). Press, but do not squeeze, to drain; pat dry with paper towels.

2. Process the peanut butter, oil, vinegar, soy sauce, honey, garlic, ginger, and jalapeño in a food processor until smooth. Combine the cabbage, carrot, radishes, scallions, and dressing in a medium bowl; toss to coat. Season with salt to taste. Cover and refrigerate; serve chilled. (The salad can be refrigerated in an airtight container for up to 2 days.)

MACARONI SALAD

WHY THIS RECIPE WORKS: Macaroni salad seems simple enough—toss elbow macaroni and a few seasonings with a mayo-based dressing. So why does this picnic salad often fall short, with mushy pasta and a bland, ho-hum dressing? We set out to make a picnic-worthy macaroni salad with tender pasta and a creamy, well-seasoned dressing.

First we had to get the pasta texture just right. To do this, we didn't drain the macaroni as thoroughly as we could have; the excess water is absorbed by the pasta as it sits and this prevents the finished salad from drying out. Also, cooking the macaroni to a point where it still has some bite left means the pasta won't get too soft when mixed with the mayonnaise. For the most flavor, we seasoned the pasta first—before adding the mayonnaise—so that the seasonings could penetrate and flavor the macaroni. Garlic powder added flavor to the salad (fresh garlic was too harsh), and lemon juice and Dijon mustard enlivened the creamy dressing.

Cool and Creamy Macaroni Salad

SERVES 8 TO 10

Don't drain the macaroni too well before adding the other ingredients—a little extra moisture will keep the salad from drying out. If you've made the salad ahead of time, simply stir in a little warm water to loosen the texture before serving.

- Table salt
- 1 pound elbow macaroni
- ½ small red onion, minced
- 1 celery rib, chopped fine
- ¼ cup minced fresh parsley leaves
- 2 tablespoons juice from 1 lemon
- 1 tablespoon Dijon mustard
- ⅛ teaspoon garlic powder
- Pinch cayenne pepper
- 1½ cups mayonnaise
- Ground black pepper

1. Bring 4 quarts water to a boil in a large pot. Stir 1 tablespoon salt and the pasta into the boiling water and cook, stirring often, until nearly tender, about 5 minutes. Drain the pasta and rinse with cold water until cool, then drain briefly so that the macaroni remains moist. Transfer to a large bowl.

2. Stir in the onion, celery, parsley, lemon juice, mustard, garlic powder, and cayenne and let sit until the flavors are absorbed, about 2 minutes. Add the mayonnaise and let sit until the salad is no longer watery, 5 to 10 minutes. Season with salt and pepper to taste and serve. (The salad can be refrigerated in an airtight container for up to 2 days.)

PASTA SALAD WITH PESTO

WHY THIS RECIPE WORKS: Pasta salad with pesto should be light and refreshing, not dry and dull. We decided to perfect pesto pasta salad—and keep it fresh, green, garlicky, and full of herbal flavor. Using a pasta shape with a textured surface, like farfalle, guaranteed that the pesto wouldn't slide off. To ensure that the pesto coated the pasta, we didn't rinse it after cooking. Instead, we spread the pasta to cool in a single layer on a baking sheet; a splash of oil helped prevent it from sticking. For the pesto, we blanched the garlic to tame its harsh bite. Lots of basil made for vibrant herb flavor, and to keep the green color from fading, we added mild-tasting baby spinach, which lent the salad a vivid green color. For a creamy, not greasy, pesto, we enriched it with mayonnaise. Lemon juice brightened the pesto's flavor, and extra pine nuts, folded into the salad, provided an additional hit of nutty flavor and a pleasant crunchy texture.

Pasta Salad with Pesto

SERVES 8 TO 10

This salad is best served the day it is made; if it's been refrigerated, bring it to room temperature before serving. The pesto can be made a day ahead—just cook the garlic in a small saucepan of boiling water for 1 minute.

- 2 medium garlic cloves, unpeeled
- Table salt
- 1 pound farfalle (bow-tie pasta)
- ¼ cup plus 1 tablespoon extra-virgin olive oil
- 3 cups packed fresh basil leaves (about 4 ounces)
- 1 cup packed baby spinach (about 1 ounce)
- ¾ cup pine nuts (3¾ ounces), toasted
- 2 tablespoons juice from 1 lemon
- ½ teaspoon ground black pepper
- 1½ ounces Parmesan cheese, finely grated (about ¾ cup), plus extra for serving
- 6 tablespoons mayonnaise
- 1 pint cherry tomatoes, quartered, or grape tomatoes, halved (optional)

1. Bring 4 quarts water to a boil in a large pot. Add the garlic to the boiling water and let cook for 1 minute. Remove the garlic with a slotted spoon and rinse under cold water; set aside to cool. Stir 1 tablespoon salt and the pasta into the boiling water and cook, stirring often, until the pasta is just past al dente. Reserve ¼ cup of the pasta cooking water, drain the pasta, toss with 1 tablespoon of the oil, spread in a single layer on a rimmed baking sheet, and cool to room temperature, about 30 minutes.

2. Peel and mince the garlic or press it through a garlic press. Process the garlic, basil, spinach, ¼ cup of the nuts, lemon juice, pepper, remaining ¼ cup oil, and 1 teaspoon salt in a food processor until smooth, scraping down the sides of the work bowl as necessary. Add the Parmesan and mayonnaise and process until thoroughly combined. Transfer the mixture to a large serving bowl. Cover and refrigerate until ready to assemble the salad.

3. Toss the pasta with the pesto, adding the reserved pasta water, 1 tablespoon at a time, until the pesto evenly coats the pasta. Fold in the remaining ½ cup nuts and the tomatoes (if using). Serve, passing extra Parmesan separately.

ANTIPASTO PASTA SALAD

WHY THIS RECIPE WORKS: We love the traditional antipasto platter served at Italian restaurants, chock-full of cured meats, cheese, and pickled vegetables. It's a full-flavored and satisfying dish—and something that we thought would translate well to a hearty pasta salad.

We quickly decided that short, curly pasta was the best shape to use, as its curves held on to the salad's other components, making for a more cohesive dish. Quickly rendering the meats in the microwave helped to keep this salad from becoming greasy. We used an increased ratio of vinegar to oil in the dressing—the sharp, acidic flavor cut the richness of the meats and cheese for a brighter-tasting salad. For well-seasoned pasta, we tossed the hot pasta with the dressing—hot pasta absorbs dressing better than cold pasta. Slicing the meat into thick strips meant that its hearty flavor wasn't lost among the other ingredients. And grating the cheese, rather than cubing it, made for evenly distributed sharp flavor throughout the salad.

Antipasto Pasta Salad

SERVES 6 TO 8

We also liked the addition of 1 cup chopped pitted kalamata olives or 1 cup jarred artichokes, drained and quartered, to this salad.

- 8 ounces sliced pepperoni, cut into ¼-inch strips
- 8 ounces thick-sliced sopresatta or salami, halved and cut into ¼-inch strips
- 10 tablespoons red wine vinegar
- 6 tablespoons extra-virgin olive oil
- 3 tablespoons mayonnaise
- 1 (12-ounce) jar pepperoncini, drained (2 tablespoons liquid reserved), stemmed, and chopped coarse
- 4 garlic cloves, minced or pressed through a garlic press (about 4 teaspoons)
- ¼ teaspoon red pepper flakes
- Table salt and ground black pepper
- 1 pound short, curly pasta, such as fusilli or campanelle
- 1 pound white mushrooms, wiped clean and quartered
- 4 ounces aged provolone cheese, grated (about 1 cup)
- 1 (12-ounce) jar roasted red peppers, drained, patted dry, and chopped coarse
- 1 cup minced fresh basil leaves

1. Bring 4 quarts water to a boil in a large pot. Place the pepperoni on a large paper towel–lined plate. Cover with another paper towel and place the sopresatta on top. Cover with another paper towel and microwave on high power for 1 minute. Discard the paper towels and set the pepperoni and sopresatta aside.

2. Whisk 5 tablespoons of the vinegar, the oil, mayonnaise, pepperoncini liquid, garlic, red pepper flakes, ½ teaspoon salt, and ½ teaspoon pepper together in a medium bowl.

3. Stir 1 tablespoon salt and the pasta into the boiling water and cook, stirring often, until the pasta is just past al dente. Drain the pasta and return it to the pot. Pour ½ cup of the dressing and the remaining 5 tablespoons vinegar over the pasta and toss to combine; season with salt and pepper to taste. Spread the pasta in a single layer on a rimmed baking sheet and cool to room temperature, about 30 minutes.

4. Meanwhile, bring the remaining dressing to a simmer in a large skillet over medium-high heat. Add the mushrooms and cook until lightly browned, about 8 minutes. Transfer to a large bowl and cool to room temperature.

5. Add the meat, provolone, peppers, basil, and pasta to the mushrooms and toss to combine. Season with salt and pepper to taste and serve.

RICE SALAD

WHY THIS RECIPE WORKS: Rice makes a light, refreshing salad when dressed properly and studded with vegetables—and it makes a nice change from pasta salad. But unlike pasta, rice can't stand up to assertive flavors or be bogged down by a heavy vinaigrette. To get rice salad just right, we would have to include a few bright, tangy ingredients and use a light hand when making the dressing.

To start out with as much flavor as possible, we toasted the rice to intensify its flavor and then boiled it in a large amount of water, as we would pasta. This method kept the rice tender when cool. To dry the rice, we spread it out on a large baking sheet—this guaranteed that the rice didn't clump or become waterlogged. As for the vinaigrette, restraint was key. We used small amounts of oil, vinegar, and seasonings to complement, but not overshadow, the grains of rice. Orange segments, slivered almonds, and chopped olives gave the salad character and textural interest. And a brief rest to blend the flavors yielded a rice salad that was bright and balanced.

Rice Salad with Oranges, Olives, and Almonds

SERVES 6 TO 8

Taste the rice as it nears the end of its cooking time; it should be cooked through and firm, but not crunchy. Be careful not to overcook the rice or the grains will be blown out.

- 1½ cups long-grain or basmati rice
- Table salt
- 2 tablespoons extra-virgin olive oil
- ¼ teaspoon grated zest plus 1 tablespoon juice from 1 orange
- 2 teaspoons sherry vinegar
- 1 small garlic clove, minced or pressed through a garlic press (about ½ teaspoon)
- ½ teaspoon ground black pepper
- 2 medium oranges, peel and pith removed, and cut into segments
- ⅓ cup chopped pitted green olives
- ⅓ cup slivered almonds, toasted
- 2 tablespoons fresh oregano leaves, minced

1. Bring 4 quarts water to a boil in a large pot. Heat a medium skillet over medium heat until hot, about 3 minutes; add the rice and toast, stirring frequently, until faintly fragrant and some grains turn opaque, about 5 minutes.

2. Stir 1½ teaspoons salt and the rice into the boiling water. Cook, uncovered, until the rice is tender but not soft, 8 to 10 minutes for long-grain rice or about 15 minutes for basmati (see note). Line a rimmed baking sheet with foil or parchment paper. Drain the rice in a colander and spread on the prepared baking sheet. Cool while preparing the salad ingredients.

3. Whisk the oil, orange zest and juice, vinegar, garlic, 1 teaspoon salt, and pepper together in a small bowl. Combine the rice, oranges, olives, almonds, and oregano in a large bowl; drizzle the dressing over the salad and toss to combine. Let stand for 20 minutes to blend the flavors, and serve.

AMERICAN POTATO SALAD

WHY THIS RECIPE WORKS: Few salads make a splash at potlucks or picnics the way potato salad does—this classic, all-American side always seems to disappear first. We wanted a recipe for a traditional, creamy (read: mayonnaise-based) potato salad that looked good—no mushy, sloppy spuds—and tasted even better.

We began by choosing red potatoes. The skin adds color to a typically monochromatic salad. We boiled them whole for best flavor and then used a serrated knife to cut the potatoes into fork-friendly chunks—the serrated edge helps prevent the skins from tearing for a nicer presentation. While the potatoes were still warm, we drizzled them with vinegar and added a sprinkle of salt and pepper; this preseasoning gave the finished salad more flavor. When the potatoes were cool, we folded in the final traditional touches—mayonnaise, pickles, and red onion—for a perfect potluck potato salad, with a creamy dressing and firm bites of potato.

American Potato Salad with Hard-Cooked Eggs and Sweet Pickles

SERVES 4 TO 6

Use sweet pickles, not relish, for the best results. For potatoes that cook through at the same rate, buy potatoes that are roughly the same size.

- 2 pounds red potatoes (about 6 medium), scrubbed (see note)
- ¼ cup red wine vinegar
- Table salt and ground black pepper
- ½ cup mayonnaise
- ¼ cup sweet pickles, chopped fine (see note)
- 3 hard-cooked eggs (see page 38), peeled and cut into ½-inch pieces
- 1 celery rib, chopped fine
- 2 tablespoons minced red onion
- 2 tablespoons minced fresh parsley leaves
- 2 teaspoons Dijon mustard

1. Place the potatoes in a large saucepan, cover with 1 inch of water, and bring to a boil over medium-high heat. Reduce the heat to medium and simmer, stirring occasionally, until the potatoes are tender (a paring knife can be slipped in and out of the potatoes with little resistance), 25 to 30 minutes.

2. Drain the potatoes and cool slightly; peel if desired. Cut the potatoes into ¾-inch pieces, using a serrated knife, while still warm, rinsing the knife occasionally in warm water to remove starch.

3. Combine the potatoes, vinegar, ½ teaspoon salt, and ¼ teaspoon pepper in a large bowl and toss gently. Cover and refrigerate until cool, about 20 minutes.

4. Meanwhile, combine the remaining ingredients and salt and pepper to taste. Add the potatoes, stir gently to combine, and serve. (The salad can be refrigerated in an airtight container for up to 1 day.)

AUSTRIAN POTATO SALAD

WHY THIS RECIPE WORKS: Austrian-style potato salad, seasoned with vinegar and mustard for a tart-and-tangy flavor, can be a welcome change of pace from traditional creamy potato salad. This style of potato salad calls on the starch from the potatoes along with an unexpected ingredient, chicken broth, to create the dressing. After cooking the sliced potatoes in broth, which we cut with an equal amount of water, we reduced the cooking liquid and mixed it with vinegar, mustard, chives, and cornichons for flavor. To give the dressing more body, and impart a rustic texture, we mashed in a small amount of our cooked potatoes. After mixing the rest of the sliced potatoes (which retained their shape but were soft and tender) with the thick vinaigrette, we had a luxurious, rich, and very different kind of potato salad.

Austrian-Style Potato Salad

SERVES 4 TO 6

If you can't find cornichons, chopped kosher dill pickles can be used in their place. To maintain its consistency, don't refrigerate the salad; it should be served within a few hours of preparation.

- 2 pounds Yukon Gold potatoes (about 4 medium), peeled, quartered, and sliced ½ inch thick
- 1 cup low-sodium chicken broth
- 2 tablespoons white wine vinegar
- 1 tablespoon sugar
- Table salt
- ¼ cup vegetable oil
- 1 small red onion, minced
- 6 cornichons, minced (about 2 tablespoons; see note)
- 2 tablespoons minced fresh chives
- 1 tablespoon Dijon mustard
- Ground black pepper

1. Bring 1 cup water, the potatoes, broth, 1 tablespoon of the vinegar, the sugar, and 1 teaspoon salt to a boil in a 12-inch skillet over high heat. Reduce the heat to medium-low, cover, and cook until the potatoes are tender (a paring knife can be slipped in and out of the potatoes with little resistance), 15 to 17 minutes. Remove the cover, increase the heat to high, and cook until the liquid has reduced, about 2 minutes.

2. Drain the potatoes in a colander set over a large bowl, reserving the cooking liquid. Set the potatoes aside. Pour off all but ½ cup cooking liquid (if ½ cup liquid does not remain, add water to make this amount). Whisk the cooking liquid, the remaining 1 tablespoon vinegar, the oil, onion, cornichons, chives, and mustard together in a large bowl.

3. Add ½ cup of the cooked potatoes to the bowl with the cooking liquid mixture and mash with a potato masher until a thick vinaigrette forms (the mixture will be slightly chunky). Add the remaining potatoes, stirring gently to combine. Season with salt and pepper to taste. Serve warm or at room temperature.

LENTIL SALADS

WHY THIS RECIPE WORKS: The most important step in making a lentil salad is perfecting the cooking of the lentils so they maintain their shape and firm-tender bite. It turns out there are two key steps. The first is to brine the lentils in warm salt water. With brining, the lentils' skins soften, which leads to fewer blowouts. The second step is to cook the lentils in the oven, which heats them gently and uniformly. Once we had perfectly cooked lentils, all we had left to do was to pair the earthy beans with a tart vinaigrette and boldly flavored mix-ins.

Lentil Salad with Olives, Mint, and Feta

SERVES 4 TO 6

French green lentils, or *lentilles du Puy*, are our preferred choice for this recipe, but it works with any type of lentil except red or yellow. Brining helps keep the lentils intact, but if you don't have time, they'll still taste good without it. The salad can be served warm or at room temperature.

- 1 cup lentils, picked over and rinsed
- Salt and pepper
- 6 cups water
- 2 cups low-sodium chicken broth
- 5 garlic cloves, lightly crushed and peeled
- 1 bay leaf
- 5 tablespoons extra-virgin olive oil
- 3 tablespoons white wine vinegar
- ½ cup pitted kalamata olives, chopped coarse
- ½ cup minced fresh mint
- 1 large shallot, minced
- 1 ounce feta cheese, crumbled (¼ cup)

1. Place lentils and 1 teaspoon salt in bowl. Cover with 4 cups warm water (about 110 degrees) and soak for 1 hour. Drain well. (Drained lentils can be refrigerated for up to 2 days before cooking.)

2. Adjust oven rack to middle position and heat oven to 325 degrees. Combine drained lentils, remaining 2 cups water, broth, garlic, bay leaf, and ½ teaspoon salt in ovensafe medium saucepan. Cover and bake until lentils are tender but remain intact, 40 minutes to 1 hour. Meanwhile, whisk oil and vinegar together in large bowl.

3. Drain lentils well; remove and discard garlic and bay leaf. Add drained lentils, olives, mint, and shallot to dressing and toss to combine. Season with salt and pepper to taste. Transfer to serving dish, sprinkle with feta, and serve.

Lentil Salad with Spinach, Walnuts, and Parmesan Cheese

Substitute sherry vinegar for white wine vinegar. Place 4 ounces baby spinach and 2 tablespoons water in bowl. Cover and microwave until spinach is wilted and volume is halved, 3 to 4 minutes. Remove bowl from microwave and keep covered for 1 minute. Transfer spinach to colander; gently press to release liquid. Transfer spinach to cutting board and chop coarse. Return to colander and press again. Substitute chopped spinach for olives and mint and ¾ cup coarsely grated Parmesan cheese for feta. Sprinkle with ⅓ cup coarsely chopped toasted walnuts before serving.

Lentil Salad with Hazelnuts and Goat Cheese

Substitute red wine vinegar for white wine vinegar and add 2 teaspoons Dijon mustard to dressing in step 2. Omit olives and substitute ¼ cup chopped parsley for mint. Substitute ½ cup crumbled goat cheese for feta and sprinkle with ⅓ cup coarsely chopped toasted hazelnuts before serving.

Lentil Salad with Carrots and Cilantro

Substitute lemon juice for white wine vinegar. Toss 2 carrots, peeled and cut into 2-inch-long matchsticks, with 1 teaspoon ground cumin, ½ teaspoon ground cinnamon, and ⅛ teaspoon cayenne pepper in bowl. Cover and microwave until carrots are tender but still crisp, 2 to 4 minutes. Substitute carrots for olives and ¼ cup minced fresh cilantro for mint. Omit shallot and feta.

CHAPTER 3

EASY SKILLET SUPPERS

PASTA FRITTATA

WHY THIS RECIPE WORKS: The classic Neapolitan pasta frittata starts with leftover cooked and sauced pasta (most often a long noodle shape) and half a dozen or so eggs beaten with salt, pepper, melted lard or butter, and grated Parmigiano-Reggiano cheese. The modest ingredients are transformed into a thick, creamy, golden-brown omelet laced with noodles. The best versions also feature small bites of meat or vegetables that contribute flavor without overly disrupting the creamy texture of the dish.

We rarely find ourselves with leftover pasta here in the test kitchen, but this dish sounded too good to pass up. Could we find a way to make a streamlined recipe that used dried pasta?

After a few tests, it was clear that angel hair was the best pasta for the job. These delicate strands brought a satisfying web of pasta to every bite without marring the tender egg texture. We found that we could cook the pasta in the same skillet we used to cook the frittata, saving time and dishes. By cooking off the water, we even skipped dirtying a strainer, and letting the pasta lightly "fry" after the water evaporated made for a lightly crispy, crunchy crust. Beating together 8 eggs provided the right balance and structure for 6 ounces of dried pasta. Gently cooking the eggs ensured that the exterior portions didn't overcook and turn rubbery while the interior came up to temperature. Three tablespoons of oil provided good richness and plenty of protection against toughness. Lastly, we added some bold flavorings, which provided richness and a bit of heat.

Pasta Frittata with Sausage and Hot Peppers

SERVES 6 TO 8

To ensure the proper texture, it's important to use angel hair pasta. We like to serve the frittata warm or at room temperature, with a green salad.

- 8 large eggs
- 1 ounce Parmesan cheese, grated (½ cup)
- 3 tablespoons extra-virgin olive oil
- 3 tablespoons coarsely chopped jarred hot cherry peppers
- 2 tablespoons chopped fresh parsley
- Salt and pepper
- 8 ounces sweet Italian sausage, casings removed, crumbled
- 2 garlic cloves, sliced thin
- 3 cups water
- 6 ounces angel hair pasta, broken in half
- 3 tablespoons vegetable oil

1. Whisk eggs, Parmesan, olive oil, cherry peppers, parsley, ½ teaspoon salt, and ½ teaspoon pepper together in large bowl until egg is even yellow color; set aside.

2. Cook sausage in 10-inch nonstick skillet over medium heat, breaking up sausage with wooden spoon, until fat renders and sausage is about half cooked, 3 to 5 minutes. Stir in garlic and cook for 30 seconds. Remove skillet from heat. Transfer sausage mixture (some sausage will still be raw) to bowl with egg mixture and wipe out skillet.

3. Bring water, pasta, vegetable oil, and ¾ teaspoon salt to boil in now-empty skillet over high heat, stirring occasionally. Cook, stirring occasionally, until pasta is tender, water has evaporated, and pasta starts to sizzle in oil, 8 to 12 minutes. Reduce heat to medium and continue to cook pasta, swirling pan and scraping under edge of pasta with rubber spatula frequently to prevent sticking (do not stir), until bottom turns golden and starts to crisp, 5 to 7 minutes (lift up edge of pasta to check progress).

4. Using spatula, push some pasta up sides of skillet so entire pan surface is covered with pasta. Pour egg mixture over pasta. Using tongs, lift up loose strands of pasta to allow egg to flow toward pan, being careful not to pull up crispy bottom crust. Cover skillet and continue to cook over medium heat until bottom crust turns golden brown and top of frittata is just set (egg below very top will still be raw), 5 to 8 minutes. Slide frittata onto large plate. Invert frittata onto second large plate and slide it browned side up back into skillet. Tuck edges of frittata into skillet with rubber spatula. Continue to cook second side of frittata until light brown, 2 to 4 minutes longer.

5. Remove skillet from heat and let stand for 5 minutes. Using your hand or pan lid, invert frittata onto cutting board. Cut into wedges and serve.

Pasta Frittata with Broccoli Rabe

Omit cherry peppers, parsley, and sausage. Heat 2 teaspoons vegetable oil in 10-inch nonstick skillet over medium heat until shimmering. Add garlic and ⅛ teaspoon red pepper flakes and cook for 1 minute. Stir in 8 ounces broccoli rabe, trimmed and cut into ½-inch pieces, 1 tablespoon water, and ¼ teaspoon salt; cover skillet and cook until broccoli rabe is crisp-tender, 2 to 3 minutes. Remove skillet from heat and add 1 tablespoon white wine vinegar. Transfer broccoli rabe to bowl with egg mixture. Proceed with recipe from step 3, cooking pasta with remaining 7 teaspoons vegetable oil.

NOTES FROM THE TEST KITCHEN

PASTA FRITTATA MADE WITHOUT LEFTOVERS

1. Add water, broken angel hair, and oil to skillet.

2. Once pasta is tender, keep cooking until water evaporates and pasta starts sizzling in oil.

3. After about 5 minutes, pasta will start to crisp (check progress by lifting up the edge).

4. Pour eggs over pasta, then gently pull up top strands to allow eggs to flow into center.

5. To brown second side, slide frittata onto plate, invert onto second plate, and return to skillet.

SKILLET BAKED ZITI

WHY THIS RECIPE WORKS: Baked ziti, a hearty combination of pasta, tomato sauce, and gooey cheese, can be time-consuming and fussy, between making the sauce, boiling the pasta, and then assembling and baking the dish. We were looking for a method that would give us the same delicious results but in less time and without watching over, or dirtying, a multitude of pots.

Instead of preparing the components of the dish separately, we found we could get all our cooking done in a skillet—including the pasta. How did we do it? We thinned the sauce with water so that the pasta cooked through in the sauce without drying out. (And the thin sauce reduced to a nicely thick consistency.) To start building the sauce, we sautéed lots of garlic with red pepper flakes, then added crushed tomatoes, water, and the ziti. When the pasta was almost tender (it would finish cooking in the oven), we added some heavy cream, for richness and body, and shredded mozzarella cheese. A little grated Parmesan boosted the cheesy flavor, and minced fresh basil and pepper were all the seasonings we needed to finish our skillet version of this family favorite.

Skillet Baked Ziti

SERVES 4

To complete this recipe in 30 minutes, preheat your oven before assembling the ingredients. If your skillet is not ovensafe, transfer the pasta mixture to a shallow 2-quart casserole dish before sprinkling with the cheese and baking. Packaged preshredded mozzarella is a real time-saver here. Penne can be used in place of the ziti.

- 1 tablespoon olive oil
- 6 medium garlic cloves, minced or pressed through a garlic press (about 2 tablespoons)
- ¼ teaspoon red pepper flakes
- Table salt
- 1 (28-ounce) can crushed tomatoes
- 3 cups water
- 12 ounces ziti (3¾ cups; see note)
- ½ cup heavy cream
- 1 ounce Parmesan cheese, grated (about ½ cup)
- ¼ cup minced fresh basil leaves
- Ground black pepper
- 4 ounces whole milk mozzarella cheese, shredded (about 1 cup; see note)

1. Adjust an oven rack to the middle position and heat the oven to 475 degrees.

2. Heat the oil in a 12-inch ovensafe nonstick skillet over medium-high heat until hot. Add the garlic, red pepper flakes, and ½ teaspoon salt and sauté until fragrant, about 1 minute. Add the crushed tomatoes, water, ziti, and ½ teaspoon salt. Cover and cook, stirring often and adjusting the heat as needed to maintain a vigorous simmer, until the ziti is almost tender, 15 to 18 minutes.

3. Stir in the cream, Parmesan, and basil. Season with salt and pepper to taste. Sprinkle the mozzarella evenly over the ziti. Transfer the skillet to the oven and bake until the cheese has melted and browned, about 10 minutes. Using potholders (the skillet handle will be hot), remove the skillet from the oven. Serve.

SKILLET CHICKEN, BROCCOLI, AND ZITI

WHY THIS RECIPE WORKS: This classic restaurant dish rarely lives up to its promise. Our challenge would lie in getting the flavors and textures just right: tender chicken, crisp broccoli, and a light, fresh sauce. We also wanted to streamline preparation for an easy weeknight dinner. First we browned pieces of skinless, boneless chicken breasts in the skillet, then we removed the chicken to build our sauce. We started with a base of sautéed onion, garlic, oregano, and red pepper flakes. And to keep all our work limited to the skillet, we cooked the pasta right in the sauce. The broccoli went in next, along with chopped sun-dried tomatoes. We then covered the skillet and simmered everything just until the broccoli turned bright green. At this point, we returned the chicken to the pan to finish cooking. A little heavy cream made the sauce silky without obscuring the flavor of the broccoli and chicken. Grated Asiago cheese enriched the sauce and gave it a pleasantly tangy flavor. And a little lemon juice added a bright note.

Skillet Chicken, Broccoli, and Ziti

SERVES 4

This recipe also works well with 8 ounces of penne. Parmesan cheese can be substituted for the Asiago.

- 1 pound boneless, skinless chicken breasts, cut into 1-inch pieces
- Table salt and ground black pepper
- 2 tablespoons vegetable or olive oil
- 1 medium onion, minced
- 3 medium garlic cloves, minced or pressed through a garlic press (about 1 tablespoon)
- ¼ teaspoon dried oregano
- ⅛ teaspoon red pepper flakes
- 8 ounces ziti (2½ cups; see note)
- 2¾ cups water
- 1⅔ cups low-sodium chicken broth
- 12 ounces broccoli florets (4 cups)
- ¼ cup oil-packed sun-dried tomatoes, rinsed and chopped coarse
- ½ cup heavy cream
- 1 ounce Asiago cheese, grated (about ½ cup), plus extra for serving (see note)
- 1 tablespoon juice from 1 lemon

1. Season the chicken with salt and pepper. Heat 1 tablespoon of the oil in a 12-inch nonstick skillet over medium-high heat until just smoking. Add the chicken in a single layer and cook for 1 minute without stirring. Stir the chicken and continue to cook until most, but not all, of the pink color has disappeared and the chicken is lightly browned around the edges, 1 to 2 minutes longer. Transfer the chicken to a clean bowl and set aside.

2. Add the remaining 1 tablespoon oil, the onion, and ½ teaspoon salt to the skillet. Return the skillet to medium-high heat and cook, stirring often, until the onion is softened, 2 to 5 minutes. Stir in the garlic, oregano, and red pepper flakes and cook until fragrant, about 30 seconds.

3. Add the ziti, 2 cups of the water, and the broth. Bring to a boil over high heat and cook until the liquid is very thick and syrupy and almost completely absorbed, 12 to 15 minutes.

4. Add the broccoli, sun-dried tomatoes, and the remaining ¾ cup water. Cover, reduce the heat to medium, and cook until the broccoli turns bright green and is almost tender, 3 to 5 minutes.

5. Uncover and return the heat to high. Stir in the cream, Asiago, and reserved chicken with any accumulated juices and continue to simmer, uncovered, until the sauce is thickened and the chicken is cooked and heated through, 1 to 2 minutes. Off the heat, stir in the lemon juice and season with salt and pepper to taste. Serve, passing more grated Asiago at the table, if desired.

SKILLET LASAGNA

WHY THIS RECIPE WORKS: Lasagna isn't usually a dish you can throw together at the last minute. Even with no-boil noodles, it takes a good amount of time to get the components just right. Our goal was to transform traditional baked lasagna into a stovetop skillet dish without losing any of its flavor or appeal.

We built a hearty, flavorful meat sauce with onions, garlic, red pepper flakes, and meatloaf mix (a more flavorful alternative to plain ground beef). A large can of diced tomatoes along with tomato sauce provided juicy tomato flavor and a nicely chunky texture. We scattered regular curly-edged lasagna noodles, broken into pieces, over the top of the sauce (smaller pieces are easier to eat and serve). We then diluted the sauce with a little water so that the noodles would cook through. After a 20-minute simmer with the lid on, the pasta was tender, the sauce was properly thickened, and it was time for the cheese. Stirring Parmesan into the dish worked well, but we discovered that the sweet creaminess of ricotta was lost unless we placed it in heaping tablespoonfuls on top of the lasagna. Replacing the lid and letting the cheese warm through for several minutes was the final step for this super-easy one-pan dish.

Skillet Lasagna

SERVES 4 TO 6

Meatloaf mix is a combination of ground beef, pork, and veal, sold prepackaged in many supermarkets. If it's unavailable, use ground beef. A skillet with a tight-fitting lid works best for this recipe. To make this dish a bit richer, sprinkle lasagna with additional shredded cheese, such as mozzarella or provolone, along with the Parmesan in step 4.

1 (28-ounce) can diced tomatoes
Water
1 tablespoon olive oil
1 medium onion, minced
Table salt
3 medium garlic cloves, minced or pressed through a garlic press (about 1 tablespoon)
⅛ teaspoon red pepper flakes
1 pound meatloaf mix (see note)
10 curly-edged lasagna noodles, broken into 2-inch lengths
1 (8-ounce) can tomato sauce
1 ounce Parmesan cheese, grated (½ cup), plus extra for serving
Ground black pepper
1 cup ricotta cheese
3 tablespoons chopped fresh basil leaves

1. Pour the tomatoes with their juice into a 4-cup liquid measuring cup. Add water until the mixture measures 4 cups.

2. Heat the oil in a 12-inch nonstick skillet over medium heat until shimmering. Add the onion and ½ teaspoon salt and cook until the onion begins to brown, 6 to 8 minutes. Stir in the garlic and red pepper flakes and cook until fragrant, about 30 seconds. Add the ground meat and cook, breaking apart the meat, until no longer pink, about 4 minutes.

3. Scatter the pasta over the meat but do not stir. Pour the diced tomatoes with their juice and the tomato sauce over the pasta. Cover and bring to a simmer. Reduce the heat to medium-low and simmer, stirring occasionally, until the pasta is tender, about 20 minutes.

4. Remove the skillet from the heat and stir in all but 2 tablespoons of the Parmesan. Season with salt and pepper to taste. Dot with heaping tablespoons of the ricotta, cover, and let stand off the heat for 5 minutes. Sprinkle with the basil and the remaining 2 tablespoons Parmesan. Serve.

SKILLET CHICKEN FAJITAS

WHY THIS RECIPE WORKS: To create indoor chicken fajitas that didn't require a slew of compensatory garnishes to be tasty, we took a fresh look at the key ingredients. For well-charred, juicy chicken we marinated boneless, skinless breasts in a potent mix of smoked paprika, garlic, cumin, cayenne, and sugar before searing them on one side and finishing them gently in a low oven. We revamped the usual bland mix of bell pepper and onion by charring poblano chiles and thinly sliced onion, and then cooking them down with cream and lime. Finally, we finished the dish with moderate amounts of complementary garnishes: pickled radish, queso fresco, and minced cilantro.

Skillet Chicken Fajitas

SERVES 4

We like to serve these fajitas with crumbled queso fresco or feta in addition to the other garnishes listed.

CHICKEN

¼ cup vegetable oil
2 tablespoons lime juice
4 garlic cloves, peeled and smashed
1½ teaspoons smoked paprika
1 teaspoon sugar
1 teaspoon salt
½ teaspoon ground cumin
½ teaspoon pepper
¼ teaspoon cayenne pepper
1½ pounds boneless, skinless chicken breasts, trimmed and pounded to ½-inch thickness

RAJAS CON CREMA

1 pound (3 to 4) poblano chiles, stemmed, halved, and seeded
1 tablespoon vegetable oil
1 onion, halved and sliced ¼ inch thick
2 garlic cloves, minced
¼ teaspoon dried thyme
¼ teaspoon dried oregano
½ cup heavy cream
1 tablespoon lime juice
½ teaspoon salt
¼ teaspoon pepper

8–12 (6-inch) flour tortillas, warmed
¼ cup minced fresh cilantro
Spicy Pickled Radishes (recipe follows)
Lime wedges

1. FOR THE CHICKEN: Whisk 3 tablespoons oil, lime juice, garlic, paprika, sugar, salt, cumin, pepper, and cayenne together in bowl. Add chicken and toss to coat. Cover and let stand at room temperature for at least 30 minutes or up to 1 hour.

2. FOR THE RAJAS CON CREMA: Meanwhile, adjust oven rack to highest position and heat broiler. Line rimmed baking sheet with aluminum foil, then arrange poblanos skin side up on baking sheet and press to flatten. Broil until skin is charred and puffed, 4 to 10 minutes, rotating baking sheet halfway through cooking. Transfer poblanos to bowl, cover, and let steam for 10 minutes. Rub most of skin from poblanos (leaving a little attached for flavor); slice into ¼-inch-thick strips. Adjust oven racks to middle and lowest positions and heat oven to 200 degrees.

3. Heat oil in 12-inch nonstick skillet over high heat until just smoking. Add onion and cook until charred and just softened, about 3 minutes. Add garlic, thyme, and oregano and cook until fragrant, about 15 seconds. Add cream and cook, stirring frequently, until reduced and cream lightly coats onion, 1 to 2 minutes. Add poblano strips, lime juice, salt, and pepper and toss to coat. Transfer vegetables to bowl, cover with foil, and place on middle oven rack. Wipe out skillet with paper towels.

4. Remove chicken from marinade and wipe off excess. Heat remaining 1 tablespoon oil in now-empty skillet over high heat until just smoking. Add chicken and cook without moving it until bottom side is well charred, about 4 minutes. Flip chicken; transfer skillet to lower oven rack. Bake until chicken registers 160 degrees, 7 to 10 minutes. Transfer to cutting board and let rest for 5 minutes; do not wash out skillet.

5. Slice chicken crosswise into ¼-inch-thick strips. Return chicken strips to skillet and toss to coat with pan juices. To serve, spoon a few pieces of chicken into center of warmed tortilla and top with spoonful of vegetable mixture, cilantro, and pickled radishes. Serve with lime wedges.

Spicy Pickled Radishes

MAKES ABOUT 1¾ CUPS

If you'd like a less spicy version of these pickled radishes, omit the seeds from the jalapeño.

- 10 radishes, trimmed and sliced thin
- ½ cup lime juice (4 limes)
- ½ jalapeño chile, stemmed and sliced thin
- 1 teaspoon sugar
- ¼ teaspoon salt

Combine all ingredients in bowl. Cover and let stand at room temperature for 30 minutes (or refrigerate for up to 24 hours).

SKILLET CHICKEN POT PIE

WHY THIS RECIPE WORKS: Quick versions of chicken pot pie are often plagued by dried-out leftover chicken, bland sauce made with canned soup, and biscuits popped out of a tube. We saw no reason why pot pie couldn't be a whole lot better. We wanted moist chicken, a richly flavored sauce, and a homemade biscuit crust.

Instead of the refrigerated biscuit dough used in most recipes, we turned to homemade biscuits, and it was easy enough to put together a simple dough for baking powder biscuits. We just whisked the dry ingredients together and stirred in heavy cream, kneaded the dough briefly, and cut it into rounds (wedges would also work fine). We then popped the biscuits into the oven to bake, while we turned to the filling.

Next, we decided to contain all our cooking to a skillet for ease of preparation. We first sautéed skinless, boneless breasts in butter, keeping the heat at medium so the exterior wouldn't toughen. We set the chicken aside after it was browned and started the sauce in the skillet with onion, celery, thyme, vermouth, and chicken broth—ingredients that contributed lots of flavor. Flour thickened the liquid, and heavy cream gave it richness and a lush texture. Gently simmering the browned chicken in this sauce not only enhanced the flavor of the sauce but also kept the chicken juicy. Using frozen peas and carrots made quick work of the vegetables. All that was left to do was to assemble our pie by placing the hot biscuits over the filling in the skillet. Our flavorful, meaty stew with tender biscuits on top was not only delicious but also fast and easy.

Skillet Chicken Pot Pie with Biscuit Topping

SERVES 4

If you don't have time to make your own biscuits for the topping, use packaged refrigerated biscuits and bake them according to the package instructions. We prefer the flavor of Pillsbury Golden Homestyle Biscuits but you can use your favorite brand (you will need anywhere from four to eight biscuits depending on their size). This pot pie can be served in a large pie plate with the biscuits arranged on top, or served directly from the skillet.

BISCUITS

- 2 cups (10 ounces) unbleached all-purpose flour, plus extra for the work surface
- 2 teaspoons sugar
- 2 teaspoons baking powder
- ½ teaspoon table salt
- 1½ cups heavy cream

FILLING

- 1½ pounds boneless, skinless chicken breasts
- Table salt and ground black pepper
- 4 tablespoons (½ stick) unsalted butter
- 1 medium onion, minced
- 1 celery rib, sliced thin
- ¼ cup unbleached all-purpose flour
- ¼ cup dry vermouth or dry white wine
- 2 cups low-sodium chicken broth
- ½ cup heavy cream
- 1½ teaspoons minced fresh thyme leaves
- 2 cups frozen pea-carrot medley, thawed

1. FOR THE BISCUITS: Adjust an oven rack to the upper-middle position and heat the oven to 450 degrees. Line a baking sheet with parchment paper and set aside.

2. Whisk the flour, sugar, baking powder, and salt together in a large bowl. Stir in the cream with a wooden spoon until a dough forms, about 30 seconds. Turn the dough out onto a lightly floured work surface and gather into a ball. Knead the dough briefly until smooth, about 30 seconds.

3. Pat the dough into a ¾-inch-thick circle. Cut the biscuits into rounds using a 2½-inch biscuit cutter or cut into eight wedges using a knife.

4. Place the biscuits on the prepared baking sheet. Bake until golden brown, about 15 minutes. Set aside on a wire rack.

5. FOR THE FILLING: While the biscuits bake, pat the chicken dry with paper towels and season with salt and pepper. Melt 2 tablespoons of the butter in a 12-inch skillet over medium heat until the foam subsides. Brown the chicken lightly on both sides, about 5 minutes total. Transfer the chicken to a clean plate.

6. Add the remaining 2 tablespoons butter to the skillet and return to medium heat until melted. Add the onion, celery, and ½ teaspoon salt and cook until the onion is softened, about 5 minutes. Stir in the flour and cook, stirring constantly, until incorporated, about 1 minute.

7. Stir in the vermouth and cook until evaporated, about 30 seconds. Slowly whisk in the broth, cream, and thyme, and bring to a simmer. Nestle the chicken into the sauce, cover, and cook over medium-low heat until the thickest part of the breasts registers 160 to 165 degrees on an instant-read thermometer, 8 to 10 minutes.

8. Transfer the chicken to a plate. Stir the peas and carrots into the sauce and simmer until heated through, about 2 minutes. When the chicken is cool enough to handle, cut or shred it into bite-size pieces and return it to the skillet. Season the filling with salt and pepper to taste.

9. FOR SERVING: Transfer the filling to a large pie plate and arrange the biscuits over the top, or serve directly from the skillet, topping individual portions with the biscuits.

SKILLET TAMALE PIE

WHY THIS RECIPE WORKS: Tamale pie—lightly seasoned, tomatoey ground beef with cornbread topping—is easy to prepare and makes a satisfying supper. But in many recipes, the filling either tastes bland and one-dimensional or turns heavy. As for the cornbread topping, it's usually from a mix and tastes like it. We wanted a skillet tamale pie with a rich, well-seasoned filling and a cornbread topping with real corn flavor.

For the beef, we found 90 percent lean ground sirloin gave us a good balance of richness and flavor. We started by sautéing minced onion and garlic. For seasoning, we used a generous amount of chili powder, which we added to the aromatics in the skillet to "bloom," or intensify, its flavor. The addition of canned black beans made our pie heartier, and canned diced tomatoes contributed additional flavor and texture. Cheddar cheese stirred into the mixture enriched the filling and also helped thicken it, and some minced fresh cilantro contributed a bright, fresh note. And to finish our pie, we skipped the cornbread mix and instead devised an easy homemade version. We spread the cornbread batter over the filling in the skillet, put the skillet in the oven to bake through, and the result was crunchy, corny topping that perfectly complemented the spicy tamale filling.

Skillet Tamale Pie

SERVES 4

Parsley can be substituted for the cilantro, if desired.

TAMALE FILLING

- 2 tablespoons vegetable oil
- 1 medium onion, minced
- 2 tablespoons chili powder
- Table salt
- 2 medium garlic cloves, minced or pressed through a garlic press (about 2 teaspoons)
- 1 pound 90 percent lean ground sirloin
- 1 (15-ounce) can black beans, drained and rinsed
- 1 (14.5-ounce) can diced tomatoes, drained
- 4 ounces cheddar cheese, shredded (about 1 cup)
- 2 tablespoons minced fresh cilantro leaves (see note)
- Ground black pepper

CORNBREAD TOPPING

- ¾ cup (3¾ ounces) unbleached all-purpose flour
- ¾ cup (3¾ ounces) yellow cornmeal
- 3 tablespoons sugar
- ¾ teaspoon table salt
- ¾ teaspoon baking powder
- ¼ teaspoon baking soda
- ¾ cup buttermilk
- 1 large egg
- 3 tablespoons unsalted butter, melted and cooled

1. Adjust an oven rack to the middle position and heat the oven to 450 degrees.

2. FOR THE TAMALE FILLING: Heat the oil in a 12-inch ovensafe skillet over medium heat until shimmering. Add the onion, chili powder, and ½ teaspoon salt and cook until the onion is softened, about 5 minutes. Stir in the garlic and cook until fragrant, about 30 seconds.

3. Stir in the ground sirloin, beans, and tomatoes and bring to a simmer, breaking up the meat with a wooden spoon, about 5 minutes. Stir the cheddar and cilantro into the filling and season with salt and pepper to taste.

4. FOR THE CORNBREAD TOPPING: Whisk the flour, cornmeal, sugar, salt, baking powder, and baking soda together in a large bowl. In a separate bowl, whisk the buttermilk and egg together. Stir the buttermilk mixture into the flour mixture until uniform. Stir in the butter until just combined.

5. Dollop the cornbread batter evenly over the filling and spread into an even layer. Bake until the cornbread is cooked through in the center, 10 to 15 minutes. Using potholders (the skillet handle will be hot), remove the skillet from the oven. Serve.

SKILLET BEEF STROGANOFF

WHY THIS RECIPE WORKS: Beef stroganoff is more often associated with bad banquet fare than with a hearty, satisfying dinner. But originally, this dish was quite elegant and was even made with filet mignon. Our goal was twofold: find a less expensive option for the beef to turn it into a within-reach weeknight supper, and bring the too-rich, often gloppy sauce back to its refined roots.

We started with the beef. Blade steaks shrank too much during cooking; sirloin tips became tender and held their shape well, but the pieces of meat crinkled up oddly. We solved that problem by pounding the meat before cutting it into strips. We first seared the meat and removed it from the pan, then sautéed mushrooms and onion in the same pan. To finish cooking the beef, we built a braising liquid with equal amounts of chicken and beef broth (beef broth alone tasted flat) and a little flour to thicken the sauce. We didn't want to overload the dish with seasonings—they would mask the flavor of the beef and mushrooms—but we found that some brandy was essential. We then returned the meat to the sauce to cook through.

To avoid cooking the noodles separately, we borrowed our method of cooking pasta directly in sauce and added the egg noodles to the braising liquid. When the noodles were tender and the beef was cooked through, we added the final touches, sour cream and lemon juice—but off the heat so that it wouldn't curdle.

Skillet Beef Stroganoff

SERVES 4

To prepare the beef, pound it with a meat pounder to an even ½-inch thickness. Slice the meat, with the grain, into 2-inch strips, then slice each piece against the grain into ½-inch strips. Brandy can ignite if added to a hot, empty skillet. Be sure to add the brandy to the skillet after stirring in the broth.

- 1½ pounds sirloin tips, pounded and cut into ½-inch strips (see note)
- Table salt and ground black pepper
- 4 tablespoons vegetable oil
- 10 ounces white mushrooms, wiped clean and sliced thin
- 1 medium onion, minced
- 2 tablespoons unbleached all-purpose flour
- 1½ cups low-sodium chicken broth
- 1½ cups beef broth
- ⅓ cup brandy (see note)
- 6 ounces wide egg noodles (4 cups)
- ⅔ cup sour cream
- 2 teaspoons juice from 1 lemon

1. Pat the beef dry with paper towels and season with salt and pepper. Heat 1 tablespoon of the oil in a 12-inch skillet over medium-high heat until just smoking. Cook half of the beef until well browned, 3 to 4 minutes per side. Transfer to a medium bowl and repeat with 1 tablespoon more oil and the remaining beef.

2. Heat the remaining 2 tablespoons oil in the now-empty skillet until shimmering. Cook the mushrooms, onion, and ½ teaspoon salt until the liquid from the mushrooms has evaporated, about 8 minutes. (If the pan becomes too brown, pour the accumulated beef juices into the skillet.) Stir in the flour and cook for 30 seconds. Gradually stir in the broths, then the brandy, and return the beef and accumulated juices to the skillet. Bring to a simmer, cover, and cook over low heat until the beef is tender, 30 to 35 minutes.

3. Stir the noodles into the beef mixture, cover, and cook, stirring occasionally, until the noodles are tender, 10 to 12 minutes. Off the heat, stir in the sour cream and lemon juice. Season with salt and pepper to taste and serve.

SKILLET-ROASTED CHICKEN DINNER

WHY THIS RECIPE WORKS: Roasted chicken and potatoes are a favorite combination for Sunday dinner. But on a busy weeknight, who has time to prepare a meal that requires at least an hour in the oven? We wanted to come up with a skillet preparation that would give us juicy, tender chicken and crispy potatoes in about half an hour.

To start, we borrowed the restaurant method of browning meat on the stovetop and finishing it in the oven. We swapped in bone-in split breasts for the whole chicken and seared the chicken in a skillet, then transferred it to a baking dish in the oven to finish cooking through.

Meanwhile, we turned to the potatoes. We chose red potatoes because their skins are tender and don't require peeling. This saved some prep time, but we couldn't get them to cook in the same amount of time as the chicken. The microwave turned out to be the solution; while the chicken was browning, we tossed the potatoes with a little olive oil, salt, and pepper and microwaved them for a few minutes to jump-start the cooking process. Placing the potatoes in a single layer in the skillet—the same one in which we'd browned the chicken—helped them cook up creamy and moist inside while their exteriors became crispy and caramelized, just when it was time to take the chicken out of the oven. Before serving, we drizzled a mixture of olive oil, lemon juice, garlic, red pepper flakes, and thyme over our chicken and potatoes for an extra hit of moisture and flavor.

Skillet-Roasted Chicken Breasts with Potatoes

SERVES 4

To complete this recipe in 30 minutes, preheat your oven before assembling the ingredients. If the split breasts are different sizes, check the smaller ones a few minutes early and remove them from the oven if they are done.

- 4 (10 to 12-ounce) bone-in, split chicken breasts
- Table salt and ground black pepper
- 6 tablespoons olive oil
- 1½ pounds red potatoes (4 to 5 medium), cut into 1-inch wedges
- 2 tablespoons juice from 1 lemon
- 1 medium garlic clove, minced or pressed through a garlic press (about 1 teaspoon)
- 1 teaspoon minced fresh thyme leaves
- Pinch red pepper flakes

1. Adjust an oven rack to the lowest position and heat the oven to 450 degrees.

2. Pat the chicken dry with paper towels and season with salt and pepper. Heat 1 tablespoon of the oil in a 12-inch nonstick skillet over medium-high heat until just smoking. Add the chicken, skin side down, and cook until deep golden, about 5 minutes.

3. Meanwhile, toss the potatoes with 1 more tablespoon of the oil, ½ teaspoon salt, and ¼ teaspoon pepper in a microwave-safe bowl. Cover tightly with plastic wrap. Microwave on high power until the potatoes begin to soften, 5 to 10 minutes, shaking the bowl (without removing the plastic) to toss the potatoes halfway through.

4. Transfer the chicken, skin side up, to a baking dish and bake until the thickest part of the breasts registers 160 to 165 degrees on an instant-read thermometer, 15 to 20 minutes.

5. While the chicken bakes, pour off any fat in the skillet, add 1 tablespoon more oil, and return to medium heat until shimmering. Drain the microwaved potatoes, then add to the skillet and cook, stirring occasionally, until golden brown and tender, about 10 minutes.

6. Whisk the remaining 3 tablespoons oil, the lemon juice, garlic, thyme, and red pepper flakes together. Drizzle the oil mixture over the chicken and potatoes before serving.

SKILLET CHICKEN AND RICE

WHY THIS RECIPE WORKS: There are lots of bad recipes out there for quick chicken and rice. Most contain leftover chicken, instant rice, and canned cream-of-something soup. We aimed to improve this dish and still deliver it quickly.

Boneless, skinless chicken breasts are definitely convenient, but we needed to prevent them from drying out. Dredging them in flour not only gave the chicken a nice brown crust but also kept the meat juicy inside. After browning the breasts on one side in a nonstick skillet, we removed them to deal with the rice. We first sautéed minced onion, garlic, and red pepper flakes in butter, then added the rice and stirred to coat the grains. Coating and toasting the rice this way before adding liquid is a technique that imparts deeper flavor and keeps the rice grains distinct and firm. We added a little white wine to the skillet for brightness. We then added chicken broth and returned the chicken to the skillet to cook through. When the chicken was done, we removed it from the skillet and finished cooking the rice. Off the heat, we added frozen peas, which cooked in a just couple of minutes, and stirred in lemon juice and sliced scallions for a fresh, bright flavor. In about 30 minutes, this dish was perfectly cooked, flavorful, and ready to serve. In addition, we developed two variations: one with cheddar and broccoli and the other with the spicy flavors of curry.

Skillet Chicken and Rice with Peas and Scallions

SERVES 4

Be sure to use chicken breasts that are roughly the same size to ensure even cooking.

- 4 (6- to 8-ounce) boneless, skinless chicken breasts, trimmed (see note)
- Table salt and ground black pepper
- ½ cup unbleached all-purpose flour
- 2 tablespoons vegetable oil
- 2 tablespoons unsalted butter
- 1 medium onion, minced
- 3 medium garlic cloves, minced or pressed through a garlic press (about 1 tablespoon)
- Pinch red pepper flakes
- 1½ cups long-grain white rice
- ½ cup dry white wine
- 4½ cups low-sodium chicken broth
- 1 cup frozen peas
- 5 scallions, sliced thin
- 2 tablespoons juice from 1 lemon
- Lemon wedges, for serving

1. Pat the chicken dry with paper towels and season with salt and pepper. Dredge the chicken in the flour to coat and shake off any excess. Heat the oil in a 12-inch nonstick skillet over medium-high heat just until smoking. Brown the chicken well on one side, about 5 minutes. Transfer the chicken to a plate and set aside.

2. Off the heat, add the butter to the skillet, and swirl to melt. Add the onion and ½ teaspoon salt and return to medium-high heat until softened, 2 to 5 minutes. Stir in the garlic and red pepper flakes and cook until fragrant, about 30 seconds. Stir in the rice thoroughly and let toast for about 30 seconds.

3. Stir in the wine and let the rice absorb it completely, about 1 minute. Stir in the broth, scraping up any browned bits. Nestle the chicken into the rice, browned side up, and add any accumulated juices. Cover and cook over medium heat until the thickest part of the chicken registers 160 to 165 degrees on an instant-read thermometer, about 10 minutes.

4. Transfer the chicken to a clean plate. Gently brush off and discard any rice clinging to the chicken, then tent the chicken with foil and set aside. Return the skillet of rice to medium-low heat, cover, and continue to cook, stirring occasionally, until the liquid is absorbed and the rice is tender, 8 to 12 minutes longer.

5. Off the heat, sprinkle the peas over the rice, cover, and let warm through, about 2 minutes. Add the scallions and lemon juice to the rice. Season with salt and pepper to taste and serve with the chicken and lemon wedges.

Skillet Chicken and Rice with Broccoli and Cheddar

SERVES 4

Be sure to use chicken breasts that are roughly the same size to ensure even cooking.

- 4 (6- to 8-ounce) boneless, skinless chicken breasts, trimmed (see note)
- Table salt and ground black pepper
- ½ cup unbleached all-purpose flour
- 3 tablespoons vegetable oil
- 1 onion, minced
- 1½ cups long-grain white rice
- 3 garlic cloves, minced or pressed through a garlic press (about 1 tablespoon)
- 4½ cups low-sodium chicken broth
- 1 (10-ounce) package frozen broccoli florets, thawed
- 4 ounces cheddar cheese, shredded (about 1 cup)
- 1 teaspoon hot sauce

1. Pat the chicken dry with paper towels and season with salt and pepper. Dredge the chicken in the flour to coat and shake off any excess. Heat 2 tablespoons of the oil in a 12-inch nonstick skillet over medium-high heat until just smoking. Brown the chicken well on one side, about 5 minutes. Transfer the chicken to a plate and set aside.

2. Add the remaining 1 tablespoon oil to the skillet and return to medium-high heat until shimmering. Add the onion and ½ teaspoon salt and cook until softened, about 5 minutes. Stir in the rice and garlic and cook until fragrant, about 30 seconds.

3. Stir in the broth, scraping up any browned bits. Nestle the chicken and any accumulated juices into the rice, browned side up. Cover and cook over medium heat until the liquid is absorbed and the thickest part of the chicken registers 160 to 165 degrees on an instant-read thermometer, about 10 minutes.

4. Transfer the chicken to a clean plate. Gently brush off and discard any rice clinging to the chicken, then tent the chicken with foil and set aside. Return the skillet of rice to medium-low heat, cover, and continue to cook, stirring occasionally, until the liquid is absorbed and the rice is tender, 8 to 12 minutes longer.

5. Off the heat, gently fold the broccoli, ½ cup of the cheddar, and the hot sauce into the rice and season with salt and pepper to taste. Sprinkle the remaining ½ cup cheddar over the top, cover, and let sit until the cheese melts, about 2 minutes. Serve with the chicken.

Skillet Curried Chicken and Rice

SERVES 4

Be sure to use chicken breasts that are roughly the same size to ensure even cooking. The heat level of curry varies from brand to brand. If your curry powder is very spicy, you may need to reduce the amount.

- 4 (6- to 8-ounce) boneless, skinless chicken breasts, trimmed (see note)
- Table salt and ground black pepper
- ½ cup unbleached all-purpose flour
- 3 tablespoons vegetable oil
- 1 onion, minced
- 1 tablespoon curry powder (see note)
- 1½ cups long-grain white rice
- 3 garlic cloves, minced or pressed through a garlic press (about 1 tablespoon)
- 4½ cups low-sodium chicken broth
- 1 cup frozen peas, thawed
- ¼ cup raisins
- ¼ cup minced fresh cilantro leaves

1. Pat the chicken dry with paper towels and season with salt and pepper. Dredge the chicken in the flour to coat and shake off any excess. Heat 2 tablespoons of the oil in a 12-inch nonstick skillet over medium-high heat until just smoking. Brown the chicken well on one side, about 5 minutes. Transfer the chicken to a plate and set aside.

2. Add the remaining 1 tablespoon oil to the skillet and return to medium-high heat until shimmering. Add the onion, curry powder, and ½ teaspoon salt and cook until softened, about 5 minutes. Stir in the rice and garlic and cook until fragrant, about 30 seconds.

3. Stir in the broth, scraping up any browned bits. Nestle the chicken and any accumulated juices into the rice, browned side up. Cover and cook over medium heat until the liquid is absorbed and the thickest part of the chicken registers 160 to 165 degrees on an instant-read thermometer, about 10 minutes.

4. Transfer the chicken to a clean plate. Gently brush off and discard any rice clinging to the chicken, then tent the chicken with foil and set aside. Return the skillet of rice to medium-low heat, cover, and continue to cook, stirring occasionally, until the liquid is absorbed and the rice is tender, 8 to 12 minutes longer.

5. Off the heat, sprinkle the peas and raisins over the rice, cover, and let warm through, about 2 minutes. Add the cilantro and gently fold into the rice. Season with salt and pepper to taste and serve with the chicken.

SKILLET JAMBALAYA

WHY THIS RECIPE WORKS: Jambalaya, a hearty mix of chicken, andouille sausage, shrimp, and rice, is typically made in a Dutch oven and can take at least an hour to prepare. We wanted a quicker, easier version without sacrificing any of the complex flavors of this Creole classic.

Bone-in, skin-on chicken thighs rather than the typical whole cut-up chicken called for in many recipes saved us time and fuss. To mimic long-simmered flavor, we browned the sausage in the skillet, added the chicken, then cooked the vegetables in some of the rendered fat. We then stirred the rice in to coat it with the fat for deep flavor. For our cooking liquid, we relied on chicken broth and clam juice (to complement the shrimp). To prevent the shrimp from overcooking, we cooked it for only a few minutes, then allowed it to finish cooking through off the heat (the residual heat is hot enough to cook it through). Entirely made in a skillet, this jambalaya makes a fast and satisfying supper.

Skillet Jambalaya

SERVES 4 TO 6

If you cannot find andouille sausage, either chorizo or linguiça can be substituted. For a spicier jambalaya, you can add 1/4 teaspoon of cayenne pepper along with the vegetables, and/or serve it with hot sauce.

- 4 bone-in, skin-on chicken thighs (about 1½ pounds), trimmed
- Table salt and ground black pepper
- 5 teaspoons vegetable oil
- ½ pound andouille sausage, halved lengthwise and sliced into ¼-inch pieces (see note)
- 1 medium onion, chopped medium
- 1 medium red bell pepper, stemmed, seeded, and chopped medium
- 5 medium garlic cloves, minced or pressed through a garlic press (about 1½ tablespoons)
- 1½ cups long-grain white rice
- 1 (14.5-ounce) can diced tomatoes, drained
- 1 (8-ounce) bottle clam juice
- 2½ cups low-sodium chicken broth
- 1 pound large shrimp (31 to 40 per pound), peeled and deveined (see page 240)
- 2 tablespoons chopped fresh parsley leaves

1. Dry the chicken thoroughly with paper towels, then season generously with salt and pepper. Heat 2 teaspoons of the oil in a 12-inch nonstick skillet over medium-high heat until just smoking. Carefully lay the chicken thighs in the skillet, skin-side down, and cook until golden, 4 to 6 minutes. Flip the chicken over and continue to cook until the second side is golden, about 3 minutes. Remove the pan from the heat and transfer the chicken to a plate. Using paper towels, remove and discard the browned chicken skin.

2. Pour off all but 2 teaspoons of the fat left in the skillet and return to medium-high heat until shimmering. Add the andouille and cook until lightly browned, about 3 minutes; transfer the sausage to a small bowl and set aside.

3. Add the remaining 3 teaspoons oil to the skillet and return to medium heat until shimmering. Add the onion, bell pepper, garlic, and 1/2 teaspoon salt; cook, scraping the browned bits off the bottom of the skillet, until the onion is softened, about 5 minutes. Add the rice and cook until the edges turn translucent, about 3 minutes. Stir in the tomatoes, clam juice, and chicken broth; bring to a simmer. Gently nestle the chicken and any accumulated juices into the rice. Cover, reduce the heat to low, and cook until the chicken is tender and cooked through, 30 to 35 minutes.

4. Transfer the chicken to a plate and cover with foil to keep warm. Stir the shrimp and sausage into the rice and continue to cook, covered, over low heat for 2 more minutes. Remove the skillet from the heat and let stand, covered, until the shrimp are fully cooked and the rice is tender, about 5 minutes. Meanwhile, shred the chicken into bite-size pieces. Stir the parsley and shredded chicken into the rice, season with salt and pepper to taste, and serve.

CHAPTER 4

ONE-DISH SUPPERS

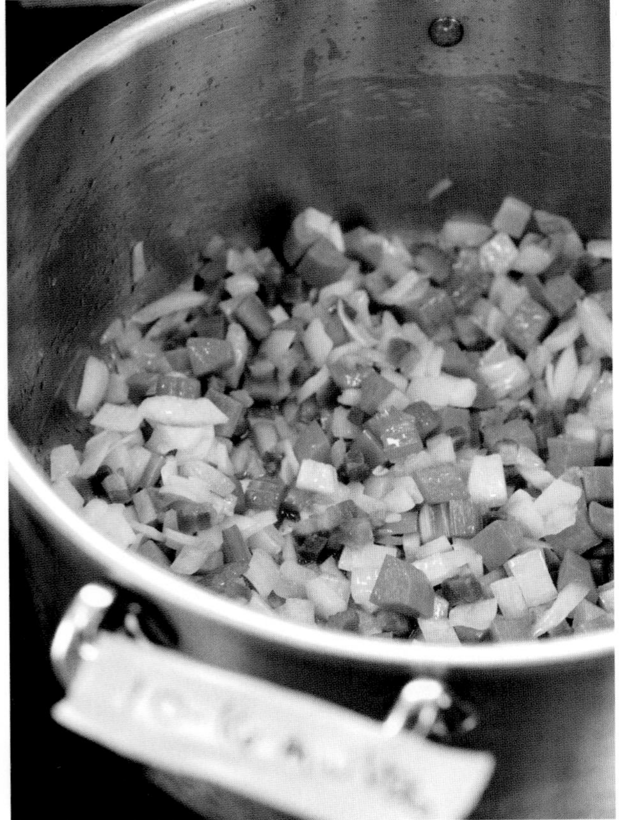

POT ROAST

WHY THIS RECIPE WORKS: The long braise that a pot roast needs can result in either a succulent roast or a dry, bland disappointment. We wanted our pot roast to be fall-apart tender with a savory sauce—a meal that would be worth the wait.

We first determined that chuck-eye is the best choice for pot roast; its fat and connective tissue break down and keep the meat moist during the long oven stay. Browning the meat first was important for flavor as well as color. Caramelizing the vegetables with a little sugar added another layer of flavor. For the braising liquid, equal amounts of beef and chicken broth tasted best; and we added just enough water for the liquid to come about halfway up the sides of the roast and prevent it from drying out. Before we moved the roast into the oven, we covered the pot with foil and then covered with the lid for a tight seal, so no steam (or flavor) escaped. The secret to tenderness is in the cooking time. Cook the meat in the oven until it reaches 210 degrees internally, then cook it for an hour longer. The reward is moist, flavorful meat that is also remarkably tender.

Simple Pot Roast

SERVES 6 TO 8

Our favorite cut for pot roast is a chuck-eye roast. Most markets sell this roast with twine tied around the center; if necessary, do this yourself. Seven-bone and top-blade roasts are also good choices for this recipe. Remember to add only enough water to come halfway up the sides of these thinner roasts, and begin checking for doneness after 2 hours. If using a top-blade roast, tie it before cooking to keep it from falling apart. Mashed or boiled potatoes are a good accompaniment to pot roast.

- 1 (3½-pound) boneless chuck-eye roast (see note)
- Table salt and ground black pepper
- 2 tablespoons vegetable oil
- 1 medium onion, chopped medium
- 1 small carrot, chopped medium
- 1 small celery rib, chopped medium
- 2 medium garlic cloves, minced or pressed through a garlic press (about 2 teaspoons)
- 2 teaspoons sugar
- 1 cup low-sodium chicken broth
- 1 cup beef broth
- 1 sprig fresh thyme
- 1–1½ cups water
- ¼ cup dry red wine

1. Adjust an oven rack to the middle position and heat the oven to 300 degrees. Thoroughly pat the roast dry with paper towels; sprinkle generously with salt and pepper.

2. Heat the oil in a large Dutch oven over medium-high heat until shimmering but not smoking. Brown the roast thoroughly on all sides, reducing the heat if the fat begins to smoke, 8 to 10 minutes. Transfer the roast to a large plate; set aside. Reduce the heat to medium; add the onion, carrot, and celery to the pot and cook, stirring occasionally, until beginning to brown, 6 to 8 minutes. Add the garlic and sugar; cook until fragrant, about 30 seconds. Add the chicken and beef broths and thyme, scraping the bottom of the pan with a wooden spoon to loosen the browned bits. Return the roast and any accumulated juices to the pot; add enough water to come halfway up the sides of the roast. Place a large piece of foil over the pot and cover tightly with the lid; bring the liquid to a simmer over medium heat, then transfer the pot to the oven. Cook, turning the roast every 30 minutes, until fully tender and a meat fork or sharp knife easily slips in and out of the meat, 3½ to 4 hours.

3. Transfer the roast to a carving board; tent with foil to keep warm. Allow the liquid in the pot to settle for about 5 minutes, then use a wide spoon to skim the fat off the surface; discard the thyme sprig. Boil over high heat until reduced to about 1½ cups, about 8 minutes. Add the red wine and reduce again to 1½ cups, about 2 minutes. Season with salt and pepper to taste.

4. Using a chef's or carving knife, cut the meat into ½-inch-thick slices, or pull apart into large pieces; transfer the meat to a warmed serving platter and pour about ½ cup sauce over the meat. Serve, passing the remaining sauce separately.

Simple Pot Roast with Root Vegetables

Add 1½ pounds carrots, sliced ½ inch thick; 1½ pounds small red potatoes, halved if larger than 1½ inches in diameter; and 1 pound parsnips, sliced ½ inch thick, to Dutch oven after cooking beef for about 3 hours, submerging them in liquid. Continue to cook until vegetables are almost tender, 30 minutes to 1 hour longer. Transfer roast to carving board; tent with foil to keep warm. Allow liquid in pot to settle for about 5 minutes, then use wide spoon to skim fat off surface; remove thyme sprig. Add wine and salt and pepper to taste; boil over high heat until vegetables are tender, 5 to 10 minutes. Using slotted spoon, transfer vegetables to warmed serving platter. Using carving knife, cut meat into ½-inch-thick slices or pull apart into large pieces; transfer meat to bowl or platter with vegetables and pour about ½ cup sauce over meat and vegetables. Serve, passing remaining sauce separately.

OLD-FASHIONED BEEF POT ROAST

WHY THIS RECIPE WORKS: Pot roast can be boring and bland, full of dry, stringy meat, stubborn bits of fat, and wan gravy. We wanted a meltingly tender roast sauced in savory, full-bodied gravy. To start, we separated the roast into two lobes, which allowed us to remove the knobs of fat that stubbornly refused to render and also shortened the cooking time. Salting the roast prior to cooking improved its flavor and allowed us to skip browning later. Sautéing the onion, celery, carrot, and garlic before we added them to the pot gave them more depth of flavor. Some recipes use water as a pot roast cooking liquid but when we tried this, the gravy turned out as you'd expect—watery. We had better luck with beef broth.

Garlic, tomato paste, red wine, thyme, and bay leaves boosted the flavor even further. The resulting gravy boasted a complex character. Finally, sealing the pot with aluminum foil before securing the lid concentrated the steam for an even simmer and fork-tender meat.

Old-Fashioned Pot Roast

SERVES 6 TO 8

To separate the roast into two pieces, simply pull apart at the natural seam and then trim away any large knobs of fat. The roast can be made up to 2 days ahead: Follow the recipe through step 4, transferring the cooked roasts to a large bowl and straining the liquid as directed in step 5. Transfer the vegetables to the bowl with the roasts, cover with plastic wrap, cut vents in the plastic, and refrigerate overnight or up to 48 hours. One hour before serving, adjust the oven rack to the middle position and heat the oven to 325 degrees. Transfer the cold roasts to a carving board, slice them against the grain into ½-inch-thick slices, place them in a 13 by 9-inch baking dish, cover tightly with foil, and bake until heated through, about 45 minutes. While the roasts heat, puree the sauce and vegetables as directed in step 5. Bring the sauce to a simmer and finish as directed in step 6 before serving with the meat.

- 1 (3½ to 4-pound) boneless chuck-eye roast, pulled into 2 pieces at the natural seam and fat trimmed (see note)
- Table salt and ground black pepper
- 2 tablespoons unsalted butter
- 2 medium onions, halved and sliced thin (about 2 cups)
- 1 large carrot, peeled and chopped medium (about 1 cup)
- 1 celery rib, chopped medium (about ¾ cup)
- 2 medium garlic cloves, minced or pressed through a garlic press (about 2 teaspoons)

- 1 cup beef broth, plus 1 to 2 cups for the sauce
- ½ cup dry red wine, plus ¼ cup for the sauce
- 1 tablespoon tomato paste
- 1 bay leaf
- 1 sprig fresh thyme plus ¼ teaspoon chopped fresh thyme leaves
- 1 tablespoon balsamic vinegar

1. Sprinkle the pieces of meat with 1½ teaspoons salt, place on a wire rack set over a rimmed baking sheet and let stand at room temperature for 1 hour.

2. Adjust an oven rack to the lower-middle position and heat the oven to 300 degrees. Heat the butter in a heavy-bottomed Dutch oven over medium heat. When the foaming subsides, add the onions and cook, stirring occasionally, until softened and beginning to brown, 8 to 10 minutes. Add the carrot and celery and continue to cook, stirring occasionally, for 5 minutes longer. Add the garlic and cook until fragrant, about 30 seconds. Stir in 1 cup of the broth, ½ cup of the wine, the tomato paste, bay leaf, and thyme sprig; bring to a simmer.

3. Season the beef generously with pepper. Using three pieces of kitchen twine, tie each piece of meat into a loaf shape for even cooking.

4. Nestle the roasts on top of the vegetables. Place a large piece of foil over the pot and cover tightly with the lid; transfer the pot to the oven. Cook the roasts until fully tender and a sharp knife easily slips in and out of the meat, 3½ to 4 hours, turning the roasts halfway through cooking.

5. Transfer the roasts to a carving board and tent loosely with foil. Strain the liquid through a fine-mesh strainer into a 4-cup liquid measuring cup. Discard the thyme sprig and bay leaf. Transfer the vegetables to a blender. Allow the liquid to settle for 5 minutes, then skim any fat off the surface. Add the remaining beef broth as necessary to bring the total amount of liquid to 3 cups. Place the liquid in the blender with the vegetables and blend until smooth, about 2 minutes. Transfer the sauce to a medium saucepan and bring to a simmer over medium heat.

6. While the sauce heats, remove the twine from the roasts and slice them against the grain into ½-inch-thick slices. Transfer the meat to a large serving platter. Stir the chopped thyme, remaining ¼ cup wine, and the balsamic vinegar into the sauce and season with salt and pepper to taste. Serve immediately, passing the sauce separately.

Old-Fashioned Pot Roast with Root Vegetables

Follow the recipe for Old-Fashioned Pot Roast, adding 1 pound carrots, peeled and cut crosswise into 2-inch pieces; 1 pound parsnips, peeled and cut crosswise into 2-inch pieces; and 1½ pounds russet potatoes, peeled, halved lengthwise, and each half quartered, to the pot in step 4 after the roasts have cooked for 3 hours. Once the pot roast and vegetables are fully cooked, transfer any large pieces of carrot, parsnip, and potato to a serving platter using a slotted spoon, cover tightly with foil, and proceed with the recipe as directed.

PRESSURE-COOKER POT ROAST

WHY THIS RECIPE WORKS: Most pressure-cooker pot roast recipes sell themselves on speed alone, often producing overcooked vegetables, fatty meat, and bland, watery gravy. In order to put the pressure cooker to work for us, we made a few key adjustments. First we split the roast into two smaller pieces to speed cooking and allow for better trimming of fat. We decreased the liquid in the pot to account for very little evaporation. And we also chose to purposefully overcook the vegetables and then puree them into the gravy for better flavor and consistency. Finally, we added some baking soda to encourage the flavorful Maillard reaction in the pressurized pot.

Pressure-Cooker Pot Roast

SERVES 6 TO 8

If using an electric pressure cooker, turn off the cooker immediately after the pressurized cooking time and let the pressure release naturally for 10 minutes; do not let the cooker switch to the warm setting. To adjust for differences among pressure cookers, cook the roasts for the recommended time, check for doneness, and, if needed, repressurize and cook up to 10 minutes longer. A half teaspoon of red wine vinegar can be substituted for the wine.

- 1 (3 ½- to 4-pound) boneless beef chuck-eye roast, pulled into 2 pieces at natural seam and trimmed of large pieces of fat
- Kosher salt and pepper
- 4 tablespoons unsalted butter, cut into 4 pieces
- 1 onion, sliced thick
- 1 celery rib, sliced thick
- 1 carrot, peeled and sliced thick
- ¼ teaspoon baking soda
- 1 cup beef broth
- 2 teaspoons soy sauce
- 2 bay leaves
- 1 tablespoon red wine
- 1 sprig fresh thyme

1. Using 3 pieces of kitchen twine per roast, tie each roast crosswise at equal intervals into loaf shape. Season roasts with salt and pepper and set aside.

2. Melt 2 tablespoons butter in pressure cooker over medium heat; refrigerate remaining 2 tablespoons butter. Add onion, celery, carrot, and baking soda to pot and cook until onion breaks down and liquid turns golden brown, about 5 minutes. Stir in broth, soy sauce, and bay leaves, scraping up any browned bits. Nestle roasts side by side on top of vegetables in cooker.

3. Lock lid in place and bring pot to high pressure over high heat, 3 to 8 minutes. As soon as indicator signals that pot has reached high pressure, reduce heat to medium-low and cook for 55 minutes, adjusting heat as needed to maintain high pressure.

4. Remove pot from heat and let pressure release naturally for 10 minutes. Quick-release any remaining pressure, then remove lid, allowing steam to escape away from you. Transfer roasts to carving board, tent with aluminum foil, and let rest for 20 minutes.

5. Meanwhile, strain liquid through fine-mesh strainer into fat separator; discard bay leaves. Transfer vegetables in strainer to blender. Let liquid settle for 5 minutes, then pour defatted liquid into blender with vegetables. Blend until smooth, about 1 minute. Transfer sauce to medium saucepan. Add wine, thyme sprig, and 2 tablespoons chilled butter and bring to boil over high heat. Cook until sauce is thickened and measures 2 cups, 5 to 8 minutes.

6. Remove twine from roasts and slice against grain into ½-inch-thick slices. Transfer meat to serving platter and season with salt to taste. Remove thyme sprig from sauce and season sauce with salt and pepper to taste. Spoon half of sauce over meat. Serve, passing remaining sauce separately.

CATALAN-STYLE BEEF STEW WITH MUSHROOMS

WHY THIS RECIPE WORKS: Supremely meaty and complexly flavored, Spanish beef stew is a little different than its American counterpart. It starts with a *sofrito*, a slow-cooked jamlike mixture of onions, spices, and herbs that builds a flavor-packed base. We normally use chuck-eye for stew, but swapped it out for boneless beef short ribs, determining that they gave us a beefier-tasting stew. We finished the stew with a mixture of toasted bread, toasted almonds, garlic, and parsley. This mixture, called a *picada*, brightened the stew's flavor and thickened the broth.

Catalan-Style Beef Stew with Mushrooms

SERVES 4 TO 6

While we developed this recipe with Albariño, a dry Spanish white wine, you can also use a Sauvignon Blanc. Remove the woody base of the oyster mushroom stems before cooking. An equal amount of quartered button mushrooms may be substituted for the oyster mushrooms. Serve the stew with boiled or mashed potatoes or rice.

STEW

- 2 tablespoons olive oil
- 2 large onions, chopped fine
- ½ teaspoon sugar
- Kosher salt and pepper
- 2 plum tomatoes, halved lengthwise, pulp grated on large holes of box grater, and skins discarded
- 1 teaspoon smoked paprika
- 1 bay leaf
- 1½ cups dry white wine
- 1½ cups water
- 1 large sprig fresh thyme
- ¼ teaspoon ground cinnamon
- 2½ pounds boneless beef short ribs, trimmed and cut into 2-inch cubes

PICADA

- ¼ cup whole blanched almonds
- 2 tablespoons olive oil
- 1 slice hearty white sandwich bread, crusts removed, torn into 1-inch pieces
- 2 garlic cloves, peeled
- 3 tablespoons minced fresh parsley

- 8 ounces oyster mushrooms, trimmed
- 1 teaspoon sherry vinegar

1. FOR THE STEW: Adjust oven rack to middle position and heat oven to 300 degrees. Heat oil in Dutch oven over medium-low heat until shimmering. Add onions, sugar, and ½ teaspoon salt; cook, stirring often, until onions are deeply caramelized, 30 to 40 minutes. Add tomatoes, smoked paprika, and bay leaf; cook, stirring often, until darkened and thick, 5 to 10 minutes.

2. Add wine, water, thyme sprig, and cinnamon to pot, scraping up any browned bits. Season beef with 1½ teaspoons salt and ½ teaspoon pepper and add to pot. Increase heat to high and bring to simmer. Transfer to oven and cook, uncovered. After 1 hour stir stew to redistribute meat, return to oven, and continue to cook, uncovered, until meat is tender, 1½ to 2 hours longer.

3. FOR THE PICADA: While stew is in oven, heat almonds and 1 tablespoon oil in 10-inch skillet over medium heat; cook, stirring often, until almonds are golden brown, 3 to 6 minutes. Using slotted spoon, transfer almonds to food processor. Return now-empty skillet to medium heat, add bread, and cook, stirring often, until toasted, 2 to 4 minutes; transfer to food processor with almonds. Add garlic and process until mixture is finely ground, about 20 seconds, scraping down bowl as needed. Transfer mixture to bowl, stir in parsley, and set aside.

4. Return again-empty skillet to medium heat. Heat remaining 1 tablespoon oil until shimmering. Add mushrooms and ½ teaspoon salt; cook, stirring often, until tender, 5 to 7 minutes. Transfer to bowl and set aside.

5. Remove bay leaf and thyme sprig. Stir picada, mushrooms, and vinegar into stew. Season with salt and pepper to taste and serve.

BEEF CARBONNADE

WHY THIS RECIPE WORKS: Most recipes for this Belgian beef, onion, and beer stew go in one of two directions: In one version, the recipe masks its genuine flavors and, in others, the recipes rigidly adhere to the "three ingredients only" rule, so the stew is pale and tasteless. We wanted hearty chunks of beef and sliced sweet onion in a thickened broth, laced with the malty flavor of beer. We found that top blade steak, which has a fair amount of marbling, provided the best texture and a "buttery" flavor that worked well alongside the onions and beer. White and red onions were too sweet in our stew; yellow onions worked better. The onions should be browned only lightly; overcaramelization caused them to disintegrate. Tomato paste gave the stew depth, as did garlic. Fresh thyme and bay

leaves provided seasoning, and a splash of cider vinegar added the right level of acidity. Beer is a staple of Belgian cooking, and we found that it's less forgiving than wine when used in a stew. The light lagers we tried resulted in pale, watery stews; better were dark ales and stouts. But beer alone often made for bitter-tasting stew, so we included some broth; a combination of chicken and beef broth gave us more solid and complex flavor.

Belgian Beef, Beer, and Onion Stew (Carbonnade à la Flamande)

SERVES 6

Top blade steaks (also called blade or flatiron steaks) are our first choice, but any boneless roast from the chuck will work. If you end up using a chuck roast, look for the chuck-eye roast, an especially flavorful cut that can easily be trimmed and cut into 1-inch pieces. Buttered egg noodles or mashed potatoes make excellent accompaniments to carbonnade.

- 3½ pounds top blade steaks, 1 inch thick, trimmed of gristle and fat and cut into 1-inch pieces (see note and page 72)
- Table salt and ground black pepper
- 3 tablespoons vegetable oil
- 2 pounds yellow onions (about 4 medium), halved and sliced ¼ inch thick
- 1 tablespoon tomato paste
- 2 medium garlic cloves, minced or pressed through a garlic press (about 2 teaspoons)
- 3 tablespoons unbleached all-purpose flour
- ¾ cup low-sodium chicken broth
- ¾ cup beef broth
- 1½ cups (12-ounce bottle or can) dark beer or stout
- 4 sprigs fresh thyme, tied with kitchen twine
- 2 bay leaves
- 1 tablespoon cider vinegar

1. Adjust an oven rack to the lower-middle position and heat the oven to 300 degrees. Dry the beef thoroughly with paper towels, then season generously with salt and pepper. Heat 2 teaspoons of the oil in a large Dutch oven over medium-high heat until beginning to smoke; add about one third of the beef to the pot. Cook without moving the pieces until well browned, 2 to 3 minutes; using tongs, turn each piece and continue cooking until the second side is well browned, about 5 minutes longer. Transfer the browned beef to a medium bowl. Repeat with 2 teaspoons more oil and half of the remaining beef. (If the drippings in the bottom of the pot are very dark, add ½ cup of the chicken or beef broth and scrape the pan bottom with a wooden spoon to loosen the browned bits; pour the liquid into the bowl with the browned beef, then proceed.) Repeat once more with 2 teaspoons more oil and the remaining beef.

2. Add the remaining 1 tablespoon oil to the now-empty Dutch oven; reduce the heat to medium-low. Add the onions, ½ teaspoon salt, and the tomato paste; cook, scraping the bottom of the pot with a wooden spoon to loosen the browned bits, until the onions have released some moisture, about 5 minutes. Increase the heat to medium and continue to cook, stirring occasionally, until the onions are lightly browned, 12 to 14 minutes. Stir in the garlic and cook until fragrant, about 30 seconds. Add the flour and stir until the onions are evenly coated and the flour is lightly browned, about 2 minutes. Stir in the broths, scraping the pan bottom to loosen any browned bits; stir in the beer, thyme, bay leaves, vinegar, browned beef with any accumulated juices, and salt and pepper to taste. Increase the heat to medium-high and bring to a full simmer, stirring occasionally; cover partially, then place the pot in the oven. Cook until a fork inserted into the beef meets little resistance, 2 to 2½ hours.

3. Discard the thyme and bay leaves. Season with salt and pepper to taste and serve. (The stew can be cooled and refrigerated in an airtight container for up to 4 days; reheat over medium-low heat.)

NOTES FROM THE TEST KITCHEN

TRIMMING BLADE STEAKS

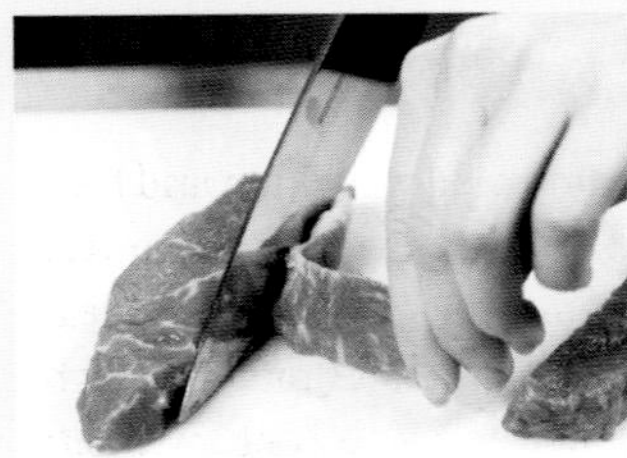

To trim blade steaks, halve each steak lengthwise, leaving the gristle on one half. Then simply cut the gristle away.

HUNGARIAN BEEF STEW

WHY THIS RECIPE WORKS: The Americanized versions of Hungarian goulash served in the United States bear little resemblance to the authentic dish. Sour cream has no place in the pot, nor do mushrooms, green peppers, or most herbs. We wanted the real deal—a simple dish of tender braised beef packed with paprika flavor.

To achieve the desired spicy intensity, some recipes call for as much as half a cup of paprika per three pounds of meat, but that much fine spice gave the dish a gritty, dusty texture. The chefs at a few Hungarian restaurants introduced us to paprika cream, a condiment as common in Hungarian cooking as the dried spice—but hard to find in the U.S. Instead, we created our own quick version by pureeing dried paprika with roasted red peppers and a little tomato paste and vinegar. This mixture imparted vibrant paprika flavor without any offensive grittiness.

As for the meat, after settling on chuck-eye roast, we bought a whole roast and cut it ourselves into uniform, large pieces to ensure even cooking. Since searing the meat first—normally standard stew protocol—competed with the paprika's brightness, we referred back to a trend we noticed in the goulash recipes gathered during research: skipping the sear. We tried this, softening the onions in the pot first, adding paprika paste, carrots, and then meat before placing the covered pot in the oven. Sure enough, the onions and meat provided enough liquid to stew the meat, and the bits of beef that cooked above the liquid line browned in the hot air. A bit of broth added near the end of cooking thinned out the stewing liquid to just the right consistency.

Hungarian Beef Stew

SERVES 6

Do not substitute hot, half-sharp, or smoked Spanish paprika for the sweet paprika in the stew, as they will compromise the flavor of the dish. Since paprika is vital to this recipe, it is best to use a fresh container. We prefer chuck-eye roast, but any boneless roast from the chuck will work. Cook the stew in a Dutch oven with a tight-fitting lid. (Alternatively, to ensure a tight seal, place a sheet of foil over the pot before adding the lid.) Serve the stew over boiled potatoes or egg noodles.

- 1 boneless chuck-eye roast (about 3½ pounds), trimmed of excess fat and cut into 1½-inch cubes (see note)
- Table salt
- 1 (12-ounce) jar roasted red peppers, drained and rinsed (about 1 cup)
- ⅓ cup sweet paprika (see note)
- 2 tablespoons tomato paste
- 1 tablespoon white vinegar

2 tablespoons vegetable oil
6 medium onions, minced (about 6 cups)
4 large carrots, peeled and cut into 1-inch-thick rounds (about 2 cups)
1 bay leaf
1 cup beef broth, warmed
¼ cup sour cream (optional)
Ground black pepper

1. Adjust an oven rack to the lower-middle position and heat the oven to 325 degrees. Sprinkle the meat evenly with 1 teaspoon salt and let stand for 15 minutes. Process the roasted peppers, paprika, tomato paste, and 2 teaspoons of the vinegar in a food processor until smooth, 1 to 2 minutes, scraping down the sides as needed.

2. Combine the oil, onions, and 1 teaspoon salt in a large Dutch oven; cover and set over medium heat. Cook, stirring occasionally, until the onions have softened but have not yet begun to brown, 8 to 10 minutes. (If the onions begin to brown, reduce the heat to medium-low and stir in 1 tablespoon water.)

3. Stir in the paprika mixture; cook, stirring occasionally, until the onions stick to the bottom of the pan, about 2 minutes. Add the beef, carrots, and bay leaf; stir until the beef is well coated. Using a rubber spatula, scrape down the sides of the pot. Cover the pot and transfer to the oven. Cook until the meat is almost tender and the surface of the liquid is ½ inch below the top of the meat, 2 to 2½ hours, stirring every 30 minutes. Remove the pot from the oven and add enough beef broth that the surface of the liquid is ¼ inch from the top of the meat (the beef should not be fully submerged). Return the covered pot to the oven and continue to cook until a fork slips easily in and out of the beef, about 30 minutes longer.

4. Skim the fat off the surface using a wide spoon; stir in the remaining 1 teaspoon vinegar and the sour cream (if using). Remove the bay leaf, season with salt and pepper to taste, and serve. (The stew can be cooled, covered tightly, and refrigerated in an airtight container for up to 2 days; wait to add the optional sour cream until after reheating. Before reheating, skim the hardened fat from the surface and add enough water to the stew to thin it slightly.)

BRAISED SHORT RIBS

WHY THIS RECIPE WORKS: Short ribs have great flavor and luscious texture, but their excess fat can be a problem since so much fat is rendered during the ribs' stint in the oven. Most recipes call for resting them in the braising liquid overnight, so that the fat solidifies into an easy-to-remove layer. However, most people don't plan their dinners days in advance and skimming such a large amount of fat off with a spoon doesn't work well enough. The meat and sauce come out greasy, no matter how diligent one's spoon-wielding. We wanted a silky, grease-free sauce and fork-tender short rib meat, all in a few hours.

The first task was to choose the right rib. Instead of traditional bone-in short ribs, we used boneless short ribs, which rendered significantly less fat than bone-in. While we didn't miss much flavor from the bones, we did want the body that the bones' connective tissue added. To solve this, we sprinkled a bit of gelatin into the sauce to restore suppleness. We also wanted to ramp up the richness of the sauce. We jump-started flavor by reducing wine with browned aromatics (onions, garlic, and carrots) before using the liquid to cook the meat. This added the right intensity, but we needed another cup of liquid to keep the meat half-submerged—the right level for braises. More wine yielded too much wine flavor; we used beef broth instead. As for the excess fat, the level was low enough that we could strain and defat the liquid in a fat separator. Reducing the liquid concentrated the flavors and made for a rich, luxurious sauce for our fork-tender boneless short ribs.

Braised Beef Short Ribs

SERVES 6

Make sure that the ribs are at least 4 inches long and 1 inch thick. If boneless ribs are unavailable, substitute 7 pounds of bone-in beef short ribs at least 4 inches long with 1 inch of meat above the bone and bone them yourself (see page 74).

3½ pounds boneless beef short ribs, trimmed of excess fat (see note)
Table salt and ground black pepper
2 tablespoons vegetable oil
2 large onions, sliced thin from pole to pole (about 4 cups)
1 tablespoon tomato paste
6 medium garlic cloves, peeled
2 cups red wine, such as Cabernet Sauvignon or Côtes du Rhône
1 cup beef broth
4 large carrots, peeled and cut crosswise into 2-inch pieces
4 sprigs fresh thyme
1 bay leaf
¼ cup cold water
½ teaspoon powdered gelatin

1. Adjust an oven rack to the lower-middle position and heat the oven to 300 degrees. Pat the beef dry with paper towels and season with 2 teaspoons salt and 1 teaspoon pepper. Heat 1 tablespoon of the oil in a large Dutch oven over medium-high heat until smoking. Add half of the beef and cook, without stirring, until well browned, 4 to 6 minutes. Turn the beef and continue to cook on the second side until well browned, 4 to 6 minutes longer, reducing the heat if the fat begins to smoke. Transfer the beef to a medium bowl. Repeat with the remaining 1 tablespoon oil and the remaining meat.

2. Reduce the heat to medium, add the onions, and cook, stirring occasionally, until softened and beginning to brown, 12 to 15 minutes. (If the onions begin to darken too quickly, add 1 to 2 tablespoons water to the pan.) Add the tomato paste and cook, stirring constantly, until it browns on the sides and bottom of the pan, about 2 minutes. Add the garlic and cook until aromatic, about 30 seconds. Increase the heat to medium-high, add the wine, and simmer, scraping the bottom of the pan with a wooden spoon to loosen the browned bits, until reduced by half, 8 to 10 minutes. Add the broth, carrots, thyme, and bay leaf. Add the beef and any accumulated juices to the pot; cover and bring to a simmer. Transfer the pot to the oven and cook, using tongs to turn the meat twice during cooking, until a fork slips easily in and out of the meat, 2 to 2½ hours.

3. Place the water in a small bowl and sprinkle the gelatin on top; let stand for at least 5 minutes. Using tongs, transfer the meat and carrots to a serving platter and tent with foil. Strain the cooking liquid through a fine-mesh strainer into a fat separator or bowl, pressing on the solids to extract as much liquid as possible; discard the solids. Allow the liquid to settle for about 5 minutes and strain off the fat. Return the cooking liquid to the Dutch oven and cook over medium heat until reduced to 1 cup, 5 to 10 minutes. Remove from the heat and stir in the gelatin mixture; season with salt and pepper to taste. Pour the sauce over the meat and carrots and serve.

NOTES FROM THE TEST KITCHEN

BONING SHORT RIBS

1. With a chef's knife as close as possible to the bone, carefully remove the meat.

2. Trim the excess hard fat and silverskin from both sides of the meat.

SLOW-COOKER BRAISED SHORT RIBS

WHY THIS RECIPE WORKS: Beef short ribs, which contain lots of fat and connective tissue, are ideal for long, slow cooking. We wanted to develop a recipe for the slow cooker that would produce meaty ribs in a rich, oniony sauce.

Thoroughly browning the ribs first gave us a good start. Next we browned lots of onions. Instead of stock or broth, we chose beer as the braising liquid, and dark beer worked best. Since flavors tend to become muted after hours in a slow cooker, we intensified the taste and color of the sauce with tomato paste and soy sauce. But we thought the dish lacked balance. We found our solution in an unusual source: prunes. They melted into the sauce and were unidentifiable, but their sweetness balanced the other flavors nicely. Livened up just before serving with some Dijon mustard and fresh thyme, these slow-cooker short ribs had the rich, complex flavor we were looking for.

Slow-Cooker Beer-Braised Short Ribs

SERVES 4 TO 6

The only way to remove fat from the braising liquid is to prepare this recipe a day or two before you want to serve it. Luckily, the short ribs actually taste better if cooked in advance and then reheated in the defatted braising liquid.

- 5 pounds English-style beef short ribs (6 to 8 ribs), trimmed of excess fat
- Table salt and ground black pepper
- 2 tablespoons vegetable oil
- 2 tablespoons unsalted butter
- 3 pounds yellow onions (about 6 medium), halved and sliced thin
- 2 tablespoons tomato paste
- 2 (12-ounce) bottles dark beer

12 pitted prunes
2 tablespoons soy sauce
2 tablespoons Minute tapioca
2 bay leaves
2 teaspoons minced fresh thyme leaves
3 tablespoons Dijon mustard
2 tablespoons minced fresh parsley leaves

1. Season the ribs with salt and pepper. Heat the oil in a 12-inch skillet over medium-high heat until just smoking. Add half of the ribs, meaty side down, and cook until well browned, about 5 minutes. Turn each rib on one side and cook until well browned, about 1 minute. Repeat with the remaining sides. Transfer the ribs to a slow-cooker insert, arranging them meaty side down. Repeat with the remaining ribs.

2. Pour off all but 1 teaspoon fat from the skillet. Add the butter and reduce the heat to medium. When the butter has melted, add the onions and cook, stirring occasionally, until well browned, 25 to 30 minutes. Stir in the tomato paste and cook, coating the onions with the tomato paste, until the paste begins to brown, about 5 minutes. Stir in the beer, bring to a simmer, and cook, scraping the browned bits from the pan bottom with a wooden spoon, until the foaming subsides, about 5 minutes. Remove the skillet from the heat and stir in the prunes, soy sauce, tapioca, bay leaves, and 1 teaspoon of the thyme. Transfer to the slow-cooker insert.

3. Set the slow cooker on low, cover, and cook until the ribs are fork-tender, 10 to 11 hours. (Alternatively, cook on high for 4 to 5 hours.) Transfer the ribs to a baking dish and strain the liquid through a fine-mesh strainer into a bowl. Cover and refrigerate for at least 8 hours or up to 2 days.

4. When ready to serve, use a spoon to skim off the hardened fat from the liquid. Place the short ribs, meaty side down, and the liquid in a Dutch oven and reheat over medium heat until warmed through, about 20 minutes. Transfer the ribs to a serving platter. Whisk the mustard and remaining 1 teaspoon thyme into the sauce and season with salt and pepper to taste. Pour 1 cup of the sauce over the ribs. Sprinkle with the parsley and serve, passing the remaining sauce separately.

NEW ENGLAND–STYLE HOME-CORNED BEEF AND CABBAGE

WHY THIS RECIPE WORKS: Corned beef and cabbage is a hearty winter favorite, but too many recipes result in overly salty beef and washed-out, mushy vegetables. To control the salt level in our beef, we eschewed commercially corned beef and set out to cure our own with an easy dry rub. We cooked our corned beef in the oven so it would benefit from the oven's slow, steady, and gentle heat. Cooking the vegetables separately in the meat's broth (while the meat rested) allowed the vegetables to be enriched by the meat's juices, but still retain their own flavor.

New England–Style Home-Corned Beef and Cabbage

SERVES 8

Leave a bit of fat attached to the brisket for better texture and flavor. A similar size point-cut brisket can be used in this recipe. The meat is cooked fully when it is tender, the muscle fibers have loosened visibly, and a skewer slides in with minimal resistance. Serve this dish with horseradish, either plain or mixed with whipped cream or sour cream, or with grainy mustard.

CORNED BEEF

½ cup kosher salt
1 tablespoon cracked black peppercorns
1 tablespoon dried thyme
2¼ teaspoons ground allspice
1½ teaspoons paprika
2 bay leaves, crumbled
1 (4- to 5-pound) beef brisket, flat cut, trimmed

VEGETABLES

1½ pounds carrots, peeled and halved crosswise, thick end halved lengthwise
1½ pounds small red potatoes
1 small rutabaga (1 pound), peeled and halved crosswise; each half cut into 6 chunks
1 small head green cabbage (2 pounds), uncored, cut into 8 wedges

1. FOR THE CORNED BEEF: Combine salt, peppercorns, thyme, allspice, paprika, and bay leaves in bowl.

2. Using metal skewer, poke about 30 holes on each side of brisket. Rub each side evenly with salt mixture. Place brisket in 2-gallon zipper-lock bag, forcing out as much air as possible. Place in 13 by 9-inch baking dish, cover with second, similar-size pan, and weight with 2 bricks or heavy cans of similar weight. Refrigerate for 5 to 7 days, turning once a day.

3. Rinse brisket and pat it dry. Place brisket in Dutch oven and cover brisket with water by 1 inch. Bring to boil over high heat, skimming any scum that rises to surface. Reduce heat to medium-low, cover, and simmer until skewer inserted in thickest part of brisket slides in and out with ease, 2 to 3 hours.

4. Adjust oven rack to middle position and heat oven to 200 degrees. Transfer meat to large platter, ladle 1 cup cooking liquid over meat, cover with aluminum foil, and place in oven to keep warm.

5. FOR THE VEGETABLES: Add carrots, potatoes, and rutabaga to Dutch oven and bring to a boil over high heat. Reduce heat to medium-low, cover, and simmer until vegetables begin to soften, about 7 minutes.

6. Add cabbage, increase heat to high and return to boil. Reduce heat to medium-low, cover, and simmer until all vegetables are tender, 13 to 18 minutes.

7. Meanwhile, remove meat from oven, transfer to carving board, and slice against grain into ¼-inch slices. Return meat to platter. Transfer vegetables to meat platter, moisten with additional broth, and serve.

HOME-CORNED BEEF WITH VEGETABLES

WHY THIS RECIPE WORKS: Making corned beef at home is actually quite simple. And though the process takes several days, it's almost entirely hands-off. After comparing wet-curing and dry-curing methods, we chose to go with the wet cure, which was considerably faster and easier, with no need for daily flipping. We soaked a flat-cut brisket for six days in a brine made with table and pink curing salts, which improved both the flavor and color of the meat. The remainder of the seasonings included brown sugar, garlic cloves, allspice berries, bay leaves, and coriander seeds—all of which put the meat a notch above commercial corned beef. After the soak, the seasoning had penetrated to the core of the meat. To break down the brisket's abundant collagen, we gently simmered the meat in a low oven after first bringing it to a simmer on the stovetop, which helped cut cooking time. As for the classic corned beef accompaniments, we added carrots, potatoes, and cabbage to the pot while the meat rested so that they simmered briefly in the seasoned cooking liquid. To add some last-minute subtle but clear depth to the dish, we filled a cheesecloth bundle with more garlic and curing spices and steeped it in the cooking liquid before serving.

Home-Corned Beef With Vegetables

SERVES 8 TO 10

Pink curing salt #1, which can be purchased online or in stores specializing in meat curing, is a mixture of table salt and nitrites; it is also called Prague Powder #1, Insta Cure #1, or DQ Curing Salt #1. In addition to the pink salt, we use table salt here. If using Diamond Crystal kosher salt, increase the salt to 1½ cups; if using Morton kosher salt, increase to 1⅛ cups.

This recipe requires six days to corn the beef, and you will need cheesecloth. Look for a uniformly thick brisket to ensure that the beef cures evenly. The brisket will look gray after curing but will turn pink once cooked.

CORNED BEEF

- 1 (4½- to 5-pound) beef brisket, flat cut
- ¾ cup salt
- ½ cup packed brown sugar
- 2 teaspoons pink curing salt #1
- 6 garlic cloves, peeled
- 6 bay leaves
- 5 allspice berries
- 2 tablespoons peppercorns
- 1 tablespoon coriander seeds

VEGETABLES

- 6 carrots, peeled, halved crosswise, thick ends halved lengthwise
- 1½ pounds small red potatoes, unpeeled
- 1 head green cabbage (2 pounds), uncored, cut into 8 wedges

1. FOR THE CORNED BEEF: Trim fat on surface of brisket to ⅛ inch. Dissolve salt, sugar, and curing salt in 4 quarts water in large container. Add brisket, 3 garlic cloves, 4 bay leaves, allspice berries, 1 tablespoon peppercorns, and coriander seeds to brine. Weigh brisket down with plate, cover, and refrigerate for 6 days.

2. Adjust oven rack to middle position and heat oven to 275 degrees. Remove brisket from brine, rinse, and pat dry with paper towels. Cut 8-inch square triple thickness of cheesecloth. Place remaining 3 garlic cloves, remaining 2 bay leaves, and remaining 1 tablespoon peppercorns in center of cheesecloth and tie into bundle with kitchen twine. Place brisket, spice bundle, and 2 quarts water in Dutch oven. (Brisket may not lie flat but will shrink slightly as it cooks.)

3. Bring to simmer over high heat, cover, and transfer to oven. Cook until fork inserted into thickest part of brisket slides in and out with ease, 2½ to 3 hours.

4. Remove pot from oven and turn off oven. Transfer brisket to large ovensafe platter, ladle 1 cup of cooking liquid over meat, cover, and return to oven to keep warm.

5. FOR THE VEGETABLES: Add carrots and potatoes to pot and bring to simmer over high heat. Reduce heat to medium-low, cover, and simmer until vegetables begin to soften, 7 to 10 minutes.

6. Add cabbage to pot, increase heat to high, and return to simmer. Reduce heat to low, cover, and simmer until all vegetables are tender, 12 to 15 minutes.

7. While vegetables cook, transfer beef to carving board and slice ¼ inch thick against grain. Return beef to platter. Using slotted spoon, transfer vegetables to platter with beef. Moisten with additional broth and serve.

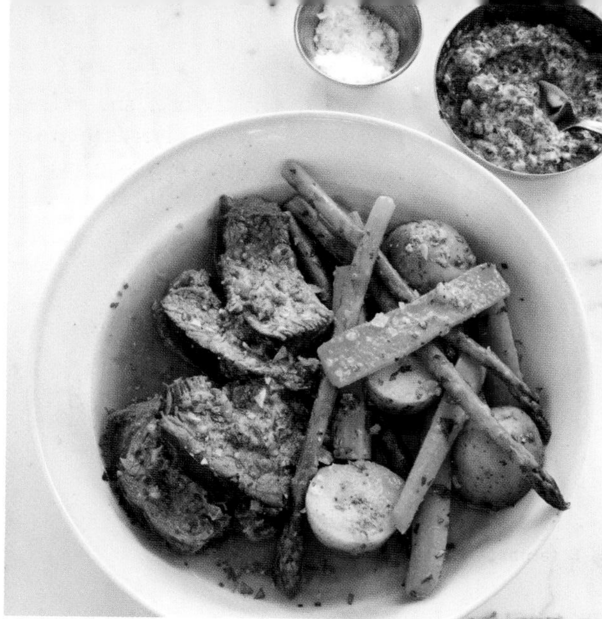

SIMPLE POT-AU-FEU

WHY THIS RECIPE WORKS: For a pot-au-feu brimming with tradition but suited to today's modern kitchen, we needed a pared-down shopping list. Boneless chuck roast beat out harder-to-find cuts of meat for its relative tenderness and big meaty flavor. Marrow bones gave the broth a buttery, beefy quality when cooked together with the meat, onion, and celery. Gently simmering the broth kept it perfectly clear. We transferred the pot to the oven partially covered to cook low and slow and, in the meantime, stirred together a sauce reminiscent of traditional pot-au-feu accompaniments. The zesty, bright combination of parsley, Dijon, chives, white wine vinegar, minced cornichon pickles, and pepper was deepened with the addition of the soft, beefy marrow extracted from the bones after cooking.

Simple Pot-au-Feu

SERVES 6 TO 8

Marrow bones (also called soup bones) can be found in the freezer section or the meat counter at most supermarkets. Use small red potatoes measuring 1 to 2 inches in diameter.

MEAT

- 1 (3½- to 4-pound) boneless beef chuck-eye roast, pulled into two pieces at natural seam and trimmed
- Kosher salt
- 1½ pounds marrow bones
- 1 onion, quartered
- 1 celery rib, sliced thin
- 3 bay leaves
- 1 teaspoon black peppercorns

PARSLEY SAUCE

- ⅔ cup minced fresh parsley
- ¼ cup Dijon mustard
- ¼ cup minced fresh chives
- 3 tablespoons white wine vinegar
- 10 cornichons, minced
- 1½ teaspoons pepper

VEGETABLES

- 1 pound small red potatoes, unpeeled, halved
- 6 carrots, peeled and halved crosswise, thick halves quartered lengthwise, thin halves halved lengthwise
- 1 pound asparagus, trimmed
- Kosher salt and pepper

Flake sea salt

1. FOR THE MEAT: Adjust oven rack to lower-middle position and heat oven to 300 degrees. Season beef with 1 tablespoon salt. Using 3 pieces of kitchen twine per piece, tie each into loaf shape for even cooking. Place beef, bones, onion, celery, bay leaves, and peppercorns in Dutch oven. Add 4 cups cold water (water should come halfway up roasts). Bring to simmer over high heat. Partially cover pot and transfer to oven. Cook until beef is fully tender and sharp knife easily slips in and out of meat (meat will not be shreddable), 3¼ to 3¾ hours, flipping beef over halfway through cooking.

2. FOR THE PARSLEY SAUCE: While beef cooks, combine all ingredients in bowl. Cover and set aside.

3. Remove pot from oven and turn off oven. Transfer beef to large platter, cover tightly with aluminum foil, and return to oven to keep warm. Transfer bones to cutting board and use end of spoon to extract marrow. Mince marrow into paste and add 2 tablespoons to parsley sauce (reserve any remaining marrow for other applications). Using ladle or large spoon, skim fat from surface of broth and discard fat. Strain broth through fine-mesh strainer into large liquid measuring cup; add water to make 6 cups. Return broth to pot. (Meat can be returned to broth, cooled, and refrigerated for up to 2 days. Skim fat from cold broth, then gently reheat and proceed with recipe.)

NOTES FROM THE TEST KITCHEN

ONE CUT IS PLENTY

Most pot-au-feu recipes call for a slew of different meats. To streamline, we settled on just one cut: chuck-eye roast, which delivers tender, beefy-tasting meat with a fraction of the effort and expense required by many classic renditions. This roast also needs very little prep.

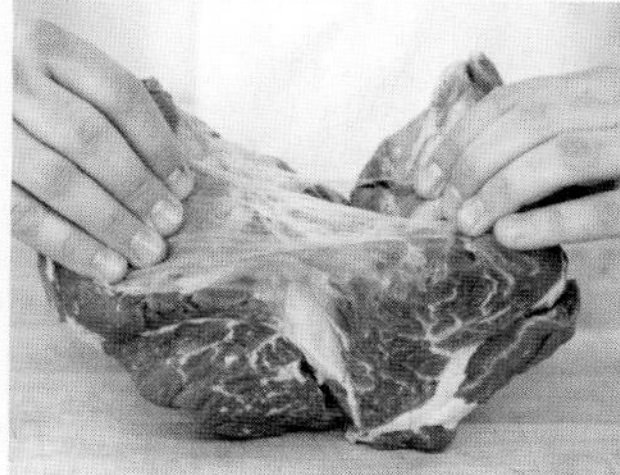

Pull roast apart at seam to make two smaller roasts and then trim any large knobs of fat.

4. FOR THE VEGETABLES: Add potatoes to broth and bring to simmer over high heat. Reduce heat to medium and simmer for 6 minutes. Add carrots and cook 10 minutes longer. Add asparagus and continue to cook until all vegetables are tender, 3 to 5 minutes longer.

5. Using slotted spoon, transfer vegetables to large bowl. Toss with 3 tablespoons parsley sauce and season with salt and pepper to taste. Season broth with salt to taste.

6. Transfer beef to cutting board, remove twine, and slice against grain ½ inch thick. Arrange servings of beef and vegetables in large, shallow bowls. Dollop beef with parsley sauce, drizzle with ⅓ cup broth, and sprinkle with flake sea salt. Serve, passing remaining parsley sauce and flake sea salt separately.

CUBAN-STYLE PICADILLO

WHY THIS RECIPE WORKS: Authentic recipes for this Cuban dish of spiced ground meat, sweet raisins, and briny olives call for hand-chopping or grinding the beef, but we wanted our version to be a quick weeknight option. Store-bought ground beef provided a convenient substitute, and supplementing it with ground pork added a subtle sweetness and complexity. Browning the meat made it tough, so we skipped the extra step and soaked the meat in a mixture of baking soda and water to ensure it remained tender. Pinching it off into sizable 2-inch chunks before adding it to the pot to simmer also kept it moist. For the spices, we settled on just oregano, cumin, and cinnamon, then bloomed them to heighten their flavor. Beef broth added a savory boost, while drained canned whole tomatoes and white wine provided brightness. Raisins and green olives were a given, but we also liked briny capers and a splash of red wine vinegar.

Cuban-Style Picadillo

SERVES 6

We prefer this dish prepared with raisins, but they can be replaced with 2 tablespoons of brown sugar added with the broth in step 2. Picadillo is traditionally served with rice and black beans. It can also be topped with chopped parsley, toasted almonds, and/or chopped hard-cooked egg.

- 1 pound 85 percent lean ground beef
- 1 pound ground pork
- 2 tablespoons water
- ½ teaspoon baking soda
- Salt and pepper
- 1 green bell pepper, stemmed, seeded, and cut into 2-inch pieces
- 1 onion, halved and cut into 2-inch pieces
- 2 tablespoons vegetable oil
- 1 tablespoon dried oregano
- 1 tablespoon ground cumin
- ½ teaspoon ground cinnamon
- 6 garlic cloves, minced
- 1 (14.5-ounce) can whole tomatoes, drained and chopped coarse
- ¾ cup dry white wine
- ½ cup beef broth
- ½ cup raisins
- 3 bay leaves
- ½ cup pimento-stuffed green olives, chopped coarse
- 2 tablespoons capers, rinsed
- 1 tablespoon red wine vinegar, plus extra for seasoning

1. Toss beef and pork with water, baking soda, ½ teaspoon salt, and ¼ teaspoon pepper in bowl until thoroughly combined. Set aside for 20 minutes. Meanwhile, pulse bell pepper and onion in food processor until chopped into ¼-inch pieces, about 12 pulses.

2. Heat oil in large Dutch oven over medium-high heat until shimmering. Add chopped vegetables, oregano, cumin, cinnamon, and ¼ teaspoon salt; cook, stirring frequently, until vegetables are softened and beginning to brown, 6 to 8 minutes. Add garlic and cook, stirring constantly, until fragrant, about 30 seconds. Add tomatoes and wine and cook, scraping up any browned bits, until pot is almost dry, 3 to 5 minutes. Stir in broth, raisins, and bay leaves and bring to simmer.

3. Reduce heat to medium-low, add meat mixture in 2-inch chunks to pot, and bring to gentle simmer. Cover and cook, stirring occasionally with 2 forks to break meat chunks into ¼- to ½-inch pieces, until meat is cooked through, about 10 minutes.

4. Discard bay leaves. Stir in olives and capers. Increase heat to medium-high and cook, stirring occasionally, until sauce is thickened and coats meat, about 5 minutes. Stir in vinegar and season with salt, pepper, and extra vinegar to taste. Serve.

Cuban-Style Picadillo with Fried Potatoes

After pulsing vegetables in food processor, toss 1 pound russet potatoes, peeled and cut into ½-inch pieces, with 1 tablespoon vegetable oil in medium bowl. Cover and microwave until potatoes are just tender, 4 to 7 minutes, tossing halfway through microwaving. Line surface of large plate with double layer of coffee filters and lightly spray with vegetable oil spray. Drain potatoes well, transfer to coffee filters, and spread in even layer. Let cool for 10 minutes; proceed with recipe from step 2. After step 3, heat 1 cup vegetable oil in large saucepan over medium-high heat until shimmering. Add cooled potatoes and cook, stirring constantly until deep golden brown, 3 to 5 minutes. Using slotted spoon, transfer potatoes to paper towel–lined plate and set aside. Add potatoes to pot with vinegar in step 4.

SHEPHERD'S PIE

WHY THIS RECIPE WORKS: Shepherd's pie, a hearty mix of meat, gravy, and mashed potatoes, can take the better part of a day to prepare. And while the dish is indeed satisfying, traditional versions are simply too rich. We wanted to scale back its preparation and lighten the dish to fit in better with modern sensibilities. Per other modern recipes, we chose ground beef as our filling over ground lamb. To prevent the beef from turning dry and crumbly, we tossed it with a little baking soda (diluted in water) before browning it. This step raises the pH level of the beef, resulting in more tender meat. An onion and mushroom gravy, spiked with Worcestershire sauce, complemented the beef filling. For the mashed potatoes, we took our cue from an Irish dish called champ and cut way back on the dairy in favor of fresh scallions, which made for a lighter, more flavorful topping that was a good match for the meat filling underneath.

Shepherd's Pie

SERVES 4 TO 6

This recipe was developed with 93 percent lean ground beef. Using ground beef with a higher percentage of fat will make the dish too greasy.

- 1½ pounds 93 percent lean ground beef
- 2 tablespoons plus 2 teaspoons water
- Salt and pepper
- ½ teaspoon baking soda
- 2½ pounds russet potatoes, peeled and cut into 1-inch chunks
- 4 tablespoons unsalted butter, melted
- ½ cup milk
- 1 large egg yolk
- 8 scallions, green parts only, sliced thin
- 2 teaspoons vegetable oil
- 1 onion, chopped
- 4 ounces white mushrooms, trimmed and chopped
- 1 tablespoon tomato paste
- 2 garlic cloves, minced
- 2 tablespoons Madeira or ruby port
- 2 tablespoons all-purpose flour
- 1¼ cups beef broth
- 2 teaspoons Worcestershire sauce
- 2 sprigs fresh thyme
- 1 bay leaf
- 2 carrots, peeled and chopped
- 2 teaspoons cornstarch

1. Toss beef with 2 tablespoons water, 1 teaspoon salt, ¼ teaspoon pepper, and baking soda in bowl until thoroughly combined. Let sit for 20 minutes.

2. Meanwhile, place potatoes in medium saucepan; add water to just cover and 1 tablespoon salt. Bring to boil over high heat. Reduce heat to medium-low and simmer until potatoes are soft and tip of paring knife inserted into potato meets no resistance, 8 to 10 minutes. Drain potatoes and return to saucepan. Return saucepan to low heat and cook, shaking pot occasionally, until any surface moisture on potatoes has evaporated, about 1 minute. Remove pan from heat and mash potatoes well with potato masher. Stir in butter. Whisk together milk and egg yolk in small bowl, then stir into potatoes. Stir in scallions and season with salt and pepper to taste. Cover and set aside.

3. Heat oil in broiler-safe 10-inch skillet over medium heat until shimmering. Add onion, mushrooms, ½ teaspoon salt, and ¼ teaspoon pepper; cook, stirring occasionally, until vegetables are just starting to soften and dark bits form on bottom of skillet, 4 to 6 minutes. Stir in tomato paste and garlic; cook until bottom of skillet is dark brown, about 2 minutes. Add Madeira and cook, scraping up any browned bits, until evaporated, about 1 minute. Stir in flour and cook for 1 minute. Add broth, Worcestershire, thyme sprigs, bay leaf, and carrots; bring to boil, scraping up any browned bits. Reduce heat to medium-low, add beef in 2-inch pieces to broth and bring to gentle simmer. Cover and cook until beef is cooked through, 10 to 12 minutes, stirring and breaking up meat chunks with 2 forks halfway through cooking. Stir cornstarch and remaining 2 teaspoons water together in bowl. Stir cornstarch mixture into filling and continue to simmer for 30 seconds. Remove thyme sprigs and bay leaf. Season with salt and pepper to taste.

4. Adjust oven rack 5 inches from broiler element and heat broiler. Place mashed potatoes in large zipper-lock bag and snip off 1 corner to create 1-inch opening. Pipe potatoes in even layer over filling, making sure to cover entire surface. Smooth potatoes with back of spoon, then use tines of fork to make ridges over surface. Place skillet on rimmed baking sheet and broil until potatoes are golden brown and crusty and filling is bubbly, 10 to 15 minutes. Let cool for 10 minutes before serving.

CHICKEN AND DUMPLINGS

WHY THIS RECIPE WORKS: Chicken and dumplings make chicken pot pie look easy: There's no disguising a leaden dumpling. Our goals were to develop a dumpling that was light yet substantial, and tender yet durable; and to develop a well-rounded recipe that, like chicken pot pie, included vegetables, therein providing the cook with a complete meal in one dish.

Dumplings can contain myriad ingredients, and there are just as many different ways to mix them. We tried them all—with disastrous results. But when we stumbled on a unique method of adding warm liquid rather than cold to the flour and fat, our dumplings were great—firm but light and fluffy. The reason? The heat expands and sets the flour so that the dumplings don't absorb liquid in the stew. The best-tasting dumplings were made with all-purpose flour, whole milk, and the chicken fat left from browning the chicken.

For the filling, we chose bone-in, skin-on chicken thighs for their deep flavor and added enough vegetables to make this dish into a meal. After browning the chicken and vegetables separately, we simmered them in the sauce until the chicken was done and the sauce thickened. We added some peas and parsley, then steamed the dumplings on top of everything until the dumplings turned light and tender.

Chicken and Dumplings

SERVES 6 TO 8

Don't use low-fat or fat-free milk in this recipe. Be sure to reserve 3 tablespoons of chicken fat for the dumplings in step 4; however, if you prefer not to use chicken fat, unsalted butter can be substituted. Start the dumpling dough only when you're ready to top the stew with the dumplings.

STEW

- 5 pounds bone-in, skin-on chicken thighs (about 12 thighs)
- Table salt and ground black pepper
- 4 teaspoons vegetable oil
- 4 tablespoons (½ stick) unsalted butter
- 4 carrots, peeled and sliced ¼ inch thick
- 2 celery ribs, sliced ¼ inch thick
- 1 medium onion, minced
- 6 tablespoons unbleached all-purpose flour
- ¼ cup dry sherry
- 4½ cups low-sodium chicken broth
- ¼ cup whole milk (see note)
- 1 teaspoon minced fresh thyme leaves
- 2 bay leaves
- 1 cup frozen green peas
- 3 tablespoons minced fresh parsley leaves

DUMPLINGS

- 2 cups unbleached all-purpose flour
- 1 tablespoon baking powder
- 1 teaspoon table salt
- 1 cup whole milk (see note)
- 3 tablespoons reserved chicken fat (see note)

1. FOR THE STEW: Pat the chicken dry with paper towels, then season with salt and pepper. Heat 2 teaspoons of the oil in a large Dutch oven over medium-high heat until just smoking. Add half of the chicken and cook until golden on both sides, about 10 minutes. Transfer the chicken to a plate and remove the browned skin. Pour off the chicken fat and reserve. Return the pot to medium-high heat and repeat with the remaining 2 teaspoons oil and the remaining chicken. Pour off and reserve any chicken fat.

2. Add the butter to the Dutch oven and melt over medium-high heat. Add the carrots, celery, onion, and ¼ teaspoon salt and cook until softened, about 7 minutes. Stir in the flour. Whisk in the sherry, scraping up any browned bits. Stir in the broth, milk, thyme, and bay leaves. Nestle the chicken, with any accumulated juices, into the pot. Cover and simmer until the chicken is fully cooked and tender, about 1 hour.

3. Transfer the chicken to a carving board. Discard the bay leaves. Allow the sauce to settle for a few minutes, then skim the fat from the surface using a wide spoon. Shred the chicken, discarding the bones, then return it to the stew.

4. FOR THE DUMPLINGS: Stir the flour, baking powder, and salt together. Microwave the milk and chicken fat in a microwave-safe bowl on high power until just warm (do not overheat), about 1 minute. Stir the warmed milk mixture into the flour mixture with a wooden spoon until incorporated and smooth.

5. Return the stew to a simmer, stir in the peas and parsley, and season with salt and pepper to taste. Following the photos, drop golf ball–sized dumplings over the top of the stew, about 1/4 inch apart (you should have about 18 dumplings). Reduce the heat to low, cover, and cook until the dumplings have doubled in size, 15 to 18 minutes. Serve.

NOTES FROM THE TEST KITCHEN

ADDING THE DUMPLINGS

1. Gather a golf ball–sized portion of the dumpling batter onto a soup spoon, then push the dumpling onto the stew using a second spoon.

2. Cover the stew with the dumplings, leaving about 1/4 inch between each.

3. When fully cooked, the dumplings will have doubled in size.

LIGHTER CHICKEN AND DUMPLINGS

WHY THIS RECIPE WORKS: A thick stew topped with sturdy dumplings makes a good cold-weather comfort food, but we wanted a version with dumplings as airy as drop biscuits in a light broth full of clean, concentrated chicken flavor.

For a streamlined rich and chickeny broth and tender meat, we poached browned chicken thighs in store-bought broth. To give our broth body, we added chicken wings to the pot. Boiling the wings converts the connective tissue in chicken wings to gelatin and thickens the broth. Dry sherry gave the broth complexity.

For light, airy dumplings sturdy enough to hold together in broth, we made some changes to our drop biscuit recipe—cutting back the buttermilk and eliminating the baking powder (which had led to overrising) were two steps in the right direction. Adding an egg white kept our dumplings from turning mushy. To help keep the dumplings intact, we waited until the broth was simmering to add them, which reduced their time in the broth and helped keep them whole. Finally, wrapping a kitchen towel around the lid of the Dutch oven trapped the moisture before it had a chance to drip down and saturate our light-as-air dumplings.

Lighter Chicken and Dumplings

SERVES 6

We strongly recommend buttermilk for the dumplings, but you can substitute 1/2 cup plain yogurt thinned with 1/4 cup milk. If you want to include white meat (and don't mind losing a bit of flavor in the process), replace 2 chicken thighs with 2 boneless, skinless chicken breast halves (about 8 ounces each). Brown the chicken breasts along with the thighs and remove them from the stew once they reach an internal temperature of 160 to 165 degrees, 20 to 30 minutes. The collagen in the wings helps thicken the stew; do not omit or substitute. Since the wings yield only about 1 cup of meat, using their meat is optional.

STEW

- 2½ pounds bone-in, skin-on chicken thighs, trimmed
- Table salt and ground black pepper
- 2 teaspoons vegetable oil
- 2 small onions, minced
- 2 carrots, peeled and cut into ¾-inch pieces
- 1 celery rib, chopped fine
- ¼ cup dry sherry
- 6 cups low-sodium chicken broth
- 1 teaspoon minced fresh thyme leaves
- 1 pound chicken wings
- ¼ cup chopped fresh parsley leaves

DUMPLINGS

- 2 cups (10 ounces) unbleached all-purpose flour
- 1 teaspoon sugar
- 1 teaspoon table salt
- ½ teaspoon baking soda
- ¾ cup cold buttermilk (see note)
- 4 tablespoons (½ stick) unsalted butter, melted and cooled
- 1 large egg white

1. FOR THE STEW: Pat the chicken thighs dry with paper towels and season with 1 teaspoon salt and 1/4 teaspoon pepper. Heat the oil in a large Dutch oven over medium-high heat until shimmering. Add the chicken thighs, skin side down, and cook until the skin is crisp and well browned, 5 to 7 minutes. Using tongs, turn the chicken pieces and brown the second side, 5 to 7 minutes longer; transfer to a large plate. Discard all but 1 teaspoon fat from the pot.

2. Add the onions, carrots, and celery to the pot. Cook, stirring occasionally, until caramelized, 7 to 9 minutes. Stir in the sherry, scraping up any browned bits. Stir in the broth and thyme. Return the chicken thighs, along with any accumulated juices, to the pot and add the chicken wings. Bring to a simmer, cover, and cook until the thigh meat offers no resistance when poked with the tip of a paring knife but still clings to the bones, 45 to 55 minutes.

3. Remove the pot from the heat and transfer the chicken to a cutting board. Allow the broth to settle for 5 minutes, then skim the fat from the surface using a wide spoon or ladle. When cool enough to handle, remove and discard the skin from the chicken. Using your fingers or a fork, pull the meat from the chicken thighs (and wings, if desired) and cut into 1-inch pieces. Return the meat to the pot.

4. FOR THE DUMPLINGS: Whisk the flour, sugar, salt, and baking soda in a large bowl. Combine the buttermilk and melted butter in a medium bowl, stirring until the butter forms small clumps. Whisk in the egg white. Add the buttermilk mixture to the dry ingredients and stir with a rubber spatula until just incorporated and the batter pulls away from the sides of the bowl.

5. Return the stew to a simmer, stir in the parsley, and season with salt and pepper to taste. Using a greased tablespoon measure (or #60 portion scoop), scoop level amounts of batter and drop them into the stew, spacing the dumplings about ¼ inch apart (you should have about 24 dumplings). Wrap the lid of the Dutch oven with a clean kitchen towel (keeping the towel away from the heat source) and cover the pot. Simmer gently until the dumplings have doubled in size and a toothpick inserted into the center comes out clean, 13 to 16 minutes. Serve immediately. (The stew can be prepared through step 3 up to 2 days in advance; bring the stew back to a simmer before proceeding with the recipe.)

BEST CHICKEN STEW

WHY THIS RECIPE WORKS: While recipes for chicken stew are few and far between, the ones we've come across are either too fussy or too fancy, or seem more soup than stew, with none of the complexity and depth we expect from the latter. We wanted to develop a chicken stew recipe that would satisfy like the beef kind—one with succulent bites of chicken, tender vegetables, and a truly robust gravy.

To start, we created an ultraflavorful gravy using chicken wings, which we later discarded. Browning the wings lent deep chicken flavor to the stew, and since wings are more about skin and bones than about meat, discarding them after they'd enriched the gravy didn't seem wasteful. A few strips of bacon, crisped in the pot before we browned the wings in the rendered fat, lent porky depth and just a hint of smoke. Soy sauce and anchovy paste, though unusual ingredients for chicken stew, lent more savory depth (without making the stew taste salty or fishy). Reducing the liquid with the aromatics at the beginning of cooking and then cooking the stew

uncovered further concentrated the flavor. To finish our hearty, savory stew, we added a splash of fresh white wine for a touch of brightness and a sprinkle of parsley for freshness.

Best Chicken Stew

SERVES 6 TO 8

Mashed anchovy fillets (rinsed and dried before mashing) can be used instead of anchovy paste. Use small red potatoes measuring 1½ inches in diameter.

- 2 pounds boneless, skinless chicken thighs, halved crosswise and trimmed
- Kosher salt and pepper
- 3 slices bacon, chopped
- 1 pound chicken wings, halved at joint
- 1 onion, chopped fine
- 1 celery rib, minced
- 2 garlic cloves, minced
- 2 teaspoons anchovy paste
- 1 teaspoon minced fresh thyme
- 5 cups chicken broth
- 1 cup dry white wine, plus extra for seasoning
- 1 tablespoon soy sauce
- 3 tablespoons unsalted butter, cut into 3 pieces
- ⅓ cup all-purpose flour
- 1 pound small red potatoes, unpeeled, quartered
- 4 carrots, peeled and cut into ½-inch pieces
- 2 tablespoons chopped fresh parsley

1. Adjust oven rack to lower-middle position and heat oven to 325 degrees. Arrange chicken thighs on baking sheet and lightly season both sides with salt and pepper; cover with plastic wrap and set aside.

2. Cook bacon in large Dutch oven over medium-low heat, stirring occasionally, until fat renders and bacon browns, 6 to 8 minutes. Using slotted spoon, transfer bacon to medium bowl. Add chicken wings to pot, increase heat to medium, and cook until well browned on both sides, 10 to 12 minutes; transfer wings to bowl with bacon.

3. Add onion, celery, garlic, anchovy paste, and thyme to fat in pot; cook, stirring occasionally, until dark fond forms on pan bottom, 2 to 4 minutes. Increase heat to high; stir in 1 cup broth, wine, and soy sauce, scraping up any browned bits; and bring to boil. Cook, stirring occasionally, until liquid evaporates and vegetables begin to sizzle again, 12 to 15 minutes. Add butter and stir to melt; sprinkle flour over vegetables and stir to combine. Gradually whisk in remaining 4 cups broth until smooth. Stir in wings and bacon, potatoes, and carrots; bring to simmer. Transfer to oven and cook, uncovered, for 30 minutes, stirring once halfway through cooking.

4. Remove pot from oven. Use wooden spoon to draw gravy up sides of pot and scrape browned fond into stew. Place over high heat, add thighs, and bring to simmer. Return pot to oven, uncovered, and continue to cook, stirring occasionally, until chicken offers no resistance when poked with fork and vegetables are tender, about 45 minutes longer. (Stew can be refrigerated for up to 2 days.)

5. Discard wings and season stew with up to 2 tablespoons extra wine. Season with salt and pepper to taste, sprinkle with parsley, and serve.

NOTES FROM THE TEST KITCHEN

BUILDING A RICH, FLAVORFUL GRAVY

1. Brown chopped bacon, then sear halved wings in rendered fat to develop meaty depth. Set bacon and wings aside.

2. Sauté aromatics, thyme, and anchovy paste in fat to create rich fond. Add chicken broth, wine, and soy sauce, then boil until liquid evaporates.

3. Cook reserved bacon and wings (with potatoes and carrots) in more broth. This extracts flavor from meats and body-enhancing collagen from wings (later discarded).

CHICKEN POT PIE

WHY THIS RECIPE WORKS: As homey as chicken pot pie sounds, this dish is a production. You've got to cook and cut up a chicken, make a sauce, parcook vegetables, and also prepare, chill, and roll out pie crust. We wanted to streamline the dish and get it on the table in 90 minutes, tops. And, we wanted a completely homemade pie (no prefab crust) full of tender, juicy chicken and bright vegetables.

To start, we swapped out a whole chicken for easy-to-poach chicken breasts—and we used the poaching liquid as the base of our sauce. But to boost the sauce's flavor, we turned to a few ingredients rich in glutamates, naturally occurring flavor compounds that accentuate savory qualities. Sautéed mushrooms, soy sauce, and tomato paste did the trick, turning into caramelized fond that gave our sauce deep flavor. Sautéing the vegetables—a medley of onions, carrots, and celery—while the chicken rested, also boosted the filling's flavor. (Later we'd add quick-cooking frozen peas straight to the filling to warm through.)

For the pot pie topping, we replaced traditional pastry with a savory crumble topping, enriched with grated cheese and pepper. To increase the crunch factor, we baked the crumble separately from the filling, then scattered it over the pot pie and slid it into the oven to warm through. Minutes later, our homemade pot pie emerged bubbling, fragrant, and topped with a crunchy, flavorful crust.

Chicken Pot Pie with Savory Crumble Topping

SERVES 6

This recipe relies on two unusual ingredients: soy sauce and tomato paste. Do not omit them. They don't convey their distinct tastes but greatly deepen the savory flavor of the filling. When making the topping, do not substitute milk or half-and-half for the heavy cream.

CHICKEN AND FILLING

- 1½ pounds boneless, skinless chicken breasts and/or thighs
- 3 cups low-sodium chicken broth
- 2 tablespoons vegetable oil
- 1 medium onion, minced
- 3 medium carrots, peeled and cut crosswise into ¼-inch-thick slices (about 1 cup)
- 2 small celery ribs, chopped fine
- Table salt and ground black pepper
- 10 ounces cremini mushrooms, stems trimmed, caps wiped clean and sliced thin
- 1 teaspoon soy sauce (see note)
- 1 teaspoon tomato paste (see note)
- 4 tablespoons (½ stick) unsalted butter
- ½ cup unbleached all-purpose flour
- 1 cup whole milk
- 2 teaspoons juice from 1 lemon
- 3 tablespoons minced fresh parsley leaves
- ¾ cup frozen baby peas

CRUMBLE TOPPING

- 2 cups (10 ounces) unbleached all-purpose flour
- 2 teaspoons baking powder
- ¾ teaspoon table salt
- ½ teaspoon ground black pepper
- ⅛ teaspoon cayenne pepper
- 6 tablespoons (¾ stick) unsalted butter, cut into ½-inch cubes and chilled
- 1 ounce Parmesan cheese, finely grated (about ½ cup)
- ¾ cup plus 2 tablespoons heavy cream (see note)

1. FOR THE CHICKEN: Bring the chicken and broth to a simmer in a covered Dutch oven over medium heat. Cook until the chicken is just done, 8 to 12 minutes. Transfer the cooked chicken to a large bowl. Pour the broth through a fine-mesh strainer into a liquid measuring cup and reserve. Do not wash the Dutch oven. Meanwhile, adjust an oven rack to the upper-middle position and heat the oven to 450 degrees.

2. FOR THE TOPPING: Combine the flour, baking powder, salt, black pepper, and cayenne in a large bowl. Sprinkle the butter pieces over the top of the flour. Using your fingers, rub the butter into the flour mixture until it resembles coarse cornmeal. Stir in the Parmesan. Add the cream and stir until just combined. Crumble the mixture into irregularly shaped pieces ranging from ½ to ¾ inch onto a parchment-lined rimmed baking sheet. Bake until fragrant and starting to brown, 10 to 13 minutes. Set aside.

3. FOR THE FILLING: Heat 1 tablespoon of the oil in the now-empty Dutch oven over medium heat until shimmering. Add the onion, carrots, celery, ¼ teaspoon salt, and ¼ teaspoon pepper; cover and cook, stirring occasionally, until just tender, 5 to 7 minutes. While the vegetables are cooking, shred the chicken into small bite-size pieces. Transfer the cooked vegetables to the bowl with the chicken; set aside.

4. Heat the remaining 1 tablespoon oil in the again-empty Dutch oven over medium heat until shimmering. Add the mushrooms; cover and cook, stirring occasionally, until the mushrooms have released their juices, about 5 minutes. Remove the cover, stir in the soy sauce and tomato paste. Increase the heat to medium-high and cook, stirring frequently, until the liquid has evaporated, the mushrooms are well browned, and a dark fond begins to form on the surface of the pan, about 5 minutes. Transfer the mushrooms to the bowl with the chicken and vegetables. Set aside.

5. Heat the butter in the again-empty Dutch oven over medium heat. When the foaming subsides, stir in the flour and cook for 1 minute. Slowly whisk in the reserved chicken broth and the milk. Bring to a simmer, scraping the pan bottom with a wooden spoon to loosen the browned bits, then continue to simmer until the sauce fully thickens, about 1 minute. Season with salt and pepper to taste. Remove from the heat and stir in the lemon juice and 2 tablespoons of the parsley.

6. Stir the chicken-vegetable mixture and peas into the sauce. Pour the mixture into a 13 by 9-inch baking dish or casserole dish of similar size. Scatter the crumble topping evenly over the filling. Bake on a rimmed baking sheet until the filling is bubbling and the topping is well browned, 12 to 15 minutes. Sprinkle with the remaining 1 tablespoon parsley and serve.

GREEK SPINACH AND FETA PIE

WHY THIS RECIPE WORKS: The roots of this savory dish run deep in Greek culture, yet most stateside versions are nothing more than soggy layers of phyllo with a sparse, bland filling. We wanted a casserole-style pie with a perfect balance of zesty spinach filling and shatteringly crisp, flaky phyllo crust—and we didn't want it to take all day. Using store-bought phyllo was an easy timesaver. Among the various spinach options (baby, frozen, mature curly-leaf), tasters favored the bold flavor of fresh curly-leaf spinach that had been microwaved, coarsely chopped, and squeezed of excess moisture. Crumbling the feta into fine pieces ensured a salty tang in every bite, while the addition of Greek yogurt buffered the assertiveness of the feta. We found that Pecorino Romano (a good stand-in for the traditional Greek hard sheep's milk cheese) added complexity to the filling and, when sprinkled between the sheets of phyllo, helped the flaky layers hold together. Using a baking sheet rather than a baking dish allowed excess moisture to easily evaporate, ensuring a crisp crust.

Greek Spinach and Feta Pie (Spanakopita)

SERVES 6 TO 8 AS A MAIN COURSE OR 10 TO 12 AS AN APPETIZER

It is important to rinse the feta; this step removes some of its salty brine, which would overwhelm the spinach. Full-fat sour cream can be substituted for whole-milk Greek yogurt.

Phyllo dough is also available in larger 14 by 18-inch sheets; if using, cut them in half to make 14 by 9-inch sheets. Don't thaw the phyllo in the microwave; let it sit in the refrigerator overnight or on the countertop for 4 to 5 hours. The filling can be made up to 24 hours in advance and refrigerated. The assembled, unbaked spanakopita can be frozen on a baking sheet, wrapped well in plastic wrap, or cut in half crosswise and frozen in smaller sections on a plate. To bake, unwrap and increase the baking time by 5 to 10 minutes.

FILLING

- 1¼ pounds curly-leaf spinach, stemmed
- ¼ cup water
- 12 ounces feta cheese, rinsed, patted dry, and crumbled into fine pieces (about 3 cups)
- ¾ cup whole-milk Greek yogurt
- 4 scallions, sliced thin
- 2 large eggs, beaten
- ¼ cup minced fresh mint leaves
- 2 tablespoons minced fresh dill leaves
- 3 medium garlic cloves, minced or pressed through a garlic press (about 1 tablespoon)
- 1 teaspoon grated zest plus 1 tablespoon juice from 1 lemon
- 1 teaspoon ground nutmeg
- ½ teaspoon ground black pepper
- ¼ teaspoon table salt
- ⅛ teaspoon cayenne pepper

PHYLLO LAYERS

- 7 tablespoons unsalted butter, melted
- 8 ounces (14 by 9-inch) phyllo, thawed
- 1½ ounces Pecorino Romano cheese, grated (¾ cup)
- 2 teaspoons sesame seeds (optional)

1. FOR THE FILLING: Place the spinach and water in a large bowl and cover with a large dinner plate. Microwave until the spinach is wilted and decreased in volume by half, about 5 minutes. Using potholders, remove the bowl from the microwave and keep covered for 1 minute. Carefully remove the plate and transfer the spinach to a colander. Using the back of a rubber spatula, gently press the spinach against the colander to release the excess liquid. Transfer the spinach to a cutting board and chop coarse. Transfer the spinach to a clean kitchen towel and squeeze to remove excess water. Place the drained spinach in a large bowl. Add the remaining filling ingredients and mix until thoroughly combined.

2. FOR THE PHYLLO LAYERS: Adjust an oven rack to the lower-middle position and heat the oven to 425 degrees. Line a rimmed baking sheet with parchment paper. Using a pastry brush, lightly brush a 14 by 9-inch rectangle in the center of the parchment with melted butter to cover an area the same size as the phyllo. Lay 1 phyllo sheet on the buttered parchment and brush thoroughly with melted butter. Repeat with 9 more phyllo sheets, brushing each with butter (you should have a total of 10 layers of phyllo).

3. Spread the spinach mixture evenly over the phyllo, leaving a ¼-inch border on all sides. Cover the spinach with 6 more phyllo sheets, brushing each with butter and sprinkling each with about 2 tablespoons Pecorino cheese. Lay 2 more phyllo sheets on top, brushing each with butter (do not sprinkle these layers with Pecorino).

4. Working from the center outward, use the palms of your hands to compress the layers and press out any air pockets. Using a sharp knife, score the spanakopita through the top 3 layers of phyllo into 24 equal pieces. Sprinkle with the sesame seeds (if using). Bake until the phyllo is golden and crisp, 20 to 25 minutes. Cool on a baking sheet for 10 minutes or up to 2 hours. Slide the spanakopita, still on the parchment, onto a cutting board. Cut into squares and serve.

MOROCCAN CHICKEN

WHY THIS RECIPE WORKS: Time-consuming techniques and esoteric ingredients make cooking authentic Moroccan chicken a daunting proposition. We wanted a recipe that was ready in an hour and relied on supermarket staples. For depth and flavor, we used a mix of white and dark meat chicken and browned the meat first. After removing the chicken from the pot, we sautéed onion, strips of lemon zest, garlic, and a spice blend in some oil and the browned bits left in the pot; this ensured that no flavor went to waste. A number of everyday spices were necessary to re-create the authentic notes in Moroccan chicken, including paprika, cumin, cayenne, ginger, coriander, and cinnamon; honey filled the bill for the missing sweetness. Greek green olives provided the meatiness and piquant flavor of hard-to-find Moroccan olives. Chopped cilantro, stirred in right before serving, was the perfect finishing touch to our exotic dinner.

Moroccan Chicken with Olives and Lemon

SERVES 4

Bone-in chicken parts can be substituted for the whole chicken. For best results, use four chicken thighs and two chicken breasts, each breast split in half; the dark meat contributes valuable flavor to the broth and should not be omitted. Use a vegetable peeler to remove wide strips of zest from the lemon before juicing it. Make sure to trim any white pith from the zest, as it can impart bitter flavor. If the olives are particularly salty, rinse them first. Serve with Simple Couscous (page 622).

- 1¼ teaspoons paprika
- ½ teaspoon ground cumin
- ½ teaspoon ground ginger
- ¼ teaspoon cayenne pepper
- ¼ teaspoon ground coriander
- ¼ teaspoon ground cinnamon
- 3 (2-inch) strips zest plus 3 tablespoons juice from 1 lemon
- 5 medium garlic cloves, minced or pressed through a garlic press (about 5 teaspoons)
- 1 (3½ to 4-pound) whole chicken, cut into 8 pieces (4 breast pieces, 2 thighs, 2 drumsticks), wings discarded, and trimmed
- Table salt and ground black pepper
- 1 tablespoon olive oil
- 1 large onion, halved and sliced ¼ inch thick
- 1¾ cups low-sodium chicken broth
- 1 tablespoon honey
- 2 medium carrots, peeled and cut crosswise into ½-inch-thick rounds, very large pieces cut into half-moons
- 1 cup cracked green olives, pitted and halved
- 2 tablespoons chopped fresh cilantro leaves

1. Combine the paprika, cumin, ginger, cayenne, coriander, and cinnamon in a small bowl and set aside. Mince 1 of the lemon zest strips, combine with 1 teaspoon of the minced garlic, and mince together until reduced to a fine paste; set aside.

2. Season both sides of the chicken pieces with salt and pepper. Heat the oil in a Dutch oven over medium-high heat until beginning to smoke. Brown the chicken pieces, skin side down, until deep golden, about 5 minutes; using tongs, flip the chicken pieces and brown on the second side, about 4 minutes longer. Transfer the chicken to a large plate; when cool enough to handle, remove and discard the skin. Pour off and discard all but 1 tablespoon fat from the pot.

3. Add the onion and the 2 remaining lemon zest strips to the pot and cook, stirring occasionally, until the onion slices have browned at the edges but still retain their shape, 5 to 7 minutes (add 1 tablespoon water if the pan gets too dark). Add the remaining 4 teaspoons garlic and cook, stirring, until fragrant, about 30 seconds. Add the spices and cook, stirring constantly, until darkened and very fragrant, 45 seconds to 1 minute. Stir in the broth and honey, scraping up the browned bits from the bottom of the pot. Add the thighs and drumsticks, reduce the heat to medium, and simmer for 5 minutes.

4. Add the carrots and breast pieces with any accumulated juices to the pot, arranging the breast pieces in a single layer on top of the carrots. Cover, reduce the heat to medium-low, and simmer until the breast pieces register 160 to 165 degrees, 10 to 15 minutes.

5. Transfer the chicken to a plate and tent with aluminum foil. Add the olives to the pot; increase the heat to medium-high and simmer until the liquid has thickened slightly and the carrots are tender, 4 to 6 minutes. Return the chicken to the pot and stir in the garlic mixture, lemon juice, and cilantro; season with salt and pepper to taste. Serve immediately.

Moroccan Chicken with Chickpeas and Apricots

Follow the recipe for Moroccan Chicken with Olives and Lemon, replacing 1 carrot with 1 cup dried apricots, halved, and replacing the olives with one 15-ounce can chickpeas, rinsed.

LATINO-STYLE CHICKEN AND RICE

WHY THIS RECIPE WORKS: The traditional way of cooking this bold-flavored cousin of American chicken and rice is time-consuming, requiring an overnight marinade of the chicken and then a long, slow stewing with rice and vegetables. Could we find a way to achieve the same results in a lot less time?

We began by choosing chicken thighs, not only for shopping convenience but also to ensure that all of the pieces would cook at the same rate—a problem when using a combination of white and dark meat. We poached the thighs in a broth preseasoned with a *sofrito*, a classic Latin American mixture of chopped onions and bell peppers. About half an hour before the chicken finished cooking, we added medium-grain rice (which we preferred over long-grain for

its creamy texture), stirring it a few times to ensure even cooking. And for maximum flavor, we devised two marinades. Before cooking, we marinated the chicken quickly in garlic, oregano, and distilled white vinegar; after cooking we tossed the cooked chicken with olive oil, vinegar, and cilantro.

We had one final dilemma: how to give the dish its traditional orange hue that comes from infusing oil with achiote, a tropical seed not readily available in local grocery stores. Adding canned tomato sauce solved the problem.

Latino-Style Chicken and Rice (Arroz con Pollo)

SERVES 4 TO 6

To keep the dish from becoming greasy, remove any visible pockets of waxy yellow fat from the chicken and most of the skin, leaving just enough to protect the meat. To use long-grain rice instead of medium-grain, increase the amount of water added in step 2 from 1/4 to 3/4 cup and add the additional 1/4 cup water in step 3 as needed. When removing the chicken from the bone in step 4, we found it better to use two spoons rather than two forks; forks tend to shred the meat, while spoons pull it apart in chunks.

- 6 medium garlic cloves, minced or pressed through a garlic press (about 2 tablespoons)
- Table salt and ground black pepper
- 1 tablespoon plus 2 teaspoons distilled white vinegar
- ½ teaspoon dried oregano
- 4 pounds bone-in, skin-on chicken thighs (about 10 thighs), trimmed (see note)
- 2 tablespoons olive oil
- 1 medium onion, minced
- 1 small green pepper, stemmed, seeded, and chopped fine
- ¼ teaspoon red pepper flakes
- ¼ cup minced fresh cilantro leaves
- 1¾ cups low-sodium chicken broth
- 1 (8-ounce) can tomato sauce
- ¼ cup water, plus more if needed (see note)
- 3 cups medium-grain rice (see note)
- ½ cup green manzanilla olives, pitted and halved
- 1 tablespoon capers
- ½ cup jarred pimentos, cut into 2 by ¼-inch strips
- Lemon wedges, for serving

1. Adjust an oven rack to the middle position and heat the oven to 350 degrees. Place the garlic and 1 teaspoon salt in a large bowl; using a rubber spatula, mix to make a smooth paste. Add 1 tablespoon of the vinegar, the oregano, and 1/2 teaspoon black pepper to the garlic-salt mixture; stir to combine. Place the chicken in the bowl with the marinade. Coat the chicken pieces evenly with the marinade; set aside for 15 minutes.

2. Heat 1 tablespoon of the oil in a Dutch oven over medium heat until shimmering. Add the onion, green pepper, and red pepper flakes; cook, stirring occasionally, until the vegetables begin to soften, 4 to 8 minutes. Add 2 tablespoons of the cilantro; stir to combine. Push the vegetables to the sides of the pot and increase the heat to medium-high. Add the chicken to the clearing in the center of the pot, skin side down, in an even layer. Cook, without moving the chicken, until the outer layer of the meat becomes opaque, 2 to 4 minutes. (If the chicken begins to brown, reduce the heat to medium.) Using tongs, flip the chicken and cook on the second side until opaque, 2 to 4 minutes more. Add the broth, tomato sauce, and water; stir to combine. Bring to a simmer; cover, reduce the heat to medium-low, and simmer for 20 minutes.

3. Add the rice, olives, capers, and 3/4 teaspoon salt; stir well. Bring to a simmer, cover, and place the pot in the oven. After 10 minutes, remove the pot from the oven and stir the chicken and rice once from the bottom up. Cover and return the pot to the oven. After another 10 minutes, stir once more, adding another 1/4 cup water if the rice appears dry and the bottom of the pot is beginning to burn. Cover and return the pot to the oven; cook until the rice has absorbed all the liquid and is tender but still holds its shape and the thickest part of the thighs registers 175 degrees on an instant-read thermometer, about 10 minutes longer.

4. Using tongs, remove the chicken from the pot; replace the lid and set the pot aside. Remove and discard the chicken skin; using two spoons, pull the meat off the bones in large chunks. Using your fingers, remove the remaining fat and any dark veins from the chicken pieces. Place the chicken in a large bowl and toss with the remaining 1 tablespoon oil, remaining 2 teaspoons vinegar, remaining 2 tablespoons cilantro, and the pimentos; season with salt and pepper to taste. Place the chicken on top of the rice, cover, and let stand until warmed through, about 5 minutes. Serve, passing the lemon wedges separately.

Latino-Style Chicken and Rice with Bacon and Roasted Red Peppers

Bacon adds a welcome layer of richness, and red peppers bring subtle sweet flavor and color to this variation. To use long-grain rice, increase the amount of water to 3/4 cup in step 2 and the salt added in step 3 to 1 teaspoon.

1. Follow the recipe for Latino-Style Chicken and Rice through step 1, substituting 2 teaspoons sweet paprika for the oregano and sherry vinegar for the white vinegar.

2. Fry 4 ounces (about 4 strips) bacon, cut into ½-inch pieces, in a Dutch oven over medium heat until crisp, 6 to 8 minutes. Using a slotted spoon, transfer the bacon to a paper towel–lined plate; pour off all but 1 tablespoon bacon fat. Continue with step 2, substituting 1 small red pepper, chopped fine, and 1 medium carrot, chopped fine, for the green pepper and sautéing the vegetables in the bacon fat.

3. Continue with the recipe, substituting ¼ cup minced fresh parsley leaves for the cilantro, omitting the olives and capers, and substituting ½ cup roasted red peppers, cut into 2 by ¼-inch strips, for the pimentos. Garnish the chicken and rice with the reserved bacon before serving.

Latino-Style Chicken and Rice with Ham, Peas, and Orange

Ham gives this variation further richness, and orange zest and juice provide a bright accent. To use long-grain rice, increase the amount of water to ¾ cup in step 2 and the salt added in step 3 to 1 teaspoon.

1. Follow the recipe for Latino-Style Chicken and Rice through step 1, substituting 1 tablespoon ground cumin for the oregano.

2. Continue with step 2, adding 8 ounces ham steak or Canadian bacon, cut into ½-inch pieces (about 1½ cups), with the onion, green pepper, and red pepper flakes.

3. With a vegetable peeler, remove three 3-inch strips of zest from 1 orange. Continue with step 3, adding the orange zest with the rice, olives, capers, and salt. Add 1 cup frozen peas to the pot with ¼ cup water, if necessary, after stirring the contents of the pot the second time.

4. In step 4, add 3 tablespoons juice from 1 orange to the bowl with the olive oil, vinegar, cilantro, and pimentos and proceed with the recipe.

CUBAN-STYLE BLACK BEANS AND RICE

WHY THIS RECIPE WORKS: Beans and rice is a familiar combination the world over, but Cuban black beans and rice is unique in that the rice is cooked in the inky concentrated liquid left over from cooking the beans, which renders the grains just as flavorful. For our own version, we expanded on this method, simmering a portion of the *sofrito* (the traditional combination of garlic, bell pepper, and onion) with our beans to infuse them with flavor and then using the liquid to cook our rice and beans together. Lightly browning the remaining sofrito vegetables and spices with rendered salt pork added complex, meaty flavor, and finishing the dish in the oven eliminated the crusty bottom that can form when the dish is cooked on the stove.

Cuban-Style Black Beans and Rice

SERVES 6 TO 8

It is important to use lean—not fatty—salt pork. If you can't find it, substitute 6 slices of bacon. If using bacon, decrease the cooking time in step 4 to 8 minutes. You will need a Dutch oven with a tight-fitting lid for this recipe. For a vegetarian version of this recipe, use water instead of chicken broth, omit the salt pork, add 1 tablespoon tomato paste with the vegetables in step 4, and increase the amount of salt in step 5 to 1½ teaspoons.

Table salt
6½ ounces dried black beans (1 cup), picked over and rinsed
2 cups low-sodium chicken broth
2 cups water
2 large green bell peppers, stemmed, seeded, and halved
1 large onion, halved at equator and peeled, root end left intact
1 head garlic, 5 medium cloves minced or pressed through a garlic press (about 5 teaspoons), remaining head halved at equator with skin left intact
2 bay leaves
1½ cups long-grain white rice
2 tablespoons olive oil
6 ounces lean salt pork, cut into ¼-inch dice (see note)
4 teaspoons ground cumin
1 tablespoon minced fresh oregano leaves
2 tablespoons red wine vinegar
2 scallions, sliced thin, for serving
Lime wedges, for serving

1. Dissolve 1½ tablespoons salt in 2 quarts cold water in a large bowl or container. Add the beans and soak at room temperature for at least 8 hours or up to 24 hours. Drain and rinse well.

2. In a Dutch oven, stir together the drained beans, broth, water, 1 bell pepper half, 1 onion half (with root end), the halved garlic head, bay leaves, and 1 teaspoon salt. Bring to a simmer over medium-high heat, cover, and reduce the heat to low. Cook until the beans are just soft, 30 to 35 minutes. Using tongs, remove and discard the pepper, onion, garlic, and bay leaves. Drain the beans in a colander set over a large bowl, reserving 2½ cups bean cooking liquid. (If you don't have enough bean cooking liquid, add water to equal 2½ cups.) Do not wash out the Dutch oven.

3. Adjust an oven rack to the middle position and heat the oven to 350 degrees. Place the rice in a large fine-mesh strainer and rinse under cold running water until the water runs clear, about 1½ minutes. Shake the strainer vigorously to remove all excess water; set the rice aside. Cut the remaining peppers and onion into 2-inch pieces and process in a food processor until broken into rough ¼-inch pieces, about 8 pulses, scraping down the bowl as necessary; set the vegetables aside.

4. In the now-empty Dutch oven, heat 1 tablespoon oil and the salt pork over medium-low heat and cook, stirring frequently, until lightly browned and rendered, 15 to 20 minutes. Add the remaining 1 tablespoon oil, the chopped bell peppers and onion, cumin, and oregano. Increase the heat to medium and continue to cook, stirring frequently, until the vegetables are softened and beginning to brown, 10 to 15 minutes longer. Add the minced garlic and cook, stirring constantly, until fragrant, about 1 minute. Add the rice and stir to coat, about 30 seconds.

5. Stir in the beans, reserved bean cooking liquid, vinegar, and ½ teaspoon salt. Increase the heat to medium-high and bring to a simmer. Cover and transfer to the oven. Cook until the liquid is absorbed and the rice is tender, about 30 minutes. Fluff with a fork and let rest, uncovered, for 5 minutes. Serve, passing the scallions and lime wedges separately.

PAELLA

WHY THIS RECIPE WORKS: Paella can be a big hit at restaurants but an unwieldy production at home. Could we re-create this Spanish classic in two hours without using any fancy equipment? The key to our paella was finding equipment and ingredients that stayed true to the dish's heritage. First, we substituted a Dutch oven for a single-purpose paella pan. Then we pared down our ingredients, dismissing lobster, diced pork, fish, rabbit, and snails. We were left with chorizo, chicken, shrimp, and mussels. We next simplified our sofrito—in this Spanish version, a combination of onions, garlic, and tomatoes—by mincing a can of drained diced tomatoes rather than seeding and grating a fresh tomato. For the rice, we found we preferred short-grain varieties. Valencia was our favorite, with Italian Arborio a close second. Sautéing the rice in the same pot used to brown the meat and make the sofrito boosted its flavor. For the cooking liquid and seasonings, we chose chicken broth, white wine, saffron, and a bay leaf. Once the rice had absorbed almost all the liquid, we added the mussels, shrimp, and peas to the mix. The result? A colorful, streamlined, yet flavorful rendition of the Spanish classic.

Paella

SERVES 6

Use a Dutch oven that is 11 to 12 inches in diameter with at least a 6-quart capacity. Dry-cured Spanish chorizo is the sausage of choice for paella, but fresh chorizo or linguiça is an acceptable substitute. *Soccarat,* a layer of crusty browned rice that forms on the bottom of the pan, is a traditional part of paella. In our version, soccarat does not develop because most of the cooking is done in the oven. We have provided instructions to develop soccarat in step 5; if you prefer, skip this step and go directly from step 4 to step 6.

- 1 pound extra-large shrimp (21 to 25 per pound), peeled and deveined (see page 240)
- Table salt and ground black pepper
- 2 tablespoons olive oil, plus extra as needed
- 8–9 medium garlic cloves, minced or pressed through a garlic press (2 generous tablespoons)
- 1 pound boneless, skinless chicken thighs (about 4 thighs), trimmed and halved crosswise
- 1 red bell pepper, stemmed, seeded, and cut pole to pole into ½-inch-wide strips
- 8 ounces Spanish chorizo, sliced ½ inch thick on the bias (see note)
- 1 medium onion, minced
- 1 (14.5-ounce) can diced tomatoes, drained, minced, and drained again
- 2 cups Valencia or Arborio rice
- 3 cups low-sodium chicken broth
- ⅓ cup dry white wine
- ½ teaspoon saffron threads, crumbled
- 1 bay leaf
- 1 dozen mussels, scrubbed and debearded
- ½ cup frozen peas, thawed
- 2 tablespoons chopped fresh parsley leaves
- 1 lemon, cut into wedges, for serving

1. Adjust an oven rack to the lower-middle position and heat the oven to 350 degrees. Toss the shrimp, ¼ teaspoon salt, ¼ teaspoon pepper, 1 tablespoon of the oil, and 1 teaspoon of the garlic in a medium bowl; cover with plastic wrap and refrigerate until needed. Season the chicken thighs with salt and pepper; set aside.

2. Heat 2 teaspoons more oil in a large Dutch oven over medium-high heat until shimmering but not smoking. Add the pepper strips and cook, stirring occasionally, until the skin begins to blister and turn spotty black, 3 to 4 minutes. Transfer the pepper to a small plate and set aside.

3. Add the remaining 1 teaspoon oil to the now-empty Dutch oven; heat the oil until shimmering but not smoking. Add the chicken pieces in a single layer; cook, without moving the pieces, until browned, about 3 minutes. Turn the pieces and brown on the second side, about 3 minutes longer; transfer the chicken to a medium bowl. Reduce the heat to medium and add the chorizo to the pot; cook, stirring frequently, until deeply browned and the fat begins to render, 4 to 5 minutes. Transfer the chorizo to the bowl with the chicken and set aside.

4. Add enough oil to the fat in the Dutch oven to equal 2 tablespoons; heat over medium heat until shimmering but not smoking. Add the onion and cook, stirring frequently, until softened, about 3 minutes; stir in the remaining garlic and cook until fragrant, about 1 minute. Stir in the tomatoes; cook until the mixture begins to darken and thicken slightly, about 3 minutes. Stir in the rice and cook until the grains are well coated with the tomato mixture, 1 to 2 minutes. Stir in the chicken broth, wine, saffron, bay leaf, and ½ teaspoon salt. Return the chicken and chorizo to the pot, increase the heat to medium-high, and bring to a boil, uncovered, stirring occasionally. Cover the pot and transfer it to the oven; cook until the rice absorbs almost all of the liquid, about 15 minutes. Remove the pot from the oven (close the oven door to retain heat). Uncover the pot; scatter the shrimp over the rice, insert the mussels, hinged side down, into the rice (so they stand upright), arrange the bell pepper strips in a pinwheel pattern, and scatter the peas over the top. Cover and return to the oven; cook until the shrimp are opaque and the mussels have opened, 10 to 12 minutes.

5. OPTIONAL: If soccarat is desired (see note), set the Dutch oven, uncovered, over medium-high heat for about 5 minutes, rotating the pot 180 degrees after about 2 minutes for even browning.

6. Let the paella stand, covered, for about 5 minutes. Discard any mussels that have not opened and the bay leaf, if it can be easily removed. Sprinkle with the parsley and serve, passing the lemon wedges separately.

GRILLED PAELLA

WHY THIS RECIPE WORKS: Grilling paella lends the dish subtle smoke flavor and a particularly rich crust and makes it a great dish for summer entertaining. In place of a traditional paella pan, we cooked ours in a large, sturdy roasting pan that maximized the amount of *socarrat*, the prized caramelized rice crust that forms on the bottom of the pan. Building a large (7-quart) fire and fueling it with fresh coals (which ignited during cooking) ensured that the heat output would last throughout cooking, but we also shortened the outdoor cooking time by using roasted red peppers and tomato paste (instead of fresh peppers and tomatoes), making an infused broth with the seasonings, and grilling (rather than searing) the chicken thighs. To ensure that the various components finished cooking at the same time, we staggered the addition of the proteins—first, the chicken thighs, followed by the shrimp, clams, and chorizo. We also deliberately placed the chicken on the perimeter of the pan, where it would finish cooking gently after grilling, and the sausage and seafood in the center, where they were partially submerged in the liquid so that they cooked through; once the liquid reduced, the steam kept them warm.

Paella on the Grill

SERVES 8

This recipe was developed with a light-colored 16 by 13.5-inch tri-ply roasting pan; however, it can be made in any heavy roasting pan that measures at least 14 by 11 inches. If your roasting pan is dark in color, the cooking times will be on the lower end of the ranges given. The recipe can also be made in a 15- to 17-inch paella pan. If littlenecks are unavailable, use 1½ pounds shrimp in step 1 and season it with ½ teaspoon salt.

- 1½ pounds boneless, skinless chicken thighs, trimmed and halved crosswise
- Salt and pepper
- 12 ounces jumbo shrimp (16 to 20 per pound), peeled and deveined (see page 240)
- 6 tablespoons extra-virgin olive oil
- 6 garlic cloves, minced
- 1¾ teaspoons smoked hot paprika
- 3 tablespoons tomato paste
- 4 cups chicken broth
- ⅔ cup dry sherry
- 1 (8-ounce) bottle clam juice
- Pinch saffron threads (optional)
- 1 onion, chopped fine
- ½ cup roasted red peppers, chopped fine
- 3 cups Arborio rice
- 1 pound littleneck clams, scrubbed
- 1 pound Spanish-style chorizo, cut into ½-inch pieces
- 1 cup frozen peas, thawed
- Lemon wedges

1. Place chicken on large plate and sprinkle both sides with 1 teaspoon salt and 1 teaspoon pepper. Toss shrimp with 1 tablespoon oil, ½ teaspoon garlic, ¼ teaspoon paprika, and ¼ teaspoon salt in bowl until evenly coated. Set aside.

2. Heat 1 tablespoon oil in medium saucepan over medium heat until shimmering. Add remaining garlic and cook, stirring constantly, until garlic sticks to bottom of saucepan and begins to brown, about 1 minute. Add tomato paste and remaining 1½ teaspoons paprika and continue to cook, stirring constantly, until dark brown bits form on bottom of saucepan, about 1 minute. Add broth, sherry, clam juice, and saffron, if using. Increase heat to high and bring to boil. Remove pan from heat and set aside.

3A. FOR A CHARCOAL GRILL: Open bottom vent completely. Light large chimney starter mounded with charcoal briquettes (7 quarts). When top coals are partially covered with ash, pour evenly over grill. Using tongs, arrange 20 unlit briquettes evenly over coals. Set cooking grate in place, cover, and open lid vent completely. Heat grill until hot, about 5 minutes.

3B. FOR A GAS GRILL: Turn all burners to high, cover, and heat grill until hot, about 15 minutes. Leave all burners on high.

4. Clean and oil cooking grate. Place chicken on grill and cook until both sides are lightly browned, 5 to 7 minutes total. Return chicken to plate. Clean cooking grate.

5. Place roasting pan on grill (turning burners to medium-high if using gas) and add remaining ¼ cup oil. When oil begins to shimmer, add onion, red peppers, and ½ teaspoon salt. Cook, stirring frequently, until onion begins to brown, 4 to 7 minutes. Add rice (turning burners to medium if using gas) and stir until grains are well coated with oil.

6. Arrange chicken around perimeter of pan. Pour broth mixture and any accumulated juices from chicken over rice. Smooth rice into even layer, making sure nothing sticks to sides of pan and no rice rests atop chicken. When liquid reaches gentle simmer, place shrimp in center of pan in single layer. Arrange clams in center of pan, evenly distributing with shrimp and pushing hinge sides of clams into rice slightly so they stand up. Distribute chorizo evenly over surface of rice. Cook, moving and rotating pan to maintain gentle simmer across entire surface of pan, until rice is almost cooked through, 12 to 18 minutes. (If using gas, heat can also be adjusted to maintain simmer.)

7. Sprinkle peas evenly over paella, cover grill, and cook until liquid is fully absorbed and rice on bottom of pan sizzles, 5 to 8 minutes. Continue to cook, uncovered, checking frequently, until uniform golden-brown crust forms on bottom of pan, 8 to 15 minutes longer. (Rotate and slide pan around grill as necessary to ensure even crust formation.) Remove from grill, cover with foil, and let stand for 10 minutes. Serve with lemon wedges.

CREOLE-STYLE GUMBO

WHY THIS RECIPE WORKS: With shrimp, sausage, and vegetables in a deeply flavored, rich brown sauce with a touch of heat, gumbo is a unique one-pot meal. We wanted a foolproof, streamlined technique for gumbo that featured a thick, smooth sauce with lots of well-seasoned vegetables, meat, and fish.

The basis of gumbo is the roux, which is flour cooked in fat. For a deep, dark roux in half the time, we heated the oil before adding the flour. We also added the roux to room-temperature shrimp stock (supplemented with clam juice) to prevent separating. Although tomatoes are traditional in gumbo, our tasters didn't think they were necessary—but garlic was, and lots of it. Some cayenne pepper added the requisite heat. We added spicy andouille sausage and simmered everything for half an hour, tossing in the shrimp only during the last few minutes of cooking. You can add filé powder if you like, but our gumbo is delicious even without it.

Creole-Style Shrimp and Sausage Gumbo

SERVES 6 TO 8

Making a dark roux can be dangerous, as the mixture reaches temperatures in excess of 400 degrees. Therefore, use a deep pot for cooking the roux and long-handled utensils for stirring it, and be careful not to splash it on yourself. One secret to smooth gumbo is adding shrimp stock that is neither too hot nor too cold to the roux. For a stock that is at the right temperature when the roux is done, start preparing it before you tend to the vegetables and other ingredients, strain it, and then give it a head start on cooling by immediately adding the ice water and clam juice. So that your constant stirring of the roux will not be interrupted, start the roux only after you've made the stock. Alternatively, you can make the stock well ahead of time and bring it back to room temperature before using it. Spicy andouille sausage is a Louisiana specialty that may not be available everywhere; kielbasa or any fully cooked smoked sausage makes a fine substitute. Gumbo is traditionally served over white rice.

- 1½ pounds small shrimp (51 to 60 per pound), shells removed and reserved
- 3½ cups ice water
- 1 (8-ounce) bottle clam juice
- ½ cup vegetable oil
- ½ cup all-purpose flour, preferably bleached
- 2 medium onions, minced
- 1 medium red bell pepper, stemmed, seeded, and chopped fine
- 1 medium celery rib, chopped fine
- 6 medium garlic cloves, minced or pressed through a garlic press (about 2 tablespoons)
- 1 teaspoon dried thyme
- Table salt
- Cayenne pepper
- 2 bay leaves
- 1 pound smoked sausage, such as andouille or kielbasa (see note), sliced ¼ inch thick
- ½ cup minced fresh parsley leaves
- 4 medium scallions, white and green parts, sliced thin
- Ground black pepper

1. Bring the reserved shrimp shells and 4½ cups water to a boil in a stockpot or large saucepan over medium-high heat. Reduce the heat to medium-low and simmer for 20 minutes. Strain the stock and add the ice water and clam juice (you should have about 2 quarts of tepid stock, 100 to 110 degrees); discard the shells. Set the stock aside.

2. Heat the oil in a Dutch oven or large, heavy-bottomed saucepan over medium-high heat until it registers 200 degrees on an instant-read thermometer, 1½ to 2 minutes. Reduce the heat to medium and gradually stir in the flour with a wooden spatula or spoon, making sure to work out any lumps that may form. Continue stirring constantly, reaching into the corners of the pan, until the mixture has a toasty aroma and is deep reddish brown, about 20 minutes. (The roux will thin as it cooks; if it begins to smoke, remove the pan from the heat and stir the roux constantly to cool slightly.)

3. Add the onions, bell pepper, celery, garlic, thyme, 1 teaspoon salt, and ¼ teaspoon cayenne to the roux and cook, stirring frequently, until the vegetables soften, 8 to 10 minutes. Add 4 cups of the reserved stock in a slow, steady stream while stirring vigorously. Stir in the remaining 4 cups of stock. Increase the heat to high and bring to a boil. Reduce the heat to medium-low, skim the foam from the surface with a wide spoon, add the bay leaves, and simmer, uncovered, skimming the foam as it rises to the surface, about 30 minutes. (The mixture can be covered and set aside for several hours. Reheat when ready to proceed.)

4. Stir in the sausage and continue simmering to blend the flavors, about 30 minutes. Stir in the shrimp and simmer until cooked through, about 5 minutes. Off the heat, stir in the parsley and scallions and season with salt, black pepper, and cayenne to taste.

CIOPPINO

WHY THIS RECIPE WORKS: Brought to San Francisco by Italian immigrants, the earliest versions of cioppino were uncomplicated affairs made by fishermen with the day's catch. Today's restaurant versions showcase a variety of fish and shellfish piled high in a bright, complex broth. Cioppino is an indulgence for a seafood lover—but many recipes are intimidating for home cooks. We wanted a restaurant-worthy cioppino in which every component was perfectly cooked but which could be on the table quickly and with minimal fuss. First, we scaled down the seafood. For the fish, halibut fillets worked perfectly—they were tender and had just enough heft. As for the shellfish, a combination of briny littleneck clams and

savory-sweet mussels had the flavors we were looking for. The only way to perfectly cook three varieties of seafood was to cook each one separately and bring them all together in the hot broth to serve. We poached the halibut in the broth while the clams and mussels steamed in a separate pan. Removing them as they opened ensured ideal doneness for each one, and using a shallow skillet made the task easy. We used white wine to steam the mussels and clams, and then added the briny cooking liquid to the stew for a boost of intense seafood flavor. Replacing the water in the broth with bottled clam juice improved the broth even further.

Cioppino

SERVES 4 TO 6

Any firm-fleshed, ¾- to 1-inch-thick whitefish (such as cod or sea bass) can be substituted for halibut. Discard clams or mussels with unpleasant odors, cracked shells, or shells that won't close. If littlenecks are not available, substitute Manila or mahogany clams, or use 2 pounds of mussels. If using only mussels, skip step 3 and cook them all at once with the butter and wine for 3 to 5 minutes.

- ¼ cup vegetable oil
- 2 large onions, chopped fine
- Salt and pepper
- ¼ cup water
- 4 garlic cloves, minced
- 2 bay leaves
- 1 teaspoon dried oregano
- ⅛–¼ teaspoon red pepper flakes
- 1 (28-ounce) can whole peeled tomatoes, drained with juice reserved, chopped coarse
- 1 (8-ounce) bottle clam juice
- 1 (1½-pound) skinless halibut fillet, ¾ to 1 inch thick, cut into 6 pieces
- 1 pound littleneck clams, scrubbed
- 1¼ cups dry white wine
- 4 tablespoons unsalted butter
- 1 pound mussels, scrubbed and debearded
- ¼ cup chopped fresh parsley
- Extra-virgin olive oil

1. Heat vegetable oil in Dutch oven over medium-high heat until shimmering. Add onions, ½ teaspoon salt, and ½ teaspoon pepper; cook, stirring frequently, until onions begin to brown, 7 to 9 minutes. Add water and cook, stirring frequently, until onions are soft, 2 to 4 minutes. Stir in garlic, bay leaves, oregano, and pepper flakes and cook for 1 minute. Stir in tomatoes and reserved juice and clam juice and bring to simmer. Reduce heat to low, cover, and simmer for 5 minutes.

2. Submerge halibut in broth, cover, and gently simmer until fish is cooked through, 12 to 15 minutes. Remove pot from heat and, using slotted spoon, transfer halibut to plate, cover with aluminum foil, and set aside.

3. Bring clams, wine, and butter to boil in covered 12-inch skillet over high heat. Steam until clams just open, 5 to 8 minutes, transferring them to pot with tomato broth as they open.

4. Once all clams have been transferred to pot, add mussels to skillet, cover, and cook over high heat until mussels have opened, 2 to 4 minutes, transferring them to pot with tomato broth as they open. Pour cooking liquid from skillet into pot, being careful not to pour any grit from skillet into pot. Return broth to simmer.

5. Stir parsley into broth and season with salt and pepper to taste. Divide halibut among serving bowls. Ladle broth over halibut, making sure each portion contains both clams and mussels. Drizzle with olive oil and serve immediately.

BEHIND THE SCENES

A PEEK INSIDE THE TEST KITCHEN FREEZER

Curious as to what we keep in our freezer? A whole lot more than you might think. In fact, we've found that some pantry staples are better preserved in the freezer. Here's a list of the more unusual items the test kitchen keeps on ice.

RIPE OR OVERRIPE BANANAS: Great to have for making banana bread or muffins, or drop them into a blender while still frozen for fruit smoothies. Peel bananas before freezing.

NUTS: Sealed in a zipper-lock freezer bag, nuts stay fresh tasting for months. And there's no need to defrost; frozen nuts chop just as easily as fresh.

HERBS: Dried bay leaves retain their potency much longer when stored in the freezer. Chopped fresh herbs such as parsley, sage, rosemary, and thyme can be covered with water in an ice cube tray and then frozen indefinitely. Keep the frozen cubes in a zipper-lock freezer bag until needed for sauces, soups, or stews. Homemade pesto can also be frozen in ice cube trays, and there's no need to add water.

BUTTER: When stored in the refrigerator, butter picks up off-odors and eventually turns rancid. You can prolong its life by storing it in the freezer. Transfer it to the refrigerator one stick at a time, as you need it.

DRY GOODS: Stored in the freezer, flour, bread crumbs, cornmeal, oats, and other grains are protected from humidity, bugs, and rancidity.

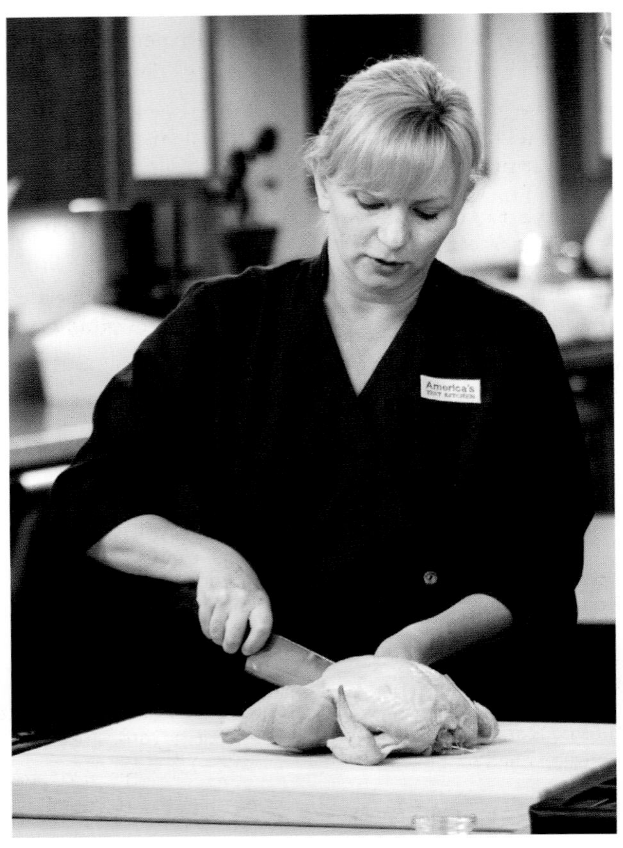

CHAPTER 5

SIMPLY CHICKEN

PERFECT POACHED CHICKEN BREASTS

WHY THIS RECIPE WORKS: Poaching can be a perfect way to gently cook delicate chicken breasts, but the standard approach can be fussy and it offers little in the way of flavor. To up the flavor ante, we added salt, soy sauce, garlic, and a bit of sugar to the poaching liquid for rich-tasting chicken. We found that our salty poaching liquid could double as a quick brine, simplifying the recipe and infusing the chicken with flavor. To ensure that the chicken cooked evenly, we used plenty of water and raised the chicken off the bottom of the pot in a steamer basket. Taking the pot off the heat partway through cooking allowed the delicate meat to cook through using residual heat and prevented overcooking. A couple of simple sauces made the perfect accompaniment.

Perfect Poached Chicken Breasts

SERVES 4

To ensure that the chicken cooks through, don't use breasts that weigh more than 8 ounces each. If desired, serve the chicken with one of our sauces (recipes follow) or in a salad or sandwiches.

- 4 (6- to 8-ounce) boneless, skinless chicken breasts, trimmed
- ½ cup soy sauce
- ¼ cup salt
- 2 tablespoons sugar
- 6 garlic cloves, smashed and peeled

1. Cover chicken breasts with plastic wrap and pound thick ends gently with meat pounder until ¾ inch thick. Whisk 4 quarts water, soy sauce, salt, sugar, and garlic in Dutch oven until salt and sugar are dissolved. Arrange breasts, skinned side up, in steamer basket, making sure not to overlap them. Submerge steamer basket in brine and let sit at room temperature for 30 minutes.

2. Heat pot over medium heat, stirring liquid occasionally to even out hot spots, until water registers 175 degrees, 15 to 20 minutes. Turn off heat, cover pot, remove from burner, and let stand until meat registers 160 degrees, 17 to 22 minutes.

3. Transfer breasts to cutting board, cover tightly with aluminum foil, and let rest for 5 minutes. Slice each breast on bias into ¼-inch-thick slices, transfer to serving platter or individual plates, and serve.

Cumin-Cilantro Yogurt Sauce

MAKES ABOUT 1 CUP

Mint may be substituted for the cilantro. This sauce is prone to curdle and thus does not reheat well; prepare it just before serving.

- 2 tablespoons extra-virgin olive oil
- 1 shallot, minced
- 1 garlic clove, minced
- 1 teaspoon ground cumin
- ⅛ teaspoon red pepper flakes
- ½ cup plain whole-milk yogurt
- ⅓ cup water
- 1 teaspoon lime juice
- Salt and pepper
- 2 tablespoons chopped fresh cilantro

Heat 1 tablespoon oil in small skillet over medium heat until shimmering. Add shallot and cook until softened, about 2 minutes. Stir in garlic, cumin, and pepper flakes and cook until fragrant, about 30 seconds. Remove from heat and whisk in yogurt, water, lime juice, and remaining 1 tablespoon oil. Season with salt and pepper to taste and cover to keep warm. Stir in cilantro just before serving.

Warm Tomato-Ginger Vinaigrette

MAKES ABOUT 2 CUPS

Parsley may be substituted for the cilantro.

- ¼ cup extra-virgin olive oil
- 1 shallot, minced
- 1½ teaspoons grated fresh ginger
- ⅛ teaspoon ground cumin
- ⅛ teaspoon ground fennel
- 12 ounces cherry tomatoes, halved
- Salt and pepper
- 1 tablespoon red wine vinegar
- 1 teaspoon packed light brown sugar
- 2 tablespoons chopped fresh cilantro

Heat 2 tablespoons oil in 10-inch nonstick skillet over medium heat until shimmering. Add shallot, ginger, cumin, and fennel and cook until fragrant, about 15 seconds. Stir in tomatoes and ¼ teaspoon salt and cook, stirring frequently, until tomatoes have softened, 3 to 5 minutes. Off heat, stir in vinegar and sugar and season with salt and pepper to taste; cover to keep warm. Stir in cilantro and remaining 2 tablespoons oil just before serving.

SAUTÉED CHICKEN WITH MUSTARD-CIDER SAUCE

WHY THIS RECIPE WORKS: Sautéed super-thin cutlets are satisfying midweek fare, except when they are tough and dry. We wanted juicy, ultra thin sautéed chicken cutlets, paired with a sauce that complements, rather than overpowers, the meat.

For evenly sized cutlets, we took a two-step approach. We halved the chicken breasts horizontally before pounding them to an even thickness under plastic wrap. Halving and pounding the breasts ensured that they cooked at the same rate, and turned out moist, tender, and juicy. To further ensure the cutlets were juicy, we browned them on only one side. And for the sauce, we kept the flavors simple, relying on the sweet, tangy combination of apple cider and cider vinegar complemented with the kick of whole grain mustard.

Sautéed Chicken Cutlets with Mustard-Cider Sauce

SERVES 4

To make slicing the chicken easier, freeze it for 15 minutes.

CHICKEN

- 4 (6- to 8-ounce) boneless, skinless chicken breasts, tenderloins removed and breasts trimmed
- Table salt and ground black pepper
- 2 tablespoons vegetable oil

MUSTARD-CIDER SAUCE

- 2 teaspoons vegetable oil
- 1 medium shallot, minced (about 3 tablespoons)
- 1¼ cups apple cider
- 2 tablespoons cider vinegar
- 2 teaspoons whole grain mustard
- 2 teaspoons minced fresh parsley leaves
- 2 tablespoons unsalted butter
- Table salt and ground black pepper

1. FOR THE CHICKEN: Adjust an oven rack to the middle position and heat the oven to 200 degrees. Halve the chicken horizontally, then cover the chicken halves with plastic wrap and use a meat pounder to pound the cutlets to an even ¼-inch thickness. Season both sides of each cutlet with salt and pepper. Heat 1 tablespoon of the oil in a 12-inch skillet over medium-high heat until just smoking. Place four cutlets in the skillet and cook without moving them until browned, about 2 minutes. Using a spatula, flip the cutlets and continue to cook until the second sides are opaque, 15 to 20 seconds. Transfer to a large heatproof plate. Add the remaining 1 tablespoon oil to the now-empty skillet and repeat to cook the remaining cutlets. Cover the plate loosely with foil and transfer it to the oven to keep warm while making the sauce.

2. FOR THE SAUCE: Off the heat, add the oil and shallot to the hot skillet. Using residual heat, cook, stirring constantly, until softened, about 30 seconds. Set the skillet over medium-high heat and add the cider and vinegar. Bring to a simmer, scraping the pan bottom with a wooden spoon to loosen any browned bits. Simmer until reduced to ½ cup, 6 to 7 minutes. Off the heat, stir in the mustard and parsley; whisk in the butter 1 tablespoon at a time. Season with salt and pepper to taste and serve immediately with the cutlets.

SAUTÉED CHICKEN CUTLETS

WHY THIS RECIPE WORKS: Sautéed chicken cutlets are a breeze to prepare, but their brief cooking time and lack of skin leaves very little fond behind with which to build a pan sauce. With this dilemma in mind, we sought out a sauce that packed big flavor and could be made before the chicken even hit the skillet. Romesco sauce—a thick, coarse Spanish concoction of roasted red peppers, toasted hazelnuts, bread, sherry vinegar, olive oil, smoked paprika, and garlic—was simple to whizz together in a food processor and boasted a bold flavor profile. Starting with those key elements, we added a touch of honey to focus the ingredients' impact and a pinch of cayenne for pleasant heat. With the pepper sauce under our belt, we used the same blueprint to create equally easy sun-dried tomato and tomatillo sauces. For the chicken, partially freezing the breasts before halving firmed them up for easy slicing. We browned the cutlets in a hot oiled pan and, in just under 3 minutes, they were ready to be served with our simple, bold red pepper sauce.

NOTES FROM THE TEST KITCHEN

MAKING CHICKEN CUTLETS

Packaged chicken cutlets from the supermarket can be ragged or uneven in thickness. You can easily make your own using boneless, skinless chicken breasts.

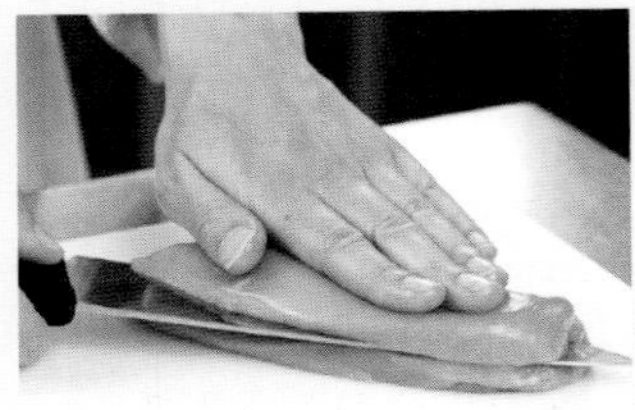

1. Remove tenderloin from underside of breast if necessary. Lay chicken smooth side up on cutting board. To make cutlets, place your hand on top of chicken and carefully slice it in half horizontally.

2. Separate breast to yield 2 cutlets between ⅜ and ½ inch thick. If necessary, pound to even thickness.

Sautéed Chicken Cutlets

SERVES 4

The cutlets will be easier to slice in half if you freeze them for about 15 minutes.

- 4 (6- to 8-ounce) boneless, skinless chicken breasts, trimmed, halved horizontally, and pounded ¼ inch thick
- Kosher salt and pepper
- 4 teaspoons vegetable oil

Pat cutlets dry with paper towels; sprinkle each side of each cutlet with ⅛ teaspoon salt and season with pepper. Heat 2 teaspoons oil in 12-inch skillet over medium-high heat until just smoking. Place 4 cutlets in skillet and cook, without moving, until browned, about 2 minutes. Flip cutlets and continue to cook until second sides are opaque, about 30 seconds. Transfer to platter and tent loosely with aluminum foil. Repeat with remaining 4 cutlets and remaining 2 teaspoons oil. Serve.

Quick Roasted Red Pepper Sauce

MAKES ABOUT 1 CUP

You will need at least a 12-ounce jar of roasted red peppers for this recipe.

- ½ slice hearty white sandwich bread, cut into ½-inch pieces
- ¼ cup hazelnuts, toasted and skinned
- 2 tablespoons extra-virgin olive oil
- 2 garlic cloves, sliced thin
- 1 cup jarred roasted red peppers, rinsed and patted dry
- 1½ tablespoons sherry vinegar
- 1 teaspoon honey
- ½ teaspoon smoked paprika
- ½ teaspoon salt
- Pinch cayenne pepper

Heat bread, hazelnuts, and 1 tablespoon oil in 12-inch skillet over medium heat; cook, stirring constantly, until bread and hazelnuts are lightly toasted, 2½ to 3 minutes. Add garlic and cook, stirring constantly, until fragrant, about 30 seconds. Transfer bread mixture to food processor and pulse until coarsely chopped, about 5 pulses. Add red peppers, vinegar, honey, paprika, salt, cayenne, and remaining 1 tablespoon oil to processor. Pulse until finely chopped, 5 to 8 pulses. Transfer to bowl and let stand for at least 10 minutes. (Sauce can be refrigerated for up to 2 days.)

Quick Sun-Dried Tomato Sauce

MAKES ABOUT 1 CUP

For the best taste and texture, make sure to rinse all the dried herbs off the sun-dried tomatoes.

- ½ slice hearty white sandwich bread, cut into ½-inch pieces
- ¼ cup pine nuts
- 2 tablespoons extra-virgin olive oil
- 2 garlic cloves, sliced thin
- 1 small tomato, cored and cut into ½-inch pieces
- ½ cup oil-packed sun-dried tomatoes, rinsed
- 2 tablespoons coarsely chopped fresh basil
- 2 tablespoons balsamic vinegar
- ½ teaspoon salt

Heat bread, pine nuts, and 1 tablespoon oil in 12-inch skillet over medium heat; cook, stirring constantly, until bread and pine nuts are lightly toasted, 2½ to 3 minutes. Add garlic and cook, stirring constantly, until fragrant, about 30 seconds. Transfer bread mixture to food processor and pulse until coarsely chopped, about 5 pulses. Add tomato, sun-dried tomatoes, basil, vinegar, salt, and remaining 1 tablespoon oil to processor. Pulse until finely chopped, 5 to 8 pulses. Transfer to bowl and let stand for at least 10 minutes. (Sauce can be refrigerated for up to 2 days.)

Quick Tomatillo Sauce

MAKES ABOUT 1 CUP

You will need at least a 15-ounce can of tomatillos for this recipe.

- ½ slice hearty white sandwich bread, cut into ½-inch pieces
- ¼ cup pepitas
- 2 tablespoons extra-virgin olive oil
- 2 garlic cloves, sliced thin
- 1 cup canned tomatillos, rinsed

2 tablespoons jarred sliced jalapeños plus 2 teaspoons brine
2 tablespoons fresh cilantro leaves
1 teaspoon honey
½ teaspoon salt

Heat bread, pepitas, and 1 tablespoon oil in 12-inch skillet over medium heat; cook, stirring constantly, until pepitas and bread are lightly toasted, 2½ to 3 minutes. Add garlic and cook, stirring constantly, until fragrant, about 30 seconds. Transfer bread mixture to food processor and pulse until coarsely chopped, about 5 pulses. Add tomatillos, jalapeños and brine, cilantro, honey, salt, and remaining 1 tablespoon oil to processor. Pulse until finely chopped, 5 to 8 pulses. Transfer to bowl and let stand for at least 10 minutes. (Sauce can be refrigerated for up to 2 days.)

BREADED CHICKEN CUTLETS

WHY THIS RECIPE WORKS: Breaded chicken cutlets, for all their apparent simplicity, can be problematic. Too often, they end up with either an underdone or burnt coating, which falls off the tasteless, rubbery chicken underneath. We wanted chicken cutlets with flavorful meat and a crunchy crust that would adhere nicely to the meat.

To ensure even cooking, we flattened the chicken breasts to ½ inch; thin enough to cook evenly, but thick enough to make a hearty, crisp cutlet. To prevent crust separation, we coated the chicken with flour, an egg and oil mixture, and flavorful, fresh bread crumbs. We then let them sit for five minutes to help set the crust. For the crispiest coating, we fried the cutlets in batches in vegetable oil. And for a tasty variation, we added Parmesan for a version of the classic Italian dish Chicken Milanese.

Breaded Chicken Cutlets

SERVES 4

If you'd rather not prepare fresh bread crumbs, use panko, the extra-crisp Japanese bread crumbs. The chicken is cooked in batches of two because the crust is noticeably more crisp if the pan is not overcrowded. Note that these cutlets are a bit thicker than others in the chapter and should not be halved horizontally.

4 (5- to 6-ounce) boneless, skinless chicken breasts, tenderloins removed and breasts trimmed
Table salt and ground black pepper
3 slices high-quality white sandwich bread, torn into quarters
¾ cup unbleached all-purpose flour
2 large eggs
1 tablespoon plus ¾ cup vegetable oil
Lemon wedges, for serving

1. Use a meat pounder to pound the chicken breasts to an even ½-inch thickness. Sprinkle the cutlets with salt and pepper and set aside. Set a large wire rack over a large baking sheet and set aside.

2. Adjust an oven rack to the lower-middle position, set a heatproof plate on the rack, and heat the oven to 200 degrees. Process the bread in a food processor until evenly fine-textured, 20 to 30 seconds. Transfer the crumbs to a pie plate or shallow dish. Spread the flour in a second plate. Beat the eggs with 1 tablespoon of the oil in a third plate.

3. Working with one cutlet at a time, dredge each cutlet in the flour, shaking off the excess. Using tongs, dip both sides of the cutlets in the egg mixture, allowing the excess to drip off. Dip both sides of the cutlets in the bread crumbs, pressing the crumbs with your fingers to form an even, cohesive coat. Place the breaded cutlets on the wire rack and allow the coating to dry for about 5 minutes.

4. Meanwhile, heat 6 tablespoons more oil in a 12-inch nonstick skillet over medium-high heat until shimmering but not smoking, about 2 minutes. Lay 2 cutlets gently in the skillet; cook until deep golden brown and crisp on the first side, gently pressing down on the cutlets with a metal spatula, about 2½ minutes. Using tongs, flip the cutlets, reduce the heat to medium, and continue to cook until the meat feels firm when pressed gently and the second side is deep golden brown and crisp, 2½ to 3 minutes longer. Line the warmed plate with a double layer of paper towels and set the cutlets on top; return the plate to the oven.

5. Discard the oil in the skillet and wipe the skillet clean with paper towels. Repeat step 4 using the remaining 6 tablespoons oil and remaining cutlets; serve with lemon wedges.

Chicken Milanese

Though Parmesan is classic in this dish, use Pecorino Romano if you prefer a more tangy flavor. Keep a close eye on the cutlets as they brown to make sure the cheese does not burn.

Follow the recipe for Breaded Chicken Cutlets, substituting ¼ cup finely grated Parmesan cheese for an equal amount of bread crumbs.

NUT-CRUSTED CHICKEN BREASTS

WHY THIS RECIPE WORKS: Adding chopped nuts to a coating is a great way to add robust flavor to otherwise lean and mild boneless, skinless chicken breasts. But nut coatings are often dense and leaden, and the rich flavor of the nuts rarely comes through. Using a combination of chopped almonds and panko bread crumbs—rather than all nuts—kept the coating light and crunchy, and the bread crumbs helped the coating adhere. Instead of frying the breaded breasts, we found that baking them in the oven was not only easier but also helped the meat stay juicy and ensured an even golden crust. But it wasn't until we cooked the coating in browned butter prior to breading the chicken that we finally achieved the deep nutty flavor we sought.

Nut-Crusted Chicken Breasts with Lemon and Thyme

SERVES 4

This recipe is best with almonds but works well with any type of nut. We prefer kosher salt in this recipe. If using table salt, reduce salt amounts by half.

- 4 (6- to 8-ounce) boneless, skinless chicken breasts, tenderloins removed and breasts trimmed
- Kosher salt
- 1 cup almonds, chopped coarse
- 4 tablespoons (½ stick) unsalted butter
- 1 medium shallot, minced (about 3 tablespoons)
- 1 cup panko bread crumbs
- 2 teaspoons finely grated zest from 1 lemon, zested lemon cut into wedges
- 1 teaspoon minced fresh thyme leaves
- ⅛ teaspoon cayenne pepper
- 1 cup unbleached all-purpose flour
- 3 large eggs
- 2 teaspoons Dijon mustard
- ¼ teaspoon ground black pepper

1. Adjust the oven rack to the lower-middle position and heat the oven to 350 degrees. Set a wire rack in a rimmed baking sheet. Pat the chicken dry with paper towels. Using a fork, poke the thickest half of the breasts 5 to 6 times and sprinkle with ½ teaspoon salt. Transfer the breasts to the prepared wire rack and refrigerate, uncovered, while preparing the coating.

2. Pulse the almonds in a food processor until they resemble coarse meal, about 20 pulses. Melt the butter in a 12-inch skillet over medium heat, swirling occasionally, until the butter is browned and releases a nutty aroma, 4 to 5 minutes. Add the shallot and ½ teaspoon salt and cook, stirring constantly, until just beginning to brown, about 3 minutes. Reduce the heat to medium-low, add the bread crumbs and ground almonds and cook, stirring often, until golden brown, 10 to 12 minutes. Transfer the panko mixture to a shallow dish or pie plate and stir in the lemon zest, thyme, and cayenne. Place the flour in a second dish. Lightly beat the eggs, mustard, and black pepper together in a third dish.

3. Pat the chicken dry with paper towels. Working with one breast at a time, dredge the chicken in the flour, shaking off the excess, then coat with the egg mixture, allowing the excess to drip off. Coat all sides of the breast with the panko mixture, pressing gently so that the crumbs adhere. Return the breaded breasts to the wire rack.

4. Bake until the chicken registers 160 degrees on an instant-read thermometer, 20 to 25 minutes. Let the chicken rest for 5 minutes before serving with the lemon wedges.

Nut-Crusted Chicken Breasts with Orange and Oregano

This version works particularly well with pistachios or hazelnuts.

Follow the recipe for Nut-Crusted Chicken Breasts with Lemon and Thyme, substituting 1 teaspoon orange zest for the lemon zest (reserving the orange wedges for the garnish) and 1 teaspoon oregano for the thyme.

STUFFED CHICKEN CUTLETS

WHY THIS RECIPE WORKS: Cutlets that are stuffed and breaded are special-occasion food. The filling moistens the chicken from the inside with a creamy, tasty sauce, while the crust makes a crunchy counterpoint. The problem is that these bundles can leak and getting the right proportion of filling to cutlet can be tricky. We wanted stuffed chicken cutlets with a creamy filling that wouldn't turn runny and flavors that would complement, not overpower, the chicken. And we wanted the crust to be crisp all over and completely seal in the filling so that none leaked out.

We pounded the chicken breasts thin so they rolled easily and cooked evenly. A combination of cream cheese and cheddar mixed with onion, garlic, and fresh thyme gave us a creamy, well-flavored filling. Thin-sliced ham added another layer of flavor to our cutlets. Before we breaded the cutlets, we chilled them in the refrigerator to help the filling set—this step prevented leaks during cooking. For perfectly cooked stuffed cutlets, we sautéed them just until brown, then moved them into the oven to finish cooking through.

Stuffed Chicken Cutlets with Ham and Cheddar

SERVES 4

To make slicing the chicken easier, freeze it for 15 minutes. The cutlets can be filled and rolled in advance, then refrigerated for up to 24 hours. To dry fresh bread crumbs, spread them out on a baking sheet and bake in a 200-degree oven, stirring occasionally, for 30 minutes. Removing some moisture from the crumbs cuts down on splattering when the breaded cutlets are pan-fried.

FILLING

- 1 tablespoon unsalted butter
- 1 small onion, minced
- 1 small garlic clove, minced or pressed through a garlic press (about ½ teaspoon)
- 4 ounces cream cheese, softened
- 1 teaspoon minced fresh thyme leaves
- 2 ounces cheddar cheese, shredded (about ½ cup)
- Table salt and ground black pepper
- 4 slices (about 4 ounces) thin-sliced cooked deli ham

CHICKEN

- 4 (5- to 6-ounce) boneless, skinless chicken breasts, tenderloins removed and breasts trimmed
- Table salt and ground black pepper
- ¾ cup unbleached all-purpose flour
- 2 large eggs
- 1 tablespoon plus ¾ cup vegetable oil
- 4 slices high-quality white sandwich bread, pulsed in a food processor to coarse crumbs and dried (see note)

1. FOR THE FILLING: Melt the butter in a medium skillet over low heat; add the onion and cook, stirring occasionally, until deep golden brown, 15 to 20 minutes. Stir in the garlic and cook until fragrant, about 30 seconds longer; set aside.

2. In a medium bowl and using an electric mixer, beat the cream cheese on medium speed until light and fluffy, about 1 minute. Stir in the onion mixture, thyme, and cheddar; season with salt and pepper to taste and set aside.

3. Following the photos, butterfly each chicken breast and pound between two sheets of plastic wrap to a uniform ¼-inch thickness. Pound the outer perimeter to ⅛ inch. Place the chicken cutlets, smooth side down, on a work surface and season with salt and pepper. Spread each cutlet with one-quarter of the cheese mixture, then place 1 slice of ham on top of the cheese, folding the ham as necessary to fit onto the surface of the cutlet. Roll up each cutlet from the tapered end, folding in the edges to form a neat cylinder. Refrigerate until the filling is firm, at least 1 hour.

4. FOR THE CHICKEN: Adjust an oven rack to the lower-middle position and heat the oven to 450 degrees. Set a large wire rack over a large baking sheet and set aside. Place the flour in a pie plate or shallow dish. Beat the eggs with 1 tablespoon of the oil in a second plate. Spread the bread crumbs in a third plate. Dredge 1 chicken roll in the flour, shaking off the excess, then coat with the egg mixture, allowing the excess to drip off. Coat all sides of the chicken roll with the bread crumbs, pressing gently so that the crumbs adhere. Place on the wire rack and repeat the flouring and breading with the remaining chicken. Allow the coating to dry for about 5 minutes. Transfer the chicken to a plate. Wipe the wire rack and baking sheet clean and set aside.

5. Heat the remaining ¾ cup oil in a 10-inch nonstick skillet over medium-high heat until shimmering, but not smoking. Using tongs, carefully add the chicken, seam side down, to the pan, and cook until medium golden brown, about 2 minutes. Turn each roll and cook until medium golden brown on all sides, 2 to 3 minutes longer. Transfer the chicken rolls, seam side down, to the now-clean wire rack on the baking sheet; bake until deep golden brown and an instant-read thermometer inserted into the center of a roll registers 160 to 165 degrees, about 15 minutes. Let stand for 5 minutes before slicing each roll crosswise on the diagonal with a serrated knife into five pieces; arrange on individual dinner plates and serve.

NOTES FROM THE TEST KITCHEN

BUTTERFLYING CHICKEN BREASTS

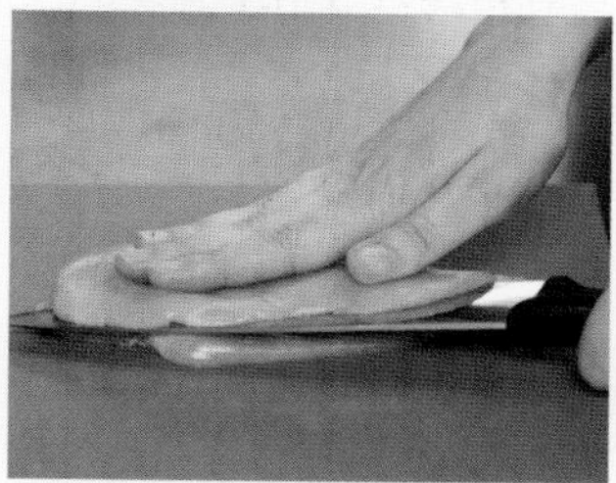

1. Starting on the thinnest side, butterfly the breast by slicing it lengthwise almost in half. Open the breast up to create a single flat breast. (To make cutlets, continue to cut through the meat until you have two cutlets.)

2. With the breast or cutlet in a zipper-lock bag or between sheets of plastic wrap, pound (starting at the center) to ¼-inch thickness. Pound the outer perimeter to ⅛ inch.

PAN-SEARED CHICKEN BREASTS

WHY THIS RECIPE WORKS: A boneless, skinless chicken breast doesn't have the bone and skin to protect it from the intensity of a hot pan. Inevitably, it emerges moist in the middle and dry at the edges, with an exterior that's leathery and tough. We wanted a boneless, skinless chicken breast that was every bit as flavorful, moist, and tender as its skin-on counterpart.

We decided to utilize a technique that we've used successfully in the test kitchen with thick-cut steaks, where we gently parcook the meat in the oven and then sear it on the stovetop. First, we salted the chicken to help it retain more moisture as it cooked. To expedite the process we poked holes in the breasts, creating channels for the salt to reach the interior of the chicken as it parcooked. We then placed the breasts in a baking dish and covered it tightly with foil. In this enclosed environment, any moisture released by the chicken stayed trapped under the foil, keeping the exterior from drying out without becoming so overly wet that it couldn't brown quickly.

The next step was figuring out how to achieve a crisp, even crust on our parcooked breasts. We turned to a Chinese cooking technique called velveting, in which meat is dipped in a mixture of oil and cornstarch to create a thin protective layer that keeps the protein moist and tender, even when exposed to ultra-high heat. We replaced the oil with butter (for flavor) and mixed flour in with the cornstarch to avoid any pasty flavor. The coating helped the chicken make better contact with the hot skillet, creating a thin, browned, crisp veneer that kept the breast's exterior as moist as the interior.

Pan-Seared Chicken Breasts

SERVES 4

For the best results, buy similarly sized chicken breasts. If your breasts have the tenderloin attached, leave it in place and follow the upper range of baking time in step 1. For optimal texture, sear the chicken immediately after removing it from the oven.

- 4 (6- to 8-ounce) boneless, skinless chicken breasts, trimmed (see note)
- 1 teaspoon table salt
- 1 tablespoon vegetable oil
- 2 tablespoons unsalted butter, melted
- 1 tablespoon unbleached all-purpose flour
- 1 teaspoon cornstarch
- ½ teaspoon ground black pepper
- 1 recipe Lemon and Chive Pan Sauce (optional; recipe follows)

1. Adjust an oven rack to the lower-middle position and heat the oven to 275 degrees. Use a fork to poke the thickest half of each breast five to six times, then sprinkle each breast with ¼ teaspoon salt. Place the chicken, skinned side down, in a 13 by 9-inch baking dish and cover tightly with foil. Bake until the chicken registers 145 to 150 degrees on an instant-read thermometer, 30 to 40 minutes.

2. Remove the chicken from the oven and transfer, skinned side up, to a paper towel–lined plate and pat dry with paper towels. Heat the oil in a 12-inch skillet over medium-high heat until smoking. While the pan is heating, whisk the butter, flour, cornstarch, and pepper together in a small bowl. Lightly brush the tops of the chicken with half of the butter mixture. Place the chicken in the skillet, coated side down, and cook until browned, 3 to 4 minutes. While the chicken browns, brush the second side with the remaining butter mixture. Using tongs, flip the chicken, reduce the heat to medium, and cook until the second side is browned and the chicken registers 160 to 165 degrees, 3 to 4 minutes. Transfer the chicken to a platter and let rest while preparing the pan sauce (if not making the pan sauce, let the chicken rest for 5 minutes before serving).

Lemon and Chive Pan Sauce

MAKES ABOUT ¾ CUP

- 1 medium shallot, minced (about 3 tablespoons)
- 1 teaspoon unbleached all-purpose flour
- 1 cup low-sodium chicken broth
- 1 tablespoon juice from 1 lemon
- 1 tablespoon minced fresh chives
- 1 tablespoon unsalted butter, chilled
- Table salt and ground black pepper

Add the shallot to the empty skillet and cook over medium heat until softened, about 2 minutes. Add the flour and cook, stirring constantly, for 30 seconds. Add the broth, increase the heat to medium-high, and bring to a simmer, scraping the pan bottom to loosen the browned bits. Simmer rapidly until reduced to ¾ cup, 3 to 5 minutes. Stir in any accumulated chicken juices, return to a simmer, and cook for 30 seconds. Off the heat, whisk in the lemon juice, chives, and butter; season with salt and pepper to taste. Spoon the sauce over the chicken and serve immediately.

ROASTED BONE-IN CHICKEN BREASTS

WHY THIS RECIPE WORKS: People often view the chicken bones and skin as a complication rather than an asset, so we resolved to devise an easy method that would deliver juicy, well-seasoned meat and crispy, brown skin. We ran into some expected problems though: The bone-in chicken breasts roasted at a high temperature achieved a crispy, brown skin, but the resulting meat was dry and bland. Cooking the chicken at a lower temperature kept the meat juicy but left the skin pale and flabby. For the best of both worlds, we adapted a cooking technique that we more commonly use for steaks: reverse searing. We started by applying salt under the skin to season the meat and help it retain moisture. Then we poked small holes in the skin to help drain excess fat. Gently baking the breasts at 325 degrees minimized moisture loss and resulted in even cooking from the breasts' thick ends to their thin ends. It also allowed the surface of the skin to dry out so that a quick sear in a hot skillet was all that was required for a crackly finish.

Roasted Bone-In Chicken Breasts

SERVES 4

Be sure to remove excess fatty skin from the thick ends of the breasts when trimming. You may serve these chicken breasts on their own or prepare a sauce (recipe follows) while the chicken roasts.

- 4 (10- to 12-ounce) bone-in chicken breasts, trimmed
- 1½ teaspoons kosher salt
- 1 tablespoon vegetable oil

1. Adjust oven rack to lower-middle position and heat oven to 325 degrees. Line rimmed baking sheet with aluminum foil. Working with 1 breast at a time, use your fingers to carefully separate chicken skin from meat. Peel skin back, leaving it attached at top and bottom of breast and at ribs. Sprinkle salt evenly over all chicken, then lay skin back in place. Using metal skewer or tip of paring knife, poke 6 to 8 holes in fat deposits in skin. Arrange breasts skin side up on prepared sheet. Roast until chicken registers 160 degrees, 35 to 45 minutes.

2. Heat 12-inch skillet over low heat for 5 minutes. Add oil and swirl to coat surface. Add chicken, skin side down, and increase heat to medium-high. Cook chicken without moving it until skin is well browned and crispy, 3 to 5 minutes. Using tongs, flip chicken and prop against side of skillet so thick side of breast is facing down; continue to cook until browned, 1 to 2 minutes longer. Transfer to platter and let rest for 5 minutes before serving.

Jalapeño and Cilantro Sauce

MAKES 1 CUP

For a spicier sauce, reserve and add some of the chile seeds to the blender.

- 1 cup fresh cilantro leaves and stems, trimmed and chopped coarse
- 3 jalapeño chiles, stemmed, seeded, and minced
- ½ cup mayonnaise
- 1 tablespoon lime juice
- 2 garlic cloves, minced
- ½ teaspoon kosher salt
- 2 tablespoons extra-virgin olive oil

Process cilantro, jalapeños, mayonnaise, lime juice, garlic, and salt in blender for 1 minute. Scrape down sides of blender jar and continue to process until smooth, about 1 minute longer. With blender running, slowly add oil until incorporated. Transfer to bowl.

CRISPY-SKINNED CHICKEN BREASTS

WHY THIS RECIPE WORKS: Perfectly cooked chicken with shatteringly crispy, flavorful skin is a rare find, so we set out to develop a foolproof recipe that would work every time. Boning and pounding the chicken breasts was essential to creating a flat, even surface to maximize the skin's contact with the hot pan. We salted the chicken to both season the meat and dry out the skin; poking holes in the skin and the meat allowed the salt to penetrate deeply. Starting the chicken in a cold pan allowed time for the skin to crisp without overcooking the meat. Weighting the chicken for part of the cooking time with a heavy Dutch oven encouraged even contact with the hot pan for all-over crunchy skin. Finally, we created silky, flavorful sauces with a bright, acidic finish, which provided the perfect foil to the skin's richness.

Crispy-Skinned Chicken Breasts with Vinegar-Pepper Pan Sauce

SERVES 2

This recipe requires refrigerating the salted meat for at least 1 hour before cooking. Two 10- to 12-ounce chicken breasts are ideal, but three smaller ones can fit in the same pan; the skin will be slightly less crispy. A boning knife or sharp paring knife works best to remove the bones from the breasts. To maintain the crispy skin, spoon the sauce around, not over, the breasts when serving.

CHICKEN

- 2 (10- to 12-ounce) bone-in split chicken breasts
- Kosher salt and pepper
- 2 tablespoons vegetable oil

PAN SAUCE

- 1 shallot, minced
- 1 teaspoon all-purpose flour
- ½ cup chicken broth
- ¼ cup chopped pickled hot cherry peppers, plus ¼ cup brine
- 1 tablespoon unsalted butter, chilled
- 1 teaspoon minced fresh thyme
- Salt and pepper

1. FOR THE CHICKEN: Place 1 chicken breast, skin side down, on cutting board, with ribs facing away from knife hand. Run tip of knife between breastbone and meat, working from thick end of breast toward thin end. Angling blade slightly and following rib cage, repeat cutting motion several times to remove ribs and breastbone from breast. Find short remnant of wishbone along top edge of breast and run tip of knife along both sides of bone to separate it from meat. Remove tenderloin (reserve for another use) and trim excess fat, taking care not to cut into skin. Repeat with second breast.

2. Using tip of paring knife, poke skin on each breast evenly 30 to 40 times. Turn breasts over and poke thickest half of each breast 5 to 6 times. Cover breasts with plastic wrap and pound thick ends gently with meat pounder until ½ inch thick. Evenly sprinkle each breast with ½ teaspoon kosher salt. Place breasts, skin side up, on wire rack set in rimmed baking sheet, cover loosely with plastic, and refrigerate for 1 hour or up to 8 hours.

3. Pat breasts dry with paper towels and sprinkle each breast with ¼ teaspoon pepper. Pour oil in 12-inch skillet and swirl to coat. Place breasts, skin side down, in oil and place skillet over medium heat. Place heavy skillet or Dutch oven on top of breasts. Cook breasts until skin is beginning to brown and meat is beginning to turn opaque along edges, 7 to 9 minutes.

4. Remove weight and continue to cook until skin is well browned and very crispy, 6 to 8 minutes. Flip breasts, reduce heat to medium-low, and cook until second side is lightly browned and meat registers 160 to 165 degrees, 2 to 3 minutes. Transfer breasts to individual plates and let rest while preparing pan sauce.

5. FOR THE PAN SAUCE: Pour off all but 2 teaspoons oil from skillet. Return skillet to medium heat and add shallot; cook, stirring occasionally, until shallot is softened, about 2 minutes. Add flour and cook, stirring constantly, for 30 seconds. Increase heat to medium-high, add broth and brine, and bring to simmer, scraping up any browned bits. Simmer until thickened, 2 to 3 minutes. Stir in any accumulated chicken juices; return to simmer and cook for 30 seconds. Remove skillet from heat and whisk in peppers, butter, and thyme; season with salt and pepper to taste. Spoon sauce around breasts and serve.

Crispy-Skinned Chicken Breasts with Lemon-Rosemary Pan Sauce

In step 5, increase broth to ¾ cup and substitute 2 tablespoons lemon juice for brine. Omit peppers and substitute rosemary for thyme.

Crispy-Skinned Chicken Breasts with Maple-Sherry Vinegar Pan Sauce

In step 5, substitute 2 tablespoons sherry vinegar for brine, 1 tablespoon maple syrup for peppers, and sage for thyme.

NOTES FROM THE TEST KITCHEN

BONING A SPLIT CHICKEN BREAST

If you want to cook boneless breasts with skin, you'll have to do a little knife work. Removing the bones allows the entire surface of the meat to lie flat and even against the pan—a must for perfectly crispy skin.

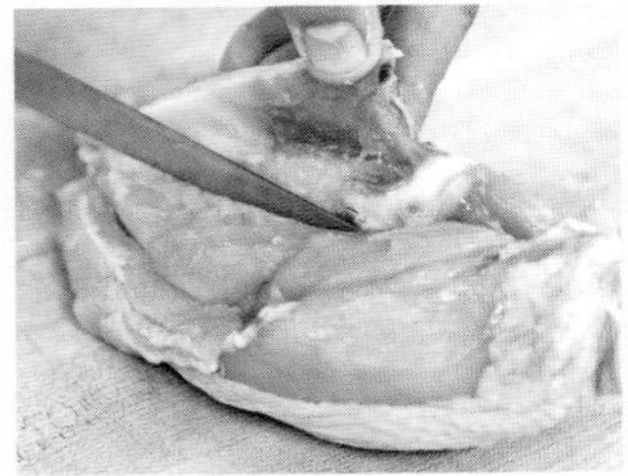

1. With chicken breast skin side down, run tip of boning or sharp paring knife between breastbone and meat, working from thick end of breast toward thin end.

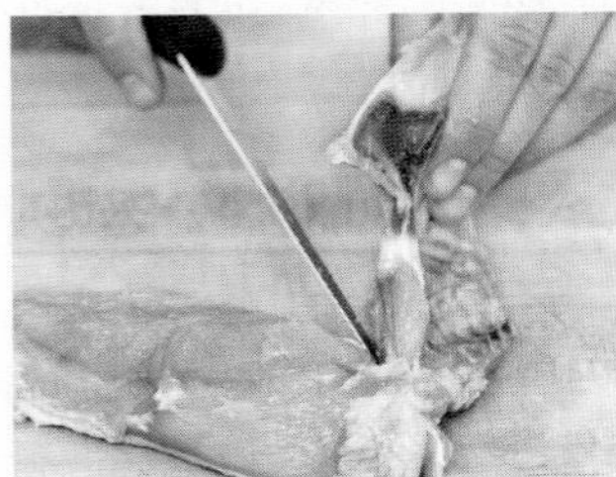

2. Angling blade slightly and following rib cage, repeat cutting motion several times to remove ribs and breastbone from breast.

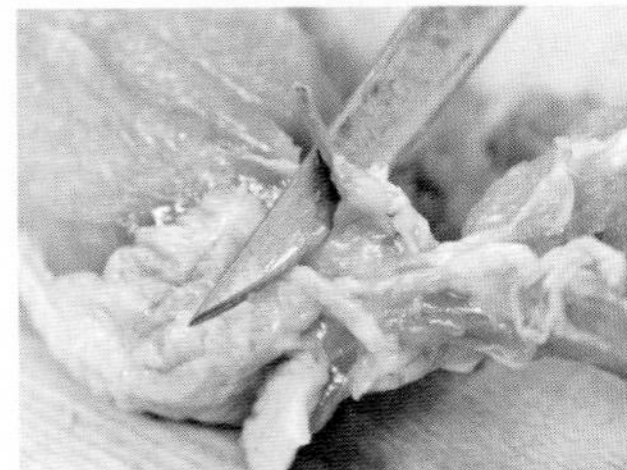

3. Find short remnant of wishbone along top edge of breast and run tip of knife along both sides of bone to separate it from meat.

CRISPY PAN-FRIED CHICKEN CUTLETS

WHY THIS RECIPE WORKS: Chicken cutlets coated in bread crumbs and pan fried are a staple weeknight meal: They're quick cooking and a crowd pleaser. But the three-step breading process of flour, egg, and crumbs is fussy, so we set out to make a streamlined version. We ditched the flour step, which made for a more delicate coating. Instead of the usual homemade bread crumbs, we swapped Japanese-style panko that we poured into a zipper-lock bag and crushed with a rolling pin, creating a perfectly even coating. To avoid any spotty browning or burned bits of panko with our second batch of cutlets, we discarded the cooking oil from the first batch and started over with fresh oil. Once done cooking, we transferred the cutlets to a paper towel–lined rack, which helped to wick away excess oil while preventing the underside from turning soggy. To punch up the flavor, we turned east for inspiration and made a Japanese barbecue-style sauce with ketchup, Worcestershire sauce, Dijon mustard, and soy sauce.

Crispy Pan-Fried Chicken Cutlets (Chicken Katsu)

SERVES 4 TO 6

Be sure to remove any tenderloins from the breasts before halving. The cutlets will be easier to slice in half if you freeze them for about 15 minutes. If you are working with 8-ounce cutlets, the skillet will initially be crowded; the cutlets will shrink slightly as they cook. The first batch of cutlets can be kept warm in a 200-degree oven while the second batch cooks. These cutlets can be sliced into ½-inch-wide strips Japanese style and served over rice with sauce (recipes follow). They can also be served in a sandwich or over a green salad.

- 2 cups panko bread crumbs
- 2 large eggs
- Salt
- 4 (6- to 8-ounce) boneless, skinless chicken breasts, trimmed, halved horizontally, and pounded ¼ inch thick
- ½ cup vegetable oil

1. Place panko in large zipper-lock bag and finely crush with rolling pin. Transfer crushed panko to shallow dish. Whisk eggs and 1 teaspoon salt in second shallow dish until well-combined.

2. Working with 1 cutlet at a time, dredge cutlet in egg mixture, allowing excess egg to drip off, then coat all sides with panko, pressing gently so crumbs adhere. Transfer cutlet to rimmed baking sheet and repeat with remaining cutlets.

3. Place wire rack in second rimmed baking sheet. Line rack with layer of paper towels. Heat ¼ cup oil and small pinch of panko in 12-inch skillet over medium-high heat. When panko has turned golden brown, place 4 cutlets in skillet. Cook without moving them until bottoms are crispy and deep golden brown, 2 to 3 minutes. Using tongs, carefully flip cutlets and cook on second side until deep golden brown, 2 to 3 minutes. Transfer cutlets to towel-lined rack and season with salt to taste. Wipe out skillet with paper towels. Repeat with remaining ¼ cup oil and 4 cutlets. Serve immediately.

Tonkatsu Sauce

MAKES ABOUT ⅓ CUP

You can substitute yellow mustard for the Dijon, but do not use a grainy mustard.

- ¼ cup ketchup
- 2 tablespoons Worcestershire sauce
- 2 teaspoons soy sauce
- 1 teaspoon Dijon mustard

Whisk all ingredients together in bowl.

Garlic-Curry Sauce

MAKES ABOUT ½ CUP

Full-fat and nonfat yogurt will both work in this recipe.

- ⅓ cup mayonnaise
- ¼ cup plain yogurt
- 2 tablespoons ketchup
- 2 teaspoons curry powder
- 1 teaspoon lemon juice
- ¼ teaspoon minced garlic

Whisk all ingredients together in bowl.

CHICKEN KIEV

WHY THIS RECIPE WORKS: Chicken Kiev is a recipe that elevates the humdrum boneless, skinless chicken breast to star status. Traditionally, the dish is a crisp fried chicken breast encasing a buttery herb sauce that dramatically oozes out when cut. But today, the dish has sunk to the level of bad banquet food—a greasy, bread crumb–coated chicken breast whose meat is dry and chalky despite the butter filling. This dish needed its greatness restored. We found that butterflying the chicken breasts, then pounding them thin—and even thinner at the edges—helped create chicken bundles that wouldn't leak the butter filling. Instead of deep-frying the chicken as is traditionally done, we chose to oven-fry the chicken. Toasting the bread crumbs prior to breading the chicken helped mimic the flavorful, golden brown crust of the original. Traditional recipes stuff the Kievs with butter spiked with nothing more than parsley and chives, but we found that minced shallots were more flavorful than chives and a small amount of tarragon added a pleasant hint of sweetness. Lemon juice tamed the rich butter with a bit of acidity and Dijon mustard provided another layer of flavor for a chicken Kiev that was anything but bland.

Chicken Kiev

SERVES 4

To make slicing the chicken easier, freeze it for 15 minutes. Unbaked, breaded chicken Kievs can be refrigerated overnight and baked the next day or frozen for up to one month. To cook frozen chicken Kievs, increase the baking time to 50 to 55 minutes (do not thaw the chicken).

HERB BUTTER

- 8 tablespoons (1 stick) unsalted butter, softened
- 1 tablespoon juice from 1 lemon
- 1 small shallot, minced (about 1 tablespoon)
- 1 tablespoon minced fresh parsley leaves
- ½ teaspoon minced fresh tarragon leaves
- ⅜ teaspoon table salt
- ⅛ teaspoon ground black pepper

CHICKEN

- 4 slices high-quality white sandwich bread, torn into quarters
- Table salt and ground black pepper
- 2 tablespoons vegetable oil
- 4 (7- to 8-ounce) boneless, skinless chicken breasts, tenderloins removed and breasts trimmed
- 1 cup unbleached all-purpose flour
- 3 large eggs, beaten
- 1 teaspoon Dijon mustard

1. FOR THE HERB BUTTER: Mix the ingredients in a medium bowl with a rubber spatula until thoroughly combined. Following the photo, form into a 2 by 3-inch rectangle on a sheet of plastic wrap; wrap tightly and refrigerate until firm, about 1 hour.

2. FOR THE CHICKEN: Adjust an oven rack to the lower-middle position and heat the oven to 300 degrees. Add half of the bread to a food processor and pulse until the bread is coarsely ground, about 16 pulses. Transfer the crumbs to a large bowl and repeat with the remaining bread. Add ⅛ teaspoon salt and ⅛ teaspoon pepper to the bread crumbs. Add the oil and toss until the crumbs are evenly coated. Spread the crumbs on a rimmed baking sheet and bake until golden brown and dry, about 25 minutes, stirring twice during the baking time. Cool to room temperature.

3. Following the photos on page 101, butterfly each chicken breast and pound between two sheets of plastic wrap to a uniform ¼-inch thickness. Pound the outer perimeter to ⅛ inch. Unwrap the herb butter and cut it into four rectangular pieces. Following the photos, place a chicken breast, cut side up, on a work surface; season both sides with salt and pepper. Place one piece of butter in the center of the bottom half of the breast. Roll the bottom edge of the chicken over the butter, then fold in the sides and continue rolling to form a neat, tight package, pressing on the seam to seal. Repeat with the remaining butter and chicken. Refrigerate the chicken, uncovered, to allow the edges to seal, about 1 hour.

NOTES FROM THE TEST KITCHEN

SHAPING THE BUTTER FOR CHICKEN KIEV

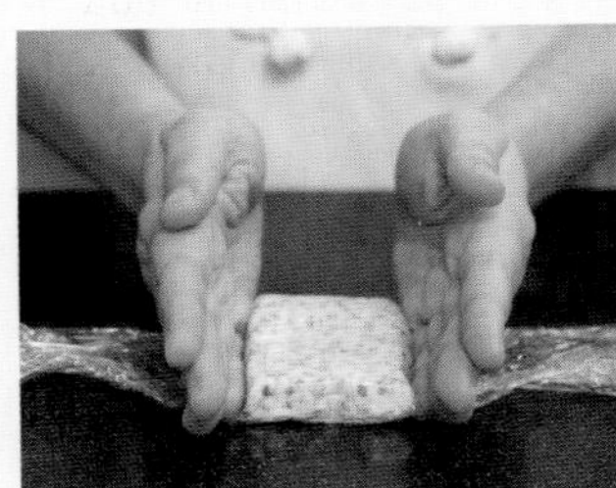

Shape the butter mixture into a 2 by 3-inch rectangle on plastic wrap, then wrap tightly and refrigerate until firm, about 1 hour.

ASSEMBLING CHICKEN KIEV

1. Cut the butter into four rectangular pieces. Place one butter piece near the tapered end of the cutlet.

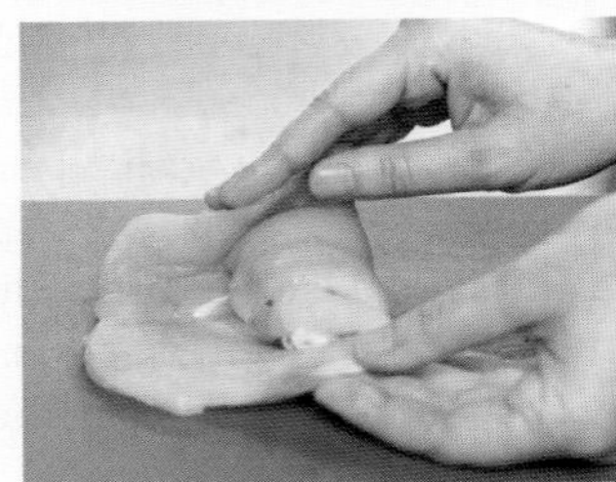

2. Roll up the tapered end of the chicken over the butter, then fold in the sides and continue rolling, pressing on the seam to seal. Repeat with the remaining butter pieces and cutlets. The chicken is now ready to be breaded.

4. Adjust an oven rack to the middle position and heat the oven to 350 degrees. Set a large wire rack over a large baking sheet and set aside. Place the flour, eggs, and bread crumbs in separate pie plates or shallow dishes. Season the flour with ¼ teaspoon salt and ⅛ teaspoon pepper; season the bread crumbs with ½ teaspoon salt and ¼ teaspoon pepper. Add the mustard to the eggs and whisk to combine. Dredge 1 chicken roll in the flour, shaking off the excess, then coat with the egg mixture, allowing the excess to drip off. Coat all sides of the chicken roll with the bread crumbs, pressing gently so that the crumbs adhere. Place on the wire rack set over a rimmed baking sheet. Repeat the flouring and breading with the remaining chicken rolls.

5. Bake until the center of the chicken registers 160 to 165 degrees on an instant-read thermometer, 40 to 45 minutes. Let rest for 5 minutes on the wire rack before serving.

CHICKEN MARBELLA

WHY THIS RECIPE WORKS: More than 25 years ago, this dinner-party mainstay put *The Silver Palate Cookbook* on the map. We wanted to retool the recipe for today's tastes. To save time and boost flavor, we ditched the original marinade and made a paste of the prunes, olives, capers, garlic, and oregano, which we spread on the chicken and caramelized into the sauce. Instead of using whole birds, which require butchering, we chose easy-prep chicken parts. To intensify the dish's meaty flavor and to create complexity, we added anchovies and red pepper flakes and browned the chicken skin in a skillet before baking it through.

Chicken Marbella

SERVES 4 TO 6

Any combination of split breasts and leg quarters can be used in this recipe.

PASTE

- ⅓ cup pitted green olives, rinsed
- ⅓ cup pitted prunes
- 3 tablespoons extra-virgin olive oil
- 2 tablespoons capers, rinsed
- 4 garlic cloves, peeled
- 3 anchovy fillets, rinsed
- ½ teaspoon dried oregano
- ½ teaspoon pepper
- ¼ teaspoon kosher salt
- Pinch red pepper flakes

CHICKEN

- 2½–3 pounds bone-in split chicken breasts and/or leg quarters, trimmed
- Kosher salt and pepper
- 2 teaspoons olive oil
- ¾ cup low-sodium chicken broth
- ⅓ cup white wine
- ⅓ cup pitted green olives, rinsed and halved
- 1 tablespoon capers, rinsed
- 2 bay leaves
- ⅓ cup pitted prunes, chopped coarse
- 1 tablespoon unsalted butter
- 1 teaspoon red wine vinegar
- 2 tablespoons minced fresh parsley

1. FOR THE PASTE: Adjust oven rack to middle position and heat oven to 400 degrees. Pulse all ingredients together in food processor until finely chopped, about 10 pulses. Scrape down bowl and continue to process until mostly smooth, 1 to 2 minutes. Transfer to bowl. (Paste can be refrigerated for up to 24 hours.)

2. FOR THE CHICKEN: Pat chicken dry with paper towels. Sprinkle chicken pieces with 1½ teaspoons salt and season with pepper.

3. Heat oil in 12-inch skillet over medium-high heat until just smoking. Add chicken, skin side down, and cook without moving until well browned, 5 to 8 minutes. Transfer chicken to large plate. Drain off all but 1 teaspoon fat from skillet and return to medium-low heat.

4. Add ⅓ cup paste to skillet and cook, stirring constantly, until fragrant and fond forms on bottom of pan, 1 to 2 minutes. Stir in broth, wine, olives, capers, and bay leaves, scraping up any browned bits. Return chicken, skin side up, to pan (skin should be above surface of liquid) and transfer to oven. Cook, uncovered, for 15 minutes.

5. Remove skillet from oven and use back of spoon to spread remaining paste over chicken pieces; sprinkle prunes around chicken. Continue to roast until paste begins to brown, breasts register 160 degrees, and leg quarters register 175 degrees, 7 to 12 minutes longer.

6. Transfer chicken to serving platter and tent loosely with aluminum foil. Remove bay leaves from sauce and whisk in butter, vinegar, and 1 tablespoon parsley; season with salt and pepper to taste. Pour sauce around chicken, sprinkle with remaining 1 tablespoon parsley, and serve.

SPANISH BRAISED CHICKEN WITH SHERRY AND SAFFRON

WHY THIS RECIPE WORKS: Nailing the classic Spanish dish called *pollo en pepitoria* hinges on achieving a balance between the richness and brightness of its creamy, nutty sherry sauce. We began with chicken thighs because their high collagen content breaks down into gelatin the longer they cook, making our slow-braised chicken tender. Onions, softened in rendered fat, created the base into which we added garlic, a bay leaf, and cinnamon. Dry, light-bodied sherries shine in savory applications, so we poured some in along with chicken broth. We also chopped canned peeled tomatoes, adding them for some bright acidity. We braised the chicken in the sauce at a gentle 300 degrees and removed the skin once the thighs were fully cooked. To finish, we poured a portion of the cooking liquid into a blender to create a *picada*, a flavorful thickener, adding chopped hard-boiled egg yolks, saffron threads, garlic, and almonds. We whirred the mixture into a thick, smooth paste. With a finishing touch of fresh lemon juice for brightness, we thickened the sauce before pouring it over the chicken. Fresh parsley and hard-boiled egg whites made for an authentic presentation.

Spanish Braised Chicken with Sherry and Saffron (Pollo en Pepitoria)

SERVES 4

Any dry sherry, such as fino or Manzanilla, will work in this dish. Serve with crusty bread.

- 8 (5- to 7-ounce) bone-in chicken thighs, trimmed
- Salt and pepper
- 1 tablespoon extra-virgin olive oil
- 1 onion, chopped fine
- 3 garlic cloves, minced
- 1 bay leaf
- ¼ teaspoon ground cinnamon
- ⅔ cup dry sherry
- 1 cup chicken broth
- 1 (14.5-ounce) can whole peeled tomatoes, drained and chopped fine
- 2 hard-cooked large eggs, peeled and yolks and whites separated
- ½ cup slivered blanched almonds, toasted
- Pinch saffron threads, crumbled
- 2 tablespoons chopped fresh parsley
- 1½ teaspoons lemon juice

1. Adjust oven rack to middle position and heat oven to 300 degrees.

2. Pat thighs dry with paper towels and season both sides of each with 1 teaspoon salt and ½ teaspoon pepper. Heat oil in 12-inch skillet over high heat until just smoking. Add thighs and brown on both sides, 10 to 12 minutes. Transfer thighs to large plate and pour off all but 2 teaspoons fat from skillet.

3. Return skillet to medium heat, add onion and ¼ teaspoon salt, and cook, stirring frequently, until just softened, about 3 minutes. Add 2 teaspoons garlic, bay leaf, and cinnamon and cook until fragrant, about 1 minute. Add sherry and cook, scraping up any browned bits, until sauce starts to thicken, about 2 minutes. Stir in broth and tomatoes and bring to simmer. Return thighs to skillet, cover, transfer to oven, and cook until chicken registers 195 degrees, 45 to 50 minutes. Transfer thighs to serving platter, remove and discard skin, and cover loosely with aluminum foil to keep warm. While thighs cook, finely chop egg whites.

4. Discard bay leaf. Transfer ¾ cup chicken cooking liquid, egg yolks, almonds, saffron, and remaining garlic to blender. Process until smooth, about 2 minutes, scraping down jar as needed. Return almond mixture to skillet. Add 1 tablespoon parsley and lemon juice; bring to simmer over medium heat. Simmer, whisking frequently, until thickened, 3 to 5 minutes. Season with salt and pepper to taste.

5. Pour sauce over chicken, sprinkle with remaining 1 tablespoon parsley and egg whites, and serve.

COQ AU RIESLING

WHY THIS RECIPE WORKS: This richer, subtler take on coq au vin swaps dry white wine for red, but creating this classic required more than just a change in wine. Sticking to tradition, we began by cutting a whole chicken into parts. To establish a meaty base, we cooked chopped bacon pieces and used the rendered fat to brown the chicken wings and back as well as the flavorful skins removed from the breasts, drumsticks, and thighs. These elements, though not part of the finished dish, contributed a rich base of flavor. A generous mirepoix of shallots, carrots, celery, and garlic, added with flour, solidified the complex flavor profile. Stirring in just 2½ cups of dry Riesling created a crisp, balanced finish. With the flavors in place, we added water, herbs, and the chicken pieces, cooking over low heat. Once cooked, we removed the chicken, discarded the back and wings, and strained the liquid to finish off the sauce. While the liquid settled, we used the empty pot to sauté white mushrooms with some of the reserved fat. We returned the liquid back to the pot, brought it to a simmer to thicken, and added tangy crème fraîche for an elegantly creamy finish.

Coq au Riesling

SERVES 4 TO 6

A dry Riesling is the best wine for this recipe, but a Sauvignon Blanc or Chablis will also work. Avoid a heavily oaked wine such as Chardonnay. Serve the stew with egg noodles or mashed potatoes.

- 1 (4- to 5-pound) whole chicken, cut into 8 pieces (4 breast pieces, 2 drumsticks, 2 thighs), wings and back reserved
- Salt and pepper
- 2 slices bacon, chopped

- 3 shallots, chopped
- 2 carrots, peeled and chopped coarse
- 2 celery ribs, chopped coarse
- 4 garlic cloves, lightly crushed and peeled
- 3 tablespoons all-purpose flour
- 2½ cups dry Riesling
- 1 cup water
- 2 bay leaves
- 6 sprigs fresh parsley, plus 2 teaspoons minced
- 6 sprigs fresh thyme
- 1 pound white mushrooms, trimmed and halved if small or quartered if large
- ¼ cup crème fraîche

1. Remove skin from chicken breast pieces, drumsticks, and thighs and set aside. Sprinkle both sides of chicken pieces with 1¼ teaspoons salt and ½ teaspoon pepper; set aside. Cook bacon in large Dutch oven over medium-low heat, stirring occasionally, until beginning to render, 2 to 4 minutes. Add chicken skin, back, and wings to pot; increase heat to medium; and cook, stirring frequently, until bacon is browned, skin is rendered, and chicken back and wings are browned on all sides, 10 to 12 minutes. Remove pot from heat and carefully transfer 2 tablespoons fat to small bowl and set aside.

2. Return pot to medium heat. Add shallots, carrots, celery, and garlic and cook, stirring occasionally, until vegetables are softened, 4 to 6 minutes. Add flour and cook, stirring constantly, until no dry flour remains, about 30 seconds. Slowly add wine, scraping up any browned bits. Increase heat to high and simmer until mixture is slightly thickened, about 2 minutes. Stir in water, bay leaves, parsley sprigs, and thyme and bring to simmer. Place chicken pieces in even layer in pot, reduce heat to low, cover, and cook until breasts register 160 degrees and thighs and legs register 175 degrees, 25 to 30 minutes, stirring halfway through cooking. Transfer chicken pieces to plate as they come up to temperature.

3. Discard back and wings. Strain cooking liquid through fine-mesh strainer set over large bowl, pressing on solids to extract as much liquid as possible; discard solids. Let cooking liquid settle for 10 minutes. Using wide shallow spoon, skim fat from surface and discard.

4. While liquid settles, return pot to medium heat and add reserved fat, mushrooms, and ¼ teaspoon salt; cook, stirring occasionally, until lightly browned, 8 to 10 minutes.

5. Return liquid to pot and bring to boil. Simmer briskly, stirring occasionally, until sauce is thickened to consistency of heavy cream, 4 to 6 minutes. Reduce heat to medium-low and stir in crème fraîche and minced parsley. Return chicken to pot along with any accumulated juices, cover, and cook until just heated through, 5 to 8 minutes. Season with salt and pepper to taste, and serve.

FILIPINO CHICKEN ADOBO

WHY THIS RECIPE WORKS: Adobo is the national dish of the Philippines, and chicken adobo is among the most popular versions. The dish consists of chicken simmered in a mixture of vinegar, soy sauce, garlic, bay leaves, and black pepper. The problem with most recipes we found was that they were aggressively tart and salty. Our secret to taming both of these elements was coconut milk. The coconut milk's richness tempered the bracing acidity of the vinegar and masked the briny soy sauce, bringing the sauce into balance. But the fat from the coconut milk and the chicken skin made the sauce somewhat greasy. To combat this, we borrowed a technique used in French bistros. We placed the meat skin side down in a cold pan and then turned up the heat. As the pan gradually got hotter, the fat under the chicken's skin melted away while the exterior browned.

Filipino Chicken Adobo

SERVES 4

Light coconut milk can be substituted for regular coconut milk. Serve this dish over rice.

- 8 (5- to 7-ounce) bone-in chicken thighs, trimmed
- ⅓ cup soy sauce
- 1 (13.5-ounce) can coconut milk
- ¾ cup cider vinegar
- 8 garlic cloves, peeled
- 4 bay leaves
- 2 teaspoons pepper
- 1 scallion, sliced thin

1. Toss chicken with soy sauce in large bowl. Refrigerate for at least 30 minutes or up to 1 hour.

2. Remove chicken from soy sauce, allowing excess to drip back into bowl. Transfer chicken, skin side down, to 12-inch nonstick skillet; set aside soy sauce.

3. Place skillet over medium-high heat and cook until chicken skin is browned, 7 to 10 minutes. While chicken is browning, whisk coconut milk, vinegar, garlic, bay leaves, and pepper into soy sauce.

4. Transfer chicken to plate and discard fat in skillet. Return chicken to skillet skin side down, add coconut milk mixture, and bring to boil. Reduce heat to medium-low and simmer, uncovered, for 20 minutes. Flip chicken skin side up and continue to cook, uncovered, until chicken registers 175 degrees, about 15 minutes. Transfer chicken to platter and tent loosely with aluminum foil.

5. Remove bay leaves and skim any fat off surface of sauce. Return skillet to medium-high heat and cook until sauce is thickened, 5 to 7 minutes. Pour sauce over chicken, sprinkle with scallion, and serve.

MAHOGANY CHICKEN THIGHS

WHY THIS RECIPE WORKS: Braising chicken thighs does an excellent job of rendering sneaky pockets of fat and producing luxurious, flavorful meat, but there is one drawback: we miss the crispy skin of roasted chicken. We wanted the best of both worlds.

We took a hybrid approach: braise for tenderness, then broil for crispy skin. We oven-braised the thighs in a flavor-infusing combination of soy sauce, sherry, white vinegar, a big piece of smashed ginger, smashed garlic, and sugar and molasses for sweetness (both would also caramelize and boost the mahogany hue). After braising for an hour, the fat was fully rendered, and although the meat was overcooked according to our usual standards, the melted connective tissue had converted to gelatin, which resulted in meat that was supple and juicy. Turning the chicken skin side up halfway through braising allowed the rendered skin to dry before broiling, which helped it crisp a little more. For a simple, streamlined finish, we used a portion of the braising liquid to make a quick sauce (thickened with a little cornstarch for body).

Mahogany Chicken Thighs

SERVES 4 TO 6

For best results, trim all visible fat and skin from the underside of the thighs. Serve with steamed rice and vegetables.

- 1½ cups water
- 1 cup soy sauce
- ¼ cup dry sherry
- 2 tablespoons sugar
- 2 tablespoons molasses
- 1 tablespoon distilled white vinegar
- 8 (5- to 7-ounce) bone-in chicken thighs, trimmed
- 1 (2-inch) piece ginger, peeled, halved, and smashed
- 6 garlic cloves, peeled and smashed
- 1 tablespoon cornstarch

1. Adjust oven rack to lower-middle position and heat oven to 300 degrees. Whisk 1 cup water, soy sauce, sherry, sugar, molasses, and vinegar together in ovensafe 12-inch skillet until sugar is dissolved. Arrange chicken, skin side down, in soy mixture and nestle ginger and garlic between pieces of chicken.

2. Bring soy mixture to simmer over medium heat and simmer for 5 minutes. Transfer skillet to oven and cook, uncovered, for 30 minutes.

3. Flip chicken skin side up and continue to cook, uncovered, until chicken registers 195 degrees, 20 to 30 minutes longer. Transfer chicken to platter, taking care not to tear skin. Pour cooking liquid through fine-mesh strainer into fat separator and let settle for 5 minutes. Heat broiler.

4. Whisk cornstarch and remaining ½ cup water together in bowl. Pour 1 cup defatted cooking liquid into now-empty skillet and bring to simmer over medium heat. Whisk cornstarch mixture into cooking liquid and simmer until thickened, about 1 minute. Pour sauce into bowl and set aside for serving.

5. Return chicken skin side up to now-empty skillet and broil until well browned, about 4 minutes. Return chicken to platter, and let rest for 5 minutes. Serve, passing reserved sauce separately.

OVEN-BARBECUED CHICKEN

WHY THIS RECIPE WORKS: Smoky, tender, and tangy, barbecued chicken is a real crowd pleaser. What do you do when a craving for this summertime favorite strikes in midwinter? Oven-barbecued chicken is the obvious solution. But while recipes for this dish abound, so do the disappointments: tough, rubbery, or unevenly cooked chicken in sauces ranging from pasty and candy-sweet to greasy, stale, thin, or commercial-tasting.

We started with boneless, skinless chicken breasts; the mild white meat is a perfect backdrop for the sauce. (Skinless breasts also meant that we wouldn't have to deal with the problem of flabby skin.) We lightly seared the chicken breasts in a skillet, then removed them from the pan to make a simple but flavorful barbecue sauce with pantry ingredients like grated onion, ketchup, Worcestershire sauce, mustard, molasses, and maple syrup. When we returned the chicken to the pan, the sauce clung nicely to the meat, thanks to the light searing we had given the chicken. We slid the chicken and sauce, still in the skillet, into the oven to cook through. Finally, for a nicely caramelized coating on the sauce, we finished the chicken under the high heat of the broiler. The result? Juicy chicken, thickly coated with a pleasantly tangy barbecue sauce.

Sweet and Tangy Oven-Barbecued Chicken

SERVES 4

Real maple syrup is preferable to imitation syrup, and "mild" or "original" molasses is preferable to darker, more bitter types. Use a rasp-style grater or the fine holes of a box grater to grate the onion. Make this recipe only in an in-oven broiler; do not use a drawer-type broiler. Broiling times may differ from one oven to another, so we urge you to check the chicken for doneness after only 3 minutes of broiling. You may also have to lower the oven rack if your broiler runs very hot. It is important to remove the chicken from the oven before switching to the broiler setting to allow the broiler element to come up to temperature.

- 1 cup ketchup
- 3 tablespoons molasses (see note)
- 3 tablespoons cider vinegar
- 2 tablespoons finely grated onion (see note)
- 2 tablespoons Worcestershire sauce
- 2 tablespoons Dijon mustard
- 2 tablespoons maple syrup (see note)
- 1 teaspoon chili powder
- ¼ teaspoon cayenne pepper
- 4 (5- to 6-ounce) boneless, skinless chicken breasts, tenderloins removed and breasts trimmed
- Table salt and ground black pepper
- 1 tablespoon vegetable oil

1. Adjust an oven rack to the upper-middle position, about 5 inches from the heating element, and heat the oven to 325 degrees. Whisk the ketchup, molasses, vinegar, onion, Worcestershire sauce, mustard, maple syrup, chili powder, and cayenne together in a small bowl; set aside. Pat the chicken dry with paper towels and season with salt and pepper.

2. Heat the oil in a 12-inch ovensafe skillet over high heat until just smoking. Add the chicken, smooth side down, and cook until very light golden, 1 to 2 minutes; using tongs, turn the chicken and cook until very light golden on the second side, 1 to 2 minutes longer. Transfer the chicken to a plate and set aside.

3. Discard the fat in the skillet; off the heat, add the sauce mixture and, using a wooden spoon, scrape up the browned bits on the bottom of the skillet. Simmer the sauce over medium heat, stirring frequently with a heatproof spatula, until the sauce is thick and glossy and a spatula leaves a clear trail in the sauce, about 4 minutes. Off the heat, return the chicken to the skillet and turn to coat thickly with the sauce; set the chicken pieces smooth side up and spoon extra sauce over each piece to create a thick coating.

4. Place the skillet in the oven and cook until the thickest part of the breasts registers 130 degrees on an instant-read thermometer, 8 to 12 minutes. Remove the skillet from the oven, turn the oven to broil, and heat for 5 minutes. Once the broiler is heated, place the skillet back in the oven and broil the chicken until the thickest part of the breasts registers 160 to 165 degrees, 3 to 8 minutes longer. Transfer the chicken to a platter and let rest for 5 minutes. Meanwhile, whisk the sauce in the skillet to recombine and transfer to a small bowl. Serve the chicken, passing the extra sauce separately.

PICNIC CHICKEN

WHY THIS RECIPE WORKS: Cold barbecued picnic chicken presents numerous challenges: the meat may be dry, the skin flabby, and the chicken covered with a sticky, messy sauce. We wanted a recipe for chicken that would be easy to pack (and eat) for a picnic; chicken with moist, tender meat flavored with robust spicy and slightly sweet barbecue flavors.

We first threw out the idea of a sticky sauce, substituting a robust dry rub (brown sugar, chili powder, paprika, and pepper) that reproduced the flavors of a good barbecue sauce. We partly solved the flabby skin problem by diligently trimming the chicken pieces as well as by slitting the skin before cooking (which allowed the excess fat to render). But the skin was still flabby from the moisture contributed by our traditional brine (we brine most poultry for better flavor and moister meat). We tried eliminating the brine, adding salt to the rub, and applying it the night before. Sure enough, when we oven-roasted the chicken the next day, we found the meat well seasoned throughout and very moist. Best of all, the skin was flavorful, delicate, and definitely not flabby.

Spice-Rubbed Picnic Chicken

SERVES 8

If you plan to serve the chicken later on the same day that you cook it, refrigerate it immediately after it has cooled, then let it come back to room temperature before serving. On the breast pieces, we use toothpicks to secure the skin, which otherwise shrinks considerably in the oven, leaving the meat exposed and prone to drying out. We think the extra effort is justified, but you can omit this step. This recipe halves easily.

- 5 pounds bone-in, skin-on chicken parts (split breasts, thighs, drumsticks, or a mix, with breasts cut into 3 pieces or halved if small), trimmed of excess fat and skin
- 3 tablespoons brown sugar
- 2 tablespoons chili powder
- 2 tablespoons sweet paprika
- 2 tablespoons kosher salt
- 2 teaspoons ground black pepper
- ¼–½ teaspoon cayenne pepper

1. Use a sharp knife to make two or three short slashes in the skin of each piece of chicken, taking care not to cut into the meat. Combine the sugar, chili powder, paprika, salt, and pepper in a small bowl and mix thoroughly. Coat the chicken pieces with the spices, gently lifting the skin to distribute the spice rub underneath but leaving it attached to the chicken. Transfer the chicken, skin side up, to a wire rack set over a large, rimmed baking sheet, lightly tent it with foil, and refrigerate for at least 6 hours or up to 24 hours.

2. If desired, secure the skin of each breast piece with two or three toothpicks placed near the edges of the skin (see note).

3. Adjust an oven rack to the middle position and heat the oven to 425 degrees. Roast the chicken until the thickest part of the smallest piece registers 140 degrees on an instant-read thermometer, 15 to 20 minutes. Increase the oven temperature to 500 degrees and continue roasting until the chicken is browned and crisp and the thickest part of the breasts registers 160 to 165 degrees, 5 to 8 minutes longer, removing the pieces from the oven and transferring them to a clean wire rack as they finish cooking. Continue to roast the thighs and/or drumsticks, if using, until the thickest part of the meat registers 175 degrees, about 5 minutes longer. Remove from the oven, transfer the chicken to a rack, and cool completely before refrigerating or serving.

PAN-ROASTED CHICKEN BREASTS

WHY THIS RECIPE WORKS: Cooking bone-in, skin-on chicken breasts can be a challenge. They are difficult to sauté or cook through on the stovetop because of their uneven shape. We wanted to find a method that would produce crisp skin, moist meat, and a quick, flavorful pan sauce.

We chose whole breasts, then split them ourselves to control their size. We brined the breasts for maximum moistness and then seared them on the stovetop before letting them cook through in a 450-degree oven. For the pan sauce, we sautéed minced shallot in the same skillet used to cook the chicken, so we could take advantage of the flavorful browned bits left in the pan. We deglazed the pan with chicken broth and vermouth, then added fresh sage for a sauce with deep herbal flavor. Butter whisked into the sauce after it had reduced lent the sauce body and richness—a perfect partner to our moist, juicy chicken.

NOTES FROM THE TEST KITCHEN

TRIMMING SPLIT CHICKEN BREASTS

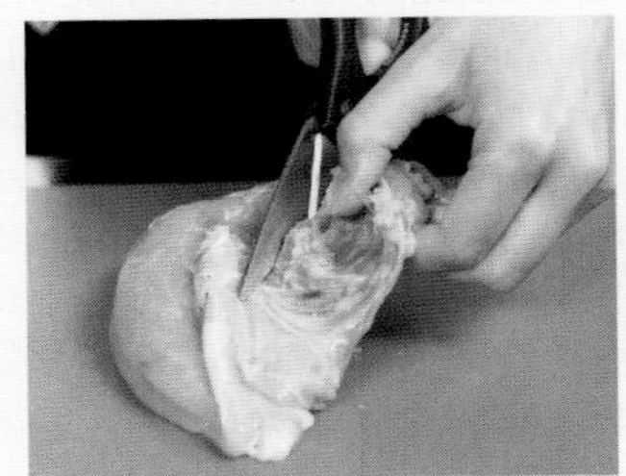

Using kitchen shears, trim off the rib sections from each breast, following the vertical line of fat from the tapered end of the breast up to the socket where the wing was attached.

Pan-Roasted Chicken Breasts with Sage-Vermouth Sauce

SERVES 4

We prefer to split whole chicken breasts ourselves because store-bought split chicken breasts are often sloppily butchered. However, if you prefer to purchase split chicken breasts, try to choose 10- to 12-ounce pieces with skin intact. If split breasts are of different sizes, check the smaller ones a few minutes early to see if they are cooking more quickly, and remove them from the skillet when they are done.

CHICKEN
- ½ cup table salt
- 2 (1½-pound) whole bone-in, skin-on chicken breasts, split in half along breast bone and trimmed of rib sections
- Ground black pepper
- 1 teaspoon vegetable oil

SAGE-VERMOUTH SAUCE
- 1 large shallot, minced (about 4 tablespoons)
- ¾ cup low-sodium chicken broth
- ½ cup dry vermouth
- 4 medium fresh sage leaves, each leaf torn in half
- 3 tablespoons unsalted butter, cut into 3 pieces
- Table salt and ground black pepper

1. FOR THE CHICKEN: Dissolve the salt in 2 quarts cold water in a large container; submerge the chicken in the brine, cover, and refrigerate for about 30 minutes. Rinse the chicken well and pat dry with paper towels. Season the chicken with pepper.

2. Adjust an oven rack to the lowest position and heat the oven to 450 degrees.

3. Heat the oil in a 12-inch ovensafe skillet over medium-high heat until beginning to smoke. Brown the chicken, skin side down, until deep golden, about 5 minutes; turn the chicken and brown until golden on the second side, about 3 minutes longer. Turn the chicken skin side down and place the skillet in the oven. Roast until the thickest part of the breasts registers 160 to 165 degrees on an instant-read thermometer, 15 to 18 minutes. Transfer the chicken to a platter, and let it rest while making the sauce. (If you're not making the sauce, let the chicken rest for 5 minutes before serving.)

4. FOR THE SAUCE: Using a potholder to protect your hands from the hot skillet handle, pour off all but 1 teaspoon of the fat from the skillet; add the shallot, then set the skillet over medium-high heat and cook, stirring frequently, until the shallot is softened, about 1½ minutes. Add the chicken broth, vermouth, and sage; increase the heat to high and simmer rapidly, scraping the skillet bottom with a wooden spoon to loosen the browned bits, until slightly thickened and reduced to about ¾ cup, about 5 minutes. Pour the accumulated chicken juices into the skillet, reduce the heat to medium, and whisk in the butter 1 piece at a time; season with salt and pepper to taste and discard the sage. Spoon the sauce around the chicken breasts and serve immediately.

SLOW-ROASTED CHICKEN PARTS

WHY THIS RECIPE WORKS: Slow roasting keeps chicken nice and juicy, but at a cost: The skin is often a bit flabby, padded with unrendered fat. For ultramoist roast chicken that boasted the shatteringly crisp skin we loved, we bypassed a whole chicken and turned to parts. We seared leg quarters and then split breasts in oil, rendering some of the fat and giving the crisping a head start. We moved the parts to a 250-degree oven, keeping the slower-cooking thighs on the back portion of the wire rack–lined sheet, facing the hotter side of the oven. While the chicken rested, we whisked together a simple pan sauce with butter, shallots, garlic, and coriander, adding a little powdered gelatin and cornstarch to give it the rich body of a jus. Before serving, we gave the skin a final crisping under the broiler.

Slow-Roasted Chicken Parts with Shallot-Garlic Pan Sauce

SERVES 8

To serve four people, halve the ingredient amounts.

- 5 pounds bone-in chicken pieces (4 split breasts and 4 leg quarters), trimmed
- Kosher salt and pepper
- ¼ teaspoon vegetable oil
- 1 tablespoon unflavored gelatin
- 2¼ cups chicken broth
- 2 tablespoons water
- 2 teaspoons cornstarch
- 4 tablespoons unsalted butter, cut into 4 pieces
- 4 shallots, sliced thin
- 6 garlic cloves, sliced thin
- 1 teaspoon ground coriander
- 1 tablespoon minced fresh parsley
- 1½ teaspoons lemon juice

1. Adjust 1 oven rack to lowest position and second rack 8 inches from broiler element. Heat oven to 250 degrees. Line rimmed baking sheet with aluminum foil and place wire rack on top. Sprinkle chicken pieces with 2 teaspoons salt and season with pepper (do not pat chicken dry).

2. Heat oil in 12-inch skillet over medium-high heat until shimmering. Place leg quarters skin side down in skillet; cook, turning once, until golden brown on both sides, 5 to 7 minutes total. Transfer to prepared sheet, arranging legs along 1 long side of sheet. Pour off fat from skillet. Place breasts skin side down in skillet; cook, turning once, until golden brown on both sides, 4 to 6 minutes total. Transfer to sheet with legs. Discard fat; do not clean skillet. Place sheet on lower rack, orienting so legs are at back of oven. Roast until breasts register 160 degrees and legs register 175 degrees, 1 hour 25 minutes to 1 hour 45 minutes. Let chicken rest on sheet for 10 minutes.

3. While chicken roasts, sprinkle gelatin over broth in bowl and let sit until gelatin softens, about 5 minutes. Whisk water and cornstarch together in small bowl; set aside.

4. Melt butter in now-empty skillet over medium-low heat. Add shallots and garlic; cook until golden brown and crispy, 6 to 9 minutes. Stir in coriander and cook for 30 seconds. Stir in gelatin mixture, scraping up any browned bits. Bring to simmer over high heat and cook until reduced to 1½ cups, 5 to 7 minutes. Whisk cornstarch mixture to recombine. Whisk into sauce and simmer until thickened, about 1 minute. Off heat, stir in parsley and lemon juice; season with salt and pepper to taste. Cover to keep warm.

5. Heat broiler. Transfer sheet to upper rack and broil chicken until skin is well browned and crisp, 3 to 6 minutes. Serve, passing sauce separately.

PERFECT ROAST CHICKEN

WHY THIS RECIPE WORKS: Most home-cooked chickens are either grossly overcooked or so underdone that they resemble an avian version of steak tartare. We wanted a method for producing perfectly roasted chicken, where the white meat cooks up juicy and tender, but with a hint of chew, and the dark meat is fully cooked, all the way to the bone.

For maximum juiciness and well-seasoned meat, we brined the chicken. And for further flavor and a moisture boost to the delicate breast, we rubbed butter under the skin and over the breast. Trussing and continuous basting both proved unnecessary for this ideal chicken. In fact, basting turned its skin greasy and chewy. We had hoped that the bird wouldn't have to be turned while cooking, but we found it was a must for even cooking. In the end, we found that roasting the bird for 15 minutes on each side and then putting it on its back rendered perfectly cooked white and dark meat as well as golden, crunchy skin.

Perfect Roast Chicken

SERVES 2 TO 3

If using a kosher chicken, skip the brining process and begin with step 2. We recommend using a V-rack to roast the chicken. If you don't have a V-rack, set the bird on a regular roasting rack and use balls of aluminum foil to keep the roasting chicken propped up on its side.

- ½ cup table salt
- ½ cup sugar
- 1 (3½- to 4-pound) whole chicken, giblets discarded (see note)
- 2 tablespoons unsalted butter, softened
- 1 tablespoon olive oil
- Ground black pepper

1. Dissolve the salt and sugar in 2 quarts cold water in a large container. Submerge the chicken in the brine, cover, and refrigerate for 1 hour.

2. Adjust an oven rack to the lower-middle position, place a roasting pan on the rack, and heat the oven to 400 degrees. Coat a V-rack with vegetable oil spray and set aside (see note). Remove the chicken from the brine, rinse well, and pat dry with paper towels.

3. Following the photo, use your fingers to gently loosen the center portion of the skin covering each breast; place the butter under the skin, directly on the meat in the center of each breast. Gently press on the skin to distribute the butter over the meat. Tuck the wings behind the back. Rub the skin with the oil, season with pepper, and place the chicken, wing side up, on the prepared V-rack. Place the V-rack in the preheated roasting pan and roast for 15 minutes.

4. Remove the roasting pan from the oven and, using two large wads of paper towels, rotate the chicken so that the opposite wing side is facing up. Return the roasting pan to the oven and roast for another 15 minutes.

5. Using two large wads of paper towels, rotate the chicken again so that the breast side is facing up and continue to roast until the thickest part of the breasts registers 160 to 165 degrees and the thickest part of the thighs registers 175 degrees on an instant-read thermometer, 20 to 25 minutes longer. Transfer the chicken to a carving board and let rest for 10 minutes. Carve the chicken and serve.

NOTES FROM THE TEST KITCHEN

APPLYING BUTTER UNDER THE SKIN

Loosen the skin on the breasts and thighs of the chicken by sliding your fingers between the skin and meat.

WEEKNIGHT ROAST CHICKEN

WHY THIS RECIPE WORKS: Roast chicken is often described as a simple dish, and it is, at least in terms of flavor—when done properly, the rich flavor and juicy meat of the chicken need little adornment. But the actual process of preparing and roasting chicken can be surprisingly complicated and time-consuming. And the most time-consuming part is salting or brining the bird, a step that ensures juiciness and well-seasoned meat. We wanted to find a way to get roast chicken on the table in just an hour without sacrificing flavor. After systematically testing the various components and steps of a typical recipe, we found we could skip complicated trussing and just tie the legs together and tuck the wings underneath. We also discovered we could skip both the V-rack and flipping the chicken by using a preheated skillet and placing the chicken breast side up; this gave the thighs a jump-start on cooking. Starting the chicken in a 450-degree oven and then turning the oven off while the chicken finished cooking slowed the evaporation of juices, ensuring moist, tender meat.

Weeknight Roast Chicken

SERVES 4

We prefer to use a 3½- to 4-pound chicken for this recipe; however this method can be used to cook a larger chicken. If roasting a larger bird, increase the cooking time in step 2 to 35 to 40 minutes. If you choose to serve the chicken with one of the pan sauces that follow, don't wash the skillet after removing the chicken. Prepare the pan sauce while resting the chicken.

1 tablespoon kosher salt
½ teaspoon ground black pepper
1 (3½- to 4-pound) whole chicken, giblets removed and discarded
1 tablespoon olive oil
1 recipe pan sauce (optional; recipes follow)

1. Adjust an oven rack to the middle position, place a 12-inch ovensafe skillet on the rack, and heat the oven to 450 degrees. Combine the salt and pepper in a bowl. Pat the chicken dry with paper towels and rub the entire surface with the oil. Sprinkle evenly all over with the salt mixture and rub in the mixture with your hands to coat evenly. Tie the legs together with twine and tuck the wing tips behind the back.

2. Transfer the chicken, breast side up, to the preheated skillet in the oven. Roast the chicken until the thickest part of the breasts registers 120 degrees and the thickest part of the thighs registers 135 degrees on an instant-read thermometer, 25 to 35 minutes. Turn off the oven and leave the chicken in the oven until the breasts register 160 degrees and the thighs register 175 degrees, 25 to 35 minutes.

3. Transfer the chicken to a carving board and rest, uncovered, for 20 minutes. Carve and serve with pan sauce.

Tarragon-Lemon Pan Sauce

MAKES ABOUT ¾ CUP

1 medium shallot, minced (about 3 tablespoons)
1 cup low-sodium chicken broth
2 teaspoons Dijon mustard
2 tablespoons unsalted butter
2 teaspoons chopped fresh tarragon leaves
2 teaspoons juice from 1 lemon
Ground black pepper

While the chicken rests, remove all but 1 tablespoon of fat from the now-empty skillet using a large kitchen spoon, leaving any browned bits and juices in the skillet. Place the skillet over medium-high heat, add the shallot, and cook until softened, about 2 minutes. Stir in the chicken broth and mustard, scraping the skillet bottom with a wooden spoon to loosen the browned bits. Cook until reduced to ¾ cup, about 3 minutes. Off the heat, whisk in the butter, tarragon and lemon juice. Season with pepper to taste; cover and keep warm.

Thyme-Sherry Vinegar Pan Sauce

MAKES ABOUT ¾ CUP

1 medium shallot, minced (about 3 tablespoons)
2 medium garlic cloves, minced or pressed through a garlic press (about 2 teaspoons)
2 teaspoons chopped fresh thyme leaves
1 cup low-sodium chicken broth
2 teaspoons Dijon mustard
2 tablespoons unsalted butter
2 teaspoons sherry vinegar
Ground black pepper

While the chicken rests, remove all but 1 tablespoon of fat from the now-empty skillet, leaving any browned bits and juices in the skillet. Place the skillet over medium-high heat, add the shallot, garlic, and thyme, and cook until softened, about 2 minutes. Stir in the chicken broth and mustard, scraping the skillet bottom with a wooden spoon to loosen the browned bits. Cook until reduced to ¾ cup, about 3 minutes. Off the heat, whisk in the butter and vinegar. Season with pepper to taste; cover and keep warm.

NOTES FROM THE TEST KITCHEN

CARVING A WHOLE CHICKEN

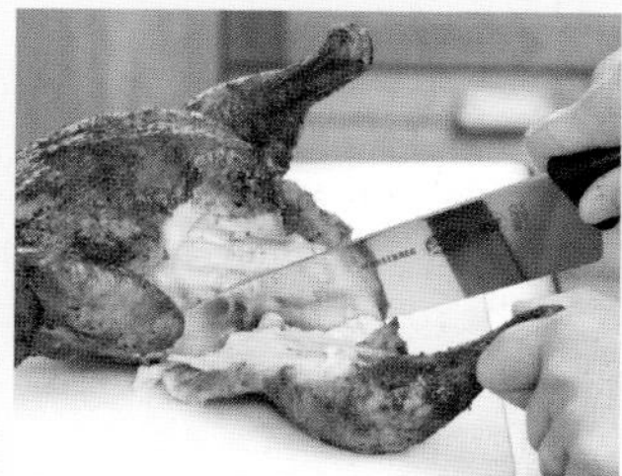

1. Cut the chicken where the leg meets the breast, then pull the leg quarter away. Push up on the joint, then carefully cut through it to remove the leg quarter.

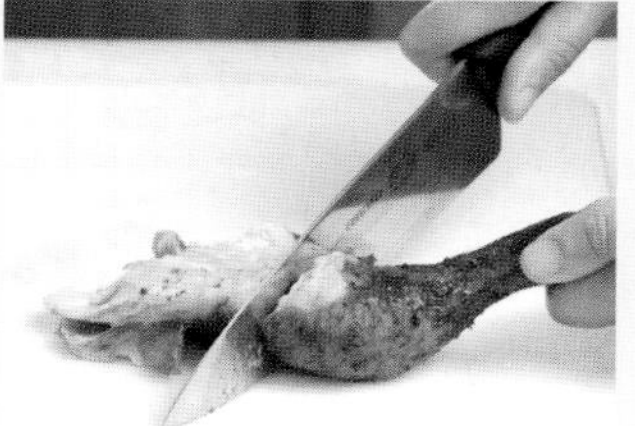

2. Cut through the joint that connects the drumstick to the thigh. Repeat on the second side to remove the other leg.

3. Cut down along one side of the breastbone, pulling the breast meat away from the bone.

4. Remove the wing from the breast by cutting through the wing joint. Slice the breast into attractive slices.

CRISP-SKINNED ROAST CHICKEN

WHY THIS RECIPE WORKS: During roasting, juices and rendered fat can accumulate beneath the chicken skin and turn it wet and flabby. We wanted a juicy roasted chicken with skin that would crackle against your teeth with every bite.

A five-step process was the solution. We first cut an incision down the chicken's back to allow fat to escape and then loosened the skin from the thighs and breasts, poking holes in the fat deposits to allow multiple channels for excess fat and juices to escape. And since skin can't brown until all the surface moisture evaporates, we added baking powder to our salt rub. This helped dehydrate the skin and enhanced the effects of our fourth step: overnight air-drying. Finally, we roasted the bird at high heat to speed the browning. To prevent our kitchen from filling with smoke from the pan drippings, we placed a sheet of foil with holes punched into it under the chicken to shield the rendered fat from direct oven heat. The final result? Roast chicken with tender, juicy meat and the crispest skin ever.

Crisp-Skinned Roast Chicken

SERVES 2 TO 3

Do not brine the bird; it will prevent the skin from becoming crisp. The sheet of foil between the roasting pan and V-rack will keep the drippings from burning and smoking.

- 1 (3½- to 4-pound) whole chicken, giblets discarded (see note)
- 1 tablespoon kosher salt or 1½ teaspoons table salt
- 1 teaspoon baking powder
- ½ teaspoon ground black pepper

1. Place the chicken, breast side down, on a work surface. Following the photos, use the tip of a sharp knife to make four 1-inch incisions along the back of the chicken. Using your fingers or the handle of a wooden spoon, separate the skin from the thighs and breast, being careful not to break the skin. Using a metal skewer, poke 15 to 20 holes in the fat deposits on top of the breast halves and thighs. Tuck the wings behind the back.

2. Combine the salt, baking powder, and pepper in a small bowl. Pat the chicken dry with paper towels and sprinkle all over with the salt mixture. Rub in the mixture with your hands, coating the entire surface evenly. Set the chicken, breast side up, in a V-rack set on a rimmed baking sheet and refrigerate, uncovered, for at least 12 hours or up to 24 hours.

3. Adjust an oven rack to the lowest position and heat the oven to 450 degrees. Using a paring knife, poke 20 holes about 1½ inches apart in a 16 by 12-inch piece of foil. Place the foil loosely in a large roasting pan. Flip the chicken so the breast side faces down, and set the V-rack in the roasting pan on top of the foil. Roast the chicken for 25 minutes.

4. Remove the roasting pan from the oven. Using two large wads of paper towels, rotate the chicken breast side up. Continue to roast until the thickest part of the breasts registers 135 degrees on an instant-read thermometer, 15 to 25 minutes.

5. Increase the oven temperature to 500 degrees. Continue to roast until the skin is golden brown and crisp and the thickest part of the breasts registers 160 to 165 degrees and the thickest part of the thighs registers 175 degrees, 10 to 20 minutes.

6. Transfer the chicken to a carving board and let rest, uncovered, for 20 minutes. Following the photos on page 115, carve the chicken and serve immediately.

NOTES FROM THE TEST KITCHEN

PREPARING CRISP ROAST CHICKEN

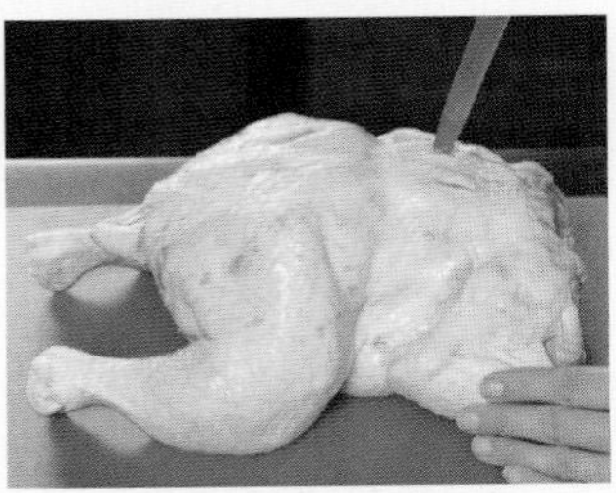

1. Cut incisions in the skin along the chicken's back for the fat to escape.

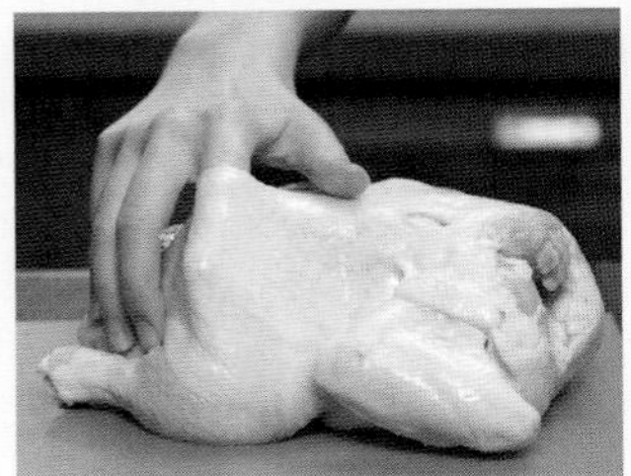

2. Loosen the skin from the thighs and breast to allow rendering fat to trickle out the openings.

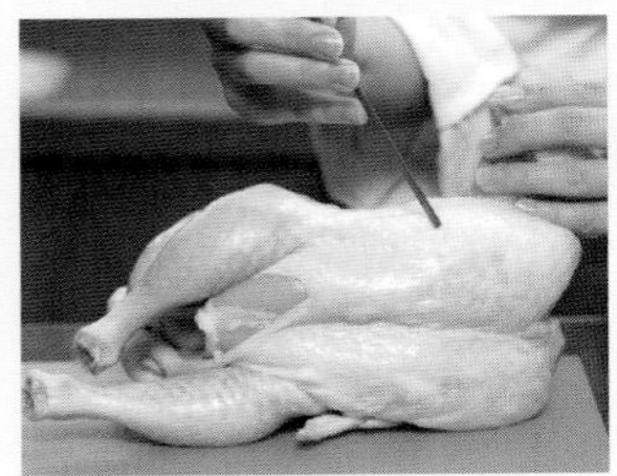

3. Poke holes in the skin of the breast and thighs to create additional channels for fat and juices to escape.

4. Rub a mixture of baking powder and salt into the skin and air-dry the chicken in the refrigerator to help the skin crisp and brown.

BROILED CHICKEN

WHY THIS RECIPE WORKS: We found that one key to getting a whole chicken on the table in about an hour was broiling. Butterflying the chicken kept it flat so that it cooked evenly under the intense direct heat, and it also helped speed up cooking. Piercing the skin at ¾-inch intervals helped the fat render and created an escape route for steam. To get the delicate white meat to finish cooking at the same time as the dark meat, we used a two-pronged approach: A preheated skillet jump-started the cooking of the leg quarters, and starting that skillet under a cold broiler slowed down the cooking of the breasts. To account for carryover cooking, we pulled the chicken from the oven when the breast meat reached 155 degrees instead of 160 degrees (the temperature we'd normally target when roasting a chicken). Finally, the simple addition of garlic and thyme sprigs to the hot pan drippings created a flavorful sauce with almost no effort.

One-Hour Broiled Chicken and Pan Sauce

SERVES 4

If your broiler has multiple settings, choose the highest one. This recipe requires a broiler-safe skillet. In step 3, if the skin is dark golden brown but the breast has not yet reached 155 degrees, cover the chicken with aluminum foil and continue to broil. Monitor the temperature of the chicken carefully during the final 10 minutes of cooking, because it can quickly overcook. Do not attempt this recipe with a drawer broiler.

- 1 (4-pound) whole chicken, giblets discarded
- 1½ teaspoons vegetable oil
- Kosher salt and pepper
- 4 sprigs fresh thyme
- 1 garlic clove, peeled and crushed
- Lemon wedges

1. Adjust oven rack 12 to 13 inches from broiler element (do not preheat broiler). Place chicken breast side down on cutting board. Using kitchen shears, cut through bones on either side of backbone. Trim off any excess fat and skin and discard backbone. Flip chicken over and press on breastbone to flatten. Using tip of paring knife, poke holes through skin over entire surface of chicken, spacing them approximately ¾ inch apart.

2. Rub ½ teaspoon oil over skin and sprinkle with 1 teaspoon salt and ½ teaspoon pepper. Flip chicken over, sprinkle bone side with ½ teaspoon salt, and season with pepper. Tie legs together with kitchen twine and tuck wings under breasts.

3. Heat remaining 1 teaspoon oil in broiler-safe 12-inch skillet over high heat until just smoking. Place chicken in skillet, skin side up, and transfer to oven, positioning skillet as close to center of oven as handle allows (turn handle so it points toward one of oven's front corners.) Turn on broiler and broil chicken for 25 minutes. Rotate skillet by moving handle to opposite front corner of oven and continue to broil until skin is dark golden brown and thickest part of breast registers 155 degrees, 20 to 30 minutes longer.

4. Transfer chicken to carving board and let rest, uncovered, for 15 minutes. While chicken rests, stir thyme sprigs and garlic into juices in pan and let stand for 10 minutes.

5. Using spoon, skim fat from surface of pan juices. Carve chicken and transfer any accumulated juices to pan. Strain sauce through fine-mesh strainer and season with salt and pepper to taste. Serve chicken, passing pan sauce and lemon wedges separately.

CLASSIC ROAST LEMON CHICKEN

WHY THIS RECIPE WORKS: Simple as it sounds, roast lemon chicken can disappoint if the chicken is dry and uninteresting, tastes nothing like lemon, or, even worse, is bursting with citric acidity. The accompanying pan sauce usually suffers a similar fate: bland and lacking lemon or overly harsh. We wanted a way to bring out the full potential of this dish. The chicken should be evenly roasted and moist, with crispy skin, and the lemon flavor should be bright and pure, with no trace of bitterness.

We brined the chicken for extra juiciness. Then we filled the chicken cavity with a cut-up lemon and garlic cloves. To further ensure a juicy bird, we found that the roasting technique was key. We started the chicken breast side down in a moderately hot oven, then flipped it breast side up, added some broth to prevent the drippings from burning, and raised the oven temperature for the remainder of the cooking time. Once the chicken was cooked, we cut it into four pieces and broiled the pieces to get an evenly crisped skin. For the truest lemon flavor, we added a squirt of fresh lemon juice to a simple pan sauce of chicken broth, butter, and fresh herbs.

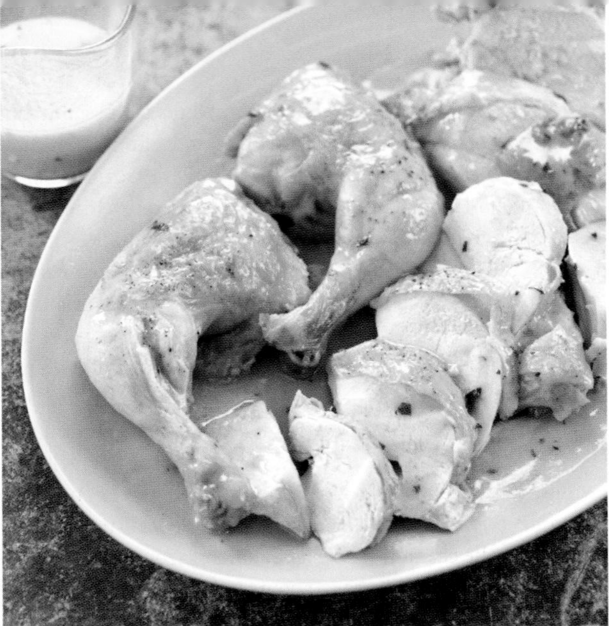

Classic Roast Lemon Chicken

SERVES 3 TO 4

If using a kosher chicken, skip the brining process and begin with step 2. Broiling the fully roasted and quartered chicken skin side up as it sits in a shallow pool of sauce crisps and browns the skin while keeping the meat succulent. If you decide to skip the broiling step, go directly from quartering the chicken to finishing the sauce with lemon juice, butter, and herbs.

- ½ cup table salt
- 1 (3½- to 4-pound) whole chicken, giblets discarded
- 2 lemons
- 6 medium garlic cloves, crushed and peeled
- 4 tablespoons (½ stick) unsalted butter, 2 tablespoons melted and 2 tablespoons chilled and cut into 2 pieces
- Ground black pepper
- 1¾ cups low-sodium chicken broth
- 1 tablespoon minced fresh parsley leaves
- 1 teaspoon minced fresh thyme leaves

1. Dissolve the salt in 2 quarts cold water in a large container. Submerge the chicken in the brine, cover, and refrigerate for 1 hour. Remove the chicken from the brine, rinse well, and pat dry with paper towels.

2. Adjust an oven rack to the lower-middle position; heat the oven to 375 degrees. Spray a V-rack with vegetable oil spray and set in a roasting pan.

3. Cut 1 of the lemons lengthwise into quarters. Place the lemon quarters and garlic in the cavity of the chicken. Brush the breast side of the chicken with 1 tablespoon of the melted butter and season generously with pepper. Place the chicken, breast side down, in the V-rack, then brush the back with the remaining 1 tablespoon melted butter and season generously with pepper.

4. Roast the chicken for 40 minutes. Remove the roasting pan from the oven; increase the oven temperature to 450 degrees. Using two large wads of paper towels, rotate the chicken breast side up; add 1 cup of the chicken broth to the roasting pan. Return the roasting pan to the oven and continue roasting until the thickest part of the breasts registers 160 to 165 degrees and the thickest part of the thighs registers 175 degrees on an instant-read thermometer, 35 to 40 minutes longer. Remove the roasting pan from the oven; tip the V-rack to let the juices from the chicken cavity run into the roasting pan. Transfer the chicken to a carving board and let rest, uncovered, while making the sauce. Remove the V-rack from the roasting pan.

5. Adjust the oven rack to the upper-middle position and heat the broiler. Skim the fat from the drippings in the roasting pan, add the remaining ¾ cup chicken broth, and set the roasting pan on a burner over high heat. Simmer the liquid, scraping the pan bottom with a wooden spoon to loosen the browned bits, until reduced to ½ cup, about 4 minutes; set aside off the heat.

6. Discard the lemons and garlic from the chicken cavity. Following photos 1 and 3 on page 115, cut the chicken into quarters. Pour the accumulated chicken juices into the roasting pan, then place the chicken quarters, skin side up, into the sauce in the roasting pan; broil the chicken until the skin is crisp and deep golden brown, 3 to 5 minutes. Transfer the chicken to a serving platter.

7. Halve the remaining lemon lengthwise; squeeze the juice of one half into the roasting pan; cut the remaining half into four wedges and set aside. Whisk the remaining 2 tablespoons butter into the sauce until combined; stir in the parsley and thyme. Season with salt and pepper to taste. Serve the chicken with the pan sauce and lemon wedges.

GLAZED ROAST CHICKEN

WHY THIS RECIPE WORKS: Glazed chicken might sound simple but actually turns up a host of troubles, as the problems inherent in roasting chicken (dry breast meat, flabby skin) are compounded by the glaze (won't stick to the meat, burns in patches, introduces moisture). We wanted evenly glazed roast chicken with crisp skin and tender meat. We started with a large roaster chicken. We separated the skin from the meat and pricked holes in the fat deposits to allow rendered fat to escape, then rubbed it with salt and baking powder—to dehydrate the skin and help it to crisp—and we roasted the chicken straddled on top of a beer can set in a roasting pan (a popular grilling technique). The technique seemed like a winner—no awkward flipping, glazing every nook and cranny was easy, and fat dripped freely out of the bird. But cutting into the chicken revealed that the breast, now exposed to the high oven heat for the entire cooking time, was dry and tough. To solve these problems, we rested the chicken before putting it in the oven for blast of heat—the skin came out crisper than before and the breast meat was perfectly cooked. Second, we thickened our glaze with cornstarch and reduced it to a syrupy consistency, then applied it before the final five minutes of roasting. The result? Moist, tender chicken with crisp, glazed skin.

Glazed Roast Chicken

SERVES 4 TO 6

For best results, use a 16-ounce can of beer. A larger can will work, but avoid using a 12-ounce can, as it will not support the weight of the chicken. A vertical roaster can be used in place of the beer can, but we recommend only using a model that can be placed in a roasting pan. Taste your marmalade before using it; if it is overly sweet, reduce the amount of maple syrup in the glaze by 2 tablespoons. Trappist Seville Orange Marmalade is the test kitchen's preferred brand.

CHICKEN

- 1 (6- to 7-pound) whole chicken, giblets discarded
- 2½ teaspoons table salt
- 1 teaspoon baking powder
- 1 teaspoon ground black pepper
- 1 (16-ounce) can beer (see note)

GLAZE

- 1 tablespoon water
- 1 teaspoon cornstarch
- ½ cup maple syrup
- ½ cup orange marmalade (see note)
- ¼ cup cider vinegar
- 2 tablespoons unsalted butter
- 2 tablespoons Dijon mustard
- 1 teaspoon ground black pepper

1. FOR THE CHICKEN: Place the chicken, breast side down, on a work surface. Following the photos on page 116, use the tip of a sharp knife to make four 1-inch incisions along the back of the chicken. Using your fingers or the handle of a wooden spoon, separate the skin from the thighs and breast, being careful not to break the skin. Using a metal skewer, poke 15 to 20 holes in the fat deposits on top of the breast halves and thighs. Tuck the wings behind the back.

2. Combine the salt, baking powder, and pepper in a small bowl. Pat the chicken dry with paper towels and sprinkle evenly all over with the salt mixture. Rub in the mixture with your hands, coating the entire surface evenly. Set the chicken, breast side up, on a rimmed baking sheet and refrigerate, uncovered, for 30 to 60 minutes. Meanwhile, adjust an oven rack to the lowest position and heat the oven to 325 degrees.

3. Open the beer can and pour out (or drink) about half of the liquid. Spray the can lightly with vegetable oil spray and place in the middle of a roasting pan. Slide the chicken over the can so the drumsticks reach down to the bottom of the can, the chicken stands upright, and the breast is perpendicular to the bottom of the pan. Roast until the skin starts to turn golden and the thickest part of the breasts registers 140 degrees on an instant-read thermometer, 75 to 90 minutes. Carefully remove the chicken and pan from the oven and increase the oven temperature to 500 degrees.

4. FOR THE GLAZE: While the chicken cooks, stir the water and cornstarch together in a small bowl until no lumps remain; set aside. Bring the remaining glaze ingredients to a simmer in a medium saucepan over medium-high heat. Cook, stirring occasionally, until reduced to ¾ cup, 6 to 8 minutes. Slowly whisk the cornstarch mixture into the glaze. Return to a simmer and cook for 1 minute. Remove the pan from the heat.

5. When the oven is heated to 500 degrees, place 1½ cups water in the bottom of the roasting pan and return to the oven. Roast until the entire chicken skin is browned and crisp, the thickest part of the breasts registers 160 to 165 degrees, and the thickest part of the thighs registers 175 degrees on an instant-read thermometer, 24 to 30 minutes. Check the chicken halfway through roasting; if the top is becoming too dark, place a 7-inch square piece of foil over the neck and wingtips of the chicken and continue to roast (if the pan begins to smoke and sizzle, add ½ cup water to the roasting pan).

6. Brush the chicken with ¼ cup of the glaze and continue to roast until browned and sticky, about 5 minutes. (If the glaze has become stiff, return to low heat to soften.) Carefully remove the chicken from the oven, transfer the chicken, still on the can, to a carving board, and brush with ¼ cup more glaze. Let rest for 20 minutes.

7. While the chicken rests, strain the juices from the pan through a fine-mesh strainer into a fat separator; allow the liquid to settle for 5 minutes. Whisk ½ cup juices into the remaining ¼ cup glaze in a saucepan and set over low heat. Using a kitchen towel, carefully lift the chicken off the can and onto a platter or carving board. Following the photos on page 115, carve the chicken, adding any accumulated juices to the sauce. Serve, passing the sauce separately.

PERUVIAN ROAST CHICKEN

WHY THIS RECIPE WORKS: Authentic versions of Peruvian garlic-lime chicken require a wood-fired oven and hard-to-find ingredients. We wanted to replicate this robustly flavored dish using an oven and supermarket staples. A paste of salt, garlic, oil, lime zest, and cumin rubbed underneath and on top of the skin produced well-seasoned meat and a heady flavor. To this basic paste we added fresh mint (replacing the black mint paste called for in authentic recipes), oregano, pepper, and minced habanero chile for tangy spice, while a little smoked paprika subtly mimicked the smokiness we were missing from the rotisserie. Roasting the chicken vertically allowed it to cook evenly, while using two different oven temperatures helped us achieve both moist meat and well-browned skin.

Peruvian Roast Chicken with Garlic and Lime

SERVES 3 TO 4

If habanero chiles are unavailable, 1 tablespoon of minced serrano chile can be substituted. Wear gloves when working with hot chiles. This recipe calls for a vertical poultry roaster. If you don't have one, substitute a 12-ounce can of beer. Open the beer and pour out (or drink) about half of the liquid. Spray the can lightly with vegetable oil spray and proceed with the recipe. Serve with Spicy Mayonnaise (recipe follows) and lime wedges.

- ¼ cup fresh mint leaves
- 6 medium garlic cloves, chopped coarse
- 3 tablespoons extra-virgin olive oil
- 1 tablespoon table salt
- 1 tablespoon ground black pepper
- 1 tablespoon ground cumin
- 1 tablespoon sugar
- 2 teaspoons smoked paprika
- 2 teaspoons dried oregano
- 2 teaspoons finely grated zest plus ¼ cup juice from 2 limes
- 1 teaspoon minced habanero chile
- 1 (3½- to 4-pound) whole chicken, giblets discarded
- 1 cup Spicy Mayonnaise (recipe follows)

1. Process all the ingredients except the chicken and mayonnaise in a blender until a smooth paste forms, 10 to 20 seconds. Following the photos, use your fingers to gently loosen the skin covering the breast and thighs; place half of the paste under the skin, directly on the meat of the breast and thighs. Gently press on the skin to distribute the paste over the meat. Spread the entire exterior surface of the chicken with the remaining paste. Tuck the wings behind the back. Place the chicken in a 1-gallon zipper-lock bag and refrigerate for at least 6 hours or up to 24 hours.

NOTES FROM THE TEST KITCHEN

FLAVORING PERUVIAN ROAST CHICKEN

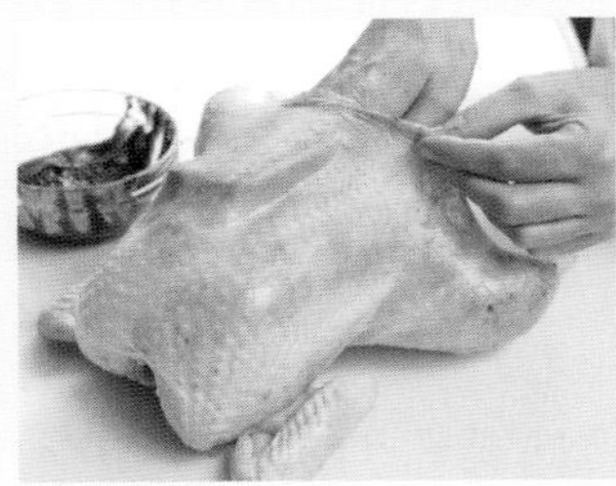

1. Use your fingers to gently loosen the chicken skin from over the thighs and breast and rub half of the paste directly over the meat.

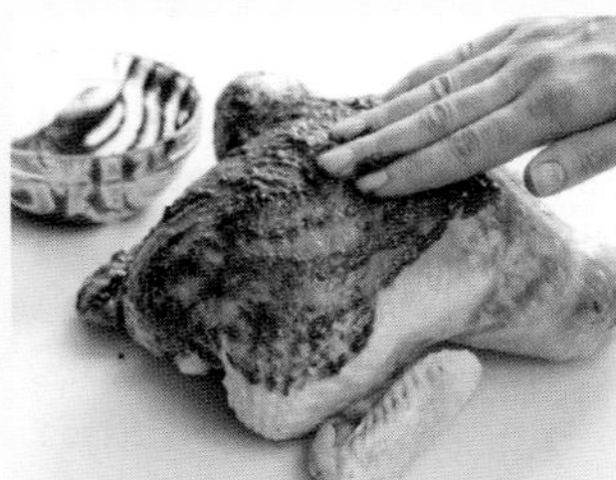

2. Spread the remaining paste over the skin of the entire chicken.

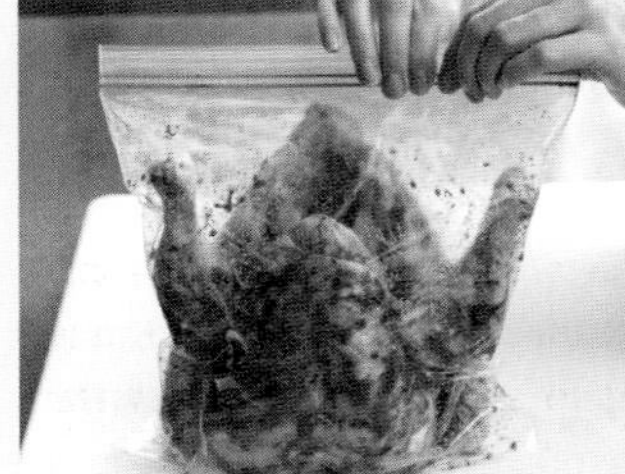

3. Place the chicken in a gallon-size zipper-lock bag; refrigerate for at least 6 or up to 24 hours.

2. Adjust an oven rack to the lowest position and heat the oven to 325 degrees. Place a vertical roaster on a rimmed baking sheet. Slide the chicken onto the vertical roaster so the drumsticks reach down to the bottom of the roaster, the chicken stands upright, and the breast is perpendicular to the bottom of the pan. Roast the chicken until the skin just begins to turn golden and the thickest part of the breast registers 140 degrees, 45 to 55 minutes. Carefully remove the chicken and the pan from the oven and increase the oven temperature to 500 degrees.

3. Once the oven has reached 500 degrees, place 1 cup water in the bottom of the baking sheet and continue to roast until the entire chicken skin is browned and crisp, the breast registers 160 degrees, and the thighs register 175 degrees, about 20 minutes, rotating the pan halfway through roasting. Check the chicken halfway through roasting; if the top is becoming too dark, place a 7-inch square piece of aluminum foil over the neck and wingtips of the chicken and continue to roast (if the pan begins to smoke and sizzle, add additional water to the pan).

4. Carefully remove the chicken from the oven and let rest, still on the vertical roaster, for 20 minutes. Using 2 large wads of paper towels, carefully lift the chicken off the vertical roaster and onto a carving board. Carve the chicken and serve, passing the Spicy Mayonnaise separately.

Spicy Mayonnaise

MAKES ABOUT 1 CUP

If you have concerns about consuming raw eggs, ¼ cup of an egg substitute can be used in place of the egg.

- 1 large egg
- 2 tablespoons water
- 1 tablespoon minced onion
- 1 tablespoon juice from 1 lime
- 1 tablespoon minced fresh cilantro leaves
- 1 tablespoon minced jarred jalapeños

1 medium garlic clove, minced or pressed through a garlic press (about 1 teaspoon)
1 teaspoon yellow mustard
¼ teaspoon table salt
1 cup vegetable oil

Process all the ingredients except the oil in a food processor until combined, about 5 seconds. With the machine running, slowly drizzle in the oil in a steady stream until a mayonnaise-like consistency is reached, scraping down the bowl as necessary.

CHICKEN MOLE POBLANO

WHY THIS RECIPE WORKS: The most famous of Mexico's *moles*, mole poblano often relies on as many as six types of chiles for its deep richness. For simplicity's sake, we pared our recipe down to two: ancho, for a robust chile base, and chipotle, for smoky, intense chile flavor. Using almond butter instead of ground almonds was a simple shortcut that lent a luxurious, velvety texture to the sauce. Just 1 ounce of chocolate added richness and depth but didn't make the sauce taste chocolaty. We added warmth and a touch of sweetness with cinnamon, cloves, and raisins. Sautéing the chiles, chocolate, and spices along with the onion and garlic deepened the flavor of the final sauce. Simmering the mole for just 10 minutes thickened the sauce to the perfect consistency. Bone-in chicken pieces worked perfectly with our mole, and removing the skin kept it from turning soggy in the sauce.

Chicken Mole Poblano

SERVES 4 TO 6

Feel free to substitute ½ teaspoon ground chipotle chile powder or ½ teaspoon minced canned chipotles in adobo sauce for the chipotle chile (we noted little difference in flavor) and add with the cinnamon in step 2. Serve with rice.

2 dried ancho chiles, stemmed, seeded, and torn into ½-inch pieces (½ cup)
½ dried chipotle chile, stemmed, seeded, and torn into ½-inch pieces (scant tablespoon)
3 tablespoons vegetable oil
1 onion, chopped fine
1 ounce bittersweet, semisweet, or Mexican chocolate, chopped coarse
½ teaspoon ground cinnamon
⅛ teaspoon ground cloves
2 garlic cloves, minced
2 cups chicken broth
1 (14.5-ounce) can diced tomatoes, drained
¼ cup raisins
¼ cup almond butter
2 tablespoons sesame seeds, plus extra for garnish, toasted
Salt and pepper
Sugar
3½ pounds bone-in chicken pieces (split breasts, legs, and/or thighs), skin removed, trimmed

1. Toast anchos and chipotle in 12-inch skillet over medium heat, stirring frequently, until fragrant, 2 to 6 minutes; transfer to plate. Add oil and onion to now-empty skillet and cook over medium-high heat until softened, 5 to 7 minutes.

2. Stir in chocolate, cinnamon, cloves, and toasted chiles and cook until chocolate is melted and bubbly, about 2 minutes. Stir in garlic and cook until fragrant, about 30 seconds. Stir in broth, tomatoes, raisins, almond butter, and sesame seeds and bring to simmer. Reduce heat to medium and simmer gently, stirring occasionally, until slightly thickened and measures about 3½ cups, about 7 minutes.

3. Transfer mixture to blender and process until smooth, about 20 seconds. Season with salt, pepper, and sugar to taste. (Sauce can be refrigerated for up to 3 days; loosen with water as needed before continuing.)

NOTES FROM THE TEST KITCHEN

MAKING MOLE POBLANO SAUCE

Mole poblano is a quintessential Mexican sauce, but traditional recipes can be very time-consuming. We streamlined the process by sautéing all of our aromatics together (rather than separately) and replacing ground almonds with almond butter for a mole with all the richness and depth of traditional versions.

1. Stem, seed, and tear chiles into ½-inch pieces. Toast chiles in 12-inch skillet over medium heat until fragrant, 2 to 6 minutes. Transfer chiles to plate.

2. Cook onion, then add chiles, spices, and chocolate. Stir in garlic, then broth, tomatoes, sesame seeds, raisins, and almond butter. Simmer until slightly thickened.

3. Transfer sauce to blender. Puree until smooth, about 20 seconds, then season with salt, pepper, and sugar to taste.

4. Adjust oven rack to middle position and heat oven to 400 degrees. Pat chicken dry with paper towels and season with salt and pepper. Arrange chicken in single layer in shallow baking dish and cover with mole sauce, turning to coat chicken evenly. Bake, uncovered, until breasts register 160 degrees, and thighs or drumsticks register 175 degrees, 35 to 45 minutes.

5. Remove chicken from oven, tent with aluminum foil, and let rest for 5 to 10 minutes. Sprinkle with extra sesame seeds and serve.

STOVETOP ROAST CHICKEN

WHY THIS RECIPE WORKS: Roasting chicken in the oven is the usual route to crisp skin and moist meat, but sometimes you want your oven for something else. Cooking chicken pieces in a skillet easily yields a flavorful pan sauce, but the skin on the chicken is often flabby and the meat unevenly cooked. We wanted to combine the best aspects of both roasted and skillet-cooked chicken. We started with four breast halves, two drumsticks, and two thighs. We tested a variety of approaches to achieve moist meat and crisp skin, but ran into numerous problems. Steaming the raw chicken in broth and then searing it in a hot pan, skin side down crisped the skin but caused it to shrink dramatically. To avoid this, we found that searing the chicken first and then steaming was the answer. After steaming, we poured off all the liquid from the pan (reserving it to use for the pan sauce) and returned the chicken to sear again skin side down. This second searing produced the deep, russet-hued crisp skin we had hoped for. After removing the finished chicken, we made our pan sauce with shallot, lemon, and herbs. This quick pan sauce was the perfect complement to our roast chicken.

Stovetop Roast Chicken with Lemon-Herb Sauce

SERVES 4

Use a splatter screen when browning the chicken.

CHICKEN

- 3½ pounds bone-in, skin-on chicken pieces (split breasts cut in half, drumsticks, and/or thighs), trimmed
- Table salt and ground black pepper
- 1 tablespoon vegetable oil
- ¾–1¼ cups low-sodium chicken broth

LEMON-HERB SAUCE

- 1 teaspoon vegetable oil
- 1 medium shallot, minced (about 3 tablespoons)
- 1 teaspoon unbleached all-purpose flour
- 1½ tablespoons minced fresh parsley leaves
- 1½ tablespoons minced fresh chives
- 1 tablespoon juice from 1 lemon
- 1 tablespoon unsalted butter, chilled
- Table salt and ground black pepper

1. FOR THE CHICKEN: Pat the chicken dry with paper towels and season with salt and pepper. Heat 2 teaspoons of the oil in a 12-inch nonstick skillet over medium-high heat until just smoking. Add the chicken pieces skin side down and cook without moving until golden brown, 5 to 8 minutes.

2. Using tongs, flip the chicken pieces skin side up. Reduce the heat to medium-low, add ¾ cup of the broth to the skillet, cover, and cook until the thickest part of the breasts registers 155 degrees and the thickest part of the thighs/drumsticks registers 170 degrees on an instant-read thermometer, 10 to 16 minutes. Transfer the chicken to a plate, skin side up.

3. Pour off the liquid from the skillet into a 2-cup measuring cup and reserve. Wipe out the skillet with paper towels. Add the remaining 1 teaspoon oil to the skillet and heat over medium-high heat until shimmering. Return the chicken pieces skin side down and cook undisturbed until the skin is deep golden brown and crisp, the thickest part of the breasts registers 160 to 165 degrees, and the thickest part of the thighs/drumsticks registers 175 degrees, 4 to 7 minutes. Transfer to a serving platter and tent loosely with foil. Using a spoon, skim any fat from the reserved cooking liquid and add enough broth to measure ¾ cup.

4. FOR THE SAUCE: Heat the oil in the now-empty skillet over low heat. Add the shallot and cook, stirring frequently, until softened, about 2 minutes. Add the flour and cook, stirring constantly, for 30 seconds. Increase the heat to medium-high, add the reserved cooking liquid, and bring to a simmer, scraping the skillet bottom with a wooden spoon to loosen any browned bits. Simmer rapidly until reduced to ½ cup, 2 to 3 minutes. Stir in any accumulated juices from the resting chicken; return to a simmer and cook for 30 seconds. Off the heat, whisk in the parsley, chives, lemon juice, and butter; season with salt and pepper to taste. Pour the sauce around the chicken and serve immediately.

RAO'S FAMOUS LEMON CHICKEN

WHY THIS RECIPE WORKS: Inspired by Rao's famous roast lemon chicken in New York City, we aspired to re-create this popular dish, while making it more accessible to home cooks. We used a mixture of white and dark meat bone-in chicken parts, instead of the small birds Rao's uses which can be difficult to find. Searing the chicken before transferring it to the oven provided flavorful fond for a pan sauce. Browning the dark meat on both sides ensured the white and dark meats cooked evenly. To get the right amount of lemony flavor, we introduced zest to the sauce right before the chicken was added. The most successful way to thicken the sauce was with flour, added to the aromatics in the beginning of cooking, which provided a full-bodied gravy. A last-minute sprinkle of oregano, parsley, and more lemon zest finished the dish, adding a fruity brightness that complemented the crisp skin, moist meat, and silky sauce.

Skillet-Roasted Chicken in Lemon Sauce

SERVES 4

We serve our version of Rao's chicken with crusty bread, but it can also be served with rice, potatoes, or egg noodles. To ensure crisp skin, dry the chicken well after brining and pour the sauce around, not on, the chicken right before serving.

- ½ cup salt
- 3 pounds bone-in chicken pieces (2 split breasts cut in half crosswise, 2 drumsticks, and 2 thighs), trimmed
- 1 teaspoon vegetable oil
- 2 tablespoons unsalted butter
- 1 large shallot, minced
- 1 garlic clove, minced
- 4 teaspoons all-purpose flour
- 1 cup chicken broth
- 4 teaspoons grated lemon zest plus ¼ cup juice (2 lemons)
- 1 tablespoon fresh parsley leaves
- 1 teaspoon fresh oregano leaves

1. Dissolve salt in 2 quarts cold water in large container. Submerge chicken in brine, cover, and refrigerate for 30 minutes to 1 hour. Remove chicken from brine and pat dry with paper towels.

2. Adjust oven rack to lower-middle position and heat oven to 475 degrees. Heat oil in ovensafe 12-inch skillet over medium-high heat until just smoking. Place chicken skin side down in skillet and cook until skin is well browned and crisp, 8 to 10 minutes. Transfer breasts to large plate. Flip thighs and legs and continue to cook until browned on second side, 3 to 5 minutes longer. Transfer thighs and legs to plate with breasts.

3. Pour off and discard fat in skillet. Return skillet to medium heat; add butter, shallot, and garlic and cook until fragrant, about 30 seconds. Sprinkle flour evenly over shallot-garlic mixture and cook, stirring constantly, until flour is lightly browned, about 1 minute. Slowly stir in broth and lemon juice, scraping up any browned bits, and bring to simmer. Cook until sauce is slightly reduced and thickened, 2 to 3 minutes. Stir in 1 tablespoon zest and remove skillet from heat. Return chicken, skin side up (skin should be above surface of liquid), and any accumulated juices to skillet and transfer to oven. Cook, uncovered, until breasts register 160 degrees and thighs and legs register 175 degrees, 10 to 12 minutes.

4. While chicken cooks, chop parsley, oregano, and remaining 1 teaspoon zest together until finely minced and well combined. Remove skillet from oven and let chicken stand for 5 minutes.

5. Transfer chicken to serving platter. Whisk sauce, incorporating any browned bits from sides of pan, until smooth and homogeneous, about 30 seconds. Whisk half of herb-zest mixture into sauce and sprinkle remaining half over chicken. Pour some sauce around chicken. Serve, passing remaining sauce separately.

BEST ROAST CHICKEN WITH ROOT VEGETABLES

WHY THIS RECIPE WORKS: Our roast chicken and root vegetables recipe ensures perfect versions of both components by calling for cooking them separately. We brined the chicken to ensure that it stayed juicy and then placed it in a preheated skillet in a hot oven. The dark meat, which needed to be cooked to a higher temperature than the white meat, stayed in contact with the pan, ensuring that it finished cooking at the same time as the more delicate breast meat. We cooked the vegetables below the chicken on a baking sheet until they were tender. Once the chicken was done, we turned the oven up to 500 degrees and finished roasting the vegetables, using the drippings left behind in the skillet to infuse them with chicken flavor. We found that a variety of vegetables worked well as long as we cut them to the same size so they cooked evenly.

Best Roast Chicken With Root Vegetables

SERVES 4 TO 6

Cooking the chicken in a preheated skillet will ensure that the breast and thigh meat finish cooking at the same time. This recipe requires brining the chicken for 1 hour before cooking. If using a kosher chicken, do not brine in step 1, but season with ½ teaspoon salt in step 3.

- 1 (3½- to 4-pound) whole chicken, giblets discarded
- Salt and pepper
- ½ cup sugar
- 1½ pounds Yukon Gold potatoes, peeled and cut into 2-inch pieces
- 12 ounces carrots, peeled, halved crosswise, thick ends halved lengthwise
- 12 ounces parsnips, peeled, halved crosswise, thick ends halved lengthwise
- 4 teaspoons extra-virgin olive oil
- ¼ cup water
- 1 teaspoon minced fresh thyme
- 1 tablespoon chopped fresh parsley

1. With chicken breast side down, use tip of sharp knife to make four 1-inch incisions along back. Using your fingers, gently loosen skin covering breast and thighs. Use metal skewer to poke 15 to 20 holes in fat deposits on top of breast halves and thighs. Dissolve ½ cup salt and sugar in 2 quarts cold water in large container. Submerge chicken in brine, cover, and refrigerate for 1 hour.

2. Adjust oven racks to upper-middle and lower-middle positions and heat oven to 450 degrees. Place 12-inch ovensafe skillet on upper rack and heat for 15 minutes. Spray rimmed baking sheet with vegetable oil spray. Arrange potatoes, carrots, and parsnips with cut surfaces down in single layer on baking sheet and cover sheet tightly with aluminum foil.

3. Remove chicken from brine and pat dry with paper towels. Combine 1 tablespoon oil and ½ teaspoon pepper in small bowl. Rub entire surface of chicken with oil-pepper mixture. Tie legs together with twine and tuck wingtips behind back.

4. Carefully remove skillet from oven (handle will be hot). Add remaining 1 teaspoon oil to skillet and swirl to coat. Place chicken breast side up in skillet. Return skillet to upper rack and place sheet of vegetables on lower rack. Cook for 30 minutes.

5. Remove vegetables from oven, remove foil, and set aside. Rotate skillet and continue to cook chicken until breast registers 160 degrees and thighs register 175 degrees, 15 to 25 minutes longer.

6. Transfer chicken to carving board and let rest, uncovered, for 20 minutes. Increase oven temperature to 500 degrees. Add water to skillet. Using whisk, stir until brown bits have dissolved. Strain sauce through fine-mesh strainer into fat separator, pressing on solids to remove any remaining liquid. Let liquid settle for 5 minutes. Pour off liquid from fat separator and reserve. Reserve 3 tablespoons fat, discarding remaining fat.

7. Drizzle vegetables with reserved fat. Sprinkle vegetables with thyme, 1 teaspoon salt, and ½ teaspoon pepper and toss to coat. Place sheet on upper rack and roast for 5 minutes. Remove sheet from oven. Using thin, sharp metal spatula, turn vegetables. Continue to roast until browned at edges, 8 to 10 minutes longer.

8. Pour reserved liquid over vegetables. Continue to roast until liquid is thick and syrupy and vegetables are tender, 3 to 5 minutes. Toss vegetables to coat, then transfer to serving platter and sprinkle with parsley. Carve chicken and transfer to platter with vegetables. Serve.

CRISP ROAST BUTTERFLIED CHICKEN

WHY THIS RECIPE WORKS: One of the major perks of a butterflied chicken is that it takes considerably less time to cook than a traditional whole bird. Additionally, flattening the chicken encourages crisp skin, since most of the skin is in contact with the hot pan. However, during our testing we found that after initially crisping up, the skin turned soggy as the chicken continued to cook skin side down in its own juices. We set out to produce perfectly cooked chicken with crisp skin that could be on the table in less than an hour. We started by heating a cast-iron skillet in a very hot oven. We then put the chicken into the preheated skillet skin side down and cooked it until the skin was golden brown. Flipping the chicken over for the remainder of the cooking time allowed us to take advantage of the hot, dry air of the oven to ensure that the skin remained crisp and intact. A simple mixture of extra-virgin olive oil, rosemary, and garlic brushed on the chicken during roasting elevated the flavor and crisped the skin further. We had four-star, perfectly browned roast chicken with spectacular skin on the table in under an hour. And as a bonus, the butterflied bird was a cinch to carve.

Crisp Roast Butterflied Chicken with Rosemary and Garlic

SERVES 4

Be aware that the chicken may slightly overhang the skillet at first, but once browned it will shrink to fit; do not use a chicken larger than 4 pounds. Serve with lemon wedges.

- 2 tablespoons extra-virgin olive oil
- 1 teaspoon minced fresh rosemary
- 1 garlic clove, minced
- 1 (3½- to 4-pound) whole chicken, giblets discarded
- Salt and pepper

1. Adjust oven rack to lowest position, place 12-inch cast-iron skillet on rack, and heat oven to 500 degrees. Meanwhile, combine 1 tablespoon oil, rosemary, and garlic in bowl; set aside.

2. With chicken breast side down, use kitchen shears to cut through bones on either side of backbone; discard backbone. Flip chicken over, tuck wingtips behind back, and press firmly on breastbone to flatten. Pat chicken dry with paper towels, then rub with remaining 1 tablespoon oil and season with salt and pepper.

3. When oven reaches 500 degrees, place chicken breast side down in hot skillet. Reduce oven temperature to 450 degrees and roast chicken until well browned, about 30 minutes.

4. Using potholders, remove skillet from oven. Being careful of hot skillet handle, gently flip chicken breast side up. Brush chicken with oil mixture, return skillet to oven, and continue to roast chicken until breast registers 160 degrees and thighs register 175 degrees, about 10 minutes. Transfer chicken to carving board, tent loosely with aluminum foil, and let rest for 15 minutes. Carve chicken and serve.

NOTES FROM THE TEST KITCHEN

BUTTERFLYING A CHICKEN

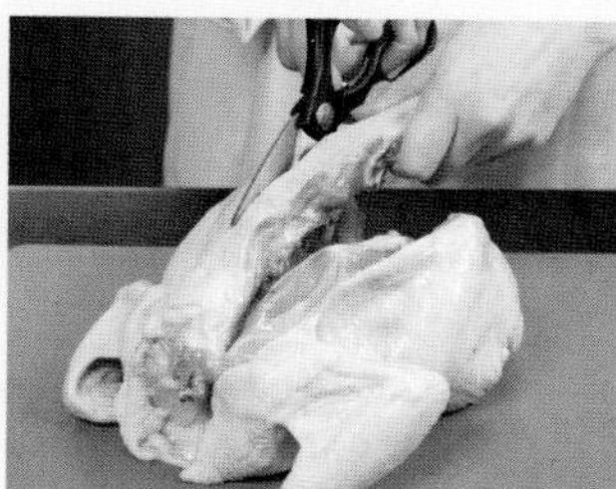

1. With the breast side down, cut along each side of the backbone and remove it.

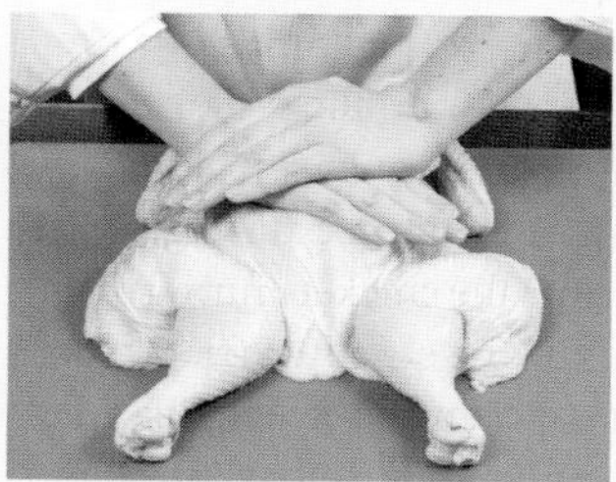

2. Turn the chicken breast side up. Open the chicken on the work surface. Use the heel of your hand to flatten the breastbone.

3. Cover the chicken with plastic wrap, then pound it with a meat pounder to a fairly even thickness.

HIGH-ROAST CHICKEN

WHY THIS RECIPE WORKS: "High roasting"—cooking a bird at temperatures in excess of 450 degrees—is supposed to produce tastier chicken with crisper skin in record time. But recipes we've tried overcook the bird while producing enough smoke to be mistaken for a five-alarm fire. We wanted to improve upon this method for a quick roasted chicken with skin that is crisp and tanned to a deep golden hue and meat that is irresistibly tender and moist. And while we were at it, we wanted roasted potatoes too.

We began by brining the chicken for moist, well-seasoned meat. Then we butterflied the chicken, which allowed for more even and faster roasting. We found that we were able to add moisture and flavor to the chicken by rubbing flavored herb butter under the skin. (Some recipes instruct rubbing the butter over the skin, but the herbs burn and the butter doesn't season the meat.) We cooked the chicken on top of a broiler pan with a bottom attached. In the bottom of the pan under the chicken, we placed a layer of potatoes. To ensure that the potatoes cooked through, we sliced them thin—⅛ to ¼ inch thick. As the chicken cooked, the potatoes absorbed the juices from the chicken and became well seasoned. In just one hour we had roast chicken with spectacularly crisp skin and moist meat—and potatoes too.

High-Roast Butterflied Chicken with Potatoes

SERVES 2 TO 3

If using a kosher bird, skip the brining process and begin with step 2. Because you'll be cooking the chicken under high heat, it's important that you rinse it thoroughly before proceeding—otherwise, the sugar remaining on the skin from the brine will caramelize and ultimately burn. For this cooking technique, russet potatoes offer the best potato flavor, but Yukon Golds develop a beautiful color and retain their shape better after cooking. Either works well in this recipe. A food processor makes quick and easy work of slicing the potatoes.

CHICKEN AND BRINE

- ½ cup table salt
- ½ cup sugar
- 1 (3½- to 4-pound) whole chicken, giblets discarded (see note)
- 1 recipe Mustard-Garlic Butter with Thyme (recipe follows)
- 1 tablespoon olive oil
- Ground black pepper

POTATOES

- 2½ pounds russet or Yukon Gold potatoes (4 to 5 medium), peeled and sliced ⅛ to ¼ inch thick (see note)
- 1 tablespoon olive oil
- ½ teaspoon table salt
- ⅛ teaspoon ground black pepper

1. FOR THE CHICKEN AND BRINE: Dissolve the salt and sugar in 2 quarts cold water in a large container. Submerge the chicken in the brine, cover, and refrigerate for 1 hour.

2. Adjust an oven rack to the lower-middle position and heat the oven to 500 degrees. Line a broiler-pan bottom with foil. Remove the chicken from the brine, rinse well, and pat dry with paper towels. Following the photos, remove the backbone from the chicken, pound the chicken to a fairly even thickness, and tuck the wings behind the back.

3. Use your fingers to gently loosen the center portion of skin covering each side of the breast. Place the butter mixture under the skin, directly on the meat in the center of each side. Gently press on the skin to distribute the butter over the meat. Rub the skin with the oil and season with pepper. Place the chicken on the broiler-pan top and push each leg up to rest between the thigh and breast.

4. FOR THE POTATOES: Toss the potatoes with the oil, salt, and pepper. Spread the potatoes in an even layer in the prepared broiler-pan bottom. Place the broiler-pan top with the chicken on top.

5. Roast the chicken until just beginning to brown, about 20 minutes. Rotate the pan and continue to roast until the skin is crisped and deep brown and the thickest part of the breasts registers 160 to 165 degrees and the thickest part of the thighs registers 175 degrees on an instant-read thermometer, 20 to 25 minutes longer. Transfer the chicken to a carving board and let rest for 10 minutes.

6. While the chicken rests, remove the broiler-pan top and, using paper towels, soak up any excess grease from the potatoes. Transfer the potatoes to a serving platter. Carve the chicken, transfer to the platter with the potatoes, and serve.

Mustard-Garlic Butter with Thyme

MAKES ABOUT 3 TABLESPOONS

- 2 tablespoons unsalted butter, softened
- 1 tablespoon Dijon mustard
- 1 medium garlic clove, minced or pressed through a garlic press (about 1 teaspoon)
- 1 teaspoon minced fresh thyme leaves
- Pinch ground black pepper

Mash all the ingredients together in a small bowl.

"STUFFED" ROAST CHICKEN

WHY THIS RECIPE WORKS: Stuffed roast chicken can be a conundrum—it's either a perfectly cooked bird filled with lukewarm stuffing (risking salmonella) or safe-to-eat stuffing packed in parched poultry. And given the small cavity of a roasting chicken, there's often no more than a few tablespoons of stuffing per person. We wanted our stuffed roast chicken to produce both flavorful white and dark chicken meat along with an ample amount of intensely flavored stuffing. And we wanted to solve the problem of cooking the stuffing to a safe temperature without drying out the delicate breast meat of the chicken.

We ensured moist, savory meat by brining the bird before we stuffed and roasted it. While the chicken was brining, we jazzed up the stuffing mix by replacing the customary onion with a thinly sliced leek, adding it along with celery, mushrooms, minced garlic, fresh sage, thyme, and parsley, and chicken broth. Our most creative solution, however, was to make an aluminum foil bowl, mound the stuffing into it, and place the chicken—after butterflying it—on top. This improvised cooking vessel allowed the stuffing to become moist and flavorful throughout from the chicken juices, while also becoming brown and chewy on the bottom. And cleanup was a snap.

"Stuffed" Roast Butterflied Chicken

SERVES 4 TO 6

If using a kosher bird, skip the brining process and begin with step 2. Use a traditional (not nonstick) roasting pan to prepare this recipe. When arranging the chicken over the stuffing, it should extend past the edges of the bowl so that most of the fat renders into the roasting pan.

- ½ cup table salt
- ½ cup sugar
- 1 (5- to 6-pound) whole chicken, giblets discarded (see note)
- 1 tablespoon olive oil
- Ground black pepper
- 1 recipe Mushroom-Leek Bread Stuffing with Herbs (recipe follows)

1. Dissolve the salt and sugar in 2 quarts cold water in a large container. Submerge the chicken in the brine, cover, and refrigerate for 1½ hours.

2. Adjust an oven rack to the lower-middle position and heat the oven to 450 degrees. Remove the chicken from the brine, rinse well, and pat dry with paper towels. Following the photos on page 125, remove the backbone from the chicken, pound the chicken to a fairly even thickness, and tuck the wings behind the back. Rub the skin with the oil and season with pepper.

3. To make the foil bowl, place two 12-inch squares of foil on top of each other. Fold the edges to construct an 8 by 6-inch bowl. Coat the inside of the bowl with vegetable oil spray, and place the bowl in a roasting pan. Gently mound and pack the stuffing into the foil bowl and position the chicken over the stuffing. Roast the chicken until just beginning to brown, about

30 minutes. Rotate the pan and continue to roast until the skin is crisped and deep golden brown, the thickest part of the breasts registers 160 to 165 degrees, and the thickest part of the thighs registers 175 degrees on an instant-read thermometer, 25 to 35 minutes longer. Transfer the chicken to a carving board and let rest for 10 minutes.

4. While the chicken rests, transfer the stuffing to a serving bowl and fluff. Cover the stuffing with foil to keep warm. Carve the chicken and serve with the stuffing.

Mushroom-Leek Bread Stuffing with Herbs

MAKES ABOUT 6 CUPS

The dried bread cubes for this stuffing can be stored in an airtight container for up to 1 week.

- 6 slices high-quality white sandwich bread, cut into ¼-inch cubes
- 2 tablespoons unsalted butter
- 1 leek, white and light green parts only, halved lengthwise, sliced ⅛ inch thick, and rinsed thoroughly
- 1 celery rib, chopped fine
- 8 ounces white mushrooms, wiped clean and chopped medium
- ¼ cup minced fresh parsley leaves
- 2 medium garlic cloves, minced or pressed through a garlic press (about 2 teaspoons)
- ½ teaspoon minced fresh sage leaves or ¼ teaspoon dried sage
- ½ teaspoon minced fresh thyme leaves or ¼ teaspoon dried thyme
- ½ cup plus 2 tablespoons low-sodium chicken broth
- 1 large egg
- ½ teaspoon table salt
- ½ teaspoon ground black pepper

1. Adjust an oven rack to the middle position and heat the oven to 250 degrees. Spread the bread cubes in a single layer on a rimmed baking sheet. Bake until thoroughly dried but not browned, about 30 minutes, stirring halfway through the baking time.

2. Meanwhile, melt the butter in a 12-inch skillet over medium-high heat. Add the leek, celery, and mushrooms and cook, stirring occasionally, until the vegetables begin to brown, 6 to 8 minutes. Stir in the parsley, garlic, sage, and thyme and cook until fragrant, about 30 seconds.

3. Whisk the broth, egg, salt, and pepper together in a large bowl. Add the bread cubes and leek-mushroom mixture and toss gently until evenly moistened and combined. Use as directed.

ROASTED CORNISH GAME HENS

WHY THIS RECIPE WORKS: Quick-cooking roasted Cornish game hens are an easy, elegant dinner option, but achieving crispy skin and tender meat in the short cooking time can be a challenge. Poking holes in the skin helped the fat to render quickly. To help the skin crisp up and brown, we used a baking powder rub and let the hens air-dry in the refrigerator overnight. To guarantee evenly golden skin, we butterflied the hens and started cooking them skin side down on a preheated baking sheet. Finally, we flipped them over for a final stint under the broiler. To season the meat inside and out, we added a light coating of kosher salt and fragrant spices on the undersides of the birds.

Roasted Cornish Game Hens

SERVES 4

This recipe requires refrigerating the salted meat for at least 4 hours or up to 24 hours before cooking (a longer salting time is preferable). If your hens weigh 1½ to 2 pounds, cook three instead of four, and extend the initial cooking time in step 5 to 15 minutes. We prefer Bell and Evans Cornish Game Hens.

- 4 (1¼- to 1½-pound) Cornish game hens, giblets discarded
- Kosher salt and pepper
- ¼ teaspoon vegetable oil
- 1 teaspoon baking powder
- Vegetable oil spray

1. Using kitchen shears and working with 1 hen at a time, with hen breast side down, cut through bones on either side of backbone; discard backbone. Lay hens breast side up on counter. Using sharp chef's knife, cut through center of breast to make 2 halves.

2. Using your fingers, carefully separate skin from breasts and thighs. Using metal skewer or tip of paring knife, poke 10 to 15 holes in fat deposits on top of breasts and thighs. Tuck wingtips underneath hens. Pat hens dry with paper towels.

3. Sprinkle 1 tablespoon salt on underside (bone side) of hens. Combine 1 tablespoon salt and oil in small bowl and stir until salt is evenly coated with oil. Add baking powder and stir until well combined. Turn hens skin side up and rub salt–baking powder mixture evenly over surface. Arrange hens skin side up and in single layer on large platter or plates and refrigerate, uncovered, for at least 4 hours or up to 24 hours.

4. Adjust oven racks to upper-middle and lower positions, place rimmed baking sheet on lower rack, and heat oven to 500 degrees.

5. Once oven is fully heated, spray skin side of hens with oil spray and season with pepper. Carefully transfer hens, skin side down, to preheated sheet and cook for 10 minutes.

6. Remove hens from oven and heat broiler. Flip hens skin side up. Transfer sheet to upper rack and broil until well browned and breasts register 160 degrees and drumsticks/thighs register 175 degrees, about 5 minutes, rotating sheet as needed to promote even browning. Transfer to platter or individual plates and serve.

Herb-Roasted Cornish Game Hens

In step 3, combine 2 tablespoons salt with 1 teaspoon dried thyme, 1 teaspoon dried marjoram, and 1 teaspoon dried crushed rosemary. Sprinkle half of salt mixture on underside of hens; add oil to remaining salt-herb mixture until mixture is evenly coated with oil. Add baking powder to oil-salt mixture and proceed with recipe.

Cumin-Coriander Roasted Cornish Game Hens

In step 3, combine 2 tablespoons salt with 2 teaspoons ground cumin, 2 teaspoons ground coriander, 1 teaspoon paprika, and 1/4 teaspoon cayenne pepper. Sprinkle half of salt mixture on underside of hens; add oil to remaining salt mixture until mixture is evenly coated with oil. Add baking powder to oil-salt mixture and proceed with recipe.

Oregano-Anise Roasted Cornish Game Hens

In step 3, combine salt with 1 teaspoon dried oregano, 1/2 teaspoon anise seeds, and 1/2 teaspoon hot smoked paprika. Sprinkle half of salt mixture on underside of hens; add oil to remaining salt mixture until mixture is evenly coated with oil. Add baking powder to oil-salt mixture and proceed with recipe.

NOTES FROM THE TEST KITCHEN

GETTING CORNISH GAME HENS TO CRISP QUICKLY AND EVENLY

Because the meat on Cornish game hens finishes cooking long before their skin crisps, we devised a few tricks to accelerate the skin's progress.

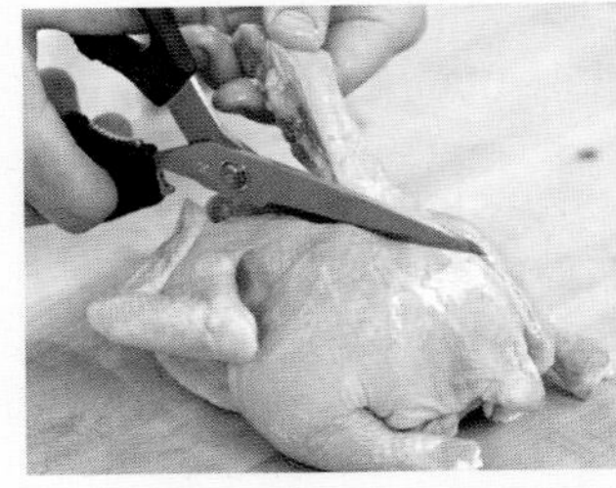

1. Cutting out the backbones and flattening the birds promotes uniform browning.

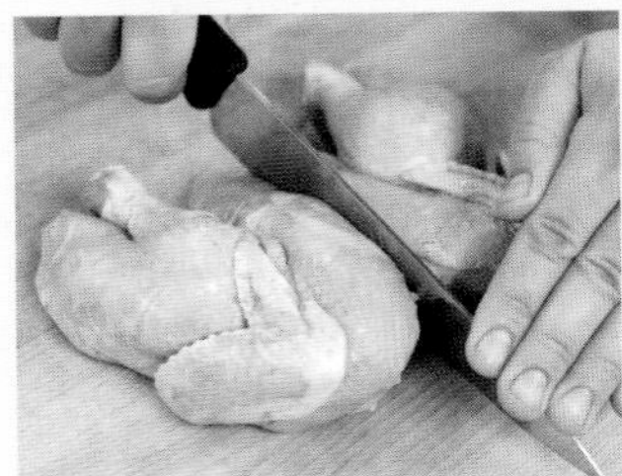

2. Halving the flattened hens (simple knife work with small birds) makes them easier to serve.

3. Loosening and poking holes in the skin allows the fat to drain during cooking, aiding crisping.

4. Rubbing the birds with salt and baking powder and then chilling them wicks away moisture.

5. Starting the birds skin side down on a preheated baking sheet effectively (and efficiently) crisps their skin.

FRIED CHICKEN

WHY THIS RECIPE WORKS: Frying chicken at home is a daunting task, with its messy preparation and spattering hot fat. In the end, the chicken often ends up disappointingly greasy, with a peeling crust and dry, tasteless meat. We wanted fried chicken worthy of the mess and splatter: moist, seasoned meat coated with a delicious, crispy mahogany crust.

We soaked chicken parts in a seasoned buttermilk brine for ultimate flavor and juiciness. Then we air-dried the brined chicken parts to help ensure a crisp skin. Flour made the crispest coating. We found that peanut oil can withstand the demands of frying and has the most neutral flavor of all the oils tested. Vegetable oil was a close runner-up. As for frying the chicken, we found that a Dutch oven worked best. With its high sides and lid, the Dutch oven minimized splatters and retained heat which helped the chicken cook through.

Crispy Fried Chicken

SERVES 4 TO 6

Avoid using kosher chicken in this recipe or it will be too salty. Maintaining an even oil temperature is key. After the chicken is added to the pot, the temperature will drop dramatically, and most of the frying will be done at about 325 degrees. Use an instant-read thermometer with a high upper range; a clip-on candy/deep-fry thermometer is fine, too, though it can be clipped to the pot only for the uncovered portion of frying.

CHICKEN

- ½ cup table salt
- ¼ cup sugar
- 2 tablespoons paprika
- 7 cups buttermilk
- 3 medium garlic heads, cloves separated and smashed
- 3 bay leaves, crumbled
- 4 pounds bone-in, skin-on chicken pieces (split breasts cut in half, drumsticks, and/or thighs), trimmed (see note)
- 3–4 quarts peanut oil or vegetable oil, for frying

COATING

- 4 cups (20 ounces) unbleached all-purpose flour
- 1 large egg
- 1 teaspoon baking powder
- ½ teaspoon baking soda
- 1 cup buttermilk

1. FOR THE CHICKEN: Dissolve the salt, sugar, and paprika in the buttermilk in a large container. Add the garlic and bay leaves, submerge the chicken in the brine, cover, and refrigerate for 2 to 3 hours.

2. Rinse the chicken well and place in a single layer on a wire rack set over a rimmed baking sheet. Refrigerate uncovered for 2 hours. (At this point, the chicken can be covered with plastic wrap and refrigerated for up to 6 more hours.)

3. Adjust an oven rack to the middle position and heat the oven to 200 degrees. In a large Dutch oven, heat 2 inches of oil over medium-high heat to 375 degrees (see note).

4. FOR THE COATING: Place the flour in a shallow dish. Whisk the egg, baking powder, and baking soda together in a medium bowl, then whisk in the buttermilk (the mixture will bubble and foam). Working with 3 chicken pieces at a time, dredge in the flour, shaking off the excess, then coat with the egg mixture, allowing the excess to drip off. Finally, coat with flour again, shake off the excess, and return to the wire rack.

5. When the oil is hot, add half of the chicken pieces to the pot, skin side down, cover, and fry until deep golden brown, 7 to 11 minutes, adjusting the heat as necessary to maintain an oil temperature of about 325 degrees. (After 4 minutes, check the chicken pieces for even browning and rearrange if some pieces are browning faster than others.) Turn the chicken pieces over and continue to cook until the thickest part of the breasts registers 160 to 165 degrees and the thickest part of the thighs or drumsticks registers 175 degrees on an instant-read thermometer, 6 to 8 minutes. Drain the chicken briefly on a paper towel–lined plate, then transfer to a clean wire rack set over a rimmed baking sheet and keep warm in the oven.

6. Return the oil to 375 degrees (if necessary) over medium-high heat and repeat with the remaining chicken pieces. Serve.

EASIER FRIED CHICKEN

WHY THIS RECIPE WORKS: Crackling-crisp, golden-brown, and juicy—what's not to love about fried chicken? In a word, frying. Heating more than a quart of fat on the stovetop can be daunting for home cooks. We wanted to find a way to prepare fried chicken without having to heat up a pot full of oil. To season the meat and ensure it turned out juicy, we soaked chicken parts in a buttermilk brine. We also incorporated baking powder, an unconventional ingredient in fried chicken, into our dredging mixture. As the chicken fried, the baking powder released carbon dioxide gas, leavening the crust and increasing its surface area, keeping it light and crisp. And while most dredging mixtures contain purely dry ingredients, we added a little buttermilk to our mixture because the small clumps of batter it formed turn ultra-crisp once fried. To streamline frying the chicken, we turned to a hybrid method where we fried the chicken until just lightly browned on both sides in less than half the amount of oil we'd typically use. Then we transferred the chicken to the oven to finish cooking through. Setting the chicken on a rack promoted air circulation all around the meat for an evenly crisp crust.

Easier Fried Chicken

SERVES 4

A whole 4-pound chicken, cut into eight pieces, can be used instead of the chicken parts. Skinless chicken pieces are also an acceptable substitute, but the meat will come out slightly drier. A Dutch oven with an 11-inch diameter can be used in place of the straight-sided sauté pan.

- 1¼ cups buttermilk
- Table salt
- Dash of hot sauce
- 3 teaspoons ground black pepper
- 1 teaspoon garlic powder
- 1 teaspoon paprika
- ¼ teaspoon cayenne pepper
- 3½ pounds bone-in, skin-on chicken parts (breasts, thighs, and drumsticks, or a mix, with breasts cut in half), trimmed of excess fat (see note)
- 2 cups unbleached all-purpose flour
- 2 teaspoons baking powder
- 1¾ cups vegetable oil

1. Whisk 1 cup of the buttermilk, 1 tablespoon salt, the hot sauce, 1 teaspoon of the black pepper, ¼ teaspoon of the garlic powder, ¼ teaspoon of the paprika, and a pinch of cayenne together in a large bowl. Add the chicken pieces and turn to coat. Refrigerate, covered, for at least 1 hour or up to overnight.

2. Adjust an oven rack to the middle position and heat the oven to 400 degrees. Whisk the flour, baking powder, 1 teaspoon salt, and the remaining 2 teaspoons black pepper, the remaining ¾ teaspoon garlic powder, the remaining ¾ teaspoon paprika, and the remaining cayenne together in a large bowl. Add the remaining ¼ cup buttermilk to the flour mixture and mix with your fingers until combined and small clumps form. Working with one piece at a time, dredge the chicken pieces in the flour mixture, pressing the mixture onto the pieces to form a thick, even coating. Place the dredged chicken on a large plate, skin side up.

3. Heat the oil in an 11-inch straight-sided sauté pan over medium-high heat to 375 degrees, about 5 minutes. Carefully place the chicken pieces in the pan, skin side down, and cook until golden brown, 3 to 5 minutes. Carefully flip the chicken pieces and continue to cook until golden brown on the second side, 2 to 4 minutes longer. Transfer the chicken to a wire rack set over a rimmed baking sheet. Bake the chicken until an instant-read thermometer inserted into the thickest part of the chicken registers 160 degrees for the breasts and 175 for the legs and thighs, 15 to 20 minutes. (Smaller pieces may cook faster than larger pieces. Remove the chicken pieces from the oven as they reach the correct temperature.) Let the chicken rest for 5 minutes before serving.

OVEN-FRIED CHICKEN

WHY THIS RECIPE WORKS: Oven-fried chicken never seems to taste as good as the real thing. The coating, often plain bread crumbs or cornflakes, never gets as crunchy or as flavorful as a deep-fried coating does. We wanted a good alternative to regular fried chicken that would have real crunch and good flavor. We soaked bone-in chicken legs and thighs in a buttermilk brine to achieve maximum juiciness. And we removed the skin from the chicken before brining because it didn't render in the oven. A mixture of eggs and mustard helped the crumbs stick to the chicken. Melba toast crumbs made the crispest coating. We baked the chicken on a wire rack set over a baking sheet that we had lined with foil. This method allowed heat to circulate around the chicken during baking, resulting in crisp chicken all over without turning.

Oven-Fried Chicken

SERVES 4

Avoid using kosher chicken in this recipe or it will be too salty. If you don't want to buy whole chicken legs and cut them into drumsticks and thighs, simply buy four drumsticks and four thighs. To make Melba toast crumbs, place the toasts in a heavy-duty zipper-lock freezer bag, seal, and pound with a meat pounder or other heavy blunt object. Leave some crumbs in the mixture the size of pebbles, but most should resemble coarse sand.

CHICKEN

- ½ cup plus 2 tablespoons table salt
- ¼ cup sugar
- 2 tablespoons paprika
- 3 medium heads garlic, cloves separated
- 3 bay leaves, crumbled
- 7 cups buttermilk
- 4 whole chicken legs, separated into drumsticks and thighs and skin removed (see note)

COATING

- ¼ cup vegetable oil
- 1 box (about 5 ounces) plain Melba toast, crushed (see note)
- 2 large eggs
- 1 tablespoon Dijon mustard
- 1 teaspoon dried thyme
- ¾ teaspoon table salt
- ½ teaspoon ground black pepper
- ½ teaspoon dried oregano
- ¼ teaspoon garlic powder
- ¼ teaspoon cayenne pepper (optional)

1. FOR THE CHICKEN: In a large zipper-lock bag, combine the salt, sugar, paprika, garlic cloves, and bay leaves. With a flat meat pounder, smash the garlic into the salt and spice mixture thoroughly. Pour the mixture into a large container. Add the buttermilk and stir until the salt and sugar are completely dissolved. Submerge the chicken in the brine and refrigerate for 2 to 3 hours. Rinse the chicken well and place on a large wire rack set over a rimmed baking sheet. Refrigerate uncovered for 2 hours. (After 2 hours, the chicken can be covered with plastic wrap and refrigerated up to 6 hours longer.)

2. Adjust an oven rack to the upper-middle position and heat the oven to 400 degrees. Line a large, rimmed baking sheet with foil and set a large wire rack over the pan.

3. FOR THE COATING: Drizzle the oil over the Melba toast crumbs in a pie plate or shallow dish; toss well to coat. Mix the eggs, mustard, thyme, salt, pepper, oregano, garlic powder, and cayenne (if using) with a fork in a second plate.

4. Working with one piece at a time, coat the chicken on both sides with the egg mixture. Set the chicken in the Melba crumbs, sprinkle the crumbs over the chicken, and press to coat. Turn the chicken over and repeat on the other side. Gently shake off the excess and place on the rack. Bake until the chicken is deep nutty brown and the thickest part of a piece registers 175 degrees on an instant-read thermometer, about 40 minutes. Serve.

BUFFALO WINGS

WHY THIS RECIPE WORKS: Buffalo wings are the ultimate bar snack. Great wings boast juicy meat, a crisp coating, and a spicy, sweet, and vinegary sauce. But dry, flabby wings are often the norm and the sauce can be scorchingly hot. We wanted perfectly cooked wings, coated in a well-seasoned sauce—good enough to serve with our creamy blue cheese dressing. We coated the wings with cornstarch for a super crisp exterior and deep-fried the wings for the best texture. Then we deepened the flavor of the traditional hot sauce by adding brown sugar and cider vinegar. For heat, we chose Frank's RedHot Original Sauce, which is traditional, but not very spicy, so we added a little Tabasco for even more kick.

Buffalo Wings

SERVES 6 TO 8

Frank's RedHot Original Sauce is not terribly spicy. We like to combine it with a more potent hot sauce, such as Tabasco, to bring up the heat.

SAUCE

- 4 tablespoons (½ stick) unsalted butter
- ½ cup Frank's RedHot Original Sauce (see note)
- 2 tablespoons Tabasco or other hot sauce, plus more to taste (see note)
- 1 tablespoon packed dark brown sugar
- 2 teaspoons cider vinegar

WINGS

- 1–2 quarts peanut oil, for frying
- 3 tablespoons cornstarch
- 1 teaspoon table salt
- 1 teaspoon ground black pepper
- 1 teaspoon cayenne pepper
- 18 chicken wings (about 3 pounds), wings separated into 2 parts at joint and wingtips removed (see photos)

VEGETABLES AND DRESSING

- 2 medium carrots, peeled and cut into thin sticks
- 4 medium celery ribs, cut into thin sticks
- 1 recipe Rich and Creamy Blue Cheese Dressing (see page 37)

1. FOR THE SAUCE: Melt the butter in a small saucepan over low heat. Whisk in the hot sauces, brown sugar, and vinegar until combined. Remove from the heat and set aside.

2. FOR THE WINGS: Heat the oven to 200 degrees. Line a baking sheet with paper towels. In a large Dutch oven fitted with a clip-on candy thermometer, heat 2½ inches of oil over medium-high heat to 360 degrees. While the oil heats, combine the cornstarch, salt, black pepper, and cayenne in a small bowl. Dry the chicken with paper towels and place the pieces in a large mixing bowl. Sprinkle the spice mixture over the wings and toss with a rubber spatula until evenly coated. Fry half of the chicken wings until golden and crisp, 10 to 12 minutes. With a slotted spoon, transfer the fried chicken wings to the prepared baking sheet. Keep the first batch of chicken warm in the oven while frying the remaining wings.

3. TO SERVE: Pour the sauce mixture into a large bowl, add the chicken wings, and toss until the wings are uniformly coated. Serve immediately with the carrot and celery sticks and blue cheese dressing on the side.

NOTES FROM THE TEST KITCHEN

CUTTING UP CHICKEN WINGS

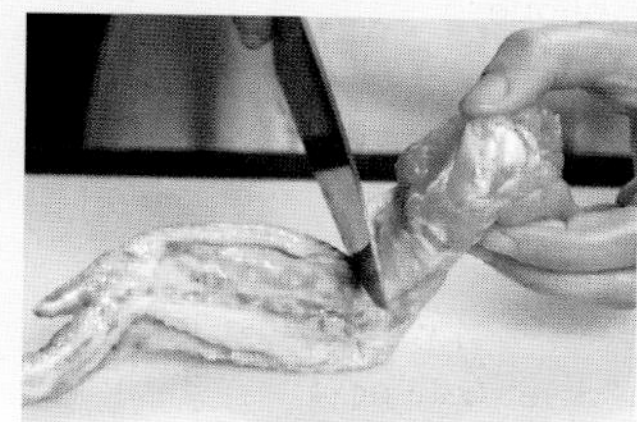
1. Cut into the skin between the larger sections of the wing until you hit the joint.

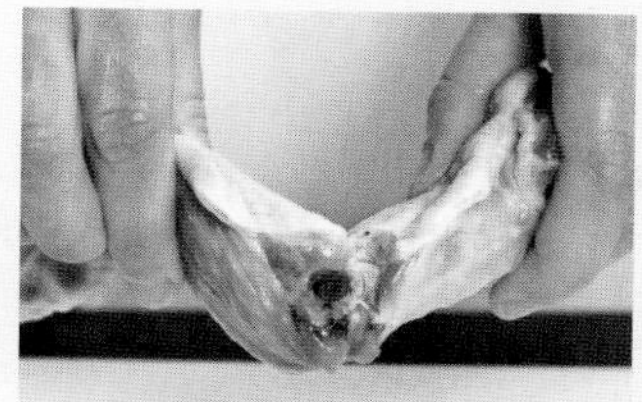
2. Bend back the two sections to pop and break the joint.

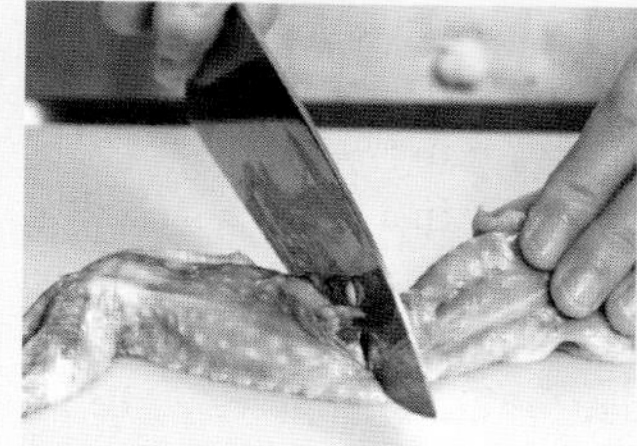
3. Cut through the skin and flesh to completely separate the two meaty portions.

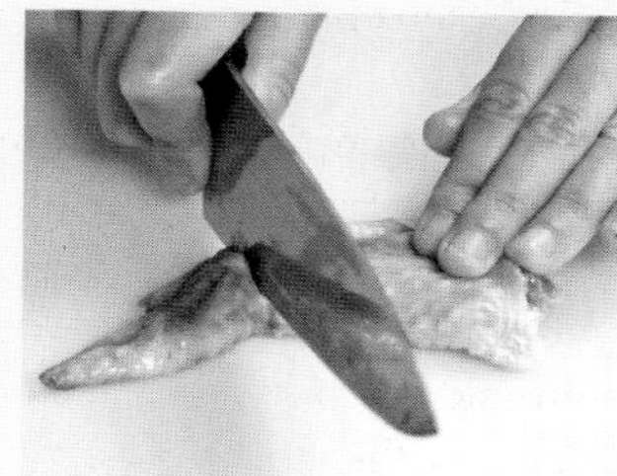
4. Hack off the wingtip and discard.

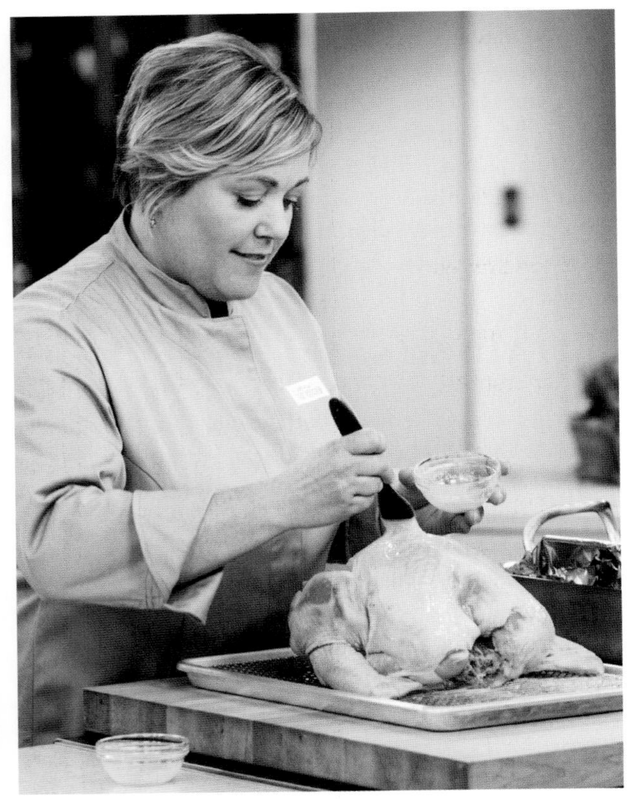

CHAPTER 6

TALKING TURKEY AND ALL THE TRIMMINGS

MORE RECIPES FOR ROUNDING OUT YOUR HOLIDAY MEAL

CLASSIC ROAST TURKEY

WHY THIS RECIPE WORKS: Few of us want to take chances when cooking the holiday bird. We wanted to find a way that guaranteed moist, flavorful meat and bronzed skin—a true holiday table centerpiece.

First we brined our turkey, which helped prevent the meat from drying out and also seasoned it right to the bone. After brining, we rinsed the bird of excess salt and let it rest on a wire rack in the refrigerator so that the skin dried out. This step helped ensure the skin would cook up crisp, not flabby. Placing the turkey on a V-rack allowed for air circulation all around so that the bird cooked evenly. And turning the turkey three times also helped to ensure even cooking. Finally, once the turkey was cooked, we waited 30 minutes before carving it. That might seem like a long time, but it allowed the juices in the turkey to redistribute so that, once carved, each slice was moist and full of flavor.

Classic Roast Turkey

SERVES 10 TO 12

Resist the temptation to tent the roasted turkey with foil while it rests on the carving board. Covering the bird will make the skin soggy.

- 2 cups table salt
- 1 (12- to 14-pound) turkey; giblets, neck, and tailpiece removed and reserved for gravy
- 2 medium onions, chopped coarse
- 2 medium carrots, chopped coarse
- 2 celery ribs, chopped coarse
- 6 sprigs fresh thyme
- 3 tablespoons unsalted butter, melted
- 1 cup water, plus more as needed
- 1 recipe Giblet Pan Gravy (recipe follows)

1. Dissolve the salt in 2 gallons cold water in a large container. Submerge the turkey in the brine, cover, and refrigerate or store in a very cool spot (40 degrees or less) for 4 to 6 hours.

2. Set a wire rack over a large rimmed baking sheet. Remove the turkey from the brine and rinse it well. Pat the turkey dry, inside and out, with paper towels. Place the turkey on the prepared baking sheet. Refrigerate, uncovered, for at least 8 hours or overnight.

3. Adjust an oven rack to the lowest position and heat the oven to 400 degrees. Line a V-rack with heavy duty foil and poke several holes in the foil. Set the V-rack in a roasting pan and spray the foil with vegetable oil spray.

4. Toss half of the onions, carrots, celery, and thyme with 1 tablespoon of the melted butter in a medium bowl and place inside the turkey. Tie the legs together with kitchen twine and tuck the wings under the bird. Scatter the remaining vegetables into the roasting pan.

5. Pour 1 cup water over the vegetable mixture. Brush the turkey breast with 1 tablespoon more melted butter, then place the turkey, breast side down, on the V-rack. Brush with the remaining 1 tablespoon melted butter.

6. Roast the turkey for 45 minutes. Remove the pan from the oven; baste with juices from the pan. With a dish towel in each hand, turn the turkey leg/thigh side up. If the liquid in the pan has totally evaporated, add another ½ cup water. Return the turkey to the oven and roast for 15 minutes. Remove the turkey from the oven again, baste, and turn the other leg/thigh side up; roast for another 15 minutes. Remove the turkey from the oven for a final time, baste, and turn it breast side up; roast until the thickest part of the breast registers 160 to 165 degrees and the thickest part of the thigh registers 175 degrees on an instant-read thermometer, 30 to 45 minutes.

7. Remove the turkey from the oven. Gently tip the turkey so that any accumulated juices in the cavity run into the roasting pan. Transfer the turkey to a carving board and let rest, uncovered, for 30 minutes. Carve the turkey and serve with the gravy.

Giblet Pan Gravy

MAKES ABOUT 6 CUPS

Complete step 1 up to a day ahead, if desired. Begin step 3 once the bird has been removed from the oven and is resting on a carving board.

- 1 tablespoon vegetable oil
- Reserved turkey giblets, neck, and tailpiece
- 1 medium onion, chopped
- 4 cups low-sodium chicken broth
- 2 cups water
- 2 sprigs fresh thyme
- 8 sprigs fresh parsley
- 3 tablespoons unsalted butter
- ¼ cup unbleached all-purpose flour
- 1 cup dry white wine
- Table salt and ground black pepper

1. Heat the oil in a large Dutch oven over medium heat until shimmering; add the giblets, neck, and tailpiece, and cook until golden and fragrant, about 5 minutes. Add the onion and continue to cook until softened, 3 to 4 minutes longer. Reduce the heat to low, cover, and cook until the turkey parts and onion release their juices, about 15 minutes. Add the broth, water, and herbs, bring to a boil, and adjust the heat to low. Simmer, uncovered, skimming any impurities that may rise to the surface, until the broth is rich and flavorful, about 30 minutes longer. Strain the broth into a large container and reserve the giblets. When cool enough to handle, chop the giblets. Refrigerate the giblets and broth until ready to use. (The broth can be stored in the refrigerator in an airtight container for up to 1 day.)

2. While the turkey is roasting, return the reserved turkey broth to a simmer. Heat the butter in a large saucepan over medium-low heat. Vigorously whisk in the flour (the mixture will froth and then thin out again). Cook slowly, stirring constantly, until nutty brown and fragrant, 10 to 15 minutes. Vigorously whisk all but 1 cup of the hot broth into the flour mixture. Bring to a boil, then continue to simmer, stirring occasionally, until the gravy is lightly thickened and very flavorful, about 30 minutes longer. Set aside until the turkey is done.

3. When the turkey has been transferred to a carving board to rest, spoon out and discard as much fat as possible from the roasting pan, leaving the caramelized herbs and vegetables. Place the roasting pan over two burners set on medium-high heat. Return the gravy to a simmer. Add the wine to the roasting pan of caramelized vegetables, scraping up any browned bits with a wooden spoon, and boil until reduced by half, about 5 minutes. Add the remaining 1 cup turkey broth and continue to simmer for 15 minutes; strain the pan juices into the gravy, pressing as much juice as possible out of the vegetables. Stir the reserved giblets into the gravy and return to a boil. Season with salt and pepper to taste and serve.

BEHIND THE SCENES

HOW BRINING SAVED THANKSGIVING

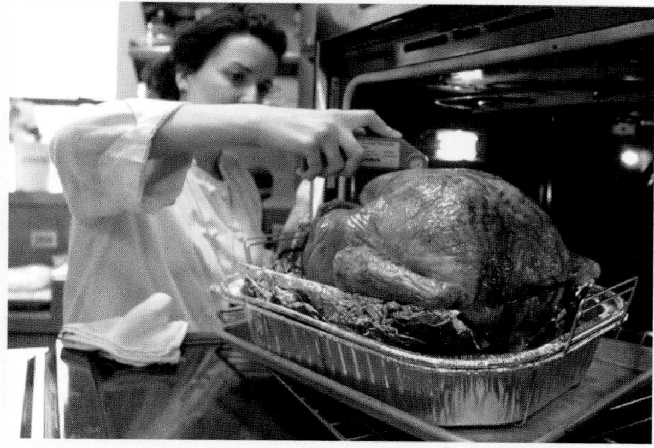

Once upon a time, the only thing the Thanksgiving turkey had going for it was tradition—and even that was tenuous, as many of us sometimes dreamed of cheating with a big buttery beef tenderloin. The problem was a familiar one. Sometimes the bird turned out juicy and flavorful, but most often, it was a dry disappointment. Passing the gravy didn't help much either. Then, 15 years ago, the test kitchen came upon an obscure technique called brining. Brining turkey involves soaking the turkey in a saltwater solution (which sometimes includes sugar) before cooking—this protects it from the ravages of heat and guarantees tender, flavorful meat from the surface all the way to the bone. (Brining does the same for other delicate white meat like chicken and pork.) How does brining work?

Simply put, the brining solution flows into the meat, distributing moisture and seasoning. In our testing, we found that while a turkey roasted straight out of its package will retain about 82 percent of its total weight after cooking, a brined turkey will retain about 93 percent of its total weight after cooking—and thus be moister and more flavorful. Once a little-known technique, brining has now become mainstream—and Thanksgiving dinners everywhere are all the better for it.

ROAST TURKEY FOR A CROWD

WHY THIS RECIPE WORKS: Unless you have access to multiple ovens, only a very large turkey will do when you've got a crowd coming to dinner. But finding a container large enough to brine a gargantuan bird can be tricky. And turning the bird in the oven, our usual method for evenly cooked meat, can be hot, heavy, and dangerous. We wanted the Norman Rockwell picture of perfection: a crisp, mahogany skin wrapped around tender, moist meat. And it had to be easy to prepare in a real home kitchen.

We chose a Butterball turkey, which has already been brined for juicy flavor (a kosher bird, which has been salted, works well too). A combination of high and low heat resulted in a tender, juicy bird with deeply browned skin. We made the meat and pan drippings more flavorful with the addition of onion, carrot, and celery. A quartered lemon added bright, clean flavor. After roasting, we allowed the turkey to rest so the juices would redistribute, but didn't tent it with foil so the skin wouldn't become soggy. Serve with Giblet Pan Gravy for a Crowd (recipe follows).

Roast Turkey for a Crowd

SERVES ABOUT 20

Rotating the bird helps produce moist, evenly cooked meat, but for the sake of ease, you may opt not to rotate it. In that case, skip the step of lining the V-rack with foil and roast the bird breast side up for the entire cooking time. Because we do not brine the bird, we had the best results with a frozen Butterball (injected with salt and water) or a kosher bird (soaked in salt water during processing).

- 3 medium onions, chopped coarse
- 3 medium carrots, chopped coarse
- 3 celery ribs, chopped coarse
- 1 lemon, quartered
- 2 sprigs fresh thyme
- 5 tablespoons unsalted butter, melted
- 1 (18- to 22-pound) frozen Butterball or kosher turkey, fully thawed (see note); giblets, neck, and tailpiece removed and reserved for gravy
- 1 cup water, plus more as needed
- 1 teaspoon table salt
- 1 teaspoon ground black pepper
- 1 recipe Giblet Pan Gravy for a Crowd (recipe follows)

1. Adjust an oven rack to the lowest position. Heat the oven to 425 degrees. Line a large V-rack with heavy-duty foil and poke several holes in the foil. Set the V-rack in a large roasting pan and spray the foil with vegetable oil spray.

2. Toss half of the onions, carrots, celery, lemon, and thyme with 1 tablespoon of the melted butter in a medium bowl and place inside the turkey. Tie the legs together with kitchen twine and tuck the wings under the bird. Scatter the remaining vegetables into the roasting pan.

3. Pour 1 cup water over the vegetable mixture. Brush the turkey breast with 2 tablespoons more of the melted butter, then sprinkle with half of the salt and half of the pepper. Place the turkey, breast side down, on the V-rack. Brush with the remaining 2 tablespoons melted butter and sprinkle with the remaining salt and pepper.

4. Roast the turkey for 1 hour. Remove the pan from the oven; baste with juices from the pan. With a dish towel in each hand, turn the turkey breast side up. If the liquid in the pan has totally evaporated, add another ½ cup water. Lower the oven temperature to 325 degrees. Return the turkey to the oven and continue to roast until the thickest part of the breast registers 160 to 165 degrees and the thickest part of the thigh registers 175 degrees on an instant-read thermometer, about 2 hours longer.

5. Remove the turkey from the oven. Gently tip the turkey up so that any accumulated juices in the cavity run into the roasting pan. Transfer the turkey to a carving board. Let rest, uncovered, for 35 to 40 minutes. Carve the turkey and serve with the gravy.

Giblet Pan Gravy for a Crowd

MAKES ABOUT 8 CUPS

Complete step 1 up to a day ahead, if desired. Begin step 3 once the bird has been removed from the oven and is resting on a carving board.

- 1 tablespoon vegetable oil
- Reserved turkey giblets, neck, and tailpiece
- 1 medium onion, unpeeled and chopped
- 6 cups low-sodium chicken broth
- 3 cups water
- 2 sprigs fresh thyme
- 8 sprigs fresh parsley
- 5 tablespoons unsalted butter
- ¼ cup plus 2 tablespoons unbleached all-purpose flour
- 1½ cups dry white wine
- Table salt and ground black pepper

1. Heat the oil in a large Dutch oven over medium heat until shimmering; add the giblets, neck, and tailpiece, and cook until golden and fragrant, about 5 minutes. Add the onion and continue to cook until softened, 3 to 4 minutes longer. Reduce the heat to low, cover, and cook until the turkey parts and onion release their juices, about 15 minutes. Add the broth, water, and herbs, bring to a boil, and adjust the heat to low. Simmer, uncovered, skimming any impurities that may rise to the surface, until the broth is rich and flavorful, about 30 minutes longer. Strain the broth into a large container and reserve the giblets. When cool enough to handle, chop the giblets. Refrigerate the giblets and broth until ready to use. (The broth can be stored in the refrigerator in an airtight container for up to 1 day.)

2. While the turkey is roasting, return the reserved turkey broth to a simmer. Heat the butter in a large saucepan over medium-low heat. Vigorously whisk in the flour (the mixture will froth and then thin out again). Cook slowly, stirring constantly, until nutty brown and fragrant, 10 to 15 minutes. Vigorously whisk all but 2 cups of the hot broth into the flour mixture. Bring to a boil, then continue to simmer, stirring occasionally, until the gravy is lightly thickened and very flavorful, about 35 minutes longer. Set aside until the turkey is done.

3. When the turkey has been transferred to a carving board to rest, spoon out and discard as much fat as possible from the roasting pan, leaving the caramelized herbs and vegetables.

Place the roasting pan over two burners set on medium-high heat. Return the gravy to a simmer. Add the wine to the roasting pan of caramelized vegetables, scraping up any browned bits with a wooden spoon, and boil until reduced by half, about 7 minutes. Add the remaining 2 cups turkey broth and continue to simmer for 15 minutes; strain the pan juices into the gravy, pressing as much juice as possible out of the vegetables. Stir the reserved giblets into the gravy and return to a boil. Season with salt and pepper to taste and serve.

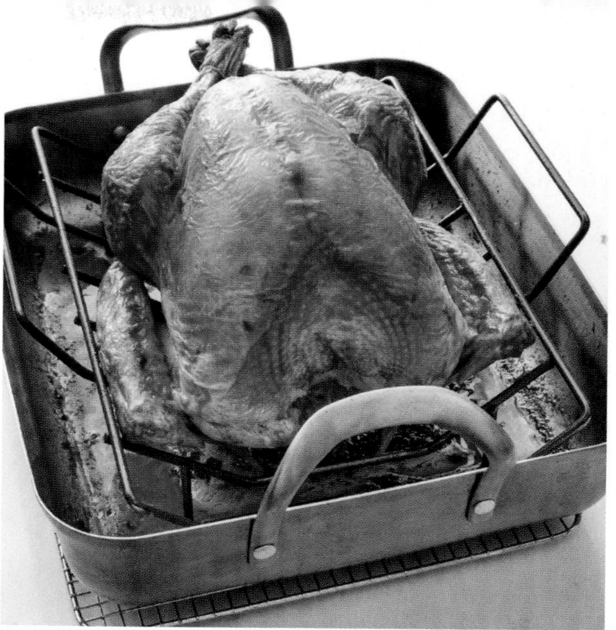

OLD-FASHIONED STUFFED TURKEY

WHY THIS RECIPE WORKS: Perfecting one aspect of a roast turkey often comes at the cost of another. Crisp skin means dry white meat. Brining adds moisture, but can turn the skin soggy. And stuffing the cavity compounds the headache, slowing the roasting time and upping the chance for uneven cooking. We wanted a turkey with everything: juicy meat, crisply burnished skin, and rich-flavored stuffing that cooked inside the bird.

For the crispiest possible skin, we opted for salting over brining. Salting initially draws moisture out of the meat, but after a long rest in the refrigerator, all the moisture gets slowly drawn back in, seasoning the meat and helping it retain moisture. Next we turned to slow roasting and started the bird in a relatively low oven, then cranked the temperature to give it a final blast of skin-crisping heat and to bring the center up to temperature. It worked beautifully, yielding breast meat that was moist and tender. For even crispier skin, we massaged it with a baking powder and salt rub. The baking powder dehydrates the skin and raises its pH, making it more conducive to browning. We also poked holes in the skin to help rendering fat escape.

And for extra flavor, we draped the bird with meaty salt pork, which we removed and drained before cranking up the heat so the bird didn't taste too smoky. To make sure the stuffing was cooked through, we started half of it in the bird (in a cheesecloth bag for easy removal) to give it meaty flavor, then combined it with the uncooked batch to finish baking it while the turkey rested.

Old-Fashioned Stuffed Turkey

SERVES 10 TO 12

Table salt is not recommended for this recipe because it is too fine. To roast a kosher or self-basting turkey (such as a frozen Butterball), do not salt it in step 1. Look for salt pork that is roughly equal parts fat and lean meat. The bread can be toasted up to 1 day in advance. Serve with Make-Ahead Turkey Gravy (recipe follows).

TURKEY

- 1 (12- to 14-pound) turkey, giblets and neck reserved for gravy, if making (see note)
- 3 tablespoons plus 2 teaspoons kosher salt (see note)
- 2 teaspoons baking powder
- 12 ounces salt pork, cut into ¼-inch-thick slices and rinsed (see note)

STUFFING

- 1½ pounds (about 15 slices) high-quality white sandwich bread, cut into ½-inch cubes (about 12 cups)
- 4 tablespoons (½ stick) unsalted butter, plus extra for the baking dish
- 1 medium onion, minced
- 2 celery ribs, chopped fine
- Kosher salt and ground black pepper
- 2 tablespoons minced fresh thyme leaves
- 1 tablespoon minced fresh marjoram leaves
- 1 tablespoon minced fresh sage leaves
- 1½ cups low-sodium chicken broth
- 1 36-inch square cheesecloth, folded in quarters
- 2 large eggs

1. FOR THE TURKEY: Following the photos on page 147, use your fingers or the handle of a wooden spoon to separate the turkey skin from the meat on the breast, legs, thighs, and back; avoid breaking the skin. Rub 1 tablespoon of the salt evenly inside the cavity of the turkey, 1½ teaspoons salt under the skin of each breast half, and 1½ teaspoons salt under the skin of each leg. Wrap the turkey tightly with plastic wrap; refrigerate for 24 to 48 hours.

2. FOR THE STUFFING: Adjust an oven rack to the lowest position and heat the oven to 250 degrees. Spread the bread cubes in a single layer on a rimmed baking sheet; bake until the edges have dried but the centers are slightly moist (the cubes should yield to pressure), about 45 minutes, stirring several times during baking. Transfer to a large bowl and increase the oven temperature to 325 degrees.

NOTES FROM THE TEST KITCHEN

STUFFING A TURKEY

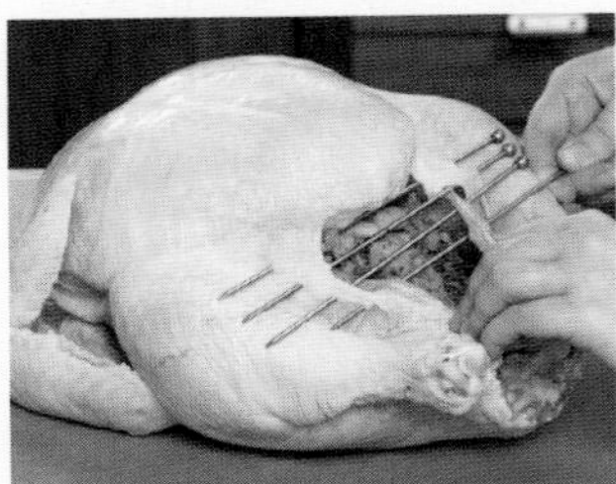

1. After placing 4 to 5 cups of the preheated stuffing into the turkey, use metal skewers (or cut bamboo skewers) and thread them through the skin on both sides of the cavity to seal the cavity shut.

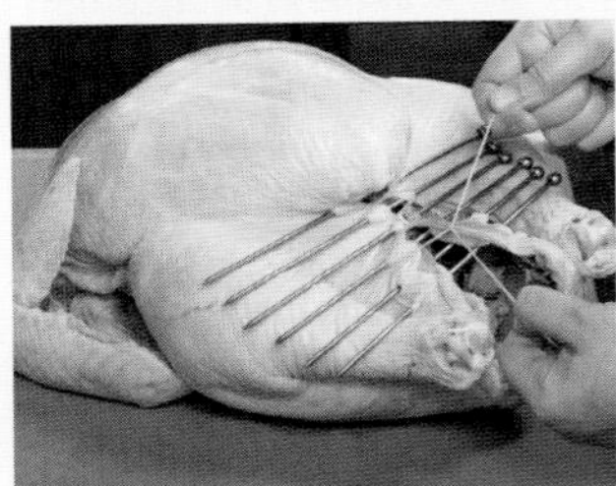

2. Center a 2-foot piece of kitchen twine on the top skewer and then cross the twine as you wrap each end of it around and under the skewers. Loosely tie the legs together with another short piece of twine.

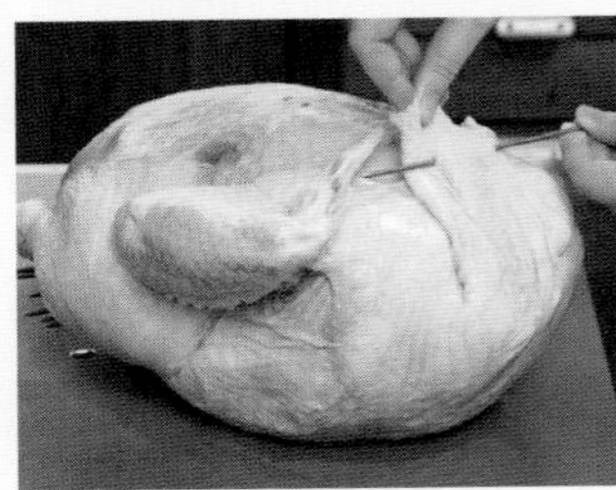

3. Flip the turkey over onto its breast. Stuff the neck cavity loosely with approximately 1 cup of stuffing. Pull the skin flap over and use a skewer to pin the flap to the turkey.

3. While the bread dries, heat the butter in a 12-inch skillet over medium-high heat; when the foaming subsides, add the onion, celery, 2 teaspoons salt, and 1 teaspoon pepper; cook, stirring occasionally, until the vegetables begin to soften and brown slightly, 7 to 10 minutes. Stir in the herbs; cook until fragrant, about 1 minute. Add the vegetables to the bowl with the dried bread; add 1 cup of the broth and toss until evenly moistened.

4. TO ROAST THE TURKEY: Combine the remaining 2 teaspoons salt and the baking powder in a small bowl. Remove the turkey from the refrigerator and unwrap. Thoroughly dry the turkey inside and out with paper towels. Using a skewer, poke 15 to 20 holes in the fat deposits on top of the breast halves and thighs, 4 to 5 holes in each deposit. Sprinkle the surface of the turkey with the salt–baking powder mixture and rub in the mixture with your hands, coating the skin evenly. Tuck the wings underneath the turkey. Line the turkey cavity with the cheesecloth, pack with 4 to 5 cups stuffing, and tie the ends of the cheesecloth together. Cover the remaining stuffing with plastic wrap and refrigerate. Using kitchen twine, loosely tie the turkey legs together. Place the turkey breast side down in a V-rack set in a roasting pan and drape the salt pork slices over the back.

5. Roast the turkey breast side down until the thickest part of the breast registers 130 degrees on an instant-read thermometer, 2 to 2½ hours. Remove the roasting pan from the oven and increase the oven temperature to 450 degrees. Transfer the turkey in the V-rack to a rimmed baking sheet. Remove and discard the salt pork. Using clean potholders or kitchen towels, rotate the turkey breast side up. Cut the twine binding the legs and remove the stuffing bag; empty into the reserved stuffing in the bowl. Pour the drippings from the roasting pan into a fat separator and reserve for gravy, if making.

6. Once the oven has come to temperature, return the turkey in the V-rack to the roasting pan and roast until the skin is golden brown and crisp, the thickest part of the breast registers 160 degrees, and the thickest part of the thigh registers 175 degrees, about 45 minutes, rotating the pan halfway through. Transfer the turkey to a carving board and let rest, uncovered, for 30 minutes.

7. While the turkey rests, reduce the oven temperature to 400 degrees. Whisk the eggs and remaining ½ cup broth together in a small bowl. Pour the egg mixture over the stuffing and toss to combine, breaking up any large chunks; spread in a buttered 13 by 9-inch baking dish. Bake until the stuffing registers 165 degrees and the top is golden brown, about 15 minutes. Carve the turkey and serve with the stuffing.

Make-Ahead Turkey Gravy

MAKES ABOUT 2 QUARTS

Note that the optional roast turkey drippings may be quite salty—add them carefully to the gravy in step 4 so the gravy does not become too salty.

- 6 turkey thighs, trimmed, or 9 wings, separated at the joints
- 2 medium carrots, chopped coarse
- 2 medium celery ribs, chopped coarse
- 2 medium onions, chopped coarse
- 1 head garlic, halved
- Vegetable oil spray
- 10 cups low-sodium chicken broth, plus extra as needed
- 2 cups dry white wine
- 12 sprigs fresh thyme
- Unsalted butter, as needed
- 1 cup unbleached all-purpose flour
- Table salt and ground black pepper
- Defatted drippings from Old-Fashioned Stuffed Turkey (page 137; optional)

1. Adjust an oven rack to the middle position and heat the oven to 450 degrees. Toss the thighs, carrots, celery, onions, and garlic together in a roasting pan and spray with vegetable oil spray. Roast, stirring occasionally, until well browned, 1½ to 1¾ hours.

2. Transfer the contents of the roasting pan to a large Dutch oven. Add the broth, wine, and thyme and bring to a boil, skimming as needed. Reduce to a gentle simmer and cook until the broth is brown and flavorful and measures about 8 cups when strained, about 1½ hours. Strain the broth through a fine-mesh strainer into a large container, pressing on the solids to extract as much liquid as possible; discard the solids. (The turkey broth can be cooled and refrigerated in an airtight container for up to 2 days or frozen for up to 1 month.)

3. Let the strained turkey broth settle (if necessary) then spoon off and reserve ½ cup of the fat that has risen to the top (add butter as needed if short on turkey fat). Heat the fat in a Dutch oven over medium-high heat until bubbling. Whisk in the flour and cook, whisking constantly, until well browned, 3 to 7 minutes.

4. Slowly whisk in the turkey broth and bring to a boil. Reduce to a simmer and cook until the gravy is very thick, 10 to 15 minutes. Add the defatted drippings (if using) to taste, then season with salt and pepper to taste and serve. (The gravy can be refrigerated in an airtight container for up to 2 days; reheat gently, adding additional chicken broth as needed to adjust the consistency).

CLASSIC ROAST STUFFED TURKEY

WHY THIS RECIPE WORKS: There is something undeniably festive about a stuffed roasted turkey, but more and more people nowadays roast turkeys unstuffed out of concern for health and safety. We wanted to find a way to safely and successfully roast a stuffed turkey, making sure that the breast meat would be succulent and the stuffing fully cooked.

At the outset, we decided to limit our turkey to a maximum of 14 pounds, because it is just too difficult to safely stuff and roast a larger bird. Often, the breast meat is a bone-dry 180 degrees by the time the stuffing reaches a safe 165 degrees. We got around this by heating the stuffing in the microwave before placing half of it in the bird to give it a head start on cooking. We baked the remaining stuffing separately in a casserole dish; this ensured that there would be enough stuffing to go around. We also brined the bird to add flavor and moisture (brining did not, as we feared, make the stuffing soggy or overly salty).

Classic Roast Stuffed Turkey

SERVES 10 TO 12

A 12- to 14-pound turkey will accommodate approximately half of the stuffing. Bake the remainder in a casserole dish while the bird rests before carving. If serving with Giblet Pan Gravy (page 134), note that you can complete step 1 up to a day ahead, if desired. Begin step 3 once the bird has been removed from the oven and is resting on a carving board.

- 2 cups table salt
- 1 (12- to 14-pound) turkey; giblets, neck, and tailpiece removed and reserved for gravy (see page 134)
- 2 medium onions, chopped coarse
- 1 medium carrot, chopped coarse
- 1 celery rib, chopped coarse
- 4 sprigs fresh thyme
- 1 cup water, plus more as needed
- 12 cups prepared stuffing (recipe follows)
- 3 tablespoons unsalted butter, plus extra for the casserole dish and foil
- ¼ cup low-sodium chicken broth
- 1 recipe Giblet Pan Gravy (page 134)

1. Dissolve the salt in 2 gallons cold water in a large container. Submerge the turkey in the brine, cover, and refrigerate or store in a very cool spot (40 degrees or less) for 4 to 6 hours.

2. Set a wire rack over a large rimmed baking sheet. Remove the turkey from the brine and rinse it well. Pat the turkey dry inside and out with paper towels. Place the turkey on the prepared baking sheet. Refrigerate, uncovered, and air-dry for at least 8 hours or overnight.

3. Adjust an oven rack to the lowest position and heat the oven to 400 degrees. Line a V-rack with heavy-duty foil and poke several holes in the foil. Set the V-rack inside a roasting pan and spray the foil with vegetable oil spray. Scatter the onions, carrot, celery, and thyme in the roasting pan. Pour 1 cup water over the vegetable mixture.

4. Place half of the stuffing in a buttered medium casserole dish, dot the surface with 1 tablespoon of the butter, cover with foil, and refrigerate until ready to use. Microwave the remaining stuffing on high power, stirring two or three times, until very hot (120 to 130 degrees on an instant-read thermometer), 6 to 8 minutes. Spoon 4 to 5 cups of stuffing into the turkey cavity until very loosely packed. Following the photos on page 138, secure the skin flap over the cavity opening with skewers. Melt the remaining 2 tablespoons butter. Tuck the wings under the bird, brush the turkey breast with half of the melted butter, then turn the turkey breast side down. Fill the neck cavity with the remaining heated stuffing and secure the skin flap over the opening. Place the turkey, breast side down, on the V-rack. Brush with the remaining butter.

5. Roast the turkey for 1 hour, then reduce the temperature to 250 degrees and roast for 2 hours longer, adding water if the pan becomes dry. Remove the pan from the oven (close the oven door) and, with a dish towel in each hand, turn the bird breast side up, and baste (the temperature of the thickest part of the breast should be 145 to 150 degrees). Increase the oven temperature to 400 degrees; continue to roast until the thickest part of the breast registers 160 to 165 degrees, the thickest part of the thigh registers 175 degrees, and the center of the stuffing registers 165 degrees on an instant-read thermometer, 1 to 1½ hours longer. Remove the turkey from the oven, transfer to a carving board, and let rest for 30 minutes.

6. Add the broth to the dish of reserved stuffing, replace the foil, and bake until hot throughout, about 20 minutes. Remove the foil; continue to bake until the stuffing forms a golden brown crust, about 15 minutes longer.

7. Carve the turkey and serve with the stuffing and the gravy.

Bread Stuffing with Bacon, Apples, Sage, and Caramelized Onions

MAKES ABOUT 12 CUPS

To dry the bread, spread the cubes out onto 2 large baking sheets and dry in a 300-degree oven for 30 to 60 minutes. Let the bread cool before using in the stuffing.

- 1 pound bacon, cut crosswise into ¼-inch strips
- 6 medium onions, sliced thin (about 7 cups)
- 1 teaspoon table salt
- 2 Granny Smith apples, peeled, cored, and cut into ½-inch cubes (about 2 cups)
- ½ cup fresh parsley leaves, chopped fine
- 3 tablespoons minced fresh sage leaves
- ½ teaspoon ground black pepper
- 3 pounds high-quality white sandwich bread, cut into ¾-inch cubes (about 12 cups)
- 1 cup low-sodium chicken broth
- 3 large eggs, lightly beaten

1. Cook the bacon in a large skillet or Dutch oven over medium heat until crisp and browned, about 12 minutes. Remove the bacon from the pan with a slotted spoon and drain on paper towels. Discard all but 3 tablespoons of the rendered bacon fat.

2. Increase the heat to medium-high and add the onions and 1/4 teaspoon of the salt. Cook the onions until golden in color, making sure to stir occasionally and scrape the sides and bottom of the pan, about 20 minutes. Reduce the heat to medium and continue to cook, stirring more often to prevent burning, until the onions are deep golden brown, another 5 minutes. Add the apples and continue to cook for another 5 minutes. Transfer the contents of the pan to a large bowl.

3. Add the parsley, sage, remaining 3/4 teaspoon salt, and the pepper to the bowl and mix to combine. Add the bread cubes.

4. Whisk the broth and eggs together in a small bowl. Pour the mixture over the bread cubes. Gently toss to evenly distribute the ingredients.

JULIA CHILD'S STUFFED TURKEY, UPDATED

WHY THIS RECIPE WORKS: In her 1989 cookbook, *The Way to Cook*, Julia Child separates a raw turkey into legs and breast to ensure that both white and dark meat are roasted to perfection. Other benefits include a quicker cook time and a small mound of rich sausage stuffing that tastes as though it has been roasted inside the bird. We loved this idea, but saw a couple of opportunities for improvement. In our version, we brined the breast to keep it juicy and flavorful. Jump-starting the cooking of the breast at 425 degrees decreased the overall cooking time, which also helped the meat to retain moisture. To make even more stuffing, we increased the amount of bread, and we swapped the sausage for the brighter flavor of dried cranberries.

Julia Child's Stuffed Turkey, Updated

SERVES 10 TO 12

This recipe calls for a natural, unenhanced turkey and requires brining the turkey breast in the refrigerator for 6 to 12 hours before cooking. If using a self-basting turkey (such as a frozen Butterball) or a kosher turkey, do not brine in step 3 and omit the salt in step 2. Trim any excess fat from the bird before cooking to ensure that the stuffing doesn't become greasy. The bottom of your roasting pan should be 7 to 8 inches from the top of the oven. In this recipe, we leave the stuffing in a warm oven while the turkey rests. If you need your oven during this time, you may opt to leave the stirred stuffing in the uncovered roasting pan at room temperature while the turkey rests and then reheat it in a 400-degree oven for 10 minutes before reassembling your turkey.

- 1 (12- to 15-pound) turkey, neck and giblets removed and reserved for gravy
- 1 teaspoon plus 2 tablespoons minced fresh sage
- Salt and pepper
- Wooden skewers
- 1½ pounds hearty white sandwich bread, cut into ½-inch cubes
- 1 tablespoon vegetable oil
- 3 tablespoons unsalted butter
- 3 onions, chopped fine
- 6 celery ribs, minced
- 1 cup dried cranberries
- 4 large eggs, beaten

1. With turkey breast side up, using boning or paring knife, cut through skin around leg quarter where it attaches to breast. Bend leg back to pop leg bone out of socket. Cut through joint to separate leg quarter. Repeat to remove second leg quarter. Working with 1 leg quarter at a time and with skin side down, use tip of knife to cut along sides of thighbone to expose bone, then slide knife under bone to free meat. Cut joint between thigh and leg and remove thighbone. Reserve thighbones for gravy.

2. Rub interior of each thigh with 1/2 teaspoon sage, 1/2 teaspoon salt, and 1/4 teaspoon pepper. Truss each thigh closed using wooden skewers and kitchen twine. Place leg quarters on large plate, cover, and refrigerate for 6 to 12 hours.

NOTES FROM THE TEST KITCHEN

DECONSTRUCTED TURKEY

Removing the leg quarters from a turkey and deboning the thighs may sound intimidating, but it really is a snap. Julia used a meat cleaver and rubber mallet to remove the backbone. But we found it easier to use only kitchen shears and a boning or paring knife, concentrating on severing the easy-to-cut ligaments, tendons, and cartilage between the bones instead of trying to hack through the bones themselves. Added bonus? Removing bones now makes it easier to carve later.

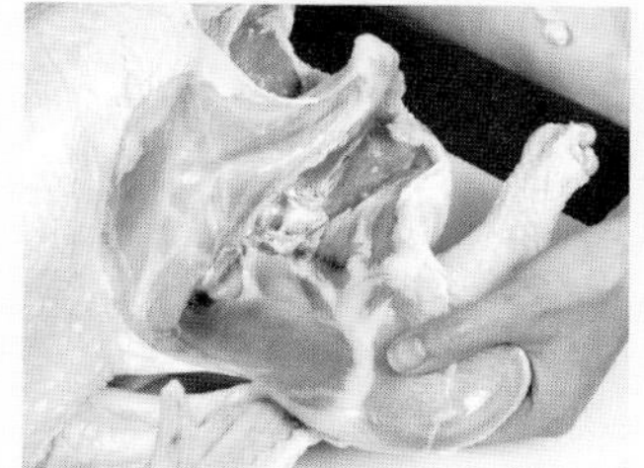

1. Using boning or paring knife, cut through skin around leg where it attaches to breast. Bend leg back to pop leg bone out of socket. Cut through joint to separate leg quarter.

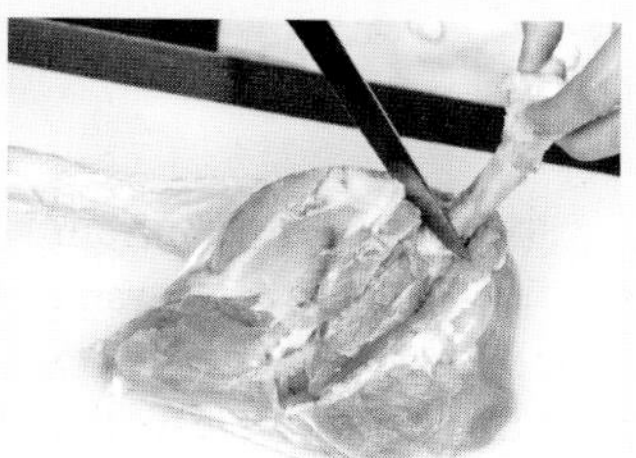

2. With tip of knife, cut along sides of thighbone to expose bone, then slide knife under bone to free meat. Without severing skin, cut joint between thigh and leg and remove thighbone.

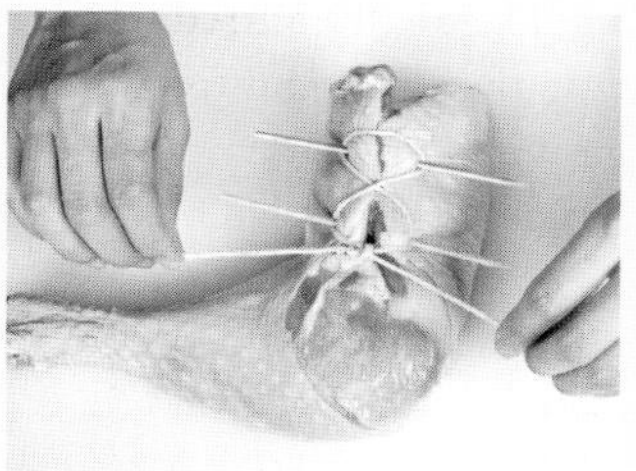

3. Rub interior of each thigh with sage, salt, and pepper. Truss thighs closed with wooden skewers and kitchen twine.

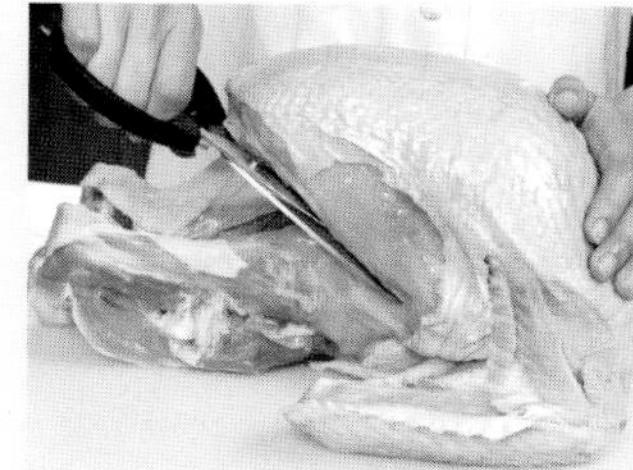

4. Using kitchen shears, cut through ribs, following line of fat running from tapered end of breast to wing joint.

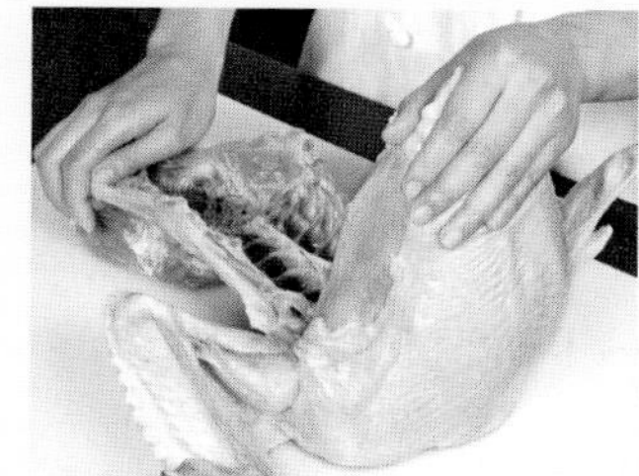

5. Using your hands, bend backbone away from breast to pop shoulder joint out of socket.

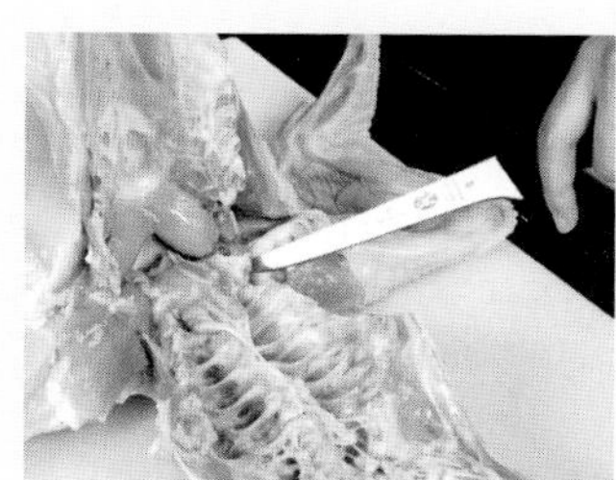

6. Cut through shoulder joint to separate back from breast.

3. Using kitchen shears, cut through ribs following vertical line of fat where breast meets back from tapered end of breast to wing joint. Using your hands, bend back away from breast to pop shoulder joint out of socket. Cut through joint between bones to separate back from breast. Reserve back for gravy. Trim excess fat from breast. Dissolve ¾ cup salt in 6 quarts cold water in large container. Submerge breast in brine, cover, and refrigerate for 6 to 12 hours.

4. Adjust oven racks to upper-middle and lower-middle positions and heat oven to 300 degrees. Spread bread cubes in even layer on 2 rimmed baking sheets and bake until mostly dry and very lightly browned, 25 to 30 minutes, stirring occasionally during baking. Transfer dried bread to large bowl. Increase oven temperature to 425 degrees.

5. While bread dries, remove breast from brine and pat dry with paper towels (leave leg quarters in refrigerator). Tuck wings behind back. Brush surface with 2 teaspoons oil. Melt butter in 12-inch nonstick ovensafe skillet over medium heat. Add onions and cook, stirring occasionally, until softened, 10 to 12 minutes. Add celery, remaining 2 tablespoons sage, and 1½ teaspoons pepper; continue to cook until celery is slightly softened, 3 to 5 minutes longer. Transfer vegetables to bowl with bread and wipe out skillet with paper towels. Place turkey breast skin side down in skillet, and roast in oven for 30 minutes.

6. While breast roasts, add cranberries and eggs to bread mixture and toss to combine (mixture will be dry). Transfer stuffing to 16 by 13-inch roasting pan and, using rubber spatula, pat stuffing into level 12 by 10-inch rectangle.

7. Remove breast from oven, and using 2 wads of paper towels, flip breast and place over two-thirds of stuffing. Arrange leg quarters over remaining stuffing and brush with remaining 1 teaspoon oil. Lightly season breast and leg quarters with salt. Tuck any large sections of exposed stuffing under bird so most of stuffing is covered by turkey. Transfer pan to oven and cook for 30 minutes.

8. Reduce oven temperature to 350 degrees. Continue to roast until thickest part of breast registers 160 to 165 degrees and thickest part of thigh registers 175 to 180 degrees, 40 minutes to 1 hour 20 minutes longer. Transfer breast and leg quarters to cutting board and let rest for 30 minutes. While turkey rests, using metal spatula, stir stuffing well, scraping up any browned bits. Redistribute stuffing over bottom of roasting pan, return to oven, and turn off oven.

9. Before serving, season stuffing with salt and pepper to taste. Mound stuffing in center of platter. Place breast on top of stuffing with point of breast resting on highest part of mound. Remove skewers and twine from leg quarters and place on each side of breast. Carve and serve.

Turkey Gravy for Julia Child's Stuffed Turkey, Updated

MAKES ABOUT 4 CUPS

If you do not have ¼ cup of reserved turkey fat in step 4, supplement with unsalted butter.

- Reserved turkey giblets, neck, backbone, and thighbones, hacked into 2-inch pieces
- 2 onions, chopped coarse
- 1 carrot, peeled and cut into 1-inch pieces
- 1 celery rib, cut into 1-inch pieces
- 6 garlic cloves, unpeeled
- 1 tablespoon vegetable oil
- 3½ cups chicken broth
- 3 cups water
- 2 cups dry white wine
- 6 sprigs fresh thyme
- ¼ cup all-purpose flour
- Salt and pepper

1. Adjust oven rack to middle position and heat oven to 450 degrees. Place turkey parts, onions, carrot, celery, and garlic in large roasting pan. Drizzle with oil and toss to combine. Roast, stirring occasionally, until well browned, 40 to 50 minutes.

2. Remove pan from oven, and place over high heat. Add broth and bring to boil, scraping up any browned bits. Transfer contents of pan to Dutch oven. Add water, wine, and thyme sprigs; bring to boil over high heat. Reduce heat to low and simmer until reduced by half, about 1½ hours.

3. Strain contents of pot through fine-mesh strainer set in large bowl. Press solids with back of spatula to extract as much liquid as possible. Discard solids. Transfer liquid to fat separator and let settle, 5 minutes.

4. Transfer ¼ cup fat to medium saucepan and heat over medium-high heat until bubbling. Whisk in flour and cook, whisking constantly, until combined and honey-colored, about 2 minutes. Gradually whisk in hot liquid and bring to boil. Reduce heat to medium-low and simmer, stirring occasionally, until thickened, about 5 minutes. Season with salt and pepper to taste. (Gravy can be refrigerated for up to 2 days.)

SLOW-ROASTED TURKEY WITH GRAVY

WHY THIS RECIPE WORKS: Roasting a whole turkey is a race to keep the white meat from drying out while the dark meat cooks through. We wanted an approach that would get our fowl from supermarket to table in just a few hours. We

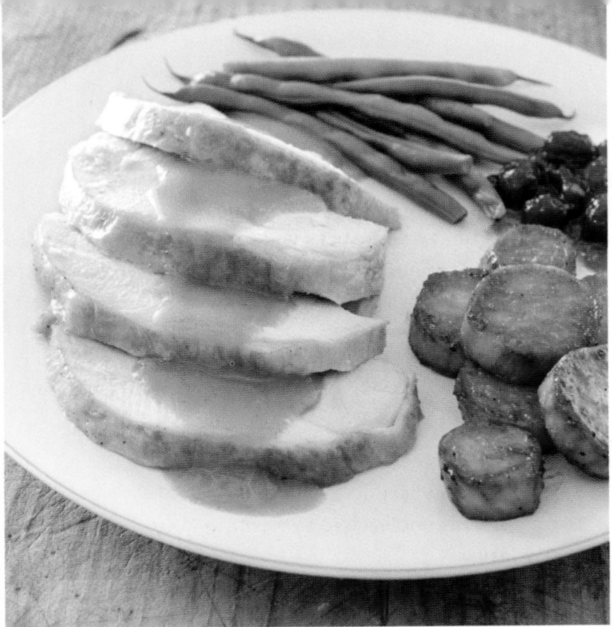

required meat as moist as prime rib and with crisp, crackling skin, and it all needed to be accompanied by rich gravy. For a greater challenge, we wanted to do it without salting the turkey or brining it, both of which take the better part of a day.

First, we roasted two nonbrined turkeys, one using our standard high-heat method and the other at 275 degrees the entire time. The outer layers of the high-heat breast dried out, but the slow-roasted breast cooked through moist, even without a brine. Coordinating the cooking between the breast and legs and thighs, however, was a problem. Instead we discovered that swapping in turkey parts for a whole turkey would help ensure the breast and thighs cooked through at about the same time. We roasted a breast and two leg quarters (thighs and drumsticks) on a rack over a baking sheet to promote air circulation. The results? Tender, juicy meat.

We next had to tackle crisping the skin. Most recipes achieve crisp skin by starting the bird in a hot oven to brown it, then lowering the heat. But that meant a higher oven temperature, which meant dried-out meat. Instead, we let the turkey cool before popping it back in the oven to crisp the skin. This turned out a perfect turkey from center to edge surrounded by flawless, crisp skin.

Slow-Roasted Turkey with Gravy

SERVES 10 TO 12

Instead of drumsticks and thighs, you may use 2 whole leg quarters, 1½ to 2 pounds each. The recipe will also work with turkey breast alone; in step 2, reduce the butter to 1½ tablespoons, the salt to 1½ teaspoons, and the pepper to 1 teaspoon. If you are roasting kosher or self-basting turkey parts, season the turkey with only 1½ teaspoons salt.

TURKEY

- 3 medium onions, chopped medium
- 3 medium celery ribs, chopped medium
- 2 medium carrots, peeled and chopped medium
- 5 sprigs fresh thyme

5 medium garlic cloves, peeled and halved
1 cup low-sodium chicken broth
1 (5- to 7-pound) whole bone-in, skin-on turkey breast, trimmed (see note)
4 pounds turkey drumsticks and thighs, trimmed (see note)
3 tablespoons unsalted butter, melted
1 tablespoon table salt
2 teaspoons ground black pepper

GRAVY

2 cups low-sodium chicken broth
3 tablespoons unsalted butter
3 tablespoons unbleached all-purpose flour
2 bay leaves
Table salt and ground black pepper

1. FOR THE TURKEY: Adjust an oven rack to the lower-middle position and heat the oven to 275 degrees. Arrange the onions, celery, carrots, thyme, and garlic in an even layer on a large rimmed baking sheet. Pour the broth into the baking sheet. Place a wire rack on top of the vegetables.

2. Pat the turkey pieces dry with paper towels. Brush the turkey pieces on all sides with the melted butter. Sprinkle the salt and pepper evenly over the turkey. Place the breast, skin side down, and the drumsticks and thighs, skin side up, on the rack on the vegetable-filled baking sheet, leaving at least ¼ inch between the pieces.

3. Roast the turkey pieces for 1 hour. With a dish towel in each hand, turn the turkey breast skin side up. Continue roasting until the thickest part of the breast registers 160 to 165 degrees the thickest part of the thigh registers 175 degrees on an instant-read thermometer, 1 to 2 hours longer. Remove the baking sheet from the oven and transfer the rack with the turkey to a second baking sheet. Allow the pieces to rest for at least 30 minutes or up to 1½ hours.

4. FOR THE GRAVY: Strain the vegetables and liquid from the baking sheet through a colander set in a large bowl. Press the solids with the back of a spatula to extract as much liquid as possible. Discard the vegetables. Transfer the liquid in the bowl to a 4-cup liquid measuring cup. Add the chicken broth to the measuring cup (you should have about 3 cups liquid).

5. In a medium saucepan, heat the butter over medium-high heat; add the flour and cook, stirring constantly, until the flour is dark golden brown and fragrant, about 5 minutes. Whisk in the broth mixture and bay leaves and gradually bring to a boil. Reduce the heat to medium-low and simmer, stirring occasionally, until the gravy is thick and reduced to 2 cups, 15 to 20 minutes. Discard the bay leaves. Remove the gravy from the heat and season with salt and pepper to taste. Keep the gravy warm.

6. TO SERVE: Heat the oven to 500 degrees. Place the baking sheet with the turkey in the oven. Roast until the skin is golden brown and crisp, about 15 minutes. Transfer the turkey to a carving board and let rest, uncovered, for 20 minutes. Carve and serve with the gravy.

CRISP-SKIN HIGH-ROAST TURKEY

WHY THIS RECIPE WORKS: High-roasting (oven-roasting at very high temperatures for the sake of speed and flavor) a turkey presents the home cook with two potential problems: billowing smoke from incinerated pan drippings and torched breast meat. We wanted to find a way to prepare a high-roast turkey with crisp, picture-perfect skin and moist, evenly cooked meat in less than two hours—without setting off the smoke alarm.

We butterflied the turkey for crisp skin and evenly cooked meat, and then roasted it on a broiler pan set over the stuffing—which absorbed the drippings. This step helped season the stuffing and kept the kitchen from filling with smoke. These techniques let us crank up the heat to get the bird done in record time. To complement our moist, crisp-skinned turkey, we made a corn bread and sausage stuffing that was both rich and easy to prepare.

Crisp-Skin High-Roast Butterflied Turkey with Sausage Dressing

SERVES 10 TO 12

The dressing can be made with corn bread or white bread, but note that they are not used in equal amounts. The turkey is roasted in a broiler pan top, or a sturdy wire rack, set in a 16 by 12-inch disposable aluminum roasting pan. If using a wire rack, choose one that measures about 17 by 11 inches so that it will span the roasting pan and sit above the dressing in the pan.

TURKEY

1 cup table salt
1 cup sugar
1 (12- to 14-pound) turkey; giblets, neck, and tailpiece removed and reserved for gravy; turkey butterflied (see photos on page 144) and backbone and rib bones reserved for gravy
1 tablespoon unsalted butter, melted

SAUSAGE DRESSING

12 cups corn bread (recipe follows) broken into 1-inch pieces (include crumbs), or 18 cups 1-inch challah or Italian bread cubes (from about 1½ loaves)
1¾ cups low-sodium chicken broth
1 cup half-and-half
2 large eggs, beaten lightly
12 ounces bulk pork sausage, broken into 1-inch pieces
3 medium onions, minced (about 3 cups)
3 celery ribs, chopped fine (about 1½ cups)
2 tablespoons unsalted butter
2 tablespoons minced fresh thyme leaves
2 tablespoons minced fresh sage leaves
3 medium garlic cloves, minced or pressed through a garlic press (about 1 tablespoon)
1½ teaspoons table salt
2 teaspoons ground black pepper
1 recipe Turkey Gravy (page 145)

1. TO BRINE THE TURKEY: Dissolve the salt and sugar in 2 gallons cold water in a large container. Submerge the turkey in the brine and refrigerate or store in a very cool spot (40 degrees or less) for 4 to 6 hours.

2. TO PREPARE THE DRESSING: While the turkey brines, adjust the oven racks to the upper-middle and lower-middle positions and heat the oven to 250 degrees. Spread the bread in an even layer on two rimmed baking sheets and dry in the oven for 50 to 60 minutes for corn bread or 40 to 50 minutes for challah or Italian bread.

3. Place the bread in a large bowl. Whisk the broth, half-and-half, and eggs together in a medium bowl; pour over the bread and toss very gently to coat so that the bread does not break into smaller pieces. Set aside.

4. Heat a 12-inch skillet over medium-high heat until hot, about 1½ minutes. Add the sausage and cook, stirring occasionally, until the sausage loses its raw color, 5 to 7 minutes. With a slotted spoon, transfer the sausage to a medium bowl. Add half the onions and celery to the fat in the skillet; sauté, stirring occasionally, over medium-high heat until softened, about 5 minutes. Transfer the onion mixture to the bowl with the sausage. Return the skillet to the heat and add the butter; when melted add the remaining onions and celery and sauté, stirring occasionally, until softened, about 5 minutes. Stir in the thyme, sage, and garlic; cook until fragrant, about 30 seconds; add the salt and pepper. Add this mixture along with the sausage and onion mixture to the bread and stir gently to combine (try not to break the bread into smaller pieces).

5. Spray a 16 by 12-inch disposable aluminum roasting pan with vegetable oil spray. Transfer the dressing to the roasting pan and spread in an even layer. Cover the pan with foil and refrigerate while preparing the turkey.

6. TO PREPARE THE TURKEY FOR ROASTING: Remove the turkey from the brine and rinse it well. Position the turkey on a broiler pan top or wire rack (see note); thoroughly pat the surface of the turkey dry with paper towels. Place the broiler pan top with the turkey on top of the roasting pan with the dressing; refrigerate, uncovered, for 8 to 24 hours.

7. TO ROAST THE TURKEY WITH THE DRESSING: Adjust an oven rack to the lower-middle position and heat the oven to 450 degrees. Remove the broiler pan top with the turkey and remove the foil from the dressing; place the broiler pan top with the turkey on the dressing in the roasting pan. Brush the turkey with the melted butter. Roast the turkey until the turkey skin is crisp and deep brown and the thickest part of the breast registers 160 to 165 degrees and the thickest part of the thigh registers 175 degrees on an instant-read thermometer, 1 hour 20 minutes to 1 hour 40 minutes, rotating the pan from front to back after 40 minutes.

8. Transfer the broiler pan top with the turkey to a carving board, tent loosely with foil, and let rest for 20 minutes. Meanwhile, adjust an oven rack to the upper-middle position, place the roasting pan with the dressing back in the oven, and bake until golden brown, about 10 minutes. Carve the turkey and serve with the dressing and gravy.

NOTES FROM THE TEST KITCHEN

PREPARING THE BUTTERFLIED TURKEY

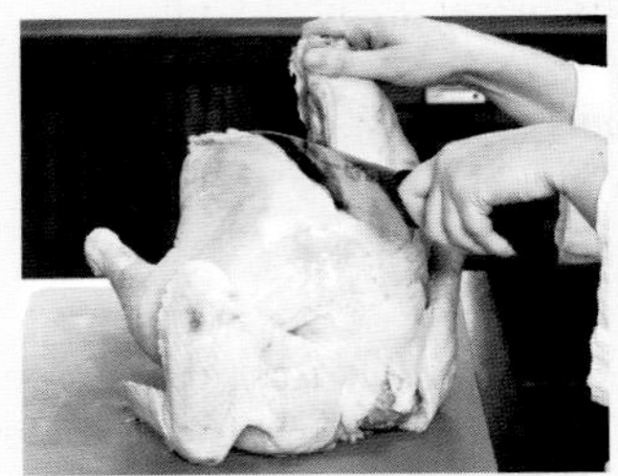

1. Holding the turkey upright with the backbone facing front, use a hacking motion to cut through the turkey directly to one side of the backbone with a chef's knife.

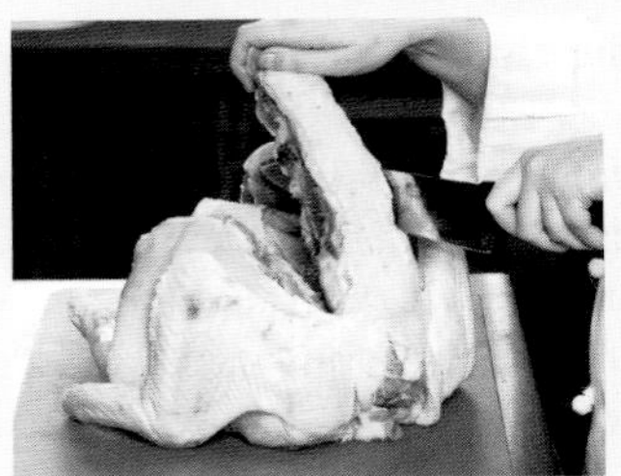

2. Holding the backbone with one hand, hack through the turkey directly to the other side of the backbone; the backbone will fall away.

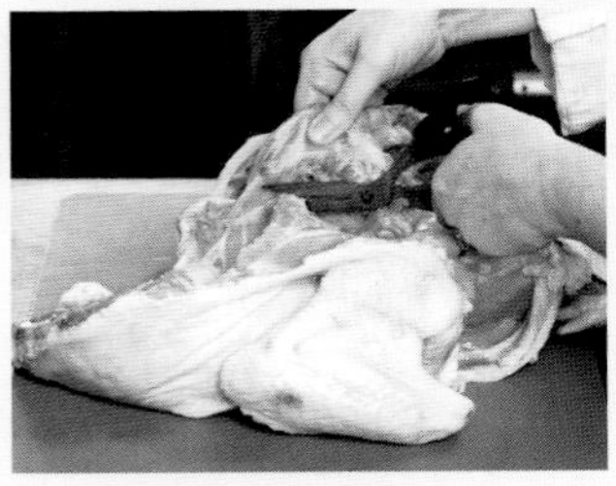

3. Using kitchen scissors, cut out the rib plate and remove any small pieces of bone.

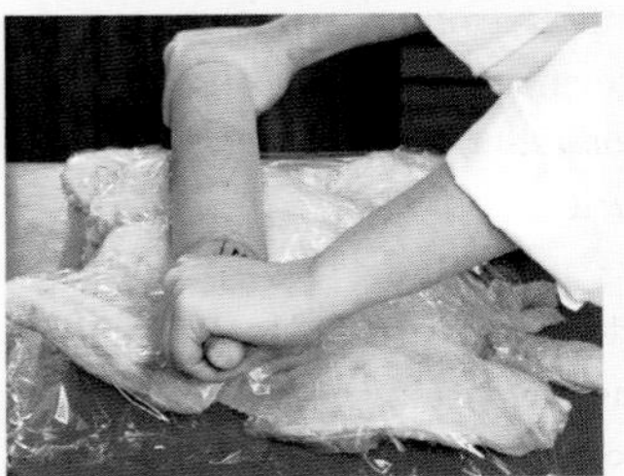

4. Place the turkey, breast side up, on a cutting board and cover with plastic wrap. With a large rolling pin, whack the breastbone until it cracks and the turkey flattens.

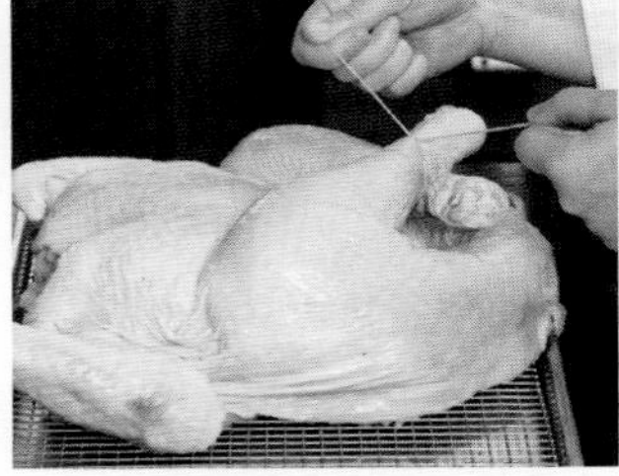

5. After brining and rinsing, place the turkey, breast side up, on a wire rack set over a rimmed baking sheet. Tuck the wings under the turkey. Push the legs up to rest between the thigh and breast. Tie the legs together.

Golden Corn Bread

MAKES ABOUT 16 CUPS CRUMBLED CORN BREAD

You need about three-quarters of this recipe for the dressing; the rest is for nibbling.

- 4 tablespoons (½ stick) unsalted butter, melted, plus extra for the baking dish
- 4 large eggs
- 1⅓ cups buttermilk
- 1⅓ cups milk
- 2 cups yellow cornmeal
- 2 cups (10 ounces) unbleached all-purpose flour
- 2 tablespoons sugar
- 4 teaspoons baking powder
- 1 teaspoon baking soda
- 1 teaspoon table salt

1. Adjust an oven rack to the middle position and heat the oven to 375 degrees. Grease a 13 by 9-inch baking dish with butter.

2. Beat the eggs in medium bowl; whisk in the buttermilk and milk.

3. Whisk the cornmeal, flour, sugar, baking powder, baking soda, and salt together in a large bowl. Push the dry ingredients up the sides of the bowl to make a well, then pour the egg and milk mixture into the well and stir with a whisk until just combined; stir in the melted butter.

4. Pour the batter into the prepared baking dish. Bake until the top is golden brown and the edges have pulled away from the sides of the pan, 30 to 40 minutes.

5. Transfer the baking dish to a wire rack and cool to room temperature before using, about 1 hour.

Turkey Gravy

MAKES ABOUT 4 CUPS

Because this gravy doesn't use drippings from the roasted turkey but instead uses the trimmings from butterflying the bird, the gravy can conveniently be made a day in advance (while the turkey brines and air-dries in the refrigerator) and then reheated before serving.

- Reserved giblets, neck, tailpiece, and backbone and rib bones from the turkey (see note)
- 2 small onions, chopped coarse
- 1 medium carrot, cut into 1-inch pieces
- 1 celery rib, cut into 1-inch pieces
- 6 garlic cloves, unpeeled
- 3½ cups low-sodium chicken broth
- 3 cups water
- 2 cups dry white wine
- 6 sprigs fresh thyme
- ¼ cup unbleached all-purpose flour
- Table salt and ground black pepper

1. Heat the oven to 450 degrees. Adjust an oven rack to the middle position. Place the turkey trimmings, onions, carrot, celery, and garlic in a large roasting pan or broiler pan bottom. Spray lightly with vegetable oil spray and toss to combine. Roast, stirring every 10 minutes, until well browned, 40 to 50 minutes.

2. Remove the pan from the oven and place over two burners set at high heat; add the chicken broth and bring to a boil, scraping up the browned bits on the bottom of the pan with a wooden spoon.

3. Transfer the contents of the pan to a large saucepan. Add the water, wine, and thyme; bring to a boil over high heat. Reduce the heat to low and simmer until reduced by half, about 1½ hours. Strain the stock into a large measuring cup or container. Cool to room temperature; cover with plastic wrap, and refrigerate until the fat congeals on the surface, about 2 hours.

4. Skim the fat from the stock using a soup spoon; reserve the fat. Pour the stock through a fine-mesh strainer to remove remaining bits of fat. Bring the stock to a simmer in a medium saucepan over medium-high heat. 5. In a second medium saucepan, heat ¼ cup reserved turkey fat over medium-high heat until bubbling; whisk in the flour and cook, whisking constantly, until combined and honey-colored, about 2 minutes. Continuing to whisk constantly, gradually add the hot stock; bring to a boil, then reduce the heat to medium-low and simmer, stirring occasionally, until slightly thickened, about 5 minutes. Season with salt and pepper to taste. (The gravy can be stored in an airtight container in the refrigerator for up to 1 day. While the turkey is resting, heat the gravy in a medium saucepan over medium heat until hot, about 8 minutes.)

EASIER ROAST TURKEY AND GRAVY

WHY THIS RECIPE WORKS: To season the meat and help it retain more juices as it cooked, we loosened the skin of the turkey and applied a mixture of salt and sugar onto the flesh. We preheated both a baking stone and roasting pan in the oven before placing the turkey in the pan. The stone absorbs heat and delivers it through the pan to the turkey's legs and thighs, which need to cook to a higher temperature than the delicate breast meat (which we protected with a foil shield). After the leg quarters had gotten a jump start on cooking, we reduced the oven temperature from 425 to 325 degrees and removed the shield to allow the breast to brown while the bird finished cooking. The boost of heat provided by the stone also helped the juices brown and reduce into concentrated drippings that can be turned into a flavorful gravy in the time that the turkey rests.

Easier Roast Turkey and Gravy

SERVES 10 TO 12

Note that this recipe requires salting the bird in the refrigerator for 24 to 48 hours. This recipe was developed and tested using Diamond Crystal Kosher Salt. If you have Morton's Kosher Salt, which is denser than Diamond Crystal, reduce the salt in step 1 to 3 tablespoons. Rub 1 tablespoon salt mixture into each breast, 1½ teaspoons into each leg, and remainder into cavity. Table salt is too fine and not recommended for this recipe. If you are roasting a kosher or self-basting turkey (such as a frozen Butterball), do not salt it; it already contains a good amount of sodium. The success of this recipe is dependent on saturating the pizza stone and roasting pan with heat. We recommend preheating the stone, pan, and oven for at least 30 minutes.

- 4 teaspoons sugar
- Kosher salt and pepper
- 1 (12- to 14-pound) turkey, neck and giblets removed and reserved for gravy
- 2½ tablespoons vegetable oil
- 1 teaspoon baking powder
- 1 small onion, chopped fine
- 1 carrot, peeled and sliced thin
- 5 sprigs fresh parsley
- 2 bay leaves
- 5 tablespoons all-purpose flour
- 3¼ cups water
- ¼ cup dry white wine

1. Combine sugar and 4 tablespoons salt in bowl. With turkey breast side up, use fingers or handle of wooden spoon to carefully separate skin from thighs and breast. Rub 4 teaspoons salt mixture under skin of each breast half, 2 teaspoons salt under skin of each leg, and remaining salt mixture into cavity. Tie legs together with kitchen twine. Place turkey on rack set in rimmed baking sheet and refrigerate uncovered for 24 to 48 hours.

2. At least 30 minutes before roasting turkey, adjust oven rack to lowest position and set pizza stone on oven rack. Place roasting pan on pizza stone and heat oven to 500 degrees. Combine 1½ teaspoons oil and baking powder in small bowl. Pat turkey dry with paper towels. Rub oil mixture evenly over turkey. Cover turkey breast with double layer of aluminum foil.

3. Remove roasting pan from oven. Place remaining 2 tablespoons oil in roasting pan. Place turkey into pan breast side up and return pan to oven. Reduce oven temperature to 425 degrees and cook for 45 minutes.

4. Remove foil shield, reduce temperature to 325 degrees, and continue to cook until breast registers 160 degrees and thighs register 175 degrees, 1 to 1½ hours longer.

5. Using spatula loosen turkey from roasting pan, transfer to carving board, and let rest uncovered for 45 minutes. While turkey rests, use wooden spoon to scrape any browned bits from bottom of roasting pan. Pour mixture through fine-mesh strainer set in bowl. Transfer drippings to fat separator and let rest 10 minutes. Reserve 3 tablespoons fat and defatted liquid (about 1 cup). Discard remaining fat.

6. Heat reserved fat in large saucepan over medium-high heat until shimmering. Add reserved neck and giblets and cook until well browned, 10 to 12 minutes. Transfer neck and giblets to large plate. Reduce heat to medium; add onion, carrot, parsley, and bay leaves; and cook, stirring frequently, until vegetables are softened, 5 to 7 minutes. Add flour and cook, stirring constantly, until flour is well coated with fat, about 1 minute. Slowly whisk in reserved defatted liquid and cook until thickened, about 1 minute. Whisk in water and wine, return neck and giblets, and bring to simmer. Simmer for 10 minutes. Season with salt and pepper to taste. Discard neck. Strain mixture through fine-mesh strainer and transfer to serving bowl. Carve turkey and arrange on serving platter. Serve with gravy.

ROAST SALTED TURKEY

WHY THIS RECIPE WORKS: Brining is the best way to guarantee a moist turkey, but it isn't always the most practical way, especially if you have limited refrigerator space. We wanted to develop an alternative method to brining that would season the meat and keep it moist. Instead of brining, we turned to salting. We wanted to make sure the salt penetrated the meat, but we didn't want to tear the skin. We found that either chopsticks or the handle of a wooden spoon worked well to help us gently separate the skin from the meat. To ensure moist breast meat, we chilled the breast by placing a small bag of ice inside the cavity against the breast and setting the turkey, breast side down, on ice. This trick brought down the temperature of the breast, thus allowing it to cook through over a longer period in the oven (more in line with the cooking time of the dark meat) without drying out.

Roast Salted Turkey

SERVES 10 TO 12

This recipe was developed and tested using Diamond Crystal Kosher Salt. If you have Morton's Kosher Salt, which is denser than Diamond Crystal, use only 4½ teaspoons of salt in the cavity, 2¼ teaspoons of salt per each half of the breast, and 1 teaspoon of salt per leg. Table salt is too fine and is not recommended for this recipe. If you are roasting a kosher or self-basting turkey (such as a frozen Butterball), do not salt it; it already contains a good amount of sodium. If serving with Giblet Pan Gravy (page 134), note that you can complete step 1 of the gravy recipe up to a day ahead, if desired. Begin step 3 once the bird has been removed from the oven and is resting on a carving board.

- 1 (12- to 14-pound) turkey; giblets, neck, and tailpiece removed and reserved for gravy (see page 134)
- 5 tablespoons kosher salt (see note)
- 1 (5-pound) bag ice cubes
- 4 tablespoons (½ stick) unsalted butter, melted
- 3 medium onions, chopped coarse
- 2 medium carrots, chopped coarse

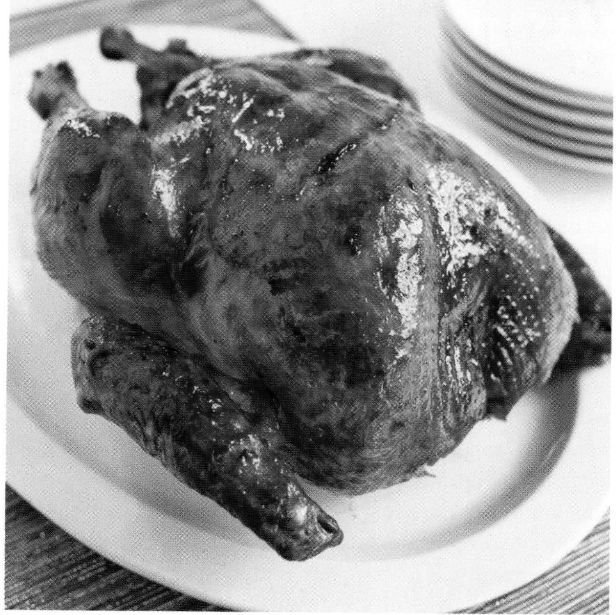

2 celery ribs, chopped coarse
6 sprigs fresh thyme
1 cup water, plus more as needed

1. Following the photos, carefully separate the turkey skin from the meat on the breast, legs, thighs, and back; avoid breaking the skin. Then rub 2 tablespoons of the salt evenly inside the cavity of the turkey, 1 tablespoon more salt under the skin of each breast half, and 1½ teaspoons more salt under the skin of each leg. Wrap the turkey tightly with plastic wrap; refrigerate for 24 to 48 hours.

2. Remove the turkey from the refrigerator. Rinse off any excess salt between the meat and skin and in the cavity, then pat dry inside and out with paper towels. Add ice to two 1-gallon zipper-lock bags until each is half full. Place the bags in a large roasting pan and lay the turkey, breast side down, on top of the ice. Add ice to two 1-quart zipper-lock bags until each is one-third full; place one bag of ice in the large cavity of the turkey and the other bag in the neck cavity. (Make sure that the ice touches the breast only, not the thighs or legs; see the photo.) Keep the turkey on ice for 1 hour (the roasting pan should remain on the counter).

3. Meanwhile, adjust an oven rack to the lowest position and heat the oven to 425 degrees. Line a large V-rack with heavy-duty foil and poke several holes in the foil. Set the V-rack in a roasting pan and spray the foil with vegetable oil spray.

4. Remove the turkey from the ice and pat dry with paper towels (discard the ice). Tuck the tips of the drumsticks into the skin at the tail to secure and tuck the wings under the bird. Brush the turkey breast with 2 tablespoons of the melted butter. Scatter the vegetables and thyme in the roasting pan and pour 1 cup water over the vegetable mixture. Place the turkey, breast side down, on the V-rack. Brush the turkey with the remaining 2 tablespoons melted butter.

5. Roast the turkey for 45 minutes. Remove the pan from the oven (close the oven door to retain the oven heat) and reduce the oven temperature to 325 degrees. With a dish towel in each hand, rotate the turkey breast side up; continue to roast until the thickest part of the breast registers 160 to 165 degrees and the thickest part of the thigh registers 175 degrees on an instant-read thermometer, 1 to 1½ hours longer. Transfer the turkey to a carving board and let rest, uncovered, for 30 minutes. Carve the turkey and serve with the gravy (see note).

NOTES FROM THE TEST KITCHEN

HOW TO SALT A TURKEY

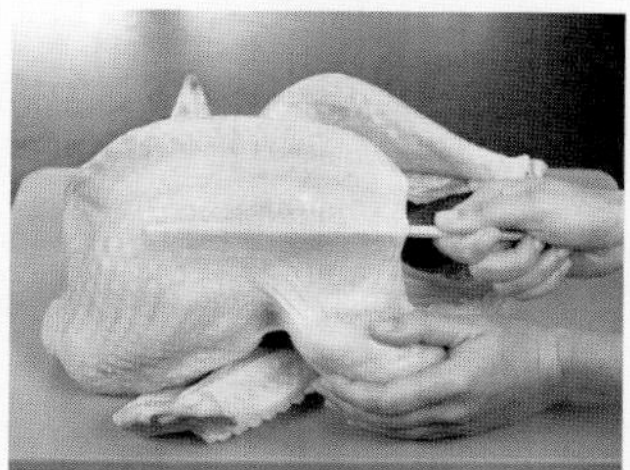

1. Use a chopstick or a thin wooden spoon handle to separate the skin from the meat over the breast, legs, thighs, and back.

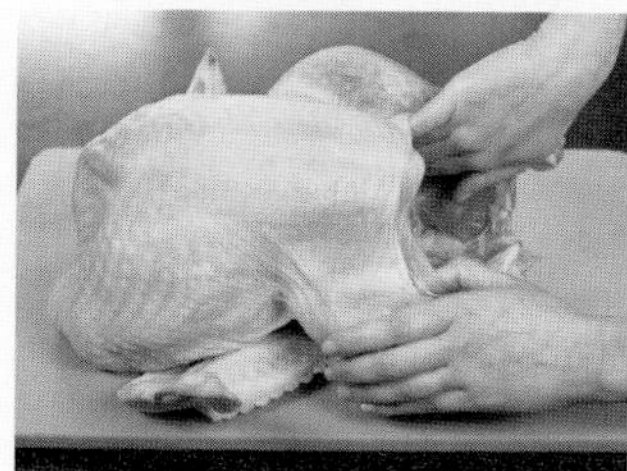

2. Rub 2 tablespoons kosher salt inside the main cavity.

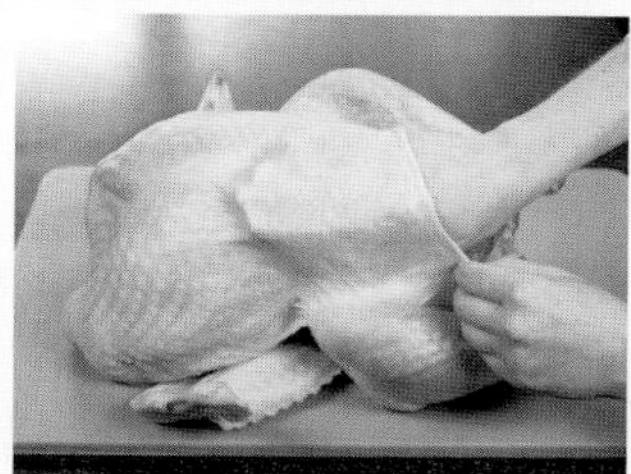

3. Lift the skin and apply 1 tablespoon kosher salt over each breast half, placing half of the salt on each end of each breast, then massaging the salt evenly over the meat.

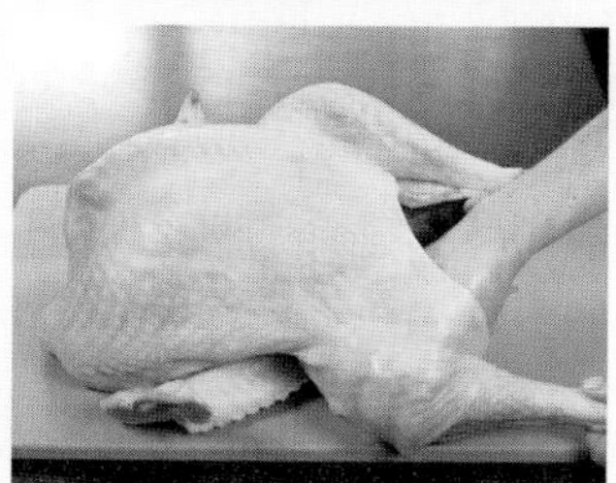

4. Apply 1½ teaspoons kosher salt over the top and bottom of each leg.

ICING THE TURKEY BREAST

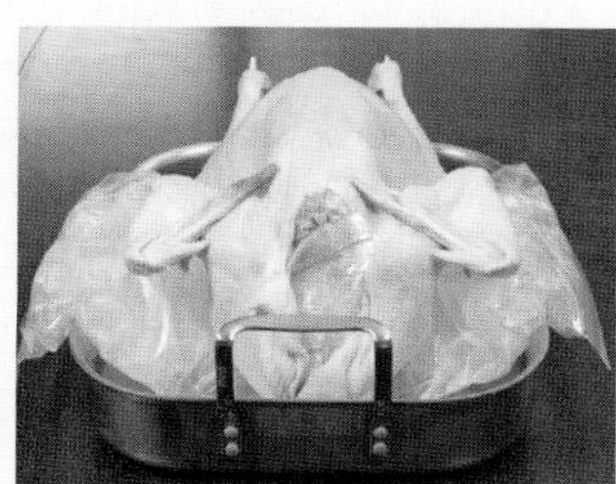

Cooling the breast down with ice ensures that it will cook more slowly than the legs and thighs, preventing the breast meat from drying out. Place bags of ice underneath the breast and inside both the large cavity and the neck area.

ROASTED BRINED TURKEY

WHY THIS RECIPE WORKS: Brining brings out the best in roasted turkey: It helps the bird retain moisture, seasons the meat, and helps the meat withstand hot oven temperatures, making for crisp skin. After brining, we let the turkey dry in the refrigerator for optimal crisping. Brushing the skin with melted butter before placing it breast-side down in a V-rack boosted its browning and added rich, buttery flavor to the finished turkey. To avoid overcooking the breast, we rotated the turkey after 45 minutes to an hour of roasting (depending on its size). This step kept the meat evenly moist and juicy. Before carving, we let the turkey rest for at least 30 minutes to give the juices time to redistribute through the meat.

Roasted Brined Turkey

SERVES 10 TO 22, DEPENDING ON TURKEY SIZE

We offer two brine formulas: one for a 4- to 6-hour brine and another for a 12- to 14-hour brine. The amount of salt used does not change with turkey size. If you're roasting a kosher or self-basting turkey, do not brine it; it already contains a good amount of sodium. Rotating the bird from a breast-side down position to a breast-side up position midway through cooking helps produce evenly cooked meat. If you're roasting a large (18- to 22-pound) bird and are reluctant to rotate it, skip the step of lining the V-rack with foil and roast the bird breast-side up for the full time.

- Salt
- 1 turkey (12–22 pounds gross weight), rinsed thoroughly, giblets and neck reserved for gravy, if making
- 4 tablespoons unsalted butter, melted

1. Dissolve 1 cup salt per gallon cold water for 4- to 6-hour brine or ½ cup salt per gallon cold water for 12- to 14-hour brine in large stockpot or clean bucket. Two gallons of water will be sufficient for most birds; larger birds may require three gallons. Add turkey and refrigerate for predetermined amount of time.

2. Set wire rack in large rimmed baking sheet. Remove turkey from brine and pat dry, inside and out, with paper towels. Place turkey on prepared baking sheet. Refrigerate, uncovered, for at least 8 hours or overnight.

3. Before removing turkey from refrigerator, adjust oven rack to lowest position; heat oven to 400 degrees for 12- to 18-pound bird or 425 degrees for 18- to 22-pound bird. Line large V-rack with heavy-duty aluminum foil and use paring knife or skewer to poke 20 to 30 holes in foil; set V-rack in large roasting pan. Tuck tips of drumsticks into skin at tail to secure; tuck wing tips behind back. Brush breast with 2 tablespoons butter. Set turkey breast side down on prepared V-rack; brush back with remaining 2 tablespoons butter. Roast 45 minutes for 12- to 18-pound bird or 1 hour for 18- to 22-pound bird.

4. Remove roasting pan with turkey from oven (close oven door to retain oven heat); reduce oven temperature to 325 degrees if roasting 18- to 22-pound bird. Using clean potholders or dish towels, rotate turkey breast side up; continue to roast until thickest part of breast registers 160 degrees and thickest part of thigh registers 175 degrees, 50 to 60 minutes longer for 12- to 15-pound bird, about 1¼ hours for 15- to 18-pound bird, or about 2 hours for 18- to 22-pound bird. Transfer turkey to carving board; let rest for 30 minutes (or up to 40 minutes for 18- to 22-pound bird). Carve and serve.

HERBED ROAST TURKEY

WHY THIS RECIPE WORKS: Throwing a bunch of herbs into the cavity of a turkey or rubbing the outside of the bird with a savory paste only flirts with great herb flavor—it doesn't infuse that flavor into each and every bite. We wanted an intensely herby turkey, one with a powerful, aromatic flavor that permeated well beyond the meat's surface.

First we tried an intense brine, but it made the bird taste more pickled than infused with herbs. Next, we pumped the paste into the bird with a syringe, which created nothing but ugly blobs of overwhelmingly strong, raw-tasting herbs. Then we tried a technique we had developed for stuffing a thick-cut pork chop. We made a vertical slit in the breast meat and, using a paring knife, created an expansive pocket by sweeping the blade back and forth. This created a void into which we could rub a small amount of herb paste. This along with three other herbal applications—underneath the skin, inside the cavity, and over the skin—made for a successful four-pronged approach that gave every bite of turkey herb flavor. The herb paste itself, balanced with small amounts of pungent herbs (sage and rosemary) and greater amounts of softer flavors (thyme and parsley), also included lemon zest for a fresh, bright note and olive oil and Dijon mustard to make it spreadable. This was a moist roast turkey packed with bright herb flavor—a fresh alternative to the usual holiday bird.

NOTES FROM THE TEST KITCHEN

APPLYING HERB PASTE TO THE TURKEY

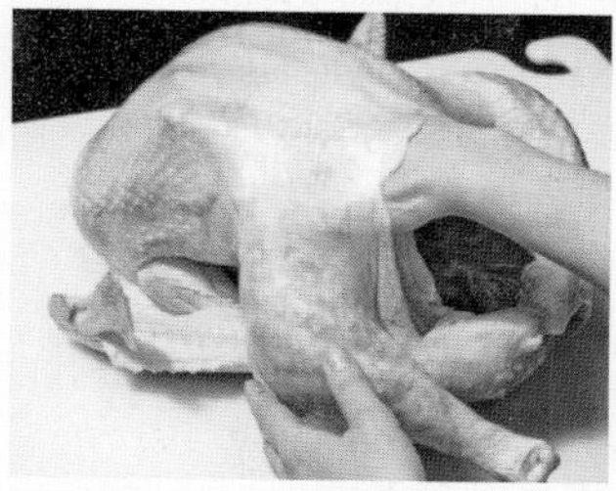

1. Carefully separate the skin from the meat on the breast, thigh, and drumstick areas.

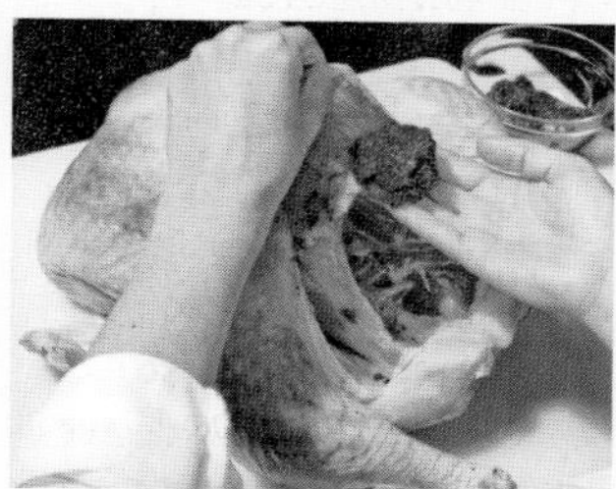

2. Rub the herb paste under the skin and directly onto the flesh, distributing it evenly.

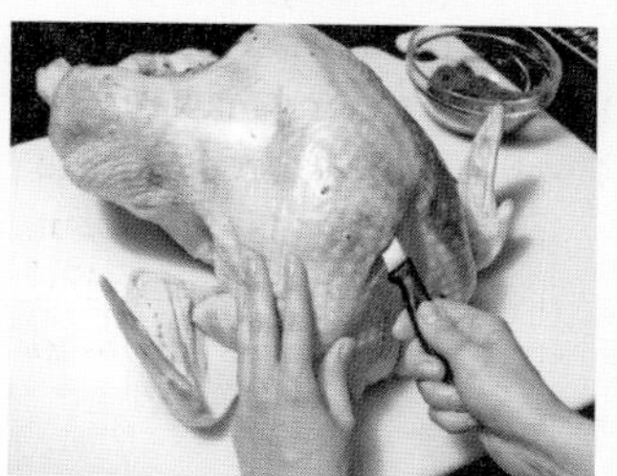

3. Make a 1½-inch slit in each breast. Swing a knife tip through the breast to create a large pocket.

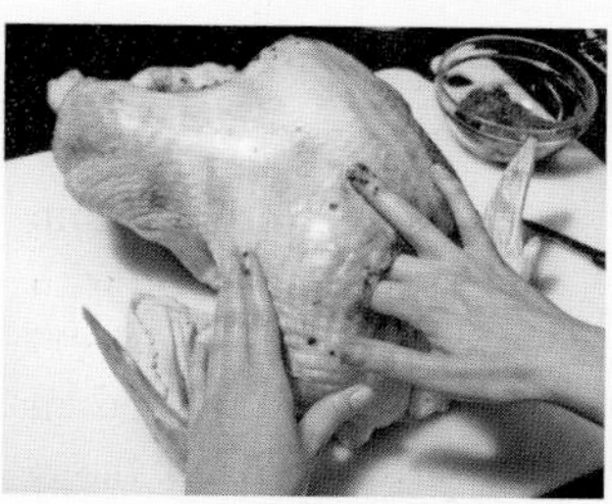

4. Place a thin layer of paste inside each pocket.

5. Rub the remaining paste inside the turkey cavity and on the skin.

Herbed Roast Turkey

SERVES 10 TO 12

If you have the time and the refrigerator space, air-drying produces extremely crisp skin and is worth the effort. After brining, rinsing, and patting the turkey dry, place the turkey, breast side up, on a wire rack set over a rimmed baking sheet and refrigerate, uncovered, for 8 to 24 hours. Proceed with the recipe. Serve with All-Purpose Turkey Gravy (recipe follows).

TURKEY AND BRINE

- 2 cups table salt
- 1 (12- to 14-pound) turkey; giblets, neck, and tailpiece removed and discarded

HERB PASTE

- 1¼ cups roughly chopped fresh parsley leaves
- 4 teaspoons minced fresh thyme leaves
- 2 teaspoons roughly chopped fresh sage leaves
- 1½ teaspoons minced fresh rosemary leaves
- 1 medium shallot, minced (about 3 tablespoons)
- 2 medium garlic cloves, minced or pressed through a garlic press (about 2 teaspoons)
- ¾ teaspoon grated zest from 1 lemon
- ¾ teaspoon table salt
- 1 teaspoon ground black pepper
- ¼ cup olive oil
- 1 teaspoon Dijon mustard
- 1 recipe All-Purpose Turkey Gravy (page 150)

1. FOR THE TURKEY AND BRINE: Dissolve the salt in 2 gallons cold water in a large container. Submerge the turkey in the brine, cover, and refrigerate or store in a very cool spot (40 degrees or less) for 4 to 6 hours.

2. Remove the turkey from the brine and rinse it well. Pat dry inside and out with paper towels. Place the turkey, breast side up, on a wire rack set over a rimmed baking sheet or roasting pan and refrigerate, uncovered, for 30 minutes. (Alternatively, air-dry the turkey; see note.)

3. FOR THE HERB PASTE: Pulse the parsley, thyme, sage, rosemary, shallot, garlic, lemon zest, salt, and pepper together in a food processor until a coarse paste is formed, 10 pulses. Add the olive oil and mustard; continue to pulse until the mixture forms a smooth paste, 10 to twelve 2-second pulses; scrape the sides of the processor bowl with a rubber spatula after 5 pulses. Transfer the mixture to a small bowl.

4. TO PREPARE THE TURKEY: Adjust an oven rack to the lowest position and heat the oven to 400 degrees. Line a large V-rack with heavy-duty foil and poke several holes in the foil. Set the V-rack in a large roasting pan and spray the foil with vegetable oil spray. Remove the turkey from the refrigerator and wipe away any water collected in the baking sheet; set the turkey, breast side up, on the baking sheet.

5. Following the photos on page 145, use your hands to carefully loosen the skin from the meat of the breast, thighs, and drumsticks. Using your fingers or a spoon, slip 1½ tablespoons of the paste under the breast skin on each side of the turkey. Using your fingers, distribute the paste under the skin over the breast, thigh, and drumstick meat.

6. Using a sharp paring knife, cut a 1½-inch vertical slit into the thickest part of each side of the breast. Starting from the top of the incision, swing the knife tip down to create a 4 to 5-inch pocket within the flesh. Place 1 tablespoon more paste in the pocket of each side of the breast; using your fingers, rub the paste in a thin, even layer.

7. Rub 1 tablespoon more paste inside the turkey cavity. Rotate the turkey breast side down; apply half the remaining herb paste to the turkey skin; flip the turkey breast side up and apply the remaining herb paste to the skin, pressing and patting to make the paste adhere; reapply the herb paste that falls onto the baking sheet. Tuck the tips of the drumsticks into the skin at the tail to secure, and tuck the wings under the bird.

8. TO ROAST THE TURKEY: Place the turkey, breast side down, on the V-rack. Roast the turkey for 45 minutes.

9. Remove the pan from the oven (close the oven door to retain the oven heat). With a dish towel in each hand, rotate the turkey breast side up. Continue to roast until the thickest part of the breast registers 160 to 165 degrees and the thickest part of the thigh registers 175 degrees on an instant-read thermometer, 50 to 60 minutes longer. Transfer the turkey to a carving board and let rest, uncovered, for 30 minutes. Following the photos, carve the turkey and serve with the gravy.

All-Purpose Turkey Gravy

MAKES ABOUT 2 CUPS

Adding drippings from the roasted turkey will enhance the flavor of the gravy.

- 1 small carrot, peeled and chopped coarse
- 1 small celery rib, chopped coarse
- 1 small onion, chopped coarse
- 3 tablespoons unsalted butter
- ¼ cup unbleached all-purpose flour
- 2 cups low-sodium chicken broth
- 2 cups beef broth
- 1 bay leaf
- 2 sprigs fresh thyme
- 5 whole black peppercorns
- Defatted pan drippings from Herbed Roast Turkey (optional; see note)
- Table salt and ground black pepper

1. Pulse the carrot into ¼-inch pieces in a food processor, about 5 pulses. Add the celery and onion and continue to pulse until all of the vegetables are chopped fine, 5 pulses.

2. Melt the butter in a large saucepan over medium-high heat. Add the vegetables and cook, stirring often, until softened and well browned, about 7 minutes. Reduce the heat to medium, stir in the flour, and cook, stirring constantly, until well browned, about 5 minutes.

3. Gradually whisk in the broths until smooth. Bring to a boil, skimming any foam that rises to the surface. Add the bay leaf, thyme, and peppercorns. Reduce the heat to medium-low and simmer, stirring occasionally, until the gravy is thickened and measures about 3 cups, 20 to 25 minutes. Stir in any juices from the roasted meat (if using) and continue to simmer the gravy as needed to re-thicken.

4. Strain the gravy through a fine-mesh strainer into a serving pitcher, pressing on the solids to extract as much liquid as possible; discard the solids. Season the gravy with salt and pepper to taste and cover to keep warm until needed.

NOTES FROM THE TEST KITCHEN

CARVING THE BREAST

The wings and legs on our Herbed Roast Turkey can be carved just as they would be on any other turkey, but the breast, which is stuffed with herb paste, needs some special attention. Here's how to ensure that every slice has a nice swirl of herbs.

1. With the wings facing toward you, cut along both sides of the breastbone, slicing from the tip of the breastbone to the cutting board.

2. Gently pull each breast half away to expose the wishbone. Then pull and remove the wishbone.

3. Using the knife tip, cut along the rib cage to remove the breast completely.

4. Place the entire breast half on a carving board and cut on the bias into thin slices. Repeat steps 3 and 4 on the other side.

BRAISED TURKEY

WHY THIS RECIPE WORKS: Separating turkey into parts and braising it for the holiday meal? It may sound heretical if you've never presented anything but a whole roasted bird at the table, but this break from tradition has a lot going for it. Roasting a large turkey is always a race to get the denser, fattier thighs and legs to come up to the ideal temperature of around 175 degrees before the leaner, more delicate breast dries out, once its temperature climbs past 160 degrees. An intact, upright bird compounds this problem because the slower-cooking thighs are shielded from the heat. So we wondered if there was an easier way to get perfectly cooked turkey on

the table without sacrificing flavor. Turkey parts provided a neat solution to the problem by giving both types of meat more even exposure to the heat—and without any cumbersome turning. Better yet, braising the pieces in a flavorful liquid created rich, ready-made gravy and infused the meat with all of its complex flavors. When we tasted this deeply flavored, moist and tender turkey, we found we didn't miss the traditional whole bird at all.

Braised Turkey

SERVES 10 TO 12

Instead of drumsticks and thighs, you may use 2 whole leg quarters, 1½ to 2 pounds each. The recipe will also work with turkey breast alone; in step 1, reduce the amount of salt and sugar to ½ cup each, and the amount of water to 4 quarts. If you are braising kosher or self-basting turkey parts, skip the brining step, and instead season the turkey parts with 1½ teaspoons salt.

BRAISED TURKEY

- Table salt and ground black pepper
- 1 cup sugar
- 1 (5- to 7-pound) whole bone-in, skin-on turkey breast, trimmed
- 4 pounds turkey drumsticks and thighs, trimmed
- 3 medium onions, chopped medium
- 3 medium celery ribs, chopped medium
- 2 medium carrots, peeled and chopped medium
- 6 medium garlic cloves, peeled and crushed
- 2 bay leaves
- 6 sprigs fresh thyme
- 6 sprigs fresh parsley
- ½ ounce dried porcini mushrooms, rinsed
- 4 tablespoons (½ stick) unsalted butter, melted
- 4 cups low-sodium chicken broth
- 1 cup dry white wine

GRAVY

- 3 tablespoons unbleached all-purpose flour
- Table salt and ground black pepper

1. FOR THE TURKEY: Dissolve 1 cup salt and the sugar in 2 gallons cold water in a large container. Submerge the turkey pieces in the brine, cover, and refrigerate for 3 to 6 hours.

2. Adjust an oven rack to the lower-middle position and heat the oven to 500 degrees. Remove the turkey from the brine and pat dry with paper towels. Toss the onions, celery, carrots, garlic, bay leaves, thyme, parsley, porcini, and 2 tablespoons of the melted butter in a large roasting pan; arrange in an even layer. Brush the turkey pieces with the remaining 2 tablespoons melted butter and season with pepper. Place the turkey pieces, skin side up, over the vegetables, leaving at least ¼ inch between the pieces. Roast until the skin is lightly browned, about 20 minutes.

3. While the turkey is roasting, bring the broth and wine to a simmer in a medium saucepan over medium heat. Cover and keep warm.

4. Remove the turkey from the oven and reduce the oven temperature to 325 degrees. Pour the broth mixture around the turkey pieces (it should come about three-quarters of the way up the legs and thighs.) Place a 12 by 16-inch piece of parchment paper over the turkey pieces. Cover the roasting pan tightly with aluminum foil. Return the covered roasting pan to the oven and cook until the breast registers 160 degrees and the thighs register 175 degrees on an instant-read thermometer, 1½ to 2 hours. Transfer the turkey to a carving board, tent loosely with foil, and let rest for 20 minutes.

5. FOR THE GRAVY: Strain the vegetables and liquid from the roasting pan through a fine-mesh strainer set in a large bowl. Press the solids with the back of a spatula to extract as much liquid as possible. Discard the vegetables. Transfer the liquid to a fat separator and allow to settle for 5 minutes. Reserve 3 tablespoons fat and measure off 3 cups broth (use any remaining broth for another use.)

6. Heat 3 tablespoons reserved turkey fat in a medium saucepan over medium-high heat; add the flour and cook, stirring constantly, until the flour is dark golden brown and fragrant, about 5 minutes. Whisk in 3 cups braising liquid and bring to a boil. Reduce the heat to medium-low and simmer, stirring occasionally, until the gravy is thick and reduced to 2 cups, 15 to 20 minutes. Remove the gravy from the heat and season with salt and pepper to taste.

7. Carve the turkey and serve, passing the gravy separately.

TURKEY BREAST EN COCOTTE WITH PAN GRAVY

WHY THIS RECIPE WORKS: Cooking turkey breast is a great alternative to tackling the whole bird; it's much easier to handle, yet still provides a substantial amount of meat. Having successfully developed a recipe for chicken en cocotte, we wondered if we could use this same method (cooking the poultry in a covered pot over low heat for an extended period of time) to get the same great results with a turkey breast—perfectly cooked, incredibly moist and tender meat. We found that bone-in breasts were more flavorful, and we decided that a 6- to 7-pound turkey breast was ideal—it's large enough to feed a small crowd (up to eight people), but small enough to fit in our 7-quart Dutch oven.To further ensure that a breast of this size easily fit into the pot, we found it helpful to trim the rib bones. Browning the turkey breast was an essential step in developing deep flavor. Adding some aromatics to the pot further rounded out the flavor, and we settled on a combination of onion, carrot, celery, garlic, thyme, and bay leaf. After 1 hour and 45 minutes, our turkey breast was done—we had an extremely tender, juicy, and moist piece of meat. After removing the turkey from the pot, we reduced the jus until it had all but evaporated, concentrating the turkey flavor, producing a mahogany fond on the bottom of the pot, and separating the fat from the jus. It was into this rendered fat that we stirred flour to make a roux. And by leaving the aromatics in the pot during the whole reduction process, we were sure to extract as much flavor from them as possible. We then added a full quart of chicken broth to the pot, brought it to a simmer, and reduced it to a proper gravy consistency. The result was a deeply flavored gravy reminiscent of Thanksgiving dinner.

Turkey Breast en Cocotte with Pan Gravy

SERVES 6 TO 8

Many supermarkets are now selling "hotel-style" turkey breasts. Try to avoid these if you can, as they still have the wings attached. If this is the only type of breast you can find, you will simply need to remove the wings before proceeding with the recipe. Be sure to use a 7- to 8-quart Dutch oven here. Don't buy a turkey breast larger than 7 pounds; it won't fit in the pot. For a smaller turkey breast, reduce the cooking time as necessary.

- 1 (6- to 7-pound) whole bone-in turkey breast
- Salt and ground black pepper
- 2 tablespoons olive oil
- 1 medium onion, chopped medium
- 1 medium carrot, chopped medium
- 1 celery rib, chopped medium
- 6 medium garlic cloves, peeled and crushed
- 2 sprigs fresh thyme
- 1 bay leaf
- ¼ cup unbleached all-purpose flour
- 4 cups low-sodium chicken broth

1. Adjust an oven rack to the lowest position and heat the oven to 250 degrees. Using kitchen shears or a chef's knife, trim the rib bones and any excess fat on both sides of the breast following the vertical line of fat. Pat the turkey dry with paper towels and season with salt and pepper.

2. Heat the oil in a large Dutch oven over medium-high heat until just smoking. Add the turkey, breast side down, and scatter the onion, carrot, celery, garlic, thyme, and bay leaf around the turkey. Cook, turning the breast on its sides and stirring the vegetables as needed, until the turkey and vegetables are well browned, 12 to 16 minutes, reducing the heat if the pot begins to scorch. Turn turkey so breast side is facing up.

3. Off the heat, place a large sheet of foil over the pot and press to seal, then cover tightly with the lid. Transfer the pot to the oven and cook until the thickest part of the breast registers 160 to 165 degrees on an instant-read thermometer, 1½ to 1¾ hours.

4. Remove the pot from the oven. Transfer the turkey to a cutting board, tent loosely with foil, and let rest while making the gravy.

5. Place the pot with the juices and vegetables over medium-high heat and simmer until almost all of the liquid has evaporated, 15 to 20 minutes. Stir in the flour and cook, stirring constantly, until browned, 2 to 5 minutes. Slowly whisk in the chicken broth, bring to a simmer, and cook, stirring often, until the gravy is thickened and measures about 2½ cups, 10 to 15 minutes.

6. Strain the gravy through a fine-mesh strainer and season with salt and pepper to taste. Carve the turkey and serve, passing the gravy separately.

GRILL-ROASTED TURKEY

WHY THIS RECIPE WORKS: Grill-roasting a turkey can be hard to manage. Cooking times can vary depending on the weather, and it's much easier to burn the bird's skin on a grill. There also remain the usual problems inherent to roasting a turkey: dry, overcooked breast meat and undercooked thighs.

But grill-roasting can produce the best-tasting, best-looking turkey ever, with crispy skin and moist meat wonderfully perfumed with smoke. We wanted to take the guesswork out of preparing the holiday bird on the grill.

Because the skin on larger birds will burn before the meat is done, we chose a small turkey (less than 14 pounds). We ditched stuffing the turkey or trussing it—both can lead to burnt skin and undercooked meat. To season the meat and help prevent it from drying out on the grill, we brined the turkey. To protect the skin and promote slow cooking, we placed the turkey on the opposite side of the glowing coals or lit gas burner. Using a V-rack also helped, as it improved air circulation. And we turned the turkey three times instead of twice; this way, all four sides received equal exposure to the hot side of the grill for evenly bronzed skin.

Grill-Roasted Turkey

SERVES 10 TO 12

If using a self-basting turkey or kosher turkey, do not brine in step 1, and season with salt after brushing with melted butter in step 2. When using a charcoal grill, we prefer wood chunks to wood chips whenever possible; substitute 6 medium wood chunks, soaked in water for 1 hour, for the wood chip packets. The total cooking time is 2 to 2½ hours, depending on the size of the bird, the ambient conditions (the bird will require more time on a cool, windy day), and the intensity of the fire.

- 1 cup salt
- 1 (12- to 14-pound) turkey, trimmed, neck, giblets, and tailpiece removed, and wings tucked behind back
- 2 tablespoons unsalted butter, melted
- 6 cups wood chips, soaked in water for 15 minutes and drained (see note)

1. Dissolve salt in 2 gallons cold water in large container. Submerge turkey in brine, cover, and refrigerate or store in very cool spot (40 degrees or less) for 6 to 12 hours.

2. Lightly spray V-rack with vegetable oil spray. Remove turkey from brine and pat dry, inside and out, with paper towels. Brush both sides of turkey with melted butter and place breast side down in prepared V-rack.

3. Using 3 large pieces of heavy-duty aluminum foil, wrap soaked chips in 3 foil packets and cut several vent holes in top.

4A. FOR A CHARCOAL GRILL: Open bottom vent halfway. Light large chimney mounded with charcoal briquettes (7 quarts). When top coals are partially covered with ash, pour into steeply banked pile against side of grill. Place 1 wood chip packet on pile of coals. Set cooking grate in place, cover, and open lid vent halfway. Heat grill until hot and wood chips are smoking, about 5 minutes.

4B. FOR A GAS GRILL: Place 1 wood chip packet directly on primary burner. Turn all burners to high, cover, and heat grill until hot and wood chips are smoking, about 15 minutes. Turn primary burner to medium-high and turn off other burner(s). (Adjust primary burner as needed during cooking to maintain grill temperature around 325 degrees.)

BEHIND THE SCENES

THE MECHANICS OF BRINING

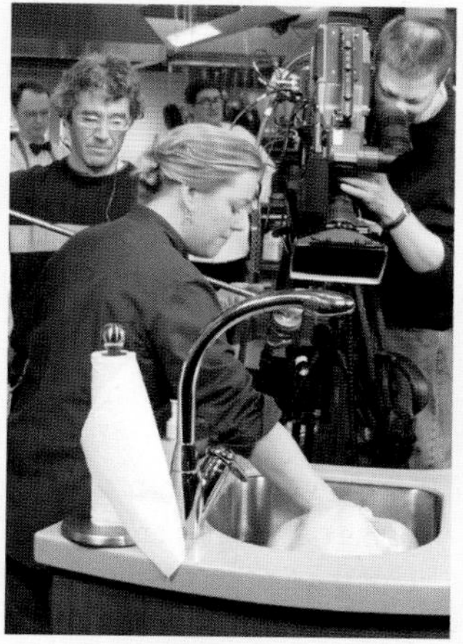

Anyone who watches our show knows that we love to brine. Brining not only helps prevent delicate meat like chicken, turkey, and pork from drying out, it also seasons the meat for better flavor. What equipment do you need for brining? A clean container that's large enough to accommodate the meat and brine. For large containers (such as a washtub or cooler) that won't fit in a refrigerator, you need ice packs to keep the temperature at 40 degrees F. For a whole chicken, the test kitchen likes to use a Cambro storage container, which is a large, clear bucket marked with level graduations—Cambros make handy containers for rising bread dough, too. (Look for these containers at restaurant supply stores or online.)

As for brining tips, we've got a few after 15 plus years. After pulling your turkey out of the brine, make sure to thoroughly pat it dry to prevent soggy skin. You can also place the turkey on a wire rack set on a baking sheet and allow it to dry overnight in the refrigerator—this will further encourage crispy skin during roasting. And as for the salt, the test kitchen prefers table salt. Kosher salt works fine, but the size of the grains varies between the two major brands, which can make recipe testing (and writing) difficult. The ratio of salt to water varies a bit from recipe to recipe, but generally the test kitchen uses 1 cup table salt to 2 gallons of water (this is enough brine for a 12- to 14-pound turkey).

5. Clean and oil cooking grate. Place V-rack with turkey on cool side of grill with leg and wing facing coal, cover (position lid vent over turkey if using charcoal), and cook for 1 hour.

6. Using potholders, transfer V-rack with turkey to rimmed baking sheet or roasting pan. If using charcoal, remove cooking grate and add 12 new briquettes and second wood chip packet to pile of coals; set cooking grate in place. If using gas, place remaining wood chip packets directly on primary burner. With wad of paper towels in each hand, flip turkey breast side up in rack and return V-rack with turkey to cool side of grill, with other leg and wing facing heat. Cover (position lid vent over turkey if using charcoal) and cook for 45 minutes.

7. Using potholders, carefully rotate V-rack with turkey (breast remains up) 180 degrees. Cover and continue to cook until breast registers 160 degrees and thighs register 175 degrees, 15 to 45 minutes longer. Transfer turkey to carving board, tent loosely with foil, and let rest for 20 to 30 minutes. Carve and serve.

SIMPLE GRILL-ROASTED TURKEY

WHY THIS RECIPE WORKS: Besides freeing up your oven for other dishes, roasting your turkey out on the grill also means that you don't have to worry about constantly monitoring the bird to ensure a perfectly juicy, tender turkey. To make grilling turkey foolproof, we divided our coals into two piles on either side of the grill so that the turkey thighs would receive the highest heat. A combination of lit coals and unlit briquettes yielded a longer-burning fire, making replenishing coals unnecessary. The addition of a pan of water stabilized the temperature inside the grill for even cooking, and a quick salt rub before grilling yielded seasoned meat and crispy skin.

Simple Grill-Roasted Turkey

SERVES 10 TO 12

Table salt is not recommended for this recipe because it is too fine. If using a kosher or self-basting turkey (such as a frozen Butterball), do not salt it in step 1. Check the wings halfway through roasting; if they are getting too dark, fold a 12 by 8-inch piece of foil in half lengthwise and then again crosswise and slide the foil between the wing and the cooking grate to shield the wings from the flame. As an accompaniment, try our Gravy for Simple Grill-Roasted Turkey (recipe follows).

- 1 (12- to 14-pound) turkey, neck and giblets removed and reserved for gravy
- Kosher salt and pepper
- 1 teaspoon baking powder
- 1 tablespoon vegetable oil
- Large disposable aluminum roasting pan (if using charcoal) or 2 disposable aluminum pie plates (if using gas)

1. Place turkey breast side down on work surface. Make two 2-inch incisions below each thigh and breast along back of turkey (4 incisions total). Using fingers or handle of wooden spoon, carefully separate skin from thighs and breast. Rub 4 teaspoons salt evenly inside cavity of turkey, 1 tablespoon salt under skin of each side of breast, and 1 teaspoon salt under skin of each leg.

2. Combine 1 teaspoon salt, 1 teaspoon pepper, and baking powder in small bowl. Pat turkey dry with paper towels and evenly sprinkle baking powder mixture all over. Rub in mixture with hands, coating entire surface evenly. Wrap turkey tightly with plastic wrap; refrigerate for 24 to 48 hours.

3. Remove turkey from refrigerator and discard plastic. Tuck wings underneath turkey. Using hands, rub oil evenly over entire surface of turkey.

4A. FOR A CHARCOAL GRILL: Open bottom vent halfway and place disposable pan filled with 3 cups water in center of grill. Arrange 1½ quarts unlit charcoal briquettes on either side of pan in even layer. Light large chimney starter two-thirds filled with charcoal briquettes (4 quarts). When top coals are partially covered with ash, pour 2 quarts of lit coals on top of each pile of unlit coals. Set cooking grate in place, cover, and open lid vent halfway. Heat grill until hot, about 5 minutes.

4B. FOR A GAS GRILL: Place 2 disposable pie plates with 2 cups water in each directly on 1 burner over which turkey will be cooked. Turn all burners to high, cover, and heat grill until hot, about 15 minutes. Turn primary burner (burner opposite pie plates) to medium and turn other burner(s) off. Adjust primary burner as needed to maintain grill temperature of 325 degrees.

5. Clean and oil cooking grate. Place turkey, breast side up, in center of charcoal grill or on cooler side of gas grill, making sure bird is over disposable pans and not over flame. Cover (placing vents over turkey on charcoal grill) and cook until breasts register 160 degrees and thighs/drumsticks register 175 degrees, 2½ to 3 hours, rotating turkey after 1¼ hours if using gas grill.

6. Transfer turkey to carving board and let rest, uncovered, for 45 minutes. Carve turkey and serve.

Gravy for Simple Grill-Roasted Turkey

MAKES 6 CUPS

- 1 tablespoon vegetable oil
- Reserved turkey neck, cut into 1-inch pieces, and giblets
- 1 pound onions, chopped coarse
- 4 cups low-sodium chicken broth
- 4 cups beef broth
- 2 small carrots, peeled and chopped coarse
- 2 small celery ribs, chopped coarse
- 6 tablespoons unsalted butter
- ½ cup all-purpose flour
- 2 bay leaves
- ½ teaspoon dried thyme
- 10 whole black peppercorns
- Salt and pepper

1. Heat oil in Dutch oven over medium-high heat until shimmering. Add turkey neck and giblets; cook, stirring occasionally, until browned, about 5 minutes. Add half of onions and cook, stirring occasionally, until softened, about 3 minutes. Reduce heat to low; cover and cook, stirring occasionally, until turkey parts and onions release their juices, about 20 minutes.

2. Add chicken broth and beef broth; increase heat to high and bring to boil. Reduce heat to low and simmer, uncovered, skimming any scum that rises to surface, until broth is rich and flavorful, about 30 minutes. Strain broth into large bowl (you should have about 8 cups), reserving giblets, if desired; discard neck. Reserve broth. If using, when cool enough to handle, remove gristle from giblets, dice, and set aside. (Broth can be refrigerated for up to 2 days.)

3. Pulse carrots in food processor until broken into rough ¼-inch pieces, about 5 pulses. Add celery and remaining onions; pulse until all vegetables are broken into ⅛-inch pieces, about 5 pulses.

4. Melt butter in now-empty Dutch oven over medium-high heat. Add vegetables and cook, stirring frequently, until softened and well browned, about 10 minutes. Reduce heat to medium; stir in flour and cook, stirring constantly, until thoroughly browned and fragrant, 5 to 7 minutes. Whisking constantly, gradually add reserved broth; bring to boil, skimming off any foam that forms on surface. Reduce heat to medium-low and add bay leaves, thyme, and peppercorns; simmer, stirring occasionally, until thickened and reduced to 6 cups, 30 to 35 minutes.

5. Strain gravy through fine-mesh strainer into clean saucepan, pressing on solids to extract as much liquid as possible; discard solids. Stir in diced giblets, if using. Season with salt and pepper to taste.

GRILL-ROASTED TURKEY BREAST

WHY THIS RECIPE WORKS: Grill-roasting a turkey breast makes a nice change from the same old oven-roasted holiday bird. And unleashing the smoky fire of the grill on mild-mannered turkey breast is bound to add great flavor. The problem is that unlike fatty pork butt or brisket, which turns moist and tender after a stint on the grill, ultra-lean turkey breast easily dries out. Plus its irregular shape can lead to uneven cooking. We wanted to develop a recipe that would deliver a grill-roasted breast with all the richness and juiciness we associate with the thighs and legs, along with crisp, well-rendered skin, and meat that was moist all the way through.

We began by salting our turkey breast. Salting, much like brining, imparts flavor and moisture to the meat. When meat is salted, its juices are initially drawn out of the flesh and beads of liquid pool on its surface. Eventually, the salty liquid slowly migrates back into the meat, keeping it moist as it cooks. We grill-roasted the turkey breast over a modified two-level fire, starting the meat over the cool side of the grill and later moving it to the hot side to finish cooking. Although most of the meat turned out moist and flavorful, there were still desiccated spots on the tapered ends of the breast and in places where the skin didn't completely cover the meat. Inspired by a restaurant technique, we reshaped our turkey breast like a roulade so that it would cook through evenly. After carefully removing the skin, we rolled the boneless turkey breast into a tight cylinder. Then we rewrapped the skin around the roulade of meat to completely cover and protect it. Our roast held its shape beautifully on the grill and, once carved, the roulade revealed moist, evenly cooked meat and crisp skin.

Grill-Roasted Boneless Turkey Breast

SERVES 6 TO 8

We prefer either a natural (unbrined) or kosher turkey breast for this recipe. Using a kosher turkey breast (rubbed with salt and rinsed during processing) or self-basting turkey breast (injected with salt and water) eliminates the need for salting in step 2. If the breast has a pop-up timer, remove it before cooking. When using a charcoal grill, we prefer wood chunks to wood chips whenever possible; substitute 1 small wood chunk, soaked in water for 1 hour, for the wood chip packet.

- ½ cup wood chips, soaked in water for 15 minutes and drained (optional)
- 1 (5- to 7-pound) whole bone-in turkey breast, trimmed
- 2 teaspoons salt
- 1 teaspoon vegetable oil
- Pepper

1. Using large piece of heavy-duty aluminum foil, wrap soaked chips, if using, in foil packet and cut several vent holes in top.

2. Remove skin from breast meat and then cut along rib cage to remove breast halves (discard bones or save for stock). Pat turkey breast halves dry with paper towels and season with salt. Stack breast halves on top of one another with cut sides facing, and alternating thick and tapered ends. Stretch skin over exposed meat and tuck in ends. Tie kitchen twine lengthwise around roast. Then tie 5 to 7 pieces of twine at 1-inch intervals crosswise along roast. Transfer roast to wire rack set in rimmed baking sheet and refrigerate for 1 hour.

3A. FOR A CHARCOAL GRILL: Open bottom vent halfway. Light large chimney starter filled with charcoal briquettes (6 quarts). When top coals are partially covered with ash, pour evenly over half of grill. Place wood chip packet, if using, on coals. Set cooking grate in place, cover, and open lid vent halfway. Heat grill until hot and wood chips are smoking, about 5 minutes.

3B. FOR A GAS GRILL: Place wood chip packet, if using, directly on primary burner. Turn all burners to high, cover, and heat grill until hot and wood chips are smoking, about 15 minutes. Turn all burners to medium-low. (Adjust burner(s) as needed during cooking to maintain grill temperature around 300 degrees.)

4. Clean and oil cooking grate. Rub surface of roast with oil and season with pepper. Place roast on grill (cool side if using charcoal). Cover (position lid vents over meat if using charcoal) and cook until roast registers 150 degrees, 40 minutes to 1 hour, turning 180 degrees halfway through cooking.

5. Slide roast to hot side of grill (if using charcoal) or turn all burners to medium-high (if using gas). Cook until roast is browned and skin is crisp on all sides, 8 to 10 minutes, rotating every 2 minutes.

6. Transfer roast to carving board, tent loosely with foil, and let rest for 15 minutes. Cut into ½-inch-thick slices, removing twine as you cut. Serve.

NOTES FROM THE TEST KITCHEN

TURNING A BONE-IN TURKEY BREAST INTO A BONELESS TURKEY ROAST

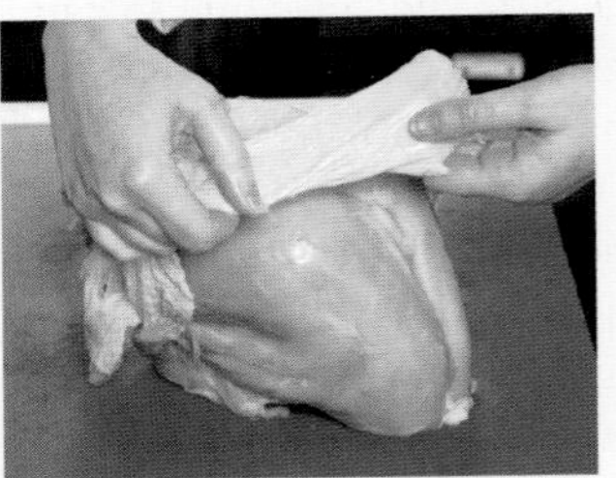

1. Starting at one side of the breast and using your fingers to separate the skin from the meat, peel the skin off the breast meat and reserve.

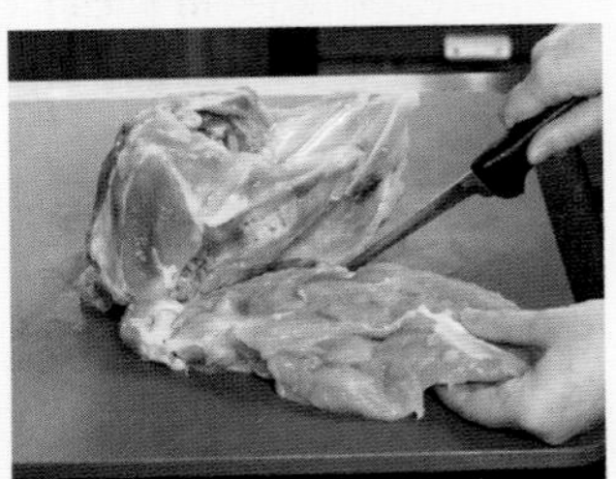

2. Using the tip of a knife, cut along the rib cage to remove each breast half completely.

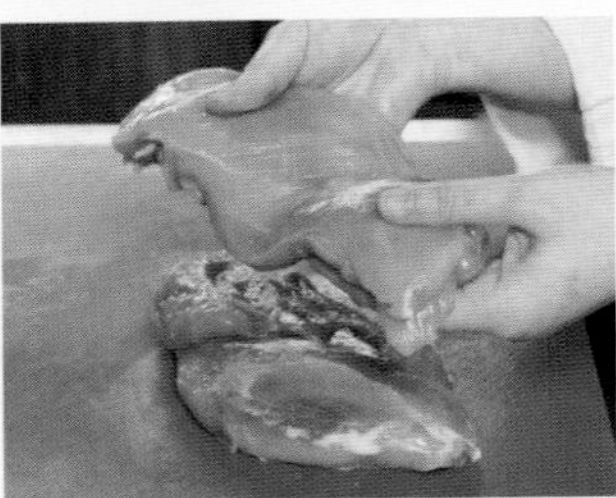

3. Arrange one breast, cut side up; top with the second breast, cut side down, the thick end over the tapered end. Drape the skin over the breasts and tuck the ends under.

4. Tie a 3-foot piece of kitchen twine lengthwise around the roast. Then, tie five to seven pieces of twine at 1-inch intervals crosswise along the roast, starting at its center, then at either end, and then filling in the rest.

CRANBERRY SAUCE

WHY THIS RECIPE WORKS: The best cranberry sauce has a clean, pure cranberry flavor, with enough sweetness to temper the assertively tart fruit but not so much that the sauce is cloying or candylike. The texture should be that of a soft gel, neither too liquidy nor too stiff, cushioning some softened but still intact berries.

For the most part, it turned out that simpler was better. We used white table sugar, which, unlike brown sugar, honey, or syrup, balanced the tartness of the cranberries without adding a flavor profile of its own. Simpler was also better when it came to liquid: water proved the best choice. We also discovered that adding just a pinch of salt brought out an unexpected sweetness in the berries, heightening the flavor of the sauce overall.

Classic Cranberry Sauce

MAKES 2¼ CUPS

If you've got frozen cranberries, do not defrost them before use; just pick through them and add about 2 minutes to the simmering time.

- 1 cup (7 ounces) sugar
- ¾ cup water
- ¼ teaspoon table salt
- 1 (12-ounce) bag cranberries, picked through (see note)

Bring the sugar, water, and salt to a boil in a medium saucepan over high heat, stirring occasionally to dissolve the sugar. Stir in the cranberries; return to a boil. Reduce the heat to medium; simmer until saucy and slightly thickened, and about two-thirds of the berries have popped open, about 5 minutes. Transfer to a medium bowl, cool to room temperature, and serve. (The cranberry sauce can be covered and refrigerated for up to 7 days; let stand at room temperature for 30 minutes before serving.)

HOLIDAY CRANBERRY CHUTNEY

WHY THIS RECIPE WORKS: There's something to be said for the simplicity of a plain old sweet-tart cranberry sauce, but sometimes we want more. To create a more complexly flavored sauce, we looked to Indian chutneys. Adding vinegar, aromatics, and spices to slow-cooked cranberries and fruit yielded a jammy relish with kick and savor.

Cranberry Chutney with Apples and Crystallized Ginger

MAKES ABOUT 3 CUPS

If using frozen cranberries, thaw them before cooking.

- 1 teaspoon vegetable oil
- 1 shallot, minced
- 2 teaspoons finely grated fresh ginger
- ½ teaspoon salt
- ⅔ cup water
- ¼ cup cider vinegar
- 1 cup packed brown sugar
- 12 ounces (3 cups) fresh or frozen cranberries
- 2 Granny Smith apples, peeled, cored, and cut into ¼-inch pieces
- ⅓ cup minced crystallized ginger

1. Heat oil in medium saucepan over medium heat until shimmering. Add shallot, fresh ginger, and salt; cook, stirring occasionally, until shallot has softened, 1 to 2 minutes.

2. Add water, vinegar, and sugar. Increase heat to high and bring to simmer, stirring to dissolve sugar. Add 1½ cups cranberries and apples; return to simmer. Reduce heat to medium-low and simmer, stirring occasionally, until cranberries have almost completely broken down and mixture has thickened, about 15 minutes.

3. Add remaining 1½ cups cranberries and crystallized ginger; continue to simmer, stirring occasionally, until cranberries just begin to burst, 5 to 7 minutes. Transfer to serving bowl and cool for at least 1 hour before serving. (Sauce can be refrigerated for up to 3 days.)

Spicy Cranberry Chutney

Increase oil to 2 teaspoons and substitute 1 stemmed and seeded red bell pepper cut into ¼-inch pieces and 2 seeded and minced jalapeño chiles for fresh ginger in step 1. Increase cooking time in step 1 to 5 minutes. Increase water to ¾ cup and omit apples and crystallized ginger.

Cranberry Chutney with Fennel and Golden Raisins

Increase oil to 2 teaspoons and substitute 1 cored fennel bulb cut into ¼-inch pieces and ½ teaspoon fennel seeds for fresh ginger in step 1. Increase cooking time in step 1 to 5 minutes. Increase water to 1 cup, omit apples, and substitute ⅓ cup golden raisins for crystallized ginger.

Cranberry-Orange Chutney

Starting with 2 oranges, remove four 2-inch-wide strips zest from 1 orange, then peel both oranges and remove segments. Set aside zest and segments. Increase fresh ginger to 4 teaspoons and add 1 teaspoon yellow mustard seeds to oil together with fresh ginger in step 1. Increase water to ¾ cup and add orange zest and segments to pot with cranberries in step 2. Omit apples and crystallized ginger.

Cranberry Chutney with Pear, Lemon, and Rosemary

Remove two 2-inch-wide strips zest from 1 lemon, then peel and remove segments. Set aside zest and segments. Substitute 2 teaspoons chopped fresh rosemary for fresh ginger. Substitute 2 peeled Bosc pears cut into ¼-inch pieces for apples; omit crystallized ginger. Add lemon zest and segments to pot with cranberries in step 2.

BAKED BREAD STUFFING

WHY THIS RECIPE WORKS: Stuffing baked in a dish definitely has appeal—you can make as much as you want and you don't have to time its doneness to coincide with the doneness of the meat—but it lacks the rich flavor from the bird's juices. As the base for our stuffing we chose ordinary sandwich bread, which we "staled" in a low oven; this would allow it to soak up plenty of liquid. To infuse the stuffing with meaty turkey flavor, we browned turkey wings on the stovetop, then we used the same pan to sauté the aromatics. When we placed the stuffing in a baking dish, we arranged the seared wings on top—as they cooked, their rendered fat infused the stuffing with rich flavor. Covering the baking dish with foil prevented the top of the stuffing from drying out, while placing a baking sheet underneath the dish protected the bottom layer from the oven's heat.

Baked Bread Stuffing with Sausage, Dried Cherries, and Pecans

SERVES 10 TO 12

Two pounds of chicken wings can be substituted for the turkey wings. If using chicken wings, separate them into 2 sections (it's not necessary to separate the tips) and poke each segment 4 to 5 times. Also, increase the amount of broth to 3 cups, reduce the amount of butter to 2 tablespoons, and cook the stuffing for only 60 minutes (the wings should register over 175 degrees at the end of cooking). Use the meat from the cooked wings to make salad or soup. The bread can be toasted up to 1 day in advance.

- 2 pounds hearty white sandwich bread, cut into ½-inch cubes (16 cups)
- 3 pounds turkey wings, divided at joints
- 2 teaspoons vegetable oil
- 1 pound bulk pork sausage
- 4 tablespoons (½ stick) unsalted butter
- 1 large onion, chopped fine
- 3 medium celery ribs, minced
- Table salt
- 2 tablespoons minced fresh thyme
- 2 tablespoons minced fresh sage
- 1 teaspoon ground black pepper
- 2½ cups low-sodium chicken broth
- 3 large eggs
- 1 cup dried cherries
- 1 cup pecan halves, toasted and chopped fine

1. Adjust the oven racks to the upper-middle and lower-middle positions and heat the oven to 250 degrees. Spread the bread cubes in an even layer on 2 rimmed baking sheets. Bake until the edges have dried but the centers are slightly moist (the cubes should yield to pressure), 45 to 60 minutes, stirring several times during baking. Transfer the dried bread to a large bowl and increase the oven temperature to 375 degrees.

2. While the bread dries, use a paring knife to poke 10 to 15 holes in each wing segment. Heat the oil in a 12-inch skillet over medium-high heat until shimmering. Add the wings in a single layer and cook until golden brown on both sides, 8 to 12 minutes. Transfer the wings to a separate bowl and set aside.

3. Return the now-empty skillet to medium-high heat, add the sausage, and cook, breaking it up into ½-inch pieces with a wooden spoon, until browned, 5 to 7 minutes. Remove the sausage with a slotted spoon and transfer to a paper towel–lined plate.

4. Melt the butter in the fat left in the skillet over medium heat. Add the onion, celery, and ½ teaspoon salt and cook, stirring occasionally, until the vegetables are softened, 7 to 9 minutes. Stir in the thyme, sage, and pepper and cook until fragrant, about 30 seconds. Stir in 1 cup of the broth, scraping up any browned bits, and bring to a simmer. Add the vegetable mixture to the bowl with the dried bread and toss to combine.

5. Grease a 13 by 9-inch baking dish. Whisk the eggs, remaining 1½ cups broth, 1½ teaspoons salt, and any accumulated juices from the wings together in a bowl. Add the egg mixture, cherries, pecans, and sausage to the bread mixture and toss to combine; transfer to the prepared baking dish. Arrange the wings on top of the stuffing, cover tightly with aluminum foil, and place the baking dish on a rimmed baking sheet.

6. Bake on the lower rack until the wings register 175 degrees, 60 to 75 minutes. (The stuffing can be held at room temperature for up to 4 hours. To finish, remove the wings from the stuffing and re-cover the stuffing tightly with foil. Heat on a rimmed baking sheet in a 375-degree oven until hot, 20 to 25 minutes. Remove the foil, fluff with a fork, and serve immediately.)

7. Remove the foil and transfer the wings to a dinner plate to reserve for another use. Gently fluff the stuffing with a fork. Let rest for 5 minutes before serving.

Baked Bread Stuffing with Leeks, Bacon, and Apple

Follow the recipe for Baked Bread Stuffing with Sausage, Dried Cherries, and Pecans, substituting 12 ounces bacon, cut into ½-inch pieces, for the sausage. In step 3, cook the bacon in a skillet until crisp, about 5 minutes. Remove the bacon with a slotted spoon and transfer to a paper towel–lined plate; pour off all but 2 tablespoons fat from the skillet. Proceed with the recipe from step 4, substituting 2 leeks, white and light green parts, sliced thin, for the onion, and 3 Granny Smith apples, cut into 1/4-inch pieces, for the dried cherries. Omit the pecans.

Baked Bread Stuffing with Fresh Herbs

Follow the recipe for Baked Bread Stuffing with Sausage, Dried Cherries, and Pecans, omitting the sausage. After the browned turkey wings have been removed in step 2, increase the butter to 6 tablespoons and melt it in the skillet over medium heat. Proceed with the recipe from step 4, substituting 3 tablespoons chopped fresh parsley for the dried cherries and pecans.

GREEN BEAN CASSEROLE

WHY THIS RECIPE WORKS: The classic combination of green beans, condensed soup, and canned onions isn't bad. But for a holiday centered on homemade food, shouldn't every dish be great? We wanted to upgrade green bean casserole to give it fresh, homemade flavor.

Our first tasting determined that we definitely needed to use fresh green beans rather than frozen or canned beans. A preliminary blanching and shocking prepared the beans to finish cooking perfectly in the casserole, enabling them to keep a consistent texture and retain their beautiful green color. For our sauce, we made a mushroom variation of the classic French velouté sauce (chicken broth thickened with a roux made from butter and flour, then finished with heavy cream). Our biggest challenge was the onion topping. Ultimately we found that the canned onions couldn't be entirely replaced without sacrificing the level of convenience we thought appropriate to the dish, but we masked their "commercial" flavor with freshly made buttered bread crumbs.

Classic Green Bean Casserole

SERVES 8 TO 10

All the components of this dish can be cooked ahead of time. The assembled casserole needs only 15 minutes in a 375-degree oven to warm through and brown.

TOPPING

- 4 slices high-quality white sandwich bread, torn into quarters
- 2 tablespoons unsalted butter, softened
- ¼ teaspoon table salt
- ⅛ teaspoon ground black pepper
- 3 cups canned fried onions (about 6 ounces)

BEANS

- Table salt
- 2 pounds green beans, ends trimmed, cut on the diagonal into 2-inch pieces
- ½ ounce dried porcini mushrooms
- 6 tablespoons (¾ stick) unsalted butter
- 1 medium onion, minced
- 3 medium garlic cloves, minced or pressed through a garlic press (about 1 tablespoon)
- 12 ounces white button mushrooms, wiped clean and sliced ¼ inch thick
- 12 ounces cremini mushrooms, wiped clean and sliced ¼ inch thick
- 2 tablespoons minced fresh thyme leaves
- ¼ teaspoon ground black pepper
- 2 tablespoons unbleached all-purpose flour
- 1 cup low-sodium chicken broth
- 2 cups heavy cream

1. FOR THE TOPPING: Pulse the bread, butter, salt, and pepper in a food processor until the mixture resembles coarse crumbs, 10 to 15 pulses. Transfer to a large bowl and toss with the onions; set aside.

2. FOR THE BEANS: Heat the oven to 375 degrees. Bring 4 quarts water to a boil in a large pot. Add 2 tablespoons salt and the beans. Cook until bright green and slightly crunchy, 4 to 5 minutes. Drain the beans and plunge immediately into a large bowl filled with ice water to stop cooking. Spread the beans out onto a paper towel–lined baking sheet to drain.

3. Meanwhile, cover the dried porcini with ½ cup hot tap water in a small microwave-safe bowl; cover with plastic wrap, cut several steam vents with a paring knife, and microwave on high power for 30 seconds. Let stand until the mushrooms soften, about 5 minutes. Lift the mushrooms from the liquid with a fork and mince using a chef's knife (you should have about 2 tablespoons). Pour the liquid through a paper towel–lined sieve and reserve.

4. Melt the butter in a large nonstick skillet over medium-high heat. Add the onion, garlic, button mushrooms, and cremini mushrooms and cook until the mushrooms release their moisture, about 2 minutes. Add the porcini mushrooms along with their strained soaking liquid, the thyme, 1 teaspoon salt, and the pepper and cook until all the mushrooms are tender and the liquid has reduced to 2 tablespoons, about 5 minutes. Add the flour and cook for 1 minute. Stir in the chicken broth and reduce the heat to medium. Stir in the cream and simmer gently until the sauce has the consistency of dense soup, about 15 minutes.

5. Arrange the beans in a 3-quart gratin dish. Pour the mushroom mixture over the beans and mix to coat the beans evenly. Sprinkle with the bread-crumb mixture and bake until the top is golden brown and the sauce is bubbling around the edges, about 15 minutes. Serve immediately.

BEHIND THE SCENES

PRESS, DON'T MINCE, YOUR GARLIC

Newly hired test cooks (many of whom are fresh out of cooking school) often do a double take when they discover a test kitchen secret. When it comes to mincing garlic, we'd rather use a garlic press to do the job. Purists may insist on mincing their garlic the old-fashioned way (a chef's knife and cutting board), but let's face it—mincing garlic is quite a chore. First, its texture is defiantly sticky, so that little bits cling tenaciously to your cutting board, knife blade, and fingers. Second, despite the diminutive size of garlic cloves, mincing a couple of them finely and evenly is a time- and labor-intensive proposition. Enter the garlic press.

Most garlic presses share a common design, comprising two handles connected by a hinge. At the end of one handle is a small perforated hopper; at the end of the other is a plunger that fits snugly inside the hopper. The garlic cloves in the hopper get crushed by the descending plunger when you squeeze the handles together and the puree is extruded through the perforations in the bottom of the hopper. In thousands of hours of use in our test kitchen, we have found that this little tool delivers speed, ease, and a comfortable separation of garlic from fingers. (See page 879 for our recommended brand of garlic press.) And there are other advantages: A good garlic press breaks down the cloves more than an average cook would with a knife, resulting in a fuller, more pungent garlic flavor. A good garlic press also ensures a consistently fine texture, which in turns means better distribution throughout the dish. Lesson learned? They don't teach you everything in cooking school.

QUICK GREEN BEAN CASSEROLE

WHY THIS RECIPE WORKS: We love traditional green bean casserole, but we wanted a streamlined technique for preparing the dish—one with tender beans in a tasty sauce worthy of a holiday spread and yet speedy enough for a last-minute supper.

Rather than using two pots—one for the beans and one for the sauce—we cooked both in just one pot, a skillet. First, we built a sauce in the skillet with onion, garlic, chicken broth, cream, and a little flour; then we added the beans along with thyme and bay leaves, covered them, and allowed them to steam until the beans were almost done. We then stirred in meaty browned cremini mushrooms and thickened the sauce by uncovering the skillet during the final phase of cooking. And instead of canned fried onions, we sprinkled crunchy fried sliced shallots over our easy, tasty skillet casserole.

Quick Green Bean "Casserole"

SERVES 8

- 3 large shallots, sliced thin (about 1 cup)
- Table salt and ground black pepper
- 3 tablespoons unbleached all-purpose flour
- 5 tablespoons vegetable oil
- 10 ounces cremini mushrooms, wiped clean and sliced ¼ inch thick
- 2 tablespoons unsalted butter
- 1 medium onion, minced
- 2 medium garlic cloves, minced or pressed through a garlic press (about 2 teaspoons)
- 1½ pounds green beans, trimmed
- 3 sprigs fresh thyme
- 2 bay leaves
- ¾ cup heavy cream
- ¾ cup low-sodium chicken broth

1. Toss the shallots with 1/4 teaspoon salt, 1/8 teaspoon pepper, and 2 tablespoons of the flour in a bowl. Heat 3 tablespoons of the oil in a 12-inch nonstick skillet over medium-high heat until smoking; add the shallots and cook, stirring frequently, until golden and crisp, about 5 minutes. Transfer the shallots with the oil to a baking sheet lined with paper towels.

2. Wipe out the skillet and return to medium-high heat. Add the remaining 2 tablespoons oil, the mushrooms, and 1/4 teaspoon salt; cook, stirring occasionally, until the mushrooms are well browned, about 8 minutes. Transfer to a plate and set aside.

3. Wipe out the skillet. Melt the butter in the skillet over medium heat, then add the onion and cook, stirring occasionally, until the edges begin to brown, about 2 minutes. Stir in the garlic and remaining 1 tablespoon flour; toss in the green beans, thyme, and bay leaves. Add the cream and chicken broth, increase the heat to medium-high, cover, and cook until the beans are partly tender but still crisp at the center, about 4 minutes. Add the mushrooms and continue to cook, uncovered, until the green beans are tender, about 4 minutes. Off the heat, discard the bay leaves and thyme; season with salt and pepper to taste. Transfer to a serving dish, sprinkle evenly with the shallots, and serve.

CANDIED SWEET POTATO CASSEROLE

WHY THIS RECIPE WORKS: Sweet potato casserole is often claimed as a must-have at the Thanksgiving table. Kids love this sweet, sticky dish, but adults long for a side dish with more restrained sweetness, rather than one that could double as dessert. We set out to develop a sweet potato casserole with a bit of a savory accent to please everyone.

For the best texture and flavor, we steamed the sweet potatoes on the stovetop with a little water, butter, and brown sugar. We kept the other flavorings simple—just salt and pepper. In the topping, we used whole pecans instead of chopped; this gave the casserole a better texture and appearance. And a little cayenne and cumin lent a hit of spice to the topping that offset the sweetness of the potato.

Candied Sweet Potato Casserole

SERVES 10 TO 12

For a more intense molasses flavor, use dark brown sugar in place of light brown sugar.

SWEET POTATOES

- 8 tablespoons (1 stick) unsalted butter, cut into 1-inch chunks
- 5 pounds sweet potatoes (about 8 medium), peeled and cut into 1-inch cubes
- 1 cup (7 ounces) packed light brown sugar (see note)
- ½ cup water
- 1½ teaspoons table salt
- ½ teaspoon ground black pepper

PECAN TOPPING

- 2 cups pecan halves
- ½ cup packed (3½ ounces) light brown sugar (see note)
- 1 egg white, lightly beaten
- ⅛ teaspoon table salt
- Pinch cayenne pepper
- Pinch ground cumin

1. FOR THE SWEET POTATOES: Melt the butter in a large Dutch oven over medium-high heat. Add the sweet potatoes, brown sugar, water, salt, and black pepper; bring to a simmer. Reduce the heat to medium-low, cover, and cook, stirring often, until the sweet potatoes are tender (a paring knife can be slipped into and out of the center of the potatoes with very little resistance), 45 to 60 minutes.

2. When the sweet potatoes are tender, remove the lid and bring the sauce to a rapid simmer over medium-high heat. Continue to simmer until the sauce has reduced to a glaze, 7 to 10 minutes.

3. FOR THE TOPPING: Meanwhile, mix all the ingredients for the topping together in a medium bowl; set aside.

4. Adjust an oven rack to the middle position and heat the oven to 450 degrees. Pour the potato mixture into a 13 by 9-inch baking dish (or a shallow casserole dish of similar size). Spread the topping over the potatoes. Bake until the pecans are toasted and crisp, 10 to 15 minutes. Serve immediately.

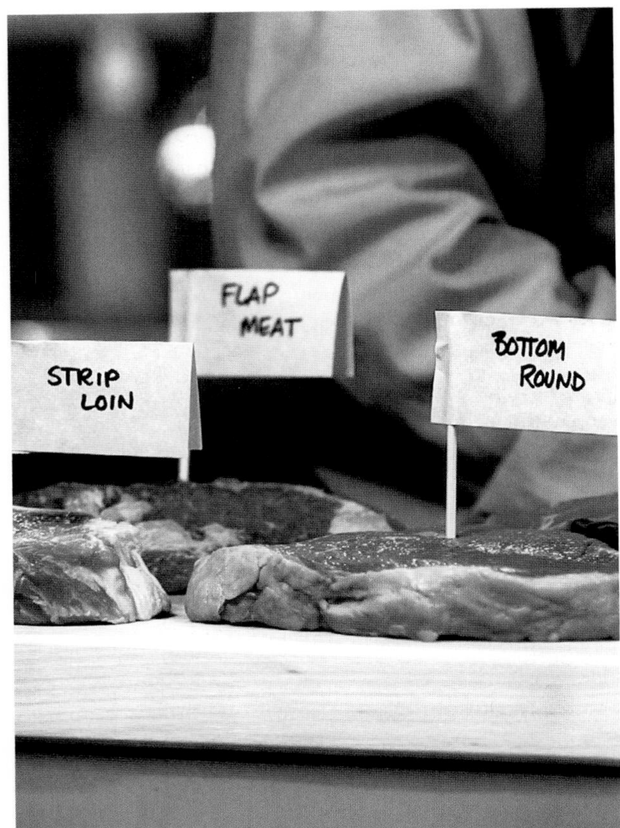

CHAPTER 7

WE'LL HAVE THE STEAK

PAN-SEARED STEAKS

WHY THIS RECIPE WORKS: The flavor of a juicy, grilled steak is hard to beat. We wanted to produce outstanding steaks—indoors—that were every bit as good as those cooked on the grill. We found that heating a heavy-bottomed skillet until very hot is essential for a good sear and, thus, a good crust. Thoroughly drying the steaks is also key—soggy steaks will steam, not sear. For best flavor, we seasoned the steaks with salt and pepper prior to cooking. And we reduced the heat before adding the steaks—the skillet was still hot, but not so hot that it burned the fond, which we used to make a pan sauce. After removing the steaks from the pan, we let them rest for five minutes, enough time to prepare the pan sauce and allow the juices in the meat to redistribute.

Pan-Seared Steaks

SERVES 4

Serve these steaks with either Red Wine Pan Sauce or Shallot Butter Sauce (recipes follow). Prepare all the sauce ingredients before starting the steaks and don't wash the skillet after cooking the steaks; the fat left in the pan will be used for the sauce. Note that the wine reduction used in the red wine sauce should be started before the steaks are cooked.

- 1 tablespoon vegetable oil
- 4 (8-ounce) boneless strip or rib-eye steaks, each 1 to 1¼ inches thick, thoroughly dried with paper towels
- Table salt and ground black pepper

1. Heat the oil in a 12-inch skillet over high heat until just smoking. Meanwhile, season both sides of the steaks with salt and pepper.

2. Lay the steaks in the pan, leaving ¼ inch of space between them; reduce the heat to medium-high and cook, not moving the steaks until well browned, about 4 minutes. Using tongs, flip the steaks; cook until the center of the steaks registers 120 degrees on an instant-read thermometer for rare (4 minutes), 125 degrees for medium-rare (5 minutes), or 130 degrees for medium (6 minutes). Transfer the steaks to a large plate, tent with foil, and let rest for 5 minutes while preparing one of the pan sauces.

Red Wine Pan Sauce

MAKES ABOUT ½ CUP

Start cooking the steaks when the wine has almost finished reducing. Use a smooth, medium-bodied, fruity wine, such as a Côtes du Rhône.

WINE REDUCTION

- 1 cup red wine (see note)
- 1 medium shallot, minced (about 3 tablespoons)
- 2 white mushrooms, wiped clean and chopped fine (about 3 tablespoons)
- 1 small carrot, chopped fine (about 2 tablespoons)
- 1 bay leaf
- 3 sprigs fresh parsley

SAUCE

- 1 medium shallot, minced (about 3 tablespoons)
- ½ cup low-sodium chicken broth
- ½ cup low-sodium beef broth
- 3 tablespoons cold unsalted butter, cut into 6 pieces
- ½ teaspoon fresh thyme leaves
- Table salt and ground black pepper

1. FOR THE WINE REDUCTION: Heat the wine, shallot, mushrooms, carrot, bay leaf, and parsley in a 12-inch skillet over low heat; cook, without simmering (the liquid should be steaming but not bubbling), until the entire mixture reduces to 1 cup, 15 to 20 minutes. Strain through a fine-mesh strainer and return the liquid (about ½ cup) to the clean skillet. Continue to cook over low heat, without simmering, until the liquid is reduced to 2 tablespoons, 15 to 20 minutes. Transfer the reduction to a bowl.

2. FOR THE SAUCE: Follow the recipe for Pan-Seared Steaks. After removing the steaks from the skillet, add the shallot and cook over low heat until softened, about 1 minute. Turn the heat to high; add the chicken and beef broths. Bring to a boil, scraping up the browned bits on the pan bottom with a wooden spoon, until the liquid is reduced to 2 tablespoons, about 6 minutes. Turn the heat to medium-low, gently whisk in the reserved wine reduction and any accumulated juices from the plate with the steaks. Whisk in the butter, one piece at a time, until melted and the sauce is thickened and glossy; add the thyme and season with salt and pepper to taste. Spoon the sauce over the steaks and serve immediately.

Shallot Butter Sauce

MAKES ABOUT ½ CUP

- 2 medium shallots, minced (about ⅓ cup)
- 4 tablespoons (½ stick) cold unsalted butter, cut into 4 pieces
- 1 teaspoon juice from 1 lemon
- 1 teaspoon minced fresh parsley leaves
- Table salt and ground black pepper

Follow the recipe for Pan-Seared Steaks. After removing the steaks from the skillet, add the shallots and cook over low heat until softened, about 1 minute. Turn the heat to medium-low; stir in the butter, scraping up the browned bits on the pan bottom with a wooden spoon. When the butter is just melted, stir in the lemon juice and parsley; season with salt and pepper to taste. Spoon the sauce over the steaks and serve immediately.

RESTAURANT-STYLE STEAK SAUCE

WHY THIS RECIPE WORKS: We love the ultra-rich flavor and glossy consistency that a classic French demi-glace (a savory, full-bodied reduction traditionally made from veal bones and stock) adds to a sauce, but making it is a time-consuming process usually left to the expertise of professional cooks. We wanted to find a shortcut for making demi-glace at home, so that we could use it as the base of a variety of great sauces for crusty, pan-seared steaks. Chopping up vegetables (to increase their surface area, thus providing more opportunity for flavorful browning) as well as adding mushrooms, tomato paste, and seasonings to red wine and beef broth was a good start, but it wasn't enough. To replicate the meaty flavor and unctuous gelatin given up by roasted bones, we sautéed ground beef with the tomato paste and stirred powdered gelatin into the final reduction. Since it was easy to freeze and use again, making a big batch of our Sauce Base was worth our while; we made enough for two recipes of steak sauce and came up with variations that would make us want to eat steak every night.

Restaurant-Style Herb Sauce for Pan-Seared Steaks

SERVES 4

We like this sauce with strip or rib-eye steaks, but it will work with any type of pan-seared steak.

- 1 recipe Pan-Seared Steaks (page 164)
- 1 small shallot, minced (about 1 tablespoon)
- ½ cup white wine
- ¼ cup Sauce Base (½ recipe; page 165)
- ¼ teaspoon white wine vinegar
- 1½ teaspoons minced fresh chives
- 1½ teaspoons minced fresh parsley leaves
- 1 teaspoon minced fresh tarragon leaves
- 1 tablespoon unsalted butter
- Table salt and ground black pepper

After transferring the steaks to a plate to rest, return the now-empty skillet to medium-low heat; add the shallot and cook, stirring constantly, until lightly browned, about 2 minutes. Add the wine and bring to a simmer, scraping the bottom of the skillet with a wooden spoon to loosen any browned bits. Add the Sauce Base, vinegar, and any accumulated juices from the steaks; return to a simmer and cook until slightly reduced, about 1 minute. Off the heat, whisk in the chives, parsley, tarragon, and butter; season with salt and pepper to taste. Spoon the sauce over the steaks and serve.

Restaurant-Style Brandy and Green-Peppercorn Sauce for Pan-Seared Steaks

SERVES 4

- 1 recipe Pan-Seared Steaks (page 164)
- 1 small shallot, minced (about 1 tablespoon)
- ½ cup brandy
- ¼ cup Sauce Base (½ recipe; page 165)
- ¼ teaspoon red wine vinegar
- ¼ cup heavy cream
- 2 tablespoons green peppercorns, rinsed
- ¼ teaspoon chopped fresh thyme leaves
- Table salt and ground black pepper

After transferring the steaks to a plate to rest, return the now-empty skillet to medium-low heat; add the shallot and cook, stirring constantly, until lightly browned, about 2 minutes. Add the brandy and bring to a simmer, scraping the bottom of the skillet with a wooden spoon to loosen any browned bits. Add the Sauce Base, vinegar, heavy cream, peppercorns, thyme, and any accumulated juices from the steaks; return to a simmer and cook until slightly reduced, about 1 minute. Off the heat, season with salt and pepper to taste. Spoon the sauce over the steaks and serve.

Restaurant-Style Port Wine Sauce for Pan-Seared Steaks

SERVES 4

- 1 recipe Pan-Seared Steaks (page 164)
- 1 small shallot, minced (about 1 tablespoon)
- ½ cup ruby port
- ¼ cup Sauce Base (½ recipe; recipe follows)
- ¼ teaspoon balsamic vinegar
- ¼ teaspoon chopped fresh thyme leaves
- 1 tablespoon unsalted butter
- Table salt and ground black pepper

After transferring the steaks to a plate to rest, return the now-empty skillet to medium-low heat; add the shallot and cook, stirring constantly, until lightly browned, about 2 minutes. Add the port and bring to a simmer, scraping the bottom of the skillet with a wooden spoon to loosen any browned bits. Add the Sauce Base, vinegar, and any accumulated juices from the steaks; return to a simmer and cook until slightly reduced, about 1 minute. Off the heat, whisk in the thyme and butter; season with salt and pepper to taste. Spoon the sauce over the steaks and serve.

Sauce Base

MAKES ½ CUP

The sauce base recipe yields more than called for in the sauce recipes; leftovers can be refrigerated in an airtight container for up to 3 days or frozen for up to 1 month.

- 1 small onion, peeled and cut into rough ½-inch pieces
- 1 small carrot, peeled and cut into rough ½-inch pieces
- 8 ounces cremini mushrooms, trimmed and halved
- 2 medium garlic cloves, peeled
- 1 tablespoon vegetable oil
- 8 ounces 85 percent lean ground beef
- 1 tablespoon tomato paste
- 2 cups dry red wine
- 4 cups beef broth
- 4 sprigs fresh thyme
- 2 bay leaves
- 2 teaspoons whole black peppercorns
- 5 teaspoons unflavored gelatin

1. Pulse the onion, carrot, mushrooms, and garlic in a food processor into ⅛-inch pieces, 10 to 12 pulses, scraping down the sides as needed.

2. Heat the oil in a Dutch oven over medium-high heat until shimmering; add the beef and tomato paste and cook, stirring frequently, until the beef is well browned, 8 to 10 minutes. Add the vegetable mixture and cook, stirring occasionally, until any exuded moisture has evaporated, about 8 minutes. Add the wine and bring to a simmer, scraping the bottom of the pot with a wooden spoon to loosen any browned bits. Add the broth, thyme, bay leaves, and peppercorns; bring to a boil. Reduce the heat and gently boil, occasionally scraping the bottom and sides of the pot and skimming fat from the surface, until reduced to 2 cups, 20 to 25 minutes.

3. Strain the mixture through a fine-mesh strainer set over a small saucepan, pressing on the solids with a rubber spatula to extract as much liquid as possible (you should have about 1 cup stock). Sprinkle the gelatin over the stock and stir to dissolve. Place the saucepan over medium-high heat and bring the stock to a boil. Gently boil, stirring occasionally, until reduced to ½ cup, 5 to 7 minutes. Remove from the heat and cover to keep warm.

CAST-IRON THICK-CUT STEAKS

WHY THIS RECIPE WORKS: We were looking for a way to make a steak with the ultimate crust entirely on the stovetop—so we turned to a cast-iron skillet, since its heat-retention properties are ideal for a perfect sear. We chose the moderately expensive boneless strip steak for its big, beefy flavor. The first step to a great sear was an evenly heated cooking surface, which we accomplished by preheating the cast-iron skillet in the oven. This also gave us time to prepare a zesty compound butter with shallot, garlic, parsley, and chives—and to let the steaks warm up to room temperature, which helped them cook more quickly and evenly. Salting the outside of the steaks while they rested pulled moisture from the steaks while also seasoning the meat, helping us get a better sear. After testing different flipping techniques and heat levels, we found that flipping the steaks every 2 minutes and transitioning from medium-high to medium-low heat partway through cooking resulted in a perfectly browned, crisp crust and a juicy, evenly cooked interior every time.

Cast-Iron Thick-Cut Steaks with Herb Butter

SERVES 4

- 2 (1-pound) boneless strip steaks, 1½ inches thick, trimmed
- Salt and pepper
- 4 tablespoons unsalted butter, softened
- 2 tablespoons minced shallot
- 1 tablespoon minced fresh parsley
- 1 tablespoon minced fresh chives
- 1 garlic clove, minced
- 2 tablespoons vegetable oil

1. Adjust oven rack to middle position, place 12-inch cast-iron skillet on rack, and heat oven to 500 degrees. Meanwhile, season steaks with salt and let sit at room temperature. Mix butter, shallot, parsley, chives, garlic, ¼ teaspoon pepper, and pinch of salt together in bowl; set aside until needed.

2. When oven reaches 500 degrees, pat steaks dry with paper towels and season with pepper. Using potholders, remove skillet from oven and place over medium-high heat; turn off oven. Being careful of hot skillet handle, add oil and heat until just smoking. Cook steaks, without moving, until lightly browned on first side, about 2 minutes. Flip steaks and continue to cook until lightly browned on second side, about 2 minutes.

3. Flip steaks, reduce heat to medium-low, and cook, flipping every 2 minutes, until steaks are well browned and meat registers 120 to 125 degrees (for medium-rare), 7 to 9 minutes. Transfer steaks to carving board, dollop 2 tablespoons herb butter on each steak, tent loosely with aluminum foil, and let rest for 5 to 10 minutes. Slice steaks into ½-inch-thick slices and serve.

Cast-Iron Thick-Cut Steaks with Blue Cheese–Chive Butter

Omit shallot and parsley. Increase chives to 2 tablespoons and add ⅓ cup crumbled mild blue cheese to butter with chives.

PAN-SEARED THICK-CUT STEAKS

WHY THIS RECIPE WORKS: A nicely charred thick-cut steak certainly looks appealing. But cutting into the steak to find that the rosy meat is confined to a measly spot in the center—with the rest a thick band of overcooked gray—is a great disappointment. We wanted to find a surefire method for pan-searing thick-cut steaks that could deliver both a flavorful crust and juicy, perfectly pink meat throughout.

We found it was essential to sear the steaks quickly to keep the meat directly under the crust from turning gray. But we'd need to take an untraditional approach for these thick-cut steaks and sear them at the end of cooking, rather than at the beginning. We began by moving the steaks straight from the fridge into a 275-degree oven, which not only warmed them to 95 degrees but also dried the meat thoroughly—dry meat is essential for a well-browned crust. At this temperature, when the steak met the hot skillet, it developed a beautiful brown crust in less than four minutes, while the rest of the meat stayed pink, juicy, and tender.

Pan-Seared Thick-Cut Steaks

SERVES 4

Rib-eye or filet mignon of similar thickness can be substituted for strip steaks. If using filet mignon, buying a 2-pound center-cut tenderloin roast and portioning it into four 8-ounce steaks yourself will produce more consistent results. If using filet mignon, increase the oven time by about 5 minutes. When cooking lean strip steaks (without an external fat cap) or filet mignon, add an extra tablespoon of oil to the pan. To serve the steaks with the Red Wine–Mushroom Pan Sauce (recipe follows), prepare all the sauce ingredients while the steaks are in the oven, and don't wash the skillet after cooking the steaks.

- 2 (1-pound) boneless strip steaks, each 1½ to 1¾ inches thick (see note)
- Table salt and ground black pepper
- 1 tablespoon vegetable oil

1. Adjust an oven rack to the middle position and heat the oven to 275 degrees. Pat the steaks dry with paper towels. Cut each steak in half vertically to create four 8-ounce steaks. Season the steaks liberally with salt and pepper; using your hands, gently shape into a uniform thickness. Place the steaks on a wire rack set over a rimmed baking sheet; transfer the baking sheet to the oven. Cook until an instant-read thermometer inserted horizontally into the center of the steaks registers 90 to 95 degrees for rare to medium-rare (20 to 25 minutes), or 100 to 105 degrees for medium (25 to 30 minutes).

2. Heat the oil in a 12-inch skillet over high heat until smoking. Place the steaks in the skillet and sear until well browned and crusty, 1½ to 2 minutes, lifting once halfway through to redistribute the fat underneath each steak. (Reduce the heat if the fond begins to burn.) Using tongs, turn the steaks and cook until well browned on the second side, 2 to 2½ minutes. Transfer the steaks to a clean rack and reduce the heat under the pan to medium. Use tongs to stand 2 steaks on their sides. Holding the steaks together, return to the skillet and sear on all edges until browned, about 1½ minutes (see photo on page 164). Repeat with the remaining 2 steaks.

3. Return the steaks to the wire rack and let rest, loosely tented with foil, for about 10 minutes. If desired, cook the sauce in the now-empty skillet. Serve immediately.

NOTES FROM THE TEST KITCHEN

SEARING TWO STEAKS AT ONCE

Use tongs to sear the sides of two steaks at the same time.

Red Wine–Mushroom Pan Sauce

MAKES ABOUT 1 CUP

Prepare all the ingredients for the pan sauce while the steaks are in the oven.

- 1 tablespoon vegetable oil
- 8 ounces white mushrooms, wiped clean and sliced thin (about 3 cups)
- 1 small shallot, minced (about 1 tablespoon)
- 1 cup dry red wine
- ½ cup low-sodium chicken broth
- 1 tablespoon balsamic vinegar
- 1 teaspoon Dijon mustard
- 2 tablespoons cold unsalted butter, cut into 4 pieces
- 1 teaspoon minced fresh thyme leaves
- Table salt and ground black pepper

Follow the recipe for Pan-Seared Thick-Cut Steaks. After removing the steaks from the skillet, pour off the fat from the skillet. Heat the oil over medium-high heat until just smoking. Add the mushrooms and cook, stirring occasionally, until beginning to brown and the liquid has evaporated, about 5 minutes. Add the shallot and cook, stirring frequently, until beginning to soften, about 1 minute. Increase the heat to high; add the red wine and broth, scraping the bottom of the skillet with a wooden spoon to loosen any browned bits. Simmer rapidly until the liquid and mushrooms are reduced to 1 cup, about 6 minutes. Add the vinegar, mustard, and any juices from the resting steaks; cook until thickened, about 1 minute. Off the heat, whisk in the butter and thyme; season with salt and pepper to taste. Spoon the sauce over the steaks and serve immediately.

Thai Chili Butter

MAKES ABOUT ⅓ CUP

Prepare all the ingredients for the butter while the steaks are in the oven. If red curry paste isn't available, increase the chili-garlic sauce to 2½ teaspoons.

4 tablespoons (½ stick) unsalted butter, softened
1 tablespoon chopped fresh cilantro leaves
2 teaspoons Asian chili-garlic sauce (preferably Thai)
1½ teaspoons thinly sliced scallion, green part only (from 1 scallion)
1 small garlic clove, minced or pressed through a garlic press (about ½ teaspoon)
½ teaspoon red curry paste (preferably Thai; see note)
2 teaspoons juice from 1 lime
Table salt

Beat the butter vigorously with a spoon until soft and fluffy. Add the cilantro, chili-garlic sauce, scallion, garlic, and red curry paste; beat to incorporate. Add the lime juice a little at a time, beating vigorously between each addition until fully incorporated. Add salt to taste. Spoon a dollop over each steak, giving it time to melt before serving.

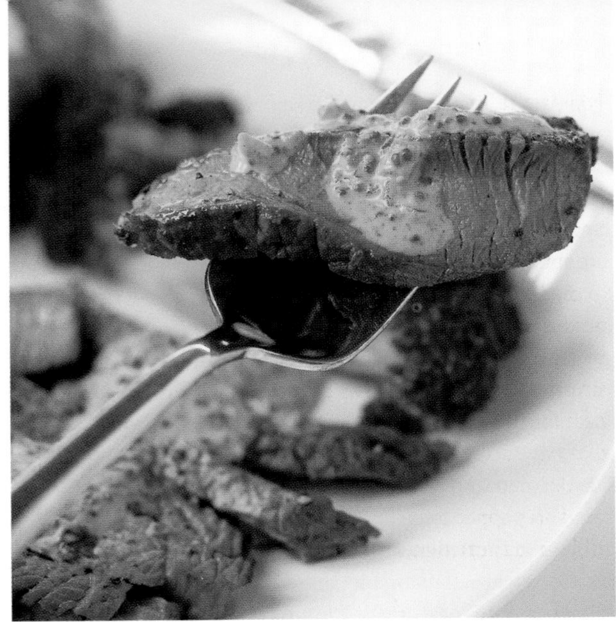

PAN-SEARED INEXPENSIVE STEAKS

WHY THIS RECIPE WORKS: Buying cheap steak can be a gamble and a lesson in confusion. Names differ from region to region, some cuts are wonderfully tender while others are hopelessly tough, and some recipes recommend cuts that are almost impossible to find, leaving the consumer to make a blind substitution. We wanted inexpensive steak with the flavor and texture to rival its pricey counterparts.

We first visited meat purveyors to learn what makes some steaks more expensive than others as well as to decipher all the different names. After sorting through the confusion, we were left with a list of 12 candidates. We cooked them as we would any steak, creating a nice sear on both sides without overcooking or allowing the browned bits in the pan to burn. Tasters judged most to be too tough and/or lacking beefy flavor, while others were livery or gamy. We tried a variety of preparation methods—salting, aging, tenderizing, marinating—but none really improved flavor and texture. In the end, two cuts earned favored status: boneless shell sirloin steak (aka top butt) and flap meat steak (aka sirloin tips). To prepare the steak, season the steaks simply with salt and pepper and start with a very hot skillet. Allow the meat to rest before slicing. Slice the steak thin, against the grain and on the bias, to ensure the tenderest meat.

Pan-Seared Inexpensive Steaks

SERVES 4

Serve these steaks with Tomato-Caper Pan Sauce or Mustard-Cream Pan Sauce (recipes follow). Prepare all of the sauce ingredients before cooking the steaks, and don't wash the skillet after removing the steaks; the sauce will use some of the fat left in the pan. To serve two instead of four, use a 10-inch skillet to cook a 1-pound steak and halve the sauce ingredients. Bear in mind that even those tasters who usually prefer rare beef preferred these steaks cooked medium-rare or medium because the texture is firmer and not quite so chewy. The times in the recipe are for 1¼-inch-thick steaks.

2 tablespoons vegetable oil
2 1-pound whole boneless shell sirloin steaks (top butt) or whole flap meat steaks, each about 1¼ inches thick
Table salt and ground black pepper

1. Heat the oil in a heavy-bottomed 12-inch skillet over medium-high heat until smoking. Meanwhile, season both sides of the steaks with salt and pepper. Place the steaks in the skillet; cook, without moving the steaks, until well browned, about 2 minutes. Using tongs, flip the steaks; reduce the heat to medium. Cook until well browned on the second side and the center of the steaks registers 125 degrees on an instant-read thermometer for medium-rare (about 5 minutes) or 130 degrees for medium (about 6 minutes).

2. Transfer the steaks to a large plate and tent loosely with foil; let rest for about 10 minutes. Meanwhile, prepare the pan sauce, if making.

3. Using a sharp chef's knife or carving knife, slice the steak about ¼ inch thick against the grain on the bias, arrange on a platter or on individual plates, and spoon some sauce (if using) over each steak; serve immediately.

Tomato-Caper Pan Sauce

MAKES ABOUT ¾ CUP

If ripe fresh tomatoes are not available, substitute 2 to 3 canned whole tomatoes, seeded and cut into ¼-inch pieces.

1 medium shallot, minced (about 3 tablespoons)
1 teaspoon unbleached all-purpose flour
2 tablespoons dry white wine
1 cup low-sodium chicken broth
2 tablespoons capers, drained
1 medium ripe tomato, seeded and cut into ¼-inch dice (about ¼ cup; see note)
¼ cup minced fresh parsley leaves
Table salt and ground black pepper

Follow the recipe for Pan-Seared Inexpensive Steaks. After removing the steaks from the skillet, pour off all but 1 tablespoon of the fat. Return the skillet to low heat and add the shallot; cook, stirring frequently, until beginning to brown, 2 to 3 minutes. Sprinkle the flour over the shallot; cook, stirring constantly, until combined, about 1 minute. Add the wine and increase the heat to medium-high; simmer rapidly, scraping up the browned bits on the pan bottom with a wooden spoon. Simmer until the liquid is reduced to a glaze, about 30 seconds; add the broth and simmer until reduced to ⅔ cup, about 4 minutes. Reduce the heat to medium; add the capers, tomato, and any meat juices that have accumulated on the plate and cook until the flavors are blended, about 1 minute. Stir in the parsley and season with salt and pepper to taste; spoon the sauce over the sliced steak and serve immediately.

Mustard-Cream Pan Sauce

MAKES ABOUT ¾ CUP

- 1 medium shallot, minced (about 3 tablespoons)
- 2 tablespoons dry white wine
- ½ cup low-sodium chicken broth
- 6 tablespoons heavy cream
- 3 tablespoons grainy Dijon mustard
- Table salt and ground black pepper

Follow the recipe for Pan-Seared Inexpensive Steaks. After removing the steaks from the skillet, pour off all but 1 tablespoon of the fat. Return the skillet to low heat and add the shallot; cook, stirring frequently, until beginning to brown, 2 to 3 minutes. Add the wine and increase the heat to medium-high; simmer rapidly, scraping up the browned bits on the pan bottom with a wooden spoon. Simmer until the liquid is reduced to a glaze, about 30 seconds; add the broth and simmer until reduced to ¼ cup, about 3 minutes. Add the cream and any meat juices that have accumulated on the plate; cook until heated through, about 1 minute. Stir in the mustard; season with salt and pepper to taste. Spoon over the sliced steak and serve immediately.

PAN-SEARED FILET MIGNON

WHY THIS RECIPE WORKS: Many cooks feel that filet mignon should be reserved for a celebratory restaurant meal. But we knew we could replicate the best restaurant filet at home, with a rich, brown crust and a tender interior, topped with a quick but luscious pan sauce.

For a great crust, we patted the steaks dry before searing them in a very hot skillet. Then we transferred the meat to a hot oven to cook through. Finishing the steak in the oven prevented the richly flavored browned bits in the bottom of the pan from burning and allowed us time to start the sauce, which can be made in minutes while the steaks rest.

Pan-Seared Filet Mignon

SERVES 4

If you are making one of the sauces, have all the sauce ingredients ready before searing the steaks, and don't wash the skillet after removing the steaks. Begin the sauce while the steaks are in the oven. To cook six steaks instead of four, use a 12-inch pan and use 6 teaspoons of olive oil.

- 4 (7- to 8-ounce) center-cut filets mignons, 1½ inches thick, each dried thoroughly with paper towels
- 4 teaspoons olive oil
- Table salt and ground black pepper

1. Adjust an oven rack to the lower-middle position, place a large rimmed baking sheet on the oven rack, and heat the oven to 450 degrees. When the oven reaches 450 degrees, heat a large skillet over high heat on the stovetop until very hot.

2. Meanwhile, rub each side of the steaks with ½ teaspoon oil and sprinkle generously with salt and pepper. Place the steaks in the hot skillet and cook, without moving the steaks, until well browned and a nice crust has formed, about 3 minutes. Turn the steaks with tongs and cook until well browned and a nice crust has formed on the second side, about 3 minutes longer. Remove the pan from the heat and use tongs to transfer the steaks to the hot baking sheet in the oven.

3. Roast until the center of the steaks registers 120 degrees on an instant-read thermometer for rare (4 to 5 minutes), 125 degrees for medium-rare (6 to 8 minutes), or 130 degrees for medium (8 to 10 minutes). Transfer the steaks to a large plate; loosely tent with foil and let rest for about 10 minutes before serving.

Madeira Pan Sauce with Mustard and Anchovies

MAKES ABOUT ⅔ CUP

If you do not have Madeira on hand, sherry makes a fine substitute. The accumulated pan juices from the steaks in the oven are incorporated into the reduction. If the steaks haven't finished cooking once the sauce has reduced, simply set the sauce aside until the steaks (and accumulated juices) are ready.

- 1 medium shallot, minced (about 3 tablespoons)
- 1 cup Madeira (see note)
- 2 anchovy fillets, minced to a paste (about 1 teaspoon)
- 1 tablespoon minced fresh parsley leaves
- 1 tablespoon minced fresh thyme leaves
- 1 tablespoon Dijon mustard
- 1 tablespoon juice from 1 lemon
- 3 tablespoons unsalted butter, softened
- Table salt and ground black pepper

Follow the recipe for Pan-Seared Filet Mignon. While the steaks are in the oven, set the skillet over medium-low heat; add the shallot and cook, stirring constantly, until softened, about 1 minute. Add the Madeira, increase the heat to high, and scrape the pan bottom with a wooden spoon to loosen the browned bits. Simmer until the liquid is reduced to about ⅓ cup, 6 to 8 minutes. Add the accumulated juices from the baking sheet and reduce the liquid 1 minute longer. Off the heat, whisk in the anchovies, parsley, thyme, mustard, lemon juice, and butter until the butter has melted and the sauce is slightly thickened. Season with salt and pepper to taste, spoon the sauce over the steaks, and serve immediately.

Argentinian-Style Fresh Parsley and Garlic Sauce (Chimichurri)

MAKES ABOUT 1 CUP

For best results use flat-leaf parsley.

- 1 cup packed fresh parsley leaves from one large bunch, washed and dried (see note)
- 5 medium garlic cloves, peeled
- ½ cup extra-virgin olive oil
- ¼ cup red wine vinegar
- 2 tablespoons water
- 1 small red onion, finely minced
- 1 teaspoon table salt
- ¼ teaspoon red pepper flakes

Pulse the parsley and garlic in a food processor, stopping as necessary to scrape down the sides of the bowl with a rubber spatula, until the garlic and parsley are chopped fine, about 20 pulses; transfer to a medium bowl. Whisk in the oil, vinegar, water, onion, salt, and red pepper flakes until thoroughly blended. Spoon about 2 tablespoons over each steak and serve. (This sauce tastes best when used fresh but can be refrigerated, with plastic wrap pressed directly on the surface, for up to 3 days.)

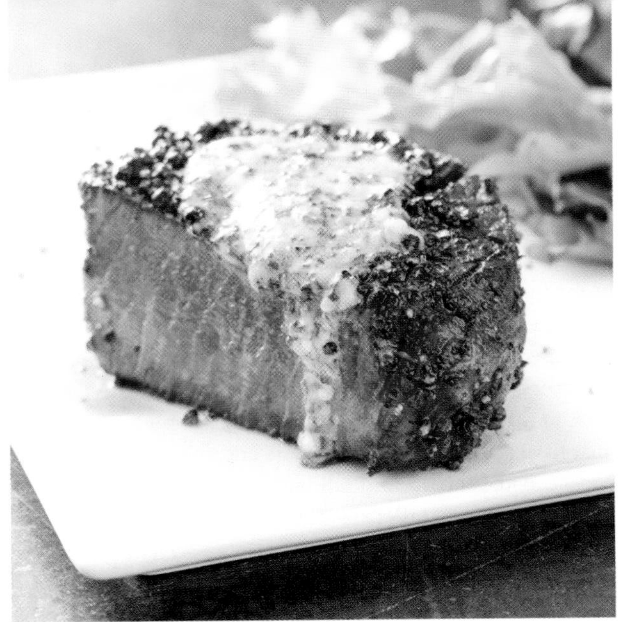

PEPPER-CRUSTED FILET MIGNON

WHY THIS RECIPE WORKS: Filet mignon is ultra-tender, but it has only mild beefy flavor. Chefs often compensate by wrapping the delicate meat in bacon or puff pastry, serving it with rich wine sauces or flavored butter, or giving it a crust of cracked black peppercorns. We decided to pursue the peppercorn approach and found several problems to solve: The peppercorns tend to fall off in the pan, interfere with the meat's browning, and—when used in sufficient quantity to create a real crust—deliver punishing pungency.

Our first step was to mellow the peppercorns' heat by gently simmering them in olive oil. We then created a well-browned and attractive pepper crust using a two-step process: First, we rubbed the raw steaks with a paste of the cooked cracked peppercorns, salt, and oil, then we pressed the paste into each steak through a sheet of plastic wrap. We let the steaks sit, covered, for an hour before cooking. The paste not only added flavor to the meat but drew out the meat's own beefy flavor. While the steaks sat wrapped and covered in paste, we had plenty of time to simmer a rich reduction sauce—though a flavored butter also made an excellent accompaniment.

Pepper-Crusted Filet Mignon

SERVES 4

If you prefer a very mild pepper flavor, drain the cooled peppercorns in a fine-mesh strainer in step 1, toss them with 5 tablespoons of fresh oil, add the salt, and proceed. Serve with Port-Cherry Reduction or Blue Cheese–Chive Butter (recipes follow).

- 5 tablespoons black peppercorns, cracked
- 5 tablespoons plus 2 teaspoons olive oil
- 1½ teaspoons table salt
- 4 (7- to 8-ounce) center-cut filets mignons, 1½ to 2 inches thick, each dried thoroughly with paper towels

1. Heat the peppercorns and 5 tablespoons of the oil in a small saucepan over low heat until faint bubbles appear. Continue to cook at a bare simmer, swirling the pan occasionally, until the pepper is fragrant, 7 to 10 minutes. Remove from the heat and set aside to cool. When the mixture is at room temperature, add the salt and stir to combine. Rub the steaks with the pepper mixture, thoroughly coating the top and bottom of each steak with the peppercorns. Cover the steaks with plastic wrap and press gently to make sure the peppercorns adhere; let stand at room temperature for 1 hour.

2. Meanwhile, adjust an oven rack to the middle position, place a rimmed baking sheet on the oven rack, and heat the oven to 450 degrees. Heat the remaining 2 teaspoons oil in a 12-inch heavy-bottomed skillet over medium-high heat until faint smoke appears. Place the steaks in the skillet and cook, without moving the steaks, until a dark brown crust has formed, 3 to 4 minutes. Using tongs, turn the steaks and cook until well browned on the second side, about 3 minutes. Remove the pan from the heat and transfer the steaks to the hot baking sheet. Roast until the center of the steaks registers 120 degrees on an instant-read thermometer for rare (3 to 5 minutes), 125 degrees for medium-rare (5 to 7 minutes), and 130 degrees for medium (7 to 9 minutes). Transfer the steaks to a wire rack and let rest, loosely tented with foil, for about 10 minutes before serving.

Port-Cherry Reduction

MAKES ABOUT 1 CUP

- 1½ cups port
- ½ cup balsamic vinegar
- ½ cup dried tart cherries
- 1 large shallot, minced (about 4 tablespoons)
- 2 sprigs fresh thyme
- 1 tablespoon unsalted butter
- Table salt

1. Combine the port, balsamic vinegar, cherries, shallot, and thyme in a medium saucepan; simmer over medium-low heat until the liquid is reduced to ⅓ cup, about 30 minutes. Set aside, covered.

2. While the steaks are resting, reheat the sauce. Off the heat, remove the thyme, then whisk in the butter until melted. Season with salt to taste. Serve, passing the sauce at the table with the steak.

Blue Cheese–Chive Butter

MAKES ABOUT ½ CUP

- 3 tablespoons unsalted butter, softened
- ⅓ cup crumbled mild blue cheese, at room temperature
- ⅛ teaspoon table salt
- 2 tablespoons minced fresh chives

Combine the butter, cheese, and salt in a medium bowl and mix with a stiff rubber spatula until smooth. Fold in the chives. While the steaks are resting, spoon 1 to 2 tablespoons of the butter on each one.

BEHIND THE SCENES

REDUCTION DEDUCTION

We've all seen recipe instructions such as "Reduce sauce to ½ cup" or "Simmer until broth is reduced to 2 cups." Those directions are clear, but when you look into a pan of sauce, can you really discern volume? Unless you have wizard-like abilities, the answer is probably "No."

Here in the test kitchen, we know that getting the right amount of sauce can make or break a dish, and to be sure of success we keep a heatproof liquid measuring cup next to the stove. As the sauce appears to be getting near the targeted amount, we pour it into the cup to get an exact measure. If it needs more time on the stove, back into the pan it goes until just the right amount is obtained. No guessing, no problem.

PAN-SEARED FLANK STEAK

WHY THIS RECIPE WORKS: Cooking flank steak indoors often poses challenges—the cut of meat is too long to fit in most skillets, and it's quite thin, so it often overcooks before the exterior is well browned. We wanted a year-round, indoor cooking method that would produce a juicy, well-browned flank steak that was cooked to medium throughout. To start, we cut the flank into four steaks that would fit neatly in the skillet, but we didn't put them there right away. Instead, we sprinkled them with salt for seasoning and sugar for browning and baked them in a very low oven until they reached 120 degrees. Then we seared them in a hot skillet to develop the crust, flipping the steaks three times instead of just once. After enriching the lean steaks with a flavorful compound butter, we sliced them thinly against the grain for maximum tenderness.

Pan-Seared Flank Steak with Mustard-Chive Butter

SERVES 4 TO 6

Open the oven as infrequently as possible in step 1. If the meat is not yet up to temperature, wait at least 5 minutes before taking its temperature again. Slice the steak as thin as possible against the grain.

1 (1½- to 1¾-pound) flank steak, trimmed
2 teaspoons kosher salt
1 teaspoon sugar
½ teaspoon pepper
3 tablespoons unsalted butter, softened
3 tablespoons chopped fresh chives
2 teaspoons Dijon mustard
½ teaspoon grated lemon zest plus 1 teaspoon juice
2 tablespoons vegetable oil

1. Adjust oven rack to middle position and heat oven to 225 degrees. Pat steak dry with paper towels. Cut steak in half lengthwise. Cut each piece in half crosswise to create 4 steaks. Combine salt, sugar, and pepper in small bowl. Sprinkle half of salt mixture on 1 side of steaks and press gently to adhere. Flip steaks and repeat with remaining salt mixture. Place steaks on wire rack set in rimmed baking sheet; transfer sheet to oven. Cook until thermometer inserted through side into center of thickest steak registers 120 degrees, 30 to 40 minutes.

2. Meanwhile, combine butter, 1 tablespoon chives, mustard, and lemon zest and juice in small bowl.

3. Heat oil in 12-inch skillet over medium-high heat until just smoking. Sear steaks, flipping every 1 minute, until brown crust forms on both sides, 4 minutes total. (Do not move steaks between flips.) Return steaks to wire rack and let rest for 10 minutes.

4. Transfer steaks to cutting board with grain running from left to right. Spread 1½ teaspoons butter mixture on top of each steak. Slice steak as thin as possible against grain. Transfer sliced steak to warm platter, dot with remaining butter mixture, sprinkle with remaining 2 tablespoons chives, and serve.

STEAK SANDWICHES

WHY THIS RECIPE WORKS: Steak sandwiches run the gamut from oversized "bombs" with greasy, gristly meat (break out the napkins) to precious restaurant concoctions (hold the truffle butter, please) with a price tag to match. We wanted to find a satisfying steak sandwich with some middle ground—easy to eat and gussied up with flavorful, but not costly, ingredients.

We started with the choice of steak, and flank steak won out over all other cuts. It's relatively inexpensive, lean, and tender, as long as the meat is cooked correctly. For a flavorful browned crust, we generously seasoned the steak with salt and pepper and then pan-seared it in a very hot skillet on both sides until browned. To keep the steak tender and juicy, we allowed the meat to rest and then sliced it thin across the grain. Soft, squishy bread needn't apply here—only a crusty French baguette or similar artisan-style bread would do. We slathered the bread with mayonnaise doctored with soy sauce, honey, garlic, and ginger. And to finish, thinly sliced onion and arugula scattered on top of the steak provided a little spicy bite.

NOTES FROM THE TEST KITCHEN

SLICING FLANK STEAK

Once the steak has rested, slice the meat across the grain into thin pieces.

Flank Steak and Arugula Sandwiches with Red Onion

SERVES 4

For juicy, tender meat, be sure to let the steak rest for 10 minutes after cooking and slice the steak thin across the grain.

1½ pounds flank steak, trimmed of excess fat and patted dry with paper towels
Table salt and ground black pepper
1 tablespoon vegetable oil
1 baguette, cut into four 5-inch lengths, each piece split into top and bottom pieces
1 recipe Garlic-Soy Mayonnaise (recipe follows)
½ small red onion, sliced thin
3 ounces arugula, stemmed, washed, and dried (about 3 cups)

1. Heat a 12-inch skillet over high heat until very hot, about 4 minutes. While the skillet is heating, season the steak generously with salt and pepper. Add the oil to the pan and swirl to coat the bottom. Lay the steak in the pan and cook without moving it until well browned, about 5 minutes. Using tongs, flip the steak; cook until well browned on the second side, about 5 minutes longer. Transfer the steak to a carving board, tent with foil, and let rest for 10 minutes. Cut the steak into ¼-inch slices on the bias against the grain.

2. Spread each baguette piece with 1 tablespoon mayonnaise; portion the steak over the bottom pieces of the bread and sprinkle with salt and pepper to taste. Evenly divide the onion and arugula over the steak; top each with a baguette piece and serve.

Garlic-Soy Mayonnaise

MAKES ABOUT ½ CUP

Blue Plate is the test kitchen's favorite brand of mayonnaise—read why on page 915.

½ cup mayonnaise
1 tablespoon soy sauce
1 teaspoon minced or grated fresh ginger

- ½ teaspoon honey
- 1 small garlic clove, minced or pressed through a garlic press (about ½ teaspoon)
- ½ teaspoon toasted sesame oil

Mix all the ingredients together in a small bowl. (The mayonnaise can be covered and refrigerated for up to 1 day.)

PUB-STYLE STEAK AND ALE PIE

WHY THIS RECIPE WORKS: Intensely savory steak pie is a classic British comfort food, but making it can be a tedious multistep procedure. Our streamlined version has all the flavor and texture of the authentic dish with less work. We skipped the traditional browning of the meat, which requires working in batches, and browned the mushrooms and onion instead, building a flavorful fond. Adding flour early in the process and limiting the amount of beef broth we added to the pot meant that the gravy formed as the meat cooked so we could bypass the usual sauce-building steps. To make sure the limited moisture didn't mean limited flavor, we added bacon, garlic, and thyme. We substituted beer for some of the broth and boosted browning with the addition of a small amount of baking soda. Our sturdy dough included an egg for added structure, which together with sour cream also contributed fat, allowing us to decrease the amount of butter. The resulting dough could go over the filling while it was hot, but it baked up flaky and substantial, the perfect complement to the rich filling.

Pub-Style Steak and Ale Pie

SERVES 6

Don't substitute bone-in short ribs; their yield is too variable. Instead, use a 4-pound chuck-eye roast, well trimmed of fat. Use a good-quality beef broth for this recipe; the test kitchen's favorite is Better Than Bouillon Roasted Beef Base. If you don't have a deep-dish pie plate, use an 8 by 8-inch baking dish and roll the pie dough into a 10-inch square. We prefer pale and brown ales for this recipe.

FILLING

- 3 tablespoons water
- ½ teaspoon baking soda
- 3 pounds boneless beef short ribs, trimmed and cut into ¾-inch chunks
- ½ teaspoon salt
- ½ teaspoon pepper
- 2 slices bacon, chopped
- 1 pound cremini mushrooms, trimmed and halved if medium or quartered if large
- 1½ cups beef broth
- 1 large onion, chopped
- 1 garlic clove, minced
- ½ teaspoon dried thyme
- ¼ cup all-purpose flour
- ¾ cup beer

CRUST

- 1 large egg, lightly beaten
- ¼ cup sour cream, chilled
- 1¼ cups (6¼ ounces) all-purpose flour
- ½ teaspoon salt
- 6 tablespoons unsalted butter, cut into ½-inch pieces and chilled

1. FOR THE FILLING: Combine water and baking soda in large bowl. Add beef, salt, and pepper and toss to combine. Adjust oven rack to lower-middle position and heat oven to 350 degrees.

2. Cook bacon in large Dutch oven over high heat, stirring occasionally, until partially rendered but not browned, about 3 minutes. Add mushrooms and ¼ cup broth and stir to coat. Cover and cook, stirring occasionally, until mushrooms are reduced to about half their original volume, about 5 minutes. Add onion, garlic, and thyme and cook, uncovered, stirring occasionally, until onion is softened and fond begins to form on bottom of pot, 3 to 5 minutes. Sprinkle flour over mushroom mixture and stir until all flour is moistened. Cook, stirring occasionally, until fond is deep brown, 2 to 4 minutes. Stir in beer and remaining 1¼ cups broth, scraping up any browned bits. Stir in beef and bring to simmer, pressing as much beef as possible below surface of liquid. Cover pot tightly with aluminum foil, then lid; transfer to oven. Cook for 1 hour.

3. Remove lid and discard foil. Stir filling, cover, return to oven, and continue to cook until beef is tender and liquid is thick enough to coat beef, 15 to 30 minutes longer. Transfer filling to deep-dish pie plate. (Once cool, filling can be covered with plastic wrap and refrigerated for up to 2 days.) Increase oven temperature to 400 degrees.

4. FOR THE CRUST: While filling is cooking, measure out 2 tablespoons beaten egg and set aside. Whisk remaining egg and sour cream together in bowl. Process flour and salt in food processor until combined, about 3 seconds. Add butter and pulse until only pea-size pieces remain, about 10 pulses. Add half of sour cream mixture and pulse until combined, about 5 pulses. Add remaining sour cream mixture and pulse until dough begins to form, about 10 pulses. Transfer mixture to lightly floured counter and knead briefly until dough comes together. Form into 4-inch disk, wrap in plastic, and refrigerate for at least 1 hour or up to 2 days.

5. Roll dough into 11-inch round on lightly floured counter. Using knife or 1-inch round biscuit cutter, cut round from center of dough. Drape dough over filling (it's OK if filling is hot). Trim overhang to ½ inch beyond lip of plate. Tuck overhang under itself; folded edge should be flush with edge of plate. Crimp dough evenly around edge of plate using your fingers or press with tines of fork to seal. Brush crust with reserved egg. Place pie on rimmed baking sheet. Bake until filling is bubbling and crust is deep golden brown and crisp, 25 to 30 minutes. (If filling has been refrigerated, increase baking time by 15 minutes and cover with foil for last 15 minutes to prevent overbrowning.) Let cool for 10 minutes before serving.

CHAPTER 8

PORK CHOPS EVERY DAY

SAUTÉED PORK CUTLETS

WHY THIS RECIPE WORKS: Lean pork cutlets are flavorless without proper browning, but by the time the cutlets take on any color, they're dry and lacking any tenderness. We wanted tender, browned cutlets with meaty flavor and a rich pan sauce to accompany them.

Instead of supermarket pork cutlets, we opted for a meatier-tasting cut: boneless country-style spare ribs. These ribs combine a large portion of the flavorful shoulder meat with minimal connective tissue and only a bit of bland tenderloin. Even better, because the ribs are sold portioned into relatively small pieces, they require little work to be fashioned into cutlets. To guard against dry meat, we brined our cutlets to help them retain moisture. A quick brine worked well, but the retained moisture kept the meat so wet that it steamed, cooking the cutlets all the way through before they had a chance to brown. To trigger faster browning, we added sugar to the brine. The sugar in the brine helped the cutlets develop a golden-brown exterior without sweetening them too much. And for an even darker crust, we cooked the cutlets in a combination of olive oil and butter. The sugars and milk proteins in the butter promoted browning and boost flavor.

Sautéed Pork Cutlets with Mustard-Cider Sauce

SERVES 4

We prefer natural to enhanced pork (pork that has been injected with a salt solution to increase moistness and flavor). If the pork is enhanced, do not brine. Look for ribs that are 3 to 5 inches long. Cut ribs over 5 inches in half crosswise before slicing them lengthwise to make pounding more manageable.

- Table salt and ground black pepper
- 1½ teaspoons sugar
- 1½ pounds boneless country-style pork spareribs, trimmed (see note)
- 1½ tablespoons unsalted butter, cut into 6 equal pieces
- 1 small shallot, minced (about 1 tablespoon)
- 1 teaspoon unbleached all-purpose flour
- 1 teaspoon dry mustard
- ½ cup low-sodium beef or chicken broth
- ¼ cup apple cider
- ½ teaspoon minced fresh sage
- 1 tablespoon olive oil
- 2 teaspoons whole-grain mustard

1. Dissolve 1 tablespoon salt and the sugar in 2 cups water in a medium bowl. Cut each pork rib lengthwise into 2 or 3 cutlets about ⅜ inch wide. Gently pound the cutlets to ¼-inch thickness between two layers of plastic wrap. Submerge the cutlets in the brine, cover with plastic wrap, and refrigerate for 30 minutes. (Do not overbrine.)

2. Meanwhile, melt 2 pieces of the butter in a small saucepan over medium heat. Add the shallot and cook until softened, about 1½ minutes. Stir in the flour and dry mustard and cook for 30 seconds. Gradually whisk in the broth, smoothing out any lumps. Stir in the cider and sage, bring to a boil, then reduce to a gentle simmer and cook for 5 minutes. Remove the pan from the heat, cover, and set aside.

3. Adjust an oven rack to the middle position and heat the oven to 200 degrees. Remove the cutlets from the brine, dry thoroughly with paper towels, and season with pepper. Heat the oil in a 12-inch skillet over medium-high heat until just smoking. Add 1 piece more butter, let it melt, then quickly lay half of the cutlets in the skillet. Cook until browned on the first side, 1 to 2 minutes.

4. Using tongs, flip the cutlets and continue to cook until browned on the second side, 1 to 2 minutes. Transfer the cutlets to a large plate and keep warm in the oven. Repeat with the remaining cutlets and 1 piece more butter.

5. Return the empty skillet to medium heat, add the reserved broth mixture, and bring to a simmer. Cook, scraping up the browned bits, until the sauce is slightly thickened and has reduced to about ½ cup, about 2 minutes. Stir in any accumulated pork juices and simmer for 30 seconds longer.

6. Off the heat, whisk in the whole-grain mustard and remaining 2 pieces butter. Season the sauce with salt and pepper to taste, spoon it over the cutlets, and serve immediately.

NOTES FROM THE TEST KITCHEN

CUTTING COUNTRY-STYLE RIBS INTO CUTLETS

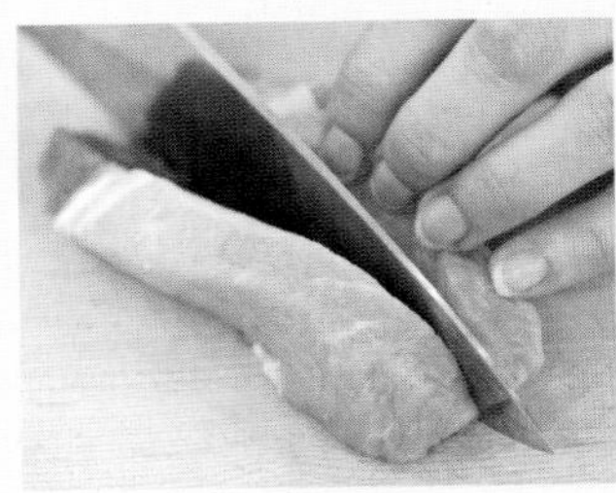

1. Slice each rib lengthwise to create 2 or 3 cutlets, each about ⅜ inch wide.

2. Lay each piece between 2 sheets of plastic wrap and pound until roughly ¼ inch thick.

CRISPY PAN-FRIED PORK CHOPS

WHY THIS RECIPE WORKS: A breaded coating can be just the thing to give lean, bland pork chops a flavor boost—but not when it turns gummy and flakes off the meat. Using boneless chops was fast and easy. Dipping the chops in cornstarch was our first step toward creating an ultra-crisp sheath. Buttermilk brought a lighter texture and tangy flavor to the breading, and minced garlic and a bit of mustard perked up the breading's flavor. Crushed cornflakes added a craggy texture to the pork chops, especially once we combined them with more cornstarch. Finally, to ensure that our breading adhered to the chops, we gave the meat a short rest and we lightly scored the pork chops before adding them to the pan.

Crispy Pan-Fried Pork Chops

SERVES 4

We prefer natural to enhanced pork (pork that has been injected with a salt solution to increase moistness and flavor) for this recipe. Don't let the chops drain on the paper towels for longer than 30 seconds, or the heat will steam the crust and make it soggy. You can substitute ¾ cup store-bought cornflake crumbs for the whole cornflakes. If using crumbs, omit the processing step and mix the crumbs with the cornstarch, salt, and pepper.

- ⅔ cup cornstarch
- 1 cup buttermilk
- 2 tablespoons Dijon mustard
- 1 medium garlic clove, minced or pressed through a garlic press (about 1 teaspoon)
- 3 cups cornflakes
- Table salt and ground black pepper
- 8 (3- to 4-ounce) boneless pork chops, ½ to ¾ inch thick, trimmed
- ⅔ cup vegetable oil
- Lemon wedges, for serving

1. Place ⅓ cup of the cornstarch in a shallow dish or pie plate. In a second shallow dish, whisk the buttermilk, mustard, and garlic until combined. Process the cornflakes, ½ teaspoon salt, ½ teaspoon pepper, and the remaining ⅓ cup cornstarch in a food processor until the cornflakes are finely ground, about 10 seconds. Transfer the cornflake mixture to a third shallow dish.

NOTES FROM THE TEST KITCHEN

HELPING THE COATING STICK

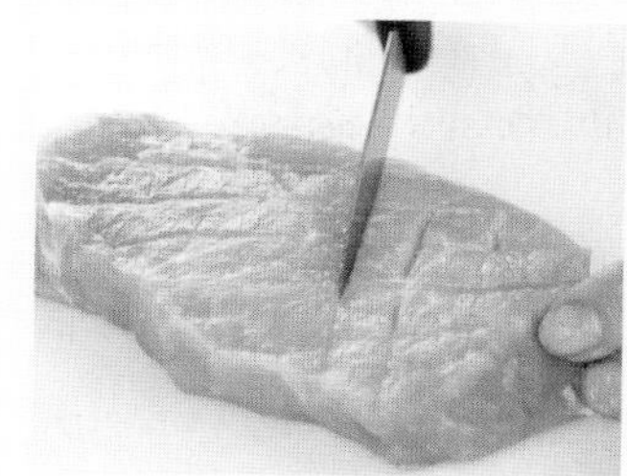

Making shallow slits on both sides of chops, spaced ½ inch apart, in a crosshatch pattern releases juices and sticky meat proteins that dampen the cornstarch, helping the cornflake coating adhere.

2. Adjust the oven rack to the middle position and heat the oven to 200 degrees. With a sharp knife, cut 1⁄16-inch-deep slits on both sides of the chops, spaced ½ inch apart, in a crosshatch pattern. Season the chops with salt and pepper. Dredge 1 chop in cornstarch; shake off the excess. Using tongs, coat with the buttermilk mixture; let excess drip off. Coat with the cornflake mixture; gently pat off excess. Transfer the coated chop to a wire rack set in a rimmed baking sheet and repeat with the remaining 7 chops. Let the coated chops stand for 10 minutes.

3. Heat ⅓ cup of the oil in a 12-inch nonstick skillet over medium-high heat until shimmering. Place 4 chops in the skillet and cook until golden brown and crisp, 2 to 5 minutes. Carefully flip the chops and continue to cook until the second side is golden brown, crispy, and the chops register 145 degrees on an instant-read thermometer, 2 to 5 minutes longer. Transfer the chops to a paper towel–lined plate and let drain for 30 seconds on each side. Transfer to a clean wire rack set in a rimmed baking sheet, then transfer to the oven to keep warm. Discard the oil in the skillet and wipe clean with paper towels. Repeat the process with the remaining ⅓ cup oil and 4 pork chops. Serve with the lemon wedges.

PAN-SEARED THICK-CUT PORK CHOPS

WHY THIS RECIPE WORKS: Pan-seared thick-cut pork chops boast a juicy interior and crisp, browned exterior. Usually, though, they aren't prepared well and fall flat on both fronts. We wanted a simple skillet-roasting recipe that would give us plump, juicy meat and a well-formed crust every time.

Instead of brining our chops, we salted the meat and let it rest for almost an hour. This helped to draw out additional moisture, which would be pulled back in later to produce juicy, well-seasoned meat. Instead of cooking our chops on the stovetop, we turned to the oven. Slow-roasting the chops at a gentle temperature broke down connective tissue and tenderized the meat. This step also dried the exterior of the chops, creating a thin outer layer that, when seared, caramelized and turned into the crisp crust that we were after. For a completely browned crust, we seared the sides of the chops as well, using tongs to hold them up on their edges. While the cooked chops rested, we created a simple wine and garlic sauce using the browned bits left behind in the pan; now, we had the perfect rich, tangy accompaniment to our chops' tender meat and crisp surface.

Pan-Seared Thick-Cut Pork Chops

SERVES 4

We prefer natural to enhanced pork (pork that has been injected with a salt solution to increase moistness and flavor) for this recipe. If using enhanced pork, skip the salting in step 1. To serve the pork chops with the Garlic and Thyme Sauce (recipe follows), have all the sauce ingredients ready to go and don't wash the skillet after browning the chops; begin the sauce, using the fat left behind from browning the chops, when you set them aside to rest.

- 4 (12-ounce) bone-in rib loin pork chops, about 1½ inches thick, trimmed of excess fat (see note)
- Table salt and ground black pepper (see note)
- 1–2 tablespoons vegetable oil

1. Adjust an oven rack to the middle position and heat the oven to 275 degrees. Pat the chops dry with paper towels. Following the photo on page 179, use a sharp knife to cut two slits, about 2 inches apart, through the outer layer of fat and silver skin of each chop (do not cut into the meat of the chops). Sprinkle each chop with ½ teaspoon salt. Place the chops on a wire rack set over a rimmed baking sheet and let stand at room temperature for 45 minutes.

2. Season the chops with pepper; transfer the baking sheet to the oven. Cook until the center of the chops registers 120 to 125 degrees on an instant-read thermometer, 30 to 45 minutes.

3. Heat 1 tablespoon oil in a 12-inch skillet over high heat until smoking. Place 2 chops in the skillet and sear until well browned, 2 to 3 minutes, lifting once halfway through to redistribute the fat underneath each chop. (Reduce the heat if the browned bits on the pan bottom start to burn.) Flip the chops and cook until the second side is well browned, 2 to 3 minutes longer. Transfer the chops to a plate and repeat with the remaining 2 chops, adding 1 tablespoon more oil if the pan is dry.

4. Reduce the heat to medium. Using tongs, stand 2 pork chops on their sides. Hold them together with the tongs, return them to the skillet, and sear the sides (do not sear the bone side) until browned and the center of the chops registers 140 to 145 degrees on an instant-read thermometer, about 1½ minutes. Repeat with the remaining 2 chops. Transfer the chops to a platter, cover loosely with foil, and let rest until the internal temperature reaches 150 degrees, about 5 minutes, or while preparing the pan sauce.

Garlic and Thyme Sauce

MAKES ABOUT ½ CUP

- 1 large shallot, minced (about 4 tablespoons)
- 2 medium garlic cloves, minced or pressed through a garlic press (about 2 teaspoons)
- ¾ cup low-sodium chicken broth
- ½ cup dry white wine
- 1 teaspoon minced fresh thyme leaves
- ¼ teaspoon white wine vinegar
- 3 tablespoons unsalted butter, chilled and cut into 3 pieces
- Table salt and ground black pepper

Follow the recipe for Pan-Seared Thick-Cut Pork Chops. Pour off all but 1 teaspoon oil from the pan used to cook the chops and return the pan to medium heat. Add the shallot and garlic and cook, stirring constantly, until softened, about 1 minute. Add the broth and wine, scraping up any browned bits. Bring to a simmer and cook until the sauce measures ½ cup, 6 to 7 minutes. Off the heat, stir in the thyme and vinegar; whisk in the butter, 1 tablespoon at a time. Season with salt and pepper to taste and serve with the pork chops.

OVEN-ROASTED PORK CHOPS

WHY THIS RECIPE WORKS: Tender, juicy pork chops make for a satisfying dinner, but most home cooks pass up thick chops at the market because they assume the cooking time will be long. However, roasting these chops in a blazing hot oven (their thickness prevents them from drying out) cuts down on cooking time and frees up the stovetop so you can make an easy pan sauce at the same time.

We chose extra-thick rib loin pork chops and flavored them with a brown sugar and salt brine. We found that our thick chops couldn't go straight into the oven—they had to be cooked in three stages. First, we seared them in a hot pan to give them a nicely browned crust, then we transferred them to a preheated pan in the oven to cook most of the way through, and finally we moved them to a platter and covered them with foil to gently come up to serving temperature (while the meat stayed moist and tender). This last step also gave us time to make a speedy lemon-caper sauce right in the pan using the fond (browned bits) left behind from searing the chops.

Oven-Roasted Pork Chops

SERVES 4

We prefer natural to enhanced pork (pork that has been injected with a salt solution to increase moistness and flavor) for this recipe. If using enhanced pork, skip the brining in step 1. To serve the pork chops with the Lemon-Caper Sauce (recipe follows), have all the sauce ingredients ready to go and don't wash the skillet after browning the chops; begin the sauce, using the fat left behind from browning the chops, after the pork chops come out of the oven and are resting.

- ¾ cup (5¼ ounces) dark brown sugar
- ¼ cup table salt
- 10 medium garlic cloves, crushed
- 4 bay leaves, crumbled
- 8 whole cloves
- 3 tablespoons whole black peppercorns, crushed
- 4 (12-ounce) bone-in rib loin pork chops, about 1½ inches thick, trimmed of excess fat (see note)
- 2 tablespoons vegetable oil

1. Dissolve the sugar and salt in 6 cups cold water in a large bowl or container. Add the garlic, bay leaves, cloves, and peppercorns. Submerge the chops in the brine, cover with plastic wrap, and refrigerate for 1 hour. Remove the chops from the brine, rinse, and pat dry with paper towels. Following the photo on page 181, use a sharp knife to cut two slits, about 2 inches apart, through the outer layer of fat and silver skin of each chop (do not cut into the meat of the chops).

2. Adjust an oven rack to the lower-middle position, place a rimmed baking sheet on the rack, and heat the oven to 450 degrees. When the oven reaches 450 degrees, heat the oil in a 12-inch skillet over high heat until shimmering. Place the chops in the skillet and cook until well browned, about 2 minutes. Flip the chops and continue to cook until the second side is well browned, about 2 minutes longer.

3. Transfer the chops to the baking sheet in the oven. Roast until the center of the chops registers 140 to 145 degrees on an instant-read thermometer, about 15 minutes, turning the chops over once halfway through the cooking time. Transfer the chops to a platter, cover loosely with foil, and let rest until the internal temperature registers 150 degrees on an instant-read thermometer, 5 to 10 minutes or while preparing the pan sauce.

Lemon-Caper Sauce

MAKES ABOUT ½ CUP

- 1 medium shallot, minced (about 3 tablespoons)
- 1 cup low-sodium chicken broth
- ¼ cup juice from 2 lemons
- 2 tablespoons capers, drained
- 3 tablespoons unsalted butter, softened

Follow the recipe for Oven-Roasted Pork Chops. After removing the chops from the pan, add the shallot and cook over medium heat until softened, about 30 seconds. Increase the heat to high and stir in the broth, scraping up any browned bits. Add the lemon juice and capers, bring to a simmer, and cook until the sauce measures ⅓ cup, 3 to 4 minutes. Off the heat, whisk in the butter; serve with the pork chops.

SKILLET-BARBECUED PORK CHOPS

WHY THIS RECIPE WORKS: One of our favorite summer flavors is that of charred, salty-sweet grilled pork chops coated with spicy barbecue sauce. But because winter sometimes seems endless, we wanted to come up with an indoor method for replicating the tangy, sweet burnished crust and juicy meat of grilled chops.

Brining the chops first ensured that our meat would be juicy and well seasoned. We quickly learned that searing the chops in a blazing hot skillet and then turning the heat down once they had developed a nice crust only made the test kitchen smoky. Instead, we coated the chops with a dry spice rub—the rub charred rather than the pork chops and gave the meat the flavor and appearance of real barbecue. To prevent the rub from blackening, we cooked the chops over medium heat and used a nonstick skillet. Homemade barbecue sauce, made with ketchup, molasses, onion, and just a few other ingredients, provided a tangy flavor that contrasted nicely with the tender meat, and some reserved spice rub gave the sauce a spicy kick. A touch of liquid smoke gave our barbecue sauce more grill flavor. Finally, we brushed our chops with a small amount of sauce for a second sear so the sauce would caramelize and intensify in flavor—just as it would on the grill.

Skillet-Barbecued Pork Chops

SERVES 4

We prefer natural to enhanced pork (pork that has been injected with a salt solution to increase moistness and flavor) for this recipe. If using enhanced pork, skip the brining in step 1 and add ½ teaspoon salt to the spice rub. Grate the onion on the large holes of a box grater. In step 5, check your chops after 3 minutes. If you don't hear a definite sizzle and the chops have not started to brown on the underside, increase the heat to medium-high and continue cooking as directed (follow the indicated temperatures for the remainder of the recipe).

PORK CHOPS

- ½ cup table salt (see note)
- 4 (8- to 10-ounce) bone-in rib loin pork chops, ¾ to 1 inch thick, trimmed of excess fat (see note)
- 4 teaspoons vegetable oil

SPICE RUB

- 1 tablespoon paprika
- 1 tablespoon brown sugar
- 2 teaspoons ground coriander
- 1 teaspoon ground cumin
- 1 teaspoon ground black pepper

SAUCE

- ½ cup ketchup
- 3 tablespoons light or mild molasses
- 2 tablespoons grated onion (see note)
- 2 tablespoons Worcestershire sauce
- 2 tablespoons Dijon mustard
- 1 tablespoon cider vinegar
- 1 tablespoon brown sugar
- 1 teaspoon liquid smoke

1. FOR THE PORK CHOPS: Dissolve the salt in 2 quarts cold water in a large bowl or container. Submerge the chops in the brine, cover with plastic wrap, and refrigerate for 30 minutes.

2. FOR THE SPICE RUB: Combine the rub ingredients in a small bowl. Measure 2 teaspoons of the mixture into a medium bowl and set aside for the sauce. Transfer the remaining spice rub to a large plate.

3. FOR THE SAUCE: Whisk the sauce ingredients in the bowl with the reserved spice mixture until thoroughly combined; set aside.

4. Remove the chops from the brine, rinse, and pat dry with paper towels. Following the photo on page 181, use a sharp knife to cut two slits, about 2 inches apart, through the outer layer of fat and silver skin of each chop (do not cut into the meat of the chops). Coat both sides of the chops with the spice rub, pressing gently so the rub adheres. Shake off the excess rub.

5. Heat 1 tablespoon of the oil in a 12-inch nonstick skillet over medium heat until just smoking. Place the chops in the skillet in a pinwheel pattern, with the ribs pointing toward the center, and cook until browned and charred in spots, 5 to 8 minutes. Flip the chops and continue to cook until the second side is browned and the center of the chops registers 130 degrees on an instant-read thermometer, 4 to 8 minutes. Remove the skillet from the heat and transfer the chops to a plate. Lightly brush the top of each chop with 2 teaspoons of the sauce.

6. Wipe out the pan with paper towels and return to medium heat. Add the remaining 1 teaspoon oil and heat until just smoking. Add the chops to the pan, sauce side down, and cook without moving them until the sauce has caramelized and charred in spots, about 1 minute. While cooking, lightly brush the top of each chop with 2 more teaspoons sauce. Flip the chops and cook until the second side is charred and caramelized and the center of the chops registers 140 to 145 degrees on an instant-read thermometer, 1 to 2 minutes.

7. Transfer the chops back to the plate, cover loosely with foil, and let rest until the center of the chops registers 150 degrees on an instant-read thermometer, about 5 minutes.

8. Meanwhile, add the remaining sauce to the pan and cook over medium heat, scraping up any browned bits, until thickened and it measures ⅔ cup, about 3 minutes. Brush each chop with 1 tablespoon of the sauce and serve, passing the remaining sauce separately.

GLAZED PORK CHOPS

WHY THIS RECIPE WORKS: Thin boneless pork chops are readily available straight from the meat case—no butcher required. Plus they cook fast and are a bargain compared to other meats. But because they do cook quickly, they're prone to overcooking. We wanted to combine the convenience and speed of thin boneless pork chops with the flavor and moist, juicy interior of their thicker, bone-in counterparts.

To cook pork chops on the stove, it's best to stick with thin chops. Before searing the chops, it's important to cut through the fat and silver skin, which create a bowing effect (especially pronounced with thin chops) as it contracts. We found the chops needed an initial quick sear—we didn't want them to cook all the way through just yet but we still wanted a nicely browned side. A sweet and sticky glaze of cider, brown sugar, soy sauce, vinegar, and mustard went into the pan to finish cooking the chops. Not only did the sauce give the chops rich flavor, but it also reduced down to a nice, thick glaze, which perfectly coated the juicy, tender chops.

Cider-Glazed Pork Chops

SERVES 4

We prefer natural to enhanced pork (pork that has been injected with a salt solution to increase moistness and flavor) for this recipe, though either will work here. If your chops are on the thinner side, check their internal temperature after the initial sear. If they are already at the 140-degree mark, remove them from the skillet and allow them to rest, covered loosely with foil, for 5 minutes, then add the accumulated juices and glaze ingredients to the skillet and proceed with step 4. If your chops are a little thicker than we specify, you may need to increase the simmering time in step 3.

GLAZE

- ½ cup distilled white vinegar or cider vinegar
- ⅓ cup (2⅓ ounces) light brown sugar
- ⅓ cup apple cider or apple juice
- 2 tablespoons Dijon mustard
- 1 tablespoon soy sauce
- Pinch cayenne pepper

PORK CHOPS

- 4 (5- to 7-ounce) boneless center-cut or loin pork chops, ½ to ¾ inch thick, trimmed of excess fat (see note)
- Table salt and ground black pepper
- 1 tablespoon vegetable oil

1. FOR THE GLAZE: Combine the glaze ingredients in a medium bowl and set aside.

2. FOR THE PORK CHOPS: Following the photo, use a sharp knife to cut two slits, about 2 inches apart, through the outer layer of fat and silver skin of each chop (do not cut into the meat of the chops). Pat the chops dry with paper towels and season with salt and pepper. Heat the oil in a 12-inch skillet over medium-high heat until smoking. Add the chops to the skillet and cook until well browned, 4 to 6 minutes. Flip the chops and cook 1 minute longer; transfer the chops to a platter and pour off any oil in the skillet. (Check the internal temperature of the thinner chops; see note.)

3. Return the chops to the skillet, browned side up, and add the glaze mixture; cook over medium heat until the center of the chops registers 140 to 145 degrees on an instant-read thermometer, 5 to 8 minutes. Remove the skillet from the heat; transfer the chops to a clean platter, cover loosely with foil, and let rest until the center of the chops registers 150 degrees on an instant-read thermometer, about 5 minutes.

4. Stir any accumulated meat juices from the plate into the glaze in the skillet and simmer, whisking constantly, until the glaze has thickened, 2 to 6 minutes. Return the chops to the skillet and turn to coat both sides with the glaze. Transfer the chops back to the plate, browned side up, spread the remaining glaze over the top, and serve.

BEHIND THE SCENES

KOSHER? YES. ENHANCED? NO.

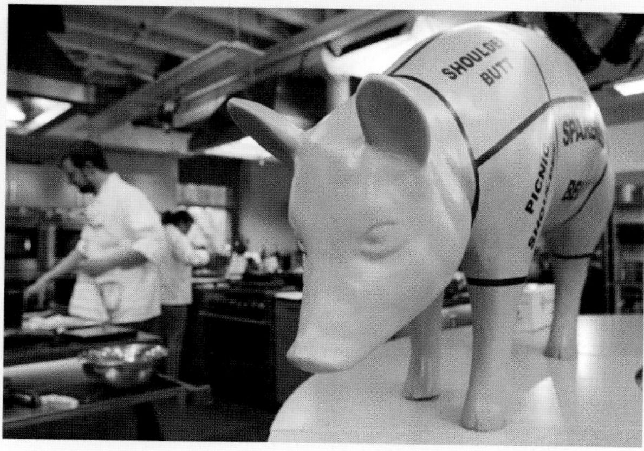

In the test kitchen we often brine chicken and pork to ensure moist, well-seasoned meat. But there are options at the store that allow you to skip this step. For chicken, that means buying a kosher bird. Koshering is a process similar to brining; it involves coating the chicken with salt to draw out any impurities. Kosher birds are also all-natural and contain no hormones or antibiotics.

Some people are surprised that pork is lean and prone to drying out. In fact, today's pork is 50 percent leaner than its 1950s counterpart, and less fat means less flavor and moisture. The industry has addressed this issue by introducing enhanced pork, which is meat injected with a solution of water, salt, and sodium phosphate. The idea is to both season the pork and prevent it from drying out. We've conducted countless tests comparing "enhanced" pork to natural pork and unequivocally prefer the latter. Natural pork has a better flavor and, if it's cooked correctly, moisture isn't an issue. We also strongly recommend brining most cuts of pork, which lends both moisture and seasoning to the meat. Manufacturers don't use the terms "enhanced" or "natural" on package labels, but if the pork has been enhanced it will have an ingredient list. Natural pork contains just pork and won't have an ingredient list. While natural pork benefits from brining, enhanced pork should not be brined because it's already pretty salty.

NOTES FROM THE TEST KITCHEN

HOW TO PREVENT CURLED PORK CHOPS

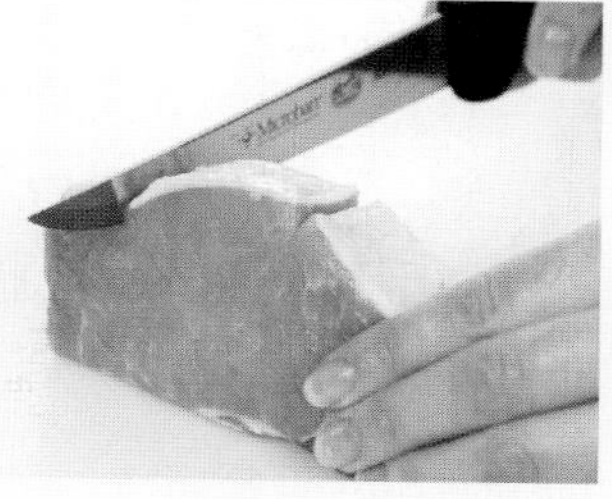

Whether your pork chops are boneless or bone-in, you can use the same technique to prevent them from buckling in a hot pan or oven. Simply cut two slits, about 2 inches apart, through one side of each chop.

SMOTHERED PORK CHOPS

WHY THIS RECIPE WORKS: Tender, flavorful chops stand up very well to rich, hearty gravy. But most of the time, the gravy misses the mark—it's either so thick you can't find the pork chop, or so thin and watery that the meat seems to be floating on the plate. We wanted a foolproof recipe for juicy chops smothered in rich gravy with a satiny, thick texture.

For a nice balance with the gravy and to allow for the best absorption of the gravy's flavors, we used thin, not thick, rib chops. Browning them well left meaty browned bits in the pan, essential for making a flavorful gravy. To build further flavor, we made a nut-brown, bacony roux. Thinly sliced yellow onions contributed a significant amount of moisture to the gravy. Garlic, thyme, and bay leaves rounded out the flavorful gravy; we skipped the salt because we had already salted the onions to encourage their browning and so they would give up liquid. For the tenderest chops, we combined the sauce and browned chops in the pan and braised them for half an hour. Not only did the lengthy braise result in moist, tender chops, it also allowed the gravy to thicken and its flavors to meld, so the chops had a rich, velvety coating when served.

Smothered Pork Chops

SERVES 4

We prefer natural to enhanced pork (pork that has been injected with a salt solution to increase moistness and flavor) for this recipe, though either will work here. Serve smothered chops with egg noodles or mashed potatoes to soak up the rich gravy.

- 3 ounces bacon (about 3 slices), cut into ¼-inch pieces
- 2 tablespoons unbleached all-purpose flour
- 1¾ cups low-sodium chicken broth
- 2 tablespoons vegetable oil, plus more as needed
- 4 (7-ounce) bone-in rib loin pork chops, ½ to ¾ inch thick, trimmed of excess fat (see note)
- Ground black pepper
- 2 medium yellow onions, halved and sliced thin (about 3½ cups)
- Table salt
- 2 tablespoons water
- 2 medium garlic cloves, minced or pressed through a garlic press (about 2 teaspoons)
- 1 teaspoon minced fresh thyme leaves
- 2 bay leaves
- 1 tablespoon minced fresh parsley leaves

1. Fry the bacon in a small saucepan over medium heat, stirring occasionally, until crisp, 8 to 10 minutes. Using a slotted spoon, transfer the bacon to a paper towel–lined plate, leaving the fat in the saucepan (you should have 2 tablespoons bacon fat; if not, add oil to make this amount). Whisk in the flour and cook over medium-low heat until golden, about 5 minutes. Whisk in the broth and bring to a boil, stirring occasionally, over medium-high heat; cover and set aside off the heat.

2. Heat 1 tablespoon of the oil in a 12-inch skillet over high heat until smoking. Pat the chops dry with paper towels. Following the photo on page 181, use a sharp knife to cut two slits, about 2 inches apart, through the outer layer of fat and silver skin of each chop (do not cut into the meat of the chops). Sprinkle each chop with ½ teaspoon pepper. Brown the chops in a single layer until browned on the first side, about 3 minutes. Flip the chops and cook until the second side is browned, about 3 minutes longer. Transfer the chops to a plate and set aside.

3. Add the remaining 1 tablespoon oil to the skillet and return to medium heat until shimmering. Add the onions, ¼ teaspoon salt, and the water, scraping up any browned bits, and cook until lightly browned, about 5 minutes. Stir in the garlic and thyme and cook until fragrant, about 30 seconds longer. Return the chops to the skillet and cover with the onions. Add the reserved sauce, the bay leaves, and any accumulated meat juices from the plate to the skillet. Cover and simmer over low heat until the chops are tender and a paring knife inserted into the chops meets little resistance, about 30 minutes.

4. Transfer the chops to a platter and cover loosely with foil. Simmer the sauce over medium-high heat, stirring frequently, until thickened, about 5 minutes. Discard the bay leaves, stir in the parsley, and season with salt and pepper to taste. Cover the chops with the sauce, sprinkle with the reserved bacon, and serve.

CRUNCHY BAKED PORK CHOPS

WHY THIS RECIPE WORKS: When done right, baked, breaded pork chops are the ultimate comfort food—juicy, tender chops covered with a well-seasoned, crunchy crust. We were on a mission to perfect these chops and avoid the common missteps of a soggy, flavorless crust, flabby meat, and a coating that just won't stay on.

We used center-cut boneless loin chops—which are easy to find and affordable—and brined them so the meat would stay moist and juicy. For the coating, only fresh bread crumbs would do; we toasted them first for crispness, then doctored them with garlic, shallots, Parmesan cheese, and minced herbs for flavor. To form a strong adhering agent for the crumbs, and prevent the chops from ending up bald in patches, we made a quick batterlike mixture by whisking flour and mustard into egg whites; whole eggs were a no-go because their higher amount of fat made for a soft, puffy layer under the bread crumbs. Baking the breaded chops on a wire rack set over a baking sheet allowed air to circulate completely around the chops, keeping the bottom crumbs crisp. Out of the oven, these chops were tender and moist, with a crisp coating that stayed put, even through some heavy knife-and-fork action.

Crunchy Baked Pork Chops

SERVES 4

We prefer natural to enhanced pork (pork that has been injected with a salt solution to increase moistness and flavor) for this recipe. If using enhanced pork, skip the brining in step 1. The breaded chops can be frozen for up to 1 week. They don't need to be thawed before baking; simply increase the cooking time in step 5 to 35 to 40 minutes.

- Table salt
- 4 (6- to 8-ounce) boneless center-cut or loin pork chops, ¾ to 1 inch thick, trimmed of excess fat (see note)
- 4 slices high-quality white sandwich bread, torn into 1-inch pieces
- 2 tablespoons vegetable oil
- 1 small shallot, minced (about 1 tablespoon)
- 3 medium garlic cloves, minced or pressed through a garlic press (about 1 tablespoon)
- Ground black pepper
- 2 tablespoons grated Parmesan cheese
- 2 tablespoons minced fresh parsley leaves
- ½ teaspoon minced fresh thyme leaves
- ¼ cup plus 6 tablespoons unbleached all-purpose flour
- 3 large egg whites
- 3 tablespoons Dijon mustard
- Lemon wedges, for serving

1. Adjust an oven rack to the middle position and heat the oven to 350 degrees. Dissolve ¼ cup salt in 4 cups cold water in a medium bowl or gallon-sized zipper-lock bag. Submerge the chops in the brine, cover the container with plastic wrap or seal the bag, and refrigerate for 30 minutes. Remove the chops from the brine, rinse, and pat dry with paper towels.

2. Meanwhile, pulse the bread in a food processor to coarse crumbs, about 8 pulses (you should have about 3½ cups crumbs). Transfer the crumbs to a rimmed baking sheet, add the oil, shallot, garlic, ¼ teaspoon salt, and ¼ teaspoon pepper, and toss until the crumbs are evenly coated with the oil. Bake until golden brown and dry, about 15 minutes, stirring twice during the baking time. (Do not turn off the oven.) Cool to room temperature. Toss the crumbs with the Parmesan, parsley, and thyme. (The bread-crumb mixture can be stored in an airtight container for up to 3 days.)

3. Place ¼ cup of the flour in a pie plate. In a second pie plate, whisk the egg whites and mustard together; add the remaining 6 tablespoons flour and whisk until almost smooth, with pea-sized lumps remaining.

4. Increase the oven temperature to 425 degrees. Spray a wire rack with vegetable oil spray and place over a rimmed baking sheet. Season the chops with pepper. Dredge 1 pork chop in the flour; shake off the excess. Using tongs, coat with the egg mixture; let the excess drip off. Coat all sides of the chop with the bread-crumb mixture, pressing gently so that a thick layer of crumbs adheres to the chop. Transfer the breaded chop to the wire rack. Repeat with the remaining 3 chops.

5. Bake until the center of the chops registers 140 to 145 degrees on an instant-read thermometer, about 20 minutes. Let rest on the rack for 5 minutes; serve with the lemon wedges.

STUFFED PORK CHOPS

WHY THIS RECIPE WORKS: Thick-cut pork chops make the perfect home for a simple stuffing. Unfortunately, most stuffed pork chops are extremely dry and bland, with a filling that looks like it's trying to escape. We wanted the stuffing to be especially flavorful and rich to offset the mildness of the pork, and we wanted the chops to be moist and juicy.

Our stuffing was easy enough to make—we used a simple combination of aromatic vegetables, herbs, and fresh bread. But the stuffing was so loose, it crumbled and spilled out over the plate when the chops were served. Clearly, we needed a binder. Instead of eggs, we chose cream, which added richness and enough moisture to bring the stuffing together. Because the stuffing didn't contain eggs, the chops could be cooked to a lower (and more palatable) internal temperature, making for tender and juicy meat. After brining the chops and creating a small "pocket" to hold the stuffing, we started them in

a skillet to develop a nice brown crust but finished cooking them through on a baking sheet in a hot oven. A sweet chutney of ginger, apples, and apple cider provided a nice contrast to the savory filling.

For an alternative to chutney, flavorful gravy (sans big roast) is ideal for draping over the stuffed chops. Thoroughly browning both the aromatic vegetables and the flour added significant flavor, as did the inclusion of two kinds of broth: beef and chicken.

Stuffed Pork Chops

SERVES 4

We prefer natural to enhanced pork (pork that has been injected with a salt solution to increase moistness and flavor) for this recipe, though either will work here. Serve these pork chops with Quick All-Purpose Gravy or Ginger-Apple Chutney (recipes follow). The gravy is best made before you start the chops and reheated as needed. If you choose to serve the chops with the chutney, prepare it in the skillet used to cook the chops while the chops are in the oven.

PORK CHOPS

- 4 (12-ounce) bone-in rib loin pork chops, about 1½ inches thick, trimmed of excess fat (see note)
- ¾ cup packed light brown sugar
- ¼ cup table salt
- Ground black pepper
- 1 tablespoon vegetable oil

STUFFING

- 3 tablespoons unsalted butter
- 1 small onion, minced
- 1 celery rib, chopped fine
- ½ teaspoon table salt
- 1 tablespoon minced fresh parsley leaves
- 2 medium garlic cloves, minced or pressed through a garlic press (about 2 teaspoons)
- 2 teaspoons minced fresh thyme leaves
- 2 slices high-quality white sandwich bread, cut into ¼-inch cubes (about 2 cups)
- 2 tablespoons heavy cream
- Ground black pepper

1. FOR THE PORK CHOPS: Following the photos on page 185, cut a small pocket through the side of each chop. Dissolve the sugar and salt in 6 cups cold water in a large bowl or container. Submerge the chops in the brine, cover with plastic wrap, and refrigerate for 1 hour.

2. FOR THE STUFFING: Melt the butter in a 12-inch skillet over medium heat. Add the onion, celery, and salt and cook until the vegetables are softened, 6 to 8 minutes. Add the parsley, garlic, and thyme and cook until fragrant, about 30 seconds. Transfer to a medium bowl and toss with the bread cubes, cream, and ⅛ teaspoon pepper. Mix, lightly pressing the mixture against the sides of the bowl, until it comes together.

3. Adjust an oven rack to the lower-middle position, place a rimmed baking sheet on the rack, and heat the oven to 450 degrees. Remove the chops from the brine, rinse, and pat dry with paper towels. Place one-quarter of the stuffing (about ⅓ cup) in the pocket of each pork chop. Season the chops with pepper.

4. Heat the oil in a 12-inch skillet over high heat until shimmering. Place the chops in the skillet and cook until well browned, about 3 minutes. Flip the chops and cook until the second side is well browned, about 2 minutes longer.

5. Transfer the chops to the baking sheet in the oven. Roast until the center of the chops registers 140 degrees on an instant-read thermometer, about 15 minutes, turning the chops over halfway through the cooking time. Transfer the chops to a plate, cover loosely with foil, and let rest for 5 to 10 minutes. Serve.

Quick All-Purpose Gravy

MAKES 2 CUPS

This gravy can be served with almost any type of meat and with mashed potatoes as well. The recipe can be doubled. If doubling it, use a Dutch oven so that the vegetables brown properly and increase the cooking times by roughly half. The finished gravy can be frozen. To thaw it, place the gravy and 1 tablespoon of water in a saucepan over low heat and slowly bring it to a simmer. It may appear broken or curdled as it thaws, but a vigorous whisking will recombine it.

- 3 tablespoons unsalted butter
- 1 onion, minced
- 1 small carrot, peeled and chopped fine
- 1 celery rib, chopped fine
- ¼ cup unbleached all-purpose flour
- 2 cups low-sodium chicken broth
- 2 cups beef broth
- 1 bay leaf
- ¼ teaspoon dried thyme
- 5 whole black peppercorns
- Table salt and ground black pepper

1. Melt the butter in a large saucepan over medium-high heat. Add the onion, carrot, and celery and cook, stirring frequently, until softened, about 7 minutes. Reduce the heat to medium, add the flour, and cook, stirring constantly, until thoroughly browned, about 5 minutes. Gradually whisk in the broths and bring to a boil, skimming off any foam that forms on the surface. Add the bay leaf, thyme, and peppercorns and simmer, stirring occasionally, until thickened and reduced to 3 cups, 20 to 25 minutes.

2. Strain the gravy through a fine-mesh strainer into a clean saucepan, pressing on the solids to extract as much liquid as possible; discard the solids. Season with salt and pepper to taste and serve with the pork chops.

NOTES FROM THE TEST KITCHEN

STUFFING PORK CHOPS

1. Using a paring knife, trim away the excess fat and connective tissue around the edge of the meat.

2. With the knife positioned as shown, insert the blade through the center of the side of the chop until the tip touches the bone.

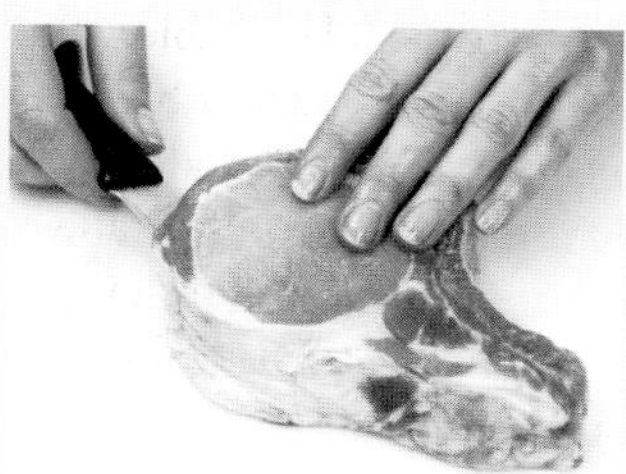

3. Swing the tip of the blade through the middle of the chop to create a pocket (the opening should be about 1 inch wide).

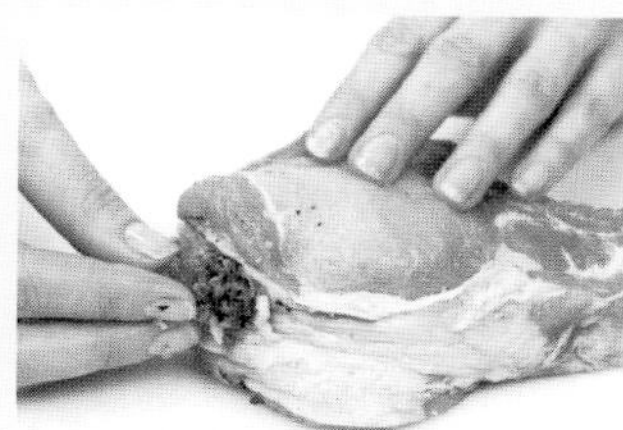

4. With your fingers, gently press the stuffing mixture into the pocket, without enlarging the opening.

Ginger-Apple Chutney

MAKES ABOUT 3½ CUPS

If you want more heat, add a little more cayenne pepper.

- 1 tablespoon vegetable oil
- 1 small onion, chopped medium
- 2 Granny Smith apples, peeled, cored, and cut into ½-inch pieces
- 1 tablespoon minced ginger
- ¼ teaspoon ground allspice
- ⅛ teaspoon cayenne pepper (see note)
- 1 cup apple cider
- ¼ cup (1¾ ounces) packed light brown sugar
- Table salt and ground black pepper

Follow the recipe for Stuffed Pork Chops. After removing the chops from the pan, pour off any fat left in the skillet. Heat the oil over medium-high heat until shimmering. Add the onion and apples and cook, stirring occasionally, until softened, about 10 minutes. Add the ginger, allspice, and cayenne and cook until fragrant, about 30 seconds. Add the cider and sugar and bring to a boil, scraping up any browned bits, until the cider is slightly thickened, about 4 minutes. Season with salt and pepper to taste and serve with the pork chops.

RED WINE–BRAISED PORK CHOPS

WHY THIS RECIPE WORKS: When braising pork chops, we found it was important to avoid lean loin chops that have a tendency to dry out when even slightly overcooked. For moist, tender chops, we began with blade chops, which, like other braising cuts, have a larger amount of fat and connective tissue. We trimmed the chops of excess fat and connective tissue to prevent buckling when cooked, and used those trimmings to build a rich and flavorful braising liquid. When the chops were done braising, we used the same liquid as the foundation for a quick and tasty sauce.

Red Wine–Braised Pork Chops

SERVES 4

Look for chops with a small eye and a large amount of marbling, as these are the best suited to braising. The pork scraps can be removed when straining the sauce in step 4 and served alongside the chops. (They taste great.)

- Salt and pepper
- 4 (10- to 12-ounce) bone-in pork blade chops, 1 inch thick
- 2 teaspoons vegetable oil
- 2 onions, halved and sliced thin
- 5 sprigs fresh thyme plus ¼ teaspoon minced
- 2 garlic cloves, peeled
- 2 bay leaves
- 1 (½-inch) piece ginger, peeled and crushed
- ⅛ teaspoon ground allspice
- ½ cup red wine
- ¼ cup ruby port
- 2 tablespoons plus ½ teaspoon red wine vinegar
- 1 cup low-sodium chicken broth
- 2 tablespoons unsalted butter
- 1 tablespoon minced fresh parsley

1. Dissolve 3 tablespoons salt in 1½ quarts cold water in large container. Submerge chops in brine, cover, and refrigerate for 30 minutes or up to 1 hour.

2. Adjust oven rack to lower-middle position and heat oven to 275 degrees. Remove chops from brine and pat dry with paper towels. Trim off meat cap and any fat and cartilage opposite rib bones. Cut trimmings into 1-inch pieces. Heat oil in Dutch oven over medium-high heat until shimmering. Add trimmings and brown on all sides, 6 to 9 minutes.

3. Reduce heat to medium and add onions, thyme sprigs, garlic, bay leaves, ginger, and allspice. Cook, stirring occasionally, until onions are golden brown, 5 to 10 minutes. Stir in wine, port, and 2 tablespoons vinegar and cook until reduced to thin syrup, 5 to 7 minutes. Add chicken broth, spread onions and pork scraps into even layer, and bring to simmer. Arrange pork chops on top of pork scraps and onions.

4. Cover, transfer to oven, and cook until meat is tender, 1¼ to 1½ hours. Remove from oven and let chops rest in pot, covered, for 30 minutes. Transfer chops to serving platter and tent with aluminum foil. Strain braising liquid through fine-mesh strainer; discard solids. Transfer braising liquid to fat separator and let stand for 5 minutes.

5. Wipe out now-empty pot with wad of paper towels. Return defatted braising liquid to pot and cook over medium-high heat until reduced to 1 cup, 3 to 7 minutes. Off heat, whisk in butter, minced thyme, and remaining ½ teaspoon vinegar. Season with salt and pepper to taste. Pour sauce over chops, sprinkle with parsley, and serve.

NOTES FROM THE TEST KITCHEN

MAKING RED WINE-BRAISED PORK CHOPS

1. The trimmed scraps from blade chops contain lots of fat and (in some cases) cartilage. Searing them builds so much flavorful browning that searing the chops themselves isn't necessary.

2. To build complex flavor, sauté the onions in the rendered pork fat until golden brown with garlic, thyme, bay leaves, ginger, and allspice.

3. To add acidity, sweetness, and complexity to the braising liquid, deglaze the pot with a combination of red wine, ruby port, and red wine vinegar.

4. Laying the chops on top of the trimmings raises them well above the liquid, where they will cook more gently and retain their flavorful juices.

FRENCH-STYLE PORK CHOPS WITH APPLES AND CALVADOS

WHY THIS RECIPE WORKS: For pork chops with big apple flavor, we took cues from the French. While our salted pork chops rested in the refrigerator, we created a base by frying up 2 slices of bacon, adding shallots and nutmeg to bloom and cook in the rendered fat. After adding a hit of Calvados, the woodsy apple brandy, we carefully ignited the sauce with a match to eliminate the alcohol's bite. We repeated this step, pouring in and flambéing a total of ½ cup of Calvados, and then rounded out the sauce's herbal, fruity flavors with apple cider, chicken broth, thyme, butter, and chopped apples. Vigorously simmering the liquid emulsified the butter. Once the sauce reduced and the apples softened, we turned our attention to the chops. After quickly browning them, we removed them from the skillet and then browned the apple rings. The apples cooked in chicken broth before we arranged the chops atop the rings, elevating the meat to finish cooking in the oven. Before serving, we strained the sauce, adding some minced thyme and cider vinegar to reinforce its apple flavor.

French-Style Pork Chops with Apples and Calvados

SERVES 4

We prefer natural pork, but if the pork is enhanced (injected with a salt solution; see page 181), decrease the salt in step 1 to ½ teaspoon per chop. To ensure that they fit in the skillet, choose apples that are approximately 3 inches in diameter. Applejack or regular brandy can be used in place of the Calvados. Before flambéing, be sure to roll up long shirtsleeves, tie back long hair, and turn off the exhaust fan and any lit burners. Use a long match or wooden skewer to flambé the Calvados. The amount of vinegar to add in step 4 will vary depending on the sweetness of your cider.

- 4 (12- to 14-ounce) bone-in pork rib chops, 1 inch thick, trimmed
- Kosher salt and pepper
- 4 Gala or Golden Delicious apples, peeled and cored
- 2 slices bacon, cut into ½-inch pieces
- 3 shallots, sliced
- Pinch ground nutmeg
- ½ cup Calvados
- 1¾ cups apple cider
- 1¼ cups chicken broth
- 4 sprigs fresh thyme, plus ¼ teaspoon minced

2 tablespoons unsalted butter
2 teaspoons vegetable oil
½–1 teaspoon apple cider vinegar

1. Evenly sprinkle each chop with ¾ teaspoon salt. Place chops on large plate, cover loosely with plastic wrap, and refrigerate for 1 hour.

2. While chops rest, cut 2 apples into ½-inch pieces. Cook bacon in medium saucepan over medium heat until crisp, 5 to 7 minutes. Add shallots, nutmeg, and ¼ teaspoon salt; cook, stirring frequently, until shallots are softened and beginning to brown, 3 to 4 minutes. Off heat, add ¼ cup Calvados and let warm through, about 5 seconds. Wave lit match over pan until Calvados ignites, then shake pan gently to distribute flames. When flames subside, 30 to 60 seconds, cover pan to ensure flame is extinguished, 15 seconds. Add remaining ¼ cup Calvados and repeat flambéing (flames will subside after 1½ to 2 minutes). (If you have trouble igniting second addition, return pan to medium heat, bring to bare simmer, and remove from heat and try again.) Once flames have extinguished, increase heat to medium-high; add cider, 1 cup broth, thyme sprigs, butter, and chopped apples; and bring to rapid simmer. Cook, stirring occasionally, until apples are very tender and mixture has reduced to 2⅓ cups, 25 to 35 minutes. Cover and set aside.

3. Adjust oven rack to middle position and heat oven to 300 degrees. Slice remaining 2 apples into ½-inch-thick rings. Pat chops dry with paper towels and evenly sprinkle each chop with pepper. Heat oil in 12-inch skillet over medium heat until just beginning to smoke. Increase heat to high and brown chops on both sides, 6 to 8 minutes total. Transfer chops to large plate and reduce heat to medium. Add apple rings and cook until lightly browned, 1 to 2 minutes. Add remaining ¼ cup broth and cook, scraping up any browned bits with rubber spatula, until liquid has evaporated, about 30 seconds. Remove pan from heat, flip apple rings, and place chops on top of apple rings. Place skillet in oven and cook until chops register 135 to 140 degrees, 11 to 15 minutes.

BEHIND THE SCENES

WHY IS THAT PORK STILL PINK?

In the test kitchen, we steer clear of dishes like Parchingly Dry Pork Chops and No-Pink Pork Loin. But there's a reason that older recipes recommend cooking pork to startlingly high internal temperatures. Years ago, when pork quality was inconsistent and trichinosis concerns ran high, pink pork was considered a safety risk, thus most recipes recommended cooking pork to 190 degrees. Today, however, the risk of trichinosis is nearly nonexistent in the United States. What's more, even when the trichinosis parasite is present, it is killed when the temperature of the meat rises to 137 degrees.

Both the U.S. Department of Agriculture and the National Pork Board recommend cooking pork to a final internal temperature of 160 degrees. If you are concerned about contamination with salmonella (which is possible in any type of meat), you must cook the pork to 160 degrees to be certain that all potential pathogens are eliminated. Unfortunately, given the leanness of today's pork, these recommendations result in dry, tough meat. (In fact, today's pork has 50 percent less fat than it did 50 years ago, which explains why older recipes that called for cooking pork to 190 degrees weren't a total disaster—all that fat kept even overcooked pork moist.)

In the test kitchen, we have found cooking modern pork beyond 150 degrees to be a waste of time and money. We cook pork to an internal temperature of 140 to 145 degrees—the meat will still be slightly rosy in the center and juicy. As the meat rests and juices are redistributed throughout the meat, the internal temperature will continue to climb to the final serving temperature of 150. Of course, if safety is your top concern, cook all meat (including pork) until it is well-done; that is, when the internal temperature reaches 160 degrees.

4. Transfer chops and apple rings to serving platter, tent loosely with aluminum foil, and let rest for 10 minutes. While chops rest, strain apple-brandy mixture through fine-mesh strainer set in large bowl, pressing on solids with ladle or rubber spatula to extract liquid; discard solids. (Make sure to use rubber spatula to scrape any apple solids on bottom of strainer into sauce.) Stir in minced thyme and season sauce with vinegar, salt, and pepper to taste. Transfer sauce to serving bowl. Serve chops and apple rings, passing sauce separately.

CHAPTER 9

ROASTS AND MORE

SLOW-ROASTED BEEF

WHY THIS RECIPE WORKS: Roasting inexpensive beef usually yields tough meat best suited for sandwiches. We wanted to take an inexpensive cut and turn it into a tender, rosy, beefy-tasting roast worthy of Sunday dinner. Our favorite cut, the eye round, has good flavor and tenderness and a uniform shape that guarantees even cooking. Next, we chose between the two classic methods for roasting meat—high and fast or low and slow. Low temperature was the way to go. Keeping the meat's internal temperature below 122 degrees as long as possible allowed the meat's enzymes to act as natural tenderizers, breaking down its tough connective tissue (this action stops at 122 degrees). Since most ovens don't heat below 200 degrees, we needed to devise a special method to lengthen this tenderizing period. We roasted the meat at 225 degrees (after searing it to give the meat a crusty exterior) and shut off the oven when the roast reached 115 degrees. The meat stayed below 122 degrees an extra 30 minutes, allowing the enzymes to continue their work before the temperature reached 130 degrees for medium-rare. As for seasoning, we found that salting the meat a full 24 hours before roasting made it even more tender and seasoned the roast throughout.

Slow-Roasted Beef

SERVES 6 TO 8

We don't recommend cooking this roast past medium. Open the oven door as little as possible and remove the roast from the oven while taking its temperature. If the roast has not reached the desired temperature in the time specified in step 3, heat the oven to 225 degrees for 5 minutes, shut it off, and continue to cook the roast to the desired temperature. For a smaller (2½- to 3½-pound) roast, reduce the amount of pepper to 1½ teaspoons. For a 4½- to 6-pound roast, cut in half crosswise before cooking to create two smaller roasts. Slice the roast as thin as possible and serve with Horseradish Cream Sauce (recipe follows), if desired.

- 1 (3½- to 4½-pound) boneless eye-round roast (see note)
- 2 teaspoons table salt
- 1 tablespoon plus 2 teaspoons vegetable oil
- 2 teaspoons ground black pepper (see note)

1. Sprinkle all sides of the roast evenly with the salt. Wrap with plastic wrap and refrigerate for 18 to 24 hours.

2. Adjust an oven rack to the middle position and heat the oven to 225 degrees. Pat the roast dry with paper towels; rub with 2 teaspoons of the oil and sprinkle all sides evenly with the pepper. Heat the remaining 1 tablespoon oil in a 12-inch skillet over medium-high heat until starting to smoke. Sear the roast until browned on all sides, 3 to 4 minutes per side. Transfer the roast to a wire rack set over a rimmed baking sheet. Roast until the center of the roast registers 115 degrees on an instant-read thermometer for medium-rare (1¼ to 1¾ hours), or 125 degrees for medium (1¾ to 2¼ hours).

3. Turn the oven off; leave the roast in the oven, without opening the door, until the center of the roast registers 130 degrees for medium-rare or 140 degrees for medium, 30 to 50 minutes longer. Transfer the roast to a carving board and let rest for 15 minutes. Slice the meat crosswise as thin as possible and serve with the sauce, if using.

Horseradish Cream Sauce

MAKES ABOUT 1 CUP

See page 913 for information on our recommended brand of prepared horseradish.

- ½ cup heavy cream, chilled
- ½ cup prepared horseradish
- 1 teaspoon table salt
- ⅛ teaspoon ground black pepper

Whisk the cream in a medium bowl until thickened but not yet holding soft peaks, 1 to 2 minutes. Gently fold in the horseradish, salt, and pepper. Transfer to a serving bowl and refrigerate for at least 30 minutes or up to 1 hour before serving.

ROAST BEEF TENDERLOIN

WHY THIS RECIPE WORKS: There's nothing like the buttery texture of a roasted beef tenderloin. Ideally, it has rosy meat all the way through and a deep brown crust; too often, though, this roast has only one or the other. We wanted a technique that produced perfectly cooked and deeply flavored meat. We opted for a center-cut piece; it's already trimmed and lacks the narrow "tail" of the whole cut. We first tried searing the meat in the oven, but it never browned evenly. Stovetop browning was better for producing a crust, but the roast still came out of the oven with a gray band. The trick was to reverse the process, first roasting the meat in the oven, then searing at the end. Lowering the oven temperature eliminated the ring of overcooked meat altogether. To add flavor to this mild cut of beef, a simple technique of salting it before roasting worked wonders; rubbing the roast with a little softened butter added richness.

A flavored butter served alongside was the final touch. With its uniformly rosy meat, deep brown crust, and beefy flavor, this beef tenderloin was worthy of its price tag.

Roast Beef Tenderloin

SERVES 4 TO 6

Ask your butcher to prepare a trimmed, center-cut Châteaubriand from the whole tenderloin, as this cut is not usually available without special ordering. If you are cooking for a crowd, this recipe can be doubled to make two roasts. Sear the roasts one after the other, wiping out the pan and adding new oil after searing the first roast. Both pieces of meat can be roasted on the same rack.

- 1 (2-pound) beef tenderloin center-cut Châteaubriand, trimmed (see note)
- 1 teaspoon table salt
- 1 teaspoon coarsely ground black pepper
- 2 tablespoons unsalted butter, softened
- 1 tablespoon vegetable oil
- 1 recipe flavored butter (recipes follow)

1. Using 12-inch lengths of kitchen twine, tie the roast crosswise at 1½-inch intervals. Sprinkle the roast evenly with the salt, cover loosely with plastic wrap, and let stand at room temperature for 1 hour. Meanwhile, adjust an oven rack to the middle position and heat the oven to 300 degrees.

2. Pat the roast dry with paper towels. Sprinkle the roast evenly with the pepper and spread the butter evenly over the surface. Transfer the roast to a wire rack set over a rimmed baking sheet. Roast until the center of the roast registers 125 degrees on an instant-read thermometer for medium-rare (40 to 55 minutes), or 135 degrees for medium (55 to 70 minutes), flipping the roast halfway through cooking.

3. Heat the oil in a 12-inch heavy-bottomed skillet over medium-high heat until just smoking. Place the roast in the skillet and sear until well browned on four sides, 1 to 2 minutes per side (a total of 4 to 8 minutes). Transfer the roast to a carving board and spread 2 tablespoons of the flavored butter evenly over the top of the roast; let rest for 15 minutes. Remove the twine and cut the meat crosswise into ½-inch-thick slices. Serve, passing the remaining flavored butter separately.

Shallot and Parsley Butter

MAKES ABOUT ½ CUP

- 4 tablespoons (½ stick) unsalted butter, softened
- 1 small shallot, minced (about 1 tablespoon)
- 1 medium garlic clove, minced or pressed through a garlic press (about 1 teaspoon)
- 1 tablespoon finely chopped fresh parsley leaves
- ¼ teaspoon table salt
- ¼ teaspoon ground black pepper

Combine all the ingredients in a medium bowl.

BEHIND THE SCENES

SALTING—THE SECRET TO JUICY ROASTS

We're big advocates of brining in the test kitchen (see "How Brining Saved Thanksgiving" on page 135). But brining works best for lean types of meat like poultry and pork. Is there an alternative to brining for fattier meats like beef? There is—salting. Salting is a kind of "dry brine" in which meat is rubbed with salt and then refrigerated for several hours. How does salting do its work? Initially, the salt draws out moisture from the meat, and this moisture mixes with the salt to form a shallow brine. Over time, the salt migrates from the shallow brine into the meat, just as it does in our usual brining technique. Once inside the meat, the salt changes the structure of the muscle fibers, allowing the meat to hold on to more water, so that it turns out juicy and well-seasoned.

We tried salting in developing our Slow-Roasted Beef (page 190) and found that salting for 24 hours worked best—the results were remarkable. In addition to the slow-cooking technique we use in this recipe, salting helped transform our bargain eye round into a tender, juicy roast that rivals beef tenderloin. (Note that smaller cuts of meat, like steak, do not need to be salted nearly as long—about 40 minutes is sufficient.)

Chipotle and Garlic Butter with Lime and Cilantro

MAKES ABOUT ½ CUP

- 5 tablespoons unsalted butter, softened
- 1 medium chipotle chile in adobo sauce, seeded and minced, with 1 teaspoon adobo sauce
- 1 medium garlic clove, minced or pressed through a garlic press (about 1 teaspoon)
- 1 teaspoon honey
- 1 teaspoon grated zest from 1 lime
- 1 tablespoon minced fresh cilantro leaves
- ½ teaspoon table salt

Combine all the ingredients in a medium bowl.

HORSERADISH-CRUSTED BEEF TENDERLOIN

WHY THIS RECIPE WORKS: A crisp horseradish crust contrasts nicely with the mild flavor of beef tenderloin, but most horseradish-crusted recipes are uninspired, and when carving time comes around, the crust falls off the meat in patches. We wanted to combine the bracing flavor of horseradish with a crisp, golden crust that would add textural contrast to rosy, medium-rare meat—and we wanted it to stick.

We chose to use a center-cut roast—also called a Châteaubriand—because its uniform shape cooks evenly. After lightly flouring the meat and applying a thin wash of egg white, we rolled the roast in crushed potato chips and panko bread crumbs mixed with horseradish, mayonnaise, shallot, garlic, and herbs. Potato chips may seem unusual, but they kept their crunch and contributed lots of flavor, particularly when we made our own by frying shredded potato in oil until browned and crisp. To make the crust adhere to the meat after being sliced, we replaced the egg white with gelatin. Because both meat and gelatin are made up of linear proteins that form tight bonds with each other, the gelatin mixture bound the bread crumbs firmly to the meat, yet yielded slightly as we cut it.

And to prevent the crust from turning soggy from meat juices released during cooking, we seared the meat in a hot skillet and let it rest so that its juices could drain off before applying the paste and the crumbs. Then we coated only the top and sides of the tenderloin, leaving an "opening" on the bottom for meat juices to escape as it roasted.

Horseradish-Crusted Beef Tenderloin

SERVES 6

If using table salt, reduce the amount in step 1 to 1½ teaspoons. Add the gelatin to the horseradish paste at the last moment or the mixture will become unspreadable. If desired, serve the roast with Horseradish Cream Sauce (page 190; you will need 2 jars of prepared horseradish for both the roast and sauce). If you choose to salt the tenderloin in advance, remove it from the refrigerator 1 hour before cooking. To make this recipe 1 day in advance, prepare it through step 3, but in step 2 do not toss the bread crumbs with the other ingredients until you are ready to sear the meat.

- 1 (2-pound) beef tenderloin center-cut Châteaubriand, trimmed of fat and silver skin
- Kosher salt (see note)
- 3 tablespoons panko (Japanese-style bread crumbs)
- 1 cup plus 2 teaspoons vegetable oil
- 1¼ teaspoons ground black pepper
- 1 small shallot, minced (about 1 tablespoon)
- 2 medium garlic cloves, minced or pressed through a garlic press (about 2 teaspoons)
- ¼ cup well-drained prepared horseradish (see note)
- 2 tablespoons minced fresh parsley leaves
- ½ teaspoon minced fresh thyme leaves
- 1 small russet potato (about 6 ounces), peeled and grated on the large holes of a box grater
- 1½ teaspoons mayonnaise
- 1½ teaspoons Dijon mustard
- ½ teaspoon powdered gelatin (see note)

1. Sprinkle the roast with 1 tablespoon salt, cover with plastic wrap, and let stand at room temperature for 1 hour or refrigerate for up to 24 hours. Adjust an oven rack to the middle position and heat the oven to 400 degrees.

2. Toss the bread crumbs with 2 teaspoons of the oil, ¼ teaspoon salt, and ¼ teaspoon of the pepper in a 10-inch nonstick skillet. Cook over medium heat, stirring frequently, until deep golden brown, 3 to 5 minutes. Transfer to a rimmed baking sheet and cool to room temperature (wipe out the skillet). Once cool, toss the bread crumbs with the shallot, garlic, 2 tablespoons of the horseradish, the parsley, and thyme.

3. Rinse the grated potato under cold water, then squeeze dry in a kitchen towel. Transfer the potatoes and remaining 1 cup oil to the skillet. Cook over high heat, stirring frequently, until the potatoes are golden brown and crisp, 6 to 8 minutes. Using a slotted spoon, transfer the potatoes to a paper towel–lined plate and season lightly with salt; let cool for 5 minutes. Reserve 1 tablespoon oil from the skillet and discard the remainder. Once the potatoes are cool, transfer to a quart-size zipper-lock bag and crush until coarsely ground. Transfer the potatoes to the baking sheet with the bread-crumb mixture and toss to combine.

4. Pat the exterior of the tenderloin dry with paper towels and sprinkle evenly with the remaining 1 teaspoon pepper. Heat the reserved 1 tablespoon oil in a 12-inch nonstick skillet over medium-high heat until just smoking. Sear the tenderloin until well browned on all sides, 5 to 7 minutes. Transfer to a wire rack set over a rimmed baking sheet and let rest for 10 minutes.

5. Combine the remaining 2 tablespoons horseradish, mayonnaise, and mustard in a small bowl. Just before coating the tenderloin, add the gelatin and stir to combine. Spread the horseradish paste on the top and sides of the meat, leaving the bottom and ends bare. Roll the coated sides of the tenderloin in the bread-crumb mixture, pressing gently so the crumbs adhere in an even layer that just covers the horseradish paste; pat off any excess.

6. Return the tenderloin to the wire rack. Roast until an instant-read thermometer inserted into the center of the roast registers 120 to 125 degrees for medium-rare, 25 to 30 minutes.

7. Transfer the roast to a carving board and let rest for 20 minutes. Carefully cut the meat crosswise into ½-inch-thick slices and serve.

ULTIMATE BEEF TENDERLOIN

WHY THIS RECIPE WORKS: Beef tenderloin is perfect holiday fare. Add a rich stuffing and you've got the ultimate main course—at least in theory. We found three problems with stuffed tenderloin. The tenderloin's thin, tapered shape made for uneven cooking; in the time it took to develop a nice crust, the meat overcooked; and "deluxe" fillings such as lobster and chanterelles were so chunky they fell out of the meat when sliced. We wanted a stuffed beef tenderloin with a deeply charred crust, a tender, rosy-pink interior, and an intensely flavored stuffing that stayed neatly rolled in the meat.

We had determined for our Roast Beef Tenderloin recipe (page 191) that a center-cut tenderloin cooks more evenly than a whole one, and its cylindrical shape had an added advantage here as it made the roast easier to stuff. But making a slit in the roast didn't give us much room for stuffing; double-butterflying the meat, to open it up like a book, gave us more space. After we stuffed, rolled, and tied it, we rubbed the roast with salt, pepper, and olive oil, which added flavor and helped develop a good crust when we seared the meat. We could fit just a cupful of stuffing in the meat, so we knew the flavors had to be intense. Chunky stuffings fell out when the roast was sliced, and anything with bread in it became a sponge that soaked up the meat juice. We finally decided on woodsy cremini mushrooms and caramelized onions, seasoned with Madeira and garlic; this combination made a savory-sweet jam-like filling that spread easily on the meat and held together well. Baby spinach added color and freshness. This roast was juicy and flavorful, and the filling was the ultimate touch of luxury.

Roast Beef Tenderloin with Caramelized Onion and Mushroom Stuffing

SERVES 4 TO 6

The roast can be stuffed, rolled, and tied a day ahead, but don't season the exterior until you are ready to cook it. This recipe can be doubled to make two roasts. Sear the roasts one after the other, cleaning the pan and adding new oil after searing the first roast. Both pieces of meat can be roasted on the same rack.

STUFFING

- 8 ounces cremini mushrooms, cleaned, stems trimmed, and broken into rough pieces
- 1½ teaspoons unsalted butter
- 1½ teaspoons olive oil
- 1 medium onion, halved and sliced ¼ inch thick
- ¼ teaspoon table salt
- ⅛ teaspoon ground black pepper
- 1 medium garlic clove, minced or pressed through a garlic press (about 1 teaspoon)
- ½ cup Madeira or sweet Marsala wine

BEEF ROAST

- 1 (2- to 3-pound) beef tenderloin center-cut Châteaubriand, trimmed and butterflied (see page 194)
- Table salt and ground black pepper
- ½ cup lightly packed baby spinach
- 3 tablespoons olive oil

HERB BUTTER

- 4 tablespoons (½ stick) unsalted butter, softened
- 1 tablespoon chopped fresh parsley leaves
- ¾ teaspoon chopped fresh thyme leaves
- 1 medium garlic clove, minced or pressed through a garlic press (about 1 teaspoon)
- 1 tablespoon whole grain mustard
- ⅛ teaspoon table salt
- ⅛ teaspoon ground black pepper

1. FOR THE STUFFING: Pulse the mushrooms in a food processor until coarsely chopped, about 6 pulses. Heat the butter and oil in a 12-inch nonstick skillet over medium-high heat. Add the onion, salt, and pepper; cook, stirring occasionally, until the onion begins to soften, about 5 minutes. Add the mushrooms and cook, stirring occasionally, until all the moisture has evaporated, 5 to 7 minutes. Reduce the heat to medium and continue to cook, stirring frequently, until the vegetables are deeply browned and sticky, about 10 minutes. Stir in the garlic and cook until fragrant, about 30 seconds. Slowly stir in the Madeira and cook, scraping the bottom of the skillet to loosen any browned bits, until the liquid has evaporated, 2 to 3 minutes. Transfer the onion-mushroom mixture to a plate and cool to room temperature.

2. FOR THE ROAST: Pat the tenderloin dry and season the cut side of the tenderloin liberally with salt and pepper. Following the photos, spread the cooled stuffing mixture over the interior of the beef, leaving a ½-inch border on all sides; press the spinach leaves on top of the stuffing. Roll the roast lengthwise, making it as compact as possible without squeezing out any filling. Evenly space eight pieces of kitchen twine (each about 14 inches) beneath the roast. Tie each strand tightly around the roast, starting with the ends.

3. In a small bowl, stir together 1 tablespoon of the olive oil, 1½ teaspoons salt, and 1½ teaspoons pepper. Rub the roast with the oil mixture and let stand at room temperature for 1 hour.

4. Adjust an oven rack to the middle position and heat the oven to 450 degrees. Heat the remaining 2 tablespoons olive oil in a 12-inch skillet over medium-high heat until smoking. Add the beef to the pan and cook until well browned on all sides, 8 to 10 minutes total. Transfer the beef to a wire rack set over a rimmed baking sheet and place in the oven. Roast until the thickest part of the roast registers 120 degrees on an instant-read thermometer for rare (16 to 18 minutes), or 125 degrees for medium-rare (20 to 22 minutes).

5. FOR THE BUTTER: While the meat roasts, combine all the ingredients in a small bowl. Transfer the tenderloin to a carving board; spread half of the butter evenly over the top of the roast. Loosely tent the roast with foil; let rest for 15 minutes. Cut the roast between the pieces of twine into thick slices. Remove the twine and serve, passing the remaining butter separately.

NOTES FROM THE TEST KITCHEN

STUFFING AND TYING A TENDERLOIN

1. Insert a chef's knife about 1 inch from the bottom of the roast and cut horizontally, stopping just before the edge. Open the meat like a book.

2. Make another cut diagonally into the thicker portion of the roast. Open up this flap, smoothing out the butterflied rectangle of meat.

3. Spread the filling evenly over the entire surface, leaving a ½-inch border on all sides. Press the spinach leaves evenly on top of the filling.

4. Using both hands, gently but firmly roll up the stuffed tenderloin, making it as compact as possible without squeezing out the filling.

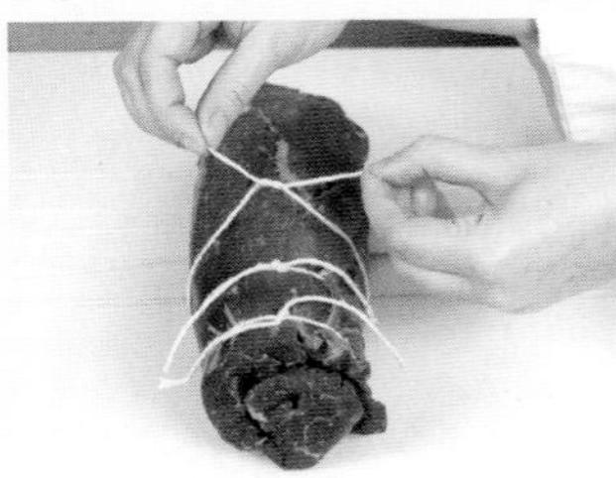

5. Evenly space eight pieces of kitchen twine (each about 14 inches) beneath the roast. Tie each strand tightly around the roast, starting with the ends.

PEPPER-CRUSTED BEEF TENDERLOIN ROAST

WHY THIS RECIPE WORKS: For a tender, rosy roast with a spicy, yet not harsh-tasting, peppercorn crust that didn't fall off, we relied on a few tricks. Rubbing the raw tenderloin with an abrasive mixture of kosher salt, sugar, and baking soda transformed its surface into a magnet for the pepper crust. To tame the heat of the pepper crust, we simmered cracked peppercorns in oil, then strained them from the oil. To replace some of the subtle flavors we had simmered away, we added some orange zest and nutmeg. With the crust in place, we gently roasted the tenderloin in the oven until it was perfectly rosy, then served it with a tangy, fruity sauce to complement the rich beef.

Pepper-Crusted Beef Tenderloin Roast

SERVES 10 TO 12

Not all pepper mills produce a coarse enough grind for this recipe. Coarsely cracked peppercorns are each about the size of a halved whole one.

- 4½ teaspoons kosher salt
- 1½ teaspoons sugar
- ¼ teaspoon baking soda
- 9 tablespoons olive oil
- ½ cup coarsely cracked black peppercorns
- 1 tablespoon finely grated orange zest
- ½ teaspoon ground nutmeg
- 1 (6-pound) whole beef tenderloin, trimmed

1. Adjust oven rack to middle position and heat oven to 300 degrees. Combine salt, sugar, and baking soda in bowl; set aside. Heat 6 tablespoons oil and peppercorns in small saucepan over low heat until faint bubbles appear. Continue to cook at bare simmer, swirling pan occasionally, until pepper is fragrant, 7 to 10 minutes. Using fine-mesh strainer, drain cooking oil from peppercorns. Discard cooking oil and mix peppercorns with remaining 3 tablespoons oil, orange zest, and nutmeg.

2. Set tenderloin on sheet of plastic wrap. Sprinkle salt mixture evenly over surface of tenderloin and rub into tenderloin until surface is tacky. Tuck tail end of tenderloin under about 6 inches to create more even shape. Rub top and side of tenderloin with peppercorn mixture, pressing to make sure peppercorns adhere. Spray three 12-inch lengths kitchen twine with vegetable oil spray; tie head of tenderloin to maintain even shape, spacing twine at 2-inch intervals.

3. Transfer prepared tenderloin to wire rack set in rimmed baking sheet, keeping tail end tucked under. Roast until thickest part of meat registers about 120 degrees for rare and about 125 degrees for medium-rare (thinner parts of tenderloin will be slightly more done), 60 to 70 minutes. Transfer to carving board and let rest for 30 minutes.

4. Remove twine and slice meat into ½-inch-thick slices. Serve.

Red Wine–Orange Sauce

MAKES 1 CUP

- 2 tablespoons unsalted butter, plus 4 tablespoons cut into 4 pieces and chilled
- 2 shallots, minced
- 1 tablespoon tomato paste
- 2 teaspoons sugar
- 3 garlic cloves, minced
- 2 cups beef broth
- 1 cup red wine
- ¼ cup orange juice
- 2 tablespoons balsamic vinegar
- 1 tablespoon Worcestershire sauce
- 1 sprig fresh thyme
- Salt and pepper

1. Melt 2 tablespoons butter in medium saucepan over medium-high heat. Add shallots, tomato paste, and sugar; cook, stirring frequently, until deep brown, about 5 minutes. Add garlic and cook until fragrant, about 1 minute. Add broth, wine, orange juice, vinegar, Worcestershire, and thyme sprig, scraping up any browned bits. Bring to simmer and cook until reduced to 1 cup, 35 to 40 minutes.

2. Strain sauce through fine-mesh strainer and return to saucepan. Return saucepan to medium heat and whisk in remaining 4 tablespoons butter, 1 piece at a time. Season with salt and pepper to taste.

Pomegranate-Port Sauce

MAKES 1 CUP

- 2 cups pomegranate juice
- 1½ cups ruby port
- 1 shallot, minced
- 1 tablespoon sugar
- 1 teaspoon balsamic vinegar
- 1 sprig fresh thyme
- Salt and pepper
- 4 tablespoons cold unsalted butter, cut into 4 pieces

Bring juice, port, shallot, sugar, vinegar, thyme sprig, and 1 teaspoon salt to simmer over medium-high heat. Cook until reduced to 1 cup, 30 to 35 minutes. Strain sauce through fine-mesh strainer and return to saucepan. Return saucepan to medium heat and whisk in butter, 1 piece at a time. Season with salt and pepper to taste.

BEEF TENDERLOIN WITH SMOKY POTATOES AND PERSILLADE RELISH

WHY THIS RECIPE WORKS: For special occasions, few cuts top a beef tenderloin. This elegant roast cooks quickly and serves a crowd, and its rich, buttery slices are fork-tender. We found that a hot oven delivered rich, roasted flavor and perfectly rosy meat without overcooking this lean cut. Tying the roast helped to ensure even cooking. The roast needed company, and small whole red potatoes were a perfect pairing. To punch up the flavor, we tossed the potatoes with smoked paprika, which added a pleasant smokiness to complement our meat, along with garlic and scallions for a deep, flavorful backbone. The tender meat needed a sauce, so we made a simple yet bold persillade relish, which featured parsley, capers, and cornichons.

Beef Tenderloin with Smoky Potatoes and Persillade Relish

SERVES 6 TO 8

We prefer to use extra-small red potatoes measuring less than 1 inch in diameter. Larger potatoes can be used, but it may be necessary to return the potatoes to the oven to finish cooking, while the roast is resting in step 5. Center-cut beef tenderloin roasts are sometimes sold as Châteaubriand.

BEEF AND POTATOES

- 1 (3-pound) center-cut beef tenderloin roast, trimmed
- Kosher salt and pepper
- 1 teaspoon baking soda
- 3 tablespoons extra-virgin olive oil
- 3 pounds extra-small red potatoes, unpeeled
- 5 scallions, minced
- 4 garlic cloves, minced
- 1 tablespoon smoked paprika
- ½ cup water

PERSILLADE RELISH

- ¾ cup minced fresh parsley
- ½ cup extra-virgin olive oil
- 6 tablespoons minced cornichons plus 1 teaspoon brine
- ¼ cup capers, rinsed and chopped coarse
- 3 garlic cloves, minced
- 1 scallion, minced
- 1 teaspoon sugar
- ¼ teaspoon salt
- ¼ teaspoon pepper

1. FOR THE BEEF AND POTATOES: Pat roast dry with paper towels. Combine 2¼ teaspoons salt, 1 teaspoon pepper, and baking soda in small bowl. Rub salt mixture evenly over roast and let stand for 1 hour. After 1 hour, tie roast with kitchen twine at 1½ inch intervals. Adjust oven rack to middle position and heat oven to 425 degrees.

2. Heat 2 tablespoons oil in 16 by 12-inch roasting pan over medium-high heat (over 2 burners, if possible) until shimmering. Add potatoes, scallions, garlic, paprika, 1 teaspoon salt, and ¼ teaspoon pepper and cook until scallions are softened, about 1 minute. Off heat, stir in water, scraping up any browned bits. Transfer roasting pan to oven and roast potatoes for 15 minutes.

3. Brush remaining 1 tablespoon oil over surface of roast. Remove roasting pan from oven, stir potato mixture, and lay beef on top. Reduce oven temperature to 300 degrees. Return pan to oven and roast until beef registers 120 to 125 degrees (for medium- rare), 45 to 55 minutes, rotating roasting pan halfway through cooking.

4. FOR THE PERSILLADE RELISH: While beef roasts, combine all ingredients in bowl.

5. Remove pan from oven. Transfer roast to carving board, tent with aluminum foil, and let rest 15 minutes. Cover potatoes left in pan with foil to keep warm. Remove twine from roast, slice into ½-inch- thick slices, and serve with potatoes and persillade relish.

FENNEL-CORIANDER TOP SIRLOIN ROAST

WHY THIS RECIPE WORKS: We wanted a holiday-caliber roast without the hefty price tag, so we set out to bring big flavor to a more affordable cut: top sirloin. We began by splitting the roast in half, creating two manageable roasts, salting the halves, and air-drying them in the refrigerator. This seasoned the meat, maximized its juiciness, and dried the surfaces for optimal browning. After 24 hours, we kickstarted the browning by quickly searing all sides of the two roasts in a skillet. Tying the roasts with kitchen twine turned the irregularly shaped roasts into two uniform cylinders. To compensate for the meat's leaner makeup, we created a rich, heavily seasoned paste that would further boost browning. We processed garlic, fennel, olive oil, and umami-boosting anchovy fillets to create a spreadable consistency, then added coriander, paprika, and oregano for extra flavor. After applying the spice paste, we roasted the meat in a 225-degree oven for 2 hours. This initial roast cooked the meat to our liking. To give it an attractive browned crust, we removed the roasts from the oven, ramped up the temperature to 500 degrees, and returned them (with twine removed) for a final crisping.

Fennel-Coriander Top Sirloin Roast

SERVES 8 TO 10

This recipe requires refrigerating the salted meat for at least 24 hours before cooking. The roast, also called a top sirloin roast, top butt roast, center-cut roast, spoon roast, shell roast, or shell sirloin roast, should not be confused with a whole top sirloin butt roast or top loin roast. Do not omit the anchovies; they provide great depth of flavor with no overt fishiness. Monitoring the roast with a meat-probe thermometer is best. If you use an instant-read thermometer, open the oven door as little as possible and remove the roast from the oven to take its temperature.

- 1 (5- to 6-pound) boneless top sirloin center-cut roast, trimmed
- 2 tablespoons kosher salt
- 4 teaspoons plus ¼ cup extra-virgin olive oil
- 4 garlic cloves, minced
- 6 anchovy fillets, rinsed and patted dry
- 2 teaspoons ground fennel
- 2 teaspoons ground coriander
- 2 teaspoons paprika
- 1 teaspoon dried oregano
- 1 teaspoon pepper
- Coarse sea salt

1. Cut roast lengthwise along grain into 2 equal pieces. Rub 1 tablespoon kosher salt over each piece. Transfer to large plate and refrigerate, uncovered, for at least 24 hours or up to 4 days.

2. Adjust oven rack to middle position and heat oven to 225 degrees. Heat 2 teaspoons oil in 12-inch skillet over high heat until just smoking. Brown 1 roast on all sides, 6 to 8 minutes. Return browned roast to plate. Repeat with 2 teaspoons oil and remaining roast. Let cool for 10 minutes.

3. While roasts cool, process garlic, anchovies, fennel, coriander, paprika, oregano, and remaining ¼ cup oil in food processor until smooth paste forms, about 30 seconds, scraping down sides of bowl as needed. Add pepper and pulse to combine, 2 to 3 pulses.

4. Using 5 pieces of kitchen twine per roast, tie each roast crosswise at equal intervals into loaf shape. Transfer roasts to wire rack set in rimmed baking sheet and rub roasts evenly with paste.

5. Roast until meat registers 125 degrees for medium-rare or 130 degrees for medium, 2 to 2¼ hours. Remove roasts from oven, leaving on wire rack, and tent loosely with aluminum foil; let rest for at least 30 minutes or up to 40 minutes.

6. Heat oven to 500 degrees. Remove foil from roasts and cut and discard twine. Return roasts to oven and cook until exteriors of roasts are well browned, 6 to 8 minutes.

7. Transfer roasts to carving board. Slice meat ¼ inch thick. Season with sea salt to taste, and serve.

BEHIND THE SCENES

GIVE THAT MEAT A REST

You'll never see anyone in the test kitchen cut into a roast, or any meat, straight from the oven. They always let it rest before slicing. Exposed to heat during cooking, proteins, which resemble coiled springs, undergo a radical transformation in which they uncoil and then reconnect to each other in haphazard structures. This process, called coagulation, is the reason that proteins become firm and lose moisture during the cooking process. The longer that proteins are exposed to heat, the tighter they coagulate and the more liquid they drive toward both the surface and the center of the meat, much like wringing a wet kitchen towel.

If you were to cut the meat immediately after removing it from the heat source, the liquid suspended between the interior proteins is driven toward the surface and would simply pool (or what many chefs call bleed) on the cutting board or plate because the proteins have not had time to relax. The best way to prevent this pooling of juices and a dry hunk of meat is to rest the roast. Although the process of coagulation is not reversible, allowing the protein molecules to relax after cooking slows the rate at which they continue to squeeze the liquid between their tight coils and increases their capacity to retain moisture. A short rest on the cutting board will decrease the amount of liquid lost during carving by about 40 percent. There's another good reason to have some patience and let your meat rest—it allows you some time to finish the other components of dinner, which is especially useful around the holidays when there are typically loads of sides to get to the table too.

Rosemary-Garlic Top Sirloin Roast

Omit fennel, coriander, paprika, and oregano. Add 3 tablespoons chopped fresh rosemary to food processor with oil in step 3. Add ¼ teaspoon red pepper flakes with pepper in step 3.

CLASSIC PRIME RIB

WHY THIS RECIPE WORKS: Most of us cook prime rib only once a year, if that, and don't want to risk experimenting with the cooking method—especially when the results are no better than mediocre. We thought that a special-occasion roast deserved better and wanted to find the best way to get the juicy, tender, rosy meat that prime rib should have.

The principal question for roasting prime rib was oven temperature, and our research turned up a wide range of recommendations. Most delivered meat that was well-done on the outside but increasingly rare toward the center—not too bad, but not exactly great. Surprisingly, the roast we cooked at a temperature of only 250 degrees was rosy from the center all the way out. Additionally, it retained more juice than a roast cooked at a higher temperature, and the internal temperature rose less during resting, so we had more control over the final degree of doneness. Searing before roasting gave us a crusty brown exterior. For seasoning, prime rib needs nothing more than salt and pepper. Now that we'd found a dependable cooking method, we could serve this once-a-year roast with confidence.

Classic Prime Rib

SERVES 6 TO 8

With two pieces of kitchen twine running parallel to the bone, tie the roast at both ends to prevent the outer layer of meat from pulling away from the rib-eye muscle and overcooking.

- 1 (7-pound; 3-rib) standing rib roast, trimmed and tied (see note)
- Table salt and ground black pepper

1. Pat the roast dry with paper towels and season with salt and pepper. Cover the roast loosely with plastic wrap and let sit at room temperature for 1 to 2 hours.

2. Adjust an oven rack to the lowest position and heat the oven to 250 degrees. Heat a large roasting pan over two burners set at medium-high heat until hot, about 4 minutes. Place the roast in the hot pan and cook on all sides until nicely browned and about ½ cup fat has rendered, 6 to 8 minutes.

3. Remove the roast from the pan. Set a wire rack in the pan, then set the roast on the rack.

4. Place the roast in the oven and roast until the meat registers 125 degrees on an instant-read thermometer for rare, 130 degrees for medium-rare, and 140 degrees for medium, 3 to 3½ hours. Remove the roast from the oven and tent with foil. Let stand for 20 to 30 minutes to allow the juices to redistribute evenly throughout the roast.

5. Remove the twine and set the roast on a carving board, with the rib bones at a 90-degree angle to the board. Following the photos, carve and serve immediately.

NOTES FROM THE TEST KITCHEN

CARVING CLASSIC PRIME RIB

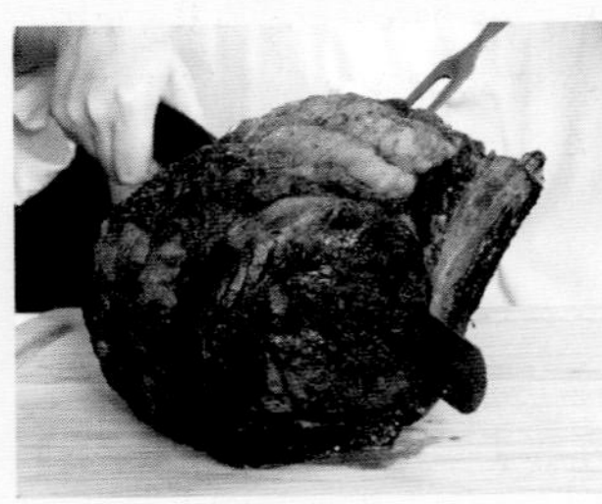

1. Using a carving fork to hold the roast in place, cut along the rib bones to sever the meat from the bones.

2. Set the roast cut side down; carve the meat across the grain into thick slices.

THE BEST PRIME RIB

WHY THIS RECIPE WORKS: The perfect prime rib should have a deep-colored, substantial crust encasing a tender, juicy rosy-pink center. To achieve superior results, we cut slits in the layer of fat to help it render efficiently, then salted the roast overnight. The long salting time enhanced the beefy flavor while dissolving some of the proteins, yielding a buttery-tender roast. To further enhance tenderness, we cooked the roast at a very low temperature, which allowed the meat's enzymes to act as natural tenderizers, breaking down its tough connective tissue. A brief stint under the broiler before serving ensured a crisp, flavorful crust.

Best Prime Rib

SERVES 6 TO 8

Look for a roast with an untrimmed fat cap (ideally ½ inch thick). We prefer the flavor and texture of Prime beef, but Choice grade will work as well. Monitoring the roast with a meat-probe thermometer is best. If you use an instant-read thermometer, open the oven door as little as possible and remove the roast from the oven while taking its temperature. If the roast has not reached the correct temperature in the time range specified in step 3, heat the oven to 200 degrees, wait for five minutes, then shut it off, and continue to cook the roast until it reaches the desired temperature.

- 1 (7-pound) first-cut beef standing rib roast (3 bones), meat removed from bones, bones reserved
- Kosher salt and pepper
- 2 teaspoons vegetable oil

1. Using sharp knife, cut slits in surface layer of fat, spaced 1 inch apart, in crosshatch pattern, being careful to cut down to, but not into, meat. Rub 2 tablespoons salt over entire roast and into slits. Place meat back on bones (to save space in refrigerator), transfer to large plate, and refrigerate, uncovered, for at least 24 hours or up to 4 days.

2. Adjust oven rack to middle position and heat oven to 200 degrees. Set wire rack in rimmed baking sheet. Heat oil in 12-inch skillet over high heat until just smoking. Sear sides and top of roast (reserving bones) until browned, 6 to 8 minutes total (do not sear side where roast was cut from bones). Place meat back on ribs so bones fit where they were cut and let cool for 10 minutes; tie meat to bones with 2 lengths of kitchen twine between ribs. Transfer roast, fat side up, to prepared wire rack and season with pepper. Roast until meat registers 110 degrees, 3 to 4 hours.

3. Turn off oven; leave roast in oven, opening door as little as possible, until meat registers about 120 degrees (for rare) or about 125 degrees (for medium-rare), 30 minutes to 1¼ hours longer.

4. Remove roast from oven (leave roast on baking sheet), tent loosely with aluminum foil, and let rest for at least 30 minutes or up to 1¼ hours.

5. Adjust oven rack to about 8 inches from broiler element and heat broiler. Remove foil from roast, form into 3-inch ball, and place under ribs to elevate fat cap. Broil until top of roast is well browned and crisp, 2 to 8 minutes.

6. Transfer roast to carving board; cut twine and remove ribs from roast. Slice meat into ¾-inch-thick slices. Season with salt to taste, and serve.

NOTES FROM THE TEST KITCHEN

PREPARING BEST PRIME RIB

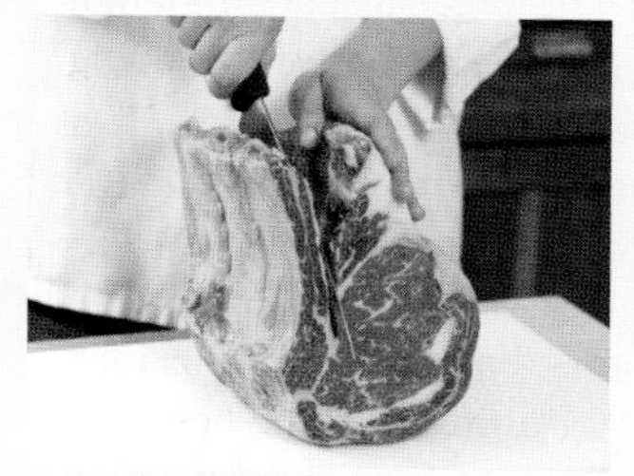

1. Removing ribs makes it easier to sear prime rib in skillet. Run sharp knife down length of bones, following contours as closely as possible to remove ribs.

2. Score fat cap in 1-inch crosshatch pattern to allow salt to contact meat directly and to improve fat rendering and crisping.

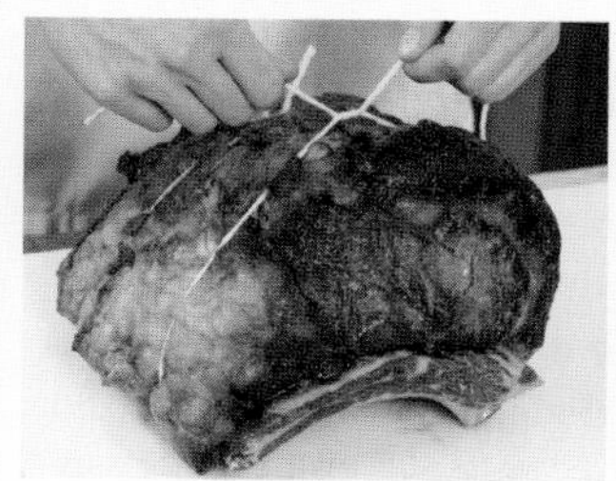

3. After searing meat, place meat back on ribs so bones fit where they were cut and let cool for 10 minutes; tie meat to bones with 2 lengths of kitchen twine between ribs. The bones provide insulation to the meat so it cooks evenly.

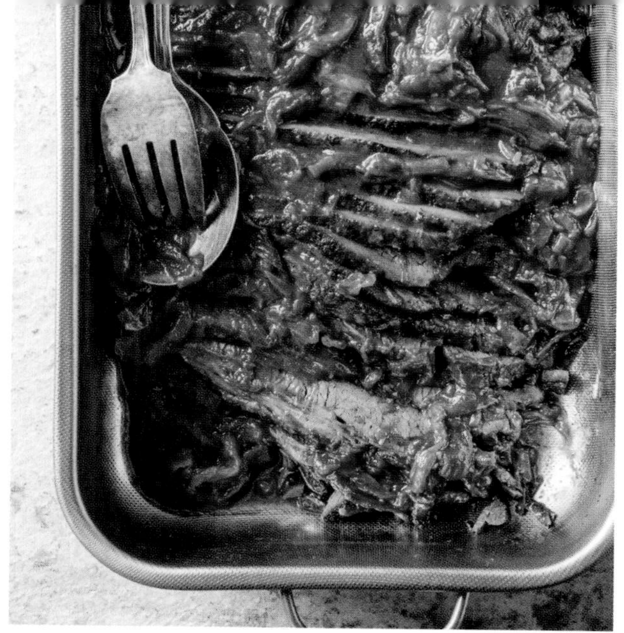

BRAISED BRISKET

WHY THIS RECIPE WORKS: Brisket is naturally flavorful, but because it is so lean, it requires long, slow braising to become tender—and the result is almost always stringy, dry meat. We wanted a better way to cook brisket so that it would remain moist, and we wanted to serve it with a flavorful sauce that would complement the beef. The fat in a piece of brisket is all on the surface; there's no marbling to keep the interior moist. We needed to find a way to get the moisture inside. We tried many different types and amounts of liquids and a variety of cooking vessels and techniques, but no matter what we did, the meat was still dry. Could the answer lie in adding moisture after the long braise? We left the meat in the sauce after cooking it, and after about an hour there was a noticeable difference. Taking this discovery further, we refrigerated the cooked meat and sauce overnight. The meat reabsorbed some of the liquid, becoming more moist and easier to carve without shredding. The sauce—based on red wine, chicken broth, and lots of onions—had improved as well; the fat had risen to the surface and congealed, making it easier to remove. All we had to do was reheat the sliced meat in the sauce, and this hearty dish was ready.

Onion-Braised Beef Brisket

SERVES 6

This recipe requires a few hours of unattended cooking. It also requires advance preparation. After cooking, the brisket must stand overnight in the braising liquid that later becomes the sauce. Defatting the sauce is essential. If the fat has congealed into a layer on top of the sauce, it can be easily removed while cold. Sometimes, however, fragments of solid fat are dispersed throughout the sauce; in this case, the sauce should be skimmed of fat after reheating. If you prefer a spicy sauce, increase the amount of cayenne to ¼ teaspoon. You will need 18-inch-wide heavy-duty foil for this recipe. If you own an electric knife, it will make easy work of slicing the cold brisket.

If you would like to make and serve the brisket on the same day, after removing the brisket from the oven in step 4, reseal the foil and let the brisket stand at room temperature for an hour. Then transfer the brisket to a carving board and continue with the recipe to strain, defat, and reheat the sauce and slice the meat; because the brisket will still be hot, there will be no need to put it back into the oven once the reheated sauce is poured over it.

- 1 (4- to 5-pound) beef brisket, preferably flat cut
- Table salt and ground black pepper
- 1 teaspoon vegetable oil, plus more as needed
- 3 large onions (about 2½ pounds), halved and sliced ½ inch thick
- 1 tablespoon brown sugar
- 3 medium garlic cloves, minced or pressed through a garlic press (about 1 tablespoon)
- 1 tablespoon tomato paste
- 1 tablespoon paprika
- ⅛ teaspoon cayenne pepper (see note)
- 2 tablespoons unbleached all-purpose flour
- 1 cup low-sodium chicken broth
- 1 cup dry red wine
- 3 bay leaves
- 3 sprigs fresh thyme
- 2 teaspoons cider vinegar (to season the sauce before serving)

1. Adjust an oven rack to the lower-middle position and heat the oven to 300 degrees. Line a 13 by 9-inch baking dish with two 24-inch-long sheets of 18-inch-wide heavy-duty foil, positioning the sheets perpendicular to each other and allowing the excess foil to extend beyond the edges of the pan. Pat the brisket dry with paper towels. Place the brisket, fat side up, on a cutting board; using a dinner fork, poke holes in the meat through the fat layer about 1 inch apart. Season both sides of the brisket liberally with salt and pepper.

2. Heat 1 teaspoon oil in a 12-inch skillet over medium-high heat until the oil just begins to smoke. Place the brisket, fat side up, in the skillet (the brisket may climb up the sides of the skillet); weight the brisket with a heavy Dutch oven or cast-iron skillet and cook until well browned, about 7 minutes. Remove the Dutch oven; using tongs, flip the brisket and cook on the second side without the weight until well browned, about 7 minutes longer. Transfer the brisket to a platter.

3. Pour off all but 1 tablespoon fat from the pan (or, if the brisket is lean, add enough oil to the fat in the skillet to equal 1 tablespoon); stir in the onions, brown sugar, and ¼ teaspoon salt and cook over medium-high heat, stirring occasionally, until the onions are softened and golden, 10 to 12 minutes. Add the garlic and cook, stirring frequently, until fragrant, about 1 minute; add the tomato paste and cook, stirring to combine, until the paste darkens, about 2 minutes. Add the paprika and cayenne and cook, stirring constantly, until fragrant, about 1 minute. Sprinkle the flour over the onions and cook, stirring constantly, until well combined, about 2 minutes. Add the broth, wine, bay leaves, and thyme, stirring to scrape up the browned bits from the pan; bring to a simmer and simmer for about 5 minutes to fully thicken.

4. Pour the sauce and onions into the foil-lined baking dish. Nestle the brisket, fat side up, in the sauce and onions. Fold the foil extensions over and seal (do not tightly crimp the foil because it must later be opened to test for doneness). Place in the oven and cook until a fork can be inserted into and removed from the center of the brisket with no resistance, 3½ to 4 hours (when testing for doneness, open the foil with caution as the contents will be steaming). Carefully open the foil and let the brisket cool at room temperature for 20 to 30 minutes.

5. Transfer the brisket to a large bowl; set a mesh strainer over the bowl and strain the sauce over the brisket. Discard the bay leaves and thyme from the onions and transfer the onions to a small bowl. Cover both bowls with plastic wrap, cut vents in the plastic with a paring knife, and refrigerate overnight.

6. About 45 minutes before serving, adjust an oven rack to the lower-middle position and heat the oven to 350 degrees. While the oven heats, transfer the cold brisket to a carving board. Scrape off and discard any congealed fat from the sauce, then transfer the sauce to a medium saucepan and heat over medium heat until warm, skimming any fat on the surface with a wide shallow spoon (you should have about 2 cups of sauce without onions; if necessary, simmer the sauce over medium-high heat until reduced to 2 cups). While the sauce heats, use an electric knife, chef's knife, or carving knife to slice the brisket against the grain into ¼-inch-thick slices, trimming and discarding any excess fat, if desired; place the slices in a 13 by 9-inch baking dish. Stir the reserved onions and the vinegar into the warmed sauce and season with salt and pepper to taste. Pour the sauce over the brisket slices, cover the baking dish with foil, and bake until heated through, 25 to 30 minutes. Serve immediately.

CUBAN BRAISED AND SHREDDED BEEF

WHY THIS RECIPE WORKS: Tender yet hearty strands of beef napped in a bright and deeply savory sauce define *ropa vieja*. For braised and shredded beef dishes, we usually turn to chuck roast and short ribs, but this Cuban specialty calls for thicker, more fibrous shreds, so we used brisket. Slicing the beef into strips made for faster cooking and easy shredding, and a quick sear before braising gave the meat some ultrasavory browning. The accompanying vegetables would get overly soft if braised, so we cooked them ahead of time, browning sliced onions and red bell peppers then using their fond (as well as the beef's) to build the sauce. A fragrant combination of minced anchovies, minced garlic, ground cumin, and dried oregano created the meaty, aromatic base to which we added dry white wine for brightness. After letting the mixture reduce, we added chicken broth, tomato sauce, and bay leaves. We cooked the brisket in this seasoned sauce for 2 hours and it emerged juicy and richly flavored. Green olives are a traditional finishing touch, so we chopped and added them to the sauce while the beef cooled, stirring them in with the cooked onions and peppers. A splash of white wine vinegar made the flavors in our perfectly chewy Cuban shredded beef pop.

Cuban Braised and Shredded Beef

SERVES 6 TO 8

Look for a brisket that is 1½ to 2½ inches thick. Serve with steamed white rice and beans. Another good accompaniment is Fried Sweet Plantains (page 615).

- 1 (2-pound) beef brisket, fat trimmed to ¼ inch
- Salt and pepper
- 5 tablespoons vegetable oil
- 2 onions, halved and sliced thin
- 2 red bell peppers, stemmed, seeded, and sliced into ¼-inch-wide strips
- 2 anchovy fillets, rinsed, patted dry, and minced
- 4 garlic cloves, minced
- 2 teaspoons ground cumin
- 1½ teaspoons dried oregano
- ½ cup dry white wine
- 2 cups chicken broth
- 1 (8-ounce) can tomato sauce
- 2 bay leaves
- ¾ cup pitted green olives, chopped coarse
- ¾ teaspoon white wine vinegar, plus extra for seasoning

1. Adjust oven rack to middle position and heat oven to 300 degrees. Cut brisket against grain into 2-inch-wide strips. Cut any strips longer than 5 inches in half crosswise. Season beef on all sides with salt and pepper. Heat 4 tablespoons oil in Dutch oven over medium-high heat until just smoking. Brown beef on all sides, 7 to 10 minutes; transfer to large plate and set aside. Add onions and bell peppers and cook until softened and pan bottom develops fond, 10 to 15 minutes. Transfer vegetables to bowl and set aside. Add remaining 1 tablespoon oil to now-empty pot, then add anchovies, garlic, cumin, and oregano and cook until fragrant, about 30 seconds. Stir in wine, scraping up any browned bits, and cook until mostly evaporated, about 1 minute. Stir in broth, tomato sauce, and bay leaves. Return beef and any accumulated juices to pot and bring to simmer over high heat. Transfer to oven and cook, covered, until beef is just tender, 2 to 2¼ hours, flipping beef halfway through cooking.

2. Transfer beef to cutting board; when cool enough to handle, shred into ¼-inch-thick pieces. Meanwhile, add olives and reserved vegetables to pot and bring to boil over medium-high heat; simmer until thickened and measures 4 cups, 5 to 7 minutes. Stir in beef. Add vinegar. Season with salt, pepper, and extra vinegar to taste; serve.

CUBAN SHREDDED BEEF

WHY THIS RECIPE WORKS: *Vaca frita* is a Cuban classic that features beef (usually flank steak) that's been boiled, shredded, and fried so that the exterior develops a deep crust; a bit of lime juice and garlic contribute the bright, tart, and robust flavors typical of Caribbean cuisine. For our recipe, we were after meat with some textural contrast—we wanted a good exterior crust, plus a moister, more tender interior. We started with a collagen-rich chuck-eye roast and cut it into 1½-inch cubes to reduce the cooking time. Gently simmering it helped keep it moist. Pounding the meat flat was much more efficient than shredding it by hand. To reinforce the beefy flavor, we fried it, along with some thin-sliced onion, in its own fat before finishing everything with a mixture of garlic, cumin, oil, and citrus juices (lime as well as orange, to mellow the lime's acidity but maintain brightness).

Cuban Shredded Beef

SERVES 4 TO 6

Use a well-marbled chuck-eye roast in this recipe. When trimming the beef, don't remove all visible fat—some of it will be used in lieu of oil later in the recipe. If you don't have enough reserved fat in step 3, use vegetable oil. This dish pairs well with rice and beans, or it can be used as a filling for tacos, empanadas, or sandwiches.

- 2 pounds boneless beef chuck-eye roast, pulled apart at seams, trimmed, and cut into 1½-inch cubes
- Kosher salt and pepper
- 3 garlic cloves, minced
- 1 teaspoon vegetable oil
- ¼ teaspoon ground cumin
- 2 tablespoons orange juice
- 1½ teaspoons grated lime zest plus 1 tablespoon juice
- 1 onion, halved and sliced thin
- 2 tablespoons dry sherry
- Lime wedges

1. Bring beef, 2 cups water, and 1¼ teaspoons salt to boil in 12-inch nonstick skillet over medium-high heat. Reduce heat to low, cover, and gently simmer until beef is very tender, about 1 hour 45 minutes. (Check beef every 30 minutes, adding water so that bottom third of beef is submerged.) While beef simmers, combine garlic, oil, and cumin in bowl. Combine orange juice and lime zest and juice in second bowl.

2. Remove lid from skillet, increase heat to medium, and simmer until water evaporates and beef starts to sizzle, 3 to 8 minutes. Using slotted spoon, transfer beef to rimmed baking sheet. Pour off and reserve fat from skillet. Rinse skillet clean and dry with paper towels. Place sheet of aluminum foil over beef and, using meat pounder or heavy sauté pan, pound to flatten beef into ⅛-inch-thick pieces, discarding any large pieces of fat or connective tissue. (Some of beef should separate into shreds. Larger pieces that do not separate can be torn in half.)

3. Heat 1½ teaspoons reserved fat in now-empty skillet over high heat. When fat begins to sizzle, add onion and ¼ teaspoon salt. Cook, stirring occasionally, until onion is golden brown and charred in spots, 5 to 8 minutes. Add sherry and ¼ cup water and cook until liquid is absorbed, about 2 minutes. Transfer onion to bowl. Return skillet to high heat, add 1½ teaspoons reserved fat, and heat until it begins to sizzle. Add beef and cook, stirring frequently, until dark golden brown and crusty, 2 to 4 minutes.

4. Reduce heat to low and push beef to sides of skillet. Add garlic mixture to center and cook, stirring frequently, until fragrant and golden brown, about 30 seconds. Remove pan from heat, add orange juice mixture and onion, and toss to combine. Season with pepper to taste. Serve immediately with lime wedges.

ROAST BUTTERFLIED LEG OF LAMB

WHY THIS RECIPE WORKS: Roast leg of lamb is both delicious and daunting. The usual bone-in or boned, rolled, and tied leg options cook unevenly and are tricky to carve. Choosing a butterflied leg of lamb did away with these problems; we simply pounded it to an even thickness and salted it for an hour to encourage juicy, evenly cooked meat. We first roasted it gently in the oven until it was just medium-rare, then we passed it under the broiler to give it a crisp crust. A standard spice rub scorched under the broiler, so we opted for a spice-infused oil which seasoned the lamb during cooking and then became a quick sauce for serving.

Roast Butterflied Leg of Lamb with Coriander, Cumin, and Mustard Seeds

SERVES 8 TO 10

We prefer the subtler flavor and larger size of lamb labeled "domestic" or "American" for this recipe. The amount of salt (2 tablespoons) in step 1 is for a 6-pound leg. If using a larger leg (7 to 8 pounds), add an additional teaspoon of salt for every pound.

LAMB

- 1 (6- to 8-pound) butterflied leg of lamb
- Kosher salt
- ⅓ cup vegetable oil
- 3 shallots, sliced thin
- 4 garlic cloves, peeled and smashed
- 1 (1-inch) piece ginger, sliced into ½-inch-thick rounds and smashed
- 1 tablespoon coriander seeds
- 1 tablespoon cumin seeds
- 1 tablespoon mustard seeds
- 3 bay leaves
- 2 (2-inch) strips lemon zest

SAUCE

- ⅓ cup chopped fresh mint
- ⅓ cup chopped fresh cilantro
- 1 shallot, minced
- 2 tablespoons lemon juice
- Salt and pepper

1. FOR THE LAMB: Place lamb on cutting board with fat cap facing down. Using sharp knife, trim any pockets of fat and connective tissue from underside of lamb. Flip lamb over, trim fat cap so it's between ⅛ and ¼ inch thick, and pound roast to even 1-inch thickness. Cut slits, spaced ½ inch apart, in fat cap in crosshatch pattern, being careful to cut down to but not into meat. Rub 2 tablespoons salt over entire roast and into slits. Let stand, uncovered, at room temperature for 1 hour.

2. Meanwhile, adjust oven racks 4 to 5 inches from broiler element and to lower-middle position and heat oven to 250 degrees. Stir together oil, shallots, garlic, ginger, coriander seeds, cumin seeds, mustard seeds, bay leaves, and lemon zest on rimmed baking sheet and bake on lower-middle rack until spices are softened and fragrant and shallots and

garlic turn golden, about 1 hour. Remove sheet from oven and discard bay leaves.

3. Thoroughly pat lamb dry with paper towels and transfer, fat side up, to sheet (directly on top of spices). Roast on lower-middle rack until lamb registers 120 degrees, 30 to 40 minutes. Remove sheet from oven and heat broiler. Broil lamb on upper rack until surface is well browned and charred in spots and lamb registers 125 degrees, 3 to 8 minutes for medium-rare.

4. Remove sheet from oven and, using 2 pairs of tongs, transfer lamb to carving board (some spices will cling to bottom of roast); tent loosely with aluminum foil and let rest for 20 minutes.

5. FOR THE SAUCE: Meanwhile, carefully pour pan juices through fine-mesh strainer into medium bowl, pressing on solids to extract as much liquid as possible; discard solids. Stir in mint, cilantro, shallot, and lemon juice. Add any accumulated lamb juices to sauce and season with salt and pepper to taste.

6. With long side facing you, slice lamb with grain into 3 equal pieces. Turn each piece and slice across grain into ¼-inch-thick slices. Serve with sauce. (Briefly warm sauce in microwave if it has cooled and thickened.)

Roast Butterflied Leg of Lamb with Coriander, Rosemary, and Red Pepper

Omit cumin and mustard seeds. Toss 6 sprigs fresh rosemary and ½ teaspoon red pepper flakes with oil mixture in step 2. Substitute parsley for cilantro in sauce.

Roast Butterflied Leg of Lamb with Coriander, Fennel, and Black Pepper

Substitute 1 tablespoon fennel seeds for cumin seeds and 1 tablespoon black peppercorns for mustard seeds in step 2. Substitute parsley for mint in sauce.

ROAST RACK OF LAMB WITH ROASTED RED PEPPER RELISH

WHY THIS RECIPE WORKS: When you really think about it, roasting a rack of lamb is a simple process, but there's a fine line between a showstopper and a dried-out disappointment. For a rack that would make us proud at our next fête, the seasoning needed to be spot-on, the meat had to be juicy, and we'd need a bold relish to serve alongside it. Starting with the lamb, carving a shallow cross-hatch into the fat cap and rubbing the racks' surfaces with a blend of kosher salt and ground cumin ensured that our lamb would be loaded with flavor. We heated the oven to 250 degrees and arranged the lamb on a wire rack–lined baking sheet. In just over an hour, our racks emerged at a rosy medium-rare with big flavor to boot. While the racks roasted in the oven, we whipped up a relish to dress up the lamb, combining chopped roasted red pepper, minced parsley, olive oil, fresh lemon juice, and minced garlic. This simple sauce steeped while the lamb cooked. Because meat always tastes best with a bit of char, we browned the racks in a skillet before slicing and serving.

Roast Rack of Lamb with Roasted Red Pepper Relish

SERVES 4 TO 6

We prefer the milder taste and bigger size of domestic lamb, but you may substitute imported lamb from New Zealand and Australia. Since imported racks are generally smaller, in step 1 season each rack with ½ teaspoon of salt and reduce the cooking time to 50 to 70 minutes. A rasp-style grater makes quick work of turning the garlic into a paste.

LAMB

- 2 racks of lamb (1¾ to 2 pounds each), fat trimmed to ⅛ to ¼ inch, rib bones frenched
- Kosher salt and pepper
- 1 teaspoon ground cumin
- 1 teaspoon vegetable oil

RELISH

- ½ cup jarred roasted red peppers, rinsed, patted dry, and chopped fine
- ½ cup minced fresh parsley
- ¼ cup extra-virgin olive oil
- ¼ teaspoon lemon juice
- ⅛ teaspoon garlic, minced to paste
- Kosher salt and pepper

1. FOR THE LAMB: Adjust oven rack to middle position and heat oven to 250 degrees. Using sharp knife, cut slits in surface layer of fat, spaced ½-inch apart, in crosshatch pattern, being careful to cut down to, but not into, meat. Combine 2 tablespoons salt and cumin in bowl. Rub ¾ teaspoon salt mixture over entire surface of each rack and into slits. Reserve remaining salt mixture for serving. Place racks, bone-side down, on wire rack set in rimmed baking sheet. Roast until meat registers 125 degrees for medium-rare or 130 degrees for medium, 1 hour 5 minutes to 1 hour 25 minutes.

2. FOR THE RELISH: While lamb roasts, combine red peppers, parsley, olive oil, lemon juice, and garlic in bowl.

Season with salt and pepper to taste. Let stand at room temperature at least 1 hour before serving.

3. Heat vegetable oil in 12-inch skillet over high heat until just smoking. Place one rack, bone-side up, in skillet and cook until well-browned, 1 to 2 minutes. Transfer to carving board. Pour off all but 1 teaspoon fat from skillet and repeat with second rack. Tent racks loosely with aluminum foil and let rest for 20 minutes. Cut between ribs to separate chops and sprinkle cut side of chops with ½ teaspoon salt mixture. Serve, passing relish and remaining salt mixture separately.

Roast Rack of Lamb with Sweet Mint-Almond Relish

Substitute ground anise for cumin in salt mixture. Omit red pepper relish. While lamb roasts, combine ½ cup minced fresh mint; ¼ cup sliced almonds, toasted and chopped fine; ¼ cup extra-virgin olive oil; 2 tablespoons red currant jelly; 4 teaspoons red wine vinegar; and 2 teaspoons Dijon mustard in bowl. Season with salt and pepper to taste. Let stand at room temperature for at least 1 hour before serving with lamb.

SAUTÉED PORK TENDERLOIN

WHY THIS RECIPE WORKS: When cooked properly, pork tenderloin has a tenderness rivaling that of beef tenderloin; unfortunately it also has ultra-mild flavor. Long marinades and hybrid searing and roasting techniques help remedy the flavor deficiency, but they take the home cook a long way from the realm of the no-fuss meal. We wanted a recipe for a fast weeknight dinner that still offered maximum flavor. We needed to deal with the tenderloin's oblong, tapered shape as well as the fact that the tenderloins (which are usually sold in a pair in a vacuum pack) were almost guaranteed to be substantially different in weight and length. The solution was to cut them into 1½-inch-thick medallions (the end pieces were scored, creating a small flap of meat that folded underneath the larger half to yield the right-sized medallion). To preserve their tidy cylindrical shape, we developed two approaches: tying the medallions or wrapping blanched bacon around them, fastened with toothpicks. We found we could create a beautiful sear on all sides of these neat packages in the time it took to reach an internal temperature of 140 to 145 degrees, and the searing process had the extra benefit of producing enough fond (flavorful browned bits) to create a few easy, flavorful pan sauces.

Thick-Cut Pork Tenderloin Medallions

SERVES 4 TO 6

We prefer natural to enhanced pork (pork that has been injected with a salt solution to increase moistness and flavor), though both will work in this recipe. Begin checking the doneness of smaller medallions 1 or 2 minutes early; they may need to be taken out of the pan a little sooner. Be sure not to rinse out the skillet if serving with a pan sauce (recipes follow).

NOTES FROM THE TEST KITCHEN

TURNING THE TAILPIECE INTO A MEDALLION

1. Score the tenderloin's tapered tail end.

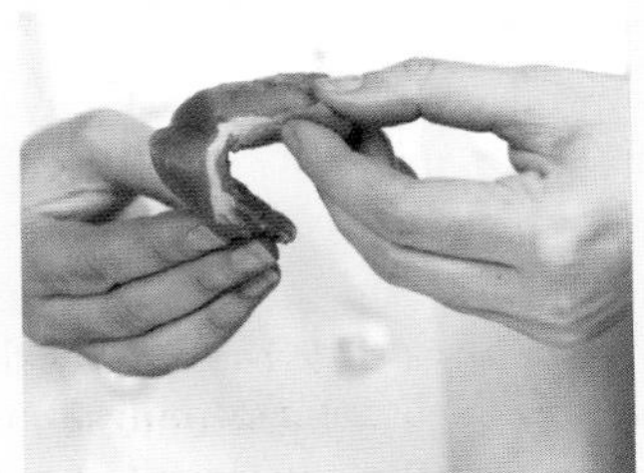

2. Fold in half at the incision.

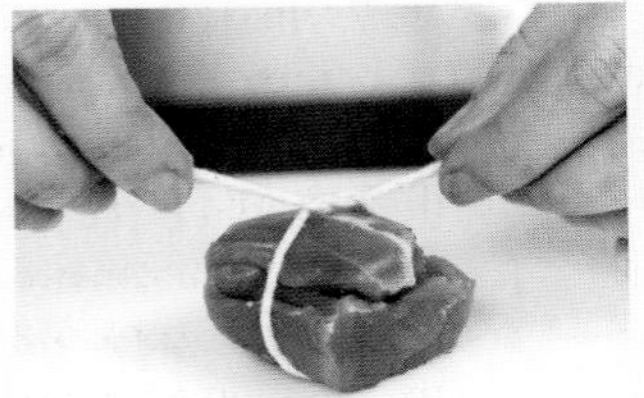

3. Tie the medallion with kitchen twine, making sure the outer surfaces are flat.

TYING THICK MEDALLIONS

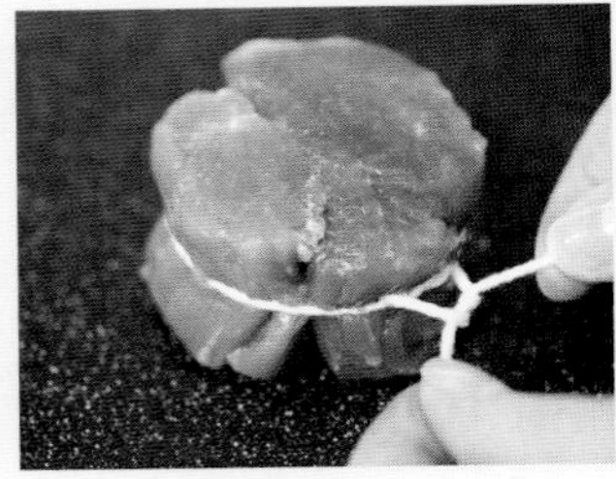

Thick medallions allow for more browning, but they can flop over in the pan. To prevent this, tie each piece with kitchen twine.

- **2 (1- to 1¼-pound) pork tenderloins, trimmed, cut crosswise into 1½-inch pieces, and tied; thinner end pieces removed and tied together (see photos)**
- **Table salt and ground black pepper**
- **2 tablespoons vegetable oil**

1. Pat the pork medallions dry and season with salt and pepper.

2. Heat the oil in a 12-inch skillet over medium-high heat until shimmering. Add the pork and cook, without moving the pieces, until well browned, 3 to 5 minutes. Turn the pork and brown on the second side, 3 to 5 minutes more. Reduce the heat to medium. Using tongs, stand each piece on its side and cook, turning the pieces as necessary, until the sides are well browned and the internal temperature registers 140 to

145 degrees on an instant-read thermometer, 8 to 12 minutes. Transfer the pork to a platter, tent loosely with foil, and let rest until the temperature registers 150 degrees on an instant-read thermometer, while making a pan sauce (recipes follow). Serve with the sauce.

Maple-Mustard Sauce

MAKES ABOUT 1 CUP

- 2 teaspoons vegetable oil
- 1 medium onion, halved and sliced thin
- 1 cup low-sodium chicken broth
- ⅓ cup maple syrup
- 3 tablespoons balsamic vinegar
- 3 tablespoons whole grain mustard
- Table salt and ground black pepper

Pour off any fat from the skillet in which the pork was cooked. Add the oil and heat the skillet over medium heat until shimmering. Add the onion and cook, stirring occasionally, until softened and beginning to brown, 3 to 4 minutes. Increase the heat to medium-high and add the broth; bring to a simmer, scraping the bottom of the skillet with a wooden spoon to loosen any browned bits. Simmer until the liquid is reduced to ½ cup, 3 to 4 minutes. Add the maple syrup, vinegar, mustard, and any juices from the resting meat and cook until thickened and reduced to 1 cup, 3 to 4 minutes longer. Season with salt and pepper to taste, pour the sauce over the pork, and serve immediately.

Apple Cider Sauce

MAKES ABOUT 1¼ CUPS

Complete step 1 of this recipe either before or during the cooking of the pork, then finish the sauce while the pork rests.

- 1½ cups apple cider
- 1 cup low-sodium chicken broth
- 2 teaspoons cider vinegar
- 1 cinnamon stick
- 4 tablespoons (½ stick) unsalted butter, cut into 4 pieces
- 2 large shallots, minced (about ½ cup)
- 1 tart apple, such as Granny Smith, peeled, cored, and diced small
- ¼ cup Calvados or apple-flavored brandy
- 1 teaspoon minced fresh thyme leaves
- Table salt and ground black pepper

1. Combine the cider, broth, vinegar, and cinnamon stick in a medium saucepan; simmer over medium-high heat until the liquid is reduced to 1 cup, 10 to 12 minutes. Remove the cinnamon stick and discard. Set the sauce aside until the pork is cooked.

2. Pour off any fat from the skillet in which the pork was cooked. Add 1 tablespoon of the butter and heat over medium heat until melted. Add the shallots and apple and cook, stirring occasionally, until softened and beginning to brown, 1 to 2 minutes. Remove the skillet from the heat and add the Calvados. Return the skillet to the heat and cook for about 1 minute, scraping the bottom of the skillet with a wooden spoon to loosen any browned bits. Add the reduced cider mixture, any juices from the resting meat, and the thyme; increase the heat to medium-high and simmer until thickened and reduced to 1¼ cups, 3 to 4 minutes. Off the heat, whisk in the remaining 3 tablespoons butter and season with salt and pepper to taste. Pour the sauce over the pork and serve immediately.

BREADED PORK CUTLETS

WHY THIS RECIPE WORKS: While classic *Wiener schnitzel* features a thin, tender veal cutlet coated in ultrafine bread crumbs and then fried until puffy and golden brown, many recipes—to avoid the toughness and high price of veal—substitute pork. But too often these recipes yield dry, tough pork cutlets with greasy coatings. We wanted tender pork cutlets with the crisp, wrinkled, puffy coating that is Wiener schnitzel's signature.

Dismissing pork chops and prepackaged cutlets, we chose tenderloin, which has a mild flavor similar to veal and isn't tough. We cut the tenderloin crosswise on an angle into four pieces, which when pounded thin gave us long, narrow cutlets that would fit two at a time in the pan. Schnitzel is breaded with a flour, egg, and bread-crumb sequence of coatings, but we had to figure out how to get the characteristic puffiness and "rumpled" appearance of the finished cutlets; with good schnitzel you should be able to slide a knife between the meat and the coating. Drying bread in the microwave produced extra-dry crumbs that helped with the crispness, and a little vegetable oil whisked into the egg helped separate the coating from the meat.

But the real breakthrough was in the frying method: Instead of sautéing the cutlets, we cooked them in a Dutch oven in an inch of oil, shaking the pot to get some of the oil over the top of the meat. The extra heat quickly solidified the egg in the coating, so that the steam from the meat couldn't escape and puffed the coating instead. With the traditional schnitzel garnishes of lemon, parsley, capers, and a sieved hard-cooked egg, these cutlets, with their tender meat and crisp coating, delivered on all fronts.

Breaded Pork Cutlets (Pork Schnitzel)

SERVES 4

To make cutlets, cut the tenderloin in half on a 20-degree angle, then cut each piece in half again at the same angle. Cut the tapered tail pieces slightly thicker than the middle ones. Using 2 cups of oil for cooking may seem like a lot, but it is necessary to get an authentic, wrinkled texture on the finished cutlets. When properly cooked, the cutlets absorb very little oil. To ensure ample room for the cutlets as they fry, it is essential to use a Dutch oven with a large surface area. Although spaetzle is the traditional side dish, boiled potatoes or egg noodles also make terrific accompaniments.

- 7 slices high-quality white sandwich bread, crusts removed, cut into ¾-inch cubes (about 4 cups)
- ½ cup unbleached all-purpose flour
- 2 large eggs
- 2 cups plus 1 tablespoon vegetable oil (see note)
- 1 (1¼-pound) pork tenderloin, trimmed of fat and silver skin and tenderloin cut on an angle into 4 equal pieces (see note)
- Table salt and ground black pepper

GARNISHES

- 1 lemon, cut into wedges
- 2 tablespoons chopped fresh parsley leaves
- 2 tablespoons capers, rinsed
- 1 large hard-cooked egg (page 38), yolk and white separated and passed separately through a fine-mesh strainer (optional)

1. Place the bread cubes on a large microwave-safe plate. Microwave on high power for 4 minutes, stirring well halfway through the cooking time. Microwave on medium power until the bread is dry and a few pieces start to lightly brown, 3 to 5 minutes longer, stirring every minute. Process the dry bread in a food processor to very fine crumbs, about 45 seconds. Transfer the bread crumbs to a shallow dish (you should have about 1¼ cups crumbs). Spread the flour in a second shallow dish. Beat the eggs with 1 tablespoon of the oil in a third shallow dish.

2. Place the pork, with one cut side down, between two sheets of plastic wrap and pound to an even thickness of between ⅛ and ¼ inch. Season the cutlets with salt and pepper. Working with one cutlet at a time, dredge the cutlets thoroughly in flour, shaking off the excess, then coat with the egg, allowing the excess to drip back into the dish to ensure a very thin coating, and coat evenly with the bread crumbs, pressing on the crumbs to adhere. Place the breaded cutlets in a single layer on a wire rack set over a baking sheet; let the coating dry for 5 minutes.

3. Heat the remaining 2 cups oil in a large Dutch oven over medium-high heat until it registers 375 degrees on an instant-read thermometer. Lay two cutlets, without overlapping, in the pan and cook, shaking the pan continuously and gently, until wrinkled and light golden brown on both sides, 1 to 2 minutes per side. Transfer the cutlets to a paper towel–lined plate and flip the cutlets several times to blot the excess oil. Repeat with the remaining cutlets. Serve immediately with the garnishes.

PAN-SEARED PORK TENDERLOIN

WHY THIS RECIPE WORKS: Because pork tenderloins are so lean, they cook relatively quickly and are therefore a good choice for an easy-to-prepare meal. But that same leanness means that the pork tends to overcook, and there's also less flavor. Although cutting the pork into medallions can alleviate some of these issues, we wanted a preparation for whole pork tenderloins that would deliver a flavor boost to this quick-cooking roast.

Simply roasted in the oven, the pork tended to dry out and never achieved the dark brown crust we wanted. We got that crust when we seared the tenderloins on the stovetop—but then the pork wasn't cooked through. A combination of searing the meat in a skillet, then transferring the pork to the oven to finish cooking, produced a flavorful crust and well-cooked meat. The browned crust added some flavor, but we wanted more. A dry rub of just salt and pepper, left on for half an hour before searing, provided enough seasoning and further encouraged a browned crust, and a pan sauce made with the browned bits left from sautéing was an additional flavor boost. Not only were these pork tenderloins delicious; they were also on the dinner table in about half an hour.

Pan-Seared Oven-Roasted Pork Tenderloin

SERVES 4

We prefer natural to enhanced pork (pork that has been injected with a salt solution to increase moisture and flavor) for this recipe. Enhanced pork can be used, but the meat won't brown as well. Because two are cooked at once, tenderloins larger than 1 pound apiece will not fit comfortably in a 12-inch skillet. If time permits, season the tenderloins up to 30 minutes before cooking; the seasonings will better penetrate the meat. The recipe will work in a nonstick or a traditional skillet. A pan sauce can be made while the tenderloins are in the oven (recipes follow); if you intend to make a sauce, make sure to prepare all of the sauce ingredients before cooking the pork.

- 2 (12- to 16-ounce) pork tenderloins, trimmed of fat and silver skin (see note)
- 1¼ teaspoons table salt
- ¾ teaspoon ground black pepper
- 2 teaspoons vegetable oil
- 1 recipe pan sauce (optional; recipes follow)

1. Adjust an oven rack to the middle position and heat the oven to 400 degrees. Sprinkle the tenderloins evenly with the salt and pepper; rub the seasoning into the meat. Heat the oil in a 12-inch skillet over medium-high heat until smoking. Place both tenderloins in the skillet; cook until well browned, about 3 minutes. Using tongs, rotate the tenderloins a quarter-turn; cook until well browned, 45 to 60 seconds. Repeat until all sides are browned, about 1 minute longer. Transfer the tenderloins to a rimmed baking sheet and place in the oven (reserve the skillet if making a pan sauce); roast until the internal temperature registers 140 to 145 degrees on an instant-read thermometer, 10 to 16 minutes. (Begin the pan sauce, if making, while the meat roasts.)

2. Transfer the tenderloins to a carving board and tent loosely with foil (continue with the pan sauce, if making); let rest until the internal temperature registers 150 degrees, 8 to 10 minutes. Cut the tenderloins crosswise into ½-inch-thick slices, arrange on a platter or individual plates, and spoon the sauce (if using) over; serve immediately.

Dried Cherry–Port Sauce with Onions and Marmalade

MAKES ABOUT ½ CUP

The flavors in this sauce are especially suited to the winter holiday season.

- 1 teaspoon vegetable oil
- 1 large onion, halved and sliced ½ inch thick (about 1½ cups)
- ¾ cup port
- ¾ cup dried cherries
- 2 tablespoons orange marmalade
- 3 tablespoons unsalted butter, cut into 3 pieces
- Table salt and ground black pepper

1. Immediately after placing the pork in the oven, add the oil to the still-hot skillet, swirl to coat, and set the skillet over medium-high heat; add the onion and cook, stirring frequently, until softened and browned around the edges, 5 to 7 minutes. (If the drippings are browning too quickly, add 2 tablespoons water and scrape up the browned bits with a wooden spoon.) Set the skillet aside off the heat.

2. While the pork is resting, set the skillet over medium-high heat and add the port and cherries; simmer, scraping up the browned bits with a wooden spoon, until the mixture is slightly thickened, 4 to 6 minutes. Add any accumulated pork juices and continue to simmer until thickened and reduced to about ⅓ cup, 2 to 4 minutes longer. Off the heat, whisk in the orange marmalade and butter, one piece at a time. Season with salt and pepper to taste.

Garlicky Lime Sauce with Cilantro

MAKES ABOUT ½ CUP

This assertive sauce is based on a Mexican sauce called *mojo de ajo*. A rasp grater is the best way to break down the garlic to a fine paste. Another option is to put the garlic through a press and then finish mincing it to a paste with a knife. If your garlic cloves contain green sprouts or shoots, remove the sprouts before grating—their flavor is bitter and hot. The initial cooking of the garlic off the heat will prevent scorching.

- 10 garlic cloves, peeled and grated to a fine paste on a rasp grater (about 2 tablespoons; see note)
- 2 tablespoons water
- 1 tablespoon vegetable oil
- ¼ teaspoon red pepper flakes
- 2 teaspoons light brown sugar
- ¼ cup chopped fresh cilantro leaves
- 3 tablespoons juice from 2 limes
- 1 tablespoon chopped fresh chives
- 4 tablespoons (½ stick) unsalted butter, cut into 4 pieces
- Table salt and ground black pepper

1. Immediately after placing the pork in the oven, mix the garlic paste with the water in a small bowl. Add the oil to the still-hot skillet and swirl to coat; off the heat, add the garlic paste and cook with the skillet's residual heat, scraping up the browned bits with a wooden spoon, until the sizzling subsides, about 2 minutes. Set the skillet over low heat and continue cooking, stirring frequently, until the garlic is sticky, 8 to 10 minutes; set the skillet aside off the heat.

2. While the pork is resting, set the skillet over medium heat; add the red pepper flakes and brown sugar to the skillet and cook until sticky and the sugar is dissolved, about 1 minute. Add the cilantro, lime juice, and chives; simmer to blend the flavors, 1 to 2 minutes. Add any accumulated pork juices and simmer for 1 minute longer. Off the heat, whisk in the butter, one piece at a time. Season with salt and pepper to taste.

MAPLE-GLAZED PORK TENDERLOIN

WHY THIS RECIPE WORKS: When done right, nothing can quite match pork tenderloin's fine-grained, buttery-smooth texture, but on its own, it can lack flavor. We thought a thick, sweet, fragrant glaze would be just the solution and decided it should feature New England's signature ingredient, maple syrup.

Getting the glaze right was comparatively easy: To temper the sweetness of the maple syrup, we added molasses, mustard, and a shot of bourbon; with a little cinnamon, cloves, and cayenne, the glaze was ready. To give the glaze something to hold on to, we rolled the tenderloins in a mixture of cornstarch and sugar before searing them. When we'd built a good crust in the skillet, we painted on some glaze and transferred the pork to the oven. It occurred to us that the painting analogy was a good one—why not put multiple coats on the tenderloins to get the best coverage? When the meat was nearly done, we put on more glaze, and we added yet another coat when the tenderloins were completely done. Finally, after letting the tenderloins rest, we glazed them one last time. Slicing into this roast revealed success: A thick maple glaze coated the meat.

Maple-Glazed Pork Tenderloin

SERVES 6

We prefer natural to enhanced pork (pork that has been injected with a salt solution to increase moistness and flavor) for this recipe. If your tenderloins are smaller than 1¼ pounds, reduce the cooking time in step 3 (and use an instant-read thermometer for best results). If the tenderloins don't fit in the skillet initially, let their ends curve toward each other; the meat will eventually shrink as it cooks. Make sure to cook the tenderloins until they turn deep golden brown in step 2 or they will appear pale after glazing. Be sure to pat off the cornstarch mixture thoroughly in step 1, as any excess will leave gummy spots on the tenderloins.

- ¾ cup maple syrup, preferably grade B
- ¼ cup light or mild molasses
- 2 tablespoons bourbon or brandy
- ⅛ teaspoon ground cinnamon
- Pinch ground cloves
- Pinch cayenne pepper
- ¼ cup cornstarch
- 2 tablespoons sugar
- 1 tablespoon table salt
- 2 teaspoons ground black pepper
- 2 (1¼- to 1½-pound) pork tenderloins (see note), trimmed of fat and silver skin
- 2 tablespoons vegetable oil
- 1 tablespoon whole grain mustard

1. Adjust an oven rack to the middle position and heat the oven to 375 degrees. Stir ½ cup of the maple syrup, the molasses, bourbon, cinnamon, cloves, and cayenne together in a 2-cup liquid measure; set aside. Whisk the cornstarch, sugar, salt, and black pepper in a small bowl until combined. Transfer the cornstarch mixture to a rimmed baking sheet. Pat the tenderloins dry with paper towels, then roll them in the cornstarch mixture until evenly coated on all sides. Thoroughly pat off the excess cornstarch mixture.

2. Heat the oil in a 12-inch heavy-bottomed nonstick skillet over medium-high heat until just beginning to smoke. Reduce the heat to medium and place both tenderloins in the skillet, leaving at least 1 inch between them. Cook until well browned on all sides, 8 to 12 minutes. Transfer the tenderloins to a wire rack set over a rimmed baking sheet.

3. Pour off the fat from the skillet and return to medium heat. Add the syrup mixture to the skillet, scraping up the browned bits with a wooden spoon, and cook until reduced to ½ cup, about 2 minutes. Transfer 2 tablespoons of the glaze to a small bowl and set aside. Using the remaining glaze, brush each tenderloin with approximately 1 tablespoon glaze. Roast the pork until the thickest part of the tenderloins registers 130 degrees on an instant-read thermometer, 12 to 20 minutes. Brush each tenderloin with another tablespoon of the glaze and continue to roast until the thickest part of the tenderloins registers 140 degrees, 2 to 4 minutes longer. Remove the tenderloins from the oven and brush each with the remaining glaze; let rest, uncovered, until the temperature reaches 150 degrees, about 10 minutes.

4. While the tenderloins rest, stir the remaining ¼ cup maple syrup and the mustard into the reserved 2 tablespoons glaze. Brush each tenderloin with 1 tablespoon mustard glaze. Transfer the meat to a carving board and slice into ¼-inch-thick pieces. Serve, passing the extra mustard glaze at the table.

BROILED PORK TENDERLOIN

WHY THIS RECIPE WORKS: An easy way to prepare quick-cooking cuts like pork tenderloin is to simply put them under the broiler. The intense heat of the broiler promises to deeply brown the exterior and cook the roast through in one fell swoop. But the problem is that recipes calling for the broiler rely on a one-size-fits-all approach, when in reality no two broilers behave exactly the same way. We wanted to figure out a way to minimize differences among broilers so every oven would produce the same richly browned, juicy pork tenderloins.

To ensure that the tip of the tenderloin cooked at the same rate as the middle, we folded the thinner tail end underneath and tied the meat at 2-inch intervals to give it a rounded shape that would cook evenly. The best browning came from cooking the roasts 4 to 5 inches from the broiler element in a disposable roasting pan, which effectively reflected the heat of the broiler. A baking soda rub further enhanced browning. To correct for differences in broilers, we started by preheating the oven to 325 degrees, then turned on the broiler at the same time that we put the pork in the oven. We pulled the roasts from the oven when they reached a slightly lower-than-normal internal temperature to account for the increased carryover cooking effect of the broiler's intense heat.

Broiled Pork Tenderloin

SERVES 4 TO 6

We prefer natural pork, but enhanced pork (injected with a salt solution) can be used. If you're using enhanced pork, reduce the amount of salt in step 2 to 1½ teaspoons. A 13 by 9-inch aluminum roasting pan that is at least 3 inches deep is critical to the success of this recipe. We do not recommend broiling the pork in a pan that is a different size or material. This lean cut can be served by itself, but it's best accompanied by a richly flavored sauce (recipes follow). We developed this recipe with an in-oven broiler; do not attempt this with a drawer broiler (the type of broiler that is below the oven compartment).

- 2 (1-pound) pork tenderloins, trimmed
- 2 teaspoons kosher salt
- 1¼ teaspoons vegetable oil
- ½ teaspoon pepper
- ¼ teaspoon baking soda
- 1 (13 by 9-inch) disposable aluminum roasting pan

1. Adjust oven rack 4 to 5 inches from broiler element and heat oven to 325 degrees. Fold thin tip of each tenderloin under about 2 inches to create uniformly shaped roast. Tie tenderloins crosswise with kitchen twine at 2-inch intervals, making sure folded tip is secured underneath. Trim any excess twine close to meat to prevent it from scorching under broiler.

2. Mix salt, oil, and pepper in small bowl until salt is evenly coated with oil. Add baking soda and stir until well combined. Rub salt mixture evenly over pork. Place tenderloins in disposable pan, evenly spaced between sides of pan and each other.

3. Turn oven to broil. Broil tenderloins for 5 minutes. Flip tenderloins and continue to broil until golden brown and meat registers 125 to 130 degrees, 8 to 14 minutes. Remove disposable pan from oven, tent loosely with aluminum foil, and let rest for 10 minutes. Remove twine, slice tenderloins into ½-inch-thick slices, and serve.

Mustard-Crème Fraîche Sauce

MAKES ABOUT 1 CUP

- ½ cup crème fraîche
- 3 tablespoons Dijon mustard
- 3 tablespoons chopped fresh parsley
- Salt and pepper

Whisk crème fraîche, mustard, and parsley together in bowl. Season with salt and pepper to taste.

Sun-Dried Tomato and Basil Salsa

MAKES ABOUT 1 CUP

- ¼ cup oil-packed sun-dried tomatoes, rinsed and chopped fine
- ¼ cup chopped fresh basil
- ¼ cup chopped fresh parsley
- ¼ cup extra-virgin olive oil
- 2 tablespoons balsamic vinegar
- 1 small shallot, minced
- Salt and pepper

Combine all ingredients in bowl and season with salt and pepper to taste.

MILK-BRAISED PORK LOIN

WHY THIS RECIPE WORKS: Braising pork in milk is an Italian technique that produces moist pork paired with a rich, savory sauce. To maximize the pork loin roast's seasoning and moisture, we brined it in salt and sugar for 90 minutes. We wanted the sauce to be loaded with porky flavor, so we rendered salt pork (simmered in water to prevent burning) before introducing the roast to the pot. We browned the roast on all sides, removed it, and then began to build the sauce, stirring together milk, garlic cloves, and sage. Adding baking soda to the pot deepened the sauce's color and enriched its savory flavors. Once the sauce had thickened, we added the roast back to the pot and transferred it to a 275-degree oven. Adding white wine brightened the sauce, and we finished it with Dijon mustard for heat and parsley for a burst of freshness.

Milk-Braised Pork Loin

SERVES 4 TO 6

The milk will bubble up when added to the pot. If necessary, remove the pot from the heat and stir to break up the foam before returning it to the heat. We prefer natural pork, but if your pork is enhanced (injected with a salt solution; see page 181), do not brine. Instead, skip to step 2.

- Salt and pepper
- ¼ cup sugar
- 1 (2- to 2½-pound) boneless pork loin roast, trimmed
- 2 ounces salt pork, chopped coarse
- 3 cups whole milk
- 5 garlic cloves, peeled
- 1 teaspoon minced fresh sage
- ¼ teaspoon baking soda
- ½ cup dry white wine
- 3 tablespoons chopped fresh parsley
- 1 teaspoon Dijon mustard

1. Dissolve ¼ cup salt and sugar in 2 quarts cold water in large container. Submerge roast in brine, cover, and refrigerate for at least 1½ hours or up to 2 hours. Remove roast from brine and pat dry with paper towels.

2. Adjust oven rack to middle position and heat oven to 275 degrees. Bring salt pork and ½ cup water to simmer in Dutch oven over medium heat. Simmer until water evaporates and salt pork begins to sizzle, 5 to 6 minutes. Continue to cook, stirring frequently, until salt pork is lightly browned and fat has rendered, 2 to 3 minutes. Using slotted spoon, discard salt pork, leaving fat in pot.

3. Increase heat to medium-high, add roast to pot, and brown on all sides, 8 to 10 minutes. Transfer roast to large plate. Add milk, garlic, sage, and baking soda to pot and bring to simmer, scraping up any browned bits. Cook, stirring frequently, until milk is lightly browned and has consistency of heavy cream, 14 to 16 minutes. Reduce heat to medium-low and continue to cook, stirring and scraping bottom of pot constantly, until milk thickens to consistency of thin batter, 1 to 3 minutes longer. Remove pot from heat.

4. Return roast to pot, cover, and transfer to oven. Cook until meat registers 140 degrees, 40 to 50 minutes, flipping roast once halfway through cooking. Transfer roast to carving board, tent with aluminum foil, and let rest for 20 to 25 minutes.

5. Once roast has rested, pour any accumulated juices into pot. Add wine and return sauce to simmer over medium-high heat, whisking vigorously to smooth out sauce. Simmer until sauce has consistency of thin gravy, 2 to 3 minutes. Off heat, stir in 2 tablespoons parsley and mustard and season with salt and pepper to taste. Slice roast into ¼-inch-thick slices. Transfer slices to serving platter. Spoon sauce over slices, sprinkle with remaining 1 tablespoon parsley, and serve.

FRENCH-STYLE POT-ROASTED PORK LOIN

WHY THIS RECIPE WORKS: *Enchaud Perigordine* is a fancy name for what's actually a relatively simple French dish: slow-cooked pork loin. Cooked in the oven in a covered casserole dish, the roast turns out incredibly moist and flavorful, with a rich jus to accompany it. At least it does when it's prepared in France. But while pigs in France are bred to have plenty of fat, their American counterparts are lean, which translates to a bland and stringy roast. To improve the flavor and texture of our center-cut loin, we lowered the oven temperature (to 225 degrees) and removed the roast from the oven when it was medium-rare. Searing just three sides of the roast, rather than all four, prevented the bottom of the roast from overcooking from direct contact with the pot. Butterflying the pork allowed us to salt a maximum amount of surface area for a roast that was thoroughly seasoned throughout. And while we eliminated the hard-to-find trotter (or pig's foot), we added butter for richness while a sprinkling of gelatin lent body to the sauce.

French-Style Pot-Roasted Pork Loin

SERVES 4 TO 6

We strongly prefer the flavor of natural pork in this recipe, but enhanced pork (injected with a salt solution) can be used. If using enhanced pork, reduce the salt to 2 teaspoons (1 teaspoon per side) in step 2. The pork can be prepared through step 2, wrapped in plastic wrap, and refrigerated for up to 2 days.

- 2 tablespoons unsalted butter, cut into 2 pieces
- 6 medium garlic cloves, sliced thin
- 1 (2½-pound) boneless center-cut pork loin roast, trimmed
- Kosher salt and ground black pepper
- 1 teaspoon sugar
- 2 teaspoons herbes de Provence
- 2 tablespoons vegetable oil
- 1 Granny Smith apple, peeled, cored, and cut into ¼-inch pieces
- 1 medium onion, chopped fine
- ⅓ cup dry white wine
- 2 sprigs fresh thyme
- 1 bay leaf
- 1 tablespoon unflavored gelatin
- ¼–¾ cup low-sodium chicken broth
- 1 tablespoon chopped fresh parsley leaves

1. Adjust an oven rack to the lower-middle position and heat the oven to 225 degrees. Melt 1 tablespoon of the butter in an 8-inch skillet over medium-low heat. Add half of the garlic and cook, stirring frequently, until golden, 5 to 7 minutes. Transfer the mixture to a bowl and refrigerate while preparing the pork.

2. Following the photos, butterfly the pork loin. Sprinkle 1 tablespoon salt evenly over both sides of the loin (½ tablespoon per side) and thoroughly rub into the pork until the surface is slightly tacky. Sprinkle the sugar evenly over the inside of the loin and then spread with the cooled toasted garlic mixture. Fold the roast back together and tie tightly with kitchen twine at 1-inch intervals. Sprinkle the tied roast evenly with the herbes de Provence and season with pepper.

3. Heat 1 tablespoon of the oil in a large Dutch oven over medium heat until just smoking. Add the roast, fat side down, and brown on the top and sides (do not the brown bottom of the roast), 5 to 8 minutes. Transfer to a large plate. Add the remaining 1 tablespoon oil, the apple, and onion; cook, stirring frequently, until the onion is softened and browned, 5 to 7 minutes. Stir in the remaining sliced garlic and cook until fragrant, about 30 seconds. Stir in the wine, thyme, and bay leaf, and cook for 30 seconds. Return the roast, fat side up, to the pot; place a large sheet of foil over the pot and cover tightly with the lid. Transfer the pot to the oven and cook until the pork registers 140 degrees on an instant-read thermometer, 50 to 90 minutes

4. Transfer the roast to a carving board, tent loosely with foil, and let rest for 20 minutes. While the pork rests, sprinkle the gelatin over ¼ cup chicken broth and let sit until the gelatin softens, about 5 minutes. Remove and discard the thyme sprigs and bay leaf from the jus. Pour the jus into a 2-cup measuring cup and, if necessary, add chicken broth to measure 1¼ cups. Return the jus to the pot and bring to a simmer over medium heat. Whisk the softened gelatin mixture, the remaining 1 tablespoon butter, and the parsley into the jus and season with salt and pepper to taste; remove from the heat and cover to keep warm. Slice the pork into ½-inch-thick slices, adding any accumulated juices to the sauce. Serve the pork, passing the sauce separately.

NOTES FROM THE TEST KITCHEN

DOUBLE-BUTTERFLYING A ROAST

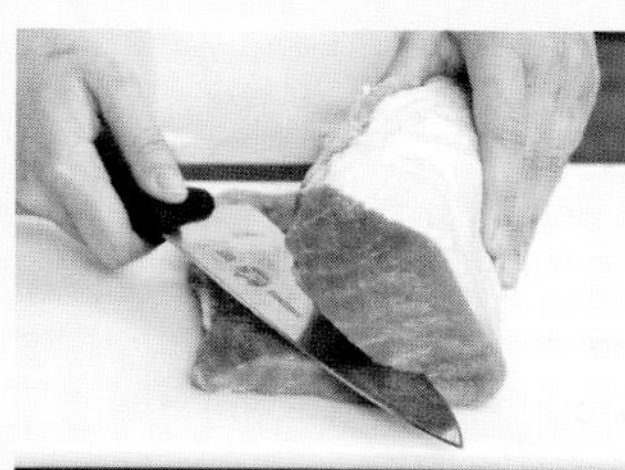

1. Holding a chef's knife parallel to the cutting board, insert the knife one-third of the way up from the bottom of the roast and cut horizontally, stopping ½ inch before the edge. Open up the flap.

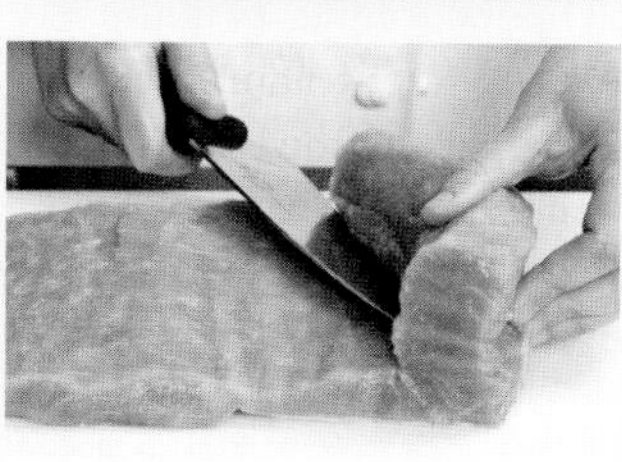

2. Make another horizontal cut into the thicker portion of the roast. Open up this flap, smoothing out the butterflied rectangle of meat.

MAPLE-GLAZED PORK ROAST

WHY THIS RECIPE WORKS: Maple-glazed pork roast often falls short of its savory-sweet promise. Many roasts turn out dry, but the glazes often present even bigger problems. Most are too thin to coat the pork properly, some are too sweet, and few have a pronounced maple flavor. We wanted a glistening roast, which, when sliced, would combine the juices from tender, well-seasoned pork with a rich maple glaze to create complex flavor in every bite. For this dish we chose a blade-end loin roast, which has a deposit of fat that helps keep the meat moist. We tied it at intervals to make a neat bundle. Searing the roast first on the stovetop was a must for a flavorful exterior. We then removed the pork so that we could use the browned bits in the skillet to build the glaze. Maple syrup, with complementary spices and cayenne pepper for heat, made a thick, clingy glaze. Instead of brushing the glaze onto the pork, however, we decided to keep things simple and returned the pork to the skillet, rolled it in the glaze to coat it, and put the whole thing into the oven. The smaller area of the skillet kept the glaze from spreading out and burning, and the glaze reduced nicely while the roast cooked. Rolling the roast in the glaze periodically ensured even coverage and resulted in a tender, juicy roast.

Maple-Glazed Pork Roast

SERVES 4 TO 6

We prefer natural to enhanced pork (pork that has been injected with a salt solution to increase moisture and flavor) for this recipe. We prefer a nonstick ovensafe skillet because it is much easier to clean than a traditional one. Whichever you use, remember that the handle will be blistering hot when you take it out of the oven, so be sure to use a potholder or oven mitt. Note that you should not trim the pork of its thin layer of fat. This dish is unapologetically sweet, so we recommend side dishes that take well to the sweetness. Garlicky sautéed greens, braised cabbage, and soft polenta are good choices.

- ⅓ cup maple syrup, preferably grade B
- ⅛ teaspoon ground cinnamon
- Pinch ground cloves
- Pinch cayenne pepper
- 1 (2½-pound) boneless blade-end pork loin roast, tied at 1½-inch intervals (see note)
- ¾ teaspoon table salt
- ½ teaspoon ground black pepper
- 2 teaspoons vegetable oil

1. Adjust an oven rack to the middle position and heat the oven to 325 degrees. Stir the maple syrup, cinnamon, cloves, and cayenne together in a measuring cup or small bowl and set aside. Pat the roast dry with paper towels, then sprinkle evenly with the salt and pepper.

2. Heat the oil in a heavy-bottomed ovensafe 10-inch nonstick skillet over medium-high heat until just beginning to smoke, about 3 minutes. Place the roast, fat side down, in the skillet and cook until well browned, about 3 minutes. Using tongs, rotate the roast a quarter-turn and cook until well browned, about 2½ minutes; repeat until the roast is well browned on all sides. Transfer the roast to a large plate. Reduce the heat to medium and pour off the fat from the skillet; add the maple syrup mixture and cook until fragrant, about 30 seconds (the syrup will bubble immediately). Turn off the heat and return the roast to the skillet; using tongs, roll the roast to coat with the glaze on all sides.

3. Place the skillet in the oven and roast until the center of the pork registers 140 to 145 degrees on an instant-read thermometer, 35 to 45 minutes, using tongs to roll and spin the roast to coat with the glaze twice during the roasting time. Transfer the roast to a carving board; set the skillet aside to cool slightly to thicken the glaze, about 5 minutes. Pour the glaze over the roast and let rest for 15 minutes longer (the center of the loin should register 150 degrees on an instant-read thermometer). Remove the twine, cut the meat into ¼-inch slices, and serve immediately.

Maple-Glazed Pork Roast with Rosemary

Follow the recipe for Maple-Glazed Pork Roast, substituting 2 teaspoons minced fresh rosemary for the cinnamon, cloves, and cayenne.

Maple-Glazed Pork Roast with Orange Essence

Follow the recipe for Maple-Glazed Pork Roast, adding 1 tablespoon fresh grated orange zest to the maple syrup along with the spices.

Maple-Glazed Pork Roast with Star Anise

Follow the recipe for Maple-Glazed Pork Roast, adding 4 star anise pods to the maple syrup along with the spices.

Maple-Glazed Pork Roast with Smoked Paprika

Follow the recipe for Maple-Glazed Pork Roast, adding 2 teaspoons smoked hot paprika to the maple syrup along with the spices.

GARLIC-STUDDED ROAST PORK LOIN

WHY THIS RECIPE WORKS: Although it has a little more fat than pork tenderloin, a center loin pork roast is still quite lean and requires special handling to roast without drying out. We sought the best way to roast this cut so that the juices would remain inside the meat, not wind up on the carving board.

It turned out that a two-step roasting process was the key to juicy pork loin. After poking slivers of garlic into the meat and rubbing the surface with a mixture of thyme, cloves, salt, and pepper for extra flavor, we refrigerated the roast overnight. The next day we cranked up the oven to 475 degrees and added the pork directly from the fridge, leaving it in the oven for just half an hour before removing it. After we rested the roast, we returned it to the oven, this time at a lower temperature, to finish cooking. The texture of the meat was remarkably tender, and it had lost very little juice. The reason this method worked was that during the rest, the middle of the roast heated by conduction from the heat absorbed by the outside of the roast. When the meat went back into the oven, the center cooked through but the outside didn't overcook. A mustard-shallot sauce provides additional moisture and flavor.

Garlic-Studded Roast Pork Loin

SERVES 4 TO 6

We prefer natural to enhanced pork (pork that has been injected with a salt solution to increase moisture and flavor) for this recipe. For extra flavor and moisture, serve the sliced roast with the mustard-shallot sauce.

- 2 teaspoons dried thyme
- 2 teaspoons table salt
- 1 teaspoon ground black pepper
- ¼ teaspoon ground cloves or allspice
- 2 large garlic cloves, peeled and cut into slivers
- 1 (2¼-pound) boneless center loin pork roast, fat trimmed to about ⅛ inch thick and roast tied at 1½-inch intervals (see note)
- 1 recipe Mustard-Shallot Sauce with Thyme (optional; recipe follows)

1. Mix together the thyme, salt, pepper, and cloves. Coat the garlic slivers in the spice mixture. Poke slits in the roast with the point of a paring knife; insert the garlic slivers. Rub the remaining spice mixture onto the meat. Tie the roast with kitchen twine into a tight cylinder. Wrap the roast in plastic wrap and refrigerate for at least 2 hours or up to 24 hours.

2. Adjust an oven rack to the middle position and heat the oven to 475 degrees. Take the meat directly from the refrigerator, remove the plastic wrap, and place it on a wire rack set in a shallow roasting pan. Roast for exactly 30 minutes.

3. Remove the meat from the oven; immediately reduce the oven temperature to 325 degrees. Insert an instant-read thermometer at one end of the roast, going into the thickest part at the center (the temperature will range from 80 to 110 degrees); let the roast rest at room temperature, uncovered, for exactly

30 minutes. (At this point the roast's internal temperature will range from 115 to 140 degrees.) After this 30-minute rest, remove the thermometer, return the meat to the oven, and roast until the thickest part of the roast reaches an internal temperature of 140 to 145 degrees, 15 to 30 minutes longer, depending on the roast's internal temperature at the end of the resting period. Since the roast may cook unevenly, take temperature readings from a couple of locations, each time plunging the thermometer into the center of the meat and waiting 15 seconds.

4. Let the roast stand at room temperature, uncovered, for 15 to 20 minutes to finish cooking. (The temperature should register 150 degrees.) Remove the twine, slice the meat thin, and serve with the sauce (if using).

Mustard-Shallot Sauce with Thyme

MAKES ABOUT 1 CUP

Start making the sauce as soon as the roast comes out of the oven for the second time. Use a grainy, or country-style, mustard in this recipe. For extra body and richness, swirl another tablespoon or two of softened butter into the finished sauce.

- 2 tablespoons unsalted butter (see note)
- 4 medium shallots, minced (about ¾ cup)
- ¾ cup dry white wine or dry vermouth
- 1 cup low-sodium chicken broth
- ¾ teaspoon minced fresh thyme leaves or ¼ teaspoon dried thyme, crumbled
- ¼ cup whole grain mustard (see note)

Melt the butter in a medium skillet over medium-high heat. Add the shallots and sauté until softened, 3 to 4 minutes. Add the wine and boil until nearly evaporated, 8 to 10 minutes. Add the broth and thyme; boil until reduced by one third, about 5 minutes. Remove the pan from the heat and stir in the mustard. Serve immediately.

PORCHETTA

WHY THIS RECIPE WORKS: As a substitute for the traditional whole pig, we opted for easy-to-find pork butt (over pork belly or a pork belly–wrapped pork loin) since it cooked up evenly and offered the right balance of meat and fatty richness. To season and flavor the porchetta thoroughly and evenly, we cut slits in the meat every few inches; coated it with salt and an intensely flavored paste of garlic, rosemary, thyme, and fennel seeds; and let it sit overnight in the refrigerator. For quicker cooking and more presentable slices, we cut the roast into two pieces and tied each into a compact cylinder. We used a two-stage cooking method: First, we covered the roasting pan with foil, which trapped steam to cook the meat evenly and more quickly and also helped keep the meat moist. We then uncovered the pan and returned it to a 500-degree oven to brown and crisp the outer layer of the roasts. For the best layer of crisp "skin" on the tops of the roasts, we cut a crosshatch in the fat cap and rubbed it with a mixture of salt, pepper, and baking soda at the same time we applied the paste to help dry it out.

Porchetta

SERVES 8 TO 10

Pork butt roast is often labeled Boston butt in the supermarket. Look for a roast with a substantial fat cap. If fennel seeds are unavailable, substitute ¼ cup of ground fennel. The porchetta needs to be refrigerated for 6 to 24 hours once it is rubbed with the paste, but it is best when it sits for a full 24 hours.

- 3 tablespoons fennel seeds
- ½ cup fresh rosemary leaves (2 bunches)
- ¼ cup fresh thyme leaves (2 bunches)
- 12 garlic cloves, peeled
- Kosher salt and pepper
- ½ cup extra-virgin olive oil
- 1 (5- to 6-pound) boneless pork butt roast, trimmed
- ¼ teaspoon baking soda

1. Grind fennel seeds in spice grinder or mortar and pestle until finely ground. Transfer ground fennel to food processor and add rosemary, thyme, garlic, 1 tablespoon pepper, and 2 teaspoons salt. Pulse mixture until finely chopped, 10 to 15 pulses. Add oil and process until smooth paste forms, 20 to 30 seconds.

2. Using sharp knife, cut slits in surface fat of roast, spaced 1 inch apart, in crosshatch pattern, being careful not to cut into meat. Cut roast in half with grain into 2 equal pieces.

3. Turn each roast on its side so fat cap is facing away from you, bottom of roast is facing toward you, and newly cut side is facing up. Starting 1 inch from short end of each roast, use boning or paring knife to make slit that starts 1 inch from top of roast and ends 1 inch from bottom, pushing knife completely through roast. Repeat making slits, spaced 1 to 1½ inches apart, along length of each roast, stopping 1 inch from opposite end (you should have 6 to 8 slits, depending on size of roast).

4. Turn each roast so fat cap is facing down. Rub sides and bottom of each roast with 2 teaspoons salt, taking care to work salt into slits from both sides. Rub herb paste onto sides and bottom of each roast, taking care to work paste into slits from both sides. Flip each roast so that fat cap is facing up. Using 3 pieces of kitchen twine per roast, tie each roast into compact cylinder.

5. Combine 1 tablespoon salt, 1 teaspoon pepper, and baking soda in small bowl. Rub fat cap of each roast with salt–baking soda mixture, taking care to work mixture into crosshatches. Transfer roasts to wire rack set in rimmed baking sheet and refrigerate, uncovered, for at least 6 hours or up to 24 hours.

6. Adjust oven rack to middle position and heat oven to 325 degrees. Transfer roasts, fat side up, to large roasting pan, leaving at least 2 inches between roasts. Cover tightly with aluminum foil. Cook until pork registers 180 degrees, 2 to 2½ hours.

7. Remove pan from oven and increase oven temperature to 500 degrees. Carefully remove and discard foil and transfer roasts to large plate. Discard liquid in pan. Line pan with foil. Remove twine from roasts; return roasts to pan, directly on foil; and return pan to oven. Cook until exteriors of roasts are well browned and interiors register 190 degrees, 20 to 30 minutes.

8. Transfer roasts to carving board and let rest for 20 minutes. Slice roasts ½ inch thick, transfer to serving platter, and serve.

TUSCAN-STYLE ROAST PORK WITH GARLIC AND ROSEMARY

WHY THIS RECIPE WORKS: The Tuscan roast pork dish known as *arista* promises to turn lean, mild pork loin into a juicy roast flavored with plenty of garlic and rosemary and featuring a deeply browned crust. Yet most versions turn out dry and bland. To boost both flavor and juiciness, we salted the meat for 1 hour before cooking, using a double-butterfly technique to expose plenty of surface area and then salting both sides and rolling it back up. This technique also allowed us to maximize the distribution of the garlic and rosemary. Briefly simmering the herb-garlic mixture before spreading it over the pork tempered any raw flavors, and using plenty of oil (which we then strained off) and a nonstick skillet kept the garlic from browning, for a fresher garlic flavor. To boost richness and enhance the overall porky flavor, we processed pancetta with the garlic and rosemary (plus red pepper flakes and lemon zest for brightness) to make a paste. Using a low oven ensured that the meat was evenly cooked from edge to center. And instead of roasting, browning, and then resting the roast under foil, we let it rest after it came out of the oven and then browned it and served it immediately; this approach helped keep the crust crispy. For a finishing touch, we made a simple, bright, rich sauce by combining the reserved strained oil with the juice from a halved lemon that we quickly caramelized in the skillet for more complex flavor.

Tuscan-Style Roast Pork with Garlic and Rosemary (Arista)

SERVES 4 TO 6

We strongly prefer natural pork in this recipe, but if enhanced pork (injected with a salt solution; see page 181) is used, reduce the salt to 2 teaspoons (1 teaspoon per side) in step 3. After applying the seasonings, the pork needs to rest, refrigerated, for 1 hour before cooking.

- 1 lemon
- ⅓ cup extra-virgin olive oil
- 8 garlic cloves, minced
- ¼ teaspoon red pepper flakes
- 1 tablespoon chopped fresh rosemary
- 2 ounces pancetta, cut into ½-inch pieces
- 1 (2½-pound) center-cut boneless pork loin roast, trimmed
- Kosher salt

1. Finely grate 1 teaspoon zest from lemon. Cut lemon in half and reserve. Combine lemon zest, oil, garlic, and pepper flakes in 10-inch nonstick skillet. Cook over medium-low heat, stirring frequently, until garlic is sizzling, about 3 minutes. Add rosemary and cook, about 30 seconds. Strain mixture through fine-mesh strainer set over bowl, pushing on garlic-rosemary mixture to extract oil. Set oil aside and let garlic-rosemary mixture cool. Using paper towels, wipe out skillet.

2. Process pancetta in food processor until smooth paste forms, 20 to 30 seconds, scraping down sides of bowl as needed. Add garlic-rosemary mixture and continue to process until mixture is homogeneous, 20 to 30 seconds longer, scraping down sides of bowl as needed.

3. Position roast fat side up. Insert knife one-third of way up from bottom of roast along 1 long side and cut horizontally, stopping ½ inch before edge. Open up flap. Keeping knife parallel to cutting board, cut through thicker portion of roast about ½ inch from bottom of roast, keeping knife level with first cut and stopping about ½ inch before edge. Open up this flap. If uneven, cover with plastic wrap and use meat pounder to even out. Sprinkle 1 tablespoon salt over both sides of roast (½ tablespoon per side) and rub into meat to adhere. Spread inside of roast evenly with pancetta-garlic paste, leaving about ¼-inch border on all sides. Starting from short side, roll roast (keeping fat on outside) and tie with twine at 1-inch intervals. Set wire rack in rimmed baking sheet and spray with vegetable oil spray. Set roast fat side up on prepared rack and refrigerate for 1 hour.

4. Adjust oven rack to middle position and heat oven to 275 degrees. Transfer roast to oven and cook until meat registers 135 degrees, 1½ to 2 hours. Remove roast from oven, tent with aluminum foil, and let rest for 20 minutes.

5. Heat 1 teaspoon reserved oil in now-empty skillet over high heat until just smoking. Add reserved lemon halves, cut side down, and cook until softened and cut surfaces are browned, 3 to 4 minutes. Transfer lemon halves to small plate.

6. Pat roast dry with paper towels. Heat 2 tablespoons reserved oil in now-empty skillet over high heat until just smoking. Brown roast on fat side and sides (do not brown bottom of roast), 4 to 6 minutes. Transfer roast to carving board and remove twine.

7. Once lemon halves are cool enough to handle, squeeze into fine-mesh strainer set over bowl. Press on solids to extract all pulp; discard solids. Whisk 2 tablespoons strained lemon juice into bowl with remaining reserved oil. Slice roast into ¼-inch-thick slices and serve, passing vinaigrette separately.

SLOW-ROASTED BONE-IN PORK RIB ROAST

WHY THIS RECIPE WORKS: A center-cut pork rib roast has a lot of potential: Some butchers call it the "pork equivalent of prime rib." Treated right, it can be truly impressive: moist, tender, and full of rich, meaty taste—and for far less money than a prime rib costs. We set out to make this cut worthy of an elegant holiday table.

To start, we pretreated the pork with a salt–brown sugar rub. The salt seasoned the meat and drew moisture into the flesh, helping to keep it juicy. The brown sugar contributed deep molasses notes and a gorgeous mahogany color, which allowed us to skip tedious searing. We also removed the bones from the meat so we could season it from all sides, then tied it back onto the bones to roast. Since heat travels more slowly through bone than through flesh, the bones helped keep the center of the roast moist. Another plus was that the finished roast, free of bones, was easier to carve. Scoring deep crosshatch marks into the fat with a sharp knife helped it melt and baste the meat during roasting. Cooking the roast in a gentle 250-degree oven ensured that the pork was evenly cooked all the way through. We crisped up the fat by blasting the roast under the broiler for a couple of minutes just prior to serving. As a finishing touch, a classic beurre rouge sauce, made with tawny port and balsamic vinegar and studded with plump dried cherries, balanced the meaty roast with echoes of fruit and herbs.

Slow-Roasted Bone-In Pork Rib Roast

SERVES 6 TO 8

This recipe requires refrigerating the salted meat for at least 6 hours before cooking. For easier carving, ask the butcher to remove the chine bone. Monitoring the roast with an oven probe thermometer is best. If you use an instant-read thermometer, open the oven door as infrequently as possible and remove the roast from the oven while taking its temperature. The sauce may be prepared in advance or while the roast rests in step 3.

- 1 (4- to 5-pound) center-cut bone-in pork rib roast, chine bone removed
- 2 tablespoons packed dark brown sugar
- 1 tablespoon kosher salt
- 1½ teaspoons pepper
- 1 recipe Port Wine–Cherry Sauce (recipe follows)

1. Using sharp knife, remove roast from bones, running knife down length of bones and following contours as closely as possible. Reserve bones. Combine sugar and salt in small bowl. Pat roast dry with paper towels. If necessary, trim thick spots of surface fat layer to about ¼-inch thickness. Using sharp knife, cut slits, spaced 1 inch apart and in crosshatch pattern, in surface fat layer, being careful not to cut into meat. Rub roast evenly with sugar mixture. Wrap roast and ribs in plastic wrap and refrigerate for at least 6 hours or up to 24 hours.

2. Adjust oven rack to lower-middle position and heat oven to 250 degrees. Sprinkle roast evenly with pepper. Place roast back on ribs so bones fit where they were cut; tie roast to bones with lengths of kitchen twine between ribs. Transfer roast, fat side up, to wire rack set in rimmed baking sheet. Roast until meat registers 145 degrees, 3 to 4 hours.

3. Remove roast from oven (leave roast on sheet), tent loosely with aluminum foil, and let rest for 30 minutes.

4. Adjust oven rack 8 inches from broiler element and heat broiler. Return roast to oven and broil until top of roast is well browned and crispy, 2 to 6 minutes.

5. Transfer roast to carving board; cut twine and remove meat from ribs. Slice meat into ¾-inch-thick slices and serve, passing sauce separately.

Port Wine–Cherry Sauce

MAKES ABOUT 1¾ CUPS

- 2 cups tawny port
- 1 cup dried cherries
- ½ cup balsamic vinegar
- 4 sprigs fresh thyme, plus 2 teaspoons minced
- 2 shallots, minced
- ¼ cup heavy cream
- 16 tablespoons unsalted butter, cut into ½-inch pieces and chilled
- 1 teaspoon salt
- ½ teaspoon pepper

1. Combine port and cherries in bowl and microwave until steaming, 1 to 2 minutes. Cover and let stand until plump, about 10 minutes. Strain port through fine-mesh strainer into medium saucepan, reserving cherries.

2. Add vinegar, thyme sprigs, and shallots to port and bring to boil over high heat. Reduce heat to medium-high and reduce mixture until it measures ¾ cup, 14 to 16 minutes. Add cream and reduce again to ¾ cup, about 5 minutes. Discard thyme sprigs. Off heat, whisk in butter, a few pieces at a time, until fully incorporated. Stir in cherries, minced thyme, salt, and pepper. Cover pan and hold, off heat, until serving. Alternatively, let sauce cool completely and refrigerate for up to 2 days. Reheat in small saucepan over medium-low heat, stirring frequently, until warm.

SLOW-COOKER PORK LOIN

WHY THIS RECIPE WORKS: Cooking a lean roast like a pork loin in a slow cooker is tricky because it can quickly turn overcooked and dry. The key to this recipe was to monitor the temperature of the roast after a few hours and take it out of the slow cooker as soon as it reached 145 degrees. Whether you're cooking a pork loin in the oven or the slow cooker, pairing the lean meat with a sauce gives it a lot more appeal. We paired our loin with both dried cranberries and whole canned cranberries. Cinnamon, orange juice, and orange zest livened up our easy-to-make sauce, which goes directly into the slow cooker. After cooking the loin, we reduced the braising liquid until it became a sweet sauce that paired perfectly with our juicy pork loin.

Slow-Cooker Pork Loin with Cranberries and Orange

SERVES 6

When choosing a pork loin, we prefer the blade-end—be sure to choose a fatter, shorter loin over a longer, skinnier one. Use a vegetable peeler to remove wide strips of zest from the orange. Make sure to trim any white pith from the zest, as it can impart a bitter flavor.

- 1 (4½- to 5-pound) boneless pork loin roast, trimmed and tied at 1-inch intervals
- Table salt and ground black pepper
- 1 tablespoon vegetable oil
- 1 (14-ounce) can whole berry cranberry sauce
- ½ cup dried cranberries
- ½ cup juice and 3 (3-inch-long) strips zest from 1 orange
- ⅛ teaspoon ground cinnamon

1. Dry the pork with paper towels and season with salt and pepper. Heat the oil in a 12-inch skillet over medium-high heat until just smoking. Brown the pork well on all sides, 7 to 10 minutes.

2. Stir the cranberry sauce, cranberries, orange juice, orange zest, and cinnamon into the slow cooker. Nestle the browned pork into the slow cooker. Cover and cook until the pork is tender and registers 140 to 145 degrees on an instant-read thermometer, about 4 hours on low.

3. Transfer the pork to a cutting board, tent loosely with aluminum foil, and let rest for 10 minutes. Let the braising liquid settle for 5 minutes, then remove the fat from the surface using a large spoon. Discard the orange zest. Transfer the braising liquid to a saucepan and simmer until reduced to 2 cups, about 12 minutes. Season with salt and pepper to taste.

4. Remove the twine from the pork, slice into ½-inch-thick slices, and arrange on a serving platter. Spoon 1 cup sauce over the meat and serve with the remaining sauce.

SLOW-ROASTED PORK SHOULDER

WHY THIS RECIPE WORKS: Although most modern pork is leaner than it used to be, this is not true of every cut. We wanted to celebrate the glories of rich old-fashioned pork with the shoulder roast (also called Boston butt or pork butt). This tough cut is loaded with intramuscular fat that builds flavor and bastes the meat during roasting; outside, its thick fat cap renders to a bronze, bacon-like crust. Plus, at around $2 per pound, the shoulder offers value.

First, we salted the meat overnight—a technique we frequently use with large, tough roasts for improved texture and flavor. This helped, but to improve the roast's flavor even more, we turned to an idea taken from Chinese barbecued pork, where the meat is rubbed with a salt and sugar rub (we preferred brown sugar over white for its subtle molasses flavor and hints of caramel). As we hoped, the sugar caramelized and helped crisp the fat cap, giving it a bronze hue. For an accompanying sauce, peaches, white wine, sugar, vinegar, and a couple of sprigs of fresh thyme added to the drippings and then reduced delivered on all fronts. To round out the sweetness, we finished it with a spoonful of whole grain mustard.

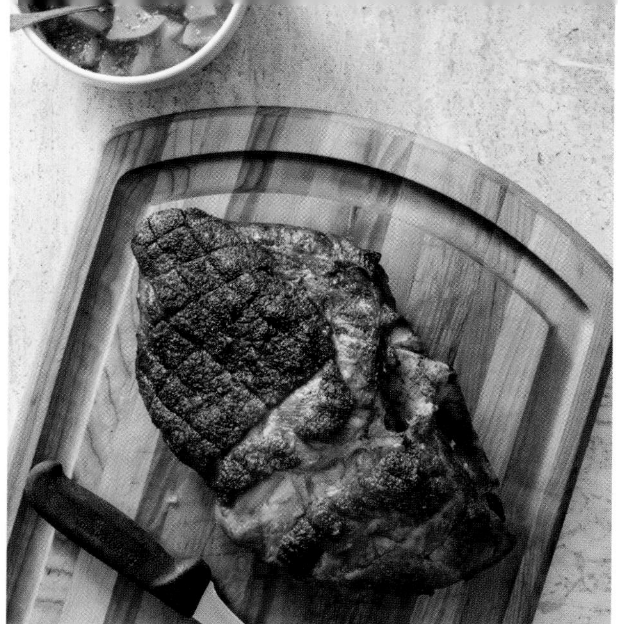

Slow-Roasted Pork Shoulder with Peach Sauce

SERVES 8 TO 12

We prefer natural pork to enhanced pork (pork that has been injected with a salt solution to increase moistness and flavor), though both will work in this recipe. Add more water to the roasting pan as necessary during the last hours of cooking to prevent the fond from burning.

PORK ROAST

- 1 (6- to 8-pound) bone-in pork butt (see note)
- ⅓ cup kosher salt
- ⅓ cup packed light brown sugar
- Ground black pepper

PEACH SAUCE

- 10 ounces frozen peaches, cut into 1-inch chunks (about 2 cups) or 2 fresh peaches cut into ½-inch wedges
- 2 cups dry white wine
- ½ cup granulated sugar
- ¼ cup plus 1 tablespoon unseasoned rice vinegar
- 2 sprigs fresh thyme
- 1 tablespoon whole grain mustard

1. FOR THE ROAST: Using a sharp knife, cut slits 1 inch apart in the fat cap of the roast in a crosshatch pattern, being careful not to cut into the meat. Combine the salt and brown sugar in a medium bowl. Rub the salt mixture over the entire pork shoulder and into the slits. Wrap the roast tightly in a double layer of plastic wrap, place on a rimmed baking sheet, and refrigerate for at least 12 hours or up to 24 hours.

2. Adjust an oven rack to the lowest position and heat the oven to 325 degrees. Unwrap the roast and brush off any excess salt mixture from the surface. Season the roast with pepper. Transfer the roast to a V-rack coated with vegetable oil spray set in a large roasting pan. Add 1 quart water to the roasting pan.

3. Cook the roast, basting twice during cooking, until the meat is extremely tender and an instant-read thermometer inserted into the roast near, but not touching, the bone registers 190 degrees, 5 to 6 hours. Transfer the roast to a carving board and let rest, loosely tented with foil, for 1 hour. Transfer the liquid in the roasting pan to a fat separator and let stand for 5 minutes. Pour off ¼ cup jus and reserve, then discard any remaining jus and fat.

4. FOR THE SAUCE: Bring the peaches, wine, granulated sugar, ¼ cup of the vinegar, the reserved defatted jus, and the thyme to a simmer in a small saucepan; cook, stirring occasionally, until reduced to 2 cups, about 30 minutes. Stir in the remaining 1 tablespoon vinegar and the mustard. Remove the thyme sprigs, cover the pan, and keep warm.

5. Using a sharp paring knife, cut around the inverted T-shaped bone, until it can be pulled free from the roast (use a clean kitchen towel to grasp the bone). Using a serrated knife, slice the roast. Serve, passing the sauce separately.

INDOOR PULLED PORK

WHY THIS RECIPE WORKS: In recipes, the phrase "indoor barbecue" is usually code for "braised in a Dutch oven with bottled barbecue sauce." Unfortunately, this results in mushy, waterlogged meat and candy-sweet sauce. We wanted moist, tender, shreddable meat with deep smoke flavor all the way through, plus a dark, richly seasoned crust, often referred to as bark.

Be it indoor or outdoor, with barbecue a good amount of fat is necessary for moisture and flavor, so we chose to use boneless Boston butt because of its high level of marbling. To mimic the moist heat of a covered grill, we came up with a dual cooking method: covering the pork for part of the oven time to speed up cooking and keep it moist, then uncovering it for the remainder of the time to help the meat develop a crust.

To achieve smoky flavor without an actual barbecue pit, we turned to liquid smoke, a natural product derived from condensing the moist smoke of smoldering wood chips. We found that adding it to our brine infused it with smoky flavor without tasting unnatural. For even more smokiness, we employed a dry rub and a wet rub, which we also fortified with smoky flavorings. To serve alongside our pork, we developed three sauces inspired by the variety of barbecue regions and styles: a classic sweet and tangy sauce, a vinegar sauce, and a mustard sauce, all of which we flavored with some of the pork's defatted cooking liquid.

Indoor Pulled Pork with Sweet and Tangy Barbecue Sauce

SERVES 6 TO 8

Sweet paprika may be substituted for smoked paprika. Covering the pork with parchment and then foil prevents the acidic mustard from eating holes in the foil. Serve the pork on hamburger rolls with pickle chips and thinly sliced onion. In place of the Sweet and Tangy Barbecue Sauce or the variations that follow, you can use 2 cups of your favorite barbecue sauce thinned with ½ cup of the defatted pork cooking liquid in step 5. The shredded and sauced pork can be cooled, tightly covered, and refrigerated for up to 2 days. Reheat it gently before serving.

PORK

- 1 cup plus 2 teaspoons table salt
- ½ cup plus 2 tablespoons sugar
- 3 tablespoons plus 2 teaspoons liquid smoke
- 1 5-pound boneless pork butt roast, cut in half horizontally
- ¼ cup yellow mustard
- 2 tablespoons ground black pepper
- 2 tablespoons smoked paprika (see note)
- 1 teaspoon cayenne pepper

SWEET AND TANGY BARBECUE SAUCE

- 1½ cups ketchup
- ¼ cup light or mild molasses
- 2 tablespoons Worcestershire sauce
- 1 tablespoon hot sauce
- ½ teaspoon table salt
- ½ teaspoon ground black pepper

1. FOR THE PORK: Dissolve 1 cup of the salt, ½ cup of the sugar, and 3 tablespoons of the liquid smoke in 1 gallon cold water in a large container. Submerge the pork in the brine, cover with plastic wrap, and refrigerate for 2 hours.

2. While the pork brines, combine the mustard and remaining 2 teaspoons liquid smoke in a small bowl; set aside. Combine the black pepper, paprika, remaining 2 tablespoons sugar, remaining 2 teaspoons salt, and cayenne in a second small bowl; set aside. Adjust an oven rack to the lower-middle position and heat the oven to 325 degrees.

3. Remove the pork from the brine and dry thoroughly with paper towels. Rub the mustard mixture over the entire surface of each piece of pork. Sprinkle the entire surface of each piece with the spice mixture. Place the pork on a wire rack set over a foil-lined rimmed baking sheet. Place a piece of parchment paper over the pork, then cover with a sheet of aluminum foil, sealing the edges to prevent moisture from escaping. Roast the pork for 3 hours.

NOTES FROM THE TEST KITCHEN

CUTTING A PORK BUTT IN HALF

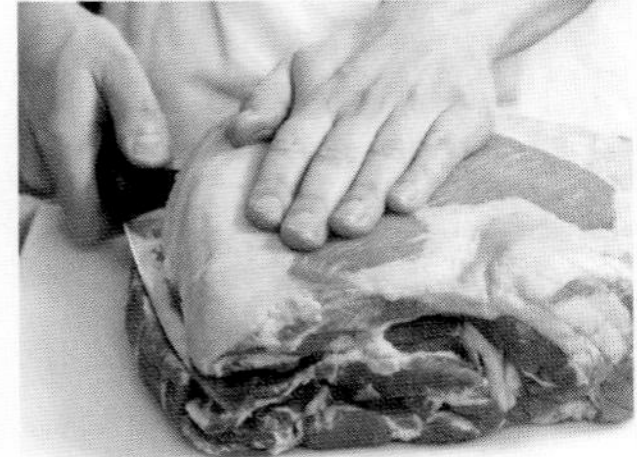

Halving the pork increases its surface area, which creates more flavorful bark. Holding your knife parallel to the cutting board, press one hand flat against the top of the pork while cutting horizontally.

4. Remove the pork from the oven; remove and discard the foil and parchment. Carefully pour off the liquid in the bottom of the baking sheet into a fat separator and reserve for the sauce. Return the pork to the oven and cook, uncovered, until well browned, tender, and the center of the roast registers 200 degrees on an instant-read thermometer, about 1½ hours. Transfer the pork to a serving dish, tent loosely with foil, and let rest for 20 minutes.

5. FOR THE SAUCE: While the pork rests, pour ½ cup of the defatted cooking liquid from the fat separator into a medium bowl; whisk in the sauce ingredients.

6. Using two forks, shred the pork into bite-size pieces. Toss with 1 cup sauce and season with salt and pepper to taste. Serve, passing the remaining sauce separately.

Lexington Vinegar Barbecue Sauce

MAKES ABOUT 2½ CUPS

- 1 cup cider vinegar
- ½ cup ketchup
- ½ cup water
- 1 tablespoon sugar
- ¾ teaspoon table salt
- ¾ teaspoon red pepper flakes
- ½ teaspoon ground black pepper

Combine all the ingredients in a medium bowl with ½ cup of the defatted cooking liquid in step 5 and whisk to combine.

South Carolina Mustard Barbecue Sauce

MAKES ABOUT 2½ CUPS

- 1 cup yellow mustard
- ½ cup white vinegar
- ¼ cup packed light brown sugar
- ¼ cup Worcestershire sauce
- 2 tablespoons hot sauce
- 1 teaspoon table salt
- 1 teaspoon ground black pepper

Combine all the ingredients in a medium bowl with ½ cup of the defatted cooking liquid in step 5 and whisk to combine.

ROAST FRESH HAM

WHY THIS RECIPE WORKS: Fresh ham is not cured like a Smithfield ham or salted and air-dried like prosciutto. It's not pressed or molded like a canned ham, and it's not smoked like a country ham. In fact, some people think there's no such thing as "fresh" ham. There is—and we wanted to find the best way to cook it for a roasted ham that boasted rich, moist meat and crackling crisp skin.

Fresh hams are large, so they're usually cut in half and sold as either the sirloin or the shank end; we chose the latter for its ease of carving. But even cut into these smaller roasts, fresh ham needs a long time in the oven, so the danger is drying out the meat. To prevent this, we brined our ham overnight. A garlic and herb rub added further flavor. We positioned the ham face down on a rack in a roasting pan; the rack allowed the heat to circulate all around the ham for more even cooking. A brief roasting at a high temperature followed by longer cooking at a lower temperature produced crunchy skin and succulent meat. The crowning touch was a sweet glaze, which we brushed on periodically while the meat roasted.

Roast Fresh Ham

SERVES 8 TO 10

Fresh ham comes from the pig's hind leg. Because a whole leg is quite large, it is usually cut into two sections. The sirloin, or butt, end is harder to carve than our favorite, the shank end. If you don't have room in your refrigerator, brine the ham in an insulated cooler or a small plastic garbage can; add five or six freezer packs to the brine to keep it well cooled.

ROAST

- 1 (6- to 8-pound) bone-in fresh half ham with skin, preferably shank end, rinsed (see note)

BRINE

- 3 cups packed brown sugar
- 2 cups table salt
- 2 heads garlic, cloves separated, lightly crushed and peeled
- 10 bay leaves
- ½ cup black peppercorns, crushed

GARLIC AND HERB RUB

- 1 cup lightly packed fresh sage leaves
- ½ cup parsley leaves
- ¼ cup olive oil
- 8 medium garlic cloves, peeled
- ½ tablespoon ground black pepper
- 1½ teaspoons table salt

GLAZE

- 1 recipe glaze (recipes follow)

1. **FOR THE ROAST:** Carefully slice through the skin and fat with a serrated knife, making a 1-inch diamond pattern. Be careful not to cut into the meat.

2. **FOR THE BRINE:** In a large container, dissolve the brown sugar and salt in 2 gallons cold water. Add the garlic, bay leaves, and crushed peppercorns. Submerge the ham in the brine and refrigerate for 8 to 24 hours.

3. Set a large disposable aluminum roasting pan on a baking sheet for extra support; place a flat wire rack in the roasting pan. Remove the ham from the brine; rinse under cold water and dry thoroughly with paper towels. Place the ham, wide cut side down, on the rack. (If using the sirloin end, place the ham skin side up.) Let the ham stand, uncovered, at room temperature for 1 hour.

4. **FOR THE RUB:** Meanwhile, adjust an oven rack to the lowest position and heat the oven to 500 degrees. Process the sage, parsley, oil, garlic, pepper, and salt in a food processor until the mixture forms a smooth paste, about 30 seconds. Rub all sides of the ham with the paste.

5. Roast the ham at 500 degrees for 20 minutes. Reduce the oven temperature to 350 degrees and continue to roast, brushing the ham with the glaze every 45 minutes, until the center of the ham registers 145 to 150 degrees on an instant-read thermometer, about 2½ hours longer. Remove from the oven and tent the ham loosely with foil and let stand until the center of the ham registers 155 to 160 degrees, 30 to 40 minutes. Carve and serve.

Cider and Brown Sugar Glaze

MAKES ABOUT 1⅓ CUPS

- 1 cup apple cider
- 2 cups packed brown sugar
- 5 whole cloves

Bring the cider, brown sugar, and cloves to a boil in a small saucepan over high heat; reduce the heat to medium-low and simmer until syrupy and reduced to about 1⅓ cups, 5 to 7 minutes. (The glaze will thicken as it cools between bastings; cook over medium heat for about 1 minute, stirring once or twice, before using.)

Spicy Pineapple-Ginger Glaze

MAKES ABOUT 1⅓ CUPS

- 1 cup pineapple juice
- 2 cups packed brown sugar
- 1 (1-inch) piece fresh ginger, grated (about 1 tablespoon)
- 1 tablespoon red pepper flakes

Bring the pineapple juice, brown sugar, ginger, and red pepper flakes to a boil in a small saucepan over high heat; reduce the heat to medium-low and simmer until syrupy and reduced to about 1⅓ cups, 5 to 7 minutes. (The glaze will thicken as it cools between bastings; cook over medium heat about for 1 minute, stirring once or twice, before using.)

Coca-Cola Glaze with Lime and Jalapeño

MAKES ABOUT 1⅓ CUPS

- 1 cup Coca-Cola
- ¼ cup juice from 2 limes
- 2 cups packed brown sugar
- 2 medium jalapeño chiles, cut crosswise into ¼-inch-thick slices

Bring the Coca-Cola, lime juice, brown sugar, and jalapeños to a boil in a small nonreactive saucepan over high heat; reduce the heat to medium-low and simmer until syrupy and reduced to about 1⅓ cups, 5 to 7 minutes. (The glaze will thicken as it cools between bastings; heat over medium heat for about 1 minute, stirring once or twice, before using.)

Orange, Cinnamon, and Star Anise Glaze

MAKES ABOUT 1⅓ CUPS

- 1 cup juice plus 1 tablespoon grated zest from 2 large oranges
- 2 cups packed brown sugar
- 4 pods star anise
- 1 (3-inch) cinnamon stick

Bring the orange juice, zest, brown sugar, star anise, and cinnamon stick to a boil in a small nonreactive saucepan over high heat; reduce the heat to medium-low and simmer until syrupy and reduced to about 1⅓ cups, 5 to 7 minutes. (The glaze will thicken as it cools between bastings; cook over medium heat for about 1 minute, stirring once or twice, before using.)

GLAZED HOLIDAY HAM

WHY THIS RECIPE WORKS: Nothing could be easier than heating up a cured ham, right? Well, we've made enough of them to know that as easy as it may be, the results are often leathery meat with an overly sweet glaze. We wanted to revisit the way to cook this roast to get moist meat accompanied by a glaze that didn't overwhelm it.

We have found that bone-in hams, labeled "with natural juices," have the best flavor, and spiral-sliced ones make carving a cinch. We knew that the longer the ham spent in the oven, the greater the chances we'd end up with dried-out meat, so we focused on reducing the cooking time. First we soaked the ham in hot water so that it wouldn't be ice-cold when it went into the oven; this step saved a full hour. Roasting the ham in an oven bag further reduced the cooking time, and using the bag had the added advantage of holding in moisture. For the glaze, we threw out the packet that came with our ham and made a fruit-based glaze with just a touch of sweetness to complement the moist, tender meat. This foolproof method will make the perfect holiday ham every time.

Glazed Spiral-Sliced Ham

SERVES 12 TO 14

You can bypass the 90-minute soaking time, but the heating time will increase to 18 to 20 minutes per pound for a cold ham. If there is a tear or hole in the ham's inner covering, wrap the ham in several layers of plastic wrap before soaking it in hot water. Instead of using the plastic oven bag, the ham may be placed cut side down in the roasting pan and covered tightly with foil, but you will need to add 3 to 4 minutes per pound to the heating time. If using an oven bag, be sure to cut slits in the bag so it does not burst.

- 1 (7- to 10-pound) spiral-sliced bone-in half ham
- 1 large plastic oven bag (see note)
- 1 recipe glaze (recipes follow)

1. Leaving the ham's inner plastic or foil covering intact, place the ham in a large container and cover with hot tap water; set aside for 45 minutes. Drain and cover again with hot tap water; set aside for another 45 minutes.

2. Adjust an oven rack to the lowest position and heat the oven to 250 degrees. Unwrap the ham; remove and discard the plastic disk covering the bone. Place the ham in the oven bag. Gather the top of the bag tightly so the bag fits snugly around the ham, tie the bag, and trim the excess plastic. Set the ham, cut side down, in a large roasting pan and cut four slits in the top of the bag with a paring knife.

3. Bake the ham until the center registers 100 degrees on an instant-read thermometer, 1 to 1½ hours (about 10 minutes per pound).

4. Remove the ham from the oven and increase the oven temperature to 350 degrees. Cut open the oven bag and roll back the sides to expose the ham. Brush the ham with one-third of the glaze and return to the oven until the glaze becomes sticky, about 10 minutes (if the glaze is too thick to brush, return it to the heat to loosen).

5. Remove the ham from the oven, transfer it to a carving board, and brush the entire ham with another third of the glaze. Let the ham rest, loosely tented with foil, for 15 minutes. While the ham rests, heat the remaining third of the glaze with 4 to 6 tablespoons of the ham juices until it forms a thick but fluid sauce. Carve and serve the ham, passing the sauce at the table.

Maple-Orange Glaze

MAKES 1 CUP

- ¾ cup maple syrup
- ½ cup orange marmalade
- 2 tablespoons unsalted butter
- 1 tablespoon Dijon mustard
- 1 teaspoon ground black pepper
- ¼ teaspoon ground cinnamon

Combine all the ingredients in a small saucepan. Cook over medium heat, stirring occasionally, until the mixture is thick, syrupy, and reduced to 1 cup, 5 to 10 minutes; set aside.

Cherry-Port Glaze

MAKES 1 CUP

- ½ cup ruby port
- ½ cup cherry preserves
- 1 cup packed dark brown sugar
- 1 teaspoon ground black pepper

Simmer the port in a small saucepan over medium heat until reduced to 2 tablespoons, about 5 minutes. Add the remaining ingredients and cook, stirring occasionally, until the sugar dissolves and the mixture is thick, syrupy, and reduced to 1 cup, 5 to 10 minutes; set aside.

CHAPTER 10

FAVORITE WAYS WITH FISH

SUPER-CRISPY OVEN-FRIED FISH

WHY THIS RECIPE WORKS: The golden brown coating and moist, flaky flesh of batter-fried fish come at a price: the oil. Cooks have turned to the oven to avoid the bother of deep-fat frying, but oven-frying often falls short. The coating never gets very crisp and the fish usually ends up overcooked. We aimed to put the crunch back into oven-frying.

We used thick fillets so that the fish and coating would finish cooking at the same time. Flaky cod and haddock provided the best contrast to the crunchy exterior we envisioned. A conventional bound breading—flour, egg, and fresh bread crumbs—wasn't as crisp as we wanted, so we toasted the bread crumbs with a little butter. (Precooking the crumbs also ensured we wouldn't have to overcook the fish to get really crunchy crumbs.) Placing the coated fish on a wire rack while baking allowed air to circulate all around the fish, crisping all sides. We boosted flavor in two ways, adding shallots and parsley to the breading and horseradish, cayenne, and paprika to the egg wash. As a final touch, we whipped up a creamy tartar sauce with mayonnaise, capers, and sweet relish.

Crunchy Oven-Fried Fish

SERVES 4

To prevent overcooking, buy fish fillets that are at least 1 inch thick. The bread crumbs can be made up to 3 days in advance and stored at room temperature in a tightly sealed container (allow to cool fully before storing). Serve the dish with Sweet and Tangy Tartar Sauce (recipe follows).

- 4 slices high-quality white sandwich bread, torn into quarters
- 2 tablespoons unsalted butter, melted
- Table salt and ground black pepper
- 2 tablespoons minced fresh parsley leaves
- 1 small shallot, minced (about 1 tablespoon)
- ¼ cup plus 5 tablespoons unbleached all-purpose flour
- 2 large eggs
- 3 tablespoons mayonnaise
- 2 teaspoons prepared horseradish (optional)
- ½ teaspoon paprika
- ¼ teaspoon cayenne pepper (optional)
- 1¼ pounds cod, haddock, or other thick whitefish fillets (1 to 1½ inches thick), cut into 4 pieces (see note)
- Lemon wedges, for serving

1. Adjust an oven rack to the middle position and heat the oven to 350 degrees. Pulse the bread, butter, ¼ teaspoon salt, and ¼ teaspoon black pepper in a food processor until the bread is coarsely ground, about 8 pulses. Transfer to a rimmed baking sheet and bake until deep golden brown and dry, about 15 minutes, stirring twice during the baking time. Cool the crumbs to room temperature, about 10 minutes. Transfer the crumbs to a pie plate and toss with the parsley and shallot. Increase the oven temperature to 425 degrees.

2. Place ¼ cup of the flour in a second pie plate. In a third pie plate, whisk together the eggs, mayonnaise, horseradish (if using), paprika, cayenne (if using), and ¼ teaspoon black pepper until combined; whisk in the remaining 5 tablespoons flour until smooth.

3. Spray a wire rack with vegetable oil spray and place over a rimmed baking sheet. Dry the fish thoroughly with paper towels and season with salt and black pepper. Dredge 1 fillet in the flour; shake off the excess. Using tongs, coat the fillet with the egg mixture. Coat all sides of the fillet with the bread-crumb mixture, pressing gently so that a thick layer of crumbs adheres to the fish. Transfer the breaded fish to the wire rack. Repeat with the remaining 3 fillets.

4. Bake the fish until the center of the fillets registers 140 degrees on an instant-read thermometer, 18 to 25 minutes. Using a thin spatula, transfer the fillets to individual plates and serve immediately with the lemon wedges.

Sweet and Tangy Tartar Sauce

MAKES ABOUT 1 CUP

This sauce can be refrigerated, tightly covered, for up to 1 week.

- ¾ cup mayonnaise
- 2 tablespoons drained capers, minced
- 2 tablespoons sweet pickle relish
- 1 small shallot, minced (about 1 tablespoon)
- 1½ teaspoons distilled white vinegar
- ½ teaspoon Worcestershire sauce
- ½ teaspoon ground black pepper

Mix all the ingredients together in a small bowl. Cover the bowl with plastic wrap and let sit until the flavors meld, about 15 minutes. Stir again before serving.

FISH AND CHIPS

WHY THIS RECIPE WORKS: The fish and chips served at most American pubs are mediocre at best. But the alternative—deep-frying fish at home—can be a hassle and a mess. Plus, by the time the fries finish frying, the fish is cold. We wanted fish with a light, crisp crust and moist interior, and we wanted to serve both the fish and the fries at their prime.

Our first challenge was to come up with a batter that not only would protect the fish as it cooked (allowing it to steam gently) but would also provide the fish with a nicely crisp contrast. We discovered that a wet batter was the most effective way to coat and protect the fish. We liked beer—the traditional choice—as the liquid component. What was the best way to keep the coating crisp? The answer was a 3–1 ratio of flour to cornstarch, along with a teaspoon of baking powder. Still, the coating was so tender it puffed away from the fish as it cooked. A final coating of flour on top of the battered fish solved the problem.

To solve the second challenge—delivering the fish and fries while both are still hot—we cooked them alternately. First, we precooked the fries in the microwave, which not only lessened cooking time but removed excess moisture that could dilute the oil and diminish crisping. Then we gave the fries their first, quick fry in hot oil. While the potatoes were draining, we battered and fried the fish. Then, as the fish drained, we gave the fries a quick final fry.

Fish and Chips

SERVES 4

For safety, use a Dutch oven with at least a 7-quart capacity. Serve with traditional malt vinegar or with Sweet and Tangy Tartar Sauce (page 224).

- 3 pounds russet potatoes (about 4 large potatoes), peeled, ends and sides squared off, and cut lengthwise into ½-inch by ½-inch fries (see page 407)
- 3 quarts plus ¼ cup peanut oil or canola oil
- 1½ cups unbleached all-purpose flour
- ½ cup cornstarch
- ½ teaspoon cayenne pepper
- ½ teaspoon paprika
- ⅛ teaspoon ground black pepper
- Table salt
- 1 teaspoon baking powder
- 1½ pounds cod or other thick whitefish fillets, such as hake or haddock, cut into eight 3-ounce pieces about 1 inch thick
- 1½ cups (12 ounces) cold beer

1. Place the cut fries in a large microwave-safe bowl, toss with ¼ cup of the oil, and cover with plastic wrap. Microwave on high power until the potatoes are partially translucent and pliable but still offer some resistance when pierced with the tip of a paring knife, 6 to 8 minutes, tossing them with a rubber spatula halfway through the cooking time. Carefully pull back the plastic wrap from the side farthest from you and drain the potatoes into a large mesh strainer set over a sink. Rinse well under cold running water. Spread the potatoes on a few clean kitchen towels and pat dry. Let rest until the fries have reached room temperature, at least 10 minutes or up to 1 hour.

2. While the fries cool, whisk the flour, cornstarch, cayenne, paprika, black pepper, and 2 teaspoons salt in a large mixing bowl; transfer ¾ cup of the mixture to a rimmed baking sheet. Add the baking powder to the bowl and whisk to combine.

3. In a large Dutch oven fitted with a clip-on candy thermometer, heat 2 quarts more oil over medium heat to 350 degrees. Add the fries to the hot oil and increase the heat to high. Fry, stirring with a mesh spider or slotted metal spoon, until the potatoes turn light golden and just begin to brown at the corners, 6 to 8 minutes. Transfer the fries to a thick paper bag or paper towels to drain.

4. Reduce the heat to medium-high, add the remaining 1 quart oil, and heat the oil to 375 degrees. Meanwhile, thoroughly dry the fish with paper towels and dredge each piece in the flour mixture on the baking sheet; transfer the pieces to a wire rack, shaking off any excess flour. Add 1¼ cups of the beer to the flour mixture in the mixing bowl and stir until the mixture is just combined (the batter will be lumpy). Add the remaining ¼ cup beer as needed, 1 tablespoon at a time, whisking after each addition, until the batter falls from the whisk in a thin, steady stream and leaves a faint trail across the surface of the batter. Using tongs, dip 1 piece of fish in the batter and let the excess run off, shaking gently. Place the battered fish back on the baking sheet with the flour mixture and turn to coat both sides. Repeat with the remaining fish, keeping the pieces in a single layer on the baking sheet.

5. When the oil reaches 375 degrees, increase the heat to high and add the battered fish to the oil with the tongs, gently shaking off any excess flour. Fry, stirring occasionally, until golden brown, 7 to 8 minutes. Transfer the fish to a thick paper bag or paper towels to drain. Allow the oil to return to 375 degrees.

6. Add all of the fries back to the oil and fry until golden brown and crisp, 3 to 5 minutes. Transfer to a fresh paper bag or paper towels to drain. Season the fries with salt to taste and serve immediately with the fish.

PAN-SEARED SALMON

WHY THIS RECIPE WORKS: We love salmon cooked on the grill, but when the weather makes grilling unpleasant or impossible, we don't want to forgo serving this flavorful fish. We wanted a great recipe for pan-seared salmon with a crisp, golden crust. Preheating the skillet over high heat and using just a teaspoon of neutral oil (butter tended to burn and was too rich) produced the brown crust we wanted—no flour or other coating was necessary. To prevent burning, we turned the heat down just after adding the fillets. Allowing plenty of space around the fillets kept them from merely steaming. We flipped the fillets when they turned opaque from the bottom to about halfway up; there was no need to shake the pan or move the fish until then. We found that removing the salmon just before it was done prevented overcooking; residual heat brought it up to serving temperature. Simply seasoned and perfectly cooked, these salmon fillets were easy to make and just as good as any cooked on the grill.

Pan-Seared Salmon

SERVES 4

To ensure uniform pieces of fish that cook at the same rate, buy a whole center-cut fillet and cut it into four pieces. With the addition of the fish fillets, the pan temperature drops; compensate for the heat loss by keeping the heat on high for 30 seconds after adding them. If cooking two or three fillets instead of the full recipe of four, use a 10-inch skillet and medium-high heat for both preheating the pan and cooking the salmon. A splatter screen helps reduce the mess of pan-searing.

- 1 (1¾- to 2-pound) skinless salmon fillet, about 1½ inches at the thickest part (see note)
- 1 teaspoon canola or vegetable oil
- Table salt and ground black pepper
- Sweet-and-Sour Chutney (recipe follows) or lemon wedges, for serving

1. Use a sharp knife to trim any whitish fat from the belly of the fillet and cut it into four equal pieces. Heat the oil in a 12-inch skillet over high heat until shimmering but not smoking. Sprinkle the salmon with salt and pepper.

2. Add the fillets, skin-side down, and cook, without moving the fillets, until the skillet regains lost heat, about 30 seconds. Reduce the heat to medium-high; continue to cook until the skin side is well browned and the bottom half of the fillets turns opaque, 4½ minutes. Turn the fillets and cook, without moving them, until they are no longer translucent on the exterior and are firm, but not hard, when gently squeezed, 3 minutes for medium-rare and 3½ minutes for medium. Remove the fillets from the skillet; let stand for 1 minute. Pat the fillets with a paper towel to absorb excess fat on the surface, if desired. Serve immediately with the chutney or the lemon wedges.

Sweet-and-Sour Chutney

MAKES ABOUT ⅓ CUP

A little of this intensely flavored condiment goes a long way.

- 1 teaspoon fennel seeds
- ½ teaspoon ground cumin
- ½ teaspoon ground coriander
- ¼ teaspoon ground cardamom
- ¼ teaspoon paprika
- ¼ teaspoon table salt
- 2 teaspoons olive oil
- ½ medium onion, minced (about ½ cup)
- ¼ cup red wine vinegar
- 1 tablespoon sugar
- 1 tablespoon minced fresh parsley leaves

Mix the fennel, cumin, coriander, cardamom, paprika, and salt in a small bowl; set aside. Heat the oil in a medium skillet over medium heat; sauté the onion until soft, 3 to 4 minutes. Add the reserved spice mixture; sauté until fragrant, about 1 minute more. Increase the heat to medium-high and add the vinegar, sugar, and 2 tablespoons water; cook until the mixture reduces by about one third and reaches a syrupy consistency, about 1½ minutes. Stir in the parsley. Serve with the salmon.

PAN-SEARED BRINED SALMON

WHY THIS RECIPE WORKS: To achieve perfectly cooked salmon, we wanted to take advantage of the intense heat of the skillet and produce a golden-brown, ultracrisp crust on the fillets while keeping their interiors moist. We first brined the fish to season it and to keep it moist. Instead of adding the fish to an already-hot skillet, we placed it in a cold, dry nonstick skillet skin side down and then turned on the heat. The skin protected the fish from drying out while cooking and later was easy to peel off and discard. Also, because the skin released fat into the pan as it cooked, no extra oil was needed to sear the second side of the fish.

Pan-Seared Brined Salmon

SERVES 4

To ensure uniform cooking, buy a 1½- to 2-pound center-cut salmon fillet and cut it into four pieces. Using skin-on salmon is important here, as we rely on the fat underneath the skin as the cooking medium (as opposed to adding extra oil). If using wild salmon, cook it until it registers 120 degrees. If you don't want to serve the fish with the skin, we recommend peeling it off the fish after it is cooked. Serve with lemon wedges or Mango-Mint Salsa or Cilantro-Mint Chutney (recipes follow).

- Kosher salt and pepper
- 4 (6- to 8-ounce) skin-on salmon fillets
- Lemon wedges

1. Dissolve ½ cup salt in 2 quarts cold water in large container. Submerge salmon in brine and let stand at room temperature for 15 minutes. Remove salmon from brine and pat dry with paper towels.

2. Sprinkle bottom of 12-inch nonstick skillet evenly with ½ teaspoon salt and ½ teaspoon pepper. Place fillets, skin side down, in skillet and sprinkle tops of fillets with ¼ teaspoon salt and ¼ teaspoon pepper. Heat skillet over medium-high heat and cook fillets without moving them until fat begins to render, skin begins to brown, and bottom ¼ inch of fillets turns opaque, 6 to 8 minutes.

3. Using tongs, flip fillets and continue to cook without moving them until centers are still translucent when checked with tip of paring knife and register 125 degrees, 6 to 8 minutes longer. Transfer fillets skin side down to serving platter and let rest for 5 minutes before serving with lemon wedges.

Mango-Mint Salsa

MAKES ABOUT 1 CUP

Adjust the salsa's heat level by reserving and adding the jalapeño seeds, if desired.

- 1 mango, peeled, pitted, and cut into ¼-inch pieces
- 1 shallot, minced
- 3 tablespoons lime juice (2 limes)
- 2 tablespoons chopped fresh mint
- 1 jalapeño chile, stemmed, seeded, and minced
- 1 tablespoon extra-virgin olive oil
- 1 garlic clove, minced
- ½ teaspoon salt

Combine all ingredients in bowl.

Cilantro-Mint Chutney

MAKES ABOUT 1 CUP

Adjust the chutney's heat level by reserving and adding the jalapeño seeds, if desired.

- 2 cups fresh cilantro leaves
- 1 cup fresh mint leaves
- ½ cup water
- ¼ cup sesame seeds, lightly toasted
- 1 (2-inch) piece ginger, peeled and sliced into ⅛-inch-thick rounds
- 1 jalapeño chile, stemmed, seeded, and sliced into 1-inch pieces
- 2 tablespoons vegetable oil
- 2 tablespoons lime juice
- 1½ teaspoons sugar
- ½ teaspoon salt

Process all ingredients in blender until smooth, about 30 seconds, scraping down sides of jar with spatula after 10 seconds.

BROILED SALMON

WHY THIS RECIPE WORKS: Cooking an entire side of salmon in the oven often results in fish that is either soggy or chalky. We wanted to pull off a crowd-pleasing side of salmon that is moist and firm, with a golden crumb crust that contrasts with the flavorful fish.

Most of the time, we achieve a crisp crust on salmon through pan-searing in a skillet on the stovetop. With a crumb crust, it made sense to use the broiler. A plain bread crumb-topping seemed bland, but when we toasted the crumbs and mixed in crushed potato chips and chopped dill, the result was a crisp and flavorful coating. To get the crumb mixture to adhere to the fish, we relied on a thin layer of mustard. One problem: The crust burned by the time the fish was cooked through. We switched gears and broiled the fish almost unadorned (save for salt, pepper, and a bit of olive oil) until it was nearly done, then spread on the mustard and crumbs for a second run under the broiler to crisp the crust. To get the fish onto a platter in one piece, we lined a baking sheet with heavy-duty foil before adding the fish, creating a sling with which we could move it. Our two-step broiling method resulted in firm, moist fish and a flavorful crunchy topping.

Broiled Salmon with Mustard and Crisp Dilled Crust

SERVES 8 TO 10

If you prefer to cook a smaller 2-pound fillet, ask to have it cut from the thick center of the fillet, not the thin tail end, and begin checking doneness a minute earlier.

- 3 slices high-quality white sandwich bread, torn into quarters
- 4 ounces plain high-quality potato chips, crushed into rough ⅛-inch pieces (about 1 cup)
- 6 tablespoons chopped fresh dill
- 1 whole side salmon fillet, about 3½ pounds, white belly fat trimmed
- 1 teaspoon olive oil
- Table salt and ground black pepper
- 3 tablespoons Dijon mustard

1. Adjust one oven rack to the top position (about 3 inches from the heat source) and the second rack to the upper-middle position; heat the oven to 400 degrees.

2. Pulse the bread in a food processor to fairly even ¼-inch pieces about the size of Grape-Nuts cereal (you should have about 1 cup), about 10 pulses. Spread the crumbs evenly on a rimmed baking sheet; toast on the lower oven rack, shaking the pan once or twice, until golden brown and crisp, 4 to 5 minutes. Toss the bread crumbs, crushed potato chips, and dill together in a small bowl; set aside.

3. Change the oven setting to broil. Cut a piece of heavy-duty foil 6 inches longer than the fillet. Fold the foil lengthwise in thirds and place lengthwise on a rimmed baking sheet; position the salmon lengthwise on the foil, allowing the excess foil to overhang the baking sheet. Rub the fillet evenly with the oil;

sprinkle with salt and pepper. Broil the salmon on the upper rack until the surface is spotty brown and the outer ½ inch of the thick end is opaque when gently flaked with a paring knife, 9 to 11 minutes. Remove the baking sheet from the oven, spread the fish evenly with the mustard, and press the bread-crumb mixture onto the fish. Return the baking sheet to the lower oven rack and continue broiling until the crust is deep golden brown, about 1 minute longer.

4. Grasping the ends of the foil sling, lift the salmon, sling and all, onto a platter. Slide an offset spatula under the thick end. Grasp the foil, press the spatula against the foil, and slide it under the fish down to the thin end, loosening the entire side of fish. Grasp the foil again, hold the spatula perpendicular to the fish to stabilize it, and pull the foil out from under the fish. Wipe the platter clean with a damp paper towel. Serve the salmon immediately.

MARINATED SALMON

WHY THIS RECIPE WORKS: Miso-marinated salmon promises firm, flavorful fish with a savory-sweet, lacquer-like exterior, but it takes 3 days to prepare. We wanted to make a dish that pulled back on the traditional approach (and shortened the process) but still achieved the depth of flavor that this dish is known for. And instead of a dense interior, we wanted fish that was silky and moist, contrasting with the texture of the crust. By reducing the marinating to between 6 and 24 hours, we found a window that allowed us to achieve such a goal. A marinade composed of miso, sugar, mirin, and sake allowed for flavor penetration, moisture retention, and better browning by firming up the fish's surface. Broiling the fish at a distance from the heating element allowed the fish to caramelize and cook to tender at the same time.

Miso-Marinated Salmon

SERVES 4

Note that the fish needs to marinate for at least 6 or up to 24 hours before cooking. Use center-cut salmon fillets of similar thickness. Yellow, red, or brown miso paste can be used instead of white.

- ½ cup white miso paste
- ¼ cup sugar
- 3 tablespoons sake
- 3 tablespoons mirin
- 4 (6- to 8-ounce) skin-on salmon fillets
- Lemon wedges

1. Whisk miso, sugar, sake, and mirin together in medium bowl until sugar and miso are dissolved (mixture will be thick). Dip each fillet into miso mixture to evenly coat all flesh sides. Place fish skin side down in baking dish and pour any remaining miso mixture over fillets. Cover with plastic wrap and refrigerate for at least 6 hours or up to 24 hours.

2. Adjust oven rack 8 inches from broiler element and heat broiler. Place wire rack in rimmed baking sheet and cover with aluminum foil. Using your fingers, scrape miso mixture from fillets (do not rinse) and place fish skin side down on foil, leaving 1 inch between fillets.

3. Broil salmon until deeply browned and centers of fillets register 125 degrees, 8 to 12 minutes, rotating sheet halfway through cooking and shielding edges of fillets with foil if necessary. Transfer to platter and serve with lemon wedges.

FLAVORFUL POACHED SALMON

WHY THIS RECIPE WORKS: When salmon is poached incorrectly, not only is it dry, but the flavor is so washed out that not even the richest sauce can redeem it. We wanted irresistibly supple salmon accented by the delicate flavor of the poaching liquid, accompanied by a simple pan sauce—all in under half an hour.

We started our tests with a classic court-bouillon, which is made by boiling water, wine, herbs, vegetables, and aromatics and then straining out the solids. But discarding all those vegetables seemed wasteful for a simple weeknight supper. Using less liquid—poaching the salmon in just enough liquid to come half an inch up the side of the fillets—allowed us to cut back on the quantity of vegetables and aromatics; in fact, a couple of shallots, a few herbs, and some wine were all we needed to solve the flavor issue. However, the part of the salmon that wasn't submerged in liquid needed to be steamed for thorough cooking, and the low cooking temperature required to poach the salmon evenly didn't create enough steam. The solution was to increase the ratio of wine to water. The additional alcohol lowered the liquid's boiling point, producing more vapor even at the lower temperature. Meanwhile, the bottom of the fillets had the opposite problem, overcooking due to direct contact with the pan. Resting the salmon fillets on top of lemon slices provided sufficient insulation. For a finishing touch, after removing the salmon, we reduced the liquid and added a few tablespoons of olive oil to create an easy vinaigrette-style sauce.

Poached Salmon with Herb and Caper Vinaigrette

SERVES 4

To ensure uniform pieces of fish that cook at the same rate, buy a whole center-cut fillet and cut it into four pieces. If a skinless whole fillet is unavailable, remove the skin yourself (see photos on page 229) or follow the recipe as directed with a skin-on fillet, adding 3 to 4 minutes to the cooking time in step 2.

- 2 lemons
- 1 large shallot, minced (about 4 tablespoons)
- 2 tablespoons minced fresh parsley leaves, stems reserved
- 2 tablespoons minced fresh tarragon leaves, stems reserved
- ½ cup dry white wine
- ½ cup water
- 1 (1¾- to 2-pound) skinless salmon fillet, about 1½ inches at the thickest part (see note)

2 tablespoons capers, rinsed and roughly chopped
2 tablespoons extra-virgin olive oil
1 tablespoon honey
Table salt and ground black pepper

1. Cut the top and bottom off 1 lemon; cut the lemon into eight to ten ¼-inch-thick slices. Cut the remaining lemon into eight wedges and set aside. Arrange the lemon slices in a single layer across the bottom of a 12-inch skillet. Scatter 2 tablespoons of the shallot and the herb stems evenly over the lemon slices. Add the wine and water.

2. Use a sharp knife to trim any whitish fat from the belly of the fillet and cut it into four equal pieces. Place the salmon fillets in the skillet, skinned side down, on top of the lemon slices. Set the pan over high heat and bring the liquid to a simmer. Reduce the heat to low, cover, and cook until the sides of the fillets are opaque but the center of the thickest part of the fillets is still translucent (or until the thickest part of the fillets registers 125 degrees on an instant-read thermometer), 11 to 16 minutes. Remove the pan from the heat and, using a spatula, carefully transfer the salmon and lemon slices to a paper towel–lined plate. Tent loosely with foil.

3. Return the pan to high heat and simmer the cooking liquid until slightly thickened and reduced to 2 tablespoons, 4 to 5 minutes. Meanwhile, combine the remaining 2 tablespoons shallot, the minced herbs, capers, olive oil, and honey in a medium bowl. Strain the reduced cooking liquid through a fine-mesh strainer into the bowl with the herb-caper mixture, pressing on the solids to extract as much liquid as possible. Whisk to combine and season with salt and pepper to taste.

4. Season the salmon lightly with salt and pepper. Using a spatula, carefully lift and tilt the salmon fillets to remove the lemon slices. Place the salmon on a serving platter or individual plates and spoon the vinaigrette over the top. Serve, passing the reserved lemon wedges separately.

NOTES FROM THE TEST KITCHEN

HOW TO SKIN A SALMON FILLET

1. Insert the blade of a sharp boning knife just above the skin about 1 inch from the end of the fillet. Cut through the nearest end, away from yourself, keeping the blade just above the skin.

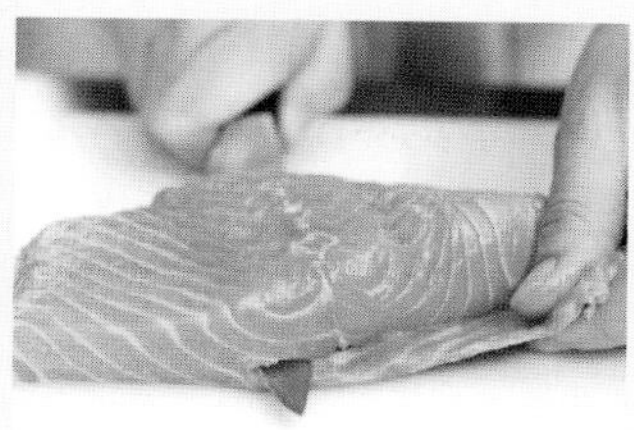

2. Rotate the fish and grab the loose piece of skin. Run the knife between the flesh and skin, making sure the knife is just above the skin, until the skin is completely removed.

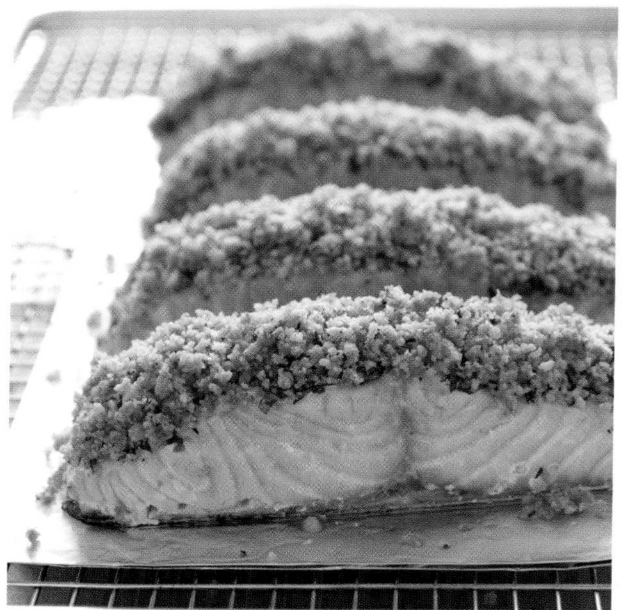

HERB-CRUSTED SALMON

WHY THIS RECIPE WORKS: Herb-crusted salmon rarely lives up to its name; it most often sports a dusty, bland sprinkling of bread crumbs and hardly any herb flavor. To make this dish the best it could be, we first brined the salmon to keep it moist (brining also inhibits the formation of the white protein albumin that appears on the fish when heated). For the herb, we thought the sweet, woodsy notes of tarragon paired especially well with our salmon. To protect its delicate flavor in the oven, we mixed the herb with mustard and mayonnaise, layered it on the fish, then sprinkled bread crumbs, which we'd seasoned with thyme, over the top. Toasting the bread crumbs in butter gave them some color and flavor. A little beaten egg helped them adhere, and a low oven kept the crust from scorching while the salmon cooked through.

Herb-Crusted Salmon

SERVES 4

For the fillets to cook at the same rate, they must be the same size and shape. To ensure uniformity, we prefer to purchase a 1½- to 2-pound center-cut salmon fillet and cut it into four pieces. Dill or basil can be substituted for the tarragon.

Salt and pepper
4 (6- to 8-ounce) skin-on salmon fillets
2 tablespoons unsalted butter
½ cup panko bread crumbs
2 tablespoons beaten egg
2 teaspoons minced fresh thyme
¼ cup chopped fresh tarragon
1 tablespoon whole-grain mustard
1½ teaspoons mayonnaise
Lemon wedges

1. Adjust oven rack to middle position and heat oven to 325 degrees. Dissolve 5 tablespoons salt in 2 quarts water in large container. Submerge salmon in brine and let stand at room temperature for 15 minutes. Remove salmon from brine, pat dry, and set aside.

2. Meanwhile, melt butter in 10-inch skillet over medium heat. Add panko and 1/8 teaspoon salt and season with pepper; cook, stirring frequently, until panko is golden brown, 4 to 5 minutes. Transfer to bowl and let cool completely. Stir in egg and thyme until thoroughly combined. Stir tarragon, mustard, and mayonnaise together in second bowl.

3. Set wire rack in rimmed baking sheet. Place 12 by 8-inch piece of aluminum foil on wire rack and lightly coat with vegetable oil spray. Evenly space fillets, skin side down, on foil. Using spoon, spread tarragon mixture evenly over top of each fillet. Sprinkle panko mixture evenly over top of each fillet, pressing with your fingers to adhere. Bake until center is still translucent when checked with tip of paring knife and registers 125 degrees (for medium-rare), 18 to 25 minutes. Transfer salmon to serving platter and let rest for 5 minutes before serving with lemon wedges.

SESAME-CRUSTED SALMON

WHY THIS RECIPE WORKS: The combination of fish and sesame shows up in cuisines from Asia to California to the Middle East. The simplest approach is to coat fillets with the seeds and then pan-sear the fish. But the duo of salmon and sesame often suffers from a common problem: Both salmon and sesame have a monotonous richness, so finishing a whole serving is a chore. We wanted a lively dish in which the salmon and sesame would be offset with bolder, brighter flavors. Brining the fish for just 15 minutes took care of any dryness. We dunked the seeds in the fish brine, which woke up the nutty flavor by infusing each with salt. Toasting the seeds gave them nice crunch. For extra sesame flavor, we "thickened" tahini with some lemon juice and used the thick paste to adhere the seeds. We also added scallion whites, lemon zest, fresh ginger, and a dash of cayenne for more layers of flavor.

Sesame-Crusted Salmon with Lemon and Ginger

SERVES 4

For even cooking, purchase fillets that are about the same size and shape. If any of your fillets have a thin belly flap, fold it over to create a more even thickness.

- Salt
- 3/4 cup sesame seeds
- 4 (6- to 8-ounce) skinless salmon fillets
- 2 scallions, white parts minced, green parts sliced thin
- 1 tablespoon grated lemon zest plus 2 teaspoons juice
- 4 teaspoons tahini
- 2 teaspoons grated fresh ginger
- 1/8 teaspoon cayenne pepper
- 1 teaspoon vegetable oil

1. Adjust oven rack to middle position and heat oven to 325 degrees. Dissolve 5 tablespoons salt in 2 quarts water. Transfer 1 cup brine to bowl, stir in sesame seeds, and let stand at room temperature for 5 minutes. Submerge fillets in remaining brine and let stand at room temperature for 15 minutes.

2. Drain seeds and place in 12-inch nonstick skillet. Cook seeds over medium heat, stirring constantly, until golden brown, 2 to 4 minutes. Transfer seeds to pie plate and wipe out skillet with paper towels. Remove fillets from brine and pat dry.

3. Place scallion whites and lemon zest on cutting board and chop until whites and zest are finely minced and well combined. Transfer scallion-zest mixture to bowl and stir in lemon juice, tahini, ginger, cayenne, and 1/8 teaspoon salt.

4. Evenly distribute half of paste over bottoms (skinned sides) of fillets. Press coated sides of fillets in seeds and transfer, seed side down, to plate. Evenly distribute remaining paste over tops of fillets and coat with remaining seeds.

5. Heat oil in now-empty skillet over medium heat until shimmering. Place fillets in skillet, skinned side up, and reduce heat to medium-low. Cook until seeds begin to brown, 1 to 2 minutes. Remove skillet from heat and, using 2 spatulas, carefully flip fillets over. Transfer skillet to oven. Bake until center of fish is translucent when checked with tip of paring knife and registers 125 degrees, 10 to 15 minutes. Transfer to serving platter and let rest for 5 minutes. Sprinkle with scallion greens and serve.

Sesame-Crusted Salmon with Lime and Coriander

Substitute 4 teaspoons lime zest for lemon zest, lime juice for lemon juice, and 1/4 teaspoon ground coriander for cayenne.

Sesame-Crusted Salmon with Orange and Chili Powder

Substitute orange zest for lemon zest, orange juice for lemon juice, and 1/4 teaspoon chili powder for cayenne.

GLAZED SALMON

WHY THIS RECIPE WORKS: The traditional method for glazed salmon calls for broiling, but reaching into a broiling-hot oven every minute to baste the fish is a hassle and, even worse, the fillets often burn if your timing isn't spot-on. We wanted a foolproof method for glazed salmon that was succulent and pink throughout while keeping the slightly crusty, flavorful browned exterior typically achieved with broiling. First we found that reducing the temperature and gently baking the fish, instead of broiling, cooked the salmon perfectly. To rapidly caramelize the exterior of the fillets before they had a chance to toughen, we sprinkled the fillets with sugar and quickly pan-seared each side before transferring them to the oven. To ensure the glaze stayed put, we rubbed the fish with a mixture of cornstarch, brown sugar, and salt before searing.

Glazed Salmon

SERVES 4

To ensure uniform pieces of fish that cook at the same rate, buy a whole center-cut fillet and cut it into 4 pieces. Prepare the glaze before you cook the salmon. If your nonstick skillet isn't ovensafe, sear the salmon as directed in step 2, then transfer it to a rimmed baking sheet, glaze it, and bake as directed in step 3. You will need a 12-inch ovensafe nonstick skillet for this recipe.

- 1 teaspoon light brown sugar
- ½ teaspoon kosher salt
- ¼ teaspoon cornstarch
- 1 (1½- to 2-pound) skin-on salmon fillet, about 1½ inches thick
- Ground black pepper
- 1 teaspoon vegetable oil
- 1 recipe glaze (recipes follow)

1. Adjust an oven rack to the middle position and heat the oven to 300 degrees. Combine the brown sugar, salt, and cornstarch in a small bowl. Use a sharp knife to remove any whitish fat from the belly of the salmon and cut the fillet into 4 equal pieces. Pat the fillets dry with paper towels and season with pepper. Sprinkle the brown sugar mixture evenly over the top of the flesh side of the salmon, rubbing to distribute.

2. Heat the oil in a 12-inch ovensafe nonstick skillet over medium-high heat until just smoking. Place the salmon, flesh side down, in the skillet and cook until well browned, about 1 minute. Using tongs, carefully flip the salmon and cook on the skin side for 1 minute.

3. Remove the skillet from the heat and spoon the glaze evenly over the salmon fillets. Transfer the skillet to the oven and cook until the fillets register 125 degrees on an instant-read thermometer (for medium-rare) and are still translucent when cut into with a paring knife, 7 to 10 minutes. Transfer the fillets to a platter or individual plates and serve.

Pomegranate-Balsamic Glaze

MAKES ABOUT ½ CUP

This fruity, tangy glaze is a perfect match for rich salmon.

- 3 tablespoons light brown sugar
- 3 tablespoons pomegranate juice
- 2 tablespoons balsamic vinegar
- 1 tablespoon whole grain mustard
- 1 teaspoon cornstarch
- Pinch cayenne pepper

Whisk the ingredients together in a small saucepan. Bring to a boil over medium-high heat; simmer until thickened, about 1 minute. Remove from the heat and cover to keep warm.

Asian Barbecue Glaze

MAKES ABOUT ½ CUP

Toasted sesame oil gives this teriyaki-like glaze rich flavor.

- 2 tablespoons ketchup
- 2 tablespoons hoisin sauce
- 2 tablespoons rice vinegar
- 2 tablespoons packed light brown sugar
- 1 tablespoon soy sauce
- 1 tablespoon toasted sesame oil
- 2 teaspoons Asian chili-garlic sauce
- 1 teaspoon minced or grated fresh ginger

Whisk the ingredients together in a small saucepan. Bring to a boil over medium-high heat; simmer until thickened, about 3 minutes. Remove from the heat and cover to keep warm.

Orange-Miso Glaze

MAKES ABOUT ½ CUP

Miso is a fermented soybean paste that adds deep flavor to foods. We prefer milder, white miso here, rather than the strong-flavored red miso.

1 teaspoon grated zest plus ¼ cup juice from 1 orange
2 tablespoons white miso
1 tablespoon light brown sugar
1 tablespoon rice vinegar
1 tablespoon whole grain mustard
¾ teaspoon cornstarch
Pinch cayenne pepper

Whisk the ingredients together in a small saucepan. Bring to a boil over medium-high heat; simmer until thickened, about 1 minute. Remove from the heat and cover to keep warm.

Soy-Mustard Glaze

MAKES ABOUT ½ CUP

Mirin, a sweet Japanese rice wine, can be found in Asian markets and the international section of most supermarkets.

3 tablespoons light brown sugar
2 tablespoons soy sauce
2 tablespoons mirin (see note)
1 tablespoon sherry vinegar
1 tablespoon whole grain mustard
1 tablespoon water
1 teaspoon cornstarch
⅛ teaspoon red pepper flakes

Whisk the ingredients together in a small saucepan. Bring to a boil over medium-high heat; simmer until thickened, about 1 minute. Remove from the heat and cover to keep warm.

OVEN-ROASTED SALMON

WHY THIS RECIPE WORKS: Roasting a salmon fillet can create a brown exterior, but often at the risk of a dry, overcooked interior. The best roasted salmon should have moist, flavorful flesh inside, with a contrasting crisp texture on the outside.

To ensure that the salmon fillets would cook evenly, we cut a whole center-cut fillet into four pieces. We roasted the fish at a low temperature and achieved the buttery flesh we were after, but no browning—and the fillets were a little mushy from the rendered fat. Taking the opposite approach, we put the fish on a preheated baking sheet and started the oven at a high temperature to firm up and brown the exterior. This gave us a crust, but we still needed to get rid of the fat; cutting slits in the skin released the fat rendered by the high heat. Lowering the temperature as soon as we put the fish in the oven enabled it to cook through gradually after the initial blast of heat, so it didn't dry out. Now we had the contrast between moist interior and crisp brown exterior that we wanted. Salmon is rich and flavorful all on its own, but we devised a couple of easy no-cook relishes that can be served alongside for even more flavor and contrast.

Oven-Roasted Salmon

SERVES 4

To ensure uniform pieces of fish that cook at the same rate, buy a whole center-cut fillet and cut it into four pieces. If your knife is not sharp enough to easily cut through the skin, try a serrated knife. It is important to keep the skin on during cooking; remove it afterward if you choose not to serve it.

1 (1¾- to 2-pound) skin-on salmon fillet, about 1½ inches at the thickest part (see note)
2 teaspoons olive oil
Table salt and ground black pepper
1 recipe relish (recipes follow)

1. Adjust an oven rack to the lowest position, place a rimmed baking sheet on the rack, and heat the oven to 500 degrees. Remove any whitish fat from the belly of the fillet and cut it into four equal pieces. Make four or five shallow slashes about an inch apart along the skin side of each piece, being careful not to cut into the flesh.

2. Pat the salmon dry with paper towels. Rub the fillets evenly with the oil and season liberally with salt and pepper. Reduce the oven temperature to 275 degrees and remove the baking sheet. Carefully place the salmon, skin-side down, on the baking sheet. Roast until the thickest part of the fillets is still translucent when cut into with a paring knife (or the thickest part of the fillets registers 125 degrees on an instant-read thermometer), 9 to 13 minutes. Transfer the fillets to individual plates or a platter. Top with relish and serve.

Tangerine and Ginger Relish

MAKES ABOUT 1¼ CUPS

4 tangerines, rind and pith removed and segments cut into ½-inch pieces (about 1 cup)
1 scallion, sliced thin (about ¼ cup)
1½ teaspoons minced or grated fresh ginger
2 teaspoons juice from 1 lemon
2 teaspoons extra-virgin olive oil
Table salt and ground black pepper

1. Place the tangerines in a fine-mesh strainer set over a medium bowl and drain for 15 minutes.

2. Pour off all but 1 tablespoon tangerine juice from the bowl; whisk in the scallion, ginger, lemon juice, and oil. Stir in the tangerines and season with salt and pepper to taste.

Fresh Tomato Relish

MAKES ABOUT 1½ CUPS

¾ pound ripe tomatoes, cored, seeded, and cut into ¼-inch dice (about 1½ cups)
2 tablespoons chopped fresh basil leaves
1 small shallot, minced (about 1 tablespoon)
1 tablespoon extra-virgin olive oil

1 teaspoon red wine vinegar
1 small garlic clove, minced or pressed through a garlic press (about ½ teaspoon)
Table salt and ground black pepper

Combine the tomatoes, basil, shallot, oil, vinegar, and garlic in a medium bowl. Season with salt and pepper to taste.

Spicy Cucumber Relish

MAKES ABOUT 2 CUPS

1 medium cucumber, peeled, seeded, and cut into ¼-inch dice (about 2 cups)
2 tablespoons minced fresh mint leaves
1 small shallot, minced (about 1 tablespoon)
1 serrano chile, seeds and ribs removed, chile minced (about 1 tablespoon)
1–2 tablespoons juice from 1 lime
Table salt

Combine the cucumber, mint, shallot, chile, 1 tablespoon of the lime juice, and 1/4 teaspoon salt in a medium bowl. Let sit at room temperature until the flavors meld, about 15 minutes. Season with additional lime juice and salt to taste.

POACHED FISH FILLETS

WHY THIS RECIPE WORKS: Restaurant-style poached fish requires a potful of pricey olive oil and promises super-moist, delicately cooked fish. Using a small skillet and flipping the fish halfway through cooking allowed us to cut back to 3/4 cup of oil, which we employed to crisp flavorful garnishes and finally blended into a vinaigrette.

Poached Fish Fillets with Crispy Artichokes and Sherry-Tomato Vinaigrette

SERVES 4

Fillets of meaty white fish like cod, halibut, sea bass, or snapper work best in this recipe. Just make sure the fillets are at least 1 inch thick. A neutral oil such as canola can be substituted for the olive oil. The onion half in step 3 is used to displace the oil; a 4-ounce porcelain ramekin may be used instead. Serve with couscous or steamed white rice.

FISH

4 (6-ounce) skinless white fish fillets, 1 inch thick
Kosher salt
4 ounces frozen artichoke hearts, thawed, patted dry, and sliced in half lengthwise
1 tablespoon cornstarch
¾ cup olive oil
3 garlic cloves, minced
½ onion, peeled

VINAIGRETTE

4 ounces cherry tomatoes
½ small shallot, peeled
4 teaspoons sherry vinegar
Kosher salt and pepper

2 ounces cherry tomatoes, cut into ⅛-inch-thick rounds
1 tablespoon minced fresh parsley

1. FOR THE FISH: Adjust oven racks to middle and lower-middle positions and heat oven to 250 degrees. Pat fish dry with paper towels and season each fillet with 1/4 teaspoon salt. Let sit at room temperature for 20 minutes.

2. Meanwhile, toss artichokes with cornstarch in bowl to coat. Heat 1/2 cup oil in 10-inch nonstick ovensafe skillet over medium heat until shimmering. Shake excess cornstarch from artichokes and add to skillet; cook, stirring occasionally, until crisp and golden, 2 to 4 minutes. Add garlic and continue to cook until garlic is golden, 30 to 60 seconds. Strain oil through fine-mesh strainer into bowl. Transfer artichokes and garlic to ovensafe paper towel–lined plate and season with salt. Do not wash strainer.

3. Return strained oil to skillet and add remaining 1/4 cup oil. Place onion half in center of pan. Let oil cool until it registers about 180 degrees, 5 to 8 minutes. Arrange fish fillets, skinned side up, around onion (oil should come roughly halfway up fillets). Spoon a little oil over each fillet, cover skillet, transfer to middle oven rack, and cook for 15 minutes.

4. Remove skillet from oven (skillet handle will be hot). Using 2 spatulas, carefully flip fillets. Cover skillet, return to middle rack, and place plate with artichokes and garlic on lower-middle rack. Continue to cook fish until it registers 130 to 135 degrees, 9 to 14 minutes longer. Gently transfer fish to serving platter, reserving 1/2 cup oil, and tent fish loosely with aluminum foil. Turn off oven, leaving plate of artichokes in oven.

5. FOR THE VINAIGRETTE: Process cherry tomatoes, shallot, vinegar, ¾ teaspoon salt, and ½ teaspoon pepper with reserved ½ cup fish cooking oil in blender until smooth, 1 to 2 minutes. Add any accumulated fish juices from platter, season with salt to taste, and blend for 10 seconds. Strain sauce through fine-mesh strainer; discard solids.

6. To serve, pour vinaigrette around fish. Garnish each fillet with warmed crisped artichokes and garlic, tomato rounds, and parsley. Serve immediately.

Poached Fish Fillets with Jalapeño Vinaigrette

To make this dish spicier, add some of the reserved chile seeds to the vinaigrette in step 5. Serve with steamed white rice.

For fish, substitute 2 jalapeño chiles, stemmed, seeded, and cut into ⅛-inch-thick rings, for artichoke hearts and reduce cornstarch to 2 teaspoons. For vinaigrette, process 4 jalapeños, stemmed, halved, and seeded (seeds reserved); ½ small shallot, peeled; 6 sprigs fresh cilantro; 8 teaspoons lime juice; and ½ teaspoon kosher salt with ½ cup reserved fish cooking oil as directed in step 5. Garnish fish with 2 tablespoons fresh cilantro leaves and ½ avocado, cut into ¼-inch pieces.

Poached Fish Fillets with Crispy Scallions and Miso-Ginger Vinaigrette

For fish, substitute 8 scallion whites, sliced ¼ inch thick, for artichoke hearts; omit garlic; and reduce cornstarch to 2 teaspoons. For vinaigrette, process 6 scallion greens, 8 teaspoons lime juice, 2 tablespoons mirin, 4 teaspoons white miso paste, 2 teaspoons minced ginger, and ½ teaspoon sugar with ½ cup reserved fish cooking oil as directed in step 5. Garnish fish with 2 thinly sliced scallion greens and 2 halved and thinly sliced radishes.

PAN-SEARED TUNA STEAKS

WHY THIS RECIPE WORKS: Moist and rare in the middle with a seared crust, pan-seared tuna is a popular entrée in restaurants. This dish is so simple that we thought it would be easy to make at home, and set out to determine the best method.

Starting with high-quality tuna—sushi grade if possible—is paramount; we prefer the flavor of yellowfin. A thickness of at least an inch is necessary for the center of the tuna to be rare while the exterior browns. Before searing the tuna in a nonstick skillet, we rubbed the steaks with oil, then coated them with sesame seeds; the oil helped the seeds stick to the fish. The sesame seeds browned in the skillet and formed a beautiful, nutty-tasting crust. We learned that tuna, like beef, will continue to cook from residual heat when removed from the stove, so when the interior of the tuna was near the desired degree of doneness (about 110 degrees on an instant-read thermometer), we transferred it to a platter.

BEHIND THE SCENES

IS THAT PAN HOT YET? SHIMMER AND SMOKE

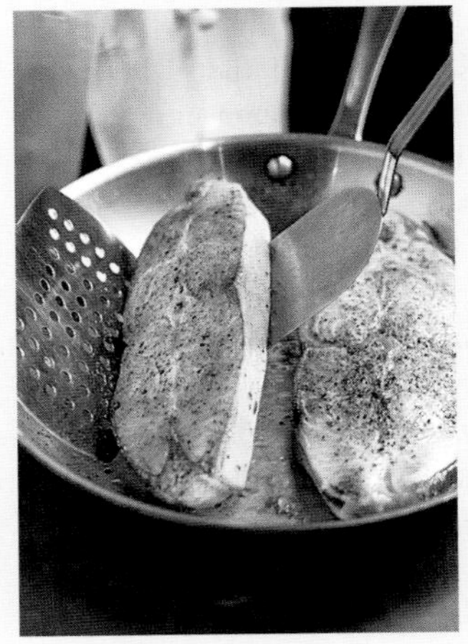

Pan-searing and sautéing both require you to heat the oil in the skillet to a certain heat level. But how do you know when the pan is hot enough? We find visual cues helpful and offer them in our recipes, as follows: When searing thick cuts of meat like a roast, steak, bone-in chop, or thick fish fillet, you want the pan *very* hot. Searing over high heat will give your food a well-browned crust. Look for wisps of smoke rising from the oil—this means the pan is ripping hot and ready. By contrast, when sautéing thin, delicate cuts of meat like cutlets, thin fish fillets, or vegetables such as onions, you want the oil to be just moderately hot. You'll know the pan is ready when the oil shimmers. Why does it make a difference? If you put a thin fillet into a smoking hot pan, the food will do more than sear—it will cook through before you've had time to flip it.

Pan-Seared Sesame-Crusted Tuna Steaks

SERVES 4

If you plan to serve the fish with the sauce or salsa (recipes follow), prepare it before cooking the fish. Most members of the test kitchen staff prefer their tuna steaks rare to medium-rare; the cooking times given in this recipe are for tuna steaks cooked to these two degrees of doneness. For tuna steaks cooked medium, observe the timing for medium-rare, then tent the steaks loosely with foil for 5 minutes before slicing. If you prefer tuna steaks cooked so rare that they are still cold in the center, try to purchase steaks that are 1½ inches thick and cook them according to the timing below for rare steaks. Bear in mind, though, that the cooking times below are estimates; check for doneness by nicking the fish with a paring knife. To cook only two steaks, use half as many sesame seeds, reduce the amount of oil to 2 teaspoons both on the fish and in the pan, use a 10-inch nonstick skillet, and follow the same cooking times.

- ¾ cup sesame seeds
- 4 (8-ounce) tuna steaks, preferably yellowfin, about 1 inch thick (see note)
- 2 tablespoons vegetable oil
- Table salt and ground black pepper
- 1 recipe sauce or salsa (recipes follow)

1. Spread the sesame seeds in a shallow baking dish or pie plate. Pat the tuna steaks dry with a paper towel; use 1 tablespoon of the oil to rub both sides of the steaks, then sprinkle them with salt and pepper. Press both sides of each steak in the sesame seeds to coat.

2. Heat the remaining 1 tablespoon oil in a 12-inch nonstick skillet over high heat until just beginning to smoke and swirl to coat the pan. Add the tuna steaks and cook 30 seconds without moving the steaks. Reduce the heat to medium-high and continue to cook until the seeds are golden brown, about 1½ minutes. Using tongs, flip the tuna steaks carefully and cook, without moving them, until golden brown on the second side and the centers register 110 degrees on an instant-read thermometer for rare (about 1½ minutes), or 120 degrees for medium-rare (about 3 minutes). Serve with Ginger-Soy Sauce with Scallions or Avocado-Orange Salsa.

Ginger-Soy Sauce with Scallions

MAKES ABOUT 1 CUP

If available, serve pickled ginger and wasabi, passed separately, with the tuna and this sauce.

- ¼ cup soy sauce
- ¼ cup rice vinegar
- ¼ cup water
- 1 medium scallion, sliced thin
- 2½ teaspoons sugar
- 2 teaspoons minced or grated fresh ginger
- 1½ teaspoons toasted sesame oil
- ½ teaspoon red pepper flakes

Combine all the ingredients in a small bowl, stirring to dissolve the sugar.

Avocado-Orange Salsa

MAKES ABOUT 1 CUP

To keep the avocado from discoloring, prepare this salsa just before you cook the tuna steaks.

- 1 large orange, cut into segments (see page 248)
- 1 ripe avocado, pitted, peeled, and diced medium (see page 414)
- 2 tablespoons minced red onion
- 2 tablespoons minced fresh cilantro leaves
- 4 teaspoons juice from 1 to 2 limes
- 1 small jalapeño chile, stemmed, seeded, and minced
- Table salt

Combine all the ingredients, including salt to taste, in a small nonreactive bowl.

PAN-ROASTED HALIBUT

WHY THIS RECIPE WORKS: Chefs often choose to braise halibut instead of pan-roasting or sautéing because this moist-heat cooking technique keeps the fish from drying out. The problem is that braising doesn't allow for browning, therefore producing a fish that the test kitchen considers bland-tasting. We didn't want to make any compromises on either texture or flavor, so we set out to develop a technique for pan-roasting halibut that would produce perfectly cooked, moist, and tender fish.

Halibut is most frequently sold as steaks, but there is quite a bit of range in size; to ensure that they cooked at the same rate, we chose steaks that were as close in size to each other as possible. We knew we could get a crust on the fish by pan-searing or oven-roasting, but neither technique proved satisfactory. A combination of the two proved best: browning on the stovetop and roasting in the oven. To be sure the steaks wouldn't overcook, we seared them on one side in a piping-hot skillet, then turned them over before placing them into the oven to finish cooking through. When they were done, the steaks were browned but still moist inside. To complement the lean fish, we paired the halibut with a rich flavored butter.

Pan-Roasted Halibut Steaks

SERVES 4 TO 6

If you plan to serve the fish with the flavored butter or vinaigrette (recipes follow), prepare it before cooking the fish. Even well-dried fish can cause the hot oil in the pan to splatter. You can minimize splattering by laying the halibut steaks in the pan gently and putting the edge closest to you in the pan first so that the far edge falls away from you.

NOTES FROM THE TEST KITCHEN

TRIMMING AND SERVING FULL HALIBUT STEAKS

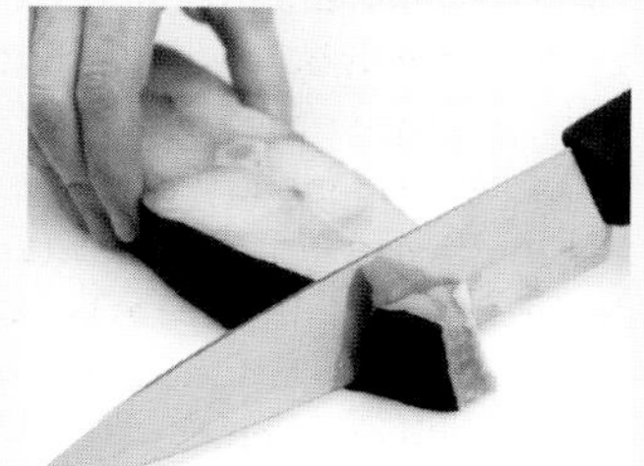

BEFORE COOKING: Cut off the cartilage at each end of the steaks to ensure that they will fit neatly in the pan and diminish the likelihood that the small bones located there will wind up on your dinner plate.

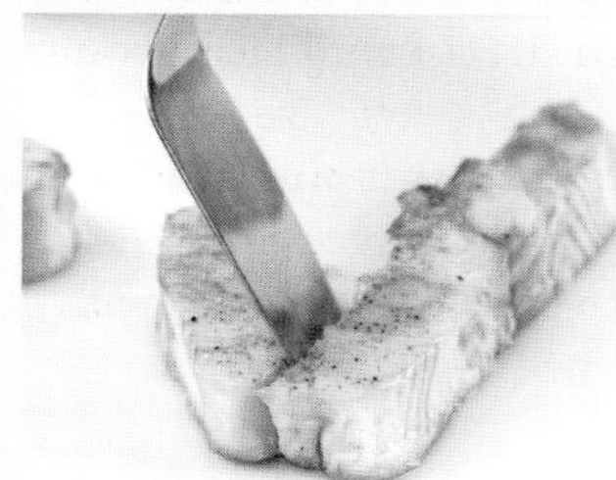

BEFORE SERVING: Remove the skin from the cooked steaks and separate the quadrants of meat from the bone by slipping a spatula gently between them.

2 tablespoons olive oil
2 (full) halibut steaks, about 1¼ inches thick and 10 to 12 inches long (about 2½ pounds total), gently rinsed, dried well with paper towels, and trimmed of cartilage at both ends (see photo on page 235)
Table salt and ground black pepper
1 recipe flavored butter or vinaigrette (recipes follow)

1. Adjust an oven rack to the middle position and heat the oven to 425 degrees. When the oven reaches 425 degrees, heat the oil in a 12-inch ovensafe skillet over high heat until the oil just begins to smoke.

2. Meanwhile, sprinkle both sides of the halibut steaks generously with salt and pepper. Reduce the heat to medium-high and swirl the oil in the pan to distribute; carefully lay the steaks in the pan and sear, without moving them, until spotty brown, about 4 minutes. (If the steaks are thinner than 1¼ inches, check browning at 3½ minutes; thicker steaks of 1½ inches may require extra time, so check at 4½ minutes.) Off the heat, flip the steaks over in the pan using two thin-bladed metal spatulas.

3. Transfer the skillet to the oven and roast until an instant-read thermometer inserted into the steaks reads 140 degrees and the fish flakes loosen and the flesh is opaque when checked with the tip of a paring knife, about 9 minutes (thicker steaks may take up to 10 minutes). Remove the skillet from the oven. Remove the skin from the cooked steaks and separate each quadrant of meat from the bones by slipping a spatula or knife gently between them (see photo). Transfer the fish to a warm platter and serve with the flavored butter or vinaigrette.

Chipotle-Garlic Butter with Lime and Cilantro

MAKES ABOUT ¼ CUP

4 tablespoons (½ stick) unsalted butter, softened
1 medium chipotle chile in adobo sauce, seeded and minced, plus 1 teaspoon adobo sauce
2 teaspoons minced fresh cilantro leaves
1 medium garlic clove, minced or pressed through a garlic press (about 1 teaspoon)
1 teaspoon honey
1 teaspoon grated zest from 1 lime
½ teaspoon table salt

Beat the butter with a fork until light and fluffy. Stir in the remaining ingredients until thoroughly combined. Dollop a portion of the butter over the pieces of hot cooked fish and allow the butter to melt. Serve immediately.

Chunky Cherry Tomato–Basil Vinaigrette

MAKES ABOUT 1½ CUPS

½ pint cherry or grape tomatoes, each tomato quartered (about 1 cup)
¼ teaspoon table salt
¼ teaspoon ground black pepper
2 medium shallots, minced (about 6 tablespoons)
6 tablespoons extra-virgin olive oil
3 tablespoons juice from 1 lemon
2 tablespoons minced fresh basil leaves

Mix the tomatoes with the salt and pepper in a medium bowl; let stand until juicy and seasoned, about 10 minutes. Whisk the shallots, oil, lemon juice, and basil together in a small mixing bowl, pour the vinaigrette over the tomatoes, and toss to combine. Pour over the pieces of hot cooked fish and serve immediately.

BRAISED HALIBUT WITH LEEKS AND MUSTARD

WHY THIS RECIPE WORKS: Braising is a technique usually reserved for tough cuts of meat, but the gentle, moist-heat cooking method also works wonders on fish. Halibut's dense flesh made it an easy fillet to manipulate and its clean, sweet flavor would pair well with a simple wine sauce. We began by gently cooking just one side of the fillets in butter in a skillet, then removing the fish to establish the braising liquid. We cooked sliced leeks in Dijon and their exuded moisture added to the thin sauce. Once the leeks had softened, we added some dry white wine, brought it to a simmer, and placed the halibut atop the vegetables with the uncooked side facing down. This arrangement allowed the parcooked side to steam while the rest of the fillet cooked through to perfection. To finish the sauce, we transferred the cooked fish and vegetables to a serving platter and let the wine sauce reduce, adding lemon juice for a burst of bright acidity.

Braised Halibut with Leeks and Mustard

SERVES 4

We prefer to prepare this recipe with halibut, but a similar firm-fleshed white fish such as striped bass or sea bass that is between ¾ and 1 inch thick can be substituted. To ensure that your fish cooks evenly, purchase fillets that are similarly shaped and uniformly thick.

4 (6- to 8-ounce) skinless halibut fillets, ¾ to 1 inch thick
Salt and pepper
6 tablespoons unsalted butter
1 pound leeks, white and light green parts only, halved lengthwise, sliced thin, and washed thoroughly
1 teaspoon Dijon mustard
¾ cup dry white wine
1 teaspoon lemon juice, plus lemon wedges for serving
1 tablespoon minced fresh parsley

1. Sprinkle fish with ½ teaspoon salt. Melt butter in 12-inch skillet over low heat. Place fish in skillet, skinned side up, increase heat to medium, and cook, shaking pan occasionally, until butter begins to brown (fish should not brown), 3 to 4 minutes. Using spatula, carefully transfer fish to large plate, raw side down.

2. Add leeks, mustard, and ½ teaspoon salt to skillet and cook, stirring frequently, until leeks begin to soften, 2 to 4 minutes. Add wine and bring to gentle simmer. Place fish, raw side down, on top of leeks. Cover skillet and cook, adjusting heat to maintain gentle simmer, until fish registers 135 to 140 degrees, 10 to 14 minutes. Remove skillet from heat and, using 2 spatulas, transfer fish and leeks to serving platter or individual plates. Tent loosely with aluminum foil.

3. Return skillet to high heat and simmer briskly until sauce is thickened, 2 to 3 minutes. Remove pan from heat, stir in lemon juice, and season with salt and pepper to taste. Spoon sauce over fish and sprinkle with parsley. Serve immediately with lemon wedges.

Braised Halibut with Carrots and Coriander

Substitute 1 pound carrots, peeled and shaved with vegetable peeler lengthwise into ribbons, and 4 shallots, halved and sliced thin, for leeks. Substitute ½ teaspoon ground coriander seed for Dijon mustard. Increase lemon juice to 1½ teaspoons and substitute cilantro for parsley.

PAN-ROASTED FISH FILLETS

WHY THIS RECIPE WORKS: Pan-roasted fish seems like a simple dish, but in reality it is usually only well executed by practiced chefs. At home, the dish often results in dry, overbaked fillets. We set out to develop a foolproof recipe for producing succulent, well-browned fillets.

From an initial round of testing, we knew we needed thick fillets; skinnier pieces end up overcooked by the time they achieved a serious sear. We then turned to a common restaurant method to cook the fish: Sear the fillet in a hot pan, flip, then transfer it to a hot oven to finish cooking. The technique was sound, but to brown the fish quickly before the hot pan had a chance to dry out the fish's exterior we turned to a sprinkling of sugar. The idea is that sugar commingles with exuded juices from the fish, accelerating browning and giving the fish a rich color and deep flavor that's anything but sweet. We dusted a few fillets with a touch of granulated sugar and placed them in a hot skillet. A well-browned crust formed almost immediately, leaving no time for the interior to dry out. And after a short stay in the oven to finish cooking through, the fish emerged well-browned, tender and moist, and best of all, not one taster detected any out-of-place sweetness.

Pan-Roasted Thick-Cut Fish Fillets

SERVES 4

Thick white fish fillets with a meaty texture, like halibut, cod, sea bass, or red snapper, work best in this recipe. Because most fish fillets differ in thickness, some pieces may finish cooking before others—be sure to immediately remove any fillet that reaches 135 degrees. You will need an ovensafe nonstick skillet for this recipe. If you can't find skinless fillets, see page 229 for information on skinning fillets. Serve with lemon wedges or one of the relishes on page 232–233.

- 4 (6 to 8-ounce) skinless white fish fillets, 1 to 1½ inches thick (see note)
- Table salt and ground black pepper
- ½ teaspoon sugar
- 1 tablespoon vegetable oil
- Lemon wedges or relish (see note), for serving

Adjust an oven rack to the middle position and heat the oven to 425 degrees. Dry the fish thoroughly with paper towels and season with salt and pepper. Sprinkle ⅛ teaspoon sugar evenly over one side of each fillet. Heat the oil in a 12-inch ovensafe nonstick skillet over high heat until smoking. Place the fillets in the skillet, sugared side down, and press down lightly to ensure even contact with the pan. Cook until browned, 1 to 1½ minutes. Using two spatulas, flip the fillets and transfer the skillet to the oven. Roast the fillets until the centers are just opaque and the fish registers 135 degrees on an instant-read thermometer, 7 to 10 minutes. Immediately transfer the fish to individual plates and serve with lemon wedges or relish.

BAKED SOLE FILLETS

WHY THIS RECIPE WORKS: We wanted a fuss-free, foolproof sole preparation that was suitable for a weeknight dinner yet impressive and elegant enough to serve to company. We found that rolling the fillets into compact bundles eased the transport from baking dish to plate and covering the baking dish with foil protected the delicate fish from the drying heat of the oven. To ramp up the fillets' mild flavor, we brushed them with Dijon mustard; seasoned them with salt, pepper, fresh herbs, and lemon zest; and drizzled them with melted butter and garlic. Then we rolled them up, drizzled them with more butter, and baked them. For texture, we added a mixture of herbs, butter, and panko bread crumbs to the sole at two intervals. We removed the foil before the fish was done cooking, basted the fillets with pan juices, topped them with most of the bread-crumb mixture, and then returned them to the oven uncovered. Just before serving, we sprinkled the remaining crumbs over the fillets.

Baked Sole Fillets with Herbs and Bread Crumbs

SERVES 6

Try to purchase fillets of similar size. If using smaller fillets (about 3 ounces each), serve 2 fillets per person and reduce the baking time in step 3 to 20 minutes. We strongly advise against using frozen fish in this recipe. Freezing can undermine the texture of the fish, making it hard to roll. Fresh basil or dill can be used in place of the tarragon.

- 3 tablespoons minced fresh parsley leaves
- 3 tablespoons minced fresh chives
- 1 tablespoon minced fresh tarragon leaves
- 1 teaspoon grated zest from 1 lemon
- 5 tablespoons unsalted butter, cut into 5 pieces
- 2 medium garlic cloves, minced or pressed through a garlic press (about 2 teaspoons)
- 6 (6-ounce) boneless, skinless sole or flounder fillets
- Table salt and ground black pepper
- 1 tablespoon Dijon mustard
- ⅔ cup panko bread crumbs
- Lemon wedges, for serving

1. Adjust an oven rack to the middle position and heat the oven to 325 degrees. Combine the parsley, chives, and tarragon in a small bowl. Reserve 1 tablespoon herb mixture; stir the lemon zest into the remaining herb mixture.

2. Heat 4 tablespoons of the butter in an 8-inch skillet over medium heat until just melted. Add half of the garlic and cook, stirring frequently, until fragrant, 1 to 2 minutes. Remove from the heat and set aside.

3. Pat the fillets dry with paper towels and season both sides with salt and pepper. Arrange the fillets, skinned side up, with the tail end pointing away from you. Spread ½ teaspoon mustard on each fillet, sprinkle each evenly with about 1 tablespoon of the herb–lemon zest mixture, and drizzle each with about 1½ teaspoons of the garlic butter. Tightly roll the fillets from the thick end to form cylinders. Set the fillets, seam side down, in a 13 by 9-inch baking dish. Drizzle the remaining garlic butter over the fillets, cover the baking dish with aluminum foil, and bake for 25 minutes. Wipe out the skillet but do not wash.

4. While the fillets are baking, melt the remaining 1 tablespoon butter in the now-empty skillet over medium heat. Add the panko and cook, stirring frequently, until the crumbs are deep golden brown, 5 to 8 minutes. Reduce the heat to low, add the remaining garlic, and cook, stirring constantly, until the garlic is fragrant and evenly distributed in the crumbs, about 1 minute. Transfer to a small bowl, stir in ¼ teaspoon salt, and season with pepper to taste. Let cool, then stir in the reserved 1 tablespoon herb mixture.

5. After the fillets have baked for 25 minutes, remove the baking dish from oven. Baste the fillets with melted garlic butter from the baking dish, sprinkle with all but 3 tablespoons of the bread crumbs, and continue to bake, uncovered, until the fillets register 135 degrees on an instant-read thermometer, 6 to 10 minutes longer. Using a thin metal spatula, transfer the fillets to plates, sprinkle with the remaining bread crumbs, and serve with the lemon wedges.

PAN-SEARED SCALLOPS

WHY THIS RECIPE WORKS: Producing, crisp-crusted restaurant-style scallops means overcoming two obstacles: chemically treated scallops and weak stovetops. We wanted to achieve superior pan-seared scallops that had a perfectly brown crust and no hint of off-flavors. We decided to work with wet scallops (those that are chemically treated with STP, a solution of water and sodium tripolyphosphate, to increase shelf life and retain moisture) first. If we could develop a good recipe for finicky wet scallops, it would surely work with premium dry (untreated) scallops. We found that waiting to add the scallops to the skillet until the oil was beginning to smoke, cooking the scallops in two batches instead of one, and switching to a nonstick skillet (so that the browned bits formed a crust on the meat instead of sticking to the skillet) were all steps in the right direction. But it wasn't until we tried a common restaurant technique—butter basting—that our scallops really improved. We seared the scallops in oil on one side and added butter to the skillet after flipping them. (Butter contains milk proteins and sugars that brown rapidly when heated.) We then used a large spoon to ladle the foaming butter over the scallops. Waiting to add the butter ensured that it had just enough time to work its browning magic on the scallops, but not enough time to burn.

Next we addressed the lingering flavor of STP. Unable to rinse it away, we decided to mask it by soaking the scallops in a saltwater brine containing lemon juice. For dry scallops, we simply skipped the soaking step and proceeded with the recipe. It produced scallops that rivaled those made on a powerful restaurant range, with golden brown exteriors and juicy and tender interiors.

Pan-Seared Scallops

SERVES 4

We strongly recommend purchasing dry scallops (those without chemical additives). If you can only find wet scallops, soak them in a solution of 1 quart cold water, ¼ cup lemon juice, and 2 tablespoons table salt for 30 minutes before proceeding with step 1, and season the scallops with pepper only in step 2. Prepare the sauce (if serving) while the scallops dry (between steps 1 and 2) and keep it warm while cooking them.

- 1½ pounds dry sea scallops (about 16 scallops), tendons removed (see note)
- Table salt and ground black pepper
- 2 tablespoons vegetable oil
- 2 tablespoons unsalted butter
- Lemon wedges or Lemon Browned Butter Sauce (recipe follows)

1. Place the scallops on a rimmed baking sheet lined with a clean kitchen towel. Place a second clean kitchen towel on top of the scallops and press gently on the towel to blot the liquid. Let the scallops sit at room temperature for 10 minutes while the towels absorb the moisture.

2. Remove the second towel and sprinkle the scallops on both sides with salt and pepper. Heat 1 tablespoon of the oil in a 12-inch nonstick skillet over high heat until just smoking. Add half of the scallops in a single layer, flat side down, and cook, without moving, until well browned, 1½ to 2 minutes.

3. Add 1 tablespoon of the butter to the skillet. Using tongs, flip the scallops and continue to cook, using a large spoon to baste the scallops with the melted butter, tilting the skillet so the butter runs to one side, until the sides of the scallops are firm and the centers are opaque, 30 to 90 seconds longer (remove the smaller scallops from the pan as they finish cooking). Transfer the scallops to a large plate and tent loosely with foil. Wipe out the skillet with a wad of paper towels and repeat with the remaining 1 tablespoon oil, remaining scallops, and remaining 1 tablespoon butter. Serve immediately with lemon wedges or sauce.

NOTES FROM THE TEST KITCHEN

ARE YOUR SCALLOPS WET OR DRY?

If you are unsure whether your scallops are wet (treated with chemicals) or dry (untreated), conduct this quick test: Place 1 scallop on a paper towel–lined, microwave-safe plate and microwave on high power for 15 seconds. If the scallop is dry, it will exude very little water. If it is wet, there will be a sizable ring of moisture on the paper towel. (The microwaved scallop can be cooked as is.)

PREPPING SCALLOPS

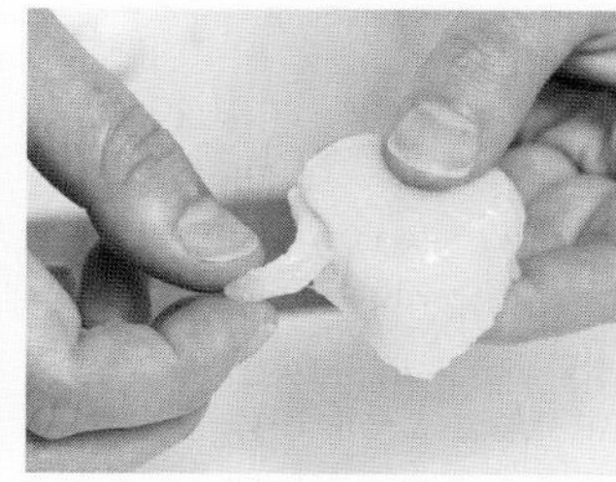

The small, crescent-shaped muscle that is sometimes attached to the scallop will be incredibly tough when cooked. Use your fingers to peel this muscle away from the sides of each scallop before cooking.

Lemon Browned Butter Sauce

MAKES ABOUT ¼ CUP

- 4 tablespoons (½ stick) unsalted butter, cut into 4 pieces
- 1 small shallot, minced (about 1½ tablespoons)
- 1 tablespoon minced fresh parsley leaves
- ½ teaspoon minced fresh thyme leaves
- 2 teaspoons juice from 1 lemon
- Table salt and ground black pepper

Heat the butter in a small heavy-bottomed saucepan over medium heat and cook, swirling the pan constantly, until the butter turns dark golden brown and has a nutty aroma, 4 to 5 minutes. Add the shallot and cook until fragrant, about 30 seconds. Remove the pan from the heat and stir in the parsley, thyme, and lemon juice. Season with salt and pepper to taste. Cover to keep warm.

PAN-SEARED SHRIMP

WHY THIS RECIPE WORKS: A good recipe for pan-seared shrimp is hard to find. Of the handful of recipes we uncovered, the majority resulted in shrimp that were either dry and flavorless or pale, tough, and gummy. We wanted shrimp that were well caramelized but still moist, briny, and tender.

We peeled the shrimp first and tried using a brine to add moisture, but found that it inhibited browning. Instead, we seasoned the shrimp with salt, pepper, and sugar, which brought out their natural sweetness and aided in browning. We cooked the shrimp in batches in a large, piping-hot skillet and then paired them with thick, glaze-like sauces with assertive ingredients and plenty of acidity as a foil for the shrimp's richness.

Pan-Seared Shrimp

SERVES 4

This recipe can also be prepared with large shrimp (31 to 40 per pound); the cooking time will be slightly shorter. Either a nonstick or a traditional skillet will work for this recipe, but a nonstick simplifies cleanup.

- 2 tablespoons vegetable oil
- 1½ pounds extra-large shrimp (21 to 25 per pound), peeled and deveined (see page 240; see note)
- ¼ teaspoon table salt
- ¼ teaspoon ground black pepper
- ⅛ teaspoon sugar

Heat 1 tablespoon of the oil in a 12-inch skillet over high heat until smoking. Meanwhile, toss the shrimp, salt, pepper, and sugar in a medium bowl. Add half of the shrimp to the pan in a single layer and cook until spotty brown and the edges turn pink, about 1 minute. Remove the pan from the heat. Using tongs, flip each shrimp and let stand until all but the very center is opaque, about 30 seconds. Transfer the shrimp to a large plate. Repeat with the remaining 1 tablespoon oil and the remaining shrimp. After the second batch has stood off the heat, return the first batch to the skillet and toss to combine. Cover the skillet and let stand until the shrimp are cooked through, 1 to 2 minutes. Serve immediately.

Pan-Seared Shrimp with Garlic-Lemon Butter

Beat 3 tablespoons softened unsalted butter with a fork in a small bowl until light and fluffy. Stir in 1 medium garlic clove, minced or pressed through a garlic press, 1 tablespoon juice from 1 lemon, 2 tablespoons chopped fresh parsley leaves, and 1/8 teaspoon salt until combined. Follow the recipe for Pan-Seared Shrimp, adding the flavored butter when returning the first batch of shrimp to the skillet. Serve with lemon wedges, if desired.

Pan-Seared Shrimp with Ginger-Hoisin Glaze

Stir 2 tablespoons hoisin sauce, 1 tablespoon rice vinegar, 1½ teaspoons soy sauce, 2 teaspoons minced or grated fresh ginger, 2 teaspoons water, and 2 scallions, sliced thin, together in a small bowl. Follow the recipe for Pan-Seared Shrimp, substituting an equal amount of red pepper flakes for the black pepper and adding the hoisin mixture when returning the first batch of shrimp to the skillet.

Pan-Seared Shrimp with Chipotle-Lime Glaze

Stir 1 chipotle chile in adobo, minced, 2 teaspoons adobo sauce, 4 teaspoons brown sugar, 2 tablespoons juice from 1 lime, and 2 tablespoons chopped fresh cilantro leaves together in a small bowl. Follow the recipe for Pan-Seared Shrimp, adding the chipotle mixture when returning the first batch of shrimp to the skillet.

NOTES FROM THE TEST KITCHEN

DEVEINING SHRIMP

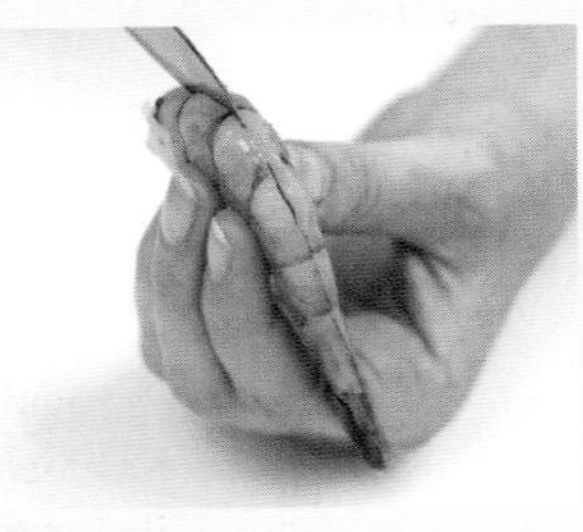

1. After removing the shell, use a paring knife to make a shallow cut along the back of the shrimp so that the vein is exposed.

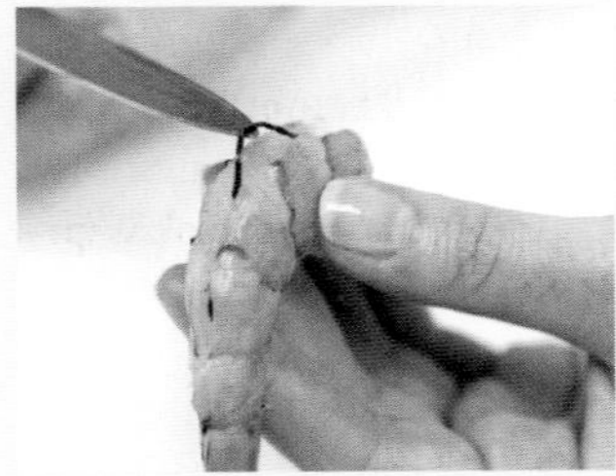

2. Use the tip of the knife to lift the vein out of the shrimp. Discard the vein by wiping the blade against a paper towel.

CRISPY SALT AND PEPPER SHRIMP

WHY THIS RECIPE WORKS: The shrimp in this Chinese restaurant specialty are noted for their spicy heat and shells so crisp they're good enough to eat. Smaller shrimp are younger and have thinner shells, so we brought home a pound of 31- to 40-count shrimp and tossed them in rice wine and salt to infuse them with well-seasoned, savory flavor. A blend of black peppercorns and lively Sichuan peppercorns, ground together, combined with sugar and cayenne established the dish's flavor profile. Coating the shrimp with this blend and some cornstarch fused the flavors to the meat while also drawing out excess moisture for maximum crisping. We fried the shrimp in batches to prevent the oil's heat from flagging. Fried jalapeño slices would add extra heat at serving, and we reinforced the dish's big flavors by reserving some of the spicy frying oil and combining it with the spice blend, minced garlic, and grated fresh ginger. We heated this seasoned oil until it browned and tossed the cooked shrimp in it, scattering in sliced scallions for a dose of freshness.

Crispy Salt and Pepper Shrimp

SERVES 4 TO 6

In this recipe the shrimp are meant to be eaten shell and all. To ensure that the shells fry up crisp, avoid using shrimp that are overly large or jumbo. We prefer 31- to 40-count shrimp, but 26- to 30-count may be substituted. Serve with steamed rice.

- 1½ pounds shell-on shrimp (31 to 40 per pound)
- 2 tablespoons Chinese rice wine or dry sherry
- Kosher salt
- 2½ teaspoons black peppercorns
- 2 teaspoons Sichuan peppercorns
- 2 teaspoons sugar
- ¼ teaspoon cayenne pepper

- 4 cups vegetable oil
- 5 tablespoons cornstarch
- 2 jalapeño chiles, stemmed, seeded, and sliced into ⅛-inch-thick rings
- 3 garlic cloves, minced
- 1 tablespoon grated fresh ginger
- 2 scallions, sliced thin on bias
- ¼ head iceberg lettuce, shredded (1½ cups)

1. Adjust oven rack to upper-middle position and heat oven to 225 degrees. Toss shrimp, rice wine, and 1 teaspoon salt together in large bowl and set aside for 10 to 15 minutes.

2. Grind black peppercorns and Sichuan peppercorns in spice grinder or mortar and pestle until coarsely ground. Transfer peppercorns to small bowl and stir in sugar and cayenne.

3. Heat oil in large Dutch oven over medium heat until oil registers 385 degrees. While oil is heating, drain shrimp and pat dry with paper towels. Transfer shrimp to bowl, add 3 tablespoons cornstarch and 1 tablespoon peppercorn mixture, and toss until well combined.

4. Carefully add one-third of shrimp to oil and fry, stirring occasionally to keep shrimp from sticking together, until light brown, 2 to 3 minutes. Using wire skimmer or slotted spoon, transfer shrimp to paper towel–lined plate. Once paper towels absorb any excess oil, transfer shrimp to wire rack set in rimmed baking sheet and place in oven. Return oil to 385 degrees and repeat in 2 more batches, tossing each batch thoroughly with coating mixture before frying.

5. Toss jalapeño rings and remaining 2 tablespoons cornstarch in medium bowl. Shaking off excess cornstarch, carefully add jalapeño rings to oil and fry until crispy, 1 to 2 minutes. Using wire skimmer or slotted spoon, transfer jalapeño rings to paper towel–lined plate. After frying, reserve 2 tablespoons frying oil.

6. Heat reserved oil in 12-inch skillet over medium-high heat until shimmering. Add garlic, ginger, and remaining peppercorn mixture and cook, stirring occasionally, until mixture is fragrant and just beginning to brown, about 45 seconds. Add shrimp, scallions, and ½ teaspoon salt and toss to coat. Line platter with lettuce. Transfer shrimp to platter, sprinkle with jalapeño rings, and serve immediately.

GARLICKY SHRIMP WITH BREAD CRUMBS

WHY THIS RECIPE WORKS: Just about every all-purpose cookbook includes a recipe for a casserole of shrimp in a sherry-garlic sauce topped with bread crumbs, but the ones we tried produced rubbery shrimp and gluey toppings. We wanted all the potent flavors and contrasting textures that the name of this dish promises—tender, moist shrimp infused with garlic and blanketed with crisp, buttery bread crumbs.

Most recipes call for cooking the shrimp twice, first poaching them on the stovetop and then baking them in the casserole dish. No wonder they're usually overdone! Our experiments with skipping the poaching weren't very successful—the shrimp were just plain bland—so we abandoned the oven altogether and decided to make the entire dish in a skillet on top of the stove. After searing the shrimp on one side, sprinkled with a pinch of sugar to promote browning, we removed them to build the sauce; we would add the shrimp back at the end to heat through and finish cooking. For the sauce, we started with garlic. Sherry alone tasted too boozy, so we cut it with clam juice, which underscored the briny flavor of the shrimp. A pinch of flour and some butter thickened the sauce, and lemon juice brightened everything up. A chewy supermarket baguette made the perfect buttery bread crumbs; sprinkled on at the last minute, they were sturdy enough to stay crisp on the saucy shrimp. Our modernized skillet "casserole" was definitely an improvement on the tired old version.

Garlicky Shrimp with Buttered Bread Crumbs

SERVES 4

Vermouth can be substituted for the sherry. If using vermouth, increase the amount to ½ cup and reduce the amount of clam juice to ½ cup. To prepare this recipe in a 10-inch skillet, brown the shrimp in three batches for about 2 minutes each, using 2 teaspoons oil per batch. Serve the shrimp with rice and either broccoli or asparagus.

- 1 (3-inch) piece baguette, cut into small pieces
- 5 tablespoons unsalted butter, cut into 5 pieces
- 1 small shallot, minced (about 1 tablespoon)
- Table salt and ground black pepper
- 2 tablespoons minced fresh parsley leaves
- 2 pounds extra-large shrimp (21 to 25 per pound), peeled and deveined (see page 240)
- ¼ teaspoon sugar
- 4 teaspoons vegetable oil
- 4 medium garlic cloves, minced or pressed through a garlic press (about 4 teaspoons)
- ⅛ teaspoon red pepper flakes
- 2 teaspoons unbleached all-purpose flour
- ⅔ cup bottled clam juice
- ⅓ cup dry sherry (see note)
- 2 teaspoons juice from 1 lemon, plus lemon wedges for serving

1. Pulse the bread in a food processor until coarsely ground, about 8 pulses; you should have about 1 cup crumbs. Melt 1 tablespoon of the butter in a 12-inch nonstick skillet over medium heat. Add the crumbs, shallot, ⅛ teaspoon salt, and ⅛ teaspoon pepper. Cook, stirring occasionally, until the bread crumbs are golden brown, 7 to 10 minutes. Stir in 1 tablespoon of the parsley and transfer to a plate to cool. Wipe out the skillet with paper towels.

2. Pat the shrimp dry with paper towels and toss with the sugar, ¼ teaspoon salt, and ¼ teaspoon pepper in a bowl. Return the skillet to high heat, add 2 teaspoons of the oil, and heat until shimmering. Add half of the shrimp in a single layer and cook until spotty brown and the edges turn pink, about 3 minutes (do not flip the shrimp). Remove the pan from heat and transfer the shrimp to a large plate. Wipe out the skillet with paper towels. Repeat with the remaining 2 teaspoons oil and remaining shrimp; transfer the shrimp to the plate.

3. Return the skillet to medium heat and add 1 tablespoon more butter. When melted, add the garlic and red pepper flakes; cook, stirring frequently, until the garlic just begins to color, about 1 minute. Add the flour and cook, stirring frequently, for 1 minute. Increase the heat to medium-high and slowly whisk in the clam juice and sherry. Bring to a simmer and cook until the mixture reduces to ¾ cup, 3 to 4 minutes. Whisk in the remaining 3 tablespoons butter, 1 tablespoon at a time. Stir in the lemon juice and remaining 1 tablespoon parsley.

4. Reduce the heat to medium-low, return the shrimp to the pan, and toss to combine. Cook, covered, until the shrimp are pink and cooked through, 2 to 3 minutes. Uncover and sprinkle with the toasted bread crumbs. Serve with the lemon wedges.

GARLICKY ROASTED SHRIMP

WHY THIS RECIPE WORKS: We loved the idea of an easy weeknight meal of juicy roasted shrimp, but getting the lean, quick-cooking shrimp to develop color and roasted flavor before they turned rubbery required a few tricks. First we chose jumbo-size shrimp, which were the least likely to dry out and overcook. Butterflying the shrimp increased their surface area, giving us more room to add flavor. After brining the shrimp briefly to help them hold on to more moisture, we tossed them in a potent mixture of aromatic spices, garlic, herbs, butter, and oil. Then we roasted them under the broiler to get lots of color as quickly as possible, elevating them on a wire rack so they'd brown all over. To further protect them as they cooked and to produce a more deeply roasted flavor, we left their shells on; the sugar- and protein-rich shells browned quickly in the heat of the oven and transferred flavor to the shrimp itself.

Garlicky Roasted Shrimp with Parsley and Anise

SERVES 4 TO 6

Don't be tempted to use smaller shrimp with this cooking technique; they will be over seasoned and prone to overcook.

- ¼ cup salt
- 2 pounds shell-on jumbo shrimp (16 to 20 per pound)
- 4 tablespoons unsalted butter, melted
- ¼ cup vegetable oil
- 6 garlic cloves, minced
- 1 teaspoon anise seeds
- ½ teaspoon red pepper flakes
- ¼ teaspoon pepper
- 2 tablespoons minced fresh parsley
- Lemon wedges

1. Dissolve salt in 1 quart cold water in large container. Using kitchen shears or sharp paring knife, cut through shell of shrimp and devein but do not remove shell. Using paring knife, continue to cut shrimp ½ inch deep, taking care not to cut in half completely. Submerge shrimp in brine, cover, and refrigerate for 15 minutes.

2. Adjust oven rack 4 inches from broiler element and heat broiler. Combine melted butter, oil, garlic, anise seeds, pepper flakes, and pepper in large bowl. Remove shrimp from brine and pat dry with paper towels. Add shrimp and parsley to butter mixture; toss well, making sure butter mixture gets into interior of shrimp. Arrange shrimp in single layer on wire rack set in rimmed baking sheet.

3. Broil shrimp until opaque and shells are beginning to brown, 2 to 4 minutes, rotating sheet halfway through broiling. Flip shrimp and continue to broil until second side is opaque and shells are beginning to brown, 2 to 4 minutes longer, rotating sheet halfway through broiling. Transfer shrimp to serving platter and serve immediately, passing lemon wedges separately.

Garlicky Roasted Shrimp with Cilantro and Lime

Annatto powder, also called achiote, can be found with the Latin American foods at your supermarket. An equal amount of paprika can be substituted.

Omit butter and increase vegetable oil to ½ cup. Omit anise seeds and pepper. Add 2 teaspoons lightly crushed coriander seeds, 2 teaspoons grated lime zest, and 1 teaspoon annatto powder to oil mixture in step 2. Substitute ¼ cup minced fresh cilantro for parsley and lime wedges for lemon wedges.

Garlicky Roasted Shrimp with Cumin, Ginger, and Sesame

Omit butter and increase vegetable oil to ½ cup. Decrease garlic to 2 cloves and omit anise seeds and pepper. Add 2 teaspoons toasted sesame oil, 1½ teaspoons grated fresh ginger, and 1 teaspoon cumin seeds to oil mixture in step 2. Substitute 2 thinly sliced scallion greens for parsley and omit lemon wedges.

SPANISH-STYLE SIZZLING GARLIC SHRIMP

WHY THIS RECIPE WORKS: Sizzling *gambas al ajillo* is a tempting dish served in tapas bars. We knew we would have to make some adjustments to re-create this dish as an appetizer to serve at home, but our work would pay off when we could savor the juicy shrimp in spicy, garlic-infused oil.

The shrimp in the Spanish original are completely submerged in oil and cooked slowly. We didn't want to use that much oil, so we added just enough to a skillet to come halfway up the sides of the shrimp. We cooked them over very low heat and turned them halfway through; these shrimp cooked as evenly as they would have if completely covered with oil. We built heady garlic flavor in three ways: We added raw minced garlic to a marinade, we browned smashed cloves in the oil in which the shrimp would be cooked, and we cooked slices of garlic along with the shrimp. We included the traditional bay leaf and red chile, and added sherry vinegar (rather than sherry) and parsley, all of which brightened the richness of the oil. Served with plenty of bread to soak up the extra juices and flavorful oil, these garlicky shrimp rival the best restaurant versions.

Spanish-Style Garlic Shrimp

SERVES 6

Serve the shrimp with crusty bread for dipping in the richly flavored olive oil. This dish can be served directly from the skillet (make sure to use a trivet) or, for a sizzling effect, transferred to an 8-inch cast-iron skillet that's been heated for 2 minutes over medium-high heat. We prefer the slightly sweet flavor of dried chiles in this recipe, but ¼ teaspoon sweet paprika can be substituted. If sherry vinegar is unavailable, use 2 teaspoons dry sherry and 1 teaspoon white vinegar.

- 14 medium garlic cloves, peeled
- 1 pound large shrimp (31 to 40 per pound), peeled, deveined (see page 240), and tails removed
- 8 tablespoons olive oil
- ½ teaspoon table salt
- 1 bay leaf
- 1 (2-inch) piece mild dried chile, such as New Mexico, roughly broken, seeds included (see note)
- 1½ teaspoons sherry vinegar (see note)
- 1 tablespoon minced fresh parsley leaves

1. Mince 2 of the garlic cloves with a chef's knife or garlic press. Toss the minced garlic with the shrimp, 2 tablespoons of the olive oil, and salt in a medium bowl. Let the shrimp marinate at room temperature for 30 minutes.

2. Meanwhile, using the flat side of a chef's knife, smash 4 more garlic cloves. Heat the smashed garlic with the remaining 6 tablespoons olive oil in a 12-inch skillet over medium-low heat, stirring occasionally, until the garlic is light golden brown, 4 to 7 minutes. Remove the pan from the heat and allow the oil to cool to room temperature. Using a slotted spoon, remove the smashed garlic from the skillet and discard.

3. Slice the remaining 8 garlic cloves thin. Return the skillet to low heat and add the sliced garlic, bay leaf, and chile. Cook, stirring occasionally, until the garlic is tender but not browned, 4 to 7 minutes. (If the garlic has not begun to sizzle after 3 minutes, increase the heat to medium-low.) Increase the heat to medium-low and add the shrimp with the marinade to the pan in a single layer. Cook the shrimp, undisturbed, until the oil starts to gently bubble, about 2 minutes. Using tongs, flip the shrimp and continue to cook until almost cooked through, about 2 minutes longer. Increase the heat to high and add the sherry vinegar and parsley. Cook, stirring constantly, until the shrimp are cooked through and the oil is bubbling vigorously, 15 to 20 seconds. Serve immediately, discarding the bay leaf.

SPANISH-STYLE TOASTED PASTA WITH SHRIMP

WHY THIS RECIPE WORKS: Traditional recipes for *fideuà* can take several hours to prepare. We wanted to speed up the process but keep the deep flavors of the classic recipes. To replace the slow-cooked fish stock of the classics, we made a quick shrimp stock using the shrimp's shells, a combination of chicken broth and water, and a bay leaf. We also streamlined the *sofrito*, the aromatic base common in Spanish cooking, by finely mincing the onion and using canned tomatoes (instead of fresh), which helped the recipe components soften and brown more quickly. The final tweak to our recipe was boosting the flavor of the shrimp by quickly marinating them in olive oil, garlic, salt, and pepper.

Spanish-Style Toasted Pasta with Shrimp

SERVES 4

In step 5, if your skillet is not broiler-safe, once the pasta is tender transfer the mixture to a broiler-safe 13 by 9-inch baking dish lightly coated with olive oil; scatter the shrimp over the pasta and stir them in to partially submerge. Broil and serve as directed. Serve this dish with lemon wedges and Aïoli (recipe follows), stirring it into individual portions at the table.

3 tablespoons plus 2 teaspoons extra-virgin olive oil
3 garlic cloves, minced
Salt and pepper
1½ pounds extra-large shrimp (21 to 25 per pound), peeled and deveined (see page 240), shells reserved
2¾ cups water
1 cup low-sodium chicken broth
1 bay leaf
8 ounces spaghettini or thin spaghetti, broken into 1- to 2-inch lengths
1 onion, chopped fine
1 (14.5-ounce) can diced tomatoes, drained and chopped fine
1 teaspoon paprika
1 teaspoon smoked paprika
½ teaspoon anchovy paste
¼ cup dry white wine
1 tablespoon chopped fresh parsley
Lemon wedges
1 recipe Aïoli (optional) (recipe follows)

1. Combine 1 tablespoon oil, 1 teaspoon garlic, ¼ teaspoon salt, and ⅛ teaspoon pepper in medium bowl. Add shrimp, toss to coat, and refrigerate until ready to use.

2. Place reserved shrimp shells, water, broth, and bay leaf in medium bowl. Cover and microwave until liquid is hot and shells have turned pink, about 6 minutes. Set aside until ready to use.

3. Toss spaghettini and 2 teaspoons oil in broiler-safe 12-inch skillet until spaghettini is evenly coated. Toast spaghettini over medium-high heat, stirring frequently, until browned and nutty in aroma (spaghettini should be color of peanut butter), 6 to 10 minutes. Transfer spaghettini to bowl. Wipe out skillet with paper towel.

4. Heat remaining 2 tablespoons oil in now-empty skillet over medium-high heat until shimmering. Add onion and ¼ teaspoon salt; cook, stirring frequently, until onion is softened and beginning to brown around edges, 4 to 6 minutes. Add tomatoes and cook, stirring occasionally, until mixture is thick, dry, and slightly darkened in color, 4 to 6 minutes. Reduce heat to medium and add remaining garlic, paprika, smoked paprika, and anchovy paste. Cook until fragrant, about 1½ minutes. Add spaghettini and stir to combine. Adjust oven rack 5 to 6 inches from broiler element and heat broiler.

5. Pour shrimp broth through fine-mesh strainer into skillet. Add wine, ¼ teaspoon salt, and ½ teaspoon pepper and stir well. Increase heat to medium-high and bring to simmer. Cook uncovered, stirring occasionally, until liquid is slightly thickened and spaghettini is just tender, 8 to 10 minutes. Scatter shrimp over spaghettini and stir shrimp into spaghettini to partially submerge. Transfer skillet to oven and broil until shrimp are opaque and surface of spaghettini is dry with crisped, browned spots, 5 to 7 minutes. Remove from oven and let stand, uncovered, for 5 minutes. Sprinkle with parsley and serve immediately, passing lemon wedges and aïoli, if using, separately.

Spanish-Style Toasted Pasta with Shrimp and Clams

Reduce amount of shrimp to 1 pound and water to 2½ cups. In step 5, cook pasta until almost tender, about 6 minutes. Scatter 1½ pounds scrubbed littleneck or cherrystone clams over pasta, cover skillet, and cook until clams begin to open, about 3 minutes. Scatter shrimp over pasta, stir to partially submerge shrimp and clams, and proceed with recipe as directed.

Aïoli

MAKES ¾ CUP

1 garlic clove, grated fine
2 large egg yolks
4 teaspoons lemon juice
¼ teaspoon salt
⅛ teaspoon sugar
Ground white pepper
¾ cup olive oil

In large bowl, combine garlic, egg yolks, lemon juice, salt, sugar, and pepper to taste until combined. Whisking constantly, very slowly drizzle oil into egg mixture until thick and creamy. Season with salt and pepper to taste.

NOTES FROM THE TEST KITCHEN

IT'S A SNAP

Since traditional short *fideos* noodles are hard to find, we came up with an easy way to break long strands into even lengths.

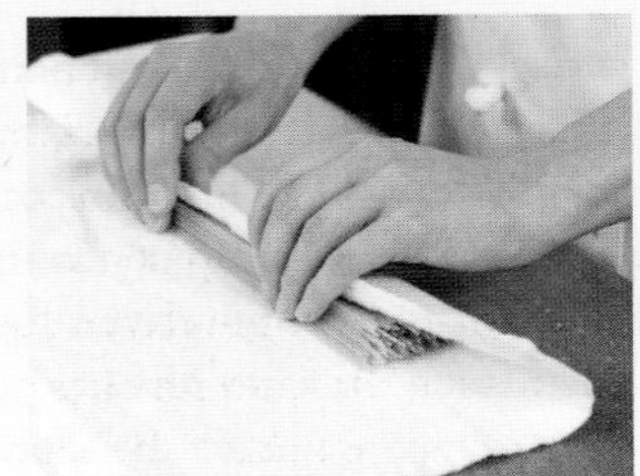

1. Loosely fold 4 ounces of spaghettini in clean dish towel, keeping pasta flat, not bunched. Position so that 1 to 2 inches of pasta rests on counter and remainder of pasta hangs off edge.

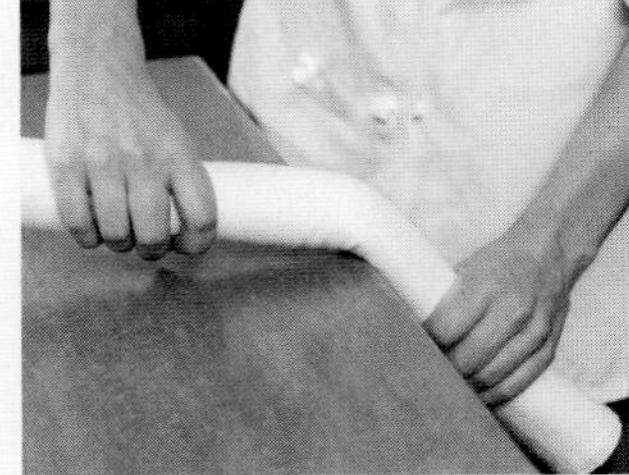

2. Pressing bundle against counter, press down on long end of towel to break strands into pieces, sliding bundle back over edge after each break.

GREEK SHRIMP

WHY THIS RECIPE WORKS: We can think of few examples where the unlikely combination of seafood and cheese marry as well as in Greece's shrimp *saganaki*. In this dish, sweet, briny shrimp are covered with a garlic-and-herb accented tomato sauce and topped with crumbles of creamy, salty feta cheese. Ordering this dish at a restaurant, however, can be a gamble. The shrimp can be tough and rubbery, the tomato sauce can turn out dull or overwhelming, and the feta can be lackluster. We set out to develop a foolproof version of this dish—one that is perfectly cooked and captures the bold and exuberant essence of Greek cuisine.

We started with the tomato sauce. Canned diced tomatoes along with sautéed onion and garlic provided our base. Dry white wine added acidity. Ouzo, the slightly sweet anise-flavored Greek liqueur, added welcome complexity when we simmered it in the sauce.

While the shrimp are typically layered with the tomato sauce and feta and baked, we found this method lacking. Since this should be a quick and easy dish, we opted to cook the shrimp right in the sauce; adding the shrimp raw to the sauce helped infuse them with the sauce's bright flavor. And for even more flavor, we marinated the shrimp with olive oil, ouzo, garlic, and lemon zest first while we made the sauce. Final touches included a generous sprinkling of feta over the sauced shrimp as well as a scattering of chopped fresh dill.

Greek-Style Shrimp with Tomatoes and Feta

SERVES 4 TO 6

This recipe works equally well with either jumbo shrimp (16 to 20 per pound) or extra-large shrimp (21 to 25 per pound); the cooking times in step 3 will vary slightly. Serve with crusty bread for soaking up the sauce.

- 1½ pounds shrimp, peeled and deveined (see page 240), tails left on, if desired (see note)
- 4 tablespoons extra-virgin olive oil
- 3 tablespoons ouzo
- 5 medium garlic cloves, minced or pressed through a garlic press (about 5 teaspoons)
- 1 teaspoon grated zest from 1 lemon
- Table salt and ground black pepper
- 1 small onion, diced medium
- ½ medium red bell pepper, stemmed, seeded, and diced medium
- ½ medium green bell pepper, stemmed, seeded, and diced medium
- ½ teaspoon red pepper flakes
- 1 (28-ounce) can diced tomatoes, drained, ⅓ cup juice reserved
- ¼ cup dry white wine
- 2 tablespoons coarsely chopped fresh parsley leaves
- 6 ounces feta cheese, preferably sheep's and/or goat's milk, crumbled (about 1½ cups)
- 2 tablespoons chopped fresh dill

1. Toss the shrimp, 1 tablespoon of the oil, 1 tablespoon of the ouzo, 1 teaspoon of the garlic, the lemon zest, ¼ teaspoon salt, and ⅛ teaspoon black pepper in a small bowl until well combined. Set aside while preparing the sauce.

2. Heat 2 tablespoons more oil in a 12-inch skillet over medium heat until shimmering. Add the onion, red and green bell peppers, and ¼ teaspoon salt and stir to combine. Cover the skillet and cook, stirring occasionally, until the vegetables release their moisture, 3 to 5 minutes. Uncover and continue to cook, stirring occasionally, until the moisture cooks off and the vegetables have softened, about 5 minutes longer. Add the remaining 4 teaspoons garlic and the red pepper flakes and cook until fragrant, about 1 minute. Add the tomatoes and reserved juice, the wine, and the remaining 2 tablespoons ouzo; increase the heat to medium-high and bring to a simmer. Reduce the heat to medium and simmer, stirring occasionally, until the flavors have melded and the sauce is slightly thickened (the sauce should not be completely dry), 5 to 8 minutes. Stir in the parsley and season with salt and pepper to taste.

3. Reduce the heat to medium-low and add the shrimp along with any accumulated liquid to the pan; stir to coat and distribute evenly. Cover and cook, stirring occasionally, until the shrimp are opaque throughout, 6 to 9 minutes for extra-large shrimp or 7 to 11 minutes for jumbo shrimp, adjusting the heat as needed to maintain a bare simmer. Remove the pan from the heat and sprinkle evenly with the feta. Drizzle the remaining 1 tablespoon oil evenly over the top and sprinkle with the dill. Serve immediately.

SHRIMP COCKTAIL

WHY THIS RECIPE WORKS: Nothing is more basic than shrimp cocktail and, given its simplicity, few dishes are more difficult to improve. Yet we set out to do just that; we wanted to work on the shrimp's flavor, the cooking method, and the cocktail sauce. Shrimp cook quickly, so there's little time to add flavor in the pan. We based our cooking liquid on shrimp stock, and added wine, lemon juice, herbs, and spices. To keep the shrimp in contact with this flavorful liquid as long as possible, we brought the mixture to a boil, turned off the heat, and then added the shrimp; the hot liquid cooked the shrimp slowly while they absorbed the stock's flavor. We determined that the classic sauce base, ketchup, was best. We added horseradish, which is the usual ingredient for spicing up the sauce, but we also included chili powder, cayenne, and lemon juice for extra spiciness.

Shrimp Cocktail

SERVES 4

When using larger or smaller shrimp, increase or decrease, respectively, the cooking times for the shrimp by one to two minutes. When using such large shrimp, we find it wise to remove the large black vein. Use horseradish from a freshly opened bottle and mild chili powder for the best flavor in the sauce.

SHRIMP

- 1 pound jumbo shrimp (16 to 20 per pound; see note), peeled, deveined (see page 240), and shells reserved
- 1 teaspoon table salt
- 1 cup dry white wine
- 4 peppercorns
- 5 coriander seeds
- ½ bay leaf
- 5 sprigs fresh parsley
- 1 sprig fresh tarragon
- 1 teaspoon juice from 1 lemon

COCKTAIL SAUCE

- 1 cup ketchup
- 1 tablespoon juice from 1 small lemon
- 2½ teaspoons prepared horseradish (see note)
- 1 teaspoon ancho or other mild chili powder (see note)
- Pinch cayenne pepper
- Table salt and ground black pepper

1. FOR THE SHRIMP: Bring the reserved shells, 3 cups water, and salt to a boil in a medium saucepan over medium-high heat; reduce the heat to low, cover, and simmer until fragrant, about 20 minutes. Strain the stock through a fine-mesh strainer, pressing on the shells to extract all the liquid.

2. Bring the stock and remaining ingredients except the shrimp to a boil in a 3- or 4-quart saucepan over high heat; boil for 2 minutes. Turn off the heat and stir in the shrimp; cover and let stand until the shrimp are firm and pink, 8 to 10 minutes. Meanwhile, fill a large bowl with ice water. Drain the shrimp, reserving the stock for another use. Immediately transfer the shrimp to the ice water to stop cooking and chill thoroughly, about 3 minutes. Remove the shrimp from the ice water and pat dry with paper towels.

3. FOR THE SAUCE: Stir all the ingredients together in a small bowl; season with salt and pepper to taste. Serve the chilled shrimp with the cocktail sauce.

BETTER SHRIMP SALAD

WHY THIS RECIPE WORKS: Most shrimp salads drown in a sea of mayonnaise, in part to hide the rubbery, flavorless boiled shrimp. We wanted perfectly cooked shrimp without the extra work of grilling, roasting, or sautéing. And we needed to coat them with the perfect deli-style dressing—something creamy but not overwhelming.

Overcooking is the culprit when shrimp turn out rubbery. We found that starting the shrimp in cold water (with lemon, parsley, tarragon, pepper, sugar, and salt), then cooking them over very gentle heat, resulted in tender shrimp. The longer cooking time infused the shrimp with the flavors of the poaching liquid. We didn't want to mask these tender, flavorful shrimp with too much dressing, so we scaled back the mayonnaise to a modest amount. Celery added a nice crunch, and shallot, herbs, and lemon juice perked up and rounded out the flavors.

Shrimp Salad

SERVES 4

This recipe can also be prepared with large shrimp (31 to 40 per pound); the cooking time will be 1 to 2 minutes shorter. The shrimp can be cooked up to 24 hours in advance, but hold off on dressing the salad until ready to serve. The recipe can be easily doubled; cook the shrimp in a 7-quart Dutch oven and increase the cooking time to 12 to 14 minutes. Serve the salad spooned over salad greens or on buttered and grilled buns.

- 1 pound extra-large shrimp (21 to 25 per pound; see note), peeled and deveined (see page 240)
- ¼ cup plus 1 tablespoon juice from 2 to 3 lemons, spent halves reserved
- 5 sprigs fresh parsley plus 1 teaspoon minced fresh parsley leaves
- 3 sprigs fresh tarragon plus 1 teaspoon minced fresh tarragon leaves
- 1 teaspoon whole black peppercorns plus ground black pepper
- 1 tablespoon sugar
- Table salt
- ¼ cup mayonnaise
- 1 small celery rib, minced (about ⅓ cup)
- 1 small shallot, minced (about 1 tablespoon)

1. Combine the shrimp, ¼ cup of the lemon juice, the reserved lemon halves, parsley sprigs, tarragon sprigs, whole peppercorns, sugar, and 1 teaspoon salt with 2 cups cold water in a medium saucepan. Place the saucepan over medium heat and cook the shrimp, stirring several times, until pink, firm to the touch, and the centers are no longer translucent, 8 to 10 minutes (the water should be just bubbling around the edge of the pan and register 165 degrees on an instant-read thermometer). Remove the pan from the heat, cover, and let the shrimp sit in the broth for 2 minutes.

2. Meanwhile, fill a medium bowl with ice water. Drain the shrimp into a colander and discard the lemon halves, herbs, and spices. Immediately transfer the shrimp to the ice water to stop the cooking and chill thoroughly, about 3 minutes. Remove the shrimp from the ice water and pat dry with paper towels.

3. Whisk together the mayonnaise, celery, shallot, remaining 1 tablespoon lemon juice, the minced parsley, and minced tarragon in a medium bowl. Cut the shrimp in half lengthwise and then each half into thirds; add the shrimp to the mayonnaise mixture and toss to combine. Season with salt and pepper to taste and serve.

Shrimp Salad with Roasted Red Pepper and Basil

This Italian-style variation is especially good served over bitter greens.

Follow the recipe for Shrimp Salad, omitting the tarragon sprigs from the cooking liquid. Replace the celery, minced parsley, and minced tarragon with ⅓ cup thinly sliced jarred roasted red peppers, 2 teaspoons rinsed capers, and 3 tablespoons chopped fresh basil leaves.

Shrimp Salad with Avocado and Orange

Avocado and orange are a refreshing addition to this salad.

Follow the recipe for Shrimp Salad, omitting the tarragon sprigs from the cooking liquid. Replace the celery, minced parsley, and minced tarragon with 4 halved and thinly sliced radishes; 1 large orange, peeled and cut into ½-inch pieces; ½ ripe avocado, cut into ½-inch pieces; and 2 teaspoons minced fresh mint leaves.

MARYLAND CRAB CAKES

WHY THIS RECIPE WORKS: Making crab cakes at home is the only way to avoid the pricey crab-flecked dough balls that pass for crab cakes in many restaurants. We wanted traditional Maryland-style crab cakes with a crisp brown exterior and well-seasoned filling that tasted of sweet crab, not filler. Fresh crabmeat provided superior taste and texture, and jumbo lump crabmeat was worth the high price tag. Pasteurized crabmeat is not quite as good, but it is less expensive. After experimenting with different binders, we settled on fine dry bread crumbs; their flavor is mild, they held the cakes together well, and they mixed easily with the crab. We used just a few tablespoons of crumbs so that the crab's flavor and texture would shine. An egg and some mayonnaise bound the cakes together. Old Bay is the traditional seasoning for crab; some herbs and white pepper were the only additions we found necessary. Carefully folding the ingredients together rather than stirring them kept the texture chunky, and a short chill in the refrigerator ensured that the cakes wouldn't fall apart. Pan-frying in vegetable oil gave our crab cakes the crisp exterior we wanted.

Maryland Crab Cakes

SERVES 4

The amount of bread crumbs you add will depend on the crabmeat's juiciness. Start with the smallest amount, adjust the seasonings, then add the egg. If the cakes won't bind at this point, add more bread crumbs, 1 tablespoon at a time. If you can't find fresh jumbo lump crabmeat, pasteurized crabmeat, though not as good, is a decent substitute. At all costs, avoid the canned crabmeat sold near canned tuna. Either a nonstick or a traditional skillet will work for this recipe, but a nonstick simplifies cleanup.

- 1 pound fresh jumbo lump crabmeat, carefully picked over to remove cartilage and shell fragments (see note)
- 4 scallions, green parts only, minced (about ½ cup)
- 1 tablespoon chopped fresh herb, such as cilantro, dill, basil, or parsley
- 1½ teaspoons Old Bay seasoning
- 2–4 tablespoons plain dry bread crumbs (see note)
- ¼ cup mayonnaise
- Table salt and ground white pepper
- 1 large egg
- ¼ cup unbleached all-purpose flour
- ¼ cup vegetable oil
- Sweet and Tangy Tartar Sauce (page 224), Creamy Chipotle Chile Sauce (recipe follows), or lemon wedges

1. Gently mix the crabmeat, scallions, herb, Old Bay, 2 tablespoons of the bread crumbs, and the mayonnaise in a medium bowl, being careful not to break up the lumps of crab. Season with salt and white pepper to taste. Carefully fold in the egg with a rubber spatula until the mixture just clings together. Add more bread crumbs if necessary.

2. Divide the crab mixture into four portions and shape each into a fat, round cake, about 3 inches across and 1½ inches high. Arrange the cakes on a baking sheet lined with waxed or parchment paper; cover with plastic wrap and chill for at least 30 minutes. (The crab cakes can be refrigerated for up to 24 hours.)

3. Place the flour in a pie plate. Lightly dredge the crab cakes in the flour. Heat the oil in a large skillet over medium-high heat until hot but not smoking. Gently place the chilled crab cakes in the skillet; pan-fry until the outsides are crisp and browned, 4 to 5 minutes per side. Serve immediately with a sauce or lemon wedges.

Creamy Chipotle Chile Sauce

MAKES ABOUT ½ CUP

The addition of sour cream makes this sauce richer than traditional tartar sauce. The chipotles add smoky and spicy flavors.

- ¼ cup mayonnaise
- ¼ cup sour cream
- 2 teaspoons canned minced chipotle chiles in adobo sauce
- 1 small garlic clove, minced or pressed through a garlic press (about ½ teaspoon)
- 2 teaspoons minced fresh cilantro leaves
- 1 teaspoon juice from 1 lime

Mix all of the ingredients in a small bowl. Cover and refrigerate until the flavors blend, about 30 minutes. (The sauce can be refrigerated for up to 2 days.)

THE BEST CRAB CAKES

WHY THIS RECIPE WORKS: We wanted to come up with a recipe for crab cakes that were chock full of sweet, plump meat delicately seasoned and seamlessly held together with a binder that didn't mask the seafood flavor. And we didn't want shopping to be an issue—we wanted our crab cakes to work with either fresh crabmeat or the pasteurized variety found at the supermarket. To highlight and enhance the crabmeat's sweetness, we bound our cakes with a delicate shrimp mousse. Classic components like Old Bay seasoning and lemon juice bolstered the crab's flavor, and panko bread crumbs helped ensure a crisp crust.

Best Crab Cakes

SERVES 4

Either fresh or pasteurized crabmeat can be used in this recipe. With packaged crab, if the meat smells clean and fresh when you first open the package, skip steps 1 and 4 and simply blot away any excess liquid. Serve the crab cakes with lemon wedges.

- 1 pound lump crabmeat, picked over for shells
- 1 cup milk
- 1½ cups panko bread crumbs
- Salt and pepper
- 2 celery ribs, chopped
- ½ cup chopped onion
- 1 garlic clove, peeled and smashed
- 1 tablespoon unsalted butter
- 4 ounces shrimp, peeled, deveined (see page 240), and tails removed
- ¼ cup heavy cream
- 2 teaspoons Dijon mustard
- 1 teaspoon lemon juice
- ½ teaspoon hot sauce
- ½ teaspoon Old Bay seasoning
- ¼ cup vegetable oil

1. Place crabmeat and milk in bowl, making sure crab is totally submerged. Cover and refrigerate for 20 minutes.

2. Meanwhile, place ¾ cup panko in small zipper-lock bag and finely crush with rolling pin. Transfer crushed panko to 10-inch nonstick skillet and add remaining ¾ cup panko. Toast over medium-high heat, stirring constantly, until golden brown, about 5 minutes. Transfer panko to shallow dish and stir in ¼ teaspoon salt and pepper to taste. Wipe out skillet.

3. Pulse celery, onion, and garlic together in food processor until finely chopped, 5 to 8 pulses, scraping down bowl as needed. Transfer vegetables to large bowl. Rinse processor bowl and blade. Melt butter in now-empty skillet over medium heat. Add chopped vegetables, ½ teaspoon salt, and ⅛ teaspoon pepper; cook, stirring frequently, until vegetables are softened and all moisture has evaporated, 4 to 6 minutes. Return vegetables to large bowl and let cool to room temperature. Rinse out pan and wipe clean.

4. Strain crabmeat through fine-mesh strainer, pressing firmly to remove milk but being careful not to break up lumps of crabmeat.

5. Pulse shrimp in now-empty food processor until finely ground, 12 to 15 pulses, scraping down bowl as needed. Add cream and pulse to combine, 2 to 4 pulses, scraping down bowl as needed. Transfer shrimp puree to bowl with cooled vegetables. Add mustard, lemon juice, hot sauce, and Old Bay; stir until well combined. Add crabmeat and fold gently with rubber spatula, being careful not to overmix, and break up lumps of crabmeat. Divide mixture into 8 balls and firmly press into ½-inch-thick patties. Place cakes in rimmed baking sheet lined with parchment paper, cover tightly with plastic wrap, and refrigerate for 30 minutes.

6. Coat each cake with panko, firmly pressing to adhere crumbs to exterior. Heat 1 tablespoon oil in now-empty skillet over medium heat until shimmering. Place 4 cakes in skillet and cook without moving them until golden brown, 3 to 4 minutes. Using 2 spatulas, carefully flip cakes. Add 1 tablespoon oil, reduce heat to medium-low, and continue to cook until second side is golden brown, 4 to 6 minutes. Transfer cakes to platter. Wipe out skillet and repeat with remaining 4 cakes and remaining 2 tablespoons oil. Serve immediately.

EASY SALMON CAKES

WHY THIS RECIPE WORKS: Most salmon cakes are mushy and overly fishy, camouflaged by gluey binders and heavy-handed seasoning. Our goal was a quick and simple recipe for salmon cakes that first and foremost tasted like salmon, with a moist, delicate texture. To simplify preparation, we broke out our food processor. Pulsing small pieces of salmon (raw was preferred over cooked, which turned fishy) allowed for more even chopping and resulted in small, discrete pieces of fish. We also found a way to ditch the egg and flour steps of the breading process. Instead, we coated the salmon cakes with panko, which we had also used as a binder.

Easy Salmon Cakes

SERVES 4

If buying a skin-on salmon fillet, purchase 1⅓ pounds fish. This will yield 1¼ pounds fish after skinning. When processing the salmon, it is OK to have some pieces that are larger than ¼ inch. It is important to avoid overprocessing the fish. Serve the salmon cakes with lemon wedges and/or tartar sauce.

- 3 tablespoons plus ¾ cup panko bread crumbs
- 2 tablespoons minced fresh parsley
- 2 tablespoons mayonnaise
- 4 teaspoons lemon juice
- 1 scallion, sliced thin
- 1 small shallot, minced
- 1 teaspoon Dijon mustard
- ¾ teaspoon salt
- ¼ teaspoon pepper
- Pinch cayenne pepper
- 1 (1¼-pound) skinless salmon fillet, cut into 1-inch pieces
- ½ cup vegetable oil

1. Combine 3 tablespoons panko, parsley, mayonnaise, lemon juice, scallion, shallot, mustard, salt, pepper, and cayenne in bowl. Working in 3 batches, pulse salmon in food processor until coarsely chopped into ¼-inch pieces, about 2 pulses, transferring each batch to bowl with panko mixture. Gently mix until uniformly combined.

2. Place remaining ¾ cup panko in shallow dish. Using ⅓-cup measure, scoop level amount of salmon mixture and transfer to baking sheet; repeat to make 8 cakes. Carefully coat each cake with bread crumbs, gently patting into disk measuring 2¾ inches in diameter and 1 inch high. Return coated cakes to baking sheet.

3. Heat oil in 12-inch skillet over medium-high heat until shimmering. Place salmon cakes in skillet and cook without moving until bottoms are golden brown, about 2 minutes. Carefully flip cakes and cook until second side is golden brown, 2 to 3 minutes. Transfer cakes to paper towel–lined plate to drain for 1 minute. Serve.

Easy Salmon Cakes with Smoked Salmon, Capers, and Dill

Reduce fresh salmon to 1 pound and salt to ½ teaspoon. Substitute 1 tablespoon minced fresh dill for parsley. Add 4 ounces finely chopped smoked salmon and 1 tablespoon chopped capers to bowl with salmon mixture.

CRAB TOWERS WITH AVOCADO AND GAZPACHO SALSAS

WHY THIS RECIPE WORKS: Sometimes a dish served in a restaurant is so delicious and impressive-looking that we just have to try to make it ourselves. A crab salad molded into towers, from the Mayflower Park Hotel in Seattle, is one such dish, but a hotel restaurant can easily handle the recipe's 35 ingredients. Was there a way to re-create the flavors and presentation at home, with fewer ingredients and a lot less effort? By breaking down the recipe for this appetizer into

NOTES FROM THE TEST KITCHEN

SEGMENTING ORANGES

1. Start by slicing a ½-inch piece from the top and bottom of the orange. With the fruit resting flat against a work surface, use a very sharp paring knife to slice off the rind, including the white pith.

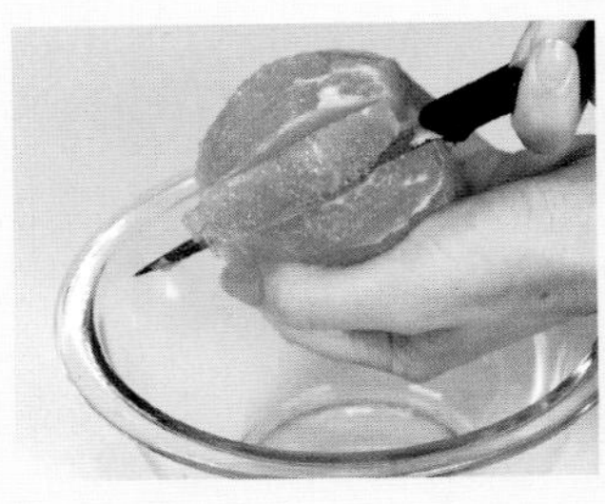

2. Slip the knife blade between a membrane and one section of the fruit and slice to the center. Turn the blade so that it is facing out and slide the blade from the center out along the membrane to completely free the section.

ASSEMBLING CRAB TOWERS

1. Place the biscuit cutter in the center of the plate and, using the back of a soup spoon, press ⅓ cup of the Avocado Salsa evenly into the cutter. Lift the cutter off the plate slightly to reveal some but not all of the avocado.

2. Holding the cutter aloft, press ⅓ cup of the Crabmeat Salad evenly into the cutter, on top of the avocado. Lift the cutter farther off the plate and press ⅓ cup of the Gazpacho Salsa evenly into the cutter, on top of the crab.

3. Gently lift the cutter up and away from the plate to reveal the crab tower. Repeat with the remaining salsas and crabmeat salad.

its components—crab salad, avocado–hearts of palm salsa, and gazpacho salsa—we were able to address each one separately. For the crab salad, we used lump crabmeat mixed with a little mayonnaise and champagne vinaigrette. We eliminated the hearts of palm from the salsa; tasters felt the avocado alone worked quite well. For the gazpacho salsa, we used only one kind of bell pepper rather than two and omitted the diced lime and orange segments that were in the original recipe; we also cut back on some of the seasonings, limiting ourselves to sherry vinegar and olive oil. Now that we'd streamlined the components, we had to assemble the dish. The restaurant uses timbale rings, but we found our workaday biscuit cutter did the job just fine.

Crab Towers with Avocado and Gazpacho Salsas

SERVES 6

You can prepare the crabmeat salad and gazpacho salsa several hours ahead of serving, but the avocado salsa should be prepared just before assembly.

CRABMEAT SALAD

- 3 tablespoons extra-virgin olive oil
- 1 tablespoon champagne vinegar
- 1 teaspoon minced or grated lemon zest
- ½ teaspoon Dijon mustard
- ½ teaspoon table salt
- ⅛ teaspoon ground black pepper
- 2 tablespoons mayonnaise
- 12 ounces lump or backfin Atlantic blue crabmeat, carefully picked over to remove cartilage and shell fragments

GAZPACHO SALSA

- 1 small yellow bell pepper, cored, seeded, and cut into ⅛-inch pieces (about ½ cup)
- ½ small cucumber, peeled if desired, seeded, and cut into ⅛-inch pieces (about ½ cup)
- 1 medium plum tomato, cored, seeded, and cut into ⅛-inch pieces (about ½ cup)
- 1 small celery rib, cut into ⅛-inch pieces (about ½ cup)
- ½ small red onion, minced (about ¼ cup)
- ½ small jalapeño chile, stemmed, seeded, and minced
- 1 tablespoon minced fresh cilantro leaves
- 2 tablespoons extra-virgin olive oil
- 1 tablespoon sherry vinegar
- ¾ teaspoon table salt
- ¼ teaspoon ground black pepper

AVOCADO SALSA

- 3 ripe avocados, pitted, peed, and cut into ¼-inch dice (page 414)
- 2 tablespoons juice from 1 lime
- ¼ teaspoon ground coriander
- ½ teaspoon table salt
- ⅛ teaspoon ground black pepper

GARNISH

1 cup frisée

2 oranges, peeled using a paring knife and segmented (optional)

1. FOR THE CRABMEAT SALAD: Whisk the olive oil, champagne vinegar, lemon zest, mustard, salt, and pepper together in a small bowl. Measure 3 tablespoons of the vinaigrette into a medium bowl and mix with the mayonnaise. Add the crabmeat to the mayonnaise mixture and toss to coat. Cover with plastic wrap and refrigerate until needed. Set the remaining vinaigrette aside.

2. FOR THE GAZPACHO SALSA: Toss the bell pepper, cucumber, tomato, celery, red onion, jalapeño, cilantro, olive oil, sherry vinegar, salt, and pepper in a medium bowl and set aside.

3. FOR THE AVOCADO SALSA: Toss the avocados, lime juice, coriander, salt, and pepper in a medium bowl and set aside.

4. TO ASSEMBLE: Place a 3-inch-wide round biscuit cutter in the center of an individual plate. Following the photos, press ⅓ cup of the Avocado Salsa into the bottom of the cutter using the back of a soup spoon. Lift the cutter off the plate slightly to reveal some but not all of the avocado. Holding the cutter aloft, press ⅓ cup of the Crabmeat Salad evenly into the cutter on top of the avocado. Lift the cutter further to reveal some but not all of the crab salad. Holding the cutter aloft, use a soup spoon to press ⅓ cup of the Gazpacho Salsa evenly into the cutter on top of the crab. Gently lift the cutter up and away from the plate to reveal the crab tower. Repeat the procedure five more times with the remaining ingredients.

5. Dress the frisée with the remaining champagne vinaigrette. Place a few sprigs of the dressed frisée on top of each crab tower and arrange the orange segments (if using) around the towers. Serve immediately.

FLAMBÉED PAN-ROASTED LOBSTER

WHY THIS RECIPE WORKS: Boiling and steaming are the usual ways of preparing lobster, and they're just fine. But we wanted an alternative cooking method that would be even tastier, and we didn't want to spend a whole lot more time in the kitchen. Our solution was a restaurant dish adapted for home cooking.

The New England restaurant chef Jasper White created a pan-roasted lobster dish that we took as our starting point. We quartered the lobsters and tossed them into a very hot skillet—shells down, so the meat wouldn't overcook—to pan-roast. The heat roasted the shells and permeated the lobster meat with intense flavor. To cook the exposed meat, we put the skillet under the broiler, returning it to the stovetop when the meat was cooked through. Now came the fun part: We flambéed the lobster with bourbon (carefully, of course!). A quick pan sauce, made in the skillet after we removed the lobsters, was the final touch; we used shallots, white wine, herbs, and, for unusual and intense flavor, the lobster tomalley.

NOTES FROM THE TEST KITCHEN

PREPARING LOBSTER FOR PAN-ROASTING

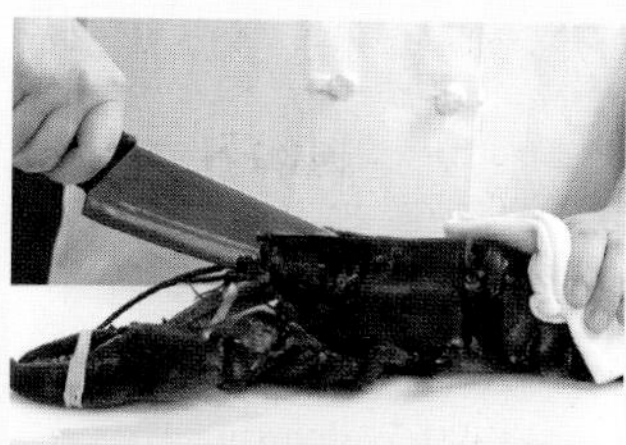

1. Freeze the lobster for 5 to 10 minutes to sedate it. Plunge a chef's knife into the body at the point where the shell forms a "T" to kill the lobster. Move the blade straight down through the head.

2. Turn the lobster around and, while holding the upper body with one hand, cut through the body toward the tail.

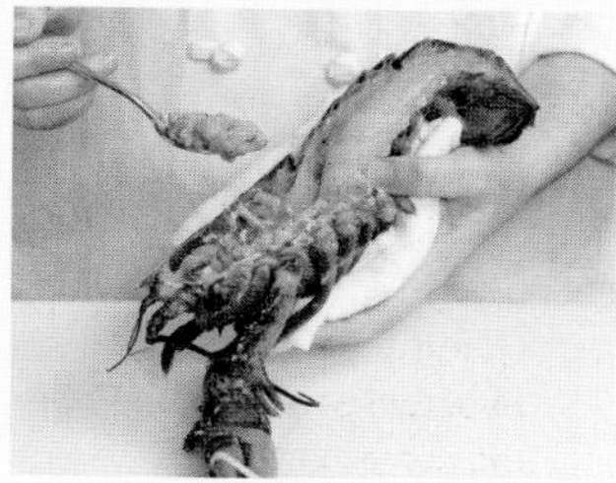

3. Remove and discard the stomach and intestinal tract. Reserve the green tomalley for the sauce, if desired.

4. Cut the tail from the body.

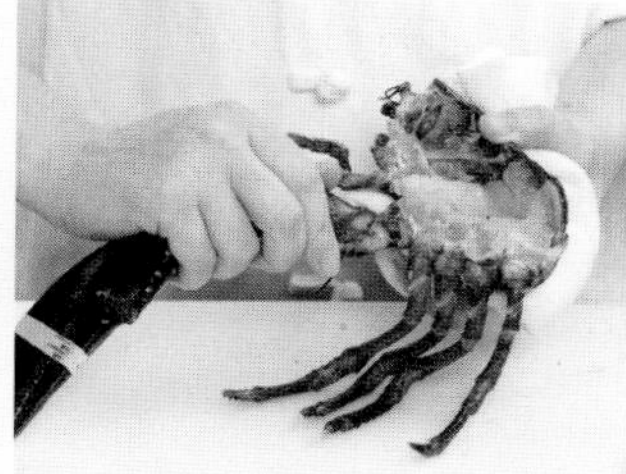

5. Twist off the claws from the body. Remove the rubber bands from the claws. (Don't be put off if the lobster continues to twitch a little; it's a reflexive movement.)

This way of cooking lobsters is a little more trouble than dunking them in a pot of boiling water, but we think the results are well worth it.

Flambéed Pan-Roasted Lobster

SERVES 2

If you want to prepare more than two lobsters, we suggest that you engage some help. This dish requires close attention, and managing multiple extremely hot pans can be tricky. Before flambéing, make sure to roll up long shirtsleeves, tie back long hair, turn off the exhaust fan (otherwise the fan may pull up the flames), and turn off any lit burners (this is critical if you have a gas stove). For equipment, you will need a large ovensafe skillet, oven mitts, a pair of tongs, and long fireplace or grill matches.

- 2 (1½- to 2-pound) live lobsters
- 2 tablespoons peanut or canola oil
- ¼ cup bourbon or cognac
- 6 tablespoons (¾ stick) unsalted butter, cut into 6 pieces
- 2 medium shallots, minced (about 6 tablespoons)
- 3 tablespoons dry white wine
- 1 teaspoon minced fresh tarragon leaves
- 1 tablespoon minced fresh chives
- Table salt and ground black pepper
- Lemon wedges, for serving (optional)

1. Use a large heavy-duty chef's knife to quarter the lobsters (see page 251). (Don't be put off if the lobsters continue to twitch a little after quartering; it's a reflexive movement.)

2. Adjust an oven rack so it is 6 inches from the broiler element and heat the broiler. Heat the peanut oil in a large ovensafe skillet over high heat until smoking. Add the lobster pieces, shell-side down, in a single layer and cook, without disturbing, until the shells are bright red and lightly browned, 2 to 3 minutes. Transfer the skillet to the broiler and cook until the tail meat is just opaque, about 2 minutes.

3. Carefully remove the pan from the oven and return it to the stovetop. Off the heat, pour the bourbon over the lobsters. Wait for 10 seconds, then light a long match and wave it over the skillet until the bourbon ignites. Return the pan to medium-high heat and shake it until the flames subside. Transfer the lobster pieces to a warmed serving bowl and tent with foil to keep warm.

4. Using tongs, remove any congealed albumin (white substance) from the skillet and add 2 tablespoons of the butter and the shallots. Cook, stirring constantly, until the shallots are softened and lightly browned, 1 to 2 minutes. Add the tomalley (if using) and white wine and stir until completely combined. Remove the skillet from the heat and add the tarragon and chives. Stirring constantly, add the remaining 4 tablespoons butter, 1 piece at a time, until fully emulsified. Season with salt and pepper to taste. Pour the sauce over the lobster pieces. Serve immediately, accompanied by the lemon wedges, if desired.

NOTES FROM THE TEST KITCHEN

REMOVING LOBSTER MEAT FROM THE SHELL

There's a lot more meat in a lobster than just the tail and claws—if you know how to get it. Here's our tried-and-true approach to extracting every last bit, no special tools needed. The method works for both hard- and soft-shell lobsters.

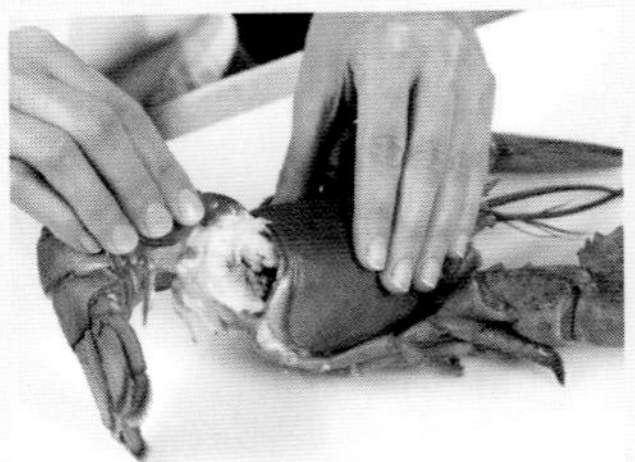

1. SEPARATE TAIL: Once cooked lobster is cool enough to handle, set it on cutting board. Grasp tail with your hand and grab body with your other hand and twist to separate.

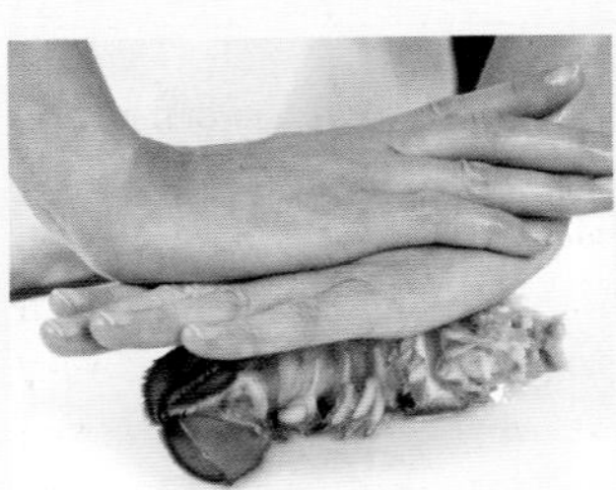

2. FLATTEN TAIL: Lay tail on its side on counter and use both hands to press down on tail until shell cracks.

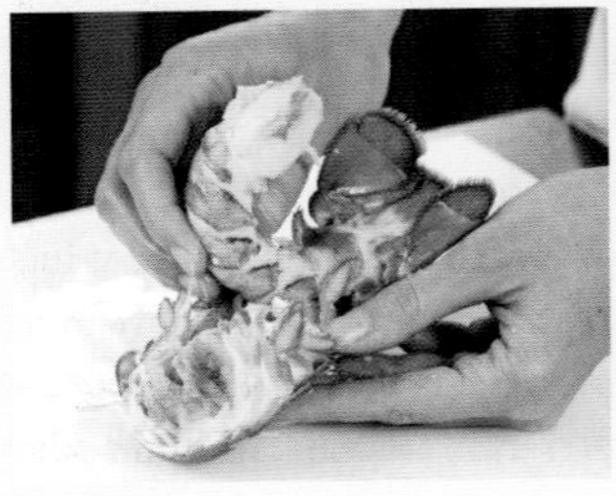

3. TAKE OUT TAIL MEAT: Hold tail, flippers facing you and shell facing down. Pull back on sides to crack open shell and remove meat. Rinse meat under water to remove green tomalley if you wish; pat meat dry with paper towels and remove dark vein.

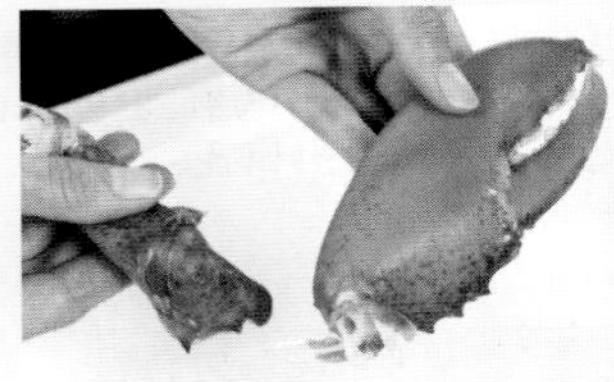

4. MOVE TO KNUCKLES: Twist "arms" to remove both claws and attached "knuckles". Twist knuckles to remove them from claw. Break knuckles at joint using back of chef's knife or lobster-cracking tool. Use handle of teaspoon to push out meat.

5. REMOVE CLAW MEAT: Wiggle hinged portion of each claw to separate. If meat is stuck inside small part, remove it with skewer. Break open claws, cracking 1 side and then flipping them to crack other side, and remove meat.

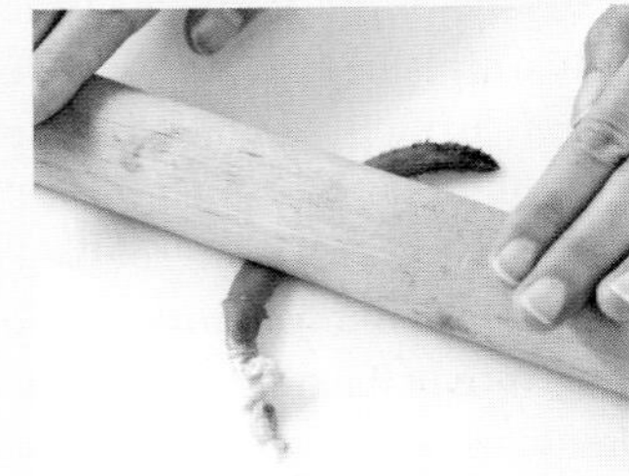

6. FINISH WITH LEGS: Twist legs to remove them. Lay legs flat on counter. Using rolling pin, start from claw end and roll toward open end, pushing out meat. Stop rolling before reaching end of legs; otherwise leg can crack and release pieces of shell.

NEW ENGLAND LOBSTER ROLL

WHY THIS RECIPE WORKS: We wanted to bring home a true New England–style lobster roll, complete with tender meat coated in a light dressing and tucked into a buttery toasted bun, but first we had to deal with the lobster. To make things easier, we sedated the lobster by placing it in the freezer for 30 minutes. Boiling was the easiest way to cook it, and removing it from the water when the tail registered 175 degrees ensured it was perfectly tender. For the lobster roll, we adhered mostly to tradition, tossing our lobster with just a bit of mayonnaise and adding a hint of crunch with lettuce leaves and a small amount of minced celery. Onion and shallot were overpowering, but minced chives offered bright herb flavor. Lemon juice and a pinch of cayenne provided a nice counterpoint to the rich lobster and mayo.

New England Lobster Roll

SERVES 6

This recipe is best when made with lobster you've cooked yourself. Use a very small pinch of cayenne pepper, as it should not make the dressing spicy. We prefer New England–style top-loading hot dog buns, as they provide maximum surface on the sides for toasting. If using other buns, butter, salt, and toast the interior of each bun instead of the exterior.

- 2 tablespoons mayonnaise
- 2 tablespoons minced celery
- 1½ teaspoons lemon juice
- 1 teaspoon minced fresh chives
- Salt
- Pinch cayenne pepper
- 1 pound lobster meat, tail meat cut into ½-inch pieces and claw meat cut into 1-inch pieces
- 2 tablespoons unsalted butter, softened
- 6 New England–style hot dog buns
- 6 leaves Boston lettuce

1. Whisk mayonnaise, celery, lemon juice, chives, ⅛ teaspoon salt, and cayenne together in large bowl. Add lobster and gently toss to combine.

2. Place 12-inch nonstick skillet over low heat. Butter both sides of hot dog buns and sprinkle lightly with salt. Place buns in skillet, with 1 buttered side down; increase heat to medium-low; and cook until crisp and brown, 2 to 3 minutes. Flip and cook second side until crisp and brown, 2 to 3 minutes longer. Transfer buns to large platter. Line each bun with lettuce leaf. Spoon lobster salad into buns and serve immediately.

Boiled Lobster

SERVES 4; YIELDS 1 POUND MEAT

To cook four lobsters at once, you will need a pot with a capacity of at least 3 gallons. If your pot is smaller, boil the lobsters in batches. Start timing the lobsters from the moment they go into the pot.

- 4 (1¼-pound) live lobsters
- ⅓ cup salt

1. Place lobsters in large bowl and freeze for 30 minutes. Meanwhile, bring 2 gallons water to boil in large pot over high heat.

2. Add lobsters and salt to pot, arranging with tongs so that all lobsters are submerged. Cover pot, leaving lid slightly ajar, and adjust heat to maintain gentle boil. Cook for 12 minutes, until thickest part of tail registers 175 degrees (insert thermometer into underside of tail to take temperature). If temperature registers lower than 175 degrees, return lobster to pot for 2 minutes longer, until tail registers 175 degrees, using tongs to transfer lobster in and out of pot.

3. Serve immediately or transfer lobsters to rimmed baking sheet and set aside until cool enough to remove meat, about 10 minutes. (Lobster meat can be refrigerated in airtight container for up to 24 hours.)

OVEN-STEAMED MUSSELS

WHY THIS RECIPE WORKS: We wanted to figure out a foolproof way to guarantee that our mussels cooked through at the same rate, so that they were all wide open and perfectly tender, even if they were different sizes. First, we moved them from the stovetop to the oven, where the even heat ensured they cooked through more gently, and we traded the Dutch oven for a large roasting pan so they weren't crowded. Covering the pan with aluminum foil trapped the moisture so the mussels didn't dry out. For a flavorful cooking liquid, we reduced white wine to concentrate its flavor and added thyme, garlic, and red pepper flakes for aromatic complexity. To avoid dirtying another pan, we simply cooked the aromatics and wine on the stovetop in the roasting pan before tossing in our mussels and transferring the pan to the oven. A few pats of butter, stirred in at the end, gave the sauce richness and body.

Oven-Steamed Mussels

SERVES 2 TO 4

Occasionally, mussels will have a harmless fibrous piece (known as the beard) protruding from between the shells. To remove it easily, trap the beard between the side of a small paring knife and your thumb and pull to remove it. The flat surface of the knife gives you some leverage to remove the beard. Unopened cooked mussels just need more cooking time. To open them, microwave briefly for 30 seconds or so. Serve mussels with crusty bread to sop up the flavorful broth.

- 1 tablespoon extra-virgin olive oil
- 3 garlic cloves, minced
- Pinch red pepper flakes
- 1 cup dry white wine
- 3 sprigs fresh thyme
- 2 bay leaves
- 4 pounds mussels, scrubbed and debearded
- ¼ teaspoon salt
- 2 tablespoons unsalted butter, cut into 4 pieces
- 2 tablespoons minced fresh parsley

1. Adjust oven rack to lowest position and heat oven to 500 degrees. Heat oil, garlic, and pepper flakes in large roasting pan over medium heat; cook, stirring constantly, until fragrant, about 30 seconds. Add wine, thyme sprigs, and bay leaves and bring to boil. Cook until wine is slightly reduced, about 1 minute. Add mussels and salt. Cover pan tightly with aluminum foil and transfer to oven. Cook until most mussels have opened (a few may remain closed), 15 to 18 minutes.

2. Remove pan from oven. Push mussels to sides of pan. Add butter to center and whisk until melted. Discard thyme sprigs and bay leaves, sprinkle parsley over mussels, and toss to combine. Serve immediately.

Oven-Steamed Mussels with Tomato and Chorizo

Omit red pepper flakes and increase oil to 3 tablespoons. Heat oil and 12 ounces Spanish-style chorizo sausage, cut into ½-inch pieces, in roasting pan until chorizo starts to brown, about 5 minutes. Add garlic and cook until fragrant, about 30 seconds. Proceed with recipe as directed, adding 1 (28-ounce) can crushed tomatoes to roasting pan before adding mussels and increasing butter to 3 tablespoons.

Oven-Steamed Mussels with Leeks and Pernod

Omit red pepper flakes and increase oil to 3 tablespoons. Heat oil; 1 pound leeks, white and light green parts only, halved lengthwise, sliced thin, and washed thoroughly; and garlic in roasting pan until leeks are wilted, about 3 minutes. Proceed with recipe as directed, omitting thyme sprigs and substituting ½ cup Pernod and ¼ cup water for wine, ¼ cup crème fraîche for butter, and chives for parsley.

Oven-Steamed Mussels with Hard Cider and Bacon

Omit garlic and red pepper flakes. Heat oil and 4 slices thick-cut bacon, cut into ½-inch pieces, in roasting pan until bacon has rendered and is starting to crisp, about 5 minutes. Proceed with recipe as directed, substituting dry hard cider for wine and ¼ cup heavy cream for butter.

NOTES FROM THE TEST KITCHEN

DEBEARDING MUSSELS

Because of the way they're cultivated, most mussels are free of the fibrous strands, or "beards," that wild mussels use to adhere to surfaces. If your mussel has a beard, hold it and use the back of a paring knife to remove it with a stern yank.

INDOOR CLAMBAKE

WHY THIS RECIPE WORKS: A clambake is perhaps the ultimate seafood meal: clams, mussels, and lobster, nestled with sausage, corn, and potatoes, all steamed together with hot stones in a sand pit by the sea. A genuine clambake is an all-day affair and, of course, requires a beach. But we wanted to re-create the great flavors of the clambake indoors, so we could enjoy this flavorful feast anywhere, without hours of preparation.

A large stockpot was the cooking vessel of choice. Many recipes suggest cooking the ingredients separately before adding them to the pot, but we found that with careful layering, we could cook everything in the same pot and have it all finish at the same time. And we didn't need to add water, because the shellfish released enough liquid to steam everything else. Sliced sausage went into the pot first (we liked kielbasa), so that it could sear before the steam was generated. Clams and mussels were next, wrapped in cheesecloth for easy removal. Then in went the potatoes, which would take the longest to cook; they were best placed near the heat source, and we cut them into 1-inch pieces to cook more quickly. Corn, with the husks left on to protect it from seafood flavors and lobster foam, was next, followed by the lobsters. It took less than half an hour for everything to cook—and we had all the elements of a clambake (minus the sand and surf) without having spent all day preparing them.

Indoor Clambake

SERVES 4 TO 6

Choose a large, narrow stockpot in which you can easily layer the ingredients. The recipe can be cut in half and layered in an 8-quart Dutch oven, but it should cook for the same amount of time. We prefer small littlenecks for this recipe. If your market carries larger clams, use 4 pounds. Mussels sometimes contain a weedy beard protruding from the crack between the two shells. It's fairly small and can be difficult to tug out of place. To remove it easily, trap the beard between the side of a small paring knife and your thumb and pull to remove it. The flat surface of the knife gives you some leverage to remove the beard.

- 2 pounds small littleneck or cherrystone clams, scrubbed (see note)
- 2 pounds mussels, scrubbed and debearded (see note)
- 1 pound kielbasa, sliced into ⅓-inch-thick rounds
- 1 pound small new or red potatoes, scrubbed and cut into 1-inch pieces
- 6 medium ears corn, silk and all but the last layer of husk removed
- 2 (1½-pound) live lobsters
- 8 tablespoons (1 stick) salted butter, melted

1. Place the clams and mussels on a large piece of cheesecloth and tie the ends together to secure; set aside. In a heavy-bottomed 12-quart stockpot, layer the sliced kielbasa, the sack of clams and mussels, the potatoes, the corn, and the lobsters on top of one another. Cover with the lid and place over high heat. Cook until the potatoes are tender (a paring knife can be slipped into and out of the center of a potato with little resistance), and the lobsters are bright red, 17 to 20 minutes.

2. Remove the pot from the heat and remove the lid (watch out for scalding steam). Remove the lobsters and set aside until cool enough to handle. Remove the corn from the pot and peel off the husks; arrange the ears on a large platter. Using a slotted spoon, remove the potatoes and arrange them on the platter with the corn. Transfer the clams and mussels to a large bowl and cut open the cheesecloth with scissors. Using a slotted spoon, remove the kielbasa from the pot and arrange it on the platter with the potatoes and corn. Pour the remaining steaming liquid in the pot over the clams and mussels. Using a kitchen towel to protect your hand, twist and remove the lobster tails, claws, and legs (if desired). Arrange the lobster parts on the platter. Serve immediately with the melted butter and napkins.

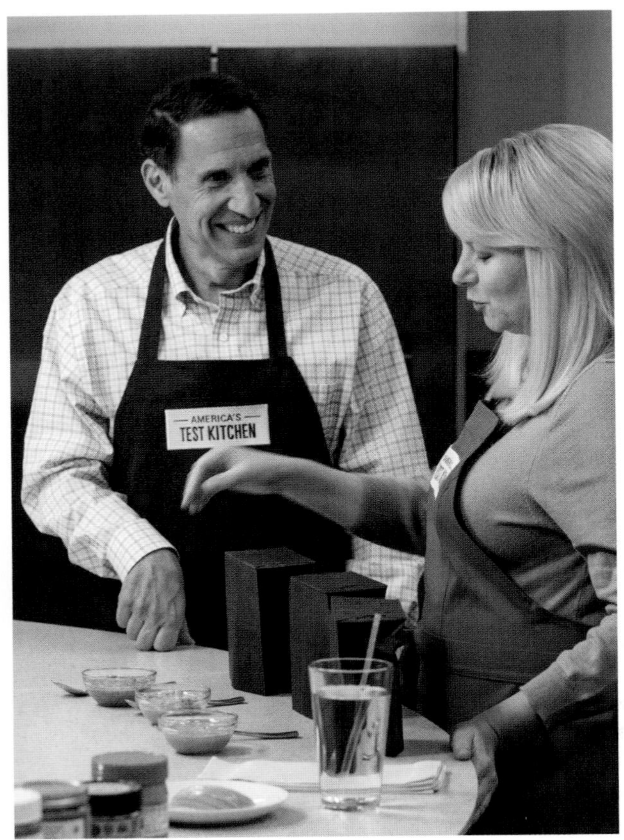

CHAPTER 11

DINNER AT THE DINER

TUNA SALAD

WHY THIS RECIPE WORKS: Tuna salads have been given a bad name by their typically mushy, watery, and bland condition. We wanted a tuna salad that was evenly textured, moist, and well seasoned. We learned that there are three keys to a great tuna salad. The first is to drain the tuna thoroughly in a colander; don't just tip the water out of the can. Next, instead of using a fork, break up the tuna with your fingers for a finer, more even texture. Finally, season the tuna before adding the mayonnaise for maximum flavor. Some additions to tuna salad are a matter of taste, but we thought that small amounts of garlic and mustard added another dimension, and minced pickle was a piquant touch. In addition to classic tuna salad, we developed a few variations that include tuna with balsamic vinegar and grapes, another with curry and apples, and a third with lime and horseradish.

Classic Tuna Salad

MAKES ABOUT 2 CUPS, ENOUGH FOR 4 SANDWICHES

Our favorite canned tuna is Wild Planet Wild Albacore. For more information on why we like this brand, see page 925.

- 2 (6-ounce) cans solid white tuna in water (see note)
- 1 small celery rib, minced (about ¼ cup)
- 2 tablespoons juice from 1 lemon
- 2 tablespoons minced red onion
- 2 tablespoons minced dill or sweet pickles
- 2 tablespoons minced fresh parsley leaves
- ½ small garlic clove, minced or pressed through a garlic press (about ½ teaspoon)
- ½ teaspoon table salt
- ¼ teaspoon ground black pepper
- ½ cup mayonnaise
- ¼ teaspoon Dijon mustard

Drain the tuna in a colander and shred with your fingers until no clumps remain and the texture is fine and even. Transfer the tuna to a medium bowl and mix in the celery, lemon juice, onion, pickles, parsley, garlic, salt, and pepper until evenly blended. Fold in the mayonnaise and mustard until the tuna is evenly moistened. (The tuna salad can be refrigerated in an airtight container for up to 3 days.)

Tuna Salad with Balsamic Vinegar and Grapes

Follow the recipe for Classic Tuna Salad, omitting the lemon juice, pickles, garlic, and parsley and adding 2 tablespoons balsamic vinegar, 6 ounces halved red seedless grapes (about 1 cup), ¼ cup lightly toasted slivered almonds, and 2 teaspoons minced thyme leaves to the tuna along with the salt and pepper.

Curried Tuna Salad with Apples and Currants

Follow the recipe for Classic Tuna Salad, omitting the pickles, garlic, and parsley and adding 1 medium firm, juicy apple, cut into ¼-inch dice (about 1 cup), ¼ cup currants, and 2 tablespoons minced fresh basil leaves to the tuna along with the lemon juice, salt, and pepper; mix 1 tablespoon curry powder into the mayonnaise before folding into the tuna.

Tuna Salad with Lime and Horseradish

Follow the recipe for Classic Tuna Salad, omitting the lemon juice, pickles, and garlic and adding 2 tablespoons juice and ½ teaspoon grated zest from 1 lime and 3 tablespoons prepared horseradish to the tuna along with the salt and pepper.

CLASSIC CHICKEN SALAD

WHY THIS RECIPE WORKS: Recipes for chicken salad are only as good as the chicken itself. If the chicken is dry or flavorless, no amount of dressing or add-ins will camouflage it. To ensure silky, juicy, and flavorful chicken, we used a method based on *sous vide* cooking (submerging vacuum-sealed foods in a temperature-controlled water bath). Our ideal formula was four chicken breasts and 6 cups of cold water heated to 170 degrees and then removed from the heat, covered, and left to stand for about 15 minutes. This yielded incomparably moist chicken that was perfect for chicken salad.

Classic Chicken Salad

SERVES 4 TO 6

To ensure that the chicken cooks through, don't use breasts that weigh more than 8 ounces or are thicker than 1 inch. Make sure to start with cold water in step 1. We like the combination of parsley and tarragon, but 2 tablespoons of one or the other is fine. This salad can be served in a sandwich or spooned over leafy greens.

- Salt and pepper
- 4 (6- to 8-ounce) boneless, skinless chicken breasts, no more than 1 inch thick, trimmed
- ½ cup mayonnaise

- 2 tablespoons lemon juice
- 1 teaspoon Dijon mustard
- 2 celery ribs, minced
- 1 shallot, minced
- 1 tablespoon minced fresh parsley
- 1 tablespoon minced fresh tarragon

1. Dissolve 2 tablespoons salt in 6 cups cold water in Dutch oven. Submerge chicken in water. Heat pot over medium heat until water registers 170 degrees. Turn off heat, cover pot, and let stand until chicken registers 165 degrees, 15 to 17 minutes.

2. Transfer chicken to paper towel–lined baking sheet. Refrigerate until chicken is cool, about 30 minutes. While chicken cools, whisk mayonnaise, lemon juice, mustard, and ¼ teaspoon pepper together in large bowl.

3. Pat chicken dry with paper towels and cut into ½-inch pieces. Transfer chicken to bowl with mayonnaise mixture. Add celery, shallot, parsley, and tarragon; toss to combine. Season with salt and pepper to taste. Serve. (Salad can be refrigerated for up to 2 days.)

Curried Chicken Salad with Cashews

Microwave 1 teaspoon vegetable oil, 1 teaspoon curry powder, and ⅛ teaspoon cayenne pepper together, uncovered, until oil is hot, about 30 seconds. Add curry oil to mayonnaise and substitute lime juice for lemon juice and 1 teaspoon grated fresh ginger for mustard in step 2. Substitute 2 tablespoons minced fresh cilantro for parsley and tarragon, and add ½ cup coarsely chopped toasted cashews and ⅓ cup golden raisins to salad with celery.

Waldorf Chicken Salad

Add ½ teaspoon ground fennel seeds to mayonnaise mixture in step 2. Substitute 1 teaspoon minced fresh thyme for parsley and add 1 peeled Granny Smith apple, cut into ¼-inch pieces, and ½ cup coarsely chopped toasted walnuts to salad with celery.

Chicken Salad with Red Grapes and Smoked Almonds

Add ¼ teaspoon grated lemon zest to mayonnaise mixture in step 2. Substitute 1 teaspoon minced fresh rosemary for tarragon, and add 1 cup quartered red grapes and ½ cup coarsely chopped smoked almonds to salad with celery.

GRILLED CHEESE SANDWICHES

WHY THIS RECIPE WORKS: The perfect grilled cheese consists of evenly melted cheese between crisp bread, but most don't turn out that way. We set out to find the keys to the ideal sandwich. We found that grating the cheese on a box grater enabled us to get an even layer of cheese onto the bread. Butter melted in the pan sometimes burned and didn't always coat the bread evenly, so we opted to butter the bread rather than the pan. And to coat the bread evenly and prevent it from tearing, we melted the butter first. Finally, we learned that the secret of a crisp exterior is low heat; the longer it takes for the bread to become golden, the crispier the bread will become—these are grilled cheese sandwiches worth the wait.

Classic Grilled Cheese Sandwiches

SERVES 2

The traditional grilled cheese sandwich usually uses a mild cheddar cheese, but our technique for this sandwich works with most any cheese. Grilled cheese sandwiches are best served hot out of the pan, though in a pinch they can be held, unsliced, for up to 20 minutes in a warm oven. If you want to make more than two sandwiches at once, get two skillets going or use an electric griddle set at medium-low (about 250 degrees), grilling 10 minutes per side. The possible variations on the basic grilled cheese sandwich are endless, but the extras are best sandwiched between the cheese. Try a few very thin slices of baked ham, prosciutto, turkey breast, or ripe, in-season tomato. Condiments such as Dijon mustard, pickle relish, or chutney can be spread on the bread instead of sandwiched in the cheese.

- 3 ounces cheese (preferably mild cheddar) or a combination of cheeses, shredded on the large holes of a box grater (about ¾ cup; see note)
- 4 slices high-quality white sandwich bread
- 2 tablespoons unsalted butter, melted

1. Heat a heavy 12-inch skillet over low to medium-low heat. Meanwhile, sprinkle the cheese evenly over two bread slices. Top each with a remaining bread slice, pressing down gently to set.

2. Brush the sandwich tops completely with half of the melted butter; place each sandwich, buttered side down, in the skillet. Brush the remaining side of each sandwich completely with the remaining butter. Cook until crisp and deep golden brown, 5 to 10 minutes per side, flipping the sandwiches back to the first side to reheat and crisp, about 15 seconds. Serve immediately.

GROWN-UP GRILLED CHEESE SANDWICHES

WHY THIS RECIPE WORKS: Melty American cheese on fluffy white bread is a childhood classic, but we wanted a grilled cheese for adults that offered more robust flavor. Aged cheddar gave us the complexity we were after, but it made for a greasy sandwich with a grainy filling. Adding a splash of wine and some Brie helped the aged cheddar melt evenly without separating or becoming greasy. Using a food processor to combine the ingredients ensured our cheese-and-wine mixture was easy to spread. A little bit of shallot ramped up the flavor without detracting from the cheese, and a smear of mustard butter livened up the bread.

Grown-Up Grilled Cheese Sandwiches with Cheddar and Shallot

SERVES 4

For the best flavor, look for a cheddar aged for about one year (avoid cheddar aged for longer; it won't melt well in this recipe). To quickly bring the cheese to room temperature, microwave the pieces until warm, about 30 seconds. The first two sandwiches can be held in a 200-degree oven on a wire rack set in a baking sheet while the second batch cooks.

- 7 ounces aged cheddar cheese, cut into 24 equal pieces, room temperature
- 2 ounces Brie cheese, rind removed
- 2 tablespoons dry white wine or dry vermouth
- 4 teaspoons minced shallot
- 3 tablespoons unsalted butter, softened
- 1 teaspoon Dijon mustard
- 8 slices hearty white sandwich bread

1. Process cheddar, Brie, and wine in food processor until smooth paste is formed, 20 to 30 seconds. Add shallot and pulse to combine, 3 to 5 pulses. Combine butter and mustard in small bowl.

2. Working on parchment paper–lined counter, divide mustard butter evenly among slices of bread. Spread butter evenly over surface of bread. Flip 4 slices of bread over and spread cheese mixture evenly over slices. Top with remaining 4 slices of bread, buttered sides up.

3. Preheat 12-inch nonstick skillet over medium heat for 2 minutes. (Droplets of water should just sizzle when flicked onto pan.) Place 2 sandwiches in skillet, reduce heat to medium-low, and cook until both sides are crisp and golden brown, 6 to 9 minutes per side, moving sandwiches to ensure even browning. Remove sandwiches from skillet and let stand for 2 minutes before serving. Repeat with remaining 2 sandwiches.

Grown-Up Grilled Cheese Sandwiches with Gruyère and Chives

Substitute Gruyère cheese for cheddar, chives for shallot, and rye sandwich bread for white sandwich bread.

Grown-Up Grilled Cheese Sandwiches with Asiago and Dates

Substitute Asiago cheese for cheddar, finely chopped pitted dates for shallot, and oatmeal sandwich bread for white sandwich bread.

Grown-Up Grilled Cheese Sandwiches with Comté and Cornichon

Substitute Comté cheese for cheddar, minced cornichon for shallot, and rye sandwich bread for white sandwich bread.

Grown-Up Grilled Cheese Sandwiches with Robiola and Chipotle

Substitute Robiola cheese, rind removed, for cheddar; 1/4 teaspoon minced canned chipotle chile in adobo sauce for shallot; and oatmeal sandwich bread for white sandwich bread.

CLASSIC MACARONI AND CHEESE

WHY THIS RECIPE WORKS: Old-fashioned macaroni and cheese takes no shortcuts. This family favorite should boast tender pasta in a smooth, creamy sauce with great cheese flavor. Too often, the dish, which is baked in the oven, dries out or curdles. We aimed to create a foolproof version.

We cooked the pasta until just past al dente and then combined it with a béchamel-based cheese sauce. For the best flavor and a creamy texture, we used a combination of sharp cheddar and Monterey Jack. We combined the cooked pasta with the sauce and heated it through on the stovetop, rather than in the oven. This step helped ensure the dish didn't dry out, but remained smooth and creamy. And to give the dish a browned topping, we sprinkled it with bread crumbs and ran it briefly under the broiler.

Classic Macaroni and Cheese

SERVES 6 TO 8

It's crucial to cook the pasta until tender—that is, just past the al dente stage. Whole, low-fat, and skim milk all work well in this recipe. The recipe may be halved and baked in an 8-inch square, broiler-safe baking dish. If desired, offer celery salt or hot sauce for sprinkling at the table.

BREAD-CRUMB TOPPING

- 6 slices high-quality white sandwich bread, torn into quarters
- 3 tablespoons cold unsalted butter, cut into 6 pieces

MACARONI AND CHEESE

- 1 tablespoon plus 1 teaspoon table salt
- 1 pound elbow macaroni
- 5 tablespoons unsalted butter
- 6 tablespoons unbleached all-purpose flour
- 1½ teaspoons dry mustard
- ¼ teaspoon cayenne pepper (optional)
- 5 cups milk (see note)
- 8 ounces Monterey Jack cheese, shredded (about 2 cups)
- 8 ounces sharp cheddar cheese, shredded (about 2 cups)

1. FOR THE BREAD-CRUMB TOPPING: Pulse the bread and butter in a food processor until coarsely ground, 10 to 15 pulses. Set aside.

2. FOR THE MACARONI AND CHEESE: Adjust an oven rack to the lower-middle position and heat the broiler. Bring 4 quarts water to a rolling boil in a large pot. Add 1 tablespoon of the salt and the macaroni and stir to separate the noodles. Cook until tender, drain, and set aside.

3. In the now-empty pot, melt the butter over medium-high heat. Add the flour, mustard, cayenne (if using), and remaining 1 teaspoon salt and whisk well to combine. Continue whisking until the mixture becomes fragrant and deepens in color, about 1 minute. Whisking constantly, gradually add the milk; bring the mixture to a boil, whisking constantly (the mixture must reach a full boil to fully thicken), then reduce the heat to medium and simmer, whisking occasionally, until thickened to the consistency of heavy cream, about 5 minutes. Off the heat, whisk in the cheeses until fully melted. Add the pasta and cook over medium-low heat, stirring constantly, until the mixture is steaming and heated through, about 6 minutes.

4. Transfer the mixture to a broiler-safe 13 by 9-inch baking dish and sprinkle with the bread crumbs. Broil until deep golden brown, 3 to 5 minutes. Cool for 5 minutes, then serve.

STOVETOP MACARONI AND CHEESE

WHY THIS RECIPE WORKS: Just about the only thing boxed macaroni and cheese has going for it is its fast prep—and the fact that kids will almost always gobble it up. We wanted a quick stovetop macaroni and cheese with an ultra-creamy texture and authentic cheese flavor—so good that it would satisfy everyone at the table.

We cooked the macaroni to just shy of al dente, then drained and combined it with butter and an egg custard mixture that included evaporated milk, eggs, hot sauce, and dry mustard. For the cheese we chose cheddar, American, or Monterey Jack—and plenty of it. We stirred the cheese into the macaroni mixture until thick and creamy and then topped the mixture with toasted homemade bread crumbs–the final touch to this easy-to-prepare family favorite.

Stovetop Macaroni and Cheese

SERVES 4

If you're in a hurry or prefer to sprinkle the dish with crumbled crackers (saltines aren't bad), you can skip the bread-crumb step.

BREAD-CRUMB TOPPING

- 3 slices high-quality white sandwich bread, torn into quarters
- 2 tablespoons unsalted butter
- Table salt

MACARONI AND CHEESE

- 2 large eggs
- 1 (12-ounce) can evaporated milk
- 2 teaspoons table salt
- ¼ teaspoon ground black pepper
- 1 teaspoon dry mustard, dissolved in 1 teaspoon water
- ¼ teaspoon hot sauce
- 8 ounces elbow macaroni (about 2 cups)
- 4 tablespoons (½ stick) unsalted butter
- 12 ounces sharp cheddar, American, or Monterey Jack cheese, shredded (about 3 cups)

1. FOR THE BREAD CRUMBS: Pulse the bread in a food processor until coarsely ground, 10 to 15 pulses. Melt the butter in a large skillet over medium heat. Add the bread crumbs and cook, tossing to coat with the butter, until the crumbs just begin to color, about 10 minutes. Season with salt to taste; set aside.

2. FOR THE MACARONI AND CHEESE: Mix the eggs, 1 cup of the evaporated milk, ½ teaspoon of the salt, the pepper, mustard mixture, and hot sauce in a small bowl; set aside.

3. Meanwhile, bring 2 quarts water to a boil in a large heavy-bottomed saucepan or Dutch oven. Add the remaining 1½ teaspoons salt and the macaroni; cook until almost tender but still a little firm to the bite. Drain and return to the pan over low heat. Add the butter; toss to melt.

4. Pour the egg mixture over the buttered noodles along with three-quarters of the cheese; stir until thoroughly combined and the cheese starts to melt. Gradually add the remaining ½ cup milk and the remaining cheese, stirring constantly, until the mixture is hot and creamy, about 5 minutes. Serve immediately, topped with the toasted bread crumbs.

ADULT MACARONI AND CHEESE

WHY THIS RECIPE WORKS: We turned to science to help make our mac and cheese creamy and smooth. We were inspired by an innovative recipe calling for adding sodium citrate, an emulsifier, to cheese to keep it smooth when heated (instead of adding flour to make a béchamel). American cheese, which contains a similar stabilizing ingredient, was the solution. But because it tastes so plain, we combined it with Gruyère and blue cheese, as well as mustard and cayenne for more sophisticated flavor. We cooked the macaroni in a smaller-than-usual amount of water, so we didn't have to drain it; the liquid that was left after the elbows were hydrated was just enough to form the base of the sauce. Rather than bake the mac and cheese, we sprinkled toasted panko bread crumbs on top to keep things simple.

Grown-Up Stovetop Macaroni and Cheese

SERVES 4

Barilla makes our favorite elbow macaroni. Because the macaroni is cooked in a measured amount of liquid, we don't recommend using different shapes or sizes of pasta. Use a 4-ounce block of American cheese from the deli counter rather than presliced cheese.

- 1¾ cups water
- 1 cup milk
- 8 ounces elbow macaroni
- 4 ounces American cheese, shredded (1 cup)
- ½ teaspoon Dijon mustard
- Small pinch cayenne pepper
- 3½ ounces Gruyère cheese, shredded (¾ cup)
- 2 tablespoons crumbled blue cheese
- ⅓ cup panko bread crumbs
- 1 tablespoon extra-virgin olive oil
- Salt and pepper
- 2 tablespoons grated Parmesan cheese

1. Bring water and milk to boil in medium saucepan over high heat. Stir in macaroni and reduce heat to medium-low. Cook, stirring frequently, until macaroni is soft (slightly past al dente), 6 to 8 minutes. Add American cheese, mustard, and cayenne and cook, stirring constantly, until cheese is completely melted, about 1 minute. Off heat, stir in Gruyère and blue cheese until evenly distributed but not melted. Cover saucepan and let stand for 5 minutes.

2. Meanwhile, combine panko, oil, ⅛ teaspoon salt, and ⅛ teaspoon pepper in 8-inch nonstick skillet until panko is evenly moistened. Cook over medium heat, stirring frequently, until evenly browned, 3 to 4 minutes. Off heat, sprinkle Parmesan over panko mixture and stir to combine. Transfer panko mixture to small bowl.

3. Stir macaroni until sauce is smooth (sauce may look loose but will thicken as it cools). Season with salt and pepper to taste. Transfer to warm serving dish and sprinkle panko mixture over top. Serve immediately.

BEHIND THE SCENES

PASS THE PEPTO, PLEASE

During the tasting lab segments, Jack asks Bridget and Julia to pick out the test kitchen's winning brands from the losers. It doesn't look hard on television, but what viewers don't know is that we film as many as 11 tasting segments in a single day. That's because it takes the production team a few hours to light the tasting lab and position the cameras. Once the crew is in place, it makes sense to keep shooting one segment after another for two days straight. That means Bridget or Julia has to do at least one—often two—tasting segments every hour, starting as early as 8 a.m. and ending around 6 p.m. So what's on the menu? Here's a sample lineup from just one day in the tasting lab: jarred anchovies, olive oil, smoked paprika, whole-milk Greek yogurt, sherry vinegar, Parmesan cheese, and almond butter.

LIGHT MACARONI AND CHEESE

WHY THIS RECIPE WORKS: Weighing in at about 650 calories and 40 grams of fat per serving, a bowl of homemade mac and cheese should really be a treat every once in a while, like a slice of cake. But the truth is, most of us like to enjoy this family favorite a little more often. We aimed to develop a lighter version of mac and cheese—macaroni in a creamy (not rubbery or grainy), cheesy sauce—with a fraction of the calories.

We slashed both fat and calories by replacing full-fat cheddar with low-fat—its flavor and texture are vastly superior to nonfat cheddar. We also swapped in 2 percent milk for the whole milk and added 2 percent evaporated milk to ensure a creamy consistency. And we found that we could eliminate butter entirely by thickening the sauce with cornstarch instead of a classic roux. In the end, we cut the calories by almost half and the fat grams by 75 percent, turning full-fat macaroni and cheese into a dish you could eat every day.

Light Macaroni and Cheese

SERVES 4 TO 6

Don't be tempted to use either preshredded or nonfat cheddar cheese in this dish—the texture and flavor of the macaroni and cheese will suffer substantially. For best results, choose a low-fat cheddar cheese that is sold in block form and has roughly 50 percent of the fat and calories of regular cheese (we like Cracker Barrel brand).

- Table salt
- 8 ounces elbow macaroni (about 2 cups)
- 1 (12-ounce) can 2 percent reduced-fat evaporated milk
- ¾ cup 2 percent milk
- ¼ teaspoon dry mustard
- ⅛ teaspoon garlic powder or celery salt (optional)
- Pinch cayenne pepper
- 2 teaspoons cornstarch
- 8 ounces 50 percent light cheddar cheese, shredded (about 2 cups; see note)

1. Bring 2½ quarts water to a boil in a large saucepan. Stir in 2 teaspoons salt and the macaroni; cook until the pasta is completely cooked and tender, about 5 minutes. Drain the pasta and leave it in the colander; set aside.

2. Add the evaporated milk, ½ cup of the 2 percent milk, the mustard, garlic powder (if using), cayenne, and ½ teaspoon salt to the now-empty saucepan. Bring the mixture to a boil, then reduce to a simmer. Whisk the cornstarch and remaining ¼ cup milk together, then whisk it into the simmering mixture. Continue to simmer, whisking constantly, until the sauce has thickened and is smooth, about 2 minutes.

3. Off the heat, gradually whisk in the cheddar until melted and smooth. Stir in the macaroni and let the macaroni and cheese sit off the heat until the sauce has thickened slightly, 2 to 5 minutes, before serving.

TURKEY TETRAZZINI

WHY THIS RECIPE WORKS: Overcooking is the inevitable fate of many casseroles, as the contents are usually cooked twice: once on their own and once again when joined with the other casserole ingredients. We wanted a casserole with a silky sauce, a generous portion of turkey meat, and noodles cooked just until done.

We found we could cut the second cooking down to just 15 minutes by baking the recipe in a shallow dish that would allow it to heat through quickly. Most recipes for turkey Tetrazzini call for a béchamel sauce, in which milk is added to a roux (a paste made from fat and flour that is then cooked on the stovetop). In switching to a velouté, which is based on chicken stock rather than milk, we brightened up the texture and the flavor. We also used less sauce than most recipes call for, giving the other ingredients a chance to express themselves. Still looking for brighter flavor, we spruced things up with a shot of sherry and a little lemon juice and nutmeg. Parmesan cheese provided tang and bite, and a full 2 teaspoons of fresh thyme helped to freshen the overall impression of the dish.

Turkey Tetrazzini

SERVES 8

Don't skimp on the salt and pepper; this dish needs aggressive seasoning.

BREAD-CRUMB TOPPING

- 6 slices high-quality white sandwich bread, torn into quarters
- 4 tablespoons (½ stick) unsalted butter, melted
- Pinch table salt
- ½ ounce Parmesan cheese, grated (about ¼ cup)

BEHIND THE SCENES

COOKS WHO CAN MAKE THE CUT

Our recipes are created by a team of test cooks—more than three dozen cooks in total—who spend their day mincing, roasting, tasting, and talking about food. So what does it take to join our army of test cooks? It goes without saying that you must love to cook. Everyone in the test kitchen has professional cooking experience (this usually includes work in a restaurant kitchen as well as a degree from one of the top cooking schools in the country). But in-depth food knowledge and cooking skills are just a start.

To get hired, you must have a passion for understanding how things work in the kitchen. A curious mind is essential, as are attention to detail and a scientific approach to problem solving. Our test cooks are continually developing hypotheses to explain how a recipe works and then devising a testing protocol to prove (or disprove) their theory. Finally, we look for cooks who understand the realities of cooking at home—with imperfect equipment, the usual distractions (kids, pets, and phone calls), and no one to wash the dishes.

So how do we find test cooks? Our test kitchen director, Erin McMurrer, has developed a bench test for potential hires—it's like an audition, with knives. Erin gives potential hires two of our published recipes and watches them as they set to work preparing them. Chop those onions when the recipe says to mince them, and you're in trouble. Use a dry measuring cup to measure milk, and you're in serious trouble. Shape cookie dough into ½-inch balls when the recipe says 1-inch balls, and you're in very serious trouble. But job candidates can save the day when the cooking is done and Erin asks them to analyze their success and failures during the bench test. A candidate who can thoughtfully examine his or her work (and figure out how to remedy problems) might just make the cut.

FILLING

- 8 tablespoons (1 stick) unsalted butter, plus extra for the baking dish
- 8 ounces white mushrooms, wiped cleaned and sliced thin (about 3 cups)
- 2 medium onions, minced
- Table salt and ground black pepper (see note)
- 12 ounces spaghetti or other long-strand pasta, strands snapped in half
- 6 tablespoons unbleached all-purpose flour
- 3 cups low-sodium chicken broth
- 1½ ounces Parmesan cheese, grated (about ¾ cup)
- ¼ cup dry sherry
- 1 tablespoon juice from 1 lemon
- 2 teaspoons minced fresh thyme leaves
- ¼ teaspoon grated nutmeg
- 2 cups frozen peas
- 4 cups leftover cooked boneless turkey or chicken meat, cut into ¼-inch pieces

1. FOR THE TOPPING: Adjust an oven rack to the middle position and heat the oven to 350 degrees. Pulse the bread in a food processor until coarsely ground, 10 to 15 pulses. Mix the bread crumbs, butter, and salt in a small baking dish; bake until golden brown and crisp, 15 to 20 minutes. Cool to room temperature and mix with the Parmesan in a small bowl. Set aside.

2. FOR THE FILLING: Increase the oven temperature to 450 degrees. Melt 2 tablespoons of the butter in a large skillet over medium heat; add the mushrooms and onions and sauté, stirring frequently, until the liquid from the mushrooms evaporates, 12 to 15 minutes. Season with salt and pepper to taste; transfer the vegetables to a medium bowl and set aside. Clean the skillet.

3. Meanwhile, bring 4 quarts water to a boil in a large pot. Add 1 tablespoon salt and the pasta and cook until al dente. Reserve ¼ cup cooking water, drain the pasta, and return to the pot with the reserved liquid.

4. Melt the remaining 6 tablespoons butter in the clean skillet over medium heat. Whisk in the flour and cook, whisking constantly, until the flour turns golden, 1 to 2 minutes. Whisking constantly, gradually add the chicken broth. Increase the heat to medium-high and simmer until the mixture thickens, 3 to 4 minutes. Off the heat, whisk in the Parmesan, sherry, lemon juice, thyme, nutmeg, and ½ teaspoon salt. Add the sauce, sautéed vegetables, peas, and turkey to the pasta and mix well; season with salt and pepper to taste.

5. Turn the mixture into a buttered 13 by 9-inch gratin dish (or other shallow ovensafe baking dish of similar size), sprinkle evenly with the reserved bread crumbs, and bake until the bread crumbs brown and the mixture is bubbly, 13 to 15 minutes. Serve immediately.

CINCINNATI CHILI

WHY THIS RECIPE WORKS: This Midwestern diner specialty is an unusual marriage of American chili and Middle Eastern spices. For an easy weeknight meal, we wanted to pare the list of ingredients down to the essentials without compromising the distinctive character of the dish.

The beef in Cincinnati Chili isn't sautéed like the beef in other chilis, so there is no way to remove the fat. To avoid greasiness, we blanched ground chuck for half a minute, which got rid of most of the fat but still left plenty of flavor. The spices used in this chili vary from recipe to recipe. We settled on a limited palette starring chili powder, oregano, cinnamon, and cocoa powder, which we bloomed in hot oil for more depth of flavor. Water and tomato sauce are the traditional base for the sauce; we added chicken broth for balance. Vinegar and brown sugar livened things up. After a long simmer, the chili was ready to be served, and we couldn't think of a better way to do it than "five-way"—over spaghetti, topped with cheddar cheese, chopped onions, and kidney beans.

Cincinnati Chili

SERVES 6 TO 8

Use canned tomato sauce for this recipe—do not use jarred spaghetti sauce.

CHILI

- 2 teaspoons table salt, plus more to taste
- 1½ pounds 80 percent lean ground chuck
- 2 tablespoons vegetable oil
- 2 medium onions, minced
- 2 medium garlic cloves, minced or pressed through a garlic press (about 2 teaspoons)
- 2 tablespoons chili powder
- 2 teaspoons dried oregano
- 2 teaspoons cocoa powder
- 1½ teaspoons ground cinnamon
- ½ teaspoon cayenne pepper
- ½ teaspoon ground allspice
- ¼ teaspoon ground black pepper
- 2 cups tomato sauce
- 2 cups low-sodium chicken broth
- 2 cups water
- 2 tablespoons cider vinegar
- 2 teaspoons dark brown sugar
- Hot sauce

ACCOMPANIMENTS

- 1 pound spaghetti, cooked, drained, and tossed with 2 tablespoons unsalted butter
- 12 ounces sharp cheddar cheese, shredded (about 3 cups)
- 1 (15-ounce) can red kidney beans, drained, rinsed, and warmed
- 1 medium onion, chopped

1. FOR THE CHILI: Bring 2 quarts water and 1 teaspoon of the salt to a boil in a large saucepan. Add the ground chuck, stirring vigorously to separate the meat into individual strands. As soon as the foam from the meat rises to the top (this takes about 30 seconds) and before the water returns to a boil, drain the meat into a strainer and set it aside.

2. Rinse and dry the empty saucepan. Set the pan over medium heat and add the oil. When the oil is warm, add the onions and cook, stirring frequently, until the onions are soft and browned around the edges, about 8 minutes. Add the garlic and cook until fragrant, about 1 minute. Stir in the chili powder, oregano, cocoa, cinnamon, cayenne, allspice, black pepper, and the remaining 1 teaspoon salt. Cook, stirring constantly, until the spices are fragrant, about 30 seconds. Stir in the tomato sauce, broth, water, vinegar, and sugar, scraping the pan bottom to remove any browned bits.

3. Add the blanched ground beef and increase the heat to high. As soon as the liquid boils, reduce the heat to medium-low and simmer, stirring occasionally, until the chili is deep red and has thickened slightly, about 1 hour. Season with salt and hot sauce to taste. (The chili can be refrigerated in an airtight container for up to 3 days. Bring to a simmer over medium-low heat before serving.)

4. TO SERVE: Divide the buttered spaghetti among individual bowls. Spoon the chili over the spaghetti and top with the cheese, beans, and onion. Serve immediately.

CHICKEN-FRIED STEAK

WHY THIS RECIPE WORKS: Although this truck-stop favorite often gets a bad rap, chicken-fried steak can be delicious when cooked just right. Poorly prepared versions feature dry, rubbery steaks that snap back with each bite, coated in damp, pale breading and topped with a bland, pasty white sauce. When cooked well, thin cutlets of beef are breaded and fried until a crisp, golden brown. The creamy gravy that accompanies the steak is well seasoned and not too thick. This was our goal.

A thin steak works best here, so we turned to cube steak and pounded the meat to an even thickness. What makes this steak special is the crisp coating. After trying a variety of coatings—Melba toast, corn flakes, panko, and the like—we determined simple was best. We dredged the steaks in heavily seasoned flour, dipped them in a thick buttermilk and egg mixture aerated with baking power and baking soda, and then returned them to the seasoned flour for a second coat. This coating fried up to an impressive dark mahogany color with a resilient texture to stand up to the gravy. For the gravy, we built in flavor by using the fried bits left in the pan after cooking the steaks and by making a roux. Onions and cayenne are traditional for the gravy, but we found that small additions of thyme and garlic also improved its flavor.

Chicken-Fried Steaks

SERVES 6

Getting the initial oil temperature to 375 degrees is key to the success of this recipe. Use an instant-read thermometer with a high upper range to check the temperature; a clip-on candy/deep-fry thermometer is also fine. If your Dutch oven measures 11 inches across (as ours does), you will need to fry the steaks in two batches.

STEAKS

- 3 cups unbleached all-purpose flour
- Table salt and ground black pepper
- ⅛ teaspoon cayenne pepper
- 1 large egg
- 1 teaspoon baking powder
- ½ teaspoon baking soda
- 1 cup buttermilk
- 6 (5-ounce) cube steaks, pounded ⅓ inch thick
- 4–5 cups peanut oil

CREAM GRAVY

- 1 medium onion, minced
- ⅛ teaspoon dried thyme
- 2 medium garlic cloves, minced or pressed through a garlic press (about 2 teaspoons)
- 3 tablespoons unbleached all-purpose flour
- ½ cup low-sodium chicken broth
- 2 cups whole milk
- ¾ teaspoon table salt
- ¼ teaspoon ground black pepper
- Pinch cayenne pepper

1. FOR THE STEAKS: Mix the flour, 5 teaspoons salt, 1 teaspoon black pepper, and the cayenne together in a large shallow dish. In a second large shallow dish, beat the egg, baking powder, and baking soda; stir in the buttermilk.

2. Set a wire rack over a large rimmed baking sheet. Pat the steaks dry with paper towels and sprinkle each side with salt and pepper. One at a time, drop the steaks into the flour and shake the dish to coat. Shake excess flour from each steak, then, using tongs, dip each steak into the egg mixture, turning to coat well and allowing the excess to drip off. Coat the steaks with flour again, shake off the excess, and place them on the wire rack.

3. Adjust an oven rack to the middle position, set a second wire rack over a second rimmed baking sheet, and place the sheet on the oven rack; heat the oven to 200 degrees. Line a large plate with a double layer of paper towels. Meanwhile, heat 1 inch of oil in a large (11-inch diameter) Dutch oven over medium-high heat to 375 degrees. Place 3 steaks in the oil and fry, turning once, until deep golden brown on each side, about 5 minutes (the oil temperature will drop to around 335 degrees). Transfer the steaks to the paper towel–lined plate to drain, then transfer them to the wire rack in the oven. Bring the oil back to 375 degrees and repeat the cooking and draining process (use fresh paper towels) with the 3 remaining steaks.

4. FOR THE GRAVY: Carefully pour the hot oil through a fine-mesh strainer into a clean pot. Return the browned bits from the strainer along with 2 tablespoons of the frying oil to the Dutch oven. Turn the heat to medium, add the onion and thyme, and cook until the onion has softened and is beginning to brown, 4 to 5 minutes. Add the garlic and cook until aromatic, about 30 seconds. Add the flour to the pan and stir until well combined and starting to dissolve, about 1 minute. Whisk in the broth, scraping any browned bits off the bottom of the pan. Whisk in the milk, salt, black pepper, and cayenne; bring to a simmer over medium-high heat. Cook until thickened (the gravy should have a loose consistency—it will thicken as it cools), about 5 minutes.

5. Transfer the chicken-fried steaks to individual plates. Spoon a generous amount of gravy over each steak. Serve immediately, passing any remaining gravy separately.

ALL-BEEF MEATLOAF

WHY THIS RECIPE WORKS: Every all-beef meatloaf we've tasted has had the same problems—chewy texture and uninteresting flavor, making it more of a hamburger in the shape of a log than bona fide meatloaf. In the past, when we wanted a great meatloaf, we turned to a traditional meatloaf mix consisting of beef, pork, and veal. Could we create an all-beef meatloaf to compete with this classic?

Supermarkets offer a wide selection of "ground beef," and after testing them alone and in combination we determined that equal parts of chuck (for moisture) and sirloin (for beefy flavor) were best. Beef has a livery taste that we wanted to subdue, and the usual dairy additions to meatloaf didn't work. Chicken broth, oddly enough, neutralized this off-flavor and provided moisture. For additional moisture and richness, we included mild-tasting Monterey Jack cheese, which also helped bind the mixture. To avoid pockets of oozing hot cheese in the meatloaf, we shredded the cheese and froze it briefly. Crushed saltines, our choice for the starchy filler, provided texture, but we felt our meatloaf needed more "sliceability." Surprisingly, gelatin gave us just the smooth, luxurious texture we sought. We seasoned the mixture with onions, celery, garlic (all sautéed), thyme, paprika, soy sauce, and mustard. A traditional ketchup glaze crowned our flavorful all-beef meatloaf.

Glazed All-Beef Meatloaf

SERVES 6 TO 8

If you can't find chuck and/or sirloin, substitute 85 percent lean ground beef.

MEATLOAF

- 3 ounces Monterey Jack cheese, shredded on the small holes of a box grater (about 1 cup)
- 1 tablespoon unsalted butter
- 1 medium onion, minced
- 1 medium celery rib, minced
- 2 teaspoons minced fresh thyme leaves
- 1 teaspoon paprika
- 1 medium garlic clove, minced or pressed through a garlic press (about 1 teaspoon)
- ¼ cup tomato juice
- ½ cup low-sodium chicken broth
- 2 large eggs
- ½ teaspoon unflavored powdered gelatin
- ⅔ cup crushed saltines
- 2 tablespoons minced fresh parsley leaves
- 1 tablespoon soy sauce
- 1 teaspoon Dijon mustard
- ¾ teaspoon table salt
- ½ teaspoon ground black pepper
- 1 pound 90 percent lean ground sirloin (see note)
- 1 pound 80 percent lean ground chuck (see note)

NOTES FROM THE TEST KITCHEN

MAKING A FREE-FORM LOAF PAN

1. Set wire rack inside rimmed baking sheet and top with 10 by 6-inch rectangle of aluminum foil.

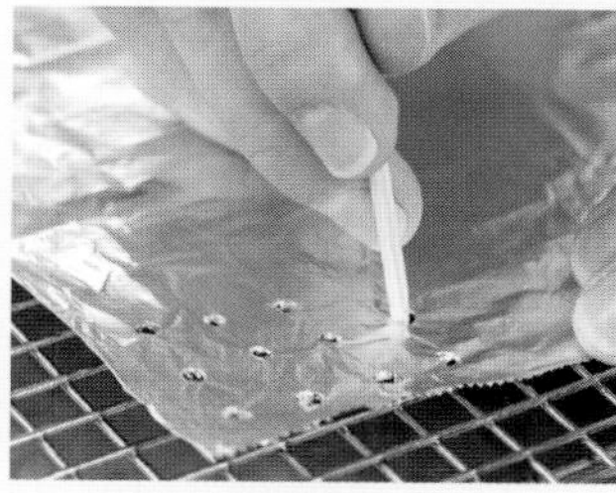

2. Using skewer, poke holes in foil, spacing them about half an inch apart.

GLAZE

- ½ cup ketchup
- ¼ cup cider vinegar
- 3 tablespoons light brown sugar
- 1 teaspoon hot sauce
- ½ teaspoon ground coriander

1. FOR THE MEATLOAF: Adjust an oven rack to the middle position and heat the oven to 375 degrees. Spread the cheese on a plate and place in the freezer until ready to use. To prepare the baking sheet, set a wire rack over a rimmed baking sheet. Fold a sheet of heavy-duty aluminum foil to form a 10 by 6-inch rectangle. Center the foil on the rack and poke holes in the foil with a skewer (about half an inch apart). Spray the foil with vegetable oil spray or use nonstick foil.

2. Melt the butter in a 10-inch skillet over medium-high heat; add the onion and celery and cook, stirring occasionally, until beginning to brown, 6 to 8 minutes. Add the thyme, paprika, and garlic and cook, stirring, until fragrant, about 1 minute. Reduce the heat to low and add the tomato juice. Cook, stirring to scrape up the browned bits from the pan, until thickened, about 1 minute. Transfer the mixture to a small bowl and set aside to cool.

3. Whisk the broth and eggs together in a large bowl until combined. Sprinkle the gelatin over the liquid and let stand for 5 minutes. Stir in the saltines, parsley, soy sauce, mustard, salt, pepper, and onion mixture. Crumble the frozen cheese into a coarse powder and sprinkle over the mixture. Add the sirloin and chuck; mix gently with your hands until thoroughly combined, about 1 minute. Transfer the meat to the foil rectangle and shape into a 10 by 6-inch oval about 2 inches high. Smooth the top and edges of the meatloaf with a moistened spatula. Bake until the center of the loaf registers 135 to 140 degrees on an instant-read thermometer, 55 to 65 minutes. Remove the meatloaf from the oven and turn on the broiler.

4. FOR THE GLAZE: While the meatloaf cooks, combine the glaze ingredients in a small saucepan; bring to a simmer over medium heat and cook, stirring, until thick and syrupy, about 5 minutes. Spread half of the glaze evenly over the cooked meatloaf with a rubber spatula; place under the broiler and cook until the glaze bubbles and begins to brown at the edges, about 5 minutes. Remove the meatloaf from the oven and spread evenly with the remaining glaze; place back under the broiler and cook until the glaze is again bubbling and beginning to brown, about 5 minutes more. Let the meatloaf cool for about 20 minutes before slicing.

CLASSIC MEATLOAF

WHY THIS RECIPE WORKS: Not all meatloaves resemble Mom's. Some recipes go the canned soup route and, frankly, taste like it. Others become gussied up with ingredients that have no place in this humble family dish—canned pineapple, sun-dried tomatoes, and the like. Our goal was not to develop the ultimate meatloaf but to bring it back to its classic roots—a tender, well-seasoned loaf smothered with tangy sweet glaze.

We started, of course, with the meat. We determined that supermarkets haven't been selling "meatloaf mix" for no reason—a mixture of ground beef chuck, ground pork, and ground veal produced the best balance of flavors and textures. A starch turned out to be a necessity for binding the meat and giving it that classic meatloaf texture; cracker crumbs, quick-cooking oatmeal, and fresh bread crumbs all worked well. To prevent the filler from drying out the meatloaf, we knew we needed to add some moisture. After trying a host of options, we determined that whole milk and plain yogurt are equally acceptable. Finally, we realized that the pan in which the meatloaf baked made a big difference. A standard loaf pan traps the fat and stews the meat, and the juice bubbles up and destroys the glaze. Baking the meatloaf free-form in a shallow baking pan gave the loaf a good crust, preserved our sweet-tart glaze, and helped the bacon topping crisp nicely.

Meatloaf with Brown Sugar–Ketchup Glaze

SERVES 6 TO 8

If you like, you can omit the bacon topping from the loaf. In this case, brush on half of the glaze before baking and the other half during the last 15 minutes of baking. If you choose not to special-order the mix of meat below, we recommend the standard meatloaf mix of equal parts beef, pork, and veal, available at most grocery stores. Lining the baking pan with foil makes for easier cleanup.

BROWN SUGAR–KETCHUP GLAZE

- ½ cup ketchup or chili sauce
- ¼ cup brown sugar
- 4 teaspoons cider vinegar or white vinegar

MEATLOAF

- 2 teaspoons vegetable oil
- 1 medium onion, chopped
- 2 medium garlic cloves, minced or pressed through a garlic press (about 2 teaspoons)
- 2 large eggs
- ½ cup whole milk or plain yogurt, plus more as needed
- 2 teaspoons Dijon mustard
- 2 teaspoons Worcestershire sauce
- 1 teaspoon table salt
- ½ teaspoon ground black pepper
- ½ teaspoon dried thyme
- ¼ teaspoon hot sauce
- 2 pounds meatloaf mix (50 percent ground chuck, 25 percent ground pork, 25 percent ground veal; see note)
- ⅔ cup crushed saltines (about 16) or quick oatmeal or 1⅓ cups fresh bread crumbs
- ⅓ cup minced fresh parsley leaves
- 6–8 ounces bacon (8 to 12 slices, depending on loaf shape) (see note)

1. FOR THE GLAZE: Mix all the ingredients together in a small saucepan; set aside.

2. FOR THE MEATLOAF: Line a 13 by 9-inch baking pan with foil; set aside. Heat the oven to 350 degrees. Heat the oil in a medium skillet over medium heat until shimmering. Add the onion and garlic; sauté until softened, about 5 minutes. Set aside to cool while preparing the remaining ingredients.

3. Mix the eggs with the milk, mustard, Worcestershire sauce, salt, pepper, thyme, and hot sauce. Combine the egg mixture with the meat in a large bowl and add the crackers, parsley, and cooked onion and garlic; mix with a fork until evenly blended and the meat mixture does not stick to the bowl. (If necessary, add more milk, a couple of tablespoons at a time, until the mixture no longer sticks.)

4. Turn the meat mixture onto a work surface. With wet hands, pat the mixture into an approximately 9 by 5-inch loaf shape. Place on the prepared baking pan. Brush with half the glaze, then arrange the bacon slices, crosswise, over the loaf, overlapping them slightly and tucking only the bacon tip ends under the loaf.

5. Bake the loaf until the bacon is crisp and the center of the loaf registers 160 degrees on an instant-read thermometer, about 1 hour. Cool for at least 20 minutes. Simmer the remaining glaze over medium heat until thickened slightly. Slice the meatloaf and serve with the extra glaze passed separately.

TURKEY MEATLOAF

WHY THIS RECIPE WORKS: Store-bought ground turkey is fine and pasty, and it produced a dense, mushy meatloaf when we simply swapped it into a traditional meatloaf recipe. We found a panade only exacerbated the mushiness. Instead, we stirred in quick oats, which added just the right amount of chew and helped open up the texture of the dense turkey. To help give the turkey's thin juices fuller body, we added cornstarch to the mix, boosted flavor with grated Parmesan cheese and butter, and used egg yolks instead of whole eggs. To avoid overwhelming the mild flavor of the meat with too many add-ins, we stirred in a modest amount of onion, as well as garlic, Worcestershire sauce, thyme, and Dijon mustard. To finish it off, we made a flavor-packed glaze and ensured that it stuck by applying a first coat to the meatloaf and letting it cook until the glaze was tacky. We then added a second coat of glaze, which stuck to this base coat in an even layer. To ensure the loaf cooked evenly, we baked it on an aluminum foil–lined wire rack set in a rimmed baking sheet.

Turkey Meatloaf with Ketchup-Brown Sugar Glaze

SERVES 4 TO 6

Do not use 99 percent lean ground turkey in this recipe; it will make a dry meatloaf. Three tablespoons of rolled oats, chopped fine, can be substituted for the quick oats; do not use steel-cut oats.

MEATLOAF

- 3 tablespoons unsalted butter
- Pinch baking soda
- ½ onion, chopped fine
- Salt and pepper
- 1 garlic clove, minced
- 1 teaspoon minced fresh thyme
- 2 tablespoons Worcestershire sauce
- 3 tablespoons quick oats
- 2 teaspoons cornstarch
- 2 large egg yolks
- 2 tablespoons Dijon mustard
- 2 pounds 85 or 93 percent lean ground turkey
- 1 ounce Parmesan, grated (½ cup)
- ⅓ cup chopped fresh parsley

GLAZE

- 1 cup ketchup
- ¼ cup packed brown sugar
- 2½ teaspoons cider vinegar
- ½ teaspoon hot sauce

1. FOR THE MEATLOAF: Adjust oven rack to upper-middle position and heat oven to 350 degrees. Line wire rack with aluminum foil and set in rimmed baking sheet. Melt butter in 10-inch skillet over low heat. Stir baking soda into melted butter. Add onion and ¼ teaspoon salt, increase heat to medium, and cook, stirring frequently, until onion is softened and beginning to brown, 3 to 4 minutes. Add garlic and thyme and cook until fragrant, about 1 minute. Stir in Worcestershire and continue to cook until slightly reduced, about 1 minute longer. Transfer onion mixture to large bowl and set aside. Combine oats, cornstarch, ¾ teaspoon salt, and ½ teaspoon pepper in second bowl.

2. FOR THE GLAZE: Whisk all ingredients in saucepan until sugar dissolves. Bring mixture to simmer over medium heat and cook until slightly thickened, about 5 minutes; set aside.

3. Stir egg yolks and mustard into cooled onion mixture until well combined. Add turkey, Parmesan, parsley, and oat mixture; using your hands, mix until well combined. Transfer turkey mixture to center of prepared rack. Using your wet hands, shape into 9 by 5-inch loaf. Using pastry brush, spread half of glaze evenly over top and sides of meatloaf. Bake meatloaf for 40 minutes.

4. Brush remaining glaze onto top and sides of meatloaf and continue to cook until meatloaf registers 160 degrees, 35 to 40 minutes longer. Let meatloaf cool for 20 minutes before slicing and serving.

Turkey Meatloaf with Apricot-Mustard Glaze

Microwave ¼ cup apricot preserves until hot and fluid, about 30 seconds. Strain preserves through fine-mesh strainer into bowl; discard solids. Stir in 2 tablespoons Dijon mustard, 2 tablespoons ketchup, and pinch salt. Proceed with recipe, substituting apricot mixture for glaze.

STUFFED PEPPERS

WHY THIS RECIPE WORKS: A vegetable can be more than just a side dish, and stuffed peppers are a perfect case in point. But slimy or too-crunchy peppers and tasteless fillings can ruin the show. We wanted to revamp this dish to be a flavorful option for a weeknight dinner. Cooking the peppers correctly is critical; they need to be sturdy enough to hold the filling but not crunchy and bitter. We found that blanching them before adding the filling gave us peppers that held their shape, had good color, and tasted sweeter. Rice is the classic stuffing for peppers, but alone it didn't have much flavor; a mixture of rice and ground beef did the trick. We cooked the rice in the water we'd used to blanch the peppers and for additional flavor, we included sautéed onion and garlic, tomatoes, cheddar cheese, and ketchup.

Classic Stuffed Bell Peppers

SERVES 4

When shopping for bell peppers to stuff, it's best to choose those with broad bases that will allow the peppers to stand up on their own. It's easier to fill the peppers after they have been placed in the baking dish because the sides of the dish will hold the peppers steady.

- Table salt
- 4 medium red, yellow, or orange bell peppers (about 6 ounces each), ½ inch trimmed off tops, cores and seeds discarded (see note)
- ½ cup long-grain white rice
- 1½ tablespoons olive oil
- 1 medium onion, minced
- 12 ounces ground beef, preferably 80 percent lean ground chuck
- 3 medium garlic cloves, minced or pressed through a garlic press (about 1 tablespoon)
- 1 (14.5-ounce) can diced tomatoes, drained, ¼ cup juice reserved
- 5 ounces Monterey Jack cheese, shredded (about 1¼ cups)
- 2 tablespoons chopped fresh parsley leaves
- Ground black pepper
- ¼ cup ketchup

1. Bring 4 quarts water to a boil in a large stockpot or Dutch oven over high heat. Add 1 tablespoon salt and the bell peppers. Cook until the peppers just begin to soften, about 3 minutes. Using a slotted spoon, remove the peppers from the pot, drain off the excess water, and place the peppers, cut side up, on paper towels. Return the water to a boil; add the rice and boil until tender, about 13 minutes. Drain the rice and transfer it to a large bowl; set aside.

2. Adjust an oven rack to the middle position and heat the oven to 350 degrees.

3. Meanwhile, heat the oil in a heavy-bottomed 12-inch skillet over medium-high heat until shimmering. Add the onion and cook, stirring occasionally, until softened and beginning to brown, about 5 minutes. Add the ground beef and cook, breaking the beef into small pieces with a spoon, until no longer pink, about 4 minutes. Stir in the garlic and cook until fragrant, about 30 seconds. Transfer the mixture to the bowl with the rice; stir in the tomatoes, 1 cup of the cheese, the parsley, and salt and pepper to taste.

4. Stir together the ketchup and the reserved tomato juice in a small bowl.

5. Place the peppers, cut side up, in a 9-inch square baking dish. Using a soup spoon, divide the filling evenly among the peppers. Spoon 2 tablespoons of the ketchup mixture over each filled pepper and sprinkle each with 1 tablespoon of the remaining ¼ cup cheese. Bake until the cheese is browned and the filling is heated through, 25 to 30 minutes. Serve immediately.

PHILLY CHEESESTEAKS

WHY THIS RECIPE WORKS: Authentic Philly cheesesteak recipes start with a rib eye and require a meat slicer and flattop griddle to achieve ultrathin slices with crisp edges. To make this sandwich at home, we needed a stand-in for the meat and a way to slice it thin to get it super-crisp, without any fancy equipment. We started by looking for a more economical cut of meat and landed on skirt steak. When partially frozen, skirt steak's thin profile and open-grained texture made for easy slicing, and its flavor was nearest to rib eye. To best approximate the wide griddle typically used in Philadelphia, we cooked the meat in two batches, letting any excess moisture drain off before giving it a final sear. Finally, to bind it all together, we let slices of American cheese melt into the meat; a bit of grated Parmesan boosted the flavor.

Philly Cheesesteaks

SERVES 4

If skirt steak is unavailable, substitute sirloin steak tips (also called flap meat). Top these sandwiches with chopped pickled hot peppers, sautéed onions or bell peppers, sweet relish, or hot sauce.

- 2 pounds skirt steak, trimmed and sliced with grain into 3-inch-wide strips
- 4 (8-inch) Italian sub rolls, split lengthwise
- 2 tablespoons vegetable oil
- ½ teaspoon salt
- ⅛ teaspoon pepper
- ¼ cup grated Parmesan cheese
- 8 slices white American cheese (8 ounces)

1. Place steak pieces on large plate or baking sheet and freeze until very firm, about 1 hour.

2. Meanwhile, adjust oven rack to middle position and heat oven to 400 degrees. Spread split rolls on baking sheet and toast until lightly browned, 5 to 10 minutes.

3. Using sharp knife, shave steak pieces as thinly as possible against grain. Mound meat on cutting board and chop coarsely with knife 10 to 20 times.

4. Heat 1 tablespoon oil in 12-inch nonstick skillet over high heat until smoking. Add half of meat in even layer and cook without stirring until well browned on 1 side, 4 to 5 minutes. Stir and continue to cook until meat is no longer pink, 1 to 2 minutes. Transfer meat to colander set in large bowl. Wipe out skillet with paper towel. Repeat with remaining 1 tablespoon oil and sliced meat.

5. Return now-empty skillet to medium heat. Drain excess moisture from meat. Return meat to skillet (discard any liquid in bowl) and add salt and pepper. Heat, stirring constantly, until meat is warmed through, 1 to 2 minutes. Reduce heat to low, sprinkle with Parmesan, and shingle slices of American cheese over meat. Allow cheeses to melt, about 2 minutes. Using heatproof spatula or wooden spoon, fold melted cheese into meat thoroughly. Divide mixture evenly among toasted rolls. Serve immediately.

JUICY GRILLED TURKEY BURGERS

WHY THIS RECIPE WORKS: To create juicy, well-textured turkey burgers, we ditched store-bought ground turkey in favor of home-ground turkey thighs, which boast more fat and flavor. To ensure that our turkey burger recipe delivered maximum juiciness, we incorporated a paste with a portion of the ground turkey, gelatin, soy sauce, and baking soda, which trapped juice within the burgers. Finally, we added coarsely chopped raw white mushrooms to keep the meat from binding together too firmly.

Juicy Grilled Turkey Burgers

SERVES 6

If you are able to purchase boneless, skinless turkey thighs, substitute 1½ pounds for the bone-in thigh. To ensure the best texture, don't let the burgers stand for more than an hour before cooking. Serve the burgers with Malt Vinegar–Molasses Burger Sauce, Chile-Lime Burger Sauce, or Apricot-Mustard Burger Sauce (recipes follow).

- 1 (2-pound) bone-in turkey thigh, skinned, boned, trimmed, and cut into ½-inch pieces
- 1 tablespoon unflavored gelatin
- 3 tablespoons low-sodium chicken broth
- 6 ounces white mushrooms, trimmed
- 1 tablespoon soy sauce
- Pinch baking soda
- 2 tablespoons vegetable oil, plus extra for brushing
- Kosher salt and pepper
- 6 large hamburger buns

1. Place turkey pieces on large plate in single layer. Freeze meat until very firm and hardened around edges, 35 to 45 minutes. Meanwhile, sprinkle gelatin over chicken broth in small bowl and let sit until gelatin softens, about 5 minutes. Pulse mushrooms in food processor until coarsely chopped, about 7 pulses, stopping and redistributing mushrooms around bowl as needed to ensure even grinding. Set mushrooms aside; do not wash food processor.

2. Pulse one-third of turkey in food processor until coarsely chopped into ⅛-inch pieces, 18 to 22 pulses, stopping and redistributing turkey around bowl as needed to ensure even grinding. Transfer meat to large bowl and repeat two more times with remaining turkey.

3. Return ½ cup (about 3 ounces) ground turkey to bowl of food processor along with softened gelatin, soy sauce, and baking soda. Process until smooth, about 2 minutes, scraping down bowl as needed. With processor running, slowly drizzle in oil, about 10 seconds; leave paste in food processor. Return mushrooms to food processor with paste and pulse to combine, 3 to 5 pulses, stopping and redistributing mixture as needed to ensure even mixing. Transfer mushroom mixture to bowl with ground turkey and use hands to evenly combine.

4. With lightly greased hands, divide meat mixture into 6 balls. Flatten into ¾-inch-thick patties about 4 inches in diameter; press shallow indentation into center of each burger to ensure even cooking. (Shaped patties can be frozen for up to 1 month. Frozen patties can be cooked straight from freezer.)

5A. FOR A CHARCOAL GRILL: Open bottom vent completely. Light large chimney starter filled with charcoal briquettes (6 quarts). When top coals are partially covered with ash, pour evenly over half of grill. Set cooking grate in place, cover, and open lid vent completely. Heat grill until hot, about 5 minutes.

5B. FOR A GAS GRILL: Turn all burners to high, cover, and heat grill until hot, about 15 minutes. Leave primary burner on high and turn off other burner(s).

6. Clean and oil cooking grate. Brush 1 side of patties with oil and season with salt and pepper. Using spatula, flip patties, brush with oil, and season second side. Place burgers over hot part of grill and cook until burgers are well browned on both sides and register 160 degrees, 4 to 7 minutes per side. (If cooking frozen burgers: After burgers are browned on both sides, transfer to cool side of grill, cover, and continue to cook until burgers register 160 degrees.)

7. Transfer burgers to plate and let rest for 5 minutes. While burgers rest, grill buns over hot side of grill. Transfer burgers to buns, add desired toppings, and serve.

Malt Vinegar–Molasses Burger Sauce

MAKES ABOUT 1 CUP

- ¾ cup mayonnaise
- 4 teaspoons malt vinegar
- ½ teaspoon molasses
- ¼ teaspoon Worcestershire sauce
- ¼ teaspoon salt
- ¼ teaspoon pepper

Whisk all ingredients together in bowl.

Chile-Lime Burger Sauce

MAKES ABOUT 1 CUP

- ¾ cup mayonnaise
- 2 teaspoons chile-garlic paste
- 2 teaspoons lime juice
- 1 scallion, sliced thin
- ¼ teaspoon fish sauce
- ⅛ teaspoon sugar

Whisk all ingredients together in bowl.

Apricot-Mustard Burger Sauce

MAKES ABOUT 1 CUP

- ¾ cup mayonnaise
- 5 teaspoons apricot preserves
- 1 tablespoon lemon juice
- 1 tablespoon Dijon mustard
- 1 tablespoon whole-grain mustard
- ¼ teaspoon salt

Whisk all ingredients together in bowl.

OLD-FASHIONED BURGERS

WHY THIS RECIPE WORKS: The burger you find at most drive-ins is a rubbery, thin, gray patty with little beef flavor. We wanted to create, at home, the classic drive-in burger. Made from freshly ground beef, cooked on a flat griddle, this style of burger is ultracrisp, ultrabrowned, and ultrabeefy. Topped with melted cheese and tangy sauce, it's the burger fast food restaurants wish they could produce.

We learned right off the bat that the thin patty typical of this burger style requires freshly ground meat. Prepackaged hamburger is ground very fine and packaged tightly, which produced dense, rubbery, and dry patties. For the meat, we settled on short ribs ground up with sirloin steak tips. Numerous grinding tests revealed that while beefiness depended on cut, juiciness corresponded to fat. Well-marbled short ribs added the perfect amount of fat to complement the beefy flavor from the sirloin tips. And if you don't have a meat grinder? The food processor worked just fine as long as the meat was first chilled in the freezer until firm but still pliable. We still had to deal with a rubbery texture caused by meat collagen proteins shrinking and tightening when exposed to heat. To fight this, the meat needed to be as loosely packed as possible—not pressed but rather gently shaped into loose patties. To top our burgers, we went back to the tried-and-true flavors of a tangy and sweet Thousand Island–style dressing, American cheese, and thinly sliced onion.

Best Old-Fashioned Burgers

MAKES 4 BURGERS

Sirloin steak tips are also labeled "flap meat" by some butchers. Flank steak can be used in its place. This recipe yields juicy medium to medium-well burgers. If doubling the recipe, process the meat in three batches in step 2. Because the cooked burgers do not hold well, fry four burgers and serve them immediately before frying more. Or cook them in two pans. Extra patties can be frozen for up to 2 weeks. Stack the patties, separated by parchment paper, and wrap them in three layers of plastic wrap. Thaw burgers in a single layer on a baking sheet at room temperature for 30 minutes before cooking.

- 10 ounces sirloin steak tips, cut into 1-inch chunks (see note)
- 6 ounces boneless beef short ribs, cut into 1-inch chunks
- Table salt and ground black pepper
- 1 tablespoon unsalted butter
- 4 soft hamburger buns
- ½ teaspoon vegetable oil
- 4 slices American cheese
- Thinly sliced onion
- 1 recipe Classic Burger Sauce (recipe follows)

1. Place the beef chunks on a baking sheet in a single layer, leaving ½ inch of space around each chunk. Freeze the meat until very firm and starting to harden around the edges but still pliable, 15 to 25 minutes.

2. Place half of the meat in a food processor and pulse until the meat is coarsely ground, 10 to 15 pulses, stopping and redistributing the meat around the bowl as necessary to ensure the beef is evenly ground. Transfer the meat to a baking sheet by overturning the bowl, without touching the meat. Repeat the grinding with the remaining meat. Spread the meat over the sheet and inspect carefully, discarding any long strands of gristle or large chunks of hard meat or fat.

NOTES FROM THE TEST KITCHEN

MAKING LOOSELY PACKED PATTIES

1. Chill meat in freezer, separating cubes by at least ½ inch, until firm but still pliable, 15 to 25 minutes. Pulse meat in food processor.

2. Spread chopped meat over baking sheet and remove any large chunks or stringy connective tissue. Gently separate meat into 4 piles.

3. Without lifting or compressing, gently form meat into thin patties with rough edges and textured surface.

3. Gently separate the ground meat into four equal mounds. Without picking the meat up, with your fingers gently shape each mound into a loose patty ½ inch thick and 4 inches in diameter, leaving the edges and surface ragged. Season the top of each patty with salt and pepper. Using a spatula, flip the patties and season the other side. Refrigerate while toasting the buns.

4. Melt ½ tablespoon of the butter in a heavy-bottomed 12-inch skillet over medium heat. Add the bun tops, cut side down, and toast until light golden brown, about 2 minutes. Repeat with the remaining ½ tablespoon butter and the bun bottoms. Set the buns aside and wipe out the skillet with paper towels.

5. Return the skillet to high heat; add the oil and heat until just smoking. Using a spatula, transfer the burgers to the skillet and cook without moving them for 3 minutes. Using the spatula, flip the burgers over and cook for 1 minute. Top each patty with a slice of the cheese and continue to cook until the cheese is melted, about 1 minute longer.

6. Transfer the patties to the bun bottoms and top with the onion. Spread 2 teaspoons of the burger sauce on each bun top. Cover the burgers with the bun tops and serve immediately.

Classic Burger Sauce

MAKES ABOUT ¼ CUP

- 2 tablespoons mayonnaise
- 1 tablespoon ketchup
- ½ teaspoon sweet pickle relish
- ½ teaspoon sugar
- ½ teaspoon white vinegar
- ¼ teaspoon ground black pepper

Whisk all the ingredients together in a small bowl.

JUICY PUB-STYLE BURGERS

WHY THIS RECIPE WORKS: Few things are as satisfying as a thick, juicy pub-style burger. But by the time the center of these hefty burgers cooks through, there is often an overcooked band of meat. We wanted a patty that was evenly rosy from center to edge. Grinding our own meat in the food processor was a must (freezing the meat until just firm helped the processor chop it cleanly), and we found that sirloin steak tips were ideal. To give the burgers just enough structure, we cut the meat into small ½-inch chunks before grinding and lightly packed the meat into patties. Melted butter improved their flavor and juiciness. Transferring the burgers from the stovetop to the oven to finish cooking eliminated the overcooked gray zone. For extra pub-style appeal, we came up with flavorful topping combinations to finish off our burgers.

Juicy Pub-Style Burgers

SERVES 4

Sirloin steak tips are also labeled as "flap meat." When stirring the butter and pepper into the ground meat and shaping the patties, take care not to overwork the meat or the burgers will become dense. For the best flavor, season the burgers aggressively just before cooking. The burgers can be topped as desired, or try one of our variations that follow. The uncooked patties can be refrigerated for up to 1 day.

- 2 pounds sirloin steak tips or boneless beef short ribs, trimmed and cut into ½-inch chunks
- 4 tablespoons unsalted butter (½ stick), melted and cooled slightly
- Table salt and ground black pepper
- 1 teaspoon vegetable oil
- 4 large hamburger buns, toasted and buttered
- 1 recipe Pub-Style Burger Sauce (optional; recipe follows)

1. Place the beef chunks on a baking sheet in a single layer. Freeze the meat until very firm and starting to harden around the edges but still pliable, 15 to 25 minutes.

2. Place one-quarter of the meat in a food processor and pulse until finely ground into 1⁄16-inch pieces, about 35 pulses, stopping and redistributing the meat around the bowl as necessary to ensure the beef is evenly ground. Transfer the meat to the baking sheet by overturning the processor bowl and without directly touching the meat. Repeat grinding with the remaining 3 batches of meat. Spread the meat over the sheet and inspect carefully, discarding any long strands of gristle or large chunks of hard meat or fat.

3. Adjust an oven rack to the middle position and heat the oven to 300 degrees. Drizzle the melted butter over the ground meat and add 1 teaspoon pepper. Gently toss with a fork to combine. Divide the meat into 4 lightly packed balls. Gently flatten into patties ¾ inch thick and about 4½ inches in diameter. Refrigerate the patties until ready to cook.

4. Season 1 side of the patties with salt and pepper. Using a spatula, flip the patties and season the other side. Heat the oil in a 12-inch skillet over high heat until just smoking. Using the spatula, transfer the burgers to the skillet and cook without moving for 2 minutes. Using the spatula, flip the burgers over and cook for 2 minutes longer. Transfer the patties to a rimmed baking sheet and bake until the burgers register 125 degrees (for medium-rare) on an instant-read thermometer, 3 to 5 minutes.

5. Transfer the burgers to a plate and let rest for 5 minutes. Transfer to the buns, top with Pub-Style Burger Sauce (if using), and serve.

Pub-Style Burger Sauce

MAKES ABOUT 1 CUP, ENOUGH TO TOP 4 BURGERS

- ¾ cup mayonnaise
- 2 tablespoons soy sauce
- 1 tablespoon dark brown sugar
- 1 tablespoon Worcestershire sauce
- 1 tablespoon minced chives
- 1 medium garlic clove, minced or pressed through a garlic press (about 1 teaspoon)
- ¾ teaspoon ground black pepper

Whisk all ingredients together in bowl.

Juicy Pub-Style Burgers with Crispy Shallots and Blue Cheese

Heat ½ cup vegetable oil and 3 thinly sliced shallots in a medium saucepan over high heat; cook, stirring frequently, until the shallots are golden, about 8 minutes. Using a slotted spoon, transfer the shallots to a paper towel–lined plate, season with table salt, and let drain until crisp, about 5 minutes. (The cooled shallots can be stored at room temperature in an airtight container for up to 3 days.) Follow the recipe for Juicy Pub-Style Burgers, topping each burger with 1 ounce crumbled blue cheese before transferring to the oven. Top with Pub-Style Burger Sauce and the crispy shallots just before serving.

Juicy Pub-Style Burgers with Peppered Bacon and Aged Cheddar

Adjust an oven rack to the middle position and heat the oven to 375 degrees. Arrange 6 bacon slices on a rimmed baking sheet and sprinkle with 2 teaspoons coarsely ground pepper. Place a second rimmed baking sheet on top of the bacon and bake until the bacon is crisp, 15 to 20 minutes. Transfer the bacon to a paper towel–lined plate and cool. Cut the bacon in half crosswise. Follow the recipe for Juicy Pub-Style Burgers, topping each burger with 1 ounce grated aged cheddar cheese before transferring to the oven. Top with Pub-Style Burger Sauce and the bacon just before serving.

Juicy Pub-Style Burgers with Sautéed Onions and Smoked Cheddar

Heat 2 tablespoons vegetable oil in a 12-inch skillet over medium-high heat until just smoking. Add 1 thinly sliced onion and ¼ teaspoon table salt; cook, stirring frequently, until softened and lightly browned, 5 to 7 minutes. Follow the recipe for Juicy Pub-Style Burgers, topping each burger with 1 ounce grated smoked cheddar cheese before transferring to the oven. Top with Pub-Style Burger Sauce and the onion just before serving.

Juicy Pub-Style Burgers with Pan-Roasted Mushrooms and Gruyère

Heat 2 tablespoons vegetable oil in a 12-inch skillet over medium-high heat until just smoking. Add 10 ounces thinly sliced cremini mushrooms, ¼ teaspoon table salt, and ¼ teaspoon pepper; cook, stirring frequently, until browned, 5 to 7 minutes. Add 1 minced shallot and 2 teaspoons minced thyme and cook until fragrant. Remove the skillet from the heat and stir in 2 tablespoons dry sherry. Follow the recipe for Juicy Pub-Style Burgers, topping each burger with 1 ounce grated Gruyère cheese before transferring to the oven. Top with Pub-Style Burger Sauce and the mushrooms just before serving.

BLACK BEAN BURGERS

WHY THIS RECIPE WORKS: As with many meatless patties, black bean burgers often get their structure from fillers that rob them of any trace of black bean flavor. We wanted that key ingredient to shine in our burgers. For convenient and reliable

beans, we turned to canned, rinsing and drying them completely to eliminate cohesion-compromising moisture. Eggs and flour served as our binding agents, and adding minced scallions, cilantro, and garlic contributed some personality. We stirred in a couple of spices with major impact—cumin and coriander—plus a hit of hot sauce for zip. In keeping with our Latin American flavor profile, we turned to the bright corn flavor of tortilla chips to build up our burger mix. After blitzing crushed chips in the food processor, we added in the beans and pulsed them into coarsely chopped pieces. We combined the beans with the flour-egg binder and refrigerated the mixture, allowing the starches to absorb some of the eggs' moisture. After an hour, we formed patties and cooked the burgers in an oiled skillet. After a quick browning on each side, these burgers were ready to serve with all of our favorite fixings.

Black Bean Burgers

SERVES 6

When forming the patties it is important to pack them firmly together. Serve the burgers with your favorite toppings or with Chipotle Mayonnaise (recipe follows).

- 2 (15-ounce) cans black beans, rinsed
- 2 large eggs
- 2 tablespoons all-purpose flour
- 4 scallions, minced (¼ cup)
- 3 tablespoons minced fresh cilantro
- 2 garlic cloves, minced
- 1 teaspoon ground cumin
- ½ teaspoon ground coriander
- ¼ teaspoon salt
- ¼ teaspoon pepper
- 1 teaspoon hot sauce (optional)
- 1 ounce tortilla chips, crushed coarse (½ cup)
- 8 teaspoons vegetable oil
- 6 burger buns

1. Line rimmed baking sheet with triple layer of paper towels and spread black beans over towels. Let stand for 15 minutes.

2. Whisk eggs and flour together in large bowl until uniform paste forms. Stir in scallions, cilantro, garlic, cumin, coriander, salt, pepper, and hot sauce, if using, until well combined.

3. Process tortilla chips in food processor until finely ground, about 30 seconds. Add black beans and pulse until beans are roughly broken down, about 5 pulses. Transfer black bean mixture to bowl with egg mixture and mix until well combined. Cover and refrigerate for at least 1 hour or up to 24 hours.

4. Divide bean mixture into 6 equal portions. Firmly pack each portion into tight ball, then flatten to 3½-inch patty. (Patties can be wrapped individually in plastic wrap, placed in a zipper-lock bag, and frozen for up to 2 weeks. Thaw patties before cooking.)

5. Heat 2 teaspoons oil in 10-inch nonstick skillet over medium heat until shimmering. Carefully lay 3 patties in skillet and cook until bottoms are well-browned and crisp, about 5 minutes. Flip patties, add 2 teaspoons oil, and cook second sides until well-browned and crisp, 3 to 5 minutes. Transfer patties to buns and repeat with remaining 3 patties and 4 teaspoons oil. Serve.

Chipotle Mayonnaise

MAKES ABOUT ⅓ CUP

- 3 tablespoons mayonnaise
- 3 tablespoons sour cream
- 2 teaspoons minced canned chipotle chile in adobo sauce
- 1 garlic clove, minced
- ⅛ teaspoon salt

Combine all ingredients. Cover and refrigerate for at least 1 hour.

VEGAN PINTO BEAN–BEET BURGERS

WHY THIS RECIPE WORKS: Vegan burgers are often bean-based; starchy, protein-packed beans taste great, hold together well, and are satisfying. Looking for a modern twist on the typical bean burger, we combined pinto beans with vibrant shredded beets, and we also packed in a generous amount of basil leaves. The result was a substantial but fresh-tasting burger with some sweetness from the beets and the bright, complementary aroma of basil. We incorporated bulgur for heft and ground nuts for meaty richness. Garlic and mustard deepened the savory flavors. While the bulgur cooked, we pulsed the other ingredients in the food processor to just the right consistency. To bind the burgers, we turned to a surprising ingredient: carrot baby food. The carrot added tackiness, and its subtle sweetness heightened that of the shredded beets; plus, it was already conveniently pureed. Panko bread crumbs further bound the mixture and helped the patties sear up with a crisp crust.

Pinto Bean–Beet Burgers

SERVES 8

When shopping, don't confuse bulgur with cracked wheat, which has a much longer cooking time and will not work in this recipe. Use a coarse grater or the shredding disk of a food processor to shred the beets.

- Salt and pepper
- ⅔ cup medium-grind bulgur, rinsed
- 1 large beet (9 ounces), peeled and shredded
- ¾ cup walnuts
- ½ cup fresh basil leaves
- 2 garlic cloves, minced
- 1 (15-ounce) can pinto beans, rinsed
- 1 (4-ounce) jar carrot baby food
- 1 tablespoon whole-grain mustard
- 1½ cups panko bread crumbs
- 6 tablespoons vegetable oil, plus extra as needed
- 8 burger buns

1. Bring 1½ cups water and ½ teaspoon salt to boil in small saucepan. Off heat, stir in bulgur, cover, and let stand until tender, 15 to 20 minutes. Drain bulgur, spread onto rimmed baking sheet, and let cool slightly.

2. Meanwhile, pulse beet, walnuts, basil, and garlic in food processor until finely chopped, about 12 pulses, scraping down sides of bowl as needed. Add beans, carrot baby food, 2 tablespoons water, mustard, 1½ teaspoons salt, and ½ teaspoon pepper and pulse until well combined, about 8 pulses. Transfer mixture to large bowl and stir in panko and cooled bulgur.

3. Adjust oven rack to middle position and heat oven to 200 degrees. Divide mixture into 8 equal portions and pack into 3½-inch-wide patties.

4. Heat 3 tablespoons oil in 12-inch nonstick skillet over medium-high heat until shimmering. Gently lay 4 patties in skillet and cook until crisp and well browned on first side, about 4 minutes. Gently flip patties and cook until crisp and well browned on second side, about 4 minutes, adding extra oil if skillet looks dry.

5. Transfer burgers to wire rack set in rimmed baking sheet and place in oven to keep warm. Wipe out skillet with paper towels and repeat with remaining 3 tablespoons oil and remaining patties. Transfer to buns and serve.

OVEN-FRIED ONION RINGS

WHY THIS RECIPE WORKS: Fried onion rings are the perfect accompaniment to burgers, barbecue, and other casual fare. But who wants the mess and smell of deep-fried onions? We wanted an oven method that produced tender, sweet onions with a super-crunchy coating.

We made a batter with buttermilk, egg, and flour, but when we put the baking sheet in the oven the batter slid right off the onions. Coating the onion rings with flour first gave the batter something to cling to. But we wanted even more crunch. For an extra layer of coating, we turned to crushed saltines and crushed potato chips. We preheated the oil in the baking sheet before adding the coated onions so they'd start crisping right away. The result: crispy, crunchy oven-fried onion rings with deep-fried flavor.

Oven-Fried Onion Rings

SERVES 4 TO 6

Slice the onions into ½-inch-thick rounds, separate the rings, and discard any rings smaller than 2 inches in diameter.

- ½ cup unbleached all-purpose flour
- 1 large egg, at room temperature
- ½ cup buttermilk, at room temperature
- ½ teaspoon table salt
- ¼ teaspoon ground black pepper
- ¼ teaspoon cayenne pepper
- 30 saltine crackers
- 4 cups kettle-cooked potato chips
- 2 large yellow onions, cut into 24 large rings (see note)
- 6 tablespoons vegetable oil

1. Adjust the oven racks to the lower-middle and upper-middle positions and heat the oven to 450 degrees. Place ¼ cup of the flour in a shallow baking dish. Beat the egg and buttermilk in a medium bowl. Whisk the remaining ¼ cup flour, the salt, black pepper, and cayenne into the buttermilk mixture. Pulse the saltines and chips together in a food processor until finely ground; place in a separate shallow baking dish.

2. Working one at a time, dredge each onion ring in the flour, shaking off the excess. Dip in the buttermilk mixture, allowing the excess to drip back into the bowl, then drop into the crumb coating, turning the ring over to coat evenly. Transfer to a large plate. (At this point, the onion rings can be refrigerated for up to 1 hour. Let them sit at room temperature for 30 minutes before baking.)

3. Pour 3 tablespoons of the oil onto each of two rimmed baking sheets. Place in the oven and heat until just smoking, about 8 minutes. Carefully tilt the heated sheets to coat evenly with the oil, then arrange the onion rings on the sheets. Bake, flipping the onion rings over and switching and rotating the baking sheets halfway through baking, until golden brown on both sides, about 15 minutes. Briefly drain the onion rings on paper towels. Serve immediately.

STEAK FRIES

WHY THIS RECIPE WORKS: Thick spears of skin-on potato, steak fries are the heartier, more rustic cousins of the crisp, skinny french fry. But getting steak fries crisp on the outside and tender inside can be tricky—soggy steak fries are too often the norm. We wanted to find a way to achieve a steak fry with hearty potato flavor and great crunch.

We found that the dense starchiness of russet potatoes makes them the best variety for frying. We got the proper ratio of crisp exterior to tender interior when we cut them into ¾-inch wedges. As for the frying oil, peanut oil was our top choice. Chilling the potatoes in cold water before frying proved to be an essential step. Prepared this way, they cooked more slowly and evenly, without burning. Even after chilling, though, our fries were overcooked when we simply fried them in oil. A two-step process worked wonders. After chilling and drying the potatoes, we par-fried them at a lower temperature to cook the interiors without browning them. Following a brief rest, we fried them again at a higher temperature to brown and crisp the exteriors. Neither greasy nor soggy, these fries boasted great flavor and crunch.

Steak Fries

SERVES 4

The potatoes must be soaked in cold water, fried once, cooled, and then fried a second time—so start this recipe at least one hour before dinner.

- 2½ pounds russet potatoes (about 4 large), scrubbed and cut lengthwise into ¾-inch-thick wedges (about 12 wedges per potato)
- 2 quarts peanut oil
- Table salt and ground black pepper

1. Place the cut potatoes in a large bowl, cover with cold water by at least 1 inch, and then cover with ice cubes. Refrigerate for at least 30 minutes or up to 3 days.

2. In a large Dutch oven fitted with a clip-on candy thermometer, heat the oil over medium-low heat to 325 degrees. (The oil will bubble up when you add the potatoes, so be sure you have at least 3 inches of room at the top of the pot.)

3. Pour off the ice and water, quickly wrap the potatoes in a clean kitchen towel, and thoroughly pat them dry. Increase the heat to medium-high and add the potatoes, one handful at a time, to the hot oil. Fry, stirring with a Chinese skimmer or large-holed slotted spoon, until the potatoes are limp and soft and have turned from white to gold, about 10 minutes. (The oil temperature will drop 50 to 60 degrees during this frying.) Use the skimmer or slotted spoon to transfer the fries to a triple thickness of paper towels to drain; let rest for at least 10 minutes. (The fries can stand at room temperature for up to 2 hours.)

4. When ready to serve the fries, reheat the oil to 350 degrees. Using the paper towels as a funnel, pour the potatoes into the hot oil. Discard the paper towels and line a wire rack with another triple thickness of paper towels. Fry the potatoes, stirring fairly constantly, until medium brown and puffed, 8 to 10 minutes. Transfer to the paper towel–lined rack to drain. Season with salt and pepper to taste. Serve immediately.

CLASSIC FRENCH FRIES

WHY THIS RECIPE WORKS: Efforts to re-create restaurant-style fries at home have always disappointed, with fries that were greasy, droopy, or burnt on the outside and raw on the inside. We wanted to find a recipe and method for the home cook that would rival those cooked by professionals—crunchy fries with deep potato flavor.

As we found in developing our recipe for Steak Fries (page 277), russet potatoes were preferred for their dense texture and hearty flavor. Because these are starchy potatoes, it was important to rinse the starch off the surface after cutting the potatoes into fries. To achieve evenly cooked fries, we first refrigerated the cut potatoes in a bowl of ice water for at least 30 minutes and then took a double-fry approach. During the first fry, because the potatoes are nearly frozen, the potatoes can cook long and slow, which ensures a soft, rich-tasting interior. A quick second fry at a higher temperature crisped and colored the exterior. We used peanut oil for frying but felt our fries lacked the flavor imparted by lard. A little strained bacon grease gave our fries a touch of meaty flavor just like those found in our favorite restaurant fries.

Classic French Fries

SERVES 4

We prefer to peel the potatoes. Leaving the skin on keeps the potato from forming those little airy blisters that we like. Peeling the potato also allows the removal of any imperfections and greenish coloring. Once the potatoes are peeled and cut, plan on at least an hour before the fries are ready to eat.

- 2½ pounds russet potatoes (about 4 large), peeled and cut into ¼-inch by ¼-inch lengths
- 2 quarts peanut oil
- ¼ cup bacon fat, strained (optional)
- Table salt and ground black pepper

1. Place the cut potatoes in a large bowl, cover with at least 1 inch of water, then cover with ice cubes. Refrigerate for at least 30 minutes or up to 3 days.

2. In a large Dutch oven fitted with a clip-on candy thermometer, heat the oil over medium-low heat to 325 degrees. (The oil will bubble up when you add the potatoes, so be sure you have at least 3 inches of room at the top of the pot.) Add the bacon grease (if using).

3. Pour off the ice and water, quickly wrap the potatoes in a clean kitchen towel, and thoroughly pat them dry. Increase the heat to medium-high and add the potatoes, one handful at a time, to the hot oil. Fry, stirring with a Chinese skimmer or large-holed slotted spoon, until the potatoes are limp and soft and have turned from white to gold, about 10 minutes. (The oil temperature will drop 50 to 60 degrees during this frying.) Use the skimmer or slotted spoon to transfer the fries to a triple thickness of paper towels to drain; let rest for at least 10 minutes. (The fries can stand at room temperature for up to 2 hours.)

4. When ready to serve the fries, reheat the oil to 350 degrees. Using the paper towels as a funnel, pour the potatoes into the hot oil. Discard the paper towels and line a wire rack with another triple thickness of paper towels. Fry the potatoes, stirring fairly constantly, until medium brown and puffed, about 1 minute. Transfer to the paper towel–lined rack to drain. Season with salt and pepper to taste. Serve immediately.

EASIER FRENCH FRIES

WHY THIS RECIPE WORKS: Our recipe for Classic French Fries works beautifully, but we'll admit that it sometimes seems like a lot of trouble. We challenged ourselves to devise a shortcut that would give us crisp, golden fries with less work. Oven-frying is the usual "quick" method, but we wanted real french fries. We started with an unorthodox procedure of starting the cut potatoes in a few cups of cold oil. To our surprise, the fries were pretty good, if a little dry. Because russets

are fairly dry, we wondered if a different type of potato would work better. Sure enough, Yukon Golds, which have more water and less starch, came out creamy and smooth inside and crisp outside. We found that leaving the fries undisturbed for 15 minutes, then stirring them, kept them from sticking and from breaking apart. Thinner batons were also less likely to stick. These fries had all the qualities of classic french fries, without all the bother.

Easier French Fries

SERVES 4

For those who like it, flavoring the oil with bacon fat gives the fries a mild meaty flavor. We prefer peanut oil for frying, but vegetable oil can be substituted. This recipe will not work with sweet potatoes or russets. Serve with dipping sauces (recipes follow), if desired.

- 2½ pounds Yukon Gold potatoes (about 6 medium), scrubbed, dried, sides squared off, and cut lengthwise into ¼-inch by ¼-inch batons (see note)
- 6 cups peanut oil (see note)
- ¼ cup bacon fat, strained (optional; see note)
- Table salt

1. Combine the potatoes, oil, and bacon fat (if using) in a large Dutch oven. Cook over high heat until the oil has reached a rolling boil, about 5 minutes. Continue to cook, without stirring, until the potatoes are pale golden and the exteriors are beginning to crisp, about 15 minutes.

2. Using tongs, stir the potatoes, gently scraping up any that stick, and continue to cook, stirring occasionally, until golden and crisp, 5 to 10 minutes longer. Using a skimmer or slotted spoon, transfer the fries to a thick paper bag or paper towels. Season with salt to taste and serve immediately.

Chive and Black Pepper Dipping Sauce

MAKES ABOUT ½ CUP

- 5 tablespoons mayonnaise
- 3 tablespoons sour cream
- 2 tablespoons chopped fresh chives
- 1½ teaspoons juice from 1 lemon
- ¼ teaspoon table salt
- ¼ teaspoon ground black pepper

Whisk all the ingredients together in a small bowl.

Belgian-Style Dipping Sauce

MAKES ABOUT ½ CUP

- 5 tablespoons mayonnaise
- 3 tablespoons ketchup
- 1 medium garlic clove, minced or pressed through a garlic press (about 1 teaspoon)
- ½ teaspoon hot sauce or more to taste
- ¼ teaspoon table salt

Whisk all the ingredients together in a small bowl.

NOTES FROM THE TEST KITCHEN

CUTTING POTATOES FOR FRENCH FRIES

1. Square off potato by cutting ¼-inch-thick slice from each of its 4 long sides.

2. Cut potato lengthwise into ¼-inch-thick planks.

3. Stack 3 or 4 planks and cut into ¼-inch-thick batons. Repeat with remaining planks.

CHAPTER 12

WHO WANTS PASTA?

PASTA WITH GARLIC AND OIL

WHY THIS RECIPE WORKS: Nothing sounds easier than pasta with olive oil and garlic, but too often this dish turns out oily or rife with burnt garlic. We were after a flawless version of this quick classic, with bright, deep garlic flavor and no trace of bitterness or harshness.

For a mellow flavor, we cooked most of the garlic over low heat until sticky and straw-colored; a modest amount of raw garlic added at the end brought in some potent fresh garlic flavor. Extra-virgin olive oil and reserved pasta cooking water helped to keep our garlic and pasta saucy. A splash of lemon juice and sprinkling of red pepper flakes added some spice and brightness to this simple, yet complex-flavored recipe.

Pasta with Garlic and Oil

SERVES 4 TO 6

For a twist on pasta with garlic and oil, try sprinkling toasted fresh bread crumbs over individual bowls, but prepare them in advance. Simply pulse two slices of high-quality white sandwich bread, torn into quarters, in a food processor to coarse crumbs. Combine with 2 tablespoons extra-virgin olive oil, season with salt and pepper, and bake on a rimmed baking sheet at 375 degrees until golden brown, 8 to 10 minutes.

- Table salt
- 1 pound spaghetti
- 6 tablespoons extra-virgin olive oil
- 12 medium garlic cloves, minced or pressed through a garlic press (about 4 tablespoons)
- ¾ teaspoon red pepper flakes
- 3 tablespoons chopped fresh parsley leaves
- 2 teaspoons juice from 1 lemon
- ½ cup grated Parmesan cheese (optional)

1. Bring 4 quarts water to a boil in a large pot. Add 1 tablespoon salt and the pasta to the boiling water and cook, stirring often, until al dente; reserve ⅓ cup of the cooking water then drain the pasta and return it to the pot.

2. Meanwhile, heat 3 tablespoons of the oil, 3 tablespoons of the garlic, and ½ teaspoon salt over low heat in a 10-inch nonstick skillet. Cook, stirring constantly, until the garlic is sticky and straw-colored, 10 to 12 minutes. Off the heat, stir in the remaining 1 tablespoon garlic, the red pepper flakes, parsley, lemon juice, and 2 tablespoons of the reserved pasta cooking water.

3. Transfer the drained pasta to a warm serving bowl; add the remaining 3 tablespoons oil and remaining reserved pasta cooking water and toss to combine. Add the garlic mixture and ¾ teaspoon salt; toss to combine. Serve, sprinkling individual bowls with Parmesan cheese, if desired.

SPAGHETTI AL LIMONE

WHY THIS RECIPE WORKS: Unaccustomed to the spotlight, lemon can turn temperamental in this quick Italian classic—unless you provide it with the perfect costars. We wanted a dish bursting with bright, bracing lemon flavor and moistened with just enough fruity olive oil to coat each delicate strand. Starting with lemon flavor, we found the window for the right amount of juice per pound of pasta was extremely small, and if we leaned more to either side, the lemon flavor became either too tart or barely noticeable. To boost the lemon's power without extra acidity, we added some grated zest to the sauce. As for the base of the sauce, we relied on an olive oil–cream sauce. The cream neutralized some of the acids in the juice while augmenting the oils responsible for the fruity, floral notes.

Spaghetti with Lemon and Olive Oil (al Limone)

SERVES 4

Letting this dish rest briefly before serving allows the flavors to develop and the sauce to thicken.

- Table salt and ground black pepper
- 1 pound spaghetti
- ¼ cup extra-virgin olive oil, plus extra for drizzling
- 1 medium shallot, minced (about 3 tablespoons)
- ¼ cup heavy cream
- 1 ounce Parmesan cheese, grated (about ½ cup), plus extra for serving
- 2 teaspoons grated zest plus ¼ cup juice from 2 lemons
- 2 tablespoons chopped fresh basil leaves

1. Bring 4 quarts water to a boil in a large pot. Add 1 tablespoon salt and the pasta to the boiling water and cook until al dente. Reserve 1¾ cups of the cooking water, then drain the pasta.

2. Heat 1 tablespoon of the oil in the now-empty pot over medium heat until shimmering. Add the shallot and ½ teaspoon salt and cook until softened, about 2 minutes. Stir in 1½ cups of the reserved cooking water and the cream, bring to a simmer, and cook for 2 minutes. Off the heat, add the drained pasta, remaining 3 tablespoons oil, Parmesan, lemon zest, lemon juice, and ½ teaspoon pepper, and toss to combine.

3. Cover and let the pasta rest for 2 minutes, tossing frequently and adding the remaining cooking water as needed to adjust the consistency. Stir in the basil and season with salt and pepper to taste. Drizzle individual portions with oil and serve, passing the additional Parmesan separately.

SPAGHETTI WITH PECORINO ROMANO AND BLACK PEPPER

WHY THIS RECIPE WORKS: With just three main ingredients (cheese, pepper, and pasta), this Roman dish makes a delicious and quick pantry supper. But in versions we tried, the creamy sauce quickly turns into clumps of solidified cheese. We wanted a sauce that was intensely cheesy but also creamy and smooth.

Our science editor explained why the cheese clumps in this dish. Cheese consists mainly of three basic substances: fat, protein, and water. When a hard cheese like Pecorino, our cheese of choice, is heated, its fat begins to melt and its proteins soften. The fat acts as a sort of glue, fusing the proteins together. In order to coat the cheese and prevent the proteins from sticking together, we needed to introduce a starch into the mix.

It occurred to us that as pasta cooks, it releases starch into the water. We reduced the amount of water to concentrate the starch and whisked some of the cooking liquid into the cheese. This helped to a point, but we found we also needed an emulsifier—something to bind together the sauce. We turned to cream. By switching the butter for cream, we created a light, perfectly smooth sauce that had all the cheese flavor we wanted. Even after sitting on the table for a full five minutes, there wasn't a clump in sight.

Spaghetti with Pecorino Romano and Black Pepper

SERVES 4 TO 6

High-quality ingredients are essential in this dish, most importantly, imported Pecorino Romano. For a slightly less rich dish, substitute half-and-half for the heavy cream. Do not adjust the amount of water for cooking the pasta; the amount used is critical to the success of the recipe. Make sure to stir the pasta frequently while cooking so that it doesn't stick to the pot. Draining the pasta water into the serving bowl warms the bowl and helps keeps the dish hot until it is served. Letting the dish rest briefly before serving allows the flavors to develop and the sauce to thicken.

- 4 ounces Pecorino Romano, grated fine (about 2 cups), plus 2 ounces grated coarse (about 1 cup), for serving
- 1 pound spaghetti
- Table salt
- 2 tablespoons heavy cream
- 2 teaspoons extra-virgin olive oil
- 1½ teaspoons ground black pepper

1. Place the finely grated Pecorino in a medium bowl. Set a colander in a large bowl.

2. Bring 2 quarts water to a boil in a large Dutch oven. Add the pasta and 1½ teaspoons salt and cook, stirring frequently, until the pasta is al dente. Drain the pasta into the colander set in the bowl, reserving the cooking water. Pour 1½ cups of the cooking water into a liquid measuring cup and discard the remainder and then place the pasta in the empty bowl.

3. Slowly whisk 1 cup of the reserved pasta water into the finely grated Pecorino until smooth. Whisk in the cream, oil, and pepper. Gradually pour the cheese mixture over the pasta, tossing to coat. Let the pasta rest for 1 to 2 minutes, tossing frequently, adjusting the consistency with the remaining ½ cup reserved pasta cooking water as needed. Serve, passing the coarsely grated Pecorino separately.

FRESH PASTA WITHOUT A MACHINE

WHY THIS RECIPE WORKS: Not everyone has a pasta machine, and rolling out pasta dough by hand is no easy task. For an easy-to-roll pasta dough (that would still cook up into delicate, springy noodles), we added six extra egg yolks and a couple of tablespoons of olive oil to our dough. In addition, we incorporated an extended resting period to allow the gluten network to relax. To roll and cut the pasta, we first divided the pasta into smaller manageable pieces, then used a rolling pin to roll the dough and a sharp knife to cut the dough into noodles.

Fresh Pasta without a Machine

MAKES 1 POUND; SERVES 4 TO 6

If using a high-protein all-purpose flour like King Arthur brand, increase the number of egg yolks to 7. The longer the dough rests in step 2, the easier it will be to roll out. When rolling out the dough, avoid adding too much flour, which may result in excessive snapback.

- 2 cups (10 ounces) all-purpose flour
- 2 large eggs plus 6 large yolks
- 2 tablespoons olive oil
- 1 tablespoon salt
- 1 recipe sauce (recipes follow)

1. Process flour, eggs and yolks, and oil together in food processor until mixture forms cohesive dough that feels soft and is barely tacky to touch, about 45 seconds. (If dough sticks to fingers, add up to ¼ cup flour, 1 tablespoon at a time, until barely tacky. If dough doesn't become cohesive, add up to 1 tablespoon water, 1 teaspoon at a time, until it just comes together; process 30 seconds longer.)

2. Turn dough ball out onto dry counter and knead until smooth, 1 to 2 minutes. Shape dough into 6-inch-long cylinder. Wrap with plastic wrap and set aside at room temperature to rest for at least 1 hour or up to 4 hours.

3. Cut cylinder crosswise into 6 equal pieces. Working with 1 piece of dough (rewrap remaining dough), dust both sides with flour, place cut side down on clean counter, and press into 3-inch square. Using heavy rolling pin, roll into 6-inch square. Dust both sides of dough lightly with flour. Starting at center of square, roll dough away from you in 1 motion. Return rolling pin to center of dough and roll toward you in 1 motion. Repeat steps of rolling until dough sticks to counter and measures roughly 12 inches long. Lightly dust both sides of dough with flour and continue rolling dough until it measures roughly 20 inches long and 6 inches wide, frequently lifting dough to release it from counter. (You should be able to easily see outline of your fingers through dough.) If dough firmly sticks to counter and wrinkles when rolled out, dust dough lightly with flour.

4. Transfer pasta sheet to clean dish towel and let stand, uncovered, until firm around edges, about 15 minutes; meanwhile, roll out remaining dough. Starting with 1 short end, gently fold pasta sheet at 2-inch intervals until sheet has been folded into flat, rectangular roll. With sharp chef's knife, slice crosswise into 3⁄16-inch-wide noodles. Use fingers to unfurl pasta and transfer to baking sheet. Repeat folding and cutting remaining sheets of dough. Cook noodles within 1 hour.

5. Bring 4 quarts water to boil in large pot. Add pasta and salt and cook, stirring often, until al dente, about 3 minutes. Reserve 1 cup cooking water, then drain pasta. Toss with sauce; serve immediately.

TO MAKE AHEAD: Follow recipe through step 4, transfer baking sheet of pasta to freezer, and freeze until pasta is firm. Transfer to zipper-lock bag and store for up to 2 weeks. Cook frozen pasta straight from freezer as directed in step 5.

Tomato and Browned Butter Sauce

MAKES 3 CUPS; ENOUGH FOR 1 POUND PASTA

- 1 (28-ounce) can whole peeled tomatoes
- 4 tablespoons unsalted butter, cut into 4 pieces
- 2 garlic cloves, minced
- ½ teaspoon sugar
- Salt and pepper
- 2 teaspoons sherry vinegar
- 3 tablespoons chopped fresh basil
- Grated Parmesan cheese

1. Process tomatoes and their juice in food processor until smooth, about 30 seconds. Melt 3 tablespoons butter in 12-inch skillet over medium-high heat, swirling occasionally, until butter is dark brown and releases nutty aroma, about 1½ minutes. Stir in garlic and cook for 10 seconds. Stir in processed tomatoes, sugar, and ½ teaspoon salt and simmer until sauce is slightly reduced, about 8 minutes. Remove pan from heat; whisk in remaining 1 tablespoon butter and vinegar. Season with salt and pepper to taste; cover to keep warm.

2. To serve, return pan to medium heat. Add pasta, ¼ cup reserved cooking water, and basil; toss to combine. Season with salt and pepper to taste and add remaining cooking water as needed to adjust consistency. Serve immediately, passing Parmesan separately.

Walnut Cream Sauce

MAKES 2 CUPS; ENOUGH FOR 1 POUND PASTA

- 1½ cups (6 ounces) walnuts, toasted
- ¾ cup dry white wine
- ½ cup heavy cream
- 1 ounce Parmesan cheese, grated (½ cup)
- Salt and pepper
- ¼ cup minced fresh chives

1. Process 1 cup walnuts in food processor until finely ground, about 10 seconds. Transfer to small bowl. Pulse remaining ½ cup walnuts in food processor until coarsely chopped, 3 to 5 pulses. Bring wine to simmer in 12-inch skillet over medium-high heat; cook until reduced to ¼ cup, about 3 minutes. Whisk in cream, ground and chopped walnuts, Parmesan, ¼ teaspoon salt, and ½ teaspoon pepper. Remove pan from heat and cover to keep warm.

2. To serve, return pan to medium heat. Add pasta, ½ cup reserved cooking water, and chives; toss to combine. Season with salt and pepper to taste and add remaining cooking water as needed to adjust consistency. Serve immediately.

NOTES FROM THE TEST KITCHEN

ROLLING AND CUTTING PASTA DOUGH BY HAND

What's the trick to turning a lump of pasta into long, silky, strands—without a pasta roller? Starting with a soft, malleable dough is half the battle. The other half: dividing the dough into small, manageable pieces and working with them one at a time.

1. Shape dough into 6-inch cylinder; wrap in plastic wrap and let rest for at least 1 hour. Divide into 6 equal pieces. Reserve 1 piece; rewrap remaining 5.

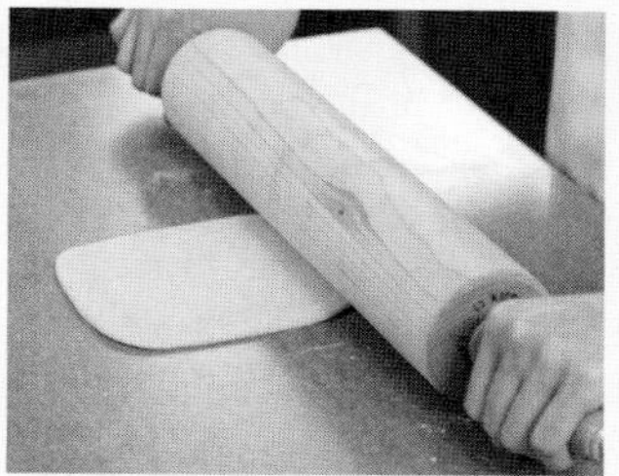

2. Working with reserved piece, dust both sides with flour, then press cut side down into 3-inch square. With rolling pin, roll into 6-inch square, then dust both sides again with flour.

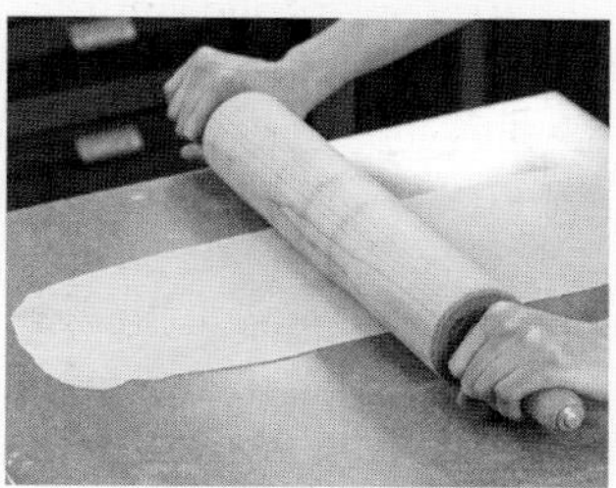

3. Roll dough to 12 by 6 inches, rolling from center of dough 1 way at a time, then dust with flour. Continue rolling to 20 by 6 inches, lifting frequently to release from counter. Transfer dough to clean dish towel and air-dry for about 15 minutes.

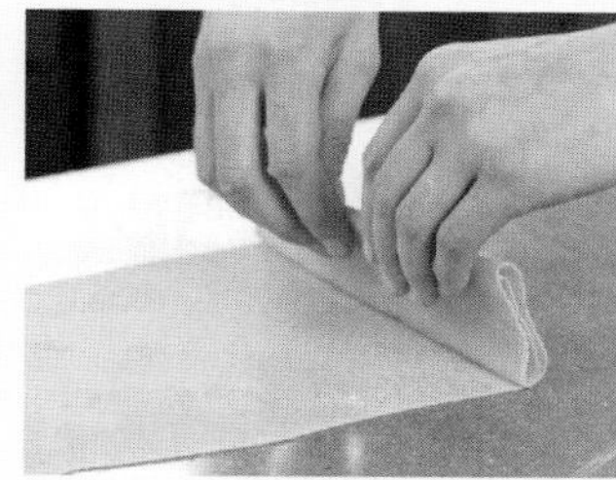

4. Starting with short end, gently fold dried sheet at 2-inch intervals to create flat, rectangular roll.

5. With sharp knife, cut into 3⁄16-inch-wide noodles.

6. Use fingers to unfurl pasta; transfer to baking sheet.

PASTA WITH FRESH TOMATOES

WHY THIS RECIPE WORKS: Fully ripe tomatoes need little else besides high-quality olive oil and a smattering of fresh herbs to become a bright, summery dressing for pasta. We set out to create the perfect raw tomato sauce—ideal for a quick yet flavorful dinner.

Selecting the ripest tomatoes guaranteed fresh flavor in the sauce, but to prevent their sweetness and acidity from taking over, we mixed in a generous amount of extra-virgin olive oil and a hefty amount of fresh herbs—you can use basil, parsley, cilantro, mint, oregano, or tarragon. We let the flavors of the tomatoes, olive oil, herbs, and some minced garlic blend while we cooked the pasta. Short pasta shapes held on to the chunky sauce nicely

Pasta with Fresh Tomatoes and Herbs

SERVES 4 TO 6

This chunky sauce works best with tubular pasta shapes, such as penne or fusilli. The success of this dish depends on using ripe, flavorful tomatoes.

- 1½ pounds ripe tomatoes (about 3 large), cored and cut into ½-inch pieces (see note)
- ¼ cup minced fresh herbs, such as basil, parsley, cilantro, mint, oregano, or tarragon
- 1 medium garlic clove, minced or pressed through a garlic press (about 1 teaspoon)
- ¼ cup extra-virgin olive oil
- Table salt and ground black pepper
- 1 pound penne, fusilli, or other short tubular pasta (see note)

1. Combine the tomatoes, herbs, garlic, oil, and salt and pepper to taste in a medium bowl. Set aside.

2. Bring 4 quarts water to a boil in a large pot. Add 1 tablespoon salt and the pasta to the boiling water and cook, stirring often, until al dente. Reserve ½ cup of the cooking water then drain the pasta and return it to the pot. Add the tomatoes and toss to combine; adjust the consistency of the sauce with the reserved pasta cooking water as needed. Serve.

PASTA AND FRESH TOMATO SAUCE

WHY THIS RECIPE WORKS: The best fresh tomato sauces capture the contrasting sweet and tart flavors of ripe tomatoes. But often, these sauces get waterlogged from the tomato juice. We wanted a cooked sauce that allowed the flavors of the traditional players—tomatoes, basil, garlic, and oil—to meld, but not become watered down. Quick cooking was the key to preserving fresh tomato flavor and creating a sauce that was both hearty and brightly flavored. To prevent unattractive pieces of curled-up tomato skin floating in our finished sauce, we simply peeled the tomatoes by boiling them and pulling off their skins. Seeded tomatoes made for a less watery start to the sauce, and cooking them down for a brief period facilitated the evaporation of any remaining liquid. Chopped fresh basil rounded out the flavors of the sauce, and a last-minute drizzle of olive oil brought a richness that complemented the sweetness of the tomatoes.

Pasta and Fresh Tomato Sauce with Garlic and Basil

SERVES 4 TO 6

To peel the tomatoes, dunk the cored tomatoes in a pot of boiling water until the skins split and begin to curl around the cored area, 15 to 30 seconds; transfer the tomatoes to a bowl of ice water, then peel off the skins with your fingers. This chunky sauce works best with tubular pasta shapes, such as penne or fusilli. If you'd like to serve it with spaghetti or linguine, puree the sauce in a blender or food processor before adding the basil. This recipe can be doubled and prepared in a 12-inch skillet.

- 3 tablespoons extra-virgin olive oil
- 2 medium garlic cloves, minced or pressed through a garlic press (about 2 teaspoons)
- 2 pounds ripe tomatoes (about 4 large), cored, peeled, seeded, and cut into ½-inch pieces (see note)
- 2 tablespoons chopped fresh basil leaves
- Table salt
- 1 pound penne, fusilli, or other short tubular pasta (see note)

1. Cook 2 tablespoons of the oil and the garlic in a 10-inch skillet over medium heat until fragrant, about 30 seconds. Stir in the tomatoes and cook over medium-high heat until the liquid released by the tomatoes evaporates and the tomato pieces form a chunky sauce, about 10 minutes. Stir in the basil and salt to taste; cover.

2. Meanwhile, bring 4 quarts water to a boil in a large pot. Add 1 tablespoon salt and the pasta to the boiling water and cook, stirring often, until al dente. Reserve ½ cup of the cooking water then drain the pasta and return it to the pot. Add ¼ cup of the reserved cooking water, the sauce, and the remaining 1 tablespoon oil and toss to combine. Adjust the consistency of the sauce with the remaining reserved pasta cooking water as needed. Serve.

BEHIND THE SCENES

TOMATOES—SKIP THE FRIDGE, PLEASE

We never store tomatoes in the refrigerator. Cold damages tomatoes in two ways: It destroys an enzyme that produces flavorful compounds, and it makes water in the tomato expand, rupturing cells and turning the flesh mealy. But what about storing a partially used tomato? We cut a dozen ripe tomatoes in two, stored half of each in the fridge, and kept the other half at room temperature (both were wrapped tightly in plastic wrap). After a few days, the halves at room temperature had begun to soften, while the refrigerated halves were still as firm as the day they were cut. Upon tasting, however, we found the refrigerated halves were bland and mealy compared with the never-refrigerated halves. Our advice? Keep cut tomatoes tightly wrapped at room temperature and consume them within a few days. The shelf life gained by refrigeration doesn't make up for the loss in flavor and texture.

PASTA WITH CREAMY TOMATO SAUCE

WHY THIS RECIPE WORKS: In the best examples of creamy tomato sauce, the acidity of fruity tomatoes is balanced with the richness of dairy; the worst deliver instant heartburn. We wanted a smooth, full-flavored tomato sauce enriched with cream, and we wanted to use canned tomatoes for convenience. Readily available, canned crushed tomatoes trumped canned whole and diced tomatoes. Before adding the tomatoes, we cooked a few tablespoons of tomato paste with some onion, garlic, and sun-dried tomatoes. A pinch of red pepper flakes, a splash of wine, and a little minced prosciutto added depth and tamed some of the sauce's sweetness; a bit of reserved uncooked crushed tomatoes and another splash of wine stirred in before serving brought the sauce's ingredients together. We added cream to the just-finished sauce to enrich it without subduing the bright tomato flavor.

Pasta with Creamy Tomato Sauce

SERVES 4 TO 6

Use high-quality crushed tomatoes; our favorite brand is SMT.

- 3 tablespoons unsalted butter
- 1 small onion, minced
- 1 ounce prosciutto, minced (about 2 tablespoons)

1 bay leaf
Pinch red pepper flakes
Table salt
3 medium garlic cloves, minced or pressed through a garlic press (about 1 tablespoon)
2 ounces oil-packed sun-dried tomatoes, drained, rinsed, patted dry, and chopped coarse (about 3 tablespoons)
2 tablespoons tomato paste
¼ cup plus 2 tablespoons dry white wine
2 cups plus 2 tablespoons crushed tomatoes (from one 28-ounce can; see note)
1 pound ziti, penne, or other short tubular pasta
½ cup heavy cream
Ground black pepper
¼ cup chopped fresh basil leaves
Grated Parmesan cheese, for serving

1. Melt the butter in a medium saucepan over medium heat. Add the onion, prosciutto, bay leaf, red pepper flakes, and ¼ teaspoon salt; cook, stirring occasionally, until the onion is very soft and beginning to turn light gold, 8 to 12 minutes. Increase the heat to medium-high, add the garlic, and cook until fragrant, about 30 seconds. Stir in the sun-dried tomatoes and tomato paste and cook, stirring constantly, until slightly darkened, 1 to 2 minutes. Add ¼ cup of the wine and cook, stirring frequently, until the liquid has evaporated, 1 to 2 minutes.

2. Add 2 cups of the crushed tomatoes and bring to a simmer. Reduce the heat to low, partially cover, and cook, stirring occasionally, until the sauce is thickened, 25 to 30 minutes.

3. Meanwhile, bring 4 quarts water to a boil in a large pot. Add 1 tablespoon salt and the pasta to the boiling water and cook, stirring often, until al dente. Reserve ½ cup of the cooking water then drain the pasta and return it to the pot.

4. Remove the bay leaf from the sauce and discard. Stir the cream, remaining 2 tablespoons crushed tomatoes, and remaining 2 tablespoons wine into the sauce; season with salt and pepper to taste. Add the sauce to the pasta and adjust the consistency of the sauce with the reserved pasta cooking water as needed. Stir in the basil and serve, passing the Parmesan separately.

NOTES FROM THE TEST KITCHEN

SHREDDING BASIL

To shred basil or other leafy herbs, simply stack several leaves on top of one another, roll them up, and slice. For basil, we find rolling leaves from tip to tail minimizes bruising and browning.

PASTA CAPRESE

WHY THIS RECIPE WORKS: The summer salad composed of creamy mozzarella, fresh basil, and sweet tomatoes has become so popular that we wanted to translate it to a simple-yet-elegant pasta dish, one in which the primary ingredients work in harmony with the pasta. Specifically, we wanted creamy pockets of milky mozzarella throughout the dish, rather than the chewy wads that can occur when cheese hits hot pasta. And we wanted to find a way to guarantee sweet tomato flavor, even when we were working with substandard tomatoes.

Supermarket mozzarella worked well in this dish; the trick was to dice and freeze it for just 10 minutes before tossing it with the hot pasta to keep the cheese soft and creamy (instead of dry and clumpy). Otherwise, handmade mozzarella (minus the freezing step) worked well. To boost the flavor of less-than-stellar tomatoes, we added a little sugar for sweetness and fresh lemon juice for brightness. Marinating the tomatoes and mozzarella with olive oil, minced shallot, salt, and a pinch of black pepper while the pasta was cooking added even more flavor. We decided not to cut corners with a substandard olive oil; because there are few flavors in this dish, the fruity nuances of a good extra-virgin olive oil really made a difference.

Pasta Caprese

SERVES 4 TO 6

This dish will be very warm, not hot. The success of this recipe depends on high-quality ingredients, including ripe, in-season tomatoes and a fruity olive oil (the test kitchen prefers Columela extra-virgin). Don't skip the step of freezing the mozzarella, as freezing prevents it from turning chewy when it comes in contact with the hot pasta. If handmade buffalo- or cow's-milk mozzarella is available (it's commonly found, packed in water, in gourmet and cheese shops), we highly recommend using it, but do not freeze it. Additional lemon juice or up to 1 teaspoon sugar can be added at the end to taste, depending on the ripeness of the tomatoes.

- ¼ cup extra-virgin olive oil (see note)
- 2–4 teaspoons juice from 1 lemon (see note)
- 1 small garlic clove, minced or pressed through a garlic press (about ½ teaspoon)
- 1 small shallot, minced (about 1 tablespoon)
- Table salt and ground black pepper
- 1½ pounds ripe tomatoes (about 3 large), cored, seeded, and cut into ½-inch dice (see note)
- 12 ounces fresh mozzarella cheese, cut into ½-inch cubes (see note)
- 1 pound penne, fusilli, or campanelle
- ¼ cup chopped fresh basil leaves
- 1 teaspoon sugar (optional; see note)

1. Whisk the oil, 2 teaspoons of the lemon juice, the garlic, shallot, ½ teaspoon salt, and ¼ teaspoon pepper together in a large bowl. Add the tomatoes and gently toss to combine; set aside. Do not marinate the tomatoes for longer than 45 minutes.

2. While the tomatoes are marinating, place the mozzarella on a plate and freeze until slightly firm, about 10 minutes. Bring 4 quarts water to a boil in a large pot. Add 1 tablespoon salt and the pasta to the boiling water and cook, stirring often, until al dente. Drain well.

3. Add the pasta and mozzarella to the tomato mixture and gently toss to combine. Let stand for 5 minutes. Stir in the basil, season with salt and pepper to taste, and add additional lemon juice or sugar, if desired. Serve immediately.

PASTA WITH RICOTTA AND SPINACH

WHY THIS RECIPE WORKS: There are many recipes that pair simple boiled pasta with spinach and ricotta as a simplified, "deconstructed" version of stuffed shells, manicotti, or ravioli. But the versions we tried lacked complexity and suffered from a gritty texture. We wanted to punch up the flavor and make this simple pasta dish an easy weeknight option. To boost the flavor of the ricotta, we mixed in some extra-virgin olive oil, salt, and pepper. Then we set out to tackle the sauce's gritty, chalky texture. Heat caused the ricotta curds to release water and coagulate, rendering the sauce grainy. To minimize this effect, we dolloped most of the ricotta on top of the pasta so that tasters got concentrated hits of cheese here and there, much as they would when eating filled pasta. We mixed the rest of the ricotta with cream (to stabilize the milk proteins), along with sautéed garlic, cayenne, and nutmeg for warmth, and used this mixture to dress the warm pasta. As for the spinach, simply tossing the coarsely chopped leaves into the pot with the pasta at the end of cooking gave us slightly wilted but still brilliant green spinach. A generous dusting of grated Parmesan cheese over the finished dish provided additional depth, and a sprinkle of lemon zest and lemon juice introduced welcome brightness. Letting the pasta sit dressed for a few minutes before serving drew out some of the pasta's starches for a creamy, velvety texture.

Fusilli with Ricotta and Spinach

SERVES 4 TO 6

We like fusilli for this recipe since its corkscrew shape does a nice job of trapping the sauce, but penne and campanelle also work well.

- 11 ounces (1⅓ cups) whole-milk ricotta cheese
- 3 tablespoons extra-virgin olive oil
- Salt and pepper
- 1 pound fusilli
- 1 pound (16 cups) baby spinach, chopped coarse
- 4 garlic cloves, minced
- ¼ teaspoon ground nutmeg
- ⅛ teaspoon cayenne pepper
- ¼ cup heavy cream
- 1 teaspoon grated lemon zest plus 2 teaspoons juice
- 1 ounce Parmesan cheese, grated (½ cup), plus extra for serving

1. Whisk 1 cup ricotta, 1 tablespoon oil, ¼ teaspoon pepper, and ⅛ teaspoon salt in medium bowl until smooth; set aside.

2. Bring 4 quarts water to boil in large pot. Add pasta and 1 tablespoon salt and cook, stirring often, until al dente. Reserve 1 cup cooking water. Stir spinach into pot with pasta and cook until wilted, about 30 seconds. Drain pasta and spinach and return them to pot.

3. While pasta cooks, heat remaining 2 tablespoons oil, garlic, nutmeg, and cayenne in saucepan over medium heat until fragrant, about 1 minute. Remove pan from heat and whisk in remaining ⅓ cup ricotta, cream, lemon zest and juice, and ¾ teaspoon salt until smooth.

4. Add ricotta-cream mixture and Parmesan to pasta and toss to combine. Let pasta rest, tossing frequently, until sauce has thickened slightly and coats pasta, 2 to 4 minutes, adjusting consistency with reserved cooking water as needed. Transfer pasta to serving platter, dot evenly with reserved ricotta mixture, and serve, passing extra Parmesan separately.

PASTA WITH TOMATOES AND OLIVES

WHY THIS RECIPE WORKS: When tomatoes are in season, there's no better time to make a simple, fresh tomato sauce. We like the classic pairing of tomatoes and olives, so we set out to make an easy, not too watery, sauce with Mediterranean flavors.

Seeding the tomatoes rid them of excess moisture and prevented a watery sauce. Instead of peeling the tomato skins, we decided to leave them on so the chopped tomatoes would have some structural integrity and not disintegrate. By making a no-cook sauce—the other components were fresh mint, chopped kalamata olives, and feta—we were able to prepare it quickly while the drained pasta waited on the sidelines. The potent olives and feta added a bright zestiness to our pasta, and the mint amplified the sauce's freshness.

Farfalle with Tomatoes, Olives, and Feta

SERVES 4 TO 6

To prevent the feta from melting into the pasta, add it only after the tomatoes have been tossed with the pasta, which gives the mixture the opportunity to cool slightly.

- Table salt
- 1 pound farfalle
- 1½ pounds ripe tomatoes (about 3 large), cored, seeded, and cut into ½-inch pieces
- ½ cup pitted kalamata olives, chopped coarse
- ¼ cup extra-virgin olive oil
- 1 tablespoon chopped fresh mint leaves
- Ground black pepper
- 6 ounces feta cheese, crumbled (about 1½ cups; see note)

1. Bring 4 quarts water to a boil in a large pot. Add 1 tablespoon salt and the pasta to the boiling water and cook, stirring often, until al dente. Reserve ½ cup of the cooking water then drain the pasta and return it to the pot.

2. Meanwhile, combine the tomatoes, olives, oil, mint, ½ teaspoon salt, and ¼ teaspoon pepper in a medium bowl. Add the sauce to the pasta and adjust the consistency of the sauce with the reserved pasta cooking water as needed. Add the feta and toss to combine. Season with salt and pepper to taste and serve.

QUICK TOMATO SAUCE

WHY THIS RECIPE WORKS: In a perfect world, garden-ripe tomatoes make the best quick tomato sauce. But that isn't realistic for most of the year. We wanted to create a complex, brightly flavored sauce with the next best alternative—canned tomatoes—that tasted of full, fruity tomatoes, in the time it took to boil pasta. Choosing the right can of tomatoes was a critical first step. Crushed tomatoes were the best choice because they would save us the step of pureeing. We also shredded a small amount of onion on a box grater before sautéing; the shredded pieces cooked faster and became sweeter more quickly. We sautéed the onion in butter, which caramelized when heated, and added garlic, sugar, and the crushed tomatoes, then simmered the sauce briefly. To make up for the lost fragrance of fresh tomatoes, we added chopped fresh basil and extra-virgin olive oil.

Quick Tomato Sauce

MAKES ABOUT 3 CUPS

This recipe makes enough to sauce a pound of pasta. High-quality canned tomatoes will make a big difference in this sauce; our preferred brand of crushed tomatoes is SMT. Grate the onion on the large holes of a box grater.

- 2 tablespoons unsalted butter
- ¼ cup grated onion (see note)
- ¼ teaspoon dried oregano
- Table salt
- 2 medium garlic cloves, minced or pressed through a garlic press (about 2 teaspoons)
- 1 (28-ounce) can crushed tomatoes (see note)
- ¼ teaspoon sugar
- 2 tablespoons chopped fresh basil leaves
- 1 tablespoon extra-virgin olive oil
- Ground black pepper

Melt the butter in a medium saucepan over medium heat. Add the onion, oregano, and ½ teaspoon salt; cook, stirring occasionally, until the liquid has evaporated and the onion is golden brown, about 5 minutes. Add the garlic and cook until fragrant, about 30 seconds. Stir in the tomatoes and sugar; bring to a simmer over high heat. Lower the heat to medium-low and simmer until slightly thickened, about 10 minutes. Off the heat, stir in the basil and oil; season with salt and pepper to taste.

BEHIND THE SCENES

USE YOUR NOODLE—PERFECT PASTA TIPS

We love pasta in the test kitchen. As a result, we're pretty opinionated about how we cook it. Here's what you need to know.

COOKING PASTA: Make sure you have all the necessary and utensils assembled before you begin. You'll need 4 quarts of water to cook 1 pound of dried pasta. Any less and the noodles may stick. Use a pot large enough to accommodate the water and pasta without boil-overs—we like an 8-quart pot. It's crucial to properly season the cooking water—we recommend 1 tablespoon table salt per 4 quarts water. Bring the water to a rolling boil before adding the salt and pasta and give it an immediate stir to prevent sticking. And don't add oil to the pot—oil will prevent sauce from sticking to the pasta.

DRAINING AND SERVING PASTA: If a sauce is too thick, we thin it with a little reserved pasta water. The trouble is, it's easy to forget to save some water. As a reminder, we place a measuring cup in the colander. As for draining pasta, just give it a shake or two. You don't want the pasta bone dry. The little bit of hot cooking water clinging to the pasta will help the sauce coat it. And if you're using a large serving bowl for the pasta, place it underneath the colander while draining the pasta. The hot water heats up the bowl, which keeps the pasta warmer longer.

MARINARA SAUCE

WHY THIS RECIPE WORKS: Making a tomato sauce with deep, complex flavor usually requires hours of simmering. We wanted to produce a multidimensional marinara sauce in under an hour, perfect for any night of the week.

Our first challenge was picking the right tomatoes. We found canned whole tomatoes, which we hand-crushed to remove the hard core, to be the best choice in terms of both flavor and texture. We boosted tomato flavor by sautéing the tomato pieces until they glazed the bottom of the pan, after which we added their liquid. We shortened the simmering time by using a skillet instead of a saucepan (the greater surface area of a skillet encourages faster evaporation and flavor concentration). Finally, we added just the right amount of sugar, red wine (we especially liked Chianti and Merlot), and, just before serving, a few uncooked canned tomatoes for texture, fresh basil for fresh herbal flavor, and olive oil for richness.

Marinara Sauce

MAKES 4 CUPS

You can figure on about 3 cups of sauce per pound of pasta. Chianti or Merlot work well for the dry red wine. Because canned tomatoes vary in acidity and saltiness, it's best to add salt, pepper, and sugar to taste just before serving. If you prefer a chunkier sauce, give it just three or four pulses in the food processor in step 4.

- 2 (28-ounce) cans whole tomatoes packed in juice
- 3 tablespoons extra-virgin olive oil
- 1 medium onion, minced
- 2 medium garlic cloves, minced or pressed through a garlic press (about 2 teaspoons)
- ½ teaspoon dried oregano
- ⅓ cup dry red wine (see note)
- 3 tablespoons chopped fresh basil leaves
- Table salt and ground black pepper
- 1–2 teaspoons sugar, as needed (see note)

1. Pour the tomatoes into a strainer set over a large bowl. Open the tomatoes with your hands and remove and discard the fibrous cores; let the tomatoes drain excess liquid, about 5 minutes. Remove ¾ cup tomatoes from the strainer and set aside. Reserve 2½ cups tomato juice and discard the remainder.

2. Heat 2 tablespoons of the olive oil in a 12-inch skillet over medium heat until shimmering. Add the onion and cook, stirring occasionally, until softened and golden around the edges, 6 to 8 minutes. Add the garlic and oregano and cook, stirring constantly, until the garlic is fragrant, about 30 seconds.

3. Add the tomatoes from the strainer and increase the heat to medium-high. Cook, stirring every minute, until the liquid has evaporated and the tomatoes begin to stick to the bottom of the pan and browned bits form around the pan edges, 10 to 12 minutes. Add the wine and cook until thick and syrupy, about 1 minute. Add the reserved tomato juice and bring to a simmer; reduce the heat to medium and cook, stirring occasionally and loosening any browned bits, until the sauce is thickened, 8 to 10 minutes.

4. Transfer the sauce to a food processor and add the reserved tomatoes; process until slightly chunky, about 8 pulses. Return the sauce to the skillet, add the basil and remaining 1 tablespoon olive oil, and season with salt, pepper, and sugar to taste. (The sauce can be refrigerated in an airtight container for up to 3 days or frozen for up to 1 month.)

MEATLESS "MEAT" SAUCE

WHY THIS RECIPE WORKS: To create a vegetarian version of an unctuous tomato-meat sauce, we started with cremini mushrooms and tomato paste—both rich sources of savory flavor. We let the food processor do the work for us, using it to chop up our mushrooms, onions, and chickpeas, which added hearty texture. Extra-virgin olive oil did double duty, cooking the mushrooms and the classic Italian aromatics of garlic, dried oregano, and red pepper flakes and enriching the sauce. To loosen the sauce without diluting its flavor, we added vegetable broth. Chopped fresh basil added an authentic finish.

Meatless "Meat" Sauce with Chickpeas and Mushrooms

MAKES 6 CUPS; ENOUGH FOR 2 POUNDS PASTA

Make sure to rinse the chickpeas after pulsing them in the food processor or the sauce will be too thick. Our favorite canned chickpeas are from Pastene, our favorite crushed tomatoes are from SMT, and our favorite tomato paste is from Goya.

- 10 ounces cremini mushrooms, trimmed
- 6 tablespoons extra-virgin olive oil
- Salt and pepper
- 1 onion, chopped
- 5 garlic cloves, minced
- 1¼ teaspoons dried oregano
- ¼ teaspoon red pepper flakes
- ¼ cup tomato paste
- 1 (28-ounce) can crushed tomatoes
- 2 cups vegetable broth
- 1 (15-ounce) can chickpeas, rinsed
- 2 tablespoons chopped fresh basil

1. Pulse mushrooms in two batches in food processor until chopped into ⅛- to ¼-inch pieces, 7 to 10 pulses, scraping down sides of bowl as needed. (Do not clean workbowl.)

2. Heat 5 tablespoons oil in Dutch oven over medium-high heat until shimmering. Add mushrooms and 1 teaspoon salt and cook, stirring occasionally, until mushrooms are browned and fond has formed on bottom of pot, about 8 minutes.

3. While mushrooms cook, pulse onion in food processor until finely chopped, 7 to 10 pulses, scraping down sides of bowl as needed. (Do not clean workbowl.) Transfer onion to pot with mushrooms and cook, stirring occasionally, until onion is soft and translucent, about 5 minutes. Combine remaining 1 tablespoon oil, garlic, oregano, and pepper flakes in bowl.

4. Add tomato paste to pot and cook, stirring constantly, until mixture is rust-colored, 1 to 2 minutes. Reduce heat to medium and push vegetables to sides of pot. Add garlic mixture to center and cook, stirring constantly, until fragrant, about 30 seconds. Stir in tomatoes and broth; bring to simmer over high heat. Reduce heat to low and simmer sauce for 5 minutes, stirring occasionally.

5. While sauce simmers, pulse chickpeas in food processor until chopped into ¼-inch pieces, 7 to 10 pulses. Transfer chickpeas to fine-mesh strainer and rinse under cold running water until water runs clear; drain well. Add chickpeas to pot and simmer until sauce is slightly thickened, about 15 minutes. Stir in basil and season with salt and pepper to taste. (Sauce can be refrigerated for up to 2 days or frozen for up to 1 month.)

PASTA PUTTANESCA

WHY THIS RECIPE WORKS: Puttanesca is a gutsy tomato sauce punctuated by the brash, zesty flavors of garlic, anchovies, olives, and capers. But too often, the sauce comes off as too fishy, too garlicky, too briny, or just plain too salty. We wanted to harmonize the bold flavors in this Neapolitan dish and not let any one preside over the others.

For a sauce with the best tomato flavor and a slightly clingy consistency, we used canned diced tomatoes and kept the cooking time to a minimum to retain their fresh flavor and their meaty texture. To tame the garlic and prevent it from burning, we soaked minced garlic in a bit of water before sautéing it. Cooking the garlic and anchovies with red pepper flakes (before adding the tomatoes) helped their flavors bloom and added a subtle heat. We chose to add the olives and capers when the sauce was finished—this prevented them from disintegrating in the sauce. Reserved tomato juice from the canned tomatoes moistened the pasta, and a last-minute addition of minced parsley preserved the fresh flavors of the sauce.

Spaghetti Puttanesca

SERVES 4 TO 6

The pasta and sauce cook in about the same amount of time, so begin the sauce just after you add the pasta to the boiling water in step 1.

- 3 medium garlic cloves, minced or pressed through a garlic press (about 1 tablespoon)
- Table salt
- 1 pound spaghetti
- 1 (28-ounce) can diced tomatoes, drained and ½ cup juice reserved
- 2 tablespoons extra-virgin olive oil, plus extra for drizzling
- 4 teaspoons minced anchovy fillets (about 8 fillets)
- 1 teaspoon red pepper flakes
- ½ cup pitted kalamata olives, chopped coarse
- ¼ cup minced fresh parsley leaves
- 3 tablespoons capers, rinsed

1. Combine the garlic with 1 tablespoon water in a small bowl; set aside. Bring 4 quarts water to a boil in a large pot. Add 1 tablespoon salt and the pasta to the boiling water and cook, stirring often, until al dente. Reserve ½ cup of the cooking water then drain the pasta and return it to the pot. Add ¼ cup of the reserved tomato juice and toss to combine.

2. Meanwhile, heat the oil, anchovies, garlic mixture, and red pepper flakes in a 12-inch skillet over medium heat. Cook, stirring frequently, until the garlic is fragrant, 2 to 3 minutes. Add the tomatoes and simmer until slightly thickened, about 8 minutes.

3. Stir the olives, parsley, and capers into the sauce. Pour the sauce over the pasta and toss to combine; adjust the consistency of the sauce with the remaining reserved tomato juice or reserved pasta cooking water as needed. Season with salt to taste, drizzle with 1 tablespoon oil, if desired, and serve immediately.

PASTA WITH TOMATO, BACON, AND ONION

WHY THIS RECIPE WORKS: There are two versions of the classic Italian pasta dish *pasta all'amatriciana*: one from Amatrice, and one from Rome. The Roman version boasts a rich sauce containing tomatoes, bacon, onion, and Pecorino Romano cheese, and generally calls for a long, tubular pasta. (The version from Amatrice adds wine, leaves out the onions, and often calls for spaghetti.) We decided to re-create the rich, hearty Roman version for the American kitchen. In Rome, the dish traditionally uses a type of bacon called *guanciale* (made from pork jowls), which is easy to find in central Italy but not so easy to locate in the States. We wanted a recipe using ingredients found locally. Thickly sliced pancetta proved a good substitute for guanciale (if you can't find pancetta, bacon works). We cut the pancetta into strips and cooked them in a skillet until crisp, then removed the pancetta to ensure it stayed crisp while we built the sauce in the remaining fat. Canned diced tomatoes, minced onion, and red pepper flakes made a flavorful, aromatic backbone to our sauce. Finally, we tossed the crisp pancetta in with the tomato sauce and pasta (traditional long-strand pasta, like bucatini or linguine, worked best) and sprinkled grated Pecorino Romano cheese on top.

Pasta with Tomato, Bacon, and Onion

SERVES 4 TO 6

This dish is traditionally made with bucatini, also called perciatelli, which appear to be thick, round strands but are actually thin, extralong tubes. Linguine works fine, too. When buying pancetta, ask the butcher to slice it ¼ inch thick; if using bacon, buy slab bacon and cut it into ¼-inch-thick slices yourself. If the pancetta that you're using is very lean, it's unlikely that you will need to drain off any fat before adding the onion.

- 2 tablespoons extra-virgin olive oil
- 6 ounces pancetta or bacon, sliced ¼ inch thick and cut into strips 1 inch long and ¼ inch wide (see note)
- 1 medium onion, minced
- ½ teaspoon red pepper flakes, or to taste
- 1 (28-ounce) can diced tomatoes, drained and juice reserved
- Table salt
- 1 pound bucatini, perciatelli, or linguine (see note)
- ⅓ cup grated Pecorino Romano cheese

1. Bring 4 quarts water to a boil in a large pot.

2. Meanwhile, heat the oil in a 12-inch skillet over medium heat until shimmering. Add the pancetta and cook, stirring occasionally, until lightly browned and crisp, about 8 minutes. Using a slotted spoon, transfer the pancetta to a paper towel–lined plate; set aside. Pour off all but 2 tablespoons of fat from the skillet. Add the onion and cook over medium heat until softened, about 5 minutes. Add the pepper flakes and cook, about 30 seconds. Stir in the tomatoes and reserved juice and simmer until slightly thickened, about 10 minutes.

3. While the sauce is simmering, add 1 tablespoon salt and the pasta to the boiling water and cook, stirring often, until al dente. Reserve ½ cup of the cooking water then drain the pasta and return it to the pot.

4. Add the pancetta to the sauce and season with salt to taste. Add the sauce to the pasta and toss over low heat to combine, about 30 seconds. Add the Pecorino and toss again. Adjust the consistency of the sauce with the reserved pasta cooking water as needed and serve immediately.

PASTA ALL'AMATRICIANA

WHY THIS RECIPE WORKS: Although the Roman version of this Italian pasta dish is understandably popular, there is another, slightly different version that hails from Amatrice, a town northeast of Rome. Rather than minced onions, the Amatrician version calls for wine in the sauce. We loved the simple concept, and knew we wanted to come up with a version that we could make at home. To create an authentic flavor profile, we first needed an alternative to hard-to-find *guanciale,* or cured pork jowl. Humble salt pork, though an unlikely solution, provided the rich, clean meatiness we were after, and proved to be a perfect foil for the bright acidity

of the wine and tomatoes. To ensure tender bites of pork throughout, we first simmered it in water to gently cook it and render fat, a step that allowed the meat to quickly turn golden once the water evaporated. Finally, to ensure the grated Pecorino Romano didn't clump in the hot sauce, we first mixed it with a little cooled rendered pork fat. Now the flavor of pork, tomato, chili flakes, and Pecorino shone through in each bite.

Pasta all'Amatriciana

SERVES 4 TO 6

Look for salt pork that is roughly 70 percent fat and 30 percent lean meat; leaner salt pork may not render enough fat. If difficult to slice, the salt pork can be put in the freezer for 15 minutes to firm up. In this dish, it is essential to use high-quality imported Pecorino Romano—not the bland domestic cheese labeled "Romano."

- 8 ounces salt pork, rind removed, rinsed thoroughly, and patted dry
- ½ cup water
- ½ teaspoon red pepper flakes
- 2 tablespoons tomato paste
- ¼ cup red wine
- 1 (28-ounce) can diced tomatoes
- 2 ounces Pecorino Romano, grated fine (1 cup)
- 1 pound spaghetti
- 1 tablespoon salt

1. Slice salt pork into ¼-inch-thick strips, then cut each strip crosswise into ¼-inch pieces. Bring pork and water to simmer in 10-inch nonstick skillet over medium heat; cook until water evaporates and pork begins to sizzle, 5 to 8 minutes. Reduce heat to medium-low and continue to cook, stirring frequently, until fat renders and pork turns golden, 5 to 8 minutes longer. Using slotted spoon, transfer salt pork to bowl. Pour off all but 1 tablespoon fat from skillet. Reserve remaining fat.

2. Return skillet to medium heat and add tomato paste and pepper flakes; cook, stirring constantly, for 20 seconds. Stir in wine and cook for 30 seconds. Stir in tomatoes and their juice and rendered pork and bring to simmer. Cook, stirring frequently, until thickened, 12 to 16 minutes. While sauce simmers, stir 2 tablespoons reserved fat and ½ cup Pecorino together in bowl to form paste.

3. Meanwhile, bring 4 quarts water to boil in large Dutch oven. Add pasta and salt and cook, stirring often, until al dente. Reserve 1 cup cooking water, then drain pasta and return it to pot.

4. Add sauce, ⅓ cup cooking water, and Pecorino mixture to pasta and toss well to coat, adding cooking water as needed to adjust consistency. Serve, passing remaining ½ cup Pecorino separately.

PENNE ARRABBIATA

WHY THIS RECIPE WORKS: *Arrabbiata* means "angry" in Italian, and one bite of this peasant-style pasta sauce will confirm that it was aptly named. To deliver an arrabbiata with complex flavor and not just searing heat, we looked beyond the tradition of using only red pepper flakes and crafted a recipe that included three different types of pepper. By supplementing pepper flakes with paprika and pickled pepperoncini, we built deep flavor while keeping the spiciness in check. Pecorino Romano, tomato paste, and anchovies, while difficult to detect in the sauce, added umami notes and richness to this traditionally simple sauce. Finally, using canned tomatoes helped bring the sauce to the table quickly and means the dish can be enjoyed year-round.

Penne Arrabbiata

SERVES 6

This recipe will work with other short tubular pastas like ziti or rigatoni.

- 1 (28-ounce) can whole peeled tomatoes
- ¼ cup extra-virgin olive oil
- ¼ cup stemmed, patted dry, and minced pepperoncini
- 2 tablespoons tomato paste
- 1 garlic clove, minced
- 1 teaspoon red pepper flakes
- 4 anchovy fillets, rinsed, patted dry, and minced to paste
- ½ teaspoon paprika
- Salt and pepper
- ¼ cup grated Pecorino Romano, plus extra for serving
- 1 pound penne

1. Pulse tomatoes and their juice in food processor until finely chopped, about 10 pulses.

2. Heat oil, pepperoncini, tomato paste, garlic, pepper flakes, anchovies, paprika, ½ teaspoon salt, and ½ teaspoon pepper in medium saucepan over medium-low heat, stirring occasionally, until deep red in color, 7 to 8 minutes.

3. Add tomatoes and Pecorino and bring to simmer. Cook, stirring occasionally, until thickened, about 20 minutes.

4. Bring 4 quarts water to boil in large pot. Add pasta and 1 tablespoon salt and cook, stirring often, until al dente. Reserve ½ cup cooking water, then drain pasta and return it to pot. Add sauce and toss to combine, adjusting consistency with reserved cooking water as needed. Season with salt and pepper to taste. Serve, passing extra Pecorino separately.

PASTA WITH CAULIFLOWER, BACON, AND BREAD CRUMBS

WHY THIS RECIPE WORKS: For an at-home version of pasta with cauliflower, a restaurant favorite, without the mountain of dirty pots and pans, we set out to streamline this recipe. We piled cauliflower florets into an oiled skillet and cooked them just enough to ensure a crisp-tender texture to contrast with the al dente pasta. Cooking the campanelle as we would a risotto—allowing the liquid to slowly absorb into the pasta—meant any of the starches we would otherwise lose after draining would stay in the pot, creating a creamy sauce. Chopped onion and minced fresh thyme established the flavorful base to which we added the uncooked campanelle and just enough chicken broth and white wine to cook the pasta, contributing complex flavor and lush texture. Once the liquid had absorbed, we stirred in the nutty cauliflower florets, plus parsley and lemon for liveliness. A sprinkling of crunchy panko crumbs cooked with salty bacon pieces offered a perfect crispy finish.

Pasta with Cauliflower, Bacon, and Bread Crumbs

SERVES 4 TO 6

Farfalle, orecchiette, or gemelli can be substituted for the campanelle. If the pasta seems too dry, stir in up to ¼ cup of hot water.

- 3 slices bacon, cut into ¼-inch pieces
- ½ cup panko bread crumbs
- Salt and pepper
- 2 tablespoons vegetable oil
- 1 large head cauliflower (3 pounds), cored and cut into 1-inch florets
- 1 onion, chopped fine
- ½ teaspoon minced fresh thyme
- 1 pound campanelle
- 5½ cups chicken broth
- ½ cup dry white wine
- 3 tablespoons minced fresh parsley
- 1 teaspoon lemon juice, plus lemon wedges for serving

1. Cook bacon in 12-inch skillet over medium-high heat until crispy, 5 to 7 minutes. Add panko and ¼ teaspoon pepper and cook, stirring frequently, until panko is well browned, 2 to 4 minutes. Transfer panko mixture to bowl and wipe out skillet.

2. Heat 5 teaspoons oil in now-empty skillet over medium-high heat until shimmering. Add cauliflower and 1 teaspoon salt; cook, stirring occasionally, until cauliflower is crisp-tender and browned in spots, 10 to 12 minutes. Remove pan from heat and cover to keep warm.

3. Heat remaining 1 teaspoon oil in Dutch oven over medium heat until shimmering. Add onion, thyme, and ½ teaspoon salt; cook, stirring frequently, until onion has softened, 4 to 7 minutes. Increase heat to high, add pasta, broth, and wine, and bring to simmer. Cook pasta, stirring frequently, until most of liquid is absorbed and pasta is al dente, 8 to 10 minutes.

4. Remove pot from heat; stir in parsley, lemon juice, and cauliflower; and season with salt and pepper to taste. Serve, passing panko mixture and lemon wedges separately.

PASTA WITH PESTO

WHY THIS RECIPE WORKS: Pasta with pesto makes for a satisfying, summery meal. But getting pesto right isn't always so easy; the sauce can be anywhere from too thin and watery to too thick and overpoweringly garlicky. Our goal was to heighten the basil and subdue the garlic flavors in pesto so that each major element balanced the next.

We started by briefly blanching whole unpeeled garlic cloves to tame their flavor and prevent them from taking over the sauce. Then we bruised the basil in a plastic bag with a meat pounder (you could also use a rolling pin) to unlock its flavor; we found that this method released the most herbal flavors from the basil. With the basil flavor boosted and the garlic toned down, it was time to process the ingredients with toasted nuts and stir in the Parmesan. Finally, we reserved some of the pasta cooking water, which was essential to thin out the pesto once it had been added to the pasta. The water also softened and blended the flavors a bit, and highlighted the creaminess of the cheese and nuts.

Farfalle with Pesto

SERVES 4 TO 6

Basil usually darkens in homemade pesto, but you can preserve the green color by adding the optional parsley. For sharper flavor, substitute 1 tablespoon finely grated Pecorino Romano cheese for 1 tablespoon of the Parmesan. For a change from farfalle, try curly shapes, such as fusilli, which can trap bits of the pesto.

- 3 medium garlic cloves, threaded on a skewer
- 2 cups packed fresh basil leaves
- 2 tablespoons fresh flat-leaf parsley leaves (optional; see note)
- ¼ cup pine nuts, walnuts, or almonds, toasted
- 7 tablespoons extra-virgin olive oil
- Table salt
- ¼ cup grated Parmesan (see note)
- 1 pound farfalle (see note)

1. Bring 4 quarts water to a boil in a large pot. Lower the skewered garlic into the water and boil for 45 seconds. Immediately run the garlic under cold water. Remove the garlic from the skewer, peel, and mince.

2. Place the basil and parsley (if using) in a zipper-lock bag and pound with the flat side of a meat pounder or a rolling pin until all the leaves are bruised.

3. Process the nuts, garlic, basil, oil, and ½ teaspoon salt in a food processor until smooth, scraping down the sides of the workbowl as necessary. Transfer the mixture to a small bowl, stir in the cheese, and season with salt to taste. (The pesto can be covered with a sheet of plastic wrap pressed against the surface and refrigerated for up to 5 days.)

4. Add 1 tablespoon salt and the pasta to the boiling water and cook, stirring often, until al dente. Reserve ½ cup of the cooking water then drain the pasta and return it to the pot. Stir in ¼ cup reserved cooking water and the pesto; adjust the consistency of the sauce with the remaining reserved pasta cooking water as needed. Serve immediately.

PASTA WITH PESTO, POTATOES, AND GREEN BEANS

WHY THIS RECIPE WORKS: The notion of putting pasta and potatoes in the same dish initially struck us as strange, but it's the preferred way to serve pesto in Liguria, Italy—the birthplace of the basil sauce. But the recipes we found needed work. The sauce was slightly grainy and the sharp, raw garlic dominated. Timing was another issue: When everything was cooked together, the green beans could be jarringly crisp and the pasta way too soft—or vice versa. How could we get all the elements of this dish to cook perfectly?

The traditional method called for cutting the potatoes into chunks and then, once cooked, vigorously mixing them with the pesto, pasta, and green beans. The agitation sloughed off their corners, which dissolved into the dish, pulling the pesto and cooking water together to form a simple sauce. Simply trading out starchy russets for creamy, waxy red potatoes eliminated graininess and made our sauce smooth. We cooked the potatoes fully, then used the starchy water to cook the pasta. As for the pesto, we toasted the garlic and pine nuts for warm, mellow flavor (then used the same skillet to quickly steam the green beans). We used plenty of pasta water to bring the sauce together. Two tablespoons of butter made it even silkier, and a splash of lemon juice brought all the flavors into focus.

Pasta with Pesto, Potatoes, and Green Beans

SERVES 6

If gemelli is unavailable, penne or rigatoni make good substitutes. Use large red potatoes measuring 3 inches or more in diameter.

- ¼ cup pine nuts
- 3 garlic cloves, unpeeled
- 1 pound large red potatoes, peeled and cut into ½-inch pieces
- Salt and pepper
- 12 ounces green beans, trimmed and cut into 1½-inch lengths
- 2 cups fresh basil leaves
- 1 ounce Parmesan cheese, grated (½ cup)
- 7 tablespoons extra-virgin olive oil
- 1 pound gemelli
- 2 tablespoons unsalted butter, cut into ½-inch pieces and chilled
- 1 tablespoon lemon juice

1. Toast pine nuts and garlic in 10-inch skillet over medium heat, stirring frequently, until pine nuts are golden and fragrant and garlic darkens slightly, 3 to 5 minutes. Transfer to bowl and let cool. Peel garlic and chop coarsely.

2. Bring 3 quarts water to boil in large pot. Add potatoes and 1 tablespoon salt and cook until potatoes are tender but still hold their shape, 9 to 12 minutes. Using slotted spoon, transfer potatoes to rimmed baking sheet. (Do not discard water.)

3. Meanwhile, bring ½ cup water and ¼ teaspoon salt to boil in now-empty skillet over medium heat. Add green beans, cover, and cook until tender, 5 to 8 minutes. Drain green beans and transfer to sheet with potatoes.

4. Process basil, Parmesan, oil, pine nuts, garlic, and ½ teaspoon salt in food processor until smooth, about 1 minute.

5. Add gemelli to water in large pot and cook, stirring often, until al dente. Set colander in large bowl. Drain gemelli in colander, reserving cooking water in bowl. Return gemelli to pot. Add butter, lemon juice, potatoes and green beans, pesto, 1¼ cups reserved cooking water, and ½ teaspoon pepper and stir vigorously with rubber spatula until sauce takes on creamy appearance. Add additional cooking water as needed to adjust consistency and season with salt and pepper to taste. Serve immediately.

BEHIND THE SCENES

PASTA PARAPHERNALIA

What's our opinion on pasta gadgets? For the most part, *fuggedaboutit*. Pasta pots with perforated inserts tend to boil over if filled with the necessary amount of water. A pot with a strainer lid might look promising, but we found that if your grip isn't secure, the lid pops off and pasta can end up all over your sink. Ditto for crescent-shaped strainer plates that fit to the edge of the pot. The only pasta tool we've come across through the years that we've actually liked is a pasta fork, which is a long-handled spoon with ridged teeth. But no need to rush out and buy one; basic tongs work just fine.

PASTA WITH TOMATO AND ALMOND PESTO

WHY THIS RECIPE WORKS: In the Sicilian village of Trapani, there's a very different kind of pesto—it's basically pesto crossed with tomato sauce. Almonds replace pine nuts, but the big difference is the appearance of fresh tomatoes—not as the main ingredient, but as a fruity, sweet accent. We wanted a recipe for a clean, bright version of this sauce, not a chunky tomato salsa or thin, watery slush.

For this uncooked sauce, fresh tomatoes were best. Cherry and grape tomatoes proved equal contenders, sharing a similar brightness and juiciness that was far more reliable than that of their larger cousins. We processed the tomatoes with a handful of basil, garlic, and toasted almonds. The almonds contributed body and thickened the sauce while retaining just enough crunch to offset the tomatoes' pulpiness; using blanched, slivered almonds avoided the muddy flavor often contributed by papery skins. We added a scant amount of hot vinegar peppers for zing, then drizzled in olive oil in a slow, steady stream to emulsify the pesto. Parmesan was stirred in for the finishing touch to this light, bright, and texturally satisfying pesto.

Pasta with Tomato and Almond Pesto (Pesto alla Trapanese)

SERVES 4 TO 6

While we prefer linguine or spaghetti, any pasta shape will work here. You may substitute ½ teaspoon of red wine vinegar and ¼ teaspoon of red pepper flakes for the pepperoncini.

- Table salt
- 1 pound linguine or spaghetti (see note)
- ¼ cup slivered almonds, toasted
- 12 ounces cherry or grape tomatoes (about 2½ cups)
- ½ cup packed fresh basil leaves
- 1 medium garlic clove, minced or pressed through a garlic press (about 1 teaspoon)
- 1 small pepperoncini (hot peppers in vinegar), stemmed, seeded, and minced (about ½ teaspoon; see note)
- Pinch red pepper flakes (optional)
- ⅓ cup extra-virgin olive oil
- 1 ounce Parmesan cheese, grated (about ½ cup), plus extra for serving

1. Bring 4 quarts water to a boil in a large pot. Add 1 tablespoon salt and the pasta to the boiling water and cook, stirring often, until al dente. Reserve ½ cup of the cooking water then drain the pasta and return it to the pot.

2. Meanwhile, process the almonds, tomatoes, basil, garlic, pepperoncini, 1 teaspoon salt, and red pepper flakes (if using) in a food processor until smooth, about 1 minute. Scrape down the sides of the workbowl with a rubber spatula. With the machine running, slowly drizzle in the oil, about 30 seconds.

3. Add the pesto and ½ cup of the Parmesan to the cooked pasta and adjust the consistency of the sauce with the reserved pasta cooking water as needed. Serve immediately, passing extra Parmesan separately.

NONTRADITIONAL PESTOS

WHY THIS RECIPE WORKS: Pesto doesn't always mean basil, pine nuts, and Parmesan. We wanted to make quick pestos with a variety of other potent ingredients, like sun-dried tomatoes, goat cheese, and kalamata olives.

For pestos that were flavorful but not harsh, we tamed the garlic by toasting unpeeled cloves in a hot skillet or replaced most of it with sun-dried tomatoes. Then we processed the garlic or sun-dried tomatoes with olive oil, nuts, cheese, and olives, among other ingredients, to create smooth sauces that cling well to pasta. And to keep the pasta moist, we made sure to reserve some of the pasta cooking water to thin the pesto.

Campanelle with Arugula, Goat Cheese, and Sun-Dried Tomato Pesto

SERVES 4 TO 6

Make sure to rinse the herbs and seasonings from the sun-dried tomatoes. Farfalle can be substituted for the campanelle.

- 1 cup oil-packed sun-dried tomatoes (one 8½-ounce jar), drained, rinsed, patted dry, and chopped coarse (see note)
- 1 ounce Parmesan cheese, grated (about ½ cup)
- 6 tablespoons extra-virgin olive oil

- ¼ cup walnuts, toasted
- 1 small garlic clove, minced or pressed through a garlic press (about ½ teaspoon)
- Table salt and ground black pepper
- 1 pound campanelle (see note)
- 1 medium bunch arugula, washed, dried, stemmed, and torn into bite-size pieces (about 6 cups)
- 3 ounces goat cheese, crumbled (about ¾ cup)

1. Process the sun-dried tomatoes, Parmesan, oil, walnuts, garlic, ½ teaspoon salt, and ⅛ teaspoon pepper in a food processor until smooth, scraping down the sides of the workbowl as necessary. Transfer the mixture to a small bowl and set aside.

2. Bring 4 quarts water to a boil in a large pot. Add 1 tablespoon salt and the pasta to the boiling water and cook, stirring often, until al dente. Reserve ¾ cup of the cooking water then drain the pasta and return it to the pot. Immediately stir in the arugula until wilted. Stir ½ cup of the reserved pasta cooking water into the pesto and add the pesto to the pasta. Toss to combine, adjusting the consistency of the sauce with the remaining reserved pasta cooking water as needed. Serve immediately, sprinkling the cheese over individual bowls.

Penne with Toasted Nut and Parsley Pesto

SERVES 4 TO 6

Toasting the unpeeled garlic in a skillet reduces its harshness and gives it a mellow flavor that works well in pesto.

- 3 medium garlic cloves, unpeeled
- 1 cup pecans, walnuts, whole blanched almonds, skinned hazelnuts, unsalted pistachios, or pine nuts, or any combination thereof, toasted
- ½ cup packed fresh parsley leaves
- 7 tablespoons extra-virgin olive oil
- 1 ounce Parmesan cheese, grated (about ½ cup)
- Table salt and ground black pepper
- 1 pound penne

1. Toast the garlic in a small skillet over medium heat, shaking the pan occasionally, until softened and spotty brown, about 8 minutes; when cool, remove and discard the skins.

2. Process the garlic, nuts, parsley, and oil in a food processor until smooth, scraping down the sides of the workbowl as necessary. Transfer the mixture to a small bowl and stir in the Parmesan; season with salt and pepper to taste.

3. Bring 4 quarts water to a boil in a large pot. Add 1 tablespoon salt and the pasta to the boiling water and cook, stirring often, until al dente. Reserve ½ cup of the cooking water then drain the pasta and return it to the pot. Stir ¼ cup of the reserved pasta cooking water into the pesto and add the pesto to the pasta. Toss to combine, adjusting the consistency of the sauce with the remaining reserved pasta cooking water as needed. Serve immediately.

Spaghetti with Olive Pesto

SERVES 4 TO 6

This black pesto is called *olivada* in Italy. Make sure to use high-quality olives in this recipe. The anchovy adds flavor but not fishiness to the pesto and we recommend its inclusion.

- 3 medium garlic cloves, unpeeled
- 1½ cups pitted kalamata olives (see note)
- 1 ounce Parmesan cheese, grated (about ½ cup), plus extra for serving
- 6 tablespoons extra-virgin olive oil
- ¼ cup packed fresh parsley leaves
- 1 medium shallot, chopped coarse (about 3 tablespoons)
- 8 large basil leaves
- 1 tablespoon juice from 1 lemon
- 1 anchovy fillet, rinsed (optional; see note)
- Table salt and ground black pepper
- 1 pound spaghetti
- Lemon wedges, for serving

1. Toast the garlic in a small skillet over medium heat, shaking the pan occasionally, until the garlic is softened and spotty brown, about 8 minutes; when cool, remove and discard the skins.

2. Process the garlic, olives, ½ cup of the Parmesan, oil, parsley, shallot, basil, lemon juice, and anchovy (if using) in a food processor, scraping down the sides of the workbowl as necessary. Transfer the mixture to a small bowl and season with salt and pepper to taste.

3. Bring 4 quarts water to a boil in a large pot. Add 1 tablespoon salt and the pasta to the boiling water and cook, stirring often, until al dente. Reserve ½ cup of the cooking water then drain the pasta and return it to the pot. Stir ¼ cup of the reserved pasta cooking water into the pesto and add the pesto to the pasta. Toss to combine, adjusting the consistency of the sauce with the remaining reserved pasta cooking water as needed. Serve immediately, passing the lemon wedges and extra Parmesan separately.

SPRING VEGETABLE PASTA

WHY THIS RECIPE WORKS: In pasta primavera, the vegetables and pasta are tossed together in a sauce made with broth and heavy cream. We love this classic, but sometimes we want a lighter, brighter version. As for the vegetables, we wanted true spring vegetables. To start, we chose asparagus and green peas, adding chives for bite and garlic and leeks for depth and sweetness. For a deeply flavored sauce that would unify the pasta and vegetables, we borrowed a technique from risotto, lightly toasting the pasta in olive oil before cooking it in broth and white wine. The sauce flavored the pasta as it cooked while the pasta added starch to the sauce, thickening it without the need for heavy cream. This nontraditional approach gave us a light but creamy sauce with sweet, grassy flavors that paired perfectly with the vegetables. This was a dish that truly tasted like spring.

Spring Vegetable Pasta

SERVES 4 TO 6

Campanelle is our pasta of choice in this dish, but farfalle and penne are good substitutes.

- 1½ pounds leeks, white and light green parts halved lengthwise, sliced ½ inch thick, and washed; 3 cups coarsely chopped dark green parts, washed
- 1 pound asparagus, tough ends trimmed, chopped coarse, and reserved, spears cut on bias into ½-inch lengths
- 2 cups frozen peas, thawed
- 4 medium garlic cloves, minced or pressed through a garlic press (about 4 teaspoons)
- 4 cups vegetable broth
- 1 cup water
- 2 tablespoons minced fresh mint leaves
- 2 tablespoons minced fresh chives
- ½ teaspoon grated zest plus 2 tablespoons juice from 1 lemon
- 6 tablespoons extra-virgin olive oil
- Table salt and ground black pepper
- ¼ teaspoon red pepper flakes
- 1 pound campanelle (see note)
- 1 cup dry white wine
- 1 ounce grated Parmesan cheese (about ½ cup), plus extra for serving

1. Bring the leek greens, asparagus trimmings, 1 cup of the peas, half of the garlic, the broth, and water to simmer in a large saucepan. Reduce the heat to medium-low and simmer gently for 10 minutes. While the broth simmers, combine the mint, chives, and lemon zest in a bowl; set aside.

2. Strain the broth through a fine-mesh strainer into a large liquid measuring cup, pressing on the solids to extract as much liquid as possible (you should have 5 cups broth; add water as needed to measure 5 cups). Discard the solids and return the broth to the saucepan. Cover and keep warm.

3. Heat 2 tablespoons of the oil in a Dutch oven over medium heat until shimmering. Add the leeks and a pinch salt and cook, covered, stirring occasionally, until the leeks begin to brown, about 5 minutes. Add the asparagus spears and cook until the asparagus is crisp-tender, 4 to 6 minutes. Add the remaining garlic and the red pepper flakes and cook until fragrant, about 30 seconds. Add the remaining 1 cup peas and continue to cook for 1 minute longer. Transfer the vegetables to a plate and set aside. Wipe out the pot.

4. Heat the remaining ¼ cup oil in the now-empty pot over medium heat until shimmering. Add the pasta and cook, stirring often, until just beginning to brown, about 5 minutes. Add the wine and cook, stirring constantly, until absorbed, about 2 minutes.

5. When the wine is fully absorbed, add the warm broth and bring to a boil. Cook, stirring frequently, until most of the liquid is absorbed and the pasta is al dente, 8 to 10 minutes. Off the heat, stir in half of the herb mixture, the vegetables, lemon juice, and ½ cup of the Parmesan. Season with salt and pepper to taste and serve immediately, passing the additional Parmesan and the remaining herb mixture separately.

SUMMER PASTA PUTTANESCA

WHY THIS RECIPE WORKS: When we make pasta puttanesca with fresh tomatoes, we want the tomatoes to share equal billing with the pungently flavorful olives and anchovies typical of this robust sauce. For a puttanesca that would make the most of a bumper crop of fresh tomatoes, we opted to use grape or cherry tomatoes, which are both excellent in summer and among the best varieties of tomatoes available year-round. To retain the fresh tomato flavor, we pureed the tomatoes and strained the juices, which we cooked down briefly to thicken the sauce. We added the tomato pulp back in at the end of cooking so we wouldn't lose the fresh tomato flavor. We traded the traditional long pasta for frilly campanelle, which held on to the coarse sauce and gave our dish a summery flair.

Summer Pasta Puttanesca

SERVES 4

We prefer to make this dish with campanelle, but fusilli and orecchiette also work. Very finely mashed anchovy fillets (rinsed and dried before mashing) can be used instead of anchovy paste. Buy a good-quality black olive, such as kalamata, Gaeta, or Alfonso.

- 3 tablespoons extra-virgin olive oil
- 4 garlic cloves, minced
- 1 tablespoon anchovy paste
- ¼ teaspoon red pepper flakes
- ¼ teaspoon dried oregano
- 1½ pounds grape or cherry tomatoes

- 1 pound campanelle
- Salt
- ½ cup pitted kalamata olives, chopped coarse
- 3 tablespoons capers, rinsed and minced
- ½ cup minced fresh parsley

1. Combine oil, garlic, anchovy paste, pepper flakes, and oregano in bowl. Process tomatoes in blender until finely chopped but not pureed, 15 to 45 seconds. Transfer to fine-mesh strainer set in large bowl and let drain for 5 minutes, occasionally pressing gently on solids with rubber spatula to extract liquid (this should yield about ¾ cup). Reserve tomato liquid in bowl and tomato pulp in strainer.

2. Bring 4 quarts water to boil in large pot. Add campanelle and 1 tablespoon salt and cook, stirring often, until al dente. Reserve 1 cup cooking water, then drain campanelle and return it to pot.

3. While campanelle is cooking, cook garlic-anchovy mixture in 12-inch skillet over medium heat, stirring frequently, until garlic is fragrant but not brown, 2 to 3 minutes. Add tomato liquid and simmer until reduced to ⅓ cup, 2 to 3 minutes. Add tomato pulp, olives, and capers; cook until just heated through, 2 to 3 minutes. Stir in parsley.

4. Pour sauce over campanelle and toss to combine, adding reserved cooking water as needed to adjust consistency. Season with salt to taste. Serve immediately.

PASTA E CECI (PASTA WITH CHICKPEAS)

WHY THIS RECIPE WORKS: *Pasta e ceci,* a sibling of *pasta e fagioli,* is a hearty and fast one-pot meal that's simple to prepare, yet packed full of satisfying flavor. To keep the cooking time to under an hour, we used canned chickpeas—along with their starchy liquid—to add even more body and flavor to the dish. Cooking the chickpeas and ditalini in the same pot blended the dish, and the additional starch released by the pasta created a silky, stick-to-your-ribs texture. We gave the chickpeas a brief head start, simmering them before adding the pasta, in order to achieve the perfect creamy softness. Using a food processor allowed us to get a finely minced *soffritto* of onions, garlic, carrot, celery, and pancetta, an addition that gave the dish a meaty backbone. And we achieved depth of flavor by adding anchovy, tomatoes, and Parmesan cheese. A last-minute addition of parsley and lemon juice provided a bright contrast just before serving.

Pasta e Ceci (Pasta with Chickpeas)

SERVES 4 TO 6

Another short pasta, such as orzo, can be substituted for the ditalini, but make sure to substitute by weight and not by volume.

- 2 ounces pancetta, cut into ½-inch pieces
- 1 small carrot, peeled and cut into ½-inch pieces
- 1 small celery rib, cut into ½-inch pieces
- 4 garlic cloves, peeled
- 1 onion, halved and cut into 1-inch pieces
- 1 (14-ounce) can whole peeled tomatoes, drained
- ¼ cup extra-virgin olive oil, plus extra for serving
- 1 anchovy fillet, rinsed, patted dry, and minced
- ¼ teaspoon red pepper flakes
- 2 teaspoons minced fresh rosemary
- 2 (15-ounce) cans chickpeas (do not drain)
- 2 cups water
- Salt and pepper
- 8 ounces (1½ cups) ditalini
- 1 tablespoon lemon juice
- 1 tablespoon minced fresh parsley
- 1 ounce Parmesan cheese, grated (½ cup)

1. Process pancetta in food processor until ground to paste, about 30 seconds, scraping down sides of bowl as needed. Add carrot, celery, and garlic and pulse until finely chopped, 8 to 10 pulses. Add onion and pulse until onion is cut into ⅛- to ¼-inch pieces, 8 to 10 pulses. Transfer pancetta mixture to large Dutch oven. Pulse tomatoes in now-empty food processor until coarsely chopped, 8 to 10 pulses. Set aside.

2. Add oil to pancetta mixture in Dutch oven and cook over medium heat, stirring frequently, until fond begins to form on bottom of pot, about 5 minutes. Add anchovy, pepper flakes, and rosemary and cook until fragrant, about 1 minute. Stir in tomatoes, chickpeas and their liquid, water, and 1 teaspoon salt and bring to boil, scraping up any browned bits. Reduce heat to medium-low and simmer for 10 minutes. Add pasta and cook, stirring frequently, until tender, 10 to 12 minutes. Stir in lemon juice and parsley and season with salt and pepper to taste. Serve, passing Parmesan and extra oil separately.

PASTA WITH ASPARAGUS

WHY THIS RECIPE WORKS: Asparagus is a natural starting point when trying to make a tomato-free vegetarian pasta sauce. Its sweet, vegetable flavor and quick-cooking nature is a terrific match to pasta. But more often than not, asparagus sauces are bland and boring. We wanted to keep it simple but make this dish livelier.

First, we focused on how to cook the asparagus. Boiling and steaming diluted the vegetable's grassy flavor, so they were out. Instead, we browned the asparagus in a hot skillet, after cutting it into bite-size pieces, for a sauce that was both quick and flavorful. The asparagus caramelized just a bit, and the heat brought out the flavors of the other ingredients, such as onions, walnuts, and garlic. To finish off the dish, we paired the asparagus with a balance of salty, sweet, and sour ingredients. In one dish, we teamed asparagus with balsamic vinegar, basil, and pecorino and in another, arugula, blue cheese, and apple worked well.

NOTES FROM THE TEST KITCHEN

TRIMMING ASPARAGUS SPEARS

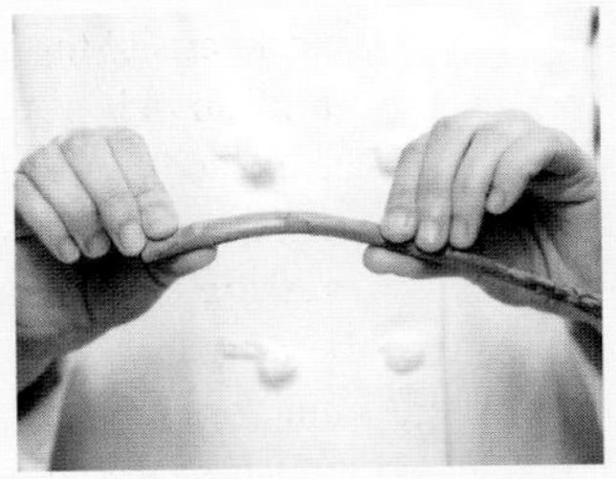

1. Before cooking asparagus, it's important to remove the tough ends. Remove one asparagus spear from the bunch and snap off the end.

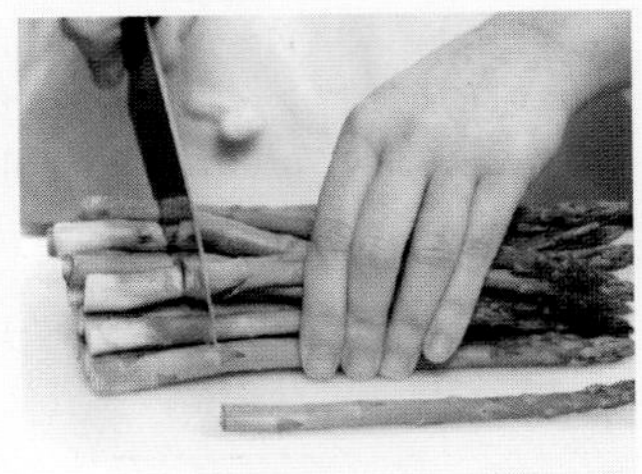

2. Using the broken asparagus as a guide, trim off the ends of the remaining spears using a chef's knife.

Campanelle with Asparagus, Basil, and Balsamic Glaze

SERVES 4 TO 6

Campanelle is a frilly trumpet-shaped pasta that pairs nicely with this sauce. If you cannot find it, fusilli works well, too. Use a vegetable peeler to shave the cheese.

- Table salt
- 1 pound campanelle (see note)
- ¾ cup balsamic vinegar
- 5 tablespoons extra-virgin olive oil
- 1 pound asparagus, tough ends trimmed (see photos), thick spears halved lengthwise and cut into 1-inch lengths
- 1 medium red onion, halved and sliced thin (about 1½ cups)
- ½ teaspoon ground black pepper
- ¼ teaspoon red pepper flakes
- 1 cup chopped fresh basil leaves
- 2 ounces Pecorino Romano cheese, shaved (about 1 cup; see note)
- 1 tablespoon juice from 1 lemon

1. Bring 4 quarts water to a boil in a large pot. Add 1 tablespoon salt and the pasta to the boiling water and cook, stirring often, until al dente. Reserve ½ cup of the cooking water then drain the pasta and return it to the pot.

2. While the pasta is cooking, bring the balsamic vinegar to a boil in an 8-inch skillet over medium-high heat; reduce the heat to medium and simmer gently until reduced to ¼ cup, 15 to 20 minutes.

3. Meanwhile, heat 2 tablespoons of the oil in a 12-inch nonstick skillet over high heat until smoking. Add the asparagus, onion, black pepper, red pepper flakes, and ½ teaspoon salt and stir to combine. Cook, without stirring, until the asparagus begins to brown, about 1 minute, then stir and continue to cook, stirring occasionally, until the asparagus is crisp-tender, about 4 minutes longer.

4. Add the asparagus mixture, basil, ½ cup of the Pecorino, the lemon juice, and the remaining 3 tablespoons oil to the pasta and toss to combine. Adjust the consistency of the sauce with the reserved pasta cooking water as needed. Serve immediately, drizzling 1 to 2 teaspoons balsamic glaze over individual servings and passing the remaining ½ cup Pecorino separately.

Cavatappi with Asparagus, Arugula, Walnuts, and Blue Cheese

SERVES 4 TO 6

Cavatappi is a short, tubular corkscrew-shaped pasta; penne is a fine substitute. The grated apple balances the other flavors in this dish.

- Table salt
- 1 pound cavatappi (see note)
- 5 tablespoons extra-virgin olive oil
- 1 pound asparagus, tough ends trimmed (see photos), thick spears halved lengthwise and cut into 1-inch lengths
- ½ teaspoon ground black pepper
- 1 cup walnuts, chopped
- 4 cups lightly packed arugula leaves from 1 large bunch, washed and dried
- 6 ounces strong blue cheese, such as Roquefort, crumbled (about 1½ cups)
- 2 tablespoons cider vinegar
- 1 Granny Smith apple, peeled, for garnish

1. Bring 4 quarts water to a boil in a large pot. Add 1 tablespoon salt and the pasta to the boiling water and cook, stirring often, until al dente. Reserve ½ cup of the cooking water then drain the pasta and return it to the pot.

2. While the pasta is cooking, heat 2 tablespoons of the oil in a 12-inch nonstick skillet over high heat until smoking. Add the asparagus, pepper, and ½ teaspoon salt and cook, without stirring, until the asparagus begins to brown, about 1 minute. Add the walnuts and continue to cook, stirring frequently, until the asparagus is crisp-tender and the nuts are toasted, about 4 minutes longer. Add the arugula and toss to wilt.

3. Add the asparagus mixture, blue cheese, vinegar, and the remaining 3 tablespoons oil to the pasta and toss to combine. Adjust the consistency of the sauce with the reserved pasta cooking water as needed. Serve immediately, grating the apple over individual servings.

PASTA WITH MUSHROOMS

WHY THIS RECIPE WORKS: Pasta with mushrooms can be watery and tasteless. But when done right, this dish transforms an ordinary box of pasta and a package of mushrooms into something special. We wanted to combine the intense flavor of sautéed mushrooms with a light cream sauce to create a woodsy, full-flavored pasta dish.

For optimum flavor and texture, we used a combination of shiitake and cremini mushrooms; cremini mushrooms provided richness and meatiness, and the shiitakes contributed hearty flavor and a pleasant, chewy texture. Cooking the mushrooms in a skillet (not in the sauce) improved their flavor; adding salt to the pan helped the mushrooms release their juices and enhanced browning. We then added chicken broth and cream to the browned bits left in the skillet after the mushrooms were removed. Garlic, shallots, and thyme rounded out the flavors of our simple sauce, and lemon juice added brightness. We added the browned mushrooms back in for a chunky sauce that paired nicely with short pasta with lots of crevices—we liked either campanelle or farfalle.

Pasta with Sautéed Mushrooms and Thyme

SERVES 4 TO 6

Vegetable broth can be substituted for the chicken broth to make this dish vegetarian. If you add the pasta to the boiling water at the same time the cremini go into the skillet, the pasta and sauce will finish at the same time.

- Table salt
- 1 pound campanelle or farfalle
- 2 tablespoons unsalted butter
- 2 tablespoons extra-virgin olive oil
- 4 large shallots, minced (about 1 cup)
- 3 medium garlic cloves, minced or pressed through a garlic press (about 1 tablespoon)
- 10 ounces shiitake mushrooms, stems discarded, caps wiped clean and sliced ¼ inch thick
- 10 ounces cremini mushrooms, wiped clean and sliced ¼ inch thick
- 1 tablespoon plus 1 teaspoon minced fresh thyme leaves
- 1¼ cups low-sodium chicken broth (see note)
- ½ cup heavy cream
- 1 tablespoon juice from 1 lemon
- Ground black pepper
- 2 ounces Parmesan cheese, grated (about 1 cup)
- 2 tablespoons minced fresh parsley leaves

1. Bring 4 quarts water to a boil in a large pot. Add 1 tablespoon salt and the pasta to the boiling water and cook, stirring often, until al dente. Reserve ½ cup of the cooking water then drain the pasta and return it to the pot.

2. Meanwhile, melt the butter with the oil over medium heat in a 12-inch skillet. Add the shallots and cook, stirring occasionally, until softened and translucent, about 4 minutes. Add the garlic and cook until fragrant, about 30 seconds. Increase the heat to medium-high; add the shiitakes and cook, stirring occasionally, for 2 minutes. Add the cremini and ½ teaspoon salt; cook, stirring occasionally, until the moisture released by the mushrooms has evaporated and the mushrooms are golden brown, about 8 minutes. Add the thyme and cook until fragrant, about 30 seconds. Transfer the mushrooms to a bowl and set aside.

3. Add the chicken broth to the skillet and bring to a boil, scraping up the browned bits. Off the heat, stir in the cream and lemon juice and season with salt and pepper to taste.

4. Add the mushrooms, chicken broth mixture, cheese, and parsley to the pasta. Toss over medium-low heat until the cheese melts and the pasta absorbs most of the liquid, about 2 minutes. Adjust the consistency of the sauce with the reserved pasta cooking water as needed and serve immediately.

QUICK MUSHROOM RAGU

WHY THIS RECIPE WORKS: We wanted a mushroom ragu that combined the naturally hearty texture of fresh mushrooms with the concentrated flavor of dried ones—and that could be on the table in about 30 minutes. Using pancetta and its fat compensated for the lean nature of the mushrooms and made our mushroom ragu meatier. Portobello mushrooms gave our dish bulk, while smoky porcini gave it concentrated flavor. Adding tomato paste and fresh crushed tomatoes to our mushrooms after they'd browned sweetened our sauce but also let the mushrooms shine through. Finally, fresh rosemary finished our dish with brightness.

Spaghetti with Quick Mushroom Ragu

SERVES 4

Use a spoon to scrape the dark brown gills from the portobellos.

- 1 cup low-sodium chicken broth
- 1 ounce dried porcini mushrooms, rinsed
- 4 ounces pancetta, cut into ½-inch pieces
- 8 ounces portobello mushroom caps, gills removed, caps cut into ½-inch pieces (about 1½ cups)
- 3 tablespoons extra-virgin olive oil
- 4 medium garlic cloves, peeled and sliced thin
- 1 tablespoon tomato paste
- 2 teaspoons minced fresh rosemary leaves
- 1 (14.5-ounce) can whole peeled tomatoes, roughly crushed by hand
- Salt and pepper
- 1 pound spaghetti
- Grated Pecorino Romano cheese

1. Microwave broth and porcini in covered bowl until steaming, about 1 minute. Let sit until softened, about 10 minutes. Drain mushrooms through fine-mesh strainer lined with coffee filter into medium bowl, reserve broth, and chop mushrooms fine.

2. Heat pancetta in 12-inch skillet over medium heat; cook, stirring occasionally, until rendered and crisp, 7 to 10 minutes. Add portobellos, chopped porcini, oil, garlic, tomato paste, and rosemary; cook, stirring occasionally, until all liquid has evaporated and tomato paste starts to brown, 5 to 7 minutes. Add reserved broth and crushed tomatoes and their juice; increase heat to high and bring to simmer. Reduce heat to medium-low and simmer until thickened, 15 to 20 minutes. Season with salt and pepper to taste.

3. While sauce simmers, bring 4 quarts water to boil in large Dutch oven. Add pasta and 1 tablespoon salt; cook, stirring often, until al dente. Reserve ½ cup cooking water, then drain pasta and return it to pot. Add sauce to pasta and toss to combine. Add reserved cooking water as needed to adjust consistency and season with salt and pepper to taste. Serve, passing Pecorino separately.

TAGLIATELLE WITH PROSCIUTTO AND PEAS

WHY THIS RECIPE WORKS: Prosciutto and Parmesan are packed with complementary flavors, so when combining them in a pasta dish, we aimed to maximize their impact. Adding prosciutto in two stages created complex, porky flavor. Mincing an ounce of prosciutto and simmering it with softened shallots and cream created a meaty sauce. We opted for tagliatelle, its long ribbons of dried egg pasta a fitting substitute for fresh pasta. We stirred together the pasta, reserved water, and the prosciutto-cream mixture, adding in strips of raw prosciutto for the meat's fruity, nutty fragrance. Grated Parmesan plus Gruyère (another nutty, aromatic cheese) worked perfectly. We used frozen peas as a sweet, bright foil to the rich sauce.

Tagliatelle with Prosciutto and Peas

SERVES 4 TO 6

We prefer imported prosciutto di Parma sliced 1/16 inch thick or domestically made prepackaged Volpi Traditional Prosciutto. Look for a hard Gruyère that is aged for at least 10 months. Pappardelle can be substituted for the tagliatelle.

- 6 ounces thinly sliced prosciutto
- 1 tablespoon unsalted butter
- 1 shallot, minced
- Salt and pepper
- 1 cup heavy cream
- 1 pound tagliatelle
- 1½ cups frozen petite peas, thawed
- 1 ounce Parmesan cheese, grated (½ cup)
- 1 ounce Gruyère cheese, grated (½ cup)

1. Slice 5 ounces prosciutto crosswise into ¼-inch-wide strips; set aside. Mince remaining 1 ounce prosciutto. Melt butter in 10-inch skillet over medium-low heat. Add shallot and ¼ teaspoon salt and cook until softened, about 2 minutes. Stir in cream and minced prosciutto and bring to simmer. Cook, stirring occasionally, until cream mixture measures 1 cup, 5 to 7 minutes. Remove pan from heat and cover to keep warm.

2. Meanwhile, bring 4 quarts water to boil in large pot. Add pasta and 1 tablespoon salt and cook, stirring often, until al dente. Reserve 2 cups cooking water, then drain pasta and return it to pot.

3. Add 1 cup reserved cooking water, cream mixture, prosciutto strips, peas, Parmesan, Gruyère, and 1 teaspoon pepper to pasta. Gently toss until pasta is well coated. Transfer pasta to serving bowl and serve immediately, adjusting consistency with remaining reserved cooking water as needed.

PASTA WITH BROCCOLI RABE AND SAUSAGE

WHY THIS RECIPE WORKS: In southern Italy, broccoli rabe and *orecchiette* (loosely translated as "little ears") is a popular combination. The trick to this pasta dish is cooking the broccoli rabe just right and limiting the number of ingredients so that at the end, you have a moist and flavorful (but not oily) pasta dish.

For a hearty, filling dish, we decided to include some Italian sausage. Tasters preferred spicy Italian sausage to the sweet variety, but if you like less heat, the sweet sausage still makes for a satisfying dish. We started by browning the sausage in a skillet. We then added the broccoli rabe and chicken broth to absorb the rich, meaty flavors in the pan; covering the pan allowed us to steam the rabe with the other sauce ingredients. Besides eliminating the need for a separate pot to blanch the rabe, this cooking method didn't wash away the pleasantly bitter flavor of this Italian vegetable. Some red pepper flakes amplified the heat from the sausage, and a drizzle of olive oil and freshly grated Parmesan cheese brought the whole dish together.

Orecchiette with Broccoli Rabe and Sausage

SERVES 4 TO 6

If you prefer to use broccoli instead of broccoli rabe in this recipe, use 2 pounds broccoli cut into 1-inch florets and increase the cooking time by several minutes. If you prefer a less spicy dish, use sweet Italian sausage.

NOTES FROM THE TEST KITCHEN

REMOVING SAUSAGE FROM ITS CASING

Italian sausage is sold in links, bulk-style tubes, and patties. If using links, remove meat from its casing before cooking so that you can crumble it into bite-size pieces. Hold sausage firmly at 1 end and squeeze meat out of opposite end.

- Table salt
- 1 pound orecchiette
- 8 ounces hot Italian sausage, casings removed (see note)
- 6 medium garlic cloves, minced or pressed through a garlic press (about 2 tablespoons)
- ½ teaspoon red pepper flakes
- 1 bunch broccoli rabe (about 1 pound), washed, trimmed, and cut into 1½-inch pieces (see note)
- ½ cup low-sodium chicken broth
- 1 tablespoon extra-virgin olive oil
- 1 ounce Parmesan cheese, grated (about ½ cup)

1. Bring 4 quarts water to a boil in a large pot. Add 1 tablespoon salt and the pasta to the boiling water and cook, stirring often, until al dente. Reserve ½ cup of the cooking water then drain the pasta and return it to the pot.

2. While the pasta is cooking, cook the sausage until browned in a 12-inch nonstick skillet over medium-high heat, breaking it into ½-inch pieces with a wooden spoon, about 3 minutes. Stir in the garlic, red pepper flakes, and ½ teaspoon salt. Cook, stirring constantly, until the garlic is fragrant, about 1½ minutes. Add the broccoli rabe and chicken broth, cover, and cook until the broccoli rabe turns bright green, about 2 minutes. Uncover and cook, stirring frequently, until most of the broth has evaporated and the broccoli rabe is tender, 2 to 3 minutes.

3. Add the sausage mixture, oil, and cheese to the pasta and toss to combine. Adjust the consistency of the sauce with the reserved pasta cooking water as needed and serve immediately.

PASTA ALLA NORCINA

WHY THIS RECIPE WORKS: *Pasta alla norcina*, from an Italian village in Umbria, features tender pasta and richly flavored pork sausage in a light cream sauce. To bring an authentic-tasting version of this dish to the American dinner table, we bypassed store-bought Italian sausage—the size of the grind and the fat levels varied too much, and the seasonings were out of place in this dish—and made our own. Brining ground pork and mixing it briefly with a spatula ensured it had a sausage-like snappy texture; rosemary, nutmeg, and garlic offered robust flavor. Adding baking soda and searing our sausage in patty form before chopping it into small pieces helped it stay juicy and tender when it finished cooking in the cream sauce. Finely chopped mushrooms provided earthy background notes, and a splash of wine balanced the richness of the dish. For the pasta, we preferred orecchiette, which cradled the chunky sauce nicely.

Pasta alla Norcina

SERVES 6

White mushrooms may be substituted for the cremini mushrooms. Short tubular or molded pastas such as mezze rigatoni or shells may be substituted for the orecchiette.

- Kosher salt and pepper
- ¼ teaspoon baking soda
- 4 teaspoons water
- 8 ounces ground pork
- 3 garlic cloves, minced
- 1¼ teaspoons minced fresh rosemary
- ⅛ teaspoon ground nutmeg
- 8 ounces cremini mushrooms, trimmed
- 7 teaspoons vegetable oil
- ¾ cup heavy cream
- 1 pound orecchiette
- ½ cup dry white wine
- 1½ ounces Pecorino Romano, grated (¾ cup)
- 3 tablespoons minced fresh parsley
- 1 tablespoon lemon juice

1. Spray large dinner plate with vegetable oil spray. Dissolve 1⅛ teaspoons salt and baking soda in water in medium bowl. Add pork and fold gently to combine; let stand for 10 minutes.

2. Add 1 teaspoon garlic, ¾ teaspoon rosemary, nutmeg, and ¾ teaspoon pepper to pork and stir and smear with rubber spatula until well combined and tacky, 10 to 15 seconds. Transfer pork mixture to greased plate and form into rough 6-inch patty. Pulse mushrooms in food processor until finely chopped, 10 to 12 pulses.

3. Heat 2 teaspoons oil in 12-inch skillet over medium-high heat until just smoking. Add patty and cook without moving it until bottom is well browned, 2 to 3 minutes. Flip patty and continue to cook until second side is well browned, 2 to 3 minutes longer (very center of patty will be raw). Remove pan from heat and transfer patty to cutting board. Using tongs to steady patty, roughly chop into ⅛- to ¼-inch pieces. Transfer meat to bowl and add cream; set aside.

4. Bring 4 quarts water to boil in large Dutch oven. Stir in orecchiette and 2 tablespoons salt and cook, stirring often, until al dente. Reserve 1½ cups cooking water, then drain orecchiette and return it to pot.

5. While orecchiette cooks, return now-empty skillet to medium heat. Add 1 tablespoon oil, mushrooms, and ⅛ teaspoon salt; cook, stirring frequently, until mushrooms are browned, 5 to 7 minutes. Stir in remaining 2 teaspoons oil, remaining 2 teaspoons garlic, remaining ½ teaspoon rosemary, and ½ teaspoon pepper; cook until fragrant, about 30 seconds. Stir in wine, scraping up any browned bits, and cook until completely evaporated, 1 to 2 minutes. Stir in meat-cream mixture and ¾ cup reserved cooking water and simmer until meat is no longer pink, 1 to 3 minutes. Remove pan from heat and stir in Pecorino until smooth.

6. Add sauce, parsley, and lemon juice to orecchiette and toss well to coat, adjusting consistency with remaining cooking water as needed. Season with salt and pepper to taste, and serve.

SHRIMP AND GARLIC WITH PASTA

WHY THIS RECIPE WORKS: In theory, garlic shrimp pasta has all the makings of an ideal weeknight meal—just toss a few quick-cooking ingredients with boiled pasta. In reality, delicate shrimp cooks fast, which translates to overcooked in a matter of seconds. Meanwhile, garlic can become bitter, depending on how it's treated. Add to that the challenge of getting a brothy sauce to coat the pasta, and this simple recipe turns into a precarious balancing act. We wanted al dente pasta and moist shrimp bound by a sauce infused with a deep garlic flavor. For the best flavor and texture, we used quick-frozen, extra-large shrimp and marinated them with minced garlic before a quick sauté in garlic oil. We also cut each shrimp into thirds before cooking to ensure that every bite of pasta had a tasty morsel of shrimp. With sweet low notes from the infused oil and brasher high notes from the garlic, we finally had a balanced garlic flavor. As for the sauce, to deglaze the pan, we preferred the clean taste of vermouth or white wine; bottled clam broth added complexity. Using a chunky tubular pasta instead of traditional linguine made it easy to find the shrimp. To get the sauce to cling to the pasta, we stirred flour into the oil just before adding the vermouth and clam juice and tossed in some cold butter to finish.

Garlicky Shrimp Pasta

SERVES 4 TO 6

Marinate the shrimp while you prepare the remaining ingredients. Any short tubular or curly pasta works well here. If you prefer more heat, use the greater amount of red pepper flakes given.

- 1 pound extra-large shrimp (21 to 25 per pound), peeled, deveined (see page 240), and each shrimp cut into 3 pieces
- 3 tablespoons olive oil
- 5 medium garlic cloves, minced or pressed through a garlic press (about 5 teaspoons), plus 4 medium garlic cloves, smashed
- Table salt
- 1 pound mezze rigatoni, fusilli, or campanelle (see note)
- ¼–½ teaspoon red pepper flakes (see note)
- 2 teaspoons unbleached all-purpose flour
- ½ cup dry vermouth or white wine
- ¾ cup clam juice
- ½ cup chopped fresh parsley leaves
- 3 tablespoons unsalted butter, cut into 3 pieces
- 1 teaspoon lemon juice, plus lemon wedges for serving
- Ground black pepper

1. Toss the shrimp, 1 tablespoon of the oil, 2 teaspoons of the minced garlic, and ¼ teaspoon salt in a medium bowl. Let the shrimp marinate at room temperature 20 minutes.

2. Heat the 4 smashed garlic cloves and the remaining 2 tablespoons oil in a 12-inch skillet over medium-low heat, stirring occasionally, until the garlic is light golden brown, 4 to 7 minutes. Remove the skillet from the heat and use a slotted spoon to remove the garlic from the skillet; discard the garlic. Set the skillet aside.

3. Bring 4 quarts water to a boil in a large pot. Add 1 tablespoon salt and the pasta to the boiling water and cook, stirring often, until al dente. Reserve ½ cup of the cooking water then drain the pasta and return it to the pot.

4. While the pasta cooks, return the skillet with the oil to medium heat; add the shrimp with the marinade to the skillet in a single layer. Cook the shrimp, undisturbed, until the oil starts to bubble gently, 1 to 2 minutes. Stir the shrimp and continue to cook until almost cooked through, about 1 minute longer. Using a slotted spoon, transfer the shrimp to a medium bowl. Add the remaining 3 teaspoons minced garlic and the red pepper flakes to the skillet and cook until fragrant, about 1 minute. Add the flour and cook, stirring constantly, for 1 minute; stir in the vermouth and cook for 1 minute. Add the clam juice and parsley; cook until the mixture starts to thicken, 1 to 2 minutes. Off the heat, whisk in the butter and lemon juice. Add the shrimp and sauce to the pasta and adjust the consistency of the sauce with the reserved pasta cooking water as needed. Season with black pepper to taste. Serve immediately, passing the lemon wedges separately.

CLASSIC SHRIMP FRA DIAVOLO

WHY THIS RECIPE WORKS: Most recipes for shrimp *fra diavolo* ("brother devil" in Italian) lack depth of flavor, with the star ingredients, shrimp and garlic, contributing little to an acidic, unbalanced tomato sauce. We wanted a classic shrimp fra diavolo with a seriously garlicky, spicy tomato sauce studded with sweet, firm shrimp.

For a streamlined procedure that would produce deep flavor, we seared the shrimp first to help them caramelize and enrich their sweetness. Following a brief sear with olive oil, salt, and red pepper flakes—the pepper flakes also benefited from the sear, as they took on toasty, earthy notes—we flambéed the shrimp with cognac. The combined forces of cognac and flame brought out the shrimp's sweet, tender notes and imbued our fra diavolo with the cognac's richness and complexity. We then sautéed the garlic slowly for a mellow nutty flavor, and reserved some raw garlic for a last-minute punch of heat and spice. Simmered diced tomatoes and a splash of white wine (balanced by a bit of sugar) completed our perfect fra diavolo in less than 30 minutes.

Classic Shrimp fra Diavolo

SERVES 4 TO 6

One teaspoon of red pepper flakes will give the sauce a little kick, but you may want to add more depending on your taste. For safety notes on flambéing, see page 408.

- Table salt
- 1 pound linguine or spaghetti
- 1 pound large shrimp (31 to 40 per pound), peeled and deveined (see page 240)
- 6 tablespoons extra-virgin olive oil
- 1 teaspoon red pepper flakes, plus more to taste (see note)
- ¼ cup cognac or brandy
- 12 medium garlic cloves, minced or pressed through a garlic press (about ¼ cup)
- 1 (28-ounce) can diced tomatoes, drained
- 1 cup dry white wine
- ½ teaspoon sugar
- ¼ cup minced fresh parsley leaves

1. Bring 4 quarts water to a boil in a large pot. Add 1 tablespoon salt and the pasta to the boiling water and cook, stirring often, until al dente. Reserve ½ cup of the cooking water then drain the pasta and return it to the pot.

2. Meanwhile, toss the shrimp with 2 tablespoons of the oil, ½ teaspoon of the red pepper flakes, and ¾ teaspoon salt. Heat a 12-inch skillet over high heat. Add the shrimp to the skillet in a single layer and cook, without stirring, until the bottoms of the shrimp turn spotty brown, about 30 seconds. Remove the skillet from the heat, flip the shrimp, and add the cognac; wait until the cognac has warmed slightly, about 5 seconds, and return the skillet to high heat. Wave a lit match over the skillet until the cognac ignites, shaking the pan to distribute the flame over the entire pan. When the flames subside (this will take 15 to 30 seconds), transfer the shrimp to a medium bowl and set aside. Let the skillet cool, off the heat, about 2 minutes.

3. Add 3 tablespoons more oil and 3 tablespoons of the garlic to the cooled skillet and cook over low heat, stirring constantly, until the garlic becomes sticky and straw colored, 7 to 10 minutes. Add the remaining red pepper flakes, ¾ teaspoon salt, the tomatoes, wine, and sugar, increase the heat to medium-high, and simmer until thickened, about 8 minutes.

4. Stir the shrimp with accumulated juices, the remaining 1 tablespoon garlic, and the parsley into the tomato sauce. Simmer until the shrimp have heated through, about 1 minute. Off the heat, stir in the remaining 1 tablespoon oil. Add ½ cup of the tomato sauce (no shrimp) to the pasta; toss to coat and adjust the consistency of the sauce with the reserved pasta cooking water as needed. Serve immediately, topping individual bowls with the sauce and shrimp.

MODERN SHRIMP FRA DIAVOLO

WHY THIS RECIPE WORKS: Shrimp *fra diavolo* is a classic 20th-century Italian American combo of shrimp, tomatoes, garlic, and hot pepper, often served over spaghetti or with crusty bread. At its best, it's lively and piquant, the tangy tomatoes countering the sweet and briny shrimp, and the pepper and garlic providing a spirited kick. Unfortunately, the spice is often so heavy-handed that it completely overwhelms the other flavors, and the fragile shrimp are often overcooked and flavorless, identifiable only by their shape. We wanted to preserve the fiery character of fra diavolo but also heighten the other flavors—particularly the brininess of the shrimp—so that they could stand up to the heat.

To build a rich, briny seafood base, we borrowed a technique from shrimp bisque: sautéing the shrimp shells in a little oil until they and the surface of the pan were spotty brown, then deglazing the pan with wine to pick up the flavorful fond. Some canned tomato liquid rounded out our shrimp "stock." To bloom the flavors of our aromatics, we sautéed some garlic, red pepper flakes, oregano, and a couple of anchovy fillets for extra savory (but not fishy) seafood flavor. We added our stock back to the aromatics and used this flavorful sauce to gently poach the shrimp. At the end of cooking, we stirred in some minced pepperoncini and their brine for a boost of tangy heat. Handfuls of chopped basil and parsley lent freshness, and a drizzle of fruity extra-virgin olive oil made for a rich finish.

Shrimp Fra Diavolo

SERVES 4

If the shrimp you are using have been treated with salt (check the bag's ingredient list), skip the salting in step 1 and add ¼ teaspoon of salt to the sauce in step 3. Adjust the amount of pepper flakes depending on how spicy you want the dish. Serve the shrimp with a salad and crusty bread or over spaghetti. If serving with spaghetti, adjust the consistency of the sauce with some reserved pasta cooking water.

- 1½ pounds large shrimp (26 to 30 per pound), peeled and deveined (see page 240), shells reserved
- Salt
- 1 (28-ounce) can whole peeled tomatoes
- 3 tablespoons vegetable oil
- 1 cup dry white wine
- 4 garlic cloves, minced
- ½–1 teaspoon red pepper flakes
- ½ teaspoon dried oregano
- 2 anchovy fillets, rinsed, patted dry, and minced
- ¼ cup chopped fresh basil
- ¼ cup chopped fresh parsley
- 1½ teaspoons minced pepperoncini, plus 1 teaspoon brine
- 2 tablespoons extra-virgin olive oil

1. Toss shrimp with ½ teaspoon salt and set aside. Pour tomatoes into colander set over large bowl. Pierce tomatoes with edge of rubber spatula and stir briefly to release juice. Transfer drained tomatoes to small bowl and reserve juice. Do not wash colander.

2. Heat 1 tablespoon vegetable oil in 12-inch skillet over high heat until shimmering. Add shrimp shells and cook, stirring frequently, until they begin to turn spotty brown and skillet starts to brown, 2 to 4 minutes. Remove skillet from heat and carefully add wine. When bubbling subsides, return skillet to heat and simmer until wine is reduced to about 2 tablespoons, 2 to 4 minutes. Add reserved tomato juice and simmer to meld flavors, 5 minutes. Pour contents of skillet into colander set over bowl. Discard shells and reserve liquid. Wipe out skillet with paper towels.

3. Heat remaining 2 tablespoons vegetable oil, garlic, pepper flakes, and oregano in now-empty skillet over medium heat, stirring occasionally, until garlic is straw-colored and fragrant, 1 to 2 minutes. Add anchovies and stir until fragrant, about

30 seconds. Remove from heat. Add drained tomatoes and mash with potato masher until coarsely pureed. Return to heat and stir in reserved tomato juice mixture. Increase heat to medium-high and simmer until mixture has thickened, about 5 minutes.

4. Add shrimp to skillet and simmer gently, stirring and turning shrimp frequently, until they are just cooked through, 4 to 5 minutes. Remove pan from heat. Stir in basil, parsley, and pepperoncini and brine and season with salt to taste. Drizzle with olive oil and serve.

LINGUINE WITH SEAFOOD

WHY THIS RECIPE WORKS: To create a seafood pasta dish with rich, savory seafood flavor in every bite (not just in the pieces of shellfish), we made a sauce with clam juice and four minced anchovies, which fortified the juices shed by the shellfish. Cooking the shellfish in a careful sequence—precooking hardier clams and mussels first and then adding the shrimp and squid during the final few minutes of cooking—ensured that every piece was plump and tender. We parboiled the linguine and then finished cooking it directly in the sauce; the noodles soaked up flavor while shedding starches that thickened the sauce so that it clung well to the pasta. Fresh cherry tomatoes, lots of garlic, fresh herbs, and lemon made for a bright, clean, complex-tasting sauce.

Linguine with Seafood (Linguine allo Scoglio)

SERVES 6

For a simpler version of this dish, you can omit the clams and squid and increase the amounts of mussels and shrimp to 1½ pounds each; you'll also need to increase the amount of salt in step 2 to ¾ teaspoon. If you can't find fresh squid, it's available frozen at many supermarkets and typically has the benefit of being precleaned. Bar Harbor makes our favorite clam juice.

- 6 tablespoons extra-virgin olive oil
- 12 garlic cloves, minced
- ¼ teaspoon red pepper flakes
- 1 pound littleneck clams, scrubbed
- 1 pound mussels, scrubbed and debearded
- 1¼ pounds cherry tomatoes (half of tomatoes halved, remaining left whole)
- 1 (8-ounce) bottle clam juice
- 1 cup dry white wine
- 1 cup minced fresh parsley
- 1 tablespoon tomato paste
- 4 anchovy fillets, rinsed, patted dry, and minced
- 1 teaspoon minced fresh thyme
- Salt and pepper
- 1 pound linguine
- 1 pound extra-large shrimp (21 to 25 per pound), peeled and deveined (see page 240)
- ½ pound squid, sliced crosswise into ½-inch-thick rings
- 2 teaspoons grated lemon zest, plus lemon wedges for serving

1. Heat ¼ cup oil in large Dutch oven over medium-high heat until shimmering. Add garlic and pepper flakes and cook until fragrant, 1 minute. Add clams, cover, and cook, shaking pan occasionally, for 4 minutes. Add mussels, cover, and continue to cook, shaking pan occasionally, until clams and mussels have opened, 3 to 4 minutes longer. Transfer clams and mussels to bowl, discarding any that haven't opened, and cover to keep warm; leave any broth in pot.

2. Add whole tomatoes, clam juice, wine, ½ cup parsley, tomato paste, anchovies, thyme, and ½ teaspoon salt to pot and bring to simmer over medium-high heat. Reduce heat to medium and cook, stirring occasionally, until tomatoes have started to break down and sauce is reduced by one-third, about 10 minutes.

3. Meanwhile, bring 4 quarts water to boil in large pot. Add pasta and 1 tablespoon salt and cook, stirring often, for 7 minutes. Reserve ½ cup cooking water, then drain pasta.

4. Add pasta to sauce in Dutch oven and cook over medium heat, stirring gently, for 2 minutes. Reduce heat to medium-low, stir in shrimp, cover, and cook for 4 minutes. Stir in squid, lemon zest, halved tomatoes, and remaining ½ cup parsley; cover and continue to cook until shrimp and squid are just cooked through, about 2 minutes longer. Gently stir in clams and mussels. Remove pot from heat, cover, and let stand until clams and mussels are warmed through, about 2 minutes. Season with salt and pepper to taste and adjust consistency with reserved cooking water as needed. Transfer to large serving dish, drizzle with remaining 2 tablespoons oil, and serve, passing lemon wedges separately.

BEHIND THE SCENES

THE TEST KITCHEN'S TOP FIVE ESSENTIAL KITCHEN TOOLS

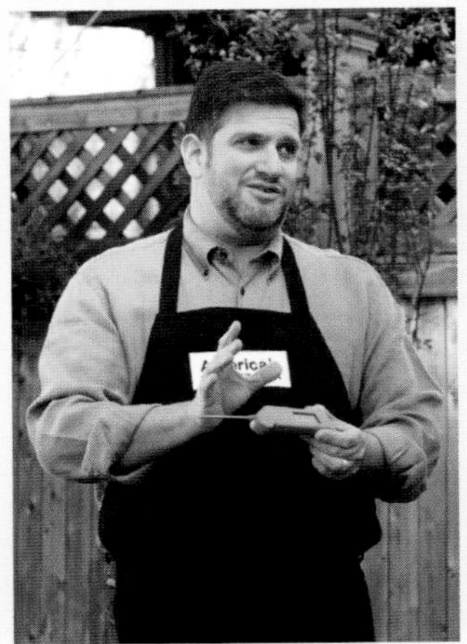

Face it: Americans are crazy about gadgets. Since the time of Benjamin Franklin, we have valued the ingenuity of the inventor who designs a simple tool that makes the execution of an everyday task easier. But as anyone who watches late-night television knows, America's love of the gadget can—and does—go too far at times. No one needs a syringe to inject marinades into meat.

So how do you know which gadgets work and which ones don't? That's where we can help. Here's our list of five gadgets you might not own, but really should. (See pages 872–903 for recommended brands.)

1. DIGITAL INSTANT-READ THERMOMETER: How else do you know when food is done? And, because it's digital, it works in seconds so your hands don't tarry in hot spots like the oven or grill.

2. LOCKING TONGS: Don't use a fork. Sturdy, long-handled tongs (with scalloped edges that won't pierce food) can turn, flip, rotate, stir, and more.

3. GARLIC PRESS: Stop kidding yourself. You're never going to mince garlic finely and evenly enough. A garlic press ensures consistent (and perfect) results every time.

4. OVEN THERMOMETER: News flash—your oven probably isn't properly calibrated. How do we know? We tested 20 home ovens and only a handful came close. You could pay big bucks to get your oven serviced by a professional or spend a few dollars on an oven thermometer so cookies don't burn and roasts are perfectly cooked.

5. KNIFE SHARPENER: Using dull knives is slow and unsafe. You wouldn't drive a car with nearly flat tires, would you? A fancy electric sharpener is nice, but even a good (and cheap) manual sharpener is far better than nothing.

RIGATONI WITH BEEF AND ONION RAGU

WHY THIS RECIPE WORKS: This rich, supple meat sauce was born out of thrift in 16th-century Naples. *La Genovese* began as a combination of beef and aromatic vegetables that were cooked down to make two meals: a savory sauce for pasta and another, separate meal of cooked beef. Later, most of the vegetables took a backseat to the onions, which became the foundation of this deeply flavorful sauce. To make the ultra-savory recipe work in a modern context, we decided to turn all the elements into one substantial sauce by shredding the meat into the sauce. To eliminate the need for intermittent stirring and monitoring during cooking, we moved the process from the stovetop to the even heat of the oven. A surprising ingredient—water—proved essential to extracting maximum flavor from the onions. We also added tomato paste for an extra boost of flavor and color. To encourage the sauce to cling to the pasta, we vigorously stirred them together so that the starch from the pasta added body to the sauce. A bit of grated Pecorino Romano brought the flavors together and added a mild tang.

Rigatoni with Beef and Onion Ragu

SERVES 6 TO 8

If marjoram is unavailable, substitute an equal amount of oregano. Pair this dish with a lightly dressed salad of assertively flavored greens.

- 1 (1- to 1¼-pound) boneless beef chuck-eye roast, cut into 4 pieces and trimmed of large pieces of fat
- Kosher salt and pepper
- 2 ounces pancetta, cut into ½-inch pieces
- 2 ounces salami, cut into ½-inch pieces
- 1 small carrot, peeled and cut into ½-inch pieces
- 1 small celery rib, cut into ½-inch pieces
- 2½ pounds onions, halved and cut into 1-inch pieces
- 2 tablespoons tomato paste
- 1 cup dry white wine
- 2 tablespoons minced fresh marjoram
- 1 pound rigatoni
- 1 ounce Pecorino Romano cheese, grated (½ cup), plus extra for serving

1. Sprinkle beef with 1 teaspoon salt and ½ teaspoon pepper and set aside. Adjust oven rack to lower-middle position and heat oven to 300 degrees.

2. Process pancetta and salami in food processor until ground to paste, about 30 seconds, scraping down sides of bowl as needed. Add carrot and celery and process 30 seconds longer, scraping down sides of bowl as needed. Transfer paste to Dutch oven and set aside; do not clean out processor bowl. Pulse onions in processor in 2 batches, until ⅛- to ¼-inch pieces form, 8 to 10 pulses per batch.

3. Cook pancetta mixture over medium heat, stirring frequently, until fat is rendered and fond begins to form on bottom of pot, about 5 minutes. Add tomato paste and cook, stirring constantly, until browned, about 90 seconds. Stir in 2 cups water, scraping up any browned bits. Stir in onions and bring to boil. Stir in ½ cup wine and 1 tablespoon marjoram. Add beef and push into onions to ensure that it is submerged. Transfer to oven and cook, uncovered, until beef is fully tender, 2 to 2½ hours.

4. Transfer beef to carving board. Place pot over medium heat and cook, stirring frequently, until mixture is almost completely dry. Stir in remaining ½ cup wine and cook for

2 minutes, stirring occasionally. Using 2 forks, shred beef into bite-size pieces. Stir beef and remaining 1 tablespoon marjoram into sauce and season with salt and pepper to taste. Remove from heat, cover, and keep warm.

5. Bring 4 quarts water to boil in large pot. Add rigatoni and 2 tablespoons salt and cook, stirring often, until just al dente. Drain rigatoni and add to warm sauce. Add Pecorino and stir vigorously over low heat until sauce is slightly thickened and rigatoni is fully tender, 1 to 2 minutes. Serve, passing extra Pecorino separately.

PASTA WITH HEARTY ITALIAN MEAT SAUCE

WHY THIS RECIPE WORKS: Traditional "Sunday gravy" is more than just meat sauce—it's a labor of love, an all-day kitchen affair, involving several types of meat, a bunch of tomatoes, and at least one Italian grandmother. We wanted to honor this meaty extravaganza but shortcut the cooking so we could get this traditional dish on the table in a reasonable amount of time. When you're using six or seven types of meat, the browning alone can take up to 40 minutes. Our first step was to limit the dish to just one kind of sausage and one pork cut—plus meatballs. Hot Italian links gave the sauce a mild kick; baby back ribs were our favorite cut of pork because they weren't too fatty and turned moist and tender in just a few hours. Meatloaf mix, a combination of ground beef, pork, and veal, produced juicy, tender meatballs, especially when mixed with a panade of bread and buttermilk. To further bump up flavor, we mixed in minced garlic, parsley, and red pepper flakes, plus an egg yolk for richness. To help the meatballs retain their shape we browned them first in a skillet before adding them to the sauce. For the tomato sauce, canned crushed tomatoes were a winner, leading to a sauce with nice thickness and bright tomato flavor. Instead of merely browning the tomato paste for 30 seconds, we cooked it until it nearly blackened, which concentrated its sweetness. The sauce was still lacking some beefy undercurrents; the best booster turned out to be the simple, straightforward addition of an ingredient rarely found in tomato sauce: beef broth.

Pasta with Hearty Italian Meat Sauce (Sunday Gravy)

SERVES 8 TO 10

We prefer meatloaf mix (a combination of ground beef, pork, and veal) for the meatballs in this recipe. Ground beef may be substituted, but the meatballs won't be as flavorful. Six tablespoons of plain yogurt thinned with 2 tablespoons of milk can be substituted for the buttermilk. Our preferred brand of crushed tomatoes is SMT. This recipe can be prepared through step 4 and then cooled and refrigerated in the Dutch oven for up to 2 days. To reheat, drizzle 1/2 cup water over the sauce (do not stir in) and warm on the lower-middle rack of a preheated 325-degree oven for 1 hour before proceeding with the recipe.

SAUCE

- 2 tablespoons olive oil
- 1 (2¼-pound) rack baby back ribs, cut into 2-rib sections
- Table salt and ground black pepper
- 1 pound hot Italian sausage links
- 2 medium onions, minced
- 1¼ teaspoons dried oregano
- 3 tablespoons tomato paste
- 4 medium garlic cloves, minced or pressed through a garlic press (about 4 teaspoons)
- 2 (28-ounce) cans crushed tomatoes (see note)
- ⅔ cup low-sodium beef broth

MEATBALLS AND PASTA

- 2 slices high-quality white sandwich bread, crusts removed and bread cut into ½-inch cubes
- ½ cup buttermilk (see note)
- ¼ cup chopped fresh parsley leaves
- 2 medium garlic cloves, minced or pressed through a garlic press (about 2 teaspoons)
- 1 large egg yolk
- Table salt
- ¼ teaspoon red pepper flakes
- 1 pound meatloaf mix (see note)
- 2 ounces thinly sliced prosciutto, minced
- 1 ounce Pecorino Romano cheese, grated (about ½ cup)
- ½ cup olive oil
- 1½ pounds spaghetti or linguine
- ¼ cup chopped fresh basil leaves
- Grated Parmesan cheese, for serving

1. FOR THE SAUCE: Adjust an oven rack to the lower-middle position and heat the oven to 325 degrees. Heat the oil in a large Dutch oven over medium-high heat until just smoking. Pat the ribs dry with paper towels and season with salt and pepper. Add half of the ribs to the pot and brown on both sides, 5 to 7 minutes total. Transfer the ribs to a large plate and repeat with the remaining ribs. After transferring the second batch of ribs to the plate, brown the sausages on all four sides, 5 to 7 minutes total. Transfer the sausages to the plate with the ribs.

2. Reduce the heat to medium, add the onions and oregano; cook, stirring occasionally, until beginning to brown, about 5 minutes. Add the tomato paste and cook, stirring constantly, until very dark, about 3 minutes. Stir in the garlic and cook until fragrant, about 30 seconds. Add the crushed tomatoes and broth, scraping up any browned bits. Return the ribs and sausage to the pot; bring to a simmer, cover, and transfer to the oven. Cook until the ribs are tender, about 2½ hours.

3. FOR THE MEATBALLS: Meanwhile, combine the bread cubes, buttermilk, parsley, garlic, egg yolk, ½ teaspoon salt, and the red pepper flakes in a medium bowl and mash with a fork until no bread chunks remain. Add the meatloaf mix, prosciutto, and Pecorino Romano to the bread mixture; mix with your hands until thoroughly combined. Divide the mixture into 12 pieces; roll into balls, transfer to a plate, cover with plastic wrap, and refrigerate until ready to use.

4. When the sauce is 30 minutes from being done, heat the oil in a large nonstick skillet over medium-high heat until shimmering. Add the meatballs and cook until well browned all over, 5 to 7 minutes. Transfer the meatballs to a paper towel–lined plate to drain briefly. Remove the sauce from the oven and skim the fat from the top with a large spoon. Transfer the browned meatballs to the sauce and gently submerge. Return the pot to the oven and continue cooking until the meatballs are just cooked through, about 15 minutes.

5. Meanwhile, bring 6 quarts water to a boil in a large pot. Add 2 tablespoons salt and the pasta to the boiling water and cook, stirring often, until al dente. Reserve ½ cup of the cooking water then drain the pasta and return it to the pot.

6. Using tongs, transfer the meatballs, ribs, and sausage to a serving platter and cut the sausages in half. Stir the basil into the sauce and season with salt and pepper to taste. Add 1 cup of the sauce and the reserved pasta cooking water to the pasta; toss to coat. Serve, passing the remaining sauce, meat platter, and Parmesan separately.

PASTA AND SLOW-SIMMERED TOMATO SAUCE WITH MEAT

WHY THIS RECIPE WORKS: Slow-simmered Italian meat sauce—the kind without meatballs—relies on pork for rich flavor. But the pork found in supermarkets is so lean, we weren't convinced that any of the options could provide enough fat and flavor. So we set out to create a flavorful meat sauce with fall-off-the-bone-tender meat that was made from readily available supermarket products. We used fattier country-style pork ribs which turned meltingly tender when cooked for a long time and added meaty flavor. Beef short ribs can also be used, but since they tend to be thicker, it's important to remember to let them cook a little longer. Red wine accentuated the meatiness of the sauce, which was built on a simple combination of sautéed onion and canned diced tomatoes.

Pasta and Slow-Simmered Tomato Sauce with Meat

SERVES 4 TO 6

This sauce can be made with either beef or pork ribs. Depending on their size, you will need 4 or 5 ribs.

- 1 tablespoon olive oil
- 1½ pounds pork spareribs or country-style ribs or beef short ribs, trimmed of fat (see note)
- Table salt and ground black pepper
- 1 medium onion, minced
- ½ cup red wine
- 1 (28-ounce) can diced tomatoes
- 1 pound ziti, rigatoni, or other short tubular pasta
- Grated Parmesan cheese, for serving

1. Heat the oil in a 12-inch skillet over medium-high heat until shimmering. Season the ribs with salt and pepper and brown on all sides, turning occasionally, 8 to 10 minutes. Transfer the ribs to a plate; pour off all but 1 teaspoon fat from the skillet. Add the onion and cook until softened, 2 to 3 minutes. Add the wine and simmer, scraping up any browned bits, until the wine reduces to a glaze, about 2 minutes.

2. Return the ribs and accumulated juices to the skillet; add the tomatoes with their juice. Bring to a boil, then reduce the heat to low, cover, and simmer gently, turning the ribs several times, until the meat is very tender and falling off the bones, 1½ hours (for pork spareribs or country-style ribs) to 2 hours (for beef short ribs).

3. Transfer the ribs to a clean plate. When cool enough to handle, remove the meat from the bones and shred, discarding the fat and bones. Return the shredded meat to the sauce. Bring the sauce to a simmer over medium heat and cook, uncovered, until heated through and slightly thickened, about 5 minutes. Season with salt and pepper to taste. (The sauce can be refrigerated in an airtight container for up to 4 days or frozen for up to 2 months.)

4. Meanwhile, bring 4 quarts water to a boil in a large pot. Add 1 tablespoon salt and the pasta to the boiling water and cook, stirring often, until al dente. Reserve ½ cup of the cooking water then drain the pasta and return it to the pot. Add the sauce to the pasta and toss to combine. Adjust the consistency of the sauce with the reserved pasta cooking water as needed. Serve immediately, passing the Parmesan separately.

SIMPLE ITALIAN-STYLE MEAT SAUCE

WHY THIS RECIPE WORKS: Old-fashioned Italian-style meat sauces are on an old-fashioned time line—they require hours of simmering. But just giving browned ground beef, onions, garlic, and canned tomatoes a quick simmer produced lackluster flavor and meat with the texture of a rubber band. We wanted a quick, weeknight meat sauce with long-simmered flavor.

Our goal required concentrated flavor and tender meat. Browned chopped onions and mushrooms gave the sauce a rich base of flavor, and browning the mushrooms made them so soft and supple they practically disappeared into the finished sauce. Deglazing the pan with tomato paste and tomato juice further boosted flavor. To tenderize the meat, we incorporated a panade—a paste of bread and milk—into the meat before cooking; we combined the panade and the meat in a food processor to avoid chili-like chunks. We cooked the meat mixture just until it lost its raw color; any longer, and the meat would have turned dry and mealy. Finishing the meat in a combination of canned diced and crushed tomatoes gave us the best mix of textures. A handful of grated Parmesan, added just before serving, lent the sauce a tangy, complex character.

Simple Italian-Style Meat Sauce

MAKES ABOUT 6 CUPS

You can figure on about 3 cups of sauce per pound of pasta. Except for ground round (which tasters found spongy and bland), this recipe will work with most types of ground beef, as long as it is 85 percent lean. Use high-quality crushed tomatoes; our favorite brand is SMT. If using dried oregano, add the entire amount with the canned tomato liquid in step 2.

- 4 ounces white mushrooms, wiped clean and broken into rough pieces
- 1 large slice high-quality white sandwich bread, torn into quarters
- 2 tablespoons whole milk
- Table salt and ground black pepper
- 1 pound 85 percent lean ground beef (see note)
- 1 tablespoon olive oil
- 1 medium onion, minced
- 6 medium garlic cloves, minced or pressed through a garlic press (about 2 tablespoons)
- 1 tablespoon tomato paste
- ¼ teaspoon red pepper flakes
- 1 (14.5-ounce) can diced tomatoes, drained, ¼ cup juice reserved
- 1 tablespoon minced fresh oregano leaves or 1 teaspoon dried oregano (see note)
- 1 (28-ounce) can crushed tomatoes (see note)
- ¼ cup grated Parmesan cheese

1. Pulse the mushrooms in a food processor until finely chopped, about 8 pulses, scraping down the sides of the workbowl as needed; transfer to a medium bowl. Add the bread, milk, ½ teaspoon salt, and ½ teaspoon black pepper to the food processor and pulse until a paste forms, about 8 pulses. Add the beef and pulse until the mixture is well combined, about 6 pulses.

2. Heat the oil in a large saucepan over medium-high heat until just smoking. Add the onion and mushrooms; cook, stirring frequently, until the vegetables are browned and dark bits form on the pan bottom, 6 to 12 minutes. Stir in the garlic, tomato paste, and red pepper flakes; cook until fragrant and the tomato paste starts to brown, about 1 minute. Add the ¼ cup reserved tomato juice and 2 teaspoons of the fresh oregano (if using dried, add the full amount), scraping the bottom of the pan with a wooden spoon to loosen the browned bits. Add the meat mixture and cook, breaking the meat into small pieces with a wooden spoon, until no longer pink, 2 to 4 minutes, making sure that the meat does not brown.

3. Stir in the diced and crushed tomatoes and bring to a simmer; reduce the heat to low and gently simmer until the sauce has thickened and the flavors have blended, about 30 minutes. Stir in the cheese and the remaining 1 teaspoon fresh oregano; season with salt and pepper to taste. (The sauce can be refrigerated in an airtight container for up to 3 days or frozen for up to 1 month.)

RAGU ALLA BOLOGNESE

WHY THIS RECIPE WORKS: Unlike meat sauces in which tomatoes dominate, Bolognese sauce is about the meat, with the tomatoes in a supporting role. We wanted a traditional recipe for this complexly flavored sauce, with rich meatiness up front and a good balance of sweet, salty, and acidic flavors. We also wanted a velvety texture that would lightly cling to the noodles. For an ultrameaty version, we used six different types of meat: ground beef, pork, and veal; pancetta; mortadella (bologna-like Italian deli meat); and chicken livers. These meats and the combination of red wine and tomato paste gave us a rich, complex sauce with balanced acidity. The addition of gelatin lent the sauce an ultra-silky texture.

Ragu alla Bolognese

MAKES ABOUT 6 CUPS

This recipe makes enough sauce for 2 pounds of pasta. Eight teaspoons of gelatin is equivalent to one (1-ounce) box of gelatin. If you can't find ground veal, use an additional ¾ pound of ground beef.

- 1 cup low-sodium chicken broth
- 1 cup beef broth
- 8 teaspoons unflavored gelatin
- 1 onion, chopped coarse
- 1 large carrot, peeled and chopped coarse
- 1 celery rib, chopped coarse
- 4 ounces pancetta, chopped
- 4 ounces mortadella, chopped
- 6 ounces chicken livers, trimmed
- 3 tablespoons extra-virgin olive oil
- ¾ pound 85 percent lean ground beef
- ¾ pound ground veal
- ¾ pound ground pork
- 3 tablespoons minced fresh sage
- 1 (6-ounce) can tomato paste
- 2 cups dry red wine
- Salt and pepper
- 1 pound pappardelle or tagliatelle
- Grated Parmesan cheese

1. Combine chicken broth and beef broth in bowl; sprinkle gelatin over top and set aside. Pulse onion, carrot, and celery together in food processor until finely chopped, about 10 pulses, scraping down bowl as needed; transfer to separate bowl. Pulse pancetta and mortadella together in now-empty food processor until finely chopped, about 25 pulses, scraping down bowl as needed; transfer to second bowl. Process chicken livers in now-empty food processor until pureed, about 5 seconds; transfer to third bowl.

2. Heat oil in Dutch oven over medium-high heat until shimmering. Add beef, veal, and pork; cook, breaking up pieces with wooden spoon, until all liquid has evaporated and meat begins to sizzle, 10 to 15 minutes. Add pancetta mixture and sage; cook, stirring frequently, until pancetta is translucent, 5 to 7 minutes, adjusting heat as needed to keep fond from burning. Add chopped vegetables and cook, stirring frequently, until softened, 5 to 7 minutes. Add tomato paste and cook, stirring constantly, until rust-colored and fragrant, about 3 minutes.

3. Stir in wine, scraping up any browned bits. Simmer until sauce has thickened, about 5 minutes. Stir in broth mixture and return to simmer. Reduce heat to low and cook at bare simmer until thickened (wooden spoon should leave trail when dragged through sauce), about 1½ hours.

4. Stir in pureed chicken livers, bring to boil, and remove from heat. Season with salt and pepper to taste; cover and keep warm.

5. Bring 4 quarts water to boil in large pot. Add pasta and 1 tablespoon salt and cook, stirring often, until al dente. Reserve ¾ cup cooking water, then drain pasta and return it to pot. Add half of sauce and cooking water to pasta and toss to combine. Transfer to serving bowl and serve, passing Parmesan separately. (Leftover sauce may be refrigerated for up to 3 days or frozen for up to 1 month.)

PASTA WITH SLOW-SIMMERED BOLOGNESE SAUCE

WHY THIS RECIPE WORKS: There are many different ways to interpret what "real" bolognese sauce is. But no matter what the ingredients are, the sauce should be hearty and rich, with plenty of meaty character.

We started simple—with just onions, carrots, and celery, sautéed in butter. Meatloaf mix provided the right amount of meatiness and kept our shopping list short. For the most tender texture, we cooked the meat just until it lost its pink color and didn't let it brown. For dairy, which is used to tenderize the meat and give the sauce a rich, appealing flavor, we used milk. Once the milk had reduced, we added white wine, which gave the sauce a delicate brightness. For the tomato element, diced canned tomatoes imparted sweet, acidic notes. Finally, we simmered the sauce at the lowest possible heat for about three hours and served it with rich, eggy fettuccine.

Fettuccine with Slow-Simmered Bolognese Sauce

SERVES 4

Don't drain the pasta of its cooking water too meticulously when using this sauce; a little water left clinging to the noodles will help distribute the very thick sauce evenly over the noodles, as will the addition of 2 tablespoons of butter along with the sauce. If doubling this recipe, increase the simmering times for the milk and the wine to 30 minutes each, and increase the simmering time once the tomatoes are added to 4 hours. You can substitute equal amounts of 80 percent lean ground beef, ground veal, and ground pork for the meatloaf mix (the total amount of meat should be ¾ pound).

- 5 tablespoons unsalted butter
- 2 tablespoons minced onion
- 2 tablespoons minced carrot
- 2 tablespoons minced celery
- ¾ pound meatloaf mix (see note)
- Table salt
- 1 cup whole milk
- 1 cup dry white wine
- 1 (28-ounce) can diced tomatoes
- 1 pound fresh or dried fettuccine
- Grated Parmesan cheese, for serving

1. Melt 3 tablespoons of the butter in a large Dutch oven over medium heat. Add the onion, carrot, and celery and cook until softened but not browned, about 6 minutes. Add the meat and ½ teaspoon salt; crumble the meat into tiny pieces with a wooden spoon. Cook, continuing to crumble the meat, just until it loses its raw color but has not yet browned, about 3 minutes.

2. Add the milk and simmer until the milk evaporates and only rendered fat remains, 10 to 15 minutes. Add the wine and simmer until the wine evaporates, 10 to 15 minutes longer. Add the tomatoes with their juice and bring to a simmer. Reduce the heat to low so that the sauce continues to simmer just barely, with an occasional bubble or two at the surface, until the liquid has evaporated, about 3 hours. Season with salt to taste. (The sauce can be refrigerated in an airtight container for up to 3 days or frozen for up to 1 month.)

3. Bring 4 quarts water to a boil in a large pot. Add 1 tablespoon salt and the pasta to the boiling water and cook, stirring often, until al dente. Reserve ½ cup of the cooking water then drain the pasta and return it to the pot. Add the sauce and remaining 2 tablespoons butter; toss to combine. Adjust the consistency of the sauce with the reserved pasta cooking water as needed. Serve, passing the Parmesan separately.

NOTES FROM THE TEST KITCHEN

IMPROVISING A FLAME TAMER

A flame tamer fits over the burner to reduce the heat to a bare simmer. To make one, take a long sheet of heavy-duty aluminum foil and shape it into a 1-inch-thick ring. Make sure the ring is of an even thickness so that the pot will rest flat on it.

PASTA WITH STREAMLINED BOLOGNESE SAUCE

WHY THIS RECIPE WORKS: Bolognese often gets its big flavor from braising ground meat and softened vegetables in slowly reducing milk, wine, and tomatoes. The process typically takes about three hours. But on a busy weeknight, we rarely have that much time to spend making dinner. We wanted to streamline Bolognese into a weeknight-friendly dinner. Using a food processor to chop the vegetables, including a big can of whole tomatoes with their juice, cut down on preparation time. To develop sweetness in the sauce without the day-long simmering, we reduced white wine in a separate pan and added it to the sauce at the end; a little bit of sugar, stirred in with the garlic to help it caramelize, amplified the sweetness. Instead of browning the ground meat, we cooked it with milk, which helped to break down and soften the meat in a short amount of time. To beef up the meaty flavor of the sauce, we added chopped pancetta, dried porcini mushrooms, and the flavorful liquid left behind from rehydrating the mushrooms. In about an hour, our sauce was ready, with all the rich meatiness of a long-simmered Bolognese.

Pasta with Streamlined Bolognese Sauce

SERVES 4 TO 6

Sweet white wines such as Gewürztraminer, Riesling, and even white Zinfandel work especially well in this sauce. To obtain the best texture, be careful not to break up the meat too much when cooking it with the milk in step 4; with additional cooking and stirring, it will continue to break up. Just about any pasta shape complements this meaty sauce, but spaghetti and linguine are the test kitchen favorites. If using pancetta that has been sliced thin rather than cut into 1-inch chunks, reduce the processing time in step 3 from 30 seconds to about 5 seconds. You can substitute equal amounts of 80 percent lean ground beef, ground veal, and ground pork for the meatloaf mix (the total amount of meat should be 1¼ pounds).

- ½ ounce dried porcini mushrooms
- 1¼ cups sweet white wine (see note)
- ½ small carrot, peeled and chopped coarse (about ½ cup)
- ½ small onion, chopped coarse (about ¼ cup)
- 3 ounces pancetta, cut into 1-inch chunks (see note)
- 1 (28-ounce) can whole tomatoes
- 1½ tablespoons unsalted butter
- 1 teaspoon sugar
- 1 small garlic clove, minced or pressed through a garlic press (about ½ teaspoon)
- 1¼ pounds meatloaf mix (see note)
- 1½ cups whole milk
- 2 tablespoons tomato paste
- Table salt
- ⅛ teaspoon ground black pepper
- 1 pound pasta (see note)
- Grated Parmesan cheese, for serving

1. Combine the porcini and ½ cup water in a small microwave-safe bowl; cover the bowl with plastic wrap, cut three vents for steam with a knife, and microwave on high power for 30 seconds. Let stand until the mushrooms have softened, about 5 minutes. Transfer the mushrooms to a second small bowl and reserve the liquid; pour the liquid through a paper towel–lined mesh strainer. Set the mushrooms and the strained liquid aside.

2. Bring the wine to a simmer in a 10-inch nonstick skillet over medium heat; reduce the heat to low and continue to simmer until the wine is reduced to 2 tablespoons, about 20 minutes. Set aside.

3. Meanwhile, pulse the carrot in a food processor until broken down into ¼-inch pieces, about 10 pulses. Add the onion and pulse until the vegetables are broken down into ⅛-inch pieces, about 10 pulses. Transfer the vegetables to a small bowl. Process the reserved mushrooms until well ground, about 15 seconds, scraping down the sides of the workbowl as needed. Transfer the mushrooms to the bowl with the vegetables. Process the pancetta until the pieces are no larger than ¼ inch, 30 to 35 seconds, scraping down the sides of the workbowl as needed; transfer to a small bowl. Pulse the tomatoes with their juice until chopped fine, about 8 pulses.

4. Melt the butter in a 12-inch skillet over medium-high heat. Cook the pancetta, stirring frequently, until well browned, about 2 minutes. Add the carrot, onion, and mushrooms and cook, stirring frequently, until the vegetables are softened but not browned, about 4 minutes. Add the sugar and garlic and cook until fragrant, about 30 seconds. Add the meat, breaking it into 1-inch pieces with a wooden spoon, and cook for about 1 minute. Add the milk and stir to break the meat into ½-inch pieces; bring to a simmer, reduce the heat to medium, and cook, stirring to break the meat into smaller pieces, until most of the liquid has evaporated and the meat begins to sizzle, 18 to 20 minutes. Stir in the tomato paste and cook until combined, about 1 minute. Add the tomatoes, reserved mushroom soaking liquid, ¼ teaspoon salt, and the pepper; bring to a simmer over medium-high heat, then reduce the heat to medium and simmer until the liquid is reduced and the sauce is thickened, 12 to 15 minutes. Stir in the reduced wine and simmer to blend the flavors, about 5 minutes.

5. Meanwhile, bring 4 quarts water to a boil in a large pot. Add 1 tablespoon salt and the pasta to the boiling water and cook, stirring often, until al dente. Reserve ½ cup of the cooking water then drain the pasta and return it to the pot. Add 2 cups of the sauce and 2 tablespoons of the reserved pasta cooking water to the pasta; toss to combine and adjust the consistency of the sauce with the remaining reserved pasta cooking water as needed. Serve immediately, topping individual bowls with ¼ cup sauce and passing the Parmesan separately.

WEEKNIGHT BOLOGNESE

WHY THIS RECIPE WORKS: To create a Bolognese sauce that could come together quickly on a busy weeknight but rival the depth and richness of a long-cooked version, we started by browning the aromatic vegetables (but not the ground beef, which would dry out and toughen if seared) to develop a flavorful fond; we also treated the ground beef with a baking soda solution to ensure that it stayed tender. Adding pancetta, which we ground and browned deeply with the aromatic vegetables, boosted the sauce's meaty flavor, and a healthy dose of tomato paste added depth and brightness. We also added Parmesan cheese, usually reserved for serving, directly to the sauce as it cooked for its umami richness. To develop concentrated flavor and a consistency that nicely coated the pasta, we boiled beef broth until it was reduced by half (mixing up a concentrated beef broth using our recommended product, Better Than Bouillon Roasted Beef Base, also works) and added it to the sauce, which then needed to simmer only 30 minutes longer. Finally, we intentionally made the sauce thin because the eggy noodles (traditionally tagliatelle or pappardelle) absorb a lot of liquid; once they have soaked up some of the sauce, it will coat the noodles beautifully.

Weeknight Tagliatelle with Bolognese Sauce

SERVES 4 TO 6

If you use our recommended beef broth, Better Than Bouillon Roasted Beef Base, you can skip step 2 and make a concentrated broth by adding 4 teaspoons paste to 2 cups water. To ensure the best flavor, be sure to brown the pancetta-vegetable mixture in step 4 until the fond on the bottom of the pot is quite dark. The cooked sauce will look thin but will thicken once tossed with the pasta. Tagliatelle is a long, flat, dry egg pasta that is about ¼ inch wide; if you can't find it, you can substitute pappardelle. Substituting other pasta may result in a too-wet sauce.

- 1 pound 93 percent lean ground beef
- 2 tablespoons water
- ¼ teaspoon baking soda
- Salt and pepper
- 4 cups beef broth
- 6 ounces pancetta, chopped coarse
- 1 onion, chopped coarse
- 1 large carrot, peeled and chopped coarse
- 1 celery rib, chopped coarse
- 1 tablespoon unsalted butter
- 1 tablespoon extra-virgin olive oil
- 3 tablespoons tomato paste
- 1 cup dry red wine
- 1 ounce Parmesan cheese, grated (½ cup), plus extra for serving
- 1 pound tagliatelle

1. Toss beef with water, baking soda, and ¼ teaspoon pepper in bowl until thoroughly combined. Set aside.

2. While beef sits, bring broth to boil over high heat in large pot (this pot will be used to cook pasta in step 6) and cook until reduced to 2 cups, about 15 minutes; set aside.

3. Pulse pancetta in food processor until finely chopped, 15 to 20 pulses. Add onion, carrot, and celery and pulse until vegetables are finely chopped and mixture has paste-like consistency, 12 to 15 pulses, scraping down sides of bowl as needed.

4. Heat butter and oil in large Dutch oven over medium-high heat until shimmering. When foaming subsides, add pancetta-vegetable mixture and ¼ teaspoon pepper and cook, stirring occasionally, until liquid has evaporated, about 8 minutes. Spread mixture in even layer in bottom of pot and continue to cook, stirring every couple of minutes, until very dark browned bits form on bottom of pot, 7 to 12 minutes longer. Stir in tomato paste and cook until paste is rust-colored and bottom of pot is dark brown, 1 to 2 minutes.

5. Reduce heat to medium, add beef, and cook, using wooden spoon to break meat into pieces no larger than ¼ inch, until beef has just lost its raw pink color, 4 to 7 minutes. Stir in wine, scraping up any browned bits, and bring to simmer. Cook until wine has evaporated and sauce has thickened, about 5 minutes. Stir in broth and Parmesan. Return sauce to simmer; cover, reduce heat to low, and simmer for 30 minutes (sauce will look thin). Remove from heat and season with salt and pepper to taste.

6. Rinse pot that held broth. While sauce simmers, bring 4 quarts water to boil in now-empty pot. Add pasta and 1 tablespoon salt and cook, stirring occasionally, until al dente. Reserve ¼ cup cooking water, then drain pasta. Add pasta to pot with sauce and toss to combine. Adjust sauce consistency with reserved cooking water as needed. Transfer to platter or individual bowls and serve, passing extra Parmesan separately.

SPAGHETTI AND MEATBALLS

WHY THIS RECIPE WORKS: One of the problems with meatballs is that they're thought of as smaller, rounder versions of hamburgers. This would be fine if meatballs were cooked to rare or medium-rare, as most hamburgers are, but meatballs are usually cooked to well-done. This can leave them flavorless, dry, and dense, so they need some help to lighten their texture. What we were after was nothing short of great meatballs: crusty and dark brown on the outside and soft and moist on the inside.

White bread soaked in buttermilk added as a binder gave the meatballs a creamy texture and an appealing tang. Eggs were also important for texture and flavor; their fats and emulsifiers added moistness and richness. Egg yolks alone worked best and kept the meatballs moist and light; the whites just made the mixture sticky and hard to handle, with no other added benefits. Adding some ground pork to the usual ground beef enhanced the flavor. Broiling dried out the meatballs; pan-frying was the best way to brown the meatballs and kept the interior moist. Finally, building the tomato sauce on top of the browned bits left in the pan after frying the meatballs made for a hearty, robust-tasting sauce.

Spaghetti and Meatballs

SERVES 4 TO 6

The shaped meatballs can be covered with plastic wrap and refrigerated for several hours ahead of serving time; fry the meatballs and make the sauce at the last minute. If you don't have buttermilk, you can substitute 6 tablespoons of plain yogurt thinned with 2 tablespoons of milk.

MEATBALLS

- 2 slices high-quality white sandwich bread, crusts removed and bread torn into small pieces
- ½ cup buttermilk (see note)
- ¾ pound 85 percent lean ground beef
- ¼ pound ground pork
- ¼ cup grated Parmesan cheese
- 2 tablespoons minced fresh parsley leaves
- 1 large egg yolk
- 1 medium garlic clove, minced or pressed through a garlic press (about 1 teaspoon)
- ¾ teaspoon table salt
- ⅛ teaspoon ground black pepper
- Vegetable oil, for pan-frying

TOMATO SAUCE AND PASTA

- 2 tablespoons extra-virgin olive oil
- 1 medium garlic clove, minced or pressed through a garlic press (about 1 teaspoon)
- 1 (28-ounce) can crushed tomatoes
- 1 tablespoon minced fresh basil leaves
- Table salt and ground black pepper
- 1 pound spaghetti
- Grated Parmesan cheese, for serving

1. **FOR THE MEATBALLS:** Mash the bread and buttermilk to a smooth paste in a large bowl. Let stand for 10 minutes.

2. Add the beef, pork, cheese, parsley, egg yolk, garlic, salt, and pepper to the mashed bread; stir gently until uniform. Gently form into 1½-inch round meatballs (about 14 meatballs). (When forming the meatballs use a light touch; if you compact the meatballs too much, they can become dense and hard.)

3. Pour the vegetable oil into a 12-inch skillet until it measures a depth of ¼ inch. Heat over medium-high heat until shimmering. Add the meatballs in a single layer and cook until nicely browned on all sides, about 10 minutes. Transfer the meatballs to a paper towel–lined plate and discard the oil left in the skillet.

4. **FOR THE SAUCE:** Add the olive oil and garlic to the skillet and cook over medium heat, scraping up any browned bits, until fragrant, about 30 seconds. Add the tomatoes with their juice, bring to a simmer, and cook until the sauce thickens, about 10 minutes. Stir in the basil and season with salt and pepper to taste. Add the meatballs and simmer, turning them occasionally, until heated through, about 5 minutes.

5. Meanwhile, bring 4 quarts water to a boil in a large pot. Add 1 tablespoon salt and the pasta to the boiling water and cook, stirring often, until al dente. Reserve ½ cup of the cooking water then drain the pasta and return it to the pot. Stir in several large spoonfuls of the tomato sauce (without meatballs) over the pasta and toss to coat. Adjust the consistency of the sauce with the reserved pasta cooking water as needed. Serve immediately, topping individual bowls with more tomato sauce and several meatballs and passing the Parmesan separately.

NOTES FROM THE TEST KITCHEN

MAKING MEATBALLS

1. Use a fork to mash the bread and buttermilk into a smooth paste.

2. Working with 3 tablespoons of the meatball mixture at a time, form the mixture into a 1½-inch ball by gently rolling it between your palms.

3. Fry the meatballs, turning every so often, until they are a crusty golden brown all over.

SPAGHETTI AND MEATBALLS FOR A CROWD

WHY THIS RECIPE WORKS: Making spaghetti and meatballs for a crowd can try the patience of even the toughest Italian grandmother. We sought an easier way. Roasting them on a wire rack made our recipe faster. Adding powdered gelatin to a mix of ground chuck and pork served to plump the meatballs and lent them a soft richness. Prosciutto gave the meatballs extra meatiness, and a panade, which we made with panko, kept the meat moist and prevented it from getting tough. To create a rich sauce, we braised the meatballs in marinara sauce for about an hour. To make sure the sauce didn't overreduce, we swapped half the crushed tomatoes in our marinara recipe for an equal portion of tomato juice.

Classic Spaghetti and Meatballs for a Crowd

SERVES 12

If you don't have buttermilk, you can substitute 1 cup whole-milk plain yogurt thinned with ½ cup whole milk. Grate the onion on the large holes of a box grater. You can cook the pasta in two separate pots if you do not have a large enough pot to cook all of the pasta together. Once cooked, the sauce and the meatballs can be cooled and refrigerated for up to 2 days. To reheat, drizzle ½ cup of water over the sauce, without stirring, and reheat on the lower-middle rack of a 325-degree oven for 1 hour.

MEATBALLS

- 2¼ cups panko bread crumbs
- 1½ cups buttermilk (see note)
- 1½ teaspoons unflavored gelatin
- 3 tablespoons water
- 2 pounds 85 percent lean ground beef
- 1 pound ground pork
- 6 ounces thinly sliced prosciutto, chopped fine
- 3 large eggs
- 3 ounces Parmesan cheese, grated (about 1½ cups)
- 6 tablespoons minced fresh parsley leaves
- 3 medium garlic cloves, minced or pressed through a garlic press (about 1 tablespoon)
- 1½ teaspoons table salt
- ½ teaspoon ground black pepper

SAUCE

- 3 tablespoons extra-virgin olive oil
- 1 large onion, grated
- 6 medium garlic cloves, minced or pressed through a garlic press (about 2 tablespoons)
- 1 teaspoon dried oregano
- ½ teaspoon red pepper flakes
- 3 (28-ounce) cans crushed tomatoes
- 6 cups tomato juice
- 6 tablespoons dry white wine
- Table salt and ground black pepper
- ½ cup minced fresh basil leaves
- 3 tablespoons minced fresh parsley leaves
- Sugar

- 3 pounds spaghetti
- 2 tablespoons table salt
- Grated Parmesan cheese, for serving

1. FOR THE MEATBALLS: Adjust the oven racks to the lower-middle and upper-middle positions and heat the oven to 450 degrees. Set 2 wire racks in 2 aluminum foil–lined rimmed baking sheets and spray the racks with vegetable oil spray.

2. Combine the bread crumbs and buttermilk in a large bowl and let sit, mashing occasionally with a fork, until a smooth paste forms, about 10 minutes. Meanwhile, sprinkle the gelatin over the water in a small bowl and allow to soften for 5 minutes.

3. Mix the ground beef, ground pork, prosciutto, eggs, Parmesan, parsley, garlic, salt, pepper, and gelatin mixture into the bread-crumb mixture using your hands. Pinch off and roll the mixture into 2-inch meatballs (about 40 meatballs total) and arrange on the prepared sheets. Bake until well browned, about 30 minutes, switching and rotating the sheets halfway through baking.

4. FOR THE SAUCE: While the meatballs bake, heat the oil in a Dutch oven over medium heat until shimmering. Add the onion and cook until softened and lightly browned, 5 to 7 minutes. Stir in the garlic, oregano, and red pepper flakes and cook until fragrant, about 30 seconds. Stir in the crushed tomatoes, tomato juice, wine, 1½ teaspoons salt, and ¼ teaspoon pepper, bring to a simmer, and cook until thickened slightly, about 15 minutes.

5. Remove the meatballs from the oven and reduce the oven temperature to 300 degrees. Gently nestle the meatballs into the sauce. Cover, transfer to the oven, and cook until the meatballs are firm and the sauce has thickened, about 1 hour.

6. Meanwhile, bring 10 quarts water to boil in a 12-quart pot. Add the pasta and salt and cook, stirring often, until al dente. Reserve ½ cup of the cooking water, then drain the pasta and return it to the pot.

7. Gently stir the basil and parsley into the sauce and season with sugar, salt, and pepper to taste. Add 2 cups of the sauce (without meatballs) to the pasta and toss to combine, adding the reserved cooking water to adjust the consistency as needed. Serve, topping individual portions with more tomato sauce and several meatballs and passing the Parmesan separately.

SAUSAGE MEATBALLS AND SPAGHETTI

WHY THIS RECIPE WORKS: For a change of pace, we wanted to use Italian sausage to create meatballs that were full of bold flavor but still tender. To temper sausage's springy texture, we added ground pork, brined with baking soda and salt to impart tenderness and help the meat retain juices. A panade made with heavy cream brought more fat into the mix, which would coat the meat's proteins and prevent them from sticking

together. Pulsing the meat mixture in a food processor cut the panade into the meat for even incorporation, and processing the meat in stages kept it from turning tough from overworking. To really highlight the bold, seasoned flavors of Italian sausage, we added a reinforcing dose of the classic spices already present in the meat: coarsely ground fennel seeds, oregano, black pepper, and red pepper flakes. We baked the meatballs in a hot oven to quickly brown them in a single batch. A simple tomato sauce was all we needed to complement the spiced-up sausage meatballs, so we sautéed garlic in oil and added both crushed tomatoes and tomato sauce for bright but smooth results. After a quick simmer, we stirred in fresh basil and added the meatballs to the pot to finish cooking.

Sausage Meatballs and Spaghetti

SERVES 4 TO 6

The fennel seeds can be coarsely ground in a spice grinder or using the bottom of a heavy skillet. Use a light touch when rolling the meatballs to prevent them from being dense. A #30 scoop, loosely filled, works well for portioning the meatballs.

MEATBALLS

- ½ teaspoon salt
- ¼ teaspoon baking soda
- 4 teaspoons water
- 12 ounces ground pork
- 2 slices hearty white sandwich bread, crusts removed, cut into ½-inch pieces
- ⅓ cup heavy cream
- ⅓ cup grated Parmesan cheese, plus extra for serving
- 2 large egg yolks
- 2 garlic cloves, minced
- 1 teaspoon fennel seeds, coarsely ground
- 1 teaspoon dried oregano
- 1 teaspoon pepper
- ½ teaspoon red pepper flakes
- 12 ounces sweet Italian sausage, casings removed and broken into 1-inch pieces

TOMATO SAUCE

- 2 tablespoons extra-virgin olive oil
- 1 garlic clove, minced
- 1 (28-ounce) can crushed tomatoes
- 1 (15-ounce) can tomato sauce
- Salt
- 1 tablespoon chopped fresh basil

- 1 pound spaghetti

1. FOR THE MEATBALLS: Adjust oven rack to upper middle position and heat oven to 500 degrees. Place wire rack in aluminum foil–lined rimmed baking sheet. Spray wire rack with vegetable oil spray.

2. Dissolve salt and baking soda in water in large bowl. Add pork and fold gently to combine; let stand for 10 minutes.

3. Pulse bread, cream, Parmesan, egg yolks, garlic, fennel seeds, oregano, pepper, and pepper flakes in food processor until smooth paste forms, about 10 pulses, scraping down sides of bowl as needed. Add pork mixture (do not wash out bowl) and pulse until mixture is well combined, about 5 pulses.

4. Transfer half of pork mixture to now-empty large bowl. Add sausage to food processor and pulse until just combined, 4 to 5 pulses. Transfer sausage-pork mixture to large bowl with pork mixture. Using your hands, gently fold together until mixture is just combined.

5. With your wet hands, lightly shape mixture into 1¾-inch round meatballs (about 1 ounce each); you should have about 24 meatballs. Arrange meatballs, evenly spaced, on prepared rack and bake until browned, about 15 minutes, rotating sheet halfway through baking.

6. FOR THE TOMATO SAUCE: While meatballs bake, heat oil in Dutch oven over medium heat until shimmering. Add garlic and cook, stirring frequently, until fragrant, about 30 seconds. Stir in crushed tomatoes, tomato sauce, and ¼ teaspoon salt and bring to boil. Reduce heat and simmer gently until slightly thickened, about 10 minutes. Stir in basil and season with salt to taste.

7. Add meatballs to sauce and gently simmer, turning them occasionally, until cooked through, 5 to 10 minutes. Cover and keep warm over low heat.

8. Bring 4 quarts water to boil in large pot. Add pasta and 1 tablespoon salt and cook, stirring often, until al dente. Reserve ½ cup cooking water, then drain pasta and return it to pot.

9. Add ½ cup sauce and ¼ cup reserved cooking water to pasta and toss to combine. Transfer pasta to large serving platter and top with meatballs and remaining sauce, adjusting consistency with remaining reserved cooking water as needed. Serve, passing extra Parmesan separately.

ITALIAN-STYLE TURKEY MEATBALLS

WHY THIS RECIPE WORKS: Our turkey meatballs rival those made from beef or pork, thanks to a few test kitchen tricks. We started with 85 or 93 percent lean turkey; these fattier options produced moister meatballs. Next, we added an egg and fresh bread crumbs to help bind the meatballs. And a stint in the fridge was key to firming up the gelatin and creating juicy texture. To boost meaty flavor, we added glutamate-rich ingredients such as Parmesan cheese, anchovies, tomato paste, and rehydrated dried shiitake mushrooms.

Italian-Style Turkey Meatballs

SERVES 4 TO 6

Serve with spaghetti.

- 1 cup chicken broth
- ½ ounce dried shiitake mushrooms
- 2 slices hearty white sandwich bread, torn into 1-inch pieces
- 1 ounce Parmesan cheese, grated (½ cup), plus extra for serving
- 1 tablespoon chopped fresh parsley
- 1½ teaspoons unflavored gelatin
- Salt and pepper
- 4 anchovy fillets, rinsed, patted dry, and minced
- 1½ pounds 85 or 93 percent lean ground turkey
- 1 large egg, lightly beaten
- 4 garlic cloves, minced
- 1 (14.5-ounce) can whole peeled tomatoes
- ½ teaspoon dried oregano
- ⅛ teaspoon red pepper flakes
- 3 tablespoons extra-virgin olive oil
- 2 tablespoons tomato paste
- ¼ cup chopped fresh basil
- Sugar

1. Microwave broth and mushrooms in covered bowl until steaming, about 1 minute. Let sit until softened, about 5 minutes. Drain mushrooms in fine-mesh strainer and reserve liquid.

2. Pulse bread in food processor until finely ground, 10 to 15 pulses; transfer bread crumbs to large bowl (do not wash processor bowl). Add Parmesan, parsley, gelatin, 1 teaspoon salt, and ¼ teaspoon pepper to bowl with bread crumbs and mix until thoroughly combined. Pulse mushrooms and half of anchovies in food processor until chopped fine, 10 to 15 pulses. Add mushroom mixture, turkey, egg, and half of garlic to bowl with bread-crumb mixture and mix with your hands until thoroughly combined. Divide mixture into 16 portions (about ¼ cup each). Using your hands, roll each portion into ball; transfer meatballs to plate and refrigerate for 15 minutes.

3. Pulse tomatoes and their juice in food processor to coarse puree, 10 to 15 pulses. Combine oregano, pepper flakes, remaining anchovies, remaining garlic, and ¼ teaspoon pepper in small bowl; set aside.

4. Heat oil in 12-inch nonstick skillet over medium-high heat until shimmering. Add meatballs and cook until well browned all over, 5 to 7 minutes. Transfer meatballs to paper towel–lined plate, leaving fat in skillet.

5. Add reserved anchovy mixture to skillet and cook, stirring constantly, until fragrant, about 30 seconds. Increase heat to high; stir in tomato paste, reserved mushroom liquid, and pureed tomatoes; and bring to simmer. Return meatballs to skillet, reduce heat to medium-low, cover, and cook until meatballs register 160 degrees, 12 to 15 minutes, turning meatballs once. Transfer meatballs to platter, increase heat to high, and simmer sauce until slightly thickened, 3 to 5 minutes. Stir in basil and season with sugar, salt, and pepper to taste. Pour sauce over meatballs and serve, passing extra Parmesan separately.

PENNE WITH VODKA SAUCE

WHY THIS RECIPE WORKS: Splashes of vodka and cream can turn run-of-the-mill tomato sauce into luxurious restaurant fare—or a heavy, boozy mistake. Despite the simple ingredients, we found recipes for penne alla vodka gave us results that varied widely. Many were absurdly rich (with more cream than tomatoes) and others were too harsh from a heavy hand with the vodka. We wanted to fine-tune this modern classic to strike the right balance of sweet, tangy, spicy, and creamy.

To achieve a sauce with the right consistency, we pureed half the tomatoes (which helped the sauce cling nicely to the pasta) and cut the rest into chunks. For sweetness, we added sautéed minced onions; for depth of flavor, we used a bit of tomato paste. We found we needed a liberal amount of vodka to cut through the richness and add "zinginess" to the sauce, but we needed to add it to the tomatoes early on to allow the alcohol to mostly (but not completely) cook off and prevent a boozy flavor. Adding a little heavy cream to the sauce gave it a nice consistency, and we finished cooking the penne in the sauce to encourage cohesiveness.

Penne with Vodka Sauce (Penne alla Vodka)

SERVES 4 TO 6

So that the sauce and pasta finish cooking at the same time, drop the pasta into the boiling water just after adding the vodka to the sauce.

- 1 (28-ounce) can whole tomatoes, drained, juice reserved
- 2 tablespoons olive oil
- ½ small onion, minced
- 1 tablespoon tomato paste
- 2 medium garlic cloves, minced or pressed through a garlic press (about 2 teaspoons)
- ¼ teaspoon red pepper flakes
- Table salt
- ⅓ cup vodka
- ½ cup heavy cream
- 1 pound penne
- 2 tablespoons minced fresh basil leaves
- Grated Parmesan cheese, for serving

1. Puree half of the tomatoes in a food processor until smooth. Dice the remaining tomatoes into ½-inch pieces, discarding the cores. Combine the pureed and diced tomatoes in a liquid measuring cup (you should have about 1⅔ cups). Add the reserved juice to equal 2 cups.

2. Heat the oil in a large saucepan over medium heat until shimmering. Add the onion and tomato paste and cook, stirring occasionally, until the onion is light golden around the edges, about 3 minutes. Add the garlic and red pepper flakes; cook, stirring constantly, until fragrant, about 30 seconds.

3. Stir in the tomatoes and ½ teaspoon salt. Remove the pan from the heat and add the vodka. Return the pan to medium-high heat and simmer briskly until the alcohol flavor is cooked off, 8 to 10 minutes; stir frequently and lower the heat to medium if the simmering becomes too vigorous. Stir in the cream and cook until hot, about 1 minute.

4. Meanwhile, bring 4 quarts water to a boil in a large pot. Add 1 tablespoon salt and the pasta to the boiling water. Cook, stirring often, until just shy of al dente. Reserve ½ cup of the cooking water then drain the pasta and return it to the pot. Add the sauce to the pasta and toss over medium heat until the pasta absorbs some of the sauce, 1 to 2 minutes. Adjust the consistency of the sauce with the reserved pasta cooking water as needed. Stir in the basil and season with salt to taste. Serve immediately, passing the Parmesan separately.

FOOLPROOF SPAGHETTI CARBONARA

WHY THIS RECIPE WORKS: This quintessential Roman pasta dish is made with simple ingredients, but the results are often disappointing. The finicky egg-based sauce (made from either whole eggs or just yolks, plus finely grated cheese) relies on the heat of the warm pasta to become lush and glossy, but that rarely happens without the addition of tons of fat. We wanted to make a classic carbonara that was foolproof but not so rich that eating a full serving was impossible.

We started by replacing the hard-to-find *guanciale*, or cured pork jowl, with good old American bacon. To approximate the meaty chew of guanciale, we cooked the bacon with a little water, which produced tender-chewy pieces. We used just a touch of the rendered fat in our sauce for consistent bacon flavor in every bite. To make a richly eggy sauce that wouldn't become dry and clumpy when mixed with the pasta, we used three eggs and an extra yolk for richness. But the real secret here was adding starch in the form of pasta water. Boiling the pasta in half the usual amount of water gave us extra starchy water to coat the proteins and fats in the cheese, preventing them from separating or clumping, making for a perfectly velvety sauce. Tossing the spaghetti with the sauce in a warm serving bowl allowed the warm pasta to gently "cook" the carbonara sauce without overcooking the eggs.

Foolproof Spaghetti Carbonara

SERVES 4

It's important to work quickly in steps 2 and 3. The heat from the cooking water and the hot spaghetti will "cook" the sauce only if used immediately. Warming the mixing and serving bowls helps the sauce stay creamy. Use a high-quality bacon for this dish; our favorites are Farmland Thick Sliced Bacon and Vande Rose Farms Artisan Dry Cured Bacon, Applewood Smoked.

- 8 slices bacon, cut into ½-inch pieces
- ½ cup water
- 3 garlic cloves, minced
- 2½ ounces Pecorino Romano, grated (1¼ cups)
- 3 large eggs plus 1 large yolk
- 1 teaspoon pepper
- 1 pound spaghetti
- 1 teaspoon salt

1. Bring bacon and water to simmer in 10-inch nonstick skillet over medium heat; cook until water evaporates and bacon begins to sizzle, about 8 minutes. Reduce heat to medium-low and continue to cook until fat renders and bacon browns, 5 to 8 minutes longer. Add garlic and cook, stirring constantly, until fragrant, about 30 seconds. Strain bacon mixture through fine-mesh strainer set in bowl. Set aside bacon mixture. Measure out 1 tablespoon fat and place in medium bowl. Whisk Pecorino, eggs and yolk, and pepper into fat until combined.

2. Meanwhile, bring 2 quarts water to boil in Dutch oven. Set colander in large bowl. Add spaghetti and salt to pot; cook, stirring frequently, until al dente. Drain spaghetti in colander set in bowl, reserving cooking water. Pour 1 cup cooking water into liquid measuring cup and discard remainder. Return spaghetti to now-empty bowl.

3. Slowly whisk ½ cup reserved cooking water into Pecorino mixture. Gradually pour Pecorino mixture over spaghetti, tossing to coat. Add bacon mixture and toss to combine. Let spaghetti rest, tossing frequently, until sauce has thickened slightly and coats spaghetti, 2 to 4 minutes, adjusting consistency with remaining reserved cooking water if needed. Serve immediately.

CLASSIC SPAGHETTI ALLA CARBONARA

WHY THIS RECIPE WORKS: Spaghetti carbonara is a mainstay on Italian restaurant menus, but the velvety, bacon-laced sauce can be elusive for the home cook. Three eggs, mixed with a combination of Pecorino-Romano and Parmesan cheeses, made a silky sauce that could cling to the spaghetti. Raw garlic gave the sauce a bit of zing without being overpowering, but we deemed heavy cream an unnecessary addition, since it weighed down the dish and dulled the cheese flavor. In place of the traditional *guanciale* (salt-cured pork jowl), we used American bacon, which we sautéed to give our dish the perfect crunch and a hint of sweetness and smoke. For added brightness, white wine was just the thing. The acidity of the wine cut through the richness of the bacon for a lighter, brighter sauce. We found that the mixing method was key to this dish; mixing the hot spaghetti with the egg and cheese mixture before gently tossing in the crispy pieces of bacon ensured that every bite was perfect.

Classic Spaghetti alla Carbonara

SERVES 4 TO 6

Although we call for spaghetti in this recipe, you can substitute linguine or fettuccine.

- ¼ cup extra-virgin olive oil
- 8 ounces (about 8 slices) bacon, halved lengthwise and cut into ¼-inch pieces
- ½ cup dry white wine
- 3 large eggs
- 1½ ounces Parmesan cheese, grated (about ¾ cup)
- ¼ cup grated Pecorino Romano cheese
- 1 large garlic clove, minced or pressed through a garlic press (about 1½ teaspoons)
- 1 pound spaghetti (see note)
- Table salt and ground black pepper

1. Adjust an oven rack to the lower-middle position, set an ovensafe serving bowl on the rack, and heat the oven to 200 degrees. Bring 4 quarts water to a boil in a large pot.

2. While the water is heating, heat the oil in a large skillet over medium heat until shimmering. Add the bacon and cook, stirring occasionally, until crisp, about 8 minutes. Add the wine and simmer until it is slightly reduced, 6 to 8 minutes. Remove from the heat and cover. Whisk the eggs, cheeses, and garlic together in a small bowl; set aside.

3. When the water comes to a boil, add 1 tablespoon salt and the pasta. Cook, stirring often, until al dente. Reserve ½ cup of the cooking water; drain the pasta. Remove the warm bowl from the oven and add the pasta. Immediately pour the egg and bacon mixtures over the pasta, season with salt and pepper to taste, and toss to coat; adjust the consistency of the sauce with the reserved pasta cooking water as needed. Serve immediately.

FETTUCCINE ALFREDO

WHY THIS RECIPE WORKS: Fettuccine Alfredo—tender pasta bathed in a silky, creamy cheese sauce—always sounds so tempting. But too often, restaurant-style fettuccine Alfredo means gargantuan portions, overcooked pasta, and a sauce that quickly congeals in the bowl (or your stomach). We were after a better Alfredo, with a luxurious sauce that remained supple and velvety from the first bite of pasta to the last. We first discovered that fresh pasta was essential as a base—dried noodles didn't hold on to the sauce, and the delicate nature of fresh pasta brought a more sophisticated tone to the dish. Turning our attention to the sauce, we found that a light hand was necessary when adding two of the richer ingredients: the cheese and the butter. Smaller amounts were sufficient to add distinctive flavor without being overwhelming. To manage the heavy cream, we reduced a portion of it, then added the remaining amount uncooked. This technique produced not only a luxurious texture but also a fresher flavor. A pinch of freshly grated nutmeg added a spicy, sweet undertone to this elegant dish.

Fettuccine Alfredo

SERVES 4 TO 6

Fresh pasta is the best choice for this dish; supermarkets sell 9-ounce containers of fresh pasta in the refrigerated section. When boiling the pasta, undercook it slightly (just shy of al dente) because the pasta cooks an additional minute or two in the sauce just before serving. Note that fettuccine Alfredo must be served immediately; it does not hold or reheat well.

- 1½ cups heavy cream
- 2 tablespoons unsalted butter
- Table salt
- ¼ teaspoon ground black pepper
- 9 ounces fresh fettuccine (see note)
- 1½ ounces Parmesan cheese, grated (about ¾ cup)
- ⅛ teaspoon grated nutmeg

1. Bring 1 cup of the heavy cream and the butter to a simmer in a medium saucepan over medium heat; reduce the heat to low and simmer gently until the mixture reduces to ⅔ cup, 12 to 15 minutes. Off the heat, stir in the remaining ½ cup cream, ½ teaspoon salt, and the pepper.

2. While the cream reduces, bring 4 quarts water to a boil in a large pot. Add 1 tablespoon salt and the pasta to the boiling water and cook, stirring often, until just shy of al dente. Reserve ¼ cup of the cooking water then drain the pasta and return it to the pot.

3. Meanwhile, return the cream mixture to a simmer over medium-high heat; reduce the heat to low and add the pasta, cheese, and nutmeg to the cream mixture. Cook over low heat, tossing the pasta to combine, until the cheese is melted, the sauce coats the pasta, and the pasta is just al dente, 1 to 2 minutes. Stir in the reserved pasta cooking water and toss to coat; the sauce may look thin but will gradually thicken as the pasta is served. Serve immediately.

SEMOLINA GNOCCHI

WHY THIS RECIPE WORKS: Unlike the pillowy dumplings we often associate with gnocchi, Roman-style semolina gnocchi bears a stronger resemblance to polenta. The dough is made from a hearty combination of semolina flour, butter, egg, and cheese. To begin, we whisked flour into hot milk with a touch of woodsy nutmeg. Butter and egg were added to boost the dough's richness. Gruyère added big flavor without watering down the mixture and minced rosemary contributed warm, savory notes. Baking powder promised great lift without compromising the texture. While some traditional recipes stamp out the gnocchi rounds like biscuits, we used a wet measuring cup to portion out the gnocchi onto a tray. Chilling the rounds before baking kept the dumplings from fusing together in the oven.

Semolina Gnocchi (Gnocchi alla Romana)

SERVES 4 TO 6

Serve as a side dish or as a light entrée topped with Quick Tomato Sauce (recipe follows).

- 2½ cups whole milk
- ¾ teaspoon salt
- Pinch ground nutmeg
- 1 cup (6 ounces) fine semolina flour
- 4 tablespoons unsalted butter
- 1 large egg, lightly beaten
- 1½ ounces Gruyère cheese, shredded (⅓ cup)
- 1 teaspoon minced fresh rosemary
- ½ teaspoon baking powder
- 2 tablespoons grated Parmesan cheese

NOTES FROM THE TEST KITCHEN

MAKING SEMOLINA GNOCCHI

By making a very stiff dough and then refrigerating the shaped dumplings before shingling them in the pan, we ensure that they don't fuse together in the oven.

1. Slowly whisk semolina into warm milk mixture. Cook over low heat until stiff dough forms. Add butter, egg, cheese, rosemary, and baking powder.

2. Use moistened ¼ cup measure to portion gnocchi, inverting onto tray.

3. Shingle gnocchi in greased 8-inch square dish, then sprinkle with Parmesan and bake.

1. Adjust oven rack to middle position and heat oven to 400 degrees. Heat milk, salt, and nutmeg in medium saucepan over medium-low heat until bubbles form around edges of saucepan. Whisking constantly, slowly add semolina to milk mixture. Reduce heat to low and cook, stirring often with rubber spatula, until mixture forms stiff mass that pulls away from sides when stirring, 3 to 5 minutes. Remove from heat and let cool for 5 minutes.

2. Stir 3 tablespoons butter and egg into semolina mixture until incorporated. (Mixture will appear separated at first but will become smooth and a bit shiny.) Stir in Gruyère, rosemary, and baking powder until incorporated.

3. Fill small bowl with water. Moisten ¼-cup dry measuring cup with water and scoop even portion of semolina mixture. Invert gnocchi onto tray or large plate. Repeat, moistening measuring cup between scoops to prevent sticking. Place tray of gnocchi, uncovered, in refrigerator for 30 minutes. (Gnocchi can be refrigerated, covered, for up to 24 hours.)

4. Rub interior of 8-inch square baking dish with remaining 1 tablespoon butter. Shingle gnocchi in pan, creating 3 rows of 4 gnocchi each. Sprinkle gnocchi with Parmesan. Bake until tops of gnocchi are golden brown, 35 to 40 minutes. Let cool for 15 minutes before serving.

Quick Tomato Sauce

MAKES ABOUT 3 CUPS

Our favorite brand of crushed tomatoes is SMT.

- 2 tablespoons unsalted butter
- ¼ cup grated onion
- 1 teaspoon minced fresh oregano or ¼ teaspoon dried
- Salt and pepper
- 2 garlic cloves, minced
- 1 (28-ounce) can crushed tomatoes
- ¼ teaspoon sugar
- 2 tablespoons chopped fresh basil
- 1 tablespoon extra-virgin olive oil

Melt butter in medium saucepan over medium heat. Add onion, oregano, and ½ teaspoon salt and cook, stirring occasionally, until onion is softened and lightly browned, 5 to 7 minutes. Stir in garlic and cook until fragrant, about 30 seconds. Stir in tomatoes and sugar, bring to simmer, and cook until slightly thickened, about 10 minutes. Off heat, stir in basil and oil and season with salt and pepper to taste.

POTATO GNOCCHI

WHY THIS RECIPE WORKS: Good potato gnocchi are something of a culinary paradox; light, airy pillows created from dense, starchy ingredients. The method is simple: knead mashed potatoes into a dough with a minimum of flour; shape; and boil for a minute. And yet the potential pitfalls are numerous (lumpy mashed potatoes, too much or too little flour, a heavy hand when kneading, and bland flavor). We wanted a foolproof recipe for impossibly light gnocchi with unmistakable potato flavor. Baking russets (parcooked in the microwave for speed and ease) produced intensely flavored potatoes—an excellent start to our gnocchi base. To avoid lumps, which can cause gnocchi to break apart during cooking, we turned to a ricer for a smooth, supple mash. While many recipes offer a range of flour to use, which ups the chances of overworking the dough (and producing leaden gnocchi), we used an exact amount based on the ratio of potato to flour so that our gnocchi dough was mixed as little as possible. And we found that an egg, while not traditional, tenderized our gnocchi further, delivering delicate pillow-like dumplings.

Potato Gnocchi with Browned Butter and Sage Sauce

SERVES 4

Gnocchi, like many baking recipes, require accurate measurement to achieve the proper texture; it's best to weigh the potatoes and flour. After processing, you may have slightly more than the 3 cups (16 ounces) of potatoes required for this recipe; do not be tempted to use more than 3 cups. If you prefer, replace the browned butter sauce with Gorgonzola-Cream Sauce or Parmesan Sauce with Pancetta and Walnuts (recipes follow).

NOTES FROM THE TEST KITCHEN

MAKING RIDGES ON GNOCCHI

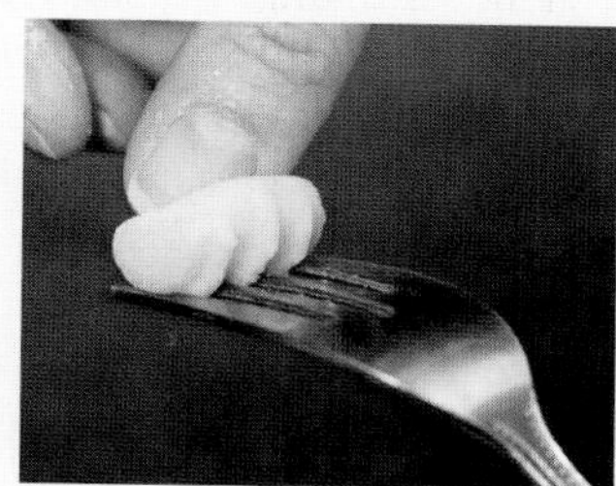

To make ridges on gnocchi, hold a fork with the tines facing down. Press each dough piece (cut side down) against the tines with your thumb to make an indentation. Roll the dumpling down the tines to create ridges on the sides.

POTATO GNOCCHI

- 2 pounds russet potatoes
- 1 large egg, lightly beaten
- ¾ cup plus 1 tablespoon (4 ounces) unbleached all-purpose flour, plus extra for the work surface
- Table salt

BROWNED BUTTER AND SAGE SAUCE

- 4 tablespoons (½ stick) unsalted butter, cut into 4 pieces
- 1 small shallot, minced (about 2 tablespoons)
- 1 teaspoon minced fresh sage leaves
- 1½ teaspoons juice from 1 lemon
- ¼ teaspoon table salt

1. FOR THE GNOCCHI: Adjust an oven rack to the middle position and heat the oven to 450 degrees. Poke each potato 8 times with a paring knife over the entire surface. Place the potatoes on a plate and microwave until slightly softened at the ends, about 10 minutes, flipping the potatoes halfway through cooking. Transfer the potatoes directly to the oven rack and bake until a skewer glides easily through the flesh and the potatoes yield to gentle pressure, 18 to 20 minutes.

2. Hold a potato with a pot holder or kitchen towel and peel with a paring knife. Process the potato through a ricer or food mill onto a rimmed baking sheet. Repeat with the remaining potatoes. Gently spread the riced potatoes into an even layer and cool for 5 minutes.

3. Transfer 3 cups (16 ounces) warm potatoes to a large bowl. Using a fork, gently stir in the egg until just combined. Sprinkle the flour and 1 teaspoon salt over the potato mixture. Using a fork, gently combine until no pockets of dry flour remain. Press the mixture into a rough dough, transfer to a lightly floured work surface and gently knead until smooth but slightly sticky, about 1 minute, lightly dusting the work surface with flour as needed to prevent sticking.

4. Line 2 rimmed baking sheets with parchment paper and dust liberally with flour. Cut the dough into 8 pieces. Lightly dust the work surface with flour. Gently roll one piece of dough into a ½-inch-thick rope, dusting with flour to prevent sticking. Cut the rope into ¾-inch lengths. Following the photo, hold a fork, with the tines facing down, in one hand and press the side of each piece of dough against the ridged surface with your thumb to make an indentation in the center; roll the dough down and off the tines to form ridges. Transfer the formed gnocchi to the prepared sheets and repeat with the remaining dough.

5. FOR THE SAUCE: Melt the butter in a 12-inch skillet over medium-high heat, swirling occasionally, until the butter is browned and releases a nutty aroma, about 1½ minutes. Off the heat, add the shallot and sage, stirring until the shallot is fragrant, about 1 minute. Stir in the lemon juice and the salt and cover to keep warm.

6. Bring 4 quarts water to a boil in a large pot. Add 1 tablespoon salt. Using the parchment paper as a sling, add half of the gnocchi and cook until firm and just cooked through, about 90 seconds (the gnocchi should float to the surface after about 1 minute). Remove the gnocchi with a slotted spoon, transfer to the skillet with the sauce, and cover to keep warm. Repeat with the remaining gnocchi and transfer to the skillet. Gently toss the gnocchi with the sauce to combine, and serve.

Gorgonzola-Cream Sauce

MAKES ABOUT 1 CUP

Adjust the consistency of the sauce with up to 2 tablespoons cooking water before adding the gnocchi to it.

- ¾ cup heavy cream
- ¼ cup dry white wine
- 4 ounces Gorgonzola cheese, crumbled (about 1 cup)
- 2 tablespoons minced fresh chives
- Table salt and ground black pepper

Bring the cream and wine to a simmer in a 12-inch skillet over medium-high heat. Gradually add the Gorgonzola while whisking constantly and cook until melted and the sauce is thickened, 2 to 3 minutes. Stir in the chives and season with salt and pepper to taste. Remove from the heat and cover to keep warm.

Parmesan Sauce with Pancetta and Walnuts

MAKES ABOUT 1 CUP

Serve gnocchi prepared with this sauce with extra grated Parmesan cheese on the side.

- ½ cup low-sodium chicken broth
- 1 ounce Parmesan cheese, grated (about ½ cup)
- ¼ cup heavy cream
- 2 large egg yolks
- ⅛ teaspoon ground black pepper
- 2 teaspoons olive oil
- 3 ounces pancetta, chopped fine
- ½ cup walnuts, chopped coarse
- Table salt

Whisk the broth, Parmesan, cream, yolks, and pepper together in a bowl until smooth. Heat the oil in a 12-inch skillet over medium heat until shimmering. Add the pancetta and cook until crisp, 5 to 7 minutes. Stir in the walnuts and cook until golden and fragrant, about 1 minute. Off the heat, gradually add the broth mixture, whisking constantly. Return the skillet to medium heat and cook, stirring often, until the sauce is thickened slightly, 2 to 4 minutes. Season with salt to taste. Remove from the heat and cover to keep warm.

BAKED CHEESY PASTA CASSEROLE

WHY THIS RECIPE WORKS: We love macaroni and cheese (who doesn't?), but sometimes we want a more sophisticated version than the typical neon orange mac and cheese. Enter the classic Italian iteration of macaroni and cheese, *pasta ai quattro formaggi*, made with four cheeses and heavy cream. We set out to make a four-cheese creamy pasta casserole with great flavor, properly cooked pasta, and a crisp bread-crumb topping.

The cheese was first up for consideration; for the best flavor and texture, we used Italian fontina, Gorgonzola, Pecorino Romano, and Parmesan cheeses. Heating the cheese and cream together made a greasy, curdled mess, so instead we built a basic white sauce (a béchamel) by cooking butter with flour and then adding cream. Combining the hot sauce and pasta with the cheese—and not cooking the cheese in the sauce—preserved the fresh flavor of the different cheeses. Knowing the pasta would spend some time in the oven, we drained it before it was al dente so it wouldn't turn to mush when baked. Topped with bread crumbs and more Parmesan, and baked briefly in a very hot oven, our pasta dinner was silky smooth and rich but not heavy—a grown-up, sophisticated version of macaroni and cheese with Italian flavors.

Creamy Baked Four-Cheese Pasta

SERVES 4 TO 6

To streamline the process, prepare the bread-crumb topping and shred, crumble, and grate the cheeses while you wait for the pasta water to boil.

- 2 slices high-quality white sandwich bread, torn into quarters
- 1 ounce Parmesan cheese, grated (about ½ cup)
- Table salt and ground black pepper
- 4 ounces Italian fontina cheese, rind removed, shredded (about 1 cup)
- 3 ounces Gorgonzola cheese, crumbled (about ¾ cup)
- 1 ounce Pecorino Romano cheese, grated (about ½ cup)
- 1 pound penne
- 2 teaspoons unsalted butter
- 2 teaspoons unbleached all-purpose flour
- 1½ cups heavy cream

1. Pulse the bread in a food processor to coarse crumbs, about 10 to 15 pulses. Transfer to a small bowl. Stir in ¼ cup of the Parmesan, ¼ teaspoon salt, and ⅛ teaspoon pepper; set aside.

2. Adjust an oven rack to the middle position and heat the oven to 500 degrees.

3. Bring 4 quarts water to a boil in a large pot. Combine the remaining ¼ cup Parmesan and the fontina, Gorgonzola, and Pecorino Romano cheeses in a large bowl; set aside. Add 1 tablespoon salt and the pasta to the boiling water and cook, stirring often.

4. While the pasta is cooking, melt the butter in a small saucepan over medium-low heat. Whisk in the flour until no lumps remain, about 30 seconds. Gradually whisk in the cream, increase the heat to medium, and bring to a boil, stirring occasionally; reduce the heat to medium-low and simmer for 1 minute longer. Stir in ¼ teaspoon salt and ¼ teaspoon pepper; cover and set aside.

5. When the pasta is just shy of al dente, drain it, leaving it slightly wet. Add the pasta to the bowl with the cheeses; immediately pour the cream mixture over, then cover the bowl and let stand for 3 minutes. Uncover the bowl and stir with a rubber spatula, scraping the bottom of the bowl, until the cheeses are melted and the mixture is thoroughly combined.

6. Transfer the pasta to a 13 by 9-inch baking dish, then sprinkle evenly with the reserved bread crumbs, pressing down lightly. Bake until the topping is golden brown, about 7 minutes. Serve immediately.

BAKED ZITI

WHY THIS RECIPE WORKS: Most versions of baked ziti seem like they went directly from the pantry into the oven, calling for little more than cooked pasta, jarred tomato sauce, a container of ricotta, and some preshredded cheese. The results: overcooked ziti in a dull, grainy sauce topped with a rubbery mass of mozzarella. We wanted to rescue baked ziti so we could have perfectly al dente pasta, a rich and flavorful sauce, and melted cheese in every bite.

For a sauce that's big on flavor and light on prep, we cooked sautéed garlic with two canned products—diced tomatoes and tomato sauce. Fresh basil and dried oregano added aromatic flavor. Just when the tomato sauce seemed perfect, we added ricotta, and a familiar problem reared its head: Rather than baking up creamy and rich, the ricotta was grainy and dulled the sauce. Cottage cheese was the best choice for a replacement—its curds have a texture similar to ricotta, but are creamier and tangier. For more flavor, we combined the cottage cheese with eggs, Parmesan, and heavy cream thickened with cornstarch. Adding this milky, tangy mixture to the tomato sauce produced a sauce that was bright, rich, and creamy.

When it came to the pasta, we undercooked it and then baked it with a generous amount of sauce for perfectly al dente pasta and plenty of sauce left to keep our baked ziti moist. As for the mozzarella, we cut it into small cubes instead of shredding it, which dotted the finished casserole with gooey bits of cheese.

Baked Ziti

SERVES 8 TO 10

We prefer baked ziti made with heavy cream, but whole milk can be substituted by increasing the amount of cornstarch to 2 teaspoons and increasing the cooking time in step 3 by 1 to 2 minutes. Our preferred brand of mozzarella is Polly-O. Part-skim mozzarella can also be used.

- 1 pound whole-milk or 1 percent cottage cheese
- 2 large eggs, lightly beaten
- 3 ounces Parmesan cheese, grated (about 1½ cups)
- Table salt
- 1 pound ziti or other short tubular pasta
- 2 tablespoons extra-virgin olive oil
- 5 medium garlic cloves, minced or pressed through a garlic press (about 5 teaspoons)
- 1 (28-ounce) can tomato sauce
- 1 (14.5-ounce) can diced tomatoes
- 1 teaspoon dried oregano
- ½ cup plus 2 tablespoons chopped fresh basil leaves
- 1 teaspoon sugar
- Ground black pepper
- ¾ teaspoon cornstarch
- 1 cup heavy cream (see note)
- 8 ounces whole-milk mozzarella cheese, cut into ¼-inch pieces (about 1½ cups; see note)

1. Adjust an oven rack to the middle position and heat the oven to 350 degrees. Whisk the cottage cheese, eggs, and 1 cup of the Parmesan together in a medium bowl; set aside. Bring 4 quarts water to a boil in a large pot. Add 1 tablespoon salt and the pasta; cook, stirring occasionally, until the pasta begins to soften but is not yet cooked through, 5 to 7 minutes. Drain the pasta and leave in the colander (do not wash the pot).

2. Meanwhile, heat the oil and garlic in a 12-inch skillet over medium heat until the garlic is fragrant but not brown, about 2 minutes. Stir in the tomato sauce, diced tomatoes, and oregano; simmer until thickened, about 10 minutes. Off the heat, stir in ½ cup of the basil and the sugar; season with salt and pepper to taste.

3. Stir the cornstarch and heavy cream together in a small bowl; transfer the mixture to the now-empty pasta pot set over medium heat. Bring to a simmer and cook until thickened, 3 to 4 minutes. Remove the pot from the heat and add the cottage cheese mixture, 1 cup of the tomato sauce, and ¾ cup of the mozzarella; stir to combine. Add the pasta and stir to coat thoroughly with the sauce.

4. Transfer the pasta to a 13 by 9-inch baking dish and spread the remaining tomato sauce evenly over the pasta. Sprinkle the remaining ¾ cup mozzarella and remaining ½ cup Parmesan over the top. Cover the baking dish tightly with foil and bake for 30 minutes.

5. Remove the foil and continue to cook until the cheese is bubbling and beginning to brown, about 30 minutes longer. Cool for 20 minutes. Sprinkle with the remaining 2 tablespoons basil and serve.

MANICOTTI

WHY THIS RECIPE WORKS: Despite being composed of a straightforward collection of ingredients (pasta, cheese, and tomato sauce), manicotti is surprisingly fussy to prepare. Blanching, shocking, draining, and stuffing slippery pasta requires a lot of patience and time. We wanted an easy-to-prepare recipe that still produced great-tasting manicotti.

Our biggest challenge was filling the slippery manicotti tubes. We solved the problem by discarding the tubes completely and spreading the filling onto a lasagna noodle, which we then rolled up. For the lasagna noodles, we found that the no-boil variety were ideal. We soaked the noodles in boiling water for 5 minutes until pliable, then used the tip of a knife to separate them and prevent sticking. For the cheese filling, we taste-tested several ricottas and found that part-skim had an ideal level of richness. Eggs, Parmesan, and an ample amount of mozzarella added richness, flavor, and structure to the ricotta filling. For a quick but brightly flavored tomato sauce, we pureed canned diced tomatoes and simmered them until slightly thickened with sautéed garlic and red pepper flakes, then finished the sauce with fresh basil.

Baked Manicotti

SERVES 6 TO 8

We prefer Barilla no-boil lasagna noodles for their delicate texture resembling fresh pasta. Note that Pasta Defino and Ronzoni brands contain only 12 no-boil noodles per package; the recipe requires 16 noodles. The manicotti can be prepared through step 5, covered with a sheet of parchment paper, wrapped in aluminum foil, and refrigerated for up to 3 days or frozen for up to 1 month. (If frozen, thaw the manicotti in the refrigerator for 1 to 2 days.) To bake, remove the parchment, replace the aluminum foil, and increase the baking time to 1 to 1¼ hours.

TOMATO SAUCE

- 2 (28-ounce) cans diced tomatoes
- 2 tablespoons extra-virgin olive oil
- 3 medium garlic cloves, minced or pressed through a garlic press (about 1 tablespoon)
- ½ teaspoon red pepper flakes (optional)
- Table salt
- 2 tablespoons chopped fresh basil leaves

CHEESE FILLING AND PASTA

- 3 cups part-skim ricotta cheese
- 4 ounces Parmesan cheese, grated (about 2 cups)
- 8 ounces whole-milk mozzarella cheese, shredded (about 2 cups)
- 2 large eggs, lightly beaten
- 2 tablespoons chopped fresh parsley leaves
- 2 tablespoons chopped fresh basil leaves
- ¾ teaspoon table salt
- ½ teaspoon ground black pepper
- 16 no-boil lasagna noodles (see note)

1. FOR THE SAUCE: Adjust an oven rack to the middle position and heat the oven to 375 degrees. Pulse 1 can of the tomatoes with their juice in a food processor until coarsely chopped, 3 to 4 pulses. Transfer to a bowl. Repeat with the remaining can of tomatoes.

2. Heat the oil, garlic, and red pepper flakes (if using) in a large saucepan over medium heat until fragrant but not brown, 1 to 2 minutes. Stir in the tomatoes and ½ teaspoon salt and simmer until thickened slightly, about 15 minutes. Stir in the basil; season with salt to taste.

3. FOR THE CHEESE FILLING: Combine the ricotta, 1 cup of the Parmesan, the mozzarella, eggs, parsley, basil, salt, and pepper in a medium bowl; set aside.

4. Pour 2 inches boiling water into a 13 by 9-inch broiler-safe baking dish. Slip the noodles into the water, one at a time, and let them soak until pliable, about 5 minutes, separating them with the tip of a knife to prevent sticking. Remove the noodles from the water and place in a single layer on clean kitchen towels. Discard the water and dry the baking dish.

5. Spread the bottom of the baking dish evenly with 1½ cups of the sauce. Using a spoon, spread ¼ cup of the cheese mixture evenly onto the bottom three-quarters of each noodle (with the short side facing you), leaving the top quarter of the noodle exposed. Roll into a tube shape and arrange in the baking dish, seam side down. Top evenly with the remaining sauce, making certain that the pasta is completely covered.

6. Cover the baking dish tightly with foil and bake until bubbling, about 40 minutes. Remove the baking dish from the oven and remove the foil. Adjust the oven rack to the uppermost position (about 6 inches from the heating element) and heat the broiler. Sprinkle the manicotti evenly with the remaining 1 cup Parmesan. Broil until the cheese is spotty brown, 4 to 6 minutes. Cool for 15 minutes; cut into pieces and serve.

NOTES FROM THE TEST KITCHEN

BAKED MANICOTTI

1. Using spoon, spread about ¼ cup of filling evenly over bottom three-quarters of each noodle, leaving top quarter of noodles exposed.

2. Starting at bottom, roll each noodle up around filling, and lay in prepared baking dish, seam side down.

SIMPLE CHEESE LASAGNA

WHY THIS RECIPE WORKS: While removing both meat and vegetables from lasagna makes it a much simpler affair, it can result in a dish lacking in texture, flavor, and stature. This recipe works by upgrading the basic components—tomato sauce, cheese, and noodles—to star players. Tomato paste, minced anchovies, grated Pecorino Romano, and a dash of sugar boosted the complexity and body of the sauce, while a small can of diced tomatoes added texture to the smoother crushed tomato base. We switched out the usual trio of cheeses for more-flavorful alternatives, replacing ricotta with cottage cheese (mixed into a no-cook sauce with heavy cream, more Pecorino Romano, and seasonings); mozzarella with fontina; and Parmesan with Pecorino Romano. To give the casserole more structure and bite, we used traditional wavy lasagna noodles but treated them like the no-boil variety by briefly soaking them in boiling water. Staggering the noodles in the dish instead of lining them up parallel to one another prevented the casserole from buckling as it baked.

Simple Cheese Lasagna

SERVES 8

Do not substitute no-boil noodles for regular noodles, as they are too thin. Alternating the noodle arrangement in step 4 keeps the lasagna from buckling. For a vegetarian version, omit the anchovies.

CHEESE SAUCE

- 4 ounces Pecorino Romano cheese, grated (2 cups)
- 8 ounces (1 cup) cottage cheese
- ½ cup heavy cream
- 2 garlic cloves, minced
- 1 teaspoon cornstarch
- ¼ teaspoon salt
- ¼ teaspoon pepper

TOMATO SAUCE

- ¼ cup extra-virgin olive oil
- 1 onion, chopped fine
- 1½ teaspoons sugar
- ½ teaspoon red pepper flakes
- ½ teaspoon dried oregano
- ½ teaspoon salt
- 4 garlic cloves, minced
- 8 anchovy fillets, rinsed, patted dry, and minced
- 1 (28-ounce) can crushed tomatoes
- 1 (14.5-ounce) can diced tomatoes, drained
- ¼ cup tomato paste
- 1 ounce Pecorino Romano cheese, grated (½ cup)

LASAGNA

- 14 curly-edged lasagna noodles
- 8 ounces fontina cheese, shredded (2 cups)
- ⅛ teaspoon cornstarch
- ¼ cup grated Pecorino Romano cheese
- 3 tablespoons chopped fresh basil

1. FOR THE CHEESE SAUCE: Whisk all ingredients in bowl until homogeneous. Set aside.

2. FOR THE TOMATO SAUCE: Heat oil in large saucepan over medium heat. Add onion, sugar, pepper flakes, oregano, and salt and cook, stirring frequently, until onions are softened, about 10 minutes. Add garlic and anchovies and cook until fragrant, about 2 minutes. Stir in crushed tomatoes, diced tomatoes, tomato paste, and Pecorino and bring to simmer. Reduce heat to medium-low and simmer until slightly thickened, about 20 minutes.

3. FOR THE LASAGNA: While sauce simmers, lay noodles in 13 by 9-inch baking dish and cover with boiling water. Let noodles soak until pliable, about 15 minutes, separating noodles with tip of paring knife to prevent sticking. Place dish in sink, pour off water, and run cold water over noodles. Pat noodles dry with clean dish towel; dry dish. Cut two noodles in half crosswise.

4. Adjust oven rack to middle position and heat oven to 375 degrees. Spread 1½ cups tomato sauce in bottom of dish. Lay 3 noodles lengthwise in dish with ends touching 1 short side, leaving space on opposite short side. Lay 1 half noodle crosswise in empty space to create even layer of noodles. Spread half of cheese sauce over noodles, followed by ½ cup fontina. Repeat layering of noodles, alternating which short side gets half noodle (alternating sides will prevent lasagna from buckling). Spread 1½ cups tomato sauce over second layer of noodles, followed by ½ cup fontina. Create third layer using 3½ noodles (reversing arrangement again), remaining cheese sauce, and ½ cup fontina.

5. Lay remaining 3½ noodles over cheese sauce. Spread remaining tomato sauce over noodles. Toss remaining ½ cup fontina with cornstarch, then sprinkle over tomato sauce, followed by Pecorino.

6. Spray sheet of aluminum foil with vegetable oil spray and cover lasagna. Bake for 35 minutes. Remove lasagna from oven and increase oven temperature to 500 degrees.

7. Remove foil from lasagna, return to oven, and continue to bake until top is lightly browned, 10 to 15 minutes longer. Let lasagna cool for 20 minutes. Sprinkle with basil, cut into pieces, and serve.

FOUR-CHEESE LASAGNA

WHY THIS RECIPE WORKS: Cheese lasagna offers an elegant alternative to meat-laden, red sauce lasagna. But some cheese lasagna is just heavy and bland, due to the use of plain-tasting cheeses. And even those with good cheese flavor can have soupy, dry, or greasy textures. We wanted a robust cheese lasagna with great structure, creamy texture, and maximum flavor.

For the best cheese flavor, we settled on a combination of fontina, Parmesan, Gorgonzola, and Gruyère cheeses. We found that making the white sauce (a béchamel) with a high ratio of flour to butter created a thick binder that provided enough heft to keep the lasagna layers together. And replacing some of the milk with chicken broth was the key to balancing the richness of the sauce and bringing the cheese flavor forward. But the real secret of a great four-cheese lasagna proved to be a fifth cheese. While ricotta didn't add much flavor, it gave the lasagna body without making the dish heavy and starchy. Our final challenge was to keep the baking time short enough to avoid harming this delicate pasta dish. Both presoaking the no-boil noodles and using a low-heat/high-heat baking method—baking at a moderate temperature and then briefly broiling to brown the top—kept the lasagna from overbaking.

Four-Cheese Lasagna

SERVES 10

It's important not to overbake the lasagna. Once the sauce starts bubbling around the edges, uncover the lasagna and turn the oven to broil. If your lasagna pan is not broiler-safe, brown the lasagna at 500 degrees for about 10 minutes. Whole milk is best in the sauce, but skim and low-fat milk also work. Supermarket-brand cheeses work fine in this recipe. The Gorgonzola may be omitted, but the flavor of the lasagna won't be as complex. We prefer Barilla no-boil lasagna noodles for their delicate texture resembling fresh pasta. Note that Pasta Defino and Ronzoni brands contain only 12 no-boil noodles per package; this recipe requires 15 noodles. This lasagna is very rich; serve small portions with a green salad.

- 6 ounces Gruyère cheese, shredded (about 1½ cups)
- 2 ounces Parmesan cheese, grated (about 1 cup)
- 1½ cups part-skim ricotta cheese
- 1 large egg, lightly beaten
- 2 tablespoons plus 2 teaspoons minced fresh parsley leaves
- ¼ teaspoon ground black pepper
- 3 tablespoons unsalted butter
- 1 medium shallot, minced (about 2 tablespoons)
- 1 medium garlic clove, minced or pressed through a garlic press (about 1 teaspoon)
- ⅓ cup unbleached all-purpose flour
- 2½ cups whole milk (see note)
- 1½ cups low-sodium chicken broth
- ½ teaspoon table salt
- 1 bay leaf
- Pinch cayenne pepper
- 15 no-boil lasagna noodles (see note)
- 8 ounces fontina cheese, rind removed, shredded (about 2 cups)
- 3 ounces Gorgonzola cheese, crumbled fine (about ¾ cup; see note)

1. Place the Gruyère and ½ cup of the Parmesan in a large ovensafe bowl. Combine the ricotta, egg, 2 tablespoons of the parsley, and the black pepper in a medium bowl. Set both bowls aside.

2. Melt the butter in a medium saucepan over medium heat; add the shallot and garlic and cook, stirring frequently, until beginning to soften, about 2 minutes. Add the flour and cook, stirring constantly, until thoroughly combined, about 1½ minutes; the mixture should not brown. Gradually whisk in the milk and broth; increase the heat to medium-high and bring to a full boil, whisking frequently. Add the salt, bay leaf, and cayenne; reduce the heat to medium-low and simmer until the sauce thickens and coats the back of a spoon, about 10 minutes, stirring occasionally with a heatproof rubber spatula or wooden spoon and making sure to scrape the bottom and corners of the saucepan.

3. Remove the saucepan from the heat and discard the bay leaf. Gradually whisk ¼ cup of the sauce into the ricotta mixture. Pour the remaining sauce over the Gruyère mixture and stir until smooth; set aside.

4. Adjust an oven rack to the upper-middle position and heat the oven to 350 degrees. Pour 2 inches boiling water into a 13 by 9-inch broiler-safe baking dish. Slip the noodles into the water, one at a time, and let them soak until pliable, about 5 minutes, separating them with the tip of a knife to prevent sticking. Remove the noodles from the water and place in a single layer on clean kitchen towels. Discard the water, dry the baking dish, and spray lightly with vegetable oil spray.

5. Spread the bottom of the baking dish evenly with ½ cup of the sauce. Place 3 noodles in a single layer on top of the sauce. Spread ½ cup of the ricotta mixture evenly over the noodles and sprinkle evenly with ½ cup of the fontina and 3 tablespoons of the Gorgonzola. Drizzle ½ cup of the sauce evenly over the cheese. Repeat the layering of noodles, ricotta, fontina, Gorgonzola, and sauce three more times. Place the final 3 noodles on top and cover completely with the remaining sauce, spreading with a rubber spatula and allowing it to spill over the noodles. Sprinkle evenly with the remaining ½ cup Parmesan.

6. Spray a large sheet of foil with vegetable oil spray and cover the lasagna; bake until the edges are just bubbling, 25 to 30 minutes, rotating the pan halfway through the baking time. Remove the foil and turn the oven to broil. Broil until the surface is spotty brown, 3 to 5 minutes. Cool for 15 minutes. Sprinkle with the remaining 2 teaspoons parsley; cut into pieces and serve.

GREAT VEGETABLE LASAGNA

WHY THIS RECIPE WORKS: For a complex vegetable lasagna with bold flavor, we started with a summery mix of zucchini, yellow squash, and eggplant, salting and microwaving the eggplant and sautéing all of the vegetables to cut down on excess moisture and deepen their flavor. Garlic, spinach, and olives added textural contrast and flavor without much work. We dialed up the typical cheese filling by switching mild-mannered ricotta for tangy cottage cheese mixed with heavy cream for richness and Parmesan and garlic for added flavor. Our creamy, quick no-cook tomato sauce brought enough moisture to our lasagna that we found that we could skip the usual step of soaking the no-boil noodles before assembling the dish.

Vegetable Lasagna

SERVES 8 TO 10

Part-skim mozzarella can also be used in this recipe, but avoid preshredded cheese, as it does not melt well. We prefer kosher salt because it clings best to the eggplant. If using table salt, reduce salt amounts by half. To make assembly easier, the roasted vegetable filling can be made ahead and stored in the refrigerator for up to one day.

TOMATO SAUCE

- 1 (28-ounce) can crushed tomatoes
- ¼ cup minced fresh basil leaves
- 2 tablespoons extra-virgin olive oil
- 2 medium garlic cloves, minced or pressed through a garlic press (about 2 teaspoons)
- 1 teaspoon kosher salt
- ¼ teaspoon red pepper flakes

CREAM SAUCE

- 8 ounces whole-milk cottage cheese (about 1 cup)
- 1 cup heavy cream
- 4 ounces Parmesan cheese, grated (about 2 cups)
- 2 medium garlic cloves, minced or pressed through a garlic press (about 2 teaspoons)
- 1 teaspoon cornstarch
- ½ teaspoon kosher salt
- ½ teaspoon ground black pepper

VEGETABLE FILLING

- 1½ pounds eggplant, peeled and cut into ½-inch pieces
- Kosher salt and ground black pepper
- 1 pound zucchini, cut into ½-inch pieces
- 1 pound yellow squash, cut into ½-inch pieces
- 5 tablespoons plus 1 teaspoon extra-virgin olive oil
- 4 medium garlic cloves, minced or pressed through a garlic press (about 4 teaspoons)
- 1 tablespoon minced fresh thyme leaves
- 12 ounces baby spinach (12 cups)
- ½ cup pitted kalamata olives, minced
- 12 ounces whole-milk mozzarella cheese, shredded (about 3 cups)

- 12 no-boil lasagna noodles
- 2 tablespoons chopped fresh basil leaves

1. FOR THE TOMATO SAUCE: Whisk all the ingredients together in a bowl; set aside.

2. FOR THE CREAM SAUCE: Whisk all the ingredients together in a separate bowl; set aside.

3. FOR THE FILLING: Adjust an oven rack to the middle position and heat the oven to 375 degrees. Toss the eggplant with 1 teaspoon kosher salt in a large bowl. Line the surface of a large plate with a double layer of coffee filters and lightly spray with vegetable oil spray. Spread the eggplant in an even layer over the coffee filters; wipe out and reserve the bowl. Microwave the eggplant, uncovered, until dry to the touch and slightly shriveled, about 10 minutes, tossing halfway through cooking. Cool slightly. Return the eggplant to the bowl and toss with the zucchini and summer squash.

4. Combine 1 tablespoon of the oil, the garlic, and thyme in a small bowl. Heat 2 tablespoons more oil in a 12-inch nonstick skillet over medium-high heat until shimmering. Add half of the eggplant mixture, ¼ teaspoon kosher salt, and ¼ teaspoon pepper and cook, stirring occasionally, until the vegetables are lightly browned, about 7 minutes. Clear the center of the skillet, add half of the garlic mixture, and cook, mashing with a spatula, until fragrant, about 30 seconds. Stir the garlic mixture into the vegetables and transfer to a medium bowl. Repeat with the remaining eggplant mixture, 2 tablespoons more oil, and the remaining garlic mixture; transfer to the bowl.

5. Heat the remaining 1 teaspoon oil in the now-empty skillet over medium-high heat until shimmering. Add the spinach and cook, stirring frequently, until wilted, about 3 minutes. Transfer the spinach to a paper towel–lined plate and drain for 2 minutes. Stir into the eggplant mixture.

6. Grease a 13 by 9-inch baking dish. Spread 1 cup of the tomato sauce evenly over the bottom of the dish. Arrange 4 noodles on top of the sauce (the noodles will overlap). Spread half of the vegetable mixture over the noodles, followed by half of the olives. Spoon half of the cream sauce over the top and sprinkle with 1 cup of the mozzarella. Repeat the layering with 4 more noodles, 1 cup more tomato sauce, the remaining vegetables, remaining olives, remaining cream sauce and 1 cup more mozzarella. For the final layer, arrange the remaining 4 noodles on top and cover completely with the remaining tomato sauce. Sprinkle with the remaining 1 cup mozzarella.

7. Cover the dish tightly with aluminum foil that has been sprayed with vegetable oil spray and bake until the edges are just bubbling, about 35 minutes, rotating the dish halfway through baking. Cool the lasagna for 25 minutes, then sprinkle with the basil and serve.

LASAGNA WITH MEAT SAUCE

WHY THIS RECIPE WORKS: Traditional meaty lasagna is one of the best comfort foods out there. Unfortunately, this hearty dish takes the better part of a day to make (not very comforting, if you ask us). The noodles must be boiled and the sauce slow-cooked. Then, once the cheese filling is mixed, the ingredients must be carefully layered before the whole thing is baked. We wanted a really good meat lasagna, with all of the rich, hearty meatiness of an all-day lasagna, but ready in a lot less time.

We made a speedy meaty tomato sauce by simmering onion, garlic, and meatloaf mix (a combination of ground beef, pork, and veal) together for about 15 minutes. Adding some heavy cream created a richer, creamier, more cohesive sauce; we stirred in pureed and diced tomatoes for a luxurious, soft sauce with chunks of tomatoes. Using no-boil lasagna noodles eliminated the tedious process of boiling and draining the pasta. For a classic cheese layer, we combined ricotta cheese, Parmesan cheese, fresh basil, and an egg, which helped thicken and bind the mixture; a layer of shredded mozzarella upped the creaminess and cheesiness of the filling. Covering the lasagna with foil before baking helped to soften the noodles; removing it during the last half-hour of baking ensured that the cheeses were properly browned.

Lasagna with Hearty Tomato-Meat Sauce

SERVES 6 TO 8

You can substitute equal amounts of 80 percent lean ground beef, ground veal, and ground pork for the meatloaf mix (the total amount of meat should be 1 pound). The assembled, unbaked lasagna will keep in the freezer for up to 2 months; wrap it tightly with plastic wrap, then foil, before freezing. To bake, defrost it in the refrigerator for up to 2 days and bake as directed, extending the covered baking time by 5 to 10 minutes.

TOMATO-MEAT SAUCE

- 1 tablespoon olive oil
- 1 medium onion, minced
- 6 medium garlic cloves, minced or pressed through a garlic press (about 2 tablespoons)
- 1 pound meatloaf mix (see note)

- ½ teaspoon table salt
- ½ teaspoon ground black pepper
- ¼ cup heavy cream
- 1 (28-ounce) can tomato puree
- 1 (28-ounce) can diced tomatoes, drained

CHEESE FILLING AND PASTA

- 1¾ cups whole-milk or part-skim ricotta cheese
- 2½ ounces Parmesan cheese, grated (about 1¼ cups)
- ½ cup chopped fresh basil leaves
- 1 large egg, lightly beaten
- ½ teaspoon table salt
- ½ teaspoon ground black pepper
- 12 no-boil lasagna noodles
- 1 pound whole-milk mozzarella cheese, shredded (about 4 cups)

1. Adjust an oven rack to the middle position and heat the oven to 375 degrees.

2. FOR THE SAUCE: Heat the oil in a large Dutch oven over medium heat until shimmering. Add the onion and cook, stirring occasionally, until softened but not browned, about 2 minutes. Add the garlic and cook until fragrant, about 2 minutes. Increase the heat to medium-high and add the meatloaf mix, salt, and pepper; cook, breaking the meat into small pieces with a wooden spoon, until the meat loses its raw color but has not browned, about 4 minutes. Add the cream and simmer, stirring occasionally, until the liquid evaporates and only rendered fat remains, about 4 minutes. Add the tomato puree and diced tomatoes and bring to a simmer; reduce the heat to low and simmer until the flavors have blended, about 3 minutes. Set aside. (The cooled sauce can be refrigerated in an airtight container for up to 2 days; reheat before assembling the lasagna.)

3. FOR THE CHEESE FILLING: Combine the ricotta, 1 cup of the Parmesan, the basil, egg, salt, and pepper in a medium bowl; set aside.

4. Spread the bottom of a 13 by 9-inch baking dish evenly with ¼ cup of the meat sauce (avoiding large chunks of meat). Place 3 noodles in a single layer on top of the sauce. Spread each noodle evenly with 3 tablespoons of the ricotta mixture and sprinkle the entire layer evenly with 1 cup of the mozzarella cheese. Spread the cheese evenly with 1½ cups of the meat sauce. Repeat the layering of noodles, ricotta, mozzarella, and sauce two more times. Place the remaining 3 noodles on top of the sauce, spread evenly with the remaining sauce, sprinkle with the remaining 1 cup mozzarella, then sprinkle with the remaining ¼ cup Parmesan. Spray a large sheet of foil with vegetable oil spray and cover the lasagna.

5. Bake for 15 minutes, then remove the foil. Continue to bake until the cheese is spotty brown and the sauce is bubbling, about 25 minutes longer. Cool the lasagna for 10 minutes; cut into pieces and serve.

BEHIND THE SCENES

A FRESH CRUSH IS BEST

We're always looking for ways to make our kitchen work more efficient and will often prep recipes in advance if we know we've got a lot of recipes to get through on a given day. But noticing that garlic can develop a particularly strong odor if minced too far in advance, we decided to run a quick test. We used garlic in three different applications: lightly cooked in Pasta with Garlic and Oil (page 282); raw, when stirred into mayonnaise; and as a subtle flavoring in a vinaigrette. For each recipe, we used freshly minced garlic, garlic that had been minced six hours in advance, and garlic that had been minced the day before. Both the six-hour-old and one-day-old minced garlic were so powerful they overwhelmed the other flavors in the dish.

Turns out, garlic flavor comes from a compound called allicin, which is not formed until after the garlic's cells are ruptured. As soon as you cut into garlic, the allicin will start to build and build until its flavor becomes overwhelmingly strong. So if you're going to prep a recipe in advance, make sure to leave the garlic cloves whole until the last minute.

CHAPTER 13

BRINGING HOME ITALIAN FAVORITES

HOMEMADE RICOTTA CHEESE

WHY THIS RECIPE WORKS: Creamy, milky, and luxuriously rich, fresh ricotta bears little-to-no resemblance to the grainy, clumpy cheese sold in supermarkets. The best part of fresh ricotta, however, is how simple it is to make at home. Using fresh homogenized and pasteurized milk yielded the most reliable results because ultra-pasteurized or ultra-heat-treated (UHT or long-life) milk wouldn't curdle properly. After lining a colander with butter muslin, we set about curdling a gallon of whole milk, heating it in a Dutch oven with salt. Once the milk reached 185 degrees, we took it off the heat and gently added the curdling agents: lemon juice and distilled white vinegar. Stirring gently and then leaving the mixture alone once the curds appeared allowed the ricotta to fully separate from the whey; adding more vinegar drew out any remaining curds from milky whey, if necessary. To finish, we emptied the pot into the colander to drain and then transferred the ricotta to a bowl to break up the curds and incorporate the whey.

Homemade Ricotta Cheese

MAKES ABOUT 2 POUNDS (4 CUPS)

For best results, don't stir the milk too hard, and be very gentle with the curds once they form.

- ⅓ cup lemon juice (2 lemons)
- ¼ cup distilled white vinegar, plus extra as needed
- 1 gallon pasteurized (not ultrapasteurized or UHT) whole milk
- 2 teaspoons salt

1. Line colander with butter muslin or triple layer of cheesecloth and place in sink. Combine lemon juice and vinegar in liquid measuring cup; set aside. Heat milk and salt in Dutch oven over medium-high heat, stirring frequently with rubber spatula to prevent scorching, until milk registers 185 degrees.

2. Remove pot from heat and slowly stir in lemon juice mixture until fully incorporated and mixture curdles, about 15 seconds. Let sit undisturbed until mixture fully separates into solid curds and translucent whey, 5 to 10 minutes. If curds do not fully separate and there is still milky whey in pot, stir in extra vinegar, 1 tablespoon at a time, and let sit another 2 to 3 minutes, until curds separate.

3. Gently pour mixture into prepared colander. Let sit, undisturbed, until whey has drained from edges of cheese but center is still very moist, about 8 minutes. Working quickly, gently transfer cheese to large bowl, retaining as much whey in center of cheese as possible. Stir well to break up large curds and incorporate whey. Refrigerate ricotta until cold, about 2 hours. Stir cheese before using. (Ricotta can be refrigerated for up to 5 days.)

FOCACCIA

WHY THIS RECIPE WORKS: Most of the focaccia we see in the States is heavy, thick, and strewn with pizza-like toppings. We wanted a lighter loaf, airy on the inside and topped with just a smattering of herbs. To start, we focused on flavor. To get the benefits of a long fermentation with minimal effort, many bakers use a "preferment" (also known as a "sponge," "starter," or *biga* in Italian): a mixture of flour, water, and a small amount of yeast that rests (often overnight) before being incorporated into the dough. We followed suit, but the interiors of the loaves weren't as tender and airy as we wanted. We wondered if our stand mixer was developing too much gluten (the strong, elastic network of cross-linked proteins that give bread its crumb structure). Instead we turned to a more gentle approach. In this method, a high hydration level (the weight of the water in relation to the weight of the flour) and a long autolysis (the dough resting process) take advantage of the enzymes naturally present in the wheat to produce the same effect as kneading. This method worked to a point—our loaves were light and airy, but squat. To improve the structure, we turned the dough at regular intervals while it proofed. To cut back on the long proofing time (three hours) and hasten gluten development, we held back the salt when mixing our dough, adding it later. We were able to shave an hour off our proofing time. To give our loaves a crisp crust, we oiled the baking pans and added coarse salt for flavor and an extra crunchy texture. This focaccia was a revelation: crackly crisp on the bottom, deeply browned on top, with an interior that was open and airy.

Rosemary Focaccia

MAKES TWO 9-INCH ROUND LOAVES

If you don't have a baking stone, bake the bread on an overturned, preheated rimmed baking sheet set on the upper-middle oven rack. The bread can be kept for up to 2 days well-wrapped at room temperature or frozen for several months wrapped in foil and placed in a zipper-lock bag.

BIGA

- ½ cup (2½ ounces) unbleached all-purpose flour
- ⅓ cup (2⅔ ounces) warm water (100–110 degrees)
- ¼ teaspoon instant or rapid-rise yeast

DOUGH

- 2½ cups (12½ ounces) unbleached all-purpose flour, plus extra for shaping
- 1¼ cups (10 ounces) warm water (100–110 degrees)
- 1 teaspoon instant or rapid-rise yeast
- Kosher salt
- 4 tablespoons extra-virgin olive oil
- 2 tablespoons chopped fresh rosemary leaves

1. FOR THE BIGA: Combine the flour, water, and yeast in a large bowl and stir with a wooden spoon until a uniform mass forms and no dry flour remains, about 1 minute. Cover the bowl tightly with plastic wrap and let stand at room temperature (about 70 degrees) overnight (at least 8 hours or up to 24 hours). Use immediately or store in the refrigerator for up to 3 days (allow to stand at room temperature for 30 minutes before proceeding with the recipe).

2. FOR THE DOUGH: Stir the flour, water, and yeast into the biga with a wooden spoon until a uniform mass forms and no dry flour remains, about 1 minute. Cover with plastic wrap and let rise at room temperature for 15 minutes.

3. Sprinkle 2 teaspoons salt over the dough; stir into the dough until thoroughly incorporated, about 1 minute. Cover with plastic wrap and let rise at room temperature for 30 minutes. Spray a rubber spatula or bowl scraper with vegetable oil spray; fold the partially risen dough over itself by gently lifting and folding the edge of the dough toward the middle. Turn the bowl 90 degrees; fold again. Turn the bowl and fold the dough six more times (for a total of eight turns). Cover with plastic wrap and let rise for 30 minutes. Repeat the folding, turning, and rising two more times, for a total of three 30-minute rises. Meanwhile, adjust an oven rack to the upper-middle position, place a baking stone on the rack, and heat the oven to 500 degrees, at least 30 minutes before baking.

4. Gently transfer the dough to a lightly floured work surface. Lightly dust the top of the dough with flour and divide it in half. Shape each piece of dough into a 5-inch round by gently tucking under the edges. Coat two 9-inch round cake pans with 2 tablespoons olive oil each. Sprinkle each pan with ½ teaspoon kosher salt. Place a round of dough in one pan, top side down; slide the dough around the pan to coat the bottom and sides, then flip the dough over. Repeat with the second piece of dough in the second pan. Cover the pans with plastic wrap and let rest for 5 minutes.

5. Using your fingertips, press the dough out toward the edges of the pan, taking care not to tear it. (If the dough resists stretching, let it relax for 5 to 10 minutes before trying to stretch it again.) Using a dinner fork, poke the entire surface of the dough 25 to 30 times, popping any large bubbles. Sprinkle the rosemary evenly over the top of the dough. Let the dough rest in the pan until slightly bubbly, 5 to 10 minutes.

NOTES FROM THE TEST KITCHEN

KEY STEPS TO MAKING FOCACCIA

1. Fold the partially risen dough over itself by gently lifting and folding the edge of the dough toward the middle. Turn the bowl 90 degrees; fold again. Turn the bowl and fold dough six more times (for a total of eight turns).

2. Cover with plastic wrap and let rise for 30 minutes. Repeat turning, folding, and rising two more times, for a total of three 30-minute rises.

3. Dust the dough with flour and divide in half. Shape the halves into 5-inch rounds. Place the rounds in the oiled pans and slide around to coat the dough. Flip and repeat. Cover the pans with plastic wrap and let rest for 5 minutes.

4. Using your fingertips, press the dough out toward the edges of the pan, taking care not to tear it. (If the dough resists stretching let it relax for 5 to 10 minutes before trying to stretch it again.)

5. Using a dinner fork, poke the surface of the dough 25 to 30 times. Deflate any remaining bubbles of dough with a fork. Sprinkle the rosemary over the dough. Let rest until slightly bubbly, 5 to 10 minutes, before baking.

6. Place the pans on the baking stone and lower the oven temperature to 450 degrees. Bake until the tops are golden brown, 25 to 28 minutes, switching the placement of the pans halfway through the baking time. Transfer the pans to a wire rack and let cool for 5 minutes. Remove the loaves from the pans and place on the wire rack. Brush the tops with any oil remaining in the pans. Cool for 30 minutes before serving.

NEAPOLITAN-STYLE PIZZA

WHY THIS RECIPE WORKS: Few dishes say "Italian" better than a slice of pizza, especially crisp-crust Neapolitan-style pizza. This style of crust is thinner than traditional parlor-style crusts, shatteringly crisp with a deeply caramelized flavor that bears no trace of raw yeast or flour.

For a pizza dough that came together quickly and easily, we turned to the food processor. Letting the dough rise slowly in the refrigerator overnight made it easier to handle the next day, and it developed good flavor from the slow fermentation. For the thinnest crust possible, we used a rolling pin. A sheet of plastic wrap on top of the dough made rolling easier; we didn't need to add more flour to prevent sticking. A bit of honey in the dough encouraged browning. This slim crust can't handle heavy toppings, nor should it. A thin layer of tomato sauce and a sprinkling of mozzarella pack lots of flavor.

Crisp Thin-Crust Pizza

SERVES 6 TO 8

Note that the pizza dough needs to be started at least 1 day before serving. Keep in mind that it is more important for the rolled dough to be of even thinness than to be a perfect circle. For topping the pizzas, we recommend buying shrink-wrapped mozzarella from the supermarket; do not use fresh because it is too moist and will make the crust soggy. If you don't have a pizza stone, bake the pizza on a rimless or overturned baking sheet that has been preheated just like the pizza stone.

DOUGH

- 1¾–2 cups (8¾ to 10 ounces) unbleached all-purpose flour, plus extra for the work surface
- ½ teaspoon instant or rapid-rise yeast
- ½ teaspoon honey
- ½ teaspoon table salt
- ¼ cup olive oil
- ¾ cup warm water (110 degrees)

TOPPINGS

- 1 cup Quick Tomato Sauce for Pizza (recipe follows)
- 8 ounces whole-milk mozzarella cheese, shredded (about 2 cups; see note)

1. FOR THE DOUGH: Pulse 1¾ cups of the flour, the yeast, honey, and salt in a food processor (fitted with the dough blade, if possible) until combined, about 5 pulses. With the machine running, pour the oil and then the water through the feed tube and process until the dough forms a ball, about 30 seconds. If after 30 seconds the dough is sticky and clings to the blade, add the remaining ¼ cup flour 1 tablespoon at a time. Turn the dough out onto a work surface.

2. Divide the dough in half and place each piece in a gallon-size, heavy-duty zipper-lock bag and seal. Refrigerate overnight or up to 48 hours.

3. TO MAKE THE PIZZA: One hour before baking the pizza, adjust an oven rack to the lowest position, set a pizza stone on the rack, and heat the oven to 500 degrees.

4. Remove the dough from the plastic bags. Set each piece in the center of a lightly floured large sheet of parchment paper. Cover each with two 18-inch lengths of plastic wrap, overlapping them in the center; let the dough rest for 10 minutes.

5. Setting one piece of dough aside, roll the other into a 14-inch round with an even thickness, using the tackiness of the dough against the parchment to help roll it. If the parchment wrinkles, flip the dough sandwich over and smooth the wrinkles with a metal bench scraper.

6. Peel the plastic wrap off the top of the rolled dough. Spread ½ cup of the tomato sauce to the edges of the dough. Sprinkle with 1 cup of the cheese.

7. Slip the dough with the parchment onto a pizza peel or rimless baking sheet. Slide the pizza, parchment and all, onto the hot pizza stone. Bake until a deep golden brown, about 10 minutes. Remove the pizza from the oven with a pizza peel or pull the parchment with the pizza onto a baking sheet. Transfer the pizza to a cutting board, slide the parchment out from under the pizza, and slide it onto a wire rack. Cool for 2 minutes until crisp; slide to a cutting board, cut into wedges, and serve.

8. While the first pizza is baking, repeat steps 5 and 6 to roll and top the second pizza; allow the baking stone to reheat for 15 minutes after baking the first pizza, then repeat step 7 to bake the second pizza.

Quick Tomato Sauce for Pizza

MAKES ABOUT 1½ CUPS

For pizza, you want the smoothest possible sauce. Start with crushed tomatoes and puree them in a food processor before cooking them with the garlic and oil. This recipe makes a bit more sauce than needed to sauce two thin-crust pizzas.

- 1 (14.5-ounce) can crushed tomatoes
- 1 tablespoon olive oil
- 1 medium garlic clove, minced or pressed through a garlic press (about 1 teaspoon)
- Table salt and ground black pepper

1. Process the tomatoes in a food processor until smooth, about 5 pulses.

2. Heat the oil and garlic in a medium saucepan over medium heat until the garlic is fragrant, about 30 seconds. Stir in the tomatoes; bring to a simmer and cook, uncovered, until the sauce thickens, about 15 minutes. Season with salt and pepper to taste.

NEW YORK–STYLE THIN-CRUST PIZZA

WHY THIS RECIPE WORKS: With home ovens that reach only 500 degrees and dough that's difficult to stretch thin, even the savviest cooks can struggle to produce parlor-quality pizza. We were in pursuit of a simple-to-make pizza with a New York–style crust: thin, crisp, and spottily charred on the exterior; tender yet chewy within. High-protein bread flour gave us a chewy, nicely tanned pizza crust and the right ratio of flour to water to yeast gave us dough that was easy to stretch and retained moisture as it baked. We kneaded the dough quickly in a food processor then let it proof in the refrigerator for 24 hours to develop its flavors. After we shaped and topped the pizza, it went onto a blazing hot baking stone to cook. Placing the stone near the top of the oven was a surprising improvement, allowing the top of the pizza to brown as well as the bottom. In minutes we had a pizza with everything in sync: a thoroughly crisp, browned crust with a slightly chewy texture, just like a good parlor slice.

New York–Style Thin-Crust Pizza

SERVES 4 TO 6

If you don't own a baking stone, bake the pizzas on a rimless or overturned baking sheet that has been preheated just like the pizza stone. If you don't own a pizza peel, stretch the dough on a large sheet of lightly floured parchment paper, transfer to a rimless or overturned baking sheet, and slide the pizza with the parchment onto the hot pizza stone. You can shape the second dough round while the first pizza bakes, but don't add the toppings until just before baking. It's important to use ice water in the dough to prevent it from overheating in the food processor. Semolina flour is ideal for dusting the peel; use it in place of bread flour if you have it. The sauce will yield more than needed in the recipe; extra sauce can be refrigerated for up to 1 week or frozen for up to 1 month.

DOUGH

- 3 cups (16½ ounces) bread flour, plus extra for the work surface
- 2 teaspoons sugar
- ½ teaspoon instant or rapid-rise yeast
- 1⅓ cups ice water
- 1 tablespoon vegetable oil
- 1½ teaspoons table salt

SAUCE

- 1 (28-ounce) can whole tomatoes, drained
- 1 tablespoon extra-virgin olive oil
- 2 medium garlic cloves, minced or pressed through a garlic press (about 2 teaspoons)
- 1 teaspoon red wine vinegar
- 1 teaspoon table salt
- 1 teaspoon dried oregano
- ¼ teaspoon ground black pepper

- 1 ounce Parmesan cheese, grated fine (about ½ cup)
- 8 ounces whole-milk mozzarella, shredded (about 2 cups)

1. FOR THE DOUGH: Pulse the flour, sugar, and yeast in a food processor (fitted with the dough blade, if possible) until combined, about 5 pulses. With the food processor running, slowly add the water; process until the dough is just combined and no dry flour remains, about 10 seconds. Let the dough sit for 10 minutes.

NOTES FROM THE TEST KITCHEN

PIZZA TOPPING TIPS

Our New York-Style Thin-Crust Pizza is great with just tomato sauce, shredded mozzarella, and Parmesan, but additional toppings are always an option—provided they're prepared correctly and added judiciously. (An overloaded pie will bake up soggy.) Here are a few guidelines for how to handle different types of toppings:

HEARTY VEGETABLES

Aim for a maximum of 6 ounces per pie, spread out in a single layer. Vegetables such as onions, peppers, and mushrooms should be thinly sliced and lightly sautéed (or microwaved for a minute or two along with a little olive oil) before using.

DELICATE VEGETABLES AND HERBS

Leafy greens and herbs like spinach and basil are best placed beneath the cheese to protect them or added raw to the fully cooked pizza.

MEATS

Proteins (no more than 4 ounces per pie) should be precooked and drained to remove excess fat. We like to poach meats like sausage (broken up into ½-inch chunks), pepperoni, or ground beef for 4 to 5 minutes in a wide skillet along with ¼ cup of water, which helps to render the fat while keeping the meat moist.

2. Add the oil and salt to the dough and process until the dough forms a satiny, sticky ball that clears the sides of the bowl, 30 to 60 seconds. Transfer the dough to a lightly oiled work surface and knead briefly by hand until smooth, about 1 minute. Shape the dough into a tight ball and place in a large, lightly oiled bowl; cover the bowl tightly with plastic wrap and refrigerate for at least 24 hours or up to 3 days.

3. FOR THE SAUCE: Process all the ingredients in the clean bowl of the food processor until smooth, about 30 seconds. Transfer to a bowl and refrigerate until ready to use.

4. TO BAKE THE PIZZA: One hour before baking, adjust an oven rack to the upper-middle position (the rack should be 4 to 5 inches from the broiler), set a baking stone on the rack, and heat the oven to 500 degrees. Transfer the dough to a clean work surface and divide in half. With cupped palms, form each half into a smooth, tight ball. Place the balls of dough on a lightly greased baking sheet, spacing them at least 3 inches apart; cover loosely with greased plastic wrap and let sit for 1 hour.

5. Coat 1 ball of dough generously with flour and place on a well-floured work surface (keep the other ball covered). Use your fingertips to gently flatten the dough into an 8-inch disk, leaving 1 inch of the outer edge slightly thicker than the center. Using your hands, gently stretch the disk into a 12-inch round, working along the edges and giving the disk quarter turns. Transfer the dough to a well-floured pizza peel and stretch into a 13-inch round. Using the back of a spoon or ladle, spread ½ cup of the tomato sauce in a thin layer over the surface of the dough, leaving a ¼-inch border around the edge. Sprinkle ¼ cup of the Parmesan evenly over the sauce, followed by 1 cup of the mozzarella. Slide the pizza carefully onto the baking stone and bake until the crust is well browned and the cheese is bubbly and beginning to brown, 10 to 12 minutes, rotating the pizza halfway through baking. Transfer the pizza to a wire rack and let cool for 5 minutes before slicing and serving. Repeat step 5 to shape, top, and bake the second pizza.

THIN-CRUST WHOLE-WHEAT PIZZA

WHY THIS RECIPE WORKS: For a whole-wheat pizza that was as crisp and chewy as traditional pizza and that offered a good, but not overwhelming, wheat flavor, we used a combination of 60 percent whole-wheat flour and 40 percent bread flour. To ensure that this higher-than-normal ratio of whole-wheat to bread flour still produced a great crust, we increased the hydration, which resulted in better gluten development and chew. To compensate for the added moisture, we employed the broiler to speed the baking process and guarantee a crisp crust and a moist, tender interior. We threw out traditional toppings, which tended to clash with the whole-wheat flavor, and opted for oil- and cream-based sauces and bold ingredients like blue cheese, pesto, and wine-braised onion.

Thin-Crust Whole-Wheat Pizza with Garlic Oil, Three Cheeses, and Basil

MAKES TWO 13-INCH PIZZAS

We recommend King Arthur brand bread flour for this recipe. Some baking stones, especially thinner ones, can crack under the intense heat of the broiler. Our recommended stone, by Old Stone Oven, is fine if you're using this technique. If you use another stone, you might want to check the manufacturer's website for guidance.

DOUGH

- 1½ cups (8¼ ounces) whole-wheat flour
- 1 cup (5½ ounces) bread flour
- 2 teaspoons honey
- ¾ teaspoon instant or rapid-rise yeast
- 1¼ cups ice water
- 2 tablespoons extra-virgin olive oil
- 1¾ teaspoons salt

GARLIC OIL

- ¼ cup extra-virgin olive oil
- 2 garlic cloves, minced
- 2 anchovy fillets, rinsed, patted dry, and minced (optional)
- ½ teaspoon pepper
- ½ teaspoon dried oregano
- ⅛ teaspoon red pepper flakes
- ⅛ teaspoon salt

- 1 cup fresh basil leaves
- 1 ounce Pecorino Romano cheese, grated (½ cup)
- 8 ounces whole-milk mozzarella cheese, shredded (2 cups)
- 6 ounces (¾ cup) whole-milk ricotta cheese

1. FOR THE DOUGH: Process whole-wheat flour, bread flour, honey, and yeast in food processor until combined, about 2 seconds. With processor running, add water and process until dough is just combined and no dry flour remains, about 10 seconds. Let dough stand for 10 minutes.

2. Add oil and salt to dough and process until it forms satiny, sticky ball that clears sides of workbowl, 45 to 60 seconds. Remove from bowl and knead on oiled countertop until smooth, about 1 minute. Shape dough into tight ball and place in large, lightly oiled bowl. Cover tightly with plastic wrap and refrigerate for at least 18 hours or up to 2 days.

3. FOR THE GARLIC OIL: Heat oil in 8-inch skillet over medium-low heat until shimmering. Add garlic; anchovies, if using; pepper; oregano; pepper flakes; and salt. Cook, stirring constantly, until fragrant, about 30 seconds. Transfer to bowl and let cool completely before using.

4. One hour before baking pizza, adjust oven rack 4½ inches from broiler element, set pizza stone on rack, and heat oven to 500 degrees. Divide dough in half. Shape each half into smooth, tight ball. Place balls on lightly oiled baking sheet, spacing them at least 3 inches apart. Cover loosely with plastic coated with vegetable oil spray; let stand for 1 hour.

5. Heat broiler for 10 minutes. Meanwhile, coat 1 ball of dough generously with flour and place on well-floured countertop. Using your fingertips, gently flatten into 8-inch disk, leaving 1 inch of outer edge slightly thicker than center. Lift edge of dough and, using back of your hands and knuckles, gently stretch disk into 12-inch round, working along edges and giving disk quarter turns as you stretch. Transfer dough to well-floured peel and stretch into 13-inch round. Using back of spoon, spread half of garlic oil over surface of dough, leaving ¼-inch border. Layer ½ cup basil leaves over pizza. Sprinkle with ¼ cup Pecorino, followed by 1 cup mozzarella. Slide pizza carefully onto stone and return oven to 500 degrees. Bake until crust is well browned and cheese is bubbly and partially browned, 8 to 10 minutes, rotating pizza halfway through baking. Remove pizza and place on wire rack. Dollop half of ricotta over surface of pizza. Let pizza rest for 5 minutes, slice, and serve.

6. Heat broiler for 10 minutes. Repeat process of stretching, topping, and baking with remaining dough and toppings, returning oven to 500 degrees when pizza is placed on stone.

Thin-Crust Whole-Wheat Pizza with Pesto and Goat Cheese

Process 2 cups basil leaves, 7 tablespoons extra-virgin olive oil, ¼ cup pine nuts, 3 minced garlic cloves, and ½ teaspoon salt in food processor until smooth, about 1 minute. Stir in ¼ cup finely grated Parmesan or Pecorino Romano and season with salt and pepper to taste. Substitute pesto for garlic oil. In step 5, omit basil leaves, Pecorino Romano, mozzarella, and ricotta. Top pizza with ½ cup crumbled goat cheese before baking.

Thin-Crust Whole-Wheat Pizza with Wine-Braised Onion and Blue Cheese

Bring 1 onion, halved through root end and sliced ⅛ inch thick, 1½ cups water, ¾ cup dry red wine, 3 tablespoons sugar, and ¼ teaspoon salt to simmer over medium-high heat in 10-inch skillet. Reduce heat to medium and simmer, stirring often, until liquid evaporates and onion is crisp-tender, about 30 minutes. Stir in 2 teaspoons red wine vinegar, transfer to bowl, and let cool completely before using. In step 5, omit garlic oil, basil leaves, Pecorino Romano, mozzarella, and ricotta. Spread ⅓ cup crème fraîche over each dough round. Top each with half of onion mixture, ½ cup coarsely chopped walnuts, and ½ cup crumbled blue cheese before baking. After letting pizza rest, top each with 2 tablespoons shredded fresh basil.

DEEP-DISH PIZZA

WHY THIS RECIPE WORKS: Unlike its thin-crust cousin, deep-dish pizza has a soft, chewy, thick crust and can stand up to substantial toppings. We wanted to try our hand at making this restaurant-style pizza at home. We were after a recipe that didn't require a lot of fuss and tasted better than takeout. Most of the allure of deep-dish pizza is in the crust, so it was important to get it right. After trying numerous ingredients and techniques, we discovered that a boiled potato gave the crust exactly the right qualities: It was soft and moist, yet with a bit of chew and good structure. The potato even made the unbaked dough easier to handle. To keep the outside of the crust from toughening during baking, we added a generous amount of olive oil to the pan before putting in the dough. Topping the pizza before it went into the oven weighed down the crust so that it didn't rise much, so we baked the crust untopped for a few minutes first. Our deep-dish crust wasn't just a platform for the topping; it had great flavor and texture of its own.

Deep-Dish Pizza with Tomatoes, Mozzarella, and Basil

SERVES 4

Prepare the topping while the dough is rising so the two will be ready at the same time. Baking the pizza in a deep-dish pan on a hot pizza stone will help produce a crisp, well-browned bottom crust. If you don't have a pizza stone, use an overturned or heavy rimless baking sheet. The amount of oil used to grease the pan may seem excessive, but it helps brown the crust while also preventing sticking. If you don't have a 14-inch deep-dish pizza pan, use two 10-inch cake pans. Grease them with 2 tablespoons oil each; divide the pizza dough in half and pat each half into a 9-inch round. Use shrink-wrapped supermarket cheese rather than fresh mozzarella.

DOUGH

- 1 medium russet potato (about 9 ounces), peeled and quartered
- 3¼–3½ cups (16¼ to 17½ ounces) unbleached all-purpose flour
- 1¾ teaspoons table salt
- 1½ teaspoons instant or rapid-rise yeast
- 6 tablespoons olive oil, plus extra for oiling the bowl (see note)
- 1 cup warm water (110 degrees)

TOPPING

- 1½ pounds plum tomatoes (5 to 6 medium), cored, seeded, and cut into 1-inch pieces
- 2 medium garlic cloves, minced or pressed through a garlic press (about 2 teaspoons)
- Table salt and ground black pepper
- 6 ounces whole-milk mozzarella cheese, shredded (about 1½ cups; see note)
- 1¼ ounces Parmesan cheese, grated (about ⅔ cup)
- 3 tablespoons shredded fresh basil leaves

1. FOR THE DOUGH: Bring 4 cups water and the potato to a boil in a small saucepan over medium-high heat; cook until tender, 10 to 15 minutes. Drain and cool until the potato can be handled; press the potato through the fine disk of a potato ricer or grate it on the large holes of a box grater. Measure 1⅓ cups lightly packed potato; discard the remaining potato.

2. Process 3¼ cups of the flour, the potato, salt and yeast in a food processor (fitted with the dough blade, if possible) until combined, about 5 seconds. With the motor running, pour 2 tablespoons of the oil and then the water through the feed tube and process until the dough comes together in a ball, about 30 seconds. If after 30 seconds the dough is sticky and clings to the blade, add the remaining ¼ cup flour 1 tablespoon at a time. Lightly coat a medium bowl with oil. Transfer the dough to the bowl; cover tightly with plastic wrap and set in a warm spot until doubled in volume, 1½ to 2 hours.

3. FOR THE TOPPING: Meanwhile, mix the tomatoes and garlic together in a medium bowl; season with salt and pepper to taste and set aside.

4. Oil the bottom of a 14-inch deep-dish pizza pan with the remaining 4 tablespoons olive oil. Remove the dough from the oven and gently punch it down; turn the dough onto a clean, dry work surface and pat it into a 12-inch round. Transfer the round to the oiled pan, cover with plastic wrap, and let rest until the dough no longer resists shaping, about 10 minutes.

5. Adjust the oven racks to the lowest and top positions, set a pizza stone on the lower rack, and heat the oven to 500 degrees. Uncover the dough and pull it into the edges and up the sides of the pan to form a 1-inch-high lip. Cover with plastic wrap; let rise in a warm, draft-free spot until doubled in size, about 30 minutes. Uncover the dough and prick it generously with a fork. Reduce the oven temperature to 425 degrees, place the pan with the pizza on the hot pizza stone, and bake until dry and lightly browned, about 15 minutes. Add the tomato mixture, followed by the mozzarella, then the Parmesan. Bake the pizza on the stone or baking sheet until the cheese melts, 10 to 15 minutes (5 to 10 minutes for 10-inch pizzas). Move the pizza to the top rack and bake until the cheese is spotty golden brown, about 5 minutes longer. Cool for 5 minutes, then, holding the pizza pan at an angle with a potholder, use a wide spatula to slide the pizza from the pan to a cutting board, cut into wedges, and serve.

CHICAGO DEEP-DISH PIZZA

WHY THIS RECIPE WORKS: Recipes for Chicago-style deep-dish pizzas—the kind with crusts like buttery pastries you can only get in Chicago pizzerias—are staunchly protected by the people who make them. We would have to invent our own recipe for the best deep-dish pizza Chicago has to offer: one that boasts a thick, crisp crust with an airy, flaky interior, and a rich taste that can hold its own under any kind of topping.

The recipes we came across in our research sounded a lot like classic pizza dough, with cornmeal added for crunch and butter for tenderness and flavor. These crusts weren't bad, but they weren't as flaky as a Chicago-made crust. To increase the flakiness factor, we turned to laminating. This baking term refers to the layering of butter and dough to create ultra-flaky pastries through a sequence of rolling and folding. A combination of adding melted butter to the dough and spreading the rolled out dough with softened butter before folding it did the trick. This crust was a huge improvement. Our only additional tweak was adding oil to each pan to crisp the edges.

With our crust all set, we turned to the toppings. Following Chicago tradition, we covered the dough with freshly shredded mozzarella and then topped the cheese with our thick, quick-to-make tomato sauce. The cheese formed a consistent barrier between the crust and our sauce, which prevented our thick, flavorful crust from turning soggy.

Chicago-Style Deep-Dish Pizza

MAKES TWO 9-INCH PIZZAS

You will need a stand mixer with a dough hook for this recipe. Place a damp kitchen towel under the mixer and watch it at all times during kneading to prevent it from wobbling off the counter. Handle the dough with slightly oiled hands to prevent sticking. The test kitchen prefers Polly-O Mozzarella; part-skim mozzarella can also be used, but avoid preshredded cheese here. Our preferred brand of crushed tomatoes is SMT. Grate the onion on the large holes of a box grater.

DOUGH

- 3¼ cups (16¼ ounces) unbleached all-purpose flour
- ½ cup (2¾ ounces) yellow cornmeal
- 2¼ teaspoons (about 1 envelope) instant or rapid-rise yeast
- 2 teaspoons sugar
- 1½ teaspoons table salt
- 1¼ cups water, room temperature
- 3 tablespoons unsalted butter, melted, plus 4 tablespoons, softened
- 1 teaspoon plus 4 tablespoons olive oil

SAUCE

- 2 tablespoons unsalted butter
- ¼ cup grated onion (see note)
- ¼ teaspoon dried oregano
- Table salt and ground black pepper

- 2 medium garlic cloves, minced or pressed through a garlic press (about 2 teaspoons)
- 1 (28-ounce) can crushed tomatoes (see note)
- ¼ teaspoon sugar
- 2 tablespoons chopped fresh basil
- 1 tablespoon extra-virgin olive oil

TOPPINGS

- 1 pound mozzarella, shredded (about 4 cups; see note)
- ¼ cup grated Parmesan cheese

1. FOR THE DOUGH: Mix the flour, cornmeal, yeast, sugar, and salt in the bowl of a stand mixer fitted with the dough hook on low speed until incorporated, about 1 minute. Add the water and melted butter and mix on low speed until fully combined, 1 to 2 minutes, scraping the sides and bottom of the bowl as needed. Increase the speed to medium and knead until the dough is glossy and smooth and pulls away from sides of the bowl, 4 to 5 minutes. (The dough will only pull away from the sides while the mixer is on. When the mixer is off, the dough will fall back to the sides.)

2. Using your fingers, coat a large bowl with 1 teaspoon of the olive oil, rubbing excess oil from your fingers onto the blade of a rubber spatula. Using the oiled spatula, transfer the dough to the oiled bowl, turning once to oil the top. Cover the bowl tightly with plastic wrap. Let the dough rise at room temperature until nearly doubled in volume, 45 to 60 minutes.

3. FOR THE SAUCE: While the dough rises, heat the butter in a medium saucepan over medium heat until melted. Add the onion, oregano, and ½ teaspoon salt and cook, stirring occasionally, until the liquid has evaporated and the onion is golden brown, about 5 minutes. Add the garlic and cook until fragrant, about 30 seconds. Stir in the tomatoes and sugar, increase the heat to high, and bring to a simmer. Lower the heat to medium-low and simmer until the sauce has reduced to 2½ cups, 25 to 30 minutes. Off the heat, stir in the basil and oil, then season with salt and pepper to taste.

4. TO LAMINATE THE DOUGH: Adjust an oven rack to the lowest position and heat the oven to 425 degrees. Using a rubber spatula, turn the dough out onto a dry work surface and roll into a 15 by 12-inch rectangle. Following the photos, use an offset spatula to spread the softened butter over the surface of the dough, leaving a ½-inch border along the edges. Starting at the short end, roll the dough into a tight cylinder. With the seam side down, flatten the cylinder into an 18 by 4-inch rectangle. Cut the rectangle in half crosswise. Working with one half, fold the dough into thirds like a business letter, then pinch the seams together to form a ball. Repeat with the remaining half of the dough. Return the dough balls to the oiled bowl, cover tightly with plastic wrap, and let rise in the refrigerator until nearly doubled in volume, 40 to 50 minutes.

5. Coat two 9-inch round cake pans with 2 tablespoons olive oil each. Transfer one dough ball to a dry work surface and roll out into a 13-inch disk about ¼ inch thick. Transfer the dough round to a cake pan by rolling the dough loosely around the rolling pin, then unrolling the dough into the pan. Lightly press the dough into the pan, working it into the corners and 1 inch up the sides. If the dough resists stretching, let it relax for 5 minutes before trying again. Repeat with the remaining dough ball.

6. For each pizza, sprinkle 2 cups of the mozzarella evenly over the surface of the dough. Spread 1¼ cups of the tomato sauce over the cheese and sprinkle 2 tablespoons of the Parmesan over the sauce for each pizza. Bake until the crust is golden brown, 20 to 30 minutes. Remove the pizza from the oven and let rest for 10 minutes before slicing and serving.

NOTES FROM THE TEST KITCHEN

MAKING CHICAGO DEEP-DISH PIZZA CRUST

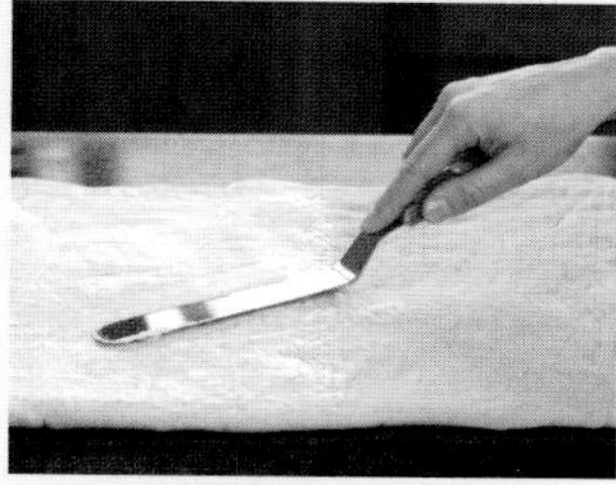

1. After rolling out the dough into a 15 by 12-inch rectangle, spread the softened butter over the dough, leaving a ½-inch border along the edges.

2. Roll the dough into a tight cylinder, starting at the short end closest to you.

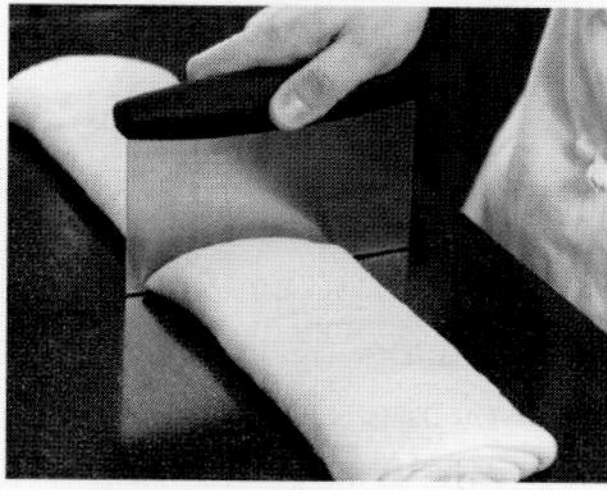

3. Flatten the dough cylinder into an 18 by 4-inch rectangle, then halve the cylinder crosswise.

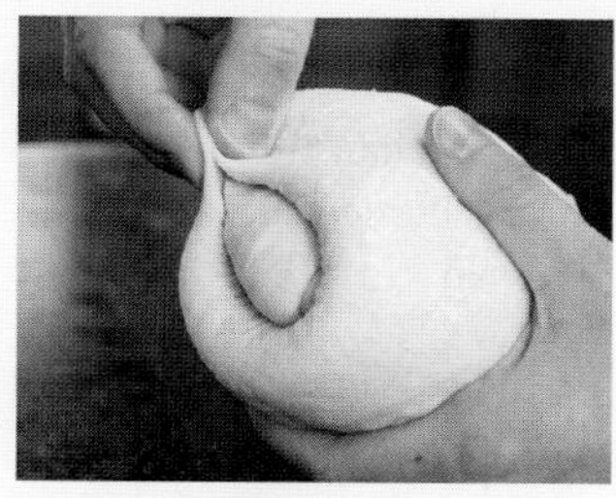

4. Fold each dough half into thirds to form a ball, pinch the seams shut, and let the dough balls rise in the refrigerator for 40 to 50 minutes.

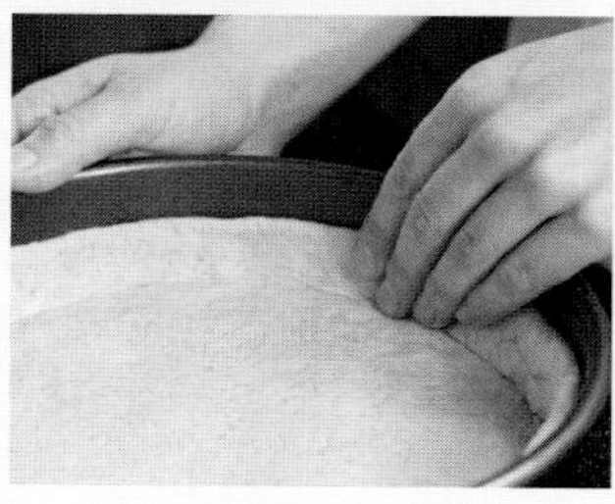

5. After rolling each ball of dough into a 13-inch disk about ¼ inch thick, transfer the dough disks to the oiled pans and lightly press the dough into the pans, working it into the corners and up the sides.

THICK-CRUST SICILIAN-STYLE PIZZA

WHY THIS RECIPE WORKS: Unlike the thin pies you can get at any pizza parlor in town, Sicilian-style pizza boasts a thick crust with a tight, even crumb and a delicately crisp underside. To replicate that golden crust in our own kitchen, we created a dough with all-purpose and semolina flours, the latter contributing the distinct yellow color and cake-like crumb. We took things slowly, adding ice water and 3 tablespoons of olive oil for a tender texture, then letting the dough rest before adding salt and kneading and shaping it into a ball. Letting the dough proof for 24 hours under plastic wrap in the refrigerator helped create flavor: The cold kept carbon dioxide from forming bubbles while the extended fermentation period allowed an array of flavor compounds to form. To ensure bubbles didn't form during the second proof, we rolled the dough out with a rolling pin, moved it onto a rimmed baking sheet, and covered it with plastic wrap and a second baking sheet. Before baking, we topped the compressed dough with a boldly seasoned, slow-cooked homemade tomato sauce and a blend of gooey mozzarella and salty, sharp Parmesan.

Thick-Crust Sicilian-Style Pizza

SERVES 6 TO 8

This recipe requires refrigerating the dough for at least 24 hours before shaping it. King Arthur all-purpose flour and Bob's Red Mill semolina flour work best in this recipe. It is important to use ice water in the dough to prevent overheating during mixing. Anchovies give the sauce depth without a discernible fishy taste; if you decide not to use them, add an additional 1/4 teaspoon of salt.

DOUGH

- 2¼ cups (11¼ ounces) all-purpose flour
- 2 cups (12 ounces) semolina flour
- 1 teaspoon sugar
- 1 teaspoon instant or rapid-rise yeast
- 1⅔ cups (13⅓ ounces) ice water
- 3 tablespoons extra-virgin olive oil
- 2¼ teaspoons salt

SAUCE

- 1 (28-ounce) can whole peeled tomatoes, drained
- 2 teaspoons sugar
- ¼ teaspoon salt
- ¼ cup extra-virgin olive oil
- 3 garlic cloves, minced
- 1 tablespoon tomato paste
- 3 anchovy fillets, rinsed, patted dry, and minced
- 1 teaspoon dried oregano
- ¼ teaspoon red pepper flakes

PIZZA

- ¼ cup extra-virgin olive oil
- 2 ounces Parmesan cheese, grated (1 cup)
- 12 ounces whole-milk mozzarella, shredded (3 cups)

1. **FOR THE DOUGH:** Using stand mixer fitted with dough hook, mix all-purpose flour, semolina flour, sugar, and yeast on low speed until combined, about 10 seconds. With machine running, slowly add water and oil until dough forms and no dry flour remains, 1 to 2 minutes. Cover with plastic wrap and let dough stand for 10 minutes.

2. Add salt to dough and mix on medium speed until dough forms satiny, sticky ball that clears sides of bowl, 6 to 8 minutes. Remove dough from bowl and knead briefly on lightly floured counter until smooth, about 1 minute. Shape dough into tight ball and place in large, lightly oiled bowl. Cover tightly with plastic wrap and refrigerate for at least 24 hours or up to 2 days.

3. **FOR THE SAUCE:** Process tomatoes, sugar, and salt in food processor until smooth, about 30 seconds. Heat oil and garlic in medium saucepan over medium-low heat, stirring occasionally, until garlic is fragrant and just beginning to brown, about 2 minutes. Add tomato paste, anchovies, oregano, and pepper flakes and cook until fragrant, about 30 seconds. Add tomato mixture and cook, stirring occasionally, until sauce measures 2 cups, 25 to 30 minutes. Transfer to bowl, let cool, and refrigerate until needed.

4. **FOR THE PIZZA:** One hour before baking pizza, place baking stone on upper-middle rack and heat oven to 500 degrees. Spray rimmed baking sheet (including rim) with vegetable oil spray, then coat bottom of a second baking sheet with oil.

Remove dough from refrigerator and transfer to lightly floured counter. Lightly flour top of dough and gently press into 12 by 9-inch rectangle. Using rolling pin, roll dough into 18 by 13-inch rectangle. Transfer dough to prepared baking sheet, fitting dough into corners. Spray top of dough with oil spray and lay sheet of plastic wrap over dough. Place second baking sheet on dough and let stand for 1 hour.

5. Remove top baking sheet and plastic wrap. Gently stretch and lift dough to fill pan. Using back of spoon or ladle, spread sauce in even layer over surface of dough, leaving ½-inch border. Sprinkle Parmesan evenly over entire surface of dough to edges followed by mozzarella.

6. Place pizza on stone; reduce oven temperature to 450 degrees and bake until bottom crust is evenly browned and cheese is bubbly and browned, 20 to 25 minutes, rotating pizza halfway through baking. Remove pan from oven and let cool on wire rack for 5 minutes. Run knife around rim of pan to loosen pizza. Transfer pizza to cutting board, cut into squares, and serve.

THE BEST GLUTEN-FREE PIZZA

WHY THIS RECIPE WORKS: Gluten-free pizza crusts are often either dense and doughy or cracker-crunchy. We wanted a gluten-free pizza crust that could hold its own against any wheat-flour crust, with a crispy exterior, a tender interior, and just enough chew. First, we developed a gluten-free flour blend that mimicked many of the properties of wheat flour. To imitate the strength and structure that gluten provides in wheat flour, we used a small amount of ground psyllium husk. To create a tender, airy crumb, we significantly increased the water in the dough and added a generous amount of baking powder. We also added a small amount of ground almond flour to introduce richness and increase crispiness without leaving the crust greasy. Since the added water made our dough sticky, we treated it like a batter and spread it onto a baking sheet with the help of a greased spatula. To ensure that the exterior of the crust didn't dry out before the interior had cooked through, we gently parbaked the crust at low heat before adding the toppings.

NOTES FROM THE TEST KITCHEN

SHAPING GLUTEN-FREE PIZZA DOUGH

Most traditional pizza dough requires a 60 percent hydration level, but gluten-free dough prepared with this ratio will be too stiff. We more than double the hydration—to 133 percent—for a gluten-free dough that can stretch and rise. But because it is so wet, it can't be shaped like traditional dough.

1. Drop batter onto parchment-lined baking sheet, then spread it into rough circle with rubber spatula. Spritz dough with vegetable oil spray.

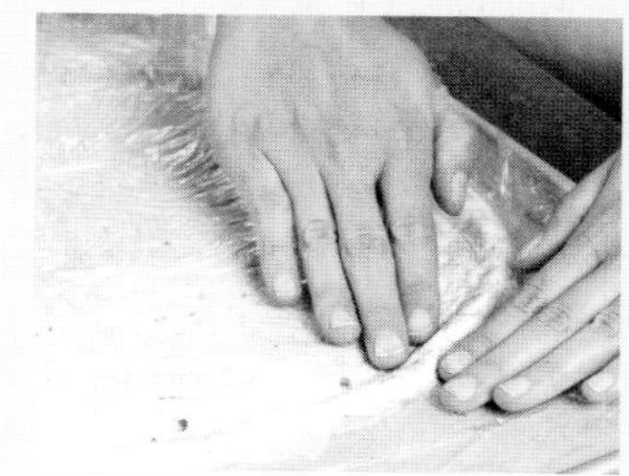

2. Cover with plastic wrap and press into even round with raised edge. To avoid gummy results, prebake crust, then top and bake to finish.

The Best Gluten-Free Pizza

MAKES TWO 12-INCH PIZZAS

This recipe requires letting the dough rise for 1½ hours and prebaking the crusts for about 45 minutes before topping and baking. If you don't have almond flour, you can process 2½ ounces of blanched almonds in a food processor until finely ground, about 30 seconds. Psyllium husk is available at natural foods stores. You can substitute 16 ounces (2⅔ cups plus ¼ cup) King Arthur Gluten-Free Multi-Purpose Flour or 16 ounces (2⅔ cup plus ½ cup) Bob's Red Mill GF All-Purpose Baking Flour for the America's Test Kitchen Gluten-Free Flour Blend. Note that pizza crust made with King Arthur will be slightly denser and not as chewy, and pizza crust made with Bob's Red Mill will be thicker and more airy and will have a distinct bean flavor.

CRUST

- 16 ounces (3⅓ cups plus ¼ cup) The America's Test Kitchen Gluten-Free Flour Blend (recipe follows)
- 2½ ounces (½ cup plus 1 tablespoon) almond flour
- 1½ tablespoons powdered psyllium husk
- 2½ teaspoons baking powder
- 2 teaspoons salt
- 1 teaspoon instant or rapid-rise yeast
- 2½ cups warm water (100 degrees)
- ¼ cup vegetable oil
- Vegetable oil spray

SAUCE

- 1 (28-ounce) can whole peeled tomatoes, drained
- 1 tablespoon extra-virgin olive oil
- 1 teaspoon red wine vinegar
- 1 garlic clove, minced
- 1 teaspoon dried oregano
- ½ teaspoon salt
- ¼ teaspoon pepper

- 1 ounce Parmesan cheese, grated fine (½ cup)
- 8 ounces whole-milk mozzarella cheese, shredded (2 cups)

1. FOR THE CRUST: Using stand mixer fitted with paddle, mix flour blend, almond flour, psyllium, baking powder, salt, and yeast on low speed until combined. Slowly add warm water and oil in steady stream until incorporated. Increase speed to medium and beat until dough is sticky and uniform, about 6 minutes. (Dough will resemble thick batter.)

2. Remove bowl from mixer, cover with plastic wrap, and let stand until inside of dough is bubbly (use spoon to peer inside dough), about 1½ hours. (Dough will puff slightly but will not rise.)

3. Adjust oven racks to middle and lower positions. Line 2 rimmed baking sheets with parchment paper and spray liberally with oil spray. Transfer half of dough to center of 1 prepared sheet. Using oil-sprayed rubber spatula, spread dough into 8-inch circle. Spray top of dough with oil spray, cover with large sheet of plastic, and, using your hands, press out dough to 11½-inch round, about ¼ inch thick, leaving outer ¼ inch slightly thicker than center; discard plastic. Repeat with remaining dough and second prepared sheet.

4. Place prepared sheets in oven and heat oven to 325 degrees. Bake dough until firm to touch, golden brown on underside, and just beginning to brown on top, 45 to 50 minutes, switching and rotating sheets halfway through baking. Transfer crusts to wire rack and let cool.

5. FOR THE SAUCE: Process all ingredients in food processor until smooth, about 30 seconds. Transfer to bowl and refrigerate until ready to use.

6. One hour before baking pizza, adjust oven rack to upper-middle position, set baking stone on rack, and heat oven to 500 degrees.

7. Transfer 1 parbaked crust to pizza peel. Using back of spoon or ladle, spread ½ cup tomato sauce in thin layer over surface of crust, leaving ¼-inch border around edge. Sprinkle ¼ cup Parmesan evenly over sauce, followed by 1 cup mozzarella. Carefully slide crust onto stone and bake until crust is well browned and cheese is bubbly and beginning to brown, 10 to 12 minutes. Transfer pizza to wire rack and let cool for 5 minutes before slicing and serving. Repeat with second crust, ½ cup tomato sauce (you will have extra sauce), remaining ¼ cup Parmesan, and remaining 1 cup mozzarella.

TO MAKE AHEAD: Extra sauce can be refrigerated for up to 1 week or frozen for up to 1 month. Parbaked and cooled crusts can sit at room temperature for up to 4 hours. Completely cooled crusts can be wrapped with plastic wrap and then aluminum foil and frozen for up to 2 weeks. Frozen crusts can be topped and baked as directed without thawing.

The America's Test Kitchen Gluten-Free Flour Blend

MAKES 42 OUNCES (ABOUT 9⅓ CUPS)

Be sure to use potato starch, not potato flour, with this recipe. Tapioca starch is also sold as tapioca flour; they are interchangeable. We strongly recommend that you use Bob's Red Mill white and brown rice flours. We also recommend that you weigh your ingredients; if you measure by volume, spoon each ingredient into the measuring cup (do not pack or tap) and scrape off the excess.

- 24 ounces (4½ cups plus ⅓ cup) white rice flour
- 7½ ounces (1⅔ cups) brown rice flour
- 7 ounces (1⅓ cups) potato starch
- 3 ounces (¾ cup) tapioca starch
- ¾ ounce (¼ cup) nonfat dry milk powder

Whisk all ingredients in large bowl until well combined. Transfer to airtight container and refrigerate for up to 3 months.

PEPPERONI PAN PIZZA

WHY THIS RECIPE WORKS: Great pan pizza—named for the pan in which the dough rises and is cooked—has an irresistible crust that's crisp on the bottom and soft and chewy in the middle. A generous amount of oil poured into the pan creates the crisp bottom; getting the soft interior is harder to figure out. We found the secret in a novel ingredient: skim milk. Milk is often used in tender yeast breads, and when we tried it in our pan pizza dough, we got a tender crust with just the right chew. Whole milk worked fine as well, but dough made with skim milk rose better and baked up especially soft and light. Just a few teaspoons of sugar gave the yeast a jump start and improved the flavor of the dough. Rising the dough in a warmed oven sped up the process to just 30 minutes. We were determined to top our pizza with the quintessential pepperoni, but when just plopped on the pizza and baked, the pepperoni floated in pools of orange grease. We tried frying it, but this made it too crisp and turned it an ugly shade of brown. The solution was to use the microwave to render the excess fat before baking. Topped with chewy, spicy pepperoni, mozzarella, and a quick, fresh tomato sauce (and ready in just 90 minutes), this pizza beat delivery hands down.

Pepperoni Pan Pizza

MAKES TWO 9-INCH PIZZAS

DOUGH

- ½ cup olive oil
- ¾ cup skim milk plus 2 additional tablespoons, warmed to 110 degrees
- 2 teaspoons sugar
- 2⅓ cups (11⅝ ounces) unbleached all-purpose flour, plus extra for the work surface
- 1 envelope instant yeast
- ½ teaspoon table salt

TOPPING

- 1 (3.5-ounce) package sliced pepperoni
- 1½ cups Quick Tomato Sauce for Pizza (page 336)
- 12 ounces shredded part-skim mozzarella cheese (about 3 cups)

NOTES FROM THE TEST KITCHEN

PAN PIZZA DOUGH WITHOUT A MIXER

In step 2 of Pepperoni Pan Pizza, mix the flour, yeast, and salt together in a large bowl. Make a well in the flour, then pour the milk mixture into the well. Using a wooden spoon, stir until the dough becomes shaggy and difficult to stir. Turn out onto a heavily floured work surface and knead, incorporating any shaggy scraps. Knead until the dough is smooth, about 10 minutes. Shape into a ball and proceed with recipe as directed.

1. TO MAKE THE DOUGH: Adjust an oven rack to the lowest position and heat the oven to 200 degrees. When the oven reaches 200 degrees, turn it off. Lightly coat a large bowl with vegetable oil spray. Coat each of two 9-inch cake pans with 3 tablespoons of the oil.

2. Mix the milk, sugar, and remaining 2 tablespoons oil in a measuring cup. Mix the flour, yeast, and salt in a stand mixer fitted with the dough hook. Turn the machine to low and slowly add the milk mixture. After the dough comes together, increase the speed to medium-low and mix until the dough is shiny and smooth, about 5 minutes. Turn the dough onto a lightly floured work surface, gently shape into a ball, and place in the greased bowl. Cover with plastic wrap and place in the warm oven until doubled in size, about 30 minutes.

3. TO SHAPE AND TOP THE DOUGH: Transfer the dough to a lightly floured work surface, divide it in half, and lightly roll each half into a ball. Working with 1 dough ball at a time, roll and shape the dough into a 9½-inch round and press into the oiled pans. Cover with plastic wrap and set in a warm spot (not in the oven) until puffy and slightly risen, about 20 minutes. Meanwhile, heat the oven to 400 degrees.

4. While the dough rises, put half of the pepperoni in a single layer on a microwave-safe plate lined with 2 paper towels. Cover with 2 more paper towels and microwave on high for 30 seconds. Discard the towels and set the pepperoni aside; repeat with new paper towels and the remaining pepperoni.

5. Remove the plastic wrap from the dough. Ladle ¾ cup of the sauce on each round, leaving a ½-inch border around the edges. Sprinkle each with 1½ cups of the cheese and top with the pepperoni. Bake until the cheese is melted and the pepperoni is browning around the edges, about 20 minutes. Remove from the oven; let the pizzas rest in the pans for 1 minute. Using a spatula, transfer the pizzas to a cutting board and cut each into 8 wedges. Serve.

PIZZA BIANCA

WHY THIS RECIPE WORKS: The Roman version of pizza has a crust like no other we've ever tasted: crisp but extraordinarily chewy. It's so good on its own that it is usually topped with just olive oil, rosemary, and kosher salt. We wanted to figure out how we could enjoy this marvel without taking a trip to Italy.

This pizza dough contains significantly more water than other styles, which is the secret to its chewy texture. But extra-wet doughs require more kneading, and we wanted to make this dish at home in a reasonable amount of time. Instead of a long knead, we let the dough rest for 20 minutes, which let us get away with just 10 minutes of kneading. After an initial rise, the dough was still sticky; we couldn't roll it out, but it was easy to pour out then press onto a baking sheet. After letting the dough rest briefly, we baked the crust, adding just kosher salt, oil, and rosemary to remain true to the authentic version.

Pizza Bianca

SERVES 6 TO 8

Serve the pizza by itself as a snack, or with soup or salad as a light entrée. Once the dough has been placed in the oiled bowl, it can be transferred to the refrigerator and kept for up to 24 hours. Bring the dough to room temperature, 2 to 2½ hours, before proceeding with step 4 of the recipe. While kneading the dough on high speed, the mixer tends to wobble and walk on the countertop. Place a towel or shelf liner under the mixer and watch it at all times while mixing. Handle the dough with lightly oiled hands. Resist flouring your fingers or the dough might stick further. This recipe was developed using an 18 by 13-inch baking sheet. Smaller baking sheets can be used, but because the pizza will be thicker, baking times will be longer. If you don't have a pizza stone, bake the pizza on a rimless or overturned baking sheet that has been preheated just like the pizza stone.

- 3 cups (15 ounces) unbleached all-purpose flour
- 1⅔ cups water, at room temperature
- 1¼ teaspoons table salt
- 1½ teaspoons instant or rapid-rise yeast
- 1¼ teaspoons sugar
- 5 tablespoons extra-virgin olive oil
- 1 teaspoon kosher salt
- 2 tablespoons whole fresh rosemary leaves

1. Mix the flour, water, and table salt in the bowl of a stand mixer fitted with the dough hook on low speed until no areas of dry flour remain, 3 to 4 minutes, occasionally scraping down the sides of the bowl. Turn off the mixer and let the dough rest for 20 minutes.

2. Sprinkle the yeast and sugar over the dough. Knead on low speed until fully combined, 1 to 2 minutes, occasionally scraping down the sides of the bowl. Increase the mixer speed to high and knead until the dough is glossy and smooth and pulls away from the sides of the bowl, 6 to 10 minutes. (The dough will pull away from the sides only while the mixer is on. When the mixer is off, the dough will fall back to the sides.)

3. Using your fingers, coat a large bowl with 1 tablespoon of the oil, rubbing the excess oil from your fingers onto the blade of a rubber spatula. Using the oiled spatula, transfer the dough to the bowl and pour 1 tablespoon more oil over the top. Flip the dough over once so that it is well coated with the oil; cover tightly with plastic wrap. Let the dough rise at room temperature until nearly tripled in volume and large bubbles have formed, 2 to 2½ hours.

4. One hour before baking the pizza, adjust an oven rack to the middle position, place a pizza stone on the rack, and heat the oven to 450 degrees.

5. Coat a rimmed baking sheet with 2 tablespoons more oil. Using a rubber spatula, turn the dough out onto the baking sheet along with any oil in the bowl. Using your fingertips, press the dough out toward the edges of the baking sheet, taking care not to tear it. (The dough will not fit snugly into corners. If the dough resists stretching, let it relax for 5 to 10 minutes before trying to stretch it again.) Let the dough rest until slightly bubbly, 5 to 10 minutes. Using a dinner fork, poke the surface of the dough 30 to 40 times and sprinkle with the kosher salt.

6. Bake until golden brown, 20 to 30 minutes, sprinkling the rosemary over the top and rotating the baking sheet halfway through baking. Using a metal spatula, transfer the pizza to a cutting board. Brush the dough lightly with the remaining 1 tablespoon oil. Slice and serve immediately.

SIMPLER GRILLED PIZZA

WHY THIS RECIPE WORKS: Most homemade versions of this restaurant classic disappoint with charred crusts and sauce and cheese that drip onto the coals. We set out to find the secret to great grilled pizza at home.

Regular pizza dough stuck to the cooking grate and burned easily. We found that the dough has to be both thinner and sturdier to work on the grill. We used high-protein bread flour to strengthen the dough, and adding water made it easier to stretch. The crust also needed more flavor to stand up to the heat of the fire, so we added extra salt, a little whole wheat flour, and some olive oil. The oil in the dough also kept the crust from sticking to the cooking grate. Salted chopped tomatoes rather than sauce and a mixture of soft fontina (which has more flavor than mozzarella) and nutty Parmesan made a flavorful but light topping that didn't weigh down the crust or make it soggy. Spicy garlic oil and a scattering of fresh basil added complexity without heaviness. Full of flavor and with a cracker-crisp crust, these grilled pizzas are as good as any we've had in a restaurant.

Grilled Tomato and Cheese Pizza

MAKES FOUR 9-INCH PIZZAS, SERVING 4 TO 6

The pizzas cook very quickly on the grill, so before you begin, be sure to have all the equipment and ingredients you need at hand. Equipment includes a pizza peel (or baking sheet), a pair of tongs, a paring knife, a large cutting board, and a pastry brush. Ingredients includes all the toppings and a small bowl of flour for dusting. The pizzas are best served hot off the grill but can be kept warm for 20 to 30 minutes on a wire rack in a 200-degree oven.

DOUGH

- 1 cup water, room temperature
- 2 tablespoons olive oil
- 2 cups (11 ounces) bread flour
- 1 tablespoon whole-wheat flour (optional)
- 2 teaspoons sugar
- 1¼ teaspoons salt
- 1 teaspoon instant or rapid-rise yeast

TOPPING

- 1½ pounds plum tomatoes, cored, seeded, and cut into ½-inch pieces
- ¾ teaspoon salt
- 6 ounces fontina cheese, shredded (1½ cups)
- 1½ ounces Parmesan cheese, grated fine (¾ cup)
- 1 recipe Spicy Garlic Oil (recipe follows)
- ½ cup chopped fresh basil
- Kosher salt

1. FOR THE DOUGH: Combine water and 2 tablespoons oil in liquid measuring cup. Pulse 1¾ cup bread flour, whole wheat flour, if using, sugar, salt, and yeast in food processor (fitted with dough blade if possible) until combined, about 5 pulses. With food processor running, slowly add water mixture; process until dough forms ball, about 1½ minutes. (If after 1½ minutes dough is sticky and clings to blade, add remaining ¼ cup flour 1 tablespoon at a time.) Transfer dough to large, lightly greased bowl; cover tightly with plastic wrap and let rise at room temperature until doubled in size, 1½ to 2 hours.

2. Gently press down on center of dough to deflate. Transfer dough to clean counter and divide into 4 equal pieces. With cupped palms, form each piece into smooth, tight ball. Set dough balls on well-floured counter. Press dough rounds by hand to flatten; cover loosely with plastic and let rest for 15 minutes.

3. FOR THE TOPPING: Meanwhile, toss tomatoes and salt in bowl; transfer to colander and drain for 30 minutes (wipe out and reserve bowl). Shake colander to drain off excess liquid; transfer tomatoes to now-empty bowl and set aside. Combine fontina and Parmesan in second bowl and set aside.

4. Gently stretch 1 dough round (keep other rounds covered) into disk about ½ inch thick and 5 to 6 inches in diameter. Roll disk out to ⅛-inch thickness, 9 to 10 inches in diameter, on well-floured sheet of parchment paper, dusting with additional flour as needed to prevent sticking. (If dough shrinks when rolled out, cover with plastic and let rest until relaxed, 10 to 15 minutes.) Dust surface of rolled dough with flour and set aside. Repeat with remaining dough rounds, stacking sheets of rolled dough on top of each other (with parchment in between) and covering stack with plastic; set aside until grill is ready.

5A. FOR A CHARCOAL GRILL: Open bottom vent completely. Light large chimney starter filled with charcoal briquettes (6 quarts). When top coals are partially covered with ash, pour evenly over three-quarters of grill. Set cooking grate in place, cover, and open lid vent completely. Heat grill until hot, about 5 minutes.

5B. FOR A GAS GRILL: Turn all burners to high, cover, and heat grill until hot, about 15 minutes. Leave primary burner on high and turn off other burner(s).

6. Clean and oil cooking grate. Lightly flour pizza peel or baking sheet; invert 1 dough round onto peel, gently stretching it as needed to retain its shape (do not stretch dough too thin; thin spots will burn quickly). Peel off and discard parchment; carefully slide round onto hotter side of grill. Immediately repeat with another dough round. Cook (covered if using gas) until tops are covered with bubbles (pierce larger bubbles with paring knife) and bottoms are grill-marked and charred in spots, 1 to 4 minutes; while rounds cook, check undersides and slide to cooler area of grill if browning too quickly. Transfer crusts to cutting board, browned sides up. Repeat with 2 remaining dough rounds.

7. Brush 2 crusts generously with garlic oil; top each evenly with one-quarter of cheese mixture and one-quarter of tomatoes. Return pizzas to hotter side of grill and cover grill with lid; cook until bottoms are well browned and cheese is melted, 2 to 6 minutes, checking bottoms frequently to prevent burning. Transfer pizzas to cutting board; repeat with remaining 2 crusts. Sprinkle pizzas with basil and season with salt to taste; cut into wedges and serve.

Spicy Garlic Oil

MAKES ENOUGH FOR 4 PIZZAS

- ⅓ cup extra-virgin olive oil
- 4 medium garlic cloves, minced or pressed through a garlic press (about 4 teaspoons)
- ½–¾ teaspoon red pepper flakes

Cook all the ingredients in a small saucepan over medium heat, stirring occasionally, until the garlic begins to sizzle, 2 to 3 minutes. Transfer to a small bowl.

ULTIMATE GRILLED PIZZA

WHY THIS RECIPE WORKS: We let the food processor do the work making the dough for our grilled pizza, before letting it proof for at least 24 hours in the refrigerator to develop complex flavor. To ensure that the dough cooked up thin, we used a tiny amount of yeast to reduce air bubbles and a relatively high percentage of water that made a relatively slack dough that easily stretched. Stretching the dough on a generously oiled baking sheet prevented it from sticking to our hands and the grill and also helped the exterior fry and crisp. To ensure that the toppings cooked quickly on a grill, we preheated the sauce and used a combination of fast-melting fresh mozzarella and finely grated Parmesan; we also sprinkled the Parmesan evenly over the dough to create a flavorful barrier against moisture before dolloping (rather than slathering on) the sauce and scattering chunks of cheese, all of which helped maintain the dough's crisp texture. To prevent a hotspot at the center that would burn the crust, we placed the coals only around the perimeter of the grill rather than in an even layer.

Ultimate Grilled Pizza

SERVES 4 TO 6

The dough must sit for at least 24 hours before shaping. We prefer the high protein content of King Arthur bread flour for this recipe, though other bread flours are acceptable. For best results, weigh your ingredients. It's important to use ice water in the dough to prevent it from overheating in the food processor. Grilled pizza cooks quickly, so it's critical to have all of your ingredients and tools ready ahead of time. We recommend pargrilling, topping, and grilling in quick succession and serving the pizzas one at a time, rather than all at once.

DOUGH

- 3 cups (16½ ounces) King Arthur bread flour
- 1 tablespoon sugar
- ¼ teaspoon instant or rapid-rise yeast
- 1¼ cups plus 2 tablespoons ice water (11 ounces)
- Vegetable oil
- 1½ teaspoons salt

SAUCE

- 1 (14-ounce) can whole peeled plum tomatoes, drained, juice reserved
- 2 tablespoons extra-virgin olive oil
- 2 teaspoons minced fresh oregano
- ¼ teaspoon red pepper flakes
- Salt
- Sugar

PIZZA

- Extra-virgin olive oil
- 3 ounces Parmesan cheese, grated (1½ cups)
- 8 ounces fresh whole-milk mozzarella cheese, torn into grape-size pieces (about 2 cups)
- 3 tablespoons shredded fresh basil
- Coarse sea salt

1. FOR THE DOUGH: Process flour, sugar, and yeast in food processor until combined, about 2 seconds. With processor running, slowly add ice water; process until dough is just combined and no dry flour remains, about 10 seconds. Let dough stand for 10 minutes.

2. Add 1 tablespoon oil and salt to dough and process until dough forms satiny, sticky ball that clears sides of bowl, 30 to 60 seconds. Transfer dough to lightly oiled counter and knead until smooth, about 1 minute. Divide dough into 3 equal pieces (about 9⅓ ounces each). Shape each piece into tight ball and transfer to well-oiled baking sheet (alternatively, place dough balls in individual well-oiled bowls). Cover tightly with plastic wrap (taking care not to compress dough) and refrigerate for at least 24 hours or up to 3 days.

3. FOR THE SAUCE: Pulse tomatoes in food processor until finely chopped, 12 to 15 pulses. Transfer to medium bowl and stir in oil, oregano, pepper flakes, reserved juice, ½ teaspoon salt, and ½ teaspoon sugar. Season with additional salt and sugar to taste, cover, and refrigerate until ready to use.

4. One hour before cooking pizza, remove tray of dough from refrigerator and let stand at room temperature.

5A. FOR A CHARCOAL GRILL: Open bottom vent halfway. Light large chimney starter three-quarters filled with charcoal briquettes (4½ quarts). When top coals are partially covered with ash, pour into ring around perimeter of grill, leaving 8-inch clearing in center. Set cooking grate in place, cover, and open lid vent halfway. Heat grill until hot, about 5 minutes.

5B. FOR A GAS GRILL: Turn all burners to high, cover, and heat grill until hot, about 15 minutes. Leave all burners on high.

6. While grill is heating, place sauce in small saucepan and bring to simmer over medium heat. Cover and keep warm.

7. FOR THE PIZZA: Clean and oil cooking grate. Pour ¼ cup oil onto center of rimmed baking sheet. Transfer 1 dough round to sheet and coat both sides of dough with oil. Using your fingertips and palms, gently press and stretch dough toward edges of sheet to form rough 16 by 12-inch oval of even thickness. Using both of your hands, lift dough and carefully transfer to grill. (When transferring dough from sheet to grill, it will droop slightly to form half-moon or snowshoe shape.) Cook (over clearing if using charcoal and covered if using gas) until grill marks form, 2 to 3 minutes. Using tongs and spatula, carefully peel dough from grill grates, then rotate dough 90 degrees and continue to cook (covered if using gas) until second set of grill marks appears, 2 to 3 minutes longer. Flip dough and cook (covered if using gas) until second side of dough is lightly charred in spots, 2 to 3 minutes. Using tongs or pizza peel, transfer crust to cutting board, inverting so side that was grilled first is facing down. Repeat with remaining 2 dough rounds, adding 1 tablespoon oil to baking sheet for each round and keeping grill cover closed when not in use to retain heat.

8. Drizzle top of 1 crust with 1 tablespoon oil. Sprinkle one-third of Parmesan evenly over surface. Arrange one-third of mozzarella pieces, evenly spaced, on surface of pizza. Dollop one-third of sauce in evenly spaced 1-tablespoon mounds over surface of pizza. Using pizza peel or overturned rimmed baking sheet, transfer pizza to grill, cover, and cook until bottom is well browned and mozzarella is melted, 3 to 5 minutes, checking bottom and turning frequently to prevent burning. Transfer pizza to cutting board; repeat with remaining 2 crusts. Sprinkle pizzas with basil, drizzle lightly with oil, and season with salt to taste. Cut into wedges and serve.

NOTES FROM THE TEST KITCHEN

DON'T SKIMP ON THE OIL

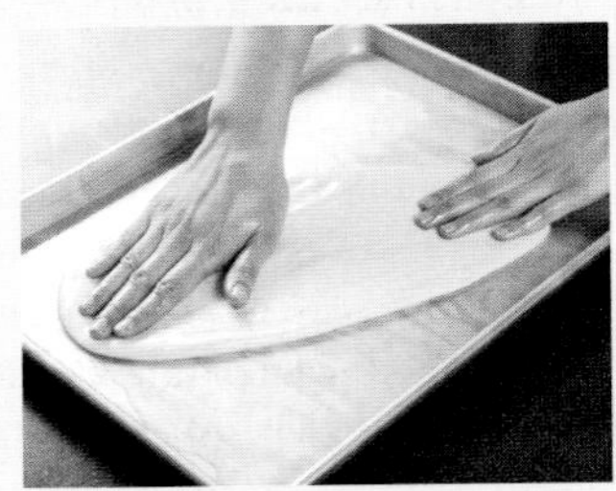

Stretching the dough in a generous amount of olive oil not only prevents it from sticking to your hands and to the cooking grate but also crisps the exterior without rendering it greasy.

NOTES FROM THE TEST KITCHEN

PREPARING TOMATO TART

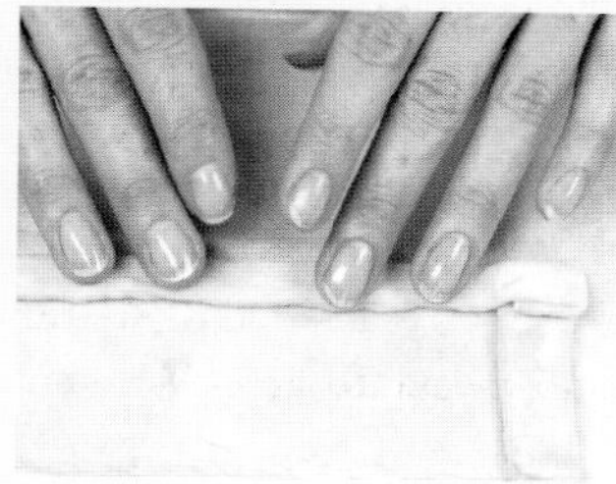

1. Fold the short edges of the pastry over by ½ inch and brush with egg. Then fold the long edges of the pastry over by ½ inch, making sure to keep the edges flush and square. Brush with egg.

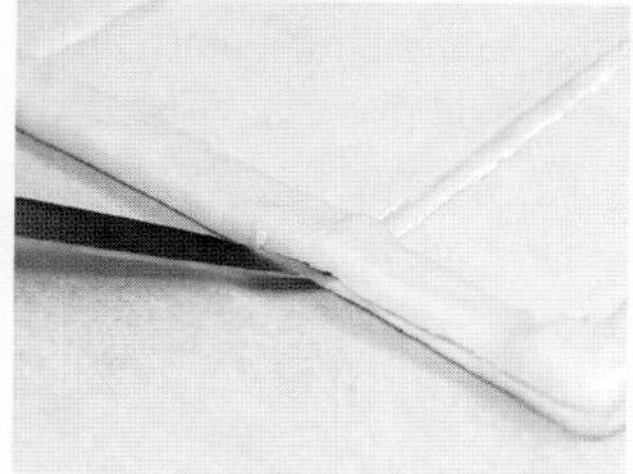

2. Using a paring knife, cut through the folded edges and corners of the tart shell.

3. After sprinkling the bottom of the tart with the Parmesan, poke the dough repeatedly with a fork. Bake the pastry shell.

4. Sprinkle the mozzarella evenly over the crust and shingle the tomatoes attractively over the mozzarella.

TOMATO TART

WHY THIS RECIPE WORKS: Falling somewhere in between pizza and quiche, tomato and mozzarella tart shares the flavors of both but features unique problems. For starters, this is not fast food, as some sort of pastry crust is required. Second, the moisture in the tomatoes almost guarantees a soggy crust. Third, despite their good looks, tomato tarts often fall short on flavor. We wanted a recipe that could easily be made at home with a solid bottom crust and great vine-ripened flavor.

Frozen puff pastry was the solution to an easy crust, and prebaking it was a start—but only a start—to solving the problem of sogginess. Sealing the puff pastry shell with an egg wash helped. Yet even with these preventive measures, the tomato juice still found its way into the crust. To extract more moisture from the tomatoes before baking the tart, we sliced and salted them, then pressed them lightly between paper towels. This removed much of the moisture. But even with a layer of grated mozzarella cheese (whole-milk worked best) between tomatoes and crust, the tart shell still came out a bit soggy. Our breakthrough came when we added a layer of grated Parmesan cheese, which sealed the crust fully and repelled moisture. After a short stay in the oven, our tart had a crisp and sturdy crust, nutty tang from the Parmesan, and rich flavors from the cheese and tomatoes.

Tomato and Mozzarella Tart

SERVES 4 TO 6

To keep the frozen dough from cracking, it's best to let it thaw slowly in the refrigerator overnight. For the best flavor, use authentic Parmesan cheese and very ripe, flavorful tomatoes. Fresh mozzarella will make the crust soggy, so be sure to use low-moisture, shrink-wrapped mozzarella.

- 1 (9 by 9½-inch) sheet frozen puff pastry, thawed (see note)
- 1 large egg, lightly beaten
- 1 ounce Parmesan cheese, grated (about ½ cup; see note)
- ½ pound plum tomatoes (2 medium), cored and sliced ¼ inch thick (see note)
- ½ teaspoon table salt
- 4 ounces whole-milk mozzarella cheese, shredded (about 1 cup; see note)
- 2 tablespoons extra-virgin olive oil
- 1 medium garlic clove, minced or pressed through a garlic press (about 1 teaspoon)
- 2 tablespoons minced fresh basil

1. Adjust an oven rack to the lowest position and heat the oven to 425 degrees. Line a large baking sheet with parchment paper. Lay the pastry in the center of the prepared baking sheet. Brush the pastry with the beaten egg. To form a rimmed crust, fold the long edges of the pastry over by ½ inch, then brush with the egg. Fold the short edges of the pastry over by ½ inch and brush with the egg. Use a paring knife to cut through the folded edges and corner of the pastry. Sprinkle the Parmesan evenly over the crust bottom. Poke the dough uniformly with a fork. Bake until golden brown and crisp, 15 to 20 minutes. Transfer to a wire rack to cool.

2. Meanwhile, spread the tomatoes over several layers of paper towels. Sprinkle with the salt and let drain for 30 minutes.

3. Sprinkle the mozzarella evenly over the crust bottom. Press excess moisture from the tomatoes, using additional paper towels. Following the photo (on page 349), shingle the tomatoes evenly over the mozzarella. Whisk the olive oil and garlic together and drizzle over the tomatoes. Bake until the shell is deep golden, 10 to 15 minutes.

4. Cool on a wire rack for 5 minutes and then sprinkle with the basil. Slide the tart onto a cutting board, slice into pieces, and serve.

GARLIC BREAD

WHY THIS RECIPE WORKS: Garlic bread is a classic accompaniment to spaghetti and meatballs, baked ziti, and countless other Italian favorites. It seems so simple, yet it often goes so wrong. We wanted to banish greasy, bland, and bitter-tasting garlic bread forever in favor of crisp toasted bread imbued with sweet, nutty garlic flavor.

Starting with the bread, we chose a substantial loaf of football-shaped Italian bread, the best quality we could find, to give us generous slices. We cut it in half horizontally, so that the surfaces would crisp up in the oven. We tamed the garlic's harshness by toasting whole cloves, which turned them rich and mellow. We cut out the step of melting butter and simply spread it, after softening and mixing in the garlic, on the bread—not too much, so the bread wouldn't be greasy or soggy. The addition of some grated Parmesan cheese was nearly undetectable, but it added a deep and complex flavor. For baking, we found that leaving the bread unwrapped on a baking sheet gave us the crispy crust we wanted, and exposure to the oven's heat further mellowed the garlic.

Classic Garlic Bread

SERVES 6 TO 8

Plan to pull the garlic bread from the oven when you are ready to serve the other dishes—it is best served piping hot.

- 9–10 medium garlic cloves, unpeeled
- 6 tablespoons (¾ stick) unsalted butter, softened
- 2 tablespoons grated Parmesan cheese
- ½ teaspoon table salt
- 1 (1-pound) loaf high-quality Italian bread (preferably football-shaped), halved horizontally
- Ground black pepper

1. Adjust an oven rack to the middle position and heat the oven to 500 degrees. Meanwhile, toast the garlic cloves in a small skillet over medium heat, shaking the pan occasionally, until fragrant and the color of the cloves deepens slightly, about 8 minutes. When cool enough to handle, peel and mince the cloves (you should have about 3 tablespoons). Using a dinner fork, mash the garlic, butter, cheese, and salt in a small bowl until thoroughly combined.

2. Spread the cut sides of the loaf evenly with the butter mixture; season with pepper to taste. Transfer the loaf halves, buttered side up, onto a rimmed baking sheet; bake, reversing the position of the baking sheet in the oven from front to back halfway through the baking time, until the surface of the bread is golden brown and toasted, 5 to 10 minutes. Cut each half into 2-inch slices; serve immediately.

REALLY GOOD GARLIC BREAD

WHY THIS RECIPE WORKS: Garlic bread is simple to make but is often a disappointment to eat, with either too much or too little garlic flavor and too crusty or too soft a texture. We briefly microwaved fresh garlic in butter and combined it with garlic powder, which provided sweet, roasty notes, some solid butter, and just a bit of cayenne and salt to make a smooth paste with just the right balance of full, complex garlic flavor. We then baked the garlic bread halves between two baking sheets to create a griddle-like set-up that crisped and browned the crust while keeping the interior soft and chewy.

Really Good Garlic Bread

SERVES 8

A 12 by 5-inch loaf of Italian bread from the bakery section of the supermarket, which has a soft, thin crust and fine crumb, works best in this recipe. We do not recommend using a rustic or crusty artisan-style loaf. A rasp-style grater makes quick work of turning the garlic into a paste. If you bake the bread on a dark baking sheet, start checking for doneness after 4 minutes after flipping the bread in step 3.

- 1 teaspoon garlic powder
- 1 teaspoon water
- 8 tablespoons unsalted butter
- ½ teaspoon salt
- ⅛ teaspoon cayenne pepper
- 4–5 garlic cloves, minced to paste (1 tablespoon)
- 1 (1-pound) loaf soft Italian bread, halved horizontally

1. Adjust oven rack to lower-middle position and heat oven 450 degrees. Combine garlic powder and water in medium bowl. Add 4 tablespoons butter, salt, and cayenne to bowl; set aside.

2. Place remaining 4 tablespoons butter in small bowl and microwave, covered, until melted, about 30 seconds. Stir in garlic and continue to microwave, covered, until mixture is bubbling around edges, about 1 minute, stirring halfway through. Transfer garlic-butter mixture to bowl with garlic powder mixture and whisk together until it forms homogenous loose paste. (If mixture melts, set aside until it solidifies before using.)

3. Spread cut sides of loaf evenly with butter mixture. Transfer bread, cut side up, to baking sheet. Bake until butter has melted into surface of bread and bread is hot, 3 to 4 minutes. Remove baking sheet from oven. Flip bread, cut side down, place second rimmed baking sheet on top and gently press. Return bread to oven, with second baking sheet on top of bread, and continue to bake until cut side of bread is golden brown and crisp, 5 to 10 minutes longer, rotating sheet halfway through baking. Transfer bread to cutting board. Using serrated knife, cut each half into 8 slices and serve immediately.

CHEESY GARLIC BREAD

WHY THIS RECIPE WORKS: Garlic bread is a balancing act between the butter, garlic, and bread. Add cheese to the mix and things get complicated. We wanted cheese-topped garlic bread that was crisp on the outside but chewy within, buttery all the way through, and with no bitter garlic aftertaste.

Supermarket baguettes already have a chewy interior and crisp crust, so we started there. Grating the garlic cloves made for a smoother butter, and to tone down the garlic's harshness we sautéed it in butter with a little water (to prevent burning). We mixed the garlic into more softened butter, spread it on our split baguette, and wrapped the bread in foil. Baking it this way "steamed" the bread and infused it with garlic-butter flavor. To crisp the crust, we took the bread out of the foil and baked it a little longer. The final adornment was the cheese; rather than shredding several different kinds ourselves, we took a shortcut and used a prepackaged mixture of shredded Italian cheeses. The last step was to run it under the broiler, which gave us both melted cheese and an extra-crisp crust.

Cheesy Garlic Bread

SERVES 6 TO 8

The serrated edges on a bread knife can pull off the cheesy crust. To prevent this, place the finished garlic bread cheese side down on a cutting board. Slicing through the crust first (rather than the cheese) will keep the cheese in place. Shredded Italian cheese blend is sold in bags in the supermarket case near other packaged cheeses.

- 5 medium garlic cloves, peeled and grated
- 8 tablespoons (1 stick) unsalted butter, softened
- ½ teaspoon water
- ¼ teaspoon table salt
- ¼ teaspoon ground black pepper
- 1 (18- to 20-inch) baguette, sliced in half horizontally
- 1½ cups shredded Italian cheese blend (see note)

1. Adjust an oven rack to the lower-middle position and heat the oven to 400 degrees. Cook the garlic, 1 tablespoon of the butter, and the water in a small nonstick skillet over low heat, stirring occasionally, until straw-colored, 7 to 10 minutes.

2. Mix the hot garlic, remaining 7 tablespoons butter, the salt, and pepper in a bowl and spread on the cut sides of the bread. Sandwich the bread back together and wrap the loaf in foil. Place on a baking sheet and bake for 15 minutes.

3. Carefully unwrap the bread and place the halves, buttered sides up, on a baking sheet. Bake until just beginning to color, about 10 minutes. Remove from the oven and set the oven to broil.

4. Sprinkle the bread with the cheese. Broil until the cheese has melted and the bread is crisp, 1 to 2 minutes. Transfer the bread to a cutting board with the cheese side facing down. Cut into pieces and serve.

FRICO

WHY THIS RECIPE WORKS: As an accompaniment to cocktails or eaten just as a snack, frico is a simple, crisp wafer of flavorful cheese, usually Montasio, that has been melted and browned. We wanted to find the secret behind great frico, and then determine the best substitute for Montasio cheese, which can be difficult to find.

Cheese simply grated into a hot pan could turn into a sticky mess, but we found that using a nonstick skillet allowed us to cook the frico without adding butter or oil. We discovered that it was easy to turn the frico to the other side once the first side was browned if we first took the skillet off the heat;

the slightly cooled cheese didn't stretch or tear when we flipped it. Turning the heat down to cook the second side gave the best results; a pan that was too hot turned the cheese bitter. Many recipes suggest Parmesan as a substitute for Montasio, but we found Asiago cheese to be a better stand-in—though the real thing is even better.

Frico

MAKES 8 LARGE WAFERS

Serve frico with drinks and a bowl of marinated olives or marinated sun-dried tomatoes. Frico is also good crumbled into a salad, crouton-style.

- 1 pound Montasio or aged Asiago cheese, grated fine (about 8 cups)

1. Sprinkle 2 ounces (about 1 cup) of the grated cheese over the bottom of a 10-inch nonstick skillet set over medium-high heat. Use a heat-resistant rubber spatula or a wooden spoon to tidy the lacy outer edges of the cheese. Cook, shaking the pan occasionally to ensure an even distribution of the cheese over the pan bottom, until the edges are lacy and toasted, about 4 minutes. Remove the pan from the heat and allow the cheese to set for about 30 seconds.

2. Using a fork on top and a heatproof spatula underneath, carefully flip the cheese wafer and return the pan to medium heat. Cook until the second side is golden brown, about 2 minutes. Slide the cheese wafer out of the pan and transfer to a plate. Repeat with the remaining cheese. Serve the frico within 1 hour.

PASTA E FAGIOLI

WHY THIS RECIPE WORKS: The American version of this hearty Italian bean-and-vegetable stew—sometimes called "pasta fazool"—often turns out bland, with mushy beans and pasta and too much tomato. And it can take hours to prepare. We wanted rich broth, perfectly cooked beans and pasta, and complex flavors—and we wanted to prepare it in a reasonable amount of time.

Substituting canned beans for dried would save the most preparation time, and we found cannellini beans to be the closest to the dried cranberry beans used in authentic recipes. We started to build deep flavor by sautéing pancetta (though bacon also works) and, for aromatics, onion, garlic, and celery. Tomatoes (diced worked better than crushed or sauce) went in next. A small amount of minced anchovies was unidentifiable but added complexity. Chicken broth diluted with water was our cooking liquid; chicken broth alone made the dish taste too much like chicken soup. A Parmesan rind added another layer of flavor. Last into the pot went the pasta. The flavors of our thick, hearty soup harmonized perfectly and, best of all, we had spent less than an hour at the stove.

Italian Pasta and Bean Soup (Pasta e Fagioli)

SERVES 8 TO 10

This soup does not hold well because the pasta absorbs the liquid, becomes mushy, and leaves the soup dry. You can, however, make the soup in two stages. Once the beans are simmered with the tomatoes, before the broth and water are added, the mixture can be cooled and refrigerated for up to 3 days. When ready to complete the soup, discard the Parmesan rind (otherwise it will become stringy), add the liquid, bring the soup to a boil, and proceed with the recipe.

- 1 tablespoon extra-virgin olive oil, plus extra for drizzling
- 3 ounces pancetta or bacon (about 3 slices), chopped fine
- 1 medium onion, minced
- 1 celery rib, chopped fine
- 4 medium garlic cloves, minced or pressed through a garlic press (about 4 teaspoons)
- 1 teaspoon dried oregano
- ¼ teaspoon red pepper flakes
- 3 anchovy fillets, minced to a paste (about 1½ teaspoons)
- 1 (28-ounce) can diced tomatoes
- 1 piece Parmesan cheese rind, about 5 inches by 2 inches
- 2 (15.5-ounce) cans cannellini beans, drained and rinsed
- 3½ cups low-sodium chicken broth
- 2½ cups water
- Table salt
- 8 ounces small pasta such as ditalini, tubetini, conchiglietti, or orzo
- 4 tablespoons chopped fresh parsley leaves
- Ground black pepper
- Grated Parmesan cheese, for serving

1. Heat the oil in a large Dutch oven over medium-high heat until shimmering. Add the pancetta and cook, stirring occasionally, until it begins to brown, 3 to 5 minutes. Add the onion and celery and cook, stirring occasionally, until the vegetables are softened, 5 to 7 minutes. Add the garlic, oregano, red pepper flakes, and anchovies and cook, stirring constantly, until fragrant, about 30 seconds. Add the tomatoes with their juice, scraping up any browned bits. Add the cheese rind and beans; bring to a boil, then reduce the heat to low and simmer to blend the flavors, 10 minutes. Add the chicken broth, water, and 1 teaspoon salt; increase the heat to high and bring to a boil. Add the pasta and cook until tender, about 10 minutes.

2. Discard the cheese rind. Off the heat, stir in 3 tablespoons of the parsley; season with salt and pepper to taste. Ladle the soup into individual bowls; drizzle each serving with olive oil and sprinkle with a portion of the remaining 1 tablespoon parsley. Serve immediately, passing the grated Parmesan separately.

ITALIAN VEGETABLE STEW (CIAMBOTTA)

WHY THIS RECIPE WORKS: Italy's ciambotta is a ratatouille-like stew chock-full of veggies that makes for a hearty one-bowl meal with nary a trace of meat. We wanted to avoid the sad fate of most recipes, which end in mushy vegetables drowning in a weak broth. To optimize the texture of the zucchini and peppers, we employed the dry heat of a skillet. To address the broth, we embraced eggplant's natural tendency to fall apart and cooked it until it completely assimilated into a thickened tomato-enriched sauce. Finally, we found that a traditional pestata of garlic and herbs provided the biggest flavor punch when added near the end of cooking.

Italian Vegetable Stew (Ciambotta)

SERVES 6 TO 8

Serve this hearty vegetable stew with crusty bread.

PESTATA

- ⅓ cup chopped fresh basil
- ⅓ cup fresh oregano leaves
- 6 garlic cloves, minced
- 2 tablespoons extra-virgin olive oil
- ¼ teaspoon red pepper flakes

STEW

- 12 ounces eggplant, peeled and cut into ½-inch pieces
- Salt
- ¼ cup extra-virgin olive oil
- 1 large onion, chopped
- 1 pound russet potatoes, peeled and cut into ½-inch pieces
- 2 tablespoons tomato paste
- 2¼ cups water
- 1 (28-ounce) can whole peeled tomatoes, drained with juice reserved, chopped coarse
- 2 zucchini (8 ounces each), halved lengthwise, seeded, and cut into ½-inch pieces
- 2 red or yellow bell peppers, stemmed, seeded, and cut into ½-inch pieces
- 1 cup shredded fresh basil

1. FOR THE PESTATA: Process all ingredients in food processor until finely ground, about 1 minute, scraping down sides as needed. Set aside.

2. FOR THE STEW: Toss eggplant with 1½ teaspoons salt in bowl. Line surface of large plate with double layer of coffee filters and lightly spray with vegetable oil spray. Spread eggplant in even layer over coffee filters. Microwave eggplant, uncovered, until dry to touch and slightly shriveled, 8 to 12 minutes, tossing once halfway through to ensure that eggplant cooks evenly.

3. Heat 2 tablespoons oil in Dutch oven over high heat until shimmering. Add eggplant, onion, and potatoes; cook, stirring frequently, until eggplant browns and surface of potatoes becomes translucent, about 2 minutes. Push vegetables to sides of pot; add 1 tablespoon oil and tomato paste to clearing. Cook paste, stirring frequently, until brown fond develops on bottom of pot, about 2 minutes. Add 2 cups water and chopped tomatoes and juice, scraping up any browned bits, and bring to boil. Reduce heat to medium, cover, and gently simmer until eggplant is completely broken down and potatoes are tender, 20 to 25 minutes.

4. Meanwhile, heat remaining 1 tablespoon oil in 12-inch skillet over high heat until smoking. Add zucchini, bell peppers, and ½ teaspoon salt; cook, stirring occasionally, until vegetables are browned and tender, 10 to 12 minutes. Push vegetables to sides of skillet; add pestata and cook until fragrant, about 1 minute. Stir pestata into vegetables and transfer vegetables to bowl. Add remaining ¼ cup water to skillet off heat, scraping up browned bits.

5. Remove Dutch oven from heat and stir reserved vegetables and water from skillet into vegetables in Dutch oven. Cover pot and let stand for 20 minutes to allow flavors to meld. Stir in basil and season with salt to taste; serve.

HEARTY TUSCAN BEAN STEW

WHY THIS RECIPE WORKS: Unlike *pasta e fagioli*, where beans and pasta share the spotlight, Tuscan bean soup boasts creamy, buttery cannellini beans in the starring role. Ideally, the beans should have a uniformly tender texture, but too often the skins are tough and the insides mealy—or the beans turn mushy. We wanted to fix the bean problem and convert this Italian classic into a hearty, rustic stew for a deeply flavorful one-pot meal.

Since the beans are the centerpiece of this stew, we concentrated on cooking them perfectly. After testing a variety of soaking times, we settled on soaking the beans overnight, a method that consistently produced the most tender and evenly cooked beans. But none of the methods we tested properly softened the skins. The answer was to soak the beans in salted water. Brining the beans, rather than the conventional approach of soaking them in plain water and then cooking them in salt water, allowed the salt to soften the skins but kept it from penetrating inside, where it could make the beans mealy. Tests showed that gently cooking the beans in a 250-degree oven produced perfectly cooked beans that stayed intact. The final trick was to add the tomatoes toward the end of cooking, since their acid interfered with the softening process. To complete our stew, we looked for other traditional Tuscan flavors, including pancetta, kale, lots of garlic, and a sprig of rosemary. And to make it even more substantial, we served the stew on a slab of toasted country bread, drizzled with fruity extra-virgin olive oil.

Hearty Tuscan Bean Stew

SERVES 8

We prefer the creamier texture of beans soaked overnight for this recipe. If you're short on time, quick-soak them: Place the rinsed beans in a large heat-resistant bowl. Bring 2 quarts water and 3 tablespoons salt to a boil. Pour the water over the beans and let them sit for 1 hour. Drain and rinse the beans well before proceeding with step 2. If pancetta is unavailable, substitute 4 ounces bacon (about 4 slices).

- Table salt
- 1 pound (about 2 cups) dried cannellini beans, picked over and rinsed
- 1 tablespoon extra-virgin olive oil, plus extra for drizzling
- 6 ounces pancetta or bacon, cut into ¼-inch pieces (see note)
- 1 large onion, chopped medium (about 1½ cups)
- 2 medium celery ribs, cut into ½-inch pieces (about ¾ cup)
- 2 medium carrots, peeled and cut into ½-inch pieces (about 1 cup)
- 8 medium garlic cloves, peeled and crushed
- 4 cups low-sodium chicken broth
- 3 cups water
- 2 bay leaves
- 1 bunch kale or collard greens (about 1 pound), stems trimmed and leaves chopped into 1-inch pieces (about 8 cups loosely packed)
- 1 (14.5-ounce) can diced tomatoes, drained
- 1 sprig fresh rosemary
- Ground black pepper
- 8 slices country white bread, each 1¼ inches thick, broiled until golden brown on both sides and rubbed with a garlic clove (optional)

1. Dissolve 3 tablespoons salt in 4 quarts cold water in a large bowl or container. Add the beans and soak at room temperature for at least 8 hours or up to 24 hours. Drain the beans and rinse well.

2. Adjust an oven rack to the lower-middle position and heat the oven to 250 degrees. Heat the oil and pancetta in a large Dutch oven over medium heat. Cook, stirring occasionally, until the pancetta is lightly browned and the fat has rendered, 6 to 10 minutes. Add the onion, celery, and carrots. Cook, stirring occasionally, until the vegetables are softened and lightly browned, 10 to 16 minutes. Stir in the garlic and cook until fragrant, about 1 minute. Stir in the broth, water, bay leaves, and soaked beans. Increase the heat to high and bring the mixture to a simmer. Cover the pot, transfer it to the oven, and cook until the beans are almost tender (the very center of the beans will still be firm), 45 minutes to 1 hour.

3. Remove the pot from the oven and stir in the kale and tomatoes. Return the pot to the oven and continue to cook until the beans and greens are fully tender, 30 to 40 minutes longer.

4. Remove the pot from the oven and submerge the rosemary sprig in the stew. Cover and let stand for 15 minutes. Discard the bay leaves and rosemary sprig and season the stew with salt and pepper to taste. If desired, use the back of a spoon to press some beans against the side of the pot to thicken the stew. Serve over the toasted bread (if using) and drizzle with olive oil.

ITALIAN WEDDING SOUP

WHY THIS RECIPE WORKS: Traditional recipes for this hearty soup featuring meatballs, tender greens, and pasta require an afternoon-long stint on the stovetop, which starts with building the *brodo*, a long-cooked broth made from the bones of meat and poultry. Wanting a quicker path to this richly flavored soup, we created a speedy yet ultrasavory broth by simmering ground beef and pork in a mixture of chicken and beef broth. Dried porcini mushrooms and Worcestershire sauce further boosted the meaty flavor. For the meatballs, we nixed the hard-to-find ground veal and stuck with ground beef and ground pork. To make up for the loss in texture from omitting the veal, we added baking powder and whipped the pork in a stand mixer to ensure the meatballs remained light, juicy, and supple. Chopped kale and ditalini, stirred in toward the end of the cooking time, became perfectly tender in a matter of minutes.

Italian Wedding Soup

SERVES 6 TO 8

Use a rasp-style grater to process the onion and garlic for the meatballs. Tubettini or orzo can be used in place of the ditalini.

BROTH

- 1 onion, chopped
- 1 fennel bulb, stalks discarded, bulb halved, cored, and chopped
- 4 garlic cloves, peeled and smashed
- ¼ ounce dried porcini mushrooms, rinsed
- 4 ounces ground pork
- 4 ounces 85 percent lean ground beef
- 1 bay leaf
- ½ cup dry white wine
- 1 tablespoon Worcestershire sauce
- 4 cups chicken broth
- 2 cups beef broth
- 2 cups water

MEATBALLS

- 1 slice hearty white sandwich bread, crusts removed, torn into 1-inch pieces
- 5 tablespoons heavy cream
- ¼ cup grated Parmesan cheese
- 4 teaspoons finely grated onion
- ½ teaspoon finely grated garlic
- Salt and pepper
- 6 ounces ground pork
- 1 teaspoon baking powder
- 6 ounces 85 percent lean ground beef
- 2 teaspoons minced fresh oregano
- 1 cup ditalini pasta
- 12 ounces kale, stemmed and cut into ½-inch pieces (6 cups)

1. FOR THE BROTH: Heat onion, fennel, garlic, porcini, pork, beef, and bay leaf in Dutch oven over medium-high heat; cook, stirring frequently, until meats are no longer pink, about 5 minutes. Add wine and Worcestershire; cook for 1 minute. Add chicken broth, beef broth, and water; bring to simmer. Reduce heat to low, cover, and simmer for 30 minutes.

2. FOR THE MEATBALLS: While broth simmers, combine bread, cream, Parmesan, onion, garlic, and pepper to taste in bowl; using fork, mash mixture to uniform paste. Using stand mixer fitted with paddle, beat pork, baking powder, and ½ teaspoon salt on high speed until smooth and pale, 1 to 2 minutes, scraping down bowl as needed. Add bread mixture, beef, and oregano; mix on medium-low speed until just incorporated, 1 to 2 minutes, scraping down bowl as needed. Using moistened hands, form heaping teaspoons of meat mixture into smooth, round meatballs; you should have 30 to 35 meatballs. Cover and refrigerate for up to 1 day.

3. Strain broth through fine-mesh strainer set over large bowl or container, pressing on solids to extract as much liquid as possible. Wipe out Dutch oven and return broth to pot. (Broth can be refrigerated for up to 3 days. Skim off fat before reheating.)

4. Return broth to simmer over medium-high heat. Add pasta and kale; cook, stirring occasionally, for 5 minutes. Add meatballs; return to simmer and cook, stirring occasionally, until meatballs are cooked through and pasta is tender, 3 to 5 minutes. Season with salt and pepper to taste and serve.

EGGPLANT PARMESAN

WHY THIS RECIPE WORKS: Frying the eggplant for this classic Italian dish not only is time-consuming but also can make the dish heavy and dull. In hopes of eliminating the grease as well as some of the prep time, we decided to cook the eggplant in the oven and see what other measures we could take to freshen up this Italian classic.

We salted and drained the eggplant slices to improve their texture. A traditional bound breading—flour, egg, and fresh bread crumbs—worked best for giving the eggplant a crisp coating. Baking the eggplant on preheated and oiled baking sheets resulted in crisp, golden brown slices. While the eggplant was in the oven, we made a quick tomato sauce using garlic, red pepper flakes, basil, and canned diced tomatoes. We layered the sauce, eggplant, and mozzarella in a baking dish and left the top layer of eggplant mostly unsauced, so that it would crisp up in the oven. Our re-engineered eggplant Parmesan was lighter and fresher tasting, and a lot less work.

Eggplant Parmesan

SERVES 6 TO 8

Use kosher salt when salting the eggplant. The coarse grains don't dissolve as readily as the fine grains of regular table salt, so any excess can be easily wiped away. It's necessary to divide the eggplant into two batches when tossing it with the salt. To be time-efficient, use the 30 to 45 minutes during which the salted eggplant sits to prepare the breading.

EGGPLANT

- 2 pounds globe eggplant (2 medium eggplants), cut crosswise into ¼-inch-thick rounds
- 1 tablespoon kosher salt (see note)
- 8 slices high-quality white sandwich bread, torn into quarters
- 2 ounces Parmesan cheese, grated (about 1 cup)
- Table salt and ground black pepper
- 1 cup unbleached all-purpose flour
- 4 large eggs
- 6 tablespoons vegetable oil

TOMATO SAUCE

- 3 (14.5-ounce) cans diced tomatoes
- 2 tablespoons extra-virgin olive oil
- 4 medium garlic cloves, minced or pressed through a garlic press (about 4 teaspoons)
- ¼ teaspoon red pepper flakes
- ½ cup coarsely chopped fresh basil leaves
- Table salt and ground black pepper

- 8 ounces whole-milk or part-skim mozzarella cheese, shredded (about 2 cups)
- 1 ounce Parmesan cheese, grated (about ½ cup)
- 10 fresh basil leaves, torn, for garnish

1. FOR THE EGGPLANT: Toss half of the eggplant slices and 1½ teaspoons of the kosher salt in a large bowl until combined; transfer the salted eggplant to a large colander set over a bowl. Repeat with the remaining eggplant and kosher salt, placing the second batch on top of the first. Let stand until the eggplant releases about 2 tablespoons liquid, 30 to 45 minutes. Spread the eggplant slices on a triple thickness of paper towels; cover with another triple thickness of paper towels. Press firmly on each slice to remove as much liquid as possible, then wipe off the excess salt.

2. While the eggplant is draining, adjust the oven racks to the upper-middle and lower-middle positions, place a rimmed baking sheet on each rack, and heat the oven to 425 degrees. Process the bread in a food processor to fine, even crumbs, about 20 to 30 seconds. Transfer the crumbs to a pie plate and stir in the Parmesan, ¼ teaspoon table salt, and ½ teaspoon pepper; set aside. Wipe out the workbowl (do not wash) and set aside.

3. Combine the flour and 1 teaspoon pepper in a large zipper-lock bag; shake to combine. Beat the eggs in a second pie plate. Place 8 to 10 eggplant slices in the bag with the flour; seal the bag and shake to coat the slices. Remove the slices, shaking off the excess flour, dip into the eggs, let the excess egg run off, then coat evenly with the bread-crumb mixture; set the breaded slices on a wire rack set over a baking sheet. Repeat with the remaining eggplant.

4. Remove the preheated baking sheets from the oven; add 3 tablespoons of the vegetable oil to each sheet, tilting to coat evenly with the oil. Place half of the breaded eggplant slices on each sheet in a single layer; bake until the eggplant is well browned and crisp, about 30 minutes, switching and rotating the baking sheets after 10 minutes, and flipping the eggplant slices with a wide spatula after 20 minutes. Do not turn off the oven.

5. FOR THE SAUCE: While the eggplant bakes, process 2 cans of the diced tomatoes in the food processor until almost smooth, about 5 seconds. Heat the olive oil, garlic, and red pepper flakes in a large heavy-bottomed saucepan over medium-high heat, stirring occasionally, until fragrant and the garlic is light golden, about 3 minutes; stir in the processed tomatoes and remaining can of diced tomatoes. Bring the sauce to a boil, then reduce the heat to medium-low and simmer, stirring occasionally, until slightly thickened and reduced, about 15 minutes (you should have about 4 cups). Stir in the basil and season with table salt and pepper to taste.

6. TO ASSEMBLE: Spread 1 cup of the tomato sauce in the bottom of a 13 by 9-inch baking dish. Layer in half of the eggplant slices, overlapping the slices to fit; distribute 1 cup more of the sauce over the eggplant; sprinkle with half of the mozzarella. Layer in the remaining eggplant and dot with 1 cup more of the sauce, leaving the majority of the eggplant exposed so it will remain crisp; sprinkle with the Parmesan and the remaining mozzarella. Bake until bubbling and the cheese is browned, 13 to 15 minutes. Cool for 10 minutes, scatter the basil over the top, and serve, passing the remaining tomato sauce separately.

EGGPLANT INVOLTINI

WHY THIS RECIPE WORKS: Eggplant *involtini* ("little bundles" in Italian) can be so complicated and messy that it makes the cook wonder whether these cheese-filled eggplant bundles are worth making. But the resulting dish—charmingly tidy involtini with homemade tomato sauce and a pleasantly cheesy filling—was too good to give up on. We wanted to come up with a version of involtini that would emphasize the eggplant and minimize the fuss.

First up for fixing: the eggplant. Generally this recipe calls for frying, but in order to fry eggplant, you must first get rid of the excess water or the eggplant will turn mushy and oily. Salting can fix this problem, but it's time-consuming. Instead, we opted for a lighter and more hands-off option: baking. We brushed the planks with oil, seasoned them with salt and pepper, and then baked them for about 30 minutes. They emerged light brown and tender, with a compact texture that was neither mushy nor sodden.

To lighten up our involtini filling, we decreased the amount of ricotta and replaced it with more flavorful Pecorino Romano, and brightened the filling with a squeeze of lemon juice. To ensure that our filling stayed creamy and didn't toughen up, we added bread crumbs to the mix. We made a bare-bones tomato sauce while the eggplant baked, then added the eggplant rolls directly to the sauce. Using a skillet meant that we could easily transfer the whole operation to the oven. We crowned the dish with an additional dusting of Pecorino and a sprinkling of basil before serving directly from the skillet.

Eggplant Involtini

SERVES 4 TO 6

Select shorter, wider eggplants for this recipe. Part-skim ricotta may be used, but do not use fat-free ricotta. Serve the eggplant with crusty bread and a salad.

- 2 large eggplants (1½ pounds each), peeled
- 6 tablespoons vegetable oil
- Kosher salt and pepper
- 2 garlic cloves, minced
- ¼ teaspoon dried oregano
- Pinch red pepper flakes
- 1 (28-ounce) can whole peeled tomatoes, drained with juice reserved, chopped coarse
- 1 slice hearty white sandwich bread, torn into 1-inch pieces
- 8 ounces (1 cup) whole-milk ricotta cheese
- 1½ ounces grated Pecorino Romano (¾ cup)
- ¼ cup plus 1 tablespoon chopped fresh basil
- 1 tablespoon lemon juice

1. Slice each eggplant lengthwise into ½-inch-thick planks (you should have 12 planks). Trim rounded surface from each end piece so it lies flat.

2. Adjust 1 oven rack to lower-middle position and second rack 8 inches from broiler element. Heat oven to 375 degrees. Line 2 rimmed baking sheets with parchment paper and spray generously with vegetable oil spray. Arrange eggplant slices in single layer on prepared sheets. Brush 1 side of eggplant slices with 2½ tablespoons oil and sprinkle with ½ teaspoon salt and ¼ teaspoon pepper. Flip eggplant slices and brush with 2½ tablespoons oil and sprinkle with ½ teaspoon salt and ¼ teaspoon pepper. Bake until tender and lightly browned, 30 to 35 minutes, switching and rotating sheets halfway through baking. Let cool for 5 minutes. Using thin spatula, flip each slice over. Heat broiler.

3. While eggplant cooks, heat remaining 1 tablespoon oil in 12-inch broiler-safe skillet over medium-low heat until just shimmering. Add garlic, oregano, pepper flakes, and ½ teaspoon salt and cook, stirring occasionally, until fragrant, about 30 seconds. Stir in tomatoes and their juice. Increase heat to high and bring to simmer. Reduce heat to medium-low and simmer until thickened, about 15 minutes. Cover and set aside.

4. Pulse bread in food processor until finely ground, 10 to 15 pulses. Combine bread crumbs, ricotta, ½ cup Pecorino, ¼ cup basil, lemon juice, and ½ teaspoon salt in medium bowl.

5. With widest short sides of eggplant slices facing you, evenly distribute ricotta mixture on bottom third of each slice. Gently roll up each eggplant slice and place seam side down in tomato sauce.

6. Bring sauce to simmer over medium heat. Simmer for 5 minutes. Transfer skillet to oven and broil until eggplant is well browned and cheese is heated through, 5 to 10 minutes. Sprinkle with remaining ¼ cup Pecorino and let stand for 5 minutes. Sprinkle with remaining 1 tablespoon basil and serve.

POLENTA

WHY THIS RECIPE WORKS: A creamy mound of hot polenta can be a comforting dish, especially when served with a stew or saucy braise. Composed of little more than cornmeal and water, it should be easy to prepare. But often it's lumpy or gummy, and getting it right requires constant stirring. We wanted the smooth, creamy texture and great corn flavor of real polenta, but without the hassle.

It turned out that the type of cornmeal made a difference in the end result, and we found that a medium-grind meal worked best. The traditional method of making polenta requires half an hour or more of constant stirring after the cornmeal is added to boiling salted water. Experimentation revealed that the way to avoid this continuous attention was very low heat. We added the cornmeal (very gradually, so it wouldn't seize up) to barely simmering water with the flame set as low as possible. With the cover on the pot to keep in moisture, the cornmeal had time to release its starches gradually and develop flavor, and we needed to stir it only every five minutes or so. Our polenta was smooth and creamy with lots of corn flavor, and we were able to serve it in half an hour without standing at the stove the whole time.

Basic Polenta

SERVES 4 TO 6

If you do not have a heavy-bottomed saucepan, you may want to use a flame tamer to manage the heat. A flame tamer can be purchased at most kitchen supply stores, or you can improvise one (see page 313). Use this polenta as the base for any stew or braise, especially Osso Buco (page 372), or serve with a chunk of Gorgonzola cheese. Cooked leafy greens also make an excellent topping for soft polenta.

- 6 cups water
- Table salt
- 1½ cups medium-grind cornmeal, preferably stone-ground
- 3 tablespoons unsalted butter, cut into large chunks
- Ground black pepper

1. Bring the water to a rolling boil in a 4-quart heavy-bottomed saucepan over medium-high heat. Reduce the heat to the lowest possible setting, add 1½ teaspoons salt, and pour the cornmeal into the water in a very slow stream from a measuring cup, all the while whisking in a circular motion to prevent lumps.

2. Cover and cook, vigorously stirring the polenta with a wooden spoon for about 10 seconds once every 5 minutes and making sure to scrape clean the bottom and corners of the pot, until the polenta has lost its raw cornmeal taste and becomes soft and smooth, about 30 minutes. Stir in the butter, season with salt and pepper to taste, and serve immediately.

MUSHROOM RISOTTO

WHY THIS RECIPE WORKS: Earthy wild mushrooms added to a basic Italian risotto make a great main course. But the difficulty, not to mention the expense, of finding exotic fungi prompted us to try our hand at reproducing these flavors with supermarket mushrooms.

Cultivated mushrooms just don't have enough flavor for a dish like this, so we turned to aromatic dried porcini, which pack quite a flavor punch. But they needed to be chopped, so for visual appeal and substantive texture we added fresh cremini. Because simmering the cremini in the rice-broth mixture would make them rubbery, we browned them in a separate skillet with some onion and garlic for added flavor, folding this mixture into the risotto only when the rice was done. We added extra wine to our basic risotto so that its acidity would balance the richness of the mushrooms, and used a decidedly un-Italian ingredient, soy sauce, to intensify the earthiness of the mushrooms and round out the flavors. Without relying on pricey fungi, we had created a risotto with the same exotic earthiness.

Mushroom Risotto

SERVES 4 TO 6

Cremini mushrooms are sometimes sold as baby bella mushrooms. If they're not available, button mushrooms make a fine, though somewhat less flavorful, substitute. Tie the thyme and parsley sprigs together with kitchen twine so they will be easy to retrieve from the pan.

- 2 bay leaves
- 6 sprigs fresh thyme (see note)
- 4 sprigs fresh parsley, plus 2 tablespoons minced parsley leaves (see note)
- 3½ cups low-sodium chicken broth
- 3½ cups water
- 1 ounce dried porcini mushrooms, rinsed in a mesh strainer under running water
- 2 teaspoons soy sauce
- 6 tablespoons (¾ stick) unsalted butter
- 1¼ pounds cremini mushrooms, wiped clean and cut into quarters if small or sixths if medium or large (see note)
- 2 medium onions, minced (about 2 cups)
- Table salt
- 3 medium garlic cloves, minced or pressed through a garlic press (about 1 tablespoon)
- 2⅛ cups Arborio rice
- 1 cup dry white wine or dry vermouth
- 2 ounces Parmesan cheese, grated fine (about 1 cup)
- Ground black pepper

1. Tie the bay leaves, thyme sprigs, and parsley sprigs together with kitchen twine. Bring the bundled herbs, chicken broth, water, porcini mushrooms, and soy sauce to a boil in a medium saucepan over medium-high heat; reduce the heat to medium-low and simmer until the dried mushrooms are softened and fully hydrated, about 15 minutes. Remove and discard the herb bundle and strain the broth through a fine-mesh strainer set over a medium bowl (you should have about 6½ cups strained liquid); return the liquid to the saucepan and keep warm over low heat. Finely mince the porcini and set aside.

2. Adjust an oven rack to the middle position and heat the oven to 200 degrees. Heat 2 tablespoons of the butter in a 12-inch nonstick skillet over medium-high heat. Add the cremini mushrooms, 1 cup of the onions, and ½ teaspoon salt; cook, stirring occasionally, until the moisture released by the mushrooms evaporates and the mushrooms are well browned, about 7 minutes. Stir in the garlic until fragrant, about 1 minute, then transfer the mushroom mixture to an ovensafe bowl and keep warm in the oven. Off the heat, add ¼ cup water to the now-empty skillet and scrape with a wooden spoon to loosen any browned bits on the pan bottom; pour the liquid from the skillet into the saucepan with the broth.

3. Melt 3 tablespoons more butter in a large saucepan over medium heat. Add the remaining 1 cup onions and ¼ teaspoon salt; cook, stirring occasionally, until the onions are softened and translucent, about 9 minutes. Add the rice and cook, stirring frequently, until the edges of the grains are transparent, about 4 minutes. Add the wine and cook, stirring frequently, until the rice absorbs the wine. Add the minced porcini and 3½ cups of the broth and cook, stirring every 2 to 3 minutes, until the liquid is absorbed, 9 to 11 minutes. Stir in ½ cup more broth every 2 to 3 minutes until the rice is cooked through but the grains are still somewhat firm at the center, 10 to 12 minutes (the rice may not require all of the broth). Stir in the remaining 1 tablespoon butter, then stir in the mushroom mixture (and any accumulated juice), cheese, and reserved chopped parsley. Season with salt and pepper to taste; serve immediately in warmed bowls.

BUTTERNUT SQUASH RISOTTO

WHY THIS RECIPE WORKS: Butternut squash and risotto should make a perfect culinary couple, but too often the squash and rice never become properly intertwined. The squash is reduced to overly sweet orange blobs or the whole dish becomes a gluey squash paste. We wanted to integrate the flavor of the squash with the risotto but still preserve their individual personalities—to create a creamy, orange-tinged rice fully infused with deep squash flavor. We started with our basic risotto recipe, then addressed the squash. We decided to brown the diced squash in a skillet and set it aside while we sautéed the aromatics and toasted the rice. We added only half of the squash with the first addition of liquid. This squash broke down somewhat during cooking and infused the rice with its flavor; the remaining squash, added when the rice was finished, retained its shape and texture. Chicken broth cut with water was the basis of the liquid, but we also simmered the squash seeds and fibers in it to intensify the squash flavor. A generous helping of white wine balanced the squash's sweetness. This creamy risotto had deep squash flavor and pleasing textures.

Butternut Squash Risotto

SERVES 4 TO 6

Infusing the chicken broth with the squash's seeds and fibers helps to reinforce the earthy squash flavor without adding more squash. We found that a 2-pound squash often yields more than the 3½ cups in step 1; this can be added to the skillet along with the squash scrapings in step 2. To make this dish vegetarian, vegetable broth can be used instead of chicken broth, but the resulting risotto will have more pronounced sweetness.

- 2 tablespoons olive oil
- 1 medium butternut squash (about 2 pounds), peeled, seeded (reserve fibers and seeds), and cut into ½-inch cubes (about 3½ cups; see note)
- ¾ teaspoon table salt
- ¾ teaspoon ground black pepper
- 4 cups low-sodium chicken broth (see note)
- 1 cup water
- 4 tablespoons (½ stick) unsalted butter
- 2 small onions, minced (about 1½ cups)
- 2 medium garlic cloves, minced or pressed through a garlic press (about 2 teaspoons)
- 2 cups Arborio rice
- 1½ cups dry white wine
- 1½ ounces Parmesan cheese, grated fine (about ¾ cup)
- 2 tablespoons minced fresh sage leaves
- ¼ teaspoon grated nutmeg

1. Heat the oil in a 12-inch nonstick skillet over medium-high heat until shimmering but not smoking. Add the squash in an even layer and cook without stirring until golden brown, 4 to 5 minutes; stir in ¼ teaspoon of the salt and ¼ teaspoon of the pepper. Continue to cook, stirring occasionally, until the squash is tender and browned, about 5 minutes longer. Transfer the squash to a bowl and set aside.

2. Return the skillet to medium heat; add the reserved squash fibers and seeds and any leftover diced squash. Cook, stirring frequently to break up the fibers, until lightly browned, about 4 minutes. Transfer to a large saucepan and add the chicken broth and water; cover the saucepan and bring the mixture to a simmer over high heat, then reduce the heat to medium-low to maintain a bare simmer.

3. Melt 3 tablespoons of the butter in the now-empty skillet over medium heat; add the onions, garlic, remaining ½ teaspoon salt, and remaining ½ teaspoon pepper. Cook, stirring occasionally, until the onions are softened, 4 to 5 minutes. Add the rice to the skillet and cook, stirring frequently, until the grains are translucent around the edges, about 3 minutes. (To prevent the rice from spilling out of the pan, stir inward, from the edges of the pan toward the center, not in a circular motion.) Add the wine and cook, stirring frequently, until the liquid is fully absorbed, 4 to 5 minutes. Meanwhile, strain the hot broth through a fine-mesh strainer into a medium bowl, pressing on the solids to extract as much liquid as possible. Return the strained broth to the saucepan and discard the solids in the strainer; cover the saucepan and set over low heat to keep the broth hot.

4. When the wine is fully absorbed, add 3 cups of the hot broth and half of the reserved squash to the rice. Simmer, stirring every 3 to 4 minutes, until the liquid is absorbed and the bottom of the pan is almost dry, about 12 minutes.

5. Stir in ½ cup more of the hot broth and cook, stirring constantly, until absorbed, about 3 minutes; repeat with additional broth until the rice is cooked through but the grains are still somewhat firm at the center. Off the heat, stir in the remaining 1 tablespoon butter, the Parmesan, sage, and nutmeg; gently fold in the remaining cooked squash. If desired, add up to ¼ cup more broth to loosen the texture of the risotto. Serve immediately in warmed bowls.

PARMESAN FARROTTO

WHY THIS RECIPE WORKS: The biggest challenge to making a satisfying *farrotto* is having it achieve the proper texture. We found that cracking about half the farro in a blender was the key to freeing enough starch from the grains to create a creamy, risotto-like consistency. Adding most of the liquid up front and cooking the farrotto in a lidded Dutch oven helped the grains cook evenly and meant we didn't have to stir constantly—just twice before stirring in the flavorings. We created variations with spring vegetables and mushrooms, which turned this simple side into a satisfying main course.

Parmesan Farrotto

SERVES 6

We prefer the flavor and texture of whole farro. Do not use quick-cooking or pearled farro. The consistency of farrotto is a matter of personal taste; if you prefer a looser texture, add more of the hot broth mixture in step 6.

- 1½ cups whole farro
- 3 cups chicken broth
- 3 cups water
- 4 tablespoons unsalted butter
- ½ onion, chopped fine
- 1 garlic clove, minced
- 2 teaspoons minced fresh thyme
- Salt and pepper
- 2 ounces Parmesan, grated (1 cup)
- 2 tablespoons minced fresh parsley
- 2 teaspoons lemon juice

1. Pulse farro in blender until about half of grains are broken into smaller pieces, about 6 pulses.

2. Bring broth and water to boil in medium saucepan over high heat. Reduce heat to medium-low to maintain gentle simmer.

3. Melt 2 tablespoons butter in large Dutch oven over medium-low heat. Add onion and cook, stirring frequently, until softened, 3 to 4 minutes. Add garlic and stir until fragrant, about 30 seconds. Add farro and cook, stirring frequently, until grains are lightly toasted, about 3 minutes.

4. Stir 5 cups hot broth mixture into farro mixture, reduce heat to low, cover, and cook until almost all liquid has been absorbed and farro is just al dente, about 25 minutes, stirring twice during cooking.

5. Add thyme, 1 teaspoon salt, and ¾ teaspoon pepper and continue to cook, stirring constantly, until farro becomes creamy, about 5 minutes.

6. Remove pot from heat. Stir in Parmesan, parsley, lemon juice, and remaining 2 tablespoons butter. Season with salt and pepper to taste. Adjust consistency with remaining hot broth mixture as needed. Serve immediately.

Farrotto with Pancetta, Asparagus, and Peas

We prefer the flavor and texture of whole farro. Do not use quick-cooking or pearled farro. The consistency of farrotto is a matter of personal taste; if you prefer a looser texture, add more of the warm broth mixture in step 5.

- 1½ cups whole farro
- 3 cups chicken broth
- 3 cups water
- 4 ounces asparagus, trimmed and cut on bias into 1-inch lengths
- 4 ounces pancetta, cut into ¼-inch pieces
- 2 tablespoons extra-virgin olive oil
- ½ onion, chopped fine
- 1 garlic clove, minced
- 1 cup frozen peas, thawed
- 2 teaspoons minced fresh tarragon
- Salt and pepper
- 1½ ounces Parmesan cheese, grated (¾ cup)
- 1 tablespoon minced fresh chives
- 1 teaspoon grated lemon zest plus 1 teaspoon juice

1. Pulse farro in blender until about half of grains are broken into smaller pieces, about 6 pulses.

2. Bring broth and water to boil in medium saucepan over high heat. Add asparagus and cook until crisp-tender, 2 to 3 minutes. Using slotted spoon, transfer asparagus to bowl and set aside. Reduce heat to low, cover broth mixture, and keep warm.

3. Cook pancetta in Dutch oven over medium heat until lightly browned and fat has rendered, about 5 minutes. Add 1 tablespoon oil and onion and cook until softened, about 5 minutes. Stir in garlic and cook until fragrant, about 30 seconds. Add farro and cook, stirring frequently, until grains are lightly toasted, about 3 minutes.

4. Stir 5 cups warm broth mixture into farro mixture, reduce heat to low, cover, and cook until almost all liquid has been absorbed and farro is just al dente, about 25 minutes, stirring twice during cooking.

5. Add peas, tarragon, ¾ teaspoon salt, and ½ teaspoon pepper and cook, stirring constantly, until farro becomes creamy, about 5 minutes. Off heat, stir in Parmesan, chives, lemon zest and juice, remaining 1 tablespoon oil, and reserved asparagus. Adjust consistency with remaining warm broth mixture as needed (you may have broth left over). Season with salt and pepper to taste. Serve.

Mushroom Farrotto

We prefer the flavor and texture of whole farro. Do not use quick-cooking or pearled farro. The consistency of farrotto is largely a matter of personal taste; if you prefer a looser texture, add more of the hot water in step 7.

- 1½ cups whole farro
- ¾ ounce dried porcini mushrooms, rinsed
- 6 cups water
- 4 tablespoons unsalted butter
- 12 ounces cremini mushrooms, trimmed and sliced thin
- Salt and pepper
- ½ onion, chopped fine
- 1 garlic clove, minced
- 2 teaspoons minced fresh thyme

1½ ounces Parmesan, grated (¾ cup)
2 tablespoons minced fresh chives
2 teaspoons sherry vinegar

1. Pulse farro in blender until about half of grains are broken into smaller pieces, about 6 pulses.

2. Microwave porcini mushrooms and 1 cup water in covered bowl until steaming, about 1 minute. Let sit until softened, about 5 minutes. Drain mushrooms in fine-mesh strainer lined with coffee filter. Transfer liquid to medium saucepan and finely chop porcini mushrooms.

3. Add remaining 5 cups water to saucepan and bring to boil over high heat. Reduce heat to medium-low to maintain gentle simmer.

4. Melt 2 tablespoons butter in large Dutch oven over medium-low heat. Add cremini mushrooms and ½ teaspoon salt and cook, stirring frequently, until moisture released by mushrooms evaporates and pan is dry, 4 to 5 minutes. Add onion and chopped porcini mushrooms and continue to cook until onion has softened, 3 to 4 minutes. Add garlic and stir until fragrant, about 30 seconds. Add farro and cook, stirring frequently, until grains are lightly toasted, about 3 minutes.

5. Stir 5 cups hot water into farro, reduce heat to low, cover, and cook until almost all liquid has been absorbed and farro is just al dente, about 25 minutes, stirring twice during cooking.

6. Add thyme, 1 teaspoon salt, and ¾ teaspoon pepper and continue to cook, stirring constantly, until farro becomes creamy, about 5 minutes.

7. Remove pot from heat. Stir in Parmesan, chives, vinegar, and remaining 2 tablespoons butter. Season with salt and pepper to taste. Adjust consistency with remaining hot water as needed. Serve immediately.

CHICKEN MARSALA

WHY THIS RECIPE WORKS: Developed in Italy after a successful 19th-century marketing campaign to promote Marsala wine from Sicily, this combination of chicken and mushrooms in wine sauce has become an Italian restaurant staple. Too often, however, the chicken is dry, the mushrooms flabby, and the sauce nondescript. We felt a rescue was in order.

We browned chicken breasts in a skillet to start and kept them warm while we prepared the mushrooms and sauce. The mushrooms went into the skillet next, but the chicken drippings burned. Our solution was to sauté some pancetta before browning the mushrooms, which rendered additional fat as well as added meaty flavor. We preferred sweet (as opposed to dry) Marsala for its depth of flavor and smooth finish. Some lemon juice tempered the Marsala's sweetness, while a little garlic and tomato paste rounded out the flavors. Finally, butter, whisked into the sauce at the end, added a rich finish and beautiful sheen.

Chicken Marsala

SERVES 4

Our wine of choice for this dish is Sweet Marsala Fine, an imported wine that gives the sauce body, soft edges, and a smooth finish. To make slicing the chicken easier, freeze it for 15 minutes.

2 tablespoons vegetable oil
1 cup unbleached all-purpose flour
4 (5- to 6-ounce) boneless, skinless chicken breasts, tenderloins removed and breasts trimmed (see note)
Table salt and ground black pepper
2½ ounces pancetta (about 3 slices), cut into pieces 1 inch long and ⅛ inch wide
8 ounces white mushrooms, wiped clean and sliced (about 2 cups)
1 medium garlic clove, minced or pressed through a garlic press (about 1 teaspoon)
1 teaspoon tomato paste
1½ cups sweet Marsala (see note)
1½ tablespoons juice from 1 lemon
4 tablespoons (½ stick) unsalted butter, cut into 4 pieces
2 tablespoons minced fresh parsley leaves

1. Adjust an oven rack to the lower-middle position, place a large ovensafe dinner plate on the oven rack, and heat the oven to 200 degrees. Heat the oil in a 12-inch skillet over medium-high heat until shimmering. Meanwhile, place the flour in a shallow baking dish or pie plate. Halve the chicken horizontally, then cover the chicken halves with plastic wrap and pound the cutlets to an even ¼-inch thickness. Pat the chicken breasts dry. Season both sides of the breasts with salt and pepper; working with one piece at a time, coat both sides with flour. Cooking the cutlets in two batches, place 4 floured cutlets in a single layer in the skillet and cook until golden brown, about 3 minutes. Using tongs, flip the cutlets and cook on the second side until golden brown and the meat feels firm when pressed with a finger, about 3 minutes longer. Transfer the chicken to the heated plate and return the plate to the oven while you cook the remaining cutlets.

2. Return the skillet to low heat and add the pancetta; sauté, stirring occasionally and scraping the pan bottom to loosen the browned bits, until the pancetta is brown and crisp, about 4 minutes. With a slotted spoon, transfer the pancetta to a paper towel–lined plate. Add the mushrooms and increase the heat to medium-high; sauté, stirring occasionally and scraping the pan bottom, until the liquid released by the mushrooms evaporates and the mushrooms begin to brown, about 8 minutes. Add the garlic, tomato paste, and cooked pancetta; sauté while stirring until the tomato paste begins to brown, about 1 minute. Off the heat, add the Marsala; return the pan to high heat and simmer vigorously, scraping the browned bits from the pan bottom, until the sauce is slightly syrupy and reduced to about 1¼ cups, about 5 minutes. Off the heat, add the lemon juice and any accumulated juices from the chicken; whisk in the butter 1 piece at a time. Season with salt and pepper to taste and stir in the parsley. Pour the sauce over the chicken and serve immediately.

BETTER CHICKEN MARSALA

WHY THIS RECIPE WORKS: In revisiting chicken Marsala, we took a new approach to fabricating and cooking chicken cutlets. First, we cut each chicken breast in half crosswise. Then, we cut the thicker half in half horizontally to make three identically sized pieces that could easily be pounded into cutlets. We salted the cutlets briefly to boost their ability to retain moisture and then dredged them in a light coating of flour, which accelerated browning and helped prevent the meat from overcooking. We seared the cutlets quickly on both sides and set them aside while we made the sauce. Our Marsala sauce used reduced dry Marsala and chicken broth, along with cremini and dried porcini mushrooms for rich flavor and gelatin for a silky texture. Once the Marsala and mushroom sauce was complete, we returned the cutlets to the pan to cook them through and wash any excess starch into the sauce, eliminating gumminess.

Better Chicken Marsala

SERVES 4 TO 6

It is worth spending a little extra for a moderately priced dry Marsala ($10 to $12 per bottle). Serve the chicken with potatoes, white rice, or buttered pasta.

- 2¼ cups dry Marsala
- 4 teaspoons unflavored gelatin
- 1 ounce dried porcini mushrooms, rinsed
- 4 (6- to 8-ounce) boneless, skinless chicken breasts, trimmed
- Kosher salt and pepper
- 2 cups chicken broth
- ¾ cup all-purpose flour
- ¼ cup plus 1 teaspoon vegetable oil
- 3 ounces pancetta, cut into ½-inch pieces
- 1 pound cremini mushrooms, trimmed and sliced thin
- 1 shallot, minced
- 1 tablespoon tomato paste
- 1 garlic clove, minced
- 2 teaspoons lemon juice
- 1 teaspoon minced fresh oregano
- 3 tablespoons unsalted butter, cut into 6 pieces
- 2 teaspoons minced fresh parsley

1. Bring 2 cups Marsala, gelatin, and porcini mushrooms to boil in medium saucepan over high heat. Reduce heat to medium-high and vigorously simmer until reduced by half, 6 to 8 minutes.

2. Meanwhile, cut each chicken breast in half crosswise, then cut thick half in half again horizontally, creating 3 cutlets of about same thickness. Place cutlets between sheets of plastic wrap and pound gently to even ½-inch thickness. Place cutlets in bowl and toss with 2 teaspoons salt and ½ teaspoon pepper. Set aside for 15 minutes.

3. Strain Marsala reduction through fine-mesh strainer, pressing on solids to extract as much liquid as possible; discard solids. Return Marsala reduction to saucepan, add broth, and return to boil over high heat. Lower heat to medium-high and simmer until reduced to 1½ cups, 10 to 12 minutes. Set aside.

4. Spread flour in shallow dish. Working with 1 cutlet at a time, dredge cutlets in flour, shaking gently to remove excess. Place on wire rack set in rimmed baking sheet. Heat 2 tablespoons oil in 12-inch skillet over medium-high heat until just smoking. Place 6 cutlets in skillet and lower heat to medium. Cook until golden brown on 1 side, 2 to 3 minutes. Flip and cook until golden brown on second side, 2 to 3 minutes. Return cutlets to wire rack. Repeat with 2 tablespoons oil and remaining 6 cutlets.

5. Return now-empty skillet to medium-low heat and add pancetta. Cook, stirring occasionally, scraping pan bottom to loosen any browned bits, until pancetta is brown and crisp, about 4 minutes. Add cremini mushrooms and increase heat to medium-high. Cook, stirring occasionally and scraping pan bottom, until liquid released by mushrooms evaporates and mushrooms begin to brown, about 8 minutes. Using slotted spoon, transfer cremini mushrooms and pancetta to bowl. Add remaining 1 teaspoon oil and shallot to pan and cook until softened, about 1 minute. Add tomato paste and garlic and cook until fragrant, about 30 seconds. Add reduced Marsala mixture, remaining ¼ cup Marsala, lemon juice, and oregano and bring to simmer.

6. Add cutlets to sauce and simmer for 3 minutes, flipping halfway through simmering. Transfer cutlets to platter. Off heat, whisk in butter. Stir in parsley and cremini mushroom mixture. Season with salt and pepper to taste. Spoon sauce over chicken and serve.

BEST CHICKEN PARMESAN

WHY THIS RECIPE WORKS: Classic chicken Parmesan should feature juicy chicken cutlets with a crisp pan-fried breaded coating, complemented by creamy mozzarella and a bright, zesty marinara sauce. But more often it ends up dry and overcooked, with a soggy crust and a chewy mass of cheese. To prevent the cutlets from overcooking, we halved them horizontally and pounded only the fatter halves thin. Then we salted them for 20 minutes to help them hold on to their moisture. To keep the crust crunchy, we replaced more than half of the sogginess-prone bread crumbs with flavorful grated Parmesan cheese. For a cheese topping that didn't turn chewy, we added some creamy fontina to the usual shredded mozzarella and ran it under the broiler for just 2 minutes to melt and brown. Melting the cheese directly on the fried cutlet formed a barrier between the crispy crust and the tomato sauce.

Best Chicken Parmesan

SERVES 4

Our preferred brand of crushed tomatoes is SMT. This recipe makes enough sauce to top the cutlets as well as four servings of pasta. Serve with pasta and a simple green salad.

SAUCE

- 2 tablespoons extra-virgin olive oil
- 2 garlic cloves, minced
- Kosher salt and pepper
- ¼ teaspoon dried oregano
- Pinch red pepper flakes
- 1 (28-ounce) can crushed tomatoes
- ¼ teaspoon sugar
- 2 tablespoons coarsely chopped fresh basil

CHICKEN

- 2 (6- to 8-ounce) boneless, skinless chicken breasts, trimmed, halved horizontally, and pounded ½ inch thick
- 1 teaspoon kosher salt
- 2 ounces whole-milk mozzarella cheese, shredded (½ cup)
- 2 ounces fontina cheese, shredded (½ cup)
- 1 large egg
- 1 tablespoon all-purpose flour
- 1½ ounces Parmesan cheese, grated (¾ cup)
- ½ cup panko bread crumbs
- ½ teaspoon garlic powder
- ¼ teaspoon dried oregano
- ¼ teaspoon pepper
- ⅓ cup vegetable oil
- ¼ cup torn fresh basil

1. FOR THE SAUCE: Heat 1 tablespoon oil in medium saucepan over medium heat until just shimmering. Add garlic, ¾ teaspoon salt, oregano, and pepper flakes; cook, stirring occasionally, until fragrant, about 30 seconds. Stir in tomatoes and sugar; increase heat to high and bring to simmer. Reduce heat to medium-low and simmer until thickened, about 20 minutes. Off heat, stir in basil and remaining 1 tablespoon oil; season with salt and pepper to taste. Cover and keep warm.

2. FOR THE CHICKEN: Sprinkle each side of each cutlet with ⅛ teaspoon salt and let stand at room temperature for 20 minutes. Combine mozzarella and fontina in bowl; set aside.

3. Adjust oven rack 4 inches from broiler element and heat broiler. Whisk egg and flour together in shallow dish or pie plate until smooth. Combine Parmesan, panko, garlic powder, oregano, and pepper in second shallow dish or pie plate. Pat chicken dry with paper towels. Working with 1 cutlet at a time, dredge cutlet in egg mixture, allowing excess to drip off. Coat all sides in Parmesan mixture, pressing gently so crumbs adhere. Transfer cutlet to large plate and repeat with remaining cutlets.

4. Heat oil in 10-inch nonstick skillet over medium-high heat until shimmering. Carefully place 2 cutlets in skillet and cook without moving them until bottoms are crispy and deep golden brown, 1½ to 2 minutes. Using tongs, carefully flip cutlets and cook on second side until deep golden brown, 1½ to 2 minutes. Transfer cutlets to paper towel–lined plate and repeat with remaining cutlets.

5. Place cutlets on rimmed baking sheet and sprinkle cheese mixture evenly over cutlets, covering as much surface area as possible. Broil until cheese is melted and beginning to brown, 2 to 4 minutes. Transfer chicken to serving platter and top each cutlet with 2 tablespoons sauce. Sprinkle with basil and serve immediately, passing remaining sauce separately.

LIGHTER CHICKEN PARMESAN

WHY THIS RECIPE WORKS: Crunchy fried chicken cutlets topped with cheese and tomato sauce, chicken Parmesan isn't exactly a dish for dieters. Not wanting to eliminate it as an option for healthy eating, we looked for a way to get the crispy coating without using all the oil.

Baking seemed to be the best alternative to frying. We toasted panko (ultracrisp Japanese-style bread crumbs) with a little oil for color and to give them "fried" flavor without the fat. Adopting the conventional breading technique of dipping the cutlets in flour (with garlic powder for flavor), then egg, then bread crumbs, we cut more calories by using only the egg whites. We baked the breasts on a wire rack until they were almost done, then topped them with tomato sauce and shredded low-fat mozzarella to finish. Leaving the breasts on the rack rather than putting them in a casserole dish ensured that they would stay crisp as they baked. Served with a little extra sauce and grated Parmesan on the side, these oven-baked chicken Parmesan cutlets were crisp and full of flavor. And with 310 calories and 8 grams of fat, they have one-third less calories and two-thirds less fat grams than traditional versions.

Lighter Chicken Parmesan

SERVES 6

If you are tight on time, you can substitute 2 cups of your favorite plain tomato sauce for the Simple Tomato Sauce. To make slicing the chicken easier, freeze it for 15 minutes.

- 1½ cups panko (Japanese-style bread crumbs)
- 1 tablespoon olive oil
- 1 ounce Parmesan cheese, grated (about ½ cup), plus extra for serving
- ½ cup unbleached all-purpose flour
- 1½ teaspoons garlic powder
- Table salt and ground black pepper
- 3 large egg whites
- 1 tablespoon water
- 3 (7- to 8-ounce) boneless, skinless chicken breasts, tenderloins removed and breasts trimmed (see note)
- 1 recipe Simple Tomato Sauce (recipe follows), warmed (see note)
- 3 ounces low-fat mozzarella cheese, shredded (about ¾ cup)
- 1 tablespoon minced fresh basil leaves

1. Adjust an oven rack to the middle position and heat the oven to 475 degrees. Combine the bread crumbs and oil in a 12-inch skillet and toast over medium heat, stirring often, until golden, about 10 minutes. Spread the bread crumbs in a shallow dish and cool slightly; when cool, stir in the Parmesan.

2. In a second shallow dish, combine the flour, garlic powder, 1 tablespoon salt, and ½ teaspoon pepper. In a third shallow dish, whisk the egg whites and water together.

3. Line a rimmed baking sheet with foil, place a wire rack over the sheet, and spray the rack with vegetable oil spray. Halve the chicken horizontally, then cover the chicken halves with plastic wrap and pound the cutlets to an even ¼-inch thickness. Pat the chicken dry with paper towels, then season with salt and pepper. Lightly dredge the cutlets in the flour, shaking off the excess. Using tongs, dip both sides of the cutlets into the egg whites and allow the excess egg to drip back into the dish. Finally, coat both sides of the chicken with the bread crumbs. Press on the bread crumbs to make sure they adhere. Lay the chicken on the wire rack.

4. Spray the tops of the chicken with vegetable oil spray. Bake until the meat is no longer pink in the center and feels firm when pressed with a finger, about 15 minutes.

5. Remove the chicken from the oven. Spoon 2 tablespoons of the sauce onto the center of each cutlet and top the sauce with 2 tablespoons of the mozzarella. Return the chicken to the oven and continue to bake until the cheese has melted, about 5 minutes. Sprinkle with the basil and serve, passing the remaining sauce and Parmesan separately.

Simple Tomato Sauce

MAKES ABOUT 2 CUPS

This easy sauce also works well with pasta.

- 1 (28-ounce) can diced tomatoes
- 4 medium garlic cloves, minced or pressed through a garlic press (about 4 teaspoons)
- 1 tablespoon tomato paste
- 1 teaspoon olive oil
- ⅛ teaspoon red pepper flakes
- 1 tablespoon minced fresh basil leaves
- Table salt and ground black pepper

Pulse the tomatoes in a food processor until mostly smooth, about 10 pulses; set aside. Cook the garlic, tomato paste, oil, and red pepper flakes in a medium saucepan over medium heat until the tomato paste begins to brown, about 2 minutes. Stir in the pureed tomatoes and cook until the sauce is thickened and measures 2 cups, about 20 minutes. Off the heat, stir in the basil and season with salt and pepper to taste. Cover and set aside until needed.

CHICKEN PICCATA

WHY THIS RECIPE WORKS: Many recipes for chicken piccata are either bland or overcomplicated, with extra ingredients that ruin the dish's simplicity. Many recipes contain just a tablespoon of lemon juice and a teaspoon of capers, neither of which provides much flavor. But chicken piccata is one of those appealing Italian recipes that taste complex but are actually easy to prepare. Our goal was properly cooked chicken with a streamlined sauce that really tasted of lemons and capers.

Many recipes suggest breading cutlets for chicken piccata, but we found that flour alone was sufficient; there was no point building a crisp crust that would end up drenched in sauce. After browning the chicken and sautéing aromatics, we deglazed the pan with chicken broth alone; although wine is sometimes suggested, we found it to be too acidic for this dish. We simmered slices from half a lemon in the broth for a few minutes; this was easier than grating the zest. For maximum lemon flavor in the sauce, we used a full quarter-cup of lemon juice, added when the sauce was nearly done so as not to blunt its impact. Butter gave the sauce body and was preferable to flour, which made it overly thick. Plenty of capers and a bit of parsley finished our ultra-lemony piccata.

Chicken Piccata

SERVES 4

To make slicing the chicken easier, freeze it for 15 minutes. If you like, use thinly sliced cutlets available at many supermarkets. These cutlets don't have any tenderloins and can be used as they are.

- 2 large lemons
- 4 boneless, skinless chicken breasts (about 1½ pounds), tenderloins removed and breasts trimmed
- Salt and ground black pepper
- ½ cup unbleached all-purpose flour
- 4 tablespoons vegetable oil
- 1 small shallot, minced (about 2 tablespoons), or 1 small garlic clove, minced (about 1 teaspoon)
- 1 cup chicken broth
- 2 tablespoons small capers, drained
- 3 tablespoons unsalted butter, softened
- 2 tablespoons minced fresh parsley leaves

1. Adjust oven rack to the lower-middle position, set large ovensafe plate on rack, and heat oven to 200 degrees.

2. Halve 1 lemon pole to pole. Trim ends from one half and cut it crosswise into slices ⅛ to ¼ inch thick; set aside. Juice remaining half and whole lemon to obtain ¼ cup juice; reserve.

3. Halve chicken horizontally, then cover chicken halves with plastic wrap and pound cutlets to even ¼-inch thickness. Sprinkle both sides of cutlets generously with salt and pepper. Place flour in shallow baking dish or pie plate. Working with 1 cutlet at a time, coat with flour and shake to remove excess.

4. Heat 2 tablespoons of oil in a heavy-bottomed 12-inch skillet over medium-high heat until shimmering. Lay half of chicken cutlets in skillet. Cook cutlets until lightly browned on first side, 2 to 3 minutes. Flip cutlets and cook until second side is lightly browned, 2 to 3 minutes longer. Remove pan from heat and transfer cutlets to plate in warm oven. Add remaining 2 tablespoons oil to now-empty skillet and heat until shimmering. Add remaining chicken cutlets and repeat.

5. Add shallot or garlic to now-empty skillet and return skillet to medium heat. Sauté until fragrant, about 30 seconds for shallot or 10 seconds for garlic. Add broth and lemon slices, increase heat to high, and scrape pan bottom with wooden spoon or spatula to loosen browned bits. Simmer until liquid reduces to about ⅓ cup, about 4 minutes. Add lemon juice and capers and simmer until sauce reduces again to ⅓ cup, about 1 minute. Remove pan from heat and swirl in butter until it melts and thickens sauce. Stir in parsley and season with salt and pepper to taste. Spoon sauce over chicken and serve immediately.

PARMESAN-CRUSTED CHICKEN BREASTS

WHY THIS RECIPE WORKS: With a short ingredient list of only chicken breasts and Parmesan cheese plus one or two binders such as eggs or flour, Parmesan-crusted chicken breasts should be straightforward. But we found pale, wet, and gummy baked versions as well as bitter and burnt pan-fried versions. We wanted moist and tender chicken coated with a thin, crispy-yet-chewy, wafer-like sheath of Parmesan cheese.

A standard breading in which we merely substituted cheese for the bread crumbs and flour was disappointing; the cheese didn't provide the dry base to which the rest of the coating would stick. So we went back to flour, with a bit of Parmesan for flavor, and we left out the egg yolks to eliminate the eggy taste. For the outermost layer, shredding the cheese on the large holes of a box grater made a sturdier, more even crust, and a little flour added to this cheese helped the coating turn crisp. Pan-frying in a nonstick skillet prevented sticking, and keeping the heat no higher than medium browned the cheese without making it bitter. These cutlets were pale golden rather than deep golden brown, but the nutty, crisp Parmesan crust was everything we hoped it would be.

Parmesan-Crusted Chicken Cutlets

SERVES 4

To make slicing the chicken easier, freeze it for 15 minutes. Note that part of the Parmesan is grated on the smallest holes of a box grater (or rasp grater) and the remaining Parmesan is shredded on the largest holes of the box grater. We like the flavor that authentic Parmigiano-Reggiano lends to this recipe. A less-expensive cheese, such as Boar's Head Parmesan cheese, can also be used, but the resulting cheese crust will be slightly saltier and chewier. Although the portion size (one cutlet per person) might seem small, these cutlets are rather rich due to the cheese content. To make eight cutlets, double the ingredients and cook the chicken in four batches, transferring the cooked cutlets to a warm oven and wiping out the skillet after each batch.

- 2 (7- to 8-ounce) boneless, skinless chicken breasts, tenderloins removed and breasts trimmed (see note)
- Table salt and ground black pepper
- 5 tablespoons unbleached all-purpose flour
- ¼ cup grated Parmesan cheese plus 6 ounces, shredded (about 2 cups; see note)
- 3 large egg whites
- 2 tablespoons minced fresh chives (optional)
- 4 teaspoons olive oil
- Lemon wedges, for serving

1. Adjust an oven rack to the middle position and heat the oven to 200 degrees. Halve the chicken horizontally, then cover the chicken halves with plastic wrap and pound the cutlets to an even ¼-inch thickness. Pat the chicken dry with paper towels and season with salt and pepper.

2. Whisk ¼ cup of the flour and the ¼ cup grated Parmesan together in a shallow dish. Whisk the egg whites and chives (if using) in a medium bowl until slightly foamy. Combine the 2 cups shredded Parmesan and remaining 1 tablespoon flour in a second shallow dish. Working with 1 chicken cutlet at a time, dredge in the flour mixture, shaking off the excess, then coat with the egg white mixture, allowing the excess to drip off. Finally, coat with the shredded Parmesan mixture, pressing gently so that the cheese adheres. Place the coated cutlets in a single layer on a wire rack set over a rimmed baking sheet.

3. Heat 2 teaspoons of the oil in a 12-inch nonstick skillet over medium heat until shimmering. Add 2 of the cutlets and cook until pale golden brown on both sides, 4 to 6 minutes in total. (While the chicken is cooking, use a thin nonstick spatula to gently separate any cheesy edges that have melted together.) Transfer to a clean wire rack set over a rimmed baking sheet and keep warm in the oven. Wipe out the skillet with paper towels. Repeat with the remaining 2 teaspoons oil and chicken. Serve with the lemon wedges.

CHICKEN FRANCESE

WHY THIS RECIPE WORKS: This fast-fading star of red-sauce Italian restaurants often features a rubbery coating and a puckery lemon sauce. Yet this quick dinner still holds promise for the home cook. We wanted our chicken to have a rich, eggy coating that would remain soft and tender yet be sturdy enough to stand up to a silky, well-balanced lemon sauce.

We found that a first coating of flour was essential for getting the egg to stick, and a little milk added to the egg prevented it from turning rubbery. A final dip into flour made a soft, delicate veneer. We sautéed the cutlets in butter for its flavor, adding a little oil to keep the butter from burning, and kept the cutlets warm in the oven while we made our sauce. Fresh lemon juice with some vermouth and chicken broth gave us the bright, fresh citrus flavor we wanted; a little sautéed shallot balanced the lemon but didn't overpower it. To get the sauce to cling to the chicken without making it soggy, we made a roux with butter and flour. Our sauce was just right, but the chicken had dried out while waiting in the oven. Our solution was to make the sauce first, then cook the chicken and finish the sauce. We think this revitalized dish deserves a place in today's home kitchens.

Chicken Francese

SERVES 4

To make slicing the chicken easier, freeze it for 15 minutes. The sauce is very lemony—for less tartness, reduce the amount of lemon juice by about 1 tablespoon.

SAUCE

- 3 tablespoons unsalted butter
- 1 large shallot, minced (about 4 tablespoons)
- 1 tablespoon unbleached all-purpose flour
- 2¼ cups low-sodium chicken broth
- ½ cup dry vermouth or white wine
- ⅓ cup juice from 2 lemons (see note)
- Table salt and ground black pepper

CHICKEN

- 4 (5- to 6-ounce) boneless, skinless chicken breasts, tenderloins removed and breasts trimmed (see note)
- Table salt and ground black pepper
- 1 cup unbleached all-purpose flour
- 2 large eggs
- 2 tablespoons milk
- 2 tablespoons unsalted butter
- 2 tablespoons olive oil
- 2 tablespoons minced fresh parsley leaves

1. Adjust an oven rack to the middle position and heat the oven to 200 degrees.

2. FOR THE SAUCE: Melt 1 tablespoon of the butter in a medium saucepan over medium heat. Add the shallot and cook, stirring occasionally, until softened, about 2 minutes. Stir in the flour and cook until light golden brown, about 1 minute. Whisk in the broth, vermouth, and lemon juice and bring to a simmer. Cook, whisking occasionally, until the sauce measures 1½ cups, about 15 minutes. Strain the sauce through a fine-mesh strainer. Return the sauce to the saucepan and set aside, discarding the solids.

3. FOR THE CHICKEN: Halve the chicken horizontally, then cover the chicken halves with plastic wrap and pound the cutlets to an even ¼-inch thickness. Pat the chicken dry with paper towels and season with salt and pepper.

4. Combine the flour, 1 teaspoon salt, and ¼ teaspoon pepper in a shallow dish and whisk the eggs and milk together in a medium bowl. Working with 1 chicken cutlet at a time, dredge in the flour, shaking off the excess, then coat with the egg mixture, allowing the excess to drip off. Finally, coat with the flour again, shaking off the excess. Place the coated chicken in a single layer on a wire rack set over a rimmed baking sheet.

5. Heat 1 tablespoon each of the butter and oil in a 12-inch nonstick skillet over medium-high heat. Add 4 of the cutlets and cook until lightly browned on one side, 2 to 3 minutes. Flip the chicken over and continue to cook until no longer pink and lightly browned on the second side, about 1 minute. Transfer the chicken to a clean wire rack set over a rimmed baking sheet and keep warm in the oven. Wipe out the skillet with paper towels. Add the remaining 1 tablespoon each of the butter and oil to the skillet and repeat with the remaining cutlets, then transfer to the oven. Wipe out the skillet with paper towels.

6. TO FINISH THE SAUCE AND SERVE: Transfer the sauce to the now-empty skillet and cook over medium-low heat until warmed, about 2 minutes. Whisk in the remaining 2 tablespoons butter, 1 tablespoon at a time, and season with salt and pepper to taste. Transfer 4 of the chicken cutlets to the skillet, turn to coat with the sauce, then transfer each serving (2 cutlets) to individual plates. Repeat with the remaining cutlets. Spoon 2 tablespoons of the sauce over each serving and sprinkle with the parsley. Serve, passing the remaining sauce separately.

CHICKEN SALTIMBOCCA

WHY THIS RECIPE WORKS: In its classic Italian form, saltimbocca is made with veal, prosciutto, and sage, but chicken is frequently substituted for the veal. The combination of flavors is meant to "jump in the mouth," as the name suggests. Preparing this dish can be complicated, but we wanted to streamline it and ensure that the flavors were well balanced.

Flouring only the chicken, rather than the chicken-prosciutto package, avoided gummy spots. The prosciutto is usually secured to the chicken with a toothpick, but we found that searing the prosciutto side of the chicken first worked as well; once browned, the two stuck together just fine. Prosciutto can overwhelm the other flavors in this dish, so it's important to use thin slices, but not so thin that they disintegrate during cooking. A single sage leaf is the usual garnish, but we wanted more sage flavor, so we sprinkled some minced fresh sage over the floured chicken before adding the prosciutto. With a simple pan sauce of vermouth, lemon juice, butter, and parsley, our chicken saltimbocca was ready to serve and full of flavor.

Chicken Saltimbocca

SERVES 4

To make slicing the chicken easier, freeze it for 15 minutes. Although whole sage leaves make a beautiful presentation, they are optional and can be left out of step 3. A single fried sage leaf is another pretty but optional garnish. Make sure to buy prosciutto that is thinly sliced, not shaved; also avoid slices that are too thick, as they won't stick to the chicken. The prosciutto slices should be large enough to fully cover one side of each cutlet.

- 4 (5- to 6-ounce) boneless, skinless chicken breasts, tenderloins removed and breasts trimmed (see note)
- ½ cup unbleached all-purpose flour
- Ground black pepper
- 1 tablespoon minced fresh sage leaves, plus 8 large leaves (optional; see note)
- 8 thin prosciutto slices (about 3 ounces; see note)
- 4 tablespoons olive oil
- 1¼ cups dry vermouth or white wine
- 2 teaspoons juice from 1 lemon
- 4 tablespoons (½ stick) unsalted butter, cut into 4 pieces and chilled
- 1 tablespoon minced fresh parsley leaves
- Table salt

1. Halve the chicken horizontally, then cover the chicken halves with plastic wrap and pound the cutlets to an even ¼-inch thickness.

2. Combine the flour and 1 teaspoon pepper in a shallow dish. Pat the chicken dry with paper towels. Dredge the chicken in the flour, shaking off any excess. Lay the cutlets flat and sprinkle evenly with the minced sage. Place 1 prosciutto slice on top of each cutlet, pressing lightly to adhere; set aside.

3. Heat 2 tablespoons of the oil in a 12-inch skillet over medium-high heat until shimmering. Add the sage leaves (if using) and cook until the leaves begin to change color and are fragrant, 15 to 20 seconds. Using a slotted spoon, transfer the sage to a paper towel–lined plate and set aside. Add 4 of the cutlets to the pan, prosciutto side down, and cook until lightly browned on one side, about 2 minutes. Flip the chicken over and continue to cook until no longer pink, 30 seconds to 1 minute. Transfer the chicken to a plate and tent loosely with

NOTES FROM THE TEST KITCHEN

MAKING CHICKEN SALTIMBOCCA

1. Flour just the chicken—not the prosciutto—before sautéing.

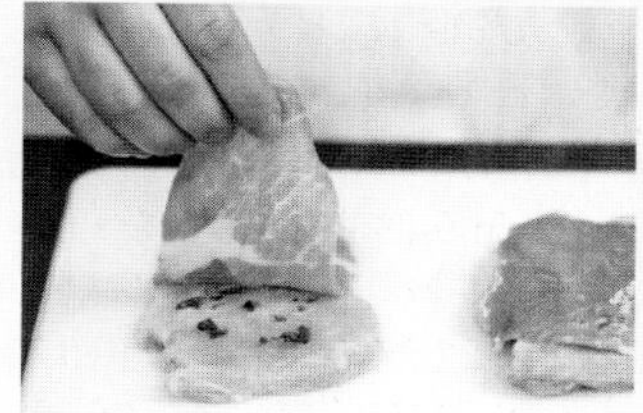

2. Sprinkle the cutlets evenly with the minced sage, then top each with a slice of prosciutto.

3. Cook the cutlets, prosciutto-side down, to help the ham adhere to the cutlets.

foil. Add the remaining 2 tablespoons oil to the skillet and repeat with the remaining 4 cutlets. Transfer to the plate and tent loosely with foil while making the sauce.

4. Pour off the excess fat from the skillet. Stir in the vermouth, scraping up any browned bits, and simmer until reduced to about ⅓ cup, 5 to 7 minutes. Stir in the lemon juice. Turn the heat to low and whisk in the butter, 1 tablespoon at time. Off the heat, stir in the parsley and season with salt and pepper to taste. Spoon the sauce over the chicken, place a sage leaf (if using) on each cutlet, and serve.

ITALIAN BRAISED CHICKEN

WHY THIS RECIPE WORKS: Chicken *canzanese* is a regional Italian braised dish that transforms tough old birds into a moist and tender meal. Today's lean, mass-produced chickens, however, turn dried-out and bland when braised. We wanted old-fashioned results with a modern-day bird: tender, juicy chicken in an intensely flavored, well-developed sauce.

To start, we swapped out young, modern chickens for meaty chicken thighs that hold up especially well to braising. Next, we turned to the sauce. We browned diced prosciutto on the stovetop until it rendered enough fat to cook the garlic, which created a rich flavor base. Then we added white wine and chicken broth, and simmered them to concentrate flavors and burn off the raw alcohol flavor. We returned the chicken to the skillet and put it into the oven, uncovered to crisp the skin. To round out the flavors, we added a quick squeeze of lemon juice, a generous pat of butter, and a sprinkling of chopped rosemary.

Chicken Canzanese

SERVES 4 TO 6

When seasoning the dish at the end, be mindful that the prosciutto adds a fair amount of salt. It is important to use a piece of thickly sliced prosciutto in this recipe; thin strips will become tough and stringy. An equal amount of thickly sliced pancetta or bacon can be used in place of the prosciutto. Serve the chicken with boiled potatoes, noodles, or polenta.

- 1 tablespoon olive oil
- 2 ounces prosciutto (¼ inch thick), cut into ¼-inch cubes (see note)
- 4 medium garlic cloves, sliced thin lengthwise
- 3 pounds bone-in, skin-on chicken thighs (about 8 thighs), trimmed
- Ground black pepper
- 2 teaspoons unbleached all-purpose flour
- 2 cups dry white wine
- 1 cup low-sodium chicken broth
- 4 whole cloves
- 1 (4-inch) sprig fresh rosemary, leaves removed and minced fine (about ½ teaspoon), stem reserved
- 12 whole fresh sage leaves
- 2 bay leaves
- ¼–½ teaspoon red pepper flakes
- 1 tablespoon juice from 1 lemon
- 2 tablespoons unsalted butter
- Table salt

1. Adjust an oven rack to the lower-middle position and heat the oven to 325 degrees. Heat 1 teaspoon of the oil in a 12-inch heavy-bottomed ovensafe skillet over medium heat until shimmering. Add the prosciutto and cook, stirring frequently, until just starting to brown, about 3 minutes. Add the garlic slices and cook, stirring frequently, until the garlic is golden brown, about 1½ minutes. Using a slotted spoon, transfer the garlic and prosciutto to a small bowl and set aside. Do not rinse the pan.

2. Increase the heat to medium-high; add the remaining 2 teaspoons oil and heat until just smoking. Pat the chicken dry with paper towels and season with black pepper. Add the chicken, skin side down, and cook without moving until well browned, 5 to 8 minutes. Using tongs, turn the chicken and brown on the second side, about 5 minutes longer. Transfer the chicken to a large plate.

3. Remove all but 2 tablespoons fat from the pan. Sprinkle the flour over the fat and cook, stirring constantly, for 1 minute. Slowly add the wine and broth; bring to a simmer, scraping the bottom of the pan with a wooden spoon to loosen the browned bits. Cook until the liquid is slightly reduced, 3 minutes. Stir in the cloves, rosemary stem, sage leaves, bay leaves, red pepper flakes, and reserved prosciutto and garlic. Nestle the chicken into the liquid, skin side up (the skin should be above the surface of the liquid), and bake, uncovered, until the meat offers no resistance when poked with a fork but is not falling off the bones, about 1 hour 15 minutes. (Check the chicken after 15 minutes; the broth should be barely bubbling. If bubbling vigorously, reduce the oven temperature to 300 degrees.)

4. Using tongs, transfer the chicken to a serving platter and tent with foil. Remove and discard the sage leaves, rosemary stem, cloves, and bay leaves. Place the skillet over high heat and bring the sauce to a boil. Cook until the sauce is reduced to 1¼ cups, 2 to 5 minutes. Off the heat, stir in the minced rosemary, lemon juice, and butter. Season with salt and pepper to taste. Pour the sauce around the chicken and serve.

BEHIND THE SCENES

SHOPPING FOR CHICKEN—WHAT YOU NEED TO KNOW

Every good chicken dish starts with high-quality, fresh chicken. But there are an overwhelming number of choices at the supermarket—so how do you recognize superior poultry? Here are a few tips the test kitchen has learned over time. If you're buying boneless, skinless chicken breasts, you should be aware that breasts of different sizes are often packaged together, and it's usually impossible to tell what you've bought until you've opened the package. If possible, buy chicken breasts individually. If that isn't an option, pound the thicker ends of the larger pieces of chicken to match those of the smaller pieces. Some breasts will still be larger than others, but pounding will help make their thickness the same and ensure even cooking. As for chicken parts—say for making a dish such as fried chicken or stew—we prefer to butcher our own birds rather than buy packaged parts. Not only is this a less expensive option, but the parts will be consistently sized. (We also use this approach with stew meat—there's no guarantee that packaged stew meat is going to be cut into even-sized pieces or be from the same cut or even the same cow!) And what about ground chicken? Prepackaged ground chicken is made from either dark or white meat or a mix of the two. Higher-end markets often grind their chicken to order, so the choice is yours. In most of our testing, we found ground white meat chicken to be exceedingly dry and almost void of flavor. The dark meat was more flavorful and juicy due to its higher fat content. For our recommended brands of chicken, see page 909.

ITALIAN GRILLED CHICKEN

WHY THIS RECIPE WORKS: Anyone who has tried to grill a whole chicken knows that it's challenging at best, and the results are often inedible. Many cuisines have developed methods to overcome the problems of chicken cooked over a fire; the Italian way is to cook the chicken under bricks. This was one method we had to try.

One attempt to grill a butterflied chicken the Italian way was enough to let us know that we needed more than just bricks to make this recipe work. We thought of brining to keep the meat moist, but it produced burnt chicken when the liquid dripped into the fire. An alternative way to retain moisture in meat is salting; we rubbed the flesh under the skin with salt, mixed with garlic, red pepper flakes, and herbs for Italian flavor. With a modified two-level fire in the grill, we cooked the chicken under preheated bricks on the cooler side, skin side down, to firm up the flesh and release fat and liquid where the fire wouldn't cause flare-ups. We flipped the chicken and finished cooking it on the hot side; another flip and a few minutes without the bricks crisped up the skin. The combination of flipping and moving the chicken from the cool side to the hot side guaranteed even cooking, and the salting had kept the meat juicy. With a finishing embellishment of a quick vinaigrette, we had perfectly cooked chicken with zesty Italian flavor, and not a burnt piece in sight.

Italian-Style Grilled Chicken

SERVES 4

Use an oven mitt or kitchen towel to safely grip and maneuver the hot bricks. You will need two standard-size bricks for this recipe. Placing the bricks on the chicken while it cooks ensures that the skin will be evenly browned and well rendered. A cast-iron skillet or other heavy pan can be used in place of the bricks.

- ⅓ cup extra-virgin olive oil
- 8 garlic cloves, minced
- 1 teaspoon grated lemon zest plus 2 tablespoons juice
- Pinch red pepper flakes
- 4 teaspoons minced fresh thyme
- 1 tablespoon minced fresh rosemary
- 1 (3½- to 4-pound) whole chicken
- Salt and pepper

1. Heat oil, garlic, lemon zest, and pepper flakes in small saucepan over medium-low heat until sizzling, about 3 minutes. Stir in 1 tablespoon thyme and 2 teaspoons rosemary and continue to cook for 30 seconds longer. Strain mixture through fine-mesh strainer set over small bowl, pushing on solids to extract oil. Transfer solids to bowl and cool; set oil and solids aside.

2. TO BUTTERFLY CHICKEN: Use kitchen shears to cut along both sides of backbone to remove it. Flatten breastbone and tuck wings behind back. Use hands or handle of wooden spoon to loosen skin over breast and thighs and remove any excess fat.

3. Combine 1½ teaspoons salt and 1 teaspoon pepper in bowl. Mix 2 teaspoons salt mixture with cooled garlic solids. Spread salt-garlic mixture evenly under skin over chicken breast and thighs. Sprinkle remaining ½ teaspoon salt mixture on exposed meat of bone side. Place chicken skin side up on wire rack set in rimmed baking sheet and refrigerate for 1 to 2 hours.

4A. FOR A CHARCOAL GRILL: Open bottom vent halfway. Light large chimney starter three-quarters filled with charcoal briquettes (4½ quarts). When top coals are partially covered with ash, pour evenly over half of grill. Set cooking grate in place, wrap 2 bricks tightly in aluminum foil, and place on cooking grate. Cover and open lid vent halfway. Heat grill until hot, about 5 minutes.

4B. FOR A GAS GRILL: Wrap 2 bricks tightly in aluminum foil and place on cooking grate. Turn all burners to high, cover, and heat grill until hot, about 15 minutes. Leave primary burner on high and turn off other burner(s). (Adjust primary burner as needed during cooking to maintain grill temperature around 350 degrees.)

5. Clean and oil cooking grate. Place chicken on cooler side of grill, skin side down, with legs facing coals and flames. Place hot bricks lengthwise over each breast half, cover, and cook until skin is lightly browned and faint grill marks appear, 22 to 25 minutes. Remove bricks from chicken. Using tongs, grip legs and flip chicken (chicken should release freely from grill; use thin metal spatula to loosen if stuck), then transfer to hot side of grill, skin side up. Place bricks over breast, cover, and cook until chicken is well browned, 12 to 15 minutes.

6. Remove bricks, flip chicken skin side down, and continue to cook until skin is well browned and breast registers 160 degrees and thighs register 175 degrees, 5 to 10 minutes longer. Transfer chicken to carving board, tent loosely with foil, and let rest for 15 minutes.

7. Whisk lemon juice, remaining 1 teaspoon thyme, and remaining 1 teaspoon rosemary into reserved oil and season with salt and pepper to taste. Carve chicken and serve, passing sauce separately.

ITALIAN SAUSAGE WITH GRAPES AND BALSAMIC VINEGAR

WHY THIS RECIPE WORKS: Italian sausage with grapes is a great example of the affinity that pork and fruit flavors have for one another. We wanted to pay homage to this simple Italian dish and highlight the attributes that make it so appealing. We used a combination of sautéing and steaming to produce sausages that were nicely browned but moist and juicy. Building the sauce in the same skillet, we cooked down seedless red grapes and thinly sliced onion until caramelized to create a sweet but complex sauce. White wine, in addition to balsamic vinegar, gave the dish acidity and complemented the grapes. Oregano and pepper contributed earthiness and a touch of spice, while a finish of fresh mint added brightness.

Italian Sausage with Grapes and Balsamic Vinegar

SERVES 4 TO 6

Serve this dish with crusty bread and salad or over polenta for a heartier meal.

- 1 tablespoon vegetable oil
- 1½ pounds sweet Italian sausage
- 1 pound red seedless grapes, halved lengthwise (3 cups)
- 1 onion, halved and sliced thin (1½ cups)
- ¼ cup water
- ⅛ teaspoon salt
- ¼ teaspoon pepper
- ¼ cup dry white wine
- 1 tablespoon chopped fresh oregano
- 2 teaspoons balsamic vinegar
- 2 tablespoons chopped fresh mint

1. Heat oil in 12-inch skillet over medium heat until shimmering. Arrange sausage links in pan and cook, turning once, until browned on both sides, about 5 minutes. Tilt skillet and carefully remove excess fat with paper towel. Distribute grapes and onion over and around sausages. Add water and immediately cover. Cook, turning sausages once, until they register between 160 and 165 degrees and onions and grapes have softened, about 10 minutes.

2. Transfer sausages to paper towel–lined plate and tent with aluminum foil. Return skillet to medium-high heat and stir salt and pepper into grape-onion mixture. Spread grape-onion mixture in even layer in skillet and cook without stirring until browned, 3 to 5 minutes. Continue to cook, stirring frequently, until mixture is well browned and grapes are soft but still retain their shape, 3 to 5 minutes longer. Reduce heat to medium, stir in wine and oregano, and cook, scraping up any browned bits, until wine is reduced by half, 30 to 60 seconds. Remove pan from heat and stir in vinegar.

3. Arrange sausages on serving platter and spoon grape-onion mixture over top. Sprinkle with mint and serve.

PORK CHOPS WITH VINEGAR AND PEPPERS

WHY THIS RECIPE WORKS: This Italian-American dish was devised when pork chops had plenty of fat to keep them juicy; the leaner pork we have today tends to dry out and ruin the dish. But the thought of succulent pork with a tangy vinegar and pepper sauce spurred us to search for a way to make this dish taste the way it should. Bone-in rib chops of medium thickness had the best flavor, and the bone helped keep the meat juicy. Brining the chops in a solution of salt and sugar added moisture and flavor, and the sugar enhanced browning. We discovered that browning the chops, removing them from the pan to build the sauce, then finishing everything together in the oven worked best to get the flavors of the sauce into the meat. We also ditched the jarred vinegar peppers, which are traditional, and made our own; they were far superior to any we'd found at the supermarket.

Pork Chops with Vinegar and Sweet Peppers

SERVES 4

We prefer natural to enhanced pork (pork that has been injected with a salt solution to increase moistness and flavor) for this recipe, though enhanced pork can be used. If using enhanced pork, skip the brining in step 1. To keep the chops from overcooking and becoming tough and dry, remove them from the oven when they are just shy of fully cooked; as they sit in the hot skillet, they will continue to cook with residual heat.

- 1 cup sugar
- Table salt and ground black pepper
- 4 (8- to 10-ounce) bone-in rib loin pork chops, ¾ to 1 inch thick, trimmed of excess fat (see note)
- 2 tablespoons olive oil
- 1 medium onion, minced
- 1 medium red bell pepper, stemmed, seeded, and cut into ¼-inch-wide strips
- 1 medium yellow bell pepper, stemmed, seeded, and cut into ¼-inch-wide strips
- 2 anchovy fillets, minced (about 1 teaspoon)
- 1 medium sprig fresh rosemary
- 2 medium garlic cloves, minced or pressed through a garlic press (about 2 teaspoons)
- ¾ cup water
- ½ cup white wine vinegar, plus 2 tablespoons to finish the sauce (optional)
- 2 tablespoons cold unsalted butter
- 2 tablespoons chopped fresh parsley leaves

NOTES FROM THE TEST KITCHEN

CUTTING BELL PEPPERS INTO MATCHSTICKS

1. Slice off the top and bottom of the pepper and remove the seeds and stem. Slice down through the side of the pepper.

2. Lay the pepper flat onto the cutting board and slice into ¼-inch-wide strips.

1. Dissolve the sugar and ½ cup salt in 2 quarts water in a large container; add the pork chops and refrigerate for 30 minutes. Remove the chops from the brine, rinse, and pat dry with paper towels. Using a sharp knife, cut two slits, about 2 inches apart, through the outer layer of fat and silver skin of each chop (do not cut into the meat of the chops). Season the chops with ¾ teaspoon pepper and set aside.

3. Set the skillet over medium-high heat. Add the onion and cook, stirring occasionally, until just beginning to soften, about 2 minutes. Add the peppers, anchovies, and rosemary; cook, stirring frequently, until the peppers just begin to soften, about 4 minutes. Add the garlic; cook, stirring constantly, until fragrant, about 30 seconds. Add the water and ½ cup of the vinegar and bring to a boil, scraping up the browned bits with a wooden spoon. Reduce the heat to medium; simmer until the liquid is reduced to about ⅓ cup, 6 to 8 minutes. Off the heat, discard the rosemary.

4. Return the pork chops, browner side up, to the skillet; nestle the chops in the peppers, but do not cover them. Add any accumulated juices to the skillet; set the skillet in the oven and cook until the center of the chops registers 140 to 145 degrees on an instant-read thermometer, 8 to 12 minutes (begin checking the temperature after 6 minutes). Using potholders, carefully remove the skillet from the oven (the handle will be very hot) and cover the skillet with a lid or foil; let stand until the center of the chops registers 150 degrees, 5 to 7 minutes. Transfer the chops to a platter or individual plates. Swirl the butter into the sauce and the peppers in the skillet; taste and stir in the remaining 2 tablespoons vinegar (if using) and the parsley. Season with salt and pepper to taste, then pour or spoon the sauce and peppers over the chops. Serve immediately.

OSSO BUCO

WHY THIS RECIPE WORKS: Osso buco, veal shanks braised in a rich sauce until tender, is incredibly rich and hearty. We felt that this time-honored recipe shouldn't be altered much, but we hoped to identify the keys to flavor so that we could perfect it.

To serve one shank per person, we searched for medium-sized shanks, and tied them around the equator to keep the meat attached to the bone for an attractive presentation. Most recipes suggest flouring the veal before browning it, but we got better flavor when we simply seared the meat, liberally seasoned with just salt and pepper. Browning in two batches enabled us to deglaze the pan twice, thus enriching the sauce. Celery, onion, and carrots formed the basis of the sauce; for the liquid we used a combination of chicken broth, white wine, and canned tomatoes. The traditional garnish of gremolata—minced garlic, lemon, and parsley—required no changes; we stirred half into the sauce and sprinkled the rest over individual servings for a fresh burst of citrus flavor.

Osso Buco

SERVES 6

To keep the meat attached to the bone during the long simmering process, tie a piece of kitchen twine around the thickest portion of each shank before it is browned. Just before serving, taste the liquid and, if it seems too thin, simmer it on the stovetop as you remove the strings from the osso buco and arrange them in individual bowls. Serve with rice or polenta.

OSSO BUCO

- 4 tablespoons vegetable oil
- 6 (8- to 10-ounce) veal shanks, 1½ inches thick, patted dry with paper towels and tied with kitchen twine at 1½-inch intervals
- Table salt and ground black pepper
- 2½ cups dry white wine
- 2 medium onions, cut into ½-inch pieces
- 2 medium carrots, cut into ½-inch pieces
- 2 medium celery ribs, cut into ½-inch pieces
- 6 medium garlic cloves, minced or pressed through a garlic press (about 2 tablespoons)
- 2 cups low-sodium chicken broth
- 2 small bay leaves
- 1 (14.5-ounce) can diced tomatoes, drained

GREMOLATA

- ¼ cup minced fresh parsley leaves
- 3 medium garlic cloves, minced or pressed through a garlic press (about 1 tablespoon)
- 2 teaspoons grated zest from 1 lemon

1. FOR THE OSSO BUCO: Adjust an oven rack to the lower-middle position and heat the oven to 325 degrees. Heat 1 tablespoon of the oil in a large Dutch oven over medium-high heat until shimmering. Meanwhile, sprinkle both sides of the shanks generously with salt and pepper. Place 3 shanks in the pan and cook until they are golden brown on one side, about 5 minutes. Using tongs, flip the shanks and cook on the second side until golden brown, about 5 minutes longer. Transfer the shanks to a bowl and set aside. Off the heat, add ½ cup of the wine to the Dutch oven, scraping the pan bottom with a wooden spoon to loosen any browned bits. Pour the liquid into the bowl with the browned shanks. Return the pot to medium-high heat, add 1 tablespoon more oil, and heat until shimmering. Brown the remaining shanks, about 5 minutes for each side. Transfer the shanks to the bowl. Off the heat, add 1 cup more wine to the pot, scraping the bottom to loosen the browned bits. Pour the liquid into the bowl with the shanks.

2. Set the pot over medium heat. Add the remaining 2 tablespoons oil and heat until shimmering. Add the onions, carrots, celery, ¼ teaspoon salt, and ⅛ teaspoon pepper and cook, stirring occasionally, until soft and lightly browned, about 9 minutes. Stir in the garlic and cook until fragrant, about 30 seconds. Increase the heat to high and stir in the broth, remaining 1 cup wine, and bay leaves. Add the tomatoes; return the veal shanks to the pot along with any accumulated juices (the liquid should just cover the shanks). Bring the liquid to a simmer. Cover the pot and transfer the pot to the oven. Cook the shanks until the meat is easily pierced with a fork but not falling off the bone, about 2 hours. (At this point the osso buco can be refrigerated for up to 2 days. Bring to a simmer over medium-low heat.)

3. FOR THE GREMOLATA: Combine the parsley, garlic, and lemon zest in a small bowl. Stir half of the gremolata into the pot, reserving the rest for garnish. Season with salt and pepper to taste. Let the osso buco stand, uncovered, for 5 minutes.

4. Using tongs, remove the shanks from the pot, cut off and discard the twine, and place 1 veal shank in each of six bowls. Ladle some of the braising liquid over each shank and sprinkle each serving with the remaining gremolata. Serve immediately.

BEEF IN BAROLO

WHY THIS RECIPE WORKS: Italian pot roast is an inexpensive cut of beef braised in wine. Full-bodied Barolo has been called the "wine of kings." It can be somewhat expensive, so this pot roast has to be special. We wanted tender meat in a rich, savory sauce that would do justice to the regal wine. A chuck-eye roast won't dry out after a long braise, but it has a line of fat in the middle that we felt was out of place in this refined dish. Separating one roast into two smaller ones enabled us to discard most of this fat before cooking. We then tied the roasts together and browned them in fat rendered from pancetta. We browned aromatics, then poured a whole bottle of wine into the pot. The Barolo's bold flavor needed something to temper it, and we liked a can of diced tomatoes. When the meat was done, we reduced the sauce and strained out the vegetables. Dark, full-flavored, and lustrous, this sauce bestowed nobility on our humble cut of meat.

Beef Braised in Barolo

SERVES 6

Don't skip tying the roasts—it keeps them intact during the long cooking time. Purchase pancetta that is cut to order, about 1/4 inch thick. If pancetta is not available, substitute an equal amount of salt pork (find the meatiest piece possible), cut it into 1/4-inch cubes, and boil it in 3 cups of water for about 2 minutes to remove excess salt. After draining, use it as you would pancetta.

- 1 (3½-pound) boneless chuck-eye roast
- Table salt and ground black pepper
- 4 ounces pancetta (about 4 slices), cut into ¼-inch cubes (see note)
- 2 medium onions, chopped medium
- 2 medium carrots, chopped medium
- 2 medium celery ribs, chopped medium
- 1 tablespoon tomato paste
- 3 medium garlic cloves, minced or pressed through a garlic press (about 1 tablespoon)
- 1 tablespoon unbleached all-purpose flour
- ½ teaspoon sugar
- 1 (750-milliliter) bottle Barolo wine
- 1 (14.5-ounce) can diced tomatoes, drained
- 1 sprig fresh thyme plus 1 teaspoon minced thyme leaves
- 1 sprig fresh rosemary
- 10 sprigs fresh parsley

1. Adjust an oven rack to the middle position and heat the oven to 300 degrees. Pull the roast apart at its major seams (delineated by lines of fat) into two halves. Use a knife as necessary. With the knife, remove the large knobs of fat from each piece, leaving a thin layer of fat on the meat. Tie three pieces of kitchen twine around each piece of meat. Thoroughly pat the beef dry with paper towels; sprinkle generously with salt and pepper. Place the pancetta in a large Dutch oven; cook over medium heat, stirring occasionally, until browned and crisp, about 8 minutes. Using a slotted spoon, transfer the pancetta to a paper towel–lined plate and reserve. Pour off all but 2 tablespoons of fat; set the Dutch oven over medium-high heat and heat the fat until beginning to smoke. Add the beef to the pot and cook until well browned on all sides, about 8 minutes total. Transfer the beef to a large plate; set aside.

2. Reduce the heat to medium; add the onions, carrots, celery, and tomato paste to the pot and cook, stirring occasionally, until the vegetables begin to soften and brown, about 6 minutes. Add the garlic, flour, sugar, and reserved pancetta; cook, stirring constantly, until combined and fragrant, about 30 seconds. Add the wine and tomatoes, scraping the bottom of the pan with a wooden spoon to loosen the browned bits; add the thyme sprig, rosemary, and parsley. Return the roast and any accumulated juice to the pot; increase the heat to high and bring the liquid to a boil, then place a large sheet of foil over the pot and cover tightly with the lid. Set the pot in the oven and cook, using tongs to turn the beef every 45 minutes, until a dinner fork easily slips in and out of the meat, about 3 hours.

3. Transfer the beef to a carving board and tent with foil to keep warm. Allow the braising liquid to settle for about 5 minutes, then, using a wide shallow spoon, skim the fat off the surface. Add the minced thyme, bring the liquid to a boil over high heat, and cook, whisking vigorously to help the vegetables break down, until the mixture is thickened and reduced to about 3½ cups, about 18 minutes. Strain the liquid through a large fine-mesh strainer, pressing on the solids with a spatula to extract as much liquid as possible; you should have 1½ cups strained sauce (if necessary, return the strained sauce to the Dutch oven and reduce to 1½ cups). Discard the solids in the strainer. Season the sauce with salt and pepper to taste.

4. Remove the kitchen twine from the meat and discard. Using a chef's knife or carving knife, cut the meat against the grain into ½-inch-thick slices. Divide the meat among warmed bowls or plates; pour about 1/4 cup sauce over each portion and serve immediately.

SHRIMP SCAMPI

WHY THIS RECIPE WORKS: Restaurant versions of shrimp scampi often run the gamut from boiled shrimp and tomato sauce on a bed of pasta to rubbery shrimp overloaded in butter or olive oil. We wanted lightly cooked, moist shrimp in a light garlic and lemon sauce.

A quick sauté in batches was all the shrimp needed to cook fully without becoming rubbery; we then set them aside to build the sauce. We cooked minced garlic briefly in butter, so as not to scorch it, then added lemon juice and vermouth for depth of flavor; the liquids also protected the garlic from burning. Additional butter thickened the sauce, and parsley and cayenne provided the finishing touches to this light, flavorful Italian favorite.

Shrimp Scampi

SERVES 4 TO 6

Serve the scampi over long pasta like linguine or spaghetti or with chewy bread to soak up the extra juices.

- 2 tablespoons olive oil
- 2 pounds extra-large shrimp (21 to 25 per pound), peeled and deveined (see page 240)
- 3 tablespoons unsalted butter
- 4 medium garlic cloves, minced or pressed through a garlic press (about 4 teaspoons)
- 2 tablespoons juice from 1 lemon
- 1 tablespoon dry vermouth
- 2 tablespoons minced fresh parsley leaves
- Pinch cayenne pepper
- Table salt and ground black pepper

1. Heat 1 tablespoon of the oil in a 12-inch skillet over high heat until shimmering. Add 1 pound of the shrimp and cook, stirring occasionally, until just opaque, about 1 minute; transfer to a medium bowl. Return the pan to high heat and repeat with the remaining 1 tablespoon oil and remaining 1 pound shrimp.

2. Return the skillet to medium-low heat; melt 1 tablespoon of the butter. Add the garlic and cook, stirring constantly, until fragrant, about 30 seconds. Off the heat, add the lemon juice and vermouth. Whisk in the remaining 2 tablespoons butter; add the parsley and cayenne, and season with salt and black pepper to taste. Return the shrimp and any accumulated juices to the skillet. Toss to combine; serve immediately.

ULTIMATE SHRIMP SCAMPI

WHY THIS RECIPE WORKS: Our new shrimp scampi recipe uses a few test kitchen tricks to ensure flavorful and well-cooked shrimp, as well as a creamy and robust sauce to pair them with. First, we brined the shrimp in salt and sugar to season them throughout and to keep them moist and juicy. Then, because sautéing the shrimp led to uneven cooking, we instead poached them in wine, a gentler approach that was more consistent. To get more shrimp flavor into the sauce, we didn't waste the shells; instead, we put them to use as the base of a stock and added wine and thyme. The key was to let it simmer for only 5 minutes, as a longer cooking time resulted in less flavor. For potent but clean garlic flavor, we used a generous amount of sliced, rather than minced, garlic. Just a teaspoon of cornstarch at the end of cooking kept the sauce emulsified and silky.

Ultimate Shrimp Scampi

SERVES 4

Extra-large shrimp (21 to 25 per pound) can be substituted for jumbo shrimp. If you use them, reduce the cooking time in step 3 by 1 to 2 minutes. We prefer untreated shrimp, but if your shrimp are treated with sodium or preservatives like sodium tripolyphosphate, skip the brining in step 1 and add ¼ teaspoon of salt to the sauce in step 4. Serve with crusty bread.

- 3 tablespoons salt
- 2 tablespoons sugar
- 1½ pounds jumbo shrimp (16 to 20 per pound), peeled, deveined (see page 240), and tails removed, shells reserved
- 2 tablespoons extra-virgin olive oil
- 1 cup dry white wine
- 4 sprigs fresh thyme
- 3 tablespoons lemon juice, plus lemon wedges for serving
- 1 teaspoon cornstarch
- 8 garlic cloves, sliced thin
- ½ teaspoon red pepper flakes
- ¼ teaspoon pepper
- 4 tablespoons unsalted butter, cut into ½-inch pieces
- 1 tablespoon chopped fresh parsley

1. Dissolve salt and sugar in 1 quart cold water in large container. Submerge shrimp in brine, cover, and refrigerate for 15 minutes. Remove shrimp from brine and pat dry with paper towels.

2. Heat 1 tablespoon oil in 12-inch skillet over high heat until shimmering. Add shrimp shells and cook, stirring frequently, until they begin to turn spotty brown and skillet starts to brown, 2 to 4 minutes. Remove skillet from heat and carefully add wine and thyme sprigs. When bubbling subsides, return skillet to medium heat and simmer gently, stirring occasionally, for 5 minutes. Strain mixture through colander set over large bowl. Discard shells and reserve liquid (you should have about 2⁄3 cup). Wipe out skillet with paper towels.

3. Combine lemon juice and cornstarch in small bowl. Heat remaining 1 tablespoon oil, garlic, pepper flakes, and pepper in now-empty skillet over medium-low heat, stirring occasionally, until garlic is fragrant and just beginning to brown at edges, 3 to 5 minutes. Add reserved wine mixture, increase heat to high, and bring to simmer. Reduce heat to medium, add shrimp, cover, and cook, stirring occasionally, until shrimp are just opaque, 5 to 7 minutes. Remove skillet from heat and, using slotted spoon, transfer shrimp to bowl.

4. Return skillet to medium heat, add lemon juice–cornstarch mixture, and cook until slightly thickened, about 1 minute. Remove from heat and whisk in butter and parsley until combined. Return shrimp and any accumulated juices to skillet and toss to combine. Serve, passing lemon wedges separately.

TUSCAN SHRIMP AND BEANS

WHY THIS RECIPE WORKS: To give this riff on Tuscan-style beans fuller seafood flavor, we made a quick concentrated stock with the shrimp shells and used it to simmer the beans. We also cooked the shrimp with the beans rather than separately and sautéed minced anchovies with the aromatics. To season the shrimp and keep them plump and juicy, we brined them briefly, added them late in the cooking process, and reduced the heat so they cooked gently. Canned beans and canned tomatoes made this dish fast and doable at any time of year; plus, the liquid from one of the cans of beans lent good body to the stew. Plenty of fresh basil and lemon juice and zest provide freshness and nice acidity.

Tuscan Shrimp and Beans

SERVES 4 TO 6

We prefer untreated shrimp, but if your shrimp are treated with added salt or preservatives like sodium tripolyphosphate, skip brining in step 1 and increase the salt to ½ teaspoon in step 3. Serve with crusty bread.

- 2 tablespoons sugar
- Salt and pepper
- 1 pound large shell-on shrimp (26 to 30 per pound), peeled, deveined (see page 240), and tails removed, shells reserved
- ¼ cup extra-virgin olive oil
- 1 onion, chopped fine
- 4 garlic cloves, peeled, halved lengthwise, and sliced thin
- 2 anchovy fillets, rinsed, patted dry, and minced
- ¼ teaspoon red pepper flakes
- 2 (15-ounce) cans cannellini beans (1 can drained and rinsed, 1 can left undrained)
- 1 (14.5-ounce) can diced tomatoes, drained
- ¼ cup shredded fresh basil
- ½ teaspoon grated lemon zest plus 1 tablespoon juice

1. Dissolve sugar and 1 tablespoon salt in 1 quart cold water in large container. Submerge shrimp in brine, cover, and refrigerate for 15 minutes. Remove shrimp from brine and pat dry with paper towels.

2. Heat 1 tablespoon oil in 12-inch skillet over medium heat until shimmering. Add shrimp shells and cook, stirring frequently, until they begin to turn spotty brown and skillet starts to brown, 5 to 6 minutes. Remove skillet from heat and carefully add 1 cup water. When bubbling subsides, return skillet to medium heat and simmer gently, stirring occasionally, for 5 minutes. Strain mixture through colander set over large bowl. Discard shells and reserve liquid (you should have about ¼ cup). Wipe skillet clean with paper towels.

3. Heat 2 tablespoons oil, onion, garlic, anchovies, pepper flakes, ¼ teaspoon salt, and ⅛ teaspoon pepper in now-empty skillet over medium-low heat. Cook, stirring occasionally, until onion is softened, about 5 minutes. Add 1 can drained beans, 1 can beans and their liquid, tomatoes, and shrimp stock and bring to simmer. Simmer, stirring occasionally, for 15 minutes.

4. Reduce heat to low, add shrimp, cover, and cook, stirring once during cooking, until shrimp are just opaque, 5 to 7 minutes. Remove skillet from heat and stir in basil and lemon zest and juice. Season with salt and pepper to taste. Transfer to serving dish, drizzle with remaining 1 tablespoon oil, and serve.

CHAPTER 14

THE FLAIR OF THE FRENCH

CLASSIC FRENCH ONION SOUP

WHY THIS RECIPE WORKS: With too many onion soups, digging through a layer of congealed cheese unearths a disappointing broth that just doesn't taste like onions. The ideal French onion soup combines a satisfying broth redolent of sweet caramelized onions with a slice of toasted baguette and melted cheese. We wanted a foolproof method for achieving extraordinarily deep flavor from the humble onion—the star of this classic soup.

The secret to a rich broth was to caramelize the onions fully. The good news is that caramelizing the onions, deglazing the pot, and then repeating this process dozens of times will keep ratcheting up the flavor. The bad news is what a laborious, hands-on process this proved to be. Fortunately, we found that if we first cooked the onions, covered, in a hot oven for two and a half hours, we only needed to deglaze the onions on the stovetop three or four times. Just one type of onion (yellow) was sufficient, but a combination of three different liquids (water, chicken broth, and beef broth) added maximum flavor. For the topping, we toasted the bread before floating it on the soup to ward off sogginess and added only a modest sprinkling of nutty Gruyère so the broth wasn't overpowered.

Classic French Onion Soup

SERVES 6

Sweet onions, such as Vidalia or Walla Walla, will make this dish overly sweet. Be patient when caramelizing the onions in step 2; the entire process takes 45 to 60 minutes. Use broiler-safe crocks and keep the rims of the bowls 4 to 5 inches from the heating element to obtain a proper gratinée of melted, bubbly cheese. If using ordinary soup bowls, sprinkle the toasted bread slices with Gruyère and return them to the broiler until the cheese melts, then float them on top of the soup. For the best flavor, make the soup a day or two in advance. Alternatively, the onions can be prepared through step 1, cooled in the pot, and refrigerated for up to 3 days before proceeding with the recipe.

SOUP

- 3 tablespoons unsalted butter, cut into 3 pieces
- 4 pounds onions (about 6 large), halved pole to pole and sliced lengthwise ¼ inch thick (see note)
- Table salt
- 2 cups water, plus extra for deglazing
- ½ cup dry sherry
- 4 cups low-sodium chicken broth
- 2 cups beef broth
- 6 sprigs fresh thyme, tied together with kitchen twine
- 1 bay leaf
- Ground black pepper

CHEESE CROUTONS

- 1 small baguette, cut on the bias into ½-inch slices
- 8 ounces Gruyère cheese, shredded (about 2 cups)

1. FOR THE SOUP: Adjust an oven rack to the lower-middle position and heat the oven to 400 degrees. Generously spray the inside of a large (at least 7-quart) Dutch oven with vegetable oil spray. Add the butter, onions, and 1 teaspoon salt to the pot. Cook, covered, for 1 hour (the onions will be moist and slightly reduced in volume). Remove the pot from the oven and stir the onions, scraping the bottom and sides of the pot. Return the pot to the oven with the lid slightly ajar and continue to cook until the onions are very soft and golden brown, 1½ to 1¾ hours longer, stirring the onions and scraping the bottom and sides of the pot after 1 hour.

2. Carefully remove the pot from the oven and place over medium-high heat. Cook the onions, stirring frequently and scraping the bottom and sides of the pot, until the liquid evaporates and the onions brown, 15 to 20 minutes, reducing the heat to medium if the onions are browning too quickly. Continue to cook, stirring frequently, until the pot bottom is coated with a dark crust, 6 to 8 minutes, adjusting the heat as necessary. (Scrape any browned bits that collect on the spoon back into the onions.) Stir in ¼ cup water, scraping the pot bottom to loosen the crust, and cook until the water evaporates and the pot bottom has formed another dark crust, 6 to 8 minutes. Repeat the process of deglazing 2 to 3 more times, until the onions are very dark brown. Stir in the sherry and cook, stirring frequently, until the sherry evaporates, about 5 minutes.

3. Stir in 2 cups water, the chicken broth, beef broth, thyme, bay leaf, and ½ teaspoon salt, scraping up any final bits of browned crust on the bottom and sides of the pot. Increase the heat to high and bring to a simmer. Reduce the heat to low, cover, and simmer for 30 minutes. Remove and discard the thyme and bay leaf, then season with salt and pepper to taste.

4. FOR THE CROUTONS: While the soup simmers, heat the oven to 400 degrees. Arrange the baguette slices in a single layer on a rimmed baking sheet and bake until dry, crisp, and golden at the edges, about 10 minutes. Set aside.

5. Adjust an oven rack 6 inches from the broiler element and heat the broiler. Set individual broiler-safe crocks on the baking sheet and fill each with about 1¾ cups of the soup. Top each bowl with one or two baguette slices (do not overlap the slices) and sprinkle evenly with the Gruyère. Broil until the cheese is melted and bubbly around the edges, 3 to 5 minutes. Cool for 5 minutes; serve.

BEHIND THE SCENES

SHEDDING TEARS IN THE TEST KITCHEN

We can't tell you how many onions we've chopped over the years. Let's just say a lot. As a result, we've shed more than a few tears. What causes cut onions to be so pesky? When an onion is cut, the cells that are damaged in the process release sulfuric compounds as well as various enzymes, notably one called sulfoxide lyase. Those compounds and enzymes, which are separated when the onion's cell structure is intact, activate and mix to form the real culprit behind crying, a volatile new compound called thiopropanal sulfoxide. When thiopropanal sulfoxide evaporates in the air, it irritates the eyes, causing redness and tears.

Through the years we've collected dozens of ideas from readers, books, and conversations with colleagues, all aimed at reducing tears while cutting onions. We finally decided to put those ideas to the test. They ranged from common sense (work underneath an exhaust fan or freeze onions for 30 minutes before slicing) to the comical (wear ski goggles or hold a toothpick in your teeth). Overall, the methods that worked best were to protect our eyes by covering them with goggles or contact lenses or to introduce a flame near the cut onions. The flame, which can be produced by either a candle or a gas burner, changes the activity of the thiopropanal sulfoxide (the volatile compound that causes tearing) by completing its oxidization. Contact lenses and goggles form a physical barrier that the vapors cannot penetrate. So if you want to keep tears at bay when handling onions, light a candle or gas burner—or put on some ski goggles, even if it does look a bit silly.

STREAMLINED FRENCH ONION SOUP

WHY THIS RECIPE WORKS: Streamlined versions of onion soup often amount to a sad crock of flavorless onions floating in super-salty beef bouillon topped with an oily blob of cheese. Or it might be just the opposite: a weak and watery affair. We wanted to make a better onion soup—a dark, rich broth, intensely flavored by an abundance of seriously cooked onions, covered by a broth-soaked crouton with a cheesy, crusty top—and we wanted to make it in record time.

We cheated from the get-go and created a simple broth with store-bought beef and chicken broths and wine. Red onions were chosen for their subtle complexity and nuance, and for the maximum flavor they offered when caramelized. Parsley, thyme, and a bay leaf rounded out the flavors and imparted freshness. To prevent the croutons from getting too soggy, we placed them atop the soup, so only the bottom was submerged. For the cheese, we liked a combination of pungent Swiss cheese topped with subdued Asiago; their flavors added some punch to our speedy but still irresistible soup.

Streamlined French Onion Soup

SERVES 6

Tie the parsley and thyme sprigs together with kitchen twine so they will be easy to retrieve from the soup pot. Use broiler-safe crocks and keep the rims of the bowls 4 to 5 inches from the heating element to obtain a proper gratinée of melted, bubbly cheese. If using ordinary soup bowls, top the toasted bread slices with the cheeses as directed in step 3 and return them to the broiler until the cheese melts, then float them on top of the soup.

SOUP

- 2 tablespoons unsalted butter
- 3 pounds red onions (about 6 medium), halved pole to pole and sliced crosswise ⅛ inch thick
- Table salt
- 6 cups low-sodium chicken broth
- 1¾ cups beef broth
- ¼ cup dry red wine
- 2 sprigs fresh parsley (see note)
- 1 sprig fresh thyme (see note)
- 1 bay leaf
- 1 tablespoon balsamic vinegar
- Ground black pepper

CHEESE CROUTONS

- 1 small baguette, cut on the bias into ½-inch slices
- 4½ ounces thinly sliced Swiss cheese
- 1½ ounces Asiago cheese, grated (about ¾ cup)

1. FOR THE SOUP: Melt the butter in a large Dutch oven over medium-high heat. Add the onions and ½ teaspoon salt and cook, stirring frequently, until the onions are reduced and syrupy and the inside of the pot is coated with a deep brown crust, 30 to 35 minutes. Add the chicken and beef broths, red wine, parsley, thyme, and bay leaf, scraping the pot bottom with a wooden spoon to loosen the browned bits, and bring to a simmer. Simmer to blend the flavors, about 20 minutes; discard the herbs. Stir in the balsamic vinegar and season with salt and pepper to taste. (The cooled soup can be refrigerated in an airtight container for up to 2 days; return to a simmer before finishing the soup with the croutons and cheese.)

2. FOR THE CROUTONS: Adjust an oven rack to the upper-middle position and heat the oven to 350 degrees. Arrange the baguette slices on a rimmed baking sheet and bake, turning once, until lightly browned, about 15 minutes. Remove the bread from the oven, carefully adjust an oven rack 6 inches from the broiler element, and heat the broiler.

3. Set individual broiler-safe crocks on the baking sheet and fill each with about 1½ cups of the soup. Top each bowl with two baguette slices and divide the Swiss cheese slices, placing them in a single layer, if possible, on the bread; sprinkle with 2 tablespoons of the grated Asiago and broil until the cheese is browned and bubbly around the edges, 7 to 10 minutes. Cool for 5 minutes; serve.

FRENCH POTATO SALAD

WHY THIS RECIPE WORKS: French potato salad is served warm or at room temperature and is composed of sliced potatoes glistening with olive oil, white wine vinegar, and plenty of fresh herbs. We wanted a potato salad that was not only pleasing to the eye but to the palate as well. The potatoes should be tender but not mushy, and the flavor of the vinaigrette should penetrate the relatively bland potatoes but not be oily or dull. We learned the hard way that to prevent torn skins and broken slices, we had to slice the potatoes before boiling them. To tone down the flavor of harsh garlic, we blanched it before mixing the vinaigrette. A little extra vinegar—more than we would normally call for in a vinaigrette—added a pleasing sharpness, while some reserved potato water added just the right amount of moisture and saltiness to the salad. Dijon mustard combined with strong herbs also perked things up. Tossing the vinaigrette with the cooked potatoes led to mangled, shabby slices, but pouring the vinaigrette over the warm potatoes on a sheet pan, then folding in the other ingredients, kept the potato slices intact.

French Potato Salad

SERVES 4 TO 6

If fresh chervil isn't available, substitute an additional ½ tablespoon minced parsley and an additional ½ teaspoon minced tarragon. For best flavor, serve the salad warm, but to make ahead, follow the recipe through step 2, cover with plastic wrap, and refrigerate. Before serving, bring the salad to room temperature, then add the shallot and herbs.

- 2 pounds red potatoes (about 6 medium or 18 small), scrubbed and sliced ¼ inch thick
- 2 tablespoons table salt
- 1 medium garlic clove, peeled and threaded on a skewer
- ¼ cup olive oil
- 1½ tablespoons champagne vinegar or white wine vinegar
- 2 teaspoons Dijon mustard
- ½ teaspoon ground black pepper
- 1 small shallot, minced (about 1 tablespoon)
- 1 tablespoon minced fresh chervil leaves (see note)
- 1 tablespoon minced fresh parsley leaves
- 1 tablespoon minced fresh chives
- 1 teaspoon minced fresh tarragon leaves

1. Place the potatoes, 6 cups cold water, and the salt in a large saucepan. Bring to a boil over high heat, then reduce the heat to medium. Lower the skewered garlic into the simmering water and blanch, about 45 seconds. Immediately run the garlic under cold tap water to stop the cooking process; remove the garlic from the skewer and set aside. Simmer the potatoes, uncovered, until tender but still firm (a paring knife can be slipped into and out of the center of a potato slice with no resistance), about 5 minutes. Drain the potatoes, reserving ¼ cup cooking water. Arrange the hot potatoes close together in a single layer on a rimmed baking sheet.

2. Press the garlic through a garlic press or mince by hand. Whisk the garlic, reserved potato cooking water, oil, vinegar, mustard, and pepper together in a small bowl until combined. Drizzle the dressing evenly over the warm potato slices; let stand for 10 minutes.

3. Meanwhile, toss the shallot and herbs gently together in a small bowl. Transfer the potatoes to a large serving bowl. Add the shallot-herb mixture and mix lightly with a rubber spatula to combine. Serve immediately.

CHEESE SOUFFLÉ

WHY THIS RECIPE WORKS: Making a truly great cheese soufflé is like finding the Holy Grail for most cooks—unattainable. But this classic French dish doesn't have to be relegated to the realm of professional chefs. We wanted a cheese soufflé with bold cheese flavor, good stature, and a light but not-too-airy texture—all without the fussiness of most recipes.

To bump up the cheese flavor without weighing down the soufflé, we added lightweight-but-flavorful Parmesan cheese to the traditional Gruyère. Reducing the amount of butter and flour also amplified the cheese flavor. Filling the soufflé dish to an inch below the rim allowed ample room for the soufflé to rise high. To get the texture just right while keeping the preparation simple, we beat egg whites to stiff peaks, and then—rather than carefully folding them into the cheese sauce—added the sauce right to the stand mixer, and beat everything until uniform. When the center reached 170 degrees, our soufflé had a perfect luscious creamy center and lightly bronzed edges.

Cheese Soufflé

SERVES 4 TO 6

Serve this soufflé with a green salad for a light dinner. Comté, sharp cheddar, or gouda cheese can be substituted for the Gruyère. To prevent the soufflé from overflowing the soufflé dish, leave at least 1 inch of space between the top of the batter and the rim of the dish; any excess batter should be discarded. The most foolproof way to test for doneness is with an instant-read thermometer. To judge doneness without an instant-read thermometer, use two large spoons to pry open the soufflé so that you can peer inside it; the center should appear thick and creamy but not soupy.

- 1 ounce Parmesan cheese, grated (½ cup)
- ¼ cup (1¼ ounces) all-purpose flour
- ¼ teaspoon paprika
- ¼ teaspoon salt
- ⅛ teaspoon cayenne pepper
- ⅛ teaspoon white pepper
- Pinch ground nutmeg
- 4 tablespoons unsalted butter
- 1⅓ cups whole milk
- 6 ounces Gruyère cheese, shredded (1½ cups)
- 6 large eggs, separated
- 2 teaspoons minced fresh parsley
- ¼ teaspoon cream of tartar

1. Adjust oven rack to middle position and heat oven to 350 degrees. Spray 8-inch round (2-quart) soufflé dish with vegetable oil spray, then sprinkle with 2 tablespoons Parmesan.

2. Combine flour, paprika, salt, cayenne, white pepper, and nutmeg in bowl. Melt butter in small saucepan over medium heat. Stir in flour mixture and cook for 1 minute. Slowly whisk in milk and bring to simmer. Cook, whisking constantly, until mixture is thickened and smooth, about 1 minute. Remove pan from heat and whisk in Gruyère and 5 tablespoons Parmesan until melted and smooth. Let cool for 10 minutes, then whisk in egg yolks and 1½ teaspoons parsley.

3. Using stand mixer fitted with whisk, whip egg whites and cream of tartar on medium-low speed until foamy, about 1 minute. Increase speed to medium-high and whip until stiff peaks form, 3 to 4 minutes. Add cheese mixture and continue to whip until fully combined, about 15 seconds.

4. Pour mixture into prepared dish and sprinkle with remaining 1 tablespoon Parmesan. Bake until risen above rim, top is deep golden brown, and interior registers 170 degrees, 30 to 35 minutes. Sprinkle with remaining ½ teaspoon parsley and serve immediately.

FRENCH ONION TART

WHY THIS RECIPE WORKS: French onion tart is similar to quiche but delivers a more refined slice of pie, with more onions than custard. But re-creating this tart at home can produce a tough and crackery crust, which is doubly disappointing after spending long hours delicately cooking the onions, making the custard, and baking the whole thing together. We wanted to simplify the crust and shorten the overall preparation time.

We found that our onions would cook in half the usual time if we left the lid on the skillet throughout cooking. And covering the onions allowed them to cook entirely in their own juices, thereby becoming tender, retaining their pure onion flavor, and cooking more evenly. We liked bacon, which acted as a crisp foil to the creamy filling, but we found a traditional custard with the bacon to be simply too rich. To resolve the issue, we reduced the number of eggs and switched out the cream for half-and-half. And to ensure the bacon stayed crisp, we sprinkled it on top of the custard. We tried several classic crust recipes, looking for one that had the intense butteriness of traditional tart dough but could still be easily patted into a tart pan. We found that using a food processor to cut cold butter completely into the flour mixture required less ice water than a conventional crust, which kept the dough firm enough to press into the pan.

French Onion and Bacon Tart

SERVES 6 TO 8

Either yellow or white onions work well in this recipe, but stay away from sweet onions, such as Vidalias, which will make the tart watery. Use a 9-inch tinned-steel tart pan; see page 886 for our recommended brand. This tart can be served hot or at room temperature and pairs well with a green salad as a main course.

CRUST

- 1¼ cups (6¼ ounces) unbleached all-purpose flour
- 1 tablespoon sugar
- ½ teaspoon table salt
- 8 tablespoons (1 stick) unsalted butter, cut into ½-inch cubes and chilled
- 2–3 tablespoons ice water

FILLING

- 4 ounces bacon (about 4 slices), halved lengthwise and cut crosswise into ¼-inch pieces
- Vegetable oil, as needed
- 1½ pounds onions (about 3 medium), halved pole to pole and cut crosswise into ¼-inch slices (about 6 cups; see note)
- ¾ teaspoon table salt
- 1 sprig fresh thyme
- 2 large eggs
- ½ cup half-and-half
- ¼ teaspoon ground black pepper

1. FOR THE CRUST: Spray a 9-inch tart pan with a removable bottom with vegetable oil spray; set aside. Pulse the flour, sugar, and salt together in a food processor until combined, about 4 pulses. Scatter the butter pieces over the flour mixture and pulse until the mixture resembles coarse sand, about 15 pulses. Add 2 tablespoons of the ice water and continue to process until large clumps of dough form and no powdery bits remain, about 5 seconds. If the dough doesn't clump, add the remaining 1 tablespoon water and pulse to incorporate, about 4 pulses. Transfer the dough to the greased tart pan and, working outward from the center, pat the dough into an even layer, sealing any cracks. Working around the edge, press the dough firmly into the corners of the pan and up the sides, using your thumb to level off the top edge. Lay plastic wrap over the dough and smooth out any bumps or shallow areas. Place the tart shell on a plate and freeze for 30 minutes.

2. Adjust an oven rack to the middle position and heat the oven to 375 degrees. Place the frozen tart shell (still in the tart pan) on a rimmed baking sheet. Gently press a piece of extra-wide heavy-duty foil that has been sprayed with vegetable oil spray against the dough and over the edges of the tart pan. Fill the shell with pie weights and bake until the top edge of the dough just starts to color and the surface of dough under the foil no longer looks wet, about 30 minutes. Remove the tart shell from the oven and carefully remove the weights and foil. Return the baking sheet with the tart shell to the oven and continue to bake, uncovered, until golden brown, 5 to 10 minutes. Set the baking sheet with the tart shell on a wire rack to cool while making the filling. (Do not turn off the oven.)

3. FOR THE FILLING: While the crust is baking, cook the bacon in a 12-inch nonstick skillet over medium heat until browned and crisp, 8 to 10 minutes. Using a slotted spoon, transfer the bacon to a paper towel–lined plate; set aside. Pour off all but 2 tablespoons bacon fat from the skillet (or add vegetable oil if needed to make this amount).

4. Add the onions, salt, and thyme to the skillet. Cover and cook until the onions release their liquid and start to wilt, about 10 minutes. Reduce the heat to low and continue to cook, covered, until the onions are very soft, about 20 minutes, stirring once or twice (if after 15 minutes the onions look wet, remove the lid and continue to cook for another 5 minutes). Remove the pan from the heat and cool for 5 minutes.

5. Whisk the eggs, half-and-half, and pepper together in a large bowl. Remove the thyme from the onions; discard. Stir the onions into the egg mixture until just incorporated. Spread the onion mixture over the bottom of the baked crust and sprinkle the reserved bacon evenly on top.

6. Bake the tart on the baking sheet until the center of the tart feels firm to the touch, 20 to 25 minutes. Set the baking sheet with the tart on a wire rack and cool for at least 10 minutes. Remove the tart pan ring, gently slide a thin-bladed spatula between the pan bottom and crust to loosen, and slide the tart onto a serving plate. Cut into wedges and serve.

PISSALADIÈRE

WHY THIS RECIPE WORKS: *Pissaladière*, the classic olive, anchovy, and onion tart from Provence, is easy enough to prepare, but each ingredient must be handled carefully. We wanted to harmonize the onions, olives, and anchovies with a crisp crust to produce a tart worthy of the finest bakery in Nice.

We made the dough in a food processor and kneaded it as little as possible to create a pizza-like dough with a cracker-like exterior and a decently chewy crumb, a dough with the structure to stand up to the heavy toppings. Bread flour was our flour of choice as it has more protein than all-purpose flour, and that translates to a more substantial chew. Using a combination of high and low heat to cook the onions—starting the onions on high to release their juices and soften them, then turning the heat to medium-low to caramelize them—gave us perfectly browned and caramelized, but not burnt, onions. Adding a bit of water before spreading them on the crust kept them from clumping. We placed the onions on top of the chopped black olives, anchovies (also chopped; whole anchovies were too overpowering), and fresh thyme leaves to protect them from burning in the oven. Diehard fish lovers can add more anchovies as a garnish if desired.

Pissaladière

MAKES 2 TARTS, SERVING 6

For the best flavor, use high-quality oil-packed anchovies; in a tasting, King Oscar was our favorite brand (see page 904). If desired, you can slow down the dough's rising time by letting it rise in the refrigerator for 8 to 16 hours in step 1; let the refrigerated dough soften at room temperature for 30 minutes before using. The caramelized onions can also be made a day ahead and refrigerated.

DOUGH

- 2 cups (11 ounces) bread flour, plus extra for dusting the work surface
- 1 teaspoon instant or rapid-rise yeast
- 1 teaspoon table salt
- 1 tablespoon olive oil, plus extra for brushing the dough and greasing hands
- 1 cup warm water (110 degrees)

CARAMELIZED ONIONS

- 2 tablespoons olive oil
- 2 pounds onions (about 4 medium), halved and sliced ¼ inch thick
- 1 teaspoon brown sugar
- ½ teaspoon table salt
- 1 tablespoon water

Olive oil

- ½ teaspoon ground black pepper
- ½ cup niçoise olives, pitted and chopped coarse
- 8 anchovy fillets, rinsed, patted dry, and chopped coarse (about 2 tablespoons), plus 12 fillets, rinsed and patted dry for garnish (optional; see note)
- 2 teaspoons minced fresh thyme leaves
- 1 teaspoon fennel seeds (optional)
- 1 tablespoon minced fresh parsley leaves (optional)

1. FOR THE DOUGH: Pulse the flour, yeast, and salt in a food processor (fitted with a dough blade, if possible) until combined, about 5 pulses. With the machine running, slowly add the oil, then the water, through the feed tube; continue to process until the dough forms a ball, about 15 seconds. Turn the dough out onto a lightly floured work surface and form it into a smooth, round ball. Place the dough in a large lightly oiled bowl and cover tightly with greased plastic wrap. Let rise in a warm place until doubled in volume, 1 to 1½ hours.

2. FOR THE CARAMELIZED ONIONS: While the dough is rising, heat the oil in a 12-inch nonstick skillet over medium-low heat until shimmering. Stir in the onions, sugar, and salt. Cover and cook, stirring occasionally, until the onions are softened and have released their juice, about 10 minutes. Remove the lid, increase the heat to medium-high, and continue to cook, stirring often, until the onions are deeply browned, 10 to 15 minutes. Off the heat, stir in the water, then transfer the onions to a bowl and set aside. Adjust the oven rack to the lowest position, set a baking stone on the rack, and heat the oven to 500 degrees. (Let the baking stone heat for at least 30 minutes but no longer than 1 hour.)

3. TO SHAPE, TOP, AND BAKE THE DOUGH: Turn the dough out onto a lightly floured work surface, divide it into two equal pieces, and cover with greased plastic wrap. Working with one piece at a time (keep the other piece covered), form each piece into a rough ball by gently pulling the edges of the dough together and pinching to seal. With floured hands, turn the dough ball seam side down. Cupping the dough with both hands, gently push the dough in a circular motion to form a taut ball. Repeat with the second piece. Brush each piece lightly with oil, cover with plastic wrap, and let rest for 10 minutes. Meanwhile, cut two 20-inch lengths of parchment paper and set aside.

4. Coat your fingers and palms generously with oil. Working with one piece of dough at a time, hold the dough up and gently stretch it to a 12-inch length. Place the dough on the parchment sheet and gently dimple the surface of the dough with your fingertips. Using your oiled palms, push and flatten the dough into a 14 by 8-inch oval. Brush the dough with oil and sprinkle with ¼ teaspoon of the pepper. Leaving a ½-inch border around the edge, sprinkle ¼ cup of the olives, 1 tablespoon of the chopped anchovies, and 1 teaspoon of the thyme evenly over the dough, then evenly scatter with half of the onions. Arrange 6 whole anchovy fillets (if using) on the tart and sprinkle with ½ teaspoon of the fennel seeds (if using). Slip the parchment with the tart onto a pizza peel (or inverted baking sheet), then slide it onto the hot baking stone. Bake until deep golden brown, 13 to 15 minutes. While the first tart bakes, shape and top the second tart.

5. Remove the first tart from the oven with a peel (or pull the parchment onto a baking sheet). Transfer the tart to a cutting board and slide the parchment out from under the tart; cool for 5 minutes. While the first tart cools, bake the second tart. Sprinkle with the parsley (if using) and cut each tart into 8 pieces before serving.

SUMMER VEGETABLE GRATIN

WHY THIS RECIPE WORKS: Layering summer's best vegetables into a gratin can lead to a memorable side dish—or a soggy mess. Juicy summer vegetables like zucchini and tomatoes can exude a torrent of liquid that washes away flavors. We wanted a simple, Provençal-style vegetable gratin, where a golden brown, cheesy topping provides a rich contrast to the fresh, bright flavor of the vegetables. The typical combination of tomatoes, zucchini, and summer squash won out. To eliminate excess moisture, we baked the casserole uncovered. Salting both seasoned and dried out the zucchini and summer squash, but proved insufficient to deal with all the tomato juice. While we could remove the watery jelly and seeds from the tomatoes, the jelly was crucial for full tomato flavor. We moved the tomatoes to the top gratin layer, which allowed them to roast and caramelize. The roasting added flavor, especially when drizzled with garlic-thyme oil. Finally, we added a layer of caramelized onions between the zucchini/squash and tomato layers and sprinkled the dish with Parmesan bread crumbs before baking.

Summer Vegetable Gratin

SERVES 6 TO 8

The success of this recipe depends on good-quality produce. Buy zucchini and summer squash of roughly the same diameter. We like the visual contrast zucchini and summer squash bring to the dish, but you can also use just one or the other. A similarly sized ovensafe gratin dish can be substituted for the 13 by 9-inch baking dish. Serve the gratin alongside grilled fish or meat, accompanied by bread to soak up any flavorful juices.

- 6 tablespoons extra-virgin olive oil
- 1 pound zucchini, ends trimmed and cut crosswise into ¼-inch-thick slices (see note)
- 1 pound yellow summer squash, ends trimmed and cut crosswise into ¼-inch-thick slices (see note)
- 2 teaspoons table salt
- 1½ pounds ripe tomatoes (3 to 4 large), cut into ¼-inch-thick slices
- 2 medium onions, halved pole to pole and sliced thin (about 3 cups)
- ¾ teaspoon ground black pepper
- 2 medium garlic cloves, minced or pressed through a garlic press (about 2 teaspoons)
- 1 tablespoon minced fresh thyme leaves
- 1 slice high-quality white sandwich bread, torn into quarters
- 2 ounces grated Parmesan cheese (about 1 cup)
- 2 medium shallots, minced (about 6 tablespoons)
- ¼ cup chopped fresh basil leaves

1. Adjust an oven rack to the upper-middle position and heat the oven to 400 degrees. Brush a 13 by 9-inch baking dish with 1 tablespoon of the oil; set aside.

2. Toss the zucchini and summer squash slices with 1 teaspoon of the salt in a large bowl; transfer to a colander set over a bowl. Let stand until the zucchini and squash release at least 3 tablespoons of liquid, about 45 minutes. Arrange the slices on a triple layer of paper towels; cover with another triple layer of paper towels. Firmly press each slice to remove as much liquid as possible.

3. Place the tomato slices in a single layer on a double layer of paper towels and sprinkle evenly with ½ teaspoon more salt; let stand for 30 minutes. Place a second double layer of paper towels on top of the tomatoes and press firmly to dry the tomatoes.

4. Meanwhile, heat 1 tablespoon more oil in a 12-inch nonstick skillet over medium heat until shimmering. Add the onions, the remaining ½ teaspoon salt, and ¼ teaspoon of the pepper; cook, stirring occasionally, until the onions are softened and dark golden brown, 20 to 25 minutes. Set the onions aside.

5. Combine the garlic, 3 tablespoons more oil, the remaining ½ teaspoon pepper, and the thyme in a small bowl. In a large bowl, toss the zucchini and summer squash in half of the oil mixture, then arrange in the greased baking dish. Arrange the caramelized onions in an even layer over the squash. Slightly overlap the tomato slices in a single layer on top of the onions. Spoon the remaining garlic-oil mixture evenly over the tomatoes. Bake until the vegetables are tender and the tomatoes are starting to brown on the edges, 40 to 45 minutes.

6. Meanwhile, process the bread in a food processor until finely ground, about 10 seconds. (You should have about 1 cup crumbs.) Combine the bread crumbs, remaining 1 tablespoon oil, the Parmesan, and shallots in a medium bowl. Remove the baking dish from the oven and increase the heat to 450 degrees. Sprinkle the bread-crumb mixture evenly on top of the tomatoes. Bake the gratin until bubbling and the cheese is lightly browned, 5 to 10 minutes. Sprinkle with the basil and cool for 10 minutes before serving.

WALKAWAY RATATOUILLE

WHY THIS RECIPE WORKS: Classic ratatouille recipes call for cutting vegetables into small pieces, labor- and time-intensive pretreatments like salting and/or pressing the vegetables to remove excess moisture, and cooking them in batches on the stovetop. Our secret to great yet easy ratatouille? Overcook some of the vegetables, barely cook the others—and let the oven do the work. Our streamlined recipe starts by sautéing onions and aromatics and then adding chunks of eggplant and tomatoes before moving the pot to the oven, where the dry, ambient heat thoroughly evaporated moisture, concentrated flavors, and caramelized some of the veggies. After 45 minutes, the tomatoes and eggplant became meltingly soft and could be mashed into a thick, silky sauce. Zucchini and bell peppers went into the pot last so that they retained some texture. Finishing the dish with fresh herbs, a splash of sherry vinegar, and a drizzle of extra-virgin olive oil tied everything together.

Walkaway Ratatouille

SERVES 6 TO 8

This dish is best prepared using ripe, in-season tomatoes. If good tomatoes are not available, substitute 1 (28-ounce) can of whole peeled tomatoes that have been drained, rinsed, and chopped coarse. Ratatouille can be served as an accompaniment to meat or fish. It can also be served on its own with crusty bread, topped with an egg, or over pasta or rice. This dish can be served warm, at room temperature, or chilled.

- ⅓ cup extra-virgin olive oil, plus extra for serving
- 2 large onions, cut into 1-inch pieces
- 8 large garlic cloves, peeled and smashed
- Salt and pepper
- 1½ teaspoons herbes de Provence
- ¼ teaspoon red pepper flakes
- 1 bay leaf
- 1½ pounds eggplant, peeled and cut into 1-inch pieces
- 2 pounds plum tomatoes, peeled and chopped coarse
- 2 small zucchini, halved lengthwise and cut into 1-inch pieces
- 1 red bell pepper, stemmed, seeded, and cut into 1-inch pieces
- 1 yellow bell pepper, stemmed, seeded, and cut into 1-inch pieces
- 2 tablespoons chopped fresh basil
- 1 tablespoon minced fresh parsley
- 1 tablespoon sherry vinegar

1. Adjust oven rack to middle position and heat oven to 400 degrees. Heat oil in Dutch oven over medium-high heat until shimmering. Add onions, garlic, 1 teaspoon salt, and ¼ teaspoon pepper and cook, stirring occasionally, until onions are starting to soften and have become translucent, about 10 minutes. Add herbes de Provence, pepper flakes, and bay leaf and cook, stirring frequently, for 1 minute. Stir in eggplant and tomatoes. Sprinkle with ½ teaspoon salt and ¼ teaspoon pepper and stir to combine. Transfer pot to oven and cook, uncovered, until vegetables are very tender and spotty brown, 40 to 45 minutes.

2. Remove pot from oven and, using potato masher or heavy wooden spoon, smash and stir eggplant mixture until broken down into sauce-like consistency. Stir in zucchini, bell peppers, ¼ teaspoon salt, and ¼ teaspoon pepper and return to oven. Cook, uncovered, until zucchini and peppers are just tender, 20 to 25 minutes.

3. Remove pot from oven, cover, and let stand until zucchini is translucent and easily pierced with tip of paring knife, 10 to 15 minutes. Using wooden spoon, scrape any browned bits from sides of pot and stir back into ratatouille. Stir in 1 tablespoon basil, parsley, and vinegar. Season with salt and pepper to taste. Transfer to large platter, drizzle with 1 tablespoon oil, sprinkle with remaining 1 tablespoon basil, and serve.

MUSHROOM AND LEEK GALETTE WITH GORGONZOLA

WHY THIS RECIPE WORKS: Most vegetable tarts rely on the same pastry dough used for fruit tarts. But vegetable tarts are more prone to leaking liquid into the crust or falling apart when the tart is sliced. We needed a crust that was extra sturdy and boasted a complex flavor of its own.

To increase the flavor of the crust and keep it tender, we swapped out part of the white flour for nutty whole wheat, and we used butter rather than shortening. To punch up its flaky texture and introduce more structure, we gave the crust a series of folds to create numerous interlocking layers. For a filling that was both flavorful and cohesive, we paired mushrooms and leeks with rich, potent binders like Gorgonzola cheese and crème fraîche.

Mushroom and Leek Galette with Gorgonzola

SERVES 6

Cutting a few small holes in the dough prevents it from lifting off the pan as it bakes. A pizza stone helps to crisp the crust but is not essential. An overturned baking sheet can be used in place of the pizza stone.

DOUGH

- 1¼ cups (6¼ ounces) all-purpose flour
- ½ cup (2¾ ounces) whole-wheat flour
- 1 tablespoon sugar
- ¾ teaspoon salt
- 10 tablespoons unsalted butter, cut into ½-inch pieces and chilled
- 7 tablespoons ice water
- 1 teaspoon distilled white vinegar

FILLING

- 1¼ pounds shiitake mushrooms, stemmed and sliced thin
- 5 teaspoons olive oil
- 1 pound leeks, white and light green parts only, sliced ½ inch thick and washed thoroughly (3 cups)
- 1 teaspoon minced fresh thyme
- 2 tablespoons crème fraîche
- 1 tablespoon Dijon mustard
- Salt and pepper

- 3 ounces Gorgonzola cheese, crumbled (¾ cup)
- 1 large egg, lightly beaten
- Kosher salt
- 2 tablespoons minced fresh parsley

1. FOR THE DOUGH: Pulse all-purpose flour, whole-wheat flour, sugar, and salt together in food processor until combined, 2 to 3 pulses. Add butter and pulse until it forms pea-size pieces, about 10 pulses. Transfer mixture to medium bowl.

2. Sprinkle water and vinegar over mixture. With rubber spatula, use folding motion to mix until loose, shaggy mass forms with some dry flour remaining (do not overwork). Transfer mixture to center of large sheet of plastic wrap, press gently into rough 4-inch square, and wrap tightly. Refrigerate for at least 45 minutes.

3. Transfer dough to lightly floured counter. Roll into 11 by 8-inch rectangle with short side of rectangle parallel to edge of counter. Using bench scraper, bring bottom third of dough up, then fold upper third over it, folding like business letter into 8 by 4-inch rectangle. Turn dough 90 degrees counterclockwise. Roll out dough again into 11 by 8-inch rectangle and fold into thirds again. Turn dough 90 degrees counterclockwise and repeat rolling and folding into thirds. After last fold, fold dough in half to create 4-inch square. Press top of dough gently to seal. Wrap in plastic and refrigerate for at least 45 minutes or up to 2 days.

4. FOR THE FILLING: Microwave mushrooms in covered bowl until just tender, 3 to 5 minutes. Transfer to colander to drain; return to bowl. Meanwhile, heat 1 tablespoon oil in 12-inch skillet over medium heat until shimmering. Add leeks and thyme, cover, and cook, stirring occasionally, until leeks are tender and beginning to brown, 5 to 7 minutes. Transfer to bowl with mushrooms. Stir in crème fraîche and mustard. Season with salt and pepper to taste. Set aside.

5. Adjust oven rack to lower-middle position, place pizza stone on rack, and heat oven to 400 degrees. Line rimmed baking sheet with parchment paper. Remove dough from refrigerator and let stand at room temperature for 15 to 20 minutes. Roll out on generously floured counter (use up to ¼ cup flour) to 14-inch circle about ⅛ inch thick. (Trim edges as needed to form rough circle.) Transfer dough to prepared baking sheet. With tip of paring knife, cut five ¼-inch circles in dough (one at center and four evenly spaced halfway from center to edge of dough). Brush top of dough with 1 teaspoon oil.

6. Spread half of filling evenly over dough, leaving 2-inch border around edge. Sprinkle with half of Gorgonzola, cover with remaining filling, and top with remaining Gorgonzola.

NOTES FROM THE TEST KITCHEN

PLEATING A FREE-FORM TART

It's surprisingly simple to create pleated edges around free-form tarts.

Gently grasp 1 edge of dough and make 2-inch-wide fold over filling. Lift and fold another segment of dough over first fold to form pleat. Repeat every 2 to 3 inches.

Drizzle remaining 1 teaspoon oil over filling. Gently grasp 1 edge of dough and fold up outer 2 inches over filling. Repeat around circumference of tart, overlapping dough every 2 to 3 inches; gently pinch pleated dough to secure but do not press dough into filling. Brush dough with egg and sprinkle evenly with kosher salt.

7. Lower oven temperature to 375 degrees. Bake until crust is deep golden brown and filling is beginning to brown, 35 to 45 minutes. Let tart cool on baking sheet on wire rack for 10 minutes. Using offset or wide metal spatula, loosen tart from parchment and carefully slide tart off parchment onto cutting board. Sprinkle with parsley, cut into wedges, and serve.

Potato and Shallot Galette with Goat Cheese

Substitute 1 pound Yukon Gold potatoes, sliced ¼ inch thick, for mushrooms and increase microwave cooking time to 4 to 8 minutes. Substitute 4 ounces thinly sliced shallots for leeks and rosemary for thyme. Increase amount of crème fraîche to ¼ cup and substitute ¼ cup chopped pitted kalamata olives and 1 teaspoon finely grated lemon zest for Dijon mustard. Substitute goat cheese for Gorgonzola.

Butternut Squash Galette with Gruyère

If desired, you can substitute rye flour for the whole-wheat flour in this recipe.

1. Microwave 6 ounces baby spinach and ¼ cup water in bowl until spinach is wilted and decreased in volume by half, 3 to 4 minutes. Using potholders, remove bowl from microwave and keep covered for 1 minute. Carefully remove plate and transfer spinach to colander. Gently press spinach with rubber spatula to release excess liquid. Transfer spinach to cutting board and chop coarse. Return spinach to colander and press again with rubber spatula; set aside.

2. Substitute 1¼ pounds butternut squash, peeled and cut into ½-inch cubes, for mushrooms and increase microwave cooking time to about 8 minutes. Substitute 1 thinly sliced red onion for leeks and ½ teaspoon minced fresh oregano for thyme. Substitute 1 teaspoon sherry vinegar for Dijon mustard and stir reserved spinach and 3 ounces shredded Gruyère cheese into filling along with crème fraîche and vinegar in step 4. Omit Gorgonzola.

SIMPLIFIED POTATO GALETTE

WHY THIS RECIPE WORKS: Pommes Anna, the classic French potato cake (or galette) in which thinly sliced potatoes are tossed with butter, tightly shingled in a skillet, and cooked slowly on the stovetop, delivers showstopping results, but it requires so much labor and time that we're willing to make it only once a year. We wanted a potato galette with a crisp, deeply bronzed crust encasing a creamy center that tastes of earthy potatoes and sweet butter—and we wanted one we could make on a weeknight.

We started by neatly arranging just the first layer of potatoes in the skillet, then casually packed the rest of the potatoes into the pan; once the galette was inverted onto the plate, only the tidy layer was visible. We swapped the traditional cast-iron skillet for a nonstick pan and achieved superior browning by starting the galette on the stovetop, then transferring it to the bottom rack of the oven. For a galette that held together but wasn't gluey, we rinsed the potatoes to rid them of excess starch, then incorporated a little cornstarch for just the right amount of adhesion. And in lieu of occasionally tamping down on the galette during cooking as in traditional recipes, we simply filled a cake pan with pie weights and set it on the galette for a portion of the baking time. A bit of fresh rosemary added another layer of earthy flavor.

Simplified Potato Galette

SERVES 6 TO 8

For the potato cake to hold together, it is important to slice the potatoes no more than ⅛ inch thick and to make sure the slices are thoroughly dried before assembling the cake. Use a mandoline slicer or the slicing attachment of a food processor to slice the potatoes uniformly thin. A pound of dried beans, rice, or coins can be substituted for the pie weights. You will need a 10-inch ovensafe nonstick skillet for this recipe.

NOTES FROM THE TEST KITCHEN

INVERTING A GALETTE

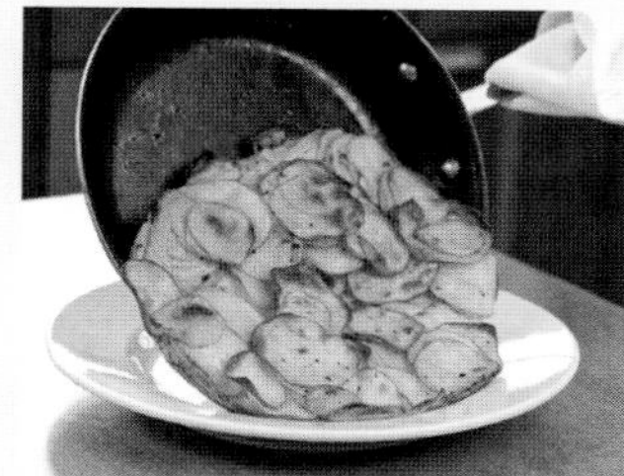

1. Using a spatula, loosen the galette and slide it out of the skillet onto a large plate.

2. Gently place a cutting board over the galette. Do not use an overly heavy board, which may crush the cake.

3. Flip the plate over so the board is on the bottom. Remove the plate, and the galette is ready to be sliced and served.

- 2½ pounds Yukon Gold potatoes, sliced ⅛ inch thick
- 5 tablespoons unsalted butter, melted
- 1 tablespoon cornstarch
- 1½ teaspoons chopped fresh rosemary leaves (optional)
- 1 teaspoon table salt
- ½ teaspoon ground black pepper

1. Adjust an oven rack to the lowest position and heat the oven to 450 degrees. Place the potatoes in a large bowl and fill with cold water. Using your hands, swirl to remove excess starch, drain, then spread the potatoes onto kitchen towels and dry thoroughly.

2. Whisk 4 tablespoons of the butter, the cornstarch, rosemary (if using), salt, and pepper together in a large bowl. Add the dried potatoes and toss to thoroughly coat. Place the remaining 1 tablespoon butter in a 10-inch ovensafe nonstick skillet and swirl to coat. Place 1 potato slice in the center of the skillet, then overlap slices in a circle around the center slice, followed by an outer circle of overlapping slices. Gently place the remaining sliced potatoes on top of the first layer, arranging so they form an even thickness.

3. Place the skillet over medium-high heat and cook until sizzling and the potatoes around the edge of the skillet start to turn translucent, about 5 minutes. Spray a 12-inch square of aluminum foil with vegetable oil spray. Place the foil, sprayed side down, on top of the potatoes. Place a 9-inch cake pan on top of the foil and fill with 2 cups pie weights. Firmly press down on the cake pan to compress the potatoes. Transfer the skillet to the oven and bake for 20 minutes.

4. Remove the cake pan and the foil from the skillet. Continue to bake until the potatoes are tender when a paring knife is inserted in the center, 20 to 25 minutes. Return the skillet to the stovetop and cook over medium heat, gently shaking the pan, until the galette releases from the sides of the pan, 2 to 3 minutes.

5. Invert the galette onto a cutting board. Using a serrated knife, gently cut into wedges and serve immediately.

POMMES ANNA

WHY THIS RECIPE WORKS: Traditional *pommes Anna* is rarely seen on home or restaurant menus these days because it takes a long time to prepare, and it is hard to remove cleanly from the pan, resulting in an unsatisfactory time-consuming and messy dish. We wanted a traditionally elegant potato cake with a crisp, deep brown crust covering the soft, creamy potato layers within.

We used a nonstick skillet to ensure easy release of our potatoes. Most recipes for pommes Anna call for clarified butter, but we decided to cut down on time and waste (a good portion of the butter is lost with clarifying) and instead tossed the sliced potatoes with melted butter. To accelerate cooking, we arranged the potatoes in elegant, layered circles in the skillet as it was heating on the stovetop; when we were done layering the slices, we pressed the potatoes with the bottom of a cake pan to compact them into a cohesive cake. To unmold, we simply inverted the potato cake onto a baking sheet and then slid it onto a serving dish.

Pommes Anna

SERVES 6 TO 8

Use a food processor fitted with a fine slicing disk or a mandoline to slice the potatoes, but do not slice them until you are ready to start assembling; see page 873 for our recommended mandoline. Remember to start timing when you begin arranging the potatoes in the skillet; they will need 30 minutes on the stovetop to brown properly no matter how quickly you arrange them.

- 3 pounds russet or Yukon Gold potatoes (about 6 medium), peeled and sliced ⅛ inch thick (see note)
- 5 tablespoons unsalted butter, melted
- ¼ cup vegetable oil or peanut oil
- Table salt and ground black pepper

1. Adjust an oven rack to the lower-middle position and heat the oven to 450 degrees. Toss the potatoes with the butter to coat.

2. Heat the oil in an ovensafe 10-inch nonstick skillet over medium-low heat. Begin timing, and arrange the potato slices in the skillet, using the most attractive slices to form the bottom layer, by placing one slice in the center of the skillet and overlapping more slices in a circle around the center slice; form another circle of overlapping slices to cover the pan bottom. Season with ¼ teaspoon salt and pepper to taste. Arrange the second layer of potatoes, working in the opposite direction of the first layer; season with ¼ teaspoon salt and pepper to taste. Repeat, layering the potatoes in opposite directions and seasoning with ¼ teaspoon salt and pepper to taste, until no slices remain (broken or uneven slices can be pieced together to form a single slice; potatoes will mound in the center of the skillet). Continue to cook until 30 minutes elapse from when you began arranging the potatoes in the skillet.

3. Using the bottom of a 9-inch cake pan, press on the potatoes firmly to compact. Cover the skillet and place in the oven; bake until the potatoes begin to soften, about 15 minutes. Uncover and continue to bake until the potatoes are tender when pierced with the tip of a paring knife and the edge of the potatoes near the skillet is browned, about 10 minutes longer. Meanwhile, line a rimless baking sheet or an inverted rimmed baking sheet with foil and spray lightly with vegetable oil spray. Carefully drain off the excess fat from the potatoes by pressing the bottom of the cake pan against the potatoes while tilting the skillet. (Be sure to use heavy potholders.)

4. Set the baking sheet, foil side down, on top of the skillet. Using potholders, hold the baking sheet in place with one hand and carefully invert the skillet and baking sheet together. Lift the skillet off the potatoes; slide the potatoes from the baking sheet onto a platter. Cut into wedges and serve immediately.

FRENCH-STYLE MASHED POTATOES

WHY THIS RECIPE WORKS: *Aligot* is French cookery's intensely rich, cheesy take on mashed potatoes. These potatoes get their elastic, satiny texture through prolonged, vigorous stirring—which can easily go awry and lead to a gluey, sticky mess. We wanted to create cheesy, garlicky mashed potatoes with a smooth, elastic texture and the same signature stretch as the French original.

After making aligot with different potatoes, we found medium-starch Yukon Golds to be the clear winner, yielding a puree with a mild, buttery flavor and a light, creamy consistency. We boiled the potatoes, then used a food processor to "mash" them. Traditional aligot uses butter and crème fraîche to add flavor and creaminess and loosen the texture before mixing in the cheese. But crème fraîche isn't always easy to find, so we substituted whole milk, which provided depth without going overboard. For the cheese, a combination of mild mozzarella and nutty Gruyère proved just right. As for the stirring, we needed to monitor the consistency closely: too much stirring and the aligot turned rubbery, too little and the cheese didn't marry with the potatoes for that essential elasticity.

French Mashed Potatoes with Cheese and Garlic (Aligot)

SERVES 6

The finished potatoes should have a smooth and slightly elastic texture. White cheddar can be substituted for the Gruyère. For richer, stretchier aligot, double the mozzarella.

- 2 pounds Yukon Gold potatoes (about 4 medium), peeled, cut into ½-inch-thick slices, rinsed well, and drained
- Table salt
- 6 tablespoons (¾ stick) unsalted butter
- 2 medium garlic cloves, minced or pressed through a garlic press (about 2 teaspoons)
- 1–1½ cups whole milk
- 4 ounces mozzarella cheese, shredded (about 1 cup; see note)
- 4 ounces Gruyère cheese, shredded (about 1 cup; see note)
- Ground black pepper

1. Place the potatoes and 1 tablespoon salt in a large saucepan; add water to cover by 1 inch. Partially cover the saucepan with a lid and bring to a boil over high heat. Reduce the heat to medium-low and simmer until the potatoes are tender and just break apart when poked with a fork, 12 to 17 minutes. Drain the potatoes and dry the saucepan.

2. Add the potatoes, butter, garlic, and 1½ teaspoons salt to a food processor. Pulse until the butter is melted and incorporated, about 10 pulses. Add 1 cup of the milk and continue to process until the potatoes are smooth and creamy, about 20 seconds, scraping down the sides of the workbowl halfway through.

3. Return the potato mixture to the saucepan and set over medium heat. Stir in the cheeses, 1 cup at a time, until incorporated. Continue to cook the potatoes, stirring vigorously, until the cheese is fully melted and the mixture is smooth and elastic, 3 to 5 minutes. If the mixture is difficult to stir and seems thick, stir in 2 tablespoons milk at a time (up to ½ cup) until the potatoes are loose and creamy. Season with salt and pepper to taste. Serve immediately.

POTATO CASSEROLE WITH BACON

WHY THIS RECIPE WORKS: This casserole of potatoes and onions is traditionally baked beneath a roast, which allows the casserole to be seasoned by the savory fat and juices of the roast. To get the same luxurious results without the roast, we started by rendering a small amount of bacon, which lent the dish a meaty flavor with a hint of smokiness. We then browned the onions in the rendered bacon fat, which gave the dish remarkable complexity.

Potato Casserole with Bacon and Caramelized Onion

SERVES 6 TO 8

Do not rinse or soak the potatoes, as this will wash away their starch, which is essential to the dish. A mandoline makes slicing the potatoes much easier. For the proper texture, make sure to let the casserole stand for 20 minutes before serving.

- 3 slices thick-cut bacon, cut into ½-inch pieces
- 1 large onion, halved and sliced thin
- 1¼ teaspoons salt
- 2 teaspoons chopped fresh thyme
- ½ teaspoon pepper
- 1¼ cups low-sodium chicken broth
- 1¼ cups beef broth
- 3 pounds Yukon Gold potatoes, peeled
- 2 tablespoons unsalted butter, cut into 4 pieces

1. Adjust oven rack to lower-middle position and heat oven to 425 degrees. Grease 13 by 9-inch baking dish.

2. Cook bacon in medium saucepan over medium-low heat until crisp, 10 to 13 minutes. Using slotted spoon, transfer bacon to paper towel–lined plate. Remove and discard all but 1 tablespoon fat from pot. Return pot to medium heat and add onion and ¼ teaspoon salt; cook, stirring frequently, until onion is soft and golden brown, about 25 minutes, adjusting heat and adding water 1 tablespoon at a time if onion or bottom of pot becomes too dark. Transfer onion to large bowl; add bacon, thyme, remaining 1 teaspoon salt, and pepper. Add broths to now-empty saucepan and bring to simmer over medium-high heat, scraping bottom of pan to loosen any browned bits.

3. Slice potatoes ⅛ inch thick. Transfer to bowl with onion mixture and toss to combine. Transfer to prepared baking dish. Firmly press down on mixture to compress into even layer. Carefully pour hot broth over top of potatoes. Dot surface evenly with butter.

4. Bake, uncovered, until potatoes are tender and golden brown on edges and most of liquid has been absorbed, 45 to 55 minutes. Transfer to wire rack and let stand for 20 minutes to fully absorb broth before cutting and serving.

POTATOES LYONNAISE

WHY THIS RECIPE WORKS: Originally conceived as a way to use up leftover boiled potatoes, potatoes Lyonnaise came to represent the best of classic French bistro cuisine: buttery, browned potato slices with strands of sweet, caramelized onion and fresh parsley—a simple yet complex skillet potato dish. Sadly, many versions are greasy and heavy rather than rich and complex. We wanted a return to the original elegant, buttery potato and onion dish—but one that didn't require leftover potatoes to make.

First, we had to choose the right potato. Yukon Golds beat out high-starch russets and low-starch Red Bliss. We precooked the potatoes in the microwave so that, once added to the skillet, they would cook through in the time they took to brown (without the microwave, the potatoes charred on the outside before cooking through). While the potatoes were in the microwave, we cooked the onions just long enough to release moisture and cook in their own juices. To finish the dish, we united the onions and potatoes in a brief sauté for the perfect melding of flavors. A sprinkling of minced parsley gave the dish a fresh taste and bright color.

Potatoes Lyonnaise

SERVES 4

Toss the potatoes halfway through the microwave session to prevent uneven cooking. If using a lightweight skillet, you will need to stir the potatoes more frequently to prevent burning.

- 3 tablespoons unsalted butter
- 1 large onion, halved pole to pole and sliced ¼ inch thick (about 3 cups)
- ½ teaspoon table salt
- 2 tablespoons water
- 1½ pounds Yukon Gold potatoes (about 3 medium), peeled and sliced crosswise into ¼-inch rounds
- ¼ teaspoon ground black pepper
- 1 tablespoon minced fresh parsley leaves

1. Melt 1 tablespoon of the butter in a 12-inch heavy nonstick skillet over medium-high heat. Add the onion and ¼ teaspoon of the salt and stir to coat; cook, stirring occasionally, until the onion begins to soften, about 3 minutes. Reduce the heat to medium and cook, covered, stirring occasionally, until the onion is light brown and soft, about 12 minutes longer, deglazing with the water when the pan gets dry, about halfway through the cooking time. Transfer to a bowl and cover. Do not wash the skillet.

2. While the onion cooks, microwave 1 tablespoon more butter on high power in a large microwave-safe bowl until melted, about 15 seconds. Add the potatoes to the bowl and toss to coat with the melted butter. Microwave on high power until the potatoes just start to turn tender, about 6 minutes, tossing halfway through the cooking time. Toss the potatoes again and set aside.

3. Melt the remaining 1 tablespoon butter in the now-empty skillet over medium-high heat. Add the potatoes and shake the skillet to distribute evenly. Cook, without stirring, until browned on the bottom, about 3 minutes. Using a spatula, stir the potatoes carefully and continue to cook, stirring every 2 to 3 minutes, until the potatoes are well browned and tender when pierced with the tip of a paring knife, 8 to 10 minutes more. Season with the remaining salt and the pepper.

4. Add the onion back to the skillet and stir to combine. Cook until the onion is heated through and the flavors have melded, 1 to 2 minutes. Transfer to a large plate, sprinkle with the parsley, and serve.

CHICKEN FRICASSEE

WHY THIS RECIPE WORKS: In search of a streamlined technique that would give this classic French braise weeknight potential and a brighter sauce, we replaced the bone-in chicken parts with the busy cook's favorite timesaver: boneless, skinless breasts and thighs. Then we found two ways to add richness that we'd lost by omitting the skin and bones: We browned the meat in butter and oil, and we browned the vegetables until they developed fond to serve as the sauce base. Increasing the amount of mushrooms boosted the fricassee's meaty flavor, while finishing the sauce with sour cream added body and tang. Whisking an egg yolk into the sour cream thickened the sauce and made it silky.

Quick Chicken Fricassee

SERVES 4 TO 6

Two tablespoons of chopped fresh parsley leaves may be substituted for the tarragon in this recipe.

- 2 pounds boneless, skinless chicken breasts and/or thighs, trimmed
- Table salt and ground black pepper
- 1 tablespoon unsalted butter
- 1 tablespoon olive oil
- 1 pound cremini mushrooms, trimmed and sliced ¼ inch thick
- 1 medium onion, chopped fine
- ¼ cup dry white wine
- 1 tablespoon unbleached all-purpose flour
- 1 medium garlic clove, minced or pressed through a garlic press (about 1 teaspoon)
- 1½ cups low-sodium chicken broth
- ⅓ cup sour cream
- 1 large egg yolk
- 2 teaspoons juice from 1 lemon
- 2 teaspoons minced fresh tarragon leaves
- ½ teaspoon freshly grated nutmeg

1. Pat the chicken dry with paper towels and season with 1 teaspoon salt and ½ teaspoon pepper. Heat the butter and oil in a 12-inch skillet over medium-high heat until the butter is melted. Place the chicken in a skillet and cook until browned, about 4 minutes. Using tongs, flip the chicken and cook until browned on the second side, about 4 minutes longer. Transfer the chicken to a large plate.

2. Add the mushrooms, onion, and wine to the now-empty skillet and cook, stirring occasionally, until the liquid has evaporated and the mushrooms are browned, 8 to 10 minutes. Add the flour and garlic; cook, stirring constantly, for 1 minute. Add the broth and bring the mixture to a boil, scraping up the browned bits from the bottom of the pan. Add the chicken and any accumulated juices to the skillet. Reduce the heat to medium-low, cover, and simmer until the breasts register 160 to 165 degrees and the thighs register 175 degrees on an instant-read thermometer, 5 to 10 minutes.

3. Transfer the chicken to a clean platter and tent loosely with foil. Whisk the sour cream and the egg yolk together in a medium bowl. Whisking constantly, slowly stir ½ cup of the hot sauce from the skillet into the sour cream mixture to temper. Stirring constantly, slowly pour the sour cream mixture into the simmering sauce. Stir in the lemon juice, tarragon and nutmeg; return to a simmer. Season with salt and pepper to taste, pour the sauce over the chicken, and serve.

STUFFED CHICKEN BREASTS

WHY THIS RECIPE WORKS: Most American cooks stuff chicken breasts with cheesy, bready fillings. French chefs, on the other hand, use a forcemeat stuffing to transform ordinary chicken breasts into a four-star affair. The French technique requires some serious labor, and includes skinning and boning a whole chicken, stuffing the breasts with the leg meat, and wrapping them up in the skin. We wanted to achieve the same flavorful package of chicken and filling—using a much simpler procedure.

Starting with boneless, skinless chicken breasts eliminated the need to bone a whole chicken. We mimicked a forcemeat stuffing by trimming a bit of meat from each chicken breast, and combining the meat with mushrooms, herbs, and leeks. Pureeing the meat trimmings created a cohesive filling that stayed put inside the chicken breasts.

Turning to the mechanics, we needed to create easy-to-roll rectangles of chicken breast to encase the stuffing. After butterflying the chicken breasts, we pounded them thin and trimmed them into a rectangular shape. The stuffing was easy to spread on the breasts, which we simply rolled up and tied with twine. Finally, we browned the chicken in a hot skillet and then added chicken broth and wine to braise the meat in the pan. Not only did the chicken stay tender when simmered, but the liquid served as a base for a simple yet intensely flavored pan sauce.

French-Style Stuffed Chicken Breasts

SERVES 4

To make slicing the chicken easier, freeze it for 15 minutes. If your chicken breasts come with the tenderloins attached, pull them off and reserve them to make the puree (along with the breast meat you will trim in step 1). Because the stuffing contains raw chicken, it is important to check its temperature in step 5.

CHICKEN AND STUFFING

- 4 (7- to 8-ounce) boneless, skinless chicken breasts, tenderloins removed and breasts trimmed (see note)
- 3 tablespoons vegetable oil
- 10 ounces white mushrooms, wiped clean and sliced thin
- 1 small leek, white part only, chopped and rinsed thoroughly (about 1 cup)
- 2 medium garlic cloves, minced or pressed through a garlic press (about 2 teaspoons)
- ½ teaspoon minced fresh thyme leaves
- 1 tablespoon juice from 1 lemon
- ½ cup dry white wine
- 1 tablespoon minced fresh parsley leaves
- Table salt and ground black pepper
- 1 cup low-sodium chicken broth

SAUCE

- 1 teaspoon Dijon mustard
- 2 tablespoons unsalted butter
- Table salt and ground black pepper

1. FOR THE CHICKEN AND STUFFING: Butterfly the chicken horizontally, stopping ½ inch from the edges so the halves remain attached, then open up each breast, cover with plastic wrap, and pound the cutlets to an even ¼-inch thickness (each cutlet should measure about 8 by 6 inches). Trim about ½ inch from the long sides of the cutlets (1½ to 2 ounces of meat per cutlet, or a total of ½ cup from all 4 cutlets) to form rectangles that measure about 8 by 5 inches. Process all the trimmings in a food processor until smooth, about 20 seconds. Transfer the puree to a medium bowl and set aside. (Do not wash the food processor bowl.)

2. Heat 1 tablespoon of the oil in a 12-inch skillet over medium-high heat until shimmering. Add the mushrooms and cook, stirring occasionally, until all the moisture has evaporated and the mushrooms are golden brown, 8 to 11 minutes. Add 1 tablespoon more oil and the leek; continue to cook, stirring frequently, until softened, 2 to 4 minutes. Add the garlic and thyme and cook until fragrant, about 30 seconds. Add 1½ teaspoons of the lemon juice and cook until all the moisture has evaporated, about 30 seconds. Transfer the mixture to the bowl of the food processor. Return the pan to the heat, add the wine, and scrape the pan bottom to loosen any browned bits. Transfer the wine to a small bowl and set aside. Rinse and dry the skillet.

3. Pulse the mushroom mixture in the food processor until roughly chopped, about 5 pulses. Transfer the mushroom mixture to the bowl with the pureed chicken. Add 1½ teaspoons of the parsley, ¾ teaspoon salt, and ½ teaspoon pepper. Using a rubber spatula, fold together the stuffing ingredients until well combined (you should have about 1½ cups stuffing).

4. Spread one-quarter of the stuffing evenly over each cutlet with a rubber spatula, leaving a ¾-inch border along the short sides of the cutlet and a ¼-inch border along the long sides. Roll each breast up as tightly as possible without squeezing out the filling and place seam side down. Evenly space three pieces of kitchen twine (each about 12 inches long) beneath each breast and tie, trimming any excess.

NOTES FROM THE TEST KITCHEN

STUFFING CHICKEN BREASTS

1. Slice each breast horizontally, stopping ½ inch from the edges so the halves remain attached.

2. Open up each breast, cover it with plastic wrap, and pound it to an even ¼-inch thickness.

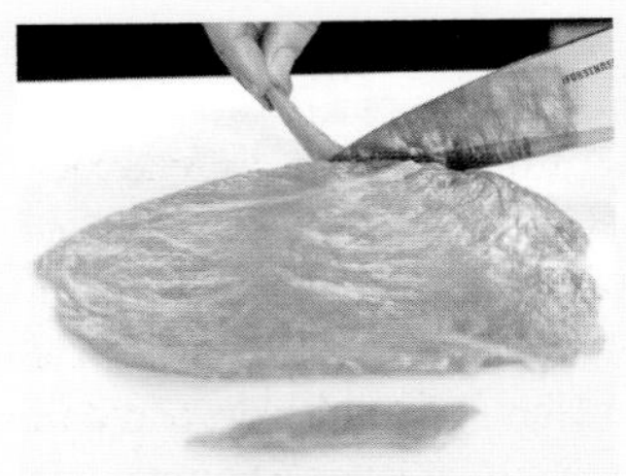

3. Trim about ½ inch from the long side of each cutlet to form an 8 by 5-inch rectangle. Reserve the trimmings for the stuffing.

4. Spread the stuffing evenly over each cutlet, leaving a ¾-inch border along the short sides and a ¼-inch border along the long sides.

5. With the short side facing you, roll up each cutlet and secure it snugly with kitchen twine.

5. Season the chicken with salt and pepper. Heat the remaining 1 tablespoon oil in the skillet over medium-high heat until just smoking. Add the chicken bundles and brown on all four sides, about 2 minutes per side. Add the broth and reserved wine to the pan and bring to a boil. Reduce the heat to low, cover the pan, and cook until the center of the chicken registers 160 to 165 degrees on an instant-read thermometer, 12 to 18 minutes. Transfer the chicken to a carving board and tent loosely with foil.

6. FOR THE SAUCE: While the chicken rests, whisk the mustard into the cooking liquid. Increase the heat to high and simmer, scraping the pan bottom to loosen the browned bits, until dark brown and reduced to ½ cup, 7 to 10 minutes. Off the heat, whisk in the butter and the remaining 1½ teaspoons parsley and 1½ teaspoons lemon juice; season with salt and pepper to taste. Remove the twine and cut each chicken bundle on the bias into six medallions. Spoon the sauce over the chicken and serve.

COQ AU VIN

WHY THIS RECIPE WORKS: Although conventional recipes for *coq au vin* take upwards of three hours to prepare, we felt that this rustic dish shouldn't be so time-consuming. After all, it's basically a chicken fricassee. We wanted to create a dish with tender, juicy chicken infused with the flavors of red wine, onions, mushrooms, and bacon in under two hours.

We decided to use chicken parts; this way, we could pick the parts we liked best. If using a mix of dark and white meat, we found it was essential to start the dark before the white, so that all the meat finished cooking at the same time and nothing was overcooked or undercooked. To thicken the stewing liquid, we sprinkled flour over the sautéed vegetables and whisked in butter toward the end of cooking; the butter also provided a nice richness in the sauce. Chicken broth added a savory note to the sauce and gave it some body; an entire bottle of red wine provided a great base of flavor. Tomato paste was a fuss-free way to add extra depth and body to the sauce, while a sprinkling of crisp, salty bacon rounded out the acidity of the wine.

Coq au Vin

SERVES 4

Use any $10 bottle of fruity, medium-bodied red wine, such as Pinot Noir, Côtes du Rhône, or Zinfandel. If using both chicken breasts and thighs/drumsticks, we recommend cutting the breast pieces in half so that each person can have some white meat and dark meat. The breasts and thighs/drumsticks do not cook at the same rate; if using both, note that the breast pieces are added partway through the cooking time. Serve with egg noodles.

- 6 ounces thick-cut bacon (about 5 slices), chopped medium
- Vegetable oil, as needed
- 4 pounds bone-in, skin-on chicken pieces (split breasts cut in half, drumsticks, and/or thighs; see note)
- Table salt and ground black pepper
- 8 ounces (about 2 cups) frozen pearl onions
- 10 ounces white mushrooms, wiped clean and quartered
- 2 medium garlic cloves, minced or pressed through a garlic press (about 2 teaspoons)
- 1 tablespoon tomato paste
- 3 tablespoons unbleached all-purpose flour
- 1 (750-milliliter) bottle medium-bodied red wine (see note)
- 2½ cups low-sodium chicken broth
- 1 teaspoon minced fresh thyme leaves or ¼ teaspoon dried
- 2 bay leaves
- 2 tablespoons unsalted butter, cut into 2 pieces, chilled
- 2 tablespoons minced fresh parsley leaves

1. Fry the bacon in a large Dutch oven over medium heat until crisp, 5 to 7 minutes. Transfer the bacon to a paper towel–lined plate, leaving the fat in the pot (you should have about 2 tablespoons; if necessary, add vegetable oil to make this amount). Set aside.

2. Pat the chicken dry with paper towels and season with salt and pepper. Return the pot with the bacon fat to medium-high heat until shimmering. Brown half of the chicken on both sides, 5 to 8 minutes per side, reducing the heat if the pan begins to scorch. Transfer the chicken to a plate, leaving the fat in the pot. Return the pot to medium-high heat and repeat with the remaining chicken; transfer the chicken to the plate.

3. Pour off all but 1 tablespoon of the fat in the pot (or add vegetable oil if needed to make this amount). Add the onions and mushrooms and cook over medium heat, stirring occasionally, until lightly browned, about 10 minutes. Stir in the garlic and tomato paste and cook until fragrant, about 30 seconds. Stir in the flour and cook for 1 minute. Stir in the wine, broth, thyme, and bay leaves, scraping up any browned bits.

4. Nestle the chicken, along with any accumulated juices, into the pot and bring to a simmer. Cover, turn the heat to medium-low, and simmer until the chicken is tender and the thickest part of the breasts registers 160 to 165 degrees on an instant-read thermometer, about 20 minutes, or the thickest part of the thighs and drumsticks registers 175 degrees on an instant-read thermometer, about 1 hour. (If using both types of chicken, simmer the thighs and drumsticks for 40 minutes before adding the breasts.)

5. Transfer the chicken to a serving dish, tent loosely with foil, and let rest while finishing the sauce. Skim as much fat as possible off the surface of the sauce and return to a simmer until the sauce is thickened and measures about 2 cups, about 20 minutes. Off the heat, remove the bay leaves, whisk in the butter, and season with salt and pepper to taste. Pour the sauce over the chicken, sprinkle with the reserved bacon and the parsley, and serve.

CHICKEN WITH 40 CLOVES OF GARLIC

WHY THIS RECIPE WORKS: In most versions of chicken with 40 cloves of garlic, the garlic is soft and spreadable, but its flavor is spiritless. The chicken is tender, but the breast meat takes on a dry, chalky quality, and its flavor is washed out. We wanted to revisit this classic French dish to make it faster and better, so it would boast well-browned, full-flavored chicken, sweet and nutty garlic, and a savory sauce.

Using a cut-up chicken rather than a whole bird ensured that the meat cooked quickly and evenly. We roasted the garlic cloves first to caramelize them and develop their flavor, then added them to the braising liquid with the chicken. Cooking it all with a two-part pan-roasting/braising technique kept the chicken moist, and finishing the chicken under the broiler made the chicken skin crispy. Some shallots and herbs added flavor to the sauce, and several roasted garlic cloves, smashed into a paste, thickened and flavored the sauce. A few tablespoons of butter, swirled in before serving, added richness.

Chicken with 40 Cloves of Garlic

SERVES 4

If using a kosher chicken, skip the brining process and begin with step 2. Avoid heads of garlic that have begun to sprout (the green shoots will make the sauce taste bitter). Tie the rosemary and thyme sprigs together with kitchen twine so they will be easy to retrieve from the pan. Serve the dish with slices of crusty baguette; you can spread them with the roasted garlic cloves.

- Table salt and ground black pepper
- 1 (3½- to 4-pound) chicken, cut into 8 pieces (4 breast pieces, 2 thighs, 2 drumsticks; see page 395) and trimmed
- 3 medium heads garlic (about 8 ounces), outer papery skins removed, cloves separated and unpeeled (see note)
- 2 medium shallots, peeled and quartered
- 1 tablespoon olive oil
- ¾ cup dry vermouth or dry white wine
- ¾ cup low-sodium chicken broth
- 2 sprigs fresh thyme (see note)
- 1 sprig fresh rosemary (see note)
- 1 bay leaf
- 2 tablespoons unsalted butter

1. Adjust an oven rack to the middle position and heat the oven to 400 degrees. Dissolve ¼ cup salt in 2 quarts cold water in a large container; submerge the chicken in the brine, cover with plastic wrap, and refrigerate for 30 minutes. Remove the chicken from the brine, rinse, and pat dry with paper towels. Season both sides of the chicken pieces with pepper.

2. Meanwhile, combine the garlic, shallots, 2 teaspoons of the olive oil, ½ teaspoon salt, and ¼ teaspoon pepper in a 9-inch pie plate; cover tightly with foil and roast until softened and beginning to brown, about 30 minutes, shaking the pan once halfway through cooking. Uncover, stir, and continue to roast, uncovered, until browned and fully tender, about 10 minutes longer, stirring once or twice. Remove from the oven and increase the oven temperature to 450 degrees.

3. Heat the remaining 1 teaspoon oil in a 12-inch ovensafe skillet over medium-high heat until smoking. Brown the chicken, skin side down, until golden, about 5 minutes; flip the chicken pieces and brown until golden on the second side, about 4 minutes longer. Transfer the chicken to a large plate and pour off the fat from the skillet. Off the heat, add the vermouth, chicken broth, thyme, rosemary, and bay leaf to the pan, scraping up any browned bits. Set the skillet over medium heat, add the garlic mixture, and return the chicken, skin side up, to the pan, nestling the pieces on top of and between the garlic cloves. Place the skillet in the oven and roast until the thickest part of the breasts registers 160 to 165 degrees on an instant-read thermometer; remove the skillet from the oven.

4. Adjust an oven rack 6 inches from the broiler element and heat the broiler. Broil the chicken to crisp the skin, 3 to 5 minutes. Remove the skillet from the oven and transfer the chicken to a serving dish. Transfer 10 to 12 garlic cloves to a fine-mesh sieve and reserve. Using a slotted spoon, scatter the remaining garlic cloves and shallots around the chicken; discard the herbs. With a rubber spatula, push the reserved garlic cloves through the sieve and into a bowl; discard the skins. Add the garlic paste to the skillet and bring the liquid to a simmer over medium-high heat, whisking to incorporate the garlic. Whisk in the butter and season with salt and pepper to taste. Serve the chicken, passing the sauce separately.

NOTES FROM THE TEST KITCHEN

CUTTING UP A WHOLE CHICKEN

Buying chicken parts is convenient, but packages often contain pieces of varying sizes. Cutting up a whole chicken yourself isn't difficult and it will guarantee evenly sized pieces of meat.

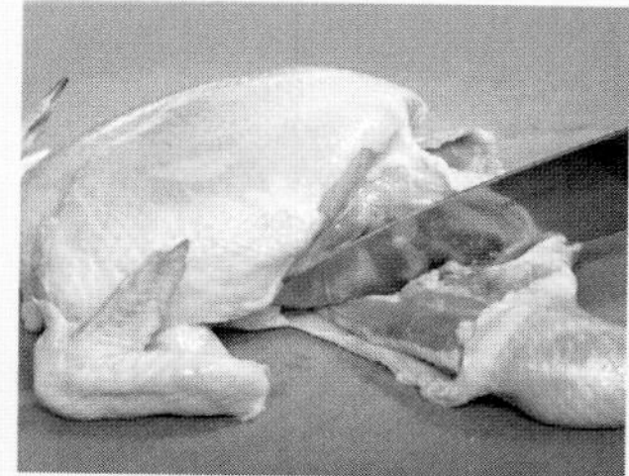

1. Using a chef's knife, cut off the legs, one at a time, by severing the joint between the leg and the body.

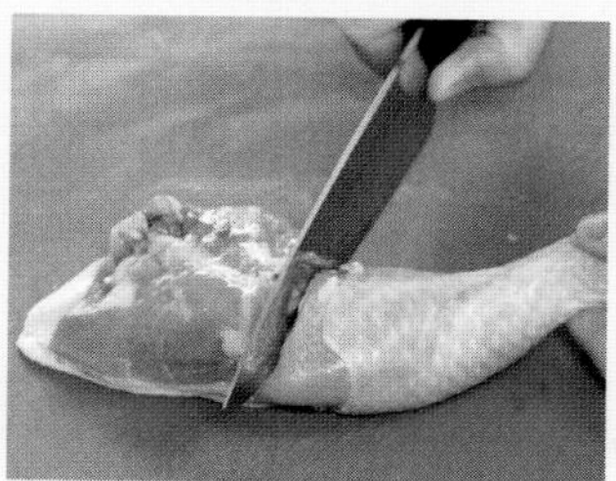

2. Cut each leg into two pieces—the drumstick and thigh—by slicing through the joint that connects them (marked by a thick white line of fat).

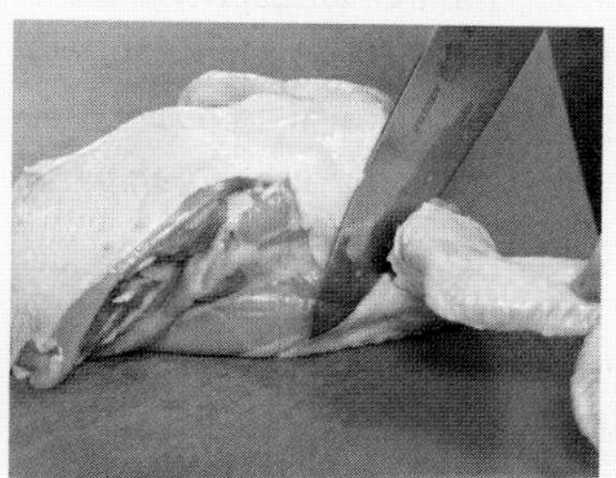

3. Flip the chicken over and remove the wings by slicing through each wing joint.

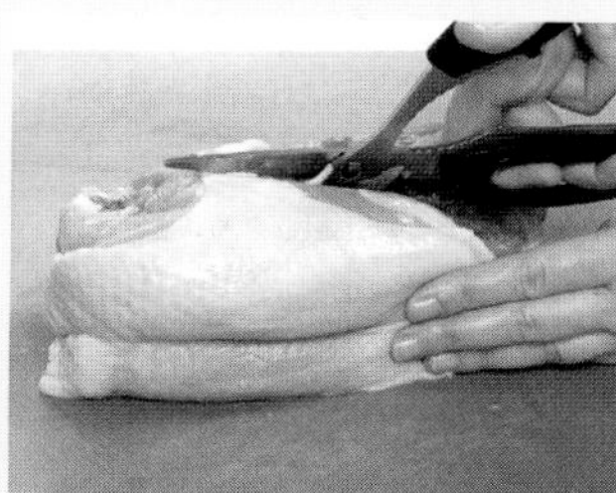

4. Turn the chicken (now without its legs and wings) on its side and, using scissors, remove the back from the chicken breast.

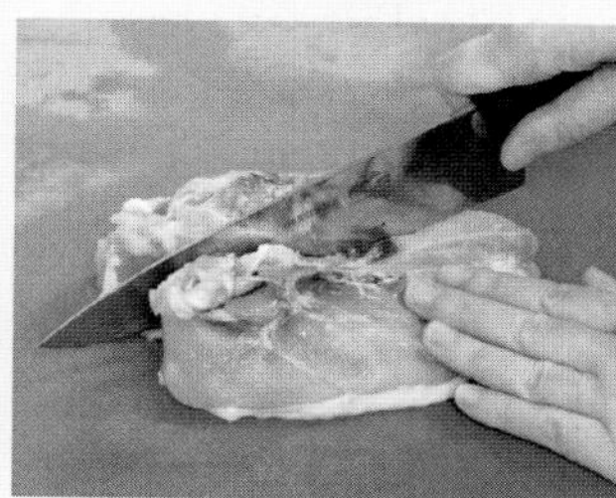

5. Flip the breast skin side down and, using a chef's knife, cut it in half through the breast plate (marked by a thin white line of cartilage), then cut each piece in half again.

FRENCH CHICKEN IN A POT

WHY THIS RECIPE WORKS: Poulet en cocotte (chicken in a pot) is a classic French specialty—at its best, it's a whole chicken baked with root vegetables in a covered pot that delivers incredibly tender and juicy meat. Sounds simple, but it's actually more challenging than throwing chicken in a pot with vegetables. One potential problem is too much moisture in the pot, which washes out the flavor; another pitfall is overcooking. We wanted chicken in a pot that delivered moist meat and satisfying flavor.

We removed the vegetables—the liquid they released made the pot too steamy—and cooked the chicken by itself (after browning it in a little oil to prevent it from sticking). We also tightly sealed the pot with foil before adding the lid. To keep the breast meat from drying out and becoming tough, we cooked the chicken very slowly. After developing the basic technique, we revisited the idea of vegetables, and found that a small amount of potently flavored aromatic vegetables could be added if they were lightly browned with the chicken to erase most of their moisture. Finally, defatting the liquid in the pot rewarded us with a richly flavored sauce.

French Chicken in a Pot

SERVES 4

The cooking times in the recipe are for a 4½- to 5-pound bird. A 3½- to 4½-pound chicken will take about an hour to cook, and a 5- to 6-pound bird will take close to 2 hours. We developed this recipe to work with a 5- to 8-quart Dutch oven with a tight-fitting lid. If using a 5-quart pot, do not cook a chicken larger than 5 pounds. If using a kosher chicken, reduce the amount of table salt to ½ teaspoon. If you choose not to serve the skin with the chicken, simply remove it before carving. The amount of sauce will vary depending on the size of the chicken; season it with about ¼ teaspoon lemon juice for every ¼ cup.

- 1 (4½- to 5-pound) whole chicken, giblets discarded, wings tucked under back (see note)
- 1 teaspoon table salt (see note)
- ¼ teaspoon ground black pepper
- 1 tablespoon olive oil
- 1 small onion, chopped medium
- 1 small celery rib, chopped medium
- 6 medium garlic cloves, peeled and trimmed
- 1 bay leaf
- 1 medium sprig fresh rosemary (optional)
- ½–1 teaspoon juice from 1 lemon (see note)

1. Adjust an oven rack to the lowest position and heat the oven to 250 degrees. Pat the chicken dry with paper towels and season with the salt and pepper.

2. Heat the oil in a large Dutch oven over medium heat until just smoking. Add the chicken, breast side down, and scatter the onion, celery, garlic cloves, bay leaf, and rosemary (if using) around the chicken. Cook until the breast is lightly browned, about 5 minutes. Flip the chicken breast side up and continue to cook until the chicken and vegetables are well browned, 6 to 8 minutes.

3. Off the heat, place a large sheet of foil over the pot and cover tightly with the lid. Transfer the pot to the oven and cook until the thickest part of the breast registers 160 to 165 degrees and the thickest part of the thighs registers 175 degrees on an instant-read thermometer, 1 hour and 20 minutes to 1 hour and 50 minutes.

4. Remove the pot from the oven. Transfer the chicken to a cutting board, tent loosely with foil, and let rest for 20 minutes. Strain the chicken juices from the pot into a fat separator, pressing on the solids to extract the liquid; discard the solids (you should have about ¾ cup juices). Let the liquid settle for 5 minutes, then pour into a saucepan and cook over low heat until hot. Carve the chicken, adding any accumulated juices to the saucepan. Season the sauce with lemon juice to taste (see note). Serve the chicken, passing the sauce separately.

FRENCH-STYLE CHICKEN AND STUFFING IN A POT

WHY THIS RECIPE WORKS: The French classic *poule au pot* is a rather unique take on stuffed chicken: Instead of being roasted, the stuffed bird is braised with vegetables in a Dutch oven to make a satisfying and hearty one-pot meal. Our first attempts gave us wan flavor and dry chicken. To ensure the pork and bread-crumb stuffing would cook through before the chicken was overdone, we skipped stuffing the bird and instead patted the stuffing into logs, wrapped them in parchment paper, and nestled them into the pot. To make room for the chicken and vegetables, we swapped out the whole bird for parts and browned them first to give the broth rich flavor. We layered them on top of the vegetables with just enough broth to cover the vegetables so the delicate breast meat could cook more gently raised above the simmering liquid. A simple herb sauce flavored with the traditional cornichons and mustard rounded out this rustic meal.

French-Style Chicken and Stuffing in a Pot

SERVES 4 TO 6

A neutral bulk sausage is best, but breakfast or sweet Italian sausage can be used. You'll need a Dutch oven with at least a 7¼-quart capacity. Use small red potatoes, measuring 1 to 2 inches in diameter. Serve this dish with crusty bread and cornichons and Dijon mustard or Herb Sauce (recipe follows).

SAUSAGE STUFFING

- 2 slices hearty white sandwich bread, crusts removed, torn into quarters
- 1 large egg
- 1 shallot, minced
- 2 garlic cloves, minced
- 2 tablespoons minced fresh parsley
- 2 tablespoons minced fennel fronds
- 2 teaspoons whole-grain mustard
- 1 teaspoon minced fresh marjoram
- ¼ teaspoon pepper
- 1 pound bulk pork sausage

CHICKEN

- 2 celery ribs, halved crosswise
- 8 sprigs plus 1 tablespoon minced fresh parsley
- 6 sprigs fresh marjoram
- 1 bay leaf
- 2 teaspoons vegetable oil
- 2 (12-ounce) bone-in split chicken breasts, trimmed
- 2 (12-ounce) bone-in chicken leg quarters, trimmed
- Salt and pepper
- 1½ pounds small red potatoes, unpeeled
- 2 carrots, peeled and cut into ½-inch lengths
- 1 fennel bulb, stalks trimmed, bulb quartered
- 8 whole peppercorns
- 2 garlic cloves, peeled
- 3–3½ cups low-sodium chicken broth

1. FOR THE SAUSAGE STUFFING: Adjust oven rack to middle position and heat oven to 300 degrees. Pulse bread in food processor until finely ground, 10 to 15 pulses. Add egg, shallot, garlic, parsley, fennel fronds, mustard, marjoram, and pepper to processor and pulse to combine, 6 to 8 pulses, scraping down sides of bowl as needed. Add sausage and pulse to combine, 3 to 5 pulses, scraping down sides of bowl as needed.

2. Place 18 by 12-inch piece of parchment paper on counter, with longer edge parallel to edge of counter. Place half of stuffing onto lower third of parchment, shaping it into rough 8 by 2-inch rectangle. Roll up sausage in parchment; gently but firmly twist both ends to compact mixture into 6- to 7-inch-long cylinder, approximately 2 inches in diameter. Repeat with second piece of parchment and remaining stuffing.

3. FOR THE CHICKEN: Using kitchen twine, tie together celery, parsley sprigs, marjoram, and bay leaf. Heat oil in large Dutch oven over medium-high heat until just smoking. Pat chicken breasts and leg quarters dry with paper towels, sprinkle with ½ teaspoon salt, and season with pepper. Add chicken, skin side down, and cook without moving it until browned, 4 to 7 minutes. Transfer chicken to large plate. Pour off and discard any fat in pot.

4. Remove Dutch oven from heat and carefully arrange celery bundle, potatoes, carrots, and fennel in even layer over bottom of pot. Sprinkle peppercorns, garlic, and ¼ teaspoon salt over vegetables. Add enough broth so that top ½ inch of vegetables is above surface of liquid. Place leg quarters on top of vegetables in center of pot. Place stuffing cylinders on either side of leg quarters. Arrange breasts on top of leg quarters. Place pot over high heat and bring to simmer. Cover, transfer to oven, and cook until breasts register 160 degrees, 60 to 75 minutes.

5. Transfer chicken and stuffing cylinders to carving board. Using slotted spoon, transfer vegetables to serving platter, discarding celery bundle. Pour broth through fine-mesh strainer into fat separator; discard solids. Let stand for 5 minutes.

6. Unwrap stuffing cylinders and slice into ½-inch-thick disks; transfer slices to platter with vegetables. Remove skin from chicken pieces and discard. Carve breasts from bone and slice into ½-inch-thick pieces. Separate thigh from leg by cutting through joint. Transfer chicken to platter with stuffing and vegetables. Pour ½ cup defatted broth over chicken and stuffing to moisten. Sprinkle with minced parsley. Serve, ladling remaining broth over individual servings.

Herb Sauce

MAKES ABOUT ½ CUP

- ⅓ cup extra-virgin olive oil
- 6 cornichons, minced
- 2 tablespoons minced fresh parsley
- 1 tablespoon minced fennel fronds
- 2 teaspoons minced shallot
- 2 teaspoons whole-grain mustard
- 1 teaspoon minced fresh marjoram
- ½ teaspoon finely grated lemon zest plus 2 tablespoons juice
- ¼ teaspoon pepper

Whisk all ingredients together in bowl. Let stand for 15 minutes before serving.

CHICKEN PROVENÇAL

WHY THIS RECIPE WORKS: Chicken *Provençal* represents the best of rustic peasant food—bone-in chicken is simmered all day in a tomatoey, garlicky herb broth. But all too often, this formula results in dry, rubbery chicken, watery or overly thick sauce, and dulled or muddied flavors. We wanted to rejuvenate this dish, and create a chicken dish that was meltingly tender, moist, and flavorful, napped in an aromatic, garlicky tomato sauce that we could mop up with a good loaf of crusty bread.

For the best flavor and most tender texture, we used bone-in chicken thighs and browned them in a sheer film of olive oil. Skinless thighs stuck to the pan, and skin-on thighs developed a flabby texture when braised later on. So we settled on a compromise—browning the thighs with the skin on (to develop rich flavor and leave browned bits in the pan), then ditching the skins prior to the braising (to avoid flabby skin). To keep the sauce from becoming greasy, we spooned off the excess fat left behind from browning the chicken, but kept enough to sauté our garlic and onion. Diced tomatoes, white wine, and chicken broth also went into the sauce. We then braised the chicken until it was meltingly tender. As for flavor enhancers, a small amount of niçoise olives added an essential brininess to the dish, and some minced anchovy made the sauce taste richer and fuller.

Chicken Provençal

SERVES 4

This dish is often served with rice or slices of crusty bread, but soft polenta is also a good accompaniment. Niçoise olives are the preferred olives here; the flavor of kalamatas and other types of brined or oil-cured olives is too potent.

- 8 (5- to 6-ounce) bone-in, skin-on chicken thighs, trimmed
- Table salt
- 1 tablespoon extra-virgin olive oil
- 1 small onion, minced
- 6 medium garlic cloves, minced or pressed through a garlic press (about 2 tablespoons)
- 1 anchovy fillet, minced (about ½ teaspoon)
- ⅛ teaspoon cayenne pepper
- 1 cup dry white wine
- 1 cup low-sodium chicken broth
- 1 (14.5-ounce) can diced tomatoes, drained
- 2½ tablespoons tomato paste
- 1½ tablespoons chopped fresh thyme leaves
- 1 teaspoon chopped fresh oregano leaves
- 1 teaspoon herbes de Provence (optional)
- 1 bay leaf
- 1½ teaspoons grated zest from 1 lemon
- ½ cup pitted niçoise olives (see note)
- 1 tablespoon chopped fresh parsley leaves

1. Adjust an oven rack to the lower-middle position and heat the oven to 300 degrees. Season both sides of the chicken thighs with salt. Heat 1 teaspoon of the oil in a large Dutch oven over medium-high heat until shimmering. Add 4 chicken thighs, skin side down, and cook, without moving, until the skin is crisp and well browned, about 5 minutes. Flip the chicken pieces and brown on the second side, about 5 minutes longer; transfer to a large plate. Repeat with the remaining 4 chicken thighs, then transfer them to the plate and set aside. Discard all but 1 tablespoon of fat from the pot.

2. Add the onion to the pot and cook, stirring occasionally, over medium heat until softened and browned, about 4 minutes. Add the garlic, anchovy, and cayenne; cook, stirring constantly, until fragrant, about 1 minute. Add the wine, scraping up any browned bits. Stir in the chicken broth, tomatoes, tomato paste, thyme, oregano, herbes de Provence (if using), and bay leaf. Remove and discard the skin from the chicken thighs, then submerge the chicken pieces in the liquid and add the accumulated chicken juices to the pot. Increase the heat to high, bring to a simmer, cover, and set the pot in the oven; cook until the chicken offers no resistance when poked with a knife but is still clinging to the bones, about 1¼ hours.

3. Using a slotted spoon, transfer the chicken to a serving platter and tent loosely with foil. Discard the bay leaf. Set the pot over high heat, stir in 1 teaspoon of the lemon zest, bring to a boil, and cook, stirring occasionally, until slightly thickened and reduced to 2 cups, about 5 minutes. Stir in the olives and cook until heated through, about 1 minute. Combine the remaining ½ teaspoon zest and the parsley. Spoon the sauce over the chicken, drizzle the chicken with the remaining 2 teaspoons oil, sprinkle with the parsley mixture, and serve.

DAUBE PROVENÇAL

WHY THIS RECIPE WORKS: *Daube Provençal,* also known as *daube niçoise,* has all the elements of the best French fare: tender beef, a luxurious sauce, and complex flavors. So why does it usually end up as beef stew with a few misplaced ingredients instead of being its own, coherent dish? We wanted to translate the flavors of Provence—olive oil, olives, garlic, wine, herbs, oranges, tomatoes, mushrooms, and anchovies—to an American home kitchen, and create a bold, brash, and full-flavored beef stew, with ingredients that married into a robust but unified dish. We started with the test kitchen's reliable set of techniques to turn tough but flavorful beef into a tender stew: Brown the beef; add the aromatics; sprinkle some flour in the pan to thicken the braising liquid; deglaze with more cooking liquid; add the meat back to the pot; and finally, cover and cook slowly in the oven until tender. Technique established, we concentrated on selecting and managing the complex blend of ingredients that defines this dish. We chose briny niçoise olives, bright tomatoes, floral orange peel, and the regional flavors of thyme and bay leaf. A few anchovies added complexity without a fishy taste, and salt pork contributed rich body. A whole bottle of wine added bold flavor and needed just a little cooking to tame its raw bite. Finally, to keep the meat from drying out during the long braising time required to create a complex-tasting sauce, we cut it into relatively large 2-inch pieces.

Daube Provençal

SERVES 4 TO 6

Serve this French beef stew with egg noodles or boiled potatoes. If niçoise olives are not available, kalamata olives, though not authentic, can be substituted. Cabernet Sauvignon is our favorite wine for this recipe, but Côtes du Rhône and Zinfandel also work. Our favorite cut of beef for this recipe is chuck-eye roast, but any boneless roast from the chuck will work. Because the tomatoes are added just before serving, it is preferable to use canned whole tomatoes and dice them yourself—uncooked, they are more tender than canned diced tomatoes. Once the salt pork, thyme, and bay leaves are removed in step 4, the daube can be cooled and refrigerated in an airtight container for up to 4 days. Before reheating, skim the hardened fat from the surface, then continue with the recipe.

- ¾ ounce dried porcini mushrooms, rinsed
- 1 (3½-pound) boneless beef chuck-eye roast, trimmed and cut into 2-inch chunks (see note)
- 1½ teaspoons table salt
- 1 teaspoon ground black pepper
- 4 tablespoons olive oil
- 5 ounces salt pork, rind removed
- 2 medium onions, halved pole to pole and cut into ⅛-inch-thick slices (about 4 cups)
- 4 large carrots, peeled and cut into 1-inch-thick rounds (about 2 cups)
- 2 tablespoons tomato paste
- 4 medium garlic cloves, peeled and sliced thin
- ⅓ cup unbleached all-purpose flour
- 1 (750-milliliter) bottle bold red wine (see note)
- 1 cup low-sodium chicken broth
- 1 cup water
- 1 cup pitted niçoise olives, drained well (see note)
- 4 strips zest from 1 orange, each strip about 3 inches long, removed with a vegetable peeler, cleaned of white pith, and cut lengthwise into thin strips
- 2 anchovy fillets, minced (about 1 teaspoon)
- 5 sprigs fresh thyme, tied together with kitchen twine
- 2 bay leaves
- 1 (14.5-ounce) can whole tomatoes, drained and cut into ½-inch cubes (see note)
- 2 tablespoons minced fresh parsley leaves

1. Combine the mushrooms and 1 cup water in a small microwave-safe bowl; cover with plastic wrap, cut three vents for steam with a knife, and microwave on high power for 30 seconds. Let stand until the mushrooms soften, about 5 minutes. Lift the mushrooms from the liquid with a fork and chop into ½-inch pieces (you should have about 4 tablespoons). Strain the liquid through a fine-mesh strainer lined with a paper towel into a medium bowl. Set the mushrooms and liquid aside.

2. Adjust an oven rack to the lower-middle position and heat the oven to 325 degrees. Dry the beef thoroughly with paper towels, then season with the salt and pepper. Heat 2 tablespoons of the oil in a large heavy-bottomed Dutch oven over medium-high heat until just smoking; add half of the beef. Cook without moving the pieces until well browned, about 2 minutes on each side, for a total of 8 to 10 minutes, reducing the heat if the fat begins to smoke. Transfer the meat to a medium bowl. Repeat with the remaining 2 tablespoons oil and the remaining beef.

3. Reduce the heat to medium and add the salt pork, onions, carrots, tomato paste, and garlic to the now-empty pot; cook, stirring occasionally, until light brown, about 2 minutes. Stir in the flour and cook, stirring constantly, about 1 minute. Slowly add the wine, gently scraping up any browned bits. Add the broth, water, and beef with any accumulated juices. Increase the heat to medium-high and bring to a simmer. Add the mushrooms and their liquid, ½ cup of the olives, the orange zest, anchovies, thyme, and bay leaves, distributing evenly and arranging the beef so it is completely covered by the liquid; partially cover the pot and place in the oven. Cook until a fork inserted in the beef meets little resistance (the meat should not be falling apart), 2½ to 3 hours.

4. Discard the salt pork, thyme, and bay leaves. Add the tomatoes and the remaining ½ cup olives; warm over medium-high heat until heated through, about 1 minute. Cover the pot and allow the stew to settle, about 5 minutes. Using a spoon, skim the excess fat from the surface of the stew. Stir in the parsley and serve.

BEEF BURGUNDY

WHY THIS RECIPE WORKS: Leave it to the French to make beef stew into an elegant affair. Unfortunately, when translated to the home kitchen, classic, intensely flavorful beef burgundy, also known as *boeuf bourguignon*, tends to lose its appeal. We've seen too many versions of this rustic French dish with tough meat or a dull sauce and no flavor complexity. We wanted to bring this dish to its earthy, robust, warm potential: satisfyingly large chunks of tender meat draped with a velvety sauce brimming with the flavor of good Burgundy wine and studded with caramelized mushrooms and pearl onions.

We started by rendering salt pork until crisp, then browned large chunks of beef chuck roast in the rendered fat. For the braising liquid, a combination of chicken broth and water, enhanced with a small amount of dried porcini mushrooms and tomato paste, provided balanced, well-rounded flavor. Using anything less than a full bottle of red wine (preferably a Burgundy, but a good Pinot Noir will suffice) left the sauce lacking and unremarkable. We deglazed the pan twice, used a roux to thicken the sauce, and then added the wine. Wrapping the aromatic vegetables in cheesecloth made it easy to remove them from the braising liquid. While the liquid reduced to a velvety sauce, we simmered pearl onions then sautéed them briefly with mushrooms to create the perfect garnish for our rich, tender beef.

Beef Burgundy

SERVES 6

Thick-cut bacon can be substituted for the salt pork; cut the bacon crosswise into ¼-inch pieces and treat it just as you would the salt pork, but note that you will have no rind to include in the vegetable and herb pouch. Boiled potatoes are the traditional accompaniment, but mashed potatoes or buttered noodles are nice as well.

STEW

- 6 ounces salt pork, trimmed of rind and rind reserved, salt pork cut into ¼-inch pieces (see note)
- 2 medium onions, chopped coarse
- 2 medium carrots, chopped coarse
- 1 medium head garlic, cloves separated and crushed but unpeeled
- 10 sprigs fresh parsley, torn into pieces
- 6 sprigs fresh thyme
- 2 bay leaves, crumbled
- ½ teaspoon black peppercorns
- ½ ounce dried porcini mushrooms, rinsed (optional)
- 1 (4- to 4½-pound) boneless beef chuck-eye roast, trimmed and cut into 2-inch chunks
- Table salt and ground black pepper

2½ cups water
4 tablespoons (½ stick) unsalted butter, cut into 4 pieces
⅓ cup unbleached all-purpose flour
1¾ cups low-sodium chicken broth
1 (750-milliliter) bottle red Burgundy or Pinot Noir
1 teaspoon tomato paste
2 tablespoons brandy
3 tablespoons minced fresh parsley leaves

ONION AND MUSHROOM GARNISH

7 ounces (about 1¾ cups) frozen pearl onions
¾ cup water
1 tablespoon unsalted butter
1 tablespoon sugar
½ teaspoon table salt
10 ounces medium white mushrooms, wiped clean and halved

1. FOR THE STEW: Bring the salt pork, reserved salt pork rind, and 3 cups water to a boil in a medium saucepan over high heat. Boil for 2 minutes, then drain well.

2. Lay a double layer of cheesecloth (each piece should measure 22 by 8 inches) in a medium bowl, placing the sheets perpendicular to each other. Place the onions, carrots, garlic, parsley pieces, thyme, bay leaves, peppercorns, porcini mushrooms (if using), and salt pork rind in the cheesecloth-lined bowl. Gather together the edges of the cheesecloth and fasten them securely with kitchen twine; trim the excess cheesecloth with scissors if necessary. Set the pouch in a large ovensafe Dutch oven. Adjust the oven rack to the lower-middle position and heat the oven to 300 degrees.

3. Cook the salt pork in a 12-inch skillet over medium heat until lightly browned and crisp, about 12 minutes. With a slotted spoon, transfer the salt pork to the pot. Pour off and reserve all but 2 teaspoons of the fat from the skillet. Pat the beef dry with paper towels and season with salt and pepper. Add half of the beef to the skillet, increase the heat to high, and brown in a single layer, turning once or twice, until deep brown, about 7 minutes; transfer the browned beef to the pot. Add ½ cup of the water to the skillet and scrape the pan with a wooden spoon to loosen the browned bits; add the liquid to the pot.

4. Heat 2 teaspoons of the reserved pork fat in the skillet over high heat until smoking. Add the remaining beef in a single layer, turning once or twice, until deep brown, about 7 minutes; transfer the browned beef to the pot. Add ½ cup more water to the skillet and scrape the pan with a wooden spoon to loosen the browned bits; add the liquid to the pot.

5. Melt the butter in the skillet over medium heat. Whisk in the flour and cook, stirring constantly, until light brown, about 5 minutes. Gradually whisk in the chicken broth and the remaining 1½ cups water. Increase the heat to medium-high and bring to a simmer, stirring frequently, until thickened; add the mixture to the pot. Add 3 cups of the wine and the tomato paste to the pot and season with salt and pepper to taste; stir to combine. Set the pot over high heat and bring to a boil; cover and place in the oven. Cook until the meat is tender, 2½ to 3 hours.

6. Remove the pot from the oven and transfer the vegetable and herb pouch to a mesh strainer; set the strainer over the pot. Using the back of a spoon, press the liquid from the pouch into the pot; discard the pouch. With a slotted spoon, transfer the beef to a medium bowl; set aside. Let the pot contents settle for about 15 minutes, then skim off and discard the fat.

7. Bring the liquid in the pot to a boil over medium-high heat. Simmer, stirring occasionally, until thickened and reduced to about 3 cups, 15 to 25 minutes.

8. FOR THE ONION AND MUSHROOM GARNISH: Meanwhile, bring the pearl onions, ½ cup of the water, the butter, sugar, and ¼ teaspoon of the salt to a boil in a 10-inch skillet over high heat. Cover, reduce the heat to medium-low, and simmer, shaking the pan occasionally, until the onions are tender, about 5 minutes. Uncover, increase the heat to high, and simmer until all the liquid evaporates, about 3 minutes. Add the mushrooms and the remaining ¼ teaspoon salt. Cook, stirring occasionally, until the liquid released by the mushrooms evaporates and the vegetables are browned, about 5 minutes. Transfer the vegetables to a bowl and set aside. Add the remaining ¼ cup water to the skillet and scrape the pan with a wooden spoon to loosen the browned bits; add the liquid to the pot with the reducing sauce.

9. When the sauce has reduced, reduce the heat to medium-low and stir in the beef, the remaining 2 tablespoons wine, the brandy, and the mushrooms and onions (and any accumulated juices). Cover the pot and cook until heated through, 5 to 8 minutes. Season with salt and pepper to taste and serve, sprinkling individual servings with the parsley.

SLOW-COOKER BEEF BURGUNDY

WHY THIS RECIPE WORKS: Given the amount of simmering time required for classic Beef Burgundy (page 399), we thought this stew could be easily morphed into a slow-cooker version that would have the same tender beef chunks and rich, earthy sauce as the original.

For a long braise, chuck roast cut into pieces is the best choice. The usual first step in making a stew is to brown the meat, but we found that we could get the same meaty flavor base from browning only half the beef. We used rendered bacon fat instead of oil; the bacon would go back into the stew at the end, lending a smoky note. Sautéed carrots and onions went into the slow-cooker insert next, with plenty of garlic, thyme, and tomato paste. As our braising liquid, beef broth tasted tinny but chicken broth worked well. We mixed it with red wine and a surprising ingredient, soy sauce, which intensified the savory flavors in the stew as well as deepened its color. To enrich the sauce, we stirred in a small amount of tapioca, a common thickening agent, in place of flour. We prepared the traditional onion and mushroom garnish separately, when the stew was almost finished cooking, and folded it in. The final touch was more red wine, which we reduced first so that it wouldn't impart a sour alcoholic taste. This slow-cooker beef burgundy had everything we would expect from the refined French original.

Slow-Cooker Beef Burgundy

SERVES 6 TO 8

Make sure to use the low setting on your slow cooker; the stew will burn on the high setting. Don't spend a lot of money for the wine in this recipe—in our testing, we found that California Pinot Noir wines in the $6 to $20 price range worked just fine. Boiled potatoes are the traditional accompaniment, but mashed potatoes or buttered noodles are nice as well.

STEW

- 8 ounces (about 8 slices) bacon, cut into ¼-inch pieces
- 1 (4-pound) boneless beef chuck-eye roast, trimmed and cut into 1½-inch chunks
- Table salt and ground black pepper
- 1 large onion, minced
- 2 carrots, peeled and minced
- 8 medium garlic cloves, minced or pressed through a garlic press (about 2 tablespoons plus 2 teaspoons)
- 2 teaspoons chopped fresh thyme leaves
- 4 tablespoons tomato paste
- 2½ cups Pinot Noir (see note)
- 1½ cups low-sodium chicken broth
- ⅓ cup soy sauce
- 3 bay leaves
- 3 tablespoons Minute tapioca
- 3 tablespoons minced fresh parsley leaves

ONION AND MUSHROOM GARNISH

- 8 ounces (about 2 cups) frozen pearl onions
- ½ cup water
- 5 tablespoons unsalted butter
- 1 tablespoon sugar
- 10 ounces white mushrooms, wiped clean and quartered
- Table salt

1. FOR THE STEW: Cook the bacon in a 12-inch skillet over medium-high heat until crisp. Using a slotted spoon, transfer the bacon to a paper towel–lined plate and refrigerate. Pour half of the bacon fat into a small bowl; set the skillet with the remaining bacon fat aside.

2. Pat the beef dry with paper towels and season with salt and pepper; place half of the beef in a slow-cooker insert. Heat the skillet with the remaining bacon fat over medium-high heat until smoking. Cook the remaining beef in a single layer until deep brown on all sides, about 8 minutes. Transfer the browned beef to the slow-cooker insert.

3. Add the reserved bacon fat to the now-empty skillet and heat over medium-high heat until shimmering. Add the onion, carrots, and ¼ teaspoon salt and cook until the vegetables begin to brown, about 5 minutes. Add the garlic and thyme and cook until fragrant, about 30 seconds. Add the tomato paste and stir until beginning to brown, about 45 seconds. Transfer the mixture to the slow-cooker insert.

4. Return the now-empty skillet to high heat and add 1½ cups of the wine, the chicken broth, and soy sauce. Simmer, scraping up any browned bits, for about 1 minute. Transfer the wine mixture to the slow-cooker insert.

5. Stir the bay leaves and tapioca into the slow-cooker insert. Set the slow cooker on low, cover, and cook until the meat is fork-tender, about 9 hours.

6. FOR THE ONION AND MUSHROOM GARNISH: Bring the pearl onions, water, butter, and sugar to a boil in a 12-inch skillet over high heat. Cover and simmer over medium-low heat until the onions are tender, about 5 minutes. Uncover, increase the heat to high, and cook until the liquid evaporates, about 3 minutes. Add the mushrooms and ¼ teaspoon salt and cook until the vegetables are browned and glazed, about 5 minutes.

7. When ready to serve, discard the bay leaves and stir in the onion and mushroom garnish and the reserved bacon. Bring the remaining 1 cup wine to a boil in a 12-inch skillet over high heat and simmer until reduced by half, about 5 minutes. Stir the reduced wine and parsley into the stew and season with salt and pepper to taste. Serve.

BEHIND THE SCENES

MISE EN PLACE—A FRENCH PHRASE EVERY HOME COOK SHOULD KNOW

When Bridget, Julia, and Becky prepare recipes on TV they always have each ingredient prepared and measured into its own glass bowl. Yes, this looks nice on television, but our test cooks follow the same procedure when the cameras aren't rolling. This practice has a fancy French name—*mise en place*, which means "to put in place"—but the concept is really quite simple. Prepare your ingredients *before* you start cooking.

To stay organized from the get-go, the test cooks measure out the amounts required in their recipes and then individually label each ingredient with its corresponding quantity, such as 1 cup unbleached all-purpose flour, 2 large egg whites, 1 cup toasted chopped walnuts, and so on. (Note that some ingredients such as onions and garlic are best prepared just before cooking, rather than in advance.) The measured and labeled ingredients are then kept together, by recipe, on large baking sheets and stored. When the test cooks are ready to cook, they grab their prepped ingredients and are ready to go. Try mise en place at home—you'll find it useful not only in helping you keep on track when tackling an involved recipe (think labor-intensive holiday meals) but also for day-to-day cooking—prepping your ingredients the night before will allow you to walk in the door after work and get dinner on the table fast. And since you can focus on what's cooking (rather than preparing ingredients), you eliminate the risk that something will burn or overcook.

MODERN BEEF BURGUNDY

WHY THIS RECIPE WORKS: We wanted to update the French classic *boeuf bourguignon* to have tender braised beef napped with a silky sauce with bold red wine flavor—without all the work that traditional recipes require. To eliminate the time-consuming step of searing the beef, we cooked the stew uncovered in a roasting pan in the oven so that the exposed meat browned as it braised. This method worked so well that we also used the oven, rather than the stovetop, to render the salt pork and to caramelize the traditional mushroom and pearl onion garnish. Salting the beef before cooking and adding some anchovy paste and porcini mushrooms enhanced the meaty savoriness of the dish without making our recipe too fussy.

Modern Beef Burgundy

SERVES 6 TO 8

If the pearl onions have a papery outer coating, remove it by rinsing them in warm water and gently squeezing individual onions between your fingertips. Two minced anchovy fillets can be used in place of the anchovy paste. To save time, salt the meat and let it stand while you prep the remaining ingredients. Serve with mashed potatoes or buttered noodles.

- 1 (4-pound) boneless beef chuck-eye roast, trimmed and cut into 1½- to 2-inch pieces, scraps reserved
- Salt and pepper
- 6 ounces salt pork, cut into ¼-inch pieces
- 3 tablespoons unsalted butter
- 1 pound cremini mushrooms, trimmed, halved if medium or quartered if large
- 1½ cups frozen pearl onions, thawed
- 1 tablespoon sugar
- ⅓ cup all-purpose flour
- 4 cups beef broth
- 1 (750-ml) bottle red Burgundy or Pinot Noir
- 5 teaspoons unflavored gelatin
- 1 tablespoon tomato paste
- 1 teaspoon anchovy paste
- 2 onions, chopped coarse
- 2 carrots, peeled and cut into 2-inch lengths
- 1 garlic head, cloves separated, unpeeled, and crushed
- 2 bay leaves
- ½ teaspoon black peppercorns
- ½ ounce dried porcini mushrooms, rinsed
- 10 sprigs fresh parsley, plus 3 tablespoons minced
- 6 sprigs fresh thyme

1. Toss beef and 1½ teaspoons salt together in bowl and let stand at room temperature for 30 minutes.

2. Adjust oven racks to lower-middle and lowest positions and heat oven to 500 degrees. Place salt pork, beef scraps, and 2 tablespoons butter in large roasting pan. Roast on lower-middle rack until well browned and fat has rendered, 15 to 20 minutes.

3. While salt pork and beef scraps roast, toss cremini mushrooms, pearl onions, remaining 1 tablespoon butter, and sugar together on rimmed baking sheet. Roast on lowest rack, stirring occasionally, until moisture released by mushrooms evaporates and vegetables are lightly glazed, 15 to 20 minutes. Transfer vegetables to large bowl, cover, and refrigerate.

4. Remove roasting pan from oven and reduce temperature to 325 degrees. Sprinkle flour over rendered fat and whisk until no dry flour remains. Whisk in broth, 2 cups wine, gelatin, tomato paste, and anchovy paste until combined. Add onions, carrots, garlic, bay leaves, peppercorns, porcini mushrooms, parsley sprigs, and thyme sprigs to pan. Arrange beef in single layer on top of vegetables. Add water as needed to

come three-quarters up side of beef (beef should not be submerged). Return roasting pan to oven and cook until meat is tender, 3 to 3½ hours, stirring after 90 minutes and adding water to keep meat at least half-submerged.

5. Using slotted spoon, transfer beef to bowl with cremini mushrooms and pearl onions; cover and set aside. Strain braising liquid through fine-mesh strainer set over large bowl, pressing on solids to extract as much liquid as possible; discard solids. Stir in remaining wine and let cooking liquid settle, 10 minutes. Using wide shallow spoon, skim fat off surface and discard.

6. Transfer liquid to Dutch oven and bring mixture to boil over medium-high heat. Simmer briskly, stirring occasionally, until sauce is thickened to consistency of heavy cream, 15 to 20 minutes. Reduce heat to medium-low, stir in beef and mushroom-onion garnish, cover, and cook until just heated through, 5 to 8 minutes. Season with salt and pepper to taste. Stir in minced parsley and serve. (Stew can be made up to 3 days in advance.)

CASSOULET

WHY THIS RECIPE WORKS: Comforting and delectable as it is, cassoulet is just too much trouble for most cooks. It can take three days to make, and the ingredients can be both hard to find and difficult to prepare. We wanted to see if there was a way to streamline the preparation of this dish without compromising its essential character.

Instead of duck confit, which is difficult to find and time-consuming to prepare, we brined chicken thighs and cooked them in bacon fat to simulate the smoky flavor and moist texture of the confit. With our mock confit lined up, the other elements fell into place. We decided on the flavorful, fatty blade-end pork roast for stewing, dried beans instead of canned beans (canned beans were out because they fell apart during cooking), and smoky kielbasa for the sausage component (the classically correct French sausage was too hard to find). We cooked the beans with onion and garlic to season them, then added some crisp bacon to infuse them with a salty smokiness. Cooking the dish entirely on the stove at a slow simmer, with a quick finish to brown our homemade croutons, gave us a quick and easy cassoulet that was worthy of the name.

Simplified Cassoulet with Pork and Kielbasa

SERVES 8

This dish can be made without brining the chicken, but we recommend that you do so. To ensure the most time-efficient preparation of the cassoulet, while the chicken is brining and the beans are simmering, prepare the remaining ingredients. Look for dried flageolet beans in specialty food stores. You can substitute a boneless Boston butt for the boneless blade-end pork loin roast. Additional salt is not necessary because the brined chicken adds a good deal of it, but if you skip the brining step, add salt to taste before serving.

CHICKEN

- 1 cup sugar
- ½ cup table salt
- 10 (5- to 6-ounce) bone-in, skin-on chicken thighs, trimmed and skin removed (see note)

BEANS

- 1 pound dried flageolet or great Northern beans, picked over and rinsed (see note)
- 1 medium onion, peeled, plus 1 small onion, minced
- 1 medium head garlic, outer papery skin removed and top ½ inch sliced off, plus 2 medium garlic cloves, minced or pressed through a garlic press (about 2 teaspoons)
- 1 teaspoon table salt
- Ground black pepper
- 6 ounces (about 6 slices) bacon, cut into ¼-inch pieces
- 1 (1-pound) boneless blade-end pork loin roast, trimmed and cut into 1-inch pieces (see note)
- 1 (14.5-ounce) can diced tomatoes, drained
- 1 tablespoon tomato paste
- 1 large sprig fresh thyme
- 1 bay leaf
- ¼ teaspoon ground cloves
- 3½ cups low-sodium chicken broth
- 1½ cups dry white wine
- ½ pound kielbasa, halved lengthwise and cut into ¼-inch slices

CROUTONS

- 6 slices high-quality white sandwich bread, cut into ½-inch cubes
- 3 tablespoons unsalted butter, melted

1. FOR THE CHICKEN: Dissolve the sugar and salt in 1 quart cold water in a gallon-size zipper-lock bag. Add the chicken, pressing out as much air as possible, seal the bag, and refrigerate for 1 hour. Remove the chicken from the brine, rinse, and pat dry with paper towels. Refrigerate until ready to use.

2. FOR THE BEANS: Bring the beans, the peeled onion, head of garlic, salt, ¼ teaspoon pepper, and 8 cups water to a boil in a large Dutch oven over high heat. Cover, reduce the heat to medium-low, and simmer until the beans are almost tender, 1¼ to 1½ hours. Drain the beans; discard the onion and garlic.

3. While the beans are cooking, fry the bacon in a large Dutch oven over medium heat until just beginning to crisp and most of the fat has rendered, 5 to 6 minutes. Using a slotted spoon, add half of the bacon to the pot with the beans; transfer the remaining bacon to a paper towel–lined plate and set aside. Increase the heat to medium-high and add half of the chicken, skinned side down; cook until lightly browned, 4 to 5 minutes. Flip the chicken thighs and cook until lightly browned on the second side, 3 to 4 minutes longer. Transfer the chicken to a large plate; repeat with the remaining thighs and set aside. Pour off all but 2 tablespoons fat from the pot. Return the pot to medium heat; add the pork pieces and cook, stirring occasionally, until lightly browned, about 5 minutes. Add the minced onion and cook, stirring occasionally, until softened, 3 to 4 minutes. Add the minced garlic, tomatoes, tomato paste, thyme, bay leaf, cloves, and pepper to taste and cook until fragrant, about 1 minute. Stir in the chicken broth and wine, scraping up any browned bits. Submerge the chicken in the pot, adding any accumulated juices, increase the heat to high, and bring to a boil. Reduce the heat to low, cover, and simmer for 40 minutes. Uncover and continue to simmer until the chicken and pork are fully tender, 20 to 30 minutes more.

4. FOR THE CROUTONS: While the chicken is simmering, adjust an oven rack to the lower-middle position and heat the oven to 400 degrees. Toss the bread cubes with the melted butter and spread out over a rimmed baking sheet. Bake until light golden brown and crisp, 8 to 12 minutes. Cool to room temperature; set aside (do not turn off the oven).

5. Gently stir the kielbasa, drained beans, and reserved bacon into the pot with the chicken and pork; remove and discard the thyme and bay leaf and season with pepper to taste (see note). Sprinkle the croutons evenly over the surface and bake, uncovered, until the croutons are deep golden brown, about 15 minutes. Let stand for 10 minutes; serve.

FRENCH-STYLE PORK STEW

WHY THIS RECIPE WORKS: In the French-style boiled dinner known as *potée*, multiple cuts of pork, sausages, and vegetables are simmered until tender, then served with their flavorful cooking liquid. We set out to turn this dish into a fork-friendly stew that was robust and satisfying, but not heavy. Pork butt, cut into chunks, became succulent and tender with the long cooking time. Supplementing it with a smoked ham shank and kielbasa gave our stew the delicate smokiness and intense porky notes found in authentic versions, plus it provided such meaty flavor and complexity that we could skip the extra step of browning the pork. Chicken broth cut with water provided a subtle flavor base that kept the flavor clean; simmering it with aromatics and seasonings added depth. For ease, we limited the traditional roster of vegetables to just three—carrots, potatoes, and cabbage—which we added toward the end of cooking so they would retain their texture. Finally, moving our stew to the oven allowed it to cook through gently and evenly.

French-Style Pork Stew

SERVES 8 TO 10

Pork butt roast, often labeled Boston butt in the supermarket, is a very fatty cut, so don't be surprised if you lose a pound or even a little more in the trimming process (the weight called for in the recipe takes this loss into account). Serve with crusty bread.

- 6 sprigs fresh parsley
- 3 large sprigs fresh thyme
- 5 garlic cloves, unpeeled
- 2 bay leaves
- 1 tablespoon black peppercorns
- 2 whole cloves
- 5 cups water
- 4 cups chicken broth
- 3 pounds boneless pork butt roast, trimmed and cut into 1- to 1½-inch pieces
- 1 meaty smoked ham shank or 2–3 smoked ham hocks (1¼ pounds)
- 2 onions, halved through root end, root end left intact
- 4 carrots, peeled, narrow end cut crosswise into ½-inch pieces, wide end halved lengthwise and cut into ½-inch pieces
- 1 pound Yukon Gold potatoes, unpeeled, cut into ¾-inch pieces

12 ounces kielbasa sausage, halved lengthwise and sliced ½ inch thick
8 cups shredded savoy cabbage
Salt and pepper
¼ cup chopped fresh parsley

1. Adjust oven rack to middle position and heat oven to 325 degrees. Cut 10-inch square of triple-thickness cheesecloth. Place parsley sprigs (fold or break to fit), thyme sprigs, garlic, bay leaves, peppercorns, and cloves in center of cheesecloth and tie into bundle with kitchen twine.

2. Bring water, chicken broth, pork butt, ham shank, onions, and herb bundle to simmer in large Dutch oven over medium-high heat, skimming off scum that rises to surface. Cover pot and place in oven. Cook until pork chunks are tender and skewer inserted into meat meets little resistance, 1¼ to 1½ hours.

3. Using slotted spoon, discard cheesecloth bundle and onion halves. Transfer shank to plate. Add carrots and potatoes to pot and stir to combine. Cover pot and return to oven. Cook until vegetables are almost tender, 20 to 25 minutes. When cool enough to handle, using two forks, remove meat from shank and shred into bite-size pieces; discard skin and bones.

4. Add shredded shank meat, kielbasa, and cabbage to pot. Stir to combine, cover, and return to oven. Cook until kielbasa is heated through and cabbage is wilted and tender, 15 to 20 minutes. Season with salt and pepper to taste, then stir in parsley. Ladle into bowls and serve.

STEAK AU POIVRE

WHY THIS RECIPE WORKS: Steak au poivre is often nothing more than uninspired skillet steak. We were after the real thing—a perfectly cooked steak with a well-seared crust of pungent, cracked peppercorns and a silky sauce.

The trick to successful steak au poivre is coating just one side of the steaks with peppercorns and cooking the steaks on the uncoated side as long as possible to promote browning and prevent scorching of the peppercorns. With the first side browned, we flipped the steaks and cooked them for less time on the peppered side. Pressing the steaks with a cake pan once they were placed in the hot skillet ensured that the peppercorns stuck. After the steaks were done to our liking, we made a simple pan sauce with a mixture of beef broth and chicken broth that we first reduced, then flavored with brandy and lemon juice. Cream made the sauce luxurious and gave it some substance; butter whisked in at the end brought silkiness.

Steak au Poivre with Brandied Cream Sauce

SERVES 4

To save time, crush the peppercorns and trim the steaks while the broth mixture simmers. Many pepper mills do not have a sufficiently coarse setting. In that case, crush peppercorns with the back of a heavy pan. See page 879 for information on our top-rated pepper mill.

4 tablespoons (½ stick) unsalted butter
1 medium shallot, minced (about 3 tablespoons)
1 cup beef broth
¾ cup low-sodium chicken broth
4 (8- to 10-ounce) strip steaks, ¾ to 1 inch thick, trimmed
Table salt
4 teaspoons black peppercorns, crushed (see note)
1 tablespoon vegetable oil
¼ cup plus 1 tablespoon brandy
¼ cup heavy cream
1 teaspoon juice from 1 lemon or 1 teaspoon champagne vinegar

1. Melt 1 tablespoon of the butter in a 12-inch skillet over medium heat. Add the shallot and cook, stirring occasionally, until softened, about 2 minutes. Add the beef and chicken broths and bring to a boil over high heat; cook until reduced to ½ cup, about 8 minutes. Transfer the broth mixture to a small bowl; wipe out the skillet with paper towels.

2. Meanwhile, pat the steaks dry with paper towels and season with salt. Sprinkle one side of each steak with 1 teaspoon of the crushed peppercorns and press them into the steaks with your fingers to adhere.

3. Heat the oil in the skillet over medium-high heat until just smoking. Carefully lay the steaks in the skillet, peppered side up. Press on the steaks with the bottom of a cake pan and cook until well-browned on the first side, 3 to 5 minutes. Flip the steaks over and continue to cook, pressing again with the cake pan, until the center of the steaks registers 120 degrees on an instant-read thermometer for rare (3 minutes), 125 degrees for medium-rare (4 minutes), or 130 degrees for medium (5 minutes). Transfer the steaks to a plate, tent loosely with foil, and let rest while making the sauce.

4. Pour off any fat left in the pan and remove any stray peppercorns. Add the broth mixture, ¼ cup of the brandy, and the cream to the skillet and bring to a boil over high heat, scraping up any browned bits. Simmer until golden brown and thickened, about 5 minutes. Off the heat, whisk in the remaining 3 tablespoons butter, the remaining 1 tablespoon brandy, the lemon juice, and any accumulated meat juices from the plate; season with salt to taste. Spoon the sauce over the steaks and serve immediately.

STEAK FRITES

WHY THIS RECIPE WORKS: Too often, steak frites in American restaurants misses the mark. The fries are usually too soggy and the steak just isn't as flavorful as it should be. We wanted to re-create the steak frites of our Parisian dreams, with perfectly cooked steak and fries that are fluffy on the inside and crisp on the outside, even when bathed in juices from the meat.

For our fries, we liked high-starch russet potatoes and found that double-cooking, or a low-temperature "blanch" in oil followed by a high-temperature "fry," yielded the crispiest exterior and fluffiest interior. Cooking multiple small batches of fries ensured that the oil's temperature wouldn't plunge too much. Soaking the potatoes in cold water before they were cooked further improved their crispiness, and a "rest" between the first and second frying allowed the fries to develop a thin coating of starch, which even further improved their crispiness. Tossing them with additional starch—in the form of cornstarch—made them perfect.

In France, steak frites is usually prepared with a cut called *entrecôte* (literally, "between the ribs"), which is a French cut you won't find in the States, but is actually quite similar to our rib-eye steak. Choosing the right size—or cutting them to fit—meant we could sear four steaks at once in a large skillet. Capped with a quick herb butter, the steaks tasted just like the bistro classic of our dreams.

Steak Frites

SERVES 4

Make sure to dry the potatoes well before tossing them with the cornstarch. For safety, use a Dutch oven with a capacity of at least 7 quarts. Use refined peanut oil (such as Planters) to fry the potatoes, not toasted peanut oil. A 12-inch skillet is essential for cooking four steaks at once. The recipe can be prepared through step 4 up to 2 hours in advance; shut off the heat under the oil, turning the heat back to medium when you start step 6. The ingredients can be halved to serve two—keep the oil amount the same and forgo blanching and frying the potatoes in batches.

HERB BUTTER

- 4 tablespoons (½ stick) unsalted butter, softened
- ½ shallot, minced (about 1 tablespoon)
- 1 tablespoon minced fresh parsley leaves
- 1 tablespoon minced fresh chives
- 1 medium garlic clove, minced or pressed through a garlic press (about 1 teaspoon)
- ¼ teaspoon table salt
- ¼ teaspoon ground black pepper

STEAK AND POTATOES

- 2½ pounds russet potatoes (about 4 large), sides squared off, cut lengthwise into ¼ by ¼-inch fries (see note)
- 2 tablespoons cornstarch
- 3 quarts peanut oil (see note)
- 1 tablespoon vegetable oil
- 2 (1-pound) boneless rib-eye steaks, cut in half
- Table salt and ground black pepper

1. FOR THE BUTTER: Combine all the ingredients in a medium bowl; set aside.

2. FOR THE POTATOES: Rinse the cut potatoes in a large bowl under cold running water until the water turns clear. Cover with cold water and refrigerate for at least 30 minutes or up to 12 hours.

3. Pour off the water, spread the potatoes onto clean kitchen towels, and thoroughly dry. Transfer the potatoes to a large bowl and toss with the cornstarch until evenly coated. Transfer the potatoes to a wire rack set over a rimmed baking sheet and let rest until a fine white coating forms, about 20 minutes.

4. Meanwhile, heat the peanut oil over medium heat to 325 degrees in a large, heavy-bottomed Dutch oven fitted with a clip-on candy thermometer.

5. Add half of the potatoes, a handful at a time, to the hot oil and increase the heat to high. Fry, stirring with a mesh spider or slotted spoon, until the potatoes start to turn from white to blond, 4 to 5 minutes. (The oil temperature will drop about 75 degrees during this frying.) Transfer the fries to a thick paper bag or paper towels. Return the oil to 325 degrees and repeat with the remaining potatoes. Reduce the heat to medium and let the fries cool while cooking the steaks, at least 10 minutes.

6. FOR THE STEAK: Heat the vegetable oil in a 12-inch skillet over medium-high heat until smoking. Meanwhile, season the steaks with salt and pepper. Lay the steaks in the pan, leaving ¼ inch between them. Cook, without moving the steaks, until well browned, about 4 minutes. Flip the steaks and continue to cook until an instant-read thermometer inserted in the center registers 120 degrees for rare to medium-rare, 3 to 7 minutes. Transfer the steaks to a large plate, top with the herb butter, and tent loosely with foil; let rest while finishing the fries.

NOTES FROM THE TEST KITCHEN

SQUARING THE SPUD

The best way to uniformly cut fries is to start by trimming a thin slice from each side of the potato. Once the potato is "squared," you can slice it into planks and then cut each plank into fries.

ONE STEAK BECOMES TWO

For steaks of the right thickness for Steak Frites (so they'll sear well without overcooking), it is necessary to buy two 1-pound steaks and cut them in half according to their thickness. If your steaks are 1¼ to 1¾ inches thick, cut them in half vertically into small, thick steaks. If your steaks are thicker than 1¾ inches, cut them in half horizontally into two thinner steaks.

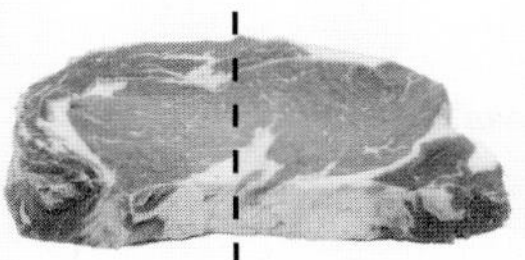

THIN STEAK
Cut in half vertically.

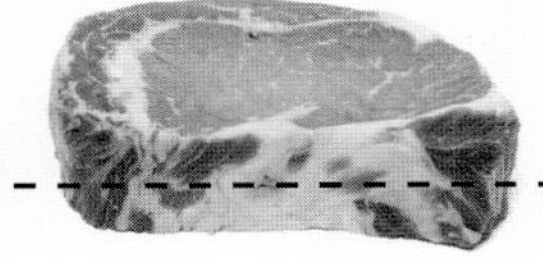

THICK STEAK
Cut in half horizontally.

7. Increase the heat under the Dutch oven to high and heat the oil to 375 degrees. Add half of the fries, a handful at a time, and fry until golden brown and puffed, 2 to 3 minutes. Transfer to a thick paper bag or paper towels. Return the oil to 375 degrees and repeat with the remaining fries. Season the fries with salt to taste and serve immediately with the steaks.

STEAK DIANE

WHY THIS RECIPE WORKS: For a different spin on the usual pan-seared steaks, we turn to the French classic, steak Diane. But the demanding rich sauce is based on an all-day veal stock reduction—and then the steaks still have to be cooked (if you have the energy, that is), and the sauce completed. We aimed to determine the right cut of steak, create a lighter, less labor-intensive sauce, and find a foolproof method for cooking the meat.

For a rich sauce base that mimicked the complexity of labor-intensive veal stock in a fraction of the time, we used a flavorful combination of sautéed tomato paste, aromatics such as garlic, onion, and carrots, both beef broth and chicken broth, red wine, peppercorns, and herbs. Omitting the traditional cream allowed the sauce to fully develop in intensity, and the inclusion of cognac gave the sauce a slightly sweet, complex flavor. For the meat, we selected strip steaks for great beefy flavor and ease of preparation. To brown the steaks evenly and develop enough fond (the flavorful browned meaty bits that cling to the pan and give pan sauces their rich, meaty flavor), we weighted the steaks with a heavy-bottomed skillet when cooking the second side.

Steak Diane

SERVES 4

If you prefer not to make the sauce base (recipe follows), mix ½ cup glace de viande with ¾ cup water and ¼ cup red wine and use this mixture in place of the base in step 2. Glace de viande is meat stock, in this case veal stock, that's been reduced to a thick syrup; we recommend Provimi Glace de Veau and CulinArte' Bonewerks Glace de Veau. Before preparing the sauce, read "Tips for Fearless Flambé" on page 408, or, if you do not wish to flambé, simmer the cognac in step 2 for 10 to 15 seconds for a slightly less sweet flavor profile.

STEAKS

- 4 (12-ounce) strip steaks, 1 to 1¼ inches thick, trimmed
- Table salt and ground black pepper
- 2 tablespoons vegetable oil

SAUCE

- 1 tablespoon vegetable oil
- 1 small shallot, minced (about 1 tablespoon)
- ¼ cup cognac
- 1 recipe Sauce Base for Steak Diane (page 408; see note)
- 2 teaspoons Dijon mustard
- 2 tablespoons unsalted butter, chilled
- 1 teaspoon Worcestershire sauce
- 2 tablespoons minced fresh chives
- Table salt and ground black pepper

1. FOR THE STEAKS: Cover the steaks with plastic wrap and use a meat pounder to pound them to an even ½-inch thickness; season them with salt and pepper. Heat 1 tablespoon of the oil in a 12-inch skillet over medium-high heat until smoking. Place 2 steaks in the skillet and cook until well browned, about 1½ minutes. Flip the steaks and weight with a heavy-bottomed pan; continue to cook until well browned on the second side, about 1½ minutes longer. Transfer the steaks to a plate and tent with foil. Add the remaining 1 tablespoon oil to the skillet and repeat with the remaining 2 steaks; transfer the second batch of steaks to the plate.

2. FOR THE SAUCE: Off the heat, add the oil and shallot to the skillet. Using the skillet's residual heat, cook, stirring frequently, until the shallot is slightly softened and browned, about 45 seconds. Add the cognac and let stand until the cognac warms slightly, about 10 seconds, then set the skillet over high heat. Wave a lit match over the skillet until the cognac ignites, shaking the skillet until the flames subside, then simmer the cognac until reduced to about 1 tablespoon, about 10 seconds.

BEHIND THE SCENES

TIPS FOR FEARLESS FLAMBÉ

Flambéing is more than just tableside theatrics: As dramatic as it looks, igniting alcohol actually helps develop a deeper, more complex flavor in sauces—thanks to flavor-boosting chemical reactions that occur only at the high temperatures reached in flambéing. But accomplishing this feat at home can be daunting. Here are some tips for successful—and safe—flambéing at home.

BE PREPARED: Turn off the exhaust fan, tie back long hair, and have a lid at the ready to smother flare-ups.

USE THE PROPER EQUIPMENT: A pan with flared sides (such as a skillet) rather than straight sides will allow more oxygen to mingle with the alcohol vapors, increasing the chance that you'll spark the desired flame. If possible, use long chimney matches, and light the alcohol with your arm extended to full length.

IGNITE WARM ALCOHOL: If the alcohol becomes too hot, the vapors can rise to dangerous heights, causing large flare-ups once lit. Inversely, if the alcohol is too cold, there won't be enough vapors to light at all. We found that heating alcohol to 100 degrees Fahrenheit (best achieved by adding alcohol to a hot pan off heat and letting it sit for five to 10 seconds) produced the most moderate, yet long-burning, flames.

IF A FLARE-UP SHOULD OCCUR: Simply slide the lid over the top of the skillet (coming in from the side of, rather than over, the flames) to put out the fire quickly. Let the alcohol cool down and start again.

IF THE ALCOHOL WON'T LIGHT: If the pan is full of other ingredients (as is the case in Crêpes Suzette, page 832), the potency of the alcohol can be diminished as it becomes incorporated. For a more foolproof flame, ignite the alcohol in a separate small skillet or saucepan; once the flame has burned off, add the reduced alcohol to the remaining ingredients.

Add the sauce base and mustard and simmer until slightly thickened and reduced to 1 cup, 2 to 3 minutes. Whisk in the butter. Off the heat, add the Worcestershire sauce, any accumulated juices from the steaks, and 1 tablespoon of the chives. Season with salt and pepper to taste.

3. Serve immediately, spooning 2 tablespoons sauce and sprinkling a portion of the remaining 1 tablespoon chives over each steak, and passing the remaining sauce separately.

Sauce Base for Steak Diane

MAKES 1¼ CUPS

This recipe yields a sauce base that is an excellent facsimile of a demi-glace, a very labor-intensive and time-consuming classic French sauce base. Because the sauce base is very concentrated, make sure to use low-sodium chicken and beef broths; otherwise, the base may be unpalatably salty.

- 2 tablespoons vegetable oil
- 4 teaspoons tomato paste
- 2 small onions, chopped medium
- 1 medium carrot, chopped medium
- 4 medium garlic cloves, peeled
- ¼ cup water
- 4 teaspoons unbleached all-purpose flour
- 1½ cups dry red wine
- 3½ cups low-sodium beef broth (see note)
- 1¾ cups low-sodium chicken broth (see note)
- 2 teaspoons black peppercorns
- 8 sprigs fresh thyme
- 2 bay leaves

1. Heat the oil and tomato paste in a Dutch oven over medium-high heat and cook, stirring constantly, until the paste begins to brown, about 3 minutes. Add the onions, carrot, and garlic and cook, stirring frequently, until the mixture is reddish brown, about 2 minutes. Add 2 tablespoons of the water and continue to cook, stirring constantly, until the mixture is well browned, about 3 minutes, adding the remaining 2 tablespoons water as needed to prevent scorching. Add the flour and cook, stirring constantly, for about 1 minute. Add the wine, scraping up the browned bits on the bottom and sides of the pot; bring to a boil, stirring occasionally (the mixture will thicken slightly). Add the beef and chicken broths, peppercorns, thyme, and bay leaves; bring to a boil and cook, uncovered, occasionally scraping the bottom and sides of the pot with a spatula, until reduced to 2½ cups, 35 to 40 minutes.

2. Strain the mixture through a fine-mesh strainer, pressing on the solids to extract as much liquid as possible; you should have about 1¼ cups. (The sauce base can be refrigerated in an airtight container for up to 3 days.)

FISH MEUNIÈRE

WHY THIS RECIPE WORKS: Fish meunière typically features pale, soggy fillets in pools of greasy sauce—that is, if the fish doesn't stick to the pan or fall apart as it is plated. We wanted perfectly cooked fillets that were delicately crisp and golden brown on the outside and moist and flavorful on the inside, napped in a buttery yet light sauce.

Whole Dover sole is the most authentic choice, but it was also hard to come by and prohibitively expensive; either sole or flounder fillets were good stand-ins. To prevent the likelihood of overcooking the fish, the fillets needed to be no less than 3/8 inch thick. The fillets must be patted dry before being seasoned with salt and pepper and dredged in flour (no need for eggs and bread crumbs). Using a nonstick skillet for pan-frying meant there was less chance for our fillets to fall apart; lubricating the pan with a mixture of oil and butter added extra insurance. Removing the pan from the heat just before the fish was cooked prevented the fish from being dry (the fish will continue to cook off the heat). Butter browned in a traditional skillet (so the changing color was easy to monitor) and brightened with lemon juice made the ideal accompaniment to our crispy, golden fillets.

Fish Meunière with Browned Butter and Lemon

SERVES 4

Try to purchase fillets that are of similar size, and avoid those that weigh less than 5 ounces because they will cook too quickly. When placing the fillets in the skillet, be sure to place them skinned side up so that the opposite side, which had bones, will brown first. To flip the fillets while cooking, use two spatulas; gently lift one side of the fillet with one spatula, then support the fillet with the other spatula and gently flip it so that the browned side faces up. A nonstick skillet ensures that the fillets will release from the pan, but for the sauce a traditional skillet is preferable because its light-colored surface will allow you to monitor the color of the butter as it browns.

FISH

- ½ cup unbleached all-purpose flour
- 4 (5- to 6-ounce) sole or flounder fillets, 3/8 inch thick (see note)
- Table salt and ground black pepper
- 2 tablespoons vegetable oil
- 2 tablespoons unsalted butter, cut into 2 pieces

BROWNED BUTTER

- 4 tablespoons (½ stick) unsalted butter, cut into 4 pieces
- 1 tablespoon chopped fresh parsley leaves
- 1½ tablespoons juice from 1 lemon
- Table salt
- Lemon wedges, for serving

1. FOR THE FISH: Adjust an oven rack to the lower-middle position, set four heatproof dinner plates on the rack, and heat the oven to 200 degrees. Place the flour in a large baking dish. Pat the fillets dry with paper towels and season with salt and pepper; let stand until the fillets are glistening with moisture, about 5 minutes. Coat both sides of the fillets with flour, shake off the excess, and place in a single layer on a rimmed baking sheet.

2. Heat 1 tablespoon of the oil in a 12-inch nonstick skillet over high heat until shimmering; add 1 tablespoon of the butter and swirl to coat the pan bottom. Carefully place 2 fillets, skinned side up, in the skillet. Immediately reduce the heat to medium-high and cook, without moving the fish, until the edges of the fillets are opaque and the bottoms are golden brown, about 3 minutes. Using two spatulas, gently flip the fillets and cook on the second side until the thickest part of the fillet easily separates into flakes when a toothpick is inserted, about 2 minutes longer. Transfer the fillets to two of the heated dinner plates, keeping them boned side up, and return the plates to the oven. Wipe out the skillet and repeat with the remaining 1 tablespoon oil, remaining 1 tablespoon butter, and the remaining fish fillets.

3. FOR THE BROWNED BUTTER: Melt the butter in a 10-inch traditional skillet over medium-high heat. Continue to cook, swirling the pan constantly, until the butter is golden brown and has a nutty aroma, 1 to 1½ minutes; remove the skillet from the heat. Remove the plates from the oven and sprinkle the fillets with the parsley. Add the lemon juice to the browned butter and season with salt to taste. Spoon the sauce over the fish and serve immediately, garnished with the lemon wedges.

CHAPTER 15

TEX-MEX TONIGHT

MARGARITAS

WHY THIS RECIPE WORKS: The typical margarita tends to be a slushy, headache-inducing concoction made with little more than ice, tequila, and artificially flavored corn syrup. We wanted a margarita with a balanced blend of fresh citrus flavors and tequila.

We found that the key was using the right proportions of alcohol and citrus juice—equal parts of each one. For a mellow, delicate flavor, we preferred reposado tequila, made from 100 percent blue agave, which is aged about 12 months. Unaged tequilas gave our margaritas a raw, harsh flavor. And those made with superpremium tequilas, which are aged up to 6 years, tasted smooth, but their distinct tannic taste dominated the cocktail. As for orange-flavored liqueurs, a lower-alcohol liqueur, such as triple sec, worked best. Mixes and bottled citrus juice had no place in our cocktail—instead we steeped lemon and lime zest in their own juice for a deep, refreshing citrus flavor. And with a bit of easy-to-dissolve superfine sugar and crushed ice, our margaritas were complete.

Fresh Margaritas

SERVES 4 TO 6

The longer the zest and juice mixture is allowed to steep, the more developed the citrus flavors will be in the finished margaritas. We recommend steeping for the full 24 hours, although the margaritas will still be great if the mixture is steeped for only the minimum 4 hours. If you're in a rush and want to serve margaritas immediately, omit the zest and skip the steeping process altogether. If you can't find superfine sugar, process an equal amount of regular sugar in a food processor for 30 seconds.

- 4 teaspoons grated zest plus ½ cup juice from 4 limes (see note)
- 4 teaspoons grated zest plus ½ cup juice from 3 lemons (see note)
- ¼ cup superfine sugar (see note)
- Pinch table salt
- 2 cups crushed ice
- 1 cup 100 percent agave tequila, preferably reposado
- 1 cup triple sec

1. Combine the lime zest and juice, lemon zest and juice, sugar, and salt in a large liquid measuring cup; cover with plastic wrap and refrigerate until the flavors meld, 4 to 24 hours.

2. Divide 1 cup of the crushed ice among 4 or 6 margarita or double old-fashioned glasses. Strain the juice mixture into a 1-quart pitcher or cocktail shaker. Add the tequila, triple sec, and the remaining 1 cup crushed ice; stir or shake until thoroughly combined and chilled, 20 to 60 seconds. Strain into the ice-filled glasses and serve immediately.

SANGRIA

WHY THIS RECIPE WORKS: Many people mistake sangria for an unruly collection of fruit awash in a sea of overly sweetened red wine. We wanted a robust, sweet-tart wine punch.

After trying a variety of red wines, we found that inexpensive wine works best. (Experts told us that the sugar and fruit called for in sangria throw off the balance of any wine used, so why spend a lot on something that was carefully crafted?) We experimented with untold varieties of fruit to put in our sangria and finally concluded that simpler is better. We preferred the straightforward tang of citrus in the form of oranges and lemons. And we discovered that the zest and pith as well as the fruit itself make an important contribution to flavor. Orange liqueur is standard in recipes for sangria, and after experimenting we found that here, as with the wine, cheaper was just fine, this time in the form of triple sec. Fortification with any other alcoholic beverage, from gin to port to brandy, simply gave the punch too much punch. What we wanted, and what we now had, was a light, refreshing drink.

Sangria

SERVES 4

Although this punch hails from Spain, it has become a mainstay on Mexican restaurant menus and pairs well with the country's spicy dishes. The longer sangria sits before drinking, the more smooth and mellow it will taste. A full day is best, but if that's impossible, give it an absolute minimum of two hours to sit. Use large, heavy, juicy oranges and lemons for the best flavor. If you can't find superfine sugar, process an equal amount of regular sugar in a food processor for 30 seconds. Doubling or tripling the recipe is fine, but you'll have to switch to a large punch bowl in place of the pitcher. An inexpensive Merlot is the best choice for this recipe.

- 2 large juice oranges, washed; one orange sliced, remaining orange juiced (see note)
- 1 large lemon, washed and sliced (see note)
- ¼ cup superfine sugar (see note)
- 1 (750-milliliter) bottle inexpensive, fruity, medium-bodied red wine, chilled (see note)
- ¼ cup triple sec

1. Add the sliced orange and lemon and the sugar to a large pitcher. Mash the fruit gently with a wooden spoon until the fruit releases some juice, but is not totally crushed, and the sugar dissolves, about 1 minute. Stir in the orange juice, wine, and triple sec; refrigerate for at least 2 hours or up to 8 hours.

2. Before serving, add 6 to 8 ice cubes and stir briskly to distribute the settled fruit and pulp; serve immediately.

NACHOS

WHY THIS RECIPE WORKS: Prepackaged shredded cheese and jars of pre-made salsa and guacamole transform nachos from something delicious into bland fast food. We wanted nachos with hot, crisp tortilla chips, plentiful cheese and toppings, and the right amount of spicy heat.

To ensure that all of the chips would be cheesy and spicy, we layered tortilla chips with a full pound of shredded cheddar cheese and sliced jalapeños. Layering the jalapeños with the cheese also helped the chiles stick to the chips. We prepared a quick homemade salsa and chunky guacamole to spoon around the edges of the hot nachos after they came out of the oven. Spoonfuls of sour cream and a sprinkling of chopped fresh scallions provided final touches. Served with lime wedges, this fresh take on nachos is light-years beyond any fast-food version of the dish.

Cheesy Nachos with Guacamole and Salsa

SERVES 4 TO 6

- 8 ounces tortilla chips
- 1 pound cheddar cheese, shredded (about 4 cups)
- 2 large jalapeño chiles, sliced thin (about ¼ cup)
- 2 scallions, sliced thin
- ½ cup sour cream
- 1 recipe One-Minute Salsa (recipe follows)
- 1 recipe Chunky Guacamole (see right)
- Lime wedges, for serving

Adjust an oven rack to the middle position and heat the oven to 400 degrees. Spread half of the chips in an even layer in a 13 by 9-inch baking dish. Sprinkle the chips evenly with 2 cups of the cheese and half of the jalapeño slices. Repeat with the remaining chips, cheese, and jalapeños. Bake until the cheese is melted, 7 to 10 minutes. Remove the nachos from the oven and sprinkle with the scallions. Along the edge of the baking dish, drop scoops of the sour cream, salsa, and guacamole. Serve immediately, passing the lime wedges separately.

One-Minute Salsa

MAKES ABOUT 1 CUP

This quick salsa can be made with either fresh or canned tomatoes. If you like, replace the jalapeño with ½ chipotle chile in adobo sauce, minced.

- 2 tablespoons chopped red onion
- 2 tablespoons fresh cilantro leaves
- 2 teaspoons juice from 1 lime
- ½ small jalapeño chile, stemmed and seeded (about 1½ teaspoons; see note)
- 1 small garlic clove, minced or pressed through a garlic press (about ½ teaspoon)
- ¼ teaspoon table salt
- Pinch ground black pepper
- 2 small ripe tomatoes, each cored and cut into eighths, or one (14.5-ounce) can diced tomatoes, drained

Pulse all the ingredients except the tomatoes in a food processor until minced, about 5 pulses, scraping down the sides of the workbowl as necessary. Add the tomatoes and pulse until roughly chopped, about 2 pulses.

GUACAMOLE

WHY THIS RECIPE WORKS: Not only eaten as a party dip, guacamole is also the traditional accompaniment to several Mexican dishes. Unfortunately, it often has so many ingredients that the primary one—the avocado—becomes overshadowed by secondary ingredients. We wanted to get back to the basics of this dish, emphasizing the avocado.

Hass avocados, the dark, pebbly-skinned type, worked best, and they needed to be perfectly ripe; they should yield slightly to a gentle squeeze. We wanted a chunky texture in our guacamole, so instead of mashing or pureeing the avocados we diced two of them and mashed one lightly. Combining the avocados gave the guacamole a chunky, cohesive texture. As for flavorings, just a bit of finely minced onion provided some bite but not overwhelming onion flavor. Lime juice was essential for its bright citrus flavor. Cumin, a jalapeño, and fresh cilantro rounded out the dip's flavors. Cool and creamy, our guacamole makes a perfect partner to a bowl of tortilla chips or a garnish to a variety of Mexican dishes.

Chunky Guacamole

MAKES 2½ TO 3 CUPS

To minimize the risk of discoloration, prepare the minced ingredients first so they are ready to mix with the avocados as soon as they are cut. Ripe avocados are essential here. To test for ripeness, try to flick the small stem off the end of the avocado. If it comes off easily and you can see green underneath it, the avocado is ripe. If it does not come off or if you see brown underneath after prying it off, the avocado is not ripe. If you like, garnish the guacamole with diced tomatoes and chopped cilantro just before serving.

NOTES FROM THE TEST KITCHEN

DICING AN AVOCADO

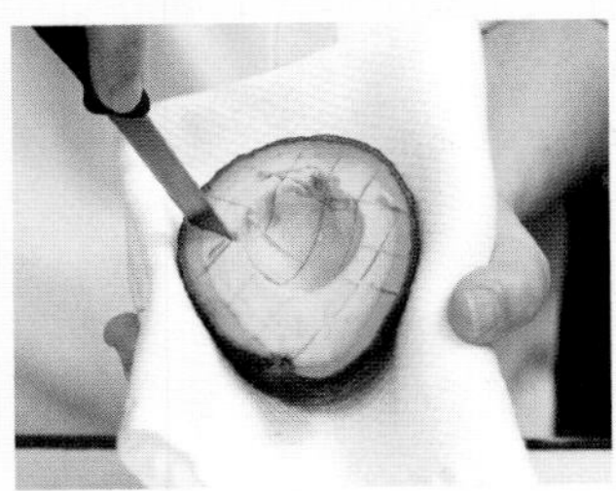

1. After halving and pitting the avocado, make ½-inch crosshatch incisions in the flesh of each half with a dinner knife, cutting down to but not through the skin.

2. Separate the diced flesh from the skin with a soup spoon, gently scooping out the avocado cubes.

- 3 medium, ripe avocados (see note)
- ¼ cup minced fresh cilantro leaves
- 2 tablespoons minced onion
- 1 small jalapeño chile, stemmed, seeded, and minced
- 1 medium garlic clove, minced or pressed through a garlic press (about 1 teaspoon)
- ½ teaspoon ground cumin (optional)
- Table salt
- 2 tablespoons juice from 1 lime

1. Halve 1 avocado, remove the pit, and scoop the flesh into a medium bowl. Mash the flesh lightly with the cilantro, onion, jalapeño, garlic, cumin (if using), and ¼ teaspoon salt with the tines of a fork until just combined.

2. Halve, pit, and cube the remaining 2 avocados. Add the cubes to the bowl with the mashed avocado mixture.

3. Sprinkle the lime juice over the diced avocado and mix the entire contents of the bowl lightly with a fork until combined but still chunky. Season with salt, if necessary, and serve. (The guacamole can be covered with plastic wrap, pressed directly onto the surface of the mixture, and refrigerated for up to 1 day. Return the guacamole to room temperature, removing the plastic wrap at the last moment, before serving.)

QUICK AND EASY QUESADILLAS

WHY THIS RECIPE WORKS: An authentic quesadilla is meant to be a quick snack, not an overstuffed tortilla with complicated fillings. We wanted a simple toasted tortilla, crisp and hot, filled with just the right amount of cheese.

We kept the tortillas crisp by lightly toasting them in a dry skillet. We then filled them with cheese and pickled jalapeños, lightly coated the tortillas with oil, and returned them to the skillet until they were well browned and the cheese was fully melted. Not yet satisfied that our recipe was speedy enough, we made the process even more convenient by switching to small 8-inch tortillas and folding them in half around the filling. This allowed us to cook two at one time in the same skillet, and the fold also kept our generous cheese filling from oozing out.

Quesadillas

MAKES 2 FOLDED 8-INCH QUESADILLAS

Cooling the quesadillas before cutting and serving them is important; straight from the skillet, the melted cheese will ooze out. Finished quesadillas can be held on a baking sheet in a 200-degree oven for up to 20 minutes.

- 2 (8-inch) flour tortillas
- 2 ounces Monterey Jack or cheddar cheese, shredded (about ½ cup)
- 1 tablespoon minced pickled jalapeños (optional)
- Vegetable oil for brushing the tortillas
- Kosher salt

1. Heat a 10-inch nonstick skillet over medium heat until hot, about 2 minutes. Place 1 tortilla in the skillet and toast until soft and puffed slightly at the edges, about 2 minutes. Flip the tortilla and toast until puffed and slightly browned, 1 to 2 minutes longer. Slip the tortilla onto a cutting board. Repeat to toast the second tortilla while assembling the first quesadilla. Sprinkle ¼ cup of the cheese and half of the jalapeños (if using) over half of the tortilla, leaving a ½-inch border around the edge. Fold the tortilla in half and press to flatten. Brush the top generously with oil, sprinkle lightly with salt, and set aside. Repeat to form the second quesadilla.

2. Place both quesadillas in the skillet, oiled sides down; cook over medium heat until crisp and well browned, 1 to 2 minutes. Brush the tops with oil and sprinkle lightly with salt. Flip the quesadillas and cook until the second sides are crisp, 1 to 2 minutes. Transfer the quesadillas to a cutting board; cool for 3 minutes, halve each quesadilla, and serve.

NOTES FROM THE TEST KITCHEN

COOKING QUESADILLAS

To cook two quesadillas at the same time, arrange the folded edges at the center of a 10-inch nonstick skillet.

TORTILLA SOUP

WHY THIS RECIPE WORKS: The classic method of making this flavorful Mexican soup is not only arduous, but it relies on a long list of ingredients, many of which are difficult, if not impossible, to find outside of specialty markets. We wanted to make an intensely and authentically flavored tortilla soup in less than one hour, using supermarket ingredients.

By breaking the soup down to its three classic components—the flavor base (tomatoes, garlic, onion, and chiles), the chicken stock, and the garnishes (including fried tortilla chips)—we found we could devise techniques and substitute ingredients that together made a compelling version of tortilla soup. We began achieving maximum flavor by composing a puree made from chipotle chiles, tomatoes, onions, garlic, jalapeños, and a cilantro/oregano substitute for the Mexican ingredient *epazote*, and then frying the puree in oil over high heat. We then added the puree to low-sodium canned chicken broth that we strained after poaching chicken in it and infusing it with onions, garlic, cilantro, and oregano. Addressing the garnish issue, we oven-toasted our lightly oiled tortilla strips instead of frying them and substituted sour cream and Monterey Jack cheese for the harder-to-find Mexican crema and cotija.

Tortilla Soup

SERVES 6

Despite its somewhat lengthy ingredient list, this recipe is very easy to prepare. If desired, the soup can be completed short of adding the shredded chicken to the pot at the end of step 3. Return the soup to a simmer over medium-high heat before proceeding. The tortilla strips and the garnishes are best prepared the day of serving.

TORTILLA STRIPS

- 8 (6-inch) corn tortillas, cut into ½-inch-wide strips
- 1 tablespoon vegetable oil
- Table salt

SOUP

- 2 bone-in, skin-on split chicken breasts (about 1½ pounds) or 4 bone-in, skin-on chicken thighs (about 1¼ pounds), skin removed and trimmed
- 8 cups low-sodium chicken broth
- 1 very large white onion (about 1 pound), peeled and quartered
- 4 medium garlic cloves, peeled
- 2 sprigs fresh epazote or 8 to 10 sprigs fresh cilantro plus 1 sprig fresh oregano
- Table salt
- 2 medium tomatoes, cored and quartered
- ½ medium jalapeño chile
- 1 chipotle chile in adobo sauce, plus up to 1 tablespoon adobo sauce
- 1 tablespoon vegetable oil

GARNISHES

- Lime wedges
- Avocado, peeled, pitted, and diced fine (see page 414)
- Cotija cheese, crumbled, or Monterey Jack cheese, diced fine
- Fresh cilantro leaves
- Jalapeño chile, minced
- Crema Mexicana or sour cream

1. FOR THE TORTILLA STRIPS: Adjust an oven rack to the middle position and heat the oven to 425 degrees. Spread the tortilla strips on a rimmed baking sheet; drizzle with the oil and toss until evenly coated. Bake until the strips are deep golden brown and crisped, about 14 minutes, rotating the pan and shaking the strips (to redistribute) halfway through baking. Season the strips lightly with salt; transfer to a plate lined with several layers of paper towels.

2. FOR THE SOUP: While the tortilla strips bake, bring the chicken, broth, 2 of the onion quarters, 2 of the garlic cloves, the epazote, and ½ teaspoon salt to a boil over medium-high heat in a large saucepan; reduce the heat to low, cover, and simmer until the chicken is just cooked through, about 20 minutes. Using tongs, transfer the chicken to a large plate. Pour the broth through a fine-mesh strainer; discard the solids in the strainer. When cool enough to handle, shred the chicken into bite-size pieces; discard the bones.

3. Puree the tomatoes, remaining 2 onion quarters, remaining 2 garlic cloves, the jalapeño, chipotle chile, and 1 teaspoon of the adobo sauce in a food processor until smooth, about 20 seconds. Heat the oil in a Dutch oven over high heat until shimmering; add the tomato-onion puree and ⅛ teaspoon salt and cook, stirring frequently, until the mixture has darkened in color, about 10 minutes. Stir the strained broth into the tomato mixture, bring to a boil, then reduce the heat to low and simmer to blend the flavors, about 15 minutes. Taste the soup; if desired, add up to 2 teaspoons more adobo sauce. Add the shredded chicken and simmer until heated through, about 5 minutes. To serve, place portions of tortilla strips in the bottom of individual bowls and ladle the soup into the bowls; pass the garnishes separately.

BLACK BEAN SOUP

WHY THIS RECIPE WORKS: Making traditional black bean soup used to be an all-day affair. Generating full flavor required hours of simmering soaked beans with numerous ingredients, including parsnips, carrots, beef bones, and smoked ham hocks. But quicker versions developed for modern kitchens often produce watery, bland, and unattractive soups. We wanted a simplified procedure that would result in an attractive, dark-colored soup full of sweet, spicy, smoky flavors and brightened with fresh garnishes.

Though convenient, canned beans couldn't compare in flavor to dried, which imparted good flavor to the broth as they simmered, and we discovered that we didn't have to soak them. A touch of baking soda in the cooking water kept the beans from turning gray. Homemade stock would be time-consuming to prepare, so we focused on adding flavor to prepared broth. Ham steak provided the smoky pork flavor of the more conventional ham hock and more meat as well. We spiced up our aromatics—carrot, celery, onion, and garlic—with lots of cumin and some red pepper flakes. We wanted a chunky texture in our soup, so we pureed it only partially, thickening it further with a slurry of cornstarch and water. Some lime juice added brightness. The customary garnishes of sour cream, avocado, red onion, cilantro, and lime wedges topped our richly flavored but easy-to-make black bean soup.

Black Bean Soup

SERVES 6

Dried beans tend to cook unevenly, so be sure to taste several beans to determine their doneness in step 1. For efficiency, you can prepare the soup ingredients while the beans simmer and the garnishes while the soup simmers. Though you do not need to offer all of the garnishes listed below, do choose at least a couple; garnishes are essential for this soup, as they add not only flavor but texture and color as well. Leftover soup can be refrigerated in an airtight container for up to 3 days; reheat it in a saucepan over medium heat until hot, stirring in additional chicken broth if it has thickened beyond your liking.

BEANS

- 1 pound (2 cups) dried black beans, rinsed and picked over
- 4 ounces ham steak, trimmed of rind
- 2 bay leaves
- 5 cups water
- ⅛ teaspoon baking soda
- 1 teaspoon table salt

SOUP

- 3 tablespoons olive oil
- 2 large onions, minced
- 3 celery ribs, chopped fine
- 1 large carrot, chopped
- ½ teaspoon table salt
- 5–6 medium garlic cloves, minced or pressed through a garlic press (about 2 tablespoons)
- 1½ tablespoons ground cumin
- ½ teaspoon red pepper flakes
- 6 cups low-sodium chicken broth
- 2 tablespoons cornstarch
- 2 tablespoons water
- 2 tablespoons juice from 1 lime

GARNISHES

- Lime wedges
- Minced fresh cilantro leaves
- Red onion, diced fine
- Avocado, peeled, pitted, and diced medium (see page 414)
- Sour cream

1. FOR THE BEANS: Place the beans, ham, bay leaves, water, and baking soda in a large saucepan with a tight-fitting lid. Bring to a boil over medium-high heat; using a large spoon, skim the foam as it rises to the surface. Stir in the salt, reduce the heat to low, cover, and simmer briskly until the beans are tender, 1¼ to 1½ hours (if necessary, add 1 cup more water and continue to simmer until the beans are tender); do not drain the beans. Discard the bay leaves. Remove the ham steak (ham steak darkens to the color of the beans), cut it into ¼-inch cubes, and set aside.

2. FOR THE SOUP: Heat the oil in a large Dutch oven over medium-high heat until shimmering but not smoking; add the onions, celery, carrot, and salt and cook, stirring occasionally, until the vegetables are soft and lightly browned, 12 to 15 minutes. Reduce the heat to medium-low and add the garlic, cumin, and red pepper flakes; cook, stirring constantly, until fragrant, about 3 minutes. Stir in the beans, bean cooking liquid, and chicken broth. Increase the heat to medium-high and bring to a boil, then reduce the heat to low and simmer, uncovered, stirring occasionally, to blend the flavors, about 30 minutes.

3. TO FINISH THE SOUP: Ladle 1½ cups of the beans and 2 cups of the liquid into a food processor or blender, process until smooth, and return to the pot. Stir together the cornstarch and water in a small bowl until combined, then gradually stir half of the cornstarch mixture into the soup; bring to a boil over medium-high heat, stirring occasionally, to fully thicken. If the soup is still thinner than desired once boiling, stir the remaining cornstarch mixture to recombine and gradually stir the mixture into the soup; return to a boil to fully thicken. Off the heat, stir in the lime juice and reserved ham; ladle the soup into bowls and serve immediately, passing the garnishes separately.

TAMALES

WHY THIS RECIPE WORKS: Tamales are small, moist corn cakes that can be stuffed with a variety of fillings, wrapped in corn husks, and steamed. Often served during the holidays, tamales are time-consuming to prepare. We wanted to simplify the process while staying true to the tamales' subtle but hearty flavor and light texture. Although masa dough (made from corn kernels that have been cooked with slaked lime, ground to a flour, and mixed with water) is traditional, it can be difficult to find. Instead, we turned to widely available masa harina, but found that when used alone, it was too fine-textured and the corn flavor was bland. Grits, on the other hand, had a granular texture similar to authentic tamales and didn't sacrifice any of the flavor. To fold the tamales, most recipes require tying each one closed, a process we found we could do without by simply folding the tamales and placing them with the seam sides facing the edges of a steamer basket. For the filling, hearty chicken thighs worked best for the long cooking time. A combination of dried ancho and New Mexican chiles resulted in a sauce with subtle spice and sweetness. Once cooked, the tamales peeled easily away from the moist rich corn cakes.

Tamales

MAKES 18 TAMALES; SERVES 6 TO 8

We found it easiest to use large corn husks that measure about 8 inches long by 6 inches wide; if the husks are small, you may need to use two per tamale and shingle them as needed to hold all of the filling. You can substitute butter for the lard if desired, but the tamales will have a distinctive buttery flavor. Be sure to use quick, not instant, grits in this recipe. For an accurate measurement of boiling water, bring a full kettle of water to a boil and then measure out the desired amount.

- 1 cup plus 2 tablespoons quick grits
- 1½ cups boiling water
- 1 cup (4 ounces) plus 2 tablespoons masa harina
- 20 large dried corn husks
- 1½ cups frozen corn, thawed
- 6 tablespoons unsalted butter, cut into ½-inch cubes and softened
- 6 tablespoons lard, softened
- 1 tablespoon sugar
- 2¼ teaspoons baking powder
- ¾ teaspoon salt
- 1 recipe Red Chile Chicken Filling (recipe follows)

1. Place grits in medium bowl, whisk in boiling water, and let stand until water is mostly absorbed, about 10 minutes. Stir in masa harina, cover, and let cool to room temperature, about 20 minutes. Meanwhile, place husks in large bowl, cover with hot water, and let soak until pliable, about 30 minutes.

2. Process masa dough, corn, butter, lard, sugar, baking powder, and salt together in food processor until mixture is light, sticky, and very smooth, about 1 minute, scraping down sides as necessary. Remove husks from water and pat dry with dish towel.

3. Working with 1 husk at a time, lay on counter, cupped side up, with long side facing you and wide end on right side. Spread ¼ cup tamale dough into 4-inch square over bottom right-hand corner, pushing it flush to bottom edge but leaving ¼-inch border at wide edge. Mound 2 scant tablespoons filling in line across center of dough, parallel to bottom edge. Roll husk away from you and over filling, so that dough surrounds filling and forms cylinder. Fold up tapered end, leaving top open, and transfer seam side down to platter.

4. Fit large pot or Dutch oven with steamer basket, removing feet from steamer basket if pot is short. Fill pot with water until it just touches bottom of basket and bring to boil. Gently lay tamales in basket with open ends facing up and seam sides facing out. Cover and steam, checking water level often and adding additional water as needed, until tamales easily come free from husks, about 1 hour. Transfer tamales to large platter. Reheat remaining sauce from filling in covered bowl in microwave, about 30 seconds, and serve with tamales.

Red Chile Chicken Filling

MAKES ENOUGH FOR 18 TAMALES

- 4 dried ancho chiles, stemmed, seeded, and torn into ½-inch pieces (1 cup)
- 4 dried New Mexican chiles, stemmed, seeded, and torn into ½-inch pieces (1 cup)
- 3 tablespoons vegetable oil
- 1 large onion, chopped
- 6 garlic cloves, minced
- ¾ teaspoon ground cumin
- ¾ teaspoon dried oregano
- Salt and pepper
- 3 cups chicken broth
- 1¼ pounds boneless, skinless chicken thighs, trimmed
- 1½ tablespoons cider vinegar
- Sugar

1. Toast anchos and New Mexican chiles in 12-inch skillet over medium heat, stirring frequently, until fragrant, 2 to 6 minutes; transfer to bowl.

2. Heat oil in now-empty skillet over medium heat until shimmering. Add onion and cook until softened, 5 to 7 minutes. Stir in garlic, cumin, oregano, ½ teaspoon salt, and toasted chiles and cook for 30 seconds. Stir in broth and simmer until slightly reduced, about 10 minutes. Transfer mixture to blender and process until smooth, about 20 seconds; return to skillet.

3. Season chicken with salt and pepper, nestle into skillet, and bring to simmer over medium heat. Cover, reduce heat to low, and cook until chicken registers 160 degrees, 20 to 25 minutes.

4. Transfer chicken to carving board and let cool slightly. Using 2 forks, shred chicken into small pieces. Stir vinegar into sauce and season with salt, pepper, and sugar to taste. Toss shredded chicken with 1 cup sauce. Reheat remaining sauce and serve with tamales.

BEEF EMPANADAS

WHY THIS RECIPE WORKS: In Latin America, crisp pastry pockets stuffed with spiced beef make a savory, light lunch. We wanted to streamline the process but still get an empanada hearty enough to take center stage at dinner, with a moist, savory filling encased in a tender crust.

To streamline the filling, we first enhanced packaged ground chuck with a milk-and-bread mixture known as a panade. As the meat and panade cooked, the starches in the panade's bread absorbed moisture from the milk and formed a gel around the protein molecules, which lubricated the meat. But to intensify the meaty flavor, we replaced the milk with an equal amount of chicken broth. To round it out we added a hefty dose of aromatics. Finally, we threw in a handful of cilantro leaves and a splash of vinegar along with chopped hard-cooked eggs, raisins, and green olives.

For our crust, we made a few Latin-inspired changes to our Foolproof Double-Crust Pie Dough (page 844), a recipe that combines butter (for flavor) and shortening (for tenderness) with water and vodka for a dough that's both workable and tender (tequila can also be substituted for the vodka). We traded some of the flour for masa harina, the ground, dehydrated cornmeal used to make Mexican tortillas and tamales. This provided nutty richness and rough-hewn texture. Finally, a quick brush of oil on the top of the empanadas gave us a shiny, crunchy crust, and preheating the baking sheet and drizzling it with oil ensured the underside of the crust got as crispy as the top.

Beef Empanadas

SERVES 4 TO 6

The alcohol in the dough is essential to the texture of the crust and imparts no flavor—do not omit it or substitute water. Masa harina can be found in the international aisle of the supermarket with other Latin foods or in the baking aisle with the flour. If you cannot find masa harina, replace it with additional all-purpose flour (for a total of 4 cups). See page 38 for instructions on how to hard-cook eggs.

NOTES FROM THE TEST KITCHEN

ASSEMBLING EMPANADAS

1. Divide the dough in half, then divide each half into six equal pieces.

2. Roll each piece of dough into a 6-inch round about ⅛ inch thick.

3. Place about ⅓ cup of the filling on each round, then brush the edges with water.

4. Fold the dough over the filling, then crimp the edges using a fork to seal.

FILLING

- 1 slice high-quality white sandwich bread, torn into quarters
- 2 tablespoons plus ½ cup low-sodium chicken broth
- 1 pound 85 percent lean ground beef
- Table salt and ground black pepper
- 1 tablespoon olive oil
- 2 medium onions, minced
- 4 medium garlic cloves, minced or pressed through a garlic press (about 4 teaspoons)
- 1 teaspoon ground cumin
- ¼ teaspoon cayenne pepper
- ⅛ teaspoon ground cloves
- ½ cup fresh cilantro leaves, chopped coarse

- 2 hard-cooked eggs (see note), chopped coarse
- ⅓ cup raisins, chopped coarse
- ¼ cup pitted green olives, chopped coarse
- 4 teaspoons cider vinegar

DOUGH

- 3 cups (15 ounces) unbleached all-purpose flour
- 1 cup (5 ounces) masa harina (see note)
- 1 tablespoon sugar
- 2 teaspoons table salt
- 12 tablespoons (1½ sticks) unsalted butter, cut into ½-inch pieces and chilled
- ½ cup cold vodka or tequila
- ½ cup cold water
- 5 tablespoons olive oil

1. FOR THE FILLING: Process the bread and 2 tablespoons of the chicken broth in a food processor until a paste forms, about 5 seconds, scraping down the sides of the bowl as necessary. Add the beef, ¾ teaspoon salt, and ½ teaspoon pepper and pulse until the mixture is well combined, 6 to 8 pulses.

2. Heat the oil in a 12-inch nonstick skillet over medium-high heat until shimmering. Add the onions and cook, stirring frequently, until beginning to brown, about 5 minutes. Stir in the garlic, cumin, cayenne, and cloves and cook until fragrant, about 1 minute. Add the beef mixture and cook, breaking the meat into 1-inch pieces with a wooden spoon, until browned, about 7 minutes. Add the remaining ½ cup chicken broth and simmer until the mixture is moist but not wet, 3 to 5 minutes. Transfer the mixture to a bowl and cool for 10 minutes. Stir in the cilantro, eggs, raisins, olives, and vinegar. Season with salt and pepper to taste and refrigerate until cool, about 1 hour.

3. FOR THE DOUGH: Pulse 1 cup of the flour, the masa harina, sugar, and salt in a food processor until combined, about 2 pulses. Add the butter and process until the mixture is homogeneous and the dough resembles wet sand, about 10 seconds. Add the remaining 2 cups flour and pulse until the mixture is evenly distributed around the bowl, 4 to 6 quick pulses. Empty the mixture into a medium bowl.

4. Sprinkle the vodka and water over the mixture. Using your hands, mix the dough until it forms a tacky mass that sticks together. Following the photo, divide the dough in half, then divide each half into six equal pieces. Transfer the dough pieces to a plate, cover with plastic wrap, and refrigerate until firm, about 45 minutes.

5. TO ASSEMBLE: Adjust the oven racks to the upper-middle and lower-middle positions, place 1 baking sheet on each rack, and heat the oven to 425 degrees. While the baking sheets are preheating, remove the dough from the refrigerator. Following the photos on page 418, roll each dough piece out on a lightly floured work surface into a 6-inch circle about ⅛ inch thick, covering each rolled-out dough round with plastic wrap while rolling out the remaining dough. Place about ⅓ cup of the filling in the center of each dough round. Brush the edges of each round with water and fold the dough over the filling. Trim any ragged edges, then crimp the edges of the empanadas shut using a fork.

6. Drizzle 2 tablespoons of the oil over the surface of each hot baking sheet, then return the sheets to the oven for 2 minutes. Brush the empanadas with the remaining 1 tablespoon oil. Carefully place 6 empanadas on each baking sheet and cook until well browned and crisp, 25 to 30 minutes, switching and rotating the baking sheets halfway through baking. Cool the empanadas on a wire rack for 10 minutes before serving. (After step 5, the empanadas can be covered tightly with plastic wrap and refrigerated for up to 2 days.)

BEEF TACOS

WHY THIS RECIPE WORKS: Tacos made from supermarket kits are disappointing substitutes for the real thing. Easy as they may be to prepare, taco fillings made with store-bought spice mixes taste flat and stale, and the shells don't taste much different than the cardboard they're packaged in. We set out to develop a recipe for toasty, not greasy, taco shells filled with a boldly spiced beef mixture and fresh toppings.

Home-fried corn tortillas made superior homemade taco shells. For the filling, we seasoned lean ground beef with onions, garlic, and spices (chili powder, cumin, coriander, and oregano). To moisten and further flavor the beef filling, we added chicken broth, brown sugar, and vinegar. Spooned into our fresh, crisp taco shells and topped with tomatoes, lettuce, avocado, Monterey Jack, onion, and cilantro, these tacos have far better flavor than taco-kit versions.

Beef Tacos

SERVES 4

Taco toppings are highly individual. We consider the ones listed below essential, but you might also want to consider diced avocado, sour cream, and chopped onion.

BEEF FILLING

- 2 teaspoons vegetable oil
- 1 small onion, minced
- 3 medium garlic cloves, minced or pressed through a garlic press (about 1 tablespoon)
- 2 tablespoons chili powder
- 1 teaspoon ground cumin
- 1 teaspoon ground coriander
- ½ teaspoon dried oregano
- ¼ teaspoon cayenne pepper
- Table salt
- 1 pound 90 percent lean ground beef
- ½ cup canned tomato sauce
- ½ cup low-sodium chicken broth
- 2 teaspoons vinegar, preferably cider vinegar
- 1 teaspoon brown sugar
- Ground black pepper

SHELLS AND TOPPINGS

- 8 Home-Fried Taco Shells (recipe follows)
- Shredded Monterey Jack cheese
- Shredded iceberg lettuce
- Diced tomatoes
- Chopped fresh cilantro leaves

1. FOR THE FILLING: Heat the oil in a medium skillet over medium heat until shimmering. Add the onion and cook, stirring occasionally, until softened, about 4 minutes. Add the garlic, spices, and ½ teaspoon salt; cook, stirring constantly, until fragrant, about 30 seconds. Add the ground beef and cook, breaking up the meat with a wooden spoon and scraping the pan bottom to prevent scorching, until the beef is no longer pink, about 5 minutes. Add the tomato sauce, broth, vinegar, and brown sugar; bring to a simmer. Reduce the heat to medium-low and simmer uncovered, stirring frequently and breaking up the meat so that no chunks remain, until the liquid has reduced and thickened (the mixture should not be completely dry), about 10 minutes. Season with salt and pepper to taste.

2. Using a wide, shallow spoon, divide the mixture evenly among the taco shells; place two tacos on each plate. Serve immediately, passing the toppings separately.

Home-Fried Taco Shells

MAKES 8 SHELLS

Fry the taco shells before you make the filling, then rewarm them in a 200-degree oven for about 10 minutes before serving.

- ¾ cup corn oil, vegetable oil, or canola oil
- 8 (6-inch) corn tortillas

1. Line a rimmed baking sheet with a double thickness of paper towels and set aside. Heat the oil in an 8-inch skillet over medium heat to 350 degrees, about 5 minutes (the oil should bubble when a small piece of tortilla is dropped in; the piece should rise to the surface in 2 seconds and be light golden brown in about 1 minute).

2. Following the photos, fry the tortillas. One at a time, place each fried taco shell on the prepared baking sheet (see note).

NOTES FROM THE TEST KITCHEN

MAKING YOUR OWN TACO SHELLS

1. Using tongs to hold the tortilla, slip half of it into the hot oil. With a metal spatula in the other hand, submerge the half in the oil. Fry until just set, but not brown, about 30 seconds.

2. Flip the tortilla and, using tongs, hold the tortilla open about 2 inches while keeping the bottom submerged in the oil. Fry until golden brown, about 1½ minutes. Flip again and fry the other side until golden brown, about 30 seconds.

3. Transfer the shell, upside down, to the paper towel-lined baking sheet to drain. Repeat with the remaining tortillas, adjusting the heat as necessary to keep the oil between 350 and 375 degrees.

STEAK TACOS

WHY THIS RECIPE WORKS: Upscale steak tacos usually get their rich, beefy flavor from the grill, but cooking outdoors isn't always possible. We wanted an indoor cooking method that would always yield steak taco meat as tender, juicy, and rich-tasting as the grilled method.

We didn't want to wrap a pricey cut of beef in a taco, so we explored inexpensive cuts and chose flank steak for its good flavor and ready availability; when sliced against the grain, it can be just as tender as pricier cuts. To add flavor, we poked holes in the meat with a fork and rubbed it with a paste of oil, cilantro, jalapeño, garlic, and scallions; salt helped draw all the flavors into the steak and ensured juiciness. Pan-searing, with a sprinkling of sugar to enhance browning, gave us a crust that mimicked the char of the grill. To maximize this effect, we cut the steak into four long pieces, which gave us more sides to brown and turn crispy. For additional flavor, we tossed the cooked steak with some marinade that we had reserved and garnished the tacos simply with onion, cilantro, and lime wedges. In Mexico, steak tacos are often served with *curtido*, a relish of pickled vegetables; we devised a quick recipe for pickled onions to accompany our good-as-grilled steak tacos.

Steak Tacos

SERVES 4 TO 6

Our preferred method for warming tortillas is to place each one over the medium flame of a gas burner until slightly charred, about 30 seconds per side. We also like toasting them in a dry skillet over medium-high heat until softened and speckled with brown spots, 20 to 30 seconds per side. For a less spicy dish, remove some or all of the ribs and seeds from the jalapeños before chopping them for the marinade. In addition to the toppings suggested below, try serving the tacos with Sweet and Spicy Pickled Onions (recipe follows), thinly sliced radish or cucumber, or salsa.

MARINADE

- ½ cup packed fresh cilantro leaves
- 3 medium scallions, roughly chopped
- 1 medium jalapeño chile, stemmed and roughly chopped (see note)
- 3 medium garlic cloves, roughly chopped
- ½ teaspoon ground cumin
- ¼ cup vegetable oil
- 1 tablespoon juice from 1 lime

STEAK

- 1 (1½- to 1¾-pound) flank steak, trimmed and cut lengthwise (with the grain) into 4 equal pieces
- 1 tablespoon kosher salt or 1½ teaspoons table salt
- ½ teaspoon sugar
- ½ teaspoon ground black pepper
- 2 tablespoons vegetable oil

TACOS

- 12 (6-inch) corn tortillas, warmed (see note)
- Fresh cilantro leaves
- Minced white onion
- Lime wedges

1. FOR THE MARINADE: Pulse the cilantro, scallions, jalapeño, garlic, and cumin in a food processor until finely chopped, 10 to 12 pulses, scraping down the sides of the workbowl as necessary. Add the oil and process until the mixture is smooth and resembles pesto, about 15 seconds, scraping down the sides as necessary. Transfer 2 tablespoons of the herb paste to a medium bowl; whisk in the lime juice and set aside.

2. FOR THE STEAK: Using a dinner fork, poke each piece of steak 10 to 12 times on each side. Place in a large baking dish; rub all sides of the steak pieces evenly with the salt and then coat with the remaining herb paste. Cover with plastic wrap and refrigerate for at least 30 minutes or up to 1 hour.

3. Scrape the herb paste off the steak and sprinkle all sides of the pieces evenly with the sugar and black pepper. Heat the oil in a 12-inch nonstick skillet over medium-high heat until smoking. Place the steak in the skillet and cook until well browned, about 3 minutes. Flip the steak and sear until the second side is well browned, 2 to 3 minutes. Using tongs, stand each piece on a cut side and cook, turning as necessary, until all cut sides are well browned and the internal steak temperature registers 125 to 130 degrees on an instant-read thermometer, 2 to 7 minutes. Transfer the steak to a cutting board and let rest for 5 minutes.

4. FOR THE TACOS: Slice the steak against the grain into ⅛-inch-thick pieces. Transfer the sliced steak to the bowl with the herb paste–lime juice mixture and toss to coat. Season with salt to taste. Spoon a small amount of the sliced steak into the center of each warm tortilla and serve immediately, passing the toppings separately.

Sweet and Spicy Pickled Onions

MAKES ABOUT 2 CUPS

The onions can be refrigerated, tightly covered, for up to 1 week.

- 1 medium red onion, halved and sliced thin (about 1½ cups)
- 1 cup red wine vinegar
- ⅓ cup sugar
- 2 jalapeño chiles, stemmed, seeded, and cut into thin rings
- ¼ teaspoon table salt

Place the onions in a medium heat-resistant bowl. Bring the vinegar, sugar, jalapeños, and salt to a simmer in a small saucepan over medium-high heat, stirring occasionally, until the sugar dissolves. Pour the vinegar mixture over the onions, cover loosely, and let cool to room temperature, about 30 minutes. Once cool, drain and discard the liquid.

SHREDDED BEEF TACOS

WHY THIS RECIPE WORKS: The Mexican taco filling called *carne deshebrada* (shredded meat) is made by braising a large cut of beef (usually brisket, chuck roast, or even flank or skirt steak) until ultra tender and then shredding the meat and tossing it with a red or green sauce. We wanted an at-home version, made with a robust *rojo* (red) sauce.

Traditionally, the beef is cooked in water, which is then discarded—along with a lot of beefy flavor. Instead, we put the braising liquid to use in the sauce. Having it pull double duty not only ensured more flavor but also streamlined the recipe. We started by swapping out the water for a bright combination of beer and cider vinegar and swapping the large roast for meaty short ribs, cut into cubes to reduce the cooking time. To skip the extra step of browning the meat in batches, we propped up the cubes on slices of onion, which allowed the meat to brown in the ambient heat, contributing deep, meaty flavor

to the sauce. Tomato paste lent savory depth, and dried ancho chiles gave it a smoky, spicy kick. Ground cumin, cinnamon, and cloves provided a warm, earthy backbone. We pureed the sauce for a silky, unctuous texture that incorporated into the shredded meat seamlessly.

For a bright, fresh topping for our tacos, we made a quick *curtido*, a cabbage slaw from El Salvador. Marinating the shredded vegetables, onion, and jalapeño in a fruity cider vinegar–based pickling liquid gave them just the right amount of punch. A sprinkling of crumbled *queso fresco* introduced the right salty, creamy finish to the tacos.

Shredded Beef Tacos (Carne Deshebrada)

SERVES 6 TO 8

Use a full-bodied lager or ale such as Dos Equis or Sierra Nevada. If you can't find queso fresco, substitute feta. If your Dutch oven does not have a tight-fitting lid, cover the pot tightly with a sheet of heavy-duty aluminum foil and then replace the lid. To warm the tortillas, place them on a plate, cover them with a damp dish towel, and microwave them for 60 to 90 seconds. The shredded beef also makes a great filling for empanadas, tamales, and chiles rellenos.

BEEF

- 1½ cups beer
- ½ cup cider vinegar
- 2 ounces (4 to 6) dried ancho chiles, stemmed, seeded, and torn into 1-inch pieces
- 2 tablespoons tomato paste
- 6 garlic cloves, lightly crushed and peeled
- 3 bay leaves
- 2 teaspoons ground cumin
- 2 teaspoons dried oregano
- Salt and pepper
- ½ teaspoon ground cloves
- ½ teaspoon ground cinnamon
- 1 large onion, sliced into ½-inch-thick rounds
- 3 pounds boneless beef short ribs, trimmed and cut into 2-inch cubes

CABBAGE-CARROT SLAW

- 1 cup cider vinegar
- ½ cup water
- 1 tablespoon sugar
- 1½ teaspoons salt
- ½ head green cabbage, cored and sliced thin (6 cups)
- 1 onion, sliced thin
- 1 large carrot, peeled and shredded
- 1 jalapeño chile, stemmed, seeded, and minced
- 1 teaspoon dried oregano
- 1 cup chopped fresh cilantro

- 18 (6-inch) corn tortillas, warmed
- 4 ounces queso fresco, crumbled (1 cup)
- Lime wedges

1. FOR THE BEEF: Adjust oven rack to lower-middle position and heat oven to 325 degrees. Combine beer, vinegar, anchos, tomato paste, garlic, bay leaves, cumin, oregano, 2 teaspoons salt, ½ teaspoon pepper, cloves, and cinnamon in Dutch oven. Arrange onion rounds in single layer on bottom of pot. Place beef on top of onion rounds in single layer. Cover and cook until meat is well browned and tender, 2½ to 3 hours.

2. FOR THE CABBAGE-CARROT SLAW: While beef cooks, whisk vinegar, water, sugar, and salt in large bowl until sugar is dissolved. Add cabbage, onion, carrot, jalapeño, and oregano and toss to combine. Cover and refrigerate for at least 1 hour or up to 24 hours. Drain slaw and stir in cilantro right before serving.

3. Using slotted spoon, transfer beef to large bowl, cover loosely with aluminum foil, and set aside. Strain liquid through fine-mesh strainer into 2-cup liquid measuring cup (do not wash pot). Discard onion rounds and bay leaves. Transfer remaining solids to blender. Let strained liquid settle for 5 minutes, then skim any fat off surface. Add water as needed to equal 1 cup. Pour liquid in blender with reserved solids and blend until smooth, about 2 minutes. Transfer sauce to now-empty pot.

4. Using two forks, shred beef into bite-size pieces. Bring sauce to simmer over medium heat. Add shredded beef and stir to coat. Season with salt to taste. (Beef can be refrigerated for up to 2 days; gently reheat before serving.)

5. Spoon small amount of beef into each warm tortilla and serve, passing slaw, queso fresco, and lime wedges separately.

SHREDDED CHICKEN TACOS

WHY THIS RECIPE WORKS: *Tinga de pollo* is typically made with cuts of meat that take several hours to turn tender—not exactly practical for a weeknight dish. We were determined to create a faster recipe that still brought authentic Mexican flavors to the table. At first, we poached chicken breast meat separately from the tomato-and-chipotle-based sauce and combined the two only briefly at the end. We realized, though, that we could achieve a deeper flavor by using boneless thighs and cooking them in the sauce. Fire-roasted tomatoes increased the sauce's smokiness, and a little brown sugar and lime juice and zest further boosted the dish's complexity. Simmering the cooked shredded chicken in the sauce for a full 10 minutes before serving gave the sauce a chance to thicken and loosened the chicken's muscle fibers so the sauce could really take hold and cling to the meat, making more cohesive tacos. Final toppings of fresh cilantro, scallions, avocado, crumbled Cotija cheese, and lime juice added the perfect amount of contrasting cool flavors.

Shredded Chicken Tacos (Tinga de Pollo)

SERVES 6

If you have a little extra time, homemade tortillas (recipe follows) will take these tacos to the next level. In addition to the Mexican-Style Pickled Vegetables (*Escabèche*) (recipe follows) and the toppings included here, Mexican *crema* (or sour cream) and minced onion are also good choices. If you can't find Cotija cheese, substitute feta. The shredded chicken mixture also makes a good topping for tostadas.

CHICKEN

- 2 pounds boneless, skinless chicken thighs, trimmed
- Salt and pepper
- 2 tablespoons vegetable oil
- 1 onion, halved and sliced thin
- 3 garlic cloves, minced
- 1 (14.5-ounce) can fire-roasted diced tomatoes
- ½ cup chicken broth
- 2 tablespoons minced canned chipotle chile in adobo sauce plus 2 teaspoons adobo sauce
- 1 teaspoon ground cumin
- ½ teaspoon brown sugar
- ¼ teaspoon cinnamon
- 1 teaspoon grated lime zest plus 2 tablespoons juice

TACOS

- 12 (6-inch) corn tortillas, warmed
- 1 avocado, halved, pitted, and cut into ½-inch pieces
- Fresh cilantro leaves
- 2 ounces Cotija cheese, crumbled (½ cup)
- 6 scallions, minced
- Lime wedges

1. FOR THE CHICKEN: Pat chicken dry with paper towels and season with salt and pepper. Heat 1 tablespoon oil in Dutch oven over medium-high heat until shimmering. Add half of chicken and brown on both sides, 3 to 4 minutes per side. Transfer to large plate. Repeat with remaining chicken.

2. Reduce heat to medium, add remaining 1 tablespoon oil to now-empty pot, and heat until shimmering. Add onion and cook, stirring frequently, until browned, about 7 minutes. Add garlic and cook until fragrant, about 1 minute. Add tomatoes and their juice, broth, chipotle and adobo sauce, cumin, sugar, and cinnamon and bring to boil, scraping bottom of pot to loosen any browned bits.

3. Return chicken to pot, reduce heat to medium-low, cover, and simmer until meat registers 195 degrees, about 15 minutes, flipping chicken after 5 minutes. Transfer chicken to cutting board.

4. Transfer cooking liquid to blender and process until smooth, 15 to 30 seconds. Return cooking liquid to pot. When cool enough to handle, use two forks to shred chicken into bite-size pieces. Return chicken to pot with cooking liquid. Cook over medium heat, stirring frequently, until sauce is thickened and clings to chicken, about 10 minutes. Stir in lime zest and juice. Season with salt and pepper to taste.

5. FOR THE TACOS: Spoon chicken into center of each warm tortilla and serve immediately, passing toppings separately.

Mexican-Style Pickled Vegetables (Escabèche)

MAKES ABOUT 2 CUPS

For a less spicy pickle, remove the seeds from the jalapeño.

- ½ teaspoon coriander seeds
- ¼ teaspoon cumin seeds
- 1 cup apple cider vinegar
- ½ cup water
- 1½ teaspoons sugar
- ¼ teaspoon salt
- 1 red onion, halved and sliced thin
- 2 carrots, peeled and sliced thin
- 1 jalapeño, stemmed and sliced thin into rings

Heat coriander seeds and cumin seeds in medium saucepan over medium heat, stirring frequently, until fragrant, about 2 minutes. Add vinegar, water, sugar, and salt and bring to boil, stirring to dissolve sugar and salt. Remove saucepan from heat and add onion, carrots, and jalapeno, pressing to submerge vegetables. Cover and let cool completely, 30 minutes. (Cooled vegetables can be refrigerated for up to 1 week.)

Corn Tortillas

MAKES ABOUT TWENTY-TWO 5-INCH TORTILLAS

Pressing the dough between a zipper-lock bag that has been cut open at the sides prevents it from sticking to the pie plate. Distribute your weight evenly over the dough when pressing. Using a clear pie plate makes it easy to see the tortilla. A tortilla press, of course, can also be used. You can find masa harina in the international aisle or near the flour.

- 2 cups (8 ounces) masa harina
- 2 teaspoons vegetable oil
- ¼ teaspoon salt
- 1¼ cups warm water, plus extra as needed

1. Cut sides of sandwich-size zipper-lock bag but leave bottom seam intact so that bag unfolds completely. Place open bag on counter and line large plate with 2 damp dish towels.

2. Mix masa, 1 teaspoon oil, and salt together in medium bowl. Using rubber spatula, stir in warm water to form soft dough. Using your hands, knead dough in bowl, adding extra warm water, 1 tablespoon at a time, until dough is soft and tacky but not sticky (texture is like Play-Doh). Cover dough and set aside for 5 minutes.

3. Meanwhile, heat remaining 1 teaspoon oil in 8-inch non-stick skillet over medium-high heat until shimmering. Using paper towel, wipe out skillet, leaving thin film of oil on bottom. Pinch off 1-ounce piece of dough (about 2 tablespoons) and roll into smooth 1¼-inch ball. Cover remaining dough with damp paper towel. Place ball in center of open bag and fold other side of bag over ball. Using clear pie plate, press down on plastic to flatten ball into 5-inch disk, rotating plastic during pressing to ensure even thickness. Working quickly, gently peel plastic away from tortilla.

4. Carefully place tortilla in skillet and cook, without moving it, until tortilla moves freely when pan is shaken, about 30 seconds. Flip tortilla and cook until edges curl and bottom surface is spotty brown, about 1 minute. Flip tortilla again and continue to cook until bottom surface is spotty brown and puffs up in center, 30 to 60 seconds. Place toasted tortilla between 2 damp dish towels; repeat shaping and cooking with remaining dough. (Cooled tortillas can be transferred to zipper-lock bag and refrigerated for up to 5 days. Reheat before serving.)

SAUSAGE AND POTATO TACOS

WHY THIS RECIPE WORKS: Juicy, seasoned Mexican chorizo is key to this classic taco, but it can be hard to find, so we devised a quick method for making our own. We started by toasting ancho chili powder, paprika, and spices in oil to intensify their flavors, and then we mixed the spiced oil into preground pork along with some cider vinegar. We cooked the mixture in a skillet and added parboiled diced potatoes to absorb the flavorful juices as they finished cooking. Mashing some of the potatoes and mixing them into the filling made it more cohesive and easier to eat. A creamy puree of tomatillos, avocado, cilantro, and jalapeños complemented the richness of the filling and was a cooling counterpoint to its spiciness.

Sausage and Potato Tacos

SERVES 4

If you can purchase a good quality Mexican-style chorizo, skip step 2 and cook the chorizo as directed in step 3. The raw onions complement the soft, rich taco filling, so we do not recommend omitting them.

FILLING

- 1 pound Yukon Gold potatoes, peeled and cut into ½-inch chunks
- Salt and pepper
- 1 tablespoon ancho chili powder
- 1 tablespoon paprika
- 1½ teaspoons ground coriander
- 1½ teaspoon dried oregano
- ¼ teaspoon ground cinnamon
- Pinch cayenne pepper
- Pinch ground allspice
- 3 tablespoons vegetable oil
- 3 tablespoons apple cider vinegar
- 1½ teaspoons sugar
- 1 garlic clove, minced
- ½ pound ground pork

SAUCE

- 8 ounces tomatillos, husks and stems removed, rinsed well and dried, and cut into 1-inch pieces
- 1 avocado, halved, pitted, and cut into 1-inch pieces
- 1–2 jalapeño chile(s), stemmed, seeded, and chopped
- ¼ cup chopped fresh cilantro leaves and stems
- 1 tablespoon lime juice
- 1 garlic clove, minced
- ¾ teaspoon salt

TACOS

- 12 (6-inch) corn tortillas, warmed
- Finely chopped white onion
- Fresh cilantro leaves
- Lime wedges

1. FOR THE FILLING: Bring 4 cups water to boil in 12-inch non-stick skillet over high heat. Add potatoes and 1 teaspoon salt. Reduce heat to medium, cover, and cook until just tender, 3 to 5 minutes. Drain and set aside. Wipe out skillet.

2. Combine chili powder, paprika, coriander, oregano, cinnamon, cayenne, allspice, ¾ teaspoon salt, ½ teaspoon pepper, and oil in now-empty skillet. Cook over medium heat, stirring constantly, until mixture is bubbling and fragrant. Remove from heat and carefully stir in vinegar, sugar, and garlic (mixture will sputter). Let stand until steam subsides and skillet cools slightly, about 5 minutes. Add pork to skillet. Mash and mix with rubber spatula until spice mixture is evenly incorporated

3. Return skillet to medium-high heat and cook pork mixture over medium-high heat, mashing and stirring until pork has broken into fine crumbles and juices are bubbling over entire surface of skillet, about 3 minutes.

4. Stir in potatoes, cover, and reduce heat to low. Cook until potatoes are fully softened and have soaked up most of the pork juices, 6 to 8 minutes, stirring halfway through cooking time.

Remove skillet from heat and, using spatula, mash approximately one-eighth of potatoes. Stir mashed potatoes into mixture until lightly coated with juices. Cover and keep warm.

5. FOR THE SAUCE: Process all ingredients in food processor until smooth, about 1 minute, scraping down sides of bowl as needed. Transfer to serving bowl.

6. FOR THE TACOS: Spoon filling into center of each warm tortilla and serve with sauce, onion, cilantro, and lime wedges.

CHICKEN FAJITAS

WHY THIS RECIPE WORKS: Too often, chicken fajitas need to be slathered with guacamole, sour cream, and salsa to compensate for the bland flavor of the main ingredients. We wanted to go back to the basics, creating a simple combination of smoky grilled vegetables and strips of chicken wrapped up in warm flour tortillas. We wanted the chicken and vegetables to be flavorful enough to make condiments unnecessary.

To boost the flavor of the chicken, we used a marinade of lime juice and oil. We added jalapeño and cilantro for some bright spice and herbal flavor, and a surprising addition—Worcestershire sauce—lent a subtle but complex savory note. We marinated the chicken only briefly, so the acid wouldn't turn the delicate chicken to mush. Bell peppers and onions are the customary vegetables, and we found that their sweet-bitter flavors contrasted well with the chicken. To prepare the vegetables for grilling, we quartered the peppers, so they'd lie flat on the grill, and cut the onion into thick rounds that would hold together during cooking. A two-level fire enabled us to grill the chicken and vegetables at the same time, the latter on the cooler part so they wouldn't burn. We saved some of the marinade to toss with everything at the end for a bright flavor burst; nestled in a warm tortilla, the smoky vegetables and well-seasoned chicken were so good on their own that we forgot all about toppings.

Grilled Chicken Fajitas

SERVES 4 TO 6

You can use red, yellow, orange, or green bell peppers in this recipe. The chicken tenderloins can be reserved for another use or marinated and grilled along with the breasts. When you head outside to grill, bring a clean dish towel in which to wrap the tortillas and keep them warm. The chicken and vegetables have enough flavor on their own, but accompaniments (guacamole, salsa, sour cream, shredded cheddar or Monterey Jack cheese, and lime wedges) can be offered at the table.

- 6 tablespoons vegetable oil
- ⅓ cup lime juice (3 limes)
- 1 jalapeño chile, stemmed, seeded, and minced
- 1½ tablespoons minced fresh cilantro
- 3 garlic cloves, minced
- 1 tablespoon Worcestershire sauce
- 1½ teaspoons packed brown sugar
- Salt and pepper
- 1½ pounds boneless, skinless chicken breasts, tenderloins removed, trimmed, pounded to ½-inch thickness
- 1 large red onion, peeled and cut into ½-inch-thick rounds (do not separate rings)
- 2 large bell peppers, quartered, stemmed, and seeded
- 8–12 (6-inch) flour tortillas

1. Whisk ¼ cup oil, lime juice, jalapeño, cilantro, garlic, Worcestershire, sugar, 1 teaspoon salt, and ¾ teaspoon pepper together in bowl. Reserve ¼ cup marinade and set aside. Add 1 teaspoon salt to remaining marinade. Place marinade and chicken in 1-gallon zipper-lock bag and toss to coat; press out as much air as possible and seal bag. Refrigerate for at least 15 minutes, flipping bag halfway through marinating. Brush both sides of onion rounds and peppers with remaining 2 tablespoons oil and season with salt and pepper to taste.

2A. FOR A CHARCOAL GRILL: Open bottom vent completely. Light large chimney starter filled with charcoal briquettes (6 quarts). When top coals are partially covered with ash, pour coals over two-thirds of grill, leaving remaining one-third empty. Set cooking grate in place, cover, and open lid vent completely. Heat grill until hot, about 5 minutes.

2B. FOR A GAS GRILL: Turn all burners to high, cover, and heat grill until hot, about 15 minutes. Leave primary burner on high and turn other burner(s) to medium.

3. Clean and oil cooking grate. Remove chicken from bag, allowing excess marinade to drip off. Place chicken on hotter side of grill, smooth side down. Cook (covered if using gas) until well browned on first side, 4 to 6 minutes. Flip and continue to cook until chicken registers 160 degrees, 4 to 6 minutes longer. Transfer chicken to cutting board, tent loosely with aluminum foil, and let rest for 5 to 10 minutes.

4. While chicken cooks, place onion rounds and peppers (skin side down) on cooler side of grill and cook until tender and charred on both sides, 8 to 12 minutes, flipping every 3 minutes. Transfer onions and peppers to cutting board with chicken.

5. Working in 2 or 3 batches, place tortillas in single layer on cooler side of grill. Cook until warm and lightly browned, about 20 seconds per side (do not grill too long or tortillas will become brittle). As tortillas are done, wrap in dish towel or large sheet of foil.

6. Separate onions into rings and place in medium bowl. Slice peppers into ¼-inch-thick strips and place in bowl with onions. Add 2 tablespoons reserved marinade and toss to combine. Slice each breast on bias into ¼-inch-thick slices, place in second bowl, and toss with remaining 2 tablespoons reserved marinade.

7. Transfer chicken and vegetables to serving platter and serve with warmed tortillas.

STEAK FAJITAS

WHY THIS RECIPE WORKS: Steak fajitas were originally made with skirt steak, but the wider availability of flank steak has made it the cut of choice for this dish. Recipes for fajitas are fairly straightforward—grill the meat and vegetables and serve them in a warm tortilla. But too often, fajitas are lackluster or ruined by unnecessary complexity. We want fajitas that boasted flawless, flavorful meat with a rosy interior and browned crust.

Marinating is often recommended as a way to tenderize flank steak, but we learned that it's plenty tender without a marinade if sliced thin against the grain after being cooked. But we did want to add flavor. A long soak turned the meat mushy, but a squeeze of lime juice and a generous dose of salt and pepper just before grilling added all the extra flavor we wanted. The tried-and-true way of cooking flank steak—over high heat for a short period of time—required no changes. We found that the meat is juicier when allowed to rest after grilling, and that gave us time to grill the vegetables. Served in tortillas with freshly made guacamole, these fajitas delivered on all fronts.

Steak Fajitas

SERVES 8

The ingredients go on the grill in order as the fire dies down: steak over a medium-hot fire, vegetables over a medium fire, and tortillas around the edge of a medium to low fire just to warm them. Make sure to cover the grilled but unsliced flank steak with foil; it will take you at least 10 minutes to get the vegetables and tortillas ready. You can use red, yellow, orange, or green bell peppers in this recipe. When you head outside to grill, bring a clean kitchen towel in which to wrap the tortillas and keep them warm. Chunky Guacamole (page 413) and fresh salsa make good accompaniments.

- 1 (2- to 2½-pound) flank steak, trimmed
- ¼ cup lime juice
- Salt and pepper
- 1 large red onion, peeled and cut into ½-inch-thick rounds (do not separate rings)
- 2 large bell peppers, quartered, stemmed, and seeded
- 8–12 (6-inch) flour tortillas

1A. FOR A CHARCOAL GRILL: Open bottom vent completely. Light large chimney starter mounded with charcoal briquettes (7 quarts). When top coals are partially covered with ash, pour evenly over half of grill. Set cooking grate in place, cover, and open lid vent completely. Heat grill until hot, about 5 minutes.

1B. FOR A GAS GRILL: Turn all burners to high, cover, and heat grill until hot, about 15 minutes.

2. Clean and oil cooking grate. Pat steak dry with paper towels and sprinkle with lime juice, salt, and pepper. Place steak on grill (hot side if using charcoal) and cook (covered if using gas) until well browned on first side, 4 to 7 minutes. Flip steak and continue to cook until meat registers 120 to 125 degrees (for medium-rare) or 130 to 135 degrees (for medium), 3 to 8 minutes. Transfer steak to cutting board, tent loosely with aluminum foil, and let rest for 10 minutes.

NOTES FROM THE TEST KITCHEN

STEMMING AND SEEDING BELL PEPPERS

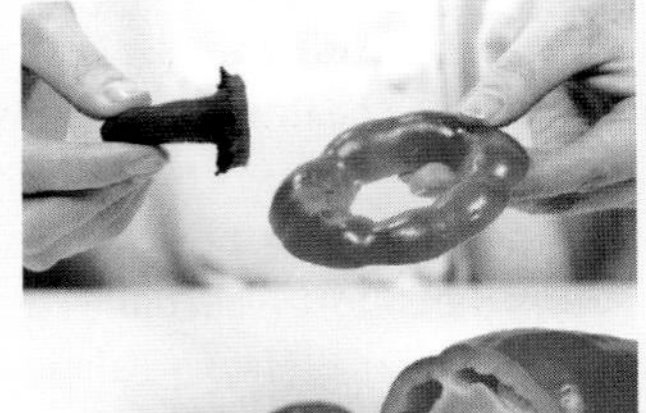

1. Slice ¼ inch from the top and bottom of each pepper and then gently remove the stem from the top lobe.

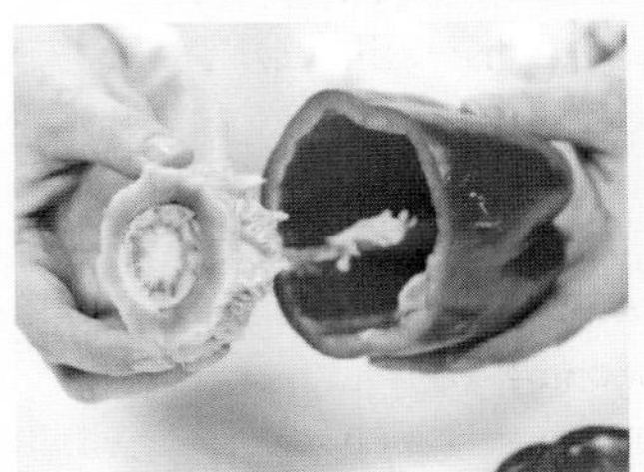

2. Pull the core out of the pepper. Make a slit down one side of the pepper and lay it flat, skin side down, in one long strip.

3. Slide a sharp knife along the inside of the pepper to remove all the ribs and seeds.

3. While steak rests, place onion rounds and peppers (skin side down) on hot side of grill (if using charcoal) or turn all burners to medium (if using gas). Cook until tender and charred on both sides, 8 to 12 minutes, flipping every 3 minutes. Transfer onions and peppers to carving board with beef.

4. Place tortillas in single layer on hot side of grill (if using charcoal) or turn all burners to low (if using gas). Cook until warm and lightly browned, about 20 seconds per side (do not grill too long or tortillas will become brittle). As tortillas are done, wrap in clean kitchen towel or large sheet of foil.

5. Separate onions into rings and slice peppers into ¼-inch strips. Slice steak, against grain, ¼-inch-thick. Transfer beef and vegetables to serving platter and serve with warmed tortillas.

CHICKEN ENCHILADAS

WHY THIS RECIPE WORKS: Chicken enchiladas are a complete meal that offers a rich and complex combination of flavors, textures, and ingredients. The problem with preparing enchiladas at home is that traditional cooking methods require a whole day of preparation. We wanted a recipe for an Americanized version of chicken enchiladas that could be made in 90 minutes from start to finish.

To save time preparing the tortillas, we sprayed them with vegetable oil spray and warmed them on a baking sheet in the oven. We created a quick chili sauce with onions, garlic, spices, and tomato sauce, and to further enhance the sauce's flavor, we poached the chicken right in the sauce. This step also made for moist, flavorful meat. And cheddar cheese spiked with canned jalapeños and fresh cilantro made a rich, flavorful filling.

Chicken Enchiladas with Red Chili Sauce

SERVES 4 TO 5

Monterey Jack can be used instead of cheddar, or for a mellower flavor and creamier texture, try farmer's cheese. Be sure to cool the chicken before filling the tortillas; otherwise the hot filling will make the enchiladas soggy.

SAUCE AND FILLING

- 1½ tablespoons vegetable oil
- 1 medium onion, chopped fine
- 3 medium garlic cloves, minced or pressed through a garlic press (about 1 tablespoon)
- 3 tablespoons chili powder
- 2 teaspoons ground coriander
- 2 teaspoons ground cumin
- 2 teaspoons sugar
- ½ teaspoon table salt
- 12 ounces boneless, skinless chicken thighs (about 4 thighs), trimmed and cut into ¼-inch-wide strips
- 2 (8-ounce) cans tomato sauce
- ¾ cup water
- 8 ounces sharp cheddar cheese (see note), shredded (about 2 cups)
- ½ cup coarsely chopped fresh cilantro leaves
- 1 (4-ounce) can pickled jalapeño chiles, drained and chopped (about ¼ cup)

TORTILLAS AND TOPPINGS

- 10 (6-inch) corn tortillas
- Vegetable oil spray
- 3 ounces sharp cheddar cheese (see note), shredded (about ¾ cup)
- ¾ cup sour cream
- 1 medium, ripe avocado, diced medium (see page 414)
- 5 romaine lettuce leaves, shredded
- Lime wedges

1. FOR THE SAUCE AND FILLING: Heat the oil in a medium saucepan over medium-high heat until shimmering. Add the onion and cook, stirring occasionally, until softened and beginning to brown, about 5 minutes. Add the garlic, chili powder, coriander, cumin, sugar, and salt and cook, stirring constantly, until fragrant, about 30 seconds. Add the chicken and cook, stirring constantly, until coated with the spices, about 30 seconds. Add the tomato sauce and water, stir to separate the chicken pieces, and bring to a simmer. Reduce the heat to medium-low and simmer, uncovered, stirring occasionally, until the chicken is cooked through and the flavors have melded, about 8 minutes. Pour the mixture through a medium-mesh strainer into a medium bowl, pressing on the chicken and onions to extract as much sauce as possible; set the sauce aside. Transfer the chicken mixture to a large plate; place in the freezer for 10 minutes to cool, then combine with the cheddar, cilantro, and jalapeños in a medium bowl.

2. Adjust the oven racks to the upper-middle and lower-middle positions and heat the oven to 300 degrees.

3. TO ASSEMBLE: Smear the bottom of a 13 by 9-inch baking dish with ¾ cup of the chili sauce. Place the tortillas in a single layer on two baking sheets. Spray both sides of the tortillas lightly with vegetable oil spray. Bake until the tortillas are soft and pliable, about 4 minutes. Transfer the warm tortillas to a work surface. Increase the oven temperature to 400 degrees. Spread ⅓ cup of the filling down the center of each tortilla. Roll each tortilla tightly by hand and place, seam side down, side by side on the sauce in the baking dish. Pour the remaining chili sauce over the top of the enchiladas. Use the back of a spoon to spread the sauce so it coats the top of each tortilla. Sprinkle the cheese down the center of the enchiladas.

4. Cover the baking dish with foil. Bake the enchiladas on the lower-middle rack until heated through and the cheese is melted, 20 to 25 minutes. Uncover and serve immediately, passing the sour cream, avocado, lettuce, and lime wedges separately.

ENCHILADAS VERDES

WHY THIS RECIPE WORKS: We love the bright taste of enchiladas verdes. But too often the green chili sauce is watery and lacks good green chile flavor. We wanted to re-create the memorable enchiladas verdes found in good Mexican restaurants: moist, tender chicken and fresh, citrusy flavors wrapped in soft corn tortillas and topped with just the right amount of melted cheese.

The chicken was easy; we poached it in chicken broth enhanced with sautéed onion, garlic, and cumin. The green sauce is based on tomatillos and chiles. Jalapeños and serranos are good for adding heat to a dish, but we wanted a more complex herbal flavor so we opted for poblanos. To get the characteristic char, which Mexican cooks achieve by roasting on a *comal*, we tossed the chiles and fresh tomatillos with a little oil and ran them under the broiler. Pulsed in a food processor and thinned with a bit of the broth left from poaching the chicken, the tomatillos and chiles formed a well-seasoned, chunky sauce. To enrich the filling, we liked pepper Jack cheese—and sprinkled more on top of the dish. To make the tortillas pliable and easy to roll, we picked up the same technique from our Chicken Enchiladas with Red Chili Sauce (page 427): We sprayed them with vegetable oil spray and baked them for a few minutes. The enchiladas required just a brief stint in the oven to heat through and melt the cheese. Garnished with sour cream, scallions, and radishes, these enchiladas may have the authentic restaurant version beat.

Enchiladas Verdes

SERVES 4 TO 6

You can substitute 3 (11-ounce) cans tomatillos, drained and rinsed, for the fresh ones in this recipe. Halve large tomatillos (more than 2 inches in diameter) and place them skin side up for broiling in step 2 to ensure even cooking and charring. If you can't find poblanos, substitute 4 large jalapeño chiles (with seeds and ribs removed). To increase the spiciness of the sauce, reserve some of the chiles' ribs and seeds and add them to the food processor in step 3.

ENCHILADAS

- 4 teaspoons vegetable oil
- 1 medium onion, chopped medium
- 3 medium garlic cloves, minced or pressed through a garlic press (about 1 tablespoon)
- ½ teaspoon ground cumin
- 1½ cups low-sodium chicken broth
- 1 pound boneless, skinless chicken breasts (2 to 3 breasts), trimmed
- 1½ pounds tomatillos (16 to 20 medium), husks and stems removed, rinsed well and dried (see note)
- 3 medium poblano chiles, halved lengthwise, stemmed, and seeded (see note)
- 1–2 teaspoons sugar
- Table salt and ground black pepper
- ½ cup coarsely chopped fresh cilantro leaves
- 8 ounces pepper Jack or Monterey Jack cheese, grated (about 2 cups)
- 12 (6-inch) corn tortillas

GARNISHES

- 2 medium scallions, sliced thin
- Thinly sliced radishes
- Sour cream

1. Adjust the oven racks to the middle and highest positions and heat the broiler. Heat 2 teaspoons of the oil in a medium saucepan over medium heat until shimmering; add the onion and cook, stirring frequently, until golden, 6 to 8 minutes. Add 2 teaspoons of the garlic and the cumin; cook, stirring frequently, until fragrant, about 30 seconds. Decrease the heat to low and stir in the broth. Add the chicken, cover, and simmer until the thickest part of the chicken registers 160 to 165 degrees on an instant-read thermometer, 15 to 20 minutes, flipping the chicken halfway through cooking. Transfer the chicken to a large bowl; place in the refrigerator to cool, about 20 minutes. Remove ¼ cup liquid from the saucepan and set aside; discard the remaining liquid.

2. Meanwhile, toss the tomatillos and poblanos with the remaining 2 teaspoons oil; arrange on a rimmed baking sheet lined with foil, with the poblanos skin side up. Broil until the vegetables blacken and start to soften, 5 to 10 minutes, rotating the pan halfway through cooking. Cool for 10 minutes, then remove the skin from the poblanos (leave the tomatillo skins intact). Transfer the tomatillos and chiles to a food processor. Decrease the oven temperature to 350 degrees. Discard the foil from the baking sheet and set the baking sheet aside for warming the tortillas.

3. Add 1 teaspoon of the sugar, 1 teaspoon salt, the remaining 1 teaspoon garlic, and the reserved ¼ cup cooking liquid to the food processor; pulse until the sauce is somewhat chunky, about 8 pulses. Taste the sauce; season with salt and pepper to taste and adjust tartness by stirring in the remaining sugar, ½ teaspoon at a time. Set the sauce aside (you should have about 3 cups).

4. When the chicken is cool, pull into shreds using your hands or two forks, then chop into small bite-size pieces. Combine the chicken with the cilantro and 1½ cups of the cheese; season with salt to taste.

5. Smear the bottom of a 13 by 9-inch baking dish with ¾ cup of the tomatillo sauce. Place the tortillas in a single layer on two baking sheets. Spray both sides of the tortillas lightly with vegetable oil spray. Bake until the tortillas are soft and pliable, 2 to 4 minutes. Increase the oven temperature to 450 degrees. Place the warm tortillas on the work surface and spread ⅓ cup of the filling down the center of each tortilla. Roll each tortilla tightly by hand and place in the baking dish, seam side down. Pour the remaining tomatillo sauce over the top of the enchiladas. Use the back of a spoon to spread the sauce so that it coats the top of each tortilla. Sprinkle with the remaining ½ cup cheese and cover the baking dish with foil.

6. Bake the enchiladas on the middle oven rack until heated through and the cheese is melted, 15 to 20 minutes. Uncover, sprinkle with the scallions, and serve immediately, passing the radishes and sour cream separately.

SPICY PORK TACOS (AL PASTOR)

WHY THIS RECIPE WORKS: In Mexico, super-thin slices of pork butt and pork fat are marinated in chiles and tomato, stacked and roasted on a spit, and shaved, hot and crispy, into a corn tortilla. To mimic this popular taco filling, which is often garnished with sweet pineapple, without any special equipment, we had to get creative. We braised ½-inch-thick slabs of pork butt in a mix of guajillo chiles, tomatoes, and spices until tender, before basting them with sauce on the grill until crisped and charred. Chopped into bite-size strips and topped with grilled pineapple, our simple homemade spicy pork filling lives up to the original.

Spicy Pork Tacos (al Pastor)

SERVES 6 TO 8

Boneless pork butt is often labeled Boston butt in the supermarket. If you can't find guajillo chiles, New Mexican chiles may be substituted, although the dish may be spicier. To warm tortillas, place them on a plate, cover with a damp dish towel, and microwave for 60 to 90 seconds. Keep tortillas covered and serve immediately.

- 10 large dried guajillo chiles, wiped clean
- 1½ cups water
- 1¼ pounds plum tomatoes, cored and quartered
- 8 garlic cloves, peeled
- 4 bay leaves
- Salt and pepper
- ¾ teaspoon sugar
- ½ teaspoon ground cumin

- ⅛ teaspoon ground cloves
- 1 (3-pound) boneless pork butt roast
- 1 lime, cut into 8 wedges
- ½ pineapple, peeled, cored, and cut into ½-inch-thick rings
- Vegetable oil
- 18 (6-inch) corn tortillas, warmed
- 1 small onion, chopped fine
- ½ cup coarsely chopped fresh cilantro

1. Toast guajillos in large Dutch oven over medium-high heat until softened and fragrant, 2 to 4 minutes. Transfer to large plate and, when cool enough to handle, remove stems.

2. Return toasted guajillos to now-empty Dutch oven, add water, tomatoes, garlic, bay leaves, 2 teaspoons salt, ½ teaspoon pepper, sugar, cumin, and cloves, and bring to simmer over medium-high heat. Cover, reduce heat, and simmer, stirring occasionally, until guajillos are softened and tomatoes mash easily, about 20 minutes.

3. While sauce simmers, trim excess fat from exterior of pork, leaving ¼-inch-thick fat cap. Slice pork against grain into ½-inch-thick slabs.

4. Transfer guajillo-tomato mixture to blender and process until smooth, about 1 minute. Strain puree through fine-mesh strainer, pressing on solids to extract as much liquid as possible. Return puree to pot, submerge pork slices in liquid, and bring to simmer over medium heat. Partially cover, reduce heat, and gently simmer until pork is tender but still holds together, 1½ to 1¾ hours, flipping and rearranging pork halfway through cooking. (Pork can be left in sauce, cooled to room temperature, and refrigerated for up to 2 days.)

5. Transfer pork to large plate, season both sides with salt, and cover tightly with aluminum foil. Whisk sauce to combine. Transfer ½ cup sauce to bowl for grilling; pour off all but ½ cup remaining sauce from pot and reserve for another use. Squeeze 2 lime wedges into sauce in pot and add spent wedges; season with salt to taste.

6A. FOR A CHARCOAL GRILL: Open bottom vent halfway. Light large chimney starter filled with charcoal briquettes (6 quarts). When top coals are partially covered with ash, pour evenly over grill. Set cooking grate in place, cover, and open lid vent halfway. Heat grill until hot, about 5 minutes.

6B. FOR A GAS GRILL: Turn all burners to high, cover, and heat grill until hot, about 15 minutes. Turn all burners to medium.

7. Clean and oil cooking grate. Brush 1 side of pork with ¼ cup reserved sauce. Place pork on 1 side of grill, sauce side down, and cook until well browned and crisp, 5 to 7 minutes. Brush pork with remaining ¼ cup reserved sauce, flip, and continue to cook until second side is well browned and crisp, 5 to 7 minutes longer. Transfer to carving board. Meanwhile, brush both sides of pineapple rings with vegetable oil and season with salt to taste. Place on other half of grill and cook until pineapple is softened and caramelized, 10 to 14 minutes; transfer pineapple to carving board.

8. Coarsely chop grilled pineapple and transfer to serving bowl. Using tongs or carving fork to steady hot pork, slice each piece crosswise into ⅛-inch pieces. Bring remaining ½ cup sauce in pot to simmer, add sliced pork, remove pot from heat, and toss to coat pork well. Season with salt to taste.

9. Spoon small amount of pork into each warm tortilla and serve, passing chopped pineapple, remaining 6 lime wedges, onion, and cilantro separately.

SPICY MEXICAN SHREDDED PORK TOSTADAS

WHY THIS RECIPE WORKS: True Mexican shredded pork, or *tinga*, is a far cry from the bland burrito-joint version often found languishing on steam tables. We set out to perfect the methods that give tinga its characteristic crisp texture and smoky tomato flavor. We wanted tender, full-flavored Mexican shredded pork that we could serve atop crisp corn tortillas or spoon into taco shells.

We trimmed and cubed a Boston butt (chosen for its good marbling and little sinew), then simmered the pieces in water that we flavored with garlic, thyme, and onion. Once the pork was tender, we drained the meat (reserving some of the cooking liquid for the sauce) and returned it to the pot to shred. The meat was so tender, it fell apart with nothing more than the pressure of a potato masher. We then sautéed the meat in a hot frying pan along with the requisite additions of finely chopped onion and oregano. Minutes later, the pork had developed crackling edges crisp enough to survive the final step of simmering in tomato sauce. Unlike American barbecue with its sweet and tangy barbecue sauce, tinga relies on a complex smoke-flavored tomato sauce. For our version, we diluted canned tomato sauce with the reserved flavorful cooking liquid from the pork and added bay leaves for herbal complexity. And for tinga's all-important smokiness, we turned to ground chipotle powder, which was a little harder to find than the other option of canned chipotle chiles in adobo sauce, but had a deeper, more complex flavor.

Spicy Mexican Shredded Pork Tostadas

SERVES 4 TO 6

The trimmed pork should weigh about 1½ pounds. The shredded pork is traditionally served on tostadas (crisp fried corn tortillas), but you can also use the meat in tacos or burritos or simply served over rice. Make sure to buy tortillas made only with corn, lime, and salt—preservatives will compromise quality. We prefer the complex flavor of chipotle powder, but two minced canned chipotle chiles can be used in its place. The pork can be prepared through step 1 and refrigerated in an airtight container for up to 2 days. The tostadas can be made up to a day in advance and stored in an airtight container.

SHREDDED PORK

- 2 pounds boneless pork butt roast, trimmed of excess fat and cut into 1-inch pieces (see note)
- 2 medium onions, 1 quartered and 1 chopped fine
- 5 medium garlic cloves, 3 peeled and smashed and 2 minced or pressed through a garlic press (about 2 teaspoons)
- 4 sprigs fresh thyme
- Table salt
- 2 tablespoons olive oil
- ½ teaspoon dried oregano
- 1 (14.5-ounce) can tomato sauce
- 1 tablespoon ground chipotle powder (see note)
- 2 bay leaves

TOSTADAS

- ¾ cup vegetable oil
- 12 (6-inch) corn tortillas (see note)
- Table salt

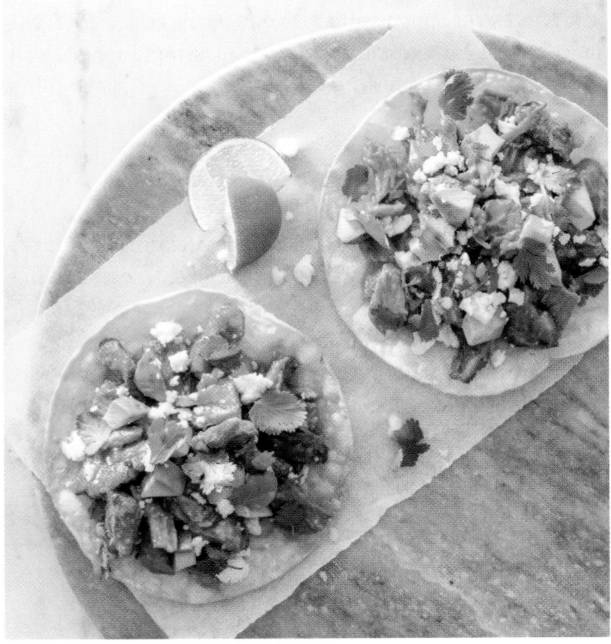

GARNISHES

- Queso fresco or feta cheese
- Fresh cilantro leaves
- Sour cream
- Diced avocado
- Lime wedges

1. FOR THE SHREDDED PORK: Bring the pork, quartered onion, smashed garlic cloves, thyme, 1 teaspoon salt, and 6 cups water to a simmer in a large saucepan over medium-high heat, skimming off any foam that rises to the surface. Reduce the heat to medium-low, partially cover, and cook until the pork is tender, 1¼ to 1½ hours. Drain the pork, reserving 1 cup cooking liquid. Discard the onion, garlic, and thyme. Return the pork to the saucepan and, using a potato masher, mash until shredded into rough ½-inch pieces; set aside.

2. Heat the olive oil in a 12-inch nonstick skillet over medium-high heat until shimmering. Add the shredded pork, chopped onion, and oregano; cook, stirring often, until the pork is well browned and crisp, 7 to 10 minutes. Add the minced garlic and cook until fragrant, about 30 seconds.

3. Stir in the tomato sauce, chipotle powder, reserved pork cooking liquid, and bay leaves; simmer until almost all the liquid has evaporated, 5 to 7 minutes. Remove and discard the bay leaves and season with salt to taste.

4. TO FRY THE TOSTADAS: Heat the vegetable oil in an 8-inch heavy-bottomed skillet over medium heat to 350 degrees. Using a fork, poke the center of each tortilla three or four times (to prevent puffing and allow for even cooking). Fry one at a time, holding a metal potato masher in the upright position on top of the tortilla to keep it submerged, until crisp and lightly browned, 45 to 60 seconds (no flipping is necessary). Drain on a paper towel–lined plate and season with salt to taste. Repeat with the remaining tortillas.

5. TO SERVE: Spoon a small amount of shredded pork onto the center of each tostada and serve, passing the garnishes separately.

MEXICAN PULLED PORK

WHY THIS RECIPE WORKS: Traditional *carnitas*, Mexico's version of pulled pork, is fried in gallons of lard or oil. The results are tasty, but who wants to deal with all that hot fat? We wanted restaurant-style carnitas—tender chunks of lightly crisped, caramelized pork, subtly accented with oregano and citrus—without the hassle of frying.

Our initial recipe for carnitas started by simmering the meat (taste tests proved boneless pork butt had the best flavor) in a seasoned broth in the oven and then sautéing it in some of the rendered fat. The flavor was OK, but too much of the pork flavor was lost when we discarded the cooking liquid. So we reduced the liquid on the stovetop (after the meat had been removed) to the consistency of a thick, syrupy glaze that was perfect for coating the meat. Broiled on a rack set over a baking sheet, the glazed meat developed a wonderfully rich flavor, and the rack allowed the excess fat to drip off. We emulated the flavor of the Mexican sour oranges used in authentic carnitas with a mixture of fresh lime and orange juices. Bay leaves and oregano provided aromatic notes, and cumin brought an earthiness that complemented the other flavors.

Mexican Pulled Pork (Carnitas)

SERVES 6

We like serving carnitas spooned into tacos, but you can also use it as a filling for tamales, enchiladas, and burritos.

PORK

- 1 (3½- to 4-pound) boneless pork butt, fat cap trimmed to ⅛ inch thick, cut into 2-inch chunks
- 1 small onion, peeled and halved
- 2 bay leaves
- 1 teaspoon dried oregano
- 1 teaspoon ground cumin
- Table salt and ground black pepper
- 2 cups water
- 2 tablespoons juice from 1 lime
- 1 medium orange, halved

TORTILLAS AND GARNISHES

- 18 (6-inch) corn tortillas, warmed (see note on page 429)
- Lime wedges
- Minced white or red onion
- Fresh cilantro leaves
- Thinly sliced radishes
- Sour cream

1. Adjust an oven rack to the lower-middle position and heat the oven to 300 degrees. Combine the pork, onion, bay leaves, oregano, cumin, 1 teaspoon salt, ½ teaspoon pepper, water, and lime juice in a large Dutch oven (the liquid should just barely cover the meat). Juice the orange into a medium bowl and remove any seeds (you should have about ⅓ cup juice). Add the juice and spent orange halves to the pot. Bring the mixture to a simmer over medium-high heat, stirring occasionally. Cover the pot and transfer it to the oven; cook until the meat is soft and falls apart when prodded with a fork, about 2 hours, flipping the pieces of meat once during cooking.

2. Remove the pot from the oven and turn the oven to broil. Using a slotted spoon, transfer the pork to a bowl; remove the orange halves, onion, and bay leaves from the cooking liquid and discard (do not skim the fat from the liquid). Place the pot over high heat (use caution, as the handles will be very hot) and simmer the liquid, stirring frequently, until thick and syrupy (a heatproof spatula should leave a wide trail when dragged through the glaze), 8 to 12 minutes. You should have about 1 cup reduced liquid.

3. Using two forks, pull each piece of pork in half. Fold in the reduced liquid; season with salt and pepper to taste. Spread the pork in an even layer on a wire rack set over a rimmed baking sheet or on a broiler pan (the meat should cover almost the entire surface of the rack or broiler pan). Place the baking sheet on the lower-middle oven rack and broil until the top of the meat is well browned (but not charred) and the edges are slightly crisp, 5 to 8 minutes. Using a wide metal spatula, flip the pieces of meat and continue to broil until the top is well browned and the edges are slightly crisp, 5 to 8 minutes longer. Serve immediately with the warm tortillas and garnishes.

MEXICAN RICE

WHY THIS RECIPE WORKS: Rice cooked the Mexican way is a flavorful pilaf-style dish, but we've had our share of soupy, greasy, or just plain bland versions. We wanted tender rice infused with well-balanced fresh flavor.

Texture proved to be the backbone of this dish. To keep the rice grains distinct, we found it important to rinse the rice of excess starch before cooking it. And sautéing the rice in vegetable oil before adding the cooking liquid produced superior grains. The best texture for the rice was achieved by properly balancing the grain-to-liquid ratio. We found that equal portions of chicken broth and fresh tomatoes were ideal for a flavorful liquid base, which we combined in a 2:1 ratio with the rice. To further guarantee the right flavor, color, and texture, we added a little tomato paste and stirred the rice midway through cooking to reincorporate the tomato mixture. The garlic and jalapeños, meanwhile, fared best sautéed and then combined with a raw puree of tomato and onion. More than a garnish, fresh cilantro, minced jalapeño, and squirt of fresh lime juice complemented the richer tones of the cooked tomatoes, garlic, and onions. Our rice was neither greasy nor soggy, and the fresh flavors and easy preparation made it a unique side dish for a weeknight dinner.

Mexican Rice

SERVES 6 TO 8

Because the spiciness of jalapeños varies from chile to chile, we try to control the heat by removing the ribs and seeds (the source of most of the heat) from those chiles that are cooked into the rice. It is important to use an ovensafe pot about 12 inches in diameter so that the rice cooks evenly and in the time indicated. The pot's depth is less important than its diameter; we've successfully used both a straight-sided sauté pan and a Dutch oven. Whichever type of pot you use, it should have a tight-fitting, ovensafe lid. Vegetable broth can be substituted for the chicken broth.

- 2 medium ripe tomatoes (about 12 ounces), cored and quartered
- 1 medium onion, preferably white, peeled and quartered
- 3 medium jalapeño chiles (see note)
- 2 cups long-grain white rice
- ⅓ cup vegetable oil
- 4 medium garlic cloves, minced or pressed through a garlic press (about 4 teaspoons)
- 2 cups low-sodium chicken broth (see note)
- 1 tablespoon tomato paste
- 1½ teaspoons table salt
- ½ cup minced fresh cilantro leaves
- Lime wedges, for serving

1. Adjust an oven rack to the middle position and heat the oven to 350 degrees. Process the tomatoes and onion in a food processor until smooth and thoroughly pureed, about 15 seconds, scraping down the bowl if necessary. Transfer the mixture to a liquid measuring cup; you should have 2 cups (if necessary, spoon off the excess so that the volume equals 2 cups). Remove the ribs and seeds from 2 of the jalapeños and discard; mince the flesh and set aside. Mince the remaining jalapeño, including the ribs and seeds; set aside.

2. Place the rice in a large fine-mesh strainer and rinse under cold running water until the water runs clear, about 1½ minutes. Shake the rice vigorously in the strainer to remove all excess water.

3. Heat the oil in a heavy-bottomed straight-sided 12-inch ovenproof sauté pan or Dutch oven with a tight-fitting lid over medium-high heat for 1 to 2 minutes. Drop 3 or 4 grains of rice into the oil; if the grains sizzle, the oil is ready. Add the rice and fry, stirring frequently, until the rice is light golden and translucent, 6 to 8 minutes. Reduce the heat to medium, add the garlic and seeded minced jalapeños, and cook, stirring constantly, until fragrant, about 1½ minutes. Stir in the pureed tomato mixture, chicken broth, tomato paste, and salt. Increase the heat to medium-high and bring to a boil. Cover the pan and transfer to the oven. Bake until the liquid is absorbed and the rice is tender, 30 to 35 minutes, stirring well after 15 minutes.

4. Stir in the cilantro and reserved minced jalapeño with seeds to taste. Serve immediately, passing the lime wedges separately.

BEST VEGETARIAN CHILI

WHY THIS RECIPE WORKS: Vegetarian chilis are often little more than a mishmash of beans and vegetables. To create a robust, complex-flavored chili—not just a bean and vegetable stew—we found replacements for the different ways in which meat adds depth and savory flavor to chili. Walnuts, soy sauce, dried shiitake mushrooms, and tomatoes added hearty savoriness. Bulgur filled out the chili, giving it a substantial texture. The added oil and nuts lent a richness to the chili, for full, lingering flavor.

Best Vegetarian Chili

SERVES 6 TO 8

We prefer to use whole dried chiles, but the chili can be prepared with jarred chili powder. If using chili powder, grind the shiitakes and oregano and add them to the pot with ¼ cup of chili powder in step 4. Pinto, black, red kidney, small red, cannellini, or navy beans can be used in this recipe, either a single variety or a combination of beans. For a spicier chili use both jalapeños. Serve with diced avocado, chopped red onion, lime wedges, sour cream, and shredded Monterey Jack or cheddar cheese.

- Salt
- 1 pound (2½ cups) dried beans, rinsed and picked over
- 2 dried ancho chiles
- 2 dried New Mexican chiles
- ½ ounce shiitake mushrooms, chopped coarse
- 4 teaspoons dried oregano
- ½ cup walnuts, toasted
- 1 (28-ounce) can diced tomatoes, drained with juice reserved
- 3 tablespoons tomato paste
- 1–2 jalapeño chiles, stemmed and chopped coarse
- 6 garlic cloves, minced
- 3 tablespoons soy sauce
- ¼ cup vegetable oil
- 2 pounds onions, chopped fine
- 1 tablespoon ground cumin
- 7 cups water
- ⅔ cup medium-grain bulgur
- ¼ cup chopped fresh cilantro

1. Bring 4 quarts water, 3 tablespoons salt, and beans to boil in Dutch oven over high heat. Remove pot from heat, cover, and let stand for 1 hour. Drain beans and rinse well.

2. Adjust oven rack to middle position and heat oven to 300 degrees. Arrange ancho and New Mexican chiles on rimmed baking sheet and toast until fragrant and puffed, about 8 minutes. Transfer to plate and let cool, about 5 minutes. Stem and seed toasted chiles. Working in batches, grind toasted chiles, shiitakes, and oregano in spice grinder or with mortar and pestle until finely ground.

3. Process walnuts in food processor until finely ground, about 30 seconds. Transfer to bowl. Process drained tomatoes, tomato paste, jalapeño(s), garlic, and soy sauce in food processor until tomatoes are finely chopped, about 45 seconds, scraping down bowl as needed.

4. Heat oil in Dutch oven over medium-high heat until shimmering. Add onions and 1¼ teaspoons salt; cook, stirring occasionally until onions begin to brown, 8 to 10 minutes. Lower heat to medium, add ground chile mixture and cumin, and cook, stirring constantly, until fragrant, about 1 minute. Add rinsed beans and water and bring to boil. Cover pot, transfer to oven, and cook for 45 minutes.

5. Remove pot from oven. Stir in bulgur, ground walnuts, tomato mixture, and reserved tomato juice. Return to oven and cook until beans are fully tender, about 2 hours.

6. Remove pot from oven, stir chili well, and let stand, uncovered, for 20 minutes. Stir in cilantro and serve. (Chili can be made up to 3 days in advance.)

BASIC CHILI

WHY THIS RECIPE WORKS: Many basic chili recipes yield a pot of under-spiced, under-flavored chili reminiscent of sloppy Joes. We wanted an easy recipe for a basic chili, made with supermarket staples, that would have some heat and great flavors—chili that would please almost everyone.

To start, we added the spices to the pan with the aromatics (bell peppers, onion, and lots of garlic) to get the most flavor, and used commercial chili powder with a boost from more cumin, oregano, cayenne, and coriander. For the meat, we found that 85 percent lean beef gave us full flavor. A combination of diced tomato and tomato puree gave our chili a well-balanced saucy backbone. We added quick-cooking canned red kidney beans with the tomatoes so that they heated through and absorbed flavor. For a rich, thick consistency, we cooked the chili with the lid on for half of the cooking time.

Beef Chili with Kidney Beans

SERVES 8 TO 10

Good choices for condiments include diced fresh tomatoes, diced avocado, sliced scallions, chopped red onion, chopped cilantro leaves, sour cream, and shredded Monterey Jack or cheddar cheese. If you are a fan of spicy food, consider using a little more of the red pepper flakes or cayenne—or both. The flavor of the chili improves with age; if possible, make it a day or up to 3 days in advance and reheat before serving. Leftovers can be frozen for up to 1 month.

- 2 tablespoons vegetable oil
- 2 medium onions, minced (about 2 cups)
- 1 medium red bell pepper, stemmed, seeded, and cut into ½-inch dice
- 6 medium garlic cloves, minced or pressed through a garlic press (about 2 tablespoons)
- ¼ cup chili powder
- 1 tablespoon ground cumin
- 2 teaspoons ground coriander
- 1 teaspoon red pepper flakes (see note)
- 1 teaspoon dried oregano
- ½ teaspoon cayenne pepper (see note)
- 2 pounds 85 percent lean ground beef
- 2 (15-ounce) cans dark red kidney beans, drained and rinsed
- 1 (28-ounce) can diced tomatoes
- 1 (28-ounce) can tomato puree
- Table salt
- Lime wedges, for serving

1. Heat the oil in a large heavy-bottomed nonreactive Dutch oven over medium heat until shimmering but not smoking. Add the onions, bell pepper, garlic, chili powder, cumin, coriander, red pepper flakes, oregano, and cayenne and cook, stirring occasionally, until the vegetables are softened and beginning to brown, about 10 minutes. Increase the heat to medium-high and add half of the beef. Cook, breaking up the pieces with a wooden spoon, until no longer pink and just beginning to brown, 3 to 4 minutes. Add the remaining beef and cook, breaking up the pieces with a wooden spoon, until no longer pink, 3 to 4 minutes.

2. Add the beans, tomatoes with juice, tomato puree, and ½ teaspoon salt. Bring to a boil, then reduce the heat to low and simmer, covered, stirring occasionally, for 1 hour. Remove the lid and continue to simmer for 1 hour longer, stirring occasionally (if the chili begins to stick to the bottom of the pot, stir in ½ cup water and continue to simmer), until the beef is tender and the chili is dark, rich, and slightly thickened. Season with salt to taste. Serve with the lime wedges and condiments (see note), if desired.

CHILI CON CARNE

WHY THIS RECIPE WORKS: Real Texas chili, made with dried chiles rather than chili powder, should have exceptional chile flavor but not overpowering heat, a smooth, rich sauce, and hearty chunks of meat. We wanted to develop the ultimate version. There are many types of dried chiles, and we chose a combination of ancho and New Mexican for a combination of earthy, fruity sweetness and crisp acidity. We got the best flavor by toasting and grinding chiles ourselves. Chuck-eye is our favored cut of beef for stews and it seemed right for our chili. We cut the meat into 1-inch chunks, which gave the chili a hearty texture. Then, we browned the meat in fat rendered from bacon, which added a smoky depth to the dish. From among the many recommended liquids to use in chili con carne, we chose plain old water—everything else diluted or competed with the flavor of the chiles. Although many "authentic" recipes include neither tomatoes nor onions, we found both to be valuable additions. To thicken the chili, we mixed in some masa harina, which also imparted a subtle corn flavor.

Chili con Carne

SERVES 6

To ensure the best chile flavor, we recommend toasting whole dried chiles and grinding them in a minichopper or spice-dedicated coffee grinder, all of which takes only 10 (very well-spent) minutes. Select dried chiles that are moist and pliant, like dried fruit. To toast and grind dried chiles: Place the chiles on a baking sheet in a 350-degree oven until fragrant and puffed, about 6 minutes. Cool, stem, and seed the pods, and tear them into pieces. Place pieces of the pods in a spice grinder and process until powdery, 30 to 45 seconds. For hotter chili, boost the heat with a pinch of cayenne pepper or a dash of hot sauce. Top with any of the following garnishes: chopped fresh cilantro leaves, minced white onion, diced avocado, shredded cheddar or Jack cheese, or sour cream.

- 3 medium ancho pods (about ½ ounce), toasted and ground (see note), or 3 tablespoons ancho chile powder
- 3 medium New Mexican pods (about ¾ ounce), toasted and ground (see note), or 3 tablespoons New Mexican chile powder
- 2 tablespoons cumin seeds, toasted in a dry skillet over medium heat until fragrant, about 4 minutes, and ground
- 2 teaspoons dried oregano, preferably Mexican
- 7½ cups water, plus extra for the masa harina or cornstarch
- 4 pounds beef chuck-eye roast, trimmed of excess fat and cut into 1-inch cubes
- Table salt
- 8 ounces bacon (about 8 slices), cut into ¼-inch pieces
- 1 medium onion, minced
- 5 medium garlic cloves, minced or pressed through a garlic press (about 5 teaspoons)
- 4–5 small jalapeño chiles, stemmed, seeded, and minced
- 1 cup canned crushed tomatoes or plain tomato sauce
- 2 tablespoons juice from 1 lime
- 5 tablespoons masa harina or 3 tablespoons cornstarch
- Ground black pepper

1. Mix the chili powders, cumin, and oregano in a small bowl and stir in ½ cup of the water to form a thick paste; set aside. Toss the beef cubes with 2 teaspoons salt in a large bowl; set aside.

2. Fry the bacon in a large Dutch oven over medium-low heat until the fat renders and the bacon crisps, about 10 minutes. Remove the bacon with a slotted spoon to a paper towel–lined plate; pour all but 2 teaspoons fat from the pot into a small bowl; set aside. Increase the heat to medium-high; sauté the meat in four batches until well browned on all sides, about 5 minutes per batch, adding 2 teaspoons more bacon fat to the pot each time as necessary. Set the browned meat aside in a large bowl.

3. Reduce the heat to medium and add 3 tablespoons more bacon fat to the now-empty pan. Add the onion and sauté until softened, 5 to 6 minutes. Add the garlic and jalapeños and sauté until fragrant, about 1 minute. Add the chili powder mixture and sauté until fragrant, 2 to 3 minutes. Add the reserved bacon and browned beef, the remaining 7 cups water, the crushed tomatoes, and lime juice. Bring to a simmer. Continue to cook at a steady simmer (lowering the heat as necessary) until the meat is tender and the juices are dark and rich and starting to thicken, about 2 hours.

4. Mix the masa harina with ⅔ cup water (or cornstarch with 3 tablespoons water) in a small bowl to form a smooth paste. Increase the heat to medium, stir in the paste, and simmer until thickened, 5 to 10 minutes. Season generously with salt and pepper to taste. Serve immediately or, for best flavor, cool slightly, cover, and refrigerate overnight or for up to 5 days. Reheat before serving.

WHITE CHICKEN CHILI

WHY THIS RECIPE WORKS: Chili made with chicken has become popular as a lighter, fresher alternative to the red kind. Though many recipes produce something more akin to chicken and bean soup, we thought there was potential to develop a rich stew-like chili with moist chicken, tender beans, and a complex flavor profile.

Ground chicken had a spongy texture and crumbly appearance, so we chose bone-in, skin-on breasts, later shredding the meat and discarding the skin and bones, and used the fat rendered from searing them to cook the aromatics. A single type of chile was one-dimensional; we used a combination of jalapeño, Anaheim, and poblano chiles, which have distinct characteristics that complemented one another. Simply sautéing the chiles with the other aromatics left them flat-tasting and too crisp, so we covered the pot and cooked them longer to soften them and deepen their flavors. Canned cannellini beans circumvented the hassle of dried beans and tasted just as good. We tried thickening the chili with masa harina, which we had used as a thickener in other chili recipes, but the texture and flavor didn't work well here. Instead, we pureed some of the chili mixture, beans, and broth, which made the chili thicker without compromising its flavor. To finish, a minced raw jalapeño stirred in before serving provided a shot of fresh chile flavor.

White Chicken Chili

SERVES 6 TO 8

Adjust the heat in this dish by adding the minced ribs and seeds from the jalapeño as directed in step 6. If Anaheim chiles cannot be found, add an additional poblano and jalapeño to the chili. This dish can also be successfully made by substituting chicken thighs for the chicken breasts. If using thighs, increase the cooking time in step 4 to about 40 minutes or

until the chicken registers 175 degrees on an instant-read thermometer. Serve the chili with sour cream, tortilla chips, and lime wedges.

- 3 pounds bone-in, skin-on chicken breast halves, trimmed
- Table salt and ground black pepper
- 1 tablespoon vegetable oil
- 3 medium jalapeño chiles (see note)
- 3 medium poblano chiles (see note), stemmed, seeded, and cut into large pieces
- 3 medium Anaheim chiles (see note), stemmed, seeded, and cut into large pieces
- 2 medium onions, cut into large pieces (about 2 cups)
- 6 medium garlic cloves, minced or pressed through a garlic press (about 2 tablespoons)
- 1 tablespoon ground cumin
- 1½ teaspoons ground coriander
- 2 (15-ounce) cans cannellini beans, drained and rinsed
- 3 cups low-sodium chicken broth
- ¼ cup minced fresh cilantro leaves
- 3 tablespoons juice from 2 limes
- 4 scallions, white and light green parts sliced thin

1. Season the chicken liberally with salt and pepper. Heat the oil in a large Dutch oven over medium-high heat until just smoking. Add the chicken, skin side down, and cook without moving until the skin is golden brown, about 4 minutes. Using tongs, turn the chicken and lightly brown the other side, about 2 minutes. Transfer the chicken to a plate; remove and discard the skin.

2. While the chicken is browning, remove and discard the ribs and seeds from 2 of the jalapeños; mince the flesh. In a food processor, pulse half of the poblanos, Anaheims, and onions until the consistency of chunky salsa, 10 to 12 pulses, scraping down the sides of the workbowl halfway through. Transfer the mixture to a medium bowl. Repeat with the remaining poblanos, Anaheims, and onions; combine with the first batch (do not wash the food processor blade or workbowl).

3. Pour off all but 1 tablespoon of the fat from the Dutch oven (adding more vegetable oil if necessary) and reduce the heat to medium. Add the minced jalapeños, chile-onion mixture, garlic, cumin, coriander, and 1/4 teaspoon salt. Cover and cook, stirring occasionally, until the vegetables soften, about 10 minutes. Remove the pot from the heat.

4. Transfer 1 cup of the cooked vegetable mixture to the now-empty food processor workbowl. Add 1 cup of the beans and 1 cup of the broth and process until smooth, about 20 seconds. Add the vegetable-bean mixture, remaining 2 cups broth, and chicken breasts to the Dutch oven and bring to a boil over medium-high heat. Reduce the heat to medium-low and simmer, covered, stirring occasionally, until the chicken registers 160 degrees (175 degrees if using thighs) on an instant-read thermometer, 15 to 20 minutes (40 minutes if using thighs).

5. Using tongs, transfer the chicken to a large plate. Stir in the remaining beans and continue to simmer, uncovered, until the beans are heated through and the chili has thickened slightly, about 10 minutes.

6. Mince the remaining jalapeño, reserving and mincing the ribs and seeds (see note), and set aside. When cool enough to handle, shred the chicken into bite-size pieces, discarding the bones. Stir the shredded chicken, cilantro, lime juice, scallions, and minced jalapeño (with seeds if desired) into the chili and return to a simmer. Season with salt and pepper to taste and serve.

HUEVOS RANCHEROS

WHY THIS RECIPE WORKS: This Mexican egg dish was devised to use up leftover salsa and tortillas for a quick but filling "rancher-style" breakfast. What you get on this side of the border, however, is often spoiled with unnecessary ingredients and muddy flavors. We wanted to use readily available ingredients to produce as authentic a version of this dish as we could.

The salsa is a crucial element, and we know from experience that jarred salsa can't compare to freshly made, so we looked for ways to maximize the flavor of our supermarket tomatoes.

We found that roasting plum tomatoes turned them more flavorful, and we thought roasting the onion and jalapeños improved their flavor as well. It was difficult to get fried eggs from the skillet onto the tortillas neatly (and without breaking the yolks), so we turned to poaching the eggs for a tidier presentation. We made things even easier by poaching them right in the simmering salsa, saving ourselves a pot to clean in the bargain. To pep up the supermarket tortillas, we brushed them with a little oil, sprinkled them with salt, and toasted them in the oven. Crisp tortillas, creamy eggs, and fiery salsa combined for a great American version of this Mexican classic.

Huevos Rancheros

SERVES 2 TO 4

To save time, make the salsa the day before and store it in the refrigerator. If you like, serve with Refried Beans (recipe follows).

- 3 jalapeño chiles, halved, seeds and ribs removed
- 1½ pounds ripe plum tomatoes (about 6 medium), cored and halved
- ½ medium onion, cut into ½-inch wedges
- 3 tablespoons vegetable oil
- 1 tablespoon tomato paste
- 2 medium garlic cloves, peeled
- Table salt
- ½ teaspoon ground cumin
- ⅛ teaspoon cayenne pepper
- 3 tablespoons minced fresh cilantro leaves
- Ground black pepper
- 1–2 tablespoons juice from 1 lime, plus an additional lime cut into wedges, for serving
- 4 (6-inch) corn tortillas
- 4 large eggs

1. Adjust an oven rack to the middle position and heat the oven to 375 degrees. Mince 1 jalapeño and set aside. In a medium bowl, combine the tomatoes, remaining 2 jalapeños, onion, 2 tablespoons of the oil, the tomato paste, garlic, 1 teaspoon salt, cumin, and cayenne; toss to mix thoroughly. Place the vegetables, cut side down, on a rimmed baking sheet. Roast until the tomatoes are tender and the skins begin to shrivel and brown, 35 to 45 minutes; cool on the baking sheet for 10 minutes. Increase the oven temperature to 450 degrees. Using tongs, transfer the roasted onion, garlic, and jalapeños to a food processor. Process until almost completely broken down, about 10 seconds, pausing halfway through to scrape down the sides of the workbowl with a rubber spatula. Add the tomatoes and process until the salsa is slightly chunky, about 15 seconds more. Add 2 tablespoons of the cilantro, and the reserved minced jalapeño, salt, pepper, and lime juice to taste.

2. Brush both sides of each tortilla lightly with the remaining 1 tablespoon oil, sprinkle both sides with salt, and place on a clean baking sheet. Bake until the tops just begin to color, 5 to 7 minutes; flip the tortillas and continue to bake until golden brown, 2 to 3 minutes more.

3. Meanwhile, bring the salsa to a gentle simmer in a 12-inch nonstick skillet over medium heat. Remove from the heat and make four shallow wells in the salsa with the back of a large spoon. Break 1 egg into a cup, then carefully pour the egg into a well in the salsa; repeat with the remaining 3 eggs. Season each egg with salt and pepper, then cover the skillet and place over medium-low heat. Cook to the desired doneness: 4 to 5 minutes for runny yolks, 6 to 7 minutes for set yolks.

4. Place the tortillas on serving plates; gently scoop one egg onto each tortilla. Spoon the salsa around each egg, covering the tortillas but leaving a portion of the eggs exposed. Sprinkle with the remaining 1 tablespoon cilantro and serve with the lime wedges.

Refried Beans

MAKES ABOUT 3 CUPS

- 2 (15-ounce) cans pinto beans, drained and rinsed
- ¾ cup low-sodium chicken broth
- ½ teaspoon table salt
- 3 ounces (about 3 slices) bacon, minced
- 1 small onion, minced (about ¾ cup)
- 1 large jalapeño chile, stemmed, seeded, and minced (about 2 tablespoons)
- ½ teaspoon ground cumin
- 2 medium garlic cloves, minced or pressed through a garlic press (about 2 teaspoons)
- 2 tablespoons minced fresh cilantro leaves
- 2 teaspoons juice from 1 lime

1. Process all but 1 cup of the beans, the broth, and salt in a food processor until smooth, about 15 seconds, scraping down the sides of the workbowl with a rubber spatula if necessary. Add the remaining beans and pulse until slightly chunky, about 10 pulses.

2. Cook the bacon in a 12-inch nonstick skillet over medium heat until the bacon just begins to brown and most of the fat has rendered, about 4 minutes; transfer to a small bowl lined with a strainer; discard the bacon and add 1 tablespoon bacon fat back to the skillet. Increase the heat to medium-high, add the onion, jalapeño, and cumin, and cook until softened and just starting to brown, 3 to 5 minutes. Stir in the garlic and cook until fragrant, about 30 seconds. Reduce the heat to medium, stir in the pureed beans, and cook until thick and creamy, 4 to 6 minutes. Off the heat, stir in the cilantro and lime juice and serve.

CHAPTER 16

LET'S DO TAKEOUT

CHINESE-STYLE CUCUMBER SALAD

WHY THIS RECIPE WORKS: Smashed cucumbers, or *pai huang gua,* is a Sichuan dish that is typically served with rich, spicy food. We started with English cucumbers, which are nearly seedless and have a thin, crisp skin. Placing them in a zipper-lock bag and smashing them into large, irregular pieces sped up a salting step that helped to expel excess water. The craggy pieces also did a better job of holding on to the dressing. Using black vinegar, an aged rice-based vinegar, added a mellow complexity to the soy and sesame dressing.

Smashed Cucumbers (Pai Huang Gua)

SERVES 4

We recommend using Chinese Chinkiang (or Zhenjiang) black vinegar in this dish because of its complex flavor. If you can't find it, you can substitute 2 teaspoons of rice vinegar and 1 teaspoon of balsamic vinegar. A rasp-style grater makes quick work of turning the garlic into a paste.

- 2 English cucumbers (about 14 ounces each)
- 1½ teaspoons kosher salt
- 4 teaspoons Chinese black vinegar
- 1 teaspoon garlic, minced to paste
- 1 tablespoon soy sauce
- 2 teaspoons toasted sesame oil
- 1 teaspoon sugar
- 1 teaspoon sesame seeds, toasted

1. Trim and discard ends from cucumbers. Cut cucumbers crosswise into three equal lengths. Place pieces in large zipper-lock bag and seal bag. Using small skillet or rolling pin, firmly but gently smash cucumbers until flattened and split lengthwise into 3 to 4 spears. Tear spears into rough 1- to 1½-inch pieces and transfer to colander set in large bowl. Toss pieces with salt and let stand for at least 15 minutes or up to 30 minutes.

2. While cucumber sits, whisk vinegar and garlic together in small bowl; let stand at least 5 minutes or up to 15 minutes.

3. Whisk soy sauce, sesame oil, and sugar into vinegar mixture until sugar has dissolved. Transfer cucumber pieces to medium bowl and discard any extracted liquid. Add dressing and sesame seeds to cucumbers and toss to combine. Serve immediately.

SCALLION PANCAKES

WHY THIS RECIPE WORKS: Scallion pancakes at Chinese restaurants tend to disappoint, so we wondered if we could end up with something better by making our own. The best scallion pancakes are crispy and browned on the outside and multilayered and delicately chewy inside. We opted for a boiling-water dough that stretched easily but did not spring back. To form alternating layers of dough and fat, we rolled the dough into a large, thin round; brushed it with a mixture of oil and flour; and sprinkled it with salt and scallions before rolling it into a cylinder. We coiled the cylinder into a spiral and then rolled it out into a round again. Making a small slit in the center of the pancake prevented steam from building up, so it laid flat and cooked evenly. A stir-together sauce complemented the richness of the pancakes.

Scallion Pancakes with Dipping Sauce

SERVES 4 TO 6

For this recipe we prefer the steady, even heat of a cast-iron skillet. A heavy stainless-steel skillet may be used, but you may have to increase the heat slightly. To make the pancakes ahead of time, stack the uncooked pancakes between layers of parchment paper, wrap them tightly in plastic wrap, and refrigerate for up to 24 hours or freeze for up to 1 month. If frozen, thaw the pancakes in a single layer for 15 minutes before cooking. These pancakes may be served as a side dish or appetizer.

DIPPING SAUCE

- 2 tablespoons soy sauce
- 1 scallion, sliced thin
- 1 tablespoon water
- 2 teaspoons rice vinegar
- 1 teaspoon honey
- 1 teaspoon toasted sesame oil
- Pinch red pepper flakes

PANCAKES

- 1½ cups (7½ ounces) plus 1 tablespoon all-purpose flour
- ¾ cup boiling water
- 7 tablespoons vegetable oil
- 1 tablespoon toasted sesame oil
- 1 teaspoon kosher salt
- 4 scallions, sliced thin

1. FOR THE DIPPING SAUCE: Whisk all ingredients together in small bowl; set aside.

2. FOR THE PANCAKES: Using wooden spoon, mix 1½ cups flour and boiling water in bowl to form rough dough. When cool enough to handle, transfer dough to lightly floured counter and knead until tacky (but not sticky) ball forms, about 4 minutes (dough will not be perfectly smooth). Cover loosely with plastic wrap and let rest for 30 minutes.

3. While dough is resting, stir together 1 tablespoon vegetable oil, sesame oil, and remaining 1 tablespoon flour. Set aside.

4. Place 10-inch cast-iron skillet over low heat to preheat. Divide dough in half. Cover one half of dough with plastic wrap and set aside. Roll remaining dough into 12-inch round on lightly floured counter. Drizzle with 1 tablespoon oil-flour mixture and use pastry brush to spread evenly over entire surface. Sprinkle with ½ teaspoon salt and half of scallions. Roll dough into cylinder. Coil cylinder into spiral, tuck end underneath, and flatten spiral with your palm. Cover with plastic and repeat with remaining dough, oil-flour mixture, salt, and scallions.

5. Roll first spiral into 9-inch round. Cut ½-inch slit in center of pancake. Place 2 tablespoons vegetable oil in skillet and increase heat to medium-low. Place one pancake in skillet (oil should sizzle). Cover and cook, shaking skillet occasionally, until pancake is slightly puffy and golden brown on underside, 1 to 1½ minutes. (If underside is not browned after 1 minute, turn heat up slightly. If it is browning too quickly, turn heat down slightly.) Drizzle 1 tablespoon vegetable oil over pancake. Use pastry brush to distribute over entire surface. Carefully flip pancake. Cover and cook, shaking skillet occasionally, until second side is golden brown, 1 to 1½ minutes. Uncover skillet and continue to cook until bottom is deep golden brown and crispy, 30 to 60 seconds longer. Flip and cook until deep golden brown and crispy, 30 to 60 seconds. Transfer to wire rack. Repeat with remaining 3 tablespoons vegetable oil and remaining pancake. Cut each pancake into 8 wedges and serve, passing dipping sauce separately.

NOTES FROM THE TEST KITCHEN

MAKING SCALLION PANCAKES

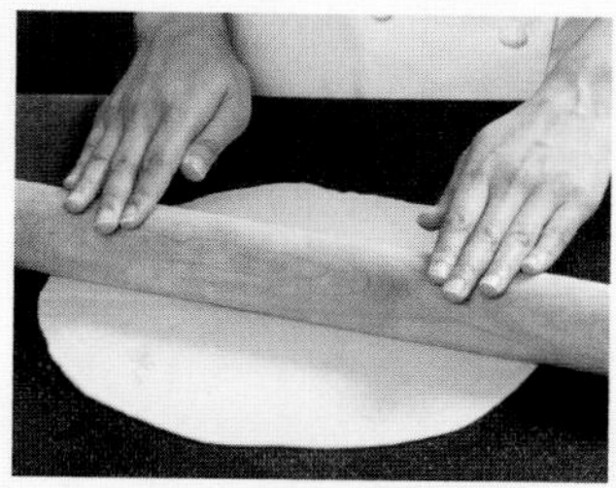

1. Roll dough into 12-inch round.

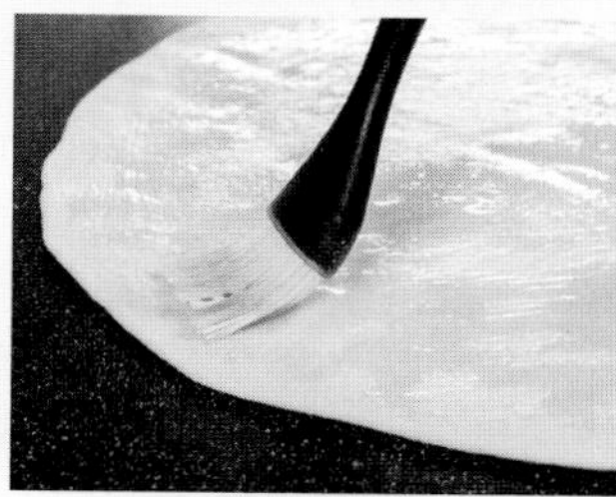

2. Brush round with oil and flour; sprinkle with salt and scallions.

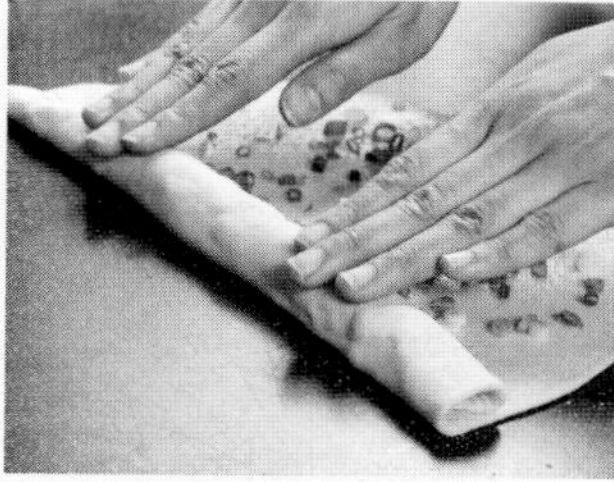

3. Roll up round into cylinder.

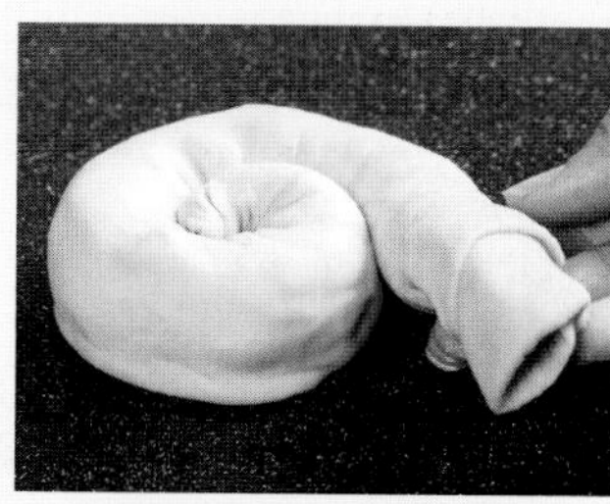

4. Coil cylinder, tucking end underneath, then flatten.

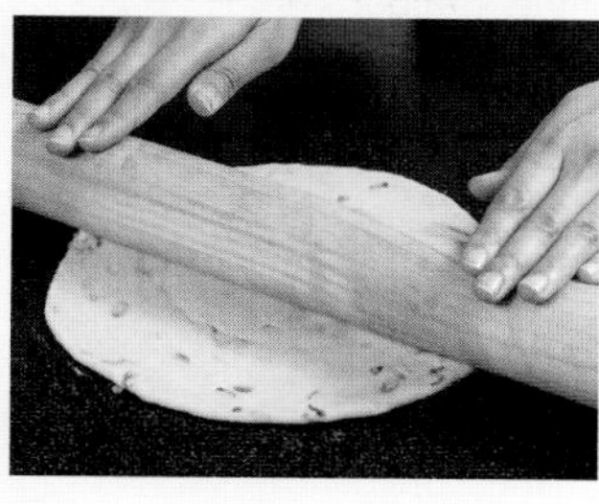

5. Roll out flattened spiral into 9-inch round; cut slit.

NOTES FROM THE TEST KITCHEN

WRAPPING POTSTICKERS

The instructions below are for round wrappers, our preferred shape. If using square wrappers, fold diagonally into a triangle (step 2) and proceed with the recipe. For rectangular wrappers, fold in half lengthwise.

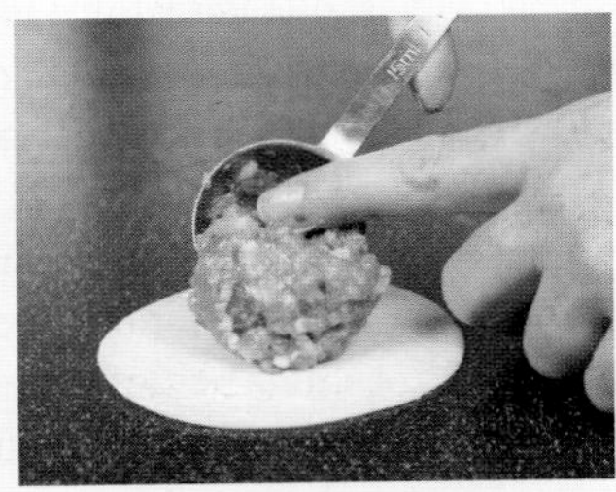

1. Place a rounded tablespoon of the filling in the center of each gyoza wrapper.

2. After moistening the edge of the wrapper, fold it in half to make a half-moon shape.

3. With your forefinger and thumb, pinch the dumpling closed, pressing out any air pockets.

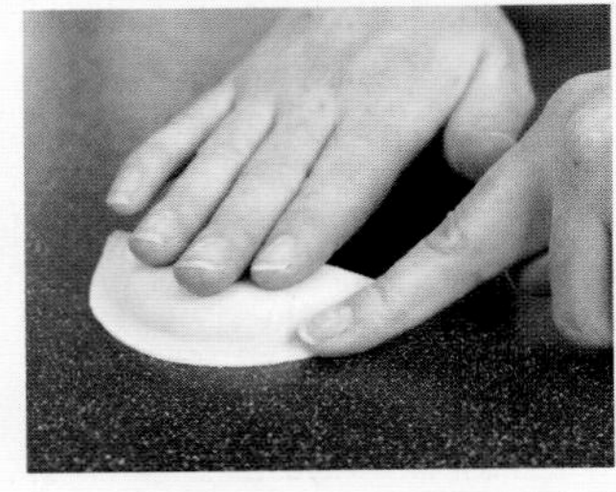

4. Place the dumpling on its side and press gently to flatten the bottom.

PERFECT POTSTICKERS

WHY THIS RECIPE WORKS: Too often, potstickers are dense, flavorless meatballs wrapped in a doughy blanket. We wanted soft, savory pillows filled with tender ground meat and crunchy cabbage and spiked with a pleasing hit of garlic, ginger, and soy. And we weren't willing to make wrappers from scratch. To lighten up the filling a bit, we increased the amount of cabbage, after first salting and draining it to get rid of excess moisture, and then added lightly beaten egg whites. For the wrappers, we found that store-bought gyoza-style wrappers and wonton wrappers both made terrific potstickers, although tasters preferred the slightly chewy texture of the gyoza-style. To keep the filling in place and the wrapper from puffing up and away from the meat during cooking, we found it best to fold each meat-filled wrapper into a half-moon, pinch the middle closed, then carefully press out any air while sealing the edges. Our final challenge was the cooking method. A sequence of browning, steaming, then cranking up the heat produced potstickers with a perfect balance of soft and crispy textures.

Potstickers with Scallion Dipping Sauce

MAKES 24 DUMPLINGS

We prefer to use gyoza wrappers. You can substitute wonton wrappers, but the cooking time and recipe yield will vary. Potstickers are best served hot from the skillet; we recommend that you serve the first batch immediately, then cook the second batch.

SCALLION DIPPING SAUCE

- ¼ cup soy sauce
- 2 tablespoons rice vinegar
- 2 tablespoons mirin or sweet sherry
- 2 tablespoons water
- 1 teaspoon chili oil (optional)
- ½ teaspoon toasted sesame oil
- 1 scallion, minced

POTSTICKERS

- 12 ounces napa cabbage (½ medium head), cored and minced
- ¾ teaspoon table salt
- 12 ounces ground pork
- 4 scallions, minced
- 2 large egg whites, lightly beaten
- 4 teaspoons soy sauce
- 1½ teaspoons minced or grated fresh ginger
- 1 medium garlic clove, minced or pressed through a garlic press (about 1 teaspoon)
- ⅛ teaspoon ground black pepper
- 24 round gyoza wrappers (see note)
- 4 teaspoons peanut or vegetable oil

1. FOR THE SAUCE: Combine all the ingredients in a small bowl and set aside. (The sauce can be refrigerated in an airtight container for up to 24 hours.)

2. FOR THE FILLING: Toss the cabbage and salt together in a colander set over a bowl and let sit until the cabbage begins to wilt, about 20 minutes. Press the cabbage gently with a rubber spatula to squeeze out excess moisture, then transfer to a medium bowl. Stir the pork, scallions, egg whites, soy sauce, ginger, garlic, and pepper into the cabbage until combined. Cover and refrigerate until the mixture is cold, at least 30 minutes or up to 24 hours.

3. Working with 4 wrappers at a time (keep the remaining wrappers covered with plastic wrap), follow the photos on page 442 to fill, seal, and shape the dumplings using a generous 1 tablespoon of the chilled filling per dumpling. Transfer the dumplings to a baking sheet. (The filled dumplings can be refrigerated for up to 24 hours in a single layer on a baking sheet wrapped tightly with plastic wrap or frozen for up to 1 month. Once frozen, the dumplings can be transferred to a zipper-lock bag to save space in the freezer; do not thaw before cooking.)

4. Brush 2 teaspoons of the peanut oil over the bottom of a 12-inch nonstick skillet and arrange half of the dumplings in the skillet, with a flat side facing down (overlapping just slightly, if necessary). Place the skillet over medium-high heat and cook the dumplings, without moving, until golden brown on the bottom, about 5 minutes.

5. Reduce the heat to low, add ½ cup water, and cover immediately. Cook until most of the water is absorbed and the wrappers are slightly translucent, about 10 minutes. Uncover, increase the heat to medium-high, and cook, without stirring, until the dumpling bottoms are well browned and crisp, 3 to 4 minutes. Slide the dumplings from the skillet onto a paper towel–lined plate, browned side down, and let drain briefly.

6. Transfer the dumplings to a platter and serve with the sauce. Let the skillet cool until just warm, then wipe out the skillet with a wad of paper towels and repeat with the remaining peanut oil and dumplings.

SHU MAI

WHY THIS RECIPE WORKS: Every so often we'll land on an exemplary version of shu mai (steamed Chinese dumplings)—one that boasts a tender, thin skin and a moist, flavorful filling. Our goal was to replicate this version at home. Our favorite restaurant dumplings rely on coarse-ground pork and shrimp. To ensure proper flavor and texture, we chose to chop the pork (boneless country-style spareribs) in a food processor rather than relying on supermarket ground pork which is often inconsistent. To prevent the meat from drying out during steaming, we mixed in a little powdered gelatin dissolved in soy sauce. As for the shrimp, we added that to the food processor, too. Dried shiitake mushrooms, minced cilantro, fresh ginger, and water chestnuts were just a few of the ingredients we relied on to round out our flavorful filling. We chose widely available egg roll skins and cut them into rounds with a biscuit cutter.

Once we added the filling and gathered the edges of the wrappers up around each one, we steamed our dumplings in a steamer basket. Served with a hot chili sauce, our dumplings were full-flavored and virtually foolproof.

Steamed Chinese Dumplings (Shu Mai)

MAKES ABOUT 40 DUMPLINGS

Do not trim the excess fat from the spareribs, as the fat contributes flavor and moistness. Use any size shrimp except popcorn shrimp; there's no need to halve shrimp smaller than 26 to 30 per pound before processing. The dumplings may be frozen for up to 3 months; cook straight from the freezer for about an extra 5 minutes. Shu mai are traditionally served with a spicy chili oil (recipe follows), or use store-bought.

- 2 tablespoons soy sauce
- ½ teaspoon unflavored powdered gelatin
- 1 pound boneless country-style pork spareribs, cut into 1-inch pieces (see note)
- ½ pound shrimp, peeled, deveined (see page 240), tails removed, and halved lengthwise (see note)
- ¼ cup chopped water chestnuts
- 4 dried shiitake mushroom caps (about ¾ ounce), soaked in hot water for 30 minutes, squeezed dry, and cut into ¼-inch dice
- 2 tablespoons cornstarch
- 2 tablespoons minced fresh cilantro leaves
- 1 tablespoon toasted sesame oil
- 1 tablespoon dry sherry or Chinese rice cooking wine (Shaoxing)
- 1 tablespoon rice wine vinegar
- 2 teaspoons sugar
- 2 teaspoons grated fresh ginger
- ½ teaspoon table salt
- ½ teaspoon ground black pepper
- 1 (1 pound) package 5½-inch square egg roll wrappers
- ¼ cup finely grated carrot (optional)

1. Combine the soy sauce and gelatin in a small bowl. Set aside to allow the gelatin to bloom, about 5 minutes.

2. Meanwhile, place half of the pork in a food processor and pulse until coarsely ground into pieces that are about ⅛ inch, about 10 pulses; transfer to a large bowl. Add the shrimp and remaining pork to the food processor and pulse until coarsely chopped into pieces that are about ¼ inch, about 5 pulses. Transfer to the bowl with the coarsely ground pork. Stir in the soy sauce mixture, water chestnuts, mushrooms, cornstarch, cilantro, sesame oil, cooking wine, vinegar, sugar, ginger, salt, and pepper until well combined.

3. Line a large baking sheet with parchment paper. Divide the egg roll wrappers into three stacks (six to seven per stack). Using a 3-inch biscuit cutter, cut two 3-inch rounds from each stack of egg roll wrappers (you should have 40 to 42 rounds). Cover the rounds with moist paper towels to prevent drying.

4. Working with six rounds at a time, brush the edges of each round lightly with water. Place a heaping tablespoon of filling in the center of each round. Following the photos, form the dumplings by crimping the wrapper around the sides of the filling and leaving the top exposed. Transfer to the prepared baking sheet, cover with a damp kitchen towel, and repeat with the remaining wrappers and filling. Top the center of each dumpling with a pinch of grated carrot (if using).

5. Cut a piece of parchment paper slightly smaller than the diameter of a steamer basket and place in the basket. Poke about 20 small holes in the parchment to allow steam to pass through and lightly coat with vegetable oil spray. Place batches of the dumplings on the parchment, making sure they are not touching. Set the steamer basket over simmering water and cook, covered, until no longer pink, 8 to 10 minutes. Serve immediately with chili oil.

Chili Oil

MAKES ABOUT ½ CUP

- 1 tablespoon soy sauce
- 2 teaspoons sugar
- ½ teaspoon table salt
- ½ cup peanut oil
- ¼ cup red pepper flakes
- 2 medium garlic cloves, peeled

Combine the soy sauce, sugar, and salt in a small bowl; set aside. Heat the oil in a small saucepan over medium heat until just shimmering and it registers 300 degrees on an instant-read thermometer. Remove the pan from the heat and stir in the red pepper flakes, garlic, and soy mixture. Let cool to room temperature, stirring occasionally, about 1 hour. Discard the garlic before storing.

NOTES FROM THE TEST KITCHEN

FILLING AND FORMING SHU MAI

1. Brush the edges of the dumpling wrapper lightly with water. Place a heaping tablespoon of filling in the center of each wrapper.

2. Pinch two opposing sides of the wrapper with your fingers. Rotate the dumpling 90 degrees, and, again, pinch the opposing sides of the wrapper with your fingers.

3. Continue to pinch the dumpling until you have eight equidistant pinches around the circumference of the dumpling.

4. Gather up the sides of the dumpling and squeeze gently at the top to create a "waist."

5. Hold the dumpling in your hand and gently but firmly pack the filling into the dumpling with a butter knife.

SHRIMP TEMPURA

WHY THIS RECIPE WORKS: A few preliminary attempts at making tempura made us see why some Japanese chefs devote their entire careers to this one technique. Success hinges almost entirely on the batter—which is maddeningly hard to get right. We wanted a recipe for perfectly cooked shrimp tempura—light, crisp, and so fresh-tasting that it barely seemed fried.

We settled on using the largest shrimp available, since it's easy to overcook small shrimp. Instead of a wok, we substituted a large Dutch oven, the test kitchen's preferred deep-frying vessel. Cooking the tempura in 400-degree oil also helped limit grease absorption. To prevent the batter from clumping on the inside curl of the shrimp, we made two shallow cuts on the underside of its flesh. For the batter, we replaced a bit of the flour with cornstarch to improve the structure and lightness. For a super tender coating, we used a combination of seltzer and vodka instead of the traditional tap water. Seltzer is a little more acidic than tap water and therefore slows down gluten development, while the vodka prevents the formation of gluten. Our tempura was now light and crisp with the essence of sweet, tender shrimp.

Shrimp Tempura

SERVES 8

Do not omit the vodka; it is critical for a crisp coating. For safety, use a Dutch oven with a capacity of at least 7 quarts. Be sure to begin mixing the batter when the oil reaches 385 degrees (the final temperature should reach 400 degrees). It is important to maintain a high oil temperature throughout cooking. If you are unable to find colossal shrimp (8 to 12 per pound), jumbo (16 to 20 per pound) or extra-large (21 to 25 per pound) may be substituted. Fry smaller shrimp in three batches, reducing the cooking time to 1½ to 2 minutes per batch.

- 3 quarts peanut or vegetable oil
- 1½ pounds colossal shrimp (8 to 12 per pound), peeled and deveined (see page 240), tails left on (see note)
- 1½ cups (7½ ounces) unbleached all-purpose flour
- ½ cup cornstarch
- 1 cup vodka (see note)
- 1 large egg
- 1 cup seltzer water
- Table salt
- 1 recipe Scallion Dipping Sauce (page 442)

1. Adjust an oven rack to the upper-middle position and heat the oven to 200 degrees. In a large, heavy Dutch oven fitted with a clip-on candy thermometer, heat the oil over high heat to 385 degrees, 18 to 22 minutes.

2. While the oil heats, make two shallow cuts about ¼ inch deep and 1 inch apart on the underside of each shrimp. Whisk the flour and cornstarch together in a large bowl. Whisk the vodka and egg together in a second large bowl, then whisk in the seltzer water.

3. When the oil reaches 385 degrees, whisk the vodka mixture into the bowl with the flour mixture until just combined (it is OK if small lumps remain). Submerge half of the shrimp in the batter. Using tongs, remove the shrimp from the batter one at a time, allowing the excess batter to drip off, and carefully place in the oil (the temperature should now be at 400 degrees). Fry, stirring with a chopstick or wooden skewer to prevent sticking, until light brown, 2 to 3 minutes. Using a slotted spoon, transfer the shrimp to a paper towel–lined plate and sprinkle with salt. Once the paper towels absorb the excess oil, transfer the shrimp to a wire rack set over a rimmed baking sheet and place in the oven to keep warm.

4. Return the oil to 400 degrees, about 4 minutes, then repeat with the remaining shrimp. Serve with the dipping sauce.

KOREAN RICE BOWL

WHY THIS RECIPE WORKS: The comforting combination of rice, vegetables, eggs, spicy sauce, and a crisp crust in Korean rice bowls, also known as *dolsot bibimbap*, is a restaurant favorite, and we wanted an efficient way to make it at home. Unfortunately, making bibimbap requires special stone bowls, a lot of sautéing, and a lot of knife work. To make a more approachable, family-style bibimbap, we substituted one enameled cast-iron Dutch oven for a set of stone bowls. To shorten the prep time and simplify the knife work involved, we decided to make three sautéed vegetable toppings instead of the usual six or more. We also turned the pickles, sauce, and vegetables into make-ahead options. Though it's traditional to rinse the rice before steaming it, after side-by-side tests we decided that skipping the rinsing saved time and ultimately made no discernible difference to the finished dish. A quickly pickled mixture of bean sprouts and cucumbers added crisp brightness in lieu of traditional kimchi.

Korean Rice Bowl (Dolsot Bibimbap)

SERVES 6

For a quick dinner, prepare the pickles, chile sauce, and vegetables a day ahead (warm the vegetables to room temperature in the microwave before adding them to the rice). You can also substitute store-bought kimchi for the pickles to save time. The Korean chile paste *gochujang* is sold in Asian markets and some supermarkets. If you can't find it, an equal amount of Sriracha can be substituted. But because Sriracha is more watery than gochujang, omit the water from the chile sauce and stir just 1 tablespoon of sauce into the rice in step 9. For a true bibimbap experience, bring the pot to the table before stirring the vegetables into the rice in step 9.

PICKLES

- 1 cup cider vinegar
- 2 tablespoons sugar
- 1½ teaspoons salt
- 1 cucumber, peeled, quartered lengthwise, seeded, and sliced thin on bias
- 4 ounces (2 cups) bean sprouts

CHILE SAUCE

- ¼ cup gochujang
- 3 tablespoons water
- 2 tablespoons toasted sesame oil
- 1 teaspoon sugar

RICE

- 2½ cups short-grain white rice
- 2½ cups water
- ¾ teaspoon salt

VEGETABLES

- ½ cup water
- 3 scallions, minced
- 3 tablespoons soy sauce
- 3 garlic cloves, minced
- 1 tablespoon sugar
- 1 tablespoon vegetable oil
- 3 carrots, peeled and shredded (2 cups)
- 8 ounces shiitake mushrooms, stemmed, caps sliced thin
- 1 (10-ounce) bag curly-leaf spinach, stemmed and chopped coarse

BIBIMBAP

- 2 tablespoons plus 2 teaspoons vegetable oil
- 1 tablespoon toasted sesame oil
- 4 large eggs

1. FOR THE PICKLES: Whisk vinegar, sugar, and salt together in medium bowl. Add cucumber and bean sprouts and toss to combine. Gently press on vegetables to submerge. Cover and refrigerate for at least 30 minutes or up to 24 hours.

2. FOR THE CHILE SAUCE: Whisk gochujang, water, oil, and sugar together in small bowl. Cover and set aside.

3. FOR THE RICE: Bring rice, water, and salt to boil in medium saucepan over high heat. Cover, reduce heat to low, and cook for 7 minutes. Remove rice from heat and let sit, covered, until tender, about 15 minutes.

4. FOR THE VEGETABLES: While rice cooks, stir together water, scallions, soy sauce, garlic, and sugar. Heat 1 teaspoon oil in Dutch oven over high heat until shimmering. Add carrots and stir until coated. Add ⅓ cup scallion mixture and cook, stirring frequently, until carrots are slightly softened and moisture has evaporated, 1 to 2 minutes. Using slotted spoon, transfer carrots to small bowl.

5. Heat 1 teaspoon oil in now-empty pot until shimmering. Add mushrooms and stir until coated with oil. Add ⅓ cup scallion mixture and cook, stirring frequently, until mushrooms are tender and moisture has evaporated, 3 to 4 minutes. Using slotted spoon, transfer mushrooms to second small bowl.

6. Heat remaining 1 teaspoon oil in now-empty pot until shimmering. Add spinach and remaining ⅓ cup scallion mixture and stir to coat spinach. Cook, stirring frequently, until spinach is completely wilted but still bright green, 1 to 2 minutes. Using slotted spoon, transfer spinach to third small bowl. Discard any remaining liquid and wipe out pot with paper towel.

7. FOR THE BIBIMBAP: Heat 2 tablespoons vegetable oil and sesame oil in now-empty pot over high heat until shimmering. Carefully add cooked rice and gently press into even layer. Cook, without stirring, until rice begins to form crust on bottom of pot, about 2 minutes. Using slotted spoon, transfer carrots, spinach, and mushrooms to pot and arrange in piles that cover surface of rice. Reduce heat to low.

8. While crust forms, heat remaining 2 teaspoons vegetable oil in 10-inch nonstick skillet over low heat for 5 minutes. Crack eggs into small bowl. Pour eggs into skillet; cover and cook (about 2 minutes for runny yolks, 2½ minutes for soft but set yolks, and 3 minutes for firmly set yolks). Slide eggs onto vegetables in pot.

9. Drizzle 2 tablespoons chile sauce over eggs. Without disturbing crust, use wooden spoon to stir rice, vegetables, and eggs until combined. Just before serving, scrape large pieces of crust from bottom of pot and stir into rice. Serve in individual bowls, passing pickles and extra chile sauce separately.

CHINESE CHICKEN LETTUCE WRAPS

WHY THIS RECIPE WORKS: This dish, popularized by chain restaurants, is based on a Cantonese dish called *sung choy bao.* Most recipes for this dish suffer from a similar fate—stringy, tasteless meat drowned in a bland sauce. To remedy this, we started with flavorful chicken thighs and marinated them in soy sauce and rice wine. To keep the meat from drying out when stir-fried, we coated it in a velvetizing cornstarch slurry, which helped it retain moisture as it cooked.

Chinese Chicken Lettuce Wraps

SERVES 4 AS A MAIN DISH OR 6 AS AN APPETIZER

To make it an entrée, serve this dish with Basic White Rice (page 453).

CHICKEN

- 1 pound boneless, skinless chicken thighs, trimmed and cut into 1-inch pieces
- 2 teaspoons Chinese rice wine or dry sherry
- 2 teaspoons soy sauce
- 2 teaspoons toasted sesame oil
- 2 teaspoons cornstarch

SAUCE

- 3 tablespoons oyster sauce
- 1 tablespoon Chinese rice wine or dry sherry
- 2 teaspoons soy sauce
- 2 teaspoons toasted sesame oil
- ½ teaspoon sugar
- ¼ teaspoon red pepper flakes

STIR-FRY

- 2 tablespoons vegetable oil
- 2 celery ribs, cut into ¼-inch pieces
- 6 ounces shiitake mushrooms, stemmed and sliced thin
- ½ cup water chestnuts, cut into ¼-inch pieces
- 2 scallions, white parts minced, green parts sliced thin
- 2 garlic cloves, minced
- 1 head Bibb lettuce (8 ounces), washed and dried, leaves separated and left whole
- Hoisin sauce

1. FOR THE CHICKEN: Place chicken pieces on large plate in single layer. Freeze meat until firm and starting to harden around edges, about 20 minutes.

2. Whisk rice wine, soy sauce, sesame oil, and cornstarch together in bowl. Pulse half of meat in food processor until coarsely chopped into ¼- to ⅛-inch pieces, about 10 pulses. Transfer meat to bowl with rice wine mixture and repeat with remaining chunks. Toss chicken to coat and refrigerate for 15 minutes.

3. FOR THE SAUCE: Whisk all ingredients together in bowl; set aside.

4. FOR THE STIR-FRY: Heat 1 tablespoon vegetable oil in 12-inch nonstick skillet over high heat until smoking. Add chicken and cook, stirring constantly, until opaque, 3 to 4 minutes. Transfer to bowl and wipe out skillet.

5. Heat remaining 1 tablespoon vegetable oil in now-empty skillet over high heat until smoking. Add celery and mushrooms; cook, stirring constantly, until mushrooms have reduced in size by half and celery is crisp-tender, 3 to 4 minutes. Add water chestnuts, scallion whites, and garlic; cook, stirring constantly, until fragrant, about 1 minute. Whisk sauce to recombine. Return chicken to skillet; add sauce and toss to combine. Spoon into lettuce leaves and sprinkle with scallion greens. Serve, passing hoisin sauce separately.

THAI PORK LETTUCE WRAPS

WHY THIS RECIPE WORKS: The classic Thai salad, *larb,* is made with finely chopped meat and nutty rice powder tossed with fresh herbs and a light dressing that embodies the cuisine's signature balance of sweet, sour, hot, and salty flavors. We aimed to develop a home-cook-friendly recipe.

Americanized recipes typically call for ground pork, but inconsistent results with supermarket ground pork inspired us to grind our own, using pork tenderloin and a food processor. To impart flavor and moisture to this lean cut, we marinated the meat in fish sauce. Toasted rice powder, which adds a nutty flavor and texture to the pork, can be found in Asian markets, but we found it was easier to just make our own by toasting rice until golden brown and grinding it in a mini food processor or with a mortar and pestle. As for the aromatic components, we found that the pungency of sliced shallots and the bright flavor of chopped mint and cilantro yielded a very flavorful salad without a trip to a specialty store. For serving, the pork is spooned into lettuce leaves and wrapped. We preferred the crisp spine, tender leaf, and mild taste of Bibb lettuce.

Thai Pork Lettuce Wraps

SERVES 6

We prefer natural pork in this recipe. If using enhanced pork (pork that has been injected with a salt solution to increase moistness and flavor), skip the marinating in step 1 and reduce the amount of fish sauce to 2 tablespoons, adding it all in step 4.

1 (1-pound) pork tenderloin, trimmed of silver skin and fat, cut into 1-inch chunks, and frozen for 20 minutes (see note)
2½ tablespoons fish sauce
1 tablespoon white rice
¼ cup low-sodium chicken broth
3 medium shallots, peeled and sliced into thin rings (about ½ cup)
3 tablespoons roughly chopped fresh mint leaves
3 tablespoons roughly chopped fresh cilantro leaves
3 tablespoons juice from 2 limes
2 teaspoons sugar
¼ teaspoon red pepper flakes
1 head Bibb lettuce, washed and dried, leaves separated and left whole

1. Pulse half of the pork in a food processor until coarsely chopped, about 6 pulses. Transfer the ground pork to a medium bowl and repeat with the remaining chunks. Stir 1 tablespoon of the fish sauce into the ground pork, cover, refrigerate, and let marinate for 15 minutes.

2. Toast the rice in a small skillet over medium-high heat, stirring constantly, until deep golden brown, about 5 minutes. Transfer to a small bowl and cool for 5 minutes. Grind the rice with a spice grinder, mini food processor, or mortar and pestle until it resembles fine meal, 10 to 30 seconds (you should have about 1 tablespoon rice powder).

3. Bring the broth to a simmer in a 12-inch nonstick skillet over medium-high heat. Add the pork and cook, stirring frequently, until about half of the pork is no longer pink, about 2 minutes. Sprinkle 1 teaspoon of the rice powder over the pork and continue to cook, stirring constantly, until the remaining pork is no longer pink, 1 to 1½ minutes longer. Transfer the pork to a large bowl and cool for 10 minutes.

4. Add the remaining 1½ tablespoons fish sauce, remaining 2 teaspoons rice powder, the shallots, mint, cilantro, lime juice, sugar, and red pepper flakes to the pork and toss to combine. Serve with the lettuce leaves, spooning the meat into the leaves at the table.

BEEF SATAY

WHY THIS RECIPE WORKS: This Southeast Asian street food should be simple enough, but more often than not it is tough, bland, and boring. We wanted tender meat that could easily be pulled apart into small bites right off the skewer, with great Southeast Asian flavors like garlic, chiles, and cilantro.

Choosing the right cut of meat proved to be more about texture than flavor. Flank steak was the winner. We used two techniques to slice it, first freezing the meat to firm it up enough to slice cleanly, then cutting the beef across the grain to keep it tender. Since the meat was so thin, cooking it was a breeze. Placing the skewered meat on a wire rack and cooking it 6 inches from the broiler's heating element proved just right. We found our marinade ingredients in the supermarket (Asian chili sauce is now commonly available) and added generous amounts of cilantro and garlic.

Beef Satay

SERVES 8 TO 10

Asian chili sauce, also called Sriracha, is available in most supermarkets. Use 6-inch-long skewers for this recipe; you'll need about 24.

¼ cup soy sauce
¼ cup peanut or vegetable oil
¼ cup packed dark brown sugar
¼ cup minced fresh cilantro leaves
4 scallions, sliced thin
2 tablespoons Asian chili sauce, or more to taste (see note)
2 medium garlic cloves, minced or pressed through a garlic press (about 2 teaspoons)
1 (1½-pound) flank steak, trimmed, halved lengthwise, frozen for 30 minutes, and sliced across the grain into ¼-inch-thick strips
1 recipe Spicy Peanut Dipping Sauce (recipe follows)

1. Combine the soy sauce, oil, sugar, cilantro, scallions, chili sauce, and garlic in a large bowl. Stir in the beef, cover, and refrigerate for 1 hour.

2. Adjust an oven rack 6 inches from the heating element and heat the broiler.

3. Weave the meat onto 6-inch bamboo skewers (one piece per skewer). Lay the skewers on a wire rack set over a rimmed baking sheet and cover the skewer ends with foil. Broil the skewers until the meat is browned, 6 to 9 minutes, flipping the skewers over halfway through. Transfer the skewers to a serving platter and serve with the peanut sauce.

Spicy Peanut Dipping Sauce

MAKES ABOUT 1½ CUPS

This sauce can be refrigerated in an airtight container for up to 24 hours; bring to room temperature before serving.

½ cup creamy peanut butter
¼ cup hot water
2 tablespoons juice from 1 lime
2 tablespoons Asian chili sauce
1 tablespoon soy sauce
1 tablespoon dark brown sugar
1 tablespoon chopped fresh cilantro leaves
2 scallions, sliced thin
1 medium garlic clove, minced or pressed through a garlic press (about 1 teaspoon)

Whisk the peanut butter and hot water together in a small bowl until smooth. Stir in the remaining ingredients.

THAI-STYLE CHICKEN SOUP

WHY THIS RECIPE WORKS: Replicating the complex flavors of Thai chicken soup at home can be difficult, since it relies on such exotica as galangal, kaffir lime leaves, lemon grass, and bird's eye chiles. We wanted a plausibly authentic version of Thai chicken soup that could be prepared with more readily available (i.e., supermarket) substitutions.

We started by making a classic version of the soup, then substituting one ingredient at a time. We developed an acceptably rich and definitely chicken-flavored broth by using equal parts chicken broth and coconut milk (adding the coconut milk in two stages: at the beginning and just before serving). We couldn't fake the flavor of lemon grass, but it proved to be easy enough to find. Our most exciting find was a "magic bullet" substitution: jarred red curry paste included all the other exotic ingredients we were missing. Just adding a dollop at the very end of cooking and whisking it with pungent fish sauce and tart lime juice allowed all the classic flavors to come through loud and clear.

Thai-Style Chicken Soup

SERVES 6 TO 8

To make slicing the chicken easier, freeze it for 15 minutes. Although we prefer the richer, more complex flavor of regular coconut milk, light coconut milk can be substituted for one or both cans. For a spicier soup, add additional red curry paste to taste.

SOUP

- 1 teaspoon peanut or vegetable oil
- 3 stalks lemon grass, bottom 5 inches only, trimmed and sliced thin (see page 479)
- 3 large shallots, chopped coarse (about ¾ cup)
- 8 sprigs fresh cilantro, chopped coarse
- 3 tablespoons fish sauce
- 4 cups low-sodium chicken broth
- 2 (14-ounce) cans coconut milk (see note)
- 1 tablespoon sugar
- 8 ounces white mushrooms, wiped clean and sliced ¼ inch thick
- 1 pound boneless, skinless chicken breasts, trimmed, halved lengthwise, and cut on the bias into ⅛-inch pieces (see note)
- 3 tablespoons juice from 2 limes
- 2 teaspoons Thai red curry paste (see note)

GARNISH

- ½ cup loosely packed fresh cilantro leaves
- 2 Thai, serrano, or jalapeño chiles, seeds and ribs removed, chiles sliced thin
- 2 scallions, sliced thin on the bias
- Lime wedges, for serving

1. Heat the oil in a large saucepan over medium heat until just shimmering. Add the lemon grass, shallots, cilantro sprigs, and 1 tablespoon of the fish sauce and cook, stirring frequently, until just softened but not browned, 2 to 5 minutes.

2. Stir in the broth and 1 can of the coconut milk and bring to a simmer over high heat. Cover, reduce the heat to low, and simmer until the flavors have blended, about 10 minutes. Pour the broth through a fine-mesh strainer, discarding the solids in the strainer. (At this point, the soup can be refrigerated in an airtight container for up to 1 day.)

3. Return the strained soup to a clean saucepan and bring to a simmer over medium-high heat. Stir in the remaining can of coconut milk and the sugar and bring to a simmer. Reduce the heat to medium, add the mushrooms, and cook until just tender, 2 to 3 minutes. Add the chicken and cook, stirring constantly, until no longer pink, 1 to 3 minutes. Remove the soup from the heat.

4. Whisk the remaining 2 tablespoons fish sauce, the lime juice, and curry paste together, then stir into the soup. Ladle the soup into individual bowls and garnish with the cilantro, chiles, and scallions. Serve with the lime wedges.

HOT AND SOUR SOUP

WHY THIS RECIPE WORKS: Authentic versions of this soup have some hard-to-find ingredients such as mustard pickle, pig's-foot tendon, and dried sea cucumber—ingredients we couldn't find in the local grocery store. Using inventory only from our local supermarket, we wanted an authentic take on hot and sour soup, including spicy, bracing, pungent elements.

We created the "hot" side of the soup with two heat sources—distinctive, penetrating white pepper and a little chili oil. For the "sour" component, we preferred the traditional Chinese black vinegar, but found that a tablespoon each of balsamic and red wine vinegar made a suitable substitution. Cornstarch turned out to be a key ingredient: A cornstarch-based slurry thickened the soup; adding cornstarch to the pork marinade gave the pork a protective sheath that kept it tender; and beating the egg with cornstarch before drizzling it into the thickened soup kept the egg light, wispy, and cohesive. Pork and tofu are the usual, easy-to-find additions to the broth, but we had to come up with substitutes for a few other classic ingredients, settling on fresh shiitakes in lieu of wood ear mushrooms and canned bamboo shoots instead of lily buds. Spicy, bracing, rich, and complex, this soup has all the flavor of the classic version.

Hot and Sour Soup

SERVES 6 TO 8

To make slicing the pork chop easier, freeze it for 15 minutes. We prefer the distinctive flavor of Chinese black vinegar; look for it in Asian supermarkets. If you can't find it, use 1 tablespoon red wine vinegar and 1 tablespoon balsamic vinegar. This soup is very spicy. For a less spicy soup, omit the chili oil altogether or add only 1 teaspoon.

- 7 ounces (½ block) extra-firm tofu
- ¼ cup soy sauce
- 3 tablespoons plus 1½ teaspoons cornstarch
- 1 teaspoon toasted sesame oil
- 1 (6-ounce) boneless center-cut pork chop (about ½ inch thick), trimmed and cut into 1-inch-long matchsticks (see note)
- 3 tablespoons plus 1 teaspoon water
- 1 large egg
- 6 cups low-sodium chicken broth
- 1 (5-ounce) can bamboo shoots, sliced into matchsticks (about 1 cup)
- 4 ounces shiitake mushrooms, stemmed, wiped clean, caps sliced ¼ inch thick
- 5 tablespoons Chinese black vinegar (see note)
- 2 teaspoons chili oil (see note)
- 1 teaspoon ground white pepper
- 3 scallions, sliced thin

1. Place the tofu in a pie plate, top with a heavy plate, and weigh down with two heavy cans. Set the tofu aside until it has released about ½ cup liquid, about 15 minutes. When drained, cut the tofu into ½-inch cubes and set aside.

2. Meanwhile, whisk 1 tablespoon of the soy sauce, 1 teaspoon of the cornstarch, and the sesame oil together in a medium bowl. Stir in the pork, cover, and let marinate for at least 10 minutes or up to 30 minutes.

3. Combine 3 tablespoons more cornstarch with 3 tablespoons of the water in a small bowl. Mix the remaining ½ teaspoon cornstarch with the remaining 1 teaspoon water in a second small bowl, then add the egg and beat with a fork until combined.

4. Bring the broth to a simmer in a large saucepan over medium-low heat. Add the bamboo shoots and mushrooms and simmer until the mushrooms are just tender, 2 to 3 minutes. Stir in the diced tofu and pork with its marinade and continue to simmer, stirring to separate any pieces of pork that stick together, until the pork is no longer pink, about 2 minutes.

5. Stir the cornstarch mixture to recombine, then add it to the soup, increase the heat to medium-high, and cook, stirring occasionally, until the soup thickens and turns translucent, about 1 minute. Stir in the remaining 3 tablespoons soy sauce, the vinegar, chili oil, and pepper and turn off the heat.

6. Without stirring the soup, use a soupspoon to slowly drizzle very thin streams of the egg mixture into the pot in a circular motion. Let the soup sit off the heat for 1 minute. Briefly return the soup to a simmer over medium-high heat, then remove from the heat immediately. Gently stir the soup once to evenly distribute the egg; ladle into individual bowls, sprinkle with the scallions, and serve.

COLD SESAME NOODLES

WHY THIS RECIPE WORKS: Cold noodles are underrated. Not as humble as they appear, these toothsome noodles tossed with shreds of tender chicken and fresh sesame sauce can be addicting if made properly. For this recipe, we set out to eliminate sticky noodles, gloppy sauce, and lackluster flavors.

We found that rinsing and tossing the noodles (either fresh Chinese noodles or dried spaghetti) with a little sesame oil after cooking prevents a rubbery texture and washes away much of their sticky starch. Boneless, skinless chicken breasts were the obvious choice for easy cooking and shredding, and broiling the meat helped retain the chicken's moisture and flavor. And for an authentic sauce, a combination of chunky peanut butter and freshly ground toasted sesame seeds was the best substitute for Asian sesame paste. After adding fresh garlic and ginger, as well as soy sauce, rice vinegar, hot sauce, and brown sugar, we achieved the perfect texture by thinning out the sauce with hot water.

Sesame Noodles with Shredded Chicken

SERVES 4 TO 6

Although our preference is for fresh Chinese noodles, we found that dried spaghetti works well, too. Because dried pasta swells so much more than fresh pasta during cooking, 12 ounces of dried spaghetti can replace 1 pound of fresh noodles.

- 5 tablespoons soy sauce
- ¼ cup sesame seeds, toasted
- ¼ cup chunky peanut butter
- 2 tablespoons rice vinegar
- 2 tablespoons light brown sugar
- 1 tablespoon minced or grated fresh ginger
- 2 medium garlic cloves, minced or pressed through a garlic press (about 2 teaspoons)
- 1 teaspoon hot sauce
- Hot water

- 1 pound fresh Chinese noodles or 12 ounces dried spaghetti (see note)
- 1 tablespoon table salt
- 2 tablespoons toasted sesame oil
- 1½ pounds boneless, skinless chicken breasts, trimmed
- 4 scallions, sliced thin on the bias
- 1 carrot, peeled and shredded

1. Process the soy sauce, 3 tablespoons of the sesame seeds, the peanut butter, vinegar, brown sugar, ginger, garlic, and hot sauce together in a blender or food processor until smooth, about 30 seconds. With the machine running, add hot water, 1 tablespoon at a time, until the sauce has the consistency of heavy cream (you should need about 5 tablespoons); set aside.

2. Position an oven rack 6 inches from the heating element and heat the broiler.

3. Bring 6 quarts water to a boil in a large pot. Add the noodles and salt and cook, stirring often, until tender, about 4 minutes for fresh and 10 minutes for dried. Drain the noodles, rinse them under cold running water until cold, then toss them with the sesame oil.

4. Set a wire rack over a foil-lined rimmed baking sheet and lightly coat the rack with vegetable oil spray. Lay the chicken on the rack and broil until lightly browned, 4 to 8 minutes. Flip the chicken over and continue to broil until the thickest part of the breast registers 160 to 165 degrees on an instant-read thermometer, 6 to 8 minutes longer. Transfer the chicken to a carving board and let rest for 5 minutes. Using two forks, shred the chicken into bite-size pieces and set aside.

5. Transfer the noodles to a large bowl, add the shredded chicken, sauce, scallions, and carrot and toss to combine. Divide the mixture among individual bowls, sprinkle with the remaining 1 tablespoon sesame seeds, and serve.

JAPANESE-STYLE STIR-FRIED NOODLES WITH BEEF

WHY THIS RECIPE WORKS: Japanese *yakisoba* stands out among noodle dishes for its sweet-savory-tangy sauce, tender meat, and hearty vegetables. For a flavor-packed noodle dish that rivaled our favorite takeout, we started with the beef. Coating bite-size strips of flank steak in baking soda and water tenderized the meat. To recreate the thick consistency and sweet, fruity flavor of yakisoba sauce, we whisked together ketchup, soy sauce, Worcestershire, brown sugar, minced garlic, minced anchovies, and rice vinegar. We cooked the remaining components in stages. Lo mein noodles (an easier supermarket find than traditional yakisoba noodles) turned tender after a few minutes in boiling water, and rinsing them under cold water after draining eliminated clingy starches. For the vegetable accompaniments to the noodles, sliced shiitakes and carrot cooked in chicken broth were an easy and traditional choice. Next, sliced napa cabbage and bright, grassy scallions cooked up quickly, followed by the slices of beef. To tie everything together, we briefly cooked the sauce, chicken broth, and noodles before tossing them with the waiting vegetables and beef. A sprinkling of homemade Sesame-Orange Spice Blend brought the authentic flavors home.

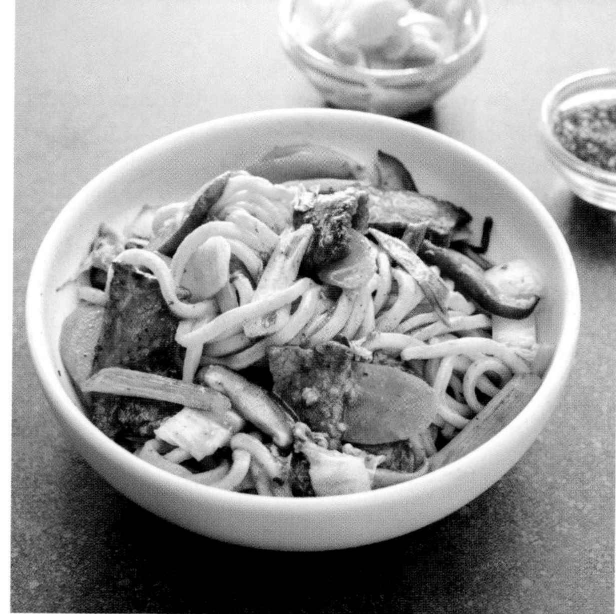

Japanese-Style Stir-Fried Noodles with Beef

SERVES 4 TO 6

This recipe calls for lo mein noodles, but use yakisoba noodles if you can find them and follow the same cooking directions. Garnish the noodles with pickled ginger (often found in the refrigerated section of the grocery store near the tofu) and our Sesame-Orange Spice Blend (recipe follows) or, if you can find it, commercial shichimi togarashi.

- ⅛ teaspoon baking soda
- 12 ounces flank steak, trimmed, sliced lengthwise into 2- to 2½-inch strips, each strip sliced crosswise ¼ inch thick
- ¼ cup ketchup
- ¼ cup soy sauce
- 2 tablespoons Worcestershire sauce
- 1½ tablespoons packed brown sugar
- 3 garlic cloves, minced
- 3 anchovy fillets, rinsed, patted dry, and minced
- 1 teaspoon rice vinegar
- 1 pound fresh or 8 ounces dried lo mein noodles
- 1 tablespoon vegetable oil
- 6 ounces shiitake mushrooms, stemmed and sliced ¼ inch thick
- 1 carrot, peeled and sliced ⅛ inch thick on bias
- ¾ cup chicken broth
- 6 cups napa cabbage, sliced crosswise into ½-inch strips
- 7 scallions, cut on bias into 1-inch lengths
- Salt

1. Combine 1 tablespoon water and baking soda in medium bowl. Add beef and toss to coat. Let sit at room temperature for 5 minutes.

2. Whisk ketchup, soy sauce, Worcestershire, sugar, garlic, anchovies, and vinegar together in second bowl. Stir 2 tablespoons sauce into beef mixture and set aside remaining sauce.

3. Bring 4 quarts water to boil in large pot. Add noodles and cook, stirring often, until almost tender (center should still be firm with slightly opaque dot), 3 to 10 minutes (cooking time will vary depending on whether you are using fresh or dry noodles). Drain noodles and rinse under cold running water until water runs clear. Drain well and set aside.

4. Heat ½ teaspoon oil in 12-inch nonstick skillet over high heat until just smoking. Add mushrooms and carrot and cook, stirring occasionally, until vegetables are spotty brown, 2 to 3 minutes. Add ¼ cup broth and cook until all liquid has evaporated and vegetables are tender, about 30 seconds. Transfer vegetables to bowl.

5. Return skillet to high heat, add ½ teaspoon oil, and heat until just smoking. Add cabbage and scallions and cook, without stirring, for 30 seconds. Cook, stirring occasionally, until cabbage and scallions are spotty brown and crisp-tender, 2 to 3 minutes. Transfer to bowl with mushrooms and carrot.

6. Return skillet to high heat, add 1 teaspoon oil, and heat until just smoking. Add half of beef in single layer. Cook, without stirring, for 30 seconds. Continue to cook, stirring occasionally, until beef is spotty brown, 1 to 2 minutes. Transfer to bowl with vegetables. Repeat with remaining beef and remaining 1 teaspoon oil.

7. Return skillet to high heat; add reserved sauce, remaining ½ cup broth, and noodles. Cook, scraping up any browned bits, until noodles are warmed through, about 1 minute. Transfer noodles to bowl with vegetables and beef and toss to combine. Season with salt to taste, and serve immediately.

Sesame-Orange Spice Blend

MAKES ¼ CUP

In addition to garnishing our stir-fry, this blend makes a great seasoning for eggs, rice, and fish. Store for up to one week.

- ¾ teaspoon grated orange zest
- 2 teaspoons sesame seeds
- 1½ teaspoons paprika
- 1 teaspoon pepper
- ¼ teaspoon garlic powder
- ¼ teaspoon ground ginger
- ⅛ teaspoon cayenne pepper

Place orange zest in small bowl and microwave, stirring every 20 seconds, until zest is dry and no longer clumping together, 1 minute 30 seconds to 2 minutes 30 seconds. Stir in sesame seeds, paprika, pepper, garlic powder, ginger, and cayenne.

FRIED RICE

WHY THIS RECIPE WORKS: Fried rice is the perfect solution for leftover rice, but it often arrives in the bowl as a soggy mess of greasy rice doused in so much flavor-disguising soy sauce that you can hardly tell the vegetables from the chicken. We wanted fried rice with firm, separate grains, and we wanted a finished dish so clean and light that we could distinguish its many different flavors in every bite.

For fried rice that is light and flavorful rather than sodden and greasy, we found it essential to start with cold, dry rice (like leftover rice). Instead of gallons of soy sauce, we added a small amount in conjunction with complex oyster-flavored sauce to yield well-seasoned but not soggy rice. Cooking the vegetables and shrimp separately ensured that everything was cooked to perfection—no rubbery shrimp or mushy peas. And frying the rice in just a couple tablespoons of oil kept it from being greasy. Lastly, we finished the dish with tender vegetables including bean sprouts and a sprinkling of scallions.

Fried Rice with Shrimp, Pork, and Shiitakes

SERVES 4 TO 6

See the Basic White Rice recipe (page 453) for tips on preparing and cooling rice.

- ½ ounce (5 to 6 medium) dried shiitake mushrooms
- ¼ cup oyster-flavored sauce
- 1 tablespoon soy sauce
- 3 tablespoons plus 1½ teaspoons peanut or vegetable oil
- 2 large eggs, lightly beaten
- 8 ounces small shrimp (51 to 60 per pound), peeled and deveined (see page 240)
- 1 cup frozen peas, thawed
- 8 ounces sliced smoked ham, cut into ½-inch pieces
- 2 medium garlic cloves, minced or pressed through a garlic press (about 2 teaspoons)
- 5 cups cold cooked white rice, large clumps broken up with fingers (see note)
- 1 cup bean sprouts
- 5 scallions, sliced thin

1. Cover the dried shiitakes with 1 cup hot tap water in a small microwave-safe bowl. Cover the bowl with plastic wrap and microwave on high power for 30 seconds. Let sit until the mushrooms soften, about 5 minutes. Lift the mushrooms from the liquid with a fork. Trim the stems, slice into ¼-inch strips, and set aside.

2. Combine the oyster-flavored sauce and soy sauce in a small bowl and set aside.

3. Heat 1½ teaspoons of the oil in a 12-inch nonstick skillet over medium heat until shimmering. Add the eggs and cook, without stirring, until they just begin to set, about 20 seconds. Scramble and break into small pieces with a wooden spoon and continue to cook, stirring constantly, until the eggs are cooked through but not browned, about 1 minute longer. Transfer the eggs to a small bowl and set aside.

4. Add 1½ teaspoons more oil to the skillet and heat over medium heat until shimmering. Add the shrimp and cook, stirring constantly, until opaque and just cooked through, about 30 seconds. Transfer the shrimp to the bowl with the eggs and set aside.

5. Add the remaining 2½ tablespoons oil to the skillet and heat over medium heat until shimmering. Add the mushrooms, peas, and ham and cook, stirring constantly, for 1 minute. Stir in the garlic and cook until fragrant, about 30 seconds. Add the rice and oyster-flavored sauce mixture and cook, stirring constantly and breaking up any rice clumps, until the mixture is heated through, about 3 minutes. Stir in the eggs, shrimp, bean sprouts, and scallions and cook until heated through, about 1 minute. Serve.

Fried Rice with Peas and Bean Sprouts

SERVES 4 TO 6

See the Basic White Rice recipe for tips on preparing and cooling rice.

- ¼ cup oyster-flavored sauce
- 1 tablespoon soy sauce
- 3 tablespoons peanut or vegetable oil
- 2 large eggs, lightly beaten
- 1 cup frozen peas, thawed
- 2 medium garlic cloves, minced or pressed through a garlic press (about 2 teaspoons)
- 5 cups cold cooked white rice, large clumps broken up with fingers (see note)
- 1 cup bean sprouts
- 5 scallions, sliced thin

1. Combine the oyster-flavored sauce and soy sauce in a small bowl and set aside.

2. Heat 1½ teaspoons of the oil in a 12-inch nonstick skillet over medium heat until shimmering. Add the eggs and cook, without stirring, until they just begin to set, about 20 seconds. Scramble and break into small pieces with a wooden spoon and continue to cook, stirring constantly, until the eggs are cooked through but not browned, about 1 minute longer. Transfer the eggs to a small bowl and set aside.

3. Add the remaining 2½ tablespoons oil to the skillet and heat over medium heat until shimmering. Add the peas and cook, stirring constantly, for 1 minute. Stir in the garlic and cook until fragrant, about 30 seconds. Add the rice and oyster-flavored sauce mixture and cook, stirring constantly and breaking up any rice clumps, until the mixture is heated through, about 3 minutes. Stir in the eggs, bean sprouts, and scallions and cook until heated through, about 1 minute. Serve.

Basic White Rice

MAKES ABOUT 5 CUPS

To rinse the rice, you can either place it in a fine-mesh strainer and rinse it under cool water or place it in a medium bowl and repeatedly fill the bowl with water while swishing the rice around, then drain off the water. In either case, you must rinse the rice until the water runs clear.

- 3 cups water
- 2 cups long-grain white rice, rinsed (see note)

1. Bring the water and rice to a boil in a large saucepan over high heat. Reduce the heat to low, cover, and cook until all the water has been absorbed, about 10 minutes. Remove the pot from the heat and let sit, covered, until the rice is tender, about 15 minutes.

2. Serve, or to make fried rice, spread the cooked rice out over a baking sheet and let cool to room temperature, about 30 minutes. (The rice can be refrigerated in an airtight container for up to 24 hours.)

FRIED BROWN RICE WITH PORK AND SHRIMP

WHY THIS RECIPE WORKS: In this dish, using brown rice instead of the more conventional white rice offered several advantages. Because of its bran, brown rice holds up well if cooked aggressively in boiling water. The bran acted as a nonstick coating on each grain, so the dish required far less oil for frying. To balance the nuttier flavor of brown rice, we used plenty of ginger, garlic, and soy sauce. For a quick version of Chinese barbecued pork to turn our fried rice into a main course, we cut boneless country-style pork ribs across the grain into bite-size slices and tossed them in hoisin sauce, honey, and five-spice powder. We chopped scallions and shrimp, beat some eggs, grated some ginger, and minced some garlic, and we were ready to stir-fry. Preparing these components in batches, starting with the shrimp and eggs and then turning to the pork, yielded perfectly cooked ingredients ready to stir together with the fried brown rice.

Fried Brown Rice with Pork and Shrimp

SERVES 6

Boiling the rice gives it the proper texture for this dish. Do not use a rice cooker. The most efficient way to make this dish is to start the rice boiling and then to assemble the remaining ingredients while the rice cooks. The stir-fry portion of this recipe moves quickly, so make sure to have all your ingredients in place before starting. This recipe works best in a nonstick skillet with a slick surface. If your skillet is a bit worn, add an additional teaspoon of oil with the eggs in step 3. Serve with a simple steamed vegetable like broccoli, bok choy, or snow peas if desired.

- 2 cups short grain brown rice
- Salt
- 10 ounces boneless country-style pork ribs, trimmed
- 1 tablespoon hoisin sauce
- 2 teaspoons honey
- ⅛ teaspoon five-spice powder
- Small pinch cayenne pepper
- 4 teaspoons vegetable oil
- 8 ounces large shrimp (26 to 30 per pound), peeled, deveined (see page 240), tails removed, and cut into ½-inch pieces
- 3 large eggs, lightly beaten
- 1 tablespoon toasted sesame oil
- 6 scallions, whites and greens separated, sliced thin on bias
- 1½ teaspoons garlic, minced
- 1½ teaspoons grated fresh ginger
- 2 tablespoons soy sauce
- 1 cup frozen peas

1. Bring 3 quarts water to boil in large pot. Add rice and 2 teaspoons salt. Cook, stirring occasionally, until rice is tender, about 35 minutes. Drain well, and return to pot. Cover and set aside.

2. While rice cooks, cut pork into 1-inch pieces, and cut each piece into ¼-inch slices against grain. Combine pork with hoisin, honey, five-spice, cayenne, and ½ teaspoon salt, and toss to coat. Set aside.

3. Heat 1 teaspoon vegetable oil in 12-inch nonstick skillet over medium-high heat until shimmering. Add shrimp in even layer and cook without moving them until bottoms are browned, about 90 seconds. Stir and continue to cook until just cooked through, about 90 seconds longer. Push shrimp to 1 side of skillet. Add 1 teaspoon vegetable oil to cleared side of skillet. Add eggs to clearing and sprinkle with ¼ teaspoon salt. Using rubber spatula, stir eggs gently until set but still wet, about 30 seconds. Stir eggs into shrimp and continue to cook, breaking up large pieces of egg, until eggs are fully cooked, about 30 seconds longer. Transfer shrimp-egg mixture to clean bowl.

4. Heat remaining 2 teaspoons vegetable oil in now-empty skillet over medium-high heat until shimmering. Add pork in even layer. Cook without moving until pork is well browned on underside, 2 to 3 minutes. Flip pork and cook without moving until pork is cooked through and caramelized on second side, 2 to 3 minutes. Transfer to bowl with shrimp-egg mixture.

5. Heat sesame oil in now-empty skillet over medium-high heat until shimmering. Add scallion whites and cook, stirring frequently, until well-browned, about 1 minute. Add ginger and garlic and cook, stirring frequently, until fragrant and beginning to brown, 30 to 60 seconds. Add soy sauce and half of rice and stir until all ingredients are fully incorporated, making sure to break up clumps of ginger and garlic. Reduce heat to medium-low and add remaining rice, pork, shrimp, eggs, and peas. Stir until all ingredients are evenly incorporated and heated through, 2 to 4 minutes. Remove from heat and stir in scallion greens. Transfer to heated platter and serve.

INDONESIAN-STYLE FRIED RICE

WHY THIS RECIPE WORKS: Chinese takeout versions of fried rice are satisfying, to be sure, but frequently leave little to the imagination. We wanted to create a less heavy version of fried rice featuring the pungent, complex flavors of Indonesia—without heading to specialty markets for all of our ingredients. The primary source of this dish's flavor is chili paste, and we were happy to discover that the ingredients for this paste (staples like chiles, shallots, brown sugar, and soy sauce) are readily available at the average supermarket. To replicate the flavor of shrimp paste—another key but hard-to-find ingredient—we used a combination of fish sauce and chopped shrimp, which we added to the skillet with the chili paste. This dish requires chilled, firm rice, but most of us don't have leftover rice sitting in our fridge. For rice with the proper consistency, we cooked it in less water and then spread it out on a baking sheet to allow it to chill quickly in the fridge.

Indonesian-Style Fried Rice (Nasi Goreng)

SERVES 4 TO 6

If Thai chiles are unavailable, substitute two serranos or two medium jalapeños. Reduce the spiciness of this dish by removing the ribs and seeds from the chiles. This dish progresses very quickly at step 4; it's imperative that your ingredients are in place by then and ready to go. If desired, serve the rice with sliced cucumbers and tomato wedges.

- 5 green or red Thai chiles, stemmed (see note)
- 7 large shallots, peeled
- 4 large garlic cloves, peeled
- 2 tablespoons dark brown sugar
- 2 tablespoons light or mild molasses
- 2 tablespoons soy sauce
- 2 tablespoons fish sauce
- Table salt
- 4 large eggs
- ½ cup vegetable oil
- 1 recipe Faux Leftover Rice (recipe follows)
- 12 ounces extra-large shrimp (21 to 25 per pound), peeled, deveined (see page 240), tails removed, and cut crosswise into thirds
- 4 large scallions, sliced thin
- 2 limes, cut into wedges

1. Pulse the chiles, 4 of the shallots, and the garlic in a food processor until a coarse paste is formed, about 15 pulses, scraping down the sides of the bowl as necessary. Transfer the mixture to a small bowl and set aside. In a second small bowl, stir together the brown sugar, molasses, soy sauce, fish sauce, and 1¼ teaspoons salt. Whisk the eggs and ¼ teaspoon salt together in a medium bowl.

2. Thinly slice the remaining 3 shallots and place in a 12-inch nonstick skillet with the oil. Cook over medium heat, stirring constantly, until the shallots are golden and crisp, 6 to 10 minutes. Using a slotted spoon, transfer the shallots to a paper towel–lined plate and season with salt to taste. Pour off the oil and reserve. Wipe out the skillet with paper towels.

3. Heat 1 teaspoon of the reserved oil in the now-empty skillet over medium heat until shimmering. Add half of the eggs to the skillet, gently tilting the pan to evenly coat the bottom. Cover and cook until the bottom of the omelet is spotty golden brown and the top is just set, about 1½ minutes. Slide the omelet onto a cutting board and gently roll up into a tight log. Using a sharp knife, cut the log crosswise into 1-inch segments (leaving the segments rolled). Repeat with 1 teaspoon more reserved oil and the remaining egg.

4. Remove the rice from the refrigerator and break up any large clumps with your fingers. Heat 3 tablespoons more reserved oil in the now-empty skillet over medium heat until just shimmering. Add the chile mixture and cook until the mixture turns golden, 3 to 5 minutes. Add the shrimp, increase the heat to medium-high, and cook, stirring constantly, until the exterior of the shrimp is just opaque, about 2 minutes. Push the shrimp to the sides of the skillet to clear the center; stir the molasses mixture to recombine and pour into the center of the skillet. When the molasses mixture bubbles, add the rice and cook, stirring and folding constantly, until the shrimp is cooked, the rice is heated through, and the mixture is evenly coated, about 3 minutes. Stir in the scallions, remove from the heat, and transfer to a serving platter. Garnish with the egg segments, fried shallots, and lime wedges; serve immediately.

Faux Leftover Rice

MAKES 6 CUPS

To rinse the rice, place it in a fine-mesh strainer and rinse under cool water until the water runs clear.

- 2 tablespoons vegetable oil
- 2 cups jasmine or long-grain white rice, rinsed (see note)
- 2⅔ cups water

Heat the oil in a large saucepan over medium heat until shimmering. Add the rice and stir to coat the grains with oil, about 30 seconds. Add the water, increase the heat to high, and bring to a boil. Reduce the heat to low, cover, and simmer until all the liquid is absorbed, about 18 minutes. Off the heat, remove the lid and place a clean kitchen towel, folded in half, over the saucepan; replace the lid. Let stand until the rice is just tender, about 8 minutes. Spread the cooked rice onto a rimmed baking sheet, set on a wire rack, and cool for 10 minutes. Transfer to the refrigerator and chill for 20 minutes.

CHICKEN TERIYAKI

WHY THIS RECIPE WORKS: Too many chicken teriyaki recipes are lackluster—they can include everything from skewered chicken chunks shellacked in a corn-syrupy sauce to overmarinated, preformed chicken breast patties. They're a long way away from the simple recipe promised in the name "teriyaki"—meaning "to shine" (referring to the sauce) and meaning "to broil." We wanted a straightforward recipe that delivered the simple and authentic result of crisp and moist, sweet and salty, glazed chicken.

First, we decided against using breast meat. Bone-in, skin-on thighs stood up best to the salty profile of the teriyaki sauce. We set a weight on top of the chicken as it cooked (we used a heavy Dutch oven), which helped to brown a greater surface area of the chicken evenly, as well as to aid in pressing out most of the fat. We also found that a quick mixture of soy sauce, sugar, mirin, and a few other flavorings made an incredible teriyaki sauce that far surpassed any we could buy in a bottle.

Chicken Teriyaki

SERVES 4

A splatter screen (or an inverted large strainer or colander) is helpful for controlling the splatter that occurs when the second side of the chicken browns. There is a fair amount of soy sauce in this dish, so there is no need to salt it before serving. Serve with Basic White Rice (page 453).

- 8 (5- to 6-ounce) bone-in, skin-on chicken thighs, trimmed
  Ground black pepper
- 2 teaspoons peanut or vegetable oil
- ½ cup soy sauce
- ½ cup sugar
- 2 tablespoons mirin or sweet sherry
- 2 teaspoons minced or grated fresh ginger
- 1 medium garlic clove, minced or pressed through a garlic press (about 1 teaspoon)
- ½ teaspoon cornstarch
- ⅛ teaspoon red pepper flakes

1. Pat the chicken thighs dry with paper towels and season with pepper. Heat the oil in a 12-inch nonstick skillet over medium-high heat until just smoking. Carefully lay the chicken in the skillet, skin side down. Weigh down the chicken with a heavy pot and cook until the skin is a deep mahogany brown and very crisp, 15 to 20 minutes. (The chicken should be moderately brown after 10 minutes. If it is very brown, reduce the heat; if it is still pale, increase the heat.)

2. Remove the weight and flip the chicken over. Reduce the heat to medium and continue to cook, without the weight, until the second side is brown and the thickest part of the thighs registers 175 degrees on an instant-read thermometer, about 10 minutes longer.

3. Meanwhile, whisk the soy sauce, sugar, mirin, ginger, garlic, cornstarch, and red pepper flakes together in a small bowl; set aside.

4. Transfer the chicken to a plate. Pour off all of the fat from the skillet. Whisk the soy mixture to recombine, then add to the skillet and return to medium heat. Return the chicken to the skillet, skin side up, and spoon the sauce over the top. Continue to simmer until the sauce is thick and glossy, about 2 minutes longer. Serve.

ORANGE-FLAVORED CHICKEN

WHY THIS RECIPE WORKS: Chinese takeout orange-flavored chicken is never as good as its name promises—too often the dish delivers ultra-thick breading wrapped around scraps of greasy, gristly, tasteless chicken bathed in an "orange" sauce that tastes likes a mixture of corn syrup and orange food coloring. We wanted substantial, well-seasoned chicken chunks with a crisp, golden brown crust, and a sauce that offered a clear hit of fresh orange flavor with balanced sweet, sour, and spicy background notes.

We chose thigh meat over breast meat for its rich flavor and tendency to remain moist when deep-fried. We marinated the chicken in a mixture of soy sauce, garlic, ginger, sugar, vinegar, fresh orange juice, and chicken broth, reserving some marinade to become the base for the final sauce. Then, we created a tender/crisp coating by dunking the marinated chicken first in egg white, then cornstarch. The egg white created a thin sheath of protein beneath the cornstarch that kept it dry, helping it to brown more readily than a wet, gluey coating would. A touch of baking soda helped the chicken pieces develop golden color during frying.

Orange-Flavored Chicken

SERVES 4

We prefer the flavor and texture of thigh meat for this recipe, though an equal amount of boneless, skinless chicken breasts can be used. Unless you have a taste for the incendiary, do not eat the whole chiles in the finished dish. Serve with Basic White Rice (page 453).

MARINADE AND SAUCE

- ¾ cup low-sodium chicken broth
- ¾ cup juice, 1½ teaspoons grated zest, and 8 strips peel (each about 2 inches long by ½ inch wide) from 2 oranges
- ½ cup packed dark brown sugar
- 6 tablespoons distilled white vinegar
- ¼ cup soy sauce
- 3 medium garlic cloves, minced or pressed through a garlic press (about 1 tablespoon)
- 1 tablespoon minced or grated fresh ginger
- ¼ teaspoon cayenne pepper
- 1½ pounds boneless, skinless chicken thighs, trimmed and cut into 1½-inch pieces (see note)

- 2 tablespoons cold water
- 1 tablespoon plus 2 teaspoons cornstarch
- 8 small whole dried red chiles (optional; see note)

COATING AND FRYING OIL

- 3 large egg whites
- 1 cup cornstarch
- ½ teaspoon baking soda
- ¼ teaspoon cayenne pepper
- 3 cups peanut or vegetable oil

1. FOR THE MARINADE AND SAUCE: Whisk the broth, orange juice, grated zest, sugar, vinegar, soy sauce, garlic, ginger, and cayenne together in a large saucepan until the sugar is fully dissolved. Transfer ¾ cup of the mixture to a medium bowl and add the chicken. Let marinate for at least 10 minutes or up to 1 hour.

2. In a small bowl, stir the cold water and cornstarch together. Bring the remaining mixture in the saucepan to a simmer over high heat. Whisk the cornstarch mixture into the sauce, bring to a simmer, and cook, stirring occasionally, until thick and translucent, about 1 minute. Off the heat, stir in the orange peel and chiles (if using) and set aside. (The sauce should measure 1½ cups.)

3. FOR THE COATING: Using a fork, lightly beat the egg whites in a shallow dish until frothy. In a second shallow dish, whisk the cornstarch, baking soda, and cayenne together until combined. Drain the chicken and pat dry with paper towels. Place half of the chicken pieces in the egg whites and turn to coat. Transfer the chicken pieces to the cornstarch mixture and coat thoroughly. Place the dredged chicken pieces on a wire rack set over a baking sheet. Repeat with the remaining chicken pieces.

4. TO FRY THE CHICKEN: Heat the oil in a Dutch oven over high heat until the oil registers 350 degrees on an instant-read or deep-fry thermometer. Carefully place half of the chicken in the oil and fry until golden brown, about 5 minutes, turning each piece with tongs halfway through. Transfer the chicken pieces to a paper towel–lined plate. Return the oil to 350 degrees and repeat with the remaining chicken.

5. TO SERVE: Reheat the sauce over medium heat until simmering, about 2 minutes. Add the chicken and gently toss until evenly coated and heated through. Serve.

THREE-CUP CHICKEN

WHY THIS RECIPE WORKS: Originating in Dadu (modern Beijing), Three-Cup Chicken, or *San Bei Ji*, was named for its sparse ingredient list, with a sauce made up of just 1 cup each of soy sauce, sesame oil, and rice wine. Now adopted by neighboring Taiwan, it has evolved into a national dish of sorts. Its robust, aromatic flavors seemed ideal for adapting for the American kitchen. While traditional recipes involve butchering a whole bird into smaller pieces, we opted for boneless, skinless thighs, which didn't require using a cleaver. The rich flavor of the thighs would stand up to the potent sauce better than that of milder breasts. Marinating the chicken in the sauce helped build deep flavor with minimal effort. We found that scallions, ginger, garlic, and red pepper flakes added even more flavor and complexity to this dish.

Three-Cup Chicken

SERVES 4

We prefer the flavor of Thai basil, but common sweet basil can be substituted. For a spicier dish, use the larger amount of red pepper flakes. Serve with Basic White Rice (page 453).

- ⅓ cup soy sauce
- ⅓ cup dry sherry
- 1 tablespoon packed brown sugar
- 1½ pounds boneless, skinless chicken thighs, trimmed and cut into 2-inch pieces
- 3 tablespoons vegetable oil
- 1 (2-inch) piece ginger, peeled, halved lengthwise, and sliced into thin half-rounds
- 12 garlic cloves, peeled and halved lengthwise
- ½–¾ teaspoon red pepper flakes
- 6 scallions, white and green parts separated and sliced thin on bias
- 1 tablespoon water
- 1 teaspoon cornstarch
- 1 cup Thai basil leaves, large leaves halved lengthwise
- 1 tablespoon toasted sesame oil

1. Whisk soy sauce, sherry, and sugar together in medium bowl. Add chicken and toss to coat; set aside.

2. Heat vegetable oil, ginger, garlic, and pepper flakes in 12-inch nonstick skillet over medium-low heat. Cook, stirring frequently, until garlic is golden brown and beginning to soften, 8 to 10 minutes.

3. Add chicken and marinade to skillet, increase heat to medium-high, and bring to simmer. Reduce heat to medium-low and simmer, stirring occasionally, for 10 minutes. Stir in scallion whites and continue to cook until chicken registers about 200 degrees, 8 to 10 minutes longer.

4. Whisk water and cornstarch together in small bowl, then whisk into sauce; simmer until sauce is slightly thickened, about 1 minute. Remove skillet from heat. Stir in basil, sesame oil, and scallion greens. Transfer to platter and serve.

KOREAN-STYLE FRIED CHICKEN

WHY THIS RECIPE WORKS: A thin, crispy exterior and a spicy-sweet-salty sauce are the hallmarks of Korean fried chicken. The biggest challenge, though, is preventing the sauce from destroying the crust. We dunked the wings (which offer a high exterior to interior ratio for maximum crunch and also cook quickly) in a loose batter of flour, cornstarch, and water, which clung nicely to the chicken and fried up brown and crispy. To help the coating withstand a wet sauce, we double-fried the wings, which removed more water from the skin than a single fry did, making the coating extra-crispy. The Korean chili paste known as *gochujang* gives our sauce the proper spicy, fermented notes, while sugar tempered the heat and garlic and ginger—cooked briefly with sesame oil—provided depth.

Korean-Style Fried Chicken

SERVES 4 TO 6 AS A MAIN DISH

A rasp-style grater makes quick work of turning the garlic into a paste. *Gochujang*, Korean hot red chili paste, can be found in Asian markets and in some supermarkets. Tailor the heat level of your wings by adjusting its amount. If you can't find gochujang, substitute an equal amount of Sriracha sauce and add only 2 tablespoons of water to the sauce. For a complete meal, serve these wings with Basic White Rice (page 453) and a vegetable.

- 1 tablespoon toasted sesame oil
- 1 teaspoon garlic, minced to paste
- 1 teaspoon grated fresh ginger
- 1¾ cups water
- 3 tablespoons sugar
- 2–3 tablespoons gochujang
- 1 tablespoon soy sauce
- 2 quarts vegetable oil
- 1 cup all-purpose flour
- 3 tablespoons cornstarch
- 3 pounds chicken wings, cut at joints, wing tips discarded

1. Combine sesame oil, garlic, and ginger in large bowl and microwave until mixture is bubbly and fragrant but not browned, 40 to 60 seconds. Whisk in ¼ cup water, sugar, gochujang, and soy sauce until smooth and set aside.

2. Heat oil in large Dutch oven over medium-high heat to 350 degrees. While oil heats, whisk flour, cornstarch, and remaining 1½ cups water in second large bowl until smooth. Set wire rack in rimmed baking sheet and set aside.

3. Place half of wings in batter and stir to coat. Using tongs, remove wings from batter one at a time, allowing any excess batter to drip back into bowl, and add to hot oil. Increase heat to high and cook, stirring occasionally to prevent wings from sticking, until coating is light golden and beginning to crisp, about 7 minutes. (Oil temperature will drop sharply after adding chicken.) Transfer wings to prepared rack. Return oil to 350 degrees and repeat with remaining wings. Reduce heat to medium and let second batch of chicken rest for 5 minutes.

4. Return oil to 375 degrees. Carefully return all chicken to oil and cook, stirring occasionally, until exterior is deep golden brown and very crispy, about 7 minutes. Transfer to rack and let stand for 2 minutes. Add chicken to reserved sauce and toss until coated. Return chicken to rack and let stand for 2 minutes to allow surface to set. Transfer to platter and serve.

CHICKEN STIR-FRY WITH CRISPY NOODLE CAKE

WHY THIS RECIPE WORKS: Stir-fries are the quintessential weeknight dinner. And while a stir-fry served on top of rice is great, a pan-fried noodle cake—crispy and crunchy on the outside and tender and chewy in the middle—offers a welcome change of pace.

For the noodle cake, we had the most success with fresh Chinese egg noodles—they made for a cohesive cake with a crunchy exterior. A nonstick skillet was crucial—it kept the cake from sticking and falling apart and allowed us to use less oil so the cake wasn't greasy. We found the best way to flip the cake in the skillet was to slide it onto a plate, invert it onto another plate, and then slide it back in the pan to finish cooking. We kept the stir-fry simple; chicken and bok choy are a classic combination. A quick marinade gave our chicken welcome flavor, and a modified version of the Chinese technique called velveting prevented the chicken from drying out over high heat.

Stir-Fried Chicken with Bok Choy and Crispy Noodle Cake

SERVES 4

To make slicing the chicken easier, freeze it for 15 minutes. Fresh Chinese noodles are often kept in the produce section of the grocery store. If you can't find them, substitute an equal amount of fresh spaghetti.

SAUCE

- ¼ cup low-sodium chicken broth
- 2 tablespoons soy sauce
- 1 tablespoon dry sherry
- 1 tablespoon oyster-flavored sauce
- 1 teaspoon sugar
- 1 teaspoon cornstarch
- ¼ teaspoon red pepper flakes

NOODLE CAKE

- 1 (9-ounce) package fresh Chinese noodles (see note)
- 1 teaspoon table salt
- 2 scallions, sliced thin
- ¼ cup peanut or vegetable oil

CHICKEN AND VEGETABLES

- 1 pound boneless, skinless chicken breasts, trimmed and sliced thin (see note)
- 1 tablespoon soy sauce
- 1 tablespoon dry sherry
- 2 tablespoons toasted sesame oil
- 1 tablespoon cornstarch
- 1 tablespoon unbleached all-purpose flour
- 2 tablespoons plus 2 teaspoons peanut or vegetable oil
- 1 tablespoon minced or grated fresh ginger
- 1 medium garlic clove, minced or pressed through a garlic press (about 1 teaspoon)
- 1 small head bok choy, stalks cut on the bias into ¼-inch pieces and greens cut into ½-inch strips
- 1 small red bell pepper, stemmed, seeded, and cut into ¼-inch strips

1. FOR THE SAUCE: Combine all the ingredients in a small bowl and set aside.

2. FOR THE NOODLE CAKE: Bring 6 quarts water to a boil in a large pot. Add the noodles and salt and cook, stirring often, until almost tender, 2 to 3 minutes. Drain the noodles, then toss them with the scallions.

3. Heat 2 tablespoons of the peanut oil in a 12-inch nonstick skillet over medium heat until shimmering. Spread the noodles evenly across the bottom of the skillet and press with a spatula to flatten into a cake. Cook until crisp and golden brown, 5 to 8 minutes.

4. Slide the noodle cake onto a large plate. Add the remaining 2 tablespoons peanut oil to the skillet and swirl to coat. Invert the noodle cake onto a second plate and slide it, browned side up, back into the skillet. Cook until golden brown on the second side, 5 to 8 minutes.

5. Slide the noodle cake onto a cutting board and let sit for at least 5 minutes before slicing into wedges and serving. (The noodle cake can be transferred to a wire rack set over a baking sheet and kept warm in a 200-degree oven for up to 20 minutes.) Wipe out the skillet with a wad of paper towels.

6. FOR THE CHICKEN AND VEGETABLES: While the noodles boil, toss the chicken with the soy sauce and sherry in a medium bowl and let marinate for at least 10 minutes or up to 1 hour. In a large bowl, whisk the sesame oil, cornstarch, and flour together. In a small bowl, mix 1 teaspoon of the peanut oil, the ginger, and garlic together.

7. Stir the marinated chicken into the sesame oil–cornstarch mixture. Heat 2 teaspoons more peanut oil in the skillet over high heat until just smoking. Add half of the chicken, break up any clumps, then cook without stirring until the meat is browned at the edges, about 1 minute. Stir the chicken and continue to cook until cooked through, about 1 minute longer. Transfer the chicken to a clean bowl and cover with foil to keep warm. Repeat with 2 teaspoons more peanut oil and the remaining chicken.

8. Add the remaining 1 tablespoon peanut oil to the skillet and return to high heat until just smoking. Add the bok choy stalks and bell pepper and cook until lightly browned, 2 to 3 minutes.

9. Clear the center of the skillet, add the ginger mixture, and cook, mashing the mixture into the pan, until fragrant, 15 to 20 seconds. Stir the ginger mixture into the vegetables, then stir in the bok choy greens and cook until beginning to wilt, about 30 seconds.

10. Stir in the chicken with any accumulated juices. Whisk the sauce to recombine, then add to the skillet and cook, tossing constantly, until the sauce is thickened, about 30 seconds. Transfer to a serving platter and serve with the noodle cake.

BEHIND THE SCENES

STIR-FRIES AT HOME? THROW OUT YOUR WOK!

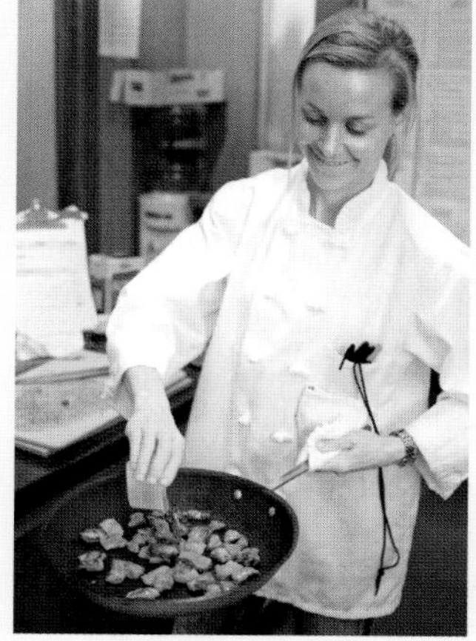

We love the theatrics of the kitchen. And few pans seem as fun to use as a wok—watching a Chinese cook stir-fry with a wok can be as exciting as catching a great drum solo at a rock concert. So imagine our disappointment when we realized woks simply don't perform as well as we thought. A wok's shape is the culprit. A wok's conical bottom is designed for a pit-style stove; the flames lick and engulf the pan, making most of the surface area hot even when food is added. But when you set a wok over a conventional stovetop, the heat becomes concentrated in the pan's bottom, and the larger surface area—the sides—simply doesn't heat as well. And when food is added to the wok, the pan's temperature drops. The results? Meat that steams instead of sears and vegetables that turn soggy, rather than crisp-tender.

What does work on a conventional stovetop? A large nonstick skillet. Its flat-bottom design allows more surface area to come in direct contact with the flat burner, delivering more heat over more parts than a wok—and enabling it to remain hot even after food is added.

To quantify their differences, we heated oil in a wok and a heavy 12-inch skillet over high heat on gas burners. Once the oil was smoking (at around 415 degrees), we added stir-fry ingredients to each pan. The wok's temperature plummeted dramatically, to 220 degrees at its center, rising only another 50 degrees over the course of cooking. The skillet's temperature dipped to 345 degrees, then recovered quickly, continuing to rise to almost 500 degrees. This higher heat translated to better browning and more flavor. The bottom line? Don't invest in a wok—use what you probably already have: a skillet. And if you want theatrics, order some concert tickets.

STIR-FRIES MADE SIMPLE

WHY THIS RECIPE WORKS: A good stir-fry made with chicken, shrimp, or tofu is more difficult to prepare than a beef or pork stir-fry because these proteins, which have less fat, are often bland. Worse, they inevitably become dry and stringy or rubbery when cooked over high heat. We aimed to create stir-fry recipes that harmonized the flavors and textures of these lighter proteins with complementary vegetables and sauces. We paired the chicken with zucchini, red bell pepper, and a zesty ginger sauce. And asparagus, yellow bell pepper, and a brightly flavored lemon sauce were a natural fit for the shrimp. We selected a slightly more assertive hot and sour sauce, along with red onion and snow peas, to enhance the mild-flavored tofu. As with most of our stir-fries, we marinated the thinly sliced chicken and shrimp, and the tofu, in a combination of soy sauce and dry sherry to add flavor. After cooking the chicken, shrimp, or tofu and removing it from the pan, we stir-fried the vegetables in batches, quickly cooked the garlic and ginger, and returned the protein to the pan along with the sauce. This final mixture needed less than a minute over medium heat to finish.

Stir-Fried Chicken and Zucchini with Ginger Sauce

SERVES 4

To make slicing the chicken easier, freeze it for 15 minutes. Serve with Basic White Rice (page 453).

SAUCE

- ¼ cup soy sauce
- 3 tablespoons minced or grated fresh ginger
- 2 tablespoons low-sodium chicken broth
- 1 tablespoon dry sherry
- ½ teaspoon sugar

CHICKEN AND VEGETABLES

- 12 ounces boneless, skinless chicken breasts, trimmed and sliced thin (see note)
- 1 tablespoon soy sauce
- 1 tablespoon dry sherry
- 2 tablespoons toasted sesame oil
- 1 tablespoon cornstarch
- 1 tablespoon unbleached all-purpose flour
- 2 tablespoons peanut or vegetable oil
- 1 tablespoon minced or grated fresh ginger
- 3 medium garlic cloves, minced or pressed through a garlic press (about 1 tablespoon)
- 2 scallions, white parts only, minced
- 2 carrots, peeled and cut into 2-inch-long matchsticks
- 1 red bell pepper, stemmed, seeded, and cut into ½-inch strips
- 1 medium zucchini, halved lengthwise and sliced ½ inch thick

1. FOR THE SAUCE: Combine all the ingredients in a small bowl and set aside.

2. FOR THE CHICKEN AND VEGETABLES: Toss the chicken with the soy sauce and sherry in a medium bowl and let marinate for at least 10 minutes or up to 1 hour. In a large bowl, whisk the sesame oil, cornstarch, and flour together. In a small bowl, mix 1 teaspoon of the peanut oil, the ginger, garlic, and scallions together.

3. Stir the marinated chicken into the sesame oil–cornstarch mixture. Heat 2 teaspoons more peanut oil in a 12-inch nonstick skillet over high heat until just smoking. Add the chicken, break up any clumps, then cook without stirring until the meat is browned at the edges, about 1 minute. Stir the chicken and continue to cook until cooked through, about 1 minute longer. Transfer the chicken to a clean bowl and cover with foil to keep warm.

4. Add the remaining 1 tablespoon peanut oil to the skillet and return to high heat until just smoking. Add the carrots and cook until beginning to soften, about 1 minute. Add the bell pepper and cook until spotty brown, about 1 minute. Add the zucchini and cook for 15 to 30 seconds, until just tender.

5. Clear the center of the skillet, add the ginger mixture, and cook, mashing the mixture into the pan, until fragrant, 15 to 20 seconds. Stir the ginger mixture into the vegetables.

6. Stir in the chicken with any accumulated juices. Whisk the sauce to recombine, then add to the skillet and cook, tossing constantly, until the sauce is thickened, about 30 seconds. Transfer to a serving platter and serve.

Stir-Fried Shrimp, Asparagus, and Yellow Pepper with Lemon Sauce

SERVES 4

One large lemon yields enough juice and zest for this sauce. Serve with Basic White Rice (page 453).

SAUCE

- 3 tablespoons juice plus ½ teaspoon zest from 1 lemon
- 2 tablespoons low-sodium chicken broth
- 1 tablespoon soy sauce
- 2 teaspoons sugar

SHRIMP AND VEGETABLES

- 1 pound medium shrimp (41 to 50 per pound), peeled and deveined (see page 240)
- 1 tablespoon soy sauce
- 1 tablespoon dry sherry
- 2 tablespoons plus 2 teaspoons peanut or vegetable oil
- 1 tablespoon minced or grated fresh ginger
- 3 garlic cloves, minced or pressed through a garlic press (about 1 tablespoon)
- 2 scallions, white parts only, minced
- 1 pound asparagus (1 bunch), tough ends trimmed, cut on the bias into 1-inch lengths
- ¼ cup water
- 1 yellow bell pepper, stemmed, seeded, and cut into ½-inch strips
- Table salt and ground black pepper
- ¼ cup chopped fresh cilantro leaves

1. FOR THE SAUCE: Combine all the ingredients in a small bowl and set aside.

2. FOR THE SHRIMP AND VEGETABLES: Toss the shrimp with the soy sauce and sherry in a medium bowl and let marinate for at least 10 minutes or up to 1 hour. In a small bowl, mix 1 teaspoon of the oil, the ginger, garlic, and scallions together.

3. Heat 2 teaspoons more oil in a 12-inch nonstick skillet over high heat until just smoking. Add the shrimp and cook without stirring until bright pink, about 1 minute. Stir the shrimp and continue to cook until cooked through, 15 to 30 seconds longer. Transfer the shrimp to a clean bowl and cover with foil to keep warm.

4. Add 1 tablespoon more oil to the skillet and return to high heat until just smoking. Add the asparagus and cook, stirring frequently, until spotty brown, about 2 minutes. Add the water, cover the pan, and lower the heat to medium. Cook the asparagus until crisp-tender, about 2 minutes. Transfer the asparagus to the bowl with the shrimp. Add the remaining 2 teaspoons oil to the skillet and return to high heat until just smoking. Add the bell pepper and cook, stirring frequently, until spotty brown, about 1½ minutes.

5. Clear the center of the skillet, add the ginger mixture, and cook, mashing the mixture into the pan, until fragrant, 15 to 20 seconds. Stir the ginger mixture into the bell pepper.

6. Stir in the asparagus and shrimp with any accumulated juices. Whisk the sauce to recombine, then add to the skillet and cook, tossing constantly, until the sauce is thickened, about 30 seconds. Season with salt and pepper to taste. Transfer to a serving platter, sprinkle with the cilantro, and serve.

Stir-Fried Tofu, Snow Peas, and Red Onion with Hot and Sour Sauce

SERVES 4

Make sure to buy firm or extra-firm tofu; silken or soft tofu will crumble if stir-fried. To promote caramelization on the exterior of the tofu, turn the cubes as little as possible so that they have time to brown on several sides. For more heat, include the jalapeño seeds and ribs when mincing. Serve with Basic White Rice (page 453).

SAUCE

- 3 tablespoons cider vinegar
- 1 tablespoon low-sodium chicken broth
- 1 tablespoon soy sauce
- 2 teaspoons sugar

TOFU AND VEGETABLES

- 1 (14-ounce) block firm or extra-firm tofu, drained and cut into 1-inch cubes (see note)
- 1 tablespoon soy sauce
- 1 tablespoon dry sherry
- 2 tablespoons plus 1 teaspoon peanut or vegetable oil
- 1 tablespoon minced or grated fresh ginger
- 3 garlic cloves, minced or pressed through a garlic press (about 1 tablespoon)
- 2 scallions, white parts only, minced
- 1 jalapeño chile, seeds and ribs removed, chile minced (see note)
- 1 medium red onion, halved and sliced thin
- 1 pound snow peas, tips and strings removed
- 2 tablespoons water

1. FOR THE SAUCE: Combine all the ingredients in a small bowl and set aside.

2. FOR THE TOFU AND VEGETABLES: Toss the tofu with the soy sauce and sherry in a medium bowl and let marinate for at least 10 minutes or up to 1 hour. In a small bowl, mix 1 teaspoon of the oil, the ginger, garlic, scallions, and jalapeño together.

3. Heat 1 tablespoon more oil in a 12-inch nonstick skillet over high heat until just smoking. Add the tofu and cook until golden brown on several sides, 2 to 3 minutes, turning as needed. Transfer the tofu to a clean bowl and cover with foil to keep warm.

4. Add the remaining 1 tablespoon oil to the skillet and return to high heat until just smoking. Add the onion and cook, stirring frequently, until beginning to brown, about 2 minutes. Add the snow peas and cook until spotty brown, about 2 minutes. Add the water, cover the pan, and lower the heat to medium. Cook the snow peas until crisp-tender, about 1 minute.

5. Clear the center of the skillet, add the ginger mixture, and cook, mashing the mixture into the pan, until fragrant, 15 to 20 seconds. Stir the ginger mixture into the vegetables.

6. Stir in the tofu. Whisk the sauce to recombine, then add to the skillet and cook, tossing constantly, until the sauce is thickened, about 30 seconds. Transfer to a serving platter and serve.

CHINESE-STYLE MAPO TOFU

WHY THIS RECIPE WORKS: Our *mapo* tofu recipe is bold in flavor, but not too spicy, and balanced, as all Sichuan dishes should be. We used cubed soft tofu, poached gently in chicken broth to help the cubes stay intact in the braise. For the sauce base, we used plenty of ginger and garlic, along with four Sichuan pantry powerhouses: Asian broad bean chili paste (*doubanjiang* or *toban djan*), fermented black beans, Sichuan chili powder, and Sichuan peppercorns. In place of the chili oil often called for, we used a generous amount of vegetable oil, extra Sichuan chili powder, and added toasted sesame oil. Finally, just the right amount of cornstarch gave the dish a velvety thickness.

Sichuan Braised Tofu with Beef (Mapo Tofu)

SERVES 4 TO 6

Ground pork can be used in place of beef, if desired. Asian broad bean chili paste (or sauce) is also known as *doubanjiang* or *toban djan*; our favorite, Pixian, is available online. Supermarket Lee Kum Kee Chili Bean Sauce is also a good option. If you can't find Sichuan chili powder, an equal amount of Korean red pepper flakes (*gochugaru*) is a good substitute. In a pinch, use 2½ teaspoons of ancho chile powder and ½ teaspoon of cayenne pepper. If you can't find fermented black beans, you can use an equal amount of fermented black bean paste or sauce or two additional teaspoons of Asian broad bean chili paste. Serve with Basic White Rice (page 453).

- 1 tablespoon Sichuan peppercorns
- 12 scallions
- 28 ounces soft tofu, cut into ½-inch cubes
- 2 cups chicken broth
- 9 garlic cloves, peeled
- 1 (3-inch) piece ginger, peeled and cut into ¼-inch rounds
- ⅓ cup Asian broad bean chili paste
- 1 tablespoon fermented black beans
- ¼ cup plus 2 tablespoons vegetable oil
- 1 tablespoon Sichuan chili powder
- 8 ounces 85 percent lean ground beef
- 2 tablespoons hoisin sauce
- 2 teaspoons toasted sesame oil
- 2 tablespoons water
- 1 tablespoon cornstarch

1. Place peppercorns in small bowl and microwave until fragrant, 15 to 30 seconds. Let cool completely. Once cool, grind in spice grinder or mortar and pestle (you should have 1½ teaspoons).

2. Using side of chef's knife, lightly crush white parts of scallions, then cut scallions into 1-inch pieces. Place tofu, broth, and scallions in large bowl and microwave, covered, until steaming, 5 to 7 minutes. Let stand while preparing remaining ingredients.

3. Process garlic, ginger, chili paste, and black beans in food processor until coarse paste forms, 1 to 2 minutes, scraping down sides of bowl as needed. Add ¼ cup vegetable oil, chili powder, and 1 teaspoon peppercorns and continue to process until smooth paste forms, 1 to 2 minutes longer. Transfer spice paste to bowl.

4. Heat 1 tablespoon vegetable oil and beef in large saucepan over medium heat; cook, breaking up meat with wooden spoon, until meat just begins to brown, 5 to 7 minutes. Transfer beef to bowl.

5. Add remaining 1 tablespoon vegetable oil and spice paste to now-empty saucepan and cook, stirring frequently, until paste darkens and oil begins to separate from paste, 2 to 3 minutes. Gently pour tofu with broth into saucepan, followed by hoisin, sesame oil, and beef. Cook, stirring gently and frequently, until dish comes to simmer, 2 to 3 minutes. Whisk water and cornstarch together in small bowl. Add cornstarch mixture to saucepan and continue to cook, stirring frequently, until thickened, 2 to 3 minutes longer. Transfer to serving dish, sprinkle with remaining peppercorns, and serve. (Mapo tofu can be refrigerated for up to 24 hours.)

STIR-FRIED BEEF AND BROCCOLI

WHY THIS RECIPE WORKS: Order beef and broccoli in most Chinese restaurants, and you are served a pile of tough meat and overcooked army-issue broccoli. Worst of all is the thick-as-pudding brown sauce, which, aside from being flavored with burnt garlic, is otherwise tasteless. We set out to rescue this dish from the tyranny of third-rate Chinese restaurants.

For the meat, we found that flank steak offered the biggest beefy taste and slicing it thin made it tender. We cooked the beef in two batches over high heat to make sure it browned and didn't steam. Then we cooked the broccoli until crisp-tender using a combination of methods—sautéing and steaming—and added some red bell pepper for sweetness and color. For the sauce, we made a simple mixture of oyster-flavored sauce, chicken broth, dry sherry, sugar, and sesame oil, which we lightly thickened with cornstarch so it clung beautifully to the beef and vegetables. Now we had it: Every component of the dish—the beef, the broccoli, and the sauce—was distinct and cooked to the best of its ability.

Stir-Fried Beef and Broccoli with Oyster Sauce

SERVES 4

To make slicing the flank steak easier, freeze it for 15 minutes. Serve with Basic White Rice (page 453).

SAUCE

- 5 tablespoons oyster-flavored sauce
- 2 tablespoons low-sodium chicken broth
- 1 tablespoon dry sherry
- 1 tablespoon light brown sugar
- 1 teaspoon toasted sesame oil
- 1 teaspoon cornstarch

BEEF AND BROCCOLI

- 1 (1-pound) flank steak, trimmed and cut into 2-inch-wide strips with the grain, then sliced across the grain into ⅛-inch-thick slices (see note)
- 3 tablespoons soy sauce
- 3 tablespoons peanut or vegetable oil
- 6 medium garlic cloves, minced or pressed through a garlic press (about 2 tablespoons)
- 1 tablespoon minced or grated fresh ginger
- 1¼ pounds broccoli, florets cut into 1-inch pieces, stems trimmed and sliced thin
- ⅓ cup water
- 1 small red bell pepper, stemmed, seeded, and cut into ½-inch pieces
- 3 scallions, sliced ½ inch thick on the bias

1. FOR THE SAUCE: Combine all the ingredients in a small bowl and set aside.

2. FOR THE BEEF AND BROCCOLI: Toss the beef with the soy sauce in a medium bowl and let marinate for at least 10 minutes or up to 1 hour. In a small bowl, mix 1 teaspoon of the peanut oil, the garlic, and ginger together.

3. Heat 2 teaspoons more peanut oil in a 12-inch nonstick skillet over high heat until just smoking. Add half of the beef, break up any clumps, then cook without stirring until the meat is browned at the edges, about 1 minute. Stir the beef and continue to cook until cooked through, about 1 minute longer. Transfer the beef to a clean bowl and cover with foil to keep warm. Repeat with 2 teaspoons more peanut oil and the remaining beef.

4. Add 1 tablespoon more peanut oil to the skillet and return to high heat until just smoking. Add the broccoli and cook for 30 seconds. Add the water, cover the pan, and lower the heat to medium. Cook the broccoli until crisp-tender, about 2 minutes. Transfer the broccoli to a paper towel–lined plate.

5. Add the remaining 1 teaspoon peanut oil to the skillet and return to high heat until just smoking. Add the bell pepper and cook, stirring frequently, until spotty brown, about 1½ minutes. Clear the center of the skillet, add the garlic mixture, and cook, mashing the mixture into the pan, until fragrant, 15 to 20 seconds. Stir the garlic mixture into the bell pepper.

6. Stir in the broccoli and beef with any accumulated juices. Whisk the sauce to recombine, then add to the skillet and cook, tossing constantly, until the sauce is thickened, about 30 seconds. Transfer to a serving platter, sprinkle with the scallions, and serve.

CHINESE PEPPER STEAK

WHY THIS RECIPE WORKS: We discovered that in order to produce a stir-fry with velvety, tender beef normally only found in Chinese restaurants, we needed to choose the right cut of meat and treat it correctly. Flank steak, cut across the grain into bite-size pieces, delivered great beef flavor and a moderate chew. Then, our combination of meat tenderizing techniques—soaking the meat briefly in a mild baking soda solution and adding some cornstarch to the marinade before flash searing the steak in a very hot pan—finished the job of delivering a supertender, restaurant-quality beef stir-fry.

Beef Stir-Fry with Bell Peppers and Black Pepper Sauce

SERVES 4

Prepare the vegetables and aromatics while the beef is marinating. Serve with Basic White Rice (page 453).

- 1 tablespoon plus ¼ cup water
- ¼ teaspoon baking soda
- 1 pound flank steak, trimmed, cut into 2- to 2½-inch strips with grain, each strip cut crosswise against grain into ¼-inch-thick slices
- 3 tablespoons soy sauce
- 3 tablespoons dry sherry or Chinese rice wine
- 3 teaspoons cornstarch
- 2½ teaspoons packed light brown sugar
- 1 tablespoon oyster sauce
- 2 teaspoons rice vinegar
- 1½ teaspoons toasted sesame oil
- 2 teaspoons coarsely ground pepper
- 3 tablespoons plus 1 teaspoon vegetable oil
- 1 red bell pepper, stemmed, seeded, and cut into ¼-inch-wide strips
- 1 green bell pepper, stemmed, seeded, and cut into ¼-inch-wide strips
- 6 scallions, white parts sliced thin on bias, green parts cut into 2-inch pieces
- 3 garlic cloves, minced
- 1 tablespoon grated fresh ginger

1. Combine 1 tablespoon water and baking soda in medium bowl. Add beef and toss to coat. Let sit at room temperature for 5 minutes.

2. Whisk 1 tablespoon soy sauce, 1 tablespoon sherry, 1½ teaspoons cornstarch, and ½ teaspoon sugar together in small bowl. Add soy sauce mixture to beef, stir to coat, and let sit at room temperature for 15 to 30 minutes.

3. Whisk remaining ¼ cup water, remaining 2 tablespoons soy sauce, remaining 2 tablespoons sherry, remaining 1½ teaspoons cornstarch, remaining 2 teaspoons sugar, oyster sauce, vinegar, sesame oil, and pepper together in second bowl.

4. Heat 2 teaspoons vegetable oil in 12-inch nonstick skillet over high heat until just smoking. Add half of beef in single layer. Cook without stirring for 1 minute. Continue to cook, stirring occasionally, until spotty brown on both sides, about 1 minute longer. Transfer to bowl. Repeat with 2 teaspoons vegetable oil and remaining beef.

5. Return skillet to high heat, add 2 teaspoons vegetable oil, and heat until just beginning to smoke. Add bell peppers and scallion greens and cook, stirring occasionally, until vegetables are spotty brown and crisp-tender, about 4 minutes. Transfer vegetables to bowl with beef.

6. Return now-empty skillet to medium-high heat and add remaining 4 teaspoons vegetable oil, scallion whites, garlic, and ginger. Cook, stirring frequently, until lightly browned, about 2 minutes. Return beef and vegetables to skillet and stir to combine.

7. Whisk sauce to recombine. Add to skillet and cook, stirring constantly, until sauce has thickened, about 30 seconds. Serve immediately.

BEEF AND VEGETABLE STIR-FRIES

WHY THIS RECIPE WORKS: More often than not, beef and vegetable stir-fries consist of chewy, gray beef, surrounded by unevenly cooked vegetables, smothered in a gloppy sauce. We wanted browned, tender beef and crisp-tender vegetables coated in deep-flavored, silky sauces.

We chose flank steak for the best texture and flavor. We thinly sliced and marinated the steak in soy sauce and sugar and cooked it over high heat to achieve a good sear. We cooked the vegetables in batches for best texture. For one stir-fry, we paired the beef with green beans, shiitakes, and a teriyaki sauce. Next, we combined the beef with a tangerine sauce, snow peas, and onion. The sauces were lightly thickened with just 1 teaspoon of cornstarch, so they clung to the beef and vegetables but were not overly thick.

Teriyaki Stir-Fried Beef with Green Beans and Shiitakes

SERVES 4

To make slicing the flank steak easier, freeze it for 15 minutes. Serve with Basic White Rice (page 453).

SAUCE

- ½ cup low-sodium chicken broth
- 2 tablespoons soy sauce
- 2 tablespoons sugar

- 1 tablespoon mirin or sweet sherry
- 1 teaspoon cornstarch
- ¼ teaspoon red pepper flakes

BEEF AND VEGETABLES

- 12 ounces flank steak, trimmed and cut into 2-inch-wide strips with the grain, then sliced across the grain into ⅛-inch-thick slices (see note)
- 2 tablespoons soy sauce
- 1 teaspoon sugar
- 2 tablespoons peanut or vegetable oil
- 1 tablespoon minced or grated fresh ginger
- 3 medium garlic cloves, minced or pressed through a garlic press (about 1 tablespoon)
- 8 ounces shiitake mushrooms, stemmed, wiped clean, caps cut into 1-inch pieces
- 12 ounces green beans, ends trimmed, cut into 2-inch lengths (see photo on page 465)
- ¼ cup water
- 3 scallions, quartered lengthwise and cut into 1½-inch pieces

1. **FOR THE SAUCE:** Combine all the ingredients in a small bowl and set aside.

2. **FOR THE BEEF AND VEGETABLES:** Toss the beef with the soy sauce and sugar in a medium bowl and let marinate for at least 10 minutes or up to 1 hour. In a small bowl, mix 1 teaspoon of the oil, the ginger, and garlic together.

3. Heat 2 teaspoons more oil in a 12-inch nonstick skillet over high heat until just smoking. Add the beef, break up any clumps, then cook without stirring until the meat is browned at the edges, about 1 minute. Stir the beef and continue to cook until cooked through, about 1 minute longer. Transfer the beef to a clean bowl and cover with foil to keep warm.

4. Add the remaining 1 tablespoon oil to the skillet and return to high heat until just smoking. Add the mushrooms and cook until beginning to brown, about 2 minutes. Add the green beans and cook, stirring frequently, until spotty brown,

3 to 4 minutes. Add the water, cover the pan, and lower the heat to medium. Cook the green beans until crisp-tender, about 2 minutes.

5. Clear the center of the skillet, add the ginger mixture, and cook, mashing the mixture into the pan, until fragrant, 15 to 20 seconds. Stir the ginger mixture into the vegetables.

6. Stir in the beef with any accumulated juices. Whisk the sauce to recombine, then add to the skillet and cook, tossing constantly, until the sauce is thickened, about 30 seconds. Stir in the scallions. Transfer to a serving platter and serve.

NOTES FROM THE TEST KITCHEN

TRIMMING GREEN BEANS QUICKLY

Line up several green beans in a row on a cutting board. Trim about ½ inch from each end, then cut the beans as directed in the recipe.

Tangerine Stir-Fried Beef with Onion and Snow Peas

SERVES 4

To make slicing the flank steak easier, freeze it for 15 minutes. Two to three oranges can be substituted for the tangerines. Note that you should zest the tangerines before juicing them. Use the larger amount of red pepper flakes if you desire a spicier dish. If available, substitute 1 teaspoon toasted and ground Sichuan peppercorns for the red pepper flakes. Serve with Basic White Rice (page 453).

SAUCE

- ¾ cup juice from 3 to 4 tangerines (see note)
- 2 tablespoons soy sauce
- 1 tablespoon light brown sugar
- 1 teaspoon toasted sesame oil
- 1 teaspoon cornstarch

BEEF AND VEGETABLES

- 12 ounces flank steak, trimmed and cut into 2-inch-wide strips with the grain, then sliced across the grain into ⅛-inch-thick slices (see note)
- 2 tablespoons soy sauce
- 1 teaspoon light brown sugar
- 2 tablespoons peanut or vegetable oil
- 1 tablespoon minced or grated fresh ginger
- 3 medium garlic cloves, minced or pressed through a garlic press (about 1 tablespoon)
- 1 tablespoon Chinese black bean sauce
- 1 teaspoon grated zest from 1 tangerine (see note)
- ¼–½ teaspoon red pepper flakes (see note)
- 1 large onion, halved and cut into ½-inch wedges
- 10 ounces snow peas, tips and strings removed
- 2 tablespoons water

1. FOR THE SAUCE: Combine all the ingredients in a small bowl and set aside.

2. FOR THE BEEF AND VEGETABLES: Toss the beef with the soy sauce and sugar in a medium bowl and let marinate for at least 10 minutes or up to 1 hour. In a small bowl, mix 1 teaspoon of the peanut oil, the ginger, garlic, black bean sauce, tangerine zest, and red pepper flakes together.

3. Heat 2 teaspoons more peanut oil in a 12-inch nonstick skillet over high heat until just smoking. Add the beef, break up any clumps, then cook without stirring until the meat is browned at the edges, about 1 minute. Stir the beef and continue to cook until cooked through, about 1 minute longer. Transfer the beef to a clean bowl and cover with foil to keep warm.

4. Add the remaining 1 tablespoon peanut oil to the skillet and return to high heat until just smoking. Add the onion and cook, stirring frequently, until beginning to brown, about 2 minutes. Add the snow peas and cook until spotty brown, about 2 minutes. Add the water, cover the pan, and lower the heat to medium. Cook the snow peas until crisp-tender, about 1 minute.

5. Clear the center of the skillet, add the ginger mixture, and cook, mashing the mixture into the pan, until fragrant, 15 to 20 seconds. Stir the ginger mixture into the vegetables.

6. Stir in the beef with any accumulated juices. Whisk the sauce to recombine, then add to the skillet and cook, tossing constantly, until the sauce is thickened, about 30 seconds. Transfer to a serving platter and serve.

CHINESE BRAISED BEEF

WHY THIS RECIPE WORKS: Chinese braised beef (also called red-cooked beef) is a slow-braised dish in which a thick, ultra-flavorful, stew-like sauce envelops tender pieces of beef. We wanted to maintain the deeply complex flavors of the original but simplify the recipe for the home kitchen.

We decided to use readily available boneless beef short ribs in place of the traditional shank of beef. To streamline the classic cooking method, we opted to skip blanching the meat, and we moved the pot from the stovetop to the even heat of the oven. A pair of thickeners—gelatin and cornstarch—added body to the sauce. Five-spice powder provided characteristic flavor without the bother of whole spices, and a combination of hoisin sauce and molasses contributed an underlying sweetness that completed the dish.

Chinese Braised Beef

SERVES 6

With its generous amount of soy sauce, this dish is meant to taste salty, which is why we pair it with Basic White Rice (page 453). A simple steamed vegetable like bok choy or broccoli completes the meal. Boneless beef short ribs require little trimming, but you can also use a 4-pound chuck roast. Trim the roast of large pieces of fat and sinew, cut it across the grain into 1-inch-thick slabs, and cut the slabs into 4 by 2-inch pieces.

- 1½ tablespoons unflavored gelatin
- 2½ cups plus 1 tablespoon water
- ½ cup dry sherry
- ⅓ cup soy sauce
- 2 tablespoons hoisin sauce
- 2 tablespoons molasses
- 3 scallions, white and green parts separated, green parts sliced thin on bias
- 1 (2-inch) piece ginger, peeled, halved lengthwise, and crushed
- 4 garlic cloves, peeled and smashed
- 1½ teaspoons five-spice powder
- 1 teaspoon red pepper flakes
- 3 pounds boneless beef short ribs, trimmed and cut into 4-inch lengths
- 1 teaspoon cornstarch

1. Sprinkle gelatin over 2½ cups water in Dutch oven and let sit until gelatin softens, about 5 minutes. Adjust oven rack to middle position and heat oven to 300 degrees.

2. Heat softened gelatin over medium-high heat, stirring occasionally, until melted, 2 to 3 minutes. Stir in sherry, soy sauce, hoisin, molasses, scallion whites, ginger, garlic, five-spice powder, and pepper flakes. Stir in beef and bring to simmer. Remove pot from heat. Cover tightly with sheet of heavy-duty aluminum foil, then lid. Transfer to oven and cook until beef is tender, 2 to 2½ hours, stirring halfway through cooking.

3. Using slotted spoon, transfer beef to cutting board. Strain sauce through fine-mesh strainer into fat separator. Wipe out pot with paper towels. Let liquid settle for 5 minutes, then return defatted liquid to now-empty pot. Cook liquid over medium-high heat, stirring occasionally, until thickened and reduced to 1 cup, 20 to 25 minutes.

4. While sauce reduces, using 2 forks, break beef into 1½-inch pieces. Whisk cornstarch and remaining 1 tablespoon water together in small bowl.

5. Reduce heat to medium-low, whisk cornstarch mixture into reduced sauce, and cook until sauce is slightly thickened, about 1 minute. Return beef to sauce and stir to coat. Cover and cook, stirring occasionally, until beef is heated through, about 5 minutes. Sprinkle scallion greens over top. Serve.

CRISPY ORANGE BEEF

WHY THIS RECIPE WORKS: Crispy orange beef has long remained a Chinese restaurant standard because its crunchy batter coating and tangy citrus sauce seem impossible in the home kitchen without a deep fryer. To make this recipe accessible without diminishing its big flavor and shatteringly crisp crust, we started with the beef. Tender flap meat cut into matchsticks maximized the surface area for extra crunch in each bite. Tossing the beef in soy sauce and cornstarch created a clingy, delicate coating and 45 minutes in the freezer dried the prepped beef's surface to boost crisping. We only needed 3 cups of oil to fry the beef to a beautiful golden brown, and thanks to the dry cornstarch coating, very little oil was absorbed, so the beef never turned greasy. For a sauce to complement the crispy beef, we recreated the bitter, citrusy tang of hard-to-find dried tangerine peels by using the juice and peels of two oranges. We whisked the fresh juice with soy sauce, molasses, dry sherry, rice vinegar, and sesame oil for a complex, complementary sauce and then, for some bite and heat, browned the peels with jalapeños in a skillet. Garlic, ginger, and red pepper flakes reinforced the spicy bite before the soy sauce mixture was added to the pan. We cooked the mixture until it thickened slightly, and then tossed in our beef along with sliced scallions for a finishing touch of brightness.

Crispy Orange Beef

SERVES 4

We prefer to buy flap meat and cut our own steak tips. Use a vegetable peeler on the oranges and make sure that your strips contain some pith. Do not use low-sodium soy sauce. Serve this dish with Basic White Rice (page 453).

- 1½ pounds beef flap meat, trimmed
- 3 tablespoons soy sauce
- 6 tablespoons cornstarch
- 10 (3-inch) strips orange peel, sliced thin lengthwise (¼ cup), plus ¼ cup juice (2 oranges)
- 3 tablespoons molasses
- 2 tablespoons dry sherry
- 1 tablespoon rice vinegar

- 1½ teaspoons toasted sesame oil
- 3 cups vegetable oil
- 1 jalapeño chile, stemmed, seeded, and sliced thin lengthwise
- 3 garlic cloves, minced
- 2 tablespoons grated fresh ginger
- ½ teaspoon red pepper flakes
- 2 scallions, sliced thin on bias

1. Cut beef with grain into 2½- to 3-inch-wide lengths. Slice each piece against grain into ½-inch-thick slices. Cut each slice lengthwise into ½-inch-wide strips. Toss beef with 1 tablespoon soy sauce in bowl. Add cornstarch and toss until evenly coated. Spread beef in single layer on wire rack set in rimmed baking sheet. Transfer sheet to freezer until meat is very firm but not completely frozen, about 45 minutes.

2. Whisk remaining 2 tablespoons soy sauce, orange juice, molasses, sherry, vinegar, and sesame oil together in bowl.

3. Line second rimmed baking sheet with triple layer of paper towels. Heat vegetable oil in large Dutch oven over medium heat until oil registers 375 degrees. Carefully add one-third of beef and fry, stirring occasionally to keep beef from sticking together, until golden brown, about 1½ minutes. Using spider, transfer beef to paper towel–lined sheet. Return oil to 375 degrees and repeat twice more with remaining beef. After frying, reserve 2 tablespoons frying oil.

4. Heat reserved oil in 12-inch skillet over medium-high heat until shimmering. Add orange peel and jalapeño and cook, stirring occasionally, until about half of orange peel is golden brown, 1½ to 2 minutes. Add garlic, ginger, and pepper flakes; cook, stirring frequently, until garlic is beginning to brown, about 45 seconds. Add soy sauce mixture and cook, scraping up any browned bits, until slightly thickened, about 45 seconds. Add beef and scallions and toss. Transfer to platter and serve immediately.

CHINESE BARBECUED PORK

WHY THIS RECIPE WORKS: For a Chinese barbecued pork recipe suited to the home kitchen, we started by slicing a boneless pork butt into strips. Our marinade of soy sauce, sherry, hoisin sauce, five-spice powder, sesame oil, ginger, and garlic introduced traditional Asian flavors, especially after we pricked the meat with a fork to enhance penetration. For optimal browning and intense flavor, we needed a two-heat process—first cooking the meat, covered, at a low temperature to render fat and then cranking up the heat to develop a burnished crust. The classic lacquered appearance was achieved by applying a ketchup-honey glaze right before broiling, which also gave our pork its traditional red color.

Chinese Barbecued Pork

SERVES 6

To facilitate cleanup, spray the rack and pan with vegetable oil spray. The pork will release liquid and fat during the cooking process, so be careful when removing the pan from the oven. If you don't have a wire rack that fits in a rimmed baking sheet, substitute a broiler pan, although the meat may not darken as much. Pay close attention to the meat when broiling—you are looking for it to darken and caramelize, not blacken. Do not use a drawer broiler; the heat source will be too close to the meat. Instead, increase the oven temperature in step 5 to 500 degrees and cook for 8 to 12 minutes before glazing and 6 to 8 minutes once the glaze has been applied; flip meat and repeat on second side. This recipe can be made with boneless country-style ribs, but the meat will be slightly drier and less flavorful. To use ribs, reduce the uncovered cooking time in step 4 to 20 minutes and increase the broiling and glazing times in step 5 by 2 to 3 minutes per side.

- 4 pounds boneless pork butt (Boston butt), cut into 8 strips and excess fat removed
- ½ cup sugar
- ½ cup soy sauce
- 6 tablespoons hoisin sauce
- ¼ cup dry sherry
- ¼ teaspoon ground white pepper
- 1 teaspoon Chinese five-spice powder
- 1 tablespoon toasted sesame oil
- 2 tablespoons grated fresh ginger (from 4- to 6-inch piece)
- 2 medium cloves garlic, minced or pressed through a garlic press (about 2 teaspoons)
- ¼ cup ketchup
- ⅓ cup honey

1. Using fork, prick pork 10 to 12 times on each side. Place pork in large plastic zipper-lock bag. Combine sugar, soy, hoisin, sherry, pepper, five-spice powder, sesame oil, ginger, and garlic in medium bowl. Measure out ½ cup marinade and set aside. Pour remaining marinade into bag with pork. Press out as much air as possible; seal bag. Refrigerate for at least 30 minutes or up to 4 hours.

2. While meat marinates, combine ketchup and honey with reserved marinade in small saucepan. Cook glaze over medium heat until syrupy and reduced to 1 cup, 4 to 6 minutes.

3. Adjust oven rack to middle position and heat oven to 300 degrees. Line rimmed baking sheet with aluminum foil and set wire rack on sheet.

4. Remove pork from marinade, letting any excess drip off, and place on wire rack. Pour ¼ cup water into bottom of pan. Cover pan with heavy-duty aluminum foil, crimping edges tightly to seal. Cook pork for 20 minutes. Remove foil and continue to cook until edges of pork begin to brown, 40 to 45 minutes.

5. Turn on broiler. Broil pork until evenly caramelized, 7 to 9 minutes. Remove pan from oven and brush pork with half of glaze; broil until deep mahogany color, 3 to 5 minutes. Using tongs, flip meat and broil until other side caramelizes, 7 to 9 minutes. Brush meat with remaining glaze and continue to broil until second side is deep mahogany, 3 to 5 minutes. Cool for at least 10 minutes, then cut into thin strips and serve.

PORK AND VEGETABLE STIR-FRIES

WHY THIS RECIPE WORKS: Pork and vegetable stir-fries, homemade or ordered out, are usually nothing more than tough, tasteless pork and barely cooked vegetables in a thick sauce. We wanted to make pork and vegetable stir-fries that had tender, flavorful pork and perfectly cooked vegetables—dishes that would taste authentic but would not have unapproachable ingredient lists. We chose pork tenderloin for our stir-fry because it is so tender. Marinating improved the pork's flavor, and cooking quickly over high heat ensured browning. Because different vegetables cook at different rates, we batch-cooked the vegetables and added aromatics (like ginger and garlic) at the end so they would cook long enough to develop their flavors but not burn. For the sauce, we used chicken broth as the backbone and added an acid like lime juice or rice vinegar to brighten the flavors. As with our other stir-fries, cornstarch created a slightly thickened sauce that lightly cloaked the pork and vegetables.

Stir-Fried Pork, Eggplant, and Onion with Garlic and Black Pepper

SERVES 4

To make slicing the pork easier, freeze it for 15 minutes. This classic Thai stir-fry is not for those with timid palates. Serve with Basic White Rice (page 453).

SAUCE

- 2½ tablespoons soy sauce
- 2½ tablespoons fish sauce
- 2½ tablespoons light brown sugar
- 2 tablespoons low-sodium chicken broth
- 2 teaspoons juice from 1 lime
- 1 teaspoon cornstarch

PORK AND VEGETABLES

- 1 (12-ounce) pork tenderloin, trimmed of fat and silver skin and cut into ¼-inch strips (see note)
- 1 teaspoon soy sauce
- 1 teaspoon fish sauce
- 3 tablespoons peanut or vegetable oil
- 12 medium garlic cloves, minced or pressed through a garlic press (about ¼ cup)
- 2 teaspoons ground black pepper
- 1 medium eggplant (1 pound), cut into ¾-inch cubes
- 1 large onion, halved and cut into ¼-inch wedges
- ½ cup chopped fresh cilantro leaves

1. FOR THE SAUCE: Combine all the ingredients in a small bowl and set aside.

2. FOR THE PORK AND VEGETABLES: Toss the pork with the soy sauce and fish sauce in a medium bowl and let marinate for at least 10 minutes or up to 1 hour. In a small bowl, mix 2 teaspoons of the oil, the garlic, and pepper together.

3. Heat 2 teaspoons more oil in a 12-inch nonstick skillet over high heat until just smoking. Add the pork, break up any clumps, then cook without stirring until the meat is browned at the edges, about 1 minute. Stir the pork and continue to cook until cooked through, about 1 minute longer. Transfer the pork to a clean bowl and cover with foil to keep warm.

4. Add 1 tablespoon more oil to the skillet and return to high heat until just smoking. Add the eggplant and cook, stirring frequently, until browned and no longer spongy, about 5 minutes. Transfer the eggplant to the bowl with the pork. Add the remaining 2 teaspoons peanut oil to the skillet and return to high heat until just smoking. Add the onion and cook until beginning to brown and soften, about 2 minutes.

5. Clear the center of the skillet, add the garlic mixture, and cook, mashing the mixture into the pan, until fragrant, 15 to 20 seconds. Stir the garlic mixture into the onion.

6. Stir in the eggplant and pork with any accumulated juices. Whisk the sauce to recombine, then add to the skillet and cook, tossing constantly, until the sauce is thickened, about 30 seconds. Transfer to a serving platter, sprinkle with the cilantro, and serve.

Stir-Fried Pork, Green Beans, and Red Bell Pepper with Gingery Oyster Sauce

SERVES 4

To make slicing the pork easier, freeze it for 15 minutes. Serve with Basic White Rice (page 453).

SAUCE

- ⅓ cup low-sodium chicken broth
- 2½ tablespoons oyster-flavored sauce
- 1 tablespoon dry sherry
- 2 teaspoons toasted sesame oil
- 1 teaspoon rice vinegar
- 1 teaspoon cornstarch
- ¼ teaspoon ground white pepper

PORK AND VEGETABLES

- 1 (12-ounce) pork tenderloin, trimmed of fat and silver skin and cut into ¼-inch strips (see note)
- 2 teaspoons soy sauce
- 2 teaspoons dry sherry
- 3 tablespoons peanut or vegetable oil
- 2 tablespoons minced or grated fresh ginger
- 2 medium garlic cloves, minced or pressed through a garlic press (about 2 teaspoons)
- 12 ounces green beans, trimmed and cut on the bias into 2-inch lengths
- ¼ cup water
- 1 large red bell pepper, stemmed, seeded, and cut into ¾-inch squares
- 3 scallions, sliced thin on the bias

1. FOR THE SAUCE: Combine all the ingredients in a small bowl and set aside.

2. FOR THE PORK AND VEGETABLES: Toss the pork with the soy sauce and sherry in a medium bowl and let marinate for at least 10 minutes or up to 1 hour. In a small bowl, mix 2 teaspoons of the peanut oil, the ginger, and garlic together.

3. Heat 2 teaspoons more peanut oil in a 12-inch nonstick skillet over high heat until just smoking. Add the pork, break up any clumps, then cook without stirring until the meat is browned at the edges, about 1 minute. Stir the pork and continue to cook until cooked through, about 1 minute longer. Transfer the pork to a clean bowl and cover with foil to keep warm.

4. Add 1 tablespoon more peanut oil to the skillet and return to high heat until just smoking. Add the green beans and cook, stirring frequently, until spotty brown, 3 to 4 minutes. Add the water, cover the pan, and lower the heat to medium. Cook the green beans until crisp-tender, about 2 minutes. Transfer the green beans to the bowl with the pork. Add the remaining 2 teaspoons peanut oil to the skillet and return to high heat until just smoking. Add the bell pepper and cook until spotty brown, about 1½ minutes.

5. Clear the center of the skillet, add the ginger mixture, and cook, mashing the mixture into the pan, until fragrant, 15 to 20 seconds. Stir the ginger mixture into the bell pepper.

6. Stir in the green beans and pork with any accumulated juices. Whisk the sauce to recombine, then add to the skillet and cook, tossing constantly, until the sauce is thickened, about 30 seconds. Transfer to a serving platter, sprinkle with the scallions, and serve.

CHINESE-STYLE PORK IN GARLIC SAUCE

WHY THIS RECIPE WORKS: Recipes for this Sichuan staple are usually imbalanced. Some taste cloyingly sweet, while others overdo it on the vinegar. And the pork is usually dry, chewy, and stringy. We wanted a version as good as anything we'd order in a Sichuan restaurant. To re-create the succulent pork found in the best restaurant stir-fries (usually achieved by low-temperature deep frying), we soaked the pork in a baking soda solution, which tenderized and moisturized the meat, and then coated it in a velvetizing cornstarch slurry, which helped it retain moisture as it cooked. Ketchup and fish sauce, both high in flavor-enhancing glutamates.

Sichuan Stir-Fried Pork in Garlic Sauce

SERVES 4 TO 6

If Chinese black vinegar is unavailable, substitute 2 teaspoons balsamic vinegar and 2 teaspoons rice vinegar. If Asian broad-bean chili paste is unavailable, substitute 2 teaspoons Asian chili-garlic paste or Sriracha sauce. Serve with Basic White Rice (page 453).

SAUCE

- ½ cup low-sodium chicken broth
- 2 tablespoons sugar
- 2 tablespoons soy sauce
- 4 teaspoons Chinese black vinegar (see note)
- 1 tablespoon toasted sesame oil
- 1 tablespoon Chinese rice wine or dry sherry
- 2 teaspoons ketchup
- 2 teaspoons fish sauce
- 2 teaspoons cornstarch

PORK

- 12 ounces boneless country-style pork ribs, trimmed
- 1 teaspoon baking soda
- 2 teaspoons Chinese rice wine or dry sherry
- 2 teaspoons cornstarch

STIR-FRY

- 2 scallions, white parts minced, green parts sliced thin
- 4 garlic cloves, minced
- 2 tablespoons Asian broad-bean chili paste (see note)
- ¼ cup vegetable oil
- 6 ounces shiitake mushrooms, stemmed and sliced thin
- 2 celery ribs, cut on bias into ¼-inch slices

1. FOR THE SAUCE: Whisk all ingredients together in bowl; set aside.

2. FOR THE PORK: Cut pork into 2-inch lengths, then cut each length into 1/4-inch matchsticks. Combine pork with 1/2 cup cold water and baking soda in bowl. Let sit at room temperature for 15 minutes.

3. Rinse pork in cold water. Drain well and pat dry with paper towels. Whisk rice wine and cornstarch together in bowl. Add pork and toss to coat.

4. FOR THE STIR-FRY: Combine scallion whites, garlic, and chili paste in bowl.

5. Heat 1 tablespoon vegetable oil in 12-inch nonstick skillet over high heat until just smoking. Add mushrooms and cook, stirring frequently, until tender, 2 to 4 minutes. Add celery and continue to cook until celery is crisp-tender, 2 to 4 minutes. Transfer vegetables to separate bowl.

6. Add remaining 3 tablespoons vegetable oil to now-empty skillet and place over medium-low heat. Add scallion-garlic mixture and cook, stirring frequently, until fragrant, about 30 seconds. Transfer 1 tablespoon scallion-garlic oil to small bowl and set aside. Add pork to skillet and cook, stirring frequently, until no longer pink, 3 to 5 minutes. Whisk sauce mixture to recombine and add to skillet. Increase heat to high and cook, stirring constantly, until sauce is thickened and pork is cooked through, 1 to 2 minutes. Return vegetables to skillet and toss to combine. Transfer to serving platter, sprinkle with scallion greens and reserved scallion-garlic oil, and serve.

PORK LO MEIN

WHY THIS RECIPE WORKS: Ordinary takeout pork lo mein invariably disappoints, with greasy flavors and sodden vegetables. We wanted a dish representative of the best that a good Chinese home cook could turn out: chewy noodles tossed in a salty-sweet sauce and accented with bits of smoky, barbecued pork and still-crisp cabbage.

First we needed to tackle the *char siu*, preferably perfecting a stir-fried version since we were already stir-frying the vegetables. Country-style pork ribs won for best cut. Though fatty, these meaty ribs have the same rich flavor of pork shoulder—but don't need to be cooked for hours since they're naturally tender. To avoid an overly greasy dish, we trimmed the fat and cut the meat into thin strips that would allow our classic Chinese marinade to penetrate effectively. A few drops of liquid smoke mimicked char siu's characteristic smoky flavor. Turning to the noodles, ones labeled "lo mein" at the Asian market won raves. Fortunately, dried linguine, cooked al dente, also worked beautifully. For the vegetables, we opted for traditional choices—cabbage, scallions, and shiitake mushrooms—stir-frying them with garlic and fresh ginger. We used our meat marinade as a sauce base, with a little chicken broth and a teaspoon of cornstarch added for body. A splash of Asian chili-garlic sauce added a little kick.

Pork Lo Mein

SERVES 4

Use a cast-iron skillet for this recipe if you have one—it will help create the best sear on the pork. If boneless pork ribs are unavailable, substitute 1½ pounds bone-in country-style ribs, followed by the next-best option, pork tenderloin. Liquid smoke provides a flavor reminiscent of the Chinese barbecued pork traditional to this dish. It is important to cook the noodles at the last minute to avoid clumping.

- 3 tablespoons soy sauce
- 2 tablespoons oyster-flavored sauce
- 2 tablespoons hoisin sauce
- 1 tablespoon toasted sesame oil
- 1/4 teaspoon Chinese five-spice powder
- 1 pound boneless country-style pork ribs, trimmed of fat and gristle, sliced crosswise into 1/8-inch pieces (see note)
- 1/4 teaspoon liquid smoke (optional; see note)
- 1/2 cup low-sodium chicken broth
- 1 teaspoon cornstarch
- 2 tablespoons plus 1 teaspoon peanut or vegetable oil
- 2 teaspoons minced or grated fresh ginger
- 2 medium garlic cloves, minced or pressed through a garlic press (about 2 teaspoons)
- 1/4 cup Chinese rice cooking wine (Shaoxing) or dry sherry
- 8 ounces shiitake mushrooms, stemmed, wiped clean, caps sliced 1/4 inch thick
- 2 bunches scallions, whites sliced thin, greens cut into 1-inch pieces
- 1 pound napa cabbage (1 small head), cored and cut into 1/2-inch strips
- 12 ounces fresh Chinese noodles or 8 ounces dried linguine
- 1 tablespoon Asian chili-garlic sauce

1. Whisk the soy sauce, oyster-flavored sauce, hoisin sauce, sesame oil, and five-spice powder together in a small bowl. Transfer 3 tablespoons of the mixture to a medium bowl and add the pork and liquid smoke (if using). Let marinate for at least 10 minutes or up to 1 hour. Whisk the broth and cornstarch into the remaining soy sauce mixture and set aside. In a small bowl, mix 1 teaspoon of the peanut oil, the ginger, and garlic together and set aside.

2. Heat 2 teaspoons more peanut oil in a 12-inch nonstick or cast-iron skillet over high heat until just smoking. Add half of the pork, break up any clumps, then cook without stirring until the meat is browned at the edges, about 1 minute. Stir the pork and continue to cook until cooked through, about 1 minute longer. Add 2 tablespoons of the wine to the skillet and cook, stirring constantly, until the liquid is reduced and the pork is well coated, 30 to 60 seconds. Transfer the pork to a clean bowl and cover with foil to keep warm. Repeat with 2 teaspoons more peanut oil, the remaining pork, and the remaining 2 tablespoons wine. Wipe out the skillet with a wad of paper towels.

3. Add 1 teaspoon more peanut oil to the skillet and return to high heat until just smoking. Add the mushrooms and cook, stirring occasionally, until light golden brown, 4 to 6 minutes. Add the scallion whites and greens and cook, stirring occasionally, until wilted, 2 to 3 minutes. Transfer the vegetables to the bowl with the pork.

4. Add the remaining 1 teaspoon peanut oil to the skillet and heat over high heat until just smoking. Add the cabbage and cook, stirring occasionally, until spotty brown, 3 to 5 minutes. Clear the center of the skillet, add the ginger mixture, and cook, mashing the mixture into the pan, until fragrant, 15 to 20 seconds. Stir the ginger mixture into the cabbage.

5. Stir in the vegetables and pork with any accumulated juices. Whisk the sauce to recombine, then add to the skillet and cook, tossing constantly, until the sauce is thickened, about 30 seconds.

6. Bring 6 quarts water to a boil in a large pot. Add the noodles and cook, stirring often, until tender, about 4 minutes for fresh and 10 minutes for dried. Drain the noodles and return them to the pot. Add the cooked stir-fry mixture and the chili-garlic sauce to the noodles and toss to combine. Transfer to a serving platter and serve.

MU SHU PORK

WHY THIS RECIPE WORKS: Mu shu pork's thin, stretchy pancakes are the hallmark of the Chinese restaurant classic, so we started there. Stirring boiling water into flour kept the dough from turning sticky and made it easy to roll. After resting the dough, we rolled it into a log and cut it into 12 pieces, pressing them into rounds and brushing one side of 6 disks with sesame oil. After placing the unoiled disks on top of the oiled ones, we rolled the doubled-up disks to a 7-inch diameter and cooked each in a warm skillet. These lightly browned, puffed pancakes were easily peeled into two thinner pancakes. We loaded up the filling with flavor-builders, first microwaving dried shiitakes in water to rehydrate them for an earthy component. We saved the shiitakes' soaking liquid to boost our sauce, whisking it with soy sauce, dry sherry, and cornstarch. To season the thinly sliced pork tenderloin, we tossed it in a blend of soy sauce, dry sherry, sugar, fresh ginger, and white pepper. Next, we scrambled 2 eggs, browned sliced scallion whites, and cooked the pork—a quick 1 to 2 minutes a side. With the pork and scrambled eggs in a bowl to the side, we finished up the vegetables. Simply heating the shiitakes and matchstick-cut bamboo shoots sufficed before adding in sliced green cabbage and scallion greens, cooking them in the mushroom liquid mixture for full umami-rich flavor. A smear of sweet and salty hoisin sauce on the pancakes tied the flavors together.

Mu Shu Pork

SERVES 4

We strongly recommend weighing the flour for the pancakes. For an accurate measurement of boiling water, bring a full kettle to a boil and then measure ¾ cup.

PANCAKES

- 1½ cups (7½ ounces) all-purpose flour
- ¾ cup boiling water
- 2 teaspoons toasted sesame oil
- ½ teaspoon vegetable oil

STIR-FRY

- 1 ounce dried shiitake mushrooms, rinsed
- ¼ cup soy sauce
- 2 tablespoons dry sherry
- 1 teaspoon sugar
- 1 teaspoon grated fresh ginger
- ¼ teaspoon white pepper
- 1 (12-ounce) pork tenderloin, trimmed, halved horizontally, and sliced thin against grain
- 2 teaspoons cornstarch
- 2 tablespoons plus 2 teaspoons vegetable oil
- 2 large eggs, beaten
- 6 scallions, white and green parts separated and sliced thin on bias
- 1 (8-ounce) can bamboo shoots, rinsed and sliced into matchsticks
- 3 cups thinly sliced green cabbage
- ¼ cup hoisin sauce

1. FOR THE PANCAKES: Using wooden spoon, mix flour and boiling water in bowl to form rough dough. When cool, transfer dough to lightly floured surface and knead until it forms ball that is tacky but no longer sticky, about 4 minutes (dough will not be perfectly smooth). Cover loosely with plastic wrap and let rest for 30 minutes.

2. Roll dough into 12-inch-long log on lightly floured surface and cut into 12 equal pieces. Turn each piece cut side up and pat into rough 3-inch disk. Brush 1 side of 6 disks with sesame oil; top each oiled side with unoiled disk and press lightly to form 6 pairs. Roll disks into 7-inch rounds, lightly flouring work surface as needed.

3. Heat vegetable oil in 12-inch nonstick skillet over medium heat until shimmering. Using paper towels, carefully wipe out oil. Place pancake in skillet and cook without moving it until air pockets begin to form between layers and underside is dry, 40 to 60 seconds. Flip pancake and cook until few light brown spots appear on second side, 40 to 60 seconds. Transfer to plate and, when cool enough to handle, peel apart into 2 pancakes. Stack pancakes moist side up and cover loosely with plastic. Repeat with remaining pancakes. Cover pancakes tightly and keep warm. Wipe out skillet with paper towel. (Pancakes can be wrapped tightly in plastic wrap, then aluminum foil, and refrigerated for up to 3 days or frozen for up to 2 months. Thaw wrapped pancakes at room temperature. Unwrap and place on plate. Invert second plate over pancakes and microwave until warm and soft, 60 to 90 seconds.)

4. FOR THE STIR-FRY: Microwave 1 cup water and mushrooms in covered bowl until steaming, about 1 minute. Let sit until softened, about 5 minutes. Drain mushrooms through fine-mesh strainer and reserve ⅓ cup liquid. Discard mushroom stems and slice caps thin.

5. Combine 2 tablespoons soy sauce, 1 tablespoon sherry, sugar, ginger, and pepper in large bowl. Add pork and toss to combine. Whisk together reserved mushroom liquid, remaining 2 tablespoons soy sauce, remaining 1 tablespoon sherry, and cornstarch; set aside.

6. Heat 2 teaspoons oil in now-empty skillet over medium-high heat until shimmering. Add eggs and scramble quickly until set but not dry, about 15 seconds. Transfer to bowl and break eggs into ¼- to ½-inch pieces with fork. Return now-empty skillet to medium-high heat and heat 1 tablespoon oil until shimmering. Add scallion whites and cook, stirring frequently, until well browned, 1 to 1½ minutes. Add pork mixture. Spread into even layer and cook without moving it until well browned on 1 side, 1 to 2 minutes. Stir and continue to cook, stirring frequently, until all pork is opaque, 1 to 2 minutes longer. Transfer to bowl with eggs.

7. Return now-empty skillet to medium-high heat and heat remaining 1 tablespoon oil until shimmering. Whisk mushroom liquid mixture to recombine. Add mushrooms and bamboo shoots to skillet and cook, stirring frequently, until heated through, about 1 minute. Add cabbage, all but 2 tablespoons scallion greens, and mushroom liquid mixture and cook, stirring constantly, until liquid has evaporated and cabbage is wilted but retains some crunch, 2 to 3 minutes. Add pork and eggs and stir to combine. Transfer to platter and top with remaining scallion greens.

8. Spread about ½ teaspoon hoisin in center of each warm pancake. Spoon stir-fry over hoisin and serve.

NOTES FROM THE TEST KITCHEN

MAKING TWO PANCAKES AT A TIME

Cooking two rounds together produces pancakes twice as fast.

1. Brush 6 disks with sesame oil. Top with unoiled disks. Press pairs together, then roll into thin rounds.

2. Heat each round until air pockets form between layers and underside is dry. Flip and cook second side.

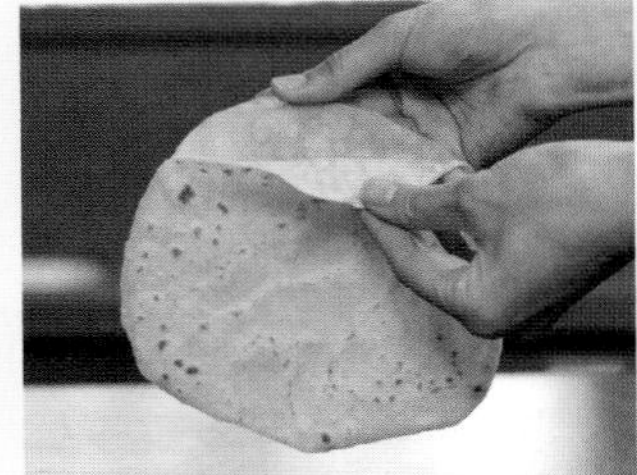

3. When pancakes are cool enough to handle, peel apart into 2 pieces.

SINGAPORE NOODLES

WHY THIS RECIPE WORKS: Singapore noodles have nothing to do with Singapore and are virtually unknown there. This light, almost fluffy stir-fry of thin, resilient rice noodles, vegetables, and shrimp is native to Hong Kong, and the name is something of a mystery. Along with the traditional Chinese flavorings of garlic, ginger, and soy, this dish prominently features curry powder. The heady spice mixture lends the dish a pervasive aroma and a pleasant chile burn. But because this dish is not saucy, the dry powder doesn't distribute evenly, leading to patchy curry flavor (and color), not to mention gritty texture. We set out to solve this problem, and also to revise the usual ratio of ingredients (mostly noodles with a smattering of veggies and protein) to make a satisfying one-dish meal.

We started with the curry powder. We knew that "blooming" the spice mix by cooking it in hot oil would release lots of complex flavor. This had the added benefit of providing a medium for the spice granules to disperse, which meant that the grittiness in the dish was gone. A spoonful of sugar dispelled lingering bitter notes. To make the noodles more manageable, we cut them after soaking to make them less tangle-prone. We also cut the shrimp into ½-inch pieces that

dispersed nicely throughout the noodles, and bulked up the protein and vegetables by adding 4 eggs (scrambled with a little salt), 4 scallions cut into ½-inch pieces, and a couple of cups of bean sprouts.

Singapore Noodles

SERVES 4 TO 6

For a spicier dish, add the optional cayenne pepper. Look for dried rice vermicelli in the Asian section of your supermarket. A rasp-style grater makes it easy to turn the garlic into a paste.

- 4 tablespoons plus 1 teaspoon vegetable oil
- 2 tablespoons curry powder
- ⅛ teaspoon cayenne pepper (optional)
- 6 ounces rice vermicelli
- 2 tablespoons soy sauce
- 1 teaspoon sugar
- 12 ounces large shrimp (26 to 30 per pound), peeled, deveined (see page 240), tails removed, and cut into ½-inch pieces
- 4 large eggs, lightly beaten
- Salt
- 1 teaspoon grated fresh ginger
- 3 garlic cloves, minced to paste
- 1 red bell pepper, stemmed, seeded, and cut into 2-inch-long matchsticks
- 2 large shallots, sliced thin
- ⅔ cup chicken broth
- 4 ounces (2 cups) bean sprouts
- 4 scallions, cut into ½-inch pieces
- 2 teaspoons lime juice, plus lime wedges for serving

1. Heat 3 tablespoons oil, curry powder, and cayenne (if using) in 12-inch nonstick skillet over medium-low heat, stirring occasionally, until fragrant, about 4 minutes. Remove skillet from heat and set aside.

2. Bring 6 cups water to boil. Place noodles in large bowl. Pour boiling water over noodles and stir briefly. Soak noodles until flexible, but not soft, about 2½ minutes, stirring once halfway through. Drain noodles briefly; do not wash bowl. Transfer noodles to cutting board. Using chef's knife, cut pile of noodles roughly into thirds. Return noodles to bowl, add curry mixture, soy sauce, and sugar; using tongs, toss until well combined. Set aside.

3. Wipe out skillet with paper towels. Heat 2 teaspoons oil in skillet over medium-high heat until shimmering. Add shrimp in even layer and cook without moving until bottom is browned, about 90 seconds. Stir and continue to cook until just cooked through, about 90 seconds longer. Push shrimp to one side of skillet. Add 1 teaspoon oil to cleared side of skillet. Add eggs to clearing, and sprinkle with ¼ teaspoon salt. Using rubber spatula, stir eggs gently until set but still wet, about 1 minute. Stir eggs into shrimp and continue to cook, breaking up large pieces of egg, until eggs are fully cooked, about 30 seconds longer. Transfer shrimp-egg mixture to second large bowl.

4. Lower heat to medium. Heat remaining 1 teaspoon oil in now-empty skillet until shimmering. Add ginger and garlic and cook, stirring constantly, until fragrant, about 15 seconds. Add bell pepper and shallots. Cook, stirring frequently, until vegetables are crisp-tender, about 2 minutes. Transfer to bowl with shrimp.

5. Return again-empty skillet to medium-high heat, add chicken broth to skillet, and bring to simmer. Add noodles and cook, stirring frequently, until liquid is absorbed, about 2 minutes. Add noodles to bowl with shrimp and vegetable mixture and toss to combine. Add bean sprouts, scallions, and lime juice, and toss to combine. Transfer to warmed platter and serve immediately, passing lime wedges separately.

NOTES FROM THE TEST KITCHEN

UNTANGLING SINGAPORE NOODLES

Two easy steps help avoid the usual "ball" of noodles that forms when you toss the rice vermicelli with the shrimp and vegetables.

1. Cutting the soaked and drained rice vermicelli into thirds makes the noodles less tangle-prone.

2. Coating the noodles with curry oil prevents them from sticking. "Blooming" the spice in oil also boosts its flavor, softens its gritty texture, and adds richness.

SHRIMP STIR-FRIES

WHY THIS RECIPE WORKS: Stir-fries are typically cooked over high heat to sear the food and develop flavor. This works well with chicken, beef, and pork, but delicate shrimp turns to rubber. We wanted a stir-fry with plump, juicy, well-seasoned shrimp in a balanced, flavorful sauce. We wondered if browning was really necessary. Abandoning the high-heat method, we turned down the burner to medium-low and gently parcooked a batch of shrimp, removed them from the skillet, then turned up the heat to sear the vegetables, sauté the aromatics, and finish cooking the shrimp with the sauce. This worked beautifully. Reversing the approach—cooking the veggies followed by the aromatics over high heat, then turning the heat down before adding the shrimp—made the process more efficient. We reduced our sweet and spicy sauce and reduced it so it tightly adhered to the shellfish.

Stir-Fried Shrimp with Snow Peas and Red Bell Pepper in Hot and Sour Sauce

SERVES 4

Serve with Basic White Rice (page 453).

- 1 pound extra-large shrimp (21 to 25 per pound), peeled, deveined (see page 240), and tails removed
- 3 tablespoons vegetable oil
- 1 tablespoon minced or grated fresh ginger
- 2 medium garlic cloves, 1 minced or pressed through a garlic press (about 1 teaspoon), 1 sliced thin
- ½ teaspoon table salt
- 3 tablespoons sugar
- 3 tablespoons white vinegar
- 1 tablespoon Asian chili-garlic sauce
- 1 tablespoon dry sherry or Chinese rice cooking wine (Shaoxing)
- 1 tablespoon ketchup
- 2 teaspoons toasted sesame oil
- 2 teaspoons cornstarch
- 1 teaspoon soy sauce
- 1 large shallot, sliced thin (about ⅓ cup)
- ½ pound snow peas or sugar snap peas, tips snapped off and strings removed
- 1 medium red bell pepper, stemmed, seeded, and cut into ¾-inch dice

1. Combine the shrimp with 1 tablespoon of the vegetable oil, the ginger, minced garlic, and salt in a medium bowl. Let the shrimp marinate at room temperature for 30 minutes.

2. Meanwhile, whisk the sugar, vinegar, chili-garlic sauce, sherry, ketchup, sesame oil, cornstarch, and soy sauce in a small bowl. Combine the sliced garlic with the shallot in a second small bowl.

3. Heat 1 tablespoon more vegetable oil in a 12-inch nonstick skillet over high heat until just smoking. Add the snow peas and bell pepper and cook, stirring frequently, until the vegetables begin to brown, 1½ to 2 minutes. Transfer the vegetables to a medium bowl.

4. Add the remaining 1 tablespoon vegetable oil to the now-empty skillet and heat until just smoking. Add the garlic-shallot mixture and cook, stirring frequently, until just beginning to brown, about 30 seconds. Reduce the heat to medium-low, add the shrimp, and cook, stirring frequently, until the shrimp are light pink on both sides, 1 to 1½ minutes. Whisk the soy sauce mixture to recombine and add to the skillet; return to high heat and cook, stirring constantly, until the sauce is thickened and the shrimp are cooked through, 1 to 2 minutes. Return the vegetables to the skillet, toss to combine, and serve.

Stir-Fried Shrimp with Garlicky Eggplant, Scallions, and Cashews

SERVES 4

To make quick work of cutting the scallions, use sharp kitchen shears. Serve with Basic White Rice (page 453).

- 1 pound extra-large shrimp (21 to 25 per pound), peeled, deveined (see page 240), and tails removed
- 3 tablespoons vegetable oil
- 6 medium garlic cloves, 1 minced or pressed through a garlic press (about 1 teaspoon), 5 sliced thin
- ½ teaspoon table salt
- 2 tablespoons soy sauce
- 2 tablespoons oyster-flavored sauce
- 2 tablespoons dry sherry or Chinese rice cooking wine (Shaoxing)
- 2 tablespoons sugar
- 1 tablespoon toasted sesame oil
- 1 tablespoon white vinegar
- 2 teaspoons cornstarch
- ⅛ teaspoon red pepper flakes
- 6 large scallions, greens cut into 1-inch pieces and whites sliced thin
- ½ cup unsalted cashews
- 1 medium eggplant (about ¾ pound), cut into ¾-inch dice

1. Combine the shrimp with 1 tablespoon of the vegetable oil, the minced garlic, and salt in a medium bowl. Let the shrimp marinate at room temperature for 30 minutes.

2. Meanwhile, whisk the soy sauce, oyster-flavored sauce, sherry, sugar, sesame oil, vinegar, cornstarch, and red pepper flakes in a small bowl. Combine the sliced garlic with the scallion whites and cashews in a small bowl.

3. Heat 1 tablespoon more vegetable oil in a 12-inch nonstick skillet over high heat until just smoking. Add the eggplant and cook, stirring frequently, until lightly browned, 3 to 6 minutes. Add the scallion greens and continue to cook until the scallion greens begin to brown and the eggplant is fully tender, 1 to 2 minutes longer. Transfer the vegetables to a medium bowl.

4. Continue with the recipe for Stir-Fried Shrimp with Snow Peas and Red Bell Pepper in Hot and Sour Sauce from step 4, replacing the garlic-shallot mixture with the garlic-scallion-cashew mixture.

KUNG PAO SHRIMP

WHY THIS RECIPE WORKS: Kung pao is meant to have a fiery personality, but many restaurant versions are dismal, featuring tiny, tough shrimp drenched in a quart of pale, greasy, bland sauce. We wanted to make this classic Sichuan stir-fry at home, with large, tender shrimp, crunchy peanuts, and an assertive, well-balanced brown sauce.

For tender, flavorful shrimp, we stir-fried marinated extra-large shrimp for just a few seconds, then added small whole red chiles and whole unsalted roasted peanuts. For vegetables, we kept things simple and added just one diced red bell pepper (tasters found other vegetables to be superfluous) and the usual aromatics, garlic and ginger. We made a potently flavored, syrupy sauce using a mixture of chicken broth, rice vinegar, toasted sesame oil, oyster-flavored sauce, hoisin sauce, and cornstarch. Stirring in sliced scallions just before serving put the final touch on our dish. We no longer need to rely on dull, gloppy restaurant renditions of this Sichuan classic.

Kung Pao Shrimp

SERVES 4

Roasted unsalted cashews can be substituted for the peanuts. Unless you have a taste for the incendiary, do not eat the whole chiles in the finished dish. Serve with Basic White Rice (page 453).

SAUCE

- ¾ cup low-sodium chicken broth
- 1 tablespoon oyster-flavored sauce
- 1 tablespoon hoisin sauce
- 2 teaspoons rice vinegar
- 2 teaspoons toasted sesame oil
- 1½ teaspoons cornstarch

SHRIMP AND VEGETABLES

- 1 pound extra-large shrimp (21 to 25 per pound), peeled and deveined (see page 240)
- 1 tablespoon Chinese rice cooking wine (Shaoxing) or dry sherry
- 2 teaspoons soy sauce
- 2 tablespoons plus 1 teaspoon peanut or vegetable oil
- 3 medium garlic cloves, minced or pressed through a garlic press (about 1 tablespoon)
- 2 teaspoons minced or grated fresh ginger
- ½ cup unsalted roasted peanuts (see note)
- 6 small whole dried red chiles (see note)
- 1 red bell pepper, stemmed, seeded, and cut into ½-inch pieces
- 3 scallions, sliced thin

1. FOR THE SAUCE: Combine all the ingredients in a small bowl and set aside.

2. FOR THE SHRIMP AND VEGETABLES: Toss the shrimp with the rice cooking wine and soy sauce in a medium bowl and let marinate for at least 10 minutes or up to 1 hour. In a small bowl, mix 1 teaspoon of the peanut oil, the garlic, and ginger together.

3. Heat 1 tablespoon more peanut oil in a 12-inch nonstick skillet over high heat until just smoking. Add the shrimp and cook until barely opaque, 30 to 40 seconds, stirring halfway through. Add the peanuts and chiles and continue to cook until the shrimp are bright pink and the peanuts have darkened slightly, 30 to 40 seconds longer. Transfer the shrimp, peanuts, and chiles to a clean bowl and cover with foil to keep warm.

4. Add the remaining 1 tablespoon peanut oil to the skillet and return to high heat until just smoking. Add the bell pepper and cook, stirring frequently, until spotty brown, about 1½ minutes. Clear the center of the skillet, add the garlic mixture, and cook, mashing the mixture into the pan, until fragrant, 15 to 20 seconds. Stir the garlic mixture into the bell pepper.

5. Stir in the peanuts, chiles, and shrimp with any accumulated juices. Whisk the sauce to recombine, then add to the skillet and cook, tossing constantly, until the sauce is thickened, about 30 seconds. Stir in the scallions, transfer to a serving platter, and serve.

VEGETABLE STIR-FRIES

WHY THIS RECIPE WORKS: Without meat, vegetable stir-fries can feel more like a side dish than a dinner. We wanted to make a satisfying, filling stir-fry—without meat.

We chose meaty portobello mushrooms as the main vegetable. We found that removing the gills kept them from tasting leathery and raw. We tried cutting them in a variety of sizes and settled on 2-inch wedges, which felt the most substantial. We cooked the mushrooms over medium-high heat until browned and tender, then added a mixture of broth, soy sauce, and sugar and reduced it to a glaze—this provided an intense flavor boost. For this stir-fry, we bulked up the amount of vegetables in our traditional stir-fries, mixing carrots, snow peas, and napa cabbage. Finally, the sauce—a mixture of broth, oyster-flavored sauce, soy sauce, cornstarch, and sesame oil—and a heavy dose of ginger tied the dish together, giving the vegetables great flavor—and nobody missed the meat!

Stir-Fried Portobellos with Ginger-Oyster Sauce

SERVES 4

Serve with Basic White Rice (see page 453).

GLAZE

- ¼ cup low-sodium chicken or vegetable broth
- 2 tablespoons soy sauce
- 2 tablespoons sugar

SAUCE

- 1 cup low-sodium chicken or vegetable broth
- 3 tablespoons oyster-flavored sauce
- 1 tablespoon soy sauce
- 1 tablespoon cornstarch
- 2 teaspoons toasted sesame oil

VEGETABLES

- ¼ cup peanut or vegetable oil
- 4 teaspoons minced or grated fresh ginger
- 2 medium garlic cloves, minced or pressed through a garlic press (about 2 teaspoons)
- 6–8 portobello mushrooms (each 4 to 6 inches), stemmed, wiped clean, gills removed, and cut into 2-inch wedges
- 4 carrots, peeled and sliced ¼ inch thick on the bias
- ½ cup low-sodium chicken or vegetable broth
- 3 ounces snow peas, tips and strings removed
- 1 pound napa cabbage (1 small head), cored and cut into ¾-inch strips
- 1 tablespoon sesame seeds, toasted (optional)

1. FOR THE GLAZE: Combine all the ingredients in a small bowl and set aside.

2. FOR THE SAUCE: Combine all the ingredients in a small bowl and set aside.

3. FOR THE VEGETABLES: In a small bowl, mix 1 teaspoon of the peanut oil, the ginger, and garlic together.

4. Heat 3 tablespoons more peanut oil in a 12-inch nonstick skillet over medium-high heat until shimmering. Add the mushrooms and cook without stirring until browned on one side, 2 to 3 minutes. Using tongs, flip the mushrooms, reduce the heat to medium, and cook until the second sides are browned and the mushrooms are tender, about 5 minutes. Increase the heat to medium-high, add the glaze, and cook, stirring frequently, until the glaze is thick and the mushrooms are coated, 1 to 2 minutes. Transfer the mushrooms to a plate. Rinse the skillet clean and dry with a wad of paper towels.

5. Add 1 teaspoon more peanut oil to the skillet and return to high heat until just smoking. Add the carrots and cook, stirring frequently, until beginning to brown, 1 to 2 minutes. Add the broth, cover the pan, and lower the heat to medium. Cook the carrots until just tender, 2 to 3 minutes. Uncover and cook until the liquid evaporates, about 30 seconds. Transfer the carrots to the plate with the mushrooms.

6. Add the remaining 1 teaspoon peanut oil to the skillet and return to high heat until just smoking. Add the snow peas and cook until spotty brown, about 2 minutes. Add the cabbage and cook, stirring frequently, until wilted, about 2 minutes.

7. Clear the center of the skillet, add the ginger mixture, and cook, mashing the mixture into the pan, until fragrant, 15 to 20 seconds. Stir the ginger mixture into the vegetables.

8. Stir in the mushrooms and carrots. Whisk the sauce to recombine, then add to the skillet and cook, tossing constantly, until the sauce is thickened, 2 to 3 minutes. Transfer to a serving platter, sprinkle with the sesame seeds (if using), and serve.

Stir-Fried Portobellos with Sweet Chili-Garlic Sauce

Follow the recipe for Stir-Fried Portobellos with Ginger-Oyster Sauce, replacing the sugar in the glaze with 2 tablespoons honey. For the sauce, increase the soy sauce to 3 tablespoons, reduce the broth to ¾ cup, and replace the oyster-flavored sauce and toasted sesame oil with 2 tablespoons honey, 1 tablespoon rice vinegar, and 1 teaspoon Asian chili sauce. Increase the garlic to 4 cloves.

THAI CHICKEN WITH BASIL

WHY THIS RECIPE WORKS: In Thailand, street vendors have mastered an alternative to traditional Chinese high-heat stir-fry, using low flames to produce complex and flavorful dishes like chicken and basil—chopped pieces of moist chicken in a bright, basil-infused sauce. We set out to create our own version.

To start, we turned to the aromatics. Because Thai stir-fries are cooked over a lower temperature, the aromatics are added at the very beginning of cooking, where they infuse the oil with their flavors. To prevent scorching, we started our aromatics (garlic, chiles, and shallots) in a cold skillet.

It was too time-consuming to chop our chicken by hand, so we turned to the food processor. To ensure moist meat, we added fish sauce to the food processor when we ground the chicken, then rested the meat in the refrigerator—the fish sauce acted as a brine, seasoning the chicken and sealing in moisture. Next, we moved on to the sauce. For our sauce base, we liked Chinese-style oyster-flavored sauce brightened with a dash of white vinegar. We spiced up the flavor of the sauce by adding a reserved tablespoon of the raw garlic-chile mixture at the end of cooking. And for intense, bright basil flavor, we cooked a portion of chopped basil with the garlic, chile, and shallot mixture, and stirred in whole basil leaves just before serving.

Thai-Style Chicken with Basil

SERVES 4

Since tolerance for spiciness can vary, we've kept our recipe relatively mild. For a very mild version, remove the seeds and ribs from the chiles. If fresh Thai chiles are unavailable, substitute 2 serranos or 1 medium jalapeño. In Thailand, crushed red pepper and sugar are passed at the table, along with extra fish sauce and white vinegar. You do not need to wash the food processor bowl after step 1. Serve with Basic White Rice (page 453) and vegetables, if desired.

- 2 cups tightly packed fresh basil leaves
- 3 garlic cloves, peeled
- 6 green or red Thai chiles, stemmed (see note)
- 2 tablespoons fish sauce, plus extra for serving
- 1 tablespoon oyster-flavored sauce
- 1 tablespoon sugar, plus extra for serving
- 1 teaspoon white vinegar, plus extra for serving
- 1 pound boneless, skinless chicken breasts, trimmed and cut into 2-inch pieces
- 3 shallots, peeled and sliced thin (about ¾ cup)
- 2 tablespoons vegetable oil
- Red pepper flakes, for serving

1. Pulse 1 cup of the basil leaves, the garlic, and chiles in a food processor until chopped fine, 6 to 10 pulses, scraping down the sides of the bowl once during processing. Transfer 1 tablespoon of the basil mixture to a small bowl, stir in 1 tablespoon of the fish sauce, the oyster-flavored sauce, sugar, and vinegar and set aside. Transfer the remaining basil mixture to a 12-inch heavy-bottomed nonstick skillet.

2. Pulse the chicken and the remaining 1 tablespoon fish sauce in the food processor until the meat is chopped into ¼-inch pieces, 6 to 8 pulses. Transfer the chicken to a medium bowl and refrigerate for 15 minutes.

3. Stir the shallots and oil into the basil mixture in the skillet. Heat the mixture over medium-low heat (the mixture should start to sizzle after about 1½ minutes; if it doesn't, adjust the heat accordingly), stirring constantly, until the garlic and shallots are golden brown, 5 to 8 minutes.

4. Add the chicken, increase the heat to medium, and cook, stirring and breaking up the chicken with a potato masher or rubber spatula, until only traces of pink remain, 2 to 4 minutes. Add the reserved basil–fish sauce mixture and continue to cook, stirring constantly, until the chicken is no longer pink, about 1 minute. Stir in the remaining 1 cup basil leaves and cook, stirring constantly, until the basil is wilted, 30 to 60 seconds. Serve immediately, passing the extra fish sauce, sugar, vinegar, and red pepper flakes separately.

THAI CURRIES

WHY THIS RECIPE WORKS: Like most Thai food, Thai curries embrace a delicate balance of tastes, textures, temperatures, and colors that come together to create a harmonious whole. Unlike Indian curries, Thai curries almost always contain coconut milk. Also, they tilt the spice balance towards fresh aromatics, which are added in the form of a paste. We wanted an authentic Thai red curry and green curry, perfumed with lemon grass, hot chiles, and coconut milk, both of which could be made easily by the home cook.

A food processor made quick work of blending together the curry pastes. For the green curry, we favored Thai green chiles (although serrano or jalapeño chiles make great substitutes), while the red curry was best with small dried red chiles and a fresh red jalapeño. Shallots, lemon grass, cilantro stems, garlic, ginger, coriander, and cumin rounded out the flavors of the pastes. And to approximate the flavor of kaffir lime leaves, we added grated lime zest. To make the curries, we skimmed the coconut cream off the coconut milk and cooked it with the curry paste—this gave our curries silky body and intense, rich flavor. We paired the green curry with chicken, broccoli, mushrooms, and bell pepper, and the red curry with shrimp, pineapple, and peanuts. All that we needed now was rice to soak up the flavorful sauce.

Thai Green Curry with Chicken, Broccoli, and Mushrooms

SERVES 4

To make slicing the chicken easier, freeze it for 15 minutes. Serve with Basic White Rice (page 453).

- 2 (14-ounce) cans unsweetened coconut milk, not shaken
- 1 recipe Green Curry Paste (recipe follows) or 2 tablespoons store-bought green curry paste
- 2 tablespoons fish sauce
- 2 tablespoons brown sugar
- 1½ pounds boneless, skinless chicken breasts, trimmed and sliced thin (see note)
- Table salt
- 8 ounces broccoli (½ small bunch), florets cut into 1-inch pieces
- 4 ounces white mushrooms, wiped clean and quartered
- 1 red bell pepper, stemmed, seeded, and cut into ¼-inch strips
- 1 Thai chile, stemmed, seeded, and quartered lengthwise (optional)
- ½ cup loosely packed fresh basil leaves
- ½ cup loosely packed fresh mint leaves
- 1 tablespoon juice from 1 lime

1. Carefully spoon off about 1 cup of the top layer of cream from one can of the coconut milk. Whisk the coconut cream and curry paste together in a large Dutch oven, bring to a simmer over high heat, and cook until almost all of the liquid evaporates, 5 to 7 minutes. Reduce the heat to medium-high and continue to cook, whisking constantly, until the cream separates into a puddle of colored oil and coconut solids, 3 to 8 minutes. Continue cooking until the curry paste is very aromatic, 1 to 2 minutes.

2. Whisk in the remaining coconut milk, the fish sauce, and sugar, bring to a simmer, and cook until the flavors meld and the sauce thickens, about 5 minutes. Season the chicken with salt, stir into the sauce, and cook until evenly coated, about 1 minute. Stir in the broccoli and mushrooms and cook until the vegetables are almost tender, about 5 minutes. Stir in the bell pepper and chile (if using) and cook until the bell pepper is crisp-tender, about 2 minutes. Off the heat, stir in the basil, mint, and lime juice. Serve.

Green Curry Paste

MAKES ABOUT ½ CUP

We strongly prefer the flavor of Thai chiles here; however, serrano and jalapeño chiles are decent substitutes. For more heat, include the chile seeds and ribs when chopping.

- ⅓ cup water
- 12 fresh green Thai, serrano, or jalapeño chiles, seeds and ribs removed, chiles chopped coarse (see note)
- 8 medium garlic cloves, peeled
- 3 medium shallots, peeled and quartered
- 2 stalks lemon grass, bottom 5 inches only, trimmed and sliced thin
- 2 tablespoons grated zest from 2 limes
- 2 tablespoons vegetable oil
- 2 tablespoons minced fresh cilantro stems
- 1 tablespoon minced or grated fresh ginger
- 2 teaspoons ground coriander
- 1 teaspoon ground cumin
- 1 teaspoon table salt

Process all the ingredients in a food processor to a fine paste, about 3 minutes, scraping down the sides of the workbowl as needed.

Thai Red Curry with Shrimp, Pineapple, and Peanuts

SERVES 4

Roasted unsalted cashews can be substituted for the peanuts. For a more authentic appearance, leave the shells on the shrimp tails. Serve with Basic White Rice (page 453).

- 2 (14-ounce) cans unsweetened coconut milk, not shaken
- 1 recipe Red Curry Paste (recipe follows) or 2 tablespoons store-bought red curry paste
- 2 tablespoons fish sauce
- 2 tablespoons brown sugar
- 1½ pounds medium shrimp (41 to 50 per pound), peeled and deveined (see page 240; see note)
- Table salt
- 1 pound peeled and cored pineapple, cut into 1-inch pieces
- 4 ounces snow peas, tips and strings removed
- 1 red bell pepper, stemmed, seeded, and cut into ¼-inch strips
- 1 Thai chile, stemmed, seeded, and quartered lengthwise (optional)
- ½ cup loosely packed fresh basil leaves
- ½ cup loosely packed fresh mint leaves
- 1 tablespoon juice from 1 lime
- ½ cup unsalted roasted peanuts, chopped coarse (see note)

1. Carefully spoon off about 1 cup of the top layer of cream from one can of the coconut milk. Whisk the coconut cream and curry paste together in a large Dutch oven, bring to a simmer over high heat, and cook until almost all of the liquid evaporates, 5 to 7 minutes. Reduce the heat to medium-high and continue to cook, whisking constantly, until the cream separates into a puddle of colored oil and coconut solids, 3 to 8 minutes. Continue cooking until the curry paste is very aromatic, 1 to 2 minutes.

2. Whisk in the remaining coconut milk, the fish sauce, and sugar, bring to a simmer, and cook until the flavors meld and the sauce thickens, about 5 minutes. Season the shrimp with salt, add them to the sauce with the pineapple, and cook, stirring occasionally, until the shrimp are almost opaque, about 4 minutes. Stir in the snow peas, bell pepper, and chile (if using) and cook until the vegetables are crisp-tender, about 2 minutes. Off the heat, stir in the basil, mint, and lime juice. Sprinkle with the peanuts and serve.

NOTES FROM THE TEST KITCHEN

CUTTING LEMON GRASS

Because of its tough outer leaves, lemon grass can be difficult to slice or mince. We like this method, which relies on a sharp knife.

1. Trim all but the bottom 5 inches of the lemon grass stalk.

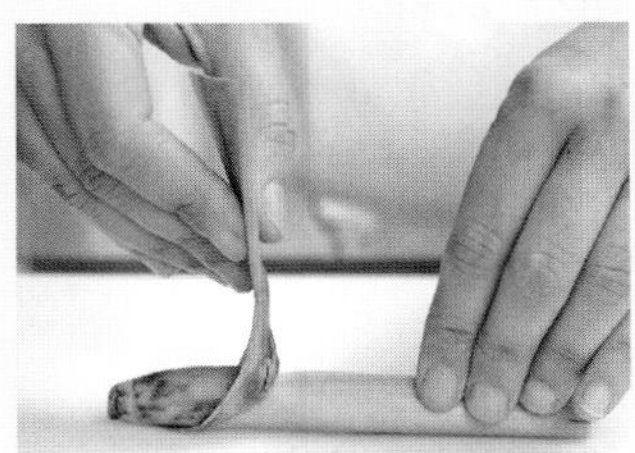

2. Remove the tough outer sheath from the trimmed lemon grass. If the lemon grass is particularly thick or tough, you may need to remove several layers to reveal the tender inner portion of the stalk.

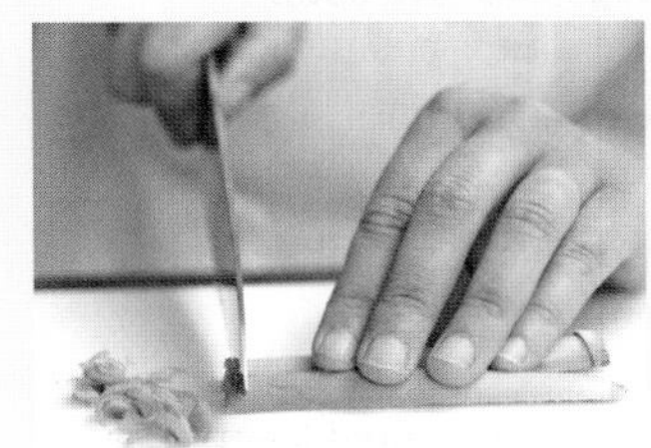

3. TO SLICE: Thinly slice the trimmed and peeled lemon grass on a slight bias. **TO MINCE:** Cut the trimmed and peeled lemon grass in half lengthwise, then mince.

Red Curry Paste

MAKES ABOUT ½ CUP

If you can't find a red jalapeño chile, you can substitute a green jalapeño. For more heat, include the jalapeño seeds and ribs when chopping.

- 8 dried small red chiles, such as Thai, japonés, or de árbol
- ⅓ cup water
- 4 medium shallots, peeled and quartered
- 2 stalks lemon grass, bottom 5 inches only, trimmed and sliced thin
- 6 medium garlic cloves, peeled
- 1 medium fresh red jalapeño chile, seeds and ribs removed, chile chopped coarse (see note)
- 2 tablespoons minced fresh cilantro stems
- 2 tablespoons vegetable oil
- 1 tablespoon grated zest from 1 lime
- 2 teaspoons ground coriander
- 1 teaspoon ground cumin
- 1 teaspoon minced or grated fresh ginger
- 1 teaspoon tomato paste
- 1 teaspoon table salt

1. Adjust an oven rack to the middle position and heat the oven to 350 degrees. Place the dried red chiles on a baking sheet and toast in the oven until fragrant and puffed, about 5 minutes. Remove the chiles from the oven and set aside to cool. When cool enough to handle, seed and stem the chiles, then break them into small pieces.

2. Process the chile pieces with the remaining ingredients in a food processor to a fine paste, about 3 minutes, scraping down the sides of the workbowl as needed.

THAI CHICKEN CURRY WITH POTATOES AND PEANUTS

WHY THIS RECIPE WORKS: Warm-spiced, savory-sweet *massaman* curry is a Thai specialty, but it presents problems for the home cook with difficult-to-find ingredients and work-intensive processes. We set out to streamline the traditional recipe. To make a deeply flavorful curry paste, we broiled chiles, garlic, and shallots per tradition, but we replaced hard-to-find galangal with readily available ginger and traded out toasted, ground whole spices for preground five-spice powder. Coconut milk and lime juice rounded out the flavor of our curry. We stuck with the traditional potatoes, onion, chicken, and peanuts, simmered in the sauce until they were tender. A final garnish of lime zest and cilantro added a splash of color and brightness.

Thai Chicken Curry with Potatoes and Peanuts

SERVES 4 TO 6

Serve the curry with jasmine rice. The ingredients for the curry paste can be doubled to make extra for future use. Refrigerate the paste for up to one week or freeze it for up to two months.

CURRY PASTE

- 6 dried New Mexican chiles
- 4 shallots, unpeeled
- 7 garlic cloves, unpeeled
- ½ cup chopped fresh ginger
- ¼ cup water
- 4½ teaspoons lime juice
- 4½ teaspoons vegetable oil
- 1 tablespoon fish sauce
- 1 teaspoon five-spice powder
- ½ teaspoon ground cumin
- ½ teaspoon pepper

CURRY

- 1 teaspoon vegetable oil
- 1¼ cups chicken broth
- 1 (13.5-ounce) can coconut milk
- 1 pound Yukon Gold potatoes, unpeeled, cut into ¾-inch pieces
- 1 onion, cut into ¾-inch pieces
- ⅓ cup dry-roasted peanuts
- ¾ teaspoon salt
- 1 pound boneless, skinless chicken thighs, trimmed and cut into 1-inch pieces
- 2 teaspoons grated lime zest
- ¼ cup chopped fresh cilantro

1. FOR THE CURRY PASTE: Adjust oven rack to middle position and heat oven to 350 degrees. Line rimmed baking sheet with aluminum foil. Arrange chiles on prepared sheet and toast until puffed and fragrant, 4 to 6 minutes. Transfer chiles to large plate. Heat broiler.

2. Place shallots and garlic on foil-lined sheet and broil until softened and skin is charred, 6 to 9 minutes.

3. When cool enough to handle, stem and seed chiles and tear into 1½-inch pieces. Process chiles in blender until finely ground, about 1 minute. Peel shallots and garlic. Add shallots, garlic, ginger, water, lime juice, oil, fish sauce, five-spice powder, cumin, and pepper to blender. Process to smooth paste, scraping down sides of blender jar as needed, 2 to 3 minutes. You should have 1 cup paste.

4. FOR THE CURRY: Heat oil in large saucepan over medium heat until shimmering. Add curry paste and cook, stirring constantly, until paste begins to brown, 2½ to 3 minutes. Stir in broth, coconut milk, potatoes, onion, peanuts, and salt, scraping up any browned bits. Bring to simmer and cook until potatoes are just tender, 12 to 14 minutes.

5. Stir in chicken and continue to simmer until chicken is cooked through, 10 to 12 minutes. Remove pan from heat and stir in lime zest. Serve, passing cilantro separately.

CURRY BEEF

WHY THIS RECIPE WORKS: Made with an orange-red paste that usually includes ground peanuts, panang curry is a sweeter, more unctuous derivative of red curry. We wanted a panang curry just as rich and flavorful as traditional versions but quicker to make, so we turned to jarred red curry paste, which contains many of the same ingredients that go into panang paste. We doctored the paste with the distinct flavors of this dish: kaffir lime leaves, fish sauce, sugar, fresh chile, and peanuts. Following the typical method, we cooked the beef (we used thin-sliced boneless beef short ribs) separately in plain water until tender. Cooking the beef separately from the sauce ensured that its flavor didn't overpower the other flavors in the dish. Once the beef was cooked (which can be done well in advance), we added it to the coconut milk–based sauce and simmered it briefly.

Panang Beef Curry

SERVES 6

Red curry pastes from different brands vary in spiciness, so start by adding 2 tablespoons and then taste the sauce and add up to 2 tablespoons more. Kaffir lime leaves are well worth seeking out. If you can't find them, substitute three 3-inch strips each of lemon zest and lime zest, adding them to the sauce with the beef in step 2 (remove the zest strips before serving). Do not substitute light coconut milk. Serve this rich dish with rice and vegetables.

- 2 pounds boneless beef short ribs, trimmed
- 2 tablespoons vegetable oil
- 2–4 tablespoons Thai red curry paste
- 1 (14-ounce) can unsweetened coconut milk
- 4 teaspoons fish sauce
- 2 teaspoons sugar
- 1 Thai red chile, halved lengthwise (optional)
- 6 kaffir lime leaves, middle vein removed, sliced thin
- ⅓ cup unsalted dry-roasted peanuts, chopped fine

1. Cut each rib crosswise with grain into 3 equal pieces. Slice each piece against grain 1/4 inch thick. Place beef in large saucepan and add water to cover. Bring to boil over high heat. Cover, reduce heat to low, and cook until beef is fork-tender, 1 to 1 1/4 hours. Using slotted spoon, transfer beef to bowl; discard water. (Beef can refrigerated for up to 24 hours; when ready to use, add it to curry as directed in step 2.)

2. Heat oil in 12-inch nonstick skillet over medium heat until shimmering. Add 2 tablespoons curry paste and cook, stirring frequently, until paste is fragrant and darkens in color to brick red, 5 to 8 minutes. Add coconut milk, fish sauce, sugar, and chile, if using; stir to combine and dissolve sugar. Taste sauce and add up to 2 tablespoons more curry paste to achieve desired spiciness. Add beef, stir to coat with sauce, and bring to simmer.

3. Rapidly simmer, stirring occasionally, until sauce is thickened and reduced by half and coats beef, 12 to 15 minutes. (Sauce should be quite thick, and streaks of oil will appear. Sauce will continue to thicken as it cools.) Add kaffir lime leaves and simmer until fragrant, 1 to 2 minutes. Transfer to serving platter, sprinkle with peanuts, and serve.

THAI CHILE BEEF

WHY THIS RECIPE WORKS: Most recipes for Thai chile beef require exotic ingredients and three hours of preparation—definitely not suitable for making midweek supper in an average American home kitchen. We wanted to create a sophisticated Thai chile beef recipe built around the traditional Thai flavors—spicy, sweet, sour, and salty—using readily available ingredients and requiring minimal cooking time.

A cheap and readily available cut—blade steak—won our taste test for its tenderness and very beefy flavor. We added the beef to our transformed stir-fry marinade—made with fish sauce for its briny flavor, white pepper for its spicy and almost gamy flavor, citrusy coriander, and a little light brown sugar for both sweetness and help in developing caramelization. With these elements, the beef only needed to marinate for 10 minutes to develop full flavor. We also wanted some heat and decided to use both a jalapeño and Asian chili-garlic paste (which added toasty garlicky flavors along with heat). More fish sauce, brown sugar, rice vinegar, fresh mint and cilantro, a few crunchy chopped peanuts, and a bright squirt of lime juice finished the dish.

Stir-Fried Thai-Style Beef with Chiles and Shallots

SERVES 4

To make slicing the blade steaks easier, freeze them for 15 minutes. If you cannot find blade steak, use flank steak; because flank steak requires less trimming, you will need only about 1 3/4 pounds. To cut a flank steak into the proper size slices for stir-frying, first cut the steak with the grain into 2-inch strips, then cut the strips against the grain into 1/8-inch-thick slices. Serve with Basic White Rice (page 453).

SAUCE

- 2 tablespoons fish sauce
- 2 tablespoons rice vinegar
- 2 tablespoons water
- 1 tablespoon light brown sugar
- 1 tablespoon Asian chili-garlic paste

BEEF AND VEGETABLES

- 2 pounds blade steaks, halved lengthwise, trimmed, and sliced into 1/8-inch-thick slices (see note)
- 1 tablespoon fish sauce
- 1 teaspoon light brown sugar
- 3/4 teaspoon ground coriander
- 1/8 teaspoon ground white pepper
- 3 tablespoons peanut or vegetable oil
- 3 medium garlic cloves, minced or pressed through a garlic press (about 1 tablespoon)
- 3 serrano or jalapeño chiles, halved, seeds and ribs removed, chiles sliced thin
- 3 medium shallots, ends trimmed, peeled, quartered lengthwise, and layers separated
- 1/2 cup fresh mint leaves, large leaves torn into bite-size pieces
- 1/2 cup fresh cilantro leaves
- 1/3 cup unsalted roasted peanuts, chopped coarse
- Lime wedges, for serving

1. FOR THE SAUCE: Combine all the ingredients in a small bowl and set aside.

2. FOR THE BEEF AND VEGETABLES: Toss the beef with the fish sauce, sugar, coriander, and white pepper in a medium bowl and let marinate for at least 10 minutes or up to 1 hour. In a small bowl, mix 1 teaspoon of the oil and the garlic together.

3. Heat 2 teaspoons more oil in a 12-inch nonstick skillet over high heat until just smoking. Add one-third of the beef, break up any clumps, then cook without stirring until the meat is browned at the edges, about 1 minute. Stir the beef and continue to cook until cooked through, about 1 minute longer. Transfer the beef to a clean bowl and cover with foil to keep warm. Repeat with 4 teaspoons more oil and the remaining beef in two batches.

4. Add the remaining 2 teaspoons oil to the skillet and return to medium heat until shimmering. Add the chiles and shallots and cook until beginning to soften, 3 to 4 minutes. Clear the center of the skillet, add the garlic mixture, and cook, mashing the mixture into the pan, until fragrant, 15 to 20 seconds. Stir the garlic mixture into the shallots and chiles.

5. Stir in the beef with any accumulated juices. Whisk the sauce to recombine, then add to the skillet and cook, tossing constantly, until the sauce is thickened, about 30 seconds. Stir in the half of the mint and half of the cilantro. Transfer to a serving platter, sprinkle with the remaining mint, remaining cilantro, and peanuts, and serve with the lime wedges.

THAI-STYLE STIR-FRIED NOODLES WITH CHICKEN

WHY THIS RECIPE WORKS: We wanted to create a version of *pad see ew*—the traditional Thai dish of chewy, lightly charred rice noodles, with chicken, crisp broccoli, and moist egg, bound with a sweet and salty soy-based sauce—that would work in the American home kitchen. We substituted supermarket ingredients for hard-to-find fresh rice noodles, Chinese broccoli, and sweet Thai soy sauce, but it was simulating the high heat of a restaurant wok burner on a lower-output home stovetop that was the real challenge. Since we were already using maximum heat, we increased the surface area by using a 12-inch nonstick skillet, and we cooked the dish in batches, combining all of the components right before serving. Most important, we found that eliminating much of the stirring in our stir-fry helped us achieve the all-important char that characterizes pad see ew.

Thai-Style Stir-Fried Noodles with Chicken and Broccolini

SERVES 4

The flat pad thai–style rice noodles that are used in this recipe can be found in the Asian section of most supermarkets. If you can't find broccolini, you can substitute an equal amount of conventional broccoli, but be sure to trim and peel the stalks before cutting.

CHILE VINEGAR

- ⅓ cup white vinegar
- 1 serrano chile, stemmed and sliced into thin rings

STIR-FRY

- 2 (6-ounce) boneless, skinless chicken breasts, trimmed and cut against grain into ¼-inch-thick slices
- 1 teaspoon baking soda
- 8 ounces (¼-inch-wide) rice noodles
- ¼ cup vegetable oil
- ¼ cup oyster sauce
- 1 tablespoon plus 2 teaspoons soy sauce
- 2 tablespoons packed dark brown sugar
- 1 tablespoon white vinegar
- 1 teaspoon molasses
- 1 teaspoon fish sauce
- 3 garlic cloves, sliced thin
- 3 large eggs
- 10 ounces broccolini, florets cut into 1-inch pieces, stalks cut on bias into ½-inch pieces (5 cups)

1. FOR THE CHILE VINEGAR: Combine vinegar and serrano in bowl. Let stand at room temperature for at least 15 minutes.

2. FOR THE STIR-FRY: Combine chicken with 2 tablespoons water and baking soda in bowl. Let sit at room temperature for 15 minutes. Rinse chicken in cold water and drain well.

3. Bring 6 cups water to boil. Place noodles in large bowl. Pour boiling water over noodles. Stir, then soak until noodles are almost tender, about 8 minutes, stirring once halfway through soaking. Drain and rinse with cold water. Drain well and toss with 2 teaspoons oil.

4. Whisk oyster sauce, soy sauce, sugar, vinegar, molasses, and fish sauce together in bowl.

5. Heat 2 teaspoons oil and garlic in 12-inch nonstick skillet over high heat, stirring occasionally, until garlic is deep golden brown, 1 to 2 minutes. Add chicken and 2 tablespoons sauce mixture, toss to coat, and spread chicken into even layer. Cook, without stirring, until chicken begins to brown, 1 to 1½ minutes. Flip chicken and cook, without stirring, until second side begins to brown, 1 to 1½ minutes. Push chicken to 1 side of skillet. Add 2 teaspoons oil to cleared side of skillet. Add eggs to clearing. Using rubber spatula, stir eggs gently and cook until set but still wet. Stir eggs into chicken and continue to cook, breaking up large pieces of egg, until eggs are fully cooked, 30 to 60 seconds. Transfer chicken mixture to bowl.

6. Heat 2 teaspoons oil in now-empty skillet until smoking. Add broccolini and 2 tablespoons sauce and toss to coat. Cover skillet and cook for 2 minutes, stirring once halfway through cooking. Remove lid and continue to cook until broccolini is crisp and very brown in spots, 2 to 3 minutes, stirring once halfway through cooking. Transfer broccolini to bowl with chicken mixture.

7. Heat 2 teaspoons oil in again-empty skillet until smoking. Add half of noodles and 2 tablespoons sauce and toss to coat. Cook until noodles are starting to brown in spots, about 2 minutes, stirring halfway through cooking. Transfer noodles to bowl with chicken mixture. Repeat with remaining 2 teaspoons oil, noodles, and sauce. When second batch of noodles is cooked, add contents of bowl back to skillet and toss to combine. Cook, without stirring, until everything is warmed through, 1 to 1½ minutes. Transfer to platter and serve immediately, passing chile vinegar separately.

PAD THAI

WHY THIS RECIPE WORKS: Ordered out, pad thai suffers from indiscriminate amounts of sugar; slick, greasy noodles; or bloated, sticky, lifeless strands that clump together. We hoped to develop a pad thai with clean, fresh, not-too-sweet flavors, perfectly cooked noodles, and plenty of plump, juicy shrimp with tender bits of scrambled egg.

Soaking the rice sticks in boiling water for 10 minutes before stir-frying made for tender but not sticky noodles. We created the salty, sweet, sour, and spicy flavor profile of pad thai by combining fish sauce, sugar, ground chiles, and vinegar. For the fresh, bright, fruity taste that is essential to the dish, we used tamarind paste, which we soaked in hot water and passed through a fine-mesh strainer to make a smooth puree. Tossed with fresh and dried shrimp and eggs, and garnished with scallions, peanuts, and cilantro, this dish is an excellent rendition of the Thai classic.

Pad Thai

SERVES 4

Although pad thai cooks very quickly, the ingredient list is long, and everything must be prepared and within easy reach at the stovetop when you begin cooking. For maximum efficiency, use the time during which the tamarind and noodles soak to prepare the other ingredients. If tamarind paste is unavailable, substitute ⅓ cup lime juice and ⅓ cup water and use light brown sugar instead of granulated sugar.

SAUCE

- ¾ cup boiling water
- 2 tablespoons tamarind paste (see note)
- 3 tablespoons fish sauce
- 3 tablespoons sugar
- 2 tablespoons peanut or vegetable oil
- 1 tablespoon rice vinegar
- ¾ teaspoon cayenne pepper

NOODLES, SHRIMP, AND GARNISH

- 8 ounces dried rice stick noodles, ⅛ to ¼ inch wide
- 2 tablespoons peanut or vegetable oil
- 12 ounces medium shrimp (41 to 50 per pound), peeled and deveined (see page 240)
- Table salt
- 1 medium shallot, minced (about 2 tablespoons)
- 3 garlic cloves, minced or pressed through a garlic press (about 1 tablespoon)
- 2 large eggs, lightly beaten
- 2 tablespoons chopped Thai salted preserved radish (optional)
- 1 tablespoon dried shrimp, chopped fine (optional)
- 3 cups bean sprouts
- ½ cup unsalted roasted peanuts, chopped coarse
- 5 scallions, green parts only, sliced thin on the bias
- ¼ cup loosely packed fresh cilantro leaves (optional)
- Lime wedges, for serving

1. FOR THE SAUCE: Combine the water and tamarind paste in a small bowl and let sit until the tamarind is softened and mushy, 10 to 30 minutes. Mash the tamarind to break it up, then push it through a fine-mesh strainer into a medium bowl to remove the seeds and fibers and extract as much pulp as possible. Stir in the remaining sauce ingredients and set aside.

2. FOR THE NOODLES, SHRIMP, AND GARNISH: Bring 4 quarts water to a boil in a large pot. Remove the boiling water from the heat, add the rice noodles, and let sit, stirring occasionally, until almost tender, about 10 minutes. Drain the noodles and set aside.

3. Heat 1 tablespoon of the oil in a 12-inch nonstick skillet over high heat until just smoking. Add the shrimp, sprinkle with ⅛ teaspoon salt, and cook without stirring until bright pink, about 1 minute. Stir the shrimp and continue to cook until cooked through, 15 to 30 seconds longer. Transfer the shrimp to a clean bowl and cover with foil to keep warm.

4. Add the remaining 1 tablespoon oil to the skillet and return to medium heat until shimmering. Add the shallot and garlic and cook, stirring constantly, until light golden brown, about 1½ minutes. Stir in the eggs and cook, stirring constantly, until scrambled and barely moist, about 20 seconds.

5. Add the noodles and the salted radish and dried shrimp (if using) to the eggs and toss to combine. Add the sauce, increase the heat to high, and cook, tossing constantly, until the noodles are evenly coated, about 1 minute.

6. Add the cooked shrimp, bean sprouts, ¼ cup of the peanuts, and all but ¼ cup of the scallions and continue to cook, tossing constantly, until the noodles are tender, about 2½ minutes. (If not yet tender add 2 tablespoons water to the skillet and continue to cook until tender.) Transfer the noodles to a serving platter, sprinkle with the remaining ¼ cup peanuts, remaining ¼ cup scallions, and cilantro (if using) and serve with the lime wedges.

EVERYDAY PAD THAI

WHY THIS RECIPE WORKS: To create a truly authentic version of pad thai with distinct sweet, sour, and salty flavors and a mix of textures, it is necessary to source hard-to-find ingredients like preserved daikon, palm sugar, and dried shrimp. We wanted to develop a recipe that maintained the integrity of the dish while using accessible ingredients. Soaking rice noodles in boiling water softened them quickly, and a sauce of sugar, fish sauce, and tamarind concentrate (also increasingly found in supermarkets) resulted in balanced flavor. Shrimp and egg bulked up the dish while bean sprouts, scallion greens, and peanuts added crunch. Finally, we pickled regular red radishes to use in place of hard-to-find preserved daikon, and we created our own faux dried shrimp by microwaving and then frying small pieces of fresh shrimp.

Everyday Pad Thai

SERVES 4

Since pad thai cooks very quickly, prepare everything before you begin to cook. Use the time during which the radishes and noodles soak to prepare the other ingredients. We recommend using a tamarind juice concentrate made in Thailand in this recipe. If you cannot find tamarind, substitute 1½ tablespoons lime juice and 1½ tablespoons water and omit the lime wedges.

CHILE VINEGAR

- ⅓ cup distilled white vinegar
- 1 serrano chile, stemmed and sliced into thin rings

STIR-FRY

- Salt
- Sugar
- 2 radishes, trimmed and cut into 1½-inch by ¼-inch matchsticks
- 8 ounces (¼-inch-wide) rice noodles
- 3 tablespoons plus 2 teaspoons vegetable oil
- ¼ cup fish sauce
- 3 tablespoons tamarind juice concentrate
- 1 pound large shrimp (26 to 30 per pound), peeled and deveined (see page 240)
- 4 scallions, white and light green parts minced, dark green parts cut into 1-inch lengths
- 1 garlic clove, minced
- 4 large eggs, beaten
- 4 ounces (2 cups) bean sprouts
- ¼ cup roasted unsalted peanuts, chopped coarse
- Lime wedges

1. FOR THE CHILE VINEGAR: Combine vinegar and chile in bowl and let stand at room temperature for at least 15 minutes.

2. FOR THE STIR-FRY: Combine ¼ cup water, ½ teaspoon salt, and ¼ teaspoon sugar in small bowl. Microwave until steaming, about 30 seconds. Add radishes and let stand for 15 minutes. Drain and pat dry with paper towels.

3. Bring 6 cups water to boil. Place noodles in large bowl. Pour boiling water over noodles. Stir, then let soak until noodles are almost tender, about 8 minutes, stirring once halfway through soaking. Drain noodles and rinse with cold water. Drain noodles well, then toss with 2 teaspoons oil.

4. Combine fish sauce, tamarind concentrate, and 3 tablespoons sugar in bowl and whisk until sugar is dissolved. Set sauce aside.

5. Remove tails from 4 shrimp. Cut shrimp in half lengthwise, then cut each half into ½-inch pieces. Toss shrimp pieces with ⅛ teaspoon salt and ⅛ teaspoon sugar. Arrange pieces in single layer on large plate and microwave at 50 percent power until shrimp are dried and have reduced in size by half, 4 to 5 minutes. (Check halfway through microwaving and separate any pieces that may have stuck together.)

6. Heat 2 teaspoons oil in 12-inch nonstick skillet over medium heat until shimmering. Add dried shrimp and cook, stirring frequently, until golden brown and crispy, 3 to 5 minutes. Transfer to large bowl.

7. Heat 1 teaspoon oil in now-empty skillet over medium heat until shimmering. Add minced scallions and garlic and cook, stirring constantly, until garlic is golden brown, about 1 minute. Transfer to bowl with dried shrimp.

8. Heat 2 teaspoons oil in now-empty skillet over high heat until just smoking. Add remaining whole shrimp and spread into even layer. Cook, without stirring, until shrimp turn opaque and brown around edges, 2 to 3 minutes, flipping halfway through cooking. Push shrimp to sides of skillet. Add 2 teaspoons oil to center, then add eggs to center. Using rubber spatula, stir eggs gently and cook until set but still wet. Stir eggs into shrimp and continue to cook, breaking up large pieces of egg, until eggs are fully cooked, 30 to 60 seconds longer. Transfer shrimp-egg mixture to bowl with scallion-garlic mixture and dried shrimp.

9. Heat remaining 2 teaspoons oil in now-empty skillet over high heat until just smoking. Add noodles and sauce and toss with tongs to coat. Cook, stirring and tossing often, until noodles are tender and have absorbed sauce, 2 to 4 minutes. Transfer noodles to bowl with shrimp mixture. Add 2 teaspoons chile vinegar, drained radishes, scallion greens, and bean sprouts and toss to combine.

10. Transfer to platter and sprinkle with peanuts. Serve immediately, passing lime wedges and remaining chile vinegar separately.

THAI GRILLED CHICKEN

WHY THIS RECIPE WORKS: This herb- and spice-rubbed chicken is served in small pieces and eaten as finger food. We wanted to develop a recipe for Thai grilled chicken to offer a refreshing change of pace from typical barbecue fare. After testing numerous rub combinations, we liked cilantro, black pepper, lime juice, garlic, coriander, and ginger. We took some of the rub and placed it in a thick layer under the skin as well as on top of it. For perfectly cooked chicken, we made a modified two-level fire, first browning the chicken directly over the coals and then moving it to the cool side of the grill to finish cooking. The true Thai flavors of this dish come through in the sauce, a classic combination of sweet and spicy. We found balance in a blend of sugar, lime juice, white vinegar, red pepper flakes, fish sauce, and garlic.

Thai-Style Grilled Chicken with Spicy Sweet-and-Sour Dipping Sauce

SERVES 4

For even cooking, the chicken breasts should be of comparable size. Some of the rub is inevitably lost to the grill, but the chicken will still be flavorful.

CHICKEN AND BRINE

- ½ cup sugar
- ½ cup salt
- 4 (12-ounce) bone-in split chicken breasts, trimmed

DIPPING SAUCE
- ⅓ cup sugar
- ¼ cup distilled white vinegar
- ¼ cup lime juice (2 limes)
- 2 tablespoons fish sauce
- 3 small garlic cloves, minced
- 1 teaspoon red pepper flakes

RUB
- ⅔ cup chopped fresh cilantro
- 12 garlic cloves, minced
- ¼ cup lime juice (2 limes)
- 2 tablespoons grated fresh ginger
- 2 tablespoons pepper
- 2 tablespoons ground coriander
- 2 tablespoons vegetable oil

- 1 disposable aluminum roasting pan (if using charcoal)

1. FOR THE CHICKEN AND BRINE: Dissolve sugar and salt in 2 quarts cold water in large container. Submerge chicken in brine, cover, and refrigerate for at least 30 minutes or up to 1 hour. Remove chicken from brine and pat dry with paper towels.

2. FOR THE DIPPING SAUCE: Whisk all ingredients together in bowl until sugar dissolves. Let stand for 1 hour at room temperature to allow flavors to meld.

3. FOR THE RUB: Combine all ingredients in small bowl; work mixture with your fingers to thoroughly combine. Slide your fingers between chicken skin and meat to loosen skin, taking care not to detach skin. Rub about 2 tablespoons rub under skin of each breast. Thoroughly rub even layer of rub onto all exterior surfaces, including bottom and sides. Place chicken in bowl, cover with plastic wrap, and refrigerate while preparing grill.

4A. FOR A CHARCOAL GRILL: Open bottom vent completely. Light large chimney starter filled with charcoal briquettes (6 quarts). When top coals are partially covered with ash, pour evenly over half of grill. Set cooking grate in place, cover, and open lid vent completely. Heat grill until hot, about 5 minutes.

4B. FOR A GAS GRILL: Turn all burners to high, cover, and heat grill until hot, about 15 minutes. Leave primary burner on high and turn other burner(s) to low.

5. Clean and oil cooking grate. Place chicken, skin side down, on hotter side of grill; cook until browned, about 3 minutes (1 to 2 minutes longer for gas grill). Using tongs, flip chicken and cook until browned on second side, about 3 minutes longer. Move chicken, skin side up, to cooler side of grill and cover with disposable pan (or close lid if using gas grill). Continue to cook until thickest part of breast (not touching bone) registers 160 degrees, 10 to 15 minutes longer. Transfer chicken to platter; let rest for 10 minutes. Serve, passing dipping sauce separately.

GRILLED THAI BEEF SALAD

WHY THIS RECIPE WORKS: This traditional Thai salad features slices of charred steak tossed with shallots, mint, and cilantro in a bright dressing. We chose flank steak for its marbling and moderate price. Grilling the steak over a modified two-level fire and flipping it just when moisture beaded on the surface yielded perfectly charred, juicy meat. Adding a fresh Thai chile, toasted cayenne, and paprika gave the dressing a fruity, fiery heat. Toasted rice powder, a traditional Thai tableside condiment that gives the dressing fuller body and a subtle crunch, is not widely available here, but we made our own by toasting rice in a skillet on the stovetop, then grinding it in a food processor, spice grinder, or even with a mortar and pestle.

Grilled Thai Beef Salad

SERVES 4 TO 6

If fresh Thai chiles are unavailable, substitute ½ serrano chile. Don't skip the toasted rice; it's integral to the texture and flavor of the dish. Any variety of white rice can be used. Toasted rice powder (*kao kua*) can also be found in many Asian markets; substitute 1 tablespoon rice powder for the white rice. Serve with Basic White Rice (page 453), if desired.

- 1 teaspoon paprika
- 1 teaspoon cayenne pepper
- 1 tablespoon white rice
- 3 tablespoons lime juice (2 limes)
- 2 tablespoons fish sauce
- 2 tablespoons water
- ½ teaspoon sugar
- 1 (1½-pound) flank steak, trimmed
- Salt and coarsely ground white pepper
- 1 seedless English cucumber, sliced ¼ inch thick on bias
- 4 shallots, sliced thin
- 1½ cups fresh mint leaves, torn
- 1½ cups fresh cilantro leaves
- 1 Thai chile, stemmed, seeded, and sliced thin into rounds

1. Heat paprika and cayenne in 8-inch skillet over medium heat; cook, shaking pan, until fragrant, about 1 minute. Transfer to small bowl. Return skillet to medium-high heat, add rice and toast, stirring constantly, until deep golden brown, about 5 minutes. Transfer to small bowl and let cool 5 minutes. Grind rice with spice grinder, mini food processor, or mortar and pestle until it resembles fine meal, 10 to 30 seconds (you should have about 1 tablespoon rice powder).

2. Whisk lime juice, fish sauce, water, sugar, and ¼ teaspoon toasted paprika mixture in large bowl and set aside.

3A. FOR A CHARCOAL GRILL: Open bottom vent completely. Light large chimney starter filled with charcoal briquettes (6 quarts). When top coals are partially covered with ash, pour in even layer over half of grill. Set cooking grate in place, cover, and open lid vent completely. Heat grill until hot, about 5 minutes.

3B. FOR A GAS GRILL: Turn all burners to high, cover, and heat grill until hot, about 15 minutes. Leave primary burner on high and turn off other burner(s).

4. Clean and oil grate. Season steak with salt and pepper. Place steak on grate over hot part of grill and cook until beginning to char and beads of moisture appear on outer edges of meat, 5 to 6 minutes. Flip steak, continue to cook on second side until meat registers 125 degrees, about 5 minutes longer. Transfer to carving board, tent loosely with aluminum foil, and rest for 10 minutes (or allow to cool to room temperature, about 1 hour).

5. Line large platter with cucumber slices. Slice meat, against grain, on bias, into ¼-inch-thick slices. Transfer sliced steak to bowl with fish sauce mixture, add shallots, mint, cilantro, chile, and half of rice powder, and toss to combine. Arrange steak over cucumber-lined platter. Serve, passing remaining rice powder and toasted paprika mixture separately.

VIETNAMESE-STYLE CARAMEL CHICKEN WITH BROCCOLI

WHY THIS RECIPE WORKS: In Vietnamese cooking, caramel sauce has a savory, bittersweet quality that gives a rich, molasses-like hue to meat, fish, and tofu alike. To prep our chicken for this flavorful sauce, we coated boneless, skinless thighs with a mixture of baking soda and water. Baking soda would help break down the muscle fibers, promising juicy, tender meat capable of taking on lots of flavor and moisture. For caramel that was savory, not sweet, we cooked sugar and water in a saucepan until the mixture took on a deep brown color and reached between 390 and 400 degrees. At that temperature, sugar molecules break down and the caramel takes on a pleasingly bitter, potent taste. We transferred the caramel to a 12-inch skillet and added fish sauce for a savory, salty punch and freshly grated ginger for spicy brightness. Simmering the boneless chicken in the sauce produced tender meat fully infused with bold Vietnamese flavor. Once the chicken was cooked, we prepared some steamed broccoli for textural and visual contrast and reduced the caramel, adding some cornstarch to further thicken and finish the sauce.

Vietnamese-Style Caramel Chicken with Broccoli

SERVES 4 TO 6

The saltiness of fish sauce can vary by brand; we recommend Red Boat. When taking the temperature of the caramel in step 2, tilt the pan and move the thermometer back and forth to equalize hot and cool spots; also make sure to have hot water at the ready. This dish is intensely seasoned, so serve it with Basic White Rice (page 453).

- 1 tablespoon baking soda
- 2 pounds boneless, skinless chicken thighs, trimmed and halved crosswise
- 7 tablespoons sugar
- ¼ cup fish sauce
- 2 tablespoons grated fresh ginger
- 1 pound broccoli, florets cut into 1-inch pieces, stalks peeled and sliced ¼ inch thick
- 2 teaspoons cornstarch
- ½ teaspoon pepper
- ½ cup chopped fresh cilantro leaves and stems

1. Combine baking soda and 1¼ cups cold water in large bowl. Add chicken and toss to coat. Let stand at room temperature for 15 minutes. Rinse chicken in cold water and drain well.

2. Meanwhile, combine sugar and 3 tablespoons water in small saucepan. Bring to boil over medium-high heat and cook, without stirring, until mixture begins to turn golden, 4 to 6 minutes. Reduce heat to medium-low and continue to cook, gently swirling saucepan, until sugar turns color of molasses and registers between 390 and 400 degrees, 4 to 6 minutes longer. (Caramel will produce some smoke during last 1 to 2 minutes of cooking.) Immediately remove saucepan

from heat and carefully pour in ¾ cup hot water (mixture will bubble and steam vigorously). When bubbling has subsided, return saucepan to medium heat and stir to dissolve caramel.

3. Transfer caramel to 12-inch skillet and stir in fish sauce and ginger. Add chicken and bring to simmer over medium-high heat. Reduce heat to medium-low, cover, and simmer until chicken is fork-tender and registers 205 degrees, 30 to 40 minutes, flipping chicken halfway through simmering. Transfer chicken to serving dish and cover to keep warm.

4. Bring 1 inch water to boil in Dutch oven. Lower insert or steamer basket with broccoli into pot so it rests above water; cover and simmer until broccoli is just tender, 4½ to 5 minutes. Transfer broccoli to serving dish with chicken.

5. While broccoli cooks, bring sauce to boil over medium-high heat and cook until reduced to 1¼ cups, 3 to 5 minutes. Whisk cornstarch and 1 tablespoon water together in small bowl, then whisk into sauce; simmer until slightly thickened, about 1 minute. Stir in pepper. Pour ¼ cup sauce over chicken and broccoli. Sprinkle with cilantro and serve, passing remaining sauce separately.

INDIAN FLATBREAD (NAAN)

WHY THIS RECIPE WORKS: Even in India, naan is considered "restaurant" bread. This may be because it calls for a traditional tandoor oven, which few home cooks own. We wanted an ideal version of this bread—light and airy, with a pliant, chewy crust—that we could easily make at home. We started with a moist dough with a fair amount of fat, which created a soft bread that was pleasantly chewy, but the real secret was the cooking method. While we thought a grill or preheated pizza stone would be the best cooking method, we discovered that they cooked the bread unevenly. A much better option was a covered skillet. The skillet delivered heat to the bottom and the top of the bread, producing loaves that were nicely charred but still moist.

Indian Flatbread (Naan)

MAKES 4 BREADS

This recipe works best with a high-protein all-purpose flour such as King Arthur brand. Do not use nonfat yogurt in this recipe. A 12-inch nonstick skillet may be used in place of the cast-iron skillet. For efficiency, stretch the next ball of dough while each naan is cooking.

- ½ cup ice water
- ⅓ cup plain whole-milk yogurt
- 3 tablespoons plus 1 teaspoon vegetable oil
- 1 large egg yolk
- 2 cups (10 ounces) all-purpose flour
- 1¼ teaspoons sugar
- ½ teaspoon instant or rapid-rise yeast
- 1¼ teaspoons salt
- 1½ tablespoons unsalted butter, melted

1. In measuring cup or small bowl, combine water, yogurt, 3 tablespoons oil, and egg yolk. Process flour, sugar, and yeast together in food processor until combined, about 2 seconds. With processor running, slowly add water mixture; process until dough is just combined and no dry flour remains, about 10 seconds. Let dough stand for 10 minutes.

2. Add salt to dough and process until dough forms satiny, sticky ball that clears sides of workbowl, 30 to 60 seconds. Transfer dough to lightly floured counter and knead until smooth, about 1 minute. Shape dough into tight ball and place in large, lightly oiled bowl. Cover tightly with plastic wrap and refrigerate for 16 to 24 hours.

3. Adjust oven rack to middle position and heat oven to 200 degrees. Place heatproof plate on rack. Transfer dough to lightly floured counter and divide into 4 equal pieces. Shape each piece into smooth, tight ball. Place dough balls on lightly oiled baking sheet, at least 2 inches apart; cover loosely with plastic coated with vegetable oil spray. Let stand for 15 to 20 minutes.

4. Transfer 1 ball to lightly floured counter and sprinkle with flour. Using hands and rolling pin, press and roll piece of dough into 9-inch round of even thickness, sprinkling dough and counter with flour as needed to prevent sticking. Using fork, poke entire surface of round 20 to 25 times. Heat remaining 1 teaspoon oil in 12-inch cast-iron skillet over medium heat until shimmering. Wipe oil out of skillet completely with paper towels. Mist top of dough lightly with water. Place dough in pan, moistened side down; mist top surface of dough with water; and cover. Cook until bottom is browned in spots across surface, 2 to 4 minutes. Flip naan, cover, and continue to cook on second side until lightly browned, 2 to 3 minutes longer. (If naan puffs up, gently poke with fork to deflate.) Flip naan, brush top with about 1 teaspoon melted butter, transfer to plate in oven, and cover plate tightly with aluminum foil. Repeat rolling and cooking remaining 3 dough balls. Once last naan is baked, serve immediately.

Quicker Indian Flatbread

This variation, which can be prepared in about 2 hours, forgoes the overnight rest, but the dough may be a little harder to roll out.

After shaping dough in step 2, let dough rise at room temperature for 30 minutes. After 30 minutes, fold partially risen dough over itself 8 times by gently lifting and folding edge of dough toward middle, turning bowl 90 degrees after each fold. Cover with plastic wrap and let rise for 30 minutes. Repeat folding, turning, and rising 1 more time, for total of three 30-minute rises. After last rise, proceed with recipe from step 3.

SAAG PANEER

WHY THIS RECIPE WORKS: *Saag paneer*, soft cubes of creamy cheese in a spicy pureed spinach sauce, is an Indian restaurant classic. We found that re-creating this dish at home wasn't so difficult. We made our own cheese by heating a combination of whole milk and buttermilk, squeezing the curds of moisture, then weighing the cheese down until it was firm enough to slice. We simply wilted the spinach in the microwave. Mustard greens gave our sauce additional complexity. Canned diced tomatoes brightened the dish. And buttery cashews gave our Indian classic a subtle nutty richness.

Indian-Style Spinach with Fresh Cheese (Saag Paneer)

SERVES 4 TO 6

To ensure that the cheese is firm, wring it tightly in step 2 and be sure to use two plates that nestle together snugly. Use commercially produced cultured buttermilk in this recipe. We found that some locally produced buttermilks didn't sufficiently coagulate the milk. Serve with basmati rice.

CHEESE

- 3 quarts whole milk
- 3 cups buttermilk
- 1 tablespoon salt

SPINACH SAUCE

- 1 (10-ounce) bag curly-leaf spinach, rinsed
- 12 ounces mustard greens, stemmed and rinsed
- 3 tablespoons unsalted butter
- 1 teaspoon cumin seeds
- 1 teaspoon ground coriander
- 1 teaspoon paprika
- ½ teaspoon ground cardamom
- ¼ teaspoon ground cinnamon
- 1 onion, chopped fine
- Salt and pepper
- 3 garlic cloves, minced
- 1 tablespoon grated fresh ginger
- 1 jalapeño chile, stemmed, seeded, and minced
- 1 (14.5-ounce) can diced tomatoes, drained and chopped coarse
- ½ cup roasted cashews, chopped coarse
- 1 cup water
- 1 cup buttermilk
- 3 tablespoons chopped fresh cilantro

1. FOR THE CHEESE: Line colander with triple layer of cheesecloth and set in sink. Bring milk to boil in Dutch oven over medium-high heat. Whisk in buttermilk and salt, turn off heat, and let stand for 1 minute. Pour milk mixture through cheesecloth and let curds drain for 15 minutes.

2. Pull edges of cheesecloth together to form pouch. Twist edges of cheesecloth together, firmly squeezing out as much liquid as possible from cheese curds. Place taut, twisted cheese pouch between 2 large plates and weigh down top plate with heavy Dutch oven. Set aside at room temperature until cheese is firm and set, at least 45 minutes. Remove cheesecloth and cut cheese into ½-inch pieces. (Left uncut, cheese can be wrapped in plastic wrap and refrigerated for up to 3 days.)

3. FOR THE SPINACH SAUCE: Place spinach in large bowl, cover, and microwave until wilted, about 3 minutes. When cool enough to handle, chop enough spinach to measure ⅓ cup and set aside. Transfer remaining spinach to blender and wipe out bowl. Place mustard greens in now-empty bowl, cover, and microwave until wilted, about 4 minutes. When cool enough to handle, chop enough mustard greens to measure ⅓ cup and transfer to bowl with chopped spinach. Transfer remaining mustard greens to blender.

4. Meanwhile, melt butter in 12-inch skillet over medium-high heat. Add cumin seeds, coriander, paprika, cardamom, and cinnamon and cook until fragrant, about 30 seconds. Add onion and ¾ teaspoon salt; cook, stirring frequently, until softened, about 3 minutes. Add garlic, ginger, and jalapeño; cook, stirring frequently, until lightly browned and just beginning to stick to pan, 2 to 3 minutes. Stir in tomatoes and cook mixture until pan is dry and tomatoes are beginning to brown, 3 to 4 minutes. Remove skillet from heat.

5. Transfer half of onion mixture to blender with greens. Add ¼ cup cashews and water; process until smooth, about 1 minute. Return puree to skillet.

6. Return skillet to medium-high heat, stir in chopped greens and buttermilk, and bring to simmer. Reduce heat to low, cover, and cook until flavors have blended, 5 minutes. Season with salt and pepper to taste. Gently fold in cheese cubes and cook until just heated through, 1 to 2 minutes. Transfer to serving dish, sprinkle with remaining ¼ cup cashews and cilantro, and serve.

NOTES FROM THE TEST KITCHEN

MAKING PANEER

Even if you've never made cheese at home, our method for making paneer is very simple, and the flavor pay-off is well worth the effort.

1. Bring milk to boil, curdle it with buttermilk, and let rest for 1 minute off heat. Pour curdled milk through cheesecloth-lined colander; let drain. Twist cheesecloth to squeeze out liquid.

2. Press cheese between plates topped with Dutch oven; let drain until firm. Slice into ½-inch pieces.

CHICKEN TIKKA MASALA

WHY THIS RECIPE WORKS: Chicken tikka masala is arguably the single most popular Indian restaurant dish in the world. Turns out, it's not an authentic Indian dish—it was invented in a London curry house. Without historical roots, there is no definitive recipe. The variations we found had mushy or dry chicken and sauces that were unbearably rich and/or overspiced. We wanted an approachable method for producing moist, tender chunks of chicken in a rich, lightly spiced tomato sauce. To season the chicken, we rubbed it with salt, coriander, cumin, and cayenne. Then we dipped it in yogurt mixed with oil, garlic, and ginger and broiled it. And since large pieces don't dry out as quickly as smaller ones under the broiler, we cooked the chicken breasts whole, cutting them into pieces only after cooking. While the chicken was cooking, we made the masala sauce. Masala means "hot spice," and the ingredients in a masala sauce depend on the whim of the cook, although tomatoes and cream are always present. We added onions, ginger, garlic, chile, and a readily available commercial garam masala spice mixture. A little tomato paste and sugar gave our sauce color and sweetness.

Chicken Tikka Masala

SERVES 4 TO 6

This dish is best when prepared with whole-milk yogurt, but low-fat yogurt can be substituted. For more heat, include the chile seeds and ribs when mincing. Serve with Rice Pilaf (see page 617).

CHICKEN

- Table salt
- ½ teaspoon ground cumin
- ½ teaspoon ground coriander
- ¼ teaspoon cayenne pepper
- 2 pounds boneless, skinless chicken breasts, trimmed
- 1 cup plain whole-milk yogurt (see note)
- 2 tablespoons vegetable oil
- 1 tablespoon minced or grated fresh ginger
- 2 medium garlic cloves, minced or pressed through a garlic press (about 2 teaspoons)

SAUCE

- 3 tablespoons vegetable oil
- 1 medium onion, minced (about 1 cup)
- 1 tablespoon garam masala
- 1 tablespoon tomato paste
- 2 medium garlic cloves, minced or pressed through a garlic press (about 2 teaspoons)
- 2 teaspoons minced or grated fresh ginger
- 1 serrano chile, seeds and ribs removed, chile minced (see note)
- 1 (28-ounce) can crushed tomatoes
- 2 teaspoons sugar
- ½ teaspoon table salt
- ⅔ cup heavy cream
- ¼ cup chopped fresh cilantro leaves

1. FOR THE CHICKEN: Combine ½ teaspoon salt, cumin, coriander, and cayenne in a small bowl. Pat the chicken dry with paper towels and sprinkle with the spice mixture, pressing gently so the mixture adheres. Place the chicken on a plate, cover with plastic wrap, and refrigerate for 30 minutes or up to 1 hour. In a large bowl, whisk the yogurt, oil, ginger, and garlic together and set aside.

2. FOR THE SAUCE: Heat the oil in a large Dutch oven over medium heat until shimmering. Add the onion and cook, stirring frequently, until softened and light golden, 8 to 10 minutes. Stir in the garam masala, tomato paste, garlic, ginger, and serrano and cook, stirring frequently, until fragrant, about 3 minutes. Add the crushed tomatoes, sugar, and salt and bring to a boil. Reduce the heat to medium-low, cover, and simmer for 15 minutes, stirring occasionally. Stir in the cream and return to a simmer. Remove the pan from the heat and cover to keep warm. (The sauce can be refrigerated in an airtight container for up to 4 days and gently reheated before adding the hot chicken.)

3. TO COOK THE CHICKEN: While the sauce simmers, position an oven rack 6 inches from the heating element and heat the broiler. Line a rimmed baking sheet or broiler pan with foil and place a wire rack over the sheet.

4. Using tongs, dip the chicken into the yogurt mixture (the chicken should be coated with a thick layer of yogurt) and arrange on the wire rack. Discard the excess yogurt mixture. Broil the chicken until lightly charred and the thickest part of the breasts registers 160 to 165 degrees on an instant-read thermometer, 10 to 18 minutes, flipping the chicken halfway through.

5. Let the chicken rest for 5 minutes, then cut into 1-inch chunks and stir into the warm sauce (do not simmer the chicken in the sauce). Stir in the cilantro, season with salt to taste, and serve.

INDIAN-STYLE CHICKEN AND RICE

WHY THIS RECIPE WORKS: Chicken biryani is a complicated (and often greasy) "gourmet" Indian dish. Chicken and rice is a simple, but unremarkable, American one-pot meal. We wanted to find a happy medium between the two.

In biryani, long-grain basmati rice takes center stage, enriched with butter, saffron, and a variety of fresh herbs and pungent spices. Pieces of tender chicken and browned onions are layered with the rice and baked until the flavors have mingled. For our recipe, we browned bone-in, skin-on chicken thighs, then removed the skin and layered them with basmati rice, lots of caramelized onions, and just the right blend of spices. To get the most flavor out of the spices, we tied them into a cheesecloth bundle and simmered them in the rice cooking water—then we added some of that water to the biryani. For a finishing touch, we added saffron, currants, and plenty of ginger and chiles.

Chicken Biryani

SERVES 4

This recipe requires a 3½- to 4-quart saucepan about 8 inches in diameter. Do not use a large, wide Dutch oven, as it will adversely affect both the layering of the dish and the final cooking times. For more heat, add the jalapeño seeds and ribs when mincing.

YOGURT SAUCE

- 1 cup whole-milk or low-fat plain yogurt
- 2 tablespoons minced fresh cilantro leaves
- 2 tablespoons minced fresh mint leaves
- 1 medium garlic clove, minced or pressed through a garlic press (about 1 teaspoon)
- Table salt and ground black pepper

CHICKEN AND RICE

- 10 cardamom pods, preferably green, smashed with a chef's knife
- 1 cinnamon stick
- 1 (2-inch) piece fresh ginger, peeled, cut into ½-inch-thick coins, and smashed
- ½ teaspoon cumin seeds
- 3 quarts water
- Table salt and ground black pepper
- 4 (5- to 6-ounce) bone-in, skin-on chicken thighs, trimmed
- 3 tablespoons unsalted butter
- 2 medium onions, halved and sliced thin
- 2 jalapeño chiles, seeds and ribs removed, chiles minced (see note)
- 4 medium garlic cloves, minced or pressed through a garlic press (about 4 teaspoons)
- 1¼ cups basmati rice
- ½ teaspoon saffron threads, lightly crumbled
- ¼ cup dried currants or raisins
- 2 tablespoons chopped fresh cilantro leaves
- 2 tablespoons chopped fresh mint leaves

1. FOR THE YOGURT SAUCE: Combine all the ingredients in a small bowl, season with salt and pepper to taste, and set aside. (The sauce can be refrigerated in an airtight container for up to 2 days.)

2. FOR THE CHICKEN AND RICE: Wrap the cardamom pods, cinnamon stick, ginger, and cumin in a small piece of cheesecloth and secure with kitchen twine. In a 3½ to 4-quart heavy-bottomed saucepan about 8 inches in diameter, bring the spice bundle, water, and 1½ teaspoons salt to a boil over medium-high heat. Reduce the heat to medium and simmer, partially covered, until the spices have infused the water, at least 15 minutes (but no longer than 30 minutes).

3. Meanwhile, pat the chicken thighs dry with paper towels and season with salt and pepper. Melt the butter in a 12-inch nonstick skillet over medium-high heat. Add the onions and cook, stirring frequently, until soft and dark brown around the edges, 10 to 12 minutes. Stir in the jalapeños and garlic and cook, stirring frequently, until fragrant, about 2 minutes. Transfer the onion mixture to a bowl, season with salt, and set aside. Wipe out the skillet with a wad of paper towels.

4. Place the chicken, skin side down, in the skillet, return the skillet to medium-high heat, and cook until well browned on both sides, 8 to 10 minutes, flipping halfway through. Transfer the chicken to a plate and remove and discard the skin. Tent loosely with foil to keep warm.

5. If necessary, return the spice-infused water to a boil over high heat. Add the rice and cook, stirring occasionally, for 5 minutes. Drain the rice through a fine-mesh strainer, reserving ¾ cup of the cooking liquid; discard the spice bundle. Transfer the rice to a medium bowl and stir in the saffron and currants (the rice will turn splotchy yellow).

6. Spread half of the rice evenly in the bottom of the saucepan using a rubber spatula. Scatter half of the onion mixture over the rice, then place the chicken thighs, skinned side up, on top of the onions; add any accumulated chicken juices. Sprinkle evenly with the cilantro and mint, scatter the remaining onion mixture over the herbs, then cover with the remaining rice. Pour the reserved 3/4 cup cooking liquid evenly over the rice.

7. Cover the saucepan and cook over medium-low heat until the rice is tender and the chicken registers 175 degrees on an instant-read thermometer, about 30 minutes (if a large amount of steam is escaping from the pot, reduce the heat to low).

8. Run a heatproof rubber spatula around the inside rim of the saucepan to loosen any affixed rice. Using a large serving spoon, spoon the biryani into individual bowls, scooping from the bottom of the pot. Serve, passing the yogurt sauce separately.

INDIAN CURRY

WHY THIS RECIPE WORKS: For many home cooks Indian cooking is a mystery, full of exotic spices and unfamiliar techniques. We hoped to bring Indian curry to the American home kitchen with a complex but not heavy-flavored curry that wouldn't take all day to prepare. Allowing the spices to cook completely provided the intense flavor we were after. We used a combination of whole spices—cinnamon sticks, cloves, green cardamom pods, black peppercorns, and a bay leaf—and toasted them in oil before adding aromatics, jalapeño, and ground spices. Instead of browning the meat), we stirred it into the pot along with crushed tomatoes and cooked the mixture until the liquid evaporated and the oil separated. This is a classic Indian technique that allows the spices to further develop their flavors in the oil, flavors which are then cooked into the meat. We then added water and simmered the mixture until the meat was tender, then stirred in the spinach and channa dal (yellow split peas) and cooked the dish until all the ingredients were melded and tender.

Indian Curry

SERVES 4 TO 6

If desired, 1½ pounds boneless, skinless chicken thighs, trimmed and cut into 3/4-inch chunks, can be substituted for the lamb. For more heat, add the jalapeño seeds and ribs when mincing. For a creamier curry, choose yogurt over the crushed tomatoes. Serve with Yogurt Sauce (page 490), Onion Relish (page 492), Cilantro-Mint Chutney (page 492), and Rice Pilaf (page 617).

SPICE BLEND

- 1½ cinnamon sticks
- 4 whole cloves
- 4 green cardamom pods
- 8 whole black peppercorns
- 1 bay leaf

CURRY

- ¼ cup vegetable oil
- 1 medium onion, halved and sliced thin
- 5 medium garlic cloves, minced or pressed through a garlic press (about 5 teaspoons)
- 1 tablespoon minced or grated fresh ginger
- 1 jalapeño chile, stemmed and halved lengthwise, seeds and ribs removed (see note)
- 2 teaspoons ground cumin
- 2 teaspoons ground coriander
- 1 teaspoon ground turmeric
- Table salt
- 1½ pounds boneless leg of lamb, trimmed and cut into ¾-inch cubes (see note)
- ⅔ cup crushed tomatoes or ½ cup plain low-fat yogurt (see note)
- 2 cups water
- 1½ pounds spinach, stemmed, washed, and chopped coarse (optional)
- ½ cup channa dal (yellow split peas)
- ¼ cup chopped fresh cilantro leaves

1. FOR THE SPICE BLEND: Combine all the ingredients in a small bowl and set aside.

2. FOR THE CURRY: Heat the oil in a Dutch oven over medium heat until shimmering. Add the spice blend and cook, stirring frequently, until the cinnamon stick unfurls and the cloves pop, about 5 seconds. Add the onion and cook, stirring occasionally, until softened, 5 to 7 minutes. Stir in the garlic, ginger, jalapeño, cumin, coriander, turmeric, and ½ teaspoon salt and cook until fragrant, about 30 seconds.

3. Stir in the lamb and the tomatoes. Bring to a simmer and cook, stirring frequently, until the liquid evaporates and the oil separates and turns orange, 5 to 7 minutes. Continue to cook until the spices are sizzling, about 30 seconds longer.

4. Stir in the water and bring to a simmer over medium heat. Reduce the heat to medium-low, cover, and cook until the lamb is almost tender, about 40 minutes.

5. Stir in the spinach (if using) and channa dal and cook until the channa dal are tender, about 15 minutes. Season with salt to taste, stir in the cilantro, and serve.

VEGETABLE CURRY

WHY THIS RECIPE WORKS: Vegetable curries can be complicated affairs, with lengthy ingredient lists and fussy techniques meant to compensate for the lack of meat. We wanted a curry we could make on a weeknight in less than an hour—without sacrificing flavor or overloading the dish with spices.

Although initially reluctant to use store-bought curry powder, we found that toasting the curry powder in a skillet turned it into a flavor powerhouse. Further experimentation proved that adding a few pinches of garam masala added even more spice flavor. To build the rest of our flavor base we started with a generous amount of sautéed onion, vegetable oil, garlic, ginger, fresh chile, and tomato paste for sweetness. When we chose our vegetables (chickpeas and potatoes for heartiness and cauliflower and peas for texture and color), we found that sautéing the spices and main ingredients together enhanced and melded the flavors. Finally, we rounded out our sauce with a combination of water, pureed canned tomatoes, and a splash of heavy cream or coconut milk.

Indian-Style Curry with Potatoes, Cauliflower, Peas, and Chickpeas

SERVES 4 TO 6

This curry is moderately spicy when made with one chile. For more heat, include the chile seeds and ribs when mincing. Serve with Yogurt Sauce (page 490), Onion Relish, Cilantro-Mint Chutney, and Rice Pilaf (page 617).

- 2 tablespoons sweet or mild curry powder
- 1½ teaspoons garam masala
- 4 tablespoons vegetable oil
- 3 medium garlic cloves, minced or pressed through a garlic press (about 1 tablespoon)
- 1 tablespoon minced or grated fresh ginger
- 1 serrano chile, seeds and ribs removed, chile minced (see note)
- 1 tablespoon tomato paste
- 1 (14.5-ounce) can diced tomatoes
- 2 medium onions, minced (about 2 cups)
- 12 ounces red potatoes (about 2 medium), scrubbed and cut into ½-inch pieces
- 1¼ pounds cauliflower (½ medium head), trimmed, cored, and cut into 1-inch florets
- 1¼ cups water
- 1 (15-ounce) can chickpeas, drained and rinsed
- Table salt
- 1½ cups frozen peas
- ¼ cup heavy cream or coconut milk

CONDIMENTS

- Onion Relish (recipe follows)
- Cilantro-Mint Chutney (recipe follows) or mango chutney

1. Toast the curry powder and garam masala in a small skillet over medium-high heat, stirring constantly, until the spices darken slightly and become fragrant, about 1 minute. Transfer the spices to a small bowl and set aside. In a separate small bowl, stir 1 tablespoon of the oil, the garlic, ginger, serrano, and tomato paste together. Pulse the tomatoes with their juice in a food processor until coarsely chopped, 3 to 4 pulses.

2. Heat the remaining 3 tablespoons oil in a large Dutch oven over medium-high heat until shimmering. Add the onions and potatoes and cook, stirring occasionally, until the onions are caramelized and the potatoes are golden brown around the edges, about 10 minutes. (Reduce the heat to medium if the onions darken too quickly.)

3. Reduce the heat to medium. Clear the center of the pot, add the garlic mixture, and cook, mashing the mixture into the pan, until fragrant, 15 to 20 seconds. Stir the garlic mixture into the vegetables. Add the toasted spices and cook, stirring constantly, for 1 minute longer. Add the cauliflower and cook, stirring constantly, until the spices coat the florets, about 2 minutes longer.

4. Add the tomatoes, water, chickpeas, and 1 teaspoon salt, scraping up any browned bits. Bring to a boil over medium-high heat. Cover, reduce the heat to medium, and cook, stirring occasionally, until the vegetables are tender, 10 to 15 minutes. Stir in the peas and cream and continue to cook until heated through, about 2 minutes longer. Season with salt to taste and serve, passing the condiments separately.

Indian-Style Curry with Sweet Potatoes, Eggplant, Green Beans, and Chickpeas

Follow the recipe for Indian-Style Curry with Potatoes, Cauliflower, Peas, and Chickpeas, substituting 12 ounces sweet potato (1 medium), peeled and cut into ½-inch pieces, for the red potatoes. Substitute 8 ounces green beans, trimmed and cut into 1-inch pieces, and 1 medium eggplant (1 pound), cut into ½-inch pieces, for the cauliflower. Omit the peas.

Onion Relish

MAKES ABOUT 1 CUP

If using a regular yellow onion, increase the sugar to 1 teaspoon. This relish can be refrigerated in an airtight container for up to 24 hours.

- 1 medium Vidalia onion, minced (about 1 cup; see note)
- 1 tablespoon juice from 1 lime
- ½ teaspoon sweet paprika
- ½ teaspoon sugar
- ⅛ teaspoon table salt
- Pinch cayenne pepper

Combine all the ingredients in a small bowl.

Cilantro-Mint Chutney

MAKES ABOUT 1 CUP

This chutney can be refrigerated in an airtight container for up to 24 hours.

- 2 cups packed fresh cilantro leaves
- 1 cup packed fresh mint leaves
- ⅓ cup plain yogurt
- ¼ cup minced onion
- 1 tablespoon juice from 1 lime
- 1½ teaspoons sugar
- ½ teaspoon ground cumin
- ¼ teaspoon table salt

Process all the ingredients together in a food processor until smooth, about 20 seconds, scraping down the sides of the workbowl as needed.

TANDOORI CHICKEN

WHY THIS RECIPE WORKS: We weren't going to let a 24-hour marinade or the lack of a 900-degree oven keep us from turning this great Indian classic into an easy weeknight dinner. Traditional tandoors produce moist, smoky meat because the heat allows protein molecules on the meat's surface to contract, trapping moisture. Juices and fat fall on the coals, creating smoky flavor. Trying to mimic the tandoor by cooking chicken in a very hot oven gave us disappointing results. Instead, we baked the chicken in a low-temperature oven until almost done, then quickly broiled it to char the exterior. To get flavor into the meat, we turned to a salt-spice rub made with garam masala, cumin, and chili powder bloomed in oil. We massaged the rub into chicken pieces to lock in juices and infuse flavor. Following a dunk in yogurt flavored with the same spice mix, the chicken was ready for the oven.

Tandoori Chicken

SERVES 4

We prefer this dish with whole-milk yogurt, but low-fat yogurt can be substituted. It is important to remove the chicken from the oven before switching to the broiler setting to allow the heating element to come up to temperature. Serve with Yogurt Sauce (page 490), Onion Relish (page 492), Cilantro-Mint Chutney (page 492), and Rice Pilaf (page 617).

- 2 tablespoons vegetable oil
- 6 medium garlic cloves, minced or pressed through a garlic press (about 2 tablespoons)
- 2 tablespoons minced or grated fresh ginger
- 1 tablespoon garam masala
- 2 teaspoons ground cumin
- 2 teaspoons chili powder
- 1 cup plain whole-milk yogurt (see note)
- ¼ cup juice from 2 limes, plus 1 lime, cut into wedges (for serving)
- 2 teaspoons table salt
- 3 pounds bone-in, skin-on chicken pieces (split breasts cut in half, drumsticks, and/or thighs), trimmed and skin removed

1. Heat the oil in an 8-inch skillet over medium heat until shimmering. Add the garlic and ginger and cook until fragrant, about 1 minute. Stir in the garam masala, cumin, and chili powder and cook until fragrant, about 30 seconds. Transfer half of the garlic-spice mixture to a medium bowl, stir in the yogurt and 2 tablespoons of the lime juice, and set aside.

2. In a large bowl, combine the remaining garlic-spice mixture, remaining 2 tablespoons lime juice, and salt. Using a sharp knife, lightly score the skin side of each piece of chicken, making two or three shallow cuts about 1 inch apart and about ⅛ inch deep. Transfer the chicken to the bowl and gently rub with the salt-spice mixture until evenly coated. Let sit at room temperature for 30 minutes.

3. Adjust an oven rack to the upper-middle position (about 6 inches from the heating element) and heat the oven to 325 degrees. Set a wire rack over a foil-lined rimmed baking sheet or broiler pan bottom.

4. Pour the yogurt mixture over the chicken and toss until the chicken is evenly coated with a thick layer. Arrange the chicken pieces, scored side down, on the prepared wire rack. Discard the excess yogurt mixture. Bake the chicken until an instant-read thermometer inserted into the thickest part of the chicken registers 125 degrees for breasts and 130 degrees for legs and thighs, 15 to 25 minutes. (Smaller pieces may cook faster than larger pieces.) Transfer the chicken to a plate.

5. Turn the oven to broil and heat for 10 minutes. Flip the chicken pieces scored side up and broil until lightly charred in spots and the thickest part of the breasts registers 165 degrees and the thickest part of the legs and thighs registers 175 degrees, 8 to 15 minutes.

6. Transfer the chicken to a serving platter, tent loosely with foil, and let rest for 5 minutes. Serve with the lime wedges.

NOTES FROM THE TEST KITCHEN

TANDOORI CHICKEN WITHOUT THE TANDOOR

1. Massage chicken pieces with salt-spice rub to lock in juices and infuse flavor.

2. Toss chicken in spiced yogurt for another layer of flavor.

3. To ensure juicy meat, bake chicken slowly in 325-degree oven until not quite cooked through.

4. For smoky flavor, briefly broil chicken until lightly charred and fully cooked.

CHAPTER 17

LET'S GET GRILLING: BEEF, PORK, AND LAMB

CLASSIC GRILLED HAMBURGERS

WHY THIS RECIPE WORKS: Burgers often come off the grill tough, dry, and bulging in the middle. We wanted a moist and juicy burger, with a texture that is tender and cohesive, not dense and heavy. Just as important, we wanted a flavorful, deeply caramelized reddish brown crust with an even surface capable of holding as many condiments as we could pile on.

Ground chuck gave us the most robustly flavored burgers when pitted head to head against burgers made from other cuts of ground beef. We selected meat with a ratio of 20 percent fat to 80 percent lean; more fat than that, and the burgers were too greasy. Burgers made with less fat lacked in juiciness and moisture. We formed the meat into 6-ounce patties that were fairly thick, with a depression in the middle. Rounds of testing taught us that indenting the center of each burger ensured that the patties would come off the grill with an even thickness instead of puffed up like a tennis ball. Cooking the burgers over the fire for just a few minutes kept them tender, and lightly oiling the cooking grate prevented them from sticking.

Grilled Hamburgers

SERVES 4

Weighing the meat on a kitchen scale is the most accurate way to portion it. If you don't own a scale, do your best to divide the meat evenly into quarters. Eighty percent lean ground chuck is our favorite for flavor, but 85 percent lean works, too.

- 1½ pounds 80 percent lean ground chuck
- 1 teaspoon salt
- ½ teaspoon pepper
- 4 hamburger rolls, toasted

1. Using hands, gently break up meat, season with salt and pepper, and toss lightly to incorporate. Divide meat into 4 portions and lightly toss 1 portion from hand to hand to form ball, then lightly flatten ball with fingertips into ¾-inch-thick patty. Press center of patty down with fingertips until it is about ½ inch thick, creating slight depression. Repeat with remaining portions.

2A. FOR A CHARCOAL GRILL: Open bottom vent completely. Light large chimney starter filled with charcoal briquettes (6 quarts). When top coals are partially covered with ash, pour evenly over grill. Set cooking grate in place, cover, and open lid vent completely. Heat grill until hot, about 5 minutes.

2B. FOR A GAS GRILL: Turn all burners to high, cover, and heat grill until hot, about 15 minutes.

3. Clean and oil cooking grate. Place burgers on grill and cook, without pressing on them, until well browned on first side, 2 to 3 minutes. Flip burgers and continue to grill, 2 to 3 minutes for rare, 2½ to 3½ minutes for medium-rare, and 3 to 4 minutes for medium.

4. Transfer burgers to serving platter, tent loosely with aluminum foil, and let rest for 5 to 10 minutes before serving on rolls.

Grilled Cheeseburgers

Since the cheese is evenly distributed in these burgers, just a little goes a long way.

Mix ¾ cup shredded cheddar, Swiss, or Monterey Jack cheese or ¾ cup crumbled blue cheese into meat with salt and pepper.

ULTIMATE GRILLED BURGERS

WHY THIS RECIPE WORKS: For us, the ideal burger has an ultra-craggy charred crust, a rich beefy taste, and an interior so juicy and tender that it practically falls apart at the slightest pressure—a particularly difficult achievement when grilling. The problem is, such a burger is pretty hard to come by. While the typical specimen may have a nicely browned crust, it's also heavy and dense with a pebbly texture that comes from using preground beef. We knew we wanted to grind our own meat to make the ultimate burger. In the test kitchen, we've found it easy to grind meat ourselves with a food processor. We trim gristle and excess fat from the meat, cut the meat into ½-inch pieces, freeze it for about 30 minutes to firm it up so that the blades cut it cleanly, and finally process it in small batches to ensure an even, precise grind. We chose to use beefy steak tips since they are decently tender, require virtually no trimming, and are relatively inexpensive. Adding a bit of butter to the food processor when grinding added richness but not buttery flavor.

To form the burgers so that they wouldn't fall apart on the grate but at the same time achieve that essential open texture, we froze them briefly before putting them on the grill. By the time they'd thawed at their centers, they had developed enough crust to ensure that they held together. A few minutes over a hot grill was all our burgers needed to achieve a

perfect medium-rare. Whether served with the classic fixings like lettuce and tomato or one of our creamy grilled-vegetable toppings, this was a grilled burger that lived up to our ideal.

Tender, Juicy Grilled Burgers

SERVES 4

This recipe requires freezing the meat twice, for a total of 65 to 80 minutes, before grilling. When stirring the salt and pepper into the ground meat and shaping the patties, take care not to overwork the meat or the burgers will become dense. Sirloin steak tips are also sold as flap meat. Serve the burgers with your favorite toppings or one of our grilled-vegetable toppings (recipes follow).

- 1½ pounds sirloin steak tips, trimmed and cut into ½-inch chunks
- 4 tablespoons unsalted butter, cut into ¼-inch pieces
- Kosher salt and pepper
- 1 (13 by 9-inch) disposable aluminum pan (if using charcoal)
- 4 hamburger buns

1. Place beef chunks and butter on large plate in single layer. Freeze until meat is very firm and starting to harden around edges but still pliable, about 35 minutes.

2. Place one-quarter of meat and one-quarter of butter cubes in food processor and pulse until finely ground into pieces size of rice grains (about 1/32 inch), 15 to 20 pulses, stopping and redistributing meat around bowl as necessary to ensure beef is evenly ground. Transfer meat to baking sheet. Repeat grinding with remaining 3 batches of meat and butter. Spread mixture over sheet and inspect carefully, discarding any long strands of gristle or large chunks of hard meat, fat, or butter.

3. Sprinkle 1 teaspoon pepper and ¾ teaspoon salt over meat and gently toss with fork to combine. Divide meat into 4 balls. Toss each between hands until uniformly but lightly packed. Gently flatten into patties ¾ inch thick and about 4½ inches in diameter. Using thumb, make 1-inch-wide by ¼-inch-deep depression in center of each patty. Transfer patties to platter and freeze for 30 to 45 minutes.

4A. FOR A CHARCOAL GRILL: Using skewer, poke 12 holes in bottom of disposable pan. Open bottom vent completely and place disposable pan in center of grill. Light large chimney starter filled two-thirds with charcoal briquettes (4 quarts). When top coals are partially covered with ash, pour into disposable pan. Set cooking grate in place, cover, and open lid vent completely. Heat grill until hot, about 5 minutes.

4B. FOR A GAS GRILL: Turn all burners to high, cover, and heat grill until hot, about 15 minutes. Leave all burners on high.

5. Clean and oil cooking grate. Season 1 side of patties liberally with salt and pepper. Using spatula, flip patties and season other side. Grill patties (directly over coals if using charcoal), without moving them, until browned and meat easily releases from grill, 4 to 7 minutes. Flip burgers and continue to grill until browned on second side and meat registers 125 degrees for medium-rare or 130 degrees for medium, 4 to 7 minutes longer.

6. Transfer burgers to plate and let rest for 5 minutes. While burgers rest, lightly toast buns on grill, 1 to 2 minutes. Transfer burgers to buns and serve.

Grilled Scallion Topping

MAKES ABOUT ½ CUP

- 2 tablespoons sour cream
- 2 tablespoons mayonnaise
- 2 tablespoons buttermilk
- 1 tablespoon cider vinegar
- 1 tablespoon minced fresh chives
- 2 teaspoons Dijon mustard
- ¼ teaspoon sugar
- Salt and pepper
- 20 scallions
- 2 tablespoons vegetable oil

1. Combine sour cream, mayonnaise, buttermilk, vinegar, chives, mustard, sugar, ½ teaspoon salt, and ⅛ teaspoon pepper in medium bowl. Set aside.

2. Toss scallions with oil in large bowl (do not wash out bowl). Grill scallions over hot fire until lightly charred and softened, 2 to 4 minutes per side. Return to bowl and let cool, 5 minutes. Slice scallions thinly, then transfer to bowl with reserved sour cream mixture. Toss to combine and season with salt and pepper to taste.

Grilled Shiitake Mushroom Topping

MAKES ABOUT ¾ CUP

- 2 tablespoons sour cream
- 2 tablespoons mayonnaise
- 2 tablespoons buttermilk
- 1 tablespoon cider vinegar
- 1 tablespoon minced fresh chives
- 2 teaspoons Dijon mustard
- ¼ teaspoon sugar
- Salt and pepper
- 8½ ounces shiitake mushrooms, stems removed
- 2 tablespoons vegetable oil

1. Combine sour cream, mayonnaise, buttermilk, vinegar, chives, mustard, sugar, ½ teaspoon salt, and ⅛ teaspoon pepper in medium bowl. Set aside.

2. Toss mushrooms with oil in large bowl (do not wash out bowl). Grill mushrooms over hot fire until lightly charred and softened, 2 to 4 minutes per side. Return to bowl and let cool, 5 minutes. Slice mushrooms thinly, then transfer to bowl with reserved sour cream mixture. Toss to combine and season with salt and pepper to taste.

Grilled Napa Cabbage and Radicchio Topping

MAKES ABOUT ¾ CUP

- 2 tablespoons sour cream
- 2 tablespoons mayonnaise
- 2 tablespoons buttermilk
- 1 tablespoon cider vinegar
- 1 tablespoon minced fresh parsley
- 2 teaspoons Dijon mustard
- ¼ teaspoon sugar
- Salt and pepper
- ¼ small head napa cabbage
- ½ small head radicchio, cut into 2 wedges
- 2 tablespoons vegetable oil

1. Combine sour cream, mayonnaise, buttermilk, vinegar, parsley, mustard, sugar, ½ teaspoon salt, and ⅛ teaspoon pepper in medium bowl. Set aside.

2. Place cabbage and radicchio wedges on rimmed baking sheet and brush with oil (do not wash sheet). Grill over hot fire until lightly charred and beginning to wilt, 2 to 4 minutes on each cut side. Return to baking sheet and let cool, 5 minutes. Slice cabbage and radicchio thinly, then transfer to bowl with reserved sour cream mixture. Toss to combine and season with salt and pepper to taste.

WELL-DONE BURGERS

WHY THIS RECIPE WORKS: We know that many backyard cooks grill their burgers to medium-well and beyond, but we aren't willing to accept the usual outcome of tough, desiccated hockey pucks with no beefy flavor. We wanted to work with supermarket ground beef to produce a tender and moist-as-can-be burger, with perfect grill marks and all, even when well-done.

Taste tests proved that well-done burgers made with 80 percent lean chuck were noticeably moister than burgers made from leaner beef, but they still weren't juicy enough. Because we couldn't force the meat to retain moisture, we opted to pack the patties with a panade, a paste made from bread and milk that's often used to keep meat loaf and meatballs moist. To punch up the flavor, we also added minced garlic and tangy steak sauce. To keep our burgers from puffing up the way most burgers do, we made use of a previous test kitchen discovery: If you make a slight depression in the center of the patty, it will puff slightly as it cooks and level out to form a flat top.

Grilled Well-Done Hamburgers

SERVES 4

Adding bread and milk to the beef creates burgers that are juicy and tender even when well-done. For cheeseburgers, follow the optional instructions below.

- 1 slice hearty white sandwich bread, crust removed, bread cut into ¼-inch pieces
- 2 tablespoons whole milk
- 2 teaspoons steak sauce
- 1 garlic clove, minced
- ¾ teaspoon salt
- ¾ teaspoon pepper
- 1½ pounds 80 percent lean ground chuck
- 6 ounces sliced cheese (optional)
- 4 hamburger buns, toasted

1. Mash bread and milk in large bowl with fork until homogeneous. Stir in steak sauce, garlic, salt, and pepper. Using hands, gently break up meat over bread mixture and toss lightly to distribute. Divide meat into 4 portions and lightly toss 1 portion from hand to hand to form ball, then lightly flatten ball with fingertips into ¾-inch-thick patty. Press center of patty down with fingertips until it is about ½ inch thick, creating slight depression. Repeat with remaining portions.

2A. FOR A CHARCOAL GRILL: Open bottom vent completely. Light large chimney starter filled with charcoal briquettes (6 quarts). When top coals are partially covered with ash, pour evenly over grill. Set cooking grate in place, cover, and open lid vent completely. Heat grill until hot, about 5 minutes.

2B. FOR A GAS GRILL: Turn all burners to high, cover, and heat grill until hot, about 15 minutes.

3. Clean and oil cooking grate. Place burgers on grill (on hot side if using charcoal) and cook, without pressing on them, until well browned on first side, 2 to 4 minutes. Flip burgers and cook 3 to 4 minutes for medium-well or 4 to 5 minutes for well-done, adding cheese, if using, about 2 minutes before reaching desired doneness and covering grill to melt cheese.

4. Transfer burgers to serving platter, tent loosely with aluminum foil, and let rest for 5 to 10 minutes before serving on buns.

Well-Done Bacon-Cheeseburgers

Most bacon burgers simply top the burgers with bacon. We also add bacon fat to the ground beef, which adds juiciness and unmistakable bacon flavor throughout the burger.

Cook 8 slices bacon in skillet over medium heat until crisp, 7 to 9 minutes. Transfer bacon to paper towel–lined plate and set aside. Reserve 2 tablespoons fat and refrigerate until just warm. Follow recipe for Grilled Well-Done Hamburgers, including optional cheese and adding reserved bacon fat to beef mixture. Top each burger with 2 slices bacon before serving.

GRILLED LAMB-STUFFED PITA WITH YOGURT SAUCE

WHY THIS RECIPE WORKS: Seasoned with warm spices and herbs, pressed between pita, and grilled, these lamb sandwiches offer a flavorful, juicy, street food–style alternative to the everyday burger on a bun. Along with traditional cumin, coriander, and onion, we added lemon zest to our meat mixture as well as cayenne for heat and paprika for its complementary pepper flavor, and swapped out neutral, grassy parsley for brighter, more aromatic cilantro. The grill helped make the pita bread really crisp, providing contrasting texture to the filling within. We started cooking with the grill lid closed to jump-start the meat and keep the pita from getting dry and tough. The lamb's fat and juices helped turn the bread supercrisp as it cooked. To help balance the richness of the sandwich, we served it with a bright and cooling yogurt-tahini sauce.

Grilled Lamb-Stuffed Pitas with Yogurt Sauce

SERVES 4 TO 6

You can substitute 85 percent lean ground beef for the ground lamb, if desired. This recipe works best with ¼-inch-thick pitas that are fresh and pliable. To determine which side of the pita is thicker, look closely at the pattern of browning across its surface; the less-fragile side is usually covered with char marks in a dotted-line pattern. Serve with a dressed green salad or with Parsley-Cucumber Salad with Feta, Pomegranate, and Walnuts (recipe follows).

SAUCE

- 1 cup plain Greek yogurt
- ½ cup minced fresh mint
- 2 tablespoons lemon juice
- 2 tablespoons tahini
- 2 tablespoons extra-virgin olive oil
- ½ teaspoon salt

SANDWICHES

- 1 onion, cut into 1-inch pieces
- 1 cup fresh cilantro leaves
- ¼ cup extra-virgin olive oil
- 1 tablespoon grated lemon zest plus 3 tablespoons juice
- 1 tablespoon ground coriander
- 1 tablespoon ground cumin
- 1 tablespoon paprika
- 2 teaspoons salt
- 1½ teaspoons pepper
- ½ teaspoon cayenne pepper
- ¼ teaspoon ground cinnamon
- 2 pounds ground lamb
- 4 (8-inch) pita breads

1. FOR THE SAUCE: Whisk all ingredients together in bowl. Set aside.

2. FOR THE SANDWICHES: Pulse onion and cilantro in food processor until finely chopped, 10 to 12 pulses, scraping down sides of bowl as needed. Transfer mixture to large bowl. Stir in oil, lemon zest and juice, coriander, cumin, paprika, salt, pepper, cayenne, and cinnamon. Add lamb and knead gently with your hands until thoroughly combined.

3. Using kitchen shears, cut around perimeter of each pita and separate into 2 halves. Place 4 thicker halves on counter with interiors facing up. Divide lamb mixture into 4 equal portions and place 1 portion in center of each pita half. Using spatula, gently spread lamb mixture into even layer, leaving ½-inch border around edge. Top each with thinner pita half. Press each sandwich firmly until lamb mixture spreads to ¼ inch from edge of pita. Transfer assembled sandwiches to large plate, cover with plastic wrap, and set aside. (Sandwiches may be held for up to 1 hour before grilling.)

4A. FOR A CHARCOAL GRILL: Open bottom vent completely. Light large chimney starter two-thirds filled with charcoal briquettes (4 quarts). When top coals are partially covered with ash, spread coals in single layer over bottom of grill. Set cooking grate in place, cover, and open lid vent completely. Heat grill until hot, about 5 minutes.

4B. FOR A GAS GRILL: Turn all burners to high, cover, and heat grill until hot, about 15 minutes. Turn all burners to medium-high.

5. Clean and oil cooking grate. Place sandwiches on grill, cover, and cook until bottoms are evenly browned and edges are starting to crisp, 7 to 10 minutes, moving sandwiches as needed to ensure even cooking. Flip sandwiches, cover grill, and continue to cook until second sides are evenly browned and edges are crisp, 7 to 10 minutes longer. Transfer sandwiches to cutting board and cut each in half crosswise. Transfer sandwiches to platter and serve, passing sauce separately.

BEHIND THE SCENES

NAKED ROAST CHICKEN AND OTHER WACKY RECIPE TESTS

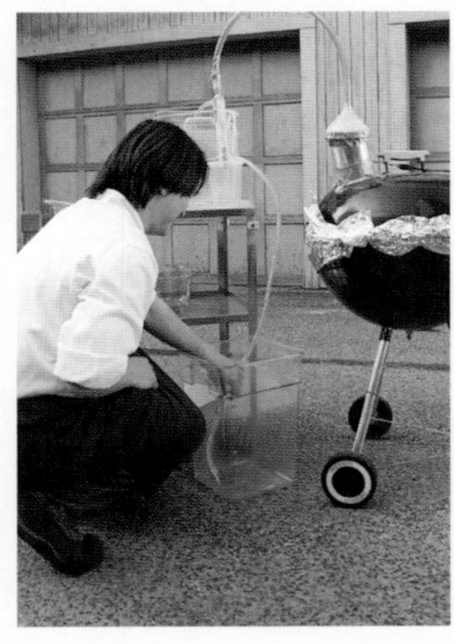

Our test cooks will do almost anything in pursuit of the perfect recipe. No idea is too silly or odd to try—not if it will make a recipe better. Here are some notable recipe tests performed over the years. Each one was deemed promising but ultimately never worked.

• Removing the skin from a chicken before it goes into the oven, pulling the skin taut with toothpicks, and then roasting the skin separately from the chicken pieces to maximize crispness. Too Hannibal Lecter.

• Cooking a roast beef in a 130-degree oven for 24 hours to maximize juiciness. Most ovens don't operate at such a low temperature, and it's probably just as well; this is a perfect recipe for food-borne illness.

• Rubbing the skin off every single chickpea to make extra-smooth hummus. Peeling chickpeas? What were we thinking?!

• Flipping a steak every 4 seconds—for a total of 176 flips over the course of the 11-minute cooking time—to ensure absolutely even heat distribution. Only cooks with Olympic aspirations need to try this.

• Attaching a still (yes, like you might devise to make moonshine) to a covered grill to make our own liquid smoke. The cost for 1 teaspoon of liquid smoke? Fifty bucks. And it didn't taste very good. Plus, this odd setup looked just a little suspicious (read: illegal) to our neighbors.

GRILLED FLANK STEAK

WHY THIS RECIPE WORKS: A common way to prepare flank steak is to marinate it in a bottle of Italian-style salad dressing. But while the resulting flavor can be interesting, the acid in the vinegar can ruin the texture, making the exterior mushy and gray. We wanted to develop a fresh, Mediterranean-style marinade without acid—a marinade that would really boost flavor without over-tenderizing the meat.

We turned to the optimal method for cooking a flank steak—use a two-level fire (which lets you move the thin part of the steak to the cooler side of the grill once it is done), cook the steak only to medium-rare to keep it from getting tough, and let the steak rest before slicing to reduce the loss of juices. Now we could concentrate on developing and applying an acid-free marinade.

Because fat carries flavor so well, we knew oil would be a key ingredient—the challenge was to infuse Mediterranean flavors (garlic, shallots, and rosemary) into the oil and then into the steak. We developed two key steps. First, we minced the aromatics and combined them with the oil in a blender to create a marinade paste. Next, we invented a novel "marinating" technique—prick the steak all over with a fork, rub it first with salt and then with the marinade paste, then let it sit for up to 24 hours. After marinating, the paste is wiped off to prevent burning, and the steak is ready for the grill. Our technique was so successful, we were free to create two more marinades—one with Asian flavors, and the other with a smoky-spicy kick.

Grilled Marinated Flank Steak

SERVES 4 TO 6

Other thin steaks with a loose grain, such as skirt steak or steak tips, can be substituted for the flank steak.

- 1 (2- to 2½-pound) flank steak, trimmed
- 1 teaspoon salt
- 1 recipe wet paste marinade (recipes follow)
- Pepper

1. Pat steak dry with paper towels and place in large baking dish. Using dinner fork, prick steak about 20 times on each side. Rub both sides of steak evenly with salt, then with paste. Cover with plastic wrap and refrigerate for at least 1 hour or up to 24 hours.

2A. FOR A CHARCOAL GRILL: Open bottom vent completely. Light large chimney starter filled with charcoal briquettes (6 quarts). When top coals are partially covered with ash, pour two-thirds evenly over grill, then pour remaining coals over half of grill. Set cooking grate in place, cover, and open lid vent completely. Heat grill until hot, about 5 minutes.

2B. FOR A GAS GRILL: Turn all burners to high, cover, and heat grill until hot, about 15 minutes.

3. Clean and oil cooking grate. Using paper towels, wipe paste off steak and season with pepper. Place steak on grill (hot side if using charcoal) and cook (covered if using gas) until well browned on first side, 4 to 6 minutes. Flip steak and cook (covered if using gas) until meat registers 120 to 125 degrees (for medium-rare) or 130 to 135 degrees (for medium), 3 to 6 minutes. If exterior of meat is browned but steak is not yet cooked through, move to cooler side of grill (if using charcoal) or turn down burners (if using gas) and continue to cook to desired doneness.

4. Transfer steak to carving board, tent loosely with aluminum foil, and let rest for 10 minutes. Slice steak ¼ inch thick against grain on bias and serve.

Garlic-Shallot-Rosemary Wet Paste Marinade

MAKES ABOUT ⅔ CUP

- 6 tablespoons olive oil
- 1 shallot, minced
- 6 garlic cloves, minced
- 2 tablespoons minced fresh rosemary

Process all ingredients in blender until smooth, about 30 seconds, scraping down bowl as needed.

Garlic-Ginger-Sesame Wet Paste Marinade

MAKES ABOUT ⅔ CUP

- ¼ cup toasted sesame oil
- 3 tablespoons grated fresh ginger
- 2 tablespoons vegetable oil
- 2 scallions, minced
- 3 garlic cloves, minced

Process all ingredients in blender until smooth, about 30 seconds, scraping down bowl as needed.

Garlic-Chile Wet Paste Marinade

MAKES ABOUT ⅔ CUP

- 6 tablespoons vegetable oil
- 6 garlic cloves, minced
- 2 scallions, minced
- 1 tablespoon minced canned chipotle chile in adobo sauce
- 1 jalapeño chile, stemmed, seeded, and minced

Process all ingredients in blender until smooth, about 30 seconds, scraping down bowl as needed.

GRILLED STUFFED FLANK STEAK

WHY THIS RECIPE WORKS: Stuffed steak originated with Italian-American cooking as a way to transform an inexpensive steak into something more exciting and colorful. But when we tried a few of the premade stuffed "pinwheels" from our local grocery store, both the stuffing and the cheese tried to make a run for it, with the cheese oozing out all over the grill, and the stuffing—which can include prosciutto, nuts, or spinach, among other things—falling out onto the grill in big clumps. We were sure we could turn this dish into an easy dinner, with tender beef and a juicy, flavorful filling that stayed in place.

Thanks to its uniform shape and good beefy taste, flank steak was clearly the best bet. To guarantee the filling stayed in place, we butterflied and pounded the steak, so we were starting with the flattest and widest surface possible. As for the filling, we eliminated bread crumbs from consideration—after grilling, they contributed a taste of burnt toast. The classic Italian-American combo of prosciutto and provolone won raves for its salty savor and the way the dry cheese melted inside the pinwheel yet turned crisp where exposed to the grill. To prevent the meat from shrinking on the grill, and squeezing the centers of the pinwheels, we rolled up our flank steak, tied it with twine, and skewered it at 1-inch intervals before slicing and grilling. The twine kept the steak from unraveling, while the skewers prevented the meat from shrinking. Finally, we had stuffing that stayed stuffed and rich, smoky beef.

NOTES FROM THE TEST KITCHEN

HOW TO BUTTERFLY AND STUFF FLANK STEAK

1. Lay the flank steak on the edge of a cutting board. Slice the steak horizontally, making sure to leave a ½-inch "hinge" along the top edge.

2. Open up the steak, cover with plastic wrap, and pound it to a 12 by 8-inch rectangle of even thickness.

3. Leaving the steak in place with the grain still running perpendicular to the edge of the cutting board, rub the steak evenly with the herb mixture, and layer it with the prosciutto and cheese, leaving a 2-inch border along the top edge.

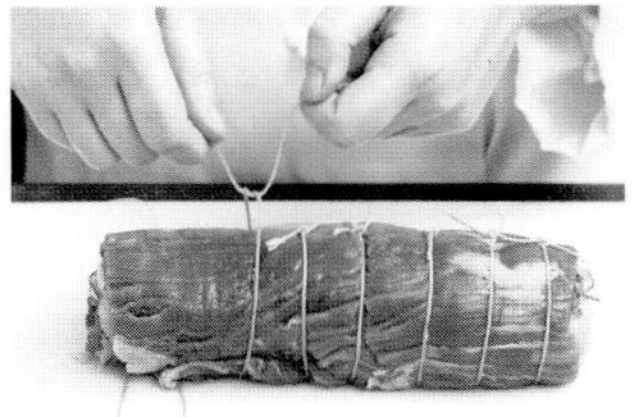

4. Roll the steak away from you into a tight log, then tie it at even 1-inch intervals. Skewer the meat directly through each string, making sure to insert the skewer through the seam in the roll to prevent the beef from unraveling during cooking.

5. Slice the beef into 1-inch-thick pinwheels. Each spiral should be held together with a skewer and a piece of twine.

Grilled Stuffed Flank Steak

SERVES 4 TO 6

Look for a flank steak measuring approximately 8 by 6 inches, with the grain running the long way. Depending on the steak's size, you may have more or less than 8 slices of meat at the end of step 2. You will need both wooden skewers and kitchen twine for this recipe.

- 2 tablespoons olive oil
- 2 tablespoons minced fresh parsley
- 1 small shallot, minced
- 2 garlic cloves, minced
- 1 teaspoon minced fresh sage
- 1 (2- to 2½-pound) flank steak, trimmed
- 4 ounces thinly sliced prosciutto
- 4 ounces thinly sliced provolone cheese
- Salt and pepper

1. Combine oil, parsley, shallot, garlic, and sage in bowl.

2. Soak 8 to 12 wooden skewers in warm water to cover (you will need 1 skewer per inch of rolled steak length) for 30 minutes. Drain, dry, and set aside.

3. Lay steak on cutting board with grain running parallel to counter edge. Cut horizontally through meat, leaving ½-inch "hinge" along top edge. Open up steak and pound flat into rough rectangle, trimming any ragged edges. Rub herb mixture evenly over opened side of steak. Lay prosciutto evenly over steak, leaving 2-inch border along top edge. Cover prosciutto with even layer of cheese, leaving 2-inch border along top edge. Starting from short edge, roll beef into tight log and place on cutting board seam side down.

4. Starting ½ inch from end of rolled steak, evenly space eight to twelve 14-inch pieces of kitchen twine at 1-inch intervals underneath steak. Tie middle piece first, then, working from outer pieces toward center, tightly tie roll and turn tied steak 90 degrees so seam is facing you.

5. Skewer beef directly through outer flap of steak near seam through each piece of twine, allowing skewers to extend ½ inch on other side. Using chef's knife, slice roll between each piece of twine into 1-inch-thick pinwheels. Season pinwheels with salt and pepper.

6A. FOR A CHARCOAL GRILL: Open bottom vent completely. Light large chimney starter three-quarters filled with charcoal briquettes (4½ quarts). When top coals are partially covered with ash, pour evenly over half of grill. Set cooking grate in place, cover, and open lid vent completely. Heat grill until hot, about 5 minutes.

6B. FOR A GAS GRILL: Turn all burners to high, cover, and heat grill until hot, about 15 minutes.

7. Clean and oil cooking grate. Place pinwheels on grill (hot side if using charcoal) and cook (covered if using gas) until well browned on both sides, 6 to 12 minutes, flipping halfway through cooking. Move pinwheels to cool side of grill (if using charcoal) or turn all burners to medium (if using gas). Cover and cook until meat registers 125 to 130 degrees (for medium-rare) or 130 to 135 degrees (for medium), 1 to 5 minutes.

8. Transfer pinwheels to serving platter, tent loosely with aluminum foil, and let rest for 5 to 10 minutes. Remove and discard skewers and twine and serve.

Grilled Stuffed Flank Steak with Spinach and Pine Nuts

Microwave 4 ounces chopped spinach, 1 tablespoon water, ½ teaspoon pepper, and ½ teaspoon salt in bowl until spinach is wilted and decreased in volume by half, 3 to 4 minutes. Cool completely, then stir in ¼ cup toasted pine nuts. Replace prosciutto with spinach mixture.

GRILLED STEAK TIPS

WHY THIS RECIPE WORKS: Steak tips have long been the darling of all-you-can-eat restaurant chains where quantity takes precedence over quality. If they're not mushy, they land on the table tough and dry. We wanted to improve this classic bar food and instill it with deep flavor and a tender texture.

To stay true to the inexpensive nature of this dish, we set our sights on finding the best affordable (read: cheap) cut of meat that would stay tender and moist during a brief stint on the grill. The best cut, we found, is what butchers call flap meat. To tenderize and flavor the meat, we used a soy sauce–based marinade and let the meat marinate for at least an hour—just the right amount of time to allow the thicker parts of the meat to become tender while preventing the thinner sections from becoming too salty. Grilling the tips over a two-level fire, which has hotter and cooler areas, helps to cook this often unevenly shaped cut evenly. We let the meat rest for five minutes after grilling to ensure juicy meat, then sliced it thin so the meat would be tender and flavorful. Lime, orange, or lemon wedges provided a bright acidic counterpoint to the steak tips.

Grilled Steak Tips

SERVES 4 TO 6

Sirloin steak tips are sometimes labeled "flap meat." A two-level fire allows you to brown the steak over the hot side of the grill, then move it to the cooler side if it is not yet cooked through. If your steak is thin, however, you may not need to use the cooler side of the grill. Serve lime wedges with the Southwestern-marinated tips and orange wedges with the tips marinated in garlic, ginger, and soy sauce.

- 1 recipe marinade (recipes follow)
- 2 pounds sirloin steak tips, trimmed
- Lime, orange, or lemon wedges

1. Combine marinade and beef in 1-gallon zipper-lock bag and toss to coat; press out as much air as possible and seal bag. Refrigerate for 1 hour, flipping bag halfway through marinating.

2A. FOR A CHARCOAL GRILL: Open bottom vent completely. Light large chimney starter filled with charcoal briquettes (6 quarts). When top coals are partially covered with ash, pour two-thirds evenly over grill, then pour remaining coals over half of grill. Set cooking grate in place, cover, and open lid vent completely. Heat grill until hot, about 5 minutes.

2B. FOR A GAS GRILL: Turn all burners to high, cover, and heat grill until hot, about 15 minutes.

3. Clean and oil cooking grate. Remove beef from bag and pat dry with paper towels. Place steak tips on grill (on hotter side if using charcoal) and cook (covered if using gas) until well browned on first side, about 4 minutes. Flip steak tips and continue to cook (covered if using gas) until meat registers 120 to 125 degrees (for medium-rare) or 130 to 135 degrees (for medium), 6 to 10 minutes longer. If exterior of meat is browned but steak is not yet cooked through, move to cooler side of grill (if using charcoal) or turn down burners to medium (if using gas) and continue to cook to desired doneness.

4. Transfer steak tips to carving board, tent loosely with aluminum foil, and let rest for 5 to 10 minutes. Slice steak tips very thin on bias and serve with lime, orange, or lemon wedges.

Southwestern Marinade

MAKES ABOUT ¾ CUP

- ⅓ cup soy sauce
- ⅓ cup vegetable oil
- 3 garlic cloves, minced
- 1 tablespoon packed dark brown sugar
- 1 tablespoon tomato paste
- 1 tablespoon chili powder
- 2 teaspoons ground cumin
- ¼ teaspoon cayenne pepper

Combine all ingredients in bowl.

Garlic, Ginger, and Soy Marinade

MAKES ABOUT ⅔ CUP

- ⅓ cup soy sauce
- 3 tablespoons vegetable oil
- 3 tablespoons toasted sesame oil
- 2 tablespoons packed dark brown sugar
- 1 tablespoon grated fresh ginger
- 2 teaspoons grated orange zest
- 1 scallion, sliced thin
- 3 garlic cloves, minced
- ½ teaspoon red pepper flakes

Combine all ingredients in bowl.

GRILLED PREMIUM STEAKS

WHY THIS RECIPE WORKS: Grilled steaks have many tempting qualities—rich, beefy flavor, a thick, caramelized crust, and almost zero cleanup or prep for the cook. But the occasional small bonfire caused by the rendered fat can leave pricey cuts of meat charred and tasting like the inside of a smokestack. We wanted to develop a surefire technique for grilling the three most popular premium steaks—strip, rib eye, and filet mignon—so they would turn out juicy and tender every time.

To get the crust we wanted, a very hot fire was essential. But we quickly learned we couldn't cook a thick steak over consistently high heat without either burning the steak or causing the fat to drip down onto the charcoal and ignite. The solution was to cook these premium steaks over a two-level fire, searing them first over high heat and then moving them to the cooler part of the grill to cook through. For the strip and rib-eye steaks, lightly oiling the cooking grate was enough to get them going and keep them from sticking, but the lean filets mignons required a bit of olive oil to encourage browning. Otherwise, we didn't fuss with our steaks before cooking them—a light seasoning with salt and pepper was sufficient.

To add a little richness to the filets mignons, we made two compound butters, one with smoked paprika and roasted red peppers, the other with lemon, parsley, and garlic—perfect for melting down the sides of the still-warm steaks.

Grilled Strip or Rib-Eye Steaks

SERVES 6

Try to buy steaks of even thickness so they cook at the same rate.

- 4 (12- to 16-ounce) strip or rib-eye steaks, with or without bone, 1¼ to 1½ inches thick
- Salt and pepper

1A. FOR A CHARCOAL GRILL: Open lid vent completely. Light large chimney starter filled with charcoal briquettes (6 quarts). When top coals are partially covered with ash, pour two-thirds evenly over grill, then pour remaining coals over half of grill. Set cooking grate in place, cover, and heat grill until hot, about 5 minutes.

1B. FOR A GAS GRILL: Turn all burners to high, cover, and heat grill until hot, about 15 minutes. Leave one burner on high and turn other burner(s) to medium.

2. Clean and oil cooking grate. Pat steaks dry with paper towels and season with salt and pepper. Place steaks on grill (hotter side if using charcoal) and cook, uncovered, until well browned on both sides, 4 to 6 minutes, flipping steaks halfway through cooking. Move steaks to cooler side of grill (if using charcoal) or turn all burners to medium (if using gas) and continue to cook until meat registers 115 to 120 degrees (for rare) or 120 to 125 degrees (for medium-rare) 5 to 8 minutes longer.

3. Transfer steaks to serving platter, tent loosely with aluminum foil, and let rest for 10 minutes before serving.

Grilled Filets Mignons

SERVES 4

We suggest serving the steaks with one of our flavored butters (recipes follow).

- 4 (7- to 8-ounce) center-cut filets mignons, 1½ to 2 inches thick, trimmed
- 4 teaspoons olive oil
- Salt and pepper

1A. FOR A CHARCOAL GRILL: Open bottom vent completely. Light large chimney starter filled with charcoal briquettes (6 quarts). When top coals are partially covered with ash, pour two-thirds evenly over grill, then pour remaining coals over half of grill. Set cooking grate in place, cover, and open lid vent completely. Heat grill until hot, about 5 minutes.

1B. FOR A GAS GRILL: Turn all burners to high, cover, and heat grill until hot, about 15 minutes. Leave all burners on high.

2. Meanwhile, pat steaks dry with paper towels and lightly rub with oil. Season steaks with salt and pepper.

3. Clean and oil cooking grate. Place steaks on grill (hotter side if using charcoal) and cook (covered if using gas) until well browned on both sides, 4 to 6 minutes, flipping halfway through cooking. Move steaks to cooler side of grill (if using charcoal) or turn all burners to medium (if using gas) and continue to cook (covered if using gas), until meat registers 115 to 120 degrees (for rare) or 120 to 125 degrees (for medium-rare), 5 to 9 minutes longer.

4. Transfer steaks to serving platter, tent loosely with aluminum foil, and let rest for 10 minutes before serving.

Roasted Red Pepper and Smoked Paprika Butter

MAKES ¼ CUP

- 4 tablespoons unsalted butter, softened
- 2 tablespoons finely chopped jarred roasted red peppers
- 1 tablespoon minced fresh thyme
- ¾ teaspoon smoked paprika
- ½ teaspoon salt
- Pinch pepper

Combine all ingredients in bowl and mix until smooth. While steaks are resting, spoon 1 tablespoon of butter on each one.

Lemon, Garlic, and Parsley Butter

MAKES ¼ CUP

- 4 tablespoons unsalted butter, softened
- 1 tablespoon minced fresh parsley
- 1 garlic clove, minced
- ½ teaspoon grated lemon zest
- ½ teaspoon salt
- Pinch pepper

Combine all ingredients in bowl and mix until smooth. While steaks are resting, spoon 1 tablespoon of butter on each one.

GRILLED FROZEN STEAKS WITH ARUGULA AND PARMESAN

WHY THIS RECIPE WORKS: It may seem too good to be true, to have a steak go from freezer to grill to plate in just 30 minutes, but not only is it possible, it's delicious. We have cooked frozen steaks indoors in a skillet to great success, but we wanted to adapt this technique for the grill. The first big challenge was choosing the right type of steak. We tried thinner flank and skirt steaks but their interiors overcooked by the time we'd achieved an ideal char on the exterior. Thicker cuts like rib-eye and strip steaks turned out to be much more successful. Additionally, as those cuts tend to have more natural flavor, all they needed was a bit of salt and pepper—a spice-heavy rub was unnecessary. We took advantage of the steaks' ultrachilled state and started them over a hot fire to develop a well-browned crust on both sides, and then we slid them to the cooler side of the grill to cook until they reached the desired internal temperature.

Grilled Frozen Steaks with Arugula and Parmesan

SERVES 4 TO 6

Use the large holes of a box grater to shred the Parmesan. Do not substitute thinner steaks for the thick-cut steaks called for in this recipe. Thinner steaks cannot be grilled successfully when taken directly from the freezer.

- 2 (1-pound) frozen boneless strip or rib-eye steaks, 1½ inches thick, trimmed
- Kosher salt and pepper
- 6 tablespoons extra-virgin olive oil
- 2 tablespoons lemon juice, plus lemon wedges for serving
- 8 ounces (8 cups) baby arugula
- 2 ounces Parmesan cheese, shredded (⅔ cup)

1A. FOR A CHARCOAL GRILL: Open bottom vent completely. Light large chimney starter mounded with charcoal briquettes (7 quarts). When top coals are partially covered with ash, pour evenly over half of grill. Set cooking grate in place, cover, and open lid vent completely. Heat grill until hot, about 5 minutes.

1B. FOR A GAS GRILL: Turn all burners to high, cover, and heat grill until hot, about 15 minutes. Leave primary burner on high and turn off other burner(s).

2. Clean and oil cooking grate. Place steaks on hotter side of grill and cook (covered if using gas) until browned and charred on first side, 5 to 7 minutes. Flip steaks, season with salt and pepper, and cook until browned and charred on second side, 5 to 7 minutes. Flip steaks, season with salt and pepper, and move to cooler side of grill, arranging so steaks are about 6 inches from heat source. Continue to cook until meat registers 115 to 120 degrees for rare or 120 to 125 degrees for medium-rare, 10 to 15 minutes longer. Transfer steaks to wire rack set in rimmed baking sheet and let rest for 5 minutes.

3. Slice steaks thin against grain. Fan slices on either side of large platter. Whisk oil, lemon juice, ¾ teaspoon salt, and ¼ teaspoon pepper together in large bowl. Add arugula and three-quarters of Parmesan and toss to combine. Arrange arugula down center of platter, allowing it to overlap steak. Sprinkle remaining Parmesan over steak and arugula. Serve with lemon wedges.

ULTIMATE CHARCOAL-GRILLED STEAKS

WHY THIS RECIPE WORKS: For a thick steak that delivered a perfectly browned crust, even doneness, and only a minimal gray band—plus, great charred flavor from the grill—we ditched the actual grill in favor of a superhot charcoal chimney. After trimming the steaks' fat caps in order to eliminate flare-ups, we scored the steaks for better browning. We salted the steaks to ensure seasoning throughout and then baked them slowly in a low oven to cook them evenly and dehydrate their surfaces. Skewering them ahead of time made for easy handling and setup. Moving to the grill, we blasted the steaks over the chimney for about 60 seconds per side, and kept the seasoning simple with just a bit of black pepper to finish.

Ultimate Charcoal-Grilled Steaks

SERVES 4

Rib-eye steaks of a similar thickness can be substituted for strip steaks, although they may produce more flare-ups. You will need a charcoal chimney starter with a 7½-inch diameter and four 12-inch metal skewers for this recipe. If your chimney starter has a smaller diameter, skewer each steak individually and cook in four batches. It is important to remove the fat caps on the steaks to limit flare-ups during grilling.

- 2 (1-pound) boneless strip steaks, 1¾ inches thick, fat caps removed
- Kosher salt and pepper

1. Adjust oven rack to middle position and heat oven to 200 degrees. Cut each steak in half crosswise to create four 8-ounce steaks. Cut 1⁄16-inch-deep slits on both sides of steaks, spaced ¼ inch apart, in crosshatch pattern. Sprinkle both sides of each steak with ½ teaspoon salt (2 teaspoons total). Lay steak halves with tapered ends flat on counter and pass two 12-inch metal skewers, spaced 1½ inches apart, horizontally through steaks, making sure to keep ¼-inch space between steak halves. Repeat skewering with remaining steak halves.

2. Place skewered steaks on wire rack set in rimmed baking sheet, transfer to oven, and cook until centers of steaks register 120 degrees, flipping steaks over halfway through cooking and removing them as they come to temperature, 1½ hours to 1 hour 50 minutes. Tent skewered steaks (still on rack) with aluminum foil.

3. Light large chimney starter filled halfway with charcoal briquettes (3 quarts). When top coals are completely covered in ash, uncover steaks (reserving foil) and pat dry with paper towels. Using tongs, place 1 set of steaks directly over chimney so skewers rest on rim of chimney (meat will be suspended over coals). Cook until both sides are well browned and charred, about 1 minute per side. Using tongs, return first set of steaks to wire rack in sheet, season with pepper, and tent with reserved foil. Repeat with second set of skewered steaks. Remove skewers from steaks and serve.

GRILLED INEXPENSIVE STEAKS

WHY THIS RECIPE WORKS: In this recipe, we used a two-stage rub to make the most of a comparatively inexpensive steak, the shell sirloin. We started with a savory rub of salt, onion powder, garlic powder, fish sauce, and tomato paste. This umami-rich rub made the steaks more savory and enhanced juiciness. For the second stage, we made our own coarsely ground rub based on toasted whole spices and dried chiles. By grinding our own spices, instead of using store-bought ground spices, we created a rub with much deeper flavor.

Grilled Steak with New Mexican Chile Rub

SERVES 6 TO 8

Shell sirloin steak is also known as top butt, butt steak, top sirloin butt, top sirloin steak, and center-cut roast. Spraying the rubbed steaks with oil helps the spices bloom, preventing a raw flavor.

STEAK

- 2 teaspoons tomato paste
- 2 teaspoons fish sauce
- 1½ teaspoons kosher salt
- ½ teaspoon onion powder
- ½ teaspoon garlic powder
- 2 (1½- to 1¾-pound) boneless shell sirloin steaks, 1 to 1¼ inches thick

SPICE RUB

- 2 dried New Mexican chiles, stemmed, seeded, and flesh torn into ½-inch pieces
- 4 teaspoons cumin seeds
- 4 teaspoons coriander seeds
- ½ teaspoon red pepper flakes
- ½ teaspoon black peppercorns
- 1 tablespoon sugar
- 1 tablespoon paprika
- ¼ teaspoon ground cloves
- Vegetable oil spray

1. FOR THE STEAK: Combine tomato paste, fish sauce, salt, onion powder, and garlic powder in bowl. Pat steaks dry with paper towels. With sharp knife, cut 1⁄16-inch-deep slits on both sides of steaks, spaced ½ inch apart, i n crosshatch pattern. Rub salt mixture evenly on both sides of steaks. Place steaks on wire rack set in rimmed baking sheet; let stand at room temperature for at least 1 hour. After 30 minutes, prepare grill.

2. FOR THE SPICE RUB: Toast chiles, cumin, coriander, pepper flakes, and peppercorns in 10-inch skillet over medium-low heat, stirring frequently, until just beginning to smoke, 3 to 4 minutes. Transfer to plate to cool, about 5 minutes. Grind spices in spice grinder or in mortar with pestle until coarsely ground. Transfer spices to bowl and stir in sugar, paprika, and cloves.

3A. FOR A CHARCOAL GRILL: Open bottom vent completely. Light large chimney starter mounded with charcoal briquettes (7 quarts). When top coals are partially covered with ash, pour two-thirds evenly over grill, then pour remaining coals over half of grill. Set cooking grate in place, cover, and open lid vent completely. Heat grill until hot, about 5 minutes.

3B. FOR A GAS GRILL: Turn all burners to high, cover, and heat grill until hot, about 15 minutes. Leave primary burner on high and turn other burner(s) to medium.

4. Clean and oil cooking grate. Sprinkle half of spice rub evenly over 1 side of steaks and press to adhere until spice rub is fully moistened. Lightly spray rubbed side of steak with vegetable oil spray, about 3 seconds. Flip steaks and repeat process of sprinkling with spice rub and coating with vegetable oil spray on second side.

5. Place steaks over hotter part of grill and cook until browned and charred on both sides and center registers 125 degrees for medium-rare or 130 degrees for medium, 3 to 4 minutes per side. If steaks have not reached desired temperature, move to cooler side of grill and continue to cook. Transfer steaks to clean wire rack set in rimmed baking sheet, tent loosely with aluminum foil, and let rest for 10 minutes. Slice meat thin against grain and serve.

Grilled Steak with Ancho Chile–Coffee Rub

Substitute 1 dried ancho chile for New Mexican chiles, 2 teaspoons ground coffee for paprika, and 1 teaspoon cocoa powder for ground cloves.

Grilled Steak with Spicy Chipotle Chile Rub

Substitute 2 dried chipotle chiles for New Mexican chiles, 1 teaspoon dried oregano for paprika, and ½ teaspoon ground cinnamon for ground cloves.

GRILLED ARGENTINE STEAKS

WHY THIS RECIPE WORKS: In Argentina, large 2-pound steaks are grilled low and slow over hardwood logs, not charcoal (and never over gas), which imbues them with a smokiness that is subtler and more complex that the typical "barbecue" flavor one comes to expect of grilled meat here in the States. With the piquant parsley, garlic, and olive oil sauce known as chimichurri served alongside, it's a world favorite. We wanted to duplicate the Argentinean method with American supermarket steaks and a kettle grill. For our choice of steak, we selected well-marbled New York strip steak for its big beefy flavor and meaty chew. To mimic a wood fire, we added unsoaked wood chunks to the perimeter of our grill fire. Setting the lid down on the grill for the first few minutes of cooking helped to quickly trap smoke flavor. To get a deep brown char on the meat without overcooking it, we used two strategies. First, we rubbed the meat with a mixture of salt and cornstarch. Salt seasons the meat and draws out moisture, as does cornstarch. Then we moved the steaks into the freezer for 30 minutes. The inside of a freezer is so dry that it often robs unprotected food of its moisture. In this instance, this was a good thing. Par-frozen steaks browned within moments of hitting the grill. Even better, these partially frozen steaks could stand about five more minutes of fire, adding up to more char and more flavor. To finish, garlicky chimichurri sauce cut through the rich, unctuous qualities of our great grilled steak.

Grilled Argentine Steaks with Chimichurri Sauce

SERVES 6 TO 8

Our preferred steak for this recipe is strip steak, also known as New York strip. A less expensive alternative is a boneless shell sirloin steak (or top sirloin steak).

SAUCE

- ¼ cup hot water
- 2 teaspoons dried oregano
- 1 teaspoon salt
- 1⅓ cups fresh parsley leaves
- ⅔ cup fresh cilantro leaves
- 6 garlic cloves, minced
- ½ teaspoon red pepper flakes
- ¼ cup red wine vinegar
- ½ cup extra-virgin olive oil

STEAKS

- 1 tablespoon cornstarch
- Salt and pepper
- 4 (1-pound) boneless strip steaks, 1½ inches thick, trimmed
- 4 (2-inch) wood chunks
- 1 (9-inch) disposable aluminum pie plate (if using gas)

1. FOR THE SAUCE: Combine water, oregano, and salt in small bowl and let sit until oregano is softened, about 15 minutes. Pulse parsley, cilantro, garlic, and pepper flakes in food processor until coarsely chopped, about 10 pulses. Add water mixture and vinegar and pulse to combine. Transfer mixture to bowl and slowly whisk in oil until emulsified. Cover with plastic wrap and let sit at room temperature for 1 hour.

2. FOR THE STEAKS: Combine cornstarch and 1½ teaspoon salt in bowl. Pat steaks dry with paper towels and place on wire rack set in rimmed baking sheet. Rub entire surface of steaks with cornstarch mixture and place steaks, uncovered, in freezer until very firm, about 30 minutes.

3A. FOR A CHARCOAL GRILL: Open bottom vent halfway. Light large chimney starter filled with charcoal briquettes (6 quarts). When top coals are partially covered with ash, pour evenly over grill. Place wood chunks around perimeter of coals. Set cooking grate in place, cover, and open lid vent halfway. Heat grill until hot and wood chips are smoking, about 5 minutes.

3B. FOR A GAS GRILL: Using metal skewer, poke holes in bottom of disposable pie plate. Place wood chunks in pie plate and set on cooking grate. Turn all burners to high, cover, and heat grill until hot, about 15 minutes. Leave all burners on high.

4. Clean and oil cooking grate. Season steaks with pepper. Place steaks on grill (alongside pie plate if using gas), cover, and cook until beginning to brown on both sides, 4 to 6 minutes, flipping halfway through cooking.

5. Flip steaks again and cook, uncovered, until well browned on first side, 2 to 4 minutes. Flip steaks once more and continue to cook until meat registers 115 to 120 degrees (for rare) or 120 to 125 degrees (for medium-rare), 2 to 6 minutes longer.

6. Transfer steaks to carving board, tent loosely with aluminum foil, and let rest for 10 minutes. Cut each steak crosswise into ¼-inch-thick slices. Transfer to serving platter and serve, passing sauce separately.

NOTES FROM THE TEST KITCHEN

GETTING PERFECT CHAR ON ARGENTINE STEAKS

To get a deep brown char on the meat without overcooking it, the meat must be completely dry. To achieve this, we use a two-pronged approach.

1. Place steaks on wire rack set in rimmed baking sheet. Rub entire surface of steaks with cornstarch mixture.

2. Place steaks, uncovered, in freezer until very firm, about 30 minutes.

MEXICAN-STYLE GRILLED STEAK

WHY THIS RECIPE WORKS: These days *carne asada* usually refers to a super charred, thin steak, but traditionally the dish involves a platter of food. Created around 1940 at the Tampico Club in Mexico City, carne asada is traditionally served with a bevy of sides. We wanted to stick close to the original while keeping it approachable for the home cook. A juicy, thin, well-charred steak was a must, and we settled on just a few extras: a salsa that would complement the meat, some quick refried beans, and simple folded enchiladas.

We decided to use skirt steak, since it stayed tender when grilled to medium (the ideal doneness for both adequate charring and tender beef). A rub made with salt and cumin gave the steaks extra flavor, and the salt dried out the steaks' exteriors to promote browning. For our grill setup, we used a disposable aluminum roasting pan with the bottom removed to corral the coals and ensure high heat for fast browning and char. A smashed clove of garlic rubbed on the steaks after grilling brought a burst of fresh garlic flavor and aroma to the meat, and a squeeze of lime before serving provided fresh citrus flavor. The fruity, slightly smoky flavor of red chile salsa complemented the steak perfectly.

Mexican-Style Grilled Steak (Carne Asada)

SERVES 4 TO 6

Two pounds of sirloin steak tips, also sold as flap meat, may be substituted for the skirt steak. Serve with Red Chile Salsa, Simple Refried Beans, and Folded Enchiladas (recipes follow), if desired.

- 2 teaspoons kosher salt
- ¾ teaspoon ground cumin
- 1 (2-pound) skirt steak, trimmed, pounded ¼ inch thick, and cut with grain into 4 equal steaks
- 1 (13 by 9-inch) disposable aluminum roasting pan (if using charcoal)
- 1 garlic clove, peeled and smashed
- Lime wedges

1. Combine salt and cumin in small bowl. Sprinkle salt mixture evenly over both sides of steaks. Transfer steaks to wire rack set in rimmed baking sheet and refrigerate, uncovered, for at least 45 minutes or up to 24 hours. Meanwhile, if using charcoal, use kitchen shears to remove bottom of disposable pan and discard, reserving pan collar.

2A. FOR A CHARCOAL GRILL: Open bottom vent completely. Light large chimney starter filled with charcoal briquettes (6 quarts). When top coals are partially covered with ash, place disposable pan collar in center of grill over bottom vent and pour coals into even layer in collar. Set cooking grate in place, cover, and open lid vent completely. Heat grill until hot, about 5 minutes.

2B. FOR A GAS GRILL: Turn all burners to high, cover, and heat grill until hot, about 15 minutes. Leave all burners on high.

3. Clean and oil cooking grate. Place steaks on grill (if using charcoal, arrange steaks over coals in collar) and cook, uncovered, until well browned on first side, 2 to 4 minutes. Flip steaks and continue to cook until well browned on second side and meat registers 130 degrees, 2 to 4 minutes longer. Transfer steaks to cutting board, tent loosely with aluminum foil, and let rest for 5 minutes.

4. Rub garlic thoroughly over 1 side of steaks. Slice steaks across grain into ¼-inch-thick slices and serve with lime wedges.

Red Chile Salsa

MAKES 2 CUPS

Guajillo chiles are tangy with just a bit of heat. Serve the salsa alongside the steak as a dipping sauce.

- 1¼ ounces dried guajillo chiles, wiped clean
- 1 (14.5-ounce) can fire-roasted diced tomatoes
- ¾ cup water
- ¾ teaspoon salt
- 1 garlic clove, peeled and smashed
- ½ teaspoon white vinegar
- ¼ teaspoon dried oregano
- ⅛ teaspoon pepper
- Pinch ground clove
- Pinch ground cumin

Toast guajillos in 10-inch nonstick skillet over medium-high heat until softened and fragrant, 1 to 2 minutes per side. Transfer to large plate and, when cool enough to handle, remove stems and seeds. Place guajillos in blender and process until finely ground, 60 to 90 seconds, scraping down sides of blender jar as needed. Add tomatoes and their juice, water, salt, garlic, vinegar, oregano, pepper, clove, and cumin to blender and process until very smooth, 60 to 90 seconds, scraping down sides of blender jar as needed. (Salsa can be stored in the refrigerator for up to 5 days or frozen for up to 1 month.)

Simple Refried Beans

MAKES ABOUT 1½ CUPS

Using the canning liquid from the beans helps develop a creamy texture.

- 2 slices bacon
- 1 small onion, chopped fine
- 2 garlic cloves, minced
- 1 (15-ounce) can pinto beans
- ¼ cup water
- Kosher salt

Heat bacon in 10-inch nonstick skillet over medium-low heat until fat renders and bacon crisps, 7 to 10 minutes, flipping bacon halfway through. Remove bacon and reserve for another use. Increase heat to medium, add onion to fat in skillet, and cook until lightly browned, 5 to 7 minutes. Add garlic and cook until fragrant, about 30 seconds. Add beans and their canning liquid and water and bring to simmer. Cook, mashing beans with potato masher, until mixture is mostly smooth, 5 to 7 minutes. Season with salt to taste, and serve.

Folded Enchiladas

SERVES 4 TO 6

Feta cheese can be substituted for the queso fresco. Guajillo chiles are tangy, with just a bit of heat.

- ⅔ ounce dried guajillo chiles, wiped clean
- 1 (8-ounce) can tomato sauce
- 1 cup chicken broth
- 1 tablespoon vegetable oil
- 1 garlic clove, peeled and smashed
- 1 teaspoon white vinegar
- ¼ teaspoon ground cumin
- Salt
- 12 (6-inch) soft corn tortillas
- Vegetable oil spray
- 1 small onion, chopped fine
- 2 ounces queso fresco, crumbled (½ cup)

1. Toast guajillos in 10-inch nonstick skillet over medium-high heat until softened and fragrant, 1 to 2 minutes per side. Transfer to large plate and, when cool enough to handle, remove stems and seeds. Place guajillos in blender and process until finely ground, 60 to 90 seconds, scraping down sides of blender jar as needed. Add tomato sauce, broth, oil, garlic, vinegar, and cumin to blender and process until very smooth, 60 to 90 seconds, scraping down sides of blender jar as needed. Season with salt to taste.

2. Place 1 cup enchilada sauce in large bowl. Spray both sides of tortillas with oil spray and stack on plate. Microwave, covered, until softened and warm, 60 to 90 seconds. Working with 1 tortilla at a time, dip into sauce in bowl to coat both sides, fold in quarters, and place in 8-inch square baking dish (enchiladas will overlap slightly in dish).

3. When ready to serve, pour remaining sauce evenly over enchiladas. Microwave enchiladas until hot throughout, 3 to 5 minutes. Sprinkle evenly with onion and queso fresco. Serve.

GRILL-ROASTED BEEF SHORT RIBS

WHY THIS RECIPE WORKS: Beef short ribs can require a lot of time and tending on the grill. We began our testing by coating our ribs with a simple spice rub. We jump-started the cooking process by giving the ribs a pit stop in the oven. In a foil-covered baking dish, the fat was rendered from the ribs, and the tough, chewy collagen began to transform into moisture-retaining gelatin. Then we headed out to the grill to complete the cooking while lacquering on one of our flavorful glazes.

Grill-Roasted Beef Short Ribs

SERVES 4 TO 6

Make sure to choose ribs that are 4 to 6 inches in length and have at least 1 inch of meat on top of the bone.

SPICE RUB

- 2 tablespoons kosher salt
- 1 tablespoon packed brown sugar
- 2 teaspoons pepper
- 2 teaspoons ground cumin
- 2 teaspoons garlic powder
- 1¼ teaspoons paprika
- ¾ teaspoon ground fennel
- ⅛ teaspoon cayenne pepper

SHORT RIBS

- 5 pounds bone-in English-style beef short ribs, trimmed
- 2 tablespoons red wine vinegar
- 1 recipe glaze (recipes follow)

1. FOR THE SPICE RUB: Combine all ingredients in bowl. Measure out 1 teaspoon rub and set aside for glaze.

2. FOR THE SHORT RIBS: Adjust oven rack to middle position and heat oven to 300 degrees. Sprinkle ribs with spice rub, pressing into all sides of ribs. Arrange ribs, bone side down, in 13 by 9-inch baking dish, placing thicker ribs around perimeter of baking dish and thinner ribs in center. Sprinkle vinegar evenly over ribs. Cover baking dish tightly with aluminum foil. Bake until thickest ribs register 165 to 170 degrees, 1½ to 2 hours.

3A. FOR A CHARCOAL GRILL: Open bottom vent halfway. Arrange 2 quarts unlit charcoal into steeply banked pile against 1 side of grill. Light large chimney starter half filled with charcoal (3 quarts). When top coals are partially covered with ash, pour on top of unlit charcoal to cover one-third of grill with coals steeply banked against side of grill. Set cooking grate in place, cover, and open lid vent halfway. Heat grill until hot, about 5 minutes.

3B. FOR A GAS GRILL: Turn all burners to high, cover, and heat grill until hot, about 15 minutes. Leave primary burner on medium and turn off other burner(s). Adjust primary burner as needed to maintain grill temperature of 275 to 300 degrees.

4. Clean and oil cooking grate. Place short ribs, bone side down, on cooler side of grill about 2 inches from flames. Brush with ¼ cup glaze. Cover and cook until ribs register 195 degrees, 1¾ to 2¼ hours, rotating and brushing ribs with ¼ cup glaze every 30 minutes. Transfer ribs to large platter, tent loosely with foil, and let rest for 5 to 10 minutes before serving.

Mustard Glaze

MAKES ABOUT 1 CUP

- ½ cup Dijon mustard
- ½ cup red wine vinegar
- ¼ cup packed brown sugar
- 1 teaspoon reserved spice rub
- ⅛ teaspoon cayenne pepper

Whisk all ingredients together in bowl.

Blackberry Glaze

MAKES ABOUT 1 CUP

- 10 ounces (2 cups) fresh or frozen blackberries
- ½ cup ketchup
- ¼ cup bourbon
- 2 tablespoons packed brown sugar
- 1½ tablespoons soy sauce
- 1 teaspoon reserved spice rub
- ⅛ teaspoon cayenne pepper

Bring all ingredients to simmer in small saucepan over medium-high heat. Simmer, stirring frequently to break up blackberries, until reduced to 1¼ cups, about 10 minutes. Strain through fine-mesh strainer, pressing on solids to extract as much liquid as possible. Discard solids.

Hoisin-Tamarind Glaze

MAKES ABOUT 1 CUP

- 1 cup water
- ⅓ cup hoisin sauce
- ¼ cup tamarind paste
- 1 (2-inch) piece ginger, peeled and sliced into ½-inch-thick rounds
- 1 teaspoon reserved spice rub
- ⅛ teaspoon cayenne pepper

Bring all ingredients to simmer in small saucepan over medium-high heat. Simmer, stirring frequently, until reduced to 1¼ cups, about 10 minutes. Strain through fine-mesh strainer, pressing on solids to extract as much liquid as possible. Discard solids.

INEXPENSIVE GRILLED ROAST BEEF

WHY THIS RECIPE WORKS: Trying to grill an uneven piece of meat usually results in a fibrous, chewy, and woefully dry roast. We wanted to turn an inexpensive cut of meat into a juicy, evenly cooked roast with a substantial, well-seasoned garlic-rosemary crust. After extensively testing five "cheap" roast beef options and subjecting each to a 24-hour salt rub, we settled on top sirloin, a beefy, relatively tender cut from the back half of the cow. To grill our roast, we set up a fire in which the coals cover one-third of the grill. In effect, this created hot zones for searing and cooler zones for gentler, indirect cooking. To prevent the meat from cooking too quickly, we placed the roast inside a disposable aluminum pan on the cooler side of the grill after searing it. Poking a few escape channels in the bottom of the aluminum allowed any liquid to drain away, preserving the meat's sear. We also found that cutting the roast into thin slices made the meat taste even more tender.

Inexpensive Grill-Roasted Beef with Garlic and Rosemary

SERVES 6 TO 8

A pair of kitchen shears works well for punching the holes in the aluminum pan. We prefer a top sirloin roast, but you can substitute a top round or bottom round roast. Start this recipe the day before you plan to grill so the salt rub has time to flavor and tenderize the meat.

- 6 garlic cloves, minced
- 2 tablespoons minced fresh rosemary
- 4 teaspoons kosher salt
- 1 tablespoon pepper
- 1 (3- to 4-pound) top sirloin roast
- 1 (13 by 9-inch) disposable aluminum roasting pan

NOTES FROM THE TEST KITCHEN

GRILLING TOP SIRLOIN ROAST

1. Place roast over hot part of grill and cook until well browned on all sides, about 10 minutes.

2. Punch fifteen ¼-inch holes in center of 13 by 9-inch disposable aluminum roasting pan in area roughly same size as roast. Place browned beef in pan.

3. Set pan over cool side of grill and cover. After about 20 minutes, rotate pan 180 degrees and continue roasting until center of roast registers 120 to 125 degrees (for medium-rare) or 130 to 135 degrees (for medium), 20 to 40 minutes more.

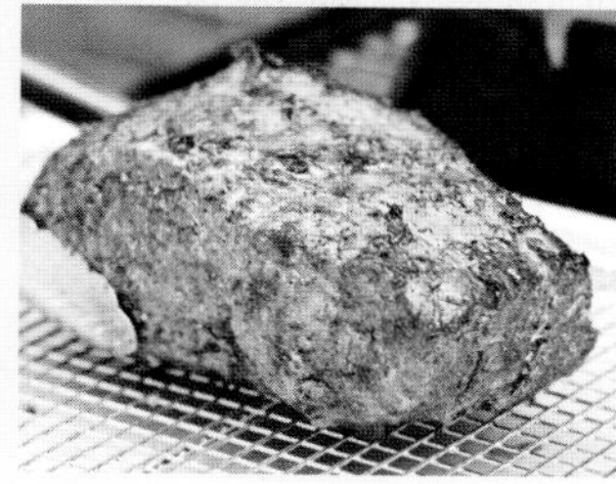

4. Transfer meat to wire rack set in rimmed baking sheet. Tent loosely with aluminum foil and let rest for 20 minutes.

1. Combine garlic, rosemary, salt, and pepper in bowl. Sprinkle all sides of roast evenly with garlic mixture, wrap tightly in plastic wrap, and refrigerate for 18 to 24 hours.

2A. FOR A CHARCOAL GRILL: Open bottom vent halfway. Light large chimney starter half filled with charcoal briquettes (3 quarts). When top coals are partially covered with ash, pour evenly over one-third of grill. Set cooking grate in place, cover, and open lid vent halfway. Heat grill until hot, about 5 minutes.

2B. FOR A GAS GRILL: Turn all burners to high, cover, and heat grill until hot, about 15 minutes.

3. Clean and oil cooking grate. Place roast on grill (hotter side if using charcoal) and cook (covered if using gas) until well browned on all sides, 10 to 12 minutes, turning as needed. (If flare-ups occur, move roast to cooler side of grill until flames die down.)

4. Meanwhile, punch fifteen ¼-inch holes in center of disposable pan in area roughly same size as roast. Once browned, place beef in pan over holes and set pan over cooler side of grill (if using charcoal) or turn primary burner to medium and other burner(s) off (if using gas). (Adjust burners as needed to maintain grill temperature of 250 to 300 degrees.) Cover and cook until meat registers 120 to 125 degrees (for medium-rare) or 130 to 135 degrees (for medium), 40 minutes to 1 hour, rotating pan halfway through cooking.

5. Transfer roast to wire rack set in rimmed baking sheet, tent loosely with aluminum foil, and let rest for 20 minutes. Transfer roast to carving board, slice thin against grain, and serve.

GRILL-ROASTED BEEF TENDERLOIN

WHY THIS RECIPE WORKS: Grilling is a great way to add flavor that enhances but doesn't overwhelm beef tenderloin's delicate beefiness. Producing deep browning was the first step toward delivering flavor. To do this without overcooking the tenderloin's interior, we rubbed the exterior of the roast with baking soda. This raised the meat's pH, which sped up browning by allowing the Maillard reaction to occur more quickly. "Grilled" flavor also depends on drippings from the food, which hit the coals (charcoal) or heat diffusers (gas), transform into new compounds, vaporize, and then waft up and stick to the meat. Because lean tenderloin produces very little in the way of drippings, we looked to an outside source: bacon. Threading three strips onto a metal skewer and placing the skewer directly over the heat source while the tenderloin cooked, low-and-slow away from direct heat, allowed the bacon to slowly render and produce the "grilled" flavor the tenderloin needed.

Grill-Roasted Beef Tenderloin

SERVES 4 TO 6

Center-cut beef tenderloin roasts are sometimes sold as Châteaubriand. You will need one metal skewer for this recipe. The bacon will render slowly during cooking, creating a steady stream of smoke that flavors the beef. Serve the roast as is or with Chermoula Sauce (recipe follows).

- 2¼ teaspoons kosher salt
- 1 teaspoon pepper
- 2 teaspoons vegetable oil
- 1 teaspoon baking soda
- 1 (3-pound) center-cut beef tenderloin roast, trimmed and tied at 1½-inch intervals
- 3 slices bacon

1. Combine salt, pepper, oil, and baking soda in small bowl. Rub mixture evenly over roast and let stand while preparing grill.

2. Stack bacon slices. Keeping slices stacked, thread metal skewer through bacon 6 or 7 times to create accordion shape. Push stack together to compact into about 2-inch length.

3A. FOR A CHARCOAL GRILL: Open bottom vent halfway. Light large chimney starter two-thirds filled with charcoal briquettes (4 quarts). When top coals are partially covered with ash, pour evenly over half of grill. Set cooking grate in place, cover, and open lid vent halfway. Heat grill until hot, about 5 minutes.

3B. FOR A GAS GRILL: Turn all burners to high, cover, and heat grill until hot, about 15 minutes. Turn primary burner to medium and turn off other burner(s). (Adjust primary burner as necessary to maintain grill temperature of 300 degrees.)

4. Clean and oil cooking grate. Place roast on hotter side of grill and cook until lightly browned on all sides, about 12 minutes. Slide roast to cooler side of grill, arranging so roast is about 7 inches from heat source. Place skewered bacon on hotter side of grill. (For charcoal, place near center of grill, above edge of coals. For gas, place above heat diffuser of primary burner. Bacon should be 4 to 6 inches from roast and drippings should fall on coals or heat diffuser and produce steady stream of smoke and minimal flare-ups. If flare-ups are large or frequent, slide bacon skewer 1 inch toward roast.)

5. Cover and cook until beef registers 120 to 125 degrees (for medium-rare), 50 minutes to 1¼ hours. Transfer roast to carving board, tent with aluminum foil, and let rest for 20 minutes. Discard twine and slice roast ½ inch thick. Serve.

Chermoula Sauce

MAKES ABOUT 1 CUP

To keep the sauce from becoming bitter, whisk in the olive oil by hand.

- ¾ cup fresh cilantro leaves
- 4 garlic cloves, minced
- 1 teaspoon ground cumin
- 1 teaspoon paprika
- ¼ teaspoon cayenne pepper
- ¼ teaspoon salt
- 3 tablespoons lemon juice
- ½ cup extra-virgin olive oil

Pulse cilantro, garlic, cumin, paprika, cayenne, and salt in food processor until coarsely chopped, about 10 pulses. Add lemon juice and pulse briefly to combine. Transfer mixture to medium bowl and slowly whisk in oil until incorporated and mixture is emulsified. Cover with plastic wrap and let stand at room temperature for at least 1 hour. (Sauce can be refrigerated for up to 2 days; bring to room temperature and rewhisk before serving.)

GRILL-ROASTED BEEF TENDERLOIN FOR A CROWD

WHY THIS RECIPE WORKS: Grilled tenderloin sounds appealing, but with a whole tenderloin going for as much as $100, uneven cooking, bland flavor, and a tough outer crust just don't cut it. We wanted it cheaper and better. At its peak, tenderloin should be an even, rosy pink throughout, have a browned, crusty exterior, and boast a well-seasoned, grilled flavor.

In need of an affordable alternative to butcher prices, we found that beef at wholesale clubs was far more wallet-friendly. Though these tenderloins needed some home butchering, they were well worth the modest time and effort it took to trim them. Flavor-enhancement came next through just an hour of salting the meat, wrapping it in plastic wrap, and letting it rest on the counter before hitting the hot coals. Tucking the narrow tip end of the tenderloin under and tying it securely gave the tenderloin a more consistent thickness that allowed it to cook through more evenly on the grill. Direct fire was too hot for the roast to endure throughout the cooking stages, so after briefly searing the meat over the coals, we moved it away from the coals for grill-roasting via indirect heat. We removed it from the grill while still rare to account for carryover cooking, and we let the meat rest before slicing to ensure the meat stayed juicy.

Grill-Roasted Beef Tenderloin for a Crowd

SERVES 10 TO 12

Beef tenderloins purchased from wholesale clubs require a good amount of trimming before cooking. At the grocery store, however, you may have the option of having the butcher trim it for you. Once trimmed, and with the butt tenderloin still attached (the butt tenderloin is the lobe attached to the large end of the roast), the roast should weigh 4½ to 5 pounds. If you purchase an already-trimmed tenderloin without the butt tenderloin attached, begin checking for doneness about 5 minutes early. When using a charcoal grill, we prefer wood chunks to wood chips whenever possible; substitute 2 medium wood chunks, soaked in water for 1 hour, for the wood chip packet (if using). Serve with Salsa Verde (recipe follows), if desired.

- 1 (6-pound) beef tenderloin, trimmed of fat and silver skin, tail end tucked and tied with kitchen twine at 2-inch intervals
- 1½ tablespoons kosher salt
- 2 cups wood chips, soaked in water for 15 minutes and drained (optional)
- 2 tablespoons olive oil
- 1 tablespoon pepper

1. Pat tenderloin dry with paper towels and rub with salt. Cover loosely with plastic wrap and let sit at room temperature for 1 hour.

2. Using large piece of heavy-duty aluminum foil, wrap soaked wood chips, if using, in foil packet and cut several vent holes in top.

3A. FOR A CHARCOAL GRILL: Open bottom vent halfway. Light large chimney starter filled with charcoal briquettes (6 quarts). When top coals are partially covered with ash, pour evenly over half of grill. Place wood chip packet, if using, on coals. Set cooking grate in place, cover, and open lid vent halfway. Heat grill until hot and wood chips are smoking, about 5 minutes.

3B. FOR A GAS GRILL: Place wood chip packet, if using, opposite primary burner. Turn all burners to high, cover, and heat grill until hot and wood chips are smoking, about 15 minutes.

4. Clean and oil cooking grate. Rub tenderloin with oil and season with pepper. Place roast on hot side of grill if using charcoal or opposite primary burner if using gas and cook (covered if using gas) until well browned on all sides, 8 to 10 minutes, turning as needed.

5. For gas grill, leave primary burner on, turning off other burner(s). (Adjust primary burner as needed during cooking to maintain grill temperature around 350 degrees.) Move roast to cool side of grill, cover (position lid vent over meat if using charcoal), and cook until meat registers 115 to 120 degrees (for rare) or 120 to 125 degrees (for medium-rare), 15 to 30 minutes.

6. Transfer roast to carving board, tent loosely with foil, and let rest for 10 to 15 minutes. Remove twine, cut into ½-inch-thick slices, and serve.

Salsa Verde

MAKES 1½ CUPS

Salsa verde is excellent with grilled or roasted meats, fish, or poultry; poached fish; boiled or steamed potatoes; or sliced tomatoes. It is also good on sandwiches.

- 2–3 slices hearty white sandwich bread, lightly toasted and cut into ½-inch pieces (about 1½ cups)
- 1 cup extra-virgin olive oil
- ¼ cup lemon juice (2 lemons)
- 4 cups parsley leaves
- ¼ cup capers, rinsed
- 4 anchovy fillets, rinsed
- 1 garlic clove, minced
- ¼ teaspoon salt

Process bread, oil, and lemon juice in food processor until smooth, about 10 seconds. Add parsley, capers, anchovies, garlic, and salt and pulse until finely chopped (mixture should not be smooth), about 5 pulses. Transfer to serving bowl. (Salsa verde can be refrigerated for up to 2 days.)

FLAT-IRON STEAKS

WHY THIS RECIPE WORKS: Smoking steaks can lend them complexity, but treating them like larger, collagen-rich barbecue cuts like brisket can overwhelm the meat's delicate flavor with too much smoke. We found that the key was using a small amount of wood chips and cooking the steaks quickly over direct heat so that they were just kissed with smoke. To make sure we had a consistent amount of smoke, we weighed the wood chips for more control over the smoke quantity. Salting the steaks for an hour before cooking ensured that the seasoning penetrated below the meat's surface, and coating them with an herb-spice rub lent an extra layer of flavor that complemented the smoke. We also grilled lemons to serve with the steaks for a hit of brightness.

Grill-Smoked Herb-Rubbed Flat-Iron Steaks

SERVES 4 TO 6

This recipe requires rubbing the steaks with salt and letting them sit at room temperature for 1 hour before cooking. You can substitute blade steaks for the flat-iron steaks, if desired. We like both cuts cooked to medium (130 to 135 degrees). We like hickory chips in this recipe, but other kinds of wood chips will work. Gas grills are not as efficient at smoking meat as charcoal grills, so we recommend using 1½ cups of wood chips if using a gas grill.

- 2 teaspoons dried thyme
- 1 teaspoon dried rosemary
- ¾ teaspoon fennel seeds
- ½ teaspoon black peppercorns
- ¼ teaspoon red pepper flakes
- 4 (6- to 8-ounce) flat-iron steaks, ¾ to 1 inch thick, trimmed
- 1 tablespoon kosher salt
- 1–1½ cups (2½–3¾ ounces) wood chips
- Vegetable oil spray
- 2 lemons, quartered lengthwise

1. Grind thyme, rosemary, fennel seeds, peppercorns, and pepper flakes in spice grinder or with mortar and pestle until coarsely ground. Transfer to small bowl. Pat steaks dry with paper towels. Rub steaks evenly on both sides with salt and place on wire rack set in rimmed baking sheet. Let stand at room temperature for 1 hour. (After 30 minutes, prepare grill.)

2. Using large piece of heavy-duty aluminum foil, wrap wood chips (1 cup if using charcoal; 1½ cups if using gas) in 8 by 4½-inch foil packet. (Make sure chips do not poke holes in sides or bottom of packet.) Cut 2 evenly spaced 2-inch slits in top of packet.

3A. FOR A CHARCOAL GRILL: Open bottom vent completely. Light large chimney starter filled with charcoal briquettes (6 quarts). When top coals are partially covered with ash, pour evenly over half of grill. Place wood chip packet on coals. Set cooking grate in place, cover, and open lid vent completely. Heat grill until hot and wood chips are smoking, about 5 minutes.

3B. FOR A GAS GRILL: Remove cooking grate and place wood chip packet directly on primary burner. Set grate in place, turn all burners to high, cover, and heat grill until hot and wood chips are smoking, about 15 minutes. Leave primary burner on high and turn other burner(s) to medium.

4. Clean and oil cooking grate. Sprinkle half of herb rub evenly over 1 side of steaks and press to adhere. Lightly spray herb-rubbed side of steaks with oil spray, about 3 seconds. Flip steaks and repeat process of sprinkling and pressing steaks with remaining herb rub and coating with oil spray on second side.

5. Place lemons and steaks on hotter side of grill, cover (position lid vent over steaks if using charcoal), and cook until lemons and steaks are well browned on both sides and meat registers 130 to 135 degrees (for medium), 4 to 6 minutes per side. (If steaks are fully charred before reaching desired temperature, move to cooler side of grill, cover, and continue to cook.) Transfer lemons and steaks to clean wire rack set in rimmed baking sheet, tent with foil, and let rest for 10 minutes. Slice steaks thin against grain and serve, passing lemons separately.

BARBECUED BRISKET

WHY THIS RECIPE WORKS: The main reason it's so hard to cook brisket is that it starts out as a very tough cut of meat. It's also big, sometimes weighing upward of 13 pounds, which is why most butchers separate it into two cuts: the "point" (the fattier of the two pieces) and the "flat" (which is leaner and also a little tougher). Slow cooking for as many as six to 12 hours at a low temperature tends to be the norm for cooking brisket, but we wanted to jump-start the cooking on the grill, to give us tender, smoky meat.

We didn't get the total cooking time below six hours, but we did make the job easier using the grill. First, we cooked the meat over the grill for two hours to let in those all-important smoky flavors; barbecuing the brisket fat side up allowed the fat to melt slowly over the meat. Then we moved it to the oven to cook for a few more hours unattended. For flavor, we turned to a dry rub; typical barbecuing methods like basting the meat or setting a pan of liquid on the cooking grate to create a moist environment just didn't work. Our grill-to-oven approach, although unconventional, gave us fork-tender meat with real barbecue flavor in about half the time it would take to cook the meat entirely on the grill.

Barbecued Whole Beef Brisket

SERVES 18 TO 24

Cooking a whole brisket, which weighs about 10 pounds, may seem like overkill. However, the process is easy, and the left-overs keep well in the refrigerator for up to 4 days. (Leave leftover brisket unsliced, and reheat the foil-wrapped meat in a 300-degree oven until warm.) Still, if you don't want to bother with a big piece of meat or if your grill has fewer than 400 square inches of cooking space, see the variation for Barbecued Half Beef Brisket (recipe follows). No matter how large or small a piece you cook, it's a good idea to save the juices the meat gives off while in the oven to enrich the barbecue sauce. If you'd like to use wood chunks instead of wood chips when using a charcoal grill, substitute 2 medium wood chunks, soaked in water for 1 hour, for the wood chip packet. You can either use store-bought barbecue sauce or our Quick Barbecue Sauce (page 533) in this recipe.

- ¼ cup paprika
- 2 tablespoons chili powder
- 2 tablespoons ground cumin
- 2 tablespoons salt
- 2 tablespoons dark brown sugar
- 1 tablespoon granulated sugar
- 1 tablespoon ground oregano
- 1 tablespoon ground black pepper
- 1 tablespoon ground white pepper
- 2 teaspoons cayenne pepper
- 1 (9- to 11-pound) whole beef brisket, fat trimmed to ¼ inch
- 2 cups wood chips
- 3 cups barbecue sauce, warmed

1. Combine paprika, chili powder, cumin, salt, brown sugar, granulated sugar, oregano, black pepper, white pepper, and cayenne in bowl. Rub brisket thoroughly with spice mixture. Wrap brisket in plastic wrap and refrigerate for at least 2 hours, or up to 2 days.

2. Just before grilling, soak wood chips in water for 15 minutes, then drain. Using large piece of heavy-duty aluminum foil, wrap soaked chips in foil packet and cut several vent holes in top.

3A. FOR A CHARCOAL GRILL: Open bottom vent halfway. Light large chimney starter half filled with charcoal briquettes (3 quarts). When top coals are partially covered with ash, pour into steeply banked pile against side of grill. Place wood chip packet on coals. Set cooking grate in place, cover, and open lid vent halfway. Heat grill until hot and wood chips are smoking, about 5 minutes.

3B. FOR A GAS GRILL: Remove cooking grate and place wood chip packet directly on primary burner. Set grate in place, turn all burners to high, cover, and heat grill until hot and wood chips are smoking, about 15 minutes. Turn primary burner to medium and turn off other burner(s). (Adjust primary burner as needed to maintain grill temperature around 275 degrees.)

4. Clean and oil cooking grate. Place brisket, fat side up, on cooler side of grill. Cover (position lid vent over meat if using charcoal) and cook for 2 hours without removing lid.

5. During final 20 minutes of grilling time, adjust oven rack to middle position and heat oven to 300 degrees. Assemble 4 by 3-foot rectangle of heavy-duty aluminum foil by piecing two, 4-foot-long pieces of foil together and folding over edges two or three times to seal.

6. Remove brisket from grill, place lengthwise in center of foil, then fold and crimp edges of foil together to completely seal brisket. Place brisket on rimmed baking sheet and cook in oven until meat is fork-tender, 3 to 3½ hours.

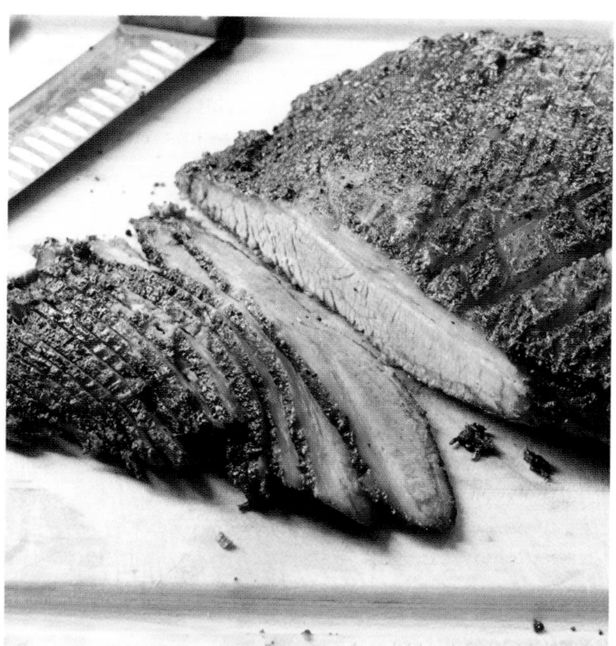

7. Remove brisket from oven, loosen foil at one end to release steam, and let rest for 30 minutes. Unwrap brisket and transfer to carving board, pouring any meat juices into fat separator. Separate meat into two sections and slice each thinly on bias against grain. Stir 1 cup of defatted juices into barbecue sauce, and serve with brisket.

Barbecued Half Beef Brisket

This smaller brisket will serve 8 to 10 people. Either a point cut or a flat cut brisket will work well here.

Substitute 4½- to 5½ pound brisket (either point cut or flat cut) for whole brisket and rub with only half of spice rub. Reduce cooking time on grill to 1½ hours and cooking time in oven to 2 hours. Reserve ½ cup of meat juices and reduce barbecue sauce to 1½ cups.

Spicy Chili Rub

MAKES ABOUT 1 CUP

If you cannot abide spicy food, reduce or eliminate the cayenne.

- 4 tablespoons paprika
- 2 tablespoons chili powder
- 2 tablespoons ground cumin
- 2 tablespoons dark brown sugar
- 2 tablespoons table salt
- 1 tablespoon ground oregano
- 1 tablespoon granulated sugar
- 1 tablespoon ground black pepper
- 1 tablespoon ground white pepper
- 2 teaspoons cayenne pepper (see note)

Combine all the ingredients in a small bowl. (The rub can be stored in an airtight container at room temperature for up to a month.)

GRILLED BONELESS PORK CHOPS

WHY THIS RECIPE WORKS: Pork chops are a prime candidate for the grill, which can imbue the lean chops with smoky, savory flavor, but too often, the results are disappointing. To produce juicy, well-charred boneless pork chops on the grill, we used a two-pronged approach. We brined the chops to improve their ability to hold on to juices during cooking, provide seasoning throughout, and increase their tenderness. To ensure we'd get a substantial browned crust before the interior overcooked, we looked to a unique coating of anchovy paste and honey. The anchovies' amino acids couple with the fructose from honey to rapidly begin the flavorful Maillard browning reaction. We developed some flavorful relishes using combinations of sweet and savory ingredients to complement the grilled chops.

Easy Grilled Boneless Pork Chops

SERVES 4 TO 6

If your pork is enhanced (see page 181), do not brine it in step 1. Very finely mashed anchovy fillets (rinsed and dried before mashing) can be used instead of anchovy paste.

- 6 (6- to 8-ounce) boneless pork chops, ¾ to 1 inch thick
- 3 tablespoons salt
- 1 tablespoon vegetable oil
- 1½ teaspoons honey
- 1 teaspoon anchovy paste
- ½ teaspoon pepper
- 1 recipe relish (optional) (recipes follow)

1. Cut 2 slits about 1 inch apart through outer layer of fat and connective tissue on each chop to prevent buckling. Dissolve salt in 1½ quarts cold water in large container. Submerge chops in brine and let stand at room temperature for 30 minutes.

2. Whisk together oil, honey, anchovy paste, and pepper to form smooth paste. Remove pork from brine and pat dry with paper towels. Using spoon, spread half of oil mixture evenly over 1 side of each chop (about ¼ teaspoon per side).

3A. FOR A CHARCOAL GRILL: Open bottom vent completely. Light chimney starter filled with charcoal briquettes (6 quarts). When top coals are partially covered with ash, pour evenly over half of grill. Set cooking grate in place, cover, and open lid vent completely. Heat grill until hot, about 5 minutes.

3B. FOR A GAS GRILL: Turn all burners to high, cover, and heat grill until hot, about 15 minutes. Leave primary burner on high and turn off other burner(s).

4. Clean and oil cooking grate. Place chops, oiled side down, over hot part of grill and cook, uncovered, until well browned on first side, 4 to 6 minutes. While chops are grilling, spread remaining oil mixture evenly over second side of chops. Flip chops and continue to cook until chops register 140 degrees, 4 to 6 minutes longer (if chops are well browned but register less than 140 degrees, move to cooler part of grill to finish cooking). Transfer chops to plate and let rest for 5 minutes. Serve with relish, if using.

Onion, Olive, and Caper Relish

MAKES ABOUT 2 CUPS

- ¼ cup olive oil
- 2 onions, cut into ¼-inch pieces
- 6 garlic cloves, sliced thin
- ½ cup pitted kalamata olives, chopped coarse
- ¼ cup capers, rinsed
- 3 tablespoons balsamic vinegar
- 2 tablespoons minced fresh parsley
- 1 teaspoon minced fresh marjoram
- 1 teaspoon sugar

- ½ teaspoon anchovy paste
- ½ teaspoon pepper
- ¼ teaspoon salt

Heat 2 tablespoons oil in 10-inch nonstick skillet over medium heat until shimmering. Add onions and cook until softened, about 5 minutes. Stir in garlic and cook until fragrant, about 30 seconds. Transfer onion mixture to medium bowl; stir in remaining 2 tablespoons oil, olives, capers, vinegar, parsley, marjoram, sugar, anchovy paste, pepper, and salt. Serve warm or at room temperature.

Tomato, Fennel, and Almond Relish

MAKES ABOUT 2 CUPS

- ¼ cup olive oil
- 1 fennel bulb, stalks discarded, bulb halved, cored, and cut into ¼-inch pieces
- 6 garlic cloves, sliced thin
- 2 tomatoes, cored and cut into ½-inch pieces
- ¼ cup green olives, pitted and chopped coarse
- 3 tablespoons sherry vinegar
- ¼ cup slivered almonds, toasted
- 3 tablespoons minced fresh parsley
- 1 teaspoon sugar
- Salt and pepper

Heat 2 tablespoons oil in 10-inch skillet over medium heat until shimmering. Add fennel and cook until slightly softened, about 5 minutes. Stir in garlic and cook until fragrant, about 30 seconds. Stir in tomatoes and continue to cook until tomatoes break down slightly, about 5 minutes. Transfer fennel mixture to medium bowl; stir in remaining 2 tablespoons oil, olives, vinegar, almonds, parsley, sugar, ¾ teaspoon salt, and ½ teaspoon pepper. Serve warm or at room temperature.

Orange, Jícama, and Pepita Relish

MAKES ABOUT 3 CUPS

- 1 orange
- ¼ cup olive oil
- 2 jalapeños, stemmed, seeded, and sliced into thin rings
- 3 shallots, sliced thin
- 6 garlic cloves, sliced thin
- 2 cups jícama, peeled and cut into ¼-inch pieces
- ¼ cup pepitas, toasted
- 3 tablespoons chopped fresh cilantro
- 3 tablespoons lime juice (2 limes)
- 1 teaspoon sugar
- Salt and pepper

Cut away peel and pith from orange. Quarter orange, then slice crosswise into ¼-inch-thick pieces. Heat 2 tablespoons oil in 10-inch skillet over medium heat until shimmering. Add jalapeños and shallots and cook until slightly softened, about 5 minutes. Stir in garlic and cook until fragrant, about 30 seconds. Transfer jalapeño-shallot mixture to medium bowl; stir in orange, jícama, pepitas, cilantro, lime juice, sugar, ¾ teaspoon salt, and ½ teaspoon pepper. Serve warm or at room temperature.

GRILLED BONE-IN PORK CHOPS

WHY THIS RECIPE WORKS: Too many grilled pork chops are burnt on the outside and raw on the inside. And even if they are cooked evenly, they can still be tough and bland. We wanted great-looking and great-tasting chops with a perfectly grilled, crisp crust and juicy, flavorful meat. What's more, we wanted our chops plump and meaty, not thin and tough.

We started with the right chops—tender and flavorful bone-in rib loin or center-cut loin chops worked best—and brined them to pump up their flavor and lock in moisture. To brown the pork chops, only a really hot fire would do. But keeping them over high heat long enough to cook through dried them out. So we grilled the chops over a two-level fire, with one side of the grill intensely hot to sear the chops, and the other only moderately hot to allow the chops to cook through without burning the exterior. So they wouldn't overcook, we pulled the chops from the grill when they were just underdone, and let the chops rest until the temperature rose to serving temperature and the juices were redistributed in the meat. A spice rub, made with potent spices and applied before grilling, added big flavor and gave our chops a nice crust.

Grilled Pork Chops

SERVES 4

Rib loin chops are our top choice for their big flavor and juiciness. The spice rub adds a lot of flavor for very little effort, but the chops can also be seasoned with pepper alone just before grilling. If the pork is enhanced (see page 181), do not brine and add 2 teaspoons salt along with spice rub or pepper.

- 3 tablespoons salt
- 3 tablespoons sugar
- 4 (12-ounce) bone-in pork rib or center-cut chops, 1½ inches thick, trimmed
- 1 recipe Basic Spice Rub for Pork Chops (recipe follows) or 2 teaspoons pepper

1. Dissolve salt and sugar in 1½ quarts cold water in large container. Submerge chops in brine, cover, and refrigerate for 30 minutes to 1 hour. Remove chops from brine and pat dry with paper towels. Rub chops with spice rub.

2A. FOR A CHARCOAL GRILL: Open bottom vent completely. Light large chimney starter filled with charcoal briquettes (6 quarts). When top coals are partially covered with ash, pour two-thirds evenly over grill, then pour remaining coals over half of grill. Set cooking grate in place, cover, and open lid vent completely. Heat grill until hot, about 5 minutes.

2B. FOR A GAS GRILL: Turn all burners to high, cover, and heat grill until hot, about 15 minutes. Leave primary burner on high and turn off other burner(s).

3. Clean and oil cooking grate. Place chops on hotter side of grill and cook (covered if using gas) until browned on both sides, 4 to 8 minutes. Move chops to cool side of grill, cover, and continue to cook, turning once, until meat registers 145 degrees, 7 to 9 minutes longer. Transfer chops to serving platter, tent loosely with aluminum foil, and let rest for 5 to 10 minutes. Serve.

Basic Spice Rub for Pork Chops

MAKES ¼ CUP

- 1 tablespoon ground cumin
- 1 tablespoon chili powder
- 1 tablespoon curry powder
- 2 teaspoons packed brown sugar
- 1 teaspoon pepper

Combine all ingredients in bowl.

GRILL-SMOKED PORK CHOPS

WHY THIS RECIPE WORKS: Getting good smoke flavor and a charred crust is an elusive grilling goal. Smokiness generally requires a lengthy exposure to a slow fire, while a charred crust requires a blast of high heat to quickly sear the exterior of the meat before the interior turns dry. We wanted chops that had it all: charred crust, ultra-moist meat, and true smoke flavor. We decided to employ a technique we had used in previous pork chop recipes: reversing the cooking by starting low and finishing with a quick sear. To reap the benefits of both high and low heat on a charcoal grill, we used a double-banked fire (made by placing a disposable aluminum pan between two mounds of coals) and started our chops under cover on the cooler center of the grill, allowing the smoke to do its job for about 25 minutes. We then applied a few coats of sauce and finished by searing them, uncovered, over hot coals.

As for arranging the chops on the grill, we found it best to rest each chop on its bone instead of laying it flat. To keep them from toppling over, we speared the chops together with skewers, making sure to leave a good inch between each one to allow smoke to circulate, then stood them upright in the center of the grill with bone, not meat, touching the grill. This allowed us to keep the chops over the fire for a full 30 minutes, after which we removed the skewers, applied the glaze, and finished the chops over hot coals for that crusty char.

Grill-Smoked Pork Chops

SERVES 4

Buy chops of the same thickness so they will cook uniformly. Use the large holes on a box grater to grate the onion for the sauce. Two medium wood chunks, soaked in water for 1 hour, can be substituted for the wood chip packet on a charcoal grill. You will need two 10-inch metal skewers for this recipe.

SAUCE

- ½ cup ketchup
- ¼ cup molasses
- 2 tablespoons grated onion
- 2 tablespoons Worcestershire sauce
- 2 tablespoons Dijon mustard
- 2 tablespoons cider vinegar
- 1 tablespoon packed light brown sugar

CHOPS

- 2 cups wood chips, soaked in water for 15 minutes and drained
- 4 (12-ounce) bone-in pork rib chops, 1½ inches thick, trimmed
- 2 teaspoons salt
- 2 teaspoons pepper
- 1 (13 by 9-inch) disposable aluminum roasting pan (if using charcoal)

1. FOR THE SAUCE: Bring all ingredients to simmer in small saucepan over medium heat and cook, stirring occasionally, until reduced to about 1 cup, 5 to 7 minutes. Transfer ½ cup sauce to small bowl and set aside remaining sauce for serving.

2. FOR THE CHOPS: Using large piece of heavy-duty aluminum foil, wrap soaked chips in foil packet and cut several vent holes in top. Pat pork chops dry with paper towels. Use sharp knife to cut 2 slits about 1 inch apart through outer layer of fat and connective tissue. Season each chop with ½ teaspoon salt and ½ teaspoon pepper. Place chops side by side, facing in same direction, on cutting board with curved rib bone facing down. Pass 2 skewers through loin muscle of each chop, close to bone, about 1 inch from each end, then pull apart to create 1-inch space between each.

3A. FOR A CHARCOAL GRILL: Open bottom vent halfway and place roasting pan in center of grill. Light large chimney starter filled with charcoal briquettes (6 quarts). When top coals are partially covered with ash, pour into 2 even piles on either side of roasting pan. Place wood chip packet on 1 pile of coals. Set cooking grate in place, cover, and open lid vent halfway. Heat grill until hot and wood chips are smoking, about 5 minutes.

3B. FOR A GAS GRILL: Place wood chip packet over primary burner. Turn all burners to high, cover, and heat grill until hot and wood chips are smoking, about 15 minutes. Turn all burners to medium-high. (Adjust burners as needed during cooking to maintain grill temperature between 300 and 325 degrees.)

4. Clean and oil cooking grate. Place skewered chops bone side down on grill (over pan if using charcoal). Cover and cook until meat registers 120 degrees, 28 to 32 minutes.

NOTES FROM THE TEST KITCHEN

SKEWERING PORK CHOPS FOR THE GRILL

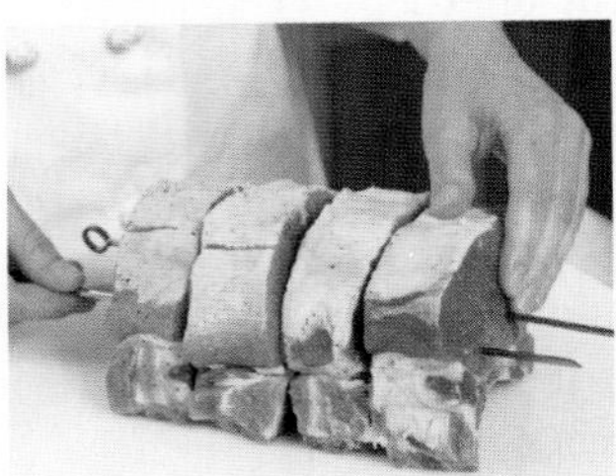

1. Pass two skewers through the loin muscle of each chop to provide stability when standing on the grill.

2. Stand the skewered chops, bone side down, on the cooking grate in the center of the grill so smoke can reach all sides.

5. Remove skewers from chops, tip chops onto flat side and brush surface of each with 1 tablespoon sauce. Transfer chops, sauce side down, to hotter parts of grill (if using charcoal) or turn all burners to high (if using gas) and cook until browned on first side, 2 to 6 minutes. Brush top of each chop with 1 tablespoon sauce, flip, and continue to cook until browned on second side and meat registers 140 degrees, 2 to 6 minutes longer.

6. Transfer chops to serving platter, tent loosely with aluminum foil, and let rest for 5 to 10 minutes. Serve, passing reserved sauce separately.

GRILLED PORK TENDERLOIN STEAKS

WHY THIS RECIPE WORKS: Although pork tenderloin medallions make for a nice presentation and offer lots of surface area to crisp and brown on the grill, they are inherently fussy: They require constant attention lest they overcook or, worse, slip through the grates. We wanted to take the spirit of the medallion approach but find a shape and a technique that, while it reliably delivered a maximum amount of flavorful, nicely browned crust, still kept this lean cut tender.

We started by cutting two tenderloin roasts in half and pounding them to an even thickness to make pork tenderloin "steaks." A two-level grill fire, with both hotter and cooler areas, allowed us to sear the steaks on the hotter side and then let them gently finish cooking on the cooler side. We added both bold seasoning and richness through a marinade. Plenty of salt ensured thorough seasoning and tender meat. Oil, lime juice and zest, garlic, fish sauce (which provided a savory boost without tasting fishy), and honey (the sugars in which would encourage browning) rounded out the marinade. We cut crosshatch marks in the steaks, which both made for extra crispy edges and allowed them to absorb even more marinade. A bit of reserved marinade, whisked with some mayo for body and cilantro for freshness, completed our tenderloin steaks.

Garlic-Lime Grilled Pork Tenderloin Steaks

SERVES 4 TO 6

Since marinating is a key step in this recipe, we don't recommend using enhanced pork (see page 181).

- 2 (1-pound) pork tenderloins, trimmed
- 1 tablespoon grated lime zest plus ¼ cup juice (2 limes)
- 4 garlic cloves, minced
- 4 teaspoons honey
- 2 teaspoons fish sauce
- ¾ teaspoon salt
- ½ teaspoon pepper
- ½ cup vegetable oil
- 4 teaspoons mayonnaise
- 1 tablespoon chopped fresh cilantro
- Flake sea salt (optional)

1. Slice each tenderloin in half crosswise to create 4 steaks total. Pound each half to ¾-inch thickness. Using sharp knife, cut ⅛-inch-deep slits spaced ½ inch apart in crosshatch pattern on both sides of steaks.

2. Whisk lime zest and juice, garlic, honey, fish sauce, salt, and pepper together in large bowl. Whisking constantly, slowly drizzle oil into lime mixture until smooth and slightly thickened. Transfer ½ cup lime mixture to small bowl and whisk in mayonnaise; set aside sauce. Add steaks to bowl with remaining marinade and toss thoroughly to coat; transfer steaks and marinade to large zipper-lock bag, press out as much air as possible, and seal bag. Let steaks sit at room temperature for 45 minutes.

3A. FOR A CHARCOAL GRILL: Open bottom vent completely. Light large chimney starter filled with charcoal briquettes (6 quarts). When top coals are partially covered with ash, pour evenly over half of grill. Set cooking grate in place, cover, and open lid vent completely. Heat grill until hot, about 5 minutes.

3B. FOR A GAS GRILL: Turn all burners to high, cover, and heat grill until hot, about 15 minutes. Leave primary burner on high and turn off other burner(s).

4. Clean and oil cooking grate. Remove steaks from marinade (do not pat dry) and place over hotter part of grill. Cook, uncovered, until well browned on first side, 3 to 4 minutes. Flip steaks and cook until well browned on second side, 3 to 4 minutes. Transfer steaks to cooler part of grill, with wider end of each steak facing hotter part of grill. Cover and cook until meat registers 140 degrees, 3 to 8 minutes longer (remove steaks as they come to temperature). Transfer steaks to cutting board and let rest for 5 minutes.

5. While steaks rest, microwave reserved sauce until warm, 15 to 30 seconds; stir in cilantro. Slice steaks against grain into ½-inch-thick slices. Drizzle with half of sauce; sprinkle with sea salt, if using; and serve, passing remaining sauce separately.

Lemon-Thyme Grilled Pork Tenderloin Steaks

Substitute grated lemon zest and juice (2 lemons) for lime zest and juice. Add 1 tablespoon minced fresh thyme to lemon mixture with garlic. Omit cilantro.

Spicy Orange-Ginger Grilled Pork Tenderloin Steaks

Reduce lime zest to 1½ teaspoons and juice to 2 tablespoons. Add 1½ teaspoons grated orange zest plus 2 tablespoons juice, 2 teaspoons grated fresh ginger, and ¼ teaspoon cayenne pepper to lime mixture with garlic.

GRILLED GLAZED PORK TENDERLOIN ROAST

WHY THIS RECIPE WORKS: Too often, delicate pork tenderloin turns out disappointing: The lean meat dries out easily, and it is plagued by uneven cooking because of its tapered shape. To make the pork cook more evenly and to create a more presentation-worthy roast, we tied two tenderloins together. Scraping the insides of the tenderloins with a fork created a sticky protein network that helped the tenderloins bind together. To ensure that our pork retained maximum juiciness, we brined the meat and cooked it mostly over indirect heat. Finally, we put together a few flavorful glazes. We made sure to use enough sugar (or ingredients containing sugar) to encourage browning, giving the pork a beautiful crust along with a flavor boost.

Grilled Glazed Pork Tenderloin Roast

SERVES 6

Since brining is a key step in having the two tenderloins stick together, we don't recommend using enhanced pork (see page 181) in this recipe.

- 2 (1-pound) pork tenderloins, trimmed
- Salt and pepper
- Vegetable oil
- 1 recipe glaze (recipes follow)

1. Lay tenderloins on cutting board, flat side (side opposite where silverskin was) up. Holding thick end of 1 tenderloin with paper towels and using dinner fork, scrape flat side lengthwise from end to end 5 times, until surface is completely covered with shallow grooves. Repeat with second tenderloin. Dissolve 3 tablespoons salt in 1½ quarts cold water in large container. Submerge tenderloins in brine and let stand at room temperature for 1 hour.

2. Remove tenderloins from brine and pat completely dry with paper towels. Lay 1 tenderloin, scraped side up, on cutting board and lay second tenderloin, scraped side down, on top so that thick end of 1 tenderloin matches up with thin end of other. Spray five 14-inch lengths of kitchen twine thoroughly with vegetable oil spray; evenly space twine underneath tenderloins and tie. Brush roast with vegetable oil and season with pepper. Transfer ⅓ cup glaze to bowl for grilling; reserve remaining glaze for serving.

3A. FOR A CHARCOAL GRILL: Open bottom vent completely. Light large chimney starter filled with charcoal briquettes (6 quarts). When top coals are partially covered with ash, pour into steeply banked pile against side of grill. Set cooking grate in place, cover, and open lid vent completely. Heat grill until hot, about 5 minutes.

3B. FOR A GAS GRILL: Turn all burners to high, cover, and heat grill until hot, about 15 minutes. Leave primary burner on high and turn off other burner(s).

4. Clean and oil cooking grate. Place roast on cooler side of grill, cover, and cook until meat registers 115 degrees, 22 to 28 minutes, flipping and rotating halfway through cooking.

5. Slide roast to hotter side of grill and cook until lightly browned on all sides, 4 to 6 minutes. Brush top of roast with about 1 tablespoon glaze and grill, glaze side down, until glaze begins to char, 2 to 3 minutes; repeat glazing and grilling with remaining 3 sides of roast, until meat registers 140 degrees.

6. Transfer roast to carving board, tent loosely with aluminum foil, and let rest for 10 minutes. Carefully remove twine and slice roast into ½-inch-thick slices. Serve with remaining glaze.

Miso Glaze

MAKES ABOUT ¾ CUP

- 3 tablespoons sake
- 3 tablespoons mirin
- ⅓ cup white miso paste
- ¼ cup sugar
- 2 teaspoons Dijon mustard
- 1 teaspoon rice vinegar
- ¼ teaspoon grated fresh ginger
- ¼ teaspoon toasted sesame oil

Bring sake and mirin to boil in small saucepan over medium heat. Whisk in miso and sugar until smooth, about 30 seconds. Remove pan from heat and continue to whisk until sugar is dissolved, about 1 minute. Whisk in mustard, vinegar, ginger, and sesame oil until smooth.

Sweet and Spicy Hoisin Glaze

MAKES ABOUT ¾ CUP

- 1 teaspoon vegetable oil
- 3 garlic cloves, minced
- 1 teaspoon grated fresh ginger
- ½ teaspoon red pepper flakes
- ½ cup hoisin sauce
- 2 tablespoons soy sauce
- 1 tablespoon rice vinegar

Heat oil in small saucepan over medium heat until shimmering. Add garlic, ginger, and pepper flakes; cook until fragrant, about 30 seconds. Whisk in hoisin and soy sauce until smooth. Remove pan from heat and stir in vinegar.

Satay Glaze

MAKES ABOUT ¾ CUP

- 1 teaspoon vegetable oil
- 1 tablespoon red curry paste
- 2 garlic cloves, minced
- ½ teaspoon grated fresh ginger
- ½ cup canned coconut milk
- ¼ cup packed dark brown sugar
- 2 tablespoons peanut butter
- 1 tablespoon lime juice
- 2½ teaspoons fish sauce

Heat oil in small saucepan over medium heat until shimmering. Add curry paste, garlic, and ginger; cook, stirring constantly, until fragrant, about 1 minute. Whisk in coconut milk and sugar and bring to simmer. Whisk in peanut butter until smooth. Remove pan from heat and whisk in lime juice and fish sauce.

SIMPLE GRILLED PORK TENDERLOIN

WHY THIS RECIPE WORKS: To produce pork tenderloin with a rich crust and a tender, juicy interior, we used a half-grill fire and seared the roast on the hotter side of the grill. This allowed the exterior to develop flavorful browning before the interior was cooked through. Then we moved the meat to the cooler side of the grill to finish cooking gently. Seasoning the meat with a mixture of salt, cumin, and chipotle chile powder added smoky, savory flavor, and a touch of sugar encouraged browning. To add bright flavor and make the most of the fire, we grilled pineapple and red onion and, while the cooked pork rested, combined them with cilantro, a serrano chile, lime juice, and a bit of reserved spice mixture to make a quick salsa.

Grilled Pork Tenderloin with Grilled Pineapple–Red Onion Salsa

SERVES 4 TO 6

We prefer unenhanced pork in this recipe, but enhanced pork (injected with a salt solution; see page 181) can be used.

PORK

- 1½ teaspoons kosher salt
- 1½ teaspoons sugar
- ½ teaspoon ground cumin
- ½ teaspoon chipotle chile powder
- 2 (12- to 16-ounce) pork tenderloins, trimmed

SALSA

- ½ pineapple, peeled, cored, and cut lengthwise into 6 wedges
- 1 red onion, cut into 8 wedges through root end
- 4 teaspoons extra-virgin olive oil
- ½ cup minced fresh cilantro
- 1 serrano chile, stemmed, seeded, and minced
- 2 tablespoons lime juice, plus extra for seasoning
- Salt

1. FOR THE PORK: Combine salt, sugar, cumin, and chile powder in small bowl. Reserve ½ teaspoon spice mixture. Rub remaining spice mixture evenly over surface of both tenderloins. Transfer to large plate or rimmed baking sheet and refrigerate while preparing grill.

2A. FOR A CHARCOAL GRILL: Open bottom vent completely. Light large chimney starter filled with charcoal briquettes (6 quarts). When top coals are partially covered with ash, pour evenly over half of grill. Set cooking grate in place, cover, and open lid vent completely. Heat grill until hot, about 5 minutes.

2B. FOR A GAS GRILL: Turn all burners to high, cover, and heat grill until hot, about 15 minutes. Leave primary burner on high and turn off other burner(s).

3. Clean and oil cooking grate. Place tenderloins on hotter side of grill. Cover and cook, turning tenderloins every 2 minutes, until well browned on all sides, about 8 minutes.

4. FOR THE SALSA: Brush pineapple and onion with 1 teaspoon oil. Move tenderloins to cooler side of grill (6 to 8 inches from heat source) and place pineapple and onion on hotter side of grill. Cover and cook until pineapple and onion are charred on both sides and softened, 8 to 10 minutes, and until pork registers 140 degrees, 12 to 17 minutes, turning tenderloins every 5 minutes. As pineapple and onion and tenderloins reach desired level of doneness, transfer pineapple and onion to plate and transfer tenderloins to carving board. Tent tenderloins with aluminum foil and let rest for 10 minutes.

5. While tenderloins rest, roughly chop pineapple. Pulse pineapple, onion, cilantro, serrano, lime juice, reserved spice mixture, and remaining 1 tablespoon oil in food processor until mixture is roughly chopped, 4 to 6 pulses. Transfer to bowl and season with salt and extra lime juice to taste.

6. Slice tenderloins crosswise ½ inch thick. Serve with salsa.

GRILLED STUFFED PORK TENDERLOIN

WHY THIS RECIPE WORKS: Pork tenderloin has many advantages that make it an ideal candidate for the grill: It's quick cooking, is extremely tender, and has a uniform shape that allows for even cooking. But this cut is also mild and lean, making it prone to drying out. Stuffing this roast solves these problems by adding flavor and moisture. For more surface area for the filling and to help prevent leaks, we pounded, filled, then rolled the tenderloins. And for our flavor filling, we pulsed bold ingredients—such as olives, sun-dried tomatoes, and porcini mushrooms—in a food processor to produce an intense paste that didn't ooze out. When it came time to fire up the grill, we found that a two-level fire, with the coals spread over half the grill, allowed the pork to cook evenly without drying out. Our last touch was a brown sugar rub on the exterior of each tenderloin, which boosted browning significantly.

Grilled Stuffed Pork Tenderloin

SERVES 6 TO 8

We prefer natural to enhanced pork (pork that has been injected with a salt solution to increase moistness and flavor; see page 181) for this recipe.

- 4 teaspoons packed dark brown sugar
- Salt and pepper
- 2 (1¼- to 1½-pound) pork tenderloins, trimmed
- 1 recipe stuffing (recipes follow)
- 1 cup baby spinach
- 2 tablespoons olive oil

1. Combine sugar, 1 teaspoon salt, and 1 teaspoon pepper in bowl. Cut each tenderloin in half horizontally, stopping ½ inch from edge so halves remain attached. Open up tenderloins, cover with plastic wrap, and pound to ¼-inch thickness. Trim any ragged edges to create rough rectangle about 10 inches by 6 inches. Season interior of pork with salt and pepper.

2. With long side of pork facing you, spread half of stuffing mixture over bottom half of pork followed by ½ cup of spinach. Roll away from you into tight cylinder, taking care not to squeeze stuffing out ends. Position tenderloin seam side down, evenly space 5 pieces kitchen twine underneath, and tie. Repeat with remaining tenderloin, stuffing, and spinach.

3A. FOR A CHARCOAL GRILL: Open bottom vent completely. Light large chimney starter filled with charcoal briquettes (6 quarts). When top coals are partially covered with ash, pour evenly over half of grill. Set cooking grate in place, cover, and open lid vent completely. Heat grill until hot, about 5 minutes.

3B. FOR A GAS GRILL: Turn all burners to high, cover, and heat grill until hot, about 15 minutes. Leave primary burner on high and turn off other burner(s). (Adjust primary burner as needed during cooking to maintain grill temperature between 325 and 350 degrees.)

4. Clean and oil cooking grate. Coat pork with oil, then rub entire surface with brown sugar mixture. Place pork on cool side of grill, cover, and cook until meat registers 140 degrees, 25 to 30 minutes, rotating pork halfway through cooking.

5. Transfer pork to carving board, tent loosely with aluminum foil, and let rest for 20 minutes. Remove twine, slice pork into ½-inch-thick slices, and serve.

Olive and Sun-Dried Tomato Stuffing

MAKES ABOUT 1 CUP

- ½ cup pitted kalamata olives
- ½ cup oil-packed sun-dried tomatoes, rinsed and chopped coarse
- 4 anchovy fillets, rinsed
- 2 garlic cloves, minced
- 1 teaspoon minced fresh thyme
- 1 teaspoon grated lemon zest
- Salt and pepper

Pulse all ingredients except salt and pepper in food processor until coarsely chopped, 5 to 10 pulses; season with salt and pepper to taste.

Porcini and Artichoke Stuffing

MAKES ABOUT 1 CUP

Avoid jarred or canned artichokes; frozen artichokes have a much fresher flavor.

- ½ ounce dried porcini mushrooms, rinsed and minced
- 3 ounces frozen artichoke hearts, thawed and patted dry (¾ cup)
- 1 ounce Parmesan cheese, grated (½ cup)
- ¼ cup oil-packed sun-dried tomatoes, rinsed and chopped coarse
- ¼ cup fresh parsley leaves
- 2 tablespoons pine nuts, toasted
- 2 garlic cloves, minced
- 1 teaspoon grated lemon zest plus 2 teaspoons juice
- Salt and pepper

Pulse all ingredients except salt and pepper in food processor until coarsely chopped, 5 to 10 pulses; season with salt and pepper to taste.

GRILLED STUFFED PORK LOIN ROAST

WHY THIS RECIPE WORKS: Center-cut pork loin is an especially lean cut, making it difficult to cook without drying out. We wanted to cook our pork loin on the grill but keep it moist using an approach other than traditional brines or sauces. We decided to use a moist, well-seasoned stuffing (and careful cooking) so our grilled pork loin would be juicy and flavorful.

We bought a short and wide roast, more square than cylindrical. This shape only required a few straight, short cuts to open to a long, flat sheet that was easy to fill and roll up. The best stuffing required both a deep flavor to counter the pork's rather bland taste and a texture thick enough to stay put. Poaching apples and cranberries in a blend of apple cider, apple cider vinegar, and spices developed a filling with the dense, chewy consistency we wanted. And this process had an added bonus—we had ample poaching liquid left, which could be reduced to a glaze. We had already decided not to give the loin a preliminary sear, which can create a tough exterior, but found we missed the brown color that searing produces. Rolling the loin in our glaze gave it a beautifully burnished finish.

Grilled Pork Loin with Apple-Cranberry Filling

SERVES 6

This recipe is best prepared with a loin that is 7 to 8 inches long and 4 to 5 inches wide and not enhanced (injected with a salt solution; see page 181). To make cutting the pork easier, freeze it for 30 minutes. If mustard seeds are unavailable, stir an equal amount of whole grain mustard into the filling after the apples have been processed. For a spicier stuffing, use the larger amount of cayenne. If you'd like to use wood chunks instead of wood chips when using a charcoal grill, substitute 2 medium wood chunks, soaked in water for 1 hour, for the wood chip packet. The pork loin can be stuffed and tied a day ahead of time, but don't season the exterior until you are ready to grill.

FILLING

- 1½ cups (4 ounces) dried apples
- 1 cup apple cider
- ¾ cup packed light brown sugar
- ½ cup cider vinegar
- ½ cup dried cranberries
- 1 large shallot, halved lengthwise and sliced thin crosswise
- 1 tablespoon grated fresh ginger
- 1 tablespoon yellow mustard seeds
- ½ teaspoon ground allspice
- ⅛–¼ teaspoon cayenne pepper

PORK

1 (2½-pound) boneless center-cut pork loin roast, trimmed
Salt and pepper

2 cups wood chips, soaked in water for 15 minutes and drained

1. FOR THE FILLING: Bring all ingredients to simmer in medium saucepan over medium-high heat. Cover, reduce heat to low, and cook until apples are very soft, about 20 minutes. Pour mixture through fine-mesh strainer set over bowl, pressing with back of spoon to extract as much liquid as possible. Return liquid to saucepan and simmer over medium-high heat until reduced to ⅓ cup, about 5 minutes; reserve for glazing. Pulse apple mixture in food processor until coarsely chopped, about 15 pulses. Transfer filling to bowl and refrigerate until needed.

2. FOR THE PORK: Position roast fat side up. Insert knife ½ inch from bottom of roast and cut horizontally, stopping ½ inch before edge. Open up this flap. Cut through thicker half of roast about ½ inch from bottom, stopping about ½ inch before edge. Open up this flap. Repeat until pork is even ½-inch thickness throughout. If uneven, cover with plastic wrap and use meat pounder to even out. Season interior with salt and pepper and spread filling in even layer, leaving ½-inch border. Roll tightly and tie with kitchen twine at 1-inch intervals. Season with salt and pepper.

3. Using large piece of heavy-duty aluminum foil, wrap soaked chips in foil packet and cut several vent holes in top.

4A. FOR A CHARCOAL GRILL: Open bottom vent halfway. Light large chimney starter three-quarters filled with charcoal briquettes (4½ quarts). When top coals are partially covered with ash, pour evenly over half of grill. Place wood chip packet on coals. Set cooking grate in place, cover, and open lid vent halfway. Heat grill until hot and wood chips are smoking, about 5 minutes.

4B. FOR A GAS GRILL: Place wood chip packet over primary burner. Turn all burners to high, cover, and heat grill until hot and wood chips are smoking, about 15 minutes. Leave primary burner on medium-high and turn off other burner(s). (Adjust primary burner as needed to maintain grill temperature of 300 to 325 degrees.)

5. Clean and oil cooking grate. Place pork, fat side up, on cooler side of grill, cover (position lid vent over roast if using charcoal), and cook until meat registers 130 to 135 degrees, 55 minutes to 1 hour 10 minutes, flipping halfway through cooking.

6. Brush roast evenly with reserved glaze. (Reheat glaze, if necessary, to make it spreadable.) Continue to cook until glaze is glossy and meat registers 145 degrees, 5 to 10 minutes longer. Transfer to carving board, tent loosely with foil, and let rest for 15 minutes. Remove twine, cut roast into ½-inch-thick slices, and serve.

NOTES FROM THE TEST KITCHEN

HOW TO STUFF A PORK LOIN

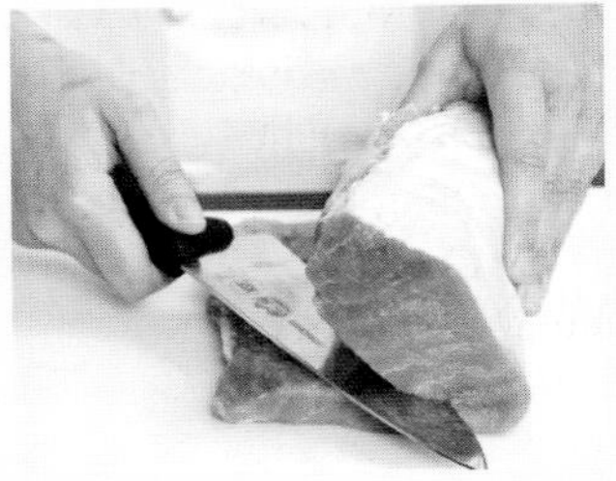

1. Position the roast fat side up. Insert a knife ½ inch from the bottom of the roast and cut horizontally, stopping ½ inch before the edge. Open up this flap.

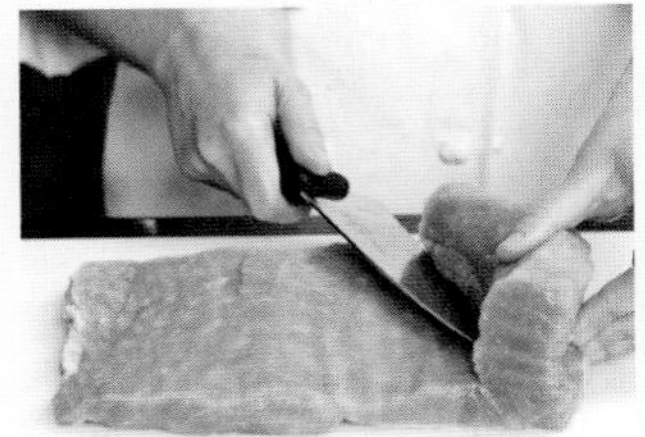

2. Cut through the thicker half of the roast about ½ inch from the bottom, stopping about ½ inch before the edge. Open up this flap.

3. Repeat until the pork loin is an even ½-inch thickness throughout. If uneven, cover with plastic wrap and use a meat pounder to even out.

4. With the long side of the meat facing you, season the meat and spread the filling, leaving a ½-inch border on all sides.

5. Starting from the short side, roll the pork loin tightly, then tie the roast with kitchen twine at 1-inch intervals.

GRILL-ROASTED PORK LOIN

WHY THIS RECIPE WORKS: When we're looking to dress up an outdoor dinner—and offer guests more than burgers or grilled chicken—we like to serve a juicy, crisp crusted pork loin. But because the roasts available at the supermarket nowadays are so incredibly lean, this cut of meat can dry out considerably when cooked with the dry heat of the grill. We planned to bring back the juiciness and produce a succulent roast with a deep brown crust and aromatic, smoke-flavored meat.

First, we chose the best cut. Our top choice—the blade-end roast—was moist and flavorful and was the hands-down winner over center-cut, sirloin, and tenderloin roasts. Brining ensured that our finished roast met with rave reviews from testers and stayed juicy and moist, and a generous coating of black pepper—or our own spicy rub—provided ample flavoring. We then used a two-step grilling process, searing the roast directly over hot coals for a nice crust and finishing it over indirect heat, so as not to overcook it. The final step was removing the roast from the grill when the internal temperature was just shy of done, then allowing it to rest until the temperature rose and the meat was juicy and tender.

Grill-Roasted Pork Loin

SERVES 4 TO 6

If the pork is enhanced (injected with a salt solution; see page 181), do not brine and add 1 tablespoon salt to the pepper or spice rub. Two medium wood chunks, soaked in water for 1 hour, can be substituted for the wood chip packet on a charcoal grill.

- ¼ cup salt
- 1 (2½- to 3-pound) boneless blade-end pork loin roast, trimmed and tied with kitchen twine at 1½-inch intervals
- 2 tablespoons olive oil
- 1 tablespoon pepper or 1 recipe spice rub (recipes follow)
- 2 cups wood chips, soaked in water for 15 minutes and drained

1. Dissolve salt in 2 quarts cold water in large container. Submerge pork loin in brine, cover, and refrigerate for 1 to 1½ hours. Remove pork from brine and pat dry with paper towels. Rub pork loin with oil and coat with pepper. Let sit at room temperature for 1 hour.

2. Using large piece of heavy-duty aluminum foil, wrap soaked chips in foil packet and cut several vent holes in top.

3A. FOR A CHARCOAL GRILL: Open bottom vent halfway. Light large chimney starter three-quarters filled with charcoal briquettes (4½ quarts). When top coals are partially covered with ash, pour evenly over half of grill. Place wood chip packet on coals. Set cooking grate in place, cover, and open lid vent halfway. Heat grill until hot and wood chips are smoking, about 5 minutes.

3B. FOR A GAS GRILL: Place wood chip packet directly on primary burner. Turn all burners to high, cover, and heat grill until hot and wood chips are smoking, about 15 minutes. Leave primary burner on high and turn off other burner(s). (Adjust primary burner as needed during cooking to maintain grill temperature between 300 and 325 degrees.)

4. Clean and oil cooking grate. Place pork loin on hot side of grill, fat side up, and cook (covered if using gas) until well browned on all sides, 10 to 12 minutes, turning as needed. Move to cool side of grill, positioning roast parallel with and as close as possible to heat. Cover (position lid vent over roast if using charcoal) and cook for 20 minutes.

5. Rotate roast 180 degrees, cover, and continue to cook until meat registers 145 degrees, 10 to 30 minutes longer, depending on thickness of roast.

6. Transfer roast to carving board, tent loosely with aluminum foil, and let rest for 15 minutes. Remove twine, cut roast into ½-inch-thick slices, and serve.

Chili-Mustard Spice Rub

MAKES ABOUT 2 TABLESPOONS

This rub packs some heat, so use the lesser amount of cayenne if you want a milder rub.

- 2 teaspoons chili powder
- 2 teaspoons dry mustard
- 1 teaspoon ground cumin
- ½–1 teaspoon cayenne pepper

Combine all ingredients in bowl.

SMOKED PORK LOIN

WHY THIS RECIPE WORKS: For a smoky, company-worthy pork roast that cooked in just a couple of hours, we looked to quick-cooking pork loin. Choosing a blade-end roast over a center-cut roast meant more fat and thus more flavor. An overnight rub of salt and brown sugar before grilling helped season the roast, kept it juicy, and delivered a nicely caramelized exterior. Low-and-slow indirect cooking was key for an evenly cooked, tender roast, so we poured lit coals over a layer of unlit coals to create a fire that wouldn't require refueling. Two cups of wood chips (in a single packet) provided just enough smoke to enhance the roast's meaty flavor without overwhelming it. A dried fruit chutney was the perfect complement to the smoky meat.

Smoked Pork Loin with Dried Fruit Chutney

SERVES 6

A blade roast is our preferred cut, but a center-cut boneless loin roast can also be used. If the pork is enhanced (injected with a salt solution; see page 181) skip step 1, but season with sugar-salt mixture in step 4. Any variety of wood chip except mesquite will work; we prefer hickory. If you'd like to use wood chunks instead of wood chips when using a charcoal grill, substitute 2 medium wood chunk(s), soaked in water for 1 hour, for the wood chip packet. To help maintain a constant charcoal grill temperature, do not remove the lid any more than necessary during cooking.

PORK

- ½ cup packed light brown sugar
- ¼ cup kosher salt
- 1 (3½- to 4-pound) blade-end boneless pork loin roast, trimmed
- 2 cups wood chips
- 1 (13 by 9-inch) disposable aluminum roasting pan (if using charcoal) or 1 (9-inch) disposable aluminum pie plate (if using gas)

CHUTNEY

- ¾ cup dry white wine
- ½ cup dried apricots, diced
- ½ cup dried cherries
- ¼ cup white wine vinegar
- 3 tablespoons water
- 3 tablespoons packed light brown sugar
- 1 shallot, minced
- 2 tablespoons grated fresh ginger
- 1 tablespoon unsalted butter
- 1 tablespoon Dijon mustard
- 1½ teaspoons dry mustard
- Kosher salt

1. FOR THE PORK: Combine sugar and salt in small bowl. Tie roast with twine at 1-inch intervals. Rub sugar-salt mixture over entire surface of roast, making sure roast is evenly coated. Wrap roast tightly in plastic wrap, set in rimmed baking sheet, and refrigerate for at least 6 hours or up to 24 hours.

2. Just before grilling, soak wood chips in water for 15 minutes, then drain. Using large piece of heavy-duty aluminum foil, wrap soaked chips in 8 by 4½-inch foil packet. (Make sure chips do not poke holes in sides or bottom of packet.) Cut 2 evenly spaced 2-inch slits in top of packet.

3A. FOR A CHARCOAL GRILL: Open bottom vent halfway. Arrange 25 unlit charcoal briquettes over half of grill and place disposable pan filled with 3 cups water on other side of grill. Light large chimney starter two-thirds filled with charcoal briquettes (4 quarts). When top coals are partially covered with ash, pour evenly over unlit briquettes. Place wood chip packet on coals. Set cooking grate in place, cover, and open lid vent halfway. Heat grill until hot and wood chips are smoking, about 5 minutes. (Adjust top and bottom vents as needed to maintain grill temperature of 300 degrees.)

3B. FOR A GAS GRILL: Remove cooking grate and place wood chip packet directly on primary burner. Place disposable pie plate filled with 1 inch water directly on other burner(s). Set grate in place, turn all burners to high, cover, and heat grill until hot and wood chips are smoking, about 15 minutes. Turn primary burner to medium and turn off other burner(s). (Adjust primary burner as needed to maintain grill temperature of 300 degrees.)

4. Clean and oil cooking grate. Unwrap roast and pat dry with paper towels. Place roast on grill (cooler side if using charcoal), directly over water pan. Cover (position lid vent over roast if using charcoal) and cook until meat registers 140 degrees, 1½ to 2 hours, rotating roast 180 degrees after 45 minutes.

5. FOR THE CHUTNEY: Combine wine, apricots, cherries, vinegar, water, sugar, shallot, and ginger in medium saucepan. Bring to simmer over medium heat. Cover and cook until fruit is softened, 10 minutes. Remove lid and reduce heat to medium-low. Add butter, Dijon, and dry mustard and continue to cook until slightly thickened, 4 to 6 minutes. Remove from heat and season with salt to taste. Transfer to bowl and let stand at room temperature.

6. Transfer roast to carving board, tent with foil, and let rest for 30 minutes. Remove and discard twine. Slice ¼ inch thick and serve, passing chutney separately.

GRILLED BONE-IN PORK ROAST

WHY THIS RECIPE WORKS: Grilling a bulky cut of meat like a pork roast may sound difficult, but we found that a tender, quick-cooking center-cut rib roast and a simple salt rub were all that we needed for a juicy grilled roast with a thick mahogany crust. We grilled it over indirect heat (on the cooler side of the grill) so it could cook through slowly, adding a single soaked wood chunk or a small amount of wood chips to the fire for a subtle tinge of smoke flavor. After a little more than an hour on the grill, our roast was tender and juicy, with plenty of rich, deep flavor. For the perfect counterpoint to the roast's richness, we whipped up a fresh orange salsa with bright citrus and fresh herbs, jalapeño, and a warm touch of cumin.

Grill-Roasted Bone-In Pork Rib Roast

SERVES 6 TO 8

If you buy a blade-end roast (sometimes called a "rib-end roast"), tie it into a uniform shape with kitchen twine at 1-inch intervals; this step is unnecessary with a center-cut roast. For easier carving, ask the butcher to remove the tip of the chine bone and to cut the remainder of the chine bone between each rib. One medium wood chunk, soaked in water for 1 hour, can be substituted for the wood chip packet on a charcoal grill.

1 (4- to 5-pound) bone-in center-cut pork rib roast, tip of chine bone removed, fat trimmed to ¼-inch thickness
4 teaspoons kosher salt
1 cup wood chips, soaked in water for 15 minutes and drained
1½ teaspoons pepper
1 recipe Orange Salsa with Cuban Flavors (optional; recipe follows)

1. Pat roast dry with paper towels. Using sharp knife, cut slits in surface fat layer, spaced 1 inch apart, in crosshatch pattern, being careful not to cut into meat. Season roast with salt. Wrap with plastic wrap and refrigerate for at least 6 hours or up to 24 hours.

2. Using large piece of heavy-duty aluminum foil, wrap soaked chips in foil packet and cut several vent holes in top.

3A. FOR A CHARCOAL GRILL: Open bottom vent halfway. Light large chimney starter filled with charcoal briquettes (6 quarts). When top coals are partially covered with ash, pour into steeply banked pile against side of grill. Place wood chip packet on coals. Set cooking grate in place, cover, and open lid vent halfway. Heat grill until hot and wood chips are smoking, about 5 minutes.

3B. FOR A GAS GRILL: Place wood chip packet over primary burner. Turn all burners to high, cover, and heat grill until hot and wood chips are smoking, about 15 minutes. Turn primary burner to medium-high and turn off other burner(s). (Adjust primary burner as needed during cooking to maintain grill temperature around 325 degrees.)

4. Clean and oil cooking grate. Unwrap roast and season with pepper. Place roast on grate with meat near, but not over, coals and flames and bones facing away from coals and flames. Cover (position lid vent over meat if using charcoal) and cook until meat registers 140 degrees, 1¼ to 1½ hours.

5. Transfer roast to carving board, tent loosely with aluminum foil, and let rest for 30 minutes. Carve into thick slices by cutting between ribs. Serve, passing salsa, if using, separately.

Orange Salsa with Cuban Flavors

MAKES ABOUT 2½ CUPS

To make this salsa spicier, add the reserved chile seeds.

½ teaspoon grated orange zest plus 5 oranges peeled and segmented; each segment quartered crosswise
½ cup minced red onion
1 jalapeño chile, stemmed, seeds reserved, and minced
2 tablespoons lime juice
2 tablespoons minced fresh parsley
1 tablespoon extra-virgin olive oil
2 teaspoons packed brown sugar
1½ teaspoons distilled white vinegar
1½ teaspoons minced fresh oregano
1 garlic clove, minced
½ teaspoon ground cumin
½ teaspoon salt
½ teaspoon pepper

Combine all ingredients in medium bowl.

GRILLED PORK KEBABS WITH HOISIN GLAZE

WHY THIS RECIPE WORKS: To bring out the best in mild pork tenderloins, we cut the meat into chunks and let them soak in salt. This simple mixture changed the structure of the raw meat's exterior proteins so that it wouldn't lose moisture on the grill. For a flavorful, sticky glaze that clung to the pork (and not to the grill), we combined five-spice powder, garlic powder, cornstarch, and hoisin sauce. Applying the glaze twice meant the pork developed great char from the sweet hoisin sauce during grilling and still had a thick, tasty coating when the kebabs were served.

Grilled Pork Kebabs with Hoisin Glaze

SERVES 4

You will need four 12-inch metal skewers for this recipe. We prefer natural pork, but if your pork is enhanced (injected with a salt solution; see page 181), do not salt it in step 1.

2 (12-ounce) pork tenderloins, trimmed and cut into 1-inch chunks
1 teaspoon kosher salt
1½ teaspoons five-spice powder
¾ teaspoon garlic powder
½ teaspoon cornstarch
4½ tablespoons hoisin sauce
Vegetable oil spray
2 scallions, thinly sliced

1. Toss pork and salt together in large bowl and let sit for 20 minutes. Meanwhile, whisk five-spice powder, garlic powder, and cornstarch together in bowl. Add hoisin to five-spice mixture and stir to combine. Set aside 1½ tablespoons hoisin mixture.

2. Add remaining hoisin mixture to pork and toss to coat. Thread pork onto four 12-inch metal skewers, leaving 1/4 inch between pieces. Spray both sides of meat generously with oil spray.

3A. FOR A CHARCOAL GRILL: Open bottom vent completely. Light large chimney starter filled with charcoal briquettes (6 quarts). When top coals are partially covered with ash, pour evenly over half of grill. Set cooking grate in place, cover, and open lid vent completely. Heat grill until hot, about 5 minutes.

3B. FOR A GAS GRILL: Turn all burners to high, cover, and heat grill until hot, about 15 minutes. Leave primary burner on high and turn off other burner(s).

4. Clean and oil cooking grate. Place skewers on hotter side of grill and grill until well charred, 3 to 4 minutes. Flip skewers, brush with reserved hoisin mixture, and continue to grill until second side is well charred and meat registers 140 degrees, 3 to 4 minutes longer. Transfer to serving platter, tent loosely with aluminum foil, and let rest for 5 minutes. Sprinkle with scallions and serve.

PULLED PORK

WHY THIS RECIPE WORKS: Pulled pork is classic summertime party food: slow-cooked pork roast, shredded and seasoned, served on the most basic of hamburger buns (or sliced white bread), with just enough of your favorite barbecue sauce, a couple of dill pickle chips, and a topping of coleslaw. However, many barbecue procedures demand the regular attention of the cook for eight hours or more. We wanted to find a way to make moist, fork-tender pulled pork without the marathon cooking time and constant attention to the grill.

After testing shoulder roasts (also called Boston butt), fresh ham, and picnic roasts, we determined that the shoulder roast, which has the most fat, retained the most moisture and flavor during a long, slow cook. We massaged a spicy chili rub into the meat, then wrapped the roast in plastic wrap and refrigerated it for at least three hours to "marinate." The roast is first cooked on the grill to absorb smoky flavor (from wood chips—no smoker required), then finished in the oven. Finally, we let the pork rest in a paper bag so the meat would steam and any remaining collagen would break down, allowing the flavorful juices to be reabsorbed. We also developed a pair of sauce recipes to please barbecue fans with different tastes.

Barbecued Pulled Pork

SERVES 8

Pulled pork can be made with a fresh ham or picnic roast, although our preference is for Boston butt. If using a fresh ham or picnic roast, remove the skin by cutting through it with the tip of a chef's knife; slide the blade just under the skin and work around to loosen it while pulling it off with your other hand. Four medium wood chunks, soaked in water for 1 hour, can be substituted for the wood chip packets on a charcoal grill. Serve on plain white bread or warmed rolls with dill pickle chips and coleslaw.

- 1 (6- to 8-pound) bone-in Boston butt roast
- 3/4 cup Dry Rub for Barbecue (recipe follows)
- 4 cups wood chips, soaked in water for 15 minutes and drained
- 1 (13 by 9-inch) disposable aluminum roasting pan
- 2 cups barbecue sauce (recipes follow)

1. Pat pork dry with paper towels, then massage dry rub into meat. Wrap meat in plastic wrap and refrigerate for at least 3 hours or up to 3 days.

2. At least 1 hour prior to cooking, remove roast from refrigerator, unwrap, and let sit at room temperature. Using 2 large pieces of heavy-duty aluminum foil, wrap soaked chips in 2 foil packets and cut several vent holes in tops.

3A. FOR A CHARCOAL GRILL: Open bottom vent halfway. Light large chimney starter three-quarters filled with charcoal briquettes (4½ quarts). When top coals are partially covered with ash, pour evenly over half of grill. Place wood chip packets on coals. Set cooking grate in place, cover, and open lid vent halfway. Heat grill until hot and wood chips are smoking, about 5 minutes.

3B. FOR A GAS GRILL: Place wood chip packets directly on primary burner. Turn all burners to high, cover, and heat grill until hot and wood chips are smoking, about 15 minutes. Turn primary burner to medium-high and turn off other burner(s). (Adjust primary burner as needed to maintain grill temperature around 325 degrees.)

4. Set roast in disposable pan, place on cool side of grill, and cook for 3 hours. During final 20 minutes of cooking, adjust oven rack to lower-middle position and heat oven to 325 degrees.

5. Wrap disposable pan with heavy-duty foil and cook in oven until meat is fork-tender, about 2 hours.

6. Carefully slide foil-wrapped pan with roast into brown paper bag. Crimp end shut and let rest for 1 hour.

7. Transfer roast to carving board and unwrap. Separate roast into muscle sections, removing fat, if desired, and tearing meat into shreds with your fingers. Place shredded meat in large bowl and toss with 1 cup barbecue sauce. Serve, passing remaining sauce separately.

Dry Rub for Barbecue

MAKES ABOUT 1 CUP

You can adjust the proportions of spices in this all-purpose rub or add or subtract a spice, as you wish.

- ¼ cup paprika
- 2 tablespoons chili powder
- 2 tablespoons ground cumin
- 2 tablespoons packed dark brown sugar
- 2 tablespoons salt
- 1 tablespoon dried oregano
- 1 tablespoon granulated sugar
- 1 tablespoon black pepper
- 1 tablespoon white pepper
- 1-2 teaspoons cayenne pepper

Combine all ingredients in small bowl.

Eastern North Carolina Barbecue Sauce

MAKES ABOUT 2 CUPS

This sauce can be refrigerated in an airtight container for up to 4 days.

- 1 cup distilled white vinegar
- 1 cup cider vinegar
- 1 tablespoon sugar
- 1 tablespoon red pepper flakes
- 1 tablespoon hot sauce
- Salt and pepper

Mix all ingredients except salt and pepper together in bowl and season with salt and pepper to taste.

Mid-South Carolina Mustard Sauce

MAKES ABOUT 2½ CUPS

This sauce can be refrigerated in an airtight container for up to 4 days.

- 1 cup cider vinegar
- 1 cup vegetable oil
- 6 tablespoons Dijon mustard
- 2 tablespoons maple syrup or honey
- 4 teaspoons Worcestershire sauce
- 1 teaspoon hot sauce
- Salt and pepper

Mix all ingredients except salt and pepper together in bowl and season with salt and pepper to taste.

SWEET AND TANGY GRILLED COUNTRY-STYLE PORK RIBS

WHY THIS RECIPE WORKS: In many ways, country-style ribs are actually more like pork chops—a point that can make them a little confusing for home cooks. Because they feature a combination of light, lean loin meat and richly flavored, fattier shoulder, the trick is figuring out how to grill them so that the white meat is juicy and the dark meat is tender. We applied a salty dry rub to boost the ribs' seasoning and help them stay moist, particularly the faster-drying light meat. We found that a doneness temperature of 150 degrees—a compromise between the usual 135 to 140 degrees required for light meat and 175 degrees for dark meat—delivered optimal results. Starting the ribs over high heat and then finishing on the cooler side of the grill ensured good browning and an evenly cooked interior. While the ribs were on the cooler side of the grill, we basted them with a sweet and tangy sauce of ketchup, molasses, Worcestershire sauce, cider vinegar, and Dijon mustard. Stirring in grated onion, minced garlic, chili powder, cayenne, and black pepper gave the sauce some depth.

Sweet and Tangy Grilled Country-Style Pork Ribs

SERVES 4 TO 6

Be sure to carefully trim the pork to reduce the number of flare-ups when the pork is grilled. This recipe requires refrigerating the spice-rubbed ribs for at least 1 hour or up to 24 hours before grilling.

PORK

- 4 teaspoons packed brown sugar
- 1 tablespoon kosher salt
- 1 tablespoon chili powder
- ⅛ teaspoon cayenne pepper
- 4 pounds bone-in country-style pork ribs, trimmed

SAUCE

- 1 cup ketchup
- 5 tablespoons molasses
- 3 tablespoons cider vinegar
- 2 tablespoons Worcestershire sauce
- 2 tablespoons Dijon mustard
- ¼ teaspoon pepper
- 2 tablespoons vegetable oil
- ⅓ cup grated onion
- 1 garlic clove, minced
- 1 teaspoon chili powder
- ¼ teaspoon cayenne pepper

1. FOR THE PORK: Combine sugar, salt, chili powder and cayenne in bowl. Rub mixture all over ribs. Wrap tightly in plastic wrap and refrigerate for at least 1 hour or up to 24 hours.

2. FOR THE SAUCE: Whisk ketchup, molasses, vinegar, Worcestershire, mustard, and pepper together in bowl. Heat oil in medium saucepan over medium heat until shimmering. Add onion and garlic; cook until onion is softened, 2 to 4 minutes. Add chili powder and cayenne and cook until fragrant, about 30 seconds. Whisk in ketchup mixture and bring to boil. Reduce heat to medium-low and simmer gently for 5 minutes. Set aside ½ cup of sauce for basting pork and reserve remaining sauce for serving. (Sauce can be refrigerated for up to 1 week.)

3A. FOR A CHARCOAL GRILL: Open bottom vent halfway. Light large chimney starter filled with charcoal briquettes (6 quarts). When top coals are partially covered with ash, pour evenly over half of grill. Set cooking grate in place, cover, and open lid vent halfway. Heat grill until hot, about 5 minutes.

3B. FOR A GAS GRILL: Turn all burners to high, cover and heat grill until hot, about 15 minutes. Leave primary burner on high and turn other burner(s) off to maintain grill temperature around 350 degrees.

4. Clean and oil cooking grate. Place ribs over hotter part of grill and cook until well browned on both sides, 4 to 7 minutes. Move ribs to cooler part of grill and brush top sides with ¼ cup sauce. Cover and cook 6 minutes. Flip ribs and brush with remaining ¼ cup sauce. Cover and continue to cook until pork registers 150 degrees, 5 to 10 minutes longer. Transfer ribs to serving platter, tent loosely with aluminum foil and let rest for 10 minutes. Serve, passing sauce separately.

KANSAS CITY RIBS

WHY THIS RECIPE WORKS: Kansas City ribs are slow-smoked pork ribs slathered in a sauce so thick, sweet, and sticky that you need a case of wet naps to get your hands clean after eating them. But authentic ribs can take all day to prepare. We knew we could come up with a faster method for Kansas City ribs—one that would produce the same fall-off-the-bone, tender smoky meat of the long-cooked original recipe.

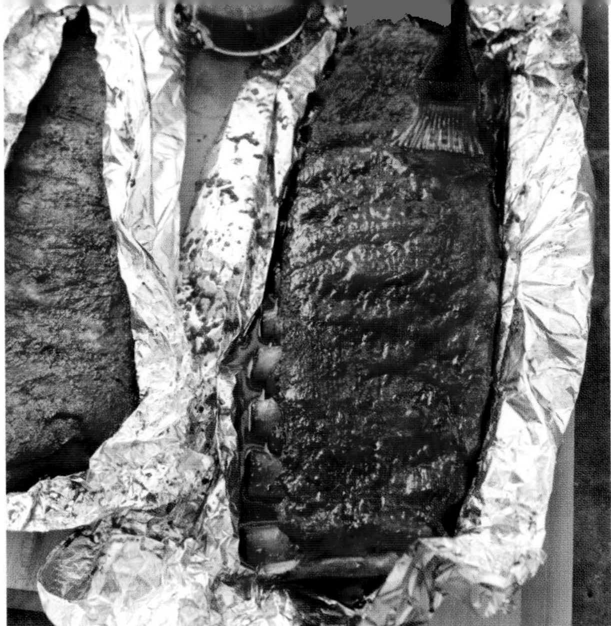

We quickly learned that spareribs, which are well marbled with fat, produce moist, tender ribs, but some racks are so big they barely fit on the grill. We turned to a more manageable cut, referred to as "St. Louis" ribs, which is a narrower, rectangular rack that offers all the taste of whole spareribs without any of the trouble. A spice rub added flavor and encouraged a savory crust on the meat.

We barbecued the ribs, covered with foil, over indirect heat for four hours—the foil traps some of the steam over the meat, so that it cooks up tender, not dry. Using wood chips on the grill imparted the meat with great smoky flavor. For sticky, saucy ribs, we brushed the ribs all over with barbecue sauce and finished them in the gentle, even heat of the oven until they were tender and falling off the bone.

Kansas City Sticky Ribs

SERVES 4 TO 6

We like St. Louis–style racks, but if you can't find them, baby back ribs will work fine; reduce the oven time in step 6 to 1 to 2 hours.

RIBS

- 3 tablespoons paprika
- 2 tablespoons brown sugar
- 1 tablespoon salt
- 1 tablespoon black pepper
- ¼ teaspoon cayenne pepper
- 2 (2½- to 3-pound) full racks pork spareribs (see note), trimmed of any large pieces of fat and membrane removed

SAUCE

- 1 tablespoon vegetable oil plus more for cooking grate
- 1 onion, minced
- Salt
- 4 cups low-sodium chicken broth

- 1 cup root beer
- 1 cup cider vinegar
- 1 cup dark corn syrup
- ½ cup light or mild molasses
- ½ cup tomato paste
- ½ cup ketchup
- 2 tablespoons brown mustard
- 1 tablespoon hot sauce
- ½ teaspoon garlic powder
- ¼ teaspoon liquid smoke
- Pepper
- 2 cups wood chips, soaked, drained, and sealed in a foil packet

NOTES FROM THE TEST KITCHEN

REMOVING THE MEMBRANE FOR KANSAS CITY RIBS

Ribs have a papery membrane on the underside that can make it hard to pull the meat off the bone. Before cooking, loosen this membrane with the tip of a paring knife and, with the aid of a paper towel, pull it off slowly, all in one piece.

1. FOR THE RIBS: Combine the paprika, sugar, salt, black pepper, and cayenne in a bowl. Pat the ribs dry with paper towels, and rub them evenly with the spice mixture. Wrap the meat in plastic wrap and let sit at room temperature for at least 1 hour, or refrigerate for up to 24 hours. (If refrigerated, let sit at room temperature for 1 hour before grilling.)

2. FOR THE SAUCE: Meanwhile, heat the oil in a large saucepan over medium heat until shimmering. Add the onion and a pinch of salt and cook until softened, 5 to 7 minutes. Whisk in the broth, root beer, vinegar, corn syrup, molasses, tomato paste, ketchup, mustard, hot sauce, and garlic powder. Bring the sauce to a simmer and cook, stirring occasionally, until reduced to 4 cups, about 1 hour. Stir in the liquid smoke. Cool to room temperature, and season with salt and pepper to taste. Measure out 1 cup of the barbecue sauce for cooking; set aside the remaining sauce for serving. (The sauce can be refrigerated in an airtight container for up to 4 days.)

3A. FOR A CHARCOAL GRILL: Open the bottom grill vents halfway. Light a large chimney starter three-quarters full with charcoal (4½ quarts, about 75 briquettes) and allow it to burn until the charcoal is partially covered with a layer of fine gray ash, about 20 minutes. Pour the coals into a steeply banked pile against 1 side of the grill and place the wood chip packet on top of the coals. Set the cooking grate in place, cover, and open the lid vents halfway. Heat the grill until hot and the wood chips begin to smoke heavily, about 5 minutes.

3B. FOR A GAS GRILL: Place the wood chip packet directly on the primary burner. Turn all the burners to high, cover, and heat the grill until hot and the wood chips begin to smoke heavily, about 15 minutes. Turn the primary burner to medium-high and turn off the other burner(s). (Adjust the primary burner as needed to maintain the grill temperature around 325 degrees.)

4. Use a grill brush to scrape the cooking grate clean. Lightly dip a wad of paper towels in oil; holding the wad with tongs, wipe the cooking grate. Place the ribs, meat side down, on the cooler side of the grill, away from the coals or flames; the ribs may overlap slightly. Place a sheet of foil on top of the ribs. Cover (positioning the lid vents over the meat if using charcoal) and cook until the ribs are deep red and smoky, about 2 hours, flipping and rotating the racks halfway through. During the final 20 minutes of grilling, adjust an oven rack to the middle position and heat the oven to 250 degrees.

5. Remove the ribs from the grill, brush them evenly with the 1 cup sauce reserved for cooking, and wrap tightly with foil. Lay the foil-wrapped ribs on a rimmed baking sheet and continue to cook in the oven until tender and a fork inserted into the ribs meets no resistance, 1½ to 2½ hours.

6. Remove the ribs from the oven and let rest, still wrapped, for 30 minutes. Unwrap the ribs and brush them thickly with 1 cup of the sauce set aside for serving. Slice the ribs between the bones and serve with the remaining sauce.

MEMPHIS DRY RUBBED PORK RIBS

WHY THIS RECIPE WORKS: Memphis pit masters pride themselves on their all-day barbecued pork ribs with a dark bark-like crust and distinctive chew. Up for a challenge, we decided to come up with our own version, but one that wouldn't involve tending a grill all day.

After failing to grill the ribs in a reasonable amount of time (less than seven hours), we opted for a grill-to-oven approach. We started first with the grill. For a fire that would maintain the key amount of indirect heat (roughly 250 to 275 degrees), we turned to a modified two-level fire where the hot coals are arranged over half the grill. In addition, we stowed a pan of water underneath the cooking grate on the cooler side of the grill, where it would absorb heat and work to keep the temperature stable, as well as help keep the meat moister. Then we transferred the ribs to a wire rack set over a rimmed baking sheet and cooked them in a moderate oven until tender and thick-crusted. We even mimicked our grill setup by pouring 1½ cups water into the rimmed baking sheet. In all, we'd shaved more than three hours off of our shortest recipe.

Memphis-Style Barbecued Spareribs

SERVES 4 TO 6

Don't remove the membrane that runs along the bone side of the ribs; it prevents some of the fat from rendering out and is authentic to this style of ribs.

- 1 recipe Spice Rub (recipe follows)
- 2 (2½- to 3-pound) racks St. Louis-style spareribs, trimmed
- ½ cup apple juice
- 3 tablespoons cider vinegar
- 1 (13 by 9-inch) disposable aluminum roasting pan (if using charcoal) or 2 (9-inch) disposable aluminum pie plates (if using gas)
- ¾ cup wood chips, soaked in water for 15 minutes and drained

1. Rub 2 tablespoons Spice Rub on each side of each rack of ribs. Let ribs sit at room temperature while preparing grill.

2. Combine apple juice and vinegar in small bowl and set aside.

3A. FOR A CHARCOAL GRILL: Open bottom vent halfway and evenly space 15 unlit charcoal briquettes on 1 side of grill. Place disposable pan filled with 2 cups water on other side of grill. Light large chimney starter one-third filled with charcoal briquettes (2 quarts). When top coals are partially covered with ash, pour evenly over unlit coals. Sprinkle soaked wood chips over lit coals. Set cooking grate in place, cover, and open lid vent halfway. Heat grill until hot and wood chips are smoking, about 5 minutes.

3B. FOR A GAS GRILL: Place soaked wood chips in pie plate with ¼ cup water and set over primary burner. Place second pie plate filled with 2 cups water on other burner(s). Turn all burners to high, cover, and heat grill until hot and wood chips are smoking, about 15 minutes. Turn primary burner to medium-high and turn off other burner(s). (Adjust primary burner as needed to maintain grill temperature of 250 to 275 degrees.)

4. Clean and oil cooking grate. Place ribs meat side down on cooler side of grill over water-filled pan. Cover (position lid vent over meat if using charcoal) and cook until ribs are deep red and smoky, about 1½ hours, brushing with apple juice mixture and flipping and rotating racks halfway through cooking. About 20 minutes before removing ribs from grill, adjust oven rack to lower-middle position and heat oven to 300 degrees.

5. Set wire rack in rimmed baking sheet and transfer ribs to rack. Brush top of each rack with 2 tablespoons apple juice mixture. Pour 1½ cups water into bottom of sheet; roast for 1 hour. Brush ribs with remaining apple juice mixture and continue to cook until meat is tender and registers 195 degrees, 1 to 2 hours. Transfer ribs to cutting board and let rest for 15 minutes. Slice ribs between bones and serve.

Spice Rub

MAKES ABOUT ½ CUP

For less spiciness, reduce the amount of cayenne to ½ teaspoon.

- 2 tablespoons paprika
- 2 tablespoons packed light brown sugar
- 1 tablespoon salt
- 2 teaspoons chili powder
- 1½ teaspoons pepper
- 1½ teaspoons garlic powder
- 1½ teaspoons onion powder
- 1½ teaspoons cayenne pepper
- ½ teaspoon dried thyme

Combine all ingredients in bowl.

RAINY DAY BARBECUED RIBS

WHY THIS RECIPE WORKS: When the craving for barbecued ribs strikes in the dead of winter, you're out of luck unless you visit the local rib joint. There are recipes for oven barbecuing, but the smoke-flavored sauce they use is no substitute for actual smoke. We wanted the real thing, but prepared indoors.

St. Louis–style ribs, trimmed of skirt meat and excess cartilage, worked best here. We started with a spice rub as we would for grilling, and found that a thin coating of mustard, ketchup, and garlic helped the rub adhere. We tried wood chips in a stovetop smoker, but we had difficulty fitting the ribs in the pan, and it's hard to find wood chips in wintertime—however, the smoke-filled kitchen was the clincher.

We gave up on wood chips and instead borrowed a Chinese cooking method of smoking over tea leaves. Lapsang Souchong tea, which has a smoky flavor and worked perfectly when ground fine. Chilling the ribs first helped prevent toughening in the oven's initial high heat. Apple juice, a common ingredient in barbecue "mops," added moisture and more flavor. And running the ribs under the broiler at the end browned and crisped them. These tender, smoky, and spicy ribs taste amazingly like those barbecued on the grill, but can be made any time of the year.

Oven-Barbecued Spareribs

SERVES 4

To make this recipe, you will need a baking stone. It's fine if the ribs overlap slightly on the wire rack. Removing the surface fat keeps the ribs from being too greasy and removing the membrane from the ribs allows the smoke to penetrate both sides of the racks and also makes the ribs easier to eat. Note that the ribs must be coated with the rub and refrigerated at least 8 hours or up to 24 hours ahead of cooking. Be careful when opening the crimped foil to add the juice, as hot steam and smoke will billow out. Serve ribs with Quick Barbecue Sauce (recipe follows), if desired.

- 6 tablespoons yellow mustard
- 2 tablespoons ketchup
- 3 garlic cloves, minced
- 3 tablespoons packed brown sugar
- 1½ tablespoons kosher salt
- 1 tablespoon sweet paprika
- 1 tablespoon chili powder
- 2 teaspoons pepper
- ½ teaspoon cayenne pepper
- 2 (2½- to 3-pound) racks St. Louis-style spareribs, trimmed, membrane removed, and each rack cut in half
- ¼ cup finely ground Lapsang Souchong tea leaves (from about 10 tea bags, or ½ cup loose tea leaves ground to a powder in a spice grinder)
- ½ cup apple juice

1. Combine mustard, ketchup, and garlic in bowl; combine sugar, salt, paprika, chili powder, pepper, and cayenne in separate bowl. Spread mustard mixture in thin, even layer over both sides of ribs; coat both sides with spice mixture, then wrap ribs in plastic and refrigerate for 8 to 24 hours.

2. Transfer ribs from refrigerator to freezer for 45 minutes. Adjust oven racks to lowest and upper-middle positions (at least 5 inches below broiler). Place baking stone on lower rack; heat oven to 500 degrees. Sprinkle ground tea evenly over bottom of rimmed baking sheet; set wire rack in baking sheet. Place ribs meat side up on rack and cover with heavy-duty aluminum foil, crimping edges tightly to seal. Place baking sheet on stone and roast ribs for 30 minutes, then reduce oven temperature to 250 degrees, leaving oven door open for 1 minute to cool. While oven is open, carefully open 1 corner of foil and pour apple juice into bottom of baking sheet; reseal foil. Continue to roast until meat is very tender and begins to pull away from bones, about 1½ hours. (Begin to check ribs after 1 hour; leave loosely covered with foil for remaining cooking time.)

3. Remove foil and carefully flip racks bone side up; place baking sheet on upper-middle rack. Turn on broiler; cook ribs until well browned and crispy in spots, 5 to 10 minutes. Flip ribs meat side up and cook until second side is well browned and crispy, 5 to 7 minutes more. Cool for at least 10 minutes before cutting into individual ribs. Serve with Quick Barbecue Sauce, if desired.

Quick Barbecue Sauce

MAKES ABOUT 1½ CUPS

Classic barbecue sauce must simmer for a long time for the whole tomatoes in it to break down. However, we found that starting with ketchup can shorten the process.

- 1 medium onion, peeled and quartered
- ¼ cup water
- 1 cup ketchup
- 5 tablespoons molasses
- 2 tablespoons cider vinegar
- 2 tablespoons Worcestershire sauce
- 2 tablespoons Dijon mustard
- 1½ teaspoons liquid smoke (optional)
- 1 teaspoon hot sauce
- ¼ teaspoon pepper
- 2 tablespoons vegetable oil
- 1 garlic clove, minced
- 1 teaspoon chili powder
- ¼ teaspoon cayenne pepper

1. Process onion and water in a food processor until pureed and mixture resembles slush, about 30 seconds. Strain mixture through fine mesh strainer into liquid measuring cup, pressing on solids with rubber spatula to obtain ½ cup juice. Discard solids.

2. Whisk onion juice, ketchup, molasses, vinegar, Worcestershire sauce, mustard, liquid smoke (if using), hot sauce, and pepper together in medium bowl.

3. Heat oil in large saucepan over medium heat until shimmering but not smoking. Add garlic, chili powder, and cayenne and cook until fragrant, about 30 seconds. Whisk in ketchup mixture and bring to a boil; reduce heat to medium-low and simmer gently, uncovered, until flavors meld and sauce is thickened, about 25 minutes. Cool sauce to room temperature before using. (Sauce can be refrigerated for up to 1 week.)

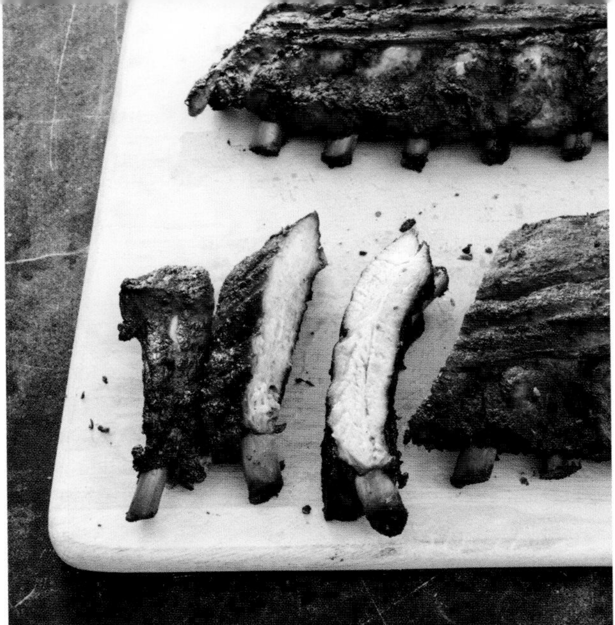

BARBECUED BABY BACK RIBS

WHY THIS RECIPE WORKS: Dry, flavorless ribs are a true culinary disaster. More often than not, baby back ribs cooked at home come out tasting like dry shoe leather on a bone. We wanted ribs that were juicy, tender, and fully seasoned, with an intense smokiness, ribs that would be well worth the time, money, and effort.

Meaty ribs—racks as close to 2 pounds as possible—provided substantial, satisfying portions. For ribs that were so good and moist they didn't even need barbecue sauce, they needed to be brined first—we used a salt, sugar, and water solution—then rubbed with a spice mix before barbecuing. Chili powder, cayenne pepper, cumin, and dark brown sugar formed a nice, crisp crust on the ribs and provided the best balance of sweet and spicy. For even more flavor, we placed wood chips or chunks on top of the coals before barbecuing and used the "low and slow" cooking method: Barbecue the ribs for a few hours on the cool side of the grill, then add fresh briquettes to the coals and continue to cook for another hour or two. This extended amount of time on the grill made for tender baby back ribs with an intensely smoky flavor.

Barbecued Baby Back Ribs

SERVES 4

For a more potent spice flavor, coat the ribs with the spice rub as directed and refrigerate them overnight, wrapped tightly in plastic wrap, If you'd like to use wood chinks rather than wood chips when using a charcoal grill, substitute 2 medium wood chunks, soaked in water for 1 hour, for the wood chip packet.

Salt and pepper
½ cup granulated sugar
2 (2-pound) racks baby back or loin back ribs, trimmed, membrane removed
1 tablespoon plus ½ teaspoon paprika
1¾ teaspoons ground cumin
1½ teaspoons chili powder
1½ teaspoons packed dark brown sugar
1 teaspoon white pepper
¾ teaspoon dried oregano
½ teaspoon cayenne pepper
2 cups wood chips, soaked in water for 15 minutes and drained

1. Dissolve ½ cup salt and granulated sugar in 4 quarts cold water in a large bowl or container. Submerge ribs in brine, cover, and refrigerate for 1 hour. Remove ribs from brine and pat dry with paper towels.

2. Combine paprika, cumin, chili powder, brown sugar, white pepper, ¾ teaspoon salt, ¾ teaspoon pepper, oregano, and cayenne in a small bowl. Rub each rack with 1 tablespoon of spice rub and refrigerate for 30 minutes. Using large piece of heavy-duty aluminum foil, wrap soaked chips in foil packet and cut several vent holes in top.

3A. FOR A CHARCOAL GRILL: Open bottom vent halfway. Light large chimney starter three-quarters filled with charcoal briquettes (4½ quarts). When top coals are partially covered with ash, pour evenly over half of grill. Place wood chip packet on coals. Set cooking grate in place, cover, and open lid vent halfway. Heat grill until hot, about 5 minutes.

3B. FOR A GAS GRILL: Place wood chip packet over primary burner. Turn all burners to high, cover, and heat grill until hot and wood chips are smoking, about 15 minutes. Leave primary burner on high and turn off other burner(s).

4. Clean and oil cooking grate. Place ribs on cooler side of grill and cook for 2 hours, covered, until grill temperature drops to about 250 degrees, flipping, switching, and rotating ribs every 30 minutes so that rack that was nearest fire is on outside. Add 10 fresh briquettes to pile of coals (if using charcoal). Cover and continue to cook (grill temperature should register 275 to 300 degrees on grill thermometer), flipping, switching, and rotating ribs every 30 minutes, until meat easily pulls away from bone, 1½ to 2 hours longer. Transfer ribs to cutting board, cut between bones to separate ribs, and serve.

GRILLED GLAZED BABY BACK RIBS

WHY THIS RECIPE WORKS: Instead of spending hours tending a grill for flavorful, tender ribs, we started ours on the stovetop, then moved them outside. Boiling is an established rib-cooking shortcut, but we found this led to unevenly cooked ribs, so we turned down the heat and simmered them; the gentler heat kept the thinner ends from overcooking and becoming dry. Salting the water prevented them from losing too much of their pork flavor to the cooking liquid. Once they reached 195 degrees, we removed our ribs from the pot, applied a flavorful glaze, and tossed them on the grill, for tender-chewy ribs that were ready in a fraction of the time.

Grilled Glazed Baby Back Ribs

SERVES 4 TO 6

Try one of the glaze recipes that follow, or use 1 cup of your favorite glaze or barbecue sauce.

- 2 tablespoons salt
- 2 (2-pound) racks baby back or loin back ribs, trimmed, membrane removed, and each rack cut in half
- 1 recipe glaze (recipes follow)

1. Dissolve salt in 2½ quarts water in Dutch oven; place ribs in pot so they are fully submerged. Bring to simmer over high heat. Reduce heat to low, cover, and cook at bare simmer until thickest part of ribs registers 195 degrees, 15 to 25 minutes. While ribs are simmering, set up grill. (If ribs come to temperature before grill is ready, leave in pot, covered, until ready to use.)

2A. FOR A CHARCOAL GRILL: Open bottom vent halfway. Light large chimney starter filled with charcoal briquettes (6 quarts). When top coals are partially covered with ash, pour evenly over grill. Set cooking grate in place, cover, and open lid vent halfway. Heat grill until hot, about 5 minutes.

2B. FOR A GAS GRILL: Turn all burners to high, cover, and heat grill until hot, about 15 minutes. Turn all burners to medium-high.

3. Clean and oil cooking grate. Remove ribs from pot and pat dry with paper towels. Brush both sides of ribs with ⅓ cup glaze. Grill ribs, uncovered, flipping and rotating as needed, until glaze is caramelized and charred in spots, 15 to 20 minutes, brushing with another ⅓ cup glaze halfway through cooking. Transfer ribs to cutting board, brush both sides with remaining glaze, tent loosely with aluminum foil, and let rest for 10 minutes. Cut ribs between bones to separate, and serve.

Hoisin-Coconut Glaze

MAKES ABOUT 1 CUP

- ⅔ cup hoisin sauce
- ⅓ cup canned coconut milk
- 3 tablespoons rice vinegar
- ¾ teaspoon pepper

Whisk all ingredients together in bowl.

Lime Glaze

MAKES ABOUT 1 CUP

- ⅔ cup lime juice (6 limes)
- ⅓ cup ketchup
- ¼ cup packed brown sugar
- 1 teaspoon salt

Whisk all ingredients together in bowl.

Spicy Marmalade Glaze

MAKES ABOUT 1 CUP

- ⅔ cup orange marmalade
- ⅓ cup cider vinegar
- 2 tablespoons hot sauce
- ¾ teaspoon salt

Whisk all ingredients together in bowl.

TEXAS BEEF RIBS

WHY THIS RECIPE WORKS: In Texas, good beef ribs are all about intense meat flavor—not just smoke and spice. The barbecue chefs we've met get this flavor just right, thanks to the assistance of massive electric smokers with automated temperature controls. But can a backyard cook replicate this Lone Star classic without the help of special equipment? We were looking for a recipe that would yield potent meat flavor with a bit of honest Texas chew—on our conventional-size grill.

We began by debating whether to trim the fatty membrane that runs along the back side of the ribs. Surprisingly, the juiciest meat with the most flavor was accomplished by the path of least resistance: simply leaving the membrane in place. The fat not only basted the ribs as they cooked but also rendered to a crisp, bacon-like texture. A simple mixture of salt, pepper, cayenne, brown sugar, and chili powder rubbed into each rack was all that it took to bring out the flavor of the meat. To turn our grill into a backyard smoker, we made a slow, even fire with a single pile of coals on one side of the grill and kept the temperature in the range of 250 to 300 degrees. About an hour and a half of slow cooking was enough to render some of the fat and make the ribs juicy, tender, and slightly toothy. When cooked any longer, as is the case with pork ribs, the meat disintegrated into messy shreds, taking on a sticky, pot-roasted sort of texture that any real Texan would immediately reject.

For real Texas-style barbecue sauce to pair with our ribs, we pulled together the usual ingredients—vinegar, onion, and molasses, to name a few—with dry mustard and chili powder for bite. Savory Worcestershire sauce added depth while tomato juice (in place of ketchup) provided tangy flavor and helped thin the sauce out.

Texas-Style Barbecued Beef Ribs

SERVES 4

Beef ribs are sold in slabs with up to seven bones, but slabs with three to four bones are easier to manage on the grill. If you cannot find ribs with a substantial amount of meat on the bones, don't bother making this recipe. One medium wood chunk, soaked in water for one hour, can be substituted for the wood chips on a charcoal grill.

TEXAS BARBECUE SAUCE

- 2 tablespoons unsalted butter
- ½ small onion, chopped fine
- 2 garlic cloves, minced
- 1½ teaspoons chili powder
- 1½ teaspoons pepper
- ½ teaspoon dry mustard
- 2 cups tomato juice
- 6 tablespoons distilled white vinegar
- 2 tablespoons Worcestershire sauce
- 2 tablespoons packed brown sugar
- 2 tablespoons molasses
- Salt

RIBS

- 3 tablespoons packed brown sugar
- 4 teaspoons chili powder
- 1 tablespoon salt
- 2 teaspoons pepper
- ½ teaspoon cayenne pepper
- 3–4 beef rib slabs (3 to 4 ribs per slab, about 5 pounds total), trimmed
- 1 cup wood chips, soaked in water for 15 minutes and drained

1. FOR THE SAUCE: Melt butter in medium saucepan over medium heat. Add onion and cook until softened, about 5 minutes. Stir in garlic, chili powder, pepper, and dry mustard and cook until fragrant, about 30 seconds. Stir in tomato juice, vinegar, Worcestershire, sugar, and molasses and simmer until sauce is reduced to 2 cups, about 20 minutes. Season with salt to taste. (Sauce can be refrigerated in airtight container for 1 week.)

2. FOR THE RIBS: Combine sugar, chili powder, salt, pepper, and cayenne in bowl. Pat ribs dry with paper towels and rub them evenly with spice mixture. Cover ribs with plastic wrap and let sit at room temperature for 1 hour.

3. Adjust oven rack to middle position and heat oven to 300 degrees. Set wire rack set in rimmed baking sheet and add just enough water to cover pan bottom. Arrange ribs on rack and cover tightly with aluminum foil. Bake until fat has rendered and meat begins to pull away from bones, about 2 hours. Using large piece of heavy-duty foil, wrap soaked chips in foil packet and cut several vent holes in top.

4A. FOR A CHARCOAL GRILL: Open bottom vent halfway. Light large chimney starter filled with charcoal briquettes (6 quarts). When top coals are partially covered with ash, pour into steeply banked pile against 1 side of grill. Place wood chip packet on coals. Set cooking grate in place, cover, and open lid vent halfway. Heat grill until hot and wood chips are smoking, about 5 minutes.

4B. FOR A GAS GRILL: Place wood chip packet directly on primary burner. Turn all burners to high, cover, and heat grill until hot and wood chips are smoking, about 15 minutes. Leave primary burner on high and turn other burner(s) off. (Adjust primary burner as needed to maintain grill temperature between 250 and 300 degrees.)

5. Clean and oil cooking grate. Place ribs meat side down on cool side of grill; ribs may overlap slightly. Cover (positioning lid vent over meat if using charcoal) and cook until ribs are lightly charred and smoky, about 1½ hours, flipping and rotating racks halfway through grilling. Transfer to cutting board, tent with foil, and let rest for 10 minutes. Serve with barbecue sauce.

GRILLED BEEF KEBABS

WHY THIS RECIPE WORKS: Most beef kebabs are disappointing, with overcooked meat and vegetables that are raw or mushy. We wanted to develop a foolproof approach to creating meaty kebabs that looked and tasted like the real thing: chunks of beef with a caramelized char on the outside and a juicy interior, all thoroughly seasoned by a marinade and paired with tender-firm vegetables. For the meat, we chose well-marbled steak tips for their beefy flavor and tender texture. For the marinade, we included salt for moisture, oil for flavor, and sugar for browning. For even more depth, we used tomato paste, a host of seasonings and herbs, and beef broth. We settled on three grill favorites for the vegetables: peppers, onions, and zucchini. Grilling the beef kebabs and vegetables on separate skewers and building a fire that has hotter and cooler areas allowed us to cook the vegetables over a lower temperature while the beef seared over the hotter area.

Grilled Beef Kebabs with Lemon and Rosemary Marinade

SERVES 4 TO 6

If you can't find sirloin steak tips, sometimes labeled "flap meat," substitute 2½ pounds of blade steak; if you use blade steak, cut each steak in half to remove the gristle. You will need four 12-inch metal skewers for this recipe. If you have long, thin pieces of meat, roll or fold them into approximate 2-inch cubes before skewering.

MARINADE

- 1 onion, chopped
- ⅓ cup beef broth
- ⅓ cup vegetable oil
- 3 tablespoons tomato paste
- 6 garlic cloves, chopped
- 2 tablespoons chopped fresh rosemary
- 2 teaspoons grated lemon zest
- 2 teaspoons salt
- 1½ teaspoons sugar
- ¾ teaspoon pepper

BEEF AND VEGETABLES

- 2 pounds sirloin steak tips, trimmed and cut into 2-inch chunks
- 1 large zucchini or summer squash, halved lengthwise and sliced 1 inch thick
- 1 large red or green bell pepper, stemmed, seeded, and cut into 1½-inch pieces
- 1 large red or sweet onion, halved lengthwise, each half cut into 4 wedges and each wedge cut crosswise into thirds

1. FOR THE MARINADE: Process all ingredients in blender until smooth, about 45 seconds. Transfer ¾ cup marinade to large bowl and set aside.

2. FOR THE BEEF AND VEGETABLES: Place remaining marinade and beef in 1-gallon zipper-lock bag and toss to coat; press out as much air as possible and seal bag. Refrigerate for at least 1 to 2 hours, flipping bag every 30 minutes.

3. Add zucchini, bell pepper, and onion to bowl with reserved marinade and toss to coat. Cover and let sit at room temperature for at least 30 minutes.

4. Remove beef from bag and pat dry with paper towels. Thread beef tightly onto two 12-inch metal skewers. Alternating pattern of zucchini, bell pepper, and onion, thread vegetables onto two 12-inch metal skewers.

5A. FOR A CHARCOAL GRILL: Open bottom vent completely. Light large chimney starter mounded with charcoal briquettes (7 quarts). When top coals are partially covered with ash, pour evenly over center of grill, leaving 2-inch gap between grill wall and charcoal. Set cooking grate in place, cover, and open lid vent completely. Heat grill until hot, about 5 minutes.

5B. FOR A GAS GRILL: Turn all burners to high, cover, and heat grill until hot, about 15 minutes. Leave primary burner on high and turn other burner(s) to medium-low.

6. Clean and oil cooking grate. Place beef skewers on grill (directly over coals if using charcoal or over hotter side of grill if using gas). Place vegetable skewers on grill (near edge of coals but still over coals if using charcoal or over cooler side of grill if using gas). Cook (covered if using gas), turning skewers every 3 to 4 minutes, until beef is well browned and registers 120 to 125 degrees (for medium-rare) or 130 to 135 degrees (for medium), 12 to 16 minutes. Transfer beef skewers to platter and tent loosely with aluminum foil. Continue to cook vegetable skewers until tender and lightly charred, about 5 minutes; serve with beef skewers.

GRILLED SHISH KEBABS

WHY THIS RECIPE WORKS: Kebabs, for all their popularity and convenience, are usually over- or undercooked, with vegetables and meat that are either burnt or raw and falling off the skewer. But kebabs are so simple, they should be a go-to grilling recipe for most home cooks; they're easy to put together and take little time on the grill, thanks to the vegetables and meat already being in bite-size pieces. We decided to revisit the kebab. So we grabbed some metal skewers and headed to the grill in search of perfectly cooked lamb and crisp, slightly charred vegetables.

To avoid the raw lamb and burnt vegetables that cooking on skewers often delivers, we cut the meat (boneless leg of lamb, trimmed of fat and silver skin) into 1-inch cubes and narrowed the vegetable field. Onions and peppers were the vegetable combination most preferred by tasters; they aren't incredibly watery like tomatoes, which were out from the beginning, and they cooked at the same rate as the meat. Marinating the meat for 2 hours added extra flavor; for the marinades, we used fruity, sweet, and spicy ingredients that stood up well to the hearty lamb.

Grilled Lamb Kebabs

SERVES 6

You can use red, yellow, orange, or green bell peppers in this recipe. You will need four 12-inch metal skewers for this recipe. If you have long, thin pieces of meat, roll or fold them into approximate 1-inch cubes before skewering.

- 1 recipe marinade (recipes follow)
- 1 (2¼-pound) shank end boneless leg of lamb, trimmed and cut into 1-inch chunks
- 1 large bell pepper, stemmed, seeded, and cut into 1-inch pieces
- 1 large red or sweet onion, peeled, halved lengthwise, each half cut into 4 wedges and each wedge cut crosswise into thirds
- Lemon or lime wedges (optional)

1. Place marinade and lamb in 1-gallon zipper-lock bag and toss to coat; press out as much air as possible and seal bag. Refrigerate for at least 2 hours or up to 24 hours, flipping bag every hour.

2. Remove lamb from bag and pat dry with paper towels. Starting and ending with meat, thread 4 pieces of meat, 3 pieces of onion (three 3-layer stacks), and 6 pieces of pepper in mixed order on four 12-inch metal skewers.

3A. FOR A CHARCOAL GRILL: Open bottom vent completely. Light large chimney starter mounded with charcoal briquettes (7 quarts). When top coals are partially covered with ash, pour evenly over grill. Set cooking grate in place, cover, and open lid vent completely. Heat grill until hot, about 5 minutes.

3B. FOR A GAS GRILL: Turn all burners to high, cover, and heat grill until hot, about 15 minutes.

4. Clean and oil cooking grate. Place skewers on grill and cook (covered if using gas), turning skewers every 3 to 4 minutes, until well browned and lamb registers 120 to 125 degrees (for medium-rare) or 130 to 135 degrees (for medium), 7 to 12 minutes.

5. Transfer skewers to serving platter, tent loosely with aluminum foil, and let rest for 5 to 10 minutes before serving with lemon wedges, if using.

Warm-Spiced Parsley Marinade with Ginger

MAKES ABOUT 1 CUP

- ½ cup olive oil
- ½ cup packed fresh parsley leaves
- 1 jalapeño chile, stemmed, seeded, and chopped coarse
- 2 tablespoons grated fresh ginger
- 3 garlic cloves, peeled
- 1 teaspoon ground cumin
- 1 teaspoon ground cardamom
- 1 teaspoon ground cinnamon
- 1 teaspoon salt
- ⅛ teaspoon pepper

Process all ingredients in food processor until smooth, about 1 minute.

Garlic and Cilantro Marinade with Garam Masala

MAKES ABOUT ¾ CUP

- ½ cup olive oil
- ½ cup fresh cilantro
- ¼ cup raisins
- 1½ tablespoons lemon juice
- 3 garlic cloves, peeled
- 1 teaspoon salt
- ½ teaspoon garam masala
- ⅛ teaspoon pepper

Process all ingredients in food processor until smooth, about 1 minute.

Sweet Curry Marinade with Buttermilk

MAKES ABOUT 1 CUP

- ¾ cup buttermilk
- 1 tablespoon lemon juice
- 3 garlic cloves, minced
- 1 tablespoon packed brown sugar
- 1 tablespoon curry powder
- 1 teaspoon red pepper flakes
- 1 teaspoon ground coriander
- 1 teaspoon chili powder
- 1 teaspoon salt
- ⅛ teaspoon pepper

Combine all ingredients in 1-gallon zipper-lock bag in which meat will marinate.

GRILLED BEEF SATAY

WHY THIS RECIPE WORKS: In the hands of American cooks, satay often comes out thick and chewy or overly marinated and mealy. To return this dish to its streetwise roots, we sliced beefy-flavored flank steak thin across the grain and threaded it onto skewers. To add flavor, we used an aromatic basting sauce consisting of authentic Thai ingredients, rather than the over tenderizing marinade used in many recipes. And to ensure that the quick-cooking beef achieved a burnished exterior, we corralled the coals in an aluminum pan in the center of the grill to bring them closer to the meat.

Grilled Beef Satay

SERVES 6

You will need ten to twelve 12-inch metal skewers for this recipe. Bamboo skewers soaked in water for 30 minutes can be substituted for metal skewers. The aluminum pan used for charcoal grilling should be at least 2¾ inches deep; you will not need the pan for a gas grill. Kitchen shears work well for punching the holes in the pan. Unless you have a very high-powered gas grill, these skewers will not be as well seared as they would be with charcoal. Serve with Peanut Sauce (recipe follows). To make it a meal, serve this dish with steamed white rice.

BASTING SAUCE

- ¾ cup regular or light coconut milk
- 3 tablespoons packed dark brown sugar
- 3 tablespoons fish sauce
- 2 tablespoons vegetable oil
- 3 shallots, minced
- 2 lemon grass stalks, trimmed to bottom 6 inches and minced
- 2 tablespoons grated fresh ginger
- 1½ teaspoons ground coriander
- ¾ teaspoon red pepper flakes
- ½ teaspoon ground cumin
- ½ teaspoon salt

BEEF

- 2 tablespoons vegetable oil
- 2 tablespoons packed dark brown sugar
- 1 tablespoon fish sauce
- 1 (1½- to 1¾-pound) flank steak, halved lengthwise and sliced on slight angle against grain into ¼-inch-thick slices
- Disposable aluminum deep roasting pan (if using charcoal)

1. FOR THE BASTING SAUCE: Whisk all ingredients together in bowl. Reserve one-third of sauce in separate bowl.

2. FOR THE BEEF: Whisk oil, sugar, and fish sauce together in medium bowl. Toss beef with marinade and let stand at room temperature for 30 minutes. Weave beef onto 12-inch metal skewers, 2 to 4 pieces per skewer, leaving 1½ inches at top and bottom of skewer exposed. You should have 10 to 12 skewers.

3A. FOR A CHARCOAL GRILL: Punch twelve ½-inch holes in bottom of disposable roasting pan. Open bottom vent completely and place roasting pan in center of grill. Light large chimney starter mounded with charcoal briquettes (7 quarts). When top coals are partially covered with ash, pour into roasting pan. Set cooking grate over coals with grates parallel to long side of roasting pan, cover, and open lid vent completely. Heat grill until hot, about 5 minutes.

3B. FOR A GAS GRILL: Turn all burners to high, cover, and heat grill until hot, about 15 minutes. Leave all burners on high.

4. Clean and oil cooking grate. Place beef skewers on grill (directly over coals if using charcoal) perpendicular to grate. Brush meat with reserved one-third of basting sauce and cook (covered if using gas) until browned, about 3 minutes. Flip skewers, brush with half of remaining basting sauce, and cook until browned on second side, about 3 minutes. Brush meat with remaining basting sauce and cook 1 minute longer. Transfer to large platter and serve with Peanut Sauce.

Peanut Sauce

MAKES ABOUT 1½ CUPS

- 1 tablespoon vegetable oil
- 1 tablespoon Thai red curry paste
- 1 tablespoon packed dark brown sugar
- 2 garlic cloves, minced
- 1 cup regular or light coconut milk
- ⅓ cup chunky peanut butter
- ¼ cup dry-roasted unsalted peanuts, chopped
- 1 tablespoon lime juice
- 1 tablespoon fish sauce
- 1 teaspoon soy sauce

Heat oil in small saucepan over medium heat until shimmering. Add curry paste, sugar, and garlic; cook, stirring constantly, until fragrant, about 1 minute. Add coconut milk and bring to simmer. Whisk in peanut butter until smooth. Remove from heat and stir in peanuts, lime juice, fish sauce, and soy sauce. Cool to room temperature.

GRILLED LAMB KOFTE

WHY THIS RECIPE WORKS: In the Middle East, kebabs called *kofte* feature ground meat, not chunks, mixed with lots of spices and fresh herbs. For ours, we started with preground lamb for convenience. Kneading the meat ensured the kofte had a sausage-like spring. To help keep the meat firm, we added a small amount of gelatin and then refrigerated it. Ground pine nuts ensured a perfect texture and prevented toughness, plus they gave the kofte a noticeably richer flavor. Hot smoked paprika, cumin, and cloves contributed warm spice notes, while parsley and mint offered bright, grassy flavors. Adding a little tahini to the tangy garlic and yogurt serving sauce gave it more complexity.

Grilled Lamb Kofte

SERVES 4 TO 6

You will need 8 (12-inch) metal skewers for this recipe. Serve with rice pilaf or make sandwiches with warm pita bread, sliced red onion, and chopped fresh mint.

YOGURT-GARLIC SAUCE

- 1 cup plain whole-milk yogurt
- 2 tablespoons lemon juice
- 2 tablespoons tahini
- 1 garlic clove, minced
- ½ teaspoon salt

KOFTE

- ½ cup pine nuts
- 4 garlic cloves, peeled
- 1½ teaspoons hot smoked paprika
- 1 teaspoon salt
- 1 teaspoon ground cumin
- ½ teaspoon pepper
- ¼ teaspoon ground coriander
- ¼ teaspoon ground cloves
- ⅛ teaspoon ground nutmeg
- ⅛ teaspoon ground cinnamon
- 1½ pounds ground lamb
- ½ cup grated onion, drained
- ⅓ cup minced fresh parsley
- ⅓ cup minced fresh mint
- 1½ teaspoons unflavored gelatin
- 1 large disposable aluminum roasting pan (if using charcoal)

1. FOR THE YOGURT-GARLIC SAUCE: Whisk all ingredients together in bowl. Set aside.

2. FOR THE KOFTE: Process pine nuts, garlic, paprika, salt, cumin, pepper, coriander, cloves, nutmeg, and cinnamon in food processor until coarse paste forms, 30 to 45 seconds. Transfer mixture to large bowl. Add lamb, onion, parsley, mint, and gelatin; knead with your hands until thoroughly combined and mixture feels slightly sticky, about 2 minutes. Divide mixture into 8 equal portions. Shape each portion into 5-inch-long cylinder about 1 inch in diameter. Using 8 (12-inch) metal skewers, thread 1 cylinder onto each skewer, pressing gently to adhere. Transfer skewers to lightly greased baking sheet, cover with plastic wrap, and refrigerate for at least 1 hour or up to 24 hours.

3A. FOR A CHARCOAL GRILL: Using skewer, poke 12 holes in bottom of disposable pan. Open bottom vent completely and place pan in center of grill. Light large chimney starter filled two-thirds with charcoal briquettes (4 quarts). When top coals are partially covered with ash, pour into pan. Set cooking grate in place, cover, and open lid vent completely. Heat grill until hot, about 5 minutes.

3B. FOR A GAS GRILL: Turn all burners to high, cover, and heat grill until hot, about 15 minutes. Leave all burners on high.

4. Clean and oil cooking grate. Place skewers on grill (directly over coals if using charcoal) at 45-degree angle to grate. Cook (covered if using gas) until browned and meat easily releases from grill, 4 to 7 minutes. Flip skewers and continue to cook until browned on second side and meat registers 160 degrees, about 6 minutes longer. Transfer skewers to platter and serve, passing yogurt-garlic sauce separately.

Grilled Beef Kofte

Substitute 80 percent lean ground beef for lamb. Increase garlic to 5 cloves, paprika to 2 teaspoons, and cumin to 2 teaspoons.

GRILLED RACK OF LAMB

WHY THIS RECIPE WORKS: With its juicy, pink meat, rich crust, and classic stand-up-straight presentation, rack of lamb is a bona fide showstopper—and it has the price tag to prove it. But grill this piece of meat improperly and you've made a very costly mistake. That's why we wanted to come up with a foolproof technique for grilling rack of lamb—one that would deliver a great crust and flavorful, tender meat, every time.

Our first challenge was choosing just the right cut. While the racks from butcher shops and high-end specialty stores cost more than those from the supermarket, they come already trimmed. And once we trimmed all the excess fat from our supermarket samples, we found this meat wasn't actually much cheaper. However, even the trimmed lamb needed additional butchering, both to remove the "cap" of fat that creates meat-scorching flare-ups and to trim away any excess meat and fat. (For perfect grilling results, we needed fairly lean racks of uniform thickness.)

To cook the lamb evenly as well as to effectively render its fat, we placed a disposable aluminum pan in the middle of the grill and heaped a small pile of coals on either side of the pan. Placing the lamb in the middle of the grill, over the pan, ensured the pan would catch the rendering fat, preventing flare-ups. A wet rub (garlic, rosemary, thyme, and olive oil) was the best way to flavor the meat—marinades turned the lamb mushy and dry rubs simply didn't work with our grilling method. For a rich crust that wasn't charred, we applied the wet rub during the last few minutes of grilling, keeping the surface crisp.

Grilled Rack of Lamb

SERVES 4 TO 6

We prefer the milder taste and bigger size of domestic lamb, but you may substitute lamb from New Zealand or Australia. Since imported racks are generally smaller, follow the shorter cooking times given in the recipe. While most lamb is sold frenched (meaning part of each rib bone is exposed), chances are there will still be some extra fat between the bones. Remove the majority of this fat, leaving an inch at the top of the small eye of meat. Also, make sure that the chine bone (along the bottom of the rack) has been removed to ensure that it will be easy to cut between the ribs after cooking. Ask the butcher to do it; it's very hard to cut off at home.

- 1 (13 by 9-inch) disposable aluminum pan (if using charcoal)
- 4 teaspoons olive oil
- 4 teaspoons chopped fresh rosemary
- 2 teaspoons chopped fresh thyme
- 2 garlic cloves, minced
- 2 (1½- to 1¾-pound) racks of lamb (8 ribs each), frenched and trimmed
- Salt and pepper

1A. FOR A CHARCOAL GRILL: Open bottom vent completely and place pan in center of grill. Light large chimney starter filled with charcoal briquettes (6 quarts). When top coals are partially covered with ash, pour into two even piles on either side of pan. Set cooking grate in place, cover, and open lid vent completely. Heat grill until hot, about 5 minutes.

1B. FOR A GAS GRILL: Turn all burners to high, cover, and heat grill until hot, about 15 minutes. Leave primary burner on high, turning off other burners.

2. Combine 1 tablespoon oil, rosemary, thyme, and garlic in bowl. Pat lamb dry with paper towels, rub with remaining teaspoon oil, and season with salt and pepper. Place racks bone side up on cooler part of grill with meaty side of racks very close to, but not quite over, hot coals or lit burner. Cover and cook until meat is lightly browned, faint grill marks appear, and fat has begun to render, 8 to 10 minutes.

3. Flip racks over, bone side down, and move to hotter parts of grill. Cook until well browned, 3 to 4 minutes. Brush racks with herb mixture. Flip racks bone side up and continue to cook until well browned, 3 to 4 minutes longer. Stand racks up and lean them against each other; continue to cook (over hotter side of grill if using charcoal) until bottom is well browned and meat registers 120 to 125 degrees (for medium-rare) or 130 to 135 degrees (for medium), 3 to 8 minutes longer.

4. Transfer lamb to carving board, tent loosely with aluminum foil, and let rest for 15 minutes. Cut between ribs to separate chops and serve.

NOTES FROM THE TEST KITCHEN

TRIMMING FAT FROM RACK OF LAMB

Use a boning or paring knife to cut away any thick portions of fat until a thin layer remains.

CHAPTER 18

LET'S GET GRILLING: POULTRY, SEAFOOD, AND VEGETABLES

GRILLED GLAZED CHICKEN BREASTS

WHY THIS RECIPE WORKS: Grilled glazed boneless chicken breasts are a quick and easy summer dinner, but too often the glaze burns or the chicken overcooks. To produce perfectly cooked chicken, we briefly brined the meat to keep it moist during cooking, and used a two-level grill fire to prevent the glaze from singeing. Lightly coating the chicken with milk powder hastened browning during the quick cooking time. We developed a variety of sweet-savory glazes that complemented but didn't overpower the chicken. A small amount of corn syrup provided a mild sweetness and just enough viscosity to help the glaze cling to the meat.

Grilled Glazed Boneless, Skinless Chicken Breasts

SERVES 4

- ¼ cup salt
- ¼ cup sugar
- 4 (6- to 8-ounce) boneless, skinless chicken breasts, trimmed
- 2 teaspoons nonfat dry milk powder
- ¼ teaspoon pepper
- Vegetable oil spray
- 1 recipe glaze (recipes follow)

1. Dissolve salt and sugar in 1½ quarts cold water. Submerge chicken in brine, cover, and refrigerate for at least 30 minutes or up to 1 hour. Remove chicken from brine and pat dry with paper towels. Combine milk powder and pepper in bowl.

2A. FOR A CHARCOAL GRILL: Open bottom vent completely. Light large chimney starter mounded with charcoal briquettes (7 quarts). When top coals are partially covered with ash, pour two-thirds evenly over half of grill, then pour remaining coals over other half of grill. Set cooking grate in place, cover, and open lid vent completely. Heat grill until hot, about 5 minutes.

2B. FOR A GAS GRILL: Turn all burners to high, cover, and heat grill until hot, about 15 minutes. Leave primary burner on high and turn other burner(s) to medium-high.

3. Clean and oil cooking grate. Sprinkle half of milk powder mixture over 1 side of chicken. Lightly spray coated side of chicken with oil spray until milk powder is moistened. Flip chicken and sprinkle remaining milk powder mixture over second side. Lightly spray with oil spray.

4. Place chicken, skinned side down, on hotter side of grill and cook until browned on first side, 2 to 2½ minutes. Flip chicken, brush with 2 tablespoons glaze, and cook until browned on second side, 2 to 2½ minutes. Flip chicken, move to cooler side of grill, brush with 2 tablespoons glaze, and cook for 2 minutes. Repeat flipping and brushing 2 more times, cooking for 2 minutes on each side. Flip chicken, brush with remaining glaze, and cook until chicken registers 160 degrees, 1 to 3 minutes. Transfer chicken to plate and let rest for 5 minutes before serving.

Spicy Hoisin Glaze

MAKES ABOUT ⅔ CUP

For a spicier glaze use the larger amount of Sriracha.

- 2 tablespoons rice vinegar
- 1 teaspoon cornstarch
- ⅓ cup hoisin sauce
- 2 tablespoons light corn syrup
- 1–2 tablespoons Sriracha sauce
- 1 teaspoon grated fresh ginger
- ¼ teaspoon five-spice powder

Whisk vinegar and cornstarch together in small saucepan until cornstarch has dissolved. Whisk in hoisin, corn syrup, Sriracha, ginger, and five-spice powder. Bring mixture to boil over high heat. Cook, stirring constantly, until thickened, about 1 minute. Transfer glaze to bowl.

Honey-Mustard Glaze

MAKES ABOUT ⅔ CUP

- 2 tablespoons cider vinegar
- 1 teaspoon cornstarch
- 3 tablespoons Dijon mustard
- 3 tablespoons honey
- 2 tablespoons corn syrup
- 1 garlic clove, minced
- ¼ teaspoon ground fennel seeds

Whisk vinegar and cornstarch together in small saucepan until cornstarch has dissolved. Whisk in mustard, honey, corn syrup, garlic, and fennel seeds. Bring mixture to boil over high heat. Cook, stirring constantly, until thickened, about 1 minute. Transfer glaze to bowl.

Coconut-Curry Glaze

MAKES ABOUT ⅔ CUP

- 2 tablespoons lime juice
- 1½ teaspoons cornstarch
- ⅓ cup canned coconut milk
- 3 tablespoons corn syrup
- 1 tablespoon fish sauce
- 1 tablespoon red curry paste
- 1 teaspoon grated fresh ginger
- ¼ teaspoon ground coriander

Whisk lime juice and cornstarch together in small saucepan until cornstarch has dissolved. Whisk in coconut milk, corn syrup, fish sauce, curry paste, ginger, and coriander. Bring mixture to boil over high heat. Cook, stirring constantly, until thickened, about 1 minute. Transfer glaze to bowl.

Miso-Sesame Glaze

MAKES ABOUT ⅔ CUP

- 3 tablespoons rice vinegar
- 1 teaspoon cornstarch
- 3 tablespoons white miso paste
- 2 tablespoons corn syrup
- 1 tablespoon sesame oil
- 2 teaspoons ginger
- ¼ teaspoon ground coriander

Whisk vinegar and cornstarch together in small saucepan until cornstarch has dissolved. Whisk in miso, corn syrup, sesame oil, ginger, and coriander. Bring mixture to boil over high heat. Cook, stirring constantly, until thickened, about 1 minute. Transfer glaze to bowl.

GRILLED BONE-IN CHICKEN BREASTS

WHY THIS RECIPE WORKS: We wanted glazed chicken breasts with tender meat and crisp, lacquered skin. Brining the bone-in chicken breasts before grilling helped ensure juicy, seasoned meat. For the glazes, we balanced sweet ingredients, like molasses and sugar, with bold flavors, like chipotle chiles, ginger, and curry powder. To keep the glazes from burning on the grill, we first seared the breasts over high heat, then moved them to the cool side of the grill, where we brushed them with the glaze in the last few minutes. For extra flavor, we reserved half of the glaze for serving.

Grilled Glazed Bone-In Chicken Breasts

SERVES 4

If using kosher chicken, do not brine in step 1, and season with salt as well as pepper. Remember to reserve half of the glaze for serving.

- ½ cup salt
- 4 (10- to 12-ounce) bone-in split chicken breasts, trimmed
- Pepper
- 1 recipe glaze (recipes follow)

1. Dissolve salt in 2 quarts cold water in large container. Submerge chicken breasts in brine, cover, and refrigerate for 30 minutes to 1 hour. Remove chicken from brine and pat dry with paper towels. Season chicken with pepper.

2A. FOR A CHARCOAL GRILL: Open bottom vent completely. Light large chimney starter filled with charcoal briquettes (6 quarts). When top coals are partially covered with ash, pour evenly over half of grill. Set cooking grate in place, cover, and open lid vent completely. Heat grill until hot, about 5 minutes.

2B. FOR A GAS GRILL: Turn all burners to high, cover, and heat grill until hot, about 15 minutes. Leave primary burner on high and turn off other burner(s). (Adjust primary burner as needed during cooking to maintain grill temperature around 350 degrees.)

3. Clean and oil cooking grate. Place chicken on hot side of grill, skin side up, and cook (covered if using gas) until lightly browned on both sides, 6 to 8 minutes, flipping halfway through cooking. Move chicken, skin side down, to cool side of grill, with thicker end of breasts facing coals and flames. Cover and continue to cook until chicken registers 150 degrees, 15 to 20 minutes longer.

4. Brush bone side of chicken generously with half of glaze, move to hot side of grill, and cook until browned, 5 to 10 minutes. Brush skin side of chicken with remaining glaze, flip chicken, and continue to cook until chicken registers 160 degrees, 2 to 3 minutes longer.

5. Transfer chicken to serving platter, tent loosely with aluminum foil, and let rest for 5 to 10 minutes before serving, passing reserved glaze separately.

Orange-Chipotle Glaze

MAKES ABOUT ¾ CUP

For a spicier glaze, use the greater amount of chipotle chiles.

- 1 teaspoon grated orange zest plus ⅔ cup juice (2 oranges)
- 1–2 tablespoons minced canned chipotle chile in adobo sauce
- 1 small shallot, minced
- 2 teaspoons minced fresh thyme
- 1 tablespoon molasses
- ¾ teaspoon cornstarch
- Salt

Combine orange zest and juice, chipotle, shallot, and thyme in small saucepan. Whisk in molasses and cornstarch, bring to simmer, and cook over medium heat until thickened, about 5 minutes. Season with salt to taste. Reserve half of glaze for serving and use remaining glaze to brush on chicken.

Soy-Ginger Glaze

MAKES ABOUT ¾ CUP

Reduce the amount of salt in the brine to ¼ cup when using this glaze.

- ⅓ cup water
- ¼ cup soy sauce
- 2 tablespoons mirin
- 1 tablespoon grated fresh ginger
- 2 garlic cloves, minced
- 3 tablespoons sugar
- ¾ teaspoon cornstarch
- 2 scallions, minced

Combine water, soy sauce, mirin, ginger, and garlic in small saucepan, then whisk in sugar and cornstarch. Bring to simmer over medium heat and cook until thickened, about 5 minutes; stir in scallions. Reserve half of glaze for serving and use remaining glaze to brush on chicken.

Curry-Yogurt Glaze

MAKES ABOUT ¾ CUP

- ¾ cup plain whole-milk yogurt
- 2 garlic cloves, minced
- 2 teaspoons grated fresh ginger
- 2 teaspoons minced fresh cilantro
- ½ teaspoon grated lemon zest
- 1½ teaspoons curry powder
- ½ teaspoon sugar
- Salt and pepper

Whisk all ingredients together in bowl and season with salt and pepper to taste. Reserve half of glaze for serving and use remaining glaze to brush on chicken.

NOTES FROM THE TEST KITCHEN

GLAZING BONE-IN CHICKEN BREASTS

To avoid charred glaze, we partially cook the chicken, then paint the glaze on in stages.

Brush bone side of chicken with glaze, then move chicken, bone side down, to hotter side of grill and cook until browned. Brush skin side with glaze and flip to brown and finish.

PREPARING BONE-IN CHICKEN BREASTS FOR CARVING

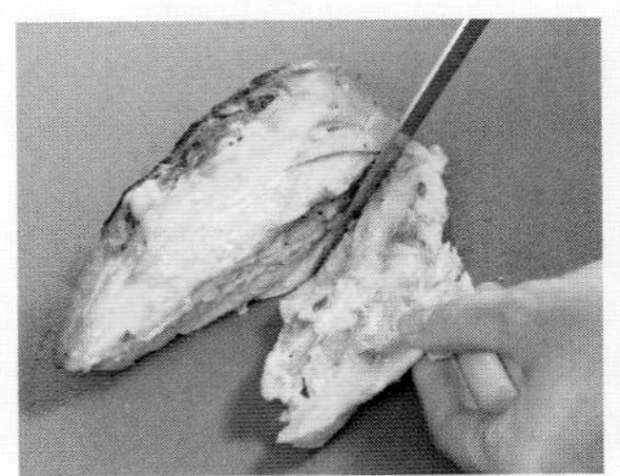

To make bone-in breasts easier to slice, we remove the meat from the bones. To start, insert tip of knife into breast just above breastbone. With tip of knife against ribs, cut along rib cage to separate meat, gently pulling away rib cage as you cut.

GRILLED STUFFED CHICKEN BREASTS

WHY THIS RECIPE WORKS: Chicken cordon bleu solves the problem of dry, mild-flavored chicken breasts with a flavorful stuffing of sharp, nutty melted cheese and salty sliced ham. We wanted to bring this concept to the grill, but leaky cheese can cause flare-ups as it drips from the chicken and into the coals. We wanted great grilled chicken breasts with a flavorful stuffing that stayed put.

Off the bat, we knew we wanted a strongly flavored stuffing for our chicken to stand up to the grill's smoke. We settled on more flavorful prosciutto and fontina cheese rather than the usual deli ham and Swiss cheese. And we chose bone-in, skin-on breasts since the skin acts as a natural protector of the meat. We butterflied the breasts—cutting them horizontally nearly halfway through so the meat opened like a book. We placed prosciutto-wrapped fontina inside, folded over the breast to enclose it and tied each breast up with kitchen twine. Encasing the fontina in prosciutto rather than layering it on top, prevented the cheese from leaking. We also chose to add a simple compound butter enlivened by shallots and tarragon for additional moisture and flavor.

Cooking the stuffed breasts over a modified two-level fire (in which all the coals are banked on one side of the grill) allowed us to first sear the breasts over the hot coals for color and flavor, then finish cooking them over more moderate indirect heat. These boneless stuffed chicken breasts were so good, we could enjoy them straight through the grilling season.

Grilled Stuffed Chicken Breasts with Prosciutto and Fontina

SERVES 4

If using kosher chicken, do not brine in step 1. You can serve the chicken on the bone, but we prefer to carve it off and slice it before serving.

- 4 (10- to 12-ounce) bone-in split chicken breasts, trimmed
- Salt and pepper
- 4 tablespoons unsalted butter, softened
- 1 shallot, minced
- 4 teaspoons chopped fresh tarragon
- 2 ounces fontina cheese, rind removed, cut into four 3 by ½-inch sticks
- 4 thin slices prosciutto

1. Using sharp knife and starting on thick side of breast closest to breastbone, cut horizontal pocket in each breast, stopping ½ inch from edge so halves remain attached. Dissolve ¼ cup salt in 2 quarts cold water in large container. Submerge chicken breasts in brine, cover, and refrigerate for 30 minutes to 1 hour. Remove chicken from brine and pat dry with paper towels. Season chicken with pepper.

2A. FOR A CHARCOAL GRILL: Open bottom vent completely. Light large chimney starter filled with charcoal briquettes (6 quarts). When top coals are partially covered with ash, pour evenly over half of grill. Set cooking grate in place, cover, and open lid vent completely. Heat grill until hot, about 5 minutes.

2B. FOR A GAS GRILL: Turn all burners to high, cover, and heat grill until hot, about 15 minutes. Leave primary burner on high and turn off other burner(s). (Adjust primary burner as needed during cooking to maintain grill temperature around 350 degrees.)

3. Meanwhile, combine butter, shallot, and tarragon in bowl. Roll each piece of fontina in 1 slice prosciutto. Spread equal amount of butter mixture inside each breast. Place 1 prosciutto-wrapped piece of fontina inside each breast and fold breast over to enclose. Evenly space 3 pieces kitchen twine (each about 12 inches long) beneath each breast and tie, trimming any excess.

4. Clean and oil cooking grate. Place chicken on hot side of grill, skin side down. Cook (covered if using gas) until well browned on first side, 4 to 6 minutes. Flip chicken and cook until second side is just opaque, about 2 minutes. Move chicken to cool side of grill, skin side up with thicker side of breasts facing coals and flames. Cover and continue to cook until chicken registers 160 degrees, 25 to 35 minutes longer.

5. Transfer chicken to carving board, tent loosely with aluminum foil, and let rest for 5 to 10 minutes. Remove twine, cut meat from bone, slice ½ inch thick, and serve.

NOTES FROM THE TEST KITCHEN

ASSEMBLING STUFFED CHICKEN BREASTS FOR GRILLING

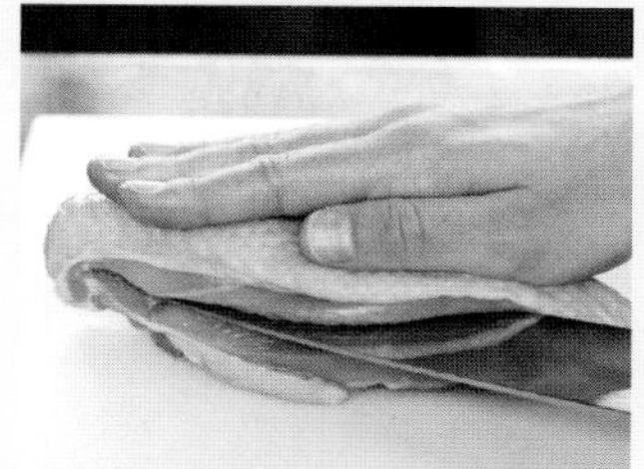

1. Starting on the thick side closest to the breastbone, cut a horizontal pocket in each breast, stopping ½ inch from the edge.

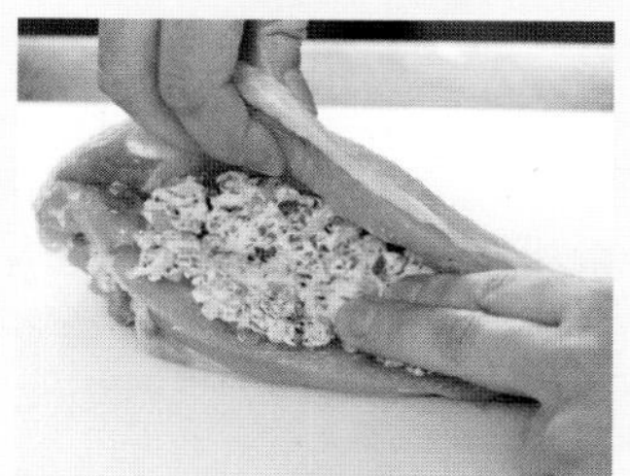

2. Spread an equal portion of compound butter inside each breast.

3. Place one prosciutto-wrapped piece of cheese inside each breast and fold the breast over to enclose.

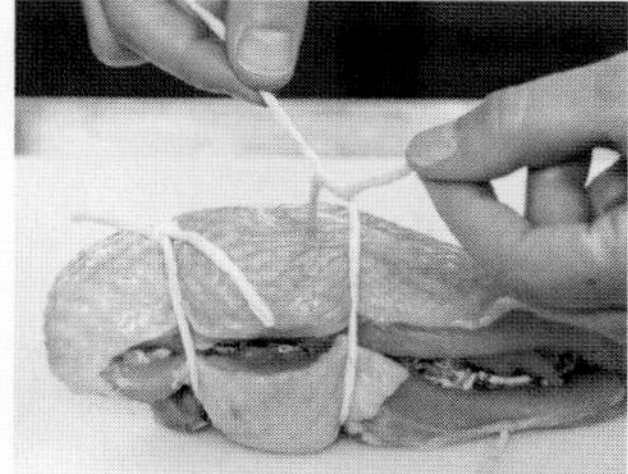

4. Tie each breast with three 12-inch pieces of kitchen twine at even intervals.

PERI PERI GRILLED CHICKEN

WHY THIS RECIPE WORKS: To bring this bold African chicken dish home, we started with a spice paste. We first blended garlic, shallot, bay leaves, lemon zest and juice, and pepper. Five-spice powder and tomato paste promised complexity, depth, and richness. Fruity-tasting arbol chiles, along with some cayenne pepper, replaced hard-to-find peri peri peppers. We tossed chicken pieces in the mixture along with chopped peanuts then let it sit overnight. The paste seasoned the meat and helped it stay juicy when cooked. We set up the grill with a cooler side and a hotter side, as well as a pan of water to help regulate the temperature. After rendering and charring the skin on the hotter side of the grill, we finished cooking the chicken on the cooler side.

Peri Peri Grilled Chicken

SERVES 6 TO 8

This recipe requires refrigerating the spice paste–coated chicken for at least 6 hours or up to 24 hours prior to cooking. When browning the chicken over the hotter side of the grill, move it away from the direct heat if any flare-ups occur. Serve with white rice.

- 4–10 arbol chiles, stemmed
- 3 tablespoons extra-virgin olive oil
- 2 tablespoons salt
- 8 garlic cloves, peeled
- 2 tablespoons tomato paste
- 1 shallot, chopped
- 1 tablespoon sugar
- 1 tablespoon paprika
- 1 tablespoon five-spice powder
- 2 teaspoons grated lemon zest plus ¼ cup juice (2 lemons)
- 1 teaspoon pepper
- ½ teaspoon cayenne pepper
- 3 bay leaves, crushed
- 6 pounds bone-in chicken pieces (breasts, thighs, and/or drumsticks), trimmed
- ½ cup dry-roasted peanuts, chopped fine
- 1 (13 by 9-inch) disposable aluminum pan (if using charcoal) or 2 (9-inch) disposable aluminum pie plates (if using gas)
- Lemon wedges

1. Process 4 arbols, oil, salt, garlic, tomato paste, shallot, sugar, paprika, five-spice powder, lemon zest and juice, pepper, cayenne, and bay leaves in blender until smooth, 10 to 20 seconds. Taste paste and add up to 6 additional arbols, depending on desired level of heat (spice paste should be slightly hotter than desired heat level of cooked chicken), and process until smooth. Using metal skewer, poke skin side of each chicken piece 8 to 10 times. Place chicken pieces, peanuts, and spice paste in large bowl or container and toss until chicken is evenly coated. Cover and refrigerate for at least 6 hours or up to 24 hours.

2A. FOR A CHARCOAL GRILL: Open bottom vent halfway and place disposable pan filled with 3 cups water on 1 side of grill. Light large chimney starter filled with charcoal briquettes (6 quarts). When top coals are partially covered with ash, pour evenly over other half of grill (opposite disposable pan). Set cooking grate in place, cover, and open lid vent halfway. Heat grill until hot, about 5 minutes.

2B. FOR A GAS GRILL: Place 2 disposable pie plates, each filled with 1½ cups water, directly on 1 burner of gas grill (opposite primary burner). Turn all burners to high, cover, and heat grill until hot, about 15 minutes. Turn primary burner to medium-high and turn off other burner(s). (Adjust primary burner as needed to maintain grill temperature between 325 and 350 degrees.)

3. Clean and oil cooking grate. Place chicken, skin side down, on hotter side of grill and cook until browned and blistered in spots, 2 to 5 minutes. Flip chicken and cook until second side is browned, 4 to 6 minutes. Move chicken to cooler side of grill and arrange, skin side up, with legs and thighs closest to fire and breasts farthest away. Cover (positioning lid vent over chicken if using charcoal) and cook until breasts register 160 degrees and legs and thighs register 175 degrees, 50 to 60 minutes.

4. Transfer chicken to serving platter, tent with aluminum foil, and let rest for 10 minutes before serving, passing lemon wedges separately.

GRILLED CHICKEN DRUMSTICKS

WHY THIS RECIPE WORKS: With the right treatment, economical chicken drumsticks can be a delicious choice for the grill. We started by soaking them in a saltwater brine to season them and help them retain their juices during cooking, then coated them with a flavorful rub. We cooked them to between 185 and 190 degrees over indirect heat, to ensure this collagen-rich cut turned tender. This also allowed the skin to render gently without the risk of flare-ups. We finished by cooking the drumsticks briefly over the coals to capture some char and crispiness.

Grilled Spice-Rubbed Chicken Drumsticks

SERVES 6

Before applying the spice rub, smooth the skin over the drumsticks so it is covering as much surface area as possible. This will help the skin render evenly and prevent the meat from drying out.

- ½ cup salt
- 5 pounds chicken drumsticks
- 1 recipe spice rub (recipes follow)

1. Dissolve salt in 2 quarts cold water in large container. Submerge drumsticks in brine, cover, and refrigerate for 30 minutes to 1 hour.

2. Place spice rub on plate. Remove drumsticks from brine and pat dry with paper towels. Holding 1 drumstick by bone end, press lightly into rub on all sides. Pat gently to remove excess rub. Repeat with remaining drumsticks.

3A. FOR A CHARCOAL GRILL: Open bottom vent halfway. Light large chimney starter filled with charcoal briquettes (6 quarts). When top coals are partially covered with ash, pour evenly over half of grill. Set cooking grate in place, cover, and open lid vent halfway. Heat grill until hot, about 5 minutes.

3B. FOR A GAS GRILL: Turn all burners to high, cover, and heat grill until hot, about 15 minutes. Leave primary burner on high and turn off other burner(s). (Adjust primary burner [or, if using three-burner grill, primary burner and second burner] as needed to maintain grill temperature between 325 and 350 degrees.)

4. Clean and oil cooking grate. Place drumsticks, skin side down, on cooler side of grill. Cover and cook for 25 minutes. Rearrange pieces so that drumsticks that were closest to edge are now closer to heat source and vice versa. Cover and cook until drumsticks register 185 to 190 degrees, 20 to 30 minutes.

5. Move all drumsticks to hotter side of grill and cook, turning occasionally, until skin is nicely charred, about 5 minutes. Transfer to platter, tent with aluminum foil, and let rest for 10 minutes. Serve.

Barbecue Spice Rub

MAKES ABOUT ⅓ CUP

You can substitute granulated garlic for the garlic powder, if desired.

- 3 tablespoons packed brown sugar
- 1 tablespoon paprika
- 1 tablespoon chili powder
- 2 teaspoons garlic powder
- ¾ teaspoon salt
- ¾ teaspoon pepper
- ¼ teaspoon cayenne pepper

Combine all ingredients in small bowl.

Jerk-Style Spice Rub

MAKES ABOUT ¼ CUP

If you can't find whole allspice berries, substitute 2 teaspoons of ground allspice.

- 1 tablespoon allspice berries
- 1 tablespoon black peppercorns
- 1½ teaspoons dried thyme
- 2 tablespoons packed brown sugar
- 2 teaspoons garlic powder
- 1½ teaspoons dry mustard
- ¾ teaspoon salt
- ¾ teaspoon cayenne pepper

Grind allspice, peppercorns, and thyme in spice grinder or mortar and pestle until coarsely ground. Transfer to bowl and stir in sugar, garlic powder, mustard, salt, and cayenne.

BEHIND THE SCENES

LIGHT MY FIRE

Don't even think of using lighter fluid to light your charcoal. Sometimes we've found that we can taste the fluid residually on grilled food—and who wants that? Electric starters are fine, but most people don't have an electrical outlet near their grill. Where does that leave you? A chimney starter. A chimney starter is a metal cylinder with a heatproof handle. Simply dump in the charcoal, light, and wait until the coals are partially covered with a layer of ash. At this point the hot coals can be poured into the grill and arranged as necessary. One thing to keep in mind when buying a chimney starter is the charcoal capacity. We like a large chimney that holds about 6 quarts of charcoal briquettes—just the right amount for grilling most foods in a large kettle grill.

JERK CHICKEN

WHY THIS RECIPE WORKS: Traditional Jamaican jerk recipes rely on island ingredients for both marinade and cooking technique. Fortunately, we were able to achieve the characteristic spicy-sweet-fresh-smoky balance with the right combination of stateside staples. Keeping the marinade pastelike and cooking the meat first over indirect heat prevented the jerk flavors from dripping or peeling off during grilling. Enhancing our hickory chip packet with a few spice-cabinet ingredients allowed our jerk chicken recipe to mimic the unique smoke of authentic pimento wood.

Jerk Chicken

SERVES 4

For a milder dish, use one seeded chile. If you prefer your food very hot, use up to all three chiles including their seeds and ribs. Scotch bonnet chiles can be used in place of the habaneros. Wear gloves when working with the chiles.

JERK MARINADE

- 1½ tablespoons whole coriander seeds
- 1 tablespoon whole allspice berries
- 1 tablespoon whole peppercorns
- 1-3 habanero chiles, stemmed, quartered, and seeds and ribs reserved, if using
- 8 scallions, chopped
- 6 garlic cloves, peeled
- 3 tablespoons vegetable oil
- 2 tablespoons soy sauce
- 2 tablespoons finely grated lime zest (3 limes), plus lime wedges for serving
- 2 tablespoons yellow mustard
- 1 tablespoon dried thyme
- 1 tablespoon ground ginger
- 1 tablespoon packed brown sugar
- 2¼ teaspoons salt
- 2 teaspoons dried basil
- ½ teaspoon dried rosemary
- ½ teaspoon ground nutmeg

CHICKEN

- 3 pounds bone-in chicken pieces (split breasts cut in half, drumsticks, and/or thighs)
- 2 tablespoons whole allspice berries
- 2 tablespoons dried thyme
- 2 tablespoons dried rosemary
- 2 tablespoons water
- 1 cup wood chips, soaked in water for 15 minutes and drained

1. FOR THE JERK MARINADE: Grind coriander seeds, allspice berries, and peppercorns in spice grinder or mortar and pestle until coarsely ground. Transfer spices to blender jar. Add habanero(s), scallions, garlic, oil, soy sauce, lime zest, mustard, thyme, ginger, sugar, salt, basil, rosemary, and nutmeg and process until smooth paste forms, 1 to 3 minutes, scraping down sides as necessary. Transfer marinade to gallon-size zipper-lock bag.

2. FOR THE CHICKEN: Place chicken pieces in bag with marinade and toss to coat; press out as much air as possible and seal bag. Let stand at room temperature for 30 minutes while preparing grill, flipping bag after 15 minutes. (Marinated chicken can be refrigerated for up to 24 hours.)

3. Combine allspice berries, thyme, rosemary, and water in bowl and set aside to moisten for 15 minutes. Using large piece of heavy-duty aluminum foil, wrap soaked chips and moistened allspice mixture in foil packet and cut several vent holes in top.

4A. FOR A CHARCOAL GRILL: Open bottom vent halfway. Arrange 1 quart unlit charcoal briquettes in single layer over half of grill. Light large chimney starter one-third filled with charcoal briquettes (2 quarts). When top coals are partially covered with ash, pour evenly over unlit briquettes, keeping coals arranged over half of grill. Place wood chip packet on coals. Set cooking grate in place, cover, and open lid vent halfway. Heat grill until hot and wood chips are smoking, about 5 minutes.

4B. FOR A GAS GRILL: Place wood chip packet over primary burner. Turn all burners to high, cover, and heat grill until hot and wood chips begin to smoke, 15 to 25 minutes. Turn primary burner to medium and turn off other burner(s).

5. Clean and oil cooking grate. Place chicken, with marinade clinging and skin side up, as far away from fire as possible, with thighs closest to fire and breasts farthest away. Cover (positioning lid vent over chicken if using charcoal) and cook for 30 minutes.

6. Move chicken, skin side down, to hotter side of grill; cook until browned and skin renders, 3 to 6 minutes. Using tongs, flip chicken pieces and cook until browned on second side and breasts register 160 degrees and thighs/drumsticks register 175 degrees, 5 to 12 minutes longer.

7. Transfer chicken to serving platter, tent loosely with foil, and let rest for 5 to 10 minutes. Serve warm or at room temperature with lime wedges.

SMOKED CHICKEN

WHY THIS RECIPE WORKS: Smoked chicken needs to be cooked for a long time to be imbued with smoke flavor, but the meat dries out easily. We wanted perfectly cooked meat with a pervasive smoky flavor and crisp skin. A salt and sugar brine guaranteed moist, well-seasoned meat. Chicken parts were easier than whole chickens; the breasts could cook evenly on the coolest part of the grill and more of the bird was exposed to the smoke and heat, adding flavor and rendering more fat from the skin. To keep the skin moist, we brushed it with oil and added a pan of water to the grill. Two wood chip packets produced the ideal amount of smoke.

Smoked Chicken

SERVES 6 TO 8

If using kosher chicken, do not brine in step 1. Two medium wood chunks, soaked in water for 1 hour, can be substituted for the wood chip packet on a charcoal grill.

- 1 cup salt
- 1 cup sugar
- 6 pounds bone-in chicken parts (breasts, thighs, and/or drumsticks), trimmed
- 3 tablespoons vegetable oil
- Pepper
- 3 cups wood chips, 1½ cups soaked in water for 15 minutes and drained, plus 1½ cups unsoaked
- 1 (16 by 12-inch) disposable aluminum roasting pan (if using charcoal) or 1 disposable aluminum pie plate (if using gas)

1. Dissolve salt and sugar in 4 quarts cold water in large container. Submerge chicken pieces in brine, cover, and refrigerate for 30 minutes to 1 hour. Remove chicken from brine and pat dry with paper towels. Brush chicken evenly with oil and season with pepper.

2. Using large piece of heavy-duty aluminum foil, wrap soaked chips in foil packet and cut several vent holes in top. Repeat with another sheet of foil and unsoaked wood chips.

3A. FOR A CHARCOAL GRILL: Open bottom vent halfway. Arrange 2 quarts unlit charcoal banked against 1 side of grill and disposable pan filled with 2 cups water on empty side of grill. Light large chimney starter half filled with charcoal briquettes (3 quarts). When top coals are partially covered with ash, pour on top of unlit charcoal, to cover one-third of grill with coals steeply banked against side of grill. Place wood chip packets on top of coals. Set cooking grate in place, cover, and open lid vent halfway. Heat grill until hot and wood chips begin to smoke, about 5 minutes.

3B. FOR A GAS GRILL: Place wood chip packets directly on primary burner. Place disposable pie plate filled with 2 cups water on other burner(s). Turn all burners to high, cover, and heat grill until hot and wood chips begin to smoke, about 15 minutes. Turn primary burner to medium-high and turn off other burner(s). (Adjust primary burner as needed to maintain grill temperature around 325 degrees.)

4. Clean and oil cooking grate. Place chicken on cool side of grill, skin side up, as far away from heat as possible with thighs closest to heat and breasts farthest away. Cover (positioning lid vents over chicken if using charcoal) and cook until breasts register 160 degrees and thighs/drumsticks register 175 degrees, 1¼ to 1½ hours.

5. Transfer chicken to serving platter, tent loosely with foil, and let rest for 5 to 10 minutes before serving.

BARBECUED CHICKEN

WHY THIS RECIPE WORKS: To produce juicy, evenly cooked chicken parts on the grill, indirect cooking is key, as it provides a hotter side for briefly searing the parts and a cooler side for them to cook through gently. We lined up the fattier leg quarters closer to the coals and the leaner white meat farther from the heat, as well as adding a water pan underneath the cooler side, to help the dark and white pieces cook slowly and evenly. Applying a simple spice rub deeply seasoned the meat, and the salt in it helped retain moisture, while brushing on a homemade sauce in stages allowed it to cling nicely to the skin and also develop layers of tangy-sweet flavor.

Sweet and Tangy Barbecued Chicken

SERVES 6 TO 8

When browning the chicken over the hotter side of the grill, move it away from any flare-ups. Try to select similar-size chicken parts for even cooking.

CHICKEN

- 2 tablespoons packed dark brown sugar
- 4½ teaspoons kosher salt
- 1½ teaspoons onion powder
- 1½ teaspoons garlic powder
- 1½ teaspoons paprika
- ¼ teaspoon cayenne pepper
- 6 pounds bone-in chicken pieces (split breasts and/or leg quarters), trimmed

SAUCE

- 1 cup ketchup
- 5 tablespoons molasses
- 3 tablespoons cider vinegar
- 2 tablespoons Worcestershire sauce
- 2 tablespoons Dijon mustard
- ¼ teaspoon pepper
- 2 tablespoons vegetable oil
- ⅓ cup grated onion
- 1 garlic clove, minced
- 1 teaspoon chili powder
- ¼ teaspoon cayenne pepper

- 1 large disposable aluminum roasting pan (if using charcoal) or 2 disposable aluminum pie plates (if using gas)

1. FOR THE CHICKEN: Combine sugar, salt, onion powder, garlic powder, paprika, and cayenne in bowl. Arrange chicken on rimmed baking sheet and sprinkle both sides evenly with spice rub. Cover with plastic wrap and refrigerate for at least 6 hours or up to 24 hours.

2. FOR THE SAUCE: Whisk ketchup, molasses, vinegar, Worcestershire, mustard, and pepper together in bowl. Heat oil in medium saucepan over medium heat until shimmering. Add onion and garlic; cook until onion is softened, 2 to 4 minutes. Add chili powder and cayenne and cook until fragrant, about 30 seconds. Whisk in ketchup mixture and bring to boil. Reduce heat to medium-low and simmer gently for 5 minutes. Set aside ⅔ cup sauce to baste chicken and reserve remaining sauce for serving. (Sauce can be refrigerated for up to 1 week.)

3A. FOR A CHARCOAL GRILL: Open bottom vent halfway and place disposable pan filled with 3 cups water on 1 side of grill. Light large chimney starter filled with charcoal briquettes (6 quarts). When top coals are partially covered with ash, pour evenly over other half of grill (opposite disposable pan). Set cooking grate in place, cover, and open lid vent halfway. Heat grill until hot, about 5 minutes.

3B. FOR A GAS GRILL: Place 2 disposable pie plates, each filled with 1½ cups water, directly on 1 burner of gas grill (opposite primary burner). Turn all burners to high, cover, and heat grill until hot, about 15 minutes. Turn primary burner to medium-high and turn off other burner(s). (Adjust primary burner as needed to maintain grill temperature of 325 to 350 degrees.)

4. Clean and oil cooking grate. Place chicken, skin side down, over hotter part of grill and cook until browned and blistered in spots, 2 to 5 minutes. Flip chicken and cook until second side is browned, 4 to 6 minutes. Move chicken to cooler side of grill and brush both sides of chicken with ⅓ cup sauce. Arrange chicken, skin side up, with leg quarters closest to fire and breasts farthest away. Cover (positioning lid vent over chicken if using charcoal) and cook for 25 minutes.

5. Brush both sides of chicken with remaining ⅓ cup sauce and continue to cook, covered, until breasts register 160 degrees and leg quarters register 175 degrees, 25 to 35 minutes longer.

6. Transfer chicken to serving platter, tent loosely with aluminum foil, and let rest for 10 minutes. Serve, passing reserved sauce separately.

BARBECUED PULLED CHICKEN

WHY THIS RECIPE WORKS: Made-from-scratch barbecued pulled chicken sandwiches often rely on boneless chicken breasts and bottled barbecue sauce. The result is a sandwich with no smoke, tough meat, and artificial flavor. We wanted to take pulled chicken sandwiches seriously—using tender, smoky meat pulled off the bone in moist, soft shreds and then tossed with a tangy, sweet sauce—but we didn't want to take all day to make them.

We chose whole chicken legs for great flavor, low cost, and resistance to overcooking. The legs cooked gently but thoroughly over indirect heat, absorbing plenty of smoke flavor along the way. Cooking the chicken to a higher-than-usual temperature also dissolved connective tissue and rendered more fat, making the meat tender and less greasy. Once the chicken finished cooking, we hand-shredded half and machine-processed the other half to produce the perfect texture—one similar to pulled pork. The chicken then just had to be combined with a thin but tangy barbecue sauce to become truly bun-worthy.

Barbecued Pulled Chicken

SERVES 6 TO 8

Chicken leg quarters consist of drumsticks attached to thighs; often also attached are backbone sections that must be trimmed away. Two medium wood chunks, soaked in water for 1 hour, can be substituted for the wood chip packet on a charcoal grill. Serve the pulled chicken on hamburger rolls or sandwich bread, with pickles and coleslaw.

CHICKEN

- 2 cups wood chips, soaked in water for 15 minutes and drained
- 1 (16 by 12-inch) disposable aluminum roasting pan (if using charcoal)
- 1 tablespoon vegetable oil
- 8 (14-ounce) chicken leg quarters, trimmed
- Salt and pepper

SAUCE

- 1 large onion, peeled and quartered
- ¼ cup water
- 1½ cups ketchup
- 1½ cups apple cider
- ¼ cup molasses

¼ cup apple cider vinegar
3 tablespoons Worcestershire sauce
3 tablespoons Dijon mustard
½ teaspoon pepper
1 tablespoon vegetable oil
1½ tablespoons chili powder
2 garlic cloves, minced
½ teaspoon cayenne pepper
Hot sauce

1. FOR THE CHICKEN: Using large piece of heavy-duty aluminum foil, wrap soaked chips in foil packet and cut several vent holes in top.

2A. FOR A CHARCOAL GRILL: Open bottom vent halfway and place roasting pan in center of grill. Light large chimney starter three-quarters filled with charcoal briquettes (4½ quarts). When top coals are partially covered with ash, pour into 2 even piles on either side of roasting pan. Place wood chip packet on 1 pile of coals. Set cooking grate in place, cover, and open lid vent halfway. Heat grill until hot and wood chips are smoking, about 5 minutes.

2B. FOR A GAS GRILL: Place wood chip packet directly on primary burner. Turn all burners to high, cover, and heat grill until hot and wood chips are smoking, about 15 minutes. Turn all burners to medium. (Adjust burners as needed during cooking to maintain grill temperature between 250 and 300 degrees.)

3. Clean and oil cooking grate. Pat chicken dry with paper towels and season with salt and pepper. Place chicken in single layer on center of grill (over roasting pan if using charcoal), skin side up, or evenly over grill (if using gas). Cover (position lid vent over meat if using charcoal) and cook until chicken registers 185 degrees, 1 to 1½ hours, rotating the chicken pieces halfway through cooking. Transfer chicken to carving board, tent loosely with foil, and let rest until cool enough to handle.

4. FOR THE SAUCE: Meanwhile, process onion and water in food processor until mixture resembles slush, about 30 seconds. Pass through fine-mesh strainer into liquid measuring cup, pressing on solids with rubber spatula (you should have ¾ cup strained onion juice). Discard solids in strainer.

5. Whisk onion juice, ketchup, cider, molasses, 3 tablespoons vinegar, Worcestershire, mustard, and ½ teaspoon pepper together in bowl. Heat oil in large saucepan over medium heat until shimmering. Stir in chili powder, garlic, and cayenne and cook until fragrant, about 30 seconds. Stir in ketchup mixture, bring to simmer, and cook over medium-low heat until slightly thickened, about 15 minutes (you should have about 4 cups of sauce). Transfer 2 cups sauce to serving bowl; leave remaining sauce in saucepan.

6. TO SERVE: Remove and discard skin from chicken legs. Using your fingers, pull meat off bones, separating larger pieces (which should fall off bones easily) from smaller, drier pieces into 2 equal piles.

7. Pulse smaller chicken pieces in food processor until just coarsely chopped, 3 to 4 pulses, stirring chicken with rubber spatula after each pulse. Add chopped chicken to sauce in saucepan. Using your fingers or 2 forks, pull larger chicken pieces into long shreds and add to saucepan. Stir in remaining 1 tablespoon cider vinegar, cover, and heat chicken over medium-low heat, stirring occasionally, until heated through, about 10 minutes. Add hot sauce to taste and serve, passing remaining sauce separately.

Barbecued Pulled Chicken for a Crowd

SERVES 10 TO 12

This technique works well on a charcoal grill but not so well on a gas grill. If your gas grill is large and can accommodate more than 8 legs, follow the master recipe, adding as many legs as will comfortably fit in a single layer.

Increase amount of charcoal briquettes to 6 quarts. Use 12 chicken legs and slot them into V-shaped roasting rack set on top of cooking grate over disposable aluminum pan. Increase cooking time in step 3 to 1½ to 1¾ hours. In step 5, remove only 1 cup of sauce from saucepan. In step 7, pulse chicken in food processor in 2 batches.

NOTES FROM THE TEST KITCHEN

BARBECUED PULLED CHICKEN FOR A CROWD

To make barbecued pulled chicken for a crowd, we found that a roasting rack with six slots was the perfect tool for the job. By sliding two legs into each slot, a total of 12 legs fit (and finish cooking) at once—plenty to feed a hungry crowd.

GRILLED CHICKEN SOUVLAKI

WHY THIS RECIPE WORKS: *Souvlaki* is basically a Greek term for meat grilled on a stick. In modern Greece, souvlaki is usually made with pork, but at Greek restaurants here in the United States, boneless, skinless chicken breast is common. The chunks of white meat are marinated in a tangy mixture of lemon juice, olive oil, oregano, parsley, and garlic before being skewered and grilled until charred. The chicken is often placed on a lightly grilled pita, slathered with a yogurt-based *tzatziki* sauce, wrapped snugly, and eaten out of hand. At least as appealing as the dish itself is how easily it translates to a home grill. The ingredients are readily available, and small chunks of boneless chicken cook quickly, making souvlaki a prime candidate for weeknight fare. Instead of a long marinating time, which made the meat mushy and didn't add much flavor, we brined the chicken for a mere 30 minutes, then tossed it with olive oil, lemon juice, dried oregano, parsley, black pepper, and honey. The honey added complexity and encouraged browning. We also reserved a bit of the mixture to season the meat after cooking. We found that the meat on the outside of the skewers cooked faster than the chunks in the middle, so we made "shields" by threading bell peppers and onions onto the ends of the skewers. For soft pita, we wrapped a stack of four pitas tightly in foil after moistening the top and bottom surfaces of the stack with water. They steamed and softened while the chicken cooked. Topped with a cool, creamy tzatziki, our chicken souvlaki makes a perfect summer dinner.

Grilled Chicken Souvlaki

SERVES 4

This *tzatziki* is fairly mild; if you like a more assertive flavor, double the garlic. A rasp-style grater makes quick work of turning the garlic into a paste. We like the chicken as a wrap, but you may skip the pita and serve the chicken, vegetables, and tzatziki with rice. You will need four 12-inch metal skewers.

TZATZIKI SAUCE

- 1 tablespoon lemon juice
- 1 small garlic clove, minced to paste
- ¾ cup plain Greek yogurt
- ½ cucumber, peeled, halved lengthwise, seeded, and diced fine (½ cup)
- 3 tablespoons minced fresh mint
- 1 tablespoon minced fresh parsley
- ⅜ teaspoon salt

CHICKEN

- Salt and pepper
- 1½ pounds boneless, skinless chicken breasts, trimmed and cut into 1-inch pieces
- ⅓ cup extra-virgin olive oil
- 2 tablespoons minced fresh parsley
- 1 teaspoon finely grated lemon zest plus ¼ cup juice (2 lemons)
- 1 teaspoon honey
- 1 teaspoon dried oregano
- 1 green bell pepper, quartered, stemmed, and seeded, each quarter cut into 4 chunks
- 1 small red onion, ends trimmed, peeled, and halved lengthwise, each half cut into 4 chunks
- 4 (8-inch) pita breads

1. FOR THE TZATZIKI SAUCE: Whisk lemon juice and garlic together in small bowl. Let stand for 10 minutes. Stir in yogurt, cucumber, mint, parsley, and salt. Cover and set aside.

2. FOR THE CHICKEN: Dissolve 2 tablespoons salt in 1 quart cold water. Submerge chicken in brine, cover, and refrigerate for 30 minutes. While chicken is brining, combine oil, parsley, lemon zest and juice, honey, oregano, and ½ teaspoon pepper in medium bowl. Transfer ¼ cup oil mixture to large bowl and set aside to toss with cooked chicken.

3. Remove chicken from brine and pat dry with paper towels. Toss chicken with remaining oil mixture. Thread 4 pieces of bell pepper, concave side up, onto one 12-inch metal skewer. Thread one-quarter of chicken onto skewer. Thread 2 chunks of onion onto skewer, and place skewer on plate. Repeat skewering remaining chicken and vegetables on 3 more skewers. Lightly moisten 2 pita breads with water. Sandwich 2 unmoistened pita breads between moistened pita breads and wrap stack tightly in lightly greased heavy-duty aluminum foil.

4A. FOR A CHARCOAL GRILL: Open bottom vent completely. Light large chimney starter mounded with charcoal briquettes (7 quarts). When top coals are partially covered with ash, pour evenly over half of grill. Set cooking grate in place, cover, and open lid vent completely. Heat grill until hot, about 5 minutes.

4B. FOR A GAS GRILL: Turn all burners to high, cover, and heat grill until hot, about 15 minutes. Leave primary burner on high and turn off other burner(s).

5. Clean and oil cooking grate. Place skewers on hotter side of grill and cook, turning occasionally, until chicken and vegetables are well browned on all sides and chicken registers 160 degrees, 15 to 20 minutes. Using fork, push chicken and vegetables off skewers into bowl of reserved oil mixture. Stir gently, breaking up onion chunks; cover with foil and let sit for 5 minutes.

6. Meanwhile, place packet of pitas on cooler side of grill. Flip occasionally to heat, about 5 minutes.

7. Lay each warm pita on 12-inch square of foil. Spread each pita with 2 tablespoons tzatziki. Place one-quarter of chicken and vegetables in middle of each pita. Roll into cylindrical shape and serve.

GRILLED LEMON CHICKEN

WHY THIS RECIPE WORKS: Grilling a whole chicken can be a recipe for disaster thanks to flare-ups caused by the fatty skin. Usually recipes address this problem with a two-stage grilling process: low heat to gently render the fat and then high heat to char the meat and crisp the skin. We found a much faster way to solve the problem: We skipped the rendering step by removing the skin before grilling. To ensure that our chicken got plenty of color and char without overcooking, we butterflied it so it was an even thickness, then we brined it in a sugar and salt solution for juicy meat. For flavor that penetrated all the way to the bone, we cut deep channels in the meat and rubbed it with lemon and herb seasoning. Basting the chicken with a flavorful butter sauce and tenting it with aluminum foil partway through cooking kept the surface moist and tender as it cooked. We quickly charred lemon wedges to squeeze over each portion before serving for even more moisture and flavor.

Grilled Lemon Chicken with Rosemary

SERVES 4

For a better grip, use a paper towel to grasp the skin when removing it from the chicken.

NOTES FROM THE TEST KITCHEN

PREPPING A WHOLE CHICKEN FOR THE GRILL

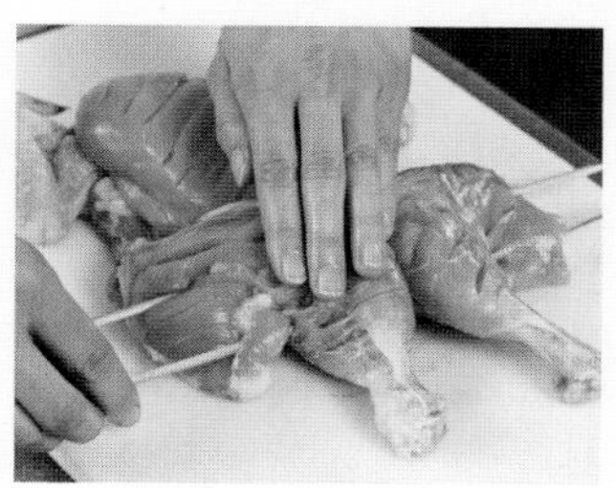

For even, fast cooking, we remove the backbone, then flip the chicken and crack and flatten the breastbone. We peel off the skin, leaving it on the wings, and deeply slash the meat. Skewers inserted through the thighs and legs provide stability.

- 1 (3½- to 4-pound) whole chicken, giblets discarded
- ¾ cup sugar
- Salt and pepper
- 2 lemons
- 1 tablespoon vegetable oil
- 2 teaspoons minced fresh rosemary
- 1½ teaspoons Dijon mustard
- 2 tablespoons unsalted butter

1. With chicken breast side down, using kitchen shears, cut through bones on either side of backbone; discard backbone. Flip chicken over and press on breastbone to flatten. Using fingers and shears, peel skin off chicken, leaving skin on wings.

2. Tuck wings behind back. Turn legs so drumsticks face inward toward breasts. Using chef's knife, cut ½-inch-deep slits, spaced ½ inch apart, in breasts and legs. Insert skewer through thigh of 1 leg, into bottom of breast, and through thigh of second leg. Insert second skewer, about 1 inch lower, through thigh and drumstick of 1 leg and then through thigh and drumstick of second leg.

3. Dissolve sugar and ¾ cup salt in 3 quarts cold water in large, wide container. Submerge chicken in brine, cover, and refrigerate for at least 30 minutes or up to 1 hour.

4. Zest lemons (you should have 2 tablespoons grated zest). Juice 1 lemon (you should have 3 tablespoons juice) and quarter remaining lemon lengthwise. Combine zest, oil, 1½ teaspoons rosemary, 1 teaspoon mustard, and ½ teaspoon pepper in small bowl; set aside. Heat butter, remaining ½ teaspoon rosemary, remaining ½ teaspoon mustard, and ½ teaspoon pepper in small saucepan over low heat, stirring occasionally, until butter is melted and ingredients are combined. Remove pan from heat and stir in lemon juice; leave mixture in saucepan.

5. Remove chicken from brine and pat dry with paper towels. With chicken skinned side down, rub ½ teaspoon zest mixture over surface of legs. Flip chicken over and rub remaining zest mixture evenly over entire surface, making sure to work mixture into slits.

6A. FOR A CHARCOAL GRILL: Open bottom vent completely. Light large chimney starter mounded with charcoal briquettes (7 quarts). When top coals are partially covered with ash, pour evenly over half of grill. Set cooking grate in place, cover, and open lid vent completely. Heat grill until hot, about 5 minutes.

6B. FOR A GAS GRILL: Turn all burners to high, cover, and heat grill until hot, about 15 minutes. Leave primary burner on high and turn off other burner(s).

7. Clean and oil cooking grate. Place chicken, skinned side down, and lemon quarters over hotter side of grill. Cover and cook until chicken and lemon quarters are well browned, 8 to 10 minutes. Transfer lemon quarters to bowl and set aside. Flip chicken over and brush with one-third of butter mixture (place saucepan over cooler side of grill if mixture has solidified). Cover chicken loosely with aluminum foil. Continue to cook, covered, until chicken is well browned on second side, 8 to 10 minutes.

8. Remove foil and slide chicken to cooler side of grill. Brush with half of remaining butter mixture, and re-cover with foil. Continue to cook, covered, until breasts register 160 degrees and thighs/drumsticks register 175 degrees, 8 to 10 minutes longer.

9. Transfer chicken to carving board, brush with remaining butter mixture, tent loosely with foil, and let rest for 5 to 10 minutes. Carve into pieces and serve with reserved lemon quarters.

GRILL-ROASTED BEER CAN CHICKEN

WHY THIS RECIPE WORKS: We wanted to know if the curious cooking method of grill-roasting chicken over a can of beer really worked. To earn our approval, this technique would have to produce a tender, juicy, and deeply seasoned bird.

We found that beer can chicken is the real deal—why? The beer in the open can simmers and turns to steam as the chicken roasts, which makes the meat remarkably juicy and rich-textured, similar to braised chicken. As an added bonus, the dry heat of the grill crisps the skin and renders the fat away. To perfect the technique, we added a few hardwood chunks or chips to the fire for smoky flavor. The best grilling setup (for a charcoal grill) proved to be banking the lit coals on either side of the grill and propping the chicken up on an open can of beer on the grill in the center, using the bird's drumsticks to form a tripod. For the gas grill, a medium fire did the trick. Finally, we found we didn't have to spend money on an expensive beer—the beer flavor wasn't really detectable in the chicken, so a cheap brew worked just fine (so does lemonade, which proved an acceptable substitute for the beer).

Grill-Roasted Beer Can Chicken

SERVES 4

Two medium wood chunks, soaked in water for 1 hour, can be substituted for the wood chip packet on a charcoal grill. If you prefer, use lemonade instead of beer; fill an empty 12-ounce soda or beer can with 10 ounces (1¼ cups) of lemonade and proceed as directed.

- 1 (12-ounce) can beer
- 2 bay leaves
- 1 (3½- to 4-pound) whole chicken
- 3 tablespoons spice rub (recipe follows)
- 2 cups wood chips, soaked in water for 15 minutes and drained
- 1 (13 by 9-inch) disposable aluminum roasting pan (if using charcoal)

1. Open beer can and pour out (or drink) about ¼ cup. With church key can opener, punch 2 more large holes in the top of can (for total of 3 holes). Crumble bay leaves into beer.

2. Pat chicken dry with paper towels. Rub chicken evenly, inside and out, with spice rub, lifting up skin over breast and rubbing spice rub directly onto meat. Using skewer, poke skin all over. Slide chicken over beer can so that drumsticks reach down to bottom of can and chicken stands upright; set aside at room temperature.

3. Using large piece of heavy-duty aluminum foil, wrap soaked chips in foil packet and cut several vent holes in top.

4A. FOR A CHARCOAL GRILL: Open bottom vent halfway and place roasting pan in center of grill. Light large chimney starter two-thirds filled with charcoal briquettes (4 quarts). When top coals are partially covered with ash, pour into 2 even piles on either side of roasting pan. Place wood chip packet on 1 pile of coals. Set cooking grate in place, cover, and open lid vent halfway. Heat grill until hot and wood chips are smoking, about 5 minutes.

4B. FOR A GAS GRILL: Place wood chip packet directly on primary burner. Turn all burners to high, cover, and heat grill until hot and wood chips are smoking, about 15 minutes. Turn all burners to medium. (Adjust burners as needed to maintain grill temperature around 325 degrees.)

5. Clean and oil cooking grate. Place chicken (with can) in center of grill (over roasting pan if using charcoal), using drumsticks to help steady bird. Cover (position lid vent over chicken if using charcoal) and cook until breast registers 160 degrees and thighs register 175 degrees, 1 to 1½ hours.

6. Using large wad of paper towels, carefully transfer chicken (with can) to tray, making sure to keep can upright. Tent loosely with foil and let rest for 15 minutes. Carefully lift chicken off can and onto carving board. Discard remaining beer and can. Carve chicken and serve.

NOTES FROM THE TEST KITCHEN

SETTING UP BEER CAN CHICKEN

With legs pointing down, slide chicken over open beer can. Two legs and beer can form tripod that steadies chicken on grill.

Spice Rub

MAKES 1 CUP

Store leftover spice rub in an airtight container for up to 3 months.

- ½ cup paprika
- 2 tablespoons kosher salt
- 2 tablespoons garlic powder
- 1 tablespoon dried thyme
- 2 teaspoons ground celery seeds
- 2 teaspoons pepper
- 2 teaspoons cayenne pepper

Combine all ingredients in bowl.

GRILL-ROASTED CORNISH GAME HENS

WHY THIS RECIPE WORKS: Grilled Cornish game hens provide an attractive, elegant alternative to grilled chicken. We wanted to develop a foolproof technique that would deliver smoky notes, crisp skin, and juicy meat infused with great flavor. By butterflying the birds we could keep all of the skin on one side, which meant it crisped more quickly when placed facing the coals. Butterflying also produced a uniformly thick bird, which promoted even cooking. We needed to secure the legs to the body to keep the skin from tearing, so we developed a special skewering procedure that stabilized the legs, made it easier to fit the birds on the cooking grate, and created a restaurant-worthy presentation. A seven-ingredient rub gave the hens a sweet and savory complexity and helped crisp the skin even further, giving it a rich mahogany hue. A quick glaze provided the crowning touch.

Grill-Roasted Cornish Game Hens

SERVES 4

To add smoke flavor to the hens, use the optional wood chips; however, when using a charcoal grill, we prefer wood chunks to wood chips whenever possible; substitute 4 medium wood chunks, soaked in water for 1 hour, for the wood chip packets. You will need four 8- to 10-inch flat metal skewers for this recipe.

- ½ cup salt
- 4 (1¼- to 1½-pound) whole Cornish game hens
- 2 tablespoons packed brown sugar
- 1 tablespoon paprika
- 2 teaspoons garlic powder
- 2 teaspoons chili powder
- 1 teaspoon ground black pepper
- 1 teaspoon ground coriander
- ⅛ teaspoon cayenne pepper
- 4 cups wood chips, soaked in water for 15 minutes and drained (optional)
- 1 (16 by 12-inch) disposable aluminum roasting pan
- 1 recipe glaze (recipes follow)

1. TO BUTTERFLY GAME HENS: Use kitchen shears to cut along both sides of backbone to remove it. With skin side down, make ¼-inch cut into bone separating breast halves. Lightly press on ribs to flatten hen. Fold wing tips behind bird to secure them.

2. Dissolve salt in 4 quarts cold water in large container. Submerge hens in brine, cover, and refrigerate for 30 minutes to 1 hour.

3. Combine sugar, paprika, garlic powder, chili powder, pepper, coriander, and cayenne in bowl. Remove hens from brine and pat dry with paper towels.

4. TO SKEWER HENS: Insert flat metal skewer ½ inch from end of drumstick through skin and meat and out other side. Turn leg so that end of drumstick faces wing, then insert tip of skewer into meaty section of thigh under bone. Press skewer all the way through breast and second thigh. Fold end of drumstick toward wing and insert skewer ½ inch from end. Press skewer so that blunt end rests against bird and stretch skin tight over legs, thighs, and breast halves. Rub hens evenly with spice mixture and refrigerate while preparing grill.

5. Using 2 large pieces of heavy-duty aluminum foil, wrap soaked chips, if using, in 2 foil packets and cut several vent holes in tops.

6A. FOR A CHARCOAL GRILL: Open bottom vent completely and place roasting pan in center of grill. Light large chimney starter filled with charcoal briquettes (6 quarts). When top coals are partially covered with ash, pour into 2 even piles on either side of roasting pan. Place 1 wood chip packet, if using, on each pile of coals. Set cooking grate in place, cover, and open lid vent completely. Heat grill until hot and wood chips are smoking, about 5 minutes.

6B. FOR A GAS GRILL: Place wood chip packets, if using, directly on primary burner. Turn all burners to high, cover, and heat grill until hot and wood chips are smoking, about 15 minutes. Turn all burners to medium. (Adjust burners as needed during cooking to maintain grill temperature around 325 degrees.)

7. Clean and oil cooking grate. Place hens in center of grill (over roasting pan if using charcoal), skin side down. Cover (position lid vent over birds if using charcoal) and cook until thighs register 160 degrees, 20 to 30 minutes.

8. Using tongs, move the birds to the hot sides of the grill (if using charcoal; 2 hens per side), keeping them skin side down, or turn all burners to high (if using gas). Cover and continue to cook until browned, about 5 minutes. Brush the birds with half of glaze, flip, and cook for 2 minutes. Brush remaining glaze over hens, flip, and continue to cook until breasts register 160 degrees and thighs register 175 degrees, 1 to 3 minutes longer.

9. Transfer hens to carving board, tent loosely with foil, and let rest for 5 to 10 minutes. Cut hens in half through the breastbone and serve.

Barbecue Glaze

MAKES ABOUT ½ CUP

- ½ cup ketchup
- 2 tablespoons brown sugar
- 1 tablespoon soy sauce
- 1 tablespoon distilled white vinegar
- 1 tablespoon yellow mustard
- 1 garlic clove, minced

Combine all ingredients in small saucepan, bring to simmer, and cook, stirring occasionally, until thickened, about 5 minutes.

Asian Barbecue Glaze

MAKES ABOUT ½ CUP

- ¼ cup ketchup
- ¼ cup hoisin sauce
- 2 tablespoons rice vinegar
- 1 tablespoon soy sauce
- 1 tablespoon toasted sesame oil
- 1 tablespoon grated fresh ginger

Combine all ingredients in small saucepan, bring to simmer, and cook, stirring occasionally, until thickened, about 5 minutes.

NOTES FROM THE TEST KITCHEN

SKEWERING GAME HENS

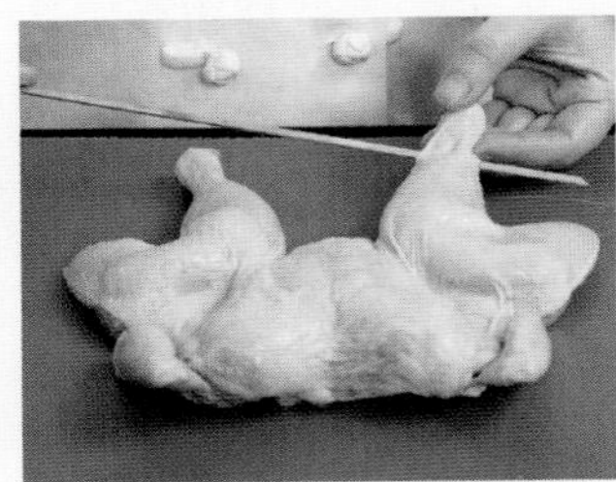

1. Insert a flat metal skewer ½ inch from the end of a drumstick through the skin and meat and out the other side.

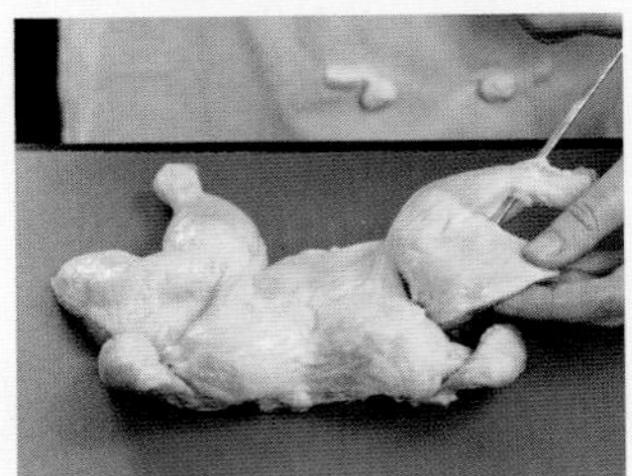

2. Turn the leg so that the end of the drumstick faces the wing, then insert the tip of the skewer into the meaty section of the thigh under the bone.

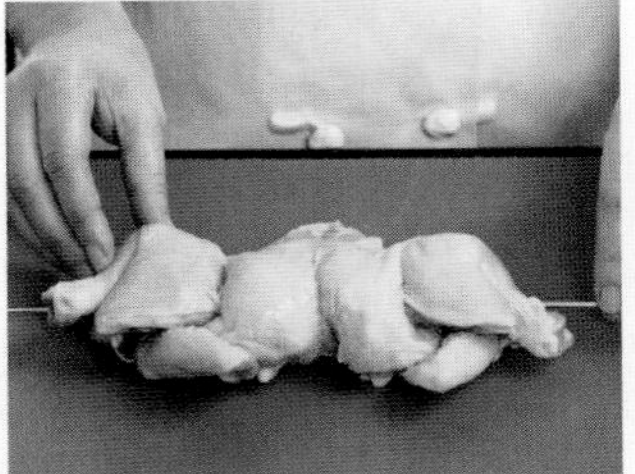

3. Press the skewer all the way through the breast and second thigh. Fold the end of the drumstick toward the wing and insert the skewer ½ inch from the end.

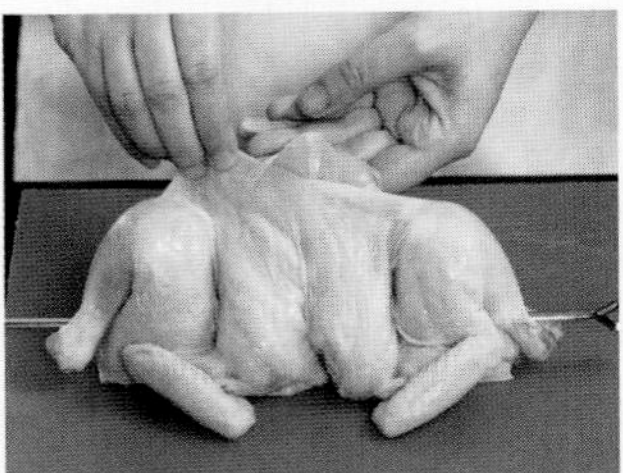

4. Press the skewer so that the blunt end rests against the bird and stretch the skin tight over the legs, thighs, and breast halves.

THAI GRILLED CORNISH GAME HENS

WHY THIS RECIPE WORKS: For our take on Thai grilled chicken, we started with Cornish hens, which are similar in size to the hens traditionally used by street vendors in Thailand. Butterflying and flattening the hens helped them cook more quickly and evenly on the grill. We created a marinade consisting of cilantro leaves and stems (a substitute for hard-to-find cilantro root), lots of garlic, white pepper, ground coriander, brown sugar, and fish sauce; thanks to its pesto-like consistency, it clung to the hens instead of sliding off. We set up a half-grill fire and started cooking the hens skin side up over the cooler side of the grill so the fatty skin had time to slowly render while the meat cooked; then we finished them over the hotter side to crisp the skin. We whipped up a version of the traditional sweet-tangy-spicy dipping sauce by combining equal parts white vinegar and sugar and simmering the mixture until it was slightly thickened and would cling nicely to the chicken. Plenty of minced garlic and Thai chiles balanced the sauce with savory, fruity heat.

Thai Grilled Cornish Game Hens with Chili Dipping Sauce (Gai Yang)

SERVES 4

The hens need to marinate for at least 6 hours before cooking (a longer marinating time is preferable). If your hens weigh 1½ to 2 pounds, grill three hens instead of four and extend the initial cooking time in step 6 by 5 minutes. If you can't find Thai chiles, substitute Fresno or red jalapeño chiles. Serve with steamed white rice.

HENS

- 4 Cornish game hens (1¼ to 1½ pounds each), giblets discarded
- 1 cup fresh cilantro leaves and stems, chopped coarse
- 12 garlic cloves, peeled
- ¼ cup packed light brown sugar
- 2 teaspoons ground white pepper
- 2 teaspoons ground coriander
- 2 teaspoons salt
- ¼ cup fish sauce

DIPPING SAUCE

- ½ cup distilled white vinegar
- ½ cup granulated sugar
- 1 tablespoon minced Thai chiles
- 3 garlic cloves, minced
- ¼ teaspoon salt

1. FOR THE HENS: Working with 1 hen at a time, place hen breast side down on cutting board and use kitchen shears to cut through bones on either side of backbone; discard backbone. Flip hen and press on breastbone to flatten. Trim off any excess fat and skin.

2. Pulse cilantro leaves and stems, garlic, sugar, pepper, coriander, and salt in food processor until finely chopped, 10 to 15 pulses; transfer to small bowl. Add fish sauce and stir until marinade has consistency of loose paste.

3. Rub hens all over with marinade. Transfer hens and any excess marinade to large zipper-lock bag and refrigerate for at least 6 hours or up to 24 hours, turning bag halfway through marinating.

4. FOR THE DIPPING SAUCE: Bring vinegar to boil in small saucepan. Add sugar and stir to dissolve. Reduce heat to medium-low and simmer until vinegar mixture is slightly thickened, 5 minutes. Remove from heat and let vinegar mixture cool to room temperature. Add chiles, garlic, and salt and stir until combined. Transfer sauce to airtight container and refrigerate until ready to use. (Sauce can be refrigerated for up to 2 weeks. Bring to room temperature before serving.)

5A. FOR A CHARCOAL GRILL: Open bottom vent completely. Light large chimney starter filled with charcoal briquettes (6 quarts). When top coals are partially covered with ash, pour evenly over half of grill. Set cooking grate in place, cover, and open lid vent completely. Heat grill until hot, about 5 minutes.

5B. FOR A GAS GRILL: Turn all burners to high, cover, and heat grill until hot, about 15 minutes. Leave primary burner and secondary burner (next to primary burner) on high and turn off other burner(s). Adjust secondary burner as needed to maintain grill temperature between 400 and 450 degrees.

6. Clean and oil cooking grate. Remove hens from bag, leaving any marinade that sticks to hens in place. Tuck wingtips behind backs and turn legs so drumsticks face inward toward breasts. Place hens, skin side up, on cooler side of grill (if using charcoal, arrange hens so that legs and thighs are facing coals). Cover and cook until skin has browned and breasts register 145 to 150 degrees, 30 to 35 minutes, rotating hens halfway through cooking.

7. Using tongs, carefully flip hens and place skin side down on hotter side of grill. Cover and cook until skin is crisp, deeply browned, and charred in spots and breasts register 160 degrees, 3 to 5 minutes, being careful to avoid burning.

8. Transfer hens, skin side up, to cutting board, tent with aluminum foil, and let rest for 10 minutes. Carve each hen in half or into 4 pieces and serve, passing dipping sauce separately.

GRILLED SALMON FILLETS

WHY THIS RECIPE WORKS: Cooking delicate salmon can be tricky. Even using a nonstick skillet, it's still easy to break the occasional fillet. Introduce that same fillet to a grill, and you've got a real challenge. We wanted grilled salmon with a tender interior and crisp skin, and with each fillet perfectly intact.

We chose thicker salmon fillets, which could stand the heat of the grill for a little while longer before the first turn. To prevent the fish from sticking, we dried the fish's exterior by wrapping it in kitchen towels and "seasoned" our cooking grate by brushing it over and over with multiple layers of oil until it developed a dark, shiny coating. After laying the fillets on the grate, we easily flipped each fillet without even the tiniest bit of sticking.

Grilled Salmon Fillets

SERVES 4

This recipe can be used with any thick, firm-fleshed white fish, including red snapper, grouper, halibut, and sea bass (cook white fish to 140 degrees, up to 2 minutes longer per side). If you are using skinless fillets, treat the skinned side of each as if it were the skin side. If desired, serve with Almond Vinaigrette or Olive Vinaigrette (recipes follow).

1 (1½- to 2-pound) skin-on salmon fillet, 1½ inches thick
Vegetable oil
Salt and pepper
Lemon wedges

1. Use sharp knife to remove any whitish fat from belly of salmon and cut fillet into 4 equal pieces. Place fillets skin side up on large plate lined with clean kitchen towel. Place second clean kitchen towel on top of fillets and press down to blot liquid. Refrigerate fish, wrapped in towels, while preparing grill, at least 20 minutes.

2A. FOR A CHARCOAL GRILL: Open bottom vent completely. Light large chimney starter two-thirds filled with charcoal briquettes (4 quarts). When top coals are partially covered with ash, pour evenly over half of grill. Set cooking grate in place, cover, and open lid vent completely. Heat grill until hot, about 5 minutes.

2B. FOR A GAS GRILL: Turn all burners to high, cover, and heat grill until hot, about 15 minutes.

3. Clean cooking grate, then repeatedly brush grate with well-oiled paper towels until grate is black and glossy, 5 to 10 times. Lightly brush both sides of fish with oil and season with salt and pepper. Place fish skin side down on hot side of grill (if using charcoal) or turn all burners to medium (if using gas) with fillets diagonal to grate. Cover and cook until skin is well browned and crisp, 3 to 5 minutes. (Try lifting fish gently with spatula after 3 minutes; if it doesn't cleanly lift off grill, continue to cook, checking at 30-second intervals, until it releases.)

4. Flip fish and continue to cook, covered, until center is still translucent when checked with tip of paring knife and registers 125 degrees (for medium-rare) and is still translucent when cut into with paring knife, 2 to 6 minutes longer. Serve immediately with lemon wedges.

Almond Vinaigrette

MAKES ABOUT ½ CUP

⅓ cup whole almonds, toasted
1 small shallot, minced
4 teaspoons white wine vinegar
2 teaspoons honey
1 teaspoon Dijon mustard
⅓ cup extra-virgin olive oil
1 tablespoon cold water
1 tablespoon chopped fresh tarragon
Salt and pepper

Place almonds in zipper-lock bag and, using rolling pin or bottom of skillet, pound until pieces no larger than ½ inch remain. Combine pounded almonds, shallot, vinegar, honey, and mustard in medium bowl. Whisking constantly, slowly drizzle in oil until smooth emulsion forms. Add water and tarragon and whisk to combine, then season with salt and pepper to taste. Whisk to recombine before serving.

Olive Vinaigrette

MAKES ABOUT ½ CUP

½ cup green or kalamata olives, pitted and chopped coarse
¼ cup extra-virgin olive oil
2 tablespoons chopped fresh parsley
1 small shallot, minced
2 teaspoons lemon juice
Salt and pepper

Combine all ingredients except salt and pepper in bowl and season with salt and pepper to taste. Whisk to recombine before serving.

GLAZED SALMON

WHY THIS RECIPE WORKS: A burnt, stuck-to-the-grill crust and flavorless interior are too often the reality of glazed salmon. But truly great glazed salmon right off the grill is a thing of beauty—the sweet glaze not only forms a glossy, deeply caramelized crust, but it also permeates the flesh, making the last bite of fish every bit as good as the first. This was the salmon that we wanted to re-create—sweet, crisp, moist, and flavorful.

Our recipe coup came early on in development—we realized that the best way to prevent the glazed salmon from sticking to the cooking grate was by not letting it touch the grate at all. We grilled the salmon fillets in individual aluminum trays set over the grill. There was no need for special equipment—we simply folded heavy-duty foil into 7 by 5-inch trays. This way, the fish still picked up great smoky flavor, but didn't stick to the cooking grate. Jelly was the best base ingredient for a sweet and sticky glaze. For the deepest flavor, we brushed some glaze over

the fish toward the end of grilling, so it caramelized, and spooned the remaining glaze, enriched with butter, over the fish just before serving.

Sweet and Saucy Glazed Salmon

SERVES 4

Be sure to spray the foil trays with vegetable oil spray. You can also use Reynolds Wrap nonstick aluminum foil and skip the vegetable oil spray.

- ½ cup jalapeño jelly
- ½ cup packed fresh cilantro leaves and stems
- 1 teaspoon grated fresh lime zest and
- 2 tablespoons fresh lime juice
- 2 scallions, chopped coarse
- 2 garlic cloves, minced
- 2 tablespoons unsalted butter
- 4 (6- to 8-ounce) skinless salmon fillets, about 1¼ inches thick
- Salt and pepper

1. Process jelly, cilantro, lime zest, lime juice, scallions, and garlic in food processor or blender to a smooth glaze. Transfer glaze to small saucepan and cook over medium heat until just bubbling, 2 to 3 minutes. Measure out and reserve ¼ cup glaze. Stir butter into remaining glaze.

2. Use heavy-duty foil to make four 7 by 5-inch trays (see photo). Coat trays with vegetable oil spray. Season fillets with salt and pepper, and brush each thoroughly, on both sides, with 1 tablespoon of the reserved ¼ cup glaze. Place fillets, skinned side up, on trays.

3A. FOR A CHARCOAL GRILL: Open bottom grill vents completely. Light large chimney starter filled with charcoal briquettes (100 briquettes; 6 quarts). When coals are hot, pour evenly over grill. Set cooking grate in place, cover, and heat grill until hot, about 5 minutes.

3B. FOR A GAS GRILL: Turn all burners to high, cover, and heat grill until hot, about 15 minutes. (Adjust the burners as needed to maintain a hot fire.)

4. Clean and oil cooking grate. Place trays on grill. Cook (covered if using gas) until glaze forms a golden brown crust, 6 to 8 minutes. Flip fillets, keeping them in trays, and spoon half of buttered glaze over salmon. Continue to cook until fish is opaque and flakes apart when gently prodded with paring knife, about 2 to 4 minutes longer.

5. Transfer trays to wire rack, tent loosely with foil, and let rest for 5 minutes. Transfer salmon to platter, spoon remaining buttered glaze over the top, and serve.

Orange-Sesame Glazed Salmon

Follow the recipe for Sweet and Saucy Glazed Salmon, substituting orange marmalade for jalapeño jelly, and lemon zest and juice for lime zest and juice, in step 1. Add 2 tablespoons oyster-flavored sauce and 1 teaspoon toasted sesame oil to food processor or blender with other glaze ingredients. Stir 1 teaspoon toasted sesame seeds into glaze with butter.

NOTES FROM THE TEST KITCHEN

MAKING FOIL TRAYS

Cut four rectangles of heavy-duty aluminum foil, then crimp the edges of each piece to make a 7 by 5-inch tray.

REMOVING SKIN FROM SALMON

1. Using tip of boning knife (or sharp chef's knife), begin to cut skin away from fish at corner of fillet.

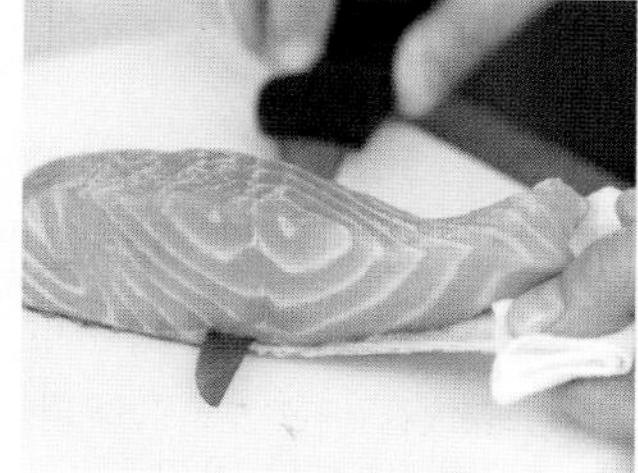

2. When enough skin is exposed, grasp it firmly with piece of paper towel, hold it taut, and carefully slice rest of skin off flesh.

Spicy Apple Glazed Salmon

Follow the recipe for Sweet and Saucy Glazed Salmon, substituting apple jelly for jalapeño jelly, and 2 tablespoons cider vinegar for lime zest and juice, in step 1. Add ½ teaspoon red pepper flakes to food processor or blender with other glaze ingredients.

BARBECUED SALMON

WHY THIS RECIPE WORKS: Store-bought smoked salmon is inconsistent in quality and also incredibly expensive—up to $8 for just 4 ounces. We wanted to create our own easy recipe for this dish that's often reserved for weekend brunch, and make moist (but not too moist), nicely crusted salmon with a hint of smoked flavor—in just two hours.

Surprisingly, impatience turned out to be the key to our success. Instead of the traditional cold-smoking technique, which keeps the salmon moist but lacks flavor, we developed a "hot-smoked" method, and kept the salmon moist by brining. We achieved full smoked salmon flavor on the grill using a whole side of salmon. To get a firm but not overly dry texture, complemented by a strong hit of smoke and wood, we slow-cooked the salmon with wood chips or chunks for more than an hour over a modified two-level fire, but kept the fish on the cooler part of the grill the whole time. Using two spatulas to transfer the cooked fish from the grill prevented it from falling apart, and cutting through the pink flesh, not the skin, to divide individual portions kept the meat intact while leaving the skin behind.

Barbecued Salmon

SERVES 4 TO 6

The cooking grate must be hot and thoroughly clean before you place the salmon on it; otherwise the fish might stick. Use foil or the back of a large rimmed baking sheet to get the fish onto the grill. If you'd like to use wood chunks instead of wood chips when using a charcoal grill, substitute 2 medium wood chunks, soaked in water for 1 hour, for the wood chip packet. If desired, serve the salmon with Horseradish Cream Sauce with Chives or Mustard-Dill Sauce (recipes follow).

- 1 cup sugar
- ½ cup salt
- 1 (2½-pound) skin-on salmon fillet
- 2 cups wood chips, soaked in water for 15 minutes and drained
- 2 tablespoons vegetable oil
- 1½ teaspoons sweet paprika
- 1 teaspoon ground white pepper

1. Dissolve sugar and salt in 7 cups cold water in gallon-size zipper-lock bag. Add salmon, seal bag, and refrigerate for 3 hours. Remove salmon from brine, pat dry with paper towels, and rub thoroughly with oil. Lay salmon skin side down on 30-inch sheet of heavy-duty aluminum foil and season top and sides with paprika and pepper.

2A. FOR A CHARCOAL GRILL: Open bottom grill vent halfway. Light large chimney starter half filled with charcoal briquettes (3 quarts). When top coals are partially covered with ash, pour evenly over half of grill. Place wood chip packet on coals. Set cooking grate in place, cover, and open lid vent completely halfway. Heat grill until hot and wood chips are smoking, about 5 minutes.

2B. FOR A GAS GRILL: Remove grill grate and place wood chip packet directly on primary burner. Set cooking grate in place, turn all burners to high, cover, and heat grill until hot and wood chips are smoking, about 15 minutes. Leave primary burner on medium and turn off other burner(s). (Adjust primary burner as needed to maintain grill temperature around 275 degrees.)

3. Clean cooking grate, then repeatedly brush grate with well-oiled paper towels until black and glossy, 5 to 10 times. Gently slide salmon off foil onto cooler side of grill, skin-side down and perpendicular to grill grate. Cover (position lid vent over meat if using charcoal) and cook until heavily flavored with smoke, about 1½ hours.

4. Using two spatulas, gently remove salmon from grill. Serve hot or at room temperature.

Horseradish Cream Sauce with Chives

MAKES ABOUT 1 CUP

- 1 cup crème fraîche or sour cream
- 2 tablespoons prepared horseradish
- 2 tablespoons minced fresh chives
- Pinch table salt

Combine the ingredients in a small bowl. (The sauce can be refrigerated in an airtight container for up to 1 day.)

Mustard-Dill Sauce

MAKES ABOUT 1 CUP

Use Dijon, honey, or grainy mustard, as desired. Depending on your choice of mustard, this sauce can be fairly hot.

- 1 cup mustard (see note)
- ¼ cup minced fresh dill

Combine the ingredients in a small bowl. (The sauce can be refrigerated in an airtight container for up to 1 day.)

BEHIND THE SCENES

HOW TO AVOID A STICKY SITUATION: PREVENTING FISH (AND MORE) FROM STICKING TO THE GRILL

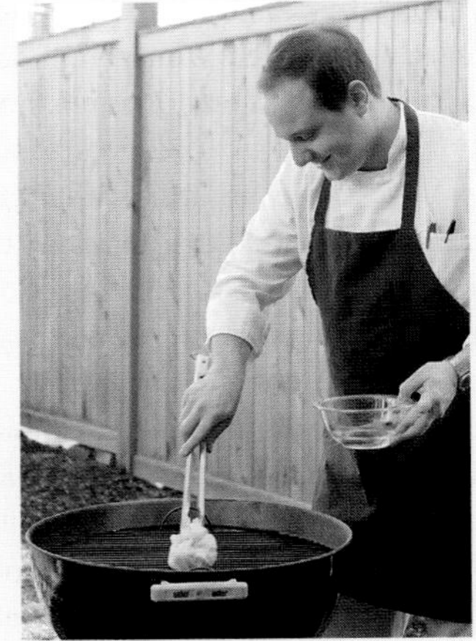

To prevent food from sticking, the cooking grate should be oiled once it is hot, after being scraped clean. Debris is more readily removed from a hot grate than a cool one, and once these stuck-on bits are gone, the grate can be more effectively slicked down with an oil-dipped wad of paper towels.

Oiling the cooking grate once it's hot also helps the oil to bond quickly to the metal and prevent proteins from sticking to the cooking grate. When oil is added to a cold cooking grate, the oil slowly vaporizes as the grill reaches the desired cooking temperature. The more the oil vaporizes, the less oil will be left on the cooking grate, making sticking more likely.

And for foods that are especially prone to sticking to the grill, like fish, multiple applications of oil work wonders. Simply apply the oil to the grate five to 10 times, re-dipping the towels in the oil between applications, until the grate is black and glossy.

One more point: Never try to take a shortcut by spraying a hot cooking grate with vegetable oil spray. You might save about 10 seconds, but you risk having a flare-up on your hands.

GRILL-SMOKED SALMON

WHY THIS RECIPE WORKS: We wanted to capture the intense, smoky flavor of hot-smoked fish and the firm but silky texture of the cold-smoked type, but we also wanted to skip specialized equipment and make this dish less of a project. We quick-cured the fish with a mixture of salt and sugar to draw moisture from the flesh, and we seasoned it inside and out. We then cooked it over a gentle fire with ample smoke to produce salmon that was sweet, smoky, and tender. We also cut our large fillet into individual serving-size portions. This ensured more thorough smoke exposure by creating more surface area. Plus, the smaller pieces of salmon were far easier to get off the grill intact than one large fillet.

Grill-Smoked Salmon

SERVES 6

Use center-cut salmon fillets of similar thickness so that they cook at the same rate. The best way to ensure uniformity is to buy a 2½- to 3-pound whole center-cut fillet and cut it into six pieces. Avoid mesquite wood chunks for this recipe. Serve the salmon with lemon wedges or with our "Smoked Salmon Platter" Sauce or Apple-Mustard Sauce (recipes follow).

- 2 tablespoons sugar
- 1 tablespoon kosher salt
- 6 (6- to 8-ounce) center-cut skin-on salmon fillets
- 2 wood chunks soaked in water for 30 minutes and drained (if using charcoal) or 2 cups wood chips, half of chips soaked in water for 15 minutes and drained (if using gas)

1. Combine sugar and salt in bowl. Set wire rack in rimmed baking sheet, set salmon on rack, and sprinkle flesh side evenly with sugar mixture. Refrigerate, uncovered, for 1 hour. With paper towels, brush any excess salt and sugar from salmon and blot dry. Return fish on wire rack to refrigerator, uncovered, while preparing grill.

2A. FOR A CHARCOAL GRILL: Open bottom vent halfway. Light large chimney starter one-third filled with charcoal briquettes (2 quarts). When top coals are partially covered with ash, pour into steeply banked pile against side of grill. Place wood chunks on top of coals. Set cooking grate in place, cover, and open lid vent halfway. Heat grill until hot and wood chunks begin to smoke, about 5 minutes.

2B. FOR A GAS GRILL: Combine soaked and unsoaked chips. Use large piece of heavy-duty aluminum foil to wrap chips into foil packet and cut several vent holes in top. Place wood chip packet directly on primary burner. Turn primary burner to high (leave other burners off), cover, and heat grill until hot and wood chips begin to smoke, 15 to 25 minutes. Turn primary burner to medium. (Adjust primary burner as needed to maintain grill temperature of 275 to 300 degrees.)

3. Clean and oil cooking grate. Fold piece of heavy-duty foil into 18 by 6-inch rectangle. Place foil rectangle over cool side of grill and place salmon pieces on foil, spaced at least ½ inch apart. Cover grill (positioning lid vent over fish if using charcoal) and cook until center of thickest part of fillet registers 125 degrees and is still translucent when checked with tip of paring knife, 30 to 40 minutes. Transfer to platter and serve, or allow to cool to room temperature.

"Smoked Salmon Platter" Sauce

MAKES 1½ CUPS

This sauce incorporates the three garnishes that are commonly served on a smoked salmon platter—hard-cooked egg, capers, and dill.

- 1 large egg yolk, plus 1 large hard-cooked egg, chopped fine
- 2 teaspoons Dijon mustard
- 2 teaspoons sherry vinegar
- ½ cup vegetable oil
- 2 tablespoons capers, rinsed, plus 1 teaspoon caper brine
- 2 tablespoons minced shallot
- 2 tablespoons minced fresh dill

Whisk egg yolk, mustard, and vinegar together in medium bowl. Whisking constantly, slowly drizzle in oil until emulsified, about 1 minute. Gently fold in capers and brine, hard-cooked egg, shallot, and dill.

Apple-Mustard Sauce

MAKES 1½ CUPS

- 2 Honeycrisp or Granny Smith apples, peeled, cored, and cut into ¼-inch dice
- ¼ cup whole-grain mustard
- 2 tablespoons Dijon mustard
- 2 tablespoons minced fresh chervil or parsley
- 1 tablespoon cider vinegar
- 1 tablespoon honey
- ¼ teaspoon salt

Combine all ingredients in bowl.

GRILLED TUNA STEAKS

WHY THIS RECIPE WORKS: Most grilled tuna steaks are either rare in the center with no char or have a great sear enveloping a dry, mealy interior. We wanted a thick layer of hot, grilled tuna with an intense smoky char wrapped around a cool, delicately flavored, tender, and moist center.

We began by selecting tuna steaks that were thick enough to stay on the grill long enough to achieve a decent crust without overcooking. Our initial test of cooking methods proved that using direct heat with a hot fire and getting the tuna on and off the grill as quickly as possible worked well. For the charred flavor we were after, we turned to an ingredient that can enhance browning—oil. Oil helped to distribute heat evenly over the surface of the fish, including those areas not actually touching the cooking grate, and it added a little fat to the lean tuna, which kept the exterior from getting too dry and stringy. But oil alone didn't infuse our fish with grill flavor. We discovered that to moisten the tuna's flesh, the oil needed to penetrate the meat's tiny muscle fibers. Instead, we turned to a vinaigrette. The dressing (and its oil) clung to the fish, moistening its exterior and solving the problem of dry flesh. To improve browning we added honey to our vinaigrette. The sugars caramelized quickly on the grill, helping deliver a perfectly browned crust on our tuna steaks.

Grilled Tuna Steaks with Vinaigrette

SERVES 6

We prefer our tuna served rare or medium-rare. If you like your fish cooked medium, observe the timing for medium-rare, then tent the steaks loosely with aluminum foil for 5 minutes before serving.

- 3 tablespoons plus 1 teaspoon red wine vinegar
- 2 tablespoons chopped fresh thyme or rosemary
- 2 tablespoons Dijon mustard
- 2 teaspoons honey
- Salt and pepper
- ¾ cup olive oil
- 6 (8-ounce) tuna steaks, 1 inch thick

1A. FOR A CHARCOAL GRILL: Open bottom vent completely. Light large chimney starter filled with charcoal briquettes (6 quarts). When top coals are partially covered with ash, pour evenly over half of grill. Set cooking grate in place, cover, and open lid vent completely. Heat grill until hot, about 5 minutes.

1B. FOR A GAS GRILL: Turn all burners to high, cover, and heat grill until hot, about 15 minutes. (Adjust burners as needed to maintain hot fire.)

2. Clean cooking grate, then repeatedly brush grate with well-oiled paper towels until grate is black and glossy, 5 to 10 times.

3. Meanwhile, whisk vinegar, thyme, mustard, honey, ½ teaspoon salt, and pinch pepper together in large bowl. Whisking constantly, slowly drizzle oil into vinegar mixture until lightly thickened and emulsified. Measure out ¾ cup vinaigrette and set aside for cooking fish. Reserve remaining vinaigrette for serving.

4. Pat fish dry with paper towels. Generously brush both sides of fish with vinaigrette and season with salt and pepper. Place fish on grill (hot side if using charcoal) and cook (covered if using gas) until grill marks form and bottom surface is opaque, 1 to 3 minutes.

5. Flip fish and cook until opaque at perimeter and translucent red at center when checked with tip of paring knife and registers 110 degrees (rare), about 1½ minutes, or until opaque at perimeter and reddish pink at center when checked with tip of paring knife and registers 125 degrees (medium-rare), about 3 minutes. Serve, passing reserved vinaigrette.

GRILLED BLACKENED RED SNAPPER

WHY THIS RECIPE WORKS: Blackened fish is usually prepared in a cast-iron skillet, but it can lead to one smoky kitchen. We thought we'd solve this issue by throwing our fish on the barbie (it works for more than just shrimp, right?). Unfortunately, this move created a host of other problems, including fish stuck to the grate, the outside of the fish being way overdone by the time the flesh had cooked through, and the skin-on fillets curling midway through cooking. We were done with the smoke—and were ready for our fillets to have a dark brown, crusty, sweet-smoky, toasted spice exterior, providing a rich contrast to the moist, mild-flavored fish inside.

The curling problem was easy to fix. We simply needed to score the skin. To prevent sticking, we made sure the grill was hot when we put the fish on and oiled the grate multiple times to ensure a clean surface. Finally, to give the fish its flavorful "blackened but not burned" coating, we bloomed our spice mixture in melted butter, allowed it to cool, and then applied the coating to the fish. Once on the grill, the spice crust acquired the proper depth and richness while the fish cooked through.

Grilled Blackened Red Snapper

SERVES 4

Striped bass, halibut, or grouper can be substituted for the snapper; if the fillets are thicker or thinner, they will have slightly different cooking times. Serve the fish with lemon wedges, Rémoulade, or Pineapple and Cucumber Salsa with Mint (recipes follow).

- 2 tablespoons paprika
- 2 teaspoons onion powder
- 2 teaspoons garlic powder
- ¾ teaspoon ground coriander
- ¾ teaspoon salt
- ¼ teaspoon cayenne pepper
- ¼ teaspoon black pepper
- ¼ teaspoon white pepper
- 3 tablespoons unsalted butter
- 4 (6- to 8-ounce) skin-on red snapper fillets, ¾ inch thick

1. Combine paprika, onion powder, garlic powder, coriander, salt, cayenne, black pepper, and white pepper in bowl. Melt butter in 10-inch skillet over medium heat. Stir in spice mixture and cook, stirring frequently, until fragrant and spices turn dark rust color, 2 to 3 minutes. Transfer mixture to pie plate and let cool to room temperature. Use a fork to break up any large clumps.

2A. FOR A CHARCOAL GRILL: Open bottom vent completely. Light large chimney starter two-thirds filled with charcoal briquettes (4 quarts). When top coals are partially covered with ash, pour evenly over half of grill. Set cooking grate in place, cover, and open lid vent completely. Heat grill until hot, about 5 minutes.

2B. FOR A GAS GRILL: Turn all burners to high, cover, and heat grill until hot, about 15 minutes.

3. Clean cooking grate, then repeatedly brush grate with well-oiled paper towels until black and glossy, 5 to 10 times.

4. Meanwhile, pat fillets dry with paper towels. Using sharp knife, make shallow diagonal slashes every inch along skin side of fish, being careful not to cut into flesh. Place fillets skin side up on large plate. Using your fingers, rub spice mixture in thin, even layer on top and sides of fish. Flip fillets over and repeat on other side (you should use all of spice mixture).

5. Place fish skin side down on grill (hot side if using charcoal) with fillets diagonal to grate. Cook until skin is very dark brown and crisp, 3 to 5 minutes. Carefully flip fish and continue to cook until dark brown and beginning to flake and center is opaque but still moist, about 5 minutes longer. Serve.

Rémoulade

MAKES ABOUT ½ CUP

The rémoulade can be refrigerated for up to 3 days.

- ½ cup mayonnaise
- 1½ teaspoons sweet pickle relish
- 1 teaspoon hot sauce
- 1 teaspoon lemon juice
- 1 teaspoon minced fresh parsley
- ½ teaspoon capers, rinsed
- ½ teaspoon Dijon mustard
- 1 small garlic clove, minced
- Salt and pepper

Pulse all ingredients in food processor until well combined but not smooth, about 10 pulses. Season with salt and pepper to taste. Transfer to serving bowl.

Pineapple and Cucumber Salsa with Mint

MAKES ABOUT 3 CUPS

To make this dish spicier, add the reserved chile seeds.

- ½ large pineapple, peeled, cored, and cut into ¼-inch pieces
- ½ cucumber, peeled, halved lengthwise, seeded, and cut into ¼-inch pieces
- 1 small shallot, minced
- 1 serrano chile, stemmed, seeds reserved, and minced
- 2 tablespoons chopped fresh mint
- 1–2 tablespoons lime juice
- ½ teaspoon grated fresh ginger
- Salt
- Sugar

Combine pineapple, cucumber, shallot, serrano, mint, 1 tablespoon lime juice, ginger, and ½ teaspoon salt in bowl and let sit at room temperature for 15 to 30 minutes. Season with lime juice, salt, and sugar to taste. Transfer to serving bowl.

BEHIND THE SCENES

ABUSE TESTS: ADAM GETS TOUGH

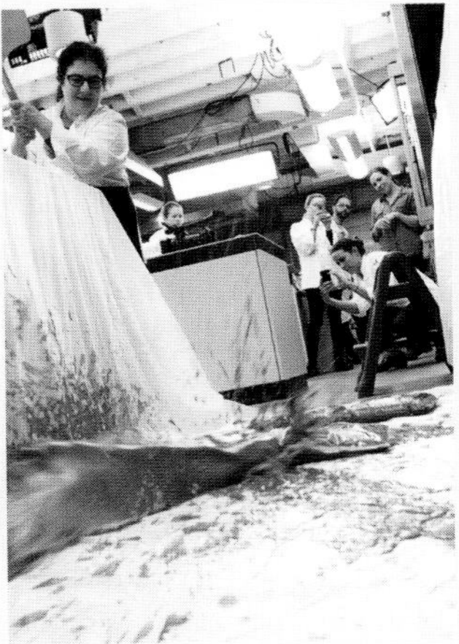

Adam and our team of equipment experts spend weeks—often months—testing leading brands to see which are worth buying. We start by answering basic performance questions—such as "Does this skillet heat evenly?" or "Is this knife sharp?"—with controlled kitchen tests. We sauté onions in every skillet in the line-up or we slice tomatoes with each knife. Once we've evaluated each brand in terms of performance (and design), it's time to assess durability. Here's where Adam and our equipment testers can get pretty creative. They devise abuse tests—the kinds of things you might do at home, even though you shouldn't—to see how products will fare.

Some abuse tests are pretty straightforward. We cut and serve lasagna baked in nonstick baking dishes with a metal spatula to see how the nonstick coating will hold up. Other tests are downright wacky. Here are some favorites over the years:

- Trying to melt rubber spatulas by leaving them in a cast-iron skillet heated to 674 degrees, then simmering the spatulas in a pot of curry for an hour to see if they would stain and absorb odors.
- Dropping sealed food storage bags filled with spaghetti sauce from a height of 3 feet onto a plastic tarp to see which bags would survive without sending sauce all over the kitchen.
- Holding our mitt-covered hands in the gas flame on a cooktop for 5 seconds to see which mitts are truly flame-resistant.

Why are Adam and his team willing to abuse kitchen equipment (and their hands) to see how products will perform during worst-case scenarios? Simple. Because we want to know which items really work, and which ones don't.

GRILLED FISH TACOS

WHY THIS RECIPE WORKS: For a fish taco with fresh, bold flavors, we fired up the grill. For simplicity we opted for skinless fillets instead of the traditional whole butterflied fish. Meaty swordfish held up on the grill better than flaky options like hake and cod. A thick paste featuring ancho and chipotle chile powders, oregano, and just a touch of citrus juice developed deep, flavorful charring on the grill without promoting sticking. Refreshing grilled pineapple salsa, avocado, and crunchy iceberg lettuce completed our tacos with flavor and texture contrasts.

Grilled Fish Tacos

SERVES 6

Mahi-mahi, tuna, and halibut fillets are all suitable substitutes for the swordfish but to ensure the best results buy 1-inch-thick fillets and cut them in a similar fashion to the swordfish.

- 3 tablespoons vegetable oil
- 1 tablespoon ancho chile powder
- 2 teaspoons chipotle chile powder
- 1 teaspoon dried oregano
- 1 teaspoon ground coriander
- 2 garlic cloves, minced
- Salt
- 2 tablespoons tomato paste
- ½ cup orange juice
- 6 tablespoons lime juice (3 limes)
- 2 pounds skinless swordfish steaks, 1 inch thick, cut lengthwise into 1-inch-wide strips
- 1 pineapple, peeled, quartered lengthwise, cored, and each quarter halved lengthwise
- 1 jalapeño chile
- 18 (6-inch) corn tortillas
- 1 red bell pepper, stemmed, seeded, and cut into ¼-inch pieces
- 2 tablespoons minced fresh cilantro, plus extra for serving
- ½ head iceberg lettuce (4½ ounces), cored and thinly sliced
- 1 avocado, halved, pitted, and sliced thin
- Lime wedges

1. Heat 2 tablespoons oil, ancho chile powder, and chipotle chile powder in 8-inch skillet over medium heat, stirring constantly, until fragrant and some bubbles form, 2 to 3 minutes. Add oregano, coriander, garlic, and 1 teaspoon salt and continue to cook until fragrant, about 30 seconds longer. Add tomato paste and, using spatula, mash tomato paste with spice mixture until combined, about 20 seconds. Stir in orange juice and 2 tablespoons lime juice. Cook, stirring constantly, until thoroughly mixed and reduced slightly, about 2 minutes. Transfer chile mixture to large bowl and cool for 15 minutes.

2. Add swordfish to bowl with chile mixture, and stir gently with rubber spatula to coat fish. Cover and refrigerate for at least 30 minutes or up to 2 hours.

3A. FOR A CHARCOAL GRILL: Open bottom vent completely. Light large chimney starter mounded with charcoal briquettes (7 quarts). When top coals are partially covered with ash, pour evenly over grill. Set cooking grate in place, cover, and open lid vent completely. Heat grill until hot, about 5 minutes.

3B. FOR A GAS GRILL: Turn all burners to high, cover, and heat grill until hot, about 15 minutes. Turn all burners to medium-high.

4. Clean cooking grate, then repeatedly brush grate with well-oiled paper towels until grate is black and glossy, 5 to 10 times. Brush both sides of pineapple with remaining 1 tablespoon oil. Place fish on half of grill. Place pineapple and jalapeño on other half. Cover and cook until fish, pineapple, and jalapeño have begun to brown, 3 to 5 minutes. Using thin spatula, flip fish, pineapple, and jalapeño over. Cover and continue to cook until second sides of pineapple and jalapeño are browned and swordfish registers 140 degrees, 3 to 5 minutes. Transfer fish to large platter, flake into pieces, and tent with aluminum foil. Transfer pineapple and jalapeño to cutting board.

5. Clean cooking grate. Place half of tortillas on grill. Grill until softened and speckled with brown spots, 30 to 45 seconds per side. Wrap tortillas in dish towel or foil to keep warm until ready to use. Repeat with remaining tortillas.

6. When cool enough to handle, finely chop pineapple and jalapeño. Transfer to medium bowl and stir in bell pepper, cilantro, and remaining 4 tablespoons lime juice. Season with salt to taste. Top tortillas with flaked fish, salsa, lettuce, and avocado. Serve with lime wedges and extra cilantro.

GRILLED SEA SCALLOPS

WHY THIS RECIPE WORKS: In theory, the blazing-hot fire of a grill is perfect for cooking scallops with an extra-crisp crust and moist interior, but in practice they're usually rubbery and overcooked by the time they develop a good sear—and they inevitably stick to the grate. For great grilled scallops, we needed to figure out how to build the biggest fire possible. The solution for a charcoal grill was a disposable aluminum pan—it allowed us to corral the coals in just the center of the grill for a tall, even, super-hot fire that gave us scallops with impressive char and juicy centers. Drying the scallops with kitchen towels before cooking helped ensure browning, and threading them onto two side-by-side skewers made them easy to flip all at once. To combat the problem of sticking, we lightly coated the scallops in a mixture of flour, cornstarch, oil, and sugar. With this simple coating, our scallops were crisp-crusted, moist and tender within, and they came off the grill without hesitation. To complement the scallops, a chile-lime vinaigrette contributed both brightness and heat, or a basil vinaigrette added a light, summery flavor.

Grilled Sea Scallops

SERVES 4

We recommend buying "dry" scallops, which don't have chemical additives and taste better than "wet." Dry scallops will look ivory or pinkish; wet scallops are bright white. If using wet scallops, soak them in a solution of 1 quart water, ¼ cup lemon juice, and 2 tablespoons salt for 30 minutes before step 1, and do not season with salt in step 3. You will need eight to twelve 12-inch metal skewers for this recipe. Double-skewering the scallops makes flipping easier. Serve with one recipe vinaigrette (recipes follow), if desired.

- 1½ pounds large dry sea scallops, tendons removed
- 1 (13 by 9-inch) disposable aluminum roasting pan
- 2 tablespoons vegetable oil
- 1 tablespoon all-purpose flour
- 1 teaspoon cornstarch
- 1 teaspoon sugar
- Salt and pepper
- Lemon wedges

1. Place scallops on rimmed baking sheet lined with clean dish towel. Place second clean dish towel on top of scallops and press gently on towel to blot liquid. Let scallops sit at room temperature, covered with towel, for 10 minutes. To double-skewer scallops, thread 4 to 6 scallops, 1 flat side down, onto 1 skewer and then place second skewer through scallops parallel to and about ¼ inch from first. Return skewered scallops to towel-lined baking sheet; refrigerate, covered with second towel, while preparing grill.

2A. FOR A CHARCOAL GRILL: Open bottom vent completely. Light large chimney starter mounded with charcoal briquettes (7 quarts). Meanwhile, poke twelve ½-inch holes in bottom of disposable pan and place in center of grill. When top coals are partially covered with ash, empty coals into pan. Set cooking grate in place, cover, and open lid vent completely. Heat grill until hot, about 5 minutes.

2B. FOR A GAS GRILL: Turn all burners to high, cover, and heat grill until hot, about 15 minutes.

3. While grill heats, whisk oil, flour, cornstarch, and sugar together in small bowl. Remove towels from scallops. Brush both sides of skewered scallops with oil mixture and season with salt and pepper.

4. Clean cooking grate, then repeatedly brush grate with well-oiled paper towels until grate is black and glossy, 5 to 10 times.

5. Place skewered scallops directly on grill (directly over hot coals if using charcoal). Cook (covered if using gas) without moving scallops until lightly browned, 2½ to 4 minutes. Carefully flip skewers and continue to cook until second side of scallops is browned, sides are firm, and centers are opaque, 2 to 4 minutes longer. Serve immediately with lemon wedges.

Chile-Lime Vinaigrette

MAKES ABOUT 1 CUP

- 1 teaspoon grated lime zest plus 3 tablespoons juice (2 limes)
- 2 tablespoons honey
- 1 tablespoon Sriracha sauce
- 2 teaspoons fish sauce
- ½ cup vegetable oil

Whisk lime zest and juice, honey, Sriracha, and fish sauce together in medium bowl until combined. Whisking constantly, slowly drizzle in oil until emulsified.

Basil Vinaigrette

MAKES ABOUT 1 CUP

- 1 cup packed fresh basil leaves
- 3 tablespoons minced fresh chives
- 2 tablespoons champagne vinegar
- 2 garlic cloves, minced
- 2 teaspoons sugar
- 1 teaspoon salt
- ½ teaspoon pepper
- ⅔ cup vegetable oil

Pulse basil, chives, vinegar, garlic, sugar, salt, and pepper in blender until roughly chopped, 5 to 7 pulses. With blender running, slowly drizzle in oil until emulsified, scraping down sides of blender jar as needed, about 1 minute.

GRILLED BACON-WRAPPED SCALLOPS

WHY THIS RECIPE WORKS: Smoky, salty bacon beautifully accents sweet, succulent scallops, and we thought taking it to the grill would make a great thing even better. We set out to make this classic appetizer into a grilled entrée.

We knew we needed to parcook the bacon to prevent the grease from dripping into the fire and incinerating our scallops. Microwaving proved a perfect solution: We layered strips of bacon between paper towels (to absorb grease) and weighed them down with a second plate to prevent curling. We wrapped each strip of bacon around two scallops for an ideal scallop to bacon ratio. Tossing the scallops in melted

butter added richness, and pressing the scallops firmly together on the skewers prevented them from spinning when flipped. A two-level fire cooked both scallops and bacon to perfection. A spritz of grilled lemon juice and a sprinkling of chopped chives gave the dish a bright finish.

Grilled Bacon-Wrapped Scallops

SERVES 4

Use ordinary bacon, as thick-cut bacon will take too long to crisp on the grill. When wrapping the scallops, the bacon slice should fit around both scallops, overlapping just enough to be skewered through both ends. We recommend buying "dry" scallops, which don't have chemical additives and taste better than "wet." Dry scallops will look ivory or pinkish; wet scallops are bright white. This recipe was developed with large sea scallops (sold 10 to 20 per pound).

- 12 slices bacon
- 24 large sea scallops, tendons removed
- 3 tablespoons unsalted butter, melted
- ½ teaspoon salt
- ⅛ teaspoon pepper
- 2 lemons, halved
- ¼ cup chopped fresh chives

1. Place 4 layers paper towels on large plate and arrange 6 slices bacon over towels in single layer. Top with 4 more paper towels and remaining 6 slices bacon. Cover with 2 layers of paper towels; place second large plate on top and press gently to flatten. Microwave until fat begins to render but bacon is still pliable, about 4 minutes. Toss scallops, butter, salt, and pepper together in bowl until scallops are thoroughly coated with butter.

2. Press 2 scallops together, side to side, and wrap with 1 slice bacon, trimming excess as necessary. Thread onto skewer through bacon. Repeat with remaining scallops and bacon, threading 3 bundles onto each of 4 skewers.

3A. FOR A CHARCOAL GRILL: Open bottom vent completely. Light large chimney starter filled with charcoal briquettes (6 quarts). When top coals are partially covered with ash, pour two-thirds evenly over half of grill, then pour remaining coals over other half of grill. Set cooking grate in place, cover, and open lid vent completely. Heat grill until hot, about 5 minutes.

3B. FOR A GAS GRILL: Turn all burners to high, cover, and heat grill until hot, about 15 minutes. Leave primary burner on high and turn other burner(s) to medium.

4. Clean and oil cooking grate. Place skewers, bacon side down, and lemon halves, cut side down, on cooler side of grill. Cook (covered, if using gas) until bacon is crispy on first side, about 4 minutes. Flip skewers onto other bacon side and cook until crispy, about 4 minutes longer. Flip skewers scallop side down and move to hot side of grill. Grill until sides of scallops are firm and centers are opaque, about 4 minutes on 1 side only. Transfer skewers to platter, squeeze lemon over, and sprinkle with chives. Serve.

GRILLED SHRIMP SKEWERS

WHY THIS RECIPE WORKS: Really great grilled shrimp—tender, moist, and flavorful—are hard to come by. Usually, they're overcooked and rubbery, giving the jaws a workout, thanks to their quick cooking time and the high temperature of the grill. Grilling shrimp in their shells can guarantee juiciness, but the seasoning tends to be lost when the shells are pulled off. We wanted tender, juicy, boldly seasoned grilled shrimp, with the flavor in the shrimp and not on our fingers.

Our decision to go with peeled shrimp for this recipe meant we had to revisit how we traditionally grilled shrimp. First we eliminated brining, which created waterlogged shrimp and hindered caramelization. Then we set the shrimp over a screaming-hot fire. This worked well with jumbo shrimp, but smaller shrimp overcooked before charring. With jumbo shrimp costing as much as $25 per pound, we decided against them. They did give us an idea, though. For our next step, we created faux jumbo shrimp by cramming a skewer with several normal-sized shrimp pressed tightly together. Our final revision was to take the shrimp off the fire before they were completely cooked (but after they had picked up attractive grill marks). We finished cooking them in a heated sauce waiting on the cool side of the grill; this final simmer gave them tons of flavor.

Grilled Shrimp Skewers

SERVES 4

The shrimp and sauce finish cooking together on the grill, so prepare the sauce ingredients while the grill is heating. To fit all of the shrimp on the cooking grate at once, you will need three 14-inch metal skewers. Serve with grilled bread.

- 1½ pounds extra-large shrimp (21 to 25 per pound), peeled and deveined (see page 240)
- 2–3 tablespoons olive oil
- Salt and pepper
- ¼ teaspoon sugar
- 1 recipe sauce (recipes follow)
- Lemon wedges

1. Pat shrimp dry with paper towels. Thread the shrimp onto 3 skewers, alternating direction of heads and tails. Brush both sides of shrimp with oil and season with salt and pepper. Sprinkle 1 side of each skewer evenly with sugar.

2A. FOR A CHARCOAL GRILL: Open bottom vent completely. Light large chimney starter filled with charcoal briquettes (6 quarts). When top coals are partially covered with ash, pour evenly over half of grill. Set cooking grate in place, cover, and open lid vent completely. Heat grill until hot, about 5 minutes.

2B. FOR A GAS GRILL: Turn all burners to high, cover, and heat grill until hot, about 15 minutes. Leave primary burner on high and turn other burner(s) to medium-low.

NOTES FROM THE TEST KITCHEN

ARRANGING SHRIMP ON A SKEWER

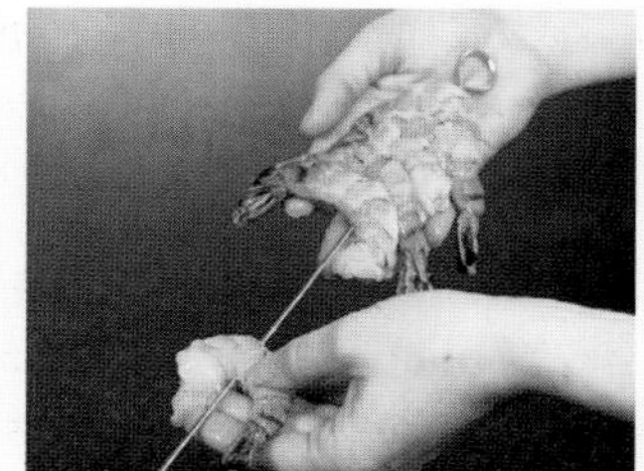

Pass the skewer through the center of each shrimp. As you add shrimp to the skewer, alternate the directions of the heads and tails for a compact arrangement of shrimp. The shrimp should fit snugly against one another.

3. Clean cooking grate, then repeatedly brush grate with well-oiled paper towels until grate is black and glossy, 5 to 10 times. Place disposable pan with sauce ingredients on hot side of grill and cook, stirring occasionally, until hot, 1 to 3 minutes. Move pan to cool side of grill.

4. Place shrimp skewers sugared side down on hot side of grill and use tongs to push shrimp together on skewers if they have separated. Cook shrimp until lightly charred, 4 to 5 minutes. Using tongs, flip and continue to cook until second side is pink and slightly translucent, 1 to 2 minutes longer.

5. Using potholder, carefully lift each skewer from grill and use tongs to slide shrimp off skewers into pan with sauce. Toss shrimp and sauce to combine. Place pan on hot side of grill and cook, stirring, until shrimp are opaque throughout, about 30 seconds. Remove from the grill, add remaining sauce ingredients, and toss to combine. Transfer to serving platter and serve with lemon wedges.

Spicy Lemon-Garlic Sauce

MAKES ABOUT ½ CUP

- 4 tablespoons unsalted butter, cut into 4 pieces
- ¼ cup lemon juice (2 lemons)
- 3 garlic cloves, minced
- ½ teaspoon red pepper flakes
- ⅛ teaspoon salt
- 1 (10-inch) disposable aluminum pie pan
- ⅓ cup minced fresh parsley

Combine butter, lemon juice, garlic, pepper flakes, and salt in aluminum pan. Cook over hot side of grill, stirring occasionally, until butter melts, about 1½ minutes. Move to cool side of grill and proceed to grill shrimp, adding parsley just before serving.

Fresh Tomato Sauce with Feta and Olives

MAKES ABOUT ½ CUP

- ¼ cup extra-virgin olive oil
- 1 large tomato, cored, seeded, and minced
- 1 tablespoon minced fresh oregano
- ⅛ teaspoon salt
- 1 (10-inch) disposable aluminum pie pan
- 4 ounces feta cheese, crumbled (1 cup)
- ⅓ cup kalamata olives, pitted and chopped fine
- 2 tablespoons lemon juice
- 3 scallions, sliced thin

Combine oil, tomato, oregano, and salt in aluminum pan. Cook over hot side of grill, stirring occasionally, until hot, about 1½ minutes. Move to cool side of grill and proceed to grill shrimp, adding feta, olives, lemon juice, and scallions just before serving.

GRILLED SHRIMP AND VEGETABLE KEBABS

WHY THIS RECIPE WORKS: Combined shrimp and vegetable kebabs are notoriously difficult to cook because the shrimp inevitably overcooks in the time it takes most vegetables to pass from raw to their crisp-tender ideal. As a result, you end up serving either overcooked shrimp or undercooked vegetables. This recipe works by pairing slower cooking jumbo shrimp with soft, quick-cooking vegetables. Mushrooms are nestled into the curve of the shrimp on the skewer to better insulate the shrimp and extend their cooking time, and the vegetables are cut to mimic the profile of the shrimp, so the entire skewer makes contact with the grill, promoting even cooking. Finally, some vegetables are precooked in the microwave before they are skewered to give them a head start. Simply seasoning with oil and pepper allows the kebabs to char beautifully on the grill, and dressing them with a fresh lemon-herb vinaigrette while they're hot from the fire finishes the dish in style.

Grilled Shrimp And Vegetable Kebabs

SERVES 4 TO 6

Small mushrooms about 1¼ to 1½ inches in diameter work best here. If using larger mushrooms, halve them before microwaving. You will need eight 12-inch metal skewers for this recipe.

SHRIMP

- Salt and pepper
- 2 tablespoons sugar
- 1½ pounds jumbo shrimp (16 to 20 per pound), peeled and deveined (see page 240)
- 3 large red or yellow bell peppers, stemmed, seeded, and cut into ¾-inch-wide by 3-inch-long strips

24 cremini mushrooms, trimmed
12 scallions, cut into 3-inch lengths
2 tablespoons vegetable oil

VINAIGRETTE

¼ cup lemon juice (2 lemons)
¼ cup extra-virgin olive oil
2 teaspoons minced fresh thyme
1 garlic clove, minced
½ teaspoon salt
¼ teaspoon Dijon mustard
⅛ teaspoon pepper

1. FOR THE SHRIMP: Dissolve 2 tablespoons salt and sugar in 1 quart cold water in large container. Submerge shrimp in brine, cover, and refrigerate for 15 minutes. Remove shrimp from brine and pat dry with paper towels.

2. Line large microwave-safe plate with double layer of paper towels. Spread half of bell peppers skin side down in even layer on plate and sprinkle with ⅛ teaspoon salt. Microwave for 2 minutes. Transfer peppers, still on towels, to cutting board and let cool. Repeat with fresh paper towels and remaining bell peppers.

3. Line second plate with double layer of paper towels. Spread mushrooms in even layer on plate and sprinkle with ⅛ teaspoon salt. Microwave for 3 minutes. Transfer mushrooms, still on towels, to cutting board and let cool.

4. Lay one shrimp on cutting board and run 12-inch metal skewer through center. Thread mushroom onto skewer through sides of cap, pushing so it nestles tightly into curve of shrimp. Follow mushroom with two pieces scallion and two pieces bell pepper, skewering so vegetables and shrimp form even layer. Repeat shrimp and vegetable sequence two more times. When skewer is full, gently press ingredients so they fit snugly together in center of each skewer. Skewer remaining shrimp and vegetables on seven more skewers for total of 8 kebabs. Brush each side of kebabs with vegetable oil and season with pepper.

5A. FOR A CHARCOAL GRILL: Open bottom vent completely. Light large chimney starter mounded with charcoal briquettes (7 quarts). When top coals are partially covered with ash, pour evenly over grill. Set cooking grate in place, cover, and open lid vent completely. Heat grill until hot, about 5 minutes.

5B. FOR A GAS GRILL: Turn all burners to high, cover, and heat grill until hot, about 15 minutes. Leave all burners on high.

6. FOR THE VINAIGRETTE: While grill heats, whisk all ingredients together in bowl.

7. Clean and oil cooking grate. Place kebabs on grill and grill (covered if using gas) until charred, about 2½ minutes. Flip skewers and grill until second side is charred and shrimp are cooked through, 2 to 3 minutes, moving skewers as needed to ensure even cooking. Transfer skewers to serving platter. Rewhisk vinaigrette and drizzle over kebabs. Serve.

GRILLED SWORDFISH SKEWERS WITH TOMATO-SCALLION CAPONATA

WHY THIS RECIPE WORKS: Swordfish is a favorite fish to grill along the Mediterranean and beyond. It has a robust taste and needs costarring ingredients with just as much oomph. We paired swordfish with a Sicilian-inspired grilled caponata relish. As a base, we grilled cherry tomatoes, lemons, and scallions alongside the swordfish and added an aromatic blend of warm spices for a potent sauce to complement the fish. Once grilled, the lemon transformed from tart and acidic to sweet. Rubbing the swordfish with ground coriander added complexity that popped with the tomato, scallions, and fresh basil.

Grilled Swordfish Skewers with Tomato-Scallion Caponata

SERVES 4 TO 6

If swordfish isn't available, you can substitute halibut. You will need six 12-inch metal skewers for this recipe.

1½ pounds skinless swordfish steaks, 1¼ to 1½ inches thick, cut into 1¼-inch pieces
5 teaspoons ground coriander
Salt and pepper
12 ounces cherry tomatoes
1 small eggplant (12 ounces), cut crosswise on bias into ½-inch-thick ovals
6 scallions, trimmed
¼ cup extra-virgin olive oil
1 tablespoon grated lemon zest, plus 2 lemons, halved
1½ tablespoons honey
2 garlic cloves, minced
1 teaspoon ground cumin
¼ teaspoon ground cinnamon
⅛ teaspoon ground nutmeg
¼ cup pitted kalamata olives, chopped
2 tablespoons minced fresh basil

1. Pat swordfish dry with paper towels, rub with 1 tablespoon coriander, and season with salt and pepper. Thread fish onto three 12-inch metal skewers. Thread tomatoes onto three 12-inch metal skewers. Brush swordfish, tomatoes, eggplant, and scallions with 2 tablespoons oil.

2A. FOR A CHARCOAL GRILL: Open bottom vent completely. Light large chimney starter filled with charcoal briquettes (6 quarts). When top coals are partially covered with ash, pour evenly over grill. Set cooking grate in place, cover, and open lid vent completely. Heat grill until hot, about 5 minutes.

2B. FOR A GAS GRILL: Turn all burners to high, cover, and heat grill until hot, about 15 minutes. Leave all burners on high.

3. Clean cooking grate, then repeatedly brush grate with well-oiled paper towels until black and glossy, 5 to 10 times. Place swordfish, tomatoes, eggplant, scallions, and lemon halves on grill. Cook (covered if using gas), turning as needed, until swordfish flakes apart when gently prodded with paring knife and registers 140 degrees and tomatoes, eggplant, scallions, and lemon halves are softened and lightly charred, 5 to 15 minutes. Transfer items to serving platter as they finish grilling and tent loosely with aluminum foil. Let swordfish rest while finishing caponata.

4. Whisk remaining 2 teaspoons coriander, remaining 2 tablespoons oil, lemon zest, honey, garlic, cumin, ¾ teaspoon salt, ¼ teaspoon pepper, cinnamon, and nutmeg together in large bowl. Microwave, stirring occasionally, until fragrant, about 1 minute. Once lemons are cool enough to handle, squeeze into fine-mesh strainer set over bowl with oil-honey mixture, extracting as much juice as possible; whisk to combine. Stir in olives.

5. Using tongs, slide tomatoes off skewers onto cutting board. Coarsely chop tomatoes, eggplant, and scallions, transfer to bowl with dressing, and gently toss to combine. Season with salt and pepper to taste. Remove swordfish from skewers, sprinkle with basil, and serve with caponata.

SHRIMP BURGERS

WHY THIS RECIPE WORKS: Shrimp burgers are a longstanding specialty in coastal towns in South Carolina and Georgia where seafood is abundant. Although the particulars may vary, a good shrimp burger should be first and foremost about the shrimp. Unfortunately, some of the shrimp burgers we've had were reminiscent of fish-flavored rubber patties; others were more bread ball than shrimp burger. We set out to develop a recipe for our ideal shrimp burger: moist, chunky yet still cohesive, and with seasoning that complements the sweet shrimp flavor but doesn't overpower it. Pan frying is the most common way to cook these burgers, but we thought they would be even better on the grill, where they could develop a nice crust.

The first issue was how to prepare the shrimp. After early testing we decided we needed a combination of textures—finely chopped shrimp to help bind the burgers, as well as some larger, bite-size chunks. We realized we could pulse the shrimp in the food processor, which resulted in an inconsistent, chunky texture. As for a binder, we wanted as little as possible. Most of the recipes we found used some combination of mayonnaise, egg, and bread crumbs, but these recipes yielded burgers with shrimp swathed in a soggy, unappealing mush. The mayonnaise was adding much-needed fat and moisture (unlike beef, shrimp have little fat of their own), but we found that we could eliminate the egg and decrease the bread crumbs. Since packing the patties makes them rubbery, we handled them as little as possible, instead allowing them to firm up in the refrigerator. Some minced scallion and parsley, lemon zest, and a touch of cayenne rounded out the flavor of our burgers. By themselves or on a bun with lettuce and tartar sauce, these burgers are sure to disappear as fast as they come off the grill.

Southern Shrimp Burgers

MAKES 4 BURGERS

Be sure to use raw, not cooked, shrimp here. Dry the shrimp thoroughly before processing, or the burgers will be mushy. Handle the burgers gently when shaping and grilling; if overhandled while being shaped, the burgers will be dense and rubbery, and if handled roughly during cooking, they will break apart. Serve with Tartar Sauce (recipe follows) or another flavored mayonnaise. If using shrimp with sodium added as a preservative, omit the salt in the recipe.

- 1 slice hearty white sandwich bread, torn into large pieces
- 1½ pounds extra-large shrimp (21 to 25 per pound), peeled, deveined (see page 240), and patted dry
- ¼ cup mayonnaise

2 scallions, minced
2 tablespoons minced fresh parsley
2 teaspoons grated fresh lemon zest
Pinch cayenne pepper
¼ teaspoon salt
⅛ teaspoon pepper

1. Pulse bread in food processor to fine crumbs, 10 to 15 pulses; transfer to bowl. Pulse shrimp in now-empty food processor until some pieces are finely minced and others are coarsely chopped, about 7 pulses. Transfer shrimp to large bowl.

2. Combine mayonnaise, scallions, parsley, lemon zest, cayenne, salt, and pepper in large bowl until uniform, then gently fold into processed shrimp until just combined. Sprinkle bread crumbs over mixture and gently fold until thoroughly incorporated.

3. Divide shrimp mixture into 4 equal portions and shape each into 1-inch-thick patty. Cover and refrigerate patties for at least 30 minutes or up to 3 hours.

4A. FOR A CHARCOAL GRILL: Open bottom grill vents completely. Light large chimney starter three-quarters full with charcoal briquettes (75 briquettes; 4½ quarts). When coals are hot, pour evenly over grill. Set cooking grate in place, cover, and heat grill until hot, about 5 minutes.

4B. FOR A GAS GRILL: Turn all burners to high, cover, and heat grill until hot, about 15 minutes. Turn all burners to medium-high. (Adjust burners as needed to maintain medium-hot fire.)

5. Clean and oil cooking grate. Lightly brush tops of burgers with oil, lay them on grill, oiled side down, and lightly brush other side with oil. Cook burgers, without pressing on them, until lightly browned and register 140 to 145 degrees, 10 to 14 minutes, flipping halfway through. Transfer burgers to platter, tent loosely with foil, and let rest for 5 minutes before serving.

Tartar Sauce

MAKES ABOUT 1 CUP

¾ cup mayonnaise
1½ tablespoons minced cornichons (about 3 large)
1 teaspoon cornichon juice
1 tablespoon minced scallion
1 tablespoon minced red onion
1 tablespoon capers, minced

Whisk all ingredients together in bowl. Cover and refrigerate until flavors meld, at least 30 minutes. (Sauce can be refrigerated for up to 4 days.)

GRILLED CORN WITH FLAVORED BUTTER

WHY THIS RECIPE WORKS: Grilled corn is a go-to summer treat, but we wanted a way to spice it up—literally. To incorporate flavorful herbs and spices into the corn, we found that a two-step approach worked best. First, we brushed the ears with vegetable oil and seared them over a hot grill fire. When the corn had a nice char, we moved the ears to a disposable pan on the grill and added a dollop of butter seasoned with herbs and other aromatic ingredients. The butter infused every kernel with extra flavor, and the disposable pan made the process simple and prevented butter-induced flare-ups on the grill.

Grilled Corn with Flavored Butter

SERVES 4 TO 6

Use a disposable aluminum roasting pan that is at least 2¾ inches deep.

1 recipe flavored butter (recipes follow)
1 (13 by 9-inch) disposable aluminum roasting pan
8 ears corn, husks and silk removed
2 tablespoons vegetable oil
Salt and pepper

1. Place flavored butter in disposable pan. Brush corn evenly with oil and season with salt and pepper to taste.

2. Grill corn over hot fire, turning occasionally, until lightly charred on all sides, 5 to 9 minutes. Transfer corn to pan and cover tightly with aluminum foil.

3. Place pan on grill and cook, shaking pan frequently, until butter is sizzling, about 3 minutes. Remove pan from grill and carefully remove foil, allowing steam to escape away from you. Serve corn, spooning any butter in pan over individual ears.

Basil and Lemon Butter

Serve with lemon wedges, if desired. We like to use a rasp grater for zesting citrus.

- 6 tablespoons unsalted butter, softened
- 2 tablespoons minced fresh basil
- 1 tablespoon minced fresh parsley
- 1 teaspoon finely grated lemon zest
- ½ teaspoon salt
- ¼ teaspoon pepper

Combine all ingredients in small bowl.

Honey Butter

This butter also works well with cornbread.

- 6 tablespoons unsalted butter, softened
- 2 tablespoons honey
- ½ teaspoon salt
- ¼ teaspoon red pepper flakes

Combine all ingredients in small bowl.

Latin-Spiced Butter

Serve with orange wedges, if desired. We like to use a rasp grater for zesting citrus.

- 6 tablespoons unsalted butter, softened
- 2 tablespoons minced fresh cilantro
- 1 tablespoon minced fresh parsley
- 1 teaspoon minced canned chipotle chile in adobo sauce
- ½ teaspoon finely grated orange zest
- ½ teaspoon salt

Combine all ingredients in small bowl.

New Orleans "Barbecue" Butter

- 6 tablespoons unsalted butter, softened
- 1 garlic clove, minced
- 1 tablespoon Worcestershire sauce
- 1 teaspoon tomato paste
- ½ teaspoon minced fresh rosemary
- ½ teaspoon minced fresh thyme
- ½ teaspoon cayenne pepper

Combine all ingredients in small bowl.

Spicy Old Bay Butter

Serve with lemon wedges, if desired.

- 6 tablespoons unsalted butter, softened
- 1 tablespoon hot sauce
- 1 tablespoon minced fresh parsley
- 1½ teaspoons Old Bay seasoning
- 1 teaspoon finely grated lemon zest

Combine all ingredients in small bowl.

MEXICAN-STYLE GRILLED CORN

WHY THIS RECIPE WORKS: In Mexico, street vendors add kick to grilled corn by slathering it with a creamy, spicy sauce. The corn takes on a sweet, charred flavor, which is heightened by the lime juice and chili powder in the cheesy sauce. We wanted to develop our own rendition of this south-of-the-border street fare. We ditched the husks, coated the ears with oil to prevent sticking, and grilled them directly on the grate. Over a single-level fire, the corn emerged nicely smoky but insufficiently charred, so we pushed all the coals to one side to create a modified two-level fire, allowing the ears to cook closer to the coals. The traditional base for the sauce is crema, a thick, soured Mexican cream. But given its spotty availability, we replaced the crema with a combination of mayonnaise and sour cream. Most recipes call for queso fresco or Cotija, but these can be hard to find. Pecorino Romano made a good substitute. We included the usual seasonings of cilantro, lime juice, garlic, and chili powder. To provide more depth, we added chili powder to the oil used for coating the corn; once heated on the grill, the chili powder bloomed with a full flavor that penetrated the corn kernels.

Mexican-Style Grilled Corn

SERVES 6

If you can find queso fresco or Cotija, use either in place of the Pecorino Romano. If you prefer the corn spicy, add the optional cayenne pepper.

- 1½ ounces Pecorino Romano cheese, grated (¾ cup)
- ¼ cup mayonnaise
- 3 tablespoons sour cream
- 3 tablespoons minced fresh cilantro
- 4 teaspoons lime juice
- 1 garlic clove, minced
- ¾ teaspoon chili powder
- ¼ teaspoon pepper
- ¼ teaspoon cayenne pepper (optional)
- 4 teaspoons vegetable oil
- ¼ teaspoon salt
- 6 ears corn, husks and silk removed

1A. FOR A CHARCOAL GRILL: Open bottom vent completely. Light large chimney starter filled with charcoal briquettes (6 quarts). When top coals are partially covered with ash, pour evenly over half of grill. Set cooking grate in place, cover, and open lid vent completely. Heat grill until hot, about 5 minutes.

1B. FOR A GAS GRILL: Turn all burners to high, cover, and heat grill until hot, about 15 minutes.

2. Meanwhile, combine Pecorino, mayonnaise, sour cream, cilantro, lime juice, garlic, ¼ teaspoon chili powder, pepper, and cayenne, if using, in large bowl and set aside. In second large bowl, combine oil, salt, and remaining ½ teaspoon chili powder. Add corn to oil mixture and toss to coat evenly.

3. Clean and oil cooking grate. Place corn on grill (hot side if using charcoal) and cook (covered if using gas) until lightly charred on all sides, 7 to 12 minutes, turning as needed. Place corn in bowl with cheese mixture, toss to coat evenly, and serve.

GRILLED POTATOES

WHY THIS RECIPE WORKS: Grilled potatoes are a summer classic, but we wanted to put a new spin on them by adding rosemary and garlic for a heartier, more savory side. We found it harder than it sounded to add garlic and rosemary flavors to plain grilled potatoes. Coating the potatoes with oil, garlic, and rosemary produced burnt, bitter garlic and charred rosemary. We wanted potent garlic and rosemary flavors in our potatoes, without bitterness and charring. We learned that we needed to introduce the potatoes to the garlic-oil mixture not once, but three times. Before cooking, we pierced the potatoes, skewered them, seasoned them with salt, brushed on a garlic-rosemary oil, and precooked them in the microwave. Then, before grilling, we brushed them again with the infused oil. After grilling, we tossed them with the garlic and rosemary oil yet again. We finally had it—tender grilled potatoes infused with the smoky flavor of the grill and enlivened with the bold flavors of garlic and rosemary.

Grilled Potatoes with Garlic and Rosemary

SERVES 4

This recipe allows you to grill an entrée while the hot coals burn down in step 4. Once that item is done, start grilling the potatoes. This recipe works best with small potatoes that are about 1½ inches in diameter. If using medium potatoes, 2 to 3 inches in diameter, cut them into quarters. If the potatoes are larger than 3 inches in diameter, cut each potato into eighths. Since the potatoes are first cooked in the microwave, use wooden skewers.

- ¼ cup olive oil
- 9 garlic cloves, minced
- 1 teaspoon chopped fresh rosemary
- Salt and pepper
- 2 pounds small red potatoes, halved and skewered
- 2 tablespoons chopped fresh chives

1. Heat oil, garlic, rosemary, and ½ teaspoon salt in small skillet over medium heat until sizzling, about 3 minutes. Reduce heat to medium-low and continue to cook until garlic is light blond, about 3 minutes. Pour mixture through fine-mesh strainer into small bowl; press on solids. Measure 1 tablespoon of solids and 1 tablespoon of oil into large bowl and set aside. Discard remaining solids but reserve remaining oil.

2. Place skewered potatoes in single layer on large plate and poke each potato several times with skewer. Brush with 1 tablespoon of strained oil and season with salt. Microwave until the potatoes offer slight resistance when pierced with paring knife, about 8 minutes, turning halfway through cooking. Transfer potatoes to baking sheet coated with 1 tablespoon of strained oil. Brush with remaining 1 tablespoon strained oil and season with salt and pepper to taste.

3A. FOR A CHARCOAL GRILL: Open bottom vent completely. Light large chimney starter filled with charcoal briquettes (6 quarts). When top coals are partially covered with ash, pour two-thirds evenly over grill, then pour remaining coals over half of grill. Set cooking grate in place, cover, and open lid vent completely. Heat grill until hot, about 5 minutes.

NOTES FROM THE TEST KITCHEN

SKEWERING POTATOES FOR THE GRILL

Place a potato half, cut side down, on the work surface and pierce through the center with a skewer. Repeat, holding the already-skewered potatoes for better leverage.

3B. FOR A GAS GRILL: Turn all burners to high, cover, and heat grill until hot, about 15 minutes. Turn all burners down to medium-high.

4. Clean and oil cooking grate. Place potatoes on grill (hotter side if using charcoal) and cook (covered if using gas) until grill marks appear, 3 to 5 minutes, flipping halfway through cooking. Move potatoes to cooler side of grill (if using charcoal) or turn all burners to medium-low (if using gas). Cover and continue to cook until paring knife slips in and out of potatoes easily, 5 to 8 minutes longer.

5. Remove potatoes from skewers and transfer to bowl with reserved garlic-oil mixture. Add chives, season with salt and pepper to taste, and toss until thoroughly coated. Serve.

TUNISIAN-STYLE GRILLED VEGETABLES

WHY THIS RECIPE WORKS: Grilling brings out the best in summer vegetables, calling forth their sweetness and adding an accent of smoke. We took inspiration from the robustly flavored Tunisian dish called *mechouia*.

We opted to use bell peppers, eggplant, zucchini, and plum tomatoes. To avoid a waterlogged salad, we halved the zucchini and eggplant and cut deep crosshatch marks in their flesh to allow them to release their moisture. We also halved the tomatoes and opened the peppers into long planks so they would cook evenly all the way through. We sprinkled the vegetables with salt and oil flavored with traditional *tabil* seasonings. The spices bloomed on the grill and became full-flavored and aromatic. More tabil, plus lemon zest and a trio of fresh herbs, brought a tangy, lively taste to our finishing vinaigrette.

Tunisian-Style Grilled Vegetables (Mechouia)

SERVES 4 TO 6

Serve as a side dish to grilled meats and fish; with grilled pita as a salad course; or with hard-cooked eggs, olives, and premium canned tuna as a light lunch. Equal amounts of ground coriander and cumin can be substituted for the whole spices.

VINAIGRETTE

- 2 teaspoons coriander seeds
- 1½ teaspoons caraway seeds
- 1 teaspoon cumin seeds
- 5 tablespoons olive oil
- ½ teaspoon sweet paprika
- ⅛ teaspoon cayenne pepper
- 3 garlic cloves, minced
- ¼ cup chopped fresh parsley
- ¼ cup chopped fresh cilantro
- 2 tablespoons chopped fresh mint
- 1 teaspoon grated lemon zest plus 2 tablespoons juice
- Salt

VEGETABLES

- 2 bell peppers (1 red and 1 green)
- 1 small eggplant, halved lengthwise
- 1 zucchini (8 to 10 ounces), halved lengthwise
- 4 plum tomatoes, cored and halved lengthwise
- Salt and pepper
- 2 medium shallots, unpeeled

1. FOR THE VINAIGRETTE: Grind coriander seeds, caraway seeds, and cumin seeds in spice grinder until finely ground. Whisk ground spices, oil, paprika, and cayenne together in bowl. Reserve 3 tablespoons oil mixture. Heat remaining oil mixture and garlic in small skillet over low heat, stirring occasionally, until fragrant and small bubbles appear, 8 to 10 minutes. Transfer to large bowl and let cool, about 10 minutes. Whisk parsley, cilantro, mint, and lemon zest and juice into oil mixture; season with salt to taste.

2. FOR THE VEGETABLES: Slice ¼ inch off tops and bottoms of bell peppers and remove cores. Make slit down 1 side of each bell pepper and then press flat into 1 long strip, removing ribs and remaining seeds with knife as needed. Using sharp knife, cut slits in flesh of eggplant and zucchini, spaced ½ inch apart, in crosshatch pattern, being careful to cut into but not through skin. Brush cut sides of bell peppers, eggplant, zucchini, and tomatoes with reserved oil mixture and season with salt to taste.

3. Grill vegetables, starting with cut sides down, over medium-hot fire, until tender and well browned and skins of bell peppers, eggplant, tomatoes, and shallots are charred, 8 to 16 minutes, turning and moving vegetables as necessary. Transfer vegetables to baking sheet as they are done. Place bell peppers in bowl, cover with plastic wrap, and let steam to loosen skins.

4. When cool enough to handle, peel bell peppers, eggplant, tomatoes, and shallots. Chop all vegetables into ½-inch pieces and transfer to bowl with vinaigrette; toss to coat. Season with salt and pepper to taste, and serve warm or at room temperature.

BABA GHANOUSH

WHY THIS RECIPE WORKS: Baba ghanoush often appears on the appetizer table as a gray, bitter, watery mass of eggplant puree. We were after a dip that had realized its potential—full of smoky eggplant flavor and brightened with garlic and lemon juice. And one certain way to produce this creation was to start off by grilling our eggplant. For the best flavor, it's imperative to start out with firm, shiny, and unblemished eggplants. We grilled the eggplants directly over a hot fire until they were wrinkled and soft. To avoid a watery texture and any bitterness, we drained the pulp of excess fluid, but didn't bother spending time deseeding the eggplants. We processed the pulp with a modest amount of garlic, tahini paste, and lemon juice for the creaminess and bright flavor that baba ghanoush is known for.

Grilled Baba Ghanoush

MAKES 2 CUPS

When buying eggplants, select those with shiny, taut, and unbruised skins and an even shape (eggplants with a bulbous shape won't cook evenly). Grill until the eggplant walls have collapsed and the insides feel sloshy when pressed with tongs. We prefer to serve baba ghanoush only lightly chilled; if cold, let it stand at room temperature for about 20 minutes before serving. Baba ghanoush does not keep well, so plan to make it the day you want to serve it. Serve with pita bread, black olives, tomato wedges, or cucumber slices.

- 2 pounds eggplant (about 2 large globe eggplants, 5 medium Italian eggplants, or 12 medium Japanese eggplants), pricked all over with fork
- 2 tablespoons tahini
- 1 tablespoon lemon juice
- 1 tablespoon extra-virgin olive oil, plus extra for serving
- 1 small garlic clove, minced
- Salt and pepper
- 2 teaspoons chopped fresh parsley

1A. FOR A CHARCOAL GRILL: Open bottom vent completely. Light large chimney starter filled with charcoal briquettes (6 quarts). When top coals are partially covered with ash, pour evenly over grill. Set cooking grate in place, cover, and open lid vent completely. Heat grill until hot, about 5 minutes.

1B. FOR A GAS GRILL: Turn all burners to high, cover, and heat grill until hot, about 15 minutes. Turn all burners to medium. (Adjust burners as needed to maintain grill temperature around 350 degrees.)

2. Clean and oil cooking grate. Set eggplants on cooking grate and cook until skins darken and wrinkle on all sides and eggplants are uniformly soft when pressed with tongs, about 25 minutes for large globe eggplants, 20 minutes for Italian eggplants, and 15 minutes for Japanese eggplants, turning every 5 minutes and reversing direction of eggplants on grill with each turn. Transfer eggplants to rimmed baking sheet and cool 5 minutes.

3. Set small colander over bowl. Trim top and bottom off each eggplant. Slit eggplants lengthwise and use spoon to scoop hot pulp from skins and place pulp in colander (you should have about 2 cups packed pulp); discard skins. Let pulp drain 3 minutes.

4. Transfer pulp to food processor. Add tahini, lemon juice, oil, garlic, ¼ teaspoon salt, and ¼ teaspoon pepper. Process until mixture has coarse, choppy texture, about 8 pulses. Season with salt and pepper to taste. Transfer to serving bowl, cover with plastic wrap flush with surface of dip, and refrigerate 45 to 60 minutes. Make trough in center of dip using large spoon and spoon olive oil into it. Sprinkle with parsley and serve.

CHAPTER 19

SIDES OF PLENTY

SIMPLE APPLESAUCE

WHY THIS RECIPE WORKS: Applesauce should taste like apples, but all too often the tart, sweet, and fruity nuances of fresh apple flavor are overpowered by sweeteners and spices, and the sauce ends up tasting like bad pie filling. The texture, too, can vary from dry and chunky to loose and thin. We wanted a smooth, thick sauce that showcases fresh apple flavor without too much sweetness or spice—the perfect partner to pork chops or as a snack.

The first step was to find the right variety of apple. We began by gathering 18 varieties and making each into applesauce. We found that Jonagold, Jonathan, Pink Lady, and Macoun varieties all produce a sauce with a pleasing balance of tart and sweet. We tried blending varieties in combination with each other, but concluded that single-variety sauces had purer, stronger character. Cooking the apples with their skins on saved us the step of peeling and enhanced the flavor of the sauce. Processing the cooked apples through a food mill, not a food processor or blender, removed the skins and produced a sauce with the silky-smooth, thick texture we were after. Adding a little water, sugar, and a pinch of salt—and no spices—resulted in a perfectly sweetened sauce that tasted first and foremost of apples.

Simple Applesauce

MAKES ABOUT 3½ CUPS

If you do not own a food mill or prefer applesauce with a coarse texture, peel the apples before coring and cutting them and, after cooking, mash them against the side of the pot with a wooden spoon or against the bottom of the pot with a potato masher. Applesauce made with out-of-season apples may be somewhat drier than sauce made with peak-season apples, so it's likely that in step 2 of the recipe you will need to add more water to adjust the texture. If you double the recipe, the apples will need 10 to 15 minutes of extra cooking time.

- 4 pounds apples (about 10 medium), preferably Jonagold, Pink Lady, Jonathan, or Macoun, unpeeled, cored, and cut into rough 1½-inch pieces (see note)
- 1 cup water, plus more as needed
- ¼ cup sugar, plus more to taste
- Pinch table salt

1. Toss the apples, water, sugar, and salt in a large Dutch oven. Cover the pot and cook the apples over medium-high heat until they begin to break down, 15 to 20 minutes, checking and stirring occasionally with a wooden spoon to break up any large chunks.

2. Process the cooked apples through a food mill fitted with the medium disk. Season with extra sugar to taste or add water to adjust the consistency as desired. Serve hot, warm, at room temperature, or chilled.

BREAD-AND-BUTTER PICKLES

WHY THIS RECIPE WORKS: We wanted a bread-and-butter pickle with a crisp texture and a balance of sweet and sour. Most recipes combine cucumbers and onions in a spiced, syrupy brine; we cut back on the sugar and added red bell pepper. Cucumbers can lose their crunch when processed in a boiling-water bath; combining several crisping techniques gave us the best results. We tossed our sliced vegetables in salt to draw out excess water. Then we added a small amount of Ball Pickle Crisp to each jar, which helps keep the natural pectin from breaking down. Next, we employed low-temperature pasteurization, which involved maintaining our pickles in a hot-water bath at a temperature of 180 to 185 degrees Fahrenheit for 30 minutes—in this temperature range micro-organisms are destroyed and pectin remains largely intact.

Bread-and-Butter Pickles

MAKES FOUR 1-PINT JARS

- 2 pounds pickling cucumbers, ends trimmed, sliced ¼ inch thick
- 1 onion, quartered and sliced thin
- 1 red bell pepper, stemmed, seeded, and cut into 1½-inch matchsticks
- 2 tablespoons canning and pickling salt
- 3 cups apple cider vinegar
- 2 cups sugar
- 1 cup water
- 1 tablespoon yellow mustard seeds
- ¾ teaspoon ground turmeric
- ½ teaspoon celery seeds
- ¼ teaspoon ground cloves
- ½ teaspoon Ball Pickle Crisp

1. Toss cucumbers, onion, and bell pepper with salt in large bowl and refrigerate for 3 hours. Drain vegetables in colander (do not rinse), then pat dry with paper towels.

2. Meanwhile, set canning rack in large pot, place four 1-pint jars in rack, and add water to cover by 1 inch. Bring to simmer over medium-high heat, then turn off heat and cover to keep hot.

3. Bring vinegar, sugar, water, mustard seeds, turmeric, celery seeds, and cloves to boil in large saucepan over medium-high heat; cover and remove from heat.

4. Place dish towel flat on counter. Using jar lifter, remove jars from pot, draining water back into pot. Place jars upside down on towel and let dry for 1 minute. Add ⅛ teaspoon Pickle Crisp to each hot jar, then pack tightly with vegetables.

5. Return brine to brief boil. Using funnel and ladle, pour hot brine over cucumbers to cover, distributing spices evenly and leaving ½ inch headspace. Slide wooden skewer along inside of jar, pressing slightly on vegetables to remove air bubbles, and add extra brine as needed.

6A. FOR SHORT-TERM STORAGE: Let jars cool to room temperature, cover with lids, and refrigerate for 1 day before serving. (Pickles can be refrigerated for up to 3 months; flavor will continue to mature over time.)

6B. FOR LONG-TERM STORAGE: While jars are warm, wipe rims clean, add lids, and screw on rings until fingertip-tight; do not overtighten. Before processing jars, heat water in canning pot to temperature between 120 and 140 degrees. Lower jars into water, bring water to 180 to 185 degrees, then cook for 30 minutes, adjusting heat as needed to maintain water between 180 and 185 degrees. Remove jars from pot and let cool for 24 hours. Remove rings, check seal, and clean rims. (Sealed jars can be stored for up to 1 year.)

NOTES FROM THE TEST KITCHEN

MAKING BREAD-AND-BUTTER PICKLES

1. We add ⅛ teaspoon of Ball Pickle Crisp to each jar before adding cucumbers and brine to help pickles retain their crispness. Pickle Crisp is simply a form of calcium chloride, which helps keep natural pectin in the cucumbers from softening.

2. It is key to have brine hot when pouring it over pickles. Be sure to distribute spices evenly between jars and leave ½ inch of headspace.

3. To remove any air bubbles trapped between layers of cucumbers, slide a wooden skewer along inside of jar and press it gently against vegetables. Once air bubbles have been dispersed, add extra brine as needed until headspace measures ½ inch.

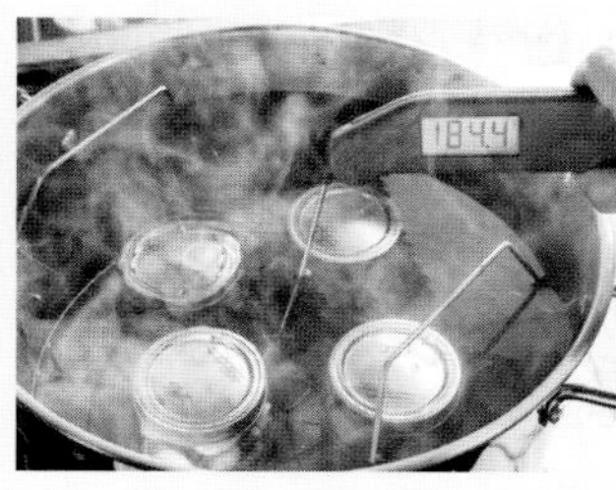

4. Using low-temperature pasteurization processing means jars of pickles need to cook in 180- to 185-degree water. If water climbs above 185, pickles will turn mushy. If water falls below 180 degrees, harmful bacteria could grow inside jars.

BROILED ASPARAGUS

WHY THIS RECIPE WORKS: Broiling can intensify the flavor of asparagus, turning it sweet and nutty. But getting the asparagus to cook through evenly can be tricky. We wanted a foolproof broiling method for turning out browned, tender spears every time.

To start, we found that with thicker asparagus, the exterior began to char before the interior of the spears became fully tender. When we used thinner spears, however, the interior was tender by the time the exterior was browned. Keeping the spears about four inches away from the broiling element allowed them to caramelize properly without charring. To encourage browning, we tossed the asparagus with olive oil before broiling. Shaking the pan with the asparagus as it cooked ensured that the spears cooked evenly. The intense dry heat of the broiler concentrated the flavor of the asparagus, and the exterior caramelization made the spears especially sweet.

Broiled Asparagus

SERVES 6

Broilers vary significantly in intensity, thus the wide range of cooking times in this recipe. Choose asparagus no thicker than ½ inch near the base for this recipe.

- 2 pounds thin asparagus (about 2 bunches), tough ends trimmed (see page 300; see note)
- 1 tablespoon olive oil
- Table salt and ground black pepper

Adjust an oven rack to the highest position (about 4 inches from the heating element) and heat the broiler. Toss the asparagus with the oil and salt and pepper to taste, then lay the spears in a single layer on a rimmed baking sheet. Broil, shaking the pan halfway through cooking to turn the spears, until the asparagus is tender and lightly browned, 6 to 10 minutes. Serve hot or warm.

PAN-ROASTED ASPARAGUS

WHY THIS RECIPE WORKS: Recipes for pan-roasted asparagus promise ease and flavor, but the results are usually disappointing: limp, greasy, and shriveled spears. We wanted a simple stovetop method that would deliver crisp, nicely browned spears.

We quickly learned to choose thick spears because thinner spears overcooked too quickly. Taking a cue from restaurant chefs who blanch asparagus first, we developed a method to lightly steam and then brown the asparagus in the same skillet. For both flavor and browning, we used olive oil and butter. Positioning half the spears in one direction and the other half in the opposite direction ensured a better fit in the pan. Browning just one side of the asparagus provided a contrast in texture and guaranteed that the asparagus were firm and tender, never limp.

Pan-Roasted Asparagus

SERVES 3 TO 4

This recipe works best with asparagus that is at least ½ inch thick near the base. If using thinner spears, reduce the covered cooking time to 3 minutes and the uncovered cooking time to 5 minutes. Do not use pencil-thin asparagus; it cannot withstand the heat and overcooks too easily.

- 1 tablespoon olive oil
- 1 tablespoon unsalted butter
- 2 pounds thick asparagus (about 2 bunches), tough ends trimmed (see page 300; see note)
- Table salt and ground black pepper
- ½ lemon (optional)

1. Heat the oil and butter in a 12-inch skillet over medium-high heat. When the butter has melted, add half of the asparagus to the skillet with the tips pointed in one direction; add the remaining asparagus with the tips pointed in the opposite direction. Using tongs, distribute the spears in an even layer (the spears will not quite fit into a single layer); cover and cook until the asparagus is bright green and still crisp, about 5 minutes.

2. Uncover and increase the heat to high; season the asparagus with salt and pepper to taste. Cook until the spears are tender and well browned along one side, 5 to 7 minutes, using the tongs to occasionally move the spears from the center of the pan to the edge of the pan to ensure all are browned. Transfer the asparagus to a dish, season with salt and pepper to taste, and squeeze the lemon half (if using) over the spears. Serve.

STIR-FRIED ASPARAGUS WITH SHIITAKE MUSHROOMS

WHY THIS RECIPE WORKS: To achieve stir-fried asparagus with a flavorful browned exterior and a crisp-tender texture, we had to start with a hot pan and only stir the asparagus occasionally. This allowed the vegetables to char and caramelize. To ensure that the asparagus cooked evenly, we diluted the sauce with water. This diluted sauce created a small amount of steam, cooking the spears through, before evaporating and leaving behind a flavorful glaze.

Stir-Fried Asparagus with Shiitake Mushrooms

SERVES 4

To allow it to brown, stir the asparagus only occasionally. Look for spears that are no thicker than ½ inch.

- 2 tablespoons water
- 1 tablespoon soy sauce
- 1 tablespoon dry sherry
- 2 teaspoons packed brown sugar
- 2 teaspoons grated fresh ginger
- 1 teaspoon toasted sesame oil
- 1 tablespoon vegetable oil
- 1 pound asparagus, tough ends trimmed (see page 300) and cut on bias into 2-inch lengths
- 4 ounces shiitake mushrooms, stemmed and sliced thin
- 2 scallions, green parts only, sliced thin on bias

1. Combine water, soy sauce, sherry, sugar, ginger, and sesame oil in bowl.

2. Heat vegetable oil in 12-inch nonstick skillet over high heat until smoking. Add asparagus and mushrooms and cook, stirring occasionally, until asparagus is spotty brown, 3 to 4 minutes. Add soy sauce mixture and cook, stirring once or twice, until pan is almost dry and asparagus is crisp-tender, 1 to 2 minutes. Transfer to serving platter, sprinkle with scallion greens, and serve.

Stir-Fried Asparagus with Red Bell Pepper

Omit soy sauce, sherry, brown sugar, ginger, and sesame oil. Reduce water to 1 tablespoon. Whisk 1 tablespoon orange juice, 1 tablespoon rice vinegar, 1 tablespoon granulated sugar, 1 teaspoon ketchup, and ½ teaspoon salt into water. Substitute 1 stemmed and seeded red bell pepper cut into 2-inch-long matchsticks for shiitakes.

Stir-Fried Asparagus with Red Onion

Omit soy sauce, sherry, ginger, and sesame oil. Whisk 4 teaspoons fish sauce, 1 tablespoon lime juice, 2 teaspoons minced fresh lemon grass, and ⅛ teaspoon red pepper flakes into water, along with sugar. Substitute ½ red onion sliced through root end into ¼-inch-thick pieces for shiitakes and 2 tablespoons chopped fresh mint for scallion greens.

BRAISED BEETS

WHY THIS RECIPE WORKS: We sought a streamlined recipe for beets that maximized their sweet, earthy flavor. To achieve this goal in less than an hour, we braised the halved beets on the stovetop in minimal water, reduced the residual cooking liquid, and added light brown sugar and vinegar. This flavor-packed glaze was just thick enough to coat the wedges of peeled beets. For flavor and texture contrast, we added toasted nuts (or pepitas), fresh herbs, and aromatic citrus zest just before serving.

Beets with Lemon and Almonds

SERVES 4 TO 6

To ensure even cooking, we recommend using beets that are of similar size—roughly 2 to 3 inches in diameter. The beets can be served warm or at room temperature. If serving at room temperature, wait until right before serving to sprinkle on the almonds and herbs.

- 1½ pounds beets, trimmed and halved horizontally
- 1¼ cups water
- Salt and pepper
- 3 tablespoons white vinegar
- 1 tablespoon packed light brown sugar
- 1 shallot, sliced thin
- 1 teaspoon grated lemon zest
- ½ cup whole almonds, toasted and chopped
- 2 tablespoons chopped fresh mint
- 1 teaspoon chopped fresh thyme

1. Place beets, cut side down, in single layer in 11-inch straight-sided sauté pan or Dutch oven. Add water and ¼ teaspoon salt; bring to simmer over high heat. Reduce heat to low, cover, and simmer until beets are tender and tip of paring knife inserted into beets meets no resistance, 45 to 50 minutes.

2. Transfer beets to cutting board. Increase heat to medium-high and reduce cooking liquid, stirring occasionally, until pan is almost dry, 5 to 6 minutes. Add vinegar and sugar, return to boil, and cook, stirring constantly with heat-resistant spatula, until spatula leaves wide trail when dragged through glaze, 1 to 2 minutes. Remove pan from heat.

3. When beets are cool enough to handle, rub off skins with paper towel or clean dish towel and cut into ½-inch wedges. Add beets, shallot, lemon zest, ½ teaspoon salt, and ¼ teaspoon pepper to glaze and toss to coat. Transfer beets to serving dish; sprinkle with almonds, mint, and thyme; and serve.

Beets with Lime and Pepitas

Omit thyme. Substitute lime zest for lemon zest, toasted pepitas for almonds, and cilantro for mint.

Beets with Orange and Walnuts

Substitute orange zest for lemon zest; walnuts, toasted and chopped, for almonds; and parsley for mint.

ROASTED BROCCOLI

WHY THIS RECIPE WORKS: Roasting can concentrate flavor to turn dull vegetables into something great, but roasting broccoli usually makes for spotty browning and charred, bitter florets. We wanted to figure out how to roast broccoli so that it turned out perfectly browned and deeply flavorful every time.

To ensure that the broccoli would brown evenly, we cut the crown into uniform wedges that lay flat on the baking sheet, increasing contact with the pan. To promote even cooking of the stem, we sliced away the exterior and cut the stalk into rectangular pieces slightly smaller than the more delicate wedges. After trial and error, we discovered that preheating the baking sheet helped the broccoli cook faster, crisping but not charring the florets, while a very hot oven delivered the best browning. Sprinkling a little sugar over the broccoli along with the salt and pepper helped it brown even more deeply. We finally had roasted broccoli with crispy-tipped florets and sweet, browned stems.

Roasted Broccoli

SERVES 4

It is important to trim away the outer peel from the broccoli stalks; otherwise they will turn tough when cooked.

- 1¾ pounds broccoli (about 1 large bunch)
- 3 tablespoons extra-virgin olive oil
- ½ teaspoon table salt
- ½ teaspoon sugar
- Ground black pepper
- Lemon wedges, for serving

1. Adjust an oven rack to the lowest position, place a large rimmed baking sheet on the rack, and heat the oven to 500 degrees. Cut the broccoli at the juncture of the florets and stems; remove the outer peel from the stalk. Cut the stalk into 2 to 3-inch lengths and each length into ½-inch-thick pieces. Cut the crowns into four wedges (if 3 to 4 inches in diameter) or six wedges (if 4 to 5 inches in diameter). Place the broccoli in a large bowl; drizzle with the oil and toss well until evenly coated. Season with the salt, sugar, and pepper to taste and toss to combine.

2. Carefully remove the baking sheet from the oven. Working quickly, transfer the broccoli to the baking sheet and spread into an even layer, placing the flat sides down. Return the baking sheet to the oven and roast until the stalks are well browned and tender and the florets are lightly browned, 9 to 11 minutes. Transfer to a dish and serve with the lemon wedges.

Roasted Broccoli with Garlic

Follow the recipe for Roasted Broccoli, adding 1 garlic clove, minced or pressed through a garlic press, to the oil before drizzling it over the broccoli in step 1.

ROASTED BRUSSELS SPROUTS

WHY THIS RECIPE WORKS: Roasting is a simple and quick way to produce Brussels sprouts that are well caramelized on the outside and tender on the inside. To ensure we achieved this balance, we started out roasting the "tiny cabbages," covered, with a little bit of water. This created a steamy environment, which cooked the vegetable through. We then removed the foil and allowed the exterior to dry out and caramelize.

Roasted Brussels Sprouts

SERVES 6 TO 8

If you are buying loose Brussels sprouts, select those that are about 1½ inches long. Quarter Brussels sprouts longer than 2½ inches; don't cut sprouts shorter than 1 inch.

- 2¼ pounds Brussels sprouts, trimmed and halved
- 3 tablespoons olive oil
- 1 tablespoon water
- Salt and pepper

1. Adjust oven rack to upper-middle position and heat oven to 500 degrees. Toss Brussels sprouts, oil, water, ¾ teaspoon salt, and ¼ teaspoon pepper together in large bowl until sprouts are coated. Transfer sprouts to rimmed baking sheet and arrange cut sides down.

2. Cover baking sheet tightly with aluminum foil and roast for 10 minutes. Remove foil and continue to cook until Brussels sprouts are well browned and tender, 10 to 12 minutes longer. Transfer to serving platter, season with salt and pepper to taste, and serve.

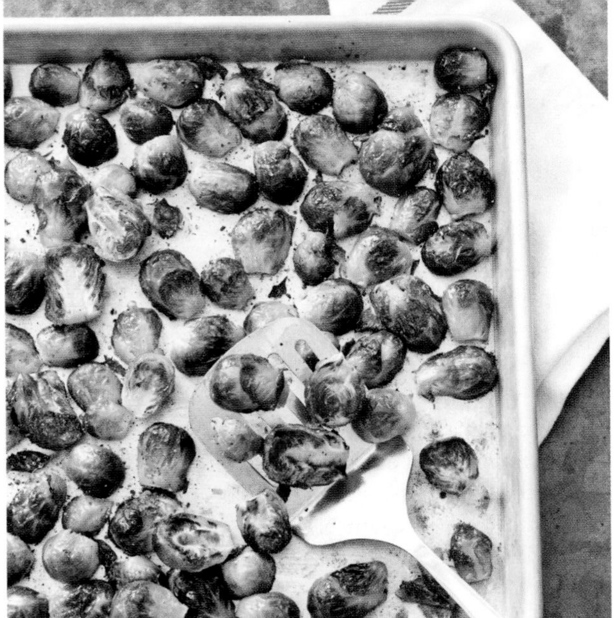

Roasted Brussels Sprouts with Garlic, Red Pepper Flakes, and Parmesan

While Brussels sprouts roast, heat 3 tablespoons olive oil in 8-inch skillet over medium heat until shimmering. Add 2 minced garlic cloves and ½ teaspoon red pepper flakes; cook until garlic is golden and fragrant, about 1 minute. Remove from heat. Toss roasted Brussels sprouts with garlic oil and season with salt and pepper to taste. Transfer to platter and sprinkle with ¼ cup grated Parmesan cheese before serving.

Roasted Brussels Sprouts with Bacon and Pecans

While Brussels sprouts roast, cook 4 slices bacon in 10-inch skillet over medium heat until crisp, 7 to 10 minutes. Using slotted spoon, transfer bacon to paper towel–lined plate and reserve 1 tablespoon bacon fat. Finely chop bacon. Toss roasted Brussels sprouts with 2 tablespoons olive oil, reserved bacon fat, chopped bacon, and ½ cup finely chopped toasted pecans. Season with salt and pepper to taste; transfer to platter and serve.

ROASTED CARROTS

WHY THIS RECIPE WORKS: Roasting carrots draws out their natural sugars and intensifies their flavor, but too often carrots shrivel up and turn jerky-like under the high heat of the oven. We wanted roasted carrots with a pleasingly al dente chew and earthy, sweet flavor.

To compensate for the oven's arid heat, we tried adding liquid to the roasting pan. While our carrots turned out moist, they weren't browned and lacked the intense roasted flavor we wanted. Our science editor then explained that no additional moisture was necessary. While a carrot's hard, woody structure doesn't suggest it, the average carrot is actually 87.5 percent water by weight. For our next test we tossed the carrots with melted butter, spread them onto a baking sheet, and covered the sheet tightly with foil. We roasted the carrots, covered, just until softened, then we removed the foil and continued to roast them to draw out their moisture and brown them. The result? Rich-tasting, tender carrots with a nutty flavor. Best of all, the technique worked just as well when we paired the carrots with other roasted root vegetables: parsnips, fennel, and shallots.

Roasted Carrots

SERVES 4 TO 6

Most bagged carrots come in a variety of sizes and must be cut lengthwise for evenly cooked results. After halving the carrots crosswise, leave small (less than ½ inch in diameter) pieces whole; halve medium pieces (½- to 1-inch diameter), and quarter large pieces (over 1 inch).

- 1½ pounds carrots, peeled, halved crosswise, and cut lengthwise if necessary (see note)
- 2 tablespoons unsalted butter, melted
- Table salt and ground black pepper

1. Adjust an oven rack to the middle position and heat the oven to 425 degrees. Line a large rimmed baking sheet with parchment or aluminum foil. In a large bowl, combine the carrots with the butter, ½ teaspoon salt, and ¼ teaspoon pepper; toss to coat. Transfer the carrots to the prepared baking sheet and spread in a single layer.

2. Cover the baking sheet tightly with foil and roast for 15 minutes. Remove the foil and continue to roast, stirring twice, until well-browned and tender, 30 to 35 minutes. Transfer to a serving platter, season with salt and pepper to taste, and serve.

Roasted Carrots and Fennel with Toasted Almonds and Lemon

Follow the recipe for Roasted Carrots, reducing the amount of carrots to 1 pound. Add ½ large fennel bulb, cored and sliced ½ inch thick, to the bowl with the carrots and roast as directed. Toss the roasted vegetables with ¼ cup toasted sliced almonds, 1 teaspoon juice from 1 lemon, and 2 teaspoons chopped fresh parsley leaves before serving in step 2.

Roasted Carrots and Parsnips with Rosemary

Follow the recipe for Roasted Carrots, reducing the amount of carrots to 1 pound. Add ½ pound peeled parsnips, cut like the carrots, and 1 teaspoon chopped fresh rosemary leaves to the bowl with the carrots and roast as directed. Toss the roasted vegetables with 2 teaspoons chopped fresh parsley leaves before serving in step 2.

QUICK ROASTED BABY CARROTS

WHY THIS RECIPE WORKS: Roasted carrots frequently end up either undercooked, with a bitter, hard center or, at the other end of the spectrum, are subjected to such intense heat that they become wan, limp, and utterly unpalatable. We wanted to release the sweetness from the carrots, yielding a caramelized exterior and a creamy, tender interior.

Roasting prepared baby carrots saved us time, because they require no cleaning or cutting. The flavor of the carrots needed a little help; plain olive oil with a little salt worked well—it neither masked the carrots' flavor nor changed their texture. Roasting the carrots uncovered at a high temperature created the caramelized exterior we were after, and using the bottom of a broiler pan prevented them from burning. We were now able to produce perfectly cooked, deeply flavorful roasted carrots in just 20 minutes.

Quick Roasted Baby Carrots

SERVES 8

When buying carrots, inspect the bag carefully for pockets of water. Bags taken from the top of the supermarket's pile are often waterlogged. This not only makes carrots mealy, it also prevents them from caramelizing properly.

- 2 pounds baby carrots (two 16-ounce bags; see note)
- 2 tablespoons olive oil
- ½ teaspoon table salt

Adjust an oven rack to the middle position and heat the oven to 475 degrees. Toss the carrots, oil, and salt in a broiler pan bottom. Spread into a single layer and roast for 12 minutes. Shake the pan to toss the carrots; continue roasting about 8 minutes longer, shaking the pan twice more, until the carrots are browned and tender. Serve.

GLAZED CARROTS

WHY THIS RECIPE WORKS: Glazing is probably the most popular way to prepare carrots, but they often turn out saccharine, with a limp and soggy or undercooked and fibrous texture. We wanted fully tender, well-seasoned carrots with a glossy and clingy—yet modest—glaze.

Peeling regular bagged carrots and cutting them on the bias yielded uniform ovals that cooked evenly. We cooked and glazed the carrots in one single operation, starting by cooking the sliced carrots in a covered skillet with chicken broth, salt, and sugar. After the carrots were cooked until almost tender, we removed the lid and turned up the heat to reduce the liquid. Finally, a little butter and a bit more sugar added to the skillet resulted in a pale amber glaze with light caramel flavor. A sprinkle of fresh lemon juice gave the dish sparkle, and a pinch of freshly ground black pepper provided depth.

Glazed Carrots

SERVES 4

We like to use a nonstick skillet here for easy cleanup, but any 12-inch skillet with a cover will work.

- 1 pound carrots (about 6 medium), peeled and sliced ¼ inch thick on the bias
- ½ cup low-sodium chicken broth
- 3 tablespoons sugar
- ½ teaspoon table salt
- 1 tablespoon unsalted butter, cut into 4 pieces
- 2 teaspoons juice from 1 lemon
- Ground black pepper

1. Bring the carrots, broth, 1 tablespoon of the sugar, and the salt to a boil in a 12-inch nonstick skillet, covered, over medium-high heat. Reduce the heat to medium and simmer, stirring occasionally, until the carrots are almost tender when poked with the tip of a paring knife, about 5 minutes. Uncover, increase the heat to high, and simmer rapidly, stirring occasionally, until the liquid is reduced to about 2 tablespoons, 1 to 2 minutes.

2. Add the remaining 2 tablespoons sugar and the butter to the skillet. Toss the carrots to coat and cook, stirring frequently, until the carrots are completely tender and the glaze is light gold, about 3 minutes. Off the heat, add the lemon juice and toss to coat. Transfer the carrots to a dish, scraping the glaze from the pan into the dish. Season with pepper to taste and serve.

SLOW-COOKED WHOLE CARROTS

WHY THIS RECIPE WORKS: We wanted a technique for cooking whole carrots that would yield a sweet and meltingly tender vegetable without the carrots becoming mushy. Cooking the tapered vegetable evenly from end to end was a challenge, so we looked to techniques that promised carrots with concentrated flavor and uniformly dense texture. Gently "steeping" the carrots in warm water, butter, and salt before cooking them firmed up the vegetable's cell walls so that they could be cooked for a long time without falling apart. We also took a tip from restaurant cooking and topped the carrots with a cartouche (a circle of parchment that sits directly on the food) during cooking to regulate the reduction of moisture. An easy relish finished the dish on a high note.

Slow-Cooked Whole Carrots

SERVES 4 TO 6

Use carrots that measure ¾ to 1¼ inches across at the thickest end. The carrots can be served plain, but we recommend topping them with Pine Nut Relish (recipe follows).

- 3 cups water
- 1 tablespoon unsalted butter
- ½ teaspoon salt
- 12 carrots (1½ to 1¾ pounds), peeled

1. Fold 12-inch square of parchment paper into quarters to create 6-inch square. Fold bottom right corner of square to top left corner to create triangle. Fold triangle again, right side over left, to create narrow triangle. Cut off ¼ inch of tip of triangle to create small hole. Cut base of triangle straight across where it measures 5 inches from hole. Open paper round.

2. Bring water, butter, and salt to simmer in 12-inch skillet over high heat. Remove pan from heat, add carrots in single layer, and place parchment round on top of carrots. Cover skillet and let stand for 20 minutes.

3. Remove lid from skillet, leaving parchment round in place, and bring to simmer over high heat. Reduce heat to medium-low and simmer until almost all water has evaporated and carrots are very tender, about 45 minutes.

4. Discard parchment round, increase heat to medium-high, and continue to cook carrots, shaking pan frequently, until they are lightly glazed and no water remains in skillet, 2 to 4 minutes longer. Transfer carrots to platter and serve.

Pine Nut Relish

MAKES ABOUT ¾ CUP

Pine nuts burn easily, so be sure to shake the pan frequently while toasting them.

- ⅓ cup pine nuts, toasted
- 1 shallot, minced
- 1 tablespoon sherry vinegar
- 1 tablespoon minced fresh parsley
- 1 teaspoon honey
- ½ teaspoon minced fresh rosemary
- ¼ teaspoon smoked paprika
- ¼ teaspoon salt
- Pinch cayenne pepper

Combine all ingredients in bowl.

BUFFALO CAULIFLOWER BITES

WHY THIS RECIPE WORKS: Deemed "better than wings" by our tasters, these crunchy, spicy vegan cauliflower bites will be the new star of your game day table. A mixture of cornstarch and cornmeal gave us an ultracrisp exterior. Because cauliflower is not naturally moist, the mixture didn't adhere; so we dunked the florets in canned coconut milk, which had the right viscosity. Frying helped achieve a crackly crust and tender interior.

Buffalo Cauliflower Bites

SERVES 4 TO 6

We used Frank's RedHot Original Cayenne Pepper Sauce, but other hot sauces can be used. Use a Dutch oven that holds 6 quarts or more for this recipe.

BUFFALO SAUCE

- ¼ cup coconut oil
- ½ cup hot sauce
- 1 tablespoon packed dark brown sugar
- 2 teaspoons cider vinegar

CAULIFLOWER

- 1–2 quarts peanut or vegetable oil
- ¾ cup cornstarch
- ¼ cup cornmeal
- Salt and pepper
- ⅔ cup canned coconut milk
- 1 tablespoon hot sauce
- 1 pound cauliflower florets, cut into 1½-inch pieces
- 1 recipe Ranch Dressing (recipe follows)

1. FOR THE BUFFALO SAUCE: Melt coconut oil in small saucepan over low heat. Whisk in hot sauce, brown sugar, and vinegar until combined. Remove from heat and cover to keep warm; set aside.

2. FOR THE CAULIFLOWER: Line platter with triple layer of paper towels. Add oil to large Dutch oven until it measures about 1½ inches deep and heat over medium-high heat to 400 degrees. While oil heats, combine cornstarch, cornmeal, ½ teaspoon salt, and ¼ teaspoon pepper in small bowl. Whisk coconut milk and hot sauce together in large bowl. Add cauliflower; toss to coat well. Sprinkle cornstarch mixture over cauliflower; fold with rubber spatula until thoroughly coated.

3. Fry half of cauliflower, adding 1 or 2 pieces to oil at a time, until golden and crisp, gently stirring as needed to prevent pieces from sticking together, about 3 minutes. Using slotted spoon, transfer fried cauliflower to prepared platter.

4. Return oil to 400 degrees and repeat with remaining cauliflower. Transfer ½ cup sauce to clean large bowl, add fried cauliflower and gently toss to coat. Serve immediately with dressing and remaining sauce.

Ranch Dressing

MAKES ABOUT ½ CUP

We strongly prefer our favorite vegan mayonnaise, Just Mayo, or our homemade Vegan Mayonnaise (recipe follows).

- ½ cup vegan mayonnaise
- 2 tablespoons unsweetened plain coconut milk yogurt
- 1 teaspoon white wine vinegar
- 1½ teaspoons minced fresh chives
- 1 ½ teaspoons minced fresh dill
- ¼ teaspoon garlic powder
- ⅛ teaspoon salt
- ⅛ teaspoon pepper

Whisk all ingredients in bowl until smooth. (Dressing can be refrigerated for up to 4 days.)

Vegan Mayonnaise

MAKES ABOUT 1 CUP

Aquafaba, the liquid found in a can of chickpeas, gives our mayo volume and emulsified body. It's devoid of off-flavors or off-textures, which was not the case when we tried creating mayo with soy milk, tofu, cashews, or miso.

- ⅓ cup aquafaba
- 1½ teaspoons lemon juice
- ½ teaspoon salt
- ½ teaspoon sugar
- ½ teaspoon Dijon mustard
- 1¼ cups vegetable oil
- 3 tablespoons extra-virgin olive oil

1. Process aquafaba, lemon juice, salt, sugar, and mustard in food processor for 10 seconds. With processor running, gradually add vegetable oil in slow, steady stream until mixture is thick and creamy, scraping down sides of bowl as needed, about 3 minutes.

2. Transfer mixture to bowl. Whisking constantly, slowly add olive oil until emulsified. If pools of oil form on surface, stop addition of oil and whisk mixture until well combined, then resume adding oil. Mayonnaise should be thick and glossy with no oil pools on surface. (Mayonnaise can be refrigerated for up to 1 week.)

CORN FRITTERS

WHY THIS RECIPE WORKS: Good corn fritters should be light—creamy in the middle and crisp on the outside. This is rarely the case, however; most corn fritters have little corn flavor and cook up dense and greasy. We wanted to make perfect corn fritters—light, crisp, and packed with fresh corn flavor.

We found that combining whole corn kernels and grated kernels worked best for visual appeal, textural contrast, and fullest corn flavor. Running the back of a knife over the cobs from which the corn had been grated helped us extract the flavorful pulp. Equal amounts of flour and cornmeal bound the mixture together without making the fritters heavy and kept the corn flavor strong. A bit of heavy cream added welcome richness. For pan-frying the cakes, vegetable oil was the cooking medium of choice for its high smoke point and neutral flavor, which didn't overpower the corn. Keeping the oil hot helped the fritters brown quickly.

Corn Fritters

MAKES TWELVE 2-INCH FRITTERS

Serve these fritters with hot sauce, salsa, or even maple syrup.

- 4 ears corn, husks and silk removed
- 1 large egg, lightly beaten
- 3 tablespoons unbleached all-purpose flour
- 3 tablespoons cornmeal
- 2 tablespoons heavy cream
- 1 small shallot, minced (about 1 tablespoon)
- ½ teaspoon salt
- Pinch cayenne pepper
- ¼ cup vegetable oil, plus more as needed

1. Stand the corn upright inside a large bowl and, using a paring knife, carefully cut the kernels from 2 ears of the corn; you should have about 1 cup. Transfer the kernels to a medium bowl. Use the back of a butter knife to scrape off any pulp remaining on the cobs and transfer it to the bowl. Grate the kernels from the remaining 2 ears of corn on the large holes of a box grater, then firmly scrape off any pulp remaining on the cobs with the back of a butter knife; you should have a generous cup of kernels and pulp. Transfer the grated kernels and pulp to the bowl with the cut kernels.

2. Mix the egg, flour, cornmeal, cream, shallot, salt, and cayenne into the corn mixture to form a thick batter.

3. Heat the oil in a 12-inch skillet over medium-high heat until almost smoking, about 2 minutes. Drop heaping tablespoons of batter into the oil (half the batter, or six fritters, should fit into the pan at once). Fry until golden brown, about 1 minute. Using a thin metal spatula, turn the fritters and fry until the second side is golden brown, about 1 minute longer. Transfer the fritters to a paper towel–lined plate. Repeat with the remaining batter, adding more oil to the skillet if necessary. Serve.

SOUTHERN CORN FRITTERS

WHY THIS RECIPE WORKS: For the lightest corn fritters, we minimized the number of fillers we added. We processed some of the kernels to act as a thickener rather than bulk up the batter with more flour or cornmeal. This step also let the fresh corn flavor shine through. Browning the corn puree in a skillet drove off excess moisture and deepened the flavor even more. Adding cayenne, nutty Parmesan cheese, and oniony chives balanced the natural sweetness of the corn, and a touch of cornstarch helped crisp the exterior and provide a textural contrast with the creamy interior.

Southern Corn Fritters

MAKES 12

Serve these fritters as a side dish with steaks, chops, or poultry or as an appetizer with a dollop of sour cream or with Red Pepper Mayonnaise, Maple-Chipotle Mayonnaise, Basil Mayonnaise, or Sriracha-Lime Yogurt Sauce (recipes follow).

- 4 ears corn, kernels cut from cobs (3 cups)
- 1 teaspoon plus ½ cup vegetable oil
- Salt and pepper
- ¼ cup all-purpose flour
- ¼ cup finely minced chives
- 2 tablespoons grated Parmesan cheese
- 1 tablespoon cornstarch
- Pinch cayenne pepper
- 1 large egg, lightly beaten

1. Process 1½ cups corn kernels in food processor to uniformly coarse puree, 15 to 20 seconds, scraping down bowl halfway through processing. Set aside.

2. Heat 1 teaspoon oil in 12-inch nonstick skillet over medium-high heat until shimmering. Add remaining 1½ cups corn kernels and ⅛ teaspoon salt, and cook, stirring frequently, until light golden, 3 to 4 minutes. Transfer to medium bowl.

3. Return skillet to medium heat, add corn puree, and cook, stirring frequently with heatproof spatula, until puree is consistency of thick oatmeal (puree clings to spatula rather than dripping off), about 5 minutes. Transfer puree to bowl with kernels and stir to combine. Rinse skillet and dry with paper towels.

4. Stir flour, 3 tablespoons chives, Parmesan, cornstarch, cayenne, ¼ teaspoon salt, and ⅛ teaspoon pepper into corn mixture until well combined. Gently stir in egg until incorporated.

5. Line rimmed baking sheet with paper towels. Heat remaining ½ cup oil in now-empty skillet over medium heat until shimmering. Drop six 2-tablespoon portions batter into skillet. Press with spatula to flatten into 2½- to 3-inch disks. Fry until deep golden brown on both sides, 2 to 3 minutes per side. Transfer fritters to prepared sheet. Repeat with remaining batter.

6. Transfer fritters to large plate or platter, sprinkle with remaining 1 tablespoon chives, and serve immediately.

Red Pepper Mayonnaise

MAKES ABOUT 1¼ CUPS

Letting the minced garlic sit in the lemon juice mellows its flavor.

- 1½ teaspoons lemon juice
- 1 clove garlic, minced
- ¾ cup jarred roasted red peppers, rinsed and patted dry
- ½ cup mayonnaise
- 2 teaspoons tomato paste
- Salt

Combine lemon juice and garlic in small bowl and let stand for 15 minutes. Process red peppers, mayonnaise, tomato paste, and lemon juice mixture in food processor until smooth, about 15 seconds, scraping down sides of bowl as needed. Season with salt to taste. Refrigerate until thickened, about 2 hours.

Maple-Chipotle Mayonnaise

MAKES ⅔ CUP

For the fullest maple flavor, use maple syrup labeled "Grade A, Dark Amber."

- ½ cup mayonnaise
- 1 tablespoon maple syrup
- 1 tablespoon minced canned chipotle in adobo sauce
- ½ teaspoon Dijon mustard

Combine all ingredients in small bowl.

Basil Mayonnaise

MAKES ¾ CUP

Blue Plate Real Mayonnaise is our favorite mayonnaise. It's one of the top-selling brands in the country, but you'll have to mail-order it unless you live in the South or Southeast. Hellmann's Real Mayonnaise, which is available nationwide (it's sold as Best Foods west of the Rockies), was our runner-up.

- ½ cup mayonnaise
- ½ cup fresh basil leaves
- 1 tablespoon water
- 1 teaspoon lemon juice
- Salt and pepper

Blend mayonnaise, basil, water, and lemon juice in blender until smooth, about 10 seconds, scraping down sides as needed. Transfer to bowl and season with salt and pepper to taste.

Sriracha-Lime Yogurt Sauce

MAKES ⅔ CUP

Our favorite Greek yogurt is Fage Total Classic Greek Yogurt.

- ½ cup plain Greek yogurt
- ½ teaspoon grated lime zest plus 1 teaspoon juice
- ½ teaspoon Sriracha sauce
- 1 tablespoon minced fresh cilantro
- Salt

Mix yogurt, lime zest and juice, Sriracha, and cilantro together in small bowl. Season with salt to taste.

BOILED CORN

WHY THIS RECIPE WORKS: For perfectly crisp, juicy corn, we figured out that the ideal doneness range is 150 to 170 degrees—when the starches have gelatinized but a minimum amount of the pectin has dissolved. Consistently cooking the corn to that temperature was easy once we realized we could use a *sous vide* method: bringing water to a boil, dropping in 6 ears of

corn, and shutting off the heat. The temperature of the water decreased quickly so the corn didn't overcook, while the temperature of the corn increased to the ideal zone. Even better, this method can accommodate between 6 and 8 ears of different sizes, and the corn can sit in the water for as long as 30 minutes without overcooking.

Boiled Corn

SERVES 4 TO 6

This recipe's success depends on using the proper ratio of hot water to corn. Use a Dutch oven with a capacity of at least 7 quarts, and bring the water to a rolling boil. Eight ears of corn can be prepared using this recipe, but let the corn sit for at least 15 minutes before serving. Serve with a flavored salt (recipes follow), if desired.

- 6 ears corn, husks and silk removed
- Unsalted butter, softened
- Salt and pepper

1. Bring 4 quarts water to boil in large Dutch oven. Turn off heat, add corn to water, cover, and let stand for at least 10 minutes or up to 30 minutes.

2. Transfer corn to large platter and serve immediately, passing butter, salt, and pepper.

Chili-Lime Salt

MAKES 3 TABLESPOONS

- 2 tablespoons kosher salt
- 4 teaspoons chili powder
- ¾ teaspoon grated lime zest

Combine all ingredients in small bowl.

Pepper-Cinnamon Salt

MAKES 2 TABLESPOONS

- 1 tablespoon kosher salt
- 1 tablespoon coarsely ground pepper
- ¼ teaspoon ground cinnamon

Combine all ingredients in small bowl.

Cumin-Sesame Salt

MAKES 3 TABLESPOONS

- 1 tablespoon cumin seeds
- 1 tablespoon sesame seeds
- 1 tablespoon kosher salt

Toast cumin seeds and sesame seeds in 8-inch skillet over medium heat, stirring occasionally, until fragrant and sesame seeds are golden brown, 3 to 4 minutes. Transfer mixture to cutting board and let cool for 2 minutes. Mince mixture fine until well combined. Transfer mixture to small bowl and stir in salt.

NEW ENGLAND BAKED BEANS

WHY THIS RECIPE WORKS: For a pot of classic New England baked beans, we made a few smart tweaks while keeping the traditional flavor. Brining the beans overnight helped jump-start hydration and also softened their skins so they cooked up tender in the oven, with few blowouts. Uncovering the pot for the last hour of cooking ensured that the liquid reduced sufficiently to coat the beans in a thick sauce. Flavorings such as molasses, brown sugar, dry mustard, bay leaf, and onion, plus one nontraditional ingredient (soy sauce), gave the beans rich flavor, while chunks of salt pork added meatiness.

New England Baked Beans

SERVES 4 TO 6

You'll get fewer blowouts if you soak the beans overnight, but if you're pressed for time, you can quick-salt-soak your beans. In step 1, combine the salt, water, and beans in a large Dutch oven and bring them to a boil over high heat. Remove the pot from the heat, cover it, and let it stand for 1 hour. Drain and rinse the beans and proceed with the recipe.

- Salt
- 1 pound (2½ cups) dried navy beans, picked over and rinsed
- 6 ounces salt pork, rinsed and cut into 3 pieces
- 1 onion, halved
- ½ cup molasses
- 2 tablespoons packed dark brown sugar
- 1 tablespoon soy sauce
- 2 teaspoons dry mustard
- ½ teaspoon pepper
- 1 bay leaf

1. Dissolve 1½ tablespoons salt in 2 quarts cold water in large container. Add beans and let soak at room temperature for at least 8 hours or up to 24 hours. Drain and rinse well.

2. Adjust oven rack to lower-middle position and heat oven to 300 degrees. Combine beans, salt pork, onion, molasses, sugar, soy sauce, mustard, pepper, bay leaf, ¼ teaspoon salt, and 4 cups water in large Dutch oven. (Liquid should cover beans by about ½ inch. Add more water if necessary.) Bring to boil over high heat. Cover pot, transfer to oven, and cook until beans are softened and bean skins curl up and split when you blow on them, about 2 hours. (After 1 hour, stir beans and check amount of liquid. Liquid should just cover beans. Add water if necessary.)

3. Remove lid and continue to cook until beans are fully tender, browned, and slightly crusty on top, about 1 hour longer. (Liquid will reduce slightly below top layer of beans.)

4. Remove pot from oven, cover, and let stand for 5 minutes. Using wooden spoon or rubber spatula, scrape any browned bits from sides of pot and stir into beans. Discard onion and bay leaf. (Salt pork can be eaten, if desired.) Let beans stand, uncovered, until liquid has thickened slightly and clings to beans, 10 to 15 minutes, stirring once halfway through. Season with salt and pepper to taste, and serve. (Beans can be refrigerated for up to 4 days.)

BOSTON BAKED BEANS

WHY THIS RECIPE WORKS: Boston baked beans are both sweet and savory, a unique combination of the simplest ingredients, unified and refined during a long simmer. Unfortunately, recipes with lengthy lists of untraditional ingredients and mushy beans abound. We wanted tender beans in a thick, smoky, slightly sweet sauce.

For depth of flavor, we started by browning a combination of salt pork and bacon in a Dutch oven. Small white beans were preferred for their creamy texture and ability to remain intact during the long simmer. Mild molasses provided just the right amount of sweetness, while brown mustard and cider vinegar added welcome notes of spice and tanginess. We removed the lid for the last hour of cooking to reduce the sauce to a syrupy, intensified consistency that perfectly napped the beans.

Boston Baked Beans

SERVES 4 TO 6

The beans can be made ahead. After cooking, cool them to room temperature and refrigerate in an airtight container for up to 4 days.

- 4 ounces salt pork, trimmed of rind and cut into ½-inch cubes
- 2 ounces (about 2 slices) bacon, cut into ¼-inch pieces
- 1 medium onion, minced
- 9 cups water
- 1 pound (2 cups) dried small white beans, rinsed and picked over
- ½ cup plus 1 tablespoon mild molasses
- 1½ tablespoons prepared brown mustard, such as Gulden's
- Table salt
- 1 teaspoon cider vinegar
- Ground black pepper

1. Adjust an oven rack to the lower-middle position and heat the oven to 300 degrees. Place the salt pork and bacon in a large Dutch oven; cook over medium heat, stirring occasionally, until lightly browned and most of the fat is rendered, about 7 minutes. Add the onion and continue to cook, stirring occasionally, until the onion is softened, 5 to 7 minutes. Add the water, beans, ½ cup of the molasses, the mustard, and 1¼ teaspoons salt; increase the heat to medium-high and bring to a boil. Cover the pot and place in the oven.

2. Bake until the beans are tender, about 4 hours, stirring once after 2 hours. Remove the lid and continue to bake until the liquid has thickened to a syrupy consistency, 1 to 1½ hours longer. Remove the beans from the oven; stir in the remaining 1 tablespoon molasses, the vinegar, and salt and pepper to taste. Serve.

DRUNKEN BEANS

WHY THIS RECIPE WORKS: To give our drunken beans a rich, complex flavor without imparting booziness or bitterness, we turned to a mixture of beer and tequila. Canned beans were out of the question because this recipe required a full-flavored bean cooking liquid that only dried beans could impart. To preserve the bacon's flavor, we removed it from the pot after crisping it (to use as a garnish). Sautéing onion, garlic, and poblano chiles in the bacon fat created a flavorful base. Off heat, we poured in the tequila and let it evaporate, cooking off some of the alcohol and leaving behind its smoky sweetness. To ensure that our beans remained intact, we brined them overnight. Cilantro leaves are a classic garnish

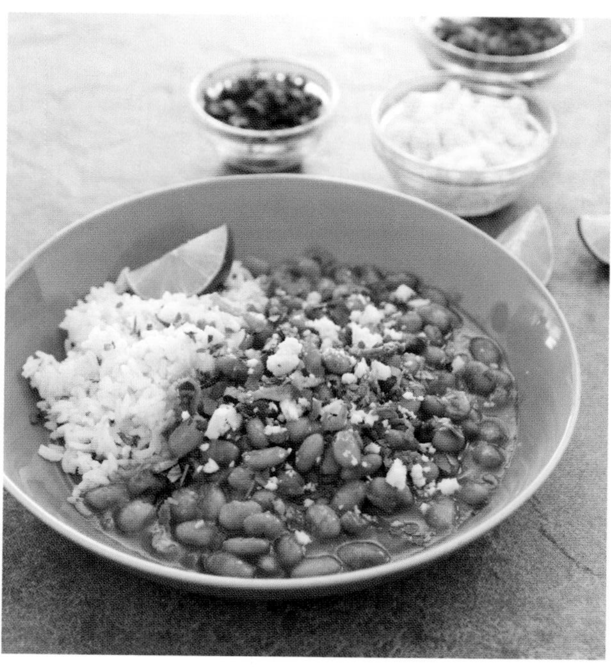

for drunken beans, but the stems also have an aromatic quality to them, so we tied the stems into a bundle and added them to the pot. We cooked the beans gently in the oven, and held back the acidic beer and tomatoes until the beans were tender. A vigorous simmer to finish caused the beans to release starches that gave the cooking liquid pleasant body.

Drunken Beans

SERVES 6 AS A MAIN DISH

You'll get fewer blowouts if you soak the beans overnight, but if you are pressed for time, you can quick-brine your beans: In step 1, combine the salt, water, and beans in a large Dutch oven and bring to a boil over high heat. Remove the pot from the heat, cover, and let stand for 1 hour. Drain and rinse the beans and proceed with the recipe. Serve with rice.

- Salt
- 1 pound (2½ cups) dried pinto beans, picked over and rinsed
- 30 sprigs fresh cilantro (1 bunch)
- 4 slices bacon, cut into ¼-inch pieces
- 1 onion, chopped fine
- 2 poblano chiles, stemmed, seeded, and chopped fine
- 3 garlic cloves, minced
- ½ cup tequila
- 2 bay leaves
- 1 cup Mexican lager
- ¼ cup tomato paste
- 2 limes, quartered
- 2 ounces Cotija cheese, crumbled (½ cup)

1. Dissolve 3 tablespoons salt in 4 quarts cold water in large bowl or container. Add beans and soak at room temperature for at least 8 hours or up to 24 hours. Drain and rinse well.

2. Adjust oven rack to lower-middle position and heat oven to 275 degrees. Pick leaves from 20 cilantro sprigs (reserve stems), mince, and refrigerate until needed. Using kitchen twine, tie remaining 10 cilantro sprigs and reserved stems into bundle.

3. Cook bacon in Dutch oven over medium heat, stirring occasionally, until crisp, 5 to 8 minutes. Using slotted spoon, transfer bacon to paper towel–lined bowl and set aside. Add onion, poblanos, and garlic to fat in pot and cook, stirring frequently, until vegetables are softened, 6 to 7 minutes. Remove from heat. Add tequila and cook until evaporated, 3 to 4 minutes. Return to heat. Increase heat to high; stir in 3½ cups water, bay leaves, 1 teaspoon salt, beans, and cilantro bundle; and bring to boil. Cover, transfer to oven, and cook until beans are just soft, 45 to 60 minutes.

4. Remove pot from oven. Discard bay leaves and cilantro bundle. Stir in beer and tomato paste and bring to simmer over medium-low heat. Simmer vigorously, stirring frequently, until liquid is thick and beans are fully tender, about 30 minutes. Season with salt to taste. Serve, passing minced cilantro, lime wedges, Cotija, and reserved bacon separately.

TO MAKE AHEAD: The finished beans can be refrigerated for up to 2 days. Before reheating, thin beans slightly with water.

BLANCHED GREEN BEANS

WHY THIS RECIPE WORKS: Most vegetable side dishes require last-minute preparation, but green beans are an ideal side dish that can be prepared largely beforehand without sacrificing texture or flavor. We wanted a foolproof way of cooking beans ahead of time and then simply reheating and seasoning them just before serving.

The easiest way to do this was to blanch the beans in salted water, shock them in ice water to stop the cooking process, and then towel-dry and refrigerate them until needed—a process that could be completed up to three days before serving. To serve, we reheated the beans in a skillet with a little water and flavored them with a butter sauce. The small amount of water came to a boil quickly and evaporated almost completely, helping to heat the beans in just a minute or two for a quick and flavorful side dish.

Blanched Green Beans

SERVES 4

Blanched and cooled beans can be refrigerated in a zipper-lock bag for up to 3 days. To blanch, dress, and serve the beans without holding them first, increase the blanching time to 5 to 6 minutes and don't bother shocking them in ice water. Instead, quickly arrange the warm, drained beans on a serving platter and top them with the sauce you've prepared as the beans blanch (recipes follow).

- 1 teaspoon table salt
- 1 pound green beans, trimmed

Bring 2½ quarts water to a boil in a large saucepan over high heat; add the salt and green beans, return to a boil, and cook until the beans are bright green and crisp-tender, 3 to 4 minutes. Drain the beans and transfer them immediately to a large bowl filled with ice water. When the beans have cooled to room temperature, drain again and dry thoroughly with paper towels. Set aside (or refrigerate) until needed.

Green Beans with Sautéed Shallots and Vermouth

- 4 tablespoons (½ stick) unsalted butter
- 4 large shallots, sliced thin (about 1 cup)
- 1 recipe Blanched Green Beans
- Table salt and ground black pepper
- 2 tablespoons dry vermouth

1. Melt 2 tablespoons of the butter in a small skillet over medium heat. Add the shallots and cook, stirring frequently, until golden brown, fragrant, and just crisp around the edges, about 10 minutes. Set the skillet aside, off the heat.

2. Heat ¼ cup water and the beans in a 12-inch skillet over high heat; cook, tossing frequently, until warmed through, 1 to 2 minutes. Season with salt and pepper to taste and arrange on a warm platter.

3. Meanwhile, return the skillet with the shallots to high heat, stir in the vermouth, and bring to a simmer. Whisk in the remaining 2 tablespoons butter, 1 tablespoon at a time, and season with salt and pepper to taste. Top the beans with the shallots and sauce and serve.

Green Beans with Toasted Hazelnuts and Browned Butter

Use a light-colored traditional saucepan instead of a darker nonstick saucepan for this recipe to easily monitor the butter's browning.

- 4 tablespoons (½ stick) unsalted butter
- ½ cup hazelnuts, toasted and chopped fine
- Table salt and ground black pepper
- 1 recipe Blanched Green Beans

1. Melt the butter in a small saucepan over medium heat and cook, swirling frequently, until brown and fragrant, 4 to 5 minutes. Add the hazelnuts and cook, stirring constantly, until fragrant, about 1 minute. Season with salt and pepper to taste.

2. Meanwhile, heat ¼ cup water and the beans in a 12-inch skillet over high heat; cook, tossing frequently, until warmed through, 1 to 2 minutes. Season with salt and pepper to taste and arrange on a warm platter. Top the beans with the hazelnuts and butter and serve.

GREEN BEANS AMANDINE

WHY THIS RECIPE WORKS: A simple dish of green beans tossed with toasted almonds and a light lemon-butter sauce, green beans amandine is refined yet not intimidating. Unfortunately, recipes too often yield limp beans swimming in pools of overly acidic sauce, with soft, pale almonds thrown on as an afterthought. We wanted to revive this side dish with tender green beans, crisp almonds, and a balanced sauce.

For maximum flavor, we toasted the almonds then added some butter to the skillet and allowed it to brown for further nuttiness. Adding some lemon juice off the heat brightened our sauce considerably. After steaming the green beans in a little water in a covered skillet until they were crisp-tender, we tossed them with our sauce for a simple, flavorful take on this classic side.

Green Beans Amandine

SERVES 8

Use a light-colored traditional skillet instead of a darker nonstick skillet for this recipe to easily monitor the butter's browning.

- ⅓ cup sliced almonds
- 3 tablespoons unsalted butter, cut into pieces
- 2 teaspoons juice from 1 lemon
- 2 pounds green beans, trimmed
- Table salt

1. Toast the almonds in a large skillet over medium-low heat, stirring often, until just golden, about 6 minutes. Add the butter and cook, stirring constantly, until the butter is golden brown and has a nutty aroma, about 3 minutes. Transfer the almond mixture to a bowl and stir in the lemon juice.

2. Add the beans, ½ cup water, and ½ teaspoon salt to the now-empty skillet. Cover and cook over medium-low heat, stirring occasionally, until the beans are nearly tender, 8 to 10 minutes. Remove the lid and cook over medium-high heat until the liquid evaporates, 3 to 5 minutes. Off the heat, add the reserved almond mixture to the skillet and toss to combine. Season with salt to taste and serve.

ROASTED GREEN BEANS

WHY THIS RECIPE WORKS: Mature supermarket green beans are often tough and dull, needing special treatment to become tender and flavorful. Braising works, but the stovetop can get awfully crowded as dinnertime approaches. Roasting is a great option for many vegetables, and we wanted to find out if this technique could help transform older green beans, giving them a flavor comparable to sweet, fresh-picked beans.

A remarkably simple test produced outstanding results: Beans roasted in a 450-degree oven with only oil, salt, and pepper transformed aged specimens into deeply caramelized, full-flavored beans. Just 20 minutes of roasting reversed the aging process (converting starch back to sugar) and encouraged flavorful browning. Just 1 tablespoon of oil was enough to lend flavor and moisture without making the beans greasy. Lining the pan with foil prevented scorching and made for easy cleanup.

Roasted Green Beans

SERVES 4

Lining the baking sheet with foil makes for easy cleanup.

- 1 pound green beans, trimmed
- 1 tablespoon olive oil
- Table salt and ground black pepper

1. Adjust an oven rack to the middle position and heat the oven to 450 degrees. Line a large rimmed baking sheet with foil; spread the beans on the baking sheet. Drizzle with the oil; using your hands, toss to coat evenly. Sprinkle with ½ teaspoon salt, toss to coat, and distribute in an even layer. Roast for 10 minutes.

2. Remove the baking sheet from the oven. Using tongs, redistribute the beans. Continue roasting until the beans are dark golden brown in spots and have started to shrivel, 10 to 12 minutes longer. Season with salt and pepper to taste and serve.

SPINACH WITH GARLIC AND LEMON

WHY THIS RECIPE WORKS: Overcooked spinach, bitter burnt garlic, and pallid lemon flavor are all too often the hallmarks of this simple side dish. Instead, we sought tender sautéed spinach, seasoned with a perfect balance of garlic and lemon.

We preferred the hearty flavor and texture of curly-leaf spinach in this classic dish. We cooked the spinach in extra-virgin olive oil with slivered garlic (lightly browned in the pan before the spinach was added), which gave the spinach a sweet nuttiness. Once the spinach was cooked, we used tongs to squeeze the spinach in a colander over the sink to get rid of all the excess moisture. As for seasoning, a squeeze of lemon juice and some grated lemon zest, as well as a pinch of red pepper flakes gave the spinach some gentle heat. And finally, a drizzle of extra-virgin olive oil boosted the fruitiness of the dish.

Sautéed Garlic-Lemon Spinach

SERVES 4

The amount of spinach may seem excessive, but the spinach wilts considerably with cooking. We like to use a salad spinner to wash and dry the spinach.

- 2 tablespoons extra-virgin olive oil, plus 1 teaspoon for drizzling
- 4 medium garlic cloves, sliced thin crosswise (about 4 teaspoons)
- 3 (10-ounce) bags curly-leaf spinach, stems removed, leaves washed and dried (see note)
- Table salt
- Pinch red pepper flakes
- ½ teaspoon grated zest plus 2 teaspoons juice from 1 lemon

1. Heat 2 tablespoons of the oil and the garlic in a large Dutch oven over medium-high heat until shimmering; cook until the garlic is light golden brown, shaking the pan back and forth when the garlic begins to sizzle, about 3 minutes. Add the spinach by the handful, using tongs to stir and coat the spinach with the oil.

2. Once all the spinach is added, sprinkle ¼ teaspoon salt, the red pepper flakes, and lemon zest over the top and continue stirring with the tongs until the spinach is uniformly wilted and glossy, about 2 minutes. Using the tongs, transfer the spinach to a colander set in a sink and gently squeeze the spinach with the tongs to release the excess liquid. Return the spinach to the Dutch oven; sprinkle with the lemon juice and stir to coat. Drizzle with the remaining 1 teaspoon olive oil and season with salt to taste. Serve.

SAUTÉED BABY SPINACH

WHY THIS RECIPE WORKS: Baby spinach is convenient—no stems to remove or grit to rinse out—but cooking often turns this tender green into a watery, mushy mess. We were determined to find a method for cooking baby spinach that would give us a worthwhile side dish. Wilting, blanching, and steaming proved to be unsuccessful in removing excess water from baby spinach, but parcooking the spinach in the microwave with a little water added to the bowl worked great. After three minutes, the spinach had softened and shrunk to half its size, thanks to the release of a great deal of liquid. But there was still more water to remove. We found that pressing the spinach against the colander before roughly chopping it on a cutting board and then pressing it again removed any remaining excess liquid. The spinach was now tender, sweet, and ready to be combined with complementary ingredients. Pairing almonds and raisins introduced bold flavors and textures that enlivened this quick-cooking green.

Sautéed Baby Spinach with Almonds and Golden Raisins

SERVES 4

If you don't have a microwave-safe bowl large enough to accommodate the entire amount of spinach, cook it in a smaller bowl in two batches. Reduce the amount of water to 2 tablespoons per batch and cook each batch for about 1½ minutes.

- 3 (6-ounce) bags baby spinach (about 18 cups)
- ¼ cup water
- 2 tablespoons extra-virgin olive oil, plus 2 teaspoons for drizzling
- ½ cup golden raisins
- 4 medium garlic cloves, sliced thin crosswise (about 4 teaspoons)
- ¼ teaspoon red pepper flakes
- Table salt
- 2 teaspoons sherry vinegar
- ⅓ cup slivered almonds, toasted

1. Place the spinach and water in a large microwave-safe bowl. Cover the bowl with a large microwave-safe dinner plate (the plate should completely cover the bowl and not rest on the spinach). Microwave on high power until the spinach is wilted and decreased in volume by half, 3 to 4 minutes. Using potholders, remove the bowl from the microwave and keep covered for 1 minute. Carefully remove the plate and transfer the spinach to a colander set in the sink. Using the back of a rubber spatula, gently press the spinach against the colander to release excess liquid. Transfer the spinach to a cutting board and roughly chop. Return to the colander and press a second time.

2. Heat 2 tablespoons of the oil, the raisins, garlic, and red pepper flakes in a 10-inch skillet over medium-high heat. Cook, stirring constantly, until the garlic is light golden brown and beginning to sizzle, 3 to 6 minutes. Add the spinach to the skillet, using tongs to stir and coat with the oil. Sprinkle with ¼ teaspoon salt and continue stirring with the tongs until the spinach is uniformly wilted and glossy, about 2 minutes. Sprinkle with the vinegar and almonds; stir to combine. Drizzle with the remaining 2 teaspoons oil and season with salt to taste. Serve.

CREAMY HERBED SPINACH DIP

WHY THIS RECIPE WORKS: Spinach dip made with sour cream and soup mixes are flat, overly salty, and stale tasting. We wanted to ditch the mix and create a rich, thick, and creamy spinach dip brimming with big, bold flavors.

We were surprised to discover that frozen spinach actually made a better-tasting dip with a vibrant, more intense flavor than one made with fresh spinach. We used a food processor to chop the spinach and then enriched it with sour cream, mayonnaise, and a mixture of fresh herbs and seasonings. The only problem was that our dip, which took just about 15 minutes to make, took almost two hours to chill. Fortunately the solution turned out to be a simple one. Instead of thawing the spinach completely, we only partially thawed it, allowing the chunks of icy spinach to thoroughly cool the dip as they broke down in the food processor. This dip is fresh-tasting, quick to make, and ready to serve immediately.

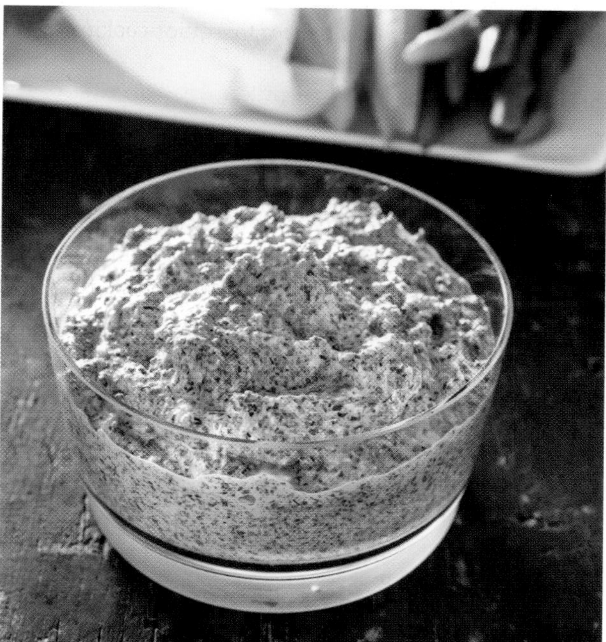

Creamy Herbed Spinach Dip

MAKES ABOUT 1½ CUPS

Partial thawing of the spinach produces a cold dip that can be served without further chilling. Instead of microwaving, the frozen spinach can also be thawed at room temperature for 1½ hours, then squeezed of excess liquid. The garlic must be minced or pressed before going into the food processor; otherwise, the dip will contain large chunks of garlic.

- 1 (10-ounce) box frozen chopped spinach
- ½ cup sour cream
- ½ cup mayonnaise
- 3 scallions, white parts only, sliced thin
- ½ cup packed fresh parsley leaves
- 1 tablespoon minced fresh dill
- 1 small garlic clove, minced or pressed through a garlic press (about ½ teaspoon; see note)
- ½ teaspoon table salt
- ¼ teaspoon ground black pepper
- ¼ teaspoon hot sauce
- ½ red bell pepper, chopped fine

1. Thaw the spinach in a microwave for 3 minutes at 40 percent power. (The edges should be thawed but not warm; the center should be soft enough to be broken into icy chunks.) Squeeze the partially frozen spinach to remove excess water.

2. Process the spinach, sour cream, mayonnaise, scallions, parsley, dill, garlic, salt, pepper, and hot sauce in a food processor until smooth and creamy, about 30 seconds. Transfer the mixture to a bowl and stir in the bell pepper; serve. (The dip can be covered with plastic wrap and refrigerated for up to 2 days.)

QUICK-COOKED TOUGH GREENS

WHY THIS RECIPE WORKS: Unlike tender greens, tougher greens such as kale, mustard, turnip, and collard greens don't have enough moisture to be wilted in a hot pan; they'll simply scorch before they wilt. Their flavor is much more assertive, even peppery in some cases, and can be overwhelming. We wanted a technique for cooking Southern-style greens that would mellow their assertive bite and render them tender—while still retaining just the right amount of chew.

Because they are relatively dry, these greens required the addition of some liquid as they cooked. Steaming the greens produced a texture tasters liked, but it didn't help tame their bitter flavor. Shallow blanching removed enough bitterness to make these assertive greens palatable, but didn't rob them of their character. After blanching the greens, we drained and then briefly cooked them with a little garlic and red pepper flakes for a spicy kick. To prevent them from becoming too dry, we added a little chicken broth to the pan for moistness and extra flavor.

Quick-Cooked Tough Greens

SERVES 4

Shallow-blanched greens should be shocked in cold water to stop the cooking process, drained, and then braised. Shocked and drained greens can be held for up to an hour before being braised.

- Table salt
- 2 pounds assertive greens, such as kale, collards, or mustard, stemmed, washed in several changes of cold water, and chopped coarse
- 3 tablespoons extra-virgin olive oil
- 3 medium garlic cloves, sliced thin crosswise (about 3 teaspoons)
- Red pepper flakes
- ⅓-½ cup low-sodium chicken broth
- Lemon wedges, for serving

1. Bring 2 quarts water to a boil in a large pot. Add 1½ teaspoons salt and the greens and stir until wilted, 1 to 2 minutes. Cover and cook until the greens are just tender, about 7 minutes. Drain the greens and pour them into a large bowl filled with ice water. Working with a handful of greens at a time, thoroughly squeeze them dry.

2. Heat the oil, garlic, and ¼ teaspoon red pepper flakes in a large skillet over medium heat until the garlic starts to sizzle, about 1 minute. Add the greens and toss to coat with the oil. Add ⅓ cup of the broth, cover, and cook over medium-high heat, adding more broth if necessary, until the greens are tender and juicy and most of the broth has been absorbed, about 5 minutes. Season with salt and additional red pepper flakes to taste. Serve with the lemon wedges.

SAUTÉED SWISS CHARD

WHY THIS RECIPE WORKS: Swiss chard, like spinach, is delicate and has an earthy flavor that mellows once cooked. A thick stalk runs through the center of each leaf, however, and can make cooking the greens a challenge. We set out to find a simple method for preparing Swiss chard—one that would yield tender, evenly cooked greens (both stalks and leaves) with deep flavor.

After testing blanching, steaming, microwaving, and wilting, the simplest, most straightforward method of cooking proved to be wilting our greens on the stovetop. First, however, we separated the leaves from the stalks and tossed the stalks, wet from washing, into the pan first. We added garlic for flavor, then added the leaves, covered the pan, and cooked, stirring occasionally, until the greens were wilted by the steam created by their own liquid. We then found that we got even better results when combining this technique with sautéing. To do this, we heated oil in the pan, then proceeded as before, adding the stalks before the leaves. Once the leaves wilted, we removed the lid, seasoned with salt and pepper, and sautéed the greens over high heat until all the liquid evaporated.

Simple Sautéed Swiss Chard

SERVES 4

A thick stalk runs through each Swiss chard leaf, so the leaf must be cut away from it.

- 3 tablespoons extra-virgin olive oil
- 2 pounds Swiss chard, stemmed, washed in several changes of cold water, stalks chopped medium and leaves chopped coarse
- 2 medium garlic cloves, minced or pressed through a garlic press (about 2 teaspoons)
- Table salt and ground black pepper
- Lemon wedges, for serving

1. Heat the oil in a large Dutch oven over medium heat until shimmering. Add the chard stalks and cook, stirring occasionally, until just tender, about 5 minutes. Add the garlic and cook until fragrant, about 30 seconds. Add the chard leaves, cover, increase the heat to medium-high, and cook, stirring occasionally, until the greens completely wilt, 2 to 3 minutes.

2. Uncover and season with salt and pepper to taste. Cook over high heat until the liquid evaporates, about 2 minutes. Serve with the lemon wedges.

ROASTED MUSHROOMS WITH PARMESAN AND PINE NUTS

WHY THIS RECIPE WORKS: Serving up a side of juicy, full-flavored roasted mushrooms started with an unusual step: brining. Soaking earthy cremini and meaty, smoky shiitakes in salty water for 10 minutes allowed the mushrooms' water-resistant proteins to break down, inviting in moisture and perfect seasoning. In order to cook the mushrooms evenly, we bypassed our stovetop in favor of oven-roasting. We spread the mushrooms on a baking sheet, drizzled them with olive oil, and roasted them for 35 minutes. After a quick stir and 10 more minutes in the oven, the mushrooms emerged deeply browned but still supremely juicy. As a final flourish before serving, we glossed them with butter and a touch of lemon juice and added Parmesan, pine nuts, and parsley to round out the side's hearty, herbal notes.

Roasted Mushrooms with Parmesan and Pine Nuts

SERVES 4

Quarter large (more than 2 inches) cremini mushrooms, halve medium (1 to 2 inches) ones, and leave small (under 1 inch) ones whole.

- Salt and pepper
- 1½ pounds cremini mushrooms, trimmed and left whole if small, halved if medium, or quartered if large
- 1 pound shiitake mushrooms, stemmed, caps larger than 3 inches halved
- 2 tablespoons extra-virgin olive oil
- 2 tablespoons unsalted butter, melted
- 1 teaspoon lemon juice
- 1 ounce Parmesan cheese, grated (½ cup)
- 2 tablespoons pine nuts, toasted
- 2 tablespoons chopped fresh parsley

1. Adjust oven rack to lowest position and heat oven to 450 degrees. Dissolve 5 teaspoons salt in 2 quarts room-temperature water in large container. Add cremini mushrooms and shiitake mushrooms to brine, cover with plate or bowl to submerge, and let stand for 10 minutes.

2. Drain mushrooms in colander and pat dry with paper towels. Spread mushrooms evenly on rimmed baking sheet, drizzle with oil, and toss to coat. Roast until liquid from mushrooms has completely evaporated, 35 to 45 minutes.

3. Remove sheet from oven (be careful of escaping steam when opening oven) and, using thin metal spatula, carefully stir mushrooms. Return to oven and continue to roast until mushrooms are deeply browned, 5 to 10 minutes longer.

4. Combine melted butter and lemon juice in large bowl. Add mushrooms and toss to coat. Add Parmesan, pine nuts, and parsley and toss. Season with salt and pepper to taste; serve immediately.

CRISPY POTATO LATKES

WHY THIS RECIPE WORKS: We wanted latkes that were light, not greasy, with buttery soft interiors and crisp outer crusts. We started with high-starch russets, shredded them, mixed them with some grated onion, then wrung the mixture out in a dish towel to rid it of excess moisture, which would prevent the latkes from crisping. To ensure that the latkes' centers were cooked before their crusts were too dark, we parcooked the potato-onion mixture in the microwave. This step also caused the starches in the potatoes to coalesce, further inhibiting the release of the potatoes' moisture when frying. We tossed the mixture with beaten egg to help bind the cakes and pan-fried them in just ¼ inch of oil. With the excess water taken care of, our latkes crisped up beautifully and absorbed minimal oil.

Crispy Potato Latkes

SERVES 4 TO 6

We prefer shredding the potatoes on the large holes of a box grater, but you can also use the large shredding disk of a food processor; cut the potatoes into 2-inch lengths first so you are left with short shreds. Serve with applesauce, sour cream, or gravlax.

- 2 pounds russet potatoes, unpeeled, scrubbed, and shredded
- ½ cup grated onion
- Salt and pepper
- 2 large eggs, lightly beaten
- 2 teaspoons minced fresh parsley
- Vegetable oil

1. Adjust oven rack to middle position, place rimmed baking sheet on rack, and heat oven to 200 degrees. Toss potatoes, onion, and 1 teaspoon salt in bowl. Place half of potato mixture in center of clean dish towel. Gather ends together and twist tightly to drain as much liquid as possible, reserving liquid in liquid measuring cup. Transfer drained potato mixture to second bowl and repeat process with remaining potato mixture. Set potato liquid aside and let stand so starch settles to bottom, at least 5 minutes.

2. Cover potato mixture and microwave until just warmed through but not hot, 1 to 2 minutes, stirring mixture with fork every 30 seconds. Spread potato mixture evenly over second rimmed baking sheet and let cool for 10 minutes. Don't wash out bowl.

3. Pour off water from reserved potato liquid, leaving potato starch in measuring cup. Add eggs and stir until smooth. Return cooled potato mixture to bowl. Add parsley, ¼ teaspoon pepper, and potato starch mixture and toss until evenly combined.

4. Set wire rack in clean rimmed baking sheet and line with triple layer of paper towels. Heat ¼-inch depth of oil in 12-inch skillet over medium-high heat until shimmering but not smoking (350 degrees). Place ¼-cup mound of potato mixture in oil and press with nonstick spatula into ⅓-inch-thick disk. Repeat until 5 latkes are in pan. Cook, adjusting heat so fat bubbles around latke edges, until golden brown on bottom, about 3 minutes. Turn and continue cooking until golden brown on second side, about 3 minutes longer. Drain on paper towels and transfer to baking sheet in oven. Repeat with remaining potato mixture, adding oil to maintain ¼-inch depth and returning oil to 350 degrees between batches. Season with salt and pepper to taste and serve immediately.

TO MAKE AHEAD: Cooled latkes can be covered loosely with plastic wrap and held at room temperature for up to 4 hours. Alternatively, they can be frozen on baking sheet until firm, transferred to zipper-lock bag, and frozen for up to 1 month. Reheat latkes in 375-degree oven until crisp and hot, 3 minutes per side for room-temperature latkes and 6 minutes per side for frozen latkes.

PATATAS BRAVAS

WHY THIS RECIPE WORKS: The best versions of *patatas bravas* showcase crispy, well-browned potatoes served with a smoky, spicy tomato-based sauce. To create an ultra-crispy crust without the need for double frying, we first parboiled russet potatoes with baking soda which helped develop into a thick crust. We also tossed the parcooked potatoes with kosher salt, which roughs up the surfaces of the potatoes, creating nooks and crannies through which steam can escape. As the steam escaped, the nooks and crannies trapped oil, making an even more substantial crust. For our sauce, tomato paste, cayenne, smoked sweet paprika, garlic, and water made a smooth, smoky, and spicy mixture, which we finished with sherry vinegar for tang. Finally, adding mayonnaise allowed us to combine the bravas sauce and another common accompaniment, *aïoli*, into a single sauce.

Patatas Bravas

SERVES 4 TO 6

While this dish is traditionally served as part of a tapas spread, it can also be served as a side dish with grilled or roasted meat. Bittersweet or smoked hot paprika can be used in place of sweet, if desired. If you make this substitution, be sure to taste the sauce before deciding how much cayenne to add, if any. A rasp-style grater makes quick work of turning the garlic into a paste.

SAUCE

- 1 tablespoon vegetable oil
- 2 teaspoons garlic, minced to paste
- 1 teaspoon smoked sweet paprika
- ½ teaspoon kosher salt
- ½–¾ teaspoon cayenne pepper
- ¼ cup tomato paste
- ½ cup water
- 2 teaspoons sherry vinegar
- ¼ cup mayonnaise

POTATOES

- 2¼ pounds russet potatoes, peeled and cut into 1-inch pieces
- ½ teaspoon baking soda
- Kosher salt
- 3 cups vegetable oil

1. FOR THE SAUCE: Heat oil in small saucepan over medium-low heat until shimmering. Add garlic, paprika, salt, and cayenne and cook until fragrant, about 30 seconds. Add tomato paste and cook for 30 seconds. Whisk in water and bring to boil over high heat. Reduce heat to medium-low and simmer until slightly thickened, 4 to 5 minutes. Transfer sauce to bowl, stir in vinegar, and let cool completely. Once cool, whisk in mayonnaise. (Sauce can be refrigerated for up to 24 hours. Bring to room temperature before serving.)

2. FOR THE POTATOES: Bring 8 cups water to boil in large saucepan over high heat. Add potatoes and baking soda. Return to boil and cook for 1 minute. Drain potatoes.

3. Return potatoes to saucepan and place over low heat. Cook, shaking saucepan occasionally, until any surface moisture has evaporated, 30 seconds to 1 minute. Remove from heat. Add 1½ teaspoons salt and stir with rubber spatula until potatoes are coated with thick, starchy paste, about 30 seconds. Transfer potatoes to rimmed baking sheet in single layer to cool. (Potatoes can stand at room temperature for up to 2 hours.)

4. Heat oil in large Dutch oven over high heat to 375 degrees. Add all potatoes (they should just be submerged in oil) and cook, stirring occasionally with wire skimmer or slotted spoon, until deep golden brown and crispy, 20 to 25 minutes.

5. Transfer potatoes to paper towel–lined wire rack set in rimmed baking sheet. Season with salt to taste. Spoon ½ cup sauce onto bottom of large platter or 1½ tablespoons sauce onto individual plates. Arrange potatoes over sauce and serve immediately, passing remaining sauce separately.

BEST BAKED POTATOES

WHY THIS RECIPE WORKS: Baked potatoes are often bland, unevenly cooked, and dependent on toppings for flavor. To produce baked potatoes with an evenly fluffy interior, ideal doneness temperature of their center should reach 205 degrees. Baking them in a hot (450-degree) oven prevented a leathery "pellicle" or film from forming underneath the peel. To season the potato skin, we coated the potatoes in salty water before baking them. We also achieved a crisp skin by painting them with vegetable oil once the potatoes were cooked through and then baking the potatoes for an additional 10 minutes.

Best Baked Potatoes

SERVES 4

Open up the potatoes immediately after removal from the oven in step 3 so steam can escape. Top them as desired, or with one of our toppings.

- Salt and pepper
- 4 (7- to 9-ounce) russet potatoes, unpeeled, each lightly pricked with fork in 6 places
- 1 tablespoon vegetable oil

1. Adjust oven rack to middle position and heat oven to 450 degrees. Dissolve 2 tablespoons salt in ½ cup water in large bowl. Place potatoes in bowl and toss so exteriors of potatoes are evenly moistened. Transfer potatoes to wire rack set in rimmed baking sheet and bake until center of largest potato registers 205 degrees, 45 minutes to 1 hour.

2. Remove potatoes from oven and brush tops and sides with oil. Return potatoes to oven and continue to bake for 10 minutes.

3. Remove potatoes from oven and, using paring knife, make 2 slits, forming X, in each potato. Using clean dish towel, hold ends and squeeze slightly to push flesh up and out. Season with salt and pepper to taste. Serve immediately.

Creamy Egg Topping

MAKES 1 CUP

- 3 hard-cooked large eggs, chopped
- 4 tablespoons sour cream
- 1½ tablespoons minced cornichons
- 1 tablespoon minced fresh parsley

- 1 tablespoon Dijon mustard
- 1 tablespoon capers, rinsed and minced
- 1 tablespoon minced shallot
- Salt and pepper

Stir together eggs, sour cream, cornichons, parsley, mustard, capers, and shallot. Season with salt and pepper to taste.

Herbed Goat Cheese Topping

MAKES ¾ CUP

Our favorite goat cheese is Laura Chenel's Chèvre Fresh Chèvre Log.

- 4 ounces goat cheese, softened
- 2 tablespoons extra-virgin olive oil
- 2 tablespoons minced fresh parsley
- 1 tablespoon minced shallot
- ½ teaspoon grated lemon zest
- Salt and pepper

Mash goat cheese with fork. Stir in oil, parsley, shallot, and lemon zest. Season with salt and pepper to taste.

Smoked Trout Topping

MAKES 1 CUP

We prefer trout for this recipe, but any hot-smoked fish, such as salmon or bluefish, may be substituted.

- 5 ounces smoked trout, chopped
- ⅓ cup crème fraîche
- 2 tablespoons minced fresh chives
- 4 teaspoons minced shallot
- 1¼ teaspoons grated lemon zest plus ¾ teaspoon lemon juice
- Salt and pepper

Stir all ingredients together and season with salt and pepper to taste.

SMASHED POTATOES

WHY THIS RECIPE WORKS: Bold flavors and a rustic, chunky texture make smashed potatoes a satisfying side dish. But good smashed potatoes are hard to find. We were after a good contrast of textures, with the rich, creamy puree of mashed potatoes accented by chunks of potato and skins. Testing revealed that low-starch, high-moisture red potatoes were the best choice for this dish. Their compact structure held up well under pressure, maintaining its integrity. The thin skins were pleasantly tender and paired nicely with the chunky potatoes. Cooked whole in salted water, the potatoes became lightly seasoned while also retaining their naturally creamy texture, as the skins protected the potato flesh from the water. For the best chunky texture, we smashed the potatoes with a rubber spatula or the back of a wooden spoon. Cream cheese and butter lent tang and body to the dish, and stirring in a little of the potato cooking water added moisture to give it a creamy consistency. Seasoned with salt, freshly ground black pepper, and chopped chives, these potatoes are a quick, no-fuss side dish.

Smashed Potatoes

SERVES 4

Try to get potatoes of equal size; if that's not possible, test the larger potatoes for doneness (use a paring knife). If only large potatoes are available, increase the cooking time by about 10 minutes.

- 2 pounds red potatoes (about 12 small), scrubbed
- Table salt
- 1 bay leaf
- 4 tablespoons (½ stick) unsalted butter, melted
- 4 ounces cream cheese, at room temperature
- 3 tablespoons minced fresh chives (optional)
- Ground black pepper

1. Place the potatoes in a large saucepan and add cold water to cover by 1 inch; add 1 teaspoon salt and the bay leaf. Bring to a boil over high heat, then reduce the heat to medium-low and simmer gently until a paring knife can be inserted into the potatoes with no resistance, 35 to 45 minutes. Reserve ½ cup of the cooking water, then drain the potatoes. Return the potatoes to the pot, discard the bay leaf, and allow the potatoes to stand in the pot, uncovered, until the surfaces are dry, about 5 minutes.

2. While the potatoes dry, whisk the melted butter and softened cream cheese in a medium bowl until smooth and fully incorporated. Add ¼ cup of the reserved cooking water, the chives (if using), ½ teaspoon pepper, and ½ teaspoon salt. Using a rubber spatula or the back of a wooden spoon, smash the potatoes just enough to break the skins. Fold in the butter–cream cheese mixture until most of the liquid has been absorbed and chunks of potatoes remain. Add more cooking water as needed, 1 tablespoon at a time, until the potatoes are slightly looser than desired (the potatoes will thicken slightly with standing). Season with salt and pepper to taste and serve.

CLASSIC MASHED POTATOES

WHY THIS RECIPE WORKS: Many people would never consider consulting a recipe when making mashed potatoes, instead adding chunks of butter and spurts of cream until their conscience tells them to stop. Little wonder then that mashed potatoes made this way are consistent only in their mediocrity. We wanted mashed potatoes that were perfectly smooth and creamy, with great potato flavor and plenty of buttery richness every time.

We began by selecting russet potatoes for their high starch content. Through trial and error, we learned to boil them whole and unpeeled—this method yielded mashed potatoes that were rich, earthy, and sweet. We used a food mill or ricer for the smoothest texture imaginable, but a potato masher can be used if you prefer your potatoes a little chunky. For smooth, velvety potatoes, we added melted butter first and then half-and-half. Melting, rather than merely softening, the butter enabled it to coat the starch molecules quickly and easily, so the potatoes turned out creamy and light.

Classic Mashed Potatoes

SERVES 4

Russet potatoes make fluffier mashed potatoes, but Yukon Golds have an appealing buttery flavor and can be used. This recipe yields smooth mashed potatoes. If you don't mind lumps, use a potato masher.

- 2 pounds russet potatoes (about 4 medium), scrubbed (see note)
- 8 tablespoons (1 stick) unsalted butter, melted
- 1 cup half-and-half, warmed
- 1½ teaspoons table salt
- Ground black pepper

1. Place the potatoes in a large saucepan and add cold water to cover by 1 inch. Bring to a boil over high heat, reduce the heat to medium-low, and simmer until the potatoes are just tender when pricked with a fork, 20 to 30 minutes. Drain the potatoes.

2. Set a ricer or food mill over the now-empty saucepan. Using a potholder (to hold the potatoes) and a paring knife, peel the skins from the potatoes. Working in batches, cut the peeled potatoes into large chunks and press or mill into the saucepan.

3. Stir in the butter until incorporated. Gently whisk in the half-and-half, and season with the salt and pepper to taste. Serve.

GARLIC AND OLIVE OIL MASHED POTATOES

WHY THIS RECIPE WORKS: The Mediterranean approach of flavoring mashed potatoes with olive oil and garlic is an appealing one, but it's not as simple as replacing the dairy with oil: olive oil can turn the texture pasty and garlic can be harsh and overpowering. We wanted to translate these bold flavors into a light and creamy mashed potato side dish that would partner well with simple grilled meats or fish.

We chose to use russets in this dish for their light, fluffy texture. We first simmered the potatoes and then put the drained, peeled, still-hot potatoes through a ricer or food mill for a smooth texture. We created a mild flavor base by slowly cooking minced garlic in oil, then heightened the garlic flavor a bit by adding just a little garlic, mashed to a paste. Fruity extra-virgin olive oil and a splash of fresh lemon juice brightened the final dish.

Garlic and Olive Oil Mashed Potatoes

SERVES 6

As this dish is denser and more intensely flavored than traditional mashed potatoes, our suggested serving size is smaller than you might expect.

- 2 pounds russet potatoes (about 4 medium), scrubbed
- 5 medium garlic cloves, minced or pressed through a garlic press (about 5 teaspoons)
- 2⅛ teaspoons table salt
- ½ cup plus 2 tablespoons extra-virgin olive oil
- ½ teaspoon ground black pepper
- 2 teaspoons juice from 1 lemon

1. Place the potatoes in a large saucepan and add cold water to cover by 1 inch. Bring to a boil over high heat; reduce the heat to medium-low and cook at a bare simmer until just tender (the potatoes will offer very little resistance when poked with a paring knife), 40 to 45 minutes.

2. Meanwhile, place 1 teaspoon of the garlic on a cutting board and sprinkle with ⅛ teaspoon of the salt. Using the flat side of a chef's knife, drag the garlic and salt back and forth across the cutting board in small circular motions until the garlic is ground into a smooth paste. Transfer to a medium bowl and set aside.

3. Place the remaining 4 teaspoons garlic in a small saucepan with ¼ cup of the oil and cook over low heat, stirring constantly, until the garlic begins to sizzle and is soft, fragrant, and golden, about 5 minutes. Transfer the oil and garlic to the bowl with the raw garlic paste.

4. Drain the cooked potatoes; set a ricer or food mill over the now-empty saucepan. Using a potholder (to hold the potatoes) and a paring knife, peel the skins from the potatoes. Working in batches, cut the peeled potatoes into large chunks and press or mill into the saucepan.

5. Add the remaining 2 teaspoons salt, the pepper, lemon juice, and remaining 6 tablespoons oil to the bowl with the cooked garlic and oil and whisk to combine. Fold the mixture into the potatoes and serve.

MASHED POTATOES WITH BLUE CHEESE AND PORT-CARAMELIZED ONIONS

WHY THIS RECIPE WORKS: When it comes to mashed potatoes, most cooks worry so much about getting the texture right that they forget about the flavor. Butter and half-and-half make for mashed potatoes that are rich tasting but not terribly exciting. Our goal was to jazz up the flavor of our classic mashed potatoes. Slowly cooking thinly sliced onions brought out their sweetness, which was further complemented by a reduced port glaze. The onions' sweetness paired well with the tanginess of blue cheese, which we stirred in just before serving.

Mashed Potatoes with Blue Cheese and Port-Caramelized Onions

SERVES 4

The port adds a sweet depth to the onions that perfectly complements the blue cheese.

ONIONS

- 1½ teaspoons unsalted butter
- 1½ teaspoons vegetable oil
- ½ teaspoon light brown sugar
- ¼ teaspoon salt
- 1 pound onions, halved and sliced ¼ inch thick
- 1 cup ruby port

POTATOES

- ¾ cup half-and-half
- 1 teaspoon chopped fresh thyme
- 2 pounds russet potatoes
- 6 tablespoons unsalted butter, melted
- 1¼ teaspoons salt
- ½ teaspoon pepper
- 4 ounces blue cheese, crumbled (1 cup)

1. FOR THE ONIONS: Heat butter and oil in 8-inch nonstick skillet over high heat until butter melts, then stir in sugar and salt. Add onions, stir to coat, and cook, stirring occasionally, until onions begin to soften and release some moisture, about 5 minutes. Reduce heat to medium and cook, stirring frequently, until onions are deeply browned and sticky, about 35 minutes longer (if onions are sizzling or scorching, reduce heat; if onions are not browning after 15 minutes, increase heat). Stir in port and continue to cook until port reduces to glaze, 4 to 6 minutes.

2. FOR THE POTATOES: While onions are cooking, bring half-and-half and thyme to boil in small saucepan; cover to keep warm.

3. Place potatoes in large saucepan and cover with 1 inch cold water. Bring to boil over high heat, reduce heat to medium-low, and simmer until potatoes are just tender (paring knife can be slipped in and out of potatoes with very little resistance), 20 to 30 minutes. Drain.

4. Set ricer or food mill over now-empty saucepan. Using potholder (to hold potatoes) and paring knife, peel skins from potatoes. Working in batches, cut peeled potatoes into large chunks and press or mill into saucepan.

5. Stir in butter until just incorporated. Add salt and pepper, then gently stir in half-and-half and blue cheese until just combined. Serve immediately topped with onions.

ULTIMATE CREAMY MASHED POTATOES

WHY THIS RECIPE WORKS: Sometimes we want a luxurious mash, one that is silky smooth and loaded with cream and butter. But there's a fine line between creamy and gluey. We wanted lush, creamy mashed potatoes, with so much richness and flavor they could stand on their own—no gravy necessary.

For a creamier, substantial mash, we found that Yukon Golds were perfect—creamier than russets but not as heavy as red potatoes. Slicing the peeled potatoes into rounds and then rinsing away the surface starch before boiling helped intensify their creamy texture without making them gluey. Setting the boiled and drained potatoes in their pot over a low flame helped further evaporate any excess moisture. Using 1½ sticks of butter and 1½ cups of heavy cream gives these potatoes luxurious flavor and richness without making the mash too thin. We found that melting the butter and warming the cream before adding them to the potatoes ensured that the finished dish arrived at the table piping hot.

Creamy Mashed Potatoes

SERVES 8 TO 10

This recipe can be cut in half, if desired.

- 4 pounds Yukon Gold potatoes (about 8 medium), scrubbed, peeled, and sliced ¾ inch thick
- 1½ cups heavy cream
- 12 tablespoons (1½ sticks) unsalted butter, cut into 6 pieces
- 2 teaspoons table salt

1. Place the potatoes in a colander and rinse under cool running water, tossing with your hands, for 30 seconds. Transfer the potatoes to a large Dutch oven, add cold water to cover by 1 inch, and bring to a boil over high heat. Reduce the heat to medium and boil until the potatoes are tender, 20 to 25 minutes.

2. Meanwhile, heat the heavy cream and butter in a small saucepan over medium heat until the butter is melted, about 5 minutes. Set aside and keep warm.

3. Drain the potatoes and return to the Dutch oven. Stir over low heat until the potatoes are thoroughly dried, 1 to 2 minutes. Set a ricer or food mill over a large bowl and press or mill the potatoes into the bowl. Gently fold in the warm cream mixture and salt with a rubber spatula until the cream is absorbed and the potatoes are thick and creamy. Serve.

FLUFFY MASHED POTATOES

WHY THIS RECIPE WORKS: In Classic Mashed Potatoes (page 600), we boil potatoes in their jackets for earthy potato flavor (and peel them while they're still hot). We don't mind this somewhat inconvenient method when we've got time to spare, but thought an easier alternative was in order.

Cooking potatoes in their skins preserves their earthy flavor and keeps the starch granules from absorbing too much water, thereby preventing gluey mashed potatoes. To give peeled potatoes the same protection, we made two alterations to our usual technique. Steaming rather than boiling the potatoes exposed the potato pieces to less water, reducing the chance of the granules swelling to the point of bursting. When they were cooked partway, we rinsed them under cold water to rid them of free amylose, the substance that results in gluey mashed potatoes, and returned them to the steamer to finish cooking. Because potatoes cooked this way are so full of rich potato flavor, we were able to use less butter and substitute whole milk for cream.

Fluffy Mashed Potatoes

SERVES 4

This recipe works best with either a metal colander that sits easily in a Dutch oven or a large pasta pot with a steamer insert. To prevent excess evaporation, it is important for the lid to fit as snugly as possible over the colander or steamer. For the lightest, fluffiest texture, use a ricer. A food mill is the next best alternative. Russets will also work in this recipe, but avoid red potatoes.

- 2 pounds Yukon Gold potatoes (about 4 medium), peeled, cut into 1-inch chunks, rinsed well, and drained (see note)
- 4 tablespoons (½ stick) unsalted butter, melted
- Table salt
- ⅔ cup whole milk, warmed
- Ground black pepper

1. Place a metal colander or steamer insert in a large pot or Dutch oven. Add enough water to barely reach the bottom of the colander. Bring the water to a boil over high heat. Add the potatoes, cover, and reduce the heat to medium-high. Cook the potatoes for 10 minutes. Transfer the colander to the sink and rinse the potatoes under cold water until no longer hot, 1 to 2 minutes. Return the colander and potatoes to the pot, cover, and continue to cook until the potatoes are soft and the tip of a paring knife inserted into the potatoes meets no resistance, 10 to 15 minutes longer. Drain the potatoes.

2. Set a ricer or food mill over the now-empty pot. Working in batches, transfer the potatoes to the hopper and process or mill, removing any potatoes stuck to the bottom. Using a rubber spatula, stir in the butter and ½ teaspoon salt until incorporated. Stir in the milk until incorporated. Season with salt and pepper to taste and serve.

BUTTERMILK MASHED POTATOES

WHY THIS RECIPE WORKS: Merely replacing butter and cream with buttermilk to create tangy, creamy buttermilk mashed potatoes doesn't work—the finished potatoes are curdled, crumbly, chalky, and dry. We wanted easy mashed potatoes with buttermilk's trademark distinctive tang, but we didn't want to sacrifice texture to get them.

Many recipes for buttermilk mashed potatoes remove so much butter that the potatoes taste lean and lack creaminess. We started by restoring just enough butter to save our mashed potatoes from this fate. We then tackled the curdling problem. Buttermilk curdles at 160 degrees, a temperature reached almost instantly when the cold liquid hits steaming-hot potatoes. By adding the butter, melted, to room-temperature buttermilk, we coated the proteins in the buttermilk and protected them from the heat shock that causes curdling. We also simplified the recipe by choosing peeled and cut Yukon Gold potatoes rather than using unpeeled russets (which we have used in other mashed potato recipes). Because Yukon Golds have less starch and are less absorbent than russets, they didn't become soggy and thinned out when simmered without their jackets.

Buttermilk Mashed Potatoes

SERVES 4

To achieve the proper texture, it is important to cook the potatoes thoroughly; they are done if they break apart when a knife is inserted and gently wiggled. Buttermilk substitutes like clabbered milk do not produce sufficiently tangy potatoes. To reduce the likelihood of curdling, the buttermilk must be brought to room temperature and mixed with cooled melted butter.

- 2 pounds Yukon Gold potatoes (about 4 medium), peeled and cut into 1-inch chunks
- Table salt
- 6 tablespoons (¾ stick) unsalted butter, melted and cooled (see note)
- ⅔ cup buttermilk, room temperature (see note)
- Ground black pepper

1. Place the potatoes in a large saucepan and add cold water to cover by 1 inch; add 1 tablespoon salt. Bring to a boil over high heat, then reduce the heat to medium and simmer until the potatoes break apart very easily when a paring knife is inserted, about 18 minutes. Drain the potatoes briefly, then immediately return them to the saucepan set on the still-hot (but off) burner.

2. Using a potato masher, mash the potatoes until a few small lumps remain. Gently mix the melted butter and buttermilk in a small bowl until combined. Add the buttermilk mixture to the potatoes; using a rubber spatula, fold gently until just incorporated. Season with salt and pepper to taste and serve.

MASHED POTATOES AND ROOT VEGETABLES

WHY THIS RECIPE WORKS: Root vegetables like carrots, parsnips, turnips, and celery root can add an earthy, intriguing flavor to mashed potatoes, but because root vegetables and potatoes have different starch levels and water content, treating them the same way creates a bad mash. We wanted a potato and root vegetable mash with a creamy consistency and a balanced flavor that highlights the natural earthiness of these humble root cellar favorites.

1. Melt the butter in a large saucepan over medium heat. Add the root vegetables and cook, stirring occasionally, until the butter is browned and the vegetables are dark brown and caramelized, 10 to 12 minutes. (If after 4 minutes the vegetables have not started to brown, increase the heat to medium-high.)

2. Add the potatoes, broth, and ¾ teaspoon salt and stir to combine. Cook, covered, over low heat (the broth should simmer gently; do not boil), stirring occasionally, until the potatoes fall apart easily when poked with a fork and all the liquid has been absorbed, 25 to 30 minutes. (If the liquid does not gently simmer after a few minutes, increase the heat to medium-low.) Remove the pan from the heat; remove the lid and allow the steam to escape for 2 minutes.

3. Gently mash the potatoes and root vegetables in the saucepan with a potato masher (do not mash vigorously). Gently fold in the half-and-half and chives. Season with salt and pepper to taste and serve.

We found that a 1:3 ratio of root vegetables to potatoes provided an optimal consistency, although the root vegetable flavor was barely recognizable. Caramelizing the root vegetables first in a little butter helped bring out their natural earthy sweetness; this step also boosted the flavor of the overall dish. To use just one pot, we first sautéed the root vegetables in butter until caramelized and then added the potatoes with a little chicken broth. This gave us great flavor, but the mash had a gluey texture. The answer was to remove the starch from the potatoes by rinsing the peeled, sliced potatoes in several changes of water ahead of time.

Mashed Potatoes and Root Vegetables

SERVES 4

Russet potatoes will yield a slightly fluffier, less creamy mash, but they can be used in place of the Yukon Gold potatoes if desired. Rinsing the potatoes in several changes of water reduces the amount of starch and prevents the mashed potatoes from becoming gluey. It is important to cut the potatoes and root vegetables into even-sized pieces so they cook at the same rate. This recipe can be doubled and cooked in a large Dutch oven. If doubling, increase the cooking time in step 2 to 40 minutes.

- 4 tablespoons (½ stick) unsalted butter
- 8 ounces carrots, parsnips, turnips, or celery root, peeled; carrots or parsnips cut into ¼-inch-thick half-moons; turnips or celery root cut into ½-inch dice (about 1½ cups)
- 1½ pounds Yukon Gold potatoes (about 3 medium), peeled, quartered lengthwise, and cut crosswise into ¼-inch-thick slices; rinsed well in 3 to 4 changes of cold water and drained well (see note)
- ⅓ cup low-sodium chicken broth
- Table salt
- ¾ cup half-and-half, warmed
- 3 tablespoons minced fresh chives
- Ground black pepper

ROASTED ROOT VEGETABLES

WHY THIS RECIPE WORKS: Roasted root vegetables develop complex flavors with just a quick toss in oil, salt, and pepper and a stint in a hot oven—until you try to roast different vegetables at the same time. We wanted a medley of vegetables that would cook through evenly. The trick was to carefully prep each vegetable according to how long it took to cook through. With each vegetable cut into the right size and shape, we could roast them together in one batch for uniformly tender results. To speed up the roasting, we briefly microwaved the vegetables, then placed them on a preheated baking sheet to jump-start the browning. A fruity salsa garnish and a rich bacon topping gave us some flavorful seasoning options.

Roasted Root Vegetables

SERVES 6

Use turnips that are roughly 2 to 3 inches in diameter. Instead of sprinkling the roasted vegetables with chopped herbs, try garnishing them with one of the toppings that follow.

- 1 celery root (14 ounces), peeled
- 4 carrots, peeled and cut into 2½-inch lengths, halved or quartered lengthwise if necessary to create pieces ½ to 1 inch in diameter
- 12 ounces parsnips, peeled and sliced 1 inch thick on bias
- 5 ounces small shallots, peeled
- Kosher salt and pepper
- 12 ounces turnips, peeled, halved horizontally, and each half quartered
- 3 tablespoons vegetable oil
- 2 tablespoons chopped fresh parsley, tarragon, or chives

1. Adjust oven rack to middle position, place rimmed baking sheet on rack, and heat oven to 425 degrees. Cut celery root into ¾-inch-thick rounds. Cut each round into ¾-inch-thick planks about 2½ inches in length.

2. Toss celery root, carrots, parsnips, and shallots with 1 teaspoon salt and pepper to taste in large microwave-safe bowl. Cover bowl and microwave until small pieces of carrot are just pliable enough to bend, 8 to 10 minutes, stirring once halfway through microwaving. Drain vegetables well. Return vegetables to bowl, add turnips and oil, and toss to coat.

3. Working quickly, remove baking sheet from oven and carefully transfer vegetables to baking sheet; spread into even layer. Roast for 25 minutes.

4. Using thin metal spatula, stir vegetables and spread into even layer. Rotate pan and continue to roast until vegetables are golden brown and celery root is tender when pierced with tip of paring knife, 15 to 25 minutes longer. Transfer to platter, sprinkle with parsley, and serve.

Bacon-Shallot Topping

MAKES ABOUT ⅓ CUP

- 4 slices bacon, cut into ¼-inch pieces
- ¼ cup water
- 2 tablespoons minced shallot
- 1 tablespoon sherry vinegar
- 2 tablespoons minced fresh chives

Bring bacon and water to boil in 8-inch skillet over high heat. Reduce heat to medium and cook until water has evaporated and bacon is crisp, about 10 minutes. Transfer bacon to paper towel–lined plate and pour off all but ½ teaspoon fat from skillet. Add shallot and cook, stirring frequently, until softened, 2 to 4 minutes. Remove pan from heat and add vinegar. Transfer shallot mixture to bowl and stir in bacon and chives. Sprinkle over vegetables before serving.

Orange-Parsley Salsa

MAKES ABOUT ½ CUP

- ¼ cup slivered almonds
- ¼ teaspoon ground cumin
- ¼ teaspoon ground coriander
- 1 orange
- ½ cup fresh parsley leaves, minced
- 2 garlic cloves, minced
- 2 teaspoons extra-virgin olive oil
- 1 teaspoon cider vinegar
- ¼ teaspoon kosher salt

1. Toast almonds in 10-inch skillet over medium-high heat until fragrant and golden brown, 5 to 6 minutes. Add cumin and coriander; continue to toast, stirring constantly, until fragrant, about 45 seconds. Immediately transfer to bowl.

2. Cut away peel and pith from orange. Use paring knife to slice between membranes to release segments. Cut segments into ¼-inch pieces. Stir orange pieces, parsley, garlic, oil, vinegar, and salt into almond mixture. Let stand for 30 minutes. Spoon over vegetables before serving.

BEHIND THE SCENES

ADAM'S EQUIPMENT HALL OF SHAME

Adam and the equipment testing team have spent thousands of hours over the past decade separating the good from the bad—and once in a while they come across gadgets and equipment that perform so poorly, they deserve special mention.

QUESADILLA MAKER: If we're going to shell out money for a gadget devoted to just one dish, it better be awfully good. This quesadilla maker, however, severely limits the amount of cheese that can be sandwiched between the tortillas. So, uh, what's the point? Unless you're on a diet, use a skillet instead.

SHRIMP BUTLER: Although this gadget is supposed to peel and devein shrimp, it only accomplishes the task partway by slitting the shell to reveal the vein. Even worse, we found that the shrimp sometimes became mangled in the machine. And since our testing, shrimp is now often sold deveined and slit for easy peeling, so a "butler" for shrimp is no longer necessary.

THERMOMETER FORK: Ouch! Put away your thermo fork and grab a pair of tongs and an instant-read thermometer instead (see our recommended brands on pages 877 and 884). Thermometer forks are designed to enable the user to move the food being cooked on the grill and take its temperature at the same time. We found this gadget awkward to use, especially when trying to flip or turn meat for even browning.

ALLIGATOR CHOPPER: This gadget claims to deliver perfectly cubed onions and elegant batons of carrots, bell peppers, or apples with one punch of the handheld chopper blades against its platform base. But too often, we found ourselves cautiously extracting suspended vegetables from the blade. We'll stick to chopping veggies the old-fashioned way—with a sharp knife and cutting board.

BANANA HANGER: Supermarkets often suspend unripe bananas from tall poles covered with small hooks. Banana hangers miniaturize this idea for the home kitchen. Sounds good, but we found no difference in the ripening time between hanging bananas . . . and simply setting them on the counter.

ROOT VEGETABLE GRATIN

WHY THIS RECIPE WORKS: For a lighter alternative to classic potato gratin, we wanted to supplement the starchy potatoes with more flavorful root vegetables—but first we needed to figure out how to cook them all evenly. To keep the potatoes from breaking down before the celery root and rutabaga slices were finished, we added dry white wine to the creamy cooking liquid. Incorporating flour into the liquid bound the layers of sliced vegetables. Dijon mustard offered a spicy, savory boost. A sprinkling of bold aromatics—chopped onion, fresh thyme, minced garlic, and black pepper—between the alternating layers infused the gratin with hearty flavors. Pressing the layers down after adding the liquid compacted the gratin, ensuring that the slices clung together nicely. A sprinkling of panko bread crumbs, Parmesan, and melted butter added with 15 minutes left in the oven created a golden crust.

Root Vegetable Gratin

SERVES 6 TO 8

Uniformly thin slices are necessary for a cohesive gratin. We recommend a mandoline for quick and even slicing, but a sharp chef's knife will also work. Because the vegetables in the gratin are tightly packed into the casserole dish, it will still be plenty hot after a 25-minute rest.

- 1 tablespoon plus 1½ cups water
- 1½ teaspoons Dijon mustard
- 2 teaspoons all-purpose flour
- Salt and pepper
- ⅔ cup dry white wine
- ½ cup heavy cream
- ½ onion, chopped fine
- 1¼ teaspoons minced fresh thyme
- 1 garlic clove, minced
- 2 pounds large Yukon Gold potatoes, peeled and sliced lengthwise ⅛ inch thick
- 1 large celery root (1 pound), peeled, quartered, and sliced ⅛ inch thick
- 1 pound rutabaga, peeled, quartered, and sliced ⅛ inch thick
- ¾ cup panko bread crumbs
- 1½ ounces Parmesan cheese, grated (¾ cup)
- 4 tablespoons unsalted butter, melted and cooled

1. Adjust oven rack to middle position and heat oven to 375 degrees. Grease 13 by 9-inch baking dish. Whisk 1 tablespoon water, mustard, flour, and 1½ teaspoons salt in medium bowl until smooth. Add wine, cream, and remaining 1½ cups water; whisk to combine. Combine onion, thyme, garlic, and ¼ teaspoon pepper in second bowl.

2. Layer half of potatoes in prepared dish, arranging so they form even thickness. Sprinkle half of onion mixture evenly over potatoes. Arrange celery root and rutabaga slices in even layer over onions. Sprinkle remaining onion mixture over celery root and rutabaga. Layer remaining potatoes over onions. Slowly pour water mixture over vegetables. Using rubber spatula, gently press down on vegetables to create even, compact layer. Cover tightly with aluminum foil and bake for 50 minutes. Remove foil and continue to bake until knife inserted into center of gratin meets no resistance, 20 to 25 minutes longer.

3. While gratin bakes, combine panko, Parmesan, and butter in bowl and season with salt and pepper to taste. Remove gratin from oven and sprinkle evenly with panko mixture. Continue to bake until panko is golden brown, 15 to 20 minutes longer. Remove gratin from oven and let stand for 25 minutes. Serve.

CAULIFLOWER GRATIN

WHY THIS RECIPE WORKS: We set out to create a cauliflower gratin that was flavorful and fresh, not rich and stodgy. We relied on cauliflower's ability to become an ultracreamy puree and used that as a sauce to bind florets together. To ensure that we had enough cauliflower to use in two ways, we used two heads. We removed the cores and stems and steamed them until soft; then blended them to make the sauce. We cut each cored head into slabs, which made for a more compact casserole and helped the florets cook more evenly. For an efficient cooking setup, we placed the cauliflower cores and stems in water in the bottom of a Dutch oven and set a steamer basket filled with the florets on top. Butter and Parmesan, plus a little cornstarch, gave the sauce a richer flavor and texture without making it too heavy, and a few pantry spices lent complexity. Tossing the florets in the sauce before placing them in the dish ensured that they were completely coated. A crisp topping of Parmesan and panko gave the gratin savory crunch, while a final garnish of minced chives added color.

Modern Cauliflower Gratin

SERVES 8 TO 10

When buying cauliflower, look for heads without many leaves. Alternatively, if your cauliflower does have a lot of leaves, buy slightly larger heads—about 2¼ pounds each. This recipe can be halved to serve 4 to 6; cook the cauliflower in a large saucepan and bake the gratin in an 8-inch square baking dish.

- 2 heads cauliflower (2 pounds each)
- 8 tablespoons unsalted butter
- ½ cup panko bread crumbs
- 2 ounces Parmesan cheese, grated (1 cup)
- Salt and pepper
- ½ teaspoon dry mustard
- ⅛ teaspoon ground nutmeg
- Pinch cayenne pepper
- 1 teaspoon cornstarch dissolved in 1 teaspoon water
- 1 tablespoon minced fresh chives

1. Adjust oven rack to middle position and heat oven to 400 degrees.

2. Pull off outer leaves of 1 head of cauliflower and trim stem. Using paring knife, cut around core to remove; halve core lengthwise and slice thin crosswise. Slice head into ½-inch-thick slabs. Cut stems from slabs to create florets that are about 1½ inches tall; slice stems thin and reserve along with sliced core. Transfer florets to bowl, including any small pieces that may have been created during trimming, and set aside. Repeat with remaining head of cauliflower. (After trimming you should have about 3 cups of sliced stems and cores and 12 cups of florets.)

3. Combine sliced stems and cores, 2 cups florets, 3 cups water, and 6 tablespoons butter in Dutch oven and bring to boil over high heat. Place remaining florets in steamer basket (do not rinse bowl). Once mixture is boiling, place steamer basket in pot, cover, and reduce heat to medium. Steam florets in basket until translucent and stem ends can be easily pierced with paring knife, 10 to 12 minutes. Remove steamer basket and drain florets. Re-cover pot, reduce heat to low, and continue to cook stem mixture until very soft, about 10 minutes longer. Transfer drained florets to now-empty bowl.

4. While cauliflower is cooking, melt remaining 2 tablespoons butter in 10-inch skillet over medium heat. Add panko and cook, stirring frequently, until golden brown, 3 to 5 minutes. Transfer to bowl and let cool. Once cool, add ½ cup Parmesan and toss to combine.

5. Transfer stem mixture and cooking liquid to blender and add 2 teaspoons salt, ½ teaspoon pepper, mustard, nutmeg, cayenne, and remaining ½ cup Parmesan. Process until smooth and velvety, about 1 minute (puree should be pourable; adjust consistency with additional water as needed). With blender running, add cornstarch slurry. Season with salt and pepper to taste. Pour puree over cauliflower florets and toss gently to evenly coat. Transfer mixture to 13 by 9-inch baking dish (it will be quite loose) and smooth top with spatula.

6. Scatter bread-crumb mixture evenly over top. Transfer dish to oven and bake until sauce bubbles around edges, 13 to 15 minutes. Let stand for 20 to 25 minutes. Sprinkle with chives and serve.

DUCK FAT–ROASTED POTATOES

WHY THIS RECIPE WORKS: For the ultimate side of roasted potatoes, we needed spuds that could take on meaty duck fat flavor and a crisp crust before drying out. Briefly boiling peeled, cut Yukon Golds in a solution of water, salt, and baking soda broke down the potatoes' pectin, causing them to release a wet starch that rapidly browns. After draining, we returned the pot to the stove to evaporate any moisture and then, off heat, stirred in enough duck fat to give the potatoes some distinct flavor. Stirring the potatoes released a thick paste that ensured a crunchy shell and roasting the pieces on a preheated baking sheet kick-started the crisping. To infuse the potatoes with richness and herbal flavors, we stirred in a mixture of rosemary and more duck fat toward the end of cooking.

Duck Fat–Roasted Potatoes

SERVES 6

Duck fat is available in the meat department in many supermarkets. Alternatively, substitute chicken fat, lard, or a mixture of 3 tablespoons of bacon fat and 3 tablespoons of extra-virgin olive oil.

3½ pounds Yukon Gold potatoes, peeled and cut into 1½-inch pieces
Kosher salt and pepper
½ teaspoon baking soda
6 tablespoons duck fat
1 tablespoon chopped fresh rosemary

1. Adjust oven rack to top position, place rimmed baking sheet on rack, and heat oven to 475 degrees.

2. Bring 10 cups water to boil in Dutch oven over high heat. Add potatoes, ⅓ cup salt, and baking soda. Return to boil and cook for 1 minute. Drain potatoes. Return potatoes to pot and place over low heat. Cook, shaking pot occasionally, until surface moisture has evaporated, about 2 minutes. Remove from heat. Add 5 tablespoons fat and 1 teaspoon salt; mix with rubber spatula until potatoes are coated with thick paste, about 30 seconds.

3. Remove sheet from oven, transfer potatoes to sheet, and spread into even layer. Roast for 15 minutes.

4. Remove sheet from oven. Using thin, sharp, metal spatula, turn potatoes. Roast until golden brown, 12 to 15 minutes. While potatoes roast, combine rosemary and remaining 1 tablespoon fat in bowl.

5. Remove sheet from oven. Spoon rosemary-fat mixture over potatoes and turn again. Continue to roast until potatoes are well browned and rosemary is fragrant, 3 to 5 minutes. Season with salt and pepper to taste. Serve immediately.

ULTIMATE ROASTED POTATOES

WHY THIS RECIPE WORKS: The aroma of roasting potatoes draws everyone into the kitchen come meal time. Too often, though, the potatoes turn out brown and leathery with a mealy interior, or worse, soft with no crisp crust at all. We wanted oven-roasted potatoes that had a crisp crust with a silky interior.

We tested using different potatoes and found that we liked Yukon Golds best. Parcooking the potatoes before subjecting them to high oven temperatures helped them develop a somewhat crisper exterior, but the browning was uneven and they still weren't crispy enough. When we switched from cubing the potatoes to slicing them thick, we created more surface area for crisping but enough heft for a creamy interior. As an added bonus, with only two surfaces to cook, we now only had to flip the potatoes once halfway through roasting. We boiled the potatoes very briefly before roasting to prevent them from breaking up on the baking sheet, and we tossed the precooked potatoes with some olive oil to rough up the exteriors and increase crispiness.

Crispy Roasted Potatoes

SERVES 4 TO 6

Note that the potatoes should be just undercooked when removed from the boiling water—this helps ensure that they will roast up crispy.

2½ pounds Yukon Gold potatoes (about 5 medium), rinsed and cut into ½-inch-thick slices
Table salt
5 tablespoons olive oil
Ground black pepper

1. Adjust an oven rack to the lowest position, place a rimmed baking sheet on the rack, and heat the oven to 450 degrees. Place the potatoes and 1 tablespoon salt in a Dutch oven; add cold water to cover by 1 inch. Bring to a boil over high heat; reduce the heat and gently simmer until the exterior of a potato has softened, but the center offers resistance when pierced with a paring knife, about 5 minutes. Drain the potatoes well, and transfer to a large bowl. Drizzle with 2 tablespoons of the oil and sprinkle with ½ teaspoon salt; using a rubber spatula, toss to combine. Drizzle with 2 tablespoons more oil and ½ teaspoon more salt; continue to toss until the exteriors of the potato slices are coated with a starchy paste.

2. Working quickly, remove the baking sheet from the oven and drizzle the remaining 1 tablespoon oil over the surface. Carefully transfer the potatoes to the baking sheet and spread them into an even layer (skin side up for the end pieces). Bake until the bottoms of the potatoes are golden brown and crisp, 15 to 25 minutes, rotating the baking sheet after 10 minutes.

3. Remove the baking sheet from the oven and, using a metal spatula and tongs, loosen the potatoes from the pan and carefully flip each slice. Continue to roast until the second side is golden and crisp, 10 to 20 minutes longer, rotating the pan as needed to ensure the potatoes brown evenly. Season with salt and pepper to taste and serve.

SKILLET-ROASTED POTATOES

WHY THIS RECIPE WORKS: Skillet-roasted potatoes often cook up unevenly, with a mixture of scorched and pallid potatoes. We wanted to be able to make truly outstanding skillet-roasted potatoes, as good as oven-roasted—extra-crisp on the outside and moist and creamy on the inside, evenly browned, and never greasy. This would be the recipe we'd turn to when we craved roasted potatoes but there was no room in the oven for the conventional kind.

The solution turned out to be choosing the right potato and cutting it uniformly. Red Bliss potatoes, cut in half if small or quartered if medium, offered a great crust and a moist interior, thanks to their high moisture content. We rinsed the cut potatoes to remove surface starch, which otherwise caused the potatoes to stick to the pan and inhibited browning. Olive oil added flavor and richness to the dish. The winning cooking technique was to first brown the potatoes over high heat, then cover and finish cooking over low heat. This allowed the insides to cook through while the outsides stayed crisp.

Skillet-Roasted Potatoes

SERVES 3 TO 4

Small and medium potatoes can be used in this recipe, but they must be cut differently. Small potatoes (1½ to 2 inches in diameter) should be cut in half and medium potatoes (2 to 3 inches in diameter) should be cut into quarters to create ¾- to 1-inch chunks. Large potatoes should not be used because the cut pieces will be uneven and won't cook at the same rate. For even cooking and proper browning, the potatoes must be cooked in a single layer and should not be crowded in the pan.

- 1½ pounds small or medium red potatoes (about 9 small or 4 to 5 medium), scrubbed, halved if small, quartered if medium (see note)
- 2 tablespoons olive oil
- ¾ teaspoon table salt
- ¾ teaspoon ground black pepper

1. Rinse the potatoes in cold water and drain well; spread on a clean kitchen towel and thoroughly pat dry.

2. Heat the oil in a 12-inch skillet over medium-high heat until shimmering. Add the potatoes, cut side down, in a single layer. Cook, without stirring, until the potatoes are golden brown (the oil should sizzle but not smoke), 5 to 7 minutes. Using tongs, turn the potatoes skin side down if halved or second cut side down if quartered. Cook, without stirring, until the potatoes are deep golden brown, 5 to 6 minutes longer. Stir the potatoes, then redistribute in a single layer. Reduce the heat to medium-low, cover, and cook until the potatoes are tender (a paring knife can be inserted into the potatoes with no resistance), 6 to 9 minutes.

3. When the potatoes are tender, sprinkle with the salt and pepper and toss gently to combine; serve.

SALT-BAKED POTATOES

WHY THIS RECIPE WORKS: Let's be honest: Sometimes baked potatoes could use a flavor boost. And instead of light and fluffy, they are often dense and crumbly. Salt-baking potatoes promises to remedy these problems. We tried burying potatoes under a mound of salt, cooking them on a bed of salt, covering them with foil, and making a salt crust on the potatoes with an egg wash. All were good, but the bed of salt was best. Moisture that escaped during baking was trapped in the pan, then absorbed by the salt, and reabsorbed by the potatoes, making their skins tender and their flesh light. Uncovering the potatoes toward the end of cooking ensured dry, crisp skin. A 13 by 9-inch baking dish provided plenty of space so we didn't crowd the potatoes, and 2½ cups of salt allowed us to thoroughly cover the bottom of the pan. A little rosemary and garlic added helped flavor the spuds.

Salt-Baked Potatoes with Roasted Garlic and Rosemary Butter

SERVES 4

Kosher salt or table salt can be used in this recipe. The salt may be sifted through a strainer to remove any solid bits and reused for this recipe. These potatoes can be prepared without the roast garlic butter and topped with your favorite potato toppings such as sour cream, chives, crumbled bacon, or shredded cheese.

- 2½ cups plus ⅛ teaspoon salt
- 4 medium russet potatoes (about 8 ounces each), well scrubbed and dried
- 2 sprigs fresh rosemary plus ¼ teaspoon minced leaves
- 1 whole garlic head, outer papery skin removed and top quarter of head cut off and discarded
- 4 teaspoons olive oil
- 4 tablespoons (½ stick) unsalted butter, softened

1. Adjust an oven rack to the middle position and heat the oven to 450 degrees. Spread the salt into an even layer in a 13 by 9-inch baking dish. Gently nestle the potatoes in the salt, broad side down, leaving space between each potato. Add the rosemary sprigs and the garlic, cut side up, to the baking dish. Cover the baking dish with aluminum foil and crimp the edges to tightly seal. Bake for 1 hour and 15 minutes; remove the pan from the oven. Increase the oven temperature to 500 degrees.

2. Carefully remove the foil. Remove the garlic head from the baking dish and set aside to cool. Brush the exposed portion of each potato with 1 teaspoon oil. Return the uncovered baking dish to the oven and continue to bake until the potatoes are tender and the skins are glossy, 15 to 20 minutes.

3. Meanwhile, once the garlic is cool enough to handle, squeeze the root end until the cloves slip out of their skins.

Using a fork, mash the garlic, butter, minced rosemary, and remaining 1⁄8 teaspoon salt to a smooth paste. Remove any clumped salt from the potatoes (holding the potatoes with a kitchen mitt if necessary), split lengthwise, top with a portion of the butter and serve immediately.

Salt-Baked Potatoes with Roasted Shallot and Thyme Butter

Follow the recipe for Salt-Baked Potatoes with Roasted Garlic and Rosemary Butter, substituting 5 crumbled bay leaves for the rosemary sprigs and 1 teaspoon chopped fresh thyme leaves for the chopped rosemary. Substitute 2 medium shallots for the garlic head.

BRAISED RED POTATOES

WHY THIS RECIPE WORKS: What if you could get red potatoes with the creamy interiors created by steaming and the crispy browned exteriors produced by roasting—without doing either? That's the result promised by recipes for braised red potatoes, but they rarely deliver. To make good on the promise, we combined halved small red potatoes, butter, and salted water (plus thyme for flavoring) in a 12-inch skillet and simmered the spuds until their interiors were perfectly creamy and the water was fully evaporated. Then we let the potatoes continue to cook in the now-dry skillet until their cut sides browned in the butter, developing the rich flavor and crisp edges of roasted potatoes. These crispy, creamy potatoes were so good they needed only a minimum of seasoning: We simply tossed them with some minced garlic (softened in the simmering water along with the potatoes), lemon juice, chives, and pepper.

Braised Red Potatoes with Lemon and Chives

SERVES 4 TO 6

Use small red potatoes measuring about 1½ inches in diameter.

- 1½ pounds small red potatoes, unpeeled, halved
- 2 cups water
- 3 tablespoons unsalted butter
- 3 garlic cloves, peeled
- 3 sprigs fresh thyme
- ¾ teaspoon salt
- 1 teaspoon lemon juice
- ¼ teaspoon pepper
- 2 tablespoons minced fresh chives

1. Arrange potatoes in single layer, cut side down, in 12-inch nonstick skillet. Add water, butter, garlic, thyme, and salt and bring to simmer over medium-high heat. Reduce heat to medium, cover, and simmer until potatoes are just tender, about 15 minutes.

2. Remove lid and use slotted spoon to transfer garlic to cutting board; discard thyme. Increase heat to medium-high and vigorously simmer, swirling pan occasionally, until water evaporates and butter starts to sizzle, 15 to 20 minutes. When cool enough to handle, mince garlic to paste. Transfer paste to bowl and stir in lemon juice and pepper.

3. Continue to cook potatoes, swirling pan frequently, until butter browns and cut sides of potatoes turn spotty brown, 4 to 6 minutes longer. Off heat, add garlic mixture and chives and toss to thoroughly coat. Serve immediately.

Braised Red Potatoes with Dijon and Tarragon

Substitute 2 teaspoons Dijon mustard for lemon juice and 1 tablespoon minced fresh tarragon for chives.

Braised Red Potatoes with Miso and Scallions

Reduce salt to ½ teaspoon. Substitute 1 tablespoon red miso paste for lemon juice and 3 thinly sliced scallions for chives.

BOILED POTATOES WITH BLACK OLIVE TAPENADE

WHY THIS RECIPE WORKS: Tapenade is an easy spread that shines as a quick go-to topping for bruschetta, pasta, or potatoes. A paste of processed pine nuts created a buttery base to keep the tapenade spreadable. Using brine-cured kalamata olives and salt-cured black olives created a perfect balance of tang. Rinsing the capers kept the salt under control. Anchovies bumped up the spread's subtle meatiness and some Dijon mustard and garlic contributed a sharp kick. We pulsed the ingredients into a finely chopped spread, stirring in olive oil by hand. Refrigerating the finished tapenade for at least 18 hours allowed the flavors to meld and develop. With our tapenade at the ready, we boiled halved red potatoes until just tender. Once drained, we folded in some of the spread. Chopped parsley and lemon juice livened the side.

Boiled Potatoes with Black Olive Tapenade

SERVES 4 TO 6

Use small red potatoes measuring about 1½ inches in diameter.

- 2 pounds small red potatoes, unpeeled, halved
- 1 tablespoon salt
- ⅓ cup Black Olive Tapenade
- 1 tablespoon lemon juice
- 1 tablespoon chopped fresh parsley
- Extra-virgin olive oil

1. Bring 6 cups water, potatoes, and salt to boil in large saucepan over medium-high heat. Reduce heat to medium-low and simmer until potatoes are just tender when pierced with knife, 10 to 15 minutes.

2. Reserve ¼ cup cooking water. Drain potatoes and return them to pan. Combine tapenade, lemon juice, and 2 tablespoons cooking water in bowl. Add tapenade mixture to potatoes and fold gently to incorporate. Add remaining 2 tablespoons cooking water as needed to adjust consistency. Transfer potatoes to serving bowl, sprinkle with parsley, drizzle with oil, and serve.

Black Olive Tapenade

MAKES ABOUT 1½ CUPS

The tapenade must be refrigerated for at least 18 hours before serving. It's important to use untoasted pine nuts in this recipe so that they provide creaminess but little flavor of their own. We prefer the rich flavor of kalamata olives, but any high-quality brine-cured black olive, such as niçoise, Sicilian, or Greek, can be substituted. Do not substitute brine-cured olives for the salt-cured olives. Serve extra tapenade as a spread with sliced crusty bread or as a dip with raw vegetables.

- ⅓ cup pine nuts
- 1½ cups pitted kalamata olives
- ½ cup pitted salt-cured black olives
- 3 tablespoons capers, rinsed
- 2 anchovy fillets, rinsed and patted dry
- 2 teaspoons Dijon mustard
- ½ garlic clove, minced
- ¼ cup extra-virgin olive oil

1. In food processor fitted with metal blade, process pine nuts until reduced to paste that clings to walls and avoids blade, about 20 seconds. Scrape down bowl to redistribute paste and process until paste again clings to walls and avoids blade, about 5 seconds. Repeat scraping and processing once more (pine nuts should form mostly smooth, tahini-like paste).

2. Scrape down bowl to redistribute paste and add olives capers, anchovies, mustard, and garlic. Pulse until finely chopped, about 15 pulses, scraping down bowl halfway through pulsing. Transfer mixture to medium bowl and stir in oil until well combined.

3. Transfer to container, cover, and refrigerate for at least 18 hours or up to 2 weeks. Bring to room temperature and stir thoroughly before serving.

SCALLOPED POTATOES

WHY THIS RECIPE WORKS: Thinly sliced potatoes layered with cream and baked until they are bubbling and browned are a classic accompaniment to baked ham or roast beef. But scalloped potatoes can occupy the oven for over two hours and still produce unevenly cooked potatoes in a heavy, curdled sauce. We wanted to minimize the cooking time while turning out layers of thinly sliced, tender potatoes, a creamy sauce, and a nicely browned, cheesy crust.

We tried using flour to thicken the sauce, but this produced a thick, pasty sauce. Instead we relied on heavy cream lightened with whole milk. To cut the cooking time, we simmered the potatoes briefly in the cream in a covered pot, before transferring the mixture to a baking dish and finishing the potatoes in the oven. We found russet potatoes had the best texture and flavor, and we sliced them thin so they formed neat layers.

Scalloped Potatoes

SERVES 8 TO 10

For the fastest and most consistent results, slice the potatoes in a food processor or on a mandoline or V-slicer.

- 2 tablespoons unsalted butter
- 1 small onion, minced
- 2 medium garlic cloves, minced or pressed through a garlic press (about 2 teaspoons)
- 4 pounds russet potatoes (about 8 medium), peeled and cut into ⅛-inch-thick slices (see note)
- 3 cups heavy cream
- 1 cup whole milk
- 4 sprigs fresh thyme
- 2 bay leaves
- 2 teaspoons table salt
- ½ teaspoon ground black pepper
- 4 ounces cheddar cheese, shredded (about 1 cup)

1. Adjust an oven rack to the middle position and heat the oven to 350 degrees. Melt the butter in a large Dutch oven over medium-high heat. Add the onion and cook until softened and lightly browned, 5 to 7 minutes. Add the garlic and cook until fragrant, about 30 seconds. Add the potatoes, cream, milk, thyme, bay leaves, salt, and pepper, and bring to a simmer. Cover, adjusting the heat as necessary to maintain a light simmer, and cook until the potatoes are almost tender (a paring knife can be slipped into and out of the center of a potato slice with some resistance), about 15 minutes.

2. Remove and discard the thyme sprigs and bay leaves. Transfer the potato mixture to a 3-quart gratin dish and sprinkle with the cheese. Bake until the cream has thickened and is bubbling around the sides, and the top is golden brown, about 20 minutes. Cool for 5 minutes before serving.

TWICE-BAKED POTATOES

WHY THIS RECIPE WORKS: Twice-baked potatoes are not difficult to make, but the process can be time-consuming, and they're plagued by chewy skins and pasty, bland fillings. We wanted to perfect the process and have twice-baked potatoes with slightly crisp, chewy skins and a rich, creamy filling.

We had a head start, having already perfected a recipe for baked potatoes. Starting there, we oiled the potatoes before baking for a crisp skin, and we let the baked potatoes cool slightly before slicing them open and removing the flesh. We found that we could prevent the hollowed-out shells from turning soggy by keeping them in the oven while making the filling. And for the filling we found it best to combine the potato with tangy dairy ingredients—sour cream and buttermilk were ideal—a small amount of butter, and sharp cheddar cheese for its bold flavor. For a perfect finish, we placed the filled potatoes under the broiler, where they turned brown and crisp.

Twice-Baked Potatoes

SERVES 6 TO 8

Most potatoes have two relatively flat, blunt sides and two curved sides. Halve the baked potatoes lengthwise so the blunt sides are down once the shells are stuffed, making the potatoes much more stable in the pan during final baking. To vary the flavor a bit, try substituting other types of cheese, such as Gruyère, fontina, or feta, for the cheddar. Yukon Gold potatoes can be substituted for the russets.

- 4 medium russet potatoes (about 8 ounces each), scrubbed, dried, and rubbed lightly with vegetable oil (see note)
- 4 ounces sharp cheddar cheese, shredded (about 1 cup; see note)
- ½ cup sour cream
- ½ cup buttermilk
- 2 tablespoons unsalted butter, softened
- 3 scallions, sliced thin
- ½ teaspoon table salt
- Ground black pepper

1. Adjust an oven rack to the upper-middle position and heat the oven to 400 degrees. Bake the potatoes on a foil-lined baking sheet until the skin is crisp and deep brown and a skewer easily pierces the flesh, about 1 hour. Transfer the potatoes to a wire rack and cool slightly, about 10 minutes. (Leave the oven on.)

2. Using an oven mitt or folded kitchen towel to handle the hot potatoes, cut each potato in half so that the long, blunt sides rest on the work surface. Using a small spoon, scoop the flesh from each half into a medium bowl, leaving a ⅛ to ¼-inch thickness of the flesh in each shell. Arrange the shells on the foil-lined baking sheet and return to the oven until dry and slightly crisp, about 10 minutes. Meanwhile, mash the potato flesh with a fork until smooth. Stir in the remaining ingredients, including pepper to taste, until well combined.

3. Remove the shells from the oven and increase the oven setting to broil. Holding the shells steady on the pan with an oven mitt or towel-protected hand, spoon the mixture into the crisped shells, mounding it slightly at the center, and return the potatoes to the oven. Broil until spotty brown and crisp on top, 10 to 15 minutes. Cool for 10 minutes and serve warm.

CRISPY SMASHED POTATOES

WHY THIS RECIPE WORKS: Crispy smashed potatoes are the best of both worlds, delivering mashed potato creaminess with the crackling crisp crust of roasted potatoes. The technique looks straightforward: Skin-on spuds are parcooked in seasoned water, drained, and squashed just shy of an inch thick. Then the potatoes are oiled, and either pan-fried on the stovetop or spread out on a baking sheet in the oven to render the roughened edges browned and crispy and the interior flesh creamy and sweet. But parcooking the potatoes (waxy, thin-skinned Red Bliss) in water diluted their flavor, so they tasted flat, rather than rich and earthy.

To fix the flavor problem and streamline the cooking method, we turned to one pan to get the job done—a baking sheet. A baking sheet's roomy cooking surface allowed us to easily prepare potatoes for four at once rather than pan-frying them in fussy batches. To soften the potatoes, we spread them out on the baking sheet, added a little water, covered the pan with foil, and baked them until tender. To smash all the potatoes at once, we used a second baking sheet, which we simply pressed evenly and firmly on top of the pan of parcooked potatoes. To crisp the potatoes we opted for olive oil to coat the baking sheet and to drizzle over the broken spuds. The result? A welcome addition to the potato rotation: browned and crunchy potato patties, full of deep, earthy flavor.

Crispy Smashed Potatoes

SERVES 4 TO 6

This recipe is designed to work with potatoes that are 1½ to 2 inches in diameter. Do not attempt it with potatoes that are over 2 inches. Remove the potatoes from the baking sheet as soon as they are done browning—they will toughen if left on the baking sheet for too long. A potato masher can also be used to "smash" the potatoes.

- 2 pounds small Red Bliss potatoes (about 18), scrubbed (see note)
- 6 tablespoons extra-virgin olive oil
- 1 teaspoon chopped fresh thyme leaves
- Kosher salt and ground black pepper

1. Adjust the oven racks to the top and bottom positions and heat the oven to 500 degrees. Spread the potatoes on a rimmed baking sheet, pour ¾ cup water into the baking sheet, and wrap tightly with aluminum foil. Cook on the bottom rack until a skewer or paring knife slips in and out of the potatoes easily, 25 to 30 minutes (poke the skewer through the foil to test). Remove the foil and cool for 10 minutes. If any water remains on the pan, blot dry with a paper towel.

2. Drizzle 3 tablespoons of the oil over the potatoes and roll to coat. Space the potatoes evenly on the baking sheet. Following the photos, place a second baking sheet on top; press down uniformly on the baking sheet until the potatoes are roughly ⅓ to ½ inch thick. Sprinkle with the thyme leaves and season generously with salt and pepper; drizzle evenly with the remaining 3 tablespoons oil. Roast the potatoes on the top rack for 15 minutes. Transfer the potatoes to the bottom rack and continue to roast until well browned, 20 to 30 minutes longer. Serve immediately.

NOTES FROM THE TEST KITCHEN

MAKING CRISPY SMASHED POTATOES

You can smash each potato by hand with a potato masher, but we found that a baking sheet smashes the potatoes all at once.

1. After rolling the cooled, oven-steamed potatoes in olive oil, space the potatoes evenly on the baking sheet and place a second baking sheet on top; press down uniformly on the baking sheet until the potatoes are roughly ⅓ to ½ inch thick.

2. Sprinkle the smashed potatoes with the thyme leaves and season generously with salt and pepper; drizzle evenly with the remaining 3 tablespoons oil. Roast as directed.

MASHED SWEET POTATOES

WHY THIS RECIPE WORKS: Mashed sweet potatoes often turn out overly thick and gluey or, at the other extreme, sloppy and loose. We wanted a recipe that would push sweet potatoes' deep, earthy sweetness to the fore and that would produce a silky puree with enough body to hold its shape on a fork.

We braised the sweet potatoes in a mixture of butter and heavy cream to impart a smooth richness. Adding a little salt brought out the sweet potatoes' delicate flavor, and just a teaspoon of sugar bolstered their sweetness. Once the potatoes were tender, we mashed them in the saucepan with a potato masher. We skipped the typical pumpkin pie seasoning and instead let the simple sweet potato flavor shine through.

Mashed Sweet Potatoes

SERVES 4

Cutting the sweet potatoes into slices of even thickness is important so that they cook at the same rate. The potatoes are best served immediately, but they can be covered tightly with plastic wrap and kept warm for 30 minutes. This recipe can be doubled and prepared in a Dutch oven; the cooking time will need to be doubled as well.

- 4 tablespoons (½ stick) unsalted butter, cut into 4 pieces
- 2 tablespoons heavy cream
- 1 teaspoon sugar
- ½ teaspoon table salt
- 2 pounds sweet potatoes (2 to 3 medium), peeled, quartered lengthwise, and cut crosswise into ¼-inch-thick slices (see note)
- Ground black pepper

1. Melt the butter in a large saucepan over low heat. Stir in the cream, sugar, and salt; add the sweet potatoes and cook, covered, stirring occasionally, until the potatoes fall apart when poked with a fork, 35 to 45 minutes.

2. Off the heat, mash the sweet potatoes in the saucepan with a potato masher or transfer the mixture to a food mill and process into a warmed serving bowl. Season with pepper to taste and serve.

SWEET POTATO FRIES

WHY THIS RECIPE WORKS: Too often, sweet potato fries simply don't do justice to their namesake. We wanted thick-cut fries with crispy exteriors and creamy interiors. Taking a cue from commercial frozen fries, we dunked the potato wedges in a slurry of water and cornstarch. Blanching the potatoes with salt and baking soda before dipping them in the slurry helped the coating stick to the potatoes, giving the fries a super-crunchy crust that stayed crispy. To keep the fries from sticking to the pan, we used a nonstick skillet, which had the added benefit of allowing us to use less oil. For a finishing touch to complement the natural sweetness of the fries, we made a spicy Belgian-style dipping sauce.

Thick-Cut Sweet Potato Fries

SERVES 4 TO 6

If your sweet potatoes are shorter than 4 inches in length, do not cut the wedges crosswise. We prefer peanut oil for frying, but vegetable oil may be used instead. Leftover frying oil may be saved for further use; strain the cooled oil into an airtight container and store it in a cool, dark place for up to one month or in the freezer for up to two months. We like these fries with our Spicy Fry Sauce (recipe follows), but they are also good served plain.

- ½ cup cornstarch
- Kosher salt
- 1 teaspoon baking soda
- 3 pounds sweet potatoes, peeled and cut into ¾-inch-thick wedges, wedges cut in half crosswise
- 3 cups peanut oil

1. Adjust oven rack to middle position and heat oven to 200 degrees. Set wire rack in rimmed baking sheet. Whisk cornstarch and ½ cup cold water together in large bowl.

2. Bring 2 quarts water, ¼ cup salt, and baking soda to boil in Dutch oven. Add potatoes and return to boil. Reduce heat to simmer and cook until exteriors turn slightly mushy (centers will remain firm), 3 to 5 minutes. Whisk cornstarch slurry to recombine. Using wire skimmer or slotted spoon, transfer potatoes to bowl with slurry.

3. Using rubber spatula, fold potatoes with slurry until slurry turns light orange, thickens to paste, and clings to potatoes.

4. Heat oil in 12-inch nonstick skillet over high heat to 325 degrees. Using tongs, carefully add one third of potatoes to oil, making sure that potatoes aren't touching one another. Fry until crispy and lightly browned, 7 to 10 minutes, using tongs to flip potatoes halfway through frying (adjust heat as necessary to maintain oil temperature between 280 and 300 degrees). Using wire skimmer or slotted spoon, transfer fries to prepared wire rack (fries that stick together can be separated with tongs or forks). Season with salt to taste and transfer to oven to keep warm. Return oil to 325 degrees and repeat in 2 more batches with remaining potatoes. Serve immediately.

Spicy Fry Sauce

MAKES ABOUT ½ CUP

For a less spicy version, use only 2 teaspoons of Asian chili-garlic sauce. The sauce can be made up to four days in advance and stored, covered, in the refrigerator.

- 6 tablespoons mayonnaise
- 1 tablespoon Asian chili-garlic sauce
- 2 teaspoons white vinegar

Whisk all ingredients together in small bowl.

FRIED SWEET PLANTAINS

WHY THIS RECIPE WORKS: In Cuban restaurants, rich, meaty dishes are often accompanied by *plátanos maduros,* or fried sweet plantains. This savory-sweet side features thick, soft slices of very ripe plantains that are fried in oil to create a caramel-like browned crust encasing a soft, sweet interior; a sprinkling of salt balances the sweetness. We deep-fry our plantains and stir the slices occasionally so that they brown evenly.

Fried Sweet Plantains (Plátanos Maduros)

SERVES 6 TO 8

Make sure to use plantains that are very ripe and black.

- 3 cups vegetable oil
- 5 very ripe black plantains (8½ ounces each), peeled and sliced on bias into ½-inch pieces
- Kosher salt

Heat oil in medium saucepan over medium-high heat until it registers 350 degrees. Carefully add one-third of plantains and cook until dark brown on both sides, 3 to 5 minutes, stirring occasionally. Using wire skimmer or slotted spoon, transfer plantains to wire rack set in rimmed baking sheet. (Do not place plantains on paper towel or they will stick.) Season liberally with salt. Repeat with remaining plantains in two more batches. Serve immediately.

ROASTED BUTTERNUT SQUASH

WHY THIS RECIPE WORKS: Taking a cue from famed chef Yotam Ottolenghi, we sought to create a savory recipe for roasted butternut squash that was simple and presentation-worthy. We chose to peel the squash thoroughly to remove not only the tough outer skin but also the rugged fibrous layer of white flesh just beneath, ensuring supremely tender squash. To encourage the squash slices to caramelize, we used a hot 425-degree oven, placed the squash on the lowest oven rack, and increased the baking time to evaporate the water. We also swapped in melted butter for olive oil to promote the flavorful Maillard reaction. Finally, we selected a mix of toppings that added crunch, creaminess, brightness, and visual appeal.

Roasted Butternut Squash with Browned Butter and Hazelnuts

SERVES 4 TO 6

For plain roasted squash omit the topping. This dish can be served warm or at room temperature. For the best texture it's important to remove the fibrous flesh just below the squash's skin.

SQUASH

- 1 large (2½- to 3-pound) butternut squash
- 3 tablespoons unsalted butter, melted
- ½ teaspoon salt
- ½ teaspoon pepper

TOPPING

- 3 tablespoons unsalted butter, cut into 3 pieces
- ⅓ cup hazelnuts, toasted, skinned, and chopped coarse
- 1 tablespoon water
- 1 tablespoon lemon juice
- Pinch salt
- 1 tablespoon minced fresh chives

1. FOR THE SQUASH: Adjust oven rack to lowest position and heat oven to 425 degrees. Using sharp vegetable peeler or chef's knife, remove skin and fibrous threads from squash just below skin (peel until squash is completely orange with no white flesh remaining, roughly ⅛ inch deep). Halve squash lengthwise and scrape out seeds. Place squash, cut side down, on cutting board and slice crosswise ½ inch thick.

2. Toss squash with melted butter, salt, and pepper until evenly coated. Arrange squash on rimmed baking sheet in single layer. Roast squash until side touching sheet toward back of oven is well browned, 25 to 30 minutes. Rotate sheet and continue to bake until side touching sheet toward back of oven is well browned, 6 to 10 minutes. Remove squash from oven and use metal spatula to flip each piece. Continue to roast until squash is very tender and side touching sheet is browned, 10 to 15 minutes longer.

3. FOR THE TOPPING: While squash roasts, melt butter with hazelnuts in 8-inch skillet over medium-low heat. Cook, stirring frequently, until butter and hazelnuts are brown and fragrant, about 2 minutes. Immediately remove skillet from heat and stir in water (butter will foam and sizzle). Let cool for 1 minute; stir in lemon juice and salt.

4. Transfer squash to large serving platter. Drizzle butter mixture evenly over squash. Sprinkle with chives and serve.

Roasted Butternut Squash with Radicchio and Parmesan

Omit topping. Whisk 1 tablespoon sherry vinegar, ½ teaspoon mayonnaise, and pinch salt together in small bowl; gradually whisk in 2 tablespoons extra-virgin olive oil until smooth. Before serving, drizzle vinaigrette over squash and sprinkle with ½ cup coarsely shredded radicchio; ½ ounce Parmesan cheese, shaved into thin strips; and 3 tablespoons toasted pine nuts.

Roasted Butternut Squash with Goat Cheese, Pecans, and Maple

Omit topping. Stir 2 tablespoons maple syrup and pinch cayenne pepper together in small bowl. Before serving, drizzle maple mixture over squash and sprinkle with ⅓ cup crumbled goat cheese; ⅓ cup pecans, toasted and chopped coarse; and 2 teaspoons fresh thyme leaves.

Roasted Butternut Squash with Tahini and Feta

Omit topping. Whisk 1 tablespoon tahini, 1 tablespoon extra-virgin olive oil, 1½ teaspoons lemon juice, 1 teaspoon honey, and pinch salt together in small bowl. Before serving, drizzle tahini mixture over squash and sprinkle with ¼ cup finely crumbled feta cheese; ¼ cup shelled pistachios, toasted and chopped fine; and 2 tablespoons chopped fresh mint.

ACORN SQUASH

WHY THIS RECIPE WORKS: Cooked properly, acorn squash develops a sweet, almost nutty flavor and moist, smooth flesh—a result that should not take hours. But after what seems like eons in the oven, acorn squash often lands on the table with little flavor and a stringy texture. We wanted better, slow-roasted acorn squash in a fraction of the time. To our astonishment, microwaving was the ideal cooking method, presenting a squash that was tender and silky smooth, with nary a trace of dryness or stringiness. Microwaved on high power for 20 minutes, the squash was perfectly cooked. It was best to halve and seed the squash before cooking. Last, we learned that when added before cooking, salt seemed to better permeate the squash. Filling in the only remaining gap, equal portions of butter and dark brown sugar gave the squash ample, but not excessive, sweetness. And for a smooth, cohesive filling mixture, combining the butter and sugar with a pinch of salt and briefly broiling the final product eliminated the nagging sticky glaze problem. Finishing the squash under the broiler also gave it a welcome roasted texture and great caramelized flavor.

Quick Roasted Acorn Squash with Brown Sugar

SERVES 4

Squash smaller than 1½ pounds will likely cook a little faster than the recipe indicates, so begin checking for doneness a few minutes early. Likewise, larger squash will take slightly longer to cook. However, keep in mind that the cooking time is largely dependent on the microwave. If microwaving the squash in Pyrex, the manufacturer recommends adding water to the dish (or bowl) prior to cooking. To avoid a steam burn when uncovering the cooked squash, peel back the plastic wrap very carefully, starting from the side that is farthest away from you.

- 2 acorn squash (about 1½ pounds each), halved pole to pole and seeded (see note)
- Table salt
- 3 tablespoons unsalted butter
- 3 tablespoons dark brown sugar

1. Sprinkle the squash halves with salt and place the halves, cut side down, in a 13 by 9-inch microwave-safe baking dish or arrange the halves in a large (4-quart) microwave-safe bowl so that the cut sides face out. (If using Pyrex, add ¼ cup water to the dish or bowl.) Cover tightly with plastic wrap, using multiple sheets, if necessary; with a paring knife, poke four steam vents in the wrap. Microwave on high power until the squash is very tender and offers no resistance when pierced with a paring knife, 15 to 25 minutes. Using potholders, remove the baking dish or bowl from the microwave and set on a clean, dry surface (avoid damp or cold surfaces).

2. While the squash is cooking, adjust an oven rack to the highest position (about 6 inches from the broiler element) and heat the broiler. Melt the butter, brown sugar, and ⅛ teaspoon salt in a small saucepan over low heat, whisking occasionally, until combined.

3. When the squash is cooked, carefully pull back the plastic wrap from the side farthest from you. Using tongs, transfer the cooked squash halves, cut side up, to a rimmed baking sheet. Spoon a portion of the butter-sugar mixture onto each squash half. Broil until brown and caramelized, 5 to 8 minutes, rotating the baking sheet halfway through the cooking time and removing the squash halves as they are done. Set the squash halves on individual plates and serve immediately.

RICE PILAF

WHY THIS RECIPE WORKS: To make rice pilaf, rice is toasted or browned in fat to build flavor before being cooked through in liquid. The result should be rice that is fragrant, fluffy, and tender. Traditional recipes insist that for a truly great pilaf you must soak or at least repeatedly rinse the rice before cooking. We wondered if there was more to making perfect rice pilaf than this.

The variables included the kind of rice to use, the ratio of rice to cooking water, and whether or not to soak the rice before cooking. Testing revealed that using basmati rice was preferable, as was using a lower amount of water than is traditional for cooking rice. The step of rinsing the rice was also important for grains that were more tender, with a slightly shinier, smoother appearance. We also sautéed the rice in plenty of butter before adding the water. After the rice was cooked, we covered it with a kitchen towel and a lid and let it steam off the heat.

Rice Pilaf

SERVES 4

If you like, olive oil can be substituted for the butter depending on what you are serving with the pilaf. For the most evenly cooked rice, use a wide-bottomed saucepan with a tight-fitting lid.

- 1½ cups basmati or long-grain rice
- 2½ cups water
- 1½ teaspoons table salt
- Pinch ground black pepper
- 3 tablespoons unsalted butter (see note)
- 1 small onion, minced (about ½ cup)

1. Place the rice in a medium bowl and add enough water to cover by 2 inches; using your hands, gently swish the grains to release the excess starch. Carefully pour off the water, leaving the rice in the bowl. Repeat four to five times, until the water runs almost clear. Using a colander or fine-mesh strainer, drain the rice; place the colander over a bowl and set aside.

2. Bring the water to a boil, covered, in a small saucepan over medium-high heat. Add the salt and pepper; cover to keep hot. Meanwhile, melt the butter in a large saucepan over medium heat; add the onion and cook until softened but not browned, about 4 minutes. Stir in the rice until coated with the butter; cook until the edges of the rice grains begin to turn translucent, about 3 minutes. Stir the hot seasoned water into the rice; return to a boil, then reduce the heat to low, cover, and simmer until all the liquid is absorbed, 16 to 18 minutes. Off the heat, remove the lid and place a clean kitchen towel folded in half over the saucepan; replace the lid. Let stand for 10 minutes; fluff the rice with a fork and serve.

WILD RICE PILAF

WHY THIS RECIPE WORKS: Sometimes wild rice turns out undercooked and difficult to chew, other times the rice is overcooked and gluey. We wanted to figure out how to turn out properly cooked wild rice every time.

Through trial and error, we learned to simmer the rice slowly in plenty of liquid, making sure to stop the cooking process at just the right moment by checking it for doneness every couple of minutes past the 35-minute mark. For a simmering liquid, we used chicken broth—its mild yet rich profile

tempered the rice's muddy flavor to a pleasant earthiness and affirmed its subdued nuttiness. To further tame the strong flavor of the wild rice, we added some white rice to the mixture, then added onions, carrots, dried cranberries, and toasted pecans for a winning pilaf.

Wild Rice Pilaf with Pecans and Dried Cranberries

SERVES 6 TO 8

Wild rice quickly goes from tough to pasty, so begin testing the rice at the 35-minute mark and drain the rice as soon as it is tender.

- 1¾ cups low-sodium chicken broth
- 2½ cups water
- 2 bay leaves
- 8 sprigs fresh thyme, divided into 2 bundles, each tied together with kitchen twine
- 1 cup wild rice, rinsed well in a strainer
- 1½ cups long-grain white rice
- 3 tablespoons unsalted butter
- 1 medium onion, minced
- 2 carrots, peeled and chopped fine
- Table salt
- ¾ cup sweetened or unsweetened dried cranberries
- ¾ cup pecans, toasted and chopped coarse
- 1½ tablespoons minced fresh parsley leaves
- Ground black pepper

1. Bring the chicken broth, ¼ cup of the water, the bay leaves, and 1 bundle of the thyme to a boil in a medium saucepan over medium-high heat. Add the wild rice, cover, and reduce the heat to low; simmer until the rice is plump and tender and has absorbed most of the liquid, 35 to 45 minutes. Drain the rice in a fine-mesh strainer. Return the rice to the saucepan; cover to keep warm and set aside.

2. While the wild rice is cooking, place the white rice in a medium bowl and add water to cover by 2 inches; gently swish the grains to release excess starch. Carefully pour off the water, leaving the rice in the bowl. Repeat four to five times, until the water runs almost clear. Drain the rice in a fine-mesh strainer.

3. Melt the butter in a medium saucepan over medium-high heat. Add the onion, carrots, and 1 teaspoon salt; cook, stirring frequently, until softened but not browned, about 4 minutes. Stir in the rinsed white rice until coated with the butter; cook, stirring frequently, until the grains begin to turn translucent, about 3 minutes. Meanwhile, bring the remaining 2¼ cups water to a boil in a small saucepan or a microwave. Add the boiling water and the second thyme bundle to the white rice; return to a boil, then reduce the heat to low, sprinkle the cranberries evenly over the rice, and cover. Simmer until all of the liquid is absorbed, 16 to 18 minutes. Off the heat, fluff the rice with a fork and discard the bay leaves and thyme bundles.

4. Combine the wild rice, white rice mixture, pecans, and parsley in a large bowl; toss with a rubber spatula until the ingredients are evenly mixed. Season with salt and pepper to taste and serve.

RICE AND PASTA PILAF

WHY THIS RECIPE WORKS: Typically, rice pilaf combines rice with pieces of vermicelli that have been toasted in butter to add richness and a nutty flavor. To produce rice that was as tender and fluffy as the pasta, we needed both elements to cook at the same rate. Jump-starting the rice by soaking it in hot water for a mere 10 minutes softened its outer coating and let it absorb water quickly. Once the pasta and rice were cooked perfectly, we let the pilaf stand for 10 minutes with a towel under the lid to absorb steam. A handful of fresh parsley lent brightness to the finished pilaf.

Rice and Pasta Pilaf

SERVES 4 TO 6

Use long, straight vermicelli or vermicelli nests.

- 1½ cups basmati or other long-grain white rice
- 3 tablespoons unsalted butter
- 2 ounces vermicelli, broken into 1-inch pieces
- 1 onion, grated
- 1 garlic clove, minced
- 2½ cups chicken broth
- 1¼ teaspoons salt
- 3 tablespoons minced fresh parsley

1. Place rice in medium bowl and cover with hot tap water by 2 inches; let stand for 15 minutes.

2. Using your hands, gently swish grains to release excess starch. Carefully pour off water, leaving rice in bowl. Add cold tap water to rice and pour off water. Repeat adding and pouring off cold water 4 to 5 times, until water runs almost clear. Drain rice in fine-mesh strainer.

3. Melt butter in saucepan over medium heat. Add pasta and cook, stirring occasionally, until browned, about 3 minutes. Add onion and garlic and cook, stirring occasionally, until onion is softened but not browned, about 4 minutes. Add rice and cook, stirring occasionally, until edges of rice begin to turn translucent, about 3 minutes. Add broth and salt and bring to boil. Reduce heat to low, cover, and cook until all liquid is absorbed, about 10 minutes. Off heat, remove lid, fold clean dish towel in half, and place over pan; replace lid. Let stand for 10 minutes. Fluff rice with fork, stir in parsley, and serve.

Herbed Rice and Pasta Pilaf

Stir ¼ cup plain whole-milk yogurt, ¼ cup minced fresh dill, and ¼ cup minced fresh chives into pilaf with parsley.

Rice and Pasta Pilaf with Golden Raisins and Almonds

Place ½ cup golden raisins in bowl and cover with boiling water. Let stand until plump, about 5 minutes. Drain and set aside. Stir 2 bay leaves and 1 teaspoon ground cardamom into rice with chicken broth. Discard bay leaves and stir raisins and ½ cup slivered almonds, toasted and chopped coarse, into rice with parsley.

Rice and Pasta Pilaf with Pomegranate and Walnuts

Omit onion and garlic. Add 2 tablespoons grated fresh ginger to pan with rice. Stir ½ teaspoon ground cumin into rice with chicken broth. Omit parsley and stir ½ cup walnuts, toasted and chopped coarse; ½ cup pomegranate seeds; ½ cup chopped fresh cilantro; and 1 tablespoon lemon juice into fluffed rice.

RICE AND LENTILS WITH CRISPY ONIONS

WHY THIS RECIPE WORKS: *Mujaddara*, the rice and beans of the Middle East, is a hearty, warm-spiced rice and lentil pilaf containing large brown or green lentils and crispy fried onion strings. We wanted a version of this dish in which all of the elements were cooked perfectly. We found that precooking the lentils and soaking the rice in hot water before combining them ensured that both components cooked evenly. For the crispiest possible onions, we removed some moisture by salting and microwaving them before frying. This allowed us to pare down the fussy process of batch-frying in several cups of oil to a single batch. And using some of the oil from the onions to dress our pilaf gave it ultrasavory depth.

Rice and Lentils with Crispy Onions (Mujaddara)

SERVES 4 TO 6

Large green or brown lentils will work interchangeably in this recipe; do not substitute smaller French lentils. When preparing the Crispy Onions, be sure to reserve 3 tablespoons of the onion cooking oil for cooking the rice and lentils.

YOGURT SAUCE

- 1 cup plain whole-milk yogurt
- 2 tablespoons lemon juice
- ½ teaspoon minced garlic
- ½ teaspoon salt

RICE AND LENTILS

- 8½ ounces (1¼ cups) green or brown lentils, picked over and rinsed
- Salt and pepper
- 1¼ cups basmati rice
- 1 recipe Crispy Onions, plus 3 tablespoons reserved oil (recipe follows)
- 3 garlic cloves, minced
- 1 teaspoon ground coriander
- 1 teaspoon ground cumin
- ½ teaspoon ground cinnamon
- ½ teaspoon ground allspice
- ⅛ teaspoon cayenne pepper
- 1 teaspoon sugar
- 3 tablespoons minced fresh cilantro

1. FOR THE YOGURT SAUCE: Whisk all ingredients together in bowl. Refrigerate while preparing rice and lentils.

2. FOR THE RICE AND LENTILS: Bring lentils, 4 cups water, and 1 teaspoon salt to boil in medium saucepan over high heat. Reduce heat to low and cook until lentils are tender, 15 to 17 minutes. Drain and set aside. While lentils cook, place rice in medium bowl and cover by 2 inches with hot tap water; let stand for 15 minutes.

3. Using your hands, gently swish rice grains to release excess starch. Carefully pour off water, leaving rice in bowl. Add cold tap water to rice and pour off water. Repeat adding and pouring off cold tap water 4 to 5 times, until water runs almost clear. Drain rice in fine-mesh strainer.

4. Heat reserved onion oil, garlic, coriander, cumin, cinnamon, allspice, ¼ teaspoon pepper, and cayenne in Dutch oven over medium heat until fragrant, about 2 minutes. Add rice and cook, stirring occasionally, until edges of rice begin to turn translucent, about 3 minutes. Add 2¼ cups water, sugar, and 1 teaspoon salt and bring to boil. Stir in lentils, reduce heat to low, cover, and cook until all liquid is absorbed, about 12 minutes.

5. Off heat, remove lid, fold clean dish towel in half, and place over pot; replace lid. Let stand for 10 minutes. Fluff rice and lentils with fork and stir in cilantro and half of crispy onions. Transfer to serving platter, top with remaining crispy onions, and serve, passing yogurt sauce separately.

Crispy Onions

MAKES 1½ CUPS

It is crucial to thoroughly dry the microwaved onions after rinsing. The best way to accomplish this is to use a salad spinner. Reserve 3 tablespoons of oil when draining the onions to use in Rice and Lentils with Crispy Onions. Remaining oil may be stored in an airtight container and refrigerated for up to 4 weeks.

- 2 pounds onions, halved and sliced crosswise into ¼-inch-thick pieces
- 2 teaspoons salt
- 1½ cups vegetable oil

1. Toss onions and salt together in large bowl. Microwave for 5 minutes. Rinse thoroughly, transfer to paper towel–lined baking sheet, and dry well.

2. Heat onions and oil in Dutch oven over high heat, stirring frequently, until onions are golden brown, 25 to 30 minutes. Drain onions in colander set in large bowl. Transfer onions to paper towel–lined baking sheet to drain. Serve.

PERSIAN-STYLE RICE

WHY THIS RECIPE WORKS: *Chelow* is a classic Iranian dish that marries a light and fluffy rice pilaf with a golden-brown, crispy crust (known as *tahdig*). Rinsing the rice and then soaking it for 15 minutes in hot salted water produced fluffy grains. Parboiling the rice and then steaming it was also essential to creating the best texture for the pilaf and the perfect crust. Steaming the grains for 45 minutes rather than the traditional hour was enough; we also wrapped the lid with a towel to absorb extra moisture. Combining a portion of the rice with thick Greek yogurt and oil created a flavorful crust, while chunks of butter enriched the pilaf portion. The yogurt also made the tahdig easier to remove from the pot, as did brushing the bottom of the pot with extra oil. Adding cumin seeds and parsley to the dish made for a more interesting and well-rounded flavor profile.

Persian-Style Rice with Golden Crust (Chelow)

SERVES 6

We prefer the nutty flavor and texture of basmati rice, but Texmati or another long-grain rice will work. For the best results, use a Dutch oven with a bottom diameter between 8½ and 10 inches. It is important not to overcook the rice during the parboiling step, as it will continue to cook during steaming. Begin checking the rice at the lower end of the given time range. Do not skip placing the pot on a damp towel in step 7—doing so will help free the crust from the pot. Serve this pilaf alongside stews or kebabs.

- 2 cups basmati rice
- Salt
- 1 tablespoon plus ¼ cup vegetable oil
- ¼ cup plain Greek yogurt
- 1½ teaspoons cumin seeds
- 2 tablespoons unsalted butter, cut into 8 cubes
- ¼ cup minced fresh parsley

1. Place rice in fine-mesh strainer and rinse under cold running water until water runs clear. Place rinsed rice and 1 tablespoon salt in medium bowl and cover with 4 cups hot tap water. Stir gently to dissolve salt; let stand for 15 minutes. Drain rice in fine-mesh strainer.

2. Meanwhile, bring 8 cups water to boil in Dutch oven over high heat. Add rice and 2 tablespoons salt. Boil briskly, stirring frequently, until rice is mostly tender with slight bite in center and grains are floating toward top of pot, 3 to 5 minutes (begin timing from when rice is added to pot).

3. Drain rice in large fine-mesh strainer and rinse with cold water to stop cooking, about 30 seconds. Rinse and dry pot well to remove any residual starch. Brush bottom and 1 inch up sides of pot with 1 tablespoon oil.

4. Whisk remaining ¼ cup oil, yogurt, 1 teaspoon cumin seeds, and ¼ teaspoon salt together in medium bowl. Add 2 cups parcooked rice and stir until combined. Spread yogurt-rice mixture evenly over bottom of prepared pot, packing it down well.

5. Stir remaining ½ teaspoon cumin seeds into remaining rice. Mound rice in center of pot on top of yogurt-rice base (it should look like small hill). Poke 8 equally spaced holes through rice mound but not into yogurt-rice base. Place 1 butter cube in each hole. Drizzle ⅓ cup water over rice mound.

6. Wrap pot lid with clean dish towel and cover pot tightly, making sure towel is secure on top of lid and away from heat. Cook over medium-high heat until rice on bottom is crackling and steam is coming from sides of pot, about 10 minutes, rotating pot halfway through for even cooking.

7. Reduce heat to medium-low and continue to cook until rice is tender and fluffy and crust is golden brown around edges, 30 to 35 minutes longer. Remove covered pot from heat and place on damp dish towel set in rimmed baking sheet; let stand for 5 minutes.

8. Stir 2 tablespoons parsley into rice, making sure not to disturb crust on bottom of pot, and season with salt to taste. Gently spoon rice onto serving platter.

9. Using thin metal spatula, loosen edges of crust from pot, then break crust into large pieces. Transfer pieces to serving platter, arranging evenly around rice. Sprinkle with remaining 2 tablespoons parsley and serve.

RED BEANS AND RICE

WHY THIS RECIPE WORKS: To replicate the traditional New Orleans red beans and rice recipe using ingredients easily found in supermarkets, we made some simple substitutions: small red beans for Camellia-brand dried red beans and bacon for hard-to-find tasso. Fine-tuning the proportions of sautéed green peppers, onions, and celery gave the recipe balance, and the right ratio of chicken broth to water added complexity to the dish.

Red Beans and Rice

SERVES 6 TO 8

If you are pressed for time you can "quick-brine" your beans. In step 1, combine the salt, water, and beans in a large Dutch oven and bring to a boil over high heat. Remove the pot from the heat, cover, and let stand 1 hour. Drain and rinse the beans and proceed with the recipe. If you can't find andouille sausage, substitute kielbasa. Tasso can be difficult to find, but if you use it, omit the bacon and paprika in step 2 and cook 4 ounces finely chopped tasso in 2 teaspoons vegetable oil until lightly browned, 4 to 6 minutes, then proceed. It is important to maintain a vigorous simmer in step 2. The beans can be cooled, covered tightly, and refrigerated for up to 2 days. To reheat, add enough water to the beans to thin them slightly.

- Salt and pepper
- 1 pound (about 2 cups) dried small red beans, picked over and rinsed
- 4 slices bacon, chopped fine
- 1 onion, chopped fine
- 1 small green bell pepper, stemmed, seeded and chopped fine
- 1 celery rib, chopped fine
- 3 garlic cloves, minced
- 1 teaspoon minced fresh thyme
- 1 teaspoon sweet paprika
- 2 bay leaves
- ¼ teaspoon cayenne pepper
- 3 cups chicken broth
- 6 cups water
- 8 ounces andouille sausage, halved lengthwise and cut into ¼-inch slices
- Basic White Rice (page 453)
- 1 teaspoon red wine vinegar, plus extra for seasoning
- 3 scallions, sliced thin
- Hot sauce (optional)

1. Dissolve 3 tablespoons salt in 4 quarts cold water in large container. Add beans and soak at room temperature at least 8 hours or up to 24 hours. Drain and rinse well.

2. Heat bacon in Dutch oven over medium heat, stirring occasionally, until browned and almost fully rendered, 5 to 8 minutes. Add onion, bell pepper, and celery; cook, stirring frequently, until vegetables are softened, 6 to 7 minutes. Stir in garlic, thyme, paprika, bay leaves, cayenne pepper, and 1/4 teaspoon black pepper; cook until fragrant, about 30 seconds. Stir in beans, broth, and water, and bring to boil over high heat. Reduce heat and vigorously simmer, stirring occasionally, until beans are just soft and liquid begins to thicken, 45 to 60 minutes.

3. Stir in sausage and 1 teaspoon vinegar and cook until liquid is thick and beans are fully tender and creamy, about 30 minutes. Season with salt, pepper, and additional vinegar to taste. Serve over rice, sprinkling with scallions and passing hot sauce separately, if using.

ALMOST HANDS-FREE RISOTTO

WHY THIS RECIPE WORKS: Classic risotto can demand half an hour of stovetop tedium for the best creamy results. Our goal was five minutes of stirring, tops.

First, we chose to cook our risotto in a Dutch oven, rather than a saucepan. A Dutch oven's thick, heavy bottom, deep sides, and tight-fitting lid are made to trap and distribute heat as evenly as possible. Typical recipes dictate adding the broth in small increments after the wine has been absorbed (and stirring constantly after each addition), but we added most of the broth at once. Then we covered the pan and simmered the rice until almost all the broth had been absorbed, stirring just twice during this time. After adding the second and final addition of broth, we stirred the pot for just a few minutes to ensure the bottom didn't cook more quickly than the top and turned off the heat. Without sitting over a direct flame, the sauce turned out perfectly creamy and the rice was thickened, velvety, and just barely chewy. To finish, we simply stirred in butter, herbs, and a squeeze of lemon juice to brighten the flavors.

Almost Hands-Free Risotto with Parmesan and Herbs

SERVES 6

This more hands-off method does require precise timing, so we strongly recommend using a timer. The consistency of risotto is largely a matter of personal taste; if you prefer a brothy risotto, add extra broth in step 4. This makes a great side dish for braised meats.

- 5 cups low-sodium chicken broth
- 1½ cups water
- 4 tablespoons (½ stick) unsalted butter
- 1 large onion, minced
- Table salt
- 1 medium garlic clove, minced or pressed through a garlic press (about 1 teaspoon)
- 2 cups Arborio rice
- 1 cup dry white wine
- 2 ounces Parmesan cheese, grated (about 1 cup)
- 1 teaspoon juice from 1 lemon
- 2 tablespoons chopped fresh parsley leaves
- 2 tablespoons chopped fresh chives
- Ground black pepper

1. Bring the broth and water to a boil in a large saucepan over high heat. Reduce the heat to medium-low to maintain a gentle simmer.

2. Heat 2 tablespoons of the butter in a large Dutch oven over medium heat. When the butter has melted, add the onion and ¾ teaspoon salt. Cook, stirring frequently, until the onion is softened but not browned, 5 to 7 minutes. Add the garlic and stir until fragrant, about 30 seconds. Add the rice and cook, stirring frequently, until the grains are translucent around the edges, about 3 minutes.

3. Add the wine and cook, stirring constantly, until fully absorbed, 2 to 3 minutes. Stir 5 cups of the warm broth mixture into the rice, reduce the heat to medium-low, cover, and simmer until almost all the liquid has been absorbed and the rice is just al dente, 16 to 19 minutes, stirring twice during cooking.

4. Add ¾ cup more broth mixture and stir gently and constantly until the risotto becomes creamy, about 3 minutes. Stir in the Parmesan. Remove the pot from the heat, cover, and let stand for 5 minutes. Stir in the remaining 2 tablespoons butter, the lemon juice, parsley, and chives. Season with salt and pepper to taste. If desired, add up to ½ cup remaining broth mixture to loosen the texture of the risotto. Serve immediately.

COUSCOUS

WHY THIS RECIPE WORKS: Although couscous traditionally serves as a sauce absorber under North African–style stews and braises, it can work equally well as a lighter, quicker alternative to everyday side dishes like rice pilaf. We wanted to develop a classic version as convenient as the box kind but much fresher tasting, as well as a handful of variations with a few flavorful add-ins. The box instructions—measure and boil water, stir in couscous, cover and let stand off heat for five minutes—gave us bland, clumpy grains. Toasting the couscous grains in butter deepened their flavor and helped them cook up fluffy and separate. And to bump up the flavor even further, we replaced half of the water with chicken broth. For our enriched variations, dried fruit, nuts, and citrus juice added textural interest and sweet, bright notes.

Simple Couscous

SERVES 4 TO 6

- 2 tablespoons unsalted butter
- 2 cups couscous
- 1 cup water
- 1 cup low-sodium chicken broth
- 1 teaspoon table salt
- Ground black pepper

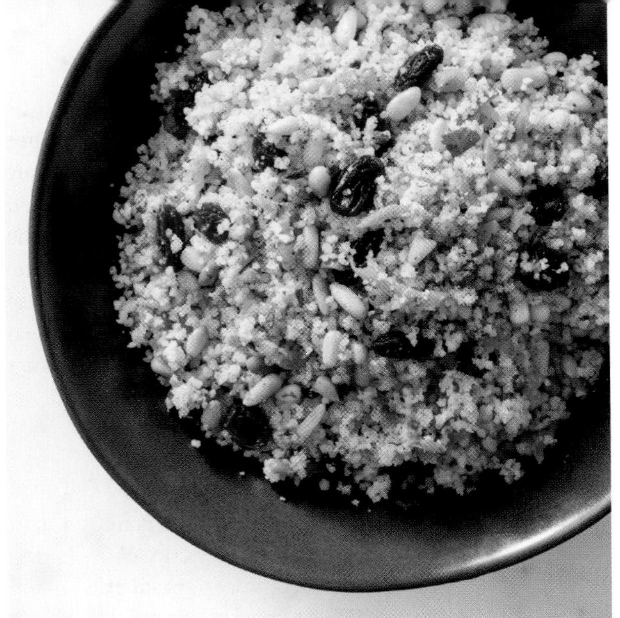

Melt the butter in a medium saucepan over medium-high heat. Add the couscous and cook, stirring frequently, until the grains are just beginning to brown, about 5 minutes. Add the water, broth, and salt and stir briefly to combine. Cover and remove the pan from the heat. Let stand until the grains are tender, about 7 minutes. Uncover and fluff the grains with a fork. Season with pepper to taste and serve.

Couscous with Dates and Pistachios

Follow the recipe for Simple Couscous, increasing the butter to 3 tablespoons and adding ½ cup chopped dates, 1 tablespoon grated fresh ginger, and ½ teaspoon ground cardamom to the saucepan with the couscous. Increase the amount of water to 1¼ cups. Stir ¾ cup coarsely chopped toasted pistachios, 3 tablespoons minced fresh cilantro leaves, and 2 teaspoons juice from 1 lemon into the couscous before serving.

Couscous with Dried Cherries and Pecans

Follow the recipe for Simple Couscous, increasing the butter to 3 tablespoons and adding ½ cup coarsely chopped dried cherries, 2 minced garlic cloves, ¾ teaspoon garam masala, and ⅛ teaspoon cayenne pepper to the saucepan with the couscous. Increase the amount of water to 1¼ cups. Stir ¾ cup coarsely chopped toasted pecans, 2 thinly sliced scallions, and 2 teaspoons juice from 1 lemon into the couscous before serving.

Couscous with Carrots, Raisins, and Pine Nuts

Follow the recipe for Simple Couscous, increasing the butter to 3 tablespoons. Once the foaming subsides, add 2 grated carrots and ½ teaspoon ground cinnamon; cook, stirring frequently, until the carrot softens, about 2 minutes. Continue with the recipe, adding ½ cup raisins to the saucepan with the couscous and increasing the water to 1¼ cups. Stir ¾ cup toasted pine nuts, 3 tablespoons minced fresh cilantro leaves, ½ teaspoon grated orange zest, and 1 tablespoon orange juice into the couscous before serving.

Couscous with Shallots, Garlic, and Almonds

Follow the recipe for Simple Couscous, increasing the butter to 3 tablespoons. Once the foaming subsides, add 3 thinly sliced shallots and cook, stirring frequently, until softened and lightly browned, about 5 minutes. Add 1 minced garlic clove and cook until fragrant, about 30 seconds. Continue with recipe, stirring 3/4 cup toasted sliced almonds, 3/4 cup minced fresh parsley, and 1/2 teaspoon grated zest and 2 teaspoons juice from 1 lemon into the couscous before serving.

SIMPLE ISRAELI COUSCOUS

WHY THIS RECIPE WORKS: Israeli couscous is nuttier than its North African cousin, thanks to the practice of drying the pasta-like pearls over a flame. To prepare pasta salad using Israeli couscous, we toasted the spheres in oil to accentuate their earthy, nutty flavor. We then added water, brought it to a boil, and cooked the couscous covered and at a simmer, allowing it to slowly and evenly absorb the liquid. To turn the finished couscous into a salad, we spread the spheres on a baking sheet to cool (and to prevent it from cooking further in its own steam). Meanwhile, we quickly pickled shallot slices, dissolving sugar in red wine vinegar over medium-high heat before removing the pan from heat, stirring in the shallots, and letting them take on more flavor as the liquid cooled. We dressed the couscous in a bold vinaigrette, whisking together olive oil, lemon juice, Dijon, and red pepper flakes. Once the couscous was coated in the vinaigrette, we finished off the salad with mint, peas, toasted pistachios, and feta.

Simple Israeli Couscous

MAKES ABOUT 4 CUPS

Warm couscous can be tossed with butter or extra-virgin olive oil and salt and pepper for a simple side dish. If you're using it in a salad, transfer the couscous to a rimmed baking sheet and let it cool completely, about 15 minutes.

- 2 cups Israeli couscous
- 1 tablespoon extra-virgin olive oil
- 2½ cups water
- ½ teaspoon salt

Heat couscous and oil in medium saucepan over medium heat, stirring frequently, until about half of grains are golden brown, 5 to 6 minutes. Carefully add water and salt; stir briefly to combine. Increase heat to high and bring to boil. Reduce heat to medium-low, cover, and simmer, stirring occasionally, until water is absorbed, 9 to 12 minutes. Remove saucepan from heat and let stand, covered, for 3 minutes. Serve.

Israeli Couscous with Lemon, Mint, Peas, Feta, and Pickled Shallots

SERVES 6

For efficiency, let the shallots pickle while you prepare the remaining ingredients.

- ⅓ cup red wine vinegar
- 2 tablespoons sugar
- Salt and pepper
- 2 shallots, sliced thin
- 3 tablespoons extra-virgin olive oil
- 3 tablespoons lemon juice
- 1 teaspoon Dijon mustard
- ⅛ teaspoon red pepper flakes
- 1 recipe Simple Israeli Couscous, cooled
- 4 ounces (4 cups) baby arugula, roughly chopped
- 1 cup fresh mint leaves, torn
- ½ cup frozen peas, thawed
- ½ cup shelled pistachios, toasted and chopped
- 3 ounces feta cheese, crumbled (¾ cup)

1. Bring vinegar, sugar, and pinch salt to simmer in small saucepan over medium-high heat, stirring occasionally, until sugar dissolves. Remove pan from heat, add shallots, and stir to combine. Cover and let cool completely, about 30 minutes. Drain and discard liquid.

2. Whisk oil, lemon juice, mustard, pepper flakes, and 1/8 teaspoon salt together in large bowl. Add cooled couscous, arugula, mint, peas, 6 tablespoons pistachios, 1/2 cup feta, and shallots and toss to combine. Season with salt and pepper to taste and transfer to serving bowl. Let stand for 5 minutes. Sprinkle with remaining 1/4 cup feta and remaining 2 tablespoons pistachios and serve.

Israeli Couscous with Tomatoes, Olives, and Ricotta Salata

SERVES 6

Crumbled feta cheese can be substituted for the ricotta salata.

- 3 tablespoons extra-virgin olive oil
- 3 tablespoons red wine vinegar
- 1 teaspoon Dijon mustard
- Salt and pepper
- 1 recipe Simple Israeli Couscous (page 623), cooled
- 12 ounces grape tomatoes, quartered
- 3 ounces ricotta salata cheese, crumbled (¾ cup)
- 2 ounces (2 cups) baby spinach, sliced ¼ inch thick
- ⅔ cup pitted kalamata olives, sliced
- 1 bunch chives, cut into ¼-inch pieces (¼ cup)
- 1½ cups basil leaves, chopped coarse
- ½ cup pine nuts, toasted

Whisk oil, vinegar, mustard, and ⅛ teaspoon salt together in large bowl. Add couscous, tomatoes, ricotta salata, spinach, olives, chives, basil, and 6 tablespoons pine nuts and toss to combine. Season with salt and pepper to taste and transfer to serving bowl. Let stand for 5 minutes. Sprinkle with ricotta salata and remaining 2 tablespoons pine nuts and serve.

QUINOA PILAF

WHY THIS RECIPE WORKS: Most recipes for quinoa pilaf turn out woefully overcooked because they call for nearly twice as much liquid as they should. We cut the water back to ensure tender grains with a satisfying bite, and gave it a stir partway through cooking to ensure the grains cooked evenly. We let the quinoa rest for several minutes before fluffing to help further improve the texture. We also pre-toasted the quinoa in a dry skillet before simmering to develop its natural nutty flavor, and finished our pilaf with a judicious amount of boldly flavored ingredients.

Quinoa Pilaf with Herbs and Lemon

SERVES 4 TO 6

If you buy unwashed quinoa, rinse the grains in a fine-mesh strainer, drain them, and then spread them on a rimmed baking sheet lined with a clean dish towel and let them dry for 15 minutes before proceeding with the recipe. Any soft herbs, such as cilantro, parsley, chives, mint, and tarragon, can be used.

- 1½ cups prewashed quinoa
- 2 tablespoons unsalted butter, cut into 2 pieces
- 1 small onion, chopped fine
- ¾ teaspoon salt
- 1¾ cups water
- 3 tablespoons chopped fresh herbs
- 1 tablespoon lemon juice

1. Toast quinoa in medium saucepan over medium-high heat, stirring frequently, until quinoa is very fragrant and makes continuous popping sound, 5 to 7 minutes. Transfer quinoa to bowl and set aside.

2. Return now-empty pan to medium-low heat and melt butter. Add onion and salt; cook, stirring frequently, until onion is softened and light golden, 5 to 7 minutes.

3. Increase heat to medium-high, stir in water and quinoa, and bring to simmer. Cover, reduce heat to low, and simmer until grains are just tender and liquid is absorbed, 18 to 20 minutes, stirring once halfway through cooking. Remove pan from heat and let sit, covered, for 10 minutes. Fluff quinoa with fork, stir in herbs and lemon juice, and serve.

Quinoa Pilaf with Chipotle, Queso Fresco, and Peanuts

Add 1 teaspoon chipotle chile powder and ¼ teaspoon ground cumin with onion and salt. Substitute ½ cup crumbled queso fresco; ½ cup roasted unsalted peanuts, chopped coarse; and 2 thinly sliced scallions for herbs. Substitute 4 teaspoons lime juice for lemon juice.

Quinoa Pilaf with Apricots, Aged Gouda, and Pistachios

Add ½ teaspoon grated lemon zest, ½ teaspoon ground coriander, ¼ teaspoon ground cumin, and ⅛ teaspoon pepper with onion and salt. Stir in ½ cup dried apricots, chopped coarse, before letting quinoa sit for 10 minutes in step 3. Substitute ½ cup shredded aged gouda; ½ cup shelled pistachios, toasted and chopped coarse; and 2 tablespoons chopped fresh mint for herbs.

FARRO SALAD

WHY THIS RECIPE WORKS: Farro comes in a few different forms, but our favorite is minimally processed whole farro, in which the germ and bran have been retained. It has a nutty flavor and chewy texture and cooks in 20 minutes, making it one of the fastest-cooking whole grains. We found that the simplest cooking method was best: Boil in salted water for about 20 minutes until tender and drain well. Its versatility makes it ideal for salads, soups, and side dishes. Extra cooked farro can be stored in the refrigerator for up to five days.

Simple Farro

MAKES 2½ CUPS

We prefer the flavor and texture of whole-grain farro. Pearled farro can be used, but cooking times vary, so start checking for doneness after 10 minutes. Do not use quick-cooking farro in this recipe. Warm farro can be tossed with butter or olive oil and salt and pepper for a simple yet hearty side dish. It can also be added to soups or, when cooled, added to salads.

- 1½ cups whole farro, rinsed
- 1 tablespoon salt

Bring 2 quarts water to boil in large saucepan. Add farro and salt. Return to boil, reduce heat, and simmer until grains are tender with slight chew, 15 to 20 minutes. Drain well. (Farro can be refrigerated for up to 5 days.)

Farro Salad with Asparagus, Sugar Snap Peas, and Tomatoes

SERVES 6

- 6 ounces asparagus, trimmed and cut into 1-inch lengths
- 6 ounces sugar snap peas, strings removed, cut into 1-inch lengths
- Salt and pepper
- 3 tablespoons extra-virgin olive oil
- 2 tablespoons lemon juice
- 2 tablespoons minced shallot
- 1 teaspoon Dijon mustard
- 1 recipe Simple Farro, room temperature
- 6 ounces cherry tomatoes, halved
- 3 tablespoons chopped fresh dill
- 2 ounces feta cheese, crumbled (½ cup)

1. Bring 2 quarts water to boil in large saucepan. Add asparagus, snap peas, and 1 tablespoon salt. Cook until vegetables are crisp-tender, 2 to 3 minutes. Using slotted spoon, transfer vegetables to rimmed baking sheet and let cool for 15 minutes.

2. Whisk oil, lemon juice, shallot, mustard, ¼ teaspoon salt, and ¼ teaspoon pepper together in large bowl. Add cooled vegetables, farro, tomatoes, dill, and ¼ cup feta to dressing and toss to combine. Season with salt and pepper to taste and transfer to serving bowl. Sprinkle salad with remaining ¼ cup feta and serve.

Warm Farro with Lemon and Herbs

SERVES 6

- 3 tablespoons unsalted butter
- 1 onion, chopped
- Salt and pepper
- 1 garlic clove, minced
- 1 recipe Simple Farro
- ¼ cup chopped fresh parsley
- ¼ cup chopped fresh mint
- 2 teaspoons lemon juice

Melt butter in 12-inch skillet over medium heat. Add onion and ¼ teaspoon salt and cook, stirring frequently, until onion is softened but not browned, 6 to 8 minutes. Add garlic and cook until fragrant, about 1 minute. Add farro and cook until warmed through, 3 to 5 minutes. Remove from heat and stir in parsley, mint, and lemon juice. Season with salt and pepper to taste, and serve.

TABBOULEH

WHY THIS RECIPE WORKS: Tabbouleh has long been a *meze* staple in the Middle East, but these days it can be found in the refrigerated section of virtually every American supermarket. Its brief (and healthful) ingredient list explains its popularity: Chopped fresh parsley and mint, tomatoes, onion, and bits of nutty bulgur are tossed with lemon and olive oil for a refreshing appetizer or side dish. It all sounds easy enough, but following a recipe or picking up a pint at the market reveals that most versions are hopelessly soggy, with flavor that is either too bold or too bland. We wanted a flavorful dish that would feature a hefty amount of parsley as well as a decent amount of bulgur.

A high ratio of chopped parsley to chopped mint put the emphasis on the bright, peppery parsley but didn't overpower the other ingredients. Bulgur is made by boiling, drying, and grinding wheat kernels, so it only needs to be soaked, not cooked. We soaked it in lemon juice to infuse it with flavor. Extra-virgin olive oil tempered the tart lemon juice. To avoid soggy tabbouleh, we salted the tomatoes, and then, rather than throw out the exuded liquid, we added it to the bulgur-soaking liquid. Two sliced scallions (preferred over red or white onion) rounded out the mix.

Tabbouleh

SERVES 4

Serve the salad with the crisp inner leaves of romaine lettuce and wedges of pita bread.

- 3 medium round tomatoes, cored and cut into ½-inch pieces
- Salt and pepper
- ½ cup medium-grind bulgur
- ¼ cup lemon juice (2 lemons)
- 6 tablespoons extra-virgin olive oil
- ⅛ teaspoon cayenne pepper
- 1½ cups chopped fresh parsley
- ½ cup chopped fresh mint
- 2 scallions, sliced thin

1. Toss tomatoes and ¼ teaspoon salt in large bowl. Transfer to fine-mesh strainer, set strainer in bowl, and let stand for 30 minutes, tossing occasionally.

2. Rinse bulgur in fine-mesh strainer under cold running water. Drain well and transfer to second bowl. Stir in 2 tablespoons lemon juice and 2 tablespoons juice from draining tomatoes. Let stand until grains are beginning to soften, 30 to 40 minutes.

3. Whisk remaining 2 tablespoons lemon juice, oil, cayenne, and ¼ teaspoon salt together in large bowl. Add drained tomatoes, soaked bulgur, parsley, mint, and scallions; toss gently to combine. Cover and let stand at room temperature until flavors have blended and bulgur is tender, about 1 hour. Toss to recombine, season with salt and pepper to taste, and serve immediately.

EGYPTIAN BARLEY SALAD

WHY THIS RECIPE WORKS: We set out to develop a recipe for a vibrantly spiced pearl barley salad with the right balance of sweetness, tang, and nuttiness. Before we could focus on building these exciting flavors, we had to find a consistent cooking method for our barley. We wanted the grains to remain distinct, rather than cohesive as in a pilaf. We turned to what we call the "pasta method," in which we simply boil the grains until tender. With our perfectly cooked barley set aside, we turned our attention back to flavor. Inspired by the flavors of Egypt, we incorporated toasty pistachios, tangy pomegranate molasses, and bright, vegetal cilantro, all balanced by warm, earthy spices and sweet golden raisins. Salty feta cheese, pungent scallions, and pomegranate seeds adorned the top of the dish for a colorful composed salad with dynamic flavors and textures.

Egyptian Barley Salad

SERVES 6 TO 8

Do not substitute hulled barley or hull-less barley in this recipe. If using quick-cooking or presteamed barley (read the ingredient list on the package to determine this), you will need to decrease the barley cooking time in step 1.

- 1½ cups pearl barley
- Salt and pepper
- 3 tablespoons extra-virgin olive oil, plus extra for serving
- 2 tablespoons pomegranate molasses
- ½ teaspoon ground cinnamon
- ¼ teaspoon ground cumin
- ⅓ cup golden raisins
- ½ cup coarsely chopped cilantro
- ¼ cup shelled pistachios, toasted and chopped coarse
- 3 ounces feta cheese, cut into ½-inch cubes (¾ cup)
- 6 scallions, green parts only, sliced thin
- ½ cup pomegranate seeds

1. Bring 4 quarts water to boil in Dutch oven. Add barley and 1 tablespoon salt, return to boil, and cook until tender, 20 to 40 minutes. Drain barley, spread onto rimmed baking sheet, and let cool completely, about 15 minutes.

2. Whisk oil, molasses, cinnamon, cumin, and ½ teaspoon salt together in large bowl. Add barley, raisins, cilantro, and pistachios and gently toss to combine. Season with salt and pepper to taste. Spread barley salad evenly on serving platter and arrange feta, scallions, and pomegranate seeds in separate diagonal rows on top. Drizzle with extra oil and serve.

NO-FUSS CREAMY POLENTA

WHY THIS RECIPE WORKS: If you don't stir polenta almost constantly, it forms intractable lumps. We wanted creamy, smooth polenta with rich corn flavor, but we wanted to find a way around the fussy process.

The prospect of stirring continuously for an hour made our arms ache, so we set out to find a way to give the water a head start on penetrating the cornmeal (we prefer the soft texture and nutty flavor of degerminated cornmeal in polenta). Our research led us to consider the similarities between cooking dried beans and dried corn. With beans, water has to penetrate the hard outer skin to gelatinize the starch within. In a corn kernel, the water has to penetrate the endosperm. To soften bean skins and speed up cooking, baking soda is sometimes added to the cooking liquid. Sure enough, a pinch was all it took to cut the cooking time in half without affecting the texture or flavor. Baking soda also helped the granules break down and release their starch in a uniform way, so we could virtually eliminate the stirring if we covered the pot and adjusted the heat to low. Parmesan cheese and butter stirred in at the last minute finishes our polenta, which is satisfying and rich.

No-Fuss Creamy Parmesan Polenta

SERVES 6 TO 8

Coarse-ground degerminated cornmeal such as yellow grits (with grains the size of couscous) works best in this recipe. Avoid instant and quick-cooking products, as well as whole grain, stone-ground, and regular cornmeal. Do not omit the baking soda—it reduces the cooking time and makes for a creamier polenta. The polenta should do little more than release wisps of steam. If it bubbles or sputters even slightly after the first 10 minutes, the heat is too high and you may need a flame tamer. A flame tamer can be purchased at most kitchen supply stores, or you can improvise your own (see page 313). For a main course, serve the polenta with a wedge of rich cheese, meat sauce, or cooked leafy greens. Served plain, the polenta makes a great accompaniment to stews and braises.

- 7½ cups water
- 1½ teaspoons table salt
- Pinch baking soda (see note)
- 1½ cups coarse-ground cornmeal (see note)
- 4 ounces Parmesan cheese, grated (about 2 cups), plus extra for serving
- 2 tablespoons unsalted butter
- Ground black pepper

1. Bring the water to a boil in a heavy-bottomed 4-quart saucepan over medium-high heat. Stir in the salt and baking soda. Slowly pour the cornmeal into the water in a steady stream, while stirring back and forth with a wooden spoon or rubber spatula. Bring the mixture to a boil, stirring constantly, about 1 minute. Reduce the heat to the lowest possible setting and cover.

2. After 5 minutes, whisk the polenta to smooth out any lumps that may have formed, about 15 seconds. (Make sure to scrape the sides and bottom of the pan.) Cover and continue to cook, without stirring, until the grains of polenta are tender but slightly al dente, about 25 minutes longer. (The polenta should be loose and barely hold its shape; it will continue to thicken as it cools.)

3. Remove from the heat, stir in the Parmesan and butter, and season with pepper to taste. Let stand, covered, for 5 minutes. Serve, passing extra Parmesan separately.

SPICED PECANS WITH RUM GLAZE

WHY THIS RECIPE WORKS: Most spiced nuts are made with a heavily sugared syrup that causes the nuts to clump awkwardly and leaves your hands in a sticky mess. We wanted to get maximum flavor and balanced sweetness with minimum mess.

We tried two popular methods—boiling the nuts in syrup and tossing them in butter—and eliminated both straight off. The former made the nuts sticky, and the latter dulled their flavor. A third method, coating the nuts with an egg white mixture, pretty much overwhelmed them with a candy-like coating. What finally worked was a light glaze made from very small amounts of liquid (we like either rum or water), sugar, and butter, which left the nuts just tacky enough to pick up an even, light coating of dry spices.

Spiced Pecans with Rum Glaze

MAKES ABOUT 2 CUPS

The spiced nuts can be stored in an airtight container at room temperature for up to 5 days.

- 2 cups raw pecan halves

SPICE MIX

- 2 tablespoons sugar
- ¾ teaspoon table salt
- ½ teaspoon ground cinnamon
- ⅛ teaspoon ground cloves
- ⅛ teaspoon ground allspice

RUM GLAZE

- 1 tablespoon rum, preferably dark, or water
- 1 tablespoon unsalted butter
- 2 teaspoons vanilla extract
- 1 teaspoon light or dark brown sugar

1. Adjust an oven rack to the middle position and heat the oven to 350 degrees. Line a rimmed baking sheet with parchment paper and spread the pecans on it in an even layer; toast until fragrant and the color deepens slightly, about 8 minutes, rotating the sheet halfway through the baking time. Transfer the baking sheet with the nuts to a wire rack.

2. FOR THE SPICE MIX: While the nuts are toasting, combine all the spice mix ingredients in a medium bowl; set aside.

3. FOR THE RUM GLAZE: Bring the rum glaze ingredients to a boil in a medium saucepan over medium-high heat, whisking constantly. Stir in the pecans and cook, stirring constantly with a wooden spoon, until almost all the liquid has evaporated, about 1½ minutes.

4. Transfer the glazed pecans to the bowl with the spice mix; toss well to coat. Return the glazed spiced pecans to the parchment-lined baking sheet to cool before serving.

CHAPTER 20

COME FOR BRUNCH

FLUFFY SCRAMBLED EGGS

WHY THIS RECIPE WORKS: Sometimes the simplest things can be the hardest to get right. Scrambled eggs are a good example. Seemingly easy to make, they can easily go wrong, and overcooking is probably the most common problem. We wanted scrambled eggs that turn out of the pan into a mound of large, soft curds—cooked enough to hold their shape but soft enough to eat with a spoon.

We learned that beating the eggs too much before cooking them can result in toughness, so we whisked our eggs just until they were combined. Milk was better than water as an addition to scrambled eggs; the sugar, proteins, and fat in milk helped create large curds, which trapped steam for that pillowy texture we were after. A nonstick skillet was a must to prevent sticking, and pan size mattered as well; if the skillet was too large, the eggs spread out in too thin a layer and overcooked. Getting the pan hot was crucial for moist, puffy curds, and constant gentle stirring—really more like pushing and folding—prevented overcooking. Cooked on the stove until they were almost done, which took only a couple of minutes, these eggs finished cooking on the way to the table, remaining moist and meltingly soft.

Fluffy Scrambled Eggs

SERVES 4

These eggs cook very quickly, so it's important to be ready to eat before you start to cook them.

- 8 large eggs
- ½ cup milk
- ½ teaspoon table salt
- Pinch ground black pepper
- 1 tablespoon unsalted butter

1. Whisk the eggs, milk, salt, and pepper together in a medium bowl until any streaks are gone and the color is pure yellow.

2. Melt the butter in a 10-inch nonstick skillet over high heat, swirling to coat the pan. Add the eggs and, using a heatproof rubber spatula, cook while gently pushing, lifting, and folding them from one side of the pan to the other as they form curds. Continue until the eggs are nicely clumped into a single mound but remain shiny and wet, 1½ to 2 minutes. Serve.

RICH AND CREAMY SCRAMBLED EGGS

WHY THIS RECIPE WORKS: Scrambled eggs often end up as either tough, dry slabs or pebbly, runny curds. We wanted foolproof rich scrambled eggs with fluffy, moist curds so creamy and light that they practically dissolved on the tongue.

The first step was to add salt to the uncooked eggs; salt dissolved some of the egg proteins so they were unable to bond when cooked, creating more tender curds. Beating the eggs until just combined, using the gentle action of a fork rather than a whisk, ensured our scramble didn't turn tough. For the intense creaminess we were after, we chose half-and-half over milk; it produced rich, clean-tasting curds that were both fluffy and stable. To replicate the richer flavor of farm-fresh eggs, we added extra yolks. Finally, when it came to the cooking process, we started the eggs on medium-high heat to create puffy curds, then finished them over low heat so they wouldn't overcook. Swapping out our 12-inch skillet for a 10-inch pan kept the eggs in a thicker layer, trapping more steam and producing heartier curds.

Rich and Creamy Scrambled Eggs

SERVES 4

It's important to follow the visual cues in this recipe, as pan thickness will affect cooking times. If using an electric stove, heat one burner on low heat and a second on medium-high heat; move the skillet between burners when it's time to adjust the heat. If you don't have half-and-half, substitute 8 teaspoons of whole milk and 4 teaspoons of heavy cream. To dress up the dish, add 2 tablespoons of chopped parsley, chives, basil, or cilantro or 1 tablespoon of dill or tarragon to the eggs after reducing the heat to low.

- 8 large whole eggs
- 2 large yolks
- ¼ cup half-and-half
- Table salt and ground black pepper
- 1 tablespoon unsalted butter, chilled

1. Beat the eggs, yolks, half-and-half, ⅜ teaspoon salt, and ¼ teaspoon pepper with a fork until the eggs are thoroughly combined and the color is pure yellow; do not over beat.

2. Heat the butter in a 10-inch nonstick skillet over medium-high heat until fully melted (the butter should not brown), swirling to coat the pan. Add the egg mixture and, using a heatproof rubber spatula, constantly and firmly scrape along the bottom and the sides of the skillet until the eggs begin to clump and the spatula just leaves a trail on the bottom of the

NOTES FROM THE TEST KITCHEN

GETTING THE TIMING RIGHT FOR RICH AND CREAMY SCRAMBLED EGGS

When your spatula just leaves a trail through the eggs, that's your cue in our dual-heat method to turn the dial from medium-high to low.

pan, 1½ to 2½ minutes. Reduce the heat to low and gently but constantly fold the eggs until clumped and just slightly wet, 30 to 60 seconds. Immediately transfer the eggs to warmed plates and season with salt to taste. Serve immediately.

Rich and Creamy Scrambled Eggs for Two

Follow the recipe for Rich and Creamy Scrambled Eggs, reducing the whole eggs to 4, the yolks to 1, the half-and-half to 2 tablespoons, and the salt and pepper to ⅛ teaspoon each. In step 2, reduce the butter to ½ tablespoon. Cook the eggs in an 8-inch skillet for 45 to 75 seconds over medium-high heat, then for 30 to 60 seconds over low heat.

HEARTY SCRAMBLED EGGS

WHY THIS RECIPE WORKS: Having perfected the technique for cooking scrambled eggs, we figured that we could make a heartier dish by simply adding other ingredients. But even a sprinkling of some sausage or vegetables discolored the eggs and made them watery. We found that cooking in stages—sautéing our aromatics and removing them, cooking the eggs, then folding in all the other ingredients off the heat—prevented discoloration and helped with the wateriness. We were able to get rid of the last bit of wateriness when we substituted a smaller amount of half-and-half—with its higher-fat, lower-water content—for the milk. Breakfast meats, crunchy vegetables, and dry leafy greens were successful additions to these eggs, so long as we avoided any that were moisture-laden. These eggs were not as fluffy as eggs without adornment, but the difference was imperceptible once we added meats and vegetables—and there were no watery puddles on the plate.

Scrambled Eggs with Bacon, Onion, and Pepper Jack Cheese

SERVES 4 TO 6

Note that you'll need to reserve 2 teaspoons of bacon fat to sauté the onion. After removing the cooked bacon from the skillet, be sure to drain it well on paper towels; otherwise, the eggs will be greasy.

- 12 large eggs
- 6 tablespoons half-and-half
- ¾ teaspoon table salt
- ¼ teaspoon ground black pepper
- 4 ounces bacon (about 4 slices), halved lengthwise, then cut crosswise into ½-inch pieces
- 1 medium onion, chopped medium
- 1 tablespoon unsalted butter
- 1½ ounces pepper Jack or Monterey Jack cheese, shredded (about ⅓ cup)
- 1 teaspoon minced fresh parsley leaves (optional)

1. Whisk the eggs, half-and-half, salt, and pepper together in a medium bowl.

2. Cook the bacon in a 12-inch nonstick skillet over medium heat, stirring occasionally, until browned, 4 to 5 minutes. Using a slotted spoon, transfer the bacon to a paper towel–lined plate; discard all but 2 teaspoons bacon fat. Add the onion to the skillet and cook, stirring occasionally, until lightly browned, 2 to 4 minutes; transfer the onion to a second plate.

3. Thoroughly wipe out the skillet with paper towels, add the butter, and melt over medium heat, swirling to coat the pan. Add the eggs and, using a heatproof rubber spatula, cook while gently pushing, lifting, and folding them from one side of the pan to the other as they form curds. Cook until large curds form but the eggs are still very moist, 2 to 3 minutes. Off the heat, gently fold in the onion, pepper Jack, and half of the bacon until evenly distributed; if the eggs are still underdone, return the skillet to medium heat for no longer than 30 seconds. Divide the eggs among individual plates, sprinkle with the remaining bacon and parsley (if using), and serve.

Scrambled Eggs with Sausage, Sweet Pepper, and Cheddar Cheese

SERVES 4 TO 6

We prefer sweet Italian sausage here, especially for breakfast, but you can certainly use spicy sausage, if desired.

- 12 large eggs
- 6 tablespoons half-and-half
- ¾ teaspoon table salt
- ¼ teaspoon ground black pepper
- 1 teaspoon vegetable oil
- 8 ounces sweet Italian sausage, casings removed, sausage crumbled into ½-inch pieces (see note)
- 1 red bell pepper, stemmed, seeded, and cut into ½-inch cubes
- 3 scallions, white and green parts separated, both sliced thin on the bias
- 1 tablespoon unsalted butter
- 1½ ounces sharp cheddar cheese, shredded (about ⅓ cup)

1. Whisk the eggs, half-and-half, salt, and pepper together in a medium bowl.

2. Heat the oil in a 12-inch nonstick skillet over medium heat until shimmering. Add the sausage and cook until beginning to brown but still pink in the center, about 2 minutes.

Add the bell pepper and scallion whites; continue to cook, stirring occasionally, until the sausage is cooked through and the pepper is beginning to brown, about 3 minutes. Spread the mixture in a single layer on a medium plate; set aside.

3. Thoroughly wipe out the skillet with paper towels, add the butter, and melt over medium heat, swirling to coat the pan. Add the eggs and, using a heatproof rubber spatula, cook while gently pushing, lifting, and folding them from one side of the pan to the other as they form curds. Cook the eggs until large curds form but the eggs are still very moist, 2 to 3 minutes. Off the heat, gently fold in the sausage mixture and cheddar until evenly distributed; if the eggs are still underdone, return the skillet to medium heat for no longer than 30 seconds. Divide the eggs among individual plates, sprinkle with the scallion greens, and serve.

PERFECT FRIED EGGS

WHY THIS RECIPE WORKS: There are two common problems when it comes to fried eggs: undercooked whites and an overcooked yolk. A hot nonstick skillet, a touch of butter, and a lid combine to produce perfectly cooked fried eggs—with crisp edges, tender whites, and runny yolks—in just a few minutes.

Perfect Fried Eggs

SERVES 2

When checking the eggs for doneness, lift the lid just a crack to prevent loss of steam should they need further cooking. When cooked, the thin layer of white surrounding the yolk will turn opaque, but the yolk should remain runny. To cook two eggs, use an 8- or 9-inch nonstick skillet and halve the amounts of oil and butter. You can use this method with extra-large or jumbo eggs without altering the timing.

- 2 teaspoons vegetable oil
- 4 large eggs
- Salt and pepper
- 2 teaspoons unsalted butter, cut into 4 pieces and chilled

1. Heat oil in 12- or 14-inch nonstick skillet over low heat for 5 minutes. Meanwhile, crack 2 eggs into small bowl and season with salt and pepper. Repeat with remaining 2 eggs and second small bowl.

2. Increase heat to medium-high and heat until oil is shimmering. Add butter to skillet and quickly swirl to coat pan. Working quickly, pour 1 bowl of eggs in 1 side of pan and second bowl of eggs in other side. Cover and cook for 1 minute. Remove skillet from burner and let stand, covered, 15 to 45 seconds for runny yolks (white around edge of yolk will be barely opaque), 45 to 60 seconds for soft but set yolks, and about 2 minutes for medium-set yolks. Slide eggs onto plates and serve.

NOTES FROM THE TEST KITCHEN

MAKING PERFECT FRIED EGGS

1. HEAT SKILLET: Heat oil in nonstick skillet over low heat for 5 minutes.

2. CRACK EGGS INTO SMALL BOWLS: While skillet heats, crack 2 eggs into small bowl. Repeat with remaining eggs and second small bowl.

3. ADD EGGS ALL AT ONCE: Increase heat. Add butter and swirl to coat pan. Working quickly, position bowls on either side of skillet and add eggs simultaneously.

4. COVER PAN, THEN FINISH OFF HEAT: Cover and cook 1 minute. Remove skillet from burner and let stand, covered, until eggs achieve desired doneness.

POACHED EGGS

WHY THIS RECIPE WORKS: A poached egg should be a neat-looking pouch of tender egg, evenly cooked all the way through, with a yolk that is barely runny. But boiling water can agitate the eggs until they are a ragged mess; we needed to figure out how to cook these eggs gently.

Our first thought was to examine the type of pan used. Most recipes require a deep saucepan, but we found that a shallow pan—a skillet—was far better: The water boiled faster, and the egg hit bottom sooner, and thus more gently, so that it could solidify before becoming stringy. A touch of vinegar lowered the boiling point of the water so that we were able to cook the eggs over more gentle heat. Our most important discovery turned out to be the importance of cooking eggs in still, not bubbling, water—as long as it was hot enough. With this in mind, we covered the skillet and turned off the heat after adding the eggs to the boiling water, allowing the residual heat to cook the eggs through. Without bubbling water to tear them apart, our poached eggs came out of the pan perfectly shaped—and cooked—with no feathery whites in sight.

Poached Eggs

MAKES 4

To get four eggs into boiling water at the same time, crack each into a small cup with a handle. Holding two cups in each hand, lower the lip of each cup just into the water and then tip the eggs into the pan.

- Table salt
- 2 tablespoons distilled white vinegar
- 4 large eggs, each cracked into a small handled cup (see note)
- Ground black pepper

1. Fill an 8- to 10-inch nonstick skillet nearly to the rim with water, add 1 teaspoon salt and the vinegar, and bring the mixture to a boil over high heat.

2. Lower the lip of each cup just into the water; tip the eggs into the boiling water, cover, and immediately remove the pan from the heat. Poach the eggs for 4 minutes for medium-firm yolks. (For firmer yolks, poach for 4½ minutes; for looser yolks, poach for 3 minutes.)

3. With a slotted spoon, carefully lift and drain each egg over the skillet. Season with salt and pepper to taste and serve.

EGGS BENEDICT

WHY THIS RECIPE WORKS: Overcoming one of the biggest challenges to poaching eggs—producing a tender, tidy white—started with draining the eggs in a colander. We also cracked the eggs into a liquid measuring cup and deposited them into the water one by one to prevent them from being jostled. Salted water with vinegar helped the whites set up quickly. Poaching the eggs in a Dutch oven filled with 6 cups of water left plenty of headspace so that steam fully cooked the notoriously gooey portion of the white. Our unconventional technique for hollandaise required whisking butter and egg yolks on the stovetop in a double boiler, creating a strong emulsion stable enough to be chilled and reheated. We served our poached eggs atop toasted English muffins and bacon, and topped them off with our velvety hollandaise.

Eggs Benedict with Perfect Poached Eggs and Foolproof Hollandaise

SERVES 4

For the best results, be sure to use the freshest eggs possible. Cracking the eggs into a colander will rid them of any watery, loose whites and result in perfectly shaped poached eggs. The hollandaise can be refrigerated in an airtight container for 3 days. Reheat in the microwave on 50 percent power, stirring every 10 seconds, until heated through, about 1 minute. You will need an instant-read thermometer to make this recipe.

HOLLANDAISE

- 8 tablespoons unsalted butter, cut into 8 pieces and softened
- 4 large egg yolks
- ⅓ cup boiling water
- 2 teaspoons lemon juice
- Pinch cayenne pepper
- Salt

EGGS

- 1 tablespoon distilled white vinegar
- Salt
- 8 large eggs

- 4 English muffins, split
- 8 slices Canadian bacon (see note)

1. FOR THE HOLLANDAISE: Whisk butter and egg yolks in large heat-resistant bowl set over medium saucepan filled with ½ inch of barely simmering water (don't let bowl touch water). Slowly add boiling water and cook, whisking constantly, until thickened and sauce registers 160 to 165 degrees, 7 to 10 minutes.

2. Off heat, stir in lemon juice and cayenne and season with salt. Cover and set aside in warm place until serving time.

3. FOR THE EGGS: Bring 6 cups water to boil in Dutch oven over high heat, and add vinegar and 1 teaspoon salt. Fill second Dutch oven halfway with water, heat over high heat until water registers 150 degrees; adjust heat as needed to maintain 150 degrees.

4. Crack 4 eggs, one at a time, into colander. Let stand until loose, watery whites drain away from eggs, 20 to 30 seconds. Gently transfer eggs to 2-cup liquid measuring cup. Remove first pot with added vinegar from heat. With lip of measuring cup just above surface of water, gently tip eggs into water, one at a time, leaving space between them. Cover pot and let stand until whites closest to yolks are just set and opaque, about 3 minutes. If after 3 minutes whites are not set, let stand in water, checking every 30 seconds, until eggs reach desired doneness. (For medium-cooked yolks, let eggs sit in pot, covered, for 4 minutes, then begin checking for doneness.)

5. Using slotted spoon, carefully lift and drain each egg over Dutch oven, then transfer to pot filled with 150-degree water and cover. Return Dutch oven used for cooking eggs to boil and repeat steps 4 and 5 with remaining 4 eggs.

6. Adjust oven rack 6 inches from broiler element and heat broiler. Arrange English muffins, split side up, on baking sheet and broil until golden brown, 2 to 4 minutes. Place 1 slice bacon on each English muffin and broil until beginning to brown, about 1 minute. Remove muffins from oven and transfer to serving plates. Using slotted spoon, carefully lift and drain each egg and lay on top of each English muffin. Spoon hollandaise over top and serve.

SOFT-COOKED EGGS

WHY THIS RECIPE WORKS: Traditional methods for making soft-cooked eggs are hit or miss. We wanted one that delivered a set white and a fluid yolk every time. Calling for fridge-cold eggs and boiling water has two advantages: It reduces temperature variables, which makes the recipe more foolproof, and it provides the steepest temperature gradient, which ensures that the yolk at the center stays fluid while the white cooks through. Using only ½ inch of boiling water instead of several cups to cook the eggs means that the recipe takes less time and energy from start to finish. Because of the curved shape of the eggs, they actually have very little contact with the water so they do not lower the water temperature when they go into the saucepan. This means that you can use the same timing for anywhere from one to six eggs without altering the consistency of the finished product.

Soft-Cooked Eggs

MAKES 4

Be sure to use large eggs that have no cracks and are cold from the refrigerator. Because precise timing is vital to the success of this recipe, we strongly recommend using a digital timer. You can use this method for one to six large, extra-large, or jumbo eggs without altering the timing. If you have one, a steamer basket makes lowering the eggs into the boiling water easier. We recommend serving these eggs in eggcups and with buttered toast for dipping, or you may simply use the dull side of a butter knife to crack the egg along the equator, break the egg in half, and scoop out the insides with a teaspoon.

4 large eggs
Salt and pepper

1. Bring ½ inch water to boil in medium saucepan over medium-high heat. Using tongs, gently place eggs in boiling water (eggs will not be submerged). Cover saucepan and cook eggs for 6½ minutes.

2. Remove cover, transfer saucepan to sink, and place under cold running water for 30 seconds. Remove eggs from pan and serve, seasoning with salt and pepper to taste.

Soft-Cooked Eggs with Salad

SERVES 2

Be sure to run the soft-cooked eggs under cold water for 30 seconds before peeling.

Combine 3 tablespoons olive oil, 1 tablespoon balsamic vinegar, 1 teaspoon Dijon mustard, and 1 teaspoon minced shallot in jar, seal lid, and shake vigorously until emulsified, 20 to 30 seconds. Toss with 5 cups assertively flavored salad greens (arugula, radicchio, watercress, or frisée). Season with salt and pepper to taste, and divide between 2 plates. Top each serving with 2 peeled soft-cooked eggs, split crosswise to release yolks, and season with salt and pepper to taste.

Soft-Cooked Eggs with Sautéed Mushrooms

SERVES 2

Be sure to run the soft-cooked eggs under cold water for 30 seconds before peeling.

Heat 2 tablespoons olive oil in large skillet over medium-high heat until shimmering. Add 12 ounces sliced white or cremini mushrooms and pinch salt and cook, stirring occasionally, until liquid has evaporated and mushrooms are lightly browned, 5 to 6 minutes. Stir in 2 teaspoons chopped fresh herbs (chives, tarragon, parsley, or combination). Season with salt and pepper to taste, and divide between 2 plates. Top each serving with 2 peeled soft-cooked eggs, split crosswise to release yolks, and season with salt and pepper to taste.

Soft-Cooked Eggs with Steamed Asparagus

SERVES 2

Be sure to run the soft-cooked eggs under cold water for 30 seconds before peeling.

Steam 12 ounces asparagus (spears about ½ inch in diameter, trimmed) over medium heat until crisp-tender, 4 to 5 minutes. Divide between 2 plates. Drizzle each serving with 1 tablespoon extra-virgin olive oil and sprinkle each serving with 1 tablespoon grated Parmesan. Season with salt and pepper to taste. Top each serving with 2 peeled soft-cooked eggs, split crosswise to release yolks, and season with salt and pepper to taste.

EGGS PIPERADE

WHY THIS RECIPE WORKS: When serving up eggs piperade for breakfast, one thing is for certain: All diners are in for a healthy serving of flavor-packed vegetables. This Basque dish serves up scrambled eggs in a vibrant sauté of tender bell peppers, onions, and tomatoes—the winning combination we love in ratatouille. We wanted our vegetables to soften but retain their structure, so we kept a close eye on our skillet. We started with the onions; as soon as the pieces began to brown in the hot oil, we brought in the aromatics: minced garlic, minced fresh thyme, paprika, and red pepper flakes. After allowing them to bloom, we introduced the peppers. Using both cubanelle and red bell peppers contributed great color and subtle sweetness. Once the peppers were just softened, coarsely chopped canned tomatoes brought in bright acidity and their juice helped meld the vegetables' flavors as the liquid reduced. Some minced fresh parsley and a touch of sherry vinegar tied the vegetables together before we turned our attention to the eggs. With the peppers and onions waiting on our serving platter, we prepared some lightly seasoned scrambled eggs, folding them in a hot oiled pan until cooked but still slightly wet. We served our sautéed vegetables and perfectly moist eggs with a final sprinkling of parsley.

Eggs Piperade

SERVES 4

We prefer to make this dish with cubanelle peppers, but green peppers can be substituted in a pinch. When serving, the eggs and pepper mixture can be served separately or the eggs can be gently folded into the pepper mixture, which is more traditional.

- 6 tablespoons extra-virgin olive oil
- 1 large onion, cut into ½-inch pieces
- 1 large bay leaf
- Salt and pepper
- 4 garlic cloves, minced
- 1 teaspoon minced fresh thyme
- 2 teaspoons paprika
- ¾ teaspoon red pepper flakes
- 3 red bell peppers (7 to 8 ounces each), stemmed, seeded, and cut into ⅜-inch strips
- 3 cubanelle peppers (3 to 4 ounces each), stemmed, seeded, and cut into ⅜-inch strips
- 1 (14-ounce) can whole peeled tomatoes, drained with ¼ cup juice reserved, chopped coarse
- 3 tablespoons minced fresh parsley
- 2 teaspoons sherry vinegar
- 8 large eggs

1. Heat 3 tablespoons oil in 12-inch nonstick skillet over medium heat until shimmering. Add onion, bay leaf, and ½ teaspoon salt and cook, stirring occasionally, until softened and just starting to brown, about 6 minutes. Add garlic, thyme, paprika, and pepper flakes and cook, stirring occasionally, until fragrant, about 1 minute. Add bell peppers, cubanelle peppers, and 1 teaspoon salt, cover, and cook, stirring occasionally, until peppers begin to soften, about 10 minutes.

2. Remove cover and stir in tomatoes and juice. Reduce heat to medium-low and cook, uncovered, stirring occasionally, until mixture appears dry and peppers are tender but not mushy, 10 to 12 minutes. Discard bay leaf; stir in 2 tablespoons parsley and vinegar. Season with salt and pepper to taste. Transfer pepper mixture to serving dish. Wipe out skillet with paper towels.

3. While pepper mixture cooks, beat eggs, 2 tablespoons oil, ½ teaspoon salt, and ¼ teaspoon pepper with fork until eggs are thoroughly combined and color is pure yellow.

4. Return now-empty skillet to medium-high heat, add remaining 1 tablespoon oil and heat until shimmering. Add egg mixture and, using rubber spatula, constantly and firmly scrape along bottom and sides of skillet until eggs begin to clump and spatula just leaves trail on bottom of pan, 30 to 60 seconds. Reduce heat to low and gently but constantly fold eggs until clumped and just slightly wet, 30 to 60 seconds. Immediately transfer eggs to serving dish with pepper mixture, sprinkle with remaining 1 tablespoon parsley, and serve.

BEHIND THE SCENES

HELP! MY RECIPE DOESN'T WORK!

It happens—even in America's Test Kitchen. Once in a while, we get a call from a viewer or reader that a recipe isn't working for them. And every time, our hearts sink. What did we do wrong? We not only test our recipes very carefully (as many as 100 times), but we also have our recipes vetted by a professional cook, and THEN we send them out to home cooks to test-drive our recipes. So why do recipes sometimes fail? The answers fall into three broad categories: substitutions, flawed equipment, or ingredient variables.

Substitutions are common (everyone does it), but if you decide to replace a key ingredient or piece of equipment, all bets are off. If you're on a diet, don't try making our crème brûlée with milk rather than cream. And don't sear four steaks in a 10-inch skillet when the recipe calls for a 12-inch pan—that is, unless you want them to taste steamed and bland. Our advice: Make the recipe once as it's written, then improvise.

Flawed equipment is harder to predict and control. Many home ovens are not properly calibrated and an oven that runs hot by 50 degrees (which is fairly common in home kitchens) will ruin many recipes. Always, always pay attention to the visual cues in our recipes, not the clock. And invest in an oven thermometer. It's cheap and will save you much frustration when cooking.

Ingredient variables are the hardest thing for us (or you) to control. Produce varies in sweetness and moisture content. The same cut of meat can have more or less fat. And brands of manufactured products are not all the same. In fact, we had trouble with a chocolate frosting recipe several years ago and realized that our recipe worked with the test kitchen's top-rated bittersweet chocolate (with 60 percent cacao) but failed when readers tried to use gourmet brands with a higher cacao content. We test all of our recipes with the ingredients that have won our blind taste tests (see pages 904 through 927). We suggest you do the same. Not only will your food taste better, but sometimes choosing the right brand can make the difference between a successful recipe and a failed one.

HOME FRIES

WHY THIS RECIPE WORKS: Whether made at home or eaten out, home fries frequently suffer from the same problems: greasy or undercooked potatoes, and bland or too-spicy flavors. We wanted a recipe that produced potatoes with a crisp crust and a tender interior. We determined that medium-starch Yukon Golds remained moist even when crisped on the outside. Attempts to cook raw diced potato in the skillet ended in failure; precooking was the way to go. We tried baking, boiling, and dicing the potatoes before frying them, but they overcooked. What finally worked was parcooking the potatoes—placing them in water and bringing them just to a boil, then immediately draining them before frying. This gave the interior of the potatoes a head start in the cooking process, but they weren't in the water long enough to absorb much liquid. The result: firm cubes of potato with crisp, browned exteriors. A combination of butter and oil worked best for frying. Onion was the perfect foil for these potatoes; we cooked it in the skillet before adding the potatoes.

Diner-Style Home Fries

SERVES 2 TO 3

If doubling this recipe, cook two batches of home fries separately. While making the second batch, keep the first batch hot and crisp by spreading the fries on a baking sheet placed in a 300-degree oven.

- 2½ tablespoons corn oil or peanut oil
- 1 medium onion, minced
- 1 pound (2 medium) Yukon Gold potatoes, scrubbed and cut into ½-inch cubes
- Table salt
- 1 tablespoon unsalted butter
- 1 teaspoon paprika (optional)
- 1 tablespoon minced fresh parsley leaves (optional)
- Ground black pepper

1. Heat 1 tablespoon of the oil in a 12-inch skillet over medium-high heat until shimmering. Add the onion and cook, stirring frequently, until browned, 8 to 10 minutes. Transfer the onion to a small bowl and set aside.

2. Meanwhile, place the potatoes in a large saucepan, cover with ½ inch of water, add 1 teaspoon salt, and bring to a boil over high heat. As soon as the water begins to boil, drain the potatoes thoroughly in a colander.

3. Heat the butter and the remaining 1½ tablespoons oil in the now-empty skillet over medium-high heat. Add the potatoes and shake the skillet to evenly distribute the potatoes in a single layer, making sure that one side of each piece is touching the surface of the skillet. Cook without stirring until one side of the potatoes is golden brown, 4 to 5 minutes, then carefully turn the potatoes, making sure the potatoes remain in a single layer. Repeat the process until the potatoes are tender and browned on most sides, turning three or four times, 10 to 15 minutes longer. Add the onions, paprika (if using), parsley (if using), ¼ teaspoon salt, and pepper to taste; serve.

surface moisture has evaporated, about 2 minutes. Remove from heat. Add butter, 1½ teaspoons salt, and cayenne; mix with rubber spatula until potatoes are coated with thick, starchy paste, about 30 seconds.

3. Remove baking sheet from oven and drizzle with 2 tablespoons oil. Transfer potatoes to baking sheet and spread into even layer. Roast for 15 minutes. While potatoes roast, combine onions, remaining 1 tablespoon oil, and ½ teaspoon salt in bowl.

4. Remove baking sheet from oven. Using thin, sharp metal spatula, scrape and turn potatoes. Clear about 8 by 5-inch space in center of baking sheet and add onion mixture. Roast for 15 minutes.

5. Scrape and turn again, mixing onions into potatoes. Continue to roast until potatoes are well browned and onions are softened and beginning to brown, 5 to 10 minutes. Stir in chives and season with salt and pepper to taste. Serve immediately.

HOME FRIES FOR A CROWD

WHY THIS RECIPE WORKS: Making home fries the traditional way requires constant monitoring while standing over a hot skillet, after which you get only three servings at most. We wanted a quicker, more hands-off method for making a larger amount. To speed things up, we developed a hybrid cooking technique: First, we parboiled diced russet potatoes, and then we coated them in oil and cooked them in a very hot oven. We discovered that boiling the potatoes with baking soda quickly broke down their exterior while leaving their insides nearly raw, ensuring home fries with a crisp, brown crust and a moist, fluffy interior. We added diced onions in the last 20 minutes of oven time and finished the home fries with chives to reinforce the onion flavor.

Home Fries for a Crowd

SERVES 6 TO 8

Don't skip the baking soda in this recipe. It's critical for home fries with just the right crisp texture.

- 3½ pounds russet potatoes, peeled and cut into ¾-inch dice
- ½ teaspoon baking soda
- 3 tablespoons unsalted butter, cut into 12 pieces
- Kosher salt and pepper
- Pinch cayenne pepper
- 3 tablespoons vegetable oil
- 2 onions, cut into ½-inch dice
- 3 tablespoons minced chives

1. Adjust oven rack to lowest position, place rimmed baking sheet on rack, and heat oven to 500 degrees.

2. Bring 10 cups water to boil in Dutch oven over high heat. Add potatoes and baking soda. Return to boil and cook for 1 minute. Drain potatoes. Return potatoes to Dutch oven and place over low heat. Cook, shaking pot occasionally, until any

BACON

WHY THIS RECIPE WORKS: A couple strips of crisp bacon are always a welcome accompaniment to a plate of eggs, but bacon requires frequent monitoring when cooked on the stovetop. The microwave produces unevenly cooked and flavorless strips, so we looked to the oven for an easier way. Bacon renders its fat while cooking, so it was important to choose a pan that would contain it; a rimmed baking sheet worked just fine, and it enabled us to cook more strips at the same time. We didn't have to turn the bacon because the heat of the oven cooked it evenly, though rotating the baking sheet front to back halfway through ensured even cooking. In comparison to the results from stovetop frying, bacon cooked in the oven wasn't quite as crisp, but it was certainly crisp enough, and it had the same great meaty flavor. Although preheating the oven and draining the bacon after cooking takes a little extra time, the payoff is that you don't have to stand at the stove while the bacon is in the oven.

Oven-Fried Bacon

SERVES 4 TO 6

A large rimmed baking sheet is important here to contain the rendered bacon fat. If cooking more than one tray of bacon, switch their oven positions once about halfway through cooking. You can use thin- or thick-cut bacon here, though the cooking times will vary.

- 12 slices bacon (see note)

Adjust an oven rack to the middle position and heat the oven to 400 degrees. Arrange the bacon slices on a rimmed baking sheet. Cook until the fat begins to render, 5 to 6 minutes; rotate the pan. Continue cooking until the bacon is crisp and browned, 5 to 6 minutes longer for thin-cut bacon, 8 to 10 minutes for thick-cut. Transfer the bacon to a paper towel–lined plate, drain, and serve.

BAKED EGGS FLORENTINE

WHY THIS RECIPE WORKS: Baked eggs can be hard to get right. We wanted a creamy, slightly runny yolk and a tender white—in the same ramekin. The answer turned out to be insulation—that is, adding a spinach cream sauce to provide a barrier between the egg and the very hot sides of the ramekin. We also found that pulling the eggs from the oven before they were done and allowing carryover cooking to finish the job, delivered first-rate baked eggs.

Baked Eggs Florentine

SERVES 6

For the eggs to cook properly, it is imperative to add them to the hot, filling-lined ramekins quickly. Prepare by cracking eggs into separate bowls or teacups while the filled ramekins are heating. Use 6-ounce ramekins with 3¼-inch diameters, measured from the inner lip. We developed this recipe using a glass baking dish; if using a metal baking pan, reduce the oven temperature to 425 degrees. This recipe can be doubled and baked in two 13 by 9-inch dishes. If doubling, increase the baking times in steps 3 and 4 by 1 minute.

- 2 tablespoons unsalted butter
- 1 large shallot, minced
- 1 tablespoon all-purpose flour
- ¾ cup half-and-half
- 10 ounces frozen spinach, thawed and squeezed dry
- 2 ounces Parmesan cheese, grated (1 cup)
- Salt and pepper
- ⅛ teaspoon dry mustard
- ⅛ teaspoon ground nutmeg
- Pinch cayenne pepper
- Vegetable oil spray
- 6 large eggs

1. Adjust oven rack to middle position and heat oven to 500 degrees.

2. Melt butter in medium saucepan over medium heat. Add shallot and cook, stirring occasionally, until softened, about 3 minutes. Stir in flour and cook, stirring constantly, for 1 minute. Gradually whisk in half-and-half; bring mixture to boil, whisking constantly. Simmer, whisking frequently, until thickened, 2 to 3 minutes. Remove pan from heat and stir in spinach, Parmesan, ¾ teaspoon salt, ½ teaspoon pepper, mustard, nutmeg, and cayenne.

3. Lightly spray six 6-ounce ramekins with oil spray. Evenly divide spinach filling among ramekins. Using back of spoon, push filling 1 inch up sides of ramekins, making shallow indentation in center of filling large enough to hold egg. Place filled ramekins in 13 by 9-inch glass baking dish. Bake ramekins until filling just starts to brown, about 7 minutes, rotating dish halfway through baking.

4. While filling is heating, crack eggs (taking care not to break yolks) into individual cups or bowls. Remove baking dish with ramekins from oven and place on wire rack. Gently pour eggs from cups into hot ramekins, centering yolk in filling. Lightly spray surface of each egg with oil spray and sprinkle each with pinch of salt. Return baking dish to oven and bake until whites are just opaque but still tremble, 6 to 8 minutes, rotating dish halfway through baking.

5. Remove dish from oven and, using tongs, transfer ramekins to wire rack. Let stand until whites are firm and set (yolks should still be runny), about 10 minutes. Serve immediately.

TO MAKE AHEAD: Follow recipe through step 3, skipping step of baking lined ramekins. Wrap ramekins with plastic wrap and refrigerate for up to 3 days. To serve, heat lined ramekins, directly from refrigerator, for additional 3 to 4 minutes (10 to 11 minutes total) before proceeding with recipe.

Baked Eggs Lorraine

Wash 1 pound leeks and slice white and light green parts thin. Cook 2 slices bacon cut into ½-inch pieces in medium saucepan over medium heat until crisp, about 10 minutes. Transfer bacon to paper towel–lined plate. Add leeks and cook until softened, about 10 minutes. Transfer leeks to plate with bacon. Proceed with recipe, omitting shallot and reducing butter to 1 tablespoon. Substitute bacon and leek mixture for spinach and ½ cup shredded Gruyère cheese for Parmesan.

FLUFFY OMELETS

WHY THIS RECIPE WORKS: A different breed than French-style rolled omelets or diner-style omelets folded into half-moons, fluffy omelets are made by baking whipped eggs in a skillet until they rise above the lip of the pan. We love their impressive height and delicate texture. But most recipes result in oozing soufflés or dry, bouncy rounds—or eggs that barely puff up at all. To give our omelet lofty height without making it tough, we folded butter-enriched yolks into stiffly whipped whites stabilized with cream of tartar. The whipped whites gave the omelet great lift while the yolks and butter kept it tender and rich-tasting. We chose light but flavorful fillings that satisfied without weighing down the omelet.

Fluffy Omelets

SERVES 2

A teaspoon of white vinegar or lemon juice can be used in place of the cream of tartar, and a hand-held mixer or a whisk can be used in place of a stand mixer. We recommend using the fillings that accompany this recipe; they are designed not to interfere with the cooking of the omelet.

- 4 large eggs, separated
- 1 tablespoon unsalted butter, melted, plus 1 tablespoon unsalted butter
- ¼ teaspoon salt
- ¼ teaspoon cream of tartar
- 1 recipe filling (recipes follow)
- 1 ounce Parmesan cheese, grated (½ cup)

1. Adjust oven rack to middle position and heat oven to 375 degrees. Whisk egg yolks, melted butter, and salt together in bowl. Place egg whites in bowl of stand mixer and sprinkle cream of tartar over surface. Fit stand mixer with whisk and whip egg whites on medium-low speed until foamy, 2 to 2½ minutes. Increase speed to medium-high and whip until stiff peaks just start to form, 2 to 3 minutes. Fold egg yolk mixture into egg whites until no white streaks remain.

2. Heat remaining 1 tablespoon butter in 12-inch ovensafe nonstick skillet over medium-high heat, swirling to coat bottom of pan. When butter foams, quickly add egg mixture, spreading into even layer with spatula. Remove pan from heat and gently sprinkle filling and Parmesan evenly over top of omelet. Transfer to oven and cook until center of omelet springs back when lightly pressed, 4½ minutes for slightly wet omelet and 5 minutes for dry omelet.

3. Run spatula around edges of omelet to loosen, shaking gently to release. Slide omelet onto cutting board and let stand for 30 seconds. Using spatula, fold omelet in half. Cut omelet in half crosswise and serve immediately.

Asparagus and Smoked Salmon Filling

MAKES ¾ CUP

- 1 teaspoon olive oil
- 1 shallot, sliced thin
- 5 ounces asparagus, trimmed and cut on bias into ¼-inch lengths
- Salt and pepper
- 1 ounce smoked salmon, chopped
- ½ teaspoon lemon juice

Heat oil in 12-inch nonstick skillet over medium-high heat until shimmering. Add shallot and cook until softened and starting to brown, about 2 minutes. Add asparagus, pinch salt, and pepper to taste, and cook, stirring frequently, until crisp-tender, 5 to 7 minutes. Transfer asparagus mixture to bowl and stir in salmon and lemon juice.

Mushroom Filling

MAKES ¾ CUP

- 1 teaspoon olive oil
- 1 shallot, sliced thin
- 4 ounces white or cremini mushrooms, trimmed and chopped
- Salt and pepper
- 1 teaspoon balsamic vinegar

Heat oil in 12-inch nonstick skillet over medium-high heat until shimmering. Add shallot and cook until softened and starting to brown, about 2 minutes. Add mushrooms, ⅛ teaspoon salt, and season with pepper to taste. Cook until liquid has evaporated and mushrooms begin to brown, 6 to 8 minutes. Transfer mixture to bowl and stir in vinegar.

Artichoke and Bacon Filling

MAKES ¾ CUP

- 2 slices bacon, cut into ¼-inch pieces
- 1 shallot, sliced thin
- 5 ounces frozen artichoke hearts, thawed, patted dry, and chopped
- Salt and pepper
- ½ teaspoon lemon juice

Cook bacon in 12-inch nonstick skillet over medium-high heat until crisp, 3 to 6 minutes. Using slotted spoon, transfer bacon to paper towel–lined plate. Pour off all but 1 teaspoon fat from skillet. Add shallot and cook until softened and starting to brown, about 2 minutes. Add artichokes, ⅛ teaspoon salt, and pepper to taste. Cook, stirring frequently, until artichokes begin to brown, 6 to 8 minutes. Transfer artichoke mixture to bowl and stir in bacon and lemon juice.

FAMILY-SIZE OMELET

WHY THIS RECIPE WORKS: An omelet is a great breakfast or brunch dish, but cooking omelets one at a time for more than a couple of people is just not practical. We wanted to find a way to make an omelet that was big enough to serve four people. We wanted it to have tender, not rubbery, eggs and a rich, cheesy filling.

Flipping a huge eight-egg omelet was clearly not going to work, so we had to find a way to cook the top of the omelet as well as the bottom. Cooking the eggs longer over lower heat resulted in an unpleasant texture. Broiling to cook the top of the eggs worked, but it dried out the omelet, and we wanted it to be creamy. Then we had the idea of covering the pan after the bottom of the eggs was set but the top was still runny, which worked like a charm. The lid trapped the heat and moisture to steam the top of the omelet, and it partially melted the cheese as well. Now we had a perfectly cooked omelet for four, with tender eggs and bits of melted cheese in every bite.

Family-Size Cheese Omelet

SERVES 4

Monterey Jack, Colby, or any other good melting cheese can be substituted for the cheddar.

- 8 large eggs
- ½ teaspoon table salt
- ⅛ teaspoon ground black pepper
- 2 tablespoons unsalted butter
- 3 ounces cheddar cheese, shredded (about ¾ cup; see note)

1. Whisk the eggs, salt, and pepper together in a medium bowl. Melt the butter in a 12-inch nonstick skillet over medium heat, swirling to coat the pan.

2. Add the eggs and cook, stirring gently in a circular motion, until the mixture is slightly thickened, about 1 minute. Following the photos, use a heatproof rubber spatula to pull the cooked edges of the egg toward the center of the pan, tilting the pan so the uncooked egg runs to the cleared edge of the pan. Repeat until the bottom of the omelet is just set but the top is still runny, about 1 minute. Cover the skillet, reduce the heat to low, and cook until the top of the omelet begins to set but is still moist, about 5 minutes.

3. Remove the pan from the heat. Sprinkle the cheddar evenly over the eggs, cover, and let sit until the cheese partially melts, about 1 minute. Slide half of the omelet onto a warmed platter using the spatula, then tilt the skillet so the remaining omelet flips over onto itself, forming a half-moon shape. Cut into wedges and serve.

NOTES FROM THE TEST KITCHEN

HOW TO MAKE AN OVERSIZED OMELET

1. Pull the cooked edges of the egg toward the center of the pan and allow the raw egg to run to the edges.

2. When the omelet is set on the bottom but still very runny on the top, cover the skillet and reduce the heat to low.

3. After the top of the omelet begins to set, sprinkle with the cheese and let the omelet rest off the heat, covered, until the cheese has partially melted.

4. After using a heatproof rubber spatula to slide half of the omelet out onto a platter, tilt the skillet so that the omelet folds over onto itself to make the traditional half-moon shape.

DENVER OMELETS

WHY THIS RECIPE WORKS: A substantial Denver omelet has become a breakfast feature in American restaurants and diners. Filled with ham and lots of vegetables in addition to cheese, it's a meal in itself. But it's hard to get the vegetables cooked without overcooking the eggs.

Cooking the filling separately, before the eggs, seemed to be the best way to avoid undercooked vegetables. In addition to the standard onion and green bell pepper, we also included red bell pepper, which made for a more colorful filling. Instead of julienning the vegetables, we finely chopped them; this made our filling easier to eat, and the peppers' skin was less intrusive. Ham steak was the easiest kind of ham to dice; it also imparted a welcome smoky flavor to the rest of the filling. For more complexity of flavor, we included garlic and parsley, which are unusual in a Denver omelet, and a dash of hot sauce livened things up without adding too much spiciness. We cooked the eggs according to our tried-and-true method, with some dairy (we used a little heavy cream, but milk worked as well) to keep the eggs from drying out, and added the warm filling just before folding the omelet onto a plate. Both components—eggs and filling—were perfectly cooked.

Denver Omelets

SERVES 2

You can make one omelet after another in the same pan, although you may need to reduce the heat. Refer to the photos for "How to Make an Oversized Omelet" on page 640—the steps are similar to the ones used here.

- 6 large eggs
- 2 tablespoons heavy cream or milk
- ½ teaspoon table salt
- ¼ teaspoon ground black pepper
- 2 tablespoons unsalted butter
- 4 ounces Monterey Jack cheese, shredded (about 1 cup)
- 1 recipe Filling for Denver Omelets (recipe follows)

1. Whisk together 3 of the eggs, 1 tablespoon of the cream, ¼ teaspoon of the salt, and ⅛ teaspoon of the pepper in a small bowl until thoroughly combined.

2. Melt 1 tablespoon of the butter in a 10-inch nonstick skillet over medium-high heat until it just begins to brown, swirling to coat the pan. Add the eggs to the skillet and cook until the edges begin to set, 2 to 3 seconds, then, with a heat-proof rubber spatula, stir in a circular motion until slightly thickened, about 10 seconds. Use the spatula to pull the cooked edges into the center, then tilt the pan to one side so that the uncooked egg runs to the edge of the pan. Repeat until the omelet is just set but still moist on the surface, 1 to 2 minutes.

3. Sprinkle ½ cup of the cheese evenly over the eggs and allow to partially melt, 15 to 20 seconds. With the handle of the pan facing you, spoon half the filling over the left side of the omelet. Following step 4 on page 640, slide the filling-topped half of the omelet onto a warmed plate using the spatula, then tilt the skillet so the remaining omelet folds over the filling in a half-moon shape; set aside. Repeat the instructions for the second omelet. Serve.

Filling for Denver Omelets

MAKES ENOUGH TO FILL 2 OMELETS

A ham steak is our top choice for this recipe, although canned ham and sliced deli ham will work. (If using sliced deli ham, add it with the garlic, parsley, and hot sauce.)

- 1 tablespoon unsalted butter
- ½ red bell pepper, stemmed, seeded, and chopped fine
- ½ green bell pepper, stemmed, seeded, and chopped fine
- 1 small onion, minced
- ¼ teaspoon table salt
- 4 ounces ham steak, diced (about 1 cup; see note)
- 1 tablespoon minced fresh parsley leaves
- 1 garlic clove, minced or pressed through a garlic press (about 1 teaspoon)
- ½ teaspoon hot sauce

Melt the butter in a 10-inch nonstick skillet over medium-high heat. Add the peppers, onion, and salt and cook, stirring occasionally, until the onion begins to soften, 5 to 7 minutes. Add the ham and cook until the peppers begin to brown, about 2 minutes. Add the parsley, garlic, and hot sauce and cook for 30 seconds. Transfer to a small bowl and cover to keep warm.

FRENCH OMELETS

WHY THIS RECIPE WORKS: In contrast to half-moon diner-style omelets, the French omelet is a pristine rolled affair. The temperature of the pan must be just right, the eggs beaten just so, and hand movements must be swift. We decided to ditch the stuffy attitude and come up with a foolproof method for making the ideal French omelet—unblemished golden yellow with an ultra-creamy texture, rolled around minimal filling.

The classic method requires a black carbon steel omelet pan and a fork, but a nonstick skillet worked fine here. Instead of a fork, which scraped our nonstick pans, bamboo skewers and wooden chopsticks gave us small curds with a silky texture. Preheating the pan for 10 minutes over low heat eliminated any hot spots. For creaminess, we added very cold butter, which dispersed evenly and fused with the eggs for a moist, rich omelet. To keep the omelet light, we found the perfect number of strokes; excessive beating unravels egg proteins, leading to denseness. We tried different heat levels, but even at medium heat, the omelet cooked so quickly it was hard to judge when it was done, so we turned off the heat when it was still runny and covered it to finish cooking. Finally, for an easy rolling method, we slid the omelet onto a paper towel and used the towel to roll the omelet into the sought-after cylinder.

French Omelets

SERVES 2

Because making these omelets is such a quick process, make sure to have all your ingredients and equipment at the ready. If you don't have skewers or chopsticks to stir the eggs in step 3, use the handle of a wooden spoon. Warm the plates in a 200-degree oven.

- 2 tablespoons unsalted butter, cut into 2 pieces
- ½ teaspoon vegetable oil
- 6 large eggs, chilled
- Table salt and ground black pepper
- 2 tablespoons shredded Gruyère cheese
- 4 teaspoons minced fresh chives

1. Cut 1 tablespoon of the butter in half. Cut the remaining 1 tablespoon butter into small pieces, transfer to a small bowl, and place in the freezer while preparing the eggs and the skillet, at least 10 minutes. Meanwhile, heat the oil in an 8-inch nonstick skillet over low heat for 10 minutes.

2. Crack 2 of the eggs into a medium bowl and separate a third egg; reserve the white for another use and add the yolk to the bowl. Add ⅛ teaspoon salt and a pinch of pepper. Break the yolks with a fork, then beat the eggs at a moderate pace, about 80 strokes, until the yolks and whites are well combined. Stir in half of the frozen butter cubes.

3. When the skillet is fully heated, use paper towels to wipe out the oil, leaving a thin film on the bottom and sides of the skillet. Add half of the reserved 1 tablespoon butter to the skillet and heat until melted. Swirl the butter to coat the skillet, add the egg mixture, and increase the heat to medium-high. Following the photos, use two chopsticks or wooden skewers to scramble the eggs using a quick circular motion to move around the skillet, scraping the cooked egg from the side of the skillet as you go, until the eggs are almost cooked but still slightly runny, 45 to 90 seconds. Turn off the heat (remove the skillet from the heat if using an electric burner) and smooth the eggs into an even layer using a heatproof rubber spatula. Sprinkle the omelet with 1 tablespoon of the Gruyère and 2 teaspoons of the chives. Cover the skillet with a tight-fitting lid and let sit, 1 minute for a runnier omelet and 2 minutes for a firmer omelet.

4. Heat the skillet over low heat for 20 seconds, uncover, and, using a heatproof rubber spatula, loosen the edges of the omelet from the skillet. Place a folded square of paper towel onto a warmed plate and slide the omelet out of the skillet onto the paper towel so that the omelet lies flat on the plate and hangs about 1 inch off the paper towel. Roll the omelet into a neat cylinder and set aside. Return the skillet to low heat and heat for 2 minutes before repeating the instructions for the second omelet starting with step 2. Serve.

NOTES FROM THE TEST KITCHEN

MAKING A FRENCH OMELET

1. Add the beaten egg mixture to the skillet and stir with chopsticks to produce small curds, which result in a silkier texture.

2. Turn off the heat while the eggs are still runny; smooth with a spatula into an even layer.

3. After sprinkling with the cheese and chives, cover so the residual heat gently finishes cooking the omelet.

4. Slide the finished omelet onto a paper towel–lined plate. Use the paper towel to lift the omelet and roll it up.

SPANISH TORTILLA

WHY THIS RECIPE WORKS: This classic Spanish omelet is immensely appealing, but can be greasy, dense, and heavy if prepared incorrectly. Typical recipes call for up to 4 cups of extra-virgin olive oil to cook the potatoes, which can lead to an overly oily—and expensive—tortilla. We wanted an intensely rich, velvety, melt-in-your-mouth egg-and-potato omelet—that didn't require using a quart of oil.

We first stuck with the traditional volume of olive oil until we could determine the proper type and ratio of ingredients. We chose starchy russet potatoes, thinly sliced, and standard yellow onions, which had a sweet, mellow flavor. We also settled on the perfect ratio of eggs to potatoes that allowed the tortilla to set firm and tender, with the eggs and potatoes melding into one another. Next we set out to reduce the amount of oil. Unfortunately, with less oil in the pan, half the potatoes were frying, while the other half were steaming. We started over with slightly firmer, less starchy Yukon Golds. With a fraction of the oil in the skillet, they were a winner: starchy enough to become meltingly tender as they cooked, but sturdy enough to stir and flip halfway through cooking with few breaks. Finally, we had to determine the best way to flip the omelet. To do this, we simply slid the tortilla out of the pan and onto one plate. Then, placing another plate upside down over the tortilla, we easily flipped the whole thing and slid the tortilla back in the pan, making a once-messy task easy and foolproof.

Spanish Tortilla with Roasted Red Peppers and Peas

SERVES 4 TO 6

Spanish tortillas are often served warm or at room temperature with olives, pickles, and Garlic Mayonnaise (recipe follows) as an appetizer. They may also be served with a salad as a light entrée. For the most traditional tortilla, omit the roasted red peppers and peas. See page 916 for our top-rated extra-virgin olive oil.

- 6 tablespoons plus 1 teaspoon extra-virgin olive oil (see note)
- 1½ pounds (3 to 4 medium) Yukon Gold potatoes, peeled, quartered, and cut into ⅛-inch-thick slices
- 1 small onion, halved and sliced thin
- 1 teaspoon table salt
- ¼ teaspoon ground black pepper
- 8 large eggs
- ½ cup jarred roasted red peppers, rinsed, dried, and cut into ½-inch pieces
- ½ cup frozen peas, thawed
- Garlic Mayonnaise (optional; recipe follows)

1. Toss 4 tablespoons of the oil, the potatoes, onion, ½ teaspoon of the salt, and the pepper in a large bowl until the potato slices are thoroughly separated and coated in oil. Heat 2 tablespoons more oil in a 10-inch nonstick skillet over medium-high heat until shimmering. Reduce the heat to medium-low, add the potato mixture to the skillet, and set the bowl aside (do not rinse). Cover and cook, stirring occasionally with a heatproof rubber spatula, until the potatoes offer no resistance when poked with a paring knife, 22 to 28 minutes (some potato slices may break into smaller pieces).

2. Meanwhile, whisk the eggs and remaining ½ teaspoon salt in the reserved bowl until just combined. Using a heatproof rubber spatula, fold the hot potato mixture, red peppers, and peas into the eggs until combined, making sure to scrape all the potato mixture out of the skillet. Return the skillet to medium-high heat, add the remaining 1 teaspoon oil, and heat until just beginning to smoke. Add the egg-potato mixture and cook, shaking the pan and folding the mixture constantly for 15 seconds; smooth the top of the mixture with a heatproof rubber spatula. Reduce the heat to medium, cover, and cook, gently shaking the pan every 30 seconds, until the bottom is golden brown and the top is lightly set, about 2 minutes.

3. Using a heatproof rubber spatula, loosen the tortilla from the pan, shaking it back and forth until the tortilla slides around. Slide the tortilla onto a large plate. Invert the tortilla onto a second large plate and slide it, browned side up, back into the skillet. Tuck the edges of the tortilla into the skillet. Return the pan to medium heat and continue to cook, gently shaking the pan every 30 seconds, until the second side is golden brown, about 2 minutes longer. Slide the tortilla onto a cutting board; cool for at least 15 minutes. Cut the tortilla into cubes or wedges and serve with Garlic Mayonnaise (if using).

Spanish Tortilla with Chorizo and Scallions

Use a cured, Spanish-style chorizo for this recipe. Portuguese linguiça is a suitable substitute.

Follow the recipe for Spanish Tortilla with Roasted Red Peppers and Peas, omitting the roasted red peppers and peas. In step 1, heat 4 ounces Spanish-style chorizo, cut into ¼-inch pieces, with 1 tablespoon oil (reduced from 2 tablespoons) in a 10-inch nonstick skillet over medium-high heat, stirring occasionally, until the chorizo is browned and the fat has rendered, about 5 minutes. Proceed with the recipe as directed, adding the potato mixture to the skillet with the chorizo and rendered fat and folding 4 thinly sliced scallions into the eggs in step 2.

Garlic Mayonnaise

MAKES ABOUT 1¼ CUPS

- 2 large egg yolks
- 2 teaspoons Dijon mustard
- 2 teaspoons juice from 1 lemon
- 1 medium garlic clove, minced or pressed through a garlic press (about 1 teaspoon)
- ¾ cup vegetable oil
- 1 tablespoon water
- ¼ cup extra-virgin olive oil
- ½ teaspoon table salt
- ¼ teaspoon ground black pepper

Process the yolks, mustard, lemon juice, and garlic in a food processor until combined, about 10 seconds. With the machine running, slowly drizzle in the vegetable oil, about 1 minute. Transfer the mixture to a medium bowl and whisk in the water. Whisking constantly, slowly drizzle in the olive oil, about 30 seconds. Whisk in the salt and pepper. (The mayonnaise can be refrigerated in an airtight container for up to 4 days.)

THICK AND HEARTY FRITTATAS

WHY THIS RECIPE WORKS: A frittata loaded with meat and vegetables often ends up dry, overstuffed, and overcooked. We wanted a frittata big enough to make a substantial meal for 6 to 8 people—with a pleasing balance of egg to filling, firm yet moist eggs, and a lightly browned crust. We started with a dozen eggs, which we found required 3 cups of cooked vegetables and meat to create the best balance. When we chose our fillings, we needed to be a little selective about the cheese—Gruyère and goat cheese both had just the right amount of moisture. Most any vegetable or meat can be added to a frittata, with two caveats: The food must be cut into small pieces, and it must be precooked to drive off excess moisture and fat. A little half-and-half added a touch of creaminess. Given the large number of eggs, we had to shorten the time the frittata spent on the stovetop so the bottom wouldn't scorch. We started the eggs on medium heat and stirred them so they could cook quickly yet evenly. With the eggs still on the wet side, we slid the skillet under the broiler until the top had puffed and browned, but removed it while the eggs in the center were still slightly wet and runny, allowing the residual heat to finish the cooking.

Asparagus, Ham, and Gruyère Frittata

SERVES 6 TO 8

A 12-inch ovensafe nonstick skillet is necessary for this recipe. Because broilers vary so much in intensity, watch the frittata carefully as it cooks.

- 12 large eggs
- 3 tablespoons half-and-half
- ½ teaspoon table salt
- ¼ teaspoon ground black pepper
- 2 teaspoons olive oil
- 8 ounces asparagus, tough ends trimmed, spears cut on the bias into ¼-inch pieces
- 4 ounces ¼-inch-thick deli ham, cut into ½-inch cubes (about ¾ cup)
- 1 medium shallot, minced (about 3 tablespoons)
- 3 ounces Gruyère cheese, cut into ¼-inch cubes (about ¾ cup)

1. Adjust an oven rack about 5 inches from the broiler element and heat the broiler. Whisk the eggs, half-and-half, salt, and pepper together in a medium bowl. Set aside.

2. Heat the oil in a 12-inch ovensafe nonstick skillet over medium heat until shimmering; add the asparagus and cook, stirring occasionally, until lightly browned and almost tender, about 3 minutes. Add the ham and shallot and cook until the shallot softens, about 2 minutes.

3. Stir the Gruyère into the eggs; add the egg mixture to the skillet and cook, using a heatproof rubber spatula to stir and scrape the bottom of the skillet, until large curds form and the spatula begins to leave a wake but the eggs are still very wet, about 2 minutes. Shake the skillet to distribute the eggs evenly and cook without stirring to let the bottom set, about 30 seconds.

4. Slide the skillet under the broiler and cook until the surface is puffed and spotty brown, yet the center remains slightly wet and runny when cut into with a paring knife, 3 to 4 minutes. Using a potholder (the skillet handle will be hot), remove the skillet from the oven and let stand for 5 minutes to finish cooking; using the spatula, loosen the frittata from the skillet and slide it onto a platter or cutting board. Cut into wedges and serve.

Leek, Prosciutto, and Goat Cheese Frittata

SERVES 6 TO 8

A 12-inch ovensafe nonstick skillet is necessary for this recipe. The goat cheese will crumble more easily if it is chilled.

- 12 large eggs
- 3 tablespoons half-and-half
- Table salt and ground black pepper
- 2 tablespoons unsalted butter
- 2 small leeks, white and light green parts only, halved lengthwise, sliced thin, and rinsed thoroughly (about 3 cups)
- 3 ounces very thinly sliced prosciutto, cut into ½-inch-wide strips
- ¼ cup chopped fresh basil leaves
- 4 ounces goat cheese, crumbled (about 1 cup; see note)

1. Adjust an oven rack about 5 inches from the broiler element and heat the broiler. Whisk the eggs, half-and-half, 1/2 teaspoon salt, and 1/4 teaspoon pepper together in a medium bowl. Set aside.

2. Melt the butter in a 12-inch ovensafe nonstick skillet over medium heat. Add the leeks and ¼ teaspoon salt; reduce the heat to low and cook, covered, stirring occasionally, until softened, 8 to 10 minutes.

3. Stir the prosciutto, basil, and ½ cup of the goat cheese into the eggs; add the egg mixture to the skillet and cook, using a heatproof rubber spatula to stir and scrape the bottom of the skillet, until large curds form and the spatula begins to leave a wake but the eggs are still very wet, about 2 minutes. Shake the skillet to distribute the eggs evenly and cook without stirring to let the bottom set, about 30 seconds.

4. Distribute the remaining ½ cup goat cheese evenly over the frittata. Slide the skillet under the broiler and cook until the surface is puffed and spotty brown, yet the center remains slightly wet and runny when cut into with a paring knife, 3 to 4 minutes. Using a potholder (the skillet handle will be hot), remove the skillet from the oven and let stand for 5 minutes to finish cooking; using the spatula, loosen the frittata from the skillet and slide it onto a platter or cutting board. Cut into wedges and serve.

QUICHE

WHY THIS RECIPE WORKS: A really good quiche should have a smooth, creamy custard in a tender pastry crust. The custard should be rich, but not overwhelmingly so, and moist, not dried out. We aimed to find a way to make this perfect pie.

We experimented with multiple combinations of egg and dairy to find the one that would provide just the right balance of richness and lightness. Eggs alone were not rich enough; whole eggs plus yolks provided the degree of richness we wanted. For the dairy component, we found that equal parts of milk and heavy cream worked best. This custard was creamy and smooth. After layering bacon and Gruyère over the bottom of the pie shell—for a classic quiche Lorraine—we poured the custard on top and baked the quiche until it was puffed and set around the edges but still jiggled in the center; the residual heat finished cooking the center without turning the top into a rubbery skin. Before serving the quiche, we let it cool on a wire rack, which is a small but important step; this allows air to circulate under the crust and prevents it from becoming soggy.

Quiche Lorraine

SERVES 8

The center of the quiche will be surprisingly soft when it comes out of the oven, but the filling will continue to set (and sink somewhat) as it cools. If the pie shell has been previously baked and cooled, place it in the heating oven for about five minutes to warm it, making sure that it does not burn.

- 1 recipe Basic Single-Crust Pie Dough (page 842), fitted into a 9-inch pie plate and chilled
- 8 ounces bacon (about 8 slices), cut into ½-inch pieces
- 2 large whole eggs plus 2 large egg yolks
- 1 cup whole milk

- 1 cup heavy cream
- ½ teaspoon table salt
- ½ teaspoon ground white pepper
- Pinch freshly grated nutmeg
- 4 ounces Gruyère cheese, shredded (about 1 cup)

1. Adjust an oven rack to the middle position and heat the oven to 375 degrees. Following the photos on page 856, line the chilled crust with a double layer of foil and fill with pie weights. Bake until the pie dough looks dry and is light in color, 25 to 30 minutes. Transfer the pie plate to a wire rack and remove the weights and foil.

2. Cook the bacon in a 12-inch nonstick skillet over medium heat until crisp, about 5 minutes. Using a slotted spoon, transfer the bacon to a paper towel–lined plate. Whisk the remaining ingredients except the Gruyère together in a medium bowl.

3. Spread the Gruyère and bacon evenly over the bottom of the warm pie shell and set the shell on the oven rack. Pour the custard mixture into the pie shell (it should come to about ½ inch below the crust's rim). Bake until light golden brown and a knife blade inserted about 1 inch from the edge comes out clean and the center feels set but still soft, 32 to 35 minutes. Transfer the quiche to a wire rack and cool. Serve warm or at room temperature.

BREAKFAST STRATA

WHY THIS RECIPE WORKS: A classic breakfast dish, strata is easy to prepare, presents a variety of flavors, can feed a crowd and, perhaps best of all, can and indeed should be made ahead of time. Too often, though, it is overloaded with fillings; we wanted a savory bread pudding with a balanced, well-seasoned filling.

Recipes recommend all kinds of bread to use; we liked supermarket French or Italian loaves, which were neutral in flavor but had a sturdy texture. Rather than cubing the bread, which is often recommended, we sliced it to retain the layered quality of the dish and let the slices dry slightly (stale bread held up better than fresh). We used whole eggs and half-and-half for the custard, with a tad more dairy than eggs, and increased the amount of custard to saturate the bread more fully. A surprisingly successful addition to the custard was white wine, which we reduced to evaporate the alcohol; it brightened all the flavors. A key to ensuring cohesiveness in the strata was weighting it while it rested for at least one hour; this way, every piece of bread absorbed some custard. We kept our fillings minimal so they wouldn't overwhelm the bread and custard, and we sautéed the filling ingredients before adding them to the casserole to keep moisture from turning the dish watery.

Breakfast Strata with Spinach and Gruyère

SERVES 6

To weigh down the assembled strata, use two 1-pound boxes of sugar, laid side by side over the plastic-covered surface. To double this recipe, use a 13 by 9-inch baking dish greased with 1½ tablespoons butter and increase the baking time in step 5 to 1 hour and 20 minutes.

- 8–10 (½-inch-thick) slices supermarket French or Italian bread
- 5 tablespoons unsalted butter, softened
- 4 medium shallots, minced (about ½ cup)
- 1 (10-ounce) package frozen chopped spinach, thawed and squeezed dry
- Table salt and ground black pepper
- ½ cup dry white wine
- 6 ounces Gruyère cheese, shredded (about 1½ cups)
- 6 large eggs
- 1¾ cups half-and-half

1. Adjust an oven rack to the middle position and heat the oven to 225 degrees. Arrange the bread in a single layer on a large baking sheet and bake until dry and crisp, about 40 minutes, turning the slices over halfway through the baking time. (Alternatively, leave the slices out overnight to dry.) Let the bread cool completely, then spread butter evenly over one side of each bread slice, using 2 tablespoons of the butter; set aside.

2. Heat 2 tablespoons more butter in a medium nonstick skillet over medium heat. Add the shallots and cook until softened, about 3 minutes; add the spinach and salt and pepper to taste and cook until the spinach is warm, about 2 minutes. Transfer to a medium bowl and set aside. Add the wine to the skillet, increase the heat to medium-high, and simmer until reduced to ¼ cup, 2 to 3 minutes; set aside.

3. Butter an 8-inch square baking dish with the remaining 1 tablespoon butter; arrange half of the bread slices, buttered-side up, in a single layer in the dish. Sprinkle half of the spinach mixture, then ½ cup of the shredded Gruyère, evenly over the bread slices. Arrange the remaining bread slices in a single layer over the cheese; sprinkle the remaining spinach mixture and ½ cup more Gruyère evenly over the bread. Whisk the eggs in a medium bowl until combined; whisk in the reduced wine, half-and-half, 1 teaspoon salt, and a pinch of pepper. Pour the egg mixture evenly over the bread layers.

4. Wrap the strata tightly with plastic wrap, pressing the wrap against the surface of the strata. Weigh the strata down (see note), and refrigerate for at least 1 hour or up to 24 hours.

5. Remove the dish from the refrigerator and let stand at room temperature for 20 minutes. Meanwhile, adjust an oven rack to the middle position and heat the oven to 325 degrees. Uncover the strata and sprinkle the remaining ½ cup Gruyère evenly over the surface; bake until both edges and center are puffed and the edges have pulled away slightly from the sides of the dish, 50 to 55 minutes. Cool on a wire rack for 5 minutes and serve.

Breakfast Strata with Sausage, Mushrooms, and Monterey Jack

To double this recipe, use a 13 by 9-inch baking dish greased with 1½ tablespoons butter and increase the baking time in step 5 to 1 hour and 20 minutes.

- 8–10 (½-inch-thick) slices supermarket French or Italian bread
- 3 tablespoons unsalted butter, softened
- 8 ounces bulk breakfast sausage, crumbled
- 3 medium shallots, minced (about 6 tablespoons)
- 8 ounces white mushrooms, wiped clean and quartered
- Table salt and ground black pepper
- ½ cup dry white wine
- 6 ounces Monterey Jack cheese, shredded (about 1½ cups)
- 6 large eggs
- 1¾ cups half-and-half
- 2 tablespoons minced fresh parsley leaves

Follow the recipe for Breakfast Strata with Spinach and Gruyère through step 1. Fry the sausage in a medium nonstick skillet over medium heat, breaking the sausage apart with a wooden spoon, until it loses its raw color and begins to brown, about 4 minutes; add the shallots and cook, stirring frequently, until softened, about 3 minutes. Add the mushrooms to the skillet and cook until the mushrooms no longer release liquid, about 6 minutes; transfer to a medium bowl and season with salt and pepper to taste. Reduce the wine as directed in step 2; continue with the recipe from step 3, adding the parsley to the egg mixture along with the salt and pepper and substituting the sausage mixture for the spinach and the Monterey Jack for the Gruyère.

BLUEBERRY PANCAKES

WHY THIS RECIPE WORKS: Blueberry pancakes sound appetizing, but they are often tough and rubbery or dense and soggy. And they inevitably take on an unappealing blue-gray hue. We wanted pancakes that cooked up light and fluffy and were studded with sweet, tangy bursts of summer's best berry.

Starting with the pancakes themselves, we determined that unbleached flour, sugar, a little salt, and both baking powder and baking soda were essential for the dry ingredients. One egg added just enough structure and richness without making the pancakes overly eggy. Buttermilk was the preferred dairy component, but since our ground rules were to use only what most home cooks would be likely to have on hand, we searched for a substitute. Lemon juice thickens milk almost to the consistency of buttermilk and adds a similar tang that tasters actually preferred. Some melted butter added to the mix prevented our pancakes from being dry and bland. Mixing the batter too strenuously leads to tough pancakes; it's time to stop mixing when there are still a few lumps and streaks of flour. Once we had great-tasting pancakes, we turned to the blueberries. Stirring them into the batter would obviously lead to smashing and those blue-gray streaks, so rather than incorporating the berries, we simply dropped some onto the batter after we'd ladled it into the skillet. Smaller wild berries are sweeter than the larger ones, but frozen berries work as well as fresh, which means we can have great blueberry pancakes any time of the year.

Blueberry Pancakes

MAKES ABOUT SIXTEEN 4-INCH PANCAKES, SERVING 4 TO 6

To make sure that frozen berries do not bleed, rinse them under cool water in a mesh strainer until the water runs clear, and then spread them on a paper towel–lined plate to dry. If you have buttermilk on hand, use 2 cups instead of the milk and lemon juice. To keep pancakes warm while cooking the remaining batter, hold them in a 200-degree oven on a greased rack set over a baking sheet.

- 2 cups milk (see note)
- 1 tablespoon juice from 1 lemon (see note)
- 2 cups (10 ounces) unbleached all-purpose flour
- 2 tablespoons sugar
- 2 teaspoons baking powder
- ½ teaspoon baking soda
- ½ teaspoon table salt
- 1 large egg
- 3 tablespoons unsalted butter, melted and cooled slightly
- 1–2 teaspoons vegetable oil
- 1 cup fresh or frozen blueberries, preferably wild, rinsed and dried (see note)

1. Whisk the milk and lemon juice together in a medium bowl or large measuring cup; set aside to thicken while preparing the other ingredients. Whisk the flour, sugar, baking powder, baking soda, and salt together in a medium bowl.

2. Whisk the egg and melted butter into the milk until combined. Make a well in the center of the dry ingredients in the bowl; pour in the milk mixture and whisk very gently until just combined (a few lumps should remain). Do not overmix.

3. Heat a 12-inch nonstick skillet over medium heat for 3 to 5 minutes; add 1 teaspoon of the oil and brush to coat the skillet bottom evenly. Pour ¼ cup batter onto three spots on the skillet; sprinkle 1 tablespoon of the blueberries over each pancake. Cook the pancakes until large bubbles begin to appear, 1½ to 2 minutes. Using a thin-bladed spatula, flip the pancakes and cook until golden brown on the second side, 1 to 1½ minutes longer. Serve and repeat with the remaining batter, using the remaining 1 teaspoon vegetable oil if necessary.

GERMAN PANCAKE

WHY THIS RECIPE WORKS: Our German pancake achieves its dramatic appearance and contrasting textures thanks to a few test kitchen tricks. First, we mixed up a simple batter containing just the right amounts of eggs, flour, and milk to produce a pancake with crispy yet tender edges and a custardy center. To produce a tall, puffy rim and an even, substantial center, we started the pancake in a cold oven and then turned the heat to 375 degrees. This allowed the center of the pancake to begin to set up before the rim got hot enough to puff up substantially. Finally, we put fruit and other ingredients on as a topping rather than baking them into the pancake. Without fruit to weigh things down, the pancake puffed dramatically and its texture remained delicate and uniform.

German Pancake

SERVES 4

A traditional 12-inch skillet may be used in place of the nonstick skillet; coat it lightly with vegetable oil spray before using. As an alternative to sugar and lemon juice, serve the pancake with maple syrup or our Brown Sugar–Apple Topping (recipe follows).

- 1¾ cups (8¾ ounces) all-purpose flour
- ¼ cup sugar
- 1 tablespoon grated lemon zest plus 1 tablespoon juice
- ½ teaspoon salt
- ⅛ teaspoon ground nutmeg
- 1½ cups milk
- 6 large eggs
- 1½ teaspoons vanilla extract
- 3 tablespoons unsalted butter

1. Whisk flour, 3 tablespoons sugar, lemon zest, salt, and nutmeg together in large bowl. Whisk milk, eggs, and vanilla together in second bowl. Whisk two-thirds of milk mixture into flour mixture until no lumps remain, then slowly whisk in remaining milk mixture until smooth.

2. Adjust oven rack to lower-middle position. Melt butter in 12-inch ovensafe nonstick skillet over medium-low heat. Add batter to skillet, immediately transfer to oven, and set oven to 375 degrees. Bake until edges are deep golden brown and center is beginning to brown, 30 to 35 minutes.

3. Transfer skillet to wire rack and sprinkle pancake with lemon juice and remaining 1 tablespoon sugar. Gently transfer pancake to cutting board, cut into wedges, and serve.

Brown Sugar–Apple Topping

MAKES ABOUT 2 CUPS

You can substitute Honeycrisp or Fuji apples for the Braeburn apples, if desired.

- 2 tablespoons unsalted butter
- ⅓ cup water
- ¼ cup packed (1¾ ounces) brown sugar
- ¼ teaspoon ground cinnamon
- ⅛ teaspoon salt
- 1¼ pounds Braeburn apples (3 to 4 apples), peeled, cored, halved, and cut into ½-inch-thick wedges, wedges halved crosswise

Melt butter in 12-inch skillet over medium heat. Add water, sugar, cinnamon, and salt and whisk until sugar dissolves. Add apples, increase heat to medium-high, and bring to simmer. Cover and cook, stirring occasionally, for 5 minutes. Uncover and continue to cook until apples are translucent and just tender and sauce is thickened, 5 to 7 minutes longer. Transfer to bowl and serve. (Topping can be refrigerated for up to 2 days.)

GERMAN APPLE PANCAKE

WHY THIS RECIPE WORKS: More akin to popovers than American pancakes, German apple pancakes are golden and puffed outside, custardy inside, with sweet apples baked right in. The dish suffers from many of the same problems as popovers, too: not enough rise, dense texture, and a too-eggy flavor. We wanted to solve these problems and get this pancake just right.

Flour and eggs are the basis of the batter; half-and-half for the dairy component imparted richness and a light texture. Sugar, salt, and vanilla completed the batter. Steam, not leavening, is what puffs the pancake, so to get the maximum rise we needed to find the right oven temperature. A very hot oven burned the exterior of the pancake; preheating the oven to a high temperature as well as preheating the pan, then lowering the temperature when the pancake went in, proved the ideal method. Granny Smith apples were our top pick if you like a little tartness; otherwise Braeburns are a good choice for their sweetness. We cooked apples with brown sugar rather than granulated for a deeper flavor, along with butter, cinnamon, and a bright touch of lemon juice. To keep the apples from being pushed out of the pan when the pancake rose, we first poured the batter around the edge of the skillet, then over the apples. Our pancake puffed spectacularly, and when we served it, every bite contained warm, tender apples.

German Apple Pancake

SERVES 4

A 10-inch ovensafe skillet is necessary for this recipe; we highly recommend using a nonstick skillet for the sake of easy cleanup, but a regular skillet will work. If you prefer tart apples, use Granny Smiths; if you prefer sweet ones, use Braeburns.

- ½ cup (2½ ounces) unbleached all-purpose flour
- 1 tablespoon granulated sugar
- ½ teaspoon table salt
- 2 large eggs
- ⅔ cup half-and-half
- 1 teaspoon vanilla extract
- 2 tablespoons unsalted butter
- 1¼ pounds Granny Smith or Braeburn apples (3 to 4 large apples), peeled, quartered, cored, and cut into ½-inch-thick slices (see note)
- ¼ cup packed (1¾ ounces) light or dark brown sugar
- ¼ teaspoon ground cinnamon
- 1 teaspoon juice from 1 lemon
- Confectioners' sugar, for dusting
- Maple syrup or Caramel Sauce (recipe follows), for serving

1. Adjust an oven rack to the upper-middle position and heat the oven to 500 degrees.

2. Whisk the flour, granulated sugar, and salt together in a medium bowl. In a second medium bowl, whisk the eggs, half-and-half, and vanilla together until combined. Add the liquid ingredients to the dry ingredients and whisk until no lumps remain, about 20 seconds; set the batter aside.

3. Melt the butter in a 10-inch ovensafe nonstick skillet over medium-high heat. Add the apples, brown sugar, and cinnamon; cook, stirring frequently with a heatproof rubber spatula, until the apples are golden brown, about 10 minutes. Off the heat, stir in the lemon juice.

4. Working quickly, pour the batter around the edge of the pan and then over the apples. Place the skillet in the oven and immediately reduce the oven temperature to 425 degrees. Bake until the pancake edges are brown and puffy and have risen above the edges of the skillet, about 18 minutes.

5. Using a potholder (the skillet handle will be hot), remove the skillet from the oven and loosen the pancake edges with a heatproof rubber spatula; invert the pancake onto a platter. Dust with confectioners' sugar, cut into wedges, and serve with maple syrup or Caramel Sauce.

Caramel Sauce

MAKES ABOUT 1½ CUPS

Cooking the sugar with some water in a covered pot helps trap moisture and ensures that the sugar will dissolve. When the hot cream mixture is added in step 3, the hot sugar syrup will bubble vigorously (and dangerously), so don't use a smaller saucepan. If you make the caramel sauce ahead, reheat it in the microwave or a small saucepan over low heat until warm and fluid.

- ½ cup water
- 1 cup (7 ounces) sugar
- 1 cup heavy cream
- ⅛ teaspoon table salt
- ½ teaspoon vanilla extract
- ½ teaspoon juice from 1 lemon

1. Place the water in a 2-quart saucepan; pour the sugar into the center of the pan, taking care not to let the sugar crystals stick to the sides of the pan. Cover and bring the mixture to a boil over high heat; once the mixture is boiling, uncover the pan and continue to boil until the sugar syrup is thick and straw-colored and registers 300 degrees on an instant-read thermometer, about 7 minutes. Reduce the heat to medium and continue to cook until the syrup is deep amber and registers 350 degrees, 1 to 2 minutes.

2. Meanwhile, bring the cream and salt to a simmer in a small saucepan over high heat (if the cream boils before the sugar syrup reaches a deep amber color, remove the cream from the heat and cover to keep warm).

3. Remove the pan with the sugar syrup from the heat; very carefully pour about one-quarter of the hot cream into it (the mixture will bubble vigorously), and let the bubbling subside. Add the remaining cream, the vanilla, and lemon juice; whisk until the sauce is smooth. (The sauce can be cooled and refrigerated in an airtight container for up to 2 weeks.)

LEMON RICOTTA PANCAKES

WHY THIS RECIPE WORKS: Light, fluffy ricotta pancakes are sophisticated enough for special occasions, but getting the balance of ingredients just right is essential for pancakes that are puffy and tender, not dense and wet. To compensate for the extra weight of the ricotta, we decreased the amount of flour and stirred four whipped egg whites into the batter. Baking soda provided extra rise and aided with browning. Bright, tangy lemon juice complemented the rich, creamy ricotta, and lemon zest enhanced the citrus flavor without watering down the batter. A touch of vanilla extract brought depth and subtle sweetness. For a company-worthy finishing touch, we draped the pancakes with a warm fruit compote.

Lemon Ricotta Pancakes

MAKES 12 (4-INCH) PANCAKES; SERVES 3 TO 4

An electric griddle set at 325 degrees can also be used to cook the pancakes. We prefer the flavor of whole-milk ricotta, but part-skim will work, too; avoid nonfat ricotta. Serve with confectioners' sugar or Pear-Blackberry Topping.

- ⅔ cup (3⅓ ounces) all-purpose flour
- ½ teaspoon baking soda
- ½ teaspoon salt
- 8 ounces (1 cup) whole-milk ricotta cheese
- 2 large eggs, separated, plus 2 large whites
- ⅓ cup whole milk
- 1 teaspoon grated lemon zest plus 4 teaspoons juice
- ½ teaspoon vanilla extract
- 2 tablespoons unsalted butter, melted
- ¼ cup (1¾ ounces) sugar
- 1–2 teaspoons vegetable oil

1. Adjust oven rack to middle position and heat oven to 200 degrees. Spray wire rack set inside rimmed baking sheet with vegetable oil spray; place in oven. Whisk flour, baking soda, and salt together in medium bowl and make well in center. Add ricotta, egg yolks, milk, lemon zest and juice, and vanilla and whisk until just combined. Gently stir in butter.

2. Using stand mixer fitted with whisk, whip egg whites on medium-low speed until foamy, about 1 minute. Increase speed to medium-high and whip whites to soft, billowy mounds, about 1 minute. Gradually add sugar and whip until glossy, soft peaks form, 1 to 2 minutes. Transfer one-third of whipped egg whites to batter and whisk gently until mixture is lightened. Using rubber spatula, gently fold remaining egg whites into batter.

3. Heat 1 teaspoon oil in 12-inch nonstick skillet over medium heat until shimmering. Using paper towels, wipe out oil, leaving thin film on bottom and sides of pan. Using ¼-cup measure or 2-ounce ladle, portion batter into pan in 3 places, leaving 2 inches between portions. Gently spread each portion into a 4-inch round. Cook until edges are set and first side is deep golden brown, 2 to 3 minutes. Using thin, wide spatula, flip pancakes and continue to cook until second side is golden brown, 2 to 3 minutes longer. Serve pancakes immediately or transfer to wire rack in preheated oven. Repeat with remaining batter, using remaining oil as needed.

Pear-Blackberry Topping

MAKES 3 CUPS

- 3 ripe pears, peeled, halved, cored, and cut into ¼-inch pieces
- 1 tablespoon sugar
- 1 teaspoon cornstarch
- Pinch salt
- Pinch ground cardamom
- 5 ounces (1 cup) blackberries, berries more than 1 inch long cut in half crosswise

Combine pears, sugar, cornstarch, salt, and cardamom in bowl and microwave until pears are softened but not mushy and juices are slightly thickened, 4 to 6 minutes, stirring once halfway through microwaving. Stir in blackberries and serve.

100 PERCENT WHOLE-WHEAT PANCAKES

WHY THIS RECIPE WORKS: Most recipes for whole-wheat pancakes call for a mix of white and whole-wheat flours, and they also call for a host of extra flavorings like spices, vanilla, fruit juice, or fruit. Why not just whole-wheat flour? We discovered that using all whole-wheat flour actually delivers light, fluffy, and tender pancakes—not the dense cakes you'd imagine—because whole-wheat flour contains slightly less gluten-forming protein than white flour and because the bran in whole-wheat flour cuts through any gluten strands that do form. Recipes for pancakes made with white flour advise undermixing to avoid dense, tough pancakes, but with whole-wheat flour we were guaranteed light and tender cakes even as we whisked our batter to a smooth, thick consistency. We saw no need to cover up whole wheat's natural flavor with other add-ins; its earthy, nutty taste proved to be the perfect complement to maple syrup. As long as we used a bag of fresh or properly stored (in the freezer) whole-wheat flour, it had just the buttery, nutty flavor we wanted.

100 Percent Whole-Wheat Pancakes

MAKES 15 PANCAKES

An electric griddle set at 350 degrees can be used in place of a skillet. If substituting buttermilk powder and water for fresh buttermilk, use only 2 cups of water to prevent the pancakes from being too wet. To ensure the best flavor, use either recently purchased whole-wheat flour or flour that has been stored in the freezer for less than 12 months. Serve with maple syrup and butter.

- 2 cups (11 ounces) whole-wheat flour
- 2 tablespoons sugar
- 1½ teaspoons baking powder

½ teaspoon baking soda
¾ teaspoon salt
2¼ cups buttermilk
5 tablespoons plus 2 teaspoons vegetable oil
2 large eggs

1. Adjust oven rack to middle position and heat oven to 200 degrees. Spray wire rack set in rimmed baking sheet with vegetable oil spray; place in oven.

2. Whisk flour, sugar, baking powder, baking soda, and salt together in medium bowl. Whisk buttermilk, 5 tablespoons oil, and eggs together in second medium bowl. Make well in center of flour mixture and pour in buttermilk mixture; whisk until smooth. (Mixture will be thick; do not add more buttermilk.)

3. Heat 1 teaspoon oil in 12-inch nonstick skillet over medium heat until shimmering. Using paper towels, carefully wipe out oil, leaving thin film on bottom and sides of pan. Using ¼-cup dry measuring cup or 2-ounce ladle, portion batter into pan in 3 places. Gently spread each portion into 4½-inch round. Cook until edges are set, first side is golden brown, and bubbles on surface are just beginning to break, 2 to 3 minutes. Using thin, wide spatula, flip pancakes and continue to cook until second side is golden brown, 1 to 2 minutes longer. Serve pancakes immediately or transfer to wire rack in oven. Repeat with remaining batter, using remaining 1 teaspoon oil as necessary.

WAFFLES

WHY THIS RECIPE WORKS: You cannot simply put pancake batter in a waffle iron and make waffles; waffles should be moist and fluffy inside and crisp and brown outside—more like a soufflé with a crust than a pancake. We wanted to find the way to achieve this archetypal waffle.

Thick batter is the secret of the crisp exterior and custardy interior of a waffle, so we used a higher proportion of flour to liquid than that of standard recipes. With buttermilk (and buttermilk makes the best-tasting waffles) there's no need for baking powder, and we found that eliminating it also helped crisp up the waffles. A small amount of cornmeal added a pleasing crunch. Separating the egg and folding the whipped white into the batter was a definite improvement; we could see the pockets of air when we cut into a waffle made this way. Like pancakes, waffles turn tough when the batter is over mixed, so we used a light hand, adding the liquid gradually and using more of a folding motion to mix. Cooked to a medium toasty brown, these waffles were everything we wanted them to be.

Buttermilk Waffles

MAKES 3 TO 4 WAFFLES, DEPENDING ON THE SIZE OF THE IRON

The secret to great waffles is a thick batter, so don't expect a pourable batter. The optional dash of cornmeal adds a pleasant crunch to the finished waffle. This recipe can be doubled or tripled. Make toaster waffles out of leftover batter—undercook the waffles a bit, cool them on a wire rack, wrap them in plastic wrap, and freeze. Pop them in the toaster for a quick breakfast. The waffles are best served fresh from the iron but can be held in an oven until all of the batter is used. As you make the waffles, place them on a wire rack set in a rimmed baking sheet, cover them with a clean kitchen towel, and place the baking sheet in a 200-degree oven.

1 cup (5 ounces) unbleached all-purpose flour
1 tablespoon cornmeal (optional; see note)
½ teaspoon table salt
¼ teaspoon baking soda
⅞ cup buttermilk
1 large egg, separated
2 tablespoons unsalted butter, melted and cooled

1. Following the manufacturer's instructions, heat a waffle iron. Whisk the flour, cornmeal (if using), salt, and baking soda together in a medium bowl. In a separate medium bowl, whisk the buttermilk, egg yolk, and melted butter together.

2. Beat the egg white with an electric mixer on medium-low speed until foamy, about 1 minute. Increase the speed to medium-high and whip the whites to stiff peaks, 2 to 4 minutes.

3. Add the liquid ingredients to the dry ingredients in a thin, steady stream while mixing gently with a rubber spatula. (Do not add the liquid faster than you can incorporate it into the batter.) Toward the end of mixing, use a folding motion to incorporate the ingredients. Gently fold the egg white into the batter.

4. Spread an appropriate amount of batter onto the waffle iron. Following the manufacturer's instructions, cook the waffle until golden brown, 2 to 5 minutes. Serve.

EASY BUTTERMILK WAFFLES

WHY THIS RECIPE WORKS: Most waffle recipes are time-consuming affairs. We wanted waffles with a crisp, golden-brown, dimpled crust surrounding a moist, fluffy interior, but for rushed morning schedules, we wanted this recipe to require little more than measuring out some flour and cracking an egg.

To get crisp, the exterior of a waffle must first become dry, and the moist steam racing past the crisping waffle as it cooked was slowing down the process. We needed a drier batter with much more leavening oomph. To do this, we took a cue from a Japanese cooking technique, tempura. In tempura batters, seltzer or club soda is often used in place of still water. The tiny bubbles of carbon dioxide released from the water inflate the batter the same way as a chemical leavener—minus the metallic taste that baking soda and powder sometimes impart. We replaced the buttermilk in our pancake recipe with a mixture of seltzer and powdered buttermilk. The resulting waffles were incredibly light, but not as crisp as we wanted. For better texture, we replaced the melted butter in the recipe with oil—melted butter, which is partly water, had been imparting moisture to the waffles, preventing them from crisping. Best of all, tasters didn't notice the swap, just the excellent flavor and wonderfully crisp texture.

Easy Buttermilk Waffles

MAKES ABOUT EIGHT 7-INCH ROUND WAFFLES

While the waffles can be eaten directly from the waffle iron, they will have a crispier exterior if rested in a warm oven for 10 minutes. Buttermilk powder is available in most supermarkets and is generally located near the dried milk products or in the baking aisle (leftover powder can be kept in the refrigerator for up to a year). Seltzer or club soda gives these waffles their light texture; use a freshly opened container for maximum lift. Avoid Perrier, which is not bubbly enough. Serve with butter and warm maple syrup.

- 2 cups (10 ounces) unbleached all-purpose flour
- ½ cup dried buttermilk powder (see note)
- 1 tablespoon sugar
- ¾ teaspoon table salt
- ½ teaspoon baking soda
- ½ cup sour cream
- 2 large eggs
- ¼ cup vegetable oil
- ¼ teaspoon vanilla extract
- 1¼ cups unflavored seltzer water or club soda (see note)

1. Adjust an oven rack to the middle position and heat the oven to 250 degrees. Set a wire rack over a rimmed baking sheet and place the baking sheet in the oven. Whisk the flour, buttermilk powder, sugar, salt, and baking soda in a large bowl to combine. Whisk the sour cream, eggs, oil, and vanilla in a medium bowl to combine. Gently stir the seltzer into the wet ingredients. Make a well in the center of the dry ingredients and pour in the wet ingredients. Gently stir until just combined. The batter should remain slightly lumpy with streaks of flour.

2. Heat a waffle iron and bake the waffles according to the manufacturer's instructions (use about ⅓ cup for a 7-inch round iron). Transfer the waffles to the rack in the warm oven and hold for up to 10 minutes before serving.

FRENCH TOAST

WHY THIS RECIPE WORKS: When it comes to French toast, the results are rarely worth the trouble. The bread is soggy, too eggy, or just plain bland. We wanted to come up with French toast that's crisp on the outside and soft and puffy on the inside, with rich, custard-like flavor every time.

We first focused on determining which type of bread fared best in a typical batter made with milk and eggs. Tasters eliminated French and Italian breads for being chewy. We then turned to white sandwich bread, which comes in two kinds: regular and hearty. Regular bread was gloppy both inside and out. Hearty bread crisped up nicely on the outside, but still had mushiness. Drying out the bread in a low oven, however, produced French toast that was crisp on the outside and velvety on the inside. As for flavor, tasters thought the French toast tasted overly eggy. We recalled a recipe that required bread dipped in milk mixed with just yolks, versus whole eggs. The yolks-only soaking liquid made a huge difference, turning the taste rich and custardlike. Research revealed that most of the flavor in eggs comes not from the yolk but from the sulfur compounds in the whites, so problem solved. For flavorings, we settled on cinnamon, vanilla, and brown sugar. For nutty butter flavor, we incorporated melted butter into the soaking liquid, warming the milk first to prevent the butter from solidifying. A final bonus—the recipe worked just as well with challah.

French Toast

SERVES 4

For best results, choose a good challah or a firm sandwich bread, such as Arnold Country Classics White or Pepperidge Farm Farmhouse Hearty White. Thomas' English Muffin Toasting Bread also works well. To prevent the butter from clumping during mixing, warm the milk in a microwave or small saucepan until warm to the touch (about 80 degrees). The French toast can be cooked all at once on an electric griddle, but may take an extra 2 to 3 minutes per side. Set the griddle temperature to 350 degrees and use the entire amount of butter for cooking. Serve with warm maple syrup.

- 8 large slices high-quality hearty white sandwich bread or challah (see note)
- 1½ cups whole milk, warmed (see note)
- 3 large egg yolks
- 3 tablespoons light brown sugar
- ½ teaspoon ground cinnamon
- 2 tablespoons unsalted butter, melted, plus 2 tablespoons for cooking
- ¼ teaspoon table salt
- 1 tablespoon vanilla extract

1. Adjust an oven rack to the middle position and heat the oven to 300 degrees. Place the bread on a wire rack set over a rimmed baking sheet. Bake the bread until almost dry throughout (the center should remain slightly moist), about 16 minutes, flipping the slices halfway through cooking. Remove the bread from the rack and let cool for 5 minutes. Return the baking sheet with the wire rack to the oven and reduce the temperature to 200 degrees.

2. Whisk the milk, egg yolks, sugar, cinnamon, 2 tablespoons melted butter, salt, and vanilla in a large bowl until well blended. Transfer the mixture to a 13 by 9-inch baking pan.

3. Soak the bread in the milk mixture until saturated but not falling apart, 20 seconds per side. Using a firm slotted spatula, pick up a bread slice and allow the excess milk mixture to drip off; repeat with the remaining slices. Place the soaked bread on another baking sheet or platter.

4. Heat ½ tablespoon of the butter in a 12-inch skillet over medium-low heat. When the foaming subsides, use a slotted spatula to transfer 2 slices of the soaked bread to the skillet and cook until golden brown, 3 to 4 minutes. Flip and continue to cook until the second side is golden brown, 3 to 4 minutes longer. (If the toast is cooking too quickly, reduce the heat slightly.) Transfer to the baking sheet in the oven. Wipe out the skillet with paper towels. Repeat cooking with the remaining bread, 2 pieces at a time, adding ½ tablespoon more butter for each batch. Serve warm.

CLASSIC BANANA BREAD

WHY THIS RECIPE WORKS: Overripe bananas are a good excuse to make banana bread, but the loaf can be dry, heavy, and bland. We wanted a banana bread with deep banana flavor, plenty of moisture, and a nice, light texture.

Very ripe, darkly speckled bananas contributed moisture as well as flavor to this bread (they're sweeter, too); unripe ones did not work. Pureeing the bananas kept the bread from rising well, so instead we mashed them thoroughly by hand. For additional moisture we included yogurt, which contributed a nice tang without masking the flavor of the bananas. The quick-bread method of mixing—melting the butter and folding the wet ingredients into the dry ones—produced a golden brown loaf and delicate texture; when we tried creaming the butter and sugar first, the bread came out more like butter cake and wasn't as golden brown. However, we found it was important not to overmix the batter; overly vigorous stirring developed excess gluten that turned the loaf tough and dense.

Classic Banana Bread

MAKES ONE 9-INCH LOAF

For best flavor, use bananas that are very ripe.

- 2 cups (10 ounces) unbleached all-purpose flour
- ¾ cup (5¼ ounces) sugar
- ¾ teaspoon baking soda
- ½ teaspoon table salt
- 3 very ripe bananas, mashed well (about 1½ cups)
- ¼ cup plain yogurt
- 2 large eggs, lightly beaten
- 6 tablespoons (¾ stick) unsalted butter, melted and cooled
- 1 teaspoon vanilla extract
- 1¼ cup walnuts, toasted and chopped coarse

1. Adjust an oven rack to the lower-middle position and heat the oven to 350 degrees. Grease and flour a 9 by 5-inch loaf pan; set aside.

2. Whisk the flour, sugar, baking soda, and salt together in a large bowl; set aside.

3. Mix the mashed bananas, yogurt, eggs, butter, and vanilla together with a wooden spoon in a medium bowl. Lightly fold the banana mixture into the dry ingredients with a rubber spatula until just combined and the batter looks thick and chunky. Fold in the walnuts. Scrape the batter into the prepared loaf pan and smooth the surface with a rubber spatula.

4. Bake until the loaf is golden brown and a toothpick inserted in the center comes out clean, about 55 minutes. Cool in the pan for 5 minutes, then transfer to a wire rack. Serve warm or at room temperature.

ULTIMATE BANANA BREAD

WHY THIS RECIPE WORKS: Recipes for ultimate banana bread abound, but because they include an overload of bananas for flavor, the bread's texture is often soggy. We wanted a moist, not mushy, loaf that tasted of banana through and through.

To impart lots of banana flavor, we needed to use a generous amount of bananas, but we needed to rid them of excess moisture. We turned to the microwave to help us out. We piled as many bananas in a bowl as we dared and zapped them in the microwave. Then we drained the now-pulpy fruit and mixed the fruit into a batter. We didn't want to toss the flavorful liquid, so we reduced it and added it into the batter as well. Like a mock extract, our reduction infused the bread with ripe, intensely fruity banana flavor.

With the flavor problem solved, a few minor tweaks completed the recipe: We exchanged the granulated sugar for light brown sugar, finding that the latter's molasses notes better complemented the bananas. Swapping out the oil for the nutty richness of butter improved the loaf further. We also added toasted walnuts to the batter, finding that their crunch provided a pleasing contrast to the rich, moist crumb. Wondering if the crust might benefit from a little embellishment, we sliced a banana and shingled it on top of the batter. A final sprinkle of sugar helped the banana slices caramelize and gave this deeply flavored loaf an enticingly crisp, crunchy top.

NOTES FROM THE TEST KITCHEN

SHINGLING THE LOAF

Layering thin bananas slices on either side of the loaf adds even more banana flavor to our bread (and brings the total number of bananas in the recipe to six). To ensure an even rise, leave a 1½-inch-wide space down the center.

Ultimate Banana Bread

MAKES ONE 9-INCH LOAF

Be sure to use very ripe, heavily speckled (or even black) bananas in this recipe. This recipe can be made using five thawed frozen bananas; since they release a lot of liquid naturally, they can bypass the microwaving in step 2 and go directly into the fine-mesh strainer. Do not use a thawed frozen banana in step 4; it will be too soft to slice. Instead, simply sprinkle the top of the loaf with sugar. The test kitchen's preferred loaf pan measures 8½ by 4½ inches; if you use a 9 by 5-inch loaf pan, start checking for doneness 5 minutes earlier than advised in the recipe. The texture is best when the loaf is eaten fresh, but it can be cooled completely and stored, covered tightly with plastic wrap, for up to 3 days.

- 1¾ cups (8¾ ounces) unbleached all-purpose flour
- 1 teaspoon baking soda
- ½ teaspoon table salt
- 6 large very ripe bananas (about 2¼ pounds), peeled (see note)
- 8 tablespoons (1 stick) unsalted butter, melted and cooled slightly
- 2 large eggs
- ¾ cup packed (5¼ ounces) light brown sugar
- 1 teaspoon vanilla extract
- ½ cup walnuts, toasted and chopped coarse (optional)
- 2 teaspoons granulated sugar

1. Adjust an oven rack to the middle position and heat the oven to 350 degrees. Spray an 8½ by 4½-inch loaf pan with vegetable oil spray. Whisk the flour, baking soda, and salt together in a large bowl.

2. Place 5 of the bananas in a microwave-safe bowl; cover with plastic wrap and cut several steam vents in the plastic with a paring knife. Microwave on high power until the bananas are soft and have released their liquid, about 5 minutes. Transfer the bananas to a fine-mesh strainer placed over a medium bowl and allow to drain, stirring occasionally, for 15 minutes (you should have ½ to ¾ cup liquid).

3. Transfer the liquid to a medium saucepan and cook over medium-high heat until reduced to ¼ cup, about 5 minutes. Return drained bananas to bowl. Stir the reduced liquid into the bananas and mash them with a potato masher until fairly smooth. Whisk in the butter, eggs, brown sugar, and vanilla.

4. Pour the banana mixture into the flour mixture and stir until just combined with some streaks of flour remaining. Gently fold in the walnuts (if using). Scrape the batter into the prepared pan. Slice the remaining banana diagonally into ¼-inch-thick slices. Following the photo, shingle the banana slices on top of either side of the loaf, leaving a 1½-inch-wide space down the center to ensure even rise. Sprinkle the granulated sugar evenly over the loaf.

5. Bake until a toothpick inserted in the center of the loaf comes out clean, 55 to 75 minutes. Cool the bread in the pan on a wire rack for 15 minutes, then remove the loaf from the pan and continue to cool on a wire rack. Serve warm or at room temperature.

CREAM SCONES

WHY THIS RECIPE WORKS: Cream scones are a far cry from humongous coffeehouse creations. They are delicate and light, much like a biscuit. We set out to perfect a technique for making these tea-time (or breakfast) favorites.

Experimentation with different kinds of flour revealed that all-purpose was the best choice for these scones, and even better, for maximum tenderness, was a lower-protein brand of flour. Butter was important for flavor, but only a modest amount or the scones would practically melt in the oven. Cream won out over buttermilk and whole milk for the liquid; it made our scones rich and kept them tender. We increased the amount of sugar from that used in traditional recipes, but only slightly to keep them from being too sweet.

The discovery that the food processor did a great job of cutting the butter into the flour was a boon, making it even easier to make these treats. Our cream scones were just right served with a bit of jam.

Cream Scones

MAKES 8 SCONES

Use a low-protein all-purpose flour, such as Gold Medal or Pillsbury. The easiest and most reliable approach to mixing the butter into the dry ingredients is to use a food processor fitted with the metal blade. If you want a light glaze on the scones, brush the tops of the scones with 1 tablespoon heavy cream and then sprinkle them with 1 tablespoon sugar just before you put them in the oven. Resist the urge to eat the scones hot out of the oven. Letting them cool for at least 10 minutes firms them up and improves their texture.

- 2 cups (10 ounces) unbleached all-purpose flour (see note)
- 3 tablespoons sugar
- 1 tablespoon baking powder
- ½ teaspoon table salt
- 5 tablespoons unsalted butter, chilled and cut into ¼-inch cubes
- ½ cup currants
- 1 cup heavy cream

1. Adjust an oven rack to the middle position and heat the oven to 425 degrees.

2. Place the flour, sugar, baking powder, and salt in a food processor and pulse to combine, about 6 pulses.

3. Scatter the butter evenly over the top and continue to pulse until the mixture resembles coarse cornmeal with a few slightly larger butter lumps, about 12 more pulses. Transfer the mixture to a large bowl and stir in the currants. Stir in the heavy cream with a rubber spatula until a dough begins to form, about 30 seconds.

4. Transfer the dough and any dry, floury bits to a work surface and knead the dough by hand just until it comes together into a rough, slightly sticky ball, 5 to 10 seconds. Cut the dough into eight wedges. Place the wedges on an ungreased baking sheet. (The baking sheet can be covered in plastic wrap and refrigerated for up to 2 hours.)

5. Bake until the scone tops are light brown, 12 to 15 minutes. Cool on a wire rack for at least 10 minutes. Serve warm or at room temperature.

BLUEBERRY SCONES

WHY THIS RECIPE WORKS: Berry scones can be a treat—moist, sweet berries throughout a tender, light biscuit—but more often the berries weigh down the scone and impart little flavor. We wanted a rich, flaky scone studded with sweet, juicy blueberries.

Starting with traditional scone recipes, we increased the amounts of sugar and butter to add sweetness and richness to our scones. A combination of sour cream and milk lent both richness and tang. But now our scones were heavier than we wanted. We found two ways to lighten them. First, we borrowed a technique from puff pastry, where the dough is turned, rolled, and folded multiple times to create layers that are forced apart by steam when baked, and added a few quick folds to our scone dough. Then, to ensure that the butter would stay as cold and solid as possible while baking, we froze the butter and grated it into the dry ingredients using a box grater. Both tricks made for lighter, flakier scones. Adding the blueberries was a challenge. If we put them into the dry ingredients, they got mashed when we mixed the dough; when we added them to the already-mixed dough, we ruined our pockets of butter when we worked the berries in. The solution was pressing the berries into the dough, rolling the dough into a log, then pressing the log into a rectangle and cutting the scones. We had successfully transformed the scone into a fruit-filled, rich yet light treat.

Blueberry Scones

MAKES 8 SCONES

It is important to work the dough as little as possible—work quickly and knead and fold the dough only the number of times called for. The butter should be frozen solid before grating. If your kitchen is hot and humid, chill the flour mixture and bowls before use. The recipe calls for two whole sticks of butter, but only 10 tablespoons are actually used (see step 1). If fresh berries are unavailable, an equal amount of frozen berries, unthawed, can be substituted. An equal amount of raspberries, blackberries, or strawberries can also be used in place of the blueberries. Cut larger berries into ¼- to ½-inch pieces before incorporating. Refrigerate or freeze leftover scones, wrapped in foil, in an airtight container. To serve, remove the foil and place the scones on a baking sheet in a 375-degree oven. Heat until warmed through and recrisped, 8 to 10 minutes if refrigerated, 16 to 20 minutes if frozen.

16 tablespoons (2 sticks) unsalted butter, frozen whole (see note)
1½ cups (about 7½ ounces) fresh blueberries, picked over (see note)
½ cup whole milk
½ cup sour cream
2 cups (10 ounces) unbleached all-purpose flour, plus extra for the work surface
½ cup (3½ ounces) sugar, plus 1 tablespoon for sprinkling
2 teaspoons baking powder
½ teaspoon table salt
¼ teaspoon baking soda
1 teaspoon grated zest from 1 lemon

1. Adjust an oven rack to the middle position and heat the oven to 425 degrees. Score and remove half of the wrapper from each stick of frozen butter. Grate the unwrapped ends on the large holes of a box grater (you should grate a total of 8 tablespoons). Place the grated butter in the freezer until needed. Melt 2 tablespoons of the remaining ungrated butter and set aside. Save the remaining 6 tablespoons butter for another use. Place the blueberries in the freezer until needed.

2. Whisk the milk and sour cream together in a medium bowl; refrigerate until needed. Whisk the flour, ½ cup of the sugar, the baking powder, salt, baking soda, and lemon zest together in a medium bowl. Add the frozen butter to the flour mixture and toss with your fingers until the butter is thoroughly coated.

3. Add the milk mixture to the flour mixture; fold with a rubber spatula until just combined. Using the spatula, transfer the dough to a liberally floured work surface. Dust the surface of the dough with flour; with floured hands, knead the dough six to eight times, until it just holds together in a ragged ball, adding flour as needed to prevent sticking.

4. Roll the dough into an approximate 12-inch square. Following the photos, fold the dough into thirds like a business letter, using a bench scraper or metal spatula to release the dough if it sticks to the work surface. Lift the short ends of the dough and fold into thirds again to form an approximate 4-inch square. Transfer the dough to a plate lightly dusted with flour and chill in the freezer for 5 minutes.

5. Transfer the dough to a floured work surface and roll into an approximate 12-inch square again. Sprinkle the blueberries evenly over the surface of the dough, then press down so they are slightly embedded in the dough. Using a bench scraper or a thin metal spatula, loosen the dough from the work surface. Roll the dough, pressing to form a tight log. Lay the log seam side down and press it into a 12 by 4-inch rectangle. Using a sharp, floured knife, cut the rectangle crosswise into four equal rectangles. Cut each rectangle diagonally to form two triangles and transfer to a parchment-lined baking sheet.

6. Brush the tops of the scones with the melted butter and sprinkle with the remaining 1 tablespoon sugar. Bake until the tops and bottoms are golden brown, 18 to 25 minutes. Transfer to a wire rack and cool for 10 minutes before serving.

NOTES FROM THE TEST KITCHEN

FOLDING AND SHAPING THE SCONES

1. Start by folding the dough into thirds (like a business letter). Then fold in the ends of the dough to form a 4-inch square. Chill the dough.

2. Reroll the dough into a 12-inch square. Press the berries into the dough.

3. Roll the dough into a jellyroll-like log to incorporate the blueberries.

4. Lay the log seam side down and press into an even 12 by 4-inch rectangle.

5. Cut the dough into eight triangular pieces.

OATMEAL SCONES

WHY THIS RECIPE WORKS: The oatmeal scones served in a typical coffeehouse are so dry and leaden that they seem like a ploy to get people to buy more coffee to wash them down. We wanted rich toasted oat flavor in a tender, flaky, not-too-sweet scone.

Whole rolled oats and quick oats performed better than instant and steel-cut oats. The rolled oats had a deeper oat flavor, but the quick-cooking oats made scones with a softer

texture; either type will work. Toasting the oats brought out their nutty flavor. We used a minimal amount of sugar and baking powder, but plenty of cold butter. A mixture of milk and heavy cream added richness without making the scones too heavy. An egg proved to be the ultimate touch of richness. Cutting the cold butter into the flour, instead of using melted butter, resulted in a lighter texture; we were careful not to overmix the dough, which toughened the scones. A very hot oven made the scones rise spectacularly and also gave them a craggy appearance; the high heat meant less time in the oven and therefore less time to dry out. You won't need a gallon of coffee to wash down these light, oaty scones.

Oatmeal Scones

MAKES 8 SCONES

Half-and-half is a suitable substitute for the milk-cream combination.

- 1½ cups (4½ ounces) old-fashioned oats or quick oats
- ¼ cup whole milk (see note)
- ¼ cup heavy cream (see note)
- 1 large egg
- 1½ cups (7½ ounces) unbleached all-purpose flour
- ⅓ cup (2⅓ ounces) sugar, plus 1 tablespoon for sprinkling
- 2 teaspoons baking powder
- ½ teaspoon table salt
- 10 tablespoons (1¼ sticks) unsalted butter, chilled and cut into ½-inch cubes

1. Adjust an oven rack to the middle position and heat the oven to 375 degrees. Spread the oats evenly on a rimmed baking sheet and toast in the oven until fragrant and lightly browned, 7 to 9 minutes; cool the oats on the baking sheet on a wire rack. Increase the oven temperature to 450 degrees. Line a second baking sheet with parchment paper. When the oats are cooled, measure out 2 tablespoons (for dusting the work surface and the dough) and set aside.

NOTES FROM THE TEST KITCHEN

CUTTING OATMEAL SCONES

After shaping scone dough into evenly thick round, use bench scraper to cut dough into 8 equal wedges.

2. Whisk the milk, cream, and egg together in a large measuring cup; remove 1 tablespoon of the mixture and reserve for glazing.

3. Pulse the flour, ⅓ cup of the sugar, the baking powder, and salt in a food processor until combined, about 4 pulses. Scatter the cold butter evenly over the dry ingredients and pulse until the mixture resembles coarse cornmeal, about 12 pulses. Transfer the mixture to a medium bowl and stir in the cooled oats. Using a rubber spatula, fold in the liquid ingredients until large clumps form. Mix the dough by hand in the bowl until the dough forms a cohesive mass.

4. Dust a work surface with half of the reserved oats, turn the dough out onto the work surface, and dust the top with the remaining oats. Gently pat into a 7-inch circle about 1 inch thick. Using a bench scraper or chef's knife, cut the dough into eight wedges and set on the prepared baking sheet, spacing the scones about 2 inches apart. Brush the surfaces with the reserved egg mixture and sprinkle with the remaining 1 tablespoon sugar. Bake until golden brown, 12 to 14 minutes; cool the scones on the baking sheet on a wire rack for 5 minutes, then transfer the scones to the rack and cool to room temperature, about 30 minutes. Serve.

Glazed Maple-Pecan Oatmeal Scones

Follow the recipe for Oatmeal Scones, toasting ½ cup chopped pecans with the oats, whisking ¼ cup maple syrup into the milk mixture, and omitting the sugar. When the scones are cooled, whisk 3 tablespoons maple syrup and ½ cup confectioners' sugar together in a small bowl until combined; drizzle the glaze over the scones.

BRITISH-STYLE CURRANT SCONES

WHY THIS RECIPE WORKS: Compared to American scones, British scones are lighter, fluffier, and less sweet; perfect for serving with butter and jam. Rather than leaving pieces of cold butter in the dry ingredients as we would with American scones, we thoroughly worked in softened butter until it was fully integrated. This protected some of the flour granules from moisture, which in turn limited gluten development and kept the crumb tender and cakey. For a higher rise, we added more than the usual amount of leavening and started the scones in a 500-degree oven to boost their lift before turning the temperature down. We brushed some reserved milk and egg on top for enhanced browning, and added currants for tiny bursts of fruit flavor throughout.

British-Style Currant Scones

MAKES 12 SCONES

We prefer whole milk in this recipe, but low-fat milk can be used. The dough will be quite soft and wet; dust your work surface and your hands liberally with flour. For a tall, even rise, use a sharp-edged biscuit cutter and push straight down; do not twist the cutter. These scones are best served fresh, but leftover scones may be stored in the freezer and reheated in a 300-degree oven for 15 minutes before serving. Serve these scones with jam as well as salted butter or clotted cream.

- 3 cups (15 ounces) all-purpose flour
- ⅓ cup (2⅓ ounces) sugar
- 2 tablespoons baking powder
- ½ teaspoon salt
- 8 tablespoons unsalted butter, cut into ½-inch pieces and softened
- ¾ cup dried currants
- 1 cup whole milk
- 2 large eggs

1. Adjust oven rack to upper-middle position and heat oven to 500 degrees. Line rimmed baking sheet with parchment paper. Pulse flour, sugar, baking powder, and salt in food processor until combined, about 5 pulses. Add butter and pulse until fully incorporated and mixture looks like very fine crumbs with no visible butter, about 20 pulses. Transfer mixture to large bowl and stir in currants.

2. Whisk milk and eggs together in second bowl. Set aside 2 tablespoons milk mixture. Add remaining milk mixture to flour mixture and, using rubber spatula, fold together until almost no dry bits of flour remain.

3. Transfer dough to well-floured counter and gather into ball. With floured hands, knead until surface is smooth and free of cracks, 25 to 30 times. Press gently to form disk. Using floured rolling pin, roll disk into 9-inch round, about 1 inch thick. Using floured 2½-inch round cutter, stamp out 8 rounds, recoating cutter with flour if it begins to stick. Arrange scones on prepared sheet. Gather dough scraps, form into ball, and knead gently until surface is smooth. Roll dough to 1-inch thickness and stamp out 4 rounds. Discard remaining dough.

4. Brush tops of scones with reserved milk mixture. Reduce oven temperature to 425 degrees and bake scones until risen and golden brown, 10 to 12 minutes, rotating sheet halfway through baking. Transfer scones to wire rack and let cool for at least 10 minutes. Serve scones warm or at room temperature.

CROISSANTS

WHY THIS RECIPE WORKS: We wanted to create an approachable croissant recipe for home bakers—one that would deliver authentic flavor. The layered structure that characterizes croissants is formed through a process called lamination. First, a basic dough of flour, water, yeast, sugar, salt, and a small amount of butter is made. Then a larger amount of butter is formed into a block and encased in the relatively lean dough. This dough and butter package is rolled out and folded multiple times (each is called a "turn") to form paper-thin layers of dough separated by even thinner layers of butter. Once baked, it's these layers that make croissants so flaky and decadent. To start, we found that more turns didn't necessarily produce more layers; we stopped at three turns, as any more produced a homogeneous bready texture. As for the star ingredient, butter, we found that great croissants demanded higher-fat European-style butter. And one essential tip we discovered during our recipe development was to give the dough a 30-minute quick freeze to firm it to the consistency of the butter, thus ensuring perfectly distinct layers.

Croissants

MAKES 22 CROISSANTS

These croissants take at least 10 hours to make from start to finish, but the process can be spread over 2 days European-style cultured butters have a higher butterfat content, which makes it easier to fold them into the dough. (Our favorite is from Plugrá.) Any brand of all-purpose flour will produce acceptable croissants, but we recommend using King Arthur All-Purpose Flour, which has a slightly higher protein content. Do not attempt to make these croissants in a room that is warmer than 80 degrees. If at any time during rolling the dough retracts, dust it lightly with flour, fold it loosely, cover it, and return it to the freezer to rest for 10 to 15 minutes. This recipe makes 22 croissants, but only 12 are baked. Shaped croissants can be evenly spaced 1 inch apart on a parchment-lined baking sheet, wrapped with plastic wrap, and frozen until solid, about 2 hours. Once frozen, transfer the croissants from the baking sheet to a zipper-lock bag. Croissants can be kept frozen for up to 2 months. Bake frozen croissants as directed from step 8, increasing the rising time by 1 to 2 hours.

- 24 tablespoons European-style unsalted butter, very cold, plus 3 tablespoons unsalted butter at room temperature (see note)
- 1¾ cups whole milk
- 4 teaspoons instant or rapid-rise yeast
- 4¼ cups (21¼ ounces) unbleached all-purpose flour (see note)
- ¼ cup (1¾ ounces) sugar
- Table salt
- 1 large egg
- 1 teaspoon cold water

1. Melt 3 tablespoons of the butter in a medium saucepan over low heat. Remove from the heat and immediately stir in the milk (the temperature should be lower than 90 degrees). Whisk in yeast; transfer the milk mixture to the bowl of a stand mixer. Add the flour, sugar, and 2 teaspoons salt. Using the mixer's dough hook, knead on low speed until a cohesive dough forms, 2 to 3 minutes. Increase the speed to medium-low and knead for 1 minute. Remove the bowl from the mixer, remove the dough hook, and cover the bowl with plastic wrap. Let the dough rest at room temperature for 30 minutes.

2. Transfer the dough to a parchment paper–lined baking sheet and shape into a 10 by 7-inch rectangle about 1 inch thick. Wrap tightly with plastic and refrigerate for 2 hours.

3. TO MAKE THE BUTTER BLOCK: While the dough chills, fold a 24-inch length of parchment in half to create a 12-inch rectangle. Following the photos, fold over 3 open sides of the rectangle to form an 8-inch square with enclosed sides. Crease the folds firmly. Place the cold butter directly on the work surface and beat with a rolling pin for about 60 seconds until the butter is just pliable, but not warm, folding the butter in on itself using a bench scraper. Beat into a rough 6-inch square. Unfold the parchment envelope. Using the bench scraper, transfer the butter to the center of the parchment square, re-folding at the creases to enclose. Turn the packet over so that the flaps are underneath and gently roll the butter packet until the butter fills the parchment square, taking care to achieve an even thickness. Refrigerate for at least 45 minutes.

4. TO LAMINATE THE DOUGH: Transfer the dough to the freezer. After 30 minutes, transfer the dough to a lightly floured work surface and roll into a 17 by 8-inch rectangle with the long side of the rectangle parallel to the edge of the work surface. Following the photos, unwrap the butter and place it in the center of the dough so that the butter and dough

NOTES FROM THE TEST KITCHEN

MAKING THE BUTTER BLOCK FOR CROISSANTS

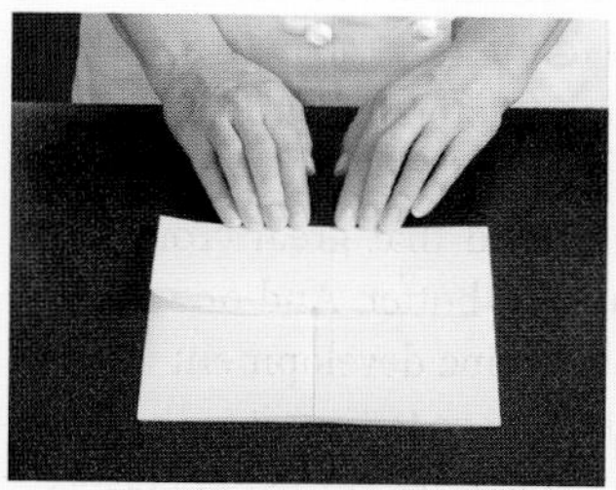

1. Fold a 24-inch length of parchment in half to create a 12-inch rectangle. Fold over 3 open sides of the rectangle to form an 8-inch enclosed square. Crease the folds firmly.

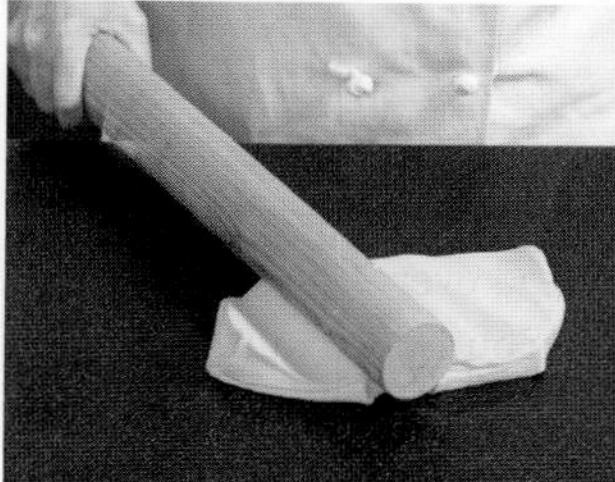

2. Using a rolling pin, beat the butter until it is just pliable, then fold the butter in on itself using a bench scraper. Beat the butter into a rough 6-inch square.

3. Unfold the envelope and, using a bench scraper, transfer the butter to the parchment, re-folding at the creases to enclose. Turn the packet over; gently roll the butter to fill the parchment square, taking care to achieve an even thickness.

LAMINATING THE CROISSANT DOUGH

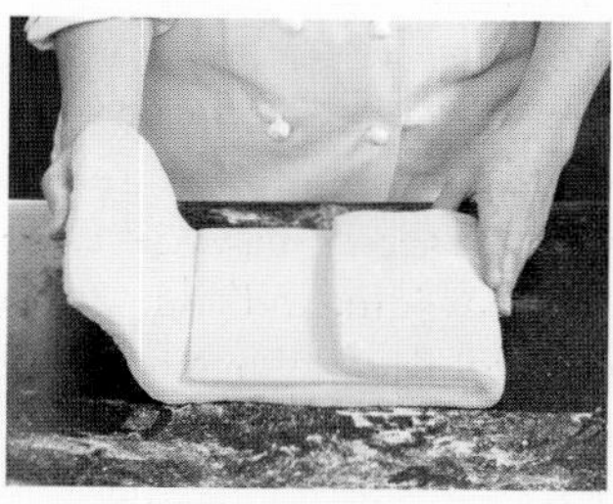

1. Roll the dough into a 17 by 8-inch rectangle. Unwrap the butter and place in the center of the dough so that the edges of the butter and dough are flush at the top and bottom. Fold two sides of the dough over the butter so they meet in the center of the butter square.

2. Using your fingertips, press the seam together. Using a rolling pin, press firmly on each open end of the packet. Roll the dough out lengthwise until it is 24 inches long and 8 inches wide.

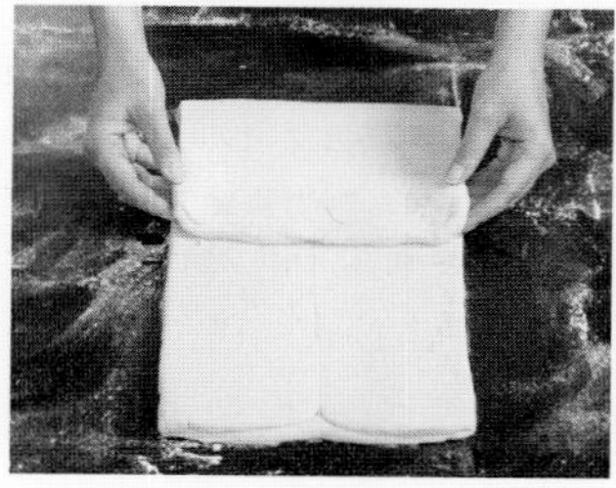

3. Starting at the bottom of the dough, fold it into thirds. Turn the dough 90 degrees; roll and fold again. Place it on a baking sheet, wrap with plastic wrap, and return to the freezer for 30 minutes. Roll and fold into thirds one more time.

are flush at the top and bottom. Fold 2 sides of the dough over the butter square so they meet in the center. Press the seam together. With the rolling pin, press firmly on each open end of the packet. Roll out the dough, perpendicular to the edge of the work surface, until it is 24 inches long and 8 inches wide. Bring the bottom third of the dough up, then fold the upper third over it, folding like a business letter into an 8-inch square. Turn the dough 90 degrees counterclockwise. Roll out the dough again, perpendicular to the edge of the work surface, into a 24 by 8-inch rectangle and fold into thirds. Place the dough on the baking sheet, wrap tightly with plastic wrap, and return to the freezer for 30 minutes.

5. Transfer the dough to a lightly floured work surface so that the top flap of the dough is facing right. Roll once more, perpendicular to the edge of the work surface, into a 24 by 8-inch rectangle and fold into thirds. Place the dough on the baking sheet, wrap tightly with plastic wrap, and refrigerate for 2 hours.

6. Transfer the dough to the freezer. After 30 minutes, transfer to a lightly floured work surface and roll into an 18 by 16-inch rectangle with the long side of the rectangle parallel

NOTES FROM THE TEST KITCHEN

SHAPING THE CROISSANTS

1. Transfer the dough from the freezer to a lightly floured work surface and roll it into an 18 by 12-inch rectangle. (If it begins to retract, fold it into thirds, wrap it, and return it to the freezer for 10 to 15 minutes.) Fold the upper half of the dough over the lower half.

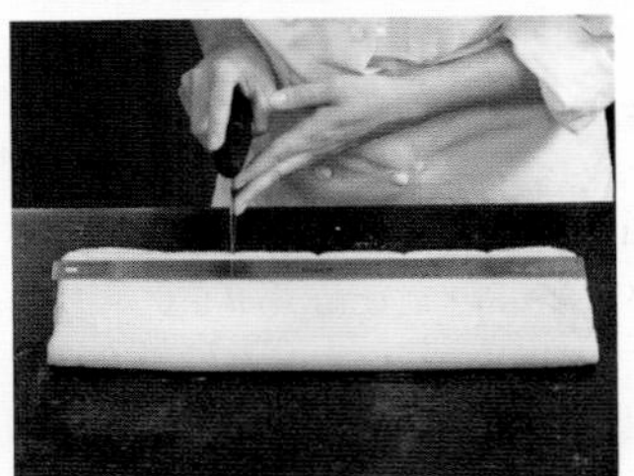

2. Using a ruler, mark the dough at 3-inch intervals along the bottom edge. Move the ruler to the top of the dough, measure in 1½ inches from the left, then use this mark to measure out 3-inch intervals.

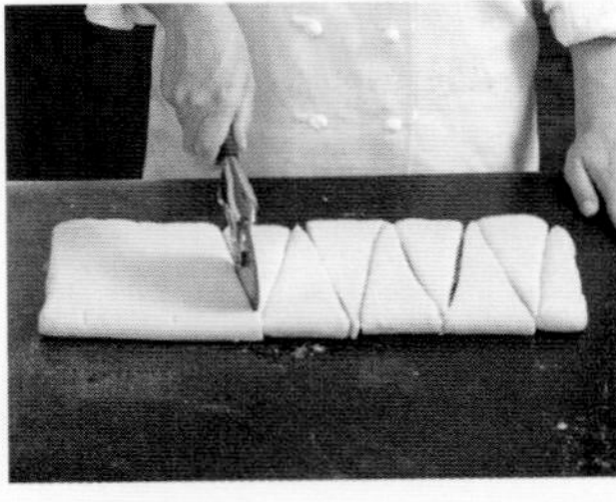

3. Using a sharp pizza wheel or knife, cut the dough into triangles from mark to mark; discard any scraps.

4. You should have 12 single triangles and 5 double triangles. Unfold the double triangles and cut in half to form 10 single triangles (making 22 triangles in all).

5. Cut a ½-inch slit in the center of the short end of a triangle. If the dough begins to soften, return it to the freezer for 10 minutes.

6. Grasp the triangle by the 2 corners on either side of the slit and stretch gently, then grasp the point and stretch.

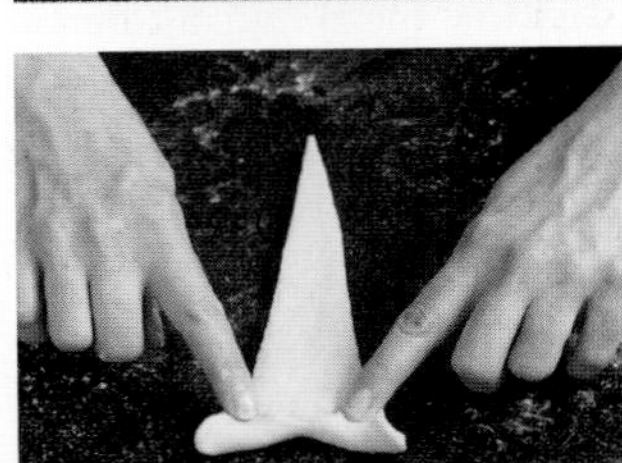

7. Place the triangle on the work surface so the point is facing toward you. Fold both sides of the slit down.

8. Positioning your palms on the folds, roll partway toward the point.

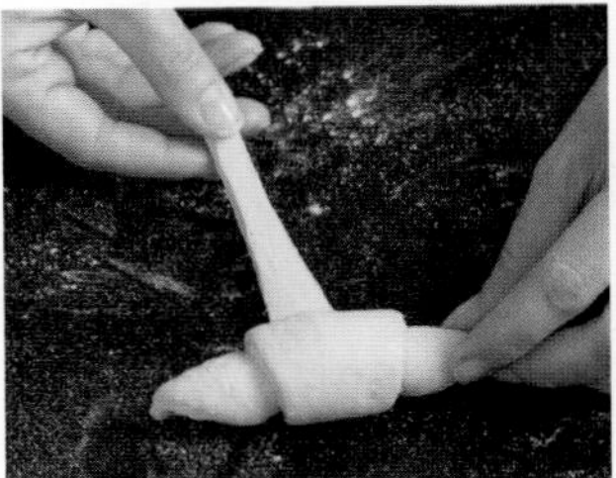

9. Gently grasp the point with one hand and stretch again. Resume rolling, tucking the point underneath.

10. Curve the ends gently toward one another to form a crescent shape. Repeat with the remaining triangles.

to the edge of the work surface. Fold the upper half of the dough over the lower half. Using a ruler, mark the dough at 3-inch intervals along the bottom edge with a bench scraper (you should have 5 marks). Move the ruler to the top of the dough, measure in 1½ inches from the left, then use this mark to measure out 3-inch intervals (you should have 6 marks). Starting at the lower left corner, use a pizza wheel or knife to cut the dough into triangles from mark to mark. You will have 12 single triangles and 5 double triangles; discard any scraps. Unfold the double triangles and cut into 10 single triangles (making 22 equal-size triangles in total). If the dough begins to soften, return to the freezer for 10 minutes.

7. TO SHAPE THE CROISSANTS: Position 1 triangle on the work surface. (Keep the remaining triangles covered with plastic while shaping.) Following the photos on page 660, cut a ½-inch slit in the center of the short end of the triangle. Grasp the triangle by 2 corners on either side of the slit and stretch gently, then grasp the bottom point and stretch. Fold both sides of the slit down. Positioning your palms on the folds, roll partway toward the point. Gently stretch the point again; continue to roll, tucking the point underneath. Curve the ends gently toward one another to create a crescent shape. Repeat with the remaining triangles.

8. Place 12 croissants on 2 parchment-lined baking sheets, leaving at least 2½ inches between the croissants, 6 croissants per sheet. Lightly wrap the baking sheets with plastic, leaving room for the croissants to expand. Let stand at room temperature until nearly doubled in size, 2½ to 3 hours. (Shaped croissants can be refrigerated on trays for up to 18 hours. Remove from the refrigerator to rise and add at least 30 minutes to the rising time.)

9. After the croissants have been rising for 2 hours, adjust the oven racks to the upper-middle and lower-middle positions and heat the oven to 425 degrees. In a small bowl, whisk together the egg, water, and a pinch of salt. Brush the croissants with the egg wash using a pastry brush. Place the croissants in the oven and reduce the temperature to 400 degrees. Bake for 12 minutes then switch and rotate the baking sheets. Continue to bake until deep golden brown, 8 to 12 minutes longer. Transfer the croissants to a wire rack and allow to cool until just warm, about 15 minutes. Serve warm or at room temperature.

BLUEBERRY MUFFINS

WHY THIS RECIPE WORKS: Blueberry muffins should be packed with blueberry flavor and boast a moist crumb. But too often, the blueberry flavor is fleeting, thanks to the fact that the berries in the produce aisle have suffered from long-distance shipping. We wanted blueberry muffins that would taste great with blueberries of any origin, even the watery supermarket kind.

To intensify the blueberry in our muffins, we tried combining blueberry jam with fresh supermarket blueberries. The muffins baked up with a pretty blue filling, but tasters thought the jam made them too sweet. To solve this, we made our own fresh, low-sugar berry jam by simmering fresh blueberries on the stovetop with a bit of sugar. Adding our cooled homemade jam to the batter along with fresh, uncooked berries gave us the best of both worlds: intense blueberry flavor and the liquid burst that only fresh berries could provide.

As for the muffin base, we found that the quick-bread method—whisking together eggs and sugar before adding milk and melted butter, and then gently folding in the dry ingredients—produced a hearty, substantial crumb that could support a generous amount of fruit. We found that an equal amount of butter and oil gave us just the right combination of buttery flavor and moist, tender texture. To make the muffins even richer, we swapped the whole milk for buttermilk. Finally, for a nice crunch, we sprinkled lemon-scented sugar on top of the batter just before baking.

Blueberry Muffins

MAKES 12 MUFFINS

For finely grated lemon zest, use a rasp grater.

LEMON-SUGAR TOPPING

- ⅓ cup (2⅓ ounces) sugar
- 1½ teaspoons finely grated zest from 1 lemon (see note)

MUFFINS

- 2 cups (about 10 ounces) fresh blueberries, picked over
- 1 teaspoon plus 1⅛ cups (8 ounces) sugar
- 2½ cups (12½ ounces) unbleached all-purpose flour
- 2½ teaspoons baking powder
- 1 teaspoon table salt
- 2 large eggs
- 4 tablespoons (½ stick) unsalted butter, melted and cooled slightly
- 4 tablespoons vegetable oil
- 1 cup buttermilk
- 1½ teaspoons vanilla extract

1. FOR THE TOPPING: Stir the sugar and lemon zest together in a small bowl until combined and set aside.

2. FOR THE MUFFINS: Adjust an oven rack to the upper-middle position and heat the oven to 425 degrees. Spray a standard-size muffin pan with vegetable oil spray. Bring 1 cup of the blueberries and 1 teaspoon of the sugar to a simmer in a small saucepan over medium heat. Cook, mashing the berries with a spoon several times and stirring frequently, until the berries have broken down and the mixture is thickened and reduced to ¼ cup, about 6 minutes. Transfer to a small bowl and cool to room temperature, 10 to 15 minutes.

3. Whisk the flour, baking powder, and salt together in a large bowl. Whisk the remaining 1⅛ cups sugar and the eggs together in a medium bowl until thick and homogeneous, about 45 seconds. Slowly whisk in the butter and oil until combined. Whisk in the buttermilk and vanilla until combined. Using a rubber spatula, fold the egg mixture and remaining 1 cup blueberries into the flour mixture until just moistened. (The batter will be very lumpy with a few spots of dry flour; do not overmix.)

4. Using a ⅓-cup measure or an ice cream scoop, divide the batter equally among the prepared muffin cups (the batter should completely fill the cups and mound slightly). Following the photos, spoon 1 teaspoon of the cooked berry mixture into the center of each mound of batter. Using a chopstick or skewer, gently swirl the berry filling into the batter using a figure-eight motion. Sprinkle the lemon sugar evenly over the muffins.

5. Bake until the muffin tops are golden and just firm, 17 to 19 minutes, rotating the pan halfway through baking. Cool the muffins in the pan for 5 minutes, then transfer them to a wire rack and cool for 5 minutes before serving.

NOTES FROM THE TEST KITCHEN

SWIRLING JAM INTO BLUEBERRY MUFFINS

1. Place 1 teaspoon of cooled berry jam in the center of each batter-filled cup, pushing it below the surface.

2. Using a chopstick, swirl the jam into the batter following a figure-eight pattern.

BRAN MUFFINS

WHY THIS RECIPE WORKS: We've made bran muffins with unprocessed wheat bran, so we know how they're supposed to look and taste. But there are so many bran cereals at the supermarket with a muffin recipe on the box that we wondered if we could achieve the same thing without a special trip to the natural foods store.

Twig-style cereal worked better than flakes, but soaking the twigs in milk, as most recipes recommend, left our muffins dense and heavy—they were soaking up all the moisture. Instead, we stirred together the wet ingredients first and then added the cereal; grinding half of the twigs in the food processor and leaving the rest whole gave us the rustic texture we wanted, and the cereal softened in just a few minutes. Whole-milk yogurt added needed moisture to the batter. Molasses and brown sugar reinforced the earthy bran flavor. To improve the texture, we swapped baking soda for baking powder and used one egg plus a yolk—two eggs made the muffins too springy. To ensure that they would soften fully, we plumped the raisins in water in the microwave. These muffins were tender and moist, rustic but not dense, with hearty bran flavor—and all the ingredients came from the supermarket.

Bran Muffins

MAKES 12 MUFFINS

The test kitchen prefers Kellogg's All-Bran Original cereal in this recipe. Dried cranberries or dried cherries may be substituted for the raisins. Low-fat or nonfat yogurt can be substituted for whole-milk yogurt, though the muffins will be slightly less flavorful.

- 1 cup raisins (see note)
- 1 teaspoon water
- 2¼ cups (5 ounces) All-Bran Original cereal (see note)
- 1¼ cups (6¼ ounces) unbleached all-purpose flour
- ½ cup (2½ ounces) whole wheat flour
- 2 teaspoons baking soda
- ½ teaspoon table salt
- 1 large whole egg plus 1 large egg yolk
- ⅔ cup packed (4⅔ ounces) light brown sugar
- 3 tablespoons mild or light molasses
- 1 teaspoon vanilla extract
- 6 tablespoons (¾ stick) unsalted butter, melted and cooled
- 1¾ cups plain whole-milk yogurt (see note)

1. Adjust an oven rack to the middle position and heat the oven to 400 degrees. Spray a standard-size muffin pan with vegetable oil spray. Combine the raisins and water in a small microwave-safe bowl, cover with plastic wrap, cut several steam vents in the plastic with a paring knife, and microwave on high power for 30 seconds. Let stand, covered, until the raisins are softened and plump, about 5 minutes. Transfer the raisins to a paper towel–lined plate to cool.

2. Process half of the bran cereal in a food processor until finely ground, about 1 minute. Whisk the flours, baking soda, and salt in a large bowl to combine; set aside. Whisk the egg and egg yolk together in a medium bowl until well combined and light-colored, about 20 seconds. Add the sugar, molasses, and vanilla; whisk until the mixture is thick, about 30 seconds. Add the melted butter and whisk to combine; add the yogurt and whisk to combine. Stir in the processed cereal and unprocessed cereal; let the mixture sit until the cereal is evenly moistened (there will still be some small lumps), about 5 minutes.

3. Add the wet ingredients to the dry ingredients and gently mix with a rubber spatula until the batter is combined and evenly moistened. Do not overmix. Gently fold the raisins into the batter. Using a ⅓-cup measure or an ice cream scoop, divide the batter evenly among the prepared muffin cups, dropping the batter to form mounds. Do not level or flatten the surfaces of the mounds.

4. Bake until the muffins are dark golden and a toothpick inserted into the center of a muffin comes out with a few crumbs attached, 16 to 20 minutes, rotating the pan halfway through the baking time. Cool the muffins in the pan for 5 minutes, then transfer to a wire rack and cool for 10 minutes before serving.

CORN MUFFINS

WHY THIS RECIPE WORKS: A corn muffin shouldn't be as sweet and fluffy as a cupcake, nor should it be dense and "corny" like corn bread. It should taste like corn, but not overpoweringly, and should be moist with a tender crumb and a crunchy top. Our mission was to come up with a recipe for these seemingly simple muffins that struck just the right balance in both texture and flavor.

The cornmeal itself proved to be an important factor, and degerminated meal just didn't have enough corn flavor. A fine-ground, whole grain meal provided better flavor and texture. Our first batches of muffins were too dry, so we experimented with various ways to add moisture; butter, sour cream, and milk provided the moisture, fat (for richness), and acidity (for its tenderizing effect) that we wanted. We tried mixing the ingredients with both the quick-bread and creaming methods; not only was the former the easier way to go, but it also resulted in less airy, cakey muffins. We got our crunchy top from a 400-degree oven. All in all, we'd resolved all of our issues with corn muffins; these were subtly sweet, rich but not dense, and with a texture that was neither cake nor corn bread.

Corn Muffins

MAKES 12 MUFFINS

Whole grain cornmeal has a fuller flavor than regular cornmeal milled from degerminated corn. To determine what kind of cornmeal a package contains, look closely at the label.

- 2 cups (10 ounces) unbleached all-purpose flour
- 1 cup (5 ounces) fine-ground, whole grain yellow cornmeal (see note)
- 1½ teaspoons baking powder
- 1 teaspoon baking soda
- ½ teaspoon table salt
- 2 large eggs
- ¾ cup (5¼ ounces) sugar
- 8 tablespoons (1 stick) unsalted butter, melted
- ¾ cup sour cream
- ½ cup milk

1. Adjust an oven rack to the middle position and heat the oven to 400 degrees. Spray a standard-size muffin pan with vegetable oil spray.

2. Whisk the flour, cornmeal, baking powder, baking soda, and salt together in a medium bowl; set aside. Whisk the eggs in a second medium bowl. Add the sugar to the eggs; whisk vigorously until thick and homogeneous, about 30 seconds; add the melted butter in three additions, whisking to combine after each addition. Add half of the sour cream and half of the milk and whisk to combine; whisk in the remaining sour cream and milk until combined. Add the wet ingredients to the dry ingredients; mix gently with a rubber spatula until the batter is just combined and evenly moistened. Do not overmix. Using a ⅓-cup measure or ice cream scoop, divide the batter evenly among the prepared muffin cups, dropping the batter to form mounds. Do not level or flatten the surface of the mounds.

3. Bake until the muffins are light golden brown and a skewer inserted into the center of the muffins comes out clean, about 18 minutes, rotating the pan halfway through the baking time. Cool the muffins in the pan for 5 minutes, then transfer to a wire rack and cool for 10 minutes before serving.

Corn and Apricot Muffins with Orange Essence

MAKES 12 MUFFINS

1. In a food processor, process ⅔ cup granulated sugar and 1½ teaspoons grated orange zest until pale orange, about 10 seconds. Transfer to a small bowl and set aside.

2. In a food processor, pulse 1½ cups (10 ounces) dried apricots for 10 pulses, until chopped fine. Transfer to a medium microwave-safe bowl; add ⅔ cup orange juice to the apricots, cover the bowl tightly with plastic wrap, and microwave on high power until simmering, about 1 minute. Let the apricots stand, covered, until softened and plump, about 5 minutes. Strain the apricots and discard the juice.

3. Follow the recipe for Corn Muffins, substituting ¼ cup packed dark brown sugar for an equal amount of the granulated sugar and stirring ½ teaspoon grated orange zest and the strained apricots into the wet ingredients before adding them to the dry ingredients. Before baking, sprinkle a portion of the orange sugar over each mound of batter. Cool the muffins in the pan for 5 minutes, then gently lift them out using the tip of a paring knife. Cool on a wire rack for 10 minutes before serving.

SAVORY CORN MUFFINS

WHY THIS RECIPE WORKS: For a corn muffin with great cornmeal flavor and proper muffin structure, we used a ratio of 2 parts cornmeal to 1 part flour for the former's big flavor and the latter's gluten-forming power. Cutting back on sugar promised a perfectly savory muffin, but we needed to keep a few tablespoons of the sweet stuff in order to boost the batter's moisture retention. To make up for the moisture that extra sugar normally provides, we used a mix of milk, butter, and sour cream for the right amount of water and fat. We incorporated extra liquid into the batter by precooking a portion of the cornmeal with additional milk to make a polenta-like porridge. With this technique, we were able to add nearly double the liquid in the batter, promising a supermoist crumb while still allowing the batter to rise into a pretty dome.

Savory Corn Muffins

MAKES 12 MUFFINS

Don't use coarse-ground or white cornmeal.

- 2 cups (10 ounces) cornmeal
- 1 cup (5 ounces) all-purpose flour
- 1½ teaspoons baking powder
- 1 teaspoon baking soda
- 1¼ teaspoons salt
- 1¼ cups whole milk
- 1 cup sour cream
- 8 tablespoons unsalted butter, melted and cooled slightly
- 3 tablespoons sugar
- 2 large eggs, beaten

1. Adjust oven rack to upper-middle position and heat oven to 425 degrees. Grease 12-cup muffin tin. Whisk 1½ cups cornmeal, flour, baking powder, baking soda, and salt together in medium bowl.

2. Combine milk and remaining ½ cup cornmeal in large bowl. Microwave milk-cornmeal mixture for 1½ minutes. Whisk thoroughly and continue to microwave, whisking every 30 seconds, until thickened to batter-like consistency (whisk will leave channel in bottom of bowl that slowly fills in), 1 to 3 minutes longer. Whisk in sour cream, melted butter, and sugar until combined. Whisk in eggs until combined. Fold in flour mixture until thoroughly combined. Using portion scoop or large spoon, divide batter evenly among prepared muffin cups (about ½ cup batter per cup; batter will mound slightly above rim).

3. Bake until tops are golden brown and toothpick inserted in center comes out clean, 13 to 17 minutes, rotating muffin tin halfway through baking. Let muffins cool in muffin tin on wire rack for 5 minutes. Remove muffins from muffin tin and let cool 5 minutes longer. Serve warm.

Savory Corn Muffins with Rosemary and Black Pepper

Whisk in 1 tablespoon minced fresh rosemary and 1½ teaspoons pepper with eggs.

CRANBERRY-NUT MUFFINS

WHY THIS RECIPE WORKS: Cranberry-nut muffins can make a quick and hearty breakfast, but all too often they are dense and leaden, with an overwhelming sour berry flavor and soggy nuts distributed haphazardly throughout. We wanted a moist, substantial muffin accented—but not overtaken—by tart cranberries and toasted, crunchy nuts. Hand mixing the batter was quick and gave our muffins enough structure to accommodate the fruit and nuts. Grinding some of the nuts and using them in place of some of the flour added complexity and nutty flavor throughout. Chopping the berries and tossing them with a little sugar toned down their tartness. Finally, adding a streusel topping added back the crunch lost from grinding up the nuts.

Cranberry-Pecan Muffins

MAKES 12 MUFFINS

If fresh cranberries aren't available, substitute frozen cranberries. Before using, place the cranberries in a microwave-safe bowl and microwave on high power until the cranberries are partially thawed, 30 to 45 seconds. Do not overthaw the cranberries.

STREUSEL TOPPING

- 3 tablespoons unbleached all-purpose flour
- 1 tablespoon packed light brown sugar
- 1 tablespoon plus 1 teaspoon granulated sugar
- Table salt
- 2 tablespoons unsalted butter, cut into ½-inch pieces, softened
- ½ cup pecan halves

MUFFINS

- 1⅓ cups (6⅔ ounces) unbleached all-purpose flour
- 1½ teaspoons baking powder
- 1 teaspoon table salt
- 1¼ cups pecan halves, toasted and cooled
- 1 cup plus 1 tablespoon (7½ ounces) granulated sugar
- 2 large eggs
- 6 tablespoons (¾ stick) unsalted butter, melted and cooled
- ½ cup whole milk
- 2 cups fresh cranberries
- 1 tablespoon confectioners' sugar

1. Adjust an oven rack to the upper-middle position and heat the oven to 425 degrees. Spray a 12-cup muffin tin with vegetable oil spray.

2. FOR THE STREUSEL: Pulse the flour, brown sugar, granulated sugar, a pinch of salt, and the butter in a food processor until the mixture resembles coarse sand, 4 to 5 pulses. Add the pecans and pulse until the pecans are chopped coarse, about 4 pulses. Transfer to a small bowl; set aside.

3. FOR THE MUFFINS: Whisk the flour, baking powder, and ¾ teaspoon of the salt together in a bowl; set aside.

4. Process the toasted pecans and granulated sugar until the mixture resembles coarse sand, 10 to 15 seconds. Transfer to a large bowl and whisk in the eggs, butter, and milk until combined. Whisk the flour mixture into the egg mixture until just moistened and no streaks of flour remain. Set the batter aside for 30 minutes to thicken.

5. Pulse the cranberries, remaining ¼ teaspoon salt, and confectioners' sugar in the food processor until very coarsely chopped, 4 to 5 pulses. Using a rubber spatula, fold the cranberries into the batter. Using an ice cream scoop or large spoon, divide the batter equally among the prepared muffin cups (the batter should completely fill the cups and mound slightly). Evenly sprinkle the streusel topping over the muffins, gently pressing into the batter to adhere. Bake until the muffin tops are golden and just firm, 17 to 18 minutes, rotating the muffin tin halfway through baking. Cool the muffins in the muffin tin on a wire rack for 10 minutes. Remove the muffins from the tin and cool for 10 minutes before serving.

OATMEAL MUFFINS

WHY THIS RECIPE WORKS: For an oatmeal muffin that is packed with oats but also has a fine, tender texture, we processed old-fashioned rolled oats into a flour in the food processor. To boost oat flavor, we first toasted the oats in a couple of tablespoons of butter and eliminated extraneous spices from the batter. To ensure a lump-free batter, we used a whisk to fold the wet and dry ingredients together and allowed the batter to sit and hydrate for 20 minutes before baking. Finally, we made an apple crisp–inspired topping of crunchy oats, nuts, and brown sugar.

Oatmeal Muffins

MAKES 12 MUFFINS

Do not use quick or instant oats in this recipe. Walnuts may be substituted for the pecans. The easiest way to grease and flour the muffin tin is with a baking spray with flour.

TOPPING

- ½ cup (1½ ounces) old-fashioned rolled oats
- ⅓ cup (1⅔ ounces) all-purpose flour
- ⅓ cup pecans, chopped fine
- ⅓ cup packed (2⅓ ounces) light brown sugar
- 1¼ teaspoons ground cinnamon
- ⅛ teaspoon salt
- 4 tablespoons unsalted butter, melted

MUFFINS

- 2 tablespoons unsalted butter, plus 6 tablespoons melted
- 2 cups (6 ounces) old-fashioned rolled oats
- 1¾ cups (8¾ ounces) all-purpose flour
- 1½ teaspoons salt
- ¾ teaspoon baking powder
- ¼ teaspoon baking soda
- 1⅓ cups packed (9⅓ ounces) light brown sugar
- 1¾ cups milk
- 2 large eggs, beaten

1. FOR THE TOPPING: Combine oats, flour, pecans, sugar, cinnamon, and salt in medium bowl. Drizzle melted butter over mixture and stir to thoroughly combine; set aside.

2. FOR THE MUFFINS: Grease and flour 12-cup muffin tin. Melt 2 tablespoons butter in 10-inch skillet over medium heat. Add oats and cook, stirring frequently, until oats turn golden brown and smell of cooking popcorn, 6 to 8 minutes. Transfer oats to food processor and process into fine meal, about 30 seconds. Add flour, salt, baking powder, and baking soda to oats and pulse until combined, about 3 pulses.

3. Stir 6 tablespoons melted butter and sugar together in large bowl until smooth. Add milk and eggs and whisk until smooth. Using whisk, gently fold half of oat mixture into wet ingredients, tapping whisk against side of bowl to release clumps. Add remaining oat mixture and continue to fold with whisk until no streaks of flour remain. Set aside batter for 20 minutes to thicken. Meanwhile, adjust oven rack to middle position and heat oven to 375 degrees.

4. Using ice cream scoop or large spoon, divide batter equally among prepared muffin cups (about ½ cup batter per cup; cups will be filled to rim). Evenly sprinkle topping over muffins (about 2 tablespoons per muffin). Bake until toothpick inserted in center comes out clean, 18 to 25 minutes, rotating muffin tin halfway through baking.

5. Let muffins cool in muffin tin on wire rack for 10 minutes. Remove muffins from muffin tin and serve or let cool completely before serving.

CRUMB CAKE

WHY THIS RECIPE WORKS: The original crumb cake was brought to New York by German immigrants; sadly, the bakery-fresh versions have all but disappeared, and most people know only the commercially baked (and preservative-laden) type. We wanted a recipe closer to the original version that could be made at home.

Most modern recipes use butter cake rather than the traditional yeast dough, which made our job that much easier. The essence of this cake is the balance between the tender, buttery cake and the thick, lightly spiced crumb topping. Starting with our favorite yellow cake recipe, we realized we needed to reduce the amount of butter or the richness would be overwhelming. We compensated for the resulting dryness by substituting buttermilk for milk, which also helped make the cake sturdy enough to support the crumbs, and we left out an egg white so the cake wouldn't be rubbery. We wanted our crumb topping to be soft and cookie-like, not a crunchy streusel, so we mixed granulated and brown sugars and melted the butter for a dough-like consistency, flavoring the mixture only with cinnamon. Broken into little pieces and sprinkled over the cake batter, our topping held together during baking and made a thick layer of moist crumbs with golden edges that didn't sink into the cake.

New York–Style Crumb Cake

SERVES 8 TO 10

Don't be tempted to substitute all-purpose flour for the cake flour; doing so will make a dry, tough cake. If you can't find buttermilk, you can use an equal amount of plain low-fat yogurt, but do not substitute powdered buttermilk because it will make a sunken cake. When topping the cake, take care to not push the crumbs into the batter. This recipe can be easily doubled and baked in a 13 by 9-inch baking dish. If doubling, increase the baking time to about 45 minutes.

CRUMB TOPPING

- ⅓ cup (2⅔ ounces) granulated sugar
- ⅓ cup packed (2⅓ ounces) dark brown sugar
- ¾ teaspoon ground cinnamon
- ⅛ teaspoon table salt
- 8 tablespoons (1 stick) unsalted butter, melted and still warm
- 1¾ cups (7 ounces) cake flour (see note)

CAKE

- 1¼ cups (5 ounces) cake flour (see note)
- ½ cup (3½ ounces) granulated sugar
- ¼ teaspoon baking soda
- ¼ teaspoon table salt
- 6 tablespoons (¾ stick) unsalted butter, cut into 6 pieces, softened but still cool
- 1 large whole egg plus 1 large egg yolk
- ⅓ cup buttermilk (see note)
- 1 teaspoon vanilla extract
- Confectioners' sugar, for dusting

1. **FOR THE CRUMB TOPPING:** Whisk the sugars, cinnamon, salt, and butter together in a medium bowl to combine. Add the flour and stir with a rubber spatula or wooden spoon until the mixture resembles a thick, cohesive dough; set aside to cool to room temperature, 10 to 15 minutes.

2. **FOR THE CAKE:** Adjust an oven rack to the upper-middle position and heat the oven to 325 degrees. Cut a 16-inch length of parchment paper or aluminum foil and fold lengthwise to a 7-inch width. Spray an 8-inch square baking dish with vegetable oil spray and fit the parchment into the dish, pushing it into the corners and up the sides; allow the excess to overhang the edges of the dish.

3. In the bowl of a stand mixer fitted with the paddle attachment, mix the flour, sugar, baking soda, and salt on low speed to combine. With the mixer running at low speed, add the butter one piece at a time; continue beating until the mixture resembles moist crumbs, with no visible butter chunks remaining, 1 to 2 minutes. Add the egg, egg yolk, buttermilk, and vanilla; beat on medium-high speed until light and fluffy, about 1 minute, scraping once if necessary.

4. Transfer the batter to the prepared baking pan; using a rubber spatula, spread the batter into an even layer. Break apart the crumb topping into large pea-size pieces, rolling them between your thumb and forefinger to form crumbs, and spread in an even layer over the batter, beginning with the edges and then working toward the center. Bake until the crumbs are golden and a wooden skewer inserted into the center of the cake comes out clean, 35 to 40 minutes. Cool on a wire rack for at least 30 minutes. Remove the cake from the pan by lifting the parchment overhang. Dust with confectioners' sugar before serving.

BLUEBERRY BOY BAIT

WHY THIS RECIPE WORKS: This coffee cake, a moist cake with blueberries and a light streusel topping, is so called because the girl who created it for the Pillsbury Grand National Baking Contest said that teenage boys found it irresistible. We tracked down a version of the contest-winning recipe and decided to see if we could improve it.

The original recipe called for shortening and granulated sugar. We swapped butter for the shortening and brown sugar for some of the granulated sugar. Both exchanges resulted in richer, deeper flavor in the cake. We doubled the amount of blueberries; half went into the cake batter and the other half on top. An extra egg in the cake batter firmed up the structure so that the extra fruit wouldn't make the cake mushy. The topping couldn't be simpler: in addition to the blueberries, just sugar and cinnamon instead of a streusel, which baked into a light, crisp, sweet coating. If the quick disappearance of this cake is any indication, it's not only teenage boys who can't refuse a second piece.

Blueberry Boy Bait

SERVES 12

If using frozen blueberries, do not let them thaw, as they will turn the batter a blue-green color.

CAKE

- 2 cups (10 ounces) plus 1 teaspoon unbleached all-purpose flour
- 1 tablespoon baking powder
- 1 teaspoon table salt
- 16 tablespoons (2 sticks) unsalted butter, softened
- ¾ cup packed (5¼ ounces) light brown sugar
- ½ cup (3½ ounces) granulated sugar
- 3 large eggs
- 1 cup whole milk
- ½ cup blueberries, fresh or frozen (see note)

TOPPING

- ½ cup blueberries, fresh or frozen (see note)
- ¼ cup (1¾ ounces) granulated sugar
- ½ teaspoon ground cinnamon

1. FOR THE CAKE: Adjust an oven rack to the middle position and heat the oven to 350 degrees. Grease and flour a 13 by 9-inch baking pan.

2. Whisk 2 cups of the flour, the baking powder, and salt together in a medium bowl. With an electric mixer, beat the butter and sugars on medium-high speed until fluffy, about 2 minutes. Add the eggs, one at a time, beating until just incorporated. Reduce the speed to medium and beat in one-third of the flour mixture until incorporated; beat in ½ cup of the milk. Beat in half of the remaining flour mixture, then the remaining ½ cup milk, and finally the remaining flour mixture. Toss the blueberries in a small bowl with the remaining 1 teaspoon flour. Using a rubber spatula, gently fold in the blueberries. Spread the batter into the prepared pan.

3. FOR THE TOPPING: Scatter the blueberries over the top of the batter. Stir the sugar and cinnamon together in a small bowl and sprinkle over the batter. Bake until a toothpick inserted in the center of the cake comes out clean, 45 to 50 minutes. Cool in the pan for 20 minutes, then turn out and place on a serving platter (topping side up). Serve warm or at room temperature. (The cake can be stored in an airtight container at room temperature for up to 3 days.)

CINNAMON BUNS

WHY THIS RECIPE WORKS: A tender, fluffy bun with a sweet filling and glaze is a brunch treat no one will turn down. Most recipes, though, require yeast, which makes them time-consuming. Eliminating the yeast would reduce the prep time substantially, so we started with the assumption that our leavener would be baking powder. A cream biscuit recipe, which could be mixed all in one bowl, was our starting point; buttermilk rather than cream (plus baking soda to balance the acidity of the buttermilk) made the interior of the buns light and airy. Melted butter restored some of the richness we had lost by eliminating the cream. A brief kneading ensured that the rolls would rise. We patted out the dough rather than rolling it out and covered it with the filling of brown and granulated sugars, cinnamon, cloves, and salt, with melted butter to help the mixture adhere. We rolled up the dough, cut the buns, and put them in a nonstick cake pan to bake. We topped the buns with a glaze of confectioners' sugar, buttermilk, and cream cheese. These cinnamon buns were on the table in less than a quarter of the time it would have taken for yeast buns—and they were just as tasty.

Quick Cinnamon Buns with Buttermilk Icing

MAKES 8 BUNS

Melted butter is used in both the filling and the dough and to grease the pan; melt the total amount (8 tablespoons) at once and measure it out as you need it. The buns are best eaten warm, but they will hold for up to 2 hours.

- 1 tablespoon unsalted butter, melted, for the pan (see note)

CINNAMON-SUGAR FILLING

- ¾ cup packed (5¼ ounces) dark brown sugar
- ¼ cup (1¾ ounces) granulated sugar
- 2 teaspoons ground cinnamon
- ⅛ teaspoon ground cloves
- ⅛ teaspoon table salt
- 1 tablespoon unsalted butter, melted (see note)

BISCUIT DOUGH

- 2½ cups (12½ ounces) unbleached all-purpose flour, plus extra for the work surface
- 2 tablespoons granulated sugar
- 1¼ teaspoons baking powder
- ½ teaspoon baking soda
- ½ teaspoon table salt
- 1¼ cups buttermilk
- 6 tablespoons (¾ stick) unsalted butter, melted (see note)

ICING

- 2 tablespoons cream cheese, softened
- 2 tablespoons buttermilk
- 1 cup (4 ounces) confectioners' sugar

1. Adjust an oven rack to the upper-middle position and heat the oven to 425 degrees. Pour 1 tablespoon of the melted butter into a 9-inch nonstick cake pan; brush to coat the pan. Spray a wire rack with vegetable oil spray and set aside.

2. FOR THE CINNAMON-SUGAR FILLING: Combine the sugars, spices, and salt in a small bowl. Add the melted butter and stir with a fork or your fingers until the mixture resembles wet sand; set the filling mixture aside.

3. FOR THE BISCUIT DOUGH: Whisk the flour, sugar, baking powder, baking soda, and salt together in a large bowl. Whisk the buttermilk and 2 tablespoons of the melted butter together in a measuring cup or small bowl. Add the liquid to the dry ingredients and stir with a wooden spoon until the liquid is absorbed (the dough will look very shaggy), about 30 seconds. Transfer the dough to a lightly floured work surface and knead until just smooth and no longer shaggy.

4. Pat the dough with your hands into a 12 by 9-inch rectangle. Brush the dough with 2 tablespoons more melted butter. Sprinkle evenly with the filling, leaving a ½-inch border of plain dough around the edges. Press the filling firmly into the dough. Using a bench scraper or metal spatula, loosen the dough from the work surface. Starting at a long side, roll the dough, pressing lightly, to form a tight log. Pinch the seam to seal. Roll the log seam side down and cut it evenly into eight pieces. With your hand, slightly flatten each piece of dough to seal the open edges and keep the filling in place. Place one roll in the center of the prepared pan, then place the remaining seven rolls around the perimeter of the pan. Brush with the remaining 2 tablespoons melted butter.

5. Bake until the edges are golden brown, 23 to 25 minutes. Use an offset metal spatula to loosen the buns from the pan. Wearing an oven mitt, place a large plate over the pan and invert the buns onto a plate. Place the greased wire rack over the plate and invert the buns onto the rack. Cool for 5 minutes.

6. FOR THE ICING: While the buns are cooling, line a rimmed baking sheet with parchment paper; set the rack with the buns over the baking sheet. Whisk the cream cheese and buttermilk together in a large nonreactive bowl until thick and smooth (the mixture will look like cottage cheese at first). Sift the confectioners' sugar over the mixture; whisk until a smooth glaze forms, about 30 seconds. Spoon the glaze evenly over the buns and serve.

STICKY BUNS

WHY THIS RECIPE WORKS: Sticky buns are often too sweet, too big, too rich—just too much. We wanted a bun that was neither dense nor bready, but tender and feathery. The sticky glaze should be gently chewy and gooey; the flavor should be warm and spicy, buttery and sweet—but just enough so that devouring one isn't a feat.

To keep the sticky bun glaze from hardening into a taffy-like shell, we hit on the idea of including cream, which kept the glaze supple. The yeast dough for these buns should be rich, so we added buttermilk, which gave the buns a complex flavor and a little acidity that balanced the sweetness. Butter and eggs enriched the dough further. After the first rise, we spread the filling—dark brown sugar, cinnamon, cloves, and butter—over the dough, rolled it, cut the individual buns, and laid them in the pan with the caramel to rise once more before being baked. We found that setting the pan (a metal nonstick pan was preferable) on a baking stone in the oven ensured that the bottoms of the buns (which would end up on top) baked completely. We wanted pecans in our sticky buns, too, but they lost their crunch when we put them into the filling or the topping. To preserve their crispness, we topped the rolls with the toasted nuts in a lightly sweetened glaze before serving.

Sticky Buns with Pecans

MAKES 12 BUNS

This recipe has four components: the dough that is shaped into buns, the filling that creates the swirl in the shaped buns, the caramel glaze that bakes in the bottom of the baking dish along with the buns, and the pecan topping that garnishes the buns once they're baked. Although the ingredient list may look long, note that many ingredients are repeated. Leftover sticky buns can be wrapped in foil or plastic wrap and refrigerated for up to 3 days, but they should be warmed through before serving. They reheat quickly in a microwave oven (for two buns, about 2 minutes at 50 percent power works well).

DOUGH

- 3 large eggs, at room temperature
- ¾ cup buttermilk, at room temperature
- ¼ cup (1¾ ounces) granulated sugar
- 1¼ teaspoons table salt
- 2¼ teaspoons (1 envelope) instant or rapid-rise yeast
- 4¼ cups (21¼ ounces) unbleached all-purpose flour, plus extra for the work surface
- 6 tablespoons (¾ stick) unsalted butter, melted and still warm

CARAMEL GLAZE

- ¾ cup packed (5¼ ounces) light brown sugar
- 6 tablespoons (¾ stick) unsalted butter
- 3 tablespoons light or dark corn syrup
- 2 tablespoons heavy cream
- Pinch table salt

CINNAMON-SUGAR FILLING

- ¾ cup packed (5¼ ounces) light brown sugar
- 2 teaspoons ground cinnamon
- ¼ teaspoon ground cloves
- Pinch table salt
- 1 tablespoon unsalted butter, melted

PECAN TOPPING

- ¼ cup packed (1¾ ounces) light brown sugar
- 3 tablespoons light or dark corn syrup
- 3 tablespoons unsalted butter
- Pinch table salt
- ¾ cup (3 ounces) pecans, toasted in a small, dry skillet over medium heat until fragrant and browned, about 5 minutes, then cooled and chopped coarse
- 1 teaspoon vanilla extract

1. FOR THE DOUGH: In the bowl of a stand mixer, whisk the eggs to combine; add the buttermilk and whisk to combine. Whisk in the granulated sugar, salt, and yeast. Add about 2 cups of the flour and the butter; stir with a wooden spoon or rubber spatula until evenly moistened and combined. Add all but about ¼ cup of the remaining flour and knead with the dough hook at low speed for 5 minutes. Check the consistency of the dough (it should feel soft and moist but should not be wet and sticky; add more flour, if necessary); knead at low speed 5 minutes longer (the dough should clear the sides of the bowl but stick to the bottom). Turn the dough out onto a lightly floured work surface; knead by hand for about 1 minute to ensure that the dough is uniform (the dough should not stick to the work surface during hand kneading; if it does, knead in additional flour 1 tablespoon at a time).

2. Lightly spray a large bowl or plastic container with vegetable oil spray. Transfer the dough to the bowl, spray the dough lightly with vegetable oil spray, then cover the bowl tightly with plastic wrap and set in a warm, draft-free spot until doubled in volume, 2 to 2½ hours.

3. FOR THE CARAMEL GLAZE: Meanwhile, combine all the glaze ingredients in a small saucepan; cook over medium heat, whisking occasionally, until the butter is melted and the mixture is thoroughly combined. Pour the mixture into a nonstick metal 13 by 9-inch baking dish; using a rubber spatula, spread the mixture to cover the surface of the baking dish; set the baking dish aside.

4. FOR THE FILLING: Combine the brown sugar, cinnamon, cloves, and salt in a small bowl and mix until thoroughly combined, using your fingers to break up any sugar lumps; set aside.

5. TO ASSEMBLE AND BAKE THE BUNS: Turn the dough out onto a lightly floured work surface. Gently shape the dough into a rough rectangle with a long side nearest you. Lightly flour the dough and roll to a 16 by 12-inch rectangle. Brush the dough with the melted butter, leaving a ½-inch border along the top edge; brush the sides of the baking dish with the butter remaining on the brush. Sprinkle the filling mixture over the dough, leaving a ¾-inch border along the top edge; smooth the filling in an even layer with your hand, then gently press the mixture into the dough to adhere. Beginning with the long edge nearest you, roll the dough into a taut cylinder. Firmly pinch the seam to seal and roll the cylinder seam side down. Very gently stretch to form a cylinder of even diameter and 18-inch length; push the ends in to create an even thickness. Using a serrated knife and gentle sawing motion, slice the cylinder in half, then slice each half in half again to create evenly sized quarters. Slice each quarter evenly into thirds, yielding 12 buns (the end pieces may be slightly smaller).

6. Arrange the buns cut side down in the prepared baking dish; cover tightly with plastic wrap and set in a warm, draft-free spot until puffy and pressed against one another, about 1½ hours. Meanwhile, adjust an oven rack to the lowest position, place a baking stone on the rack, and heat the oven to 350 degrees.

7. Place the baking pan on the baking stone; bake until golden brown and the center of the dough registers 180 degrees on an instant-read thermometer, 25 to 30 minutes. Cool on a wire rack for 10 minutes; invert onto a rimmed baking sheet, large rectangular platter, or cutting board. With a rubber spatula, scrape any glaze remaining in the baking pan onto the buns; cool while making the pecan topping.

8. FOR THE PECAN TOPPING: Combine the brown sugar, corn syrup, butter, and salt in a small saucepan and bring to a simmer over medium heat, whisking occasionally to thoroughly combine. Off the heat, stir in the pecans and vanilla until the pecans are evenly coated. Using a soupspoon, spoon a heaping tablespoon of nuts and topping over the center of each sticky bun. Continue to cool until the sticky buns are warm, 15 to 20 minutes. Pull apart or use a serrated knife to cut apart the sticky buns; serve.

PERFECT STICKY BUNS

WHY THIS RECIPE WORKS: Sticky buns look inviting, but most are dry and overly sweet, with a topping that threatens your dental work. We wanted a version that fulfilled its promise. To make a softer, more tender, and moist sticky bun, we added a cooked flour-and-water paste to the dough. The paste traps water, so the dough isn't sticky or difficult to work with, and the increased hydration converts to steam during baking, which makes the bread fluffy and light. The added water also keeps the crumb moist and tender. To ensure that the soft bread wouldn't collapse under the weight of the topping, we strengthened the crumb by adding a resting period and withholding the sugar and salt until the gluten was firmly established. Dark corn syrup plus water was the key to a gooey, sticky topping that was substantial enough to sit atop the buns without sinking in but not so firm that it presented a danger to our teeth.

Perfect Sticky Buns

MAKES 12 BUNS

These buns take about 4 hours to make from start to finish. For dough that is easy to work with and produces light, fluffy buns, we strongly recommend that you measure the flour for the dough by weight. The slight tackiness of the dough aids in flattening and stretching it in step 6, so resist the urge to use a lot of dusting flour. Rolling the dough cylinder tightly in step 7 will result in misshapen rolls; keep the cylinder a bit slack. Bake these buns in a metal, not glass or ceramic, baking pan. We like dark corn syrup and pecans here, but light corn syrup may be used, and the nuts may be omitted, if desired.

FLOUR PASTE

- ⅔ cup water
- ¼ cup (1⅓ ounces) bread flour

DOUGH

- ⅔ cup milk
- 1 large egg plus 1 large yolk
- 2¾ cups (15⅛ ounces) bread flour
- 2 teaspoons instant or rapid-rise yeast
- 3 tablespoons granulated sugar
- 1½ teaspoons salt
- 6 tablespoons unsalted butter, softened

TOPPING

- 6 tablespoons unsalted butter, melted
- ½ cup packed (3½ ounces) dark brown sugar
- ¼ cup (1¾ ounces) granulated sugar
- ¼ cup dark corn syrup
- ¼ teaspoon salt
- 2 tablespoons water
- 1 cup pecans, toasted and chopped (optional)

FILLING

- ¾ cup packed (5¼ ounces) dark brown sugar
- 1 teaspoon ground cinnamon

1. FOR THE FLOUR PASTE: Whisk water and flour together in small bowl until no lumps remain. Microwave, whisking every 25 seconds, until mixture thickens to stiff, smooth, pudding-like consistency that forms mound when dropped from end of whisk into bowl, 50 to 75 seconds.

2. FOR THE DOUGH: In bowl of stand mixer, whisk flour paste and milk together until smooth. Add egg and yolk and whisk until incorporated. Add flour and yeast. Fit stand mixer with dough hook and mix on low speed until all flour is moistened, 1 to 2 minutes. Let stand for 15 minutes. Add sugar and salt and mix on medium-low speed for 5 minutes. Stop mixer and add butter. Continue to mix on medium-low speed for 5 minutes longer, scraping down dough hook and sides of bowl halfway through (dough will stick to bottom of bowl).

3. Transfer dough to lightly floured counter. Knead briefly to form ball and transfer seam side down to lightly greased bowl; lightly coat surface of dough with vegetable oil spray and cover bowl with plastic wrap. Let dough rise until just doubled in volume, 40 minutes to 1 hour.

4. FOR THE TOPPING: While dough rises, grease 13 by 9-inch metal baking pan. Whisk melted butter, brown sugar, granulated sugar, corn syrup, and salt together in medium bowl until smooth. Add water and whisk until incorporated. Pour mixture into prepared pan and tilt pan to cover bottom. Sprinkle evenly with pecans, if using.

5. FOR THE FILLING: Combine sugar and cinnamon in small bowl and mix until thoroughly combined; set aside.

6. Turn out dough onto lightly floured counter. Press dough gently but firmly to expel air. Working from center toward edge, pat and stretch dough to form 18 by 15-inch rectangle with long edge nearest you. Sprinkle filling over dough, leaving 1-inch border along top edge; smooth filling into even layer with your hand, then gently press mixture into dough to adhere.

7. Beginning with long edge nearest you, roll dough into cylinder, taking care not to roll too tightly. Pinch seam to seal and roll cylinder seam side down. Mark gently with knife to create 12 equal portions. To slice, hold strand of dental floss taut and slide underneath cylinder, stopping at first mark. Cross ends of floss over each other and pull. Slice cylinder into 12 portions and transfer, cut sides down, to prepared baking pan. Cover tightly with plastic wrap and let rise until buns are puffy and touching one another, 40 minutes to 1 hour. (Buns may be refrigerated immediately after shaping for up to 14 hours. To bake, remove baking pan from refrigerator and let sit until buns are puffy and touching one another, 1 to 1½ hours.) Meanwhile, adjust oven racks to lowest and lower-middle positions. Place rimmed baking sheet on lower rack to catch any drips and heat oven to 375 degrees.

8. Bake buns on upper rack until golden brown, about 20 minutes. Tent with aluminum foil and bake until center of dough registers at least 200 degrees, 10 to 15 minutes longer. Let buns cool in pan on wire rack for 5 minutes. Place rimmed baking sheet over buns and carefully invert. Using spoon, scoop any glaze from baking pan onto buns. Let cool for at least 10 minutes longer before serving.

NOTES FROM THE TEST KITCHEN

ROLLING DOUGH FOR STICKY BUNS

Because these sticky buns bake up so soft and fluffy, it's important to roll the dough loosely when forming the cylinder in step 7. If rolled too tightly, the buns will expand upward.

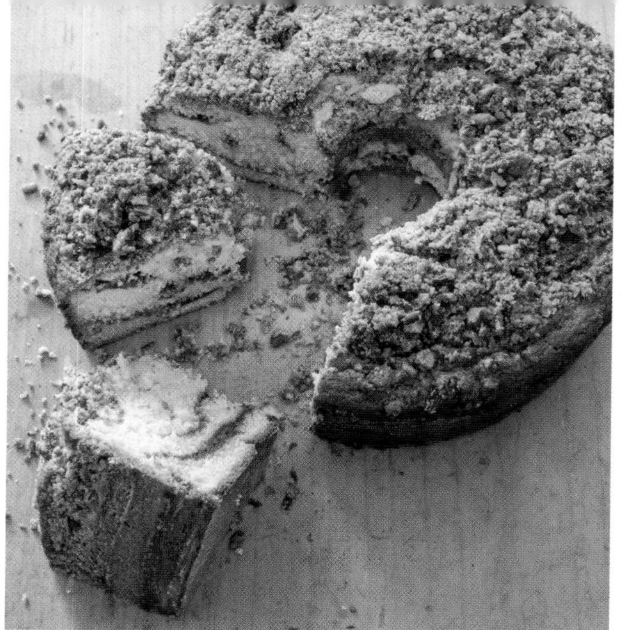

SOUR CREAM COFFEE CAKE

WHY THIS RECIPE WORKS: Sour cream coffee cakes should be buttery and rich. But some recipes yield a heavy cake that borders on greasy. We wanted a pleasantly rich cake with lots of streusel. All-purpose flour gave us a better texture than the cake flour specified in many recipes. For richness, we used plenty of butter, sour cream, and eggs; the eggs also contributed a tight crumb. Baking powder and baking soda were necessary to make this hefty batter rise. Rather than creaming the butter and sugar, which made the cake too light and airy, we cut softened butter and some of the sour cream into the dry ingredients, then added the eggs and the rest of the sour cream. In addition to the streusel in the middle of the cake, we wanted more on top, so we started with a mixture of brown and granulated sugars and added a big hit of cinnamon and some flour (to keep the streusel from congealing). We then divided the mixture—some for the interior streusel layers, which we sweetened further with more brown sugar, and the rest for the topping. To the latter, we added pecans and butter; the nuts toasted as the cake baked, so we didn't have to toast them first. With two layers of streusel in our moist, rich cake and another layer on top with toasty, crunchy nuts, this was a coffee cake worth getting up for.

Sour Cream Coffee Cake with Brown Sugar–Pecan Streusel

SERVES 12 TO 16

A 10-inch tube pan is best for this recipe.

STREUSEL

- ¾ cup (3¾ ounces) unbleached all-purpose flour
- ¾ cup (5¼ ounces) granulated sugar
- ½ cup packed (3½ ounces) dark brown sugar
- 2 tablespoons ground cinnamon
- 1 cup pecans, chopped
- 2 tablespoons unsalted butter, chilled and cut into 2 pieces

CAKE

- 12 tablespoons (1½ sticks) unsalted butter, softened but still cool, cut into ½-inch cubes, plus 2 tablespoons softened butter, for greasing the pan
- 4 large eggs
- 1½ cups sour cream
- 1 tablespoon vanilla extract
- 2¼ cups (11½ ounces) unbleached all-purpose flour
- 1¼ cups (8¾ ounces) granulated sugar
- 1 tablespoon baking powder
- ¾ teaspoon baking soda
- ¾ teaspoon table salt

1. FOR THE STREUSEL: In a food processor, process the flour, granulated sugar, ¼ cup of the brown sugar, and the cinnamon until combined, about 15 seconds. Transfer 1¼ cups of the flour-sugar mixture to a small bowl; stir in the remaining ¼ cup brown sugar and set aside to use for the streusel filling. Add the pecans and butter to the flour-sugar mixture in the food processor; pulse until the nuts and butter resemble small pebbly pieces, about 10 pulses; set aside.

2. FOR THE CAKE: Adjust an oven rack to the lowest position and heat the oven to 350 degrees. Grease a 10-cup tube pan with 2 tablespoons of the softened butter. Whisk the eggs, 1 cup of the sour cream, and the vanilla together in a medium bowl until combined.

3. Mix the flour, granulated sugar, baking powder, baking soda, and salt in the bowl of a stand mixer on low speed until combined, about 30 seconds. Add the remaining 12 tablespoons butter and remaining ½ cup sour cream; mix on low speed until the dry ingredients are moistened and the mixture resembles wet sand, with a few large butter pieces remaining, about 1½ minutes. Increase the speed to medium and beat until the batter comes together, about 10 seconds, scraping down the sides of the bowl with a rubber spatula as necessary. Lower the speed to medium-low and gradually add the egg mixture in three additions, beating for 20 seconds after each addition and scraping down the sides of the bowl as necessary. Increase the speed to medium-high and beat until the batter is light and fluffy, about 1 minute.

4. Using a rubber spatula, spread 2 cups of the batter in the bottom of the prepared pan, smoothing the surface. Sprinkle evenly with ¾ cup of the streusel filling without butter or nuts. Repeat with 2 cups more batter and the remaining ¾ cup streusel filling without butter or nuts. Spread the remaining batter over, then sprinkle with the streusel topping with butter and nuts.

5. Bake until the cake feels firm to the touch and a long toothpick or skewer inserted into the center comes out clean (bits of sugar from the streusel may cling to the tester), 50 to 60 minutes. Cool the cake in the pan on a wire rack for 30 minutes. Invert the cake onto a rimmed baking sheet (the cake will be streusel side down); remove the tube pan, place a wire rack on top of the cake, and reinvert the cake streusel side up. Cool to room temperature, about 2 hours. Cut into wedges and serve. (The cake can be wrapped in foil and stored at room temperature for up to 5 days.)

CREAM CHEESE COFFEE CAKE

WHY THIS RECIPE WORKS: This brunch staple is fraught with pitfalls—from dry, bland cake to lackluster fillings that sink to the bottom as they cook. We wanted a rich, moist cake with a texture that could support a tangy swirl of cream cheese filling.

We assembled a batter of flour, granulated sugar, salt, butter, eggs, whole milk, and baking powder and settled on a straightforward creaming method: Beat softened butter with sugar, then add the eggs, milk, and dry ingredients. The resulting cake was full of flavor and capable of supporting our cheese filling—but it was also a bit dry. To add moisture, we replaced the milk with rich sour cream, added baking soda, and upped the amount of butter. Our cake now had a lush texture as well as subtle acidity—a perfect backdrop for the cheese filling. We settled on a base mixture of softened cream cheese and sugar and added lemon juice to cut the richness and a hint of vanilla extract for depth of flavor. To prevent graininess, we incorporated some of the cake batter into the cheese. The filling not only stayed creamy, but it fused to the cake during baking, eliminating gaps that had afflicted our earlier tests. For a topping, we decided upon a crisp yet delicate coating of sliced almonds, sugar, and lemon zest. As it baked, the topping formed a glistening, crackly crust on our now-perfect coffee cake.

Cream Cheese Coffee Cake

SERVES 12 TO 16

Leftovers should be stored in the refrigerator, covered tightly with plastic wrap. For optimal texture, allow the cake to return to room temperature before serving.

LEMON SUGAR–ALMOND TOPPING

- ¼ cup (1¾ ounces) sugar
- 1½ teaspoons finely grated zest from 1 lemon
- ½ cup sliced almonds

CAKE

- 2¼ cups (11¼ ounces) unbleached all-purpose flour
- 1⅛ teaspoons baking powder
- 1⅛ teaspoons baking soda
- 1 teaspoon table salt
- 10 tablespoons (1¼ sticks) unsalted butter, softened but still cool
- 1 cup (7 ounces) plus 7 tablespoons sugar
- 1 tablespoon finely grated zest plus 4 teaspoons juice from 1 to 2 lemons
- 4 large eggs
- 5 teaspoons vanilla extract
- 1¼ cups sour cream
- 8 ounces cream cheese, softened

1. FOR THE TOPPING: Adjust an oven rack to the middle position and heat the oven to 350 degrees. Stir together the sugar and lemon zest in a small bowl until combined and the sugar is moistened. Stir in the almonds; set aside.

NOTES FROM THE TEST KITCHEN

MAKING CREAM CHEESE COFFEE CAKE

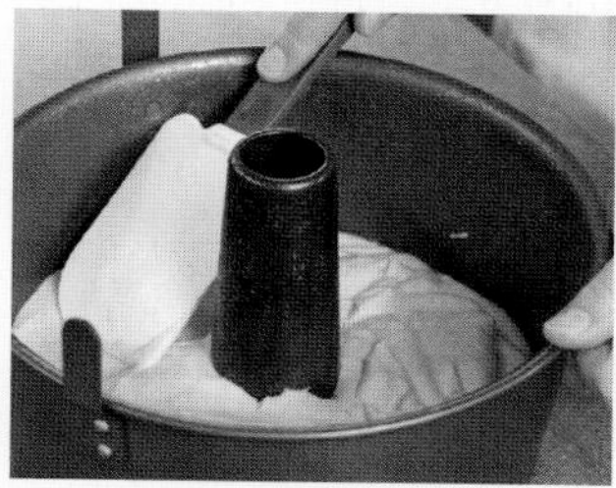

1. Reserve 1¼ cups of the batter, then fill the pan with the remaining batter; smooth the top.

2. Beat ¼ cup of the reserved batter with the filling ingredients; spoon the filling evenly over the batter.

3. Top the filling with the remaining 1 cup reserved batter; smooth the top.

4. Using a figure-8 motion, swirl the filling into the batter. Tap the pan on the counter.

5. Sprinkle the lemon sugar–almond topping onto the batter, then gently press to adhere.

2. FOR THE CAKE: Spray a 10-inch tube pan with vegetable oil spray. Whisk the flour, baking powder, baking soda, and salt together in a medium bowl; set aside. In a stand mixer fitted with the paddle attachment, beat the butter, 1 cup plus 2 tablespoons of the sugar, and the lemon zest at medium speed until light and fluffy, about 3 minutes, scraping down the sides and bottom of the bowl with a rubber spatula. Add the eggs one at a time, beating well after each addition, about 20 seconds, and scraping down the beater and sides of the bowl as necessary. Add 4 teaspoons of the vanilla and mix to combine. Reduce the speed to low and add one-third of the flour mixture, followed by half of the sour cream, mixing until incorporated after each addition, 5 to 10 seconds. Repeat, using half of the remaining flour mixture and all of the remaining sour cream. Scrape the bowl and add the remaining flour mixture; mix at low speed until the batter is thoroughly combined, about 10 seconds. Remove the bowl from the mixer and fold the batter once or twice with a rubber spatula to incorporate any remaining flour.

3. Reserve 1¼ cups of the batter and set aside. Spoon the remaining batter into the prepared pan and smooth the top. Return the now-empty bowl to the mixer and beat the cream cheese, remaining 5 tablespoons sugar, lemon juice, and remaining 1 teaspoon vanilla on medium speed until smooth and slightly lightened, about 1 minute. Add ¼ cup of the reserved batter and mix until incorporated. Spoon the cheese filling mixture evenly over the batter, keeping the filling about 1 inch from the edges of the pan; smooth the top. Spread the remaining 1 cup reserved batter over the filling and smooth the top. With a butter knife or offset spatula, gently swirl the filling into the batter using a figure-eight motion, being careful not to drag the filling to the bottom or edges of the pan. Firmly tap the pan on the counter two or three times to dislodge any bubbles. Sprinkle the lemon sugar–almond topping evenly over the batter and gently press into the batter to adhere.

4. Bake until the top is golden and just firm and a long skewer inserted into the cake comes out clean (a skewer will be wet if inserted into the cheese filling), 45 to 50 minutes. Remove the pan from the oven and firmly tap on the counter two or three times (the top of the cake may sink slightly). Cool the cake in the pan on a wire rack for 1 hour. Gently invert the cake onto a rimmed baking sheet (the cake will be topping side down); remove the tube pan, place a wire rack on top of the cake, and invert the cake sugar side up. Cool to room temperature, about 1½ hours, before serving.

CHUNKY GRANOLA WITH DRIED FRUIT

WHY THIS RECIPE WORKS: Store-bought granola suffers from many shortcomings. It's often loose and gravelly and/or infuriatingly expensive. We wanted to make our own granola at home, with big, satisfying clusters and crisp texture. The secret was to firmly pack the granola mixture into a rimmed baking sheet before baking. Once it was baked, we had a granola "bark" that we could break into crunchy lumps of any size.

Almond Granola with Dried Fruit

MAKES ABOUT 9 CUPS

Chopping the almonds by hand is the first choice for superior texture and crunch. If you prefer not to hand chop, substitute an equal quantity of slivered or sliced almonds. (A food processor does a lousy job of chopping whole nuts evenly.) Use a single type of your favorite dried fruit or a combination. Do not use quick oats.

- ⅓ cup maple syrup
- ⅓ cup packed (2⅓ ounces) light brown sugar
- 4 teaspoons vanilla extract
- ½ teaspoon salt
- ½ cup vegetable oil
- 5 cups (15 ounces) old-fashioned rolled oats
- 2 cups (10 ounces) raw almonds, chopped coarse
- 2 cups raisins or other dried fruit, chopped

1. Adjust oven rack to upper-middle position and heat oven to 325 degrees. Line rimmed baking sheet with parchment paper.

2. Whisk maple syrup, brown sugar, vanilla, and salt in large bowl. Whisk in oil. Fold in oats and almonds until thoroughly coated.

3. Transfer oat mixture to prepared baking sheet and spread across sheet into thin, even layer (about ⅜ inch thick). Using stiff metal spatula, compress oat mixture until very compact. Bake until lightly browned, 40 to 45 minutes, rotating pan once halfway through baking. Remove granola from oven and cool on wire rack to room temperature, about 1 hour. Break cooled granola into pieces of desired size. Stir in dried fruit. (Granola can be stored in airtight container for up to 2 weeks.)

Pecan-Orange Granola with Dried Cranberries

Add 2 tablespoons finely grated orange zest and 2½ teaspoons ground cinnamon to maple syrup mixture in step 2. Substitute coarsely chopped pecans for almonds. After granola is broken into pieces, stir in 2 cups dried cranberries.

Spiced Walnut Granola with Dried Apple

Add 2 teaspoons ground cinnamon, 1½ teaspoons ground ginger, ¾ teaspoon ground allspice, ½ teaspoon freshly grated nutmeg, and ½ teaspoon pepper to maple syrup mixture in step 2. Substitute coarsely chopped walnuts for almonds. After granola is broken into pieces, stir in 2 cups chopped dried apples.

Tropical Granola with Dried Mango

Reduce vanilla extract to 2 teaspoons and add 1½ teaspoons ground ginger and ¾ teaspoon freshly grated nutmeg to maple syrup mixture in step 2. Substitute coarsely chopped macadamias for almonds and 1½ cups unsweetened shredded coconut for 1 cup oats. After granola is broken into pieces, stir in 2 cups chopped dried mango or pineapple.

Hazelnut Granola with Dried Pear

Substitute coarsely chopped, skinned hazelnuts for almonds. After granola is broken into pieces, stir in 2 cups chopped dried pears.

TEN-MINUTE STEEL-CUT OATMEAL

WHY THIS RECIPE WORKS: Most oatmeal fans agree that the steel-cut version of the grain offers the best flavor and texture, but many balk at the 40-minute cooking time. We decreased the cooking time to only 10 minutes by stirring steel-cut oats into boiling water the night before. This enabled the grains to hydrate and soften overnight. In the morning, more water (or fruit juice or milk) was added and the mixture was simmered for 4 to 6 minutes, until thick and creamy. A brief resting period off the heat ensured the perfect consistency.

Ten-Minute Steel-Cut Oatmeal

SERVES 4

The oatmeal will continue to thicken as it cools. If you prefer a looser consistency, thin the oatmeal with boiling water. Customize your oatmeal with toppings such as brown sugar, toasted nuts, maple syrup, or dried fruit.

- 4 cups water
- 1 cup steel-cut oats
- ¼ teaspoon salt

1. Bring 3 cups water to boil in large saucepan over high heat. Remove pan from heat; stir in oats and salt. Cover pan and let stand overnight.

2. Stir remaining 1 cup water into oats and bring to boil over medium-high heat. Reduce heat to medium and cook, stirring occasionally, until oats are softened but still retain some chew and mixture thickens and resembles warm pudding, 4 to 6 minutes. Remove pan from heat and let stand for 5 minutes. Stir and serve, passing desired toppings separately.

Apple-Cinnamon Steel-Cut Oatmeal

Increase salt to ½ teaspoon. Substitute ½ cup apple cider and ½ cup whole milk for water in step 2. Stir ½ cup peeled, grated sweet apple, 2 tablespoons packed dark brown sugar, and ½ teaspoon ground cinnamon into oatmeal with cider and milk. Sprinkle each serving with 2 tablespoons coarsely chopped toasted walnuts.

Carrot-Spice Steel-Cut Oatmeal

Increase salt to ¾ teaspoon. Substitute ½ cup carrot juice and ½ cup whole milk for water in step 2. Stir ½ cup finely grated carrot, ¼ cup packed dark brown sugar, ⅓ cup dried currants, and ½ teaspoon ground cinnamon into oatmeal with carrot juice and milk. Sprinkle each serving with 2 tablespoons coarsely chopped toasted pecans.

Cranberry-Orange Steel-Cut Oatmeal

Increase salt to ½ teaspoon. Substitute ½ cup orange juice and ½ cup whole milk for water in step 2. Stir ½ cup dried cranberries, 3 tablespoons packed dark brown sugar, and ⅛ teaspoon ground cardamom into oatmeal with orange juice and milk. Sprinkle each serving with 2 tablespoons toasted sliced almonds.

Banana-Coconut Steel-Cut Oatmeal

Increase salt to ½ teaspoon. Substitute 1 cup canned coconut milk for water in step 2. Stir ½ cup toasted shredded coconut, 2 diced bananas, and ½ teaspoon vanilla extract into oatmeal before serving.

Peanut, Honey, and Banana Steel-Cut Oatmeal

Increase salt to ½ teaspoon. Substitute ½ cup whole milk for ½ cup water in step 2. Stir 3 tablespoons honey into oatmeal with milk and water. Add ¼ cup of peanut butter and 1 tablespoon unsalted butter to oatmeal after removing from heat in step 2. Stir 2 diced bananas into oatmeal before serving. Sprinkle each serving with 2 tablespoons coarsely chopped toasted peanuts.

FRUIT SALAD

WHY THIS RECIPE WORKS: A bowl of cut-up fresh fruit is a nice complement to the sweets and heavier egg dishes at a brunch, but it can be a little boring without additional flavors. Yogurt-based sauces mask the fresh flavors of the fruit, and sweet syrups make the fruit too much like a dessert. We were looking for a lighter, more flavorful alternative. We adapted a French dressing called a *gastrique,* a reduction of an acidic liquid with sugar that usually accompanies savory dishes made with fruit. It's a simple technique, and our experiments with reducing different types of acid—wine, citrus juice, and balsamic vinegar—were an unqualified success. We were able to use additional flavorings in the dressing, such as spices, extracts, and citrus zests, that would complement the flavors of the fruit. Served at room temperature or chilled, fresh fruit bathed in a light but sweet-tart dressing is not only delicious but easy to make.

Strawberries and Grapes with Balsamic and Red Wine Reduction

MAKES ABOUT 6 CUPS

An inexpensive balsamic vinegar is fine for use in this recipe. Save high-quality vinegar for other preparations in which the vinegar is not cooked.

- ¾ cup balsamic vinegar (see note)
- ¼ cup dry red wine
- ¼ cup sugar
- Pinch table salt
- 1 tablespoon grated zest plus 1 tablespoon juice from 1 lemon
- ¼ teaspoon vanilla extract
- 3 whole cloves
- 1 quart strawberries, hulled and halved lengthwise (about 4 cups)
- 9 ounces large seedless red or black grapes, each grape halved pole to pole (about 2 cups)

1. Simmer the vinegar, wine, sugar, and salt in a small saucepan over high heat until syrupy and reduced to ¼ cup, about 15 minutes. Off the heat, stir in the lemon zest and juice, vanilla, and cloves; steep for 1 minute to blend the flavors and strain.

2. Combine the strawberries and grapes in a medium bowl; pour the warm dressing over the fruit and toss to coat. Serve at room temperature, or cover with plastic wrap, refrigerate for up to 4 hours, and serve chilled.

Nectarines, Blueberries, and Raspberries with Champagne-Cardamom Reduction

MAKES ABOUT 6 CUPS

Dry white wine can be substituted for the champagne.

- 1 cup champagne (see note)
- ¼ cup sugar
- Pinch table salt
- 1 tablespoon grated zest plus 1 tablespoon juice from 1 lemon
- 5 cardamom pods, crushed
- 3 medium nectarines (about 18 ounces), cut into ½-inch wedges (about 3 cups)
- 1 pint blueberries
- ½ pint raspberries

1. Simmer the champagne, sugar, and salt in a small saucepan over high heat until syrupy, honey-colored, and reduced to ¼ cup, about 15 minutes. Off the heat, stir in the lemon zest and juice and cardamom; steep for 1 minute to blend the flavors and strain.

2. Combine the nectarines, blueberries, and raspberries in a medium bowl; pour the warm dressing over the fruit and toss to coat. Serve at room temperature, or cover with plastic wrap, refrigerate for up to 4 hours, and serve chilled.

Honeydew, Mango, and Blueberries with Lime-Ginger Reduction

MAKES ABOUT 6 CUPS

Be sure to zest one of the limes before juicing. Cantaloupe can be used in place of honeydew, although the color contrast with the mango won't be as vivid.

1 cup juice plus 1 tablespoon grated zest from 8 limes (see note)
¼ cup sugar
Pinch table salt
1 (1-inch) piece fresh ginger, peeled and minced (about 1 tablespoon)
1 tablespoon juice from 1 lemon
½ small honeydew melon (see note), seeds and rind removed, cut into 1-inch pieces (about 2 cups)
1 mango (about 10 ounces), peeled and cut into ½-inch pieces (about 1½ cups)
1 pint blueberries

1. Simmer the lime juice, sugar, and salt in a small saucepan over high heat until syrupy, honey-colored, and reduced to 1/4 cup, about 15 minutes. Off the heat, stir in the lime zest, ginger, and lemon juice; steep for 1 minute to blend the flavors and strain.

2. Combine the melon, mango, and blueberries in a medium bowl; pour the warm dressing over the fruit and toss to coat. Serve at room temperature, or cover with plastic wrap, refrigerate for up to 4 hours, and serve chilled.

CLASSIC STRAWBERRY JAM

WHY THIS RECIPE WORKS: Strawberry jam is a universal favorite. Naturally low in pectin, strawberries are often cooked too long, causing the fruit to lose its bright flavor. We shortened the cooking time by cutting the strawberries into smaller pieces and then mashing them to release their juices and jump-start the cooking process. Shredded apple added natural pectin and fresh flavor to the mix. Lemon juice added acidity to balance the sugar's sweetness and helped the natural pectin to gel. Small, fragrant berries produce the best jam.

Classic Strawberry Jam

MAKES FOUR 1-CUP JARS

For safety reasons, be sure to use bottled lemon juice, not fresh-squeezed juice, in this recipe.

3 pounds strawberries, hulled and cut into ½-inch pieces (10 cups)
3 cups sugar
1¼ cups peeled and shredded Granny Smith apple (1 large apple)
2 tablespoons bottled lemon juice

1. Place 2 small plates in freezer to chill. Set canning rack in large pot, place four 1-cup jars in rack, and add water to cover by 1 inch. Bring to simmer over medium heat, then turn off heat and cover to keep hot.

2. In Dutch oven, crush strawberries with potato masher until fruit is mostly broken down. Stir in sugar, apple, and lemon juice and bring to boil, stirring often, over medium-high heat. Once sugar is completely dissolved, boil mixture, stirring and adjusting heat as needed, until thickened and registers 217 to 220 degrees, 20 to 25 minutes. (Temperature will be lower at higher elevations.) Remove pot from heat.

3. To test consistency, place 1 teaspoon jam on chilled plate and freeze for 2 minutes. Drag your finger through jam on plate; jam has correct consistency when your finger leaves distinct trail. If runny, return pot to heat and simmer for 1 to 3 minutes longer before retesting. Skim any foam from surface of jam using spoon.

4. Place dish towel flat on counter. Using jar lifter, remove jars from pot, draining water back into pot. Place jars upside down on towel and let dry for 1 minute. Using funnel and ladle, portion hot jam into hot jars, leaving 1/4 inch headspace. Slide wooden skewer along inside edge of jar and drag upward to remove air bubbles.

5A. FOR SHORT-TERM STORAGE: Let jam cool to room temperature, cover, and refrigerate until jam is set, 12 to 24 hours. (Jam can be refrigerated for up to 2 months.)

5B. FOR LONG-TERM STORAGE: While jars are hot, wipe rims clean, add lids, and screw on rings until fingertip-tight; do not overtighten. Return pot of water with canning rack to boil. Lower jars into water, cover, bring water back to boil, then start timer. Cooking time will depend on your altitude: Boil 10 minutes for up to 1,000 feet, 15 minutes for 1,001 to 3,000 feet, 20 minutes for 3,001 to 6,000 feet, or 25 minutes for 6,001 to 8,000 feet. Turn off heat and let jars sit in pot for 5 minutes. Remove jars from pot and let cool for 24 hours. Remove rings, check seal, and clean rims. (Sealed jars can be stored for up to 1 year.)

NOTES FROM THE TEST KITCHEN

KEYS TO STRAWBERRY JAM SUCCESS

Stir sugar, shredded apple, and lemon juice into mashed berries and bring mixure to a vigorous boil. Boil mixture vigorously until it has thickened and registers between 217 and 220 degrees (at sea level).

To test jam's consistency, place 1 teaspoon of hot jam on a chilled plate and freeze it for 2 minutes. Drag your finger through the chilled jam on the plate; jam has the correct consistency when your finger leaves a distinct trail.

CHOCOLATE HAZELNUT SPREAD

WHY THIS RECIPE WORKS: Much as we love Nutella, we couldn't resist making our own homemade version of the habit-forming chocolate-hazelnut spread. Without the additives and palm oil, we hoped for a spread with a texture closer to natural peanut butter with a deeply nutty, chocolaty punch. After blanching raw hazelnuts in water and baking soda, we immediately transferred them to ice water. Their skin was easily removed by rubbing with a dish towel. Roasting the hazelnuts on a baking sheet brought out their buttery fragrance and toasty, nutty flavor. The remaining steps were as easy as pulling out our food processor and whirling the nuts into a smooth paste before adding in sugar, cocoa, oil, vanilla, and salt.

Chocolate Hazelnut Spread

MAKES 1½ CUPS

Hazelnut oil work best to reinforce the spread's flavors, but walnut and vegetable oils are also passable.

- 2 cups hazelnuts
- 6 tablespoons baking soda
- 1 cup (4 ounces) confectioners' sugar
- ⅓ cup (1 ounce) unsweetened cocoa powder
- 2 tablespoons hazelnut oil
- 1 teaspoon vanilla extract
- ⅛ teaspoon salt

1. Fill large bowl halfway with ice and water. Bring 4 cups water to boil. Add hazelnuts and baking soda and boil for 3 minutes. Transfer nuts to ice bath with slotted spoon, drain, and slip skins off with dish towel.

2. Adjust oven rack to middle position and heat oven to 375 degrees. Place hazelnuts in single layer on rimmed baking sheet and roast until fragrant and golden brown, 12 to 15 minutes, rotating sheet halfway through roasting.

3. Process hazelnuts in food processor until oil is released and smooth, loose paste forms, about 5 minutes, scraping down sides of bowl often.

4. Add sugar, cocoa, oil, vanilla, and salt and process until fully incorporated and mixture begins to loosen slightly and becomes glossy, about 2 minutes, scraping down sides of bowl as needed.

5. Transfer spread to jar with tight-fitting lid. Chocolate hazelnut spread can be stored at room temperature or refrigerated for up to 1 month.

MEXICAN HOT CHOCOLATE

WHY THIS RECIPE WORKS: For an always-ready Mexican hot chocolate mix that delivered rich texture, indulgent taste, and a touch of heat, we needed our chocolate to come in two forms. Cocoa powder is loaded with chocolate flavor and made for a thick drink, and unsweetened chocolate promised a creamy, smooth texture. Nonfat dry milk powder introduced a creamy sweetness to the blend plus a bit of extra thickening, further boosted with some cornstarch. Vanilla extract and salt heightened the chocolate's flavor. To infuse the mix with some heat, we added ground cinnamon, ancho chile powder, and cayenne. Whizzing the ingredients in the food processor created a fine, even powder that would stay combined during storage.

Mexican Hot Chocolate

MAKES 3 CUPS OF MIX; ENOUGH FOR TWELVE 1-CUP SERVINGS

Our preferred unsweetened chocolate is Hershey's Unsweetened Baking Bar. Both natural and Dutch-processed cocoa will work in this recipe. Our favorite natural cocoa powder is Hershey's Natural Cocoa Unsweetened; our favorite Dutch-processed cocoa powder is Droste Cocoa. For one serving of hot chocolate, heat 1 cup of whole, 2 percent low-fat, or 1 percent low-fat milk in a small saucepan over medium heat until it starts to steam and bubbles appear around the edge of the saucepan. Add ¼ cup of hot chocolate mix and continue to heat, whisking constantly, until simmering, 2 to 3 minutes longer. Pour the hot chocolate into a mug and serve.

- 1 cup (7 ounces) sugar
- 6 ounces unsweetened chocolate, chopped fine
- 1 cup (3 ounces) unsweetened cocoa powder
- ½ cup (1½ ounces) nonfat dry milk powder
- 5 teaspoons cornstarch
- 1 teaspoon vanilla extract
- ¾ teaspoon kosher salt
- 1 teaspoon ground cinnamon
- ¾ teaspoon ancho chile powder
- Pinch cayenne pepper

Process all ingredients in food processor until ground to powder, 30 to 60 seconds. Transfer to airtight container and store at room temperature for up to 2 months.

CHAPTER 21

PLEASE PASS THE BREAD

CREAM BISCUITS

WHY THIS RECIPE WORKS: With a high rise, light texture, and rich flavor, fresh-from-the-oven biscuits tend to disappear quicker than cookies in the test kitchen. So it's a shame that many prospective bakers pass them up, just because the recipe calls for the strenuous step of cutting butter into flour, or the messy move of rolling out dough time and again to get every last piece into a round for the baking sheet. We wanted to make great biscuits that cut out these extra steps and used a basic combination of heavy cream, flour, baking powder, and salt.

Instead of cutting butter into flour, we included a generous amount of heavy cream in our biscuits, which gave them a lighter and more tender texture. Kneading for just 30 seconds was enough to get our dough smooth and uniform. We used an extra bit of cream to soak up all the last bits of flour in the bowl, ensuring that nothing was wasted. To enhance the light flavor of our biscuits, we added a small amount of sugar. All there was left to do was shape them, then pop them into the oven immediately to keep them from spreading. Although it is easy enough to pat out this dough and cut it into rounds with a biscuit cutter, we devised a second strategy of simply pressing the dough into an 8-inch cake pan, turning out the dough, and then slicing it into wedges.

Cream Biscuits

MAKES 8 BISCUITS

Bake the biscuits immediately after cutting them; letting them stand for any length of time can decrease the leavening power and thereby prevent the biscuits from rising properly in the oven.

- 2 cups (10 ounces) unbleached all-purpose flour, plus extra for the work surface
- 2 teaspoons sugar
- 1 teaspoon baking powder
- ½ teaspoon table salt
- 1½ cups heavy cream

1. Adjust an oven rack to the upper-middle position and heat the oven to 425 degrees. Line a large rimmed baking sheet with parchment paper. Whisk the flour, sugar, baking powder, and salt together in a medium bowl.

2. Add 1¼ cups of the cream to the flour mixture and stir with a wooden spoon until a dough forms, about 30 seconds. Transfer the dough to a lightly floured work surface, leaving all dry, floury bits behind in the bowl. Add the remaining ¼ cup cream, 1 tablespoon at a time, to the bowl, mixing with a wooden spoon after each addition, until all the loose flour is just moistened; add these moistened bits to the dough. Knead the dough briefly just until smooth, about 30 seconds.

3. Pat the dough into a ¾-inch-thick circle or press it into an 8-inch cake pan and turn it out onto a lightly floured surface. Cut the biscuits into rounds using a 2½-inch biscuit cutter or into eight wedges using a knife. Place the rounds or wedges onto the prepared baking sheet and bake until golden brown, about 15 minutes. Serve immediately.

Cream Biscuits with Fresh Herbs

Use the herb of your choice in this variation.

Follow the recipe for Cream Biscuits, adding 2 tablespoons minced fresh herbs to the flour mixture in step 1. Proceed as directed.

Cheddar Biscuits

Follow the recipe for Cream Biscuits, adding 2 ounces sharp cheddar cheese, shredded (about ½ cup), to the flour mixture in step 1. Proceed as directed, increasing the baking time to 18 minutes.

BEST DROP BISCUITS

WHY THIS RECIPE WORKS: Drop biscuits have many things going for them: a crisp outer crust, a tender, flaky interior, and a simple, no-nonsense method. There's only one problem—they're often not very good. Too many are dense, gummy, and doughy or, on the flip side, lean and dry. Drop biscuits should, by nature, be simple to make and tender. We wanted a biscuit that could be easily broken apart and eaten piece by buttery piece.

Identifying the best ingredients was the first task. While oil-based biscuits were easy to work with, they lacked flavor, so butter was a must. Replacing the usual milk with buttermilk helped heighten flavor; the biscuits now had a rich, buttery tang and were crisper on the exterior and fluffier on the interior. Choosing the right leavener was also important. We needed a substantial amount, but too much baking powder left a metallic taste. Since we'd added buttermilk, we could replace some of the baking powder with baking soda (buttermilk provides the acid that soda needs to act), which gave us the rise we needed without the metallic bitterness. Once the ingredients had been identified, we were left with only one problem. Properly combining the butter and buttermilk required that both ingredients be at just the right temperature; if they weren't, the melted butter clumped in the buttermilk. But when we had trouble avoiding this, we made a batch with lumpy buttermilk anyway. The result was a surprisingly better biscuit, slightly higher and with better texture. The water in the lumps of butter (butter is 20 percent water) had turned to steam in the oven, helping create additional height.

Best Drop Biscuits

MAKES 12 BISCUITS

A ¼-cup (#16) portion scoop can be used to portion the batter. To refresh day-old biscuits, heat them in a 300-degree oven for 10 minutes.

- 2 cups (10 ounces) unbleached all-purpose flour
- 2 teaspoons baking powder
- 1 teaspoon sugar
- ¾ teaspoon table salt
- ½ teaspoon baking soda
- 1 cup buttermilk, chilled
- 8 tablespoons (1 stick) unsalted butter, melted and cooled slightly, plus 2 tablespoons melted butter for brushing the biscuits

1. Adjust an oven rack to the middle position and heat the oven to 475 degrees. Line a large rimmed baking sheet with parchment paper. Whisk the flour, baking powder, sugar, salt, and baking soda together in a large bowl. Combine the buttermilk and 8 tablespoons of the melted butter in a medium bowl, stirring until the butter forms small clumps.

2. Add the buttermilk mixture to the dry ingredients and stir with a rubber spatula until just incorporated and the batter pulls away from the sides of the bowl. Using a greased ¼-cup measuring cup, scoop a level amount of batter and drop onto the prepared baking sheet. Repeat with the remaining batter, spacing the biscuits about 1½ inches apart. Bake until the tops are golden brown and crisp, 12 to 14 minutes.

3. Brush the biscuit tops with the remaining 2 tablespoons melted butter. Transfer to a wire rack and cool for 5 minutes before serving.

PUMPKIN BREAD

WHY THIS RECIPE WORKS: Although most recipes for pumpkin bread are pleasantly sweet and spicy, they're nothing to write home about. For a bread with rich pumpkin flavor and enough spices to enhance rather than overwhelm the flavor of our pumpkin, we used a few strategies. To rid canned pumpkin puree of its raw flavor and bring out its richness, we cooked it on top of the stove just until it began to caramelize. To replace some of the lost moisture from cooking the puree and offset some of the sweetness, we added softened cream cheese to the mix. A modest hand with spices and a sweet streusel sprinkled over the top of the loaf gave us perfect pumpkin bread.

Pumpkin Bread

MAKES 2 LOAVES

The test kitchen's preferred loaf pan measures 8½ by 4½ inches; if using a 9 by 5-inch loaf pan, start checking for doneness 5 minutes early.

TOPPING

- 5 tablespoons packed (2¼ ounces) light brown sugar
- 1 tablespoon all-purpose flour
- 1 tablespoon unsalted butter, softened
- 1 teaspoon ground cinnamon
- ⅛ teaspoon salt

BREAD

- 2 cups (10 ounces) all-purpose flour
- 1½ teaspoons baking powder
- ½ teaspoon baking soda
- 1 (15-ounce) can unsweetened pumpkin puree
- 1 teaspoon salt
- 1½ teaspoons ground cinnamon
- ¼ teaspoon ground nutmeg
- ⅛ teaspoon ground cloves
- 1 cup (7 ounces) granulated sugar
- 1 cup packed (7 ounces) light brown sugar
- ½ cup vegetable oil
- 4 ounces cream cheese, cut into 12 pieces
- 4 large eggs
- ¼ cup buttermilk
- 1 cup walnuts, toasted and chopped fine

1. FOR THE TOPPING: Using fingers, mix all ingredients together in bowl until well combined and topping resembles wet sand; set aside.

2. FOR THE BREAD: Adjust oven rack to middle position and heat oven to 350 degrees. Grease two 8½ by 4½-inch loaf pans. Whisk flour, baking powder, and baking soda together in bowl.

3. Combine pumpkin puree, salt, cinnamon, nutmeg, and cloves in large saucepan over medium heat. Cook mixture, stirring constantly, until reduced to 1½ cups, 6 to 8 minutes. Remove pot from heat; stir in granulated sugar, brown sugar, oil, and cream cheese until combined. Let mixture stand for 5 minutes. Whisk until no visible pieces of cream cheese remain and mixture is homogeneous.

4. Whisk together eggs and buttermilk. Add egg mixture to pumpkin mixture and whisk to combine. Fold flour mixture into pumpkin mixture until combined (some small lumps of flour are OK). Fold walnuts into batter. Scrape batter into prepared pans. Sprinkle topping evenly over top of each loaf. Bake until skewer inserted in center of loaf comes out clean, 45 to 50 minutes. Let loaves cool in pans on wire rack for 20 minutes. Remove loaves from pans and let cool for at least 1½ hours. Serve warm or at room temperature.

Pumpkin Bread with Candied Ginger

Substitute ½ teaspoon ground ginger for cinnamon in topping. Fold ⅓ cup minced crystallized ginger into batter after flour mixture has been added in step 4.

ZUCCHINI BREAD

WHY THIS RECIPE WORKS: In the health food–crazed 1960s and '70s, recipes for zucchini bread popped up everywhere. With bits of healthy green vegetable speckling the crumb, the bread was a sweet treat you could not only enjoy but also feel virtuous about eating. But zucchini can also be a liability, as too much leads to a soggy loaf. That's why, in spite of the oft-stated goal of using up surplus squash, most recipes top out at a mere 10 to 12 ounces. And despite being associated with a health-food movement, the recipes tend to call for copious amounts of oil that turn the loaf greasy and overly rich.

We found that coarsely grated, thoroughly squeezed squash produced a crumb that was super moist but not gummy. This had the added benefit of removing some of the key compounds in zucchini—called Amadori compounds—which are responsible for zucchini's vegetal flavor, giving our loaf a sweet, mildly earthy (but not vegetal) flavor. For deeper flavor, we switched from granulated sugar to molasses-y brown sugar, increased the cinnamon to 1 tablespoon, and added nutmeg and vanilla. Swapping some of the all-purpose flour for whole-wheat gave the loaf even better structure and ensured that it wasn't soggy.

Zucchini Bread

MAKES 1 LOAF

Use the large holes of a box grater to shred the zucchini. The test kitchen's preferred loaf pan measures 8½ by 4½ inches; if you use a 9 by 5-inch loaf pan, start checking for doneness 5 minutes early.

- 1½ pounds zucchini, shredded
- 1¼ cups (8¾ ounces) packed brown sugar
- ¼ cup vegetable oil
- 2 large eggs
- 1 teaspoon vanilla extract
- 1½ cups (7½ ounces) all-purpose flour
- ½ cup (2¾ ounces) whole-wheat flour
- 1 tablespoon ground cinnamon
- 1½ teaspoons salt
- 1 teaspoon baking powder
- 1 teaspoon baking soda
- ½ teaspoon ground nutmeg
- ¾ cup walnuts, toasted and chopped (optional)
- 1 tablespoon granulated sugar

1. Adjust oven rack to middle position and heat oven to 325 degrees. Grease 8½ by 4½-inch loaf pan.

2. Place zucchini in center of clean dish towel. Gather ends together and twist tightly to drain as much liquid as possible, discarding liquid (you should have ½ to ⅔ cup liquid). Whisk brown sugar, oil, eggs, and vanilla together in medium bowl. Fold in zucchini.

3. Whisk all-purpose flour, whole-wheat flour, cinnamon, salt, baking powder, baking soda, and nutmeg together in large bowl. Fold in zucchini mixture until just incorporated. Fold in walnuts, if using. Pour batter into prepared pan and sprinkle with granulated sugar.

4. Bake until top bounces back when gently pressed and toothpick inserted in center comes out with a few moist crumbs attached, 65 to 75 minutes. Let bread cool in pan on wire rack for 30 minutes. Remove bread from pan and cool completely on wire rack. Serve.

Zucchini Bread with Walnuts and Dried Cherries

Substitute cocoa powder for cinnamon and ground cloves for nutmeg. Add ¾ cup dried cherries, chopped, to batter with walnuts in step 3.

BOSTON BROWN BREAD

WHY THIS RECIPE WORKS: When colonists started making this unyeasted, one-bowl bread in the 18th century, most cooking was done over an open hearth—a tricky environment for bread baking. To get around this, brown bread was steamed in lidded tin pudding molds in a kettle of simmering water over an open fire, giving the loaves a distinctive shape and a smooth, crustless exterior—and keeping the whole-grain crumb remarkably moist. To get the right balance of flavor in our brown bread, we combined whole-wheat flour, rye flour, and finely ground cornmeal in equal amounts. Molasses, the traditional sweetener, added the right hint of bitterness. Baking soda and baking powder reacted with the acid in the batter to lighten the bread, and melted butter added some richness. We steamed the batter on the stovetop in two 28-ounce tomato cans, which produced moist loaves inside and out.

Boston Brown Bread

MAKES 2 SMALL LOAVES; SERVES 6 TO 8

BPA-free 28-ounce tomato cans are a good substitute for traditional (but increasingly uncommon) coffee cans. This recipe requires two empty 28-ounce cans. Use cans that are labeled "BPA-free." We prefer Quaker white cornmeal in this recipe, though other types will work; do not use coarse grits. Any style of molasses will work except for blackstrap. This recipe requires a 10-quart or larger stockpot that is at least 7 inches deep. Brown bread is traditionally served with baked beans but is also good toasted and buttered.

- ¾ cup (4⅛ ounces) rye flour
- ¾ cup (4⅛ ounces) whole-wheat flour
- ¾ cup (3¾ ounces) fine white cornmeal
- 1¾ teaspoons baking soda
- ½ teaspoon baking powder
- 1 teaspoon salt
- 1⅔ cups buttermilk
- ½ cup molasses
- 3 tablespoons butter, melted and cooled slightly
- ¾ cup raisins

1. Bring 3 quarts water to simmer in large stockpot over high heat. Fold two 16 by 12-inch pieces of aluminum foil in half to yield two rectangles that measure 8 by 12 inches. Spray 4-inch circle in center of each rectangle with vegetable oil spray. Spray insides of two clean 28-ounce cans with vegetable oil spray.

2. Whisk rye flour, whole-wheat flour, cornmeal, baking soda, baking powder, and salt together in large bowl. Whisk buttermilk, molasses, and melted butter together in second bowl. Stir raisins into buttermilk mixture. Add buttermilk mixture to flour mixture and stir until combined and no dry flour remains. Evenly divide batter between cans. Wrap tops of cans tightly with prepared foil, positioning sprayed side of foil over can openings.

3. Place cans in stockpot (water should come about halfway up sides of cans). Cover pot and cook, maintaining gentle simmer, until skewer inserted in center of loaves comes out clean, about 2 hours. Check pot occasionally and add hot water as needed to maintain water level.

4. Using jar lifter, carefully transfer cans to wire rack set in rimmed baking sheet and let cool for 20 minutes. Slide loaves from cans onto rack and let cool completely, about 1 hour. Slice and serve. (Bread can be wrapped tightly in plastic wrap and stored at room temperature for up to 3 days or frozen for up to 2 weeks.)

IRISH SODA BREAD

WHY THIS RECIPE WORKS: Authentic Irish soda bread has a tender, dense crumb and a rough-textured, thick crust—definitely a departure from the more common Americanized soda bread, which is closer to a supersized scone. We wanted to try our hand at the authentic version of this bread, which relies on a simple ingredient list of flour, baking soda, salt, and buttermilk. A loaf made with all-purpose flour produced a doughy, heavy bread with an overly thick crust. To soften the crumb, we added some cake flour. A version made with all cake flour, however, was heavy and compact. A ratio of 3 parts all-purpose flour to 1 part cake flour proved best. With only the flour, buttermilk, baking soda, and salt, our bread was lacking in flavor and still tough. Traditionally, very small amounts of butter and sugar are sometimes added, so we felt justified in using a minuscule amount of each. The sugar added flavor without making the bread sweet, and the butter softened the dough without making it overly rich.

Irish Soda Bread

MAKES 1 LOAF

If you do not have a cast-iron skillet, the bread can be baked on a baking sheet, although the crust won't be quite as crunchy. Soda bread is best eaten on the day it is baked but does keep well covered and stored at room temperature for a couple of days, after which time it will become dry.

- 3 cups (15 ounces) unbleached all-purpose flour
- 1 cup (4 ounces) cake flour
- 2 tablespoons sugar
- 1½ teaspoons baking soda
- 1½ teaspoons cream of tartar
- 1½ teaspoons table salt
- 2 tablespoons unsalted butter, softened, plus 1 tablespoon melted butter for brushing the loaf (optional)
- 1¾ cups buttermilk

1. Adjust an oven rack to the middle position and heat the oven to 400 degrees. Whisk the flours, sugar, baking soda, cream of tartar, and salt together in a large bowl. Add the softened butter and rub it into the flour using your fingers until it is completely incorporated. Make a well in the center of the flour mixture and add 1½ cups of the buttermilk. Work the buttermilk into the flour mixture using a fork until the dough comes together in large clumps and there is no dry flour in the bottom of the bowl, adding up to ¼ cup more buttermilk, 1 tablespoon at a time, until all the loose flour is just moistened. Turn the dough onto a lightly floured work surface and pat together to form a 6-inch round. The dough will be scrappy and uneven.

2. Place the dough in a 12-inch cast-iron skillet. Score a deep cross, about 5 inches long and ¾ inch deep, on the top of the loaf and place in the oven. Bake until nicely browned and a knife inserted in the center of the loaf comes out clean, 40 to 45 minutes. Remove from the oven and brush with the melted butter (if using). Cool for at least 30 minutes before slicing.

Whole-Wheat Soda Bread

This variation is known as brown bread in Ireland. The dough will be sticky and you may need to add a small amount of all-purpose flour as you mix it.

Follow the recipe for Irish Soda Bread, reducing the unbleached all-purpose flour to 1½ cups (7½ ounces) and the cake flour to ½ cup (2 ounces) and increasing the sugar to 3 tablespoons. Add 1½ cups (8¼ ounces) whole-wheat flour and ½ cup toasted wheat germ with the flours, sugar, baking soda, cream of tartar, and salt in step 1.

QUICK CHEESE BREAD

WHY THIS RECIPE WORKS: Run-of-the-mill cheese bread is both dry and greasy, with almost no cheese flavor. We wanted to create a rich loaf topped with a bold, crust. We started with all-purpose flour and added whole milk and sour cream for a creamy flavor and moist texture. Just a few tablespoons of butter added enough richness without greasiness, and using less fat made the texture heartier. A single egg gave rise and structure without an overly eggy flavor. As for cheese, small chunks of Asiago or cheddar mixed into the dough offered rich, cheesy pockets throughout the bread; a moderate amount added plenty of flavor without weighing it down. For added cheesy flavor and a crisp crust, we coated the pan and sprinkled the top of the loaf with shredded Parmesan.

Quick Cheese Bread

MAKES ONE 8-INCH LOAF

If using Asiago, choose a mild supermarket cheese that yields to pressure when pressed. Aged Asiago that is as firm as Parmesan is too sharp and piquant for this bread. If, when testing the bread for doneness, the toothpick comes out with what looks like uncooked batter clinging to it, try again in a different, but still central, spot; if the toothpick hits a pocket of cheese, it may give a false indication.

- 3 ounces Parmesan cheese, shredded on the large holes of a box grater (about 1 cup)
- 3 cups (15 ounces) unbleached all-purpose flour
- 1 tablespoon baking powder
- 1 teaspoon table salt
- ¼ teaspoon cayenne pepper
- ⅛ teaspoon ground black pepper
- 4 ounces extra-sharp cheddar cheese, cut into ½-inch cubes, or mild Asiago (see note), crumbled into ¼- to ½-inch pieces (about 1 cup)
- 1¼ cups whole milk
- 3 tablespoons unsalted butter, melted
- 1 large egg, lightly beaten
- ¾ cup sour cream

1. Adjust an oven rack to the middle position and heat the oven to 350 degrees. Spray an 8½ by 4½-inch loaf pan with vegetable oil spray; sprinkle ½ cup of the Parmesan evenly over the bottom of the pan.

2. Whisk the flour, baking powder, salt, cayenne, and black pepper together in a large bowl. Using a rubber spatula, mix in the cheddar, breaking up clumps. Whisk the milk, melted butter, egg, and sour cream together in a medium bowl. Using a rubber spatula, gently fold the wet ingredients into the dry ingredients until just combined (the batter will be heavy and thick); do not overmix. Scrape the batter into the prepared loaf pan; smooth the surface with a rubber spatula. Sprinkle the remaining ½ cup Parmesan evenly over the surface.

3. Bake until deep golden brown and a toothpick inserted in the center comes out clean, 45 to 50 minutes. Cool on a wire rack for 5 minutes; invert the loaf onto the wire rack, then turn right side up and continue to cool until warm, about 45 minutes. Cut into slices and serve.

Quick Cheese Bread with Bacon, Onion, and Gruyère

Cook 5 ounces (about 5 slices) bacon, cut into ½-inch pieces, in a 10-inch nonstick skillet over medium heat, stirring occasionally, until crisp, about 8 minutes. Using a slotted spoon, transfer the bacon to a paper towel–lined plate and pour off all but 3 tablespoons fat from the skillet. Add ½ cup minced onion to the skillet and cook, stirring frequently, until softened, about 3 minutes; set the skillet with the onion aside. Follow the recipe for Quick Cheese Bread, substituting Gruyère for the cheddar, adding the bacon and onion to the flour mixture with the cheese, and omitting the butter.

ALL-PURPOSE CORNBREAD

WHY THIS RECIPE WORKS: Cornbread can be sweet and cakey (the Northern version) or savory and light (the Southern version). We wanted a combination of the two. And most important, we wanted our cornbread to be bursting with corn flavor.

The secret to cornbread with real corn flavor was pretty simple: Use corn, not just cornmeal. While fresh corn was best, we wanted to be able to make this cornbread year round. We found that frozen kernels were nearly as good as fresh, and pureeing the kernels in a food processor made them easy to use while minimizing tough, chewy kernels. For flavoring, buttermilk provided a tangy flavor, while light brown sugar enhanced the naturally sweet flavor of the corn. Baking the bread at a higher than conventional temperature produced a crunchy crust full of toasted corn flavor.

All-Purpose Cornbread

MAKES ONE 8-INCH SQUARE

Before preparing the baking dish or any of the other ingredients, measure out the frozen corn kernels and let them stand at room temperature until thawed. When corn is in season, fresh cooked kernels can be substituted for the frozen corn. This recipe was developed with Quaker yellow cornmeal; a stone-ground whole-grain cornmeal will work but will yield a drier and less tender cornbread. We prefer a Pyrex glass baking dish because it yields a nice golden brown crust, but a metal baking dish (nonstick or traditional) will also work. The cornbread is best served warm; leftovers can be wrapped in foil and reheated in a 350-degree oven for 10 to 15 minutes.

- 1½ cups (7½ ounces) unbleached all-purpose flour
- 1 cup (about 5 ounces) yellow cornmeal (see note)
- 2 teaspoons baking powder
- ¾ teaspoon table salt
- ¼ teaspoon baking soda
- 1 cup buttermilk
- ¾ cup frozen corn kernels, thawed (see note)
- ¼ cup packed (1¾ ounces) light brown sugar
- 2 large eggs
- 8 tablespoons (1 stick) unsalted butter, melted and cooled slightly

1. Adjust an oven rack to the middle position and heat the oven to 400 degrees. Spray an 8-inch square baking dish with vegetable oil spray. Whisk the flour, cornmeal, baking powder, salt, and baking soda together in a medium bowl until combined; set aside.

2. Process the buttermilk, thawed corn kernels, and brown sugar in a food processor or blender until combined, about 5 seconds. Add the eggs and process until well combined (corn lumps will remain), about 5 seconds longer.

3. Using a rubber spatula, make a well in the center of the dry ingredients; pour the wet ingredients into the well. Begin folding the dry ingredients into the wet ingredients, giving the mixture only a few turns to barely combine; add the melted butter and continue folding until the dry ingredients are just moistened. Pour the batter into the prepared baking dish; smooth the surface with a rubber spatula. Bake until deep golden brown and a toothpick inserted in the center comes out clean, 25 to 35 minutes. Cool on a wire rack for 10 minutes; invert the cornbread onto the wire rack, then turn right side up and continue to cool until warm, about 10 minutes longer. Cut into pieces and serve.

Spicy Jalapeño-Cheddar Cornbread

Follow the recipe for All-Purpose Cornbread, reducing the table salt to ½ teaspoon; add ⅜ teaspoon cayenne pepper, 1 medium jalapeño chile, seeds and ribs removed, minced, and 2 ounces sharp cheddar cheese, shredded (about ½ cup), to the flour mixture in step 1 and toss well to combine. Reduce the brown sugar to 2 tablespoons and sprinkle 2 ounces more sharp cheddar, shredded (about ½ cup), over the batter in the baking dish just before baking.

FRESH CORN CORNBREAD

WHY THIS RECIPE WORKS: For cornbread packed with fresh, concentrated corn flavor, we pureed fresh corn kernels and cooked them down into a "corn butter" that we incorporated into the batter. Buttermilk added tang, while egg yolks and a little bit of extra butter ensured that the bread would be moist.

Fresh Corn Cornbread

SERVES 6 TO 8

We prefer to use a well-seasoned cast-iron skillet in this recipe, but an ovensafe 10-inch skillet can be used in its place. Alternatively, in step 4 you can add 1 tablespoon of butter to a 9-inch cake pan and place it in the oven until the butter melts, about 3 minutes.

- 1⅓ cups (6⅔ ounces) stone-ground cornmeal
- 1 cup (5 ounces) all-purpose flour
- 2 tablespoons sugar
- 1½ teaspoons baking powder
- ¼ teaspoon baking soda
- 1¼ teaspoons salt
- 3 ears corn, kernels cut from cobs (2¼ cups)
- 6 tablespoons unsalted butter, cut into 6 pieces
- 1 cup buttermilk
- 2 large eggs plus 1 large yolk

1. Adjust oven rack to middle position and heat oven to 400 degrees. Whisk cornmeal, flour, sugar, baking powder, baking soda, and salt together in large bowl.

2. Process corn kernels in blender until very smooth, about 2 minutes. Transfer puree to medium saucepan (you should have about 1½ cups). Cook puree over medium heat, stirring constantly, until very thick and deep yellow and it measures ¾ cup, 5 to 8 minutes.

3. Remove pan from heat. Add 5 tablespoons butter and whisk until melted and incorporated. Add buttermilk and whisk until incorporated. Add eggs and yolk and whisk until incorporated. Transfer corn mixture to bowl with cornmeal mixture and, using rubber spatula, fold together until just combined.

4. Melt remaining 1 tablespoon butter in 10-inch cast-iron skillet over medium heat. Scrape batter into skillet and spread into even layer. Bake until top is golden brown and toothpick inserted in center comes out clean, 23 to 28 minutes. Let cool on wire rack for 5 minutes. Remove cornbread from skillet and let cool for 20 minutes before cutting into wedges and serving.

SOUTHERN CORNBREAD

WHY THIS RECIPE WORKS: Classic Southern cornbread is made in a ripping hot skillet greased with bacon fat, which causes it to develop a thin, crispy crust as the bread bakes. The resulting bread is moist and tender, with the aroma of toasted corn and the subtle flavor of dairy. Traditionally, Southern-style cornbread is made from white cornmeal and has only trace amounts of sugar and flour. We wanted to perfect the proportions of ingredients and come up with our own crusty, savory Southern-style cornbread baked in a cast-iron skillet.

Departing from tradition, we chose yellow cornmeal over white—cornbreads made with yellow cornmeal consistently had a more potent corn flavor than those made with white cornmeal. We chose a rustic method to incorporate the cornmeal—combining part of the cornmeal with boiling water to create a cornmeal "mush." Cornbread that started with some mush had the most corn flavor, and it also produced a fine, moist crumb. We then stirred the buttermilk and egg into the mush before adding the remaining cornmeal and other dry ingredients. As for sugar, a small amount enhanced the natural sweetness of the corn. Finally, we poured the batter into a hot, greased cast-iron skillet to bake until crusty and fragrant.

Southern Cornbread

MAKES ONE 8-INCH LOAF

Cornmeal mush of just the right texture is essential to this bread. Make sure that the water is at a rapid boil when it is added to the cornmeal. And for an accurate measurement of boiling water, bring a kettle of water to a boil, then measure out the desired amount. Though we prefer to make cornbread in a preheated cast-iron skillet, a 9-inch round cake pan or 9-inch square baking pan, greased lightly with butter and not preheated, will also produce acceptable results if you double the recipe and bake the bread for 25 minutes. For our top-rated cast-iron skillet, see page 875.

- 4 teaspoons bacon drippings or vegetable oil
- 1 cup (about 5 ounces) yellow cornmeal, preferably stone-ground
- 2 teaspoons sugar
- 1 teaspoon baking powder
- ½ teaspoon table salt
- ¼ teaspoon baking soda
- ⅓ cup boiling water (see note)
- ¾ cup buttermilk
- 1 large egg, lightly beaten

1. Adjust an oven rack to the lower-middle position and heat the oven to 450 degrees. Add the bacon drippings to an 8-inch cast-iron skillet and place the skillet in the heating oven.

2. Place ⅓ cup of the cornmeal in a medium bowl. Whisk the remaining ⅔ cup cornmeal, the sugar, baking powder, salt, and baking soda together in a small bowl; set aside.

3. Add the boiling water to the ⅓ cup cornmeal and stir to make a stiff mush. Whisk in the buttermilk gradually, breaking up lumps until smooth, then whisk in the egg. When the oven is preheated and the skillet is very hot, add the dry ingredients to the cornmeal mush and stir until just moistened. Carefully remove the skillet from the oven (skillet handle will be hot). Pour the hot bacon fat from the pan into the batter and stir to incorporate, then quickly pour the batter into the heated skillet. Bake until golden brown, about 20 minutes. Remove from the oven and immediately turn the cornbread onto a wire rack. Cool for 5 minutes; serve.

BEHIND THE SCENES

WEIGHING IN ON WEIGHTS AND MEASURES

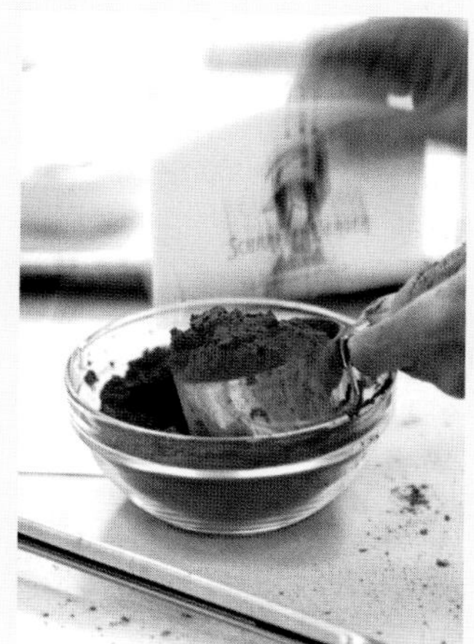

Variations in measurement can have a significant effect on baked goods. To prove this point, we asked 10 home cook volunteers to measure out 1 cup of flour and 3 tablespoons of water. The weights of the measured flour and water varied by as much as 20 percent! From these findings, we recommend three things to guarantee more consistent results from your baked goods:

WEIGH FLOUR: Don't rely on cup measurements alone. (One cup of all-purpose flour weighs 5 ounces; 1 cup of bread or whole-wheat flour weighs 5½ ounces; and 1 cup of cake flour weighs 4 ounces.)

USE THE RIGHT MEASURING CUP: Liquid measurements should be made in a liquid cup measure (not a dry cup measure). To measure accurately, place the cup on a level surface and bring your eyes down to the level of the measurement markings. Add liquid until the bottom of the curved top surface of the liquid (called the meniscus)—not the edges of the surface, which can cling and ride up the walls of the measuring cup—is level with the measurement marking.

BE PRECISE: When measuring tablespoon or teaspoon amounts of liquid, make sure that the teaspoon is completely filled and that there is no excess liquid clinging to the bottom of the spoon after pouring.

POTATO BURGER BUNS

WHY THIS RECIPE WORKS: Mashed potatoes are hefty and substantial, but in recipes for potato rolls, they give the crumb a light, tender, moist texture. That's because the starches in potatoes dilute the gluten-forming proteins in flour, which weakens the structural network of the dough and makes it softer, moister, and more tender. For the lightest potato rolls, we combined ½ pound of mashed russet potatoes with high-protein bread flour. This created a potato roll dough with a stable structure, producing rolls that were not only perfectly risen but also light and airy.

Potato Burger Buns

MAKES 9 ROLLS

Don't salt the cooking water for the potatoes. A pound of russet potatoes should yield just over 1 very firmly packed cup (½ pound) of mash. To ensure optimum rise, your dough should be warm; if your potatoes or potato water are too hot to touch, let cool before proceeding with the recipe. This dough looks very dry when mixing begins but will soften as mixing progresses. If you prefer, you may portion the rolls by weight in step 5 (2.75 ounces of dough per roll).

- 1 pound russet potatoes, peeled and cut into 1-inch pieces
- 2 tablespoons unsalted butter, cut into 4 pieces
- 2¼ cups (12⅓ ounces) bread flour
- 1 tablespoon sugar
- 2 teaspoons instant or rapid-rise yeast
- 1 teaspoon salt
- 2 large eggs, 1 lightly beaten with 1 teaspoon water and pinch salt
- 1 tablespoon sesame seeds (optional)

1. Place potatoes in medium saucepan and add water to just cover. Bring to boil over high heat; reduce heat to medium-low and simmer until potatoes are cooked through, 8 to 10 minutes.

2. Transfer 5 tablespoons cooking water to bowl to cool; drain potatoes. Return potatoes to saucepan and place over low heat. Cook, shaking pot occasionally, until any surface moisture has evaporated, about 1 minute. Remove from heat. Process potatoes through ricer or food mill or mash well with potato masher. Measure 1 very firmly packed cup potatoes and transfer to bowl. Reserve any remaining potatoes for another use. Stir in butter until melted.

3. Combine flour, sugar, yeast, and salt in bowl of stand mixer. Add warm potato mixture to flour mixture and mix with hands until combined (some large lumps are OK). Add 1 egg and reserved potato water; mix with dough hook on low speed until dough is soft and slightly sticky, 8 to 10 minutes.

4. Shape dough into ball and place in lightly greased container. Cover tightly with plastic wrap and allow to rise at room temperature until almost doubled in volume, 30 to 40 minutes.

5. Turn out dough onto counter, dusting with flour only if dough is too sticky to handle comfortably. Pat gently into 8-inch square of even thickness. Using bench scraper or chef's knife, cut dough into 9 pieces (3 rows by 3 rows). Separate pieces and cover loosely with plastic.

6. Working with 1 piece of dough at a time and keeping remaining pieces covered, form dough pieces into smooth, taut rounds. (To round, set piece of dough on unfloured work surface. Loosely cup hand around dough and, without applying pressure to dough, move hand in small circular motions. Tackiness of dough against work surface and circular motion should work dough into smooth, even ball, but if dough sticks to hands, lightly dust fingers with flour.) Cover rounds with plastic and allow to rest for 15 minutes.

7. Line 2 rimmed baking sheets with parchment paper. On lightly floured surface, firmly press each dough round into 3½-inch disk of even thickness, expelling large pockets of air. Arrange on prepared baking sheets. Cover loosely with plastic and let rise at room temperature until almost doubled in size, 30 to 40 minutes. While rolls rise, adjust oven racks to middle and upper-middle positions and heat oven to 425 degrees.

8. Brush rolls gently with egg wash and sprinkle with sesame seeds, if using. Bake rolls until deep golden brown, 15 to 18 minutes, rotating and switching baking sheets halfway through baking. Transfer baking sheets to wire racks and let cool for 5 minutes. Transfer rolls from baking sheets to wire racks. Serve warm or at room temperature.

Potato Dinner Rolls

MAKES 12 ROLLS

Line rimmed baking sheet with parchment paper. In step 5, divide dough square into 12 pieces (3 rows by 4 rows). Shape pieces into smooth, taut rounds as directed in step 6. Transfer rounds to prepared baking sheet and let rise at room temperature until almost doubled in size, 30 to 40 minutes. Bake on upper-middle rack until rolls are deep golden brown, 12 to 14 minutes, rotating baking sheet halfway through baking.

RUSTIC DINNER ROLLS

WHY THIS RECIPE WORKS: The remarkably crisp crust of European-style dinner rolls is what keeps these rolls in the domain of professionals, who typically rely on a steam-injected oven to expose the developing crust to moisture. We wanted to create a reliable recipe for rustic dinner rolls with a crisp crust and chewy crumb that looked—and tasted—like they came from an artisanal bakery.

We baked our first batch using bread flour, but when we broke the rolls open, we found a dense, bland crumb beneath a leathery crust. The flavor was easy to improve—we replaced a few tablespoons of bread flour with whole-wheat flour, which contributed earthiness, while honey added sweetness. A little extra yeast improved the crumb slightly, but not enough; making the dough wetter was the fix. Lots of water in the dough created more steam bubbles during baking, which produced an airier crumb. Giving the dough a couple of turns also encouraged the yeast to produce more carbon dioxide, creating more bubbles and a lighter crumb.

As for baking, we came up with a two-step baking process to mimic a steam-injected oven: First, we misted the rolls with water before baking them for an even crisper crust. We then partially baked them in a cake pan at a high temperature to help set their shape. Halfway through baking, we removed the cake pan from the oven, lowered the temperature, pulled the rolls apart, and returned them to the oven spaced out on a baking sheet for uniformly golden rolls with the crust and crumb we were looking for.

Rustic Dinner Rolls

MAKES 16 ROLLS

Because this dough is sticky, keep your hands well floured when handling it. Use a spray bottle to mist the rolls with water. The rolls will keep for up to 2 days at room temperature stored in a zipper-lock bag. To recrisp the crust, place the rolls in a 450-degree oven for 6 to 8 minutes. The rolls will keep frozen for several months wrapped in foil and placed in a large zipper-lock freezer bag. Thaw the rolls at room temperature and recrisp using the instructions above.

- 1½ cups plus 1 tablespoon water, at room temperature
- 2 teaspoons honey
- 1½ teaspoons instant or rapid-rise yeast
- 3 cups plus 1 tablespoon (16½ ounces) bread flour, plus extra for the dough and work surface
- 3 tablespoons whole-wheat flour
- 1½ teaspoons table salt

1. Whisk the water, honey, and yeast in the bowl of a stand mixer until well combined, making sure no honey sticks to the bottom of the bowl. Add the flours and mix on low speed with the dough hook until a cohesive dough is formed, about 3 minutes. Cover the bowl with plastic wrap and let sit at room temperature for 30 minutes.

2. Remove the plastic wrap and sprinkle the salt evenly over the dough. Knead on low speed for 5 minutes. (If the dough

creeps up on the attachment, stop the mixer and scrape it down.) Increase the speed to medium and continue to knead until the dough is smooth and slightly tacky, about 1 minute. If the dough is very sticky, add 1 to 2 tablespoons flour and continue mixing for 1 minute. Lightly oil a medium bowl; transfer the dough to the bowl and cover with plastic wrap. Let the dough rise in a warm, draft-free place until doubled in size, about 1 hour.

3. Fold the dough over itself; rotate the bowl a quarter turn and fold again. Rotate the bowl again and fold once more. Cover with plastic wrap and let rise for 30 minutes. Repeat the folding, replace the plastic wrap, and let the dough rise until doubled in size, about 30 minutes. Spray two 9-inch round cake pans with vegetable oil spray and set aside.

4. Transfer the dough to a floured work surface and sprinkle the top with more flour. Using a bench scraper, cut the dough in half and gently stretch each half into a 16-inch log. Divide each log into quarters, then each quarter into two pieces (you should have 16 pieces total), and dust the top of each piece with more flour. With floured hands, gently pick up each piece and roll it in your palms to coat with flour, shaking off the excess, and place in the prepared cake pan. Arrange eight dough pieces in each cake pan, placing one piece in the middle and the others around it, with the long side of each piece running from the center of the pan to the edge and making sure the cut side faces up. Loosely cover the cake pans with plastic wrap and let the rolls rise until doubled in size, about 30 minutes (the dough is ready when it springs back slowly when pressed lightly with a knuckle). Thirty minutes before baking, adjust an oven rack to the middle position and heat the oven to 500 degrees.

5. Remove the plastic wrap from the cake pans, spray the rolls lightly with water, and place in the oven. Bake until the tops of the rolls are brown, 10 minutes, then remove them from the oven. Reduce the oven temperature to 400 degrees; using kitchen towels or oven mitts, invert the rolls from both cake pans onto a rimmed baking sheet. When the rolls are cool enough to handle, turn them right side up, pull apart, and space evenly on the baking sheet. Continue to bake until the rolls develop a deep golden brown crust and sound hollow when tapped on the bottom, 10 to 15 minutes, rotating the baking sheet halfway through baking. Transfer the rolls to a wire rack and cool to room temperature, about 1 hour.

AUTHENTIC BAGUETTES

WHY THIS RECIPE WORKS: A great baguette is hard to come by, at least outside of France. The ideal: a moist, wheaty interior punctuated with irregular holes and a deeply browned crust so crisp it shatters into millions of tiny shards.

For the ideal structure and open crumb, we opted for a hybrid mixing approach: We mixed the dough in a stand mixer, then folded the dough several times during the initial proofing. As for fermentation, the best flavor (and most convenient method) was a slow rise in the fridge. At least 24 hours, or up to 72, produced the most flavorful loaves.

As a bonus, this dough could be portioned out to make baguettes as desired within that window. Some sifted wheat flour provided extra depth of flavor without any bitterness. The key to shaping was a three-stage process, starting with pressing the dough into a square and then rolling it like a log. Leaving the ends of the loaves unsealed until the very end allowed air bubbles to escape. For slashes with the right wide almond shape, we found that we needed to keep the blade at a shallow angle while making the cuts, about 30 degrees to the work surface. Using a *lame*, which has a slightly curved blade, made this job easy and also created a ridge, or "ear" along the edge of the slash that baked up deliciously crisp. For a shatteringly crisp crust, we covered the bread with a disposable roasting pan while it baked to allow it to begin cooking in its own steam, which promoted good color and flavor as well as crispiness.

Authentic Baguettes at Home

MAKES FOUR 15-INCH-LONG BAGUETTES

We recommend using a *couche*, *lame*, flipping board, and diastatic malt powder for this recipe (see right for more information). You will also need a baking stone and a baking peel (see page 887 for our recommended brands). If you can't find King Arthur all-purpose flour, substitute bread flour, not another all-purpose flour. For best results, weigh your ingredients. This recipe makes enough dough for four loaves, which can be baked anytime during the 24- to 72-hour window after placing the dough in the fridge.

- ¼ cup (1⅓ ounces) whole-wheat flour
- 3 cups (15 ounces) King Arthur all-purpose flour
- 1 teaspoon instant or rapid-rise yeast
- 1 teaspoon diastatic malt powder (optional; see page 690)
- 1½ teaspoons salt
- 1½ cups (12 ounces) water
- 2 (16 by 12-inch) disposable aluminum roasting pans

1. Sift whole-wheat flour through fine-mesh strainer into bowl of stand mixer; discard bran remaining in strainer. Add all-purpose flour; yeast; malt, if using; and salt to mixer bowl. Fit stand mixer with dough hook, add water, and knead on low speed until cohesive dough forms and no dry flour remains, 5 to 7 minutes. Transfer dough to lightly oiled large bowl, cover with plastic wrap, and let rest at room temperature for 30 minutes.

2. Holding edge of dough with your fingertips, fold dough over itself by gently lifting and folding edge of dough toward center. Turn bowl 45 degrees; fold again. Turn bowl and fold dough 6 more times (total of 8 folds). Cover with plastic and let rise for 30 minutes. Repeat folding and rising every 30 minutes, 3 more times. After fourth set of folds, cover bowl tightly with plastic and refrigerate for at least 24 hours or up to 72 hours.

3. Transfer dough to lightly floured counter, pat into 8-inch square (do not deflate), and divide in half. Return 1 piece of dough to container, wrap tightly with plastic, and refrigerate (dough can be shaped and baked anytime within 72-hour window). Divide remaining dough in half crosswise, transfer to lightly floured rimmed baking sheet, and cover loosely with plastic. Let rest for 45 minutes.

4. On lightly floured counter, roll each piece into loose 3- to 4-inch-long cylinder; return to floured baking sheet and cover with plastic. Let rest at room temperature for 30 minutes.

5. Lightly mist underside of couche with water, drape over inverted baking sheet and dust with flour. Gently press 1 piece of dough into 6 by 4-inch rectangle on lightly floured counter, with long edge facing you. Fold upper quarter of dough toward center and press gently to seal. Rotate dough 180 degrees and repeat folding step to form 8 by 2-inch rectangle.

6. Fold dough in half toward you, using thumb of your other hand to create crease along center of dough, sealing with heel of your hand as you work your way along the loaf. Without pressing down on loaf, use heel of your hand to reinforce seal (do not seal ends of loaf).

7. Cup your hand over center of dough and roll dough back and forth gently to tighten (it should form dog-bone shape).

8. Starting at center of dough and working toward ends, gently and evenly roll and stretch dough until it measures 15 inches long by 1¼ inches wide. Moving your hands in opposite directions, use back and forth motion to roll ends of loaf under your palms to form sharp points.

9. Transfer dough to floured couche, seam side up. Gather edges of couche into 2 pleats on either side of loaf, then cover loosely with large plastic garbage bag.

10. Repeat steps 4 through 9 with second piece of dough and place on opposite side of pleat. Fold edges of couche over loaves to cover completely, then carefully place sheet inside bag, and tie or fold under to enclose.

11. Let stand until loaves have nearly doubled in size and dough springs back minimally when poked gently with your fingertip, 45 to 60 minutes. While bread rises, adjust oven rack to middle position, place baking stone on rack, and heat oven to 500 degrees.

12. Line pizza peel with 16 by 12-inch piece parchment paper with long edge perpendicular to handle. Unfold couche, pulling from ends to remove pleats. Gently pushing with side of flipping board, roll 1 loaf over, away from other loaf, so it is seam side down. Using your hand, hold long edge of flipping board between loaf and couche at 45-degree angle, then lift couche with your other hand and flip loaf seam side up onto board.

NOTES FROM THE TEST KITCHEN

BAGUETTE BAKER'S KIT

Baguettes require a few specialty items, though we did find some alternatives. For more information on these items, see pages 896 and 897.

COUCHE: To proof baguettes, bakers cradle them in the folds of a piece of heavy linen called a *couche*. It maintains their shape while wicking away moisture, and the fabric releases the dough without tugging it out of shape. Our favorite is the **San Francisco Baking Institute 18˝ Linen Canvas (Couche)** ($8 for a 36 by 18-inch couche). Alternatively, use a double layer of 100 percent linen tea towels at least 16 inches long and 12 inches wide.

FLIPPING BOARD: To move baguettes from the couche to the oven, professional bakers use a flipping board or transfer peel. While these boards aren't expensive ($12 from breadtopia.com), a homemade substitute, made by taping two 16 by 4-inch pieces of cardboard together with packaging tape, works equally well.

LAME: For the proper almond-shaped slashes, with one edge that bakes up into a crispy ridge, you must cut the loaf at a low angle, something much more easily done with the curved blade of a *lame*. Our favorite, the **Breadtopia Bread Lame** ($9.50), scored baguettes perfectly (we did have to choke up a bit on the long handle), and its blades are easy to change (it came with five extras). Alternatively, an unused box cutter blade will work.

DIASTATIC MALT POWDER: Because of the long proofing time, nearly all the sugars in this dough will be consumed by the yeast. Since sugars are responsible for browning and caramelization, this will leave the crust pale and dull-tasting. Adding diastatic malt powder, a naturally occurring enzyme that converts the starches in flour into sugar, guarantees a supply of sugar at baking time and thus a crust that browns quickly and deeply. It's not critical, but it definitely makes a difference. Purchase diastatic malt powder (available from Amazon, $7.63 for 1 pound), not plain malt powder or malt syrup.

NOTES FROM THE TEST KITCHEN

SHAPING AND BAKING BAGUETTES

Once your dough has gone through the initial rising, folding, and resting stages, it's ready to be shaped. For more information on the *couche* and *lame*, see pages 896 and 897.

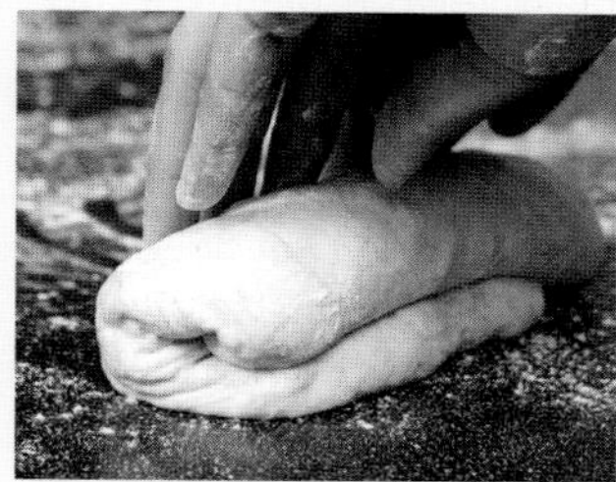

1. On lightly floured counter, roll each piece of refrigerated and rested dough into loose 3- to 4-inch-long cylinder. Move dough to floured baking sheet and cover with plastic. Let rest at room temperature for 30 minutes.

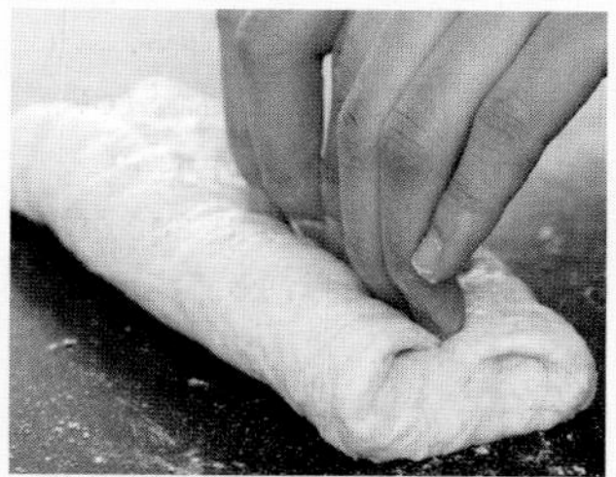

2. Gently press 1 piece of dough into 6 by 4-inch rectangle with long edge facing you. Fold upper quarter of dough toward center and press gently to seal. Rotate dough 180 degrees and repeat folding step to form 8 by 2-inch rectangle.

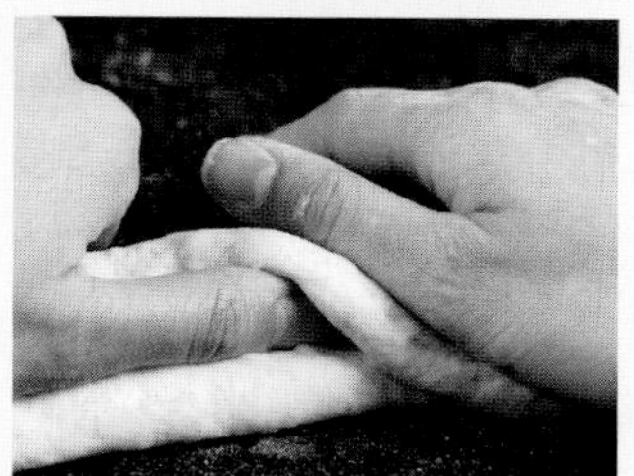

3. Fold dough in half toward you, using thumb of your other hand to create crease along center of dough, sealing with heel of your hand as you work your way along the loaf. Do not seal ends of loaf.

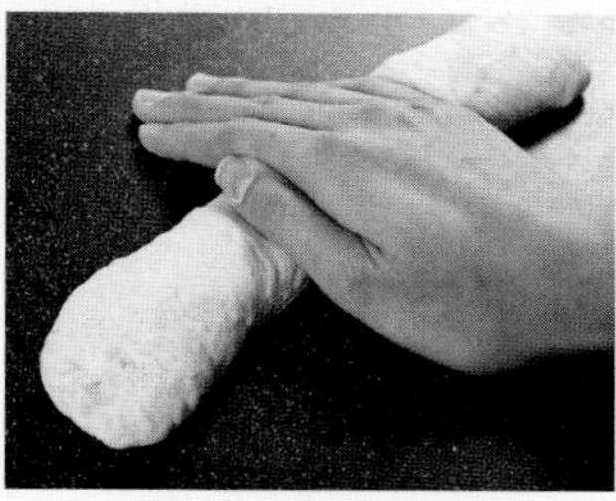

4. Cup your hand over center of dough and roll dough back and forth gently to form dog-bone shape. Working toward ends, gently roll and stretch dough until it measures 15 inches long by 1¼ inches wide.

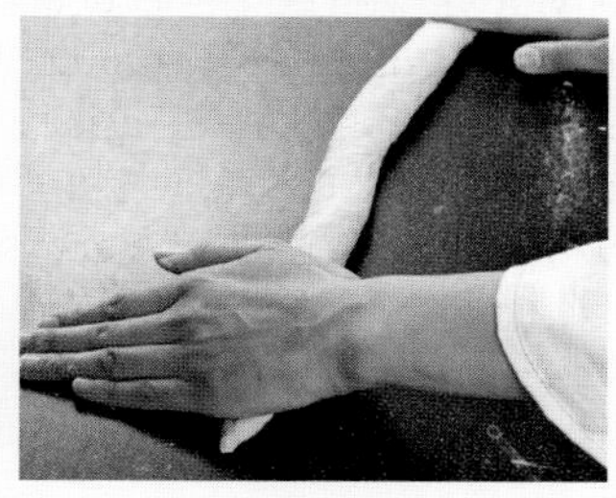

5. Moving your hands in opposite directions, use back and forth motion to roll ends of loaf under your palms to form sharp points.

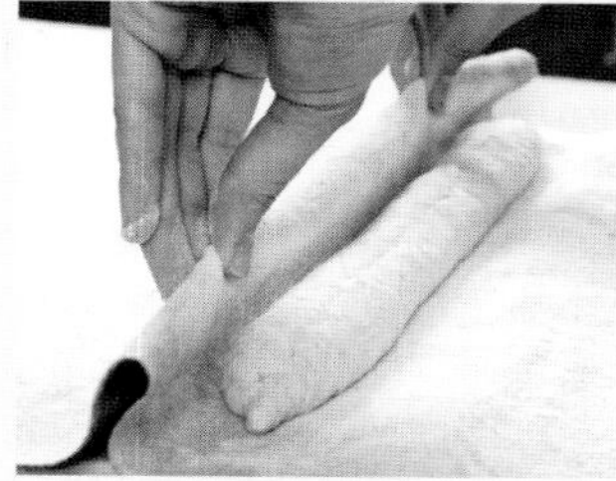

6. Transfer dough to floured couche, seam side up. On either side of loaf, pinch edges of couche into pleat. Cover loosely with large plastic garbage bag.

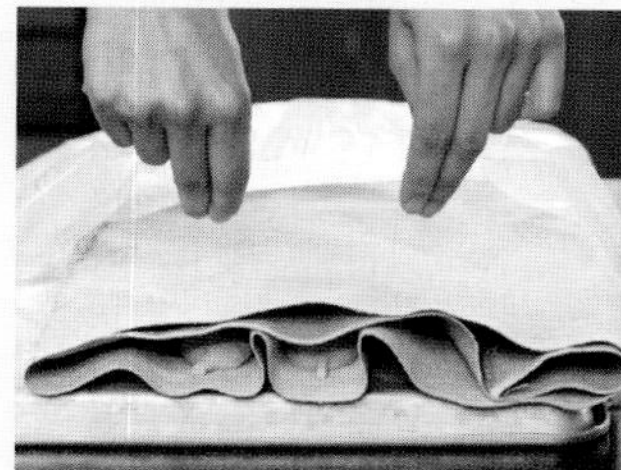

7. Place second loaf on opposite side of pleat. Fold edges of couche over loaves to cover, then carefully place sheet inside bag, and tie or fold under to enclose. Let rise for 45 to 60 minutes. While bread rises, preheat baking stone.

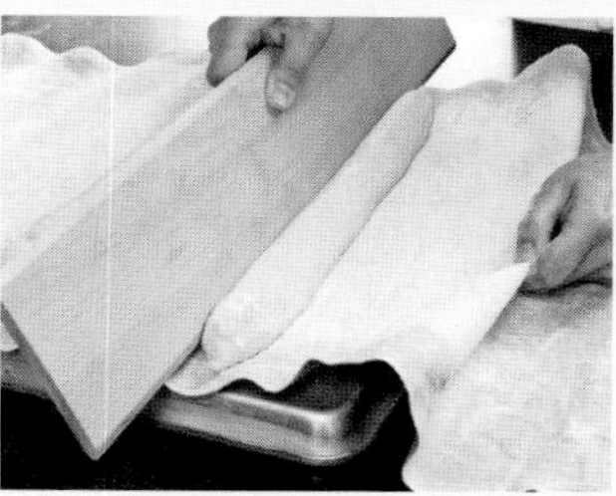

8. Unfold couche. For each loaf, use flipping board to roll loaf over so it is seam side down. Hold long edge of flipping board between loaf and couche at 45-degree angle. Lift couche and flip loaf seam side up onto board. Invert loaf onto parchment-lined peel.

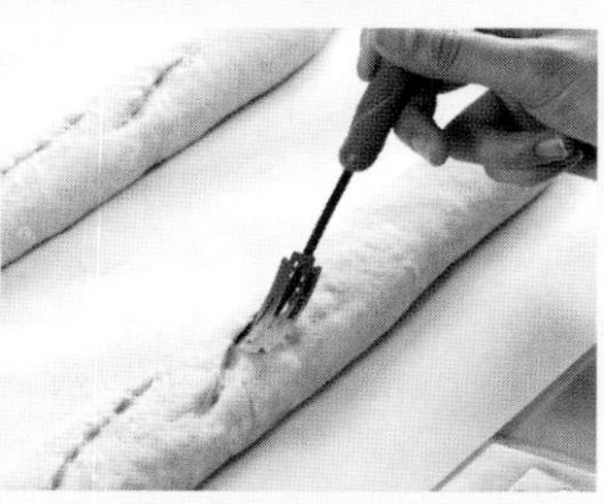

9. Holding lame concave side up at 30-degree angle to loaf, make series of three 4-inch-long, ½-inch-deep slashes along length of each loaf, using swift, fluid motion, overlapping each slash slightly.

10. Transfer loaves, on parchment, to baking stone, cover with stacked inverted disposable pans, and bake for 5 minutes. Carefully remove pans and bake until loaves are evenly browned, 12 to 15 minutes longer, rotating parchment halfway through baking.

---

13. Invert loaf onto parchment-lined peel, seam side down, about 2 inches from long edge of parchment, then use flipping board to straighten loaf. Repeat with remaining loaf, leaving at least 3 inches between loaves.

14. Holding lame concave side up at 30-degree angle to loaf, make series of three 4-inch-long, ½-inch-deep slashes along length of loaf, using swift, fluid motion, overlapping each slash slightly. Repeat with second loaf.

15. Transfer loaves, on parchment, to baking stone, cover with stacked inverted disposable pans, and bake for 5 minutes. Carefully remove pans and bake until loaves are evenly browned, 12 to 15 minutes longer, rotating parchment halfway through baking. Transfer to cooling rack and let cool for at least 20 minutes before serving. Consume within 3 to 4 hours.

RUSTIC COUNTRY BREAD

WHY THIS RECIPE WORKS: Authentic rustic country bread should be made with little more than flour, water, yeast, and salt. We aimed to develop a reliable recipe for a big, crusty, pleasant loaf—made the old-fashioned way.

We decided to focus our tests around using a sponge starter—a mixture of flour, water, and yeast, left to ferment and then combined with additional flour, water, and other ingredients. A sponge starter gave our bread a complex flavor that yeast alone could not provide. We soon learned that bread with a high water content produces a chewier texture. So we ended up working with a wet dough, to which we could add more flour if necessary. This wet dough was tricky to work with but resulted in a bread with a texture so rough, chewy, and substantial that it was a meal all by itself. For a finishing touch, we added whole-wheat and rye flours to the ingredients to enhance this bread's full flavor.

Rustic Country Bread

MAKES 1 ROUND LOAF

Because of its high water content, the bread will be gummy if pulled from the oven too soon. To ensure the bread's doneness, make sure its internal temperature reads 210 degrees by inserting an instant-read thermometer into the loaf. The crust should be very dark brown, almost black. Leftover bread can be wrapped in a double layer of plastic wrap and stored at room temperature for up to 3 days; wrapped with an additional layer of aluminum foil, the bread can be frozen for up to one month. To recrisp the crust, place the unwrapped bread in a 450-degree oven for 10 minutes (frozen bread should be thawed at room temperature before recrisping).

SPONGE

- 1 cup water, at room temperature
- ½ teaspoon instant or rapid-rise yeast
- 1 cup (5½ ounces) bread flour
- 1 cup (5½ ounces) whole-wheat flour

DOUGH

- 3–3½ cups (16½ to 19¼ ounces) bread flour, plus extra for the dough and work surface
- ½ cup (2¾ ounces) rye flour
- 1⅓ cups water, at room temperature
- 2 tablespoons honey
- 2 teaspoons table salt

1. FOR THE SPONGE: Combine the water and yeast in a medium bowl and stir until the yeast is dissolved. Add the flours and stir with a rubber spatula to create a stiff, wet dough. Cover the bowl with plastic wrap and let sit at room temperature for at least 5 hours or up to 24 hours. (The sponge can be refrigerated for up to 24 hours; return to room temperature before continuing with the recipe.)

2. FOR THE DOUGH: Using a rubber spatula, combine 3 cups of the bread flour, the rye flour, water, honey, and sponge in the bowl of a stand mixer. Knead the dough on low speed with the dough hook until smooth, about 15 minutes, adding the salt during the final 3 minutes. If more flour is needed, add the remaining ½ cup bread flour, 1 tablespoon at a time, until the dough clears the sides of the bowl but sticks to the bottom. Lightly oil a large bowl; transfer the dough to the bowl and cover with plastic wrap. Let the dough rise until tripled in size, about 2 hours.

3. Transfer the dough to a lightly floured work surface. Flour the top of the dough. With floured hands, shape the dough into a round by pulling the edges into the middle and gathering it loosely together. Transfer the dough, seam side down, to an inverted baking sheet lined with parchment paper. Cover with plastic wrap and let rise until almost doubled in size, about 45 minutes. (The dough should barely spring back when poked with a knuckle.)

4. Meanwhile, adjust an oven rack to the lower-middle position, place a baking stone on the rack, and heat the oven to 450 degrees at least 30 minutes before baking.

5. Use a razor blade or sharp knife to cut three slashes on the top of the dough. With scissors, trim the excess parchment around the dough. Lightly spray the dough with water.

6. Carefully slide the parchment with the dough onto the baking stone using a jerking motion. Bake until the crust is very dark brown and the center registers 210 degrees on an instant-read thermometer, 35 to 40 minutes, rotating the bread halfway through baking (see note). Turn the oven off, open the oven door, and let the bread remain in the oven 10 minutes longer. Remove from the oven, transfer to a wire rack, and cool to room temperature, about 2 hours.

ALMOST NO-KNEAD BREAD

WHY THIS RECIPE WORKS: The no-knead method of bread making first came to our attention in an article on baker Jim Lahey in the *New York Times*. The article claimed that Lahey's method produces artisanal-style loaves with minimum effort. Lahey uses two approaches to replace kneading (the mechanical process that forms gluten, which gives bread structure): a very high hydration level (85 percent—meaning that for every 10 ounces of flour, there are 8.5 ounces of water) and a 12-hour autolysis period that allows the flour to hydrate and rest before the dough is kneaded. After the dough is briefly kneaded, it is baked in a covered Dutch oven; the lid trapped released steam, creating a springy loaf. By finishing the baking with the loaf uncovered, we created a beautifully browned crust.

However, as we baked loaf after loaf, we found two big problems: The dough didn't have enough structure, and it lacked flavor. To give the dough more strength (and make it easier to handle), we lowered the hydration and added the bare minimum of kneading time (under a minute) to compensate. To solve the lack of flavor, we needed to introduce two elements that a starter adds to artisan breads: an acidic tang with vinegar and a shot of yeasty flavor with beer.

NOTES FROM THE TEST KITCHEN

MAKING ALMOST NO-KNEAD BREAD

1. Mix the dough by stirring the wet ingredients into the dry ingredients with a rubber spatula, then leave the dough to rest for 8 to 18 hours.

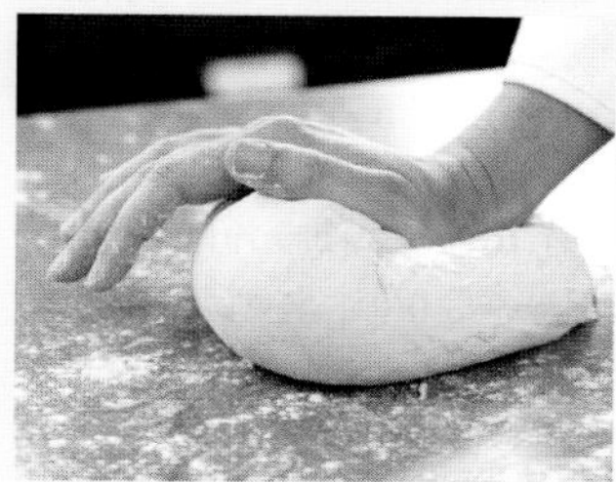

2. Turn the dough out onto a lightly floured surface and knead the dough 10 to 15 times.

3. After kneading the dough, shape it into a ball by pulling the edges into the middle.

4. Transfer the loaf, seam side down, to a large sheet of greased parchment and, using the paper, transfer it to a Dutch oven. Mist the bread with vegetable oil spray, cover it loosely with plastic, and let it rise until doubled in size, about 2 hours.

5. Sprinkle the dough with flour and cut a ½-inch-deep X into the loaf. Cover the pot, place it in the oven, and turn the oven to 425 degrees. Bake for 30 minutes, then remove the lid and bake until the loaf registers 210 degrees.

Almost No-Knead Bread

MAKES 1 ROUND LOAF

Use a mild-flavored lager, such as Budweiser (mild nonalcoholic lager also works). In step 3, start the 30-minute timer as soon as you put the bread in the cold oven. Do not wait until the oven has preheated to start your timer or the bread will burn. The bread is best eaten the day it is baked, but it can be wrapped in aluminum foil and stored in a cool, dry place for up to two days.

- 3 cups (15 ounces) all-purpose flour
- 1½ teaspoons salt
- ¼ teaspoon instant or rapid-rise yeast
- ¾ cup plus 2 tablespoons water, room temperature
- 6 tablespoons mild-flavored lager
- 1 tablespoon distilled white vinegar
- Vegetable oil spray

1. Whisk flour, salt, and yeast together in large bowl. Add water, lager, and vinegar. Using rubber spatula, fold mixture, scraping up dry flour from bottom of bowl, until shaggy ball forms. Cover bowl with plastic wrap and let dough sit at room temperature for at least 8 hours or up to 18 hours.

2. Lay 18 by 12-inch sheet of parchment paper on counter and coat lightly with vegetable oil spray. Transfer dough to lightly floured counter and knead by hand to form smooth, round ball, 10 to 15 times. Shape dough into ball by pulling edges into middle. Transfer dough, seam side down, to center of parchment and spray surface of dough with oil spray. Pick up dough by lifting parchment overhang and lower into heavy-bottomed Dutch oven (let any excess parchment hang over pot edge). Cover loosely with plastic and let rise at room temperature until dough has doubled in size and does not readily spring back when poked with finger, about 2 hours.

3. Adjust oven rack to middle position. Remove plastic from pot. Lightly flour top of dough and, using razor blade or sharp knife, make one 6-inch-long, ½-inch-deep slit along top of dough. Cover pot and place in oven. Heat oven to 425 degrees. Bake bread for 30 minutes.

4. Remove lid and continue to bake until loaf is deep brown and registers 210 degrees, 20 to 30 minutes. Carefully remove bread from pot; transfer to wire rack and let cool completely, about 2 hours.

BEST SOURDOUGH BREAD

WHY THIS RECIPE WORKS: Making one's own sourdough culture (starter) is a commitment, but one that's rewarding—even addictive. For a simple, straightforward sourdough starter, we began by mixing all-purpose flour with whole-wheat flour, which provided extra nutrition for the developing bacteria and yeasts. We then added enough water to form a wet dough and let it sit at room temperature. After 3 days or so, when it started to show signs of life in the form of gas bubbles and a pungent aroma, we began a routine of daily feedings, mixing some of the culture with fresh flour and water. After 10 to 14 days, it smelled pleasantly yeasty and doubled in volume 8 to 12 hours after refreshing, a sure sign that it was mature enough to use. For a simple recipe in which to use the culture, we developed a sourdough version of our Almost No-Knead Bread, which rises overnight and is baked in a Dutch oven. We also came up with an easy way to maintain the culture between uses. We found we could refresh the food supply just once a week by letting the culture sit for 5 hours at room temperature after feeding it and then moving it to the refrigerator for storage.

Sourdough Starter

MAKES ABOUT 2 CUPS

It's okay to occasionally miss a daily feeding in step 2, but don't let it go for more than 48 hours. For the best results, weigh your ingredients and use organic flour and bottled or filtered water to create the starter. Once the starter is mature, all-purpose flour should be used to maintain it. Placing the starter in a glass bowl will allow for easier observation of activity beneath the surface. Discarding some starter before each feeding gets rid of waste and keeps the amount of starter manageable.

- 4½ cups (24¾ ounces) whole-wheat flour
- 5 cups (25 ounces) all-purpose flour, plus extra for maintaining starter
- Water, room temperature

1. Combine whole-wheat flour and all-purpose flour in large container. Using wooden spoon, mix 1 cup (5 ounces) flour mixture and ⅔ cup (5⅓ ounces) room-temperature water in glass bowl until no dry flour remains (reserve remaining flour mixture). Cover with plastic wrap and let sit at room temperature until bubbly and fragrant, 48 to 72 hours.

2. FEED STARTER: Measure out ¼ cup (2 ounces) starter and transfer to clean bowl or jar; discard remaining starter. Stir ½ cup (2½ ounces) flour mixture and ¼ cup (2 ounces) water into starter until no dry flour remains. Cover with plastic wrap and let sit at room temperature for 24 hours.

3. Repeat step 2 every 24 hours until starter is pleasantly aromatic and doubles in size 8 to 12 hours after being refreshed, about 10 to 14 days. At this point starter is mature and ready to be baked with, or it can be moved to storage. (If baking, use starter once it has doubled in size during 8- to 12-hour window. Use starter within 1 hour after it starts to deflate once reaching its peak.)

4A. TO STORE AND MAINTAIN MATURE STARTER: Measure out ¼ cup (2 ounces) starter and transfer to clean bowl; discard remaining starter. Stir ½ cup (2½ ounces) all-purpose flour and ¼ cup (2 ounces) room-temperature water into starter until no dry flour remains. Transfer to clean container that can be loosely covered (plastic container or mason jar with its lid inverted) and let sit at room temperature for 5 hours. Cover and transfer to refrigerator. If not baking regularly, repeat process weekly.

4B. TO PREPARE FOR BAKING: Eighteen to 24 hours before baking, measure out ½ cup (4 ounces) starter and transfer to clean bowl; discard remaining starter. Stir 1 cup (5 ounces) all-purpose flour and ½ cup (4 ounces) room-temperature water into starter until no dry flour remains. Cover and let sit at room temperature for 5 hours. Measure out amount of starter called for in bread recipe and transfer to second bowl. Cover and transfer to refrigerator for at least 12 hours or up to 18 hours. Remaining starter should be refrigerated and maintained as directed.

Almost No-Knead Sourdough Bread

MAKES 1 LARGE ROUND LOAF

We prefer King Arthur all-purpose flour here; if you can't find it, you can substitute bread flour. For the best results, weigh your ingredients. The dough can rise at room temperature in step 3 (instead of in the oven), but it will take 3 to 4 hours. Do not wait until the oven has preheated in step 4 to start timing 30 minutes or the bread will burn.

- 3⅔ cups (18⅓ ounces) King Arthur all-purpose flour
- 1¾ teaspoons salt
- 1½ cups plus 4 teaspoons (12⅔ ounces) water, room temperature
- ⅓ cup (3 ounces) mature sourdough starter

1. Whisk flour and salt together in medium bowl. Whisk room-temperature water and starter in large bowl until smooth. Add flour mixture to water mixture and stir using wooden spoon, scraping up dry flour from bottom of bowl, until dough comes together, and then knead by hand in bowl until shaggy ball forms and no dry flour remains. Cover bowl with plastic wrap and let sit at room temperature for at least 12 hours or up to 18 hours.

2. Lay 12 by 12-inch sheet of parchment paper on counter and spray generously with vegetable oil spray. Transfer dough to lightly floured counter and knead 10 to 15 times. Shape dough into ball by pulling edges into middle. Transfer dough, seam side down, to center of parchment. Pick up dough by lifting parchment edges and lower into heavy-bottomed Dutch oven. Cover with plastic wrap.

3. Adjust oven rack to middle position and place loaf pan or cake pan in bottom of oven. Place Dutch oven on middle rack and pour 3 cups of boiling water into pan below. Close oven

door and let dough rise until doubled in size and does not readily spring back when poked with your floured finger, 2 to 3 hours.

4. Remove Dutch oven and water pan from oven; discard plastic from Dutch oven. Lightly flour top of dough and, using razor blade or sharp knife, make one 7-inch-long, ½-inch-deep slit along top of dough. Cover pot and place on middle rack in oven. Heat oven to 425 degrees. Bake bread for 30 minutes (starting timing as soon as you turn on oven).

5. Remove lid and continue to bake until bread is deep brown and registers 210 degrees, 20 to 30 minutes longer. Carefully remove bread from pot; transfer to wire rack and let cool completely before serving.

NO-KNEAD BRIOCHE

WHY THIS RECIPE WORKS: The average brioche recipe is 50 percent butter, and the high fat content can make the brioche incredibly tender—or it can cause the dough to separate into a greasy mess. For rich, tender brioche without the hassle of painstakingly adding softened butter to the dough little by little as it is kneaded, we melted the butter and added it directly to the eggs. Then we dispensed with the stand mixer and opted for an equally effective no-knead approach that lets time do most of the work: An overnight rest in the fridge developed both structure and flavor. We used two simple loaf pans and then, to build structure and ensure an even, fine crumb, we shaped the dough into four tight balls before placing two in each pan. The dough can also be divided to make brioche buns or traditionally shaped loaves using fluted brioche molds.

No-Knead Brioche

MAKES 2 LOAVES

High-protein King Arthur Bread Flour works best with this recipe, though other bread flours will suffice. The test kitchen's preferred loaf pan measures 8½ by 4½ inches; if you use a 9 by 5-inch pan, start checking for doneness 5 minutes earlier. If you don't have a baking stone, bake the bread on a preheated rimmed baking sheet.

- 3¼ cups (17¾ ounces) bread flour
- 2¼ teaspoons instant or rapid-rise yeast
- 1½ teaspoons salt
- 7 large eggs (1 lightly beaten with pinch salt)
- ½ cup water, room temperature
- ⅓ cup (2⅓ ounces) sugar
- 16 tablespoons unsalted butter, melted and cooled slightly

1. Whisk flour, yeast, and salt together in large bowl. Whisk 6 eggs, water, and sugar together in medium bowl until sugar has dissolved. Whisk in butter until smooth. Add egg mixture to flour mixture and stir with wooden spoon until uniform mass forms and no dry flour remains, about 1 minute. Cover bowl with plastic wrap and let stand for 10 minutes.

2. Holding edge of dough with your fingertips, fold dough over itself by gently lifting and folding edge of dough toward middle. Turn bowl 45 degrees; fold again. Turn bowl and fold dough 6 more times (total of 8 folds). Cover with plastic and let rise for 30 minutes. Repeat folding and rising every 30 minutes, 3 more times. After fourth set of folds, cover bowl tightly with plastic and refrigerate for at least 16 hours or up to 48 hours.

3. Transfer dough to well-floured counter and divide into 4 equal pieces. Working with 1 piece of dough at a time, pat dough into 4-inch disk. Working around circumference of dough, fold edges of dough toward center until ball forms. Flip dough over and, without applying pressure, move your hands in small circular motions to form dough into smooth, taut round. (If dough sticks to your hands, lightly dust top of dough with flour.) Repeat with remaining dough. Cover dough rounds loosely with plastic and let rest for 5 minutes.

4. Grease two 8½ by 4½-inch loaf pans. After 5 minutes, flip each dough ball so seam side is facing up, pat into 4-inch disk, and repeat rounding step. Place 2 rounds, seam side down, side by side into prepared pans and press gently into corners. Cover loaves loosely with plastic and let rise at room temperature until almost doubled in size (dough should rise to about ½ inch below top edge of pan), 1½ to 2 hours. Thirty minutes before baking, adjust oven rack to middle position, place baking stone on rack, and heat oven to 350 degrees.

5. Remove plastic and brush loaves gently with remaining 1 egg beaten with salt. Set loaf pans on stone and bake until golden brown and internal temperature registers 190 degrees, 35 to 45 minutes, rotating pans halfway through baking. Transfer pans to wire rack and let cool for 5 minutes. Remove loaves from pans, return to wire rack, and let cool completely before slicing and serving, about 2 hours.

No-Knead Brioche Buns

MAKES 10 BUNS

1. Line 2 rimmed baking sheets with parchment paper. Transfer dough to well-floured counter and divide into 10 equal pieces. Working with 1 piece of dough at a time, pat dough into disk. Working around circumference of dough, fold edges of dough toward center until ball forms. Flip dough over and, without applying pressure, move your hands in small circular motions to form dough into smooth, taut round. (Tackiness of dough against counter and circular motion should work dough into smooth, even ball, but if dough sticks to your hands, lightly dust top of dough with flour.) Repeat with remaining dough.

2. Arrange buns on prepared sheets, five per sheet. Cover loosely with plastic and let rise at room temperature until almost doubled in size, 1 to 1½ hours. Thirty minutes before baking, adjust oven racks to upper-middle and lower-middle positions and heat oven to 350 degrees.

3. Remove plastic and brush rolls gently with remaining 1 egg beaten with salt. Bake until golden brown and internal temperature registers 190 degrees, 15 to 20 minutes, rotating and switching sheets halfway through baking. Transfer sheets to wire rack and let cool for 5 minutes. Transfer buns to wire rack. Serve warm or at room temperature.

No-Knead Brioche à Tête

MAKES 2 LOAVES

Traditional loaves of *brioche à tête* achieve their fluted sides and conical shape from a brioche mold.

1. Transfer dough to well-floured counter and divide into 2 equal pieces. Remove golf ball–size piece of dough from each. Pat 2 large pieces of dough into 4-inch disks and 2 small pieces of dough into ½-inch disks. Working with 1 piece of dough at a time, work around circumference of dough; fold edges of dough toward center until ball forms. Flip dough over and, without applying pressure, move your hands in small circular motions to form dough into smooth, taut round. (Tackiness of dough against counter and circular motion should work dough into smooth, even ball, but if dough sticks to your hands, lightly dust top of dough with flour.) Repeat with remaining dough. Cover dough rounds loosely with plastic and let rest for 5 minutes.

2. Grease two 8- to 8½-inch fluted brioche pans. After 5 minutes, flip each dough ball so seam side is facing up, pat into 4-inch and ½-inch disks, and repeat rounding step. Place larger rounds, seam side down, into prepared pans and press gently into corners. Place smaller rounds, seam side down, in center of larger rounds, pushing down gently so only top halves of smaller rounds are showing. Cover loaves loosely with plastic and let rise at room temperature until almost doubled in size (dough should rise to about ½ inch below top edge of pan), 1½ to 2 hours. Thirty minutes before baking, adjust oven rack to middle position, place baking stone on rack, and heat oven to 350 degrees.

3. Remove plastic and brush loaves gently with remaining 1 egg beaten with salt. Set pans on stone and bake until golden brown and internal temperature registers 190 degrees, 35 to 45 minutes, rotating pans halfway through baking. Transfer pans to wire rack and let cool for 5 minutes. Remove loaves from pans, return to wire rack, and let cool completely before slicing and serving, about 2 hours.

CINNAMON SWIRL BREAD

WHY THIS RECIPE WORKS: This American classic frequently disappoints due to either precious little cinnamon flavor or, just as bad, a gloppy, oozing filling reminiscent of sticky buns. The bread itself is often an afterthought of pedestrian white bread, or else it's a cakey, dense affair. We swapped in an airy, cottony Japanese white bread called *shokupan* and created a filling with a balanced mixture of cinnamon, confectioners' sugar, and vanilla. To ensure that our filling stayed put and could be tasted with every bite, we traded the traditional swirl shape for a simple yet elegant Russian braid.

Cinnamon Swirl Bread

MAKES 2 LOAVES

To achieve the proper dough consistency, make sure to weigh your ingredients. The dough will appear very wet and sticky until the final few minutes of kneading; do not be tempted to add supplemental flour.

DOUGH

- 8 tablespoons unsalted butter
- 3¾ cups (20⅔ ounces) bread flour
- ¾ cup (2¾ ounces) nonfat dry milk powder
- ⅓ cup (2⅓ ounces) granulated sugar
- 1 tablespoon instant or rapid-rise yeast
- 1½ cups (12 ounces) water, heated to 110 degrees
- 1 large egg, lightly beaten
- 1½ teaspoons salt
- 1½ cups (7½ ounces) golden raisins

FILLING

- 1 cup (4 ounces) confectioners' sugar
- 3 tablespoons ground cinnamon
- 1 teaspoon vanilla extract
- ½ teaspoon salt
- 1 large egg, lightly beaten with pinch salt

1. FOR THE DOUGH: Cut butter into 32 pieces and toss with 1 tablespoon flour; set aside to soften while mixing dough. Whisk remaining flour, milk powder, sugar, and yeast together in bowl of stand mixer fitted with dough hook. Add water and egg and mix on medium-low speed until cohesive mass forms, about 2 minutes, scraping down bowl as needed. Cover mixing bowl with plastic wrap and let stand for 20 minutes.

2. Adjust oven rack to middle position and place loaf or cake pan on bottom of oven. Grease large bowl. Remove plastic from mixer bowl, add salt, and mix on medium-low speed until dough is smooth and elastic and clears sides of bowl, 7 to 15 minutes. With mixer running, add butter a few pieces at a time, and continue to knead until butter is fully incorporated and dough is smooth and elastic and clears sides of bowl, 3 to 5 minutes longer. Add raisins and mix until incorporated, 30 to 60 seconds. Transfer dough to prepared bowl and, using bowl scraper or rubber spatula, fold dough over itself by gently lifting and folding edge of dough toward middle.

NOTES FROM THE TEST KITCHEN

WEAVING CINNAMON SWIRL BREAD, RUSSIAN-STYLE

The benefit of a Russian braid—other than good looks—is that it solves the gapping that plagues swirl breads. The twisted shape tightly seals the pieces of dough together while providing plenty of escape routes for the excess air that would otherwise compress the dough and create tunnels in the loaf.

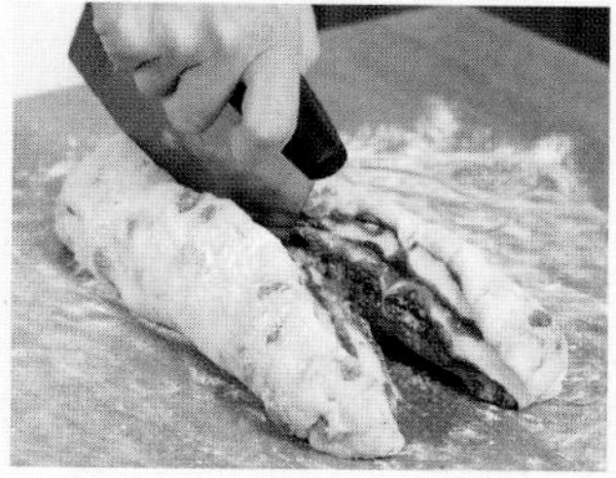

1. Using bench scraper or sharp chef's knife, cut filled dough in half lengthwise. Turn halves so cut sides are facing up.

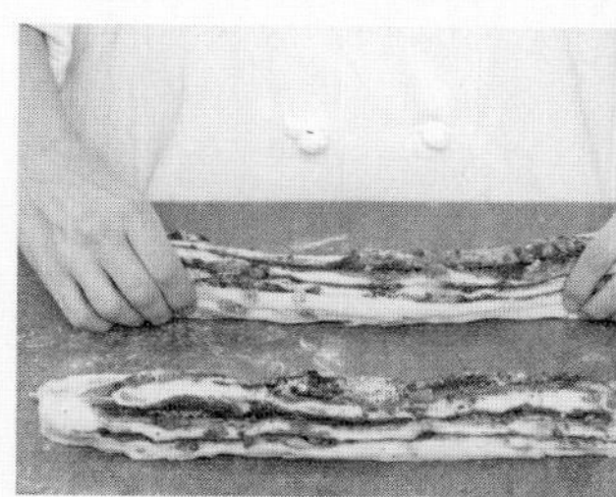

2. With cut sides up, stretch each half into 14-inch length.

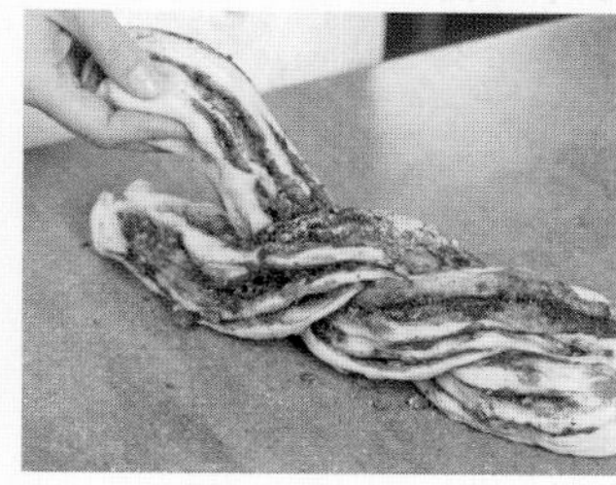

3. Pinch 2 ends of strips together. To braid, take left strip of dough and lay it over right strip of dough. Repeat braiding, keeping cut sides face up, until pieces are tightly twisted. Pinch ends together.

Turn bowl 90 degrees; fold again. Turn bowl and fold dough 6 more times (total of 8 folds). Cover tightly with plastic and transfer to middle rack of oven. Pour 3 cups boiling water into loaf pan in oven, close oven door, and allow dough to rise for 45 minutes.

3. Remove bowl from oven and gently press down on center of dough to deflate. Repeat folding (making total of 8 folds), re-cover, and return to oven until doubled in volume, about 45 minutes.

4. FOR THE FILLING: Whisk all ingredients together in bowl until well combined; set aside.

5. Grease two 8½ by 4½-inch loaf pans. Transfer dough to lightly floured counter and divide into 2 pieces. Working with 1 piece of dough, pat into rough 6 by 11-inch rectangle. With short side facing you, fold long sides in like a business letter to form 3 by 11-inch rectangle. Roll dough away from you into ball. Dust ball with flour and flatten with rolling pin into 7 by 18-inch rectangle with even ¼-inch thickness. Using spray bottle, spray dough lightly with water. Sprinkle half of filling mixture evenly over dough, leaving ¼-inch border on sides and ¾-inch border on top and bottom; spray filling lightly with water. (Filling should be speckled with water over entire surface.) With short side facing you, roll dough away from you into firm cylinder. Turn loaf seam side up and pinch closed; pinch ends closed. Dust loaf lightly on all sides with flour and let rest for 10 minutes. Repeat with second ball of dough and remaining filling.

6. Working with 1 loaf at a time, use bench scraper to cut loaf in half lengthwise; turn halves so cut sides are facing up. Gently stretch each half into 14-inch length. Line up pieces of dough and pinch 2 ends of strips together. Take piece on left and lay over piece on right. Repeat, keeping cut side up, until pieces of dough are tightly twisted. Pinch ends together. Transfer loaf, cut side up, to prepared loaf pan; push any exposed raisins into seams of braid. Repeat with second loaf. Cover loaves loosely with plastic, return to oven, and allow to rise for 45 minutes. Remove loaves and water pan from oven; heat oven to 350 degrees. Allow loaves to rise at room temperature until almost doubled in size, about 45 minutes (tops of loaves should rise about 1 inch over lip of pans).

7. Brush loaves with egg mixture. Bake until crust is well browned, about 25 minutes. Reduce oven temperature to 325 degrees, tent loaves with aluminum foil, and continue to bake until internal temperature registers 200 degrees, 15 to 25 minutes longer.

8. Transfer pans to wire rack and let cool for 5 minutes. Remove loaves from pans, return to rack, and cool to room temperature before slicing, about 2 hours.

CIABATTA

WHY THIS RECIPE WORKS: Unless your source is an artisanal bakery, most loaves of ciabatta available just aren't any good. Some lack flavor, others are too flat, and still others have holes so big there's hardly any bread. Ideally, this Italian loaf should boast a crisp, flavorful crust, a full and tangy flavor, and a chewy, open crumb. Uninterested in yet another lackluster loaf from the supermarket, we decided to make our own.

We started with the flour selection—whole-wheat, bread, or all-purpose? We preferred all-purpose, which is made from both hard and soft wheat and has less protein than bread flour, producing loaves with a more open, springy texture. The next step was to build flavor through the sponge (or *biga* in Italian), which we also used in our Rustic Country Bread (page 692). As it ferments, the yeast in the biga produces lactic and acetic acids as by-products, which give the bread its characteristic sourness. Kneading the sponge and remaining dough ingredients in a stand mixer for only a few minutes produced loaves that spread out instead of rising, so we turned to a combination of kneading and folding the dough over itself a few times before letting it rest. This two-step process gave the dough structure but also supported oversized holes. Adding a small amount of milk, which contains a protein that slightly weakens the gluten strands, remedied the problem and took down the size of those big bubbles.

To avoid extra handling of the dough, we formed the loaves,

then moved them to parchment paper and slid the parchment onto the baking surface after another rest. We opted to bake the loaves at a cooler temperature than 500 degrees (as most recipes recommend). A final enhancement was to spray the loaves with water in the first minutes of baking for a crisper crust and loaves that rose a bit higher.

Ciabatta

MAKES 2 LOAVES

As you make this bread, keep in mind that the dough is wet and very sticky. The key to manipulating it is working quickly and gently; rough handling will result in flat, tough loaves. When possible, use a large rubber spatula or bowl scraper to move the dough. If you have to use your hands, make sure they are well floured. Because the dough is so sticky, it must be prepared in a stand mixer. If you don't have a baking stone, bake the bread on an overturned and preheated rimmed baking sheet set on the lowest oven rack. Leftover bread can be wrapped in a double layer of plastic wrap and stored at room temperature for up to 3 days; wrapped with an additional layer of aluminum foil, the bread can be frozen for up to 1 month. To recrisp the crust, place the unwrapped bread in a 450-degree oven for 6 to 8 minutes (frozen bread should be thawed at room temperature before recrisping).

SPONGE

- 1 cup (5 ounces) unbleached all-purpose flour
- ⅛ teaspoon instant or rapid-rise yeast
- ½ cup water, at room temperature

DOUGH

- 2 cups (10 ounces) unbleached all-purpose flour, plus extra for the dough and work surface
- 1½ teaspoons table salt
- ½ teaspoon instant or rapid-rise yeast
- ¾ cup water, at room temperature
- ¼ cup milk, at room temperature

1. FOR THE SPONGE: Combine the flour, yeast, and water in a medium bowl and stir with a wooden spoon until a uniform mass forms, about 1 minute. Cover the bowl tightly with plastic wrap and let stand at room temperature (about 70 degrees) for at least 8 hours or up to 24 hours.

2. FOR THE DOUGH: Place the sponge and dough ingredients in the bowl of a stand mixer fitted with the paddle attachment. Mix on low speed until roughly combined and a shaggy dough forms, about 1 minute; scrape down the sides of the bowl as necessary. Increase the speed to medium-low and continue mixing until the dough becomes a uniform mass that collects on the paddle and pulls away from the sides of the bowl, 4 to 6 minutes. Change to the dough hook and knead the bread on medium speed until smooth and shiny (the dough will be very sticky), about 10 minutes. (If the dough creeps up on the attachment, stop the mixer and scrape it down.) Transfer the dough to a large bowl and cover tightly with plastic wrap. Let the dough rise at room temperature until doubled in size, about 1 hour. (The dough should barely spring back when poked with a knuckle.)

3. Spray a rubber spatula or bowl scraper with vegetable oil spray; fold the partially risen dough over itself by gently lifting and folding the edge of the dough toward the middle. Turn the bowl 90 degrees; fold again. Turn the bowl and fold the dough six more times (for a total of eight turns). Cover with plastic wrap and let rise for 30 minutes. Repeat folding, replace the plastic wrap, and let rise until doubled in size, about

NOTES FROM THE TEST KITCHEN

MAKING CIABATTA

1. After mixing the dough and allowing it to rest, turn the partially risen dough by folding it in on itself to gently encourage more gluten development. Let it rest again, then repeat this step.

2. Transfer the dough to a lightly floured surface and halve it with a bench scraper.

3. Press each half into a rough 12 by 6-inch rectangle.

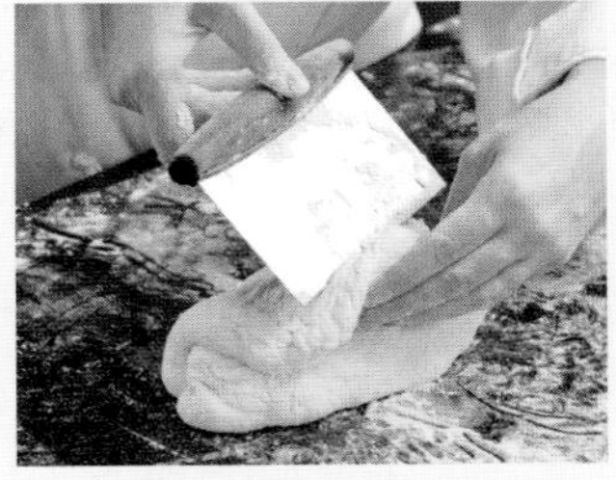

4. Fold each dough half like a business letter into a 7 by 4-inch loaf. Transfer each loaf, seam side down, to sheets of parchment, dust with flour, and cover with plastic wrap. Let rest for 30 minutes.

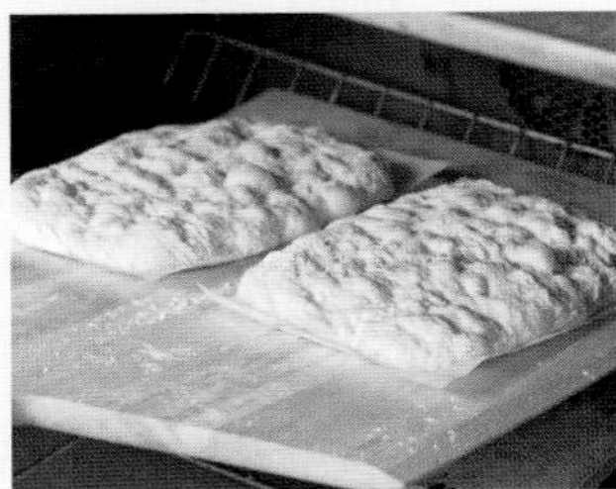

5. Use floured fingertips to evenly poke the entire surface of each loaf to form a 10 by 6-inch rectangle; spray the loaves lightly with water. Transfer the loaves, parchment and all, onto the hot baking stone and bake.

30 minutes longer. Meanwhile, adjust an oven rack to the lower-middle position, place a baking stone on the rack, and heat the oven to 450 degrees at least 30 minutes before baking.

4. Cut two 12 by 6-inch pieces of parchment paper and liberally dust with flour. Transfer the dough to a floured work surface, being careful not to deflate it completely. Liberally flour the top of the dough and divide it in half with a bench scraper. Turn one piece of dough cut side up and dust with flour. Following the photos on page 698, with well-floured hands, press the dough into a rough 12 by 6-inch shape. Fold the shorter sides of the dough toward the center, overlapping them like a business letter to form a 7 by 4-inch loaf. Repeat with the second dough piece. Gently transfer each loaf, seam side down, to the parchment sheets, dust with flour, and cover with plastic wrap. Let the loaves sit at room temperature for 30 minutes (the surface of the loaves will develop small bubbles).

5. Slide the parchment with the loaves onto an inverted rimmed baking sheet or pizza peel. Using floured fingertips, evenly poke the entire surface of each loaf to form a 10 by 6-inch rectangle; spray the loaves lightly with water. Carefully slide the parchment with the loaves onto the baking stone using a jerking motion. Bake, spraying the loaves with water twice more during the first 5 minutes of baking time, until the crust is a deep golden brown and the center of the loaves registers 210 degrees on an instant-read thermometer, 22 to 27 minutes. Transfer to a wire rack, discard the parchment, and cool the loaves to room temperature, about 1 hour, before slicing and serving.

EASY SANDWICH BREAD

WHY THIS RECIPE WORKS: A freshly baked loaf of bread is one of life's great pleasures. But most people don't have 4 hours to devote to mixing dough, waiting for it to rise, kneading, shaping, and baking. Could we find a quicker way? We started with basic batter bread, which relies on a high hydration level and a single rise, but falls short on flavor. Adding melted butter was a good start toward a tastier loaf, and substituting some whole-wheat flour provided nutty depth. Swapping the rest of the all-purpose flour for bread flour lent better structure. We also traded 1 tablespoon of honey for sugar, which contributed complexity and encouraged browning. Two 20-minute proofs were enough for flavor development. Adding salt only after the initial rise allowed the bread to rise high. An egg wash before baking and a brush of melted butter provided a shiny, tender crust.

Easy Sandwich Bread

MAKES 1 LOAF

The test kitchen's preferred loaf pan measures 8½ by 4½ inches; if using a 9 by 5-inch pan, check for doneness 5 minutes early. To prevent the loaf from deflating as it rises, do not let the batter come in contact with the plastic wrap. This loaf is best eaten the day it is made, but leftovers may be wrapped in plastic wrap and stored for up to two days at room temperature or frozen for up to one month.

- 2 cups (11 ounces) bread flour
- 6 tablespoons (2 ounces) whole-wheat flour
- 2¼ teaspoons instant or rapid-rise yeast
- 1¼ cups plus 2 tablespoons warm water (120 degrees)
- 3 tablespoons unsalted butter, melted
- 1 tablespoon honey
- ¾ teaspoon salt
- 1 large egg, lightly beaten with 1 teaspoon water and pinch salt

1. In bowl of stand mixer, whisk bread flour, whole-wheat flour, and yeast together. Add 1¼ cups warm water, 2 tablespoons melted butter, and honey. Fit stand mixer with paddle and mix on low speed for 1 minute. Increase speed to medium and mix for 2 minutes. Scrape down bowl and paddle with greased rubber spatula. Continue to mix 2 minutes longer. Remove bowl and paddle from mixer. Scrape down bowl and paddle, leaving paddle in batter. Cover with plastic wrap and let batter rise in warm place until doubled in size, about 20 minutes.

2. Adjust oven rack to lower-middle position and heat oven to 375 degrees. Spray 8½ by 4½-inch loaf pan with vegetable oil spray. Dissolve salt in remaining 2 tablespoons warm water. When batter has doubled, attach bowl and paddle to mixer. Add salt-water mixture and mix on low speed until water is mostly incorporated, about 40 seconds. Increase speed to medium and mix until thoroughly combined, about 1 minute, scraping down paddle if necessary. Transfer batter to prepared pan and smooth surface with greased rubber spatula. Cover and leave in warm place until batter reaches ½ inch below edge of pan, 15 to 20 minutes. Uncover and let rise until center of batter is level with edge of pan, 5 to 10 minutes longer.

3. Gently brush top of risen loaf with egg mixture. Bake until deep golden brown and loaf registers 208 to 210 degrees, 40 to 45 minutes. Using clean dish towels, carefully invert bread onto wire rack. Reinvert loaf and brush top and sides with remaining 1 tablespoon melted butter. Let cool completely before slicing.

WHOLE-WHEAT SANDWICH BREAD

WHY THIS RECIPE WORKS: Most whole-wheat bread recipes turn out either squat bricks or white bread in disguise. We wanted a nutty, light-textured sandwich loaf. We started with a good white-flour recipe and worked our way backward to "unrefine" it. We made a series of white bread loaves, replacing different amounts of all-purpose flour with whole-wheat to find the highest percentage of whole-wheat flour we could use before the texture suffered, landing on 60 percent. We also substituted bread flour for the all-purpose flour. Next, we soaked the flour overnight in milk, with some wheat germ for added flavor. This softened the grain's fiber, kept the dough moist, and coaxed out some sweetness. Finally, we turned to a sponge, a mixture of flour, water, and yeast left to sit overnight to develop a full range of flavor. Adding honey lent complexity and swapping out some of the butter for vegetable oil cut the richness.

Best Whole-Wheat Sandwich Bread

MAKES TWO 8-INCH LOAVES

If you don't have a stand mixer, you can mix the dough by hand following the instructions on page 701. If you don't have a baking stone, bake the bread on an overturned and preheated rimmed baking sheet set on the lowest oven rack. The bread can be wrapped in a double layer of plastic wrap and stored at room temperature for up to 3 days. Wrapped with an additional layer of aluminum foil, the bread can be frozen for up to 1 month.

SPONGE

- 2 cups (11 ounces) bread flour
- 1 cup water, heated to 110 degrees
- ½ teaspoon instant or rapid-rise yeast

SOAKER

- 3 cups (16½ ounces) whole-wheat flour
- ½ cup wheat germ
- 2 cups whole milk

DOUGH

- 6 tablespoons unsalted butter, softened
- ¼ cup honey
- 2 tablespoons instant or rapid-rise yeast
- 2 tablespoons vegetable oil
- 4 teaspoons table salt

1. FOR THE SPONGE: Combine the flour, water, and yeast in a large bowl and stir with a wooden spoon until a uniform mass forms and no dry flour remains, about 1 minute. Cover the bowl tightly with plastic wrap and let sit at room temperature for at least 8 hours or up to 24 hours.

2. FOR THE SOAKER: Combine the flour, wheat germ, and milk in a separate large bowl and stir with a wooden spoon until a shaggy mass forms, about 1 minute. Transfer the dough to a lightly floured work surface and knead by hand until smooth, 2 to 3 minutes. Return the soaker to the bowl, cover tightly with plastic wrap, and refrigerate for at least 8 hours or up to 24 hours.

3. FOR THE DOUGH: Tear the soaker apart into 1-inch pieces and place in the bowl of a stand mixer fitted with the dough hook. Add the sponge, butter, honey, yeast, oil, and salt and mix on low speed until a cohesive mass starts to form, about 2 minutes. Increase the speed to medium and knead until the dough is smooth and elastic, 8 to 10 minutes. Transfer the dough to a lightly floured work surface and knead by hand to form a smooth, round ball, about 1 minute. Place the dough in a large, lightly greased bowl. Cover tightly with plastic wrap and let rise at room temperature for 45 minutes.

4. Gently press down on the center of the dough to deflate. Spray a rubber spatula or bowl scraper with vegetable oil spray; fold the partially risen dough over itself by gently lifting and folding the edge of the dough toward the middle. Turn the bowl 90 degrees; fold again. Turn the bowl and fold the dough 6 more times (for a total of 8 folds). Cover tightly with plastic wrap and allow to rise at room temperature until doubled in size, about 45 minutes.

5. Grease two 8½ by 4½-inch loaf pans. Transfer the dough to a well-floured work surface and divide in half. Press 1 piece of the dough into a 17 by 8-inch rectangle, with the short side facing you. Roll the dough toward you into a firm cylinder, keeping the roll taut by tucking it under itself as you go. Turn the loaf seam side up and pinch it closed. Place the loaf seam side down in a prepared pan, pressing gently into the corners. Repeat with the second piece of dough. Cover the loaves loosely with greased plastic wrap and let rise at room temperature until nearly doubled in size, 1 to 1½ hours (the top of the loaves should rise about 1 inch over the lip of the pan).

6. Thirty minutes before baking, adjust the oven racks to the middle and lowest positions, place a baking stone on the middle rack, place an empty loaf pan or other heatproof pan on the bottom rack, and heat the oven to 400 degrees. Bring 2 cups water to boil on the stovetop.

7. Using a sharp serrated knife or a single-edge razor blade, make one ¼-inch-deep slash lengthwise down the center of each loaf. Working quickly, pour the boiling water into the empty loaf pan in the oven and set the loaves on the baking stone. Reduce the oven temperature to 350 degrees. Bake until the crust is dark brown and the loaves register 200 degrees on an instant-read thermometer, 40 to 50 minutes, rotating the loaves front to back and side to side halfway through baking. Transfer the pans to a wire rack and let cool for 5 minutes. Remove the loaves from the pans, return to the rack, and let cool to room temperature, about 2 hours, before slicing and serving.

NOTES FROM THE TEST KITCHEN

MIXING WHOLE-WHEAT SANDWICH DOUGH BY HAND

Stir the wet and dry ingredients together along with the sponge with a stiff rubber spatula until the dough comes together and looks shaggy. Transfer the dough to a clean work surface and knead by hand to form a smooth, round ball, 15 to 25 minutes, adding additional flour if necessary to prevent the dough from sticking to the work surface. Proceed with the recipe as directed.

FOLDING AND FORMING WHOLE-WHEAT SANDWICH BREAD

1. Deflate the center of the dough, then fold it in on itself. Turn the bowl 90 degrees; fold again. Repeat for a total of 8 folds. Let rise for 45 minutes.

2. Halve the dough and pat each portion into an 8 by 17-inch rectangle, with the short side facing you.

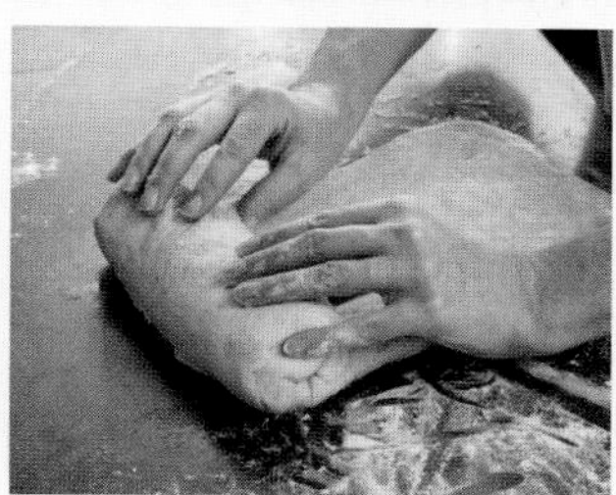

3. Roll each sheet toward you into a tight cylinder. Keep the roll taut by tucking it under itself as you go. Pinch the seams to seal.

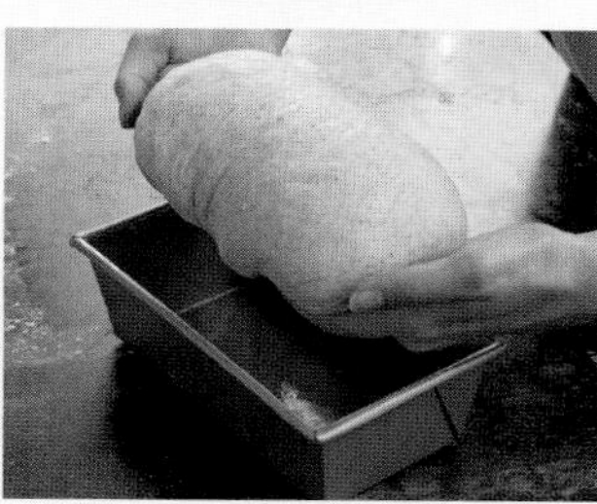

4. Place each loaf seam side down in the prepared loaf pans. Let the dough rise until almost doubled in size, 60 to 90 minutes.

5. Using a knife, make a shallow slash down the center of each loaf to stop the bread from tearing when it rises. Bake for 40 to 50 minutes.

MULTIGRAIN BREAD

WHY THIS RECIPE WORKS: Although multigrain bread often has great flavor, the quantity of ingredients weighs it down so much that the loaf becomes dense and heavy. On the other end of the spectrum are loaves with a sandwich-style texture but so little grain that they're hard to distinguish from white bread. We wanted a multigrain bread with great flavor and balanced texture. Our first challenge was to develop more gluten in the dough. Because the protein content of any flour is an indicator of how much gluten it will produce, we thought first to switch out all-purpose flour for bread flour, but this move only made the bread chewier. The solution was twofold: long kneading preceded by an autolyse, a resting period just after the initial mixing of water and flour that gives flour time to hydrate. This combination also made the dough easier to work with. The result was a loaf that baked up light yet chewy, without being tough. To incorporate grains into the bread, we used a one-stop-shopping alternative: packaged seven-grain hot cereal. To soften the grains, we made a thick porridge with the cereal before adding it to the dough. A final step of rolling the shaped loaves in oats yielded a finished, professional look.

Multigrain Bread

MAKES TWO 8-INCH LOAVES

Don't confuse seven-grain hot cereal mix with boxed, cold breakfast cereals that may also be labeled "seven-grain." Our favorite brands of seven-grain mix are Bob's Red Mill and Arrowhead Mills. Leftover bread can be wrapped in a double layer of plastic wrap and stored at room temperature for up to 3 days; wrapped with an additional layer of aluminum foil, the bread can be frozen for up to 1 month. For an accurate measurement of boiling water, bring a kettle of water to a boil, then measure out the desired amount. See page 885 for information on our top-rated loaf pan.

- 1¼ cups (6¼ ounces) seven-grain hot cereal mix (see note)
- 2½ cups boiling water (see note)
- 3 cups (15 ounces) unbleached all-purpose flour, plus extra for the dough and work surface
- 1½ cups (8¼ ounces) whole-wheat flour
- ¼ cup honey
- 4 tablespoons (½ stick) unsalted butter, melted and cooled slightly
- 1 envelope (2¼ teaspoons) instant or rapid-rise yeast
- 1 tablespoon table salt
- ¾ cup unsalted pumpkin seeds or sunflower seeds
- ½ cup old-fashioned rolled oats or quick oats

1. Place the cereal mix in the bowl of a stand mixer and pour the boiling water over it; let stand, stirring occasionally, until the mixture cools to 100 degrees and resembles thick porridge, about 1 hour. Whisk the flours together in a medium bowl.

2. Once the grain mixture has cooled, add the honey, melted butter, and yeast and stir to combine. Attach the bowl to a stand mixer fitted with the dough hook. With the mixer running on low speed, add the flours, ½ cup at a time, and knead until the dough forms a ball, 1½ to 2 minutes; cover the bowl with plastic wrap and let the dough rest for 20 minutes. Add the salt and knead on medium-low speed until the dough clears the sides of the bowl, 3 to 4 minutes (if it does not clear the sides, add 2 to 3 tablespoons additional all-purpose flour and continue mixing); continue to knead the dough for 5 more minutes. Add the seeds and knead for another 15 seconds. Transfer the dough to a floured work surface and knead by hand until the seeds are dispersed evenly and the dough forms a smooth, taut ball. Place the dough in a greased container with a 4-quart capacity; cover with plastic wrap and allow to rise until doubled in size, 45 to 60 minutes.

3. Adjust an oven rack to the middle position and heat the oven to 375 degrees. Spray two 9 by 5-inch loaf pans with vegetable oil spray. Transfer the dough to a lightly floured work surface and pat into a 12 by 9-inch rectangle; cut the dough in half crosswise with a knife or bench scraper. With a short side facing you, starting at the farthest end, roll one dough piece into a log, keeping the roll taut by tucking it under itself as you go. Seal the loaf by pinching the seam together gently with your thumb and forefinger; repeat with the remaining dough. Spray the loaves lightly with water or vegetable oil spray. Roll each dough log in oats to coat evenly and place, seam side down, in the greased loaf pans, pressing gently into the corners; cover lightly with plastic wrap and let rise until almost doubled in size, 30 to 40 minutes. (The dough should barely spring back when poked with a knuckle.) Bake until the center of the loaves registers 200 degrees on an instant-read thermometer, 35 to 40 minutes. Remove the loaves from the pans and cool on a wire rack before slicing, about 3 hours.

NEW YORK BAGELS

WHY THIS RECIPE WORKS: For the chewy center and crackly-crisp shell of an authentic New York bagel, we needed to take the obvious steps—mixing flour, water, yeast and salt; shaping the dough into rings; letting the rings proof—and add some extra at-home finesse. For a fine, uniform crumb with plenty of chew, the dough's gluten network needed tightening. Mixing vital wheat gluten with bread flour elevated the gluten and ice water kept the dough cool during mixing. Dissolving malt syrup in the water ahead of time infused the dough with distinct malty flavor. Flattening, rolling, and twisting the dough into a compact spiral stressed it, eliminating air pockets and promising a bagel with substantial chew. After the bagels proofed in the refrigerator, we boiled them in an alkaline mixture of water, sugar, and baking soda to wake up the yeast and cook some of the surface starches for a glossy, crisp crust. Preheating a baking stone in the oven created a hearth-like cooking environment while the bagels boiled. We arranged them on a wire rack–lined rimmed baking sheet and placed the sheet directly on the baking stone. Before leaving the bagels to bake, we poured boiling water into the bottom of the sheet for plenty of steam. A flip halfway through baking ensured even browning.

New York Bagels

MAKES 8 BAGELS

This recipe requires refrigerating the shaped bagels for 16 to 24 hours before baking them. This recipe works best with King Arthur bread flour, although other bread flours will work. Vital wheat gluten and malt syrup are available in most supermarkets in the baking and syrup aisles, respectively. If you cannot find malt syrup, substitute 4 teaspoons of molasses. The bagels are best eaten within a day of baking; fully cooled bagels can be transferred to heavy-duty zipper-lock bags and frozen for up to one month.

- 1 cup plus 2 tablespoons ice water (9 ounces)
- 2 tablespoons malt syrup
- 2⅔ cups (14⅔ ounces) bread flour
- 4 teaspoons vital wheat gluten
- 2 teaspoons instant or rapid-rise yeast
- 2 teaspoons salt
- ¼ cup (1¼ ounces) cornmeal
- ¼ cup (1¾ ounces) sugar
- 1 tablespoon baking soda

1. Stir ice water and malt syrup together in 2-cup liquid measuring cup until malt syrup has fully dissolved. Process flour, wheat gluten, and yeast in food processor until combined, about 2 seconds. With processor running, slowly add ice water mixture; process until dough is just combined and no dry flour remains, about 20 seconds. Let dough stand for 10 minutes.

2. Add salt to dough and process, stopping processor and redistributing dough as needed, until dough forms shaggy mass that clears sides of workbowl (dough may not form one single mass), 45 to 90 seconds. Transfer dough to unfloured counter and knead until smooth, about 1 minute. Divide dough into 8 equal pieces (3½ ounces each) and cover loosely with plastic wrap.

3. Working with 1 piece of dough at a time and keeping remaining pieces covered, form dough pieces into smooth, taut rounds. (To round, set piece of dough on unfloured counter. Loosely cup your hand around dough and, without applying pressure to dough, move your hand in small circular motions. Tackiness of dough against counter and circular motion should work dough into smooth, even ball, but if dough sticks to your hands, lightly dust your fingers with flour.) Let dough balls rest on counter, covered, for 15 minutes.

4. Sprinkle rimmed baking sheet with cornmeal. Working with 1 dough ball at a time and keeping remaining pieces covered, coat dough balls lightly with flour and then, using your hands and rolling pin, pat and roll dough balls into 5-inch rounds. Starting with edge of dough farthest from you, roll into tight cylinder. Starting at center of cylinder and working toward ends, gently and evenly roll and stretch dough into 8- to 9-inch-long rope. Do not taper ends. Rolling ends of dough under your hands in opposite directions, twist rope to form tight spiral. Without unrolling spiral, wrap rope around your fingers, overlapping ends of dough by about 2 inches under your palm, to create ring shape. Pinch ends of dough gently together. With overlap under your palm, press and roll seam using circular motion on counter to fully seal. Transfer rings to prepared sheet and cover loosely with plastic, leaving at least 1 inch between bagels. Let bagels stand at room temperature for 1 hour. Cover sheet tightly with plastic and refrigerate for at least 16 hours or up to 24 hours.

5. One hour before baking, adjust oven rack to upper-middle position, place baking stone on rack, and heat oven to 450 degrees.

6. Bring 4 quarts water, sugar, and baking soda to boil in large Dutch oven. Set wire rack in rimmed baking sheet and spray rack with vegetable oil spray.

7. Transfer 4 bagels to boiling water and cook for 20 seconds. Using wire skimmer or slotted spoon, flip bagels over and cook 20 seconds longer. Using wire skimmer or slotted spoon, transfer bagels to prepared wire rack, with cornmeal side facing down. Repeat with remaining 4 bagels.

8. Place sheet with bagels on preheated baking stone and pour ½ cup boiling water into bottom of sheet. Bake until tops of bagels are beginning to brown, 10 to 12 minutes. Using metal spatula, flip bagels and continue to bake until golden brown, 10 to 12 minutes longer. Remove sheet from oven and let bagels cool on wire rack for at least 15 minutes. Serve warm or at room temperature.

Bagel Toppings

Place ½ cup poppy seeds, sesame seeds, caraway seeds, dehydrated onion flakes, dehydrated garlic flakes, or coarse/pretzel salt in small bowl. Press tops of just-boiled bagels (side without cornmeal) gently into topping and return to wire rack, topping side up.

NOTES FROM THE TEST KITCHEN

SHAPING BAGELS LIKE A PRO

Thoroughly working the dough during shaping helps a New York bagel develop its characteristic chew.

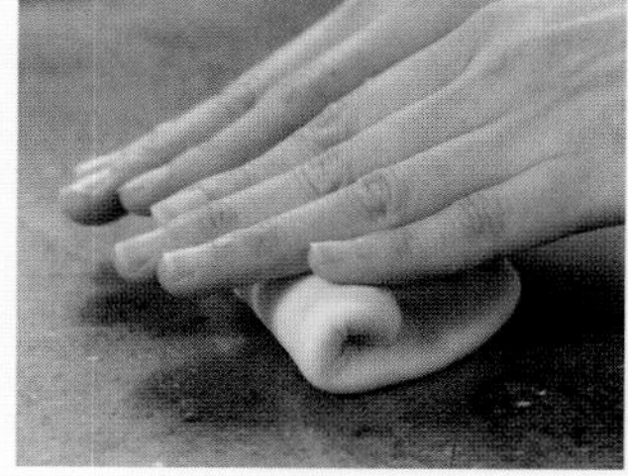

1. Pat and roll dough ball (lightly coated with flour) with rolling pin into 5-inch round. Roll into tight cylinder, starting with far side of dough.

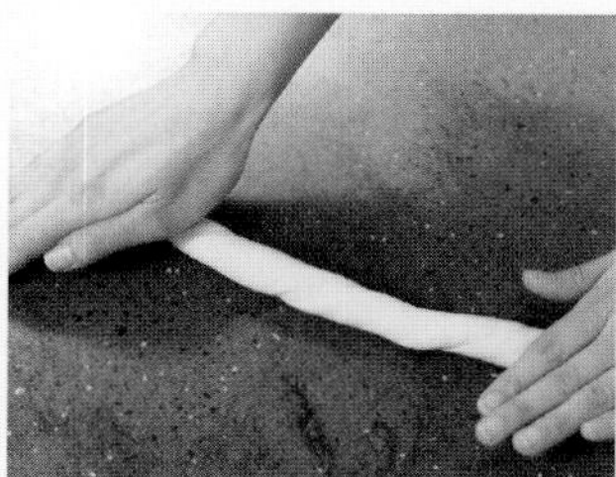

2. Roll and stretch dough into 8- to 9-inch-long rope, starting at center of cylinder (don't taper ends). Twist rope to form tight spiral by rolling ends of dough under hands in opposite directions.

3. Wrap rope around fingers, overlapping ends by 2 inches, to create ring. Pinch ends together. Press and roll seam (positioned under your palm) using circular motion on counter to fully seal.

CHAPTER 22

COOKIE JAR FAVORITES

CHEWY SUGAR COOKIES

WHY THIS RECIPE WORKS: Traditional recipes for sugar cookies require obsessive attention to detail. The butter must be at precisely the right temperature and it must be creamed to the proper degree of airiness. Slight variations in measures can result in cookies that spread or cookies that become brittle and hard upon cooling. We didn't want a cookie that depended on such a finicky process, we wanted an approachable recipe for great sugar cookies that anyone could make anytime. We melted the butter so our sugar cookie dough could easily be mixed together with a spoon—no more fussy creaming. Replacing a portion of the melted butter with vegetable oil ensured a chewy cookie without affecting flavor. And incorporating an unusual addition, cream cheese, into the cookie dough kept our cookies tender, while the slight tang of the cream cheese made for a rich, not-too-sweet cookie.

Chewy Sugar Cookies

MAKES ABOUT 24 COOKIES

The final dough will be slightly softer than most cookie doughs. For best results, handle the dough as briefly and gently as possible when shaping the cookies. Overworking the dough will result in flatter cookies.

- 2¼ cups (11¼ ounces) unbleached all-purpose flour
- 1 teaspoon baking powder
- ½ teaspoon baking soda
- ½ teaspoon table salt
- 1½ cups (10½ ounces) sugar, plus ⅓ cup for rolling
- 2 ounces cream cheese, cut into 8 pieces
- 6 tablespoons (¾ stick) unsalted butter, melted and still warm
- ⅓ cup vegetable oil
- 1 large egg
- 1 tablespoon whole milk
- 2 teaspoons vanilla extract

1. Adjust an oven rack to the middle position and heat the oven to 350 degrees. Line 2 large rimmed baking sheets with parchment paper. Whisk the flour, baking powder, baking soda, and salt together in a medium bowl. Set aside.

2. Place 1½ cups of the sugar and the cream cheese in a large bowl. Place the remaining ⅓ cup sugar in a shallow baking dish or pie plate and set aside. Pour the warm butter over the sugar and cream cheese and whisk to combine (some small lumps of cream cheese will remain but will smooth out later). Whisk in the oil until incorporated. Add the egg, milk, and vanilla; continue to whisk until smooth. Add the flour mixture and mix with a rubber spatula until a soft homogeneous dough forms.

3. Divide the dough into 24 equal pieces, about 2 tablespoons each. Using your hands, roll each piece of dough into a ball (see note). Working in batches, roll the balls in sugar to coat and set on the prepared baking sheet, 12 dough balls per sheet. Using the bottom of a drinking glass, flatten the dough balls until 2 inches in diameter. Sprinkle the tops of the cookies evenly with the remaining sugar, using 2 teaspoons for each sheet. (Discard the remaining sugar.)

4. Bake the cookies, one sheet at a time, until the edges are set and beginning to brown, 11 to 13 minutes, rotating the sheet after 7 minutes. Cool the cookies on the baking sheet for 5 minutes; using a wide metal spatula, transfer the cookies to a wire rack and cool to room temperature.

BROWN SUGAR COOKIES

WHY THIS RECIPE WORKS: Simple sugar cookies, while classic, can seem too basic—even dull—at times. We wanted to turn up the volume on the sugar cookie by switching out the granulated sugar in favor of brown sugar. We had a clear vision of this cookie. It would be oversized, with a crackling crisp exterior and a chewy interior. And, like Mick Jagger, this cookie would scream "brown sugar."

We wanted butter for optimal flavor, but the traditional creaming method (creaming softened butter with sugar until fluffy, beating in an egg, and then adding the dry ingredients) gave us a cakey texture. Cutting the butter into the flour produced crumbly cookies. What worked was first melting the butter. We then tweaked the amount of eggs, dark brown sugar, flour, and leavener to give us a good cookie, but we wanted even more brown sugar flavor. We made progress by rolling the dough balls in a combination of brown and granulated sugar and adding a healthy amount of vanilla and table salt. But our biggest success came from an unlikely refinement. Browning the melted butter added a complex nuttiness that made a substantial difference.

Brown Sugar Cookies

MAKES ABOUT 24 COOKIES

Avoid using a nonstick skillet to brown the butter. The dark color of the nonstick coating makes it difficult to gauge when the butter is sufficiently browned. Use fresh brown sugar, as hardened brown sugar will make the cookies too dry. Achieving the proper texture—crisp at the edges and chewy in the middle—is critical to this recipe. Because the cookies are so dark, it's hard to judge doneness by color. Instead, gently press halfway between the edge and center of the cookie. When it's done, it will form an indentation with slight resistance. Check early and err on the side of underdone.

- 14 tablespoons (1¾ sticks) unsalted butter
- 2 cups packed (14 ounces) dark brown sugar (see note)
- ¼ cup (1¾ ounces) granulated sugar
- 2 cups plus 2 tablespoons (about 10⅔ ounces) unbleached all-purpose flour
- ½ teaspoon baking soda
- ¼ teaspoon baking powder
- ½ teaspoon table salt
- 1 large whole egg
- 1 large egg yolk
- 1 tablespoon vanilla extract

1. Melt 10 tablespoons of the butter in a 10-inch skillet over medium-high heat, about 2 minutes. Continue to cook, swirling the pan constantly until the butter is dark golden brown and has a nutty aroma, 1 to 3 minutes. Transfer the browned butter to a large heatproof bowl. Stir the remaining 4 tablespoons butter into the hot butter to melt; set aside for 15 minutes.

2. Meanwhile, adjust an oven rack to the middle position and heat the oven to 350 degrees. Line 2 large baking sheets with parchment paper. In a shallow baking dish or pie plate, mix ¼ cup of the brown sugar and the granulated sugar, rubbing the mixture between your fingers until well combined; set aside. Whisk the flour, baking soda, and baking powder together in a medium bowl; set aside.

3. Add the remaining 1¾ cups brown sugar and the salt to the bowl with the cooled butter; mix until no sugar lumps remain, about 30 seconds. Scrape down the bowl with a rubber spatula; add the whole egg, egg yolk, and vanilla and mix until fully incorporated, about 30 seconds. Scrape down the bowl. Add the flour mixture and mix until just combined, about 1 minute. Give the dough a final stir to ensure that no flour pockets remain and the ingredients are evenly distributed.

4. Divide the dough into 24 portions, each about 2 tablespoons, rolling them between your hands into balls about 1½ inches in diameter. Working in batches, drop 12 dough balls into the baking dish with the sugar mixture and toss to coat. Set the dough balls on the prepared baking sheet, spacing them about 2 inches apart; repeat with the second batch of 12.

5. Bake one sheet at a time until the cookies are browned and still puffy and the edges have begun to set but the centers are still soft (the cookies will look raw between the cracks and seem underdone), 12 to 14 minutes, rotating the baking sheet halfway through the baking time. Do not overbake.

6. Cool the cookies on the baking sheet for 5 minutes; using a wide metal spatula, transfer the cookies to a wire rack and cool to room temperature.

SNICKERDOODLES

WHY THIS RECIPE WORKS: With their crinkly tops and liberal dusting of cinnamon sugar, snickerdoodles are a New England favorite. Cream of tartar is essential to these cookies, as it provided their subtle tang, and, when combined with baking soda, it created a short-lived leavening effect that caused the cookies to rise and fall quickly while baking, leaving them with a distinctive crinkly appearance. We found that using equal amounts of shortening and butter gave us nicely shaped cookies that were chewy and buttery. Rolling the balls of dough in cinnamon sugar—a full tablespoon for warm spice flavor—imparted a spicy sweet crunch to the cookies. For the best results, we baked the cookies one sheet at a time and pulled them from the oven just as they were beginning to brown but were still soft and puffy in the middle. They continued to cook as they cooled on the baking sheet and were perfectly done and chewy once cooled.

Snickerdoodles

MAKES 24 COOKIES

Cream of tartar is essential to the flavor of these cookies, and it works in combination with the baking soda to give the cookies lift; do not substitute baking powder. For the best results, bake only one sheet of cookies at a time.

- 2½ cups (12½ ounces) all-purpose flour
- 2 teaspoons cream of tartar
- 1 teaspoon baking soda
- ½ teaspoon salt
- 8 tablespoons unsalted butter, softened
- 8 tablespoons vegetable shortening
- 1½ cups (10½ ounces) sugar, plus ¼ cup for rolling
- 2 large eggs
- 1 tablespoon ground cinnamon

1. Adjust oven rack to middle position and heat oven to 375 degrees. Line 3 baking sheets with parchment paper. Whisk flour, cream of tartar, baking soda, and salt together in bowl.

2. Using stand mixer fitted with paddle, beat butter, shortening, and 1½ cups sugar together on medium speed until light and fluffy, about 3 minutes. Beat in eggs, one at a time, until incorporated, about 30 seconds, scraping down bowl as needed.

3. Reduce speed to low and slowly add flour mixture until combined, about 30 seconds. Give dough final stir by hand to ensure no flour pockets remain.

4. Combine remaining ¼ cup sugar and cinnamon in shallow dish. Working with 2 tablespoons dough at a time, roll into balls, then roll in sugar to coat; measure and space 2 inches apart on prepared baking sheets. (Dough balls can be frozen for up to 1 month; bake frozen cookies in 300-degree oven for 18 to 20 minutes.)

5. Bake cookies, 1 sheet at a time, with 8 cookies per sheet, until edges are just set and beginning to brown but centers are still soft, puffy, and cracked (cookies will look raw between cracks and seem underdone), 8 to 12 minutes, rotating sheet halfway through baking. Let cookies cool on sheet for 10 minutes, then transfer to wire rack and let cool completely before serving.

MOLASSES SPICE COOKIES

WHY THIS RECIPE WORKS: Molasses spice cookies are often miserable specimens, no more than flat, tasteless cardboard rounds of gingerbread. They can be dry and cakey without the requisite chew; others are timidly flavored with molasses and scantily spiced. We wanted to create the ultimate molasses spice cookie—soft, chewy, and gently spiced with deep, dark molasses flavor. We also wanted it to have the traditional cracks and crinkles so characteristic of these charming cookies.

We started with all-purpose flour and butter for full, rich flavor. Using just the right amount of molasses and brown sugar and flavoring the cookies with a combination of vanilla, ginger, cinnamon, cloves, black pepper, and allspice gave these spiced cookies the warm tingle that we were after. We found that to keep the cookies mild, using a light or mild molasses was imperative; but if it's a stronger flavor you want, dark molasses is in order. We pulled the cookies from the oven when they still looked a bit underdone; residual heat finished the baking and kept the cookies chewy and moist.

Molasses Spice Cookies

MAKES ABOUT 22 COOKIES

For best flavor, make sure that your spices are fresh. Light or mild molasses gives the cookies a milder flavor; for a stronger flavor, use dark molasses. Either way, measure molasses in a liquid measure. If you find that the dough sticks to your palms as you shape the balls, moisten your hands occasionally in a bowl filled with cold tap water and shake off the excess. Bake the cookies one sheet at a time; if baked two sheets at a time, the cookies started on the bottom rack won't develop attractive crackly tops. Remove the cookies from the oven when they still look slightly raw and underbaked.

- ⅓ cup (2⅓ ounces) granulated sugar, plus ½ cup for coating
- 2¼ cups (11¼ ounces) unbleached all-purpose flour
- 1 teaspoon baking soda
- 1½ teaspoons ground cinnamon
- 1½ teaspoons ground ginger
- ½ teaspoon ground cloves
- ¼ teaspoon ground allspice
- ¼ teaspoon ground black pepper
- ¼ teaspoon table salt
- 12 tablespoons (1½ sticks) unsalted butter, softened
- ⅓ cup packed (2⅓ ounces) dark brown sugar
- 1 large egg yolk
- 1 teaspoon vanilla extract
- ½ cup light or dark molasses (see note)

1. Adjust an oven rack to the middle position and heat the oven to 375 degrees. Line 2 large baking sheets with parchment paper. Place ½ cup of the granulated sugar in a shallow baking dish or pie plate; set aside.

2. Whisk the flour, baking soda, spices, and salt together in a medium bowl; set aside.

3. In a stand mixer fitted with the paddle attachment, beat the butter, brown sugar, and remaining ⅓ cup granulated sugar on medium-high speed until light and fluffy, about 3 minutes. Decrease the speed to medium-low and add the egg yolk and vanilla; increase the speed to medium and beat until incorporated, about 20 seconds. Decrease the speed to medium-low and add the molasses; beat until fully incorporated, about 20 seconds, scraping down the bowl once with a rubber spatula. Decrease the speed to low and add the flour mixture; beat until just incorporated, about 30 seconds, scraping down the bowl once. Give the dough a final stir to ensure that no flour pockets remain. The dough will be soft.

4. Divide the dough into 22 portions, each about 1 tablespoon, and roll them between your hands into balls about 1¼ to 1½ inches in diameter. Working in batches, drop five dough balls into the baking dish with the sugar and toss to coat. Set the dough balls on the prepared baking sheets, spacing them about 2 inches apart. Repeat with the remaining dough.

5. Bake one sheet at a time, rotating the baking sheets halfway through the baking time, until the cookies are browned, still puffy, and the edges have begun to set but the centers are still soft (the cookies will look raw between the cracks and seem underdone), about 11 minutes. Do not overbake.

6. Cool the cookies on the baking sheets for 5 minutes; using a wide metal spatula, transfer the cookies to a wire rack and cool to room temperature.

Molasses Spice Cookies with Dark Rum Glaze

If the glaze is too thick to drizzle, whisk in up to an additional ½ tablespoon rum.

Follow the recipe for Molasses Spice Cookies. Whisk 1 cup (4 ounces) confectioners' sugar and 2½ tablespoons dark rum together in a medium bowl until smooth. Drizzle or spread the glaze using the back of a spoon on the cooled cookies. Allow the glazed cookies to dry for at least 15 minutes.

CLASSIC CHOCOLATE CHIP COOKIES

WHY THIS RECIPE WORKS: Rich and buttery, with their soft cores and crispy edges, chocolate chip cookies are the American cookie-jar standard. Since Nestlé first began printing the recipe for Toll House cookies on the back of chocolate chip bags in 1939, generations of bakers have packed them into lunches and taken them to potlucks. But we wondered if this was really the best that a chocolate chip cookie could be. We wanted something more than the standard bake sale offering; we wanted a moist and chewy cookie with crisp edges and deep notes of toffee and butterscotch to balance its sweetness.

Melting the butter before combining it with the other ingredients gave us the chewy texture we wanted, and browning a portion of it added nutty flavor. Upping the brown sugar enhanced chewiness, while a combination of one whole egg and one egg yolk gave us supremely moist cookies. For the crisp edges and deep toffee flavor, we allowed the sugar to dissolve and rest in the melted butter. We baked the cookies until golden brown and just set, but still soft in the center. The resulting cookies were crisp, chewy, and gooey with chocolate and boasted a complex medley of sweet, buttery, caramel, and toffee flavors.

Classic Chocolate Chip Cookies

MAKES ABOUT 16 LARGE COOKIES

Avoid using a nonstick skillet to brown the butter; the dark color of the nonstick coating makes it difficult to gauge when the butter is browned. Use fresh, moist brown sugar instead of hardened brown sugar, which will make the cookies dry. This recipe works with light brown sugar, but the cookies will be less full-flavored. For our winning brand of chocolate chips, see page 910. If you're using smaller baking sheets, put fewer cookies on each sheet and bake them in batches.

- 1¾ cups (8¾ ounces) unbleached all-purpose flour
- ½ teaspoon baking soda
- 14 tablespoons (1¾ sticks) unsalted butter
- ¾ cup packed (5¼ ounces) dark brown sugar (see note)
- ½ cup (3½ ounces) granulated sugar
- 1 teaspoon table salt
- 2 teaspoons vanilla extract
- 1 large whole egg
- 1 large egg yolk
- 1¼ cups (7½ ounces) semisweet chocolate chips or chunks (see note)
- ¾ cup chopped pecans or walnuts, toasted (optional)

1. Adjust an oven rack to the middle position and heat the oven to 375 degrees. Line 2 large baking sheets with parchment paper.

2. Whisk the flour and baking soda together in a medium bowl; set aside.

3. Heat 10 tablespoons of the butter in a 10-inch skillet over medium-high heat until melted, about 2 minutes. Continue cooking, swirling the pan constantly until the butter is dark golden brown and has a nutty aroma, 1 to 3 minutes. Transfer the browned butter to a large heatproof bowl. Add the remaining 4 tablespoons butter and stir until completely melted.

4. Add the sugars, salt, and vanilla to the melted butter; whisk until fully incorporated. Add the whole egg and egg yolk; whisk until the mixture is smooth with no sugar lumps remaining, about 30 seconds. Let the mixture stand for 3 minutes, then whisk for 30 seconds. Repeat the process of resting and whisking two more times until the mixture is thick, smooth, and shiny. Using a rubber spatula, stir in the flour mixture until just combined, about 1 minute. Stir in the chocolate chips and nuts (if using), giving the dough a final stir to ensure that no flour pockets remain.

5. Divide the dough into 16 portions, each about 3 tablespoons. Place the cookies on the prepared baking sheets, spacing them about 2 inches apart.

6. Bake one sheet at a time, rotating the sheet halfway through the baking time, until the cookies are golden brown and still puffy, and the edges have begun to set but the centers are still soft, 10 to 14 minutes. Transfer the baking sheet to a wire rack; cool to room temperature.

THICK AND CHEWY CHOCOLATE CHIP COOKIES

WHY THIS RECIPE WORKS: Nowadays, chocolate chip cookies sold in gourmet shops and cafés always come jumbo-sized (think saucer plate). These cookies are incredibly appealing and satisfying—thick and chewy rounds loaded with as many chocolate chips as they can hold. We wanted our own version that retained the soft and tender texture of these café cookies, even after a day or two (not that they'd be hanging around that long).

One key element in achieving this cookie was melting the butter, which created a product with a chewy texture. But to keep the cookie from becoming tough, we had to add a little extra fat, which we did in the form of an egg yolk; the added fat acts a tenderizer and prevents the cookies from hardening after several hours. The usual suspects of all-purpose flour, baking soda, an egg, brown sugar, and granulated sugar made an appearance in our cookie recipe, and vanilla provided a light flavor. A good amount of chocolate chips guaranteed that every bite was rich and chocolaty. Finally, we formed the dough into balls, then pulled each ball into two pieces and rejoined them with the uneven surface facing up; now our cookies had the rustic, craggy appearance we wanted.

Thick and Chewy Chocolate Chip Cookies

MAKES ABOUT 18 LARGE COOKIES

To ensure the proper texture, cool the cookies on the baking sheets. See page 876 for our top-rated baking sheet.

- 2 cups plus 2 tablespoons (about 10⅔ ounces) unbleached all-purpose flour
- ½ teaspoon baking soda
- ½ teaspoon table salt
- 12 tablespoons (1½ sticks) unsalted butter, melted and cooled
- 1 cup packed (7 ounces) light or dark brown sugar
- ½ cup (3½ ounces) granulated sugar
- 1 large whole egg
- 1 large egg yolk
- 2 teaspoons vanilla extract
- 1½ cups (9 ounces) semisweet chocolate chips

1. Adjust the oven racks to the upper-middle and lower-middle positions and heat the oven to 325 degrees. Line 2 large baking sheets with parchment paper.

2. Whisk the flour, baking soda, and salt together in a medium bowl; set aside.

3. In a stand mixer fitted with the paddle attachment, beat the butter and sugars at medium speed until smooth, about 1 minute. Add the whole egg, egg yolk, and vanilla and beat on medium-low speed until fully incorporated, about 30 seconds, scraping down the bowl and beater as needed with a rubber spatula. Add the dry ingredients and mix on low speed until combined, about 30 seconds. Mix in the chocolate chips until just incorporated.

4. Divide the dough into 18 portions, each about ¼ cup, and roll them between your hands into balls. Holding one dough ball with your fingers, pull the dough apart into two equal halves. Rotate the halves 90 degrees and, with the jagged surfaces facing up, join the halves together at their base, again forming a single ball, being careful not to smooth the dough's uneven surface. Place the cookies on the prepared baking sheets, spacing them about 2½ inches apart.

5. Bake until the cookies are light golden brown and the edges start to harden but the centers are still soft and puffy, 15 to 18 minutes, switching and rotating the baking sheets halfway through the baking time. Cool the cookies on the baking sheets.

THIN, CRISPY CHOCOLATE CHIP COOKIES

WHY THIS RECIPE WORKS: Too often, thin and crispy chocolate chip cookies are brittle and crumbly or tough and lacking flavor. We wanted cookies that were thin and packed a big crunch without breaking teeth or shattering into a million pieces when eaten. And they had to have the simple, gratifying flavors of deeply caramelized sugar and rich butter. For cookies with a notable butterscotch flavor and sufficient crunch, we turned to a combination of light brown sugar and white sugar. Next we focused on the thickness of our cookies. When butter is creamed with sugar, air cells are created in the batter; these cells expand during baking, leading to cookies that rise—and cookies with height were not what we wanted. So we used melted butter and milk to create a batter that would spread (not rise) in the oven, resulting in cookies with the perfect thin crispiness. A bit of baking soda and corn syrup promoted maximum browning and caramelization, and vanilla and salt gave our cookies the best flavor.

Thin and Crispy Chocolate Chip Cookies

MAKES ABOUT 40 COOKIES

The dough, en masse or shaped into balls and wrapped well, can be refrigerated for up to 2 days or frozen for up to 1 month; bring it to room temperature before baking.

- 1½ cups (7½ ounces) unbleached all-purpose flour
- ¾ teaspoon baking soda
- ¼ teaspoon table salt
- 8 tablespoons (1 stick) unsalted butter, melted and cooled
- ½ cup (3½ ounces) granulated sugar
- ⅓ cup packed (2⅓ ounces) light brown sugar
- 2 tablespoons light corn syrup
- 1 large egg yolk
- 2 tablespoons milk
- 1 tablespoon vanilla extract
- ¾ cup (4½ ounces) semisweet chocolate chips

1. Adjust an oven rack to the middle position and heat the oven to 375 degrees. Line 2 large baking sheets with parchment paper.

2. Whisk the flour, baking soda, and salt together in a medium bowl; set aside.

3. In a stand mixer fitted with the paddle attachment, beat the melted butter, granulated sugar, brown sugar, and corn syrup at low speed until thoroughly blended, about 1 minute. Add the egg yolk, milk, and vanilla; mix until fully incorporated and smooth, about 1 minute, scraping down the bowl and beater as needed. With the mixer still running on low, slowly add the dry ingredients and mix until just combined. Do not over beat. Add the chocolate chips and mix until evenly distributed throughout the batter, about 5 seconds.

4. Divide the dough into 40 portions, each about 1 tablespoon, and roll them between your hands into balls. Place the cookies on the prepared baking sheets, spacing them about 2 inches apart. Bake, one sheet at a time, until the cookies are deep golden brown and flat, about 12 minutes, switching and rotating the baking sheets halfway through the baking time.

5. Cool the cookies on the baking sheet for 3 minutes. Using a wide metal spatula, transfer the cookies to a wire rack and cool to room temperature.

BEHIND THE SCENES

A RULE TO COOK BY

Contrary to what you may think, the test kitchen isn't packed with the latest high-tech kitchen gadgets. In fact, one of our favorite gadgets isn't even found in a kitchenware store. Wondering why that cake didn't rise properly? Or why those cookies ran together? Did your expensive steak overcook? Pull out a ruler. It can prove that the 8-inch cake pan you are using is actually 9 inches, that the cookies have been spaced together too closely, and that the supposedly 1-inch-thick steak the butcher sold you is only ½ inch thick. We prefer 18-inch stainless steel rulers, which can be thrown right into the dishwasher. They can be purchased at any office supply store for about $4.

GLUTEN-FREE CHOCOLATE CHIP COOKIES

WHY THIS RECIPE WORKS: Chocolate chip cookies are a classic favorite, but most gluten-free versions turn out crumbly, gritty, and greasy. Using the test kitchen's gluten-free flour blend, we set out to create a gluten-free cookie that would be as good as the original version. Cutting back on butter helped to minimize greasiness. Melting the butter, rather than creaming (as called for in traditional recipes), gave the cookies a chewier texture. Some xanthan gum helped give the cookies structure, allowing them to hold together. To alleviate grittiness, we added more liquid in the form of milk and let the batter rest for 30 minutes so that the starches had time to hydrate and soften. Upping the ratio of brown sugar to granulated sugar made our cookies crispy on the edges and chewy in the center, and also gave the cookies more complex, toffee-like flavor.

Gluten-Free Chocolate Chip Cookies

MAKES ABOUT 24 COOKIES

Not all brands of chocolate chips are processed in a gluten-free facility, so read labels carefully. We highly recommend you weigh the ingredients for this recipe, rather than rely on cup measurements. You can substitute 8 ounces (¾ cup plus ⅔ cup) King Arthur Gluten-Free Multi-Purpose Flour or 8 ounces (1½ cups plus 2 tablespoons) Bob's Red Mill GF All-Purpose Baking Flour for the ATK Blend. Note that cookies made with King Arthur will spread more and be more delicate, while cookies made with Bob's Red Mill will spread more and have a distinct bean flavor.

- 8 ounces (1¾ cups) The America's Test Kitchen Gluten-Free Flour Blend (page 344)
- 1 teaspoon baking soda
- ¾ teaspoon xanthan gum
- ½ teaspoon salt
- 8 tablespoons unsalted butter, melted
- 5¼ ounces (¾ cup packed) light brown sugar
- 2⅓ ounces (⅓ cup) granulated sugar
- 1 large egg
- 2 tablespoons milk
- 1 tablespoon vanilla extract
- 7½ ounces (1¼ cups) semisweet chocolate chips

1. Whisk flour blend, baking soda, xanthan gum, and salt together in medium bowl; set aside. Whisk melted butter, brown sugar, and granulated sugar together in large bowl until well combined and smooth. Whisk in egg, milk, and vanilla and continue to whisk until smooth. Stir in flour mixture with rubber spatula and mix until soft, homogeneous dough forms. Fold in chocolate chips. Cover bowl with plastic wrap and let dough rest for 30 minutes. (Dough will be sticky and soft.)

2. Adjust oven rack to middle position and heat oven to 350 degrees. Line 2 baking sheets with parchment paper. Using 2 soupspoons and working with about 1½ tablespoons of dough at a time, portion dough and space 2 inches apart on prepared sheets. Bake cookies, 1 sheet at a time, until golden brown and edges have begun to set but centers are still soft, 11 to 13 minutes, rotating sheet halfway through baking.

3. Let cookies cool on sheet for 5 minutes, then transfer to wire rack. Serve warm or at room temperature. (Cookies are best eaten on day they are baked, but they can be cooled and placed immediately in airtight container and stored at room temperature for up to 1 day.)

CHOCOLATE COOKIES

WHY THIS RECIPE WORKS: Cookie recipes that trumpet their extreme chocolate flavor always leave us a bit suspicious. While they provide plenty of intensity, these over-the-top confections also tend to be delicate and crumbly, more like cakey brownies than cookies. We set out to make an exceptionally rich chocolate cookie that we could sink our teeth into—without having it fall apart.

Our first batch, with modest amounts of cocoa powder and melted chocolate, baked up too cakey and tender—just what we didn't want. The chocolate was the culprit; its fat was softening the dough. Cutting out the chocolate made the cookies less cakey and tender, and more like cookies. To restore chocolate flavor without adding too much fat, we increased the cocoa powder and reduced the flour. Using an egg white rather than a whole egg gave us the structure we wanted, and adding dark corn syrup gave the cookies a nice chewiness and lent a hint of caramel flavor. For more richness, we folded in chopped bittersweet chocolate; the chunks stayed intact and added intense chocolate flavor. A dip in granulated sugar before baking gave the cookies a sweet crunch and an attractive crackled appearance once they were out of the oven.

Chocolate Cookies

MAKES ABOUT 16 COOKIES

We recommend using one of the test kitchen's favorite baking chocolates, Ghirardelli Bittersweet Chocolate or Callebaut Intense Dark Chocolate, but any high-quality dark, bittersweet, or semisweet chocolate will work. Light brown sugar can be substituted for the dark, as can light corn syrup for the dark, but with some sacrifice in flavor.

- ⅓ cup (2⅓ ounces) granulated sugar, plus ½ cup for coating
- 1½ cups (7½ ounces) unbleached all-purpose flour
- ¾ cup Dutch-processed cocoa powder
- ½ teaspoon baking soda
- ¼ teaspoon plus ⅛ teaspoon table salt
- ½ cup dark corn syrup (see note)
- 1 large egg white
- 1 teaspoon vanilla extract
- 12 tablespoons (1½ sticks) unsalted butter, softened
- ⅓ cup packed (2⅓ ounces) dark brown sugar (see note)
- 4 ounces bittersweet chocolate, chopped into ½-inch pieces (see note)

1. Adjust the oven racks to the upper-middle and lower-middle positions and heat the oven to 375 degrees. Line 2 large baking sheets with parchment paper. Place ½ cup of the granulated sugar in a shallow baking dish or pie plate. Whisk the flour, cocoa powder, baking soda, and salt together in a medium bowl. Whisk the corn syrup, egg white, and vanilla together in a small bowl.

2. In a stand mixer fitted with the paddle attachment, beat the butter, brown sugar, and remaining ⅓ cup granulated sugar at medium-high speed until light and fluffy, about 2 minutes. Decrease the speed to medium-low, add the corn syrup mixture, and beat until fully incorporated, about 20 seconds, scraping down the bowl and beater as needed with a rubber spatula. Decrease the speed to low, add the flour mixture and chopped chocolate, and mix until just incorporated, about 30 seconds, scraping down the bowl and beater as needed. Give the dough a final stir to ensure that no pockets of flour remain. Chill the dough for 30 minutes to firm slightly (do not chill longer than 30 minutes).

3. Divide the dough into 16 equal portions, each a generous 2 tablespoons, and roll them between your hands into balls about 1½ inches in diameter. Working in batches, drop eight dough balls into the baking dish with the sugar and toss to

coat. Place the dough balls on the prepared baking sheet, spacing them about 2 inches apart; repeat with the second batch of eight. Bake, switching and rotating the sheets halfway through the baking time, until the cookies are puffed and cracked and the edges have begun to set but the centers are still soft (the cookies will look raw between the cracks and seem underdone), 10 to 11 minutes. Do not overbake.

4. Cool the cookies on the baking sheets for 5 minutes; using a wide metal spatula, transfer the cookies to a wire rack and cool to room temperature.

DOUBLE-CHOCOLATE COOKIES

WHY THIS RECIPE WORKS: Our goal in creating a traditional double-chocolate cookie recipe seemed more like a fantasy: The first bite of the cookie would reveal a center of hot fudge sauce, the texture would call to mind chocolate bread pudding, and the overall flavor would be of deep and complex chocolate. Was it possible?

In the end, the fulfillment of our fantasy relied on very basic ingredients: chocolate, sugar, eggs, butter, flour, baking powder, and salt. We used a modified creaming method with minimal beating to produce moist cookies that weren't cakey, and we let the batter rest for a half-hour to develop a certain fudginess. Ingredient proportions were all-important—for moist, rich cookies, we used more chocolate than flour. The more highly processed semisweet chocolate tasted smoother and richer than unsweetened, and Dutch-processed cocoa and instant coffee further enriched the chocolate flavor. At last, we had a cookie that was both rich and soft, with an intense chocolaty center.

Thick and Chewy Double-Chocolate Cookies

MAKES ABOUT 42 COOKIES

To melt the chocolate using a microwave, heat it at 50 percent power for 2 minutes; stir the chocolate and continue heating until melted, stirring once every additional minute. Resist the urge to bake the cookies longer than indicated; they may appear underbaked at first but will firm up as they cool.

- 2 cups (10 ounces) unbleached all-purpose flour
- ½ cup Dutch-processed cocoa powder
- 2 teaspoons baking powder
- ½ teaspoon table salt
- 16 ounces semisweet chocolate, chopped
- 4 large eggs
- 2 teaspoons vanilla extract
- 2 teaspoons instant coffee or espresso powder
- 10 tablespoons (1¼ sticks) unsalted butter, softened
- 1½ cups packed (10½ ounces) light brown sugar
- ½ cup (3½ ounces) granulated sugar

1. Whisk the flour, cocoa powder, baking powder, and salt together in a medium bowl; set aside.

2. Melt the chocolate in a medium heatproof bowl set over a saucepan of barely simmering water, stirring occasionally, until smooth; set aside to cool slightly. Whisk the eggs and vanilla together in a medium bowl, sprinkle the coffee powder over the top to dissolve, and set aside.

3. In a stand mixer fitted with the paddle attachment, beat the butter and sugars at medium speed until combined, about 45 seconds; the mixture will look granular. Decrease the speed to low, gradually add the egg mixture, and mix until incorporated, about 45 seconds. Add the melted chocolate in a steady stream and mix until combined, about 40 seconds, scraping down the bowl and beater as needed with a rubber spatula. With the mixer still running on low, add the dry ingredients and mix until just combined. Do not over beat. Cover the bowl of dough with plastic wrap and let stand at room temperature until the consistency is scoopable and fudge-like, about 30 minutes.

4. Meanwhile, adjust the oven racks to the upper-middle and lower-middle positions and heat the oven to 350 degrees. Line 2 baking sheets with parchment paper. Divide the dough into 42 equal portions, each about 2 tablespoons, and roll them between your hands into balls about 1¾ inches in diameter. Set the dough balls on the prepared baking sheets, spacing them about 1½ inches apart.

5. Bake two sheets at a time, switching and rotating the baking sheets halfway through the baking time, until the edges have just begun to set but the centers are still very soft, about 10 minutes. Cool the cookies on the baking sheets for 10 minutes; using a wide metal spatula, transfer the cookies to a wire rack and cool to room temperature.

Thick and Chewy Triple-Chocolate Cookies

The addition of chocolate chips will slightly increase the yield of the cookies.

Follow the recipe for Thick and Chewy Double-Chocolate Cookies, adding 2 cups (12 ounces) semisweet chocolate chips to the batter after the dry ingredients are incorporated in step 3.

CHOCOLATE CRINKLE COOKIES

WHY THIS RECIPE WORKS: The name says it all—these cookies are as much about looks as they are about flavor. Rolled in powdered sugar before going in the oven, chocolate crinkle cookies (aka earthquakes) form dark chocolaty fissures that break through the bright white surface during baking. They're eye-catching, with an irresistible deep chocolaty richness to back it up. Or at least, that's how they should be. Too often, these cookies turn out tooth-achingly sweet, with just a couple of wide gaping cracks instead of a crackly surface. We wanted a cookie with deep chocolate flavor and only enough sweetness to balance the chocolate's bitterness; a moist and tender—but not gooey—interior; and plenty of small irregular crinkly fissures breaking through a bright-white surface.

For the best chocolate flavor, we used a combination of unsweetened chocolate and cocoa powder, which got an additional flavor boost from espresso powder. Using brown sugar instead of granulated lent a more complex, tempered sweetness with a bitter molasses edge that complemented the chocolate. A combination of both baking powder and baking soda gave us cookies with the right amount of lift and spread and contributed to a crackly surface. But the real key was rolling the cookies in granulated sugar before the traditional powdered sugar. It not only helped produce the perfect crackly exterior by creating a "shell" that broke into numerous fine fissures as the cookie rose and spread, but it also helped the powdered sugar coating stay in place. We finally had chocolate crinkle cookies that lived up to their name.

Chocolate Crinkle Cookies

MAKES 22 COOKIES

Both natural and Dutch-processed cocoa will work in this recipe. Our favorite brand of natural cocoa is Hershey's Natural Cocoa Unsweetened; our favorite Dutch-processed cocoa is Droste Cocoa.

- 1 cup (5 ounces) all-purpose flour
- ½ cup (1½ ounces) unsweetened cocoa powder
- 1 teaspoon baking powder
- ¼ teaspoon baking soda
- ½ teaspoon salt
- 1½ cups packed (10½ ounces) brown sugar
- 3 large eggs
- 4 teaspoons instant espresso powder (optional)
- 1 teaspoon vanilla extract
- 4 ounces unsweetened chocolate, chopped
- 4 tablespoons unsalted butter
- ½ cup (3½ ounces) granulated sugar
- ½ cup (2 ounces) confectioners' sugar

1. Adjust oven rack to middle position and heat oven to 325 degrees. Line 2 baking sheets with parchment. Whisk flour, cocoa, baking powder, baking soda, and salt together in bowl.

2. Whisk brown sugar, eggs, espresso powder (if using), and vanilla together in large bowl. Microwave chocolate and butter in bowl at 50 percent power, stirring occasionally, until melted, 2 to 3 minutes.

3. Whisk chocolate mixture into egg mixture until combined. Fold in flour mixture until no dry streaks remain. Allow dough to sit at room temperature, 10 minutes.

4. Place granulated sugar and confectioners' sugar in two separate shallow baking dishes or pie plates. Divide dough into 2-tablespoon portions and roll into balls (or use #30 scoop). Drop balls of dough directly into granulated sugar and roll to coat. Transfer balls to confectioners' sugar and roll to coat. Evenly space dough balls on prepared baking sheets, 11 dough balls per sheet.

5. Bake cookies, 1 sheet at a time, until cookies are puffed and cracked and edges have begun to set but centers are still soft (cookies will look raw between cracks and will seem underdone), about 12 minutes, rotating sheet halfway through baking. Cool completely on baking sheet before serving.

PEANUT BUTTER COOKIES

WHY THIS RECIPE WORKS: Recipes for peanut butter cookies tend to fall into one of two categories: sweet and chewy with a mild peanut flavor, and sandy and crumbly with a strong peanut flavor. What we wanted, of course, was the best of both worlds—that is, cookies that were crisp on the edges and chewy in the center, with lots of peanut flavor.

First off, we had to determine the amount and type of sugar. Granulated sugar was necessary for crisp edges and chewy centers, while dark brown sugar enriched the peanut flavor. As for flour, too little resulted in an oily cookie, whereas too much made for dry cookies. Baking soda contributed to browning and amplified the peanut flavor and baking powder provided lift, making both leaveners necessary. Extra-crunchy peanut butter also helped the cookie rise and achieve a crisper edge and a softer center. But the best way to get the true peanut flavor we sought was to use peanuts and salt. Adding some roasted, salted peanuts, ground in a food processor, and then adding still more salt (directly to the batter as well in the form of salted rather than unsalted butter) produced a strong roasted nut flavor without sacrificing anything in terms of texture.

Peanut Butter Cookies

MAKES ABOUT 36 COOKIES

These cookies have a strong peanut flavor that comes from extra-crunchy peanut butter as well as from roasted salted peanuts that are ground in a food processor and worked into the dough. In our testing, we found that salted butter brings out the flavor of the nuts. If using unsalted butter, increase the salt to 1 teaspoon.

- 2½ cups (12½ ounces) unbleached all-purpose flour
- ½ teaspoon baking soda
- ½ teaspoon baking powder
- ½ teaspoon table salt
- 16 tablespoons (2 sticks) salted butter, softened (see note)
- 1 cup packed (7 ounces) dark brown sugar
- 1 cup (7 ounces) granulated sugar
- 1 cup extra-crunchy peanut butter, at room temperature
- 2 large eggs
- 2 teaspoons vanilla extract
- 1 cup (5 ounces) roasted salted peanuts, ground in a food processor to resemble bread crumbs, about 14 pulses

1. Adjust the oven racks to the upper-middle and lower-middle positions and heat oven to 350 degrees. Line 2 large baking sheets with parchment paper.

2. Whisk the flour, baking soda, baking powder, and salt together in a medium bowl; set aside.

3. In a stand mixer fitted with the paddle attachment, beat the butter and sugars at medium speed until light and fluffy, about 2 minutes, scraping down the bowl and beater as needed with a rubber spatula. Add the peanut butter and mix until fully incorporated, about 30 seconds; add the eggs, one at a time, and the vanilla and mix until combined, about 30 seconds. Decrease the speed to low and add the dry ingredients; mix until combined, about 30 seconds. Mix in the ground peanuts until just incorporated.

4. Divide the dough into 36 portions, each a generous 2 tablespoons, and roll them between your hands into balls about 2 inches in diameter. Place the dough balls on the prepared baking sheets, spacing them about 2½ inches apart. Press each dough ball twice, at perpendicular angles, with a dinner fork dipped in cold water to make a crisscross design.

5. Bake, switching and rotating the sheets halfway through the baking time, until the cookies are puffy and slightly brown around the edges but not on top, 10 to 12 minutes; the cookies will not look fully baked. Cool the cookies on the baking sheets for 5 minutes; using a wide metal spatula, transfer the cookies to a wire rack and cool to room temperature.

PEANUT BUTTER SANDWICH COOKIES

WHY THIS RECIPE WORKS: We wanted a cookie so packed with peanut flavor that it needed no crosshatch to identify it. In the research for our testing, we found that peanut butter flavor molecules can be trapped by flour in baked applications, so we ratcheted up the flavor's intensity by sandwiching an uncooked peanut butter filling between our cookies. Adding a full cup of confectioners' sugar to the filling made it firm enough to stay in place, and we balanced the sweetness with a relatively low-sugar cookie component. Extra liquid and extra baking soda gave our cookies the thin, flat dimensions and sturdy crunch that are vital to a sandwich cookie.

Peanut Butter Sandwich Cookies

MAKES 24 COOKIES

Do not use unsalted peanut butter for this recipe.

COOKIES

- 1¼ cups (6¼ ounces) raw peanuts, toasted and cooled
- ¾ cup (3¾ ounces) all-purpose flour
- 1 teaspoon baking soda
- ½ teaspoon salt
- 3 tablespoons unsalted butter, melted
- ½ cup creamy peanut butter
- ½ cup (3½ ounces) granulated sugar
- ½ cup packed (3½ ounces) light brown sugar
- 3 tablespoons whole milk
- 1 large egg

FILLING

- ¾ cup creamy peanut butter
- 3 tablespoons unsalted butter
- 1 cup (4 ounces) confectioners' sugar

1. FOR THE COOKIES: Adjust oven racks to upper-middle and lower-middle positions and heat oven to 350 degrees. Line 2 baking sheets with parchment paper. Pulse peanuts in food processor until finely chopped, about 8 pulses. Whisk flour, baking soda, and salt together in bowl. Whisk melted butter, peanut butter, granulated sugar, brown sugar, milk, and egg together in second bowl. Stir flour mixture into peanut butter mixture with rubber spatula until combined. Stir in peanuts until evenly distributed.

2. Using #60 scoop or tablespoon measure, place 12 mounds, evenly spaced, on each prepared baking sheet. Using damp hand, flatten mounds until 2 inches in diameter.

3. Bake until deep golden brown and firm to touch, 15 to 18 minutes, switching and rotating baking sheets halfway through baking. Let cookies cool on baking sheets for 5 minutes. Transfer cookies to wire rack and let cool completely, about 30 minutes. Repeat portioning and baking remaining dough.

NOTES FROM THE TEST KITCHEN

FILLING COOKIES EVENLY

1. Using #60 scoop or tablespoon measure, portion warm filling onto bottom cookies (turned upside down).

2. Rather than spreading filling with knife or offset spatula, top bottom cookie with second cookie and press gently until filling spreads to edges.

4. FOR THE FILLING: Microwave peanut butter and butter together until butter is melted and warm, about 40 seconds. Using rubber spatula, stir in confectioners' sugar until combined.

5. TO ASSEMBLE: Place 24 cookies upside down on counter. Place 1 level tablespoon (or #60 scoop) warm filling in center of each cookie. Place second cookie on top of filling, right side up, pressing gently until filling spreads to edges. Allow filling to set for 1 hour before serving. Assembled cookies can be stored at room temperature for up to 3 days.

Peanut Butter Sandwich Cookies with Honey-Cinnamon Filling

Omit butter from filling. Stir 5 tablespoons honey and ½ teaspoon ground cinnamon into warm peanut butter before adding confectioners' sugar.

Peanut Butter Sandwich Cookies with Milk Chocolate Filling

Reduce peanut butter to ½ cup and omit butter from filling. Stir 6 ounces finely chopped milk chocolate into warm peanut butter until melted, microwaving for 10 seconds at a time if necessary, before adding confectioners' sugar.

CLASSIC CHEWY OATMEAL COOKIES

WHY THIS RECIPE WORKS: Many oatmeal cookies are dry, cakey, and overly spiced. To make ours dense and chewy, we combined unsaturated fat (vegetable oil) and saturated fat (butter) in a ratio of nearly 3 to 1, and we decreased the proportion of flour. Adding an extra egg yolk boosted moistness and richness, while a touch more salt than most recipes call for tempered the sweetness and complemented the oaty flavor. Most recipes call for using a stand mixer, but we found this counterproductive to our goal of chewy, dense cookies because the mixer beats air into the dough. Instead we made our dough by hand, melting the butter for easier mixing. Browning the butter delivered more complexity, and blooming a small amount of cinnamon in the butter rounded out its flavor. Raisins added pops of brightness and reinforced the chewy texture.

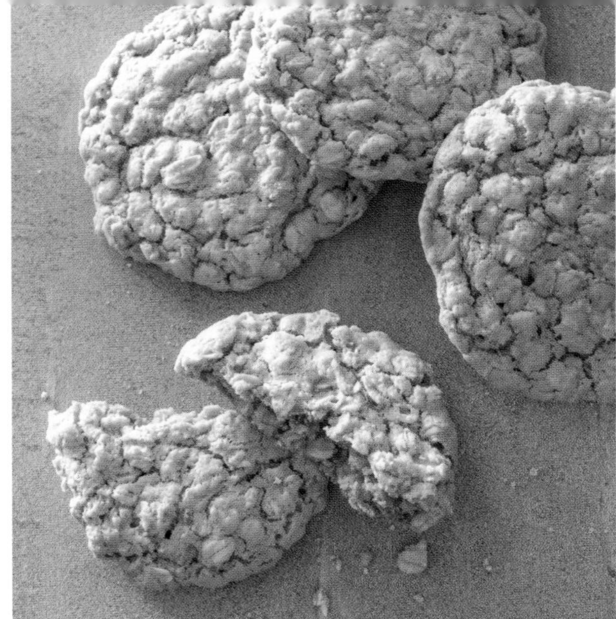

Classic Chewy Oatmeal Cookies

MAKES 20 COOKIES

Regular old-fashioned rolled oats worked best in this recipe. Do not use extra-thick rolled oats. For cookies with just the right amount of spread and chew, we strongly recommend that you weigh your ingredients. If you omit the raisins, the recipe will yield 18 cookies.

- 1 cup (5 ounces) all-purpose flour
- ¾ teaspoon salt
- ½ teaspoon baking soda
- 4 tablespoons unsalted butter
- ¼ teaspoon ground cinnamon
- ¾ cup packed (5¼ ounces) dark brown sugar
- ½ cup (3½ ounces) granulated sugar
- ½ cup vegetable oil
- 1 large egg plus 1 large yolk
- 1 teaspoon vanilla extract
- 3 cups (9 ounces) old-fashioned rolled oats
- ½ cup raisins (optional)

1. Adjust oven rack to middle position and heat oven to 375 degrees. Line 2 rimmed baking sheets with parchment paper. Whisk flour, salt, and baking soda together in medium bowl; set aside.

2. Melt butter in 8-inch skillet over medium-high heat, swirling pan occasionally, until foaming subsides. Continue to cook, stirring and scraping bottom of pan with heatproof spatula, until milk solids are dark golden brown and butter has nutty aroma, 1 to 2 minutes. Immediately transfer browned butter to large heatproof bowl, scraping skillet with spatula. Stir in cinnamon.

3. Add brown sugar, granulated sugar, and oil to bowl with butter and whisk until combined. Add egg and yolk and vanilla and whisk until mixture is smooth. Using wooden spoon, stir in flour mixture until fully combined, about 1 minute. Add oats and raisins, if using, and stir until evenly distributed (mixture will be stiff).

4. Divide dough into 20 portions, each about 3 tablespoons (or use #24 cookie scoop). Arrange dough balls 2 inches apart on prepared sheets, 10 dough balls per sheet. Using your damp hand, press each ball into 2½-inch disk.

5. Bake, 1 sheet at a time, until cookie edges are set and lightly browned and centers are still soft but not wet, 8 to 10 minutes, rotating sheet halfway through baking. Let cookies cool on sheet on wire rack for 5 minutes; using wide metal spatula, transfer cookies to wire rack and let cool completely.

CHEWY OATMEAL-RAISIN COOKIES

WHY THIS RECIPE WORKS: Big, moist, and craggy, oatmeal raisin cookies are so good and so comforting, but also so hard to get just right. Too often, they have textural issues and other times the flavor is off, with cookies that lack any sign of oatiness. We wanted an oversize, chewy cookie with buttery oat flavor. After numerous rounds of testing, we discovered three key changes that made a significant difference in the research recipes we uncovered. First, we substituted baking powder for baking soda, which gave the dough more lift and made the cookies less dense and a bit chewier. Second, we eliminated the cinnamon recommended in lots of recipes; by taking away the cinnamon, we revealed more oat flavor. We wanted some spice, however, and chose nutmeg, which has a cleaner, subtler flavor that we like with oats. Finally, we increased the sugar in our cookies, and this made a huge difference in terms of texture and moistness.

Big and Chewy Oatmeal-Raisin Cookies

MAKES ABOUT 18 LARGE COOKIES

If you prefer a less sweet cookie, you can reduce the granulated sugar to ¾ cup, but you will lose some crispness. Do not overbake these cookies. The edges should be brown, but the rest of the cookie should be very light in color.

- 1½ cups (7½ ounces) unbleached all-purpose flour
- ½ teaspoon table salt
- ½ teaspoon baking powder
- ¼ teaspoon freshly grated nutmeg
- 16 tablespoons (2 sticks) unsalted butter, softened
- 1 cup packed (7 ounces) light brown sugar
- 1 cup (7 ounces) granulated sugar (see note)
- 2 large eggs
- 3 cups (9 ounces) old-fashioned oats
- 1½ cups raisins (optional)

1. Adjust the oven racks to the upper-middle and lower-middle positions and heat the oven to 350 degrees. Line 2 large baking sheets with parchment paper. Whisk the flour, salt, baking powder, and nutmeg together in a medium bowl; set aside.

2. In a stand mixer fitted with the paddle attachment, beat the butter and sugars at medium speed until light and fluffy, about 2 minutes. Add the eggs, one at a time, and mix until combined, about 30 seconds.

3. Decrease the speed to low and slowly add the dry ingredients until combined, about 30 seconds. Mix in the oats and raisins (if using) until just incorporated.

4. Divide the dough into 18 portions, each a generous 2 tablespoons, and roll them between your hands into balls about 2 inches in diameter. Place the dough balls on the prepared baking sheets, spacing them about 2 inches apart.

5. Bake, switching and rotating the sheets halfway through the baking time, until the cookies turn golden brown around the edges, 22 to 25 minutes. Cool the cookies on the baking sheets for 2 minutes; using a wide metal spatula, transfer the cookies to a wire rack and cool to room temperature.

Big and Chewy Oatmeal-Date Cookies

Follow the recipe for Big and Chewy Oatmeal-Raisin Cookies, substituting 1½ cups chopped dates for the raisins.

THIN AND CRISPY OATMEAL COOKIES

WHY THIS RECIPE WORKS: Thin and crispy oatmeal cookies can be irresistible—crunchy and delicate, these cookies really let the flavor of the oats take center stage. But the usual ingredients that give thick, chewy oatmeal cookies great texture—generous amounts of sugar and butter, a high ratio of oats to flour, raisins, and nuts—won't all fit in a thin, crispy cookie. We wanted to adjust the ingredients to create a crispy, delicate cookie in which the simple flavor of buttery oats really stands out. Given this cookie's simplicity, creating a rich butter flavor was critical, so we kept almost the same amount of butter as in our standard big, chewy oatmeal cookie, but we scaled back the amount of sugar. During baking, large carbon dioxide bubbles created by the baking soda and baking powder caused the cookies to puff up, collapse, and spread out, producing the thin, flat cookies. Baking the cookies until they were fully set and evenly browned from center to edge made them crisp throughout but not tough.

Thin and Crispy Oatmeal Cookies

MAKES ABOUT 24 COOKIES

To ensure that the cookies bake evenly and are crisp throughout, bake them one sheet at a time. Place them on the baking sheet in three rows, with three cookies in the outer rows and two cookies in the center row. If you reuse a baking sheet, allow the cookies on it to cool for at least 15 minutes before transferring them to a wire rack, then reline the sheet with fresh parchment before baking more cookies. We developed this recipe using Quaker Old Fashioned Oats. Other brands of old-fashioned oats can be substituted but may cause the cookies to spread more. Do not use instant or quick oats.

- 1 cup (5 ounces) unbleached all-purpose flour
- ¾ teaspoon baking powder
- ½ teaspoon baking soda
- ½ teaspoon table salt
- 14 tablespoons (1¾ sticks) unsalted butter, softened but still cool
- 1 cup (7 ounces) granulated sugar
- ¼ cup packed (1¾ ounces) light brown sugar
- 1 large egg
- 1 teaspoon vanilla extract
- 2½ cups (7½ ounces) old-fashioned oats (see note)

1. Adjust an oven rack to the middle position and heat the oven to 350 degrees. Line 3 large baking sheets with parchment paper. Whisk the flour, baking powder, baking soda, and salt in a medium bowl; set aside.

2. In a stand mixer fitted with the paddle attachment, beat the butter and sugars at medium-low speed until just combined, about 20 seconds. Increase the speed to medium and continue to beat until light and fluffy, about 1 minute longer, scraping down the bowl and beater as needed with a rubber spatula. Add the egg and vanilla and beat on medium-low until fully incorporated, about 30 seconds, scraping down the bowl and beater as needed. Decrease the speed to low, add the flour mixture, and mix until just incorporated and smooth, about 10 seconds. With the mixer still running on low, gradually add the oats and mix until well incorporated, about 20 seconds. Give the dough a final stir to ensure that no flour pockets remain and the ingredients are evenly distributed.

3. Divide the dough into 24 portions, each about 2 tablespoons, and roll them between your hands into balls. Place the cookies on the prepared baking sheets, spacing them about 2½ inches apart, eight dough balls per sheet (see note). Using your fingertips, gently press each dough ball to a ¾-inch thickness.

4. Bake one sheet at a time until the cookies are deep golden brown, the edges are crisp, and the centers yield to slight pressure when pressed, 13 to 16 minutes, rotating the sheet halfway through the baking time. Cool the cookies completely on the sheet.

Salty Thin and Crispy Oatmeal Cookies

We prefer the texture and flavor of a coarse-grained sea salt, like Maldon or *fleur de sel*, but kosher salt can be used. If using kosher salt, reduce the amount sprinkled over the cookies to ¼ teaspoon.

Follow the recipe for Thin and Crispy Oatmeal Cookies, reducing the amount of salt in the dough to ¼ teaspoon. Lightly sprinkle ½ teaspoon coarse sea salt evenly over the flattened dough balls before baking.

ULTIMATE OATMEAL COOKIES

WHY THIS RECIPE WORKS: Oatmeal cookies can be great vehicles for additional flavors, but it's easy to get carried away and overload the dough with a crazy jumble of ingredients resulting in a poorly textured cookie monster. Our ultimate oatmeal cookie would have just the right amount of added ingredients and an ideal texture—crisp around the edges and chewy in the middle.

We wanted to add four flavor components—sweet, tangy, nutty, and chocolaty—to the underlying oat flavor. Bittersweet chocolate, dried sour cherries (or cranberries), and toasted pecans gave the right balance of flavors. We also analyzed the cookie dough ingredients and discovered that cookies made with brown sugar were moister and chewier than cookies made with granulated sugar. A combination of baking powder and baking soda (we doubled the usual amount) produced cookies that were light and crisp on the outside, but chewy, dense, and soft in the center. Finally, we focused on appearance to decide when to remove the cookies from the oven—they should be set but still look wet between the fissures; if they look matte rather than shiny, they've been overbaked.

Chocolate-Chunk Oatmeal Cookies with Pecans and Dried Cherries

MAKES ABOUT 16 LARGE COOKIES

We like these cookies made with pecans and dried sour cherries, but walnuts or skinned hazelnuts can be substituted for the pecans, and dried cranberries for the cherries. Quick oats used in place of the old-fashioned oats will yield a cookie with slightly less chewiness. These cookies keep for 4 to 5 days stored in an airtight container or zipper-lock bag, but they will lose their crisp exterior and become uniformly chewy after a day or so. To recrisp the cookies, place them on a baking sheet and in a 425-degree oven for 4 to 5 minutes. Make sure to let the cookies cool on the baking sheet for a few minutes before removing them, and eat them while they're warm.

- 1¼ cups (6¼ ounces) unbleached all-purpose flour
- ¾ teaspoon baking powder
- ½ teaspoon baking soda
- ½ teaspoon table salt
- 1¼ cups (3¾ ounces) old-fashioned oats (see note)
- 1 cup (4 ounces) pecans, toasted and chopped (see note)
- 1 cup dried sour cherries, chopped coarse (see note)
- 4 ounces bittersweet chocolate, chopped into chunks about the size of chocolate chips (about ¾ cup)
- 12 tablespoons (1½ sticks) unsalted butter, softened
- 1½ cups packed (10½ ounces) brown sugar, preferably dark
- 1 large egg
- 1 teaspoon vanilla extract

1. Adjust the oven racks to the upper-middle and lower-middle positions and heat the oven to 350 degrees. Line 2 large baking sheets with parchment paper.

2. Whisk the flour, baking powder, baking soda, and salt together in a medium bowl. In a second medium bowl, stir together the oats, pecans, cherries, and chocolate.

3. In a stand mixer fitted with the paddle attachment, beat the butter and sugar at medium speed until no sugar lumps remain, about 1 minute, scraping down the bowl and beater as needed with a rubber spatula. Add the egg and vanilla and beat on medium-low until fully incorporated, about 30 seconds, scraping down the bowl and beater as needed. Decrease the speed to low, add the flour mixture, and mix until just combined, about 30 seconds. With the mixer still running on low, gradually add the oat-nut mixture; mix until just incorporated. Give the dough a final stir to ensure that no flour pockets remain and the ingredients are evenly distributed.

4. Divide the dough into 16 portions, each about ¼ cup, and roll them between your hands into balls; stagger eight balls on each prepared baking sheet, spacing them about 2½ inches apart. Using your fingertips, gently press each dough ball to a 1-inch thickness. Bake the cookies for 20 to 22 minutes, switching and rotating the baking sheets halfway through the baking time, until the cookies are medium brown and the edges have begun to set but the centers are still soft (the cookies will seem underdone and will appear raw, wet, and shiny in the cracks).

5. Cool the cookies on the baking sheets for 5 minutes; using a wide metal spatula, transfer the cookies to a wire rack and cool to room temperature.

GINGERSNAPS

WHY THIS RECIPE WORKS: We wanted to put the "snap" back in gingersnap cookies. This meant creating a cookie that not only breaks cleanly in half and crunches satisfyingly with every bite but also has an assertive ginger flavor and heat. The key to texture was reducing the moisture in the final baked cookie. We achieved this by reducing the amount of sugar (which holds on to moisture), increasing the baking soda (which created cracks in the dough where more moisture could escape), and lowering the oven temperature (which increased the baking time.) For flavor we doubled the normal amount of dried ginger but also added fresh ginger, black pepper, and cayenne to ensure our cookie had real "snap."

Gingersnaps

MAKES 80 1½-INCH COOKIES

For the best results, use fresh spices. For efficiency, form the second batch of cookies while the first batch bakes. The 2 teaspoons of baking soda are essential to getting the right texture.

- 2½ cups (12½ ounces) all-purpose flour
- 2 teaspoons baking soda
- ½ teaspoon salt
- 12 tablespoons unsalted butter
- 2 tablespoons ground ginger
- 1 teaspoon ground cinnamon
- ¼ teaspoon ground cloves
- ¼ teaspoon pepper
- Pinch cayenne pepper
- 1¼ cups packed (8¾ ounces) dark brown sugar
- ¼ cup molasses
- 2 tablespoons finely grated fresh ginger
- 1 large egg plus 1 large yolk
- ½ cup (3½ ounces) granulated sugar

1. Whisk flour, baking soda, and salt together in bowl. Heat butter in 10-inch skillet over medium heat until melted. Lower heat to medium-low and continue to cook, swirling pan frequently, until foaming subsides and butter is just beginning to brown, 2 to 4 minutes. Transfer butter to large bowl and whisk in ground ginger, cinnamon, cloves, pepper, and cayenne. Let cool slightly, about 2 minutes. Add brown sugar, molasses, and fresh ginger to butter mixture and whisk to combine. Add egg and yolk and whisk to combine. Add flour mixture and stir until just combined. Cover dough tightly with plastic wrap and refrigerate until firm, about 1 hour.

2. Adjust oven racks to upper-middle and lower-middle positions and heat oven to 300 degrees. Line 2 baking sheets with parchment paper. Place granulated sugar in shallow dish. Divide dough into heaping teaspoon portions; roll dough into 1-inch balls. Working in batches of 10, roll balls in sugar to coat. Evenly space dough balls on prepared baking sheets, 20 dough balls per sheet.

3. Place 1 sheet on upper rack and bake for 15 minutes. Transfer partially baked top sheet to lower rack, rotating 180 degrees, and place second sheet of dough balls on upper rack. Continue to bake until cookies on lower tray just begin to darken around edges, 10 to 12 minutes longer. Remove lower sheet of cookies and transfer upper sheet to lower rack, rotating 180 degrees, and continue to bake until cookies begin to darken around edges, 15 to 17 minutes longer. Slide baked cookies, still on parchment, to wire rack and let cool completely before serving. Let baking sheets cool slightly and line with parchment again. Repeat step 2 with remaining dough balls. (Cooled cookies can be stored at room temperature for up to 2 weeks.)

TO MAKE AHEAD: Dough can be refrigerated for up to 2 days or frozen for up to 1 month. Let frozen dough thaw overnight in refrigerator before proceeding with recipe. Let dough stand at room temperature for 30 minutes before shaping.

FLORENTINE LACE COOKIES

WHY THIS RECIPE WORKS: Wafer-thin almond Florentines have a reputation for being fussy and unpredictable, but these elegant, confection-like cookies have undeniable appeal. To make our recipe foolproof, we ground the almonds and decreased the flour to allow the cookies to spread more. Instead of getting out a thermometer to make the caramel-like base of the dough, we removed the pan from the heat when the sugar mixture thickened and began to brown. Substituting orange marmalade for the usual candied orange peel and corn syrup produced a more concentrated, complex citrus flavor. A flourish of faux-tempered chocolate completed the professional pastry shop effect.

Florentine Lace Cookies

MAKES 24 COOKIES

It's important to cook the cream mixture in the saucepan until it is thick and starting to brown at the edges; undercooking will result in a dough that is too runny to portion. Do not be concerned if some butter separates from the dough while you're portioning the cookies. For the most uniform cookies, use the flattest baking sheets you have and make sure that your parchment paper lies flat. When melting the chocolate, pause the microwave and stir the chocolate often to ensure that it doesn't get much warmer than body temperature.

- 2 cups slivered almonds
- ¾ cup heavy cream
- 4 tablespoons unsalted butter, cut into 4 pieces
- ½ cup (3½ ounces) sugar
- ¼ cup orange marmalade
- 3 tablespoons all-purpose flour
- 1 teaspoon vanilla extract
- ¼ teaspoon grated orange zest
- ¼ teaspoon salt
- 4 ounces bittersweet chocolate, chopped fine

1. Adjust oven racks to upper-middle and lower-middle positions and heat oven to 350 degrees. Line 2 baking sheets with parchment paper. Process almonds in food processor until they resemble coarse sand, about 30 seconds.

2. Bring cream, butter, and sugar to boil in medium saucepan over medium-high heat. Cook, stirring frequently, until mixture begins to thicken, 5 to 6 minutes. Continue to cook, stirring constantly, until mixture begins to brown at edges and is thick enough to leave trail that doesn't immediately fill in when spatula is scraped along pan bottom, 1 to 2 minutes longer (it's OK if some darker speckles appear in mixture). Remove pan from heat and stir in almonds, marmalade, flour, vanilla, orange zest, and salt until combined.

3. Drop 6 level tablespoons dough at least 3½ inches apart on prepared sheets. When cool enough to handle, use damp fingers to press each portion into 2½-inch circle.

4. Bake until deep brown from edge to edge, 15 to 17 minutes, switching and rotating sheets halfway through baking. Transfer cookies, still on parchment, to wire racks and let cool. Let baking sheets cool for 10 minutes, line with fresh parchment, and repeat portioning and baking with remaining dough.

5. Microwave 3 ounces chocolate in bowl at 50 percent power, stirring frequently, until about two-thirds melted, 1 to 2 minutes. Remove bowl from microwave, add remaining 1 ounce chocolate, and stir until melted, returning to microwave for no more than 5 seconds at a time to complete melting if necessary. Transfer chocolate to small zipper-lock bag and snip off corner, making hole no larger than 1/16 inch.

6. Transfer cooled cookies directly to wire racks. Pipe zigzag of chocolate over each cookie, distributing chocolate evenly among all cookies. Refrigerate until chocolate is set, about 30 minutes, before serving. (Cookies can be stored at cool room temperature for up to 4 days.)

COCONUT MACAROONS

WHY THIS RECIPE WORKS: Not that long ago, macaroons (cone-shaped cookies flavored with shredded coconut) were quite elegant and very popular. But today, they have deteriorated into lackluster mounds of beaten egg whites and

coconut shreds or, at their worst, nothing more than a baked mixture of condensed milk and sweetened coconut. We set out to create a great coconut macaroon, with a pleasing texture and real, honest coconut flavor.

When we began looking at recipes for modern coconut macaroons, we found that they varied widely, some calling for vanilla or almond extract in addition to different kinds of coconut and sweeteners. We knew that narrowing the field when it came to the coconut and other flavorings would make a big difference in both taste and texture. After rounds of testing, we determined that unsweetened shredded coconut resulted in a less sticky, more appealing texture. But sweetened shredded coconut packed more flavor than the unsweetened coconut, so we decided to use both; together they worked very well in the cookie. To add one more layer of coconut flavor, we tried cream of coconut and hit the jackpot. As for the structure of our cookie, a few egg whites and some corn syrup ensured that the macaroons held together well and were moist and pleasantly chewy.

Triple-Coconut Macaroons

MAKES ABOUT 48 COOKIES

Cream of coconut, available canned, is a very sweet product commonly used in piña colada cocktails. Be sure to mix the can's contents thoroughly before using, as the mixture separates upon standing. Unsweetened desiccated coconut is commonly sold in natural foods stores and Asian markets. If you are unable to find any, use all sweetened flaked or shredded coconut, but reduce the amount of cream of coconut to ½ cup, omit the corn syrup, and toss 2 tablespoons cake flour with the coconut before adding the liquid ingredients. For larger macaroons, shape haystacks from a generous ¼ cup of batter and increase the baking time to 20 minutes.

- 1 cup cream of coconut (see note)
- 2 tablespoons light corn syrup
- 4 large egg whites
- 2 teaspoons vanilla extract
- ½ teaspoon table salt
- 3 cups unsweetened, shredded, desiccated (dried) coconut (see note)
- 3 cups sweetened flaked or shredded coconut

1. Adjust the oven racks to the upper-middle and lower-middle positions and heat the oven to 375 degrees. Line 2 baking sheets with parchment paper and lightly spray the parchment with vegetable oil spray.

2. Whisk the cream of coconut, corn syrup, egg whites, vanilla, and salt together in a small bowl; set aside. Combine the unsweetened and sweetened coconuts in a large bowl; toss together, breaking up clumps with your fingertips. Pour the liquid ingredients over the coconut and mix with a rubber spatula until evenly moistened. Chill for 15 minutes.

3. Drop heaping tablespoons of batter onto the prepared baking sheets, spacing them about 1 inch apart. Using moistened fingertips, form the cookies into loose haystacks. Bake until light golden brown, about 15 minutes, switching and rotating the sheets halfway through the baking time.

4. Cool the cookies on the baking sheets until slightly set, about 2 minutes; using a wide metal spatula, transfer the cookies to a wire rack and cool to room temperature.

Chocolate-Dipped Triple-Coconut Macaroons

Using the two-stage melting process for the chocolate helps ensure that it will be at the proper consistency for dipping the cookies. To melt the 8 ounces of chocolate in a microwave, heat it at 50 percent power for 2 minutes; stir the chocolate and continue heating until melted, stirring once every additional minute.

Follow the recipe for Triple-Coconut Macaroons. Cool the baked macaroons to room temperature; line two large baking sheets with parchment paper. Chop 10 ounces semisweet chocolate; melt 8 ounces of the chocolate in a small heatproof bowl set over a saucepan of barely simmering water, stirring occasionally, until smooth. Off the heat, stir in the remaining 2 ounces of chocolate until smooth. Holding a macaroon by its pointed top, dip the bottom ½ inch up the sides in the chocolate, scrape off the excess, and place the macaroon on the prepared baking sheet. Repeat with the remaining macaroons. Refrigerate until the chocolate sets, about 15 minutes.

HOLIDAY SPRITZ COOKIES

WHY THIS RECIPE WORKS: Spritz cookies, those golden-swirled holiday cookies, often end up bland, gummy, and tasteless. How come they never taste as good as they look? Unfortunately, this Scandinavian treat has fallen victim to many recipe modifications, such as the use of vegetable shortening instead of butter, an overload of eggs, and an excess of starchy confectioners' sugar. We set out to spruce up spritz cookies and make them light, crisp, buttery treats—the life of any holiday party. The success of these confections rests primarily in the management of a finicky ingredient list. Carefully balancing the butter, sugar, flour, egg yolk, heavy cream (just a drop), vanilla, and salt is the only recipe for success—a few simple ingredients gathered in the proper proportions. Creaming the butter and sugar in the traditional fashion worked well and produced a dough light enough to easily press or pipe the cookies. As for shaping, either a cookie press or a pastry bag can be used—it's up to you.

Spritz Cookies

MAKES ABOUT 72 SMALL COOKIES

If using a pastry bag, use a star tip to create the various shapes. For stars, a ½ to ⅝-inch tip (measure the diameter of the tip at the smallest point) works best, but for rosettes and S shapes, use a ⅜-inch tip. To create stars, see the photo; stars should be about 1 inch in diameter. To create rosettes, pipe the dough while moving the bag in a circular motion, ending at the center of the rosette; rosettes should be about 1¼ inches in diameter. To create S shapes, pipe the dough into compact S's; they should be about 2 inches long and 1 inch wide. If you make an error while piping, the dough can be scraped off the baking sheet and re-piped.

We had the best results baking these cookies one sheet at a time. When reusing a baking sheet, make sure that it has completely cooled before forming more cookies on it. Unbaked dough can be refrigerated in an airtight container for up to 4 days; to use, let it stand at room temperature until softened, about 45 minutes. Baked cookies will keep for more than a week if stored in an airtight container or zipper-lock bag.

- 1 large egg yolk
- 1 tablespoon heavy cream
- 1 teaspoon vanilla extract
- 16 tablespoons (2 sticks) unsalted butter, softened but still cool
- ⅔ cup (4⅔ ounces) granulated sugar
- ¼ teaspoon table salt
- 2 cups (10 ounces) unbleached all-purpose flour

1. Adjust an oven rack to the middle position and heat the oven to 375 degrees. Line 2 large baking sheets with parchment paper. Whisk the egg yolk, cream, and vanilla in a small bowl until combined; set aside.

2. In a stand mixer fitted with the paddle attachment, beat the butter, sugar, and salt at medium-high speed until light and fluffy, about 3 minutes, scraping down the bowl and beater as needed with a rubber spatula. With the mixer running at medium speed, add the yolk-cream mixture and beat until incorporated, about 30 seconds. With the mixer running at low speed, gradually beat in the flour until combined, scraping down the bowl and beater as needed. Give the dough a final stir to ensure that no flour pockets remain.

3. If using a cookie press to form the cookies, follow the manufacturer's instructions to fill the press. If using a pastry bag (see note), fit it with a star tip and fill the bag with half of the dough. Press or pipe cookies onto the prepared baking sheet, spacing them about 1½ inches apart, refilling the cookie press or pastry bag as needed. Bake one sheet at a time, until the cookies are light golden brown, 10 to 12 minutes, rotating the baking sheet halfway through the baking time. Cool the cookies on the baking sheet for 10 to 15 minutes; using a metal spatula, transfer them to a wire rack and cool to room temperature.

Spritz Cookies with Lemon Essence

Follow the recipe for Spritz Cookies, adding 1 teaspoon juice from 1 lemon to the yolk-cream mixture in step 1 and adding 1 teaspoon finely grated zest from 1 lemon to the butter along with the sugar and salt in step 2.

Almond Spritz Cookies

Grind ½ cup sliced almonds and 2 tablespoons of the flour in a food processor until powdery and evenly fine, about 12 pulses; combine the almond mixture with the remaining flour. Follow the recipe for Spritz Cookies, substituting ¾ teaspoon almond extract for the vanilla.

NOTES FROM THE TEST KITCHEN

PIPING SPRITZ COOKIES

Using a ½-inch star tip, hold the bag at a 90-degree angle to the baking sheet and pipe the dough straight down, about 1 inch in diameter. If you make an error while piping, the dough can be scraped off the baking sheet and re-piped.

SABLÉ COOKIES

WHY THIS RECIPE WORKS: During the holidays, these French butter cookies offer sophistication and style. That is, if you can capture their elusive sandy texture (*sablé* is French for sandy), which separates them from sturdy American butter cookies. Most of the sablé recipes we came across had only slight differences in ingredient proportions—but they all baked up without the delicate crumbliness that defines this cookie. To create the hallmark sandy texture of sablés—light, with an inviting granular quality similar to shortbread—we would have to do some detective work. We started with a basic recipe using the typical method of creaming butter and sugar, then adding egg and flour. We found that we needed to decrease the liquid in the dough so there would be less moisture to dissolve the sugar particles. Cutting back on butter helped, as did the inclusion of a hard-cooked egg yolk, an addition we came across in our research. Adding the mashed yolk during creaming eliminated moisture and perfected the texture of the cookies. Brushing the cookies with a beaten egg white and sprinkling them with coarse sugar before baking added a delicate crunch and an attractive sparkle.

Sablés (French Butter Cookies)

MAKES ABOUT 40 COOKIES

Turbinado sugar is commonly sold as Sugar in the Raw. Demerara sugar, sanding sugar, or another coarse sugar can be substituted. Make sure the cookie dough is well chilled and firm so that it can be uniformly sliced. After the dough has been wrapped in parchment, it can be double-wrapped in plastic wrap and frozen for up to 2 weeks.

- 1 large egg
- 10 tablespoons (1¼ sticks) unsalted butter, softened
- ⅓ cup plus 1 tablespoon (2¾ ounces) granulated sugar
- ¼ teaspoon table salt
- 1 teaspoon vanilla extract
- 1½ cups (7½ ounces) unbleached all-purpose flour
- 1 large egg white, lightly beaten with 1 teaspoon water
- 4 teaspoons turbinado sugar (see note)

1. Place the egg in a small saucepan, cover with water by 1 inch, and bring to a boil over high heat. Remove the pan from the heat, cover, and let sit for 10 minutes. Meanwhile, fill a small bowl with ice water. Using a slotted spoon, transfer the egg to the ice water and let stand for 5 minutes. Crack the egg and peel the shell. Separate the yolk from the white; discard the white. Press the yolk through a fine-mesh strainer into a small bowl.

2. In a stand mixer fitted with the paddle attachment, beat the butter, granulated sugar, salt, and cooked egg yolk on medium speed until light and fluffy, about 4 minutes, scraping down the bowl and beater as needed with a rubber spatula. Decrease the speed to low, add the vanilla, and mix until incorporated. Stop the mixer; add the flour and mix on low speed until just combined, about 30 seconds. Using a rubber spatula, press the dough into a cohesive mass.

NOTES FROM THE TEST KITCHEN

FORMING SPIRAL COOKIES

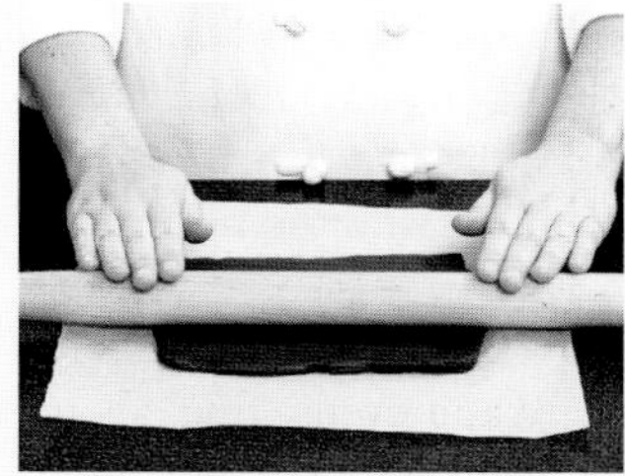

1. Halve each batch of dough. Roll out each portion on parchment paper into an 8 by 6-inch rectangle, ¼ inch thick. Briefly chill the dough until firm enough to handle.

2. Using a bench scraper, place one plain cookie dough rectangle on top of one chocolate dough rectangle. Repeat to make two double rectangles.

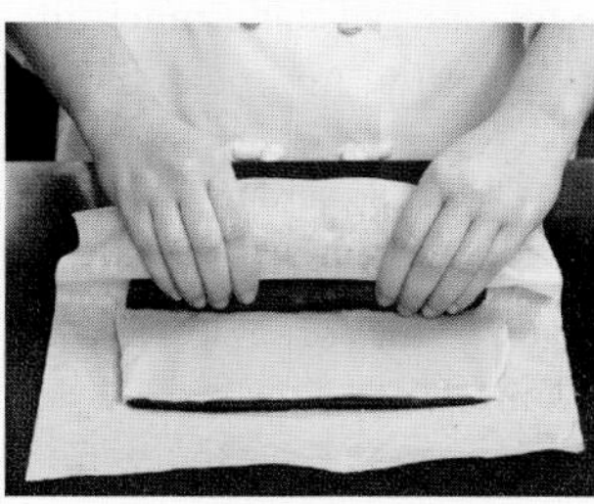

3. Roll out each double rectangle on parchment into a 9 by 6-inch rectangle (if too firm, let rest until malleable). Then, starting at the long end, roll each into a tight log.

4. Twist the ends of the parchment to seal. Chill the logs for 1 hour. Slice the logs into ¼-inch-thick rounds.

FORMING PRETZEL COOKIES

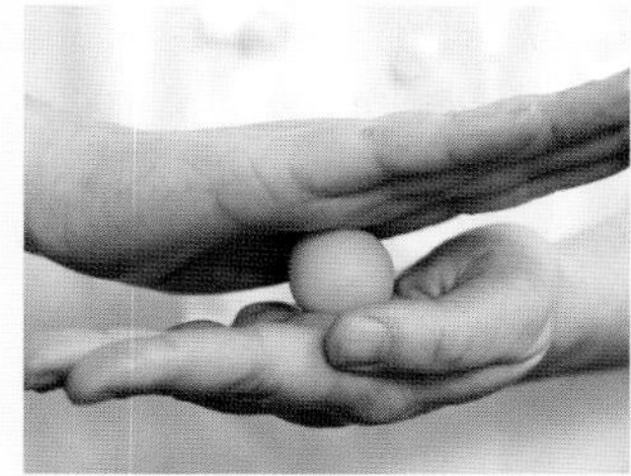

1. Slice slightly chilled dough into ¼-inch-thick rounds and roll into balls.

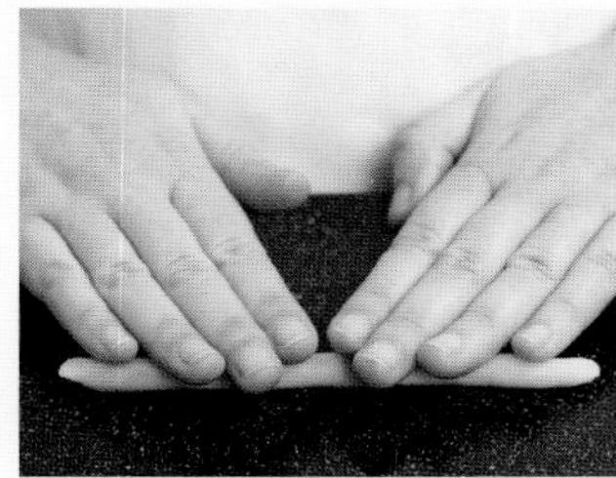

2. Roll each ball into a 6-inch rope, tapering the ends.

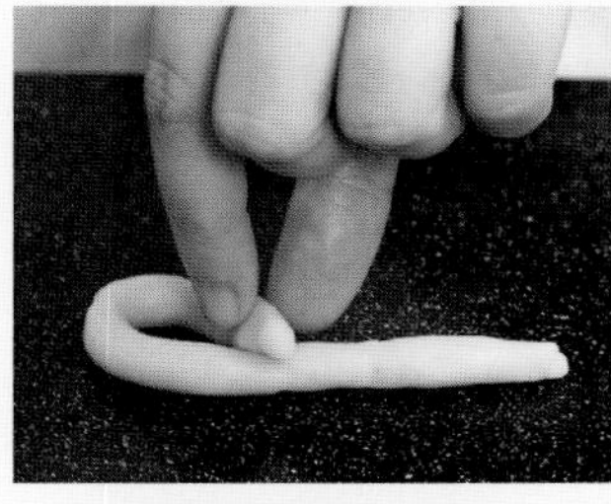

3. Pick up one end of the rope and cross it over to form half of a pretzel shape.

4. Bring the second end over to complete the pretzel shape.

3. Divide the dough in half; roll each piece into a log about 6 inches long and 1¾ inches in diameter. Wrap each log in a 12-inch square of parchment paper and twist the ends to seal and firmly compact the dough into a tight cylinder. Chill until firm, about 1 hour.

4. Adjust the oven racks to the upper-middle and lower-middle positions and heat the oven to 350 degrees. Line 2 large baking sheets with parchment paper. Using a chef's knife, slice the dough into ¼-inch-thick rounds, rotating the dough so that it won't become misshapen from the weight of the knife. Place the cookies 1 inch apart on the baking sheets. Using a pastry brush, gently brush the cookies with the egg white mixture and sprinkle evenly with the turbinado sugar.

5. Bake until the centers of the cookies are pale golden brown with edges slightly darker than the centers, about 15 minutes, switching and rotating the baking sheets halfway through the baking time. Cool the cookies on the baking sheets for 5 minutes; using a thin metal spatula, transfer the cookies to a wire rack and cool to room temperature. (The cookies can be stored between sheets of parchment paper in an airtight container for up to 1 week.)

Chocolate Sablés

Follow the recipe for Sablés, reducing the flour to 1⅓ cups (6⅔ ounces) and adding ¼ cup Dutch-processed cocoa powder with the flour in step 2.

Black and White Spiral Cookies

MAKES ABOUT 80 COOKIES

Follow the recipes for Sablés and Chocolate Sablés through step 2. Following the "Forming Spiral Cookies" photos on page 723, form the dough into spiral logs. Proceed with the Sablés recipe from step 4, slicing the logs into ¼-inch-thick rounds, omitting the egg white mixture and turbinado sugar in both recipes, and baking as directed.

Chocolate Sandwich Cookies

MAKES ABOUT 40 COOKIES

Follow the recipe for Sablés through step 3. In step 4, slice one dough log into ⅛-inch-thick rounds, omitting the egg white mixture and turbinado sugar. Bake the cookies as directed in step 5, reducing the baking time to 10 to 13 minutes. Repeat with the second dough log. When all the cookies are completely cool, melt 3½ ounces dark or milk chocolate and cool slightly. Spread the melted chocolate on the bottom of one cookie. Place a second cookie on top, slightly off-center, so some chocolate shows. Repeat with the remaining melted chocolate and cookies.

Vanilla Pretzel Cookies

MAKES ABOUT 40 COOKIES

Follow the recipe for Sablés through step 3, increasing the vanilla extract to 1 tablespoon and reducing the chilling time to 30 minutes (the dough will not be fully hardened). Slice the dough into ¼-inch-thick rounds and roll into balls. Roll each ball into a 6-inch rope, tapering the ends. Following the "Forming Pretzel Cookies" photos on page 723, form the ropes into pretzel shapes. Proceed with the recipe, brushing with the egg white mixture, sprinkling with the turbinado sugar, and baking as directed.

HOLIDAY ROLLED COOKIES

WHY THIS RECIPE WORKS: Baking holiday cookies should be a fun endeavor but so often it's an exercise in frustration. The dough clings to the rolling pin, it rips and tears as it is rolled out, and the tactic of moving the dough in and out of the fridge to make it easier to work with turns a simple one-hour process into a half-day project. We wanted a simple recipe that would yield a forgiving, workable dough, producing cookies that would be sturdy enough to decorate yet tender enough to be worth eating.

Our first realization was that we had to use enough butter to stay true to the nature of a butter cookie but not so much that the dough became greasy. All-purpose flour had enough gluten to provide structure, while superfine sugar provided a fine, even crumb and a compact, crisp cookie. Cream cheese—a surprise ingredient—gave the cookies flavor and richness without altering their texture.

Glazed Butter Cookies

MAKES ABOUT 38 COOKIES

If you cannot find superfine sugar, process granulated sugar in a food processor for 30 seconds. If desired, the cookies can be finished with sprinkles or other decorations immediately after glazing (see page 726).

BUTTER COOKIE DOUGH

- 2½ cups (12½ ounces) unbleached all-purpose flour
- ¾ cup (5⅔ ounces) superfine sugar (see note)
- ¼ teaspoon table salt
- 16 tablespoons (2 sticks) unsalted butter, cut into 16 pieces, softened
- 2 tablespoons cream cheese, at room temperature
- 2 teaspoons vanilla extract

GLAZE

- 1 tablespoon cream cheese, at room temperature
- 3 tablespoons milk
- 1½ cups (6 ounces) confectioners' sugar

1. FOR THE COOKIES: In a stand mixer fitted with the paddle attachment, mix the flour, sugar, and salt at low speed until combined, about 5 seconds. With the mixer running on low, add the butter 1 piece at a time; continue to mix until the mixture looks crumbly and slightly wet, 1 to 2 minutes longer. Beat in the cream cheese and vanilla until the dough just begins to form large clumps, about 30 seconds.

2. Knead the dough by hand in the bowl, about two to three turns, until it forms a large, cohesive mass. Transfer the dough to a clean work surface and divide it into two even pieces. Press each piece into a 4-inch disk, wrap the disks in plastic wrap, and refrigerate until the dough is firm but malleable, about 30 minutes. (The disks can be refrigerated for up to 3 days or frozen for up to 2 weeks; defrost in the refrigerator before using.)

3. Adjust an oven rack to the middle position and heat the oven to 375 degrees. Working with one piece of dough at a time, roll out the dough to an even ⅛-inch thickness between 2 large sheets of parchment paper; slide the rolled dough, still on the parchment, onto a baking sheet and refrigerate until firm, about 10 minutes.

4. Line 2 large baking sheets with parchment paper. Working with 1 sheet of dough at a time, cut into desired shapes using cookie cutters and place the cookies on the prepared sheet, spacing them about 1½ inches apart. Bake 1 sheet at a time, until the cookies are light golden brown, about 10 minutes, rotating the sheet halfway through the baking time. (The dough scraps can be patted together, chilled, and rerolled once.) Cool the cookies on the baking sheet for 3 minutes; using a wide metal spatula, transfer the cookies to a wire rack and cool to room temperature.

5. FOR THE GLAZE: Whisk the cream cheese and 2 tablespoons of the milk together in a medium bowl until combined and no lumps remain. Add the confectioners' sugar and whisk until smooth, adding the remaining 1 tablespoon milk as needed until the glaze is thin enough to spread easily. Using the back of a spoon, drizzle or spread a scant teaspoon of the glaze onto each cooled cookie. Allow the glazed cookies to dry for at least 30 minutes.

NOTES FROM THE TEST KITCHEN

CUTTING AND FILLING JAM SANDWICHES

1. Using a 2-inch round fluted cookie cutter, cut out cookies from one piece of the dough.

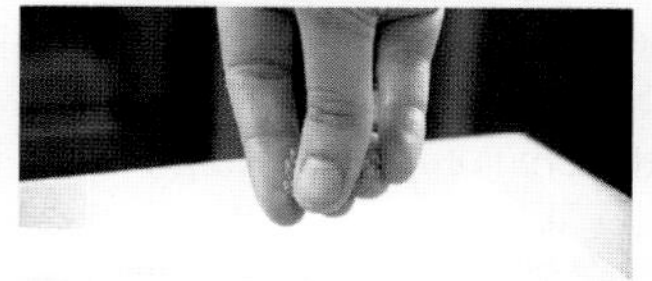

2. Sprinkle the second piece of rolled dough evenly with turbinado sugar and cut out 2-inch rounds.

3. Using a ¾-inch round fluted cookie cutter, cut out the centers of the sugared rounds.

4. When the cookies have cooled, spread the reduced jam on the solid cookies, then place the cut-out cookies on top.

Jam Sandwiches

MAKES ABOUT 30 COOKIES

See the photos to prepare these cookies. Turbinado sugar is commonly sold as Sugar in the Raw. Demerara sugar, sanding sugar, or another coarse sugar can be substituted.

- 1 recipe Butter Cookie Dough, prepared through step 3
- 2 tablespoons turbinado sugar (see note)
- 1¼ cups (12 ounces) raspberry jam, strained, simmered until reduced to 1 cup, and cooled to room temperature

1. Line 2 large baking sheets with parchment paper. Using a 2-inch round fluted cookie cutter, cut rounds from 1 piece of rolled dough and bake on a prepared sheet in a 375-degree oven, rotating the baking sheet halfway through the baking time, until the cookies are light golden brown, 8 to 10 minutes.

2. Sprinkle the second piece of rolled dough evenly with the sugar.

3. Using a 2-inch round fluted cookie cutter, cut rounds of sugar-sprinkled dough. Using a ¾-inch round fluted cookie cutter, cut out the centers of the sugared rounds. Place the cookies on a prepared sheet and bake, rotating the baking sheet halfway through the baking time, until the cookies are light golden brown, about 8 minutes.

4. When the cookies have cooled, spread 1 teaspoon jam on the top of each solid cookie, then cover with a cut-out cookie. Let the filled cookies stand until set, about 30 minutes.

Lime-Glazed Coconut Snowballs

MAKES ABOUT 40 COOKIES

- 1 recipe Butter Cookie Dough, with 1 teaspoon grated lime zest added with the dry ingredients, prepared through step 2
- 1 recipe Glaze, with 3 tablespoons juice from 2 limes substituted for the milk
- 1½ cups sweetened shredded coconut, pulsed in a food processor until finely chopped, about 15 pulses

1. Line 2 baking sheets with parchment paper. Roll the dough between your hands into 1-inch balls. Place the balls on the prepared sheets, spacing them about 1½ inches apart. Bake one sheet at a time in a 375-degree oven until lightly browned, about 12 minutes. Cool to room temperature.

2. Dip the tops of the cookies into the glaze and scrape off the excess, then dip them into the coconut. Place the cookies on a wire rack and let stand until the glaze sets, about 20 minutes.

Chocolate-Cherry Bar Cookies with Hazelnuts

MAKES ABOUT 50 COOKIES

- 1 recipe Butter Cookie Dough, with 1 cup chopped dried cherries added with the dry ingredients, prepared through step 2
- 1½ cups (9 ounces) semisweet chocolate chips
- 1½ cups (6 ounces) hazelnuts, toasted, skinned, and chopped

1. Adjust an oven rack to the lower-middle position and heat the oven to 375 degrees. Line a 17 by 12-inch rimmed baking sheet with parchment paper. Press the dough evenly into the prepared sheet and bake until golden brown, about 20 minutes, rotating the sheet halfway through the baking time.

2. Immediately after removing the baking sheet from the oven, sprinkle evenly with the chocolate chips; let stand to melt, about 3 minutes.

3. Using an offset spatula, spread the chocolate into an even layer, then sprinkle the chopped hazelnuts evenly over the chocolate. Cool on a wire rack until just warm, 15 to 20 minutes.

4. Using a pizza wheel, cut on the diagonal into 1½-inch diamonds. Transfer the cookies to a wire rack to cool completely.

NOTES FROM THE TEST KITCHEN

DECORATING GLAZED BUTTER COOKIES

1. For a smooth, evenly glazed cookie, spoon a little glaze on the center of the cookie, then spread it out in an even layer using the back of a spoon.

2. After glazing the cookies, sprinkle with crushed candy canes, colored sugar, or chopped nuts.

3. To add detail to a cut-out cookie, make a piping bag by spooning some glaze into a zipper-lock bag, pushing the glaze to a bottom corner, and snipping off the corner of the bag with scissors.

4. After you've piped outlines onto a cookie, go back and fill in with colored glazes.

5. Use the zipper-lock bag to pipe small dots on the cookie, then top with shiny bead-like decorations. When set, the glaze will hold the beads in place.

BEST SHORTBREAD

WHY THIS RECIPE WORKS: When made well, shortbread, with its moderately sweet, buttery flavor and distinctive sandy texture, is the perfect partner to a cup of tea or served alongside fruit for dessert, but often shortbread turns out bland and chalky. We wanted superlative shortbread with an alluring tawny brown crumb and pure, buttery richness.

In initial tests, we tinkered with various mixing methods and found that reverse creaming—mixing the flour and sugar before adding the butter, creating less aeration—yielded the most reliable results. To smooth out an objectionable granular texture, we swapped the white sugar for confectioners' sugar. Still, our shortbread was unpleasantly tough. The problems were gluten and moisture. Gluten, the protein matrix that lends baked goods structure and chew, forms naturally when liquid and all-purpose flour are combined, even without kneading. The liquid in our recipe was coming from butter, which contains 20 percent water. To curb gluten development, we replaced some of our flour with powdered old-fashioned oats. We ground some oats to a powder and supplemented it with a modest amount of cornstarch (using all oat powder muted the buttery flavor). The cookies were now perfectly crisp and flavorful, with an appealing hint of oat flavor.

As for the moisture problem, we took a hint from recipes from historic cookbooks: We cooked the dough briefly, then shut off the heat and let it sit in the still-warm oven. The batch was dry through and through, with an even golden brown exterior. Crisp and buttery, our shortbread was anything but bland.

NOTES FROM THE TEST KITCHEN

FORMING AND BAKING THE SHORTBREAD

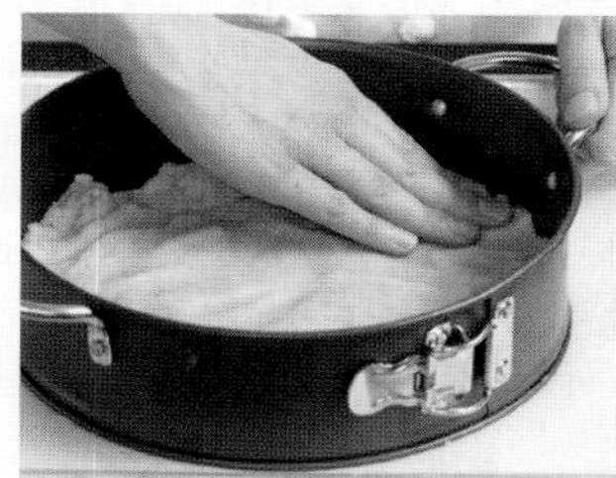

1. Press the dough into a closed springform pan collar; smooth with the back of a spoon.

2. Cut a hole in the center of the dough with a 2-inch biscuit cutter and remove the round of dough—place it on the baking sheet next to the collar; replace the cutter in the hole.

3. Open the collar, but leave it in place. Bake 5 minutes at 450 degrees, then 10 to 15 minutes at 250 degrees.

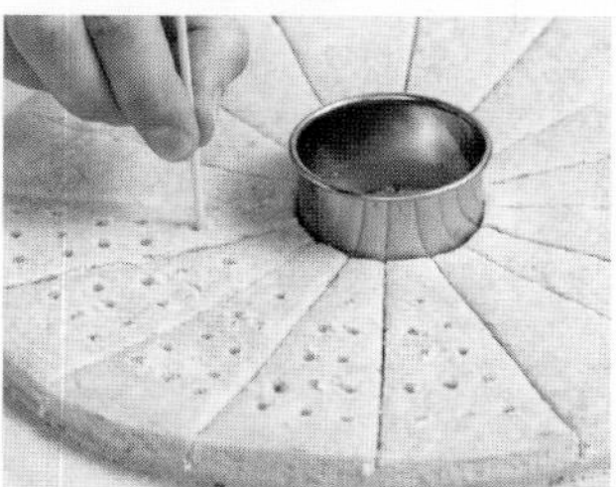

4. Score the partially baked shortbread into wedges, then poke 8 to 10 holes in each wedge.

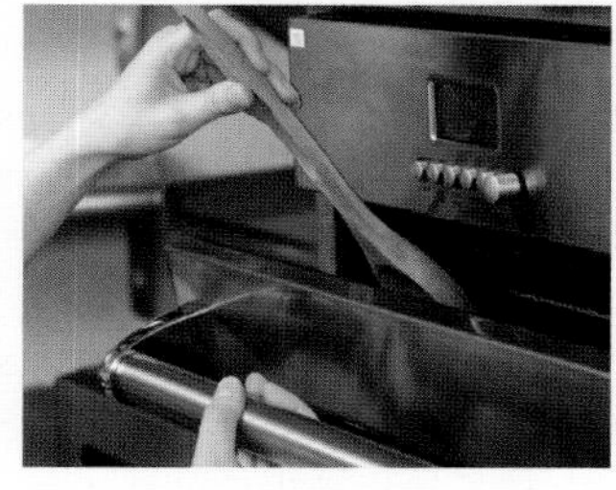

5. Return the shortbread to the turned-off oven to dry; prop the door open with a wooden spoon or stick.

Best Shortbread

MAKES 16 WEDGES

Use the collar of a springform pan to form the shortbread into an even round. Mold the shortbread with the collar in the closed position, then open the collar, but leave it in place. This allows the shortbread to expand slightly but keeps it from spreading too far. The extracted round of dough in step 2 is baked alongside the rest of the shortbread. Wrapped well and stored at room temperature, the shortbread will keep for up to 7 days.

- ½ cup (1½ ounces) old-fashioned oats
- 1½ cups (7½ ounces) unbleached all-purpose flour
- ¼ cup cornstarch
- ⅔ cup (2⅔ ounces) confectioners' sugar
- ½ teaspoon table salt
- 14 tablespoons (1¾ sticks) unsalted butter, chilled, cut into ⅛-inch-thick slices

1. Adjust an oven rack to the middle position and heat the oven to 450 degrees. Pulse the oats in a spice grinder or blender until reduced to a fine powder, about ten 5-second pulses (you should have ¼ to ⅓ cup oat flour). In a stand mixer fitted with the paddle attachment, mix the oat flour, all-purpose flour, cornstarch, sugar, and salt on low speed until combined, about 5 seconds. Add the butter to the dry ingredients and continue to mix on low speed until the dough just forms and pulls away from the sides of the bowl, 5 to 10 minutes.

2. Place an upside-down (the grooved edge should be at the top) collar of a 9- or 9½-inch springform pan on a parchment-lined rimmed baking sheet (do not use the springform pan bottom). Following the photos, press the dough into the collar in an even ½-inch-thick layer, smoothing the top of the dough with the back of a spoon. Place a 2-inch biscuit cutter in the center of the dough and cut out the center. Place the extracted round alongside the springform collar on the baking sheet and replace the cutter in the center of the dough. Open the springform collar, but leave it in place.

3. Bake the shortbread for 5 minutes, then reduce the oven temperature to 250 degrees. Continue to bake until the edges turn pale golden, 10 to 15 minutes longer. Remove the baking sheet from the oven; turn off the oven. Remove the springform pan collar; use a chef's knife to score the surface of the shortbread into 16 even wedges, cutting halfway through the shortbread. Using a wooden skewer, poke 8 to 10 holes in each wedge. Return the shortbread to the oven and prop the door open with the handle of a wooden spoon, leaving a 1-inch gap at the top. Allow the shortbread to dry in the turned-off oven until pale golden in the center (the shortbread should be firm but giving to the touch), about 1 hour.

4. Transfer the baking sheet to a wire rack; cool the shortbread to room temperature, at least 2 hours. Cut the shortbread at the scored marks to separate and serve.

NUT CRESCENT COOKIES

WHY THIS RECIPE WORKS: When nut crescent cookies are well made, they can be delicious: buttery, nutty, slightly crisp, slightly crumbly, with a melt-in-your mouth quality. Too often, however, they turn out bland and dry. We wanted to develop a recipe that would put them back in their proper place.

The ratio of 1 cup butter to 2 cups flour in almost all of the recipes we looked at is what worked for us. We tried three kinds of sugar in the batter: granulated, confectioners', and superfine. The last resulted in just what we wanted: cookies that melted in our mouths. In determining the amount, we had to remember that the cookies would be sweetened once more by their traditional coating of confectioners' sugar. Before rolling them, we let the cookies cool to room temperature; coating them with sugar while still warm results in the pasty outer layer we wanted to avoid.

Pecan or Walnut Crescent Cookies

MAKES ABOUT 48 SMALL COOKIES

If you cannot find superfine sugar, you can obtain a close approximation by processing regular granulated sugar in a food processor for about 30 seconds. If you don't have a food processor, you can finely grind the chopped nuts by rolling them between two large sheets of plastic wrap with a rolling pin, applying moderate pressure, until broken down to a coarse cornmeal-like texture.

- 2 cups (8 ounces) whole pecans or walnuts, chopped fine
- 2 cups (10 ounces) unbleached all-purpose flour
- ½ teaspoon table salt
- 16 tablespoons (2 sticks) unsalted butter, softened
- ⅓ cup (2½ ounces) superfine sugar (see note)
- 1½ teaspoons vanilla extract
- 1½ cups (6 ounces) confectioners' sugar

1. Adjust the oven racks to the upper-middle and lower-middle positions and heat the oven to 325 degrees. Line 2 large baking sheets with parchment paper.

2. Whisk 1 cup of the chopped nuts, the flour, and salt together in a medium bowl; set aside. Process the remaining 1 cup chopped nuts in a food processor (see note) until they are the texture of coarse cornmeal, 10 to 15 seconds (do not over process). Stir the nuts into the flour mixture and set aside.

3. In a stand mixer fitted with the paddle attachment, beat the butter and superfine sugar at medium-low speed until light and fluffy, about 2 minutes; add the vanilla, scraping down the bowl and beater with a rubber spatula. Add the flour mixture and beat on low speed until the dough just begins to come together but still looks scrappy, about 15 seconds. Scrape down the bowl and beater again with a rubber spatula; continue beating at low speed until the dough is cohesive, 6 to 9 seconds longer. Do not over beat.

4. Divide the dough into 48 portions, each about 1 tablespoon, and roll them between your hands into 1¼-inch balls. Roll each ball between your palms into a rope that measures 3 inches long. Place the ropes on the prepared baking sheets and turn up the ends to form a crescent shape. Bake until the tops are pale golden and the bottoms are just beginning to brown, 17 to 19 minutes, switching and rotating the baking sheets halfway through the baking time.

5. Cool the cookies on the baking sheets for 2 minutes; using a wide metal spatula, transfer the cookies to a wire rack and cool to room temperature, about 30 minutes. Place the confectioners' sugar in a shallow baking dish or pie plate. Working with three or four cookies at a time, roll the cookies in the sugar to coat them thoroughly; gently shake off the excess. (The cookies can be stored in an airtight container for up to 5 days.) Before serving, roll the cookies in the confectioners' sugar again and tap off the excess.

Almond or Hazelnut Crescent Cookies

Almonds can be used raw for cookies that are light in both color and flavor or toasted to enhance the almond flavor and darken the crescents.

Follow the recipe for Pecan or Walnut Crescent Cookies, substituting 1¾ cups (7¾ ounces) whole blanched almonds (toasted, if desired) or 2 cups (8 ounces) toasted, skinned hazelnuts for the pecans or walnuts. If using almonds, add ½ teaspoon almond extract along with the vanilla extract.

MERINGUE COOKIES

WHY THIS RECIPE WORKS: A classic meringue cookie may have only two ingredients—egg whites and sugar—but it requires precise timing. Otherwise, you'll end up with a meringue that's as dense as Styrofoam or weepy, gritty, and cloyingly sweet. A great meringue cookie should emerge from the oven glossy and white, with a shatteringly crisp texture that dissolves instantly in your mouth.

We chose a basic French meringue over a fussier Italian meringue. The French version, in which egg whites are whipped with sugar, is the simpler of the two; the Italian meringue, in which hot sugar syrup is poured into the whites, produces cookies that are dense and candy-like. The key to

glossy, evenly textured meringue was adding the sugar at just the right time—when the whites have been whipped enough to gain some volume, but still have enough free water left in them for the sugar to dissolve completely. Surprisingly, we found that cream of tartar wasn't necessary. Without it, the whites formed more slowly, giving a wider time frame in which to add the sugar. It was also important to form the cookies in a uniform shape, so we piped them from either a pastry bag or a zipper-lock bag with a corner cut off.

Meringue Cookies

MAKES ABOUT 48 SMALL COOKIES

Meringues may be a little soft immediately after being removed from the oven but will stiffen as they cool. To minimize stickiness on humid or rainy days, allow the meringues to cool in a turned-off oven for an additional hour (for a total of 2 hours) without opening the door, then transfer them immediately to airtight containers and seal. Cooled cookies can be kept in an airtight container for up to 2 weeks.

- ¾ cup (5¼ ounces) sugar
- 2 teaspoons cornstarch
- 4 large egg whites
- ¾ teaspoon vanilla extract
- ⅛ teaspoon table salt

1. Adjust the oven racks to the upper-middle and lower-middle positions and heat the oven to 225 degrees. Line 2 large baking sheets with parchment paper. Combine the sugar and cornstarch in a small bowl.

2. In a stand mixer fitted with the whisk attachment, beat the egg whites, vanilla, and salt together at high speed until very soft peaks start to form (the peaks should slowly lose their shape when the whip is removed), 30 to 45 seconds. Decrease the speed to medium and slowly add the sugar mixture in a steady stream down the side of the mixer bowl (the process should take about 30 seconds). Stop the mixer and scrape down the sides and bottom of the bowl with a rubber spatula. Increase the speed to high and beat until glossy and stiff peaks have formed, 30 to 45 seconds.

3. Working quickly, place the meringue in a pastry bag fitted with a ½-inch plain tip or a large zipper-lock bag with ½ inch of the corner cut off. Pipe meringues into 1¼-inch-wide mounds about 1 inch high on the baking sheets, six rows of four meringues on each sheet. Bake for 1 hour, switching and rotating the baking sheets halfway through the baking time. Turn off the oven and allow the meringues to cool in the oven for at least 1 hour. Remove the meringues from the oven and let cool to room temperature before serving, about 10 minutes.

Chocolate Meringue Cookies

Follow the recipe for Meringue Cookies, gently folding 2 ounces finely chopped bittersweet chocolate into the meringue mixture at the end of step 2.

Toasted Almond Meringue Cookies

Follow the recipe for Meringue Cookies, substituting ½ teaspoon almond extract for the vanilla extract. In step 3, sprinkle the meringues with ⅓ cup coarsely chopped toasted almonds and 1 teaspoon coarse sea salt, such as Maldon (optional), before baking.

BISCOTTI

WHY THIS RECIPE WORKS: We wanted biscotti that were hard and crunchy, but not hard to eat, and bold in flavor. To keep the crumb crisp, we used just a small amount of butter (4 tablespoons), and to keep the biscotti from being too hard, we ground some of the nuts to a fine meal, which helped minimize gluten development in the crumb. To ensure bold flavor in a biscuit that gets baked twice, we increased the quantities of almond extract and of the aromatic herbs and spices used in our variations, such as anise, rosemary, lavender, cardamom, and cloves.

Almond Biscotti

MAKES 30 COOKIES

The almonds will continue to toast while the biscotti bake, so toast the nuts only until they are just fragrant.

- 1¼ cups whole almonds, lightly toasted
- 1¾ cups (8¾ ounces) all-purpose flour
- 2 teaspoons baking powder
- ¼ teaspoon salt
- 2 large eggs, plus 1 large white beaten with pinch salt
- 1 cup (7 ounces) sugar
- 4 tablespoons unsalted butter, melted and cooled
- 1½ teaspoons almond extract
- ½ teaspoon vanilla extract
- Vegetable oil spray

1. Adjust oven rack to middle position and heat oven to 325 degrees. Using ruler and pencil, draw two 8 by 3-inch rectangles, spaced 4 inches apart, on piece of parchment paper. Grease baking sheet and place parchment on it, marked side down.

2. Pulse 1 cup almonds in food processor until coarsely chopped, 8 to 10 pulses; transfer to bowl and set aside. Process remaining ¼ cup almonds in food processor until finely ground, about 45 seconds. Add flour, baking powder, and salt; process to combine, about 15 seconds. Transfer flour mixture to second bowl. Process 2 eggs in now-empty food processor until lightened in color and almost doubled in volume, about 3 minutes. With processor running, slowly add sugar until thoroughly combined, about 15 seconds. Add melted butter, almond extract, and vanilla and process until combined, about 10 seconds. Transfer egg mixture to medium bowl. Sprinkle half of flour mixture over egg mixture and, using spatula, gently fold until just combined. Add remaining flour mixture and chopped almonds and gently fold until just combined.

3. Divide batter in half. Using floured hands, form each half into 8 by 3-inch rectangle, using lines on parchment as guide. Spray each loaf lightly with oil spray. Using rubber spatula lightly coated with oil spray, smooth tops and sides of rectangles. Gently brush tops of loaves with egg white wash. Bake until loaves are golden and just beginning to crack on top, 25 to 30 minutes, rotating pan halfway through baking.

4. Let loaves cool on baking sheet for 30 minutes. Transfer loaves to cutting board. Using serrated knife, slice each loaf on slight bias into ½-inch-thick slices. Lay slices, cut side down, about ¼ inch apart on wire rack set in rimmed baking sheet. Bake until crisp and golden brown on both sides, about 35 minutes, flipping slices halfway through baking. Let cool completely before serving. Biscotti can be stored in airtight container for up to 1 month.

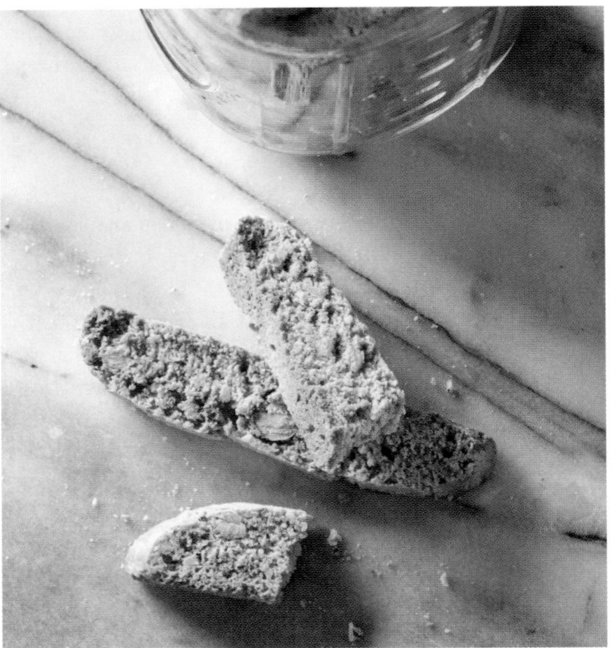

Anise Biscotti

Add 1½ teaspoons anise seeds to flour mixture in step 2. Substitute anise-flavored liqueur for almond extract.

Hazelnut-Orange Biscotti

Substitute lightly toasted and skinned hazelnuts for almonds. Add 2 tablespoons minced fresh rosemary to flour mixture in step 2. Substitute orange-flavored liqueur for almond extract and add 1 tablespoon grated orange zest to egg mixture with butter.

Hazelnut-Lavender Biscotti

Substitute lightly toasted and skinned hazelnuts for almonds. Add 2 teaspoons dried lavender flowers to flour mixture in step 2. Substitute 1½ teaspoons water for almond extract and add 2 tablespoons grated lemon zest to egg mixture with butter.

Pistachio-Spice Biscotti

Substitute shelled pistachios for almonds. Add 1 teaspoon ground cardamom, ½ teaspoon ground cloves, ½ teaspoon pepper, ¼ teaspoon ground cinnamon, and ¼ teaspoon ground ginger to flour mixture in step 2. Substitute 1 teaspoon water for almond extract and increase vanilla extract to 1 teaspoon.

BLONDIES

WHY THIS RECIPE WORKS: Blondies are first cousins to both brownies and chocolate chip cookies. Although blondies are baked in a pan like brownies, the flavorings are similar to those in chocolate chip cookies. They're sometimes laced with nuts and chocolate chips or butterscotch chips. But even with these extras, blondies can be pretty bland, floury, and dry. We set out to fix the blondie so it would be chewy but not dense, sweet but not cloying, and loaded with nuts and chocolate. We found that the key to chewy blondies was using melted, not creamed, butter because the creaming process incorporated too much air into the batter. Light brown sugar lent the right amount of molasses flavor. And combined with vanilla extract and salt, the light brown sugar developed a rich butterscotch flavor. To add both texture and flavor, we included chocolate chips and pecans. We also tried butterscotch chips, but we found that they did little for this recipe. On a whim, we included white chocolate chips with the semisweet chips, and we were surprised that they produced the best blondie yet.

Blondies

MAKES 36 BARS

If you have trouble finding white chocolate chips, chop a bar of white chocolate into small chunks.

- 1½ cups (7½ ounces) unbleached all-purpose flour
- 1 teaspoon baking powder
- ½ teaspoon table salt
- 1½ cups packed (10½ ounces) light brown sugar

12 tablespoons (1½ sticks) unsalted butter, melted and cooled
2 large eggs
1½ teaspoons vanilla extract
1 cup (4 ounces) pecans, toasted and chopped coarse
½ cup (3 ounces) semisweet chocolate chips
½ cup (3 ounces) white chocolate chips (see note)

1. Adjust an oven rack to the middle position and heat the oven to 350 degrees. Line a 13 by 9-inch baking pan with 2 pieces of foil (see the photos on page 732) and spray with vegetable oil spray.

2. Whisk the flour, baking powder, and salt together in a medium bowl; set aside.

3. Whisk the brown sugar and melted butter together in a medium bowl until combined. Add the eggs and vanilla and mix well. Using a rubber spatula, fold the dry ingredients into the egg mixture until just combined. Do not overmix. Fold in the nuts and semisweet and white chocolate chips and turn the batter into the prepared pan, smoothing the top with a rubber spatula.

4. Bake until the top is shiny and cracked and feels firm to the touch, 22 to 25 minutes. Transfer the pan to a wire rack and cool completely. Loosen the edges with a paring knife and lift the bars from the pan using the foil sling. Cut into 2 by 1½-inch bars.

Congo Bars

If you have trouble locating unsweetened shredded coconut, try a natural foods store or an Asian market. Keep a close eye on the coconut when toasting, as it can burn quickly.

Toast 1½ cups unsweetened shredded coconut on a rimmed baking sheet on the middle oven rack at 350 degrees, stirring two to three times, until light golden, 4 to 5 minutes. Transfer to a small bowl to cool. Follow the recipe for Blondies, adding the toasted coconut with the chocolate chips and nuts in step 3.

CLASSIC BROWNIES

WHY THIS RECIPE WORKS: Chewy and chocolaty, brownies should be a simple and utterly satisfying affair. But too often, brownies are heavy, dense, and remarkably low on chocolate flavor. We wanted old-fashioned brownies that had serious chocolate flavor. They had to be the simple treats we enjoyed in our youth—Mom's brownies—but altered to cater to adult tastes.

To get that tender texture and delicate chew, we shelved the all-purpose flour in favor of cake flour; a bit of baking powder further lightened the crumb. Getting the number of eggs just right prevented our brownies from being cakey or dry. As for chocolatiness, plenty of unsweetened chocolate provided maximum chocolate flavor—not too sweet, with profound chocolate notes. Nailing the baking time was essential—too little time in the oven and the brownies were gummy and underbaked, too much time and they were dry. Finally, for nut-lovers, we toasted pecans and topped the brownies with them just before baking; baked inside the brownies, they steamed and got soft.

Classic Brownies

MAKES 24 BROWNIES

Be sure to test for doneness before removing the brownies from the oven. If underbaked (the toothpick has batter clinging to it), the texture of the brownies will be dense and gummy; if overbaked (the toothpick comes out completely clean), the brownies will be dry and cakey. To melt the chocolate using a microwave, heat it with the butter at 50 percent power for 2 minutes; stir the chocolate and continue heating until melted, stirring once every additional minute.

1¼ cups (5 ounces) cake flour
¾ teaspoon baking powder
½ teaspoon table salt
6 ounces unsweetened chocolate, chopped fine
12 tablespoons (1½ sticks) unsalted butter, cut into 6 pieces
2¼ cups (15¾ ounces) sugar
4 large eggs
1 tablespoon vanilla extract
1 cup (4 ounces) pecans or walnuts, toasted and coarsely chopped (optional)

1. Adjust an oven rack to the middle position and heat the oven to 325 degrees. Line a 13 by 9-inch baking pan with 2 pieces of foil (see the photos on page 732) and spray with vegetable oil spray.

2. Whisk the flour, baking powder, and salt in a medium bowl until combined; set aside.

3. Melt the chocolate and butter in a medium heatproof bowl set over a saucepan of barely simmering water, stirring occasionally, until smooth. Off the heat, gradually whisk in the sugar. Add the eggs, one at a time, whisking after each

NOTES FROM THE TEST KITCHEN

MAKING A FOIL SLING

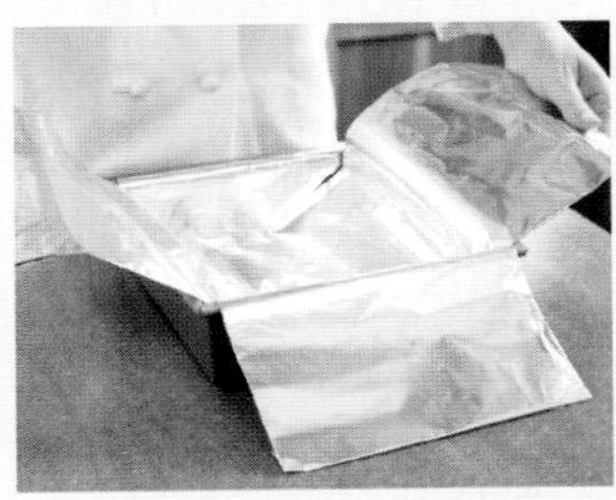

1. Place two sheets of aluminum foil perpendicular to each other in the baking pan, with the extra foil hanging over the edges of the pan.

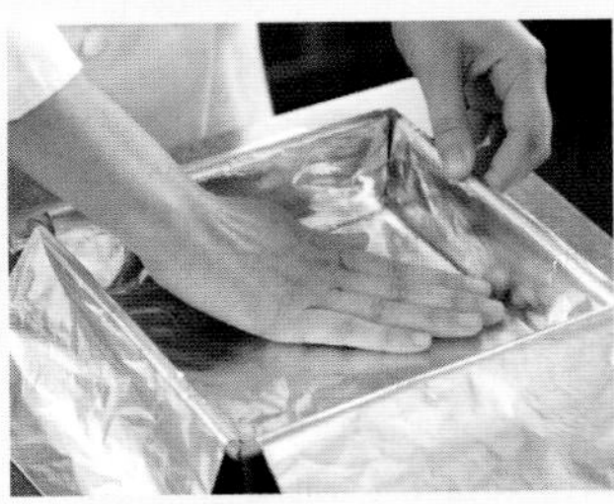

2. Push the foil into the corners and up the sides of the pan, smoothing out any wrinkles in the foil.

3. After the bars or brownies have baked and cooled, use the foil sling to lift and transfer them to a cutting board before cutting into squares.

addition, until thoroughly combined. Whisk in the vanilla. Add the flour mixture in three additions, folding with a rubber spatula until the batter is completely smooth and homogeneous.

4. Transfer the batter to the prepared pan; using a spatula, spread the batter into the corners of the pan and smooth the surface. Sprinkle the toasted nuts (if using) evenly over the batter. Bake until a toothpick or wooden skewer inserted into the center of the brownies comes out with a few moist crumbs attached, 30 to 35 minutes. Cool on a wire rack to room temperature, about 2 hours; loosen the edges with a paring knife and lift the brownies from the pan using the foil sling. Cut the brownies into 2-inch squares and serve. (The brownies can be stored in an airtight container at room temperature for up to 3 days.)

FUDGY BROWNIES

WHY THIS RECIPE WORKS: Classic Brownies (page 731) boast a balance of cakey and chewy. We wanted a brownie that was distinctly chewy and fudgy—a moist, dark brownie with a firm, smooth texture. To develop a rich, deep chocolate flavor, we ultimately found it necessary to use three types of chocolate. Unsweetened chocolate laid a solid, intense foundation; semisweet chocolate provided a mellow, even somewhat sweet, flavor; and cocoa powder smoothed out any rough edges introduced by the unsweetened chocolate and added complexity to what can be the bland flavor of semisweet chocolate. We focused on flour, butter, and eggs to arrive at the chewy texture we wanted. Too little flour and the batter was goopy; too much made the brownies dry and muted the flavor. We melted the butter instead of creaming softened butter with the sugar and eggs; as with our Classic Brownies, the melted butter produced a more dense and fudgy texture.

Fudgy Triple-Chocolate Brownies

MAKES 64 SMALL BROWNIES

To melt the chocolates in a microwave, heat them with the butter at 50 percent power for 2 minutes; stir the chocolate and continue heating until melted, stirring once every additional minute. Either Dutch-processed or natural cocoa powder works well in this recipe. These brownies are very rich, so we prefer to cut them into very small squares for serving.

- 5 ounces semisweet or bittersweet chocolate, chopped
- 2 ounces unsweetened chocolate, chopped
- 8 tablespoons (1 stick) unsalted butter, cut into quarters
- 3 tablespoons cocoa powder (see note)
- 3 large eggs
- 1¼ cups (8¾ ounces) sugar
- 2 teaspoons vanilla extract
- ½ teaspoon table salt
- 1 cup (5 ounces) unbleached all-purpose flour

1. Adjust an oven rack to the lower-middle position and heat the oven to 350 degrees. Following the photos, line an 8-inch square baking pan with 2 pieces of foil and spray with vegetable oil spray.

2. Melt the chocolates and butter in a medium heatproof bowl set over a saucepan of barely simmering water, stirring occasionally, until smooth. Whisk in the cocoa powder until smooth. Set aside to cool slightly.

3. Whisk the eggs, sugar, vanilla, and salt together in a medium bowl until combined, about 15 seconds. Whisk the warm chocolate mixture into the egg mixture. Using a wooden spoon, stir in the flour until just combined. Transfer the batter to the prepared pan; using a spatula, spread the batter into the corners and smooth the surface. Bake until slightly puffed and a toothpick or wooden skewer inserted into the center of the brownies comes out with a few moist crumbs attached, 35 to 40 minutes. Cool the brownies on a wire rack to room temperature, about 2 hours; loosen the edges with a paring knife and lift the brownies from the pan using the foil sling. Cut the brownies into 1-inch squares and serve. (Do not cut the brownies until ready to serve; the brownies can be wrapped in plastic wrap and refrigerated for up to 5 days.)

Triple-Chocolate Espresso Brownies

Follow the recipe for Fudgy Triple-Chocolate Brownies, whisking in 1½ tablespoons instant espresso or coffee powder along with the cocoa powder in step 2.

CHEWY BROWNIES

WHY THIS RECIPE WORKS: Brownies are a tricky business: Homemade recipes have better flavor, while boxed mixes claim best texture. Our goal was clear: a homemade brownie with chewiness to rival the boxed-mix standard—but flush with a rich, deep chocolate flavor. Boxed brownie mixes derive their chewy texture from the right combination of saturated (solid) and unsaturated (liquid) fats. Unsaturated vegetable oil and powdered solid fat combine in a ratio designed to deliver maximum chew. To get the same chew at home, we tested and tested until we finally homed in on the ratio that produced the chewiest brownie. To combat greasiness, we replaced some of the oil with egg yolks, whose emulsifiers prevented fat from separating and leaking out during baking. We focused on flavor next. Because unsweetened chocolate contains a similar ratio of saturated and unsaturated fat to butter, we could replace some of the butter with unsweetened chocolate, thereby providing more chocolate flavor. Espresso powder improved the chocolate taste as well. And finally, folding in bittersweet chocolate chunks just before baking gave our chewy, fudgy brownies gooey pockets of melted chocolate and rounded out their complex chocolate flavor.

Chewy Brownies

MAKES 2 DOZEN 2-INCH BROWNIES

For an accurate measurement of boiling water, bring a full kettle of water to a boil, then measure out the desired amount. For the chewiest texture, it is important to let the brownies cool thoroughly before cutting. If your baking dish is glass, cool the brownies for 10 minutes, then remove them promptly from the pan (otherwise, the superior heat retention of glass can lead to overbaking). While any high-quality chocolate can be used, our preferred brands of bittersweet chocolate are Callebaut Intense Dark Chocolate and Ghirardelli Bittersweet Chocolate. Our preferred brand of unsweetened chocolate is Hershey's.

- ⅓ cup (1 ounce) Dutch-processed cocoa powder
- 1½ teaspoons instant espresso (optional)
- ½ cup plus 2 tablespoons boiling water (see note)
- 2 ounces unsweetened chocolate (see note), chopped fine
- ½ cup plus 2 tablespoons vegetable oil
- 4 tablespoons (½ stick) unsalted butter, melted
- 2 large whole eggs plus 2 large egg yolks
- 2 teaspoons vanilla extract
- 2½ cups (17½ ounces) sugar
- 1¾ cups (8¾ ounces) unbleached all-purpose flour
- ¾ teaspoon table salt
- 6 ounces bittersweet chocolate (see note), cut into ½-inch pieces

1. Adjust an oven rack to the lowest position and heat the oven to 350 degrees. Following the photos on page 732, line a 13 by 9-inch baking pan with a foil sling, lightly coat with vegetable oil spray, and set aside.

2. Whisk the cocoa, espresso powder (if using), and boiling water together in a large bowl until smooth. Add the unsweetened chocolate and whisk until the chocolate is melted. Whisk in the oil and melted butter. (The mixture may look curdled.) Add the whole eggs, egg yolks, and vanilla and continue to whisk until smooth and homogeneous. Whisk in the sugar until fully incorporated. Add the flour and salt and mix with a rubber spatula until combined. Fold in the bittersweet chocolate pieces.

3. Scrape the batter into the prepared pan and bake until a toothpick inserted halfway between the edge and the center comes out with just a few moist crumbs attached, 30 to 35 minutes. Transfer the pan to a wire rack and cool for 1½ hours.

4. Loosen the edges with a paring knife and lift the brownies from the pan using the foil sling. Return the brownies to the wire rack and let cool completely, about 1 hour. Cut into 2-inch squares and serve. (The brownies can be stored in an airtight container at room temperature for up to 4 days.)

CREAM CHEESE BROWNIES

WHY THIS RECIPE WORKS: Rich, decadent cream cheese brownies are hard to get just right: They are plagued by chalky cream cheese, dry brownie, and uneven distribution of each element. To fix these issues, we started with a cakey brownie, which would absorb some of the moisture from the cream cheese. Unsweetened chocolate gave us the most intense chocolate flavor, and a bit of extra sugar eliminated bitter notes. For the cream cheese swirl, we mixed in some sour cream for tang and richness. Dolloping the cream cheese into the brownie batter made for unevenly dispersed swirls; we fixed this problem by layering some of the brownie batter, then the cream cheese, then dolloping more brownie batter on top and giving the whole construction a few quick swirls with a knife.

Cream Cheese Brownies

MAKES SIXTEEN 2-INCH BROWNIES

To accurately test the doneness of the brownies, be sure to stick the toothpick into the brownie portion, not the cream cheese. Leftover brownies should be stored in the refrigerator. Let leftovers stand at room temperature for 1 hour before serving.

CREAM CHEESE FILLING

- 4 ounces cream cheese, cut into 8 pieces
- ½ cup sour cream
- 2 tablespoons sugar
- 1 tablespoon all-purpose flour

BROWNIE BATTER

- ⅔ cup (3⅓ ounces) all-purpose flour
- ½ teaspoon baking powder
- ½ teaspoon salt
- 4 ounces unsweetened chocolate, chopped fine
- 8 tablespoons unsalted butter
- 1¼ cups (8¾ ounces) sugar
- 2 large eggs
- 1 teaspoon vanilla extract

1. FOR THE CREAM CHEESE FILLING: Microwave cream cheese until soft, 20 to 30 seconds. Add sour cream, sugar, and flour and whisk to combine. Set aside.

2. Adjust oven rack to middle position and heat oven to 325 degrees. Make foil sling for 8-inch square baking pan by folding 2 long sheets of aluminum foil so each is 8 inches wide. Lay sheets of foil in pan perpendicular to each other, with extra foil hanging over edges of pan. Push foil into corners and up sides of pan, smoothing foil flush to pan. Grease foil.

3. FOR THE BROWNIE BATTER: Whisk flour, baking powder, and salt together in bowl and set aside. Microwave chocolate and butter in bowl at 50 percent power, stirring occasionally, until melted, 1 to 2 minutes.

4. Whisk sugar, eggs, and vanilla together in medium bowl. Add melted chocolate mixture (do not clean bowl) and whisk until incorporated. Add flour mixture and fold to combine.

5. Transfer ½ cup batter to bowl used to melt chocolate. Spread remaining batter in prepared pan. Spread cream cheese filling evenly over batter.

6. Microwave bowl of reserved batter until warm and pourable, 10 to 20 seconds. Using spoon, dollop softened batter over cream cheese filling, 6 to 8 dollops. Using knife, swirl batter through cream cheese filling, making marbled pattern, 10 to 12 strokes, leaving ½-inch border around edges.

7. Bake until toothpick inserted in center comes out with a few moist crumbs attached, 35 to 40 minutes, rotating pan halfway through baking. Let cool in pan on wire rack for 1 hour.

8. Using foil overhang, lift brownies out of pan. Return brownies to wire rack and let cool completely, about 1 hour. Cut into 2-inch squares and serve.

FUDGY LOW-FAT BROWNIES

WHY THIS RECIPE WORKS: We have tried many recipes for "healthy" brownies, but it usually takes just one bite to regret the effort. Either the texture is incredibly dry or the chocolate flavor is anemic. We wanted a moist, fudgy, chocolaty brownie that had a lower fat and calorie count than a traditional brownie, which can weigh in at over 200 calories and 12 grams of fat.

We knew the richness and flavor would have to come from somewhere if we were cutting back on butter and unsweetened chocolate. We started our tests with "alternative" ingredients, such as prune puree, applesauce, and yogurt, but they resulted in everything from oddly flavored brownies to flavorless hockey pucks. We had more success replacing some of the butter with low-fat sour cream, which yielded moist, fudgy brownies. A blend of cocoa powder and bittersweet chocolate (which has less fat per ounce than unsweetened chocolate) added deep chocolate flavor. And to boost both the brownies' chocolate flavor and moisture without adding any fat, we used a shot of chocolate syrup. Our brownies were now rich and decadent, but with half the calories (just 110 per serving) and less than half the fat (only 4.5 grams) of traditional brownies.

Fudgy Low-Fat Brownies

MAKES 16 BROWNIES

For a truly fudgy consistency, don't overbake the brownies; as soon as a toothpick inserted into the center comes out with moist crumbs attached, the brownies are done. If the toothpick emerges with no crumbs, the brownies will be cakey. To melt the chocolate in a microwave, heat it with the butter at 50 percent power for 2 minutes; stir and continue heating until melted, stirring once every additional minute.

- ¾ cup (3¾ ounces) unbleached all-purpose flour
- ⅓ cup Dutch-processed cocoa powder
- ½ teaspoon baking powder
- ¼ teaspoon table salt
- 2 ounces bittersweet chocolate, chopped
- 2 tablespoons unsalted butter
- 1 cup (7 ounces) sugar
- 2 tablespoons low-fat sour cream
- 1 tablespoon chocolate syrup
- 2 teaspoons vanilla extract
- 1 large whole egg
- 1 large egg white

1. Adjust an oven rack to the middle position and heat the oven to 350 degrees. Line an 8-inch square baking pan with 2 pieces of foil (see photos on page 732) and spray with vegetable oil spray.

2. Whisk the flour, cocoa powder, baking powder, and salt together in a medium bowl. Melt the chocolate and butter in a large heatproof bowl set over a saucepan of barely simmering water, stirring occasionally, until smooth. Set aside to cool slightly, 2 to 3 minutes. Whisk in the sugar, sour cream, chocolate syrup, vanilla, whole egg, and egg white. Using a rubber spatula, fold the dry ingredients into the chocolate mixture until combined.

3. Transfer the batter to the prepared pan; using a spatula, spread the batter into the corners and smooth the surface. Bake until slightly puffed and a toothpick or wooden skewer inserted into the center of the brownies comes out with a few moist crumbs attached, 20 to 25 minutes. Cool the brownies on a wire rack to room temperature, about 1 hour. Loosen the edges with a paring knife and lift the brownies from the pan using the foil sling. Cut the brownies into 2-inch squares and serve. (Do not cut the brownies until ready to serve; the brownies can be wrapped in plastic wrap and refrigerated for up to 3 days.)

MILLIONAIRE'S SHORTBREAD

WHY THIS RECIPE WORKS: Millionaire's shortbread has a lot going for it: a crunchy shortbread base topped with a chewy, caramel-like layer, all covered in shiny, snappy chocolate. We wanted foolproof methods for producing all three layers. We started by making a quick pat-in-the-pan shortbread with melted butter. Sweetened condensed milk was important to the creaminess of the middle layer, but we needed to add a little heavy cream to keep it from separating. Gently heating the chocolate in the microwave and stirring in grated chocolate created a firm top layer, which made a suitably elegant finish for this rich yet refined cookie.

Millionaire's Shortbread

MAKES 40 COOKIES

For a caramel filling with the right texture, monitor the temperature with an instant-read thermometer. We prefer Ghirardelli 60% Cacao Bittersweet Chocolate Premium Baking Bar for this recipe. Grating a portion of the chocolate is important for getting the chocolate to set properly; the small holes on a box grater work well for this task. Stir often while melting the chocolate and don't overheat it.

CRUST

- 2½ cups (12½ ounces) all-purpose flour
- ½ cup (3½ ounces) granulated sugar
- ¾ teaspoon salt
- 16 tablespoons unsalted butter, melted

FILLING

- 1 (14-ounce) can sweetened condensed milk
- 1 cup packed (7 ounces) brown sugar
- ½ cup heavy cream
- ½ cup corn syrup
- 8 tablespoons unsalted butter
- ½ teaspoon salt

CHOCOLATE

- 8 ounces bittersweet chocolate (6 ounces chopped fine, 2 ounces grated)

1. FOR THE CRUST: Adjust oven rack to lower-middle position and heat oven to 350 degrees. Make foil sling for 13 by 9-inch baking pan by folding 2 long sheets of aluminum foil; first sheet should be 13 inches wide and second sheet should be 9 inches wide. Lay sheets of foil in pan perpendicular to each other, with extra foil hanging over edges of pan. Push foil

into corners and up sides of pan, smoothing foil flush to pan. Combine flour, sugar, and salt in medium bowl. Add melted butter and stir with rubber spatula until flour is evenly moistened. Crumble dough evenly over bottom of prepared pan. Using your fingertips and palm of your hand, press and smooth dough into even thickness. Using fork, pierce dough at 1-inch intervals. Bake until light golden brown and firm to touch, 25 to 30 minutes. Transfer pan to wire rack. Using sturdy metal spatula, press on entire surface of warm crust to compress (this will make finished bars easier to cut). Let crust cool until it is just warm, at least 20 minutes.

2. FOR THE FILLING: Stir all ingredients together in large, heavy-bottomed saucepan. Cook over medium heat, stirring frequently, until mixture registers between 236 and 239 degrees (temperature will fluctuate), 16 to 20 minutes. Pour over crust and spread to even thickness (mixture will be very hot). Let cool completely, about 1½ hours.

3. FOR THE CHOCOLATE: Microwave chopped chocolate in bowl at 50 percent power, stirring every 15 seconds, until melted but not much warmer than body temperature (check by holding in palm of your hand), 1 to 2 minutes. Add grated chocolate and stir until smooth, returning to microwave for no more than 5 seconds at a time to finish melting if necessary. Spread chocolate evenly over surface of filling. Refrigerate shortbread until chocolate is just set, about 10 minutes.

4. Using foil overhang, lift shortbread out of pan and transfer to cutting board; discard foil. Using serrated knife and gentle sawing motion, cut shortbread in half crosswise to create two 6½ by 9-inch rectangles. Cut each rectangle in half to make four 3½ by 9-inch strips. Cut each strip crosswise into 10 equal pieces. (Shortbread can be stored at room temperature, between layers of parchment, for up to 1 week.)

RASPBERRY SQUARES

WHY THIS RECIPE WORKS: Raspberry squares are one of the best, and easiest, bar cookies to prepare, especially since the filling is ready-made (a jar of raspberry preserves). But sometimes the proportions are uneven, leaving one parched from too much sandy crust, or with a puckered face from an overload of tart filling. We were after a buttery, tender, golden brown crust and crumb topping with just the right amount of sweet and tart raspberry preserves in the middle.

For the tender, almost (but not quite) sandy crumb, we had to get the right combination of ingredients, especially the butter and sugar. Too much butter made the raspberry squares greasy, but too little left them on the dry side. We found that equal amounts of white and light brown sugar made for a deeper flavor than white alone; oats and nuts made a subtle contribution to flavor while also adding some textural interest. For a golden brown bottom crust, we prebaked it before layering it with raspberry preserves and sprinkling on the top crust, which was a small amount of the reserved bottom crust mixture.

Raspberry Squares

MAKES 25 SQUARES

For a nice presentation, trim ¼ inch off the outer rim of the uncut baked block. The outside edges of all cut squares will then be neat.

- 1½ cups (7½ ounces) unbleached all-purpose flour
- 1¼ cups (3¾ ounces) quick oats
- ½ cup pecans or almonds, chopped fine
- ⅓ cup (2⅓ ounces) granulated sugar
- ⅓ cup packed (2⅓ ounces) light brown sugar
- ¼ teaspoon baking soda
- ¼ teaspoon table salt
- 12 tablespoons (1½ sticks) unsalted butter, cut into 12 pieces and softened
- 1 cup raspberry preserves

1. Adjust an oven rack to the lower-middle position and heat the oven to 350 degrees. Line a 9-inch square baking pan with 2 pieces of foil (see the photos on page 732) and spray with vegetable oil spray.

2. Whisk the flour, oats, nuts, sugars, baking soda, and salt together in a large bowl. In a stand mixer fitted with the paddle attachment, beat the flour mixture and butter at low speed until well blended and the mixture resembles wet sand, about 2 minutes.

3. Transfer two-thirds of the mixture to the prepared pan. Press the crumbs evenly and firmly into the bottom of the pan. Bake until just starting to brown, about 20 minutes. Using a rubber spatula, spread the preserves evenly over the hot crust; sprinkle the remaining flour mixture evenly over the preserves. Bake until bubbling around the edges and the top is golden brown, about 30 minutes, rotating the pan halfway through the baking time. Cool on a wire rack to room temperature, 1 to 1½ hours. Lift the bars from the baking pan using the foil sling; cut the bars into 25 squares and serve.

KEY LIME BARS

WHY THIS RECIPE WORKS: Key lime pie is a luscious, bright, summery dessert, but like all pies, it's not very portable. Thus, we decided to bring all the essence of Key lime pie to a Key lime bar, creating a cookie that balanced tart and creamy flavors as well as soft and crispy textures.

To support our handheld bars, we needed a thicker, sturdier crust, which required more crumbs and butter than used in traditional pie crust. Tasters found the traditional graham cracker flavor too assertive in such a crust and preferred the more neutral flavor of animal crackers. As for the filling, it also had to be firmer. By adding cream cheese and an egg yolk to the usual sweetened condensed milk, lime juice, and lime zest, we created a firm, rich filling that didn't fall apart when the bars were picked up. Two issues remained: Were Key limes really key? Did we need a topping? While testers preferred Key lime juice to regular lime juice by a narrow margin, regular juice was judged acceptable, especially considering that we needed to squeeze far fewer regular limes (three) than Key limes (20) to get the same amount of juice. For a topping, a heavy streusel was rejected. The favorite was an optional toasted-coconut topping.

Key Lime Bars

MAKES 16 BARS

If you cannot find fresh Key limes, use regular (Persian) limes. Do not use bottled lime juice. Grate the zest from the limes before juicing them, avoiding the bitter white pith that lies just beneath the outermost skin. The optional coconut garnish adds textural interest and tames the lime flavor for those who find it too intense. The recipe can be doubled and baked in a 13 by 9-inch baking pan; you will need a double layer of extra-wide foil for the pan (each sheet about 20 inches in length) and should increase the baking times by a minute or two.

CRUST

- 5 ounces animal crackers
- 3 tablespoons brown sugar
- Pinch table salt
- 4 tablespoons (½ stick) unsalted butter, melted and cooled slightly

FILLING

- 2 ounces cream cheese, at room temperature
- 1 tablespoon grated zest from 1 lime
- Pinch table salt
- 1 (14-ounce) can sweetened condensed milk
- 1 large egg yolk
- ½ cup juice from about 20 Key limes or from about 3 Persian limes (see note)

GARNISH (OPTIONAL)

- ¾ cup sweetened shredded coconut, toasted until golden and crisp (see note)

1. Adjust an oven rack to the middle position and heat the oven to 325 degrees. Line an 8-inch square baking pan with 2 pieces of foil (see the photos on page 732) and spray with vegetable oil spray.

2. FOR THE CRUST: Pulse the animal crackers in a food processor until broken down, about 10 pulses; process the crumbs until evenly fine, about 10 seconds (you should have about 1¼ cups crumbs). Add the brown sugar and salt; process to combine, 10 to 12 pulses (if large sugar lumps remain, break them apart with your fingers). Drizzle the butter over the crumbs and pulse until the crumbs are evenly moistened with the butter, about 10 pulses. Press the crumbs evenly and firmly into the bottom of the prepared pan. Bake until deep golden brown, 18 to 20 minutes. Cool on a wire rack while making the filling. Do not turn off the oven.

3. FOR THE FILLING: While the crust cools, in a medium bowl, stir the cream cheese, zest, and salt with a rubber spatula until softened, creamy, and thoroughly combined. Add the sweetened condensed milk and whisk vigorously until incorporated and no lumps of cream cheese remain; whisk in the egg yolk. Add the lime juice and whisk gently until incorporated (the mixture will thicken slightly).

NOTES FROM THE TEST KITCHEN

ZESTING CITRUS

Hold a rasp-style grater upside down with the fruit on the bottom and the inverted grater on the top. This method is neater and makes it easy to see exactly how much zest you have.

4. Pour the filling into the crust; spread to the corners and smooth the surface with a rubber spatula. Bake until set and the edges begin to pull away slightly from the sides, 15 to 20 minutes. Cool on a wire rack to room temperature, 1 to 1½ hours. Cover with foil and refrigerate until thoroughly chilled, at least 2 hours.

5. Loosen the edges with a paring knife and lift the bars from the baking pan using the foil sling; cut the bars into 16 squares. Sprinkle with the toasted coconut (if using) and serve. (Leftovers can be refrigerated for up to 2 days; the crust will soften slightly. Let the bars stand at room temperature for about 15 minutes before serving.)

Triple Citrus Bars

Using three types of citrus (orange, lemon, and lime) gives these bars a slightly more complex, floral flavor.

Follow the recipe for Key Lime Bars, substituting 1½ teaspoons each grated lime zest, lemon zest, and orange zest for the lime zest, and using 6 tablespoons lime juice, 1 tablespoon lemon juice, and 1 tablespoon orange juice in place of all the lime juice.

PECAN BARS

WHY THIS RECIPE WORKS: Pecan bars usually take the lead from pecan pie and are more about a thick, custardy filling than the pecans. We wanted a bar cookie that emphasized the star ingredient. For the filling, we increased the amount of pecans to a full pound and tossed them in a thick mixture of brown sugar, corn syrup, and melted butter for an easy dump-and-stir filling that spread itself evenly in the heat of the oven. Using so many nuts gave these pecan bars a variety of textures; depending on the bite, some parts were chewy and some crunchy—a quality we enjoyed. Instead of making a crust using cold butter in a food processor, we found that melted butter helped form an easy press-in crust with no special equipment necessary. And after we eliminated the wet custardy filling, we discovered the crust also didn't need parbaking. A final sprinkling of flaky sea salt as the bars came out of the oven elevated the flavor and appearance of this nutty treat.

Ultranutty Pecan Bars

MAKES 24 BARS

It is important to use pecan halves, not pieces. The edges of the bars will be slightly firmer than the center. If desired, trim ¼ inch from the edges before cutting into bars. Toast the pecans on a rimmed baking sheet in a 350-degree oven until fragrant, 8 to 12 minutes, shaking the sheet halfway through.

CRUST

- 1¾ cups (8¾ ounces) all-purpose flour
- 6 tablespoons (2⅔ ounces) granulated sugar
- ½ teaspoon salt
- 8 tablespoons unsalted butter, melted

TOPPING

- ¾ cup packed (5¼ ounces) light brown sugar
- ½ cup light corn syrup
- 7 tablespoons unsalted butter, melted and hot
- 1 teaspoon vanilla extract
- ½ teaspoon salt
- 4 cups (1 pound) pecan halves, toasted
- ½ teaspoon flake sea salt (optional)

1. FOR THE CRUST: Adjust oven rack to lowest position and heat oven to 350 degrees. Make foil sling for 13 by 9-inch baking pan by folding 2 long sheets of aluminum foil; first sheet should be 13 inches wide and second sheet should be 9 inches wide. Lay sheets of foil in pan perpendicular to each other, with extra foil hanging over edges of pan. Push foil into corners and up sides of pan, smoothing foil flush to pan. Lightly spray foil with vegetable oil spray.

2. Whisk flour, sugar, and salt together in medium bowl. Add melted butter and stir with wooden spoon until dough begins to form. Using your hands, continue to combine until no dry flour remains and small portion of dough holds together when squeezed in palm of your hand. Evenly scatter tablespoon-size pieces of dough over surface of pan. Using your fingertips and palm of your hand, press and smooth dough into even thickness in bottom of pan.

3. FOR THE TOPPING: Whisk sugar, corn syrup, melted butter, vanilla, and salt together in medium bowl until smooth (mixture will look separated at first but will become homogeneous), about 20 seconds. Fold pecans into sugar mixture until nuts are evenly coated.

NOTES FROM THE TEST KITCHEN

HOW TO TOAST NUTS

Nuts (especially irregularly shaped ones) toast more evenly in the oven, but the stovetop is more convenient for amounts less than 1 cup. To avoid overbrowning, transfer toasted nuts to a plate to cool.

IN THE OVEN
Spread nuts in single layer on rimmed baking sheet and toast in 350-degree oven until fragrant and slightly darkened, 8 to 12 minutes, shaking sheet halfway through.

ON THE STOVETOP
Place nuts in single layer in dry skillet set over medium heat and toast, stirring frequently, until fragrant and slightly darkened, 3 to 5 minutes.

4. Pour topping over crust. Using spatula, spread topping over crust, pushing to edges and into corners (there will be bare patches). Bake until topping is evenly distributed and rapidly bubbling across entire surface, 23 to 25 minutes.

5. Transfer pan to wire rack and lightly sprinkle with flake sea salt, if using. Let bars cool completely in pan on rack, about 1½ hours. Using foil overhang, lift bars out of pan and transfer to cutting board. Cut into 24 bars. (Bars can be stored at room temperature for up to 5 days.)

BAKLAVA

WHY THIS RECIPE WORKS: Baklava is rich with butter, sugar, and nuts, but it can be too soggy and too sweet. We wanted our baklava to be crisp, flaky, and buttery, light yet decadent, filled with fragrant nuts and spices, and sweetened just assertively enough. To achieve this goal, we sprinkled store-bought phyllo dough with three separate layers of nuts (a combination of almonds and walnuts) flavored with cinnamon and cloves and clarified butter for even browning. Fully cutting the baklava rather than just scoring it before baking helped it to absorb the sugar syrup. A low oven and slow baking time proved best. Finally, allowing the baklava to stand overnight before serving improved both its flavor and texture.

Baklava

MAKES 32 TO 40 PIECES

A straight-sided traditional (not nonstick) metal baking pan works best for making baklava; the straight sides ensure that the pieces will have nicely shaped edges, and the surface of a traditional pan will not be marred by the knife during cutting, as would a nonstick surface. If you don't have this type of pan, a glass baking dish will work. Make sure that the phyllo is fully thawed before use; leave it in the refrigerator overnight or on the countertop for four to five hours. When assembling, use the nicest, most intact phyllo sheets for the bottom and top layers; use sheets with tears or ones that are smaller than the size of the pan in the middle layers, where their imperfections will go unnoticed.

SUGAR SYRUP

- 1¼ cups granulated sugar
- ¾ cup water
- ⅓ cup honey
- 1 tablespoon lemon juice from 1 lemon, plus 3 strips zest, removed in large strips with vegetable peeler
- 1 cinnamon stick
- 5 whole cloves
- ⅛ teaspoon salt

NUT FILLING

- 8 ounces blanched slivered almonds
- 4 ounces walnuts
- 1¼ teaspoons ground cinnamon
- ¼ teaspoon ground cloves
- 2 tablespoons granulated sugar
- ⅛ teaspoon salt

PASTRY AND BUTTER

24 tablespoons (3 sticks) unsalted butter, cut into 1-inch pieces
1 pound frozen phyllo, thawed (see note)

1. FOR THE SUGAR SYRUP: Combine syrup ingredients in small saucepan and bring to full boil over medium-high heat, stirring occasionally to ensure that sugar dissolves. Transfer to 2-cup liquid measuring cup and set aside to cool while making and baking baklava; when syrup is cool, discard spices and lemon zest. (Cooled syrup can be refrigerated in airtight container for up to 4 days.)

2. FOR THE NUT FILLING: Pulse almonds in food processor until very finely chopped, about twenty 1-second pulses; transfer to medium bowl. Pulse walnuts in food processor until very finely chopped, about fifteen 1-second pulses; transfer to bowl with almonds and toss to combine. Measure out 1 tablespoon nuts and set aside for garnish. Add cinnamon, cloves, sugar, and salt; toss well to combine.

3. TO ASSEMBLE AND BAKE: Melt butter in small saucepan over medium-low heat. Remove pan from heat and let stand for 10 minutes. Using spoon, carefully skim off foam from surface. Spoon butterfat into bowl, leaving water and milk solids in saucepan and tipping saucepan gently and only when it becomes necessary. Brush 13 by 9-inch traditional (not nonstick) baking pan with some of melted butter. Adjust oven rack to lower-middle position and heat oven to 300 degrees. Unwrap and unfold phyllo on large cutting board; carefully smooth with hands to flatten. Using baking pan as guide, cut sheets crosswise with chef's knife, yielding two roughly evenly sized stacks of phyllo (one may be narrower than other). Cover with plastic wrap, then damp dish towel to prevent drying.

4. Place one phyllo sheet (from wider stack) in bottom of baking pan and brush until completely coated with butter. Repeat with 7 more phyllo sheets (from wider stack), brushing each with butter.

5. Evenly distribute about 1 cup nuts over phyllo. Cover nuts with phyllo sheet (from narrower stack) and dab with butter (phyllo will slip if butter is brushed on). Repeat with 5 more phyllo sheets (from narrower stack), staggering sheets slightly if necessary to cover nuts, and brushing each with butter. Repeat layering with additional 1 cup nuts, 6 sheets phyllo, and remaining 1 cup nuts. Finish with 8 to 10 sheets phyllo (from wider stack), using nicest and most intact sheets for uppermost layers and brushing each except final sheet with butter. Use palms of hands to compress layers, working from center outward to press out any air pockets. Spoon 4 tablespoons butter on top layer and brush to cover all surfaces. Use bread knife or other serrated knife with pointed tip in gentle sawing motion to cut baklava into diamonds, rotating pan as necessary to complete cuts. (Cut on bias into eighths on both diagonals.)

6. Bake until golden and crisped, about 1½ hours, rotating baking pan halfway through baking. Immediately after removing baklava from oven, pour cooled syrup over cut lines until about 2 tablespoons remain (syrup will sizzle when it hits hot pan); drizzle remaining syrup over surface. Garnish center of each piece with pinch of reserved ground nuts. Cool to room temperature on wire rack, about 3 hours, then cover with foil and let stand at least 8 hours before serving. (Once cooled, baklava can be served, but flavor and texture improve if left to stand at least 8 hours. Baklava can be wrapped tightly in foil and kept at room temperature for up to 10 days.)

Pistachio Baklava with Cardamom and Rose Water

Omit honey, lemon zest, and cinnamon in sugar syrup and increase sugar to 1¾ cups. Substitute 10 whole peppercorns for cloves and stir in 1 tablespoon rose water after discarding peppercorns. Substitute 2¾ cups shelled pistachios for almonds and walnuts and 1 teaspoon ground cardamom for cinnamon and cloves in nut filling.

CHOCOLATE TRUFFLES

WHY THIS RECIPE WORKS: The problem with many homemade truffles is that they have a dry, grainy texture. There are three keys to creating creamy, silky-smooth truffles. First, start with melted chocolate. Melting the chocolate before adding the cream allowed us to stir—rather than whisk—the two together, reducing the incorporation of air that can cause grittiness. Second, add corn syrup and butter. Corn syrup smoothed over the gritty texture of the sugar, and butter introduced silkiness. Finally, cooling down the ganache gradually before chilling prevented the formation of grainy crystals.

Chocolate Truffles

MAKES 64 TRUFFLES

In step 5, running your knife under hot water and wiping it dry makes cutting the chocolate easier. We recommend using Callebaut Intense Dark L-60-40NV or Ghirardelli Bittersweet Chocolate Baking Bar. If giving the truffles as a gift, set them in 1½-inch candy cup liners in a gift box and keep them chilled.

GANACHE

- 2 cups (12 ounces) bittersweet chocolate, roughly chopped
- ½ cup heavy cream
- 2 tablespoons light corn syrup
- ½ teaspoon vanilla extract
- Pinch salt
- 1½ tablespoons unsalted butter, cut into 8 pieces and softened

COATING

- 1 cup (3 ounces) Dutch-processed cocoa
- ¼ cup (1 ounce) confectioners' sugar

1. FOR THE GANACHE: Lightly coat 8-inch baking dish with vegetable oil spray. Make parchment sling by folding 2 long sheets of parchment so that they are as wide as baking pan. Lay sheets of parchment in pan perpendicular to each other, with extra hanging over edges of pan. Push parchment into corners and up sides of pan, smoothing flush to pan.

2. Microwave chocolate in medium bowl at 50 percent power, stirring occasionally, until mostly melted and a few small chocolate pieces remain, 2 to 3 minutes; set aside. Microwave cream in measuring cup until warm to touch, about 30 seconds. Stir corn syrup, vanilla, and salt into cream and pour mixture over chocolate. Cover bowl with plastic wrap, set aside for 3 minutes, and then stir with wooden spoon to combine. Stir in butter, one piece at a time, until fully incorporated.

3. Using rubber spatula, transfer ganache to prepared pan and set aside at room temperature for 2 hours. Cover pan and transfer to refrigerator; chill for at least 2 hours. (Ganache can be stored, refrigerated, for up to 2 days.)

4. FOR THE COATING: Sift cocoa and sugar through fine-mesh strainer into large bowl. Sift again into large cake pan and set aside.

5. Gripping overhanging parchment, lift ganache from pan. Cut ganache into sixty-four 1-inch squares (8 rows by 8 rows). (If ganache cracks during slicing, let sit at room temperature for 5 to 10 minutes and then proceed.) Dust hands lightly with cocoa mixture to prevent ganache from sticking and roll each square into ball. Transfer balls to cake pan with cocoa mixture and roll to evenly coat. Lightly shake truffles in hand over pan to remove excess coating. Transfer coated truffles to airtight container and repeat until all ganache squares are rolled and coated. Cover container and refrigerate for at least 2 hours or up to 1 week. Let truffles sit at room temperature for 5 to 10 minutes before serving.

Hazelnut-Mocha Truffles

Substitute 2 tablespoons Frangelico (hazelnut-flavored liqueur) and 1 tablespoon espresso powder for vanilla. For coating, omit confectioners' sugar and use enough cocoa to coat hands while shaping truffles. Roll shaped truffles in 1½ cups finely chopped toasted hazelnuts.

BEHIND THE SCENES

ERIN KNOWS BEST

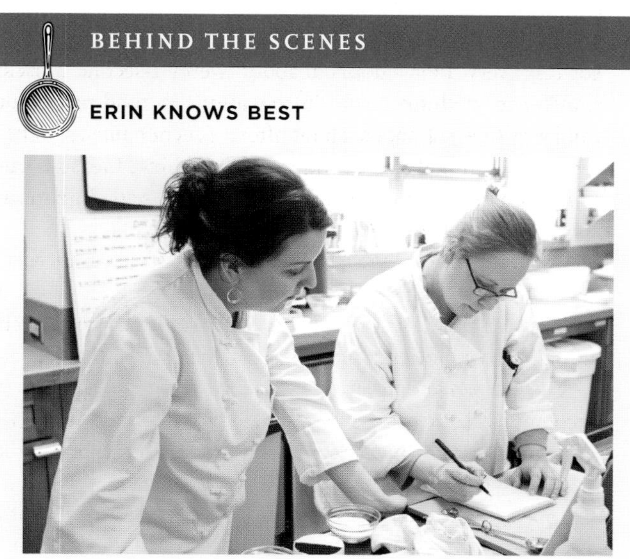

Erin McMurrer is our test kitchen director. She oversees all the recipe testing and development in the test kitchen, but one of her most important jobs is to keep an eye on new test cooks to make sure they're keeping up with test kitchen standards. And like the proverbial mother with eyes in the back of her head, Erin doesn't miss much. You'll often hear her issuing gentle admonitions to new test cooks throughout the day. Where do the test cooks sometimes fall short? Cutting vegetables into perfect dice? Filleting fish properly? Efficiently frenching racks of lamb? Not even close. They sometimes neglect to thoroughly scrape out the contents of their measuring cups. Other than the waste factor, there is a second important reason Erin wants to make sure all the ingredients make it into the mixing bowl—it can often make or break a recipe.

To prove this point, we baked two batches of molasses spice cookies. In one batch we used a rubber spatula to scrape every last bit of molasses (an especially viscous ingredient) from the measuring cup and in the other, we simply poured the molasses from the cup, which left some residue behind (nearly 2 tablespoons!). The results were remarkable. The cookies made with less molasses were less flavorful and they were also dry and cakey as opposed to the cookies using the full amount of molasses, which were richly flavored, moist, and chewy.

So whether you're a test cook or home cook, heed Erin's advice and take a few extra minutes to scrape out your measuring cups—it makes a difference.

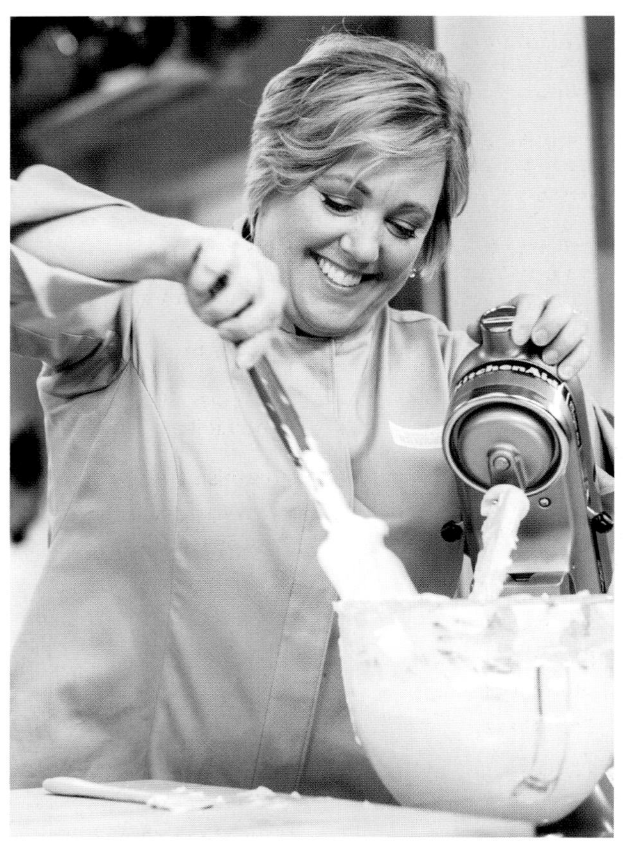

CHAPTER 23

A PIECE OF CAKE

OLIVE OIL CAKE

WHY THIS RECIPE WORKS: We wanted our simple olive oil cake to have a light yet plush crumb, with a subtle but noticeable olive oil flavor. Whipping the sugar with whole eggs, rather than just the whites, produced a fine texture that was airy but sturdy enough to support the olive oil–rich batter. To emphasize the defining flavor, we opted for a good-quality extra-virgin olive oil and accentuated its fruitiness with a tiny bit of lemon zest. Sugar created a crackly topping that added a touch of sweetness and sophistication.

Olive Oil Cake

SERVES 8 TO 10

For the best flavor, use a fresh, high-quality extra-virgin olive oil. If your springform pan is prone to leaking, place a rimmed baking sheet on the oven floor to catch any drips. Leftover cake can be wrapped in plastic wrap and stored at room temperature for up to three days.

- 1¾ cups (8¾ ounces) all-purpose flour
- 1 teaspoon baking powder
- ¾ teaspoon salt
- 3 large eggs
- 1¼ cups (8¾ ounces) plus 2 tablespoons sugar
- ¼ teaspoon grated lemon zest
- ¾ cup extra-virgin olive oil
- ¾ cup milk

1. Adjust oven rack to middle position and heat oven to 350 degrees. Grease 9-inch springform pan. Whisk flour, baking powder, and salt together in bowl.

2. Using stand mixer fitted with whisk attachment, whip eggs on medium speed until foamy, about 1 minute. Add 1¼ cups sugar and lemon zest, increase speed to high, and whip until mixture is fluffy and pale yellow, about 3 minutes. Reduce speed to medium and, with mixer running, slowly pour in oil. Mix until oil is fully incorporated, about 1 minute. Add half of flour mixture and mix on low speed until incorporated, about 1 minute, scraping down bowl as needed. Add milk and mix until combined, about 30 seconds. Add remaining flour mixture and mix until just incorporated, about 1 minute, scraping down bowl as needed.

3. Transfer batter to prepared pan; sprinkle remaining 2 tablespoons sugar over entire surface. Bake until cake is deep golden brown and toothpick inserted in center comes out with few crumbs attached, 40 to 45 minutes. Transfer pan to wire rack and let cool for 15 minutes. Remove side of pan and let cake cool completely, about 1½ hours. Cut into wedges and serve.

ANGEL FOOD CAKE

WHY THIS RECIPE WORKS: At its heavenly best, an angel food cake should be tall and perfectly shaped, have a snowy-white, tender crumb, and be encased in a thin, delicate golden crust. The difficulty with making a great angel food cake is that it requires a delicate balance of ingredients and proper cooking techniques. In particular, since this cake is leavened only with beaten egg whites, it is critical that you whip them correctly. Over beaten egg whites produce a flatter cake.

First, we found it key to create a stable egg-white base, starting the whites at medium-low speed just to break them up into a froth and increasing the speed to medium-high speed to form soft, billowy mounds. Next, the sugar should be added, a tablespoon at a time. Once all the sugar is added, the whites become shiny and form soft peaks when the beater is lifted. A delicate touch is required when incorporating the remaining ingredients, such as the flour, which should be sifted over the batter and gently folded in. Angel food cakes are baked in a tube pan. We like to use a tube pan with a removable bottom but a pan without one can be lined with parchment paper. We avoid greasing the sides of the pan so that the cake can climb up and cling to the sides as it bakes—a greased pan will produce a disappointingly short cake. Follow our instructions and you'll be rewarded with the perfect tall, light yet firm angel food cake.

Angel Food Cake

SERVES 10 TO 12

If your tube pan has a removable bottom, you do not need to line it with parchment. Angel food cake can be served plain or dusted with confectioners' sugar.

- 1½ cups (10½ ounces) sugar
- ¾ cup (3 ounces) cake flour
- 12 large egg whites, at room temperature
- 1 teaspoon cream of tartar
- ¼ teaspoon table salt
- 1½ teaspoons juice from 1 lemon
- 1½ teaspoons vanilla extract
- ½ teaspoon almond extract

1. Adjust an oven rack to the lower-middle position and heat the oven to 325 degrees. Line the bottom of a 16-cup tube pan with parchment paper but do not grease. Whisk ¾ cup of the sugar and the flour together in a medium bowl.

2. In a stand mixer fitted with the whisk attachment, whip the egg whites and cream of tartar together on medium-low speed until foamy, about 1 minute. Increase the mixer speed to medium-high and whip the whites to soft, billowy mounds, about 1 minute. Gradually whip in the salt and remaining ¾ cup sugar, 1 tablespoon at a time, about 1 minute. Continue to whip the whites until they are shiny and form soft peaks, 1 to 3 minutes.

3. Whisk the lemon juice and extracts into the whipped whites by hand. Sift ¼ cup of the flour mixture over the top of the whites, then gently fold to combine with a large rubber spatula until just a few streaks of flour remain. Repeat with the remaining flour mixture, ¼ cup at a time.

4. Scrape the batter into the prepared pan and smooth the top. Wipe any drops of batter off the sides of the pan and lightly tap the pan against the countertop two or three times to settle the batter. Bake the cake until golden brown and the top springs back when pressed firmly, 50 to 60 minutes.

5. Invert the tube pan over a large metal kitchen funnel or the neck of a sturdy bottle (or, if your pan has "feet" that rise above the top edge of the pan, simply let the cake rest upside down). Cool the cake completely, upside down, 2 to 3 hours.

6. Run a small knife around the edge of the cake to loosen. Gently tap the pan upside down on the countertop to release the cake. Peel off the parchment paper, turn the cake right side up onto a serving platter, and serve.

CHOCOLATE BUNDT CAKE

WHY THIS RECIPE WORKS: A Bundt cake is the pinnacle of cake-baking simplicity. With its decorative shape, this cake doesn't require frosting or fussy finishing techniques. We wanted a cake that would deliver that moment of pure chocolate ecstasy with the first bite—a chocolate Bundt cake that tastes every bit as good as it looks, with a fine crumb, moist texture, and rich chocolate flavor.

We intensified the chocolate flavor by using both bittersweet chocolate and natural cocoa and dissolving them in boiling water, which "bloomed" their flavor. We used sour cream and brown sugar instead of white to add moisture and flavor. Finally, we further enhanced flavor with a little espresso powder and a generous amount of vanilla extract, both of which complemented the floral nuances of the chocolate.

Rich Chocolate Bundt Cake

SERVES 12

We prefer natural cocoa here because Dutch-processed cocoa will result in a compromised rise. For an accurate measurement of boiling water, bring a kettle of water to a boil, then measure out the desired amount. The cake can be served with just a dusting of confectioners' sugar but is easily made more impressive with lightly sweetened whipped cream and raspberries.

- 12 tablespoons (1½ sticks) unsalted butter, softened, plus 1 tablespoon, melted, for the pan
- ¾ cup natural cocoa powder, plus 1 tablespoon for the pan (see note)
- 6 ounces bittersweet chocolate, chopped coarse
- 1 teaspoon instant espresso powder (optional)
- ¾ cup boiling water (see note)
- 1 cup sour cream, at room temperature
- 1¾ cups (8¾ ounces) unbleached all-purpose flour
- 1 teaspoon table salt
- 1 teaspoon baking soda
- 2 cups packed (14 ounces) light brown sugar
- 1 tablespoon vanilla extract
- 5 large eggs, at room temperature
- Confectioners' sugar, for dusting (see note)

1. Stir together the 1 tablespoon melted butter and 1 tablespoon of the cocoa in a small bowl until a paste forms. Using a pastry brush, coat all the interior surfaces of a standard 12-cup Bundt pan. (If the mixture becomes too thick to brush on, microwave it for 10 to 20 seconds, or until warm and softened.) Adjust an oven rack to the lower-middle position and heat the oven to 350 degrees.

2. Combine the remaining ¾ cup cocoa, the chocolate, and espresso powder (if using) in a medium heatproof bowl. Pour the boiling water over and whisk until smooth. Cool to room temperature; then whisk in the sour cream. Whisk the flour, salt, and baking soda in a second bowl to combine.

3. In a stand mixer fitted with the paddle attachment, beat the remaining 12 tablespoons butter, the brown sugar, and vanilla on medium-high speed until pale and fluffy, about 3 minutes. Reduce the speed to medium and add the eggs one at a time, mixing for about 30 seconds after each addition and scraping down the bowl with a rubber spatula after the first two additions. Reduce to medium-low speed (the batter may appear separated); add about one-third of the flour mixture and half of the chocolate mixture and mix until just incorporated, about 20 seconds. Scrape the bowl and repeat using half of the remaining flour mixture and all of the remaining chocolate mixture; add the remaining flour mixture and beat until just incorporated, about 10 seconds. Scrape the bowl and mix on medium-low speed until the batter is thoroughly combined, about 30 seconds.

4. Transfer the batter to the prepared pan, smoothing the top with a rubber spatula. Lightly tap the pan against the countertop two or three times to settle the batter. Bake until a toothpick inserted into the center comes out with a few crumbs attached, 45 to 50 minutes, rotating the pan halfway through the baking time. Cool the cake in the pan on a wire rack for 10 minutes, then invert the cake directly onto the wire rack; cool to room temperature, about 2 hours. Dust with confectioners' sugar, transfer to a serving platter, cut into slices, and serve.

CIDER-GLAZED APPLE BUNDT CAKE

WHY THIS RECIPE WORKS: We managed to pack the equivalent of 4½ pounds of fruit into our apple cake and its glaze. Baking the thick, dense batter in a Bundt pan rather than a round pan allowed heat to flow through the center of the cake, ensuring that it baked evenly edge to edge. Mixing reduced apple cider into the batter, brushing it onto the cake, and using it to flavor the icing drizzled on top provided layers of pervasive apple flavor. Minimizing the spices allowed true apple flavor to shine.

Cider-Glazed Apple Bundt Cake

SERVES 12 TO 16

For the sake of efficiency, we recommend that you begin boiling the cider before assembling the rest of the ingredients. Reducing the cider to exactly 1 cup is important to the success of this recipe. If you accidentally over-reduce the cider, make up the difference with water. Baking spray that contains flour can be used to grease and flour the pan. We like the tartness of Granny Smith apples in this recipe, but any variety of apple will work. You may shred the apples with the large shredding disc of a food processor or with the large holes of a box grater.

- 4 cups apple cider
- 3¾ cups (18¾ ounces) all-purpose flour
- 1½ teaspoons salt
- 1½ teaspoons baking powder
- ½ teaspoon baking soda
- ¾ teaspoon ground cinnamon
- ¼ teaspoon ground allspice
- ¾ cup (3 ounces) confectioners' sugar
- 16 tablespoons (2 sticks) unsalted butter, melted
- 1½ cups packed (10½ ounces) dark brown sugar
- 3 large eggs
- 2 teaspoons vanilla extract
- 1½ pounds Granny Smith apples, peeled, cored, and shredded (3 cups)

1. Boil cider in 12-inch skillet over high heat until reduced to 1 cup, 20 to 25 minutes. While cider is reducing, adjust oven rack to middle position and heat oven to 350 degrees. Grease and flour 12-cup nonstick Bundt pan. Whisk flour, salt, baking powder, baking soda, cinnamon, and allspice together in large bowl until combined. Place confectioners' sugar in small bowl.

2. Add 2 tablespoons reduced cider to confectioners' sugar, and whisk to form smooth icing. Cover icing with plastic wrap and set aside. Pour ½ cup reduced cider into large bowl. Set remaining 6 tablespoons reduced cider aside to brush over baked cake.

3. Add butter, brown sugar, eggs, and vanilla to ½ cup cider reduction and whisk until smooth. Pour cider mixture over flour mixture, and stir with rubber spatula until almost fully combined (some streaks of flour will remain). Stir in apples and any accumulated juices until evenly distributed. Transfer mixture to prepared Bundt pan and smooth top. Bake until skewer inserted in center of cake comes out clean, 55 to 65 minutes.

4. Transfer pan to wire rack set in rimmed baking sheet. Brush exposed surface of cake lightly with 1 tablespoon reserved cider reduction. Allow cake to cool for 10 minutes. Invert cake onto wire rack. Brush top and sides with remaining 5 tablespoons reserved cider reduction. Cool cake for 20 minutes. Stir icing to loosen, and drizzle over cake. Cool cake completely, at least 2 hours, before serving. (Leftover cake may be wrapped loosely and stored at room temperature for up to three days.)

MARBLED BLUEBERRY BUNDT CAKE

WHY THIS RECIPE WORKS: Oversize, bland cultivated blueberries wreak havoc in a cake. The berries refuse to stay suspended in the batter and burst into bland, soggy pockets in the heat of the oven. We solved these problems by pureeing the fruit, seasoning it with sugar and lemon, and bumping up its natural pectin content with low-sugar pectin for a thickened, fresh-tasting filling that can be swirled throughout the cake.

Marbled Blueberry Bundt Cake

SERVES 12

Spray the pan well in step 1 to prevent sticking. If you don't have baking spray with flour, mix 1 tablespoon melted butter and 1 tablespoon flour into a paste and brush inside the pan. For fruit pectin we recommend both Sure-Jell for Less or No Sugar Needed Recipes and Ball RealFruit Low or No-Sugar Needed Pectin. If using frozen berries, thaw them before blending in step 3. This cake can be served plain or with Lemon Glaze or Cinnamon Whipped Cream (recipes follow).

CAKE

- 3 cups (15 ounces) all-purpose flour
- 1½ teaspoons baking powder
- ¾ teaspoon baking soda
- 1 teaspoon salt
- ½ teaspoon ground cinnamon
- ¾ cup buttermilk
- 2 teaspoons grated lemon zest plus 3 tablespoons juice
- 2 teaspoons vanilla extract
- 3 large eggs plus 1 large yolk, room temperature
- 18 tablespoons (2¼ sticks) unsalted butter, softened
- 2 cups (14 ounces) sugar

FILLING

- ¾ cup (5¼ ounces) sugar
- 3 tablespoons low- or no-sugar-needed fruit pectin
- Pinch salt
- 10 ounces (2 cups) fresh or thawed frozen blueberries
- 1 teaspoon grated lemon zest plus 1 tablespoon juice

1. FOR THE CAKE: Adjust oven rack to lower-middle position and heat oven to 325 degrees. Heavily spray 12-cup nonstick Bundt pan with baking spray with flour. Whisk flour, baking powder, baking soda, salt, and cinnamon together in large bowl. Whisk buttermilk, lemon zest and juice, and vanilla together in medium bowl. Gently whisk eggs and yolk to combine in third bowl.

2. Using stand mixer fitted with paddle, beat butter and sugar on medium-high speed until pale and fluffy, about 3 minutes, scraping down bowl as needed. Reduce speed to medium and beat in half of eggs until incorporated, about 15 seconds. Repeat with remaining eggs, scraping down bowl after incorporating. Reduce speed to low and add one-third of flour mixture, followed by half of buttermilk mixture, mixing until just incorporated after each addition, about 5 seconds. Repeat using half of remaining flour mixture and all of remaining buttermilk mixture. Scrape down bowl, add remaining flour mixture, and mix at medium-low speed until batter is thoroughly combined, about 15 seconds. Remove bowl from mixer and fold batter once or twice with rubber spatula to incorporate any remaining flour. Cover bowl with plastic wrap and set aside while preparing filling (batter will inflate a bit).

3. FOR THE FILLING: Whisk sugar, pectin, and salt together in small saucepan. Process blueberries in blender until mostly smooth, about 1 minute. Transfer ¼ cup puree and lemon zest to saucepan with sugar mixture and stir to thoroughly combine. Heat sugar-blueberry mixture over medium heat until just simmering, about 3 minutes, stirring frequently to dissolve sugar and pectin. Transfer mixture to medium bowl and let cool for 5 minutes. Add remaining puree and lemon juice to cooled mixture and whisk to combine. Let sit until slightly set, about 8 minutes.

4. Spoon half of batter into prepared pan and smooth top. Using back of spoon, create ½-inch-deep channel in center of batter. Spoon half of filling into channel. Using butter knife or small offset spatula, thoroughly swirl filling into batter (there should be no large pockets of filling remaining). Repeat swirling step with remaining batter and filling.

5. Bake until top is golden brown and skewer inserted in center comes out with no crumbs attached, 60 to 70 minutes. Let cake cool in pan on wire rack for 10 minutes, then invert cake directly onto wire rack. Let cake cool for at least 3 hours before serving.

Lemon Glaze

MAKES ABOUT 2 CUPS

This glaze can be used with Marbled Blueberry Bundt Cake or another Bundt cake.

- 3–4 tablespoons lemon juice (2 lemons)
- 2 cups (8 ounces) confectioners' sugar

1. While cake is baking, whisk together 3 tablespoons lemon juice and sugar until smooth, gradually adding more lemon juice as needed until glaze is thick but still pourable (mixture should leave faint trail across bottom of mixing bowl when drizzled from whisk).

2. After cake has been removed from pan and inverted onto wire rack set in baking sheet, pour half of glaze over warm cake and let cool for 1 hour. Pour remaining glaze evenly over cake and continue to let cool to room temperature, at least 2 hours longer.

Cinnamon Whipped Cream

MAKES ABOUT 2 CUPS

For the best texture, whip the cream until soft peaks just form. Do not over whip.

- 1 cup heavy cream
- 2 tablespoons confectioners' sugar
- ¼ teaspoon ground cinnamon
- Pinch salt

Using stand mixer fitted with whisk, whip all ingredients on medium-low speed until foamy, about 1 minute. Increase speed to high and whip until soft peaks form, 1 to 3 minutes.

LEMON BUNDT CAKE

WHY THIS RECIPE WORKS: Lemons are tart, brash, and aromatic. Why, then, is it so hard to capture their assertive flavor in a straightforward Bundt cake? The flavor of lemon juice is drastically muted when exposed to the heat of an oven, and its acidity can wreak havoc on the delicate nature of baked goods. We wanted to develop a Bundt cake with potent lemon flavor without ruining its texture.

We developed a battery of tests challenging classic lemon Bundt cake ingredient proportions, finally deciding to increase the butter and to replace the milk with buttermilk. We also found that creaming was necessary to achieve a light and even crumb. But we still needed to maximize the lemon flavor; we couldn't get the flavor we needed from lemon juice alone without using so much that the cake fell apart when sliced. We turned to zest and found that three lemons' worth gave the cake a perfumed lemon flavor, though we needed to give the zest a brief soak in lemon juice to eliminate its fibrous texture. The final challenge was the glaze, and a simple mixture of lemon juice, buttermilk, and confectioners' sugar made the grade.

Lemon Bundt Cake

SERVES 12

The cake has a light, fluffy texture when eaten the day it is baked, but if well wrapped and held at room temperature overnight its texture becomes more dense—like that of pound cake—the following day.

CAKE

- 18 tablespoons (2¼ sticks) unsalted butter, at room temperature, plus 1 tablespoon, melted, for the pan
- 3 cups (15 ounces) unbleached all-purpose flour, plus 1 tablespoon for the pan
- 3 tablespoons grated zest plus 3 tablespoons juice from 3 lemons
- 1 teaspoon baking powder
- ½ teaspoon baking soda
- 1 teaspoon table salt
- ¾ cup buttermilk
- 1 teaspoon vanilla extract
- 3 large eggs plus 1 large egg yolk, at room temperature
- 2 cups (14 ounces) granulated sugar

GLAZE

- 2 cups (8 ounces) confectioners' sugar
- 2–3 tablespoons juice from 1 lemon
- 1 tablespoon buttermilk

1. FOR THE CAKE: Adjust an oven rack to the lower-middle position and heat the oven to 350 degrees. Stir together the 1 tablespoon melted butter and 1 tablespoon of the flour in a small bowl until a paste forms. Using a pastry brush, coat all the interior surfaces of a standard 12-cup Bundt pan. (If the mixture becomes too thick to brush on, microwave it for 10 to 20 seconds, or until warm and softened.) Mince the lemon zest to a fine paste (you should have about 2 tablespoons). Combine the zest and lemon juice in a small bowl; set aside to soften, 10 to 15 minutes.

2. Whisk the remaining 3 cups flour, the baking powder, baking soda, and salt in a large bowl. Combine the lemon juice mixture, buttermilk, and vanilla in a medium bowl. In a small bowl, gently whisk the whole eggs and yolk to combine.

In a stand mixer fitted with the paddle attachment, beat the remaining 18 tablespoons butter and the granulated sugar at medium-high speed until pale and fluffy, about 3 minutes. Reduce to medium speed and add half of the eggs, mixing until incorporated, about 15 seconds; scrape down the bowl with a rubber spatula. Repeat with the remaining eggs; scrape down the bowl again. Reduce to low speed; add about one-third of the flour mixture, followed by half of the buttermilk mixture, mixing until just incorporated after each addition (about 5 seconds). Repeat using half of the remaining flour mixture and all of the remaining buttermilk mixture. Scrape down the bowl and add the remaining flour mixture; mix at medium-low speed until the batter is thoroughly combined, about 15 seconds. Transfer the batter to the prepared pan, smoothing the top with a rubber spatula. Lightly tap the pan against the countertop two or three times to settle the batter.

3. Bake until the top is golden brown and a toothpick inserted into the center comes out with no crumbs attached, 45 to 50 minutes, rotating the pan halfway through the baking time.

4. FOR THE GLAZE: While the cake is baking, whisk the confectioners' sugar, 2 tablespoons of the lemon juice, and the buttermilk until smooth, adding more lemon juice gradually as needed until the glaze is thick but still pourable. Cool the cake in the pan on a wire rack set over a baking sheet for 10 minutes, then invert the cake directly onto the rack. Pour half of the glaze over the warm cake and cool for 1 hour; pour the remaining glaze evenly over the top of the cake and continue to cool to room temperature, at least 2 hours. Cut into slices and serve.

LEMON POUND CAKE

WHY THIS RECIPE WORKS: Pound cakes often turn out spongy, rubbery, heavy, and dry—and lemon pound cakes often lack true lemon flavor. We wanted to produce a superior pound cake (fine-crumbed, rich, moist, and buttery) while making the process as simple and foolproof as possible.

After less-than-successful results with a stand mixer and a hand mixer, we turned to the food processor to mix our cake. It ensured a perfect emulsification of the eggs, sugar, and melted butter (we found that a blender worked, too). Cake flour produced a tender crumb, but our cake was still a bit heavy. We fixed matters with the addition of baking powder, which increased lift and produced a consistent, fine crumb. Finally, in addition to mixing lemon zest into the cake batter, we glazed the finished cake with lemon sugar syrup—but first we poked holes all over the cake to ensure that the tangy, sweet glaze infused the cake with a blast of bright lemon flavor.

Lemon Pound Cake

MAKES ONE 8-INCH LOAF, SERVING 8

You can use a blender instead of a food processor to mix the batter. To add the butter, remove the center cap of the lid so it can be drizzled into the whirling blender with minimal splattering. This batter looks almost like a thick pancake batter and is very fluid.

CAKE

- 16 tablespoons (2 sticks) unsalted butter, plus 1 tablespoon, softened, for the pan
- 1½ cups (6 ounces) cake flour, plus 1 tablespoon for the pan
- 1 teaspoon baking powder
- ½ teaspoon table salt
- 1¼ cups (8¾ ounces) sugar
- 2 tablespoons grated zest plus 2 teaspoons juice from 1 lemon
- 4 large eggs, at room temperature
- 1½ teaspoons vanilla extract

GLAZE

- ½ cup (3½ ounces) sugar
- ¼ cup juice from 2 lemons

1. FOR THE CAKE: Adjust an oven rack to the middle position and heat the oven to 350 degrees. Grease an 8½ by 4½-inch loaf pan with 1 tablespoon of the softened butter; dust with 1 tablespoon of the flour, tapping out the excess. In a medium bowl, whisk together the remaining 1½ cups flour, the baking powder, and salt; set aside.

2. Melt the remaining 16 tablespoons butter in a small saucepan over medium heat. Whisk the melted butter thoroughly to reincorporate any separated milk solids.

3. In a food processor, pulse the sugar and zest until combined, about 5 pulses. Add the lemon juice, eggs, and vanilla; process until combined, about 5 seconds. With the machine running, add the melted butter through the feed tube in a steady stream (this should take about 20 seconds). Transfer the mixture to a large bowl. Sift the flour mixture over the egg mixture in three additions, whisking gently after each addition until just combined.

4. Pour the batter into the prepared pan and bake for 15 minutes. Reduce the oven temperature to 325 degrees and continue to bake until deep golden brown and a toothpick inserted in the center comes out clean, about 35 minutes, rotating the pan halfway through the baking time. Cool in the pan for 10 minutes, then turn onto a wire rack. Poke the top and sides of the cake throughout with a toothpick. Cool to room temperature, at least 1 hour. (The cooled cake can be wrapped tightly in plastic wrap and stored at room temperature for up to 5 days.)

5. FOR THE GLAZE: While the cake is cooling, bring the sugar and lemon juice to a boil in a small saucepan, stirring occasionally to dissolve the sugar. Reduce the heat to low and simmer until thickened slightly, about 2 minutes. Brush the top and sides of the cake with the glaze and cool to room temperature.

APPLESAUCE CAKE

WHY THIS RECIPE WORKS: Applesauce cakes run the gamut from dense, chunky fruitcakes to gummy "health" cakes without much flavor. We wanted a moist and tender cake that actually tasted like its namesake.

It was easy to achieve the looser, more casual crumb that is best suited to a rustic snack cake. Since this texture is similar to that of quick breads and muffins, we used the same technique, i.e., mixing the wet ingredients separately and then gently adding the dry ingredients by hand. The harder challenge was to develop more apple flavor—simply adding more applesauce made for a gummy cake and fresh apples added too much moisture. But two other sources worked well. Apple cider, reduced to a syrup, contributed a pleasing sweetness and a slight tang without excess moisture. And plumping dried apples in the cider while it was reducing added even more apple taste without making the cake chunky. With such great apple flavor, we didn't want the cake to be too sweet or rich, so we rejected the idea of topping the cake with a glaze or frosting. But we found we liked the modicum of textural contrast provided by a simple sprinkling of spiced granulated sugar.

Applesauce Snack Cake

SERVES 9

This recipe can be easily doubled and baked in a 13 by 9-inch baking dish. If doubling the recipe, give the cider and dried apple mixture about 20 minutes to reduce, and bake the cake for about 45 minutes. The cake is very moist, so it is best to err on the side of overdone when testing its doneness. The test kitchen prefers the rich flavor of cider, but apple juice can be substituted.

- 1 cup apple cider (see note)
- ¾ cup (2 ounces) dried apples, cut into ½-inch pieces
- 1½ cups (7½ ounces) unbleached all-purpose flour
- 1 teaspoon baking soda
- ⅔ cup (4⅔ ounces) sugar
- ½ teaspoon ground cinnamon
- ¼ teaspoon ground nutmeg
- ⅛ teaspoon ground cloves
- 1 cup unsweetened applesauce, at room temperature
- 1 large egg, at room temperature, lightly beaten
- ½ teaspoon table salt
- 8 tablespoons (1 stick) unsalted butter, melted and cooled slightly
- 1 teaspoon vanilla extract

1. Adjust an oven rack to the middle position and heat the oven to 325 degrees. Cut a 16-inch length of parchment paper or foil and fold lengthwise to a 7-inch width. Grease an 8-inch square baking dish and fit the parchment into the dish, pushing it into the corners and up the sides; allow the excess to overhang the edges of the dish.

2. Bring the cider and dried apples to a simmer in a small saucepan over medium heat; cook until the liquid evaporates and the mixture appears dry, about 15 minutes. Cool to room temperature.

3. Whisk the flour and baking soda in a medium bowl to combine; set aside. In a second medium bowl, whisk the sugar, cinnamon, nutmeg, and cloves together. Measure 2 tablespoons of the sugar-spice mixture into a small bowl and set aside for the topping.

4. In a food processor, process the cooled dried-apple mixture and applesauce until smooth, 20 to 30 seconds, scraping down the sides of the bowl as needed; set aside. Whisk the egg and salt in a large bowl to combine. Add the sugar-spice mixture and whisk continuously until well combined and light colored, about 20 seconds. Add the butter in three additions, whisking after each addition. Add the applesauce mixture and vanilla and whisk to combine. Add the flour mixture to the wet ingredients; using a rubber spatula, fold gently until just combined and evenly moistened.

5. Transfer the batter to the prepared pan, smoothing the top with a rubber spatula. Lightly tap the pan against the countertop two or three times to settle the batter. Sprinkle the reserved 2 tablespoons sugar-spice mixture evenly over the batter. Bake until a toothpick inserted into the center comes out clean, 35 to 40 minutes, rotating the pan halfway through the baking time. Cool the cake to room temperature in the pan on a wire rack, about 2 hours. Remove the cake from the pan by lifting the parchment overhang and transfer to a cutting board. Cut the cake into squares and serve.

OATMEAL CAKE

WHY THIS RECIPE WORKS: While we love the broiled icing on this classic snack cake, we find that the cake itself is often dense, gummy, and bland. And the icing isn't always perfect, either; it can be saccharine sweet and tend toward greasiness. We wanted a moist, not dense, cake with buttery undertones topped by a broiled icing that features chewy coconut, crunchy nuts, and a butterscotch-like flavor.

We solved the problem of denseness by replacing some of the brown sugar with granulated sugar—less moist than brown sugar, granulated sugar lightened the cake's texture. We also reduced the proportion of flour to oats, using the minimum amount of flour needed to keep the cake from collapsing into crumbs. The cake was now sufficiently light, and its more moderate sweetness made it better suited to a sugary icing. We still had to tackle the gumminess, however, which was created partly by soaking the oats in water; the hydrated oats were a sticky mess when we stirred them into the batter. But simply folding in dried oats didn't work—they never fully hydrated during baking, and tasted raw and chewy in the finished cake. The answer proved to be soaking the oats in room-temperature rather than boiling water, minimizing the amount of released starch. As for the type of oats, quick-cooking worked best. Unlike the cake, the icing only required a few tweaks. Cutting back on the sugar brought the sweetness in line, using melted butter (rather than creaming the butter into the sugar) simplified the recipe, and adding a splash of milk made the icing more pliable. Keeping the cake about 9 inches from the heating element produced the "crun-chewy" texture we wanted.

Oatmeal Cake with Broiled Icing

SERVES 9

Do not use old-fashioned or instant oats for this recipe. Be sure to use a metal baking dish; glass pans are not recommended when broiling. If you have a drawer-style broiler (underneath the oven), position the rack as far as possible from the broiler element and monitor the icing carefully as it cooks in step 5. A vertical sawing motion with a serrated knife works best for cutting through the crunchy icing and tender crumb.

CAKE

- 1 cup (3 ounces) quick-cooking oats (see note)
- ¾ cup water, at room temperature
- ¾ cup (3¾ ounces) unbleached all-purpose flour
- ½ teaspoon baking soda
- ½ teaspoon baking powder
- ½ teaspoon table salt
- ¼ teaspoon ground cinnamon
- ⅛ teaspoon ground nutmeg
- 4 tablespoons (½ stick) unsalted butter, softened
- ½ cup (3½ ounces) granulated sugar
- ½ cup packed (3½ ounces) light brown sugar
- 1 large egg, at room temperature
- ½ teaspoon vanilla extract

BROILED ICING

- ¼ cup packed (1¾ ounces) light brown sugar
- 3 tablespoons unsalted butter, melted and cooled
- 3 tablespoons milk
- ¾ cup sweetened shredded coconut
- ½ cup (2½ ounces) pecans, chopped

1. FOR THE CAKE: Adjust an oven rack to the middle position and heat the oven to 350 degrees. Cut two 16-inch lengths of aluminum foil and fold both lengthwise to 5-inch widths. Grease an 8-inch square metal baking dish. Fit the foil pieces into the baking dish, one overlapping the other, pushing them into the corners and up the sides of the pan; allow the excess to overhang the pan edges. Spray the foil lightly with vegetable oil spray.

2. Combine the oats and water in a medium bowl and let sit until the water is absorbed, about 5 minutes. In a second medium bowl, whisk the flour, baking soda, baking powder, salt, cinnamon, and nutmeg together.

3. In the bowl of a stand mixer fitted with the paddle attachment, beat the butter and sugars on medium speed until combined and the mixture has the consistency of damp sand, 2 to 4 minutes, scraping down the bowl with a rubber spatula halfway through mixing. Add the egg and vanilla; beat until combined, about 30 seconds. Add the flour mixture in two additions and mix until just incorporated, about 30 seconds. Add the soaked oats and mix until combined, about 15 seconds.

4. Give the batter a final stir with a rubber spatula to make sure it is thoroughly combined. Transfer the batter to the prepared pan and lightly tap it against the countertop two or three times to settle the batter; smooth the surface with the spatula. Bake the cake until a toothpick inserted into the center comes out with a few crumbs attached, 30 to 35 minutes, rotating the pan halfway through the baking time. Cool the cake slightly in the pan, at least 10 minutes.

5. FOR THE BROILED ICING: While the cake cools, adjust an oven rack about 9 inches from the broiler element and heat the broiler. In a medium bowl, whisk the brown sugar, melted butter, and milk together; stir in the coconut and pecans. Spread the mixture evenly over the warm cake. Broil until the topping is bubbling and golden, 3 to 5 minutes.

6. Cool the cake in the pan for 1 hour. To remove the cake from the pan, pick up the overhanging edges of the foil and transfer the cake to a platter. Gently push the side of the cake with a knife and remove the foil, one piece at a time. Cut the cake into squares and serve.

PEAR-WALNUT UPSIDE-DOWN CAKE

WHY THIS RECIPE WORKS: Pears are sometimes referred to as the queen of fruit, but, despite their subtle floral flavor and graceful shape, their popularity in desserts has always been a distant second to apples. We were determined to create an elegant cake that really showcased the pears. We settled on Bosc pears; since they have dense flesh, they hold their shape after baking. Cutting the pears into wedges allowed them to be baked raw but still be manageable to eat with the cake. Instead of a sweet, somewhat dense yellow cake, we made a walnut-based cake, which was light but sturdy, earthy-tasting and less sweet, and visually attractive. Lining the cake pan (a light-colored pan helped the cake cook more evenly) with parchment and removing the cake from

the pan after 15 minutes—good practice for any upside-down cake—allowed the top to set while preventing the bottom of the cake from steaming and turning soggy.

Pear-Walnut Upside-Down Cake

SERVES 8 TO 10

We strongly recommend baking this cake in a light-colored cake pan with sides that are at least 2 inches tall. If using a dark-colored pan, start checking for doneness at 1 hour, and note that the cake may dome in the center and the topping may become too sticky. Serve with crème fraîche or lightly sweetened whipped cream.

TOPPING

- 4 tablespoons unsalted butter, melted
- ½ cup packed (3½ ounces) dark brown sugar
- 2 teaspoons cornstarch
- ⅛ teaspoon salt
- 3 ripe but firm Bosc pears (8 ounces each)

CAKE

- 1 cup walnuts, toasted
- ½ cup (2½ ounces) all-purpose flour
- ½ teaspoon salt
- ¼ teaspoon baking powder
- ⅛ teaspoon baking soda
- 3 large eggs
- 1 cup (7 ounces) granulated sugar
- 4 tablespoons unsalted butter, melted
- ¼ cup vegetable oil

1. FOR THE TOPPING: Adjust oven rack to middle position and heat oven to 300 degrees. Grease 9-inch round cake pan and line bottom with parchment paper. Pour melted butter over bottom of pan and swirl to evenly coat. Combine sugar, cornstarch, and salt in small bowl and sprinkle evenly over melted butter.

2. Peel, halve, and core pears. Set aside 1 pear half and reserve for other use. Cut remaining 5 pear halves into 4 wedges each. Arrange pears in circular pattern around cake pan with tapered ends pointing inward. Arrange two smallest pear wedges in center.

3. FOR THE CAKE: Pulse walnuts, flour, salt, baking powder, and baking soda in food processor until walnuts are finely ground, 8 to 10 pulses. Transfer walnut mixture to bowl.

4. Process eggs and sugar in now-empty processor until very pale yellow, about 2 minutes. With processor running, add melted butter and oil in steady stream until incorporated. Add walnut mixture and pulse to combine, 4 to 5 pulses. Pour batter evenly over pears (some pear may show through; cake will bake up over fruit).

5. Bake until center of cake is set and bounces back when gently pressed and toothpick inserted in center comes out clean, 1 hour 10 minutes to 1¼ hours, rotating pan after 40 minutes. Let cake cool in pan on wire rack for 15 minutes. Carefully run paring knife or offset spatula around sides of pan. Invert cake onto wire rack set in rimmed baking sheet; discard parchment. Let cake cool for about 2 hours. Transfer to serving platter, cut into wedges, and serve.

NOTES FROM THE TEST KITCHEN

UNMOLDING UPSIDE-DOWN CAKES

If an upside-down cake is turned out of the pan too quickly, the bottom of the cake steams and turns gummy; if the cake cools completely in the pan, the fruit will stick.

Our approach is to line the pan with parchment paper, which ensures that the fruit releases cleanly; let the cake rest in the pan for just 15 minutes before turning it out onto a rack.

APPLE UPSIDE-DOWN CAKE

WHY THIS RECIPE WORKS: Ever since canned pineapple was introduced into this country in the early 1900s, pineapple has been synonymous with upside-down cake. But at one time, upside-down cakes were made with seasonal fruit, such as apples. We loved the idea of resurrecting apple upside-down cake. We wanted a rich buttery cake topped with tightly packed, burnished, sweet apples.

We started our testing with choosing the type of apple. Most apples turned mushy and watery and were simply too sweet, but crisp, tart Granny Smiths made the cut. Following the lead of recipes found in our research, we shingled the apples in the pan and poured the cake batter over the top. But once baked and inverted, our apple layer was shrunken and dry. The solution turned out to be increasing the number of apples, for a hefty layer of fruit.

This effort yielded better results, but we found the apples to be overcooked, so we turned to a method uncovered in our recipe for Deep-Dish Apple Pie (page 847)—we pre-cooked half the apples by sautéing them on the stovetop, then we cut the remainder thin, so they baked through evenly. For the butter cake, we tested milk, buttermilk, yogurt, and sour cream. Sour cream won hands down—its subtle tang balanced the sweetness of the cake and complemented the caramelized apples. And another addition—cornmeal—gave the cake a hint of earthy flavor and a pleasantly coarse texture. Our final discovery came when we attempted to release the cake cleanly from the pan. Typical recipes instruct a 5 to 10-minute cooling period, but we found that a full 20 minutes was required to allow the apple filling to set. And turning the cake out onto a rack to finish cooling let the bottom of the cake breathe, preventing sogginess, which is typical of so many upside-down cakes.

Apple Upside-Down Cake

SERVES 8

We like the slight coarseness that cornmeal adds to the cake, but it's fine to omit it. Golden Delicious apples can be substituted for the Granny Smiths. You will need a 9-inch nonstick cake pan with sides that are at least 2 inches high; anything shallower and the cake will overflow. Alternatively, a 10-inch ovensafe stainless steel skillet (don't use cast iron) can be used to both cook the apples and bake the cake, with the following modifications: Cook the apples in the skillet and set them aside while mixing the batter (it's OK if the skillet is still warm when the batter is added) and increase the baking time by 7 to 9 minutes. If you don't have either a 2-inch-high cake pan or an ovensafe skillet, use an 8-inch square pan.

TOPPING

- 4 tablespoons (½ stick) unsalted butter, cut into 4 pieces, plus extra for the pan
- 4 Granny Smith apples (about 2 pounds), peeled and cored (see note)
- ⅔ cup packed (4⅔ ounces) light brown sugar
- 2 teaspoons juice from 1 lemon

CAKE

- 1 cup (5 ounces) unbleached all-purpose flour
- 1 tablespoon cornmeal (optional; see note)
- 1 teaspoon baking powder
- ½ teaspoon table salt
- ¾ cup (5¼ ounces) granulated sugar
- ¼ cup packed (1¾ ounces) light brown sugar
- 2 large eggs, at room temperature
- 6 tablespoons (¾ stick) unsalted butter, melted and cooled slightly
- ½ cup sour cream
- 1 teaspoon vanilla extract

1. FOR THE TOPPING: Butter the bottom and sides of a nonstick 9-inch-wide by 2-inch-high round cake pan; set aside. Adjust an oven rack to the lowest position and heat the oven to 350 degrees.

2. Halve the apples from pole to pole. Cut 2 apples into ¼-inch-thick slices; set aside. Cut the remaining 2 apples into ½-inch-thick slices. Melt the butter in a 12-inch skillet over medium-high heat. Add the ½-inch-thick apple slices and cook, stirring two or three times, until the apples begin to caramelize, 4 to 6 minutes. (Do not fully cook the apples.) Add the ¼-inch-thick apple slices, brown sugar, and lemon juice; continue cooking, stirring constantly, until the sugar dissolves and the apples are coated, about 1 minute longer. Transfer the apple mixture to the prepared pan and lightly press into an even layer. Set aside while preparing the cake.

3. FOR THE CAKE: Whisk the flour, cornmeal (if using), baking powder, and salt together in a medium bowl; set aside. Whisk the sugars and eggs together in a large bowl until thick and homogeneous, about 45 seconds. Slowly whisk in the butter until combined. Add the sour cream and vanilla; whisk until combined. Add the flour mixture and whisk until just combined. Pour the batter into the pan and spread evenly over the fruit. Lightly tap the pan against the countertop two or three times to settle the batter. Bake until the cake is golden brown and a toothpick inserted into the center comes out clean, 35 to 40 minutes, rotating the pan halfway through the baking time.

4. Cool the pan on a wire rack for 20 minutes. Run a small knife around the sides of the cake to loosen. Place a wire rack over the cake pan. Holding the rack tightly, invert the cake pan and wire rack together; lift off the cake pan. Place the wire rack over a baking sheet or large plate to catch any drips. If any fruit sticks to the pan bottom, remove and position it on top of the cake. Cool the cake for 20 minutes (or longer to cool it completely), then transfer it to a serving platter, cut into pieces, and serve.

Apple Upside-Down Cake with Almond

Follow the recipe for Apple Upside-Down Cake, combining ⅓ cup finely ground toasted almonds with the flour and adding 1 teaspoon almond extract with the sour cream and vanilla in step 3.

Apple Upside-Down Cake with Lemon and Thyme

Follow the recipe for Apple Upside-Down Cake, adding 1 teaspoon finely grated lemon zest and 1 teaspoon finely chopped fresh thyme leaves with the sour cream and vanilla in step 3.

FRENCH APPLE CAKE

WHY THIS RECIPE WORKS: For our own version of this classic French dessert, we wanted the best of both worlds: a dessert with a custardy, apple-rich base beneath a light, cake-like topping. To ensure that the apple slices softened fully, we microwaved them briefly to break the enzyme responsible for firming up pectin. And to create two differently textured layers from one batter, we divided the batter and added egg yolks to one part to make the custardy base and added flour to the rest to form the cake layer above it.

French Apple Cake

SERVES 8 TO 10

The microwaved apples should be pliable but not completely soft when cooked. To test for doneness, take one apple slice and try to bend it. If it snaps in half, it's too firm; microwave it for an additional 30 seconds and test again. If Calvados is unavailable, 1 tablespoon of apple brandy or white rum can be substituted.

- 1½ pounds Granny Smith apples, peeled, cored, cut into 8 wedges, and sliced ⅛ inch thick crosswise
- 1 tablespoon Calvados
- 1 teaspoon lemon juice
- 1 cup (5 ounces) plus 2 tablespoons all-purpose flour
- 1 cup (7 ounces) plus 1 tablespoon granulated sugar
- 2 teaspoons baking powder
- ½ teaspoon salt
- 1 large egg plus 2 large yolks
- 1 cup vegetable oil
- 1 cup whole milk
- 1 teaspoon vanilla extract
- Confectioners' sugar

1. Adjust oven rack to lower-middle position and heat oven to 325 degrees. Spray 9-inch springform pan with vegetable oil spray. Place prepared pan on rimmed baking sheet lined with aluminum foil. Place apple slices in microwave-safe pie plate, cover, and microwave until apples are pliable and slightly translucent, about 3 minutes. Toss apple slices with Calvados and lemon juice and let cool for 15 minutes.

2. Whisk 1 cup flour, 1 cup granulated sugar, baking powder, and salt together in bowl. Whisk egg, oil, milk, and vanilla together in second bowl until smooth. Add dry ingredients to wet ingredients and whisk until just combined. Transfer 1 cup batter to separate bowl and set aside.

3. Add egg yolks to remaining batter and whisk to combine. Using spatula, gently fold in cooled apples. Transfer batter to prepared pan; using offset spatula, spread batter evenly to pan edges, gently pressing on apples to create even, compact layer, and smooth surface.

4. Whisk remaining 2 tablespoons flour into reserved batter. Pour over batter in pan and spread batter evenly to pan edges and smooth surface. Sprinkle remaining 1 tablespoon granulated sugar evenly over cake.

5. Bake until center of cake is set, toothpick inserted in center comes out clean, and top is golden brown, about 1¼ hours. Transfer pan to wire rack; let cool for 5 minutes. Run paring knife around sides of pan and let cool completely, 2 to 3 hours. Dust lightly with confectioners' sugar, cut into wedges, and serve.

CARROT CAKE

WHY THIS RECIPE WORKS: A relic of the health food craze, carrot cake was once heralded for its use of vegetable oil in place of butter and carrots as a natural sweetener. Sure, the carrots add some sweetness, but they also add a lot of moisture, which is why carrot cake is invariably soggy. And oil? It makes this cake dense and, well, oily. We didn't want a greasy cake. We wanted a moist, rich cake with a tight and tender crumb and balanced spice.

We started with all-purpose flour—cake flour proved too delicate to support the grated carrots that get mixed in. For lift, we liked a combination of baking soda and baking powder. Some carrot cakes use a heavy hand with the spices and taste too much like spice cake. We took a conservative approach and used modest amounts of cinnamon, nutmeg, and cloves. After trying varying amounts of grated carrots, we settled on 3 cups for a pleasantly moist texture. One and one-half cups of vegetable oil gave us a rich, but not greasy, cake. Cream cheese frosting is the perfect partner to carrot cake—we enriched our version with sour cream for extra tang and vanilla for depth of flavor.

Carrot Cake

SERVES 15 TO 18

You can serve the cake right out of the pan, in which case you'll only need 3 cups of frosting for the top of the cake.

- 2½ cups (12½ ounces) unbleached all-purpose flour
- 1¼ teaspoons ground cinnamon
- 1¼ teaspoons baking powder
- 1 teaspoon baking soda
- ½ teaspoon table salt
- ½ teaspoon ground nutmeg
- ⅛ teaspoon ground cloves
- 4 large eggs, at room temperature
- 1½ cups (10½ ounces) granulated sugar
- ½ cup packed (3½ ounces) light brown sugar
- 1½ cups vegetable oil
- 1 pound carrots (about 6 medium), peeled and grated (about 3 cups)
- 4 cups Cream Cheese Frosting (recipe follows; see note)

1. Adjust an oven rack to the middle position and heat the oven to 350 degrees. Grease a 13 by 9-inch baking pan, then line the bottom with parchment paper. Whisk the flour, cinnamon, baking powder, baking soda, salt, nutmeg, and cloves together in a medium bowl.

2. In a large bowl, whisk the eggs and sugars together until the sugars are mostly dissolved and the mixture is frothy. Continue to whisk, while slowly drizzling in the oil, until thoroughly combined and emulsified. Whisk in the flour mixture until just incorporated. Stir in the carrots.

3. Give the batter a final stir with a rubber spatula to make sure it is thoroughly combined. Scrape the batter into the prepared pan, smooth the top, and lightly tap the pan against the countertop two or three times to settle the batter. Bake the cake until a toothpick inserted in the center comes out with a few moist crumbs attached, 35 to 40 minutes, rotating the pan halfway through the baking time.

4. Cool the cake completely in the pan, set on a wire rack, about 2 hours. Run a small knife around the edge of the cake and flip the cake out onto a wire rack. Peel off the parchment paper, then flip the cake right side up onto a serving platter. Spread the frosting evenly over the top and sides of the cake and serve.

Cream Cheese Frosting

MAKES ABOUT 4 CUPS

If the frosting becomes too soft to work with, let it chill in the refrigerator until firm.

- 2 (8-ounce) packages cream cheese, softened
- 10 tablespoons (1¼ sticks) unsalted butter, cut into chunks and softened
- 2 tablespoons sour cream
- 1½ teaspoons vanilla extract
- ¼ teaspoon table salt
- 2 cups (8 ounces) confectioners' sugar

1. Beat the cream cheese, butter, sour cream, vanilla, and salt together in a large bowl with an electric mixer on medium-high speed until smooth, 2 to 4 minutes.

2. Reduce the mixer speed to medium-low, slowly add the confectioners' sugar, and beat until smooth, 4 to 6 minutes. Increase the mixer speed to medium-high and beat until the frosting is light and fluffy, 4 to 6 minutes.

LIGHT CARROT CAKE

WHY THIS RECIPE WORKS: Although carrot cake sounds healthy, most versions tip the scales at 500 calories and 31 grams of fat per slice. We wanted to create a moist and rich carrot cake and we wanted the cake to be lighter in both calories and fat.

We made four significant changes to satisfy our goal of a tasty dessert we could enjoy more than once in a while. We reduced the amount of oil from 1½ cups to ½ cup and also reduced the number of eggs from four to three. We whipped air into the eggs to keep the cake from being dense and leaden. And, finally, we replaced the cream cheese and butter in the frosting with Neufchâtel reduced-fat cream cheese and mixed it by hand to prevent it from being runny. In the end, we reduced the calories to 350 and the fat grams to 13 and still had a cake that was tender, moist, and flavorful.

Light Carrot Cake

SERVES 16

You can use either the large holes of a box grater or the large-holed shredding disk in a food processor for grating the carrots. Use a metal cake pan, not a glass or Pyrex pan, for best results. This cake is terrific with our Light Cream Cheese Frosting (recipe follows) or a simple dusting of confectioners' sugar.

- 2½ cups (12½ ounces) unbleached all-purpose flour
- 1¼ teaspoons baking powder
- 1 teaspoon baking soda
- 1¼ teaspoons ground cinnamon
- ½ teaspoon ground nutmeg
- ½ teaspoon table salt
- ⅛ teaspoon ground cloves
- 3 large eggs, at room temperature
- 1 cup packed (7 ounces) light brown sugar
- 1 cup (7 ounces) granulated sugar
- ½ cup vegetable oil
- 1 pound carrots (about 6 medium), peeled and grated (about 3 cups; see note)

1. Adjust an oven rack to the middle position and heat the oven to 350 degrees. Grease a 13 by 9-inch cake pan, then line the bottom with parchment paper. Whisk the flour, baking powder, baking soda, cinnamon, nutmeg, salt, and cloves together in a medium bowl.

2. Beat the eggs, brown sugar, and granulated sugar together in a large bowl with an electric mixer on medium speed until the mixture turns thick and creamy, 1 to 3 minutes. Reduce the mixer speed to low and slowly beat in the oil until thoroughly combined and emulsified, 30 to 60 seconds.

3. Sift half the flour mixture over the batter and gently whisk in by hand. Repeat with the remaining flour mixture and continue to whisk the batter gently until most of the lumps are gone (do not overmix). Using a rubber spatula, gently stir in the carrots.

4. Pour the batter into the prepared pan and smooth the top. Bake until a wooden skewer inserted into the center of the cake comes out with a few moist crumbs attached, 35 to 40 minutes, rotating the pan halfway through the baking time.

5. Cool the cake completely in the pan, about 2 hours. Run a paring knife around the edge of the cake and flip the cake out onto a wire rack. Peel off the parchment paper, then flip the cake right side up onto a serving platter. If desired, spread the frosting (see note) evenly over the top and sides of the cake and serve.

Light Cream Cheese Frosting

MAKES ABOUT 2 CUPS

- 12 ounces Neufchâtel (⅓ less fat) cream cheese, softened
- 1 teaspoon vanilla extract
- 1½ cups (6 ounces) confectioners' sugar

Mix the cream cheese and vanilla together in a large bowl with a rubber spatula. Add the confectioners' sugar and stir until thoroughly combined and smooth.

NOTES FROM THE TEST KITCHEN

TESTING FOR DONENESS

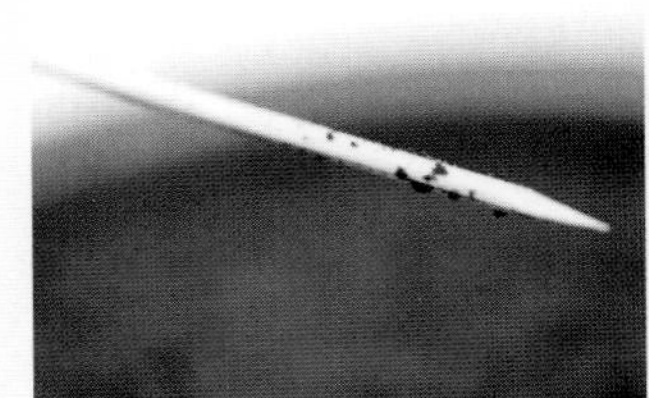

As a rule of thumb, we pull our cakes out of the oven when there are just a few crumbs still clinging to the skewer (wooden skewers work best). The residual heat will continue to bake the cake to perfection.

CARROT LAYER CAKE

WHY THIS RECIPE WORKS: This American classic has a lot going for it: moist cake, delicate spices, tangy cream cheese frosting. But its presentation could use some refinement. We wanted to reengineer humble carrot cake as a four-tier, nut-crusted confection that could claim its place among the most glamorous desserts. To start, we found that baking this cake in a half sheet pan meant that it baked and cooled in far less time than a conventional layer cake, and—cut into quarters—it produced four thin, level layers that did not require splitting or trimming. Extra baking soda raised the pH of the batter, ensuring that the coarsely shredded carrots softened during the shortened baking time. Buttermilk powder in the frosting reinforced the tangy flavor of the cream cheese.

Carrot Layer Cake

SERVES 10 TO 12

Shred the carrots on the large holes of a box grater or in a food processor fitted with the shredding disk. Do not substitute liquid buttermilk for the buttermilk powder. To ensure the proper spreading consistency for the frosting, use cold cream cheese. If your baked cake is of an uneven thickness, adjust the orientation of the layers as they are stacked to produce a level cake. Assembling this cake on a cardboard cake round trimmed to about a 6 by 8-inch rectangle makes it easy to press the pecans onto the sides of the frosted cake.

CAKE

- 1¾ cups (8¾ ounces) all-purpose flour
- 2 teaspoons baking powder
- 1 teaspoon baking soda
- 1½ teaspoons ground cinnamon
- ¾ teaspoon ground nutmeg
- ½ teaspoon salt
- ¼ teaspoon ground cloves
- 1¼ cups packed (8¾ ounces) light brown sugar
- ¾ cup vegetable oil
- 3 large eggs
- 1 teaspoon vanilla extract
- 2⅔ cups shredded carrots (4 carrots)
- ⅔ cup dried currants

FROSTING

- 3 cups (12 ounces) confectioners' sugar
- 16 tablespoons unsalted butter, softened
- ⅓ cup buttermilk powder
- 2 teaspoons vanilla extract
- ¼ teaspoon salt
- 12 ounces cream cheese, chilled and cut into 12 equal pieces
- 2 cups (8 ounces) pecans, toasted and chopped coarse

1. FOR THE CAKE: Adjust oven rack to middle position and heat oven to 350 degrees. Grease 18 by 13-inch rimmed baking sheet, line with parchment paper, and grease parchment. Whisk flour, baking powder, baking soda, cinnamon, nutmeg, salt, and cloves together in large bowl.

2. Whisk sugar, oil, eggs, and vanilla together in second bowl until mixture is smooth. Stir in carrots and currants. Add flour mixture and fold with rubber spatula until mixture is just combined.

3. Transfer batter to prepared sheet and smooth surface with offset spatula. Bake until center of cake is firm to touch, 15 to 18 minutes. Cool in pan on wire rack for 5 minutes. Invert cake onto wire rack (do not remove parchment), then reinvert onto second wire rack. Cool cake completely, about 30 minutes.

4. FOR THE FROSTING: Using stand mixer fitted with paddle, beat sugar, butter, buttermilk powder, vanilla, and salt together on low speed until smooth, about 2 minutes, scraping down bowl as needed. Increase speed to medium-low; add cream cheese, 1 piece at a time; and mix until smooth, about 2 minutes.

5. Transfer cooled cake to cutting board, parchment side down. Using sharp chef's knife, cut cake and parchment in half crosswise, then lengthwise into 4 even quarters.

6. Place 6 by 8-inch cardboard rectangle on cake platter. Place 1 cake layer, parchment side up, on cardboard and carefully remove parchment. Using offset spatula, spread ⅔ cup frosting evenly over top, right to edge of cake. Repeat with 2 more layers of cake, pressing lightly to adhere and frosting each layer with ⅔ cup frosting. Top with last cake layer and spread 1 cup frosting evenly over top. Spread remaining frosting evenly over sides of cake. (It's fine if some crumbs show through frosting on sides, but if you go back to smooth top of cake, be sure that spatula is free of crumbs.)

7. Hold cake with 1 hand and gently press chopped pecans onto sides with other hand. Chill for at least 1 hour before serving. (The frosted cake can be refrigerated for up to 24 hours before serving.)

SPICE CAKE

WHY THIS RECIPE WORKS: The problem with spice cakes? Spice. Some variations suffer from spice overload, which makes them gritty and dusty. Others are so lacking in spice flavor that it seems as if a cinnamon stick has only been waved in their general direction. We wanted an old-fashioned, moist, and substantial spice cake with spices that were warm and bold without being overpowering. We needed a less-than-tender cake, one with a substantial and open crumb that could stand up to the spices. We found that all-purpose flour, rather than cake flour, added volume and heft. Butter and eggs contributed richness. We bloomed the spices in butter, a process that intensified their aromas and gave the cake a heightened spice impact throughout. We used the classic mixture of cinnamon, cloves, cardamom, allspice, and nutmeg, but found that a tablespoon of grated fresh ginger and a couple of tablespoons of molasses gave the cake an extra zing. And reserving a little of the spice mixture to add to the cream cheese frosting united the frosting and the cake.

Spice Cake

SERVES 15 TO 18

Using fresh ginger instead of dried ground ginger gives this cake a brighter flavor. You can serve the cake right out of the pan, in which case you'll only need 3 cups of frosting for the top of the cake.

- 1 tablespoon ground cinnamon
- ¾ teaspoon ground cardamom
- ½ teaspoon ground allspice
- ½ teaspoon ground cloves
- ¼ teaspoon ground nutmeg
- 16 tablespoons (2 sticks) unsalted butter, cut into 16 pieces and softened
- 2¼ cups (11¼ ounces) all-purpose flour
- ½ teaspoon baking powder
- ½ teaspoon baking soda
- ½ teaspoon table salt
- 2 large whole eggs plus 3 large egg yolks, at room temperature
- 1 teaspoon vanilla extract
- 1¾ cups (12¼ ounces) sugar
- 2 tablespoons light or mild molasses
- 1 tablespoon minced or grated fresh ginger (see note)
- 1 cup buttermilk, room temperature
- 4 cups Cream Cheese Frosting (page 755; see note)

1. Adjust an oven rack to the middle position and heat the oven to 350 degrees. Grease a 13 by 9-inch baking pan, then line the bottom with parchment paper.

2. Combine the cinnamon, cardamom, allspice, cloves, and nutmeg in a small bowl; reserve ½ teaspoon of the spice mixture for the frosting. Melt 4 tablespoons of the butter in a small skillet over medium heat and continue to cook, swirling the pan constantly, until the butter is light brown, 3 to 6 minutes. Stir in the spice mixture and cook until fragrant, about 15 seconds. Set the mixture aside to cool slightly.

3. In a medium bowl, whisk the flour, baking powder, baking soda, and salt together. In a small bowl, whisk the whole eggs, egg yolks, and vanilla together.

4. In a stand mixer fitted with the paddle attachment, beat the remaining 12 tablespoons butter, the sugar, and molasses on medium-high speed until light and fluffy, 3 to 6 minutes; scrape down the bowl with a rubber spatula. Beat in the ginger, cooled butter-spice mixture, and half of the egg mixture until combined, about 30 seconds. Beat in the remaining egg mixture until combined, about 30 seconds, and scrape down the bowl again.

5. Reduce the mixer speed to low and beat in one-third of the flour mixture, followed by half of the buttermilk. Repeat with half of the remaining flour mixture and the remaining buttermilk. Beat in the remaining flour mixture until just combined; scrape down the bowl.

6. Give the batter a final stir with a rubber spatula to make sure it is thoroughly combined. Scrape the batter into the prepared pan, smooth the top, and lightly tap the pan against the countertop two or three times to settle the batter. Bake the cake until a toothpick inserted in the center comes out with a few moist crumbs attached, 30 to 35 minutes, rotating the pan halfway through the baking time.

7. Cool the cake completely in the pan, set on a wire rack, about 2 hours. Run a small knife around the edge of the cake and flip the cake out onto a wire rack. Peel off the parchment paper, then flip the cake right side up onto a serving platter. Stir the reserved spice mixture into the frosting, spread the frosting evenly over the top and sides of the cake, and serve.

BEST ALMOND CAKE

WHY THIS RECIPE WORKS: Simple, rich almond cake makes a sophisticated dessert, but traditional European versions can be heavy and dense. For a slightly cakier version with plenty of nutty flavor, we swapped out traditional almond paste for toasted blanched sliced almonds and added a bit of almond extract for extra depth. Lemon zest in the batter provided citrusy brightness. For a lighter crumb, we increased the flour slightly and added baking powder. Making the batter in a food processor broke down some of the protein structure in the eggs, ensuring that the cake had a level, not domed, top. We swapped some butter for oil and lowered the oven temperature to produce an evenly baked, moist cake. For a crunchy finishing touch, we topped the cake with sliced almonds and a sprinkle of lemon zest–infused sugar.

Best Almond Cake

SERVES 8 TO 10

If you can't find blanched sliced almonds, grind slivered almonds for the batter and use unblanched sliced almonds for the topping. Serve plain or with Orange Crème Fraîche (recipe follows).

- 1½ cups plus ⅓ cup blanched sliced almonds, toasted
- ¾ cup (3¾ ounces) all-purpose flour
- ¾ teaspoon salt
- ¼ teaspoon baking powder
- ⅛ teaspoon baking soda
- 4 large eggs
- 1¼ cups (8¾ ounces) plus 2 tablespoons sugar
- 1 tablespoon plus ½ teaspoon grated lemon zest (2 lemons)
- ¾ teaspoon almond extract
- 5 tablespoons unsalted butter, melted
- ⅓ cup vegetable oil

1. Adjust oven rack to middle position and heat oven to 300 degrees. Grease 9-inch round cake pan and line with parchment paper. Pulse 1½ cups almonds, flour, salt, baking powder, and baking soda in food processor until almonds are finely ground, 5 to 10 pulses. Transfer almond mixture to bowl.

2. Process eggs, 1¼ cups sugar, 1 tablespoon lemon zest, and almond extract in now-empty processor until very pale yellow, about 2 minutes. With processor running, add melted butter and oil in steady stream, until incorporated. Add almond mixture and pulse to combine, 4 to 5 pulses. Transfer batter to prepared pan.

3. Using your fingers, combine remaining 2 tablespoons sugar and remaining ½ teaspoon lemon zest in small bowl until fragrant, 5 to 10 seconds. Sprinkle top of cake evenly with remaining ⅓ cup almonds followed by sugar-zest mixture.

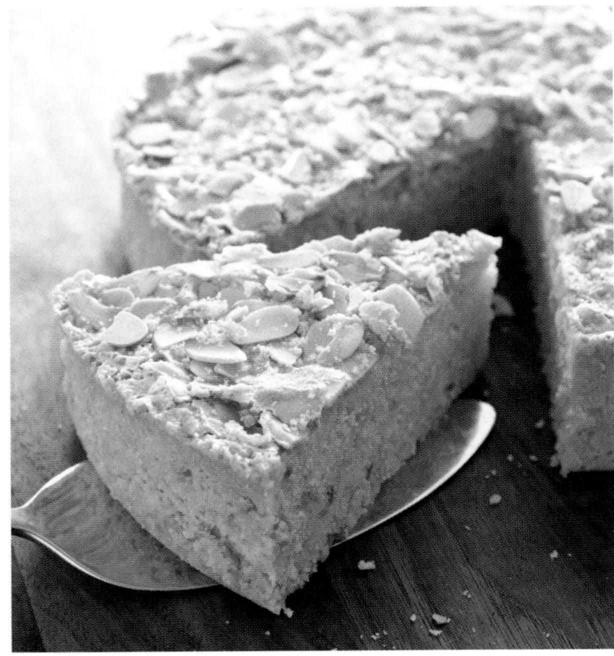

4. Bake until center of cake is set and bounces back when gently pressed and toothpick inserted in center comes out clean, 55 to 65 minutes, rotating pan after 40 minutes. Let cake cool in pan on wire rack for 15 minutes. Run paring knife around sides of pan. Invert cake onto greased wire rack, discard parchment, and reinvert cake onto second wire rack. Let cake cool, about 2 hours. Cut into wedges and serve. (Store cake in plastic wrap at room temperature for up to 3 days.)

Orange Crème Fraîche

MAKES ABOUT 2 CUPS

- 2 oranges
- 1 cup crème fraîche
- 2 tablespoons sugar
- ⅛ teaspoon salt

Remove 1 teaspoon zest from 1 orange. Cut away peel and pith from oranges. Slice between membranes to release segments and cut segments into ¼-inch pieces. Combine orange pieces and zest, crème fraîche, sugar, and salt in bowl and mix well. Refrigerate for 1 hour.

GÂTEAU BRETON

WHY THIS RECIPE WORKS: The rich, dense texture of gâteau Breton lies somewhere between shortbread and pound cake. To avoid introducing too much air into the batter of our French butter cake, which would lead to a fluffy, airy texture, we creamed the butter and sugar for only 3 minutes before adding the egg yolks and flour. Briefly freezing a layer of the batter in the cake pan helped us spread a bright homemade apricot filling onto the batter. The pan then went back into the freezer to firm so that the top layer of batter could also easily be added. All that was left to do was pretty up the cake with an egg wash and diamond-patterned design.

Gâteau Breton with Apricot Filling

SERVES 8

We strongly prefer the flavor of California apricots in the filling. Mediterranean (or Turkish) apricots can be used, but increase the amount of lemon juice to 2 tablespoons. This cake is traditionally served plain with coffee or tea but can be dressed up with fresh berries, if desired.

FILLING

- ⅔ cup water
- ½ cup dried California apricots, chopped
- ⅓ cup (2⅓ ounces) sugar
- 1 tablespoon lemon juice

CAKE

- 16 tablespoons (2 sticks) unsalted butter, softened
- ¾ cup plus 2 tablespoons (6⅛ ounces) sugar
- 6 large egg yolks (1 lightly beaten with 1 teaspoon water)
- 2 tablespoons dark rum
- 1 teaspoon vanilla extract
- 2 cups (10 ounces) all-purpose flour
- ½ teaspoon salt

1. **FOR THE FILLING:** Process water and apricots in blender until uniformly pureed, about 2 minutes. Transfer puree to 10-inch nonstick skillet and stir in sugar. Set skillet over medium heat and cook, stirring frequently, until puree has darkened slightly and rubber spatula leaves distinct trail when dragged across bottom of pan, 10 to 12 minutes. Transfer filling to bowl and stir in lemon juice. Refrigerate filling until cool to touch, about 15 minutes.

2. **FOR THE CAKE:** Adjust oven rack to lower-middle position and heat oven to 350 degrees. Grease 9-inch round cake pan.

3. Using stand mixer fitted with paddle, beat butter on medium-high speed until smooth and lightened in color, 1 to 2 minutes. Add sugar and continue to beat until pale and fluffy, about 3 minutes longer. Add 5 egg yolks, one at a time, and beat until combined. Scrape down bowl, add rum and vanilla, and mix until incorporated, about 1 minute. Reduce speed to low, add flour and salt, and mix until flour is just incorporated, about 30 seconds. Give batter final stir by hand.

4. Spoon half of batter into bottom of prepared pan. Using small offset spatula, spread batter into even layer. Freeze for 10 minutes.

5. Spread ½ cup filling in even layer over chilled batter, leaving ¾-inch border around edge (reserve remaining filling for another use). Freeze for 10 minutes.

6. Gently spread remaining batter over filling. Using offset spatula, carefully smooth top of batter. Brush with egg yolk wash. Using tines of fork, make light scores in surface of cake, spaced about 1½ inches apart, in diamond pattern, being careful not to score all the way to sides of pan. Bake until top is golden brown and edges of cake start to pull away from sides of pan, 45 to 50 minutes. Let cake cool in pan on wire rack for 30 minutes. Run paring knife between cake and sides of pan, remove cake from pan, and let cool completely on rack, about 1 hour. Cut into wedges and serve.

Gâteau Breton with Prune Filling

Increase water to 1 cup, substitute 1 cup pitted prunes for apricots, and omit sugar. Bring water and prunes to simmer in small saucepan over medium heat. Reduce heat to medium-low and cook until all liquid is absorbed and prunes are very soft, 10 to 12 minutes. Remove saucepan from heat, add lemon juice, and stir with wooden spoon, pressing prunes against side of saucepan, until coarsely pureed. Transfer filling to bowl and refrigerate until cool to touch, about 15 minutes.

STRAWBERRY CREAM CAKE

WHY THIS RECIPE WORKS: What could possibly ruin the heavenly trio of cake, cream, and ripe strawberries? How about soggy cake, bland berries, and squishy cream? We wanted a sturdy cake, a firm filling, and strawberry flavor fit for a starring role—a cake that would serve a formal occasion better than a simple strawberry shortcake.

To start, we had to solve three crucial problems. First, we realized that tender butter cakes couldn't support a substantial strawberry filling, so we developed a chiffon-style cake that combined the rich flavor of a butter cake with the light-yet-sturdy texture of a sponge cake. Second, we made a flavorful berry "mash" with half of the berries and then reduced the macerated juice in a saucepan (with a little kirsch) to help concentrate and round out the flavor. We sliced the rest of the berries and placed them around the edges of the cake for visual appeal. Another problem arose when the cake was sliced: The filling squirted out and the layers fell apart. To correct the problem, we reduced the number of layers from four to three and fortified the whipped-cream filling with cream cheese. This filling stayed put and didn't mar the glorious layers of this spectacular summertime cake.

Strawberry Cream Cake

SERVES 8 TO 10

You will need a cake pan with straight sides that are at least 2 inches high.

CAKE

- 1¼ cups (5 ounces) cake flour, plus extra for the pan
- 1½ teaspoons baking powder
- ¼ teaspoon table salt
- 1 cup (7 ounces) sugar
- 5 large eggs (2 whole and 3 separated), at room temperature
- 6 tablespoons (¾ stick) unsalted butter, melted and cooled slightly
- 2 tablespoons water
- 2 teaspoons vanilla extract

STRAWBERRY FILLING

- 2 pounds fresh strawberries (medium or large, about 2 quarts), washed, dried, and stemmed
- 4–6 tablespoons sugar
- 2 tablespoons kirsch
- Pinch table salt

WHIPPED CREAM

- 8 ounces cream cheese, at room temperature
- ½ cup (3½ ounces) sugar
- 1 teaspoon vanilla extract
- ⅛ teaspoon table salt
- 2 cups heavy cream

1. FOR THE CAKE: Adjust an oven rack to the lower-middle position and heat the oven to 325 degrees. Grease and flour a 9-inch-wide by 2-inch-high round cake pan or 9-inch springform pan and line it with parchment paper. Whisk the flour, baking powder, salt, and all but 3 tablespoons of the sugar in a mixing bowl. Whisk in 2 whole eggs and 3 yolks (reserving the whites), the butter, water, and vanilla; whisk until smooth.

2. In the clean bowl of a stand mixer fitted with the whisk attachment, beat the remaining 3 egg whites at medium-low speed until frothy, 1 to 2 minutes. With the machine running, gradually add the remaining 3 tablespoons sugar, increase the speed to medium-high, and beat until soft peaks form, 60 to 90 seconds. Stir one-third of the whites into the batter to lighten; add the remaining whites and gently fold into the batter until no white streaks remain. Transfer the batter to the prepared pan, smoothing the top with a rubber spatula. Lightly tap the pan against the countertop two or three times to settle the batter. Bake until a toothpick inserted into the center comes out clean, 30 to 40 minutes, rotating the pan halfway through the baking time. Cool the cake in the pan on a wire rack for 10 minutes, then invert onto the wire rack and peel off the parchment. Invert the cake again and cool completely on the rack, about 2 hours.

3. FOR THE STRAWBERRY FILLING: Halve 24 of the best-looking berries and reserve. Quarter the remaining berries; toss with 4 to 6 tablespoons sugar (depending on the sweetness of the berries) in a medium bowl and let sit for 1 hour, stirring occasionally. Strain the juices from the berries and reserve (you should have about ½ cup). In a food processor, give the macerated berries 5 pulses (you should have about 1½ cups). In a small saucepan over medium-high heat, simmer the reserved juices and the kirsch until syrupy and reduced to about 3 tablespoons, 3 to 5 minutes. Pour the reduced syrup over the processed, macerated berries, add the salt, and toss to combine. Set aside until the cake has cooled.

NOTES FROM THE TEST KITCHEN

BUILDING A STRAWBERRY CREAM CAKE

1. With a serrated knife, use a sawing motion to cut the cake into three layers, rotating the cake as you go.

2. Place sliced berries evenly around the edges (they will be visible once the layers are assembled).

3. Cover the center of the cake completely with half of the pureed strawberries.

4. Spread one-third of the whipped cream over the berries, leaving a ½-inch border. Repeat the layering.

5. Press the last layer into place, spread with the remaining cream, and decorate with the remaining berries.

4. FOR THE WHIPPED CREAM: When the cake has cooled, place the cream cheese, sugar, vanilla, and salt in the clean bowl of a stand mixer fitted with the whisk attachment. Whisk at medium-high speed until light and fluffy, 1 to 2 minutes, scraping down the bowl with a rubber spatula as needed. Reduce the speed to low and add the heavy cream in a slow, steady stream; when almost fully combined, increase the speed to medium-high and beat until the mixture holds stiff peaks, 2 to 2½ minutes more, scraping down the bowl as needed (you should have about 4½ cups).

5. TO ASSEMBLE THE CAKE: Line the edges of a cake platter with strips of parchment paper to keep the platter clean. Following the photos, use a serrated knife to cut the cake horizontally into three even layers. Place the bottom layer on the platter and arrange a ring of 20 strawberry halves, cut sides down and stem ends facing out, around the perimeter of the cake layer. Pour one-half of the pureed berry mixture (about ¾ cup) in the center, then spread to cover any exposed cake. Gently spread about one-third of the whipped cream (about 1½ cups) over the berry layer, leaving a ½-inch border from the edge. Place the middle cake layer on top and press down gently (the whipped cream layer should become flush with the cake edge). Repeat with 20 additional strawberry halves, the remaining berry mixture, and half of the remaining whipped cream; gently press the last cake layer on top. Spread the remaining whipped cream over the top; decorate with the remaining cut strawberries. Remove the parchment strips from the platter and serve.

RASPBERRY CHARLOTTE

WHY THIS RECIPE WORKS: Raspberry charlotte is a showstopping dessert, but the traditional steps are so labor intensive that many home cooks shy away. We wanted to deliver a creamy filling and tender cake without the hassle, so we started from the inside out where a bright raspberry curd would serve as the filling's base. First, we sprinkled gelatin over water—just enough to eventually give the filling some spring without turning it to Jell-O. We mashed raspberries with sugar, butter, and salt in a saucepan and cooked the mixture to break down the berries. Whisking cornstarch into the egg yolks prevented curdling as the hot raspberry mixture was added in. The curd slowly formed once we brought the raspberry-yolk mixture back to the stove, whisking constantly. We poured the curd into the gelatin mixture through a sieve to remove the berries' seeds, stirring the filling together and letting it cool and thicken. The cake base and sides are traditionally made with ladyfingers, but we preferred the tender, rich texture (and superior structure) of chiffon cake. For easy assembly, we baked one round cake and one square cake, using the round as the bottom and slicing the square cake into strips to line the walls of a springform pan. Before assembling, we spread the cakes with a zesty, bright spread of raspberry jam boosted with lemon-soaked gelatin. We lightened the filling before pouring it into the cake ring by whipping heavy cream to soft peaks, whisking a third of it into the curd and folding the rest in to finish. After pouring in and smoothing the top of the filling, we created a dramatic marbled pattern with the remaining jam.

Raspberry Charlotte

SERVES 12 TO 16

It is fine to use frozen raspberries in the filling. Thaw frozen berries completely before using and use any collected juices, too. It is important to measure the berries for the filling by weight. If you wish to garnish the top of the charlotte with berries, arrange 1 to 1½ cups fresh berries (depending on size) around the edge of the assembled charlotte before refrigerating. For clean, neat slices, dip your knife in hot water and wipe it dry before each slice.

FILLING

- 1¼ teaspoons unflavored gelatin
- 2 tablespoons water
- 3 large egg yolks (reserve whites for cake)
- 2 teaspoons cornstarch
- 1 pound (3¼ cups) fresh or thawed frozen raspberries
- ⅔ cup (4⅔ ounces) sugar
- 2 tablespoons unsalted butter
- Pinch salt
- 1¾ cups heavy cream

JAM MIXTURE

- ½ teaspoon unflavored gelatin
- 1 tablespoon lemon juice
- ½ cup seedless raspberry jam

CAKE

- ⅔ cup (2⅔ ounces) cake flour
- 6 tablespoons (2⅔ ounces) sugar
- ¾ teaspoon baking powder
- ⅛ teaspoon salt
- ¼ cup vegetable oil
- 1 large egg plus 3 large egg whites (reserved from filling)
- 2 tablespoons water
- 1 teaspoon vanilla extract
- ¼ teaspoon cream of tartar

1. FOR THE FILLING: Sprinkle gelatin over water in large bowl and set aside. Whisk egg yolks and cornstarch together in medium bowl until combined. Combine raspberries, sugar, butter, and salt in medium saucepan. Mash lightly with whisk and stir until no dry sugar remains. Cook over medium heat, whisking frequently, until mixture is simmering and raspberries are almost completely broken down, 4 to 6 minutes.

2. Remove raspberry mixture from heat and, whisking constantly, slowly add ½ cup raspberry mixture to yolk mixture to temper. Whisking constantly, return tempered yolk mixture to mixture in saucepan. Return saucepan to medium heat and cook, whisking constantly, until mixture thickens and bubbles, about 1 minute. Pour through fine-mesh strainer set over gelatin mixture and press on solids with back of ladle or rubber spatula until only seeds remain. Discard seeds and stir raspberry mixture until gelatin is dissolved. Set aside, stirring occasionally, until curd is slightly thickened and reaches room temperature, at least 30 minutes or up to 1 hour 15 minutes.

3. FOR THE JAM MIXTURE: Sprinkle gelatin over lemon juice in small bowl and let sit until gelatin softens, about 5 minutes. Heat jam in microwave, whisking occasionally, until hot and fluid, 30 to 60 seconds. Add softened gelatin to jam and whisk until dissolved. Set aside.

4. FOR THE CAKE: Adjust oven rack to upper-middle position and heat oven to 350 degrees. Lightly grease 8-inch round cake pan and 8-inch square baking pan, line with parchment paper, and lightly grease parchment. Whisk flour, sugar, baking powder, and salt together in medium bowl. Whisk oil, whole egg, water, and vanilla into flour mixture until smooth batter forms.

5. Using stand mixer fitted with whisk, whip egg whites and cream of tartar on medium-low speed until foamy, about 1 minute. Increase speed to medium-high and whip until soft peaks form, 2 to 3 minutes. Transfer one-third of egg whites to batter; whisk gently until mixture is lightened. Using rubber spatula, gently fold remaining egg whites into batter.

6. Pour 1 cup batter into round pan and spread evenly. Pour remaining batter into square pan and spread evenly. Place pans on rimmed baking sheet and bake until cakes spring back when pressed lightly in center and surface is no longer sticky, 8 to 11 minutes (round cake, which is shallower, will be done before square cake). Cakes should not brown.

7. Let cakes cool in pans on wire rack for 5 minutes. Invert round cake onto wire rack. Carefully remove parchment, then reinvert onto second wire rack. Repeat with square cake. Let cool completely, at least 15 minutes.

8. Place round cake in center of serving platter. Spread with 2 tablespoons jam mixture. Place ring from 9-inch springform pan around cake, leaving equal space on all sides. Leave clasp of ring slightly loose. Using sharp chef's knife, trim ⅛ inch off all edges of square cake. Spread square cake with 2 tablespoons jam mixture. Cut cake in half. Cut each half lengthwise into two pieces to make four equal-size long strips. Place cake strips vertically around round cake, jam side in, taking care to nestle ends together neatly. Fasten clasp of springform ring.

9. Using stand mixer fitted with whisk, whip cream on medium-low speed until foamy, about 1 minute. Increase speed to high and whip until soft peaks form, 1 to 2 minutes.

Transfer one-third of whipped cream to curd; whisk gently until mixture is lightened. Using rubber spatula, gently fold in remaining cream until mixture is homogenous.

10. Pour filling into cake ring and spread evenly to edge. (Surface of filling will be above edge of cake.) Drizzle remaining jam mixture over surface of filling. Using knife, swirl jam through surface of filling, making marbled pattern. Refrigerate for at least 5 hours or up to 24 hours.

11. To unmold, run thin knife around edge of ring (just ½ inch down). Release ring and lift to remove. Let stand at room temperature for 20 minutes before slicing and serving.

NOTES FROM THE TEST KITCHEN

ASSEMBLING RASPBERRY CHARLOTTE

Our charlotte requires 2 cakes—one round cake as the base and a square cake, cut into strips, to line the sides. We construct our charlotte inside the ring of a springform pan, right on the serving platter.

1. Spread round cake with jam mixture and place springform pan ring around cake. Spread square cake with jam mixture, cut into strips, and place strips vertically around round cake. Fasten clasp of ring.

2. Whip cream and fold into curd, then pour filling into cake-lined pan.

3. Drizzle remaining jam mixture over cake and swirl.

SUMMER PEACH CAKE

WHY THIS RECIPE WORKS: Marrying cake with fresh summer peaches, this dessert is a bakery favorite, yet most versions are plagued by soggy cake and barely noticeable peach flavor. We wanted a buttery cake that was moist and not at all soggy, with a golden-brown exterior and plenty of peach flavor. Roasting chunks of peaches tossed in sugar and a little lemon juice helped concentrate their flavor and expel excess moisture before we combined them with our cake batter. However, during roasting, the peach chunks became swathed in a flavorful but unpleasantly gooey film. Coating our roasted peaches in panko bread crumbs before combining them with the batter ensured the film was absorbed by the crumbs, which then dissolved into the cake during baking. To amplify the peach flavor, we tossed the fruit with peach schnapps before roasting, and a little almond extract added to the batter lent a subtle complementary note. Fanning peach slices (macerated with a little more of the schnapps) over the top, sprinkled with almond extract–flavored sugar for a light glaze, ensured our cake looked as good as it tasted.

Summer Peach Cake

SERVES 8

To crush the panko bread crumbs, place them in a zipper-lock bag and smash them with a rolling pin. If you can't find panko, ¼ cup of plain, unseasoned bread crumbs can be substituted. Orange liqueur can be substituted for the peach schnapps. If using peak-of-season, farm-fresh peaches, omit the peach schnapps.

- 2½ pounds peaches, halved, pitted, and cut into ½-inch wedges
- 5 tablespoons peach schnapps (see note)
- 4 teaspoons juice from 1 lemon
- 6 tablespoons plus ⅓ cup (5 ounces) granulated sugar
- 1 cup (5 ounces) unbleached all-purpose flour
- 1¼ teaspoons baking powder
- ¾ teaspoon table salt
- ½ cup packed (3½ ounces) light brown sugar
- 2 large eggs, at room temperature
- 8 tablespoons (1 stick) unsalted butter, melted and cooled
- ¼ cup sour cream
- 1½ teaspoons vanilla extract
- ¼ teaspoon plus ⅛ teaspoon almond extract
- ⅓ cup panko bread crumbs, crushed fine (see note)

1. Adjust an oven rack to the middle position and heat the oven to 425 degrees. Line a rimmed baking sheet with aluminum foil and spray with vegetable oil spray. Grease and flour a 9-inch springform pan. Gently toss 24 peach wedges with 2 tablespoons of the schnapps, 2 teaspoons of the lemon juice, and 1 tablespoon of the granulated sugar in a bowl; set aside.

2. Cut the remaining peach wedges crosswise into 3 chunks. In a large bowl, gently toss the chunks with the remaining 3 tablespoons schnapps, remaining 2 teaspoons lemon juice, and 2 tablespoons more granulated sugar. Spread the peach chunks in a single layer on the prepared baking sheet and bake until the exuded juices begin to thicken and caramelize at the edges of the pan, 20 to 25 minutes. Transfer the pan to a wire rack and let the peaches cool to room temperature, about 30 minutes. Reduce the oven temperature to 350 degrees.

3. Whisk the flour, baking powder, and salt together in a bowl. Whisk ⅓ cup more granulated sugar, the brown sugar, and eggs together in a bowl until thick and thoroughly combined, about 45 seconds. Slowly whisk in the butter until combined. Add the sour cream, vanilla, and ¼ teaspoon of the almond extract; whisk until combined. Add the flour mixture and whisk until just combined.

4. Pour half of the batter into the prepared pan. Using an offset spatula, spread the batter evenly to the pan edges and smooth the top. Sprinkle the crushed panko evenly over the cooled peach chunks and gently toss to coat. Arrange the peach chunks on the batter in the pan in an even layer, gently pressing the peaches into the batter. Gently spread the remaining batter over the peach chunks and smooth the top. Arrange the reserved peach wedges, slightly overlapped, in a ring over the surface of the batter, placing the smaller wedges in the center. Stir the remaining 3 tablespoons granulated sugar and the remaining ⅛ teaspoon almond extract together in a small bowl until the sugar is moistened. Sprinkle the sugar mixture evenly over the top of the cake.

5. Bake until the center of the cake is set and a toothpick inserted in the center comes out clean, 50 to 60 minutes. Transfer the pan to a wire rack and let cool for 5 minutes. Run a thin knife between the cake and the sides of the pan; remove the sides of the pan. Let the cake cool completely, 2 to 3 hours, before serving.

CLASSIC GINGERBREAD

WHY THIS RECIPE WORKS: Most recipes for gingerbread suffer from a dense, sunken center, and flavors range from barely gingery to spicier than a curry dinner. Our ideal gingerbread should be moist through and through and utterly simple. Focusing on flavor first, we bumped up the ginger with both a hefty dose of ground ginger and grated fresh ginger. Cinnamon and freshly ground pepper produced a complex, lingering heat. Dark stout, gently heated to minimize its booziness, had a bittersweet flavor that brought out the caramel undertones of the molasses. Finally, swapping out the butter for vegetable oil and replacing some of the brown sugar with granulated let the spice flavors come through. To prevent a sunken center, we looked at our leaveners first. Baking powder isn't as effective at leavening if too many other acidic ingredients are present in the batter. Incorporating the baking soda with the wet ingredients instead of the other dry ones helped to neutralize those acidic ingredients before they got incorporated into the batter and allowed the baking powder to do a better job. While stirring is typically the enemy of tenderness since it develops the flour's gluten, our batter was so loose that vigorous stirring actually gave our gingerbread the structure necessary to further ensure the center didn't collapse. With that, we had a flawless cake with plenty of spice and warmth.

Classic Gingerbread Cake

SERVES 8

This cake packs potent yet well-balanced spice. If you prefer less spice, you can decrease the amount of ground ginger to 1 tablespoon. Avoid opening the oven door until the minimum baking time has elapsed. Serve the gingerbread plain or with lightly sweetened whipped cream.

- ¾ cup stout, such as Guinness
- ½ teaspoon baking soda
- ⅔ cup molasses
- ¾ cup (5¼ ounces) packed light brown sugar
- ¼ cup (1¾ ounces) granulated sugar
- 1½ cups (7½ ounces) unbleached all-purpose flour
- 2 tablespoons ground ginger
- ½ teaspoon baking powder
- ½ teaspoon table salt
- ¼ teaspoon ground cinnamon
- ¼ teaspoon ground black pepper
- 2 large eggs, at room temperature
- ⅓ cup vegetable oil
- 1 tablespoon grated fresh ginger

1. Adjust an oven rack to the middle position and heat the oven to 350 degrees. Grease an 8-inch square baking pan, line with parchment paper, grease the parchment, and flour the pan.

2. Bring the stout to a boil in a medium saucepan over medium heat, stirring occasionally. Remove from the heat and stir in the baking soda (the mixture will foam vigorously). When the foaming subsides, stir in the molasses, brown sugar, and granulated sugar until dissolved; set aside. Whisk the flour, ground ginger, baking powder, salt, cinnamon, and pepper together in a large bowl.

3. Transfer the stout mixture to a second large bowl. Whisk in the eggs, oil, and grated ginger until combined. Whisk the wet mixture into the flour mixture in thirds, stirring vigorously until completely smooth after each addition.

4. Scrape the batter into the prepared pan, smooth the top with a rubber spatula, and gently tap the pan on the counter to release any air bubbles. Bake until the top of the cake is just firm to the touch and a toothpick inserted into the center comes out clean, 35 to 45 minutes. Let the cake cool in the pan on a wire rack, about 1½ hours, before serving.

COCONUT LAYER CAKE

WHY THIS RECIPE WORKS: Too often, a coconut cake is just plain white cake with plain white frosting sprinkled with shredded coconut, lacking any real coconut flavor. Coconut cake should be perfumed inside and out with the cool, subtle, mysterious essence of coconut. Its layers of snowy white cake should be moist and tender, with a delicate, yielding crumb, and the icing a silky, gently sweetened coat covered with a deep drift of downy coconut.

For this type of cake, we found a traditional butter cake to be best. To infuse this cake with maximum coconut flavor, we relied on coconut extract and cream of coconut in the cake and the buttercream icing. We also coated the cake with a generous amount of shredded coconut for more flavor and textural interest.

Coconut Layer Cake

SERVES 10 TO 12

Be sure to use cream of coconut (such as Coco López), and not coconut milk here. If you like, before decorating, toast the shredded coconut in a 350-degree oven, stirring often, until golden, about 10 minutes. Toasting the coconut, which is optional, adds a golden halo to the finished cake, as well as a nutty flavor.

CAKE

- 2¼ cups (9 ounces) cake flour, plus extra for the pans
- ¾ cup cream of coconut (see note)
- 5 large egg whites plus 1 large egg, at room temperature
- ¼ cup water
- 1 teaspoon coconut extract
- 1 teaspoon vanilla extract
- 1 cup (7 ounces) granulated sugar
- 1 tablespoon baking powder
- ¾ teaspoon table salt
- 12 tablespoons (1½ sticks) unsalted butter, cut into 12 pieces and softened

FROSTING

- 2 tablespoons heavy cream
- 1 teaspoon coconut extract
- 1 teaspoon vanilla extract
- Pinch table salt
- 16 tablespoons (2 sticks) unsalted butter, cut into chunks and softened
- ¼ cup cream of coconut (see note)
- 3 cups (12 ounces) confectioners' sugar
- 2 cups sweetened shredded coconut (see note)

1. FOR THE CAKE: Adjust an oven rack to the middle position and heat the oven to 325 degrees. Grease and flour two 9-inch round cake pans, then line the bottoms with parchment paper. Whisk the cream of coconut, egg whites, whole egg, water, and extracts together in a medium bowl.

2. In a stand mixer fitted with the paddle attachment, mix the flour, granulated sugar, baking powder, and salt on low speed until combined, about 30 seconds. Increase the speed to medium and beat the butter into the flour mixture, one piece at a time, about 30 seconds. Continue to beat the mixture until it resembles moist crumbs, about 1 minute.

3. Beat in all but ½ cup of the cream of coconut mixture, then increase the mixer speed to medium and beat the batter until smooth, light, and fluffy, about 1 minute. Reduce the mixer speed to low and slowly beat in the remaining cream of coconut mixture until the batter is combined, about 30 seconds.

4. Scrape the batter into the prepared pans, smooth the tops, and lightly tap the pans against the countertop two or three times to settle the batter. Bake the cakes until a toothpick inserted in the center comes out with a few crumbs attached, 30 to 35 minutes, rotating the pans halfway through the baking time.

5. Cool the cakes in the pans for 10 minutes. Run a small knife around the edge of the cakes, then flip them out onto a wire rack. Peel off the parchment paper, flip the cakes right side up, and cool completely before frosting, about 2 hours.

6. FOR THE FROSTING: In a small bowl, stir the cream, extracts, and salt together. In a stand mixer fitted with the paddle attachment, beat the butter and cream of coconut together on medium-high speed until smooth, about 20 seconds. Reduce the mixer speed to medium-low and gradually beat in the confectioners' sugar, then continue to beat until smooth, about 2 minutes. Beat in the cream mixture. Increase the mixer speed to medium-high and beat until the mixture is light and fluffy, about 4 minutes.

7. Line the edges of a cake platter with strips of parchment paper to keep the platter clean while you assemble the cake. Place one of the cake layers on the platter. Spread 1 cup of the frosting over the cake, right to the edges. Place the other cake layer on top and press lightly to adhere. Frost the cake with the remaining frosting. Press the coconut into the sides of the cake and sprinkle it over the top. Remove the parchment strips from the platter before serving.

EASY CARAMEL CAKE

WHY THIS RECIPE WORKS: A Southern favorite, caramel cake boasts a rich toffee-flavored caramel frosting spread over yellow cake layers. But the best part—the caramel frosting that develops a thin, crystalline crust on its exterior while remaining silky-smooth closer to the cake—is notoriously troublesome to make. We wanted an easier, even foolproof, caramel icing that would stay creamy long enough to frost a two-layer cake. First, we needed a cake sturdy enough to support the thick frosting. Using the reverse creaming method—beating the butter into the dry ingredients—and switching from cake flour to all-purpose flour gave us a tender, fine-crumbed cake with enough structure. For a truly easy frosting, we simmered brown sugar and butter before adding cream, and rather than use a candy thermometer we relied on simple visual cues to know when to add the cream and when to remove the mixture from the heat. To ensure that the frosting wouldn't stiffen before we frosted the cake, we beat in a little softened butter. The fat from the butter kept the frosting soft and spreadable for a few precious extra minutes. After about 30 minutes, it transformed into the classic coating of frosting that we were after.

Easy Caramel Cake

SERVES 8

In step 5, the cooled frosting stays soft and spreadable longer than with other recipes, but it will harden over time. If the frosting does begin to stiffen, you can microwave it for about 10 seconds (or until it returns to a spreadable consistency).

CAKE

- ½ cup buttermilk, at room temperature
- 4 large eggs, at room temperature
- 2 teaspoons vanilla extract
- 2¼ cups (11¼ ounces) unbleached all-purpose flour
- 1½ cups (10⅓ ounces) granulated sugar
- 1½ teaspoons baking powder
- ½ teaspoon baking soda
- ¾ teaspoon table salt
- 16 tablespoons (2 sticks) unsalted butter, cut into 16 pieces and softened

FROSTING

- 12 tablespoons (1½ sticks) unsalted butter, cut into 12 pieces and softened
- 2 cups packed (14 ounces) dark brown sugar
- ½ teaspoon table salt
- ½ cup heavy cream
- 1 teaspoon vanilla extract
- 2½ cups (10 ounces) confectioners' sugar, sifted

1. FOR THE CAKE: Adjust an oven rack to the middle position and heat the oven to 350 degrees. Grease and flour two 9-inch cake pans, then line the bottoms with parchment paper. Whisk the buttermilk, eggs, and vanilla in a large measuring cup. With an electric mixer on low speed, mix the flour, granulated sugar, baking powder, baking soda, and salt until combined. Beat in the butter, 1 piece at a time, until only pea-size pieces remain. Pour in half of the buttermilk mixture and beat over medium-high speed until light and fluffy, about 1 minute. Slowly add the remaining buttermilk mixture to the bowl and beat until incorporated, about 15 seconds.

2. Scrape equal amounts of the batter into the prepared pans and bake until golden and a toothpick inserted in the center comes out clean, 20 to 25 minutes. Cool the cakes in the pans for 10 minutes, then turn out onto wire racks. Cool completely, at least 1 hour.

3. FOR THE FROSTING: Following the photo, heat 8 tablespoons of the butter, the brown sugar, and salt in a large saucepan over medium heat until small bubbles appear around the perimeter of the pan, 4 to 8 minutes. Whisk in the cream and cook until the ring of bubbles reappears, about 1 minute. Off the heat, whisk in the vanilla.

4. Transfer the hot frosting mixture to a bowl and, with the electric mixer on low speed, gradually mix in the confectioners' sugar until incorporated. Increase the speed to medium and beat until the frosting is pale brown and just warm, about 5 minutes. Add the remaining butter, 1 piece at a time, and beat until light and fluffy, about 2 minutes.

5. Line the edges of a cake platter with strips of parchment paper to keep the platter clean. Place 1 cake round on a serving platter. Spread ¾ cup of the frosting over the cake, then top with the second cake round. Spread the remaining frosting evenly over the top and sides of the cake. Serve.

NOTES FROM THE TEST KITCHEN

GETTING THE TIMING RIGHT FOR CARAMEL

When a ring of bubbles appears around the perimeter of the pan, it's time to add the cream.

CHOCOLATE-CARAMEL LAYER CAKE

WHY THIS RECIPE WORKS: Many chocolate-caramel cakes barely contain enough caramel flavor to merit the name. To ensure a hit of caramel flavor in each and every bite, we sandwiched three layers of thick but spreadable caramel filling between layers of deep, dark, moist chocolate cake. We started with a simple chocolate cake recipe and added a little extra water and swapped melted butter for more neutral-tasting vegetable oil. Combining the dry ingredients and wet ingredients separately before whisking them together could not have been easier, and greasing and then lining two cake pans with parchment paper made for a clean release after baking. For a not-too-sweet caramel that was spreadable but thick enough to stand out between the layers, we cooked it until it turned dark (but not burnt) and added extra butter to ensure that it set up at room temperature without any unpleasant oozing. Because the cake and filling both had deep, rich flavors, we determined that the frosting could afford to be on the slightly sweeter side. Using a food processor, we combined softened butter, confectioners' sugar, cocoa powder, corn syrup (for a guaranteed smooth texture), vanilla, and melted bittersweet chocolate. For a dramatic layered look, we split our two cake rounds in half, creating four layers, and sandwiched our lush caramel filling between each before spreading the thick chocolate frosting over the sides and top of the cake.

Chocolate-Caramel Layer Cake

SERVES 12

Baking spray with flour can be used to grease and flour the pans. Both natural and Dutch-processed cocoa will work in this recipe. Our favorite natural cocoa is Hershey's Natural Cocoa Unsweetened; our favorite Dutch-processed cocoa is Droste Cocoa. When taking the temperature of the caramel in steps 3 and 4, remove the pot from heat and tilt the pan to one side. Use your thermometer to stir the caramel back and forth to equalize hot and cool spots and make sure you are getting an accurate reading. When cooking the caramel in step 4, be sure the caramel is between 240 and 245 degrees to ensure a filling with the correct consistency.

CAKE

- 1½ cups (7½ ounces) all-purpose flour
- ¾ cup (2¼ ounces) unsweetened cocoa powder
- 1½ cups (10½ ounces) granulated sugar

- 1¼ teaspoons baking soda
- ¾ teaspoon baking powder
- ¾ teaspoon salt
- ¾ cup buttermilk
- ½ cup water
- ¼ cup vegetable oil
- 2 large eggs
- 1 teaspoon vanilla extract

CARAMEL FILLING

- 1¼ cups (8¾ ounces) granulated sugar
- ¼ cup light corn syrup
- ¼ cup water
- 1 cup heavy cream
- 8 tablespoons unsalted butter, cut into 8 pieces
- 1 teaspoon vanilla extract
- ¾ teaspoon salt

FROSTING

- 16 tablespoons unsalted butter, softened
- ¾ cup (3 ounces) confectioners' sugar
- ½ cup (1½ ounces) unsweetened cocoa powder
- Pinch salt
- ½ cup light corn syrup
- ¾ teaspoon vanilla extract
- 6 ounces bittersweet chocolate, melted and cooled

- ¼-½ teaspoon coarse sea salt (optional)

1. FOR THE CAKE: Adjust oven rack to middle position and heat oven to 325 degrees. Grease two 9-inch round cake pans, line with parchment paper, grease parchment, and flour pans. Sift flour and cocoa into large bowl. Whisk in sugar, baking soda, baking powder, and salt. Whisk buttermilk, water, oil, eggs, and vanilla together in second bowl. Whisk buttermilk mixture into flour mixture until smooth batter forms. Divide batter evenly between prepared pans and smooth tops with rubber spatula.

2. Bake until toothpick inserted in center comes out clean, 22 to 28 minutes, rotating and switching pans halfway through baking. Let cakes cool in pans on wire rack for 15 minutes. Remove cakes from pans, discard parchment, and let cool completely on rack, at least 2 hours.

3. FOR THE CARAMEL FILLING: Lightly grease 8-inch square baking pan. Combine sugar, corn syrup, and water in medium saucepan. Bring to boil over medium-high heat and cook, without stirring, until mixture is amber colored, 8 to 10 minutes. Reduce heat to low and continue to cook, swirling saucepan occasionally, until dark amber, 2 to 5 minutes longer. (Caramel will register between 375 and 380 degrees.)

4. Off heat, carefully stir in cream, butter, vanilla, and salt (mixture will bubble and steam). Return saucepan to medium heat and cook, stirring frequently, until smooth and caramel reaches 240 to 245 degrees, 3 to 5 minutes. Carefully transfer caramel to prepared pan and let cool until just warm to touch (100 to 105 degrees), 20 to 30 minutes.

5. FOR THE FROSTING: Process butter, sugar, cocoa, and salt in food processor until smooth, about 30 seconds, scraping down sides of bowl as needed. Add corn syrup and vanilla and process until just combined, 5 to 10 seconds. Scrape down sides of bowl, then add chocolate and pulse until smooth and creamy, 10 to 15 seconds. (Frosting can be made 3 hours in advance. For longer storage, cover and refrigerate frosting. Let stand at room temperature for 1 hour before using.)

6. Using long serrated knife, score 1 horizontal line around sides of each cake layer; then, following scored lines, cut each layer into 2 even layers.

7. Using rubber spatula or large spoon, transfer ⅓ of caramel to center of 1 cake layer and use small offset spatula to spread over surface, leaving ½-inch border around edge. Repeat with remaining caramel and 2 of remaining cake layers. (Three of your cake layers should be topped with caramel.)

8. Line edges of cake platter with 4 strips of parchment to keep platter clean. Place 1 caramel-covered cake layer on platter. Top with second caramel-covered layer. Repeat with third caramel-covered layer and top with final layer. Spread frosting evenly over sides and top of cake. Carefully remove parchment strips. Let cake stand for at least 1 hour. (Cake can be made up to 2 days in advance and refrigerated. Let stand at room temperature for at least 5 hours before serving.) Sprinkle with coarse sea salt, if using. Cut and serve.

LEMON LAYER CAKE

WHY THIS RECIPE WORKS: Most versions of lemon layer cake are poorly executed concoctions of heavy cake stacked with filling and frosting that taste more like butter than lemon. We wanted an old-fashioned cake in which tangy, creamy lemon filling divides layers of tender, delicate cake draped in sweet frosting—an ideal contrast of sweet and tart.

Most layer cakes are substantial butter cakes, but we suspected that the light, fresh flavor of lemon would be better served by something more ethereal. After trying a sponge cake and a classic yellow cake, we found that a white butter cake was the perfect compromise: a cake nicely flavored by butter yet light enough for our flavors, with a fine crumb and tender texture.

Lemon layer cake is often filled with lemon-scented buttercream, but this filling can mute the lemon flavor and make the cake far too rich. We preferred the brightness of lemon curd. We also wanted something lighter than buttercream for our frosting, eventually landing on an old-fashioned classic: seven-minute icing. We needed to make some adjustments, as the traditional version was a little too sweet, slightly thick, and required holding a handheld mixer for longer than was comfortable. We cut back on the sugar and added a squeeze of lemon juice to solve the first two problems. After some trial and error, we learned that if we heated the mixture to at least 160 degrees and then transferred it to the stand mixer for whipping (rather than holding a hand mixer for seven minutes), the end result was just as billowy and shiny as the old-fashioned version.

Lemon Layer Cake with Fluffy White Icing

SERVES 10 TO 12

You will need a cake pan with straight sides that are at least 2 inches high. For neater slices, dip a knife into hot water before cutting the cake.

LEMON CURD FILLING

- 1 cup juice from about 6 lemons
- 1 teaspoon powdered gelatin
- 1½ cups (10½ ounces) sugar
- ⅛ teaspoon table salt
- 4 large whole eggs plus 6 large egg yolks (reserve the egg whites for the cake)
- 8 tablespoons (1 stick) unsalted butter, cut into ½-inch cubes and frozen

CAKE

- 2¼ cups (9 ounces) cake flour, plus extra for the pans
- 1 cup whole milk, at room temperature
- 6 large egg whites, at room temperature
- 2 teaspoons vanilla extract
- 1¾ cups (12¼ ounces) sugar
- 4 teaspoons baking powder
- 1 teaspoon table salt
- 12 tablespoons (1½ sticks) unsalted butter, cut into 12 pieces, softened but still cool

FLUFFY WHITE ICING

- 1 cup (7 ounces) sugar
- 2 large egg whites, at room temperature
- ¼ cup water
- 1 tablespoon juice from 1 lemon
- 1 tablespoon corn syrup

1. FOR THE FILLING: Measure 1 tablespoon of the lemon juice into a small bowl; sprinkle the gelatin over the top. Heat the remaining lemon juice, the sugar, and salt in a medium saucepan over medium-high heat, stirring occasionally, until the sugar dissolves and the mixture is hot but not boiling. Whisk the eggs and yolks in a large bowl. Whisking constantly, slowly pour the hot lemon-sugar mixture into the eggs, then return the mixture to the saucepan. Cook over medium-low heat, stirring constantly with a heatproof spatula, until the mixture registers 170 degrees on an instant-read thermometer and is thick enough to leave a trail when the spatula is scraped along the pan bottom, 4 to 6 minutes. Immediately remove the pan from the heat and stir in the gelatin mixture until dissolved. Stir in the frozen butter until incorporated. Pour the filling through a fine-mesh strainer into a bowl (you should have 3 cups). Lay a sheet of plastic wrap directly on the surface and refrigerate until firm enough to spread, at least 4 hours.

2. FOR THE CAKE: Adjust an oven rack to the middle position and heat the oven to 350 degrees. Grease and flour two 9-inch-wide by 2-inch-high round cake pans and line with parchment paper. In a 2-cup liquid measure or medium bowl, whisk together the milk, egg whites, and vanilla.

3. In a stand mixer fitted with the paddle attachment, mix the flour, sugar, baking powder, and salt at low speed until combined, about 30 seconds. With the mixer running at low speed, add the butter one piece at a time; continue beating until the mixture resembles moist crumbs with no visible butter chunks. Add all but ½ cup of the milk mixture to the crumbs and beat at medium speed until the mixture is pale and fluffy, about 1½ minutes. With the mixer running at low speed, add the remaining ½ cup milk mixture; increase the speed to medium and beat for 30 seconds more. Stop the mixer and scrape the sides of the bowl. Return the mixer to medium speed and beat for 20 seconds longer. Divide the batter evenly between the pans, smoothing the tops with a rubber spatula. Lightly tap the pan against the countertop two or three times to settle the batter.

4. Bake until a toothpick inserted in the center of the cakes comes out clean, 23 to 25 minutes, rotating the pans halfway through the baking time. Cool the cakes in the pans on a wire rack for 10 minutes. Run a small knife around the edges of the cakes, then flip them out onto a wire rack. Peel off the parchment paper, flip the cakes right side up, and cool completely before frosting, about 2 hours.

5. TO ASSEMBLE: Line the edges of a cake platter with strips of parchment paper to keep the platter clean while you assemble the cake. Use a serrated knife to cut each cake horizontally into two even layers. Place the bottom layer of one cake on the platter. Using a spatula, spread 1 cup of the lemon filling evenly on the cake, leaving a ½-inch border around the edge. Carefully place the upper cake layer on top of the filling. Spread 1 cup of the filling on top; repeat using the remaining filling and cake layers. Smooth out any filling that has leaked from the sides of the cake; cover with plastic wrap and refrigerate while making the icing.

6. FOR THE ICING: Combine all the ingredients in the bowl of a stand mixer or a large heatproof bowl and set over a medium saucepan filled with 1 inch of barely simmering water (do not let the bowl touch the water). Cook, stirring constantly, until the mixture registers 160 degrees on an instant-read thermometer, 5 to 10 minutes. Remove the bowl from the heat and transfer the mixture to a stand mixer fitted with the whisk attachment. Beat on medium speed until soft peaks form, about 5 minutes. Increase the speed to medium-high and continue to beat until the mixture has cooled to room temperature and stiff peaks form, 5 minutes longer. Using a spatula, spread the frosting evenly over the top and sides of the cake. Remove the parchment strips from the platter and serve.

OLD-FASHIONED BIRTHDAY CAKE

WHY THIS RECIPE WORKS: White layer cakes have been the classic birthday cake for more than 100 years. White cake is simply a basic butter cake made with egg whites instead of whole eggs. The whites produce the characteristic color, and they are also supposed to make the cake soft and fine-grained—that's what we wanted. Unfortunately, the white cakes that we have baked over the years, though good enough, always fell short of our high expectations. They came out a little dry and chewy—one might say cottony—and we noticed that they were riddled with tunnels and small holes. What were we doing wrong?

Every traditional recipe for white cake calls for stiffly beaten egg whites folded into the batter at the end. We began to suspect that it was the beaten egg whites that were forming the large air pockets and those unsightly holes in the baked cakes. We solved this problem by mixing the egg whites with the milk before beating them into the flour-and-butter mixture. The results were fantastic. The cake was not only fine-grained and free from holes but, to our surprise, it was also larger and lighter than the ones we'd prepared with beaten whites. And the method couldn't be simpler, quicker, or more foolproof. To make this cake birthday-special, we iced it with an easy butter frosting and added a layer of raspberry jam and chopped toasted almonds.

Classic White Layer Cake with Butter Frosting and Raspberry-Almond Filling

SERVES 10 TO 12

There will be enough frosting left to pipe a border around the base and top of the cake; to decorate the cake more elaborately, you should make 1½ times the frosting recipe. If desired, finish the sides of the cake with 1 cup of sliced almonds.

CAKE

- 2¼ cups (9 ounces) cake flour, plus extra for the pans
- 1 cup whole milk, at room temperature
- 6 large egg whites, at room temperature
- 1 teaspoon vanilla extract
- 1 teaspoon almond extract
- 1¾ cups (12¼ ounces) granulated sugar
- 4 teaspoons baking powder
- 1 teaspoon table salt
- 12 tablespoons (1½ sticks) unsalted butter, cut into 12 pieces and softened

FROSTING AND FILLING

- 16 tablespoons (2 sticks) unsalted butter, softened
- 4 cups (1 pound) confectioners' sugar
- 1 tablespoon vanilla extract
- 1 tablespoon milk
- Pinch table salt
- ½ cup (2¼ ounces) blanched slivered almonds, toasted and chopped coarse
- ⅓ cup seedless raspberry jam

1. FOR THE CAKE: Adjust an oven rack to the middle position and heat the oven to 350 degrees. Grease and flour two 8- or 9-inch round cake pans, then line the bottoms with parchment paper. Whisk the milk, egg whites, and both extracts together in a small bowl.

2. In a stand mixer fitted with the paddle attachment, mix the flour, sugar, baking powder, and salt together on low speed until combined, about 30 seconds. Increase the speed to medium-low and beat the butter into the flour mixture, one piece at a time, about 30 seconds. Continue to beat the mixture until it resembles moist crumbs, about 1 minute.

3. Beat in all but ½ cup of the milk mixture, then increase the mixer speed to medium and beat until smooth, light, and fluffy, about 1 minute. Reduce the mixer speed to low and slowly beat in the remaining ½ cup milk mixture until the batter looks slightly curdled, about 15 seconds.

4. Give the batter a final stir with a rubber spatula to make sure it is thoroughly combined. Scrape the batter into the prepared pans, smooth the tops, and lightly tap the pans against the countertop two or three times to settle the batter. Bake the cakes until a toothpick inserted in the center comes out with a few crumbs attached, 20 to 25 minutes, rotating the pans halfway through the baking time.

5. Cool the cakes in the pans for 10 minutes. Run a small knife around the edge of the cakes, then flip them out onto a wire rack. Peel off the parchment paper, flip the cakes right side up, and cool completely before frosting, about 2 hours.

6. FOR THE FROSTING AND FILLING: In the bowl of a stand mixer fitted with the paddle attachment, beat the butter, confectioners' sugar, vanilla, milk, and salt on low speed until the sugar is moistened, about 30 seconds. Increase the speed to medium-high; beat, stopping twice to scrape down the bowl, until creamy and fluffy, about 1½ minutes.

7. Line the edges of a cake platter with strips of parchment to keep the platter clean while you assemble the cake. Place one cake layer on the platter. Combine ½ cup of the frosting with the almonds in a small bowl. Spread the almond frosting over the first layer. Carefully spread the jam on top, then cover with the second cake layer. Spread the remaining frosting evenly over the top and sides of the cake. Remove the parchment strips from the platter before serving.

NOTES FROM THE TEST KITCHEN

LINING CAKE PANS

1. Trace the outline of the bottom of the pan onto a sheet of parchment paper. Cut out the outline, cutting on the inside of the line so that the round fits snugly inside the pan.

2. Fit the trimmed piece of parchment into the pan.

CLASSIC YELLOW LAYER CAKE

WHY THIS RECIPE WORKS: Traditional yellow layer cake should melt in the mouth and taste of butter and eggs. But many recipes we tried came out crumbly, sugary, and hard. And the flavor? It tasted merely sweet. We wanted a yellow cake that was tender and buttery and could stand up to a slathering of frosting, if desired.

Most versions of yellow layer cake rely on the classic 1–2–3–4 formula (1 cup butter, 2 cups sugar, 3 cups flour, and four eggs—plus milk, baking powder, vanilla, and salt) and follow the classic way of mixing together the ingredients—creaming the butter and sugar, adding the eggs one at a time, and finally adding the milk and dry ingredients alternately. This worked okay, but we wanted something easier for this cake. The two-stage method fit the bill. In this technique, the dry ingredients are combined and then two-thirds of the milk and eggs are added and beaten until thick and fluffy. Then in the second stage, the rest of the milk and eggs are poured in and the batter is beaten again. This technique is simpler and quicker, and produced a tender cake. The flavor still needed some improvement. We tackled the proportions of the ingredients, increasing the butter, eggs, and sugar. This cake turned out fine-grained, soft, and meltingly rich—just what we wanted. As for the frosting, we chose a traditional vanilla buttercream. Rich with egg yolks, butter, sugar, and corn syrup for sheen, this supple frosting is the perfect complement to our cake.

Classic Yellow Layer Cake with Vanilla Buttercream

SERVES 8 TO 10

Cake flour gives this buttery yellow cake its tender crumb; do not substitute all-purpose flour. When making the buttercream, make sure that the sugar mixture is poured into the egg yolks while still hot. For a decorative finish, press toasted sliced almonds on the sides of the cake.

CAKE

- 1¾ cups (7 ounces) cake flour (see note), plus extra for the pans
- ½ cup whole milk, at room temperature
- 4 large eggs, at room temperature
- 2 teaspoons vanilla extract
- 1½ cups (10½ ounces) sugar
- 2 teaspoons baking powder
- ¾ teaspoon table salt
- 16 tablespoons (2 sticks) unsalted butter, cut into 16 pieces and softened

VANILLA BUTTERCREAM

- 6 large egg yolks, at room temperature
- ¾ cup (5¼ ounces) sugar
- ½ cup light corn syrup
- 2½ teaspoons vanilla extract
- ¼ teaspoon table salt
- 4 sticks unsalted butter, cut into chunks and softened

1. FOR THE CAKE: Adjust an oven rack to the middle position and heat the oven to 350 degrees. Grease and flour two 8- or 9-inch round cake pans, then line the bottoms with parchment paper. Whisk the milk, eggs, and vanilla together in a small bowl.

2. In a stand mixer fitted with the paddle attachment, whisk the flour, sugar, baking powder, and salt together on low speed until combined, about 30 seconds. Increase the speed to medium-low and beat the butter into the flour mixture, one piece at a time, about 30 seconds. Continue to beat the mixture until it resembles moist crumbs, about 1 minute.

3. Beat in all but ½ cup of the milk mixture, then increase the mixer speed to medium and beat the batter until smooth, light, and fluffy, about 1 minute. Reduce the mixer speed to low and slowly beat in the remaining ½ cup milk mixture until the batter looks slightly curdled, about 15 seconds.

4. Give the batter a final stir with a rubber spatula to make sure it is thoroughly combined. Scrape the batter into the prepared pans and smooth the tops with a rubber spatula. Lightly tap the pans against the countertop two or three times to settle the batter. Bake the cakes until a toothpick inserted in the center comes out with a few crumbs attached, 20 to 25 minutes, rotating the pans halfway through the baking time.

5. Cool the cakes in the pans for 10 minutes. Run a small knife around the edge of the cakes, then flip them out onto a wire rack. Peel off the parchment paper, flip the cakes right side up, and cool completely before frosting, about 2 hours.

6. FOR THE FROSTING: Whip the egg yolks in a large bowl with an electric mixer on medium speed until slightly thickened and pale yellow, 4 to 6 minutes.

7. Meanwhile, bring the sugar and corn syrup to a boil in a small saucepan over medium heat, stirring occasionally to dissolve the sugar, about 3 minutes.

8. Without letting the hot sugar mixture cool off, turn the mixer to low and slowly pour the warm sugar syrup into the whipped egg yolks without hitting the side of the bowl or the beaters. Increase the mixer speed to medium-high and whip the mixture until it is light and fluffy and the bowl is no longer warm, 5 to 10 minutes.

9. Reduce the mixer speed to medium-low and add the vanilla and salt. Gradually add the butter, one piece at a time, until completely incorporated, about 2 minutes. Increase the mixer speed to medium-high and whip the buttercream until smooth and silky, about 2 minutes. (If the mixture looks curdled, wrap a hot wet towel around the bowl and continue to whip until smooth, 1 to 2 minutes.)

10. Line the edges of a cake platter with strips of parchment to keep the platter clean while you assemble the cake. Place one cake layer on the platter. Spread 1½ cups of the frosting evenly across the top of the cake with a spatula. Place the second cake layer on top, then spread the remaining frosting evenly over the top and sides of the cake. Remove the parchment strips from the platter before serving.

FLUFFY YELLOW CAKE

WHY THIS RECIPE WORKS: It's easy to create a supremely fluffy layer cake with additives, but most cakes made entirely from natural ingredients are either unpleasantly dense or too fragile to support layers of frosting. We wanted a frosted yellow layer cake with an ethereal texture and the great flavor of real butter and eggs.

Chiffon cakes are especially weightless, springy, and moist. But unlike butter cakes, they are too light to stand up to a serious slathering of frosting. We decided to blend the two types of cake. We adapted a chiffon technique (using a large quantity of whipped egg whites to get a high volume and light texture) to combine the ingredients from our butter cake recipe. This worked beautifully, creating a light, porous cake that was hefty

enough to hold the frosting's weight. But the cake lacked moistness and some tenderness. A combination of fats (butter plus vegetable oil), kept the butter flavor intact while improving the moistness of the cake. For extra tenderness, we increased the sugar and substituted buttermilk for milk. The buttermilk not only introduced a new flavor dimension, but also allowed us to replace some of the baking powder with a little baking soda to ensure an even rise.

As for the frosting, a fluffy chocolate frosting is the perfect partner to this cake. A hefty amount of cocoa powder combined with melted chocolate gave the frosting a deep chocolate flavor. A combination of confectioners' sugar and corn syrup made it smooth and glossy. To keep the frosting from separating and turning greasy, we moved it out of the stand mixer and into the food processor. The faster machine minimized any risk of over beating, as it blended the ingredients quickly without melting the butter or incorporating too much air. The result is a thick, fluffy chocolate frosting that spreads like a dream.

Fluffy Yellow Layer Cake with Milk Chocolate Frosting

SERVES 10 TO 12

Bring all the ingredients to room temperature before beginning. For the frosting, cool the chocolate to between 85 and 100 degrees before adding it to the butter mixture. The frosting can be made 3 hours in advance. For longer storage, refrigerate the frosting, covered, and let it stand at room temperature for 1 hour before using.

CAKE

- 2½ cups (10 ounces) cake flour, plus extra for the pans
- 1¾ cups (12¼ ounces) granulated sugar
- 1¼ teaspoons baking powder
- ¼ teaspoon baking soda
- ¾ teaspoon table salt
- 1 cup buttermilk, at room temperature
- 10 tablespoons (1¼ sticks) unsalted butter, melted and cooled slightly
- 3 tablespoons vegetable oil
- 2 teaspoons vanilla extract
- 6 large egg yolks plus 3 large egg whites, at room temperature

FROSTING

- 20 tablespoons (2½ sticks) unsalted butter, softened
- 1 cup (4 ounces) confectioners' sugar
- ¾ cup Dutch-processed cocoa powder
- Pinch table salt
- ¾ cup light corn syrup
- 1 teaspoon vanilla extract
- 8 ounces milk chocolate, melted and cooled slightly (see note)

1. FOR THE CAKE: Adjust an oven rack to the middle position and heat the oven to 350 degrees. Grease and flour two 9-inch-wide by 2-inch-high round cake pans and line with parchment paper. Whisk the flour, 1½ cups of the granulated sugar, the baking powder, baking soda, and salt together in a large bowl. In a 4-cup liquid measuring cup or medium bowl, whisk together the buttermilk, melted butter, oil, vanilla, and egg yolks.

2. In a stand mixer fitted with the whisk attachment, beat the egg whites at medium-high speed until foamy, about 30 seconds. With the machine running, gradually add the remaining ¼ cup granulated sugar; continue to beat until stiff peaks just form, 30 to 60 seconds (the whites should hold a peak but the mixture should appear moist). Transfer to a bowl and set aside.

NOTES FROM THE TEST KITCHEN

FROSTING A LAYER CAKE

1. Dollop a portion of frosting in the center of the cake and spread into an even layer right to the edge.

2. Lay the second layer on top. Brush away any large crumbs, dollop more frosting in the center, and spread slightly over the edge.

3. Gather a few tablespoons of frosting onto the top of the spatula, then gently smear it onto the side of the cake. Repeat to frost the sides completely.

4. For smooth sides, gently run the edge of the spatula around the cake. Or, to create billows in the frosting, press the back of a soup spoon into the frosting, then twirl the spoon as you lift it away.

3. Add the flour mixture to the now-empty mixing bowl. With the mixer still fitted with the whisk attachment, and running at low speed, gradually pour in the butter mixture and mix until almost incorporated (a few streaks of dry flour will remain), about 15 seconds. Stop the mixer and scrape the whisk and the sides of the bowl. Return the mixer to medium-low speed and beat until smooth and fully incorporated, 10 to 15 seconds.

4. Using a rubber spatula, stir one-third of the whites into the batter to lighten, then add the remaining whites and gently fold into the batter until no white streaks remain. Divide the batter evenly between the prepared pans, smoothing the tops with a rubber spatula. Lightly tap the pans against the countertop two or three times to settle the batter.

5. Bake until the cake layers begin to pull away from the sides of the pans and a toothpick inserted into the centers comes out clean, 20 to 22 minutes, rotating the pans halfway through the baking time. Cool the cakes in the pans on a wire rack for 10 minutes. Run a small knife around the edge of the cakes, then flip them out onto a wire rack. Peel off the parchment paper, flip the cakes right side up, and cool completely before frosting, about 2 hours.

6. FOR THE FROSTING: In a food processor, process the butter, confectioners' sugar, cocoa, and salt until smooth, about 30 seconds, scraping down the sides of the bowl as needed. Add the corn syrup and vanilla and process until just combined, 5 to 10 seconds. Scrape down the sides of the bowl, then add the chocolate and process until smooth and creamy, 10 to 15 seconds. The frosting can be used immediately or held (see note).

7. Line the edges of a cake platter with strips of parchment to keep the platter clean while you assemble the cake. Place one cake layer on the platter. Spread 1½ cups of the frosting evenly across the top of the cake with a spatula. Place the second cake layer on top, then spread the remaining frosting evenly over the top and sides of the cake. Remove the parchment strips from the platter before serving.

OLD-FASHIONED CHOCOLATE LAYER CAKE

WHY THIS RECIPE WORKS: Over the years, chocolate cakes have become denser, richer, and squatter. Many contemporary cakes are so intense that just a few forkfuls satisfy. These cakes taste great—it's hard to imagine a bad chocolate cake—but sometimes we'd rather have a real piece of cake, not a fudge-like confection. We wanted an old-style, mile-high chocolate layer cake with a tender, airy, open crumb and a soft, billowy frosting.

The mixing method was the key to getting the right texture. After trying a variety of techniques, we turned to ribboning, a popular old-fashioned method used for cakes like genoise (a moist, light sponge cake). Ribboning involves whipping eggs with sugar until they double in volume, then adding the butter, dry ingredients, and milk. The egg foam aerated the cake, giving it both structure and tenderness. To achieve a moist cake with rich chocolate flavor, we once again looked to historical sources, which suggested using buttermilk and making a "pudding" with a mixture of chocolate, water, and sugar. We simply melted unsweetened chocolate and cocoa powder in hot water over a double boiler, then stirred in sugar until it dissolved. Turning to the frosting, we wanted to combine the best elements of classic chocolate frostings: the intense chocolate flavor of a ganache (a mixture of chocolate and cream) and the volume of a meringue or buttercream. The solution turned out to be a simple reversal of the conventional ganache procedure: We poured cold (rather than heated) cream into warm (rather than room-temperature) chocolate, waited for it to cool to room temperature, then whipped until fluffy.

Old-Fashioned Chocolate Layer Cake with Chocolate Frosting

SERVES 10 TO 12

For a smooth, spreadable frosting, use chopped semisweet chocolate, not chocolate chips—chocolate chips contain less cocoa butter than bar chocolate and will not melt as readily. As for other bar chocolate, bittersweet chocolate that is 60 percent cacao can be substituted but it will produce a stiffer, but still spreadable, frosting. Bittersweet chocolate with 70 percent cacao, however, should be avoided—it will produce a frosting that is crumbly and it will not spread. For best results, don't make the frosting until the cakes are cooled, and use the frosting as soon as it is ready. If the frosting gets too cold and stiff to spread easily, wrap the mixer bowl with a towel soaked in hot water and mix on low speed until the frosting appears creamy and smooth.

CAKE

- 1¾ cups (8¾ ounces) unbleached all-purpose flour, plus extra for the pans
- 4 ounces unsweetened chocolate, chopped coarse
- ¼ cup Dutch-processed cocoa powder
- ½ cup hot water
- 1¾ cups (12¼ ounces) sugar
- 1½ teaspoons baking soda
- 1 teaspoon table salt
- 1 cup buttermilk
- 2 teaspoons vanilla extract
- 4 large whole eggs plus 2 large egg yolks, at room temperature
- 12 tablespoons (1½ sticks) unsalted butter, very soft

FROSTING

- 1 pound semisweet chocolate, chopped fine (see note)
- 8 tablespoons (1 stick) unsalted butter
- ⅓ cup (2⅓ ounces) sugar
- 2 tablespoons corn syrup
- 2 teaspoons vanilla extract
- ¼ teaspoon table salt
- 1¼ cups heavy cream, chilled

1. FOR THE CAKE: Adjust an oven rack to the middle position and heat the oven to 350 degrees. Grease and flour two 9-inch-wide by 2-inch-high round cake pans and line with parchment paper. Combine the chocolate, cocoa powder, and hot water in a medium heatproof bowl set over a saucepan filled with 1 inch of barely simmering water, stirring occasionally until smooth. Add ½ cup of the sugar to the chocolate mixture and stir until thick and glossy, 1 to 2 minutes. Remove the bowl from the heat and set aside to cool.

2. Whisk the flour, baking soda, and salt in a medium bowl. Combine the buttermilk and vanilla in a small bowl. In the bowl of a stand mixer fitted with the whisk attachment, whisk the whole eggs and egg yolks on medium-low speed until combined, about 10 seconds. Add the remaining 1¼ cups sugar, increase the speed to high, and whisk until fluffy and lightened in color, 2 to 3 minutes. Replace the whisk with the paddle attachment. Add the cooled chocolate mixture to the egg-sugar mixture and mix on medium speed until thoroughly incorporated, 30 to 45 seconds, pausing to scrape down the sides of the bowl with a rubber spatula as needed. Add the softened butter 1 tablespoon at a time, mixing for about 10 seconds after each addition. Add about one-third of the flour mixture followed by half of the buttermilk mixture, mixing until incorporated after each addition (about 15 seconds). Repeat, using half of the remaining flour mixture and all of the remaining buttermilk mixture (the batter may appear separated). Scrape down the sides of the bowl and add the remaining flour mixture; mix at medium-low speed until the batter is thoroughly combined, about 15 seconds. Remove the bowl from the mixer and fold the batter once or twice with a rubber spatula to incorporate any remaining flour. Divide the batter evenly between the prepared pans, smoothing the tops with a rubber spatula. Lightly tap the pans against the countertop two or three times to settle the batter.

3. Bake the cakes until a toothpick inserted into the center comes out with a few crumbs attached, 25 to 30 minutes, rotating the pans halfway through the baking time. Cool the cakes in the pans on a wire rack for 15 minutes. Run a small knife around the edge of the cakes, then flip them out onto a wire rack. Peel off the parchment paper, flip the cakes right side up, and cool completely before frosting, about 2 hours.

4. FOR THE FROSTING: Melt the chocolate in a heatproof bowl set over a saucepan containing 1 inch of barely simmering water, stirring occasionally until smooth. Remove from the heat and set aside. Meanwhile, heat the butter in a small saucepan over medium-low heat until melted. Increase the heat to medium; add the sugar, corn syrup, vanilla, and salt and stir with a heatproof spatula until the sugar is dissolved, 4 to 5 minutes. Add the melted chocolate, butter mixture, and cream to the clean bowl of a stand mixer and stir to thoroughly combine.

5. Place the mixer bowl over an ice bath and stir the mixture constantly with a rubber spatula until the frosting is thick and just beginning to harden against the sides of the bowl, 1 to 2 minutes (the frosting should be at 70 degrees). Place the bowl on a stand mixer fitted with the paddle attachment and beat on medium-high speed until the frosting is light and fluffy, 1 to 2 minutes. Stir with a rubber spatula until completely smooth.

6. Line the edges of a cake platter with strips of parchment to keep the platter clean while you assemble the cake. Place one cake layer on the platter. Spread 1½ cups of the frosting evenly across the top of the cake with a spatula. Place the second cake layer on top, then spread the remaining frosting evenly over the top and sides of the cake. Remove the parchment strips from the platter before serving.

CHOCOLATE SHEET CAKE

WHY THIS RECIPE WORKS: Sheet cakes, for all their simplicity, can still turn out dry, sticky, or flavorless and, on occasion, can even sink in the middle. We wanted a simple, dependable recipe that delivered a moist yet tender cake. We started with the mixing method—testing everything from creaming butter to beating yolks, whipping whites, and gently folding together everything in the end. The best of the lot was the most complicated to make, so we took a step back. The simplest technique we tried was simply whisking all the ingredients together without beating, creaming, or whipping. The recipe needed work, but the approach was clearly a good match for the simple all-purpose nature of a sheet cake. First we added buttermilk and baking soda to lighten the batter. To increase the chocolate flavor, we reduced the sugar, flour, and butter. To further deepen the chocolate taste, we used semisweet chocolate in addition to the cocoa. We baked the cake at a low temperature for 40 minutes to produce a perfect cake with a flat top. Though this cake can be frosted with almost anything, we like a classic American milk chocolate frosting, which pairs well with the darker flavor of the cake.

Chocolate Sheet Cake with Easy Chocolate Frosting

SERVES 15 TO 18

We prefer Dutch-processed cocoa for the deeper chocolate flavor it gives the cake. The frosting needs about an hour to cool before it can be used, so begin making it when the cake comes out of the oven. You can also serve the cake lightly dusted with confectioners' sugar or with lightly sweetened whipped cream.

CAKE

- 12 tablespoons (1½ sticks) unsalted butter
- ¾ cup cocoa powder, preferably Dutch-processed (see note)
- 1¼ cups (6¼ ounces) unbleached all-purpose flour
- ½ teaspoon baking soda
- ¼ teaspoon table salt
- 8 ounces semisweet chocolate, chopped
- 4 large eggs, at room temperature
- 1½ cups (10½ ounces) granulated sugar
- 1 teaspoon vanilla extract
- 1 cup buttermilk

FROSTING

- ½ cup heavy cream
- Pinch table salt
- 1 tablespoon light or dark corn syrup
- 10 ounces milk chocolate, chopped
- ½ cup (2 ounces) confectioners' sugar
- 8 tablespoons (1 stick) cold unsalted butter, cut into 8 pieces

1. FOR THE CAKE: Adjust an oven rack to the middle position and heat the oven to 325 degrees. Grease a 13 by 9-inch baking pan, then line the bottom with parchment paper.

2. Sift together the cocoa, flour, baking soda, and salt in a medium bowl; set aside. Melt the chocolate and butter in a heatproof bowl set over a saucepan filled with 1 inch of barely simmering water, stirring occasionally until smooth. Whisk together the eggs, sugar, and vanilla in a medium bowl. Whisk in the buttermilk until smooth.

3. Whisk the chocolate into the egg mixture until combined. Whisk in the dry ingredients until the batter is smooth and glossy. Pour the batter into the prepared pan; bake until firm in the center when lightly pressed and a toothpick inserted in the center comes out clean, about 40 minutes, rotating the pan halfway through the baking time. Let the cake cool completely in the pan, set on a wire rack, about 2 hours. Run a small knife around the cake and flip the cake out onto a wire rack. Peel off the parchment paper, then flip the cake right side up onto a serving platter.

4. FOR THE FROSTING: Heat the cream, salt, and corn syrup in a microwave-safe measuring cup on high power until simmering, about 1 minute, or bring to a simmer in a small saucepan over medium heat.

5. Place the chocolate in a food processor. With the machine running, gradually add the hot cream mixture through the feed tube; process for 1 minute after the cream has been added. Stop the machine; add the confectioners' sugar and process to combine, about 30 seconds. With the machine running, add the butter through the feed tube one piece at a time; process until incorporated and smooth, about 20 seconds longer.

6. Transfer the frosting to a medium bowl and cool at room temperature, stirring frequently, until thick and spreadable, about 1 hour. Spread the frosting evenly over the top and sides of the cake and serve.

SIMPLE CHOCOLATE SHEET CAKE

WHY THIS RECIPE WORKS: For a simple cake that boasted deep chocolate flavor and color, we used a combination of Dutch-processed cocoa and melted bittersweet chocolate; the cocoa offered pure, assertive chocolate flavor while the chocolate contributed complexity as well as fat and sugar. Neutral-tasting oil allowed the chocolate flavor to shine. To minimize cleanup, we mixed the wet and dry ingredients directly into the saucepan where we'd melted the chocolate with cocoa and milk. A milk chocolate ganache frosting contrasted nicely with the deeper flavor of the cake. To make the ganache thick, rich, and creamy, we added plenty of softened butter to the warm chocolate-cream mixture, refrigerated the frosting to cool it quickly so that it would spread nicely, and gave it a quick whisk to smooth it out and lighten its texture.

Simple Chocolate Sheet Cake with Milk Chocolate Frosting

SERVES 12

While any high-quality chocolate can be used here, our preferred bittersweet chocolates are Ghirardelli 60% Cacao Bittersweet Chocolate Premium Baking Bar and Callebaut Intense Dark Chocolate, L-60-40NV, and our favorite milk chocolate is Dove Silky Smooth Milk Chocolate. We recommend making this cake with a Dutch-processed cocoa powder; our favorite is from Droste. Using a natural cocoa powder will result in a drier cake.

CAKE

- 1½ cups (10½ ounces) granulated sugar
- 1¼ cups (6¼ ounces) all-purpose flour
- ½ teaspoon baking soda
- ½ teaspoon salt
- 1 cup whole milk
- 8 ounces bittersweet chocolate, chopped fine
- ¾ cup (2¼ ounces) Dutch-processed cocoa powder
- ⅔ cup vegetable oil
- 4 large eggs
- 1 teaspoon vanilla extract

FROSTING

- 1 pound milk chocolate, chopped
- ⅔ cup heavy cream
- 16 tablespoons (2 sticks) unsalted butter, cut into 16 pieces and softened

1. FOR THE CAKE: Adjust oven rack to middle position and heat oven to 325 degrees. Lightly spray 13 by 9-inch baking pan with vegetable oil spray. Whisk sugar, flour, baking soda, and salt together in medium bowl; set aside.

2. Combine milk, chocolate, and cocoa in large saucepan. Place saucepan over low heat and cook, whisking frequently, until chocolate is melted and mixture is smooth. Remove from heat and let cool slightly, about 5 minutes. Whisk oil, eggs, and vanilla into chocolate mixture (mixture may initially look curdled) until smooth and homogeneous. Add sugar mixture and whisk until combined, making sure to scrape corners of saucepan.

3. Transfer batter to prepared pan; bake until firm in center when lightly pressed and toothpick inserted in center comes out with few crumbs attached, 30 to 35 minutes, rotating pan halfway through baking. Let cake cool completely in pan on wire rack before frosting, 1 to 2 hours.

4. FOR THE FROSTING: While cake is baking, combine chocolate and cream in large heatproof bowl set over saucepan filled with 1 inch barely simmering water, making sure that water does not touch bottom of bowl. Whisk mixture occasionally until chocolate is uniformly smooth and glossy, 10 to 15 minutes. Remove bowl from saucepan. Add butter, whisking once or twice to break up pieces. Let mixture stand for 5 minutes to finish melting butter, then whisk until completely smooth. Refrigerate frosting, without stirring, until cooled and thickened, 30 minutes to 1 hour.

5. Once cool, whisk frosting until smooth. (Whisked frosting will lighten in color slightly and should hold its shape on whisk.) Spread frosting evenly over top of cake. Cut cake into squares and serve out of pan. (Leftover cake can be refrigerated in airtight container for up to 2 days.)

GERMAN CHOCOLATE CAKE

WHY THIS RECIPE WORKS: Most German chocolate cake recipes are similar, if not identical, to the one on the German's Sweet Chocolate box. Our tasters found several shortcomings in this recipe. It produced a cake that was too sweet, with chocolate flavor that was too mild, and with a texture so listless that the filling and cake together formed a soggy, sweet mush. We wanted a cake that was less sweet and more chocolaty than the original, but we didn't want to sacrifice the overall blend of flavors and textures that makes German chocolate cake so appealing in the first place.

The first order of business was to scale back the recipe by one quarter, which allowed us to fit the batter into two cake pans, thereby producing a cake with four thinner layers rather than three thicker layers. After testing, we discovered that the texture of the cake actually improved when we used whole eggs instead of laboriously separating the eggs, beating the whites, and folding them into the batter. We increased chocolate flavor with a combination of cocoa powder and good-quality semisweet or bittersweet chocolate. By adjusting the level and proportions of the sugar (both brown and white) and butter in the cake and filling, as well as toasting the pecans, we finished the necessary adjustments to create a definitely easier-to-make cake, with better texture and flavor than the original.

German Chocolate Cake

SERVES 12 TO 16

When you assemble the cake, the filling should be cool or cold. To be time-efficient, first make the filling, then use the refrigeration time to prepare, bake, and cool the cakes. For an accurate measurement of boiling water, bring a kettle of water to a boil, then measure out the desired amount. Note that the toasted pecans are stirred into the filling just before assembly to keep them from becoming soft and soggy.

FILLING

- 4 large egg yolks, at room temperature
- 1 (12-ounce) can evaporated milk
- 1 cup (7 ounces) granulated sugar
- ¼ cup packed (1¾ ounces) light brown sugar
- 6 tablespoons (¾ stick) unsalted butter, cut into 6 pieces
- ⅛ teaspoon table salt
- 2 teaspoons vanilla extract
- 2⅓ cups sweetened shredded coconut
- 1½ cups (6 ounces) finely chopped pecans, toasted (see note)

CAKE

- 4 ounces semisweet or bittersweet chocolate, chopped fine
- ¼ cup Dutch-processed cocoa powder
- ½ cup boiling water (see note)
- 2 cups (10 ounces) unbleached all-purpose flour, plus extra for the pans
- ¾ teaspoon baking soda
- 12 tablespoons (1½ sticks) unsalted butter, softened

- 1 cup (7 ounces) granulated sugar
- ⅔ cup packed (4⅔ ounces) light brown sugar
- ¾ teaspoon table salt
- 4 large whole eggs, at room temperature
- 1 teaspoon vanilla extract
- ¾ cup sour cream, at room temperature

1. FOR THE FILLING: Whisk the egg yolks in a medium saucepan; gradually whisk in the evaporated milk. Add the sugars, butter, and salt and cook over medium-high heat, whisking constantly, until the mixture is boiling, frothy, and slightly thickened, about 6 minutes. Transfer the mixture to a bowl, whisk in the vanilla, then stir in the coconut. Cool until just warm, cover with plastic wrap, and refrigerate until cool or cold, at least 2 hours or up to 3 days. (The pecans are stirred in just before cake assembly.)

2. FOR THE CAKE: Adjust an oven rack to the lower-middle position; heat the oven to 350 degrees. Combine the chocolate and cocoa in a small bowl; pour the boiling water over and let stand to melt the chocolate, about 2 minutes. Whisk until smooth; set aside until cooled to room temperature.

3. Meanwhile, grease and flour two 9-inch-wide by 2-inch-high round cake pans and line with parchment paper. Sift the flour and baking soda into a medium bowl or onto a sheet of parchment or waxed paper.

4. In a stand mixer fitted with the paddle attachment, beat the butter, sugars, and salt at medium-low speed until the sugar is moistened, about 30 seconds. Increase the speed to medium-high and beat until the mixture is light and fluffy, about 4 minutes, scraping down the bowl with a spatula halfway through. With the mixer running at medium speed, add the eggs one at a time, beating well after each addition and scraping down the bowl halfway through. Beat in the vanilla; increase the speed to medium-high and beat until light and fluffy, about 45 seconds. With the mixer running at low speed, add the chocolate mixture, then increase the speed to medium and beat until combined, about 30 seconds, scraping down the bowl once (the batter may appear curdled). Add about one-third of the flour mixture, followed by half of the sour cream, mixing until just incorporated after each addition (about 5 seconds). Repeat using half of the remaining flour mixture and all of the remaining sour cream. Scrape down the bowl and add the remaining flour mixture; mix at medium-low speed until the batter is thoroughly combined, about 15 seconds. Divide the batter evenly between the prepared cake pans, smoothing the tops with a rubber spatula. Lightly tap the pans against the countertop two or three times to settle the batter.

5. Bake the cakes until a toothpick inserted into the centers comes out clean, about 30 minutes, rotating the pans halfway through the baking time. Cool the cakes in the pans on a wire rack for 10 minutes. Run a small knife around the edges of the cakes, then flip them out onto a wire rack. Peel off the parchment, flip the cakes right side up, and cool completely before frosting, about 2 hours.

6. TO ASSEMBLE: Stir the toasted pecans into the chilled filling. Line the edges of a cake platter with strips of parchment paper to keep the platter clean while you assemble the cake. Use a serrated knife to cut each cake horizontally into two even layers. Place one bottom layer on the platter. Spread about 1 cup of the filling evenly across the top of the cake with a spatula. Carefully place the upper cake layer on top of the filling; repeat using the remaining filling and cake layers. Remove the parchment strips before serving.

CHOCOLATE CUPCAKES

WHY THIS RECIPE WORKS: Cupcakes shouldn't be complicated, but homemade versions can take a lot of time and store-bought mixes don't deliver good chocolate flavor. We wanted the consummate chocolate cupcake—one with a rich, buttery flavor, a light, moist, cakey texture, and just the right amount of sugar—but we wanted it to be almost as quick and easy to make as the cupcakes that come from a box.

For the mixing method, we found that the melted-butter method often used for mixing muffins, quick breads, and brownies—a method that requires no mixer and no time spent waiting for butter to soften—worked best. The same procedure won out over the more conventional creaming method for our cupcakes, delivering a light texture with a tender, fine crumb. Moving on to tackle our desire for deep chocolate flavor, we found that a combination of cocoa powder and bittersweet chocolate delivered deep chocolate flavor and that mixing the cocoa powder with the butter and chocolate as they melted (rather than adding the cocoa to the dry ingredients) made the chocolate flavor even stronger and richer. Sour cream gave our cupcakes moistness and a little tang, while just the right amounts of baking soda and baking powder helped them rise to a gently domed shape that was perfect for frosting.

Dark Chocolate Cupcakes

MAKES 12 CUPCAKES

Store leftover cupcakes (frosted or unfrosted) in the refrigerator, but let them come to room temperature before serving.

- 8 tablespoons (1 stick) unsalted butter, cut into 4 pieces
- 2 ounces bittersweet chocolate, chopped
- ½ cup cocoa powder, preferably Dutch-processed
- ¾ cup (3¾ ounces) unbleached all-purpose flour
- ¾ teaspoon baking powder
- ½ teaspoon baking soda
- 2 large eggs, at room temperature
- ¾ cup (5¼ ounces) sugar
- 1 teaspoon vanilla extract
- ½ teaspoon table salt
- ½ cup sour cream
- 1 recipe Easy Vanilla Bean Buttercream, Easy Chocolate Buttercream, or Easy Coffee Buttercream (recipes follow)

1. Adjust an oven rack to the lower-middle position and heat the oven to 350 degrees. Line a standard-size muffin pan with baking cup liners.

2. Melt the butter, chocolate, and cocoa in a medium heat-proof bowl set over a saucepan filled with 1 inch of barely simmering water, stirring occasionally. Set aside to cool until just warm to the touch.

3. Whisk the flour, baking powder, and baking soda in a small bowl to combine.

4. Whisk the eggs in a medium bowl to combine; add the sugar, vanilla, and salt and whisk until fully incorporated. Add the cooled chocolate mixture and whisk until combined. Sift about one-third of the flour mixture over the chocolate mixture and whisk until combined; whisk in the sour cream until combined, then sift the remaining flour mixture over the batter and whisk until homogeneous and thick.

5. Divide the batter evenly among the muffin cups. Bake until a toothpick or wooden skewer inserted into the center of the cupcakes comes out clean, 18 to 20 minutes, rotating the pan halfway through the baking time.

6. Cool the cupcakes in the pan on a wire rack until cool enough to handle, about 15 minutes. Carefully lift each cupcake from the muffin pan and set on a wire rack. Cool to room temperature before icing, about 30 minutes. To frost: Mound about 2 tablespoons of icing on the center of each cupcake. Using a small spatula or butter knife, spread the icing to the edge of the cupcake, leaving a slight mound in the center.

Easy Vanilla Bean Buttercream

MAKES ABOUT 1½ CUPS, ENOUGH TO FROST 12 CUPCAKES

If you prefer to skip the vanilla bean, increase the extract to 1½ teaspoons. Any of the buttercream frostings can be made ahead and refrigerated; if refrigerated, however, the frosting must stand at room temperature to soften before use. If using a hand-held mixer, increase mixing times significantly (by at least 50 percent).

- 10 tablespoons (1¼ sticks) unsalted butter, softened
- ½ vanilla bean, halved lengthwise (see note)
- 1¼ cups (5 ounces) confectioners' sugar
- Pinch table salt
- 1 tablespoon heavy cream
- ½ teaspoon vanilla extract

In a stand mixer fitted with the whisk attachment, beat the butter at medium-high speed until smooth, about 20 seconds. Using a paring knife, scrape the seeds from the vanilla bean into the butter and beat the mixture at medium-high speed to combine, about 15 seconds. Add the confectioners' sugar and salt and beat at medium-low speed until most of the sugar is moistened, about 45 seconds. Scrape down the bowl and beat at medium speed until the mixture is fully combined, about 15 seconds. Scrape down the bowl, add the heavy cream and vanilla extract, and beat at medium speed until incorporated, about 10 seconds, then increase the speed to medium-high and beat until light and fluffy, about 4 minutes, scraping down the bowl once or twice.

Easy Chocolate Buttercream

Follow the recipe for Easy Vanilla Bean Buttercream, omitting the vanilla bean and heavy cream and reducing the sugar to 1 cup. After beating in the vanilla extract, reduce the speed to low and gradually beat in 4 ounces melted and cooled semi-sweet or bittersweet chocolate.

Easy Coffee Buttercream

Follow the recipe for Easy Vanilla Bean Buttercream, omitting the vanilla bean and dissolving 1½ teaspoons instant espresso powder in the heavy cream and vanilla extract.

ULTIMATE CHOCOLATE CUPCAKES

WHY THIS RECIPE WORKS: A cupcake catch-22 befalls bakery and homemade confections alike: If the cupcakes are packed with decent chocolate flavor, their structure can be too crumbly for out-of-hand consumption. Conversely, if the cakes balance moisture and tenderness without crumbling, the core elements—cake and frosting—are barely palatable. We wanted a moist, tender (but not crumbly) crumb capped with just enough creamy, not-too-sweet frosting.

Figuring that a cupcake is just a pint-size cake, we made cupcakes using our favorite chocolate cake recipe. Tasters liked the real chocolate flavor, but their crumbly texture made them impossible to eat without a fork. Though we were loath to compromise the chocolate's intensity, we knew that to strengthen the batter we had to cut back on both kinds of chocolate. We tweaked the ingredients to achieve a perfectly portable batch of cupcakes before we turned our attention to working in more chocolate without disrupting the batter's structure. Mixing the cocoa with hot coffee eked out more chocolate flavor. To make the chocolate even more pronounced, we replaced the butter with more neutral-flavored vegetable oil.

Next, we tried enhancing the structure of the cupcake. That would give us a base for adding back extra chocolate without over tenderizing. To do this, we substituted bread flour for all-purpose flour. Specifically engineered for gluten development, bread flour turned out a cupcake that was markedly less crumble-prone, but not tough. For a final chocolate burst, we spooned ganache onto the cupcakes before baking, which gave them a truffle-like center. A velvety buttercream with just enough sweetness crowned the cake perfectly.

Ultimate Chocolate Cupcakes with Ganache Filling

MAKES 12 CUPCAKES

Use a high-quality bittersweet or semisweet chocolate for this recipe, such as one of the test kitchen's favorite baking chocolates, Callebaut Intense Dark Chocolate or Ghirardelli Bittersweet Chocolate. Though we highly recommend the ganache filling, you can omit it for a more traditional cupcake.

GANACHE FILLING

- 2 ounces bittersweet chocolate, chopped fine (see note)
- ¼ cup heavy cream
- 1 tablespoon confectioners' sugar

CHOCOLATE CUPCAKES

- 3 ounces bittersweet chocolate, chopped fine (see note)
- ⅓ cup (1 ounce) Dutch-processed cocoa powder
- ¾ cup hot coffee
- ¾ cup (4⅛ ounces) bread flour
- ¾ cup (5¼ ounces) granulated sugar
- ½ teaspoon table salt
- ½ teaspoon baking soda
- 6 tablespoons vegetable oil
- 2 large eggs
- 2 teaspoons white vinegar
- 1 teaspoon vanilla extract
- 1 recipe Creamy Chocolate Frosting (recipe follows)

1. FOR THE GANACHE FILLING: Place the chocolate, cream, and confectioners' sugar in a medium microwave-safe bowl. Microwave until the mixture is warm to the touch, 20 to 30 seconds. Whisk the mixture until smooth, then refrigerate until just chilled, no longer than 30 minutes.

2. FOR THE CUPCAKES: Adjust an oven rack to the middle position and heat the oven to 350 degrees. Line a standard-size muffin pan (cups have ½-cup capacity) with baking cup liners. Place the chocolate and cocoa in a medium bowl. Pour the hot coffee over the mixture and whisk until smooth. Refrigerate until completely cool, about 20 minutes. Whisk the flour, granulated sugar, salt, and baking soda together in a medium bowl and set aside.

3. Whisk the oil, eggs, vinegar, and vanilla into the cooled chocolate-cocoa mixture until smooth. Add the flour mixture and whisk until smooth.

4. Divide the batter evenly among the muffin pan cups. Place one slightly rounded teaspoon of the ganache filling on top of each cupcake. Bake until the cupcakes are set and just firm to the touch, 17 to 19 minutes. Cool the cupcakes in the muffin pan on a wire rack until cool enough to handle, about 10 minutes. Carefully lift each cupcake from the muffin pan and set on a wire rack. Cool to room temperature before frosting, about 1 hour.

5. TO FROST: Mound 2 to 3 tablespoons of the frosting on the center of each cupcake. Use a small icing spatula or butter knife to ice each cupcake. (The cupcakes can be made up to 24 hours in advance and stored unfrosted in an airtight container.)

Creamy Chocolate Frosting

MAKES ABOUT 2¼ CUPS

Cool the chocolate to between 85 and 100 degrees before adding it to the frosting. If the frosting seems too soft after adding the chocolate, chill it briefly in the refrigerator and then rewhip it until creamy.

- ⅓ cup (2⅓ ounces) sugar
- 2 large egg whites
- Pinch salt
- 12 tablespoons (1½ sticks) unsalted butter, cut into 12 pieces and softened
- 6 ounces bittersweet chocolate, melted and cooled (see note)
- ½ teaspoon vanilla extract

1. Combine the sugar, egg whites, and salt in the bowl of a stand mixer, then place the bowl over a pan of simmering water. Whisking gently but constantly, heat the mixture until slightly thickened and foamy and it registers 150 degrees on an instant-read thermometer, 2 to 3 minutes.

2. Using the whisk attachment, beat the mixture on medium speed in a stand mixer until it reaches the consistency of shaving cream and is slightly cooled, 1 to 2 minutes. Add the butter, one piece at a time, until smooth and creamy. (The frosting may look curdled after half of the butter has been added; it will smooth with additional butter.) Once all the butter is added, add the cooled melted chocolate and the vanilla and mix until combined. Increase the mixer speed to medium-high and beat until light, fluffy, and thoroughly combined, about 30 seconds, scraping the beater and sides of the bowl with a rubber spatula as necessary. (The frosting can be made up to 24 hours in advance and refrigerated in an airtight container. When ready to frost, place the frosting in a microwave-safe container and microwave briefly until just slightly softened, 5 to 10 seconds. Once warmed, stir until creamy.)

CHOCOLATE TORTE

WHY THIS RECIPE WORKS: Sachertorte, the classic Viennese dessert with layers of chocolate cake sandwiching apricot jam and enrobed in a creamy-rich chocolate glaze, always sounds more promising than it typically is in reality—dry, flavorless cake and sweet jam with little fruity complexity, all covered in a glaze that is nothing more than a thin, overly sugary coating. We set out to create a rich, deeply chocolaty dessert using Sachertorte as the inspiration, giving it our own spin by pairing the chocolate with raspberries.

For a rich, fudgy base, we started by baking our Flourless Chocolate Cake (page 781) in two 9-inch pans, so we could sandwich the two cakes together rather than deal with halving a single delicate cake. But when we tried to stack the layers, the dense cake tore and fell apart. Adding ground nuts gave it the structure it needed, plus a good boost of flavor. Since we were using the food processor to grind the nuts, we tweaked our cake recipe so that it could be prepared using the same appliance. The winning approach for our filling was to combine jam with lightly mashed fresh berries for a tangy-sweet mixture that clung to the cake. For the glaze, we kept things simple, melting bittersweet chocolate with heavy cream to create a rich-tasting, glossy ganache that poured smoothly over the cake. For simple but tasty decorating, we dotted fresh raspberries around the top of the torte and pressed sliced, toasted almonds along its sides.

Chocolate-Raspberry Torte

SERVES 12 TO 16

Be sure to use cake pans with at least 2-inch-tall sides.

CAKE

- 8 ounces bittersweet chocolate, chopped fine
- 12 tablespoons (1½ sticks) unsalted butter, cut into ½-inch pieces
- 2 teaspoons vanilla extract
- ¼ teaspoon instant espresso powder
- 1¾ cups (6⅛ ounces) sliced almonds, toasted
- ¼ cup (1¼ ounces) unbleached all-purpose flour
- ½ teaspoon table salt
- 5 large eggs, at room temperature
- ¾ cup (5¼ ounces) sugar

FILLING

- 2½ ounces (½ cup) raspberries, plus 16 individual raspberries
- ¼ cup seedless raspberry jam

GLAZE

- 5 ounces bittersweet chocolate, chopped fine
- ½ cup plus 1 tablespoon heavy cream

1. FOR THE CAKE: Adjust an oven rack to the middle position and heat the oven to 325 degrees. Grease and flour two 9-inch round cake pans, line the bottoms with parchment paper, then grease and flour the parchment. Melt the chocolate and butter in a large heatproof bowl set over a saucepan filled with 1 inch of simmering water, stirring occasionally until smooth. Remove from the heat and let cool to room temperature, about 30 minutes. Stir in the vanilla and espresso powder.

2. Pulse ¾ cup of the almonds in a food processor until coarsely chopped, 6 to 8 pulses, and set aside. Process the remaining 1 cup almonds until very finely ground, about 45 seconds. Add the flour and salt and continue to process until combined, about 15 seconds. Transfer the almond-flour mixture to a medium bowl. Process the eggs until lightened in color and almost doubled in volume, about 3 minutes. With the processor running, slowly add the sugar and process until thoroughly combined, about 15 seconds. Using a whisk, gently fold the egg mixture into the chocolate mixture until some streaks of egg remain. Sprinkle half of the almond-flour mixture over the chocolate mixture and gently whisk until just combined. Sprinkle with the remaining almond-flour mixture and gently whisk until just combined.

3. Divide the batter evenly between the prepared pans and smooth the tops with a rubber spatula. Bake until the center is firm and a toothpick inserted in the center comes out with a few moist crumbs attached, 14 to 16 minutes. Transfer the cakes to a wire rack and let cool completely in the pans, about 30 minutes.

4. Run a paring knife around the sides of the cakes to loosen and invert the cakes onto cardboard rounds cut the same size as the diameter of the cake; discard the parchment. Using a wire rack, turn 1 cake right side up, then slide from the rack back onto the cardboard round.

5. FOR THE FILLING: Place ½ cup of the raspberries in a medium bowl and coarsely mash with a fork. Stir in the raspberry jam until just combined.

NOTES FROM THE TEST KITCHEN

DECORATING CHOCOLATE-RASPBERRY TORTE

1. With the fully assembled cake placed on a cardboard round, hold the bottom of the cake in one hand and gently press the chopped nuts onto its side with the other hand.

2. Place one raspberry on the cake at 12 o'clock, then another at 6 o'clock. Place a third berry at 9 o'clock and a fourth at 3 o'clock. Continue to place raspberries directly opposite each other until all have been arranged in an evenly spaced circle.

6. TO ASSEMBLE THE TORTE: Spread the raspberry mixture onto the cake layer that is right side up. Top with the second cake layer, leaving it upside down. Transfer the assembled cake, still on the cardboard round, to a wire rack set in a rimmed baking sheet.

7. FOR THE GLAZE: Melt the chocolate and cream in a medium heatproof bowl set over a saucepan filled with 1 inch of simmering water, stirring occasionally until smooth. Remove from the heat and gently whisk until very smooth. Pour the glaze onto the center of the assembled cake. Using an offset spatula, spread the glaze evenly over the top of the cake, letting it drip down the sides. Spread the glaze along the sides of the cake to coat evenly.

8. Using a fine-mesh strainer, sift the reserved chopped almonds to remove any fine bits. Holding the bottom of the cake on the cardboard round with 1 hand, gently press the sifted almonds onto the cake sides with the other hand. Arrange the remaining 16 raspberries around the circumference. Refrigerate the cake on the rack until the glaze is set, at least 1 hour or up to 24 hours (if refrigerating the cake for more than 1 hour, let sit at room temperature for about 30 minutes before serving). Transfer the cake to a platter and serve.

FLOURLESS CHOCOLATE CAKE

WHY THIS RECIPE WORKS: While all flourless chocolate cake recipes share common ingredients (chocolate, butter, and eggs), the techniques used to make them vary, as do the results. You can end up with anything from a fudge brownie to a bittersweet chocolate soufflé. We wanted something dense, moist, and ultra-chocolaty.

We started with the type of chocolate. A cake made with unsweetened chocolate was neither smooth nor silky enough for this kind of cake. Bittersweet or semisweet chocolate was ideal, with deep chocolate flavor and a smooth texture. Next we turned to the eggs—we compared cakes made with room temperature eggs and eggs taken straight from the fridge. The batter made with chilled eggs produced a denser foam and the resulting cake boasted a smooth, velvety texture. And the gentle, moist heat of a water bath further preserved the cake's lush texture.

Flourless Chocolate Cake

SERVES 12 TO 16

This cake is best when baked a day ahead to mellow its flavor. Even though the cake may not look done, pull it from the oven when an instant-read thermometer registers 140 degrees. (Do not let the tip of the thermometer hit the bottom of the pan.) It will continue to firm up as it cools. If you use a 9-inch springform pan instead of the preferred 8-inch pan, reduce the baking time to 18 to 20 minutes. See page 910 for our top-rated brands of chocolate.

- 8 large eggs, chilled
- 1 pound bittersweet or semisweet chocolate, chopped (see note)
- ½ pound (2 sticks) unsalted butter, cut into ½-inch chunks
- ¼ cup strong coffee
- Confectioners' sugar or cocoa powder, for decoration

1. Adjust an oven rack to the lower-middle position and heat the oven to 325 degrees. Grease an 8-inch springform pan, then line the bottom with parchment paper. Wrap the outside of the pan with two 18-inch-square pieces of heavy-duty foil; set the springform pan in a roasting pan. Bring a kettle of water to a boil.

2. In a stand mixer fitted with the whisk attachment, beat the eggs at medium speed until doubled in volume, about 5 minutes.

3. Meanwhile, melt the chocolate and butter in a large heatproof bowl set over a saucepan filled with 1 inch of barely simmering water until smooth, stirring once or twice; stir in the coffee. Using a large rubber spatula, fold one-third of the egg mixture into the chocolate mixture until only a few streaks of egg are visible; fold the remaining egg mixture, in two additions, until the batter is totally homogeneous.

4. Scrape the batter into the prepared pan and smooth the surface with the spatula. Set the roasting pan on the oven rack and pour in enough boiling water to come about halfway up the sides of the pan. Bake until the cake has risen slightly, the edges are just beginning to set, a thin glazed crust (like a brownie) has formed on the surface, and an instant-read thermometer inserted halfway through the center of the cake registers 140 degrees, 22 to 25 minutes. Remove the pan from the water bath and set on a wire rack; cool to room temperature. Cover and refrigerate overnight to mellow the flavors. (The cake can be covered and refrigerated for up to 4 days.)

5. About 30 minutes before serving, remove the springform pan sides, then flip the cake out onto the wire rack. Peel off the parchment and flip the cake right side up onto a serving platter. Lightly dust the cake with confectioners' sugar or unsweetened cocoa powder, if desired, and serve.

HOT FUDGE PUDDING CAKE

WHY THIS RECIPE WORKS: Those who have eaten hot fudge pudding cake know its charms: moist, brownie-like chocolate cake sitting on a pool of thick, chocolate pudding–like sauce, baked together in one dish, as if by magic. Served warm with vanilla ice cream, this cake has a flavor that more than makes up for its homespun looks. We set out to master this humble dessert. Pudding cake is made by sprinkling brownie batter with a mixture of sugar and cocoa, then pouring hot water on top, and baking. To bump up the chocolate flavor, we used a combination of Dutch-processed cocoa and bittersweet chocolate. We also added instant coffee to the water that is poured over the batter to cut the sweetness of the cake. We baked the cake slow and low to promote a good top crust and a silky sauce. And we found that letting the cake rest for 20 to 30 minutes before eating allows the sauce to become pudding-like and the cake brownie-like.

Hot Fudge Pudding Cake

SERVES 8

If you have cold brewed coffee on hand, it can be used in place of the instant coffee and water, but to make sure it isn't too strong, use 1 cup of cold coffee mixed with ½ cup of water. Serve the cake warm with vanilla or coffee ice cream.

- 2 teaspoons instant coffee powder (see note)
- 1½ cups water
- 1 cup (7 ounces) granulated sugar
- ⅔ cup Dutch-processed cocoa powder
- ⅓ cup packed (2⅓ ounces) brown sugar
- 6 tablespoons (¾ stick) unsalted butter
- 2 ounces bittersweet or semisweet chocolate, chopped
- ¾ cup (3¾ ounces) unbleached all-purpose flour
- 2 teaspoons baking powder
- ⅓ cup whole milk
- 1 tablespoon vanilla extract
- ¼ teaspoon table salt
- 1 large egg yolk, at room temperature

1. Adjust an oven rack to the lower-middle position and heat the oven to 325 degrees. Lightly grease an 8-inch square glass or ceramic baking dish. Stir the instant coffee into the water; set aside to dissolve. Stir together ⅓ cup of the granulated sugar, ⅓ cup of the cocoa, and the brown sugar in a small bowl, breaking up large clumps with your fingers; set aside. Melt the butter, the remaining ⅓ cup cocoa, and the chocolate in a small bowl set over a saucepan filled with 1 inch of barely simmering water; whisk until smooth and set aside to cool slightly. Whisk the flour and baking powder in a small bowl to combine; set aside. Whisk the remaining ⅔ cup granulated sugar, the milk, vanilla, and salt in a medium bowl until combined; whisk in the egg yolk. Add the chocolate mixture and whisk to combine. Add the flour mixture and whisk until the batter is evenly moistened.

2. Pour the batter into the prepared baking dish and spread evenly to the sides and corners. Sprinkle the cocoa-sugar mixture evenly over the batter (the cocoa mixture should cover the entire surface of the batter); pour the coffee mixture gently over the cocoa mixture. Bake until the cake is puffed and bubbling and just beginning to pull away from the sides of the baking dish, about 45 minutes, rotating the pan halfway through the baking time. (Do not overbake.) Cool the cake in the dish on a wire rack for about 25 minutes and serve.

Individual Hot Fudge Pudding Cakes

Follow the recipe for Hot Fudge Pudding Cake, heating the oven to 400 degrees and lightly greasing eight 6- to 8-ounce ramekins; set the ramekins on a baking sheet. Divide the batter evenly among the ramekins (about ¼ cup per ramekin) and level with the back of a spoon; sprinkle about 2 tablespoons cocoa-sugar mixture over the batter in each ramekin. Pour 3 tablespoons coffee mixture over the cocoa-sugar mixture in each ramekin. Bake until puffed and bubbling, about 20 minutes. (Do not overbake.) Cool the pudding cakes for about 15 minutes before serving (the cakes will fall as they cool).

BITTERSWEET CHOCOLATE ROULADE

WHY THIS RECIPE WORKS: A chocolate roulade can be a baker's nightmare—a hard-to-roll cake with a dry texture and a filling that won't stay put. We wanted a recipe for a true showcase roulade, a cake with a velvety texture and deep chocolate flavor, a thick, rich filling, and a decadent icing that covers it all.

We used bitter- or semisweet chocolate for maximum chocolate flavor. Six eggs gave our cake great support. A combination of cocoa and flour provided further structure and extra chocolate flavor. Once the cake was baked, we cooled it briefly in the pan, then unmolded it onto a kitchen towel rubbed with cocoa to prevent sticking. While the cake was still warm, we rolled it up with the towel inside, cooled it briefly, and then unrolled the cake—this method gave the cake a "memory" so it could be filled and re-rolled. For the filling, we made a simple espresso-flavored cream with just four ingredients, including the lush Italian cream cheese, mascarpone. Mascarpone provided both structural support and rich flavor. For the icing, we chose dark chocolate ganache, made with bittersweet chocolate and cognac for complex flavor.

Bittersweet Chocolate Roulade

SERVES 8 TO 10

We suggest that you make the filling and ganache first, then make the cake while the ganache is setting up. Or, if you prefer, the cake can be baked, filled, and rolled—but not iced—then wrapped in plastic wrap and refrigerated for up to 24 hours. If serving this cake in the style of a holiday yule log, make wood-grain striations in the ganache with a fork. The roulade is best served at room temperature.

¼ cup (1¼ ounces) unbleached all-purpose flour, plus extra for the pan
6 ounces bittersweet or semisweet chocolate, chopped fine
2 tablespoons cold unsalted butter, cut into 2 pieces
2 tablespoons cold water
¼ cup Dutch-processed cocoa powder, sifted, plus 1 tablespoon for unmolding
⅛ teaspoon table salt
6 large eggs, at room temperature and separated
⅓ cup (2⅓ ounces) sugar
1 teaspoon vanilla extract
⅛ teaspoon cream of tartar
1 recipe Espresso-Mascarpone Cream (recipe follows)
1 recipe Dark Chocolate Ganache (recipe follows)

1. Adjust an oven rack to the upper-middle position and heat the oven to 400 degrees. Spray a 17½ by 12-inch rimmed baking sheet with vegetable oil spray, cover the pan bottom with parchment paper, and spray the parchment with vegetable oil spray; dust with flour and tap out the excess.

2. Heat the chocolate, butter, and water in a small heatproof bowl set over a saucepan filled with 1 inch of barely simmering water, stirring occasionally until smooth. Set aside to cool slightly. Sift ¼ cup of the cocoa, the flour, and salt together into a small bowl and set aside.

3. In a stand mixer fitted with the whisk attachment, beat the egg yolks at medium-high speed until just combined, about 15 seconds. With the mixer running, add half of the sugar. Continue to beat, scraping down the sides of the bowl as necessary, until the yolks are pale yellow and the mixture falls in a thick ribbon when the whisk is lifted, about 8 minutes. Add the vanilla and beat to combine, scraping down the bowl once, about 30 seconds. Turn the mixture into a medium bowl; wash and dry the mixer bowl and whisk attachment.

4. In the clean bowl with the clean whisk attachment, beat the egg whites and cream of tartar at medium speed until foamy, about 30 seconds. With the mixer running, add about 1 teaspoon more sugar; continue beating until soft peaks form, about 40 seconds. Gradually add the remaining sugar and beat until the egg whites are glossy and hold stiff peaks when the whisk is lifted, about 1 minute longer. Do not over beat.

5. Stir the chocolate mixture into the egg yolks. With a rubber spatula, stir one-quarter of the egg whites into the chocolate mixture to lighten it. Fold in the remaining egg whites until almost no streaks remain. Sprinkle the cocoa-flour mixture over the top and fold in quickly but gently.

6. Pour the batter into the prepared pan; using a spatula and working quickly, even the surface and smooth the batter into the pan corners. Lightly tap the pan against the countertop two or three times to settle the batter. Bake until the center of the cake springs back when touched with a finger, 8 to 10 minutes, rotating the pan halfway through the baking time. Cool the cake in the pan on a wire rack for 5 minutes.

7. While the cake is cooling, lay a clean kitchen towel over the work surface and sift the remaining 1 tablespoon cocoa over the towel; rub the cocoa into the towel. Run a small knife around the baking sheet to loosen the cake. Flip the cake onto the towel and peel off the parchment.

8. Roll the cake, towel and all, into a jellyroll shape. Cool for 15 minutes, then unroll the cake and towel. Using a spatula, immediately spread the filling evenly over the cake, almost to the edges. Roll up the cake gently but snugly around the filling. Set a large sheet of parchment paper on an overturned rimmed baking sheet and set the roulade, seam side down, on top. Trim both ends on the diagonal. Spread the ganache evenly over the roulade. Use a fork to make wood-grain striations, if desired, on the surface of the ganache before the icing has set. Refrigerate the cake, on the baking sheet, uncovered, to slightly set the icing, about 20 minutes.

9. Carefully slide two wide metal spatulas under the cake and transfer the cake to a serving platter. Cut into slices and serve.

Espresso-Mascarpone Cream

MAKES ABOUT 2½ CUPS

Mascarpone is a fresh Italian cheese. Its flavor is unique—mildly sweet and refreshing. It is sold in small containers in some supermarkets as well as most gourmet stores, cheese shops, and Italian markets.

½ cup heavy cream
2 teaspoons espresso powder or instant coffee
6 tablespoons confectioners' sugar
16½ ounces mascarpone cheese (generous 2 cups)

1. Bring the cream to a simmer in a small saucepan over high heat. Off the heat, stir in the espresso and confectioners' sugar; cool slightly.

2. With a spatula, beat the mascarpone in a medium bowl until softened. Gently whisk in the cooled cream mixture until combined. Cover with plastic wrap and refrigerate until ready to use.

Dark Chocolate Ganache

MAKES ABOUT 1½ CUPS

If your kitchen is cool and the ganache becomes too stiff to spread, set the bowl over a saucepan of simmering water, then stir briefly until it is smooth and icing-like.

- ¾ cup heavy cream
- 2 tablespoons unsalted butter
- 6 ounces high-quality bittersweet or semisweet chocolate, chopped
- 1 tablespoon cognac

Microwave the cream and butter in a microwave-safe measuring cup on high power until bubbling, about 1½ minutes. (Alternatively, bring to a simmer in a small saucepan over medium-high heat.) Place the chocolate in a food processor. With the machine running, gradually add the hot cream mixture and cognac through the feed tube and process until smooth and thickened, about 3 minutes. Transfer the ganache to a medium bowl and let stand at room temperature for 1 hour, until spreadable (the ganache should have the consistency of soft icing).

TRIPLE-CHOCOLATE MOUSSE CAKE

WHY THIS RECIPE WORKS: Triple chocolate mousse cake is a truly decadent dessert. Most times, though, the mousse texture is exactly the same from one layer to the next and the flavor is so rich it's hard to finish more than a few forkfuls. We set out to tweak this showy confection. By finessing one layer at a time, we aimed to create a triple-decker that was incrementally lighter in texture—and richness. For simplicity's sake, we decided to build the whole dessert, layer by layer, in the same springform pan. For a base layer that had the heft to support the upper two tiers, we chose flourless chocolate cake instead of the typical mousse. Folding egg whites into the batter helped lighten the cake without affecting its structural integrity. For the middle layer, we started with a traditional chocolate mousse, but the texture seemed too heavy when combined with the cake, so we removed the eggs and cut back on the chocolate a bit—this resulted in the lighter, creamier layer we desired. And for the crowning layer to our cake, we made an easy white chocolate mousse by folding whipped cream into melted white chocolate—and to prevent the soft mousse from oozing during slicing, we added a little gelatin to the mix.

Triple-Chocolate Mousse Cake

SERVES 12 TO 16

This recipe requires a springform pan at least 3 inches high for all three layers to fit. It is imperative that each layer is made in sequential order. Cool the base completely before topping with the middle layer. We recommend Ghirardelli Bittersweet Chocolate for the base and middle layers; our other recommended brand of chocolate, Callebaut Intense Dark Chocolate, may be used but will produce drier, slightly less sweet results. Our preferred brand of white chocolate is Guittard Choc-Au-Lait White Chips. For best results, chill the mixer bowl before whipping the heavy cream. For neater slices, clean the knife thoroughly between slices.

BASE LAYER

- 6 tablespoons (¾ stick) unsalted butter, cut into 6 pieces
- 7 ounces bittersweet chocolate, chopped fine (see note)
- ¾ teaspoon instant espresso powder
- 4 large eggs, at room temperature and separated
- 1½ teaspoons vanilla extract
- Pinch table salt
- ⅓ cup packed (2⅓ ounces) light brown sugar, crumbled with fingers to remove lumps

MIDDLE LAYER

- 5 tablespoons hot water
- 2 tablespoons cocoa powder, preferably Dutch-processed
- 7 ounces bittersweet chocolate, chopped fine (see note)
- 1½ cups heavy cream, chilled
- 1 tablespoon granulated sugar
- ⅛ teaspoon table salt

TOP LAYER

- ¾ teaspoon powdered gelatin
- 1 tablespoon water
- 6 ounces white chocolate, chopped fine (see note)
- 1½ cups heavy cream, chilled
- Shaved chocolate or cocoa powder, for serving (optional)

1. **FOR THE BASE LAYER:** Adjust an oven rack to the middle position and heat the oven to 325 degrees. Grease the bottom and sides of a 9-inch-wide by 3-inch-high round springform

pan. Melt the butter, chocolate, and espresso powder in a large heatproof bowl set over a saucepan filled with 1 inch of barely simmering water, stirring occasionally until smooth. Remove from the heat and cool the mixture slightly, about 5 minutes. Whisk in the egg yolks and vanilla; set aside.

2. In a stand mixer fitted with the whisk attachment, beat the egg whites and salt at medium speed until frothy, about 30 seconds. Add half of the brown sugar and beat until combined, about 15 seconds. Add the remaining brown sugar and beat at high speed until soft peaks form when the whisk is lifted, about 1 minute longer, scraping down the sides of the bowl halfway through. Using a whisk, fold one-third of the beaten egg whites into the chocolate mixture to lighten. Using a rubber spatula, fold in the remaining egg whites until no white streaks remain. Carefully transfer the batter to the prepared pan, gently smoothing the top with a spatula.

3. Bake until the cake has risen, is firm around the edges, and the center has just set but is still soft (the center of the cake will spring back after pressing gently with a finger), 13 to 18 minutes. Transfer the cake to a wire rack to cool completely, about 1 hour. (The cake will collapse as it cools.) Do not remove the cake from the pan.

4. FOR THE MIDDLE LAYER: Combine the hot water and cocoa powder in a small bowl; set aside. Melt the chocolate in a large heatproof bowl set over a saucepan filled with 1 inch of barely simmering water, stirring occasionally until smooth. Remove from the heat and cool slightly, 2 to 5 minutes.

5. In the clean bowl of a stand mixer fitted with the whisk attachment, whip the heavy cream, sugar, and salt at medium speed until it begins to thicken, about 30 seconds. Increase the speed to high and whip until soft peaks form when the whisk is lifted, 15 to 60 seconds. Whisk the cocoa powder mixture into the melted chocolate until smooth. Using a whisk, fold one-third of the whipped cream mixture into the chocolate mixture to lighten. Using a rubber spatula, fold in the remaining whipped cream mixture until no white streaks remain. Spoon the mousse into the springform pan over the cooled cake and lightly tap the pan against the countertop two or three times to settle the mousse; gently smooth the top with a spatula. Wipe the inside edge of the pan with a damp cloth to remove any drips. Refrigerate the cake for at least 15 minutes while preparing the top layer.

6. FOR THE TOP LAYER: In a small bowl, sprinkle the gelatin over the water; let stand for at least 5 minutes. Place the white chocolate in a medium bowl. Bring ½ cup of the cream to a simmer in a small saucepan over medium-high heat. Remove from the heat; add the gelatin mixture and stir until fully dissolved. Pour the cream mixture over the white chocolate and whisk until the chocolate is melted and the mixture is smooth, about 30 seconds. Cool to room temperature, stirring occasionally, 5 to 8 minutes (the mixture will thicken slightly).

7. In the bowl of a stand mixer fitted with the whisk attachment, whip the remaining 1 cup cream at medium speed until it begins to thicken, about 30 seconds. Increase the speed to high and whip until soft peaks form when the whisk is lifted, 15 to 60 seconds. Using a whisk, fold one-third of the whipped cream into the white chocolate mixture to lighten. Using a rubber spatula, fold the remaining whipped cream into the white chocolate mixture until no white streaks remain. Spoon the white chocolate mousse into the pan over the bittersweet chocolate mousse layer. Smooth the top with a spatula. Return the cake to the refrigerator and chill until set, at least 2½ hours.

8. TO SERVE: Garnish the top of the cake with chocolate curls or dust with cocoa (if using). Run a thin knife between the cake and sides of the springform pan; remove the sides of the pan. Run the cleaned knife along the outside of the cake to smooth the sides. Serve.

CHOCOLATE VOLCANO CAKES WITH ESPRESSO ICE CREAM

WHY THIS RECIPE WORKS: A common restaurant dessert, volcano cake, or molten chocolate cake, is an intensely chocolate cake that boasts a warm, liquid center. In addition to its great flavor and alluring contrasting textures, the cake can often be made ahead and baked just before serving. The make-ahead appeal of such a cake inspired us to master this dessert for the home cook.

The initial recipes we tried revealed a host of problems with this cake—unbalanced chocolate flavor and a soggy or dry texture were just a few issues we faced. After testing various chocolates, we settled on a combination of bittersweet chocolate and unsweetened chocolate—this gave us maximum chocolate flavor. Chocolate alone seemed a little flat, so we added Grand Marnier for another layer of flavor. Whole eggs and egg yolks contributed richness and cornstarch helped make the batter remarkably stable. To help the cakes fall right out of the ramekins without a struggle, we buttered and sugared the ramekins before pouring in the batter. The cakes alone were great, but we felt they were even better when accompanied by a cold, creamy scoop of doctored "espresso" ice cream.

Chocolate Volcano Cakes with Espresso Ice Cream

SERVES 8

Use a bittersweet bar chocolate in this recipe, not chips—the chips include emulsifiers that will alter the cakes' texture. The cake batter can be mixed and portioned into the ramekins, wrapped tightly with plastic wrap, and refrigerated up to 24 hours in advance. The cold cake batter should be baked straight from the refrigerator.

ESPRESSO ICE CREAM

- 2 pints coffee ice cream, softened
- 1½ tablespoons finely ground espresso beans

CAKES

- 10 tablespoons (1¼ sticks) unsalted butter, cut into ½-inch pieces, plus extra for the ramekins
- 1½ cups (10½ ounces) granulated sugar, plus extra for the ramekins
- 8 ounces bittersweet chocolate, chopped fine (see note)
- 2 ounces unsweetened chocolate, chopped fine
- 2 tablespoons cornstarch
- 3 large eggs plus 4 large egg yolks, at room temperature
- 2 teaspoons Grand Marnier (or other orange-flavored liqueur)
- Confectioners' sugar, for dusting the cakes

1. FOR THE ICE CREAM: Transfer the ice cream to a medium bowl and, using a rubber spatula, fold in the ground espresso until incorporated. Press a sheet of plastic wrap directly on the ice cream to prevent freezer burn and return it to the freezer. (The ice cream can be prepared up to 24 hours ahead.)

2. FOR THE CAKES: Lightly coat eight 4-ounce ramekins with butter. Dust with sugar, tapping out any excess, and set aside.

3. Melt the bittersweet and unsweetened chocolates and the 10 tablespoons butter in a large heatproof bowl set over a pan filled with 1 inch of barely simmering water, stirring occasionally until smooth. In a large bowl, whisk the 1½ cups sugar and cornstarch together. Add the chocolate mixture and stir to combine. Add the whole eggs, egg yolks, and Grand Marnier and whisk until fully combined. Using a ½-cup measure, scoop the batter into each of the prepared ramekins. (The ramekins can be covered tightly with plastic wrap and refrigerated for up to 24 hours.)

4. Adjust an oven rack to the upper-middle position and heat the oven to 375 degrees. Place the filled ramekins on a rimmed baking sheet and bake until the tops of the cakes are set, have formed shiny crusts, and are beginning to crack, 16 to 20 minutes.

5. Transfer the ramekins to a wire rack and cool slightly, about 2 minutes. Run a small knife around the edge of each cake. Using a towel to protect your hand from the hot ramekins, invert each cake onto a small plate, then immediately invert again right side up onto eight individual plates. Sift confectioners' sugar over each cake. Remove the ice cream from the freezer and scoop a portion next to each cake. Serve immediately.

CHOCOLATE-ESPRESSO DACQUOISE

WHY THIS RECIPE WORKS: We made this elaborate and impressive-looking dessert more approachable by reworking the meringue and buttercream, making them simpler and more foolproof. We swapped the traditional individually piped layers of meringue for a single sheet that was trimmed into layers after baking, and we shortened the usual 4-plus hours of oven time by increasing the oven temperature. While many recipes call for a Swiss or French buttercream made with a hot sugar syrup, we opted for a German buttercream. With equal parts pastry cream and butter, this option required no hot syrup and it enabled us to use up the egg yolks left over from the meringue.

Chocolate-Espresso Dacquoise

SERVES 10 TO 12

The components in this recipe can easily be prepared in advance. Use a rimless baking sheet or an overturned rimmed baking sheet to bake the meringue. Instant coffee may be substituted for the espresso powder. To skin the hazelnuts, simply place the warm toasted nuts in a clean dish towel and rub gently. We recommend Ghirardelli Bittersweet Chocolate Baking Bar with 60 percent cacao for this recipe.

MERINGUE

- ¾ cup blanched sliced almonds, toasted
- ½ cup hazelnuts, toasted and skinned
- 1 tablespoon cornstarch
- ⅛ teaspoon salt
- 1 cup (7 ounces) sugar
- 4 large egg whites, room temperature
- ¼ teaspoon cream of tartar

BUTTERCREAM

- ¾ cup whole milk
- 4 large egg yolks
- ⅓ cup (2⅓ ounces) sugar
- 1½ teaspoons cornstarch
- ¼ teaspoon salt
- 2 tablespoons amaretto or water
- 1½ tablespoons instant espresso powder
- 16 tablespoons unsalted butter, softened

GANACHE

- 6 ounces bittersweet chocolate, chopped fine
- ¾ cup heavy cream
- 2 teaspoons corn syrup

- 12 whole hazelnuts, toasted and skinned
- 1 cup blanched sliced almonds, toasted

1. FOR THE MERINGUE: Adjust oven rack to middle position and heat oven to 250 degrees. Using ruler and pencil, draw 13 by 10½-inch rectangle on piece of parchment paper. Grease baking sheet and place parchment on it, marked side down.

2. Process almonds, hazelnuts, cornstarch, and salt in food processor until nuts are finely ground, 15 to 20 seconds. Add ½ cup sugar and pulse to combine, 1 to 2 pulses.

3. Using stand mixer fitted with whisk, whip egg whites and cream of tartar on medium-low speed until foamy, about 1 minute. Increase speed to medium-high and whip whites to soft, billowy mounds, about 1 minute. With mixer running at medium-high speed, slowly add remaining ½ cup sugar and continue to whip until glossy, stiff peaks form, 2 to 3 minutes. Fold nut mixture into egg whites in 2 batches. With offset

spatula, spread meringue evenly into 13 by 10½-inch rectangle on parchment, using lines on parchment as guide. Using spray bottle, evenly mist surface of meringue with water until glistening. Bake for 1½ hours. Turn off oven and allow meringue to cool in oven for 1½ hours. (Do not open oven during baking and cooling.) Remove from oven and let cool to room temperature, about 10 minutes. (Cooled meringue can be kept at room temperature, tightly wrapped in plastic wrap, for up to 2 days.)

4. FOR THE BUTTERCREAM: Heat milk in small saucepan over medium heat until just simmering. Meanwhile, whisk yolks, sugar, cornstarch, and salt in bowl until smooth. Remove milk from heat and, whisking constantly, add half of milk to yolk mixture to temper. Whisking constantly, return tempered yolk mixture to remaining milk in saucepan. Return saucepan to medium heat and cook, whisking constantly, until mixture is bubbling and thickens to consistency of warm pudding, 3 to 5 minutes. Transfer pastry cream to bowl. Cover and refrigerate until set, at least 2 hours or up to 24 hours. Before using, warm gently to room temperature in microwave at 50 percent power, stirring every 10 seconds.

5. Stir together amaretto and espresso powder; set aside. Using stand mixer fitted with paddle, beat butter at medium speed until smooth and light, 3 to 4 minutes. Add pastry cream in 3 batches, beating for 30 seconds after each addition. Add amaretto mixture and continue to beat until light and fluffy, about 5 minutes longer, scraping down bowl thoroughly halfway through mixing.

NOTES FROM THE TEST KITCHEN

ASSEMBLING THE DACQUOISE

Here's how to assemble the three different components of dacquoise—cooled, baked meringue; buttercream; and ganache—into a dessert that looks like it was made in a professional bakery.

1. Using serrated knife and gentle, repeated scoring motion, trim edges of cooled meringue to form 12 by 10-inch rectangle.

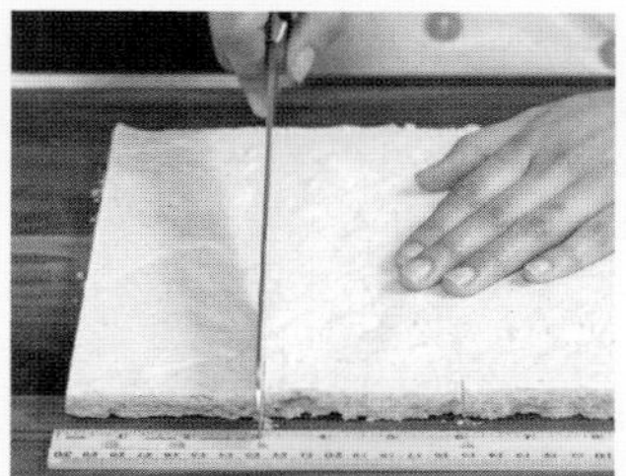

2. With long side of meringue parallel to counter, mark top and bottom edges at 3-inch intervals.

3. Repeatedly score surface by gently drawing knife from top mark to corresponding bottom mark until cut through. Repeat to make four 10 by 3-inch strips.

4. Place 3 strips on wire rack and spread ¼ cup ganache evenly over each. Refrigerate for 15 minutes. Spread remaining strip with ½ cup buttercream.

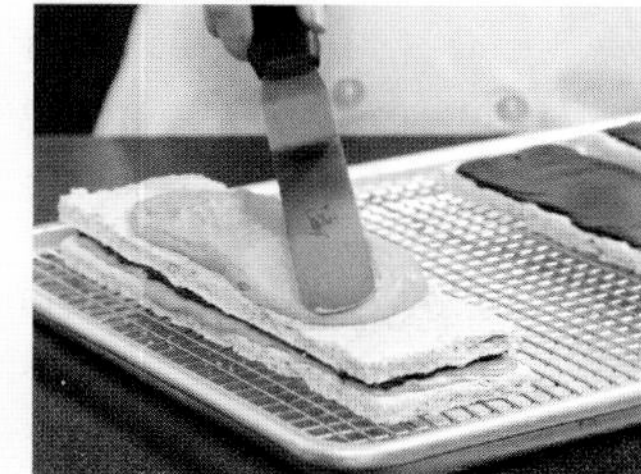

5. Invert one ganache-coated strip on top of buttercream-coated strip and press gently. Spread top with buttercream. Repeat twice to form 4 layers.

6. Lightly coat sides of cake with half of remaining buttercream; coat top with remaining buttercream. Smooth edges and surfaces; refrigerate until firm.

7. Pour ganache over top of cake and spread in thin, even layer, letting excess flow down sides. Spread thinly across sides.

8. Place toasted whole hazelnuts in line on top of cake and gently press sliced almonds onto sides.

6. FOR THE GANACHE: Place chocolate in heatproof bowl. Bring cream and corn syrup to simmer in small saucepan over medium heat. Pour cream mixture over chocolate and let stand for 1 minute. Stir mixture until smooth. Set aside to cool until chocolate mounds slightly when dripped from spoon, about 5 minutes.

7. Carefully invert meringue and peel off parchment. Reinvert meringue and place on cutting board. Using serrated knife and gentle, repeated scoring motion, trim edges of meringue to form 12 by 10-inch rectangle. Discard trimmings. With long side of rectangle parallel to counter, use ruler to mark both long edges of meringue at 3-inch intervals. Using serrated knife, score surface of meringue by drawing knife toward you from mark on top edge to corresponding mark on bottom edge. Repeat scoring until meringue is fully cut through. Repeat until you have four 10 by 3-inch rectangles. (If any rectangles break during cutting, use them as middle layers.)

8. Place 3 rectangles on wire rack set in rimmed baking sheet. Using offset spatula, spread ¼ cup ganache evenly over surface of each meringue. Refrigerate until ganache is firm, about 15 minutes. Set aside remaining ganache.

9. Using offset spatula, spread top of remaining rectangle with ½ cup buttercream; place on wire rack with ganache-coated meringues. Invert 1 ganache-coated meringue, place on top of buttercream, and press gently to level. Repeat, spreading meringue with ½ cup buttercream and topping with inverted ganache-coated meringue. Spread top with buttercream. Invert final ganache-coated meringue on top of cake. Use 1 hand to steady top of cake and spread half of remaining buttercream to lightly coat sides of cake, then use remaining buttercream to coat top of cake. Smooth until cake resembles box. Refrigerate until buttercream is firm, about 2 hours. (Once buttercream is firm, assembled cake may be wrapped tightly in plastic and refrigerated for up to 2 days.)

10. Warm remaining ganache in heatproof bowl set over barely simmering water, stirring occasionally, until mixture is very fluid but not hot. Keeping assembled cake on wire rack, pour ganache over top of cake. Using offset spatula, spread ganache in thin, even layer over top of cake, letting excess flow down sides. Spread ganache over sides in thin layer (top must be completely covered, but some small gaps on sides are OK).

11. Garnish top of cake with hazelnuts. Holding bottom of cake with 1 hand, gently press almonds onto sides with other hand. Chill on wire rack, uncovered, for at least 3 hours or up to 12 hours. Transfer to platter. Cut into slices with sharp knife that has been dipped in hot water and wiped dry before each slice. Serve.

TIRAMISÙ

WHY THIS RECIPE WORKS: There's a reason restaurant menus (Italian or not) offer tiramisù. Delicate ladyfingers soaked in a spiked coffee mixture layered with a sweet, creamy filling make an irresistible combination. Preparing tiramisù, however, can be labor intensive. Some versions are overly rich with ladyfingers that turn soggy. We wanted to avoid these issues and find a streamlined approach—one that highlights the luxurious combination of flavors and textures that have made this dessert so popular. Instead of hauling out a double boiler to make the fussy custard-based filling (called *zabaglione*), we instead simply whipped egg yolks, sugar, salt, rum, and mascarpone together. Salt heightened the filling's subtle flavors. And to lighten the filling, we chose whipped cream instead of egg whites. For the coffee soaking mixture, we combined strong brewed coffee and espresso powder (along with more rum). To moisten the ladyfingers so that they were neither too dry nor too saturated, we dropped them one at a time into the spiked coffee mixture and rolled them over to moisten the other side for just a couple of seconds. For best flavor and texture, we discovered that it was important to allow the tiramisù to chill in the refrigerator for at least six hours.

Tiramisù

SERVES 10 TO 12

Brandy and even whiskey can stand in for the dark rum. The test kitchen prefers a tiramisù with a pronounced rum flavor; for a less potent rum flavor, halve the amount of rum added to the coffee mixture in step 1. Do not allow the mascarpone to warm to room temperature before using it; it has a tendency to break if allowed to do so.

- 2½ cups strong brewed coffee, at room temperature
- 9 tablespoons dark rum (see note)
- 1½ tablespoons instant espresso powder
- 6 large egg yolks, at room temperature
- ⅔ cup (4⅔ ounces) sugar
- ¼ teaspoon table salt
- 1½ pounds mascarpone (generous 3 cups; see note)

- ¾ cup heavy cream, chilled
- 14 ounces (42 to 60, depending on size) dried ladyfingers
- 3½ tablespoons cocoa powder, preferably Dutch-processed
- ¼ cup grated semisweet or bittersweet chocolate (optional)

1. Stir together the coffee, 5 tablespoons of the rum, and the espresso powder in a wide bowl or baking dish until the espresso dissolves; set aside.

2. In a stand mixer fitted with the whisk attachment, beat the egg yolks at low speed until just combined. Add the sugar and salt and beat at medium-high speed until pale yellow, 1½ to 2 minutes, scraping down the sides of the bowl with a rubber spatula once or twice. Add the remaining 4 tablespoons rum and beat at medium speed until just combined, 20 to 30 seconds; scrape the bowl. Add the mascarpone and beat at medium speed until no lumps remain, 30 to 45 seconds, scraping down the sides of the bowl once or twice. Transfer the mixture to a large bowl and set aside.

3. In the now-empty mixer bowl (no need to clean the bowl), beat the cream at medium speed until frothy, 1 to 1½ minutes. Increase the speed to high and continue to beat until the cream holds stiff peaks, 1 to 1½ minutes longer. Using a rubber spatula, fold one-third of the whipped cream into the mascarpone mixture to lighten, then gently fold in the remaining whipped cream until no white streaks remain. Set the mascarpone mixture aside.

4. Working one at a time, drop half of the ladyfingers into the coffee mixture, roll, remove, and transfer to a 13 by 9-inch glass or ceramic baking dish. (Do not submerge the ladyfingers in the coffee mixture; the entire process should take no longer than 2 to 3 seconds for each cookie.) Arrange the soaked cookies in a single layer in the baking dish, breaking or trimming the ladyfingers as needed to fit neatly into the dish.

5. Spread half of the mascarpone mixture over the ladyfingers; use a rubber spatula to spread the mixture to the sides and into the corners of the dish and smooth the surface. Place 2 tablespoons of the cocoa in a fine-mesh strainer and dust the cocoa over the mascarpone.

6. Repeat the dipping and arrangement of the ladyfingers; spread the remaining mascarpone mixture over the ladyfingers and dust with the remaining 1½ tablespoons cocoa. Wipe the edges of the dish with a dry paper towel. Cover with plastic wrap and refrigerate for 6 to 24 hours. Sprinkle with the grated chocolate (if using); cut into pieces and serve chilled.

Tiramisù with Cooked Eggs

This recipe involves cooking the yolks in a double boiler, which requires a little more effort and makes for a slightly thicker mascarpone filling, but the results are just as good as with our traditional method. You will need an additional ⅓ cup heavy cream.

Follow the recipe for Tiramisù through step 1. In step 2, add ⅓ cup cream to the egg yolks after the sugar and salt; do not whisk in the rum. Set the bowl with the yolks over a medium saucepan containing 1 inch gently simmering water; cook, constantly scraping along the bottom and sides of the bowl with a heatproof spatula, until the mixture coats the back of a spoon and registers 160 degrees on an instant-read thermometer, 4 to 7 minutes. Remove from the heat and stir vigorously to cool slightly, then set aside to cool to room temperature, about 15 minutes. Whisk in the remaining 4 tablespoons rum until combined. Transfer the bowl to a stand mixer fitted with the whisk attachment, add the mascarpone, and beat at medium speed until no lumps remain, 30 to 45 seconds. Transfer the mixture to a large bowl and set aside. Continue with the recipe from step 3, using the full amount of cream specified (¾ cup).

BOSTON CREAM PIE

WHY THIS RECIPE WORKS: This triple-component dessert deserved a revival—if only we could make the filling foolproof and keep the glaze from cracking off. A hot-milk sponge cake made a good base because it didn't require any finicky folding or separating of eggs. Baking the batter in two pans eliminated the need to slice a single cake horizontally before adding the filling. We used butter to firm up our pastry cream, and added corn syrup to heavy cream and melted chocolate to make a smooth glaze that clung to the top of our Boston Cream Pie and dripped artistically down its sides.

Wicked Good Boston Cream Pie

SERVES 8 TO 10

Chill the assembled cake for at least 3 hours to make it easy to cut and serve.

PASTRY CREAM

- 2 cups half-and-half
- 6 large egg yolks
- ½ cup (3½ ounces) sugar
- Pinch salt
- ¼ cup all-purpose flour
- 4 tablespoons cold unsalted butter, cut into four pieces
- 1½ teaspoons vanilla extract

CAKE

- 1½ cups (7½ ounces) all-purpose flour
- 1½ teaspoons baking powder
- ¾ teaspoon salt
- ¾ cup whole milk
- 6 tablespoons unsalted butter
- 1½ teaspoons vanilla extract
- 3 large eggs
- 1½ cups (10½ ounces) sugar

GLAZE

- ½ cup heavy cream
- 2 tablespoons light corn syrup
- 4 ounces bittersweet chocolate, chopped fine

1. FOR THE PASTRY CREAM: Heat half-and-half in medium saucepan over medium heat until just simmering. Meanwhile, whisk yolks, sugar, and salt in medium bowl until smooth. Add flour to yolk mixture and whisk until incorporated. Remove half-and-half from heat and, whisking constantly, slowly add ½ cup to yolk mixture to temper. Whisking constantly, return tempered yolk mixture to half-and-half in saucepan.

2. Return saucepan to medium heat and cook, whisking constantly, until mixture thickens slightly, about 1 minute. Reduce heat to medium-low and continue to simmer, whisking constantly, 8 minutes.

3. Increase heat to medium and cook, whisking vigorously, until bubbles burst on surface, 1 to 2 minutes. Remove saucepan from heat; whisk in butter and vanilla until butter is melted and incorporated. Strain pastry cream through fine-mesh strainer set over medium bowl. Press lightly greased parchment paper directly on surface and refrigerate until set, at least 2 hours and up to 24 hours.

4. FOR THE CAKE: Adjust oven rack to middle position and heat oven to 325 degrees. Lightly grease two 9-inch round cake pans with vegetable oil spray and line with parchment. Whisk flour, baking powder, and salt together in medium bowl. Heat milk and butter in small saucepan over low heat until butter is melted. Remove from heat, add vanilla, and cover to keep warm.

5. In stand mixer fitted with whisk attachment, whip eggs and sugar at high speed until light and airy, about 5 minutes. Remove mixer bowl from stand. Add hot milk mixture and whisk by hand until incorporated. Add dry ingredients and whisk until incorporated.

6. Working quickly, divide batter evenly between prepared pans. Bake until tops are light brown and toothpick inserted in center of cakes comes out clean, 20 to 22 minutes.

7. Transfer cakes to wire rack and cool completely in pan, about 2 hours. Run small plastic knife around edge of pans, then invert cakes onto wire rack. Carefully remove parchment, then reinvert cakes.

8. TO ASSEMBLE: Place one cake round on large plate. Whisk pastry cream briefly, then spoon onto center of cake. Using offset spatula, spread evenly to cake edge. Place second layer on pastry cream, bottom side up, making sure layers line up properly. Press lightly on top of cake to level. Refrigerate cake while preparing glaze.

9. FOR THE GLAZE: Bring cream and corn syrup to simmer in small saucepan over medium heat. Remove from heat and add chocolate. Whisk gently until smooth, 30 seconds. Let stand, whisking occasionally, until thickened slightly, about 5 minutes.

10. Pour glaze onto center of cake. Use offset spatula to spread glaze to edge of cake, letting excess drip decoratively down sides. Chill finished cake for 3 hours before slicing. Cake may be made up to 24 hours before serving.

NEW YORK–STYLE CHEESECAKE

WHY THIS RECIPE WORKS: The ideal New York cheesecake should be a tall, bronze-skinned, and dense affair. The flavor should be pure and minimalist, sweet and tangy, and rich. But many recipes fall short, with textures that range from fluffy to rubbery and leaden, and flavors that are starchy or overly citrusy. We wanted to perfect New York cheesecake. After trying a variety of crusts, we settled on the classic graham cracker crust—a simple combination of graham crackers, butter, and sugar. For the filling, cream cheese, boosted by the extra tang of a little sour cream, delivered the best flavor. A little lemon juice and vanilla added just the right sweet, bright accents without calling attention to themselves. A combination of eggs and egg yolks yielded a texture that was dense but not heavy. We found that the New York method worked better for this cheesecake than the typical water bath—baking the cake in a hot oven for 10 minutes then in a low oven for a full 90 minutes yielded the satiny texture we were after.

New York Cheesecake

SERVES 12

For neater slices, clean the knife thoroughly between slices. Serve as is or with Strawberry Topping (recipe follows). If you are concerned about the precision of your oven's temperature, try our Foolproof New York Cheesecake, page 791.

CRUST

- 8 whole graham crackers, broken into 1-inch pieces
- 7 tablespoons unsalted butter, melted and cooled
- 3 tablespoons sugar

FILLING

- 2½ pounds cream cheese, cut into chunks and softened
- 1½ cups (10½ ounces) sugar
- ⅛ teaspoon table salt
- ⅓ cup sour cream
- 2 teaspoons juice from 1 lemon
- 2 teaspoons vanilla extract
- 6 large eggs plus 2 large egg yolks, at room temperature

1. FOR THE CRUST: Adjust an oven rack to the middle position and heat the oven to 325 degrees. Process the graham cracker pieces in a food processor to fine, even crumbs, about 30 seconds. Sprinkle 6 tablespoons of the melted butter and the sugar over the crumbs and pulse to incorporate. Sprinkle the mixture into a 9-inch springform pan. Press the crumbs firmly into an even layer using the bottom of a measuring cup. Bake the crust until fragrant and beginning to brown, 10 to 15 minutes. Cool the crust to room temperature, about 30 minutes.

2. FOR THE FILLING: Meanwhile, increase the oven temperature to 500 degrees. In the bowl of a stand mixer fitted with the paddle attachment, beat the cream cheese on medium-low speed until smooth, 1 to 3 minutes. Scrape down the bowl and beaters as needed.

3. Beat in ¾ cup of the sugar and the salt until incorporated, 1 to 3 minutes. Beat in the remaining ¾ cup sugar until incorporated, 1 to 3 minutes. Beat in the sour cream, lemon juice, and vanilla until incorporated, 1 to 3 minutes. Beat in the whole eggs and egg yolks, two at a time, until combined, 1 to 3 minutes.

4. Being careful not to disturb the baked crust, brush the inside of the prepared springform pan with the remaining 1 tablespoon melted butter. Set the pan on a rimmed baking sheet. Carefully pour the filling into the pan. Bake the cheesecake for 10 minutes.

5. Without opening the oven door, reduce the oven temperature to 200 degrees and continue to bake until the center of the cheesecake registers 150 degrees on an instant-read thermometer, about 1½ hours.

6. Transfer the cheesecake to a wire rack and run a knife around the edge of the cake. Cool the cheesecake until just barely warm, 2½ to 3 hours, running a knife around the edge of the cake every hour or so. Wrap the pan tightly in plastic wrap and refrigerate until cold, about 3 hours.

7. To unmold the cheesecake, wrap a wet, hot kitchen towel around the cake pan and let sit for 1 minute. Remove the sides of the pan and carefully slide the cake onto a cake platter. Let the cheesecake sit at room temperature for 30 minutes before serving.

Strawberry Topping

MAKES ABOUT 6 CUPS

This accompaniment to cheesecake is best served the same day it is made.

- 2 pounds fresh strawberries, cleaned, hulled, and cut lengthwise into ¼ to ⅛-inch slices
- ½ cup (3½ ounces) sugar
- Pinch table salt
- 1 cup strawberry jam
- 2 tablespoons juice from 1 lemon

1. Toss the berries, sugar, and salt in a medium bowl; let stand until the berries have released their juices and the sugar has dissolved, about 30 minutes, tossing occasionally to combine.

2. Process the jam in a food processor until smooth, about 8 seconds; transfer to a small saucepan. Bring the jam to a simmer over medium-high heat; simmer, stirring frequently, until dark and no longer frothy, about 3 minutes. Stir in the lemon juice; pour the warm liquid over the strawberries and stir to combine. Let cool, then cover with plastic wrap and refrigerate until cold, at least 2 hours or up to 12 hours. To serve, spoon a portion of topping over each slice of cheesecake.

FOOLPROOF NEW YORK CHEESECAKE

WHY THIS RECIPE WORKS: Our original New York Cheesecake (page 790) has a luxurious texture and brown surface, but some ovens yielded inconsistent cakes. To revise our recipe for everyone's ovens, we first created a pastry–graham cracker hybrid crust that wouldn't become soggy. Pulsing graham crackers, sugar, flour, and salt with melted butter coated the starches, making a crisp crust. Straining and resting the filling released bubble-producing air pockets. New York–style cheesecakes usually start in a hot oven before the temperature is dropped, but we found the time it took for the oven temperature to change varied. We flipped the order, baking at a low temperature to set the filling and then removing it before ramping up the oven's heat. Once the oven hit 500 degrees, we put the cheesecake on the upper rack to brown. This cheesecake would now have the same texture, flavor, and appearance no matter what oven was used.

Foolproof New York Cheesecake

SERVES 12 TO 16

This cheesecake takes at least 12 hours to make (including chilling), so we recommend making it the day before serving. An accurate oven thermometer and instant-read thermometer are essential. To ensure proper baking, check that the oven thermometer is holding steady at 200 degrees and refrain from frequently taking the temperature of the cheesecake (unless it is within a few degrees of 165, allow 20 minutes between checking). Keep a close eye on the cheesecake in step 5 to prevent overbrowning.

CRUST

- 6 whole graham crackers, broken into pieces
- ⅓ cup packed (2⅓ ounces) dark brown sugar
- ½ cup (2½ ounces) all-purpose flour
- ¼ teaspoon salt
- 7 tablespoons unsalted butter, melted

FILLING

- 2½ pounds cream cheese, softened
- 1½ cups (10½ ounces) granulated sugar
- ⅛ teaspoon salt
- ⅓ cup sour cream
- 2 teaspoons lemon juice
- 2 teaspoons vanilla extract
- 6 large eggs plus 2 large egg yolks

1. FOR THE CRUST: Adjust oven racks to upper-middle and lower-middle positions and heat oven to 325 degrees. Process cracker pieces and sugar in food processor until finely ground, about 30 seconds. Add flour and salt and pulse to combine, 2 pulses. Add 6 tablespoons melted butter and pulse until crumbs are evenly moistened, about 10 pulses. Brush bottom of 9-inch springform pan with ½ tablespoon melted butter. Using your hands, press crumb mixture evenly into pan bottom. Using flat bottom of measuring cup or ramekin, firmly pack crust into pan. Bake on lower-middle rack until fragrant and beginning to brown around edges, about 13 minutes. Transfer to rimmed baking sheet and set aside to cool completely. Reduce oven temperature to 200 degrees.

2. FOR THE FILLING: Using stand mixer fitted with paddle, beat cream cheese, ¾ cup sugar, and salt at medium-low speed until combined, about 1 minute. Beat in remaining ¾ cup sugar until combined, about 1 minute. Scrape beater and bowl well; add sour cream, lemon juice, and vanilla and beat at low speed until combined, about 1 minute. Add egg yolks and beat at medium-low speed until thoroughly combined, about 1 minute. Scrape bowl and beater. Add whole eggs two at a time, beating until thoroughly combined, about 30 seconds after each addition. Pour filling through fine-mesh strainer set in large bowl, pressing against strainer with rubber spatula or back of ladle to help filling pass through strainer.

3. Brush sides of springform pan with remaining ½ tablespoon melted butter. Pour filling into crust and set aside for 10 minutes to allow air bubbles to rise to top. Gently draw tines of fork across surface of cake to pop air bubbles that have risen to surface.

4. When oven thermometer reads 200 degrees, bake cheesecake on lower rack until center registers 165 degrees, 3 to 3½ hours. Remove cake from oven and increase oven temperature to 500 degrees.

5. When oven is at 500 degrees, bake cheesecake on upper rack until top is evenly browned, 4 to 12 minutes. Let cool for 5 minutes; run paring knife between cheesecake and side of springform pan. Let cheesecake cool until barely warm, 2½ to 3 hours. Wrap tightly in plastic wrap and refrigerate until cold and firmly set, at least 6 hours.

6. To unmold cheesecake, remove sides of pan. Slide thin metal spatula between crust and pan bottom to loosen, then slide cheesecake onto serving plate. Let cheesecake stand at room temperature for about 30 minutes. To slice, dip sharp knife in very hot water and wipe dry between cuts. Serve. (Leftovers can be refrigerated for up to 4 days.)

LIGHT CHEESECAKE

WHY THIS RECIPE WORKS: Of all the desserts that people long for in low-fat form, cheesecake is probably the most popular—but it's also the most difficult to lighten. Why? One modest slice of cheesecake boasts nearly 600 calories and about 40 grams of fat. Start removing the fat and sugar in the cake and flavor and texture can suffer terribly, as evidenced by the light recipes we tried. These cheesecakes were rubbery, gummy, and full of artificial flavors. We set out to develop a light cheesecake worth eating.

Three key steps produced our desired results. We replaced full-fat cream cheese and sour cream with a combination of light cream cheese, low-fat cottage cheese, and low-fat yogurt cheese. And to ensure a firm, not loose, filling, we drained the cottage cheese—this rid it of excess moisture. We cut the fat further by using a reduced number of whole eggs instead of whole eggs and yolks. And, finally, we pureed the filling in a food processor for an ultra smooth texture. The result? A rich, creamy cheesecake with about half the calories and three-quarters less fat than the original.

Light New York Cheesecake

SERVES 12

You can buy low-fat yogurt cheese (also called *labne*) or make your own with low-fat yogurt—allow at least 10 hours for the yogurt to drain. To make 1 cup yogurt cheese, line a fine-mesh strainer with 3 paper coffee filters or a double layer of cheesecloth. Spoon 2 cups of plain low-fat yogurt into the lined strainer, cover, and refrigerate for 10 to 12 hours (about 1 cup of liquid will have drained out of the yogurt to yield 1 cup yogurt cheese). Serve cake as is, or with Strawberry Topping (page 791).

CRUST

- 9 whole graham crackers, broken into 1-inch pieces
- 4 tablespoons (½ stick) unsalted butter, melted
- 1 tablespoon sugar

FILLING

- 1 pound 1 percent cottage cheese
- 1 pound light cream cheese, cut into chunks and softened
- 8 ounces (1 cup) low-fat yogurt cheese (see note)

1½ cups (10½ ounces) sugar
1 tablespoon vanilla extract
1 teaspoon grated zest from 1 lemon
¼ teaspoon table salt
3 large eggs, at room temperature

1. FOR THE CRUST: Adjust an oven rack to the middle position and heat the oven to 325 degrees. Process the graham cracker pieces in a food processor to fine, even crumbs, about 30 seconds. Mix the cracker crumbs, melted butter, and sugar together, then pour into a 9-inch springform pan. Press the crumbs firmly into an even layer using the bottom of a measuring cup. Bake the crust until fragrant, 10 to 15 minutes. Cool on a wire rack, about 30 minutes.

2. FOR THE FILLING: Meanwhile, increase the oven temperature to 500 degrees. Line a medium bowl with a clean dish towel or several layers of paper towels. Spoon the cottage cheese into the bowl and let drain for 30 minutes.

3. Process the drained cottage cheese in a food processor until smooth and no visible lumps remain, about 1 minute, scraping down the bowl as needed. Dollop the cream cheese and yogurt cheese into the food processor and continue to process until smooth, 1 to 2 minutes, scraping down the bowl as needed. Add the sugar, vanilla, lemon zest, and salt and continue to process until smooth, about 1 minute. With the processor running, add the eggs one at a time and continue to process until smooth.

4. Being careful not to disturb the baked crust, spray the insides of the springform pan with vegetable oil spray. Set the pan on a rimmed baking sheet. Pour the processed cheese mixture into the cooled crust and bake for 10 minutes.

5. Without opening the oven door, reduce the oven temperature to 200 degrees and continue to bake until the center of the cheesecake registers 150 degrees on an instant-read thermometer, about 1½ hours.

6. Transfer the cake to a wire rack and run a paring knife around the edge of the cake. Cool until barely warm, 2½ to 3 hours, running a paring knife around the edge of the cake every hour or so. Wrap the pan tightly in plastic wrap and refrigerate until cold, about 3 hours.

7. To unmold the cheesecake, wrap a wet, hot kitchen towel around the springform pan and let stand for 1 minute. Remove the sides of the pan. Blot any excess moisture from the top of the cheesecake with paper towels and slide onto a cake platter. Let the cheesecake stand at room temperature for about 30 minutes before slicing.

PUMPKIN CHEESECAKE

WHY THIS RECIPE WORKS: Those who suffer from pumpkin pie ennui embrace pumpkin cheesecake as "a nice change," but the expectations are low. Textures run the gamut from dry and dense to wet, soft, and mousse-like. Flavors veer from far too cheesy and tangy to pungently overspiced to totally bland. We wanted a creamy pumpkin cheesecake with a velvety smooth texture that tasted of sweet, earthy pumpkin as well as tangy cream cheese, that struck a harmonious spicy chord, and, of course, that had a crisp, buttery, cookie-crumb crust. For a cookie crust that complemented the earthy, warm flavors of pumpkin, we spiced up a graham cracker crust with ginger, cinnamon, and cloves. For a smooth and creamy texture, we blotted canned pumpkin puree with paper towels to remove excess moisture—this solved the sogginess issue. For dairy, we liked heavy cream, not sour cream, for added richness. We also preferred white sugar to brown, which tended to overpower the pumpkin flavor. Whole eggs, vanilla, salt, lemon juice, and a moderate blend of spices rounded out our cake. And for a smooth, velvety texture, we baked the cheesecake in a water bath in a moderate oven.

Spiced Pumpkin Cheesecake

SERVES 12

Be sure to buy unsweetened canned pumpkin, not pumpkin pie filling, which is preseasoned and sweetened. For neater slices, clean the knife thoroughly between slices.

CRUST

8 whole graham crackers, broken into 1-inch pieces
7 tablespoons unsalted butter, melted and cooled
3 tablespoons sugar
½ teaspoon ground ginger
½ teaspoon ground cinnamon
¼ teaspoon ground cloves

FILLING

1 (15-ounce) can pumpkin puree (see note)
1⅓ cups (9⅓ ounces) sugar
1 teaspoon ground cinnamon
½ teaspoon ground ginger
¼ teaspoon ground nutmeg
¼ teaspoon ground cloves
¼ teaspoon ground allspice
½ teaspoon table salt
1½ pounds cream cheese, cut into chunks and softened
1 tablespoon juice from 1 lemon
1 tablespoon vanilla extract
5 large eggs, at room temperature
1 cup heavy cream

1. FOR THE CRUST: Adjust an oven rack to the middle position and heat the oven to 325 degrees. Process the graham cracker pieces in a food processor to fine, even crumbs, about 30 seconds. Sprinkle 6 tablespoons of the melted butter, the sugar, and spices over the crumbs and pulse to incorporate. Sprinkle the mixture into a 9-inch springform pan. Press the crumbs firmly into an even layer using the bottom of a measuring cup. Bake the crust until fragrant and beginning to brown, 10 to 15 minutes. Let the crust cool to room temperature, about 30 minutes. Once cool, wrap the outside of the pan with two sheets of heavy-duty foil and set in a large roasting pan lined with a dish towel. Bring a kettle of water to a boil.

2. FOR THE FILLING: Pat the pumpkin puree dry with several layers of paper towels. Whisk the sugar, spices, and salt together in a small bowl.

3. In a stand mixer fitted with the paddle attachment, beat the cream cheese on medium-low speed until smooth, about 1 minute. Scrape down the bowl and beaters as needed.

4. Beat in half of the sugar mixture until incorporated, about 1 minute. Beat in the remaining sugar mixture until incorporated, about 1 minute. Beat in the dried pumpkin, lemon juice, and vanilla until incorporated, about 1 minute. Beat in the eggs, one at a time, until combined, about 1 minute. Beat in the heavy cream until incorporated, about 1 minute.

5. Being careful not to disturb the baked crust, brush the inside of the springform pan with the remaining 1 tablespoon melted butter. Carefully pour the filling into the pan. Set the roasting pan, with the cheesecake, on the oven rack and pour the boiling water into the roasting pan until it reaches about halfway up the sides of the pan. Bake the cheesecake until the center registers 150 degrees on an instant-read thermometer, about 1½ hours.

6. Cool the cheesecake in the roasting pan for 45 minutes, then transfer to a wire rack and cool until barely warm, 2½ to 3 hours, running a knife around the edge of the cake every hour or so. Wrap the pan tightly in plastic wrap and refrigerate until cold, about 3 hours.

7. To unmold the cheesecake, wrap a wet, hot kitchen towel around the cake pan and let sit for 1 minute. Remove the sides of the pan and carefully slide the cake onto a cake platter. Let the cheesecake sit at room temperature for 30 minutes before serving.

LEMON CHEESECAKE

WHY THIS RECIPE WORKS: Cheesecake is decadently rich. We love it in its unadulterated form, but sometimes the fresh flavor of citrus can take cheesecake to a refreshing new level. We aimed to develop a creamy cheesecake with a bracing but not overpowering lemon flavor.

Graham crackers, our usual cookie for cheesecakes, were too overpowering for the filling's lemon flavor. Instead, we turned to biscuit-type cookies, such as animal crackers, for a mild-tasting crust that allowed the lemon flavor of the cheesecake to shine. For maximum lemon flavor, we ground lemon zest with a portion of the sugar. This released its flavorful oils dramatically. Grinding the zest also improved the filling's texture (minced lemon zest baked up into fibrous bits in the cake). Heavy cream, in addition to cream cheese, provided richness, and vanilla rounded out the flavors. For ultimate creaminess, we baked the cake in a water bath. And finally, for an additional layer of bright lemon flavor, we topped off the cake with lemon curd.

Lemon Cheesecake

SERVES 12

Be sure to zest the lemons before juicing them. For neater slices, clean the knife thoroughly between slices.

CRUST

- 5 ounces Nabisco Barnum's Animal Crackers or Social Tea Biscuits
- 7 tablespoons unsalted butter, melted and cooled
- 3 tablespoons sugar

FILLING

- 1¼ cups (8¾ ounces) sugar
- 1 tablespoon grated zest from 1 lemon
- 1½ pounds cream cheese, cut into chunks and softened
- ¼ teaspoon table salt
- ¼ cup juice from 2 lemons
- 2 teaspoons vanilla extract
- 4 large eggs, at room temperature
- ½ cup heavy cream

CURD

- ⅓ cup juice from 2 lemons
- ½ cup (3½ ounces) sugar
- Pinch table salt
- 2 large whole eggs plus 1 large egg yolk
- 2 tablespoons unsalted butter, cut into ½-inch pieces and frozen
- 1 tablespoon heavy cream
- ¼ teaspoon vanilla extract

1. FOR THE CRUST: Adjust an oven rack to the middle position and heat the oven to 325 degrees. Process the cookies in a food processor to fine, even crumbs, about 30 seconds. Sprinkle 6 tablespoons of the melted butter and the sugar over the crumbs and pulse to incorporate. Sprinkle the mixture into a 9-inch springform pan. Press the crumbs firmly into an even layer using the bottom of a measuring cup. Bake the crust until fragrant and beginning to brown, 10 to 15 minutes. Let the crust cool to room temperature, about 30 minutes. Once cool, wrap the outside of the pan with two sheets of heavy-duty foil and set in a large roasting pan lined with a dish towel. Bring a kettle of water to a boil.

2. FOR THE FILLING: Process ¼ cup of the sugar and the lemon zest in a food processor until the sugar is yellow and the zest is very fine, about 15 seconds. Pulse in the remaining 1 cup sugar to combine.

3. In a stand mixer fitted with the paddle attachment, beat the cream cheese on medium speed until smooth, about 1 minute. Scrape down the bowl and beaters as needed.

4. Beat in half of the lemon sugar and the salt until incorporated. Beat in the remaining lemon sugar until incorporated, about 1 minute. Beat in the lemon juice and vanilla until incorporated, about 1 minute. Beat in the eggs, one at a time, until combined, about 1 minute. Beat in the heavy cream until incorporated, about 1 minute.

5. Being careful not to disturb the baked crust, brush the inside of the prepared springform pan with the remaining 1 tablespoon melted butter. Carefully pour the filling into the pan. Set the roasting pan, with the cheesecake, on the oven rack and pour the boiling water into the roasting pan until it reaches about halfway up the sides of the springform pan. Bake the cheesecake until the center registers 150 degrees on an instant-read thermometer, about 1½ hours.

6. Cool the cheesecake in the roasting pan for 45 minutes, then transfer to a wire rack and cool until barely warm, 2½ to 3 hours, running a knife around the edge of the cake every hour or so. Wrap the pan tightly in plastic wrap and refrigerate until cold, about 3 hours.

7. FOR THE CURD: Meanwhile, cook the lemon juice, sugar, and salt together in a small saucepan over medium-high heat until the sugar dissolves and the mixture is hot (do not boil). In a medium bowl, whisk the whole eggs and egg yolk together until combined, then slowly whisk in the hot lemon mixture to temper. Return the mixture to the saucepan and cook over medium-low heat, stirring constantly, until the mixture is thickened and a spatula scraped along the bottom of the pan leaves a trail (170 degrees on an instant-read thermometer), 2 to 4 minutes.

8. Off the heat, stir in the frozen butter until melted and incorporated, then stir in the cream and vanilla. Strain the curd through a fine-mesh strainer into a small bowl. Press plastic wrap directly on the surface of the curd and refrigerate until needed.

9. TO FINISH THE CAKE: When the cheesecake is cold, spoon the lemon curd over the top of the cake and spread into an even layer. Wrap the pan tightly in plastic wrap and refrigerate until the curd and cake have set, at least 5 hours.

10. To unmold the cheesecake, wrap a wet, hot kitchen towel around the cake pan and let sit for 1 minute. Remove the sides of the pan and carefully slide the cake onto a cake platter. Let the cheesecake sit at room temperature for 30 minutes before serving.

LEMON PUDDING CAKES

WHY THIS RECIPE WORKS: Despite the appeal of a single batter that produces two texturally distinct layers, lemon pudding cake can be unpredictable, sporting underbaked cake or grainy pudding. We wanted lots of lemon flavor, tender cake, and rich, creamy pudding. Whipping the egg whites to soft peaks and decreasing the amount of flour gave us the best ratio of pudding to cake. Baking powder gave the cake layer some lift, while also producing a golden top. Using a cold water bath in a large roasting pan prevented the pudding from curdling while still allowing the cake to cook through. By infusing the milk and cream with lemon zest, we achieved maximum lemon flavor without a disruption in the smooth texture of the dessert. We finished off the cakes with a sweet, fruity blueberry compote to complement the tart lemon flavor.

Lemon Pudding Cakes

SERVES 6

To take the temperature of the pudding layer, touch the probe tip to the bottom of the ramekin and pull it up ¼ inch. The batter can also be baked in an 8-inch square glass baking dish. We like this dessert served at room temperature, but it can also be served chilled (the texture will be firmer). Spoon Blueberry Compote (recipe follows) over the top of each ramekin or simply dust with confectioners' sugar.

- 1 cup whole milk
- ½ cup heavy cream
- 3 tablespoons grated lemon zest plus ½ cup juice (3 lemons)
- 1 cup (7 ounces) sugar
- ¼ cup (1¼ ounces) all-purpose flour
- ½ teaspoon baking powder
- ⅛ teaspoon salt
- 2 large eggs, separated, plus 2 large whites
- ½ teaspoon vanilla extract

1. Adjust oven rack to middle position and heat oven to 325 degrees. Bring milk and cream to simmer in medium saucepan over medium-high heat. Remove pan from heat, whisk in lemon zest, cover pan, and let stand for 15 minutes. Meanwhile, fold dish towel in half and place in bottom of large roasting pan. Place six 6-ounce ramekins on top of towel and set aside pan.

2. Strain milk mixture through fine-mesh strainer into bowl, pressing on lemon zest to extract liquid; discard lemon zest. Whisk ¾ cup sugar, flour, baking powder, and salt in second bowl until combined. Add egg yolks, vanilla, lemon juice, and milk mixture and whisk until combined. (Batter will have consistency of milk.)

3. Using stand mixer fitted with whisk, whip egg whites on medium-low speed until foamy, about 1 minute. Increase speed to medium-high and whip whites to soft, billowy mounds, about 1 minute. Gradually add remaining ¼ cup sugar and whip until glossy, soft peaks form, 1 to 2 minutes.

4. Whisk one-quarter of whites into batter to lighten. With rubber spatula, gently fold in remaining whites until no clumps or streaks remain. Ladle batter into ramekins (ramekins should be nearly full). Pour enough cold water into roasting pan to come one-third of way up sides of ramekins. Bake until cake is set and pale golden brown and pudding layer registers 172 to 175 degrees at center, 50 to 55 minutes.

5. Remove pan from oven and let ramekins stand in water bath for 10 minutes. Transfer ramekins to wire rack and let cool completely. Serve.

Blueberry Compote

MAKES ABOUT 1 CUP

To use fresh blueberries, crush one-third of them against the side of the saucepan with a wooden spoon after adding them to the butter and then proceed as directed.

- 1 tablespoon unsalted butter
- 10 ounces (2 cups) frozen blueberries
- 2 tablespoons sugar, plus extra for seasoning
- Pinch salt
- ½ teaspoon lemon juice

Melt butter in small saucepan over medium heat. Add blueberries, 2 tablespoons sugar, and salt; bring to boil. Lower heat and simmer, stirring occasionally, until thickened and about one-quarter of juice remains, 8 to 10 minutes. Remove pan from heat and stir in lemon juice. Season with extra sugar to taste.

BAKED ALASKA

WHY THIS RECIPE WORKS: Though making a baked Alaska can be intimidating to some, the dessert is essentially a dressed-up ice cream cake that's no more difficult to make than any other version. Plenty of insulation was the key to a baked Alaska that is toasty on the outside but still firm at the center. Most recipes use cake only as a base, but we used it to encase the ice cream entirely, thereby decreasing the amount of meringue by more than one-third without sacrificing heat resistance. To further improve the balance, we added cocoa to our cake, boosting flavor without adding sweetness. Rather than packing softened ice cream into a mold (refrozen ice cream can be icy, and it can be hard to match cake pans and bowls), we simply cut the cardboard off two pints of firm ice cream and stuck them together to form the core of our dessert. We opted for coffee ice cream, which complements the flavor of the cake and the sweetness of the meringue perfectly.

Baked Alaska

SERVES 8

Coffee ice cream provides the best contrast with sweet meringue in this recipe, but other flavors may be substituted, if desired. A high-quality ice cream such as Häagen-Dazs works best because it is slower to melt. To ensure the proper texture when serving, it is necessary to remove the cake from the freezer before making the meringue. This recipe leaves just enough leftover cake and ice cream to make an additional for-two version (recipe follows).

- 2 (1-pint) containers coffee ice cream

CAKE

- 1 cup (4 ounces) cake flour
- ⅓ cup (1 ounce) unsweetened cocoa powder
- ⅔ cup (4⅔ ounces) sugar
- 1½ teaspoons baking powder
- ¼ teaspoon salt
- ½ cup vegetable oil
- 6 tablespoons water
- 4 large eggs, separated

MERINGUE

- ¾ cup (5¼ ounces) sugar
- ⅓ cup light corn syrup
- 3 large egg whites
- 2 tablespoons water
- Pinch salt
- 1 teaspoon vanilla extract

1. Lay 12-inch square sheet of plastic wrap on counter and remove lids from ice cream. Use scissors to cut cardboard tubs from top to bottom. Peel away cardboard and discard. Place ice cream blocks on their sides in center of plastic with wider ends facing each other. Grasp each side of plastic and firmly press blocks together to form barrel shape. Wrap plastic tightly around ice cream and roll briefly on counter to form uniform cylinder. Place cylinder, standing on end, in freezer until completely solid, at least 1 hour.

2. FOR THE CAKE: Adjust oven rack to middle position and heat oven to 350 degrees. Lightly grease 18 by 13-inch rimmed baking sheet, line with parchment paper, and lightly grease parchment. Whisk flour, cocoa, ⅓ cup sugar, baking powder, and salt together in large bowl. Whisk oil, water, and egg yolks into flour mixture until smooth batter forms.

3. Using stand mixer fitted with whisk attachment, whip egg whites on medium-low speed until foamy, about 1 minute. Increase speed to medium-high and whip whites to soft, billowy mounds, about 1 minute. Gradually add remaining ⅓ cup sugar and whip until glossy, soft peaks form, 1 to 2 minutes. Transfer one-third of egg whites to batter; whisk gently until mixture is lightened. Using rubber spatula, gently fold remaining egg whites into batter.

4. Pour batter into prepared sheet; spread evenly. Bake until cake springs back when pressed lightly in center, 10 to 13 minutes. Transfer cake to wire rack and let cool for 5 minutes. Run knife around edge of sheet, then invert cake onto wire rack. Carefully remove parchment, then reinvert cake onto second wire rack. Let cool completely, at least 15 minutes.

5. Transfer cake to cutting board with long side of rectangle parallel to edge of counter. Using serrated knife, trim ¼ inch off left side of cake and discard. Using ruler, measure 4½ inches from cut edge and make mark with knife. Using mark as guide, cut 4½-inch rectangle from cake. Trim piece to create 4½ by 11-inch rectangle and set aside. (Depending on pan size and how much cake has shrunk during baking, it may not be necessary to trim piece to measure 11 inches.)

Measure 4 inches from new cut edge and make mark. Using mark as guide, cut 4-inch rectangle from cake. Trim piece to create 4 by 10-inch rectangle, wrap rectangle in plastic, and set aside. Cut 3½-inch round from remaining cake and set aside (biscuit cutter works well). Save scraps for Bonus Baked Alaska.

6. Unwrap ice cream. Trim cylinder to 4½ inches in length and return remainder to freezer for Bonus Baked Alaska. Place ice cream cylinder on 4½ by 11-inch cake rectangle and wrap cake around ice cream. (Cake may crack slightly.) Place cake circle on one end of cylinder. Wrap entire cylinder tightly in plastic. Place cylinder, standing on cake-covered end, in freezer until cake is firm, at least 30 minutes.

7. Unwrap cylinder and place on cutting board, standing on cake-covered end, and cut in half lengthwise. Unwrap reserved 4 by 10-inch cake rectangle and place halves on top, ice cream side down, with open ends meeting in middle. Wrap tightly with plastic and press ends gently to close gap between halves. Return to freezer for at least 2 hours and up to 2 weeks.

8. FOR THE MERINGUE: Adjust oven rack to upper-middle position and heat oven to 500 degrees. Spray wire rack set in rimmed baking sheet with vegetable oil spray. Unwrap cake and place on rack. Combine sugar, corn syrup, egg whites, water, and salt in bowl of stand mixer; place bowl over saucepan filled with 1 inch simmering water, making sure that water does not touch bottom of bowl. Whisking gently but constantly, heat until sugar is dissolved and mixture registers 160 degrees, 5 to 8 minutes.

9. Place bowl in stand mixer fitted with whisk attachment. Beat mixture on medium speed until bowl is only slightly warm to touch, about 5 minutes. Increase speed to high and beat until mixture begins to lose its gloss and forms stiff peaks, about 5 minutes. Add vanilla and beat until combined.

10. Using offset spatula, spread meringue over top and sides of cake, avoiding getting meringue on rack. Use back of spoon to create peaks all over meringue.

11. Bake until browned and crisp, about 5 minutes. Run offset spatula or thin knife under dessert to loosen from rack, then use two spatulas to transfer to serving platter. To slice, dip sharp knife in very hot water and wipe dry after each cut. Serve immediately.

Bonus Baked Alaska

SERVES 2

Our Baked Alaska recipe leaves just enough leftover cake and ice cream to make an additional for-two version.

From remaining cake, cut two 3⅓-inch rounds and one 11 by 2-inch strip. Place leftover ice cream disk on top of 1 cake round. Wrap strip of cake around sides of disk. Place remaining cake round on top, wrap tightly in plastic, and freeze. Following step 10, spread meringue over cake and bake as directed.

NOTES FROM THE TEST KITCHEN

BUILDING A NEW BAKED ALASKA

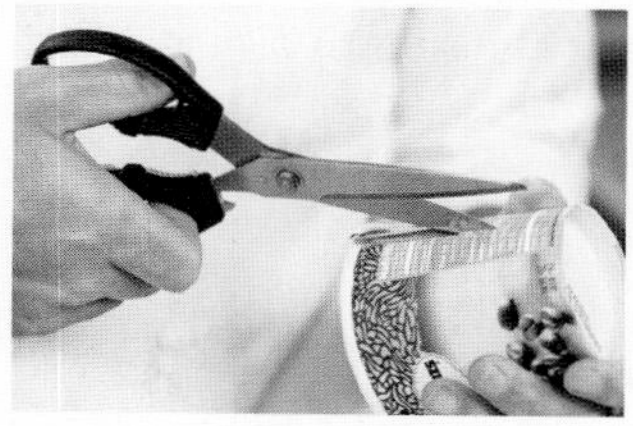

1. Cut ice cream tubs from top to bottom and peel away cardboard. Place blocks on plastic wrap on their sides with wider ends facing each other.

2. Wrap plastic tightly around ice cream and roll on counter to form even cylinder. Place in freezer, standing on end, for 1 hour.

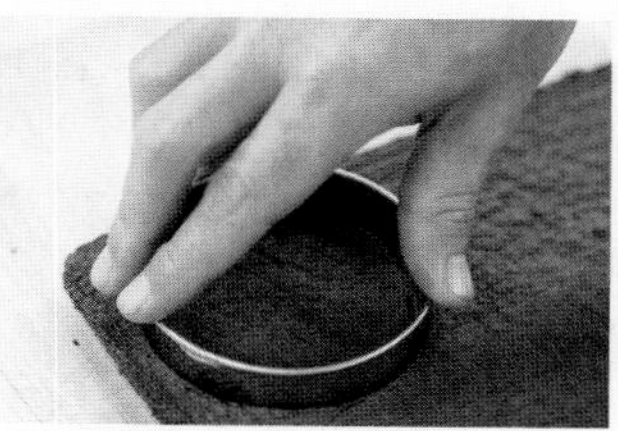

3. Trim ¼ inch off left side of cake. Cut 4½ by 11-inch rectangle, 4 by 10-inch rectangle, and 3½-inch round. Save scraps for Bonus Baked Alaska.

4. Unwrap ice cream and trim cylinder to 4½ inches in length. Return remainder to freezer.

5. Place ice cream on 11 by 4½-inch cake rectangle and wrap cake around ice cream. Place cake circle on 1 end of cylinder. Wrap in plastic. Freeze, standing on cake-covered end, for 30 minutes.

6. Unwrap cylinder, stand on cake-covered end, and cut in half lengthwise. Place halves on 10 by 4-inch rectangle, ice cream side down, with open ends meeting in middle.

CHAPTER 24

PUDDINGS, SOUFFLÉS, AND MORE

BREAD PUDDING

WHY THIS RECIPE WORKS: Contemporary versions of this humble dish vary in texture, from mushy porridge to chewy, desiccated cousins of overcooked holiday stuffing. We wanted a dessert as refined as any French soufflé. We chose challah for its rich flavor, cut the bread into cubes, toasted them until lightly browned, and soaked them with basic custard. Once the cubes were saturated, we transferred them to a baking dish and slid our pudding into a low-temperature oven to prevent curdling. The custard turned out creamy and smooth, but not as set as we'd have liked. Adding another egg or two would help, but it already tasted somewhat eggy. It turns out that eggy flavor comes from the sulfur compounds in egg whites. We got rid of the whites and just used the yolks. We now had a luscious, silky custard with no trace of egginess. For a crackly crust, we dotted the top of the pudding with additional toasted bread cubes. Then we brushed it with melted butter and sprinkled it with a flavorful mixture of white and brown sugar before transferring it to the oven. The crunchy, buttery, sugary crust was the perfect partner to the satiny-smooth custard that lay below.

Classic Bread Pudding

SERVES 8 TO 10

Challah is an egg-enriched bread that can be found in most bakeries and supermarkets. If you cannot find challah, a firm high-quality sandwich bread such as Arnold Country Classics White or Pepperidge Farm Farmhouse Hearty White may be substituted. If desired, serve this pudding with softly whipped cream or with Bourbon–Brown Sugar Sauce (recipe follows). Store leftovers tightly wrapped in the refrigerator. To retain a crisp top crust when reheating leftovers, cut the bread pudding into squares and heat, uncovered, in a 450-degree oven until warmed through, 6 to 8 minutes.

- 2 tablespoons light brown sugar
- ¾ cup (5¼ ounces) plus 1 tablespoon granulated sugar
- 1 (14-ounce) loaf challah bread, cut into ¾-inch cubes (about 10 cups; see note)
- 9 large egg yolks
- 4 teaspoons vanilla extract
- ¾ teaspoon table salt
- 2½ cups heavy cream
- 2½ cups milk
- 2 tablespoons unsalted butter, melted

1. Adjust the oven racks to the middle and lower-middle positions and heat the oven to 325 degrees. Combine the brown sugar and 1 tablespoon of the granulated sugar in a small bowl; set aside.

2. Spread the bread cubes in a single layer on two rimmed baking sheets. Bake, tossing occasionally, until just dry, about 15 minutes, switching the baking sheets halfway through the baking time. Cool the bread cubes for about 15 minutes; set aside 2 cups.

3. Whisk the egg yolks, remaining ¾ cup sugar, the vanilla, and salt together in a large bowl. Whisk in the cream and milk until combined. Add the remaining 8 cups cooled bread cubes and toss to coat. Transfer the mixture to a 13 by 9-inch baking dish and let stand, occasionally pressing the bread cubes into the custard, until the cubes are thoroughly saturated, about 30 minutes.

4. Spread the reserved bread cubes evenly over the top of the soaked bread mixture and gently press into the custard. Using a pastry brush, dab the melted butter over the top of the unsoaked bread pieces. Sprinkle the brown sugar mixture evenly over the top. Place the bread pudding on a rimmed baking sheet and bake on the middle rack until the custard has just set and pressing the center of the pudding with your finger reveals no runny liquid, 45 to 50 minutes. (An instant-read thermometer inserted into the center of the pudding should read 170 degrees.) Transfer to a wire rack and cool until the pudding is set and just warm, about 45 minutes. Serve.

Bourbon–Brown Sugar Sauce

MAKES ABOUT 1 CUP

- ½ cup packed (3½ ounces) light brown sugar
- 7 tablespoons heavy cream
- 2½ tablespoons unsalted butter
- 1½ tablespoons bourbon

Whisk the brown sugar and heavy cream in a small saucepan over medium heat until combined. Continue to cook, whisking frequently, until the mixture comes to a boil, about 5 minutes. Whisk in the butter and bring the mixture back to a boil, about 1 minute. Remove from the heat and whisk in the bourbon. Cool to just warm; serve with the bread pudding.

SLOW-COOKER CHOCOLATE BREAD PUDDING

WHY THIS RECIPE WORKS: Making bread pudding in a slow cooker may seem like a stretch, but we were determined to make a company-worthy version in the slow cooker that boasted both decadence and hands-off (and oven-freeing) convenience. Getting the texture of this dessert just right was the real challenge; early tests yielded mushy or dry puddings, not the creamy and moist texture we were after. After testing various types of bread, we agreed challah, with its rich flavor, had the upper hand. We cut the bread into cubes and toasted it in the oven before adding it to the slow cooker. This extra step dried out the bread so it would be able to soak up as much custard as possible. Once toasted, we transferred the bread to the slow cooker and added the custard (a combination of egg yolks, milk, heavy cream, sugar, and vanilla). Pressing the bread into the custard ensured every cube soaked up its share. A chocolate bread pudding seemed like the right indulgent route to take, and opting for Nutella as our chief chocolaty component took our recipe to the next level. To give our recipe another chocolaty boost, we stirred in chocolate chips, which melted into the pudding and made this dessert that much more decadent.

Chocolate-Hazelnut Slow-Cooker Bread Pudding

SERVES 8 TO 10

- 1 (14-ounce) loaf challah bread, cut into 1-inch cubes (about 12 cups; see note on page 800)
- ½ cup chocolate chips
- 2 cups heavy cream
- 2 cups whole milk
- 9 large egg yolks
- 1 cup Nutella
- ¾ cup plus 1 tablespoon (5⅔ ounces) granulated sugar
- 4 teaspoons vanilla extract
- ¾ teaspoon table salt
- 2 tablespoons light brown sugar

1. Following the photos, line the slow cooker with an aluminum foil collar, then line with a foil sling, and spray with vegetable oil spray. Adjust the oven rack to the middle position and heat the oven to 225 degrees. Spread the bread over a rimmed baking sheet and bake, shaking the pan occasionally, until dry and crisp, about 40 minutes. Let the bread cool slightly, then transfer to a very large bowl.

2. Mix the chocolate chips into the dried bread; transfer to the prepared slow cooker. Whisk the cream, milk, egg yolks, Nutella, ¾ cup of the granulated sugar, the vanilla, and salt together in a bowl, then pour the mixture evenly over the bread. Press gently on the bread to submerge.

3. Mix the remaining 1 tablespoon granulated sugar with the brown sugar then sprinkle over the top of the casserole. Cover and cook until the center is set, about 4 hours on low. Let cool for 30 minutes before serving.

NOTES FROM THE TEST KITCHEN

PREPARING THE SLOW COOKER

1. TO MAKE A FOIL COLLAR: Layer and fold sheets of heavy-duty foil until you have a six-layered foil rectangle that measures roughly 16 inches long by 4 inches wide. Press the collar into the back side of the slow-cooker insert.

2. TO MAKE A FOIL SLING: Fit two large sheets of heavy-duty foil into the slow cooker, perpendicular to one another and hanging over the edges of the slow cooker. Use the overhanging foil to lift the dish out of the slow cooker fully intact.

STOVETOP RICE PUDDING

WHY THIS RECIPE WORKS: At its best, rice pudding is lightly sweet and tastes of its primary component, rice. At its worst, the rice flavor is lost to cloying sweetness, overcooked milk, and a pasty, leaden consistency. We wanted a rice pudding with intact, tender grains bound loosely in a subtly sweet, creamy pudding.

For simple, straightforward rice flavor, we avoided aromatic rices like basmati and jasmine. Arborio rice, used for risotto, was stiff and gritty. Overall, medium-grain rice produced the best texture (with long-grain rice a close second). We found that cooking the rice in water rather than milk left its flavor intact. After the rice absorbed the water, we added sugar and equal amounts of milk and half-and-half, which delivered the proper degree of richness; the eggs and butter found in other recipes were just too overpowering. When we cooked the rice in water with the lid on the pan, then removed the lid while the rice simmered in the milk mixture, we got the results we wanted: distinct, tender grains of rice in a milky, subtly sweet sauce.

Stovetop Rice Pudding

SERVES 6 TO 8

We prefer pudding made with medium-grain rice, but long-grain rice works, too.

- 2 cups water
- 1 cup medium-grain rice (see note)
- ¼ teaspoon table salt
- 2½ cups whole milk
- 2½ cups half-and-half
- ⅔ cup (4⅔ ounces) sugar
- ½ cup raisins
- 1½ teaspoons vanilla extract
- 1 teaspoon ground cinnamon

1. Bring the water to a boil in a large saucepan. Stir in the rice and salt, cover, and simmer over low heat, stirring once or twice, until the water is almost fully absorbed, 15 to 20 minutes.

2. Stir in the milk, half-and-half, and sugar. Increase the heat to medium-high and bring to a simmer, then reduce the heat to maintain a simmer. Cook, uncovered and stirring frequently, until the mixture starts to thicken, about 30 minutes. Reduce the heat to low and continue to cook, stirring every couple of minutes to prevent sticking and scorching, until a spoon is just able to stand up in the pudding, about 15 minutes longer.

3. Remove from the heat and stir in the raisins, vanilla, and cinnamon. Serve warm, at room temperature, or chilled. (To store, press plastic wrap directly onto the surface of the pudding and refrigerate for up to 2 days. If serving at room temperature or chilled, stir in up to 1 cup warm milk, 2 tablespoons at a time, as needed to loosen before serving.)

Coconut Rice Pudding

To toast the coconut, spread it out on a rimmed baking sheet and toast it in a 325-degree oven, stirring often, until light golden, 10 to 15 minutes.

Follow the recipe for Stovetop Rice Pudding, substituting coconut milk for the whole milk and garnishing with 1 cup shredded sweetened coconut, toasted, before serving.

BEST BUTTERSCOTCH PUDDING

WHY THIS RECIPE WORKS: For butterscotch pudding with rich, bittersweet flavor, we made butterscotch sauce by cooking butter, brown and white sugar, corn syrup, lemon juice, and salt together into a dark caramel. Because making caramel can be finicky—it can go from caramelized to burnt in a matter of seconds—we used a two-step process that gave us a larger window in which to gauge the doneness of the caramel. We first brought the mixture to a rolling boil and then we reduced the heat to a low simmer where it slowly came up to temperature and we could stop the cooking at just the right moment. To turn our butterscotch into pudding, we ditched the classical (yet time-consuming) tempering method in favor of a revolutionary technique that calls for pouring the boiling caramel sauce directly over the thickening agents (egg yolks and cornstarch thinned with a little milk). The result is the sophisticated bittersweet flavor of traditional butterscotch with less mess and fuss.

Best Butterscotch Pudding

SERVES 8

When taking the temperature of the caramel in step 1, tilt the pan and move the thermometer back and forth to equalize hot and cool spots. Work quickly when pouring the caramel mixture over the egg mixture in step 4 to ensure proper thickening. Serve the pudding with lightly sweetened whipped cream.

- 12 tablespoons unsalted butter, cut into ½-inch pieces
- ½ cup (3½ ounces) granulated sugar
- ½ cup packed (3½ ounces) dark brown sugar
- ¼ cup water
- 2 tablespoons light corn syrup
- 1 teaspoon lemon juice
- ¾ teaspoon salt
- 1 cup heavy cream
- 2¼ cups whole milk
- 4 large egg yolks
- ¼ cup cornstarch
- 2 teaspoons vanilla extract
- 1 teaspoon dark rum

1. Bring butter, granulated sugar, brown sugar, water, corn syrup, lemon juice, and salt to boil in large saucepan over medium heat, stirring occasionally to dissolve sugar and melt butter. Once mixture is at full rolling boil, cook, stirring occasionally, for 5 minutes (caramel will register about 240 degrees). Immediately reduce heat to medium-low and gently simmer (caramel should maintain steady stream of lazy bubbles—if not, adjust heat accordingly), stirring frequently, until mixture is color of dark peanut butter, 12 to 16 minutes longer (caramel will register about 300 degrees and should have slight burnt smell).

2. Remove pan from heat; carefully pour ¼ cup cream into caramel mixture and swirl to incorporate (mixture will bubble and steam); let bubbling subside. Whisk vigorously and scrape corners of pan until mixture is completely smooth, at least 30 seconds. Return pan to medium heat and gradually whisk in remaining ¾ cup cream until smooth. Whisk in 2 cups milk until mixture is smooth, making sure to scrape corners and edges of pan to remove any remaining bits of caramel.

3. Meanwhile, microwave remaining ¼ cup milk until simmering, 30 to 45 seconds. Whisk egg yolks and cornstarch together in large bowl until smooth. Gradually whisk in hot milk until smooth; set aside (do not refrigerate).

4. Return saucepan to medium-high heat and bring mixture to full rolling boil, whisking frequently. Once mixture is boiling rapidly and beginning to climb toward top of pan, immediately pour into bowl with yolk mixture in 1 motion (do not add gradually). Whisk thoroughly for 10 to 15 seconds (mixture will thicken after a few seconds). Whisk in vanilla and rum. Spray piece of parchment paper with vegetable oil spray and press on surface of pudding. Refrigerate until cold and set, at least 3 hours. Whisk pudding until smooth before serving.

PANNA COTTA

WHY THIS RECIPE WORKS: Though its name is lyrical, the literal translation of panna cotta, "cooked cream," does nothing to suggest its ethereal qualities. In fact, panna cotta is not cooked at all. Neither is it complicated with eggs, as is a custard. Instead, sugar and gelatin are melted in cream and milk, and the whole mixture is then turned into individual ramekins and chilled. Panna cotta is more often found on restaurant menus, but we wanted a version for the home cook—one that would guarantee a pudding with the rich flavor of cream and vanilla and a delicate texture.

After trying several different recipes, we concluded that we needed a higher proportion of cream to milk to achieve the creamiest flavor and texture. The amount of gelatin proved critical—too much turned the panna cotta rubbery; it needs to be just firm enough to unmold, so we used a light hand. And because gelatin sets more quickly at cold temperatures, we minimized the amount of heat by softening the gelatin in cold milk, then heating it very briefly until it was melted. To avoid premature hardening, we gradually added cold vanilla-infused cream to the gelatin mixture and stirred everything over an ice bath to incorporate the gelatin. Chilled until set and served with a raspberry sauce, our panna cotta was creamy, smooth, and light.

Panna Cotta

SERVES 8

A vanilla bean gives the panna cotta the deepest flavor, but 2 teaspoons of vanilla extract can be used instead. If you like, you can omit the Raspberry Coulis and simply serve the panna cotta with lightly sweetened berries. Though traditionally unmolded, panna cotta may be chilled and served in wine glasses and sauced on top. If you would like to make the panna cotta a day ahead, decrease the amount of gelatin to 2½ teaspoons, and chill the filled wine glasses or ramekins for 18 to 24 hours.

- 1 cup whole milk
- 2¾ teaspoons gelatin (see note)
- 3 cups heavy cream
- 1 vanilla bean, halved lengthwise (see note)
- 6 tablespoons sugar
- Pinch table salt
- Raspberry Coulis (recipe follows)

1. Pour the milk into a medium saucepan; sprinkle the surface evenly with the gelatin and let stand for 10 minutes. Meanwhile, turn the contents of two ice cube trays (about 32 cubes) into a large bowl; add 4 cups cold water. Pour the cream into a large measuring cup or pitcher. With a paring knife, scrape the vanilla seeds into the cream; place the pod in the cream along with the seeds and set the mixture aside. Set eight 4-ounce ramekins on a rimmed baking sheet.

2. Heat the milk and gelatin mixture over high heat, stirring constantly, until the gelatin is dissolved and the mixture registers 135 degrees on an instant-read thermometer, about 1½ minutes. Off the heat, add the sugar and salt; stir until dissolved, about 1 minute.

3. Stirring constantly, slowly pour the cream with the vanilla into the saucepan containing the milk, then transfer the mixture to a medium bowl and set the bowl over the ice water bath. Stir frequently until thickened to the consistency of eggnog and the mixture registers 50 degrees on an instant-read thermometer, about 10 minutes. Strain the mixture into a large measuring cup or pitcher, then distribute evenly among the ramekins. Cover the baking sheet with plastic wrap, making sure that the plastic does not mar the surface of the cream; refrigerate until just set (the mixture should wobble when shaken gently), about 4 hours.

4. To serve, spoon a portion of the raspberry coulis onto eight individual serving plates. Pour 1 cup boiling water into a small wide-mouthed bowl, dip a ramekin filled with panna cotta into the water for 3 seconds and lift the ramekin out of the water. With a moistened finger, press lightly on the periphery of the panna cotta to loosen the edges. Dip the ramekin back into the hot water for another 3 seconds. Invert the ramekin over your palm and loosen the panna cotta by cupping your fingers between the panna cotta and the edges of the ramekin. Gently lower the panna cotta onto a serving plate with the coulis. Repeat the process with the remaining ramekins of panna cotta. Serve.

Raspberry Coulis

MAKES ABOUT 1½ CUPS

- 24 ounces (about 5 cups) frozen raspberries
- ⅓ cup (2⅓ ounces) sugar
- ¼ teaspoon juice from 1 lemon
- Pinch table salt

1. Place the frozen raspberries in a 4-quart saucepan. Cover and simmer over medium-high heat, stirring occasionally, for 10 to 12 minutes. Add the sugar and increase the heat to high. Boil for 2 minutes.

2. Strain the berries through a fine-mesh strainer into a bowl, using a rubber spatula to push the berries through the strainer; discard the seeds. Stir in the lemon juice and salt. Cover and refrigerate until chilled, at least 2 hours or up to 3 days.

CRÈME BRÛLÉE

WHY THIS RECIPE WORKS: Crème brûlée is all about the contrast between the crisp sugar crust and the silky custard underneath. But too often the crust is either stingy or rock-hard and the custard is heavy and tasteless. Because crème brûlée requires so few ingredients, we knew that finding just the right technique would be key in creating the quintessential version of this elegant dessert.

The texture of the custard should not be firm but rather soft and supple. The secret, we found, is using egg yolks—and lots of them—rather than whole eggs. Heavy cream gave the custard a luxurious richness. Sugar, a vanilla bean, and a pinch of salt were the only other additions. Despite instructions in many recipes to use scalded cream, we found that this technique was more likely to result in overcooked custard, so we thought we would leave the ingredients cold. The downside, however, was that we needed heat to extract flavor from the vanilla bean and dissolve the sugar. Our compromise was to heat only half of the cream with the sugar and vanilla bean and add the remaining cream cold, which worked perfectly. For the crust, we used crunchy turbinado sugar, which was easy to spread on the baked and chilled custards. A propane or butane torch worked better than the broiler for caramelizing the sugar, and because the blast of heat inevitably warms the custard beneath the crust, we chilled our crèmes brûlées once more before serving.

Classic Crème Brûlée

SERVES 8

Separate the eggs and whisk the yolks after the cream has finished steeping; if left to sit, the surface of the yolks will dry and form a film. A vanilla bean gives the custard the deepest flavor, but 2 teaspoons of vanilla extract, whisked into the yolks in step 4, can be used instead. The best way to judge doneness is with an instant-read thermometer. For the caramelized sugar crust, we recommend turbinado or Demerara sugar. Regular granulated sugar will work, too, but use only 1 scant teaspoon on each ramekin or 1 teaspoon on each shallow fluted dish. It's important to use 4- to 5-ounce ramekins.

- 4 cups heavy cream, chilled
- ⅔ cup (4⅔ ounces) granulated sugar
- Pinch table salt
- 1 vanilla bean, halved lengthwise (see note)
- 12 large egg yolks (see note)
- 8–12 teaspoons turbinado or Demerara sugar (see note)

1. Adjust an oven rack to the lower-middle position and heat the oven to 300 degrees.

2. Combine 2 cups of the cream, the sugar, and salt in a medium saucepan. With a paring knife, scrape the seeds from the vanilla bean into the pan, submerge the pod in the cream, and bring the mixture to a boil over medium heat, stirring occasionally to ensure that the sugar dissolves. Take the pan off the heat and let steep for 15 minutes.

3. Meanwhile, place a kitchen towel in the bottom of a large baking dish or roasting pan and arrange eight 4- or 5-ounce ramekins (or shallow fluted dishes) on the towel (making sure they do not touch). Bring a kettle or large saucepan of water to a boil.

4. After the vanilla bean has steeped, stir in the remaining 2 cups cream to cool down the mixture. Whisk the egg yolks in a large bowl until broken up and combined. Whisk about 1 cup of the cream mixture into the yolks until loosened and combined; repeat with 1 cup more cream. Add the remaining cream and whisk until evenly colored and thoroughly combined. Strain the mixture through a fine-mesh strainer into a large measuring cup or pitcher (or clean medium bowl); discard the solids in the strainer. Pour or ladle the mixture into the ramekins, dividing it evenly among them.

5. Carefully place the baking dish with the ramekins on the oven rack; pour the boiling water into the dish, taking care not to splash water into the ramekins, until the water reaches two-thirds of the way up the sides of the ramekins. Bake until the centers of the custards are just barely set and are no longer sloshy and register 170 to 175 degrees on an instant-read thermometer, 30 to 35 minutes (25 to 30 minutes for shallow fluted dishes). Begin checking the temperature about 5 minutes before the recommended time.

6. Transfer the ramekins to a wire rack and cool to room temperature, about 2 hours. Set the ramekins on a rimmed baking sheet, cover tightly with plastic wrap, and refrigerate until cold, at least 4 hours or up to 4 days.

7. Uncover the ramekins; if condensation has collected on the custards, blot the moisture with a paper towel. Sprinkle each with about 1 teaspoon turbinado sugar (1½ teaspoons for shallow fluted dishes); tilt and tap each ramekin for even coverage. Ignite a torch and caramelize the sugar. Refrigerate the ramekins, uncovered, to rechill, 30 to 45 minutes (but no longer); serve.

Espresso Crème Brûlée

Place ¼ cup espresso beans in a zipper-lock bag and crush lightly with a rolling pin or meat pounder until coarsely cracked. Follow the recipe for Classic Crème Brûlée, substituting the cracked espresso beans for the vanilla bean and whisking 1 teaspoon vanilla extract into the egg yolks in step 4 before adding the cream.

CRÈME CARAMEL

WHY THIS RECIPE WORKS: This simple, classic French dessert is essentially a baked custard, but what makes it really stand out is the caramel sauce. We found that making the caramel is relatively simple; what we needed to address was the custard, which should be silky smooth, modestly sweet, and firm but not rubbery.

We discovered that the proportion of egg whites to yolks in the custard was critical for the texture. Too many whites caused the custard to solidify too much, and too few left it almost runny. We settled on a formula of three whole eggs and two yolks. Light cream and milk for the dairy component provided the proper amount of richness. For contrast with the sweet caramel, we kept the amount of sugar in the custard to a minimum. The caramel comes together quickly; sugar is dissolved in water and cooked until caramel-colored. Baking the ramekins in a water bath was essential for even cooking and ensured a delicate custard; a dish towel on the bottom of the pan stabilized the ramekins and prevented the bottoms of the custards from overcooking. When we unmolded our crème caramel on serving plates, the sweet caramel sauce bathed the rounds of perfectly cooked custard.

Classic Crème Caramel

SERVES 8

You can vary the amount of sugar in the custard to suit your taste. Most tasters preferred the full ⅔ cup, but you can reduce that amount to as little as ½ cup to create a greater contrast between the custard and the caramel. Cook the caramel in a pan with a light-colored interior, since a dark surface makes it difficult to judge the color of the syrup. Caramel can leave a real mess in a pan, but it is easy to clean. Simply boil water in the pan for 5 to 10 minutes to loosen the hardened caramel.

CARAMEL

- ⅓ cup water
- 2 tablespoons light corn syrup
- ¼ teaspoon juice from 1 lemon
- 1 cup (7 ounces) sugar

CUSTARD

- 1½ cups whole milk
- 1½ cups light cream
- 3 large eggs, plus 2 large yolks
- ⅔ cup (4⅔ ounces) sugar (see note)
- 1½ teaspoons vanilla extract
- Pinch table salt

1. **FOR THE CARAMEL:** Combine the water, corn syrup, and lemon juice in a 2 to 3-quart saucepan. Pour the sugar into the center of the saucepan, taking care not to let the sugar granules touch the sides of the pan. Gently stir with a clean spatula to moisten the sugar thoroughly. Bring to a boil over medium-high heat and cook, without stirring, until the sugar is completely dissolved and the liquid is clear, 6 to 10 minutes. Reduce the heat to medium-low and continue to cook (swirling occasionally) until the caramel darkens to a honey color, 4 to 5 minutes longer. Remove the pan immediately from the heat and, working quickly but carefully (the caramel is above 300 degrees and will burn if it touches your skin), pour a portion of the caramel into each of eight ungreased 6-ounce ramekins. Allow the caramel to cool and harden, about 15 minutes. (The caramel-coated ramekins can be covered with plastic wrap and refrigerated for up to 2 days; return to room temperature before adding the custard.)

2. **FOR THE CUSTARD:** Adjust an oven rack to the middle position and heat the oven to 350 degrees. Heat the milk and cream in a medium saucepan over medium heat, stirring occasionally, until steam appears and/or the mixture registers 160 degrees on an instant-read thermometer, 6 to 8 minutes; remove from the heat. Meanwhile, gently whisk the whole eggs, egg yolks, and sugar in a large bowl until just combined. Off the heat, gently whisk the warm milk mixture, vanilla, and salt into the eggs until just combined but not at all foamy. Strain the mixture through a fine-mesh strainer into a large measuring cup or pitcher (or clean medium bowl); set aside.

3. Bring a kettle or large saucepan of water to a boil. Meanwhile, place a kitchen towel in the bottom of a large baking dish or roasting pan. Arrange the ramekins on the towel (making sure they do not touch). Divide the reserved custard mixture among the ramekins and carefully place the baking dish on the oven rack. Pour the boiling water into the dish, taking care not to splash water into the ramekins, until the water reaches halfway up the sides of the ramekins; cover the entire pan loosely with aluminum foil. Bake until a paring knife inserted halfway between the center and the edge of the custards comes out clean, 35 to 40 minutes. Transfer the custards to a wire rack and cool to room temperature. (The custards can be covered with plastic wrap and refrigerated for up to 2 days.)

4. To unmold, slide a paring knife around the perimeter of each ramekin, pressing the knife against the side of the dish. Hold a serving plate over the top of the ramekin and invert; set the plate on a work surface and shake the ramekin gently to release the custard. Repeat with the remaining ramekins and serve.

LATIN AMERICAN–STYLE FLAN

WHY THIS RECIPE WORKS: The Latin style of this baked custard isn't light and quivering like its European counterparts. It is far richer and more densely creamy, with a texture somewhere between pudding and cheesecake. It also boasts a more deeply caramelized, toffee-like flavor. The custard gets its thick, luxurious texture from canned milk—evaporated as well as sweetened condensed. But in many recipes, much of the caramel sticks to the bottom of the pan, and the custard is stiff with an unpleasantly thick skin where the flan is exposed to the direct heat of the oven. We got to work on a version that was as dense and rich-tasting as it was creamy.

We realized that the high protein content of canned milk products was to blame for the stiff texture. Removing one egg from the mix helped, but not enough. To further improve creaminess, we added 1/2 cup of fresh milk. Wrapping the cake pan in foil before baking prevented the skin from forming on top, and reducing the oven temperature ensured that the custard baked evenly. We also switched from a shallow cake pan to a loaf pan, which produced a gorgeous, tall flan less prone to cracking. Adding a bit of water to the warm caramel and then letting the baked flan sit overnight helped more of the caramel to come out of the dish, creating a substantial layer of gooey caramel.

Perfect Latin Flan

SERVES 8 TO 10

This recipe should be made at least 1 day before serving. We recommend an 8½ by 4½-inch loaf pan for this recipe. If your pan is 9 by 5 inches, begin checking for doneness at 1 hour and 15 minutes. You may substitute 2 percent milk for the whole milk, but do not use skim milk. Serve the flan on a platter with a raised rim to contain the liquid caramel.

- ⅔ cup (4⅔ ounces) sugar
- ¼ cup water plus 2 tablespoons warm tap water
- 2 large eggs, plus 5 large yolks
- 1 (14-ounce) can sweetened condensed milk
- 1 (12-ounce) can evaporated milk
- ½ cup whole milk
- 1½ tablespoons vanilla extract
- ½ teaspoon salt

1. Stir together sugar and 1/4 cup water in medium heavy saucepan until sugar is completely moistened. Bring to boil over medium-high heat, 3 to 5 minutes, and cook without stirring until mixture begins to turn golden, another 1 to 2 minutes. Gently swirling pan, continue to cook until sugar is the color of peanut butter, 1 to 2 minutes. Remove from heat and swirl pan until sugar is reddish-amber and fragrant, 15 to 20 seconds. Carefully swirl in 2 tablespoons warm tap water until incorporated; mixture will bubble and steam. Pour caramel into 8½ by 4½-inch loaf pan; do not scrape out saucepan. Set loaf pan aside.

2. Adjust oven rack to middle position and heat oven to 300 degrees. Line bottom of 13 by 9-inch baking pan with dish towel, folding towel to fit smoothly, and set aside. Bring 2 quarts water to boil.

3. Whisk eggs and yolks until combined. Add sweetened condensed milk, evaporated milk, whole milk, vanilla, and salt, and whisk until incorporated. Strain mixture through fine-mesh strainer into prepared loaf pan.

4. Cover loaf pan tightly with aluminum foil and place in prepared baking pan. Place baking pan in oven and carefully pour boiling water into pan. Bake until center of custard jiggles slightly when shaken and custard registers 180 degrees, 1¼ to 1½ hours. Remove foil and leave custard in water bath until loaf pan has cooled to room temperature. Wrap loaf pan tightly with plastic wrap and chill overnight or up to 4 days.

5. To unmold, slide paring knife around edges of pan. Invert serving platter on top of pan and turn pan and platter over. When flan is released, remove loaf pan. Use rubber spatula to scrape residual caramel onto flan. Slice and serve. Leftover flan may be covered loosely and refrigerated for up to 4 days.

Coffee Flan

Whisk 4 teaspoons of instant espresso powder into the egg-milk mixture until dissolved.

Orange-Cardamom Flan

Whisk 2 tablespoons orange zest and 1/4 teaspoon ground cardamom into the egg-milk mixture before straining.

Almond Flan

Reduce vanilla to 1 tablespoon and whisk 1 teaspoon almond extract into the egg-milk mixture.

CHOCOLATE POTS DE CRÈME

WHY THIS RECIPE WORKS: Classic *pots de crème* can be finicky and laborious, requiring a hot water bath that threatens to splash the custards every time the pan is moved. In addition, the individual custards don't always cook at the same rate. We wanted a user-friendly recipe that delivered a decadent dessert with a satiny texture and intense chocolate flavor.

First we moved the dish out of the oven, concentrating on an unconventional approach in which the custard is cooked on the stovetop in a saucepan, then poured into ramekins. Our next challenge was developing the right amount of richness and body, which we did by choosing a combination of heavy cream and half-and-half, along with egg yolks only, for maximum richness. For intense chocolate flavor, we focused on bittersweet chocolate—and a lot of it. Our chocolate content was at least 50 percent more than in any other recipe we had encountered.

Chocolate Pots de Crème

SERVES 8

We prefer pots de crème made with 60 percent bittersweet chocolate (our favorite brands are Callebaut Intense Dark Chocolate and Ghirardelli Bittersweet Chocolate), but 70 percent bittersweet chocolate can also be used. If using a 70 percent bittersweet chocolate, reduce the amount of chocolate to 8 ounces. An instant-read thermometer is the most reliable way to judge when the custard has reached the proper temperature. However, you can also judge the progress of the custard by its thickness. Dip a wooden spoon into the custard and run your finger across the back. The custard is ready when it coats the spoon and a line drawn maintains neat edges. The pots de crème (minus the whipped cream garnish) can be covered tightly with plastic wrap and refrigerated for up to 3 days.

POTS DE CRÈME

- 10 ounces bittersweet chocolate, chopped fine (see note)
- 5 large egg yolks
- 5 tablespoons sugar
- ¼ teaspoon table salt
- 1½ cups heavy cream
- ¾ cup half-and-half
- 1 tablespoon vanilla extract
- ½ teaspoon instant espresso powder mixed with 1 tablespoon water

WHIPPED CREAM AND GARNISH

- ½ cup heavy cream, chilled
- 2 teaspoons sugar
- ½ teaspoon vanilla extract
- Cocoa, for dusting (optional)
- Chocolate shavings, for sprinkling (optional)

1. FOR THE POTS DE CRÈME: Place the chocolate in a medium heatproof bowl; set a fine-mesh strainer over the bowl and set aside.

2. Whisk the egg yolks, sugar, and salt together in a medium bowl until combined, then whisk in the heavy cream and half-and-half. Transfer the mixture to a medium saucepan. Cook the mixture over medium-low heat, stirring constantly and scraping the bottom of the pot with a wooden spoon, until it is thickened and silky and registers 175 to 180 degrees on an instant-read thermometer, 8 to 12 minutes. (Do not let the custard overcook or simmer.)

3. Immediately pour the custard through the strainer over the chocolate. Let the mixture stand to melt the chocolate, about 5 minutes. Whisk gently until smooth, then whisk in the vanilla and dissolved espresso. Divide the mixture evenly among eight 5-ounce ramekins. Gently tap the ramekins against the counter to remove any air bubbles.

4. Cool the pots de crème to room temperature, then cover with plastic wrap and refrigerate until chilled, at least 4 hours or up to 3 days. Before serving, let the pots de crème stand at room temperature for 20 to 30 minutes.

5. FOR THE WHIPPED CREAM AND GARNISH: Using an electric mixer, whip the cream, sugar, and vanilla on medium-low speed until small bubbles form, about 30 seconds. Increase the speed to medium-high and continue to whip the mixture until it thickens and forms stiff peaks, about 1 minute. Dollop each pot de crème with about 2 tablespoons of the whipped cream and garnish with cocoa and/or chocolate shavings (if using). Serve.

Milk Chocolate Pots de Crème

Milk chocolate behaves differently in this recipe than bittersweet chocolate, and more of it must be used to ensure that the custard sets. And because of the increased amount of chocolate, it's necessary to cut back on the amount of sugar so that the custard is not overly sweet.

Follow the recipe for Chocolate Pots de Crème, substituting 12 ounces milk chocolate for the 10 ounces bittersweet chocolate. Reduce the amount of sugar to 2 tablespoons and proceed as directed.

CHOCOLATE PUDDING

WHY THIS RECIPE WORKS: Homemade chocolate pudding often suffers either from lackluster chocolate flavor, caused by a dearth of chocolate, or a grainy texture, caused by too much cocoa butter. We were after chocolate pudding that tasted deeply of chocolate and was thickened to a perfectly silky, creamy texture.

We found that using a moderate amount of bittersweet chocolate in combination with unsweetened cocoa and espresso powder helped us achieve maximum chocolate flavor. Cornstarch proved the right thickener for our pudding; using mostly milk, and just half a cup of heavy cream, along with three egg yolks ensured that our pudding had a silky smooth texture. Salt and vanilla enhanced the chocolate flavor for the perfect classic chocolate pudding.

Creamy Chocolate Pudding

SERVES 6

We recommend using one of the test kitchen's favorite baking chocolates, Callebaut Intense Dark Chocolate or Ghirardelli Bittersweet Chocolate, for this recipe, but any high-quality dark, bittersweet, or semisweet chocolate will work. This recipe was developed using a 60 percent cacao chocolate. Using a chocolate with a higher cacao percentage will result in a thicker pudding. Low-fat milk (1 percent or 2 percent) may be substituted for the whole milk with a small sacrifice in richness. Do not use skim milk as a substitute. Serve the pudding with lightly sweetened whipped cream and chocolate shavings.

- 2 teaspoons vanilla extract
- ½ teaspoon instant espresso powder
- ½ cup (3½ ounces) sugar
- 3 tablespoons Dutch-processed cocoa powder
- 2 tablespoons cornstarch
- ¼ teaspoon table salt
- 3 large egg yolks
- ½ cup heavy cream
- 2½ cups whole milk (see note)
- 5 tablespoons unsalted butter, cut into 8 pieces
- 4 ounces bittersweet chocolate, finely chopped (see note)

1. Stir together the vanilla extract and espresso powder in a bowl; set aside. Whisk the sugar, cocoa, cornstarch, and salt together in a large saucepan. Whisk in the egg yolks and cream until fully incorporated, making sure to scrape the corners of the saucepan. Whisk in the milk until incorporated.

2. Place the saucepan over medium heat and cook, whisking constantly, until the mixture is thickened and bubbling over the entire surface, 5 to 8 minutes. Cook for 30 seconds longer, remove from the heat, add the butter and chocolate, and whisk until melted and fully incorporated. Whisk in the vanilla mixture.

3. Strain the pudding through a fine-mesh strainer into a bowl. Place lightly greased parchment paper against the surface of the pudding, and place in a refrigerator to cool, at least 4 hours. Serve. (The pudding can be refrigerated for up to 2 days.)

CHOCOLATE MOUSSE

WHY THIS RECIPE WORKS: Rich, creamy, and dense, chocolate mousse can be delicious but too filling after a few mouthfuls. On the other hand, light and airy mousse usually lacks deep chocolate flavor. We wanted chocolate mousse with both a light, meltingly smooth texture and a substantial chocolate flavor.

To start, we addressed the mousse's dense, heavy texture. Most recipes for chocolate mousse contain butter. Could we do without it? We eliminated the butter and found that our mousse tasted less heavy. We further lightened the mousse's texture by reducing the number of egg whites and yolks. To make up for the lost volume of the eggs, we whipped the cream to soft peaks before adding it to the chocolate.

Next we tackled the mousse's flavor. We maximized the chocolate flavor with a combination of bittersweet chocolate and cocoa powder. And to further deepen the chocolate flavor, we found that a small amount of instant espresso powder, salt, and brandy did the trick.

Dark Chocolate Mousse

SERVES 6 TO 8

When developing this recipe, we used our winning brands of dark chocolate, Callebaut Intense Dark Chocolate and Ghirardelli Bittersweet Chocolate, which each contain about

60 percent cacao. If you want to use a chocolate with a higher percentage of cacao, see our variation, Premium Dark Chocolate Mousse (recipe follows). If you choose to make the mousse a day in advance, let it sit at room temperature for 10 minutes before serving. Serve with very lightly sweetened whipped cream and chocolate shavings, if desired.

- 8 ounces bittersweet chocolate, chopped fine (see note)
- 5 tablespoons water
- 2 tablespoons cocoa powder, preferably Dutch-processed
- 1 tablespoon brandy
- 1 teaspoon instant espresso powder
- 2 large eggs, separated
- 1 tablespoon sugar
- ⅛ teaspoon table salt
- 1 cup plus 2 tablespoons heavy cream, chilled

1. Melt the chocolate with the water, cocoa powder, brandy, and espresso powder in a medium heatproof bowl set over a saucepan filled with 1 inch of barely simmering water, stirring frequently until smooth. Remove from the heat.

2. Whisk the egg yolks, 1½ teaspoons of the sugar, and the salt in a medium bowl until the mixture lightens in color and thickens slightly, about 30 seconds. Pour the melted chocolate into the egg mixture and whisk until combined. Cool until just warmer than room temperature, 3 to 5 minutes.

3. Using an electric mixer, whip the egg whites at medium-low speed until frothy, 1 to 2 minutes. Add the remaining 1½ teaspoons sugar, increase the mixer speed to medium-high, and whip until soft peaks form when the whisk is lifted, about 1 minute. Whisk the last few strokes by hand, making sure to scrape any unbeaten whites from the bottom of the bowl. Using the whisk, stir about one-quarter of the whipped egg whites into the chocolate mixture to lighten it; gently fold in the remaining egg whites with a rubber spatula until a few white streaks remain.

4. In the now-empty bowl, whip the heavy cream at medium speed until it begins to thicken, about 30 seconds. Increase the speed to high and whip until soft peaks form when the whisk is lifted, about 15 seconds more. Using a rubber spatula, fold the whipped cream into the mousse until no white streaks remain. Spoon the mousse into six to eight individual serving dishes or goblets. Cover with plastic wrap and refrigerate until set and firm, at least 2 hours or up to 24 hours. Serve.

Chocolate-Orange Mousse

For best flavor, the orange zest needs to steep in the heavy cream overnight, so plan accordingly. Garnish each serving of mousse with a thin strip of orange zest, if desired.

Follow the recipe for Dark Chocolate Mousse with the following changes: Start by bringing the heavy cream to a simmer in a medium saucepan. Remove from the heat and transfer to a liquid measuring cup; add 3 strips orange zest (each about 2 inches long and ½ inch wide). Cool until just warm, cover, and refrigerate overnight. Remove and discard the zest; add more heavy cream, if necessary, to equal 1 cup plus 2 tablespoons. Continue with step 1, reducing the amount of water to 4 tablespoons and omitting the brandy. Once the chocolate is melted, stir in 2 tablespoons Grand Marnier and proceed as directed in step 2.

Chocolate-Raspberry Mousse

Chambord is our preferred brand of raspberry-flavored liqueur for this recipe. Serve the mousse with fresh raspberries, if desired.

Follow the recipe for Dark Chocolate Mousse, reducing the amount of water to 4 tablespoons, omitting the brandy, and, once the chocolate is melted at the end of step 1, stirring in 2 tablespoons raspberry-flavored liqueur.

Premium Dark Chocolate Mousse

This recipe is designed to work with a boutique chocolate that contains a higher percentage of cacao than the Callebaut or Ghirardelli chocolate recommended for our Dark Chocolate Mousse.

Follow the recipe for Dark Chocolate Mousse, replacing the bittersweet chocolate (containing about 60 percent cacao) with an equal amount of bittersweet chocolate containing 62 to 70 percent cacao. Increase the amount of water to 7 tablespoons, add 1 egg (for a total of 3 eggs), and increase the amount of sugar to 3 tablespoons (adding the extra 2 tablespoons sugar to the chocolate mixture in step 1).

LOW-FAT CHOCOLATE MOUSSE

WHY THIS RECIPE WORKS: When presented with the challenge of developing a low-fat chocolate mousse, we admit we were daunted. After all, traditional chocolate mousse gets its lush, creamy texture and decadent richness chiefly from heavy cream—and lots of it. We wanted to ditch the cream but preserve the rich chocolate flavor and silky, fluffy texture.

We found the solution in an Italian meringue (egg whites beaten until fluffy, and then cooked in hot sugar syrup). It made a fat-free base that mimicked the volume and texture of a traditional mousse made with heavy cream. Semisweet chocolate and Dutch-processed cocoa added rich chocolate flavor, and a surprise ingredient—melted white chocolate chips—mellowed and rounded out the flavors of each.

Low-Fat Chocolate Mousse

SERVES 6

The meringue and chocolate mixture are combined in two stages so the meringue doesn't collapse. For the best texture, chill the mousse overnight. The mousse can be refrigerated for up to 4 days.

- 4 ounces semisweet chocolate, broken into pieces
- ⅓ cup white chocolate chips
- 2 tablespoons Dutch-processed cocoa powder
- 6 tablespoons plus ½ cup water
- 1 teaspoon vanilla extract
- ½ cup (3½ ounces) sugar
- 3 large egg whites
- ¼ teaspoon cream of tartar

1. Melt the semisweet chocolate, white chocolate, cocoa powder, 6 tablespoons of the water, and the vanilla in a medium bowl set over a pot of barely simmering water, stirring until smooth. Set aside to cool slightly.

2. Bring the remaining ½ cup water and the sugar to a vigorous boil in a small saucepan over high heat. Boil until slightly thickened and large bubbles rise to the top, about 4 minutes. Remove from the heat.

3. With an electric mixer on medium-low speed, beat the egg whites in a large bowl until frothy, about 1 minute. Add the cream of tartar and beat, gradually increasing the speed to medium-high, until the whites hold soft peaks, about 2 minutes. With the mixer running, slowly pour the hot syrup into the whites (avoid pouring the syrup onto the beaters or it will splash). Increase the speed to high and beat until the meringue has cooled to just warm and becomes very thick and shiny, 2 to 3 minutes.

4. Whisk one-third of the meringue into the chocolate mixture until combined, then whisk in the remaining meringue. Spoon the mousse into six 6-ounce ramekins or pudding cups. Cover tightly with plastic wrap. Chill overnight.

FRESH STRAWBERRY MOUSSE

WHY THIS RECIPE WORKS: There's a good reason that strawberry mousse recipes aren't very prevalent: The berries contain lots of juice that can easily ruin the texture of a mousse that should be creamy and rich. Plus, the fruit flavor produced by most strawberry mousse recipes is too subtle. To achieve a creamy yet firm texture without losing the strawberry flavor, we replaced some of the cream with cream cheese. We processed the berries into small pieces and macerated them with sugar and a little salt to draw out their juice. We then reduced the released liquid to a syrup before adding it to the mousse, which standardized the amount of moisture in the dessert and also concentrated the berry flavor. Fully pureeing the juiced berries contributed bright, fresh berry flavor. A dollop of lemon whipped cream made for a tangy finish, and extra diced strawberries made for a pretty presentation.

Fresh Strawberry Mousse

SERVES 4 TO 6

This recipe works well with supermarket strawberries and farmers' market strawberries. In step 1, be careful not to overprocess the berries. If you like, substitute 1½ pounds (5¼ cups) of thawed frozen strawberries for fresh strawberries. If using frozen strawberries skip step 1 (do not process berries). Proceed with the recipe, adding the ½ cup of sugar and the salt to the whipped cream in step 4. For more-complex berry flavor, replace the 3 tablespoons of raw strawberry juice in step 2 with strawberry or raspberry liqueur. In addition to the diced berries, or if you're using frozen strawberries, you can serve the mousse with Lemon Whipped Cream (recipe follows).

- 2 pounds strawberries, hulled (6½ cups)
- ½ cup (3½ ounces) sugar
- Pinch salt
- 1¾ teaspoons unflavored gelatin
- 4 ounces cream cheese, cut into 8 pieces and softened
- ½ cup heavy cream, chilled

1. Cut enough strawberries into ¼-inch dice to measure 1 cup; refrigerate until ready to garnish. Pulse remaining strawberries in food processor in 2 batches until most pieces are ¼ to ½ inch thick (some larger pieces are fine), 6 to 10 pulses. Transfer strawberries to bowl and toss with ¼ cup sugar and salt. (Do not clean processor.) Cover bowl and let strawberries stand for 45 minutes, stirring occasionally.

2. Strain processed strawberries through fine-mesh strainer into bowl (you should have about ⅔ cup juice). Measure out 3 tablespoons juice into small bowl, sprinkle gelatin over juice, and let sit until gelatin softens, about 5 minutes. Place remaining juice in small saucepan and cook over medium-high heat until reduced to 3 tablespoons, about 10 minutes. Remove pan from heat, add softened gelatin mixture, and stir until gelatin has dissolved. Add cream cheese and whisk until smooth. Transfer mixture to large bowl.

3. While juice is reducing, return strawberries to now-empty processor and process until smooth, 15 to 20 seconds. Strain puree through fine-mesh strainer into medium bowl, pressing on solids to remove seeds and pulp (you should have about 1⅔ cups puree). Discard any solids in strainer. Add strawberry puree to juice-gelatin mixture and whisk until incorporated.

4. Using stand mixer fitted with whisk, whip cream on medium-low speed until foamy, about 1 minute. Increase speed to high and whip until soft peaks form, 1 to 3 minutes. Gradually add remaining ¼ cup sugar and whip until stiff peaks form, 1 to 2 minutes. Whisk whipped cream into strawberry mixture until no white streaks remain. Portion into dessert dishes and chill for at least 4 hours or up to 48 hours. (If chilled longer than 6 hours, let mousse sit at room temperature for 15 minutes before serving.) Serve, garnishing with reserved diced strawberries.

Lemon Whipped Cream

MAKES ABOUT 1 CUP

If preferred, you can replace the lemon with lime.

- ½ cup heavy cream
- 2 tablespoons sugar
- 1 teaspoon finely grated lemon zest plus 1 tablespoon juice

Using stand mixer fitted with whisk, whip cream on medium-low speed until foamy, about 1 minute. Add sugar and lemon zest and juice, increase speed to medium-high, and whip until soft peaks form, 1 to 3 minutes.

GRAND MARNIER SOUFFLÉ

WHY THIS RECIPE WORKS: Home cooks are wary of attempting soufflés, which have the reputation of being difficult and temperamental and so are relegated to being eaten only in restaurants. The reality, however, is that they are relatively easy to make. To prove the point, we set out to develop a reliable recipe for a classic Grand Marnier soufflé.

The best soufflés have a crusty top layer above the rim of the dish and a contrasting rich, creamy, almost-fluid center, so we needed to produce height without making the entire dish foamy. For the base we began with a *bouillie*—a paste of flour and milk. Butter kept the egginess at bay, and increasing the usual amount of flour prevented the frothiness we wanted to avoid. An equal number of egg whites and yolks was the right proportion for rise versus richness. Adding a little sugar and some cream of tartar to the whites while we whipped them stabilized the whites so that they would hold their structure. We discovered that the sugar must be added gradually and partway through the beating process, not at the beginning, or the soufflé will not rise properly and will taste too sweet. We also found it important to remove the soufflé from the oven while the center was still loose and moist to prevent overcooking. With a luxuriously creamy interior and crusty top, our foolproof soufflé is an impressive dessert that can easily be made at home.

Grand Marnier Soufflé

SERVES 6 TO 8

Make the soufflé base and immediately begin beating the whites before the base cools too much. Once the whites have reached the proper consistency, they must be used at once. Do not open the oven door during the first 15 minutes of baking time; as the soufflé nears the end of its baking, you may check its progress by opening the oven door slightly. (Be careful here; if your oven runs hot, the top of the soufflé may burn.) A quick dusting of confectioners' sugar is a nice finishing touch, but a soufflé waits for no one, so be ready to serve it immediately.

SOUFFLÉ DISH PREPARATION

- 1 tablespoon unsalted butter, softened
- ¼ cup sugar
- 2 teaspoons sifted cocoa powder

SOUFFLÉ

- 5 tablespoons unbleached all-purpose flour
- ½ cup (3½ ounces) sugar
- ¼ teaspoon table salt
- 1 cup whole milk
- 2 tablespoons unsalted butter, at room temperature
- 5 large eggs, separated
- 1 tablespoon grated zest from 1 orange
- 3 tablespoons Grand Marnier
- ⅛ teaspoon cream of tartar

1. TO PREPARE THE SOUFFLÉ DISH: Adjust an oven rack to the upper-middle position and heat the oven to 400 degrees. Grease a 1½-quart porcelain soufflé dish with the butter, making sure to coat all of the interior surfaces. Stir the sugar and cocoa together in a small bowl; pour into the buttered soufflé dish and shake to coat the bottom and sides with a thick, even coating. Tap out the excess and set the dish aside.

2. FOR THE SOUFFLÉ: Whisk the flour, ¼ cup of the sugar, and the salt in a small saucepan. Gradually whisk in the milk, whisking until smooth and no lumps remain. Bring the mixture to a boil over high heat, whisking constantly, until thickened and the mixture pulls away from the sides of the pan, about 3 minutes. Scrape the mixture into a medium bowl; whisk in the butter until combined. Whisk in the yolks until incorporated; stir in the orange zest and Grand Marnier.

3. Using an electric mixer, whip the egg whites, cream of tartar, and 1 teaspoon more sugar at medium-low speed until combined, about 10 seconds. Increase the speed to medium-high and whip until frothy and no longer translucent, about 2 minutes. With the mixer running, sprinkle in half of the remaining sugar; continue whipping until the whites form soft, billowy peaks, about 30 seconds. With the mixer still running, sprinkle in the remaining sugar and whip until just combined, about 10 seconds. The whites should form soft peaks when the beater is lifted but should not appear Styrofoam-like or dry.

4. Using a rubber spatula, immediately stir one-quarter of the beaten whites into the soufflé base to lighten until almost no white streaks remain. Scrape the remaining whites into the base and fold in the whites with a balloon whisk until the mixture is just combined, gently flicking the whisk after scraping up the sides of the bowl to free any of the mixture caught in the whisk. Gently pour the mixture into the prepared dish and run your index finger through the mixture, tracing the circumference about ½ inch from the side of the dish, to help the soufflé rise properly. Bake until the surface of the soufflé is deep brown, the center jiggles slightly when shaken, and the soufflé has risen 2 to 2½ inches above the rim of the dish, 20 to 25 minutes. Serve immediately.

Grand Marnier Soufflé with Grated Chocolate

A rotary cheese grater is the perfect tool for grating the chocolate, though a box grater works well, too.

Finely grate ½ ounce bittersweet chocolate (you should have about ⅓ cup). Follow the recipe for Grand Marnier Soufflé, folding the grated chocolate into the soufflé base along with the beaten egg whites.

CHILLED LEMON SOUFFLÉ

WHY THIS RECIPE WORKS: "Chilled lemon soufflé" can be interpreted in many ways, from cooled baked pudding cake to lemony, eggy foam. But no matter what the desired outcome, what typically results is a dense, rubbery mass or a mouthful of tart egg white foam. The delicate balance of ingredients is hard for home cooks to get right. We wanted to perfect the unusual marriage of cream and foam, sweet and sour, high lemony notes and rich custard.

A starting point of egg whites, gelatin, sugar, and lemon juice had none of the creaminess we desired, so we cooked a custard base of milk, egg yolks, and sugar, adding a little cornstarch to prevent the yolks from curdling. To our custard we then added lemon juice and gelatin (to stabilize the mixture so it would set up while chilling). Because this was to be a soufflé, not a pudding, we lightened the custard with whipped cream and beaten egg whites. The egg yolks and dairy tended to mute the lemon flavor, so for more citrus punch we included grated lemon zest. Now we had the balance of flavor and texture that we sought: a satisfying but light custard with bright lemon flavor.

Chilled Lemon Soufflé

SERVES 4 TO 6

To make this lemon soufflé "soufflé" over the rim of the dish, use a 1-quart soufflé dish and, following the photo on page 814, make a foil collar for it before beginning the recipe. For those less concerned about appearance, this dessert can be served from any 1½-quart serving bowl. For the best texture, serve the soufflé after 1½ hours of chilling. It may be chilled for up to 6 hours; though the texture will stiffen slightly because of the gelatin, it will taste just as good.

- ½ cup juice plus 2½ teaspoons grated zest from 3 lemons
- 1 (¼-ounce) package gelatin
- 1 cup whole milk
- ¾ cup (5¼ ounces) sugar
- 5 large egg whites plus 2 large egg yolks, at room temperature
- ¼ teaspoon cornstarch
- Pinch cream of tartar
- ¾ cup heavy cream
- Mint, raspberries, confectioners' sugar, or finely chopped pistachios, for garnish (optional)

1. Place the lemon juice in a small bowl; sprinkle the gelatin over and set aside.

2. Heat the milk and ½ cup of the sugar in a medium saucepan over medium-low heat, stirring occasionally, until steaming and the sugar is dissolved, about 5 minutes. Meanwhile, whisk the egg yolks, 2 tablespoons more sugar, and the cornstarch in a medium bowl until pale yellow and thickened. Whisking constantly, gradually add the hot milk to the yolks. Return the milk-egg mixture to the saucepan and cook, stirring constantly, over medium-low heat until the foam has dissipated to a thin layer and the mixture thickens to the consistency of heavy cream and registers 185 degrees on an instant-read thermometer, about 4 minutes. Pour the mixture through a fine-mesh strainer into a medium bowl; stir in the lemon juice mixture and zest. Set the bowl with the custard in a large bowl of ice water; stir occasionally to cool.

3. While the custard mixture is chilling, use an electric mixer to whip the egg whites and cream of tartar on medium speed until foamy, about 1 minute. Increase the speed to medium-high; gradually add the remaining 2 tablespoons sugar and continue to whip until glossy and the whites hold soft peaks when the beater is lifted, about 2 minutes longer. Do not over whip. Remove the bowl containing the custard mixture from the ice water bath; gently whisk in about one-third of the egg whites, then fold in the remaining whites with a large rubber spatula until almost no white streaks remain.

4. In the same mixer bowl, whip the cream on medium-high speed until soft peaks form when the beater is lifted, 2 to 3 minutes. Fold the cream into the custard and egg-white mixture until no white streaks remain.

5. Pour into a 1½ quart soufflé dish or bowl (see note). Chill until set but not stiff, about 1½ hours; remove the foil collar, if using, and serve, garnishing if desired.

Chilled Lemon Soufflé with White Chocolate

The white chocolate in this variation subdues the lemony kick.

Follow the recipe for Chilled Lemon Soufflé, adding 2 ounces chopped white chocolate to the warm custard before adding the lemon juice mixture and the zest. Stir until melted and fully incorporated.

Individual Chilled Lemon Soufflés

Follow the recipe for Chilled Lemon Soufflé, dividing the batter equally among eight ¾-cup ramekins (filled to the rim) or six 6-ounce ramekins with foil collars (see photo).

LEMON POSSET

WHY THIS RECIPE WORKS: Lemon posset is a silky, rich British dessert with bright citrus flavor. We found that using just the right proportions of sugar and lemon juice was the key to custard with a smooth, luxurious consistency and a bright enough flavor to balance the richness of the cream. Lemon zest was essential to making the lemon flavor even more prominent. For a posset with an optimally dense, firm set, we reduced the cream-sugar mixture to 2 cups to evaporate some of the water before adding the lemon juice, which in turn caused the mixture to solidify. Letting the warm mixture rest for 20 minutes before straining and portioning allowed the flavors to meld even more and ensured a silky-smooth consistency. Pairing the dessert with fresh berries for textural contrast helps keep it from feeling overly rich.

Lemon Posset with Berries

SERVES 6

This dessert requires portioning into individual servings. Reducing the cream mixture to exactly 2 cups creates the best consistency. Transfer the liquid to a 2-cup heatproof liquid measuring cup once or twice during boiling to monitor the amount. Do not leave the cream unattended, as it can boil over easily.

- 2 cups heavy cream
- ⅔ cup (4⅔ ounces) sugar
- 1 tablespoon grated lemon zest plus
- 6 tablespoons juice (2 lemons)
- 1½ cups (7½ ounces) blueberries or raspberries

1. Combine cream, sugar, and lemon zest in medium saucepan and bring to boil over medium heat. Continue to boil, stirring frequently to dissolve sugar. If mixture begins to boil over, briefly remove from heat. Cook until mixture is reduced to 2 cups, 8 to 12 minutes.

2. Remove saucepan from heat and stir in lemon juice. Let sit until mixture is cooled slightly and skin forms on top, about 20 minutes. Strain through fine-mesh strainer into bowl; discard zest. Divide mixture evenly among 6 individual ramekins or serving glasses.

3. Refrigerate, uncovered, until set, at least 3 hours. Once chilled, possets can be wrapped in plastic wrap and refrigerated for up to 2 days. Unwrap and let sit at room temperature for 10 minutes before serving. Garnish with berries and serve.

MAKE-AHEAD CHOCOLATE SOUFFLÉS

WHY THIS RECIPE WORKS: A chocolate soufflé is a grand dessert to serve dinner guests, but most cooks wouldn't risk the anxiety of all the last-minute preparation when entertaining. It seemed a shame to cross this dessert off the list of possibilities for a dinner party, so we challenged ourselves to find a way to make it in advance. We wanted the chocolate to be front and center, so we used a base of egg yolks beaten with sugar, with no flour or milk to mute the chocolate flavor. Instead of the equal number of egg yolks and whites that worked for our Grand Marnier Soufflé (page 811), two extra whites were necessary to lighten and lift our chocolaty base. Now that we had the flavor and texture we wanted, it was time to address the problem of making the soufflés ahead of time. To our amazement, the answer was simple: freezing. Adding a little confectioners' sugar to the egg whites helped stabilize them so they held up better in the freezer, and individual ramekins produced better results than a single large soufflé dish. Now we could make our dinner party dessert ahead of time, confident that we could pull perfectly risen, rich chocolate soufflés from the oven at the end of the meal.

Make-Ahead Chocolate Soufflés

SERVES 6 TO 8

The yolk whipping time in step 3 depends on the type of mixer you use; a stand mixer will take about 3 minutes, and a hand-held mixer will take about 8 minutes. If using 6-ounce ramekins, reduce the cooking time to 20 to 22 minutes. See the photo for making a collar for the ramekins.

RAMEKIN PREPARATION
- 2 tablespoons unsalted butter, softened
- 2 tablespoons granulated sugar

SOUFFLÉS
- 8 ounces bittersweet or semisweet chocolate, chopped coarse
- 4 tablespoons (½ stick) unsalted butter, cut into ½-inch pieces
- 1 tablespoon Grand Marnier
- ½ teaspoon vanilla extract
- ⅛ teaspoon table salt
- 6 large egg yolks plus 8 large egg whites
- ⅓ cup (2⅓ ounces) granulated sugar
- ¼ teaspoon cream of tartar
- 2 tablespoons confectioners' sugar

1. FOR THE RAMEKINS: Grease the inside of eight 8-ounce ramekins with the softened butter, then coat the inside of each dish evenly with the granulated sugar.

2. FOR THE SOUFFLÉS: Melt the chocolate and butter together in a medium heatproof bowl set over a saucepan filled with 1 inch of barely simmering water, stirring frequently until smooth. Remove from the heat and stir in the Grand Marnier, vanilla, and salt; set aside.

3. Using an electric mixer, whip the egg yolks and granulated sugar at medium speed until the mixture triples in volume and is thick and pale yellow, 3 to 8 minutes (see note). Fold the yolk mixture into the chocolate mixture. Thoroughly clean and dry the mixing bowl and the beaters.

4. Using the clean beaters, whip the egg whites at medium-low speed until frothy, 1 to 2 minutes. Add the cream of tartar, increase the mixer speed to medium-high, and whip until soft peaks form when the beaters are lifted, 1 to 2 minutes. Add the confectioners' sugar and continue to whip until stiff peaks form, 2 to 4 minutes (do not over whip). Whisk the last few strokes by hand, making sure to scrape any unwhipped whites from the bottom of the bowl.

5. Vigorously stir one-quarter of the whipped egg whites into the chocolate mixture. Gently fold the remaining whites into the chocolate mixture until just incorporated. Carefully spoon the mixture into the prepared ramekins almost to the rim, wiping the excess filling from the rims with a wet paper towel. If making a foil collar for the ramekins, see the photo. (To serve right away, bake as directed in step 7, reducing the baking time to 12 to 15 minutes.)

6. TO STORE: Cover each ramekin tightly with plastic wrap and then foil and freeze for at least 3 hours or up to 1 month. (Do not thaw before baking.)

7. TO BAKE AND SERVE: Adjust an oven rack to the lower-middle position and heat the oven to 400 degrees. Unwrap the frozen ramekins and spread them out on a baking sheet. Bake the soufflés until fragrant, fully risen, and the exterior is set but the interior is still a bit loose and creamy, about 25 minutes. (To check the interior, use two spoons to pull open the top of one and peek inside.) Serve immediately.

Make-Ahead Mocha Soufflés

Follow the recipe for Make-Ahead Chocolate Soufflés, adding 1 tablespoon instant coffee or espresso powder dissolved in 1 tablespoon hot water to the melted chocolate with the vanilla in step 2.

NOTES FROM THE TEST KITCHEN

MAKING A FOIL COLLAR

Baking our individual chocolate soufflés from the freezer gives them a high rise and a domed top, just as we like them. But placing a collar around the ramekins yields an even higher rise with an iconic, perfectly flat top.

Secure a strip of foil that has been sprayed with vegetable oil spray around each ramekin so that it extends 2 inches above the rim (do this after the ramekins have been filled). You can tape the foil collar to the dish to prevent it from slipping.

SKILLET SOUFFLÉ

WHY THIS RECIPE WORKS: Having taken the mystique out of soufflé making and even developing a recipe for making soufflés ahead of time, we wondered if we could take our expertise one step further. If we could make a soufflé in a skillet, we would guarantee that this great dessert was in the realm of everyday cooking.

We theorized that the heat on the stovetop would activate the batter and ensure an even rise from the egg whites. To determine what to use for the soufflé base, we pitted the bases used in our other soufflés—béchamel and *bouillie*—against a simpler base of whipped egg yolks. All tasted fine, but the whipped egg yolks were so much less complicated that we decided to start there. A little flour added to the yolks kept the soufflé creamy rather than foamy. We decided that lemon would be the best flavoring, since it would shine through the eggy base well; lemon juice and zest provided bright, natural citrus flavor. We beat the egg whites separately, adding sugar partway through, folded them into the egg-lemon base, and poured the mixture into a buttered ovensafe skillet. After a few minutes on the stovetop the soufflé was just set around the edges and on the bottom (and the crust that eventually formed on the bottom was a bonus our tasters applauded), so we moved the skillet to the oven to finish. A few minutes later our soufflé was puffed, golden on top, and creamy in the middle—a successful transformation from fussy to easy.

Skillet Lemon Soufflé

SERVES 6

Don't open the oven door during the first 7 minutes of baking, but do check the soufflé regularly for doneness during the final few minutes in the oven. Be ready to serve the soufflé immediately after removing it from the oven. Using a 10-inch traditional (not nonstick) skillet is essential to getting the right texture and height in the soufflé.

- 5 large eggs, separated
- ¼ teaspoon cream of tartar
- ⅔ cup (4⅔ ounces) granulated sugar
- ⅛ teaspoon table salt
- ⅓ cup juice plus 1 teaspoon grated zest from 2 lemons
- 2 tablespoons unbleached all-purpose flour
- 1 tablespoon unsalted butter
- Confectioners' sugar, for dusting

1. Adjust an oven rack to the middle position and heat the oven to 375 degrees. Using an electric mixer, whip the egg whites and cream of tartar together on medium-low speed until foamy, about 1 minute. Slowly add ⅓ cup of the granulated sugar and the salt, then increase the mixer speed to medium-high, and continue to whip until stiff peaks form, 3 to 5 minutes. Gently transfer the whites to a clean bowl and set aside.

2. Using an electric mixer (no need to wash the mixing bowl), whip the egg yolks and the remaining ⅓ cup granulated sugar together on medium-high speed until pale and thick, about 1 minute. Whip in the lemon juice, zest, and flour until incorporated, about 30 seconds.

3. Fold one-quarter of the whipped egg whites into the yolk mixture until almost no white streaks remain. Gently fold in the remaining egg whites until just incorporated.

4. Melt the butter in a 10-inch ovensafe skillet over medium-low heat. Swirl the pan to coat it evenly with the melted butter, then gently scrape the soufflé batter into the skillet and cook until the edges begin to set and bubble slightly, about 2 minutes.

5. Transfer the skillet to the oven and bake the soufflé until puffed, the center jiggles slightly when shaken, and the surface is golden, 7 to 11 minutes. Using a potholder (the skillet handle will be hot), remove the skillet from the oven. Dust the soufflé with the confectioners' sugar and serve immediately.

Skillet Chocolate-Orange Soufflé

Grating the chocolate fine is key here; we find it easiest to use either a rasp grater or the fine holes of a box grater.

Follow the recipe for Skillet Lemon Soufflé, substituting 1 tablespoon grated zest from 1 orange for the lemon zest and ⅓ cup orange juice for the lemon juice. Gently fold 1 ounce finely grated bittersweet chocolate (about ½ cup) into the soufflé batter after incorporating all of the whites in step 3.

VANILLA ICE CREAM

WHY THIS RECIPE WORKS: Homemade vanilla ice cream is never as creamy or dense as the impossibly smooth "super-premium" ice cream found at gourmet markets or high-end ice cream shops. Instead of thick, dense, and velvety, ice cream made at home invariably turns out crumbly, fluffy, and icy. We wanted an incredibly creamy custard-based vanilla ice cream that would rival any pricey artisanal batch.

Creating smooth ice cream means reducing the size of the ice crystals; the smaller they are, the less perceptible they are. Our first move was to replace some of the sugar in our custard base with corn syrup, which interferes with crystal formation, making for a super-smooth texture. To speed up the freezing process, further ensuring small ice crystals, we froze a portion of the custard prior to churning, then mixed it with the remaining refrigerated custard. Finally, instead of freezing the churned ice cream in a tall container, we spread it into a thin layer in a cold metal baking pan and chilled it, which allowed the ice cream to firm up more quickly and delivered the flawlessly smooth texture we were after.

Homemade Vanilla Ice Cream

MAKES ABOUT 1 QUART

Two teaspoons of vanilla extract can be substituted for the vanilla bean; stir the extract into the cold custard in step 3. An instant-read thermometer is critical for the best results. Using a prechilled metal baking pan and working quickly in step 4 will help prevent melting and refreezing of the ice cream and will speed the hardening process. If using a canister-style ice cream maker, be sure to freeze the empty canister at least 24 hours and preferably 48 hours before churning. For self-refrigerating ice cream makers, prechill the canister by running the machine for 5 to 10 minutes before pouring in the custard. The ice cream can be stored for up to 5 days.

- 1 vanilla bean
- 1¾ cups heavy cream
- 1¼ cups whole milk
- ½ cup plus 2 tablespoons (4⅖ ounces) sugar
- ⅓ cup light corn syrup
- ¼ teaspoon table salt
- 6 large egg yolks

1. Place an 8- or 9-inch-square metal baking pan in the freezer. Cut the vanilla bean in half lengthwise. Using the tip of a paring knife, scrape out the vanilla seeds. Combine the vanilla bean, seeds, cream, milk, ¼ cup plus 2 tablespoons of the sugar, the corn syrup, and salt in a medium saucepan. Heat over medium-high heat, stirring occasionally, until the mixture is steaming steadily and registers 175 degrees on an instant-read thermometer, 5 to 10 minutes. Remove the saucepan from the heat.

2. While the cream mixture heats, whisk the egg yolks and the remaining ¼ cup sugar in a bowl until smooth, about 30 seconds. Slowly whisk 1 cup of the heated cream mixture into the egg yolk mixture. Return the mixture to the saucepan and cook over medium-low heat, stirring constantly, until the mixture thickens and registers 180 degrees, 7 to 14 minutes. Immediately pour the custard into a large bowl and let cool until no longer steaming, 10 to 20 minutes. Transfer 1 cup of the custard to a small bowl. Cover both bowls with plastic wrap. Place the large bowl in the refrigerator and the small bowl in the freezer and cool completely, at least 4 hours or up to 24 hours. (The small bowl of custard will freeze solid.)

3. Remove the custards from the refrigerator and freezer. Scrape the frozen custard from the small bowl into the large bowl of custard. Stir occasionally until the frozen custard has fully dissolved. Strain the custard through a fine-mesh strainer and transfer to an ice cream maker. Churn until the mixture resembles thick soft-serve ice cream and registers about 21 degrees, 15 to 25 minutes. Transfer the ice cream to the frozen baking pan and press plastic wrap on the surface. Return to the freezer until firm around the edges, about 1 hour.

4. Transfer the ice cream to an airtight container, pressing firmly to remove any air pockets, and freeze until firm, at least 2 hours, before serving.

FROZEN YOGURT

WHY THIS RECIPE WORKS: We wanted to make frozen yogurt that put the tart, fresh flavor of yogurt up front and had the texture of a dense, creamy premium ice cream. We found that Greek yogurt produced a chalky frozen yogurt, so instead we used regular plain yogurt that we had strained of excess liquid (the whey) to help minimize the number of ice crystals. Swapping in a few tablespoons of Lyle's Golden Syrup for some of the granulated sugar not only gave us a frozen yogurt with fewer ice crystals but also one that was more scoopable straight from the freezer. This is because about half of Lyle's sugar is invert sugar (the other half is glucose). Unlike granulated sugar, which is made up of large sucrose molecules, invert sugar is made up of the "small sugars" glucose and fructose, which are much better at depressing the freezing point, which kept more of the water in the frozen yogurt base in liquid form for a smoother, more scoopable final product. The final step in managing the water in our base was to trap some of it using unflavored gelatin. By dissolving and heating just 1 teaspoon of gelatin in a portion of the strained whey, we prevented water molecules from joining together and forming large ice crystals.

Frozen Yogurt

MAKES ABOUT 1 QUART

We prefer the flavor and texture that Lyle's Golden Syrup lends this frozen yogurt, but light corn syrup may be substituted. Any brand of whole-milk yogurt will work in this recipe. Low-fat yogurt can be used, but the results will be less creamy and less flavorful. If more than 1¼ cups of whey drains from the yogurt in step one, simply stir the extra back in.

- 1 quart plain whole-milk yogurt
- 1 teaspoon unflavored gelatin
- ¾ cup sugar
- 3 tablespoons Lyle's Golden Syrup
- ⅛ teaspoon salt

1. Line colander or fine-mesh strainer with triple layer of cheesecloth and place over large bowl or measuring cup. Place yogurt in colander, cover with plastic wrap (plastic should not touch yogurt), and refrigerate until 1¼ cups whey has drained from yogurt, at least 8 hours and up to 12 hours.

2. Discard ¾ cup of drained whey. Sprinkle gelatin over remaining ½ cup whey in bowl and let sit until gelatin softens, about 5 minutes. Microwave until mixture is bubbling around edges and gelatin dissolves, about 30 seconds. Let cool for 5 minutes. In large bowl, whisk sugar, Lyle's Golden Syrup, salt, drained yogurt, and cooled gelatin mixture together until sugar is completely dissolved. Cover and refrigerate (or place bowl over ice bath) until yogurt mixture registers 40 degrees or less.

3. Churn yogurt mixture in ice cream maker until mixture resembles thick soft-serve frozen yogurt and registers about 21 degrees, 25 to 35 minutes. Transfer frozen yogurt to airtight container and freeze until firm, at least 2 hours. Serve. (Frozen yogurt can be stored for up to 5 days.)

Ginger Frozen Yogurt

Stir 1 tablespoon grated fresh ginger and 1 teaspoon ground ginger into whey-gelatin mixture as soon as it is removed from microwave. After mixture has cooled for 5 minutes, strain through fine-mesh strainer, pressing on solids to extract all liquid. Proceed with recipe as directed.

Orange Frozen Yogurt

Substitute ½ cup fresh orange juice for ½ cup whey in step 2. Stir ½ teaspoon grated orange zest into whey-gelatin mixture as soon as it is removed from microwave.

Strawberry Frozen Yogurt

Substitute ¾ cup strawberry puree for ½ cup whey in step 2.

RASPBERRY SORBET

WHY THIS RECIPE WORKS: For our raspberry sorbet recipe, we super-chilled the base and used just the right ratio of sweeteners to water to ensure the finest-textured ice crystals possible. We also bumped up the berries' natural amount of pectin to give the sorbet stability both in the freezer and out.

Raspberry Sorbet

MAKES 1 QUART

Super-chilling part of the sorbet base before transferring it to the ice cream maker will keep ice crystals to a minimum. If using a canister-style ice cream maker, be sure to freeze the empty canister for at least 24 hours and preferably 48 hours before churning. For self-refrigerating ice cream makers, prechill the canister by running the machine for five to 10 minutes before pouring in the sorbet mixture. Allow the sorbet to sit at room temperature for five minutes to soften before serving. Fresh or frozen berries may be used. If using frozen berries, thaw them before proceeding. Make certain that you use Sure-Jell engineered for low- or no-sugar recipes (packaged in a pink box) and not regular Sure-Jell (in a yellow box).

- 1 cup water
- 1 teaspoon Sure-Jell for Less or No Sugar Needed Recipes
- ⅛ teaspoon salt
- 1¼ pounds (4 cups) raspberries
- ½ cup (3½ ounces) plus 2 tablespoons sugar
- ¼ cup light corn syrup

1. Combine water, Sure-Jell, and salt in medium saucepan. Heat over medium-high heat, stirring occasionally, until Sure-Jell is fully dissolved, about 5 minutes. Remove saucepan from heat and allow mixture to cool slightly, about 10 minutes.

2. Process raspberries, sugar, corn syrup, and water mixture in blender or food processor until smooth, about 30 seconds. Strain mixture through fine-mesh strainer, pressing on solids to extract as much liquid as possible. Transfer 1 cup mixture to small bowl and place remaining mixture in large bowl. Cover both bowls with plastic wrap. Place large bowl in refrigerator and small bowl in freezer and cool completely, at least 4 hours or up to 24 hours. (Small bowl of base will freeze solid.)

3. Remove mixtures from refrigerator and freezer. Scrape frozen base from small bowl into large bowl of base. Stir occasionally until frozen base has fully dissolved. Transfer mixture to ice cream maker and churn until mixture has consistency of thick milkshake and color lightens, 15 to 25 minutes.

4. Transfer sorbet to airtight container, pressing firmly to remove any air pockets, and freeze until firm, at least 2 hours. Serve. (Sorbet can be frozen for up to 5 days.)

Raspberry–Lime Rickey Sorbet

Reduce water to ¾ cup. Add 2 teaspoons grated lime zest and ¼ cup lime juice to blender with raspberries.

Raspberry-Port Sorbet

Substitute ruby port for water in step 1.

Raspberry Sorbet with Ginger and Mint

Substitute ginger beer for water in step 1. Add 2-inch piece of peeled and thinly sliced ginger and ¼ cup mint leaves to blender with raspberries. Decrease amount of sugar to ½ cup.

CHAPTER 25

CLASSIC FRUIT DESSERTS

STRAWBERRY SHORTCAKES

WHY THIS RECIPE WORKS: While some cooks like to spoon strawberries over pound cake, sponge cake, and even angel food cake, our idea of strawberry shortcake definitely involves a biscuit. We wanted a juicy strawberry filling and mounds of freshly whipped cream sandwiched in between a lightly sweetened, tender biscuit.

While eggs are not traditional, we found that one whole egg gave our biscuits a light, tender texture. And we used just enough dairy (half-and-half or milk) to bind the dough together. A modest amount of sugar yielded a lightly sweetened biscuit. For the strawberries, we wanted to avoid both a mushy puree and dry chunks of fruit. We found our solution in a compromise—mashing a portion of the berries and slicing the rest for a chunky, juicy mixture that didn't slide off the biscuit. And lightly sweetened whipped cream, flavored with vanilla, provided a cool, creamy contrast to the berries and biscuits.

Strawberry Shortcakes

SERVES 6

Start the recipe by preparing the fruit, then set the fruit aside while preparing the biscuits to allow the juices to become syrupy.

FRUIT

- 8 cups (40 ounces) strawberries, hulled
- 6 tablespoons sugar

SHORTCAKE

- 2 cups (10 ounces) unbleached all-purpose flour, plus extra for the work surface and biscuit cutter
- 5 tablespoons sugar
- 1 tablespoon baking powder
- ½ teaspoon table salt
- 8 tablespoons (1 stick) unsalted butter, cut into ½-inch pieces and chilled
- ½ cup plus 1 tablespoon half-and-half or milk
- 1 large whole egg, lightly beaten
- 1 large egg white, lightly beaten

WHIPPED CREAM

- 1 cup heavy cream, chilled
- 1 tablespoon sugar
- 1 teaspoon vanilla extract

1. **FOR THE FRUIT:** Crush 3 cups of the strawberries in a large bowl with a potato masher. Slice the remaining 5 cups of berries and stir them into the crushed berries along with the sugar. Set aside until the sugar has dissolved and the berries are juicy, at least 30 minutes or up to 2 hours.

2. **FOR THE SHORTCAKE:** Adjust an oven rack to the lower-middle position and heat the oven to 425 degrees. Line a large baking sheet with parchment paper. Pulse the flour, 3 tablespoons of the sugar, the baking powder, and salt in a food processor until combined. Sprinkle the butter pieces over the top and pulse until the mixture resembles coarse meal, about 15 pulses. Transfer the mixture to a large bowl.

3. Whisk the half-and-half and lightly beaten whole egg together in a small bowl, then stir into the flour mixture with a rubber spatula until large clumps form. Turn the dough onto a lightly floured work surface and knead lightly until it comes together.

4. Pat the dough into a 9 by 6-inch rectangle, about ¾ inch thick. Do not overwork the dough. Using a floured 2¾-inch biscuit cutter, cut out six dough rounds. Arrange the shortcakes on the prepared baking sheet, spaced about 1½ inches apart. Brush the tops with the lightly beaten egg white and sprinkle evenly with the remaining 2 tablespoons sugar. (The unbaked shortcakes can be covered with plastic wrap and refrigerated for up to 2 hours.)

5. Bake until the shortcakes are golden brown, 12 to 14 minutes, rotating the sheet halfway through the baking time. Transfer the sheet to a wire rack and cool the shortcakes until warm, about 10 minutes.

6. **FOR THE WHIPPED CREAM:** In a medium bowl, whip the cream, sugar, and vanilla with an electric mixer on medium-low speed until frothy, about 1 minute. Increase the speed to high and continue to whip until the cream forms soft peaks, 1 to 3 minutes.

7. **TO ASSEMBLE:** When the shortcakes have cooled slightly, split them in half horizontally. Place each shortcake bottom on an individual plate, spoon a portion of the berries over each bottom, dollop with whipped cream, and cap with the shortcake tops. Serve immediately.

CHERRY COBBLER

WHY THIS RECIPE WORKS: Most cherry cobblers are no more than canned pie filling topped with dry, heavy biscuits. We wanted a filling that highlighted the unique, sweet-tart flavor of sour cherries and, on top, we wanted a tender, feather-light biscuit crust.

Because fresh sour cherries are so hard to find most of the year, we picked jarred Morello cherries—easy to find and available year-round. Embellishing the cherries with cherry juice, cinnamon, and vanilla was a step in the right direction but the filling still tasted a bit flat, so we switched out some of the juice for red wine and replaced the vanilla with almond extract. The resulting sauce was better, but a little thin. A small amount of cornstarch thickened the filling nicely. As for the biscuits, we favored buttermilk biscuits, which have a light and fluffy texture. To ensure nicely browned biscuits that didn't become soggy over the filling, we parbaked them on their own ahead of time, then slid the biscuits over the warm cherry filling and put it in the oven to finish cooking.

Sour Cherry Cobbler

SERVES 12

Use the smaller amount of sugar in the filling if you prefer your fruit desserts on the tart side and the larger amount if you like them sweet. Serve with vanilla ice cream or lightly sweetened whipped cream.

BISCUIT TOPPING

- 2 cups (10 ounces) unbleached all-purpose flour
- ½ cup (3½ ounces) sugar
- ½ teaspoon baking powder
- ½ teaspoon baking soda
- ½ teaspoon table salt
- 6 tablespoons (¾ stick) unsalted butter, cut into ½-inch pieces and chilled
- 1 cup buttermilk

FILLING

- 8 cups jarred Morello cherries from 4 (24-ounce) jars, drained, 2 cups juice reserved
- ¾–1 cup (5¼ to 7 ounces) sugar (see note)
- 3 tablespoons plus 1 teaspoon cornstarch
- Pinch table salt
- 1 cup dry red wine
- 1 (3-inch) cinnamon stick
- ¼ teaspoon almond extract

1. Adjust an oven rack to the middle position and heat the oven to 425 degrees. Line a large baking sheet with parchment paper.

2. FOR THE BISCUIT TOPPING: Pulse the flour, 6 tablespoons of the sugar, the baking powder, baking soda, and salt in a food processor until combined. Sprinkle the butter pieces over the top and pulse until the mixture resembles coarse meal, about 15 pulses. Transfer the mixture to a large bowl; add the buttermilk and stir with rubber spatula until combined. Using a greased ¼-cup measure ice cream scoop, scoop 12 biscuits onto the prepared baking sheet, spacing them 1½ inches apart. Sprinkle the biscuits evenly with the remaining 2 tablespoons sugar and bake until lightly browned, about 15 minutes, rotating the sheet halfway through baking. (Do not turn the oven off.)

3. FOR THE FILLING: Meanwhile, arrange the drained cherries in an even layer in a 13 by 9-inch glass baking dish. Combine the sugar, cornstarch, and salt in a medium saucepan. Stir in the reserved cherry juice and wine and add the cinnamon stick; cook over medium-high heat, stirring frequently, until the mixture simmers and thickens, about 5 minutes. Discard the cinnamon stick, stir in the almond extract, and pour the hot liquid over the cherries in the baking dish.

4. TO BAKE: Arrange the hot biscuits in three rows of four biscuits over the warm filling. Bake the cobbler until the filling is bubbling and the biscuits are deep golden brown, about 10 minutes. Transfer the baking dish to a wire rack and cool for 10 minutes; serve.

Fresh Sour Cherry Cobbler

Morello or Montmorency cherries can be used in this cobbler made with fresh sour cherries. Do not use sweet Bing cherries. If the cherries do not release enough juice after 30 minutes in step 1, add cranberry juice to make up the difference.

- 1¼ cups (8¾ ounces) sugar
- 3 tablespoons plus 1 teaspoon cornstarch
- Pinch table salt
- 8 cups (4 pounds) fresh sour cherries, pitted, juice reserved (see note)
- 1 cup dry red wine
- Cranberry juice, as needed (see note)
- 1 recipe Biscuit Topping
- 1 (3-inch) cinnamon stick
- ¼ teaspoon almond extract

1. Whisk the sugar, cornstarch, and salt together in a large bowl; add the cherries and toss well to combine. Pour the wine over the cherries; let stand for 30 minutes. Drain the cherries in a colander set over a medium bowl. Combine the drained and reserved juices (from pitting the cherries); you should have 3 cups (if not, add cranberry juice to make this amount).

2. Meanwhile, prepare and bake the biscuit topping.

3. Arrange the drained cherries in an even layer in a 13 by 9-inch glass baking dish. Bring the juices, wine, and cinnamon stick to a simmer in a medium saucepan over medium-high heat, stirring frequently, until the mixture thickens, about 5 minutes. Discard the cinnamon stick, stir in the almond extract, and pour the hot juices over the cherries in the baking dish.

4. Arrange the hot biscuits in three rows of four biscuits over the warm filling. Bake the cobbler until the filling is bubbling and the biscuits are deep golden brown, about 10 minutes. Transfer the baking dish to a wire rack and cool for 10 minutes; serve.

BLUEBERRY COBBLER

WHY THIS RECIPE WORKS: Too often, blueberry cobbler means a filling that is too sweet, overspiced, and unappealingly thick. We wanted a not-too-thin, not-too-thick filling where the blueberry flavor would be front and center. And over the fruit, we wanted a light, tender biscuit topping that could hold its own against the fruit filling, with an ingredient list simple enough to allow the blueberries to play a starring role.

We prepared a not-too-sweet filling using 6 cups of fresh berries and less than a cup of sugar. Cornstarch worked well as a thickener—it thickened the fruit's juice without leaving a starchy texture behind. A little lemon and cinnamon were all that were needed to enhance the filling without masking the blueberry flavor. For the topping, ease of preparation was our guiding principle, so we made light, rustic drop biscuits enriched with a little cornmeal. Adding the biscuit topping to the cobbler after the filling had baked on its own allowed the biscuits to brown evenly and cook through. A sprinkling of cinnamon sugar on the dropped biscuit dough added a pleasing sweet crunch.

Blueberry Cobbler

SERVES 6 TO 8

While the blueberries are baking, prepare the ingredients for the topping, but do not stir the wet ingredients into the dry ingredients until just before the berries come out of the oven. A standard or deep-dish 9-inch pie plate works well; an 8-inch square baking dish can also be used. Vanilla ice cream or lightly sweetened whipped cream is the perfect accompaniment. To reheat leftovers, put the cobbler in a 350-degree oven for 10 to 15 minutes, until heated through.

FILLING

- ½ cup (3½ ounces) sugar
- 1 tablespoon cornstarch
- Pinch ground cinnamon
- Pinch table salt
- 6 cups (30 ounces) fresh blueberries, rinsed and picked over
- 1½ teaspoons grated zest plus 1 tablespoon juice from 1 lemon

BISCUIT TOPPING

- 1 cup (5 ounces) unbleached all-purpose flour
- ¼ cup (1¾ ounces) plus 2 teaspoons sugar
- 2 tablespoons stone-ground cornmeal
- 2 teaspoons baking powder
- ¼ teaspoon baking soda
- ¼ teaspoon table salt
- 4 tablespoons (½ stick) unsalted butter, melted
- ⅓ cup buttermilk
- ½ teaspoon vanilla extract
- ⅛ teaspoon ground cinnamon

1. Adjust an oven rack to the lower-middle position and heat the oven to 375 degrees.

2. FOR THE FILLING: Whisk the sugar, cornstarch, cinnamon, and salt together in a large bowl. Add the berries and mix gently with a rubber spatula until evenly coated; add the lemon zest and juice and mix to combine. Transfer the berry mixture to a 9-inch glass pie plate, place the pie plate on a rimmed baking sheet, and bake until the filling is hot and bubbling around the edges, about 25 minutes.

3. FOR THE BISCUIT TOPPING: Meanwhile, whisk the flour, ¼ cup of the sugar, the cornmeal, baking powder, baking soda, and salt together in a large bowl. Whisk the melted butter, buttermilk, and vanilla together in a small bowl. Mix the remaining 2 teaspoons sugar with the cinnamon in a second small bowl and set aside. One minute before the berries come out of the oven, add the wet ingredients to the dry ingredients; stir with a rubber spatula until just combined and no dry pockets remain.

4. TO ASSEMBLE AND BAKE: Remove the berries from the oven; increase the oven temperature to 425 degrees. Divide the biscuit dough into eight equal pieces and place them on the hot berry filling, spacing them at least ½ inch apart (they should not touch). Sprinkle each mound of dough evenly with the cinnamon sugar. Bake until the filling is bubbling and the biscuits are golden brown on top and cooked through, 15 to 18 minutes. Transfer the cobbler to a wire rack; cool for 20 minutes and serve.

PEACH CRISP

WHY THIS RECIPE WORKS: There is seldom anything crisp about most crisps. This simple fruit dessert usually comes out of the oven with a soggy, mushy topping—quite a letdown from the ideal of a warm, fruity filling covered in a crunchy, sweet topping. We set out to make peach crisp that wouldn't disappoint, one with the perfect balance of nicely thickened filling and a lightly sweetened, crisp topping.

We tried everything from Grape-Nuts to cookie crumbs and found the ideal topping mixture to be chopped nuts, butter, and flour. Cutting the butter into the flour was crucial for creating a crisp topping, and we found that a food processor was ideally suited to producing a mixture that resembled crumbly wet sand. Another issue to tackle was sugar: what kind and how much. White sugar alone was too bland, while brown sugar on its own was too strong tasting. A 50–50 mix of the two proved to be the perfect combination. We decided not to use too much sugar in the fruit filling so there would be some contrast with the topping. And we nixed the idea of a thickener—the filling without one had a nicely bright fresh fruit flavor and the topping remained crisp whether we used one or not.

Peach Crisp

SERVES 4 TO 6

Lightly sweetened whipped cream or vanilla ice cream is the perfect accompaniment, especially if serving the crisp warm. A standard or deep-dish 9-inch pie plate works well; an 8-inch square baking dish can also be used.

TOPPING

- 6 tablespoons unbleached all-purpose flour
- ¼ cup packed (1¾ ounces) light brown sugar
- ¼ cup (1¾ ounces) granulated sugar
- ¼ teaspoon ground cinnamon
- ¼ teaspoon ground nutmeg
- ¼ teaspoon table salt
- 5 tablespoons unsalted butter, cut into ½-inch pieces and chilled
- ¾ cup (about 4 ounces) coarsely chopped pecans, walnuts, or almonds

FILLING

- 3 pounds peaches (6 to 8 medium), peeled, pitted, and cut into ½-inch slices
- ¼ cup (1¾ ounces) granulated sugar
- ½ teaspoon grated zest plus 1½ tablespoons juice from 1 lemon

1. FOR THE TOPPING: Pulse the flour, sugars, cinnamon, nutmeg, and salt in a food processor until combined. Sprinkle the butter pieces over the top and pulse until the mixture resembles coarse meal, about 15 pulses. Add the nuts and pulse until the mixture clumps together and resembles wet sand, about 5 pulses; do not overmix. Transfer the mixture to a bowl and refrigerate while preparing the filling, at least 15 minutes.

2. FOR THE FILLING: Adjust an oven rack to the lower-middle position and heat the oven to 375 degrees. Combine the peaches, sugar, zest, and juice in a large bowl and toss gently to combine. Transfer the peach mixture to a 9-inch glass pie plate, place the pie plate on a rimmed baking sheet, and sprinkle the chilled topping evenly over the top.

3. Bake for 40 minutes. Increase the oven temperature to 400 degrees and continue to bake until the filling is bubbling and the topping is deep golden brown, about 5 minutes longer. Serve warm.

Peach Crisp for a Crowd

SERVES 10

Follow the recipe for Peach Crisp, doubling all the ingredients and using a 13 by 9-inch baking dish. Increase the baking time to 55 minutes and bake at 375 degrees without increasing the oven temperature.

CHERRY CLAFOUTI

WHY THIS RECIPE WORKS: For a clafouti that featured juicy cherries in every bite (and no pits to get in the way, as most traditional recipes have), we pitted and halved the cherries. To concentrate their flavor and prevent excess moisture from leaking into the custard, we roasted them in a hot oven for 15 minutes and then tossed them with a couple of teaspoons of absorbent flour. To recover the slightly spicy, floral flavor the pits contributed, we added ⅛ teaspoon of cinnamon to the flour. We found that too much flour made the custard too bready, whereas an excess of dairy made it too loose. Ultimately, we settled on a moderate amount of each for a tender yet slightly resilient custard void of pastiness. Switching from a casserole dish to a preheated 12-inch skillet gave us better browning and made the custard easy to slice and serve. A last-minute sprinkle of granulated sugar added a touch of sweetness and a delicate crunch.

Cherry Clafouti

SERVES 6 TO 8

We prefer whole milk in this recipe, but 1 or 2 percent low-fat milk may be substituted. Do not substitute frozen cherries for the fresh cherries.

- 1½ pounds fresh sweet cherries, pitted and halved
- 1 teaspoon lemon juice
- 2 teaspoons plus ½ cup (2½ ounces) all-purpose flour
- ⅛ teaspoon ground cinnamon
- 4 large eggs
- ⅔ cup (4⅔ ounces) plus 2 teaspoons sugar
- 2½ teaspoons vanilla extract
- ¼ teaspoon salt
- 1 cup heavy cream
- ⅔ cup whole milk
- 1 tablespoon unsalted butter

1. Adjust oven racks to upper-middle and lowest positions; place 12-inch ovensafe skillet on lower rack and heat oven to 425 degrees. Line rimmed baking sheet with aluminum foil and place cherries, cut side up, on sheet. Roast cherries on upper rack until just tender and cut sides look dry, about 15 minutes. Transfer cherries to medium bowl, toss with lemon juice, and let cool 5 for minutes. Combine 2 teaspoons flour and cinnamon in small bowl; dust flour mixture evenly over cherries and toss to coat thoroughly.

2. While cherries roast, whisk eggs, ⅔ cup sugar, vanilla, and salt in large bowl until smooth and pale, about 1 minute. Whisk in remaining ½ cup flour until smooth. Whisk in cream and milk until incorporated.

3. Remove skillet (skillet handle will be hot) from oven and set on wire rack. Add butter and swirl to coat bottom and sides of skillet (butter will melt and brown quickly). Pour batter into skillet and place cherries evenly over top (some will sink). Transfer skillet to lower rack and bake until clafouti puffs and surface is golden brown (edges will be dark brown), and center registers 195 degrees, 18 to 22 minutes, rotating skillet halfway through baking. Transfer skillet to wire rack, and let cool for 25 minutes. Sprinkle evenly with remaining 2 teaspoons sugar. Slice into wedges and serve.

RASPBERRY GRATIN

WHY THIS RECIPE WORKS: Quicker than a crisp and dressier than a shortcake, a gratin is a layer of fresh fruit piled into a shallow baking dish, dressed up with bread crumbs, and run under a broiler. The topping browns and the fruit is warmed just enough to release a bit of juice. We wanted to find the quickest, easiest route to this pleasing dessert.

We started with perfect raspberries: ripe, dry, unbruised, and clean. Tossing the sweet-tart berries with just a bit of sugar and kirsch (a clear cherry brandy; vanilla extract can be substituted) provided enough additional flavor and sweetness. For the topping, we combined soft white bread, brown sugar, cinnamon, and butter in the food processor and topped the berries with the fluffy crumbs. Instead of broiling the gratin, which can produce a crust that's burnt in spots, we simply baked it. We found that a moderately hot oven gave the berries more time to soften and browned the crust more evenly.

Simple Raspberry Gratin

SERVES 4 TO 6

If you prefer, you can substitute blueberries, blackberries, or strawberries for part or all of the raspberries. If using strawberries, hull them and slice them in half lengthwise if small or into quarters if large. Later in the summer season, ripe, peeled peaches or nectarines, sliced, can be used in combination with the blueberries or raspberries.

- 4 cups (20 ounces) fresh or frozen (not thawed) raspberries (see note)
- 1 tablespoon granulated sugar
- 1 tablespoon kirsch or vanilla extract (optional)
- Pinch table salt
- 3 slices high-quality white sandwich bread, torn into quarters
- ¼ cup packed (1¾ ounces) light or dark brown sugar
- 2 tablespoons unsalted butter, softened
- Pinch ground cinnamon

1. Adjust an oven rack to the lower-middle position and heat the oven to 400 degrees. Gently toss the raspberries, granulated sugar, kirsch (if using), and salt in a medium bowl. Transfer the mixture to a 9-inch glass pie plate.

2. Pulse the bread, brown sugar, butter, and cinnamon in a food processor until the mixture resembles coarse crumbs, about 10 pulses. Sprinkle the crumbs evenly over the fruit and bake until the crumbs are deep golden brown, 15 to 20 minutes. Transfer to a wire rack; cool for 5 minutes and serve.

FRESH BERRY GRATIN

WHY THIS RECIPE WORKS: Gratins can be very humble, as in our Simple Raspberry Gratin, where the topping is little more than sweetened bread crumbs. Or they can be a bit more sophisticated, as when they are topped with the foamy Italian custard called zabaglione. Zabaglione is made with just three simple ingredients—egg yolks, sugar, and alcohol—but it requires constant watching so that the mixture doesn't overcook. It also needs to be whisked just long enough to transform the egg yolks to the ideal thick, creamy texture. We were after a foolproof method for this topping for a gratin that could serve as an elegant finale to a special summer meal.

We chose to make individual gratins—perfect for entertaining—and settled on raspberries, strawberries, blueberries, and blackberries. We tossed the berries with sugar and a pinch of salt to draw out their juices and let the mixture

sit while we worked on the custard. To prevent scrambled eggs, we kept the heat low; for the right texture, we didn't stop whisking when soft peaks formed—instead we waited until the custard became slightly thicker. As for flavor, tasters thought that zabaglione made with the traditional Marsala wine was a bit sweet and cloying on top of the berries. We switched to a crisp, dry Sauvignon Blanc and found that its clean flavor allowed the berries to shine. However, with that change, our zabaglione was almost runny. After trying to thicken it with cornstarch and gelatin (with disappointing results), we turned to whipped cream. After carefully folding a few tablespoons of whipped cream into the cooked and slightly cooled zabaglione base, we spooned it over the berries. Finally, we sprinkled the custard with a mixture of brown and white sugar before broiling for a crackly, caramelized crust.

Individual Fresh Berry Gratins with Zabaglione

SERVES 4

When making the zabaglione, make sure to cook the egg mixture in a glass bowl over water that is barely simmering; glass conducts heat more evenly and gently than metal. If the heat is too high, the yolks around the edges of the bowl will start to scramble. Constant whisking is required. Do not use frozen berries for this recipe. You will need four shallow 6-inch gratin dishes, but a broiler-safe pie plate or gratin dish can be used instead. To prevent scorching, pay close attention to the gratins when broiling.

BERRY MIXTURE

- 3 cups (about 15 ounces) mixed berries (raspberries, blueberries, blackberries, and strawberries; strawberries hulled and halved lengthwise if small, quartered if large), at room temperature (see note)
- 2 teaspoons granulated sugar
- Pinch table salt

ZABAGLIONE

- 3 large egg yolks
- 3 tablespoons granulated sugar
- 3 tablespoons dry white wine, such as Sauvignon Blanc
- 2 teaspoons light brown sugar
- 3 tablespoons heavy cream, chilled

1. FOR THE BERRY MIXTURE: Toss the berries, sugar, and salt together in a medium bowl. Divide the berry mixture evenly among four shallow 6-ounce gratin dishes set on a rimmed baking sheet; set aside.

2. FOR THE ZABAGLIONE: Whisk the egg yolks, 2 tablespoons plus 1 teaspoon of the granulated sugar, and the wine together in a medium glass bowl until the sugar is dissolved, about 1 minute. Set the bowl over a saucepan of barely simmering water and cook, whisking constantly, until the mixture is frothy. Continue to cook, whisking constantly, until the mixture is slightly thickened, creamy, and glossy, 5 to 10 minutes (the mixture will form loose mounds when dripped from the whisk). Remove the bowl from the saucepan and whisk constantly for 30 seconds to cool slightly. Transfer the bowl to the refrigerator and chill until the egg mixture is completely cool, about 10 minutes.

3. Meanwhile, adjust an oven rack 6 inches from the broiler element and heat the broiler. Combine the brown sugar and the remaining 2 teaspoons granulated sugar in a small bowl.

4. Whisk the heavy cream in a large bowl until it holds soft peaks, 30 to 90 seconds. Using a rubber spatula, gently fold the whipped cream into the cooled egg mixture. Spoon the zabaglione over the berries and sprinkle the sugar mixture evenly on top; let stand at room temperature for 10 minutes, until the sugar dissolves.

5. Broil the gratins until the sugar is bubbly and caramelized, 1 to 4 minutes. Serve immediately.

Individual Fresh Berry Gratins with Lemon Zabaglione

Follow the recipe for Individual Fresh Berry Gratins with Zabaglione, replacing 1 tablespoon of the wine with 1 tablespoon juice from 1 lemon and adding 1 teaspoon grated zest from 1 lemon to the yolk mixture in step 2.

BAKED APPLES

WHY THIS RECIPE WORKS: This homey dessert is often plagued with a mushy texture and one-dimensional, cloyingly sweet flavor. We wanted baked apples that were tender and firm with a filling that perfectly complemented their sweet, tart flavor. We knew picking the right variety of apple was paramount to our success and, after extensive testing, we arrived at a surprising winner: Granny Smith was the best apple for the job, with its firm flesh and tart, fruity flavor. To ensure that our fruit avoided even the occasional collapse, we peeled the apples after cutting off the top.

The skin traps steam from the extra moisture released by the breakdown of the apples' interior cells, and removing it allows the steam to escape and the apple to retain its tender-firm texture. Sautéing our apples cut side down intensified their flavor. Our filling base of dried cranberries, brown sugar, and pecans benefited from some finessing by way of cinnamon, orange zest, and a pat of butter. We intensified the nuttiness with chewy rolled oats, and diced apple was an obvious addition. A melon baller helped us to scoop out a spacious cavity that accommodated plenty of filling. We then capped off the filled apples with the tops we had previously lopped off. Once in the oven, the apples were basted with an apple cider and maple syrup sauce and emerged full of flavor.

Best Baked Apples

SERVES 6

If you don't have an ovensafe skillet, transfer the browned apples to a 13 by 9-inch baking dish and bake as directed. The recipe calls for seven apples; six are left whole and one is diced and added to the filling. Serve the apples with vanilla ice cream, if desired.

- 7 large (about 6 ounces each) Granny Smith apples (see note)
- 6 tablespoons (¾ stick) unsalted butter, softened
- ⅓ cup dried cranberries, chopped coarse
- ⅓ cup coarsely chopped pecans, toasted
- ¼ cup packed (1¾ ounces) brown sugar
- 3 tablespoons old-fashioned oats
- 1 teaspoon finely grated zest from 1 orange
- ½ teaspoon ground cinnamon
- Pinch table salt
- ⅓ cup maple syrup
- ⅓ cup plus 2 tablespoons apple cider

1. Adjust an oven rack to the middle position and heat the oven to 375 degrees. Peel, core, and cut 1 apple into ¼-inch dice. Combine 5 tablespoons of the butter, the cranberries, pecans, brown sugar, oats, orange zest, cinnamon, salt, and diced apple in a large bowl; set aside.

2. Shave a thin slice off the bottom (blossom end) of the remaining 6 apples to allow them to sit flat. Cut the top ½ inch off the stem end of the apples and reserve. Peel the apples and use a melon baller or small measuring spoon to remove a 1½-inch-diameter core, being careful not to cut through the bottom of the apple.

3. Melt the remaining 1 tablespoon butter in a 12-inch ovensafe nonstick skillet over medium heat. Once the foaming subsides, add the apples, stem side down, and cook until the cut surface is golden brown, about 3 minutes. Flip the apples, reduce the heat to low, and spoon the filling inside, mounding the excess filling over the cavities; top with the reserved apple caps. Add the maple syrup and ⅓ cup of the cider to the skillet. Transfer the skillet to the oven and bake until a skewer inserted into the apples meets little resistance, 35 to 40 minutes, basting every 10 minutes with the maple syrup mixture in the skillet.

4. Transfer the apples to a serving platter. Stir up to 2 tablespoons of the remaining cider into the sauce in the skillet to adjust the consistency. Pour the sauce over the apples and serve.

APPLE CRISP

WHY THIS RECIPE WORKS: Most apple crisp recipes are what you'd expect—unevenly cooked fruit and an unremarkable topping that rarely lives up to its crisp moniker. We wanted an exemplary apple crisp—a lush (but not mushy) sweet-tart apple filling covered with truly crisp morsels of buttery, sugary topping.

For apple crisp, we prefer crisp apples such as Golden Delicious, because they are hardier and turn tender but not mushy. But they posed two problems. One, their mellower, more honeyed flesh lacked fruity punch. And while complete apple blowouts had been averted, the apples were still cooking unevenly. Stirring the fruit helped solve the problem but donning oven mitts to reach into a hot oven and stir bubbling fruit was a hassle. Instead, we turned to softening our fruit on the stovetop—in a skillet. The shallow, flared shape of the skillet also encouraged evaporation, browning, and better flavor overall. But to improve the flavor further, we turned to apple cider, first reducing it in the skillet to a syrupy consistency. This super-potent reduction contributed an intense, almost *tarte Tatin*–like fruity depth.

As for the topping, we added brown sugar to white to play up the apples' caramel notes. Rolled oats gave the topping character and chew. Chopped pecans not only improved the crunch factor, but added rich flavor as well. We then slid the skillet into the oven for a quick browning and to finish cooking the apples.

Skillet Apple Crisp

SERVES 6 TO 8

If your skillet is not ovensafe, prepare the recipe through step 3 and then transfer the filling to a 13 by 9-inch baking dish. Top the filling as directed and bake for an additional 5 minutes. We like Golden Delicious apples for this recipe, but any sweet, crisp apple such as Honeycrisp or Braeburn can be substituted. Do not use Granny Smith apples in this recipe. While old-fashioned oats are preferable in this recipe, quick-cooking oats can be substituted. Serve the apple crisp warm or at room temperature with vanilla ice cream or whipped cream.

TOPPING

- ¾ cup (3¾ ounces) unbleached all-purpose flour
- ¾ cup (3 ounces) pecans, chopped fine
- ¾ cup (2¼ ounces) old-fashioned oats (see note)
- ½ cup packed (3½ ounces) light brown sugar
- ¼ cup (1¾ ounces) granulated sugar
- ½ teaspoon ground cinnamon
- ½ teaspoon table salt
- 8 tablespoons (1 stick) unsalted butter, melted

FILLING

- 3 pounds Golden Delicious apples (about 7 medium), peeled, cored, halved, and cut into ½-inch-thick wedges (see note)
- ¼ cup (1¾ ounces) granulated sugar
- ¼ teaspoon ground cinnamon (optional)
- 1 cup apple cider
- 2 teaspoons juice from 1 lemon
- 2 tablespoons unsalted butter

1. FOR THE TOPPING: Adjust an oven rack to the middle position and heat the oven to 450 degrees. Combine the flour, pecans, oats, brown sugar, granulated sugar, cinnamon, and salt in a medium bowl. Stir in the butter until the mixture is thoroughly moistened and crumbly. Set aside while preparing the fruit filling.

2. FOR THE FILLING: Toss the apples, sugar, and cinnamon (if using) together in a large bowl; set aside. Bring the cider to a simmer in a 12-inch ovensafe skillet over medium heat; cook until reduced to ½ cup, about 5 minutes. Transfer the reduced cider to a bowl or liquid measuring cup; stir in the lemon juice and set aside.

3. Heat the butter in the now-empty skillet over medium heat. When the foaming subsides, add the apple mixture and cook, stirring frequently, until the apples are beginning to soften and become translucent, 12 to 14 minutes. (Do not fully cook the apples.) Remove the pan from the heat and gently stir in the cider mixture until the apples are coated.

4. Sprinkle the topping evenly over the fruit, breaking up any large chunks. Place the skillet on a baking sheet and bake until the fruit is tender and the topping is deep golden brown, 15 to 20 minutes. Cool on a wire rack until warm, at least 15 minutes, and serve.

APPLE BROWN BETTY

WHY THIS RECIPE WORKS: In its most basic form, apple brown betty contains only four ingredients: apples, bread crumbs, sugar, and butter. Sadly, this simple combination inevitably results in a soggy, mushy mess—not the classic Colonial dish of tender, lightly spiced chunks of apple topped with toasted bread crumbs. We decided it was time to give "Betty" a serious makeover. For a lightly sweetened, crisp topping, we toasted white sandwich bread crumbs with butter and a bit of sugar. The sweet/tart combination of Granny Smith and Golden Delicious apples made a not-too-sweet apple filling. Instead of baking the dessert, we prepared it in a skillet on the stovetop and cooked the apples in two batches to ensure even cooking. After preparing the bread crumbs, we removed them from the pan and caramelized the apples. Adding brown sugar to the apples along with ginger and cinnamon gave the dessert a deepened, lightly spiced flavor. The addition of apple cider to the fruit brought moisture and a further dimension of apple flavor; a bit of lemon juice brightened the filling. For a thicker filling, we added a portion of the toasted bread crumbs to the apples and reserved the remainder for sprinkling over the top.

Skillet Apple Brown Betty

SERVES 6 TO 8

If your apples are especially tart, omit the lemon juice. If, on the other hand, your apples are exceptionally sweet, use the full amount. Leftovers can be refrigerated in an airtight container; topped with vanilla yogurt, they make an excellent breakfast.

BREAD CRUMBS

- 4 slices high-quality white sandwich bread, torn into quarters
- 3 tablespoons unsalted butter, cut into 4 pieces
- 2 tablespoons packed light brown sugar

FILLING

- ¼ cup packed (1¾ ounces) light brown sugar
- ¼ teaspoon ground ginger
- ¼ teaspoon ground cinnamon
- Pinch table salt
- 3 tablespoons unsalted butter
- 1½ pounds Granny Smith apples (about 3 large), peeled, cored, and cut into ½-inch cubes (about 4 cups)
- 1½ pounds Golden Delicious apples (about 3 large), peeled, cored, and cut into ½-inch cubes (about 4 cups)
- 1¼ cups apple cider
- 1–3 teaspoons juice from 1 lemon (see note)

1. FOR THE BREAD CRUMBS: Pulse the bread, butter, and sugar in a food processor until coarsely ground, 5 to 7 pulses. Transfer the bread crumbs to a 12-inch skillet and toast over medium heat, stirring constantly, until they are deep golden brown, 8 to 10 minutes. Transfer to a paper towel–lined plate; wipe out the skillet.

2. FOR THE FILLING: Combine the sugar, spices, and salt in a small bowl. Melt 1½ tablespoons of the butter in the now-empty skillet over high heat. Stir in the Granny Smith apples and half of the sugar mixture. Distribute the apples in an even layer and cook, stirring two or three times, until medium brown, about 5 minutes; transfer to a medium bowl. Repeat with the remaining butter, the Golden Delicious apples, and the remaining sugar mixture, returning the first batch of apples to the skillet when the second batch is done.

3. Add the apple cider to the skillet and scrape the bottom and sides of the pan with a wooden spoon to loosen the browned bits; cook until the apples are tender but not mushy and the liquid has reduced and is just beginning to thicken, 2 to 4 minutes.

4. Remove the skillet from the heat; stir in the lemon juice (if using) and ⅓ cup of the toasted bread crumbs. Using a wooden spoon, lightly flatten the apples into an even layer in the skillet and evenly sprinkle with the remaining toasted bread crumbs. Spoon the warm betty into individual bowls and serve with vanilla ice cream, if desired.

APPLE STRUDEL

WHY THIS RECIPE WORKS: Most modern phyllo-based versions of strudel have tough layers of phyllo on the underside, while the sheets on top shatter before you even cut a slice. Meanwhile, fillings collapse and leak everywhere, despite the bread crumbs supposedly added to soak up liquid and prevent leaking (instead, they just make the filling taste pasty). We parcooked the apples in the microwave to activate an enzyme that sets the pectin in the fruit and allows them to bake without collapsing. We stirred in ultradry panko bread crumbs instead of homemade toasted crumbs since we could use less of them to soak up a comparable amount of liquid (thus avoiding pastiness). To avoid a compressed, tough underside, we used fewer sheets of phyllo and changed the typical wrapping technique so the seam was on the top instead of on the bottom. We were able to minimize the flyaways on top by dusting a small amount of confectioners' sugar between the phyllo layers so that they fused in the oven, and by slicing our strudel while it was warm. Making two smaller strudels simplified assembly.

Apple Strudel

SERVES 6

Gala apples can be substituted for Golden Delicious. Phyllo dough is also available in larger 18 by 14-inch sheets; if using, cut them in half to make 14 by 9-inch sheets. Thaw phyllo in the refrigerator overnight or on the counter for 4 to 5 hours; don't thaw it in the microwave.

- 1¾ pounds Golden Delicious apples, peeled, cored, and cut into ½-inch pieces
- 3 tablespoons granulated sugar
- ½ teaspoon grated lemon zest plus 1½ teaspoons juice
- ¼ teaspoon ground cinnamon
- ¼ teaspoon ground ginger
- Salt
- 3 tablespoons golden raisins
- 1½ tablespoons panko bread crumbs
- 7 tablespoons unsalted butter, melted
- 14 (14 by 9-inch) phyllo sheets, thawed
- 1 tablespoon confectioners' sugar, plus extra for serving

1. Toss apples, granulated sugar, lemon zest and juice, cinnamon, ginger, and ⅛ teaspoon salt together in large bowl. Cover and microwave until apples are warm to touch, about 2 minutes, stirring once halfway through microwaving. Let apples stand, covered, for 5 minutes. Transfer apples to colander set in second large bowl and let drain, reserving liquid. Return apples to bowl; stir in raisins and panko.

2. Adjust oven rack to upper-middle position and heat oven to 375 degrees. Spray rimmed baking sheet with vegetable oil spray. Stir ⅛ teaspoon salt into melted butter.

3. Place 16½ by 12-inch sheet of parchment paper on counter with long side parallel to edge of counter. Place 1 phyllo sheet on parchment with long side parallel to edge of counter. Place 1½ teaspoons confectioners' sugar in fine-mesh strainer (rest strainer in bowl to prevent making mess). Lightly brush sheet with melted butter and dust sparingly with confectioners' sugar. Repeat with 6 more phyllo sheets, melted butter, and confectioners' sugar, stacking sheets one on top of the other as you go.

4. Arrange half of apple mixture in 2½ by 10-inch rectangle 2 inches from bottom of phyllo and about 2 inches from each side. Using parchment, fold sides of phyllo over filling, then fold bottom edge of phyllo over filling. Brush folded portions of phyllo with reserved apple liquid. Fold top edge over filling, making sure top and bottom edges overlap by about 1 inch. (If they do not overlap, unfold, rearrange filling into slightly narrower strip, and refold.) Press firmly to seal. Using thin metal spatula, transfer strudel to 1 side of prepared baking sheet, facing seam toward center of sheet. Lightly brush top and sides of strudel with half of remaining apple liquid. Repeat process with remaining phyllo, melted butter, confectioners' sugar, filling, and apple liquid. Place second strudel on other side of prepared sheet, with seam facing center of sheet.

5. Bake strudels until golden brown, 27 to 35 minutes, rotating sheet halfway through baking. Using thin metal spatula, immediately transfer strudels to cutting board. Let cool for 3 minutes. Slice each strudel into thirds and let cool for at least 20 minutes. Serve warm or at room temperature, dusting with extra confectioners' sugar before serving.

EASY APPLE STRUDEL

WHY THIS RECIPE WORKS: Apple strudel, lightly spiced apples in a thin, flaky pastry, is meant to be savored by the forkful, preferably with a strong cup of coffee. We wanted all the flavor and charm of this apple dessert, but we didn't want to bother with the hours of preparation the paper-thin dough requires. So we set out to simplify this classic dessert while keeping the rich apple filling and as much of the crisp, flaky texture as possible.

Replacing homemade strudel dough with purchased phyllo dough made for a crust with perfect flaky layers in a fraction of the time. We brushed the phyllo sheets with melted butter to keep them crisp and flaky. A combination of Golden Delicious and McIntosh apples, sliced thin, gave us a filling with layered apple flavor and just the right texture. A small amount of bread crumbs, browned in butter, thickened the filling without weighing it down. Golden raisins, plumped on the stove with Calvados (apple brandy), added a sophisticated, fruity dimension to the apple filling; for brightness and to lighten the filling, we added in some fresh lemon juice. We found that the phyllo on most strudels, including this one, curled and shattered as it cooled; sprinkling sugar between the layers of phyllo "glued" them together in the oven and prevented this problem.

Easy Apple Strudel

SERVES 6

The best ways to thaw the phyllo are in the refrigerator overnight or at room temperature for 3 to 4 hours; it doesn't defrost well in the microwave. Make sure that the phyllo sheets you use for the strudel are not badly torn. If they have small cuts or tears in the same location (sometimes an entire package sustains cuts in the same spot), when forming the strudel, flip alternating layers so that the cuts will not line up, thereby creating a weak spot that can cause the strudel to burst during baking. To make the fresh bread crumbs, process one slice of high-quality white sandwich bread in a food processor until fine, 20 to 30 seconds. Serve the strudel warm with Tangy Whipped Cream (recipe follows) or regular whipped cream.

NOTES FROM THE TEST KITCHEN

ASSEMBLING EASY APPLE STRUDEL

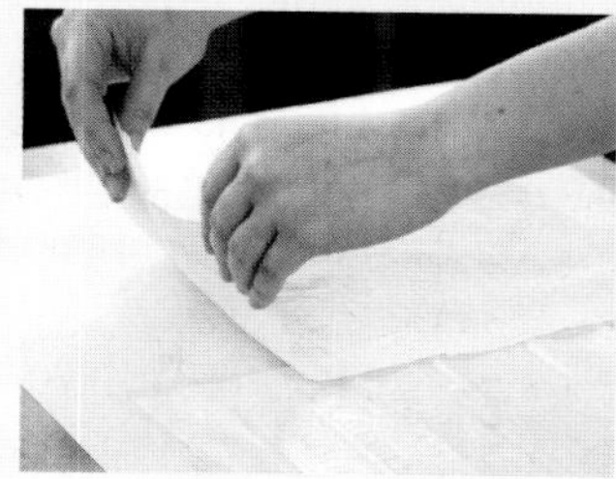

1. Brush 1 sheet of phyllo with melted butter and sprinkle with sugar. Place another sheet of phyllo next to it, overlapping the sheets. Brush with more butter and sprinkle with sugar. Repeat this process four times.

2. Mound the filling along the bottom edge of the phyllo, leaving a 2½-inch border on the bottom and a 2-inch border on the sides.

3. Fold the dough on the sides over the apples. Fold the dough on the bottom over the apples and continue to roll the dough around the filling to form the strudel.

4. After the strudel has been assembled and rolled, gently lay it seam side down on the prepared baking sheet.

- ½ cup golden raisins
- 2 tablespoons Calvados or apple cider
- 8 tablespoons (1 stick) unsalted butter, melted and cooled
- ¼ cup fresh bread crumbs (see note)
- 1 pound Golden Delicious apples (about 2 large), peeled, cored, and sliced ¼ inch thick
- 1 medium McIntosh apple, peeled, cored, and sliced ¼ inch thick
- ¼ cup (1¾ ounces) plus 2 tablespoons granulated sugar
- ⅓ cup finely chopped walnuts (optional), toasted
- ¼ teaspoon ground cinnamon
- ⅛ teaspoon table salt
- 1 teaspoon juice from 1 lemon
- 10 (14 by 9-inch) sheets phyllo, thawed (see note)
- 1½ teaspoons confectioners' sugar

1. Adjust an oven rack to the lower-middle position and heat the oven to 475 degrees. Line a large baking sheet with parchment paper. Bring the raisins and Calvados to a simmer in a small saucepan over medium heat. Cover, remove from the heat, and let stand until needed.

2. Combine 1 tablespoon of the butter and the bread crumbs in a small skillet and cook over medium heat, stirring frequently, until golden brown, about 2 minutes. Transfer the bread crumbs to a small bowl and set aside.

3. Drain off and discard any remaining liquid from the raisins. Toss the apples, raisins, bread crumbs, ¼ cup of the granulated sugar, the walnuts (if using), cinnamon, salt, and lemon juice in a large bowl to combine.

4. Melt the remaining 7 tablespoons butter. Place a large sheet of parchment paper horizontally on a work surface. Following the photos on page 829, lay 1 sheet of phyllo on the left side of the sheet of parchment paper, then brush with melted butter and sprinkle with ½ teaspoon more of the granulated sugar. Place another sheet of phyllo on the right side of the parchment, overlapping the sheets by 1 inch, then brush with more butter and sprinkle with sugar. Repeat this process with the remaining 8 sheets of phyllo, more butter, and more sugar. Mound the filling along the bottom edge of the phyllo, leaving a 2½-inch border on the bottom and a 2-inch border on the sides. Fold the dough on the sides over the apples. Fold the dough on the bottom over the apples and continue to roll the dough around the filling to form the strudel.

5. Place the strudel, seam side down, on the prepared baking sheet; brush with the remaining butter and sprinkle with the remaining 1 teaspoon sugar. Cut four 1-inch crosswise vents into the top of the strudel and bake until golden brown, 15 minutes. Transfer the baking sheet to a wire rack and cool until warm, about 40 minutes.

6. Dust the strudel with the confectioners' sugar before serving; slice with a serrated knife and serve warm or at room temperature.

Tangy Whipped Cream

MAKES ABOUT 2 CUPS

Adding sour cream to whipped cream mimics the pleasantly tart flavor of the rich French-style whipped cream, crème fraîche.

- 1 cup heavy cream
- ½ cup sour cream
- 1 tablespoon sugar
- 1 teaspoon vanilla extract

Whip the heavy cream and sour cream in a large bowl with an electric mixer on medium-low speed until frothy, about 1 minute. Add the sugar and vanilla. Increase the mixer speed to high and continue to whip until the cream forms soft peaks, 1 to 3 minutes.

APPLE PANDOWDY

WHY THIS RECIPE WORKS: Apple pandowdy harks back to Colonial-era New England—the dessert takes a more rustic approach to apple pie in that it features just one pastry crust, placed on top of a lightly sweetened apple filling. During or after baking, the pastry is broken and pushed into the filling—a technique known as "dowdying." We found the idea of an easier approach to apple pie very appealing—no fussy crimping and only one piece of pastry dough to roll out, so we set out to make our own version—one with a flaky crust and tender, juicy apples.

For a juicy apple filling with bright fruit flavor, we added cider to the apples and sweetened the filling with maple syrup—the tart intensity of the cider deepened the apple flavor and maple syrup's rich character added the right degree of sweetness. Both additions also made for a pleasantly saucy filling. Parcooking the apples in a skillet until caramelized before adding the other ingredients helped to deepen their flavor. For the crust, we cut a standard pie crust into squares after rolling it over the fruit right in the skillet—this encouraged a multitude of crispy edges that contrast nicely with the tender fruit and recall (in a less dowdy way) the broken-up crusts of a traditional pandowdy.

Skillet Apple Pie

SERVES 6 TO 8

If your skillet is not ovensafe, precook the apples and stir in the cider mixture as instructed, then transfer the apples to a 13 by 9-inch baking dish. Roll out the dough to a 13 by 9-inch rectangle and cut the crust and bake the pandowdy as instructed. If you do not have apple cider, reduced apple juice may be used as a substitute; simmer 1 cup apple juice in a small saucepan over medium heat until reduced to ½ cup (about 10 minutes). Serve the pandowdy warm or at room temperature with vanilla ice cream or whipped cream. Use a combination of sweet, crisp apples such as Golden Delicious and firm, tart apples such as Cortland or Empire.

CRUST

- 1 cup (5 ounces) unbleached all-purpose flour, plus extra for the work surface
- 1 tablespoon sugar
- ½ teaspoon table salt
- 2 tablespoons vegetable shortening, chilled
- 6 tablespoons (¾ stick) unsalted butter, cut into ¼-inch pieces and chilled
- 3–4 tablespoons ice water

FILLING

- ½ cup apple cider
- ⅓ cup maple syrup
- 2 tablespoons juice from 1 lemon
- 2 teaspoons cornstarch
- ⅛ teaspoon ground cinnamon (optional)
- 2 tablespoons unsalted butter
- 2½ pounds sweet and tart apples (about 4 large), peeled, cored, and cut into ½-inch-thick wedges (see note)
- 1 large egg white, lightly beaten
- 2 teaspoons sugar

1. FOR THE CRUST: Pulse the flour, sugar, and salt in a food processor until combined, about 4 pulses. Add the shortening and pulse until the mixture has the texture of coarse sand, about 10 pulses. Sprinkle the butter pieces over the flour mixture and pulse until the mixture is pale yellow and resembles coarse crumbs, with the butter bits no larger than small peas, about 10 pulses. Transfer the mixture to a medium bowl.

2. Sprinkle 3 tablespoons of the ice water over the mixture. With a rubber spatula, use a folding motion to mix, pressing down on the dough until the dough is slightly tacky and sticks together, adding up to 1 tablespoon more ice water if the dough does not come together. Flatten the dough into a 4-inch disk. Wrap the disk in plastic wrap and refrigerate for at least 1 hour or up to 2 days. Let the dough stand at room temperature for 15 minutes before rolling.

3. FOR THE FILLING: Adjust an oven rack to the upper-middle position (between 7 and 9 inches from the heating element) and heat the oven to 500 degrees. Whisk the cider, syrup, lemon juice, cornstarch, and cinnamon (if using) together in a medium bowl until smooth. Melt the butter in a 12-inch ovensafe skillet over medium-high heat. Add the apples and cook, stirring two or three times, until the apples begin to caramelize, about 5 minutes. (Do not fully cook the apples.) Remove the pan from the heat, add the cider mixture, and gently stir until the apples are well coated. Set aside to cool slightly.

4. TO ASSEMBLE AND BAKE: Roll the dough out on a lightly floured work surface to an 11-inch circle. Roll the dough loosely around the rolling pin and unroll over the apple filling. Brush the dough with the egg white and sprinkle with the sugar. With a sharp knife, gently cut the dough into six pieces by making one vertical cut followed by two evenly spaced horizontal cuts (perpendicular to the first cut). Bake until the apples are tender and the crust is a deep golden brown, about 20 minutes, rotating the skillet halfway through the baking time. Cool for 15 minutes and serve.

BANANAS FOSTER

WHY THIS RECIPE WORKS: Although the New Orleans dessert bananas Foster is quick and simple, with few ingredients (butter, brown sugar, rum, and bananas), things can go wrong. Sometimes the bananas are overcooked and mushy. Or the sauce can be too thin, overly sweet, or taste too strongly of alcohol. We wanted to fix these issues and come up with a quick, reliable dessert with tender bananas and a flavorful but not boozy sauce.

First we kept the amounts of butter and brown sugar in check—most recipes use a high ratio of butter to brown sugar, which makes for a thin, greasy sauce. For the rum, we found that a small amount was just enough to impart a definite rum flavor without turning the dessert into a cocktail. We decided to add some rum to the sauce and use the rest to flambé the bananas. We also enhanced the sauce with a little cinnamon and lemon zest, which added some complexity. As for the bananas, we cooked them in the sauce until soft, flipping them over halfway through cooking so they turned out tender, not mushy.

Bananas Foster

SERVES 4

While the bananas cook, scoop the ice cream into individual bowls so they are ready to go once the sauce has been flambéed. Before preparing this recipe, read "Tips for Fearless Flambé" on page 408.

- 4 tablespoons (½ stick) unsalted butter
- ½ cup packed (3½ ounces) dark brown sugar
- 1 (3-inch) cinnamon stick
- 1 (2-inch) strip zest from 1 lemon
- 4 tablespoons dark rum
- 2 large, firm, ripe bananas, peeled and quartered
- 1 pint vanilla ice cream, divided among four bowls

1. Combine the butter, sugar, cinnamon stick, zest, and 1 tablespoon of the rum in a 12-inch skillet. Cook over medium-high heat, stirring constantly, until the sugar dissolves and the mixture has thickened, about 2 minutes.

2. Reduce the heat to medium and add the bananas to the pan, spooning some sauce over each quarter. Cook until the bananas are glossy and golden on the bottom, about 1½ minutes. Flip the bananas; continue to cook until very soft but not mushy or falling apart, about 1½ minutes longer.

3. Off the heat, add the remaining 3 tablespoons rum and allow the rum to warm slightly, about 5 seconds. Wave a lit match over the pan until the rum ignites, shaking the pan to distribute the flame over the entire pan. When the flames subside (this will take 15 to 30 seconds), discard the cinnamon stick and zest and divide the bananas and sauce among the four bowls of ice cream. Serve.

CRÊPES SUZETTE

WHY THIS RECIPE WORKS: Classic French restaurants have mastered the fiery theatrics of this tableside treat—a sophisticated combination of crêpes, oranges, liqueur, and a showy flambé. We wanted to develop a recipe that would comfortably guide the home cook through the flambé process so this dessert could be prepared for an elegant dinner party. For a foolproof flambé that didn't create a frightening fireball or, conversely, didn't burn at all, we ignited the cognac alone in the skillet before building the sauce. We enriched a reduction of butter, sugar, and fresh orange juice with additional orange juice, fresh orange zest, and triple sec. For tender but sturdy crêpes that would stand up to the sauce without turning soggy, we skipped the usual resting of the batter, meant to relax the gluten, before cooking. Then, once the crêpes were cooked, we sprinkled them with sugar and ran them under the broiler for a sweet and crunchy coating.

Crêpes Suzette

SERVES 6

Note that it takes a few crêpes to get the heat of the pan right; your first two or three will almost inevitably be unusable. (To allow for practice, the recipe yields about 16 crêpes; only 12 are needed for the dish.) A dry measuring cup with a ¼-cup capacity is useful for portioning the batter. We prefer crêpes made with whole milk, but low-fat or skim milk can also be used. Before preparing this recipe, read "Tips for Fearless Flambé" on page 408.

CRÊPES

- 3 large eggs
- 1½ cups whole milk (see note)
- 1½ cups (7½ ounces) unbleached all-purpose flour
- ½ cup water
- 5 tablespoons unsalted butter, melted, plus extra for brushing the pan
- 3 tablespoons sugar
- 2 tablespoons cognac
- ½ teaspoon table salt

ORANGE SAUCE

- 4 tablespoons cognac
- 1¼ cups juice plus 1 tablespoon finely grated zest from 3 to 4 large oranges
- 6 tablespoons (¾ stick) unsalted butter, cut into 6 pieces
- ¼ cup (1¾ ounces) sugar
- 2 tablespoons orange-flavored liqueur, preferably triple sec

1. **FOR THE CRÊPES:** Combine the eggs, milk, flour, water, melted butter, sugar, cognac, and salt in a blender until a smooth batter forms, about 10 seconds. Transfer the batter to a medium bowl.

2. Using a pastry brush, brush the bottom and sides of a 10-inch nonstick skillet very lightly with melted butter and heat the skillet over medium heat. When the butter stops sizzling, tilt the pan slightly to the right and begin pouring in a scant ¼ cup batter. Continue to pour the batter in a slow, steady stream, rotating your wrist and twirling the pan slowly counterclockwise until the pan bottom is covered with an even layer of batter. Cook until the crêpe starts to lose its opaqueness and turns spotty light golden brown on the bottom, loosening the crêpe from the side of the pan with a heatproof rubber spatula, 30 seconds to 1 minute. To flip the crêpe, loosen the edge with the spatula and, with your fingertips on the top side, slide the spatula under the crêpe and flip. Cook until dry on the second side, about 20 seconds.

3. Place the cooked crêpe on a plate and repeat the cooking process with the remaining batter, brushing the pan very lightly with butter before making each crêpe. As they are done, stack the crêpes on a plate (you will need 12 crêpes). (The crêpes can be double-wrapped in plastic wrap and refrigerated for up to 3 days; bring them to room temperature before making the sauce.)

4. **FOR THE ORANGE SAUCE:** Adjust an oven rack to the lower-middle position and heat the broiler. Add 3 tablespoons of the cognac to a broiler-safe 12-inch skillet; heat the pan over medium heat just until the vapors begin to rise from the cognac, about 5 seconds. Remove the pan from the heat and wave a lit match over the pan until the cognac ignites, shaking the pan until the flames subside, about 15 seconds; reignite if the flame dies too soon.

5. Add 1 cup of the orange juice, the butter, and 3 tablespoons of the sugar and simmer briskly over high heat, stirring occasionally, until many large bubbles appear and the mixture reduces to a thick syrup, 6 to 8 minutes (you should have just over ½ cup sauce). Transfer the sauce to a small bowl; do not wash the skillet. Stir the remaining ¼ cup orange juice, zest, liqueur, and the remaining 1 tablespoon cognac into the sauce; cover.

6. **TO ASSEMBLE:** Fold each crêpe in half, then in half again to form a wedge shape. Arrange nine folded crêpes around the edge of the now-empty skillet, with the rounded edges facing inward, overlapping as necessary to fit. Arrange the remaining three crêpes in the center of the pan. Sprinkle the crêpes evenly with the remaining 1 tablespoon sugar. Broil until the sugar caramelizes and the crêpes turn spotty brown, about 5 minutes. (Watch the crêpes constantly to prevent scorching; turn the pan as necessary.) Carefully remove the pan from the oven and pour half of the sauce over the crêpes, leaving some areas uncovered. Transfer the crêpes to individual serving dishes and serve immediately, passing the extra sauce separately.

CLASSIC CRÊPES

WHY THIS RECIPE WORKS: A crêpe is nothing but a thin pancake cooked quickly on each side and wrapped around a sweet or savory filling, but it has a reputation for being difficult. We wanted an easy method for crêpes that were thin and delicate yet rich and flavorfully browned in spots.

Finding the perfect ratio of milk to flour and sugar gave us rich-tasting, lightly sweet pancakes. We were surprised to find that neither the type of flour nor the mixing method seemed to matter, and a plain old 12-inch nonstick skillet worked as well as a specialty crêpe pan. What does matter is heating the pan properly (over low heat for at least 10 minutes), using the right amount of batter (we settled on ¼ cup), and flipping the crêpe at precisely the right moment, when the edges appear dry, matte, and lacy. To transform our perfectly cooked crêpes into decadent desserts, we whipped up a few sweet fillings: the simple classic of sugar and lemon; a decadent chocolate and orange; and a banana and Nutella sure to please kids and adults alike.

Crêpes with Sugar and Lemon

SERVES 4

The crêpes will give off steam as they cook, but if at any point the skillet begins to smoke, remove it from the heat immediately and turn down the heat. Stacking the crêpes on a wire rack allows excess steam to escape so they won't stick together. To allow for practice, the recipe yields 10 crêpes; only eight are needed for the filling.

- ½ teaspoon vegetable oil
- 1 cup (5 ounces) unbleached all-purpose flour
- 1 teaspoon sugar, plus 8 teaspoons for sprinkling
- ¼ teaspoon table salt
- 1½ cups whole milk
- 3 large eggs
- 2 tablespoons unsalted butter, melted and cooled
- Lemon wedges, for serving

1. Heat the oil in a 12-inch nonstick skillet over low heat for at least 10 minutes.

NOTES FROM THE TEST KITCHEN

MAKING A CRÊPE

1. Pour ¼ cup batter into far side of skillet.

2. Tilt and shake skillet gently until batter evenly covers bottom of skillet.

3. Gently slide spatula underneath edge of crêpe, grasp edge with your fingertips, and flip crêpe.

2. While the skillet is heating, whisk the flour, 1 teaspoon of the sugar, and the salt together in a medium bowl. In a separate bowl, whisk together the milk and eggs. Add half of the milk mixture to the dry ingredients and whisk until smooth. Add the butter and whisk until incorporated. Whisk in the remaining milk mixture until smooth.

3. Using a paper towel, wipe out the skillet, leaving a thin film of oil on the bottom and sides of the pan. Increase the heat to medium and let the skillet heat for 1 minute. After 1 minute, test the heat of the skillet by placing 1 teaspoon of the batter in the center; cook for 20 seconds. If the mini crêpe is golden brown on the bottom, the skillet is properly heated; if it is too light or too dark, adjust the heat accordingly and retest.

4. Pour ¼ cup batter into the far side of pan and tilt and shake gently until the batter evenly covers the bottom of the pan. Cook the crêpe without moving until the top surface is dry and the edges are starting to brown, loosening the crêpe from the side of the pan with a rubber spatula, about 25 seconds. Gently slide the spatula underneath the edge of the crêpe, grasp the edge with your fingertips, and flip the crêpe. Cook until the second side is lightly spotted, about 20 seconds. Transfer the cooked crêpe to a wire rack, inverting so the spotted side is facing up. Return the pan to the heat and heat for 10 seconds before repeating with the remaining batter. As the crêpes are done, stack on the wire rack.

5. Transfer the stack of crêpes to a large plate and invert a second plate over the crêpes. Microwave until the crêpes are warm, 30 to 45 seconds (45 to 60 seconds if the crêpes have cooled completely). Remove the top plate and wipe dry with a paper towel. Sprinkle half of the top crêpe with 1 teaspoon sugar. Fold the unsugared bottom half over the sugared half, then fold into quarters. Transfer the sugared crêpe to a second plate. Continue with the remaining crêpes. Serve immediately, passing the lemon wedges separately.

Crêpes with Chocolate and Orange

Follow the recipe for Crêpes with Sugar and Lemon, omitting the 8 teaspoons sugar for sprinkling and the lemon wedges. Using your fingertips, rub 1 teaspoon finely grated orange zest into ¼ cup sugar. Stir in 2 ounces finely grated bittersweet chocolate. In step 5, sprinkle 1½ tablespoons of the chocolate-orange mixture over half of each crêpe. Fold the crêpes into quarters. Serve immediately.

Crêpes with Bananas and Nutella

Follow the recipe for Crêpes with Sugar and Lemon, omitting the 8 teaspoons sugar for sprinkling and the lemon wedges. In step 5, spread 2 teaspoons Nutella over half of each crêpe, followed by eight to ten ¼-inch-thick banana slices. Fold the crêpes into quarters. Serve immediately.

SUMMER PUDDING

WHY THIS RECIPE WORKS: If any food speaks of summer, the English dessert called summer pudding does. Ripe, fragrant, lightly sweetened berries are gently cooked to coax out their juices and then packed into a bowl lined with slices of bread. The berry juices soak and soften the bread to make it meld with the fruit. We set out to master this summertime classic.

Instead of lining the mold with bread and then filling it with berries, we opted to layer bread (cut out with a biscuit cutter) and berries together in ramekins; this way, the layers of bread on the inside would almost melt into the fruit. Combining the berries—we used strawberries, raspberries, blueberries, and blackberries—with sugar and lemon juice, and gently cooking the mixture for just five minutes, released just the right amount of juice and offset the tartness of the berries. Fresh bread became too gummy in the pudding, but day-old bread had just the right consistency. We used potato bread; its even, tight-crumbed, tender texture and light sweetness was a perfect match for the berries (challah makes a good substitute). To ensure that the puddings would come together and hold their shape, we weighted and refrigerated them for at least eight hours.

Individual Summer Berry Puddings

SERVES 6

The bread should be dry to the touch but not brittle. If working with fresh bread, dry the slices by heating them on an oven rack in a single layer in a 200-degree oven for about 1 hour, flipping them once halfway through the time. For this recipe, you will need six 6-ounce ramekins and a round cookie cutter of a slightly smaller diameter than the ramekins. If you don't have the right size cutter, use a paring knife and the bottom of a ramekin (most ramekins taper toward the bottom) as a guide for trimming the rounds. Challah will need to be cut into slices about ½ inch thick; if both potato bread and challah are unavailable, use high-quality white sandwich bread. Summer pudding can be made up to 24 hours before serving; held any longer, the berries begin to lose their freshness. Lightly sweetened whipped cream is the perfect accompaniment.

- 4 cups (20 ounces) strawberries, hulled and sliced
- 2 cups (about 10 ounces) raspberries
- 1 cup (about 5 ounces) blueberries
- 1 cup (about 5 ounces) blackberries
- ¾ cup (5¼ ounces) sugar
- 2 tablespoons juice from 1 lemon
- 12 slices stale potato bread, challah, or high-quality white sandwich bread (see note)

1. Cook the strawberries, raspberries, blueberries, blackberries, and sugar in a large saucepan over medium heat, stirring occasionally, until the berries begin to release their juice and the sugar has dissolved, about 5 minutes. Off the heat, stir in the lemon juice; cool to room temperature.

2. While the berries are cooling, spray six 6-ounce ramekins with vegetable oil spray and place on a rimmed baking sheet. Use a cookie cutter to cut out 12 bread rounds that are slightly smaller in diameter than the ramekins.

3. Using a slotted spoon, place ¼ cup of the fruit mixture in each ramekin. Lightly soak one bread round in the fruit juice in the saucepan and place on top of the fruit in a ramekin; repeat with five more bread rounds and the remaining ramekins. Diving the remaining fruit among the ramekins. Lightly soak one bread round in the juice and place on top of the fruit in a ramekin (it should sit above the lip of the ramekin); repeat with the remaining five bread rounds and the remaining ramekins. Pour the remaining fruit juice over the bread and cover the ramekins loosely with plastic wrap. Place a second baking sheet on top of the ramekins and weight it with heavy cans. Refrigerate the puddings for at least 8 hours or up to 24 hours.

4. Remove the cans and baking sheet and uncover the puddings. Loosen the puddings by running a paring knife around the edge of each ramekin, unmold into individual bowls, and serve immediately.

Large Summer Berry Pudding

SERVES 6 TO 8

You will need a 9 by 5-inch loaf pan for this recipe. Because there is no need to cut out rounds for this version, you will need only about 8 slices bread, depending on their size.

Follow the recipe for Individual Summer Berry Puddings through step 1. While the berries are cooling, spray a 9 by 5-inch loaf pan with vegetable oil spray, line it with plastic wrap, and place it on a rimmed baking sheet. Trim the crusts from the bread and trim the slices to fit in a single layer in the loaf pan (you will need about 2½ slices per layer; there will be three layers). Using a slotted spoon, spread about 2 cups of the fruit mixture evenly over the bottom of the prepared pan. Lightly soak enough bread slices for one layer in the fruit juice in the saucepan and place on top of the fruit. Repeat with two more layers of fruit and bread. Pour the remaining fruit juice over the bread and cover loosely with plastic wrap. Place a second baking sheet on top of the loaf pan and weight it with heavy cans. Refrigerate the pudding for at least 8 hours or up to 24 hours. Remove the cans and baking sheet and uncover the pudding. Invert the pudding onto a serving platter, remove the loaf pan and plastic wrap, slice, and serve.

CARAMELIZED PEARS

WHY THIS RECIPE WORKS: Pears and blue cheese are a classic combination, but we wanted to up the flavor ante with another component—caramel. We had encountered this triple play in restaurants, where a caramel sauce is draped over seared pears, and a modest amount of pungent blue cheese provides a nice contrast to the dessert's sweetness. We decided to adapt this dish so it would be easy for the home cook to get it just right (meaning no mushy pears and no sticky, overcooked caramel).

To streamline the recipe, we cooked the pears right in the caramel sauce, instead of separately, saving time and eliminating some dirty dishes. We brought water and sugar (the basis for caramel sauce) to a boil in a skillet and slid the pears into the hot mixture to cook in the browning caramel. We added cream to the pan to transform the sticky sugar syrup into a smooth sauce that clung lightly to the pears. After removing the pears, we were able to season the sauce left in the skillet with just the right amount of black pepper and salt. For an attractive presentation, we stood the pears upright on a plate (we had already trimmed the bottom off each pear for a flat base) and drizzled the caramel sauce around them, then added wedges of strong blue cheese—the perfect foil to the sweet caramel.

Caramelized Pears with Blue Cheese and Black Pepper-Caramel Sauce

SERVES 6

Any type of pear can be used in this recipe, but the pears must be firm to withstand the heat. If desired, the pears can be served upright on a large platter instead of on individual plates, with the warm caramel sauce and the blue cheese

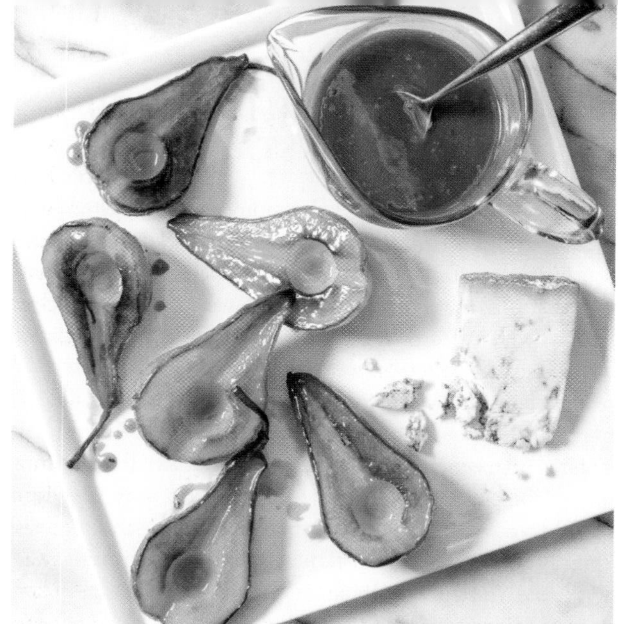

passed separately. Many pepper mills do not have a sufficiently coarse setting; in that case, crush peppercorns with the back of a heavy pan or a rolling pin. See page 879 for information on our top-rated pepper mill.

- ⅓ cup water
- ⅔ cup (4⅔ ounces) sugar
- 3 ripe, firm pears, halved, cored, and ¼ inch trimmed off the bottom (see note)
- ⅔ cup heavy cream
- Table salt
- ¼ teaspoon black peppercorns, crushed (see note)
- 3 ounces strong blue cheese (such as Stilton), cut into 6 wedges

1. Pour the water into a 12-inch nonstick skillet, then pour the sugar into the center of the pan, being careful not to let it hit the sides of the pan. Bring to a boil over high heat, stirring occasionally, until the sugar is fully dissolved and the liquid is bubbling. Add the pears to the skillet, cut side down, cover, reduce the heat to medium-high, and cook until the pears are almost tender and a paring knife inserted into the center of the pears meets slight resistance, 13 to 15 minutes.

2. Uncover, reduce the heat to medium, and cook until the sauce is golden brown and the cut sides of the pears are beginning to brown, 3 to 5 minutes. Pour the heavy cream around the pears and cook, shaking the pan until the sauce is a smooth, deep caramel color and the cut sides of the pears are golden brown, 3 to 5 minutes.

3. Off the heat, transfer the pears, cut side up, to a wire rack set over a rimmed baking sheet and cool slightly. Season the sauce left in the pan with salt to taste and the crushed peppercorns, then transfer it to a small bowl.

4. Carefully (the pears will still be hot) stand each pear half upright on an individual plate and arrange a wedge of the blue cheese beside it. Drizzle the caramel sauce over the plate and the pear. Serve immediately.

ROASTED PEARS WITH DRIED APRICOTS AND PISTACHIOS

WHY THIS RECIPE WORKS: Tender, caramelized roasted pears are a delightfully simple dessert, but it took a two-step cooking process to perfect their texture. To eliminate any excess moisture that might weigh down the fruit, we cooked our peeled, halved pears in butter in a hot skillet. Once the pears began to brown, we transferred the skillet to the oven for 30 minutes. We plated the fork-tender fruit and started in on the sauce, deglazing the pan with white wine and adding sweet dried apricots, sugar, cardamom, and salt, plus a pat of butter for a creamy dimension. A touch of lemon juice stirred in once the liquid had thickened contributed citrusy brightness, and a sprinkling of pistachios, added right at serving, gave the dessert some toasty, textural contrast.

Roasted Pears with Dried Apricots and Pistachios

SERVES 4 TO 6

Select pears that yield slightly when pressed. We prefer Bosc pears in this recipe, but Comice and Bartlett pears also work. The fruit can be served as is or with vanilla ice cream or plain Greek yogurt.

- 2½ tablespoons unsalted butter
- 4 ripe but firm Bosc pears (6 to 7 ounces each), peeled, halved, and cored
- 1¼ cups dry white wine
- ½ cup dried apricots, quartered
- ⅓ cup (2⅓ ounces) sugar
- ¼ teaspoon ground cardamom
- ⅛ teaspoon salt
- 1 teaspoon lemon juice
- ⅓ cup pistachios, toasted and chopped

1. Adjust oven rack to middle position and heat oven to 450 degrees. Melt 1½ tablespoons butter in ovensafe 12-inch skillet over medium-high heat. Place pear halves, cut side down, in skillet. Cook, without moving them, until pears are just beginning to brown, 3 to 5 minutes.

2. Transfer skillet to oven and roast pears for 15 minutes. Using tongs, flip pears and continue to roast until fork easily pierces fruit, 10 to 15 minutes longer (skillet handle will be hot).

3. Using tongs, transfer pears to platter. Return skillet to medium-high heat and add wine, apricots, sugar, cardamom, salt, and remaining 1 tablespoon butter. Bring to vigorous simmer, whisking to scrape up any browned bits. Cook until sauce is reduced and has consistency of maple syrup, 7 to 10 minutes. Remove pan from heat and stir in lemon juice.

4. Pour sauce over pears, sprinkle with pistachios, and serve.

Roasted Apples with Dried Figs and Walnuts

Substitute Gala apples for pears, red wine for white wine, dried figs for apricots, ¾ teaspoon pepper for cardamom, and walnuts for pistachios.

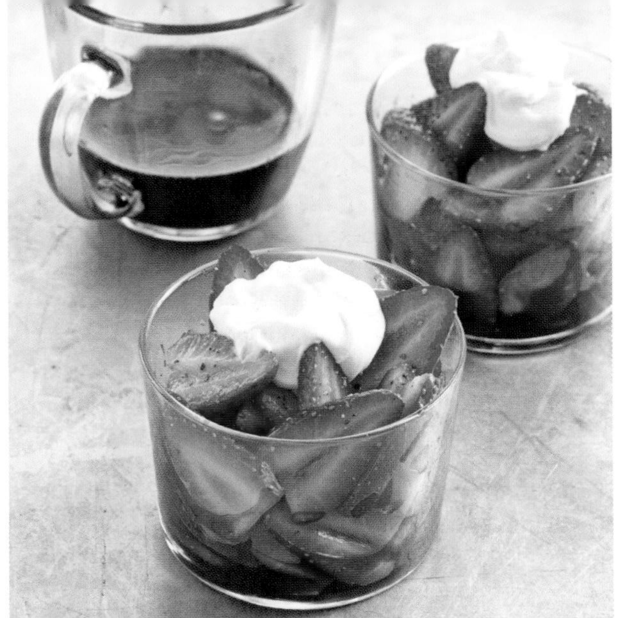

STRAWBERRIES WITH BALSAMIC VINEGAR

WHY THIS RECIPE WORKS: Strawberries with balsamic vinegar may sound a bit trendy, but this combination actually goes back in time—hundreds of years at least—to northern Italy. We wanted to pay homage to this time-honored tradition and create our own dessert, with the vinegar enhancing but not overwhelming the flavor of bright, summer berries.

We didn't want to pay big bucks for a super-pricey balsamic vinegar, so we opted to use an inexpensive vinegar. To coax big flavor out of our bargain balsamic, we simmered it with some sugar to approximate the syrupy texture of an aged vinegar. Next we tried to enhance the flavor with honey or vanilla, but these flavors were too overpowering; a squirt of fresh lemon juice brought just the right amount of brightness. We tossed the berries with light brown sugar—rather than the traditional granulated sugar—for the most complex flavor. Once we mixed the sliced berries and sugar together, it took about 15 minutes for the sugar to dissolve and the berries to release their juice; if the strawberries sat any longer than this, they continued to soften and became quite mushy.

Strawberries with Balsamic Vinegar

SERVES 6

If you don't have light brown sugar on hand, sprinkle the berries with an equal amount of granulated sugar. Serve the berries and syrup as is or with a scoop of vanilla ice cream or a dollop of lightly sweetened whipped cream.

- ⅓ cup balsamic vinegar
- 2 teaspoons granulated sugar
- ½ teaspoon juice from 1 lemon
- 6 cups (30 ounces) strawberries, hulled, sliced lengthwise ¼ inch thick if large, halved or quartered if small
- ¼ cup packed (1¾ ounces) light brown sugar (see note)
- Ground black pepper

1. Bring the vinegar, granulated sugar, and lemon juice to a simmer in a small saucepan over medium heat. Simmer until the syrup is reduced by half (about 3 tablespoons), about 3 minutes. Transfer to a small bowl and cool completely.

2. Gently toss the berries and brown sugar in a large bowl. Let stand until the sugar dissolves and the berries exude some juice, 10 to 15 minutes. Pour the vinegar syrup over the berries, add pepper to taste, and toss to combine. Serve immediately.

BERRY FOOL

WHY THIS RECIPE WORKS: Traditionally, fruit fool is made by folding pureed stewed fruit (traditionally gooseberries) into sweet custard. Modern fool recipes skip the traditional custard and use whipped cream. But whipped cream blunts the fruit flavor and is too light and insubstantial—or, worse, it can turn the dessert soupy. We wanted a dessert with intense fruitiness and rich body—and we wanted to use raspberries or strawberries rather than the traditional gooseberries.

Gooseberries are naturally high in pectin—when exposed to heat, sugar, and acid, pectin breaks down and causes fruit to thicken, which made them ideal for fruit fool. We wanted to use raspberries and strawberries, which are low in pectin, so our first challenge was to thicken the fruit properly. We turned to gelatin to thicken our berries, but used a judicious hand (just 2 teaspoons), softening the gelatin in some uncooked berry puree, and then combined the softened mixture with some heated puree to help melt and distribute the gelatin. The result? A smooth, thickened puree with intense fruit flavor.

Now we just needed a richer, sturdier cream base to partner with the fruit puree. We liked the ease of using whipped cream rather than custard, so why not make whipped cream more custard-like? Combined with sour cream, the mixture was airy yet substantial, and the sour cream added just the right touch of richness, along with a tangy undertone. For even more fruit flavor, we layered the fruit puree and cream base with fresh berries that had been macerated in sugar to release excess juice. Finally, topping the dessert with crumbled sweet wheat crackers added a pleasant, nutty contrast.

Berry Fool

SERVES 6

Blueberries or blackberries can be substituted for raspberries in this recipe. You may also substitute frozen fruit for fresh, but there will be a slight compromise in texture. If using frozen fruit, reduce the amount of sugar in the puree by 1 tablespoon. The thickened fruit puree can be made up to 4 hours in advance; just make sure to whisk it well in step 4 to break up any clumps before combining it with the whipped cream. For the best results, chill your beater and bowl before whipping the cream. We like the granular texture and nutty flavor of Carr's Whole Wheat Crackers, but graham crackers or gingersnaps will also work.

- 2 quarts strawberries (about 2 pounds), washed, dried, and stemmed
- 1 pint raspberries (about 12 ounces), washed and dried (see note)
- ½ cup (3½ ounces) plus 4 tablespoons sugar
- 2 teaspoons unflavored powdered gelatin
- 1 cup heavy cream
- ¼ cup sour cream
- ½ teaspoon vanilla extract
- 4 Carr's Whole Wheat Crackers, crushed fine (about ¼ cup; see note)
- 6 sprigs fresh mint (optional)

1. Process 1 quart of the strawberries, ½ pint of the raspberries, and ½ cup of the sugar in a food processor until the mixture is completely smooth, about 1 minute. Strain the berry puree through a fine-mesh strainer into a 4-cup liquid measuring cup (you should have about 2½ cups puree; reserve any excess for another use). Transfer ½ cup of the puree to a small bowl and sprinkle the gelatin over the top; stir until the gelatin is incorporated and let stand for at least 5 minutes. Heat the remaining 2 cups puree in a small saucepan over medium heat until it begins to bubble, 4 to 6 minutes. Remove the pan from the heat and stir in the gelatin mixture until dissolved. Transfer the gelatin-puree mixture to a medium bowl, cover with plastic wrap, and refrigerate until cold, about 2 hours.

2. Meanwhile, chop the remaining 1 quart strawberries into rough ¼-inch pieces. Toss the strawberries, remaining ½ pint raspberries, and 2 tablespoons more sugar together in a medium bowl. Set aside for 1 hour.

3. Place the cream, sour cream, vanilla, and remaining 2 tablespoons sugar in the chilled bowl of a stand mixer. Beat on low speed until bubbles form, about 30 seconds. Increase the mixer speed to medium and continue beating until the beaters leave a trail, about 30 seconds. Increase the mixer speed to high; continue beating until the mixture has nearly doubled in volume and holds stiff peaks, about 30 seconds. Transfer ⅓ cup of the whipped cream mixture to a small bowl and set aside.

4. Remove the thickened berry puree from the refrigerator and whisk until smooth. With the mixer running at medium speed, slowly add two-thirds of the puree to the whipped cream mixture; mix until incorporated, about 15 seconds. Using a spatula, gently fold in the remaining thickened puree, leaving streaks of puree.

5. Transfer the uncooked berries to a fine-mesh strainer; shake gently to remove any excess juice. Divide two-thirds of the berries evenly among six tall parfait or sundae glasses. Divide the creamy berry mixture evenly among the glasses, followed by the remaining uncooked berries. Top each glass with the reserved plain whipped cream mixture. Sprinkle with the crushed crackers and garnish with mint sprigs (if using). Serve immediately.

RHUBARB FOOL

WHY THIS RECIPE WORKS: A fool is a quick, everyday dessert that just so happens to have a quaint and quirky British name. We decided to try our hand at this simple dessert—cooked fruit with whipped cream folded in—using rhubarb as the foundation. Although fool is in itself no culinary feat, the challenges lie in the rhubarb, with its sometimes overpowering sourness and tendency to cook into a thick, drab gray mess. We knew that before we could finalize a fool, we would have to tame the rhubarb. We wanted the perfect balance—pinkish-red, sweet/tart, toothsome fruit mixed with light cream. Baking, stewing, and sautéing the rhubarb all led to gray, mushy fruit. Eventually, we hit on soaking the rhubarb in cold water for 20 minutes—this removed some of the bitterness—and simmering it with orange juice. For the whipped cream, we decided that a soft-to-medium peak gave the fool just enough body. For the best presentation and flavor, we arranged the rhubarb and whipped cream in layers rather than folding the two elements together, making for a pleasing contrast of color and flavor.

Rhubarb Fool

SERVES 8

For a more elegant presentation, use a pastry bag to pipe the whipped cream into individual glasses. To make one large fool, double the recipe and layer the rhubarb and whipped cream in a 12-cup glass bowl.

- 2¼ pounds rhubarb, trimmed and cut into 6-inch lengths
- ⅓ cup juice from 1 large orange
- 1 cup (7 ounces) plus 2 tablespoons sugar
- Pinch table salt
- 2 cups heavy cream, chilled

1. Soak the rhubarb in cold water for 20 minutes. Drain, pat dry with paper towels, and cut crosswise into ½-inch-thick pieces.

2. Bring the orange juice, ¾ cup of the sugar, and the salt to a boil in a medium saucepan over medium-high heat. Add the rhubarb and return to a boil, then reduce the heat to medium-low and simmer, stirring two or three times, until the rhubarb begins to break down and is tender, 7 to 10 minutes. Transfer the rhubarb to a large bowl, cool to room temperature, cover with plastic wrap, and refrigerate until cold, at least 1 hour or up to 24 hours.

3. Whip the cream and remaining 6 tablespoons sugar in a large bowl with an electric mixer on medium-low speed until frothy, about 1 minute. Increase the speed to high and continue to whip until the cream forms soft peaks, 1 to 3 minutes.

4. To assemble, spoon about ¼ cup rhubarb into each of eight 8-ounce glasses, then layer about ¼ cup whipped cream on top. Repeat, ending with a dollop of cream; serve. (The fools can be refrigerated, covered with plastic wrap, for up to 6 hours.)

Strawberry-Rhubarb Fool

Follow the recipe for Rhubarb Fool, substituting 4 cups strawberries, hulled and quartered, for 1¼ pounds of the rhubarb and adding the strawberries to the saucepan with the rhubarb in step 2.

SUMMER BERRY TRIFLE

WHY THIS RECIPE WORKS: Trifles usually look a lot better than they taste because busy cooks simplify the complicated preparation by subbing in shortcut ingredients like storebought cake and pudding from a box. We wanted to streamline, but not shortchange, the components so that the entire trifle could be made from scratch in just a few hours. We added a little extra flour to a classic chiffon cake so we could bake it in an 18 by 13-inch sheet, which baked and cooled much more quickly than the traditional tall chiffon cake, and we prevented our pastry cream from turning runny during assembly by adding a little more cornstarch. We mashed one-third of the berries so their juices would provide moisture to the cake. A bit of cream sherry added a sophisticated layer of flavor.

Summer Berry Trifle

SERVES 12 TO 16

For the best texture, this trifle should be assembled at least 6 hours before serving. Use a glass bowl with at least a 3½-quart capacity; straight sides are preferable.

PASTRY CREAM

- 3½ cups whole milk
- 1 cup (7 ounces) sugar
- 6 tablespoons cornstarch
- Pinch salt
- 5 large egg yolks (reserve whites for cake)
- 4 tablespoons unsalted butter, cut into ½-inch pieces and chilled
- 4 teaspoons vanilla extract

CAKE

- 1⅓ cups (5⅓ ounces) cake flour
- ¾ cup (5¼ ounces) sugar
- 1½ teaspoons baking powder
- ¼ teaspoon salt
- ⅓ cup vegetable oil
- ¼ cup water
- 1 large egg
- 2 teaspoons vanilla extract
- 5 large egg whites (reserved from pastry cream)
- ¼ teaspoon cream of tartar

FRUIT FILLING

- 1½ pounds strawberries, hulled and cut into ½-inch pieces (4 cups), reserving 3 halved for garnish
- 12 ounces (2⅓ cups) blackberries, large berries halved crosswise, reserving 3 whole for garnish
- 12 ounces (2⅓ cups) raspberries, reserving 3 for garnish
- ¼ cup (1¾ ounces) sugar
- ½ teaspoon cornstarch
- Pinch salt

WHIPPED CREAM

- 1 cup heavy cream
- 1 tablespoon sugar
- 1 tablespoon plus ½ cup cream sherry

1. FOR THE PASTRY CREAM: Heat 3 cups milk in medium saucepan over medium heat until just simmering. Meanwhile, whisk sugar, cornstarch, and salt together in medium bowl. Whisk remaining ½ cup milk and egg yolks into sugar mixture until smooth. Remove milk from heat and, whisking constantly, slowly add 1 cup to sugar mixture to temper. Whisking constantly, return tempered sugar mixture to milk in saucepan.

2. Return saucepan to medium heat and cook, whisking constantly, until mixture is very thick and bubbles burst on surface, 4 to 7 minutes. Remove saucepan from heat; whisk in butter and vanilla until butter is melted and incorporated. Strain pastry cream through fine-mesh strainer set over medium bowl. Press lightly greased parchment paper directly on surface and refrigerate until set, at least 2 hours or up to 24 hours.

3. FOR THE CAKE: Adjust oven rack to middle position and heat oven to 350 degrees. Lightly grease 18 by 13-inch rimmed baking sheet, line with parchment, and lightly grease parchment. Whisk flour, sugar, baking powder, and salt together in medium bowl. Whisk oil, water, egg, and vanilla into flour mixture until smooth batter forms.

4. Using stand mixer fitted with whisk, whip reserved egg whites and cream of tartar on medium-low speed until foamy, about 1 minute. Increase speed to medium-high and whip until soft peaks form, 2 to 3 minutes. Transfer one-third of whipped egg whites to batter; whisk gently until mixture is lightened. Using rubber spatula, gently fold remaining egg whites into batter.

5. Pour batter into prepared sheet; spread evenly. Bake until top is golden brown and cake springs back when pressed lightly in center, 13 to 16 minutes.

6. Transfer cake to wire rack; let cool for 5 minutes. Run knife around edge of sheet, then invert cake onto wire rack. Carefully remove parchment, then reinvert cake onto second wire rack. Let cool completely, at least 30 minutes.

7. FOR THE FRUIT FILLING: Place 1½ cups strawberries, 1 cup blackberries, 1 cup raspberries, sugar, cornstarch, and salt in medium saucepan. Place remaining berries (except those reserved for garnish) in large bowl; set aside. Using potato masher, thoroughly mash berries in saucepan. Cook over medium heat until sugar is dissolved and mixture is thick and bubbling, 4 to 7 minutes. Pour over berries in bowl and stir to combine. Set aside.

8. FOR THE WHIPPED CREAM: Using stand mixer fitted with whisk, whip cream, sugar, and 1 tablespoon sherry on medium-low speed until foamy, about 1 minute. Increase speed to high and whip until soft peaks form, 1 to 2 minutes.

9. Trim ¼ inch off each side of cake; discard trimmings. Using serrated knife, cut cake into 24 equal pieces (each piece about 2½ inches square).

10. Briefly whisk pastry cream until smooth. Spoon ¾ cup pastry cream into trifle bowl; spread over bottom. Shingle 12 cake pieces, fallen domino–style, around bottom of trifle, placing 10 pieces against dish wall and 2 remaining pieces in center. Drizzle ¼ cup sherry evenly over cake. Spoon half of berry mixture evenly over cake, making sure to use half of liquid. Using back of spoon, spread half of remaining pastry cream over berries, then spread half of whipped cream over pastry cream (whipped cream layer will be thin). Repeat layering with remaining 12 cake pieces, sherry, berries, pastry cream, and whipped cream. Cover bowl with plastic wrap and refrigerate for at least 6 hours or up to 36 hours. Garnish top of trifle with reserved berries and serve.

CHAPTER 26

KEEP YOUR FORK—THERE'S PIE!

BASIC PIE DOUGH

WHY THIS RECIPE WORKS: Basic pie dough often contains vegetable shortening, which makes the dough easier to handle and yields a crust that is remarkably flaky. The primary issue with vegetable shortening crusts, however, is that they lack flavor. We set out to master basic pie dough by determining the right fat, the right proportion of fat to flour, and the right method for combining them.

Flakiness is important to a crust, but so is flavor—and nothing beats butter. We experimented with a variety of combinations and ultimately settled on a proportion of 3 parts butter to 2 parts shortening as optimal for both flavor and texture. We also settled on a ratio of 2 parts flour to 1 part fat. This crust is relatively high in fat, but we found that the 2–1 proportion produces dough that is easier to work with and a baked crust that is more tender and flavorful than any other. You can make this pie dough by hand, but the food processor is faster and easier and does the best job of cutting the fat into the flour.

Basic Double-Crust Pie Dough

MAKES ENOUGH FOR ONE 9-INCH PIE

The dough, wrapped tightly in plastic wrap, can be refrigerated for up to 2 days or frozen for up to 1 month. If frozen, let the dough thaw completely on the counter before rolling it out.

- 2½ cups (12½ ounces) unbleached all-purpose flour, plus extra for the work surface
- 2 tablespoons sugar
- 1 teaspoon table salt
- ½ cup vegetable shortening, cut into ½-inch pieces and chilled
- 12 tablespoons (1½ sticks) unsalted butter, cut into ¼-inch pieces and chilled
- 6–8 tablespoons ice water

1. Process the flour, sugar, and salt together in a food processor until combined. Scatter the shortening over the top and process until the mixture resembles coarse cornmeal, about 10 seconds. Scatter the butter pieces over the top and pulse the mixture until it resembles coarse crumbs, about 10 pulses. Transfer the mixture to a large bowl.

2. Sprinkle 6 tablespoons of the ice water over the mixture. Stir and press the dough together, using a stiff rubber spatula, until the dough sticks together. If the dough does not come together, stir in the remaining water, 1 tablespoon at a time, until it does.

3. Divide the dough into two even pieces. Turn each piece of dough onto a sheet of plastic wrap and flatten each into a 4-inch disk. Wrap each piece tightly in plastic wrap and refrigerate for 1 hour. Before rolling the dough out, let it sit on the counter to soften slightly, about 10 minutes.

NOTES FROM THE TEST KITCHEN

ROLLING AND FITTING PIE DOUGH

1. Lay the disk of dough on a lightly floured work surface and roll the dough outward from its center into a 12-inch circle. Between every few rolls, give the dough a quarter turn to help keep the circle nice and round.

2. Toss additional flour underneath the dough as needed to keep the dough from sticking to the work surface.

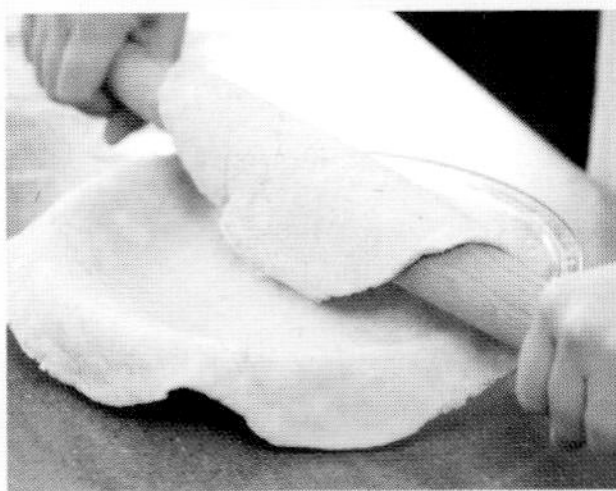

3. Loosely roll the dough around the rolling pin, then gently unroll it over the pie plate.

4. Lift the dough and gently press it into the pie plate, letting the excess hang over the plate. For a double-crust pie, cover the crust lightly with plastic wrap and refrigerate for at least 30 minutes. To crimp a single-crust pie, see page 825.

Hand Mixed Basic Double-Crust Pie Dough

Freeze the butter in its stick form until very firm. Whisk the flour, sugar, and salt together in a large bowl. Add the chilled shortening and press it into the flour using a fork. Grate the frozen butter on the large holes of a box grater into the flour mixture, then cut the mixture together using two butter or dinner knives, until the mixture resembles coarse crumbs. Follow the recipe for Basic Double-Crust Pie Dough, adding the water as directed.

Basic Single-Crust Pie Dough

MAKES ENOUGH FOR ONE 9-INCH PIE

The dough, wrapped tightly in plastic wrap, can be refrigerated for up to 2 days or frozen for up to 1 month. If frozen, let the dough thaw completely on the counter before rolling it out.

- 1¼ cups (6¼ ounces) unbleached all-purpose flour, plus extra for the work surface
- 1 tablespoon sugar
- ½ teaspoon table salt
- 3 tablespoons vegetable shortening, cut into ½-inch pieces and chilled
- 5 tablespoons unsalted butter, cut into ¼-inch pieces and chilled
- 4–6 tablespoons ice water

1. Process the flour, sugar, and salt together in a food processor until combined. Scatter the shortening over the top and process until the mixture resembles coarse cornmeal, about 10 seconds. Scatter the butter pieces over the top and pulse the mixture until it resembles coarse crumbs, about 10 pulses. Transfer the mixture to a medium bowl.

2. Sprinkle 4 tablespoons of the ice water over the mixture. Stir and press the dough together, using a stiff rubber spatula, until the dough sticks together. If the dough does not come together, stir in the remaining water, 1 tablespoon at a time, until it does.

3. Turn the dough onto a sheet of plastic wrap and flatten into a 4-inch disk. Wrap the dough tightly in plastic wrap and refrigerate for 1 hour. Before rolling the dough out, let it sit on the counter to soften slightly, about 10 minutes.

4. Following the photos on page 842, roll the dough into a 12-inch circle and fit it into a pie plate. Following the photos at right, trim, fold, and crimp the edge of the dough. Wrap the dough-lined pie plate loosely in plastic wrap and place in the freezer until the dough is fully chilled and firm, about 30 minutes, before using.

Hand Mixed Basic Single-Crust Pie Dough

Freeze the butter in its stick form until very firm. Whisk the flour, sugar, and salt together in a medium bowl. Add the chilled shortening and press it into the flour using a fork. Grate the frozen butter on the large holes of a box grater into the flour mixture, then cut the mixture together using two butter or dinner knives, until the mixture resembles coarse crumbs. Follow the recipe for Basic Single-Crust Pie Dough, adding the water as directed.

Single-Crust Pie Dough for Custard Pies

We like rolling our single-crust dough in fresh graham cracker crumbs because it adds flavor and crisp textural appeal to many of our custard pies.

Crush 3 whole graham crackers to fine crumbs. (You should have about ½ cup crumbs.) Follow the recipe for Basic Single-Crust Pie Dough, dusting the work surface with the graham cracker crumbs instead of flour. Continue sprinkling the dough with the crumbs, both underneath and on top, as it is being rolled out.

NOTES FROM THE TEST KITCHEN

CRIMPING A SINGLE-CRUST PIE DOUGH

For a traditional single-crust pie, you need to make an evenly thick edge before crimping. Trim the pie dough so that it hangs over the pie plate by ½ inch, then tuck the dough underneath itself to form a tidy, even edge that sits on the lip of the pie plate.

FOR A FLUTED EDGE: Use the index finger of one hand and the thumb and index finger of the other to create fluted ridges perpendicular to the edge of the pie plate.

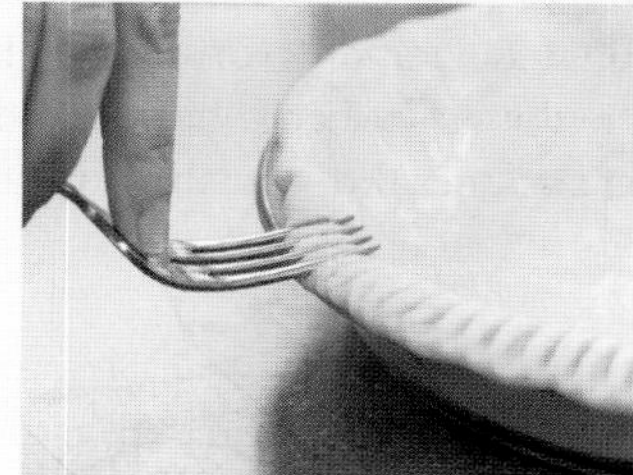

FOR A RIDGED EDGE: Press the tines of a fork into the dough to flatten it against the rim of the pie plate.

ALL-BUTTER PIE DOUGH

WHY THIS RECIPE WORKS: All-butter pie doughs possess great flavor, but they often fail to be flaky and are notoriously difficult to work with. We wanted an all-butter pie pastry that was easier to mix, handle, and roll, producing a pie crust with all the tenderness and flavor that the description "all-butter" promises.

We initially tried to make the dough easier to handle by reducing the amount of butter, but this resulted in bland flavor and dry texture. Rather than adding back the subtracted butter, we experimented with other forms of fat, including heavy cream, cream cheese, and sour cream. We found that sour cream not only added flavor but, because acid reduces gluten development, also helped keep the dough tender and flaky. And to mix the dough, we used a food processor, which brought the ingredients together quickly and evenly.

All-Butter Double-Crust Pie Dough

MAKES ENOUGH FOR ONE 9-INCH PIE

Freezing the butter for 10 to 15 minutes is crucial to the flaky texture of this crust. If preparing the dough in a very warm kitchen, refrigerate all of the ingredients before making the dough. The dough, wrapped tightly in plastic wrap, can be refrigerated for up to 2 days or frozen for up to 1 month. If frozen, let the dough thaw completely on the counter before rolling it out.

⅓ cup ice water, plus extra as needed
3 tablespoons sour cream
2½ cups (12½ ounces) unbleached all-purpose flour, plus extra for the work surface
1 tablespoon sugar
1 teaspoon table salt
16 tablespoons (2 sticks) unsalted butter, cut into ¼-inch pieces and frozen for 10 to 15 minutes (see note)

1. Mix ⅓ cup of the ice water and the sour cream in a small bowl until combined. Process the flour, sugar, and salt together in a food processor until combined. Following the photos, scatter the butter pieces over the top and pulse the mixture until the butter is the size of large peas, about 10 pulses.

2. Pour half of the sour cream mixture over the flour mixture and pulse until incorporated, about 3 pulses. Repeat with the remaining sour cream mixture. Pinch the dough with your fingers; if the dough feels dry and does not hold together, sprinkle 1 to 2 tablespoons more ice water over the mixture and pulse until the dough forms large clumps and no dry flour remains, 3 to 5 pulses.

3. Divide the dough into two even pieces. Turn each piece of dough onto a sheet of plastic wrap and flatten each into a 4-inch disk. Wrap each piece tightly in plastic wrap and refrigerate for 1 hour. Before rolling the dough out, let it sit on the counter to soften slightly, about 10 minutes.

NOTES FROM THE TEST KITCHEN

MAKING ALL-BUTTER DOUBLE-CRUST PIE DOUGH

1. Pulse the butter and flour mixture together in a food processor until the butter is the size of large peas, about 10 pulses.

2. After adding the sour cream and water mixture, pinch the dough with your fingers. If the dough is dry and does not hold together, sprinkle 1 to 2 tablespoons ice water over the mixture and pulse 3 to 5 times.

3. Divide the dough into two pieces and flatten each into a 4-inch disk. Wrap the disks tightly in plastic wrap and refrigerate for 1 hour. Before rolling the dough out, let it sit on the counter to soften slightly, about 10 minutes.

Hand Mixed All-Butter Double-Crust Pie Dough

Freeze the butter in its stick form until very firm. Whisk the flour, sugar, and salt together in a large bowl. Grate the frozen butter on the large holes of a box grater into the flour mixture, then cut the mixture together using two butter or dinner knives, until the mixture resembles coarse crumbs. Follow the recipe for All-Butter Double-Crust Pie Dough, adding the liquid as directed, stirring it with a rubber spatula.

FOOLPROOF PIE DOUGH

WHY THIS RECIPE WORKS: Unless you're a practiced pie baker, it's hard to get the same results every time. While we think our All-Butter Pie Dough (page 843) and Basic Pie Dough (page 842) are great, we wanted a recipe for pie dough that rolls out easily every time and produces a tender, flaky crust. The first step was to determine the right fat. As with our basic dough, a combination of butter and shortening provided the best balance of flavor and tenderness. Once again, the best tool to cut the fat into the flour was the food processor. To ensure the butter was incorporated evenly, we skipped cutting it into pieces and made a paste instead. Rather than starting with all the flour in the processor, we put aside 1 cup of flour and processed the remaining 1½ cups with all of the fat until it formed a unified paste. We added the reserved flour to the bowl and pulsed it until it was just evenly distributed. Finally, we tackled the tenderness issue, which is partially determined by the amount of water added. For the dough to roll easily, it needs a generous amount of water, but more water makes crusts tough. We found the answer in the liquor cabinet: vodka. While gluten (the protein that makes crust tough) forms readily in water, it doesn't form in ethanol, and vodka is 60 percent water and 40 percent ethanol. So adding ¼ cup of vodka produced a moist, easy-to-roll dough that stayed tender. (The alcohol vaporizes in the oven, so you won't taste it in the baked crust.)

Foolproof Double-Crust Pie Dough

MAKES ENOUGH FOR ONE 9-INCH PIE

Vodka is essential to the tender texture of this crust and imparts no flavor—do not substitute water. This dough is moister than most standard pie doughs and will require lots of flour to roll out (up to ¼ cup). The dough, wrapped tightly in plastic wrap, can be refrigerated for up to 2 days or frozen for up to 1 month. If frozen, let the dough thaw completely on the counter before rolling it out.

2½ cups (12½ ounces) unbleached all-purpose flour, plus extra for the work surface (see note)
2 tablespoons sugar
1 teaspoon table salt
12 tablespoons (1½ sticks) unsalted butter, cut into ¼-inch pieces and chilled
½ cup vegetable shortening, cut into 4 pieces and chilled
¼ cup vodka, chilled (see note)
¼ cup ice water

1. Process 1½ cups of the flour, the sugar, and salt together in a food processor until combined. Scatter the butter and shortening over the top and continue to process until incorporated and the mixture begins to form uneven clumps with no remaining floury bits, about 15 seconds.

2. Scrape down the workbowl and redistribute the dough evenly around the processor blade. Sprinkle the remaining 1 cup flour over the dough and pulse until the mixture has broken up into pieces and is evenly distributed around the bowl, 4 to 6 pulses.

3. Transfer the mixture to a medium bowl. Sprinkle the vodka and water over the mixture. Stir and press the dough together, using a stiff rubber spatula, until the dough sticks together.

4. Divide the dough into two even pieces. Turn each piece of dough onto a sheet of plastic wrap and flatten each into a 4-inch disk. Wrap each piece tightly in plastic wrap and refrigerate for 1 hour. Before rolling the dough out, let it sit on the counter to soften slightly, about 10 minutes.

Foolproof Single-Crust Pie Dough

MAKES ENOUGH FOR ONE 9-INCH PIE

Vodka is essential to the tender texture of this crust and imparts no flavor—do not substitute water. This dough is moister than most standard pie doughs and will require lots of flour to roll out (up to ¼ cup). The dough, wrapped tightly in plastic wrap, can be refrigerated for up to 2 days or frozen for up to 1 month. If frozen, let the dough thaw completely on the counter before rolling it out.

- 1¼ cups (6¼ ounces) all-purpose flour
- 1 tablespoon sugar
- ½ teaspoon salt
- 6 tablespoons unsalted butter, cut into ¼-inch pieces and chilled
- 4 tablespoons vegetable shortening, cut into 2 pieces and chilled
- 2 tablespoons vodka, chilled
- 2 tablespoons ice water

1. Process ¾ cups of the flour, the sugar, and salt together in a food processor until combined. Scatter the butter and shortening over the top and continue to process until incorporated and the mixture begins to form uneven clumps with no remaining floury bits, about 10 seconds.

2. Scrape down the workbowl and redistribute the dough evenly around the processor blade. Sprinkle the remaining ½ cup flour over the dough and pulse until the mixture has broken up into pieces and is evenly distributed around the bowl, 4 to 6 pulses.

3. Transfer the mixture to a medium bowl. Sprinkle the vodka and water over the mixture. Stir and press the dough together, using a stiff rubber spatula, until the dough sticks together.

4. Turn the dough onto a sheet of plastic wrap and flatten into a 4-inch disk. Wrap tightly in plastic wrap and refrigerate for 45 minutes or up to 2 days. Before rolling the dough out, let it sit on the counter to soften slightly, about 10 minutes.

BEHIND THE SCENES

YOU CAN NEVER HAVE ENOUGH RECIPES FOR PIE DOUGH

Viewers of our television show and readers of our recipes may wonder why we revisit the same recipes (roast chicken, mashed potatoes, and pie dough, to name a few) and develop alternate versions of them. Simply put, personal choice is a big factor. Take pie dough. There are few recipes that divide the test kitchen like the humble pie crust. Some in the test kitchen are purists when it comes to pie dough—they wouldn't dream of using anything but an all-butter dough. The flavor of our All-Butter Pie Dough (page 843) is undeniably buttery and delicious, but let's face it—this dough can be difficult to work with and isn't quite as flaky as a pie dough made with vegetable shortening. Next are the cooks who prefer the ease of working with a dough made with vegetable shortening as well as butter, like our Basic Pie Dough (page 842). Vegetable shortening, such as Crisco, is made from vegetable oil that has been hydrogenated, a process in which hydrogen gas is pumped into vegetable oil so it solidifies. Adding vegetable shortening makes the dough easier to work with and it does a good job of lightening and tenderizing the dough. That said, this pie dough still takes some patience to roll out.

The problem is that most pie dough recipes are stingy with the water (and thus really hard to roll out). Adding more water may seem to help matters, but once baked, the resulting crust is tougher. So to solve this problem, we developed a third pie dough, based on our Basic Pie Dough but with an unlikely ingredient—vodka.

While gluten (the protein that makes crust tough) forms readily in water, it doesn't form in ethanol, and vodka is 60 percent water and 40 percent ethanol. So adding ¼ cup of vodka and ¼ cup of water produces a moist, easy-to-roll dough that stays tender because the alcohol vaporizes in the oven, leaving the final crust with only about 6 tablespoons of water. This dough bakes into a crust that is tender and flavorful and that rolls out easily every time. For those in the test kitchen who demand an easy-to-roll pie dough, this is their dream recipe. (And for those who aren't practiced bakers and make a pie maybe once a year around the holidays, this dough makes a lot of sense.) Does that mean we're through developing pie doughs? Maybe, maybe not.

GRAHAM CRACKER CRUST

WHY THIS RECIPE WORKS: Saving time is always a good idea—just as long as you're not sacrificing quality. But while store-bought graham cracker pie crusts are tempting (all you have to do is fill, chill, then serve), they taste stale and bland. We wanted a fresh-tasting homemade crust that wasn't too sweet, with a crisp texture.

Turns out, a classic graham cracker crust couldn't be easier to make: Combine crushed crumbs with a little butter and sugar to bind them, then use a measuring cup or flat-bottomed glass to pack the crumbs into the pie plate. And producing a perfect graham cracker crust has a lot to do with the type of graham crackers used. After experimenting with the three leading brands, we discovered subtle but distinct differences among them and found that these differences carried over into crumb crusts made with each kind of cracker. Here in the test kitchen, we prefer Nabisco Original Graham Crackers for their hearty molasses flavor.

Graham Cracker Crust

MAKES ENOUGH FOR ONE 9-INCH PIE

We don't recommend using store-bought graham cracker crumbs here as they can often be stale. Be sure to note whether the crust needs to be warm or cool before filling (the pie recipes will specify) and plan accordingly.

- 8 whole graham crackers, broken into 1-inch pieces
- 5 tablespoons unsalted butter, melted and cooled
- 3 tablespoons sugar

1. Adjust an oven rack to the middle position and heat the oven to 325 degrees. Process the graham cracker pieces in a food processor to fine, even crumbs, about 30 seconds. Sprinkle the butter and sugar over the crumbs and pulse to incorporate.

2. Sprinkle the mixture into a 9-inch pie plate. Following the photo, use the bottom of a measuring cup to press the crumbs into an even layer on the bottom and sides of the pie plate. Bake until the crust is fragrant and beginning to brown, 13 to 18 minutes. Following the particular pie recipe, use the crust while it is still warm or let it cool completely.

NOTES FROM THE TEST KITCHEN

MAKING A GRAHAM CRACKER OR COOKIE CRUST

Press the crumb mixture firmly and evenly across the bottom of the pie plate, using the bottom of a measuring cup. Then tightly pack the crumbs against the sides of the pie plate, using your thumb and the measuring cup simultaneously.

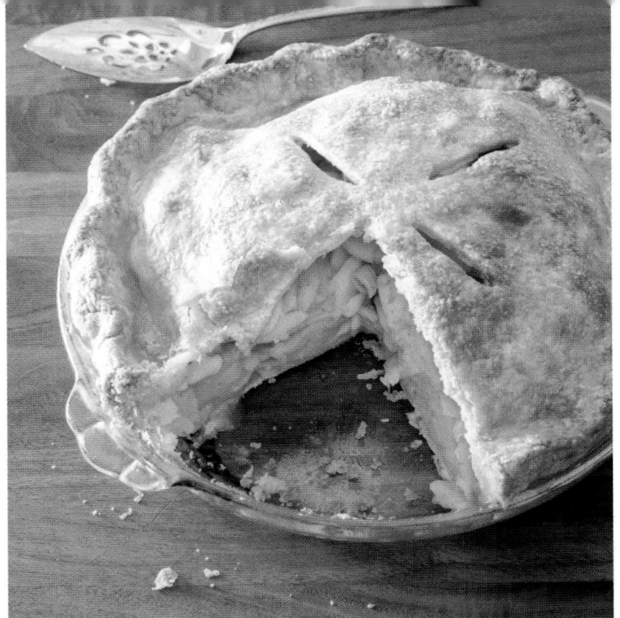

APPLE PIE

WHY THIS RECIPE WORKS: In the test kitchen, we have found that it's difficult to produce an apple pie with a filling that is tart as well as sweet and juicy. We wanted to develop a classic apple pie recipe—one with the clean, bright taste of apples that could be made year-round, based on apple types that are always available in the supermarket.

To arrive at the tartness and texture we were after, we had to use two kinds of apples in our pie, Granny Smith and McIntosh. The Grannies could be counted on for tartness and for keeping their shape during cooking; the Macs added flavor, and their otherwise frustrating tendency to become mushy was a virtue, providing a nice, juicy base for the harder Grannies. While many bakers add butter to their apple pie fillings, we found that it dulled the fresh taste of the apples and so did without it. Lemon juice, however, was essential, counterbalancing the sweetness of the apples. To give the apples the upper hand, we settled on quite modest amounts of cinnamon, nutmeg, and allspice.

Classic Apple Pie

SERVES 8

You can use All-Butter Double-Crust Pie Dough (page 843), Basic Double-Crust Pie Dough (page 842), or Foolproof Double-Crust Pie Dough (page 844) for this pie. The pie is best eaten when cooled to room temperature, or even the next day. Serve with vanilla ice cream or lightly sweetened whipped cream.

- 1 recipe double-crust pie dough (see note)
- 2 tablespoons unbleached all-purpose flour, plus extra for the work surface
- ¾ cup (5¼ ounces) plus 1 tablespoon sugar

- 1 teaspoon grated zest plus 1 tablespoon juice from 1 lemon
- ¼ teaspoon table salt
- ¼ teaspoon ground nutmeg
- ¼ teaspoon ground cinnamon
- ⅛ teaspoon ground allspice
- 2 pounds firm McIntosh apples (about 4 large), peeled, cored, and sliced ¼ inch thick
- 1½ pounds Granny Smith apples (about 3 large), peeled, cored, and sliced ¼ inch thick
- 1 large egg white, lightly beaten

1. Following the photos on page 842, roll one disk of dough into a 12-inch circle on a lightly floured work surface, then fit it into a 9-inch pie plate, letting the excess dough hang over the edge; cover with plastic wrap and refrigerate for 30 minutes. Roll the other disk of dough into a 12-inch circle on a lightly floured work surface, then transfer to a parchment-lined baking sheet; cover with plastic wrap and refrigerate for 30 minutes.

2. Adjust an oven rack to the lowest position and heat the oven to 500 degrees.

3. Mix the flour, ¾ cup of the sugar, the zest, salt, nutmeg, cinnamon, and allspice together in a large bowl. Add the lemon juice and apples and toss until combined. Spread the apples with their juice into the dough-lined pie plate, mounding them slightly in the middle. Following the photos on page 848, loosely roll the second piece of dough around the rolling pin and gently unroll it over the pie. Trim, fold, and crimp the edges, and cut four vent holes in the top. Brush the dough with the egg white and sprinkle with the remaining 1 tablespoon sugar.

4. Place the pie on a rimmed baking sheet, reduce the oven temperature to 425 degrees, and bake until the crust is golden, about 25 minutes. Reduce the oven temperature to 375 degrees, rotate the baking sheet, and continue to bake until the juices are bubbling and the crust is deep golden brown, 35 to 45 minutes longer. Cool the pie on a wire rack to room temperature, about 4 hours. Serve.

Apple Pie with Crystallized Ginger

Follow the recipe for Classic Apple Pie, adding 3 tablespoons chopped crystallized ginger to the apple mixture.

Apple Pie with Dried Fruit

Toss 1 cup raisins, dried sweet cherries, or dried cranberries with the lemon juice plus 1 tablespoon applejack, brandy, or cognac. Follow the recipe for Classic Apple Pie, adding the dried fruit and liquid to the apple mixture.

Apple Pie with Fresh Cranberries

Follow the recipe for Classic Apple Pie, increasing the sugar to 1 cup (7 ounces) and adding 1 cup fresh or frozen cranberries to the apple mixture.

DEEP-DISH APPLE PIE

WHY THIS RECIPE WORKS: The problem with deep-dish apple pie is that the apples are often unevenly cooked and the exuded juice leaves the apples swimming in liquid, producing a bottom crust that is pale and soggy. Then there is the gaping hole left between the apples (which are shrunken from the loss of all that moisture) and the arching top crust, making it impossible to slice and serve a neat piece of pie. We wanted our piece of deep-dish pie to be a towering wedge of tender, juicy apples, fully framed by a buttery, flaky crust. Precooking the apples solved the shrinking problem, helped the apples hold their shape, and prevented juices from collecting in the bottom of the pie plate, giving us a nicely browned bottom crust. All that was left to do was to choose the right combination of apples and stir in a little brown sugar, salt, lemon, and cinnamon, for flavor and sweetness.

Deep-Dish Apple Pie

SERVES 8

You can use All-Butter Double-Crust Pie Dough (page 843), Basic Double-Crust Pie Dough (page 842), or Foolproof Double-Crust Pie Dough (page 844) for this pie. Use a combination of tart and sweet apples for this pie. Good choices for tart are Granny Smiths, Empires, or Cortlands; for sweet we recommend Golden Delicious, Jonagolds, or Braeburns. Serve with vanilla ice cream or lightly sweetened whipped cream.

- 1 recipe double-crust pie dough (see note)
- Unbleached all-purpose flour, for the work surface
- 2½ pounds firm tart apples (about 5 large), peeled, cored, and sliced ¼ inch thick (see note)
- 2½ pounds firm sweet apples (about 5 large), peeled, cored, and sliced ¼ inch thick (see note)
- ½ cup (3½ ounces) plus 1 tablespoon granulated sugar
- ¼ cup packed (1¾ ounces) light brown sugar
- ½ teaspoon grated zest plus 1 tablespoon juice from 1 lemon
- ¼ teaspoon table salt
- ⅛ teaspoon ground cinnamon
- 1 large egg white, lightly beaten

1. Following the photos on page 842, roll one disk of dough into a 12-inch circle on a lightly floured work surface, then fit it into a 9-inch pie plate, letting the excess dough hang over the edge; cover with plastic wrap and refrigerate for 30 minutes. Roll the other disk of dough into a 12-inch circle on a lightly floured work surface, then transfer to a parchment-lined baking sheet; cover with plastic wrap and refrigerate for 30 minutes.

2. Toss the apples, ½ cup of the granulated sugar, the brown sugar, zest, salt, and cinnamon together in a Dutch oven. Cover and cook over medium heat, stirring frequently, until the apples are tender when poked with a fork but still hold their shape, 15 to 20 minutes. Transfer the apples and their juice to a rimmed baking sheet and cool to room temperature, about 30 minutes.

3. Adjust an oven rack to the lowest position and heat the oven to 425 degrees. Drain the cooled apples thoroughly through a colander, reserving ¼ cup of the juice. Stir the lemon juice into the reserved ¼ cup apple juice.

4. Spread the apples into the dough-lined pie plate, mounding them slightly in the middle, and drizzle with the lemon juice mixture. Following the photos, loosely roll the second piece of dough around the rolling pin and gently unroll it over the pie. Trim, fold, and crimp the edges and cut four vent holes in the top. Brush the dough with the egg white and sprinkle with the remaining 1 tablespoon sugar.

5. Place the pie on a rimmed baking sheet and bake until the crust is golden, about 25 minutes. Reduce the oven temperature to 375 degrees, rotate the baking sheet, and continue to bake until the juices are bubbling and the crust is deep golden brown, 30 to 40 minutes longer. Cool the pie on a wire rack until the filling has set, about 2 hours; serve slightly warm or at room temperature.

NOTES FROM THE TEST KITCHEN

MAKING A DOUBLE-CRUST PIE

1. Loosely roll the chilled top crust around the rolling pin, then gently unroll it over the filled pie crust bottom.

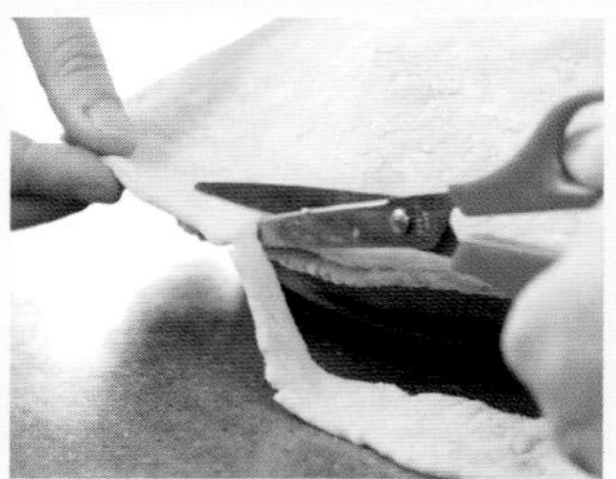

2. Using scissors, trim all but ½ inch of the dough overhanging the edge of the pie plate.

3. Press the top and bottom crusts together, then tuck the edges underneath.

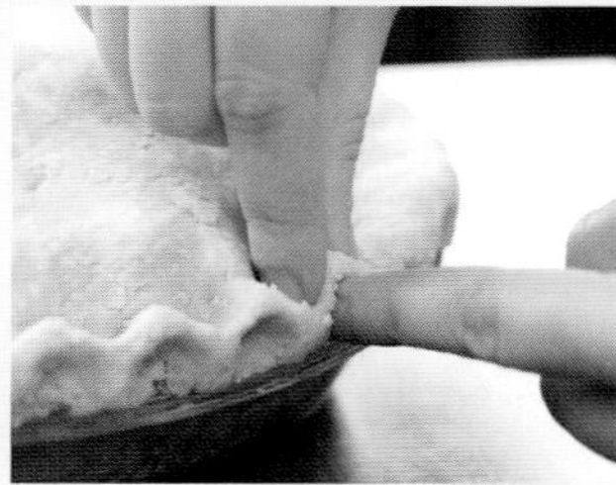

4. Crimp the dough evenly around the edge of the pie, using your fingers. Cut vent holes attractively in the center of the top crust with a paring knife (drier pies only require four vents, while very juicy pies require eight vents).

FRESH PEACH PIE

WHY THIS RECIPE WORKS: Juicy summer peaches often produce soupy peach pies, and the amount of moisture changes from pie to pie. To control the moisture, we macerated the peaches to draw out some of their juices and then added a measured amount back to the filling. Cornstarch and pectin helped hold the filling together without making it gluey or bouncy, and mashing some of the peaches helped make neat, attractive slices. A buttery, tender lattice-top crust allowed moisture to evaporate and made for an impressive presentation.

Fresh Peach Pie

SERVES 8

If your peaches are too soft to withstand the pressure of a peeler, cut a shallow X in the bottom of the fruit, blanch them in a pot of simmering water for 15 seconds, and then shock them in a bowl of ice water before peeling. For fruit pectin we recommend both Sure-Jell for Less or No Sugar Needed Recipes and Ball RealFruit Low or No-Sugar Needed Pectin. For illustrations of our no-weave lattice, see page 849.

- 3 pounds peaches, peeled, quartered, and pitted, each quarter cut into thirds
- ½ cup (3½ ounces) plus 3 tablespoons sugar
- 1 teaspoon grated lemon zest plus 1 tablespoon juice
- ⅛ teaspoon salt
- 2 tablespoons low- or no-sugar-needed fruit pectin
- ¼ teaspoon ground cinnamon
- Pinch ground nutmeg
- 1 recipe Pie Dough for Lattice-Top Pie (recipe follows)
- 1 tablespoon cornstarch

1. Toss peaches, ½ cup sugar, lemon zest and juice, and salt in medium bowl. Let stand at room temperature for at least 30 minutes or up to 1 hour. Combine pectin, cinnamon, nutmeg, and 2 tablespoons sugar in small bowl and set aside.

2. Remove dough from refrigerator. Before rolling out dough, let it sit on counter to soften slightly, about 10 minutes. Roll 1 disk of dough into 12-inch circle on lightly floured counter. Transfer to parchment paper–lined baking sheet. With pizza wheel, fluted pastry wheel, or paring knife, cut round into ten 1¼-inch-wide strips. Freeze strips on sheet until firm, about 30 minutes.

3. Adjust oven rack to lowest position, place rimmed baking sheet on rack, and heat oven to 425 degrees. Roll other disk of dough into 12-inch circle on lightly floured counter. Loosely roll dough around rolling pin and gently unroll it onto 9-inch pie plate, letting excess dough hang over edge. Ease dough into plate by gently lifting edge of dough with your hand while pressing into plate bottom with your other hand. Leave any dough that overhangs plate in place. Wrap dough-lined pie plate loosely in plastic wrap and refrigerate until dough is firm, about 30 minutes.

4. Meanwhile, transfer 1 cup peach mixture to small bowl and mash with fork until coarse paste forms. Drain remaining peach mixture through colander set in large bowl. Transfer

peach juice to liquid measuring cup (you should have about ½ cup liquid; if liquid measures more than ½ cup, discard remainder). Return peach pieces to bowl and toss with cornstarch. Transfer peach juice to 12-inch skillet, add pectin mixture, and whisk until combined. Cook over medium heat, stirring occasionally, until slightly thickened and pectin is dissolved (liquid should become less cloudy), 3 to 5 minutes. Remove skillet from heat, add peach pieces and peach paste, and toss to combine.

5. Transfer peach mixture to dough-lined pie plate. Remove dough strips from freezer; if too stiff to be workable, let stand at room temperature until malleable and softened slightly but still very cold. Lay 2 longest strips across center of pie perpendicular to each other. Using 4 shortest strips, lay 2 strips across pie parallel to 1 center strip and 2 strips parallel to other center strip, near edges of pie; you should have 6 strips in place. Using remaining 4 strips, lay each one across pie parallel and equidistant from center and edge strips. If dough becomes too soft to work with, refrigerate pie and dough strips until dough firms up.

6. Trim overhang to ½ inch beyond lip of pie plate. Press edges of bottom crust and lattice strips together and fold under. Folded edge should be flush with edge of pie plate. Crimp dough evenly around edge of pie using your fingers. Using spray bottle, evenly mist lattice with water and sprinkle with remaining 1 tablespoon sugar.

7. Place pie on rimmed baking sheet and bake until crust is set and begins to brown, about 25 minutes. Reduce oven temperature to 375 degrees, rotate sheet, and continue to bake until crust is deep golden brown and filling is bubbly at center, 30 to 40 minutes longer. Let pie cool on wire rack for 3 hours before serving.

Pie Dough for Lattice-Top Pie

MAKES ENOUGH FOR ONE 9-INCH PIE

- 3 cups (15 ounces) all-purpose flour
- 2 tablespoons sugar
- 1 teaspoon salt
- 7 tablespoons vegetable shortening, cut into ½-inch pieces and chilled
- 10 tablespoons unsalted butter, cut into ¼-inch pieces and frozen for 30 minutes
- 10–12 tablespoons ice water

1. Process flour, sugar, and salt in food processor until combined, about 5 seconds. Scatter shortening over top and process until mixture resembles coarse cornmeal, about 10 seconds. Scatter butter over top and pulse until mixture resembles coarse crumbs, about 10 pulses. Transfer to bowl.

2. Sprinkle 5 tablespoons ice water over flour mixture. With rubber spatula, use folding motion to evenly combine water and flour mixture. Sprinkle 5 tablespoons ice water over mixture and continue using folding motion to combine until small portion of dough holds together when squeezed in palm of your hand, adding up to 2 tablespoons remaining ice water if necessary. (Dough should feel quite moist.) Turn out dough onto clean, dry counter and gently press together into cohesive ball. Divide dough into 2 even pieces and flatten each into 4-inch disk. Wrap disks tightly in plastic wrap and refrigerate for 1 hour or up to 2 days.

NOTES FROM THE TEST KITCHEN

BUILDING A "NO-WEAVE" LATTICE TOP

Making a lattice top for our Fresh Peach Pie can be intimidating. But it need not be if you use our simple technique: Freeze strips of dough and then arrange them in a particular order over the filling. Done properly, our approach gives the illusion of a woven lattice with less effort.

1. Roll dough into 12-inch circle, transfer to parchment paper-lined baking sheet, and cut into ten 1¼-inch-wide strips with a fluted pastry wheel, pizza wheel, or paring knife. Freeze for 30 minutes.

2. Lay 2 longest strips perpendicular to each other across center of pie to form cross. Place 4 shorter strips along edges of pie, parallel to center strips.

3. Lay 4 remaining strips between each edge strip and center strip. Trim off excess lattice ends, press edges of bottom crust and lattice strips together, and fold under.

STRAWBERRY PIE

WHY THIS RECIPE WORKS: Because uncooked berries shed so much liquid, the filling for strawberry pie is usually firmed up with a thickener, which produces results that range from stiff and bouncy to runny and gloppy. We wanted a strawberry pie featuring fresh berries lightly held together by a sheer, glossy glaze in a buttery shell. We knew that the success of our strawberry pie hinged on getting the thickener just right. When none of the thickeners we tried worked on their own, we decided to use a combination of two: pectin (in the form of a homemade strawberry jam) and cornstarch. By themselves, pectin produced a filling that was too firm and cornstarch one that was too loose, but together they created just the right supple, lightly clingy glaze. Fresh, flavorful strawberries make this dessert a perfect summery treat.

Fresh Strawberry Pie

SERVES 8

To account for any imperfect strawberries, the ingredient list calls for several more ounces of berries than will be used in the pie. If possible, seek out ripe, farmers' market–quality berries. Make sure to thoroughly dry the strawberries after washing. Make certain that you use fruit pectin engineered for low- or no-sugar recipes (we recommend Sure-Jell Premium Fruit Pectin) and not regular pectin; otherwise, the glaze will not set properly. The pie is at its best after two or three hours of chilling; as it continues to chill, the glaze becomes softer and wetter, though the pie will taste just as good.

- 1 recipe Foolproof Single-Crust Pie Dough (page 845), fitted into a 9-inch pie plate and chilled
- 3 pounds strawberries, hulled (9 cups)
- ¾ cup (5¼ ounces) sugar
- 2 tablespoons cornstarch
- 1½ teaspoons Sure-Jell for low-sugar recipes (see note)
- Pinch table salt
- 1 tablespoon juice from 1 lemon
- 1 cup heavy cream, cold
- 1 tablespoon sugar

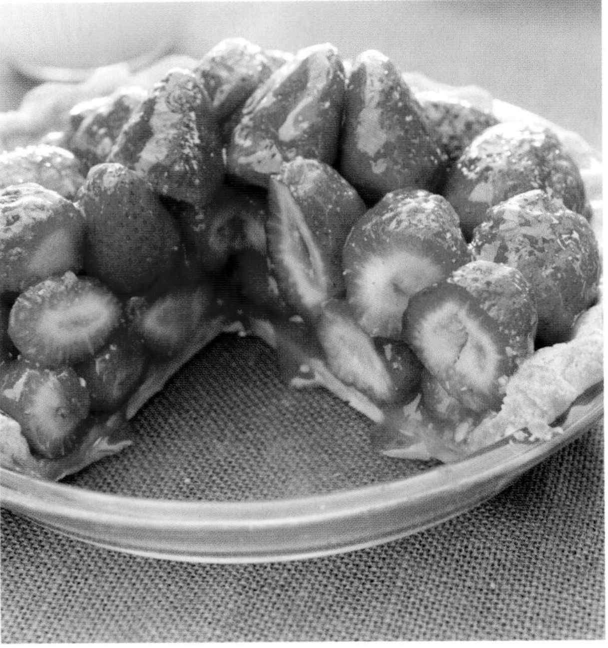

1. Adjust an oven rack to the middle position and heat the oven to 375 degrees. Following the photos on page 856, line the chilled pie shell with a double layer of foil and fill with pie weights.

2. Bake until the pie dough looks dry and is light in color, 25 to 30 minutes. Remove the weights and foil and continue to bake the crust until deep golden brown, 10 to 12 minutes longer. Transfer the pie plate to a wire rack and let cool completely, about 1 hour.

3. Select 6 ounces misshapen, underripe, or otherwise unattractive berries, halving those that are large; you should have about 1½ cups. Process the berries in a food processor to a smooth puree, 20 to 30 seconds, scraping down the bowl as needed (you should have about ¾ cup puree).

4. Whisk the sugar, cornstarch, Sure-Jell, and salt together in a medium saucepan. Stir in the berry puree, making sure to scrape the corners of the pan. Cook over medium-high heat, stirring constantly, and bring to a boil. Boil, scraping the bottom and sides of the pan to prevent scorching, for 2 minutes to ensure that the cornstarch is fully cooked (the mixture will appear frothy when it first reaches a boil, then will darken and thicken with further cooking). Transfer the glaze to a large bowl and stir in the lemon juice; let cool to room temperature.

5. Meanwhile, pick over the remaining berries and measure out 2 pounds of the most attractive ones; halve only any extra-large berries. Add the berries to the bowl with the glaze and fold gently with a rubber spatula until the berries are evenly coated. Scoop the berries into the cooled prebaked pie shell, piling into a mound. If any cut sides face up on top, turn them face down. If necessary, rearrange the berries so that holes are filled and the mound looks attractive. Refrigerate the pie until the filling is chilled and has set, about 2 hours. Serve within 5 hours of chilling.

6. Just before serving, beat the cream and sugar with an electric mixer on low speed until small bubbles form, about 30 seconds. Increase the speed to medium; continue beating until the beaters leave a trail, about 30 additional seconds. Increase the speed to high; continue beating until the cream is smooth, thick, and nearly doubled in volume and forms soft peaks, 30 to 60 seconds.

7. Cut the pie into wedges and serve with whipped cream.

STRAWBERRY-RHUBARB PIE

WHY THIS RECIPE WORKS: The key to pairing sweet strawberries and tart rhubarb in a pie is to keep their high water content in check. Microwaving rhubarb pieces with sugar allowed them to shed some liquid. We tossed in some of our cut strawberries to macerate among the microwaved

rhubarb and used the juices to create a jammy filling. We cooked the rest of the cut strawberries in the liquid, softening them until they were easy to mash into a jam. Adding tapioca to the filling mixture gelatinized the juices, protecting the crust from turning soggy. A sugary crust offered a contrast to the tart rhubarb, and brushing the surface with water before sprinkling it with sugar ensured the granules stayed put during baking.

Strawberry-Rhubarb Pie

SERVES 8

This dough is unusually moist and requires a full ¼ cup of flour when rolling it out to prevent it from sticking. Rhubarb varies in the amount of trimming required. Buy 2 pounds to ensure that you end up with 7 cups of rhubarb pieces. For tips on crimping the dough, see page 843. If desired, serve the pie with whipped cream or ice cream.

CRUST

- 2½ cups (12½ ounces) all-purpose flour
- 2 tablespoons sugar, plus 3 tablespoons for sprinkling
- 1 teaspoon salt
- 12 tablespoons unsalted butter, cut into ¼-inch slices and chilled
- ½ cup vegetable shortening, cut into 4 pieces and chilled
- ¼ cup vodka, chilled
- ¼ cup cold water, plus extra for brushing

FILLING

- 2 pounds rhubarb, trimmed and cut into ½-inch pieces (7 cups)
- 1¼ cups (8¾ ounces) sugar
- 1 pound strawberries, hulled, halved if less than 1 inch, quartered if more than 1 inch (3 to 4 cups)
- 3 tablespoons instant tapioca

1. FOR THE CRUST: Process 1½ cups flour, 2 tablespoons sugar, and salt in food processor until combined, about 5 seconds. Scatter butter and shortening over top and process until incorporated and mixture begins to form uneven clumps with no remaining floury bits, about 15 seconds.

2. Scrape down sides of bowl and redistribute dough evenly around processor blade. Sprinkle remaining 1 cup flour over dough and pulse until mixture has broken up into pieces and is evenly distributed around bowl, 4 to 6 pulses.

3. Transfer mixture to large bowl. Sprinkle vodka and cold water over mixture. Using rubber spatula, stir and press dough until it sticks together.

4. Divide dough in half. Turn each half onto sheet of plastic wrap and form into 4-inch disk. Wrap disks tightly in plastic and refrigerate for 1 hour. Let chilled dough sit on counter to soften slightly, about 10 minutes, before rolling. (Wrapped dough can be refrigerated for up to 2 days or frozen for up to 1 month. If frozen, let dough thaw completely on counter before rolling.)

5. FOR THE FILLING: While dough chills, combine rhubarb and sugar in bowl and microwave for 1½ minutes. Stir and continue to microwave until sugar is mostly dissolved, about 1 minute longer. Stir in 1 cup strawberries and set aside for 30 minutes, stirring once halfway through.

6. Drain rhubarb mixture through fine-mesh strainer set over large saucepan. Return drained rhubarb mixture to bowl and set aside. Add remaining strawberries to rhubarb liquid and cook over medium-high heat until strawberries are very soft and mixture is reduced to 1½ cups, about 10 to 15 minutes. Mash berries with fork (mixture does not have to be smooth). Add strawberry mixture and tapioca to drained rhubarb mixture and stir to combine. Set aside.

7. Roll 1 disk of dough into 12-inch circle on well-floured counter. Loosely roll dough around rolling pin and gently unroll onto 9-inch pie plate, letting excess dough hang over edge. Ease dough into plate by gently lifting edge of dough with your hand while pressing into plate bottom with your other hand. Wrap dough-lined plate loosely in plastic and refrigerate until dough is firm, about 30 minutes.

8. Roll other disk of dough into 12-inch circle on well-floured counter, then transfer to parchment paper–lined baking sheet; cover with plastic and refrigerate for 30 minutes. Adjust rack to middle position and heat oven to 425 degrees.

9. Transfer filling to chilled dough-lined plate and spread into even layer. Loosely roll remaining dough round around rolling pin and gently unroll it onto filling. Trim overhang to ½ inch beyond lip of plate. Pinch edges of top and bottom crusts firmly together. Tuck overhang under itself; folded edge should be flush with edge of plate. Crimp dough evenly around edge of plate using your fingers or butter knife. Brush surface thoroughly with extra water and sprinkle with 3 tablespoons sugar. Cut eight 2-inch slits in top crust.

10. Place pie on parchment-lined rimmed baking sheet and bake until crust is set and begins to brown, about 25 minutes. Rotate pie and reduce oven temperature to 375 degrees; continue to bake until crust is deep golden brown and filling is bubbling, 30 to 40 minutes longer. If edges of pie begin to get too brown before pie is done, cover loosely with aluminum foil. Let cool on wire rack for 2½ hours before serving.

BLUEBERRY PIE

WHY THIS RECIPE WORKS: If the filling in blueberry pie doesn't jell, a sliced wedge can collapse into a soupy puddle topped by a sodden crust. Too much thickener and the filling can be so dense that cutting into it is like slicing through gummi bears. We wanted a pie that had a firm, glistening filling full of fresh, bright flavor and still-plump berries.

To thicken the pie, we favored tapioca because it didn't mute the fresh yet subtle blueberry flavor as cornstarch and flour did. The back of the tapioca box recommended 6 tablespoons, but this produced a stiff, congealed mass. Cooking and reducing half of the berries helped us cut down on the tapioca required, but not enough. A second inspiration came from a peeled and grated Granny Smith apple. Apples are high in pectin, a type of carbohydrate that acts as a thickener when cooked. Combined with a modest 2 tablespoons of tapioca, the apple thickened the filling to a soft, even consistency that was neither gelatinous nor slippery. The crust posed a much simpler challenge. As with all of our fruit pies, baking on a rimmed baking sheet on the bottom oven rack produced a crisp, golden bottom crust. And we found a fast, easy alternative to a lattice top in a small biscuit cutter, which we used to cut out circles in the top crust before transferring the dough onto the pie. The attractive, unusual-looking top crust vented the steam from the berries as successfully as a classic lattice top.

Blueberry Pie

SERVES 8

You can use All-Butter Double-Crust Pie Dough (page 843), Basic Double-Crust Pie Dough (page 842), or Foolproof Double-Crust Pie Dough (page 844) for this pie. This recipe was developed using fresh blueberries, but unthawed frozen blueberries (our favorite brands are Wyman's and Cascadian Farm) will work as well. In step 3, cook half the frozen berries over medium-high heat, without mashing, until reduced to 1¼ cups, 12 to 15 minutes. Grind the tapioca to a powder in a spice grinder or mini food processor. If using pearl tapioca, reduce the amount to 5 teaspoons. Serve with vanilla ice cream or lightly sweetened whipped cream.

- 1 recipe double-crust pie dough (see note)
- Unbleached all-purpose flour, for the work surface
- 6 cups (30 ounces) fresh blueberries (see note)
- 1 Granny Smith apple, peeled, cored, and shredded on the large holes of a box grater
- ¾ cup (5¼ ounces) sugar
- 2 tablespoons instant tapioca, ground (see note)
- 2 teaspoons grated zest plus 2 teaspoons juice from 1 lemon
- Pinch table salt
- 2 tablespoons unsalted butter, cut into ¼-inch pieces
- 1 large egg white, lightly beaten

1. Following the photos on page 842, roll one disk of dough into a 12-inch circle on a lightly floured work surface, then fit it into a 9-inch pie plate, letting the excess dough hang over the edge; cover with plastic wrap and refrigerate for 30 minutes.

2. Roll the other disk of dough into a 12-inch circle on a lightly floured work surface. Following the photo, use a 1¼-inch round biscuit cutter to cut a round from the center of the dough. Cut 6 more rounds from the dough, 1½ inches from the edge of the center hole and equally spaced around the center hole. Transfer the dough to a parchment-lined baking sheet; cover with plastic wrap and refrigerate for 30 minutes.

3. Place 3 cups of the berries in a medium saucepan and set over medium heat. Using a potato masher, mash the berries several times to release the juices. Continue to cook, stirring

NOTES FROM THE TEST KITCHEN

MAKING A CUT-OUT CRUST

1. Use a 1¼-inch round biscuit cutter (or spice jar lid) to cut holes in the dough.

2. The cut-out crust vents the steam from the berry filling and is an easy alternative to a lattice-top pie.

frequently and mashing occasionally, until about half of the berries have broken down and the mixture is thickened and reduced to 1½ cups, about 8 minutes. Cool slightly.

4. Adjust an oven rack to the lowest position and heat the oven to 400 degrees.

5. Place the shredded apple in a clean kitchen towel and wring dry. Transfer the apple to a large bowl and stir in the cooked berries, remaining 3 cups uncooked berries, sugar, tapioca, lemon zest and juice, and salt until combined. Spread the mixture into the dough-lined pie plate and scatter the butter pieces over the top.

6. Following the photos on page 848, loosely roll the second piece of dough around the rolling pin and gently unroll it over the pie. Trim, fold, and crimp the edges. Brush the dough with the egg white.

7. Place the pie on a rimmed baking sheet and bake until the crust is golden, about 25 minutes. Reduce the oven temperature to 350 degrees, rotate the baking sheet, and continue to bake until the juices are bubbling and the crust is deep golden brown, 35 to 50 minutes longer. Cool the pie on a wire rack to room temperature, about 4 hours. Serve.

SUMMER BERRY PIE

WHY THIS RECIPE WORKS: A fresh berry pie might seem like an easy-to-pull-off summer dessert, but most of the recipes we tried buried the berries in gluey thickeners or embedded them in bouncy gelatin. We wanted a simple pie with great texture and flavor. We started with the test kitchen's quick and easy homemade graham cracker crust. For the filling, we used a combination of raspberries, blackberries, and blueberries. After trying a few different methods, we found a solution that both bound the berries in the graham cracker crust and intensified their bright flavor. We processed a portion of berries in the food processor until they made a smooth puree, then we thickened the puree with cornstarch. Next, we tossed the remaining berries with warm jelly for a glossy coat and a shot of sweetness. Pressed gently into the puree, the berries stayed put and tasted great.

Summer Berry Pie

SERVES 8

Feel free to vary the amount of each berry as desired as long as you have 6 cups of berries total; do not substitute frozen berries here. Serve with lightly sweetened whipped cream.

- 2 cups (10 ounces) raspberries (see note)
- 2 cups (10 ounces) blackberries (see note)
- 2 cups (10 ounces) blueberries (see note)
- ½ cup (3½ ounces) sugar
- 3 tablespoons cornstarch
- ⅛ teaspoon table salt
- 1 tablespoon juice from 1 lemon
- 1 recipe Graham Cracker Crust (page 846), baked and cooled
- 2 tablespoons red currant or apple jelly

1. Gently toss the berries together in a large bowl. Process 2½ cups of the berries in a food processor until very smooth, about 1 minute (do not under-process). Strain the puree through a fine-mesh strainer into a small saucepan, pressing on the solids to extract as much puree as possible (you should have about 1½ cups); discard the solids.

2. In a small bowl, whisk the sugar, cornstarch, and salt together, then whisk into the strained puree. Bring the puree to a boil over medium heat, stirring constantly, and cook until it is as thick as pudding, about 7 minutes. Off the heat, stir in the lemon juice and set aside to cool slightly.

3. Pour the warm berry puree into the baked and cooled pie crust. Melt the jelly in a small saucepan over low heat, then pour over the remaining 3½ cups berries and toss to coat. Spread the berries evenly over the puree and lightly press them into the puree. Cover the pie loosely with plastic wrap and refrigerate until the filling is chilled and set, about 3 hours. Serve chilled or at room temperature.

CHERRY PIE

WHY THIS RECIPE WORKS: Great cherry pie is typically made with sour cherries because their soft, juicy flesh and bright, punchy flavor isn't dulled by oven heat or sugar. But cherry season is cruelly short and chances are the cherries that are available are the sweet variety. Sweet cherries have mellower flavors and meaty, firm flesh—traits that make them ideal for eating straight off the stem but don't translate well to baking. Our challenge was obvious: Develop a recipe for sweet cherry pie with all the intense, jammy flavor and softened but still intact fruit texture of the best sour cherry pie.

To mimic the bright, tart flavor of a sour cherry pie filling, we supplemented sweet cherries with chopped plums, which are tart and helped tame the cherries' sweet flavor. To fix the texture problem, we cut the cherries in half to expose their sturdy flesh. This step encouraged the cherries to soften and give up their juices. A splash of bourbon and lemon juice also offset the sweetness and added flavorful depth. To keep the filling juicy, rather than dry, we switched out the typical lattice pie crust in favor of a traditional top crust, which prevented any moisture from evaporating.

Sweet Cherry Pie

SERVES 8

You can use All-Butter Double-Crust Pie Dough (page 843), Basic Double-Crust Pie Dough (page 842), or Foolproof Double-Crust Pie Dough (page 844) for this recipe. The tapioca should be measured first, then ground in a coffee grinder or food processor for 30 seconds. If you are using frozen fruit, measure it frozen, but let it thaw before filling the pie. If not, you run the risk of partially cooked fruit and undissolved tapioca.

- 1 recipe double-crust pie dough (see note)
- Unbleached all-purpose flour, for the work surface
- 2 red plums, halved and pitted
- 6 cups (about 2 pounds) pitted sweet cherries or 6 cups pitted frozen cherries, halved (see note)
- ½ cup (3½ ounces) sugar
- ⅛ teaspoon table salt
- 1 tablespoon juice from 1 lemon
- 2 teaspoons bourbon (optional)
- 2 tablespoons instant tapioca, ground (see note)
- ⅛ teaspoon ground cinnamon (optional)
- 2 tablespoons unsalted butter, cut into ¼-inch pieces
- 1 large egg, lightly beaten with 1 teaspoon water

1. Following the photos on page 842, roll one disk of the dough into a 12-inch circle on a lightly floured work surface, then fit it into a 9-inch pie plate, letting the excess dough hang over the edge; cover with plastic wrap and refrigerate for 30 minutes. Roll the other disk of dough into a 12-inch circle on a lightly floured work surface, then transfer to a parchment-lined baking sheet; cover with plastic wrap and refrigerate for 30 minutes.

2. Adjust an oven rack to the lowest position and heat the oven to 400 degrees. Process the plums and 1 cup of the halved cherries in a food processor until smooth, about 1 minute, scraping down the sides of the bowl as necessary. Strain the puree through a fine-mesh strainer into a large bowl, pressing on the solids to extract the liquid; discard the solids. Stir in the remaining 5 cups halved cherries, sugar, salt, lemon juice, bourbon (if using), tapioca, and cinnamon (if using) into the puree; let stand for 15 minutes.

3. Transfer the cherry mixture, including all the juices, to the dough-lined plate. Scatter the butter pieces over the fruit. Following the photos on page 848, loosely roll the second piece of dough around the rolling pin and gently unroll it over the pie. Trim, fold, and crimp the edges, and cut eight evenly spaced vent holes in the top. Brush the dough with the egg mixture. Freeze the pie for 20 minutes.

4. Place the pie on a rimmed baking sheet and bake for 30 minutes. Reduce the oven temperature to 350 degrees and continue to bake until the juices bubble and the crust is deep golden brown, 35 to 50 minutes longer.

5. Cool the pie on a wire rack to room temperature, about 4 hours, before serving.

PUMPKIN PIE

WHY THIS RECIPE WORKS: Too often, pumpkin pie appears at the end of a Thanksgiving meal as a grainy, overspiced, canned-pumpkin custard encased in a soggy crust. We wanted to create a pumpkin pie recipe destined to be a new classic: velvety smooth, packed with pumpkin flavor, and redolent of just enough fragrant spices.

Canned pumpkin contains moisture, which dilutes a pie's flavor. To maximize flavor, we concentrated this liquid by cooking the pumpkin with sugar and spices, then whisked in heavy cream, milk, and eggs. This improved the flavor and the hot filling let the custard firm up quickly in the oven, preventing it from soaking into the crust. For spices, we chose nutmeg, cinnamon, and, surprisingly, freshly grated ginger. Sugar and maple syrup sweetened things, but tasters still craved a more complex pie. On a whim, we added mashed roasted yams to the filling and tasters appreciated the deeper flavor. To streamline the recipe we switched to canned candied yams and cooked them with the pumpkin. To keep the custard from curdling, we started the pie at a high temperature for 10 minutes, followed by a reduced temperature for the remainder of the baking time. This cut the baking time to less than one hour and the dual temperatures produced a creamy pie fully and evenly cooked from edge to center.

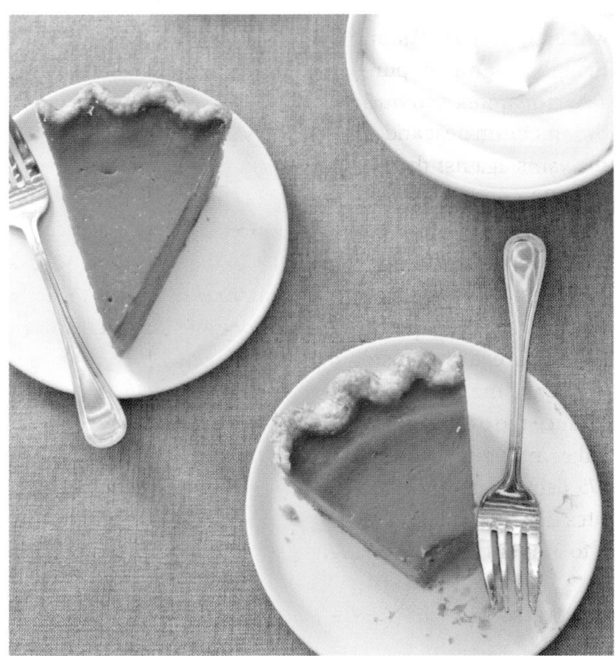

Pumpkin Pie

SERVES 8

If candied yams are unavailable, regular canned yams can be substituted. When the pie is properly baked, the center 2 inches of the pie should look firm but jiggle slightly. The pie finishes cooking with residual heat; to ensure that the filling sets, cool it at room temperature and not in the refrigerator. The crust and filling must both be warm when the filling is added. Serve with lightly sweetened whipped cream.

- 1 recipe Basic Single-Crust Pie Dough (page 842), fitted into a 9-inch pie plate and chilled
- 1 cup heavy cream
- 1 cup whole milk
- 3 large whole eggs plus 2 large egg yolks
- 1 teaspoon vanilla extract
- 1 (15-ounce) can pumpkin puree
- 1 cup candied yams, drained (see note)
- ¾ cup (5¼ ounces) sugar
- ¼ cup maple syrup
- 2 teaspoons grated or minced fresh ginger
- 1 teaspoon table salt
- ½ teaspoon ground cinnamon
- ¼ teaspoon ground nutmeg

1. Adjust an oven rack to the middle position and heat the oven to 375 degrees. Following the photos on page 856, line the chilled pie shell with a double layer of foil and fill with pie weights.

2. Bake until the pie dough looks dry and is light in color, 25 to 30 minutes. Remove the weights and foil and continue to bake the crust until deep golden brown, 10 to 12 minutes longer. Transfer the pie plate to a wire rack. (The crust must still be warm when the filling is added.)

3. While the pie shell is baking, whisk the cream, milk, whole eggs, egg yolks, and vanilla together in a medium bowl. Bring the pumpkin puree, yams, sugar, maple syrup, ginger, salt, cinnamon, and nutmeg to a simmer in a large saucepan over medium heat and cook, stirring constantly and mashing the yams against the sides of the pot, until thick and shiny, 15 to 20 minutes.

4. Remove the pan from the heat and whisk in the cream mixture until fully incorporated. Strain the mixture through a fine-mesh strainer set over a medium bowl, using the back of a ladle or spatula to press the solids through the strainer. Whisk the mixture, then transfer to the warm prebaked pie crust.

5. Bake the pie on a rimmed baking sheet for 10 minutes. Reduce the oven temperature to 300 degrees and continue to bake until the edges of the pie are set and the center registers 175 degrees on an instant-read thermometer, 25 to 45 minutes longer. Cool the pie on a wire rack to room temperature, 2 to 3 hours, before serving.

PECAN PIE

WHY THIS RECIPE WORKS: Pecan pies can be overwhelmingly sweet, with no real pecan flavor. And they too often turn out curdled and separated. What's more, the weepy filling makes the bottom crust soggy and leathery. The fact that the crust usually seems underbaked to begin with doesn't help matters. We wanted to create a recipe for a not-too-sweet pie with a smooth-textured filling and a properly baked bottom crust.

We tackled this pie's problems by using brown sugar and reducing the amount, which helped bring out the pecan flavor. We also partially baked the crust, which kept it crisp. We found that it's important to add the hot filling to a warm pie crust as this helps keep the crust from getting soggy. In addition, we discovered that simulating a double boiler when you're melting the butter and making the filling is an easy way to maintain gentle heat, which helps ensure that the filling doesn't curdle.

Pecan Pie

SERVES 8

The crust must still be warm when the filling is added. To serve the pie warm, cool it thoroughly so that it sets completely, then warm it in a 250-degree oven for about 15 minutes and slice. Serve with vanilla ice cream or lightly sweetened whipped cream.

- 1 recipe Basic Single-Crust Pie Dough (page 842), fitted into a 9-inch pie plate and chilled
- 6 tablespoons (¾ stick) unsalted butter, cut into 1-inch pieces
- 1 cup packed (7 ounces) dark brown sugar
- ½ teaspoon table salt
- 3 large eggs
- ¾ cup light corn syrup
- 1 tablespoon vanilla extract
- 2 cups (8 ounces) pecans, toasted and chopped into small pieces

NOTES FROM THE TEST KITCHEN

BLIND BAKING A PIE CRUST

1. Line the chilled pie shell with a double layer of aluminum foil, covering the edges to prevent burning.

2. Fill the shell with pie weights and bake until dry and light in color. After baking, carefully remove the weights and let the crust cool (for a partially baked crust) or continue to bake until deep golden brown (for a fully baked crust).

1. Adjust an oven rack to the middle position and heat the oven to 375 degrees. Following the photos, line the chilled pie shell with a double layer of foil and fill with pie weights. Bake until the pie dough looks dry and is light in color, 25 to 30 minutes. Transfer the pie plate to a wire rack and remove the weights and foil. Adjust the oven rack to the lower-middle position and reduce the oven temperature to 275 degrees. (The crust must still be warm when the filling is added.)

2. Melt the butter in a heatproof bowl set in a skillet of water maintained at just below a simmer. Remove the bowl from the skillet and stir in the sugar and salt until the butter is absorbed. Whisk in the eggs, then the corn syrup and vanilla until smooth. Return the bowl to the hot water and stir until the mixture is shiny and hot to the touch and registers 130 degrees on an instant-read thermometer. Off the heat, stir in the pecans.

3. Pour the pecan mixture into the warm pie crust. Bake the pie until the filling looks set but yields like Jell-O when gently pressed with the back of a spoon, 50 to 60 minutes. Cool the pie on a wire rack until the filling has firmed up, about 2 hours; serve slightly warm (see note) or at room temperature.

Triple Chocolate Chunk Pecan Pie

SERVES 8

Use either just one type of chocolate listed or a combination of two or three types. See page 910 for information on our top-rated brands of chocolate. The crust must still be warm when the filling is added.

- 1 recipe Basic Single-Crust Pie Dough (page 842), fitted into a 9-inch pie plate and chilled
- 3 tablespoons unsalted butter, cut into 3 pieces
- ¾ cup packed (5¼ ounces) dark brown sugar
- ½ teaspoon table salt
- 2 large eggs
- ½ cup light corn syrup
- 1 teaspoon vanilla extract
- 1 cup (4 ounces) pecans, toasted and chopped coarse
- 6 ounces semisweet, milk, and/or white chocolate, chopped coarse (see note)

1. Adjust an oven rack to the middle position and heat the oven to 375 degrees. Following the photos, line the chilled pie shell with a double layer of foil and fill with pie weights. Bake until the pie dough looks dry and is light in color, 25 to 30 minutes. Transfer the pie plate to a wire rack and remove the weights and foil. Adjust the oven rack to the lower-middle position and reduce the oven temperature to 275 degrees. (The crust must still be warm when the filling is added.)

2. Melt the butter in a heatproof bowl set in a skillet of water maintained at just below a simmer. Remove the bowl from the skillet and stir in the sugar and salt until the butter is absorbed. Whisk in the eggs, then the corn syrup and vanilla until smooth. Return the bowl to the hot water and stir until the mixture is shiny and hot to the touch and registers 130 degrees on an instant-read thermometer. Off the heat, stir in the pecans.

3. Pour the pecan mixture into the warm pie crust. Scatter the chocolate over the top and lightly press it into the filling with the back of a spoon. Bake the pie until the filling looks set but yields like Jell-O when gently pressed with the back of a spoon, 50 to 60 minutes. Cool the pie on a wire rack until the filling has firmed up, about 2 hours; serve slightly warm or at room temperature.

KEY LIME PIE

WHY THIS RECIPE WORKS: Some of us have been served Key lime pie in restaurants and found it disappointing, usually harsh and artificial tasting. We wanted a recipe for classic Key lime pie with a fresh flavor and silky filling. Traditional Key lime pie is usually not baked; instead, the combination of egg yolks, lime juice, and sweetened condensed milk firms up when chilled because the juice's acidity causes the proteins in the eggs and milk to bind.

Although we had suspected that the sweetened condensed milk was the party guilty of giving Key lime pies their "off" flavor, we found that the real culprit was the lime juice—bottled, reconstituted lime juice, that is. When we substituted the juice and zest from fresh limes, the pie became an entirely different experience: pungent and refreshing, cool and yet creamy, and very satisfying. We also discovered that while the pie filling will set without baking (most recipes call only for mixing and then chilling), it set much more nicely after being baked for only 15 minutes. We tried other, more dramatic, departures from the "classic" recipe—folding in egg whites, substituting heavy cream for condensed milk—but they didn't work. Just two seemingly minor adjustments to the recipe made all the difference in the world.

Key Lime Pie

SERVES 8

We found that tasters could not tell the difference between pies made with regular supermarket limes (called Persian limes) and true Key limes. Since Persian limes are easier to find and juice, we recommend them. You need to make the filling first, then prepare the crust.

PIE

- 4 large egg yolks
- 4 teaspoons grated zest plus ½ cup juice from 3 or 4 limes (see note)
- 1 (14-ounce) can sweetened condensed milk
- 1 recipe Graham Cracker Crust (page 846)

TOPPING (OPTIONAL)

- 1 cup heavy cream, chilled
- ¼ cup (1 ounce) confectioners' sugar

1. FOR THE PIE: Whisk the egg yolks and lime zest together in a medium bowl until the mixture has a light green tint, about 2 minutes. Whisk in the condensed milk until smooth, then whisk in the lime juice. Cover the mixture and set aside at room temperature until thickened, about 30 minutes.

2. Meanwhile, prepare and bake the crust. Transfer the pie plate to a wire rack and leave the oven at 325 degrees. (The crust must still be warm when the filling is added.)

3. Pour the thickened filling into the warm pie crust. Bake the pie until the center is firm but jiggles slightly when shaken, 15 to 20 minutes. Let the pie cool slightly on a wire rack, about 1 hour, then cover loosely with plastic wrap and refrigerate until the filling is chilled and set, about 3 hours.

4. FOR THE TOPPING (IF USING): Before serving, whip the cream and sugar together in a large bowl with an electric mixer on medium-low speed until frothy, about 1 minute. Increase the mixer speed to high and continue to whip until the cream forms soft peaks, 1 to 3 minutes. Spread the whipped cream attractively over the top of the pie and serve.

LEMON MERINGUE PIE

WHY THIS RECIPE WORKS: Most everybody loves lemon meringue pie—at least the bottom half of it. The most controversial part is the meringue. On any given day it can shrink, bead, puddle, deflate, burn, sweat, break down, or turn rubbery. We wanted a pie with a crisp, flaky crust and a rich filling that would balance the airy meringue, without blocking the clear lemon flavor. The filling should be soft but not runny; firm enough to cut but not stiff and gelatinous. Most important, we wanted a meringue that didn't break down and puddle on the bottom or "tear" on top.

We consulted a food scientist, who told us that the puddling underneath the meringue is from undercooking. The beading on top of the pie is from overcooking. We discovered that if the filling is piping hot when the meringue is applied, the underside of the meringue will not undercook; if the oven temperature is relatively low, the top of the meringue won't overcook. Baking the pie in a relatively cool (325-degree) oven also produces the best-looking, most evenly baked meringue. To further stabilize the meringue and keep it from weeping (even on hot, humid days), we beat in a small amount of cornstarch.

Lemon Meringue Pie

SERVES 8

Make the pie crust, let it cool, and then begin work on the filling. As soon as the filling is made, cover it with plastic wrap to keep it hot and then start working on the meringue topping. You want to add hot filling to the pie crust, apply the meringue topping, and then quickly get the pie into the oven.

- 1 recipe Single-Crust Pie Dough for Custard Pies (page 843), fitted into a 9-inch pie plate and chilled

FILLING

- 1½ cups water
- 1 cup (7 ounces) sugar
- ¼ cup (1 ounce) cornstarch
- ⅛ teaspoon table salt
- 6 large egg yolks
- 1 tablespoon grated zest plus ½ cup juice from 3 lemons
- 2 tablespoons unsalted butter, cut into 2 pieces

MERINGUE

- ⅓ cup water
- 1 tablespoon cornstarch
- ½ cup (3½ ounces) sugar
- ¼ teaspoon cream of tartar
- 4 large egg whites
- ½ teaspoon vanilla extract

1. Adjust an oven rack to the middle position and heat the oven to 375 degrees. Following the photos on page 856, line the chilled pie shell with a double layer of foil and fill with pie weights. Bake until the pie dough looks dry and is light in color, 25 to 30 minutes. Remove the weights and foil and continue to bake the crust until deep golden brown, 10 to 12 minutes longer. Cool the crust to room temperature. Reduce the oven temperature to 325 degrees.

2. FOR THE FILLING: Bring the water, sugar, cornstarch, and salt to a simmer in a large saucepan over medium heat, whisking constantly. When the mixture starts to turn translucent, whisk in the egg yolks, 2 at a time. Whisk in the lemon zest and juice and the butter. Return the mixture to a brief simmer, then remove the pan from the heat. Lay a sheet of plastic wrap directly on the surface of the filling to keep warm and prevent a skin from forming.

3. FOR THE MERINGUE: Bring the water and cornstarch to a simmer in a small saucepan and cook, whisking occasionally, until thickened and translucent, 1 to 2 minutes. Set aside off the heat to cool slightly.

4. Combine the sugar and cream of tartar in a small bowl. In a large bowl, whip the egg whites and vanilla together with an electric mixer on medium-low speed until foamy, about 1 minute. Increase the mixer speed to medium-high, add the sugar mixture, 1 tablespoon at a time, and whip the whites until shiny and soft peaks form, 1 to 3 minutes. Add the cornstarch mixture, 1 tablespoon at a time, and continue to whip the meringue to stiff peaks, 1 to 3 minutes longer.

5. Meanwhile, remove the plastic wrap from the filling and return to very low heat during the last minute or so of beating the meringue (to ensure the filling is hot).

6. Pour the warm filling into the pie crust. Using a rubber spatula, immediately distribute the meringue evenly around the edge and then the center of the pie, attaching the meringue to the pie crust to prevent shrinking. Use the back of a spoon to create attractive swirls and peaks in the meringue. Bake until the meringue is golden brown, about 20 minutes. Cool the pie on a wire rack until the filling has set, about 2 hours. Serve.

LEMON CHIFFON PIE

WHY THIS RECIPE WORKS: We love the elegant simplicity of lemon chiffon pie but found the gelatin used in most recipes difficult to work with. We use a combination of cornstarch and gelatin to get a creamy pie and add a burst of lemon flavor by tucking a layer of lemon curd beneath the chiffon. Our graham cracker crust adds just a hint of flavor and is a crisp contrast to the soft and fluffy filling.

Lemon Chiffon Pie

SERVES 8 TO 10

Before cooking the curd mixture, be sure to whisk thoroughly so that no clumps of cornstarch or streaks of egg white remain. Pasteurized egg whites can be substituted for the 3 raw egg whites. Serve with lightly sweetened whipped cream.

CRUST

- 9 whole graham crackers
- 3 tablespoons sugar
- ⅛ teaspoon salt
- 5 tablespoons unsalted butter, melted

FILLING

- 1 teaspoon unflavored gelatin
- 4 tablespoons water
- 5 large eggs (2 whole, 3 separated)
- 1¼ cups (8¾ ounces) sugar
- 1 tablespoon cornstarch
- ⅛ teaspoon salt
- 1 tablespoon grated lemon zest plus ¾ cup juice (4 lemons)
- ¼ cup heavy cream
- 4 ounces cream cheese, cut into ½-inch pieces, softened

1. FOR THE CRUST: Adjust oven rack to lower-middle position and heat oven to 325 degrees. Process graham crackers in food processor until finely ground, about 30 seconds (you should have about 1¼ cups crumbs). Add sugar and salt and pulse to combine. Add melted butter and pulse until mixture resembles wet sand.

2. Transfer crumbs to 9-inch pie plate. Press crumbs evenly into bottom and up sides of plate. Bake until crust is lightly browned, 15 to 18 minutes. Allow crust to cool completely.

3. FOR THE FILLING: Sprinkle ½ teaspoon gelatin over 2 tablespoons water in small bowl and let sit until gelatin softens, about 5 minutes. Repeat with second small bowl, remaining ½ teaspoon gelatin, and remaining 2 tablespoons water.

4. Whisk 2 eggs and 3 yolks together in medium saucepan until thoroughly combined. Whisk in 1 cup sugar, cornstarch, and salt until well combined. Whisk in lemon zest and juice and heavy cream. Cook over medium-low heat, stirring constantly, until thickened and slightly translucent, 4 to 5 minutes (mixture should register 170 degrees). Stir in 1 water-gelatin mixture until dissolved. Remove pan from heat and let stand for 2 minutes.

5. Remove 1¼ cups curd from pan and pour through fine-mesh strainer set in bowl. Transfer strained curd to prepared pie shell (do not wash out strainer or bowl). Place filled pie shell in freezer. Add remaining water-gelatin mixture and cream cheese to remaining curd in pan and whisk to combine. (If cream cheese does not melt, briefly return pan to low heat.) Pour through strainer into now-empty bowl.

6. Using stand mixer, whip 3 egg whites on medium-low speed until foamy, about 2 minutes. Increase speed to medium-high and slowly add remaining ¼ cup sugar. Continue whipping until whites are stiff and glossy, about 4 minutes. Add curd–cream cheese mixture and whip on medium speed until few streaks remain, about 30 seconds. Remove bowl from mixer and, using spatula, scrape sides of bowl and stir mixture until no streaks remain. Remove pie shell from freezer and carefully pour chiffon over curd, allowing chiffon to mound slightly in center. Refrigerate for at least 4 hours or up to 2 days before serving.

COCONUT CREAM PIE

WHY THIS RECIPE WORKS: Most recipes for this diner dessert are nothing more than a redecorated vanilla cream pie. A handful of coconut shreds stirred into the filling or sprinkled on the whipped cream might be enough to give it a new name, but certainly not enough to give it flavor. We wanted a coconut cream pie with the exotic and elusive flavor of tropical coconut rather than a thinly disguised vanilla custard.

We found that using not-too-sweet graham crackers made a crust with a delicate, cookie-like texture that didn't overshadow the coconut filling. For the filling, we started with a basic custard, using a combination of unsweetened coconut milk and whole milk. For more coconut flavor, we stirred in unsweetened shredded coconut and cooked it so the shreds softened slightly in the hot milk. Lastly, we topped the pie with simple sweetened whipped cream and dusted it with crunchy shreds of toasted coconut.

Coconut Cream Pie

SERVES 8

Do not use low-fat coconut milk here because it does not have enough flavor. Also, don't confuse coconut milk with cream of coconut. The filling should be warm—neither piping hot nor room temperature—when poured into the cooled pie crust. To toast the coconut, place it in a small skillet over medium heat and cook, stirring frequently, for 3 to 5 minutes. It burns quite easily, so keep a close eye on it.

FILLING

- 1 (14-ounce) can coconut milk (see note)
- 1 cup whole milk
- ½ cup (1¼ ounces) unsweetened shredded coconut
- ⅔ cup (4⅔ ounces) sugar
- ¼ teaspoon table salt
- 5 large egg yolks
- ¼ cup (1 ounce) cornstarch
- 2 tablespoons unsalted butter, cut into 2 pieces
- 1½ teaspoons vanilla extract

- 1 recipe Graham Cracker Crust (page 846), baked and cooled

TOPPING

- 1½ cups heavy cream, chilled
- 1½ tablespoons sugar
- 1½ teaspoons dark rum (optional)
- ½ teaspoon vanilla extract
- 1 tablespoon unsweetened shredded coconut, toasted (see note)

1. FOR THE FILLING: Bring the coconut milk, whole milk, shredded coconut, ⅓ cup of the sugar, and the salt to a simmer in a medium saucepan over medium-high heat, stirring occasionally.

2. As the milk mixture begins to simmer, whisk the remaining ⅓ cup sugar, the egg yolks, and cornstarch together in a separate bowl. Slowly whisk 1 cup of the simmering coconut milk mixture into the yolk mixture to temper, then slowly whisk the tempered yolks back into the simmering saucepan. Reduce the heat to medium and cook, whisking vigorously, until the mixture is thickened and a few bubbles burst on the surface, about 30 seconds.

3. Off the heat, whisk in the butter and vanilla. Cool the mixture until just warm, stirring often, about 5 minutes.

4. Pour the warm filling into the baked and cooled pie crust. Lay a sheet of plastic wrap directly on the surface of the filling and refrigerate the pie until the filling is chilled and set, about 4 hours.

5. FOR THE TOPPING: Before serving, whip the cream, sugar, rum (if using), and vanilla together with an electric mixer on medium-low speed until frothy, about 1 minute. Increase the mixer speed to high and continue to whip until the cream forms soft peaks, 1 to 3 minutes. Spread the whipped cream attractively over the top of the pie and sprinkle with the toasted coconut.

CHOCOLATE CREAM PIE

WHY THIS RECIPE WORKS: Chocolate cream pies can look superb but are often gummy, gluey, overly sweet, and impossible to slice. We wanted a voluptuously creamy pie, with a well-balanced chocolate flavor somewhere between milkshake and melted candy bar, and a delicious, easy-to-slice crust.

After testing every type of cookie on the market, we hit on pulverized Oreos and a bit of melted butter for the tastiest, most tender, sliceable crumb crust. We found that the secret to perfect chocolate cream pie filling was to combine two different types of chocolate for a deeper, more complex flavor. Bittersweet or semisweet chocolate provides the main thrust of flavor, and intensely flavored unsweetened chocolate lends depth. One ounce of unsweetened chocolate may not seem like much, but it gives this pie great flavor. We also discovered that the custard's texture depended upon carefully pouring the egg yolk mixture into simmering half-and-half, then whisking in butter.

Chocolate Cream Pie

SERVES 8

For the best chocolate flavor and texture, we recommend Callebaut semisweet chocolate or Hershey's Special Dark and Hershey's unsweetened chocolate. Other brands of chocolate sandwich cookies may be substituted for the Oreos, but avoid any "double-filled" cookies because the proportion of cookie to filling won't be correct. Do not combine the egg yolks and sugar in advance of making the filling—the sugar will begin to break down the yolks, and the finished cream will be pitted.

CRUST

- 16 Oreo cookies, broken into rough pieces (see note)
- 4 tablespoons (½ stick) unsalted butter, melted and cooled

FILLING

- 2½ cups half-and-half
- ⅓ cup (2⅓ ounces) sugar
- Pinch table salt
- 6 large egg yolks
- 2 tablespoons cornstarch
- 6 tablespoons (¾ stick) unsalted butter, cut into 6 pieces
- 6 ounces semisweet or bittersweet chocolate, chopped fine (see note)
- 1 ounce unsweetened chocolate, chopped fine (see note)
- 1 teaspoon vanilla extract

TOPPING

- 1½ cups heavy cream, chilled
- 2 tablespoons sugar
- ½ teaspoon vanilla extract

1. FOR THE CRUST: Adjust an oven rack to the middle position and heat the oven to 350 degrees. Pulse the cookies in a food processor until coarsely ground, about 15 pulses, then continue to process to fine, even crumbs, about 15 seconds. Sprinkle the butter over the crumbs and pulse to incorporate.

2. Sprinkle the mixture into a 9-inch pie plate. Following the photo on page 846, use the bottom of a measuring cup to press the crumbs into an even layer on the bottom and sides of the pie plate. Bake until the crust is fragrant and looks set, 10 to 15 minutes. Transfer the crust to a wire rack and cool completely.

3. FOR THE FILLING: Bring the half-and-half, 3 tablespoons of the sugar, and the salt to a simmer in a medium saucepan over medium-high heat, stirring occasionally.

4. As the half-and-half mixture begins to simmer, whisk the egg yolks, cornstarch, and remaining sugar together in a medium bowl until smooth. Slowly whisk about 1 cup of the simmering half-and-half mixture into the yolk mixture to temper, then slowly whisk the tempered yolks back into the simmering saucepan. Reduce the heat to medium and cook, whisking vigorously, until the mixture is thickened and a few bubbles burst on the surface, about 30 seconds.

5. Off the heat, whisk in the butter and chocolates until completely smooth and melted. Stir in the vanilla. Pour the warm filling into the baked and cooled pie crust. Lay a sheet of plastic wrap directly on the surface of the filling and refrigerate the pie until the filling is chilled and set, about 4 hours.

6. FOR THE TOPPING: Before serving, whip the cream, sugar, and vanilla together with an electric mixer on medium-low speed until frothy, about 1 minute. Increase the mixer speed to high and continue to whip until the cream forms soft peaks, 1 to 3 minutes. Spread the whipped cream attractively over the top of the pie.

CLASSIC TART DOUGH

WHY THIS RECIPE WORKS: The problem with most tarts is the crust—it's usually either too tough or too brittle. While regular pie crust is tender and flaky, classic tart crust should be fine-textured, buttery-rich, crisp, and crumbly—it is often described as being shortbread-like. We set out in the test kitchen to achieve the perfect tart dough, one that we could use in several of our tart recipes.

We found that using a full stick of butter made tart dough that tasted great and was easy to handle, yet still had a delicate crumb. Instead of using the hard-to-find superfine sugar and pastry flour that many other recipes call for, we used confectioners' sugar and all-purpose flour to achieve a crisp texture. Rolling the dough and fitting it into the tart pan was easy, and we had ample dough to patch any holes.

Classic Tart Dough

MAKES ENOUGH FOR ONE 9-INCH TART

Tart crust is sweeter, crisper, and less flaky than pie crust—it is more similar in texture to a cookie. The dough, wrapped tightly in plastic wrap, can be refrigerated for up to 2 days or frozen for up to 1 month. If frozen, let the dough thaw completely on the counter before rolling out.

- 1 large egg yolk
- 1 tablespoon heavy cream
- ½ teaspoon vanilla extract
- 1¼ cups (6¼ ounces) unbleached all-purpose flour
- ⅔ cup (2⅔ ounces) confectioners' sugar
- ¼ teaspoon table salt
- 8 tablespoons (1 stick) unsalted butter, cut into ¼-inch pieces and chilled

NOTES FROM THE TEST KITCHEN

MAKING A TART SHELL

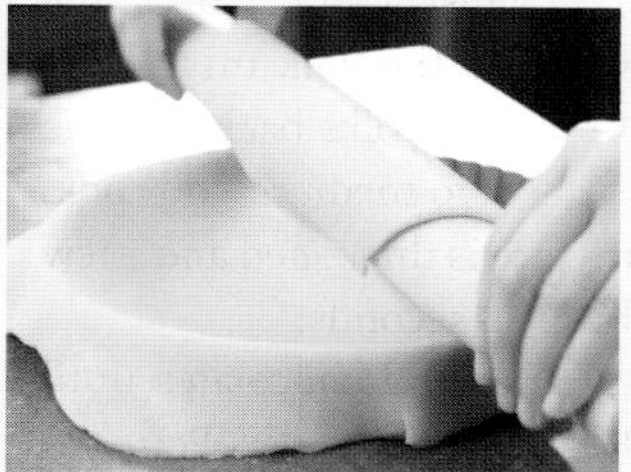

1. After rolling the dough out into an 11-inch circle on a lightly floured work surface, wrap it loosely around the rolling pin and unroll the dough over a 9-inch tart pan with a removable bottom.

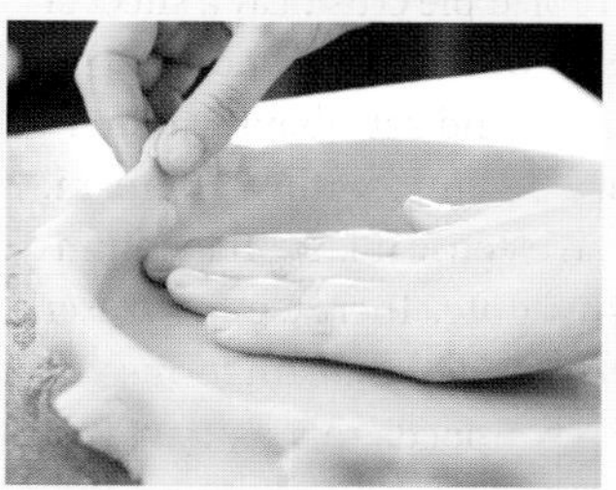

2. Lifting the edge of the dough, gently ease the dough into the pan. Press the dough into the corners and fluted sides of the pan.

3. Run the rolling pin over the top of the tart pan to remove any excess dough and make a clean edge.

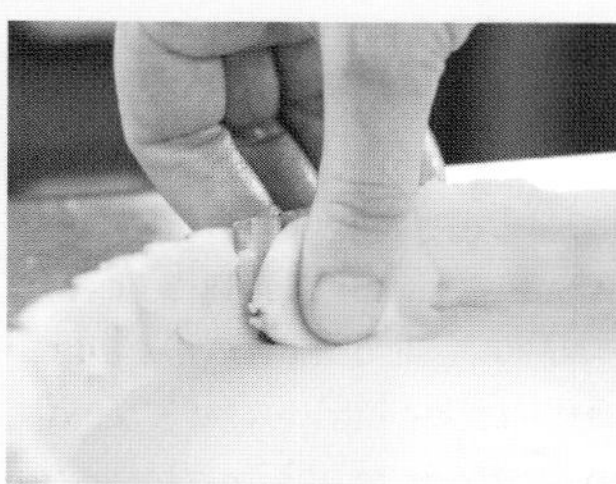

4. If parts of the edge are too thin, reinforce them by pressing in some of the excess dough. If the edge is too thick, press some of the dough up over the edge of the pan and trim it away.

1. Whisk the egg yolk, cream, and vanilla together in a small bowl. Process the flour, sugar, and salt together in a food processor until combined. Scatter the butter pieces over the top and pulse until the mixture resembles coarse cornmeal, about 15 pulses.

2. With the machine running, add the egg mixture through the feed tube and continue to process until the dough just comes together around the processor blade, about 12 seconds.

3. Turn the dough onto a sheet of plastic wrap and flatten into a 6-inch disk. Wrap the dough tightly in plastic wrap and refrigerate for 1 hour. Before rolling the dough out, let it sit on the counter to soften slightly, about 10 minutes.

LEMON TART

WHY THIS RECIPE WORKS: Despite its apparent simplicity, there is much that can go wrong with a lemon tart. It can slip over the edge of sweet into cloying; its tartness can grab at your throat; it can be gluey or eggy or, even worse, metallic-tasting. Its crust can be too hard, too soft, too thick, or too sweet. We wanted a proper tart, one in which the filling is baked with the shell. For us, that meant only one thing: lemon curd. For just enough sugar to offset the acid in the lemons, we used 3 parts sugar to 2 parts lemon juice, plus a ¼ cup of lemon zest. To achieve a curd that was creamy and dense with a vibrant lemony yellow color, we used a combination of whole eggs and egg yolks. We cooked the curd over direct heat, then whisked in cold butter. And for a smooth texture, we strained the curd and stirred in heavy cream just before baking.

Lemon Tart

SERVES 8 TO 10

Once the lemon curd ingredients have been combined, cook the curd immediately; otherwise it will have a grainy finished texture. Dust with confectioners' sugar before serving, or serve with lightly whipped cream.

- 1 recipe Classic Tart Dough
- Unbleached all-purpose flour, for the work surface
- 7 large egg yolks plus 2 large whole eggs
- 1 cup (7 ounces) sugar
- ¼ cup grated zest plus ⅔ cup juice from 4 to 5 lemons
- Pinch table salt
- 4 tablespoons (½ stick) unsalted butter, cut into 4 pieces
- 3 tablespoons heavy cream

1. Roll the dough out to an 11-inch circle on a lightly floured work surface and, following the photos, fit it into a 9-inch tart pan with a removable bottom. Set the tart pan on a large plate and freeze the tart shell for 30 minutes.

2. Adjust an oven rack to the middle position and heat the oven to 375 degrees. Set the tart pan on a large baking sheet. Press a double layer of foil into the frozen tart shell and over the edges of the pan and fill with pie weights. Bake until the tart shell is golden brown and set, about 30 minutes, rotating the baking sheet halfway through.

3. Carefully remove the weights and foil and continue to bake the tart shell until it is fully baked and golden, 5 to 10 minutes longer. Transfer the tart crust with the baking sheet to a wire rack and cool the tart shell slightly while making the filling.

4. Whisk the egg yolks and whole eggs together in a medium saucepan. Whisk in the sugar until combined, then whisk in the lemon zest and juice and salt. Add the butter and cook over medium-low heat, stirring constantly, until the mixture thickens slightly and registers 170 degrees on an instant-read thermometer, about 5 minutes. Immediately pour the mixture through a fine-mesh strainer into a bowl and stir in the cream.

5. Pour the lemon filling into the warm tart shell. Bake the tart on the baking sheet until the filling is shiny and opaque and the center jiggles slightly when shaken, 10 to 15 minutes. Let the tart cool completely on the baking sheet, about 1½ hours. To serve, remove the outer metal ring of the tart pan, slide a thin metal spatula between the tart and the tart pan bottom, and carefully slide the tart onto a serving platter or cutting board.

THE BEST SUMMER FRUIT TART

WHY THIS RECIPE WORKS: By trading the traditional rolled pastry and pastry cream filling for easier, faster alternatives, we produced a fresh fruit tart that is as appealing to make as it is to eat. Stirring melted butter into the dry ingredients yielded a malleable dough that could be pressed into the pan; for extra flavor, we browned the butter first and added back water that we lost so that there was enough moisture to help the flour form gluten (the protein network that would give the dough structure). A mix of mascarpone cheese, melted white baking chips, and lime juice and zest gave us a quick-to-make filling that was lush and creamy but also tangy and firm enough to slice cleanly. Arranging thin-sliced peaches in lines that radiated from the center of the tart to its outer edge created cutting guides between which we artfully arranged a mix of berries. These cutting guides ensured that we could slice the tart into neat portions without marring the arrangement of the fruit. An apricot preserves and lime juice glaze brightened the fruit, and gave the tart a polished, professional look.

The Best Summer Fruit Tart

SERVES 8

This recipe calls for extra berries to account for any bruising. Ripe, unpeeled nectarines can be substituted for the peaches, if desired. Use white baking chips here, not white chocolate bars, which contain cocoa butter and will result in a loose filling. Be sure to use a light hand when dabbing on the glaze as too much force will dislodge the fruit. If the glaze begins to solidify while dabbing, microwave it for 5 to 10 seconds.

CRUST

- 1 cup (6 ounces) all-purpose flour
- ¼ cup (1¾ ounces) sugar
- ⅛ teaspoon salt
- 10 tablespoons unsalted butter
- 2 tablespoons water

TART

- ⅓ cup (2 ounces) white baking chips
- ¼ cup heavy cream
- 1 teaspoon grated lime zest plus 7 teaspoons juice (2 limes)
- Pinch salt
- 6 ounces (¾ cup) mascarpone, room temperature
- 2 ripe peaches, peeled
- 20 ounces (4 cups) raspberries, blackberries, and blueberries
- ⅓ cup apricot preserves

1. FOR THE CRUST: Adjust oven rack to middle position and heat oven to 350 degrees. Whisk flour, sugar, and salt together in bowl. Melt butter in small saucepan over medium-high heat, swirling pan occasionally, until foaming subsides. Continue to cook, stirring and scraping bottom of pan with heatproof spatula, until milk solids are dark golden brown and butter has nutty aroma, 1 to 3 minutes. Remove pan from heat and add water. When bubbling subsides, transfer butter to bowl with flour mixture, scraping pan with spatula. Stir until mixture is well combined. Transfer dough to 9-inch tart pan with removable bottom and let dough rest until warm to the touch, about 10 minutes.

2. Use hands to evenly press and smooth dough over bottom and up side of pan (using two-thirds of dough for bottom crust and remaining third for side). Place tart pan on wire rack set in rimmed baking sheet. Bake until crust is golden brown, 25 to 30 minutes, rotating pan halfway through baking. Let cool completely, about 1 hour. (Cooled crust can be wrapped loosely in plastic wrap and stored at room temperature for up to 24 hours before filling.)

3. FOR THE TART: Microwave baking chips, cream, lime zest, and salt in medium bowl, stirring every 10 seconds, until chips are melted, 30 to 60 seconds. Whisk in one-third of mascarpone to cool mixture, then whisk in 6 teaspoons lime juice and remaining mascarpone until smooth. Transfer filling to cooled tart shell and smooth into even layer.

4. Place peach stem side down on cutting board. Placing knife just to side of pit, cut down to remove one side of peach. Turn peach 180 degrees and cut off opposite side. Slice off remaining 2 sides. Arrange pieces cut side down on cutting board and slice into ¼-inch thick half-moon shapes. Repeat with second peach. Select the 24 best slices.

5. Arrange 8 berries, evenly spaced, around outer edge of tart. Using berries as guide, arrange 8 sets of 3 peach slices in filling, slightly overlapping them with rounded side up, starting at center and ending on right side of each berry at outer edge of tart. Arrange remaining berries in attractive pattern between peach slices, covering as much of filling as possible and keeping fruit in even layer.

6. Microwave preserves and remaining 1 teaspoon lime juice in small bowl until fluid, 20 to 30 seconds. Strain mixture through fine-mesh strainer. Using pastry brush, gently dab mixture over fruit, avoiding crust. Refrigerate tart for 30 minutes.

7. Remove outer metal ring of tart pan. Insert thin metal spatula between crust and pan bottom to loosen tart; carefully slide tart onto serving platter. Let tart sit at room temperature for 15 minutes. Using peaches as guide, cut into wedges and serve. (Tart can be refrigerated for up to 24 hours. If refrigerated for more than 1 hour, let tart sit at room temperature for 1 hour before serving.)

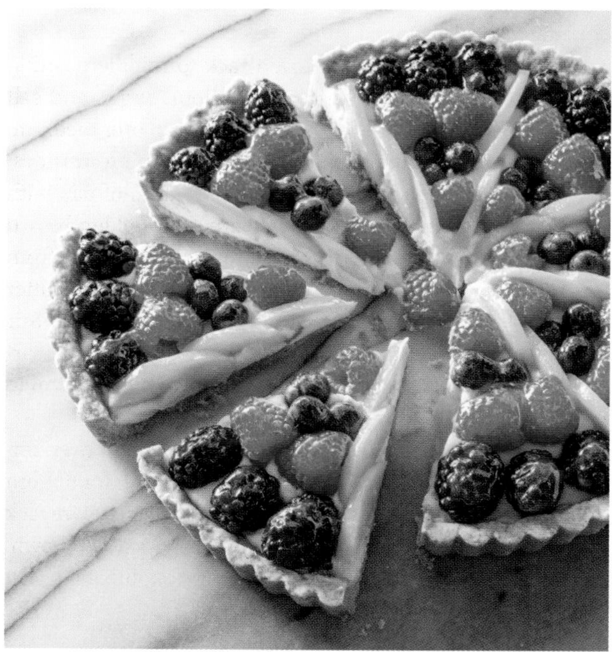

FRESH FRUIT TART WITH PASTRY CREAM

WHY THIS RECIPE WORKS: Fresh fruit tarts usually offer little substance beyond their dazzling beauty, with rubbery or institutionalized pudding fillings, soggy crusts, and underripe, flavorless fruit. We set out to create a buttery, crisp crust filled with rich, lightly sweetened pastry cream, topped with fresh, glistening fruit. We started with our classic tart dough as the crust and baked it until it was golden brown. We then filled the tart with pastry cream, made with half-and-half that was enriched with butter and thickened with just enough cornstarch to keep its shape without becoming gummy. For the fruit, we chose a combination of kiwi, which we peeled and sliced into half-moons, raspberries, and blueberries. We found that it was important not to wash the berries, as washing causes them to bruise and bleed and makes for a less than attractive tart. The finishing touch: a drizzle with a jelly glaze for a glistening presentation.

Fresh Fruit Tart with Pastry Cream

SERVES 8 TO 10

The pastry cream can be made a day or two in advance, but do not fill the prebaked tart shell until just before serving. Once filled, the tart should be topped with fruit, glazed, and served within half an hour or so. Don't wash the berries or they will lose their flavor and shape.

PASTRY CREAM

- 2 cups half-and-half
- ½ cup (3½ ounces) sugar
- Pinch table salt
- 5 large egg yolks
- 3 tablespoons cornstarch
- 4 tablespoons (½ stick) unsalted butter, cut into 4 pieces
- 1½ teaspoons vanilla extract

TART SHELL AND FRUIT

- 1 recipe Classic Tart Dough (page 861)
- Unbleached all-purpose flour, for the work surface
- 2 large kiwis, peeled, halved lengthwise, and sliced ⅜ inch thick
- 2 cups (10 ounces) raspberries (see note)
- 1 cup (5 ounces) blueberries (see note)
- ½ cup red currant or apple jelly

1. FOR THE PASTRY CREAM: Bring the half-and-half, 6 tablespoons of the sugar, and the salt to a simmer in a medium saucepan over medium-high heat, stirring occasionally.

2. As the half-and-half mixture begins to simmer, whisk the egg yolks, cornstarch, and remaining 2 tablespoons sugar together in a medium bowl until smooth. Slowly whisk about 1 cup of the simmering half-and-half mixture into the yolks to temper, then slowly whisk the tempered yolks back into the simmering saucepan. Reduce the heat to medium and cook, whisking vigorously, until the mixture is thickened and a few bubbles burst on the surface, about 30 seconds.

3. Off the heat, stir in the butter and vanilla. Transfer the mixture to a medium bowl, lay a sheet of plastic wrap directly on the surface, and refrigerate the pastry cream until chilled and firm, about 3 hours.

4. FOR THE TART SHELL AND FRUIT: Roll the dough out to an 11-inch circle on a lightly floured work surface and, following the photos on page 861, fit it into a 9-inch tart pan with a removable bottom. Set the tart pan on a large plate and freeze the tart shell for 30 minutes.

5. Adjust an oven rack to the middle position and heat the oven to 375 degrees. Set the tart pan on a large baking sheet. Press a double layer of foil into the frozen tart shell and over the edges of the pan and fill with pie weights. Bake until the tart shell is golden brown and set, about 30 minutes, rotating the baking sheet halfway through.

6. Carefully remove the weights and foil and continue to bake the tart shell until it is fully baked and golden, 5 to 10 minutes longer. Transfer the tart shell with the baking sheet to a wire rack and cool the tart shell completely, about 1 hour.

7. Spread the chilled pastry cream evenly over the bottom of the cooled tart shell. Shingle the kiwi slices around the edge of the tart, then arrange three rows of raspberries inside the kiwi. Finally, arrange a mound of blueberries in the center.

8. Melt the jelly in a small saucepan over medium-high heat, stirring occasionally to smooth out any lumps. Using a pastry brush, dab the melted jelly over the fruit. To serve, remove the outer metal ring of the tart pan, slide a thin metal spatula between the tart and the tart pan bottom, and carefully slide the tart onto a serving platter or cutting board.

Mixed Berry Tart with Pastry Cream

Follow the recipe for Fresh Fruit Tart with Pastry Cream, omitting the kiwi and adding 2 cups (10 ounces) extra berries (including blackberries or quartered strawberries). Combine the berries in a large plastic bag and toss them gently to mix. Carefully spread the berries in an even layer over the tart. Glaze and serve as directed.

FREE-FORM FRUIT TART

WHY THIS RECIPE WORKS: Few things are better than a summer fruit pie, but that takes time (and skill). What we wanted was simpler: a buttery, flaky crust paired with juicy summer fruit—with half the work of a regular pie. A free-form tart (a single layer of buttery pie dough folded up around fresh fruit) seemed the obvious solution.

Without the support of a pie plate, tender crusts are prone to leak juice, and this results in soggy bottoms. For our crust, we used a high proportion of butter to flour, which provided the most buttery flavor and tender texture without compromising the structure. We then turned to a French technique in pastry making called *fraisage*. To begin, butter is only partially cut into the dry ingredients. Then, with the heel of the hand, the cook presses the barely mixed dough firmly against the counter. As a result, the chunks of butter are pressed into long, thin sheets that create lots of flaky layers when the dough is baked. We rolled the dough into a 12-inch circle for a crust that was thick enough to contain a lot of fruit but thin enough to bake evenly and thoroughly. We placed the fruit in the middle, then lifted the dough up and back over the fruit and pleated it loosely to allow for shrinkage. The bright summer fruit needed only the simple addition of sugar.

Free-Form Summer Fruit Tart

SERVES 6

The dough, wrapped tightly in plastic wrap, can be refrigerated for up to 2 days or frozen for up to 1 month. If frozen, let the dough thaw completely on the counter before rolling it out. Though we prefer a tart made with a mix of stone fruits and berries, you can use only one type of fruit if you prefer. Taste the fruit before adding sugar to it; use the lesser amount if the fruit is very sweet, more if it is tart. However much sugar you use, do not add it to the fruit until you are ready to fill and form the tart. Serve with vanilla ice cream, lightly sweetened whipped cream, or crème fraîche.

RUSTIC TART DOUGH

- 1½ cups (7½ ounces) unbleached all-purpose flour, plus extra for the work surface
- ½ teaspoon table salt
- 10 tablespoons (1¼ sticks) unsalted butter, cut into ½-inch pieces and chilled
- 4–6 tablespoons ice water

FILLING

- 1 pound peaches, nectarines, apricots, or plums, pitted and sliced into ½-inch-thick wedges (see note)
- 1 cup (5 ounces) blueberries, raspberries, or blackberries (see note)
- 3–5 tablespoons plus 1 tablespoon sugar (see note)

1. FOR THE RUSTIC TART DOUGH: Process the flour and salt in a food processor until combined. Scatter the butter pieces over the top and pulse until the mixture resembles

coarse bread crumbs and the butter pieces are about the size of small peas, about 10 pulses. Continue to pulse, adding the water through the feed tube 1 tablespoon at a time, until the dough begins to form small curds that hold together when pinched with your fingers (the dough will be crumbly), about 10 pulses.

2. Following the photos, turn the dough crumbs out onto a lightly floured work surface and gather into a rectangular-shaped pile. Starting at the farthest end, use the heel of your hand to smear a small amount of dough against the work surface. Continue to smear the dough until all the crumbs have been worked. Gather the smeared crumbs together in another rectangular-shaped pile and repeat the process. Flatten the dough into a 6-inch disk, wrap it tightly in plastic wrap, and refrigerate for 1 hour. Before rolling the dough out, let it sit on the counter to soften slightly, about 10 minutes.

3. Roll the dough into a 12-inch circle between two large sheets of floured parchment paper. Slide the dough, still between the parchment sheets, onto a large baking sheet and refrigerate until firm, about 20 minutes.

4. FOR THE FILLING: Adjust an oven rack to the middle position and heat the oven to 375 degrees. Gently toss the fruit and sugar together in a large bowl. Remove the top sheet of parchment paper from the dough. Mound the fruit in the center of the dough, leaving a 2½-inch border around the edge. Following photo 2 on page 868, and being careful to leave a ½-inch border of dough around the fruit, fold the outermost 2 inches of dough over the fruit, pleating it every 2 to 3 inches as needed; gently pinch the pleated dough to secure, but do not press the dough into the fruit. Working quickly, brush the dough with water and sprinkle evenly with the additional 1 tablespoon sugar.

5. Bake the tart until the crust is deep golden brown and the fruit is bubbling, about 1 hour, rotating the baking sheet halfway through.

NOTES FROM THE TEST KITCHEN

MIXING A FLAKY DOUGH

1. Starting at one end of the rectangular pile of dough, smear a small amount of the dough against the work surface with the heel of your hand. Repeat this process (called fraisage) until the rest of the buttery crumbs have been worked.

2. Gather the smeared bits into another rectangular pile and repeat the smearing process until all of the crumbs have been worked again. This second time won't take as long and will result in large flakes of dough.

6. Cool the tart on the baking sheet on a wire rack for 10 minutes, then use the parchment paper to gently transfer the tart to a wire rack. Use a metal spatula to loosen the tart from the parchment and remove the parchment. Cool the tart on the rack until the juices have thickened, about 25 minutes. Serve warm or at room temperature.

APPLE GALETTE

WHY THIS RECIPE WORKS: The French tart known as an apple galette should have a flaky crust and a layer of shingled caramelized apples. But it's challenging to make a crust strong enough to hold the apples and still be eaten out of hand—most recipes create a tough, bland crust. Choosing the right flour put us on the right track. All-purpose flour contained too much gluten; it made the pastry tough. Lower-protein pastry flour created a flaky and sturdy pastry. As pastry flour is hard to find, we mixed regular all-purpose flour with instant flour. Technique also proved to be important. We used the French fraisage method of blending butter into dough (see page 864). We found that any thinly sliced apple would work, although we slightly preferred Granny Smith.

Apple Galette

SERVES 10 TO 12

The most common brands of instant flour are Wondra and Shake & Blend; they are sold in canisters in the baking aisle. The galette can be made without instant flour, using 2 cups unbleached all-purpose flour and 2 tablespoons cornstarch; however, you might have to increase the amount of ice water. The dough, wrapped tightly in plastic wrap, can be refrigerated for up to 2 days or frozen for up to 1 month. If frozen, let the dough thaw completely on the counter before rolling out. Serve with ice cream, whipped cream, or crème fraîche.

DOUGH

- 1½ cups (7½ ounces) unbleached all-purpose flour, plus extra for the work surface
- ½ cup (2½ ounces) instant flour (see note)
- ½ teaspoon table salt
- ½ teaspoon sugar
- 12 tablespoons (1½ sticks) unsalted butter, cut into ¼-inch pieces and chilled
- 7–9 tablespoons ice water

TOPPING

- 1½ pounds Granny Smith apples (about 3 large), peeled, cored, and sliced ⅛ inch thick
- 2 tablespoons unsalted butter, cut into ¼-inch pieces
- ¼ cup (1¾ ounces) sugar
- 3 tablespoons apple jelly

NOTES FROM THE TEST KITCHEN

PREPARING APPLE GALETTE

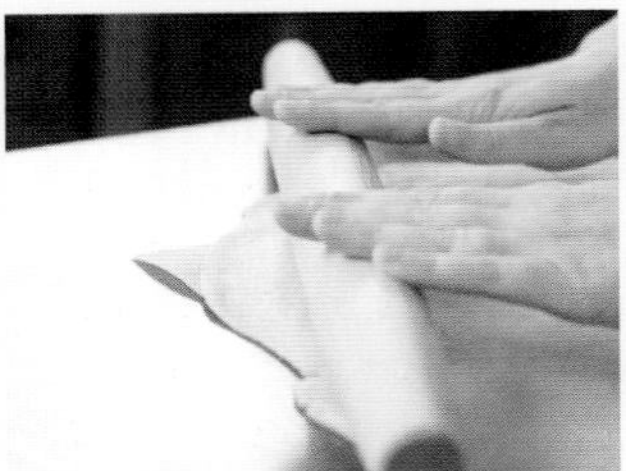

1. Cut a piece of parchment to measure exactly 16 by 12 inches, then roll the dough out on top of the parchment until it just overhangs the edge and is about ⅛ inch thick.

2. Trim the dough so that the edges are even with the parchment paper. We use the parchment as a guide to cut a perfectly even rectangle of dough from which we can make a large thin crust.

3. Roll up 1 inch of each edge to create a ½-inch-thick border. This border is decorative and helps keep the apple slices in place.

4. Slide the parchment and dough onto a rimmed baking sheet. Starting in one corner, shingle the apple slices in tidy rows on the diagonal over the dough, overlapping each row by a third.

1. FOR THE DOUGH: Process the flours, salt, and sugar together in a food processor until combined. Scatter the butter pieces over the top and pulse until the mixture resembles coarse cornmeal, about 15 pulses. Continue to pulse, adding the water through the feed tube 1 tablespoon at a time until the dough begins to form small curds that hold together when pinched with your fingers (the dough will be crumbly), about 10 pulses.

2. Following the photos on page 865, turn the dough crumbs onto a lightly floured work surface and gather into a rectangular-shaped pile. Starting at the farthest end, use the heel of your hand to smear a small amount of dough against the work surface. Continue to smear the dough until all the crumbs have been worked. Gather the smeared crumbs together in another rectangular-shaped pile and repeat the process. Press the dough into a 4-inch square, wrap it tightly in plastic wrap, and refrigerate for 1 hour. Before rolling the dough out, let it sit on the counter to soften slightly, about 10 minutes.

3. Adjust an oven rack to the middle position and heat the oven to 400 degrees. Cut a piece of parchment to measure exactly 16 by 12 inches. Following the photos, roll the dough out over the parchment, dusting with flour as needed, until it just overhangs the parchment. Trim the edges of the dough even with the parchment. Roll the outer 1 inch of the dough up to create a ½-inch-thick border. Slide the parchment paper with the dough onto a large rimmed baking sheet.

4. FOR THE TOPPING: Starting in one corner of the tart, shingle the apple slices onto the crust in tidy diagonal rows, overlapping them by a third. Dot with the butter and sprinkle evenly with the sugar. Bake the tart until the bottom is deep golden brown and the apples have caramelized, 45 to 60 minutes, rotating the baking sheet halfway through.

5. Melt the jelly in a small saucepan over medium-high heat, stirring occasionally to smooth out any lumps. Brush the glaze over the apples and let the tart cool slightly on the baking sheet for 10 minutes. Slide the tart onto a large platter or cutting board and slice the tart in half lengthwise, then crosswise into square pieces. Serve warm or at room temperature.

FRENCH APPLE TART

WHY THIS RECIPE WORKS: Classically elegant French apple tart is little more than apples and pastry, but such simplicity means that imperfections like tough or mushy apples, unbalanced flavor, and a sodden crust are hard to hide. We wanted a foolproof way to achieve tender apples and a flavorful, buttery crust. We parbaked our quick pat-in-pan dough for a cookie-like texture that gave the tart a sturdy base. For intense fruit flavor, we packed the tart with a whopping 5 pounds of Golden Delicious apples. We cooked half into a concentrated puree, which we made more luxurious with butter and apricot preserves. For textural contrast, we sliced and parcooked the remaining apples and used them to adorn the top. A thin coat of preserves and a final stint under the broiler provided an attractively caramelized finish.

French Apple Tart

SERVES 8

You may have extra apple slices after topping the tart in step 6. If you don't have a potato masher, you can puree the applesauce in a food processor. For the best flavor and texture, be sure to bake the crust thoroughly. The tart is best served the day it is assembled. To ensure that the outer ring of the pan releases easily from the tart, avoid getting apple puree and apricot glaze on the crust.

CRUST

- 1⅓ cups (6⅔ ounces) all-purpose flour
- 5 tablespoons (2¼ ounces) sugar
- ½ teaspoon salt
- 10 tablespoons unsalted butter, melted

FILLING

- 10 Golden Delicious apples (8 ounces each), peeled and cored
- 3 tablespoons unsalted butter
- 1 tablespoon water
- ½ cup apricot preserves
- ¼ teaspoon salt

1. FOR THE CRUST: Adjust 1 oven rack to lowest position and second rack 5 to 6 inches from broiler element. Heat oven to 350 degrees. Whisk flour, sugar, and salt together in bowl. Add melted butter and stir until dough forms. Using your hands, press two-thirds of dough into bottom of 9-inch tart pan with removable bottom. Press remaining dough into fluted sides of pan. Press and smooth dough with your hands to even thickness. Place pan on wire rack set in rimmed baking sheet and bake on lowest rack, until crust is deep golden brown and firm to touch, 30 to 35 minutes, rotating pan halfway through baking. Set aside until ready to fill.

2. FOR THE FILLING: Cut 5 apples lengthwise into quarters and cut each quarter lengthwise into 4 slices. Melt 1 tablespoon butter in 12-inch skillet over medium heat. Add apple slices and water and toss to combine. Cover and cook, stirring occasionally, until apples begin to turn translucent and are slightly pliable, 3 to 5 minutes. Transfer apples to large plate, spread into single layer, and set aside to cool.

3. While apples cook, microwave apricot preserves until fluid, about 30 seconds. Strain preserves through fine-mesh strainer into small bowl, reserving solids. Set aside 3 tablespoons strained preserves for brushing tart.

4. Cut remaining 5 apples into ½-inch-thick wedges. Melt remaining 2 tablespoons butter in now-empty skillet over medium heat. Add remaining strained apricot preserves, reserved apricot solids, apples, and salt. Cover and cook, stirring occasionally, until apples are very soft, about 10 minutes.

5. Mash apples to puree with potato masher. Continue to cook, stirring occasionally, until puree is reduced to 2 cups, about 5 minutes.

6. Transfer apple puree to baked tart shell and smooth surface. Select 5 thinnest slices of sautéed apple and set aside. Starting at outer edge of tart, arrange remaining slices, tightly overlapping in concentric circles. Bend reserved slices to fit in center. Bake tart, still on wire rack in sheet, on lowest rack, for 30 minutes. Remove tart from oven and heat broiler.

7. While broiler heats, warm reserved preserves in microwave until fluid, about 20 seconds. Brush evenly over surface of apples, avoiding tart crust. Broil tart, checking every 30 seconds and turning as necessary, until apples are attractively caramelized, 1 to 3 minutes. Let tart cool for at least 1½ hours. Remove outer metal ring of tart pan, slide thin metal spatula between tart and pan bottom, and carefully slide tart onto serving platter. Cut into wedges and serve.

TO MAKE AHEAD: Baked crust, apple slices, and apple puree can be made up to 24 hours in advance. Apple slices and puree should be refrigerated separately. Assemble tart with refrigerated apple slices and puree and bake as directed, adding 5 minutes to baking time.

NOTES FROM THE TEST KITCHEN

MAKING AN APPLE ROSETTE

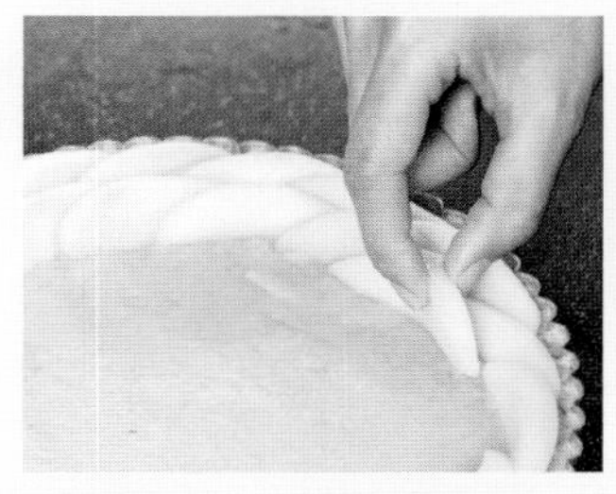

1. Starting at edges and working toward center, arrange most of the cooled sautéed apple slices in tightly overlapping concentric circles.

2. Bend remaining slices to fit in center.

FREE-FORM APPLE TART

WHY THIS RECIPE WORKS: Apple tarts are easier to make than apple pie, but they have their problems: The filling can dry out owing to the lack of a top crust, and the dough can be limp and tacky. We wanted a simple free-form tart with moist, flavorful apples neatly contained by a flaky, easy-to-handle dough.

Off the bat, we decided to borrow the crust from our Free-Form Summer Fruit Tart recipe (see page 864)—it's sturdy yet flaky, with a great buttery flavor. As with our Classic Apple Pie (see page 846), we favored a combination of Granny Smith and McIntosh apples. To ensure that the apples cooked through in a short amount of time, we sliced them 1/4 inch thick. All the apples needed in the way of flavor enhancement was lemon juice, sugar, and cinnamon.

Free-Form Apple Tart

SERVES 6

Serve with vanilla ice cream or lightly sweetened whipped cream.

- 1 pound Granny Smith apples (about 2 large), peeled, cored, and sliced ¼ inch thick
- 1 pound McIntosh apples (about 2 large), peeled, cored, and sliced ¼ inch thick
- ½ cup (3½ ounces) plus 1 tablespoon sugar
- 1 tablespoon juice from 1 lemon
- ⅛ teaspoon ground cinnamon
- 1 recipe Rustic Tart Dough (page 864), rolled into a 12-inch circle and chilled

1. Adjust an oven rack to the middle position and heat the oven to 375 degrees. Toss the apples, 1/2 cup of the sugar, the lemon juice, and cinnamon together in a large bowl.

2. Remove the top sheet of parchment paper from the dough. Following the photos, stack some of the apples into a circular wall, leaving a 2½-inch border around the edge. Fill in the middle of the tart with the remaining apples. Being careful to leave a ½-inch border of dough around the fruit, fold the outermost 2 inches of dough over the fruit, pleating it every 2 to 3 inches as needed; gently pinch the pleated dough to secure, but do not press the dough into the fruit. Working quickly, brush the dough with water and sprinkle evenly with the remaining 1 tablespoon sugar.

3. Bake the tart on a large rimmed baking sheet until the crust is deep golden brown and the apples are tender, about 1 hour, rotating the baking sheet halfway through.

4. Cool the tart on the baking sheet on a wire rack for 10 minutes, then use the parchment paper to gently transfer the tart to the wire rack. Use a metal spatula to loosen the tart from the parchment and remove the parchment. Cool the tart on the rack until the juices have thickened, about 25 minutes. Serve warm or at room temperature.

NOTES FROM THE TEST KITCHEN

MAKING A FREE-FORM APPLE TART

1. Discard the top piece of parchment. Stack the apple slices into a circular wall, leaving a 2½-inch border of dough. Fill the center with the remaining apples.

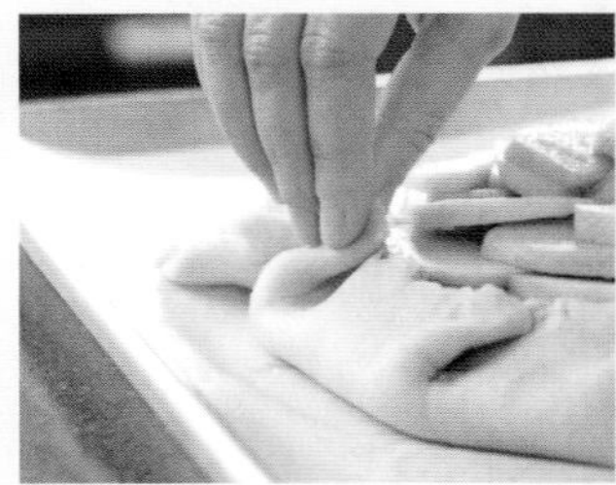

2. Fold 2 inches of the dough up over the fruit, leaving a ½-inch border between the fruit and the edge of the tart shell. This ½-inch space helps prevent the tart juices from leaking through the folds in the shell.

TARTE TATIN

WHY THIS RECIPE WORKS: Making a true *tarte Tatin* requires an investment of time and a certain amount of skill. Traditionally, the apples are cooked in a skillet until caramelized, then topped with homemade pastry and cooked in the oven. Before serving, the tart is masterfully flipped onto a serving platter. Yes, this version is great, but we wanted to simplify it enough for a weeknight dessert.

We first baked a sheet of store-bought puff pastry until it was beautifully golden brown. While the pastry baked, we caramelized the apples in a skillet until they were tender. We then spooned the apples over the pastry, arranging them in three even rows with a ½-inch border around the outside of the pastry. As a final touch, we created a simple sauce by adding heavy cream and Grand Marnier to the juices left behind after the apples were cooked.

30-Minute Tarte Tatin

SERVES 6 TO 8

To get this dessert on the table in 30 minutes, peel the apples while the oven preheats and the pastry thaws, and then bake the pastry while the apples are caramelizing. This dessert is especially good with Tangy Whipped Cream (page 830).

- 1 (9½ by 9-inch) sheet frozen puff pastry, thawed
- 8 tablespoons (1 stick) unsalted butter
- ¾ cup (5¼ ounces) sugar
- 2 pounds Granny Smith apples (about 4 large), peeled, quartered, and cored
- ¼ cup heavy cream
- 2 tablespoons Grand Marnier, spiced rum, or Calvados (optional)

1. Adjust an oven rack to the middle position and heat the oven to 400 degrees. Line a rimmed baking sheet with parchment paper. Unfold the puff pastry, lay it on the prepared baking sheet, and bake until golden brown and puffed, 15 to 20 minutes, rotating the baking sheet halfway through. Transfer the baked pastry sheet to a serving platter and press lightly to flatten if domed.

2. Meanwhile, melt the butter in a 12-inch nonstick skillet over high heat. Remove the pan from the heat and sprinkle evenly with the sugar. Lay the apples in the skillet, return the skillet to high heat, and cook until the juice in the pan turns a rich amber color and the apples are caramelized, about 15 minutes, turning the apples halfway through.

3. Remove the apples from the pan one at a time and arrange in three overlapping rows on the baked pastry sheet, leaving a ½-inch border. Spoon about half of the pan juice over the apples.

4. Whisk the cream and Grand Marnier (if using) into the remaining juice in the pan and bring to a simmer. Pour some sauce over the tart and serve, passing the remaining sauce separately.

Pear Tatin

We like to use Bosc or Bartlett pears here because they maintain their shape nicely when cooked. If you have it on hand, substitute Poire William (or other pear liqueur) for the Grand Marnier.

Follow the recipe for 30-Minute Tarte Tatin, substituting 2 pounds Bosc or Bartlett pears for the apples. Increase the cooking time by 5 to 10 minutes if necessary.

BEST CHOCOLATE TART

WHY THIS RECIPE WORKS: For us, a great chocolate tart should possess deep chocolate flavor, a rich, lush texture, and a sophisticated presentation. First we made a custardy filling by melting intense dark chocolate into hot cream, adding eggs, and baking. To enrich the filling's flavor, we added some butter and a little instant espresso to echo the bittersweetness of the chocolate. Because custards tend to curdle under high heat, we baked the tart in a very low 250-degree oven for a smooth and silky texture. To make our tart a showstopper, we topped it with a simple glossy glaze of chocolate, cream, and corn syrup. A classic sweet pastry dough flavored with ground almonds made the perfect complement to the chocolate filling.

Best Chocolate Tart

SERVES 12

Toasted and skinned hazelnuts can be substituted for the almonds. Use good-quality dark chocolate containing a cacao percentage between 60 and 65 percent; our favorites are Ghirardelli 60% Cacao Bittersweet Chocolate and Callebaut Intense Dark Chocolate, L-60-40NV. Let tart sit at room temperature for 30 minutes before glazing in step 6. The tart can be garnished with chocolate curls or with a flaky coarse sea salt, such as Maldon. Serve with lightly sweetened whipped cream; if you like, flavor the whipped cream with cognac or vanilla extract.

CRUST

- 1 large egg yolk
- 2 tablespoons heavy cream
- ½ cup sliced almonds, toasted
- ¼ cup (1¾ ounces) sugar
- 1 cup (5 ounces) all-purpose flour
- ¼ teaspoon salt
- 6 tablespoons unsalted butter, cut into ½-inch pieces

FILLING

- 1¼ cups heavy cream
- ½ teaspoon instant espresso powder
- ¼ teaspoon salt
- 9 ounces bittersweet chocolate, chopped fine
- 4 tablespoons unsalted butter, cut into thin slices and softened
- 2 large eggs, lightly beaten, room temperature

GLAZE

- 3 tablespoons heavy cream
- 1 tablespoon light corn syrup
- 2 ounces bittersweet chocolate, chopped fine
- 1 tablespoon hot water

1. FOR THE CRUST: Beat egg yolk and cream together in small bowl. Process almonds and sugar in food processor until nuts are finely ground, 15 to 20 seconds. Add flour and salt; pulse to combine, about 10 pulses. Scatter butter over

flour mixture; pulse to cut butter into flour until mixture resembles coarse meal, about 15 pulses. With processor running, add egg yolk mixture and process until dough forms ball, about 10 seconds. Transfer dough to large sheet of plastic wrap and press into 6-inch disk; wrap dough in plastic and refrigerate until firm but malleable, about 30 minutes. (Dough can be refrigerated for up to 3 days; before using, let stand at room temperature until malleable but still cool.)

2. Roll out dough between 2 large sheets of plastic into 11-inch round about ⅜ inch thick. (If dough becomes too soft and sticky to work with, slip it onto baking sheet and refrigerate until workable.) Place dough round (still in plastic) on baking sheet and refrigerate until firm but pliable, about 15 minutes.

3. Adjust oven rack to middle position and heat oven to 375 degrees. Spray 9-inch tart pan with removable bottom with vegetable oil spray. Keeping dough on sheet, remove top layer of plastic. Invert tart pan (with bottom) on top of dough round. Press on tart pan to cut dough. Using both hands, pick up sheet and tart pan and carefully invert both, setting tart pan right side up. Remove sheet and peel off plastic; reserve plastic. Roll over edges of tart pan with rolling pin to cut dough. Gently ease and press dough into bottom of pan, reserving scraps. Roll dough scraps into ¾-inch rope (various lengths are OK). Line edge of tart pan with rope(s) and gently press into fluted sides. Line tart pan with reserved plastic and, using measuring cup, gently press and smooth dough to even thickness (sides should be about ¼ inch thick). Using paring knife, trim any excess dough above rim of tart; discard scraps. Freeze dough-lined pan until dough is firm, 20 to 30 minutes.

4. Set dough-lined pan on baking sheet. Spray 12-inch square of aluminum foil with oil spray and press foil, sprayed side down, into pan; fill with 2 cups pie weights. Bake until dough is dry and light golden brown, about 25 minutes, rotating sheet halfway through baking. Carefully remove foil and weights and continue to bake until pastry is rich golden brown and fragrant, 8 to 10 minutes longer. Let cool completely on baking sheet on wire rack.

5. FOR THE FILLING: Heat oven to 250 degrees. Bring cream, espresso powder, and salt to simmer in small saucepan over medium heat, stirring once or twice to dissolve espresso powder and salt. Meanwhile, place chocolate in large heatproof bowl. Pour simmering cream mixture over chocolate, cover, and let stand for 5 minutes to allow chocolate to soften. Using whisk, stir mixture slowly and gently (so as not to incorporate air) until homogeneous. Add butter and continue to whisk gently until fully incorporated. Pour beaten eggs through fine-mesh strainer into chocolate mixture; whisk slowly until mixture is homogeneous and glossy. Pour filling into tart crust and shake gently from side to side to distribute and smooth surface; pop any large bubbles with toothpick or skewer. Bake tart, on baking sheet, until outer edge of filling is just set and very faint cracks appear on surface, 30 to 35 minutes; filling will still be very wobbly. Let cool completely on baking sheet on wire rack. Refrigerate, uncovered, until filling is chilled and set, at least 3 hours or up to 18 hours.

6. FOR THE GLAZE: Thirty minutes before glazing, remove tart from refrigerator. Bring cream and corn syrup to simmer in small saucepan over medium heat; stir once or twice to combine. Remove pan from heat, add chocolate, and cover. Let stand for 5 minutes to allow chocolate to soften. Whisk gently (so as not to incorporate air) until mixture is smooth, then whisk in hot water until glaze is homogeneous, shiny, and pourable. Working quickly, pour glaze onto center of tart. To distribute glaze, tilt tart and allow glaze to run to edge. (Spreading glaze with spatula will leave marks on surface.) Pop any large bubbles with toothpick or skewer. Let cool completely, about 1 hour.

7. Remove outer ring from tart pan. Insert thin-bladed metal spatula between crust and pan bottom to loosen tart; slide tart onto serving platter. Cut into wedges and serve.

NOTES FROM THE TEST KITCHEN

FITTING DELICATE PASTRY INTO A TART PAN

After your dough has been refrigerated, follow these easy steps to get it into the tart pan. This novel method works with any tart dough, but it is especially helpful when working with higher-fat, more fragile pastry.

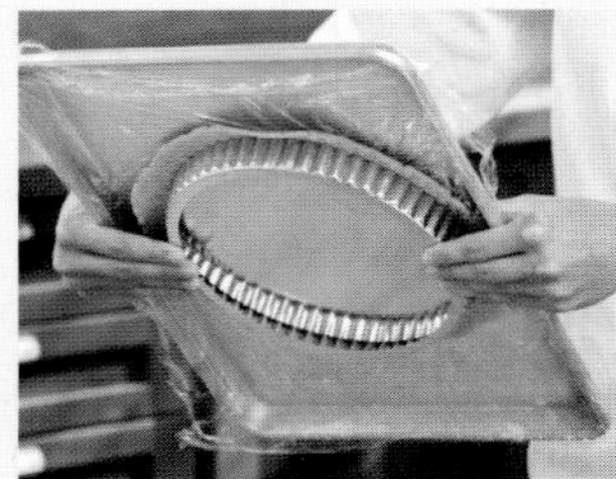

1. Invert tart pan (with bottom) onto dough round. Press down on tart pan to perforate dough. Invert baking sheet, holding tart pan in place, then set down so that tart pan is right side up. Remove baking sheet and plastic wrap.

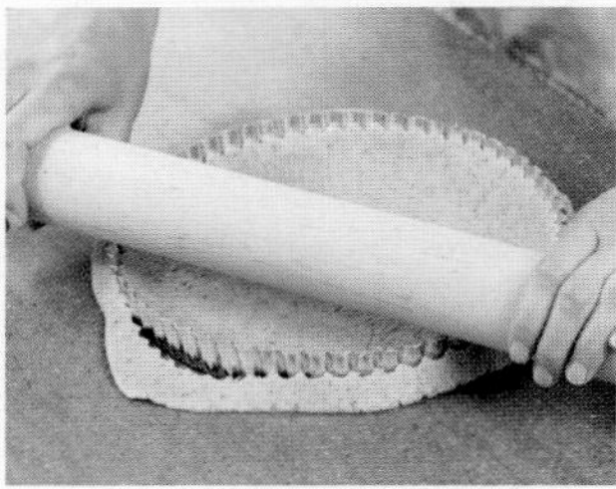

2. Roll over dough edges with rolling pin to cut off excess, reserving scraps. Gently press dough into bottom of pan in even layer.

3. Roll dough scraps into ¾-inch rope(s). Line fluted edges of pan with ropes and press evenly into sides.

THE AMERICA'S TEST KITCHEN SHOPPING GUIDE

SHOPPING FOR EQUIPMENT

With a well-stocked kitchen, you'll be able to take on any recipe. But with so much equipment out there on the market, how do you figure out what's what? Price often correlates with design, not performance. Over the years, our test kitchen has evaluated thousands of products. We've gone through copious rounds of testing and have identified the most important attributes in every piece of equipment, so when you go shopping you'll know what to look for. And because our test kitchen accepts no support from product manufacturers, you can trust our ratings. Prices in this chart are based on shopping at online retailers and will vary. See AmericasTestKitchen.com for updates to these testings.

KNIVES AND MORE	ITEM	WHAT TO LOOK FOR	TEST KITCHEN FAVORITES
MUST-HAVE ITEMS 	CHEF'S KNIFE	• High-carbon stainless-steel knife • Thin, curved 8-inch blade • Lightweight • Comfortable grip and nonslip handle	Victorinox Fibrox Pro 8-Inch Chef's Knife $24.95
 MUST-HAVE ITEMS	SERRATED KNIFE	• 10-inch blade • Fewer broader, deeper, pointed serrations • Thinner blade angle • Comfortable, grippy handle • Medium weight	Mercer Culinary Millennia 10″ Wide Bread Knife $22.10
 MUST-HAVE ITEMS	SLICING KNIFE	• Tapered 12-inch blade for slicing large cuts of meat • Oval scallops (called a granton edge) carved into blade • Fairly rigid blade with rounded tip	Victorinox 12″ Fibrox Pro Granton Edge Slicing/Carving Knife $54.65
 MUST-HAVE ITEMS	PARING KNIFE	• Sharp, lightweight, slightly flexible blade • Comfortable, secure handle • Blade between 3 and 3¼ inches long	Victorinox Swiss Army Fibrox Pro 3¼″ Spear Point Paring Knife $9.47
	SERRATED PARING KNIFE	• Thin blade with razor-sharp serrations for safe, precise slicing • Hefty but nimble	Wüsthof Classic 3.5-Inch Fully Serrated Paring Knife $59.95 Best Buy: Victorinox Serrated Paring Knife $5.95
	STEAK KNIVES	• Super-sharp, straight-edged blade • Sturdy—not wobbly—blade	Victorinox Swiss Army 6-Piece Rosewood Steak Set, Spear Point, Straight Edge $170.74 for set of 6 Best Buy: Chicago Cutlery Walnut Tradition 4-Piece Steak Knife Set $17.95 for set of 4
	SANTOKU KNIFE	• Solid but light feel • Fine, level cuts providing good precision and control	Misono UX10 Santoku 7.0″ $179.50

KNIVES AND MORE	ITEM	WHAT TO LOOK FOR	TEST KITCHEN FAVORITES
	BONING KNIFE	• 6-inch blade • Narrow, highly maneuverable and razor-sharp blade • Comfortable grip and nonslip handle	**Victorinox 6-Inch Fibrox Pro Flexible Boning Knife** $27.20
	MEAT CLEAVER	• Relatively light and evenly balanced • 7¼-inch thin blade with acute angle • Long handle	**Shun Classic Meat Cleaver** $149
	VEGETABLE CLEAVER	• Slim blade for slicing through thick, hard vegetables • Lightweight	**MAC Japanese Series 6½-Inch Japanese Vegetable Cleaver** $95
	HYBRID CHEF'S KNIFE	• High-carbon stainless-steel knife • Lightweight • Thin blade that tapers from spine to cutting edge and from handle to tip	**Masamoto VG-10 Gyutou, 8.2″** $136.50
	CARBON-STEEL KNIFE	• 8-inch blade • Sloping ergonomic handle • Narrow, razor-sharp blade	**Bob Kramer 8″ Carbon Steel Chef's Knife by Zwilling J.A. Henckels** $299.95 Best Buy: **Togiharu Virgin Carbon Steel Gyutou, 8.2″** $98.50
	MANDOLINE	• Razor-sharp blade(s) • Hand guard to shield fingers • Gripper tongs to grasp food • Measurement-marked dial for precision cuts • Storage for extra blades	**Swissmar Börner Original V-Slicer Plus Mandoline** $29.99
	CARVING BOARD	• Trenches can contain ½ cup of liquid • Large and stable enough to hold large roasts • Midweight for easy carrying, carving, and cleaning	**J.K. Adams Maple Reversible Carving Board** $69.95
MUST-HAVE ITEM	CUTTING BOARD	• Roomy work surface at least 20 by 15 inches • Teak board for minimal maintenance • Durable edge-grain construction (wood grain runs parallel to surface of board)	**Proteak Edge Grain Teak Cutting Board** $84.99

KNIVES AND MORE	ITEM	WHAT TO LOOK FOR	TEST KITCHEN FAVORITES
MUST-HAVE ITEM	KNIFE SHARPENER	• Reliable notch removal and diamond sharpening material in electric sharpeners • Clear, precise user instructions • Easy and comfortable to use	Electric: **Chef'sChoice Trizor XV Knife Sharpener** $149.99 Electric, Best Buy: **Chef'sChoice Diamond Sharpener for Asian Knives** $79.99 Manual: **Chef'sChoice Pronto Manual Diamond Hone Asian Knife Sharpener** $49.99
	UNIVERSAL KNIFE BLOCK	• Heavy, ultrastable block with rotating base • Durable bamboo exterior for easy cleaning • Well-placed, medium-strength magnets for easy knife attachment	**Design Trifecta 360 Knife Block** $248.64
	MAGNETIC KNIFE STRIP	• Medium strength magnets to hold knives with just the right amount of pull • Easy to install and clean • Bamboo surface that is gentle on blades	**Messermeister 16.75-inch Bamboo Knife Magnet** $59.95
	CUT-RESISTANT GLOVE	• Tightly woven fabric for durability • Stretchy fabric for comfortable fit • Fits either right or left hand	**Microplane Specialty Series Cut Resistant Glove** $14.95

POTS AND PANS	ITEM	WHAT TO LOOK FOR	TEST KITCHEN FAVORITES
MUST-HAVE ITEMS	TRADITIONAL SKILLET	• Thick aluminum core speeds up cooking • Steeply angled handle allows for better leverage • Good to have smaller (8- or 10-inch) skillets too	**All-Clad 12-Inch Stainless Fry Pan with Lid** $96.85
MUST-HAVE ITEMS	NONSTICK SKILLET	• Dark, nonstick surface • 12- or 12½-inch diameter, thick bottom • Comfortable, ovensafe handle • Cooking surface of at least 9 inches • Good to have smaller (8- or 10-inch) skillets too	**OXO Good Grips Non-Stick 12-Inch Open Frypan** $39.99
	CARBON-STEEL SKILLET	• Affordable • Thick, solid construction; ergonomically angled handle • Sides flared up just right for easy access but high enough to contain splashes	**Matfer Bourgeat Black Steel Round Frying Pan, 11⅞"** $44.38

POTS AND PANS	ITEM	WHAT TO LOOK FOR	TEST KITCHEN FAVORITES
	CAST-IRON SKILLET Traditional	• Thick bottom and straight sides • Roomy interior (cooking surface of 9¼ inches or more) • Preseasoned	**Lodge Classic Cast Iron Skillet, 12″** $33.31
	Enameled	• Balanced weight, wide pour spouts, and oversized helper handle for comfortable use • Durable, satiny surface that does not require preseasoning • Easy to clean	**Le Creuset Signature 11¾″ Iron Handle Skillet** $179.95 Best Buy: **Mario Batali by Dansk 12″ Open Sauté Pan** $59.95
	ECO-FRIENDLY SKILLET	• PFOA-free (perfluorooctanoic acid) surfaces are nonstick and more durable than silicone coatings • Roomy interior (cooking surface of 9 inches or more) NOTE: We prefer our favorite nonstick skillet for its superior performance.	**Scanpan Professional 12.5-Inch Fry Pan** $129.95
MUST-HAVE ITEM	DUTCH OVEN	• Enameled cast iron or stainless steel • Capacity of at least 6 quarts • Diameter of at least 9 inches • Tight-fitting lid • Wide, sturdy handles	Heavier Choice: **Le Creuset 7¼-Quart Round French Oven** $359.99 Best Buy: **Cuisinart 7 Qt. Round Covered Casserole** $121.94
	DUTCH OVEN, INNOVATIVE	• Large capacity • Sturdy, thick base • Silicone oil chamber in base spreads heat slowly and evenly • Good heat retention	**Pauli Cookware Never Burn Sauce Pot, 10 Quart** $229.99
MUST-HAVE ITEM	SAUCEPAN Large	• Steady heating and good visibility to monitor browning • Stay-cool, easy to grip handle • Helper handle for extra grabbing point	**All Clad 4 Quart Stainless Steel Sauce Pan with Loop Helper Handle** $179.13 Best Buy: **Cuisinart MultiClad Unlimited Dishwasher Safe 4-Quart Saucepan with Cover** $65.12

POTS AND PANS	ITEM	WHAT TO LOOK FOR	TEST KITCHEN FAVORITES
MUST-HAVE ITEMS	SAUCEPAN Small	• Heavy, solid, well-priced • Easy to control • Shallow shape and generous diameter	**Calphalon Contemporary Nonstick 2½ Quart Shallow Saucepan with Cover** $39.95
	RIMMED BAKING SHEET	• Light-colored surface (heats and browns evenly) • Sturdy but lightweight pan • Dimensions of 18 by 13 inches • Good to have at least two	**Nordic Ware Bakers Half Sheet** $14.97
	SAUTÉ PAN	• Aluminum core surrounded by layers of stainless steel • Relatively lightweight • 9¾-inch diameter • Stay-cool helper handle	**All-Clad Stainless 3-Quart Tri-Ply Sauté Pan** $224.95 Best Buy: **Cuisinart MultiClad Pro Stainless 3½-Quart Sauté Pan with Helper and Cover** $78.13
	OMELET PAN	• Gently sloped sides for easy turning and rolling of omelets • Nonstick finish • Heavy construction for durability and even heat distribution • 8-inch size for French omelets	**Original French Chef Omelette Pan** $139.95
	PAELLA PAN	• Shallow, wide shape maximizes the surface area of the paella • Distributes heat evenly	**Matfer Bourgeat Black Steel Paella Pan** $49.98
	CANNING POT	• Comfortable, grippy handles • Clear lid that allows user to easily monitor contents	**Victorio Stainless Steel Multi-Use Canner** $75.19
MUST-HAVE ITEM	STOCKPOT	• 12-quart capacity • Thick bottom to prevent scorching • Wide body for easy cleaning and storage • Flat or round handles that extend at least 1¾ inches	**All-Clad Stainless 12-Quart Stock Pot** $389.95 Best Buy: **Cuisinart Chef's Classic Stainless 12-Quart Stock Pot** $69.99

POTS AND PANS	ITEM	WHAT TO LOOK FOR	TEST KITCHEN FAVORITES
MUST-HAVE ITEM	ROASTING PAN	• At least 15 by 11 inches • Stainless-steel interior with aluminum core for even heat distribution • Upright handles for easy gripping • Light interior for better food monitoring	**Calphalon Contemporary Stainless Roasting Pan with Rack** $99.99
	V-RACK	• Fixed, not adjustable, to provide sturdiness • Tall, vertical handles positioned on long side of rack	**All-Clad Nonstick Large Rack** $24.95
	GRILL PAN	• Cast-iron pan with enamel coating for heat retention and easy cleanup • Tall ridges (4- to 5.5-mm high) to keep food above rendered fat • Generous cooking area	**Staub 12-Inch American Square Grill Pan and Press** $219.95, including press Best Buy: **Lodge Square Grill Pan and Lodge Ribbed Panini Press** $18.97, grill pan $14.58, panini press
	COOKWARE SET	• Fully clad stainless steel with aluminum core for even heat distribution • Moderately heavy, durable construction • Lids included • Ideal mix of pans includes 12-inch skillet, 10-inch skillet, 2-quart saucepan, 4-quart saucepan, 8-quart stockpot	**All-Clad Stainless Steel Cookware Set, 10-piece** $799.95 Best Buy: **Tramontina 18/10 Stainless Steel TriPly-Clad Cookware Set, 8-piece** $144.97

HANDY TOOLS	ITEM	WHAT TO LOOK FOR	TEST KITCHEN FAVORITES
MUST-HAVE ITEMS	KITCHEN SHEARS	• Take-apart scissors (for easy cleaning) • Super-sharp blades • Sturdy construction • Work for both right- and left-handed users	**Kershaw Taskmaster Shears/ Shun Multi-Purpose Shears** $49.95 Best Buy: **J.A. Henckels International Kitchen Shears—Take Apart** $14.95
MUST-HAVE ITEMS	TONGS	• Scalloped edges • Slightly concave pincers • Length of 12 inches (to keep your hand far from the heat) • Open and close easily	**OXO Good Grips 12-Inch Locking Tongs** $12.09
	WOODEN SPOON	• Slim yet broad bowl • Stain-resistant bamboo • Comfortable handle	**SCI Bamboo Wood Cooking Spoon** $2.40

HANDY TOOLS	ITEM	WHAT TO LOOK FOR	TEST KITCHEN FAVORITES
MUST-HAVE ITEM	SLOTTED SPOON	• Lightweight • Wide, shallow bowl • Thin-edged bowl • Long, comfortable handle	**Cuisinart Stainless Steel Slotted Spoon** $9.12
	BASTING SPOON	• Thin, shallow bowl • Handle at least 9 inches in length • Slight dip from handle to bowl	**Rösle Basting Spoon with Hook Handle** $28.95
	SPOONULA	• Lightweight thanks to lightly textured silicone material and gently rounded handle • Odor-resistant • Vibrant color hides stains	**Starpack Premium Silicone Spoonula** $8.49
MUST-HAVE ITEMS	ALL-AROUND SPATULA	• Head about 3 inches wide and 5½ inches long • 11 inches in length (tip to handle) • Long, vertical slots • Useful to have a metal spatula to use with traditional cookware and plastic for nonstick cookware	Metal: **Wüsthof Gourmet Slotted Turner/Fish Spatula** $34.95 Best Buy: **OXO Good Grips Flexible Turner—Steel** $7.99 Plastic: **Matfer Bourgeat Pelton Spatula** $8.23
MUST-HAVE ITEMS	SILICONE SPATULA	• Firm enough for scraping and scooping • Fits neatly into tight corners • Straight sides and wide, flat blade to ensure no food is left unmixed	**Di Oro Living Seamless Silicone Spatula-Large** $10.97 Best Large: **Rubbermaid 13.5" High-Heat Scraper** $14.50
MUST-HAVE ITEMS	OFFSET SPATULA	• Flexible blade offset to a roughly 30-degree angle • Enough usable surface area to frost the radius of a 9-inch cake • Comfortable handle	**OXO Good Grips Bent Icing Knife** $9.99
	COOKIE SPATULA	• Small, silicone blade with thin, flexible edge • Angled handle	**OXO Good Grips Cookie Spatula** $6.99
	JAR SPATULA	• Slim, flexible head maneuvers tight corners and edges • Strong enough to lift heavy food • Seamless silicone for easy cleaning and comfortable feel	**GIR Skinny Spatula** $12.95 Best Buy: **OXO Good Grips Silicone Jar Spatula** $5.95

HANDY TOOLS	ITEM	WHAT TO LOOK FOR	TEST KITCHEN FAVORITES
MUST-HAVE ITEM	ALL-PURPOSE WHISK	• At least 10 wires • Wires of moderate thickness • Comfortable rubber handle • Balanced, lightweight feel	**OXO Good Grips 11-Inch Balloon Whisk** $9.99
	FLAT WHISK	• Comfortable to use for longer periods • Grippy TPE handle • Tines with good rigidity and spacing	**OXO Good Grips Flat Whisk** $6.95
MUST-HAVE ITEMS	PEPPER MILL	• Easy-to-adjust, clearly marked grind settings • Efficient, comfortable grinding mechanism • Generous capacity	**Cole & Mason Derwent Gourmet Precision Pepper Mill** $40
MUST-HAVE ITEMS	LADLE	• Stainless steel • Hook handle • Pouring rim to prevent dripping • Handle 9 to 10 inches in length	**Rösle Hook Ladle with Pouring Rim** $34 Best Buy: **OXO Good Grips Brushed Stainless Steel Ladle** $9.99
MUST-HAVE ITEMS	CAN OPENER	• Easy to attach • Smooth and comfortable turning motions • Pulls off removed lid for safe and easy disposal	**Fissler Magic Smooth-Edge Can Opener** $29
	JAR OPENER	• Strong, sturdy clamp grip • Adjusts quickly to any size jar	**Amco Swing-A-Way Jar Opener** $5.99
MUST-HAVE ITEM	GARLIC PRESS	• Large capacity that holds multiple garlic cloves • Long handle and short distance between pivot point and plunger	**Kuhn Rikon Stainless Steel Epicurean Garlic Press** $39.95
	SERRATED FRUIT PEELER	• Comfortable grip and nonslip handle • Sharp blade	**Messermeister Serrated Swivel Peeler** $5.50
MUST-HAVE ITEM	VEGETABLE PEELER	• Sharp, carbon steel blade • 1-inch space between blade and peeler to prevent jamming • Lightweight and comfortable	**Kuhn Rikon Original Swiss Peeler** $3.50

HANDY TOOLS	ITEM	WHAT TO LOOK FOR	TEST KITCHEN FAVORITES
MUST-HAVE ITEMS	AVOCADO SLICER	• Compact • Relatively comfortable to hold • Double-headed configuration with knife on one end and slicer on the other	**OXO Good Grips 3-in-1 Avocado Slicer** $9.95
	RASP GRATER	• Sharp teeth (require little effort or pressure when grating) • Maneuverable over round shapes • Comfortable handle	**Microplane Classic Zester Grater** $12.35
	GRATER	• Four super-sharp grating planes framed by tough plastic, making it easy to handle • Large holes for quick, flawless mozzarella grating and fine holes for perfect shredded ginger or Parmesan	**Microplane Specialty Series 4-Sided Box Grater** $34.95
	ROTARY GRATER	• Barrel at least 2 inches in diameter • Classic turn-crank design • Comfortable handle • Simple to disassemble for easy cleanup	**Zyliss All Cheese Grater** $19.95
	MANUAL CITRUS JUICER	• Hand-held squeezer with comfortable handle • Durable, plastic exterior • Large, slat-like holes for efficient draining	**Chef'n FreshForce Citrus Juicer** $23.04
	ICE CREAM SCOOP	• Comfortable handle • Gently curved bowl for easy releasing • Scoop warms on contact with your hand to slightly melt ice cream	**Zeroll Original Ice Cream Scoop** $18.44
	MEAT POUNDER	• At least 1½ pounds in weight • Vertical handle for better leverage and control	**Norpro GRIP-EZ Meat Pounder** $17.50
	BENCH SCRAPER	• Sturdy blade • Comfortable handle with plastic, rubber, or nylon grip	**Dexter-Russell 6″ Dough Cutter/Scraper—Sani-Safe Series** $7.01
	BOWL SCRAPER	• Curved shape with comfortable grip • Rigid enough to move dough but flexible enough to scrape up batter • Thin, straight edge doubles as dough cutter or bench scraper	**iSi Basics Silicone Scraper Spatula** $5.99

HANDY TOOLS	ITEM	WHAT TO LOOK FOR	TEST KITCHEN FAVORITES
	ROLLING PIN	• Moderate weight (1 to 1½ pounds) • 19-inch straight barrel • Slightly textured wooden surface to grip dough for easy rolling	**J.K. Adams Plain Maple Rolling Dowel** $13.95
MUST-HAVE ITEMS	MIXING BOWLS Stainless Steel	• Lightweight and easy to handle • Durability • Conducts heat well for double boiler	**Vollrath Economy Stainless Steel Mixing Bowls** $2.90, 1.5 quart $4.50, 3 quart $6.90, 5 quart
	Glass	• Tempered to increase impact and thermal resistance • Can be used in microwave • Durability	**Pyrex Smart Essentials Mixing Bowl Set with Colored Lids** $27.98 for 4-bowl set
	MINI PREP BOWLS	• Wide, shallow bowls are easy to hold, fill, empty, and clean • Can be used in the microwave and oven	**Anchor Hocking 6-Piece Nesting Prep Bowl Set** $11
	BOWL STABILIZER	• Firmly attaches bowls to every work surface in the kitchen • Accommodates bowls from 6 to 21 inches in diameter • Forms a tight seal in double boilers	**Staybowlizer** $19.95
MUST-HAVE ITEM	OVEN MITT	• Form-fitting and not overly bulky for easy maneuvering • Machine washable • Flexible, heat-resistant material	**Kool-Tek 15-Inch Oven Mitt by KatchAll** $44.95 each
	JAR LIFTER	• Spring-loaded hinge that pops grabbers open when handles are released • Broad, molded handles comfortable and secure • Does not rust	**Ball Secure-Grip Jar Lifter** $10.99
	COOKIE PRESS	• Produces visually appealing, uniform cookies • Withstands prolonged use with no decline in performance • Consistently produces cookies with intact designs without dough jamming	**Marcato Biscuit Maker** $42

HANDY TOOLS	ITEM	WHAT TO LOOK FOR	TEST KITCHEN FAVORITES
	PASTRY BRUSH	• Silicone bristles (heat-resistant, durable, and easy to clean) • Perforated flaps (to trap liquid) • Angled head to reach tight spots • Comfortable handle	**OXO Good Grips Silicone Pastry Brush** $6.99
	SPLATTER SCREEN	• Diameter of at least 13 inches • Lollipop-shaped design • Tightly woven mesh face	**Progressive Prepworks Splatter Screen** $11.67
	BOUILLON STRAINER/ CHINOIS	• Conical shape • Depth of 7 to 8 inches • At least one hook on rim for stability	**Winco Reinforced Extra Fine Mesh Bouillon Strainer** $33.78
MUST-HAVE ITEMS	COLANDER	• 4- to 7-quart capacity • Metal ring attached to the bottom for stability • Many holes for quick draining • Small holes so pasta doesn't slip through	**RSVP International Endurance Precision Pierced 5 Qt. Colander** $25.99
MUST-HAVE ITEMS	FINE-MESH STRAINER	• Roomy, medium-depth basket with fine, stiff mesh • Long wide hook and rounded steel handle	**Rösle Fine Mesh Strainer, Round Handle, 7.9 inches, 20 cm** $45
	SPIDER SKIMMER	• Long handle for protection from hot water and oil • Well-balanced and easy to maneuver	**Rösle Wire Skimmer Skimmer** $41.68
	COLLAPSIBLE MINI COLANDER	• Large, comfortable, rubberized grip • Perfectly sized webbed basket	**Progressive International Collapsible Mini Colander** $13.70
	FOOD MILL	• Interchangeable disks for fine, medium, and coarse purees • Easy to turn	**RSVP Classic Rotary Food Mill** $24.95
	FAT SEPARATOR	• Bottom-draining model • Detachable bowl for easy cleaning • Strainer for catching solids	**Cuisipro Fat Separator** $33.95

HANDY TOOLS	ITEM	WHAT TO LOOK FOR	TEST KITCHEN FAVORITES
MUST-HAVE ITEMS	POTATO MASHER	• Solid mashing disk with small holes • Comfortable grip	**Zyliss Stainless Steel Potato Masher** $12.99
	SALAD SPINNER	• Ergonomic and easy-to-operate hand pump • Wide base for stability • Flat lid for easy cleaning and storage	**OXO Good Grips Salad Spinner** $29.99
	STEAMER BASKET	• Stainless-steel basket with feet • Roomy and collapsible	**OXO Good Grips Pop-Up Steamer** $16.99
	MORTAR AND PESTLE	• Heavy, stable base with tall, narrow walls • Rough interior to help grip and grind ingredients • Comfortable, heavy pestle	**Frieling "Goliath" Mortar and Pestle Set** $49.95
	INNOVATIVE MORTAR AND PESTLE	• Heavy ceramic ball quickly crushes spices and garlic • Dishwasher-safe	**Jamie Oliver Flavour Shaker** $29.95

MEASURING EQUIPMENT	ITEM	WHAT TO LOOK FOR	TEST KITCHEN FAVORITES
MUST-HAVE ITEMS	DRY MEASURING CUPS	• Accurate measurements • Easy-to-read measurement markings • Stack and store neatly • Durable measurement markings • Stable when empty and filled • Handles perfectly flush with cups	**OXO Good Grips Stainless Steel Measuring Cups** $19.99
	LIQUID MEASURING CUP	• Crisp, unambiguous markings that include ¼- and ⅓-cup measurements • Heatproof, sturdy cup with handle • Good to have in a variety of sizes (1, 2, and 4 cups)	**Pyrex 2-Cup Measuring Cup** $5.99
	ADJUSTABLE MEASURING CUP	• Plunger-like bottom (with a tight seal between plunger and tube) that you can set to correct measurement, then push up to cleanly extract sticky ingredients (such as shortening or peanut butter) • 1- or 2-cup capacity • Dishwasher-safe	**KitchenArt Adjust-A-Cup Professional Series, 2-Cup** $12.95

MEASURING EQUIPMENT	ITEM	WHAT TO LOOK FOR	TEST KITCHEN FAVORITES
MUST-HAVE ITEMS	MEASURING SPOONS	• Long, comfortable handles • Rim of bowl flush with handle (makes it easy to "dip" into a dry ingredient and "sweep" across the top for accurate measuring) • Slim design	**Cuisipro Stainless Steel Measuring Spoons Set** $11.95
	KITCHEN RULER	• Stainless steel and easy to clean • 18 inches in length • Large, easy-to-read markings	**Empire 18-Inch Stainless Steel Ruler** $8.49
	DIGITAL SCALE	• Easy-to-read display not blocked by weighing platform • At least 7-pound capacity • Accessible buttons • Gram-to-ounce conversion feature • Roomy platform	**OXO Good Grips 11 lb Food Scale with Pull Out Display** $49.95 Best Buy: **Ozeri Pronto Digital Multifunction Kitchen and Food Scale** $11.79

THERMOMETERS AND TIMERS	ITEM	WHAT TO LOOK FOR	TEST KITCHEN FAVORITES
MUST-HAVE ITEMS	INSTANT-READ THERMOMETER	• Digital model with automatic shut-off • Quick-response readings in 10 seconds or fewer • Wide temperature range (-40 to 450 degrees) • Long stem that can reach interior of large cuts of meat • Water-resistant	**ThermoWorks Thermapen Mk4** $99 Best Buy: **ThermoWorks ThermoPop** $29
	OVEN THERMOMETER	• Clearly marked numbers for easy readability • Large, sturdy base • Large temperature range (up to 600 degrees)	**CDN Pro Accurate Oven Thermometer** $8.70
	MEAT PROBE/ CANDY/ DEEP-FRY THERMOMETER	• Digital model • Easy-to-read console • Intuitive design and ovensafe probe	**ThermoWorks ChefAlarm** $59 Best Buy: **Polder Classic Digital Thermometer/Timer** $24.99
	REFRIGERATOR/ FREEZER THERMOMETER	• Accurate and customizable • Alerts when temperatures remain outside safe zone for over 30 minutes	**ThermoWorks Fridge/Freezer Alarm** $22.99
	REMOTE THERMOMETER	• Easy to customize • Reports accurate readings from up to 120 feet from its base	**Oregon Scientific Grill-Right Bluetooth BBQ Thermometer** $48.62

THERMOMETERS AND TIMERS	ITEM	WHAT TO LOOK FOR	TEST KITCHEN FAVORITES
MUST-HAVE ITEM	KITCHEN TIMER	• Lengthy time range (1 second to at least 10 hours) • Able to count up after alarm goes off • Easy to use and read • Able to track multiple events	**OXO Good Grips Triple Timer** $19.99

BAKEWARE	ITEM	WHAT TO LOOK FOR	TEST KITCHEN FAVORITES
MUST-HAVE ITEMS	GLASS BAKING DISH	• Large handles • Lightweight • Easy to grip and maneuver	**Pyrex Easy Grab 3-Quart Oblong Baking Dish** $7.29
	METAL BAKING PAN	• Dimensions of 13 by 9 inches • Straight sides • Nonstick coating for even browning and easy release of cakes and bar cookies	**Williams-Sonoma Goldtouch Nonstick Rectangular Cake Pan, 9" x 13"** $32.95
	SQUARE BAKING PAN	• Straight sides • Light gold or dark nonstick surface for even browning and easy release of cakes • Good to have both 9-inch and 8-inch square pans	**Williams-Sonoma Goldtouch Nonstick 8-Inch Square Cake Pan** $21
	ROUND CAKE PAN Best All Around	• Best for cake • Straight sides • Light finish for tall, evenly baked cakes • Nonstick surface for easy release	**Nordic Ware Naturals Nonstick 9-Inch Round Cake Pan** $14.32
	Best for Browning	• Dark finish is ideal for pizza and cinnamon buns • Nonstick	**Chicago Metallic Non-Stick 9" Round Cake Pan** $10.97
	PIE PLATE	• Glass promotes even browning and allows progress to be monitored • ½-inch rim (makes it easy to shape decorative crusts) • Shallow angled sides prevent crusts from slumping • Good to have two	**Pyrex Bakeware 9-Inch Pie Plate** $8.16
	LOAF PAN	• Light gold or dark nonstick surface for even browning and easy release • Good to have both 8½ by 4½-inch and 9 by 5-inch pans	**Williams-Sonoma Goldtouch Nonstick Loaf Pan** $21

BAKEWARE	ITEM	WHAT TO LOOK FOR	TEST KITCHEN FAVORITES
	SPRINGFORM PAN	• Tight seal between band and bottom of pan prevents leakage • Raised base makes cutting and removing slices easy • Light finish for controlled, even browning	**Williams-Sonoma Goldtouch Springform Pan, 9"** $49.95 Best Buy: **Nordic Ware 9" Leakproof Springform Pan** $16.22
	MUFFIN TIN	• Easy to hold and turn • Oversize rim for secure grasping • Gold finish for perfectly browned baked goods	**OXO Good Grips Non-Stick Pro 12-Cup Muffin Pan** $24.99
	COOLING RACK	• Grid-style rack with tightly woven bars • Six feet on three bars for extra stability • Should fit inside standard 18 by 13-inch rimmed baking sheet • Dishwasher-safe	**Libertyware Half Size Sheet Pan Cooling Rack** $15.99 for set of two ($7.99 each)
	BAKER'S COOLING RACK	• Sturdy rack • Four collapsible shelves • Unit folds down for easy storage	**Linden Sweden Baker's Cooling Rack** $17.99
	BISCUIT CUTTERS	• Sharp edges • A set with a variety of sizes	**Ateco 5357 11-Piece Round Cutter Set** $14.95
	BUNDT PAN	• Thick, easy-to-grip handles • Deep, well-defined ridges that produce perfect cakes	**Nordic Ware Anniversary Bundt Pan** $30.99
	MINI BUNDT PAN	• Tray-style model with six ¾-cup molds • Silver platinum nonstick surface for even browning and easy release • Clearly defined ridges	**Nordic Ware Platinum Anniversary Bundtlette Pan** $40
	TART PAN	• Nonstick coating for easy transfer • Professional-looking edges • If you bake a lot, it's good to have multiple sizes, though 9 inches is standard	**Matfer Steel Non-stick Fluted Tart Mold with Removable Bottom 9½"** $27

MUST-HAVE ITEMS

BAKEWARE	ITEM	WHAT TO LOOK FOR	TEST KITCHEN FAVORITES
	TUBE PAN	• Heavy pan (at least 1 pound) • Heavy bottom for leak-free seal • Dark nonstick surface for even browning and easy release • 16-cup capacity • Feet on the rim	**Chicago Metallic Professional Nonstick Angel Food Cake Pan with Feet** $19.95
	PULLMAN LOAF PAN	• Squared-off pan (4 by 4 inches) • Nonstick aluminized steel for easy cleanup • Light surface for even browning	**USA Pan 13 by 4-Inch Pullman Loaf Pan and Cover** $33.95
	BAKER'S EDGE PAN	• Attached cutting grid • Dark nonstick surface for easy release	**Baker's Edge Brownie Pan** $34.95
	SOUFFLÉ DISH	• Round dish with straight sides • Not-too-thick side walls	**HIC 64-Ounce Soufflé** $15.12
	BAKING STONE	• Substantial but not too heavy to handle • Dimensions of 16 by 14 inches • Clay, not cement, for evenly browned crusts	**Old Stone Oven Pizza Baking Stone** $59.95
	BAKING PEEL	• Polymer coating guards against moisture • Innovative cloth conveyer belt	**EXO Polymer Sealed Super Peel** $54.95 Best Buy: **Pizzacraft 14" Wood Pizza Peel** $27.31

SMALL APPLIANCES	ITEM	WHAT TO LOOK FOR	TEST KITCHEN FAVORITES
MUST-HAVE ITEM	FOOD PROCESSOR	• 14-cup capacity • Sharp and sturdy blades • Wide feed tube • Should come with basic blades and discs: steel blade, dough blade, shredding/slicing disc	**Cuisinart Custom 14-Cup Food Processor** $199.99

SMALL APPLIANCES	ITEM	WHAT TO LOOK FOR	TEST KITCHEN FAVORITES
	STAND MIXER	• Planetary action (stationary bowl and single mixing arm) • Powerful motor • Bowl size of at least 4½ quarts • Slightly squat bowl to keep ingredients in beater's range • Should come with basic attachments: paddle, dough hook, metal whisk	**KitchenAid Pro Line Series 7-Qt Bowl Lift Stand Mixer** $549.95 Best Buy: **KitchenAid Classic Plus Stand Mixer** $199.99
	HANDHELD MIXER	• Lightweight model • Slim wire beaters without central post • Variety of speeds	**KitchenAid 5-Speed Ultra Power Hand Mixer** $69.99 Best Buy: **Cuisinart PowerSelect 3-Speed Hand Mixer** $26.77
	BLENDER	• Mix of straight and serrated blades at different angles • Jar with curved base • At least 44-ounce capacity • Heavy base for stability	**Vitamix 5200** $449 Best Midpriced: **Breville The Hemisphere Control** $199.95
	PERSONAL BLENDER	• Quick and effective blending thanks to sharp, six-pronged blades angled both up and down • Travel lid well-designed with drinking spout and hinged arm that seals tight	**Ninja Nutri Ninja Pro** $89
	IMMERSION BLENDER	• Grippy rubber handle • Easy to change speeds	**Braun Multiquick 5 Hand Blender** $59.99
	ELECTRIC EGG COOKER	• Boiling capacity of seven eggs • Well-fitting lid, not too tight, for safety • Audible timer • Easy to use	**West Bend Automatic Egg Cooker** $24.99

SMALL APPLIANCES	ITEM	WHAT TO LOOK FOR	TEST KITCHEN FAVORITES
	ELECTRIC GRIDDLE	• Large cooking area (about 21 by 12 inches) • Attached pull-out grease trap (won't tip over) • Nonstick surface for easy cleanup	**Broilking Professional Griddle** $99.99
	ELECTRIC JUICER	• Ideal for making a large amount of fruit or vegetable juice • Centrifugal, not masticating, model for fresher-tasting juice • 3-inch-wide feed tube • Easy to assemble and clean	**Breville Juice Fountain Plus** $149.99
	ADJUSTABLE ELECTRIC KETTLE	• Heats water to a range of different temperatures • Automatic shutoff • Separate base for cordless pouring • Visible water level	**Zojirushi Micom Water Boiler & Warmer** $114.95
	COFFEE MAKER	• Thermal carafe that keeps coffee hot and fresh with capacity of at least 10 cups • Short brewing time (6 minutes is ideal) • Copper, not aluminum, heating element • Easy-to-fill water tank • Clear, intuitive controls	**Technivorm Moccamaster 10-Cup Coffee Maker with Thermal Carafe** $299 Best Buy: **Bonavita 8-Cup Coffee Maker with Thermal Carafe** $189.99
	ESPRESSO MACHINE	• Compact, well-made machine • Consistent, excellent espresso • Easy adjustment of flavor, temperature, and shot strength • Simple attached steam wand with silicone grip for easy cleaning • Clear display and well-designed controls	**Gaggia Anima Automatic Coffee Machine** $690.06 Best for DIY Types: **Breville BES870XL Barista Express Espresso Machine** $578
	MANUAL PASTA MACHINE	• Laser-sharp noodle attachment for perfectly shaped pasta • Wide and narrow thickness settings • Easy-to-use dial	**Marcato Atlas 150 Wellness Pasta Machine** $69.25

SMALL APPLIANCES	ITEM	WHAT TO LOOK FOR	TEST KITCHEN FAVORITES
	PORTABLE INDUCTION BURNER	• Large cooking surface for even heating of pans • Basic push buttons and dial controls for ease of use	**Max Burton Induction Cook Top** $124.25
	WARMING TRAY	• Features a range of heat settings to keep food at a safe serving temperature • Keeps food hot for 4 hours • Stay-cool handles for easy maneuvering • Easily wipes clean and is cool after use in 20 minutes' time	**BroilKing Professional Stainless Warming Tray** $126.06 Best Buy: **Oster Stainless Steel Warming Tray** $38.15
	ICE CREAM MAKER	• Compact size for easy storage • Simple to use and clean • Produces dense, smooth ice cream	**Cuisinart Frozen Yogurt, Ice Cream, and Sorbet Maker** $53.99
	ICE CREAM CONE MAKER	• Easy to use • Solidly constructed • Channel around edge to catch excess batter for easy cleanup	**Chef's Choice 838 Waffle Cone Express** $49.95
	STOVETOP PRESSURE COOKER	• Solidly built • Stovetop model with low sides and wide base for easy access and better browning and heat retention • Easy-to-read pressure indicator	**Fissler Vitaquick 8½-Quart Pressure Cooker** $279.95 Best Buy: **Fagor Duo 8-Quart Stainless Steel Pressure Cooker** $109.95
	SLOW COOKER	• At least 6-quart capacity • Insert handles • Clear lid to see progress of food • Dishwasher-safe insert • Intuitive control panel with programmable timer and warming mode	**KitchenAid 6-Quart Slow Cooker with Solid Glass Lid** $99.99
	RICE COOKER	• Produces tender-chewy white, brown, and sushi rice • Digital timer with clear audio alert and a delayed-start function • Removable lid for hassle-free cleanup • Small countertop footprint	**Aroma 8-Cup Digital Rice Cooker and Food Steamer** $29.92

SMALL APPLIANCES	ITEM	WHAT TO LOOK FOR	TEST KITCHEN FAVORITES
	TOASTER OVEN	• Quartz heating elements for steady, controlled heat • Roomy but compact interior • Simple to use	**The Smart Oven by Breville** $249.95 Best Buy: **Hamilton Beach Set & Forget Toaster Oven with Convection Cooking** $99.99
	WAFFLE IRON	• Indicator lights and audible alert • Makes two waffles at a time • Six-point dial for customizing waffle doneness	**Cuisinart Double Belgian Waffle Maker** $99.95

GRILLING EQUIPMENT	ITEM	WHAT TO LOOK FOR	TEST KITCHEN FAVORITES
	GAS GRILL	• Large main grate • Built-in thermometer • Two burners for varying heat levels (three is even better) • Made of thick, heat-retaining materials such as cast aluminum and enameled steel	**Weber Spirit E-310 Gas Grill** $499
	CHARCOAL GRILL	• Sturdy construction for maintaining heat • Well-designed cooking grate, handles, lid, and wheels • Generous cooking and charcoal capacity • Well-positioned vents to control air flow • Gas ignition instantly and easily lights coals • Ash catcher for easy cleanup	**Weber Performer Deluxe Charcoal Grill** $399 Best Buy: **Weber Original Kettle Premium Charcoal Grill, 22-Inch** $149
	SMOKER	• Large cooking area • Water pan • Multiple vents for precise temperature control	**Weber Smokey Mountain Cooker 18″** $298.95
	CHIMNEY STARTER	• 6-quart capacity • Holes in the canister so air can circulate around the coals • Sturdy construction • Heat-resistant handle • Dual handle for easy control	**Weber Rapidfire Chimney Starter** $14.99

GRILLING EQUIPMENT	ITEM	WHAT TO LOOK FOR	TEST KITCHEN FAVORITES
	GRILL TONGS	• 16 inches in length • Scalloped, not sharp and serrated, edges • Open and close easily • Lightweight • Moderate amount of springy tension	**OXO Good Grips 16-Inch Locking Tongs** $14.99
	GRILL BRUSH	• Long handle (about 14 inches) • Large woven-mesh detachable stainless-steel scrubbing pads	**Grill Wizard 18-Inch China Grill Brush** $31.50
	GRILL GRATE CLEANING BLOCK	• Use for once-per-season grill reconditioning • Pumice scrubber to strip all accumulated gunk even from cold grates	**GrillStone Value Pack Cleaning Kit by Earthstone International** $9.99
	BASTING BRUSH	• Silicone bristles • Angled brush head • Handle 8 to 13 inches in length • Heat-resistant	**Elizabeth Karmel Super Silicone Angled BBQ Brush** $9.16
	SKEWERS	• Flat and metal • 3⁄16 inch thick	**Norpro 12-Inch Stainless Steel Skewers** $6.85 for set of 6
	GRILL GLOVES	• Excellent heat protection • Gloves, rather than mitts, for dexterity • Long sleeves to protect forearms	**Steven Raichlen Ultimate Suede Grilling Gloves** $29.99 per pair
	GRILL LIGHTER	• Flexible neck • Refillable chamber with large, easy-to-read fuel window • Comfortable grip	**Zippo Flexible Neck Utility Lighter** $18.35
	OUTDOOR GRILL PAN	• Narrow slits and raised sides so food can't fall through or off • Sturdy construction with handles	**Weber Professional-Grade Grill Pan** $19.99

GRILLING EQUIPMENT	ITEM	WHAT TO LOOK FOR	TEST KITCHEN FAVORITES
	GRILL GRATE SET	• Stainless-steel grate for 22½-inch charcoal grill • Removable inner circle of grate can be replaced with crosshatched sear grate (shown), griddle, or wok (sold separately)	**Weber 7420 Gourmet BBQ System Sear Grate Set** $54.99
	PIZZA GRILLING KIT	• Metal collar that elevates the grill's lid • Brings grill heat to over 900 degrees • Cutout that lets you insert pizzas without losing heat	**KettlePizza Pro 22 Kit** $299.95
	STOVETOP SMOKER	• Sliding snug, flat metal lid • Large drip tray • Rack with parallel wires • Stay-cool handle	**Camerons Stovetop Smoker** $54.95
	SMOKER BOX	• Cast iron for slow heating and steady smoke • Easy to fill, empty, and clean	**GrillPro Cast Iron Smoker Box by Onward Manufacturing Company** $12.79
	GRILLING BASKET FOR WHOLE FISH	• Two-piece metal cage with nonstick coating to keep fish from sticking • Wires less than 2 inches apart to secure both large and small fish • Removable handle for easy cleanup	**Charcoal Companion Ultimate Nonstick Fish-Grilling Basket** $24.99
	VERTICAL ROASTER	• Helps poultry cook evenly • 8-inch shaft keeps chicken above fat and drippings in pan • Attached basin catches drippings for pan sauce • Sturdy construction	**Vertical Roaster with Infuser by Norpro** $22.11 Best Buy: **Elizabeth Karmel's Grill Friends Porcelain Chicken Sitter** $11.99
	CHARCOAL STARTERS	• Relatively water-resistant • Ignite easily without impacting food flavor	**Weber Lighter Cubes** $3.29 for 24 cubes ($0.14 per cube)

SPECIALTY PIECES	ITEM	WHAT TO LOOK FOR	TEST KITCHEN FAVORITES
	APPLE CORER	• Sharp, serrated barrel edges • Blade diameter measuring ¾ to 1 inch	**Cuisipro Apple Corer** $9.95
	GRAPEFRUIT KNIFE	• Sturdy, lightweight handle • Gently angled blade for precise cutting	**Messermeister Pro-Touch 4-Inch Grapefruit Knife** $15.39
	STRAWBERRY HULLER	• Huller with four spring-loaded metal prongs that slice out leaves, stem, and core • Easy and safe to use • Compact for easy storage	**StemGem Strawberry Hull Remover by Chef'n** $7.95
	PINEAPPLE SLICER	• Corkscrew design • Easy to use • Narrow slicing base for easy storage	**OXO Good Grips Stainless Steel Ratcheting Pineapple Slicer** $19.99
	CORN STRIPPER	• Safer than using chef's knife • Attached cup to catch kernels • Comfortable grip and sharp blade	**OXO Good Grips Corn Stripper** $11.99
	MANUAL NUT CHOPPER	• Sharp, sturdy stainless steel chopping tines • Dishwasher-safe	**Prepworks from Progressive Nut Chopper with Non-Skid Base** $11.70
	NUTCRACKER	• Lever-style model • Solidly built • Extra-long handle for good leverage and easy cracking	**Get Crackin' Heavy Duty Steel Lever Nutcracker** $35.99

SPECIALTY PIECES	ITEM	WHAT TO LOOK FOR	TEST KITCHEN FAVORITES
	SPIRAL SLICER (SPIRALIZER)	• Includes three blades that are stored in the base • Stabilizing suction cups make for safer slicing • Pronged to hold fruit and vegetables against blade for optimal spiralizing • Large rectangular chamber accommodates vegetables up to 10 inches long or 7 inches thick	**Paderno World Cuisine Tri-Blade Plastic Spiral Vegetable Slicer** $33.24
	TORTILLA PRESS	• Wood or heavy cast iron • Large pressing surface of 8 inches • Easy to use	**La Mexicana Tortilladora de Madera Barnizada/ Mesquite Tortilla Press** $64.95 Best Buy: **Imusa Cast Iron Tortilla Press** $23.99
	STOVETOP GRIDDLE	• Anodized aluminum for even heating • Nonstick coating • Lightweight (about 4 pounds) • Heat-resistant loop handles • At least 17 by 9 inches (large enough to span two burners) • Pour spout for draining grease	**Anolon Advanced Double Burner Griddle** $68.99
	MILK FROTHER	• Easy to use and clean • Immersion blender–style wand • Battery operated	**Aerolatte Milk Frother** $19.99
	OYSTER KNIFE	• Sturdy, flat blade with slightly curved tip for easy penetration • Slim, nonstick handle for secure, comfortable grip	**R. Murphy New Haven Oyster Knife with Stainless Steel Blade** $16.65
	SEAFOOD SCISSORS	• Thin, curved blades to fit into shells • Strong and sturdy	**RSVP International Endurance Seafood Scissors** $14.99
	SILICONE MICROWAVE LID	• Thin, silicone round to cover splatter-prone food during microwave heating • Easy to clean • Doubles as jar opener	**Piggy Steamer** $18
	RECIPE HOLDER	• Holds pages at perfect angle for viewing • Compact yet sturdy • Strong magnet	**Recipe Rock by Architec** $9.99

SPECIALTY PIECES	ITEM	WHAT TO LOOK FOR	TEST KITCHEN FAVORITES
	OIL MISTER	• Clear plastic makes it easy to monitor oil level • Consistent, fine spray • Easy to refill • Dishwasher-safe (top shelf only)	**Mastrad Oil and Flavor Mister** $17.29
	MICROWAVE RICE COOKER	• Sturdy and compact • 6-cup capacity • Easy to clean	**Progressive International Microwave Rice Cooker Set** $8.99
	MICROWAVE CHIP MAKER	• Perforated 11-inch silicone disk that holds 15 to 20 chips • Slicer that produces wafer-thin chips	**Topchips Chips Maker** $19.99
	PIPING SET	• Large bag (about 18 inches in length) for easier gripping and twisting • Contains all of the essentials: twelve 16-inch pastry bags; four plastic couplers; and the following Wilton tips: #4 round, #12 round, #70 leaf, #103 petal, #2D large closed star, #1M open star	**Test Kitchen Self-Assembled à La Carte Decorating Set** $15.32
	CHEESE WIRE	• Comfortable plastic handles • Narrow wire	**Fante's Handled Cheese Wire** $2.99
	PIZZA CUTTER	• Comfortable, soft-grip handle • Thumb guard to protect fingers	**OXO Good Grips 4" Pizza Wheel** $12.99
	BAKING PEEL	• Wood board • Pastry cloth threaded through board makes it essentially nonstick when well-floured • Gentle touch for bread loaves	**Super Peel by EXO Products, Inc.** $55
	COUCHE	• Maintains baguettes' shape and wicks moisture effectively • Fabric easily releases dough	**San Francisco Baking Institute 18-Inch Linen Canvase (Couche)** $8 for 36 x 18-inch couche

SPECIALTY PIECES	ITEM	WHAT TO LOOK FOR	TEST KITCHEN FAVORITES
	LAME	• Scores baguettes cleanly and evenly • Easy to change blades	**Breadtopia Bread Lame** $9.50
	POTATO RICER	• Hopper with many holes so more food can travel through • Comfortable handles • Easy to assemble and clean	**RSVP International Potato Ricer** $13.95
	PANCAKE BATTER DISPENSER	• Tall plastic cylinder • Easy to use • Heat-resistant silicone tip	**Tovolo Pancake Pen** $9.95
	INSULATED ICE CREAM KEEPER	• Foam-core insulated base and gel pack-lined lid • Can hold 1 pint of ice cream • Keeps ice cream frozen for 90 minutes	**Zak! Designs Ice Cream Tubbie** $10.12
	QUICK POPSICLE MAKER	• Easy to fill, transport, and store • Easy to remove and clean pops • Long, grippy, reusable popsicle sticks	**Zoku Classic Pop Molds** $15.45
	CUPCAKE AND CAKE CARRIER	• Fits both round and square cakes and cupcakes • Snap locks • Nonskid base • Collapses for easy storage	**Progressive Collapsible Cupcake and Cake Carrier** $29.95
	PIE CARRIER	• Collapsible plastic tote expands to accommodate larger pies • Large, nonstick base	**Prepworks Collapsible Party Carrier** $23.81 Best Buy: **Pyrex Portables Pie Carrier with 9" Pie Plate** $11.88
	REVOLVING CAKE STAND	• Tall stand with excellent visibility and comfort • Easy to carry • Rotates quickly and smoothly	**Winco Revolving Cake Decorating Stand** $29.98

SPECIALTY PIECES	ITEM	WHAT TO LOOK FOR	TEST KITCHEN FAVORITES
	CREAM WHIPPER	• Rubber grip • Responsive lever for effortless control	**ISI Gourmet Whip** $99.27
	SPICE/COFFEE GRINDER	• Electric, not manual, grinders • Deep bowl to hold ample amount of coffee beans • Easy-to-control texture of grind • Good to have two, one each for coffee grinding and spice grinding	**Krups Fast-Touch Coffee Mill, Model 203** $19.99
	MOKA POT	• Classic design that uses steam pressure to force hot water from bottom chamber up through coffee grounds • Stovetop, not electric, model • Easy to use	**Bialetti Moka Express, 3 cups** $24.95
	FRENCH PRESS	• Fine-mesh filter to eliminate sediment • Insulated pot to keep coffee hot • Smooth, simple, dishwasher-safe parts for easy cleanup	**Bodum Columbia French Press Coffee Maker, Double Wall, 8 Cup** $79.95
	COLD BREW COFFEE MAKER	• Easy to use • Produces smooth, rich-tasting cold brew concentrate • Enough concentrate to make sixty-four 4-ounce cups of coffee	**Toddy Cold Brew System** $34.95
	MANUAL ESPRESSO MAKER	• Includes milk foamer, measuring scoop, and adapter for making two shots simultaneously • Easy and intuitive to use	**ROK Manual Espresso Maker** $150

SPECIALTY PIECES	ITEM	WHAT TO LOOK FOR	TEST KITCHEN FAVORITES
	INNOVATIVE TEAPOT	• Contained ultrafine-mesh strainer keeps tea leaf dregs separate • One-piece design for easy cleaning	**ingenuiTEA by Adagio Teas** $14.95
	TEA MACHINE	• Perforated tea basket for thorough infusion • Programmable temperature and steep times • Fully automated brewing • Dishwasher-safe accessories	**Breville Tea Maker** $249.99 Best Buy: **Cuisinart PerfecTemp Programmable Tea Steeper & Kettle** $99
MUST-HAVE ITEM	WINE OPENER	• Durable waiter's corkscrew design • Teflon-coated worm • Ergonomically curved body and hinged fulcrum	**Pulltap's Classic Evolution Corkscrew by Pulltex** $39.95 Best Buy: **Trudeau Double Lever Corkscrew** $12.99
	ELECTRIC WINE OPENER	• Sturdy, quiet corkscrew • Broad base that rests firmly on bottle	**Cuisinart Cordless Wine Opener with Vacuum Sealer** $39.95
	WINE AERATOR	• Long, tubelike design that exposes wine to air as it is being poured • Neat, hands-free aerating	**Nuance Wine Finer** $19.95
	WINE SAVER	• Minimizes amount of contact wine has with air • Easy, reliable mechanism • Keeps wine drinkable for at least one month	**Air Cork The Wine Preserver** $24.95
	CHAMPAGNE SAVER	• Inexpensive • Attaches with an easy one-handed motion • Fits easily in the fridge	**Cilio Champagne Bottle Sealer** $7.50

SPECIALTY PIECES	ITEM	WHAT TO LOOK FOR	TEST KITCHEN FAVORITES
	COCKTAIL SHAKER	• Leakproof and easy to use • Domed top doubles as a 1- and 2-ounce jigger • Comfortable grip • Wide mouth for effortless filling, muddling, and cleaning • Includes reamer attachment	Best Cobbler Style Shaker: **Tovolo Stainless Steel 4-in-1 Cocktail Shaker** $29.99 Best Boston Style Shaker: **The Boston Shaker Professional Boston Shaker, Weighted** $14.50
	SILICONE ICE CUBE TRAY	• Sturdy silicone construction • Large cubes that keep drinks from tasting watered-down	**Tovolo King Cube Silicone Ice Cube Tray** $7.95
	COOLER	• Insulating layer of plastic lining • Lightweight, durable, sturdy, and easy to move, even when full • Easy to clean	**California Cooler Bags T-Rex Large Collapsible Rolling Cooler** $75
	INSULATED FOOD CARRIER	• Designed to carry two 13 by 9-inch baking dishes • Sturdy, expandable frame • Insulation keeps food above 140 degrees for more than 3 hours	**Rachael Ray Expandable Lasagna Lugger** $26.95
	WINE CARRIER	• Reusable and washable • Folds up for easy transport • Fits taller and wider bottles	**VinniBag** $28
	INSULATED SHOPPING TOTE	• Shoulder straps for easy toting • Insulation keeps groceries at a food-safe temperature for 2 hours in a 90-degree room	**Rachael Ray ChillOut Thermal Tote** $17.99
	SELTZER MAKER	• Easy to use and easy-to-control level of fizz • Cartridges carbonate up to 60 liter-size bottles	**SodaStream Source Starter Kit** $99.95

SPECIALTY PIECES	ITEM	WHAT TO LOOK FOR	TEST KITCHEN FAVORITES
	SOUS VIDE MACHINE	• Slowly cooks vacuum-sealed food in water bath at precise temperatures • Easy to set up and use • Quiet	**Anova One** $199
	VACUUM ROBOT	• Easy to use and program • Recharging dock • Efficient, grid-pattern cleaning program • Unique shape fits into corners and along walls	**Neato Botvac D80** $499.99
	NEW GENERATION KITCHEN TRASH CANS	• Sleek, spacious frame • Foot pedal flips lid open completely and allows it to close slowly when released • Fingerprint-proof stainless-steel exterior • Easy bag changes	**Simplehuman Rectangular Step Trash Can Fingerprint-Proof Brushed Stainless Steel, 50 Liter/13 Gallon** $180 Best Buy: **Sterilite Lift-Top Wastebasket** $17.99
	COMPOST BUCKET	• Plastic pail to collect food scraps for composter • Carbon filter prevents odors from escaping and allows oxygen to enter so decomposition can occur • Easy-to-open lid that latches securely in place • 2.4-gallon capacity	**Exaco Trading Kitchen Compost Waste Collector** $19.98

KITCHEN SUPPLIES	ITEM	WHAT TO LOOK FOR	TEST KITCHEN FAVORITES
	FIRE EXTINGUISHER	• Fast and effective • Powerful spray	**Kidde ABC Multipurpose Home Fire Extinguisher** $25.99
	PLASTIC WRAP	• Clings tightly and resticks well • Packaging with sharp teeth that aren't exposed (to avoid snags on clothing and skin) • Adhesive pad to hold cut end of wrap	**Glad Cling Wrap Clear Plastic** $1.20 per 100 square feet

KITCHEN SUPPLIES	ITEM	WHAT TO LOOK FOR	TEST KITCHEN FAVORITES
	PLASTIC WRAP DISPENSERS	• Concealed metal teeth for easy, clean cuts • Slightly elevated for easier wrapping	**Stretch-Tite Wrap'n Snap 7500 Dispenser** $22
	FOOD STORAGE BAGS	• Thick plastic and tight seal • Order online at webrestaurantstore.com	**Elkay Plastics Ziplock Heavy Weight Freezer Bag** $9.69 for 100 bags
	PARCHMENT COOKING BAGS	• Bags easy to fill and fold	**PaperChef Culinary Parchment Cooking Bags** $7.98 for 10 bags
	CHEESE STORAGE WRAPS	• Two-ply wax-coated paper • Easy to fill and fold	**Formaticum Cheese Bags and Cheese Paper** $9 for 15 bags $9 for 15 sheets with stickers
	FOOD STORAGE CONTAINER	• Snap-style seal with ridge on underside to ensure tight seal • Low, flat rectangle for easy storage and more efficient heating and chilling • Made of plastic free of BPA (bisphenol-A)	**Snapware Airtight** $7.99 for 8-cup rectangle
	DRY FOOD STORAGE CONTAINER	• Sturdy, spacious, and simple to use and clean • Available in a range of sizes • Note: lid sold separately	**Cambro 6-Quart Square Storage Container** $23.74 ($16.67 for container, $7.07 for lid)
	SOAP-FILLED DISH BRUSH	• Handle for easy gripping and to keep hands dry • Tight seal to prevent soap from leaking	**OXO Steel Soap Squirting Dish Brush** $11.99
MUST-HAVE ITEM	ALL-PURPOSE CLEANER	• Natural, green product • Cuts through grease and food splatters quickly and efficiently • Pleasant, not overpowering, scent	**Method All-Purpose Natural Surface Cleaner (French Lavender)** $3.79 for 28 oz

KITCHEN SUPPLIES	ITEM	WHAT TO LOOK FOR	TEST KITCHEN FAVORITES
	CAST-IRON POT SCRUBBER	• 5-inch square of chain mail made of 316-grade stainless steel • Ideal for cleaning cast-iron cookware and all other cookware surfaces except nonstick	**Knapp Made Small Ring CM Scrubber** $19.98
	HEAVY-DUTY HANDLED SCRUB BRUSH	• Short, stiff bristles • Built-in scraper • Compact size • Thick nonslip handle	**Caldrea Dishwashing Brush** $5
MUST-HAVE ITEM	DISH TOWEL	• Thin cotton for absorbency and flexibility • Dries glassware without streaks • Washes clean without shrinking	**Williams-Sonoma Striped Towels, Set of 4** $19.95
	PAPER TOWEL HOLDER	• Sturdy, secure, and easy to carry • Angled arm uses spring-loaded tension and tilts to accommodate rolls of all sizes	**Simplehuman Tension Arm Paper Towel Holder** $24.99
	APRON	• Adjustable neck strap and long strings • Full coverage; chest area reinforced with extra layer of fabric • Stains wash out completely	**Bragard Travail Bib Apron** $27.95
MUST-HAVE ITEM	LIQUID DISH SOAP	• High concentration of surfactants to wash away oil • Clean scent	**Mrs. Meyer's Clean Day Liquid Dish Soap, Lavender** $3.99 for 16 ounces
	LAUNDRY STAIN REMOVER	• Clear instructions • Contains enzymes and surfactants to eliminate old and new stains from fabric • Stained fabrics emerged bright as new	**OxiClean Versatile Stain Remover** $8.59 for 3-pound tub

SHOPPING FOR INGREDIENTS

Using the best ingredients is one way to guarantee success in the kitchen. But how do you know what to buy? Shelves are filled with a dizzying array of choices—and price does not equal quality. Over the years, the test kitchen's blind-tasting panels have evaluated thousands of ingredients, brand by brand, side by side, plain and in prepared applications, to determine which brands you can trust and which brands to avoid. In the chart that follows, we share the results, revealing our top-rated choices and the attributes that made them stand out among the competition. And because our test kitchen accepts no support from product manufacturers, you can trust our ratings. See AmericasTestKitchen.com for updates to these tastings.

ITEM	TEST KITCHEN FAVORITES	WHY WE LIKE IT
ANCHOVIES	**King Oscar—Flat Fillets in Olive Oil**	• Right amount of salt • Savory without being fishy • Firm, meaty texture • Minimal bones • Aged 4 to 6 months
APPLESAUCE	**Musselman's Lite**	• An unusual ingredient, sucralose, sweetens this applesauce without overpowering its fresh, bright apple flavor • Pinch of salt boosts flavor above weak, bland, and too-sweet competitors • Coarse, almost chunky texture, not slimy like applesauces sweetened with corn syrup
BACON, SUPERMARKET	**Farmland Thick Sliced** and **Plumrose Premium Thick Sliced**	• Good balance of saltiness and sweetness • Smoky and full flavored • Very meaty, not too fatty • Crisp and hearty texture
BARBECUE SAUCE, SUPERMARKET	**Bull's-Eye Original**	• Spicy, fresh tomato taste • Good balance of tanginess, smokiness, and sweetness • Robust flavor from molasses • Sweetened with sugar and molasses, not high-fructose corn syrup, which caramelizes and burns quickly
BARBECUE SAUCE, HIGH-END	**Pork Barrel Original**	• Generous amounts of vinegar, salt, chili paste, and liquid smoke for bold spicy flavor • Tangy kick • Good body
BEANS, CANNED BAKED	**B&M Vegetarian**	• Firm and pleasant texture with some bite • Sweetened with molasses for complexity and depth

	ITEM	TEST KITCHEN FAVORITES	WHY WE LIKE IT
	BEANS, CANNED BLACK	**Bush's Best**	• Clean, mild, and slightly earthy flavor • Firm, almost al dente texture, not mushy or pasty • Good amount of salt
	BEANS, CANNED CHICKPEAS	**Pastene**	• Firm yet tender texture bests pasty and dry competitors • Clean chickpea flavor • Enough salt to enhance but not overwhelm the flavor
	BEANS, CANNED WHITE	**Goya**	• Well seasoned, with both sweet and savory flavor • Ultracreamy and smooth texture with a nice firm bite • Big and meaty beans
	BEANS, DRIED WHITE	**Rancho Gordo Classic Cassoulet Bean**	• Creamy and smooth texture • Fresh taste • Nutty and sweet flavors
	BEANS, REFRIED	**Taco Bell Home Originals**	• Well-seasoned mixture • Super-smooth texture, not overly thick, pasty, or gluey
	BREAD, WHITE SANDWICH	**Arnold Country Classics**	• Subtle sweetness, not tasteless or sour • Perfect structure, not too dry or too soft
	BREAD, WHOLE-WHEAT SANDWICH	**Arnold Whole Grains**	• Mild sweetness • Tender and chewy
	BREAD CRUMBS	**Ian's Original Style**	• Crisp, with a substantial crunch • Not too delicate, stale, sandy, or gritty • Oil-free and without seasonings or undesirable artificial flavors

	ITEM	TEST KITCHEN FAVORITES	WHY WE LIKE IT
	BROTH, BEEF	**Better Than Bouillon**	• Deep, savory profile with rich notes • Contains flavor-enhancing ingredients such as yeast extract
	BROTH, VEGETABLE	**Orrington Farms**	• Good robust, savory flavor without bitter or cloying off-flavors • Contains flavor boosters like salt and yeast extract
	BROTH, VEGETABLE, LOW-SODIUM	**Edward & Sons Low Sodium Not-Chick'n Natural Bouillon Cubes**	• Mild, chicken-y flavor • Unctuous, meaty body • Lends a clean, fresh flavor to risottos and vegetable soups
	BROWNIE MIX	**Ghirardelli Chocolate Supreme** and **Barefoot Contessa**	• Rich, balanced chocolate flavor from both natural and Dutch-processed cocoa • Moist, chewy, and fudgy with perfect texture
	BUTTER, ALMOND	**Jif Creamy**	• Homogeneous, creamy texture • Clean and distinct almond flavor • Well seasoned with salt and sugar • Made with almonds that are blanched and roasted
	BUTTER, UNSALTED	**Plugrá European-Style**	• Sweet and creamy • Complex tang and grassy flavor • Moderate amount of butterfat so that it's decadent and glossy but not so rich that baked goods are greasy
	CHEESE, AMERICAN	**Boar's Head**	• Nutty, sharp, tangy flavor • Superthin slices for perfect melting • Tender, slightly soft texture
	CHEESE, BRIE	**Fromager d'Affinois**	• Buttery, earthy flavor with gooey, silky texture • Soft, pillowy rind

	ITEM	TEST KITCHEN FAVORITES	WHY WE LIKE IT
	CHEESE, CHEDDAR, ARTISANAL	**Milton Creamery Prairie Breeze** Runner-Up: **Cabot Cellars at Jasper Hill Clothbound**	• Earthy complexity with nutty, buttery, and fruity flavors • Dry and crumbly with crystalline crunch, not rubbery or overly moist • Aged no more than 12 months to prevent overly sharp flavor
	CHEESE, CHEDDAR, EXTRA-SHARP	**Cabot Private Stock** Runner-Up: **Cabot Extra-Sharp**	• Balance of salty, creamy, and sweet flavors • Considerable but well-rounded sharpness, not overwhelming • Firm, crumbly texture, not moist, rubbery, or springy • Aged at least 12 months for complex flavor
	CHEESE, CHEDDAR, PRESLICED	**Tillamook Presliced Sharp**	• Slightly crumbly, not rubbery or processed, texture characteristic of block cheddar • Strong, tangy, and salty flavor, not bland or too mild
	CHEESE, CHEDDAR, REDUCED-FAT	**Cracker Barrel Reduced Fat Sharp**	• Ample creaminess • Strong cheesy flavor • Good for cooking
	CHEESE, CHEDDAR, SHARP	**Cabot Vermont**	• Nutty, smoky, caramel flavor • Firm, crumbly texture, not moist, rubbery, or springy • Aged a minimum of 9 months for complex flavor
	CHEESE, COTTAGE	**Hood Country Style**	• Rich, well-seasoned, and buttery flavor • Velvety, creamy texture • Pillowy curds
	CHEESE, CREAM, ARTISANAL	**Zingerman's Creamery**	• Supercreamy and smooth texture • Impressive depth of flavor
	CHEESE, CREAM, SUPERMARKET	**Philadelphia Brick Original**	• Rich, tangy, and milky flavor • Thick, creamy texture, not pasty, waxy, or chalky
	CHEESE, FETA	**Real Greek**	• Complex, balanced flavor with perfect salt levels • Silky texture that's tender but firm enough to maintain its presence when baked or stirred into salads

	ITEM	TEST KITCHEN FAVORITES	WHY WE LIKE IT
	CHEESE, FONTINA For Cheese Plate	**Fontina Val d'Aosta**	• Strong, earthy aroma • Somewhat elastic texture with small irregular holes • Grassy, nutty flavor—but can be overpowering in cooked dishes
	For Cooking	**Italian Fontina**	• Semisoft, super-creamy texture • Mildly tangy, nutty flavor • Melts well
	CHEESE, GOAT	**Laura Chenel's Chèvre**	• Rich-tasting, grassy, tangy flavor • Salt content enhances flavor and texture • Smooth and creamy both unheated and baked
	CHEESE, GRUYÈRE	**1655 Le Gruyère AOP**	• Aged for 12 to 14 months • High fat and low moisture content provide dense, fudgy texture • Excellent crystalline structure
	CHEESE, MASCARPONE	**Polenghi Mascarpone**	• Made with all cream and no milk • Soft and creamy but able to hold shape in desserts • Perfect consistency
	CHEESE, MOZZARELLA	**Polly-O Whole Milk**	• Creamy and milky with hint of salt • Melts and adheres well
	CHEESE, PARMESAN, PRE-SHREDDED	**Sargento Artisan Blends Shredded Parmesan Cheese**	• Mix of small and large shreds • Blends 10- and 18-month-aged Parmesan • Reminded tasters of "freshly shredded" Parmesan atop pasta
	CHEESE, PARMESAN, SUPERMARKET	**Boar's Head Parmigiano-Reggiano**	• Rich and complex flavor balances tanginess and nuttiness • Dry, crumbly texture yet creamy with a crystalline crunch, not rubbery or dense • Aged a minimum of 12 months for better flavor and texture
	CHEESE, PEPPER JACK	**Boar's Head with Jalapeño**	• Buttery, tangy cheese • Clean, balanced flavor with assertive spice

ITEM	TEST KITCHEN FAVORITES	WHY WE LIKE IT
CHEESE, PROVOLONE	**Provolone Vernengo**	• Bold, nutty, and tangy flavor, not plasticky or bland • Firm, dry texture
CHEESE, RICOTTA	**Belgioso Whole Milk**	• Slightly sweet flavor • Dense, luscious consistency • Rich but not overwhelming in manicotti
CHEESE, SWISS For Cheese Plate	**Edelweiss Creamery Emmentaler Switzerland** Runner-Up: **Emmi Kaltbach Cave-Aged Emmentaler Switzerland AOC**	• Subtle flavor with sweet, buttery, nutty, and fruity notes • Firm yet gently giving texture, not rubbery • Aged longer for better flavor, resulting in larger eyes • Mildly pungent yet balanced
For Cooking	**Boar's Head Gold Label Switzerland**	• Mild nutty flavor • Smooth texture when melted
For Cheese Plate or Cooking	**Emmi Emmentaler Cheese AOC**	• Creamy texture • Salty mildness preferable for grilled cheese sandwiches
CHICKEN, BREASTS, BONELESS, SKINLESS	**Bell & Evans Air Chilled**	• Juicy and tender with clean chicken flavor • Not salted or brined • Air-chilled • Aged on bone for at least 12 hours after slaughter for significantly more tender meat
CHICKEN, WHOLE	**Mary's Free Range Air Chilled** (also sold as Pitman's) Runner-Up: **Bell & Evans Air Chilled Premium Fresh**	• Great, savory chicken flavor • Very tender • Air-chilled for minimum water retention and cleaner flavor
CHILI POWDER	**Morton & Bassett**	• Blend of chile peppers with added seasonings, not assertively hot, overly smoky, or one-dimensional • Balance of sweet and smoky flavors • Potent but not overwhelming

	ITEM	TEST KITCHEN FAVORITES	WHY WE LIKE IT
	CHOCOLATE, DARK	**Ghirardelli 60% Cacao Bittersweet Chocolate Premium Baking Bar** Runner-Up: **Callebaut Intense Dark Chocolate, L-60-40NV**	• Creamy texture, not grainy or chalky • Dark, bold flavor with notes of cherries, wine, and smoke • Balance of sweetness and bitterness
	CHOCOLATE, DARK CHIPS	**Ghirardelli 60% Cacao Bittersweet**	• Intense, complex flavor beats one-dimensional flavor of competitors • Low sugar content highlights chocolate flavor • High amount of cocoa butter ensures creamy, smooth texture, not gritty and grainy • Wider, flatter shape and high percentage of fat help chips melt better in cookies
	CHOCOLATE, MILK	**Dove Silky Smooth**	• Intense, full, rich chocolate flavor • Super-creamy texture from abundant milk fat and cocoa butter • Not overwhelmingly sweet
	CHOCOLATE, MILK CHIPS	**Hershey's**	• Bold chocolate flavor outshines too-sweet, weak chocolate flavor of other chips • Complex with caramel and nutty notes • Higher fat content makes texture creamier than grainy, artificial competitors
	CHOCOLATE, UNSWEETENED	**Hershey's Unsweetened Baking Bar**	• Well-rounded, complex flavor • Assertive chocolate flavor and deep notes of cocoa
	CHOCOLATE, WHITE CHIPS	**Guittard Choc-Au-Lait**	• Creamy texture, not waxy or crunchy • Silky smooth meltability from high fat content • Complex flavor like high-quality real chocolate, no artificial or off-flavors
	CINNAMON	**Morton & Bassett Spices**	• Perfectly balanced sweet and spicy • Desirable, mellow flavor when baked into cinnamon rolls and on pita chips
	COCOA POWDER	**Hershey's Natural Unsweetened**	• Full, strong chocolate flavor • Complex flavor with notes of coffee, cinnamon, orange, and spice

	ITEM	TEST KITCHEN FAVORITES	WHY WE LIKE IT
	COCONUT MILK	**Aroy-D**	• Velvety, luxurious texture that's not too thick • Tastes strongly of coconut but doesn't overwhelm other ingredients
	COFFEE, DECAF	**Maxwell House Original Roast**	• Smooth, mellow flavor without being acidic or harsh • Complex, with a slightly nutty aftertaste • Made with only flavorful Arabica beans
	COFFEE, MEDIUM ROAST	**Peet's Coffee Café Domingo** and **Millstone Breakfast Blend**	• Extremely smooth but bold-tasting with a strong finish • Rich chocolate and toast flavors • Few defective beans and low acidity
	CORNMEAL	**Arrowhead Mills Organic Yellow**	• Clean, pure corn flavor comes from using whole-grain kernels • Ideal texture resembling slightly damp, fine sand, not too fine or too coarse
	COUSCOUS, ISRAELI	**Roland**	• Large pearls with a firm, springy texture • Sweet, toasty flavor • Sold in an airtight jar
	CRABMEAT	**Phillips Premium Crab Jumbo**	• Moist, plump, meaty chunks • Taste comparable to freshly picked crabmeat
	CURRY POWDER	**Penzeys Sweet**	• Balanced, neither too sweet nor too hot • Complex and vivid earthy flavor, not thin, bland, or one-dimensional NOTE: Available through Amazon.com or mail order (800-741-7787, Penzeys.com).
	DINNER ROLLS, FROZEN	**Pepperidge Farm Stone Baked Artisan French**	• Pleasantly wheaty and yeasty flavor • Chewy, tender insides and crispy crust • Tastes closest to fresh homemade

ITEM	TEST KITCHEN FAVORITES	WHY WE LIKE IT
FIVE-SPICE POWDER	**Frontier Natural Products Co-Op**	• Woodsy, sweet, and aromatic taste • Harmonious flavor with a nice spice kick
FLOUR, ALL-PURPOSE	**King Arthur Unbleached Enriched**	• Fresh, toasty flavor • No metallic taste or other off-flavors • Consistent results across recipes • Made tender, flaky pie crust, hearty biscuits, crisp cookies, and chewy, sturdy bread
	Pillsbury Unbleached Enriched	• Clean, toasty, and hearty flavor • No metallic or other off-flavors • Consistent results across recipes • Made flaky pie crust, chewy cookies, and tender biscuits, muffins, and cakes
FLOUR, WHOLE-WHEAT	**King Arthur Premium**	• Finely ground for hearty but not overly coarse texture in bread and pancakes • Sweet, nutty flavor
GIARDINIERA	**Pastene**	• Sharp, vinegary tang • Crunchy mix of vegetables • Mellow heat that's potent but not overpowering
HAM, BLACK FOREST DELI	**Dietz & Watson**	• Good texture • Nice ham flavor
HAM, PROSCIUTTO	**Volpi Traditional** Best Buy: **Del Duca**	• Tender and buttery flavor • Silky and supple texture • Very thin slices

	ITEM	TEST KITCHEN FAVORITES	WHY WE LIKE IT
	HAM, SPIRAL-SLICED, HONEY-CURED	**Johnston County Spiral-Sliced Smoked**	• Good balance of smokiness and sweetness • Moist, tender yet firm texture, not dry or too wet • Classic ham flavor
	HOISIN SAUCE	**Kikkoman**	• Balances sweet, salty, pungent, and spicy flavors • Initial burn mellows into harmonious and aromatic blend without bitterness
	HORSERADISH	**Boar's Head**	• No preservatives, just horseradish, vinegar, and salt (found in refrigerated section) • Natural flavor and hot without being overpowering
	HOT DOGS	**Nathan's Famous**	• Meaty, robust, and hearty flavor, not sweet, sour, or too salty • Juicy but not greasy • Firm, craggy texture, not rubbery, mushy, or chewy
	HOT FUDGE SAUCE	**Hershey's**	• True fudge flavor, not weak or overly sweet • Thick, smooth, and buttery texture
	HOT SAUCE	**Huy Fong** Runner-Up: **Frank's RedHot Original**	• Right combination of punchy heat, saltiness, sweetness, and garlic • Full, rich flavor • Mild heat that's not too hot
	HUMMUS	**Sabra Classic**	• Nutty, earthy flavor • Thick, creamy texture • Clean flavor of tahini

ITEM	TEST KITCHEN FAVORITES	WHY WE LIKE IT
ICE CREAM BARS	**Dove Bar Vanilla Ice Cream with Milk Chocolate**	• Rich, prominent chocolate flavor • Thick, crunchy chocolate coating • Dense, creamy ice cream with pure vanilla flavor • Milk chocolate, not coconut oil, listed first in coating ingredients
ICE CREAM, CHOCOLATE	**Turkey Hill Premium Dutch Chocolate**	• Smooth, creamy texture • Well-rounded chocolate flavor • Clean aftertaste with no bitterness
ICE CREAM, VANILLA	**Ben & Jerry's**	• Complex yet balanced vanilla flavor from real vanilla extract • Sweetness solely from sugar rather than corn syrup • Creamy richness from both egg yolks and small amount of stabilizers
ICED TEA, BLACK Loose Leaf	**Tazo Iced**	• Distinctive flavor with herbal notes • Balanced level of strength and astringency
Bottled, with Lemon	**Lipton PureLeaf with Lemon**	• Bright, balanced, and natural tea and lemon flavors • Uses concentrated tea leaves to extract flavor
KETCHUP	**Heinz Organic** Best Buy: **Hunt's**	• Clean, pure sweetness from sugar, not high-fructose corn syrup • Bold, harmonious punch of saltiness, sweetness, tang, and tomato flavor
LEMONADE	**Natalie's Natural**	• Natural-tasting lemon flavor without artificial flavors or off-notes • Perfect balance of tartness and sweetness, unlike many overly sweet competitors • Contains 20% lemon juice
MACARONI & CHEESE	**Kraft Homestyle Dinner Classic**	• Reinforces flavor with blue and cheddar cheeses • Uses creamy, clingy liquid cheese sauce • Dry noodles, rather than frozen, for substantial texture and bite • Crunchy, buttery bread-crumb topping

	ITEM	TEST KITCHEN FAVORITES	WHY WE LIKE IT
	MAPLE SYRUP	**Grade A Dark Amber**	• Rich caramel flavor and deep molasses-like hue NOTE: We found that all Grade A Dark Amber maple syrups at supermarkets taste similar, so our advice is to buy the cheapest all-maple product available.
	MAYONNAISE	**Blue Plate Real**	• Great balance of taste and texture • Richer, deeper flavor from using egg yolks alone (no egg whites) • Short ingredient list that's close to homemade
	MAYONNAISE, LIGHT	**Hellmann's Light**	• Bright, balanced flavor close to full-fat counterpart, not overly sweet like other light mayos • Not as creamy as full-fat but passable texture NOTE: Hellmann's is known as Best Foods west of the Rocky Mountains.
	MAYONNAISE, VEGAN	**Hampton Creek Just Mayo, Original**	• Tangy taste and smooth, supercreamy texture • Tasters liked it as much as Hellmann's Real Mayonnaise when tasted side by side
	MEXICAN LAGER	**Tecate**	• Light bodied and straw colored • Crisp and clean with lingering bitterness • Refreshing citrusy flavor
	MIRIN (JAPANESE RICE WINE)	**Mitoku Organic Mikawa Sweet Rice Seasoning** Best Buy: **Eden Mirin Rice Cooking Wine**	• Good straight up or in teriyaki sauce • Balanced flavors with woodsy overtones and smoky aftertaste
	MOLASSES	**Brer Rabbit All Natural Unsulphured Mild Flavor**	• Acidic yet balanced • Strong and straightforward raisin-y taste • Pleasantly bitter bite

	ITEM	TEST KITCHEN FAVORITES	WHY WE LIKE IT
	MUSTARD, COARSE-GRAIN	**Grey Poupon Harvest** and **Grey Poupon Country**	• Spicy, tangy burst of mustard flavor • High salt content amplifies flavor • Contains no superfluous ingredients that mask mustard flavor • Big, round seeds add pleasant crunch • Just enough vinegar, not too sour or thin
	MUSTARD, DIJON	**Trois Petits Cochons Moutarde de Dijon**	• Potent, bold, and very hot, not weak or mild • Good balance of sweetness, tanginess, and sharpness • High ratio of mustard seeds for balanced but impactful heat
	MUSTARD, YELLOW	**Annie's Naturals Organic**	• Lists mustard seeds second in the ingredients for rich mustard flavor • Good balance of heat and tang • Relatively low salt content
	OATS, ROLLED	**Bob's Red Mill Old-Fashioned**	• Toasty, nutty flavor • Hearty, tender
	OATS, STEEL-CUT	**Bob's Red Mill Organic Steel-Cut**	• Rich and complex oat flavor with buttery, earthy, nutty, and whole-grain notes • Creamy yet toothsome texture • Moist but not sticky NOTE: Not recommended for baking.
	OLIVE OIL, EXTRA-VIRGIN, CALIFORNIA	**California Olive Ranch Arbequina**	• Round and full, sweet olive flavor with little bitterness or pungency • Complex with fruity, nutty, and buttery notes and fresh, pure olive aftertaste
	OLIVE OIL, EXTRA-VIRGIN, PREMIUM	**Gaea Fresh Extra Virgin**	• Buttery, smooth, lemony, sweet olive fruitiness • Nicely balanced • Aroma like tomato stems with a lightly peppery aftertaste
	OLIVE OIL, EXTRA-VIRGIN, SUPERMARKET	**California Olive Ranch Everyday Extra Virgin Olive Oil**	• Complex finish with fresh flavors • Aromatic and fruity, not bland or bitter • Clean taste, comparable to a fresh-squeezed olive • Outshines bland, greasy competitors

ITEM	TEST KITCHEN FAVORITES	WHY WE LIKE IT
 OLIVES, PIMENTO-STUFFED GREEN	**Mezzetta Super Colossal Spanish Queen**	• Meaty and juicy • Bright taste when cooked • Calcium chloride helps to firm flesh
 ORANGE JUICE	**Natalie's 100%**	• Squeezed within 24 hours of shipping • Superfresh taste with no flavor manipulation • Gentler pasteurization helps retain fresh-squeezed flavor • Pleasantly variable flavor with notes of guava and mango
 OYSTER CRACKERS	**Sunshine Krispy**	• Wheaty, toasty flavor • Flaky, delicate crackers that retain their crispness in soup
 PANCAKE MIX	**Hungry Jack Buttermilk**	• Flavorful balance of sweetness and tang well-seasoned with sugar and salt • Light, extra fluffy texture • Requires vegetable oil (along with milk and egg) to reconstitute the batter
 PAPRIKA, SMOKED	**Simply Organic**	• Deep, rich smoky taste • Balanced flavor • Made in Spain according to traditional methods
 PAPRIKA, SWEET	**The Spice House Hungarian Sweet**	• Complex flavor with earthy, fruity notes • Bright and bold, not bland and boring • Rich, toasty aroma NOTE: Available only through mail order, The Spice House (312-274-0378, TheSpiceHouse.com).
 PASTA, CHEESE RAVIOLI, SUPERMARKET	**Rosetto**	• Creamy, plush, and rich blend of ricotta, Romano, and Parmesan cheeses • Pasta with nice, springy bite • Perfect dough-to-filling ratio
 PASTA, CHEESE TORTELLINI, SUPERMARKET	**Barilla Three Cheese**	• Robustly flavored filling from combination of ricotta, Emmentaler, and Grana Padano cheeses • Tender pasta that's sturdy enough to withstand boiling but not so thick that it becomes doughy

ITEM	TEST KITCHEN FAVORITES	WHY WE LIKE IT
PASTA, EGG NOODLES	**Pennsylvania Dutch Wide**	• Balanced, buttery taste with no off-flavors • Light and fluffy texture, not gummy or starchy
PASTA, ELBOW MACARONI	**Barilla**	• Rich, wheaty taste with no off-flavors • Pleasantly hearty texture, not mushy or chewy • Ridged surface and slight twist in shape hold sauce especially well
PASTA, LASAGNA NOODLES		
No-Boil	**Barilla**	• Taste and texture of fresh pasta • Delicate, flat noodles
Whole-Wheat	**Bionaturae Organic**	• Complex nutty, rich wheat flavor • Substantial chewy texture without any grittiness
PASTA, PENNE	**Mueller's**	• Hearty texture, not insubstantial or gummy • Wheaty, slightly sweet flavor, not bland
PASTA, SPAGHETTI	**De Cecco No. 12**	• Rich, nutty, wheaty flavor • Firm, ropy strands with good chew, not mushy, gummy, or mealy • Semolina flour for resilient texture • Dried at moderately low temperature for 18 hours to preserve flavor
PASTA, SPAGHETTI, GLUTEN-FREE	**Jovial Gluten Free Brown Rice Pasta**	• Springy texture • Clean-tasting flavor • No off-flavors or gumminess
PASTA, SPAGHETTI, WHOLE-WHEAT	**Bionaturae Organic**	• Chewy, firm, and toothsome, not mushy or rubbery • Full and nutty wheat flavor

ITEM	TEST KITCHEN FAVORITES	WHY WE LIKE IT
PASTA SAUCE, JARRED	**Bertolli Tomato and Basil**	• Fresh-cooked, balanced tomato flavor, not overly sweet • Pleasantly chunky, not too smooth or pasty • Not overseasoned with dry herbs like competitors
PASTA SAUCE, PREMIUM	**Victoria Marinara**	• Nice, bright acidity that speaks of real tomatoes • Robust flavor comparable to homemade
PEANUT BUTTER, CREAMY	**Skippy**	• Smooth, creamy, and spreadable • Good balance of sweet and salty flavors
PEPPERCORNS, BLACK Artisanal	**Kalustyan's Indian Tellicherry**	• Enticing and fragrant, not musty, aroma with flavor to back it up and moderate heat • Fresh, complex flavor at once sweet and spicy, earthy and smoky, fruity and floral NOTE: Available only by mail order, Kalustyan's (800-352-3451, Kalustyans.com).
Supermarket	**Morton & Bassett Organic Whole**	• Spicy but not too hot • Sharp, fresh, classic pepper flavor
PEPPERCORNS, SICHUAN	**Dean & DeLuca** Best Buy: **Savory Spice Shop**	• Fresh, potent aroma with floral, citrus, herbal, and black tea notes • Sharp, zippy tingling effect
PEPPERONI	**Margherita Italian Style**	• Nice balance of meatiness and spice • Tangy, fresh flavor with hints of fruity licorice and peppery fennel • Thin slices with the right amount of chew

ITEM	TEST KITCHEN FAVORITES	WHY WE LIKE IT
PEPPERS, ROASTED RED	**Dunbars Sweet**	• Balance of smokiness and sweetness • Mild, sweet, and earthy red pepper flavor • Firm texture, not slimy or mushy • Packed in simple yet strong brine of salt and water without distraction of other strongly flavored ingredients
PICKLES, BREAD-AND-BUTTER	**Bubbies**	• Subtle, briny tang • All-natural solution that uses real sugar, not high-fructose corn syrup
PICKLES, WHOLE KOSHER DILL	**Boar's Head**	• Authentic, garlicky flavor and firm, snappy crunch • Balanced salty, sour, and garlic flavors • Fresh and refrigerated, not processed and shelf-stable
PORK, PREMIUM	**Snake River Farms American Kurobuta (Berkshire)**	• Deep pink tint, which indicates higher pH level and more flavorful meat • Tender texture and juicy, intensely porky flavor
POTATO CHIPS	**Lay's Kettle Cooked Original**	• Big potato flavor, no offensive off-flavors • Perfectly salted • Slightly thick chips that aren't too delicate or brittle • Not too greasy
POTATO CHIPS, REDUCED FAT	**Cape Cod 40% Reduced Fat**	• Real potato flavor with excellent crunch and texture • Contain only potatoes, canola oil, and salt • With less sodium than many competitors, they have just the right balance of salt
PRESERVES, APRICOT	**Smucker's**	• Deep, authentic apricot taste • Visible fruit suspended in spreadable jam • Sweetened with sugar and syrup rather than with flavor-muting fruits
PRESERVES, RASPBERRY	**Smucker's**	• Clean, strong raspberry flavor, not too tart or sweet • Not overly seedy • Ideal, spreadable texture, not too thick, artificial, or overprocessed

	ITEM	TEST KITCHEN FAVORITES	WHY WE LIKE IT
	PRESERVES, STRAWBERRY	**Welch's**	• Big, distinct strawberry flavor • Natural-tasting and not overwhelmingly sweet • Thick and spreadable texture, not runny, slimy, or too smooth
	RELISH, SWEET PICKLE	**Cascadian Farm**	• Piquant, sweet flavor, lacks out-of-place flavors such as cinnamon and clove present in competitors • Fresh and natural taste, free of yellow dye #5 and high-fructose corn syrup • Good texture, not mushy like competitors
	RICE, ARBORIO	**RiceSelect**	• Creamier than competitors • Smooth grains • Characteristic good bite of Arborio rice in risotto where al dente is ideal
	RICE, BASMATI	**Tilda Pure**	• Very long grains expand greatly with cooking, a result of being aged for a minimum of one year, as required in India • Ideal, fluffy texture, not dry, gummy, or mushy • Nutty taste with no off-flavors • Sweet aroma
	RICE, BROWN	**Lundberg Organic Brown Long-Grain**	• Firm yet tender grains • Bold, toasty, nutty flavor
	RICE, JASMINE	**Dynasty**	• Floral fragrance • Separate, toothsome grains
	RICE, LONG-GRAIN WHITE	**Lundberg Organic Long-Grain**	• Nutty, buttery, and toasty flavor • Distinct, smooth grains that offer some chew without being overly chewy
	RICE, READY, WHITE	**Minute Ready to Serve**	• Parboiled long-grain white rice that is ready in less than 2 minutes • Toasted, buttery flavor • Firm grains with al dente bite
	RICE, WILD	**Goose Valley**	• Plump grains • Firm texture • Woodsy flavor

ITEM	TEST KITCHEN FAVORITES	WHY WE LIKE IT
SALSA, HOT	**Pace Hot Chunky**	• Good balance of bright tomato, chile, and vegetal flavors • Chunky, almost crunchy texture, not mushy or thin • Spicy and fiery but not overpowering
SALT	**Maldon**	• Light and airy texture • Delicately crunchy flakes • Not so coarse as to be overly crunchy or gritty nor so fine as to disappear
SAUCE, FISH	**Red Boat 40° N**	• Intensely rich and flavorful thanks to an abundance of protein • High in sodium but not overly salty
SAUSAGE, BREAKFAST	**Jimmy Dean Fully Cooked Original**	• Nice and plump with crisp golden crust • Good balance of sweetness and spiciness with hints of maple • Tender, super-juicy meat, not rubbery, spongy, or greasy
SAUSAGE, KIELBASA	**Wellshire Farms**	• Deeply smoked and distinctive garlicky flavor • Nice, coarse texture
SMOKED SALMON	**Spence & Co. Traditional Scottish Style**	• Subtle smoky flavor balanced with clean fresh salmon taste • Thinly sliced for easy eating • Firm and flaky, even when cooked • Uniformly silky and buttery thanks to manufacturer's trimming of pellicle
SOUP, CANNED CHICKEN NOODLE	**Muir Glen Organic**	• Organic chicken and vegetables and plenty of seasonings give it a fresh taste and spicy kick • Firm, not mushy, vegetables and noodles • No off-flavors
SOUP, CANNED TOMATO	**Progresso Vegetable Classics**	• Includes fresh, unprocessed tomatoes, not just tomato puree like some competitors • Tangy, slightly herbaceous flavor • Balanced seasoning and natural sweetness • Medium body and slightly chunky texture

ITEM	TEST KITCHEN FAVORITES	WHY WE LIKE IT
SOY SAUCE	**Kikkoman**	• Good salty-sweet balance • Long fermentation (6–8 months) • Simple ingredient list (wheat, soybeans, water, and salt) with no added sugar or flavor enhancers
STOCK, CHICKEN	**Swanson**	• Rich, meaty flavor • More robust and savory than unsalted version
STOCK, CHICKEN, UNSALTED	**Swanson Unsalted**	• Subtle and clean-tasting with mellow chicken flavor • High percentage of meat-based proteins
SWEETENED CONDENSED MILK	**Borden Eagle Brand** and **Nestlé Carnation**	• Made with whole milk • Creamy in desserts and balances more assertive notes with other ingredients
TAHINI	**Ziyad**	• Distinct, intense sesame flavor • Smooth, fluid consistency made creamy, buttery hummus
TARTAR SAUCE	**Legal Sea Foods**	• Creamy, nicely balanced sweet-tart base • Lots of vegetable chunks
TEA, BLACK For Plain Tea	**Twinings English Breakfast**	• Bright, bold, and flavorful yet not too strong • Fruity, floral, and fragrant • Smooth, slightly astringent profile preferred for tea without milk
For Tea with Milk and Sugar	**Tetley British Blend**	• Clean, strong taste • Caramel notes and pleasant bitterness • Full, deep, smoky flavors • Good balance of flavor and intensity • More astringent profile stands up to milk

ITEM	TEST KITCHEN FAVORITES	WHY WE LIKE IT
TERIYAKI SAUCE	**Annie Chun's All Natural**	• Distinct teriyaki flavor without offensive or dominant flavors, unlike competitors • Smooth, rich texture, not too watery or gluey
TOFU, FIRM	**Nasoya Organic Firm**	• Delicate, clean soy flavor • Consistent, even texture that holds its shape and offers right amount of chew when cooked
TOMATOES, CANNED CRUSHED	**SMT**	• Bright and sweet, full tomato flavor • Added diced tomatoes contribute a firm, tender texture
TOMATOES, CANNED DICED	**Hunt's**	• Bright, fresh tomato flavor that balances sweet and tart • Firm yet tender texture
TOMATOES, CANNED FIRE-ROASTED	**DeLallo**	• Intense smoky flavor • Natural tomato texture
TOMATOES, CANNED PUREED	**Muir Glen Organic**	• Full tomato flavor without any bitter, sour, or tinny notes • Pleasantly thick, even consistency, not watery or thin
TOMATOES, CANNED WHOLE	**Muir Glen Organic Peeled**	• Pleasing balance of bold acidity and fruity sweetness • Firm yet tender texture, even after hours of simmering
TOMATO PASTE	**Goya**	• Bright, robust tomato flavor • Balance of sweet and tart flavors

ITEM	TEST KITCHEN FAVORITES	WHY WE LIKE IT
TORTILLA CHIPS	**On the Border Cafe Style**	• Buttery, sweet corn flavor, not bland, artificial, or rancid • Sturdy yet crunchy and crisp texture, not brittle, stale, or cardboardlike
TORTILLAS, FLOUR	**Old El Paso 6-Inch**	• Thin and flaky texture, not doughy or stale • Slightly rich and buttery
TOSTADAS, CORN	**Mission Tostadas Estilo Casero**	• Crisp, crunchy texture • Good corn flavor • Flavor and texture that are substantial enough to stand up to hearty toppings
TUNA, CANNED	**Wild Planet Wild Albacore**	• Rich, fresh-tasting, and flavorful, not fishy • Hearty, substantial chunks of tuna
TUNA, CANNED PREMIUM	**Nardin Bonito Del Norte Ventresca Fillets** Best Buy: **Tonnino Ventresca Yellowfin in Olive Oil**	• Creamy, delicate meat and tender yet firm fillets • Full, rich tuna flavor
TURKEY, HERITAGE	**Mary's Free-Range Heritage** Best Buy: **Heritage Turkey Farm**	• Distinct layer of fat below the skin for moist, flavorful meat • Long-legged with an angular breast and almost bluish-purple dark meat (the sign of a well-exercised bird)
TURKEY, SUPERMARKET	**Mary's Free-Range Non-GMO Verified** Best Buy: **Plainville Farms**	• Juicy, moist texture • Rich, colorful turkey taste

	ITEM	TEST KITCHEN FAVORITES	WHY WE LIKE IT
	VANILLA BEANS	McCormick Madagascar	• Moist, seed-filled pods • Complex, robust flavor with caramel notes
	VANILLA EXTRACT	McCormick Pure	• Strong, rich vanilla flavor where others are weak and sharp • Complex flavor with spicy, caramel notes and a sweet undertone
	VEGETABLE OIL, ALL-PURPOSE	Crisco Blends	• Unobtrusive, mild flavor for stir-frying and sautéing and for use in baked goods and in uncooked applications such as mayonnaise and vinaigrette • Neutral taste and absence of fishy or metallic flavors when used for frying
	VINEGAR, APPLE CIDER	Heinz Filtered	• Good balance of sweet and tart • Distinct apple flavor with a floral aroma and assertive, tangy qualities
	VINEGAR, BALSAMIC, SUPERMARKET	Bertolli	• Syrupy texture when used in a vinaigrette • Notes of apple, molasses, and dried fruit when served plain
	VINEGAR, RED WINE	Laurent Du Clos	• Crisp red wine flavor balanced by stronger than average acidity and subtle sweetness • Complex yet pleasing taste from multiple varieties of grapes

ITEM	TEST KITCHEN FAVORITES	WHY WE LIKE IT
VINEGAR, SHERRY	**Napa Valley Naturals Reserve**	• Slightly sweet with just the right amount of tang • Boasts flavors ranging from "lemony" to "smoky"
VINEGAR, WHITE WINE	**Napa Valley Naturals Organic**	• High levels of acidity and sweetness • Made from a wine based on crisp-tasting Trebbiano grapes
YOGURT, FROZEN, SUPERMARKET	**TCBY Classic Vanilla Bean**	• Balanced sweetness • Straightforward vanilla flavor • Smooth texture
YOGURT, GREEK NONFAT	**Fage Total**	• Smooth, creamy consistency, not watery or puddinglike from added thickeners such as pectin or gelatin • Pleasantly tangy, well-balanced flavor, not sour or metallic
YOGURT, GREEK WHOLE-MILK	**Fage Total**	• Rich taste and satiny texture, not thin, watery, or soupy • Buttery, tangy flavor
YOGURT, WHOLE-MILK	**Brown Cow Cream Top Plain**	• Rich, well-rounded flavor, not sour or bland • Especially creamy, smooth texture, not thin or watery • Higher fat content contributes to flavor and texture

CONVERSIONS AND EQUIVALENTS

Some say cooking is a science and an art. We would say that geography has a hand in it, too. Flour milled in the United Kingdom and elsewhere will feel and taste different from flour milled in the United States. So, while we cannot promise that the loaf of bread you bake in Canada or England will taste the same as a loaf baked in the States, we can offer guidelines for converting weights and measures. We also recommend that you rely on your instincts when making our recipes. Refer to the visual cues provided. If the bread dough hasn't "come together in a ball," as described, you may need to add more flour—even if the recipe doesn't tell you so. You be the judge.

The recipes in this book were developed using standard U.S. measures following U.S. government guidelines. The charts below offer equivalents for U.S. and metric (U.K.) measures. All conversions are approximate and have been rounded up or down to the nearest whole number.

EXAMPLES:

1 teaspoon = 4.929 milliliters, rounded up to 5 milliliters

1 ounce = 28.349 grams, rounded down to 28 grams

VOLUME CONVERSIONS

U.S.	METRIC
1 teaspoon	5 milliliters
2 teaspoons	10 milliliters
1 tablespoon	15 milliliters
2 tablespoons	30 milliliters
¼ cup	59 milliliters
⅓ cup	79 milliliters
½ cup	118 milliliters
¾ cup	177 milliliters
1 cup	237 milliliters
1¼ cups	296 milliliters
1½ cups	355 milliliters
2 cups	473 milliliters
2½ cups	591 milliliters
3 cups	710 milliliters
4 cups (1 quart)	0.946 liter
1.06 quarts	1 liter
4 quarts (1 gallon)	3.8 liters

WEIGHT CONVERSIONS

OUNCES	GRAMS
½	14
¾	21
1	28
1½	43
2	57
2½	71
3	85
3½	99
4	113
4½	128
5	142
6	170
7	198
8	227
9	255
10	283
12	340
16 (1 pound)	454

CONVERSIONS FOR INGREDIENTS COMMONLY USED IN BAKING

Baking is an exacting science. Because measuring by weight is far more accurate than measuring by volume, and thus more likely to achieve reliable results, in our recipes we provide ounce measures in addition to cup measures for many ingredients. Refer to the chart below to convert these measures into grams.

INGREDIENT	OUNCES	GRAMS
Flour		
1 cup all-purpose flour*	5	142
1 cup cake flour	4	113
1 cup whole-wheat flour	5½	156
Sugar		
1 cup granulated (white) sugar	7	198
1 cup packed brown sugar (light or dark)	7	198
1 cup confectioners' sugar	4	113
Cocoa Powder		
1 cup cocoa powder	3	85
Butter†		
4 tablespoons (½ stick, or ¼ cup)	2	57
8 tablespoons (1 stick, or ½ cup)	4	113
16 tablespoons (2 sticks, or 1 cup)	8	227

* U.S. all-purpose flour, the most frequently used flour in this book, does not contain leaveners, as some European flours do. These leavened flours are called self-rising or self-raising. If you are using self-rising flour, take this into consideration before adding leavening to a recipe.

† In the United States, butter is sold both salted and unsalted. We generally recommend unsalted butter. If you are using salted butter, take this into consideration before adding salt to a recipe.

OVEN TEMPERATURES

FAHRENHEIT	CELSIUS	GAS MARK
225	105	¼
250	120	½
275	135	1
300	150	2
325	165	3
350	180	4
375	190	5
400	200	6
425	220	7
450	230	8
475	245	9

CONVERTING TEMPERATURES FROM AN INSTANT-READ THERMOMETER

We include doneness temperatures in many of our recipes, such as those for poultry, meat, and bread. We recommend an instant-read thermometer for the job. Refer to the table above to convert Fahrenheit degrees to Celsius. Or, for temperatures not represented in the chart, use this simple formula:

Subtract 32 degrees from the Fahrenheit reading, then divide the result by 1.8 to find the Celsius reading.

EXAMPLE:

"Roast chicken until thighs register 175 degrees."

To convert:

175° F - 32 = 143°

143° ÷ 1.8 = 79.44°C, rounded down to 79°C

INDEX

Note: Page references in *italics* indicate photographs.

B

D

E

F

G

H

L

M

N

O

P

Q

R

S

T

U

V

Lincoln Christian College
P9-DIG-863
For Reference
Not to be taken
from this library
DICTIONARY OF AMERICAN HISTORY

DICTIONARY OF
AMERICAN HISTORY

VOLUME I

DICTIONARY OF AMERICAN HISTORY

JAMES TRUSLOW ADAMS
Editor in Chief

R. V. COLEMAN
Managing Editor

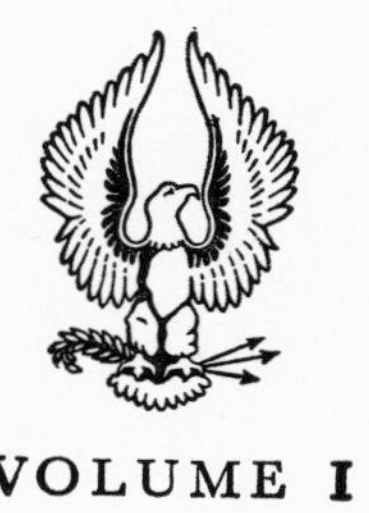

VOLUME I

SECOND EDITION
REVISED

NEW YORK
CHARLES SCRIBNER'S SONS

C–12.66

Printed in the United States of America
Library of Congress Catalog Card Number 44–1876

Advisory Council

Foreword

AMERICA has never before been so interested in its history as it is today. The many tercentenaries in recent years have helped us to realize that we have a past and are no longer young. That past is essentially our own, different from that of other nations. We have developed a distinct American culture.

In the last few decades our history has been almost completely rewritten. New facts have been discovered; new interests have developed. A generation ago historians had done the merest spade work in many departments of our national life. They were still chiefly concerned with political and military events. Today our whole culture is their province, and the public which reads history has widened with the widening of the historian's vision. Moreover a knowledge of history has become essential to an understanding of much in the daily press and in the radio broadcasts, recording the events of our world hour by hour. Advertisers, sensitive barometers of public interest, have taken to using historical material in their advertisements. History is no longer the concern of a few. If the interests of scholars have broadened, so has the use of the results of their researches, until historical facts are sought for in business offices as well as in halls of learning.

Until now the facts of the new history have not been readily available. They are scattered through thousands of volumes of general histories or special studies. There has been an increasingly insistent demand for some one source to which an inquirer might go to find, and quickly, what he wishes to know as to specific facts, events, trends or policies in our American past, without searching for hours, perhaps unsuccessfully, through stacks of books, even should he have access to them. It is this need which the *Dictionary of American History* is intended to fill.

Work on it began in the latter part of 1936 and has progressed steadily ever since. The editorial program started with the compilation of a vast index of proposed subjects, in which several hundred historians, representing all interests and all sections of the country, together with many historical societies, co-operated. This preliminary step was followed by an intensive sifting process which resulted in a tentative list of some six thousand topics. This list, with the suggested number of words for each article, was then printed and again presented to all of those who were co-operating. On the basis of the advice and criticisms received, the list was again carefully revised, and the assigning of subjects to authors was begun.

More than a thousand historians, representing a cross section of American historical scholarship, have joined in the writing of the five to six thousand articles which will be found in the completed work. The intent has been to have each article written by the historian in whose field it properly falls. In the case of certain specialized subjects, the articles have been contributed by men in closest touch with the facts. Thus Admiral Byrd wrote the account of his Polar flights; General John J. Pershing wrote that of the American Expeditionary Forces; Gutzon Borglum wrote of his colossal sculptures in the Black Hills; and Doctor Arthur E. Morgan wrote the articles on Flood Control and the Tennessee Valley Authority.

Throughout the long and complicated editorial process, emphasis has constantly been placed on the fact that this is a "dictionary" and not a collection of essays or even an encyclopædia. In general, the articles are brief, each dealing with a separate, and definite, aspect of our history. There are, however, a considerable number of "covering articles," each of which not only presents its broader subject in an orderly sequence, but, by cross references, guides the reader to the various supporting or related articles in which the individual phases of the subject are treated in more detail. Thus, if the reader wishes to know only the general succession of events, he does not have to piece them together from scores of separate articles; but if, on the other hand, he wishes information about only one aspect of the subject he will find it, indexed under the name by which it is usually identified.

This arrangement, which it is hoped will be found extremely useful, has involved one of the most difficult and meticulously painstaking portions of the editorial work — that of making constant cross references either by exact citation or, more generally, by the symbol qv (*quod vide*, "which see"; qqv being used for the plural). Where in one article there may be even a casual reference to a related subject, the reader is referred to that article in case he desires to follow the line of investigation. Thus, on "International Law" the investigator will find a 1500-word covering article by Professor Charles G. Fenwick of Bryn Mawr College. As he reads the article he will find a reference to the "foreign policy" of the United States, from which a *qv* will carry him to an article on this subject by Professor Samuel Flagg Bemis of Yale University. A few lines farther along there is a reference to "recognition," from which a *qv* carries him to an article on the "Policy of Recognition" by Professor George D. Harmon of Lehigh University. Then the reader comes upon such aspects of international law as "neutrality," "belligerent," "contraband" and "blockade," to separate articles on which he is guided by the symbol *qqv*. Somewhat farther along, a cross reference takes him to an article on "Recognition of the Latin-American Republics" by Professor Dana G. Munro of Princeton University; while a reference to the Monroe Doctrine carries him to an article on that subject by Professor Dexter Perkins of the University of Rochester. "Naturalization" is mentioned, and a *qv* leads the reader to an article on the topic by Professor Robert Phillips of Purdue University. In the same way, he is referred to articles on "Continuous Voyage" by Professor Richard W. Van Alstyne of Chico State College, and on "The *Alabama*" by Professor Allan Nevins of Columbia University. A cross reference and a *qv* direct the reader to articles on the "Fourteen Points" and the "Treaty of Versailles," both by Professor Bernadotte E. Schmitt of the University of Chicago; also to an article on the "League of Nations" by Professor Harold S. Quigley of the University of Minnesota. From a reference to the "Open Door" the reader is led to an article on this subject by Doctor Stanley K. Hornbeck of the Department of State; and from a reference to the "Briand-Kellogg Pact" to an article on that topic by Professor Benjamin H. Williams of the University of Pittsburgh. In the last paragraph, where the "Pan-American Conferences" are referred to, there is a cross reference to an article on these conferences by Professor A. Curtis Wilgus of George Washington University. Similarly, in each of the articles to which the reader is referred he will discover references to yet other related subjects. Thus, without going outside these volumes the student will find an almost inexhaustible mine of collateral material — contributed in each case by a recognized authority.

This breaking down of larger topics into their component parts, for immediate reference, has also been one of the difficult editorial tasks. In every case we have tried to choose the caption which would most likely occur to the reader in searching for a subject of which he has a general idea but not specific knowledge. For example, if he should wish to learn about the frequently mentioned undefended frontier between Canada and the United States he would probably never find it were it indexed only under the heading "Rush-Bagot Agreement." He will find it in the *Dictionary of American History* not only from that caption but also from one reading "Canadian Boundary, Disarmament of." The system of breaking down articles in this way, for ready reference, has naturally called for conciseness in treatment if the work as a whole were not to become too bulky, but each author has had the opportunity of retaining his individual flavor within this necessary restriction.

It is obvious that every item in history could not find a place. Every town, city, college, and so on, could not be mentioned though each has its own story of local interest. Lines have had to be drawn. Although exclusions may occasionally appear arbitrary to some, they have been made only after the most careful consideration, and upon advice from competent scholars.

The items in the brief bibliographies have been selected, so far as possible, with a view to accessibility in the average library. References do not include volumes, chapters or page numbers if the subject may easily be found in the work referred to; but in those cases in which there might be difficulty, exact citations are provided.

We owe the deepest gratitude to the thousand and more scholars who have given us their unselfish and wholehearted co-operation. We have already spoken of the way in which great numbers of the articles have had to be made to dovetail into one another. Frequently the author of one has not seen some other closely connected with it. The fitting together has of necessity been part of the editorial duties and could not have been accomplished had not the contributors, many of them among the most eminent scholars in the country, shown understanding of the difficulties, and assisted, by their unfailing courtesy as well as unflagging patience. It is impossible to acknowledge our full debt to them.

We also wish to express to the members of the Advisory Council our great appreciation of their help in planning the work and shaping its policy, as well as for their advice and criticism in connection with the articles proposed for inclusion, and their constant oversight of, and interest in, the broad details of the work as it progressed.

We are deeply indebted to Mr. Paul M. Angle of the Illinois State Historical Library and to Doctor Will D. Howe for reading the entire proof of the five volumes and making most helpful suggestions.

As Editor in Chief I also desire to bear testimony to the invaluable work done by the Managing Editor, Mr. R. V. Coleman. His broad knowledge of American history, his understanding of the relations of its parts and periods, his wide acquaintance among the scholars and historical institutions of the country, and his editorial skill, have alone made this work possible.

We have happily been assisted by a most competent and loyal staff. As the volumes now near completion we wish to say how much we owe to the Associate Editors, Mr. Thomas Robson Hay and Doctor Ralph Foster Weld, and to assure them of our recognition of their constant and valuable assistance. A work of this sort, more complex than the user may realize, calls for the most watchful care in every detail to avoid those pitfalls which every historian realizes lie in his way. To those who have done so much to help us with these many problems we extend our appreciative thanks: to E. Graham Platt, Frances B. Gallagher, Marion G. Barnes and Roger Hart, who have been associated with the work from beginning to end; and to all those others who in one way or another and at one time and another have assisted.

To sum up, the *Dictionary of American History* is the result of the labor of some four years and of the collaboration of well over a thousand persons — historians and those who have made history — representing every part of the country and every phase of its life. We send it out now to the public with the hope that it will prove worthy of the scholarship of the nation and be useful to all its people, of all ages and of all vocations.

JAMES TRUSLOW ADAMS

Jan. 2, 1940

Note to the Reader

The symbols *q.v.* (*quod vide*, "which see") and *qq.v.* (the plural of *q.v.*) indicate that there are separate articles on the subjects so marked. In general, these articles should easily be found under natural phrasings of the titles, but, if there is difficulty, the Index may prove helpful.

DICTIONARY OF AMERICAN HISTORY

A. B. Plot — Comstock Lode

A. B. Plot (1823–24). The political enmity between Sen. Ninian Edwards of Illinois and William H. Crawford, Secretary of the Treasury, produced this "plot." Crawford had employed the unstable western banks to collect public land revenues in fluctuating banknote currencies. This policy, though justifiable, resulted in losses to the government, while he doubtless used his banking connections to advance his political influence. In 1823 the Washington *Republican,* a Calhoun organ, published a series of articles signed A. B. which attacked Crawford for malfeasance in his relations with certain banks, and accused him of suppressing letters on the subject for which the House had called. These articles were written by Edwards; while some thought he desired to damage Crawford in the 1824 presidential campaign, J. Q. Adams believed the real object was to remove W. W. Seaton and Joseph Gales, Crawford supporters, from the post of public printers. Early in 1824, while on his way west as the newly appointed Minister to Mexico, Edwards sent formal charges against Crawford to the House. He was at once recalled to testify before an investigating committee of seven, resigning his ministership. The committee report not only exonerated Crawford but left Edwards' reputation severely blemished.

[T. C. Pease, *The Frontier State 1818-48, Centennial History of Illinois;* Ninian W. Edwards, *History of Illinois from 1778 to 1833 and Life and Times of Ninian W. Edwards;* J. E. D. Shipp, *Giant Days, or the Life and Times of William H. Crawford.*]

ALLAN NEVINS

A. B. C. Conference, THE, met at Niagara Falls May–July, 1914, after Argentina, Brazil and Chile tendered mediation to prevent a conflict between the United States and the Huerta regime in Mexico (*see* Vera Cruz, 1914). The conference failed because Carranza, victorious in recent battles, rejected its proposal for a provisional government chosen by agreement between the contending factions. Huerta, however, resigned on July 15 and Carranza assumed the presidency on Aug. 22. (*See also* Mexican Relations.)

[*Foreign Relations of the United States,* 1914.]

DANA G. MUNRO

A. E. F. *See* American Expeditionary Forces.

Abbot Downing Coach. *See* Concord Coach.

Abenaki, THE, were in colonial times a loose confederacy of Algonkian[qv] tribes occupying the present state of Maine and southern New Brunswick. In a restricted sense the term applied to the Indians of the Kennebec River (and sometimes in a wider sense it covered all the Algonkian tribes of the Atlantic coast). The New England settlers generally called them Tarrateens. Under missionary influence they were active allies of the French against the northern New England settlements, which they ravaged repeatedly, notably during King William's War[qv]. After the Peace of Utrecht[qv] the French maintained their influence, and in consequence of the resumption of irregular attacks on border settlements the New Englanders in 1724 destroyed Norridgewock[qv] on the Kennebec, the center of the French mission to the Abenaki. The Kennebec population was dispersed, mainly to Canada, where their principal settlement developed on the St. Francis River near its juncture with the St. Lawrence. The Penobscot and Passamaquoddy, and the Malecite to the east of them, did not move to Canada, and in 1749 the Penobscot made their peace with the English. Some Indians returned to Norridgewock, but it was attacked in 1749, and in 1754 its inhabitants migrated again to St. Francis, which, although ravaged in 1759 by Robert Rogers'

Rangers (*see* St. Francis, Rogers' Expedition Against), has remained the principal home of the remnants of the Abenaki tribe.

[F. W. Hodge, *Handbook of American Indians North of Mexico.*] REGINALD G. TROTTER

Abilene, Kans., an early cow town, was established by Joseph G. McCoy in 1867 as a depot to which Texas cattle might be driven for shipment by rail to Kansas City (*see* Abilene Trail; *also* Chisholm Trail). Attempts of trail drivers[qv] to reach market in 1866 had largely failed due to the hostility of the settlers of Missouri and eastern Kansas, who feared the introduction of Texas fever. Located on the Kansas Pacific Railway[qv] west of all settlement, Abilene was for two or three years a popular shipping point until the westward advance of settlers forced the drovers to new cow towns[qv] farther west.

[Joseph G. McCoy, *Historic Sketches of the Cattle Trade and Southwest.*] EDWARD EVERETT DALE

Abilene Trail, The, was a cattle trail leading from Texas to Abilene[qv], Kans. Its exact route is disputed owing to its many offshoots, but it crossed the Red River a little east of Henrietta, Tex., and continued north across the Indian Territory[qv] to Caldwell, Kans., and on past Wichita[qv] and Newton to Abilene. The first herds were probably driven over it in 1866, though it was not named until Abilene was established in 1867. EDWARD EVERETT DALE

Ab-Initio Movement, The, was a controversy that originated during Reconstruction[qv] in Texas in 1866. In the constitutional convention of that year the question arose, "Was secession null and void from the beginning (*ab-initio*) or became null and void as a result of the war?" The staunch unionists or radicals took the position that it was null and void from the beginning and therefore all laws based upon secession were null and void and all public and private relations based upon such laws were null and void. This contention was rejected by the governor, military officers, both constitutional conventions and by the Republican State Convention, but it seriously divided the party of Reconstruction. Two brothers assumed leadership of the respective groups, Morgan Hamilton of the Ab-Initios and ex-Gov. A. J. Hamilton of the anti-ab-initios. This heated controversy continued over a period of three years. A. J. Hamilton and the conservatives finally emerged victorious but not until compromise had been made.

[C. W. Ramsdell, *Reconstruction in Texas.*] J. G. SMITH

Ableman v. Booth, 1859 (21 How. 506), provided Chief Justice Taney with an opportunity for a masterly analysis of Federal and state powers. Sherman Booth, sentenced to jail by a Federal court for assisting in the rescue of a fugitive slave at Milwaukee, was released on a writ of habeas corpus[qv] issued by a judge of the Supreme Court of Wisconsin on the ground that the Fugitive Slave Act[qv] was unconstitutional. The case was carried to the United States Supreme Court[qv] which rendered a unanimous opinion pronouncing the Fugitive Slave Act valid and forbidding a state to interfere with Federal prisoners by habeas corpus writs.

[J. B. McMaster, *History of the People of the United States*, Vol. VIII; C. B. Swisher, *Roger B. Taney;* Homer Cummings and Carl McFarland, *Federal Justice.*] JOHN G. VAN DEUSEN

Abolition Movement, The. The first recorded vote against slavery in the United States was that on Feb. 18, 1688, by the Monthly Meeting of the Germantown, Pa., Society of Friends (*see* Quakers). Long before that, even in 1624, protests were heard against slavery in the colonies, both in the South and in the North. When the Revolution came, it was plain to increasing numbers that slavery was inconsistent with the sentiments of the Declaration of Independence[qv]. In Jefferson's first draft of that document the slave trade[qv] was described as a "cruel war against human nature itself, violating its most sacred rights of life and liberty." Negroes were freed on enlisting in the Continental armies, in which many served.

The early formation of antislavery societies[qv] during and immediately after the Revolution showed the strength of the opposition to slavery which waxed until the invention of Eli Whitney's cotton gin[qv] in 1793 enthroned King Cotton[qv], made slaves valuable, and, together with the Missouri Compromise[qv], caused the dying out of antislavery sentiment. With each year of cotton prosperity the bitterness against all who attacked the human property of the South rose. Still James G. Birney, William Swaim, Cassius M. Clay, John Rankin, John G. Fee, and other Southerners worked steadily in the South for Abolition.

For the corresponding appearance in the North by 1830 of a militant antislavery movement[qv] there were various reasons, among them the general awakening of a more humanitarian[qv] spirit as shown by the reforming of jails, hospitals and orphanages, the growth of the temperance movement[qv], and the beginning of the agitation for women's rights and suffrage[qqv]. At this time there appeared a number of leaders and agitators, among the first being Benjamin Lundy, who in turn inspired William Lloyd Garrison, the founding of whose *Liberator*qv, with his determined announcement: "I will be as harsh as truth and as uncompromising as justice . . . I will not retreat a single inch, and I will be heard," brought about instant repercussions in the South. Within a year the legislature of Georgia offered a reward of $5000 for Garrison's "arrest and conviction."

The Garrison wing was uncompromisingly for immediate emancipation, refused to act politically, violently denounced all who disagreed with its policies, had little to do with the Middle Western and political movements and was as offensive to the moderate wing as to the slaveholders. At first the Church in the North was hostile to the Abolitionists (*see* Slavery, Attitude of Churches to); every church in Boston was closed to them. But gradually there appeared a group of great preachers, such as Theodore Parker, William Ellery Channing, Samuel J. May, and, later, Henry Ward Beecher and others, to espouse the cause of the slave. Other outstanding leaders were Theodore D. Weld, Wendell Phillips, Albert Gallatin, and John Quincy Adams then in the House of Representatives, although he refused to ally himself directly with the Abolition movement. Soon Abolitionists entered Northern state legislatures and Congress, in which, prior to 1835, there was only one, William Slade of Vermont.

Thereafter Abolition was in politics to dominate everything until Emancipationqv. To this end the annexation of Texas, the war with Mexico, the Fugitive Slave Law, the Kansas-Nebraska Act, "Bleeding Kansas," the determination of the slaveholders to extend their "peculiar system"qqv, all contributed and gave the Abolitionists their opportunity to appeal to the conscience of the nation and keep the country in a turmoil. To this, two books contributed enormously, Harriet Beecher Stowe's *Uncle Tom's Cabin*qv (1852) and Hinton Rowan Helper's *The Impending Crisis of the South*qv (1859). From 1850 on, the history of Abolition is the history of the nation, and John Brown's Harpers Ferry raidqv the curtain-raiser to the bloody years which ended in April, 1865.

[G. H. Barnes, *The Antislavery Impulse.*]

OSWALD GARRISON VILLARD

Abolitionist Literature extended from 1820 to the Civil Warqv and included many varieties, namely: newspapers, published letters, the *Annual Reports* and other publications of the antislavery societiesqv, sermons and addresses condemning slaveryqv, the narratives and lives of escaped slaves and kidnapped free Negroes, William Lloyd Garrison's *Thoughts on African Colonization* (1832), a denunciation of the principles and purposes of the American Colonization Societyqv, some popular poems of John Greenleaf Whittier and James Russell Lowell and others, *The Liberty Minstrel* (a collection of songs by George W. Clark which passed through several editions), extended analyses and denunciations of the Fugitive Slave Act of 1850qv (some of which were reprinted several times), *Uncle Tom's Cabin*qv and subsequent works by Harriet Beecher Stowe, and the Rev. W. M. Mitchell's *Underground Railroad* (1860), which gave a glimpse at the secret methods of helping the runaways.

The great number of antislavery newspapers began with Charles Osborn's *Philanthropist* (1820) and Benjamin Lundy's *Genius of Universal Emancipation*qv (1821), both originating at Mt. Pleasant, Ohio, and *The Castigator* (1824) at Ripley, Ohio. *Letters on American Slavery* (1826) by the Rev. John Rankin passed through five editions by 1838. Having read the little book, Garrison became Rankin's "disciple." The Rev. Samuel Crothers, Rankin's contemporary and not distant neighbor, also abhorred slavery, as shown in his *Life and Writings* (1857). Antislavery societies became numerous in the North after 1832 and often had hundreds of members, by whom their *Annual Reports* were read. These abolitionistsqv also read such publications as *The Anti-Slavery Almanac,* Theodore Dwight Weld's *Slavery as It Is, The Anti-Slavery Manual, The Cabinet of Freedom, The Liberty Bell,* Jay's *View of the Action of the Federal Government on Slavery,* Horace Mann's *Slavery: Letters and Speeches,* E. B. Chase's *Teachings of Patriots and Statesmen,* and the memoirs of escaped slaves, including Frederick Douglas' *My Bondage and My Freedom,* C. E. Stevens' *Anthony Burns,* the *Narrative of Henry Box Brown,* and J. R. Giddings' *The Exiles of Florida;* also the few but stirring memoirs of abductors of slaves. Occasionally a runaway's narrative sold up to 10,000 copies. *Uncle Tom's Cabin* (1852) quickly made a "mass appeal" and intensified Northern hatred of the Fugitive Slave Law of 1850. Mrs. Stowe's *Key to Uncle Tom's Cabin* (1853) fed fuel to the fire, and her *Dred* increased the excitement over the Kansas struggleqv and the assault on Charles Sumner (*see* Brooks-Sumner Affair).

[*Ohio State Archæological and Historical Quarterly,* July, 1937; A. B. Hart, *Slavery and Abolition;* Henry Wilson,

Rise and Fall of the Slave Power in America; and the publications referred to above.]

WILBUR H. SIEBERT

Abominations, Tariff of. *See* Tariff of Abominations.

Abraham, Plains of, on the west side of the city of Quebec, were named after Abraham Martin, a Quebec pilot, who once owned part of the land. They were the scene, in 1759, of the battle (*see* Quebec, Capture of) that brought an end to the dream of French empire in North America, and, incidentally, resulted in the death of two great generals, Wolfe and Montcalm. The site is now a Canadian national park.

LAWRENCE J. BURPEE

Abraham Lincoln, Fort, was built by Gen. George A. Custer in 1873, on the Missouri River, just below Heart River. Fort McKean, on top a hill above this fort, was an infantry post, and though built first, was usually considered part of Fort Abraham Lincoln. In 1895 the fort was abandoned. Fort Lincoln was authorized the same year to be built near the city of Bismarck, N. Dak., as an eight-company post. Buildings were constructed in 1903, but the post was abandoned until 1927. It is the only surviving military post in North Dakota.

[L. F. Crawford, *History of North Dakota.*]

CARL L. CANNON

Absentee Ownership, as commonly conceived, is a type of organization where management and direction are separated in whole or in part from actual ownership. Usually the owner is not present where operations are carried on, although, upon occasions, he may be on the spot. Such conditions are as old as the centuries. At the very beginning of American settlement there existed in colonization, or trading, companies, resident owners—in most cases largely a fiction—and directing owners, who lived in England. In very early times, in the southern colonies, the need of continually taking up new land imposed upon owners a system of direction by means of which some holdings were managed by overseers. These persons were often ex-indentured servants who had been trained to plantation conditions. In later plantation days, notably after the great development of cotton as a commercial crop, the management of plantations by overseers became a rather common occurrence. Some shipping ventures in New England properly belong in the class of agent direction. Captains and crews of merchant vessels were sometimes merely contract representatives of the actual owners, or operated under some kind of share system, by means of which they obtained some of the profits in the ventures.

It is in recent times, however, that the question of absentee ownership has become a live question. Two fields in which it is an issue are in farm tenancy^qv^ and in the growth of the industrial corporation. The corporation idea is as old as Roman law, perhaps in its "entity" aspect, as old as the human race. The concept was preserved in the mediæval municipal corporation, and adapted, notably in the 19th century, to business practices. The significant fact in this development is that the corporation became a kind of little republic with management vested in representatives of stockholders (directors), the stockholders themselves taking no part in the management. In fact, stockholders may be dispersed over wide areas, as with such large organizations as General Motors^qv^. Such development has been made possible by the use of evidences of property—stock, bonds, notes, mortgages, leases. In American practice, at least in the earlier days of the Constitution, the corporate form was looked upon with suspicion, possibly as an outward and visible sign of monopoly^qv^. The earliest corporations in the United States were in turnpikes, banking, and shipping ventures, where the need of large capital and limited liability made this form desirable. The first organizations of this type came into existence under special charter; it was not until the decade 1840 to 1850 that the states began to grant charters of general incorporation. In the banking field, free banking^qv^ is an illustration; but after 1860 the corporation was to an ever increasing extent adopted for industrial and commercial purposes. Out of the corporate idea has developed in quite recent times the concept of trusteeship. This applies not only to financial institutions, but more and more to industrial and commercial companies. That is to say, that the directors occupy a position of trust and confidence with respect to stockholders.

Some idea of the growth of the corporate form is seen by its use in manufacture. By the census of 1929 some 210,000 establishments were in this form. They turned out goods worth over $69,000,000,000. A similar condition exists in mining, forestry, commerce, finance, and transport. Another view is contained in the value of listed securities on the New York Stock Exchange^qv^. On June 30, 1938, the value of listed bonds was over $49,000,000,000. The total shares of listed stock were 1,426,800,000,000 with a market value of over $41,900,000,000. This says nothing about shares listed on the Curb and other exchanges.

Shortly before the panic of 1929[qv] corporate farming was beginning to make considerable headway. Stocks and bonds were sold in many communities. Such enterprises were organized after the manner of industrial corporations, with directors, general managers, superintendents, foremen, and general run of workers. In another aspect farming presents a case of absentee ownership, namely, in the various types of tenancy. This condition has been increasing over the last thirty years. In 1930, 42.4% of American farms were operated by tenants. Whether or not this condition is socially desirable is a debatable question. Some investigators have suggested that, in many cases, tenancy is only a temporary status. The young man starts as a tenant, gradually accumulates funds, and ultimately becomes an owner. Besides tenancy, in 1930, about 55,000 farms in this country were operated by managers. Mechanization of farms, the condition of the terrain in some areas, and the kinds of crops are factors in determining the type of management.

[P. A. Bruce, *Economic History of Virginia in the Seventeenth Century;* W. B. Weeden, *Economic and Social History of New England, 1620-1789*, Vol. II; *Hunt's Merchants' Magazine*, volumes from 1840 to 1850 relative to the Corporation.]

ISAAC LIPPINCOTT

Absentee Voting was first permitted to Union soldiers in the field during the Civil War, and some states today restrict such voting to persons in the military or naval service of the government. Beginning, however, with Vermont (1896) and Kansas (1901, 1911), nearly all states have enacted laws permitting civilians who expect to be absent from their home precincts on an election day—including traveling salesmen, government officials, railway and steamship employees, and college and university students—to cast ballots either before leaving home or *in absentia*. The more generous laws also permit absentee voting on account of illness or disability.

[P. O. Ray, *Introduction to Political Parties and Practical Politics*, 3rd ed.]

P. ORMAN RAY

Abundant Life, The More, a phrase of scriptural flavor used by President Franklin D. Roosevelt in his address before the Inter-American Conference for the Maintenance of Peace, Buenos Aires, Argentina, Dec. 1, 1936, to signify the improved living conditions and enlarged cultural and economic opportunities available to the whole world through the maintenance in the Western Hemisphere of constitutional representative government based on faith in God.

[F. D. Roosevelt, *The Public Papers and Addresses*, Vol. V.]

STANLEY R. PILLSBURY

Academic Freedom represents the traditional right of the scholar to study and teach as his conscience may dictate. It was reflected in the chartered special privileges of scholars and universities in Europe and England, and developed in the several countries in accordance with their general views regarding freedom.

In the United States the early colleges and universities[qv] were under ecclesiastical leadership, and occasionally difficulties arose from philosophical independence. However, some colonial colleges by charter provisions prohibited religious tests, and laid foundations for freedom not only from political but also from ecclesiastical authority.

During the 19th century four developments made academic freedom an important issue. First, the emphasis upon research which accompanied the change of many colleges into universities, either in organization or in spirit, raised controversial questions. Second, the impact of scientific research and philosophic speculation upon religious belief produced tension. The evolutionary theory[qv], for example, was a focal center of this issue for about fifty years. Third, the development of private philanthropy as the basis for the support of colleges and universities led in some instances to attempts to please actual or prospective donors by limitations upon teaching and research. Fourth, state support and control of universities raised problems when professors were critical of measures or policies of the state government. With local exceptions, however, the struggle for academic freedom was won.

A new phase occurred with the rise of the state and the growth of political control of social and economic matters. It reached an acute stage with the World War, and since that time has been chronic because of the appearance of the self-conscious totalitarianism of Communism, Fascism, and Nazism, all which reject the basic assumptions of academic freedom. These developments made the academic community more jealous of its rights; fears aroused by real or fancied penetration of Communistic or Fascist ideals, thought to be fostered by some members of faculties, led to conflicts and occasional incidents. Thus far, with relatively few local exceptions, academic freedom has been maintained.

HENRY M. WRISTON

Academies. There have been three types of secondary schools in the United States: the Latin grammar school[qv] of the Colonial Period; the academy which began about the middle of the 18th century and continued for nearly a century; and the public high school[qv]. The Latin grammar school was displaced by the academy and the academy was largely displaced by the public high school.

An early school of this kind grew out of the work of Benjamin Franklin in Philadelphia. Most of the early academies, however, seem to have been the fruits of denominational interests, and most of them were private institutions, although some states undertook to provide for county systems of academies. They were also under the control of self-perpetuating boards of trustees, were often chartered by the legislatures of the various states and had the right to own and control property, to receive gifts and endowments, and to engage and dismiss their teachers. These institutions went by a variety of names, such as academy, institution, seminary, collegiate institute, and sometimes college. There were academies for boys, academies for girls, and in some cases these schools were co-educational. Tuition fees were usually charged but occasionally the legislature would charter an academy or grant it other privileges with the provision that poor children should be taught gratuitously. The academy movement spread widely. It was reported that by 1830 there were 1000 such incorporated institutions in the United States and within two decades probably more than 6000, instructing more than 260,000 pupils.

The academies stimulated interest in the training of teachers and may be considered the forerunner of the normal schools[qv]. Many became the nuclei from which collegiate institutions developed. They served also to encourage the education of girls and women. Variants of the academy appeared in the manual labor schools and in military schools.

[Edgar W. Knight, *Education in the United States.*]

EDGAR W. KNIGHT

Acadia and the Acadians. The name Acadia, whether of European origin or a derivative of the Indian word *Aquoddiake,* was first applied in letters-patent to the grant obtained by Pierre de Guast, Sieur de Monts, from the King of France, Nov. 18, 1603. The boundaries of Acadia, never clearly defined, roughly embraced the North American coast from Cape Breton to the shores below the Hudson (40° to 46° N. Lat.) and overlapped considerably the land claimed by England by virtue of Cabot's discovery (*see* Cabot, Voyages) and Sir Humphrey Gilbert's possessory claim in the 16th century. Such was the basis for the conflicting claims of England and France to North America which resulted in a hundred and fifty years of predatory warfare, during which time Acadia, unproductive and desolate, was traded back and forth between the two powers as English and French diplomats sought to adjust the balance of losses and acquisitions elsewhere.

Although by the Treaty of Utrecht, 1713[qv], "all Nova Scotia with its ancient boundaries" was ceded to England, French empire builders saw the advantage of tacitly narrowing the indefinite limits of Nova Scotia to what is now the peninsula bearing that name, and England, faced with the necessity of holding the land from the Kennebec to the St. Croix, came to view the French inhabitants of the peninsula, the Acadians, with alarm. By 1755 new colonial wars had broken out. The Acadians, both the victims and oftentimes the participators in maundering warfare, charged by the English with disloyalty undoubtedly fostered by Jesuit priests, were believed to menace the English colonial possessions from within. By an act of extreme severity, immortalized by Longfellow in his *Evangeline*[qv], over 4000 of these Acadians were uprooted from their homes and dispersed to other English colonies, principally Maryland and Virginia. Some made their way to the West Indies and Louisiana (*see* Acadians in Louisiana). Many found their way back, however, and today their descendants may be found in Nova Scotia as well as in Madawaska, Maine.

[F. Parkman, *A Half-Century of Conflict* and his *Montcalm and Wolfe;* J. B. Brebner, *New England's Outpost.*]

ELIZABETH RING

Acadian Coast, THE, is the section of Louisiana along the Mississippi River settled by the exiled Acadians[qv] after about 1760. While applying particularly to the present parish of St. James, the term is sometimes used to designate the scattered Acadian settlements on the Mississippi as far as the mouth of Red River.

[C. Gayarré, *History of Louisiana;* A. Fortier, *Louisiana,* Cyclopedic.]

WALTER PRICHARD

Acadians in Louisiana, THE. It is not known that any of the Acadians came directly from their homeland to Louisiana. They came in irregular groups and at irregular intervals, having first attempted to settle at other places without success. Some came by ship to New Orleans from the New England and Atlantic seaboard colonies, but the majority came overland, from Maryland, Pennsylvania, and Virginia, by trail across the mountains and by flatboat[qv] down the Tennessee, the Ohio, and the Mississippi rivers. This accounts for the fact that some came after the first deportation, while others did not arrive until 1766. From New Orleans they were first sent some fifty miles up the river to what is now St. James Parish (county) and gave the name of Acadian Coast[qv] to that section of the river. Others pushed up the river as far as Pointe Coupée[qv], in the parish of that name. Later arrivals were sent westward into southern Louisiana, from 70 to 100 miles from New Orleans, along Bayou Lafourche and Bayou Teche, into the region protected by the frontier *postes* of Attakapas and Opelousas.

At the former *poste* they largely founded the town of Saint Martinville, which soon became and has remained the center of the Acadian life in Louisiana. Land was given them in this frontier region, they built their homes and furnished them largely with handmade furniture that may still be seen throughout south Louisiana. An industrious and prolific people, in this genial climate they rapidly increased in numbers and spread westward into the parish which bears their name, Acadia, and the surrounding territory. They and their descendants have been largely farmers, but some became merchants and stock raisers, while some entered the professions. In the region of the Teche and Lafourche they developed a characteristic culture that exists today despite modern changes.

Until the last three decades their language was almost entirely French, and they developed a characteristic dialect which has been the subject of recent interesting study. For many years their newspapers were published in French. However, public education has, during the present century, taken rapid hold among them, the speaking and study of English is compulsory in all schools, so that all of the present generation know and speak English, though French is still the family tongue. The French press has disappeared.

Saint Martinville is one of the most charming towns in Louisiana, and a Mecca for tourists. Here on the banks of the Teche stands the "Evangeline Oak," and nearby in the churchyard of Saint Martin is the grave of Evangeline[qv], marked by a life-size bronze statue, for here lived Emmeline Labiche, the original of Longfellow's heroine. Not far distant is the Evangeline State Park, a beautiful tract along the Teche, where there is preserved a typical Acadian farm dwelling, furnished as they originally stood.

No record was kept of the numbers of Acadians who arrived in Louisiana. Dudley LeBlanc, in his *True Story of the Acadians,* states that 2500 came by way of France, and that the total number was 5000. This appears to be an exaggeration for the total number deported is given as 5788, by Ficklin. In 1787, which was thirty-two years after the beginning of the deportations, Gov. Miro of Louisiana had a census of the Acadians taken, and reported the number in the province as 1587. It would appear that the number did not exceed 2000 altogether, or at most 2500. Today they number more than 300,000, and their region is the most densely populated section of the state.

[Alcée Fortier, *Louisiana Studies;* Margaret A. Johnston, *In Acadia;* Alcée Fortier, Acadians, in *Louisiana,* Cyclopedic; Charles Gayarré, *History of Louisiana.*]

J. FAIR HARDIN

Acceptance Business and Foreign Trade. A bank acceptance is a time bill of exchange[qv], drawn on a bank and accepted by it. The Federal Reserve Act[qv] granted member banks the privilege of accepting drafts against them arising from the domestic shipment or storage of goods, or from the exportation or importation of goods and the storage or shipment thereof in or between foreign nations.

The development of dollar acceptances during the World War enabled United States bankers to gain practically all of our import and export financing, and eventually to engage in the financing of trade between European nations. Since 1920 most of the foreign patronage has returned to European bankers, although American shippers continued to use dollar acceptances almost exclusively. Approximately 75% of current United States bankers' acceptances have arisen from the importation, exportation, or shipment of our goods in foreign trade.

[W. R. Burgess, *The Reserve Banks and the Money Market.*]

FRANK PARKER

Acceptance Speech. *See* Notification Speech.

Accidents. In an average year, only four diseases kill more people than accidents. Accidents lead all causes of death for both sexes between the ages of three and twenty-one, and among males from three to forty. Among males of all ages, heart disease alone kills a greater number, while among females, accidents rank between sixth and seventh as a cause of death. While man has always suffered from accidental injuries, with the introduction of factory systems and the development of machines, railroads, automobiles, and hundreds of mechanical devices, an era fraught with many new and unforeseen hazards was ushered in. It was not so many years ago, however, that serious thought concerning accident prevention started to supersede the old philosophy that mishaps were acts of God.

Probably the first step in the control of untoward events were mechanical safeguards. In 1833, Stephenson suggested steam whistles for locomotives. It was in 1868 that Westinghouse perfected the first air brake, and the first test of automatic car couplers was made in 1885. By 1893, standard safety equipment was required on all railroad trains through the adoption of the Federal Safety Appliance Act. It was not before 1900, however, that railroads began to organize definite campaigns against accidents.

It was about this time, shortly before the first workmen's compensation[qv] laws were passed, that some industrial plants began to practise organized accident prevention. In 1912, a small group of men interested in accident prevention met in Milwaukee, under the Association of Iron and Steel Electrical Engineers. This group decided that by exchanging ideas on a co-operative basis, much greater progress might be made in the control of accidents. Out of this meeting was evolved the idea for a national association that would act as a clearing house for the best ideas in accident prevention. At a convention called in New York City for the following year, the National Safety Council for Industrial Safety was formally organized. With the automobile had come the problem of public safety, and in 1915 the name was changed to the National Safety Council and the constitution altered to include a national program of public as well as industrial safety.

The motor age has brought an enormously increased accident toll. In 1937 there were 39,500 traffic deaths, 1,360,000 personal injuries and an economic loss of $1,700,000,000. This toll is four fifths as great as American losses in the World War, and is equivalent to the destruction of a city like Waltham, Mass., or Santa Monica, Calif.

Deaths from home accidents each year rank second only to traffic fatalities. In 1937 they caused 32,500 deaths and 4,700,000 non-fatal injuries. About 140,000 of these were permanent disabilities.

Each year since 1913 has seen considerable improvement in industrial safety. At that time there were about 35,000 workers killed yearly in occupational accidents, although fewer persons were working then than now. In 1937, there were 19,500 occupational deaths, a reduction of 44% since 1913.

[Stewart Holbrook, *Let Them Live.*]

W. H. CAMERON

Accomac. *See* Bacon's Rebellion.

Ackia, Battle of. On May 26, 1736, the Chickasaws[qv] decisively defeated the French under Bienville at Ackia, near present Tupelo, Miss. This defeat reduced French prestige in that quarter, where French and English traders were engaged in a contest for control of Indian trade. (*See also* Chickasaw-French War.)

[J. F. H. Claiborne, *Mississippi, as a Province, Territory and State;* Charles Gayarré, *History of Louisiana;* Dunbar Rowland, *History of Mississippi.*]

WALTER PRICHARD

Acoma is the name of both an Indian tribe and its pueblo, perched on a bold rock extending 357 feet into the air in Valencia County, N. Mex. It was discovered by the Spanish in 1539 and at one time had a large population. The Indians gained subsistence by cultivating gardens near the base of the rock which they reached by a dizzy trail cut in the rock. In 1599 the rock was scaled by the Spaniards who, after a three days' battle, killed about 1500 Acoma, or half the tribe.

[F. W. Hodge, *Handbook of American Indians.*]

CARL L. CANNON

Acre Right. *See* Cabin Right.

Act for the Impartial Administration of Justice, The (one of the Coercion Acts[qv]), passed by Parliament in May, 1774, provided that whenever the governor of Massachusetts doubted whether a person accused of misconduct in suppressing a riot or executing the law could secure a fair trial in Massachusetts, he might, with consent of the Council, transfer the trial to another colony or to Great Britain. This act—known in America as the "Murder Act"—aroused the colonists' apprehensions that the British government intended to establish a military despotism by giving British soldiers the privilege of shooting down Whigs with impunity.

[C. H. Van Tyne, *The Causes of the War of Independence.*]

JOHN C. MILLER

Acting. *See* Drama, The American.

Active Case, The, known as Olmstead et als. v. Rittenhouse's Executives, raised the question of prerogative as between Federal and state courts. Olmstead of Connecticut and others seized the British sloop *Active* (1777), which was later captured by the Pennsylvania armed brig *Convention,* commanded by Houston. Award of prize money[qv] to Houston and his crew by state courts of Pennsylvania was set aside by the Supreme Court (1809) after a bitter dispute regarding jurisdiction.

WHEELER PRESTON

Acts of Trade. *See* Navigation Acts, The.

Adair v. U. S., 1908 (208 U. S. 161). In violation of a Federal law of 1898, William Adair, acting for the L. & N. Railroad[qv], dismissed O. B.

Coppage because he was a member of a labor union. The Supreme Court declared this law unconstitutional because it violated the right of personal liberty and of property guaranteed by the Fifth Amendment[qv].

[Charles Warren, *The Supreme Court in the United States.*]

E. MERTON COULTER

Adams, Fort (Miss.), built 1798–99 by Maj. Thomas Freeman eight miles above the 31st parallel on the east bank of the Mississippi River (Loftus Heights[qv]), was an earthwork, magazine, and barracks for boundary defense (*see* Southern Boundary, Survey of the) against the Spanish, just removed from Natchez[qv] and confined to Louisiana and Florida (*see* Pinckney's Treaty). It was the United States port of entry on the Mississippi.

Here Gen. James Wilkinson negotiated a treaty with the Choctaws (Dec. 12, 1801) for resurveying the British line from the Yazoo southward marking limits of the Natchez District, and for a road (Natchez Trace) through Choctaw country to the Chickasaws, thence to Nashville[qqv]. Negotiations for a road to Mobile were opened but abandoned for fear of Spanish hostility. Wilkinson completed the resurvey in 1803. Congress appropriated $6000 for the Trace (1806). After American acquisition of Louisiana and Florida[qqv], Fort Adams was abandoned.

[Dunbar Rowland, *Mississippi*, Vol. I; American State Papers, *Indian Affairs*, Vol. I; C. E. Carter, Territorial Papers of the United States, Vol. V, *The Territory of Mississippi.*]

MACK SWEARINGEN

Adams Express Company. In 1839 Alvin Adams, a produce merchant ruined by the panic of 1837[qv], began carrying letters, small packages and valuables for patrons between Boston and Worcester. He had at first a partner named Burke, who soon withdrew, and as Adams & Company, Adams rapidly extended his territory to New York, Philadelphia and other eastern cities. By 1847 he had penetrated deeply into the South, and by 1850 he was shipping by rail and stagecoach to St. Louis. In 1854 his company was reorganized as the Adams Express Company. Meanwhile, a subsidiary concern, Adams & Company of California, had been organized in 1850 and spread its service all over the Pacific Coast; but not being under Adams' personal management, it was badly handled, and failed in 1854, causing a panic which shook California to its depths. The South was almost entirely covered by the Adams express service in 1861, when the Civil War necessitated the splitting off of another company, which, for politic reasons, was given the name of Southern. There was a mysterious kinship between the two ever afterward, they having joint offices at common points. Southern stock was never quoted in the market, and it was even charged by some Adams stockholders that the Southern was secretly owned by the Adams. The parent company held a strong position from New England and the mid-Atlantic coast to the far Western plains. Its stock holdings were enormous. In 1910 it was the second largest stockholder in the Pennsylvania Railroad[qv] and the third largest in the New Haven, besides owning large blocks of American Express, Norfolk & Western and other shares. Its ante bellum employment of Allan Pinkerton to solve its robbery problems was a large factor in building up that noted detective agency[qv]. Along with the other expresses, it merged its shipping interests into the American Railway Express Company, but continued its corporate existence as a wealthy investment trust.

[Alvin F. Harlow, *Old Waybills.*]

ALVIN F. HARLOW

Adams-Onís Treaty, THE, signed at Washington, Feb. 22, 1819, by John Quincy Adams, Secretary of State, and Luis de Onís, Spanish Minister, closed the first era of United States expansion by providing for the cession of East Florida[qv], the abandonment of the controversy over West Florida[qv], which had previously been seized by the United States (*see* Mobile Seized, 1813), and a boundary delineation along the Sabine River from the Gulf of Mexico to the 32nd parallel, N. Lat., thence north to the Red River, along it to the 100th parallel, W. Long., north to the Arkansas, along it to its source, thence directly north or south as the case might be to the 42nd parallel, N. Lat., and west on that line to the Pacific Ocean (*see* Oregon Question, The). The United States assumed claims of its own citizens against Spain, prorating them down to a maximum of $5,000,000. Non-conflicting articles of Pinckney's Treaty of 1795[qv] were to remain in force. Spanish goods received certain tariff privileges in Florida ports.

Spain, weakened by European wars and colonial revolutions, was obliged to sacrifice her interests, especially after Andrew Jackson's seizure of Spanish property in the Floridas in 1818 (*see* Arbuthnot and Ambrister, Case of). Other nations declined to assist Spain in the negotiations. Ferdinand VII's ministers at first refused to ratify the treaty, using as a pretext the nullification of certain land grants made by Ferdinand in the Floridas. Evasion failed, and after a revolt made Ferdinand a constitutional monarch in 1820, his council was obliged to approve the treaty. Ratifications were exchanged at Washington on Feb. 22, 1821. (*See also* Louisiana Purchase, Boundaries of.)

[Hunter Miller, *Treaties and Other International Acts of the United States of America.*]

PHILIP COOLIDGE BROOKS

Adamson Act, The, enacted under Administration pressure backed by a strike threat, was passed Sept. 2, 1916. It established, in place of a ten, an eight-hour day[qv] for railroad trainmen. The alternative of 100 miles of run remained unchanged. The railroads claimed the law raised wages rather than regulated hours, as normal operation required over eight hours work. The law was upheld, in Wilson v. New (243 U. S. 332), as hour legislation in the interests of interstate commerce[qv].

[J. R. Commons and J. B. Andrews, *Principles of Labor Legislation.*]

JAMES D. MAGEE

Adding Machine. *See* Business, Mechanical Devices Used in.

"Address of the Southern Delegates" (1848). Southern delegates in Congress, aroused by hostile resolutions on slavery, called a caucus for Dec. 23, 1848. John C. Calhoun submitted an address "moderate in manner" but calculated to unite the South which, with three amendments that did not "affect the truth of its narrative, or materially change its character," was finally adopted on Jan. 22, 1849, after Berrien's substitute had been rejected. Calhoun's address relates entirely to the sectional contest over slavery and recounts the aggressions of the North on the South. These aggressions were of two kinds: nullification of constitutional guarantees for the return of fugitive slaves[qv]; and the exclusion of slavery and Southerners from the common territories (*see* Wilmot Proviso). Calhoun maintained that these aggressions threatened ultimate abolition and the complete overturn of Southern society unless the South united and brought them to an end. Less than half the Southern delegates signed the address and it accomplished little. (*See also* Tarpley Letter, The.)

[T. H. Benton, *Thirty Years' View;* John C. Calhoun, *Works,* Vol. VI; G. P. Garrison, *Westward Extension;* W. M. Meigs, *Life of John Caldwell Calhoun.*]

FLETCHER M. GREEN

Addyston Pipe Company Case, The, 1899 (175 U. S. 211). The Supreme Court, by a unanimous decision based on the Sherman Anti-Trust Act[qv], permanently enjoined six producers of cast-iron pipe from continuing an agreement eliminating competition among themselves. Justice Peckham, speaking for the Court, denied that the decision in the Knight case[qv] obtained, saying that here was a definite conspiracy to interfere with the flow of interstate commerce and a positive scheme to limit competition and fix prices. This decision indicated that the Sherman Anti-Trust Act possessed "teeth" and tended to restrain similar activities.

[Eliot Jones, *The Trust Problem in the United States;* W. Z. Ripley, *Trusts, Pools and Corporations;* L. B. Evans, *Leading Cases on Constitutional Law.*]

ALLEN E. RAGAN

Adena Prehistoric Culture, The, a type of Mound Builder[qv] culture, takes its name from a mound at Adena, Ohio. It apparently existed in southern Ohio and adjacent parts of Kentucky, West Virginia and Indiana. The culture is characterized by shapely conical mounds, burials in log cists (usually without cremation), skill in carving small objects in the round, the use of tubular pipes, and a limited use of copper for ornamental purposes. No dwelling sites have been found.

[Henry Clyde Shetrone, *The Mound-Builders.*]

EUGENE H. ROSEBOOM

Adkins v. Children's Hospital, 1923 (261 U. S. 525), was a Supreme Court decision holding invalid an act of Congress creating a Minimum Wage[qv] Board to "ascertain" and "fix" adequate wages for women employees in the District of Columbia.

The question before the Court was whether the act of Congress constituted a deprivation of "life, liberty or property without due process of law" under the Fifth Amendment. The Court held by a vote of five to three that the act was an unjustified interference by Congress with the freedom of employer and employee to contract as they pleased. Taft, Sanford and Holmes, dissenting, took the view that the Fifth Amendment did not stand in the way of reasonable legislation calculated to correct admitted evils. The case was expressly overruled by West Coast Hotel Company v. Parrish[qv] (57 Sup. Ct. 578), 1937.

[Roscoe Pound and others, *The Supreme Court and Minimum Wage Legislation.*]

GEORGE W. GOBLE

Administrative Agency. *See* Congress, The Regulatory Powers of.

Administrative and Political Divisions. *See* Local Government.

Administrative Discretion, Delegation of. Delegation of discretionary power to administrative officials has accompanied the increase in functions of government, particularly regulatory functions, during the past half century. Legislative motives for the delegation have been numerous and varied—to avoid tedious, technical decisions necessary in regulation[qv], to employ a more expert personnel and less formal procedure in discovering facts than is possible in courts of law, to provide continuing, preventive regulation of an elastic character, and even to disguise legislative failure to make a clear-cut decision on questions of policy. Discretionary power has been delegated to the President, governors of states, and municipal executives; but more frequently, where regulation directly affecting the public is involved, authority has been granted to responsible heads of departments or to independent commissions. For example, the Secretaries of Agriculture and Labor, the Interstate Commerce and Federal Trade Commissions[qqv], state directors of banking, state public utility commissions, and local health officers or boards of health exercise important discretionary powers.

Although discretion is commonly labeled "quasi-legislative" or "quasi-judicial"[qv], the classification is chiefly one of convenience; for many (quasi-legislative) rules are made after investigation of a judicial character, and many administrative (quasi-judicial) orders to individuals serve to define a general rule of conduct by establishing precedents. According to American constitutional law, legislatures may not delegate discretionary authority without anchoring it to a basic policy and setting limits to the swing of judgment. As interpreted by the courts this rule has not been a serious check to delegation of power. However, the traditional review by law courts of administrative decisions affecting private rights has greatly curtailed the discretion of administrative officials (*see* Judicial Review). The courts have not only asserted their right to settle questions of law, but have freely substituted their judgment for that of designated officials in deciding questions of fact. Consequently the findings of expert bodies are not infrequently set aside, and their determinations commonly lack finality. Administrative regulation has tended to become a preliminary to the formal judicial prosecution and trial which it was intended to replace (*see* Administrative Justice).

[John Dickinson, *Administrative Justice and the Supremacy of Law.*]

GEORGE A. GRAHAM

Administrative Justice or administrative adjudication is a term applied to the procedure whereby the rights of individuals are determined by administrative agencies[qv] rather than by regular courts of law. This procedure is sometimes referred to as "regulation by government" in contrast to "regulation by law."

To some extent, administrative adjudication has existed in the United States from the first. For example, the Patent Office, the Land Office, the Post Office Department and the Treasury Department[qqv] have throughout their existence exercised what amount to judicial powers in some instances. Since early history there have similarly been examples of administrative adjudication in the states, particularly in relation to such matters as taxes and public health.

Since about 1890 there has been a remarkable development of administrative justice. This has been due to the vast increase in the regulatory activity of both the state and Federal governments. As a result, by 1919 Massachusetts had 216 administrative agencies and New York had 187. Each of the other states usually had two score or more. These agencies became responsible for a vast amount of adjudication in relation to banks and other financial institutions, public utilities, sanitation and public health, employment of women and children, conditions of work, industrial accidents, taxes, and so forth. In the period since the World War there has been much improvement in the machinery of administration, at least in those states which have followed the lead of Illinois which in 1917 adopted a comprehensive plan for administrative reorganization. In the reorganized departments which are few in number (ten in Illinois), the practice has been to include special boards to perform quasi-judicial[qv] as well as quasi-legislative functions.

In the Federal Government likewise, there has been a rapid growth of administrative agencies exercising quasi-judicial functions. First are those which are located within other governmental organizations, as, for example, the Board of Appeals created in 1933 in the Veterans' Administration, and the Government Contract Board created in 1936 in the Department of Labor. Another classification consists of independent agencies whose chief function is regulation, such as the Interstate Commerce Commission created in 1887, the Federal Trade Commission set up in 1914, the Securities and Exchange Commission and the Federal Communications Commission both of which came into existence in 1934, the Federal Reserve Board created in 1933, and the National Labor Relations Board authorized by a 1935 act of Congress[qqv]. Under another classification are regular courts of law which have been assigned the functions of reviewing administrative decisions. For example, under the Radio Act of 1927, Congress assigned to the Court of Appeals of the District of Columbia the authority to review the decisions of the Federal Radio Commission. This function was continued in 1934 in relation to the Federal Communications Commission.

Under a separate classification is the United States Tariff Commission[qv] which was created in 1916. It exercises quasi-judicial power in relation to unfair practices in connection with imports. Still another classification includes those agencies in which are vested licensing powers. An example is the Civil Aeronautics Authority created in 1938 to replace a bureau within the Department of Commerce. A separate classification must be given to the Comptroller General[qv] of the United States who, since 1921, has performed a judicial function in reviewing governmental accounts. A separate classification should also be given to executive officials such as the Secretaries of Agriculture, the Interior, and of Labor who, in recent years, have been assigned important functions in connection with administrative adjudication.

Among the most important of the agencies are those which are referred to as independent administrative courts. These agencies perform no functions other than those of a quasi-judicial nature. These administrative courts are the Court of Claims[qv], created in 1855; the Court of Customs and Patents Appeals, created in 1929; and the Board of Tax Appeals, created in 1924.

The development of administrative justice has been not only rapid but haphazard. General procedural rules have not been developed. Rules of evidence vary from those used in regular courts to practically no rules at all. Some administrative agencies hold formal hearings while others are very informal. Most agencies assume jurisdiction of their own volition while in other instances administrative adjudication is initiated by formal or informal complaints by interested parties. Usually the decisions of administrative tribunals can be appealed to regular courts, but in some cases their findings are final, at least as to "fact" if not as to "law." Decisions of some agencies are self-enforcing while those of others require an order from a regular court in order to secure enforcement. Obviously, there is much need for reform in the whole field of administrative justice in the interest of uniformity, efficiency and fair dealing.

[Frederick F. Blachly and Miriam E. Oatman, *Administrative Legislation and Adjudication;* John Dickinson, *Administrative Justice and the Supremacy of Law in the United States.*]

ERIK MCKINLEY ERIKSSON

Administrative Reorganization, THE MOVEMENT FOR, had its real beginning in 1910 when President Taft appointed a commission to study the matter. No action resulted. In 1918 Congress passed the Overman Act[qv] under which President Wilson accomplished some reorganization. In 1921 a committee was appointed to investigate proposals for administrative reform but again nothing important was accomplished. In his annual messages to Congress, President Hoover strongly urged on Congress the necessity of reorganization in the interests of efficiency and economy. On June 30, 1932, he was granted the right to reorganize subject to Congressional approval. In the following December he issued eleven executive orders, providing for extensive reorganization but, on Jan. 19, 1933, they were rejected by the House of Representatives. Subsequently, on March 3, 1933, President Hoover signed a bill empowering his successor for a period of two years to reorganize the administration as he saw fit. President Franklin D. Roosevelt issued forty-one executive orders under this law but failed to bring about any far-reaching reorganization. For a time the matter was dropped but on Jan. 12, 1937, the President again asked for broad reorganization powers. On March 29, 1939, Congress completed action on a bill granting him a limited power to reorganize.

[L. F. Schmeckebier, Organization of the Executive Branch of the National Government of the United States, *American Political Science Review*, XXVII-XXIX (1933-35); The President's Committee, *Administrative Management.*]

ERIK MCKINLEY ERIKSSON

Admirals. The highest rank in the American navy until 1862 was captain, for commodore was merely a courtesy title for a captain in charge of more than one ship. Admiral was thought to savor of aristocracy. But in 1862, Congress, in order to honor Farragut for his victory at New Orleans (1862)[qv], made him a rear admiral, and after Mobile (1864)[qv], a vice admiral. In 1866 he was made an admiral for life. Three years after Farragut's death in 1870, David D. Porter, who had been a vice admiral since 1866, was appointed admiral, which grade he retained till his death in 1891. In 1899 George Dewey was made Admiral of the Navy and remained so until he died in 1917. Controversy over the battle of Santiago[qv] prevented the award of admiral or vice admiral to either Sampson or Schley.

When the navy was expanded in 1915, Congress made provision for the rank of admiral and vice admiral to be held temporarily by the officers in first and second command respectively of the principal fleets, and in 1916 the rank, pay, and privileges of an admiral were assigned to the Chief of Naval Operations, who was to outrank all the rest. As in the Spanish-American

War, the close of the World War brought disputes regarding the relative merits of the various fleet commanders and Washington bureau chiefs. These jealousies prevented any naval officer from being granted the coveted right to fly permanently the four-starred admiral's flag.

[L. P. Lovette, *Naval Customs, Traditions, and Usage.*]

WALTER B. NORRIS

Admiralty Law and Courts. In the American colonies in the 17th century admiralty jurisdiction was generally exercised by the ordinary common law courts, although governors had the right to commission courts of vice admiralty; but by the end of the century royal patents were being issued for the establishment of vice admiralty courts, beginning in New York in 1696. In addition to the jurisdiction of the English admiralty courts over such matters as prize, wreck, salvage, insurance, freight and passenger contracts, bottomry, charter parties and seamen's wages, the colonial vice admiralty courts enforced the Acts of Trade[qv]. Piracy, which originally was under the jurisdiction of the admiralty, was in the colonies normally dealt with by courts specially commissioned by the crown to deal with particular cases. Procedure in vice admiralty was *in rem* rather than *in personam*. As the vice admiralty courts exercised summary jurisdiction and did not have trial by jury, they attained a considerable degree of unpopularity among that element in the colonies opposed to the Acts of Trade, and in some colonies writs of prohibition were frequently issued by the common law courts against the vice admiralty on the ground that the latter court was incompetent to act in particular litigation. As a rule such writs were obeyed. Common law courts throughout the colonial period, as, for example, the Mayor's Court of New York City, continued to exercise a good deal of admiralty jurisdiction.

After the Revolution most of the states erected their own courts of admiralty, really continuing the provincial courts, but the Federal Convention gave to the Federal courts "all cases of admiralty and maritime jurisdiction." Among the anachronisms surviving down to the 20th century in American admiralty law has been the privilege of the shipowner to limit liability after a disaster to whatever the value of the vessel or wreckage may be after the occurrence of the act. The *Titanic* and *Morro Castle* are two notorious examples of the application of this rule. The evolution of the doctrine of continuous voyage[qv] by the Federal courts during the Civil War provided Great Britain during the World War with a convenient precedent to justify the seizure of our ships bound for neutral ports on the ground that their ultimate destination was Germany.

[C. M. Andrews, Introduction to the Records of the Vice Admiralty Court of Rhode Island, *American Legal Records*, Vol. III; H. J. Crump, *Colonial Admiralty Jurisdiction in the 17th Century;* F. R. Sanborn, *Origins of the Early English Maritime and Commercial Law;* C. M. Hough, ed., *Reports of Cases in the Vice Admiralty of the Province of New York and in the Court of Admiralty of the State of New York.*]

RICHARD B. MORRIS

Admission of States. *See* States, Admission of.

Adobe Houses are structures made of earth and used principally in the Rocky Mountain plateau and in southwestern United States. The method came from North Africa via Spain and was introduced by the Spanish conquerors into the Southwest in the 16th century. Most of the Spanish mission buildings were made of this material. Wet clay and chopped hay or other fibrous material were mixed and the mass tramped with the bare feet. This was moulded into brick and sun dried. The walls were laid up with mud mortar. In the Rocky Mountain plateau adobe houses were made by moulding clay directly into the wall instead of making it into bricks. Adobe was widely used to build forts and trading posts as far east and north as Nebraska. Adobe was corrupted to "dobie" by the Americans. Since 1900 there has been a revival of adobe construction.

EVERETT DICK

Adobe Walls, The Battle of, was fought at the buffalo hunters' trading post by that name, on the north side of the Canadian River, in the Panhandle of Texas, June 27, 1874. The hide hunt was on, and the Adobe Walls post, established by hunters and traders from Dodge City[qv], Kans., was the southern outpost.

The Comanche, Cheyenne and Kiowa[qqv] were concentrated in Indian Territory, but during the spring of 1874 made several raids into Texas. Concentrating on the hunters who were killing their source of food, clothing and shelter, several hundred Indians attacked Adobe Walls. But they could not stand up against the fire of the Sharp's[qv] buffalo guns, and though three of the hunters were killed, the Indians, after losing heavily, abandoned the attack.

[Olive K. Dixon, *Life of Billy Dixon;* R. N. Richardson, in *The Panhandle-Plains Historical Review, 1931.*]

J. EVETTS HALEY

Adult Education is the name, borrowed from English usage, given to an American movement having its origins in the tradition of free speech[qv] inherent in the New England town meetings[qv] of the 17th century. The movement may be traced through the rise of the mechanics institutes in the early 19th century, the flowering of the lyceum movement[qv] in the eighteen-thirties and eighteen-forties, the foundation of the Philadelphia Extension Society in 1876, and the subsequent growth of the free public library[qv] and university extension movements. The term "adult education" did not come into general use in the United States until 1924, when the Carnegie Corporation[qv] of New York initiated a series of exploratory studies based on considerations similar to those contained in the findings of the epoch-making British Ministry of Reconstruction Report of 1919.

Following the publication of the American studies, two national and four regional conferences of adult educators were held, resulting in the founding at Chicago in 1926 of the American Association for Adult Education. The Association acts as a clearing house for information, an agency for the sponsorship and conduct of experiments and demonstrations, of studies and researches, and as the publisher of various materials on the philosophy and methods employed in the movement. It also publishes the quarterly *Journal of Adult Education*. It is currently (1938) engaged in a five-year study of the social significance of adult education, the findings being published from time to time in book form. Some forty subfields of adult education are under examination.

It is estimated that some 27,000,000 Americans, one third of the adult population, participate more than sporadically in some form of adult education, enormous increases during the economic depression (*see* Panic of 1929) being attributable to increased leisure time due to shortened working hours and to the large relief[qv] effort of the Federal Government in this field. The range of activities extends from radio[qv] listening individually and in groups, at one extreme, to post-graduate professional courses and conferences, at the other. Wide variations exist in the program offerings, the movement including provisions for the illiterate and the barely literate as well as services for collegiate alumni. Commonly included in the adult education enrollment are those who take part in rural adult education through the agricultural extension offerings of the land-grant colleges and the U. S. Department of Agriculture (*see* Agricultural Education), 7,000,000 strong; library patrons pursuing reading according to plan, numbering 1,000,000; members of men's and women's clubs participating in educational activities, 1,250,000; lyceum, Chautauqua and lecture course members[qqv], 1,000,000; subscribers to private correspondence school courses, 1,250,000; indoor recreation groups, 2,100,000; participants in public school offerings, in the regular evening elementary and high schools involving both cultural work and vocational offerings, 2,000,000; and those taking part in emergency relief classes of all types, numbering 2,250,000.

In addition, the open forum movement includes 500,000; churches and religious groups enroll 300,000; university extension 350,000; and various forms of vocational education, mainly for younger adults, 600,000. Smaller but highly important groups comprise workers' education, museum course attendants, foreign-born organization memberships, music groups including orchestras and choral societies, parent education, Negro groups, settlement[qv] and neighborhood groups, little theater[qv] organizations exclusive of audiences, corporation school enrollees, Civilian Conservation Corps[qv] Camp members, prisoners in penal institutions, and students in thousands of special schools for adults, etc.

The development of adult education in America, having been chiefly in the hands of a large number of private voluntary organizations, has been on the whole free from troublesome problems of censorship and control. Such questions have arisen in late years, however, as the tax-supported ventures in the field suddenly assumed large numerical proportions. However, the more farseeing of the school administrators, in responding to the new demand for adult education, are wisely forming advisory committees and local councils representative of many adult interests. These groups are expected to influence the program offerings in the direction of liberality of point of view, allowing for the full and free discussion of controversial subjects.

Important beginnings have been made in conducting the basic psychological, sociological and educational research necessary for a full understanding of adult instructional problems. Important contributions have been made by Prof. E. L. Thorndike and his associates at Teachers College, Columbia University, in determining the learning ability of adults at various age levels and also in determining adult interests. Studies and researches at the University of Chicago have done much to identify the interests of adult readers. Sociological studies made in rural districts by Prof. Edmund deS. Brunner of Teachers College, Columbia, have likewise contributed to an increasing fund of knowledge of adult education needs as have also such urban studies as R. S. and H. M. Lynd's *Middletown*.

American adult education has been described

as a "bourgeois" movement in contrast with European adult education, which even in Great Britain is much more representative of the working classes than of the population generally. In the United States adult education is regarded more as a right than as a privilege, and opportunities are usually as much available to the "middle class" as to working men and their families. The much more widespread opportunity for free child education through the adolescent years even to young manhood and young womanhood is accountable for this difference from the European scene.

Proponents of the movement assert that it bears a direct and important relationship to the effective functioning of the democratic form of government envisaged by the founders of the United States, and trace their obligation to the public back to the considerations set forth by Jay, Hamilton, and Madison in the Federalist^{qv} papers. Adult educators are outspoken in their support of a liberal position on political, economic, and social issues, but generally concur in the belief that their responsibility for the education of the adult student stops with due and careful preparation of the individual for social action rather than extending to social action itself. The leaders of the movement have conscientiously avoided any political flavor or affiliation in their adult education work.

[Dorothy Canfield Fisher, *Why Stop Learning?;* Morse A. Cartwright, *Ten Years of Adult Education;* Dorothy Hewitt and Kirtley Mather, *Adult Education—A Dynamic for Democracy;* Mary L. Ely, *Adult Education in Action.*]

MORSE A. CARTWRIGHT

Adulteration. The first federal recognition of the duty of the United States Government to protect consumers was evidenced by the Tea Inspection Act of March 2, 1897. Nine years later, the Pure Food and Drugs Act[qv] prohibited the adulteration of drugs, confectionery and foods, detailing those acts which constituted violation. The next step taken was the passage of an act forbidding transportation or sale of adulterated insecticides or fungicides within the territories as well as importation into the United States (36 U. S. 331). Shortly thereafter, the importation of adulterated grass and grain seeds was prohibited (37 U. S. 507). Various states forbid the adulteration of certain articles, e.g., California prohibits the sale or offering for sale of debased quicksilver.

[Publications of Consumers Research, Inc., and of Consumers Union, both give information concerning adulteration of specific items in commerce.]

ROBERT G. RAYMER

Adventists, OR MILLERITES, were followers of William Miller (1782–1849) who, during 1831–44, preached that, according to Daniel's and Ezra's prophecies, at Christ's second coming in 1844 fire would destroy the earth. The advent failing to materialize and opposition from existing sects becoming intolerant, a new church, Adventist, developed in 1845. The adherents believed in Christ's personal, visible return, the necessity for repentance and faith to obtain salvation, a physical resurrection, and a millennium spanning the period between the first and second resurrections. This organization finally disintegrated to form five extant groups, among them the Advent Christian Church and the Seventh-day Adventists[qv].

[I. C. Wellcome, *History of the Second Advent Message and Mission, Doctrine and People;* G. D. Hagstotz, *Seventh-day Adventists in the British Isles*, 1878-1933; M. E. Olsen, *A History of the Origin and Progress of the Seventh-day Adventists.*]

G. D. HAGSTOTZ

Adventure, THE, was a sloop built in the winter of 1791–92 at Clayoquot on Nootka Sound by Captains Asa Gray and John Kendrick of Boston who were on an exploring and trading expedition in the Northwest. It was the first American sailing vessel built on the Pacific coast.

[K. Coman, *Economic Beginnings of the Far West.*]

CARL L. CANNON

Adventurers. Colonization demanded labor and capital. Settlers had to be transported across a hostile sea, properly equipped to build life anew in a virgin land, and supplied with food until self-sustaining. Many were able to help themselves, venturing both life and money. Many others in their poverty were dependent upon financial assistance. The demands upon capital were heavy.

The term "adventurer" runs far back into English history when there appeared a body of traders known as "merchant adventurers." The very name, adventurer, denoted a new age and spirit in mercantile life. With money to invest, these enterprising merchants sought opportunities beyond England's shores. They adventured or risked their capital in foreign trade. Groups of merchant adventurers existed in Bristol, London, York, Chester and other leading ports.

These adventurers supplied the capital and enterprise which built up England's profitable commercial dominion in the Old World in the 16th century. The New World offered new opportunities. The merchants of Bristol aided Gilbert's futile colonial venture in Newfoundland in 1583 and a few London merchants assisted Raleigh[qv] in his ill-fated attempt to settle Roanoke Island in 1585. A larger capital was necessary and the familiar device of the joint-stock company was employed (*see* Trading Companies). Adventurers of Plymouth subscribed to the stock of the Plymouth Company[qv] whose colonial effort in Maine in 1607 promptly failed. London adventurers took stock in the company which by persistent effort succeeded in making Virginia a permanent colony (*see* Virginia Company of London). A group of London merchants risked their capital in aiding the Pilgrims to settle the colony of Plymouth[qv] in 1620. The colony of Massachusetts[qv] originated in an association of merchants living in and about Dorchester[qv], England. Not all those who risked their capital were merchants. The charter of 1609 to the Virginia Company of London incorporated fifty-six companies of the city of London and 659 persons gathered from various walks of life.

[C. M. Andrews, *Colonial Period of American History;* C. P. Nettels, *Roots of American Civilization.*]

WINFRED T. ROOT

Advertisements, Early American (1704–1830), were usually of the legal notice variety with a slight amount of display or illustration. The *Boston News Letter*[qv] in its third issue, May 1–8, 1704, carried a notice of real estate for sale, and two notices of lost articles. Soon there were also runaways to be advertised, and slaves for sale. These were set solid as other matter, though with a larger initial letter. Franklin in 1735 used larger type at the head of a notice; and somewhat later began the use of small woodcuts—of ships, Negroes, horses, etc.—to give variety and interest to the page. Notices were usually column width, and the larger were elongated squares. Shortage of paper led printers to discourage large notices, and to set a limit to the size of cuts.

These advertisements furnish valuable information for social and economic history. Commodities listed by merchants and manufacturers show the variety of imports and extent of manufactures, as well as consumers' tastes. Details of transportation and communication are found in notices of the sailings of ships, of post-routes, and later of stage, canal, and steamboat schedules. Beginnings of the professions are indicated by such notices as Paul Revere's offer to make false teeth (1768), and those offering the services of barbers, school teachers and dancing masters. Morals of an earlier generation are revealed by advertisements for runaway apprentices and slaves, and by offers of slaves for sale, often with detailed descriptions; and when the head of a family inserted a notice for a wet nurse, or informed the public not to trust the wife who had left his "bed and board." Lotteries[qv], theatrical entertainments, horse races[qv], and exhibitions of animals were recorded in advertisements; while cultural advance was indicated by notices of schools, musical organizations, libraries and lists of books for sale.

[Frank Presbrey, *The History and Development of Advertising.*]

MILTON W. HAMILTON

Advertising, National. Up to the time of the Civil War, advertising in America was mainly local, in such forms as signs, posted bills, cards, pamphlets, handbills and brief notices in the newspapers. Many merely identified a seller and listed his wares. Others aimed to bring together a specific need and a supply, and were often inserted by the prospective buyer, as in "Lost and Found" and "Wanted" advertisements. Even retailers' advertisements seldom contained much salesmanship before the adoption of the one-price policy.

Among manufacturers, almost the only ones who advertised were the proprietors of patent medicines[qv]. Most families resorted to self-medication, especially in districts where doctors were scarce and not readily accessible. There was a lively demand for sarsaparillas, bitters, liniments, pills, and panaceas. Such items had a low transportation cost, a high profit margin to manufacturer and retailer, and enjoyed a good repeat sale. However, the task of inducing the first purchase required aggressive salesmanship. Medical advertising was usually full of sensational and exaggerated claims; much of it was fraudulent.

Medical advertisers used every available medium. A favorite form was the almanac[qv], since it was likely to be kept for reference throughout the year. The newspapers[qv] were almost the only periodicals available. Their values varied greatly and their rates were elastic. The difficulty of bargaining for space in them was partly solved by the emergence of the advertising agency[qv]. The agent could secure the lowest possible rate and handle the details of billing and checking; later he undertook other services.

After the Civil War the agricultural papers and religious papers[qqv] enjoyed a brief importance. The general magazines at this period were not highly regarded as advertising media, and most of the influential ones did not welcome advertising. Some inserted only advertisements of books issued by their own publishing house. But in the eighteen-eighties, the magazines began to be more receptive to advertisers whose products and claims they considered acceptable. Because they had a country-wide circulation of well-to-do people, and were comparatively free from objectionable medical advertising, they rose rapidly toward a position of leadership in national advertising.

By this time American inventive genius had brought forth many new types of articles, and the network of railroads had made it possible to ship them to all the states of the Union. Manufacturers of cameras, fountain pens, typewriters, bicycles and a host of other new articles found the magazine a convenient medium for educating the public regarding their products. Manufacturers of new types of old articles like shaving soap, or of articles that were not habitually used, like chocolate and canned soup, widened their markets by magazine advertising. Brands of staple articles competed for the consumers' choice. Service industries used institutional advertisements to build good-will for their organizations and methods.

The growth of national advertising was aided by the constantly increasing efficiency of transportation, by the cheapness of periodicals, by the gradual transition from home-made to factory-made products, and by the change from buying in bulk to buying in packages. Advertising, in turn, exerted a reciprocal action in hastening these changes. This action was most obvious in the field of periodical publishing, where early in the 20th century advertising had become the chief source of income. It made possible 2-cent newspapers of forty-eight or more pages, and 5-cent weeklies with as much editorial content as the old 35-cent monthlies.

Advertising in the small "standard-size" (6″ x 9″) magazine soon reached a point of saturation. Advertisements in a thick segregated advertising section had a poor chance of being seen. Advertisers turned to the larger size flat publications, with reading matter distributed through the advertising section. Many of the older magazines changed their formats to meet the advertisers' wishes; others suspended. The losses were largely offset by the rise of new periodicals of various kinds, notably class publications with audiences selected on the basis of vocation or leisure interests.

The volume of national advertising continued to grow, with few setbacks, for the first three decades of the 20th century. During the World War it was an important aid in selling Liberty Bonds[qv] and in popularizing Government policies, including such policies as refraining from white bread and other articles needed for war purposes (*see* Food Administration, 1917–19). In 1929 the highest peak of national advertising was reached in an issue of the *Saturday Evening Post* containing 272 pages, of which about 168 were advertising pages (many in four colors) with a total cost of $1,579,408. The actual advertising cost per inch of space, on the basis of audience reached, was lower than that of most magazines of the 19th century, for the publication reached nearly three million families. The *Post* circulation has since then exceeded the three million mark, but its volume of advertising has never since equalled that of 1929.

The only medium that has consistently grown in volume of advertising since 1929 is the radio[qv]. This had first become available in 1922 but did not become significant until about 1930. Many advertisers have sponsored coast-to-coast broadcasts; a much larger number have had programs that reached all the thickly populated areas. Although radio advertising appeals through the ear and hence is not a direct competitor of advertising that appeals through the eye, it probably took parts of the advertising budget that would otherwise have been spent in newspaper, magazine and outdoor advertising. Nevertheless the newspaper continued to hold its leadership in manufacturers' advertising, with the magazine in second place, but by decreasing margins.

Even during the most prosperous period, national advertisers faced several obstacles that tended to lessen the efficiency of their advertising. Among them were: (1) the increased competition for attention; (2) the decline of public faith in advertising, due partly to the percentage of fraud and misrepresentation; (3) the competition of wholesalers and retailers.

The keen competition for the eye and ear of the public led to more scientific study. Market research was invoked to discover the number and character of consumers, their wants and habits, and the most efficient channels for reaching them. Psychologists examined buying motives and the ways to appeal to them. Methods of pre-testing copy were devised. Every part of the art and technique of advertising was analyzed. Courses in advertising were offered in universities. Before 1900 there was practically no literature of advertising, and only a few books before 1910. Since then, hundreds of volumes have been published covering every phase of the subject.

Although the better magazines and newspapers used every precaution to exclude fraudulent advertisers, these still found media for transmitting their messages. To eliminate them altogether, the Associated Advertising Clubs (later called the Advertising Federation of America) adopted the motto "Truth in Advertising" in 1911 and appointed a Vigilance Committee to see that fraudulent advertisers were prosecuted and punished according to law. This work was later systematized in the Better Business Bureaus in fifty-five cities, financed mainly by advertisers and publishers. Several states made false advertising a misdemeanor. The Federal Government, through the Post Office Department, the Department of Agriculture and the Federal Trade Commission[qqv], also stamped out some of the most serious evils. During the depression years, however, the frantic search for stimulants to buying caused some relapses into objectionable forms of advertising.

The competition of middlemen manifested itself most disturbingly in price-cutting on nationally advertised brands, and the promotion of private brands[qv]. Although the nationally advertised brands seldom allowed an abnormally large profit margin, they were frequently used as "loss-leaders" by large-scale dealers. This practice made them less acceptable to dealers who could not afford to meet the price cuts. A remedy was sought in Fair Trade Laws which legalized price maintenance[qv] of resale prices. Before the passage of these, however, many wholesalers and dealers (including some of the most drastic price-cutters) had established their own private brands. These usually required more personal sales effort, but were relatively free from price comparisons. Some manufacturers succeeded in getting the co-operation of dealers in making their advertising effective. In fields where price-cutting and private branding were not prevalent, national advertising did not usually result in an increase in the number of competitive brands. On the contrary, the number tended to decrease, as the brands that received little popular support were eliminated. The survivors were not invariably the most extensive or persuasive advertisers; often—as in automobiles and automobile accessories—they were those that had gauged more accurately the wants of consumers and adapted their product and messages to them.

[Frank Presbrey, *History and Development of Advertising;* Paul T. Cherington, *The Consumer Looks at Advertising;* H. J. Kenner, *The Fight for Truth in Advertising.*]

G. B. HOTCHKISS

Advertising Agency. The modern advertising agency appears to have originated in the activities of independent space brokers early in the 19th century. Some of these were free-lance advertising salesmen, or conveniently situated business men (such as post-masters) who as a sideline accepted advertisements for insertion in various newspapers. Probably the earliest to make space brokerage his sole business was Volney B. Palmer. Shortly after 1840 he had offices in Boston, New York and Philadelphia, and represented himself as a duly accredited agent to receive advertisements and subscriptions for "most of the best papers published in the United States and Canada." He assumed no responsibility for collecting money from the advertiser, but charged the publisher 25% for his service in selling the space.

Another agent, John L. Hooper, who began business in New York about the same time as Palmer, or a little later, inaugurated a policy that eventually became standard practice with agencies. He assumed the financial risk of paying the publisher himself and then collecting from the advertisers. By the time of the Civil War, at least twenty agencies were operating in the larger cities.

In 1865, George P. Rowell invented his "List System" which consisted in buying space at wholesale and selling at retail. His offer was "an-inch-of-space-a-month-in-one-hundred-papers-for-one-hundred-dollars." Similar methods were adopted by other agents and applied to other kinds of periodicals, such as religious papers, farm papers, and general magazines[qqv]. The system was an important factor in the early development of magazine advertising, but ultimately was abandoned, and the commission basis of payment was re-established.

Throughout the early period, the chief service of the agent was that of buying space more efficiently than the advertiser could do it. Newspapers varied tremendously in advertising values and the publishers' claims of circulation were notoriously unreliable. Only an expert space-buyer could determine the value of advertising space in a given medium, and buy it at the lowest price. Secret knowledge of values and rates, together with bargaining ability, remained the chief assets of the advertising agent until 1869. In that year appeared the first volume of Rowell's American Newspaper Directory. This listed 5411 publications in the United States and 367 in Canada, with estimates of their circulation. Subsequent issues of this directory, and other media directories and services, gradually made information about circulations more accessible and reliable. Space-buying had become a minor function of most agencies by 1914, when the Audit Bureau of Circulations was established to secure accurate and systematic information regarding the quantity and quality of circulation of periodicals.

In the meantime, the agencies were developing new and valuable services. Through their experience in placing advertising they accumulated funds of knowledge about planning and executing campaigns. They wrote copy, designed the pictorial and typographic display, supervised the art work, and handled the production of material used in the actual printing of the advertisements. Many agencies added research departments and departments for handling such media as industrial publications, direct mail, and radio. Although most of these services could be performed by the advertiser himself, the bulk of national advertisers and many local advertisers found it expedient to employ the expert knowledge of an agency.

Thus the advertising agents approached a professional status. However, they were in the anomalous position of regarding the advertisers as their clients, while receiving most of their compensation from the media in the form of a commission. The amount of this varied in the eighteen-eighties and eighteen-nineties, but ultimately became standardized at 15% for most newspapers and magazines. The amount of service rendered to the advertiser was not so easily fixed. Moreover, the competition for desirable clients resulted occasionally in "splitting commissions" or otherwise rebating a part of the compensation.

To correct such practices and other forms of unfair competition, local associations of agencies were formed, and in 1917 a national organization, known as the American Association of Advertising Agencies. This included in its membership the majority of the "fully recognized" agencies in the country. An agency was "recognized" by a publisher when he granted it the commission on space purchased through it. To secure such recognition, an agency usually had to demonstrate its financial strength, its expert ability, its possession of several substantial clients, and its freedom from alliances with either publishers or advertisers.

The Association of Agencies adopted a code of Standards of Practice in 1924 by which the members agreed to refrain from unfair competition or rebates, from submitting speculative plans or copy, and from preparing or handling any advertising of an untruthful, indecent, or objectionable character. The commission system remained a target for criticisms by large advertisers. At their instigation, the Federal Trade Commission[qv] brought suit against the Association, together with several publishers' associations, as a conspiracy in restraint of trade[qv], but after lengthy investigation and litigation the suit was dismissed. Nevertheless, the powerful Association of National Advertisers recommended a change to a more flexible system, and steps in that direction have been taken by some agencies.

[George P. Rowell, *Forty Years an Advertising Agent;* Frank Presbrey, *History and Development of Advertising.*]

G. B. HOTCHKISS

Aeolus. One of the early experiments in railroad cars, the yachtlike *Aeolus* was designed to sail before the wind. It was tried on the Baltimore & Ohio Railroad[qv] in 1830. On one occasion the *Aeolus* failed to stop when it reached the end of the finished track, and ran into an embankment.

[Edward Hungerford, *The Story of the Baltimore and Ohio Railroad.*]

FRANK FREIDEL

Aeronautics. *See* Aviation; Balloons.

African Company, Royal, THE (1672–1750), was one of a series of trading companies granted a monopoly of the African slave trade[qv]. In 1672 it took over the charter and African trading posts of the Company of Royal Adventurers to Africa established by the Duke of York and associates in 1662. In 1697 its monopoly was destroyed when independent merchants were permitted to engage in the trade upon payment for fourteen years of export duties which were turned over to the company to maintain its posts. From this time the trade was largely absorbed by the independents. During the 18th century most of the slaves were carried to the West Indies and North America in ships owned by Bristol, Liverpool and colonial merchants. The company endeavored to prevent independent traders from bargaining directly with native dealers. Most of the Negroes it secured were sold to the independents, to the English South Sea Company after it was granted the Asiento[qv] (1713), or even to foreign traders. The destruction of the monopoly, the competition of independent traders, the expense of maintaining its posts, and the imposition of poll duties on slave importations by Virginia, South Carolina, Jamaica and Barbados, all proved so disastrous to the company, that, in spite of annual grants by Parliament of £10,000 beginning in 1729, its affairs were wound up in 1750. By that year, of the 155 British ships in the trade, twenty were North American, nearly half from Rhode Island.

[L. H. Gipson, *The British Empire before the American Revolution.*]

CHARLES F. MULLETT

African Methodist Episcopal Church. The oldest and largest denomination of colored Methodists[qv], organized in 1816 with Richard Allen as its first Bishop. The origin of this body was the result of friction in St. George's Methodist Episcopal Church in Philadelphia, due to a feeling of race discrimination and a consequent conviction on the part of the colored members that they would enjoy a larger measure of freedom in worship and service by themselves. The denomination grew in the first decade slowly, reaching a membership of nearly 10,000, but after the close of the Civil War increased rapidly and now claims a membership of more than 500,000. In doctrine and polity it differs little from the mother church.

[Matthew Simpson, *Cyclopedia of Methodism;* Benjamin E. Mays and Joseph William Nicholson, *The Negro's Church.*]

C. H. STACKPOLE

Agamenticus. Successively known as Bristol (1632), Agamenticus (1641), Gorgeana (1642), and York (1652), this early Maine settlement, equidistant from Mt. Agamenticus and the Piscataqua River, has the distinction of being the first municipal corporation in America (1642), created so by Sir Ferdinando Gorges whose special favor the settlement enjoyed. Settled about 1624, it was one of the few substantial settlements in the province of Maine during the trying period of colonial wars^{qv}.

[C. E. Banks, *History of York, Maine.*]

ELIZABETH RING

Agent, Colonial. *See* Colonial Agent, The.

Agrarian Movement, The. Efforts on the part of the rural classes to better their lot by concerted political action have been almost a constant quantity in American history. Even in colonial times the southern planters, forced to exchange their produce for British manufactures on terms that left them permanently in debt to British merchants, protested to the point of revolt against the imperial regulations that they blamed for their distress. From their point of view the American Revolution was a movement to free American agriculture from the tyranny of British commercialism. Independence was no sooner won, however, than in some of the northern states the debt-ridden farmers of the back-country launched a similar protest against the political power of the well-to-do seaboard merchants. The latter, frightened by such episodes as Shays' Rebellion^{qv} in Massachusetts and the paper money craze in Rhode Island (*see* Trevett v. Weeden; Paper Money), joined with the creditor classes generally in a movement to provide a national government strong enough to keep order and protect property. The Constitution^{qv} of the United States was the result.

Differences between the devotees of commerce and of agriculture speedily produced a two-party political system^{qv} for the new republic. The Federalists^{qv}, under the effective leadership of Alexander Hamilton, made it their business to head off money inflation, establish the national credit, keep open the lanes of commerce, and minimize the rights of the states (*see* States' Rights), in which occasionally the agrarians had the upper hand. When the need for more revenue required the levying of an excise^{qv} tax, they singled out whiskey^{qv}, a by-product of the back-country farms, to bear the burden. These policies the Republicans (*see* Republican Party, Jeffersonian), equally well led by the agriculturally minded Thomas Jefferson, criticized with increasing vehemence. When the "Revolution of 1800" made Jefferson President, the more offensive Federalist measures were repealed, and a new course, definitely favorable to agriculture, was charted. The purchase of Louisiana added new territory for the agricultural interest to exploit, while such measures as the Embargo and Non-intercourse^{qqv} gravely jeopardized the welfare of commerce. Under Jefferson's successor, Madison, the War of 1812^{qv} was fought, less to safeguard American commerce on the high seas than to end the British and Indian menace to the westward march of agriculture, and to pave the way for the conquest by farmers and planters of Canada and Florida.

Ironically, the commercial restrictions that preceded and accompanied the War of 1812 resulted in a new and formidable challenge to the supremacy of the agriculturalists. Domestic manufacturing, essential because commerce had languished, soon revealed possibilities of profit that could not be ignored. Factories, particularly in the Northeast, multiplied with amazing rapidity, and the agricultural interests, scarcely aware of what had been going on, awoke to find themselves almost displaced by factory owners and their satellites in the control of the Republican (Jeffersonian) party. Soon the very party that Jefferson had founded was chartering a new national bank (*see* Bank of the U. S., First and Second), adopting a protective tariff^{qv} and giving serious consideration to a nation-wide program of internal improvements^{qv}. Jacksonian Democracy^{qv} was in no small degree the inevitable response of the agriculturalists to this challenge of the industrialists, and with the elevation of "Old Hickory"^{qv} to the presidency—"the Revolution of 1828"—much of the lost ground was recovered. The Bank was destroyed, the tariff was reduced, and the burdensome problem of internal improvements was relegated to the states and to individuals.

The solidarity of the agricultural front was not to be maintained for long. The planters of the South, now obedient to the dictates of "King

Agrarian

Cotton"[qv] and devoted as never before to the system of slave labor, had little in common with the small free farmers who owned the West. Both wished for expansion (*see* Manifest Destiny), and they cheerfully joined hands against the Indians and against the Mexicans to take what they wanted. But each hoped to exclude the other from the spoils of war. The small free farmers wished a small-free-farmer West; the slave-owning planters wished a slave-owning-planter West. The southern planters, however, were far more gifted at the game of politics than their western rivals, and for a generation after Jackson left office they maintained an unbroken ascendancy in the national councils.

Distaste for the policies of the slave-holding South at length drove the free-farmer West into an open alliance with the industrial Northeast. The fruit of this union was a new Republican party, which promised to the West free lands, to the Northeast a protective tariff, and to both a Pacific railroad[qqv]. Rather than submit to such a program the South fought, and lost, the Civil War. With southern protests stilled, the other sections voted themselves what they had promised, and, for good measure, a new national banking[qv] system as well. Slavery[qv] itself was abolished.

The leadership of the re-united nation fell naturally to the industrialists. This was not due solely to the War, for the rising tide of industrialism was world-wide, not merely national. In the United States, as elsewhere, population tended more and more to concentrate in cities; and whole new industries such as steel and oil[qqv], virtually unknown before the Civil War, extended the field of industrial operations far into the West and South. Against this growing strength of the industrialists the agriculturalists found it difficult to unite. Farmers in the industrialized sections ministered to the local city markets, and tended to accept without protest both the policies and the prices that were offered them, while the farmers of West and South, with their economic interests at best somewhat divergent, overcame with difficulty the rancors let loose by war.

The same forces that had been at work to transform industry, however, were bringing about a revolution in agriculture. The old system of production for use, to which the small free farmer had long been accustomed, gradually gave way to a system of production for sale. New machines transformed each farm into a kind of factory, designed often-times to turn out a highly specialized product. The farmers of the Northwest concentrated on wheat, or corn, or live stock, or dairy products[qqv]. The farmers of the South still pinned their faith mainly to tobacco and cotton[qqv]. Fruit-growers appeared in the Far West. All were dependent upon the railroads for transportation, upon the banks for credit, upon the merchants for all those necessities of life that farmers no longer produced for themselves, upon nation-wide or world-wide markets for the prices of the things they had to sell. Land values, thanks in part to the greater economy of production with the new machines and in part to the disappearance of the frontier[qv], rose persistently. But farm mortgages also mounted, tenantry increased (*see* Farmer, Tenant), and each cycle of depression left the rural classes worse off, relatively, than they had been before.

Out in the upper Mississippi Valley, where the cost of transportation ate up all the grain growers' profits, and down in the reconstructed South, where the crop-lien system had forced the cotton growers into virtual peonage, the "embattled farmers" began fumblingly and reluctantly to unite in their own defense. Through their experiences with the Granger movement, the Greenback movement, and the Farmers' Alliances[qqv], they learned that, if only they could stand together as voters, they might force the governments of state and nation to restrain the railroads and the trusts[qqv], to scale down debts by some form of money inflation[qv], and to protect in general the farmers' interests. They discovered, too, that by co-operation in marketing, in purchasing, and even in manufacturing they might hope, with adequate management, to help themselves. Efforts to unite the rural classes into a People's Party[qv] that would take over the government and administer it directly in the farmers' interest failed during the 1890's, but the drift toward closer organization and co-operation went on.

During the 20th century the rural classes brought persistent pressure upon state governments to attain desired ends. In Wisconsin, for example, the LaFollette progressives[qv], composed mainly of rural voters, captured the Republican organization, instituted the primary system[qv] of making nominations for office, established close supervision of railroads and public utilities[qv], and reformed the system of taxation. The Farmers' Nonpartisan League[qv] in North Dakota, Minnesota and other northwestern states attempted with less complete success to bring about state operation of elevators, flour mills, and other businesses deemed guilty of taking unfair advantages of the farmers. Alliances with labor became increasingly common, and paved the way for such organizations as the Farmer-Labor party of Minnesota[qv], and the Farmer-Labor-Progressive federation of Wisconsin. In the South the rural whites, increasingly rebellious against the exactions of country storekeepers and landlords, put their trust in the promises of such demagogic leaders as James K. Vardaman and Theodore G. Bilbo of Mississippi, the "Hon. Jeff." Davis of Arkansas, and Huey P. Long of Louisiana. Numerous agricultural organizations, such as the American Society of Equity, the Farmers' Union, and the American Farm Bureau Federation, appeared both in the South and in the West. Most of these orders emphasized almost equally the need of political pressure and of farmer-owned business co-operatives[qv].

On the national front the agriculturalists regained much of the unity they had known before the Civil War. Republican "insurgents" from the Northwest worked together with southern Democrats from agricultural regions against the high protective rates of the Payne-Aldrich tariff[qv], and during Wilson's administration helped inaugurate a generous Federal farm loan system[qv]. When the overexpansion of agriculture during the World War led to a drastic deflation at its close, a congressional "Farm Bloc," aided by pressure from a multitude of agricultural organizations the country over, began an agitation for farm relief that led eventually to the establishment under Hoover of the short-lived Federal Farm Board[qv], and under F. D. Roosevelt of the Agricultural Adjustment Administration[qv]. Both measures had as their main objective the stabilization of farm incomes at a high enough level to insure farmers a profitable return for their labor and investments. When in 1936 the United States Supreme Court held the "A.A.A." unconstitutional, the New Deal[qv] substituted for it a soils conservation[qv] policy designed to gain the same end in another way.

[Charles A. and Mary R. Beard, *The Rise of American Civilization;* Edward Wiest, *Agricultural Organization in the United States.*]

JOHN D. HICKS

Agricultural Adaptation to the Plains. The Great Plains, with sub-humid climate, wind, heat, high rate of evaporation, and lack of timber, presented agricultural problems new to the experience of settlers of Anglo-American descent. Three approaches were employed: pastoral, irrigation and dry land farming. The pastoral period was represented especially by the live stock boom (1865–1886). Next came the small farmer invasion of the 1880's. The drouth[qv] decade beginning in 1886 brought the irrigation[qv] boom. Especially difficult was the problem of the transitional country between humid and arid regions which could employ traditional methods during wet cycles but desperately needed the full technique of dry land farming in dry periods. Out of the conflict of ideals and objectives the inhabitants of the Plains worked out their destiny. No lasting stabilization had been reached, however, when the technological revolution of the 1920's and the drouth and depression of the 1930's brought a prolonged test of the soundness of current practices.

In a humid climate timber and water are available to all, and self-sufficiency is possible. The instruments to sustain life had to be brought to the Plains from outside: railroads, weapons (revolver and repeating rifle), barbed-wire fencing, windmills, fuel and farm machinery[qqv]—all products of the industrial revolution[qv]. Nature limited the variety of production and enforced specialization; cash crops were necessary to enable farmers to buy the necessities of life. Thus the Plains civilization was founded on regional interdependence.

The early phases of the live stock industry were abnormal, based on native cattle, the supply of which was soon exhausted, pastured upon public land[qv] without charge. Later came fenced public range and improved breeding. A permanent cattle and sheep industry required the transition to privately owned land, sometimes supplemented by public range; improved breeds of stock adapted to the region; and the production of some irrigated or drouth-resistant hay and feed crops for winter and drouth feeding. Significantly, in order to survive, the live stock interest found it necessary to compromise with field crop agriculture.

The small farmer invasion of the Plains in the 1880's was based on the 160-acre family size farm idea, with a mixed farm-crop program of the more humid East. Experience demonstrated that a larger unit was necessary. Farmers had to learn to ridge the soil against the prevailing winds or to leave it rough and trashy to prevent it from blowing. They had to devise means of working the soil quickly, when moisture was available, and to prepare it to receive and conserve moisture most effectively. Some systems involved summer-fallowing, some insisted on diversified farming, but no fixed procedure was applicable to all regions of the plains and intermountain area, and the extensive experimental work done during the drouth period of the 1930's superseded much of the earlier practices. Conventional moldboard plows gave way in part or altogether during the 1890's to disc machinery which left the ground relatively rough, the trash on top, and worked drier ground, or to the lister which ridged the ground. During the 1930's, the chisel tool, or the small bottomed lister, with damming attachment (sometimes called the basin tool or basin lister), found favor over the disc machinery or regular lister among many operators.

The problem of speeding up tillage operations was partly met by the lister, but not until the tractor[qv] was perfected and became available for general use after the World War could it be said to have been solved. As summer-fallowing became more widely accepted as part of dry land farming practice, tools for fallow cultivation were emphasized. Although some preferred the new type chisel tool, special tools or attachments for listers were developed such as the duck-foot, the spring-tooth and the rod-weeder. During the 1920's, extensive experimental work was done with seeding tools; deep-furrow and semi-deep-furrow drills, either disc or shoe types; the chisel tools; varying widths of spacing between the rows; varying widths of furrows in which the seed was scattered in the rows; varying degrees of ridging of ground between the rows to prevent blowing of the soil and to catch rain and snow until the crop made sufficient growth to cover the ground. Some of the most advanced machines of 1937 were combination tools, incorporating in one piece of machinery, the chisel or lister, the fallowing attachments, and the seeding accessories.

The harvesting of short-stemmed small grain required special machinery also. The header and, about the turn of the century, the convertible header-binder reached the size limits of horse-driven machinery. After the World War, mechanical power made practical the combine[qv] (header-thresher) which reduced harvesting and threshing to a single operation. It is significant that the farmers themselves and the implement makers achieved most of this adaptation and invention through a process of private trial-and-error experiment, governmental agencies contributing only a minor role, and even that only in the later stages and mostly in those departments where exact scientific knowledge, procedures and equipment were necessary, such as plant breeding and insect and disease controls. One of the most remarkable features of the history of the Great Plains region was the marvelous resourcefulness, persistence, and optimism of the inhabitants in adaptational experimentation.

The original crop program of the small Plains farmer was transplantation of his accustomed planning from the humid East, especially corn and oats[qqv] as the principal crops. Hard spring wheats[qv] eventually supplanted these as well as the soft varieties of wheat in the northern Plains during the late 1870's and 1880's, assisted by the development of the purifier and the roller grinding machinery for handling hard wheats in the flour mills[qv]. In the southwest Plains drouth-resistant hard winter wheat was introduced from Russia in 1873 (*see* Wheat, Turkey Red), spreading during the drouth period of the 1890's, and after 1900 was supplemented by new introductions and the development of varieties by both governmental agencies and private individuals. The sorghums came to provide forage and grain crops in place of corn, being introduced from Africa and Asia, a few varieties of the saccharine sorghums as early as the 1850's, and the grain types such as milo and kaffir later in the century, feterita in 1906 and sudan grass in 1909.

Irrigation was subject to drastic limitations, because the area from which water could be drawn was itself arid. In any event, only a small percentage of the area could have water from the surface supply and this type of project was restricted to the valleys near the sources of the streams. Ground water supplies were limited by the same moisture deficiency for the area, and by the depth of wells and the cost of pumping. Large scale pumping projects were not practical as they were for surface-water reclamation projects, therefore each farmer must install his own equipment if he practised irrigation farming. Thus the Plains area proper could receive little direct benefit from irrigation of either type. It was primarily either a live stock or a dry land farming area, or a combination of them. The indirect benefits of irrigation were nevertheless vital to supplement other economic activities and to achieve balances within the Plains and Mountain area as a whole.

[H. E. Briggs, The development of agriculture in territorial Dakota, *Culver-Stockton Quarterly*, 7 (1931): 1-37; L. C. Aicher, Damming attachments for listers, *30 Biennial Report* of the Kansas State Board of Agriculture, 35: 78-82; C. R. Bell, The history of American wheat improvement, *Agricultural History*, 4 (April 1930): 48-71; E. C. Chilcott, Dry farming in the Great Plains area, *Yearbook*, U. S. Dept. of Agric., 1907; E. C. Chilcott, Some misconceptions concerning dry farming, *Yearbook*, U. S. Dept. of Agric., 1911; E. C. Chilcott, Preventing soil blowing on the Southern Plains, *Farmers' Bulletin*, U. S. Dept. of Agric., No. 1771 (1937); John S. Cole, Implements and methods to control soil blowing on the Northern Great Plains, *Farmers' Bulletin*, U. S. Dept. of Agric., No. 1797 (1938); Carter Goodrich, et al., *Migration and economic opportunity;* A. L. Hallstead, Reducing risks in wheat growing, *30 Biennial Report* of the Kansas State Board of Agriculture, 35:98-110; Henrietta Larson, *The Wheat Market and the Farmer in Minnesota, 1858-1900;* C. P. Loomis, The human ecology of the Great Plains area, *Proceedings* of the Oklahoma Academy of Science, 1937; Angus McDonald, Erosion and its control in Oklahoma Territory, U. S. Dept. of Agriculture, *Misc. publication*, No. 301; James C. Malin, Adaptation of the agricultural system to sub-humid environment, *Agricultural History*, 10 (July 1936): 118-41; James C. Malin, The turnover of farm population in Kansas, *Kansas Historical Quarterly*, 4 (Nov. 1935): 339-72; John H. Parker, Wheat improvement in Kansas, *29 Biennial Report* of the Kansas State Board of Agriculture, 34: 39-64; H. S. Schell, Drought and agriculture in eastern South Dakota in the eighteen-eighties, *Agricultural History*, 5 (October 1931): 162-80; R. C. Smith, Upsetting the balance of nature with special reference to Kansas and the Great Plains, *Science*, 75 (June 24, 1932): 649-54; W. E. Smythe, *Conquest of Arid America;* A. T. Steinel and D. W. Working, *History of Agriculture in Colorado;* A. F. Swanson, The development of sorghum culture in Kansas, *29 Biennial Report* of the Kansas State Board of Agriculture, 34: 165-74; W. P. Webb, *The Great Plains;* E. J. Wickson, *Rural California;* John A. Widtsoe, *Dry Farming.*]

JAMES C. MALIN

Agricultural Adjustment Administration (1933). The Agricultural Adjustment Act of 1933 was an emergency[qv] measure of the New Deal[qv]. In 1932 the platform of the Democratic party pledged the extension and "development of the farm co-operative movement and effective control of crop surpluses." Thus, it was at the instigation of Secretary of Agriculture Henry Wallace that President F. D. Roosevelt called representative farm leaders to Washington on March 10, 1933. Six days later the Chief Executive sent to Congress a bill drafted by the conference.

In his message of March 16, the President pointed out that while the measure followed "a new and untrod path," "an unprecedented condition" called for a "new means to rescue agriculture." By May 10 Congress had agreed to the provisions of the farm bill, and two days later the President signed the measure proposing to "relieve the existing national economic emergency by increasing agricultural purchasing power." The statute emphasized the emergency situation and attempted to increase farm income and to reduce farm surpluses. Using the years 1909–14 as a base period, the administrators hoped to establish and maintain a balance between production and consumption of agricultural products.

Included in the statute were provisions relative to credit extension and relief for farm mortgages; but more particularly the Secretary of Agriculture was given extensive authority to reduce productive acreage and to foster marketing quotas. To effect the program farm surpluses were removed from the market and prices were to be increased by placing restraints on production. Immediate payments were made to farmers participating in the program.

The much discussed tax levied upon processors was to "obtain revenue for extraordinary expenses incurred by reason of the national economic emergency." The tax was to help defray the administrative costs of carrying out the provisions of the enactment. And agreements drawn up by participating farmers were to prevent produce from burdening markets. To help administer the act, state and local committees, or associations of producers, were to assist the Federal officials. This was a concession to avoid the criticism of centralization. The entire plan was to be financed by an appropriation of $100,000,000.

After the Agricultural Adjustment Act was in operation three years the Supreme Court in 1936 declared, in U. S. v. Butler[qv], that the statute was unconstitutional. (*See also* Rickert Rice Mills v. Fontenot.) It was held that the regulation of agriculture did not come within the jurisdiction of Congress, but was instead a function properly belonging to the states. Following this declaration, Congress enacted a Soil Conservation and Domestic Allotment[qv] program for farm relief.

[Henry Wallace, *New Frontiers;* Edwin G. Nourse and others, *Three Years of the Agricultural Adjustment Act;* 48 U. S. Statutes at Large, p. 31.]

BENJAMIN F. SHAMBAUGH

Agricultural Adjustment Administration Act of 1938. This act was the result of the unconstitutionality of previous New Deal[qv] farm legislation and the success of the Soil Conservation and Domestic Allotment Act[qv] passed in 1936. During the first session of the Seventy-fifth Congress an extension of the soil conservation plan was given consideration. Through the summer of 1937 hearings of farm leaders were conducted in various states; but the second session adjourned while the farm bill was still in the hands of a conference committee.

In his message of Jan. 3, 1938, President F. D. Roosevelt emphasized the work of the conference committee and hoped that a "sound, consistent measure" would be adopted. After some debate in Congress the President, on Feb. 16, signed the measure providing "for the conservation of national soil resources."

The Soil Conservation Act was to be continued as a permanent farm policy; and to promote the program, national acreage allotments were to be fixed at a point "to give production sufficient for domestic consumption, for exports, and for reserve supplies." To induce farmers to operate within the allotments, payments were to be made by the Government. In order that "an adequate and balanced flow of agricultural commodities" might be maintained, the statute incorporated a method for storing produce in years of shortage. Four research laboratories are to be established at Peoria, Ill., in the New Orleans area, in the Philadelphia area, and in the San Francisco area, to study farm needs. And if two thirds of the farmers participating in the program agreed, marketing quotas in tobacco, corn, wheat, cotton, and rice might be fixed by the Secretary of Agriculture.

[*Laws of Congress*, 75th Cong., 3rd Sess., Chap. 30; *Congressional Record*, 75th Cong., 3rd Sess., Appendix, p. 810.]

BENJAMIN F. SHAMBAUGH

Agricultural Education has developed in four interrelated lines. Collegiate instruction while tried in a few states during the 1850's was definitely established by Federal endowment in the Morrill Land-Grant Act^qv^ of 1862. Before 1890 curriculum and method were uncertain and relatively ineffective. Subject matter was not verified and organized and teaching methods were not systematized. Technical courses were grouped about the departments of agricultural chemistry, applied botany, and "agriculture" which included the various branches of farm organization and practice. The requirement of manual labor by most of the institutions emphasized training in practical skill at the expense of scientific principles.

By the 1890's transforming influences were in operation. Experiment stations^qv^ were establishing information and differentiating it into special fields, and contributing to the extension and perfecting of the laboratory method. Textbooks and reference works based upon American conditions and needs were multiplying. Short courses, general and special, were set off from the regular course and met an increasing demand. A series of conventions culminating in the formation of the Association of American Agricultural Colleges and Experiment Stations (renamed Association of Land-Grant Colleges and Universities) in 1887 brought an interchange of ideas and experiences. The "Second Morrill Act" of 1890 gave more adequate endowment and encouraged the states to provide regular educational support.

Graduate study in agriculture has attained to standardized achievement through the research organization and technique of the experiment station. Agricultural research involving special application of the basic sciences has paralleled the growth of these sciences. With the recent emphasis upon the problems of rural economy and society especial attention has been given to the application of the social sciences.

Efforts to bring existing information directly to the farmers were made early in the 19th century by the agricultural societies^qv^ through their exhibitional fairs and lecturers. From the 1870's the colleges combined with the state boards in conducting farmers' institutes^qv^. Early in the 20th century reading courses, demonstrational trains and co-operative regional projects were introduced. The whole extension program was modernized and unified by the Smith-Lever Act^qv^ of 1914 (supplemented by the Capper-Ketcham Act of 1928) which makes the college the directing and clearing center for the main lines of extension effort: county agents, boys' and girls' clubs, extension specialists and home economics demonstrators.

From the manual labor schools of the 1820's efforts had been made from time to time to teach agriculture at the secondary level but it was only with the development of the agricultural phase of the vocational educational work provided for in the Smith-Hughes Act^qv^ of 1917 (supplemented by the George-Deen Act of 1936) that this type of vocational high school was given assured place. Except for a limited utilization of materials in the teaching of the common branches agriculture has not entered the elementary curriculum.

[A. C. True, *A History of Agricultural Education in the United States;* E. P. Cubberley, *Public Education in the United States.*]

EARLE D. ROSS

Agricultural Experiment Stations were established to provide instructional materials for the colleges and to investigate occupational problems. Organization and method were modeled upon European stations and the work of state chemists. The first station was founded by Connecticut in 1875 and by 1887 fourteen states had definite organizations and in thirteen others the colleges conducted equivalent work. The Bussey Institution at Harvard (since 1871) and the Houghton Farm at Cornwall, N. Y. (1876–88), were privately endowed stations. Through the combined efforts of the colleges and the Department of Agriculture the Federal Hatch Act of 1887 provided an annual subvention for the stations. This aid has been increased by the Adams Act (1906) and the Purnell Act (1925).

[A. C. True and V. A. Clark, *The Agricultural Experiment Stations in the United States;* A. C. True, *A History of Agricultural Experimentation and Research in the United States.*]

EARLE D. ROSS

Agricultural Implements. *See* Farm Machinery.

Agricultural Societies, as an educational and as a political force, have vitally affected the progress of agriculture. During the post-Revolutionary years the low status of American agriculture prompted the forming of societies which, through meetings, premiums and publications, sought to stimulate improvement. The earliest society devoted exclusively to agriculture was the Philadelphia Society for Promoting Agriculture, organized in March, 1785. Washington and Franklin were members. In August, 1785, the Agricultural Society of South Carolina had its beginning. Agricultural societies followed in Maine (1787), in New York (1791), in Massachusetts (1792), and in Connecticut (1794). The Columbian Agricultural Society (D. C.), the first society to hold an agricultural exhibition, was formed in 1809. In 1817 the Albemarle (Va.) Agricultural Society was created under the leadership of Thomas Jefferson, with James Madison as its president.

The county agricultural fair[qv] received a great impetus as an educational agency in the Berkshire Agricultural Society movement, which, originating in 1810 on the initiative of Elkanah Watson, of Pittsfield, Mass., during the next twenty years swept New England and spread south and west. After a lull between 1830 and 1850, county societies experienced a renaissance in the decade 1850–60, when also many state societies began to exert an influence on legislation. The United States Agricultural Society, the first real national association, organized in 1852, was instrumental in the creation of the United States Department of Agriculture[qv], in 1862.

Economic disturbances following the Civil War occasioned the "agrarian movement"[qv], from which came organizations aimed at greater economic security for the farmer. Chief among these was the National Grange[qv], or Patrons of Husbandry, formed in 1867, through the efforts of Oliver H. Kelley. Engaging a secret fraternal ritual and embracing both men and women, the Grange undertook a program that was economic and political in purpose as well as educational and social.

Since 1900 the outstanding developments in agricultural organization have been: (1) farmers' co-operatives[qv], essentially economic in purpose, reported in the last census to have handled in 1929, for 825,000 farms, purchases and sales valued at over $1,000,000,000; and (2) the farm bureau[qv], primarily educational and partly political, whose county units became the local co-operating agencies of the agricultural extension service established by Congress in 1914.

[O. H. Kelley, *Origin and Progress of the Order of Patrons of Husbandry;* O. M. Kile, *The Farm Bureau Movement;* A. C. True, *History of Agricultural Education in the United States, 1785-1925;* R. H. True, *Sketch of the History of the Philadelphia Society for Promoting Agriculture;* R. H. True, *The Early Development of Agricultural Societies in the United States,* Agr. Hist. Soc. Papers, No. 3.]

CARL R. WOODWARD

Agricultural Wheel, THE, was a movement started in 1882, by W. W. Tedford, farmer and school teacher, to improve farming conditions. In 1886 it became the National Agricultural Wheel, and in 1889 merged with the National Farmers' Alliance[qv] and Co-operative Union of America.

[I. M. Tarbell, *Nationalizing of Business.*]

CARL L. CANNON

Agriculture. The nations of Europe that participated in the colonization of North America were influenced by various motives. A leading one with Spain was the hope of obtaining a generous supply of the precious metals. The dominant motive of France was the acquisition of wealth through the trade in furs and peltries, natural products of America's woods and streams.

Britain felt these motives too, and also another which affected her rivals as well, namely, the hope of making significant explorations leading to the nation's enrichment through commerce. But Britain in the 17th century had large groups of persons who for their own and the nation's benefit needed to emigrate. This fact differentiated her colonizing activity from that of the other powers and resulted in the establishment of agriculture as the leading industry in the British colonies.

This agriculture, in the first instance, was necessarily a kind of subsistence farming. Men were thrown upon their own resources in the presence of abundant, cheap, and fertile soil. By clearing and cultivating some of this land, keeping livestock to live on natural grasses and on browse, roots, nuts, acorns, etc., and by associating household industries with farming, men could hope to make a living in primitive fashion. The doing of this became the regular procedure of many thousands of colonists, especially those who settled in New England. The habits, the skills, the bodily strength and moral fiber guaranteeing survival under such conditions, were developed as fixed traits of American character, and became essential conditions of the westward movement which led to the conquest of the continent for agriculture, and ultimately for the culture appropriate to enlightened living. As population pushed westward toward new frontiers, the subsistence farmer was usually the true "pioneer"; however, his movements may have been suggested or directed by fur traders, promoters of transportation, or other commercial agencies.

Virginians, the first English colonists, began like those of Plymouth to farm for the sake of a

Agriculture 27

livelihood. But the planting of tobacco[qv] quickly changed the agriculture of that colony in large part to the business type of farming under the planting and slave labor economy. The Virginians, in the item of tobacco, had hit upon a crop for which there was an adequate cash market in England, the necessary condition to make farming a business. Land was easy to procure; capital could be derived from the crops; labor was provided at first by indentured white servants[qv], drawn from the poorest class of immigrants, and finally by African slaves[qv]. The temptation to increase land holdings, enlarge the labor group, strengthen management, and multiply its profits was such that great plantations inevitably resulted with all the social, economic and political concomitants of such a system.

The plantation type[qv] of agriculture came to have a powerful appeal for social and political reasons, so that even when its economic soundness was in doubt it continued to flourish as movement westward in the Southern states took place. The greatest single economic cause of its expansion, after tobacco, indigo and rice[qqv] had reached the limits of profitable cultivation in Virginia, the Carolinas and Georgia, was the production of short staple cotton[qv], ginned by machinery. For that product the demand, during a certain period, seemed unlimited, cotton being the chief export of the United States; and plantations spread over the most available lands in all the states of the lower South. The number of small and moderate-size farms, mainly subsistence homesteads[qv], in that region was always much greater than the number of plantations, but the plantations and their owners dominated the area economically, socially and politically.

Planters and their families constituted a farming aristocracy modeled in colonial times upon the English country gentry. Pretentious houses, elegant furniture and rich plate, spectacular turnouts, and stables of superior saddle horses were among the evidences of their distinction. They dispensed a generous hospitality, visited much, leaving overseers in charge of their farming operations and their slaves; they devoted much time to public affairs, educated their children in the best schools and colleges. For many years, prior to the Civil War, the Southern planting class was the leading group in national politics as well as in the affairs of their several states. Washington, Jefferson, Madison, Monroe and Jackson, among the Presidents, belonged to the Southern planter class.

Both the primitive subsistence farming and big business farming of the plantation type exploited the soil[qv], robbing it of its fertility and causing it to waste away through erosion. By owning vast areas and continually opening up new fields, planters were able to maintain themselves for several generations during which "old fields," covered with weeds, bramble, and finally a crop of young timber, expanded apace. Northern subsistence farmers, on their smaller areas, followed courses not greatly dissimilar. New fields were opened until the entire area, in many cases, had been cleared and soon the farm as a whole was a reluctant producer. Before the close of the 18th century the farms of southern New England could no longer be made to yield profitable crops of wheat[qv], and so the people lived on bread made of a mixture of corn and rye, "rye and injun," as it was called. It was haphazard farming at best.

So long as the absence of a cash market for farm products deprived the people of an incentive to better farming, the primitive methods persisted. The change was brought about through the growth of towns and cities based on commerce and industry, the promotion of foreign trade, and the opening of roads, canals and other means of transportation[qqv] enabling farmers of the interior to reach the seacoast with their products. The planters of the South had an advantage in that ocean-going vessels could ascend the rivers, docking at the planters' wharves. Earliest improvement, of course, came to the farms nearest the port cities, Boston, New Haven, New York, Philadelphia. High prices for grain in Europe during the Napoleonic wars gave a notable stimulus to wheat growing, both North and South. The progress of manufacturing during and after the War of 1812, marked by the rapid growth of city populations, dependent for supplies upon the farms, gave a powerful and permanent impulse to agricultural improvement, "better farming." Now began the general agitation of the subject by organized groups known as agricultural societies[qv], the establishment of an agricultural press, the widespread attention to English books on farming, the beginnings of the importation from England of improved livestock, the general awakening of the American newspapers to the needs of their rural constituencies. The *American Farmer,* begun at Baltimore in 1819, was the first American farm journal[qv]. It soon had a large number of imitators, especially in the North.

This period, also, was marked by a particularly rapid movement of population into what was destined to become the greatest farming area of the United States, the Middle West. Indiana, Illinois and Missouri gained the status of statehood by 1820. Michigan, Iowa and Wis-

Agriculture

consin were destined to follow within the space of a single generation. This extraordinary westward movement[qv] tended to revolutionize agricultural conditions. The Government's land laws were liberalized so that it was practically possible for settlers to buy good farm land at $1.25 per acre, and a pre-emption[qv] right was soon added as a further concession to settlers. New transportation agencies, the steamboat, perfected for use on western rivers by 1817, the great canals of which the most important was the Erie Canal completed in 1825, and the beginnings of railroads[qqv], partially removed the handicaps of western farmers and brought them, with their fresh fertile lands, in partial competition with farmers of the East. The latter could not survive, save on the lowest subsistence plane from which they had already gradually risen, without a determined and well-directed policy of agricultural improvement.

Such improvement, since Northeastern farms generally required fertilization, called for emphasis upon the production of livestock—cattle, hogs, sheep, and to some extent, horses. The demand of the cities for meat, for butter and cheese (*see* Dairy Industry), wool to feed the factory spindles, and horses to draw coaches and drays was such that a policy of livestock[qv] improvement and better management also could be logically based upon it. It seemed the way to save the agriculture of the Northeastern states. But a livestock economy required more land than did the primitive subsistence farming. The old 50, 75, or 100 acre farms were found to be uneconomical for keeping herds and flocks of sufficient size to pay dividends.

The conjunction of the new farming, based on livestock, in the Northeast, with the opening of vast new and fertile wheat-growing areas in the Middle West, was a principal cause of the large emigration from older states to newer in that period. Owners of farms that were too small sold to their neighbors and went west, as did the sons and daughters of thousands of farm households, attracted by the ease with which farms could be made on the open lands, and fortunes acquired through wheat growing. The latter industry, in turn, under the impulsion of new machinery for harvesting and cultivation, steadily tended toward an enlarged scale of operations (*see* Farm Machinery).

The phenomenon of open-land farming with wheat as the money crop was a new one. The valleys of the Delaware and Susquehanna rivers, the earlier wheat centers, had originally been wooded. The Genesee valley furnished the foretaste of what the West would supply in seemingly endless abundance—rich, level, grass-covered lands, easily subdued to cultivation. The difficulty was that such lands, equally with the timbered lands, quickly became conditioned against wheat, yielding ever more meager returns to the cultivator. Besides, the very ease of cultivation proved a disadvantage, for the open-land farmer was tempted to break up his entire farm in a few years in order to have the maximum amount of wheat to sell. Consequently, the wheat farms on the open lands "ran down," and in a short time became unprofitable.

The remedy was obvious: a different kind of farming, with livestock, feed crops, and fertilization as the watchwords (*see* Diversification, Agricultural). Thousands of the earlier wheat growers, wedded to their vocation, simply sold out and went farther west to raise wheat under more favorable, that is, newer, conditions, and on a larger scale. Genesee valley wheat farmers, not a few, removed first to Wisconsin or Iowa, then to Minnesota or the Red River valley, and finally to the Palouse country of Washington, increasing their holdings and their product at each remove. Others, realizing that soil robbery is a losing game, adopted the new farming and remade their former wheat farms into stock and dairy farms. Thus it was that agricultural improvement moved westward at the remove of about one generation behind the pioneer settlers.

The westward movement brought into view two new phases of big-business farming in addition to the planting system characteristic of the South. These were, first, large-scale cattle raising under the open ranching or grazing system and, second, bonanza wheat farming on the Great Plains by the machine method.

Ranching was a development, under new and favorable conditions, of practices which were already old at the middle of the 19th century. The business of cattle raising was normal to all peaceful frontiers, and in the piedmont[qv] district of Virginia, North and South Carolina, cowpens and cattle trails, as well as cowboys, were well understood phenomena of the 18th century. The vast supply of Spanish cattle which fell to the United States upon the annexation of Texas[qv], and the gradual pacification of Indian tribes over enormous stretches of the Great Plains, which were covered with nutritious grasses, gave the new impetus to the open-range cattle business[qv] which had its greatest development in the period 1865 to 1885. The cattle kings, owners of herds numbering thousands, lorded it over customary ranges embracing sometimes hundreds of thousands of acres of government land. Private control of a few hundred acres dominating watering privileges was all that was necessary to bring about such control.

Ranchers were the nabobs of the grazing states and territories, as the planters were of the cotton and tobacco states, although due to their sparse numbers and isolation they did not dominate all life in the manner of the planters, nor did they constitute an acknowledged aristocracy. In some respects the ranchers' position was quite as precarious as that of the planters. Not only did their profits depend on the price of beef and the cost of marketing, but quite as much on weather and on cattle diseases. Untimely rains in the fall spoiled the grass for winter feeding. But blizzards[qv] such as visited nearly the entire grazing area in the winter of 1885–86 decimated the herds and brought universal bankruptcy to the owners. Foot-and-mouth disease, Texas fever, and murrain to which ranch cattle were subject, and sometimes an epidemic of cattle thieving, played havoc with a business that, with luck, made surer profits than any other phase of agriculture.

Cattle ranchers also had to reckon with the sheep ranchers who were rival contenders for the range, especially in the rough land areas; and when the pressure of population made the Great Plains an object of desire to farmers, who had the legal support of the Federal Government, the doom of the open range became assured. Cattle ranching continues, but under far different conditions. The rancher now generally owns or leases his range lands. He puts up winter feed and protects his cattle against storms. His herd is no longer composed of lanky Texas longhorns[qv], but of blocky, compact beef-breed varieties like the Herefords, Shorthorns, or Galloways. The ranches have become big stock farms.

Sheep[qv] ranching at times was more profitable than cattle ranching. The mountain areas are best adapted to sheep, and under the herding system—a man with a wagon in charge of thousands of sheep—the cost of raising them was extraordinarily low, so that large profits rewarded good management.

The bonanza wheat farms[qv] were made possible by the existence in a few regions like the Red River valley, the Palouse country, and the Great Valley of California, of practically unlimited stretches of unusually enduring fertile soil, which could be counted on to grow profitable wheat crops for many successive years. With some thousands of acres of such land, bought at a cheap price, with capital to procure machinery, work stock, and labor, the manager could ordinarily count on very large profits. At least that was true during the period of very heavy European demand for American wheat, which lasted from the 1840's down to recent times. The substitution of tractors[qv] for horse power, with implements of cultivation adapted to the newer power, and the combine[qv] instead of the self-binder and the threshing machine to harvest the crop, have made profits possible on the cheaper lands even at very much less than the traditionary "dollar a bushel" for wheat.

Great improvements have been made in the process of wheat growing, as in cattle raising. Government research in seed breeding, and in the discovery of varieties best suited to different types of soil and climate like the dry and high plateau lands, also in methods of cultivation and conditions of marketing, have affected the business to a considerable extent. Recently, the Government's attempt at crop control has been an element to be reckoned with (*see* Agricultural Adjustment Administration). The chief problem under present world conditions is in the tendency of wheat growers to oversupply the market, foreign purchases having declined sharply since 1920 and the domestic market being insufficient to absorb the bumper crops of good years. Under adverse conditions, however, it is clear that the larger capitalistic growers have the advantage over small growers, their costs of production being lower. Nevertheless, the advance in farm land prices has resulted in breaking up many of the greatest wheat-growing units. There is no longer a Dalrymple farm in the Red River valley of North Dakota with its spectacular procession of scores of self-binders reaping a single great field. The size of big wheat farms in the Palouse area today is frequently gauged by the capacity of a unit of machinery, the combine setting the standard.

A major proportion of all wheat grown now is produced on farms that are under 1000 acres in extent. Farms over that size, however, exist to a considerable number, especially in the states of the Pacific Northwest. The annual production for a number of years prior to the World War was between 500,000,000 and 600,000,000 bushels. In 1938 the crop is estimated at 800,000,000.

Tremendous strides in agricultural improvement were made in England during the second half of the 18th century, in the benefits of which the United States shared in the 19th. The body of information accumulated in books became directly available to Americans, and in addition the intercourse of Americans with English farming enthusiasts had a certain influence toward inspiring the imitation of the better British farming methods. It was partly personal contacts that created the better farming agitation through the press, and through organization.

Nevertheless, most of this British material was a systematization of the results of common-sense practice rather than a body of scientific knowledge. It was not until the science of chemistry began to be applied to the problems of agriculture that we have the true beginnings of a science of agriculture. The practical commencement was made in 1803, when Sir Humphry Davy gave his lectures on "the connection of chemistry with vegetable physiology," published ten years later as *Elements of Agricultural Chemistry*. Boussingault in France and Justus Liebig in Germany, especially the latter, advanced the science enormously through experimentation and publication, and in 1843 J. B. Lawes founded the world-famous Rothamsted station in England, securing as chief coadjutor the chemist, J. H. Gilbert.

Americans quickly availed themselves of the scientific knowledge obtainable in England, Scotland, Holland, Germany and France; and, with their genius for organization, produced a magnificent system of agricultural schools and of experiment stations[qqv] which European countries have a right to envy. In short, before the close of the 19th century America was in possession of the equipment for making its agriculture as nearly professional as is possible in an activity compounded of science, business and habitual practice. Within the present century the progress of organization has gone forward till practically every farmer in every county of the forty-eight states has at his command not only the best scientific aids in print, but the advice of a scientifically trained farm expert, and schools in which his children can learn the science of farming.

Despite all this, despite the enormous outlay made by the Federal Government and by the states in the interest of improved and scientific agriculture, it is a truism to say that most Americans continue to farm in traditional ways instead of following the guidance furnished by science, although the proportion of these is gradually decreasing. The Government's land policies of the past have had much to do with conditioning unfavorably the agriculture of the present; for example, in permitting the homesteading[qv] of lands unfitted for permanent cultivation, permitting forest destruction, the overgrazing of grasslands and forest land, etc.

The Government's land policy[qv] was framed for farmers going into the fertile, well-watered, wooded, or open lands of the Middle West. It was ill adapted to the needs of cattle ranchers who wished to utilize the high plains for grazing, their best use. For the Middle Westerner a homestead of 160 acres would insure a family's living; a section, 640 acres, would constitute a large estate. The rancher, however, needed for his business, in order to make it pay, a township, possibly more than a township, covered with the sparse buffalo grass.

A multitude of problems must be solved before farming in America can be brought to its ideal perfection professionally, and as a way of living.

[Everett E. Edwards, *A Bibliography of the History of Agriculture*, Department of Agriculture Miscellaneous Publication No. 84, 1930; Percy Wells Bidwell, *Rural Economy in New England;* Percy Wells Bidwell and John I. Falconer, *History of Agriculture in the Northern United States, 1620-1860;* L. C. Gray, *History of Agriculture in the Southern United States to 1860;* U. B. Phillips, *Life and Labor in the Old South;* A. O. Craven, The Agricultural Reformers of the Ante-Bellum South, *American Historical Review*, 1928; Joseph Schafer, *The Social History of American Agriculture;* A. C. True, *History of Agricultural Education; Report of the Country Life Commission*, Washington, 1909; B. H. Hibbard, *A History of the Public Land Policies.*]

JOSEPH SCHAFER

Agriculture, Credit for. *See* Farm Credit Agencies, Federal.

Agriculture, Department of. A Federal organization devoted exclusively to agriculture was anticipated in the activities carried on by the Patent Office[qv] from 1836 to 1862. These activities were begun by the Commissioner of Patents, who, independently of his office, assumed responsibility for the distribution of new and valuable seeds among farmers in 1836. Three years later this work received official recognition when Congress made a small appropriation to the Patent Office for "collecting and distributing seeds, prosecuting agricultural investigations, and procuring agricultural statistics." For the first twenty years, the Patent Office was primarily concerned with the collection of agricultural statistics and the purchase and distribution of seeds. In 1854 the agricultural work received a scientific emphasis with the employment of a chemist, botanist and entomologist, and with the establishment of a garden for experiments.

Rapid urbanization, need for increased production during the Civil War, and pressure from agricultural societies[qv] caused the establishment, by the organic act of May 5, 1862, of a Department of Agriculture headed by a commissioner. Under the commissioners, from 1862 to 1889, the department passed through its formative period. The scope of its work was constantly extended, and as it became specialized, various administrative units were set up to carry out the functions theretofore performed by individuals, which later developed into the bureaus of the present day. The gathering and disseminating of agricultural information and the distributing of seeds was continued, while the scientific work of the divisions of Chemistry, Entomology and Botany, which were created shortly after the establishment of the department, was supplemented by the creation of new divisions, such as Microscopy in 1871, Forestry in 1880, Veterinary in 1883, Economic Ornithology and Mammalogy in 1886, Pomology in 1886, and Vegetable Physiology and Pathology in 1887. The success of the Bureau of Animal Industry, established in 1884, in combating animal diseases and its notable scientific achievements in the theory of diseases hastened the department's elevation to cabinet status in 1889.

With cabinet status, the department passed into its expansive period, in which its work came to cover almost every phase of agricultural endeavor. Its activities are carried on through an organization of ever-increasing complexity, which at present is headed by the Secretary, assisted by general administrative officers working through the following offices: Land Use Co-ordination, Personnel, Budget and Finance, Operation, Solicitor, Information, and Experiment Stations; through the following bureaus: Agricultural Economics, Animal Industry, Biological Survey, Chemistry and Soils, Dairy Industry, Entomology and Plant Quarantine, Federal Surplus Commodities, Home Economics, Plant Industry, Public Roads, and Weather; through the following services: Forest, Extension, and Soil Conservation; through the following administrations: Agricultural Adjustment, Commodity Exchange, Farm Security, and Food and Drug; and through the following corporations: Federal Surplus Commodities, and Federal Crop Insurance.

These activities, in general, fall into several classes: 1. Research activities, which predominate in most bureaus, and which relate to various physical phenomena, such as those connected with soils, climate, etc., to various biological phenomena, which in agriculture have been developed into highly specialized phases such as genetics, plant and animal pathology, agronomy, horticulture, dairying and animal husbandry, and to various social phenomena arising from the production, distribution and consumption of agricultural commodities. Planning activities are consolidated in the Bureau of Agricultural Economics, and incorporate erosion control, rehabilitation, price stability, marketing, production adjustment, security of farm tenure, forest wild life and soil conservation. As a result of the Hatch Act of 1887, the department through the Office of Experiment Stations co-ordinates and directs similar research activities of the agricultural colleges throughout the country. 2. Extension and information activities, which relate to the dissemination of information resulting from the research activities of the department and of state agricultural colleges, and which are carried out co-operatively by the Extension Service and the states through county agents, as a result of the Smith-Lever Actqv of 1914. 3. Eradication or control of plant and animal diseases and pests, attempted chiefly by the Bureau of Entomology and Plant Quarantine and the Bureau of Animal Industry. 4. Service activities, such as weather reporting by the Weather Bureau, which was transferred to the department from the War Department in 1891, crop reporting by the Bureau of Agricultural Economics, forest administration by the Forest Service, and wild-life-refuge administration by the Bureau of Biological Survey. 5. Administration of regulatory laws, which began with the inspection and quarantine of livestock in 1884 and which now include more than fifty laws, pertaining, among other matters, to the safeguarding of the food and drug supply, to the inspection of commodities in interstate shipment, to the maintenance of commodity standards, to the supervision of packers, stockyards, and of commodity exchanges. 6. Road construction, carried out co-operatively by the Bureau of Public Roads and the states, as a result of the Federal Aid Road Act of 1916qv. 7. Emergency-adjustment work carried on in consequence of numerous important Congressional enactments during the Roosevelt administration, resulting in various programs designed to promote the conservation of the basic resources of the country: greater security of tenure, and the efficient production, distribution and utilization of agricultural products.

[Francis G. Caffey, *A Brief Statutory History of the United States Department of Agriculture*, U. S. Department of Agriculture, Office of the Solicitor, Washington, 1916; Arthur P. Chew, *The Response of Government to Agriculture*, Washington, 1937; M. S. Eisenhower and Arthur P. Chew, *The United States Department of Agriculture: Its Structure and Functions*, U. S. Department of Agriculture, Miscellaneous Publication No. 88, 2nd rev., Washington, 1934; Charles H. Greathouse, *Historical Sketch of the United States Department of Agriculture: Its Objects and Present Organization*, U. S. Department of Agriculture, Division of Publication, Bulletin No. 3, 2nd rev., Washington, 1907; James M. Swank, *The Department of Agriculture: Its History and Objects*, U. S. Department of Agriculture, Report No. 7, Washington, 1872; William L. Wanlass, *The United States Department of Agriculture: A Study in Administration;* Edward Wiest, *Agricultural Organization in the United States.*]

T. R. SCHELLENBERG

Agriculture, European Influences upon. Having an abundance of land and a scarcity of labor the early settlers in America reverted, in general, to the system of extensive husbandry so common in Europe centuries earlier. The nucleated village plan was transplanted to New England and New France but elsewhere scattered homesteads were generally preferred. The modified feudal system introduced in the proprietary colonies broke down and the manors became great plantations. In the Illinois country[qv] the French established a form of the European land system with commons and cultivated common fields. The row culture, so characteristic of American agriculture, was adopted, along with maize, from the Indian. The field-grass system of Europe awaited more mature settlements. The field tools after the early 19th century were developed to fit local conditions and with slight influence from abroad.

The colonists on their rich lands generally disregarded the advanced English ideas on agriculture but when their soils[qv] began to show signs of exhaustion, the more progressive farmers turned to England for guidance. Except for Jared Eliot, who followed English thought, the principal agricultural writers who influenced America until well into the 19th century were Englishmen. Coke of Holkham was influential in introducing the agricultural county fair[qv] into America. He also sent Devon cattle, particularly for the foundation of the Patterson herd in Maryland. Sir John Sinclair and Arthur Young of the English Board of Agriculture were in correspondence with Washington, Jefferson and others and stimulated the formation of agricultural societies[qv] in America and the adoption of improved practices. After 1815, however, America turned its face inward and developed a strong feeling of nationalism and self-confidence. European influence waned but the work of the soil chemist, Johnston of Edinburgh, was widely known and highly regarded in America near the middle of the 19th century. Later in the century much breeding livestock[qv] was imported for the improvement of American flocks and herds.

[L. C. Gray, *History of Agriculture in the Southern United States to 1860;* N. S. B. Gras, *A History of Agriculture;* R. C. Loehr, The Influence of English Agriculture upon American Agriculture, 1775-1825, *Agricultural History,* 11:3-15.]

RUSSELL H. ANDERSON

Agriculture, Government Control of. In 1932 the index number of the Federal Bureau of Agricultural Economics, expressing the ratio of prices received by farmers for the commodities they sold in relation to prices paid for the goods they purchased, was 53 as compared with 100 on a five-year base, August, 1909–July, 1914. In his campaign utterances in the fall of 1932, Gov. Franklin D. Roosevelt of New York severely condemned the farm relief[qv] measures of the Hoover administration, and promised the farmers of the nation that if elected President he would immediately call their leaders together to formulate a plan upon which they could agree as best for the improvement of agricultural conditions. Toward that objective, the President-elect had Henry Morgenthau, Jr., who was at that time Chairman of the Advisory Committee on Agriculture in New York State, meet with some fifty agricultural leaders in Washington on Dec. 12, 1932. The results of this conference were presented in the form of amendments to the Jones Bill and came before the last lame duck[qv] Congress, but a House and a Senate hostile toward each other prevented any definite action.

On March 10, 1933, Secretary of Agriculture Henry A. Wallace called a meeting of representative farm leaders in Washington, and the deliberations of this group, together with the technical assistance of agricultural specialists, resulted in the Agricultural Adjustment Act[qv] which was approved by the President on May 12, 1933. This measure was composed of three parts: (1) that granting authority to the President, through the Secretary of Agriculture, to take steps to increase agricultural purchasing power by means of raising farm income; (2) another empowering the Farm Credit Administration (*see* Farm Credit Agencies) to lighten the load of farm mortgages; and (3) the granting of certain unusual powers to the President (*see* Presidents, Special Powers Granted to) with regard to the national currency and credit. The act provided, upon ratification by referenda of the farmers concerned, authority to establish quotas for limiting the production by individual farmers of certain leading agricultural commodities considered as basic. No penalties were provided in the act for those who did not care to enter into such a voluntary contract, but such penalties were established for the cotton grower in the separate Bankhead Cotton Act[qv] of 1934 and for the tobacco grower in the similar Kerr Tobacco Act. The principle employed in the act was that of rewarding the farmer by benefit payments for his compliance. The measure was self-financing through processing taxes collected by the Bureau of Internal Revenue from the first domestic processor of each of the basic commodities.

On Jan. 6, 1936, the original Agricultural Adjustment Act was declared unconstitutional by the United States Supreme Court on the grounds that agriculture is a purely local activity and that Federal attempts to control its production were in violation of the Tenth Amendment (*see* Constitution) and hence constituted an interference with rights the states had reserved to themselves. In place of the annulled measure, the Soil Conservation and Domestic Allotment Act[qv] was enacted by the Congress on Feb. 29, 1936. The emphasis in this measure was on soil conservation, and the objective was sought by rewarding the farmer for balancing his production between "soil depleting" and "soil conserving" crops and practices. Provision was made, however, for restoration of parity in the purchasing power of the farmer at as rapid a rate as the Secretary of Agriculture determined to be practicable; and, undoubtedly, it was hoped that the response of the farmers would be sufficiently general to bring about an effective control of agricultural production. That this hope was in vain was made apparent by a bumper crop of wheat in 1937, and in the same year, the largest cotton crop ever before produced in this country.

Faced again with the threat of overwhelming farm surpluses, the Congress on Feb. 16, 1938, replaced the Soil Conservation and Domestic Allotment Act of 1936 by the Agricultural Adjustment Act of 1938[qv]. This measure provided for the continuation of the soil conservation program inaugurated in 1936. In addition, however, it authorized national acreage allotments set at levels designed to bring about production ample for domestic consumption, for exports and for reserve supplies; marketing quotas for commercial producers of cotton, wheat, corn, tobacco and rice; the systematic storage, with the assistance of government loans, of food and feed surpluses in years of big yields and the release of these in lean years; and beginning in 1939, crop insurance for wheat, the premiums to be paid in kind. Marketing quotas were to be invoked upon the appearance of designated surpluses which promised to be burdensome, and were to be effective then only upon approval of a two-thirds majority of the farmers concerned. Once the marketing quotas were established, heavy penalties were provided for noncompliance. Funds for carrying out the provisions of the act were to be provided through appropriations from the Treasury of the United States.

[Mordecai Ezekiel and Louis H. Bean, *Economic Bases for the Agricultural Adjustment Act*, U. S. Dept. of Agriculture, December, 1933; Agricultural Adjustment Administration, *Achieving a Balanced Agriculture;* Reports of the Agricultural Adjustment Administration; Wilson Gee, *American Farm Policy; Agricultural Adjustment Act*, Publication No. 10, H. R. 3835, 73rd Congress, approved May 12, 1933; *Soil Conservation and Domestic Allotment Act*, Publication No. 461, S. 3780, 74th Congress, approved Feb. 29, 1936; *Agricultural Adjustment Act of 1938*, Publication No. 430, H. R. 8505, 75th Congress, approved Feb. 16, 1938.]

WILSON GEE

Agriculture, The Influence of Transportation on. In the opening of new settlements away from the coast this varied with the relative value of the products raised. Wheat, wool, butter and cheese bore the cost of transportation better than corn and oats[qqv] for example. Western Pennsylvania could haul whiskey but not grain to the seaboard (*see* Whiskey Insurrection).

Early settlers across the mountains complained bitterly when the Spanish interfered with their outlet down the Mississippi (*see* Mississippi River, Free Navigation of). Further development of this area led to a demand for a trade way which would permit a commercial agriculture, and trade connections with the East. The first such highway, the Erie Canal[qv], opened the wheat lands of western New York and led to a shift from grain to livestock in New England. But the highway which carried Genesee wheat brought settlers and a market to the lake country. The influx of settlers absorbed the produce for some years but exports of wheat began in 1835 from Ohio and steadily grew in volume, with profitable shipment limited to the area near Lake Erie.

The Cumberland Road[qv] greatly reduced the time of travel overland to the Ohio, but few products could bear the cost of hauling over the mountains. The road facilitated the entry of settlers and the steamboat[qv] supplied them with goods. The southern outlet gave the Mississippi and Ohio lands a marked advantage over the lake country until the opening of the Erie Canal. As connections were made between the systems, as the Illinois and Michigan Canal[qv], much of the traffic turned toward the lakes. Corn could bear the cost of wagon transport some thirty miles and wheat about fifty, thus much of the interior remained on a subsistence basis until the coming of the railway[qv] net which placed practically the whole Middle West within reach of a market. The South lacked such a network of railroads but had numerous navigable rivers.

Beyond the Mississippi such trails as the Oregon and Santa Fe[qqv] had fostered trade and led some settlers into the far West, but commercial agriculture in most instances awaited the railroad. When the railroad reached Abilene[qv], Kans., in 1867, it tapped the growing cattle empire of the Southwest which now spread to the northern plains (*see* Cow Country). Wheat raisers pressed westward and later, with the extension of the railroad into the Dakotas and the development of new milling machinery, they opened up the northern wheat belt.

When the railroads were opening up new markets, farmers welcomed them as outstanding benefactors. In the eighteen-seventies, when the farmers of the older sections began to suffer from low prices and relatively high freight rates, they sought to place the blame for their troubles upon the railroads and grain elevators[qv]. Illinois began the crusade against them with a regulating act in 1870 and other states followed with similar "Granger" laws[qv]. In their zeal the states overstepped their powers under the Constitution and the problem, outlined by the efforts of the states, was placed before Congress which passed the Interstate Commerce Act[qv] in 1887.

Since 1920 the motor truck[qv] has been an important factor in the transportation of farm products, particularly fruit, vegetables, livestock and milk. It has taken a commanding position within a range of 150 miles and has won much traffic at greater distances. In connection with radio marketing service it has had a stabilizing influence, reducing day-to-day fluctuations. The influence of the motor truck has been largely in the distribution of products although it has led to some shifts of producing areas by restoring more of the advantages of proximity to market.

[H. U. Faulkner, *Economic History of the United States;* R. H. Anderson, New York Agriculture Meets the West, *Wisconsin Magazine of History*, Dec. 1932,-Mar., 1933; S. J. Buck, *The Granger Movement.*]

RUSSELL H. ANDERSON

Aguayo Expedition, THE (1720–22). Marquis San Miguel de Aguayo, governor of Coahuila[qv] and Texas, left Monclova in 1720 with an expedition of 500 soldiers to re-establish the Spanish missions and presidios in East Texas which had been abandoned in 1719 because of trouble with the French at Natchitoches[qv]. Joined by eighty refugees at San Antonio, Aguayo continued northeastward, re-established six missions and fortified Adaes (now Robeline, La.) near the French. On his return in 1722, he erected a mission near the site of LaSalle's Fort St. Louis[qv]. Thus Aguayo in effect put an end to French claims in Texas.

[Eleanor Buckley, The Aguayo Expedition in Texas and Louisiana, *Texas Historical Quarterly*, Vol. XV.]

L. W. NEWTON

Ague, OR SHAKES AND AGUE, THE, was a disease of malarial origin prevalent on the frontier from the Appalachian to the Rocky Mountains. It was thought to be caused by the dew or by gases from newly plowed virgin soil. The patient was afflicted with chills lasting an hour or two, succeeded by a fever, severe headache, and delirium lasting six to eight hours. Then came a devitalizing sweat and temporary recovery only to be followed by the same process in from one to three days. Hardly a person in low territory escaped it. Quinine was the best of innumerable remedies.

[Everett Dick, *The Sod-House Frontier.*]

EVERETT DICK

Air Commerce Act of 1926, THE. *See* Civil Aeronautics Act.

Air Conditioning. The only air conditioning known in the 19th century consisted of hot air or steam heating and ventilating fans. Cotton mills, to keep down lint, learned to use a fine water spray, which both moistened and cooled the air. In 1897 Joseph McCreary patented an air washer which also cooled and humidified to some extent. In 1906 Stuart W. Cramer devised an automatic humidity control, and Willis H. Carrier invented an improved air washer which automatically controlled temperature. Other improvements followed. After 1920 artificial cooling of theaters in summer increased rapidly, and no large new theaters were erected without complete air conditioning. In other buildings the improvement came more slowly. After 1930 the conditioning of railway trains came to be more and more an expected service.

[Earl Vernon Hill, *Aerology for Amateurs and Others; Scientific American*, 1897-1938.]

ALVIN F. HARLOW

Air Mail. The first test of air-mail service was made in May, 1918, when the United States Army and the Post Office Department together set up an experimental line between New York and Washington, using army pilots. After three months, the Post Office assumed entire control of the line, and employed civilian aviators. This route was too short to give the plane much advantage over the railway, and did not continue long. Other disconnected lines were tried, between New York and Cleveland, Cleveland and Chicago, Chicago and Omaha, but all had the same fault—they were too short to attract mail at high rates. In 1920 the Post Office Department installed a service between New York and San Francisco, whereon the planes flew only by daylight, the mail being transferred from them at dusk to railway trains and rushed on, to take to the air again early next morning. This was replaced on July 1, 1924, by a continuous, day-and-night service across the continent. In 1926–

27 the Department turned the handling over to private corporations as contractors. Branch lines and north-and-south lines were rapidly added. In 1930 when two new routes—New York to Los Angeles via St. Louis and Los Angeles to Atlanta—were designated, there were only two bids for the former contract and one for the latter. Charging that there had been collusion among air-line owners in the bidding, Postmaster-General Farley on Feb. 9, 1934, canceled all air mail contracts, and for four months army planes carried the mail, while an official investigation was conducted. There were several fatal accidents to army fliers. New contracts were signed in June, and the service, which by this time covered the United States pretty thoroughly and connected with lines to Canada, the West Indies, Mexico, Central and South America, was returned to private planes.

In 1935 regular mail service was established across the Pacific between San Francisco and Manila, and in 1939 transatlantic service between New York and London.

[Alvin F. Harlow, *Old Post Bags;* Paul T. David, *The Economics of Air Mail Transportation.*]

ALVIN F. HARLOW

Air Navigation Agreements, International. The United States did not ratify the Convention Relating to the Regulation of Air Navigation, negotiated at the Paris Peace Conference in 1919, which created the Commission Internationale de Navigation Aérienne. In 1923, at the Pan-American Conference[qv] in Santiago, the United States took a prominent role in negotiations that finally led to the signing of the Pan-American Convention of Commercial Aviation in 1928. While the United States has refrained from participation in multipartite agreements regarding public air law with European countries, it has participated in conferences for the codification of private air law such as the Warsaw Conference of 1930, and is usually represented on the Comité International Technique d'Experts Juridique Aériens. The United States has numerous bipartite agreements with such countries as Canada, Mexico, Cuba and the Latin-American states which regulate flights over the territories of the signatory powers.

[Kenneth Colegrove, *International Control of Aviation.*]

KENNETH COLEGROVE

Air Photography. The first American aerial photograph was a view of Boston taken from a captive balloon by J. W. Black on Oct. 13, 1860. Few attempts to follow up Black's work were made in the next fifty years, the balloon photographs of W. N. Jennings made in the early eighteen-nineties, and the development of kite photography by W. A. Eddy (1895) being the most important exceptions. The advent of the airplane resulted in further efforts. The earliest photographs from airplanes in this country were probably made in 1911. The first airplane photograph used as a newspaper illustration is said to have been a view of fire-destroyed Springfield, Mass., taken on Jan. 26, 1914.

During the World War, rapid developments in aerial cameras were made both at home and abroad. The marked improvement in aerial photographic technique resulting from these developments led, by 1920, to extensive photographic mapping by a number of public and private agencies. As a result, up to April 1, 1938, 1,505,100 square miles of continental United States had been mapped photographically for various bureaus of the Department of Agriculture, the United States Coast and Geodetic Survey and the United States Geological Survey.

[Robert Taft, *Photography and the American Scene;* Sherman M. Fairchild, Aerial Photography, *Annals of the American Academy*, 1927, Vol. 131, pp. 49-55; H. K. Baisley, Aerial Photography, *Annual Report of the Smithsonian Institution*, 1936, pp. 383-390; *Photogrammetric Engineering*, 1938, Vol. 4, No. 3, pp. 169-207.]

ROBERT TAFT

Airplane, THE. *See* Aviation.

Airplane Disasters, in the United States, have accompanied the progress of aviation as indeed of all other modes of transportation. In 1908, while airplane flights were still in the experimental stage, Orville Wright crashed his plane, killing his passenger, Lt. Selfridge, in a demonstration before the War Department at Fort Myer. In 1911, John J. Montgomery, of Santa Clara College in California, whose experiments contributed much to the art of gliding, was killed in one of his machines. The conquest of the Atlantic and the Pacific was accomplished only after numerous disasters. Several fatal accidents attended the contest to win the Orteig prize for the first nonstop flight from New York to Paris over the Atlantic; in 1926, René Fonck crashed his plane when taking off from Roosevelt Field and two of his crew were burned to death, and in 1927 the French aviators, Nungesser and Coli, were lost over the Atlantic when attempting the more difficult east-to-west crossing. The Dole race (*see* Airplane Races) from Oakland to Hawaii in August, 1927, cost ten lives when several planes crashed, two disappeared over the Pacific and two planes were lost while searching for them. In 1937, the gallant woman aviator, Amelia Earhart, and her navigator were lost in the Pacific on a flight around the world when flying the lap between New Guinea and Howland Island. In January, 1938, the veteran Capt. Edwin C. Musick and his crew of six, on the *Samoan Clipper,* disappeared when making a trial flight for the new Pan-American Airways service from Pago Pago Harbor to Auckland, New Zealand.

In commercial flying, every year following the inception of scheduled routes has taken its toll of accidents and deaths. In the period of 1918–26, when the Post Office Department flew the mail, there were thirty-nine fatalities (thirty being pilots and nine passengers) in the 11,835,080 miles flown. In the ten years of 1928 to 1937, when the carriage of the mails as well as passengers was by transport companies, there were 353 fatalities in a total of 488,348,434 miles of flying over scheduled routes.

The death of Sen. Bronson M. Cutting, in 1935, in the crash of a transcontinental airliner in Missouri, led the United States Senate to cause an investigation of airplane accidents and to recommend more rigid governmental regulation. Previous to the Civil Aeronautics Act of 1938[qv], the Secretary of Commerce and the Director of the Bureau of Commerce were responsible for the enforcement of regulations for air safety, while investigation boards were appointed each time an accident occurred. Under the act of 1938 responsibility for regulation was concentrated in the Civil Aeronautics Authority, while a permanent Air Safety Board investigated and reported upon all accidents in air commerce.

[*Annual Report of the Director of Aeronautics to the Secretary of Commerce; Air Commerce Bulletin; Senate Report No. 185,* 75th Congress, 1st session.]

KENNETH COLEGROVE

Airplane Races played a prominent role in stimulating the development of aircraft as well as in arousing popular interest in aeronautical progress. At the first large air meet or exhibition held in the United States at Los Angeles in January, 1910, Glenn H. Curtiss made a new world's record for speed with a passenger in the plane, flying at a rate of fifty-five miles an hour. In the same year he won the prize of $10,000 offered by the *New York Herald* for the first flight from Albany to New York, while his pupil, Charles K. Hamilton, won the prize offered by the *New York Times* and the Philadelphia *Public Ledger* for the first flight between the two cities and return in twenty-four hours. The *New York Times* also offered a prize of $25,000 for the first flight between New York and Chicago completed in seven days, and the Chicago *Evening Post* duplicated the prize. For several years after the World War, the Pulitzer Trophy offered by the editor of the *St. Louis Post-Dispatch* and the *New York World* stimulated aeronautical achievement. In 1920, in a race under the auspices of the Aero Club of America, held at Mitchel Field, Garden City, Lt. C. C. Mosley won the trophy with a speed of 156 miles per hour over a closed course. In the race of 1921, at Omaha, the trophy and a world record were won by Bert Acosta with a speed of 176 miles, while in 1923, at St. Louis, the trophy was won by Lt. A. J. Williams at a speed of 243 miles per hour.

The Orteig prize of $25,000 for the first nonstop flight between New York and Paris over the Atlantic, offered in 1919, was not won until 1927 by Charles A. Lindbergh (*see* Lindbergh Flies Across the Atlantic). An innovation in aerial racing in America was the Dole race in 1927, when a planter of Hawaii offered prizes of $25,000 and $10,000 for the first and second airplanes to reach Hawaii from Oakland. In previous competitions, such as the Orteig prize, the competitors were unrestricted as to the time of departure; in the Dole race, all competitors were to take off at approximately the same time, on Aug. 12, which was postponed to Aug. 16 because of weather conditions. The race cost heavily in human lives. Three flyers were killed in preliminary flights. Two planes were lost over the Pacific, and two others disappeared in the search for them resulting in seven more deaths. Of the fifteen planes entering the contest only eight took off, and only two reached Hawaii. The winning plane was piloted by Maj. Arthur Goebel with Lt. William Davis as navigator, in a flight of twenty-five hours and seventeen minutes. The loss of life in the Dole race provoked so much criticism that proposals for similar races across the Atlantic were frowned upon by many aeronautic experts. In the Bendix Transcontinental Speed Dash, held each year since 1929, the contestants take off from Burbank at frequent intervals on the same day.

In 1922 the formation of the National Aeronautic Association placed air races upon a sound basis. The first national air races under its auspices were held in 1923 at St. Louis with an attendance of 50,000 on the last day of the races. Since then the air races have been held generally on the week-end of Labor Day each September. At the races in Cleveland in 1938 a crowd of 79,000 witnessed the three-day events. The principal trophies were the Bendix Transcontinental Speed Dash between Burbank, Calif., and Bendix, N. J., the Greve Trophy Race for speed in traveling 200 miles in twenty laps over a ten-mile course and the Thompson Trophy for speed in a race of 300 miles of thirty laps over a ten-mile course. The purses for these races totalled respectively, $30,000, $25,000 and $45,000.

[*Aircraft Year Book*, published by the Aeronautical Chamber of Commerce of America; *Aviation; Aero Digest.*]

KENNETH COLEGROVE

Airports. The establishment of air routes for mail, passenger and express service in the years following the World War required the building of fields for the take off and landing of aircraft, and, at the terminals, hangars for storing and servicing the aircraft. Most of the fields used by the army and navy as well as those of the aeronautical manufacturers were not located convenient to large cities. To facilitate air traffic, in 1918, the municipality of St. Louis appropriated $28,000 to level a field. This was but a beginning and eventually several million dollars were devoted to the construction of a municipal airport. Among other cities which constructed, owned and operated airports were: Newark, Chicago, Pittsburgh, Cleveland, Wichita, Minneapolis, Oakland, San Francisco and Seattle. Other cities such as Philadelphia, Los Angeles (Burbank) and Miami depended upon commercially owned or operated airports. Within a decade every city that was a terminal of an air route was equipped with an airport having cement runways, large hangars and ground stations for radio communication. By 1927, there were 864 municipal and private airports. In that year, under the Air Commerce Act of 1926*qv*, the Department of Commerce assumed the regulation of the Federal system of airways, and the department undertook the encouragement of the development of airports, the building of intermediate landing fields and the encouragement of the airmarking of cities. At the same time the department conducted experimentation with aids to air navigation, such as the transmission by radio teletypewriter, carrying this device to the point where reliability equal to land wire operation was attained permitting the transmission of meteorological information to aircraft while in flight. By 1938, when the Civil Aeronautics Authority took over the regulation of the Federal airways, the governmental agency had established Airway Traffic Control offices and taken responsibility for the operation of such stations in the airports at Newark, Cleveland, Chicago, Pittsburgh, Detroit, Washington, Burbank and Oakland. At this time there were 2376 airports and landing fields in the United States. Of these, 787 were municipal airports, 49 were state-operated airports, 434 commercial airports, 267 intermediate landing fields, 637 marked auxiliary fields, 61 army airdromes, 25 naval air stations, 91 private fields and 25 government fields. For night flying, 717 airports were equipped. In the three years following 1935 the Works Progress Administration*qv* expended over $93,000,000 of Federal funds on the improvement of airports.

[*Annual Report of the Director of Aeronautics; Annual Report of the Secretary of Commerce; U. S. Department of Commerce: Descriptions of Airports and Landing Fields in the United States, 1938; Aircraft Year Book*, published by the Aeronautical Chamber of Commerce; Joseph H. Wenneman, *Municipal Airports.*]

KENNETH COLEGROVE

Airways are air routes designated for regular travel by aircraft carrying mail, passengers and express and for itinerant aircraft between terminal cities and laid out over the best flying terrain. Prior to the World War, in the United States as in Europe, there were no air routes in continuous operation, save for a few seasonal short lines occasionally operated since 1911 in connection with air meets and exhibitions and other special arrangements. In 1918 an experimental air-mail*qv* route was started by the Post Office Department between Washington, D. C., and New York. In 1920, the Department opened the transcontinental air mail route between New York, Chicago and San Francisco. A route from St. Louis to Minneapolis was initiated in 1920. In the same year foreign mail contract routes were opened between Seattle and Victoria in Canada, and between Key West and Havana in Cuba. Since then every year has witnessed extensions or improvements in the air-mail service. With the lighting of the airway between Salt Lake City and San Francisco, night-flying permitted the carriage of air mail by continuous flight from New York to the Pacific coast without the necessity of grounding the planes after sunset.

In 1926, under the Air Commerce Act*qv*, a Federal airways system was inaugurated, the Secretary of Commerce being charged with the establishment and maintenance of civil airways and their equipment, with intermediate landing fields, beacon lights, signal and radio range beacons, and other aids to air navigation. In 1926 the Federal Government relinquished the operation of the air mails to commercial companies which carried the mails under contract at pound rates on the same basis as that carried by land and water. The contract constituted a generous subsidy to encourage the development of passenger and express transportation in the air in addition to air-mail carriage. Today, practically all air routes are those over which not only the mails, but also passengers and express, are carried by commercial planes. In 1927 the Department of Commerce, with an appropriation of $300,000, controlled 1386 miles of lighted airways, with 32 lighted intermediate landing fields and 107 airway beacons, maintained by 134 employees. By 1937 the Department was authorized to expend some $5,000,000 per year on Federal airways, which now included 22,399 miles of lighted routes, 280 intermediate landing fields, 1916 beacon lights, 82 radio communication stations, 164 radio range stations, 55 radio marker stations and 13,885 teletypewriter circuits, maintained by 1538 employees. In 1923 the scheduled miles flown over American air routes were 5,870,489. By 1927 it had increased to 76,996,165. In 1938 the establishment and the supervision of the Federal airways were transferred from the Department of Commerce to the Administration of the Civil Aeronautics Authority.

Expansion of air routes beyond the United States received an impetus when, in 1927, the Pan American Airways Corporation inaugurated air lines to Latin-American countries. Soon it maintained regular schedules from New York to Bermuda, from Miami to the West Indies and along the east coast of South America to Buenos Aires, from Miami to Panama and to Santiago along the west coast of South America, and from Brownsville and Los Angeles to Mexico City. In 1934 Pan American Airways began operations in Alaska and Canada, and in 1935 a Pacific service, which soon included a regular schedule from San Francisco to Hong Kong and the Philippines by way of Hawaii, and to New Zealand.

[*Annual Report of the Director of Aeronautics; Annual Report of the Secretary of Commerce; Air Commerce Bulletin; Aircraft Year Book*, published by the Aeronautical Chamber of Commerce of America; *Annual Report to Stockholders of the Pan American Airways Corporation.*]

KENNETH COLEGROVE

Aisne Defensive, THE (May 27–June 5, 1918), was a sequel of the operations on the Somme in March, the Germans making a new attack southward between Soissons and Reims with the intention of drawing French reserves south so that they could renew their attacks in the north. The attack was successful even beyond their hopes, and reached the Marne near Chateau Thierry, only forty miles from Paris. The Germans then attempted to establish a bridgehead on the Marne, and also to push westward toward Paris; both efforts were unsuccessful. Two American divisions took part in the defense—the Third opposing the crossing of the Marne, and the Second being very heavily engaged at the Bois de Belleau[qv] and at Vaux, west of Chateau Thierry[qv].

[John J. Pershing, *Final Report as Commander-in-Chief, A.E.F.;* Oliver L. Spaulding, *The United States Army in War and Peace.*]

OLIVER LYMAN SPAULDING

Aisne-Marne Operation, THE (July 18–Aug. 6, 1918), was the Franco-American counter-offensive, following the German offensive of July 15 in the Marne salient (*see* Aisne Defensive). The French Tenth Army (Mangin) opened the attack, striking eastward into the salient just south of Soissons. The main attack was made by the XX Corps, with three divisions in front line, two American and one Moroccan. The Germans were taken by surprise, and their outpost line made little resistance, but the line soon stiffened and the fighting was severe. It was not until the 21st that control of the Soissons-Chateau Thierry highway was gained. The total penetration was eight miles.

From July 21 on, the armies farther east joined in the advance—the Sixth (Degoutte) and the Fifth (Berthelot), along both faces of the salient. With the Sixth Army there were two American corps headquarters—the I (Liggett) and the III (Dickman)—and eight American divisions. The Germans conducted their retreat skillfully, making an especially strong stand on the Ourcq on July 28. But early in August they were back behind the Vesle.

The operations since July 15 had changed the whole aspect of the war. A German offensive had been suddenly stopped in mid-career, and the advance changed to a retreat. The Marne salient had ceased to exist, and the Germans were never again able to undertake a serious offensive.

[John J. Pershing, *Final Report as Commander-in-Chief, A.E.F.;* Oliver L. Spaulding, *The United States Army in War and Peace.*]

OLIVER LYMAN SPAULDING

Aix-la-Chapelle, Treaty of (Oct. 18, 1748), ended the War of the Austrian Succession (*see* King George's War). The chief term which concerned American history was the restoration of Louisburg[qv] to France, which irritated the New Englanders who had been active in the capture. The peace was merely an intermission in the protracted struggle for control of the St. Lawrence and Mississippi basins. Its final phase, the French and Indian War[qv], began in 1754.

[*Cambridge History of British Foreign Policy*, Vol. IX.]

EDMUND K. ALDEN

Akron, THE. *See* Dirigibles.

Akron Law, The (Feb. 8, 1847), resulted from a movement for a better public school system in Akron, Ohio. The Ohio General Assembly passed a special law for the city, which provided for an elected board of education of six members, the organization of the city as a single school district, free admission of all children to the public schools, the adoption of a system for the classification of pupils and their promotion by examinations, and local taxation for financing the schools. The law was broadened in 1848 to apply to any incorporated town, if the voters by a two-thirds vote chose to adopt the plan. In 1849 a general law, modeled on the Akron Law, reduced this requirement to a majority vote, required that schools be kept in operation not less than thirty-six nor more than forty-four weeks per year, and limited to four mills the amount of taxes to be raised for school purposes in any one year. In 1850 townships and special districts were permitted to make use of this system. Thus the Akron Law, with some modifications, came to be applied generally throughout the state.

[Edward A. Miller, The History of Educational Legislation in Ohio before 1850, *Ohio Archaeological and Historical Quarterly*, XXVII (Jan., 1918), 1-271.]

EUGENE H. ROSEBOOM

Alabama. The roots of Alabama's history reach back to the beginnings of contact between Europe and North America. Some of the earliest Spanish explorers visited the Alabama coast, and DeSoto[qv] in 1540 explored the interior of the state. Alabama was the patrimony of three of the celebrated royal houses of Europe. The Spanish founded at least two temporary settlements on its soil in 1559. The French occupied it from 1702 to 1763; the British from 1763 to 1783; and the Spanish again held the southern portion of it from 1783 to 1813. Spain held the strip below parallel 31° and the United States all above that line (*see* Southern Boundary, Survey of). The Spanish base at Mobile[qv] was crushed out in 1813. In 1817 the Alabama Territory was organized out of the Mississippi[qv] Territory, of which it had been a part since 1798, and was admitted to the Union as a state, Dec. 14, 1819.

Alabama was settled principally by farmers, planters and professional men. An unique incident in its settlement was the founding of a colony of prominent Napoleonic exiles at Demopolis in 1817. The social and economic life of the state prior to 1860 was like that of the cotton[qv] South generally. Agriculture was the dominant interest, and the plantation system[qv] flourished in all of its glory. Alabama ranked second as a cotton-producing state in 1860.

Prior to 1860 politics was colorful. Many professional politicians, who had held high official stations in other states, moved into Alabama and jousted with each other for position and leadership. The Democratic and Whig parties[qqv] sprang up and under able leadership stimulated a vigorous political life. The Democratic party dominated, but the Whigs kept up a spirited contest and exerted a large influence. Though local questions, such as the State Bank and state aid to railroads, gave rise to sharp contests, politics usually revolved around national questions. The people generally supported Jefferson's agrarian policies and the South's cause in slavery[qv]. Andrew Jackson was the idol of the masses but Calhoun and Clay had many followers. The states' rights[qv] sentiment grew apace after the Creek Indian[qv] controversy of 1832–33, and became robust under the impact of sectionalism[qv] between 1845 and 1860. William L. Yancey and his colleagues put the state in the front ranks of defense of southern rights. The exponents of sectional reconciliation, headed by Henry W. Hilliard, however, stayed the progress toward secession for a decade (*see* Compromise of 1850).

Alabama seceded from the Union in 1861, and the Confederate Government was organized and set up at Montgomery, since known as the "Cradle of the Confederacy." During the war that followed, its soldiers distinguished themselves in battle and prominent men held high places in the civil and military counsels of the Confederacy. The cost of the war was terrific. Property losses, including slaves, have been estimated at $500,000,000. The white population was frightfully decimated, and more than 437,000 slaves were freed and for many years had small part in rebuilding the state. When the war was over Alabamians earnestly sought restoration to the Union. They set up a state government under President Johnson's plan of reconstruction, but this plan was repudiated by Congress and the people were subjected again to enervating uncertainty and to military oppression (*see* Reconstruction). The state was restored to the Union under the Congressional plan in 1868. This plan resulted in six years of ignorant and corrupt government at the hands of adventurers from the North (*see* Carpet-Baggers) and poor local whites and Negroes, that in some respects was more costly than the war itself. When home rule was restored in 1875 the state debt amounted to $32,000,000 and the local debt to about $20,000,000, much of which was fraudulent and was repudiated.

Besides the debt load, reconstruction gave the state the one-party system. The Democratic party has dominated since 1875. The maintenance of white supremacy[qv] was the prime objective in politics prior to 1901. The populist[qv] outburst of the 1890's came dangerously near to giving the Negro voters the balance of power. This experience led to the disfranchisement of most of the Negroes by the Constitution of 1901, which also introduced some other notable changes. Besides the suffrage provisions, it extended the term of executive and legislative officials from two to four years and made executive officers ineligible to succeed themselves; it created the office of lieutenant-governor, reduced the powers of local government, and enlarged the powers of the legislature over corporations.

Politics since 1890, broadly speaking, has been an affair between the conservative and progressive wings of the Democratic party. These groups have battled over such public questions as taxation, education, prohibition, methods of nominating officers, and the regulation of corporations. In recent years the progress of the state in public health and child welfare work has been conspicuous.

Though there has been a notable rise in mining and manufacturing since 1900, agriculture still dominates, and the people are largely rural. Only 28.1% of the population was urban in 1930. Cotton is still the leading crop.

[T. P. Abernethy, *The Formative Period in Alabama;* A. B. Moore, *History of Alabama.*] A. B. MOORE

Alabama, THE. In June, 1861, Capt. J. D. Bulloch reached England as Confederate agent[qv] to contract with private builders for warships. He first obtained the *Florida*[qv], and on May 15, 1862, a second and more powerful ship, the *Alabama,* was launched at Liverpool. The United States Minister, C. F. Adams, who had previously demanded the detention of the *Florida,* now presented, on June 23, what he thought full evidence of the illegal character of the *Alabama;* but the British authorities were deplorably slow and the sudden insanity of a law-officer of the crown caused a five-day delay. Finally orders were telegraphed to hold the vessel, but she had already sailed under pretense of a trial trip. Earl Russell and other Cabinet members felt a sincere desire to keep her from leaving, and deeply regretted the evasion. Guns, munitions and coal were brought her at the Azores, and she became the terror of American vessels. Under Capt. Raphael Semmes, before her destruction in June, 1864, in the English channel (*see Kearsarge-Alabama* Fight), she sunk, burned, or captured more than sixty ships.

[Ephraim D. Adams, *Great Britain and the American Civil War;* Allan Nevins, *Hamilton Fish.*] ALLAN NEVINS

Alabama Claims, THE. American grievances against Great Britain during and just after the Civil War all clustered about this generic phrase; but they filled a broad category. The Queen's proclamation of neutrality, giving the South belligerent rights, was regarded by Secretary Seward and most Northerners as hasty and unfriendly. The Confederate cruisers, built or armed by Britons, not only destroyed American shipping, but did indirect damage by driving insurance rates high and forcing many American ships under foreign flags. The Confederates raised large sums of money in Great Britain and outfitted blockade runners[qv] there.

Early in the war Seward instructed Minister C. F. Adams to lay before the British Government, with a demand for redress, the losses caused by the *Alabama*[qv]. As a result the British authorities showed greater care. In April, 1863, they halted the *Alexandra* when Adams proved she was intended for the Confederacy; in September, Russell issued orders to detain the two armored rams which Laird[qv] was building. Only one other ship, the *Shenandoah*[qv], clearly violated the British neutrality laws and she only after refitting at Melbourne. Ultimately, the United States entered claims against Great Britain for damage wrought by eleven vessels, totalling $19,021,000. Of these the damage done by the *Alabama* was estimated at $6,547,609; that by the *Shenandoah* at $6,488,320; and that by the *Florida*[qv] at $3,698,609. The American claims were repeated from time to time but met no response until 1868. The Johnson-Clarendon Convention[qv], signed that year under Seward's close supervision, made no mention of the *Alabama* damages but provided for a settlement of all Anglo-American claims since 1853. Partly because of the unpopularity of the Johnson Administration, the Convention was overwhelmingly defeated by the Senate (April 13, 1869). Sumner seized the opportunity to make a speech reviewing the whole American case against Great Britain. He declared that the *Alabama* and other cruisers had not only done heavy damage, direct and indirect, but with the Queen's proclamation and other moral and material support given by England to the South had doubled the duration of the war. His object in thus implying that the total American bill reached $2,125,000,000 was to lay a basis for demands which could be met only by the cession of Canada. Fortunately Hamilton Fish, becoming Secretary of State in March, 1869, took a saner position. Playing for time, he soon adopted the view that the whole set of *Alabama* claims could be met by the payment of a moderate lump sum, an apology, and a definition of maritime international law meeting American wishes. When he mildly urged Canadian independence, the British Government refused to admit that the two questions could be connected. The impasse between the two nations was brief. Great Britain advanced to a more conciliatory position when Lord Granville succeeded Clarendon as Foreign Minister, and when the Franco-Prussian War and Russia's denunciation of her Black Sea pledges threatened European complications. Washington became more amenable when Canada showed distinct hostility to the United States, when the Santo Domingo[qv] controversy destroyed Sumner's influence over Grant, and when financial interests pressed for a settlement. With Sir John Rose, a Canadian prominent in London, acting as intermediary, Fish and Granville decided that a joint commission should settle the whole nexus of disputes—Canadian fisheries, northwestern boundary[qqv] and Alabama Claims. The Commission, meeting under Fish and Earl DeGrey, drew up the Treaty of Washington[qv] (signed May 8, 1871), which expressed British regret for the escape of the *Alabama* and other cruisers, laid down three rules of maritime neutrality, and provided for submission of the Alabama Claims to a board of five arbitrators, American, British, Italian, Swiss and Brazilian. This tribunal decided Sept. 14, 1872, that Great Britain had failed in her duties as a neutral, and awarded the United States $15,500,000 in gold to meet her direct damages, all indirect claims having been excluded. American opinion accepted the award as adequate.

[John Bassett Moore, *International Arbitrations*, I; S. F. Bemis, ed., *American Secretaries of State*, VII; Bancroft Davis, *Mr. Fish and the Alabama Claims;* Caleb Cushing, *The Treaty of Washington;* Allan Nevins, *Hamilton Fish.*]

ALLAN NEVINS

Alabama Platform, The, adopted by the Democratic state convention in 1848 and approved by other southern groups, was W. L. Yancey's answer to Wilmot Proviso and squatter sovereignty[qqv] principles. It demanded congressional protection of slavery in the Mexican Cession. Rejected by the National Democratic convention of 1848, the principle was incorporated in the majority report at Charleston in 1860 (*see* Campaigns of 1848 and 1860). When that convention disrupted, it became the basic issue of the southern Democratic party.

[C. P. Denman, *The Secession Movement in Alabama.*]

WENDELL H. STEPHENSON

Alabamo, The Battle of (April 25, 1541). Breaking up winter quarters in the Indian village, Chicacilla, Hernando DeSoto[qv] marched his forces to seize the Indian fort at Alabamo, Miss., on the Yazoo River. After a bitter fight, he captured the fort and killed most of its garrison.

[Lambert A. Wilmer, *The Life, Travels and Adventures of Ferdinand DeSoto, Discoverer of the Mississippi;* Theodore Irving, *The Conquest of Florida by Hernando DeSoto.*]

ROBERT S. THOMAS

Alamance, Battle of. To punish and suppress the Regulators of North Carolina[qv], Governor Tryon ordered Gen. Hugh Waddell to Hillsborough with a force of about 1000 militia. The Regulators to the number of 2000 had assembled on the Alamance River, about one-half without arms, and with no officer higher than captain. The provincial army had artillery and was adequately equipped. The battle, fought May 16, 1771, lasted two hours and ended in disaster to the Regulators. The provincials lost nine killed and sixty-one wounded while the Regulators had about twenty killed and a greater number wounded. As a result of their defeat, many of the Regulators migrated to the trans-Alleghany region, to Tennessee[qv] in particular.

[E. W. Caruthers, *Life of Rev. David Caldwell.*]

SAMUEL C. WILLIAMS

Alamo, Siege and Fall of the (Feb. 23 to March 6, 1836). When the revolting province of Texas swept its soil clear of weak Mexican garrisons in 1835 the commander-in-chief, Sam Houston, ordered a concentration on the theory that the Mexicans would return (*see* Texas Revolution). He recommended the destruction and abandonment of the fortifications at San Antonio. For this cautious counsel Houston was deposed from command. A twenty-seven-year-old lawyer, Lt.-Col. William Barret Travis, found himself in joint command, with James Bowie, of about 145 men at San Antonio when on Feb. 23 Santa Anna appeared with between 6000 and 7000 men.

Travis and Bowie could have retreated safely. Instead they moved into the stout-walled Alamo Mission, answered a demand for surrender with a cannon shot and sent couriers for reinforcements. A message signed by Travis read: "I have sustained a continual Bombardment and cannonade for 24 hours and have not lost a man. . . . Our flag still proudly waves from the wall. I shall never surrender or retreat. . . . VICTORY OR DEATH." On the eighth day of battle thirty-two recruits crept through the Mexican lines, the last reinforcements the garrison was to receive. This brought their number to about 187. Though suffering from want of sleep, and with ammunition running low, the Texans had lost the services of only one man, Bowie, ill and disabled by a fall.

At four in the morning of March 6, the thirteenth day of battle, Santa Anna stormed the Alamo on all sides. The first and second assaults were broken up. Day was dawning when the Mexicans attacked again. The Texans' guns were hot, their ammunition nearly out and, though casualties had not been numerous, men were dropping from exhaustion. The walls were breached. From building to building and room to room in the mission compound the defenders fought, clubbing rifles and drawing knives. The last point taken was the church. There fell David Crockett and twelve volunteers who had followed him from Tennessee.

By eight o'clock the last of the 187 defenders was dead, though the Mexicans spared about thirty noncombatants. Mexican losses were about 1500 killed and died of wounds.

The first effect of the butchery was to sow panic through Texas, precipitating a flight of the civil population and of the government toward United States soil. Inwardly raging against Travis' disastrous stand, Houston gathered an army. Six weeks later, marching to meet Santa Anna, Houston paraded his men and in an impassioned address abjured them to "Remember the Alamo!" With that cry on their lips they vanquished the Mexicans at San Jacinto[qv], establishing the independence of the Texas Republic[qv].

[Marquis James, *The Raven.*]

MARQUIS JAMES

Alaska. The discovery and occupation of Alaska climaxed an eastward expansion trend of Russia, which, beginning about the middle of the 16th century, in a hundred years had gained a firm footing in the great river valleys of Siberia and given the Czar at least a shadowy claim as far east as Bering Sea.

From Okhotsk in the south and Anadirsk in the north, as centers of operation, the peninsula of Kamchatka was reduced to subjection and when rumors of the existence of another land, across a narrow sea, created a ferment of interest among navigators, Peter the Great set exploration in motion. As one of the last important acts of his reign, Peter inaugurated an expedition headed by Vitus Bering, a Danish sea captain, with the Russian Tchirikoff as second. The object was to determine the geographical relation of northeastern Asia to the American continent. On Aug. 8, 1728, three years after leaving St. Petersburg, Bering in the ship *Gabriel* rounded the northeastern point of Asia, proving that the continents of Asia and America were distinct and separate. That they were not far apart in that latitude was indicated by various signs.

A new expedition in 1741 resulted in the discovery of Alaska's mainland, together with some of the islands between Alaska and Kamchatka. Then followed the fur traders from Kamchatka whose activities quickly disclosed much of the Alaskan coast and her most obvious sources of wealth.

Independent Russian fur traders, bitter rivals for the profits of the trade, not only threatened to destroy the fur-bearing animals but made the coasts and inlets of Alaska frequent scenes of bloodshed. A natural result was the concentration of the business, at first in the hands of a few large companies and finally, in 1799, in a monopoly called the Russian American Fur Company[qv], chartered for a term of twenty years. The charter granted exclusive rights of trade from N. Lat. 55° to Bering Strait, including the "Aleutian, Kurile, and other islands situated in the northeastern ocean." The company was also empowered to make discoveries, north and south, and to occupy them for Russia; and to trade with neighboring people.

The company's success was due largely to its Alaskan manager, Alexander Baranoff. He established a central station at the island of Sitka, built ships for the trade and for expansion southward, finally occupying a port and territory in California. Failing in a plan to provide vessels for the China-Russian trade, he entered into an agreement with John Jacob Astor by which Alaska would be supplied with needed goods, including foodstuffs, in exchange for furs which Astor would sell in Canton. Later, the company made a similar agreement with the Hudson's Bay Company[qv]. Receiving full supplies of grain from Oregon, the California post, Fort Ross, was sold in 1841 to Capt. John A. Sutter.

When the company's charter was renewed in 1821, it professed to grant rights extending to N. Lat. 51°. This gave rise to controversies with both the United States and Great Britain, and finally to treaties with both delimiting the Russian claims (*see* Alaska Boundary Question).

The Russian government in 1867, disturbed over the prospect of war with Britain and not willing to extend the company's charter again, sold the territory to the United States (*see* Alaska, The Purchase of). The price paid was $7,200,000.

"Seward's folly," as American newspapers were fond of calling Alaska, was badly neglected by a government whose people generally regarded the country as a liability rather than an asset. One resource, the seal crop on the Pribilof Islands[qv], was leased to the Alaska Commercial Company[qv]. A better contract entered into with the North American Commercial Company in 1890 gave the Government a revenue from that source alone which guaranteed the repayment of the purchase price of Alaska. Pelagic sealing, however, has caused great losses and created international complications.

Sealing questions, and the fisheries (*see* Seal Fisheries), interested Congress. But the Klondike[qv] placer discoveries in 1896 caused a gold rush reminiscent of California in 1849. Alaskan streams began to be prospected in earnest, and great quartz deposits like those at Juneau were opened. Alaska became a land of adventure, romance and riches, which could no longer be neglected by the Government.

Control through army and navy had proved unsatisfactory. The first regular government was established in 1884. Alaska became a civil and judicial district, with an appointive governor, a judge, a district attorney, a clerk of court, a marshal and four United States commissioners. With some modifications, that arrangement continued down to 1912. Alaska was then given a senate and house of representatives elected from four judicial districts, each district choosing four representatives for two years, two senators for four years. Juneau is the capital of the territory. Alaska has had a delegate in Congress since 1906.

The leading industries of the territory are the fisheries, products of which in 1934 aggregated nearly $42,000,000; and mining, $16,721,000. A Matanuska colonization project was begun in 1936.

[H. H. Bancroft, *History of Alaska;* Joseph Schafer, *The Pacific Slope and Alaska.*]

JOSEPH SCHAFER

Alaska, The Purchase of. Three alleged movements for the sale of Alaska before 1867 are disclosed by documents in the Soviet Foreign Office: in 1854, during the Crimean War, to prevent England from seizing the territory; in 1856, when Senator Gwin of California and Secretary of State Marcy proposed its sale to this country; and in 1860, when President Buchanan contemplated its purchase. There is no record of these movements in the Department of State.

On Dec. 28, 1866, Russia decided to sell Alaska to the United States because of the financial decline of the Russian American Company[qv] and Russia's disinclination to administer Alaska and inability to defend it, and in order to avoid future difficulties with the United States. *Ca.* March 9, 1867, the Russian Minister, Edouard de Stoeckl, broached the subject to Secretary of State Seward, who readily agreed. On March 30, 1867, a treaty was signed conveying Alaska to the United States for $7,200,000. The Senate on April 9 gave its advice and consent to ratification out of gratitude for Russia's having sent its fleet to American waters in 1863 (*see* Russian Fleets, Visit of), supposedly as a demonstration against England and France, which were sympathetic to the Confederacy. Ratifications were exchanged June 20, 1867, and the treaty was proclaimed that day. The formal transfer took place at Sitka, Oct. 18, 1867.

The motives which induced Seward to purchase Alaska are not altogether clear, but we know that prior to the Civil War he had envisioned the United States as coextensive with the North American continent and that after the War he had embarked upon a program of expansion. While he was engaged in this program, Stoeckl appeared with the offer of Alaska. As Alaska fitted into his plan of expansion, Seward probably purchased it for that reason.

[Victor J. Farrar, *The Annexation of Russian America to the United States;* Frank A. Golder, The Purchase of Alaska, in *American Historical Review*, Vol. XXV, April, 1920.]

VICTOR J. FARRAR

Alaska Boundary Question, The. Maps of Alaska, American, English, Russian, French or Spanish, dated after the treaty of 1825 between Russia and England, all represented southern Alaska as a thirty-mile-wide strip parallel to the coast. That is what the treaty stipulated in establishing a boundary between Russian territory and British. The line was to start from the southernmost point of Prince of Wales Island in N. Lat. 54° 40′, ascend along Portland Channel to latitude 56°, then follow a supposititious "range of mountains" running parallel to the coast to the intersection of the 141° of longitude; thence north on that parallel to the Arctic Ocean. If the supposed range of mountains at any point was found to lie more than ten marine leagues from the ocean, then the line was to follow "the sinuosities of the coast" and not more than ten marine leagues therefrom. Since such mountains were nonexistent, the thirty-mile strip was always reckoned as Russian, later American territory.

The Klondike[qv] placer mines, discovered in the upper Yukon country in 1896, were found to lie east of longitude 141°, therefore in British territory. The only practicable way to reach the

Klondike was by ascending Lynn Canal to its head, thence following one of several passes to the Yukon. It would have been of vast importance to British interests to gain a duty-free entrance through Lynn Canal which they would have if the inlet could be shown to extend far into British territory: impossible, however, on the theory that the line of demarcation ran, at the distance of thirty miles, parallel to the "sinuosities of the coast."

Now there began to appear Canadian maps representing an entirely different theory of the boundary line. This was based on a "coast" defined as international law defines the three-mile limit, namely, sinuosities except at inlets, then "headland to headland." This clash of theories made the Alaska boundary question. It was adjudicated under a treaty stipulating that the findings of a joint commission[qv], three American lawyers and three British, should be accepted as final. The commission met in London during the summer of 1903 and found by majority vote in favor of the American claim.

[*Alaskan Boundary Tribunal*, *Proceedings*, 58th Cong., 2nd Sess., Senate No. 102.]

JOSEPH SCHAFER

Alaska Boundary Tribunal. The claim of the Canadians that the boundary of the Alaska panhandle should be so redrawn as to give them the heads of the principal salt-water inlets resulted in the convention of 1903 between Great Britain and the United States. By its terms provision was made for submitting the seven questions at issue to a tribunal of "six impartial jurists of repute." President Roosevelt, who was authorized to appoint three, chose George Turner, Henry Cabot Lodge and Elihu Root, all of disputed impartiality. His Britannic Majesty appointed two prominent Canadians, Sir Louis A. Jetté and A. B. Aylesworth, and Lord Alverstone, Lord Chief Justice of England. The Tribunal met in London, Sept. 3 to Oct. 20, 1903, and after considering lengthy written and oral argument voted (the two Canadians dissenting) against the main Canadian contention. In response to angry charges, Lord Alverstone insisted that his decision had been purely judicial. Although this may have been true, it is clear that President Roosevelt tried to influence his vote by strong indirect pressure.

[A. L. P. Dennis, *Adventures in American Diplomacy.*]

THOMAS A. BAILEY

Alaska Commercial Company (incorporated 1868), a Pacific Coast enterprise with offices at San Francisco, was organized by groups of eastern and western capitalists for the exploitation of the seal fishery[qv] in Alaskan waters. Congress leased it a twenty-year monopoly (May 1, 1870) to kill seals on the Pribilof Islands[qv]. It is now (1939) a trading company.

[H. H. Bancroft, *History of Alaska.*]

LLOYD C. M. HARE

Alaska-Pacific-Yukon Exposition, Seattle, 1909, was a notable achievement of the Pacific Northwest. The Federal Government spent $600,000 for exhibits on the Philippines, Hawaii and Alaska to reveal to the American people, by the first comprehensive demonstration, the peoples, arts and industries of these possessions. Japan presented the largest foreign exhibit she had ever attempted; China and Oceania were well represented. An estimated $20,000,000, secured by taxation, appropriations, gifts and revenues, was spent on the entire exposition. It was a minor, but a highly successful, American exposition.

FRANK MONAGHAN

Alaska Railroad, THE, was authorized by Congress March 12, 1914, to connect one or more of the open harbors on the southern coast of Alaska with the navigable waters, coal fields and agricultural lands of the interior. Commenced in 1915 under general supervision of the Secretary of the Interior and technical supervision of the Alaska Engineering Commission, the 612 miles of road was completed in 1923, and has since been in operation. The main line (470 miles) extends from Seward to Fairbanks. The enterprise has been financed, and is owned, by the National Government.

[Annual reports of the Secretary of the Interior; O. F. Ohlson, The Alaska Railroad, *Baldwin Locomotives*, IX, 19-30 (April 1931); *United States Daily*, March 20, 1930, p. 198.]

P. ORMAN RAY

Albany. In September, 1609, Henry Hudson moored his ship, the *Half Moon*[qv], near the site of the present city of Albany. No serious attempt at settlement was made, however, until the spring of 1624, when the Dutch West India Company[qv] sent over a group of eighteen families, mostly Walloons[qv], who built Fort Orange on the site of the present steamboat square. During the years 1630–36 the colony was augmented by the arrival of groups of colonists sent over by Kiliaen van Rensselaer, who had been granted a large tract of land near Fort Orange. In 1652 the village of about 100 houses, which had grown up in the protection of the fort, was declared independent of the Patroon's colony, and became known as Beverwyck. Shortly afterward, the fur trade, which had been under the control of the

Dutch West India Company, having been thrown open to the citizens, rapidly increased.

On Sept. 24, 1664, Fort Orange surrendered to the English and Beverwyck became Albany, after the Scotch title of the Duke of York. On July 22, 1686, Governor Dongan granted the city a charter. For many years Albany was the key in the regulation of Indian affairs. Since the early days of the colony relations with the Iroquois[qv] had been friendly. During the period of the colonial wars many conferences including the famous Albany Congress[qv] of 1754 were held there. The fur trade continued to be important.

On the eve of the Revolution Albany was a prosperous city of 3000 inhabitants, laid out in a wide strip along the Hudson. The Albanians entered into the struggle with ardor. The position of the city made it strategically important, and throughout the war the inhabitants were in fear of attack. The year 1777 was an anxious one. Burgoyne advanced toward the city by way of Lake Champlain and St. Leger by way of the Mohawk (*see* British Campaign of 1777). At the request of Gen. Schuyler the lead window weights were melted down and made into bullets. The surrender of Burgoyne and retreat of St. Leger relieved the anxiety of the people, but conditions in the city were wretched. It was crowded with refugees and sick or wounded soldiers. In addition a conspiracy among the Negroes, British prisoners and Tories[qv] was feared. News of the Provisional Peace was received with great rejoicing, and the citizens set to work with zest to build up their neglected trade. By a law enacted on March 10, 1797, Albany became the capital of the State of New York. Fulton's steamboat, turnpikes, the Erie and Champlain Canals, railroads[qqv], improved highways and the creation of the Port of Albany have contributed to the city's modern historical importance.

[Codman Hislop, *Albany, Dutch, English and American.*]

A. C. FLICK

Albany Congress, THE (1754), called by order of the British government for the purpose of conciliating the Iroquois[qv] and securing their support in the war against France, was more notable for the plans that it made than for its actual accomplishments. In June commissioners from New York, Massachusetts, Rhode Island, Connecticut, Pennsylvania, New Hampshire and Maryland met with the chiefs of the Six Nations[qv]. Encroachment on their lands, the trade of Albany with Canada, and the removal of Johnson (later Sir William Johnson) from the management of their affairs had aroused a dangerous spirit of disaffection among the Indians. Gifts and promises were bestowed and the alliance renewed, but the Iroquois went away only half satisfied.

For the better defense of the colonies and control of Indian affairs it had long been felt that a closer union was needed than occasional meetings of governors or commissioners. Discussion of such a union now became one of the principal subjects of the congress. Massachusetts indeed had granted her delegates authority to "enter into articles of union . . . for the general defense of his majesty's subjects." The plan adopted was one proposed by Benjamin Franklin and frequently referred to at the time as the "Albany Plan." It provided for a voluntary union of the colonies with "one general government," each colony to retain its own separate existence and government. The new government was to be administered by a President General appointed by the crown and a Grand Council of Delegates from the several colonial assemblies, members of the Council to hold office for three years. This federal government was given exclusive control of Indian affairs including the power to make peace and declare war, regulate Indian trade, purchase Indian lands for the crown, raise and pay soldiers, build forts, equip vessels, levy taxes and appropriate funds. The home government disapproved this plan because it was felt that it encroached on the royal prerogative. The colonies disapproved of it because it did not allow them sufficient independence. Nevertheless this Albany plan was to have far-reaching results. It paved the way for the Stamp Act Congress of 1765 and for the Continental Congress of 1774[qqv]. And when, during the troubled days which followed, the need of a closer union was felt, there was a definite plan to serve as a guide in the deliberations of the representatives of the colonies.

[E. B. O'Callaghan, ed., *Documentary History of the State of New York.*]

A. C. FLICK

Albany Convention, THE (1689–90), was a convention of the civil and military officers of Albany, which, convening on Aug. 1, 1689, set itself up as an emergency government until the pleasure of William and Mary should be made known. Fearful of attack by the French, the convention sought a promise of aid from Jacob Leisler[qv], who had seized control of southern New York, but was rebuffed by Leisler, whose subsequent demand that he be recognized as commander-in-chief was rejected. Badly frightened by a French attack on Schenectady[qv], the convention sought aid from New England and in the spring yielded to renewed demands from Leisler.

[V. H. Paltsits, Transition from Dutch to English Rule, in Flick, *History of the State of New York*, Vol. II.] A. C. FLICK

Albany Regency, THE, was the first American political machine[qv]. It was organized (1820) under Martin Van Buren, and acquired its name because his first aides, residing in Albany and nearby, managed the machine during his absence in the United States Senate. The Regency developed party discipline and originated the control of party conventions[qv] through officeholders and others subservient to it. The spoils system[qv] was the core of its philosophy. The Regency waned when Van Buren's star set in 1848.

[Denis Tilden Lynch, *An Epoch and a Man, the Times of Martin Van Buren;* Denis Tilden Lynch, *The Growth of Political Parties, 1777-1850.*]

DENIS TILDEN LYNCH

Albatross, THE, was the Yankee-owned ship which brought to W. P. Hunt, partner of the Pacific Fur Company[qv], at its Astoria[qv] post, news of the outbreak of the War of 1812. Hunt chartered the ship and removed the furs from Astoria to avoid possible British capture, thus abandoning the first American fur post on the Columbia River[qv].

[H. M. Chittenden, *History of the American Fur Trade.*]

CARL L. CANNON

Albemarle, THE, Confederate ram[qv], built on the Roanoke River, under command of James W. Cooke on April 19, 1864, sank the gunboat *Southfield,* put the *Miami* to flight, and captured Plymouth, N. C. On May 5 she fought indecisively Capt. Melancton Smith's seven blockaders at the mouth of the Roanoke. But on the night of Oct. 27 Lt. William B. Cushing, with fifteen men in a small launch, bearing a torpedo ingeniously attached to a spar, sank her.

[J. Thomas Scharf, *History of the Confederate States Navy;* E. M. H. Edwards, *Commander William Barker Cushing.*] CHARLES LEE LEWIS

Albemarle and Chesapeake Canal, THE, was built by a corporation in 1856–60 to afford inland navigation between Chesapeake Bay and Albemarle Sound. It is really two canals, thirty miles apart; one eight and one-half miles long, connecting Elizabeth River with North Landing River in Virginia, the other five and one-half miles long, connecting Currituck Sound with North River in North Carolina.

ALVIN F. HARLOW

Albemarle Settlements. The first permanent settlement in what is now North Carolina was made in the Albemarle Sound region about the middle of the 17th century by Virginians, in quest of good lands. In 1653 the Virginia Assembly granted Roger Green a tract of land on Roanoke River south of Chowan, to be located "next to those persons who have had a former grant." In 1662 George Durant purchased lands from the Indians in this region, and there is evidence to indicate that others had done the same. When it was learned that the Albemarle settlements were not included in the Carolina[qv] proprietary grant of 1663, a new charter was granted in 1665, which included them. Government was instituted in Albemarle in 1664 and within a decade settlements extended from the Chowan River to Currituck Sound. (*See also* Cape Fear River Settlements.)

[R. D. W. Connor, *North Carolina: Rebuilding an Ancient Commonwealth.*] HUGH T. LEFLER

Albuquerque, N. Mex., originated, April, 1706, as the Spanish villa "San Felipe de Albuquerque," named for King Philip V and the Viceroy, Duke of Albuquerque. It was on the Chihuahua Trail[qv] and dominated the Rio Abajo (down river) part of the province. Exposed to Apache and Navajo[qqv] inroads, the settlers were "reduced" (1779) to the plaza arrangement which survives in "Old Town."

New Albuquerque started a century later (1880) a mile to the east, as a railroad center. That year, the Santa Fé system (*see* Atchison, Topeka and Santa Fé Railway) built down the Rio Grande and the Atlantic and Pacific[qv] headed westward over the old United States survey (1853) along the 35th parallel. Connection southeast into Texas came only in 1907. In recent years the automobile and airplane also have made Albuquerque an important crossroads of transcontinental routes.

[L. B. Bloom, Albuquerque and Galisteo, in *New Mexico Historical Review,* X (1935); C. F. Coan, *History of New Mexico.*] LANSING B. BLOOM

Alcaldes, THE, were mayors of Mexican towns. Under the American provisional government in California these officers were recognized by military governors and continued in office until 1850.

[T. H. Hittell, *History of California.*]

WILLIAM S. LEWIS

Alcatraz, a thirty-five-acre island in San Francisco Bay, was first used in 1886 by the War Department as a place of confinement for long-term military prisoners. In 1907 it was designated Pacific Branch of the United States Military Prison; later, as Pacific Branch United States Disciplinary Barracks. Transferred to the Department of Justice in 1934, Alcatraz is now the penitentiary in which are confined the more dangerous and difficult types of persons convicted of federal crimes.

[C. M. Tuteur, Alcatraz—the Prison Island, *San Francisco Police and Peace Officers Journal*, XV; S. Bates, *Prisons and Beyond.*] P. ORMAN RAY

Alder Gulch, Mont. Gold was discovered on Alder Gulch, and the first stampede reached there June 6, 1863. The people lived in brush wickyups, dug-outs[qqv] and rocks, but later a town sprang up which was named Virginia City[qv]. The diggings[qv] were the richest gold placer deposits ever discovered and in three years $30,000,000 was taken from them.

[G. Stuart, *Forty Years on the Frontier.*] CARL L. CANNON

Aldrich Commission. *See* National Monetary Commission.

Aldrich-Vreeland Emergency Currency Law, THE, enacted May 30, 1908, as a result of the so-called "bankers' panic" of 1907[qv], aimed to give elasticity to the currency through the next six years, by permitting national banks[qv] to issue circulating notes on securities additional to Federal bonds. It permitted issuance, under strict supervision, of additional currency, on bonds of states, cities, towns and counties, and on commercial paper. A tax graduated up to 10% discouraged abundant issues. The Act also created a National Monetary Commission[qv] to investigate systems of money and banking abroad and to advise Congress of desirable changes in the American banking system.

[*U. S. Statutes at Large*, Vol. 35.] JEANNETTE P. NICHOLS

Aleutian Islands, THE, were discovered in 1741 by Vitus Bering, commissioned in 1725 by Peter the Great to lead a Russian expedition to determine whether Asia joined America. Michael Novidiskoff, probably the first fur trader in Alaska, reached Attu in 1745. Then began a lucrative trade with the native Aleuts in the pelts of the fur seal and the sea otter[qqv]. The port of Unalaska[qv], founded in 1761, became one of the three Russian settlements in Alaska, and had 25 white and 125 half-breed inhabitants in 1867 when Alaska was purchased by the United States. In 1881, when the United States Government determined to protect the fur seals by prohibiting the pelagic or open-sea killing, the far-reaching extent of the Aleutian Islands was the basis of the American claim that the Bering Sea constituted a *mare clausum*[qv]. (*See also* Bering Sea Fisheries.)

[Henry W. Clark, *History of Alaska.*] KENNETH COLEGROVE

Alexandria, Va., on the Potomac River, below Washington, was an important trading center until early in the 19th century, particularly as a tobacco warehousing and deep-sea shipping port. Incorporated in 1748, on an original grant of 6000 acres, awarded in 1669, the site was owned for a century by the Alexander family. It was situated on the main stage route, the King's Highway, running southward into Virginia. Braddock[qv] departed from there on his fatal expedition. The Fairfax Resolves[qv] were signed in Alexandria, July 18, 1774. From 1791 to 1846 Alexandria was under exclusive Federal jurisdiction as part of the District of Columbia. Jefferson's Embargo Act[qv] destroyed its tobacco trade. During the Civil War it was occupied by Union troops. Alexandria was the home of Lee and other prominent Virginia families. In recent years its colonial architecture has attracted much interest.

[Mary G. Powell, *The History of Old Alexandria, Virginia.*] ETHEL ARMES

Alexandria Conference, THE (March 28, 1785), between Maryland and Virginia, concerned navigation and commerce in Chesapeake Bay and the Potomac and Pocomoke rivers. Scheduled for Alexandria for March 21, it actually met at Washington's invitation at Mount Vernon. Daniel of St. Thomas Jenifer, Thomas Stone and Samuel Chase represented Maryland, George Mason and Alexander Henderson, Virginia. In ratifying the agreement, Maryland urged the inclusion of Pennsylvania and Delaware, while Virginia urged a meeting of all the states to adopt uniform commercial regulations. This produced the Annapolis Convention[qv], the origin of the Convention of 1787[qv].

[J. Thomas Scharf, *History of Maryland.*] WALTER B. NORRIS

Alfalfa. Spanish explorers probably first brought seed of this legume to the Americas in the 16th century. It was grown in Mexico and later became established in Peru and Chile. Attempts by colonists along the Atlantic seaboard to grow it met with indifferent success. George Washington planted a field of alfalfa in 1794.

Development of alfalfa as a great forage crop of the United States dates from about 1850, when seed from Chile or Peru was introduced into California by gold seekers. It moved into Utah, thence to Colorado, Kansas and Nebraska and by 1900 had reached Illinois and Ohio.

Alfalfa found its most favorable environment in the great Mississippi Valley and in mountain regions of the West. Of eleven and one-half million acres harvested in the United States in 1934, over seven and one-half million acres were grown in fourteen North Central States, bounded on the east by Ohio and by Colorado on the west. Value of the 18,742,093 tons of alfalfa hay produced in the United States that year was $268,298,614.

Alfalfa, in common with other legumes, serves as a host for bacteria which possess the ability to extract nitrogen from the air and render it available in the soil to other plants. This soil-improving characteristic, combined with its forage value, makes it one of the great economic crops and favorably influences the development of a well-diversified type of agricultural and livestock production, essential to a stabilized and profitable farming industry.

[*Yearbook of Agriculture, 1937*, United States Department of Agriculture; *Alfalfa in Kansas*, Kansas State Board of Agriculture; Charles V. Piper, *Forage Plants and their Culture.*]

ARTHUR CAPPER

Algeciras, Conference at. France made agreements with England and Spain in 1904 which allowed her to increase her influence in Morocco. Germany, angered because she was not consulted, demanded a conference of the signatories of the Morocco agreement negotiated at Madrid[qv] in 1880. Among the signatories was the United States to whom the German government now appealed for an extension of the open-door policy[qv] to Morocco. President Theodore Roosevelt, in an attempt to obtain a peaceful solution, helped Germany by persuading England and France to attend a conference at Algeciras, Spain, in 1906. In the conference, however, the Germans appeared so uncompromising that Roosevelt supported France, which in the end won out by obtaining a privileged position in Morocco. The United States Senate ratified the resulting treaty but declared that this action was taken solely to protect American interests and should not be interpreted as an abandonment of a non-intervention policy[qv] toward Europe.

[E. N. Anderson, *First Moroccan Crisis;* A. L. P. Dennis, *Adventures in American Diplomacy.*]

LYNN M. CASE

Algiers, United States War with. *See* Barbary Wars, The (1801–05) (1815).

Algonquin (ALGONKIN), THE, is a generic term for a linguistic stock or basic group of Indians having a wide distribution, their territory reaching from Newfoundland to the Rocky Mountains and from isolated areas in California to Pamlico Sound. This great family embraced numerous tribes and groups of tribes having a common linguistic affinity. The Algonquin were first met in Canada where the Weskarini provided the name now applied to the whole. The western group embraced the Blackfoot confederacy and the Arapaho and Cheyenne[qqv]; the extensive northern division the Chippewa[qv], the Missasaga, Nipissing, Abittibi, Algonkin and probably the Cree[qv]. The northeastern division embraced the Montagnais group, the Abnaki[qv], including the Micmac, Malecite, Passamaquoddy, Arosaguntacook, Sokoki, and Norridgewock. The central division embraced the Sauk, Fox, Kickapoo, Mascoutin, Pottawatomie, the Illinois branch of the Miami group which included the Peoria, Kaskaskia, Cahokia, Tamaroa and Michigamea, the Miami group proper, including the Miami, Piankashaw and Wea[qqv]. The eastern division embraced all the Atlantic coast Algonquian tribes, such as the Pennacook, Massachusetts, Wampanoag, Narragansett, Nipmuc, Montauk, Mohegan, Mahican, Wappinger, Delaware, Shawnee[qqv], Nanticoke, Conoy, Powhatan and Pamlico.

The Algonquian tribes were the first to sustain the shock of French and English penetration and suffered greatly from wars with the Iroquois[qv]. Most of the tribes except those of the north were sedentary and carried on agriculture with varying degrees of intensity. They possessed a degree of manual skill and their mental qualities are not to be despised. Among their great leaders were such men as Tecumseh, Pontiac, Samoset, Massasoit, King Philip, Powhatan and Nimham. Many eastern tribesmen embraced Christianity early in the colonial period.

[Hodge, *Handbook of American Indians.*]

ARTHUR C. PARKER

Alien and Sedition Acts, THE, were enacted by Congress (1798) because of threatened war with France, and the desire of the Federalists[qv] to insure against Jeffersonian Republican[qv] success at the polls. The presence in the country of a considerable number of alien Frenchmen favorable to the Republicans, and intemperate newspaper opposition to the Federalists, were the principal factors in prompting these laws.

The act of June 18 decreed that instead of

five years, aliens must reside in the country fourteen years before naturalization, and must declare such intention five years before applying for citizenship. This law was repealed by the Republicans (Jeffersonian) in 1802. The act of June 25, which expired in 1800 and was not renewed, empowered the President to deport any aliens he deemed dangerous to public peace. The third act, of July 6, was the most defensible. It empowered the President, in time of war, to arrest, imprison, or banish aliens with whose motherland this country might be at war. In the two years of its existence, it was never applied, but many French were frightened into leaving the country. The principal objection to these laws was the arbitrary power they granted the executive.

The Sedition Act of July 14 made it a high misdemeanor "unlawfully to combine and conspire" in order to oppose legal measures of the Government, to interfere with an officer in the discharge of his duty, to engage in or abet "insurrection, riot, or unlawful assembly or combination." The penalty was a fine of not more than $5000 and imprisonment up to five years. The publication of false or malicious writing against the nation, the President or Congress, was punishable by a fine of not more than $2000 and imprisonment not exceeding two years. The anti-Federalists^qv^ held that this act was unconstitutional. Of all the Federalist leaders, only John Marshall opposed it openly. A decision of the Supreme Court in 1882 supports the view that the Sedition Act was unconstitutional. It is noteworthy that the act was used to punish Republican editors who had criticized President Adams, while the diatribes of Federalists against Vice-President Jefferson were ignored. Ten individuals, all Republicans, were fined and imprisoned under the Sedition Act. The most notable was Dr. Thomas Cooper, later president of South Carolina College. He paid $400 and spent six months in prison for saying that when Adams took office he "was hardly in the infancy of political mistake: even those who doubted his capacity thought well of his intentions . . . nor had he yet interfered, as President of the United States, to influence the decision of a court of justice." Many others were tried but not convicted. In some cases the Federalist judges, especially Justice Samuel Chase, displayed violent partisan bias against the accused. As the public began to treat the victims of these prosecutions as martyrs and popular heroes, the Federalists realized their mistake and ceased to enforce the act. Four decades later, Congress refunded some of the fines.

The most conspicuous result of these four laws was the evocation of protests from many states. The extreme protest was voiced in the Virginia and Kentucky Resolutions[qv] written, respectively, by Madison and Jefferson.

[J. S. Bassett, *The Federalist System.*]

MILLEDGE L. BONHAM, JR.

Alien Contract Labor Law, THE, enacted by Congress Feb. 26, 1885, was supplemented by later ones, notably that of 1907, as amended by that of 1910. The object was to prevent the lowering of wage standards by importing indigent and dependent laborers. The original Act excepted certain groups, such as domestic labor, artists, and lecturers. The Act of 1903 extended the exceptions to any "recognized learned profession," including teachers. Violation of these acts involves both penal and civil liability.

C. SUMNER LOBINGIER

Alien Landholding. The common-law disability of aliens to inherit lands in the United States has always been removable by statute and by treaty. Alienage occasioned by the Revolution was excepted by the Definitive Treaty of Peace[qv], which also required Congress to "recommend to the State Legislatures" restitution of confiscated estates. The Jay Treaty[qv] went a step farther by guaranteeing existing titles wherever held, and treating British subjects, with respect thereto, as equal to citizens. But this did not hold for lands thereafter acquired, nor for other than British aliens. The Convention of 1800[qv] removed the disability of alienage for French citizens in all the states. A treaty with Switzerland (1850) similarly affected Swiss citizens. But in the absence of such a treaty state laws applied, as in Kansas where the disability was expressed in the state Constitution. In California, on the other hand, the Constitution authorized aliens to acquire, transmit, and inherit property equally with citizens; and this, like similar provisions in other states, was upheld by the Supreme Court. The vast increase in European immigration after the mid-19th century stimulated a contrary sentiment. In 1887 Congress passed an act prohibiting aliens (natural or corporate), from acquiring lands in the territories or District of Columbia "except . . . by inheritance or . . . in the ordinary course of justice." In Nebraska, where an Englishman named Scully had bought large areas, an act was passed in 1889 prohibiting non-resident aliens or foreign corporations, with certain exceptions, "from acquiring title to or taking or holding any lands." The Washington State Constitution prohibiting ownership of lands by aliens who have not declared their intention of becoming citizens was judicially upheld; but an Arkansas act of 1925, similar in scope, was annulled as infringing the state prohibition of "distinction . . . between resident aliens and citizens in regard to . . . property."

C. SUMNER LOBINGIER

Alien Property. During the Revolution several colonies sequestrated British debts[qv] and refused to restore right of suit (*see* Confiscation of Property). The United States in 1802 settled British claims, and subsequently by treaties with many countries affirmed the general doctrine of inviolability of enemy alien property during war. But in 1917 Congress authorized the conveyance of such property to a Custodian as trustee for management and "if necessary" for sale, to prevent its use by the enemy. Later the idea of trusteeship changed and the property was sold freely at very low prices, even after the Armistice. Several thousand coveted German chemical patents were bought (at $50 each!) by The Chemical Foundation, organized for this purpose by a former Alien Property Custodian and associates. By a series of acts since 1921, notably the Settlement of War Claims Act[qv] of 1928, Congress has compensated Austrians and Hungarians in full. Of German property seized by the Custodian, 80% has been returned. The balance was to have been settled out of bonds deposited by Germany by Agreement of 1930, but in default since 1931. For ships and certain other property used by the Government, Germans have been paid 50%, the remainder being held up as above.

[Annual Reports of the Secretary of the Treasury, 1930, 1934, 1936.] FRANK A. SOUTHARD, JR.

Aliens. *See* Naturalization.

Aliens, Legislation Regarding. The alien problem confronted the United States practically from the beginning. In its earliest form it concerned mainly natives and foreign-born who had elected to remain British subjects after independence (*see* Loyalists). The Definitive Treaty of Peace, 1783[qv], guaranteed immunity, to those electing to remain British, from prosecutions "for the part . . . taken in the war," from "loss or damage in . . . person, liberty or property" and from continued imprisonment on the same account. It likewise authorized creditors to recover debts which had been sequestered in the Colonies; but this was not carried out and the Jay Treaty[qv] waived for each signatory future rights of confiscation[qv]. Such waiver was likewise made in many subsequent treaties and those rights were not actually exercised by the United States for nearly a century and a quarter. The right of aliens to enter and settle was virtually unlimited by legislation before 1882 and that of naturalization[qv] was extended to aliens by the First Congress. American insistence upon the right of expatriation[qv] was in fact a cause of the War of 1812. The Fourteenth Amendment[qv] to the Federal Constitution, forbidding any state to "deny to any person within its jurisdiction the equal protection of the laws," purported to place aliens virtually on a par with citizens regarding civil rights[qv]. A lower Federal court in California declared unconstitutional a state statute forbidding Chinese to fish in streams of that state; but the Supreme Court upheld a Pennsylvania act of 1909 prohibiting resident aliens from killing wild game or owning firearms, as infringing neither the Fourteenth Amendment nor the Italian (1871) or Swiss (1855) Treaty. In some of the western states, e.g., Nebraska, aliens who had declared their intention to become citizens were permitted to vote; but such legislation was generally repealed during or after the World War.

C. SUMNER LOBINGIER

All American Canal, THE, scheduled for completion in 1939, at a cost of $38,000,000, will divert Colorado River water at Imperial Dam, 23 miles above the Mexican border, and carry it 80 miles to the Imperial Valley and 130 miles to the Coachella Valley, Calif., for irrigation, replacing a canal traversing Mexican territory. An apportionment negotiated by Secretary of Interior Ray Lyman Wilbur in 1930 entitles these areas to 3,850,000 acre feet annually, plus a share of any excess water. Mexico will not be served by this canal, but will divert from the river independently.

[Ray Lyman Wilbur and Northcutt Ely, *The Hoover Dam Contracts.*] NORTHCUTT ELY

All Quiet Along the Potomac, a poem first published as "The Picket Guard" by Mrs. Ethelind Eliot Beers in *Harper's Weekly,* Nov. 30, 1861. It refers to official telegrams reporting "all is quiet tonight" to the Secretary of War by Maj. Gen. George B. McClellan.

[George W. Stimpson, *Popular Questions Answered.*]

FRED A. EMERY

Allatoona Pass, Battle at (Oct. 5, 1864). After the fall of Atlanta[qv] Hood (C.) moved his army northward to destroy Sherman's (U.) communications. Sherman followed. Hood detached French's (C.) division to destroy a railroad bridge. On his march French stopped to destroy stores at Allatoona and attacked Federal troops stationed there, but without success. The popular song, "Hold the Fort," was based on messages exchanged between Corse (U.) at Allatoona and Sherman.

[*Battles and Leaders of the Civil War,* Vol. IV.]
THOMAS ROBSON HAY

Alleghenies, Routes across. The steep eastern escarpment of the Allegheny Mountains, about 3000 feet high, extending from the Mohawk valley to the Tennessee River was a serious impediment to the westward movement[qv]. Routes across the Alleghenies depended upon gaps and approaches to these along the tributaries of rivers. Probably buffalo first trod these routes. Later the Indians followed them as trails. In turn they were used by white explorers and fur traders.

The Susquehanna with its West Branch extending close to the Allegheny River furnished a route much used by the Indians, though whites other than fur traders made little use of it during the early period. The branches of the Juniata River led to two historic routes across the Alleghenies, one, the Frankstown Path, much used by Pennsylvania fur traders, and the other, the Traders Path, followed by Forbes' Expedition[qv] and the Pennsylvania Road. From the Potomac at Wills Creek ran the route over the Alleghenies, used by Gist, Washington, and Braddock. From the headwaters of the Potomac also ran a route over the mountains much used in later times as the Northwestern Pike. The headwaters of the James River determined a route overland to branches of the Great Kanawha, one branch of which, the New River, also provided a route from the headwaters of the Roanoke River. Farthest south Cumberland Gap[qv] offered easy passage from eastern Tennessee to central Kentucky making possible the much used Wilderness Road[qv]. In the light of the extensive use made of Forbes' Road, Braddock's Road[qqv] and the Wilderness Road in the westward movement, probably no routes in the United States are more properly known as historic highways.

Even in the age of railways and automobile highways, topography is dominant, and the transportation of the 20th century follows closely the old routes across the Alleghenies.

[Archer Butler Hulbert, *Historic Highways of America;* Alfred P. James, Approaches to the Early History of Western Pennsylvania, *Western Pennsylvania Historical Magazine,* XIX (1936), 203.]
ALFRED P. JAMES

Allegheny Portage Railway, THE, spanned the thirty-six miles between Hollidaysburg and Johnstown to link the eastern and western canals of the Pennsylvania System[qv]. Constructed in 1831–35 when the ascent of 1400 feet from Hollidaysburg to Blair's Gap, at the summit of the Allegheny Mountains, within 10.1 miles seemed a prohibitive gradient for a continuous roadbed, the railway consisted of eleven level stretches and ten inclined planes, five on each side of the crest. The planes were operated by stationary engines. Locomotives quickly replaced horses as motive power. In 1856 the planes were superseded by a continuous railway. The Portage Railroad was sold to the Pennsylvania Railroad[qv] in 1857 and shortly abandoned.

[W. B. Wilson, *History of the Pennsylvania Railroad Company.*]
E. DOUGLAS BRANCH

Allegheny River, THE, rises in Potter County, Pa., and flows in an arc through New York and back into Pennsylvania, where it unites with the Monongahela[qv] to form the Ohio. About 350 miles long, it is navigable by small steamboats for about 150 miles. It was considered by the French and early English explorers as a part of the Ohio River. The Delaware and Shawnee[qqv] settled along its course soon after 1720; white settlement followed after 1790. It was an important highway for settlers and freight in the keelboat and flatboat[qqv] era. Its name is probably a corruption of *Alligewi-hanna,* "stream of the Alligewi," from a tribe that Indian tradition says once inhabited the region.
LELAND D. BALDWIN

Alliance, Farmers'. *See* Farmers' Alliance, The.

Alliance, THE, was a Continental frigate[qv], thirty-six guns, built in Salisbury, Mass., 1778. She carried Lafayette and Thomas Paine to France. Her first commander, Landais, showed doubtful loyalty in the *Bonhomme Richard-Serapis* engagement[qv]. Barry cruised in her from 1780 through the last sea fight of the Revolution with the *Sybil,* March 10, 1783.

[G. W. Allen, *Naval History of the American Revolution.*]
WALTER B. NORRIS

Almanacs. In Colonial days the almanac was a publication of prime importance second only to the Bible and widely used by farmers. Beginning as a publication of astronomical information and prophecy, it later grew into one of culture, occupying the position in the 18th century later taken by the magazine.

The first almanac printed in America was entitled *An Almanac Calculated for New England,* by Mr. Pierce, printed by Stephen Daye at Cambridge in 1639; in 1676 an almanac was published in Boston; in 1686 in Philadelphia, Samuel Atkins, "A student in the mathematics and astrology," compiled *The American Messenger.*

Almanacs were published in New York in 1697, in Rhode Island in 1728, and in Virginia in 1731. In content these almanacs were similar to earlier ones in Europe containing prophecies concerning human beings and the weather, based on astrology. The early almanacs were preserved from year to year and the blank spaces used for diaries, recording accounts, and attempts at poetry.

The most famous of the early almanacs are *The Astronomical Diary and Almanac* published by Ames in Boston (1725–64); and *Poor Richard's Almanac*[qv] by Franklin in Philadelphia (1732–57). The latter was unequalled in reputation for proverbs, wit, and wisdom, not all original. Nathaniel Ames, in his *Astronomical Diary and Almanac,* furnished perhaps a greater versatility than appeared in any other almanac of the century. Its tide charts, solar table calculations and eclipses, and changes of the moon were definite assets.

Foreign language almanacs were widely used. A prominent example was *The Hoch Deutsch Americanische* in 1739 and various almanacs published by the Pennsylvania Germans[qv].

In the 19th century, almanacs were frequently issued for political and other propaganda and advertising purposes as indicated by the *Sun Anti-Masonic Almanac* (1831); *Harrison Almanacs* (1840–41); *Henry Clay Almanac* (1844); *General Taylor's Rough and Ready Almanac* (1848); *Cass and Butler Almanac* (1849); *Common School Almanac* (1842); *Temperance Almanac* (1834).

The Confederate Almanac and Register (1862) and *Uncle Sam's Union Almanac* (1863) gave military statistics somewhat as did *Hutchin's Almanac* of New York in the later 18th century.

Comic almanacs in the eighteen-thirties; *Josh Billings' Almanac* in 1870; *Fithian's Silk Growers Almanac* in 1840; *The Poultry Breeder's Almanac* of 1856 and the *Phrenological Almanac* of 1841 are typical of the times.

All the outstanding religious denominations published almanacs giving denominational statistics and other information. Medical almanacs of all types have been widely distributed. Encyclopedic information is well served by almanacs published by newspapers of which that of the *Tribune* (1846) and the later *World Almanac* are examples.

[Thomas, *History of Printing in America.*]

H. H. SHENK

Alphabetical Agencies. A term first applied to the numerous Government agencies set up under authority of Congress, beginning in March, 1933, to administer the New Deal[qv] relief and recovery measures. It soon became customary to refer to them by the initials of their respective titles, e.g., N.R.A. (National Recovery Administration), A.A.A. (Agricultural Adjustment Administration), F.C.A. (Farm Credit Administration), T.V.A. (Tennessee Valley Authority), S.E.C. (Securities and Exchange Commission), P.W.A. (Public Works Administration), W.P.A. (Works Progress Administration), C.C.C. (Civilian Conservation Corps)[qqv]. Later, Government agencies that antedated the New Deal were similarly referred to, e.g., I.C.C. (Interstate Commerce Commission), F.T.C. (Federal Trade Commission) and R.F.C. (Reconstruction Finance Corporation)[qqv].

[L. F. Schmeckebier, *New Federal Organizations;* S. C. Wallace, *The New Deal in Action.*]

P. ORMAN RAY

Alphadelphia Association, THE, was a Fourierist[qv] community established in Comstock township, Kalamazoo County, Mich., in 1844. A German, Dr. H. R. Schetterly, was the leading spirit. Three thousand acres of land were purchased, a large "mansion" built, and at one time probably 300 members were admitted. The common property was valued at $43,897.21 in 1846. It was disbanded in 1848.

[*Michigan Pioneer and Historical Collections,* Vol. V, 406-12.]

WILLIS DUNBAR

Alta California. Under Spain (1533–1822) California embraced the whole Pacific coast of North America from Cape San Lucas to the Oregon country. Till the middle 18th century it was frequently represented on maps as an island some 3000 miles long. Early in the 18th century the Jesuit Father Kino proved by actual exploration that the southern portion of the area was a peninsula and the rest of it mainland. Thereafter the peninsula came to be called Baja (Lower) and the rest Alta (Upper) California.

[C. E. Chapman, *California, The Spanish Period;* H. E. Bolton, *Outpost of Empire.*]

HERBERT E. BOLTON

Alta Vela Claim. This was a flimsy claim against the Dominican Government by American adventurers ejected on the eve of the unsuccessful Spanish reoccupation (1861–65) of the guano island by that name located some fifteen miles south of the Dominican Republic. It has both a sinister and an auspicious significance in United States political history because former Secretary of State Jeremiah S. Black resigned as defending counsel in the impeachment[qv] trial of President

Andrew Johnson in 1868 when the latter would not order Secretary of State Seward to approve the claim.

[Samuel Flagg Bemis, *Diplomatic History of the United States.*]

SAMUEL FLAGG BEMIS

Alton Petroglyphs. Near the present town of Alton, Ill., Marquette in 1673 saw painted upon the face of a rocky bluff the figure of a monster which terrified him and interested later travelers until its destruction about 1856. Called "Piasa" by the Indians, the figure was that of an imaginary bird legendary with many tribes.

[F. W. Hodge, *Handbook of American Indians.*]

CLARK WISSLER

Aluminum. From its discovery in 1825 to 1886, the year in which Charles Martin Hall perfected an electrolytic process for its reduction, aluminum was a costly metal. Its chief qualities were lightness, a high degree of resistance to corrosion, good electrical and heat conductivity, and good reflectivity for light and heat; it was considered as a material which would enjoy great usefulness if its price could be brought down. Prior to Hall's invention, aluminum sold for $8 a pound, and at one time had sold as high as $545 a pound. Now (1938) it costs approximately twenty cents a pound, and in 1937, 292,000,000 pounds of aluminum were made in the United States alone.

Hall, a native of Ohio and a graduate of Oberlin College, was twenty-two years old at the time he discovered the new process. After vainly attempting to interest a number of manufacturers, he went to Pittsburgh in 1888, and there discussed the possibilities of making aluminum on a commercial scale with Capt. Alfred E. Hunt, head of the Pittsburgh Testing Laboratory. Hunt immediately grasped the significance of the discovery, and in a few weeks was able to interest a group of men in forming a company to exploit the invention. The sum of $20,000 was raised for this purpose, and the Pittsburgh Reduction Company came into being.

The uses of the metal were at first confined to novelties, but constant research improved the product, and its applications were widened with every passing year. The addition of small amounts of other metals to aluminum produced various grades of alloys which could be used in an infinite number of ways, greatly widening the metal's sphere of influence.

In 1907 the name of the Pittsburgh Reduction Company was changed to that of the Aluminum Company of America, in order to identify the firm more closely with the product it manufactured. The virgin metal, of which this firm is the sole producer in the United States, is taken by thousands of fabricators and made into tens of thousands of commodities. The first large field which aluminum entered was that of cooking utensils, but today only a fraction of the annual tonnage is earmarked for this purpose. Aluminum and its alloys find their largest use in the field of transportation, where they are employed in the manufacture of airplanes, bus and truck bodies, stream-lined trains, street and subway cars, railroad cars, automobiles, vessels of various types, engines, outboard motors, motorcycles and bicycles.

Aluminum alloys of high strength are used in the construction of bridge floor systems, dragline booms and buckets, shovel dippers, heavy-duty dump trucks, hopper cars, flood bulkheads, mine skips, and man cages. Because it is inert to many chemicals, aluminum is used in the form of tanks, carboys, and other types of containers. Many dairies use aluminum tanks, while a number of important American breweries are equipped with aluminum fermenting and storage tanks, wort coolers, yeast tubs and beer barrels.

[Edwards, Frary and Jeffries, *The Aluminum Industry.*]

C. C. CARR

Amana Community, The. Consisting of approximately fifteen hundred people, living in seven villages and owning twenty-six thousand acres of land in one of the garden spots of Iowa, the Amana Community had for nearly a century conducted the most successful experiment in communism recorded in the annals of American history. Then in 1932 by unanimous vote this community reorganized as a joint stock company where stockholders are both owners and employees.

Born of religious enthusiasm, this unique community was founded in 1714 as the Community of True Inspiration in protest against the arbitrary rule of church and state. For mutual protection the Inspirationists congregated on several large estates in south Germany. But high rents and unfriendly governments forced them to seek a new home in America.

Under the leadership of Christian Metz the Inspirationists crossed the Atlantic in the early eighteen-forties and settled near Buffalo in Erie County, N. Y. Here they laid out six villages, called the place Ebenezer, built mills and factories, tilled the soil, and formally adopted communism as a way of life.

The rapid expansion of nearby Buffalo threatened that isolation which the Inspirationists had sought in the New World. And so, after twelve years at Ebenezer they moved to the frontier state of Iowa where they located in Iowa County, incorporated as the "Amana Society," and once more built houses, churches, schools, stores and mills, and continued their community life of "brothers all" through communism.

With the passing of years, the frontier disappeared, isolation became impossible, memories of the founding forefathers faded, the old idealism grew dim, spiritual enthusiasms waned, and in the midst of world depression in the early nineteen-thirties, the Community of True Inspiration faced a setting sun.

The crisis was met with intelligent leadership which realized that it would be impossible to maintain an 18th-century culture in the competitive gear of a machine age. And so, church and state were separated and the community was reorganized on the basis of co-operative capitalism in which the old communism is simply overtone.

[Bertha M. H. Shambaugh, *Amana, The Community of True Inspiration*, and *Amana That Was and Amana That Is*, published by The State Historical Society of Iowa.] BERTHA M. H. SHAMBAUGH

Ambassadors. The grade of ambassador is the highest rank in the diplomatic service*qv*. An ambassador has direct access, when desired, to a sovereign. The United States did not appoint officers of this rank until the close of the 19th century, contenting itself with ministers. The first ambassador of the United States was Thomas F. Bayard of Delaware, commissioned to Great Britain on March 30, 1893. The first ambassador to the United States was Sir Julian Pauncefote of Great Britain, who was presented to President Cleveland on April 11, 1893. Following this exchange of ambassadors between the United States and Great Britain, similar officers were appointed and received for the principal European powers. The first ambassador to Japan was Luke E. Wright of Tennessee, appointed Jan. 25, 1906; to China, Nelson T. Johnson of Oklahoma, appointed Sept. 17, 1935. The first ambassador of the United States to a Latin-American republic was Powell Clayton of Arkansas, who received his commission on Dec. 8, 1898. Although Matías Romero, who had long held the post of minister to the United States, had been appointed as first ambassador from Mexico with a commission dated Dec. 5, 1898, and arrangements had been made for the presentation of his credentials, his death prevented his reception; consequently the first ambassador received for a Latin-American republic was Manuel de Azpíroz of Mexico, who was presented to the President on March 30, 1899. Ambassadors today (1939) represent the United States in the following countries—the date of inception of the office is indicated in parentheses: Argentina (1914), Belgium (1919), Brazil (1905), Chile (1914), China (1935), Colombia (1938), Cuba (1923), France (1893), Germany (1893), Great Britain (1893), Italy (1893), Japan (1906), Mexico (1898), Panama (1939), Peru (1919), Poland (1919), Russia (1898), Spain (1913), Turkey (1906), and Venezuela (1938).

SAMUEL FLAGG BEMIS

Ambrister. *See* Arbuthnot and Ambrister, Case of.

Ambulance Companies. During Gen. Grant's attack on Fort Donelson*qv* in February, 1862, four ambulance companies and four field hospitals were organized by Surgeon H. S. Hewitt. As provisional organizations they were used to remove the wounded to field hospitals. Maj. Jonathan Letterman later fathered the formation of an expanded ambulance corps, large enough to serve for every battlefield need. In the World War, ambulance companies, organized with the assistance of the American Red Cross*qv*, were successfully used as units of divisional sanitary trains.

[*The Medical Department of the United States Army in the World War; Medical and Surgical History of the War of the Rebellion;* both compiled in the Office of the Surgeon General, United States Army.]

ROBERT S. THOMAS

Amelia Island Affair. The Embargo*qv* Act (1807) and the abolishment of the American slave trade*qv* (1808) made Amelia Island, on the coast of Spanish Florida*qv*, a resort for smugglers*qv* with sometimes as many as 300 square-rigged vessels in its harbor.

To Amelia in June, 1817, came one Gregor McGregor, styling himself the "brigadier general" of the United Provinces of the New Granada and Venezuela and general-in-chief of the armies of the two Floridas. He left for Nassau in September, but his followers were soon joined by Luis Aury, formerly associated with McGregor in South American adventures, but later leader of a piratical band on Galveston Island, Texas. Aury assumed control of Amelia, got a legislature elected, set a committee to drawing a constitution, and invited all Florida to unite in throwing off the Spanish yoke. The United States becoming tired of having its laws violated sent a naval force which captured Amelia Island Dec. 23, 1817, and put an end to the miniature republic.

The island was returned to the Spaniards prior to 1821.

[Carolina Mays Brevard, *History of Florida;* James Parton, *Andrew Jackson.*] W. T. CASH

Amen Corner was a celebrated niche in the corridor of the old Fifth Avenue Hotel (1859–1908), New York City, where politicians and reporters gathered to discuss coming political events. It was here that Sen. Thomas C. Platt's "Sunday School Class" was held in the late eighteen-nineties, and when the Senator announced his decisions his associates would say "Amen."

[*The Autobiography of Thomas Collier Platt,* compiled and edited by Louis J. Lang.]

HAROLD F. GOSNELL

Amendment Clause of the Constitution, THE, was adopted by the Convention of 1787*qv* with little controversy. It is contained in Article V of the United States Constitution. It provides two methods for the proposal of Amendments: either by a two-thirds vote of both Houses of Congress or, on the application of the legislatures of two-thirds of the states, Congress shall call a convention for proposing Amendments. In either case Amendments must be ratified in one of two ways: either by action of the legislatures of three-fourths of the states or by conventions in three-fourths of the same. Congress is empowered to provide either one of these methods of ratification.

During the entire one hundred and fifty years of our history under the Constitution the only method used for amendment, with but one exception, has been the proposal by Congress, and the ratification by the state legislatures. The exception was the Twenty-first Amendment*qv* which by direction of Congress was ratified by conventions in the states. From time to time changes in the method of ratification have been suggested in order that there might be some sort of popular vote upon the question. Up to the present time (1939) this has not resulted in any formal Amendment being passed by Congress.

[Edward S. Corwin, *The Constitution and What It Means Today.*] WILLIAM STARR MYERS

Amendments to the Constitution, to the number of twenty-one, may be said to have been made on seven different occasions.

Amendments I to X may be considered almost a part of the original Constitution. That document contained no Bill of Rights*qv*. The prevailing feeling in the Convention of 1787*qv* was that it was unnecessary to have one since the new government had no authority to interfere with the inalienable rights of individuals which already existed under the English Common Law. On the other hand, many states felt it to be necessary that definite provisions should be included in the Constitution which specifically would make safe the rights of individuals. For this reason the conventions in Massachusetts, New York and a number of other states ratified the Constitution (*see* Constitution, Ratification of the) with the recommendation that a Bill of Rights be added by the amending process when the new government was established. Various states proposed a total of 189 Amendments, many of which were upon like subjects. Twelve Amendments were finally proposed by Congress on Sept. 25, 1789. Ten of these were declared ratified by the necessary number of states on Dec. 15, 1791. They form a Bill of Rights and bind the National Government, but do not limit the powers of the states.

The Eleventh Amendment*qv* was proposed by Congress on Sept. 5, 1794, and was declared ratified on Jan. 8, 1798. It provided that the judicial power of the United States should not be construed to extend to any suit in law or equity against any one of the United States by citizens of another state or by citizens or subjects of any foreign state.

The Twelfth Amendment*qv* was proposed by Congress on Dec. 12, 1803, and declared ratified on Sept. 25, 1804. It was largely the result of the controversy following the tie in the election of Jefferson and Burr in 1800 (*see* Campaign of 1800), and provides primarily that presidential electors*qv* shall make a separate designation in their choice for President and Vice-President*qqv*.

The Thirteenth, Fourteenth, and Fifteenth Amendments*qqv* were the result of the Civil War struggle and may be considered as part of the same process. The Thirteenth Amendment was proposed by Congress on Feb. 1, 1865, and declared ratified on Dec. 18 of the same year. It abolished slavery*qv* and involuntary servitude. The Fourteenth Amendment was proposed by Congress on June 16, 1866, and declared ratified on July 22, 1868. It provided that national citizenship be primary and state citizenship derived therefrom. The most important provisions deal with the privileges or immunities of citizens, "due process of law," and the equal protection of the laws*qqv*. Other sections are mainly of historical interest since they provide for matters arising immediately out of the Civil War. The Fifteenth Amendment resulted in the enfranchisement of the Negroes*qv*. It was proposed by Congress on Feb. 26, 1869, and was declared ratified on March 30, 1870.

The Sixteenth and Seventeenth Amendments[qqv] were the result of the so-called Progressive movement[qv] during the early years of the 20th century. The Sixteenth Amendment empowers Congress to levy a national income tax[qv], was proposed by Congress on July 12, 1909, and was declared ratified on Feb. 25, 1913. The Seventeenth Amendment provides for the election of the United States Senators[qv] by direct vote of the people. It was proposed on May 16, 1912, and was declared ratified on May 31, 1913.

The World War exerted a profound effect upon the thought of our people and it was during the time when its influence still was of primary importance that the Eighteenth and Nineteenth Amendments[qqv] were adopted. The Eighteenth or "Prohibition"[qv] Amendment was proposed on Dec. 18, 1917, and declared ratified on Jan. 29, 1919. The Nineteenth or Woman's Suffrage[qv] Amendment was proposed on June 4, 1919, and declared ratified on Aug. 18, 1920.

The latest two Amendments may be described as the direct results of the New Deal[qv] movement. The Twentieth Amendment[qv] provides that the terms of the President and Vice-President shall begin on Jan. 20 and those of senators and representatives on Jan. 3 of the appropriate years. It was proposed on March 2, 1932, and was ratified on Feb. 6, 1933.

The Twenty-first Amendment[qv] repealed the Eighteenth or "Prohibition" Amendment by means of conventions in the states. It passed Congress on Feb. 20, 1933, and was declared ratified on Dec. 5 of the same year. It is the only Amendment in which the ratification by state conventions has been authorized and required by the action of Congress.

[Edward S. Corwin, *The Constitution and What It Means Today.*] WILLIAM STARR MYERS

"America." *See* "My Country, 'Tis of Thee."

America, Discovery of. "Traditionally, the history of America begins with the 'discovery' in 1492. Now, that date does mark an important episode—the first piloting of sailing vessels across the Atlantic Ocean, an episode comparable with the first piloting of airplanes across the same sea. But neither was a feat of discovery." (Edgar Lee Hewett.) In other words, America was populated before the continents were "discovered" by western Europeans. It is the consensus of opinion of anthropologists at the present time, that man did not develop, indigenously, in America, but that early man came from the Mongoloid groups of central Asia and probably "discovered" and entered North America by way of Alaska, either by crossing Bering Strait, or possibly by an isthmus or other land bridge which may have existed at the time.

About the year 1000 A.D. roving Norsemen[qv], starting from the Scandinavian colonies in Greenland, may have reached the coast of North America anywhere between Labrador and the Chesapeake. If they did, they left no undisputed archæologic evidences of their visit. The legends of the voyages of Leif Ericsson and Thorfinn Karlsefne depend upon three manuscripts of sagas written more than three hundred years after the possible "discovery" of that part of America which Leif called "Vinland the Good." Admitting Leif to have been the "discoverer" of America, Edward Channing aptly said, "The history of America would have been precisely what it has been if Leif Ericsson had never been born and if no Northman had ever steered his knǫrr west of Iceland."

On the other hand, it is an undisputed historic fact that on Aug. 3, 1492, the Genoese, Christopher Columbus, sailed from Palos, Spain, under the authority of the King and Queen of that country. On Oct. 11, 1492, he saw, and the next day Columbus and his party landed on, some island in the Bahamas which the Indians called Guanahani, and which Columbus rechristened San Salvador. Its exact identity today has never been conclusively established, but many good scholars have accepted Watling Island as his first landfall. Following this Columbus made three other voyages to the New World (1495, 1499 and 1502), during which he touched the coasts of South and Central America. But it must be remembered there is a documented story that one of the factors which induced Columbus to make his voyage was his actually meeting with, or knowledge of, a Spanish pilot who brought back news of having been wrecked on an island far west of the Madeiras as early as 1484.

Possibly independently, John Cabot[qv] sailed from Bristol, England, in May, 1497, and some time in June probably discovered the continent of North America. In 1499, Alonso de Ojeda and Juan de la Cosa visited South America, and with them went Americus Vespucius who wrote such popular accounts of his own deeds that the German geographer, Martin Waldseemüller, coined the word "America"[qv] in a book published in 1507. The inevitability of the so-called discovery of America by Europeans is illustrated by the fact that the Portuguese, Pedro Cabral, in 1500, tried to reach India by way of the African coast, and was accidentally blown to the west where unintentionally he reached the coast of Brazil.

The island of Espagnola (Hispaniola-Santo Domingo) became the Spanish outpost from which further discoveries of the mainland were made. Thence Vasco Nuñez de Balboa went to Central America, crossed the Isthmus of Panama and discovered the Pacific Ocean, Sept. 25, 1513. The eastern coast of the mainland of North America had been seen and was cartographically traced by 1502. On Easter Sunday, 1513, Juan Ponce de Leon[qv], from Espagnola, found his way to the site of the present city of St. Augustine, Fla. Francisco Gordillo coasted as far north as Cape Fear (1521) and Lucas Vasquez de Ayllon[qv] followed and got as far as the James River in Virginia (1526). Meantime Hernando Cortés had landed in Mexico and conquered it in one of a series of the most amazing expeditions in all history (1519). Panfilo de Narvaez[qv] explored western Florida, and possibly Georgia (1528–36) while his treasurer Alvar Nuñez Cabeza de Vaca[qv] walked overland from Pensacola Bay, Fla., to the Gulf of California. In 1539 Hernando de Soto[qv] took an expedition from Tampa Bay, Fla., marched north to the Savannah River, turned west and proceeded overland until he reached the Mississippi in 1541.

By this time Antonio de Mendoza[qv] had become viceroy of New Spain (Mexico, as opposed to Peru) and from his bailiwick, Franciscan[qv] friars were pushing up into what is now "The Southwest"[qv] of the United States. Fray Marcos de Niza (1539) brought back such reports that Francisco Vasquez de Coronado[qv] started out in April of 1540 on an expedition which took him as far north as central Kansas (1541).

So much for the Spaniards. Meantime the French had entered the field of exploration. Giovanni da Verrazzano, acting under the favor of Francis I, came to North America in 1524 and possibly saw the Lower Bay of New York. Jacques Cartier coasted Labrador in 1534, and in the next year entered and explored the St. Lawrence to the La Chine Rapids above Quebec. The discovery of much of the present area of the United States from the north was the work of Samuel de Champlain[qv], who found Maine in 1603–4, and Cape Cod in 1605, and got as far as central New York State in 1615.

Last, but most effective of the discovering nations was England. The Hawkins—William, John, and James—roamed the West Indies. Sir Francis Drake[qv] doubled Cape Horn and reached the coast of California, near, if not at, San Francisco Bay in June, 1579. In 1602 Bartholomew Gosnold reached the coast of Maine near Cape Porpoise, skirted Cape Cod (which he named) and found Narragansett Bay. George Weymouth in 1605 sighted Nantucket and then headed north to find the coast of Maine in the neighborhood of Monhegan and the Gorges Islands.

Mention should be made of an alleged discovery of America by Swedes and Norwegians from Greenland in the 13th century, through Hudson Bay and the Red River of the North into the present State of Minnesota. This theory rests on an inscribed stone and certain artifacts which need further study (*see* Kensington Stone, The). There are also stories of pre-Columbian discoveries of America by the Chinese, Welsh, Irish, Phœnicians and others. These are all legendary.

[Justin Winsor, *Narrative and Critical History of America;* Edward Channing, *History of the United States,* Vol. I.]

RANDOLPH G. ADAMS

America, THE, is an American yacht which in 1851 won the trophy cup presented by the Royal Yacht Squadron, the famous America's Cup. She served later as a Confederate despatch boat, was captured, served as practice ship at the Naval Academy, defended the Cup in 1870, was sold to Gen. B. F. Butler in 1873, and in 1917 to Charles H. W. Foster of the Eastern Yacht Club. She was permanently docked at the Naval Academy in 1921.

[J. S. Hughes, *Famous Yachts;* W. M. Thompson, *The Yacht America.*]

LOUIS H. BOLANDER

America, The Name. The earliest explorers and historians designated America as the "Indies," the "West Indies," or the "New World," and these terms remained the favorites in Spain and Portugal for over two centuries. Amerigo Vespucci was little known there, but beyond the Pyrenees the chief source of information on the discoveries was his account of his voyages, translated into Latin. A coterie of scholars at St. Dié, in Lorraine, chiefly Martin Waldseemüller and Mathias Ringmann, printed this in 1507 in *Cosmographiae Introductio,* a small work designed to accompany and explain a wall map and globe executed by Waldseemüller. In their work two names were suggested for the new "fourth part" of the world, one *Amerige* (pronounced "A-meri-gay," with the *-ge* from the Greek, meaning "earth"), and the other *America* (in the feminine form, parallel to *Europa* and *Asia*). The latter form was placed on Waldseemüller's maps of 1507, and their wide circulation brought about the gradual adoption of the name. Waldseemüller was aware of only South America as a continent, but Mercator in 1538 extended the designation to both continents.

Although Vespucci was not responsible for the giving of the name, the injustice to Columbus has aroused a series of protests since 1535. Various impossible origins of America have been suggested—that it comes from a native Indian word, from a sheriff of Bristol named Richard Ameryk, etc. The etymology of *Amerigo* can be traced to the old Germanic, meaning "ruler of the home." The name America is today highly ambiguous, since it often, as determined by the context, refers to the United States alone.

[Edward Gaylord Bourne, The Naming of America, in *American Historical Review*, Vol. X (1904), 41–51.]

ALLEN WALKER READ

American Academy of Arts and Letters, THE, founded in 1904 to protect and foster literature and the fine arts[qv], limits its membership to fifty, chosen from the larger National Institute of Arts and Letters. Among past and present members are counted many of the most distinguished Americans in letters and arts, including music.

JAMES TRUSLOW ADAMS

American Antislavery Societies. The first two American antislavery societies were the New York "Society for the Promoting of the Manumission[qv] of Slaves" and the "Pennsylvania Society for Promoting the Abolition of Slavery, the Relief of Free Negroes unlawfully held in Bondage and Improving the Condition of the African Race." Under their auspices the first convention of Abolition societies was held in Philadelphia in January, 1794. The Pennsylvania society was created in April, 1775, less than a week before the clash at Lexington and Concord[qv]; Benjamin Franklin and Dr. Benjamin Rush were among its presidents. John Jay, later Chief Justice, was the first president of the New York society on its organization in 1785. Other state societies were organized in Delaware, 1788, Maryland, 1789, Rhode Island and Connecticut, 1790, Virginia, 1791, and New Jersey, 1792. There were also Abolition societies in Charlestown, Md., and Winchester, Va., and one for the State of Kentucky. The older societies withered and died after the Missouri Compromise[qv] of 1820.

The militant Garrisonian Abolition movement[qv] led to the formation of the New England Anti-Slavery Society[qv] later called the Massachusetts Anti-Slavery Society, on Jan. 6, 1832, and the National Anti-Slavery Society in Philadelphia, Dec. 6, 1833. The New York Anti-Slavery Society was mobbed on the day of its organization, Oct. 21, 1835. From then on such organizations multiplied rapidly throughout the North. In 1835 there were 200; by 1840, 2000 auxiliary societies with a membership between 150,000 and 200,000. The American Anti-Slavery Society came to life in 1833. (*See* Antislavery Movement.)

[G. H. Barnes, *The Antislavery Impulse, 1830-1844.*]

OSWALD GARRISON VILLARD

American Automobile Association, THE, was organized March 4, 1902, in Chicago, Ill., by representatives of nine automobile clubs. Winthrop E. Scarritt, of the Automobile Club of America (New York City), was chosen first president.

The purposes of the A.A.A., as outlined in the formal call for organization, included: enactment of liberal motor vehicle laws; protection of legal rights of motor vehicle users; improvement of public highways; "development and introduction of the automobile"; equitable regulation of racing and endurance tests; and the provision of a medium for "counsel and interchange of information, ideas, and suggestions tending to the development and advancement of the art."

One of the earliest activities of the A.A.A. was the sponsoring, during the period 1905–13, of national reliability runs, popularly known as the "Glidden Tours." The A.A.A. also sponsored the good roads movement[qv] which resulted in the establishment of the Federal aid system[qv].

Gradually the motor clubs lost nearly all of their early social aspect and became primarily service and civic organizations. At the close of 1937 there were approximately 750 motor clubs, state associations, and motor club branches, with about 800,000 members, federated under the A.A.A. banner.

RICHARD W. TUPPER

American Bible Society, THE, was organized in New York City in 1816 by delegates from thirty-one local societies. Elias Boudinot was elected president. Its purpose was to produce and distribute the Scriptures in all languages and in all lands. Its work has continually prospered and expanded, and is furthered by a number of auxiliary and co-operating societies.

By the close of 1936 the whole Bible had been published in 176 languages, the New Testament in 214, portions or selections in 601 more, so that the Scriptures have now been published in 991 languages and dialects. During the year 1936 through its various agencies at home and abroad the Society put in circulation, in upwards of forty countries, a total of more than 7,760,000 Bibles, Testaments, Gospels and portions. A much appreciated feature of the Society's service is its ministry to the blind[qv]. Since the beginning of such work more than 125,000 embossed volumes in twenty-five languages and systems have been published.

The Society has a number of well-organized agencies in home and foreign lands. It is interdenominational, is governed by its own duly elected officers, managers, and committees, and asks for the observance of a Bible Sunday each year.

[Annual Reports of the American Bible Society.]

C. H. STACKPOLE

American Bottom, THE, narrow Mississippi River flood plain extending roughly 100 miles between Chester and Alton, Ill., took its name jointly perhaps from the first American settlers in the Old Northwest[qv] and from serving as part of the territorial boundary before the Louisiana Purchase[qv]. Site of pre-eminent burial and ceremonial mounds[qv], the bluff-hemmed strip became a lifeline of white population in the wilderness with settlements at Cahokia, Kaskaskia, Fort de Chartres, Bellefontaine[qqv], and Prairie du Rocher among others. Frontier travelers found the pond-dotted flat "miasmatic" but "extremely fertile."

[L. C. Beck, *Gazetteer of Illinois and Missouri;* H. I. Priestly, *The Coming of the White Man;* W. K. Moorehead and M. M. Leighton, *The Cahokia Mounds;* C. W. Alvord, *Cahokia Records, 1778-1790.*]

IRVING DILLIARD

American Colonization Society, THE (1817–1912), labored to remove free Negroes[qv] from the United States to Liberia[qv], and in addition, aided in manumitting[qv] slaves and in suppressing the slave trade[qv]. Local branches in every state, the churches and, in some cases, state legislatures supplied the money necessary to buy slaves, transport them, and establish them in Liberia. The Society transported 6000 Negroes between 1821 and 1867. Lack of funds, internal dissension and the opposition of extremists, North and South, hampered the efforts of the Society after 1840. After 1865 the Society functioned chiefly as trustee for the Liberian settlement.

[E. L. Fox, *The American Colonization Society, 1817-1840.*]

ELIZABETH W. MEADE

American Eagle, THE. *See* Eagle, The American.

American Expeditionary Forces, THE. This term was used to designate the American troops serving in Europe during the World War. The declaration of war found us without plans for organizing a force that would be capable of offensive action in modern warfare. On May 26, 1917, Maj. Gen. John J. Pershing, who had been selected by President Wilson to command our land forces abroad, was directed to proceed with his staff to France. Shortly after his arrival, convinced that military assistance on a vast scale would be necessary to Allied success, Gen. Pershing cabled the War Department that its minimum undertaking should contemplate 1,000,000 men in France by the following May, and that plans should be based on an ultimate force of 3,000,000. When the Armistice[qv] came, approximately 2,000,000 men had been transported to Europe, where they were trained, subsisted and equipped through their own supply system, and took a decisive part in bringing the war to a successful conclusion.

In the spring and early summer of 1918 a series of powerful German offensives threatened defeat of the Allies. In the crisis Gen. Pershing placed the entire resources of the American Expeditionary Forces at the disposal of the Allied High Command, postponing until July 24, 1918, the formation of the American First Army.

The assistance we gave the Allies in combat began in May with the capture of Cantigny[qv] by an American division in the first independent American offensive operation of the war. This was followed early in June by the entrance into battle of two divisions that stopped the German advance on Paris near Chateau-Thierry[qv]. In July two American divisions, with one Moroccan division, formed the spearhead of the counter-attack against the Chateau-Thierry salient, which marked the turning point of the war. Approximately 300,000 American troops were engaged in this Second Battle of the Marne. In the middle of September the American First Army of 550,000 men reduced the St. Mihiel[qv] salient. The latter part of September our Meuse-Argonne offensive[qv] was begun. After forty-seven days of intense fighting, this great battle ended brilliantly for our First and Second Armies on Nov. 11. More than 1,200,000 American soldiers had participated.

With the cessation of hostilities, attention was immediately turned to repatriating the troops. By the end of August, 1919, the last American division had embarked, leaving only a small force in occupied Germany, and on Sept. 1, 1919, Gen. Pershing and his staff sailed for the United States. (*See* World War.)

JOHN J. PERSHING

American Expeditionary Forces in Italy. As tangible proof of American co-operation, the Italian Minister of War urged that American units be sent to Italy. The 332nd Infantry Regiment, the 331st Field Hospital, and the 102nd Base Hospital were so despatched. With headquarters at Treviso, the 332nd Infantry made numerous marches to the front line, there to be observed by Austrians and Italians. The regiment participated in the attack to force a crossing of the Piave River[qv] (Oct. 26, 1918), and in the Battle of the Tagliamento River[qv] (Nov. 4). In March, 1919, American troops sailed from Italy.

[Cablegrams exchanged between War Department and Gen. Pershing; Letters from Chief, American Military Mission to Italy; Records of Supreme War Council; Regimental records, 332nd Infantry; all on file in United States War Department.]

ROBERT S. THOMAS

American Express Company. In 1850 two express companies then operating in the Northeast, Wells, Butterfield & Company and Livingston, Fargo & Company, were united to form a joint stock association with a capital of $150,000 known as the American Express Company. Henry Wells and William G. Fargo were the real governing geniuses of the company, and Wells became its first president. It operated on important lines in New England, followed the Great Lakes into the Midwest and Northwest, and even thrust fingers into Canada. It played no small part in the commercial development of the State of Michigan. Its incorporators organized Wells, Fargo & Company[qv] in 1852 as a sister organization for the western half of the country. The United States Express Company was organized in 1854 as a subsidiary, but in the course of two decades the two companies drifted apart and became sharp competitors. In 1915 the American operated on 61,500 miles of steam and electric railroads, water and stage lines, this being the second largest territory among the express companies. In 1918 all the companies merged their shipping interests in the American Railway Express Company, the American Express Company continuing as a banking and tourist bureau. In 1929 the Railway Express Agency, owned by the railroads, took over the American Railway Express Company.

[Alvin F. Harlow, *Old Waybills.*]

ALVIN F. HARLOW

American Federation of Labor. A federation of autonomous craft and industrial unions, chiefly the former, organized in 1886. The A. F. of L. was a reorganization of the Federation of Organized Trades and Labor Unions of the United States and Canada (1881). The object of the new federation was to promote vigorous independent trade unionism[qv] based upon craft autonomy, as opposed to the centrally controlled unionism of the Knights of Labor[qv] (1869). Each of the federation's constituent unions has its own government, determines its own policies, and conducts its own financial affairs. The federation has no powers except those conceded by its member unions through a written constitution and the annual convention. Craft autonomy with loose federation for the administration of common interests and the promotion of common purposes is the foundation of the A. F. of L. structure.

The organic unit of the federation is the local union. These locals are integrated in national or international unions. To achieve greater economic and political unity and power, A. F. of L. unions have formed city central labor unions or local federations. Even within the same industry, co-ordinating councils have been set up, such as the building trades councils. These deal with jurisdictional disputes between member unions and in other ways promote common interests. Crowning the structure of the federation is the Executive Council, consisting of a president, several vice-presidents, a treasurer and a secretary, which administers the affairs of the federation in the interim between conventions.

The general object of the A. F. of L. is continued improvement of the economic status of wage-earners. Thus far its accomplishments have been confined largely to the ranks of skilled workers. Its aim is attained chiefly through the medium of collective bargaining[qv] in the industrial field. To secure and make effective the method of collective bargaining, such weapons as the strike, boycott, picketing[qqv] and union labels are employed.

Sustained leadership has been a factor in the steady growth of the federation. Although serious losses in membership have occurred in each period of depression, the total membership increased from less than 200,000 in 1886 to approximately 4,100,000 in 1920. The membership in 1938 is estimated at 2,861,000. Since 1935 the leadership of the federation has been in serious conflict with the Committee for Industrial Organization[qv] over the issue of industrial versus craft unionism.

[American Federation of Labor, *History, Encyclopedia, Reference Book;* Selig Perlman, *A History of Trade Unionism in the United States;* Samuel Gompers, *Seventy Years of Life and Labor;* Lewis L. Lorwin, *The American Federation of Labor.*]

GORDON S. WATKINS

American Flag. *See* Flag of United States, The.

American Forces in Germany. *See* Army of Occupation (1918–23).

American Fur Company, THE, was incorporated for a period of twenty-five years, under the laws of the State of New York by an act passed on April 6, 1808. Its capital stock was not to exceed $1,000,000 for two years; thereafter it might not exceed $2,000,000. John Jacob Astor was the sole stockholder. From being a poor immigrant German lad in 1784, Astor had risen by 1808 to a position where he felt he could challenge unaided and successfully the two great fur-trading companies of Canada that were securing a large part of their furs within the limits of the United States—the North West Company[qv], with a capital of $1,200,000, and the Michilimackinac Company, capitalized at about $800,000. All that he needed was incorporation as a company. This might seem presumption on Astor's part, but events were to prove that his belief in himself was justified.

To get control of the fur trade of the Great Lakes[qv], the American Fur Company first came to an agreement with the North West Company and the Michilimackinac Company, whereby the South West Fur Company[qv], representing the three companies, was constituted Jan. 28, 1811, to last for five years. It was to confine its operations to the region south of the Canadian frontier. The War of 1812 stopped the normal course of the fur trade and by 1817 Astor was able to buy out his partners in the South West Company at a very low price. Thereupon the Northern Department of the American Fur Company was established, with headquarters at Mackinac[qv].

The next aim of the Company was to secure the St. Louis and Missouri River trade. In 1817 it made a tentative arrangement with powerful St. Louis firms, but it was not until 1822 that the Company established its own branch in St. Louis. This became known as the Western Department of the American Fur Company.

Still another obstacle to be overcome in securing monopoly of the fur trade of the United States was the abolition of the system of United States trading factories, which had been in existence since 1796 and which were a step in the direction of a safe, enlightened and humane Indian policy[qv]. However, they could compete successfully with Astor for the trade and so he determined to get rid of them. With the aid of such interested men as Lewis Cass and Thomas Hart Benton, he campaigned successfully. In 1822 the system was abolished (*see* Factory System, The Indian).

Private traders and other companies were treated in the same high-handed manner. Competition was stifled by fair means or foul. An act excluding foreigners from the trade was passed by Congress in 1816, probably at the instigation of the American Fur Company. In 1824 Congress passed another act, designating certain places at which trade might be carried on, which greatly hampered the Company's competitors while favoring the Company men.

In 1827 the greatest rival of the Company united with it—the Columbia Fur Company[qv]—which operated between the upper Mississippi and the upper Missouri, and known henceforth as the Upper Missouri Outfit of the American Fur Company.

By 1828 the Company had a virtual monopoly of the fur trade of the United States. In 1834, however, it became politic for the Company to withdraw from the Rocky Mountain area. In that year, too, Astor withdrew from the Company, whose charter had lapsed in April, 1833, though no notice had been taken of that fact. During the last decade of its existence, the Company made profits and declared dividends of over $1,000,000. After 1817 the Company had consisted (till 1823) of Astor, Ramsay Crooks, and Robert Stuart. After 1823 and until 1827 the only new partners were the St. Louis firms. In 1827 the Columbia Fur Company's men were added. In 1834 Astor sold out his interests: those in the Western Department to Pratte, Chouteau[qv] and Company; and those in the Northern Department to a group headed by Ramsay Crooks. This second group, of some ten stockholders, now became the American Fur Company. It lasted till 1842. During these eight years Ramsay Crooks was president of the Company. Its operations were confined roughly to the area between Detroit, the Ohio and the Red River of the North. It built vessels on the upper Great Lakes, established extensive fisheries on Lake Superior, marketed the furs of the St. Louis firm of Pratte, Chouteau and Company (after 1838 Pierre Chouteau, Jr., and Company), tried desperately to oust such important rivals as W. G. and G. W. Ewing of Fort Wayne and maintained something of a banking business throughout the area of its operations. After its failure in 1842 it seems to have been reconstituted once more in 1846 as a commission house. Its papers end for all practical purposes in 1847.

[Kenneth W. Porter, *John Jacob Astor, Business Man;* Grace Lee Nute, Papers of the American Fur Company, in *American Historical Review*, April, 1927.]

GRACE LEE NUTE

American Historical Association, THE, was formed at Saratoga, N. Y., on Sept. 9, 1884, and incorporated by act of Congress on Jan. 4, 1889, with headquarters in Washington. From the first it exerted a constructive influence in the organization of research, classification of official archives and in promoting the study of neglected fields. Its activities have been carried on chiefly through the *American Historical Review* (founded in 1895, taken over in 1898) and through standing committees, like the Historical Manuscripts Commission (1895) and the Public Archives Commission (1899). Significant reports have been issued by special committees, notably the Committees of Seven and of Eight on history in the secondary and elementary schools (published, 1899, 1909), the Commission on the Social Studies (in fifteen parts, 1932–37) and the Committee on Bibliography (*A Guide to Historical Literature,* 1931). Important publications have also been made through the Littleton-Griswold, the Beveridge and the Revolving funds. In 1903 a Pacific Coast Branch was founded, which since 1932 has issued the *Pacific Historical Review.*

[*Papers of the American Historical Association,* 1885-91; *Annual Reports,* Government Printing Office, 1890; J. F. Jameson, The American Historical Association, 1884-1909, *American Historical Review,* XV, 1-20.]

HENRY E. BOURNE

American Iron and Steel Institute, with its predecessor organizations, is one of the oldest trade associations in the United States, dating back to 1855. It assumed its present form in 1908, with Judge Elbert H. Gary, chairman of the United States Steel Corporation[qv], as its first president. Its development was in response to the need for a co-operative agency in the iron and steel industry[qv] for collecting and disseminating statistics and information, carrying on investigations, providing a forum for the discussion of problems and generally advancing the interests of the industry.

[Joseph H. Foth, *Trade Associations.*]

JOHN W. HILL

American Joint Commission to France. *See* France, American Joint Commission to.

American Labor Party, THE, arose during April, 1936, as a New York State unit of Labor's Non-Partisan League sponsored by John L. Lewis of the Committee for Industrial Organization[qv], Maj. G. L. Berry of the Pressmen's Union and Sidney Hillman of the Amalgamated Clothing Workers. The Party acting independently aided the re-election of President F. D. Roosevelt and Gov. Lehman of New York in 1936, and contributed to Mayor LaGuardia's re-election in November, 1937. Primarily a pressure group[qv], the American Labor Party has preferred to support those behind a program of social legislation rather than to enter independent candidates.

[P. W. Ward, The Coming Labor Party, *The Nation,* April 15, 1936.]

HARVEY WISH

American Legion, THE, is an organization of veterans of the World War. Any person who served in active duty in the army, navy, marine corps or coast guard[qqv] of the United States forces between April 6, 1917, and Nov. 11, 1918, and who received an honorable discharge, is eligible to membership. Also, the mothers, wives, daughters and sisters of Legion members are eligible to auxiliary membership. Col. Theodore Roosevelt, Jr., is given credit for first suggesting such an organization. On Feb. 16, 1919, some twenty men of the American Expeditionary Forces[qv] met in Paris, and had dinner together. "At that dinner the American Legion was born." Two subsequent organization meetings followed; one held in Paris, March 15–17, 1919; and the second in St. Louis, Mo., May 8–10, 1919. The Paris Caucus was attended by 1000 representative officers and enlisted men of the A. E. F. Col. Bennett C. Clark presided at this meeting, and an executive committee was appointed to confer with a similar executive committee in the United States to plan for the St. Louis Caucus. At the St. Louis meeting, May 8–10, 1919, final steps were taken to incorporate the American Legion. It was chartered by act of Congress, Sept. 16, 1919.

Early in its history, the American Legion announced the primary objectives for which it would strive. It declared itself a patriotic organization of the first order, and dedicated its efforts to "God and Country." Relief for the wounded and disabled veterans[qv] was placed first in its program. In 1922, it succeeded in having the United States Veterans Bureau[qv] established. Also, it secured the organization of a National Rehabilitation Service, to see that every veteran received proper hospital care and treatment, and adequate compensation. The Legion soon made itself felt as a pressure group[qv] in national politics. As early as 1920 the National Legislative Committee reported that it had secured the passage of bills embodying a fourfold bonus[qv] plan; a bill that raised the monthly allowance of disabled men; and an amendment to the Civil Service Law[qv], giving preference to honorably discharged soldiers, sailors and marines, seeking Federal positions.

In 1922 the American Legion inaugurated a child welfare[qv] program, and in 1925 it turned its attention to the aid and care of orphans of veterans. Another activity sponsored by the Legion was that of community service. By 1926 this veterans' organization had some 10,000 local posts scattered throughout the country, and each post was called upon to assist in programs looking toward civic improvements. A list of the projects included the creation of parks and playgrounds, the building of hospitals, the enlargement of public welfare work, safety-first campaigns, the organization of Junior Baseball Leagues and similar undertakings. In 1928, the Legion undertook another form of activity, known as that of giving emergency relief. Chief aid was given to the flood sufferers of the Mississippi Valley following the devastating floods of 1927 and 1928 (*see* Floods). This same service was repeated during the later floods of 1936 and 1937. As the Legion grew older and increased in membership (it had 1,053,909 paid up members in 1931), it expanded its program of activities. It became especially active in a nation-wide child welfare campaign in 1929–30. It threw its influence behind the child labor[qv] amendment then pending in forty-four states, and urged the passage of a bill providing for universal service of all able-bodied citizens, and for the conscription of wealth in time of war.

Early in the depression years of the 1930's the Legion adopted a program calling for the immediate payment of the Adjusted Service Certificates at face value (*see* Bonus). In 1934 a large home in Washington, D. C., was purchased (the National Headquarters of the American Legion are in Indianapolis, Ind.), to house the rehabilitation and legislative activities of the Legion. The campaign for the immediate payment of the bonus was vigorously pushed throughout the sessions of the 74th Congress. The Vinson Bill, as the act came to be known, finally passed both House and Senate in January, 1936, only to be vetoed by President Roosevelt. The veto was, however, promptly overridden, the vote in the House being 346 to 59, and in the Senate 76 to 16–"Thus ending in victory the years of efforts on the part of the Legion to obtain immediate payment of the certificates as an act of justice to World War veterans." Following this victory, and with the approach of the twentieth anniversary of its organization, the Legion announced that it was dedicating itself anew to a nation-wide program of public service. The aims listed include, Americanism, peace, national defense, neutrality, universal service, youth training, child welfare, community service, care of the disabled, protection of war widows and orphans, highway safety and the preservation of law and order.

[G. S. Wheat, *Story of the American Legion;* Marquis James, *History of the American Legion;* Marcus Duffield, *King Legion;* Knowlton Durham, *Billions for Veterans;* and *Reports of the Annual National Conventions of the American Legion.*]

JOHN W. OLIVER

American Liberty League, THE, was organized in August, 1934, with the express purpose of fighting radicalism[qv] and defending property rights and the United States Constitution. Among its organizers were many lifelong, though conservative Democrats, but it was clearly inimical to the "New Deal"[qv] and, because of this and its many wealthy members, was denounced by the F. D. Roosevelt administration as reactionary.

[Fifty-Eight Lawyers, *United States Law Review,* Vol. 69, pp. 505, 613; Vol. 70, p. 22.]

ALVIN F. HARLOW

American Management Association. A professional association for business executives. Organized in 1913 in personnel field. Took present name in 1923 and broadened scope. Personnel, Insurance, Financial, Marketing, Office, Production and General Management divisions hold annual conferences and publish papers. *Management Review, Personnel* and *Business Conditions and Forecasts* are published. The Association makes no profit, does no lobbying and advances no propaganda. Its interests are practical solution of management problems and development of the science of management.

[*The American Management Association and its Predecessors,* Special paper No. 17.]

ALVIN E. DODD

American-Mexican Mixed Claims Commissions, THE. Behind United States-Mexican relations lies the constant question of unsettled damage claims. The first joint commission (1839–42) settled American claims with awards totaling $2,026,139.68. Payments were interrupted by revolution, and Mexico failed to ratify another claims convention (1843). The question thus became a factor in the Mexican War[qv]. By the Treaty of Guadalupe Hidalgo[qv] the United States paid, through a special (American) commission, claims against Mexico for $3,250,000, including the fraudulent Gardiner award[qv]. A second joint commission (1869–76) settled 2025 claims arising 1848–68 with awards to Mexico of $150,498.41 (167 cases) and to United States $4,125,622.20 (186 cases), including interest on the Pious Fund[qv].

The Bucareli Conference (Mexico City, 1923), which arranged for recognition of the Obregon government, brought two joint commissions. A general claims commission (1923–31) awarded $2,599,166.10, plus interest, to the United States, and $39,000 to Mexico, and disposed of 148 out of 2781 claims arising since 1868. Agrarian claims were excluded when the commission was renewed (1932). By executive agreement (1934) the commission reported its findings to both governments (1937) for agreement by direct negotiations. The special (Revolutionary, 1910–20) claims commission met twice (1926 and 1931), hearing and dismissing two claims. Mexico refused (1932) to renew the commission, but settled the claims (1935) for $5,448,020.14. A special (American) commission was then established (1935) to settle with claimants by 1938.

[F. S. Dunn, *Diplomatic Protection of Americans in Mexico;* A. H. Feller, *Mexican Claims Commissions, 1923-34.*]

HAROLD E. DAVIS

American (or Know-Nothing) Party, THE, enjoyed a meteoric career during the 1850's. It was founded in New York in 1849 as a secret patriotic society known as the Order of the Star Spangled Banner, but experienced little success until after 1852. Expansion from that time on was so rapid that by 1854 a national organization could be perfected.

This phenomenal growth was due partly to the charm of secrecy with which the party clothed itself. Members were initiated and sworn not to reveal its mysteries; their universal answer to questions was "I know nothing about it," thus giving their organization its popular name: the Know-Nothing Party. All who joined were pledged to vote only for natives, to work for a twenty-one-year probationary period preceding naturalization, and to combat the Catholic Church.

More important in accounting for the party's success was the period in which it thrived. Older party lines had been disrupted by the Kansas-Nebraska Act[qv] and many voters, unwilling to cast their lot either with proslavery Democrats or antislavery Republicans, found refuge with the Know-Nothings. At this time, too, anti-Catholic sentiment, long fostered by churches, societies and the press, was reaching its height. The American Party attracted thousands of persons who sincerely believed that Catholicism and immigration menaced their land.

These factors account for the startling strength shown by the party. In the elections of 1854 and 1855 it was successful in a number of New England and border states and its supporters fully expected to carry the country in 1856.

By this time, however, the slavery issue had caused a split in Know-Nothing ranks. A proslavery resolution, pushed through the 1855 convention by Southern delegates, caused a lasting breach and the American Party entered the election of 1856[qv] so hopelessly divided that its presidential candidate, Millard Fillmore, carried only the State of Maryland. This crushing defeat and the growing sectional antagonism over slavery brought about the party's rapid end.

[L. D. Scisco, *Political Nativism in New York State;* L. F. Schmeckebier, *History of the Know-Nothing Party in Maryland;* M. E. Thomas, *Nativism in the Old Northwest, 1850-1860;* Ray Allen Billington, *The Protestant Crusade.*]

RAY ALLEN BILLINGTON

American Peace Society, THE (Washington, D. C.), was founded upon the initiative of William Ladd, in New York City, May 8, 1828. It was formed by the merging of many state and local societies, of which the oldest dated from 1815. Ladd was an advocate of a "Congress and High Court of Nations." Since 1828 the Society has regularly published a periodical, now called *World Affairs.*

A. CURTIS WILGUS

American Philosophical Society, THE, was founded by Benjamin Franklin in 1743 "for the promotion of useful knowledge among the British plantations in America." It is the oldest learned society[qv] in America and from its foundation to the present time has included in its membership the leading scientists, scholars, statesmen and public servants of this country and some of the most illustrious of foreign lands. Membership is limited to 500.

Its publications are the *Proceedings,* the *Transactions,* the *Memoirs* and the annual *Year Book.* The Library includes more than 80,000 volumes, 50,000 pamphlets and 5500 maps in addition to a rich collection of MSS. including the largest existing collection of Frankliniana. During the years 1934–38 the Society distributed nearly 300 grants in aid[qv] of research of an aggregate sum of about $347,000. The total endowment is approximately $5,000,000.

EDWIN GRANT CONKLIN

American Protective Association, THE, a secret anti-Catholic society, was founded at Clinton, Iowa, in 1887 by Henry F. Bowers. It grew slowly in the Middle West until the Panic of 1893[qv] brought home to natives the economic rivalry of second generation immigrants and this, combined with rural antagonism toward urban Catholics, the effective propaganda of nativistic[qv] newspapers and speakers, revived Catholic demands for a share in public school funds, and political instability following the Democratic victory in 1892 attracted a million members by 1896. This voting strength was utilized to gain control of local Republican organizations and carry elections throughout the Middle West but in 1896 the Association split over the question of supporting William McKinley, and its members deserted rapidly amidst the greater excitement of the free silver^qv^ campaign. It lingered on despite steadily declining support until 1911.

[H. J. Desmond, *The A.P.A. Movement. A Sketch.*]

RAY ALLEN BILLINGTON

American Railway Association, THE, had its inception in meetings of General Managers and ranking railway operating officials known as Time Table Conventions, the first of which was held on Oct. 1, 1872, at Louisville, Ky. In 1875 the group changed its name to General Time Convention and in October, 1891, to American Railway Association. In January, 1919, ten separate groups of operating officers were amalgamated with the association and carried on their activities as divisions, sections or committees of the larger group.

[American Railway Association, Historical Statement; Present Activities, Aug. 15, 1921.]

HARVEY WALKER

American Railway Union, THE, was started by Eugene V. Debs^qv^ in June, 1893, in an attempt to unite all railroad workers. In June, 1894, it ordered its members not to handle Pullman cars in sympathy with the Pullman shop strikers^qv^. Violence resulting, President Cleveland sent troops to stop interference with the mails. The union officers were jailed for violating an injunction secured by the railroads under the Sherman Act^qv^. The strike was lost, and the union collapsed.

[McAlister Coleman, *Eugene V. Debs.*]

JAMES D. MAGEE

American Republican Party, THE, a minor nativistic^qv^ political organization, was launched in New York in June, 1843, largely as a protest against immigrant voters and officeholders. In 1844 it carried municipal elections in New York City and Philadelphia and expanded so rapidly that by July, 1845, a national convention was called. This convention changed the name to the Native American Party and drafted a legislative program calling for a twenty-one-year period preceding naturalization^qv^ and other sweeping reforms in the naturalization machinery. Failure to force congressional action on these proposals, combined with the growing national interest in the Mexican problem, led to the party's rapid decline.

[L. D. Scisco, *Political Nativism in New York State;* Ray Allen Billington, *The Protestant Crusade.*]

RAY ALLEN BILLINGTON

American Republics, Bureau of. *See* Pan-American Union, The.

American Revolution. *See* Revolution, American.

American Sugar Refining Company, THE, has been since its incorporation in New Jersey, Jan. 10, 1891, the largest business unit in the sugar refining industry. Like its predecessor, the Sugar Refineries Company (1887), it consolidated most of the existing plants with a view to cost reduction and price control and for many years carried the popular sobriquet, "The Sugar Trust"^qv^. The Supreme Court declared in the much-cited Knight case^qv^, March 24, 1894, that its purchase of the stock of competitors was not a combination in restraint of trade^qv^. The combination expanded horizontally for about twenty years as new competitors arose; later it expanded vertically, undertaking the production of cane and raw sugar in Cuba and acquiring lumber interests. The company was investigated by the Industrial Commission in 1900 and by a special congressional committee in 1911–12. Federal suit for its dissolution begun in 1910 was terminated by consent decree announced Dec. 21, 1921, when it was stated that its effective control of refined sugar had dropped from 72% to 24%.

[Jenks and Lauck, *The Trust Problem.*]

LELAND H. JENKS

American System, a term applied by Henry Clay, in his tariff speech of March 30–31, 1824, by which he sought to justify the greater measure of protection that he was trying to secure in the tariff bill under discussion. His object was to create a home market and "to lay the foundations of a genuine American policy"; he wished to check the decline of American industry and offered a remedy which, he said, "consists in modifying our foreign policy, and in adopting a genuine American system." By this he proposed to eliminate the dependence upon the foreign market with the result that American industries would flourish and a home market for the surplus of agricultural products would develop. Such a program was presumed to offer attractions not only to the eastern manufacturer but also to the western farmer. Implicit in the arrangement was the availability of more revenue for internal improvements^qv^, upon which Clay had already taken a leading position.

Since Clay became known as "the father of the American system," the practice soon developed of applying this label to collateral measures for which he stood. With his tariff^{qv} and internal improvement policies was combined his proposal to have the national government distribute among the states the proceeds of the sale of public lands[qv]. Clay's contemporary biographer, Calvin Colton, declared (I, 428) : "There are collateral measures, and measures of affinity, having more or less of an intimate connection. There are numerous measures of result emanating from this system. But internal improvement, and protection of American interests, labor, industry and arts, are commonly understood to be the LEADING measures, which constitute the AMERICAN SYSTEM."

[C. Colton, *The Life and Times of Henry Clay;* T. H. Clay, *Henry Clay.*]

ARTHUR C. COLE

American Telephone and Telegraph Company. Thomas Sanders of Haverhill, Mass., and Gardiner G. Hubbard of Cambridge each supplied one half the funds necessary to finance Alexander Graham Bell in the experiments which led to his obtaining patents on the telephone[qv] (1875–76), with the understanding that the three owned the patents jointly. After the telephone became a workable instrument, the three patentees organized on July 9, 1877, a joint stock concern known as the Bell Telephone Company, with Hubbard as trustee, to whom all patent rights were assigned. Thomas A. Watson, who had been Bell's faithful assistant all through the experiments, was given a tenth interest. On Feb. 12, 1878, the New England Telephone Company was organized to control the business in that territory. The need for more capital and a better organization to cover the country led to the organization of a new Bell Telephone Company minus Hubbard's trusteeship and with a capital of $450,000 in the summer of 1878. Technical improvements devised by others were bought and incorporated with the Bell instrument. A group of new stockholders headed by William H. Forbes now came into virtual control of the company's policy and these desired unity of all telephone interests. Accordingly on Feb. 17, 1879, the National Bell Telephone Company, capitalized at $850,000, was organized and took over the existing Bell and New England companies.

A period of litigation over telephone patents followed, the Bell's chief opponent being the Western Union Telegraph Company[qv], which had bought Edison's and other patent rights. The Western Union capitulated to the Bell company on Nov. 10, 1879. A new and enormously larger corporation to control the nation-wide business through the ownership of many small companies was now desired. On March 20, 1880, the American Bell Telephone Company was organized, with a capital of $7,350,000. As the telephone became more efficient, the American Telephone and Telegraph Company was organized Feb. 28, 1885, with a capital of $100,000, to build and operate long-distance lines. For fifteen years the latter was a subsidiary company, but in 1900 the American Bell passed out of existence, and the American Telephone and Telegraph became a great holding company for city and regional organizations, as well as the owner of long lines. In 1909 this company took over the Western Union Telegraph Company, but the Government, under the Sherman Anti-Trust Act[qv], forced the separation of the two companies in 1913.

[Alvin F. Harlow, *Old Wires and New Waves.*]

ALVIN F. HARLOW

American Tobacco Case, THE. In this decision, 1911 (221 U. S. 106), the Supreme Court, following the same line of reasoning as in the Standard Oil[qv] decision of the same year, found that the American Tobacco Company had attempted to restrain commerce and monopolize the tobacco business in violation of the Sherman Anti-Trust Act[qv]. "Restraint of trade"[qv], the Court declared, did not embrace "all those normal and usual contracts essential to individual freedom, and the right to make which was necessary in order that the course of trade might be free," but on the other hand, in view of "the general language of the statute, and the public policy which it manifested, there was no possibility of frustrating that policy by resorting to any disguise or subterfuge of form, since resort to reason rendered it impossible to escape by any indirection the prohibitions of the statute."

[E. D. Durand, *The Trust Problem;* J. A. McLaughlin, *Cases on the Federal Anti-Trust Laws of the United States;* W. W. Willoughby, *The Constitutional Law of the United States.*]

W. A. ROBINSON

American Tract Society, THE, organized in New York City (1825) for the dissemination of Christian literature in leaflet form, co-ordinated the activities of numerous local societies. It is interdenominational and is governed by an executive committee. It soon took rank with the American Bible Society[qv]. During its history a total publication of 834,873,708 copies of Christian literature has been produced and distributed. Colporteurs have visited two and one-half million families. Five hundred tracts in thirty languages have recently been put in circulation.

[*Methodist Year Book,* 1934.]

C. H. STACKPOLE

Americanism. By an Apostolic Letter, entitled *Testem benevolentiæ* (from the first two words of the text), addressed by Leo XIII to the American hierarchy on Jan. 22, 1899, the pontiff, while expressing praise for the progress Catholicism had made in the United States, took occasion to point out some dogmatic and moral tendencies which he signaled out for correction. The three main points of discussion were: the adaptation of Christian teaching to our advancing civilization, freedom of spirit in matters of faith and of Christian life, and the division of virtues into active and passive. Principal among these was the alleged effort on the part of some American ecclesiastics to have the Church adapt her teaching to contemporary religious thought. Hence the name as used in the Brief. The term "Americanism" is vague, although it was defined at the time as "a spirit that is democratic, tolerant, anti-mediæval, up-to-date, individualistic, believing chiefly in good works, and lastly, very ultramontane" (Adrian Fortescue, *Folia Fugitiva,* N. Y., 1907, 276). The Latin and English Text of the Brief will be found in the *American Catholic Quarterly Review,* XXIV (April, 1899), 184–201.

[Peter Guilday, The Church in the United States: 1870–1920, *Catholic Historical Review,* January, 1921.]

PETER GUILDAY

Americanization began on the first frontier. Traders and settlers, from the beginning, adapted their food, clothing, shelter, religion, warfare, education, agriculture, transportation and trade to the environment and to Indian modes. The process became more marked along the mid-18th century frontier where Scotch-Irish and Germans met pioneers from the eastern settlements and rubbed elbows with the Indians and with the Indian traders, producing a new American society in flux, characterized by religious emotionalism and by an optimistic democracy. The war spirit of the American Revolution and of the War of 1812 molded the diverse elements into a vigorous nationality.

Jacksonian Democracy[qv] after 1825 furnished a new instrument of Americanization in such local party organizations as Tammany Hall[qv]. The common school revival in the 1830's and the rapid spread of academies[qv] which followed caught up and Americanized the foreign-born in the movement for general education. From the earliest times foreign-born Americans like Albert Gallatin had pointed the way to Americanization, but beginning with the years immediately preceding the Civil War, the German foreign language press, led by such men as Francis Lieber, assumed an increasingly important but contradictory role of keeping alive German consciousness and directing it toward Americanization. Nativism[qv] in the 1850's emphasized the problem of Americanization but contributed nothing to its solution.

Civil War army service Americanized the German and Irish immigrants of the 1850's, and post-war expansion also assisted, especially by employment in railroad construction and in the growing industries. But increasing immigration[qv] and the change in the sources of the immigration after 1890 presented new problems of assimilation[qv]. Homesteaders living under frontier conditions were easily Americanized by the common schools, Protestant churches, the labor and dangers of pioneer life and democratic political organizations, but it was more difficult with the new immigrants herded into rapidly growing city slums or into mining and manufacturing towns. Since much of the new immigration was Roman or Orthodox Catholic or Jewish, Protestant churches came to play a less important part in its Americanization. During the 1880's settlement houses[qv] began to Americanize the community life of the slums with a program of neighborliness. Mutual benefit societies and national cultural organizations became common. But no consciously organized program of Americanization appeared, until attention was directed to the seriousness of the situation by the Immigration Commission (1911).

The World War found 15,000,000 European-born immigrants in the United States, including 3,000,000 adults who could not speak English, and 9,000,000 who read foreign newspapers exclusively. New York City alone had half a million non-English speaking inhabitants. The drive for Americanization started in Cleveland July 4, 1914, with the organization of the first Americanization day. By 1915 at least 150 cities observed such a day and in the same year a national Americanization Committee was organized. In April, 1918, a conference on Americanization was called by the Secretary of the Interior. Soon state and city committees were established, and Americanization schools appeared throughout the country. Trade unions[qv], instead of assisting in the process, discouraged Americanization by discriminating against foreign-born membership. Americanization seemed also to weaken family life by encouraging a second generation revolt against family and church and their Old World moral codes.

Two other aspects of Americanization may be noticed briefly: that of the Indians, accomplished through trade, missions, treaties, reservations, schools, finally culminating in the Dawes Act of 1887[q.v.], and the less conscious Americanization of the Negro through missions, schools, slavery and post-slavery economic exploitation.

[Emory Bogardus, *Essentials of Americanization;* J. W. Jenks and W. J. Lauck, *Immigration Problem;* R. E. Park and H. A. Miller, *Old World Traits Transplanted.*]

HAROLD E. DAVIS

American's Creed, THE. In a nation-wide contest (1917) for "the best summary of American political faith," this 100-word composite of fundamental expressions by the builders of the republic was compiled by William Tyler Page, who received the award of $1000, which was offered by the city of Baltimore as "the home of the Star-Spangled Banner[q.v.]."

[*The Book of the American's Creed.*]

MATTHEW PAGE ANDREWS

America's Cup Races, THE. *See* Yacht Racing.

Amiens, The Treaty of, signed March 27, 1802 (after agreement in October, 1801, on preliminary articles) between France and Great Britain, ended the war declared by France on Feb. 1, 1793, and terminated the first phase of the wars of the French Revolution. Its significance for American history is that it afforded a short breathing spell in the controversy with the belligerents over neutral rights, and offered an interval of peace during which Napoleon turned to the newly acquired province of Louisiana as a field for the building of a great colonial empire. On the eve of war again with Great Britain in 1803, he sold Louisiana[q.v.] to the United States to cash in on the territory before it should be captured by superior British sea power.

[Henry Adams, *History of the United States during the First Administration of Thomas Jefferson,* Vols. I, II.]

SAMUEL FLAGG BEMIS

Amish Mennonites, THE, are followers of Jacob Amman. They separated from the Mennonites[q.v.] in Europe in the late 17th century because of a strict interpretation of the practice of "avoidance" and "shunning," i.e., ostracizing, socially and religiously, violators of church rule.

Ultraconservatism is the chief characteristic of their cult. They use hooks and eyes instead of buttons, wear beards but ban the mustache, the badge of the soldier.

They first appeared in Pennsylvania about 1714, and now (1939) have settlements in Pennsylvania, Iowa, Maryland, Indiana, Illinois, Ohio, Delaware, Kansas, Michigan, Missouri, Montana, Nebraska, Oklahoma, Oregon and Virginia.

[C. H. Smith, *The Mennonite Immigration to Pennsylvania.*]

H. H. SHENK

***Amistad* Case** (1839). The fifty-four slaves on this Spanish schooner mutinied near Cuba, murdered part of the crew, and caused the remainder to sail into Long Island Sound and the jurisdiction of American courts. Piracy charges were quashed but some salvage claims awarded by legal proceedings in Connecticut. In 1841 the Supreme Court declared the Negroes free. Private charity provided their transportation back to Africa. This case offers an interesting comparison with the *Creole* affair[q.v.].

[J. W. Barber, *A History of the Amistad Captives.*]

JARVIS M. MORSE

Amite, Battle of, was a skirmish fought on the Amite River in Mississippi Territory, August, 1808, between a party of nineteen frontier settlers and a marauding band of thirty Choctaw Indians[q.v.] who were committing depredations in that vicinity. Regular troops and militia were called out, but the Indians disappeared.

[Dunbar Rowland, ed., *Mississippi* (Cyclopedic), I.]

WALTER PRICHARD

Amnesty (1862–98). Proclamations issued by President Lincoln, primarily as war measures, and by President Johnson as aids to Reconstruction[q.v.], extended pardon and re-enfranchisement, with certain exceptions and restrictions, to those then in or who had been in rebellion against the United States Government (*see* Civil War). The constitutional meaning of amnesty was not clearly understood, but it was thought to be a sort of general or group pardon. Although the word does not appear in the Constitution, Congress, in the Confiscation Act[q.v.], July 17, 1862, granted to the President the right of "amnesty." Lincoln made no use of this privilege until after the Union victory at Chattanooga[q.v.], when, Dec. 8, 1863, he issued his first amnesty proclamation, supplementing it, March 26, 1864, with another restricting the scope of the first. On May 29, 1865, Johnson proclaimed amnesty and pardon to a degree sufficient to provide an adequate number of "rebels" to man the restored state governments. As Johnson's contest with the Radical Republicans[q.v.] became more bitter, Congress determined to reconstruct the South in its own way. On Jan. 7, 1867, it angrily repealed the amnesty grant authorized in the Confiscation Act, and then, in the third reconstruction act, July 19, 1867, repeated its stand that a presidential pardon did not re-enfranchise. Johnson, denying the right thus to abrogate his presidential power of pardon[qv], issued three more amnesty proclamations—Sept. 7, 1867, July 4, 1868, and Dec. 25, 1868—the last granting general amnesty without the formality of oath. These, however, were mere gestures so far as the franchise was concerned because Congress, in the Fourteenth Amendment[qv], adopted July 28, 1868, had finally secured control of the authority to grant amnesty, at least to the extent of restoring the right to hold office. Henceforth amnesty would be extended by legislative statute rather than by executive proclamation.

Under the Fourteenth Amendment over 150,000 persons were barred from holding office unless Congress, by a two-thirds vote, should remove their disabilities. During the next few years much time was spent in enacting individual amnesty acts, mostly applying to those ex-Confederates who were willing to join the radical party. In order to satisfy public demand and to aid in Grant's re-election (*see* Campaign of 1872), Congress, on May 22, 1872, passed a general amnesty act, which re-enfranchised all except between 500 and 750 who had been high officials in the Confederate Government. Thereafter, individual disability bills dribbled through each congressional session, the last being passed Feb. 24, 1897. By an act of June 6, 1898, final amnesty was granted, by removing the disabilities from those still barred by the provisions of Section 3 of the Fourteenth Amendment.

[J. T. Dorris, *Pardon and Amnesty During the Civil War and Reconstruction;* J. G. Randall, *Constitutional Problems Under Lincoln;* William A. Russ, Jr., *Congressional Disfranchisement,* an unpublished doctoral dissertation deposited at the Library of the University of Chicago.]

WILLIAM A. RUSS, JR.

Amnesty (1919 f.). Soon after the close of the World War the Federal authorities began liberating and amnesting the many conscientious objectors[qv] to military service and other violators (including deserters) of war-time legislation. From Fort Leavenworth[qv], where more than 2000 were confined, the Secretary of War discharged 113 in January, 1919. Other liberations followed and by 1922 the work was practically done. Sometimes prisoners' disabilities were removed by order of the President, as in the case of Harold S. Gray, whom President Wilson ordered "dishonorably" discharged from Alcatraz on Aug. 23, 1919. As late as March 5, 1924, President Coolidge granted "amnesty and pardon to all persons" under conviction, or who might thereafter be convicted, of desertion.

[Mrs. Lucy Robbins, *War Shadows: A Documentary Story of the Struggle for Amnesty;* Norman Thomas, *The Conscientious Objector in America; U. S. Statutes at Large,* Vol. 40, pt. 2.]

JONATHAN T. DORRIS

Amundsen Polar Expeditions. Roald Engelbregt Gravning Amundsen gained his first experience as an explorer in the Belgian Antarctic Expedition, 1897–99. He led the first expedition to sail through the Northwest Passage[qv] from the Atlantic to the Pacific, a feat he accomplished in the sloop *Gjöa,* 1903–6. He discovered the South Pole in December, 1911, beating Capt. Scott to the goal by a month. He sailed through the Northeast Passage from Norway to Alaska in the *Maud,* 1918–20, on an unsuccessful attempt to drift across the Pole from the New Siberian Islands. In an effort to attain the North Pole with Lincoln Ellsworth by airplane from Spitsbergen in 1925 he reached latitude 88°. With Ellsworth and Col. Nobile he navigated the airship *Norge,* from Spitsbergen to Alaska in 1926. He was lost in 1928 while flying across the Arctic wastes in search of the missing *Italia's* crew.

[Amundsen, *The North West Passage; The South Pole; Nordöst Passagen; My Life as an Explorer;* Amundsen and Ellsworth, *Our Polar Flight; First Crossing of the Polar Sea.*]

N. M. CROUSE

Amusements. In the early colonial period, the recreational opportunities available were naturally limited. The harsh conditions of pioneer life demanded of all classes a concentration on work which left little leisure for amusements, and under the stress of economic circumstance any "mispense of time" was rigorously prohibited in both Jamestown and Plymouth[qqv]. As conditions improved, a gradual change was effected but in New England normal recreational developments were further impeded by the religious prejudice of Puritanism[qv]. Colonial leaders in both Massachusetts and Connecticut vigorously attempted to suppress almost all kinds of amusements, with bans not only on the theater[qv], card playing, horse racing[qv], but also on tavern sports and dancing. No conflict between pleasure and conscience inhibited the fox-hunting, horse-racing, cockfighting[qv] planters of Virginia and South Carolina. They enjoyed such opportunities for diversion as came their way without thought as to whether they might be inspired by God or the Devil, but New Englanders tended to look with suspicion upon play in any guise whatsoever and indulged in recreation with sober restraint.

The spirit of Puritanism was, however, not proof against the growing demand for recreation, as economic security and leisure increased. Throughout the colonies a predominantly agricultural population found relief from the tedium of farm work in the festivities attendant upon training days and elections; at house raisings and husking bees[qv]; at country dances and at such tavern sports as bowling, shuffle board and quoits—activities which were always enlivened by a plentiful flow of spirituous liquors. Hunting and fishing were everywhere enjoyed; shooting matches had a great popularity and other rural pastimes found favor in New England as in the Middle and Southern Colonies. In the colonial cities and on southern plantations[qqv], the more wealthy enjoyed a social life in which elaborate dining and wining, card playing, concerts and frequent balls and assemblies were predominant features. The theater was restricted to New York, Philadelphia and the South, but otherwise New England had gone far toward discarding earlier restraints as the 18th century progressed and the colonial period drew to its close.

After the Revolution, and for the first quarter of the 19th century, there was no marked change in the recreational scene, but the gradual industrialization of the country and the growth of urban populations were soon to have far-reaching effects. Deprived of the simple pleasures of country life, the great mass of city dwellers became more and more dependent upon the commercial amusements which rapidly developed to meet this increasing need. The restraints of religious prejudice, inherent in what is called Puritanism, and the feeling, natural to a young and expanding country, that everything else should be subordinated to work, gave foreign visitors of the first half of the 19th century the impression that Americans took no time for play; but there was evidence to the contrary on every hand.

The theater[qv] became an important element in the amusement scene, not only in the larger cities but in smaller towns throughout the country. And it had a popular appeal, reflected in both admission charges and the type of entertainment it offered, which it had not had in colonial days. The second quarter of the century also witnessed the development of amusements even more frankly adapted to the popular taste: variety theaters, minstrel shows[qv], dancing halls and the beginnings of amusement parks. The peripatetic showmen and animal exhibitors of earlier days joined forces to produce the modern circus[qv], and traveling shows began to tour the country, bringing a new form of entertainment to rural as well as urban communities. For the wealthy, social life in the cities became more pretentious, summer resorts sprang up, but the really significant fact in the development of amusements in the first half of the 19th century was their increasing democratization. The new vogue for popular, commercialized entertainment was graphically symbolized in the career of P. T. Barnum[qv].

The rise of sports[qv] also began just before the Civil War, although it was in the 1870's and 1880's that they became really important. Informal sports had always been popular in rural communities but the cities called for organization, and the crowds which were attracted by the opportunity to get a vicarious satisfaction out of watching others play soon led to commercialization. Horse races on occasion drew as many as 50,000 spectators; boating and yachting races[qv] had an immense vogue, restricted as far as participation was concerned to the wealthy, but providing a spectacle for thousands; pedestrian races were popular, and while prize fighting[qv] had not yet escaped the odium which clung to it throughout the bare-knuckle days, it began to awaken intense popular interest. The 1850's saw the beginnings of baseball[qv], with amateur clubs springing up in New York and other cities, pointing the way to a development which was soon to make it the national game.

After the Civil War what we now term spectator sports made still greater advances, emphasized by the professionalization of baseball, but there was also far more widespread participation in sports. The successive introduction of new games provided healthy outdoor amusement for thousands. Archery, croquet, roller skating and then lawn tennis swept the country, for the first time bringing women into sports activity; football[qv] developed as a college sport with the adoption of national rules of play; and baseball was more widely played on sand lots and country fields. Bicycling[qv] became an outdoor activity for hundreds of thousands. The complaint that spectator sports were playing a far larger role in the life of the people than participant sports was widely heard before the close of the century, but great masses of people played themselves, favoring the games for which little or no equipment was necessary and organization not essential. Always there were hunting and fishing, skating and sleigh-riding in the winter, informal ball games, bowling, quoits, shooting matches, pitching horseshoes. . . .

At the same time, commercial amusements served to supplement to an increasing extent the informal activities of social life. Visits and entertaining, club life, reading, card playing, music, country excursions, picnics and the more elaborate functions of the socially elect constituted the non-athletic amusements of most of the people most of the time, as they always must, but city life was still responsible for needs of which commercial showmen took full advantage. There was further expansion of the theater in the last half of the 19th century, with stock companies and well-known players touring the country; concerts and opera, the establishment of vaudeville circuits, and bigger and better circuses. Dancing halls multiplied; amusement parks were established not only near the large cities but wherever trolley lines could bring together paying customers; there was a great increase in bowling alleys and billiard parlors. Amusement was becoming an important business.

For all this expansion, the beginning of the 20th century nevertheless brought about a further transformation in the general pattern of the country's recreational life more important than anything which had heretofore taken place. The machine which had made possible the new leisure of men and women of the working classes, and had thereby created the need for commercial amusements, was itself adapted to recreational activities. The automobile, the moving picture and the radio[qqv] were rapidly to become the principal sources of entertainment for the American people as a whole. Spectator sports drew ever greater crowds with baseball, prize fighting, college football, athletic meets and professional hockey gaining in popularity; participation in sports grew apace with the new popularity of tennis, golf and skiing; national parks[qv] and city playgrounds providing new facilities for outdoor recreation. But automobile pleasure riding, attendance at the movies and listening to the radio were to dominate the modern amusement scene. By the end of the third decade of the century, they accounted for by far the greater part of the national expenditure on amusements, a figure which has been estimated as high as $10,000,000,000 a year.

FOSTER RHEA DULLES

***Amy Warwick* Admiralty Case,** 1863 (2 Black 635). This was one of the Prize Cases[qv] in which the Supreme Court upheld the power of the President to recognize the existence of a civil war and thereupon to establish a blockade[qv], without awaiting congressional action.

[Charles Warren, *The Supreme Court in United States History.*]

CHARLES FAIRMAN

Anaconda Copper, one of the largest copper mining[qv] companies of the world, and the principal producer of the Butte district of Montana, was organized in 1881 as The Anaconda Silver Mining Company, Marcus Daly having persuaded James B. Haggin, Lloyd Tevis and George Hearst to purchase for $30,000 the small Anaconda silver mine, then only sixty feet deep. The ore contained just enough copper to facilitate the recovery of the silver for which it was being worked, but at greater depth it became evident that its principal content was copper. A copper smelter was erected in 1884 and 3000 tons of ore was being treated daily by 1889. Continuing to expand through the purchase of other mines it was reorganized as the Anaconda Mining Company in 1891, with a capital of $25,000,000. The Hearst interests were sold to the Exploration Company, London, and the company was reorganized in 1895 as the Anaconda Copper Mining Company, three quarters of the stock having been bought by the Amalgamated Copper Company. In 1910 its capitalization was increased to $150,000,000 to take over all the properties of the Amalgamated in the Butte district and some of the William A. Clark interests, the purchase being completed by 1915 and the Amalgamated dissolved. By 1937 it had an authorized capital of $600,000,000 and was operating in Chile, Peru and Poland as well as in the United States.

[H. J. Stevens, *The Copper Handbook.*]

T. T. READ

Anæsthesia. Though it had been known from ancient times that certain narcotic[qv] preparations would deaden pain and though Sir Humphrey Davy had suggested in 1800 that nitrous oxide (popularly called "laughing gas") might be used in surgery, no anæsthesia was ever administered in an operation until 1842. On March 30, 1842, Dr. Crawford W. Long used sulphuric ether on a patient in Jefferson, Ga., and removed without pain a tumor from the back of his neck. Though local prejudice was strong against this practice, Long later used ether in performing a number of other operations, but he published no statement of the fact. In December, 1844, Dr. Horace Wells, a dentist of Hartford, Conn., having likewise discovered that "laughing gas" was an anæsthesia, had it administered to himself and had a tooth extracted without pain. In 1846 Dr. W. T. G. Morton, a

Boston dentist and a former associate of Wells, using sulphuric ether, performed a like act. Soon thereafter he administered ether in an operation in the Massachusetts General Hospital. A long contest over the question of priority in the use of an anæsthesia has followed, complicated further by the claims of Charles T. Jackson, a Boston chemist.

[J. T. Flexner, *Doctors on Horseback;* Frances L. Taylor, *Crawford W. Long and the Discovery of Ether Anesthesis;* F. R. Packard, *History of Medicine in the United States.*]

E. MERTON COULTER

Anahuac, Attack on (June, 1832). Anahuac was a Mexican military post on the east shore of Galveston Bay. To effect the release of William B. Travis and other Americans held there, a group of American settlers in Texas attacked the place. The resulting negotiations led the Texans to declare for the Santa Anna party in Mexico. The incident was an important preliminary to the Texas Revolution[qv].

[E. C. Barker, *Mexico and Texas, 1821-1835.*]

E. C. BARKER

Ananias Club, THE, was an expression employed by the press in 1906–7 to avoid the "short and ugly word" (liar) in connection with the "mutual accusations of inveracity" which arose between President Theodore Roosevelt and Sen. Tillman of South Carolina over the railway rate bill and later during the controversy between Roosevelt and the "nature fakers."

[Mark Sullivan, *Our Times*, Vol. III.]

ROSCOE R. HILL

Anarchists. The leading exponent of philosophical anarchism in the United States was Benjamin R. Tucker. In his magazine *Liberty,* published in Boston, he defined anarchism as the law of equal liberty, with self-interest the supreme law for man, abolition of the state to be achieved by education and passive resistance. His theories were set forth in *Instead of a Book* (1893). Another, an insurgent school, leaned to the Bakunin-Kropotkin theory that the state belongs to a low stage of evolution and must disappear since the trend of social progress is toward more and more liberty. It saw evolution and revolution as alternating processes, revolution and political assassination as an accelerated evolution and belonging to the unity of nature. While this school did not advocate deeds of violence it did not condemn, and sometimes condoned them. To it belonged John J. Most, who, after expulsion from Germany in 1878 and imprisonment in England for incendiary utterances in his periodical, *Freiheit,* made his home in New York. Until 1883, anarchists and socialists[qv] belonged to the same organizations, though theoretically they were diametrically opposed. In 1887, in Chicago, following the Haymarket riot[qv], four men who confessed themselves anarchists but denied bomb throwing were hanged. It was a young Russian immigrant, Emma Goldman, a gifted orator, who in 1889 became an active leader of the insurgent school. She championed an anarchist of the deed, Alexander Berkman, when, having attempted the life of Henry C. Frick, he was sentenced to twenty-two years' imprisonment. When President McKinley was shot, Sept. 6, 1901, by another anarchist of the deed, Leon Czolgosz, Emma Goldman became the object of suspicion when she published an essay explaining the deed in its social and psychological aspect. In 1906 she published an anarchist magazine, *Mother Earth,* which Berkman edited on his release.

In July, 1917, Berkman and Emma Goldman were sentenced to two years in the penitentiary, with $10,000 fine and deportation to Russia for their activities in the Anti-Conscription agitation. Since then the movement seems to have died.

[E. V. Zenkner, *Anarchism;* Dr. Paul Eltzbacher, *Anarchism.*]

CHARLES J. FINGER

Ancient, Fort, the name given a large prehistoric earthwork in Ohio. Earthern walls from six to twenty feet high enclose the top of an irregular plateau; area about 100 acres. Experts place it in the mound building[qv] period and consider it a ceremonial structure instead of a fortification.

[H. C. Shetrone, *The Mound Builders.*]

CLARK WISSLER

Andaste, THE, so named by the Jesuit Fathers, were prominent in the 17th-century history of the Susquehanna basin which they entered earlier from the Ohio. Though of Iroquoian[qv] stock, enmity with Iroquois kinsmen aligned them with northern Hurons[qv]. Identified with Smith's *Sasquesahanoughs* (1608), Champlain's *Carantouannais* (1615), the *Minquas* of early Swedish fur trade (1637), the *Conestogas* whose fort formed the crux of Pennsylvania-Maryland boundary disputes[qv], in 1676 they precipitated Bacon's Rebellion[qv] and their own virtual extermination.

[J. S. Clark, *Aboriginal History of the Susquehanna.*]

ELSIE MURRAY

Anderson v. Dunn (6 Wheaton 204, 1821). The right of the House of Representatives to charge, hear and punish contempt[qv], and detain, arrest and imprison those so charged, was unanimously upheld on the analogy of the right of the judiciary to punish contempt—for the self-preservation of the institutions of the state.

PHILLIPS BRADLEY

Andersonville Prison (February, 1864–April, 1865) in Georgia was the largest and best-known of Confederate military prisons[qv]. Hastily established because the number of prisoners constituted a military danger and was a serious drain on the food supplies of Richmond, no adequate preparations were made for housing the captives. The poverty of the Confederacy, a defective transportation system and the concentration of all resources on the army, prevented the prison officials supplying barracks, cooked food, clothing or medical care to their charges. The prison consisted solely of a log stockade of sixteen and one-half acres (later enlarged to twenty-six acres) through which ran a stream of water. Rations to the prisoners generally consisted of corn meal and beans, and seldom included meat. Bad sanitary conditions, lack of cooking facilities, poor food, crowding and exposure soon produced respiratory diseases, diarrhœa and scurvy[qv]. The inadequate medical staff, without drugs, could not cope with the situation. During the summer the number of prisoners increased to 31,678. There are 12,912 graves in the National Cemetery at Andersonville. Estimates place the total number of deaths at even higher figures. In September, the approach of Sherman's army caused the removal of all well prisoners to Charleston, S. C. Only enlisted men were confined in Andersonville; commissioned officers were held at Macon, Ga.

To the prisoners and to their friends in the North it appeared that the Confederates were deliberately murdering the captives. As a result of this belief, Capt. Henry Wirz, commander of the interior of the prison, was tried in August, 1865, on charges of murder and conspiring with Jefferson Davis to murder. Although found guilty by a military commission, and hanged, Nov. 10, 1865, subsequent investigation has revealed much in Wirz's favor. For many years Andersonville prison was a vital element in the "bloody shirt"[qv] issue in politics.

[W. B. Hesseltine, *Civil War Prisons: A Study in War Psychology.*]

W. B. HESSELTINE

André Is Captured. Maj. John André, adjutant-general of the British Army in North America during the Revolution, was entrusted by Sir Henry Clinton with the correspondence between the British Headquarters and the American traitor, Brig.-Gen. Benedict Arnold[qv], in the years 1779–80. On Sept. 21, 1780, he met Arnold at Joshua Hett Smith's house, just south of West Point on the Hudson, to complete the arrangements for the betrayal of West Point[qv] to the British. He had arrived on the British vessel *Vulcan* which anchored opposite Haverstraw. While Arnold and André were in conference, American artillery fire compelled the *Vulcan* to fall down-stream. Having lost his means of transport, André was persuaded to change his costume for a disguise and carry the treasonable papers back overland by horseback. He crossed the Hudson, started down the east bank, and was captured (Sept. 23) by three American irregulars, John Paulding, Isaac van Wart and David Williams who searched him, discovered the papers and turned him over to the American army. André explained himself to Washington, and Sir Henry Clinton demanded his release on the ground that he had gone to consult with Arnold under a flag of truce, which was true. But, in fact, his conduct had made him a spy, as he said in his own words: "The events of coming within an Enemy's posts and of changing my dress which led me to my present Situation were contrary to my own Inclination as they were to your [Clinton's] orders. . . ." He was tried before a court-martial (Sept. 29), of which Maj. Gen. Nathanael Greene was the president, convicted of being a spy and ordered to be hanged. Washington refused to intercede in his behalf, and he was executed on Oct. 2, 1780, at Tappan, N. Y.

[W. Abbatt, *Crisis of the Revolution.*]

RANDOLPH G. ADAMS

Andrews' Raid. On April 12, 1862, twenty-two Union spies attempted to destroy the strategic railroad between Atlanta and Chattanooga. After a race in the engine *General* they were captured by men from the pursuing engine *Texas*. Eight were subsequently hanged.

[John R. Hornady, *Atlanta, Yesterday, Today, and Tomorrow.*]

HAYWOOD J. PEARCE, JR.

Andros Regime. *See* New England, Dominion of.

Anglican Church. *See* Church of England in the Colonies, The.

Anglo-American Relations properly date from the year 1783, when the Definitive Treaty of Peace[qv] was ratified. It was, at first, the hope of the British Ministry that some sort of an intimate alliance might be immediately worked out with the United States, for the old imperial relationship. This would leave the United States independent, in complete free trade with the Empire, bound by a close naval alliance to furnish seamen and ships. The peace commissioners at Paris proved unamenable to this, and it fell flat.

During the period of the Confederation[qv], 1783–89, the imperfect constitutional organization of the United States, and the resulting national weakness, placed it at the mercy of British commercial preponderance and diplomatic calculation. John Adams, first minister of the United States to Great Britain, tried in vain to secure a treaty of commerce, as well as an adjustment of issues connected with non-fulfillment of the Treaty of Peace. These comprised British retention of the strategic military posts on American soil along the newly established river-and-lake boundary (*see* Border Forts), the failure of the Federal Government promptly and perfectly to execute articles of the treaty relating to the payment of private pre-war debts (*see* British Debts) and the prevention of further confiscations and discriminations against returning Loyalists[qv]. The existing commercial situation was entirely satisfactory to Great Britain, with the Americans now taking nine-tenths of their imports from England but automatically excluded by the fact of independence from trade with the British colonial dominions. There was no danger of retaliatory tariffs or commercial discrimination against British commerce so long as the government of the Confederation lacked control over interstate and foreign commerce. Meanwhile the internal weaknesses of the Confederation presaged to secret British observers an impending break-up. In London there seemed no necessity for a treaty. Great Britain would not even send a diplomatic representative to the United States.

The political miracle of the Constitution[qv] and the establishment of the new national Government under President George Washington saved independence and crystalized American nationality in permanent form. The outbreak of the French Revolution at this same time presently gave rise to a series of European wars that completely absorbed British attention and energies for the next twenty-five years. Stiffened American nationality, with control over foreign and interstate commerce, and a resolution to police the Western Indians and reduce them to national authority, gave the British government more respect for the authority and independence of the United States and led to the exchange of diplomatic representatives in 1791. A movement in the new Congress for discriminatory tariffs against British goods and ships precipitated this despatch of a British minister to Philadelphia.

The instructions of the first British minister, George Hammond, were to talk the Government of the United States out of commercial discrimination and to offer to make a general treaty only on condition of the establishment of a neutral Indian barrier state[qv], under British influence. This plan was frustrated by the innate patriotism of even the pro-British elements in the United States, and by the exigencies of the international situation in Europe, where war broke out between England and France in 1793. The United States, on its side, wanted neutrality. The frontier situation and British arbitrary naval seizures produced a war scare in the spring of 1794 but this was settled by Jay's Treaty[qv], which was a decisive turning point in Anglo-American relations and indeed in the history of the United States. It was the price which Washington's Government, under Federalist[qv] advice, paid to British sea power for the redemption of American territory and for a breathing spell of peace to secure the newly established nationality and financial stability which depended on Anglo-American commerce for its revenues.

All attempts at a negotiated basis of Anglo-American relations during the Napoleonic wars fell down as the system of retaliations was built up between the Leviathan of the Seas and the Colossus of the Land, each trying desperately to destroy the other by the most deadly weapons at his disposal. American administration reprisals at British naval practice, such as the Non-Importation Act, the Embargo and the Non-Intercourse Act[qqv], only served to damage American commerce and to align the United States as a supplement to Napoleon's Continental System (*see* Napoleon's Decrees). The "retaliatory" British blockade and the practice of impressment[qqv], especially the latter, fired American public opinion with the old hostility to England, although not to the extent of war. It is to be noted that, when war was declared in 1812, the very coastal constituencies of Congress, which had been most oppressed by British naval practice, voted against war; this was presumably because war trade on British sufferance, as controlled by the British navy for British supply and profit, was to them preferable to war and the ruin of trade. What tipped the scales in favor of a declaration of war was the vote of the members from the Southern and the new Western states (*see* War Hawks). The United States was lucky to get out of the war without the loss of territory (*see* War of 1812).

The Peace of Ghent[qv], ratified in 1815, was really a compromise peace on the basis of the *status quo ante bellum.* It settled none of the issues, like impressment and the freedom of the seas[qv], which had helped to cause the war. But it did settle the permanence of the northern frontier, and England proved willing to extend the frontier, by the Convention of 1818[qv], on the line of 49° N. Lat. as far as the Rocky Mountains, leaving the opposing claims in the Pacific Northwest still unsettled (*see* Oregon Question). A naval limitations agreement in 1817 (*see* Great Lakes, Agreement for Disarmament on the), ratified subsequently by the Senate, demilitarized the Great Lakes. It has remained in effect ever since, and the principle of disarmament has been extended in practice all along the frontier.

Two other great diplomatic settlements were necessary in the generation after Ghent to harmonize completely Anglo-American frontier relations: the settlement of the Northeastern frontier dispute by the Webster-Ashburton Treaty of 1842[qv], and the termination of the long contention for dominion over Oregon. Webster's concessions in the Northeast were compensated by the victory of American diplomacy, on the eve of the war with Mexico[qv], in settling the Northwestern territorial question by the Oregon Treaty of 1846[qv], which continued the line of 49° N. Lat. straight through to the Pacific Ocean, reserving for British subjects trading with the Hudson's Bay Company[qv] the right to navigate the Columbia River[qv]. The achievement of this line was a diplomatic victory rather than the "compromise" that it is sometimes represented to be. The United States had always refused to take less than 49°. Great Britain had not consistently refused to take less than the line of the Columbia River, which was the basis of her claim. The exact line through the channels out to the open sea became a matter of dispute subsequent to 1846 and involved the sovereignty of the San Juan[qv] archipelago at the entrance to Puget Sound. These islands were adjudged to the United States by the Alabama Claims arbitration of 1871, provided for in the Treaty of Washington[qqv].

In the mid-century there were three other serious issues between the United States and Great Britain: the regulation of the suppression of the African slave trade[qv] on the high seas, the Texas question and the Isthmian question (*see* Panama Canal). Both countries had abolished the African slave trade. Great Britain had negotiated treaties with the principal maritime powers providing for the mutual right of visit and search[qv] of ships suspected of engaging in the slave trade. The United States refused to make such a treaty unless Great Britain would at the same time expressly abandon the practice of impressment. After much diplomatic discussion, the British government explicitly disavowed any right of visit and search in time of peace but insisted that it was proper to visit a vessel suspected of flying the American flag illegally; otherwise slavers could cover themselves by that flag with impunity. The United States consistently maintained that ships flying its flag illegally could be searched and even captured and punished but there must be no mistake made in molesting a real American vessel. This uncompromising attitude by both parties created incidents and obstructed the strict policing of this nefarious commerce.

Undoubtedly, the influence of the Southern slave states in the American Congress made it impossible for the Federal Government to reach an agreement with England, because in 1862, after the secession of the Southern states and the outbreak of the American Civil War[qqv], Secretary of State Seward promptly concluded a convention with Great Britain, providing for the mutual right of visit and search in specified waters off the coasts of Africa and Cuba, with mixed courts at Sierra Leone, Cape Town and New York, composed of an equal number of judges from each party for the trial of offenders. The passage of time and the growth of American power had wiped away any possibility of renewal by Great Britain of the obnoxious and humiliating practice of impressment.

Slavery, too, played a prominent part in the Texas question. It was the purpose of British diplomacy to prevent Texas from becoming annexed to the United States, and in a friendly way to press for the ultimate abolition of slavery there. An independent Texas would be an alternate source, indispensably needed, of cotton to keep British textile mills operating, in case difficulties with the United States should ever shut off that source. Further, Texas as a sovereign state would be outside the American tariff walls and, presumably, a free-trade market for British manufactures (*see* Webster-Ashburton Treaty). On the eve of the war between the United States and Mexico, British diplomacy had negotiated a treaty between Texas and Mexico, providing for Mexican recognition of Texan independence upon the condition of Texas never being annexed to any third state. This treaty was never ratified, and annexation[qv] in 1845 definitely ended the Texas question. Great Britain's attitude about Texas, however, did much to offset the appeasement of feeling wrought by the Webster-Ashburton settlement of 1842 and the Oregon Treaty of 1846.

The Isthmian question involved the control of the route of a future canal. American expansion into Texas, the war with Mexico and the alliance with New Granada (Colombia) annoyed Great Britain, which sought to block American influence on the Isthmus, by securing control of strategic points at both termini of the Nicaraguan canal route (*see* Bidlack-Mallarino Treaty). Anglo-American tension on the Isthmus reached almost the point of war in 1850, but was adjusted by the Clayton-Bulwer Treaty[qv] of that year, one of the most embarrassing international engagements which the United States has ever ratified. This treaty placed any future Isthmian canal under the joint control of the United States and Great Britain and provided that there should never be any discrimination in traffic charges against the citizens or subjects of either party to the canal treaty.

It was indeed a fortunate occurrence that on the outbreak of the Civil War Anglo-American relations had been cleared of any serious controversy, for the war served to embitter feelings between the two peoples. Great Britain allowed Southern cruisers to be constructed and fitted out from British ports, whence they proceeded to spread havoc in the merchant marine[qv] of the United States, the destruction of which would not displease British maritime interests. In the famous *Trent* case[qv] Great Britain protested to the point of an ultimatum against American seizure of disloyal subjects from British ships on the high seas. The conformance of the United States to British demands, albeit justified on technical grounds, saved peace with England and strengthened the American point of view against the old British practice of impressment. Although the cotton shortage, caused by the blockade of Southern ports, and Southern embargoes on cotton export, brought great hardship to the masses of British textile employees, Great Britain acquiesced in the imperfect Union blockade because it established a valuable Anglo-American precedent for the employment by Great Britain in any future contingency of an imperfect blockade of her own in a war in which the United States might be neutral. British diplomacy cashed in heavily on this precedent during the period of American neutrality in the first three years of the World War.

Despite their sufferings, the British working classes, to whom slavery was hateful, sympathized ardently with the cause of the Union. After the Civil War the United States successfully demanded the arbitration with Great Britain of British responsibilities for the equipment and consequent depredations of the Confederate cruisers, the *Alabama*[qv] and ships of her class. For this the Geneva Arbitration of 1871 awarded a total of $15,500,000. At the same time, various British claimants received $1,929,819, in awards of a General Claims Commission, and the Halifax Mixed Commission[qv] awarded $5,500,000 as additional compensation to Great Britain for fishery concessions in British territorial waters that had been extended without compensation in 1866, upon the expiration of the Canadian Reciprocity Treaty of 1854[qv].

The Geneva adjudication was one of several Anglo-American arbitrations which cleared away the controversies which arose during the generation after the Civil War. The attempt of the United States to control the seal fisheries[qv] in Bering Sea met the protests of the British against the exercise of sovereign rights on the high seas, even for the protection and preservation of marine life. The ensuing arbitration of 1892 gave a clear-cut decision against the United States, whose case had been greatly prejudiced by earlier traditional American protests in favor of the freedom of the seas.

In 1895 President Grover Cleveland startled the world with his spectacular ultimatum insisting that Great Britain arbitrate a long-standing boundary dispute between British Guiana and the republic of Venezuela. It was President Cleveland's conviction that Great Britain would violate the Monroe Doctrine[qv] if she exploited the boundary dispute to expand her territory on the American continents at the expense of an American republic. The rise of German naval power and its threat to the British Empire, graphically signalized by the Kaiser's telegram of congratulations to President Krueger of the Transvaal on the eve of the Boer War, together with the ever-present exposure of the Canadian flank of empire, speedily induced Great Britain to accept Cleveland's ultimatum and arbitrate her controversy (advantageously, it proved) with the United States (*see* Venezuela Boundary Controversy). Since then Great Britain has accepted the Monroe Doctrine as a permanent part of her foreign policy and has consistently striven for an *entente cordiale* with the United States, as a means of strengthening her diplomatic and even military resources to deal with controversies and wars that threaten her intimately in the Old World. This approach is illustrated by the cordial tone of British diplomacy and public opinion during the Spanish-American War[qv]. In line with the improvement of

Anglo-American relations and the new cordial tone, Great Britain prevailed upon Canada to submit to arbitration her dispute over the Alaskan boundary[qv]. At the same time, British policy profited heavily by the American Open Door policy[qv] in China, which was as British in its origin as it was American, and certainly more to the advantage of Great Britain than to the United States. There is no documentary evidence yet presented of an explicit bargain diplomatically, by which Great Britain got out of the Caribbean, and the United States got into the Far East, but it was implicit in the general situation.

The last great controversy to be cleared up between the United States and England was the historic dispute over fishing privileges on the Atlantic coast of British North America, which was compromised by the arbitral decision of 1910 (*see* Fisheries Dispute). Since then the United States and Great Britain have enjoyed general treaties of arbitration and conciliation and have been pledged to peace by the Briand-Kellogg Pact[qv]. Since both of them are powers whose vital interests dictate peace, and each of whom would have much to lose by the defeat of the other, they tend to drift together in the face of common danger.

The inveterate friendship of Anglo-American relations and the common outlook on danger made the United States and its people highly sympathetic to the British cause at the outbreak of the World War. Other factors inclined toward a neutrality more benevolent to Great Britain than to Germany and her allies: a common cultural background, a common tradition of liberal constitutionalism, a common language, highly conducive to skillful British propaganda (as contrasted with clumsy German propaganda and misunderstanding of American history), and an economic tie-up in the shape of munitions supply and heavy subscriptions to the war loans of Britain and her allies. These factors made the United States want Great Britain to win, rather than Germany, particularly because the United States had little to lose if Great Britain should win and much to lose if Germany, which had never recognized the Monroe Doctrine, should triumph. All of this predisposed the United States toward the Allied cause but the precipitation of war occurred only when Germany added the challenge of unrestricted submarine warfare.

During the World War the United States, as a belligerent, did not desert, technically speaking, its traditional stand for the freedom of the seas; but after the war, in 1927, by an exchange of notes, the United States, while carefully reserving its principles in the premises, released Great Britain from claims for maritime captures and interferences with American neutral commerce, 1914 to 1917.

Anglo-American relations since the World War, while cordial, have not been passionately friendly. The principal outstanding issues today are: discriminations against American commerce wrought by inter-imperial preference treaties (like that of Ottawa, 1932) and Great Britain's default on her pledge to pay her war debt[qv] while insisting that the United States observe its pledge, inherited from the old Clayton-Bulwer Treaty and reincorporated in the Hay-Pauncefote Treaty[qv] of 1902, not to levy any higher traffic charges on foreign ships than on American ships going through the Panama Canal[qv], control and defense of which, since 1902, consented to by Great Britain, is at the cost of the American taxpayer, as is also payment of the defaulted loans to Great Britain. It should always be remembered that of the approximately $4,277,000,000 loaned to Great Britain, $581,000,000 is a peace debt loaned after Nov. 11, 1918. To these grits in the present smoothness of Anglo-American relations must be added the disappointment experienced when Great Britain refused to act with the United States for the solution of the Manchurian crisis of 1931 to 1933. Many observers feel that here started the chain of aggressions which extended itself in the Rhineland, Abyssinia, Spain, Austria and Czechoslovakia at the expense of the democratic powers, and which seems to unleash a future of dismay for them.

The existing issues are small and capable of settlement by wise and resolute statesmen, if there are such. The commercial question has recently been adjusted, at this writing, by the new trade agreements of 1938: between the United States and Canada, and between the United States and Great Britain and her crown colonies. More than ever Great Britain and the United States need each other's friendship. More than ever each has much to lose by the other's defeat and little to fear from the other's prosperity and success. More than ever the culture, the freedom and the ideals of each great people are threatened by new ideologies and auguries in the international world.

[Samuel Flagg Bemis, *A Diplomatic History of the United States;* Ephraine D. Adams, *Great Britain and the American Civil War;* Frank L. Owsley, *King Cotton Diplomacy;* William Archibald Dunning, *The British Empire and the United States.*]

SAMUEL FLAGG BEMIS

Anglo-Chinese War (1839–42), American Interests in the, center about the initiative of Commodore Lawrence Kearny[qv] that led to opening several Chinese ports to American commerce. Arriving off Canton with the *Constellation* and *Boston* in March, 1842, Kearny found the war, precipitated by the opium[qv] dispute, nearly ended. He cultivated friendly relations with both sides and when the victorious British demanded special trade privileges, he pleaded with the Chinese for equal privileges being granted Americans. This principle was accepted by the Chinese and formed the basis of our first treaty with China negotiated by Caleb Cushing[qv] at Canton in 1844.

[C. O. Paullin, *Diplomatic Negotiations of American Naval Officers.*] DUDLEY W. KNOX

Anglophobia and Anglomania. Historically the attitude of mind described by these words goes back to the period of the Confederation[qv]; but these particular descriptive terms first became part of the American vocabulary in the decade between 1880 and 1890. The terms were exploited by partisans in the Democratic and Republican parties[qqv] alike. The anglomaniac was popularly described as an aristocrat, usually from the East, who aped English manners, read English books and favored an Anglo-American alliance. The Murchison letter[qv] episode of the presidential election of 1888[qv] indicates how the politicians took advantage of the feeling against the anglophile.

The anglophobe was more articulate than the anglomaniac and was much more in evidence in the 1890's. In the Middle West there existed the traditional anti-English attitude, supplemented by the political hostility of the Populist[qv] group. The cheap-money group declared that England alone stood in the way of universal bimetallism[qv]; and the Populist orators demanded war against this great "money empire." Racial groups, especially the Irish-American and German-American, were generally anglophobe, and their attitude of hostility toward England was especially notable during the Boer War.

The work of such statesmen as John Hay and James Bryce helped to soften some of the animosities developed by the anti-British group, but despite these efforts there was a strong outburst against England when the repeal of the Panama Tolls Act[qv] was before Congress.

Before America's entry into the World War the feelings of the two groups were intensified by events connected with the struggle over neutral rights. Ambassador Walter Hines Page was pictured as an anglomaniac by one faction while William Randolph Hearst was considered an anglophobe. America's entry into the war naturally brought a temporarary truce between the groups. Despite some recurrence of feeling in the post-war period, there has been no such intensive partisanship as that characterizing the turn of the century.

[B. A. Reuter, *Anglo-American Relations During the Spanish American War.*] THEODORE G. GRONERT

Anián, Strait of. A mythical strait, supposed to connect the Atlantic and Pacific, sought by the Spaniards in the 16th and 17th centuries. In 1601 they tried to find a harbor on it beyond Quivira[qv] for direct intercourse with Spain. Until 1742 the Gulf of California was believed by many to join the west end of the strait.

[C. E. Chapman, *A History of California: Spanish Period.*] LANSING B. BLOOM

Annapolis. *See* Naval Academy, United States.

Annapolis Convention, THE, was the precursor of the Constitutional Convention of 1787[qv]. On Sept. 11, 1786, twelve commissioners from New York, New Jersey, Pennsylvania, Delaware and Virginia met in the State House at Annapolis, Md., to discuss reform of the vexatious restrictions placed upon interstate commerce by the various states. Among those present were Alexander Hamilton, John Dickinson and James Madison. The convention took no action except to recommend that a larger convention be held in Philadelphia the following May.

[A. C. McLaughlin, *The Confederation and the Constitution.*] WALTER B. NORRIS

Annapolis Royal. *See* Port Royal (N. S.).

Annexation of Territory. No specific provision was made in the Constitution for the annexation of territory. It is doubtful that the Fathers in 1783 contemplated expansion across the empty continent beyond the ample boundaries set down in the Definitive Treaty of Peace[qv]. All the region beyond the Mississippi, north of the Great Lakes and south of 31° N. Lat., then remained in the hands of strong European monarchies. But Europe's distresses were America's advantage. The wars which followed the outbreak of the French Revolution and convulsed the Old World from 1793–1815 exhausted the energies of Great Britain and Spain, and also of France which had intervened in Louisiana in 1800–1803, and enabled the United States first to clear its own territory of foreign troops and then to expand. By the twin treaties of Washington's administration, Jay's Treaty with England (1794) and Pinckney's Treaty with Spain (1795)[qqv], the West was cleared. Practice discovered four different means of annexation, all of which proved to be constitutional. A lucky break in the European constellation of 1800–1803 enabled President Jefferson unexpectedly by treaty to purchase the vast territory of Louisiana[qv] and thus to annex it to the United States. After 1815 England was so exhausted that, as Castlereagh said, she needed a long period of repose; reposing she made a boundary treaty in 1818 (*see* Convention of 1818) which accepted the line of 49° N. Lat. to the Rocky Mountains and acknowledged the equal claim of the United States to the Pacific Northwest. Spain, harassed by South American revolutions, in 1819 gave up Florida to the United States in a treaty which also established a most favorable transcontinental frontier line from Texas to California (*see* Adams-Onís Treaty).

These new boundaries were soon expanded in both directions: to the southwest, by the annexation of Texas[qv], and by the purchase of Mexican territory in the Treaty of Guadalupe Hidalgo[qv], 1848, following a war the fundamental cause of which was the Texas question; to the northwest, by the Oregon Treaty[qv] in which England recognized full American sovereignty south of 49° to the Pacific Ocean. Great Britain was opposed to both of these expansions, but preferred to accept them because at that time she was not in a position really to fight, either for Texas or Oregon. In 1853 the United States bought from Mexico a comparatively small strip of territory, the Gadsden Purchase[qv].

It will be noted that this expansion of territory took place in three ways: by treaties of purchase; by treaties for frontier settlements; and by joint resolution of annexation, accepted by the republic of Texas reciprocally in 1845.

Two other treaties of purchase vastly expanded American territory: Alaska[qv], from Russia in 1867 (Russia preferred to sell an unprofitable colony rather than see it some day conquered by the British navy), and the Philippines[qv] from Spain in 1899, as a result of the war of 1898. In the same treaty of peace Puerto Rico and Guam[qqv] were ceded as an outright conquest. The Hawaiian Islands[qv] were meanwhile annexed by joint resolution of Congress, which was reciprocally voted by the Hawaiian legislature, as in the case of Texas. The Danish West Indies[qv] were acquired by a treaty of purchase in 1917. A number of small islands in the Atlantic and Pacific (*see* Pacific Islands) have been annexed by presidential proclamation (a fourth means of annexation). Annexation of the Philippines, accomplished by a treaty of peace and purchase, is being undone by an act of Congress (*see* Philippine Independence).

[Samuel Flagg Bemis, *A Diplomatic History of the United States.*]

SAMUEL FLAGG BEMIS

Antarctic Exploration. *See* Byrd's Polar Flights; Wilkes Exploring Expedition, 1838–42.

Antelope, THE, a Spanish vessel taken March, 1820, by an American privateer, was seized by a United States revenue cutter with a cargo of slaves captured from Spanish and Portuguese ships. Vessel and Africans were claimed by Spanish and Portuguese vice-consuls on behalf of their citizens. Chief Justice Marshall, declaring for the United States Supreme Court that the African slave trade was not contrary to the law of nations, that the American cruiser had no right of search[qv] and seizure in a time of peace, and that it was not the duty of the United States to execute the penal laws of another country, directed that the slaves be restored to the foreigner in possession at the time of the capture.

[10 Wheaton 66.]

LIONEL H. LAING

Anthracite, or hard coal, is a solid fuel characterized by a very high percentage of fixed carbon and a low percentage of volatile matter. Although anthracitic coals are mined in limited quantities in Arkansas, Colorado, New Mexico, Virginia and Washington, the term "anthracite" usually is applied only to the output from an elongated area of approximately 480 square miles in eastern Pennsylvania.

The existence of Pennsylvania anthracite was known to colonists as early as 1763. Obadiah Gore used it successfully in a smithy forge in Wilkes-Barre in 1769, and anthracite was shipped to the Carlisle arsenal in 1776. Jesse Fell, also of Wilkes-Barre, demonstrated its industrial fuel possibilities in nail manufacturing in 1788; twenty years later he put it in the domestic picture by burning it on an open grate with natural draft.

Progress, nevertheless, was slow. Wood, plentiful and cheap, was the preferred household fuel. Acceleration in industrial demand had to wait upon the manufacturing growth of the new nation. Canals, and later railroads[qqv], had to be developed as marketing adjuncts to mining operations. Between 1807 and 1820, total output aggregated only 12,000 net tons; the 1,000,000-ton mark was not reached until 1837 and annual production did not touch 10,000,000 tons until 1863.

Thereafter the long-term trend continued steadily upward, culminating in the war-time peak of 99,611,811 tons in 1917. Long before that peak, however, bituminous coal[qv] had far outstripped anthracite in the industrial markets. Today, anthracite is primarily a domestic fuel; over 85% of the output is used for heating services.

Here, too, competition is taking its toll. Strikes (*see* Anthracite Strike, 1902), increasing mine costs and transportation charges in the early years of the 20th century shrank the areal market while actual tonnage was showing no alarming downward trends. More recently, and particularly since 1927, competition with other fuels in what is now its major market—the New England and Middle Atlantic states—has still further curtailed anthracite consumption, scaling down output from established mines to 51,745,000 tons in 1937. In the campaign to stop these losses and recover vanished markets, the greatest gains have been made in the sale of the smaller sizes of anthracite adaptable for use in household stokers.

[*Mineral Resources of the United States*, U. S. Geological Survey, 1879-1923; U. S. Bureau of Mines, 1924-31; *Minerals Yearbook*, U. S. Bureau of Mines, 1932-38; Eliot Jones, *The Anthracite Coal Combination in the United States;* Hudson Coal Co., *The Story of Anthracite.*]

SYDNEY A. HALE

Anthracite Strike (1902). In May, 1902, after vain efforts to secure an agreement, 150,000 anthracite[qv] miners, members of the United Mine Workers[qv], under the leadership of John Mitchell, went on strike for higher wages, shorter hours and recognition of the union. Most of the mines were owned by corporations which also controlled the coal-carrying railroads. Though the strike forced a complete shutdown, practically paralyzing the industry, the owners refused any dealings with the striking miners. There was little violence and because they had real grievances, the miners won a large measure of public sympathy and support. As winter approached acute coal shortage developed. A widespread public demand arose for prompt settlement. Prices rose steadily. The coal operators still refused to meet the miners' representatives, their spokesman, George F. Baer, declaring in June: "We will give no consideration to any plan of arbitration or mediation or to any interference on the part of any outside party." On July 17 Baer wrote: "The rights and interests of the laboring men will be protected and cared for, not by the labor agitators, but by the Christian men to whom God in his infinite wisdom has given the control of the property interests of the country." Two months later, Baer again stated the operators would not yield. Soon afterwards President Theodore Roosevelt intervened and called for a conference of the warring elements. The operators resented this action and accused the President of failure to send troops to protect the mines from violence. Of this charge, the President was not guilty, as the governor of Pennsylvania had refused to call for Federal troops; instead he called out the Pennsylvania Guard. The situation was becoming dangerous. After a secret, but unsuccessful, attempt had been made to intercede through a commission of which ex-President Cleveland was to be chairman, the President was ready to send regular troops, even to take over and operate the mines. This determination was allowed to be known and as a result the owners and operators yielded and in a stormy conference agreed to a committee of arbitration to be appointed by the President. The miners returned to work and, March 18, 1903, the commission awarded them a 10% increase in wages and other concessions. This strike is notable in that it emphasized that in struggles between capital and labor, the interests of a third party, the public, are paramount.

[John R. Commons, *History of Labour in the United States.*]

THOMAS ROBSON HAY

Anthracite-Tidewater Canals. Anthracite was discovered in northeastern Pennsylvania in the latter 18th century, but for years it could be gotten to market only by floating it in arks or flatboats[qqv] down the turbulent streams flowing out of the coal region—a difficult and expensive method. Josiah White in 1818 improved the upper Lehigh River with dams, but this not proving adequate, he built the Lehigh Canal, completing it to the Delaware River at Easton in 1829. From there the Delaware Division of the Pennsylvania Canals continued the haul to tidewater at Bristol. Later, some of the coal crossed New Jersey to New York Harbor through the Morris Canal[qv], built 1824–32. The Schuylkill Canal, completed in 1825, was not conceived as a coal carrier, but it became one of the greatest in the country. The Delaware & Hudson[qv], built 1825–29, hauled coal out of the Lackawanna region, which was also served by the North Branch of the Pennsylvania State Canals[qv], following down the Susquehanna, transferring some of its coal at Middletown to the Union Canal[qv], whence it passed via the Schuylkill to Philadelphia and New York; or it carried on to Columbia, where the Susquehanna & Tidewater (built 1835–38) took over and hauled the coal down to Baltimore, sometimes through the Chesapeake & Delaware Canal^qv^, Delaware River and Delaware & Raritan Canal^qv^ to New York. These canals in their heyday, during the 1860's and 1870's, may each have carried from 1,000,000 to 3,000,000 tons yearly; but the greater speed of the railroads destroyed them, one by one. The Lehigh-Delaware was the longest-lived of all. In 1931, after it had transported nearly 50,000,000 tons of anthracite, not to mention other freight, all in horse-drawn boats, its traffic was abandoned.

[Alvin F. Harlow, *Old Towpaths.*]

ALVIN F. HARLOW

Anti-Bank Movement of the West, THE. Opposition to banks of issue existed from the beginning of such institutions in America in the late 18th century. It was a marked characteristic of the Jeffersonian^qv^ movement. After the panic of 1837^qv^, however, the sentiment reached the stage of a movement to abolish banks. It was rooted in Jacksonian fear, debtor distress, and a bullionist or "hard money"^qv^ theory (*see* Jacksonian Democracy).

The movement was centered in the new Jacksonian states of the Mississippi Valley and reached its climax in the constitutional conventions of the 1840's and 1850's. Between 1845 and 1863 banks were abolished at one time in Illinois, Wisconsin, Iowa, Missouri, Arkansas, Louisiana, Texas and the Pacific Coast.

The movement is properly interpreted as an early example of agrarian^qv^ protest similar to the Populist^qv^ movement of a later date.

[L. C. Helderman, *National and State Banks: A Study of Their Origins.*]

L. C. HELDERMAN

Antietam, The Battle of (Sept. 17, 1862). Early in September, 1862, Gen. Lee's (C.) Army of Northern Virginia^qv^ crossed the Potomac into Maryland (*see* Maryland, Invasion of). He concentrated at Frederick, then sent Jackson's corps south to take Harpers Ferry, and Longstreet's westward across the South Mountain^qv^. On the 14th McClellan's (U.) Army of the Potomac^qv^ forced the mountain passes.

Lee began to concentrate toward the Potomac, and took position at Sharpsburg, on the Antietam Creek. While Longstreet was assembling here, Lee heard that Jackson had captured Harpers Ferry^qv^, and took the bold decision to stand and fight behind the creek, with the Potomac at his back. Longstreet took the right of the line; Jackson's troops, as they arrived, the left.

McClellan planned to strike Lee's left with three corps (Hooker's, Mansfield's and Sumner's); to follow this blow with an attack by Burnside's corps on the Confederate right; and to hold Porter's and Frankin's corps, with Pleasonton's cavalry, in reserve in the center.

But Hooker, Mansfield and Sumner attacked successively, not simultaneously, and each in turn was beaten. Burnside's attack on the other flank came still later. Longstreet's line had been weakened to reinforce Jackson, for Lee had no real reserve; hence Burnside made some progress at first, but when fully engaged he was struck in flank by A. P. Hill's (C.) division, the last of Jackson's troops returning from Harpers Ferry. Burnside was driven back to the bridge by which he had crossed the creek, and darkness ended the fighting.

On the 18th Lee stood fast and McClellan did not renew his attack. On the 19th Lee effected his withdrawal across the Potomac. The numbers engaged are uncertain; perhaps a fair estimate is 50,000 Federal, 40,000 Confederate. But this was Lee's entire strength, and McClellan had 20,000 in reserve, never used. The losses may be estimated as 12,000 Federal, 9000 Confederate.

[Official Records, War of the Rebellion; *Battles and Leaders of the Civil War;* J. C. Palfrey, *The Antietam and Fredericksburg.*]

OLIVER LYMAN SPAULDING

Anti-Federalists, THE, were opponents of ratification of the Constitution^qv^ (1781–88), who feared loss of individual liberty and state rights^qv^. After 1793 they became identified with the Jeffersonian Republican Party^qv^.

WHEELER PRESTON

Anti-Horse Thief Association, THE, was organized at Fort Scott, Kans., in 1859 to provide protection against marauders thriving on border warfare^qv^. It resembled vigilance societies^qv^ in organization and methods. After the Civil War gangs of outlaws made their hideaways in the inadequately policed Indian Territory^qv^ and preyed on the livestock, chiefly horses, of the neighboring states. During the period 1869 to 1875 officers were unable to cope with the bandits, and few sheriffs ventured south of the Marion County line, 150 miles north of the Indian Territory. The organization spread to other sections of the state as necessity arose, and probably to other states, but eventually turned into a social organization.

[E. Dick, *Sod House Frontier;* J. A. McClellan, Joseph McClellan, in *Kansas Historical Collection,* Vol. 17.]

CARL L. CANNON

Anti-Imperialists. This term was applied to American leaders who opposed colonial expansion after the Spanish-American War[qv]. Sen. George Frisbie Hoar and other New England Republicans were strong Anti-Imperialists, but refused to desert their party on the issue. A number of liberals joined the Anti-Imperialism League, which in 1900 threw its support to William Jennings Bryan.

[W. R. Thayer, *Life and Letters of John Hay.*]

THEODORE G. GRONERT

Anti-Masonic Movements. Suspicion of secret societies[qv] was marked at an early date, but the fact that Washington and other patriots were Masons[qv] seemed proof that the Order was not dangerous. In 1826, however, when the Morgan Trials[qv] aroused western New York there was a widespread reaction, which assumed national importance with the organization of the Anti-Masonic party. Many Masons renounced their vows, membership in New York dwindling from 20,000 to 3000 between 1826 and 1836. The number of lodges was reduced from 507 before 1826, to 48 in 1832. In Vermont the Grand Lodge voted down a proposal for dissolution, but agreed to receive charters from chapters desiring to surrender them, and provided that funds of such lodges should go to the state public school fund. Many congregations were divided, especially Presbyterian, Baptist, Methodist and Congregational[qqv]. Masons were excluded from membership, and pastors were barred from their pulpits. In Pennsylvania, Anti-Masonry found favor among Quakers, Mennonites, Dunkards, Moravians and some Lutheran and German Reformed groups[qqv]. A Vermont law of 1833 forbade extrajudicial oaths; and elsewhere Masons were deprived of local office and dropped from jury rolls.

Anti-Masonic newspapers were an index of the rapid growth of the Anti-Masonic party. Charging intimidation of printers and suppression of facts of the Morgan Trials, party leaders urged the establishment of "free presses." Thurlow Weed, who in 1828 had started the Rochester *Anti-Masonic Enquirer,* was given financial backing in 1830 for his *Albany Evening Journal,* the principal party organ. In 1832 there were forty-six Anti-Masonic papers in New York and fifty-five in Pennsylvania. In September, 1831, a national Anti-Masonic convention was held at Baltimore, naming William Wirt of Maryland for President. This, the first "third party"[qv], only drew support from Clay, and helped the sweep for Jackson in 1832. It received seven electoral votes from Vermont. The party also gained adherents in Pennsylvania, Ohio, New Jersey, Massachusetts, Connecticut and Rhode Island; but only Pennsylvania, through the leadership of Thaddeus Stevens, and Vermont elected Anti-Masonic governors. In the late 1830's the excitement subsided, or was replaced by the antislavery[qv] agitation. By 1838 the party had merged with the Whigs[qv].

After the Civil War there was another movement directed against secret societies. The National Christian Association was founded at Aurora, Ill., in 1868 to oppose secret orders, "Jesuitism, Mormonism, atheism, spiritualism and free love"[qv]. It maintained a national organization and published a weekly, *The Christian Cynosure* (1867–71). This crusade was unsuccessful, and the 1880's and 1890's witnessed a great increase of fraternal orders.

[J. C. Palmer, *The Morgan Affair and Anti-Masonry;* Charles McCarthy, *The Anti-Masonic Party; The Anti-Masonic Scrapbook,* 1883.]

MILTON W. HAMILTON

Anti-Monopoly Parties (1873–76), sometimes called Independent or Reform parties, were organized by farmers, especially Grange[qv] members, in Indiana, Illinois, Michigan, Wisconsin, Minnesota, Iowa, Missouri, Kansas, Nebraska, California and Oregon. Their platforms demanded government reform, economy and reduced taxation; all but two also demanded state regulation of corporations, particularly railroads. In some states the new parties fused with the Democrats[qv]; thus they had some success in Iowa, and elected the whole state ticket in Wisconsin. In other states, as in Oregon, and to some extent in Illinois, they remained independent and won local victories. In Illinois, Kansas and California they secured the election of "Reformers" as United States senators. In Wisconsin, Iowa and Minnesota, in 1874, the Anti-Monopolists obtained enactment of "Granger" railroad laws[qv]. Though these were soon repealed or moderated, their passage evoked court decisions establishing the right of states to regulate railway corporations. The Anti-Monopoly parties did not survive the presidential campaign of 1876[qv].

[S. J. Buck, *The Granger Movement;* S. J. Buck, Independent Parties in the West, in *Essays in American History Dedicated to Frederick Jackson Turner.*]

SOLON J. BUCK

Antinomian Controversy, THE, was a theological dispute begun in Boston by Mistress Anne Hutchinson in the fall of 1636. She had been a parishioner and devout admirer of John Cotton in Boston, England, and with her husband followed him to the new Boston, where they were admitted to membership in the First Church. She was exceptionally intelligent, learned and eloquent, and began innocently to repeat on week days to small gatherings the substance of Cotton's sermons, but soon commenced delivering opinions of her own. At the height of her influence about eighty persons were attending lectures in her house.

She caused turmoil by putting a different conclusion from that maintained by the clergy upon the doctrine of the Covenant of Grace. The standard view held that the elect entered a Covenant with God on the condition of their believing in Christ, in return for which God contracted to give them salvation, but that thereafter the justified saints devoted themselves to good works, not in order to merit redemption, but as evidence of their having been called. Mrs. Hutchinson declared that stating the matter thus put too much emphasis upon "works" and denied the fundamental Protestant tenet of salvation by faith alone. Consequently she preached that the believer received into his soul the very substance of the Holy Ghost and that no value whatsoever adhered to conduct as a sign of justification.

This conclusion made for a disregard of morality such as Protestant theologians had everywhere endeavored to resist, and it could clearly lead to disastrous social consequences; the New England clergy, recognizing in her teachings a form of "Antinomianism," i.e., a discarding of the moral law, could not possibly have tolerated her. She made matters worse by accusing all the clergy except Cotton of preaching a Covenant of Works, so that Winthrop says it began to be as common in Massachusetts to distinguish the party of works and the party of grace "as in other countries between Protestants and papists." Thus she threatened to split the colony into factions, particularly when she was supported by her brother-in-law, the Rev. John Wheelwright, and the young governor, Harry Vane. The other clergy and magistrates believed that the existence of the whole enterprise was at stake; led by John Winthrop, and employing consummately clever tactics, they regained control of the government in May, 1637, then proceeded to disarm Anne's partisans and suppress the movement. Anne was examined by a synod of the ministers, which found her guilty of eighty erroneous opinions; John Cotton publicly repudiated her. Wheelwright was banished to New Hampshire; Anne was arraigned before the General Court, where she boasted of having received explicit revelations from the Holy Ghost, a possibility which no orthodox Protestant community could for a moment admit. She was excommunicated from the First Church in March, 1638, John Cotton pronouncing sentence upon her, and banished from the colony by the Court, whereupon she fled to Rhode Island.

[C. F. Adams, *Antinomianism in the Colony of Massachusetts Bay; Three Episodes of Massachusetts History;* Perry Miller, *Orthodoxy in Massachusetts;* E. S. Morgan, The Case Against Anne Hutchinson, *New England Quarterly,* X, 635-649, 1937.]

PERRY MILLER

Anti-Poverty Societies supported Henry George's view that involuntary poverty resulted from human laws; they were formed in New York City (1887) and other cities.

WHEELER PRESTON

Anti-Rent Agitation, THE, which swept New York, 1839–46, was a culmination of the resentment of farmers against the leasehold system[qv], whereby the great landlords and land companies collected yearly tribute in produce, labor or money, and exacted a share ("quarter sales") of one quarter or one third of the amount realized from the sale of a leasehold. In 1839, when the heirs of Stephen Van Rensselaer tried to collect some $400,000 in back rent, the farmers rebelled. Gov. Seward called out the militia and issued a proclamation of warning. This sobered the rioters and ended the so-called "Helderberg War." Similar disturbances, however, soon broke out in the counties south of Albany.

In Columbia and Delaware Counties groups of men disguised as Indians tarred and feathered sheriffs and deputies who attempted to serve writs of ejectment. The murder of Deputy Sheriff Steele, August, 1845, led Gov. Wright to proclaim Delaware County in a state of insurrection. Anti-rent secret societies spread rapidly and became a political influence. The constitution of 1846 prohibited new feudal tenures and a court decision declared "quarter sales" illegal. There followed a general conversion of old leases into fee simple ownership.

[E. P. Cheney, The Antirent Movement, in A. C. Flick, *History of the State of New York,* Vol. VI.]

A. C. FLICK

Anti-Saloon League, THE, was founded at Oberlin, Ohio, May 24, 1893. Creating this statewide organization was the idea of the Rev. H. H. Russell. This "Ohio plan" was copied by many states and in 1895 a national organization, the Anti-Saloon League of America, was established at the Calvary Baptist Church, Washington, D. C. Soliciting and securing aid from the Protestant Evangelical churches, the league grew rapidly and came to regard itself as the "Church in Action Against the Saloon."

Theoretically, the co-operating churches possess the ultimate authority within the league. In fact, however, real control is exercised by the national executive committee and the national board of directors. The board, composed of not less than two nor more than five representatives from each state, is chosen by the state boards. The executive committee, when the board is not in session, exercises all the powers of the board. The General Superintendent, appointed by the board, exercises general supervision over national and state affairs and nominates the state superintendents who are theoretically selected by the state boards. Both state and national organizations employ legislative agents and attorneys who act as lobbyists for the league. Wayne B. Wheeler was national legislative superintendent from 1920 to 1927.

Prior to the Eighteenth Amendment*qv* the league centered its attention upon destroying the liquor traffic by legislation. To this end it sought and obtained local option*qv*, county option, state prohibition, regulation of interstate liquor shipments and finally national prohibition*qv*. Following national prohibition the league sought by propaganda and pressure to achieve enforcement and the maintenance of this policy. For the first time in its history it was completely on the defensive. Accused of responsibility for the development of bootleg*qv* gangs, disrespect for law and all of the undesirable social practices of the post-war period, the league slowly lost support. The depression of 1929 brought a diminution in the league's revenues. Faced by a public willing to try anything which might re-establish prosperity, and weakened internally, it lost ground rapidly, suffering its final indignity in 1933 when the Eighteenth Amendment was repealed. Since that date it has not been significant in national politics and has returned to its original program of persuasion and local option.

[E. H. Cherrington, *History of the Anti-Saloon League;* Peter Odegard, *Pressure Politics;* Justin Stewart, *Wayne Wheeler, Dry Boss.*]

DAYTON E. HECKMAN

Antislavery. Antislavery sentiment varied all the way from the mildest doubts as to the wisdom of chattel slavery to a militant movement to abolish it without compensation and without delay. It was conditioned upon forces that worked in fields as diverse as the legal and political, the religious and moral, the social and economic and the more vaguely sentimental and humanitarian. An antislavery attitude was implicit in the English legal system as it stood on the eve of American colonization, by which time the remnants of slavery under the feudal system had disappeared. Even the early colonial statutes recognizing slavery*qv* put numerous qualifications upon its status. If Protestantism as such did not debar slavery, at least its more radically democratic sects, like the Quakers*qv* and various Puritan groups, did denounce it. They marshaled moral and religious arguments against the institution, the Quakers stressing the implications of the doctrine of human brotherhood. The influence of John Locke*qv* led 18th-century commentators to include personal freedom as one of the natural and inalienable rights of man; the exploitation of such theories during the American Revolution included a strong challenge to slavery on humanitarian grounds, which penetrated the ranks of many of the Southern slaveholders themselves.

From the earliest days of the institution there were those who condemned it on social and economic grounds, as a wasteful and more expensive system making for unwilling workmen and a prejudice against honest toil and one which degraded the poor and elevated a small slavocracy*qv*. In the ante-bellum period others attributed to slavery responsibility for the economic backwardness of the South and the "thriftlessness, desolation and debasement" (Abbott, *South and North,* 329–330) that prevailed in that section. In the 1850's Lincoln and others charged the extreme defenders of slavery with an attack, under their "mudsill" theory, upon the white man's charter of liberty, the Declaration of Independence*qv*. Slavery was also held responsible for the political situation under which an oligarchy of a few thousand slaveholders came to rule the million whites of the South and exercised a dominant influence in national politics. On this ground Northern sentiment came to be aroused to an attempt to check the spread of slavery and its political power, by preventing its further extension into the territories. (*See* Missouri Compromise; Compromise of 1850.)

Throughout the duration of slavery, particularly in its later years, there were those who sentimentalized over the unfortunate lot of the poor slave toiling in bondage; they pictured the cruelty and injustice of harsh masters and overseers and other evils, real or imagined, connected with the system. The horrors of the slave traffic, the hapless plight of the fugitive, hunted by bloodthirsty pursuers and their baying bloodhounds, the thrilling rescues of captives from proslavery mobs bent upon carrying their victims back into bondage became the stock in trade of sentimental arguments, literary and oral. (*See* Fugitive Slave Act; Dred Scott Case; *Uncle Tom's Cabin,* Influence of; Underground Railway.)

With the outbreak of the Civil War, Northern

sentiment increasingly charged slavery with responsibility for the attempt to destroy the Union. Out of this situation arose an increasing demand for the extinction of slavery, root and branch.

[J. Macy, *The Anti-Slavery Crusade.*]

ARTHUR C. COLE

Antislavery Literature became a force in the latter half of the 18th century as an expression of the egalitarianism then dominant in England. By 1800, through the essays of Quakers[qv] like John Woolman, and of humanitarians[qv] like Thomas Jefferson, Benjamin Franklin and Thomas Paine, the abstract right of the Negro slave to freedom on both religious and political grounds had become part of our literary tradition. During the next three decades the rise of cotton[qv] and the opening of the Southwest to slavery[qv] led to sectional[qv] divergence. By 1832 Southern tradition viewed slavery as a permanent institution, while Northern opinion still condemned it "in the abstract." (*See* Proslavery; Antislavery.)

During the ensuing decade, militant organization of antislavery sentiment produced an enormous volume of antislavery tracts, but the controversy over immediatist doctrine[qv], imported here from the contemporary British movement, gave to most of them only ephemeral value. Aside from some brilliant writing in the antislavery periodicals, notably the *Liberator*[qv], effective work during this decade was largely done by the antislavery orators, such as Wendell Phillips and Theodore Dwight Weld.

By the 1840's, however, immediatism was triumphant; slavery was no longer an abstract wrong, but a concrete horror; and the Slave Power was the enemy of mankind. In this new tradition, Whittier wrote his greatest poems for freedom and James Russell Lowell published his *Biglow Papers*[qv]. In 1851 Harriet Beecher Stowe embalmed the tradition for all time in her novel, *Uncle Tom's Cabin*[qv].

Toward the close of the 1850's economic tracts against slavery appeared to supplement the humanitarian literature: Helper's *Impending Crisis*[qv] (1857) and Olmsted's travel narratives, especially his *Journey in the Seaboard Slave States* (1856). The Civil War put an end to significant antislavery literature.

[M. N. Work, *A Bibliography of the Negro in Africa and America.*]

GILBERT HOBBS BARNES

Antislavery Literature and the Mails. Antislavery literature was barred from the mails in the South in 1835. It was excluded by indirect means, and not by law, although a bill for the purpose was debated in the Senate, failing of passage on June 8, 1836, by six votes. The American Anti-Slavery Society[qv] had mailed thousands of copies of its publications to individuals in the Southern states. On July 29 and 30, 1835, members of an indignant mob removed a mass of these papers from the post office at Charleston, S. C., and burned them. Postmaster-General Amos Kendall subsequently wrote the Charleston postmaster and others in the South, unofficially sanctioning their removal of antislavery papers. Postmasters or other citizens thereupon prevented the delivery of such literature. Feeling grew bitter throughout the country and violent means were used to silence unwelcome opinions. Denying the abolitionists[qv] the use of the mails was unwise in that it enabled them to add to their basic arguments the issue of a deprivation of their civil rights.

[J. B. McMaster, *A History of the People of the United States*, Vol. VI.]

ROBERT P. LUDLUM

Antislavery Movement, THE, in the United States may be defined as the history of organized propaganda against Negro slavery[qv]. This movement was but one of a complex of forces affecting slavery, which included economic developments both North and South, the pull and haul of sectional politics (*see* Sectionalism), changing creeds in both religion and social philosophy, and even the fortuitous course of public events. Before 1830, one or the other of these forces so overshadowed earlier forms of antislavery organization as to make them negligible (*see* Missouri Compromise); but after that date a new type of organization appeared which made history. Begun originally to promote interdenominational enterprises such as the distribution of Bibles and tracts (*see* American Tract Society), this new type of organization during the previous decade had spread to temperance, prison reform[qqv] and similar moral causes. By 1830 it had become a major force in the American scene.

Though each cause was organized separately as a national society, the whole movement was administered through interlocking directorates by a relatively small number of philanthropists and clergymen, who were regularly re-elected at annual conventions of delegates from the nation, which met in New York each May. Between conventions, the societies propagandized their reforms through tracts and weekly newspapers, and through traveling agents (*see* Antislavery Literature). Among the ruling philanthropists, the most influential were the brothers Arthur and Lewis Tappan, wealthy New York merchants;

and among the agents, incomparably the most eloquent and successful was Theodore Weld.

This whole movement was copied slavishly, in some cases even as to names, from like organizations in Great Britain. It was to be expected, therefore, that shortly after British philanthropists started a parliamentary drive, in 1830, for the immediate abolition of slavery in the West Indies (*see* Immediatism), the Tappans should organize a similar movement here. In June, 1831, they published plans for an American Anti-Slavery Society[qv]; during the next two years they laid its foundations throughout the North; and in December, 1833, they launched it at Philadelphia.

During its first two years, the Society's drive against slavery, in the form of a monster pamphlet[qv] campaign, met with little but hostility. This was largely because the pamphlets advocated immediate emancipation, which was everywhere interpreted as meaning "to turn the slave loose, regardless of consequences." Actually, the "watchword" of immediate emancipation was adopted in order to identify the American with the British movement; and the phrase was officially defined as meaning merely that "measures looking toward ultimate emancipation be immediately begun." But the failure of the pamphlet campaign clearly showed, as Channing, New England liberal, remarked, that "it is a fatal mistake for a party to choose a watchword which almost certainly conveys a wrong sense and needs explanation."

Meanwhile, however, Theodore Weld, at Lane Seminary in Cincinnati, at Oberlin and in New York, had been training a corps of agents in a new technique of antislavery agitation, revivalistic in character and essentially religious in its appeal. So successful were they that in 1836 the national society abandoned its pamphlet drive, and took over their support. During the remainder of the decade these new agents converted whole communities to the duty of denouncing slavery as a sin. (*See* Proslavery.)

The chief activity of these new converts was securing signatures from their neighbors on petitions to Congress for antislavery objects. The fact that Southern Congressmen opposed their reception in the House made petitions a prime means of propaganda; and when John Quincy Adams championed their cause in Congress, the question of their reception became a national issue (*see* Petitions, Antislavery). More and more of the efforts and resources of the converts went into local petition campaigns; and the national society, thus deprived of funds and functions, withered away. In 1840 it ceased in all but name.

Two years later, antislavery sentiment in districts converted by Weld's agents had become so strong that their representatives in Congress, led by Joshua Giddings, decided to break with the party program and attack slavery systematically upon the floor of the House. Under Weld's guidance—he was now in Washington—they succeeded, and thereby established still another type of antislavery organization, an insurgent bloc[qv] in Congress.

Though the insurgents' program in Congress was determined largely by the course of public events, they furthered systematic propaganda by means of a weekly newspaper, *The National Era,* which was established in Washington with Lewis Tappan's aid. Through its columns they directed antislavery workers in the field, and published effective tracts and documents. Here first appeared the greatest tract of the movement, *Uncle Tom's Cabin*[qv].

As the number of insurgents increased, friction with party leaders grew intolerable. The time inevitably came when they broke with their parties and established the final form of antislavery organization, first as the Free Soil party[qv], then as the antislavery wing of the Republican party[qv].

[G. H. Barnes, *The Antislavery Impulse,* 1830-44; F. J. Klingberg, *The Antislavery Movement in England.*]

GILBERT HOBBS BARNES

Antisuffragists, those opposed to suffrage for women. The first antisuffrage group was organized by women in Washington in 1871. Other groups were formed in Eastern states from time to time but the movement made little progress in the West. In 1911 women organized The National Association Opposed to Woman Suffrage and in 1913 the Men's Antisuffrage Association was organized in New York. The organizations disappeared with the ratification of the Nineteenth Amendment[qv] in 1920. (*See also* Woman Suffrage.)

[Ida Husted Harper, *History of Woman Suffrage,* Vol. V.]

HALLIE FARMER

Antisyndicalist Laws. Beginning with Idaho in 1917, criminal syndicalism laws have been passed in twenty-one states and two territories. These laws define criminal syndicalism[qv] as "the doctrine which advocates crime, sabotage, violence, or other unlawful methods of terrorism as a means of accomplishing industrial and political reform." The immediate cause of such legislation was the activity of the Industrial Workers of the World[qv], which advocated sabotage and other forms of direct action among the miners, lumber workers and agricultural laborers of the West and Northwest. During the period of the

World War obstruction by the I. W. W. was greatly feared. Following the war, considerable hysteria developed as a result of the organization of the Communist party[qv] of America. Antisyndicalist laws represented an attempt to suppress all subversive[qv] activities. Under these laws criminal syndicalism is a felony. State supreme courts have upheld these statutes and the United States Supreme Court has approved them as valid exercise of police power[qv]. Reversal of sentences by higher state courts has been common, and state executives have issued numerous pardons.

[P. F. Brissenden, *The I.W.W.: a Study in American Syndicalism.*]

GORDON S. WATKINS

Antitrust Laws. The industrial life in the United States started under a regime of *laissez faire*[qv] and, for many years, no attempt was made to regulate business of any kind. The rapid growth of population, the introduction of the factory system with large-scale production, the development of the corporate form of business organization, the extension of transportation systems and protection from foreign competition all contributed to the growth of what has generally come to be known as the trust[qqv]. In reality it has taken many forms, such as the trust proper, in which the shares of stock of several independent firms are placed in the hands of a trustee who manages the business for the good of the group; the holding company[qv], in which the parent company owns a controlling interest in subsidiary companies; the merger, in which the actual properties of former companies are consolidated into one business; and the trade agreement, in which several firms reach an agreement as to the business practices which they will follow. In the formation of these big businesses many unfair practices were used, such as cutthroat competition, rebates and repression of patents. The public reaction to such practices, together with the antagonism to the monopolies[qv] which resulted, led to the demand for regulation.

The Sherman Antitrust Act[qv], passed in 1890, was the first formal result of the demand for regulation. This declared all combinations in restraint of trade[qv] to be illegal and penalties were provided for violation. Because of the extreme provisions of the act, little was done in the way of its enforcement and the Supreme Court adopted the "rule of reason"[qv] in 1911. Under this the decree was set forth that the act applied only to those combinations in business which resulted in unreasonable restraints upon trade. Throughout these years of inactivity the trust movement grew rapidly.

The failure of the Sherman Act to accomplish satisfactory regulation resulted in the passage of the Clayton Act and the Federal Trade Commission Act[qqv] in 1914. These acts recognize that combinations in themselves are not necessarily evil, but that certain practices should be prohibited. The Clayton Act prohibited certain types of price discriminations and the use of tying contracts; regulations were placed upon the use of the holding company; under certain conditions, one person was not allowed to be a director in two or more companies engaged in commerce; and directors in corporations were to be held personally liable for illegal activities. The work of the Federal Trade Commission is that of investigation of business practices to the end that unfair competition may be prevented. It does not have final jurisdiction but can press its charges before the courts. It often acts, moreover, in an advisory capacity as to the legality of contemplated business practices.

The National Industrial Recovery Act[qv] was passed in 1933. Under this, codes were drawn for different industries which set forth the type of combination and business practices which each expected to use. Much dissatisfaction arose over the codes and many modifications would have had to be made had not the Supreme Court declared the act unconstitutional. At present (1939) the legislation of 1914 prevails although legislation has granted immunity from its application to certain types of business. In general, the present attitude is to recognize the possible advantages of big business, but to set up standards of conduct and to see that they are enforced.

[Gemmill and Blodgett, *Economics.*]

MERLIN H. HUNTER

Anza Expedition, THE (Oct. 23, 1775–Jan. 4, 1776), was sent out by Antonio Bucareli, Viceroy of New Spain, to provide Alta California[qv] with the white population essential to its occupation in face of English and Russian threats. Led by Juan Bautista de Anza, who in 1774 had proved that a route existed from Sonora to California, 244 persons crossed the Colorado desert and reached San Gabriel. Local jealousies prevented Anza from founding the city he laid out but his capable lieutenant, José Joaquin Moraga, Sept. 17, 1776, dedicated a presidio[qv] on the site of modern San Francisco and there, Oct. 9, 1776, was started the mission San Francisco de Asís.

[H. E. Bolton, *Anza's California Expeditions.*]

OSGOOD HARDY

Apache, Fort, Incident at (Sept. 13, 1886). Chiricahua and Mimbreno Apaches living near Fort Apache were believed aiding hostile bands in the summer of 1886. September 13, Col. J. F. Wade summoned the Apaches[qv] to the fort, for counting, surrounded them with troops and shipped them wholesale to Fort Marion, Fla., to be interned.

[Nelson A. Miles, *Personal Recollections.*]

PAUL I. WELLMAN

Apache, THE, was a name applied to a number of banded warlike tribes in New Mexico, Arizona and west Texas, belonging to the Athapascan family. After the Spanish conquest the tribes increased and extended into northern Mexico. From their homes in the mountains they raided Mexicans and Americans alike, and became notoriously expert at hiding, trailing, ambushing and shooting. Apache campaigns were bloody and prolonged. Some bands were practically exterminated before they surrendered and the name has become synonymous with treachery and cruelty. F. W. Hodge believes some of their later hostilities were due to mismanagement. Their famous chiefs were Cochise[qv], Victorio and Geronimo[qv]. The Chiricahua tribe held out longest; Geronimo was not captured until 1886, and a few bands were still at large in 1900.

[F. W. Hodge, *Handbook of American Indians.*]

CARL L. CANNON

Apache Pass Expedition (Feb. 4–23, 1861). Cochise, a chief of the Chiricahua Apaches, was arrested Feb. 5, 1861, by Lt. George N. Bascom, 7th Infantry, on an unproved charge of having captured a boy. He escaped, led attacks on a nearby stage station and on a wagon train, captured three men and offered to exchange one of his prisoners for Indians held by Bascom. Bascom demanded all three. On his way to Bascom's relief, Asst. Surgeon B. J. D. Irwin captured three Indians. It was later learned that Cochise had killed his prisoners, and six Indians were hanged in retaliation. This incident was the reputed origin of the long warfare (1861–74) against Cochise.

[Don Russell, in *Winners of the West,* December, 1936.]

DON RUSSELL

Apalache Massacre, THE (1704), was an episode in Queen Anne's War[qv]. Having failed to take St. Augustine, Fla. (1702), ex-Gov. James Moore of Carolina with 50 Englishmen and 1000 Indians invaded the Apalache district in western Florida, defeating Capt. Mexia's force of 30 Spaniards and 400 Apalaches, destroying all (i.e., 13) but one of the Franciscan[qv] mission settlements and carrying off considerable loot including about 1400 Christian Indians.

[J. T. Lanning, *The Spanish Missions of Georgia.*]

FRANCIS BORGIA STECK

Apartment Houses. The word apartment has only recently come into its present use. In England it means a house let to tenants or lodgers. In the United States it is difficult to distinguish between apartments and tenements[qv]. In New England any house or apartment rented is called a tenement. The usual definition of an apartment is a division of a building designed to be used by an individual or a group of individuals living together. An apartment is usually of better construction, pays higher rentals and if over three stories is equipped with elevator[qv].

The apartment has come into use in the United States within the last thirty-five years and prevails mainly in large cities where land values are high and congestion of population prevails. Families desiring to avoid the responsibilities connected with maintaining an individual home prefer apartments. The new methods of construction have made possible the building of large numbers of apartments on small lots and still provide light and air as well as many comforts.

There are no statistical figures which distinguish tenements from apartments. Nor is there a legal way of precise differentiation. Apartments being multifamily dwellings accommodating three or more families we can only present the conditions and trends regarding multifamily dwellings built within a certain period of time. In 255 of the largest cities of the country, of all dwellings built during 1921 only 24.42% were multiple dwellings while in 1928 the multifamily dwellings increased to 53.74% of all the dwellings built in that year. In the cities of the Middle Atlantic states the proportion of such construction increased from 35% in 1921 to 70% in 1928.

Families desiring to combine home ownership with the advantages of apartment house living bought co-operative apartments. There are (1938) about 200 such apartments in New York and many others throughout the country. In 1930 there were 3,615,379 families living in apartments or multifamily dwellings or 12.1% of all the families of the United States. The number is constantly growing.

The largest increase in multifamily dwellings has taken place in the cities of over 100,000 population, the great metropolitan centers and their suburbs and the cities between 25,000 and 50,000 population. The apartment hotel is a new development in the larger cities and embodies the advantages of an apartment with many of the services afforded by hotels.

[Reports of the Dodge Corporation; Coleman Woodbury, *Apartment House Increases and Attitudes Towards Ownership.*]

CAROL ARONOVICI

Apia, Disaster of. On March 16, 1889, one British, three American and three German warships were crowded into Apia Harbor, ready for hostilities due to the German attempt to set up a protectorate under a puppet native king. A hurricane swept in, destroying the German *Eber, Adler* and the *Olga,* with the loss of 134 men; the U. S. *Trenton* and the *Vandalia,* with a loss of fifty-two lives. The U. S. *Nipsic* was run ashore. The British *Calliope* escaped by steaming out to sea. The Berlin Conference followed, establishing for Samoa[qv] a tripartite government.

[G. H. Ryden, *The Foreign Policy of the United States in Relation to Samoa.*]

J. W. ELLISON

Apostolic Delegation, THE, was established in Washington, D. C., by Pope Leo XIII, Jan. 24, 1893. Archbishop Satolli, representative of the Holy See at the World's Columbian Exposition[qv], was appointed as the first Apostolic Delegate. Since an attempt to establish formal diplomatic relations with the United States had been prudently abandoned in 1837, Pope Leo XIII did not accredit the Apostolic Delegate to the Government, but to the Catholic Church in the United States.

[*Catholic Encyclopedia,* Vol. IX; *The Ecclesiastical Review,* December, 1936.]

T. E. HEWITT

Appalachian Mountains, As Boundary. *See* Proclamation of 1763, The; Quebec Act, The; Indian Barrier State (Proposed).

***Appam* Case,** 1917 (243 U. S. 124). On Jan. 15, 1916, a German cruiser captured the above named British merchantman on the high seas and took her into Hampton Roads, Va. There her British crew was released by order of the American Government and on February 16 the shipowner filed a libel in the proper United States District Court, which ultimately decreed restitution of ship and cargo. On appeal by the German government to the Supreme Court the decree was affirmed on the ground that the capture, being a prize[qv], of which the lower court had jurisdiction, the ship's detention in port was a breach of American neutrality, unauthorized by any treaty.

C. SUMNER LOBINGIER

Appeal of the Independent Democrats, THE, a manifesto issued in January, 1854, was inspired by the Kansas-Nebraska Bill[qv], then pending. The signers, led by Sen. Salmon P. Chase, were free soilers[qv]. Chase had tried to convert Northern Democrats into a Wilmot Proviso[qv] party. Now, by a master stroke, precisely timed, he helped to create the Republican party[qv]. The "Appeal" was sincere and effective, though it contained exaggerated statements and unsound prophecies relative to the possible influence of the Douglas measure on the spread of slavery.

[*Congressional Globe,* 33rd Congress, 1st Session, 281-282.]

WILLIAM O. LYNCH

Appeals from Colonial Courts. In the latter part of the 17th century the new colonial charters[qv], proprietary and royal, reserved for the King in Council the right to hear cases on appeal from provincial courts where the sum litigated exceeded £300 sterling. In the New England colonies particularly the appellate authority was at best grudgingly conceded, as the Connecticut and Rhode Island charters made no provision for judicial review. At times, as in the case of Frost v. Leighton (1739), an order of the Privy Council[qv] was deliberately ignored by the Massachusetts authorities. Pending appeals, executions of the colonial courts were suspended. Such appeals were both costly and protracted.

Through this appellate procedure the Privy Council sought to bring the legal systems of the colonies into conformity with that of England, particularly in such matters as the rules of evidence and the jury system. Major issues of colonial policy were reviewed in litigation brought on appeal, notably Indian relations, the colonial currency laws and intestate succession. Currency practices in the colonies were more generally dealt with by the Privy Council under its authority to disallow colonial legislation or by Parliament (*see* Royal Disallowance). In the suit of the Virginia clergy instituted to recover back salaries resulting from the disallowance of the "two penny act"[qv], the Council, in view of the constitutional storms raised by the Stamp Act[qv], was prompted by political considerations to dismiss the appeal on a technicality. In the notable case of Winthrop v. Lechmere the Council held the Connecticut custom of divisible descent of intestate estates[qv] invalid as contrary to the common law, but reversed itself in Clark v. Tousey and in the Massachusetts case of Phillips v. Savage, a great victory for egalitarian property concepts in New England.

[G. A. Washburne, *Imperial Control of the Administration of Justice in the Thirteen American Colonies;* R. B. Morris, *Studies in the History of American Law.*]

RICHARD B. MORRIS

Apple Culture. The apple (*Pyrus Malus*), indigenous to southwestern Asia and adjacent Europe, thrives in temperate zones. Cultivated since the beginning of civilization, it is today the most important commercial pomological fruit. The world area in cultivated apples in 1932 was estimated at 6,940,000 acres, planted in about 415,000,000 trees, yielding a yearly average of 550,000,000 bushels. Thirty-five per cent of the world's acreage and crop is found in the United States.

Europe's best varieties were introduced in America by the early settlers. The French planted apples in Acadia and along the St. Lawrence about 300 years ago. The English and the Dutch introduced apples on the Atlantic seaboard as early as 1630. In Virginia, apples were grafted on wild stocks as early as 1647. In 1726 Chief Justice Dudley, of Massachusetts, wrote: "Our apples are, without doubt, as good as those of England, and fairer to look to." During the colonial period, Massachusetts, New York, Pennsylvania and Virginia grew quantities of apples for cider and for export as well. In 1790–91 the United States exported to England 12,352 barrels of apples, valued at $12,352. A number of new varieties were developed in America; in 1869 Charles Downing listed 1856 varieties.

Indians, traders, missionaries, settlers, carried the fruit to the frontier. Spanish missionaries planted apples in California in the 18th century. Apple culture in the Pacific Northwest was introduced in 1826, at Vancouver, Wash., by the Hudson's Bay Company. In 1847, Henderson Luelling brought his famous "traveling nursery" overland from Iowa. He established the first nursery in the Northwest, and introduced some of the best varieties of apples. During the gold rush, Oregon exported to California quantities of apples, which sold for as much as 75 cents to $5 each.

With the increase of population and adequate transportation facilities, the Pacific Coast and the entire country began to grow apples on a large scale. Practically every state grows apples; from twenty-five to forty states ship the fruit. The leading apple states in 1932 were: Washington, 30,960,000 bushels; New York, 22,197,000; Pennsylvania, 9,537,000; California, 9,045,000; Virginia, 7,830,000; Maine, 5,800,000; Ohio, 5,145,000; Oregon, 4,950,000; Idaho, 4,200,000; West Virginia, 4,191,000; New Jersey, 3,640,000; Massachusetts, 3,525,000. The apple industry, except on the Pacific Coast, is not as well organized as that of other fruits. It is confronted with severe competition on the domestic market and from tariff barriers abroad.

[L. H. Bailey, *The Standard Cyclopedia of Horticulture;* Bailey, *The Apples of New York.*]

J. W. ELLISON

Appleseed, Johnny. As the American frontier moved into Ohio, Indiana and Illinois, the settlers were deprived of fruit until orchards could be grown. Since the people lacked money, they could not have bought young trees were nurseries available; and horticulture languished. John Chapman therefore consecrated himself from 1801 to 1847 to the mission of bringing seed from Pennsylvania and planting flowers and fruits, especially apple seed in the forests to be ready for the free use of the settlers when they arrived. Meager documentary evidence and rich tradition have preserved Chapman's fame under the sobriquet of Johnny Appleseed.

[W. A. Duff, *Johnny Appleseed, an Ohio Hero;* Henry Chapin, *The Adventures of Johnny Appleseed; Kansas Horticultural Society Report*, 1922-23, pp. 137-40; *Harper's Magazine*, November, 1871, pp. 830-36.]

BLISS ISELY

Appointment, Council of. *See* Council of Appointment, New York, The.

Appointments and the Appointing Power. In the thirteen colonies appointment was a crown prerogative vested in the governor. In practice, however, the colonial assemblies[qv], in control of the purse, assumed the power of appointing the treasurer. In some colonies they came to control administration by appointing their own commissions of Indian affairs, intercolonial relations and military matters, even dictating the appointment and removal of military officers.

Long before the Revolution some legislatures were claiming the right to make all nominations by appropriating the salary not to the office but to a specified person. Independence removed virtually all restraint upon appointment by the legislature, even the governor being their appointee by all the first state constitutions except in Massachusetts and New York. By 1787 Americans generally thought of their executives as titular, political chiefs not properly concerned with administration and appointments.

The Federal Constitution[qv] departed radically from prevailing theory and practice in vesting the appointing power in the President[qv]. When the first Congress concluded that the Senate[qv] held no check on the President's power of removal[qv] his evolution into the administrative chief was inevitable.

Early Presidents made relatively few removals but the Four Years Law (1820) established a fixed term for numerous Federal officials. Taking advantage of consequent expirations President Jackson introduced (1829) rotation in office^{qv} in order to democratize the official personnel by overthrowing the prevailing aristocracy of office holders. The practice rapidly degenerated into a vicious spoils system^{qv} and persisted scarcely challenged until the Civil Service Reform^{qv} movement secured passage of the Pendleton Act^{qv} (1883) which authorized a classified list of Federal officials to be recruited on the basis of merit^{qv}.

In 1867 Congress had passed a Tenure of Office Act^{qv} to prevent President Johnson from packing the civil service with appointees who might sabotage the congressional reconstruction program. It made each dismissal contingent upon the Senate's confirmation of a successor. Worsted in bitter controversies over dismissals by Presidents Hayes (1877–8) and Cleveland (1885), the Senate initiated a measure repealing (1887) the Tenure of Office Act.

In 1925 the Supreme Court in Myers v. U. S.^{qv} (272 U. S. 106) confirmed the prevalent popular opinion that the President had unlimited power of dismissal of executive appointees, but in 1934 they modified their opinion in Humphrey's Executor v. U. S.^{qv} (295 U. S. 602) by holding that he could dismiss members of a quasi legislative or quasi judicial agency^{qv} such as the Federal Trade Commission^{qv} only for reasons specified in the statute creating it.

[F. J. Goodnow, *Comparative Administrative Law.*]

W. E. BINKLEY

Appomattox, former courthouse (county seat) of the county of the same name in Virginia, and scene of the surrender of the Confederate Army of Northern Virginia to the Union Army of the Potomac^{qqv}, April 9, 1865, is twenty miles ESE. of Lynchburg. Gen. R. E. Lee, commanding the Confederate forces which evacuated Petersburg and Richmond^{qqv} on the night of April 2–3, had planned to withdraw into North Carolina, via Danville, and to join Gen. Joseph E. Johnston; but on the third day of retreat, Lee found the Federals across his front at Jetersville, on the Richmond and Danville Railroad. As he was dependent on the railways for supplies, he determined to move westward across country to the Southside Railroad at Farmville, where he hoped to procure rations for a march to Lynchburg. Thence he would turn south again toward Danville. En route to Farmville, Lee was attacked heavily on April 6, at Sayler's (Sailor's) Creek^{qv}, where he lost about 6000 men. The next day at Farmville he was again assailed before he could victual all his troops. By that time, long marches without food had so depleted the Confederate ranks that Gen. Grant addressed Lee a proposal for the surrender of the army. Lee did not consider the situation altogether hopeless and pushed on toward Lynchburg by the Richmond Stage Road. When the army bivouacked around Appomattox Courthouse on the evening of April 8, the reflection of Federal campfires against the clouds showed that the surviving Confederates, now reduced to two small corps, were surrounded on three sides. Lee closed his column and prepared to cut his way out, but, when he found the next morning that the corps of John B. Gordon faced impossible odds on the Stage Road, he sent a flag of truce to Gen. Grant. A suggestion that the army break into small bands and attempt to slip through the enveloping lines was rejected by Gen. Lee on the ground that it would carry a hopeless struggle into country that had escaped the ravages of war. After some delay in communicating with Gen. Grant, who had made his dispositions with the greatest skill, Lee rode, about 1 P.M., into the village and, at the house of Maj. Wilmer McLean, formally arranged the surrender of all forces then under arms in Virginia. Gen. Grant's generous terms, which allowed officers to retain their side arms and provided for the parole of all surrendered troops, were executed with the least humiliation to the defeated army. A full day's rations were issued the prisoners of war. When the troops marched into an open field to lay down their weapons and their flags, April 12, the Federal guard presented arms. The number of Confederate infantrymen surrendered at Appomattox with arms in their hands was 7892; the total number of troops paroled was 28,231. In an interview with Lee on April 10, Grant sought to prevail on the Confederate commander to advise that all the remaining Confederate troops cease resistance, but Lee insisted that this was a question to be decided by the civil authorities.

[U. S. Grant, *Personal Memoirs*, Vol. 2; *Battles and Leaders of the Civil War*, Vol. 4; D. S. Freeman, *R. E. Lee*, Vol. 4.]

DOUGLAS SOUTHALL FREEMAN

Apportionment, Constitutional, signifies the distribution of legislative membership among established units of government, usually allocated with more or less exactness upon an equality of population. The Federal Constitution^{qv} requires that representatives be apportioned among the several states according to population. Since 1842, they have been chosen in single member districts (*see* District, Congressional); the boundaries of these districts are fixed by state law. In the Senate[qv], the equality of states is a constituent element of American federalism. The result is greatly to overrepresent the agricultural sections of the country. The practice in respect to state legislative apportionment has been largely conditioned by the democratic idea of equality, which holds that representatives should be allocated among districts containing substantially an equal number of persons. The application of this theory, in earlier days, was reasonably satisfactory, as many counties and towns were equal in population and similar in interest. The basis of representation[qv] in the lower house of the legislature is usually the county. In simplest form, each county is a separated district with one representative. The town is the basis of representation in New England; the ancient practice survives of allowing each town, regardless of size, at least one representative. The upper house of the legislature is formed by a grouping of counties or by a division of the more populous ones into districts, with approximately equal population. In municipal government[qv], the ward was, for many years, the unit of representation, with one or two aldermen from each ward. The modern types of city government provide, however, for election-at-large of the municipal legislative body.

Periodic reapportionment for the House of Representatives[qv] is made after each census[qv]. Provision is made in most state constitutions[qv] for legislative reapportionment every ten years. Constitutional provisions in respect to this practice are mandatory in form, but no effective method exists to force a legislature to act if it does not wish to do so. The continuation of existing apportionment results; this often perpetuates a very unequal arrangement. Should the legislature fail to act, apportionment by state executive or by local officials is authorized in several states. Although emphasis upon a mathematically accurate population distribution of seats may be exaggerated, where counties or towns are given equality of representation, regardless of population, or where a limitation is placed on the number of representatives from one county, the basis of apportionment is decidedly unfair. Rural sections thus become overrepresented and extreme discrimination exists against urban areas. The legislative gerrymander[qv] develops various forms of discrimination, partisan, sectional or rural and urban in character. In application, therefore, a conflict often occurs in the theories of territorial representation and of population representation, with results thoroughly inconsistent with American principles of government.

[W. Anderson, *American City Government;* W. F. Dodd, *State Government,* 2nd Ed.]

THOMAS S. BARCLAY

Apprenticeship. A system by which a youth bound himself to a master workman for a period of years in exchange for maintenance and training in a craft. Known in ancient times, it was elaborated by the mediæval guilds. The general principles of an English act of 1562, defining the relations of master and apprentice, were adopted in the American colonies, where both voluntary and compulsory apprenticeship existed. In the latter case, poor children were bound out to masters for support and trade-training. Massachusetts Bay by a General Court Order (1642) required all masters to teach apprentices to read, as well as the principles of religion. This was the first compulsory education law in America, and was followed by similar enactments in Connecticut (1650), New Haven (1655) and New Plymouth (1671). It was extended to New York by the Duke of York's Laws[qv] of 1665.

The privileges and duties of master and apprentice were defined in a form of contract called an "indenture" (*see* Indentured Servants). During the 19th century the system gradually receded with the advance of machinery, factories and technical schools. It still continues in some degree, however, in certain skilled trades, as well as in trade-union regulations.

[R. A. Bray, *Boy Labour and Apprenticeship;* R. F. Seybolt, *Apprenticeship and Apprenticeship Education in Colonial New England and New York;* Samuel McKee, *Labor in Colonial New York.*]

RALPH FOSTER WELD

Appropriations by Congress. The Constitution gives Congress exclusive control over the public purse, the only limitations being restriction of army appropriations to a two-year period and the veto power[qv] of the President. The latter, however, is ineffective since it can be exercised only in regard to an entire bill.

Appropriations fall under three heads—permanently specific, permanent and annual. Theoretically the bulk of appropriations is of the last type, to insure close control of expenditures; but in practice many fall ouside this category. Permanent specific appropriations (rivers and harbors, public buildings, fortifications, etc.) are available until the amount provided is exhausted. Permanent appropriations (interest and sinking-fund charges, judicial salaries, etc.) continue annually until the authorizing act is repealed. Deficiency bills^qv^ provide additional funds whenever appropriations prove inadequate.

Although there is no constitutional provision to the effect, it has been customary for such bills to originate in the House of Representatives. The Senate in 1856 unsuccessfully attempted to share this function. The first appropriation bill (1780), prepared by the House sitting as the Committee of the Whole^qv^, was thirteen lines in length and covered four items. To take financial leadership away from the Treasury where it had largely rested during Hamilton's secretaryship, the Committee on Ways and Means^qv^ was established (1796) and given power to prepare and introduce financial measures. This group was superseded by the Committee on Appropriations in 1865. Thereafter special appropriation committees were appointed from time to time until finally (1880) eight additional committees were submitting appropriation legislation. Since there were by this time fourteen regular bills containing hundreds of items each, the division of authority and responsibility encouraged logrolling, pork-barrel^qqv^ legislation, inconsistency and waste. This condition was furthered by Congressional insistence that its appropriations were mandatory, that the Government was required to spend the full amount of any fund provided, and that unexpended balances could not be shifted to other uses. The situation called for revision and reform, so in 1911 a commission was appointed to consider the advisability of a national budget. In spite of a favorable report the Budget and Accounting Act^qv^ was not passed until 1921. This authorized the President, assisted by the Bureau of the Budget, to prepare and submit an annual budget to Congress. While acceptance of these estimates is optional, Congress in its appropriations has adhered rather closely to them. Congress has thus retained its final authority over expenditures while control has been unified and estimates based on demonstrated need.

[D. S. Alexander, *History and Procedure of the House of Representatives;* C. G. Haines and B. M. Haines, *Principles and Problems of Government;* D. R. Dewey, *Financial History of the United States.*]

W. B. LOCKLING

Aqueducts. Of both types of aqueducts—those carrying canals across streams and gorges and those supplying water to cities—America has constructed some notable specimens. On the many canals^qv^ built in the United States before 1850 there were some fine stone-arched aqueducts, such as those by which the Erie^qv^ crossed the Genesee River at Rochester and the Mohawk at Little Falls, the Morris Canal's^qv^ crossing of the Passaic River and the Chesapeake and Ohio's^qv^ over the Monocacy. Many canal aqueducts, however, were just huge, leaky wooden troughs supported by stone piers and wooden trusses or—in the case of two on the Delaware and Hudson^qv^—supported by cables; in effect, suspension bridges^qv^. Nearly all of these structures of both types have passed out of existence.

The first public water supply^qv^ for cities, around the beginning of the 19th century, was obtained from wells^qv^ or near-by streams. New York City in 1837–43 built the first great aqueduct in America for this purpose, a masonry conduit bringing 72,000,000 gallons daily from the Croton River, forty-one miles distant. A new Croton aqueduct was built in 1885–90—nearly all tunnel, well-nigh an air line, and only 30.87 miles long. At the time of construction, it was our greatest engineering feat. Both these were surpassed by the Catskill aqueduct, opened in 1917, which has its head in the Ashokan Reservoir, ninety-two and one-half miles from the city. It passes under the Hudson River by an inverted siphon which descends to 1100 feet below the surface of the water. The Los Angeles aqueduct, built 1908–13, is the longest in existence, bringing 259,000,000 gallons daily from the Owens River, 235 miles distant. For a quarter century after 1910, San Francisco toiled at completing the great aqueduct which conveys its water from the Hetch-Hetchy Valley, 168 miles distant.

ALVIN F. HARLOW

Aquidneck Island. An Indian name for Rhode Island^qv^, the largest of the islands in Narragansett Bay. The island's purchase from the Narragansett sachems was witnessed by Roger Williams on March 24, 1638.

[S. G. Arnold, *History of Rhode Island.*]

ARTHUR R. BLESSING

Arabian Gold in our colonies (after 1685)—mostly *pagodas,* from the India pagodas on their reverse side, or gold *mohurs* of India or Persia—was captured by our colonial pirates from Arabian or Indian ships in the Arabian Sea. New York merchants got much more by trading with the Madagascar pirates; and these "Arabian" gold coins were common in New York, Philadelphia and Rhode Island in 1690. Pirate Avery in 1698 brought his huge "Arabian" loot to the West Indies, whence our colonies got their supply of specie.

[F. W. Clarke, *Weights, Measures and Money of All Nations;* Charles J. Bullock, *The Monetary History of the United States;* George Francis Dow and John Henry Edmonds, *The Pirates of the New England Coast;* John Harris, *Collection of Voyages.*]

GEORGE WYCHERLEY

***Arabic* Case.** On Aug. 19, 1915, a German submarine torpedoed without warning the British White Star passenger liner, *Arabic,* with the loss of two United States citizens. This attack occurred soon after the exchanges of notes that followed the torpedoing similarly of the *Lusitania*qv, in which the United States had insisted that the lives of noncombatants could not lawfully be put in jeopardy by the capture or destruction of unresisting merchantmen. The German act indicated that it was still uncertain whether Germany had accepted the American position. After seeking to justify the attack on the ground that the *Arabic* was attempting to ram the submarine, the German government disavowed the act and offered indemnity. Claims of United States citizens arising out of this and similar cases were eventually adjudicated by the Mixed Claims Commission, United States and Germany, following the war between the two nations. (*See also* World War.)

[*Foreign Relations of the United States, 1915 Supplement.*]

SAMUEL FLAGG BEMIS

Aranda Memorial, The, was a statement said to have been presented by Pedro Pablo Abarca de Bolea, Count of Aranda, to Charles III of Spain in 1783 or 1784. In the Memorial appear statements of regret that Spain and France entered the war in behalf of the American colonies. It contains a striking prediction that the new "federated republic" will become an "irresistible colossus" endangering Spain's possession. Hence the author suggested that new kingdoms, bound to Spain by marriage and commercial ties, be created from the Spanish colonies. By some historians Aranda's authorship of the Memorial has been questioned.

[Arthur P. Whitaker, The Pseudo-Aranda Memoir of 1783, in *The Hispanic American Historical Review,* August, 1937; Almon R. Wright, The Aranda Memorial, Genuine or Forged, *ibid.*, November, 1938.]

ALMON R. WRIGHT

Aranjuez, The Convention of (April 12, 1779), provided for the entrance of Spain, as an ally of France, into the war against Great Britain (*see* Revolution, American), in case Great Britain should reject (which she did) Spain's impossibly intrusive offer of mediation. Spain and France made a pact to fight the war jointly, and not to negotiate peace separately, and in any peace Gibraltar was to go to Spain. Other desirable acquisitions were stipulated for both allies out of anticipated conquests from Great Britain.

[Samuel Flagg Bemis, *Diplomacy of the American Revolution.*]

SAMUEL FLAGG BEMIS

Arapaho, The, a large and important plains tribe, and a branch of the Algonquinqv family, ranged from the head of the North Platte River to the Arkansas, when first encountered by the whites. Formerly they lived, according to tradition, east of the Missouri, probably in Minnesota. In warfare they associated themselves with the Cheyenneqv who were good fighters with a strong tribal organization and culture. Most white observers of the 1850's and 1860's found the Arapaho dirty, lazy and immoral to a degree. In war they were formidable enemies, especially under Cheyenne leadership, but they were more friendly and hospitable than their allies in times of peace. Some members of the tribe participated in the Fort Fetterman fight, raids in western Kansas, the Beecher Island fight, the Washita massacre, and a few were in the Custer fight on the Little Big Hornqqv. They attended the Medicine Lodge Treaty of 1867qv at which it was proposed to move them south of the Arkansas. In early days the Santa Fé tradeqv was greatly harassed by raids from this tribe.

[F. W. Hodge, *Handbook of the American Indians;* G. B. Grinnell, *Fighting Cheyennes.*]

CARL L. CANNON

Arbella, The, was flagship of the "Winthrop Fleet" on which, between April 8 and June 12, 1630, Gov. Winthrop, other members of the Company and Puritan emigrants transported themselves and the Charter of the Massachusetts Bay Companyqv from England to Salem, thereby giving legal birth to the commonwealth of Massachusetts. (*See* Great Migration.)

[*Winthrop's Journal;* C. M. Andrews, *The Colonial Period of American History.*]

RAYMOND P. STEARNS

Arbitration, Commercial. The Charter of the New York Chamber of Commerce (1768) provided that the body could arbitrate business disputes. Its first arbitration plan failed because there was no method of enforcement; the second and third plans undertook too much. The fourth attempt profited by previous experiences and incorporated features from European commercial courts, stock exchanges, trading bodies and other organizations. This plan has become a model for such undertakings in this country. In the meantime, commercial arbitration was started by the Philadelphia Chamber of Commerce in 1801, the Boston Chamber of Commerce in 1836, the Boston Board of Trade in 1854, and by other bodies in Memphis, New Orleans, Chicago, Baltimore, St. Louis, Cincinnati, Indianapolis and elsewhere. When a dispute arises, a board selected from a list of arbitrators, with representatives of the disputants, hears evidence and renders a decision, which the parties have agreed in advance to respect. The award is set aside only because of fraud, corruption, misconduct or the exceeding of power by the arbitrators. Otherwise, it is adhered to as scrupulously as a court decision. The plan is generally regarded as an economical and effective substitute for litigation in commercial disputes.

[William George Bruce, *Commercial Organizations.*]

PAUL T. CHERINGTON

Arbitration, Industrial. Disputes between employers and employees are usually settled by joint conference under the terms of a trade agreement, mediation, conciliation[qv], voluntary arbitration, compulsory investigation or compulsory arbitration.

Conciliation and mediation are essentially the same process. Mediation takes place when an outside person or agency intercedes to suggest a peaceable settlement. Conciliation usually takes the form of a joint conference of the representatives of the disputants, according to the terms of a trade agreement, but it may be the result of the good offices of an outsider. Arbitration may be voluntary or compulsory, depending upon whether or not the submission of the dispute to settlement is required by law.

Mediation, conciliation and voluntary arbitration are the predominant methods of settling labor disputes in the United States. The most important agency of mediation and conciliation here is the Conciliation Service of the United States Department of Labor, established March 4, 1913. State conciliation and mediation agencies have been relatively unimportant.

Most states provide for voluntary arbitration, but in this field also Federal agencies have been much more important. In peace times the latter have been developed largely in one industry—railroading. The settlement of labor disputes in this industry has been provided for under the terms of a series of significant laws including the Act of 1888, the Erdman Act of 1898, the Newlands Act of 1913, the Esch-Cummins Transportation Act of 1920[qv] and the Watson-Parker Act of 1926 (*see* Railroad Mediation Acts). Under the last-named law collective bargaining[qv] is recognized and a comprehensive system of adjustment is created. Temporary regional bipartisan Boards of Adjustment are established to encourage settlement of disputes by the parties themselves. Cases not settled by the Boards of Adjustment go to the Board of Mediation, which is composed of five salaried members appointed by the President of the United States and removable by him for cause. Although conciliation is stressed, voluntary arbitration is provided for. By consent of the disputants the controversy may be submitted to Boards of Arbitration created for each case and consisting of from three to six men, depending upon the decision of the parties. If either party protests the award, the case is argued in a circuit court the decision of which is final unless the disputants agree to modification. The act also provides that if the permanent Board of Mediation fails to conciliate the parties or to secure arbitration it must notify the President that an emergency exists which threatens disruption of interstate commerce. The President may, if he deems it necessary, appoint an Emergency Board of Investigation which has compulsory fact-finding powers and reports to him within thirty days. From the time such a board is created no strike, lockout[qqv] or change of condition in employment may take place for sixty days. The President may publicize the findings, if he sees fit, but they are not binding on the disputants after the specified time limit expires.

Compulsory investigation was first given prominence in the United States in 1915, when Colorado passed a law patterned after the Canadian Industrial Disputes Investigation Act of 1907. Under the Colorado Act the Industrial Commission is empowered to settle disputes in "public interest" industries through compulsory investigation of facts. Strikes and lockouts are prohibited for thirty days, the findings may be publicized, and public opinion is relied upon to force compliance with the findings of the commission. This act has been less successful than the Canadian law, but it has contributed to the growth of conciliation and peace. Many other states have statutes providing for compulsory investigation, but they have not been successfully executed.

Compulsory arbitration with compulsory acceptance of the award has been attempted seriously by only one state. In 1920 Kansas created a Court of Industrial Relations consisting of three judges appointed for three years by the governor. In all industries "affected with a public interest" lockouts, strikes, boycotts, picketing[qqv] and other methods of industrial warfare were prohibited. The court could require the submission of evidence and render a decision concerning wages, hours, working conditions, working rules and similar matters. The criteria established to guide the action of the court involved a "fair" wage and healthful employment conditions for employees, "fair" profits for employers, and "fair" prices for consumers. Any enterprise under its jurisdiction could be taken over and operated by the court, if necessary. The orders of the court were to be effective for at least sixty days, at the end of which time employers or employees could appeal for a rehearing either before the Industrial Court or the Supreme Court of Kansas. Unless the award was modified after examination of the new evidence, it was binding upon both parties. A fine of not more than $1000 or imprisonment of not more than one year, or both, was imposed on individuals guilty of willful disobedience of the court's orders; a fine of $5000 or imprisonment of two years, or both, was imposed on officers of unions and corporations or employers' associations guilty of instigating violations. Some parts of the act were declared unconstitutional by the United States Supreme Court, and continued opposition by employers and employees caused the legislature in 1925 to abolish the court and transfer its functions to the Public Service Commission, which has never exercised them. While the act still is on the statute books it is practically a dead letter.

[J. R. Commons and J. B. Andrews, *Principles of Labor Legislation;* International Labour Office, *The Conciliation and Arbitration of Industrial Disputes;* D. A. McCabe and G. E. Barnett, *Mediation, Investigation, and Arbitration in Industrial Disputes;* U. S. Bureau of Labor Statistics, Bulletin 322, *Kansas Court of Industrial Relations.*]

GORDON S. WATKINS

Arbitration, International, may be defined in general terms as the submission of a controversy to persons not parties to the dispute with the understanding that the decision of the arbitrators shall be regarded as final. It involves, therefore, a controversy which it has not been possible to settle by direct negotiation; the creation of a special tribunal to decide the dispute; an understanding in respect to the precise issues to be arbitrated; determination of the procedure to be followed; and in some cases an agreement upon the special rules of law to be applied to the decision of the case. In recent years arbitration has come to be distinguished from "judicial settlement" which is a similar reference of a controversy to a permanent court rather than to a tribunal constituted for the particular case.

The history of arbitration in modern times may be said to begin with the Jay Treaty[qv] of 1794 by which the United States and Great Britain agreed to submit to arbitration three groups of disputes arising from the terms of the Definitive Treaty of Peace[qv], 1783. While the arbitrations carried out in pursuance of the terms of the Jay Treaty could not all be described as successful, yet the precedent of recourse to arbitration was established, and the United States continued during the 19th century the policy of arbitrating disputes which seemed susceptible of settlement by that procedure. The successful arbitration of the Alabama Claims[qv] dispute not only strengthened the United States in its faith in the procedure of arbitration, but it had a wide influence in impressing upon other nations the possibility of the peaceful settlement of disputes by that method. Again in 1892 the United States and Great Britain agreed to arbitrate the Bering Sea seal fisheries dispute[qv], the results of which, while not immediately successful, led ultimately to a constructive solution of the problem of protecting the fisheries. Following the creation of the Hague Permanent Court of Arbitration[qv] a number of disputes were arbitrated by tribunals constituted by selection from the general list of the court, the most important of which were the Mexican Pious Fund Case[qv] and the North Atlantic Coast Fisheries Case. The recent arbitration of the *I'm Alone* Case[qv] was before a mixed commission[qv] of two members.

Side by side with the actual practice of arbitration has been the growth of an elaborate series of agreements looking to the arbitration of future disputes. As early as 1848, in the Treaty of Guadalupe Hidalgo[qv], the United States agreed with Mexico that if any disagreement should thereafter arise between them they would endeavor to settle it by peaceful negotiations and that, if these should fail, then "by the arbitration of commissioners appointed on each side," unless this procedure were incompatible with the nature of the difference or the circumstances of the case.

By the close of the 19th century numerous treaties of "general arbitration," as distinct from the arbitration of specific disputes, were entered into among the Latin American states. This movement received an additional impulse from the adoption at the Hague Peace Conference of 1899[qv] of a broad provision recognizing that in questions of a legal nature and in the interpretation and application of treaties arbitration was the most effective and equitable means of settling disputes which diplomacy had failed to settle. In 1903 Great Britain and France concluded a general treaty which served as a model for numerous subsequent treaties. The chief problem presented by treaties of this general character was that, since it was impossible to foresee what particular disputes might arise in the future, it was necessary to qualify them so as to leave loopholes of escape from the obligation in case a dispute arose which one of the parties would not be willing to arbitrate. In the so-called Root Treaties of 1908[qv] the United States agreed with the other contracting parties that differences which might arise of a legal nature or relating to the interpretation of treaties should be referred to the Hague Permanent Court of Arbitration, "provided, nevertheless, that they do not affect the vital interests, the independence, or the honor of the two contracting states and do not concern the interests of third parties." Three years later President Taft sought to conclude a new series of arbitration treaties in which the obligation to arbitrate was made to extend to "justiciable" disputes, which were defined as disputes susceptible of decision by the application of the principles of law or equity. These treaties failed of ratification because the President objected to a reservation entered by the Senate which would have made it necessary for the President to submit to the Senate in each particular case the question whether the character of the dispute came within the terms of the treaty.

In view of the difficulties met with by President Taft in the negotiation of an arbitration treaty along more liberal lines than the Root Treaties of 1908, Secretary Bryan undertook in 1913–15 to negotiate a series of treaties designated as Treaties for the Advancement of Peace (*see* Bryan Treaty Model). These treaties were phrased so as to cover all disputes not otherwise settled by negotiation; but instead of providing for arbitration, which would have necessitated exceptions and qualifications, they called for the submission of the dispute to a permanent international commission for "investigation and report."

At the close of the World War the United States took part in the formulation of the Covenant of the League of Nations[qv], Article XIII of which provided for the submission to arbitration of any dispute which the members of the League might recognize as being "suitable for submission to arbitration." The alternative to arbitration was the submission of the dispute to "inquiry" by the Council of the League. Four groups of disputes were enumerated as "generally suitable" for submission to arbitration. A subsequent amendment to this article offered the alternative of submission of the dispute to "judicial settlement." In the succeeding years it became the custom, in the conclusion of peace treaties such as those signed at Locarno[qv] in 1925, to tie up provisions for arbitration with provisions for conciliation and for judicial settlement, leaving to the parties the option of one or other of those methods of peaceful settlement. In the Briand-Kellogg Pact[qv] the agreement merely recites that the contracting parties will never seek the settlement of disputes "except by pacific means."

In 1929 the General Treaty of Inter-American Arbitration was signed by representatives of all of the twenty-one American republics except Argentina. The treaty calls for the submission to arbitration of questions "juridical in their nature," and it specifies under that head the four groups of disputes enumerated in Article XIII of the Covenant of the League of Nations and in Article XXXVI of the Statute of the Permanent Court of International Justice. Two exceptions are entered: controversies within the "domestic jurisdiction" of the parties and controversies affecting states not parties to the treaty. The terms of this treaty were incorporated into the Convention to Co-ordinate Existing Treaties signed at Buenos Aires in 1936 (*see* Peace Conference at Buenos Aires, 1936).

Closely associated with the development of the obligation to arbitrate have been the various efforts to create a permanent international court before which disputes might be brought for settlement. Most of the arbitrations of the 19th century were held before mixed arbitration tribunals, composed as a rule of an equal number of judges chosen by each of the disputants, with an umpire chosen by agreement between the national judges. The umpire was thus made to carry the responsibility for the decision; while the tribunals themselves were ephemeral in character, so that their decisions had little weight as precedents. At the Hague Peace Conference of 1899 the Convention for the Pacific Settlement of International Disputes was signed, which created the Hague Permanent Court of Arbitration, consisting of a list of judges appointed by the signatory powers to the number of four each. From this list special tribunals of five judges were to be constituted when a case for arbitration arose. At the second Hague Conference of 1907 the United States delegation endeavored to bring about the establishment of a more permanent court, known as the Judicial Arbitration Court, which would sit continuously and build up a system of international jurisprudence in the form of precedents having something of the force of law. Due to the failure to agree upon the choice of judges the court never became a reality; but the draft convention providing for it had influence upon the Advisory Committee of Jurists which met at The Hague in 1920 and prepared the draft of the Statute of the Permanent Court of International Justice. Reference of a dispute to the Permanent Court is described as "judicial settlement" as distinct from "arbitration"; and the court renders a "decision" as distinct from an arbitral "award."

[J. B. Moore, *A History and Digest of the International Arbitrations to which the United States has been a Party, 1898; International Adjudications*, Modern Series, 1929–.]

CHARLES G. FENWICK

Arbor Day, Origin of. On the motion of J. Sterling Morton the Nebraska State Board of Agriculture designated the tenth day of April, 1872, as a day to plant trees, naming it Arbor Day. Later the state legislature changed the day to April 22, the birthday of Morton, and made it a legal holiday[qv]. Other states followed this example.

[Addison E. Sheldon, *Nebraska Old and New.*]

EVERETT DICK

Arbuthnot and Ambrister, Case of. An incident of Gen. Andrew Jackson's raid into East Florida[qv] in 1818. Believing himself tacitly authorized to seize the Floridas in view of Spain's delay in diplomacy, Jackson attacked the Seminole Indians[qv] in Spanish territory. At St. Mark's, Fla., he captured Alexander Arbuthnot, a Scotch trader who had warned the Indians to escape. At the village of Chief Bowlegs on the Suwanee River he captured Robert Ambrister, an English trader, who had plotted an Indian uprising. After courts-martial, Ambrister was shot and Arbuthnot hanged, both at St. Mark's on April 29, 1818. The British government took no action, but Spain protested the invasion. Secretary of State John Quincy Adams vigorously defended Jackson in his published despatches to the United States Minister at Madrid, and thus helped to force Spanish signature of the Adams-Onís Treaty[qv] of Feb. 22, 1819, which included the cession of East Florida.

[John S. Bassett, *Life of Andrew Jackson.*]

PHILIP COOLIDGE BROOKS

Archæology, North American. In North America the term archæology covers research into the culture of native peoples living before the 16th century, the time level separating the historic from the prehistoric. In the study of living natives, or Indians, historical methods are used, but for those living before the 16th century the method is that of archæology. The primary objective is the discovery of time sequences in cultures and peoples. Such chronologies are expressed in successive changes in artifacts or in typological differences. The empirical determination of time sequence in artifacts is by super-position; i.e., when in undisturbed deposits, one type of artifact is found consistently above another, the lower one is the older. For example, in some rock-shelters and cave entrances east of the Mississippi, pottery[qv] is found in the upper levels only: certain shell heaps along the Atlantic coast show the same sequence. It is evident, therefore, that in this part of North America there is a pre-pottery period, followed by one of pottery, extending into the 16th century, or historic time. In southwestern United States a similar pre-pottery period has been demonstrated, but in parts of California and northward along the Pacific coast belt no pottery is found nor was any made in historic time.

Pre-pottery time can be subdivided in the Ohio Valley and the Ozark Mountains by the appearance of cultivated plants. Thus, in certain rock-shelters, seeds of the cultivated sunflower, gourd and pigweed appear at a given level, later these give way to maize[qv] and pottery. So the first people to occupy these shelters were hunters who may have gathered some wild seeds but knew nothing of agriculture; later, hunters who cultivated certain local plants for their seeds lived here. Finally, maize was introduced from the south, but this was also the period of pottery. Agriculture in southwestern United States seems to have begun with maize and pottery and on the Pacific side of the continent where no pottery is found, there was no agriculture.

In southwestern United States and in parts of Mexico it is possible to subdivide the pottery period because styles in form and decoration changed frequently. The super-position of these styles in refuse heaps gives the time order of their appearance. Thus for parts of Arizona and New Mexico, the following culture periods have been established: Basket-Maker III, Pueblo I, II, III, IV and V, as subdivisions of the pottery period. These are culture periods because many other types of artifacts change in unison with pottery styles. In other words, in this area, pottery styles are the indicators of culture sequence.

To integrate fully such archæological sequences in cultures with historical chronology, actual dates are necessary. Surprisingly enough, this has been found possible by the tree-ring[qv] method where timbers used in buildings have been preserved by favorable climate or by charring in fire. For contiguous parts of New Mexico and Arizona this method gives exact dates for artifacts and ruins grouped typologically, or in culture periods, as follows: Pueblo V, since 1700; Pueblo IV, 1350–1700; Pueblo III, 950–1350; Pueblo II, 600–950; Pueblo I, 100–600; Basket-Maker III, ?–100 A.D. Undated are Basket-Maker I and II.

In Mexico and Central America certain ruins and the cultures they represent bear inscription dates whose correlations with our own calendar are still in doubt. Hence, the one sure chronology for North America is the one given above. Whether the remainder of the United States can be correlated with this remains to be seen.

A sequence without dates has been established for the Mississippi Valley, as: (8) Historic Period; (7) Proto-historic Period; (6) Mississippi Culture; (5) Woodland Culture; (4) Maize and Pottery Culture; (3) Pre-maize Agriculture; (2) Hunters of modern fauna; (1) Hunters of extinct fauna. Periods 4 to 8 have been traced over most of the country between Kansas and the Atlantic, 3 and 2 are known in Kentucky and the Ozarks and 1 in New Mexico, Colorado, and Nebraska.

[Clark Wissler, *The American Indian;* Cole and Deuel, *Rediscovering Illinois.*]

CLARK WISSLER

Archangel, American Troops at. After the Russian revolution (1917) the Allies sent a joint expedition, under British command, to co-operate with the White Russians at Murmansk and Archangel against the Bolshevist forces. By President Wilson's order American troops, eventually numbering 5100, participated. On Sept. 4, 1918, the 339th Infantry and auxiliary units reached Archangel with other Allied forces. The mission of the Allies was limited to protecting the ports and surrounding territory. The Americans guarded a front of 450 miles south and east of Archangel, and between September, 1918, and May, 1919, suffered more than 500 casualties. The last American troops withdrew from north Russia in July, 1919.

[*Final Report of General John J. Pershing; Order of Battle of the United States Land Forces in the World War.*]

JOSEPH MILLS HANSON

Architecture, American, has presented a succession of styles which, with one exception, were echoes of contemporary architectural fashions in England, France and Italy. Beneath this superficiality, American genius and energy have expressed themselves through vast resources of native raw building materials, the richest and most diversified in the world. As a result, the United States has produced an architecture varied in style and quality. It has made contributions to the science of building of which one, at least, is epoch-making: skeleton steel construction with its overwhelming daughter the skyscraper^qv^. In consequence of these abilities and opportunities, and its vast wealth, the United States, in the early years of the 20th century, achieved a pre-eminent position in world architecture which it is still holding, perhaps precariously.

The Spanish, Dutch, Swedish and English settlers of the eastern North American coast ignored such aboriginal models as huts and wigwams^qv^, and sought to reproduce the architecture of the fatherland. The predominance of English dominion and influence made the architecture of this region essentially English, which in the 17th century was Elizabethan and Jacobean. Our first houses had such English characteristics as the overhanging second story, steep gabled roofs, leaded glass casement sash, a huge central chimney and in all likelihood half-timbered walls, soon to be clapboarded against the rigors of New England climate. These are all mediæval characteristics hardly yet affected by the Renaissance. Typical examples are the Parson Capen House, Toppsfield (1683), the House of Seven Gables, Salem, and the Paul Revere House, Boston. Perhaps less than 100 remain. In the South the few surviving 17th-century buildings were built of brick^qv^, which eliminated the overhang, as in the John Rolfe House at Smith's Fort (1651), Bacon's Castle, Surry County, (1676), and St. Luke's Church, Isle of Wight County (1632), all in Virginia. The faint Dutch and Swedish influence in the Middle Colonies was shortly overwhelmed by the weight of English culture and tradition. We therefore find in succession, after the "Early American," echoes of the robust Renaissance of Sir Christopher Wren, as in the public buildings of Williamsburg^qv^; the simpler dignity of the early Georges in Independence Hall^qv^ and Christ Church, Philadelphia; and the delicacy of the Adam period in the later days of George III, as in Homewood, Baltimore, the Russell House, Charleston, and McIntire's work in Salem; covering in all a period approximately from 1700 to 1800.

It must not be inferred that the American adaptation of these English fashions was without originality or power. In the transatlantic voyage all of the European styles have undergone a sea change that have made them in many cases representative of the New World. This is particularly true of the Colonial style. Here the modest scale of the buildings, the lack of money, the availability of pine, the absence of professional architects and a certain inherent taste shared by aristocrat and craftsman alike produced an architecture of which any land at any time could justly be proud.

The American Revolution, and Thomas Jefferson's residence in France from 1784 to 1789, profoundly influenced American architecture. The source of inspiration was turned from England to France, and beyond that to ancient Rome. The professional architect appeared in Bulfinch, Thornton and Hoban. Jefferson was a near-professional. His capitol building in Richmond (1789) introduced the columned and pedimented portico. His house, Monticello, and the University of Virginia (1818) made him the father of the Post-Colonial, Federal, or Republican style (as it is variously called) dated usually from 1790 to 1820. Other monuments of this style are the earliest portions of the Capitol in Washington, the old City Hall, New York (1803), the White House[qv] (1818), and the State House, Boston.

In the later years of the 18th century ancient Greek architecture was revived as a result of the published researches of the British architects Stuart and Revett. A furious vogue of the Greek style followed. It came to America through Benjamin Latrobe, an English architect, who built the Bank of North America[qv] in Philadelphia (1799–1801) in pure Greek style and started a fashion that spread throughout the land. The classic mania accompanied the pioneers. Its invasion of the wilderness is one of the most extraordinary phenomena in our architectural history. The covered wagon, along with rifle and plowshare, found room for the portico of the Parthenon. Although architects like Strickland, Mills and Walter built many state capitols, exchanges and institutes, the new style was essentially an architecture of the Handbooks, little volumes with drawings and minute directions for reproducing the Greek. They were on every gentleman's table and in the breeches pocket of every carpenter. Æsthetically its contribution was one of charm and dignity. Its best monument, perhaps, is Girard College, in Philadelphia, built by Thomas U. Walter in 1833. Churches usually followed the type established in colonial days, but with Greek detail. Among the government structures in the Greek style in Washington, the Treasury building is the best. There were a vast number of houses, a splendid example of which is the James F. D. Lanier House (1844), in Madison, Ind. Among the contributions to the science of building introduced in this period was "balloon construction," invented in Chicago (1837), which revolutionized frame construction for wooden buildings, and is universally used today. The Greek style was moribund in the 1850's, the Civil War finished it.

The ideals of the Greek Revival were completely repudiated in the architecturally chaotic years between 1855 and 1880. In the 1850's comfort and safety just achieved in ocean travel sent scores of our "merchant princes" and their families to Europe. They observed the Gothic Revival in full blast in England, and in France the sophisticated classicism of the Second Empire. Both were brought back to America along with the latest in clothes and cooking. It was a period of great material expansion and pride of purse, and there was a rush of building for a public whose attitude toward art, while enthusiastic, was naïve and provincial. The result demonstrated the difficulty of imitating and adapting such complicated models, especially by untrained architects. It is in fact the nadir of our national taste and in architecture has appropriately been called the Parvenu style. Its apotheosis was the Centennial Exposition in Philadelphia (1876)[qv]. The period has scarcely a single creative idea to its credit which has survived.

In the Parvenu period buildings inspired by contemporary French architecture came first. They are characterized by heavy mansard roofs, elaborate cornices, often of galvanized iron, debased detail and an indiscriminate use of the orders. The high and narrow ideal permeated the structure. Ornament and elaborations as evidence of cost were cachets of elegance and taste. The "cast iron front" appeared on our commercial buildings, and residences with "brown stone fronts" and high stoops lined our fashionable avenues. As the French type of classic was the favorite for masonry construction, so the English Gothic Revival, or Mid-Victorian, was used for lesser buildings, often of wood. It had the curious Italian tinge which the writings of Ruskin had given it. As used in Villa architecture and in the Cottage style it called upon the jig saw to perform wonders in intricate and often charming scroll work. The cupola and the porte-cochère were popular in both varieties of the Parvenu and the high and narrow motive prevailed as well. The performances of the Gothic type were much superior to the essays in European classic; Memorial Hall at Harvard and New Old South Church in Boston demonstrate this, as do countless modest houses.

Jibes at our domestic art by foreign guests at the Centennial Exposition in 1876, as well as ex-

amples of foreign craftsmanship exhibited there, gave us pause; and at this critical moment appeared H. H. Richardson, graduate of the École des Beaux Arts in Paris, who leaped into fame with the building of Trinity Church in Boston (1879). Its style was French Romanesque, practically unknown in America. The popularity of this new fashion was almost equal to that of the Greek Revival, although it was held at bay in New York City by Richard M. Hunt and the youthful firm of McKim, Mead and White, who held by the classic tradition, of which they almost alone were worthy interpreters.

The heavy Romanesque was essentially an architecture of stone. For the wooden house of the ordinary citizen our architects eagerly followed some talented young English architects in what was called Free Classic, or Queen Anne, alike, in its Romanticism, to the Romanesque Revival. The turning lathe replaced the jig saw, and our houses between 1880 and 1893 were picturesque jumbles of steep roofs, balconies, gables, dormers and many chimneys, built in all sorts of materials. Shingles for walls, stucco and plate glass windows made their bow and the high and narrow motive made way for the low and broad. With all its faults the Queen Anne style was more truly indigenous than any since the Colonial.

The great gift of the period, however, had nothing to do with style, unless begotten of the virile strength of the Romanesque Revival. In 1884, Maj. William Le Baron Jenney built the Home Insurance Building in Chicago. In this structure the front, rear and court walls above the second floor, as well as the floors, were supported by a skeleton of wrought and cast iron, beams and columns. In the Tacoma Building built by Holabird and Roche (1887), a steel skeleton extended from the ground, the steel columns resting on isolated foundations. These were the first skyscrapers, progenitors of a mighty brood.

When the World's Columbian Exposition[qv] was conceived, the Commission of Architects decided to build in the classic style. Although there were contributing factors such as the growth of architectural education, this great World's Fair of 1893 in Chicago was the principal cause of the revolt that made Romanesque and Queen Anne not only out of fashion but taboo. The classic urge which succeeded was really eclectic; any historic style if correctly done was *au fait*. The new dispensation included in addition to architecture landscape gardening, mural painting and sculpture. This Eclectic period extended through the World War and has been called the Golden Age of American architecture; not the purest but certainly the most sumptuous of our modes. Undisturbed by wars or rumors of wars in a period of unexampled prosperity, completely sure of itself, it revived not only the splendor that was Rome, but that which was Italy, France, England and Spain to boot! Whatever may have been false in its philosophy, it developed the science of building as had not been done since the Middle Ages.

Its largest product was the skyscraper[qv], which at the same time spelled an engineering triumph and an æsthetic failure. The job of adapting an ancient style to the great height of a modern steel skeleton was too much for the men of the Golden Age, and they admitted it. In other fields the eclectics were more successful. Being school men, their planning was excellent; so much so that norms were developed for office buildings, hotels, libraries, banks, railway stations, schools, churches, etc., which still persist. In buildings of moderate height where classic proportions were suitable, such as the Boston Public Library by McKim, Mead and White, almost perfection was achieved. A list of the masterpieces of the Golden Age would be extensive. To cite the Palace of Fine Arts, World's Fair, Chicago, by Charles B. Atwood; the Pennsylvania Station, New York; the Harkness Memorial at Yale, by James Gamble Rogers; St. Thomas' Church, New York, by Cram and Goodhue; Lincoln Memorial, Washington, by Henry Bacon, merely scratches the surface. Ralph Adams Cram and Bertram Goodhue revolutionized ecclesiastical architecture with a fresh and brilliant interpretation of the Gothic. D. H. Burnham, city planner, made architecture Big Business, and planned a new Chicago and San Francisco. The American city was rebuilt in those years of mellow fruitfulness. The first super-skyscraper, the Woolworth Building in New York, was built by Cass Gilbert in 1917. By following the Gothic principle of verticality it somewhat redeemed the many failures of the misapplied classic.

In 1922 the Chicago *Tribune* held a competition for its proposed building, thirty stories high. The second prize, by Eliet Saarinen, was generally accepted by architects as the long looked for solution of the riddle of the skyscraper. It became the chosen formula for skyscraper and super-skyscraper alike. The *Daily News* Building, by Raymond Hood; Rockefeller Center (seventy stories); Chicago Board of Trade, by Holabird and Root; and the Empire State Building (eighty-four stories), by Shreve, Lamb and Harmon, illustrated the new dispensation and mark, perhaps, its culmination.

An important element in the solution of the skyscraper was the Functional or International style, which saw its birth in the work and principles of Louis Sullivan of Chicago as first expressed in the Transportation Building in the World's Fair of 1893. Receiving no hearing during the Golden Age, though kept alive by Frank Lloyd Wright and the Chicago School, it assumed importance in Holland and Germany just before the World War, and returned to America triumphantly in our post-war building boom. The International style is puritan in its purpose. It would purge from architecture falsities in expression, the use of historic styles and all ornament, unless it be "significant." It revolutionizes the concept of architecture in that a building is not an expression of mass but of volume in which walls become but an enclosing skin for the rooms (volumes) within. Our architecture, which has been molluscan for thousands of years, now becomes vertebrate. Such a concept calls for new building materials, and the manufacturers, who in America have always marched side by side (and sometimes a step ahead) with the architects, are producing them ready to his hand.

The International style has conquered nearly every field in commercial building, though the Gothic in ecclesiastical architecture and Colonial in the domestic field hold somewhat precariously their lines. The restoration of colonial Williamsburg (1927–36) has greatly strengthened the Colonial in popularity. As the well-loved style has been somewhat chastened and streamlined, it may survive.

Nevertheless the Functional or International style seems to be elected to represent the new era. Its contributions in the utilities such as kitchen arrangement and equipment, furniture and lighting; in construction with its advance in reinforced concrete and prefabrication and in the creation of new building materials give it the leadership aside from style. Its greatest successes have been so far in buildings of specialized functions such as factories, airdromes, casinos, etc. Its abhorrence of ornament marks it as a "puritan movement" and especially adaptable for world expression. Hence its excellent name, the International style.

The last great expression of the spirit of the Renaissance, that beauty is its own excuse for being, occurred in the San Francisco Exposition of 1915 (*see* Panama-Pacific International Exposition). It is of arresting significance that the International style was selected without question for the great exposition in New York in 1939[qv], "The World of Tomorrow."

[M. S. Briggs, *The Homes of the Pilgrim Fathers in England and America;* H. D. Eberlein, *Architecture of Colonial America;* R. A. Cram, *American Church Building of Today;* G. H. Edgell, *American Architecture of Today;* T. F. Hamlin, *American Spirit in Architecture;* Fiske Kimball, *American Architecture*, and *Domestic Architecture of the American Colonies and the Early Republic;* Howard Major, *Domestic Architecture of the Early American Republic: the Greek Revival;* Lewis Mumford, *Sticks and Stones;* Rexford Newcomb, *Old Mission Churches and Historic Homes of California;* R. W. Sexton, *American Commercial Buildings of Today;* T. E. Tallmadge, *Story of Architecture in America.*]

THOMAS E. TALLMADGE

Archive War, The, was a contest between Austin and Houston, Tex., in 1842, over the state archives. Austin had been designated as the capital in 1839 but President Houston, after a Mexican raid on San Antonio in 1842, fearing the archives might be lost, undertook to remove them to Houston. The citizens of Austin overtook the wagons and forced them to be returned to Austin.

[H. H. Bancroft, *History of the North Mexican States and Texas*, Vol. II.]

J. G. SMITH

Archives. The body of records and papers officially produced or received by a government, a governmental agency, an institution, an organization, or a firm in the conduct of its affairs and filed or preserved by it or its legitimate successors for record purposes constitutes its archives. The term is sometimes applicable to the papers of a family or an individual, but such collections usually lack the organic character of true archives. Collections of historical manuscripts assembled by an agency or individual rather than received or produced in the transaction of affairs are not archives, even though they contain official documents. Although archives are preserved primarily for administrative purposes, they constitute a fundamental basis of knowledge of the history, not only of the agency whose records they are, but also of the people in their social and economic relationships.

The national archives of the United States, consisting of the records of all the agencies of the Federal Government, are, of course, of outstanding importance for American history. Although most nations long ago made special provisions for the preservation and administration of their non-current records, the United States until recently left them in the custody of the agencies that had accumulated them, with the result that some were inadvertently destroyed and many were stored in unsuitable places where they were subject to deterioration and were practically inaccessible to scholars or officials. In 1926 Congress made provision for the construction of an Archives Building in Washington, which, though not fully completed until 1937, was occupied in 1935. The agency known as The National Archives was set up in 1934 to have the custody and administration of the records transferred to the building, and the Archivist was given authority to inspect any records of the Federal Government. Under his direction a comprehensive survey was made of the records in Washington, and a similar survey of Federal records outside Washington was made as a Works Progress Administration[qv] project with The National Archives as a co-operating sponsor. The mass of information assembled by these surveys is on file at The National Archives.

Among the more important records already (1938) transferred to the Archives Building are the Senate files to 1929 with some exceptions, most of the records of the State Department to 1906, the centralized records of the army to 1912, the records of the Attorney General and the Justice Department to 1903, records of the Office of Indian Affairs from 1795 to 1907, records of pensions based on military or naval service from 1817 to 1917, and records of most of the emergency World War agencies. With a few exceptions, the records at The National Archives are available for consultation, and photostatic or microfilm reproductions of them can be obtained at low cost. A guide to these records, revised from time to time, is published by The National Archives.

Most of the states preceded the Federal Government in making some provision for the centralization of non-current records, but these provisions are extremely diverse and frequently inadequate. Usually the functions of an archival agency are performed by the state historical society, the state library, a state department of archives and history, a state historical commission, or the Secretary of State. Independent archival agencies have recently been established in a few states, but they usually have historical as well as strictly archival functions. In Illinois, however, the archives agency, though a branch of the state library, is separately administered and has its own building. In most of the states vast quantities of non-current records remain in the custody of the offices that accumulated them. The Public Archives Commission set up by the American Historical Association[qv] in 1899 brought about the compilation and publication in the *Annual Reports* of the Association of guides to the archives of all but a few of the states; but most of these guides are now out of date. More comprehensive guides or inventories of state archives are now being compiled by the Historical Records Survey set up by the Works Progress Administration in 1936.

The non-current records of counties and other local governments have been sadly neglected. In a few states such records have been assembled in part in central depositories, and in a few they are inspected from time to time by a state official. Inventories have been published of the county records of Illinois and California, and more complete inventories of local records throughout the country now being compiled by the Historical Records Survey will serve to open up to historians a tremendous mass of original material for the history of the American people.

The archives of semipublic and private organizations have also been neglected, as a rule, after they ceased to be of current value; but a few religious organizations, educational institutions and business firms have made special provision for the preservation and use for historical purposes of their records. In this field again, the Historical Records Survey is rendering valuable services in inventorying church records and other non-public archival material throughout the country.

The archives of foreign governments also include material of great importance for American history. This is especially true of those of England, France and Spain for the colonial and Revolutionary periods; but students of the foreign relations of the United States find pertinent material in the archives of practically every country. Fortunately for the historian, a series of guides to material for American history in foreign archives has been compiled and published by the Carnegie Institution of Washington[qv], and much of this material is available in the form of reproductions at the Library of Congress[qv].

As a result of the establishment of The National Archives, the expansion of state archival activities and the work of the Historical Records Survey, interest in archival problems was greatly increased and the need was felt for a professional organization to promote their solution. This need was met by the establishment in 1936 of the Society of American Archivists, which launched a quarterly magazine, *The American Archivist,* in 1938.

[C. H. Van Tyne and W. G. Leland, *Guide to the Archives of the Government of the United States in Washington;* Archivist of the United States, *Annual Reports;* C. M. Gates, The Administration of State Archives, in *Pacific Northwest Quarterly,* January, 1938; Business Historical Society, *The Preservation of Business Records.*]

SOLON J. BUCK

Arctic Exploration. *See* Polar Expeditions.

Argonauts of California. *See* Forty-Niners.

***Argus-Pelican* Engagement** (1813). Off St. David's Head, Wales, on August 14, the British brig *Pelican,* captured the American brig *Argus.* The American loss was six killed and seventeen wounded; the British had two killed and five wounded.

[Theodore Roosevelt, *The Naval War of 1812.*]

CHARLES LEE LEWIS

Arickaree, Fight on the. *See* Beecher Island, Battle of, 1868.

Arikara, THE, Caddoan people, primitive inhabitants of central South Dakota, were strongly entrenched on Missouri River for centuries before white exploration. They lived in substantial houses in stockaded villages, and cultivated extensive gardens. They were expelled by the Sioux^qv^ August, 1794, and settled near present Mobridge, S. Dak. A remnant is now at Fort Berthold.

[DeLand, *Aborigines of South Dakota,* Vol. 3, South Dakota Historical Collections.] DOANE ROBINSON

Arizona, the forty-eighth state admitted to the Union, is the fifth in area. The southwestern one third of the state is chiefly low desert, sloping toward the Gila and Colorado rivers and the Gulf of California; the northeastern two thirds being the high mountain deserts and forest lands of the Colorado plateau. Arizona contains some of the oldest human habitations in the United States, some Indian towns and cliff dwellings^qv^ dating back 1000 years or more. A considerable population of sedentary Pima^qv^ and Yuma Indians occupied towns and irrigated lands in the Gila valley, wherein they were often on the defensive against the attacks of Apache^qv^ and other highland tribes.

Opinions differ as to who were the first white visitors to Arizona. Padres Juan de la Asunción and Pedro Nazal are said to have reached it in 1538, and Fray Marcos de Niza probably entered it in 1539. It is certain that Francisco Vásquez de Coronado's^qv^ Spanish army crossed it en route to Cíbola^qv^ (Zuñi, in New Mexico), in 1540; while detachments from his expedition reached the Colorado mouth and discovered the Hopi^qv^ Indian towns and the Grand Canyon^qv^. In 1583, Antonio de Espejo seems to have worked gold deposits near Prescott, and in 1604–6 Juan de Oñate^qv^, conqueror of New Mexico, crossed northern Arizona and descended the Colorado to the Gulf. Franciscan^qv^ missionaries were at work among the Hopis of northeastern Arizona between 1629 and 1680. Padre Eusebio Francisco Kino and other Jesuits^qv^ penetrated southern Arizona from 1691 onward, founding Mission San Xavier del Bac in 1700 and other Pima missions soon afterward. A Pima revolt^qv^ in 1750–53 led to the establishment of a Spanish presidio^qv^ at Tubac^qv^ in 1752, moved to the Spanish and Indian settlement of San Agustín de Tucson in 1776. The Jesuits, expelled in 1767, were replaced by Franciscans, who maintained a feeble hold upon the missions until about 1828. During Mexican rule, 1821–56, the only important white settlements in Arizona were at Tubac and Tucson in the Santa Cruz valley, nearly all others having been abandoned because of frequent Apache raids.

Anglo-American fur trappers penetrated Arizona by way of the Gila valley as early as 1826, and were fairly common visitors thereafter. The Mexican War^qv^ saw the passage of a number of American military expeditions through the Gila valley from New Mexico to California, one of which, the Mormon Battalion^qv^, captured Tucson Dec. 16, 1846. The Treaty of Guadalupe Hidalgo^qv^, Feb. 2, 1848, left nearly all of Arizona south of the Gila a part of the Mexican state of Sonora. The region north of the Gila became part of New Mexico Territory under the act of Congress of Sept. 9, 1850. Explorations for a proposed Pacific coast railway, 1848–53, seemed to indicate the acquisition of the southern Gila valley as necessary for such a line. Accordingly, the Gadsden Purchase^qv^ was negotiated with Mexico, Dec. 30, 1853, by which Arizona between the Gila and the present Mexican boundary was added to New Mexico, official possession being taken at Tucson, March 10, 1856.

In 1856 a convention at Tucson petitioned Congress to grant separate territorial status to Arizona, but the movement was defeated. Texan Confederate troops occupied southern Arizona for a few months in 1862; but after their expulsion, Congress, on Feb. 24, 1863, established the Federal territory of Arizona (including at first the southern tip of Nevada). A movement for statehood took definite shape on Oct. 2, 1891, with the framing of a constitution by the legislature, at Phoenix, the new territorial capital. Nearly twenty years later, Aug. 21, 1911, President Taft gave a new state constitution his approval, conditioned upon the elimination of a clause providing for the recall^qv^ of judges; and the acceptance of this condition led to Arizona's formal admission as a state, Feb. 14, 1912, although the troublesome provision was soon restored. George W. P. Hunt was the first state governor, and served seven terms in that office.

[T. E. Farish, *History of Arizona;* J. H. McClintock, *Arizona, Prehistoric, Aboriginal, Pioneer, Modern.*]

RUFUS KAY WYLLYS

Ark* and the *Dove, The, were the two vessels which brought the first colonists, about 200 in number, to Maryland^qv^. These pioneers left England at the suggestion of and under instruction from Cecil Calvert, to whom, on June 20, 1632, Charles I had granted a charter which conferred proprietary powers and authorized the colonization of the territory in the vicinity of the Chesapeake Bay. Sailing from Cowes, on the Isle of Wight, on Nov. 22, 1633, the *Ark* and the *Dove* laid their course to the Chesapeake by way of the Canary Islands and the West Indies. Entering the Potomac during the first week in March, 1634, they explored the northern bank of this river until, on March 27, it was finally decided to make the first permanent settlement on a river which empties into the Potomac not very far from its mouth. This settlement was and still is known as St. Mary's.

[C. C. Hall, *Narratives of Early Maryland, 1633-1684.*]

RAPHAEL SEMMES

Arkansas. The first white man to visit the region known as Arkansas was DeSoto^qv^ (1541). Next came Marquette and Jolliet (1673) and then LaSalle and Tonti (1682)^qqv^, who came to take possession of the Mississippi Valley for the French. In 1686 Tonti founded Arkansas Post^qv^, the first permanent settlement in the region. The name "Arkansas" is derived from that of a tribe of Indians living west of the Mississippi and north of the Arkansas rivers. It appears on a map of 1718 as "Akansas." Capt. Zebulon Pike spelled it "Arkansaw" (1811) and it so appears in some government documents, but "Arkansas" came into general use. The Arkansas legislature of 1881 adopted the pronunciation Ark' an saw.

This region became American territory with the purchase of Louisiana^qv^ (1803). When the State of Louisiana was admitted to the Union in 1812 Arkansas District became a part of Missouri Territory and then a separate territory of the first type in 1819, when Missouri applied for statehood. Arkansas Post was the first capital, but Little Rock soon took its place. The growth of the population was slow at first, but some energetic leaders soon got the territory advanced to the third stage with a bicameral legislature^qv^ elected by the people. The same class of ambitious leaders rushed it into statehood (1836), ahead of time, measured by the population. One reason for the rush was to get banks. The first legislature created two, a State Bank and the Real Estate Bank (private). These banks, which were underwritten by the state, soon failed and left a debt of $3,000,000 for the state to pay.

Most of the people who settled in Arkansas came from the older South. Some brought their slaves with them. Cotton growing became the leading industry. Henry M. Rector, a defender of slavery, was elected governor in 1860 and he moved for secession^qv^. The state convention submitted "secession" or "co-operation" to be voted on in August, but after the bombardment of Fort Sumter^qv^ and Lincoln's call for troops, the convention reassembled and seceded with only one dissenting vote. Isaac Murphy cast that vote and he became the first loyal governor in 1864. Although the state government had been organized under Lincoln's plan of reconstruction, Arkansas subsequently had to endure four years of congressional Reconstruction which left the state and counties heavily in debt with no money in the state treasury (*see* Joint Committee on Reconstruction). A new constitution was drawn up in 1874 and Augustus H. Garland was elected governor. In politics Arkansas has always been Democratic except for the Reconstruction period, although the agrarian movement^qv^ attained considerable strength in the 1880's and 1890's. A large part of the debt left by the Reconstructionists was repudiated in 1884 as illegal (*see* Repudiation of State Debts); also the unliquidated part of the debt of the Real Estate Bank for the same reason. The initiative and referendum^qqv^ were adopted in 1910 and have been used extensively, sometimes for good, sometimes for ill. An extensive road-building program, since 1915, and other expenditures left the state with a bonded indebtedness of about $165,000,000, the heaviest debt per capita and in proportion to wealth in the Union. It was advantageously refunded in 1933 and the state soon began to call bonds before they were due.

The constitution of 1868 provided for a public school system and this has been carried out. The state has a university, four separate agricultural colleges and two separate teacher-training colleges.

[D. T. Herndon, ed., *Centennial History of Arkansas;* Josiah H. Shinn, *Pioneers and Makers of Arkansas History;* T. S. Staples, *Reconstruction in Arkansas;* David Y. Thomas, *Arkansas in War and Reconstruction;* David Y. Thomas, ed., *Arkansas and Its People.*]

DAVID Y. THOMAS

***Arkansas*, Destruction of the Ironclad** (1862). After the *Arkansas* passed through the Federal fleet before Vicksburg^qv^ to co-operate in Breckinridge's attempt to recapture Baton Rouge^qv^, her machinery became disabled when within five miles of her destination, and she was run ashore and blown up to escape Federal capture, Aug. 5, 1862.

[*War of the Rebellion Records,* Naval Series, XXIII, 293; A. Fortier, *History of Louisiana.*]

WALTER PRICHARD

Arkansas, French Post and Mission at. When LaSalle[qv] laid claim to the entire Mississippi Valley for France in 1682 he granted to Henry de Tonti a large concession at the Quapaw villages on the Arkansas River, and in 1686 Tonti established the Arkansas Post as the earliest French settlement in the lower Mississippi Valley. In 1689 Tonti established a Catholic mission at the post, and by 1700 Jean Couture[qv], who was left in command of the post, had developed an extensive trade with the English of Carolina. The subsequent history of the coast is obscure until the Western Company[qv] took possession of Louisiana in 1718 and John Law sent 700 German colonists to develop his large concession on the Arkansas River. But Law's venture collapsed a few years later, and his colonists abandoned the settlement and located at the "German Coast" (*see* Côte des Allemand) near New Orleans. When French Louisiana was divided into nine districts in 1721, Arkansas Post became the administrative center for the Arkansas District, and in 1722 Benard de la Harpe strengthened the stockade and placed a regular garrison there. Arkansas Post remained important until the end of the French regime in 1762 as the administrative and commercial center of the extensive Arkansas District and as the site of a Jesuit mission[qv].

[Dallas T. Herndon, ed., *Centennial History of Arkansas;* David Y. Thomas, ed., *Arkansas and Its People: A History, 1541-1930;* M. W. Benjamin, French History of Arkansas, in *Publications of the Arkansas Historical Association,* II (1908); Charles Gayarré, *History of Louisiana.*]

WALTER PRICHARD

Arkansas, Great Bend of the, was an important landmark on the Santa Fé trail[qv], marking the first point at which the river was encountered, 278 miles from Independence[qv], and roughly half way to Bent's Fort[qv], which was 530 miles. At Walnut Creek, which joined the Arkansas at the apex of the bend, travelers commonly encountered the first fringe of the buffalo[qv] herds, and Pawnee Rock[qv], fifteen miles beyond, was regarded as the beginning of the hostile Indian country. One hundred miles from Walnut Creek was the Cimarron Crossing where a short cut to Santa Fé could be obtained.

[Col. Henry Inman, *The Old Santa Fé Trail.*]

PAUL I. WELLMAN

Arkansas, THE. Akensas, Akansas, Acansa, a tribe of Indians belonging to the southwestern Siouan[qv] family. They called themselves O guah-pa or Akapa, signifying "those going down stream." They were mound builders[qv]. By De Soto's[qv] time, 1541, they were in the lower Arkansas valley. DeSoto's chroniclers called them Pacaha and Capaha. The early French explorers called them Arkansea. LaSalle[qv] and Tonti found them living in three villages near the mouth of the Arkansas River, in 1683. The Arkansas were tall, well-shaped, non-warlike, agricultural people. From the Arkansas Post[qv], France controlled their trade and made alliances with them. As a result of the Anglo-American westward movement[qv], they were pushed west and south. The remnant of the tribe, now called Quapaw, is in northeastern Oklahoma.

[F. W. Hodge, ed., *Handbook of American Indians;* G. R. Thwaites, *Early Western Travels, 1748-1846.*]

ANNA LEWIS

Arkansas Post, Battle of. Arkansas Post (Fort Hindman) was fortified by the Confederates for the protection of Little Rock. After the repulse of Sherman's (U.) attack upon Vicksburg[qv] (Dec. 29, 1862) it was considered essential to capture the post. Gen. John A. McClernand, with 30,000 men backed by Admiral David D. Porter's fleet of ironclads[qv], forced Gen. Thomas J. Churchill to surrender Jan. 11, 1863.

[David Y. Thomas, *Arkansas in War and Reconstruction.*]

DAVID Y. THOMAS

Arkansas River, known to the early French as Rivière des Ark or d'Ozark, derived its name from the Arkansas Indians[qv] who lived on its banks. The river was first discovered and explored by DeSoto[qv] in 1541 on his journey into the Southwest. The French explorers, Jolliet and Marquette[qv], reached its mouth in 1673, in their search for a river "coming in from California on the southern sea." The Arkansas Post[qv], established in 1686 by Henry Tonti, was the first permanent settlement in Arkansas River region, and around the post centers the early history of the river.

Arkansas River to the French was the highway leading into the Spanish Southwest—Taos and Santa Fé[qqv]. French traders preferred waterways as highways. The headwaters of the Arkansas were in Spanish territory. The Spanish explorer Uribarri in 1696 called the upper Arkansas by the name Rio Napestle, probably of native Indian origin. This name was applied to the river by the Spanish until the 19th century. The treaty with Spain in 1819 (*see* Adams-Onís Treaty) made the Arkansas River west of the 100th meridian a part of the western boundary of the United States. The name Arkansas, which had applied only to lower reaches of the stream, was carried westward by American traders and trappers and succeeded in replacing the name Rio Napestle, or Napeste.

Arkansas River was navigable with keelboats[qv] as far west as Grand River. In early days "Arkansas" and "Ozark" were used interchangeably and were applied to Arkansas River, the mountains north of it and the post near its mouth.

[A. B. Thomas, *Spanish Exploration of Oklahoma, 1599-1792;* Anna Lewis, *Along the Arkansas.*]

ANNA LEWIS

Arkansas River Route, THE, was the mountain or Pikes Peak division of the Santa Fé Trail[qv], which avoided the dangerous Jornada[qv] desert of the Cimarron cut-off. Instead of turning south at Cimarron Crossing near the present site of Dodge City[qv], this route followed up the Arkansas River to old Bent's Fort[qv] near present-day La Junta and there turned southwesterly to the mountains and crossed the difficult Raton Pass[qv]. Choice was now open to continue southward rejoining the other Trail and going through Las Vegas to Santa Fé, or to proceed westward, past the Maxwell Ranch, along the base of the mountains and over the range to Taos[qv]. The Trail then followed the Rio Grande down to Santa Fé[qv]. The Arkansas River Route, though longer, was extensively used because of the importance of Bent's Fort, the trading center of the trappers and Indians; the presence of water and the demand for freight at the settlements along the way. Also it was the route to the Colorado goldfields of 1858 (*see* Pikes Peak Gold Rush) and later and to Denver-Auraria[qv].

[Henry Inman, *The Old Santa Fé Trail.*]

MALCOLM G. WYER

"Arkansas Traveler," THE, is not only the best-known piece of folklore that Arkansas can lay claim to but the favorite of all old-time breakdown fiddle tunes in America. The rollicky dialogue and the rollickier tune go back to the days of Davy Crockett, but the author of neither has been determined. Newspapers, books and articles of commerce have taken the title. As the tradition goes, a stranger traveling in Arkansas comes to a roofless tavern before which the proprietor sits fiddling. "Where does this road go?" asks the stranger. "It's never gone anywhar since I been here," the squatter answers, going on fiddling. Finally, after more such colloquy, the stranger asks, "Why don't you play the rest of that tune?" Immediately the squatter makes the stranger dismount and play. This "turn of the tune" brings forth civil, though still comical, answers, whiskey, food, shelter, horse provender, a hospitality having all the gusto of a country hoe-down.

[Fred W. Allsopp, *Folklore of Romantic Arkansas,* Vol. II.]

J. FRANK DOBIE

Arks were known also as flatboats[qv], broadhorns, Kentucky or Orleans boats, etc. These craft until 1860 carried a large part of the downstream traffic on the rivers of the West. They were cheaply constructed of green wood, shaped like boxes with raked bows, roofed over in whole or in part, and were sold for lumber or firewood at their destinations. They were steered by a long oar, and two or more sweeps, or broadhorns, were used to move them into or out of the current. Three to five men constituted the crew. They averaged about fifteen by fifty feet and held forty to fifty tons of flour.

[Leland D. Baldwin, *The Keelboat Age on Western Waters.*]

LELAND D. BALDWIN

Arkwright Machinery. A spinning machine developed, rather than invented, by Richard Arkwright in England about 1770. It was a marked improvement over earlier forms of spinning machines. The English government prohibited the exportation of machines or drawings but a young immigrant, Samuel Slater, carried the idea to Providence, R. I., and under his direction Almy and Brown constructed a set of Arkwright machines carrying seventy-two spindles. These were installed in 1790 in a small building at the Falls of Pawtucket which still (1938) stands. This introduced the modern factory to this country. (*See also* Machines.)

[Dexter S. Kimball, *Principles of Industrial Organization.*]

DEXTER S. KIMBALL

Arlington National Shrine is on the Virginia bank of the Potomac, directly opposite Washington, D. C. Originally part of the estate of George Washington, it passed to his adopted son, G. W. Parke Custis. In 1831 Robert E. Lee married Mary Ann Custis. Mrs. Lee inherited a life interest in the estate, which after her death was to go to her eldest son, G. W. Custis Lee.

Upon the outbreak of the Civil War, the estate was seized by the United States, which acquired an alleged tax title, built a fort and hospital on the site and used the grounds as a cemetery. In 1882, after suit which reached the Supreme Court, G. W. Custis Lee was declared the legal owner of the property. The matter was settled by paying Custis Lee $150,000 indemnity.

The estate has become the site of one of the most important shrines maintained by the United States. In the cemetery are buried the dead of every war since the Revolution. Arlington House has been restored and a Memorial Amphitheater erected. After the World War the Tomb of the Unknown Soldier^qv^ was added.

[J. T. Faris, *Historic Shrines of America.*]

L. C. HELDERMAN

"Arm in Arm" Convention. *See* National Union ("Arm in Arm") Convention.

Armaments. *See* Defense, National.

Armed Neutrality, THE, had its origin (1780) at the Court of Catherine II, Empress of Russia, who desired to free neutral trade from the interference of belligerents. Her declaration sought to overturn the "Rule of 1756"^qv^ and secure for neutrals the freedom of navigation even to the ports of belligerents; it restricted the category of contraband^qv^ to munitions and the essential instruments of war; it asserted as an established rule of international law^qv^ the principle that "free ships make free goods"^qv^, and set forth a new theory of blockade^qv^. The declaration was followed by the arming of the neutrals of northern Europe to protect their commerce in accordance with the principles to which they had subscribed.

The United States on Oct. 5, 1780, accepted unreservedly the rules of the Armed Neutrality as a basis for its instructions to the commanders of its armed vessels. This action by Congress was intended to pave the way for the United States to become a party to the League of Neutrals. Francis Dana was appointed minister to Russia to secure the twin objectives of recognition of the independence of the United States and its admission "as a party to the convention for maintaining the freedom of the seas"^qv^. His mission was in vain. The United States could not, while a belligerent, become a party to the Armed Neutrality, and Catherine II refused to receive Dana as long as the independence of the colonies was not recognized by Great Britain. The Definitive Treaty of Peace^qv^ in 1783 altered the situation, and the primary object of the mission to Russia was removed. Madison pointed out that, although Congress approved the principles of the Armed Neutrality, it would be "unwise to become a party to a confederacy which might thereafter complicate the interests of the United States with the politics of Europe." Congress finally resolved (June 12, 1783) upon a clear distinction between the principles of the Armed Neutrality and a confederation for their enforcement. That the United States should have escaped from participation in a confederacy of this sort was fortunate. All the members of the Armed Neutrality abandoned, upon the very next opportunity of their becoming belligerents, the creed which they had sought to enforce by arms when they were neutrals. Whatever advantage might have been gained for American commerce by membership in the league would not have compensated for the political embarrassments of such an alliance.

[W. S. Carpenter, The United States and the League of Neutrals of 1780, *American Journal of International Law*, XV, pp. 511-522.]

WILLIAM S. CARPENTER

Armies, Disbanding of the. *See* Demobolization.

Arminianism, the Reformed theology which arose in opposition to the prevailing Calvinism^qv^, received its name from Jacobus Arminius (1560–1609), a mild and liberal-spirited Dutch theologian. It places chief emphasis upon man's freedom and holds that God's sovereignty is so exercised as to be co-operable with the freedom of man. Introduced into America in the early 18th century, its influence spread rapidly in spite of able opposition. Those who accepted it became the advocates of a larger tolerance. On the frontier it made even more rapid headway than elsewhere, since it emphasized the natural human duties rather than speculative theology and the equality of all men in the sight of God, rather than limited grace and the possibility of salvation only for the few, which was the Calvinistic position.

[G. L. Curtiss, *Arminianism in History.*]

WILLIAM W. SWEET

Armistice of November 11, 1918. On Oct. 4, 1918, the German government appealed to President Wilson for an armistice with a view to peace on the basis of the Fourteen Points^qv^. As a prerequisite, Wilson insisted on the practical democratization of the German government and hinted openly at the abdication of William II. Gen. Pershing, the American commander in France, wished to continue the war until Germany was thoroughly beaten, but the Allied commanders, including Marshal Foch, agreed to an armistice and Wilson accepted this view. On Nov. 5, the United States notified Germany that the Fourteen Points were accepted as the basis of peace, subject to two reservations: (1) the freedom of the seas^qv^ was not to be discussed;

(2) Germany must make reparation for the damage done to the property of Allied nationals during the war. The terms of armistice were communicated to Germany on Nov. 8 and signed on Nov. 11 at 5 A.M., to take effect at 11 A.M. Germany had to evacuate all territory west of the Rhine, which was to be occupied by Allied troops; a neutral zone was established ten kilometers east of the Rhine. Germany surrendered large quantities of artillery, machine guns, airplanes, motor trucks and railway rolling stock, as well as most of her navy: it was made impossible for her to resume fighting. She had also to renounce the treaties of Brest-Litovsk and Bucharest and to withdraw her troops from Russia, Rumania and Turkey. The blockade was to continue until peace was made, and a blanket financial reservation was added that "any future claims and demands of the Allies and the United States of America remain unaffected." The armistice was for one month, and was renewed from time to time until peace was signed.

[Charles Seymour, *American Diplomacy during the World War.*]

BERNADOTTE E. SCHMITT

Armor Plate. Credit for the first proposal for an iron-plated ship (*see* Ironclad Warship, Development of) belongs to an American, Col. John Stevens, of Hoboken, N. J., who, early in the War of 1812, designed a floating battery[qv] protected with iron plates. In 1820 Col. Stevens fired thirty-two pound shot at seventy yards without damage against targets protected with iron one-half inch thick, and in July, 1841, his sons, Edwin A. and John C. Stevens, fired sixty-four pound solid shot at thirty yards without damage against targets protected with wrought-iron boiler plates riveted together to four and one-half inches thickness. Steel supplanted wrought iron for armor plate in 1876, the first all-steel plates being made at Creusot, France. The Creusot process was brought to the United States in 1887 by the Bethlehem Steel Company. In 1890 tests at Annapolis proved definitely the superiority of steel over compound (wrought iron faced with steel) plates. In 1891 the Harvey process increased the resistance of steel by nearly 50%, but was supplanted by the Krupp process in 1900.

[J. P. Baxter, *Introduction of the Iron-Clad Warship;* William Hovgaard, *Modern History of Warships;* United States Naval Institute, *Proceedings*, July, 1883.]

LOUIS H. BOLANDER

Armour and Company, one of the world's largest meat and slaughtering establishments, arose from the partnership of John Plankinton and Philip D. Armour in a meat-packing and grain business established at Milwaukee in 1863. Shortly after the Civil War Armour became interested in a grain commission business in Chicago. In 1868 a meat-packing plant was added to the Chicago business, which in 1870 took the name of Armour and Company. Its growth was due to a vast emporium of livestock, railway transportation systems, the vigor and ability of leaders, the building of stockyards and to the growing use of refrigerator cars in transporting meats. Armour's first plant outside of Chicago was opened at Omaha in 1898. Armour and Company of Delaware was formed in 1922 to facilitate financing and administration. Armour and Company of Illinois, incorporated in 1900, showed an inventory in 1936 of 14 packing, 17 produce and creamery houses, 203 branch places, 7 foreign branch houses, a working capital of $112,291,000 and annual sales of $749,000,000.

[Howard C. Hill, Development of Chicago as a . . . Meat Packing Industry, *Mississippi Valley Historical Review*, X, December, 1923.]

LOUIS PELZER

Armstrong, Fort (1816–36), was one of a chain of frontier defenses erected after the War of 1812. It was located at the foot of Rock Island[qv], in the Mississippi River, five miles from the principal Sauk and Fox[qqv] village on Rock River, Ill. Of stone and timber construction, 300 feet square, the fort was commenced in May, 1816, and completed the following year. It was garrisoned until 1836, usually by two companies of United States regulars.

[D. W. Flagler, *History of the Rock Island Arsenal;* Stephen H. Long, *Voyage in a Six-Oared Skiff to the Falls of Saint Anthony in 1817*, Minnesota Historical Society Collections, II, Part I.]

PAUL M. ANGLE

Army, Confederate. Officially, the "Army of the Confederate States of America" was the small regular force established by an act of the Confederate Provisional Congress, March 6, 1861, to consist of one corps of engineers, one of artillery, six regiments of infantry, one of cavalry and four staff departments (adjutant and inspector general's, quartermaster general's, subsistence and medical). This force, incompletely organized when war began, was soon overshadowed by the volunteer forces known officially as "the provisional army." Other acts of Feb. 28 and March 6 authorized the President to assume control over military operations, to accept state forces and 100,000 volunteers for twelve months. By the end of April President Jefferson Davis had called for 82,000 men. On May 8 Congress authorized enlistments[qv] for the war and on Aug. 8, four more states having joined the Confederacy, 400,000 volunteers for one or three years' service. After the passage of the first conscription act in April, 1862 (*see* Confederacy, Conscription in the; Conscription), men were taken into the provisional army directly without the necessary aid of the state authorities.

The highest office in the Regular Army was that of brigadier general until Congress, on May 16, 1861, established the rank of general in order to give higher Confederate commanders control over major generals of state troops in the field. On Aug. 31 Davis nominated and the Congress confirmed Samuel Cooper, Albert Sidney Johnston, R. E. Lee, Joseph E. Johnston and G. T. Beauregard as generals of the Regular Army. On April 12, 1862, Braxton Bragg became a general in that army and in May, 1864, E. Kirby Smith a general in the provisional army. Major generals in the provisional army, under the act of Feb. 28, 1861, were first appointed in May of that year. In September, 1862, the rank of lieutenant general in the provisional army was created.

Serious difficulties were encountered in arming, clothing and feeding the troops. Most of the arms available in May, 1861, were obsolete or inferior and even these could not supply all the men. There was little powder. Only one foundry could cast cannon and only one small powder mill was in operation. The chief reliance for improved arms was in purchases abroad, but getting them through the blockade[qv] was a slow, risky and expensive process. The Government made contracts with private firms for arms, set up its own arsenals and powder mills. Shoes, clothing and blankets were hard to procure, for wool and leather were scarce and importations did not fill requirements. Food supplies, much more plentiful in the South, were often reduced by weak transportation facilities. By 1863 horses and mules had become scarce, thus reducing the mobility of the cavalry, artillery and baggage trains. Although the Confederate soldier was often poorly armed, clothed and fed, discipline in the larger armies was good and morale high until near the end.

The Confederacy[qv] was divided into military departments, fluctuating in number and extent, under commanders responsible only to the War Department and the President. Prompt co-ordination between these departments was often lacking. Other than President Davis himself, there was no commander-in-chief until R. E. Lee was appointed on Feb. 6, 1865, although Lee had been Davis' military adviser for a short time early in 1862 and Braxton Bragg from February to October, 1864.

Because of incomplete surviving records the number of enlistments in the Confederate armies has long been in dispute. Southern writers have estimated them at from 600,000 to 800,000 men, some Northern students at from 1,100,000 to 1,500,000. This last figure is obviously too high for a white population of about 5,000,000. The United States Census for 1860 indicates approximately 1,100,000 men of military age in the seceded states, but these figures are deceptive. Many sections where hostility to the Confederacy developed furnished few soldiers; other large areas were soon overrun by the Union armies. Apparently more men from the seceded states went into the Union Army[qv] than came to the Confederate colors from the non-seceding slave states. Exemptions, details for industrial work and other evasions of service cut down enlistments. Probably between 800,000 and 900,000 actually enrolled, but so many were never in service at any given date. Consolidated returns in the War Department showed:

	Total present and absent	*Total present*	*Total effective present for duty*
Dec. 31, 1862	449,439	304,015	253,208
Dec. 31, 1863	464,646	277,970	233,586
Dec. 31, 1864	400,787	196,016	154,910

Liberal allowances for scattered commands not reported and for irregular organizations would not bring the total enrolled to more than 600,000 at any of these dates. The state militia, serving short terms, uncertain in number and of dubious value, probably fell short of 100,000 at any given date. Losses from battle, disease, capture and desertion so reduced the numbers with the colors that only 174,223 surrendered in April and May, 1865.

[*War of the Rebellion: Official Records of the Union and Confederate Armies; Statutes at Large of the Confederate States;* T. L. Livermore, *Numbers and Losses in the Civil War in America, 1861-65;* R. H. McKim, *The Numerical Strength of the Confederate Army.*]

CHARLES W. RAMSDELL

Army, Enlistment in. *See* Enlistment; Enlistment in the Union Army.

Army, Peace-Time Work. The work of the army in time of peace is so inconspicuous that the country at large seldom hears of it, and yet so multifarious that it is difficult to describe. It falls into two great classes—that work which the army does in its own preparation for war, and that which it does for others.

The activity which attracts the public attention is that concerned with parades[qv], horse shows and similar displays. This all comes within the "preparation" class; for while winning horse show, polo or parade trophies does not prepare for war, the ability to win them makes for discipline and for maintenance of mobility in the field. But the more direct preparation is obscure. The public sees troop columns and truck trains on their way to maneuvers, but knows nothing of the long preparation and laborious execution of the maneuvers themselves. The same is true on a smaller scale of the ordinary daily field exercises of a regiment or garrison. And even the daily housekeeping duties of the army are no small task. The captain who is personally responsible for shelter, clothing, subsistence, discipline, training and recreation of a hundred or more men, the training and health of as many horses, the upkeep of a small fleet of motor vehicles and the accountability for $100,000 or more of Government property, is a busy man.

Such preparatory work is not done by the Regular Army for itself alone. It has always been charged with a somewhat vague responsibility for assisting the National Guard[qv], and for several generations has handled such military instruction as was given in schools and colleges. But since the World War it has been very definitely charged with responsibility for instruction and inspection of the National Guard; for the entire training of the newly formed Officers' Reserve Corps[qv], including the Air Corps Reserve, which furnishes so many of our commercial pilots; for systematic and uniform instruction of the Reserve Officers' Training Corps[qv]; and for the conduct of innumerable Citizens' Military Training Camps[qv].

The other phase of army peace-time work is connected with emergencies of all kinds. From the beginning of our history the Army has fixed the frontier line, guarded it, explored beyond it, pushed it forward as the advance of settlement demanded, established communications by road, rail, wire and radio, aided the civil authority in maintaining order, given relief in fire, flood, famine and catastrophes of all kinds, e.g., the Black Hawk War, the Union Pacific Railway, Sitting Bull, Geronimo, the opening and organization of Alaska, the San Francisco fire, the Panama Canal, the conquering of the yellow and typhoid fevers, the Civilian Conservation Corps[qqv].

[Oliver L. Spaulding, *The United States Army in War and Peace.*]

OLIVER LYMAN SPAULDING

Army, Union (1861–65). When Fort Sumter[qv] was fired on, the United States had an army barely exceeding 16,000 enlisted men and officers, and the effectiveness of this organization was soon lessened by the resignations of Lee and other Southern officers. Northern states were feverishly passing laws for the raising, equipping and training of volunteers[qv] for three years of the war. And by April, 1861, the governors had offered some 300,000 such troops to the Federal Government. But President Lincoln, though determined to restore the Union by force, would not assemble Congress before July 4. Without new legislation there was no authority for an increase in the army, so all the recruiting fervor of the early spring was wasted.

The 75,000 militia, called for on April 15, could be used for only three months, and hence were rushed into battle at Bull Run[qv] in a futile effort to show the strength of the Union before their enlistment should expire. The lesson of Bull Run finally aroused Federal activity as it had not been stirred by the earlier agitation in the states. On July 22, 1861, and following, Congress authorized the creation of a volunteer army of 500,000 men and legalized the President's call of May 3 for 42,000 three-year volunteers and 22,700 regulars. The Regular Army at an authorized strength of 42,000, which was halfway approximated, was used throughout the war for border defense against the Indians. The volunteer army, with which the war was fought, was officered mainly by political generals chosen by the governors, and in the early months, at least, by regimental officers elected by the enlisted men. The result was a needlessly slow development of discipline and efficiency. Also, the competition of state governments with the War Department in bidding for uniforms, munitions, food and supplies led to a scandalous series of contract grafts, high prices and shoddy products (*see* Army Contracts).

The volunteering spirit so cooled off after Bull Run that the remainder of 1861 had passed before an acceptable army could be whipped into rudimentary shape. By the middle of 1862 the first army had been so badly depleted by disease and battle that on July 2 an additional 300,000 volunteers were called for, the governors again being left to care for recruiting and management of the new contingents till they were mustered into service. The troops were urgently needed and on Aug. 4, when volunteering proved sluggish, a draft[qv] of 300,000 nine months' militia was ordered under terms of an act of July 17, 1862. As a direct means of getting soldiers this draft proved a failure, only about 65,000 men being provided. But Federal, state and local bounties lured enough volunteers during the next few months to tide over the emergency.

Early in 1863 it was seen that continued heavy casualties, desertions[qqv], the expiration of short-term enlistments and scanty volunteering was likely to cause a collapse of the army before the close of the year. Consequently, the Enrollment Act of March 3, 1863, was passed to provide men by draft. The act was intended mainly to stimulate volunteering by threat of conscription[qv], thus encouraging the states and localities to avoid this stigma by the offering of adequate bounties[qv]. Men of means were given an easy escape from the draft by the payment of a $300 commutation fee or the hiring of substitutes[qv]. By a later amendment the commutation fee was limited to conscientious objectors[qv], but substitution was permitted till the end of the war. The direct product of two years of repeated drafting was about 50,000 conscripts and 120,000 substitutes. But in the same period over a million volunteers were procured by bounties. Thus for the last half of the war the army was relieved from the constant danger of extinction which had threatened the first half.

The total effective strength of the army on Jan. 1, 1863, before Federal conscription was begun, was just under 700,000. On May 1, 1865, at its highest point, the number was nearly 800,000. Including all men not fit for active service, each of these figures would be increased by about 200,000. The commissioning of 2537 generals alone (including brevet brigadiers) for an army of this size may be taken as an indication of the part spoilsman politics played in army organization. Nevertheless, after the first year the weeding out of incapable officers in high positions went on apace, proved capacity began to replace political favoritism and regimental elections for minor officers, and a tolerable degree of discipline was evolved. Contract grafts continued to lessen the efficiency of the army, but in a diminishing degree. An obtuse policy of the War Department prevented the supplying of the soldiers with modern weapons, which were available to the Union but not to the Confederacy, thus further restricting military efficiency.

[F. A. Shannon, *The Organization and Administration of the Union Army, 1861-1865.*]

FRED A. SHANNON

Army, United States. The United States Army is distinctly different from other armies, in origin, organization and employment.

It is modeled primarily upon the English; for when English colonists arrived in America they brought with them not only their civil but their military institutions. In England, as elsewhere in Europe, the land forces were made up primarily of regular, that is to say professional, troops; of these there were several classes, but their distinguishing characteristic was that they were directly under the orders of the king, whether or not they were directly raised by him; and that they were available for service anywhere that he might direct.

Besides these there were in many countries, and notably in England, nonprofessional, part-time, militia troops, intended primarily for local use in defense of the territory.

When English colonies were established in America or elsewhere, they were entitled, as British territory, to defense by the king's troops; and garrisons of those troops were sent to them at the king's discretion. Each colony also raised its own militia[qv], for preservation of order and defense of the frontier. When a special emergency arose a special expedition was formed, made up of the king's troops, local militia and local irregulars formed for the occasion.

When the American colonies rebelled, the king's troops suddenly became not friends but enemies. Nothing was left to the colonies but their own militia, with such new troops as they might see fit to form. These troops were subject, not to any central government, but each troop unit to its own colonial government. When the New England contingents assembled at Boston there was no real command, but only voluntary co-operation—which might answer for a time, in an inactive situation, but could not work for long.

When Washington joined, a central command was assured, but there was still no permanency of forces. Each colony dealt with its own; discipline, training, pay and supply were all chaotic. The only answer was to form a new force, responsible to Congress only, not to any state. This new force was the Continental Army[qv], which now took the place corresponding to that of the old British regulars. The force at large continued a mixed force, including Continentals, separate militia for each colony and new levies of various kinds.

At the end of the Revolutionary War the militia regiments went back to their own states, where most of them were disbanded; but a few regiments now forming part of our National Guard[qv] are continuations of these Revolutionary units. The Continentals had always been looked upon as a wartime expedient, and the entire force was promptly disbanded, with one interesting exception. Certain military stores were on hand, at West Point and Fort Pitt[qqv], and it was necessary to provide for guarding them until they could be disposed of. Hence one company of artillery was retained in service for that purpose. The company selected happened to be the one formerly commanded by Alexander Hamilton; and Hamilton's Battery is still in service, as Battery "D," 5th Field Artillery.

But hardly had the Continental troops been discharged when it was found that the Federal Government needed troops of its own, not of any state. The Whiskey Rebellion[qv] in western Pennsylvania placed the Government in the humiliating position of having to borrow troops from the states to enforce its own laws; and the Indians on the northwestern frontiers, in Ohio, Indiana and Michigan, proved too serious a problem to leave to local forces. So a new Regular Army was built up. Our oldest infantry regiment, now numbered as the Third, dates back to 1784; and we have many troop units almost as old.

This gives us our traditional military system: a small Regular Army under the exclusive control of the National Government; varying forces of militia in each state, responsible solely to the state in peace, but capable of passing under Federal control in war. The limitation upon the use of British militia still remained among our state troops—they could not be ordered abroad. In our case, many of the militia construed this limitation so strictly that they even questioned the authority of the United States to order them outside their own states. This point was raised so often during the War of 1812[qv] that on one occasion Gen. Jackson, having raised some entirely new troops and offered them to the Government, explained that they were "volunteers and not militia, and had no constitutional scruples."

In the Mexican War[qv] the force of state troops required was not large. The Regular Army was expanded, and various new regiments were raised under the authority of the United States. These new regiments were called regular, because they belonged to no state, but they were not permanent troops, and were disbanded upon conclusion of peace.

In the Civil War[qv], on the other hand, the little regular force was not a drop in the bucket. All that existed were used, and the only complaint was that there were not more of them; but the war was fought chiefly by state troops, raised and officered by the states and then mustered into the Federal service. Many individual regular officers, of course, were assigned to duty with these troops, which helped the new forces, but contributed to the disintegration of the old.

This procedure, of disregarding regular troops and raising state troops, became thoroughly familiar to all the people during the Civil War. Without thinking of merits and demerits, the country at large came to look upon it as the natural and proper way of raising troops. The Spanish War was comparatively a small effort, and the leading men in the Government, both civil and military, were nearly all men of Civil War experience; the old plan was followed, as a matter of course, and apparently without conscious weighing of other plans.

A complication arose at the close of hostilities with Spain. We had inherited an insurrection in the Philippines[qv], and many of the troops sent there were state troops enlisted for the war with Spain. They continued, loyally and cheerfully, to serve in the insurrection, but palpably it was unfair to expect them to do so indefinitely; and we had recourse to the Mexican War expedient of raising temporary troops under Federal, not state, authority. In this case we called them, not temporary regulars, but United States Volunteers, and they served until additional regular troops could be authorized and raised.

We had become familiar, then, with four classes of troops; the Regular Army, always in service, subject to the Federal Government alone, and kept almost as busy in peace as in war; temporary regulars or United States Volunteers, like the regulars but authorized only by special acts of Congress for war times; state troops, under the jurisdiction of the states only; and state troops mustered into the service of the United States for specific purposes.

When it came to the great mobilization for the World War[qv] we utilized all these classes, and much in the same manner as before. The Regular Army was greatly expanded, and at the same time it was called upon for heavy details of officers and men to form a nucleus for the new troops, badly disrupting the old. State troops were called for, and mustered into the service of the United States; they were then so completely reorganized as to leave little sign of their old form. A new National Army[qv], of temporary troops under United States control, was formed. Such was the haste to get troops into the field that the possibilities of orderly expansion were overlooked; so many divisions were organized that when one was to go overseas it almost always had to be filled up by drafts from others, leaving those others to go through the whole organization process again.

At the close of the war a drastic reorganization was made, with a view to obviating the difficulties encountered. The state troops, now called the National Guard, were placed on a more systematic basis, and provision was made for more simple and rapid transformation into United States troops. The National Army, of course, had disappeared, but provision was made for a corps of reserve officers, to maintain its tradition and to prepare the way for the prompt mobilization of a new one. The Regular Army was given a new system of organization and command, and was reduced to a peace basis; but a large number of additional officers, not required by the Regular Army organization itself, was added to furnish instructors for the National Guard and for the reserve officers, and to set up a scheme of school training for officers and officer candidates. This expansion of the Regular Army lists, of course, did provide for the needs in question, but it enormously reduced the amount of troop duty that an officer can do, and threw more emphasis upon theoretical study and less upon practical troop work than we had ever tried before.

The school system just mentioned calls for a word of explanation. It consists of elementary professions schools in all regular troop units; special schools for officers of each arm; a command and staff school at Fort Leavenworth for selected officers of all arms; and a War College[qv] at Washington for instruction in the mechanism of the War Department staff and of the highest troop units in the field. To keep up the numbers of the reserve officers required under the general scheme the old system of military instruction in high schools and colleges was improved and systematized, taking the form of a Reserve Officers' Training Corps[qv]. To provide noncommissioned officers for any new force to be raised, the Citizens' Military Training Camps[qv] were formed, operating every summer. A few of the attendants at these camps, who attend for four summers, are commissioned as reserve officers, on the same basis as graduates of the R.O.T.C.

This whole system is in operation, and is under trial, particularly with respect to the number of troops that can be efficiently raised in a given time. It will be noted that while nearly all the details have been changed, the general scheme is that under which we have always raised our armies in past wars. It is still too early to predict how, in its present form, it will succeed under stress; or to judge to what extent, if any, the whole plan will require reconstruction to meet modern conditions.

[Oliver L. Spaulding, *The United States Army in War and Peace;* National Defense Act with Amendments, *House of Representatives Document*, 1935; Hearings on National Defense, House of Representatives, March, 1927; Burnside Report on Reorganization of the Army, *Senate Report 555*, Dec. 12, 1878.]

OLIVER LYMAN SPAULDING

Army, United States, Insignia of Rank in. The origin of insignia of rank in our army dates from the period of Washington's variously clad Continental Army[qv], wherein it became necessary to devise badges in order to indicate rank. Washington's order read, "As the Continental Army has unfortunately no uniforms, and consequently many inconveniences must arise from not being able to distinguish the commissioned officers from the privates, it is desired that some badges of distinction may be immediately provided; for instance that the field officers may have red or pink colored cockades in their hats. the captains yellow or buff, and the subalterns green. They are to furnish themselves accordingly. The sergeants may be distinguished by an epaulette or stripe of red cloth sewed upon their right shoulder, the corporals by one of green." Just prior to the issuance of this order, Washington directed that "the general officers and their aides-de-camp will be distinguished in the following manner: The Commander in Chief by a light-blue ribband worn across his heart between his coat and waistcoat; the Major and Brigadier General by a pink ribband worn in like manner; the Aides-de-Camp by a green ribband." Major Generals' sleeves were to be distinguished from Brigadier Generals' by a "broad purple ribband." Thus began the indications of rank in our army. Such markings now extend, through varying devices, from the Second Lieutenant's single gold bar to the General's four silver stars, and through a variety of chevrons for noncommissioned rank.

[Col. Robert E. Wyllie, *The Romance of Military Insignia.*]

ROBERT S. THOMAS

Army Contracts have been used as the chief instruments through which the American armed forces have been supplied with materiel since the Revolution. A dubious fame had been won by these contracts as early as 1777, when the states were urged by the Continental Congress[qv] to fix prices on clothing in order to forestall large profits gained from "sharping and extortion." In 1781, when the harassed Congress adopted the European system of supply, a single civilian contractor might become virtually dictator of the army's movements. Buying supplies and transporting them to the troops, the contractor was inclined not only to stint on quality but to await a favorable market and favorable weather. Bitter criticism during the War of 1812 and the Florida Indian campaigns led in 1818 to an attempt to halt corruption and to promote efficiency by the adoption of a strengthened staff system. Public notice and inspection were required and staff members were prohibited from profiting personally on purchases or sales.

But the first months of the Civil War saw collusion, fraud and favoritism at their worst. Contracts, made at exorbitant prices, were sold to subcontractors and the profits pocketed without risk; the Government bought its own cast-off arms; troops were clad in shoddy which disintegrated under their eyes. A congressional investigation resulted in restrictive legislation, passed early in 1862, requiring competitive bidding and written contracts, prohibiting subletting and subjecting contractors to court-martial in cases of indictment for fraud. Government inspection was tightened up, with the result that the worst abuses were eliminated, although unreasonable profits continued, laying the foundations of many American fortunes.

The effect of legislation and regulation produced by these experiences came to a head in the World War and proved as obstructive under modern conditions as their lack had earlier proved scandalous. The War Department unwound itself from peace-time red tape hardly a month before the armistice signaled the end of the war. Nevertheless, the World War was remarkably free from contract scandals. Although $17,480,000,000 was disbursed from April 6, 1917, to June 1, 1919, of which $9,850,000,000 was spent on contract by the Quartermaster Corps and Ordnance Department alone, Congress in 1919–20 found little evidence of graft or collusion. Congressional criticism centered around the cost-plus[qv] contract, an emergency instrument ultimately prohibited. To offset profits, price-fixing[qv] was attempted and excess-profits taxes[qv] were applied, measures which were only partially successful. In this war, however, the contractor was in no position to bargain on equal terms, for the Government, with its massive purchasing power, perfected propaganda techniques and the legal right to commandeer productive facilities, was in a position superior even to that of the giant corporation.

[L. C. Hatch, *The Administration of the American Revolutionary Army;* M. M. McKee, Service of Supply in the War of 1812, *Quartermaster Review,* Vol. VI; F. A. Shannon, *The Organization and Administration of the Union Army;* J. F. Crowell, *Government War Contracts.*]

WAYNE C. GROVER

Army General Staff, DEVELOPMENT OF THE. In the period of our colonial wars, when our military institutions were being formed from those of England, the staff of an army consisted primarily of a Quartermaster General and an Adjutant General, each with a staff of his own to handle details. The Quartermaster General assisted the commander in preparing operations plans, and in the execution of these plans collected information and arranged marches and quarters. The supply service (*see* Army Supply) was under his direction. The Adjutant General dealt with the internal economy of troop units.

During the 19th century the Quartermaster General became a supply officer only, while the term General Staff was used to signify all general officers and members of staff departments, not belonging to regiments. The staff departments reported direct to the Secretary of War, and the nominal Commanding General of the army had little authority over them.

In 1903, by act of Congress upon recommendation of Secretary Root, a General Staff Corps was formed. In place of a Commanding General of the army a Chief of Staff was provided, issuing orders to the whole army in the name of the Secretary of War.

This system being new to us, no really efficient organization was worked out for some years. Finally, in the American Expeditionary Forces[qv] in France, a system was adopted assimilating our General Staff organization very closely to the French. Meanwhile a different system had been adopted in the War Department[qv], and at the end of the war it became necessary to choose between the two. The A.E.F. system was decided upon, with some modifications.

Our General Staff now consists of five divisions, one dealing with personnel administration, one with military intelligence, one with organization and training, one with supply and transportation and one with war plans. It differs from the other types described above, in that they are essentially army agencies, dealing exclusively with intelligence and operations and having nothing to do with War Department administration. Ours is distinctly a War Department agency, controlling the entire administration of the army.

[Oliver L. Spaulding, *The United States Army in War and Peace.*]

OLIVER LYMAN SPAULDING

Army Hospitalization may be defined as the process of providing shelter, care and other environmental factors needed to restore the disabled to health and physical fitness. The Surgeon General of the army is the head of the Medical Department. He is charged among his other duties and responsibilities with the supervision of the administration of all establishments for the care, treatment and transportation of the sick and wounded personnel of the military establishment under the immediate direction of the War Department, as prescribed by the Secretary of War.

The first hospital for sick soldiers in the territory now known as the United States was established on Manhattan Island in 1658. During the American Revolution, because of the poverty and meager resources of the country, little was done in hospital building. The sick and wounded were at first evacuated to various types of houses. Later there were provided log huts so built that air could penetrate the crevices. These huts were without floors, the ground being hardened or baked with heat. Each hut accommodated eight to twelve men. During the War of 1812, in addition to previous hospital facilities, a general hospital was established constituting forty wards containing between 700 and 800 patients. The patients were segregated according to surgical cases and various other diseases. Profiting by the experience of the British government during the Crimean War, this country during the Civil War developed the most perfect system of army hospitals ever known up to that time. It consisted of the pavilion type of general hospital. Each pavilion constituted a single ward of not more than fifty beds, isolated from adjacent buildings. An improvement to this type of building was made at the time of the Spanish-American War. The Letterman General Hospital at San Francisco was among the best. Still greater improvements were made in the pavilion type of hospital during the World War, and today there are available for use at any time, plans and specifications for standardized pavilion hospitals appropriate for both the Zone of the Interior and the Theater of Operations requirements.

During peace only station and general hospitals care for army patients. The station hospital, varying greatly in bed capacity, serves only the local station or post. Its facilities depend in general upon the size of the command served. General hospitals provide general and special, rather than local and ordinary, needs. They are organized, equipped and staffed to afford better facilities than can be given in station hospitals. In time of war, peace-time hospitals are augmented by leasing existing buildings and sites and by the erection of new buildings in the Theater of Operations and the Zone of the Interior. All hospitals established in the Zone of the Interior to meet local mobilization needs are designated either station or general hospitals, while hospitals in the Theater of Operations are classed as mobile and fixed hospitals. The mobile hospitals (hospital companies or troops, surgical hospitals, evacuation hospitals and convalescent hospitals) accompany the armies in the Combat Zone and are equipped with sufficient tentage for sheltering patients, but utilize existing buildings when possible. The fixed hospitals (station hospitals, general hospitals, hospital centers and convalescent camps) are units in the Communication Zone to which the sick and wounded are sent for definitive treatment. Casualties requiring prolonged treatment or considered a permanent loss as a military asset are transferred to station and general hospitals in the Zone of the Interior.

[*The Medical Service of the Corps and Army*, published by the Medical Field Service School, Carlisle Barracks, Pa.; *The Medical Service of the Field Forces*, published by the Medical Field Service School, Carlisle Barracks, Pa.]

CHARLES M. WALSON

Army of Occupation (1918–23). As part of the Allied Army of Occupation, the American Third Army, commanded by Maj. Gen. Joseph T. Dickman, crossed into Germany in December, 1918, taking station in the North Sector of the Coblenz bridgehead. Units of the Third Army were stationed at various points within the American area and engaged in duties of occupation and training, including participation in civil administration of occupied territory, until July 2, 1919, when the Third Army was discontinued. It was succeeded by the "American Forces in Germany."

Maj. Gen. Edward F. McGlachlin, Jr., assumed command of this newly designated force until July 8, 1919, when its permanent commander, Maj. Gen. Henry T. Allen, reported. From January, 1920, Gen. Allen worked in conjunction with the Rhineland High Commission. At noon on Jan. 27, 1923, American troops having left the Coblenz area, Gen. Allen relinquished command of the American area.

[Henry T. Allen, *The Rhineland Occupation.*]

ROBERT S. THOMAS

Army on the Frontier. This term applies to the activities of the United States Army stationed near the frontier settlements from the beginning of national existence until about 1890, the end of the settlers' frontier. The principal functions performed by this army were: 1, guarding the frontier settlements from hostile Indians; 2, aiding the settlement of the West by developing and protecting the communication between the older settlements and the frontier, by exploring the West, constructing roads and defending the overland trails, water routes and later telegraph and railroad lines; and 3, policing the frontier until the civil governments could maintain order.

The western movement[qv] of settlers brought conflict with the Indians. Scores of Indian wars and campaigns were fought by the army. Some of the more notable Indian wars were: the Northwest Indians, 1790–95 and 1811–13; Seminole Wars in Florida, 1817–18, 1835–42 and 1856; Black Hawk War, 1832; Sioux War, 1862–67; War of the Plains Indians, 1863–69; Sioux and Cheyenne War of 1876–79; and Apache Wars, 1861–90[qqv]. These wars were fought by the regular infantry and cavalry regiments occasionally aided by state militia and volunteers. The frontier soldiers were usually stationed in posts at strategic points defending the routes of communications, settlements and Indian reservations. The strength of this army, about one half of the Regular Army in time of peace, ranged from 1423 troops in 1790 in the Northwest Territory[qv] to over 26,000 in 1868, which was the height of the Indian wars on the Great Plains. The frontier posts had on the average a garrison of 200 troops. By 1867 over 100 posts were scattered throughout the West. As the Indian wars ended, after 1870, these posts were rapidly abandoned.

The army supplies were carried by boats, steamboats, ox and mule trains, pack mules and horses and later by railroads, which stimulated the development of trade, farming and ranching. The difficulty of supplying these remote army posts encouraged farming and urban enterprises around the posts, the beginning of permanent settlements.

The daily life of the frontier soldier was a hardy one. The soldiers built their shelter, escorted travelers, emigrants, and wagon trains on the trails, aided and protected surveying parties, constructed thousands of miles of trails and roads, supplied needy emigrants, patrolled trails and railroad lines, guarded river navigation, protected government and private property from hostile Indians and outlaws, assisted and fed friendly Indians, fought hostile Indians and gave police assistance to the weak civil authorities on the frontier. Their shelters were usually log, stone, adobe or sod huts constructed largely by their own labor. The hardships of the soldiers, the miserable quarters, inferior food and the lonely life encouraged many desertions.

The army on the frontier disagreed with the Indian Bureau[qv] and the frontier civil authorities over the Indian policy[qv]. The frontiersmen in general demanded the destruction or removal of the Indians (*see* Indian Removals). The Indian Bureau attempted to protect the Indians, and the army to coerce them. When the Indians revolted the army made war upon the entire Indian tribe, punishing the innocent with the guilty, even to the extent of killing women and children in raids on villages or camps. The Indian Bureau and the army officials accused each other of being responsible for the Indian wars.

[C. Goodwin, *Trans-Mississippi West;* G. W. Manypenny, *Our Indian Wards;* N. A. Miles, *Serving the Republic;* F. L. Paxson, *History of the American Frontier,* and *The Last American Frontier;* R. E. Reigel, *America Moves West;* J. Winsor, *The Westward Movement.*]

RAYMOND L. WELTY

Army Posts, THE, of the United States Army[qv] played an important part in the westward extension of the frontier[qv]. In the older eastern states they became centers for recruiting and drilling troops and guardians of the coast line at strategic points. These older forts followed European models of construction, and accommodations for the soldiers, officers and their wives were usually comfortable. Not so those of the frontier, which were often in advance or on the fringe of the settled regions and were usually speedily constructed by the soldiers themselves. Jefferson introduced the factory or trading system[qv] in connection with the establishment of army posts as a means of dealing with the Indians. Settlements grew up around these posts and after their abandonment, usually after a period of a few years, towns of the same name frequently remained. Important treaties with the Indians were very often made at the forts, or at points near them under military protection. Many of these treaties were negotiated by the officers themselves.

A study of the extension of forts westward will show that they were usually slightly in advance of the frontier line of settlement and at some periods were constructed more rapidly than at others. The period after the War of 1812 was one in which forts were rapidly advanced throughout the old Northwest[qv] into territory formerly claimed by the British. As Spain and Mexico were pushed back in the Southwest, army posts followed, until by 1845 a line of eleven forts extended from Lake Superior to the Gulf of Mexico.

Indian raids during the Civil War on the Great Plains and the extension of mail routes and later railroads to the Pacific necessitated the buildings of forts at strategic points. Regular Army forts accommodating usually from two to six companies with artillery were supplemented by minor temporary or lightly held centers designated as camps or cantonments. These last were usually little more than huts or shelters and often merely wooded, grassed and watered areas suitable for a few days' stay.

The usual form for the larger posts, which indicates a fairly permanent station for troops, was in the form of a quadrangle constructed around a parade ground, with the officers' quarters, barracks, post traders and hospital on one side and the stables and quartermaster's supplies on the other. The ends of the quadrangle might be occupied by the guard house, company kitchens and work shops, and farther back by the laundress' quarters. Not all new forts had such elaborate equipment.

Despite the lack of the amenities, life at some of these frontier posts was pleasant—in peace times—for the younger set. Young West Pointers brought out their wives, who maintained as far as possible the social standards of their old homes, and "post hops," riding and hunting parties and card games were enjoyed. Wild game was often plentiful but this asset of the larder was supplemented when necessary by cattle drives[qv] from the east and south, thus introducing cattle to the Great Plains. Gardens and farms were laid out around the posts to provide vegetables, grains and forage, and thus it was demonstrated that the prairies were not sterile because they had no trees. Flour mills were constructed at certain posts such as Snelling and Atkinson[qqv].

Most garrisons had post schools, libraries, newspapers and magazines. Plays were given and some of the most accurate and colorful literature of the new territory appears in the memoirs of army officers and even of their wives. After the abandonment of a post the buildings were usually sold and the land ceded or auctioned off. In a few cases the area was made into a national reserve.

[H. P. Beers, *Western Military Frontier;* U. S. War Department, Surgeon General Official Circular No. 8, *Report of the Hygiene of the United States Army with a Description of Military Posts.*]

CARL L. CANNON

Army School System. Such schooling as was available in the United States Army prior to and following the Civil War was obtained in Lyceum courses: assemblies at which selected officers presented prepared papers. The army was then scattered throughout the country in small isolated garrisons, much of the time in actual field duty. There was no definite educational system or policy.

The Garrison School, supervised by the War Department, replaced the Lyceum system and continued until the World War. A school of artillery instruction was begun at Fortress Monroe in 1824. In 1881 a School of Application for Infantry and Cavalry, now Command and General Staff School, was established at Fort Leavenworth, Kans. This was the first definite step to secure a bona fide system of instruction and has served as the basis for the army's school policies. The Army War College[qv], Washington, D. C., established in 1901, laid the cornerstone of our modern military educational system.

World War experience brought about the establishment of branch schools—the Special Service Schools. These constitute the backbone of the system; in them the officer learns the fundamentals of his arm.

Schooling is compulsory and continuous throughout an officer's service. Troop Schools and Special Service Schools which provide basic courses are usually attended by all officers of the particular service.

The General Service Schools are the Leavenworth School, the Army War College and the Army Industrial College. Attendance is by selection.

Every officer aspires for Leavenworth. Courses are for regular officers, with shorter courses for the National Guard and Officer's Reserve Corps[qqv]. The school prepares officers for command and general staff[qv] duty.

Only a few attend the War College, graduation from which completes the officer's education; the mission of the War College is to train officers in the operations of the army and higher echelons; and to instruct in those political, economic and social matters which influence the conduct of war.

The Army Industrial College situated in Washington, D. C., is limited to officers of the Regular Army. It trains officers in the wartime needs of industrial organization and mobilization of material; technique of wartime procurement of military supplies, etc.

W. M. GRIMES

Army Supply. As now used in the American Army, the word "supply," in its broadest sense, indicates all military stores and services furnished by one branch of the army for the use of another. This includes food, clothing, shelter, transportation, weapons, ammunition, equipment of all kinds, purchase, pay, hospitalization[qv], labor, etc. These supply functions of the army are divided between the several branches of the staff known, generally, as the Supply Departments or the Supply Services and are grouped under the supervision of a General Staff[qv] officer known as the Assistant Chief of Staff for Supply.

Beginning in the Revolution and until a comparatively recent date, the principal supply functions of the army, as above defined, were divided between the Quartermaster Department, the Subsistence Department, the Pay Department, the Corps of Engineers, the Ordnance Department and the Medical Department. The Signal Corps was added in 1863 and the Chemical Warfare Service in 1920.

The Corps of Engineers, the Signal Corps and the Chemical Warfare Service not only furnish supplies to other arms, but also perform a distinctive combat function of their own, so that, to this extent, they belong to the Line of the army.

Under the act of Aug. 24, 1912, the Quartermaster Department, the Subsistence Department and the Pay Department were merged into one branch, known as the Quartermaster Corps. Later, in 1920, the old Pay Department was taken away from the Quartermaster Corps and with added duties became the Finance Department.

During the World War the Supply Services, while continuing in a general way to perform their old duties, were largely superseded in the War Department by a branch of the General Staff known as the Division of Purchase, Storage and Traffic.

In France a somewhat similar organization was created under the name of the Services of Supply, with headquarters at Tours and entirely separated from Gen. Pershing's headquarters at Chaumont (*see* American Expeditionary Forces). During the course of the war, a number of changes were made in this organization, but, generally speaking, it provided for a redistribution of the old supply functions into the following groups: the Quartermaster Department, the Transportation Department, the Motor Transport Corps, the Army Service Corps, the Division of Construction and Forestry, the Division of Engineer Supplies, the Division of Light Railways, the Ordnance Department, the Gas Service, the Medical Department, the Finance Department, the General Purchasing Board and the War Risk Insurance.

After the World War there was another reorganization of the Supply Departments in Washington. In effect, they resumed their old functions under their old names, with the addition of the Chemical Warfare Service, but were coordinated by an Assistant Chief of Staff for Supply.

In addition to this there was created a procurement agency in the office of the Assistant Secretary of War which is charged with the general supervision of procurement of military stores in time of peace and with the mobilization of industry in time of war.

In the more restricted sense, the word "supplies" is used in the army to indicate military stores and does not include personal services.

[Gen. Johnson Hagood, *The Services of Supply.*]

JOHNSON HAGOOD

Army War College, THE, is the highest seat of instruction in, and culmination of, the educational system of the United States Army[qv]; it trains selected officers for high command and the higher General Staff[qv] duties; and ninety Regular Army and a limited number of Navy and Marine Corps officers pursue a one-year course. Organized in 1901 by Secretary of War Root, until creation of the General Staff of the army in 1903, it performed the functions of that body, continuing as a part thereof until the World War.

J. L. DEWITT

Arnold Betrays the Cause. Brig. Gen. Benedict Arnold of the Continental Army had fought gallantly for the American cause from Ticonderoga (1775) to Saratoga (1777)[qqv]. But by the spring of 1779 several motives led him to open up a treasonable correspondence with the British headquarters in New York. These were (1) irritation at repeated slights by Congress, (2) resentment at the authorities of Pennsylvania who had court-martialed him, (3) need for money and (4) opposition to the French alliance of 1778[qv]. Throughout the rest of 1779 and 1780 he transmitted military intelligence about the American Army to the British. July 12, 1780, he "accepted the command at West Point as a post in which I can render the most essential services" [to the British]. He demanded from the British £20,000 in case he could betray West Point and £10,000 in case he failed but himself went over to the British. Negotiations were carried on with Maj. John André[qv], adjutant general of the British army. The latter visited Arnold at a point between the British and American lines Sept. 21, 1780. On Sept. 23, when returning from this meeting, André was captured by the Americans, and the incriminating documents found in his stocking were sent to Gen. Washington, who happened to be in the neighborhood. News of André's capture was also sent to Arnold, thus giving him time to escape down the Hudson River to the British before he could be arrested for treason. He became a brigadier general in the British army, went to England after the defeat of the British and died there June 14, 1801.

[I. N. Arnold, *Life of Benedict Arnold;* W. Abbatt, *Crisis of the Revolution.*]

RANDOLPH G. ADAMS

Arnold's March to Quebec. In the summer of 1775 Col. Benedict Arnold went to Cambridge, Mass., and laid before Commander in Chief George Washington a plan for attacking Canada. Washington was sympathetic. The old classic route by way of Lakes George and Champlain and the Richelieu River was assigned to Gen. Richard Montgomery. News of another passage by way of the Kennebec and Chaudière rivers had reached Washington. This route was assigned to a force under Arnold. On Sept. 19 Arnold's command left Newburyport, Mass., and went by sea to and up the Kennebec where 200 bateaux had been ordered to be ready. With these Arnold headed up the river. Made of green wood and ill-adapted to the upper rushing waters of the Kennebec, these bateaux were a tactical blunder which, however, did not daunt Arnold. Neither did he hesitate when Maj. Roger Enos turned back with one-fourth of the little army. On up the Dead River, full of ice and through snowstorms, with insufficient food and clothing, Arnold led his force. Oct. 28 found them going across the carrying place which was actually the divide between the St. Lawrence and Atlantic watersheds. Arnold plunged ahead with an advance guard while the remainder were reduced to eating dogs and shoeleather. At Sertigan, Arnold arranged for supplies which refreshed his exhausted detachment so that they were able to go down the Chaudière and reach the St. Lawrence on Nov. 9, 1775. In the meantime Montgomery had reached Montreal, but Arnold went on across the St. Lawrence and was actually in front of Quebec before Montgomery arrived. Guy Carleton, the British commander at Montreal, evacuated that place and got into Quebec before Montgomery could join Arnold on Dec. 2. Carleton had 1200 men while the combined American forces numbered scarcely 1000. Nevertheless, in a blinding snowstorm, Montgomery and Arnold assaulted Quebec on the night of Dec. 31, 1775. The effort failed, Montgomery was killed and Arnold wounded. Arnold's march through the wilderness of Maine has been regarded as a classic of perseverance and determination in the face of extreme hardship.

[J. H. Smith, *Arnold's March from Cambridge to Quebec,* and *Our Struggle for the Fourteenth Colony.*]

RANDOLPH G. ADAMS

Arnold's Raid in Virginia. In December of 1780 Commander in Chief Sir Henry Clinton of the British armies in North America determined to send an expedition into Virginia. Its purpose was to conduct desultory raids into the tidewater region of that state and to block the mouth of the Chesapeake. The command was given to the traitor, Benedict Arnold, because Clinton admired his intrepidity and believed he could induce some more Americans to desert. Leaving Sandy Hook on Dec. 20–21 and arriving at Hampton Roads Dec. 30, Arnold seized the small boats on the James River and pushed up that stream to Westover. Sending Simcoe's Rangers ahead, the force was moved on to Richmond, which Arnold occupied after a skirmish on Jan. 5, 1781. He destroyed the iron foundry at Westham and the American stores at Richmond. Arnold then re-embarked on the James and fell down to Portsmouth, which he fortified and whence he sent various marauding and pillaging expeditions into the neighborhood until March, when he was joined and outranked by Maj. Gen. William Phillips. In April Phillips and Arnold started another expedition up the James, reaching City Point on the 24th, whence they proceeded overland to Petersburg where 1000 hogsheads of tobacco were destroyed, as were the small boats on the Appomattox. Arnold then returned to Osborn's on the James where he destroyed a small American fleet, marched to Manchester where 1200 hogsheads of tobacco were destroyed, thence to Warwick where the flour magazines and mills were burned. In May the force fell down to Westover, thence to Brandon. Throughout these movements the British were harassed by the inferior forces of Lafayette and Wayne. Phillips died at Petersburg on May 13, 1781, and the chief command momentarily devolved on Arnold again. But at this time Lord Cornwallis came up with his superior forces and joined the detachment of Phillips and Arnold to his for the campaign of the summer of 1781.

[J. G. Simcoe, *Journal of the Operations of the Queen's Rangers.*]

RANDOLPH G. ADAMS

Aroostook War, The, was an undeclared and bloodless "war," from February to May, 1839, occasioned by the failure of the United States and Great Britain to determine the boundary between New Brunswick and what is now Maine (*see* Northeast Boundary). In 1820 Maine became a state. Almost immediately, ignoring the British contention that all land north of Mars Hill, in Aroostook, was British, the Maine legislature, jointly with Massachusetts, made grants to settlers along both branches of the Aroostook River. In 1831 Madawaska, in the disputed area, was incorporated by Maine. Finally, in January, 1839, Rufus McIntire was appointed land agent, with authority to take a posse into the disputed area and oust Canadians. Within two months 10,000 Maine troops were either encamped along the Aroostook River or were on their way there. At the insistence of Maine congressmen, the Federal Government voted a force of 50,000 men and $10,000,000 in the event of war. To prevent a clash Gen. Winfield Scott was despatched to negotiate a truce with the lieutenant governor of New Brunswick. This he did, and Great Britain, convinced of the seriousness of the situation, agreed to a boundary commission, whose findings were incorporated in the Webster-Ashburton Treaty[qv].

[H. S. Burrage, *Maine and the Northeastern Boundary Controversy.*]

ELIZABETH RING

Arpent, THE, is an old French unit of land measure, both linear and superficial, now standardized in Louisiana at 192 English feet, or a square of that dimension (equal to approximately five sixths of an acre). French colonial land grants were described as fronting a given number of arpents on a river or bayou by forty arpents in depth and containing a certain number of superficial arpents.

WALTER PRICHARD

Arrest. "The course of development (under the common law) seems to have been outlawry, vengeance, hue and cry[qv], arrest." The first three stages had passed before the colonization of America, though arrest without warrant "survives from the hue and cry" (not abolished in England until 1827) and is here the oldest form. Such arrest is still permitted by an officer or private citizen, of one who is about to commit, is committing or has committed a crime in the former's presence. In certain cases an officer may make such an arrest on suspicion. Suspected aliens were formerly arrested by immigration inspectors without warrant; but the practice was finally discontinued as "illegal." Arrest upon a warrant issued by a justice of the peace became the usual practice in England and the common law, as carried to the colonies, generally required a warrant.

But arrest was not confined to criminal procedure. The civil writ of *capias ad satisfaciendum,* e.g., was executed by imprisoning defendant until debt and costs were paid; that practice continued in England until 1869. "From time immemorial members of Parliament were privileged from arrest during the sessions of that body" (67 Neb. 75); but its act of 1770, sponsored by Lord Mansfield, limited the privilege to civil arrest (207 U. S. 438) and seven years later language of that act was embodied in the Articles of Confederation[qv] (V), a decade thereafter in the Federal Constitution[qv] (I, 6, paragraph I) and subsequently in many state constitutions; but in none does the exemption extend to other civil process (293 U. S. 76) in the absence of an express provision, which, however, has been enacted in some states. "When the Constitution was adopted arrests in civil suits were still common in America" (293 U. S. 83). Indeed, the United States Circuit Court for the Rhode Island district, with Chief Justice Jay presiding in 1792, annulled, as impairing the obligation of contracts[qv], a state statute exempting a debtor from arrest during a moratorium. Statutes are still in force in some states authorizing the arrest of a delinquent debtor, especially one guilty of fraud; but in others a state constitutional ban of imprisonment for debt has been held to preclude such arrest (106 Ala. 35), and it is not permitted in Federal courts except in enforcing a state law (U. S. Code § 843). Differing in its nature and origin from the common-law arrest is the "attachment" for contempt in disobeying an order of a chancery court (e.g., an injunction[qv]). Always obnoxious to the champions of labor, such jurisdiction in Federal courts has been somewhat curtailed by the acts of Congress of 1914 (Clayton Act[qv]) and 1932 (Norris-LaGuardia Act[qv]); but the power to "attach" for contempt remains and in some state courts even decrees for alimony are thus enforced, despite the constitutional prohibition of imprisonment for debt[qv].

[Wilgus, Arrest without a Warrant, *Mich. L. Rev. XXII,* 545; Warren, *History of the Supreme Court; Corpus Juris,* 2, VI, 568-712; Executions against the Body, etc., *Encyc. Pl. & Pr. VIII,* 584.]

C. SUMNER LOBINGIER

Arrest, Arbitrary, during the Civil War. Freedom from arbitrary arrest, guaranteed in the writ of habeas corpus[qv], has become synonymous in Anglo-Saxon tradition with civil liberty[qv]. The right to restrict this freedom nevertheless is recognized in England as a parliamentary function and in the United States as a constitutional exercise of power in time of "rebellion or invasion." Until 1861 this Federal right had never been exercised, but the Civil War brought widespread restrictions of civil liberty. In order to cope with antiwar activities (*see* Copperheads), President Lincoln issued several proclamations by which the privilege of the writ of habeas corpus was suspended, first within limited areas and later (Sept. 24, 1862) throughout the entire nation.

The President's control of arbitrary arrest was frequently questioned, especially by Chief Justice Taney, who held (*ex parte* Merryman[qv]) that the legislative branch rather than the executive had this constitutional authority. Lincoln ably defended himself against dictatorship charges in various open letters, however (*see* Birchard Letter; Corning Letter). Executive control was maintained and extended, even after Congress required (March 3, 1863) that political prisoners either be released or subjected to regular judicial procedure. The Department of State and later the War Department administered arrests. Passports were required, a secret service[qv] was organized and Union officers and local police co-operated in apprehending suspects. Political prisoners were detained without hearing and usually released after brief imprisonment. Trial by military commissions, such as in the Vallandigham and Milligan cases[qqv], was exceptional. Although the authority for such commissions was not questioned by the Supreme Court during the war, their use outside the war zone for the trial of civilians was declared unconstitutional after the war.

The number of arrests for antiwar activities is not known exactly. One official list with 13,535 names is incomplete, while on the other hand Alexander Johnston's guess of 38,000 is exaggerated. No authoritative total has ever been reached. One famous series of arrests included the mayor and a judge of Baltimore and certain members of the Maryland legislature. Equally important, however, was the imprisonment of a number of Northern editors and several public men including Congressman Henry May, ex-Gov. Morehead of Kentucky, the mayor of Washington and two of Buchanan's diplomats (C. J. Faulkner and G. W. Jones) returning from abroad.

The Confederacy likewise made summary arrests to suppress disloyalty. Success was small, however, not only because political prisoners became popular martyrs, but because Confederate policy met the additional resistance of state-rights[qv] opposition in numerous localities.

[J. G. Randall, *Constitutional Problems under Lincoln;* F. L. Owsley, *State Rights in the Confederacy.*]

MARTIN P. CLAUSSEN

Arrowsmith's Map. A MAP EXHIBITING ALL THE NEW DISCOVERIES IN THE INTERIOR PART OF NORTH AMERICA, was published in London, Jan. 1, 1795, by Aaron Arrowsmith, "Hydrographer to His Majesty." A large-scale map on a globular projection, it was printed on six sheets, measuring when joined 48½ x 57 inches. From notes furnished by members of the Hudson's Bay Company[qv], numerous additions and corrections were made on the basic map. More than seventeen editions were published between 1795 and 1850, first by the author and later by his two sons, which attest the accuracy and importance of the map.

[Charles O. Paullin's *Atlas of the Historical Geography of the United States.*]

LLOYD A. BROWN

Arsenals. An arsenal is primarily an establishment for the manufacture, repair, storage or issue of arms and all military equipment whether for land or naval service. The first arsenal in the United States was established at Carlisle, Pa., in 1776. In 1838 the Ordnance Department[qv] of the army was placed in charge of armories and arsenals. At present there are nineteen permanent stations maintained, six of which are manufacturing units, and, as such, are looked upon as arsenals in the strict sense of the word—these are Frankford, Pa., Picatinny, N. J., Rock Island, Ill., Springfield, Mass., Watervliet, N. Y., and Watertown, Mass. The remaining thirteen stations are designated not for manufacturing, but for handling, storage and issue of ordnance material for the army.

[*History of Arsenals*, Compiled and filed in the Office, Chief of Ordnance, War Department, Washington, D. C.]

ROBERT S. THOMAS

Art. Jeremiah Dummer (1645–1718) the first known American-born artist, added accomplishment as painter to proficiency in silversmithing. The names of many early immigrant artists are lost to record. Three generations of the Duyckinck family gave painters to the New York district, Evert Duyckinck (1621–1702) having arrived at New Amsterdam from Holland in 1638. Authenticated works of the following are well known: Pieter Vanderlyn (1687–1778), a Dutchman who painted portraits at Kingston and Albany; Gustavus Hesselius (1682–1755), a Swede who worked in Pennsylvania and Maryland; Jeremiah Theus (1719–74), an exceptionally gifted artist, Swiss-born, who worked in Charleston; and the Scot, John Smibert (1688–1751), who came from England under patronage of Bishop Berkeley and settled in Boston.

Through the same period there was widespread anonymous production of naively conceived or so-called "primitive" portraits, now appreciated for the special charm of their stiff but intuitively rhythmic design and their arbitrarily decorative coloring. These "folk art" masterpieces are considered by some as nearer to the beginning of a native tradition of art than the more numerous portraits painted in the European fashion. The primitive feeling can be traced continuously, in the works of such untutored painters as the Quaker preacher, Edward Hicks (1780–1849), and even into the 20th century in the naive canvases of John Kane.

Robert Feke and Joseph Badger were competent portraitists of the northern colonies in the middle 18th century. The fashionable native painters of the following fifty years were Ralph Earl (1751–1801); John Singleton Copley (1738–1815), who deserted America in 1774 and became a successful painter in London; and Gilbert Stuart (1755–1828), most talented of the native painters in the international tradition, who made a success in London, but returned in 1793 or 1794, and produced the portraits of Washington now seen, in originals or copies, in innumerable galleries. Benjamin West (1738–1820), born in America, went early to England, and succeeded Sir Joshua Reynolds as president of the Royal Academy. His paintings were unimportant, but he influenced American art through his teaching. Among his pupils were John Trumbull (1756–1843), painter of portraits and large-canvas historical scenes; Charles Willson Peale (1741–1827), whose sons Rembrandt and Raphael also became important painters; and the inventors, Robert Fulton and Samuel F. B. Morse (1791–1872).

In the early 19th century landscape became prominent, along with allegorical and historical pieces, still-lifes and even *genre*. Miniature painting was reaching its highest point; Edward Green Malbone (1777–1807) is considered the greatest American master, and Charles Fraser (1782–1860) his worthiest follower. Henry Inman, William Sidney Mount, Eastman Johnson, George Caleb Bingham and J. G. Brown exploited familiar native-scene and story-telling pictures.

The realistic portrait tradition was continued by Thomas Sully (1783–1872), Samuel Lovett Waldo (1783–1861), Chester Harding (1792–1866), and John Neagle (1796–1865). More creative was John James Audubon, with his *Birds of America*. Washington Allston was superlatively praised for his religious and historical canvases, but his reputation has declined. Landscape was developed by Thomas Doughty, Thomas Cole and Jasper Cropsey of the Hudson River School; by John Frederick Kensett; by Asher B. Durand; and by Frederick Edwin Church. With George Inness (1825–94) American landscape art touched maturity, in atmospheric works comparable to those of the Barbizon School in France. Alexander Wyant and Homer D. Martin were contemporaries of Inness.

Before the century-end, certain painters emerged as typically American in their vigor and forthrightness, most notably Winslow Homer (1836–1910) and Thomas Eakins (1844–1916). Greater in stature because more universal were the expatriate, James McNeill Whistler (1834–1903), deeply inventive, a pioneer of Modernism; Albert Pinkham Ryder, an unappreciated mystic, finally recognized as the most original artist in American history; and John H. Twachtman, who added to a brilliant but fragile Impressionism a formal magic almost Oriental. Others whose names survive were Ralph Blakelock, George Fuller, John LaFarge, Frank Duveneck, William Merritt Chase and Mary Cassatt.

Childe Hassam, Ernest Lawson and Frederick C. Frieseke carried on the ideals of the Impressionist school in the face of the growing post-Impressionist revolution of the early 20th century. The unchallenged fashionable painter of the time was John Singer Sargent, but his reputation later dwindled. By 1910 a vigorous revolt against fashionable elegance and sentimentality was staged by a group of realists led by Robert Henri, John Sloan, George Luks and, later, George Bellows. A more inventive group turned to follow the post-Impressionist trend (as marked out by the French leader Cézanne); John Marin, Walt Kuhn, Max Weber, John Carroll, Maurice Sterne and Henry Mattson, in particular, combining native originality with the new internationally developed æsthetic, served to bring the body of American art to unquestioned creative maturity.

The history of sculpture is far less significant as a native manifestation. In the colonial period such things as weather vanes and ships' figureheads were produced, along with the commoner architectural ornamentation and gravestones. In the early national period William Rush (1756–1833) was famous for his figureheads; John Frazee (1790–1852) was best known for tombstones and mantels; while the greatest figure was Samuel McIntire (1757–1811), celebrated for wood carving on furniture, doorways and mantels.

The sculptors born after 1800, affected by the neo-Classicism of European studios, were likely to spend their best years in Italy, as did Horatio Greenough, William Wetmore Story and Hiram Powers (1805–73), whose *Greek Slave* became internationally celebrated. These expatriates had little to do with American life, but a clay-modeller, John Rogers (1829–1904), scored with naturalistic depictions of everyday living. His enlarged mantelpiece compositions, known as Rogers groups, constitute the most distinctive American sculptured product up to 1880.

By that time a few monumental sculptors were finding a market, most notably John Quincy Adams Ward (1830–1910), and the French-trained Augustus Saint-Gaudens (1848–1907), the most graceful and proficient realist of his era and often named as America's foremost sculptor. Other figures of this group were Herbert Adams, Frederick MacMonnies, Gutzon Borglum, Lorado Taft, Paul Bartlett and Daniel Chester French. Borglum, with his colossal sculpture[qv], is now carrying on an experiment in mountain-side rock carving. Most original sculptor of that generation was George Grey Barnard (1863–1938); but the transition to modern ideals was completed only in the work of Gaston Lachaise (1882–1935).

The early history of print-making is concerned less with art values than with topographical and other practical interests. Two phenomena of the mid-19th century are notable: the high artistic merit of the Currier and Ives prints[qv]; and the achievement of the American-born artist, James McNeill Whistler, as the foremost etcher of his time. Soon after 1900 Joseph Pennell was popular for his purely illustrational etchings and lithographs. Many painters turned their hands to the copper and stone mediums; among their works the lithographs of George Bellows are most original. There had been a time when American reproductive engraving on wood had been the world's finest, and there developed after 1910 an extension into finely creative work in this medium, as in the prints of Thomas Nason.

Many have felt that American originality and feeling for beauty have found expression chiefly in the utilitarian arts. Household utensils and furniture[qv] from the earliest colonial periods are marked by simple rhythmic beauty, with feeling for characteristic values in materials, whether wood or metal or clay. As the colonies advanced culturally, the imported classic style was adopted in ornamentation, with an accent recognizably American (as seen also in architecture[qv]). In the fields of commercial handicrafts, early American silverware and pewterware are outstanding, as is the native glass[qv]. Distinctive needlework and weaving developed among the home crafts.

When the machine took over task after task formerly accomplished by hand, the first result was a flood of mass-produced objects defaced with ornament badly copied from handicraft originals. Late in the 19th century there was a widespread attempt to improve standards, particularly by encouraging the purchase of hand-made goods as against machine-made, an effort fostered by innumerable "arts and crafts" societies. A more rational approach to the problem has come since 1900 in the separation of the handicrafts from the mass-production crafts, which in turn have been recognized as having values and style-marks—even an æsthetic—of their own, so that a new profession, "industrial design," has emerged, concerned exclusively with the application of art principles to objects characteristically suited to duplication by the machine.

[H. Cahill and A. H. Barr, Jr., editors, *Art in America: a Complete Survey;* S. Isham and R. Cortissoz, *The History of American Painting;* F. F. Sherman, *Early American Painting.*]

SHELDON CHENEY

Art Collections of America. The Philadelphia Academy of Fine Arts, established in 1805 in Independence Hall (removed to a new building in 1876) was the first public art museum in the United States. The Boston Athenæum, opened in 1827, lent most of its collection to the new Museum of Fine Arts, opened in that city in 1876. The private collection of John Varden, begun in Washington about 1829, was transferred to the National Institution for the Promotion of Science in 1841 and thence to the Smithsonian Institution[qv] in 1862, becoming a part of the new United States National Museum. The Brooklyn Institute of Arts and Sciences, founded under another name in 1823, established a museum in 1889 and opened its large art building in 1897. Great expositions[qv] have displayed remarkable assemblings of art in permanent buildings which remained as museums—such as that at Philadelphia, 1876 (Pennsylvania Museum of Art); Buffalo, 1901 (Buffalo Fine Arts Academy); St. Louis, 1904 (City Art Museum, founded 1879); San Francisco, 1915 (San Francisco Museum of Art). Other great establishments are the Metropolitan Museum of Art in New York, those at Cincinnati, founded in 1869; Detroit (1882); Worcester, Mass. (1896), etc. The new American millionaire in the latter 19th century almost inevitably collected—often vicariously, by agents who scoured Europe and the Orient—some form or all forms of art, preferably paintings. Some of these private collections later enriched great museums—as that of J. Pierpont Morgan, the most of which went to the Metropolitan after his death in 1913 and that of William A. Clark, copper magnate (1839–1925), which fell to the Corcoran Art Gallery. Some by bequest became individual museums—notably those of W. W. Corcoran, founded in Washington in 1869 while the collector was still alive, of Charles L. Freer (died 1919) in Washington, of Henry E. Huntington at San Marino, Calif. (opened in 1928), of Henry C. Frick, New York, 1931, and Andrew W. Mellon, given to the National Government and endowed in 1937. Many were sold and dispersed after the owner's death; that of Charles T. Yerkes, traction magnate, sold in 1910, brought $2,707,866, a record sum. That of William Salomon in 1923 brought $1,288,705 and of Elbert H. Gary (1928), $2,297,763. So rapid was the movement of Europe's art treasures to public and private galleries in America around the beginning of the 20th century and thereafter that European art lovers were appalled by it. Lord Leverhulme's collection was even sent bodily to the United States and sold in 1926, bringing $1,274,000.

[Frederic A. Lucas, *Glimpses of Early Museums;* Lewis Barrington and L. C. Everard, *Handbook of American Museums.*]

ALVIN F. HARLOW

Article Ten of the League of Nations*ᵠᵛ* Covenant was of wholly American origin and was regarded by President Wilson as an extension of the Monroe Doctrine*ᵠᵛ* to the whole world. In Wilson's mind the undertaking "to preserve as against external aggression the territorial integrity and existing political independence of all Members of the League" was not a pledge to go to war in advance of congressional consideration and decision. He interpreted the obligations of the article as moral, not legal.

Opponents of the covenant in the Senate made Article X their principal target. They argued that it was not the proper business of the United States to guarantee either new boundaries or old empires or to intervene in cases of revolution against oppression. They contended that moral obligations would be found as binding as legal ones. Consequently the Senate adopted a ponderous reservation repudiating any obligation under the article except as the Congress should provide in any particular case. This was unacceptable to President Wilson not for its legal effect but for its embodiment of an attitude destructive to the principle of international responsibility. He contemplated territorial change accomplished through the peaceful operation of Article XIX rather than the traditional resort to violence.

[D. F. Fleming, *The United States and the League of Nations, 1918-1920.*]

HAROLD S. QUIGLEY

Articles of Confederation. The Continental Congress*ᵠᵛ* decided even before independence that it was necessary to set up a confederacy based upon a written instrument. Several plans appeared in the press and the subject was embraced in R. H. Lee's motion of June 7, 1776, on independence (*see* Declaration of Independence). On June 11 Congress voted to appoint a committee. This body set to work at once and on July 12 reported through John Dickinson a set of Articles of Confederation, of which eighty copies were printed for the use of members. Congress was so engrossed in war problems, however, that debates on the scheme dragged through more than a year. The principal disputes raged over the questions whether taxes should be apportioned according to the gross number of inhabitants counting slaves or excluding them—the South of course wishing them excluded; whether large and small states should have equality in voting; whether Congress should be given the right to regulate Indian affairs; and whether Congress should be permitted to fix the western boundaries of those states which claimed to the Mississippi. On Nov. 15, 1777, Congress finally approved a draft and sent it to the states, on the understanding that all must ratify it before it went into effect. This draft, declared a circular letter of Congress, "is proposed as the best which could be adapted to the circumstances of all; and as that alone which affords any tolerable prospect of a general ratification."

The Articles did not become the law of the land until March 1, 1781. Nine states ratified as early as July, 1778, but several of the smaller ones held back because of the question of western lands*ᵠᵛ*. Maryland in particular had urged that these lands be regarded as a common possession of all the states, and felt aggrieved when the Articles contained a clause declaring that no state should be deprived of territory for the benefit of the United States. She first declared that she would not ratify until her powerful neighbor, Virginia, ceased to advance extravagant western claims. But when New York had yielded and Virginia seemed certain to do so, Maryland on March 1, 1781, signed the Articles through her delegates, and made them effective.

Although the Articles have been harshly criticized and the very shrewdest critics at the time saw their inadequacy, they were generally regarded in 1781 as offering a sound national constitution. They provided for a "perpetual union" or "firm league of friendship" between the states. Each remained sovereign and independent, and retained every right not expressly ceded by the Articles to the general government. A single agency of government was established—a Congress; the states were to appoint from two to seven delegates annually to it, and each state was to have one vote. Rhode Island thus obtained a parity with New York or Virginia. The costs of government and defense were to be defrayed from a common treasury, to which the states were to contribute in proportion to the value of their surveyed land and improvements. The states were likewise to supply quotas of troops, in proportion to the white inhabitants of each, upon congressional requisitions. To Congress was entrusted the management of foreign affairs, of war and of the postal service; it was empowered to borrow money, emit bills of credit, and determine the value of coin; it was to appoint naval officers and superior military officers, and control Indian affairs. But none of these powers was to be exercised save by vote of a majority of all states, and the more important could not be exercised save by the vote of nine. On paper, almost every important national authority was turned over to Congress save three: the authority to raise money directly, the authority to enlist troops directly and the authority to regulate commerce. But the paper powers proved to be very different from actual power.

It soon became evident that Congress was doomed to fail in its attempts to make the Articles workable. These attempts consisted chiefly in requests to the states for money that was never paid, pleas for troops which filled no army ranks, and petitions for special powers which the states never granted. At various points the powers of the states were supposedly limited. They were forbidden to enter into treaties, confederations, or alliances, to meddle with foreign affairs, or to wage war without congressional consent, unless invaded. Most important of all, they were to give to free inhabitants of other states all the privileges and immunities of their own citizens. A citizen of South Carolina, for example, who removed to Boston, at once became a citizen of Massachusetts. Interstate extradition of criminals was also provided. The states could impose duties, but not any which conflicted with the treaty stipulations of Congress. They were required to "abide by the determinations of Congress" on all subjects which the Articles left to that body. The states did respect each other's rights to a considerable extent (when two or more of them fell out, any one could submit the dispute to Congress). But they failed lamentably to respect the needs and requests of the National Government. They refused to do what they should have done, especially in supplying money and men; they frequently did what they should have refrained from doing. A circular prepared by Congress not long after Maryland's ratification in 1781 declared: "The inattention of the States has almost endangered our very existence as a people."

Demands for amendment and invigoration of the Articles were made even before they became effective. New Jersey served notice on Congress Feb. 3, 1780, for example, that it was absolutely necessary to give the nation power to regulate commerce and to fix duties on imports. A committee which reported May 3, 1781, pointed to the chief defect of the Articles—the fact that they gave Congress no power to enforce its measures, and suggested a new article authorizing the employment of armed forces to compel recalcitrant states "to fulfill their Federal engagements." This would have led straight to civil war, and the plan failed. The years 1782–86 witnessed earnest efforts by Congress to obtain state consent to a Federal impost, which would have furnished a stable revenue; earnest efforts also were made to obtain from the states a sufficient control over shipping to enable it to wage commercial warfare with nations discriminating against the United States. But some states, notably New York and Rhode Island, long proved stubborn; others were tardy; and when they did act, their laws were found to conflict. Again, while the states were bound to respect the treaties made by Congress, several of them indulged in gross violations of the Definitive Treaty of Peaceᵠᵛ. The close of the year 1786 found the Articles of Confederation in widespread discredit, and many national leaders eager to find a wholly new basis for union. Yet the Articles, soon to give way to the Constitutionᵠᵛ, should not be regarded with contempt. They had served as a stepping-stone to a new order; as John Marshall said later, they had preserved the idea of union until national wisdom could adopt a more efficient system. Had they not been agreed upon in time, the states might have fallen asunder after Yorktown.

[A. C. McLaughlin, *The Confederation and the Constitution;* Allan Nevins, *The American States During and After the Revolution.*]

ALLAN NEVINS

Articles of War, The. These in general establish Federal military law, limited, personal and not territorial, criminal and punitive rather than civil, administered solely by military personnel, and not subject to review by civilian courts except to test jurisdiction (Swain v. U. S., 165 U. S. 553). Save for "any person" in contempt (Art. 32) or "found lurking or acting as a spy" (Art. 82), they affect only precisely defined "persons subject to military law." Entrance of such persons into service effects a definite "change of status" (*In re* Morrissey, 137 U. S. 157) and deprives them of many otherwise normal rights. Under Constitutional authority, Congress enacts

Articles of War for "the government and regulation" of the army, and the President by Executive Order specifies rules of procedure, modes of proof and limits of punishment. These Articles deal chiefly with strictly military offenses, although they also cover acts considered felonies in civilian courts (Arts. 92 & 93) and in addition "crimes or offenses not capital" (Art. 96).

June 30, 1775, the Continental Congress[qv] enacted our first Articles, based largely on British of 1765 and the Massachusetts of April 5, 1775. Amplified in 1776 and supplemented in 1786 regarding administrative details, Congress adopted them into Federal law Sept. 29, 1789 (1 Stat. 95), and by act of April 10, 1806 (2 Stat. 359) revised and adapted them into Constitutional conformity. These 1806 Articles, supplemented during the Civil War and restated in the Revised Statutes of 1874, remained in force until the acts of June 3 and Aug. 29, 1916 (39 Stat. 200 and 650) completely revised and modernized the full military code. Detailed study of World War experiences produced important amendments on June 4, 1920 (41 Stat. 759), which emphasized and extended legal rights of soldiers under charges and provided various means of obviating excessive trials.

[G. Glenn, *The Army and the Law; Manual for Courts-Martial, United States Army*, 1921.]

ELBRIDGE COLBY

Artillery, THE AMERICAN, dates from the Revolution, when a Massachusetts regiment and a Rhode Island company joined in the siege of Boston[qv], June, 1775. Its guns then, and long thereafter, were maneuvered by men hauling on drag ropes. A new regiment under Col. Henry Knox took over artillery duties in January, 1776. Knox transported from Ticonderoga[qv] the cannon which forced the evacuation of Boston (March 17). When Washington moved to New York, he left an artillery company in the captured coast defenses. Four regiments organized in 1777 constituted the regular artillery during the rest of the war.

An artillery battalion manned guns, but served chiefly as infantry, under Harmar, St. Clair and Wayne[qqv] against western Indians, 1790–94. Our first system of coast defenses[qv] brought new duties to the artillery (1794). When the War of 1812 came, small artillery detachments were scattered from Maine to New Orleans and Mackinac. There were three artillery regiments. One, of light artillery, was mounted as horse artillery, but soon lost its horses for want of forage. No coast defense succumbed to naval attack. In 1821 the artillery was reorganized into four regiments. One company in each was to be light artillery. The four companies were not mounted until 1838–39. They made brilliant records in the Mexican War. Gen. Scott mounted four more at Puebla (1847); but three fourths of the artillery served as infantry. In the Civil War fifty-six out of sixty companies were mounted, of which about twenty-two were horse batteries. In the Spanish-American War coast companies were mounted as siege artillery. In 1901 the artillery lost its regimental formation and became a corps under a chief. The Field and Coast were separated in 1907; the Coast was given a chief and the Field organized into regiments. The Coast was given a regimental organization for A.E.F. units in 1917 and for all units in 1924. A chief of Field Artillery was designated in 1918.

[William E. Birkhimer, *Historical Sketch of the Artillery, United States Army;* W. L. Haskin, *The History of the First Regiment of Artillery;* W. A. Ganoe, *History of the United States Army.*]

S. C. VESTAL

"As goes Maine, so goes the Union," a saying based upon the supposed accuracy of Maine's September election as a political barometer for the country, was originated by the Whigs after the presidential election of 1840[qqv].

[Claude E. Robinson, Maine—Political Barometer, *Political Science Quarterly*, June, 1932.]

ROBERT E. MOODY

Ash Hollow, Battle of (Sept. 3, 1855). To punish the Sioux Indians for the Grattan massacre on the California Trail, Gen. Harney left Fort Leavenworth[qqv], Kans., Aug. 5, with 1200 troops. Proceeding west of Fort Kearny[qv], Nebr., he encountered Little Thunder's band at Ash Hollow. The Indians fought desperately but were nearly exterminated, losing 136 killed.

[*South Dakota Historical Collections*, Vols. I and II.]

JOSEPH MILLS HANSON

Ashburton Treaty. *See* Webster-Ashburton Treaty of 1842.

Ashby's Gap. A pass in the Blue Ridge Mountains of Virginia leading from the Shenandoah Valley into eastern Virginia, often used by Confederate and Federal armies in the several valley campaigns. In June, 1863, J. E. B. Stuart's cavalry held this gap to prevent Hooker interfering with Lee's army in the march that led to Gettysburg.

[*Battles and Leaders of the Civil War*, III.]

W. N. C. CARLTON

Ashley Expeditions, The, three in number, were for the purpose of launching the Rocky Mountain Fur Company in competition with the Hudson's Bay Company*qqv* and the older established American companies. The more important results were the exploration of vast areas of the Rocky Mountain Northwest, the firmer hold of American interests on the disputed Northwest country and the development of some of the more noted "mountain men,"*qv* including Jedediah Smith, Etienne Provost, Jim Bridger, Milton Sublette, Hugh Glass and Thomas Fitzpatrick.

Organized in St. Louis in 1822 the first expedition, commanded by Andrew Henry, Ashley's lieutenant, came to grief near Great Falls, Mont., where he was attacked by the Blackfeet*qv* and driven out of the country. Ashley headed another expedition in the following spring, only to be attacked by the Arikaras*qv*, on the Missouri, and forced to retreat with heavy loss. Reinforced, the third expedition, in charge of Jedediah Smith*qv*, pushed on to the Yellowstone, penetrated to the Green River Valley, the Utah trapping grounds, and learned from the Crow Indians the important location of South Pass*qv*, the effective discovery of which dates from that time. The party returned with a rich cache of furs, and Ashley set forth on a return winter trip. He crossed the Continental Divide by Bridger's Gap, and reached the Green River near the crossing of the Oregon Trail*qqv*. Bridger in the previous autumn had discovered Great Salt Lake*qv*. The first mountain trappers' rendezvous*qv* was held in June and Ashley returned in the fall of 1825 with a fortune in furs.

[H. M. Chittenden, *History of American Fur Trade;* W. J. Ghent, *Early Far West;* H. C. Dale, *Ashley-Smith Expeditions.*]

CARL L. CANNON

Asia, Trade with, began immediately after the Revolution. The *Empress of China* sailed from New York for Canton on Feb. 22, 1784, and within a decade American vessels were calling regularly at Calcutta and Bombay, trading on the pepper coast of Sumatra, making port in Java and lading tea and silks from Canton. It was a trade which played an important part in reviving the commerce cut off by British navigation laws, and it brought new wealth to the enterprising merchants of New York, Philadelphia, Boston, Salem, Baltimore and Providence. Trade with the Far East*qv*, from its very inception, held out the bright promise of bringing to the United States products which the colonies had depended on England to supply, and of providing a new market for American exports.

The trade with China*qv*, concentrated in the port of Canton, was the most important branch of this commerce. Silks, nankeens and tea were the products sought by the American ships, with tea becoming virtually the sole import by the 1840's. In order to supplement American exports with other goods suitable for the Chinese market, American merchant seamen developed the fur trade of the Northwest Coast*qv* and scoured the islands of the South Pacific. Development of our early trade with China was an important factor in the settlement of Oregon*qv*. It led to the opening up of relations with Hawaii*qv*, and served to build up that general interest in the Pacific*qv* which was an influential motive in our acquisition of California*qv*. The potentialities of the markets of the East as an outlet for American produce and manufactures won a hold upon popular imagination a century ago which bore little relation to the statistics of actual trade.

After its first period of dramatic growth, total trade with Asia underwent a relative decline. In the middle of the century, exports were valued at $3,028,000, or only 2.1% of our total exports in comparison with 3.6% in 1821, while imports, valued at $12,434,000, represented 7.2% of total imports in comparison with 9.8% in 1821. With the "opening" of Japan by Commodore Matthew C. Perry*qv*, in 1854, a new market and a new source of imports became available. The rapid emergence of Japan as an economic and commercial power of the first rank provided the United States with a valuable outlet for its exports, primarily raw cotton, which was exchanged largely for silk. By the end of the century trade with Asia as a whole had regained its relative importance in our total commerce, and succeeding years witnessed its further growth to a position of the utmost importance. In the pre-depression period of 1926–30 average annual exports to Asia were valued at $573,973,000, or no less than 12% of our entire export trade, while average annual imports were valued at $1,192,632,000, or 29.6% of total imports.

The potentialities of the trade with China, despite disappointment in its actual development and the statistical evidence of Japan's greater importance both as a market and as a source of imports, have served as the primary factor in the formulation of our economic and political policies in the Pacific. The desire to promote this commerce was largely responsible for American territorial expansion in Alaska, Hawaii, Samoa and the Philippines*qqv*. It led to Secretary Hay's pronouncement of the Open Door policy*qv* in 1899. During the present century, the potential trade of China has intensified an interest in the preservation of that country's territorial and political integrity which has repeatedly brought the United States into serious controversy with Japan. American trade with Asia has been even more important in its bearing upon our political relations in the Pacific than in its significance for our general economic development.

[Tyler Dennett, *Americans in Eastern Asia.*]

FOSTER RHEA DULLES

Asiento, THE (1713), was a license granted to the English South Sea Company by the Spanish government, as a result of the Treaty of Utrecht[qv], whereby the company was given the exclusive right to sell a total of 144,000 Negro slaves in the Spanish colonies during thirty years or at the rate of 4800 a year (*see* African Company, Royal). For this privilege the company paid the Spanish crown $200,000.

A. CURTIS WILGUS

Assassinations, Political, were all too frequent in the mid-West and far West in pioneer days, and in the South even in later decades. In 1839 a member of the Wisconsin territorial legislature, James R. Vineyard, shot another member, Charles C. P. Arndt, to death in the Assembly chamber. In Kentucky and some other states, politics engendered the most violent acrimony, and personal encounters, killings and duels were not uncommon. The assassination of President Lincoln[qv] was the first of great political consequence in the United States. Two other Presidents were also murdered. Bitter quarrels among Republican leaders in 1880 over patronage had its effect upon the brain of a man named Charles J. Guiteau, who annoyed President James A. Garfield from the day of his inauguration, March 4, 1881, with importunities for a consular position. On July 2 he armed himself and shot the President down as he was passing through the Pennsylvania station in Washington, accompanied by Secretary Blaine. Mr. Garfield lingered for weeks, and finally, because of the heat of Washington, was removed to Elberon, N. J., where he died on Sept. 19. William McKinley was the third presidential victim. On Sept. 6, 1901, as he stood, shaking hands with a line of visitors to the Pan-American Exposition[qv] at Buffalo, N. Y., he was shot by Leon Czolgosz, a young anarchist who had been influenced by the propaganda of Emma Goldman and others. Mr. McKinley died on Sept. 14. Among the most noted of American political assassinations was that of William Goebel[qv], claimant to the governorship of Kentucky in 1900. Another was that of Edward W. Carmack, of Tennessee, who had just left the United States Senate and become editor of the Nashville *Tennesseean.* He was shot on a street in Nashville by Robin Cooper, son of a prominent political opponent, Col. Duncan Cooper, who accompanied his son to the killing. The Coopers were convicted of murder, but immediately pardoned by Gov. Malcolm Patterson. United States Senator Huey P. Long of Louisiana, a bizarre and dynamic character who had built a powerful political machine in that state and thereby aroused some violent antagonisms, was fatally shot in the Capitol building at Baton Rouge on Sept. 8, 1935, by Dr. C. A. Weiss, a dentist, son-in-law of a prominent anti-Long leader. Weiss was immediately shot dead by Long's ever-present bodyguard. Sen. Long died on the following day.

[E. Benjamin Andrews, *History of the United States.*]

ALVIN F. HARLOW

Assay Offices. Assaying is done at all the Federal mints[qv], but special plants were established at New York in 1853, at Boise, Idaho, 1869; Helena, Mont., 1874; Deadwood, S. Dak., and Seattle, Wash., 1896, and Salt Lake City, Utah, 1908, for the receipt, testing, melting, and refining of gold and silver bullion and foreign coins, and recasting into bars, ingots or discs. The early mints established at New Orleans, La., Charlotte, N. C., and Denver, Colo., were later turned into assay offices.

[Jesse P. Watson, *The Bureau of the Mint.*]

ALVIN F. HARLOW

Assembly, The Right of, is guaranteed against interference by Congress in the Federal Constitution, and is supplemented by state constitutional provisions imposing similar restrictions upon state legislatures. In no place is the right absolute, but is subject to supervision in its exercise by local government officials. The right of assembly will not be sustained where its exercise threatens to disrupt the government or destroy the public peace. Here the assembly clearly becomes unlawful.

The Supreme Court in U. S. v. Cruikshank[qv] (1876) held that the right of the people peaceably to assemble for lawful purposes, with the obligation on the part of the states to afford them protection, existed long before the adoption of the Constitution. It had existed in English law from "time out of mind" as a distinct, separate and independent right. That the right was so recognized was made evident by the numerous statutes which restricted and regulated its use.

A statute passed by Parliament in the reign of George I fixed the limitations upon the right of assembly which are still observed in this country. According to this act, the right of assembly cannot be maintained if the meeting is for an unlawful purpose or is conducted in a tumultuous manner. Most of the cases in which the right has been challenged fall into the second category. Four notorious cases of the last century which come under the heading of unlawful assembly involved four different motives. These were a meeting in Philadelphia of the proposed "Native American Party,"[qv] 1844 (*see* Philadelphia Riots, The); the "Astor Place Riots"[qv] in New York City, 1849, concerning a performance at the Astor Place Opera House; the disapproval of a stringent liquor law in the State of Maine, 1855, by a meeting in Portland, and the "Anarchists' Case" of 1886 (*see* Haymarket Affair, The), arising from an attempt of the workingmen in Chicago to introduce the eight-hour day. Each of these cases contained the essential elements of an unlawful assembly, in fact they were almost riots. In more recent years, most of the cases of unlawful assembly have developed from meetings of communists and strikers[qqv].

The practical decision whether or not an assembly is unlawful rests with the local police authorities. The chief of police or other official is supposed to exercise his fair and honest discretion. His action is subject to review by the courts but relief from the courts, if relief is merited, is at best uncertain (*see* Police Power).

[Jarrett and Mund, The Right of Assembly, *New York University Law Quarterly Review*, IX, pp. 1-38.]

WILLIAM S. CARPENTER

Assessment of Candidates. *See* Political Assessments.

Assimilation. As applied to immigration and cognate matters, the word is here used as signifying genuine absorption; the real incorporation of an individual into the idealistic and cultural fabric of American life, much as food is digested and becomes organically part of the human body. It is the culmination of a process which logically begins when the immigrant first sets foot on American soil, yet which may not end with the immigrant himself, but only with his children or even his children's children. Naturalization[qv], the legal act of conferring citizenship upon an alien, is only a step in the process, and often a very short step. The term Americanization[qv], being logically limited to the foreign born, does not fully coincide with assimilation in the word's larger meaning.

Despite the stoppage of mass-immigration for nearly two decades through a series of measures culminating with the Johnson Act[qv] of 1924, the assimilation of the foreign born and their progeny is far from complete. Many groups still exist, both in the cities and over the countryside, whose members remain essentially foreign-minded even unto the third generation. This, however, is a waning factor which promises to vanish in the relatively near future. More widespread and far more serious is the large element of native-born persons, especially in the large cities and industrial centers of the Northeast, who are cultural and spiritual nondescripts. Such persons usually speak English and have an American veneer in material externals such as clothing and forms of amusement. However, they are not American in the deeper sense. Though they have generally rejected the customs and ideas of their foreign-born forebears, and have thus lost their ancestral heritage, they have not acquired American culture and ideals.

These nondescript urban masses, with no genuine loyalties, traditional roots or cultural and idealistic standards, are not merely a heavy handicap on their local communities; they are likewise a grave problem for the nation as a whole. Inevitably restless and discontented, they are prone to crime and to ultra-radical agitation.

[Edward R. Lewis, *America: Nation or Confusion;* Gino Speranza, *Race or Nation.*]

LOTHROP STODDARD

Assiniboine, Fort (1834–35), post of the American Fur Company[qv], west of Fort Union, was, for a time, the head of steamboat navigation on the Missouri, and a depot for inland trade with the Assiniboine, Piegan and Blackfeet Indians[qqv].

[H. M. Chittenden, *The American Fur Trade of the Far West.*]

PAUL C. PHILLIPS

Assiniboine or Stone Indians, The, of Siouan[qv] stock, left the parent nation in the 17th century, and shortly after 1800 settled on the upper Missouri. By the Treaty of Fort Laramie in 1851[qv] they were assigned a reservation between the Missouri and Yellowstone rivers. In the 1870's they were moved to the Fort Peck and Fort Belknap[qqv] reservations.

[Edward T. Denig, Indian Tribes of the Upper Missouri, in 46th *Annual Report* of the Bureau of American Ethnology; F. W. Hodge, *Handbook of American Indians.*]

PAUL C. PHILLIPS

Assistance Clause, THE. Election laws[qv], providing for the choice of an "honest and capable man" from each major party to "assist any voter in the preparation of his ballot when from any cause he is unable to do so" (Delaware, 1891) or for the voter's choice of "any qualified voter in the election district" for the same purpose (Pennsylvania, 1891), soon facilitated the delivery of bribed votes. Party members, serving as assistants, influenced the marking of ballots and rewarded the "fixed" voters with the token (pin, tag, acorn) for which the promised bribe would be paid. The 20th century saw increasing state legislation to abolish the assistants and check fraud in connection with bona fide assistance to disabled voters.

[J. A. Woodburn, *Political Parties and Party Problems in the United States*, 3rd ed.; J. A. Salter, *Boss Rule.*]

BAYRD STILL

Assistant. The Massachusetts Bay Company Charter (1629)[qv] provided eighteen assistants elected yearly by the "freemen"[qv] (stockholders). Seven, with the governor (or deputy governor), constituted a quorum ("Court of Assistants") to manage the Company's ordinary affairs. When the Company became a commonwealth in Massachusetts, an assistant became a "magistrate." Until deputies were admitted (1634), the Court of Assistants was the colony's sole legislature. As the colony's constitution matured, the assistants held four functions, legislative, executive, judicial and "consultative" (i.e., the governor's "standing council" with extensive powers "in the vacancy of the General Court"[qv]). The Connecticut Charter (1662) provided twelve assistants with similar powers.

[H. L. Osgood, *The American Colonies in the Seventeenth Century.*]

RAYMOND P. STEARNS

"Associated Loyalists" of New England, or Loyal Associated Refugees, consisted of various associations formed by Col. Edward Winslow, Jr., in Rhode Island during its occupation by the British (December, 1776–October, 1779), to chastise the Americans for losses and indignities. They made several raids in Long Island Sound, capturing vessels, cattle and prisoners.

[W. H. Siebert, Loyalist Troops of New England, *The New England Quarterly*, IV, No. 1.]

WILBUR H. SIEBERT

Associated Power. Owing to traditional fear of entangling alliances[qv] this was the official designation of our relationship to the Allies after entering the World War on their side in 1917.

JAMES TRUSLOW ADAMS

Associated Press. As early as 1827, the newspapers of New York had combined in sending reporters in rowboats to meet incoming ships off Sandy Hook, get European news and send it to the city by carrier pigeon or by semaphore telegraph from Staten Island or Coney Island, several hours before the ship docked. This combination became known as the New York Associated Press. After the invention of the electric telegraph[qv] and the extension of the wires to Halifax, where the Cunard steamers touched, the association brought European news to New York two days sooner than by ship. The various telegraph companies installed news services of their own in the latter 1840's and fought the New York combination for several years; but gradually they yielded, and the Associated Press, at it came to be called, extended its service until it covered the country. After 1860 it had almost complete control of the news situation in the United States and Canada, and was bitterly vituperated in Congress and elsewhere as a ruthless monopoly. Between 1880 and 1900 there were wars and mutations, the United Press[qv], a Chicago Associated Press and a Western Associated Press being involved. A new corporation was organized in 1900, and held the leadership of its predecessor. An attack upon it under the Sherman Antitrust Law[qv] caused its membership rules to be made more liberal in 1915, and its members were permitted to use other press services also.

[Victor Rosewater, *History of Cooperative News-Gathering in the United States;* Melville E. Stone, *Fifty Years a Journalist.*]

ALVIN F. HARLOW

Associations represent one of the most effective pieces of revolutionary machinery used in the American Revolution. Before the Stamp Act[qv] the colonies were already familiar through merchant societies and political clubs with the idea of organization by agreement and pledge of support for some particular purpose. It was therefore an easy step for them, after the passage of that act, to use the device in nonimportation[qv] and nonconsumption agreements as a means of economic compulsion on the Mother Country, enforced by another form of association, the Sons of Liberty[qv]. Local organizations were early linked up through committees of correspondence[qv] into an intercolonial association of the "true Sons of Liberty" whose chief aim appears to have been to keep a watchful eye on suspected enemies of the colonial cause. By 1773 nonimportation agreements and the Sons of Liberty had practically faded out of the picture, but came forcibly to the fore again when Parliament that year passed the act permitting the East India Company^qv^ to export its tea to America without paying the usual English duties. Upon the passing of the Boston Port Bill following the Tea Party, the First Continental Congress^qqv^ in 1774 adopted the famous "Association," the members pledging themselves and their constituents not to import, export or consume British goods until their grievances were redressed. The pledgers in this case provided the commercial boycott as sanction against both states and individuals who refused to join or broke their agreements. After the outbreak of hostilities, associations, both loyalist and patriot, were spontaneously formed, pledging the signers to serve their cause with their lives. During the course of the war, both England and her colonies found the association idea an effective device for recruiting troops.

[Carl Becker, *The Eve of the Revolution.*]

VIOLA F. BARNES

Associators, THE, were a military organization formed by Franklin, Nov. 21, 1747, to defend the Port of Philadelphia. Revolting against the pacific policy of the Quakers^qv^, they formed military companies and erected two batteries on the Delaware. The Associators disbanded after the peace of Aix-la-Chapelle^qv^ in 1748.

[Scharf and Westcott, *History of Philadelphia.*]

JULIAN P. BOYD

Assumption of, and Funding of, Revolutionary Debt. At the time of the organization of the American National Government under the United States Constitution it was found that the national debt consisted of the following: foreign debt, $11,710,378; to domestic creditors, $42,414,085, including $2,000,000 of unliquidated debt. Alexander Hamilton as Secretary of the Treasury proposed to pay this at par in order that the credit of the National Government might be established, though the domestic debt had been selling as low as 25%. This was finally agreed to after much popular opposition, since it meant that speculators who had bought up the securities would make large profits. In addition Hamilton also desired that the National Government should assume the payment of the debts incurred by the individual states in carrying on the Revolutionary War. This assumption of the state debts would increase the national debt by $18,271,786. From this proposal arose the celebrated "assumption" issue.

Some of the states had paid part of their Revolutionary War debt while others had paid but little, also some states were in far better financial condition than others, since they had suffered but little from the direct effects of the war. The State of New York was in peculiarly advantageous position if an assumption measure was proposed. It was among the largest of the debtors, but aside from this obligation was in an unusually strong financial situation, due to the sale of public lands and the careful investment of state funds. The Southern states whose population was smaller than that of the Northern states were especially hostile to this assumption, which would place increased taxation for its payment upon the entire country, themselves included. Hamilton rightly claimed that assumption of the state debts would cause the creditors holding these securities to look to the National Government for their payment, and thus increase their support of the new government at the expense of the states. He favored this as a strong believer in nationalism^qv^.

At the same time quite a controversy arose concerning the location of the new national capital^qv^. The Southern states were especially anxious that it be placed on the banks of the Potomac River while other locations such as sites on the Susquehanna River in Pennsylvania and the Delaware River in New Jersey were advocated by the people of the Middle and Northern states. The issue of assumption was at first defeated in Congress but finally, with the assistance of Jefferson, Hamilton procured an agreement by which Southern votes in Congress were secured for the assumption of state debts in return for Northern votes to locate the national capital on the banks of the Potomac River at the present city of Washington, D. C. This agreement was accomplished by the adroit action of Thomas Jefferson, then Secretary of State, who invited the Secretary of the Treasury, Alexander Hamilton, to dine with him at his home. Also, a few other friends were present at this social meeting for an informal conference. Jefferson, himself, stated that reasonable men could form a compromise by mutual satisfaction, which compromise was to save the Union. Since it would take time to build the national capital it was further agreed that the Government, then located at New York, should be transferred to Philadelphia for ten to fifteen years, and after that to the present site of the national capital city at Washington.

As a result of this informal agreement both the measures with regard to the assumption of state debts and the location of the national capital were carried through Congress in the spring of 1790.

[J. S. Bassett, *A Short History of the United States;* Gilbert Chinard, *Thomas Jefferson;* S. McKee, ed., *Hamilton's Papers on Public Credit, Commerce, Finance.*]

WILLIAM STARR MYERS

Astor Fur Company. *See* American Fur Company, The.

Astor Place Riot, THE, in New York, May 10, 1849, grew out of long-standing jealousy between the American actor, Edwin Forrest, and the English tragedian, William Charles Macready, and was essentially an expression of anti-British feeling mingled with class hatred. When police failed to disperse a pro-Forrest mob outside the Astor Place Opera House where Macready was playing *Macbeth,* the militia was called out; violence and many casualties followed.

[M. J. Moses, *The Fabulous Forrest.*]

STANLEY R. PILLSBURY

Astoria. John Jacob Astor planned an organized fur trade[qv] on a continental scale some time before American occupation of the upper Missouri country. To his American Fur Company[qv], chartered in 1808, he added the Pacific Fur Company[qv], organized in 1810, and proceeded to extend his organization from St. Louis to the mouth of the Columbia[qv]. Two expeditions were sent to the latter point: one by sea, and the other along the route of Lewis and Clark[qv]. The sea-going party, under Capt. Jonathan Thorn, embarked Sept. 6, 1810, in the *Tonquin*[qv] and after a stormy voyage reached the Columbia, Mar. 23, 1811. Within three weeks Astoria was established under the direction of Duncan McDougal, acting resident agent. In June Capt. Thorn and a trading party were massacred by Indians in Nootka Sound, and the lone white survivor blew up the ship *Tonquin,* killing himself and many Indians.

July 15, 1811, a party of Canadians sent by the North West Company[qv] to forestall the Americans, arrived at Astoria. In January, 1812, a second party came from the rival North West Company post on the Spokane River. Then came the Astor Overlanders, thirty-four in number. They had left St. Louis March 12, 1811, under the leadership of Wilson Price Hunt, and had traveled up the Missouri and westward through the country of the Crows[qv], over the Continental Divide to the Snake River, thence to the Columbia and the Pacific, where they arrived Feb. 15, 1812. In May, the Astor ship, *Beaver,* arrived. Activities were extended inland to the mouth of the Okanagan, to the Spokane, and to the Snake River. Robert Stuart and a small party of eastbound Astor Overlanders set out with dispatches for Mr. Astor in New York, June 29, 1812, ascended the Snake River to its head, became the first white men to cross the South Pass[qv], wintered on the Platte, and arrived in St. Louis April 30, 1813. They did not return, for news of the War of 1812 sounded the doom of the Astor enterprise. While Hunt was absent, McDougal and his associates, whose sympathies were with the British, sold all the Astor interests on the Columbia to the North West Company. Hunt returned to find Astoria in rival hands, the post renamed Fort George, and the British flag flying where the Stars and Stripes had been. Astoria was restored to the United States in 1818 in accordance with the Treaty of Ghent[qv]. (*See* Oregon Question.)

[H. M. Chittenden, *The American Fur Trade of the Far West.*]

CARL P. RUSSELL

Atarés Massacre, THE, was the shooting of fifty men, mostly Americans, by the Spaniards, in Havana, Aug. 16, 1851. Belonging to the López filibustering expedition[qv] they were executed as pirates.

[H. Portell-Vilá, *Historia de Cuba en sus relaciones con los Estados Unidos,* Vol. I.]

HERMINIO PORTELL-VILÁ

Atchison, Kans., named for Sen. David R. Atchison of Missouri, was the headquarters of the proslavery movement in Kansas from its establishment in 1854. The *Squatter Sovereign,* published at Atchison, was the most outspoken of all the proslavery papers. Abolition sympathizers were tarred and feathered or driven from the vicinity by threats. Atchison citizens were active in the "Wakarusa War"[qv] and other border difficulties of 1855–57 (*see* Border War). They formed a unit of the proslavery "army" which, May 21, 1856, captured Lawrence[qv], the abolition headquarters, and destroyed the *Herald of Freedom* office, and the Free State Hotel.

[William G. Cutler, *The History of Kansas.*]

PAUL I. WELLMAN

Atchison, Topeka and Santa Fé Railway is the corporate title of one of the largest transport systems in America, owning 13,000 miles of main line stretching from Chicago into Kansas, across the southeast corner of Colorado into New Mexico, thence across Arizona to touch the coast at San Francisco, Los Angeles and San Diego. It has also a line branching to Galveston.

The initiative of Cyrus Holliday led to the chartering in Kansas, Feb. 15, 1859, of the Atchison and Topeka, rechartered in 1863 as the

Atchison, Topeka and Santa Fé Railroad. Actual building of the track beyond the Kansas border was begun in 1868, financed by T. J. Peters, of Cincinnati, who quickly sold securities to Eastern capitalists so that by 1869 control passed to Henry Keyes, of Newbury, Vt., as president of the concern. Later, Thomas Nickerson and W. B. Strong made the road a powerful factor in the development of the Southwest.

Increase in the cattle business helped the road to weather the Panic of 1873[qv] and in the later years of that decade building was resumed. As construction toward Santa Fé proceeded the road became involved in serious competition with the Denver and Rio Grande[qv] over territory. Santa Fé was reached in 1880, and a transcontinental link by connection with the Southern Pacific[qv] at Deming, N. Mex., was completed, March, 1881. Agreements with that company permitted building an independent track to Needles, where the Santa Fé bridged the Colorado River. West of that point, short lines already built were purchased and united to give entry to Los Angeles and San Diego, while a new track running northwest from Barstow, Calif., entered San Francisco.

The expense of construction into a newly settled country (long stretches of the line lie through deserts still very sparsely inhabited) coupled with the general financial depression of the early 1890's brought bankruptcy, which was followed by reorganization and sale to the Atchison, Topeka & Santa Fé Railway Company, chartered Dec. 12, 1895.

[R. E. Riegel, *The Story of the Western Railroads.*]

ROBERT G. RAYMER

Atherton Company. Maj. Humphrey Atherton, Gov. John Winthrop, the younger, and an incongruous intercolonial group of speculators formed a company which, by purchase from the Indians (1659) and foreclosure of a questionable Indian mortgage (1662), claimed title to nearly all the Narragansett country. Jurisdiction over the area was disputed between Connecticut and Rhode Island, whose charter claims conflicted; and the company, by supporting Connecticut and selling land to settlers, precipitated armed "incidents" and rendered vain all attempts at decision until the Board of Trade[qv] (1727) gave Rhode Island jurisdiction and left the company's heirs no tenable claims to the land.

[Edward Field, *State of Rhode Island and Providence Plantations . . .; Records of the Proprietors of the Narragansett, otherwise called the Fones Record.*]

RAYMOND P. STEARNS

Atkinson, Fort (Kansas) was one of the early posts located by the United States Government along the Santa Fé trail[qv]. It was built in Ford County on the Arkansas River by Maj. Hoffman in 1850, of sod. For this reason it was called Fort Sod and later Fort Sodom. It was besieged on one occasion by Comanches and Kiowas[qqv] but was relieved. Abandoned in 1853, it was later temporarily reoccupied, but was permanently abandoned in October, 1854. Other forts of this name were located in Florida, Iowa (near Council Bluffs), Nebraska and Wisconsin.

[F. W. Blackmar, *Kansas;* F. B. Heitman, *Historical Register of U. S. Army.*]

CARL L. CANNON

Atlanta, Capture and Burning of (1864). On Sept. 1, 1864, Gen. Sherman (U.) telegraphed President Lincoln: "Atlanta is ours and fairly won." Sherman had finally forced Hood (C.) out of the city (*see* Atlanta Campaign). The Confederate Army concentrated to the southward. All people remaining in Atlanta were deported. After a brief rest Hood started northward (*see* Hood's Tennessee Campaign). Sherman followed, but soon returned to Atlanta. On Nov. 16, 1864, the famous March to the Sea[qv] was begun.

Before setting out, Sherman ordered the complete destruction of the town. "Behind us," he wrote, "lay Atlanta smouldering and in ruins, the black smoke rising high in air and hanging like a pall over the ruined city." No city during the Civil War was so nearly completely annihilated.

[W. T. Sherman, *Memoirs*, Vol. II.]

THOMAS ROBSON HAY

Atlanta Campaign, The (May to September, 1864). The Union advance southward to Atlanta began, May 5, 1864, simultaneously with Grant's advance to Richmond (*see* Wilderness, Battles of the). Sherman's (U.) army numbered 110,000 men; Johnston's (C.) half that number. Sherman's superiority enabled him, with little risk, to maneuver Johnston from one position to another. If Johnston was to save his army and prevent Sherman from taking Atlanta, he could not afford to stand and fight unless conditions were favorable. He considered doing this at Cassville, half way to Atlanta, but his subordinate commanders believed the risk too great. Ten days later a fierce battle took place at New Hope Church[qv].

As the Confederates retreated nearer to Atlanta, fighting became more frequent. At Kenesaw Mountain[qv], Sherman made a frontal attack against prepared positions, but was everywhere repulsed. The flanking operations were resumed. By July 6 Sherman had moved so near Atlanta that Johnston transferred his army south of the Chattahoochee River, into prepared positions along Peachtree Creek[qv]. On July 17 Johnston was relieved by a subordinate, Hood (C.), because he had "failed to arrest the advance of the enemy" (*see* Davis-Johnston Controversy). On July 20 Hood violently attacked, but was repulsed with heavy losses. The attack was resumed, but was again repulsed. Sherman's renewal of his flanking movements to cut Hood's line of supply and force him out of Atlanta brought on the battle of Ezra Church[qv]. During August, Sherman edged closer to Hood's supply line. By the 31st he was across it. Hood evacuated Atlanta, Sept. 1; Sherman's troops moved into the city, Sept. 2 (*see* Atlanta, The Capture and Burning of). The campaign was over.

[*Battles and Leaders of the Civil War.*]

THOMAS ROBSON HAY

Atlantic and Pacific Railroad. This land-grant railroad was chartered on July 27, 1866, to run along the 31st parallel, from Springfield, Mo., by way of the Indian Territory[qv], northern Texas and Albuquerque and across the Colorado River at Needles. The road was to receive twenty sections of land per mile in the states traversed (except Texas) and forty sections in the territories. Railroad building had reached Vinita, Indian Territory, when the Panic of 1873[qv] brought an end to operations. In 1876 the company was reorganized as a part of the St. Louis and San Francisco, but still cash for construction was not forthcoming. Four years later the Atchison, Topeka and Santa Fé[qv] bought a half interest in the old Atlantic and Pacific. Before through trains were run from California to St. Louis in 1883 it was necessary to reach a settlement with the Southern Pacific[qv], which had built a line across California to Needles.

[Robert E. Riegel, *The Story of the Western Railroads.*]

DAN E. CLARK

Atlantic Cable. The laying of the Atlantic Cable was mainly due to the perseverance of Cyrus W. Field. A company was organized in 1854. A survey of the cable route followed. The British and American Governments loaned ships for the expeditions. A broken cable frustrated the efforts of 1857 and likewise efforts made in June of 1858. A later attempt in July met with success and by Aug. 5, 1858, the cable was laid. England and America rejoiced. President Buchanan and Queen Victoria exchanged greetings. Records of these early cable messages, cut in paper, are preserved at the Smithsonian Institution in Washington. Enthusiasm in America reached a culmination in early September when a great ovation was given Field in New York. But on Sept. 1 the cable ceased to function properly. For a time the experiment was much discredited.

During the Civil War capital was raised with great difficulty. Nevertheless, in July, 1865, the steamer *Great Eastern*[qv] began laying a cable which broke after two-thirds of it had been laid. Success crowned the efforts of 1866 and shortly after the cable of 1865 was recovered and operated. (*See also* Cables, Transatlantic; Pacific Cable.)

[Isabella Field Judson, *Cyrus W. Field—His Life and Work.*]

PHILIP G. AUCHAMPAUGH

Atlantic Coast Line Railroad, one of the most important railway systems of the South operating its main line between Richmond, Va., and Tampa, Fla. It was originally the Richmond and Petersburg Railroad, chartered by the State of Virginia in 1836 and received its present name in 1900 when other roads operating in the Southeast were consolidated with it.

[J. W. Starr, *One Hundred Years of American Railroading.*]

HALLIE FARMER

Atlantic Fisheries Dispute. *See* Fisheries Dispute, Arbitration of.

Atrocities in War. No war has been fought which did not produce its quota of brutality stories, narrations of savage, cruel and brutal deeds, shocking to those who, in the quiet calm of natural, peace conditions, read of them on the printed page. It is folly for any nation to try to dismiss the charge of perpetrating atrocities as complete falsehood. It is equally foolish to believe entirely the horror stories circulated during war. Upon investigation, these rumors frequently collapse entirely or are reduced to almost negligible minimums. Characterizations of atrocities extend throughout the gamut of human imaginations or fiendishness—bombardment of open towns, private houses, noncombatants, hospitals, orphan asylums and mercy stations; use of explosive bullets which burst within the human body and tear their way outward; employment of poison gas; massacre and mistreatment of enemy wounded and prisoners and of noncombatant civilians; rape; staking out of victims; crucifixion; eye gouging; tongue severing and splitting; hacking off of hands and feet; sexual mutilation; impaling and many other forms of brutality.

During the Revolution we suffered inhuman treatment of our men held prisoners aboard the nefarious British prison ships*qv* in Wallabout Bay, Long Island. In our naval wars, the record shows we were more sinned against than sinning and this is equally true of the Mexican War. If we discount the charge against us for the use of the "water cure"*qv* in the Philippine Islands, the Civil War brings out the worst charges and countercharges against us, charges in which we, perforce, stand self-accused since only our own people are involved. Stories of Libby Prison, Andersonville*qqv*, Salisbury and others in the South are matched by tales of equal brutality in Northern prisons such as Elmira, Camp Chase and Rock Island*qqv*. In fairness, it should be remembered that, materially, the South was ill-equipped to handle great numbers of prisoners. A Southern writer commenting upon prison fare, shelter and the like stated that the only difference between Union prisoners in a Southern camp and Confederate soldiers in the ranks was that the latter were free. When Grant (U.) refused any longer to exchange prisoners, conditions in the already overcrowded Southern prisons rapidly became intolerable. To ascribe a systematic, preconceived policy of atrocity either to Union or Confederate Governments is ridiculous.

In the World War our late entry made us the scapegoat which automatically inherited credit or discredit for all the moth-eaten charges that had already gone the rounds. In the alien press, for purposes of propaganda, the American devil had ascribed to him all the fiendish acts with which the "Aussies" from down under, the "Ladies of Hell" from Scotland, the territorials from Morocco and our neighbors from Canada had been charged from 1914 to 1917—we were simply a new target for old ammunition. Solemn documentary proofs of outrages were printed in "Brown Books" to be refuted by the opposition in "White Books" with equally weighty statements. Usually, specific and thorough investigations of alleged atrocities committed disclosed a normal 90% error, sometimes revealing even that the charges were supported by forged documents and faked photographs.

The dum-dum or explosive bullet cannot be explained away; nor can the use of poison gas, but use of the former has never been authentically charged or proved against us and the latter was forced upon us as a weapon of war by Germany's first use of it in 1915 (*see* Chemical Warfare).

[Asa B. Isham, *Prisoners of War and Military Prisons;* R. Randolph Stevenson, *The Southern Side, or Andersonville Prison;* Southern Society Historical Papers, Vol. I, March and April, 1876; Jefferson Davis, *Andersonville and Other War Prisons;* Anthony M. Keiley, *Prisoner of War, or Five Months Among the Yankees;* The Right Flanker, MS. sheets circulated among Southern prisoners in Fort LaFayette, N. Y.; Henry M. Davidson, *Fourteen Months in Southern Prisons;* Clay W. Holmes, *The Elmira Prison Camp;* William H. Knauss, *The Story of Camp Chase;* Robert H. Kellogg, *Life and Death in Rebel Prisons;* Frank E. Moran, *Bastiles of the Confederacy;* Isaac W. K. Handy, *United States Bonds;* N. P. Chipman, *The Horrors of Andersonville Rebel Prison;* A. O. Abbott, *Prison Life in the South;* A. M. Reiley, *In Vinculis;* J. Ogden Murray, *The Immortal Six Hundred;* George Taylor, *Martyrs to the Revolution in the British Prison Ships;* Rev. R. Livesey, *A Relic of the Revolution;* Joseph Bedier, *German Atrocities;* Carl P. Dennett, *Prisoners of the Great War;* Foreign Relations of the United States, World War Supplement volume.]

ROBERT S. THOMAS

Attainder, now obsolete in all democratic governments, is a summary legal procedure whereby all the ordinary civil rights of the defendant are waived, the state proceeding against him by "bill," or legislative act. An attainted person suffered the loss of offices, property and usually life; his children losing the inheritance of the estate and their noble rank, if any. The Constitution of the United States specifically prohibits the enactment of bills of attainder.

[T. P. Taswell-Langmead, *English Constitutional History.*]

BEN R. BALDWIN

Attorney General of the United States. *See* Justice, Department of.

Aubry's Ride. Francis Xavier Aubry, after a successful trading venture in Santa Fé in 1848, determined to bring out a second caravan in the same year and allowed himself eight days to ride back to Missouri. Doubts being expressed by his friends, he wagered a considerable sum on his ability to do so. Riding hard, his horse gave out on the Arkansas, but he pushed on fifteen or twenty miles to Mann's Fort, secured a remount, pressed onward, was pursued by Indians near Pawnee Fork, but reached Independence within less than the time specified.

[G. D. Brewerton, *Overland with Kit Carson.*]

CARL L. CANNON

Auburn (N. Y.) Prison System. The details of the separate or silent system were originally worked out in the prison being erected by New York at Auburn in the years following 1819. An act of that year and another of 1821 called for individual cells to displace the discredited congregate system. Rows of cells, 3½ x 7 x 7 feet in size, were erected in tiers, back to back, forming a cell block which was inclosed by the outer walls of the building. The plan differed strikingly from the Pennsylvania solitary pattern[qv], but could trace a distant descent from the plans of the *maison de force* at Ghent. The cells provided separate sleeping quarters, from which the convicts marched in lockstep to the shops of contractors located in the prison yard. Strict rules of silence were enforced at all times. Religious services were conducted in chapels. The system was designed to isolate the convicts from each other and to encourage them to penitence without sacrificing the value of their labor. The fact that convict labor[qv] was thus available to the enterprising pioneers of the factory system in America helped to make Auburn the favorite pattern for state prisons[qv] during the next half-century.

[Blake McKelvey, *American Prisons.*]

BLAKE MCKELVEY

Auctions. Sale by auction is a method of sale which was known to the Romans and at the time of the discovery of America the traders and merchants of European nations were familiar with its use. When the chief colonial cities reached some commercial importance, auctions became a part of their trading organizations. As early as 1729 Pennsylvania regulated auctions, New York followed in 1761 and Massachusetts enacted such a law in 1780. The Federal Government passed laws levying duties on sales at auction in 1794 and in 1813. From 1795 to 1801 the total value of goods sold at auction in the United States, with exceptions as provided in the law of 1794, was $64,996,278.

Auctions, however, were more important after the War of 1812 than they were before. This was due largely to the restrictions on commerce previous to and during the war which resulted in an unusual demand for goods. When peace was declared there was a rush for the American market and resort was had to the quickest and most convenient method of sale which often proved to be the auction. The preference for the auction method of sale seriously disturbed the business of American importers and jobbers. From one-half to three-fourths of the cargoes entering New York were on foreign account and instead of this merchandise passing through the trade channel of importer-jobber-retailer-consumer, it came accompanied by an agent and passed through the trade channel of auction-retailer-consumer, thus eliminating the importer and jobber.

The importers and jobbers did not sit idly by and watch this serious inroad on the business which they had customarily controlled. For fifteen years they attacked the auctions with petitions, pamphlets and ballots and although they were never successful in getting Congress to pass a bill restricting and regulating auctions, they were successful with the legislatures of the important commercial states.

The auction method of sale declined in importance after 1830 and did not again reach its former estate. The number of people following the occupation of an auctioneer, however, increased from 890 in 1850 to 4281 in 1930. The volume of sales made by 461 auction companies engaged in the wholesale distribution of commodities in 1929 was $373,775,525, about thirty-four times the total of all auction sales in 1800, but this amounted to only about one half of 1% of the total value of commodities sold at wholesale.

[Fred M. Jones, *Middlemen in the Domestic Trade of the United States 1800-1860.*]

FRED M. JONES

Audubon Societies, NATIONAL ASSOCIATION OF. This organization, for many years the foremost in the wild-life-conservation field, was incorporated Jan. 5, 1905. Primarily concerned with conservation education, it came into being as a federation of a number of dissociated state and local Audubon clubs which, in turn, had stemmed from the original "Audubon Society," first formed in 1886 by Dr. George Bird Grinnell, editor of *Forest and Stream.* This group consisted largely of school children, reached a total membership of about 50,000 and was abandoned in 1889 for lack of funds; memberships were based on pledges not to kill or injure "any wild bird not used for food" and not to make use of wild-bird plumage as an article of fashion or household furniture. No dues were charged.

One of the association's major projects has been the formation and maintenance of Junior Audubon Clubs, of which more than 150,000 have been established, with nearly 6,000,000 members. Each of these children has been provided, at less than cost, with literature designed to arouse an interest in wild life—especially birds—and its protection; the printed material has totaled more than 300,000,000 pages with more than 57,000,000 colored pictures. Besides this literature, the association distributes much miscellaneous printed material and publishes a magazine, *Bird-Lore.* Its adult education work has largely consisted in stimulating an interest in threatened forms of wild life and promoting an understanding of the biological principles behind their conservation. The association has also maintained a number of bird sanctuaries[qv].

[T. Gilbert Pearson, *Adventures in Bird Protection.*]

WILLIAM VOGT

Aughwick, Indian village on the Juniata River near the site of Shirleysburg, Pa., became in 1753 headquarters for George Croghan, trader and agent for Pennsylvania among western Indians. Friendly Indians, refugees from the vicinity of Fort Duquesne^qv^, were maintained at Aughwick and left there to join Braddock's expedition^qv^ in 1755.

[C. A. Hanna, *The Wilderness Trail;* C. Hale Sipe, *Indian Wars of Pennsylvania.*]

SOLON J. BUCK

Augusta, Fort, named for George III's mother. Constructed by Pennsylvania in 1756, at the site of present Sunbury, to defend the frontier after Braddock's defeat^qv^, and to forestall the French who supposedly intended to fortify the forks of the Susquehanna, it protected frontiersmen from Indians and Tories until abandoned after 1780.

[*Report of the Commission to Locate the Site of the Frontier Forts of Pennsylvania,* 2 volumes, Harrisburg, 1896.]

WILLIAM A. RUSS, JR.

Augusta, Ga., was founded (1735) by Gen. James Edward Oglethorpe at the head of navigation on the Savannah River. Until 1773 it remained the northwestern outpost of Georgia, dominating Indian trade and relations. Largely loyalist, it fell twice into British hands (1779, 1780–81). For a short period, ending in 1795, it was the state capital. There a convention ratified the United States Constitution. Upland cotton and steam transportation made it, temporarily, the greatest inland cotton market in the world. A government arsenal and a large powder mill made it a major source of supply for Confederate armies during the Civil War.

[E. M. Coulter, *A Short History of Georgia.*]

CHESTER McA. DESTLER

Augusta, THE, was a British vessel which, in 1777, led the attack against Commodore Hazelwood's fleet defending Fort Mercer^qv^ on the Delaware. The Americans resisted, forcing a British retreat. Defense construction may have caused channel changes, and the *Augusta* grounded. The Revolutionists attacked and, on Oct. 23, the *Augusta* exploded, losing over sixty men.

[Gardner W. Allen, *Naval History of the American Revolution.*]

JULIAN P. BOYD

Augusta, The Congress of (1763), took place Nov. 5–10, in response to orders from the British government to the governors of Virginia, North and South Carolina and Georgia that they collect representatives of the southern Indians (Creeks, Cherokees, Choctaws, Chickasaws, and Catawbas^qqv^), inform them that the French and Indian War^qv^ had ended, and bring about a general settlement on trade and boundary difficulties. The governors from these colonies (lieutenant governor from Virginia) and John Stuart, Superintendent of Indian Affairs^qv^ in the Southern District, met 700 Indians at Augusta, signed a treaty of friendship, and secured therein important land cessions in Georgia from the Creeks.

[C. C. Jones, Jr., *History of Georgia,* Vol. II W. B. Stevens, *History of Georgia,* Vol. II; *Journal of the Southern Congress held at Augusta in Georgia, 1763.*]

E. MERTON COULTER

Augusta, The Treaty of (1773), was made by Gov. James Wright, of Georgia, and John Stuart, Superintendent of Indian Affairs^qv^ in the Southern District, with chiefs of the Creek and Cherokee nations^qqv^, at the suggestion of the Indians, who were hopelessly in debt to various groups of white traders. By this agreement Georgia was ceded two tracts of land, one between the Altamaha and Ogeechee rivers and the other lying between the upper stretches of the Ogeechee and Savannah rivers, comprising in all more than 2,100,000 acres, and from the sale of these lands the traders were to be paid. A great influx of settlers was attracted here just before the Revolution.

[C. C. Jones, Jr., *History of Georgia,* Vol. II; W. B. Stevens, *History of Georgia,* Vol. II; George White, *Historical Collections of Georgia;* R. and G. Watkins, eds., *Digest of the Laws of the State of Georgia.*]

E. MERTON COULTER

Augusta County, Va., named in honor of Princess Augusta, wife of the Prince of Wales, was erected on Nov. 1, 1738, from that portion of Orange County lying beyond the Blue Ridge. The newly created county was to remain part of the parent county until the number of inhabitants warranted the establishment of a separate government, which was not until Oct. 30, 1745. Territorially it included the present states of Kentucky, Ohio, Indiana, Illinois, nearly all of West Virginia and a part of western Pennsylvania. Here the Virginians came into conflict with Pennsylvania's claims, for both colonies had settlers in those parts of Pennsylvania west of the Alleghenies. Becoming alarmed at the influx of Virginia settlers, Pennsylvania had erected, on Feb. 26, 1773, Westmoreland County, which included all of the present counties of Westmoreland, Fayette, Greene, Washington and parts of Allegheny, Beaver, Indiana and Armstrong. In

1774–75 Virginia created the District of West Augusta, which claimed the land of the newly created Westmoreland County. In 1776 Virginia attempted to strengthen title to these lands by dividing West Augusta into three new counties: Ohio, Yohogania and Monongalia. These conflicting jurisdictional claims produced the Pennsylvania-Virginia Boundary dispute[qv] which was not settled until 1780. The immense territory of Augusta County was thus cut down, first by the creation of Botetourt County in 1769, Fincastle in 1772, the three counties in West Augusta and later encroachments until it reached its present-day status.

[Jos. A. Waddell, *Annals of Augusta County, Virginia, from 1726 to 1871;* Edgar W. Hassler, *Old Westmoreland: A History of Western Pennsylvania during the Revolution;* Boyd Crumrine, *The County Court for the District of West Augusta, Virginia.*]

R. J. FERGUSON

Auraria (Colo.), established in October, 1858, was one of the towns started at the juncture of Cherry Creek and the South Platte, following gold discoveries earlier that summer (*see* Pikes Peak Gold Rush). In April, 1860, it was consolidated with Denver[qv], its rival, on the opposite bank of Cherry Creek.

[J. C. Smiley, *History of Denver.*]

MALCOLM G. WYER

Aurora, THE, a Philadelphia newspaper founded in 1790 by Benjamin Franklin Bache as the *General Advertiser.* When Freneau's *National Gazette*[qv] suspended, the *Aurora* took its place as the Jeffersonian Republican[qv] mouthpiece. It was notorious for its violent personal abuse and its attacks on Washington's administration, including the charge that the President had violated the Constitution and including also forged letters of Washington.

[B. Faÿ, *The Two Franklins.*]

JULIAN P. BOYD

Austin Colony, Texas. On Jan. 17, 1821, the Spanish authorities in Mexico granted to Moses Austin permission to settle 300 families in Texas. After the death of the grantee, and after Mexico's successful revolt from Spain, the Mexican provisional government confirmed this concession to Stephen F. Austin, the "Father of Texas." Subsequently the younger Austin obtained contracts to settle 900 additional families, most of whom he had introduced by 1833. Austin's colonies formed the nucleus of the Anglo-American occupation of Texas.

[E. C. Barker, *The Life of Stephen F. Austin.*]

E. C. BARKER

Austria, Treaty of Peace with (1921). After the Senate had refused to ratify the Treaty of Versailles[qv], the Treaty of Saint-Germain-en-Laye was not submitted to it. On July 2, 1921, a joint resolution of Congress declared at an end the state of war existing with Austria-Hungary since Dec. 7, 1917; it also affirmed the rights of the United States arising from its participation in the war, the terms of the armistice[qv] or the Treaty of Saint-Germain, and as one of the principal Allied and Associated Powers, and provided for the retention of all property seized in wartime until Austria had satisfied all claims for losses suffered by American nationals since 1914. The Treaty of Vienna (Aug. 24, 1921), based on this resolution, provided that the United States should enjoy the rights of Parts V, VI, VIII, IX, X, XI, XII, XIV of the Treaty of Saint-Germain, but should not be bound by Parts I (League of Nations), II, III, IV and XIII (Labor); further, the United States was privileged, but not bound, to participate in the Reparation Commission[qv]. The treaty was ratified by Austria on Oct. 8, 1921, and by the United States on Oct. 21, 1921.

BERNADOTTE E. SCHMITT

Auto Racing. The first road race occurred at Chicago in 1895, with a record of 7.5 miles per hour. Speedways were introduced in 1907–8. The classic 500-mile race is held each Decoration Day at the Indianapolis 2.5-mile paved track, constructed in 1909–10, where the record in 1938 was 117.20 miles per hour. Speed tests are made at Daytona Beach and Bonneville (Utah) salt flats. A record of 368.85 miles per hour was achieved (1939) at Bonneville. Over 150 races are held annually in the United States under rules of the Contest Board of the American Automobile Association.

ROSCOE R. HILL

Automobile, THE, was not invented by any one person but was evolved through the efforts of many experimenters in several nations. So early as 1787 Oliver Evans, of Philadelphia, petitioned the Maryland legislature for a patent on the manufacture and operation of steam-propelled vehicles, and in 1804 he ran through the streets of Philadelphia a strange vehicle consisting of a large wagon which carried, and was driven by, a steam-propelled flatboat. However, largely because of the atrocious roads of the period and because of concentration on railroad development, little progress was made in this country until almost the close of the 19th century and automotive development got its real start abroad.

In the 1830's steam-driven stage coaches—ponderous, clumsy and rough—were operating on regular schedules along several routes in England but eventually they were driven from the road by excessive toll charges and restrictive legislation. Most of the real progress was made in Germany: in 1876 Dr. A. N. Otto built a four-cycle internal combustion hydrocarbon motor, the same in principle as those used in motor vehicles today; in 1885 Gottfried Daimler built the first motorcycle, and in 1886 Carl Benz built the first automobile powered by a gasoline engine. The French quickly took up their ideas and by 1895 the French firm of Panhard & Lavassor was producing horseless vehicles on a commercial scale.

Meanwhile, activity in America was practically dormant, with most of the experimentation during the period being concentrated on heavy steam-propelled traction engines. After 1890, however, American pioneers began working in homes and workshops, borrowing heavily on the ideas of their European colleagues, and by 1900 they had laid the basis for a new industry. Authorities differ over the somewhat empty question as to which of the United States experimenters deserves precedence, but the weight of evidence places Charles and Frank Duryea first, in 1892; Henry Ford second in 1893, Elwood Haynes in 1894, with R. E. Olds, Alexander Winton and Charles P. King following closely. At any rate, the Duryea cars were the first American vehicles to prove themselves in competition: a Duryea road wagon won the first road race held in this country—the *Times-Herald* contest run over the snow-covered streets of Chicago on Thanksgiving Day in 1895—and the following year three of the four Duryea entries took all the money in the New York-to-Irvington race.

The first automotive trade journal, *The Horseless Age,* was launched with a good deal of temerity by E. P. Ingersoll in 1895, but the industry was to remain largely in the experimental stage until the close of the century. The next decade saw phenomenal advances in the art of road transportation. Twelve manufacturing firms in 1900 turned out 4000 vehicles; by 1910 there were sixty-nine companies in the field and their annual production had leaped to 181,000. This whole decade was marked by tremendous enthusiasm and intense activity: automobile clubs were formed; a dozen or more reliability runs were staged each year; a craze for speed contests of all kinds sprang up on both sides of the Atlantic—climaxed by the fantastic race around the world from New York to Paris in 1908; strenuous campaigns for construction of good roads[qv] were undertaken; legislators puzzled and wrangled over laws to govern the new form of transportation; extravagant claims for their products were made by the makers in screaming advertisements; and controversy between car owners and horse owners reached a furious crescendo.

Most of the firms started during this period operated on little more than a shoestring, using credit advanced by the supply companies, demanding advance payments and cash on delivery from dealers, and financing expansion through reinvestment of profits. The Ford Motor Company[qv] started business with a capital of $28,000; the Hudson Motor Car Company, with "considerably less than that." Very little actual manufacturing was done by these early companies; rather their job was to buy the parts ready-made, assemble them and sell the resultant vehicles as quickly as possible. Mortality among the automobile firms was very high: of the sixty-nine companies making cars in 1910, only eight still survived in 1938—Packard, started in 1900, Ford and Cadillac in 1903, Studebaker and Buick in 1904, Willys-Overland in 1908 and General Motors[qv] and Hudson in 1909.

Naturally enough, the tremendous profits realized by a few of the companies gave rise to many promotional ventures, based largely on hopes and extravagant claims, and a number of companies capitalized at many millions of dollars sprang into the picture only to crash and disappear almost immediately. Of all the large promotions, only two persisted for any appreciable length of time, and one of these—the Electric Vehicle Company—was sustained for some years by its ownership of the Selden patent[qv].

This patent was the storm center of a court battle that dragged on in the courts for eight years and was a vital factor in influencing the early development of the automobile industry. In 1879 George B. Selden, of Rochester, N. Y., filed application for a patent on a gasoline-propelled vehicle, but purposely kept the matter pending so that the patent was not granted until 1895. It eventually came into the possession of the Electric Vehicle Company which immediately began infringement proceedings. After one legal set-back, practically all the major manufacturers, with the exception of Ford, capitulated, forming themselves into the Association of Licensed Automobile Manufacturers. At length, the appeals court ruled that, while the patent was valid, it was not being infringed and therefore not enforceable. The principal effect of the Selden patent was to teach the manufacturers the value of co-operation and to give them a healthy fear of patent litigation, thus laying the groundwork for the cross-licensing agreement that has kept the automobile industry almost free of the patent difficulties which have plagued so many other lines of enterprise.

In 1910–11 the industry experienced a temporary set-back; twenty firms dropped out of existence and the curve of production increase slacked off considerably. Almost immediately, however, the automobile makers began improving production methods: mass-production[qv] techniques were perfected, phenomenal reductions were made in the man-hours of labor per car, and prices were slashed. Automobile purchasing again shot upward and by 1920 there were eighty-four firms engaged in automobile production, making in that year 1,906,000 cars valued at $1,809,000,000. During this period, American makers obtained dominance of the world markets, exports of passenger cars and trucks during 1920 totaling 142,000, while imports, which had begun back in 1895, dropped almost to the vanishing point.

The installment plan[qv] of car purchasing, instituted on a large scale shortly after the World War, proved a tremendous stimulant. The low prices obtaining in the used-car market aided in providing individual transportation for the lower-income groups and intensive road-building added further to the popularity of motor vehicles. Although the number of manufacturing firms dropped steadily, declining from a high of eighty-eight in 1921 to twenty in 1937, passenger car registrations continued rapidly upward, losing ground only during the depression years, 1930–33. In 1937, when more than 5,000,000 vehicles valued at nearly $3,000,000,000 were produced, there were approximately 30,000,000 motor vehicles registered in the United States, of which 25,500,000 were passenger cars. This represented 70% of all motor vehicles in use throughout the world and was equivalent to one vehicle for each four persons living in this country.

This tremendous motorization has profoundly affected many phases of American life. It has driven the horse from the highway, wrecking the $50,000,000 carriage and buggy-building industry in the process. It has brought about the construction of nearly 1,000,000 miles of improved highways. The motor vehicle has robbed the railroads of much of their passenger traffic and some of their freight, but it has provided them with 4,000,000 carloads of automotive freight annually and has given them a flexible instrument for delivery to and from the stations.

The automobile industry gives direct and semidirect employment to some 6,000,000 workers, with total wage payments since 1900 estimated at $82,000,000,000. It is the principal consumer of many important commodities such as steel, rubber, plate glass, nickel and lead, and is responsible for the tremendous expansion of the oil industry, which produces more than a billion barrels of crude petroleum a year.

Politically, the motor vehicle exerts continuous pressure for less local and more national governmental control. It produces more than a billion and a half dollars in taxes a year, most of which goes toward road-building. It has worked against sectionalism[qv] and provincialism and has been a major factor in integrating the nation. It has created a major social problem by causing some 40,000 deaths and 1,000,000 injuries yearly.

To the farmer, the motor vehicle has brought more centralized educational facilities, lower transportation costs on his produce, quicker medical attention, more social intercourse and greater ease in obtaining his supplies. To the city dweller, it has brought a new means of leisure-utilization, freedom from mass-transportation herding and a method of periodic escape from urban surroundings. It has hastened suburban development and is beginning to cause disintegration of congested business districts.

Practically every prosperous family owns a motor car; a startlingly large percentage of the poorest families own them. Like the bathtub, the telephone and the radio[qqv], it has become an essential element in the American way of living.

[J. R. Doolittle, *The Romance of the Automobile Industry;* R. C. Epstein, *The Automobile Industry.*]

RICHARD W. TUPPER

Auttose, The Battle of (Nov. 29, 1813). As an aid to Jackson in his campaign against the Creeks[qv], Gen. John Floyd, commanding 940 Georgia militia and several hundred friendly Creeks, crossed the Chattahoochee River into Alabama. On Nov. 29 he attacked Auttose, a Creek Indian village on the Tallapoosa River near Tookabatchee[qv], and drove the Creeks from their villages, burned their houses and killed 200, losing but 11 killed and 54 wounded himself.

[Henry Adams, *History of the United States of America.*]

ROBERT S. THOMAS

Avery Salt Mine is located near New Iberia, La. Although a brine spring was discovered in 1791, it was not until May, 1862, that the existence of a rock salt mass was revealed. The Confederate government worked the mine until the Union forces seized it in April, 1863.

ELLA LONN

Avery's Trace. In 1787 the North Carolina legislature provided for a lottery[q.v.] the proceeds of which should be used in cutting a way across the Cumberland Mountains in the Tennessee country in order to connect Washington District with the Cumberland settlements[qq.v.]. Peter Avery blazed and cut a trace through the sites of the present towns of Harriman, Monterey and Cookeville where the descent of the western escarpment of the Cumberland plateau began. The Cherokees[q.v.] claimed the region traversed by the trace and demanded toll for its use. Guards of militia became necessary where the party of travelers was not large or not well armed.

[W. E. McElwee, The Old Road, *The American Historical Magazine*, Vol. VIII.] SAMUEL C. WILLIAMS

Averysboro, Battle of (March 16, 1865). Hardee's corps of Gen. J. E. Johnston's Confederate Army, retreating through North Carolina, entrenched at this village and gave a portion of Sherman's (U.) Army, under Slocum and Kilpatrick, a determined resistance for several hours; but inferiority in numbers compelled his retreat during the night.

[*Battles and Leaders of the Civil War.*] ALVIN F. HARLOW

Aviation. While Lilienthal and Pilcher were carrying on experiments with gliding in Europe between 1890 and 1900, Octave Chanute was doing the same in the United States. At precisely the same period, Ader in France, Maxim in England, and, in the United States, Samuel P. Langley, secretary of the Smithsonian Institution, were endeavoring to solve the problem of a power-driven glider. Ader and Maxim gave it up. Langley continued his experiments from 1887 until 1903, at which time the Government withdrew support from his experiments upon the wrecking of his last model. Wilbur and Orville Wright, operators of a bicycle repair shop in Dayton, Ohio, had about 1896 begun experiments, and in 1903 achieved short power-driven flights at Kittyhawk[q.v.] Island, N. C. On Oct. 5, 1905, they accomplished a flight of twenty-four miles, the aeroplane—as it was called for many years before the word was modified to airplane—remaining in the air thirty-eight minutes and three seconds. Wilbur Wright spent a part of 1908 in France and gave aviation a strong impetus there. The United States Government accepted its first plane (it had a speed of forty miles per hour) from the Wright brothers in 1909. This and all other machines constructed in America for a number of years thereafter were biplanes.

In 1908 the biplane of Glenn H. Curtiss won recognition, and in the following year won the prize in an international contest in France for the fastest time—15 minutes, 56 1/5 seconds—over a course of 20 kilometers. In 1910 Curtiss flew from Albany to New York harbor, 142 miles, stopping three times for oil and fuel, at an average speed of forty-nine miles per hour. He produced a seaplane in 1911 which won for him the Aero Club of America trophy. At the beginning of the World War the United States was pre-eminent in seaplane construction. The Wright brothers had obtained broad patents, and there was much litigation with Curtiss and others, the Wrights' claims for the most part being upheld. Curtiss opened an aviation school and did much to spread the knowledge of the science. For several years all flights were either experimental or exhibitions at county fairs and elsewhere by individual aviators who owned their machines. A shocking number of these pioneers were killed in accidents (*see* Airplane Disasters).

In 1911 William R. Hearst offered a prize of $50,000 for a flight across the United States within thirty days, elapsed time. Galbraith P. Rogers attempted it with a plane having a 40-horse-power motor. He limped from town to town, his longest flight being but 133 miles, fell frequently, replaced many parts and finally, after sixty-eight days, reached California in another plane than the one with which he started. His elapsed time was forty-nine days. Thereafter, aviation began to make more rapid strides. May 2–3, 1923, Lts. Kelley and Macready of the United States Army flew nonstop from New York to San Diego in twenty-six hours and fifty minutes. In 1924 Russell L. Maugham reduced this to twenty-one hours forty-eight minutes, making six stops. In 1929 Frank Hawks crossed the continent eastward in a trifle over nineteen hours, and westward in seventeen hours thirty-eight minutes sixteen seconds. In 1930 he did the journey in twelve hours twenty-five minutes. In 1938 Howard R. Hughes flew from Los Angeles to Newark in seven hours twenty-eight minutes and twenty-five seconds. Lincoln Beachy's altitude record of 11,642 feet in 1912 was surpassed by Capt. Schroeder in 1918 with 28,000 feet, by the same man in 1920 with 36,000, by Lt. Macready in 1921 with 40,800 feet and by Lt. Soucek in 1930 with 43,166 feet.

The first plane to cross the Atlantic was the United States Navy's NC-4 (1919)[q.v.], one of three which attempted a flight via Newfoundland, the Azores and Portugal; the other two were wrecked en route. In June of that year two Englishmen, Alcock and Brown, flew the 1600 miles from Newfoundland to Ireland, but the 3600-mile solo flight of Charles A. Lindbergh[qv] from New York to Paris, May 20–21, 1927, was considered a milestone in aviation history. Two weeks later Clarence Chamberlin with a passenger flew nonstop from New York to a point in Germany, 3923 miles. For years European flyers tried in vain to cross the Atlantic in a westerly direction, and many were lost in the attempts; but by 1938 this had come to be a commonplace affair. In 1924 two army planes out of four (two being wrecked on the way) went around the globe, passing the Pacific via Alaska and Kamtchatka, and the Atlantic via Scotland, the Orkney Islands and Iceland. Their actual flying time was only 15 days and 11 hours, but they consumed 175 days, all told, in making the tour. In 1931 Wiley Post and Harold Gatty encircled the globe in eight days sixteen hours, and in 1933 Post did it alone in seven days eighteen hours and forty-nine minutes. This record was eclipsed by Howard R. Hughes, who, with a crew of four, accomplished the feat in July, 1938, in three days nineteen hours.

The United States Army used planes for scouting in the Mexican border troubles in 1916. Early in the World War several American flyers joined the Lafayette Escadrille[qv], and when the United States entered the war, American planes and men did notable work on the French and Italian fronts. Meanwhile, American factories were supplying many planes to other nations. It was during the war, on May 15, 1918, that the Post Office Department started the first experimental air-mail plane[qv] between New York and Washington. This carrying very soon passed into private hands, and the mail planes began carrying passengers—a traffic which grew within a few years to enormous proportions. The first goods other than letters to be sent by air were motion-picture news films carried by private planes. In 1927 the American Railway Express Company began carrying small packages by plane in a limited way. Rates at first were enormously high—at one time $10 per pound for 1000 miles—but they declined rapidly and the service developed with even greater speed. By 1934 not only small but heavy freight up to the size of an automobile was being carried all over the United States, and through Mexico and the West Indies to all parts of South America. After 1930 the great majority of machines built in the United States were monoplanes. Speeds had risen to 200 and even 300 miles per hour. On Jan. 1, 1930, there were 1279 airports[qv] in the United States; in 1938 there were 3000 such ports. Mail and passenger service was begun between the United States and South America in 1930, across the Pacific to Asia in 1935 and across the Atlantic in 1939.

[John Goldstrom, *A Narrative History of Aviation;* Chelsea Fraser, *The Story of Aircraft.*]

ALVIN F. HARLOW

"Awakening," Second, is the name usually given the great religious revival[qv] which swept over the United States in the latter 18th and early 19th centuries, following an era of extreme religious deadness. In the East it centered in the colleges where religion had been in sad plight with infidelity rampant among the students. President Dwight at Yale met the issue squarely and in chapel sermons and classroom discussions he won the respect of the students and prepared the way for a renewed religious interest. A revival began in 1802 which resulted in the conversion of a third of the student body. The Awakening spread to other colleges and soon a stream of young college graduates was entering every form of Christian work, particularly the Christian ministry and education and Home and Foreign mission[qqv] enterprises.

In the West the Awakening was attended with great emotional excitement, under the preaching of such evangelists[qv] as James McGready, Barton W. Stone and William McKendree. No churches were large enough to hold the vast crowds which assembled to hear the evangelists and as a result the camp-meeting[qv] evolved. While at first largely a Presbyterian movement, the revival soon became interdenominational and spread rapidly throughout the West. Though greatly increasing church membership and raising the standard of Western morals, there were some unfortunate results, such as excessive emotionalism and church schisms.

[Catharine C. Cleveland, *The Great Revival in the West, 1797-1805.*]

WILLIAM W. SWEET

Axes, Frontier. From the early contacts of Europeans with Indians in the 15th century, through all periods of fur trade and other commerce, the Indian demanded and received the iron axe and hatchet. The French in the 17th century distributed great numbers of axes with light polls and long blades, a type known as the French trade axe. Records show, however, that Holland and England both supplied this same "Biscay" hatchet. The tree-felling axe brought by Frenchmen for their own use was a large counterpart of the popular trade axe, with heavy blade and light poll. The axe taken to Jamestown and Plymouth differed little from that of the French, but before a century had passed, there had developed from this British tool a better-balanced Anglo-American implement with lengthened poll and somewhat shortened blade. Before 1776 American makers had developed the characteristic American axe with heavy squared poll that outweighed the bit, a tool unknown in other parts of the world. The Indian, however, refused to recognize the greater efficiency of this new axe and as long as frontier relationships endured the "French trade axe" persisted.

[Harold A. Innis, *The Fur Trade in Canada;* Henry C. Mercer, Ancient Carpenters Tools, *Old Time New England*, Vol. XV.]

CARL P. RUSSELL

Ayllon, Expeditions of. In 1521 Vasquez de Ayllon sent from the West Indies an exploring expedition which visited the present Carolina coast, returning therefrom with a number of captured natives. In 1526 de Ayllon sailed in three caravels with 600 prospective settlers, Negro slaves, scores of horses and orders to seek the ever-elusive Northwest Passage^qv^. The name of his settlement, San Miguel de Gualdape, is recorded, but its site has yet to be determined, some scholars having placed it south of Cape Hatteras, while others have placed it within the Chesapeake, either on the James or the Potomac. Since the most extended account refers to severe cold, acceptance thereof would point to the more northerly site. The Spaniards suffered all the ills subsequently endured by the English at Jamestown^qv^ in the form of malarial fevers, dissensions and Indian assaults. The settlement was abandoned and the survivors returned to the West Indies.

[Elroy M. Avery, *A History of the United States*, Vol. I.]

MATTHEW PAGE ANDREWS

Ayubale (Ayaville), Battle of (Dec. 14, 1703), was a frontier engagement between a force of 50 whites and 1000 Indians under ex-Gov. James Moore of South Carolina and the defenders of the Spanish mission at Ayubale, near Tallahassee. Moore, who as governor (1700–1703) had failed in an attempt to take the fort at St. Augustine, was given command of the expedition into Apalache^qv^ to redeem his failure. He took Ayubale, devastated a wide area, badly crippled the Spanish in Florida and carried away 1300 Apalache Indian captives (or 600, according to the Spanish estimate), settling as Carolina dependents, on the east side of the lower course of the Savannah River, those not sold as slaves.

[D. D. Wallace, *History of South Carolina;* J. T. Lanning, *Spanish Missions in Georgia.*]

D. D. WALLACE

Ayuntamiento, THE, or ***Cabildo,*** is a Spanish and Spanish-American municipal council, with administrative, legislative and judicial functions. Citizens sometimes joined it in open meeting, or *cabildo abierto.* Many cities in the United States, including St. Augustine, Fla., San Antonio, Tex., and Los Angeles, Calif., have been governed by *ayuntamientos,* which still survive in republican Spanish America.

[C. E. Chapman, *Colonial Hispanic America: a History.*]

CHARLES EDWARD CHAPMAN and
ROBERT HALE SHIELDS

Azilia, Margravate of, designates the fantastic scheme of Sir Robert Montgomery to establish "a New Colony to the South of Carolina." Despite activities in Britain, he and others failed to settle the area between the Savannah and the Altamaha rivers, the Golden Islands region, within the three years conditioning his grant of 1717 from the Carolina proprietors^qv^.

[V. W. Crane, *The Southern Frontier, 1670-1732.*]

H. B. FANT

Aztalan, an Indian village of moderate antiquity, was located near Lake Mills, Wis., on the Crawfish. The inhabitants, a people of Middle Mississippi Valley culture, lived on seeds, nuts, berries, molluscs, fish, birds and animals. Cannibalism was practised. Arts and crafts were well advanced, and pottery and implement manufacture was carried on. The village was protected by a wall of palisades with watch towers at regular intervals; within were rectangular and circular mud-plastered wooden houses. The earthwork enclosure was first described by N. F. Hyer in the *Milwaukee Advertiser* in 1836; it was surveyed and described by Dr. I. A. Lapham in *The Antiquities of Wisconsin* in 1855 and excavated by the Milwaukee Public Museum, 1919–20, 1932.

[Milwaukee Public Museum, *Aztalan.*]

CHARLES E. BROWN

Babcock Tester. *See* Dairy Industry.

Bachelor Houses. To protect the colony from being burdened with the indigent and to maintain moral standards, Connecticut as early as 1636 forbade heads of families from entertaining single young men without permission. Nor could an unmarried young man keep home alone without consent under penalty of a fine. The Connecticut Code of 1650 (*see* Ludlow's Code) and the New Haven laws of 1656 extended this prohibition to single persons of either sex. Similarly strict laws against strangers are found in the Massachusetts codes of 1641, 1648 and 1660.

[E. W. Capen, *The Historical Development of the Poor Law of Connecticut.*] RICHARD B. MORRIS

Backwoods and Back Country. The term backwoodsman was not applied to those who, in the first century of our colonization, settled in the wilder portions of New England. It did not become common until pioneers began advancing the frontier farther south—moving into and beyond the mountains of Pennsylvania, Virginia and the Carolinas, regions which came to be known to the Coast states as the back country. For generations after the great westward movement[qv] beginning about 1769–70, this back country, comprising the present Middle West, West Virginia, Kentucky, Tennessee and other inland areas farther south, was predominantly forest. Until after 1800 roads fit for wheeled vehicles were rare and short, and most traveling was done by water or mere horse trail. There were still only a few small cleared areas in what is now Kentucky in 1776 when the settlers chose two agents to ask protection of Virginia, with the result that "Kentucky County"[qv] was created, and in the following year sent two burgesses to the Virginia legislature. Backwoodsmen under George Rogers Clark (*see* Clark's Northwest Campaign) took Kaskaskia and Vincennes[qqv]. In Tennessee they first organized the Watauga Association and then the State of Franklin[qqv]. An undisciplined but, as usual, efficient army of them annihilated Ferguson's force at the Battle of King's Mountain[qv]. Later, under their idol, Andrew Jackson, they fought the Creek War and won the Battle of New Orleans[qqv]. Their prowess in war bred in them a group consciousness and pride. When Jackson was inaugurated in 1829 they flocked to Washington and made the occasion, including the White House reception, so turbulent and uproarious that old Federalists and Whigs[qqv] thought the era of mob rule had come. The word backwoodsman acquired during that period an opprobrium which it never afterwards lost.

[Theodore Roosevelt, *The Winning of the West;* E. Douglas Branch, *Westward;*. Seymour Dunbar, *History of Travel in America.*] ALVIN F. HARLOW

Bacon's Rebellion (1675–76) had its roots in the autocratic government of Gov. Berkeley of Virginia and the resentment of the small landholders when Berkeley refused to defend the colonists adequately against murderous attacks by Indians. The building of forts and additional taxes did not satisfy those who desired direct action. When 300 men volunteered to go against the savages, Berkeley declared them rebels and ordered them to return. Although the majority, fearing the governor, obeyed, sixty followed Nathaniel Bacon, a planter who had settled on the western frontier of the province. Bacon attacked the Indians and killed 150.

Berkeley yielded to the popular demand for a new assembly, which inaugurated reforms giving the freeholders a greater share in government. Bacon, coming to Jamestown with 500 men, demanded a commission to fight the Indians and was supported by the House of Burgesses and the governor's council. Berkeley again yielded, but when Bacon departed the governor called upon the militia of two counties to suppress the upstart planter. Failing in this, Berkeley fled to Accomac County, across Chesapeake Bay, in the vain hope of finding supporters in that royalist section.

Bacon returned from his expedition against the Indians, assumed leadership and called a new assembly. During his absence on another expedition against the Indians, Berkeley returned to Jamestown with 600 men. Bacon hastened back, defeated Berkeley's force and the governor once more fled to Accomac. In the midst of Bacon's preparations for invading Accomac he was stricken with fever and died. After his death the rebellion collapsed. The aged governor executed some of Bacon's followers in spite of royal pardon. He was soon recalled by the king.

[C. M. Andrews, *Colonial Self-Government;* H. L. Osgood, *The American Colonies in the 17th Century.*]

PERCY SCOTT FLIPPIN

Bad Axe, Battle of (Aug. 2, 1832). The Sauk and Fox Indians[qqv], dissatisfied with lands to which the Federal Government had moved them, recrossed the Mississippi in April, 1832, and, under the leadership of Black Hawk[qv], revolted against the whites. They were finally penned up against the Mississippi River at the mouth of the Bad Axe River, midway between Prairie du Chien and La Crosse, Wis., and there completely defeated by an American force of 400 regular infantry and 900 militia, commanded by Gen. Henry Atkinson.

[Frank E. Stevens, *The Black Hawk War.*]

ROBERT S. THOMAS

Badlands of South Dakota were created by precipitation of volcanic ash, sand and Fuller's earth, perhaps borne by wind, from eruptions in the far Northwest which buried several hundred square miles more than 300 feet in depth. Water erosion carved this material into many fantastic forms. The precipitation engulfed vast herds of antediluvian monsters where they were feeding in the swamps, the remains of which were later exposed by erosion. The Federal Government has established the region as "The Badlands National Monument" and has built a system of highways into the more scenic regions of the park. The Badlands were discovered by fur traders early in the 19th century and for more than 100 years scientific societies, museums and educational institutions have been busily engaged in unearthing the paleontological treasures, so long entombed. Included in these relics are fossil mammoths, elephants, Brontotheriums, Protoceras, camels, horses and many of the Carnivora whose descendants are still extant. In these fastnesses the Sioux took refuge when pursued by the army in the Messiah War[qv] of 1890.

[The White River Badlands, *Bulletins 5 and 13*, South Dakota School of Mines.] DOANE ROBINSON

Bagot-Rush Agreement. *See* Great Lakes, Agreement for Disarmament on the.

Bahama Islands, THE, although granted to the Carolina proprietors[qv] in 1670, were passed by during the most active age of colonization and had only a meager development before 1718. Pirates found their innumerable harbors most convenient. After 1718, with separation from the Carolinas, colonists increased and pirates diminished; nevertheless illegal trading still featured the economic life. In the preliminaries of the American Revolution, the islanders supported the American opponents of British policy and later aided them with military supplies. During the 19th century American interest in the Bahamas was sustained in numerous ways. They figured extensively in the blockade running[qv] during the Civil War. More recently, American investments in the islands' fruit production and an ever-increasing number of tourists have brought close relations. The prohibition[qv] experiment greatly stimulated American interest, and the islanders have sought by various attractions to maintain the contacts thus inaugurated.

[C. Atchley, *The West Indies.*]

CHARLES F. MULLETT

Bailey v. Drexel Furniture Company (259 U. S. 20) was a case in which the United States Supreme Court (1922) invalidated an act of Congress (1919) levying a tax of 10% upon the net profits of business concerns employing children under the age of sixteen. The Supreme Court held that the measure was not a valid exercise of the taxing power, since it was an attempt to bring under congressional control matters whose regulation belongs solely to the states. (*See also* Child Labor Cases.)

P. ORMAN RAY

Baker's Cabin Massacre, THE (April 30, 1774), a cause of Dunmore's War[qv], was the cold-blooded murder of some six or seven unarmed Mingo[qv] Indians by a party of unscrupulous whites at Baker's Cabin, about fifteen miles above present Steubenville, Ohio, on the Virginia side of the Ohio River. Logan[qv], the Mingo chief, went on the warpath, charging that his sister and other near relatives had been killed.

[R. G. Thwaites and Louise Phelps Kellogg, *A Documentary History of Dunmore's War.*]

EUGENE H. ROSEBOOM

Bakeshop Case, THE. *See* Lochner v. New York.

Balance of Trade. Following the mercantilistic[qv] tradition, an excess of merchandise exports over imports is usually called a "favorable" balance of trade, and the reverse an "unfavorable" balance, the original assumption being that the difference was paid in specie, the acquisition of which made a nation economically strong. This theory is fallacious but persistent. It confuses money with wealth and is incompatible with any demand-and-supply theory of the value of money. It leaves out of consideration all "invisible" items like capital loans, shipping charges, tourist expenditures, immigrant remittances and interest payments. Inclusion of these is necessary to calculate the more significant balance of international payments. In the long run the value of the wealth (including bullion[qv]) and services flowing out of a country tends to equal that of those flowing in except for excesses of bad debts or other losses in one direction or the other.

The American colonies had an "unfavorable" balance of trade because they were a new country and the settlers were constantly buying on credit or depending on England for capital for new undertakings. Mercantilistic England encouraged our extractive industries and discouraged manufacturing. In 1770 the colonies south of Pennsylvania had a nearly even trade balance with England; Pennsylvania and those north imported eight times as much from England as they exported to her, making up the difference largely by a very "favorable" trade balance with the West Indies[qv] and by their carrying business.

After the Revolution we still wanted English manufactures but found difficulty paying for them because England's markets were closed to many of our products and trade with the British West Indies was illegal. The new trade to China[qv], treaties with Prussia and Sweden and finally Jay's Treaty[qv] improved matters a little, but the development of cotton growing and the outbreak in 1793 of what soon became the Napoleonic wars helped much more. Both France and England bought heavily of our agricultural products and made increasing use of our shipping services. Between 1790 and 1807 our merchant marine[qv] engaged in foreign trade tripled. After 1806 England took successful steps to stop our commercial growth and from this the War of 1812[qv] developed. Following the war foreign manufactured goods flooded our markets and hurt our infant industries. Protection[qv] sentiment increased, producing progressively higher tariffs[qv] in 1816, 1824 and 1828. Thereafter rates fell (except in 1842). Higher tariffs here and abroad, a post-war depression and the greater interest in developing the West all cut down the rate of growth of our foreign commerce and its relative importance to domestic commerce. Foreign trade picked up after 1830. Europeans, particularly the English, invested approximately $250,000,000, much of it in our internal improvements[qv]. This ended abruptly with the Panic of 1837[qv] and defalcation by several states. Between 1838 and 1849 our trade balance was slightly "favorable." During the 1850's both imports and exports (notably cotton) expanded rapidly until the Civil War. Foreign trade[qv] declined during the war because of the Northern blockade[qv] and activity of the Southern cruisers.

During the prosperity following the war our foreign trade grew from $405,000,000 in 1865 to $1,164,000,000 in 1873. The Homestead Act[qv], wars in Europe, immigration[qv], railroad building[qv] and increasing use of agricultural machinery caused a rise in food exports. A five-year depression began in 1873. In 1874 our trade balance again became "favorable," largely because interest payments on foreign capital here exceeded new foreign investments. The annual balance has been "favorable" ever since 1876 except for 1888 and 1889. A great expansion of foreign trade began after 1897. Then our capital loans abroad grew nearly as fast as foreign loans to us. Tourist expenditures and immigrant remittances became important.

During the World War we supplied the Allies with enormous quantities of food and war materials. Between July 1, 1914, and Dec. 31, 1919, our trade balance was "favorable" by $18,600,000,000, $4,000,000,000 being paid in specie, $2,600,000,000 in returned securities, and the balance in capital loans, three-quarters governmental (*see* Debts, Foreign). In 1916 we ceased being a debtor nation and became a creditor.

The 1920's were a prosperous era. Since our high tariffs made imports difficult, the only way to continue to sell abroad was to make heavy loans. We loaned $12,000,000,000 during the decade, while foreigners invested $7,000,000,000 here. Of course a loss occurred from scaling down the war debts[qv]. Notable borrowers were Latin-American nations whose prospects were sometimes too optimistically regarded, and Germany, who was thereby helped to pay reparations[qv] to the Allies (*see* Dawes Plan; Young Plan), who in turn were able to pay us on their war debts. Then came the crash of 1929. Numerous Latin-American nations, largely dependent on the marketing of one or two commodities, defaulted. Our loans to Germany declined, and after the Hoover moratorium[qv] in 1931 Germany ceased paying reparations and the Allies gradually stopped paying their debts. Losses on foreign investments, however, were no greater proportionately than on domestic ones.

Foreign trade improved after 1933. Devaluation of the dollar stimulated exports, retarded imports and greatly increased our large stock of gold. Since 1934 numerous reciprocal trade treaties[qv] have lowered our tariff walls slightly and encouraged the flow of trade. This is desirable for many reasons, one being to help our debtors pay us. After a nation has been a creditor for some time it should usually receive back annually more in interest and returned principal than it makes in new loans. The United States is on the verge of having an "unfavorable" trade balance for this reason.

[J. P. Young, *International Trade and Finance;* E. L. Bogart, *Economic History of the American People;* C. Lewis, *America's Stake in International Investments;* Dept. of Commerce, *The Balance of International Payments;* also, *Statistical Abstract.*]

DONALD L. KEMMERER

Balcones Escarpment, The, is a geologic fault extending across Texas from Del Rio to Red River west of Denison. Visible on the surface eastward from Del Rio and northeastward from San Antonio to Austin, it continues below the surface to the east of Waco and Fort Worth. It very nearly divides Texas into two geographical regions.

L. W. NEWTON

Balfour and Viviani-Joffre Missions (1917). After the United States entered the World War, a mission headed by Arthur James Balfour, British foreign secretary, and another by René Viviani, French minister of justice, and Marshal Joffre, former commander of the French armies, visited the United States. The British discussed questions of the purchase of war materials, military equipment, merchant tonnage and co-operation of the British and American navies; they proposed the sending of American troops to France to be trained and incorporated in the British and French armies. Joffre, on the other hand, urged the creation of an American Army, even though this might take longer, and this plan was adopted. Balfour discussed terms of peace with House and then with Wilson, but it is not clear whether he disclosed specifically the terms of the "secret treaties" between the Allies.

[Blanche E. C. Dugdale, *Arthur James Balfour;* C. Seymour, *The Intimate Papers of Colonel House;* Frederic Palmer, *Newton D. Baker;* W. G. Lyddon, *British War Missions to the United States, 1914-1918.*]

BERNADOTTE E. SCHMITT

Balize was a pilot village and fortification (1722), on the principal mouth (then usually called Southeast Pass) of the Mississippi, about a half-mile from the Gulf of Mexico and nearly a mile below the bar at the entrance (then) to the river proper, roughly 110 miles from New Orleans. Built by the French as first line of defense for Louisiana, it afforded slight protection because the mud would not hold strong works, there was frequent demolition by storms and floods and other passes were negotiable by light craft. The Spanish maintained it, but the United States abandoned it for defenses some thirty miles upstream (Forts Jackson and St. Philip[qv]).

[P. de Charlevoix, *Histoire et description générale de la nouvelle France,* Vol. VI.] MACK SWEARINGEN

Ballads, American. When Prof. George Lyman Kittredge wrote, in the introduction of a volume of selections from Francis James Child's monumental work, *The English and Scottish Popular Ballads* (1904), that "A ballad is a song that tells a story or a story told in song" only one collection of American folk songs[qv] had been published (*Allen's Slave Songs of the United States,* 1867). Since that time more than 100 titles have been added to the literature of American balladry. Not all of the items in these books, of course, fit the definition of a ballad but they indicate the great richness of America's heritage of traditional balladry and an astonishing fertility in the production of indigenous folk songs. Versions of the so-called Child ballads have been found all over the United States, along with large numbers of the 18th and 19th century come-all-ye's. Often these ballads have been adapted to the locale that has preserved them and always new ballads have grown out of the traditional matrix. Among people, whether untutored or educated, whose lives are isolated, the desire for entertainment usually breeds songs that tell stories. American frontiers have been lonely.

In subject matter the ancient ballads and the indigenous product are generally widely different. The former sing of the highborn lady, the men of fortune and renown, while their American prototypes, composed by hard-handed miners, mountaineers, cowboys, sailors and lumberjacks, follow the pattern of the come-all-ye's and are peopled with working-class characters. Undoubtedly the most popular of indigenous types are the occupational ballads, the bad-man ballad, the murder ballad and the vulgar or bawdy ballad. In the occupational ballad the singer celebrates the hardships or the glories of some type of work or else he recounts a feat of daring, the tragic death of a worker, or some comic incident of camp life. "Foreman James Monroe," "James Bird," "The Buffalo Skinners," "Red Iron Ore," "Joe Bowers,"[qv] "Casey Jones" and "The Erie Canal" are familiar examples.

As the English loved Robin Hood because he took from the rich to give to the poor, so the American folk singer has commemorated Jesse James, Sam Bass, Pancho Villa and others. Indeed, the sympathies of the folk singer have always been with the rebel against society. Thus the 19th-century American ballad persistently attributes crime to the influence of a bad environment ("liquor and bad company") and then is likely to quote the criminal's confession where he apologizes for his deed. White ballads ordinarily run in this vein, although in the case of such horrible murders as that of Pearl Bryant or in the feud songs of the Southern mountains, the singers express their indignation at the deeds.

The vulgar ballad has, of course, not found its way into published collections, but there is no question as to the universal popularity of this type from the forecastle to the college campus. Transmitted by word of mouth and finding no occupational or class barriers, these ballads usually have fine tunes and are often couched in fresh and vigorous language.

American Negro ballads stand in a class by themselves, for while the main body of Negro songs are not strictly narrative in form, the race has produced America's most original and interesting narrative songs in English—"John Henry," "Frankie," "Casey Jones," "Po' Laz'us." Perhaps these Negro songs do not equal in grace and finish the older English lays, but in them are found the same fresh imagery, the same direct and incisive narrative technique along with new interest in the internal emotional problems of the characters. Certain work ballads, such as "Po' Laz'us" and "John Henry," orally composed and transmitted in big construction camps, have an epic vigor. Moreover, while the pioneer or occupational isolation that produced the best white ballads has been broken, the Negro community has kept its folk solidarity and has responded fruitfully to the influence of the radio and the phonograph by producing new songs of high quality.

America's heritage of Spanish, French and German ballads has been the subject of fruitful study in recent years. Surviving ballads in other foreign languages have received too little notice. The Library of Congress through aid from the Rockefeller Foundation and the Carnegie Institution has accumulated the music from field transcriptions of more than 5000 American folk songs and the work now goes forward from Government appropriations.

[Carl Sandburg, *The American Song Bag;* John A. and Alan Lomax, *American Ballads and Folk Songs.*]

JOHN A. LOMAX

Ballinger-Pinchot Controversy, THE (1909–11), was a bitter contention over the conservation^qv^ of natural resources. Early in the Taft administration an order of former President Roosevelt withdrawing from sale certain public lands^qv^ containing water power^qv^ sites in Montana and Wyoming was cancelled. Chief Forester Gifford Pinchot protested and publicly charged Secretary of the Interior Richard A. Ballinger with favoritism toward corporations seeking water power sites. Pinchot defended L. R. Glavis, Land Office investigator, dismissed for accusing Ballinger of favoring the Cunningham syndicate's claims to valuable Alaskan mineral lands. Pinchot likewise was dismissed. A joint congressional investigating committee^qv^ exonerated Ballinger. But failing to regain public confidence, Ballinger resigned. The incident widened the cleavage in the Republican party^qv^.

[F. A. Ogg, *National Progress.*]

GLENN H. BENTON

Balloons. The first balloon ascent in America was made by a Frenchman, Jean Pierre Blanchard, Jan. 9, 1793, at Philadelphia, in the presence of President Washington. In 1785 an American, Dr. John Jeffries, with Blanchard, made the first balloon crossing of the English Channel. John Wise, of Lancaster, Pa., was the most prominent American balloonist before the Civil War. His most successful flight was in 1859 from St. Louis to Henderson, N. Y., covering a distance of 809 miles in twenty hours. In June, 1861, a balloonist, Thaddeus S. C. Lowe, offered his services to the Federal Government. He organized an aeronautic corps, built five balloons, and rendered useful service in reconnaissance at Bull Run, in the Peninsula Campaign and at Chancellorsville^qqv^. During the World War captive balloons were used by the army for field reconnaissance and fire control, and by the navy for spotting submarines below the water's surface. The United States Weather Bureau^qv^ uses small, unmanned balloons for studying the direction and strength of air currents and for recording atmospheric conditions in the upper air.

[R. H. Upson and C. De F. Chandler, *Free and Captive Balloons; American Historical Review,* July, 1937.]

LOUIS H. BOLANDER

Ballot, THE. Originally derived from the Italian *ballotta,* a little ball used for secret voting, the word ballot is now applied to the voting papers, commonly called "tickets," used in elections. Historically ballots followed *viva-voce* choice of public officials. Common during colonial and post-revolutionary days the *viva-voce* method was defended as manly and open, placing a premium upon the practice of independent citizenship. It was attacked vigorously, however, because it permitted the wholesale intimidation of poorer electors. After innumerable state-wide controversies revolving around these opposing views, some of which persisted well into the 19th century, the older open method was everywhere supplanted by the ballot.

The ballots first used in American elections were provided by candidates or party committees. Occasionally they were tampered with in personal or factional interest ("phony ballots"); often they were voted under conditions making secrecy impossible. During the '70's and '80's of the last century election frauds of this character became rampant, especially in large cities. Reform was sought and in large measure achieved by the Australian ballot system under which ballots are provided and their genuineness guaranteed by the state. First used in the Louisville, Ky., municipal election of 1888, this system has now spread to all the states of the Union with four exceptions.

Owing to the inclusion of candidates for national, state and local offices, also to the choice by popular vote of executive and judicial as well as of legislative officials, the ballots used are long and complicated. Against this evil the Short-Ballot movement has made considerable progress. In form the ballots used in our states are either (1) of the party-column type, with or without emblems (*see* Emblems, Party); or (2) of the Massachusetts type in which candidates are grouped according to offices; or (3) of the Pennsylvania or hybrid type. Since 1892 voting by ballots has been giving way before the voting machine[qv] which is now in use in more than thirty states.

[E. C. Evans, *History of the Australian Ballot System.*]

ROBERT C. BROOKS

Ball's Bluff, Battle of (Oct. 21, 1861). Inconsequential as a military affair, this engagement had important results. Col. E. D. Baker (U.), Senator from Oregon, a personal friend of President Lincoln, was killed; the Union troops, through mismanagement, were defeated. Discontented Radicals[qv] and a critical public blamed McClellan (U.). Congress inaugurated the Committee on the Conduct of the War[qv] to investigate Ball's Bluff and other Union failures. McClellan, on orders from the Secretary of War, arrested Gen. C. P. Stone (U.), charged with responsibility both for the defeat and for Baker's death. No formal charges were ever made. After six months' imprisonment Stone was released by a special provision in the Confiscation Act, July 17, 1862[qv]. The Army of the Potomac (U.)[qv] questioned their leader's ability. "A fatal hesitation took possession" of McClellan. A movement against Richmond was deferred pending further preparation.

[*Battles and Leaders of the Civil War.*]

THOMAS ROBSON HAY

Baltimore, Battle of (Sept. 12, 1814). After the burning of Washington[qv], a British land force of 8000, commanded by Gen. Ross, attempted to capture Baltimore. Ross, killed in battle, was successfully opposed by a force of Maryland and Pennsylvania militia and volunteers.

[B. J. Lossing, *Pictorial Field Book of the War of 1812.*]

ROBERT S. THOMAS

Baltimore, Md. It was almost 100 years after the landing of the colonists at St. Mary's[qv] in 1634, the first settlement in Maryland, that Baltimore was founded, in 1729, on the Patapsco River, a tributary of the Chesapeake Bay. The new settlement was named in honor of Charles Calvert, fifth proprietor of Maryland, who held the hereditary title of Baron Baltimore, of Baltimore, in Ireland. While political and religious factors account in part for the founding of St. Mary's and of Annapolis, in 1649, the founding of Baltimore was due to the desire of the inhabitants of Baltimore County, in which the proposed town was located, to have a port in that vicinity. The site chosen on the Patapsco had an excellent harbor near grain and tobacco lands.

Although at first Baltimore grew very slowly, near the close of the 18th century the town ranked third in commercial importance, being surpassed in trade by only two ports, Philadelphia and New York. During the Revolution and the War of 1812, privateers[qv] built and manned in Baltimore played a conspicuous part. The bombardment by a British fleet of Fort McHenry[qv], which defended the town during the War of 1812, inspired Francis Scott Key to write the "Star Spangled Banner".[qv] After this war, the experience and knowledge gained by shipbuilders in that conflict and during the Revolution enabled them to develop a type of merchant vessel known as the Baltimore clipper[qv]. By the construction of the Baltimore and Ohio Railroad[qv], chartered in 1827, Baltimore retained much of the trans-Allegheny trade which the completion of the Erie Canal[qv] had threatened to divert. Baltimore prospered in the period between the War of 1812 and the Civil War. From the wealth acquired from trade, especially with the South, there arose a merchant class which dispensed a lavish but gracious hospitality.

[C. C. Hall, *Baltimore, Its History and Its People.*]

RAPHAEL SEMMES

***Baltimore* Affair,** The (Oct. 15, 1891), was an attack by a Chilean mob in Valparaiso upon a party of 116 sailors on shore leave from the U. S. S. *Baltimore;* two Americans were killed and several others seriously wounded. This hostility emerged from the mistaken feeling that the United States had sympathized unduly with the *Balmacedistas* whom the Congressionalists had overthrown. The new government did not punish the assailants and offered neither apology nor explanation until President Harrison laid the matter before Congress. This was the nearest the United States has ever come to actual conflict with a South American nation.

[H. C. Evans, *Chile and Its Relations with the United States.*]

OSGOOD HARDY

Baltimore and Ohio Railroad, The, was chartered Feb. 28, 1827, and built from Baltimore to the Ohio to counteract the prosperity that canals[qv] were bringing to the rival cities of Philadelphia and New York. It was planned originally to operate throughout its entire length by horsepower; with relay stations each ten miles for changes of steeds. The road was surveyed by United States Army engineers. Work on it progressed slowly and it was not until Christmas 1853 that it was completed to Wheeling, Va.

Steam power was first used in 1829–30. Interesting experiments were conducted in the development of locomotives and cars. The road played a dramatic role in the Civil War, particularly in and about Harpers Ferry^qv^. John W. Garrett, president of the road (1858–84), extended it westward to Cincinnati, St. Louis and Chicago; and eastward to Philadelphia and (by trackage rights) to New York.

[Edward Hungerford, *The Story of the Baltimore and Ohio Railroad.*]

EDWARD HUNGERFORD

Baltimore Bell Teams took their name from the small bells suspended in metal arches over the hames to speed the horses and sound warning on narrow, crooked roads. These teams hauled country produce to Baltimore and returned with goods for homes and local merchants. Such teams made regular trips from points as far southwest as Knoxville, Tenn., and operated till 1850 or later when they were superseded by canals and railroads. A few bell teams survive, chiefly on mountainous roads.

JOHN W. WAYLAND

Baltimore Clipper, THE, was a term applied to the fast topsail schooners developed in and around the Chesapeake Bay in the Revolutionary period and (later) to the square-rigged vessels having the same general lines which were built in the Chesapeake region. In post-Revolutionary days they came into general notice largely because their speed enabled them to be used effectively both in privateering^qv^ and in the slave trade^qv^. *Ann McKim* (1833) was the ultimate expression of the type and by some is regarded as the link between the Baltimore clipper and the clipper ship^qv^. Her length (143 feet) was great by prevailing standards compared to her beam (31 feet). She had the characteristic Baltimore clipper drag in that she drew eleven feet forward and seventeen aft. Her stem was sharp but her greatest beam was so far forward that she was bluffer bowed than the later clipper ship. Her freeboard was low and her carrying capacity was small and hence she was primarily a speed model. The three masts were tall and light with a sharp rake, but she was ship-rigged with courses, topsails, topgallant sails and royals on each mast.

[Howard Irving Chappelle, *The Baltimore Clipper, Its Origin and Development;* Jacques and Helen LaGrange, *Clipper Ships of America and Great Britain.*]

HAMILTON OWENS

Baltimore Councils, Provincial and Plenary. Ecclesiastical legislation in the Roman Catholic Church^qv^ of the United States began with a synod of the priests under Bishop John Carroll of Baltimore in 1791. The regulations adopted served to administer Church affairs until 1829, when the first Provincial Council of Baltimore was held. There were seven of these Councils (1829, 1833, 1837, 1840, 1843, 1846 and 1849). By the year 1852 the Church had been divided into several provinces and while provincial councils were held in these provinces under their archbishops, three plenary councils were held in Baltimore in 1852, 1866 and 1884. The legislation of these three national assemblies was concerned with explanations of Catholic faith, with regulations for the administration of the sacraments, with feasts and fast days, with clerical life and discipline, ecclesiastical property tenure and with Catholic education and social welfare agencies.

[Peter Guilday, *A History of the Councils of Baltimore: 1791-1884.*]

PETER GUILDAY

Baltimore Fire, THE (Feb. 7–8, 1904), the third greatest conflagration in American history, destroyed most of the central business district, over an area of 150 acres. Damages were estimated at $50,000,000 to $100,000,000. Better streets and more fire protection were indirect results.

[H. D. Northrup, *World's Greatest Calamities.*]

W. C. MALLALIEU

***Baltimore* Incident,** THE (Nov. 16, 1798). While convoying merchant vessels to Havana during naval hostilities with France^qv^, Capt. Isaac Phillips in the United States sloop *Baltimore* encountered a British squadron. Facing superior force, and with strict injunctions to avoid conflict with British vessels, Phillips, under protest, submitted to the mustering of his crew and the removal of all seamen without papers showing American citizenship (*see* Impressment of Seamen). Fifty-five were taken off, but only five were finally retained. Phillips was afterward summarily dismissed from the navy, and stringent orders were issued requiring American national vessels to resist forcibly any similar insult to the flag.

[G. W. Allen, *Our Naval War with France.*]

ALLAN WESTCOTT

Baltimore Riot, THE (April 19, 1861), occurred when Pennsylvania and Massachusetts militia, en route to Washington, were attacked by Baltimoreans who considered them invaders. The railroad was not continuous through Baltimore, horses drawing the cars from one terminal to the other. After a few troops had gone through, the connecting tracks were blocked with anchors and other obstacles, which forced later contingents to march. The crowd pursued them with stones, bricks and a few pistol shots. The militia, who had broken into a run, fired backward over their shoulders and forward at the people lining the street ahead of them. The mayor endeavored to quiet the crowd and finally, near the Washington terminal, the police succeeded in holding the people back until the troops entrained. Four militiamen and twelve civilians were killed and an unknown number wounded.

[George W. Brown, *Baltimore and the Nineteenth of April, 1861.*] GEORGE FREDERICK ASHWORTH

Bandits. Highway robbery was comparatively rare before 1800, and usually consisted of the holdup of a traveler or a late walker by a solitary rough; the professional bandit was unknown. After 1800, holdups of mail coaches and post riders took place occasionally, sometimes with violence. A mail carrier was killed in Illinois in 1810 and a stagecoach driver near Baltimore in 1830. In the Middle West there were river pirates such as those of Cave-in Rock^qv^, and between 1795 and 1800 the Harpe^qv^ brothers in Kentucky, and a little later the murderous John A. Murrell in the same region—he was one of those who robbed travelers along the Natchez Trace^qv^—were much feared. The Gold Rush^qv^ brought the scum of all the Western Hemisphere and Australia to California, and from 1850 on, robbery of stagecoaches^qv^, mounted express messengers and others was common. With the opening of the Idaho^qv^ gold mines in 1860, robbery began there and developed into a virtual reign of terror. From there, some of the outlaws moved to the new Montana gold mines in 1863, where they robbed and murdered until virtually eliminated by Vigilantes^qv^ two years later. In the 1860's and 1870's robbery was a commonplace in California, among the widely scattered Nevada mining camps, and in the Sierra Nevada passes. "Shotgun messengers," cool and deadly marksmen, rode on stagecoaches beside the drivers, to protect express and mail, and there were some hot battles between them and the brigands. The opening of the Black Hills^qv^ gold mines in 1876 launched another era of robbery, in which Sam Bass earned a reputation which he later enhanced by train robbery^qv^ in Texas.

East of the Mississippi banditry was a minor evil before the Civil War (1861–65), money being handled casually by express with little thought of danger; but a wave of lawlessness followed the war. A party of amateur robbers concealed themselves in a supposedly locked express car leaving New York on a January night in 1866, and decamped from it in Connecticut with $700,000 in cash, bonds and jewels. The first train holdup of record was perpetrated Oct. 6, 1866, in southern Indiana by the four Reno brothers, who had drifted into crime during the war. They and their gang continued these attacks, thus becoming the first organized band of train robbers in history. Train robbery next appeared in western Tennessee and Kentucky and in Nevada; and in 1873 the James-Younger gang took to it. The career of this band continued for ten years thereafter, or until Jesse James' death in 1883 (*see* Northfield Bank Robbery). They were succeeded in that region by the Daltons, whose career was finally ended in their attempted robbery of the banks at Coffeyville, Kans., Oct. 5, 1892, when two Dalton brothers and two others of the gang were killed and another Dalton captured. Bill Doolin carried on a remnant of the gang for three years thereafter. During the 1880's the Southwest swarmed with bandits and rough characters; stage and train robberies were numerous, even cowboys and townsmen of hitherto honest record sometimes taking to crime. Rube Burrow, a farm hand, was one who attained great notoriety as a train robber in Texas, Mississippi and Alabama, 1886–91, his career being ended by death. Around the end of the century the Hole-in-the-Wall gang, from an impregnable lair in the Wyoming mountains, harassed the Union Pacific Railroad^qv^. Dynamiting of express cars held by stubborn messengers began. During the decade 1890–99, the *Express Gazette* said that there had been 261 train robberies, in which eighty-eight persons were killed and eighty-six wounded. Express cars now began to be built of heavier steel, carrying massive built-in safes, with time locks or combinations known only at terminals. "Arsenal cars," guarded by squads of heavily armed men, began running on important routes. Through these measures train robbery became more difficult and gradually less common.

The World War and the passage of the Eighteenth Amendment^qv^ gave banditry a new impetus. Bootleggers^qv^ were preyed upon by "hijackers," who, from the violent seizure of truckloads of liquor, proceeded later to the capture of loads of silks, cigars and other valuable freight. Bank and payroll holdups and the robbery of jewelers were of daily occurrence, frequently accompanied by murder—this partly due to the fact that the robbers were now often half-crazed from the use of heroin. Organized gangs, such as those of John Dillinger, Alvin Karpis and "Pretty Boy" Floyd, functioned again, turning their hands either to robbery or kidnaping[qv]. The Federal Bureau of Investigation[qv] and the new but well-organized state police forces began, however, to make crime more hazardous. Dillinger was killed by Federal agents in Chicago in 1934, as were more than a dozen others of the most notorious brigands in the country during that year and the previous one.

[Alvin F. Harlow, *Old Waybills;* Oliver G. Swan, *Frontier Days;* Herbert Corey, *Farewell, Mr. Gangster. America's War on Crime.*]

ALVIN F. HARLOW

Bank, Federal Reserve. *See* Federal Reserve System.

Bank Deposits. Prior to the Civil War, banks and note issue powers were considered as more or less synonymous, with deposits holding a place of secondary importance except in some of the large cities. Statistics of bank deposits are fragmentary for this early period. Some data, however, are available.

The First Bank of the United States (*see* Bank of the United States) had $8,500,000 of individual deposits in January, 1809, and $5,900,000 two years later. Deposits of the Second Bank of the United States fluctuated between $5,100,000 and $22,800,000 in the years 1817 to 1836 inclusive. Statistics for other banks are not available for this period. Between 1837 and 1860, deposits of state banks[qv] ranged between $56,000,000 and $260,000,000, being generally below $100,000,000 prior to 1850 and above that figure after 1850. These figures do not include savings deposits, which amounted to $149,000,000 in 1860.

Since the establishment of the National Banking System, commercial deposits have assumed a place of far greater importance than bank notes as a medium of exchange. Between 1866 and 1913 national banks[qv] were the most important group of commercial banking institutions. Deposits of these banks increased with a high degree of regularity from $564,617,000 in 1866 to $6,051,689,000 in 1913. The latter figure compared with national bank note issues of but $727,079,000.

After 1913, with the establishment of the Federal Reserve System[qv], bank deposits increased rapidly. In June, 1914, total deposits for all banks of the country were $18,566,000,000, the deposits of state and mutual savings banks totaling about twice those of national banks. Deposits of all banks grew steadily from 1914 to 1930, reaching a total of $54,954,000,000 in the latter year. Then, as a result of the great depression (*see* Panic of 1929), this figure shrank to just under $38,000,000,000 in June, 1933, since which date it has again increased to more than $52,000,000,000 in 1937.

The figures just given include deposits in savings banks, as well as savings and time deposits in commercial banks. Perhaps the best figures to show the extent to which checking deposits are used as a medium of exchange are those for "demand deposits adjusted," as calculated for member banks of the Federal Reserve System. Since Dec. 31, 1917 (when this figure is first available), these deposits have increased from $9,972,000,000 to $20,387,000,000 on Dec. 31, 1937.

[J. T. Holdsworth, *The First Bank of the United States;* A. B. Hepburn, *A History of Currency in the United States;* Annual Reports of the Comptroller of the Currency; Annual Reports of the Federal Reserve Board.]

FREDERICK A. BRADFORD

Bank Failures. American financial history has been characterized by the greatest instability of any nation. The record of its bank failures from the beginning of the Federal period to the bank crisis of 1933[qv] constitutes the severest possible indictment of our methods. Compared to that of England or Canada the record is one of an appalling failure of either private business to regulate itself or of government to regulate in the public interest.

The statistics of state bank[qv] failures (1789–1863) are inadequate, but the losses were unquestionably large. John Jay Knox estimated the losses to note holders, alone, at 5% per annum. Even the famous Free Bank System[qv] of New York (1838) showed a record of fifty-seven failures. It is not possible to estimate the losses to depositors and stockholders for the period. It must be noted, however, that the note issue function of banks was then the most important.

The establishment of the National Banking System[qv] did not materially reduce the disaster. Most of the failures since 1863, to be sure, have been state banks but the list of national bank failures leaves nothing about which to boast. By 1882 eighty-seven national banks were in the hands of receivers and over 400 had gone into voluntary liquidation. In 1893, alone, the number of failures was over 600. Between 1893 and the establishment of the Federal Reserve System[qv] not a single year passed without a failure. From the creation of the Federal Reserve System until 1920 only one year passed without a national bank failure, 1918.

In the prosperous period of the 1920's the record did not improve. The number of failures for the period 1920–33 continued to illustrate the glaring defects of the American system of private business and government regulation. The period saw 11,000 failures as against one in Canada and none in England. In 1930 came the largest bank failure in American history—the Bank of the United States in New York.

The new legislation since 1933, particularly the limited Federal insurance of deposits (*see* Federal Deposit Insurance Corporation), has made the greatest improvement in our record of bank failures. Our banking structure, however, is still far from perfect. The history of bank failures in America is a testimony to the patience of the American people.

[John Jay Knox, *History of Banking in the United States.*]

LEONARD C. HELDERMAN

Bank for International Settlements, THE, evolved from the Hague Agreement of Jan. 20, 1930, which in turn was predicated on the report in March, 1929, of the Committee of Reparation Experts headed by Owen D. Young (*see* Young Plan). The bank was incorporated in and received its charter from Switzerland on Feb. 25, 1930. On March 31, 1937, there were thirty-nine stockholding banks, twenty-four scattered over Europe, fourteen in a syndicate led by the Industrial Bank of Japan, Tokio, and the First National Bank of New York. The bank began business May 17, 1930, with an authorized capital of $100,000,000, of which $25,000,000 was paid in at the outset. The board of directors is composed of the governors of the central banks of Belgium, France, Germany, Great Britain, Italy, Japan and a representative from the United States in addition to seven persons designated by each of the foregoing governors and nine directors elected by the other stockholding banks.

The chief objectives of the bank are to promote the co-operation of central banks, to provide additional facilities for international financial operations and to act as trustee in connection with international financial settlements entrusted to it. To achieve these objectives, the bank may perform practically all the functions ordinarily performed by a central bank, except that it is specifically interdicted from issuing notes, accepting bills of exchange, making advances to governments, or opening current accounts in the name of governments, or acquiring the predominant interest in any business enterprise.

[P. Einzig, *The Bank for International Settlements.*]

FRANK PARKER

Bank Notes have had wide use in the United States since the beginnings of the country. Prior to the introduction of national bank notes[qv] in 1863 the circulation consisted of state bank issues and notes of the United States banks (*see* Bank of the United States) during their chartered existences. Since 1866 state banks[qv] have been effectively prevented from issuing notes by a 10% Federal tax and, since 1913, Federal Reserve notes have assumed first place among bank-note issues of the country. Since 1935 the latter have been the only bank notes in general circulation.

[D. R. Dewey, *Financial History of the United States;* A. B. Hepburn, *A History of Currency in the United States.*]

FREDERICK A. BRADFORD

Bank of Augusta v. Earle, 1839 (13 Peters 519), involved the right of a Georgia bank to recover on a bill of exchange purchased in Alabama. The Supreme Court, speaking through Justice Taney, held that though a state might exclude the creature of another state, yet in the silence of any positive rule it would be presumed that foreign corporations were by comity permitted to make contracts. Taney's opinion became the leading authority on the law of foreign corporations.

[Charles Warren, *The Supreme Court in United States History;* G. C. Henderson, *The Position of Foreign Corporations in American Constitutional Law.*]

CHARLES FAIRMAN

Bank of Commerce v. New York City, 1863 (2 Black 620). The Supreme Court held that the state could not tax capital invested in Federal securities—thereby strengthening the financial position of the Government in the midst of the Civil War.

[T. R. Powell, Indirect Encroachment on Federal Authority by the Taxing Power of the States, 31 and 32, *Harvard Law Review;* Charles Warren, *The Supreme Court in United States History.*]

CHARLES FAIRMAN

Bank of North America, THE, the country's first Government incorporated bank, was chartered by the Continental Congress[qv] in 1781 and commenced operations in Philadelphia on Jan. 7, 1782. Organized by Robert Morris, the bank supplied vital financial aid to the Government during the closing months of the American Revolution. Original depositors and stockholders included Thomas Jefferson, Alexander Hamilton, Benjamin Franklin, John Paul Jones, James Monroe, John Jay and Stephen Decatur.

[A. W. Whittlesey, *Highlights in the 125-Year History of The Pennsylvania Company.*]

A. W. WHITTLESEY

Bank of State of South Carolina, THE. *See* South Carolina, The State Bank of.

Bank of the United States, FIRST AND SECOND. An act incorporating the subscribers to the Bank of the United States was approved by Washington and became law on Feb. 25, 1791. Under the provisions of the law the bank, which was to be located in Philadelphia, was to have a capital of $10,000,000, composed of 25,000 shares of $400 par value. One fifth of the capital was subscribed by the Government, the rest by private investors. Private subscriptions were limited to 1000 shares, and no shareholder was to have more than thirty votes. Foreign shareholders were not permitted to vote by proxy.

The management of the bank was vested in a board of twenty-five directors, elected by the shareholders. The board of directors was authorized to elect a president who was to receive compensation, the directors serving without pay. Only American citizens might be directors of the bank.

The bank was empowered to carry on a commercial banking business, was not permitted to deal in commodities or real estate and was limited in the interest it might charge on loans to 6%. The bank was authorized to issue circulating notes up to $10,000,000, the amount of its capital.

The Bank of the United States opened its doors for business on Dec. 12, 1791. It was efficiently managed and furnished the country, through its main office and eight branches, with sound banking service throughout its chartered life of twenty years. The bank served satisfactorily as fiscal agent for the Government and exerted a salutary controlling influence on the note issues of the state banks[qv] by refusing to accept state bank notes that were not redeemable in specie. In spite of the manifest advantages of a national bank, the charter of the First Bank was not renewed in 1811, doubt as to its constitutionality being the controlling factor. The bank therefore wound up its affairs, eventually paying shareholders $434 on each share held.

After a brief and unsatisfactory period of state banking, the Second Bank of the United States was incorporated under a law of April 10, 1816. The charter provisions were similar to those of the First Bank except that the capital and note issue limits were increased to $35,000,000. The President of the United States was also authorized to appoint five of the twenty-five directors.

The Second Bank was badly managed under its first president, William Jones, who retired in 1819. Langdon Cheeves, who succeeded Jones, spent his administration in getting the bank back to a sound position. In 1823 Nicholas Biddle assumed the presidency, and from then until 1833 the bank was well and capably managed, extending sound banking service to the country through its main office and twenty-five branches.

A dispute between Biddle and President Jackson led to the withdrawal of Government deposits in 1833 (*see* Removal of Deposits) and a severe contraction of the bank's business. Efforts to obtain a renewal of the Second Bank's charter proved futile and the institution ceased to function as a national bank upon the expiration of its charter in 1836.

[J. T. Holdsworth and D. R. Dewey, *The First and Second Banks of the United States;* R. C. H. Catterall, *The Second Bank of the United States.*]

FREDERICK A. BRADFORD

Bank of the United States v. Halstead, 1825 (10 Wheaton 51), concerned the applicability of state legislation regulating the procedural processes to Federal courts within the respective states. The Court upheld the power of Federal courts to alter forms of proceedings to meet changing conditions on general (implied) grounds relating to the judicial power and from specific legislative grants.

PHILLIPS BRADLEY

Bank of the United States v. Planters' Bank of Georgia (9 Wheaton 904). Mr. Chief Justice Marshall here (1824) enunciated the rule that a suit against a corporation chartered and partly owned by a state was not a suit against the state itself. "It is, we think, a sound principle that when a government becomes a partner in any trading company, it divests itself, so far as concerns the transactions of that company, of its sovereign character, and takes that of a private citizen." The rule was later applied to banks wholly owned by a state (*see* Briscoe v. Bank of the Commonwealth of Kentucky, 11 Peters 257).

[A. J. Beveridge, *John Marshall.*]

PHILLIPS BRADLEY

Bank Robbery. Bank burglars were but little heard of until the discovery of western gold in 1849. The Civil War gave another impetus to all forms of crime, including bank burglary. The burglars of those days occasionally rented a vacant store near the bank and from it tunneled underground to and through the vault wall; but they more frequently overpowered or corrupted the bank's night watchman and then picked or solved the vault's combination lock. The robbery of the Manhattan Savings Institution in New York of $2,747,000 in cash and securities in 1878 was a notable example of the last-named method. The introduction of the time lock by James Sargent in 1874 was a deterrent, and the gradual development during the next three decades of still better locks and almost impregnable steel vaults finally well-nigh eliminated bank burglary. In its stead, aided by the automobile, came the bank holdup, first introduced to America by the James gang at Liberty, Mo., in 1866. In two decades, 1914-34, 2500 banks were robbed in the United States—422 of them during the year ending Aug. 31, 1934. By that time, Federal and state police and detective agencies were reaching new high levels of efficiency and the yearly number of robberies began to decline. (*See also* Bandits.)

[Thomas Byrnes, *Professional Criminals of America;* Richard Wilmer Rowan, *The Pinkertons;* Herbert Corey, *Farewell, Mr. Gangster.*]

ALVIN F. HARLOW

Bankhead Cotton Act, The, approved April 21, 1934, was designed to supplement the cotton production control provisions of the Agricultural Adjustment Act of 1933[qv]. While not actually placing limits upon the growing of cotton by individual farmers, the act established a national quota and levied a tax of 50% of the central market price (but not less than five cents per pound) upon cotton ginned in excess of the individual quota. This tax was the essence of the act. Following the decision of the Supreme Court invalidating the Agricultural Adjustment Act, Congress repealed the Bankhead Act (Feb. 10, 1936).

[Agricultural Adjustment, 1933 to 1935, U. S. Dept. of Agriculture. Washington: 1936.]

R. P. BROOKS

Banking. The fundamental functions of a modern bank are discounting, receiving deposits and lending its credit in the form of "created" deposits or bank notes.

There were no banks in this sense in colonial times, but there were loan offices or land banks, which made loans on real-estate security with limited issues of legal tender[qv] notes.

Robert Morris founded the first bank in the United States, the Bank of North America[qv], chartered Dec. 31, 1781. It greatly assisted the financing of the closing years of the Revolution. The second bank was the Bank of Massachusetts, chartered Feb. 7, 1784, and the third was the Bank of New York which began without a charter June 9, 1784. By 1800 there were twenty-six state banks[qv] and by 1811 there were eighty-eight.

Alexander Hamilton's financial program included a central bank to serve as a fiscal agent, provide a depository for public money, and be a regulator of the currency. Accordingly, the First Bank of the United States (*see* Bank of the United States), the fifth bank chronologically, was founded Feb. 25, 1791. Its sound but unpopular policy of promptly returning bank notes[qv] for redemption and refusing those of non-specie-paying banks, together with a political feud, were largely responsible for the narrow defeat of its recharter bill in 1811. Between 1811–16 people and Government were dependent on state banks whose number increased to 246. Nearly all but the New England banks suspended specie payments in September, 1814, because of the war and their own unregulated credit expansion.

The need for a new central bank was soon realized, and the Second Bank of the United States was established April 10, 1816, with a twenty-year charter. Like its predecessor it incurred the enmity of state banks by constantly requiring them to redeem in specie[qv]. This policy, President Jackson's prejudice against banks and monopolies and Biddle's tactless decision to let rechartering be an issue in the 1832 election (*see* Campaign of 1832) led to the bank's demise. After Sept. 26, 1833, the Government made all its deposits with the "pet banks"[qv] until the independent treasury system was set up.

The country, again without a regulator of bank currency, entered upon a period of loose banking practice. Banks loaned heavily on real estate and resorted to many subterfuges to avoid redeeming their notes in specie. Conditions were especially bad in Michigan where the term "wildcat bank"[qv] probably originated. Everywhere bank tellers had to consult newspapers for the current discounts on bank notes and turn to the latest bank-note detectors to distinguish the hundreds of counterfeits and notes of failed banks. In these "dark decades" of banking there were, however, a few bright spots which offered some protection to note holders. There were the Suffolk Banking System of Massachusetts (1819–56), which kept New England notes at par; the moderately successful Safety Fund (1829–66) and Free Banking[qqv] (1838–66) systems of New York, the latter copied in fourteen other states; the Indiana (1834–59) and Ohio (1845–66) state banks; and the Louisiana Banking System[qv]

(1842–62) which was the first to require a minimum per cent of specie reserve behind liabilities.

Secretary of the Treasury Chase began agitating for an improved banking system in 1861, one important motive for which was the desire to widen the market for government bonds[qv]. The National Currency Act creating the National Banking System[qv] was passed Feb. 25, 1863, and completely revised June 3, 1864. It was based on several recent reforms, especially the Free Banking System's idea of bond-backed notes. The reserve requirements for bank notes were high and real-estate loans were forbidden. State banks at first saw little reason to join, so in 1865 Congress levied a prohibitive 10% tax on their bank notes, effective July 1, 1866, which drove most of these banks into the new system. There were 1644 national banks by Oct. 1, 1866. The use of checks had been increasing in popularity in the more settled districts before the Civil War and the desire of all banks to evade the new restrictions on notes doubtless speeded up the shift to this more convenient form of bank credit. The proportion of state banks increased again, exceeding the national after 1894. Improvements of state banking laws began about 1887.

The National Banking System had two major faults. One was inelasticity of the bond-secured bank notes. The other was decentralization of deposit reserves. There were three classes of national banks, and the lesser ones kept part of their reserves in their own vaults and deposited the rest at interest with the larger, especially with the New York City banks which, in turn, loaned a considerable part on the call money market. In times of uncertainty the lesser banks demanded their outside reserves, call money rates soared, security prices tobogganed and many good as well as weak banks were ruined by runs.

After the panic of 1907 Congress passed the Aldrich-Vreeland Act to permit emergency bank note issues and established the National Monetary Commission to investigate foreign banking systems and suggest reforms[qqv]. The Aldrich Bill, proposed in 1912, provided for a central bank with fifteen branches, but was never passed. The Federal Reserve Act, passed Dec. 23, 1913 (*see* Federal Reserve System), was the product of many compromises. It created twelve regional central banks co-ordinated by a Federal Reserve Board. All national banks had to join: others might. Comparatively few but the largest have. To correct the fault of reserve decentralization member banks have to keep all legal reserves

against deposits with their district Federal Reserve Bank. To provide a sound and elastic currency the act created the Federal Reserve notes, specifically backed by at least 40% gold and by other assets, originally intended to be chiefly short-time commercial paper. Federal Reserve banks can expand or contract credit by rediscount rate changes and open market operations[qv]. Some of these ideas were borrowed from Europe and aroused skepticism. The new system began operations Nov. 14, 1914, and convincingly proved its worth during the World War.

Although the system permitted limited real-estate and farm loans, it assisted chiefly commercial banking. Therefore agriculture was given twelve regional banks of rediscount for five- to forty-year loans by the Federal Farm Loan Act of July 17, 1916, and twelve more for nine months to three-year loans by the Agricultural Credits Act of March 4, 1923. These and other institutions were consolidated under the Federal Farm Credit Administration in 1933 (*see* Farm Credit Agencies, Federal).

Some authorities consider the easy credit policy of the Federal Reserve Board and the tendency of banks to invest, even speculate, heavily in capital securities, because of the unavailability of sufficient commercial paper, to have been an important cause of the 1928–29 boom and collapse. During 1921–29 there were 5714 bank failures[qv] and during 1930–32 there were 5102 more. Yet no reforms of consequence were passed. The Reconstruction Finance Corporation[qv], set up Jan. 22, 1932, helped stave off disaster temporarily, but the publicity of its loans and the strained condition of banks after four years of depression brought on the bank crisis of 1933[qv] culminating in the nationwide bank moratorium[qv] of March 6. The Franklin Roosevelt administration closed 2113 weak banks and enacted allegedly remedial legislation. The Banking Act of 1933[qv] divorced commercial and investment banking and set up a temporary Federal Deposit Insurance Corporation[qv]. The latter helped restore public confidence in banks. The Banking Act of August, 1935[qv], made deposit insurance permanent, eased restrictions on real-estate loans, enabling members to compete with state banks, lowered the quality of paper on which member banks might borrow, reorganized the Federal Reserve Board and renamed it the Board of Governors, and authorized it to increase legal reserves up to a maximum of doubling if necessary. Such a doubling was effected because our bank reserve percentages had increased so much, largely by reason of heavy gold imports and a small demand for bank loans, as to place a feared dangerous expansion of bank credit beyond the control of the Federal Reserve authorities. Legal reserves were reduced about one eighth after April 16, 1938, to induce credit expansion.

The recent trend in this country has been toward more government control of banking. A rapidly growing portion of banks' earning assets is in government bonds. At the end of 1938 two fifths of our 15,200 banks, holding over two thirds of the banking assets, were inside the Federal Reserve System, and 13,654 belonged to the Federal Deposit Insurance Corporation.

[H. White, *Money and Banking;* J. T. Holdsworth, *The First Bank of the U. S.;* R. C. Catterall, *The Second Bank of the U. S.;* D. R. Dewey, *State Banking Before the Civil War;* G. E. Barnett, *State Banks and Trust Companies;* E. W. Kemmerer, *The A B C of the Federal Reserve System,* 11th ed.; F. A. Bradford, *Money and Banking;* A. S. Pratt and Sons, *Digest of Federal Banking Laws; Annual Report of the Comptroller of Currency; The Federal Reserve Bulletin.*]

DONALD L. KEMMERER

Banking, Branch and Group. The First Bank of the United States (*see* Bank of the United States) had eight branches; the Second Bank had twenty-nine. Thereafter, what meager developments there were in branch banking before the 20th century took place under state authority.

The Federal Reserve Act of 1913 permitted foreign branches to a limited degree; in 1918 state banks having branches and wanting to join the Federal Reserve System[qv] were authorized to keep them; and the McFadden-Pepper Act[qv] of 1927 allowed national banks to set up a limited number of branches in the parent bank's city provided the state permitted branch banking.

During the 1920's hundreds of small state banks failed because of dependence on a single local crop or industry. Canadian and English experience indicated that branch banking offered a partial solution. Accordingly, the Banking Act of 1933[qv] permitted national banks to establish branches, under certain restrictions, in states allowing branch banking. This has attracted a few score state banks into the national system.

In 1936 eighteen states permitted state-wide branch banking, and seventeen permitted it within limited areas. California had the most highly developed systems. At the end of 1938 the 15,200 commercial banks in the United States had only 3581 branches, 1499 being national. Federal Reserve Banks had twenty-five branches.

Where branch banking is prohibited or discouraged, resort is sometimes had to group or chain banking, the distinction between them being that chains are owned by one or more individuals, and groups are owned by holding companies. The Banking Act of 1933 brought any group under Federal supervision if it owned even one member bank of the Federal Reserve System. At the end of 1937 there were 461 groups operating a total of 883 banks and having deposits of over $6,000,000,000.

[G. T. Cartinhour, *Branch, Group and Chain Banking;* D. R. Dewey, *State Banking Before the Civil War;* J. S. Lawrence, *Banking Concentration in the U. S.;* S. D. Southworth, *Branch Banking in the U. S.;* R. B. Westerfield, *Money, Credit and Banking; Annual Report of the Board of Governors of the Federal Reserve System;* F. A. Bradford, *Money and Banking.*]

DONALD L. KEMMERER

Banking, State. *See* State Banking.

Banking Acts of 1933 and 1935. The Banking Act of 1933, approved June 16, 1933, contained three groups of provisions as follows: (a) provisions designed to increase the power of the Federal Reserve Board[qv] to control credit, especially with respect to loans to brokers and customers secured by stocks and bonds; (b) provisions dealing with the commercial banks, of which by far the most important was the one providing for the insurance of bank deposits under the supervision of the Federal Deposit Insurance Corporation[qv]; and (c) provisions designed to separate commercial and investment banking functions by prohibiting commercial banks from operating investment affiliates and by prohibiting investment banking houses from carrying on a deposit banking business.

The Banking Act of 1935, approved Aug. 23, 1935, contained three titles. Title I amended the deposit insurance provisions of the Banking Act of 1933. Title II provided for a rather drastic reorganization of the Federal Reserve Board and changed the name of that body to the Board of Governors of the Federal Reserve System. Certain changes were also made in the management of the Federal Reserve banks. Powers over discount and open market operations[qv] of the Reserve banks were increased and centralized in the Board of Governors, and the discount base was very materially broadened. Title III contained a series of technical amendments to the banking laws governing the operations of the commercial banks.

[F. A. Bradford, *Money and Banking.*]

FREDERICK A. BRADFORD

Banking Crisis of 1933, THE, was the outcome of the large number of bank failures[qv] during the years 1931–32, combined with the wave of hoarding which swept the country and markedly weakened the banking structure. The attempts of the Reconstruction Finance Corporation[qv] to avoid final disaster were in large measure nullified by the publication of the names of borrowing banks, a procedure not calculated to restore confidence to frightened depositors.

Banking difficulties in Michigan finally caused Gov. William A. Comstock to declare a bank moratorium[qv] in that state on Feb. 14, 1933. Alarm quickly spread to neighboring states. Moratoria were declared in four other states by the end of February, and in seventeen additional states during the first three days of March. Finally, on March 4, banks in the remaining states closed their doors and the country was left devoid of banking facilities.

The situation was serious and prompt action was imperative. Congress, called in special session by President Roosevelt, passed the Emergency Banking Act of 1933 on March 9, thus providing machinery for reopening the banks. Under this act, only sound banks were to be reopened while those of questionable soundness were to be placed in the hands of conservators, to be opened later if conditions permitted.

The bank moratorium, which had been proclaimed by the President on March 6, was extended a few days to permit the provisions of the act to be put into effect. Sound banks were reopened on March 13, 14 and 15. By the latter date, banks controlling about 90% of the banking resources of the country were again in operation and the banking crisis of 1933 was at an end.

[J. I. Bogen and M. Nadler, *The Banking Crisis;* F. A. Bradford, *Money and Banking;* L. Sullivan, *Prelude to Panic.*]

FREDERICK A. BRADFORD

Bankruptcy Laws usually follow in the wake of a depression. The English bankruptcy legislation of Queen Anne's reign doubtless inspired the clause in the Federal Constitution (I, 8, 4) authorizing Congress "to establish . . . uniform laws on the subject of bankruptcies throughout the United States." This power, while it left the states free to pass insolvency legislation operative only within their respective limits, reserved the national field for Congress. It was nearly a dozen years, however, after the Federal Government was organized, before the power was exercised and then but meagerly. The act of 1800, mainly for bankers and merchants, failed to provide for voluntary bankruptcy and was repealed in 1803. Following the panic of 1837[qv], Congress passed a second act in 1841. It was an improvement on the first, in providing for voluntary bankruptcy, but was of even briefer duration, being repealed in 1843. The third act, that of 1867, remained in force until 1878. The panic of 1893[qv] and subsequent years furnished the background for the more elaborate and, as it has proved, permanent, legislation of 1898 (30 U. S. Statutes 544). Though amended in 1903, 1906, 1910, 1933, 1934 and 1938 its main provisions are still in force, after over forty years, and have been supplemented by rules and forms prescribed by the Supreme Court. The depression beginning in 1929[qv] occasioned substantial additions. The Municipal Bankruptcy Act of May 24, 1934, authorized local tax units to readjust their obligations where a substantial majority of creditors approve. The act of June 7, 1934, permits corporate reorganization under court supervision with consent of a majority of the creditors. (The amendment's moratorium clause was declared unconstitutional, 295 U. S. 555.) But the Chandler Act of June 22, 1938, has been pronounced "the first thoroughgoing revision" of the American bankruptcy statute in forty years. Sec. 77B of the original 1898 act, dealing with corporate reorganizations, was enlarged into a new chapter (X) and the S.E.C. (Securities and Exchange Commission) has created a new division which acts in an advisory capacity to the courts in such cases.

[*Collier on Bankruptcy*, 3d ed., 1934; *Am. Bar Ass'n Jnl.*, XXIV, 875, 880; U. of Chicago *L. Rev.*, V, I, 272, 398.]

C. SUMNER LOBINGIER

Banks, Land. *See* Farm Credit Agencies, Federal.

Banks, National, were first organized under the act of Feb. 25, 1863, entitled "An Act to provide a National Currency, secured by a pledge of United States stocks, and to provide for the circulation and redemption thereof." This act provided that any five or more natural persons might organize a national banking association by complying with certain routine requirements of the law and by fulfilling the minimum capital requirements which the law specified.

The act of 1863 was not a success. As late as Oct. 5, 1863, only sixty-six national banks had been organized, while the number of state banks[qv] was more than 1400. Consequently, the law was repealed and a new act, bearing the same title (the title National Bank Act was adopted in 1874), was passed and became law on June 3, 1864. It bore the same provisions relative to the organization of national banks as that of 1863.

Under the act of 1864 national banks might be organized with a minimum capital of from

$50,000 to $200,000, depending upon the location of the bank. Such banks might issue notes secured by government bonds and were authorized by law to carry on a strictly commercial banking business.

By October, 1864, the number of national banks had reached 508, but not until the passage of an act of March 3, 1865, imposing a 10% tax on the circulation of state bank notes, did the number of national banks increase rapidly. On Oct. 2, 1865, there were 1513 national banks, and the number had increased to 1644 a year later.

After 1866 the number of national banks increased steadily to 7509 in October, 1913, just prior to the passage of the Federal Reserve Act[qv]. At that time the national banks carried on the great bulk of the commercial banking business of the country. From 1913 on the number of national banks increased to 8249 in 1922, after which the number declined steadily to 5293 in June, 1937. However, the number of state and private banks[qv] also declined sharply. Total banking strength, as measured by total assets, of national banks increased slightly as compared with state and private banks between 1914 and 1937.

Since the establishment of the Federal Reserve System[qv], national banks have been permitted to carry on savings and trust business in order to allow them to compete with state banking institutions.

[C. F. Dunbar, *Theory and History of Banking;* F. A. Bradford, *Money and Banking;* Comptroller of the Currency, *Annual Reports.*]

FREDERICK A. BRADFORD

Banks, Postal Savings. *See* Postal Savings Banks.

Banks, Private, the original form of banking historically, are strictly defined as individuals or partnerships engaged in any of the functions of banking—deposit, exchange, loan, discount or sale of securities. Like any private business their obligations were originally protected by the personal liability of the individual or partnership. They were the product of the era of *laissez-faire*[qv] and developed in America on the model of the great English "houses."

With the growth of social control of business—and banking was one of the earliest areas of economic life to yield to this—the number of private banks has declined. Some states prohibit their operations entirely and in all there has been an increasing tendency to subject them to the same control as corporations[qv] and curtail the field of their operations. The function of note issue has been taken over by the Federal Government.

They continued to exist because of a real need for their services, the lack of regulation, and a tradition of personal integrity. Perhaps the most famous "house" of private bankers in America has been that of J. P. Morgan.

Some of the banks which developed before the Civil War with charters for speculative businesses such as railroads, insurance companies, canal companies, etc., may be regarded as private banks. An example of these was The Manhattan Company, organized ostensibly for the purpose of supplying New York City with water. Another example was "George Smith's Bank" of Milwaukee, which, organized to carry on insurance, converted itself into a bank.

[L. C. Helderman, *National and State Banks.*]

LEONARD C. HELDERMAN

Banks, Savings. The earliest savings bank in the United States, and the first legally sanctioned savings bank in the world, was the Provident Institution for Savings in Boston, which received a charter on Dec. 13, 1816. The Philadelphia Savings Fund Society began business on Dec. 2, 1816, but did not receive a charter until Feb. 25, 1819. Between 1816 and 1820 nine mutual savings banks were chartered, two in Massachusetts, two in Rhode Island, two in New York and one each in Pennsylvania, Connecticut and Maryland.

From these early beginnings the number of mutual savings banks grew to 634 in 1914 (June 30) with deposits of nearly $4,000,000,000. Since 1914 the number of such banks has decreased to 564 (1937), but deposits have increased to slightly over $10,000,000,000. These banks are located in eighteen states, but four fifths of them are in New York and New England.

After the Civil War stock savings banks were organized in various states. By June 30, 1915, the number of these banks had reached 1529. By 1935, however, the number had declined to 341, since which year separate reports for such banks have not been published. The total of savings deposits in stock savings banks in 1935 was slightly over $700,000,000. Other savings deposits are held in the savings departments of national banks, state banks and trust companies.

[F. J. Sherman, *The Modern Story of Mutual Savings Banks;* Comptroller of the Currency, *Annual Reports.*]

FREDERICK A. BRADFORD

Banks, State. *See* State Banks.

Banks, Wildcat, were the unsound state banks[qv] on the frontiers after 1800 and especially in the

1830's and 1840's. Since they profited by keeping their bank notes in circulation, some of them located at remote places (among the wildcats) where it was difficult to present the notes for redemption. There were many evils. Charter granting was mixed with politics and sometimes graft. Capital was often composed of promissory notes. Many banks had little specie. Loans were made recklessly, particularly to land speculators. Redemption of notes was evaded. Circulation was unsatisfactory. Good bank notes were at a discount outside the town of issue, and there were counterfeits, raised notes and notes of closed banks. The confusion was so great that businessmen had to refer to "bank note reporters" to determine the value of a note. The crises of 1818, 1837, 1841 and 1857 were marked by failures of these banks.

[Horace White, *Money and Banking.*]

JAMES D. MAGEE

Bannock War, THE (1878), was the last major uprising of Indians in the Pacific Northwest. It was waged by approximately 1500 malcontents, principally Bannocks and Paiutes^{qv}. Gen. O. O. Howard's troops engaged most of the hostiles, who, dissatisfied with reservation policies in Idaho and Oregon, fought under Chiefs Buffalo Horn and Egan. In the skirmishes, about eighty Indians and approximately fifty whites were slain. The majority of Indian prisoners were transferred to Yakima Reservation, Washington Territory, in 1879.

[G. F. Brimlow, *The Bannock Indian War of 1878;* R. Ross Arnold, *Indian Wars of Idaho.*]

GEORGE F. BRIMLOW

Baptists, the most numerous Protestant body in the United States, originated in England in the early 17th century and are not to be confused with the Anabaptists. They hold to five great principles: (1) separation of Church and State; (2) complete independence of the congregation; (3) the Scriptures as supplying the only standard of faith; (4) church membership based on a religious experience; and (5) immersion as the only Scriptural form of baptism. It has generally been held that Roger Williams was the father of the American Baptists and the church he founded at Providence (1638) was the mother church of the denomination in America. This is disputed, however, by recent Baptist historians, who have shown that Williams and his associates, though rebaptized, were not immersed. Rhode Island, however, became the center for the propagation of Baptist views and the first American college founded by Baptists was established at Warren, R. I., in 1764 (*see* Brown University). Baptists were severely persecuted in the New England colonies, outside Rhode Island, though after 1691 a larger degree of toleration was secured. Up until the Great Awakening[qv] Baptists flourished most in the Middle Colonies, due largely to English and Welsh immigration. The first Baptist Association in America, made up of five churches, was formed in Philadelphia in 1707. In 1742 this body adopted a Calvinistic Confession of Faith, and from that time forward the majority of American Baptists have been Calvinistic[qv] in their theology. By 1740 there were more than fifty Baptist churches in the colonies, the largest number being in New York, Pennsylvania, Maryland and Virginia.

As a result of the Great Awakening, the Separate, or revivalistic, Baptists, led by uneducated and unsalaried farmer-preachers, grew very rapidly in Virginia and North Carolina. This type of evangelism was particularly effective among the lower economic classes. By the end of the Revolution the southern Baptists were both numerous and influential. Separation of Church and State[qv] being one of the great Baptist principles, they naturally took a prominent part in the struggle to establish complete religious liberty in America. In both New England and Virginia, where that struggle was most severe, the Baptists were in the lead. Due largely to the farmer-preacher type of ministry, the Baptists proved one of the most effective of the churches in following moving population, and their churches were planted widely on every frontier.

In 1814 the General Convention of the Baptist Denomination in the United States for Foreign Missions was formed and in 1832 a similar organization for Home Missions was established. Opposition to missions[qv] developed on the frontier and after 1818 an antimission schism occurred, often called "Hard-Shells." Since Baptists were numerous in both North and South a slavery controversy arose, which in 1844–45 led to the formation of a Southern Baptist Convention. Since the Civil War the number of Negro Baptists has grown rapidly, largely due to the ease with which Baptist churches can be formed and the pageantry which they make of the rite of baptism by immersion. There are now more than 3,000,000 Negro Baptists, while white Baptists are twice as numerous in the South as in the North.

[A. H. Newman, *A History of the Baptist Churches in the United States;* W. W. Sweet, *Religion on the American Frontier: The Baptists.*]

WILLIAM W. SWEET

Baptists, Seventh Day. These literal Bible-followers, accepting the seventh day for Sabbath, started in Newport, R. I. (1671). A German group at Ephrata[qv], Pa., later joined them. They have 6807 members and sixty-eight churches in twenty-one states.

AUGUSTUS H. SHEARER

Bar Association, American, was organized in 1878, with members from all states in the Union, one of its primary objects being the improvement of legal education. It has exerted much influence in national legislation. To relieve pressure upon the Supreme Court calendar, it proposed and planned the United States Circuit Court of Appeals, created by Congress in 1891. It planned the consolidation of the United States Circuit and District Courts, accomplished in 1911. In 1920 it began taking an active part in the movement to provide legal aid for poor litigants. It fought the proposed Child Labor Amendment[qv] to the Constitution, but approved the uniform child labor laws of 1930.

[M. Louise Rutherford, *The Influence of the American Bar Association on Public Opinion and Legislation.*]

ALVIN F. HARLOW

Barataria is the name of a bay, a lake and a bayou on the Gulf coast of Louisiana, sixty miles south of New Orleans and forty miles west of the mouth of the Mississippi. The Barataria region is inseparably connected in history and legend with the smuggling operations of Jean and Pierre Lafitte, who maintained headquarters there from 1810 to 1815. Though regarded as pirates[qv] by the United States, the Lafittes claimed to operate as privateers[qv] under letters of marque and reprisal[qv] issued by the Republic of Cartagena, on the northern coast of South America, which had declared its independence from Spain in 1810. (*See also* Galveston Pirates.)

[Lyle Saxon, *Lafitte the Pirate.*]

WALTER PRICHARD

Barbados, settled in 1627, traded extensively—and not always legitimately—with New England, New York and Virginia throughout the colonial period, mainly exchanging sugar, cotton, molasses and ginger for foodstuffs. Moreover, many settlers went from Barbados to the Carolinas. Since the Revolution, the island has had little contact with this continent.

[C. Atchley, *The West Indies.*]

CHARLES F. MULLETT

Barbary Wars, THE (1801–5; 1815). After the Revolution the United States, following the example of European nations, made annual payments to the piratical Barbary States, Morocco, Algiers, Tripoli and Tunis, for unmolested transit of merchantmen through the Mediterranean. Constant difficulties, however, ensued, such as the episode of the *George Washington*[qv], and in 1801 Tripoli declared war and seized several Americans and their vessels. The war, entirely naval except for the Derna Expedition[qv], was very feebly prosecuted by the commanders first dispatched, Commodores Dale and Morris, but in 1803 Edward Preble was sent out with the *Constitution, Philadelphia*[qqv] and several brigs and schooners. His arrival galvanized the entire force into vigorous action. Making a naval demonstration before Tangiers which brought the Emperor of Morocco to make amends for treaty violations, Preble set up a strict blockade of Tripoli itself. Here on Oct. 31, 1803, the *Philadelphia* ran on a reef just outside the harbor and was captured by the Tripolitans, who a few days later floated her and anchored her under the guns of the citadel. But on Feb. 16, 1804, Stephen Decatur and eighty other officers and men recaptured and burned her in a daring night attack.

During August and September, 1804, Preble, in addition to blockading, harassed the Tripolitan shipping and fortifications with frequent attacks, in which the small gunboats fearlessly entered the harbor to enable the crews to board and capture piratical craft while the larger ships kept up a protective fire on batteries. Such activity reached a climax on Sept. 4, when the *Intrepid*[qv] with its cargo of gunpowder and explosive shells was maneuvered into the harbor at night. Apparently the explosion occurred prematurely, for all the participants were killed and little damage was done to the Tripolitan shipping.

When, soon after, Preble was relieved by Commodore Samuel Barron, and he in turn the next spring by Commodore John Rodgers, the Bey was ready to conclude peace. He was partly induced to this by the success of the Derna Expedition, which had captured Derna and was threatening to march on Tripoli itself. The treaty, somewhat hastily concluded, June 4, 1805, abolished all annual payments, but provided for $60,000 ransom money for the officers and crew of the *Philadelphia.*

Although payments were continued to the other Barbary States, the absence of American naval vessels in the years preceding the War of 1812 encouraged Algiers to seize American merchantmen such as the *Mary Ann,* for which $18,000 was paid Algiers, and to threaten others such as the *Alleghany,* where an increased payment was demanded and secured. Immediately after the termination of the war, Decatur and Bainbridge were ordered to the Mediterranean with an overwhelming force (*see* Decatur's Cruise to Algiers). By June, 1815, within forty days from his departure from New York, Decatur, the first to arrive, had achieved his immediate mission. Capturing the Algerian flagship *Mashuda* in a running fight off Cape de Gat and appearing off Algiers, he demanded and secured a treaty humiliating to the once proud piratical state—no future payments, restoration of all American property, the emancipation of all Christian slaves escaping to American men-of-war, civilized treatment to prisoners of war and $10,000 for a merchantman recently seized. As Tunis and Tripoli were forced to equally hard terms and an American squadron remained in the Mediterranean, the safety of American commerce was assured.

[G. W. Allen, *Our Navy and the Barbary Corsairs.*]

WALTER B. NORRIS

Barbecue. An outdoor entertainment distinguished by the serving of meat cooked, often as whole carcasses, on racks over open pits of coals. Apparently originating in Virginia about 1700, probably in connection with local fairs where foot-races, dancing, fiddling contests and other sport and pastimes were engaged in, the barbecue was especially popular on the southwestern frontier. During the first period of nationalism the universal celebration of the Fourth of July[qv] did much to shape the barbecue as an institution. Beeves were donated, and meat, bread, condiments and often beer or lemonade were served free to all comers. There were oratory (*see* Frontier Oratory), music, dancing and various sports, including tournaments, roping contests and other equestrian games. Candidates for public office were invited to expound their platforms, and they and their partisans were quick to take advantage of the barbecue as a campaigning device.

The barbecue survives in the West and Southwest, largely as a social institution.

MODY C. BOATRIGHT

Barbed Wire. "Free grass" and the open range[qv] were doomed by advancing values and population. Without absolute control of his land and stock, no ranchman could afford extensive improvement. If he provided ample water, the stock belonging to other men would tramp out his range in getting to it; if he bought high-grade bulls, his neighbors would get the use of them, while at the same time scrub bulls of other brands ran with his cows. Colorado alone of the range states enforced laws against scrub breeders.

Cattle, some rovers always excepted, would after being located normally remain on a given range; but drouths and blizzards made them drift, a hundred—sometimes two hundred—miles. Moreover, open range meant open road for thieves. "Slick" wire would not hold range stock; plank fences were too expensive; hedges of *bois d'arc,* wild roses and other growth proved impracticable. Only small bunches of cattle could thrive under herd, and herding was costly; the line-riders of the big outfits were helpless when northers and blizzards struck.

Following various patents on barbed wire, in 1873 J. F. Glidden, a prairie farmer of Illinois, gave it commercial practicability and the next year sold the first piece. Factories developed. Fencing proceeded outward from privately owned land near settlements. John W. Gates in the late 1870's put up a "bob" wire fence on Alamo Plaza in San Antonio to demonstrate its being "bull proof and horse high." Before the plains were fenced into pastures, cowmen co-operated to build drift fences across long distances. By 1890 most of the range land under private ownership had been fenced, but it was decades later before some of the Federal and state lands of Western states were fenced.

With fencing came wire-cutting "wars" in Texas and elsewhere, brought on by men accustomed to using land without owning it and resentful of being shut out. Many big outfits fenced in vast tracts to which they had no right. Bigfoot Wallace used to say, "Bob wire played hell with Texas." But barbed wire came to stay. It revolutionized the whole range industry, cutting off trail driving[qv] and free grazing, making the improvement of breeds and the watering of the range by wells and tanks inevitable. It developed stock-farming. (*See also* Windmills.)

[W. P. Webb, *The Great Plains.*]

J. FRANK DOBIE

Barbed Wire Patent Case, The (143 U. S. 275, 1892), settled a long dispute as to patent rights for the invention of barbed wire (twisted wire with coiled barb) between the assignees of Joseph Glidden and Jacob Haish. The latter claimed that exclusive rights could not be set up because there were various types of barbed wire in local use at the time the Glidden patent was granted. The court decided, however, in favor of this patent on the ground that Glidden had "taken the final step in the invention which has turned a failure into a (commercial) success. In the law of patents it is the last step that wins."

PHILLIPS BRADLEY

Bargemen is a term that was used interchangeably with keelboatmen, bargers and keelers, and applied to men engaged in operating river boats that traveled upstream as distinct from flatboats. French bargemen and American bargemen employed on the Missouri and upper Mississippi were also hunters and trappers. Most full-time bargemen worked on the lower Mississippi and the Ohio and its tributaries. After 1820 they gradually disappeared as the steamboat, turnpike and railroad took over transportation.

The bargemen were traditionally the roughest element in the West, prodigious drinkers, fighters, gamblers, pranksters and workers, and the respectable elements along the rivers are said to have lived in terror of them. Their chief pleasuring resorts were New Orleans, Natchez, St. Louis, Shawneetown and Louisville. They wore red shirts as a sort of occupational badge. A number of bargemen were famous in their day and Mike Fink became the hero of a cycle of legends.

[Leland D. Baldwin, *The Keelboat Age on Western Waters.*]

LELAND D. BALDWIN

Barnburners was the nickname of a faction of the Democratic party[qv] in New York State in the 1840's. They were first called Radicals and were the progressive element in the party. The name "Barnburner" was given them as early as 1843, and accepted by them at the State Democratic Convention of 1847. It was based on the story of the Dutch farmer who was willing to burn his barn to get rid of the rats. They opposed further expenditures for canals[qv], wanted a limitation on the state debt, and a direct state tax. They advocated a Constitutional Convention, and when it was called in 1846, they controlled it. In national affairs, they favored the Wilmot Proviso[qv] and opposed the extension of slavery[qv]. They seceded from the State Convention of 1847 and from the 1848 Democratic National Convention. They nominated Martin Van Buren for President and then united with the Free Soilers[qv]. This movement defeated Cass, the Democratic candidate. After this election they gradually returned to the Democratic party, but when the Republican party[qv] was formed most of the younger Barnburners joined, bringing elements of leadership and voting strength.

[H. D. A. Donovan, *The Barnburners.*]

AUGUSTUS H. SHEARER

Barn-raising is a custom representative of the combination of co-operative labor and social festivity common in frontier days. The custom still survives in some sections. (*See* picture and description of a barn-raising in York County, Pa., in *The Harrisburg Patriot,* Jan. 7, 1938.)

Before the day set for the barn-raising, carpenters cut the lumber. Great care is exercised, lest, on the day of the barn-raising, the pieces do not fit perfectly, and the carpenter's reputation be ruined in the sight of the men of the entire district.

On the day of the great event, all the neighboring farmers, with their families, assemble. In the morning all the men co-operate in erecting, with the simplest of tools, the framework of the barn. Prizes are sometimes offered for the exhibition of the greatest feat of strength. Dinner prepared by the combined efforts of the women present is then served. Later the occasion takes on a more strictly social aspect. The program usually includes games, athletic events and a dance. Wrestling, jumping competition and prize fighting have been common.

Barn-raisings have had most significance in sections of the Middle and West Central states where large structures were erected.

[Bristow, *Old Time Tales of Warren County, Pa.*]

H. H. SHENK

Barnstorming. In 1815, at the instance of N. L. Usher, of Lexington, Ky., a theatrical troup, which included Noah M. Ludlow, was led by Samuel Drake from Albany into the West. They often slept in barns and played in theaters that were little better than barns. William Turner, James Caldwell, Collins and Jones, Sol Smith, Mary Duff and Eliza Riddle were among the barnstormers who brought contemporary farce and melodrama as well as Shakespeare and Sheridan to Cincinnati, St. Louis, Nashville, New Orleans, and many smaller frontier centers in the days before railroads. By analogy, itinerant fliers and stunt pilots about 1912–22 were also called barnstormers.

[Noah Miller Ludlow, *Dramatic Life as I Found It;* William Dunlap, *A History of the American Theatre;* William Carson, *The Theatre on the Frontier.*]

HARVEY L. CARTER

Barnum's Museum. In December, 1841, P. T. Barnum bought Scudder's American Museum at Broadway and Ann Street, New York. This he enlarged as Barnum's American Museum, open weekdays at sunrise, with a single fee of twenty-five cents; exhibiting not only thousands of curios and relics but also living curiosities and "transient novelties"; with a "Lecture Room" seating 3000, in which plays were given. Fire destroyed building and contents, July 13, 1865. Barnum's less-famous New American Museum, opened Nov. 13, 1865, on Broadway between Spring and Prince streets, was also burned (1868).

[Bryan's edition of Barnum's autobiography, *Struggles and Triumphs.*]

G. S. BRYAN

Barrage. A curtain of fire, moving or stationary, designed to protect friendly troops while advancing or while in position. A *box* barrage forms three sides of a square and is customarily used to protect troops while making a raid on a portion of the enemy's line; a *rolling* barrage (referred to by the infantry as "creeping") is timed to lift its angle of fire and move forward as the infantry advances under its protection; an *anti-aircraft* barrage is defensive in character and is designed to protect a given area from enemy aircraft; a *balloon* barrage is a floating curtain of piano wire, suspended from captive balloons, used notably in the defense of London during the World War.

ROBERT S. THOMAS

Barrier Forts, Attack on (1856), was the first use of armed force against China by the United States. On Nov. 15, during intermittent warfare between the Chinese and the British, Commander Foote, in a small boat below Canton, was fired upon by the Barrier Forts. On the 20th, Foote retaliated by attacking the forts with a force of 287 sailors and marines, spiking the guns and blowing up the walls. The American loss was seven killed and twenty-two wounded. Although Secretary of State Marcy criticized the action as hasty, Foote's aggressiveness secured greater safety for Americans trading in China.

[J. M. Hoppin, *Life of Andrew Hull Foote.*]

WALTER B. NORRIS

Barron v. Baltimore. The issue in this case was whether the first ten amendments to the Federal Constitution[qv], and in particular the due process[qv] clause of the Fifth, were intended as restrictions on state as well as Federal authority. In 1833, in the last case participated in by John Marshall, the Supreme Court[qv] held that in view of the history of the adoption of the bill of rights[qv], the prohibitions were directed against the Federal Government but not against the states.

[A. C. McLaughlin, *A Constitutional History of the United States.*]

LEONARD C. HELDERMAN

Barter, strictly, is the exchange of goods for goods without using money, e.g., furs were obtained from the Indians for beads, liquor, firearms, etc. As the people on the frontier usually lacked money they bartered horses, farms, tobacco, etc. Less strictly but more importantly, barter is involved in transactions carried on in terms of money which utilize goods for part of the payment. The farmer's wife trades butter and eggs for groceries. The accounts are kept in money, but actually it is an exchange of goods for goods. Many real-estate deals are of this nature. The old radio or auto is part payment for the new one. Many security transactions involve giving old securities for new ones. Clearing houses of banks and stock exchanges involve a similar procedure. They offset the debits and the credits and pay only balances.

[B. M. Anderson, Jr., *The Value of Money.*]

JAMES D. MAGEE

Bartlett's (John Russell) Explorations were made in the years 1850, 1851, 1852 and 1853 in Texas, New Mexico, California and adjacent Mexican states, as United States Commissioner on the Mexican boundary question. Scientists accompanied the party and the results were published with interesting illustrations in 1854.

[H. R. Wagner, *Plains and the Rockies;* Bartlett, *Personal Narrative.*]

CARL L. CANNON

Bascom, Fort, was established on the Canadian River in New Mexico in 1868 by Gen. Getty acting under Gen. Sheridan's orders. Its purpose was to protect the frontier against raids of the Cheyenne, Kiowa, Comanche and Arapaho Indians[qqv]. It was abandoned in 1870.

[C. C. Rister, *Southwestern Frontier, 1865-1881.*]

CARL L. CANNON

Baseball evolved from the various bat-and-ball games which the early settlers in this country brought with them from England. It was the offshoot of a children's game actually called baseball in the 18th century, the old English game of rounders, and New England town ball. The origin of the modern game is often traced to new developments supposedly introduced by Abner Doubleday at Cooperstown, N. Y., in 1839, but there is no authentic evidence that he brought about any change in existing methods of play. A more important date in baseball's early history was the adoption in 1845 of a codified set of rules, embodying the more important features of the modern game, by the Knickerbocker Club of New York.

As in the case of every new sport introduced in the 19th century, baseball was at first a prerogative of the well-to-do, the gentleman amateur. But more democratic clubs than the old

Knickerbockers soon began to be organized in and about New York, and in the 1850's baseball was slowly reaching out to a wider public. It gradually superseded all older forms of the traditional ball game, although New England continued for some time to play town ball, and before the Civil War over fifty clubs were members of the National Association of Base Ball Players. Games were being played on regular schedule which attracted admission-paying spectators. When the champion Excelsiors, of Brooklyn, returned from a triumphal tour through the Eastern states, one of their games drew an estimated attendance of 15,000.

The Civil War interrupted this inter-club competition, but it provided a tremendous impetus for the growth of the game throughout the country. It was played everywhere behind the lines, and with the end of the war it was taken back by the demobilized soldiers to their home communities. Membership in the National Association jumped to 202 clubs in 1866. "The game of baseball," a contemporary sports writer stated in that year, "has now become, beyond question, the leading feature in the outdoor sports of the United States."

Professionalism began to invade the ranks of the players. The local club's desire to win led to the hiring of skilled players, and when the Cincinnati Red Stockings, a wholly professional team, toured the country in 1869 and won every game, the way was paved for the organization of baseball along new lines. The amateurs withdrew from the National Association and the professionals formed an organization of their own. Its failure to prevent gambling, the bribing of players, and operation of illegal pools for a time cast baseball under the shadow of intense public disapproval. The game was almost killed. But with the organization of the National League of Professional Baseball Clubs in 1876, made up of teams in New York, Philadelphia, Hartford, Boston, Chicago, Louisville, Cincinnati and St. Louis, professional baseball had a controlling body which effectively put its house in order. The National League stabilized the professional game, restored public confidence in the honesty of the regularly scheduled matches among league teams and gave all baseball a new standing in popular estimation.

Since that date it has continued to expand both as a professional game, drawing every year millions of spectators, and as an amateur sport played by thousands of teams throughout the entire country. While the National League worked out the immensely complicated system of major and minor leagues, franchises, player contracts and other business controls which still govern the professional game, colleges, high schools, Y. M. C. A.'s and local clubs organized amateur nines which competed with the keenest rivalry. Baseball became the national game because in its modern development it was a distinctively American product, and because it aroused both spectator and player interest to a greater degree than any other sport. While the professional has always held the spotlight, and in almost every way dominated the game, baseball has its roots in the small-town park, the village playing field and the city's vacant lot.

Until the opening of the 20th century, the National League had no real rival in the professional world. For a time it faced the competition of the American Association, and in 1889–90 the National Brotherhood of Base Ball Players represented a short-lived attempt on the part of the players themselves to take over control of the game. It was not until the organization of the American League ten years later, however, that two almost equally powerful major leagues were in competition. Their successful division of the field and the establishment, in 1903, of the National Commission brought about still further stabilization of the game, and inauguration that same year of the World Series, between the champions of the two leagues, added still more to popular interest in the game.

In the 1890's it was estimated that paid attendance at the games of the hundred-odd professional clubs organized under the National Agreement totaled approximately 8,000,000 annually. Two decades later A. G. Spalding placed the total for all major and minor league games at close upon 26,000,000, the majors accounting for 6,000,000. Neither estimate included attendance at college, high school or local amateur games. In the 1930's the broad, all-inclusive figure for annual attendance at baseball games has been estimated as high as 50,000,000. Obviously, exact statistics on the number of persons either playing or watching baseball are unobtainable. In recent years baseball has had to face far heavier competition from other sports, but its continuing popularity is attested on all sides. Among the contributing factors, both in baseball's growth and in its present standing, has been the immense publicity which has been given the professional game ever since the first reports of local contests began to appear in the New York papers of mid-century.

[A. G. Spalding, *America's National Game.*]

FOSTER RHEA DULLES

Basketball has the unique feature of being the

one popular sport played in this country which is truly American in its origins. It was invented, in 1891, by James Naismith, an instructor at the Y. M. C. A. Training School in Springfield, Mass. His purpose was to introduce an active but not too rough game which could be played indoors, without elaborate equipment, to take the place of outdoor sports curtailed by winter weather. It proved so practical that it spread rapidly. It was taken up by schools, colleges, athletic clubs and industrial organizations, while a modified game for women became equally popular in girls' schools and colleges. It today has its professional as well as amateur teams, although it remains primarily an amateur sport for young people, and it has been estimated that more people watch basketball than any other sport in the United States.

[John A. Krout, *Annals of American Sport.*]

FOSTER RHEA DULLES

Bateau, THE, was in general a keelless, flat-bottomed, sharp-ended craft, built of plank, and propelled by oars, setting poles or square sails and steered by oar or rudder. Large bateaux employed eighteen or twenty rowers and carried forty tons or more. Missouri bateaux were often called Mackinaw boats[qv]. Bateaux were superseded on the Ohio and Mississippi before 1800 by keelboats[qv].

[Leland D. Baldwin, *The Keelboat Age on Western Waters.*]

LELAND D. BALDWIN

Bathtubs and Bathing. The first mention of the use of bathtubs in the United States dates back to the early 1820's. The most advanced installation took place in Philadelphia between 1832 and 1837 when the Stephen Girard Estate built a row of model houses. This was made possible by the water supply provided by the Schuylkill Water Works. The water rate for a bathtub in 1836 was $3.00 per year. In that year, despite an effort to ban them on sanitary grounds (their use was prohibited between Nov. 1 and March 15 as a health measure), Philadelphia had 1530 bathtubs. In 1845 Boston made their use unlawful, except on the advice of a physician. Hartford, Providence and Wilmington made heavy water charges for their use.

The "rain bath" was introduced during the middle of the 19th century. In 1850 Harper and Gillespie of Philadelphia installed the first bathtub in the White House, for President Fillmore. It was not replaced until President Cleveland's administration.

By 1860 most first-class New York hotels had bathtubs. In 1930 there were bathtubs in 16% of the farm homes and 87.5% of the non-farm homes in the United States.

CAROL ARONOVICI

Baton Rouge (La.). Founded by the French about 1720 as an important military and trading post, it became English in 1763, Spanish in 1783 and was annexed to the United States as a part of the Louisiana Purchase in 1810, after the successful West Florida Revolution (*see* Baton Rouge, Seizure of). In 1822 it became the United States military post and arsenal for the southwestern district, and remained such until 1877, except during a part of the Civil War (*see* Baton Rouge, Battle of).

[A. Fortier, *Louisiana,* Cyclopedic, I.]

WALTER PRICHARD

Baton Rouge, Battle of (Aug. 5, 1862). To regain control of the lower Mississippi, the Confederates planned to recapture Baton Rouge, La., then occupied by Union forces. Breckinridge's (C.) land forces were to be supported by the ironclad ram, *Arkansas*[qv]. He attacked the town from the east and forced the Union troops to the levee where their gunboats protected them. Unsupported by the *Arkansas,* which had broken down, Breckinridge withdrew.

[Alcée Fortier, *A History of Louisiana.*]

W. B. HATCHER

Baton Rouge, Seizure of (1810). Baton Rouge, on the Mississippi River, was in a portion of Spanish West Florida (between the Mississippi and the Perdido) to which the United States mistakenly asserted title as a part of the Louisiana Purchase[qv], but of which it had not attempted to take possession. In September, 1810, American settlers in West Florida[qv] seized Baton Rouge, organized a convention, declared their independence of Spain, and invited the United States to annex their territory. President Madison disregarded their pretensions to independence, but promptly gave orders for the occupation of West Florida as territory belonging to the United States and Baton Rouge was occupied by American troops early in December, 1810.

[I. J. Cox, *The West Florida Controversy.*]

JULIUS W. PRATT

Battery, THE, southwestern tip of Manhattan Island and site of Dutch fortifications, so called because of the battery of cannon constructed there in 1693 by Gov. Fletcher. Later, it became a public park and was a popular pleasure ground and favorite promenade of New York citizens in the 18th and early 19th centuries. By 1858 it had fallen into disuse but by filling in it has been extended to an area of twenty-one acres including the Aquarium and historic landmarks.

[J. G. Wilson, *Memorial History of the City of New York.*]

A. C. FLICK

Battle Fleet, Cruise of the, Round the World (1907–9), was undertaken by order of President Theodore Roosevelt as a demonstration of national strength. The fleet, consisting of sixteen American battleships, sailed from Hampton Roads, Va., bound for San Francisco, on Dec. 16, 1907, under the command of Rear Admiral Robley D. Evans, by way of Rio de Janeiro and Magellan Strait. On May 6, 1908, the fleet reached San Francisco where, on May 9, Admiral Evans was relieved by Rear Admiral Charles M. Thomas. Five days later Admiral Thomas turned over his command to Rear Admiral Charles S. Sperry, who sailed from San Francisco for Hawaii on July 7. The squadron visited New Zealand, Australia, the Philippines, China and Japan, finally returning by way of the Suez Canal and the Mediterranean. It reached Hampton Roads on Feb. 22, 1909, after an absence of 434 days, of which 190 were spent in actual cruising. A month had been spent in Magdalena Bay in target practice and another month in Manila Bay in battle practice. The Battle Fleet visited every continent on the globe, sailed over every navigable ocean, and crossed the equator four times. The officers of the Fleet were entertained and feted by the rulers of nearly all countries visited, and naval greetings were exchanged with the warships of fourteen different nations.

[Franklin Matthews, *With the Battle Fleet;* Franklin Matthews, *Back to Hampton Roads;* R. D. Evans, *An Admiral's Log.*]

LOUIS H. BOLANDER

Battle Fleet, United States. *See* Fleet, The United States.

"Battle Hymn of the Republic," one of the most popular and inspiring of American patriotic hymns, was written (1861) by Mrs. Julia Ward Howe.

In the autumn of 1861 Mrs. Howe and her husband were in Washington, D. C., interested in hospital work under the Sanitary Commission[qv]. They had been outside the city on a mission in connection with their work and were returning in a carriage through an exceedingly dark night. They met a regiment of troops which was marching up the road and singing the familiar song known as "John Brown's Body," the music of which was written by William Steffe about 1852. Mrs. Howe remarked as the soldiers were passing that these were poor words to be set to such a glorious tune. Dr. Howe replied, "Julia, why do you not write better ones?" Mrs. Howe continued to turn the matter over in her mind and awakened from her sleep late that night when the words suddenly came to her, beginning "Mine eyes have seen the glory of the coming of the Lord." She arose and wrote down the entire hymn.

The poem was printed in the *Atlantic Monthly* for February, 1862. It at once became popular and spread over the entire country. Not only is it in all collections of patriotic American songs but is included in the hymnals of a number of churches as well.

[J. E. Richards and M. H. Elliott, *Julia Ward Howe,* Vol. I.]

WILLIAM STARR MYERS

Battleships. *See* Warships.

Battleships, Dummy. On Feb. 24, 1863, a scow with turret of tar-smeared barrel staves, wooden guns, clay furnace, pork barrel funnel and ludicrous mottoes painted across its false paddle box, floated down the Mississippi River by Federal seamen, caused the Confederates below Vicksburg to destroy the newly captured ironclad *Indianola.* A similar dummy released on a flood tide, Feb. 20, 1865, drew fire from Confederate batteries along Cape Fear River for several hours. The success of these facetious experiments was largely due to the sensation created by the monitor type of battleship.

[Richard S. West, Jr., *The Second Admiral, A Life of David Dixon Porter.*]

RICHARD S. WEST, JR.

Batts-Fallam Expedition (1671) was an expedition sent out from Fort Henry (site of Petersburg, Va.) by Col. Abraham Wood for the "finding out the waters on the other side of the mountains in order to discovery of the South sea." The leader was Capt. Thomas Batts, and the expedition was journalized by Robert Fallam. The party of five, including an Appamattox Indian chief, set out Sept. 1, 1671, crossed the Blue Ridge and the Allegheny range and pushed down the valley of Wood's (New) River to where that stream reaches the line of West Virginia, Sept. 17.

[C. W. Alvord and Lee Bidgood, *The First Explorations of the Trans-Allegheny Region.*]

SAMUEL C. WILLIAMS

Baumes Law, THE, one of a series of amendments to the New York Penal Code, sponsored by Sen. Caleb H. Baumes of Newburgh, was passed by the legislature in 1926, to combat the so-called crime wave that swept the country in the aftermath of the World War. Its provision for a life sentence for fourth offenders was then widely acclaimed, but is now regarded as arbitrary and frequently unjustified.

[National Commission on Law Observance and Enforcement, *Report.*]

W. BROOKE GRAVES

Bay Path, The, was a trail from the Connecticut River to Massachusetts Bay at or near Boston. Conversely, the same trail from the Bay to the Connecticut River would be the Connecticut Path. Some writers reserve the name Bay Path for such a trail in Massachusetts and that of Connecticut Path for one in Connecticut. There seems no question that from 1648 there was the New Path westward through Weston, Sudbury, Marlboro, Worcester, Brookfield and Brimfield to Springfield. Similarly, there is no question that after 1683 a Path ran southwestward from the vicinity of Boston to Woodstock, Conn., and thence westward to Hartford. Obviously the New Path was not used by the earliest settlers in the Connecticut Valley, but some claim that the second or southern route was the Old Path which was used by the Hooker party in 1636 and by the other early colonists. There is, however, considerable evidence that the Old Path followed a middle route coinciding in part with the eastern section of the second Path and with the portion of the New Path west of Brimfield. Competent recent authorities have tended to accept this middle route as the original Old Path used in the 1630's. But it must be admitted that the evidence is incomplete and not incontrovertible. On the other hand, the existence of the second route earlier than 1683 is not adequately supported by contemporary evidence. It is even possible that the original Old Path did not follow exactly any one of the three routes. All three routes assume a Path between Springfield and Hartford which would have been on the east bank of the Connecticut at least as far south as East Windsor.

[Florence S. M. Crofut, *Guide to History and Historical Sites of Connecticut;* Mathias Spiess in *Manchester* (Conn.) *Evening Herald*, Oct. 19, 1934; Levi B. Chase, *The Bay Path and Along the Way.*]

GEORGE MATTHEW DUTCHER

Bay Psalm Book, The, so called from its origin in Massachusetts Bay Colony^qv^, was the earliest book known to have been printed within the present boundaries of the United States. Begun in 1639 and finished in 1640, it was printed in Cambridge, Mass., by Stephen Daye, the first printer of the English colonies. Eleven copies are known to exist of which six are imperfect.

[C. Evans, *American Bibliography;* J. T. Winterich, *Early American Books.*]

CARL L. CANNON

Bayard-Chamberlain Treaty, The, drafted by a joint commission at Washington, Feb. 15, 1888, was intended to clarify the respective powers and rights of Great Britain and the United States in the waters of Newfoundland and the adjacent provinces. The Treaty of Washington^qv^, extending valuable privileges to American fishermen in Canadian waters, had been abrogated as of July 1, 1885, and more stringent and somewhat obscure provisions of the Convention of 1818^qv^ were now effective. Rigorous enforcement by the Canadian authorities, seizure and forfeiture of American vessels, retaliatory legislation, jingoistic fulminations by press and politicians, had created a situation which threatened peaceful relations. The new treaty provided for a joint commission to define American rights in Canadian waters, recognized exclusive Canadian jurisdiction in bays whose outlets were less than six miles in width, remedied several minor American grievances and promised further concessions should the United States remove tariff duties on Canadian fish. The Senate rejected the treaty on Aug. 21, 1888, but more than twenty years later when the protracted fisheries dispute^qv^ was arbitrated at The Hague, the substance of several of its more significant provisions appears in the award which that tribunal rendered against American claims.

[Joseph I. Doran, *Our Fishery Rights in the North Atlantic;* Allan Nevins, *Grover Cleveland.*]

W. A. ROBINSON

Bayard v. Singleton (N. C. Superior Court, 1787). This case is important because it is the first reported decision under a written constitution overruling a law as unconstitutional. (Four years earlier than cases cited in 1 Kent. Com., 450; State v. Glenn, 52 N. C. 324.) The defendant moved dismissal of the case according to an act of the legislature which required the courts to dismiss, upon affidavit, suits against persons holding forfeited Tory (enemy alien) estates. The court overruled the motion and declared that the constitution of the state gives every man a right to a decision concerning property by jury trial. If the legislature could thus alter or repeal the constitution it would thereby destroy its own existence, and might even take away, summarily, one's life.

[*North Carolina Reports*, I; H. T. Lefler, *North Carolina History told by Contemporaries.*] ROBERT W. WINSTON

Baynton, Wharton and Morgan (1763–98) was a firm of Philadelphia merchants which virtually monopolized the rich western trade at the close of the French and Indian War[qv] and which by its contacts in Philadelphia, Lancaster, Pittsburgh, Kaskaskia[qv] and London exploited the West in one of the most significant commercial enterprises of the day. Before the legal opening of Indian trade, it sent the first cargo of goods westward (1765) under protection of passes by George Croghan[qv], Deputy Superintendent for Indian affairs. This premature attempt to capture Indian trade infuriated the "Black Boys"[qv] who attacked the pack train and destroyed the shipment. Soon, however, the firm had 600 pack horses and wagons on the road between Philadelphia and Pittsburgh and some 300 boatmen on the Ohio.

Its unscrupulous business methods, Gen. Gage's curtailment of Indian trading posts and his restrictions on the Indian department, together with the collapse of trade due to illicit French suppliers and the growing competition of another Philadelphia firm, David Franks and Company, combined to cause a sharp decline in its fortunes during 1767. The company entered into voluntary receivership and withdrew completely from the Illinois trading venture in 1772.

To recoup its losses and those of the "Suff'ring Traders"[qv] of 1763, Baynton, Wharton and Morgan, with the firm of Simon, Trent, Levy and Franks, organized The Indiana Company[qv] to secure land grants for losses incurred through Indian attacks. Wharton and Trent represented their respective firms. Sir William Johnson's ingenious handling of the Indians at Fort Stanwix[qv] in 1768 resulted in the Six Nations[qv] ceding to this company 2,500,000 acres of land, now a part of West Virginia. Immediate objections arose, royal confirmation was withheld and Wharton and Trent were sent to London to negotiate for The Indiana Company. Here the claims of other groups brought about the formation of the Grand Ohio Company[qv] or Walpole Company (1769) in which the Indiana land grant was merged, but Wharton excluded Baynton and Morgan, thus incurring their bitter enmity. The outbreak of the Revolution caused this project to collapse. (*See also* Vandalia Company.)

[A. T. Volwiler, *George Croghan and the Westward Movement, 1741-1782.*] JULIAN P. BOYD

Bayonne Decree, The. *See* Napoleon's Decrees.

Bayou Teche Expedition was a Federal raid directed by Gen. Banks in April and May, 1863, from Brashear City (Berwick Bay) to Alexandria, La., on Red River, to disperse the Confederate state government at Opelousas and to prevent Confederate reinforcements being sent from that quarter to Vicksburg[qv], then besieged by Gen. Grant.

[A. Fortier, *History of Louisiana*, IV.] WALTER PRICHARD

Beall's Raid on Lake Erie (Sept. 19, 1864) was an unsuccessful attempt to capture the revenue cutter *Michigan* and free Confederate prisoners on Johnson's Island[qv], Sandusky Bay, Ohio.

[J. F. Rhodes, *History of the United States from the Compromise of 1850*, Vol. V.] CHARLES H. COLEMAN

Bear Flag Revolt, The (1846), climaxed a decade of suspicion and jealousy between the Anglo-Californians of the Sacramento Valley and the Mexican authorities. Unlike the American residents of Monterey and Los Angeles, many of whom were closely connected with prominent California families through business relations, friendship or even marriage, the American residents of northern central California formed a community by themselves. Restive under Mexican rule and over-anxious to assert their racial superiority, they had a deep-seated fear of their fate if the California authorities should get them completely under control.

Some color was indeed given to this fear by the treatment accorded the fur traders Smith and Pattie in the previous decade and especially by the deportation in 1840 of Isaac Graham and some forty of his friends. Accordingly it is not surprising that, when the settlers learned of the Hawk's Peak episode[qv] and Frémont's expulsion from California in March, 1846, they should have believed the rumors that the government planned to seize and expel all foreigners in the province.

Uneasiness gave place to alarm when the news came (later proved false) that 250 Californians were advancing on Sacramento. The Americans immediately repaired to Frémont's quarters at the Marysville Buttes where, in the middle of May, he had encamped on his return from Oregon. This much criticized defiance of the local authorities by Frémont was declared by him to be "the first step in the conquest of California." The next step was the seizure, early in June, by

Ezekial Merritt and a dozen other Americans of a large band of government horses which Gen. Castro had obtained from Gen. M. G. Vallejo at Sonoma and which were being driven to San José by way of Sutter's Fort^qv^. This was an act of war and it was decided that the third step must be the capture of Sonoma, the chief stronghold of the Californians north of the Bay Region. The actual capture of the quiet little pueblo at early dawn, June 14, 1846, was a rather ludicrous affair; "To whom shall we surrender?", demanded the kindly general's wife. After a scene of no little confusion and considerable imbibing of Vallejo's wine, simple articles of capitulation were arranged and signed.

Then followed the erection of the Republic of California under the leadership of William B. Ide. To signalize it, William Todd designed a flag from a piece of unbleached cloth five feet long and three feet wide. Facing a red star was a grizzly bear which gave both the flag and the republic its familiar name. A proclamation setting forth the justification and purposes of the revolution was prepared; but before the new government could get under way, July 10, 1846, the American flag was officially sent to Sonoma.

The actual accomplishments of the Bear Flag Revolt were thus of little importance, but had not the Mexican War^qv^ intervened, either "Ide or Frémont might have stood out as the creator of a new republic, the Sam Houston of the Pacific Coast."

[R. G. Cleland, *A History of California: the American Period;* W. B. Ide, *Who Conquered California?*]

OSGOOD HARDY

Bear Paw Mountains, Indian Fight at (Oct. 3–5, 1877). At the end of their long campaign starting in Idaho, June, 1877, the Nez Percé Indians^qv^ under Joseph (Hinmaton-yalatkit) were surrounded by Col. Miles' command in the Bear Paws of northern Montana. After a brave three days' resistance, Joseph surrendered, ending the Nez Percé War^qv^.

[Nelson A. Miles, *Personal Recollections.*]

PAUL I. WELLMAN

Bear River, Calif., gold deposits were discovered in July, 1848, some six months after the strike at Sutter's^qv^ mill. Some of the most picturesque mining camps in California collected on the river and its tributaries, including Red Dog, Dutch Flat and You Bet.

[O. C. Coy, *Gold Days.*]

CARL L. CANNON

Bear River, Utah, Battle of (Jan. 29, 1863). Indians, on friendly terms with the Mormons^qv^, had preyed upon Overland Mail Route^qv^ emigrants for fifteen years. To subdue and control them Col. P. E. Connor led California troops from Camp Douglas to Bear River. There, with scarcely 200 effectives, he fought four hours against 300 well-armed Indians, smashing their villages, capturing their animals and stores, and killing over 200 of them. His own loss was fifteen killed and forty-eight wounded.

[*War of the Rebellion—Official Records of the Union and Confederate Armies,* Series I, Vol. L, Parts I and II.]

ROBERT S. THOMAS

Bears, Bear Hunters and Bear Stories. When Lewis and Clark^qv^ in 1806 returned from their historic expedition, they published to the world, along with other wonders, accounts of the grizzly bear and its ferocity. A naturalist named it *Ursus horribilis*—and in hunters' stories the grizzly has ever since been *horrible,* though his familiar names, "Old Ephraim" and "Moccasin Joe," indicate truthful modifications of the reputation. The grizzly certainly would fight when cornered, and often he imagined himself cornered when he wasn't. Stories like that of Hugh Glass and his hand-to-hand fight with a grizzly became an enduring part of American lore. The fights between bulls and grizzlies arranged by early Californians were an American counterpart to English "bear baiting" but more heroic.

The discovery of the grizzly increased the fame of the more widespread black bear, known, indeed, to have killed a few men, though the "bear hug" is a fable. Bear hunters became a type as distinct as keelboatmen^qv^ or Indian fighters. In 1827 David Crockett of Tennessee was sent to Congress almost purely on his reputation as a "bar hunter"; he killed 105 bears in one season —and was soon talked of for the Presidency. Empowered by mother wit, he so narrated his exploits with bears that his autobiography remains an American classic. "Mighty hunters" like Wade Hampton of South Carolina followed Crockett. The tall tale has had no richer subject than the bear.

By 1925 dangerously approaching extinction, the grizzly lives on, not only in national parks but more nationally in the paintings of Western artists like Frederick Remington and Charles M. Russell, in many books, and in folk talk. Black Bruin's range has become exceedingly restricted, but he is known wherever nursery books and sportsman magazines are read or country people tell stories.

[J. Cecil Alter, *James Bridger;* Theodore H. Hittell, *The Adventures of James Capen Adams;* Joaquin Miller,

True Bear Stories; John G. Neihardt, *The Song of Hugh Glass;* Theodore Roosevelt, *The Wilderness Hunter;* Wm. H. Wright, *The Grizzly Bear.*]

J. FRANK DOBIE

Beaubien Land Claim, THE, was an effort to homestead a portion of the Fort Dearborn[qv] military reservation at Chicago. The claimant, Jean Baptiste Beaubien, had long lived on the tract as a trader, and in 1835 he entered some seventy-five acres of it at the land office. The commandant ignored this title and a prolonged legal contest ended in its rejection by the United States Supreme Court in 1839. Immense wealth hinged upon the issue and the contest aroused intense local public interest.

[*U. S. Reports,* 13 Peters, 498-518; Henry H. Hurlbut, *Chicago Antiquities.*]

M. M. QUAIFE

Beaufort, S. C., founded in 1711 on Port Royal Island in a region where Spanish, French and English had previously failed to maintain themselves, was the second permanent settlement in South Carolina.

[H. A. M. Smith, Beaufort, the Original Plan and Early Settlers, *S. C. Hist. and Gen. Mag.,* IX, 141-160, 1908.]

FRANCIS B. SIMKINS

Beauharnois, Fort, a French post and Jesuit[qv] mission, was erected in 1727 on Lake Pepin to keep the Sioux[qv] from attacking France's new line of communication between Lake Superior[qv] and the West; and to prevent the Sioux from allying with the Foxes[qv]. It was practically abandoned in 1728.

[Pierre Margry, ed., *Découvertes et Établissements des Français,* VI.]

GRACE LEE NUTE

Beaver Dam Creek, Battle of. *See* Mechanicsville, Battle of.

Beaver Dams, Battle of (June 24, 1813). Col. Boerstler with a detachment of about 600 men left Fort George[qv], the evening of the 23d, under orders to march by way of Queenston, Ont., to the De Cou house to disperse FitzGibbon's British irregulars and Indians. On the 24th the Americans were ambushed a little east of Beaver Dams and forced to surrender.

[Louis L. Babcock, *The War of 1812 on the Niagara Frontier.*]

ROBERT W. BINGHAM

Beaver Hats. America produced quantities of beaver fur, but men's beaver hats were all imported until the middle of the 17th century or after. Virginia in 1662 sought to stimulate manufacture by offering a subsidy of ten pounds of tobacco for every good hat made from native fur or wool. But once begun, hat manufacture grew rapidly. By 1731 the hatmakers of London were complaining to Parliament that New England and New York were producing 10,000 hats annually and exporting them not only to British possessions, but to Spain, Portugal, the West Indies, etc. In 1732 Parliament forbade American makers to export hats, even among the American colonies. Seven years' apprenticeship was also required and no Negroes were permitted to work at the trade. New England calmly ignored or evaded the law, which remained in force until the Revolutionary War. Silk hat manufacture began in earnest about 1835 and soon forced beaver out.

[H. H. Manchester, *Sixty Centuries of Hatmaking;* J. Leander Bishop, *History of American Manufactures, 1608-1860.*]

ALVIN F. HARLOW

Beaver Money (1849). Lack of currency in the Pacific Northwest led to the private coinage of gold dust into coins called "beaver money" because a beaver was pictured on each coin. They were also stamped with their weight, the initials of the partners of the issuing company, and the date 1849. These illegal, but useful, coins quickly disappeared from circulation because they contained 8% more gold than the United States coins.

[Charles H. Carey, *A General History of Oregon Prior to 1861.*]

ROBERT MOULTON GATKE

Beaver Trade. *See* various articles on the Fur Trade.

Becknell's Expeditions. William Becknell, sometimes referred to as the "Father of the Santa Fé Trail," set out from Franklin, Mo., for Santa Fé, N. Mex., June 10, 1821, on a trading expedition. He is believed by most authorities to be the first American merchant to reach the New Mexican capital after the establishment of Mexican independence. After a profitable trade he returned in January, 1822. His success was responsible for the rapid development of commercial relations with Santa Fé. He later made a second trip in which he departed from the regular trail by the Cimarron Division. This trip was memorable in that wagons were first used on the plains.

[W. J. Ghent, *Early Far West;* Wm. Becknell, *Journal of Santa Fé Expedition, 1821.*]

CARL L. CANNON

Bedford, Fort (Bedford, Pa.). Fort Raystown, built in 1757 by Col. John Armstrong as a frontier defense, was in July, 1758, much enlarged and strengthened by Col. Henry Bouquet for the use of the Forbes Expedition^qv^. Here Bouquet was joined in September by Gen. Forbes and the Virginia troops under Col. George Washington for the advance along the Forbes Road^qv^, which began four miles westward. Rechristened Fort Bedford (1759), it was the principal depot for supplies and troops between Carlisle and Fort Pitt^qv^. The fort withstood a six weeks' siege during Pontiac's Conspiracy^qv^, but in 1769 was bloodlessly yielded to James Smith's "Black Boys"^qv^. Dilapidated, it was abandoned before the Revolution.

[*Report of . . . the Frontier Forts of Pennsylvania,* I.]

E. DOUGLAS BRANCH

Bedini Riots, THE, were public demonstrations against the Papal Nuncio, Monsignor Gaetano Bedini, on Dec. 31, 1853, and Jan. 14, 1854, on the occasion of his visit to Cincinnati, Ohio. Nativistic, Know-Nothing^qqv^ and anti-Catholic prejudice had been aroused by press and speeches, prior to his arrival. On the night of Dec. 31 a disorderly mob marched to the Cathedral Rectory, but was dispersed after rioting had broken out and one citizen and one policeman had been injured fatally. The demonstration on Jan. 14 was attended by no fighting, but an effigy of Monsignor Bedini was burned and threats were made against the Catholic clergy and churches.

[M. E. Thomas, *Nativism in the Old Northwest.*]

ALFRED G. STRITCH

Beech Seal. A term applied to one of the popular methods of punishment employed by the Green Mountain Boys^qv^ during the controversial days when Vermont was known as the New Hampshire Grants^qv^ and the settlers rose in resentment against the efforts of New York to evict them from their lands, chastising offending agents with the pliable twigs of the wilderness, thereby ironically setting their seal, in allusion to the Great Seal of New Hampshire, upon their backs.

[Zadock Thompson, *History of Vermont.*]

LEON W. DEAN

Beecher Island, Battle of (1868). Col. George A. Forsyth, leading fifty experienced scouts, in search of Indians who had pillaged western Kansas, encamped, Sept. 16, 1868, on the Arickaree River, fifteen miles south of Wray, Colo. Attacked next morning by about 1000 Cheyennes and Sioux^qqv^, led by Roman Nose, the scouts moved onto a sandy island and with butcher knives and tin plates scooped out rifle pits. In the first Indian charge, Roman Nose fell, Forsyth was wounded, and Lt. F. H. Beecher was killed. The Indians made several unsuccessful charges, then settled to a siege. Despite wounds, death and the stifling odor from their dead horses, the scouts held on. Emissaries eluded the Indians at night and sought help. On the ninth day troops arrived. Five scouts were dead, eighteen wounded and the remainder almost exhausted.

[Geo. A. Forsyth, *The Story of the Soldier.*]

LEROY R. HAFEN

Beecher's Bibles was the term applied during the Kansas troubles^qv^ to Sharps Rifles^qv^. In March, 1856, at New Haven, Henry Ward Beecher addressed a meeting at which a subscription was taken to equip a company of free-state emigrants to Kansas. Beecher said that for slave holders in Kansas a Sharps Rifle was a greater moral argument than a Bible. The first rifle was subscribed by Prof. Benjamin Silliman, of the Yale College faculty, the second by the pastor of the church in which the meeting was held and Mr. Beecher pledged the last twenty-five for Plymouth Church, Brooklyn.

[J. F. Rhodes, *History of the United States.*]

JAMES ELLIOTT WALMSLEY

Beef Trust Cases. In 1902 three large packers —Swift, Armour^qv^ and Morris—formed the National Packing Company in an effort to secure control of packing houses in Kansas City, East St. Louis and Omaha. The Government promptly attacked these and three other concerns, charging monopolistic practices which had resulted in a large degree of control over the slaughtering and packing of meat. In 1905 the Supreme Court (196 U. S. 394) upheld the Government for the most part, but failed to order dissolution of the National Packing Company, and monopolistic practices continued. Thereupon the Government sought an injunction, but the individuals involved successfully pleaded immunity from criminal prosecution because they had previously been compelled to testify against themselves. In 1910 further attacks on the packers were again unsuccessful, but in 1920, after an extensive Federal Trade Commission^qv^ investigation, the packers agreed to dispose of their varied stockyards interests, their retail meat markets and the wholesaling of lines not directly related to meat packing^qv^.

[Harry W. Laidler, *Concentration of Control in American Industry.*]

R. E. WESTMEYER

Beekman Patent, The, granted April 22, 1697, by Gov. Fletcher to Col. Henry Beekman, was a tract sixteen miles square in Dutchess County, N. Y., embracing the present towns of Beekman, Union Vale, a portion of La Grange, and nearly all of Pawling and Dover. The death of Bellomont, Fletcher's successor, cut short an attempt to vacate the patent as an "extravagant grant." A new patent for the same land was issued by Cornbury in 1703.

[Frank Hasbrouck, *History of Dutchess County.*]

A. C. FLICK

Beer. *See* Brewing.

Bees, Husking, Quilting, etc. In the New England and Middle colonies and on the early and Midwestern frontiers various communal activities formed an important exception to the ordinarily individualistic habits of American farm families. The motivation was both economic and social. Log rollings and barn raisings*qv* necessitated collective effort; corn husking and threshing*qv* were most efficiently done by common endeavor. Machinery and specialized labor ended all these practices except for the threshing ring which continues where farms are not large and farming is diversified. Corn husking, cradling, threshing among men, sewing, quilting, apple paring among women, roused the competitive spirit, made sport of work, and gave public recognition to the champion worker. Courting opportunities were afforded the young people. The finder of a red ear at a husking bee was awarded an extra pull at the jug. Sociability, neighborliness and conversation were promoted. The educational counterparts of these activities were spelling bees*qv* and ciphering matches. Maple sugaring-offs in the North and cane sorghum boilings in the South made party occasions of work. The round-up in the cattle country was an adaptation of the same general principle. Competitive aspects survive in rodeos*qv* and various contests at agricultural fairs*qv*.

[P. W. Bidwell and J. I. Falconer, *History of Agriculture in the Northern United States, 1620-1860.*]

HARVEY L. CARTER

Beet Sugar. Though sugar beets were grown experimentally near Philadelphia about 1830 there is no record that sugar was made from them. A small factory built in Massachusetts eight years later proved a failure. Soon afterwards Mormon*qv* pioneers erected a mill in Utah but only succeeded in making syrup. After the Civil War high sugar prices encouraged experiments with both sorghum and beets. Machinery was imported from Germany and France for beet factories in Illinois, Iowa and Wisconsin, where a few tons of sugar were made, and a larger project was promoted in California. During the 1870's Maine and Delaware offered a bonus for beet sugar manufactured within their limits, and factories were built at Portland and Wilmington. Small establishments were also erected elsewhere in the East, but none lasted more than a few seasons. By 1880, however, the industry was on a commercial basis in California, and soon thereafter Spreckles, a sugar millionaire from Hawaii, and the Oxnards, prominent refiners, erected factories in California and Nebraska. In 1892, when the output reached 14,000 tons, representatives of six companies met in San Francisco and formed an association to promote the industry.

By 1910 more beet than cane sugar was made in the continental United States. Ten years later the output exceeded 1,000,000 tons and in 1936–37 it reached nearly 1,700,000 tons.

Today eighty or more active factories in sixteen states buy beets under contract from nearly 90,000 farmers. Climatic and soil conditions, the varying profit of competing crops and distance from the coastal cane sugar refineries, which make a product chemically identical with beet sugar, favor the concentration of the industry in the mountain states, where Colorado leads the nation's output, and in California, Michigan and Nebraska. Beet pulp, a by-product of sugar manufacture, is used for feeding cattle and fits into the economy of stock-raising communities. Many minors and immigrants, especially from Mexico, work in the beet fields during the crop season. The United States ranks next to Russia and Germany as the largest beet sugar producing country and even under present quota limitations makes more than one-tenth of the world's supply.

[U. S. Census reports; U. S. Department of Agriculture reports; U. S. Beet Sugar Association, records; V. S. Clark, *History of Manufactures in the United States.*]

VICTOR S. CLARK

Belgian Relief (1914–19) was the means by which some 7,300,000 Belgian civilians, inside the German army lines during the World War*qv*, received necessary food imports through the naval blockade. Created as a temporary committee in October, 1914, by a group of Americans, with the approval of their government, The Commission for Relief in Belgium (C.R.B.) became the neutral channel through which more than 5,100,000 tons of provisions and supplies passed into Belgium and were distributed by local Belgian committees. From 1915 some 1,800,000

French civilians in the occupied areas of northern France were included in the relief.

The functions of the C.R.B. were to secure basic foodstuffs by purchase or gift, to transport these commodities into Belgium and to guarantee their equitable distribution under the supervision of American or neutral volunteer workers. Delicate semidiplomatic relationships with belligerent and neutral powers, and public opinion widely mobilized, kept the door to Belgium open. Relief requirements were met by gifts amounting to $52,000,000 in cash and kind collected by volunteer committees in America, the British Empire and elsewhere, by British and French government subsidies totaling $314,000,000 and by American Government loans of $380,000,000 made to Belgium and France in 1917–19. Altogether the C.R.B. disbursed $894,797,000 with an administrative expense of less than half of 1% (.43%). The price level of breadstuffs in Belgium remained about 15% below commercial prices in surrounding countries.

From October, 1914, to July, 1919, Herbert Hoover, with his associates, directed and controlled the complicated operations.

[G. I. Gay and H. H. Fisher, *Public Relations of the Commission for Relief in Belgium;* G. I. Gay, *Statistical Review of Relief Operations.*]

PERRIN C. GALPIN

Belknap, Fort (Tex.), named for William G. Belknap, was built in 1850 on the Salt Fork of the Brazos River to afford frontier protection; also to guard the "Lower Indian Reserve" set aside by Texas. The tribes on the Reserve were the Caddo, Anadarkho, Waco, Tahwaccaro and Tonkawa.

[J. Pike, *Scout and Ranger*, ed. Carl L. Cannon.]

CARL L. CANNON

Belknap Scandal, THE (1876), was one of the series of scandals which marked Grant's second administration. Secretary of War W. W. Belknap's first wife agreed to secure a lucrative post tradership at Fort Sill[qv] for C. P. March of New York on condition that she should receive one-half the profits. The trader at the post paid March $12,000 a year not to take the place and March paid $6000 to Mrs. Belknap. After her death he paid the money to the Secretary. Just before a House investigation committee moved to impeach him, Belknap resigned. The impeachment trial in April and May resulted in acquittal, largely on the ground that the Senate had no jurisdiction over a resigned officer.

[W. B. Hesseltine, *Ulysses S. Grant, Politician.*]

W. B. HESSELTINE

Bell Telephone Company. *See* American Telephone and Telegraph Company.

Belle Isle, an island in the James River at Richmond used as a prison for enlisted men captured by the Confederacy. In use continuously after the Battle of Bull Run[qv], the prison held approximately 10,000 men by the end of 1863. At that time, because the prisoners constituted a drain on the food supply and were the objectives of several cavalry raids (*see* Dahlgren's Raid), the captives were sent to a new prison at Andersonville[qv], Ga.

[W. B. Hesseltine, *Civil War Prisons.*]

W. B. HESSELTINE

Belleau Wood, Battle of (June 2–July 7, 1918). The German 7th Army, under von Boehn, driving southward from the Chemin des Dames toward Paris, on May 31 approached the Marne at Chateau-Thierry[qv]. Just west of there the American 2nd Division (Bundy) hastened into support of the French 21st Corps (Degoutte), the left corps of Duchesne's French 6th Army. Forcing back minor French units, by June 3 the Germans uncovered the American front line, which stood fast and stopped them. On June 6 the Americans assumed the offensive. Against bitter resistance the 4th (Marine) Brigade (Harbord) recaptured Bouresches and the southern edge of the Bois de Belleau, while on its right the 3rd Infantry Brigade (Lewis) advanced nearly to Vaux.

Continuing their local offensive, the Americans took most of Belleau Wood on June 8–11, and despite desperate counterattacks completed its capture June 21. At noon, July 1, following an intense artillery preparation, the 3rd Infantry Brigade stormed Vaux and La Roche Wood. The division front, everywhere established on favorable ground, was turned over to the American 26th Division, July 9, the 2nd Division retiring to a support position.

[Charles R. Howland, *A Military History of the World War;* Joseph M. Hanson, *History of the American Combat Divisions, The Stars and Stripes.*]

JOSEPH MILLS HANSON

Bellefontaine was the first permanent settlement of English-speaking people in the Old Northwest[qv]. The spring which gave it its name, "la belle fontaine," was located a short distance south of the present town of Waterloo, Ill. The first settlers, mainly veterans who had served with George Rogers Clark, established themselves with their families at Bellefontaine in the fall of 1779. At an election held there in 1782 fifteen Americans voted. The Federal census of 1800 enumerated 286 inhabitants, making Bellefontaine the third largest settlement in the Illinois Territory. As Illinois became more populous, Bellefontaine, never a compact village, gradually lost its identity.

[C. W. Alvord, *Kaskaskia Records, 1778-1790;* C. W. Alvord, *The Illinois Country, 1673-1818.*]

PAUL M. ANGLE

Bellefontaine, Fort or Cantonment (1805–26), on the south side of the Missouri, four miles from its junction with the Mississippi, was built under direction of Gen. James Wilkinson, in the fall of 1805, by Lt. Col. Jacob Kingsbury and two companies of the First Infantry. Constructed on low land near Coldwater Creek, where a fine spring gave name to the place, it was moved after the flood of 1810 to the top of the hill and there served as military headquarters for the Middle West until the erection of Jefferson Barracks[qv] in 1826.

[Kate L. Gregg, Building of the First American Fort West of the Mississippi, *Missouri Historical Review*, July, 1936.]

KATE L. GREGG

Bellevue War, THE. W. W. Brown, who kept a hotel at Bellevue, Jackson County, Iowa, was believed to be the leader of a gang of outlaws in that vicinity. When Sheriff William A. Warren attempted to arrest Brown and several other men on April 1, 1840, a fight resulted. Four of the posse and three of the alleged bandits (including Brown) were killed and thirteen of Brown's band were captured. The following day the citizens voted on the penalty, dropping white beans in a box for hanging, red beans for whipping. The red beans predominated and the men were flogged and sent down the river.

[Harvey Reid, *Thomas Cox;* John C. Parish, White Beans for Hanging, in *The Palimpsest*, Vol. I.]

RUTH A. GALLAHER

Belligerents are states or organized communities which are engaged in lawful warfare. Strictly speaking, only sovereign states are legally qualified to declare war and to acquire the status of belligerents and to exercise in consequence the rights of belligerents in respect to neutral powers. But international law[qv] has frequently recognized the *de facto* belligerent status of protectorates and other dependent states; and it has also found it necessary to accord belligerent status to colonies in rebellion against the mother country and to other "insurgent" communities which have been able to establish control over a definite area of territory and to maintain a separate government or *de facto* independence over a period of time. Recognition by third states of the belligerency of an insurgent community gives to the insurgents the right to apply in their regard the law of contraband and blockade[qqv] and otherwise to exercise the rights of land and naval warfare. The recognition by President Monroe in 1822 of the belligerency of certain of the South and Central American colonies preceded the recognition of their independence (*see* Monroe Doctrine). A sharp controversy developed between the United States and Great Britain in 1861 over the recognition by the latter of the belligerency of the Confederate States, Great Britain claiming that the earlier establishment of a blockade by President Lincoln had been itself a recognition of their belligerency (*see* Prize Cases; Alabama Claims). In the case of the *Ambrose Light* a United States Circuit Court held in 1885 that acts of warfare committed by unrecognized insurgents were acts of piracy; but this position has been sharply criticized. The recognition by the United States on Sept. 3, 1918, of a "state of belligerency" between the Czech army and the Central Powers was based upon the necessities of war rather than upon the *de facto* character of the Czech government.

[H. W. Briggs, *The Law of Nations: Cases, Documents and Notes;* C. G. Fenwick, *International Law.*]

C. G. FENWICK

Belmont, Mo., Battle of (Nov. 7, 1861), was Grant's (U.) first Civil War battle and first defeat. Frémont ordered the attack on Belmont to prevent Polk at Columbus, Ky., from aiding the Confederates in Missouri. Steaming from Cairo, Ill., Grant landed five miles above Belmont and drove Gen. G. J. Pillow's men to the river and set fire to their camp. Polk, crossing with re-enforcements and aided by the Columbus batteries, drove Grant to his transports.

[U. S. Grant, *Personal Memoirs; Battles and Leaders of the Civil War.*]

W. C. MALLALIEU

Beloved Woman. This was a title bestowed by the Cherokee[qv] Indians on an outstanding woman of the tribe, who was thereby entitled to speak in councils and to decide the fate of captives. The most famous of these was Nancy Ward who frequently, like her uncle the great Chief Attakullakulla, proved her friendship for the white people.

SAMUEL C. WILLIAMS

Belt, Indian. *See* Wampum Belt, The.

Beltrán-Espejo Expedition, THE. When the

soldier-escort of the Rodríguez expedition[qv] returned from "New Mexico" (1582), the Franciscans[qv] on the frontier at Santa Bárbara (southern Chihuahua) were alarmed for the safety of two missionaries who had remained at Puaráy. With fifteen volunteer soldiers Fray Bernardino Beltrán started north (November, 1582) to rescue his colleagues. Upon reaching the Pueblo country, he learned that they had been killed; but the soldiers refused to return before exploring the country.

We have no account from Beltrán regarding what happened; our knowledge rests on later statements of soldiers, especially Luxán and Espejo. The latter, desiring to emulate Hernán Cortés by developing a "new" Mexico, largely financed the expedition and tried to dominate it. His report added much detailed information of the Pueblo country and people; his exaggerations regarding population, resources and mining prospects were somewhat discounted by Luxán.

The expedition failed in its immediate objective, but its favorable reports of the country strengthened the resolve of secular and religious authorities to colonize and evangelize New Mexico.

[G. P. Hammond and A. Rey, eds., *Luxán: The Espejo Expedition into New Mexico;* H. E. Bolton, ed., *Spanish Exploration in the Southwest.*]

LANSING B. BLOOM

Bemis Heights, Battles of. *See* Freeman's Farm, Battles of.

Bender Family, THE, consisted of a middle-aged man and wife, son and daughter (though the parentage is questioned) who settled in a prairie cabin in southeastern Kansas in 1871. Here they fed and lodged passing travelers, and killed an occasional one for his money. Suspicion fell upon them and they fled in May, 1873, barely escaping a citizens' posse. They were pursued into the Indian Territory[qv], but their fate remains a mystery. At least eleven bodies were found buried near their cabin.

[John T. James, *The Benders in Kansas.*]

ALVIN F. HARLOW

Benefactions and Gifts, strictly, include bequests but are best considered to be philanthropic donations made during the lifetime of donors. In 1889 Andrew Carnegie wrote: "The day is not far distant when the man who dies leaving behind him millions of available wealth, which were free for him to administer during life, will pass away 'unwept, unhonored, and unsung,' no matter to what use he leaves the dross which he cannot take with him. Of such as these the public verdict will be: The man who dies thus rich dies disgraced."

Carnegie distributed $350,000,000, or nine tenths of his wealth, during his lifetime in countless gifts including 8000 church organs, 3000 libraries, appropriations to 500 universities and colleges, and eight foundations (1896–1916) capitalized at $280,500,000. John D. Rockefeller's benefactions included $600,000,000 to five foundations (1901–23). The John D. Rockefellers, father and son, gave $50,000,000 to the University of Chicago; Sen. and Mrs. Leland Stanford $25,000,000 to Stanford University; George Eastman more than $25,000,000 to the University of Rochester and the Massachusetts Institute of Technology. The history of large American benefactions in the 1900's includes such other names as Jules S. Bache, George F. Baker, Curtis Bok, George G. and Ella S. Booth, Henry Buhl, Jr., Dr. Godfrey Cabot, James Couzens, James B. Duke, Henry Ford, Henry C. Frick, Charles Garland, Murry and Simon Guggenheim, Edward S. and Stephen V. Harkness, Charles Hayden, Anna T. Jeanes, Augustus Juilliard, W. K. Kellogg, Atwater Kent, S. S. Kresge, Lucius N. Littauer, John Markle, Israel Matz, Andrew W. Mellon, Gordon McKay, Gustav Oberlaender, Horace H. Rackham, Julius Rosenwald, Mrs. Russell Sage, Leopold Schepp, Caroline Stokes, Mrs. Henry A. Strong, Frank K. Sturgis, Charles R. Walgreen, Mrs. William Ziegler.

The donor of smaller sums contributes locally to various social welfare agencies and bodies, educational and religious institutions, perhaps a community trust or chest. For the decade 1921–30 the John Price Jones Corporation estimates the total charitable budget for the nation at more than twenty and three-quarters billions, of which foundations and community trusts may have contributed 9.16%. Of this huge sum, education received the largest share (43%); race relations, less than 1%. For the years 1930–37 American benefactions and gifts probably exceeded four and one-half billions. State and Federal distribution of great sums raised through borrowing and taxation has doubtless decreased but has not yet irreparably impaired the flow of private benefactions.

[Andrew Carnegie, *The Gospel of Wealth;* Frederick P. Keppel, *The Foundation, Its Place in American Life;* Hollis, *Philanthropic Foundations and Higher Education.*]

HOWARD J. SAVAGE

Benefit of Clergy was originally a plea exempting the clergy from criminal process of the

English royal courts, but ultimately it was a commutation of the death sentence in certain felonies for all prisoners who could read, which last requirement was dropped by the 18th century. In colonial times it was in general use in the South and occasionally in New England, notably in the famous "Boston Massacre"^{qv} case. Statutes abolishing this privilege appear after the Revolution, but until the eve of the Civil War it was still allowed in the Southern states, where its use meant sparing a master's valuable property in his slave.

[A. L. Cross, Benefit of Clergy in the American Criminal Law, Mass. Hist. Soc., *Proceedings*, LXI, 154-181.]

RICHARD B. MORRIS

Benning, Fort, Ga. Camp Benning (redesignated as Fort Benning in 1922) was established near Columbus, Ga., during the World War. By consolidation of the Small Arms Firing School (Camp Perry, Ohio), the Infantry School (Fort Sill, Okla.) and the Machine Gun School (Augusta, Ga.), the present model Infantry School was established at Benning in 1920.

[Charles J. Sullivan, *Army Posts and Towns;* William A. Ganoe, *The History of the United States Army.*]

ROBERT S. THOMAS

Bennington, Battle of (Aug. 16, 1777). Toward the middle of August Gen. Burgoyne^{qv} planned a raid on the American stores at Bennington. His purpose was fourfold: to encourage the loyalists^{qv}; frighten New England; replenish his stock of provisions; and mount a regiment of heavily equipped German dragoons. Accordingly, these dragoons, lumbering along on foot in their enormous jack boots and stiff leather breeches, were made the nucleus of the raiding force, which, under the command of the German Col. Baum, amounted, with Tories^{qv}, Canadians, Indians and a handful of English, to about 800 men. On nearing Bennington, Baum, learning that Gen. Stark had assembled about 1600 troops at Bennington to oppose him, sent to Burgoyne for reinforcements. Col. Breyman, with 500 men, was accordingly sent to his assistance. In the meantime Gen. Stark, hearing of Baum's advance, marched to meet him. On Aug. 15 it rained, and both armies remained in their lines. The following afternoon Stark attacked. Baum's command was too widely dispersed. His auxiliaries were scattered and his regulars, hastily entrenched on a hill overlooking the Walloomsac, were surrounded and most of them captured. In the meantime Breyman, ignorant of what was going on, approached. Stark, reinforced by Col. Warner with 350 men, re-formed and attacked. The Germans retreated and were pursued until dark. The Americans took about 700 prisoners. The fortunate outcome of the engagement did much to improve the morale of the American forces.

[H. B. Dawson, *Battles of the United States;* Hoffman Nickerson, *The Turning Point of the Revolution.*]

A. C. FLICK

Benton, Fort (1850–65). After 1830 the American Fur Company^{qv} established several trading posts near the navigation-head of the Missouri River. One of these, Fort Lewis (established 1844), a large, bastioned, log structure, was moved in 1846 to the site of the present town of Fort Benton, Mont., where it retained its original name until 1850, when it was renamed for Thomas Hart Benton, who allegedly saved the company from prosecution for selling whiskey to the Indians. The post was subsequently rebuilt with adobe bricks. During the Montana gold rush, beginning in 1862, Fort Benton became a main port of entry to the mines. A town with the same name sprang up around it and the fur company sold out to a mercantile firm in 1865.

[H. M. Chittenden, *The American Fur Trade* and *Early Steamboat Navigation on the Missouri River;* A. J. Craven, ed., Affairs at Fort Benton from Lt. Bradley's Journal, in *Contributions to Hist. Soc. of Mont.*, Vol. III.]

JAY MONAGHAN

Bentonville, Battle of (March 19, 1865). Gen. J. E. Johnston (C.), in command of the small Confederate force in the Carolinas, hoping to prevent a junction of Sherman (U.) and Grant (U.), here attacked the left wing of Sherman's army, which was moving rapidly northward (*see* Carolinas, Sherman's March through). Though outnumbered, Johnston succeeded in fighting a drawn battle, but lost at least 2600 men. Desultory fighting occurred during the next two days, but by the night of the 21st most of Sherman's army was concentrated at the spot, and Johnston retired.

[*Battles and Leaders of the Civil War.*]

ALVIN F. HARLOW

Bent's Fort, first known as Fort William, was founded by William Bent and partners about 1832, on the north bank of the Arkansas, some seven miles east of present La Junta, Colo. The founders are said to have previously built a temporary stockade farther up the river. Located on the mountain branch of the Santa Fé Trail^{qv}, Bent's Fort participated in both the mountain fur trade^{qv} and the overland commerce to Santa Fé, becoming the outstanding trading post of the Southwest. It was rectangular in form, about 180 by 135 feet. The walls, of gray adobe^{qv}, were two to four feet thick and fifteen high, with bastions at two diagonal corners. Within, low earth-roofed rooms faced an interior court. An adjoining adobe corral housed stock and equipment.

Cheyennes and Arapahoes^{qqv} brought buffalo robes and skins for barter at the fort and from it white traders carried wares to Indian villages. An annual wagon train^{qv} freighted furs to Missouri and returned with Indian goods. The fort outfitted trappers and traders, sheltered early travelers, was a depot for military expeditions before and during the Mexican War^{qv}. William Bent married a Cheyenne woman, reared his family at the fort and became Colorado's first citizen. According to unverified tradition, the Government desired the fort, but offered an inadequate price. Bent thereupon deserted the fort and partially destroyed it in 1849. Moving forty miles down the river, he erected Bent's New Fort, 1853. This structure, built of stone, he leased to the Government in 1859. Next year additional barracks were built and the post was named Fort Wise, after the governor of Virginia. In 1861 the name was changed to Fort Lyon, honoring Gen. Nathaniel Lyon. Floods endangering the buildings in 1866, Fort Lyon was moved up the river to its present location.

[G. B. Grinnell, *Bent's Old Fort and Its Builders.*]

LEROY R. HAFEN

Berea College Case, THE (1908), upheld the right of a state to require the separation of Negroes and whites in private schools; held that the right to give instruction is a property right^{qv} whenever such service is "rendered for compensation"; also held that it is a "part of one's liberty as guaranteed against hostile state action by the Constitution." Another case (1912), sometimes also referred to as the Berea College Case, dealt with tax exemption of service properties of educational institutions and held that the state cannot tax such properties.

[Berea College v. Kentucky, 211 U. S. 45; Commonwealth v. Berea College, 149 Ky. 95.]

EDGAR W. KNIGHT

Bergen Prizes (1779). Capt. Landais of the *Alliance*^{qv}, an American vessel of John Paul Jones' squadron in European waters, captured three British merchantmen (*Betsy, Union, Charming Polly*) in 1779. Bad weather forced Landais into Bergen, Norway. England requested and obtained restoration of the vessels from the Danish-Norwegian government. Jones, in person, demanded indemnification at Copenhagen. The Danish Premier, Count Bernstorff, negotiated with the United States for years. It was proved finally that an Anglo-Danish treaty (1660) obligated Denmark to England, hence under international law^{qv} she could not be forced to indemnify the United States. Congress reimbursed Landais in 1806 and the heirs of Jones in 1848.

[S. J. M. P. Fogdall, *Danish-American Diplomacy, 1776-1920.*]

S. P. FOGDALL

Bering Sea Fisheries. *See* Seal Fisheries.

Berlin, The Treaty of (1921), is the separate peace treaty between the United States and Germany, entered into after the Senate rejected the Treaty of Versailles^{qv}. This Treaty of Berlin is unique, first, because of its brevity, and secondly, because it is an "index-treaty," in that its provisions merely refer to provisions of the Treaty of Versailles which are either accepted or rejected by the United States. Provisions thus taken over were those with respect to colonies, disarmament, reparations and responsibility for the war. The most important features rejected were the League of Nations, the International Labor Organization^{qqv} and the boundaries provisions. Approximately two thirds of the Treaty of Versailles, including its harshest provisions, was thus accepted by the United States through the Treaty of Berlin.

[Treaty of Berlin, in *U. S. Treaty Series,* No. 658; Treaty of Versailles, in *International Conciliation,* No. 142, September, 1919.]

CLARENCE A. BERDAHL

Berlin Decree. *See* Napoleon's Decrees.

***Bermuda* Admiralty Case.** In 1861 Confederate agents in Liverpool were loading a British steamer, the *Bermuda,* with munitions for the Confederate Army when United States Minister Adams learned of it, and notified Foreign Secretary Russell. Russell replied that the Crown Admiralty law officers found the evidence insufficient to warrant interference; their law applied only to the equipment of vessels to be used as transports or cruisers, and not to the nature of the cargo. The *Bermuda* sailed, and safely ran the blockade^{qv} into Savannah (*see* Destination, Enemy, and Continuous Voyage).

[*Claims of the United States against Great Britain,* Civil War, Vol. I, pp. 759-61.]

ALVIN F. HARLOW

Bermudas, THE, have had close contacts with America from the first settlement by colonists shipwrecked on their way to Virginia in 1609 (*see* Somers' Voyage), down to the present day. From 1612 to 1615 the islands were included under the Virginia Company[qv] charter, but thereafter they had a separate history, first as a company colony and then under royal control. The settlers concentrated on tobacco (*see* Tobacco Contract, The) and the colony developed rapidly. Throughout the colonial period there was considerable trade with the mainland where, in addition, many Bermudans sought opportunities denied them in the islands. During the Revolutionary era the inhabitants opposed British colonial policy and sent delegates to the Continental Congress[qv] to secure relief from the trade embargo against loyal colonies. They achieved their end by furnishing powder and other supplies to the rebels.

[Hudson Strode, *The Story of Bermuda.*]

CHARLES F. MULLETT

Bernard, Fort, was a small trading post between Horse Creek and Fort Laramie[qv] on the Oregon Trail[qv]. It was noted by many overland emigrants before and after the California gold rush[qv] of 1849, but there is no definite information about the owner or how long it continued. A trappers' trail from Bent's Fort[qv] on the south joined the Oregon Trail at this post. Taos and Santa Fé[qqv] traders freighted flour here to trade to emigrants bound for the coast.

[A. B. Hulbert, *Forty-Niners.*]

CARL L. CANNON

Bessemer Steel. *See* Iron and Steel Industry.

Best Sellers. Any book which outsells its competitors, or the author of such a book, is named a best seller. Unhappily sharp trade practices and the suppression of actual sales figures tend to render the term meaningless in present-day publishers' advertising. Through the years, however, certain books have outdistanced others; their records are fairly well authenticated. *The Holy Bible*[qv], distributed in every known dialect, probably outdistances all other books; certainly its circulation in the United States is highest. Second in volume is Noah Webster's *Blue-Backed Speller*[qv] of which nearly 100,000,000 copies have been sold. Other schoolbooks, like *The New-England Primer,* "Peter Parley's" and *McGuffey's Readers*[qqv], sold beyond the million mark in the first half of the 19th century. Tract society publications frequently reached astonishing totals. Mason L. Weems' *Life of Washington* (1800), which the author peddled over the country, was reprinted some fifty times. The first American novel to reach a sale totaling a million copies was Harriet Beecher Stowe's *Uncle Tom's Cabin*[qv] (1852), often considered the firebrand of the Civil War. The largest sale of any work of fiction has been attained by the Rev. Dr. Charles Monroe Sheldon's *In His Steps* (1899), which, because of a defective copyright, was issued simultaneously by sixteen different publishers. Other novels with a circulation of a million and a half or more include Mark Twain's *Tom Sawyer* (1876), Lew Wallace's *Ben Hur* (1880), Owen Wister's *The Virginian* (1902), Jack London's *Call of the Wild* (1903), Harold Bell Wright's *The Winning of Barbara Worth* (1911) and Gene Stratton Porter's *The Girl of the Limberlost* (1909), *The Harvester* (1911), *Freckles* (1912) and *Laddie* (1913). Novels selling beyond a million copies include E. N. Westcott's *David Harum* (1898), J. W. Fox, Jr.'s *The Little Shepherd of Kingdom Come* (1903) and *The Trail of the Lonesome Pine* (1908) and Margaret Mitchell's *Gone with the Wind* (1936). Many other novels passed the half-million mark. Among college textbooks Edwin C. Woolley's *Handbook of Composition* (1907) and Richard T. Ely's *Principles of Economics* (1904) have sold more than a million copies and after thirty years still command large sales. Similarly leading its field is *The Boston Cooking School Cook Book* (1896). The book clubs in recent years have tended to bring into temporary prominence books thus distributed and to give them a factitious best-seller appearance.

HARRY R. WARFEL

Betharaba, the first town planted by German Moravians[qv] from Pennsylvania in Wachovia, N. C., was begun in 1753. Its early settlers were noted for advanced agricultural practices, especially their "Medicine Garden," which produced over fifty kinds of herbs. Betharaba grew slowly and today (1938) it is only a small village, known locally as "Old Town."

[J. H. Clewell, *History of Wachovia.*]

HUGH T. LEFLER

Bethel Community (1844–79) was a minor communistic experiment established in Shelby County, Mo., by William Keil accompanied by followers (chiefly German) from Ohio and Pittsburgh, Pa. Keil preached moral living, subscribing to no religious faith, and dominated an unincorporated, self-sustaining, orderly, prosperous community which expanded to four towns. Property and labor were shared, though private earnings were allowed. A sister colony was fostered in Aurora, Ore., in 1855. Both dissolved, dividing their property upon Keil's death.

[Robert J. Hendricks, *Bethel and Aurora.*]

FLOYD C. SHOEMAKER

Bethesda, House of Mercy, was what Rev. George Whitefield called the orphanage and school that he began to build near Savannah, 1740. Although his Georgia project outlived the great Awakener, it faltered before 1800. Savannah's venerable Union Society, sponsor of present Bethesda, revived the use of the site for orphanage purposes, 1855.

[E. W. G. Boogher, *Secondary Education in Georgia, 1732-1858.*]

H. B. FANT

Bible, THE. It is a fact of large historical importance that the appearance of the two most widely used of the early English translations of the Bible was contemporaneous with the beginnings of English colonization of America. The Genevan Bible, the work of exiled Protestant scholars who had fled to Geneva to escape Queen Mary's persecutions, was in fact the Puritan's Bible. Its convenient size and relative cheapness, together with its verse divisions and Calvinistic notes, gave it an immense popularity. From the date of its first publication in 1560 to 1640 it passed through 160 editions, and was, undoubtedly, the Bible most used by the first two generations of American Puritans*qv*. Even after the appearance of the King James or Authorized version (1611) the Genevan Bible continued to hold its own, though doubtless the Authorized version found greater favor outside New England. The availability of these two great versions from the beginning of colonization helps to explain the influence exerted by the Bible in American colonial life. Taking the colonial period as a whole the Bible was easily first in its moral and cultural influence upon the plain people of English speech.

The Bible in German, printed by Christopher Sower, Sr., the Dunker printer of Germantown, in 1740–43, the first Bible to appear in a European language in America, exercised a corresponding influence upon the growing number of German colonists.

The nation confronted no more serious problem after independence than that connected with the western movement of the population. Among the questions to be decided upon the immense stage of the West was whether the nation was to be Christian or pagan in its outlook. And no single factor had a larger part in determining what direction the nation would take than the widespread distribution of the Bible throughout the West, by such agencies as the American Bible Society (1816), the American Tract Society*qqv* (1825), and the American Sunday School Union (1824). These agencies, together with the direct influence exerted by the evangelical churches, made the Bible a necessity in almost every American home. As a result of the great revivals*qv* which swept over the nation from the beginning of the last century until near its end, Bible reading and study in the home as well as in the Sabbath Schools and denominational colleges was stressed as the best means of cultivating the Christian life. Family worship became a practice in tens of thousands of American homes, where a chapter of the Bible was read, a hymn sung, and a prayer offered as a part of the daily family routine. The Young Men's and Young Women's Christian Associations*qqv*, from their formation, stressed Bible study.

The Bible has had an important part in advancing every reform movement in American history, as witness the antislavery, temperance and peace movements*qqv*. Unfortunately it has also been used to support glaring evils, to oppose progress, and has given birth to numerous erratic movements, and in too many instances to superstitious practices.

It is an opinion widely held at the present time that Bible reading and study has greatly declined and that there has been a corresponding decrease in its influence. Certainly the old emphasis upon Bible reading in the home has greatly lessened. If this is true, it is doubtless due in large part to the fact that the Bible is no longer considered the infallible guide in every department of life as it once was. Yet the Bible still is in great demand and exercising a wide influence, as indicated by the fact that the American Bible Society published 323,109 Bibles and 413,826 Testaments in 1933, and the Press-Radio Bible Service served newspapers having a daily circulation of more than 14,000,000 copies.

[P. Marion Simms, *The Bible in America.*]

WILLIAM W. SWEET

Bible Commonwealth is a term which has been applied by modern historians to the Puritan colonies of Massachusetts and New Haven, where the right to vote was limited to church members and an effort was made to bring all activities into harmony with the Bible. This effort is best illustrated by *An Abstract of the Lawes of New England . . .* (London, 1641), a code prepared by John Cotton which became the basis for the government of the New Haven Colony*qv*. With the exception of the chapters dealing with inheritance and crime, the provisions of this code were not biblical but were based upon the early practices of Massachusetts. Insofar as possible, however, all provisions were supported by marginal scriptural citations.

[I. M. Calder, *The New Haven Colony.*]

ISABEL M. CALDER

Bibles, Printing of. The first book printed within the limits of the present United States of which any copy survives was a portion of the Bible (the so-called *Bay Psalm Book*[qv], Cambridge, Mass., 1640). The first complete Bible produced was John Eliot's translation into an Algonquian language printed at Cambridge in 1663 (second edition, 1685). In 1688 William Bradford projected the printing of a Bible in Philadelphia, but nothing came of it or of John Fleeming's proposal in Boston in 1770. Partly because the printing of the King James version was an Oxford monopoly, three editions of Martin Luther's Bible in German appeared in America (Germantown, Christopher Sower, 1743, 1763, 1776) before any were printed in English. Robert Aitken published the first American Bible in English in Philadelphia, 1781–82. Isaiah Thomas is responsible for the legend of an English Bible printed surreptitiously in Boston about 1752, but no such book was attested by contemporaries, nor is any copy known to exist. Thomas printed the first Greek New Testament, Worcester, 1800. The first printing of the Douai version (Roman Catholic) was in Philadelphia in 1790.

[E. B. O'Callaghan, *List of editions of the Holy Scriptures . . . printed in America previous to 1860.*]

RANDOLPH G. ADAMS

Bicameral Legislatures. The bicameral system has always dominated in the United States, in both state and nation. In the Federal Congress, in addition to the established English precedent, there was the fact that the representative character of the two houses was quite different, as a result of one of the major compromises of the Convention of 1787[qv]. The large states won representation on the basis of population in the House; the small states, fearful that this would place them at the mercy of the large states, won equality of representation in the Senate, as well as the constitutional guarantee that no state should be deprived of its equal representation without its consent—which means in fact, never. The bicameral principle is, therefore, firmly established in the Federal Government.

In the states, bicameralism has been universally in effect, with the specific exceptions here noted. After independence was achieved, three states set up or retained existing unicameral legislatures[qv]; with the exception of Vermont, these lasted only a few years:

Georgia 1777–1789
Pennsylvania 1701–1789
Vermont 1776–1836

In the years immediately preceding our entry into the World War, there was considerable agitation for unicameralism; several governors recommended it, and several states voted on it, rejecting it by substantial majorities. The movement was resumed when Nebraska in 1934 adopted such a constitutional amendment, effective in 1937.

In the cities the bicameral system, with a large common council and a smaller select council, universally prevailed, down to the period of the Muckrakers and the Progressive movement[qqv]. At present, all of the city councils are unicameral, nearly all with a small membership. The spread of unicameralism in the cities has been used as an argument for its extension among the states.

[Daniel B. Carroll, *The Unicameral Legislature of Vermont;* David L. Colvin, *The Bicameral Principle in the New York Legislature;* Hastings B. Lees-Smith, *Second Chambers in Theory and Practice;* Robert Luce, *Legislative Assemblies;* Dorothy Schaffter, *The Bicameral System in Practice;* John P. Senning, *The Unicameral Legislature;* W. F. Willoughby, *Principles of Legislative Organization and Administration.*]

W. BROOKE GRAVES

Bicycling. Invented largely in France and England, bicycles had their first vogue in America in the late 1860's. The sudden popularity soon collapsed but was revived a decade later when Albert A. Pope began importing them from England and later manufacturing them. Chiefly through his efforts, which included continuous propaganda for better roads, bicycling became, during the 1880's and 1890's, one of the most popular of American sports[qv]. Change in design and model made bicycling more practical. Their use was thus widened to include business as well as pleasure. Bicycling as a sport reached its height in the late 1890's. After that it was pushed into the background by motor cycles and motor cars and by the development of golf, tennis, and other outdoor sports. The bicycle continued as an adjunct of business and in the middle 1930's it experienced a revival in both fields.

[*Thirteenth Census 1910*, Vol. X, pp. 825 ff.]

H. U. FAULKNER

Biddle Mission to Panama and Bogotá, The. Charles A. Biddle, sent by President Jackson to Nicaragua, Guatemala and Panama to determine expediency of Isthmian canal negotiations, secured from New Granada a concession (June 22, 1836) for himself and associates to construct a trans-isthmian road or railway, and for steam navigation of Chagres River. Jackson, infuriated because of Biddle's use of a governmental mission to secure a private concession, disclaimed official connection with the affair. Biddle's death (Dec. 21, 1836) saved him a presidential reprimand.

[E. T. Parks, *Colombia and the United States, 1765-1934.*]

E. T. PARKS

Bidlack-Mallarino Treaty of 1846, THE, between the United States and New Granada (Colombia), removed tariff discrimination against American commerce, and provided for the guarantee of the neutrality of the Isthmus of Panama "with a view that the free transit . . . [across it] may not be interrupted." New Granada's rights of sovereignty over the Isthmus were also guaranteed.

On thirteen occasions (1856–1903) American troops were landed to protect the transit route. In 1903 President Theodore Roosevelt argued that this treaty "vested in the United States a substantial property right" in the Isthmus. When Panama^qv^ seceded (Nov. 3, 1903) it was held by the American Government that the covenant ran with this land (*see* Hay-Bunau-Varilla Treaty, The).

[H. C. Hill, *Roosevelt and the Caribbean;* E. T. Parks, *Colombia and the United States.*]

E. T. PARKS

Big Black River, Battle at (May 17, 1863). After his defeat at Champion's Hill^qv^, Pemberton (C.) retreated to the Big Black River. It was hoped the bridge could be held long enough to permit the army to cross before Grant (U.) could attack in force. Everything was in confusion; there seemed to be no leadership. On the morning of May 17 Grant's advance troops appeared. Pemberton was driven in retreat into Vicksburg^qv^.

[F. V. Greene, *The Mississippi.*]

THOMAS ROBSON HAY

Big Bone Lick, THE, is in Boone County, Ky., one and one-half miles east from the Ohio River. The earliest known white man to visit this place was Capt. Charles Lemoyne de Longeuil, who came in 1729. Christopher Gist^qv^ visited it in 1751; and in 1773 James Douglas, a Virginia surveyor, described the animal remains which he found on the surface. Here were found the bones of mastodon, Arctic elephant and other animals of the Glacial Age. In 1803 and 1806 Dr. William Goforth made a collection of fossils which he entrusted to the English traveler, Thomas Ashe. Ashe in turn sold these to the Royal College of Surgeons in London, and to private Irish and Scotch collectors. Thomas Jefferson made a collection of some of the bones, and natural history museums at Lexington, Cincinnati, Philadelphia and Boston collected the remaining skeletons. The large pre-historic animals were attracted to the Big Bone Lick by the seepage of brine from an underlying basal coal measure. Pioneers found that 500 gallons of this water made one bushel of salt.

[W. R. Jillson, *Big Bone Lick.*]

T. D. CLARK

Big Bottom Massacre, MUSKINGUM RIVER, OHIO (Jan. 2, 1791). Shawnee^qv^ Indians surprised a new settlement on the Muskingum, stormed the blockhouse and killed eleven men, one woman and two children. Three settlers were captured while four others escaped into the woods. The Ohio Company of Associates^qv^ acted immediately after this outrage to provide greater protection for settlers.

[*American State Papers,* Class II, Indian Affairs.]

ROBERT S. THOMAS

Big Brother Movement. In 1904, following an appeal by Ernest K. Coulter to the Men's Club of the Central Presbyterian Church of New York City, forty men each agreed to take an interest in and render assistance to one boy brought into the Children's Court. At present 355 volunteer Big Brother organizations enlist the services of 15,000 Catholics, Jews and Protestants in an intensive personal effort to prevent juvenile delinquency. In 1934 the movement aided 64,000 children in 100 cities in 36 states and 6 Canadian provinces, and claimed that 97% turned their back permanently on crime.

[William F. McDermott, When a Feller Needs a Friend, *Reader's Digest,* Sept., 1936.]

DONALD G. BISHOP

Big Hole, Battle of the, was fought in the Big Hole Basin, Mont., Aug. 9, 1877, during the Joseph campaign. Col. John Gibbon attacked Joseph's camp at daybreak, burning lodges and killing men, women and children. The surviving Nez Percés drove the soldiers back, captured a howitzer and ammunition, wounded Gibbon and disabled or killed sixty-nine soldiers; then withdrew during the night. (*See* Nez Percé War.)

[H. H. Bancroft, *History of Washington, Idaho and Montana.*]

WILLIAM S. LEWIS

Big Horn Mountains, THE, are a range of the Rocky Mountains lying mainly in north central Wyoming, but extending into southern Montana. Discovered in 1743 by Chevalier Vérendrye, they were early frequented by American fur traders. In 1811 they were crossed by Wilson Price Hunt and the overland Astoria[qv] expedition. Here in 1866 occurred the so-called Fetterman massacre[qv], and in 1876 Custer's force was annihilated in the Battle of the Little Big Horn[qv].

DAN E. CLARK

Big Knives or Long Knives was a term used by the western Indians to designate the English colonists. After 1750 it was restricted to the colonists of Virginia, in contradistinction to those of New York and Pennsylvania. George Rogers Clark[qv] spoke of himself and men as "Big Knives," or Virginians, in his speeches to the Indians in 1778 after the capture of Illinois. In the latter part of the Revolution, down to and during the War of 1812, the term was used to designate Americans. The origin is thought to have been the use of steel knives and swords by the colonists, perhaps contrasted with the stone knives of the primitive Indians.

[R. G. Thwaites, *Daniel Boone.*]

LOUISE PHELPS KELLOGG

Big Moccasin Gap, in extreme southwestern Virginia, admitted Daniel Boone and other pioneers through the Clinch Mountains into Kentucky. Not far from it were the blockhouses, built by Capt. John Anderson in 1777, where parties formed for the journey over the Wilderness Road[qv]. The line established by the Treaty of Lochaber[qv], 1768, and surveyed by John Donelson[qv] in 1770 crossed the road near this Gap.

[W. A. Posey, *The Wilderness Road;* A. B. Hulbert, *Boone's Wilderness Road.*]

JONATHAN T. DORRIS

Big Tree Treaty (1797). Robert Morris' agreement with the Holland Land Company[qv] required the acquisition of the Indian title. At Big Tree (Geneseo, N. Y.) with the sanction of the United States Government, the Senecas[qv], by a treaty concluded Sept. 15, ceded to Morris all of their land west of the Genesee River, except about 200,000 acres, for the sum of $100,000 to be invested in United States Bank stock.

[P. D. Evans, *The Holland Land Company.*]

ROBERT W. BINGHAM

Biglow Papers, THE. Originally these were nine satirical poems in Yankee dialect directed against the Mexican War, which, in the opinion of their author, James Russell Lowell, had as its object the acquisition of slave territory. From 1846 to 1848 the jingling rhymes like "What Mr. Robinson Thinks" spread from newspaper to newspaper. In 1848 Lowell gathered the nine poems into a collection, embroidering them with elaborations until the original intent of the lyrics was all but lost. To Hosea Biglow was added the pundit editor Parson Wilbur, who was endless in his comment. Written in haste, with youthful extravagance and zeal, the satires sparkle with fun and at times bite like acid.

Beginning in 1862, Lowell ran in the *Atlantic Monthly* a second series of the papers, this time satirizing the South. Some of the lyrics, like "Jonathan to John," display flashes of the old-time fire, but the poet, less youthful now, had to force himself into the satiric mood. The jingles of Hosea Biglow with their misspellings could not voice the national tragedy. As a result the final collection, 1867, with its chaos of embellishment, its beautiful nature poetry, and its long essay on Yankee dialect, is, unlike the first series, hardly to be rated as primarily satiric.

FRED LEWIS PATTEE

Bill of Rights. The first ten Amendments to the Constitution[qv] of the United States are generally referred to as the national Bill of Rights. At the time the Constitution was submitted to the people in 1787 (*see* Constitution, Ratification of the) there was much criticism of the document due to the fact that it did not contain a Bill of Rights. The explanation of this goes back to the original English common-law idea of government. According to this, individual rights exist of themselves as inborn and inalienable. The Constitution and government are merely an added protection to those rights which the people already possess. This idea underlies today the governments not only of Great Britain and the United States, but also those of the self-governing British Commonwealths.

In contrast to this should be mentioned the doctrine and belief that were and still are prevalent in other countries, such as the states of Continental Europe, which are under what might be termed a prerogative type of government. Even the most free of these countries in their written Constitutions make statements of individual rights that are based on the underlying thought that these rights are the gift of the state. Thus we find the Constitution of Switzerland (Article 55), "The freedom of the press is guaranteed. However, cantonal laws shall enact the necessary provisions to avoid abuse; these provisions shall be submitted to the approval of the Federal Council. The Confederation may also fix penalties in order to prevent abuses directed against itself or its authorities." This provision is characteristic of the most enlightened European democracies and is in direct contrast to the British and American common-law idea of protection for already existing, inalienable rights.

Naturally there was a general feeling among those who made the Constitution and who were advocating its adoption that a Bill of Rights was unnecessary, since it might grant rights that already existed or merely prohibit the Government from interfering with these rights, which it had no authority to do. Alexander Hamilton, in *The Federalist*[qv], No. 84, wrote: " 'We, the people[qv] of the United States . . .' is a better recognition of popular rights than volumes of those aphorisms which make the principal figure in several of our State bills of rights, and which would sound much better in a treatise of ethics than in a constitution of government. . . . The truth is, after all the declamation we have heard, that the Constitution is itself, in every rational sense, and to every useful purpose, a bill of rights."

In contrast to this was a widespread popular feeling that it would be wise to make a definite statement of these fundamental rights since such a statement would have a beneficial and restraining influence on the minds of both rulers and the people and also might serve as a definite basis for future court decisions in protecting these rights. This feeling, amounting to a conviction, went back to the old British tradition inherited by the colonists from the Revolution of 1688. This great change in the government of England and her colonies had as one important result the Declaration of Rights of 1689 which formed the basis for the later American Bill of Rights.

Massachusetts, Virginia, New York and several other states ratified the new Constitution with the recommendation that a Bill of Rights be added which should specifically safeguard individual rights. This was done by the First Congress in the form of twelve proposed Amendments which, after some delay, were passed by that body on Sept. 25, 1789. Of the twelve Amendments submitted, ten were declared ratified by the necessary number of states on Dec. 15, 1791. They bind the National Government alone, but do not limit the power of the individual states. The material for these Amendments was drawn in large part from the Virginia Declaration of Rights[qv] which was adopted by a

Virginia convention composed of members of the colonial House of Burgesses which met at Williamsburg in 1776. The preparation of this Declaration was in large part the work of George Mason. In a sense, it was intended to serve as an original compact for society by stating permanent and fundamental truths. Also, it was intended to be the basis for a new society and government to be independently organized in America. In plain language it stated specific and fundamental principles with regard to jury trial, cruel and unusual punishments, search warrants, freedom of the press, the subordination of military to civil power; the derivation of all authority from the people, who have an inalienable right to reform an evil government; the doctrine of the separation of executive, legislative and judicial powers; and it declared for a full grant of religious freedom. Likewise it stated that all men should have the franchise[qv] who had sufficient evidence of permanent common interests with the community.

Jefferson soon thereafter drew upon it when he wrote the Declaration of Independence[qv], and it not only became the basis for these first Amendments to the Constitution but also furnished a model for the various Bills of Rights adopted soon after by other colonies and offered the basis for the later Bills of Rights in many of the present state constitutions (*see* Bills of Rights, State).

The First Amendment provides that "Congress shall make no law respecting an establishment of religion, or prohibiting the free exercise thereof; or abridging the freedom of speech or of the press[qqv]; or the right of the people peaceably to assemble[qv], and to petition[qv] the government for a redress of grievances." These are among the most fundamental rights to be preserved in a free government. In contrast to the above quotation from the Swiss Constitution, they prohibit interference with individual rights that already exist.

More specifically they mean that the National Government has nothing to do with religion as such. The right of fair discussion of men and measures does not mean free license of utterance, but the right of a person to express his or her thoughts depends on the thoughts themselves and on time and place. The right on the part of citizens to meet peaceably for consultation in respect to public affairs and to petition for a redress of grievances is implied in the very idea of popular government. It is true that the right of petition has lost much both in use and influence during more recent years. This is due to the extension of the means for expression of the popular will or protest, by universal suffrage. On the other hand, it still holds great potential value as a ready means of popular influence upon the course of legislation or administration in time of crisis.

Amendment II provides: "A well-regulated militia being necessary to the security of a free State, the right of the people to keep and bear arms shall not be infringed." This may be summarized as the right to bear arms in common defense but not to carry such arms as the individual may desire in order to use them in private conflict.

The Third Amendment provides: "No soldier shall, in time of peace, be quartered[qv] in any house without the consent of the owner, nor in time of war, but in a manner to be prescribed by law," and the Fourth Amendment provides for the security of the people "in their persons, houses, papers and effects, against unreasonable searches and seizures"[qv]. These two Amendments are designed to protect the people against any acts of illegal force by the National Government that may infringe their personal rights.

The four Amendments numbered V, VI, VII and VIII control legal proceedings in the Federal courts and constitute a statement of the rights of accused persons by guaranteeing to them the rule of common law.

The provisions of Amendment V are: "No person shall be held to answer for a capital, or otherwise infamous crime, unless on a presentment or indictment of a grand jury, except in cases arising in the land or naval forces, or in the militia, when in actual service in time of war or public danger; nor shall any person be subject for the same offense to be twice put in jeopardy of life or limb; nor shall be compelled in any criminal case to be a witness against himself, nor be deprived of life, liberty, or property, without due process[qv] of law; nor shall private property be taken for public use, without just compensation." The most important clause of this Amendment is that guaranteeing "due process of law" to every citizen under Federal law. This means "that the accused person be given the right to a fair hearing in a tribunal having jurisdiction of his case." (E. S. Corwin.)

Amendment VI lays down certain provisions that are designed to secure this due process of law. It provides that "in all criminal prosecutions the accused shall enjoy the right to a speedy and public trial, by an impartial jury of the State and district wherein the crime shall have been committed, which district shall have been previously ascertained by law, and to be informed of the nature and cause of the accusation; to be confronted with the witness against him; to have compulsory process for obtaining witnesses in his favor, and to have the assistance of counsel for his defence."

Amendment VII provides that "in suits at common law, where the value in controversy shall exceed twenty dollars, the right of trial by jury shall be preserved, and no fact tried by a jury shall be otherwise re-examined in any court of the United States, than according to the rules of the common law." This Amendment restricts the power of the Supreme Court of the United States in reviewing questions of fact upon appeal from lower Federal courts. Amendment VIII requires that "excessive bail shall not be required, nor excessive fines imposed, nor cruel and unusual punishments inflicted." The wording of this Amendment is taken almost verbatim from the English Bill of Rights of 1689.

The last two Amendments in the Bill of Rights numbered IX and X form a final restraint upon the National Government and require it to be one of enumerated powers only. Thus Amendment IX states that "the enumeration in the Constitution of certain rights shall not be construed to deny or disparage others retained by the people," and Amendment X states that "the powers not delegated to the United States by the Constitution, nor prohibited by it to the States, are reserved to the States respectively or to the people." It would seem that the sovereign people of the United States are ultimately the ones who enumerate the rights and reserve them to the states or to the people. In other words, as stated in the Preamble to the Constitution, "We, the people of the United States," did "ordain and establish" the Constitution, with the result that legally and politically it may be said that the United States *is* a Nation, rather than the more grammatical expression that the United States are a nation.

As may be imagined, the various provisions of the Bill of Rights have been called into question on numerous occasions, especially in time of war, but by origin, historic development and acceptance they have been rooted so deeply in the minds and consciences of the American people that their validity is essentially as strong and as universally accepted at the present time as in any period in our history. Any seeming infringement of them immediately arouses strong and overwhelming political opposition.

[F. W. Maitland, *The Constitutional History of England;* A. V. Dicey, *The Law of the Constitution;* E. S. Corwin, *The Constitution and What It Means Today;* Allan Nevins, *The American States during and after the Revolution 1775-1789;* Helen Hill, *George Mason.*]

WILLIAM STARR MYERS

Billeting, or quartering of military troops, was a European practice rarely resorted to in America. Regiments usually camped out or occupied forts and barracks erected at colonial expense. Increased troop arrivals during the French and Indian War made it an issue, beginning in New York and Philadelphia, in 1756. To shelter soldiers, the Mutiny Act[qv] of 1765 required colonial governments, when barracks did not avail, to billet troops in inns, barns and uninhabited houses, and furnish certain provisions. As "a common resort of arbitrary princes," billeting aroused resistance in Charleston (1764), New York (1766), and Boston (1768), largely arising from unwillingness to accede to any money legislation by Parliament and to any military enforcement of unpopular measures. This resistance fed on traditional British aversion to standing armies. Billeting, though paid for, led directly to the Boston Massacre[qv]. The Quartering Act[qv] of 1774, designed to permit billeting within Boston, had little to do with the final issue, which was already joined. Billeting was objected to in the Declaration of Independence[qv] and was prohibited in the Bill of Rights[qv] as stated in the Third Amendment to the Constitution.

[C. M. Clode, *Military Forces of the Crown;* C. H. Van Tyne, *Causes of the War of Independence;* G. O. Trevelyan, *The American Revolution;* W. C. Abbott, *New York in the American Revolution;* Edward McCrady, *History of South Carolina under the Royal Government, 1719-76.*]

ELBRIDGE COLBY

Bills of Credit is a term applied to non-interest-bearing government obligations which circulate as money, although commonly applied in this country to issues by the colonies and, later, by the Continental Congress[qv] and states during the Revolutionary War[qv]. Since the establishment of the National Government, such issues have been known as Treasury notes[qv] or United States notes.

Bills of credit in the colonies began with an issue of £7000, shortly increased to £40,000, in Massachusetts in 1690. This was followed by similar action by New Hampshire, Rhode Island, Connecticut, New York and New Jersey before 1711, South Carolina in 1712, Pennsylvania in 1723, Maryland in 1734, Delaware in 1739, Virginia in 1755 and Georgia in 1760. In most cases the bills were issued to excess and depreciated sharply in value. Parliament finally prohibited such paper currency, in New England in 1751, and in the other colonies in 1764.

As soon as the colonies broke away from the mother country, they again began to emit bills of credit in large amounts. The Continental Congress, unable to obtain necessary funds from other sources, authorized $241,552,780 of bills from 1775 to 1779 inclusive, while the various states put out $209,524,776 of bills during the same period.

[D. R. Dewey, *Financial History of the United States.*]

FREDERICK A. BRADFORD

Bills of Rights, State. In American history the Bill of Rights adopted by the State of Virginia in 1776 preceded those of the other states, and also was the model upon which the national Bill of Rights[qv], the first ten Amendments of the United States Constitution, was drawn up. The Virginia Declaration[qv], in large part, was the work of George Mason and was adopted on June 12 by the colonial House of Burgesses which met as a convention. The Virginia document was in large part a restatement of English principles drawn from such sources as Magna Carta, the Petition of Rights and the Bill of Rights. It still stands in practically the original form at the beginning of the sixth or present Constitution of the State of Virginia, which was formed in 1902.

While other and later constitutions of the various states have copied the Virginia provisions in large part, they also have added other provisions according to local or contemporary needs. The second great Bill of Rights in point of time was "The Declaration of Rights of the Commonwealth of Massachusetts" which was adopted in 1780. It was stated in thirty provisions while that of Virginia was stated in sixteen. The Massachusetts Bill of Rights goes into greater detail than that of Virginia, stressing such things as the right of the people to bear arms, a condemnation of *ex post facto* laws, bills of attainder[qv], and the quartering[qv] of soldiers in time of peace. The Puritan religious influence is shown in the statement that "it is the right as well as the duty of all men in society, publicly, and at stated seasons, to worship the Supreme Being, the great Creator and Preserver of the universe." The final article is a more lengthy and specific statement of the principle of Separation of Powers[qv]. This Bill of Rights also stands as a part of the original Constitution of Massachusetts and still remains in force today.

The Bills of Rights in other or later-formed states show the results of contemporary events and influence and are often much more lengthy. Thus, slavery is prohibited in the Bill of Rights of the State of Maryland; also in the State of Nevada, and in almost all the Southern states. This is a direct result of the Civil War and Reconstruction^{qv} period. Also, the Constitution of the State of New Mexico contains such an odd and legally questionable statement as the following, that "the people of the State have the sole and exclusive right to govern themselves as a free, sovereign and independent State."

While many of the Bills of Rights of the various states set forth matters which are never questioned and establish prohibitions of powers already beyond the competence of the state governments, yet there is no doubt that their effect in general is healthy and constructive. They specifically state and emphasize the fundamental principles upon which American government and society are founded.

[E. S. Corwin, *The Constitution and What It Means Today;* Allan Nevins, *The American States during and after the Revolution, 1775-1789.*]

WILLIAM STARR MYERS

Biloxi was the first establishment in and capital of Louisiana. Settled by Pierre le Moyne, Sieur d'Iberville, in 1699, with 200 French colonists, it has been relocated once at least, but still exists, approximately on its original site, on the Mississippi Gulf Coast, fifty miles west of Mobile Bay. When New Orleans was made Louisiana's capital in 1722, Biloxi ceased to be important. (*See also* Maurepas, Fort.)

[Robert Lowry and William H. McCardle, *A History of Mississippi.*]

MACK SWEARINGEN

Bimetallism. Under the coinage act of April 2, 1792, a system of bimetallism was established in the United States. The law provided for a gold dollar unit of 24.75 grains fine and a silver dollar of 371.25 grains fine. This thus established the mint ratio of gold to silver at 1 to 15. The act provided for the minting of gold coins of $10, $5 and $2.50 denomination, and silver coins of the denomination of one dollar, half-dollar, quarter-dollar, disme and half-disme. Copper cents and half-cents were also provided for.

In fundamentals the act of 1792 followed recommendations contained in Alexander Hamilton's report. This report, in turn, consisted in large measure of an able selection of the more workable proposals of earlier reports by Jefferson (1784), the Grand Committee (1785), and the Board of Treasury (1786). Strangely enough, Hamilton's chief creative proposal, for the elimination of foreign coins, was disregarded entirely in the act of 1792.

It seems probable that the adoption of a bimetallic system in 1792 resulted from a lack of knowledge regarding the principles of subsidiary coinage^{qv}. Hamilton, along with other financial experts of the time, could not conceive of fractional silver coins with a bullion^{qv} value less than their face value as money. Consequently, since fractional gold coins were impractical, Hamilton felt that the choice lay between a single silver standard and a bimetallic standard. As Hamilton in fact approved of a gold standard^{qv}, he recommended a bimetallic system, thinking that gold coin would be used for major transactions while silver would circulate in the fractional denominations. Moreover, when Hamilton submitted his report, the leading countries of the world had some form of bimetallism, the single gold standard not being adopted by England until twenty-five years later.

In accordance with the familiar principle of Gresham's Law, under which the cheaper metal drives out the dearer, gold did not circulate to any great extent after the adoption of the coinage act of 1792. After 1793, the market ratio of gold to silver was above 1 to 15 steadily in succeeding years. By 1812 the market ratio of gold to silver had reached 1 to 16, the mint ratio being fixed by law at 1 to 15. The mint ratio thus overvalued silver by making it worth one-fifteenth as much as gold (when used as money), while in the market silver was worth only one-sixteenth as much as gold. This being the case, it paid to take silver to the mint to be coined into money, while gold was more valuable for use as a metal or for shipment to foreign countries.

The United States was accordingly on a silver standard in practice from the early part of the 19th century on until 1834. The desire of Eastern business interests for a gold coinage plus a wish to develop newly discovered gold mines in North Carolina and Georgia were probably the chief forces leading to the passage of the act of June 28, 1834, which, by reducing the fine weight of the gold dollar to 23.2 grains, altered the mint ratio to 16.002 to 1. Nearly three years later the act of Jan. 18, 1837, for technical reasons, increased the fine weight of the gold dollar to 23.22 grains, thus changing the mint ratio slightly to 15.988 to 1.

The laws of 1834 and 1837 overvalued gold at the mint, but the discrepancy between the mint and market ratios was not sufficient to cause silver to disappear from circulation for some years. By the late 1840's, however, business was hampered by the disappearance from circulation of much of the fractional silver, which was full-weight coin and hence tended to be melted up and used as metal since the mint ratio overvalued gold. This difficulty was finally overcome by the passage of the coinage act of

Feb. 21, 1853, which provided for short-weight silver coins and thereby permitted the circulation of silver in the fractional denominations and gold coin for larger transactions. In practice the act of 1853 permitted the operation of a single gold standard, although legally the country still maintained bimetallism, since the law permitted the free coinage of silver dollars at the mint, even though it was not profitable to take advantage of this provision.

Because of the inflation[qv] following the issuance of greenbacks[qv] during the Civil War, both gold and fractional silver disappeared from circulation. In spite of the fact that the country remained on a paper (greenback) standard until 1879, the coinage laws were revised and recodified in 1873.

The act of Feb. 12, 1873, marked the end of legal bimetallism in the United States. The silver dollar was dropped from the list of coins which could be freely struck at the mint. Thus, with no free coinage of silver, the single gold standard was legally established in the United States.

The dropping of the silver dollar in 1873 was not the outcome of a design to put the United States on a gold standard. As a result of the overvaluation of gold at the mint, silver had not been presented for coinage into dollars for many years. Congress, accordingly, deeming this coin to be unpopular and unwanted, merely struck it off the list without giving a thought to the fact that this action legally established a single gold standard.

Shortly after 1873, the market ratio of silver to gold changed so that coinage of silver dollars would have again been profitable. The silver interests raised a hue and cry about "The Crime of '73,"[qv] which demonetized silver, although the accusation of a crime or conspiracy had no basis in fact.

From 1875 on, the silver interests have been strong enough to obtain silver legislation[qv] in their favor, although they have not succeeded in bringing back bimetallism. William Jennings Bryan ran for President in 1896 (*see* Campaign of 1896) on a platform advocating a return to bimetallism at the old ratio of 16 to 1 (accurately 15.988 to 1), but was defeated both in that year and in 1900.

In 1933, the silver interests obtained the inclusion (in the Thomas Inflation Amendment[qv] of May 12) of a clause permitting the President to re-establish bimetallism at such a mint ratio as he should designate. Fortunately, to date, no such action has been taken by the President.

[N. Carothers, *Fractional Money;* J. L. Laughlin, *History of Bimetallism in the United States.*]

FREDERICK A. BRADFORD

Bingham Purchase. In 1786, when Massachusetts, which then included Maine, disposed of large tracts of unsettled lands in Maine by lottery, William Bingham, a wealthy Philadelphia banker, drew several townships and purchased others, with a total area of 1,000,000 acres. Gen. Henry Knox had signed a contract to buy another tract of 1,000,000 acres, but his duties as Secretary of War prevented his developing it, and Bingham took that over also.

ALVIN F. HARLOW

Biographic Writing, American, reaches as far back as Cotton Mather's *Life of His Excellency Sir William Phips,* published in London in 1697; autobiographic writing may be said to date from Capt. John Smith's *True Relation* (1608). But unlike history, biographic writing produced no works of permanent importance until after the Revolution. The first three books worthy of notice—for Parson Weems' lives of Washington and Marion are not biographies but romances—are John Marshall's five-volume *Life of Washington* (1804–7); William Wirt's *Life of Patrick Henry* (1817); and Benjamin Franklin's *Autobiography* in the version presented by Temple Franklin (1817). Marshall's book, clumsily written, full of plagiarisms from various annalists and showing a strong Federalist[qv] bias, contains enough factual value to make it still useful; Wirt's volume, hasty, inaccurate and not devoid of inventions, was excellently written and for its time had real merit. Franklin's work is of course a classic. From these beginnings American biography rapidly multiplied the number of its titles, but before the Civil War yielded few works of permanent worth. Washington Irving's *History of the Life and Voyages of Christopher Columbus,* which appeared in four volumes in 1828, represented independent research in Spanish archives and was so beautifully written that it may still be read with pleasure. Jared Sparks set to work in the 1830's with more industry than literary talent or scientific method. His *Life of Gouverneur Morris* in three volumes (1832) and his *Life of Washington* in one (1837), were esteemed excellent in their day, but were without lasting qualities. His *Library of American Biography,* appearing in two series (1834–38, 1844–47) had more merit; a collection of brief filiopietistic memoirs of worthies of the colonial and early national period, it was naturally uneven, but filled a glaring gap and contained some biographies that are still of value. Meanwhile, George Tucker had written a two-volume life of Thomas Jefferson (1834) of more than mediocre quality. Irving's *Life of Washington* (five volumes, 1855–59) was thought worthy of its great theme and remained unsurpassed till the end of the century, though he dismissed the post-Revolutionary years briefly. Charles Francis Adams in the 1850's published a really admirable life of John Adams. In 1862–63 Pierre M. Irving's four-volume *Life and Letters of Washington Irving* furnished the first ample and spirited biography of an American writer.

After the Civil War biography rapidly became too ample and voluminous to permit of summarization. It attracted the talents of the ablest men of letters, as Oliver Wendell Holmes' memoirs of Emerson and Motley and Henry James' life of Hawthorne testify. Writers of note, the first being James Parton with his lives of Jefferson, Burr, Jackson, Greeley and others, gave their whole energies to it. With Henry Adams' *Life of Albert Gallatin* (1879) modern methods of historical research and criticism began to be applied to political biography; and with the ten-volume *Abraham Lincoln: A History* by John G. Nicolay and John Hay biography became more monumental in character. By the beginning of the 20th century it had easily eclipsed history in the interest of American readers.

[William P. Trent, John Erskine, Stuart P. Sherman and Carl Van Doren, eds., *The Cambridge History of American Literature.*]

ALLAN NEVINS

Birch Coulee, Battle of. Early Sept. 2, 1862, Sioux Indians attacked the camp near Birch Coulee, Minn., of a mixed force of 170 men commanded by Maj. Joseph R. Brown, despatched from Fort Ridgely to bury Sioux War[qv] victims. After thirty hours and sixty casualties, the detachment was relieved by Col. H. H. Sibley's main army.

[W. W. Folwell, *A History of Minnesota.*]

WILLOUGHBY M. BABCOCK

Birchard Letter, THE (June 29, 1863), was a public letter to M. Birchard and eighteen other Ohio Democrats in which President Lincoln defended the administration's treatment of antiwar agitators, and offered to release C. L. Vallandigham[qv] if a majority of those to whom the letter was addressed would subscribe to certain pledges in connection with the prosecution of the Civil War.

[Nicolay and Hay, *Complete Works of Abraham Lincoln.*]

PAUL M. ANGLE

Birch-bark. The bark of the paper birch (*Betula papyrifera*) was used by Indians of the Great Lakes country and adjacent Canada for covering canoes, wigwams, food containers, and cooking vessels. A kettle of this bark will boil food safely, if it does not touch the flames. Small sheets of birch-bark were used for picture writing with a stylus by the Ojibway and a few other Indians. Its use for canoes and shelters extended into Alaska, thence to Siberia.

[W. J. Hoffman, *The Beginnings of Writing;* J. H. Saloman, *Indian Crafts and Lore.*]

CLARK WISSLER

Bird Sanctuaries may be defined as areas in which unnaturally favorable conditions are maintained, by manipulation of environment, for breeding, migrating and wintering birds. Their establishment began in the United States, in 1900, when William Dutcher, Chairman of the Bird Protection Committee of the American Ornithologists' Union, with funds provided by Abbott H. Thayer, the bird painter, employed wardens to protect gulls, terns and other water birds against millinery hunters, who had slaughtered these birds until they faced extermination.

From that time, prime movers in the establishment of bird sanctuaries have been the Audubon Societies[qv] and the Bureau of Biological Survey of the United States Department of Agriculture. Hundreds of sanctuaries have also been set aside by states and individuals but many of them scarcely deserve the name; a survey of nearly a hundred small bird sanctuaries, by Dr. L. E. Hicks, "showed that fully 80% actually contained less bird life after being so designated than before." This was usually the result of too great human interference.

It has been generally true that sanctuaries have been created in response to undeniable needs—initially to protect plume and millinery species, latterly for the harassed and reduced waterfowl.

Two methods have been used by the Audubon Societies in setting up sanctuaries. Permanent areas, such as the Paul J. Rainey Wild Life Sanctuary of 26,000 acres in Louisiana, have been intensively managed for the benefit of their denizens. In other regions the juxtaposition of birds and an Audubon warden has constituted sanctuaries; this system has the advantage of reducing costs consequent on land ownership, and making it possible for guardians to follow their flocks much as herders follow sheep. Under the ownership system, protection is based upon state and Federal conservation laws and trespass statutes; under the latter system, wardens depend entirely on conservation laws. At the present time (1938) a chain of twenty-four Audubon sanctuaries extends from Maine to Texas.

The Federal Government's bird sanctuary program, initiated in 1903, was given a tremendous impetus during the administrations of Franklin D. Roosevelt when more than 230 waterfowl refuges included more than 6,524,000 acres. Vast though this area seems, it is still an inadequate substitute for the more than 100,000,000 acres of once valuable wild-life habitats, turned into wild-life deserts by drainage.

[Anonymous, *Wildlife and the Land:* 75th Congress, 1st Session; T. Gilbert Pearson, in *Fifty Years' Progress of American Ornithology.*]

WILLIAM VOGT

Bird's Invasion of Kentucky (1780) constituted but one phase of an extensive series of operations planned by the British for the year 1780, whereby the entire West, from Canada to Florida, was to be swept clear of both Spaniards and colonists (*see* British Plan of Campaign in the West, 1780). From Detroit, Capt. Bird led an Indian army, accompanied by a few white men, against the settlers of Kentucky. The settlements of Martin's Station and Ruddle's Station were easily overwhelmed, but lack of provisions compelled a retreat. Over 300 prisoners were carried back to Detroit.

[M. M. Quaife, When Detroit Invaded Kentucky, in *Burton Historical Collection Leaflet,* IV, 17-32.]

M. M. QUAIFE

Bird's Point, Mo., neighbor to both Charleston, Mo., and Cairo, Ill., is opposite the mouth of the Ohio River. Of strategic importance in guarding both rivers, it was first fortified by the Spanish in 1795. Col. U. S. Grant was in command of this district for a time, and a few skirmishes took place here during the Civil War.

[Louis Houck, *History of Missouri;* U. S. Grant, *Personal Memoirs; War of the Rebellion Records,* Ser. I, Vol. 3.]

STELLA M. DRUMM

Birth Control. The American birth rate in 1800 was about 50 per 1000 population per year. It gradually fell to about thirty by 1900, and in recent years has approximated sixteen. While the motives leading to this change have arisen from our rising standards of living, the chief instrumentality of the change has been the increased use of mechanical and chemical contraceptives.

In 1802 Malthus taught that man must either limit his reproduction through "moral restraint" or suffer from vice, misery and starvation. In 1822 the "neo-Malthusian" movement began to advocate "preventives" in place of "moral restraint." This has come to be the modern "birth-control movement." Its most influential publication of the 19th century was *The Fruits of Philosophy,* by Dr. Charles Knowlton of Massachusetts, in 1832. The sale of this tract in England led to a famous trial which exonerated the distributors. But in the United States the propaganda was somewhat checked by the Federal Obscenity Law of 1873 and subsequent state enactments. Anthony Comstock was a leader in the suppression. Since 1914, when Margaret Sanger was arrested for distributing her *Family Limitation,* there has been continuous warfare between the birth-control movement and those who would use the obscenity laws to prevent the further spread of contraceptive information or devices. During all this time, despite the questionable legality, contraception has continued to spread. In recent years the legal restrictions have relaxed, mainly through judicial reinterpretations of the law rather than repeal. Nevertheless, the Massachusetts Supreme Court in 1938 compelled the closing of the Boston clinic. The American Birth Control League, the central organization of many local bodies which support clinics and which are commonly known as "maternal health," or "maternal welfare" leagues, in 1938 reported the existence of some 374 birth-control clinics in the United States. The number grows continually. In 1939 the American Birth Control League amalgamated with the other major national organization in this field, the Birth Control Clinical Research Bureau, to form the new "Birth Control Federation of America," with headquarters in New York City. The Roman Catholic Church, a major opponent of the movement, has given approval of the "rhythm method" of contraception.

[D. D. Bromley, *Birth Control, Its Use and Abuse;* N. H. Himes, *Medical History of Contraception.*]

JOSEPH K. FOLSOM

Bishop Hill Colony, a theocratic communistic colony, was founded in Henry County, Ill., in 1846 by Eric Janson who brought there some 1500 emigrants from Sweden where they had been persecuted because of their conversion to perfectionism^qv^. The colony was incorporated in 1853 and was dissolved in 1860. In 1879 many members of the former colony lost their farms to liquidate its debts and the costs of years of litigation.

[G. M. Stephenson, *The Religious Aspects of Swedish Immigration;* M. A. Mikkelsen, *The Bishop Hill Colony;* Johns Hopkins University, *Studies in Historical and Political Science,* Vol. 10.]

G. M. STEPHENSON

Bison. *See* Buffalo, The.

Bit. An archaic term for a currency value of one eighth of a dollar, used chiefly in the South and Southwest, when depreciation of colonial paper money, problems of exchange, coinage and lack of specie caused the circulation of the Spanish real, a silver coin of that value.

[Neil Carothers, *Fractional Money.*]

JOHN FRANCIS, JR.

Bituminous, or soft coal, the major source of power and heat in this country, is mined in twenty-nine states. Approximately 90% of the output, however, comes from thirteen states east of the Mississippi River, with two—Pennsylvania and West Virginia—producing about half the national total. Bituminous statistics usually include lignite and also anthracitic coals mined outside the Pennsylvania anthracite region. In 1936 coal in these two categories accounted for 3,630,000 tons out of a bituminous total of 439,088,000 tons.

French explorers of the Mississippi Valley were the first to mention coal in this country. Jolliet^{qv} and Marquette discovered coal between the present cities of Utica and Ottawa, Ill., in 1673. Commercial mining of bituminous coal, however, started in the Richmond Basin of Virginia about 1750. Illinois mining did not begin until sixty years later, with operations in Jackson County—many miles south of the original discoveries. A small tonnage was reported for Maryland in 1820, but continuous records do not begin until 1842. Kentucky officially entered the picture in 1828, Ohio ten years later and Pennsylvania in 1840.

Bituminous production did not pass anthracite[qv] in annual tonnage until 1870. From that time the general trend was steadily upward until the peak of 1917 when 579,386,000 tons were mined. Two major factors contributed to the phenomenal growth from the 17,371,000-ton total of 1870: these were the rapid development of rail transportation and the industrialization of the nation which set in after the close of the Civil War. Approximately 80% of the output of a normal year is consumed by the railroads, public utilities and general industry. From the standpoint of tonnage, however, the quantity of bituminous coal used directly or indirectly for heating services exceeds that of anthracite.

In recent years increasing competition from oil[qv] and hydroelectric power and the renascence of natural gas[qv] have served as checks upon the continued growth of bituminous coal. Probably even more important in turning down the production curve has been the increased efficiency in utilization by large industrial consumers. Despite these checks, bituminous coal was the source of 45% of the energy consumed in 1937. This percentage, however, understates the importance of coal since most of the crude petroleum and natural gas, which together contributed 40.2% of the total energy supply, do not come into direct competition with coal.

Steady progress in lightening the task of the worker has marked the history of the bituminous coal industry. An eight-hour day[qv] was written into union wage agreements in 1898 (*see* United Mine Workers). Many nonunion operators also adopted that standard so that by 1920, 97.1% of the workers were on an eight-hour basis. Even at the trough of the depression in 1932, the percentage held close to 92. With the advent of N.R.A.[qv], the percentage jumped to 99.8 and the standard work-week was cut from 48 to 40 hours under a government-sponsored agreement effective Oct. 2, 1933. On April 1, 1934, the maximum work-week was further reduced to 35 hours.

The mine mule is yielding to the electric locomotive; operations where animal haulage is now employed are exceptional. Pick mining also is disappearing; in 1891 only 5.3% of the tonnage was undercut by machine, by 1936 the figure was 84.8%. Even more spectacular gains have been made in replacing hand shoveling into cars underground with machine loading. Improvements in cleaning and sizing also have kept pace. Stripping, one of the earliest forms of mining, has assumed new importance with the development of large-capacity equipment.

[*Mineral Resources of the United States*, U. S. Geological Survey, 1879-1923; U. S. Bureau of Mines, 1924-31; *Minerals Yearbook*, U. S. Bureau of Mines, 1932-38.]

SYDNEY A. HALE

Black Ball Line, THE, was the first and most celebrated of the lines of transatlantic sailing packets[qv] from New York. Its popular nickname came from the black disc carried on the foretopsail and the house flag. On Oct. 27, 1817, came the announcement of regular monthly sailings. Service started at Liverpool on Jan. 4, 1818, and at New York the next day. In 1822 it was increased to semimonthly sailings with eight ships. It was started by five New York textile and cotton merchants, all but one of whom were Quakers[qv]. Jeremiah Thompson is credited with the original idea. After 1834 it was operated by Capt. Charles H. Marshall. The line continued for exactly sixty years, terminating in 1878. During that time forty-three different ships were used.

[R. G. Albion, *Square-Riggers on Schedule.*]

ROBERT G. ALBION

Black Belt, THE, is a crescent-shaped area extending along the Alabama River in Alabama and up the Tombigbee in northeastern Mississippi. About three fourths of its 5000 square miles lies in Alabama, including seventeen counties which make up nearly one fourth the entire area of the state. This region derives its name from the black soil which is prevalent here in contrast to the red clays to the north and south. The Black Belt is a prairie which lies much lower than the surrounding country due to the decomposition of the soft limestone rock which underlies the soil. This rock decomposition has given it a remarkably fertile soil which makes it one of the best agricultural regions of the entire South.

That portion of the Black Belt which lies in Alabama was first opened for settlement by the Creek[qv] cession of 1816. However, the pioneers were suspicious of the unusual black soil and it was not until the Jacksonian migration of the 1830's that the region began to be settled. The Mississippi portion was opened at this time, too, as the Choctaw and Chickasaw[qqv] moved west of the Mississippi. On account of the high fertility of the soil and the accessibility to market at Mobile it was inevitable that the Black Belt should become a plantation region producing great crops of cotton[qv] by slave labor. The slave population, in fact, at one time reached 87% of the whole, and thus afforded an additional justification of the name. From 1830 to 1860 the Black Belt of Alabama was the most prosperous portion of the state, held the most slaves, produced the most cotton, and was the bulwark of the Whig party[qv]. All the rivers of Alabama, except the Tennessee, water the region, and three of the five state capitals—Cahaba, Tuscaloosa and Montgomery—were located there.

With the coming of the Civil War, the Black Belt turned from cotton production to the raising of foodstuffs and furnished throughout the war a great part of the food supplies for the Confederate armies. As it had almost no railroad connections with the West or North it remained practically untouched by the Northern armies. After the war it again became the leading cotton-producing region of the South until 1880. In recent times, unable to meet the competition of Texas cotton, it has turned more and more to diversified farming and the raising of food crops, although still the principal cotton region east of the Mississippi.

[T. P. Abernethy, *The Formative Period in Alabama;* U. B. Phillips, *American Negro Slavery.*]

R. S. COTTERILL

Black Boys, THE, were Pennsylvania frontiersmen who, in 1763, 1765 and 1769, came together under the leadership of James Smith to defend the frontier against the Indians, and who, in 1765, burned a pack-horse train belonging to Baynton, Wharton and Morgan[qv] engaged in the Indian trade (*see* Sideling Hill).

[A. T. Volwiler, *George Croghan and the Westward Movement;* Neil Swanson, *The First Rebel.*]

JULIAN P. BOYD

Black Codes, THE, were laws passed in the ex-Confederate states in 1865–66, which dealt with the status of the Negro as affected by the abolition of slavery. As a rule, the laws were not organized as a separate code, in the usual sense of the word, but were statutes in the different states which dealt with vagrancy, apprenticeship, penalty for crime, property rights, etc. For the most part they adapted old principles on these subjects to the new conditions. The Negro was defined usually as "a person of color," one who had a certain degree of African blood, usually fixed at one eighth. Intermarriage between the races was forbidden. Marital relations and family responsibilities were legalized. Vagrancy laws attempted to force Negroes to work when many wished to "enjoy their freedom." Apprentice laws aimed to provide for orphans and the destitute young by hiring them out, usually to their former owners. Labor contracts provided means by which the Negroes might be held to steady labor, such as was required for the production of staple crops. Laws gave to the Negroes the ordinary civil rights to sue and be sued, and to give testimony in court, but only in cases involving Negroes. The laws varied greatly among the states, being most restrictive to the Negro in Mississippi and South Carolina, where the colored population largely outnumbered the white.

From the point of view of the South the laws were constructive measures to prevent complete chaos when the whole social system embodied in slavery was suddenly destroyed. From the point of view of the North the legislation expressed an attempt to revive slavery under another guise. The black codes furnished evidence to the already dissatisfied Radical Republicans[qv] that the state governments set up by President Johnson gave inadequate security to the permanence of Union victory, and so encouraged their demand for more thorough reconstruction[qv] by Congress (*see* Civil Rights Act; Fourteenth Amendment).

[W. A. Dunning, *Reconstruction, Political and Economic.*]

C. MILDRED THOMPSON

Black Friday (Sept. 24, 1869) was the climactic day of an effort by Jay Gould, James Fisk, Jr., Abel Rathbone Corbin and one or two associates to corner the ready gold supply of the United States. The nation then being on a paper-money basis, gold was dealt in as a speculative commodity on the New York exchange. Gould and Fisk first enlisted Corbin, who had married President Grant's sister; they then drew the new head of the New York Sub-Treasury, Daniel Butterfield, into the scheme, and unsuccessfully tried to involve Grant's private secretary, Horace Porter. On June 15, 1869, they entertained Grant on Fisk's Bristol Line steamboat, attempted to learn the Treasury's gold policy, and argued that it was important to keep gold high in order to facilitate sales of American grain in Europe. Grant was noncommittal. A gold corner did not seem difficult if government nonintervention could be assured, for New York banks in the summer of 1869 held only about $14,000,000 in gold, not more than a million was in local circulation and time would be required to bring more from Europe. On Sept. 2 Gould began buying gold on a large scale; on the 15th Fisk began buying heavily and soon forced the price from 135 to 140. The movement excited much suspicion and fear and on the 13th the *New York Tribune* declared it the "clear and imperative duty" of the Treasury to sell gold and break up the conspiracy. Secretary Boutwell visited New York but decided not to act; meanwhile Grant had gone to Washington, Pa., and was out of touch until he returned to Washington on Sept. 22. On the 23d, with gold at 144, the New York panic grew serious.

The climax of Black Friday found Fisk driving gold higher and higher, business profoundly disturbed throughout the nation, and the New York gold room a pandemonium as scores were ruined. As the price rose to 160 Boutwell in Washington urged the sale of three millions of the gold reserve, Grant suggested five, and the Secretary telegraphed an order to sell four. Gould, perhaps forewarned by Butterfield, had already begun selling and gold sank rapidly to 135; Fisk immediately found means to repudiate his contracts. The episode caused heavy indirect losses to business and placed an ugly smirch on the Grant administration.

[F. C. Hicks, ed., *High Finance in the Sixties;* G. S. Boutwell, *Reminiscences of Sixty Years in Public Affairs;* James Schouler, *History of the United States*, VII.]

ALLAN NEVINS

Black Hand. The Italian Mafia or Black Hand was a Sicilian secret society of a type fairly common since the Middle Ages. Its discipline was drastic, members being put to death for crimes against the society quite as ruthlessly as persons of whom the society disapproved. Attempts in Italy to suppress the organization caused many members to emigrate to the Southern states; it is best known here because of the famous incident in New Orleans, in 1891, caused by the ruthless murder of Chief of Police David C. Hennessey. (*See* Mafia Incident.)

[William E. Curtis, *The United States and Foreign Powers;* W. Brooke Graves, *American State Government.*]

W. BROOKE GRAVES

Black Hawk Purchase, The, was the closing episode of the Black Hawk War[qv] and marked the first cession of land in Iowa. The treaty, negotiated by Gen. Winfield Scott and Gov. John Reynolds of Illinois, on the present site of Davenport, Iowa, was signed at Fort Armstrong[qv] on Rock Island on Sept. 21, 1832. Nine Sauks[qv] (including Keokuk) and twenty-four Foxes[qv] signed the treaty. Black Hawk was held captive in Jefferson Barracks[qv] at the time and did not sign the treaty which paid the red man fourteen cents an acre for 6,000,000 acres of land. The Indians ceded a tract about fifty miles wide along the Mississippi from the southern boundary of the Neutral Ground[qv] to the Missouri line. An oblong tract of 400 square miles was reserved for Keokuk and his followers as a reward for remaining out of the war. The Indians were to receive an annuity of $20,000 in specie for thirty years. The Government agreed to maintain one black- and gunsmith shop for three decades, and deliver forty kegs of tobacco and forty barrels of salt yearly for the same period. The treaty set aside $40,000 for the just debts of the Indians and restricted Black Hawk and his followers. The Indians agreed to remove by June 1, 1833, the date marking the beginning of legal settlement in Iowa.

[W. J. Petersen, The Terms of Peace, in *The Palimpsest*, 13: 74-89.]

WILLIAM J. PETERSEN

Black Hawk War, The (1832), was waged chiefly in Illinois and Wisconsin between the United States and a faction of the Sauk and Fox Indians[qqv] led by Chief Black Hawk, whose home village was near Rock Island, Ill. In November, 1804, certain spokesmen of the two tribes had ceded to the Government their title to 50,000,000 acres of land, comprising the northwestern half of Illinois and much of southwestern Wisconsin and eastern Missouri. The validity of this cession was hotly denied by Black Hawk, who was supported by a formidable fraction of the two tribes. The issue became acute in 1831, when squatters pre-empted the site of Black Hawk's village, and the Chief threatened forcible resistance. An army of regulars and Illinois militia was embodied, however, and before this threat of force Black Hawk yielded and withdrew to the Iowa side of the Mississippi.

Early in 1832 he recrossed the river with several hundred followers, intent on joining the friendly Winnebago[qv] and raising a crop of corn. Gen. Atkinson ordered him to return to Iowa, and since he did not comply, the war was on. Black Hawk slowly retired up Rock River, the white forces pursued, and numerous killings and minor activities took place. Before long Black Hawk perceived the futility of his foray into Illinois and made proffers of peace, which were ignored. The remnant of his despairing followers was pursued westward across southern Wisconsin to the mouth of Bad Axe[qv] River, where, on Aug. 3, they were practically annihilated. At Fort Armstrong[qv], in September, Gen. Scott compelled the Winnebago to cede their possessions in Wisconsin and the Sauks and Foxes to cede all of eastern Iowa, by way of punishment for the war (*see* Black Hawk Purchase).

[*Autobiography of Black Hawk;* Frank E. Stevens, *The Black Hawk War.*]

M. M. QUAIFE

Black Hills, THE, lying chiefly in South Dakota and skirting over into southeastern Wyoming, are formed by an upthrust of the archean rock through the overlying strata to a maximum height of 7242 feet above sea level. Mount Harney is the granite (archean) core of the upthrust. Passing from the surrounding prairie through the foothills to Mount Harney, the explorer walks over the upcrop of each strata which rises in regular order: the shales, redbeds (gypsum), sandstone, schists, limestones, and granite as they are folded back, affording an unusual opportunity to study the geological formations underlying the region. The Black Hills were embraced within the Great Sioux Reservation as defined by the Laramie Treaty of 1868[qv]. Gold was found in the Hills by miners accompanying Gen. Custer's expedition of 1874 which set out from Fort Abraham Lincoln[qv] (Bismarck) to find a practicable highway to Fort Laramie[qv]. The "discovery" created much excitement, but the Federal Government sought to protect the rights of the Indians until they had been duly extinguished by treaty. When early efforts to accomplish this release failed by reason of the refusal of the Sioux[qv] to agree upon reasonable terms, the Government raised the embargo and gold hunters rushed into the diggings in vast numbers. This invasion led to the Black Hills War, the high feature of which was the destruction of Custer's army on the Little Bighorn[qv] in June, 1876. After this affair the Government forced a treaty of relinquishment and civil government was established.

The miners first assembled at Custer, where 15,000 passed the winter of 1875–76. Gold having been found in Deadwood Gulch, there was a stampede from Custer to the new diggings early in 1876 and Deadwood became in a day the most exciting and picturesque gold camp on the continent. The diggings at that time were entirely in placer gravel, but before autumn the Homestake lead had been located and passed into the hands of San Francisco capitalists. The Homestake Gold Mine was developed and for sixty-two years has yielded fabulous sums. Its engineers believe its stores of ore cannot be depleted for scores of years to come.

There are extensive gold deposits in and about Keystone and that region is very heavily mineralized. Mica, spodumine, ambligonite, feldspar, arsenic, gold, silver and galena are produced in commercial values. More than 100 valuable minerals are present. Custer State Park is very extensive and scenically attractive. President Coolidge, with his staff, made it his summer home in 1927. The Needles Highway and Iron Mountain road within the park are nationally popular.

On Mount Rushmore, of the Harney Range, in the park, the Federal Government is nearing the completion of a colossal national memorial, consisting of massive sculptures of Washington, Lincoln, Jefferson and Theodore Roosevelt, by Gutzon Borglum[qv]. The memorial is located essentially in the center of the North American Continent, upon the highest range between Pikes Peak and the Matterhorn.

DOANE ROBINSON

Black-Horse Cavalry, THE, is the name applied to a bipartisan group of corruptionists in the New York legislature which during the last quarter of the 19th century preyed particularly on corporations. It usually blackmailed by introducing bills against the corporations which would be killed if sufficient money were forthcoming.

[Theodore Roosevelt, *An Autobiography.*]

HAROLD ZINK

Black Jack, Battle of (June 2, 1856), was the first engagement of the Kansas Border War[qv]. John Brown had committed the massacre of Potawatomie[qv] Creek. In retaliation a Missouri band under Capt. Pate seized two of Brown's sons. Brown attacked Pate at Black Jack, near Baldwin, Kans. After minor casualties on each side Pate surrendered with twenty-one men. Both bands were dispersed by Col. Sumner of the Regular Army. Fighting revived, extended throughout the Border and merged at last in the Civil War.

[W. E. Connelley, *Standard History of Kansas and Kansans.*]

WILLIAM M. BALCH

Black Laws. Ohio enacted laws in 1804 and 1807, compelling registration of all Negroes in the state, forbidding any free Negro to remain without giving $500 bond against his becoming a public charge, denying validity to a Negro's testimony in trials where whites were involved, etc. These laws were an issue in the state campaign of 1846, and in the legislative session of 1848–49, with the Free Soil party[qv] leading the attack upon them, they were repealed.

[Charles B. Galbreath, *History of Ohio.*]

ALVIN F. HARLOW

Black Legion, THE (*ca.* 1936), a secret organization which sought to usurp the functions of government in Michigan and adjoining states, first attracted public notice by its "execution," May 12, 1936, of Charles A. Poole of Detroit. The resultant criminal prosecutions and sweeping expression of public condemnation soon drove the order into obscurity and, possibly, to dissolution.

[See Detroit newspaper files, 1936-37, especially *Detroit News,* April 22, 1937.]

M. M. QUAIFE

Black Legs is a term now used in a general sense which once had a special significance, being associated peculiarly with the history of "Natchez-Under-the-Hill." It referred to professional gamblers possessing large capital, associated in perfectly organized gangs which robbed, murdered and plundered with impunity in the early period of the Old Southwest.

[Robert Coates, *The Outlaw Years.*]

JAMES W. SILVER

Black Patch War, THE, resulted from attempts of Kentucky and Tennessee tobacco growers to overcome monopolistic control of markets and prices. By 1906 producers were sufficiently organized to threaten control of the "Trust." In the "Black Patch" or "dark fired" tobacco area, which embraced counties in southwestern Kentucky and adjoining districts in Tennessee, aggressive methods imposed by association members, and retaliation by non-members, resulted in much violence. During 1907 and 1908 "night riding"[qv] by the "Silent Brigade" was prevalent. Speculation in warehouse receipts, increased production in unrestricted areas, adverse court decisions and general friction, hostility and suspicion doomed the movement to deterioration.

[John G. Miller, *The Black Patch War;* B. H. Hibbard, *Marketing Agricultural Products.*]

FRED COLE

Black Rock, Bombardment of (Oct. 13, 1812). In reprisal for the capture of two British sloops by a small American naval force, Black Rock (at the northern end of the village of Buffalo) was subjected to a heavy bombardment. The short range of the guns on the American shore prevented an effective answer and considerable damage to the village was caused. During the bombardment news came of the American defeat at Queenston Heights[qv] and a week's armistice was arranged to permit the burial of the killed.

[L. L. Babcock, *The War of 1812 on the Niagara Frontier;* R. W. Bingham, *The Cradle of the Queen City.*]

JULIAN PARK

Black Swamp, THE, is a term once applied to much of northwestern Ohio but more accurately to an area lying chiefly in the drainage basin of the Maumee River, including all or parts of a dozen present-day counties. Most of this region was once under the waters of Lake Erie. It is so level and swampy that drainage difficulties, the prevalence of malarial diseases and its general inaccessibility for a long time retarded settlement. After 1850, when drainage and transportation problems began to be solved, the region underwent a rapid development and today constitutes one of the richest farming sections of the state.

[Henry Howe, *Historical Collections of Ohio,* Vol. II.]

EUGENE H. ROSEBOOM

***Black Warrior* Affair,** THE. The *Black Warrior,* a vessel in the American coastwise trade, touched at Havana, Cuba, Feb. 28, 1854, on her eighteenth voyage to New York. In technical conformity with law, but contrary to informal agreements, a cargo manifest was demanded. Failing this, the ship was seized, but was restored to her owners on payment of a $6000 fine, subsequently remitted. The controversy called forth able papers by William L. Marcy, Secretary of State, but the tactics of Pierre Soulé, American minister to Spain, temporarily threatened war. Linked somewhat with the Ostend

Manifesto[qv], the issue hung fire until August, 1855, when Spain paid an indemnity of $53,000.

[*See* sketch of William L. Marcy, by H. B. Learned, in *The American Secretaries of State and Their Diplomacy* series, edited by Samuel Flagg Bemis, Vol. VI; A. A. Ettinger, *The Mission to Spain of Pierre Soulé.*]

LOUIS MARTIN SEARS

Blackburn's Ford, Battle at (July 18, 1861). On his advance to Bull Run[qv] McDowell (U.) ordered Tyler's division to reconnoiter toward Manassas Junction. Tyler found Longstreet's (C.) brigade in position behind Bull Run at Blackburn's Ford, attacked, and was decisively repulsed. The morale of McDowell's army suffered from this initial reverse.

[*Battles and Leaders of the Civil War,* Vol. I; *Official Records, Union and Confederate Armies,* Vol. II.]

JOSEPH MILLS HANSON

Blackfeet, THE, a confederacy of the Siksika proper, Bloods and Piegan sub-tribes, so called because of the color of their moccasins, are members of the Algonquian[qv] linguistic family and thus related to the eastern timber tribes. Acquiring the horse, they appear to have migrated to the Northwest, adopted the culture of the plains tribes and, existing chiefly on buffalo meat, come to occupy a territory some 300 miles in width along the eastern slope of the Rocky Mountains between the North Saskatchewan River, Canada, and the southern headwaters of the Missouri in Montana. They had great herds of horses and were in frequent conflict with neighboring tribes. While hostile to the white man in early days, they never waged actual war against the United States. In 1855 they were located in part on a reservation in northwest Montana where their descendants now reside.

[F. W. Hodge, *Handbook of American Indians;* G. B. Grinnell, *Blackfoot Lodge Tales.*]

JOHN FRANCIS, JR.

Blacklisting is the practice of circulating among employers the names of union members, labor agitators, strikers, or persons otherwise distasteful. Such information may be furnished one employer by another upon request, or possibly by an employers' association serving as a sort of clearinghouse. Blacklisting is a long-standing antiunion employer technique; the aggressive unionism of the 1830's faced a widespread blacklisting; the railroads maintained blacklists in the 1860's. In part, at least, the blacklist provoked the secret organizations of labor in the 1870's, the outstanding example of which was the Knights of Labor[qv]. Many states, beginning in the 1880's, at one time or another, endeavored to prohibit or restrict the practice, but the secret methods open to employers made detection virtually impossible. Proof was practically out of the question. Hence, in 1926, Commons and Andrews wrote "Blacklisting is legal in the United States to all intents and purposes." This remained the case so long as the right to discharge workers for union activity and membership remained legally unchallenged. The National Labor Relations Act[qv] of 1935, which prohibited discharge for union activity, clarified this general situation.

[Commons and Andrews, *Principles of Labor Legislation;* A. G. Taylor, *Labor Problems and Labor Law;* Commons and associates, *History of Labor in the United States.*]

HERBERT MAYNARD DIAMOND

Blacksmith, THE. In colonial times the blacksmith was an important factor of the community. The first colony at Jamestown[qv], Va., in 1607, brought over a blacksmith. Plymouth Colony[qv] in 1626 enacted, "no smiths shall use their science or Trade . . . for any streangers . . . til . . . the necessity of the Colony be served." About 1635 Lynn assigned a blacksmith twenty acres. In 1642 Plymouth ordered smiths to "repaire armes speedyly," and to take corn for their pay. Secretary van Tienhoren in 1650 wrote that New Netherland[qv] required "a blacksmith conversant with the treatment of horses and cattle." In 1694 a blacksmith's apprentice at Elizabeth, Va., after seven years' service, was to receive a full set of tools and clothing.

The blacksmith did the ironwork for implements, tools and the household. As roads were developed, horseshoes, horseshoeing and tires became important.

In 1810 Pennsylvania reported 2562 blacksmith shops, doing $1,572,627 worth of work. In 1850 the United States had 100,000 blacksmiths and whitesmiths, besides gunsmiths and machinists.

The blacksmith shop was the meeting place of all trades, where the blacksmith often led the discussions. Thomas Hazard, whose diary for 1777–81 is published, was a village philosopher. Nathanael Greene worked in his father's foundry before becoming a Revolutionary general. Elihu Burritt, the peace advocate, was called "The Learned Blacksmith." Longfellow wrote "The Village Blacksmith" in eulogy of his own ancestor. Henry Ward Beecher came from a line of blacksmiths. R. H. Stoddard, the writer, and Robert Collyer, the clergyman, started as blacksmiths.

HERBERT MANCHESTER

Blackstock's Hill, Battle of. *See* Enoree, Battle of.

Blackwater, Battle of (Dec. 18, 1861). While campaigning against the Confederate Gen. Sterling Price in Missouri, part of Gen. Pope's command, under Col. J. C. Davis, surrounded an enemy force south of Milford at the mouth of Clear Creek (vicinity of Warrensburg), and compelled its surrender. This was part of Pope's campaign to strip Price of supplies and munitions.

[*War of the Rebellion, Official Records of the Union and Confederate Armies*, Series I, Vol. VIII.]

ROBERT S. THOMAS

Bladensburg, Battle of (Aug. 24, 1814). Maj. Gen. Robert Ross, with 4500 British troops, landed on the Patuxent River in Maryland, Aug. 19–20, thus compelling Commodore Joshua Barney to destroy his gunboat flotilla in that river. The British force then turned toward Washington. About 6000 District and Maryland militia, a few regulars and Barney's seamen constituted the defensive force under Maj. Gen. William Winder. Ross reached Bladensburg Aug. 24. Across the river, on rising ground, Winder hastily and unskilfully posted his army, already worn down by three days' futile maneuvering, sleepless nights and scanty food. The British advanced steadily under artillery fire, drove back the American light troops after crossing the bridge, and approached the second line. Showers of Congreve rockets so terrified the raw militia that two regiments disintegrated immediately. A Baltimore regiment offered some resistance but broke when ordered to fall back. Barney's naval contingent, firing eighteen-pounders, checked Ross for a time, retreating only when its flanks were uncovered by fleeing infantry supports, its ammunition expended and Barney wounded. A general retirement, ordered by Winder, was effected in fair order, the British being too exhausted to pursue vigorously. Halting briefly at Capitol Hill, the Americans marched on to Georgetown. Ross entered Washington and burned the Capitol, presidential mansion and public buildings. President Madison, Secretary of War Armstrong, Secretary of State Monroe and Attorney General Rush were on the field during part of the battle. American losses were insignificant, those of the British rather severe. A congressional investigation whitewashed all concerned, but the uselessness of undisciplined militia against British regulars was again demonstrated. Winder was exculpated by a court of inquiry, and Armstrong, made the scapegoat by the public, was compelled to resign. Failure of the administration to adopt defensive measures in time may be considered the true explanation of the disaster. (*See also* Washington Burned.)

[J. S. Williams, *History of the Invasion and Capture of Washington;* American State Papers, Military Affairs, I, 524-599.]

CHARLES WINSLOW ELLIOTT

Bladensburg Duelling Field was five miles from Washington, but in the jurisdiction of Maryland, where statutes against duelling were more lax than in the District of Columbia. Thirty to fifty duels were fought there by statesmen, military and naval officers and civilians from 1802 until 1851. The most famous were the mortal wounding of Commodore Decatur by Commodore Barron (1820) and the killing of Sen. A. T. Mason of Virginia by his brother-in-law J. M. McCarty (1819).

[D. C. Seitz, *Some Famous Duels.*]

RICHARD J. PURCELL

Bland-Allison Act, The (Feb. 28, 1878), was the first of several United States Government subsidies to silver producers in depression periods. The five-year depression following the Panic of 1873[qv] caused cheap-money advocates (led by Representative R. P. Bland of Missouri) to join with silver-producing interests in urging return to bimetallism[qv]. The silver dollar had been omitted from the list of coins by a mint reform act, which lent itself to the political soubriquet of "The Crime of '73,"[qv] and silver[qv] had depreciated with other commodities. The allies demanded restoration of free coinage of silver at "16–1," approximately $1.29 an ounce.

Free coinage, as the symbol of justice for the poor, was seized upon by greenbackers[qv] and others determined to prevent resumption of specie payments[qv] and to make government obligations payable in silver. When Bland's bill for free coinage, passed by the House, jeopardized Secretary of the Treasury Sherman's plans for resuming specie payments, Sherman substituted limited purchases for free coinage, through a Senate amendment sponsored by Sen. W. B. Allison of Iowa. The producers accepted the arrangement as likely to restore silver to $1.29.

The law required Government purchase, at market prices, of $2,000,000 to $4,000,000 worth of silver bullion monthly, and coinage into legal tender "16–1" dollars, exchangeable for $10 silver certificates receivable for public dues and reissuable. The President was directed to arrange an international bimetallic conference to meet within six months. These provisions signified:—victory for producers over inflationists, defeat of international bimetallists by national bimetallists, a drain on the Treasury through the customs in times of uncertainty and failure for the conference.

[H. B. Russell, *International Monetary Conferences.*]

JEANNETTE P. NICHOLS

Blast Furnaces, Early. From the earliest days of English colonization, Englishmen pointed out that the smelting of iron in the New World for England's manufacturers would be advantageous to the mother country in view of the diminishing English forests which furnished fuel for the production of iron. The first attempt to build blast furnaces in the colonies was made in Virginia by the London Company[qv]. The project was not successful. The Puritans[qv] in Massachusetts established the first successful ironworks as early as 1644 (*see* Iron Industry, Early, Furnaces and Forges). The colonial iron industry, however, made slow progress in the 17th century.

Not until the 18th century did the smelting of iron in America become important. The colonial iron industry then went through a process of remarkable development. By the outbreak of the American Revolution there were more blast furnaces in the American colonies than in England and Wales, and American furnaces produced more pig iron and castings than English furnaces.

Colonial blast furnaces were patterned after those of the mother country. Built of stone, they were usually about twenty-five feet square at the bottom and from twenty-five to thirty feet high. Although square, they were larger at the bottom than at the top; thus they resembled truncated pyramids. The blast, forced through a single tuyère into the furnace, was produced by large bellows driven by water power. Before 1800 blowing cylinders were substituted for bellows at a number of furnaces. American furnaces continued to use charcoal fuel and cold blast until just before 1840 when some ironmasters began using anthracite[qv] coal. Later, coke displaced anthracite and charcoal as a furnace fuel. The early iron industry was the foundation upon which the great iron and steel industry[qv] of the present was established.

[Arthur C. Bining, *British Regulation of the Colonial Iron Industry;* Arthur C. Bining, *Pennsylvania Iron Manufacture in the Eighteenth Century;* V. S. Clark, *History of Manufactures in the United States, 1607-1860.*]

ARTHUR C. BINING

Blease Movement in South Carolina, THE, developed in the 1900's from the failure of the Tillman Movement[qv] to satisfy the ambitions of the white masses. By studiously imitating Ben Tillman's vehement attacks on Negroes, aristocrats and clerical politicians, Cole L. Blease became something of the popular idol Tillman had formerly been. Elected governor in 1910, his administration was bizarre, but not criminal. He pardoned extravagantly and answered the snubs of the opposition with abusive language. Although the combined opposition of Tillman and the upper classes could not prevent his reelection in 1912, his influence thereafter declined and his repeated attempts to win high office usually ended in failure. Blease lacked a constructive program and the prudence of a successful organizer. But his agitations had permanently quickened the political consciousness of the cotton-mill operatives and other poor whites.

[D. D. Wallace, *The History of South Carolina.*]

FRANCIS B. SIMKINS

Bleeding Kansas. *See* Border War, 1854–59.

Blennerhassett Island in the Ohio River below the mouth of the Little Kanawha River, an Indian rendezvous, was first known as Backus Island for Elijah Backus who purchased it in 1792. It is famous as the site of Blennerhassett House, where Aaron Burr and Harman Blennerhassett, who purchased the north end of the island in 1798, are alleged to have plotted treason against the United States. (*See* Burr Conspiracy, The.)

[William H. Safford, *The Life of Harman Blennerhassett.*]

CHARLES H. AMBLER

Blessing of the Bay, second seaworthy vessel built in what is now the United States, preceded only by the *Virginia,* a thirty-ton pinnace built by the Popham Colony[qv] at the mouth of the Kennebec River, Maine, in 1607. The *Blessing of the Bay,* a thirty-ton bark, mostly of locust, was built at a cost of £145 for John Winthrop at Mistick (now Medford), Mass., by Robert Molton and other shipwrights sent to New England in 1629 by the Company of the Massachusetts Bay[qv], and was launched July 4, 1631. She went to sea Aug. 31, 1631, and carried on a coastwise trade as far south as the Dutch town of New Amsterdam[qv] (New York).

[John Robinson and G. F. Dow, *Sailing Ships of New England;* W. B. Weeden, *Economic and Social History of New England.*]

R. W. G. VAIL

Blind, THE. The first school for the blind to be set up in the United States was in New York City in 1832, and the second, though organized in 1829, was opened in Boston a few months later than the New York school. The third school was in Philadelphia in 1833. These three schools were all under private societies, with state appropriations to assist in their support. In 1837 a school was established in Ohio as a state institution; and from this time on nearly all the schools brought into being have been of like character. Besides the public institutions in which blind children are boarded and given care, there have been started in a number of cities day schools, more on the order of the regular public schools, the first being in Chicago in 1900. Home teaching carried into the homes of blind persons began formally in Connecticut in 1893. It is now carried on more or less definitely in about half of the states. Special industrial establishments or workshops number close to fourscore. The first one was in connection with the school in Boston in 1840. The initial independent shop was in Philadelphia in 1874. A little more than twenty special homes for the adult blind have been founded, the first being in Philadelphia, New York City and St. Louis, all started in 1868.

For the blind in general, there has been provided raised print, consisting in the largest part of a system of dots. In 1868 there was invented a special form known as New York Point, and in 1878 a system called American Braille, a modification of the original European Braille. In 1932 an agreement was reached calling for the use, with slight modifications, of English or European Braille.

In 1855 there was established at Louisville, Ky., the American Printing House for the Blind, which in 1879 began to receive an annual subsidy from the Federal Government. There are now several other printing plants. About twoscore periodicals are published in raised print, the chief of which is the *Matilda Ziegler Magazine for the Blind,* established in 1907. In 1868 a special library for the blind was begun at the Boston Public Library, a plan that has now extended to different cities. In 1896 a state library for the blind was inaugurated by New York. In 1897 a department for the blind was created at the Library of Congress at Washington.

Before the adoption of the Social Security^qv law in 1936, pensions were provided by law in a little over one half of the states. The first were introduced in the city of New York in 1866, and in the state of Ohio in 1898. Through the Social Security law pensions are now available in the larger number of states. Private associations doing various forms of social service for the blind are found in many cities, the first in New York in 1905. Such bodies are also found in most of the states, Massachusetts coming first in 1903. Public commissions or other agencies for the blind, with like purposes, are found in a little more than half of the states, the first general one being in Massachusetts in 1903.

[Harry Best, *Blindness and the Blind in United States.*]

HARRY BEST

Blizzards. This word is applied to snowstorms or drifting snow accompanied by severe cold and strong winds. It probably first appeared in print in this sense about 1870, but was widely used by 1880.

The most famous blizzard in American history is that of March 11, 1888, in the northeastern states. The streets of New York City were piled with twelve feet of snow in many places; in Herald Square the drift was thirty feet deep. There were no means of transportation except sleighs. Fires started and burned themselves out because fire-fighting apparatus could not move through the streets. A food panic threatened, as thousands were marooned in their homes. The Stock Exchange suspended business, telegraph communication was cut, and railroads stopped running. For a while the East River was frozen over. This blizzard took an unknown number of lives, including that of Sen. Roscoe Conkling, and caused a property loss of $25,000,000.

Another famous blizzard was in Kansas in January, 1886. Almost 100 lives were lost, and stock by the thousands perished. Animals drifted with the storm until caught by fences or other obstructions, and froze to death in the drifts. After the storm bodies of stock, rabbits, antelope and even wolves were found huddled together.

More than 200 people were said to have perished in the Dakotas and adjoining states during the blizzard of Jan. 12, 1888. In that storm the wind attained a velocity of sixty miles an hour, the temperature falling 60° in twenty-four hours.

The storm of May 3–4, 1905, in the Dakotas, caught stockmen and homesteaders unprepared. Stock had already been turned out on the ranges and had shed their winter coats, and fruit trees were in blossom. When the blizzard came, great drifts were piled in the streets of Rapid City. Stock were driven blindly before the wind, over canyon walls, and into the draws where they were buried deep in the drifts. This storm caused greater livestock loss than any other in the history of the region.

On Dec. 4–5, 1913, Denver, Colo., experienced its worst blizzard. Due to the comparatively high air temperatures, however, there was little suffering as a result of the unusually heavy snowfall.

On Jan. 27, 1922, a severe snowstorm occurred on the Middle Atlantic seaboard. In Washington, D. C., it was known as the Knickerbocker storm, because the collapse of the roof of the Knickerbocker Theater killed nearly 100 persons.

The blizzard of Feb. 13–14, 1923, was one of the worst on record in the Dakotas and Minnesota, marked by unusually low temperatures. Notwithstanding ample warnings from the Weather Bureau, good telephone connections and better housing than in the old days, more than twenty people froze to death.

One of the worst blizzards since 1886 swept the Plains states on March 26–27, 1931, and was especially severe in Colorado and Kansas.

[*Bulletin of the American Meteorological Society*, *4*, p. 45; *9*, p. 55; *10*, p. 78; *11*, p. 47; *12*, p. 72. *Tycos-Rochester* Oct., 1928, p. 150; April, 1931, p. 70; April, 1932, p. 66; Jan., 1933, p. 34.]

RICHMOND T. ZOCH

Blockade is the effective cutting off of communications to a port by a blockading squadron to such an extent that communications are rendered dangerous. Since the close of the Revolution the blockade has played an important part in American naval and diplomatic history. The United States has always maintained that a blockade to be valid and binding must be maintained by a force strong enough to make it effective. This was first announced in the Treaty Plan of the Continental Congress of 1784. During the Napoleonic wars the United States protested to Great Britain and other Powers against blockades in name only. In his war message to Congress, June 1, 1812, President James Madison declared that "pretended blockades" under the name of "orders in council"*qv* had been used as a pretext for plundering American commerce. In 1814 he issued a proclamation against the "paper" British blockade of the Atlantic coast, claiming that it was not effective and formed no lawful obstacle for neutral shipping. The first American treaty to define a valid blockade was made with Colombia in 1824, when a blockaded port was defined as one "actually attacked by a belligerent force capable of preventing the entry of the Neutral."

At the outbreak of the Mexican War*qv* the naval commanders in the Gulf and on the Pacific coast were ordered to blockade as many Mexican ports as they could effectually. During the Civil War*qv* the Federal Navy maintained a blockade of the ports of the Confederate states*qv*, the most extensive in history. In the Spanish-American War*qv* the Navy maintained a blockade of all Cuban ports and of San Juan, Puerto Rico. The United States Naval War Code of 1900 reiterated the principle of a valid blockade as did the Declaration of London of 1909*qv*. In 1915 the British and French governments declared that they would "detain and take into port ships carrying goods of presumed enemy destination, ownership, or origin." This declaration was made effective by a British order in council of March 11, 1915, and by a French decree of March 13. The American Government on Oct. 21, 1915, protested against thus detaining American shipping, claiming that their blockade was ineffective and illegal, and that it involved a curtailment of neutral trading rights. When the United States entered the war the Navy assisted in maintaining the blockade of Germany's coast until the Armistice. (*See also* Foreign Policy.)

[U. S. Department of State, *Policy of the United States Toward Maritime Commerce in War*, 2 Vols.; C. C. Soule and C. McCauley, *International Law for Naval Officers*, 3rd ed.]

LOUIS H. BOLANDER

Blockade Runners, Confederate. With the number of violations of the blockade estimated at 8250 and the risk of capture averaging one in six, the trade proved highly lucrative. The value to the Confederacy is told in the record of 1,250,000 bales of cotton run out; in 600,000 small arms and other munitions, in the endless supplies of provisions, clothing, hospital stores, manufactures and luxuries run in. The goods entering the Confederacy were valued at $200,000,000. Except for the blockade runners the armies would more than once have been on the verge of starvation; except for the increasing stringency of the blockade they would probably have enabled the South to win its independence. They kept a Federal squadron of 600 vessels occupied. Furthermore, they afforded the one means of outside communication. On the debit side must be ranged the facts that the traffic drained away the gold, thus contributing to depreciation of Confederate currency; that it drew attention to the ports, probably precipitating attacks upon their defenses; that the yellow fever scourge in Wilmington was traceable to a blockade runner; and that the traffic, stimulating a hunger for speculation and the riotous living of the blockade-running gentry, demoralized many citizens.

[F. C. Bradlee, *Blockade Running During the Civil War;* F. L. Owsley, *King Cotton Diplomacy;* J. R. Soley, *The Blockade and the Cruisers.*]

ELLA LONN

"Blocks of Five." This phrase acquired notoriety during the Harrison-Cleveland election of 1888 when Dudley, Republican campaign treasurer, issued a circular on Oct. 24, to Indiana followers that they "divide the floaters into blocks of five" each in charge of a trusted leader with the necessary bribes who would insure the proper delivery of the vote.

[Ellis P. Oberholtzer, *A History of the United States Since the Civil War*, V.]

HARVEY WISH

Blocs, as the term is used in the United States, are members of legislative bodies who, disregarding party lines, agree to act together for certain special purposes, and set up an organization to accomplish these purposes. The co-operation of legislators with similar interests, such as the tariff or silver, has occurred throughout our history, but deliberately organized blocs are relatively recent, beginning with the Farm Bloc, organized in May, 1921.

This Farm Bloc consisted of about twenty-five senators from the West and South who organized for the purpose of promoting legislation on behalf of agriculture. Committees were appointed to deal with different subjects; and a program of legislation was worked out, involving at least twenty bills. At the same time a similar bloc was organized in the House with approximately 100 members who could be counted on to act together. These Senate and House blocs for a time held the balance of power in each house, and had considerable success in securing the legislation they desired. They gradually broke up, however, and by 1928 had practically ceased to exist as organized groups.

In December, 1922, a Progressive Bloc was organized, under the leadership of Sen. LaFollette (Rep., Wis.). With somewhat the same membership as the Farm Bloc, it operated differently in that it was a joint bloc of Senate and House members. It forced some modifications in congressional procedure and secured some concessions to the progressive viewpoint in legislation, but with the death of Sen. LaFollette in 1925 tended gradually to disintegrate.

After the election of 1934 another group of approximately 100 members of the House organized into a Progressive, or Liberal, Bloc, primarily to give militant support to President F. D. Roosevelt's New Deal[qv] program. Other blocs include a Bonus Bloc, a Farm Tariff Bloc, a Wet Bloc, a Dry Bloc and a Far Western Bloc.

[W. F. Willoughby, *Principles of Legislative Organization and Administration;* Arthur Capper, *The Agricultural Bloc;* Basil M. Manly, Organizing to Fight Corporate Rule, *LaFollette's Magazine*, Dec., 1922.]

CLARENCE A. BERDAHL

"Blood Is Thicker than Water." Commodore Tattnall, in command of the American Squadron in Far Eastern waters, made this adage a part of American history when explaining why he had given aid to the British squadron in an attack on Taku forts at the mouth of the Pei-ho, June 25, 1859, thereby infringing strict American neutrality.

[Tyler Dennett, *Americans in Eastern Asia.*]

KEITH CLARK

Bloody Angle, THE, at Spottsylvania (May 12, 1864), was the climax in the first phase of Grant's (U.) Wilderness Campaign[qv]. Union troop movements indicated Grant planned a heavy attack. Lee (C.) was uncertain where the blow would fall. Early in the morning Grant moved in force against "the salient," or "Bloody Angle" in Lee's line. Because of surprise, lack of artillery and the force of the onslaught "the salient" was overrun. To restore the broken line and save his army, Lee proposed to lead the counterattack. Officers and men remonstrated, crying "General Lee to the rear." Lee's example fired his troops with intense ardor. The opposing lines met; the Union advance was halted and forced back. Lee put in every available man. All day and far into the night the battle raged. Neither side could advance. Early next morning Lee retired to prepared positions. The fighting ceased.

[*Battles and Leaders of the Civil War.*]

THOMAS ROBSON HAY

Bloody Island was a sand bar in the Mississippi River, opposite St. Louis, Mo., which became densely wooded and a rendezvous for duelists. Appearing first above water in 1798 its continuous growth menaced St. Louis Harbor. In 1837 Capt. Robert E. Lee, of U. S. A. Engineers, devised and established a system of dikes and dams that washed out the western channel and ultimately joined the island to the Illinois shore.

[Stella M. Drumm, Robert E. Lee and the Improvement of the Mississippi River, in *Missouri Historical Society Collections*, Vol. 6.]

STELLA M. DRUMM

Bloody Marsh, The Battle of (July 7, 1742), was the principal and decisive engagement in the war of Jenkins' Ear[qv]. In the summer of 1742 a Spanish force collected in Havana and St. Augustine, consisting of about fifty sails and a number of men, estimated in contemporary accounts to be from 2800 to 4000, invaded Georgia. They made a landing preparatory to attacking Frederica^qv^, the strongest English settlement in Georgia. Oglethorpe immediately marched out a hurriedly organized force and attacked. He routed the Spaniards, and in the retreat he posted in ambush on the edge of a marsh three platoons and a company of Highlanders. When a group of about 400 Spaniards unsuspectingly marched into the glade, Oglethorpe's forces attacked them and killed about 200 and forced the remainder to retreat to the south end of the island. A few days later the whole remaining force returned to Florida.

[W. B. Stevens, *A History of Georgia;* C. C. Jones, *A History of Georgia;* H. E. Bolton and M. Ross, *The Debatable Land; Collections of the Georgia Historical Society,* III.]

E. MERTON COULTER

"Bloody Monday" was the name given the election riots, Aug. 6, 1855, in Louisville, Ky. These riots grew out of the bitter rivalry between the Democrat and Know-Nothing parties[qqv]. Rumors were started that foreigners and Catholics had interfered with the process of voting. A street fight occurred, twenty-two persons were killed, scores were injured and much property was destroyed by fire.

[W. H. Perrin, J. H. Battle, G. C. Kniffen, *Kentucky, History of the State; The Louisville Journal,* Aug. 6-15, 1855.]

T. D. CLARK

Bloody Pond, N. Y., Battle of (Sept. 8, 1755). The British expedition, which under the command of Col. William Johnson was to capture Crown Point[qv], had proceeded no farther than the southern extremity of Lake George, when word was received of the approach of a body of French and Indians commanded by Baron Dieskau (*see* Lake Champlain in the French and Indian War). The following morning a detachment of 1000 men was sent out to reconnoiter, and a hasty attempt made to fortify the camp. The reconnoitering party fell into an ambush and the survivors retreated with difficulty to the English camp. A fierce attack on the camp followed, but was beaten off and the French were forced to retreat. Just before the final rout, several hundred Canadians and Indians left the field and returned to plunder the scene of the morning fight. They were resting near a forest pool when they were attacked by a scouting party from Fort Edward[qv]. After a short but bloody fight, the Canadians and Indians fled. The bodies of the dead were thrown into the pool, which henceforth was called Bloody Pond.

[F. Parkman, *Montcalm and Wolfe,* Vol. I.]

A. C. FLICK

Bloody Run, Battle of (July 31, 1763). Pontiac's siege of Detroit[qv] began May 9, 1763. On July 29 Capt. James Dalzel brought a detachment of 280 soldiers to the relief of the garrison. Dalzel was eager to attack Pontiac in his camp at the Grand Marais, and Maj. Gladwin, the commandant, reluctantly granted his permission. In the night of July 30–31, 250 redcoats marched eastward along the river road to surprise Pontiac. Instead, the column was itself furiously assailed at Parent's Creek (ever since called Bloody Run) and driven back to the fort in several hours of furious fighting. Dalzel was slain and sixty of his followers were killed or wounded.

[*See* Maj. John Duncan's narrative, in *Canadian Historical Review,* XII, 183-88.]

M. M. QUAIFE

Bloody Shirt, THE, usually found in the expression, "waving the bloody shirt." It is used to describe the attempts made in political campaigns (especially in 1872 and 1876) by radical Republicans[qv] to defeat the Democrats[qv] by impassioned oratory designed to keep alive the hatreds and prejudices of the Civil War period.

Perhaps the most reasonable explanation of the origins of the phrase is the Scotch tradition that after the massacre of Glenfurin, 220 widows rode to Stirling Tower, each bearing aloft on a spear the bloody shirt of her murdered husband, thus arousing the people to take vengeance on their enemies.

[W. A. Dunning, *Reconstruction, Political and Economic.*]

HALLIE FARMER

Bloomer Dress, THE, a loosely fitting costume of knee-length dress and "Turkish" trousers buttoned at the ankle, was introduced in Seneca Falls, N. Y., by Elizabeth Smith Miller in February, 1851, and popularized by Amelia Bloomer, editor of a feminist journal, *The Lily.* For its physical comfort and as a symbol of the suffrage movement[qv], the dress survived six years of ridicule but was extinguished by the revival of the hoopskirt.

[E. D. Branch, The Lily and the Bloomer, *The Colophon,* Dec., 1932.]

E. DOUGLAS BRANCH

Blount Conspiracy, THE, takes its name from William Blount, United States Senator from Tennessee in 1796–97. It was connected with the Yazoo land frauds[qv] of 1796 and its main purpose seems to have been to raise the value of Western lands by driving the Spaniards out of Louisiana and Florida[qqv]. This was to be accomplished by a land force of Western frontiersmen and Indians with the aid of a British fleet. The British minister in the United States, Robert Liston, gave the conspirators some encouragement and sent one of them to London. The conspiracy was exposed when an incriminating letter written by Blount to one of his agents fell into the hands of the administration and was transmitted by President Adams to the Senate (July 3, 1797). Blount was promptly expelled from that body. Impeachment[qv] proceedings against him were considered but dropped because of his expulsion. The exposure of the conspiracy had repercussions in the domestic politics and foreign relations of the United States, and there is some reason to believe that Aaron Burr's later conspiracy[qv] was connected with this one.

[Arthur P. Whitaker, *The Mississippi Question, 1795-1803.*]

ARTHUR P. WHITAKER

"Blue and Gray," THE, are familiar names for the armies of the North and South during the Civil War, derived from the fact that the Union Army wore blue uniforms while the Confederates wore gray. As sectional hatred has died, these terms have superseded the harsher names of the 19th century.

FRED B. JOYNER

Blue Eagle Emblem, THE, was a blue-colored representation of the American "thunder bird," with outspread wings, which was proclaimed on July 20, 1933, as the symbol of industrial recovery by Hugh S. Johnson, the head of the National Recovery Administration[qv]. All who accepted the President's Re-employment Agreement or a special Code of Fair Competition were permitted to display a poster on which was reproduced the Blue Eagle together with the announcement, "Member N.R.A. We Do Our Part." On Sept. 5, 1935, following the invalidation of the compulsory code system, the emblem was abolished and its future use as a symbol was prohibited.

[Hugh S. Johnson, *The Blue Eagle from Egg to Earth.*]

ERIK McKINLEY ERIKSSON

Blue Laws. Rev. Samuel A. Peters originated the account of the so-called Blue Laws of Connecticut in *A General History of Connecticut, by a Gentleman of the Province,* published in London in 1781. The term was taken up by various later editors of the laws to refer specifically to the legislation of the New Haven Colony[qv]. Such instances as punishments of a rebellious child by being forced to work for his father as a prisoner with a lock on his leg, and of a young unmarried couple by a fine of twenty shillings for kissing, were considered typical Blue Laws. Despite some distortions, it is perfectly true that rather rigid Sabbath, sex, and sumptuary regulations prevailed generally in Puritan New England. But Blue Laws were not original among the Puritans[qv] nor unique with them in this country. To some degree Blue Laws could be found in every one of the American colonies. Compulsory church attendance and laws forbidding sports, travel and work on the Sabbath were found in the South as well, perhaps the most sweeping Sunday law being the Georgia act of 1762. Blue Laws became in the main dead letters after the Revolution, but in more recent times there has been an attempt to revive them all along the line. National prohibition, anti-cigarette legislation, the activities of the Lord's Day Alliance and other groups attest to the survival of the Blue Law spirit to some degree.

[G. Myers, *Ye Olden Blue Laws;* F. E. Baldwin, *Sumptuary Legislation and Personal Regulation in England.*]

RICHARD B. MORRIS

Blue Licks, Battle of (Aug. 19, 1782). An engagement between 182 Kentucky pioneers and 240 Indians and Canadians, in the British service, raiding into Kentucky from the Ohio country and the vicinity of Detroit. It occurred near the Lower Blue Lick Springs on the Middle Fork of Licking River. A precipitate attack was launched by Kentuckians, from several pioneer "Stations," against the foe lying in ambush. After a fierce conflict of a few minutes, the right wing of the Kentuckians gave way and the entire body retreated in confusion, with a loss of about seventy killed and captured. The loss of the Indians and Canadians was never definitely ascertained. Notwithstanding the adverse outcome of the battle, no invasion by Indians in force ever afterwards occurred within the borders of Kentucky.

[Bennett H. Young, *History of the Battle of the Blue Licks;* Samuel M. Wilson, *Battle of the Blue Licks.*]

SAMUEL M. WILSON

Blue Lights. American frigates under Stephen Decatur prepared to run out of the harbor of New London, Conn., during the War of 1812[qv]. Decatur saw blue lights burning near the mouth of the river in sight of the British blockaders. Convinced that these were signals to betray his plans he abandoned the project. Suspicion was directed against the peace men and the odious epithet of "Bluelight Federalists" long was applied to extreme Federalists.

[James Schouler, *History of the United States of America.*]

CHARLES MARION THOMAS

Blue Lodges were secret proslavery societies formed in western Missouri during 1854 to thwart Northern antislavery designs to make Kansas a free territory under the Kansas-Nebraska Act[qv]. They not only promoted the migration of proslavery settlers to Kansas but occasionally crossed the border to participate in the election of proslavery members to the territorial government.

[L. W. Spring, *Kansas, the Prelude to the War for the Union.*]

ASA E. MARTIN

Blue Ridge Tunnel, THE, piercing the mountain under Rockfish Gap, between Afton and Waynesboro, Va., was constructed in 1850–58 by the Blue Ridge Railroad, the State of Virginia and the Virginia Central Railroad, at a cost of $488,000. It was for some time the longest tunnel in America. In 1870 it was acquired by the Chesapeake & Ohio Railroad.

[William Couper, *Claudius Crozet, 1789-1864.*]

JOHN W. WAYLAND

Blue Sky Laws. This term is applied to legislative enactments designed to prevent the fraudulent flotation or sale of corporate stocks and bonds. Kansas enacted the first Blue Sky Law in May, 1911, and this statute was followed by similar ones in forty-five other states. There are three types of these laws: (1) Fraud statutes, the principle of which is to follow and punish the security swindler under the criminal law; (2) Dealers-license statutes, which endeavor to prevent fraud by restricting security traffic to carefully selected professional dealers, as well as by revoking licenses for violation of the statute; and (3) Specific approval statutes, regulating and controlling only the securities sought to be sold within the state, through specific permits of sale. Blue Sky Laws have been supplemented by the Securities Act of 1933, and the Securities Exchange Act of 1934[qv], which regulate and control interstate dealings in securities and the operation of the organized security exchanges respectively.

[*Corporation Manual,* U. S. Corporation Co.]

FRANK PARKER

Bluebacks, Confederate Paper Currency, were first issued under an act approved one month after the establishment of the Confederate Government. From an initial issue of $1,000,000, the Treasury notes grew to $800,000,000 by April 1, 1864, when deflationary measures were taken which reduced the outstanding currency to $480,036,095 on Oct. 1, 1864.

[*The Confederate Soldier in the Civil War*: a compilation, see appendix containing extensive reproductions of Confederate Treasury notes; *Reports of the Secretary of the Treasury to the Confederate Congress,* 1861-1865.]

WILLIAM M. ROBINSON, JR.

Bluegrass Country, THE, comprises some 8000 square miles of east central Kentucky. It is bounded by the Ohio River on the north and the Knobs on the east, south and west. The terrain, with some exceptions, has a gracefully undulating surface over a limestone foundation. The land is specially adapted to the growth of bluegrass, for which the region has been named. The inner portion with Lexington[qv] at the center is a beautiful district of shaded, winding roads, fine farms and prosperous villages and towns.

To this region came the first settlers of Kentucky in one of the greatest migrations of American history. Over the Wilderness Road[qv], by way of Cumberland Gap[qv], trekked most of these multitudes. Here the pioneers, Daniel Boone and Simon Kenton became national heroes. At Harrodsburg[qv] the first permanent settlement in Kentucky was made; at Boonesborough[qv] the first Anglo-Saxon government west of the Alleghenies was organized; at Lexington the first college (Transylvania) in the West was established; at "Ashland" lived Henry Clay, the Great Pacificator; to Transylvania came Jefferson Davis to study; and to Lexington came Abraham Lincoln to court Mary Todd. These and many other places and incidents in the Bluegrass Country constitute a historic environment probably unequaled in the Mississippi valley.

[Thomas D. Clark, *A History of Kentucky;* Darrell Haug Davis, *Geography of the Blue Grass Region of Kentucky.*]

JONATHAN T. DORRIS

Bluestem Pastures, THE, prior to 1929 called Flint Hills, is a region in east central Kansas about 50 miles east-to-west (Wilson to Marion counties) and about 130 miles north-to-south (Potawatomie County to the south line), extending into Oklahoma to include that part of Osage County which lies between the Verdegris and the Arkansas rivers, where the region is called the Osage pastures. Originally all eastern Kansas was covered mostly with bluestem grasses, but because of the hilly character of the country and the presence of extensive outcroppings of limestone rock, settlement left this part of the area largely in grass. During the later 1880's the pastures were fenced and served not only the local herds but the transient herds from the Southwest, which by this time were moved by rail instead of by the long drive. The bluestem is unusually rich in feed value for grass-fattening livestock during the spring and early summer, and eventually the region became the most important pasture country in the central prairie-plains area. Supplemented by the corn and alfalfa lands of the valleys, the region became also an important breeding center and the home of the great herds of W. J. Todd, Dan Casement and R. H. Hazlett.

As procedure became standardized, the shipments of southwestern cattle northward to the grasslands were made during April and May, and from pasture to market or feed lot from midsummer to fall. Some were pastured on lease by southwestern owners, some were bought outright by pasture owners and other were handled by commission houses. During the 1920's pasture rents varied from six to twelve dollars per head for the season, on the basis of three to five acres per head. The volume of this cattle movement from Texas alone during the years 1925–31 averaged 222,225 to the Kansas Bluestem and 122,319 to the Osage pastures. The peak shipments during the period were in 1927, when the numbers were 267,562 and 152,331 respectively. In 1930 the estimated cattle movement from the Southwest was: Texas, 360,000; New Mexico, 120,000; and Arizona, 90,000. The destination of most of these was the Kansas-Oklahoma pastures. The volume of this movement exceeded that of the old trail days, and when allowance is made for the number then diverted for stocking the northern ranges and for Indian and army contracts, the commercial beef shipments to packing centers through the bluestem pastures, although not so spectacular, represented annually several times as many cattle, as well as a finer quality of meat than the earlier period.

[F. A. Buechel, Eight years of livestock shipments in Texas, 1925-1932, Part I: Cattle and calves, *Bureau of Business Research*, Research Monograph No. 10, Austin, University of Texas, 1933; H. R. Hilton, The bluestem-limestone pastures of Kansas, *26th Biennial Report of the Kansas State Board of Agriculture*, 31, 1927-28, 187-194; T. W. Morse, In the Flint Hills of Kansas, *24th Biennial Report of the Kansas State Board of Agriculture*, 29, 1923-24, 171-175; R. H. Wilcox, et al., Factors in the cost of producing beef in the Flint Hills, *U. S. Department of Agriculture*, Department Bulletin 1454, Washington, Government Printing Office, 1926.]

JAMES C. MALIN

Bluffton Movement, THE (1844), in South Carolina, was an attempt to invoke "separate state action" against the tariff of 1842, after Calhoun's failure to secure the presidential nomination and the Northern Democrats' abandonment of the South on the tariff^qv^ had apparently destroyed hope for relief within the Democratic party. Though many of the "Blufftonites" undoubtedly contemplated disunion, the object of their leader, Robert Barnwell Rhett, seems rather to have been a "reform" of the Union giving further safeguards to Southern interests. The movement collapsed within a short time, largely through its repudiation by Calhoun.

[Laura A. White, *Robert Barnwell Rhett; Father of Secession.*]

JAMES W. PATTON

Blunder, Fort. *See* Rouse's Point, Boundary Controversy.

Board of Trade and Plantations, THE, was the main British colonial office from its creation, May 15, 1696, until the eve of the American Revolution. It replaced the older committee of the Privy Council, called Lords of Trade and Plantations^qv^. It was a paid board of five members, the chief officers of state being also ex officio members. It had charge of poor relief in England, regular commercial relations with other nations, the enforcement of the trade and navigation acts^qv^, the general supervision of colonial administration, the examination of colonial laws to see that they were not harmful to British interests nor contrary to the English common law. It heard and investigated complaints of merchants and recommended imperial legislation in its field. It supervised the negotiation of important commercial treaties and kept in touch with the regular consular service. Its voluminous records today are the chief source for American colonial history in its imperial aspects. (*See* Colonial Policy, The British.)

The Board was a part of the regular political party system and its members changed with the usual party shifts. Most of its business articulated with the office of the Secretary of State for the Southern Department, consequently the activities of the Board varied with the practices and desires of the Secretary of State. Under a dominant character like Newcastle it had little power—most of the business being transferred directly to Newcastle's office. In 1748 George Dunk, Earl of Halifax, was appointed president of the Board. He began at once to make his position important. Investigations were made and reports compiled of what had been going on in America for the past thirty years. Plans were developed for strengthening the position of the royal governors^qv^. Instructions were revised, judges were made dependent upon the crown for their salaries and their terms of office, and the struggle began between the agents of the crown and the leaders of the colonial legislatures. By his energy, Halifax made himself practically a secretary of state for the colonies, secured control of the colonial patronage and was admitted to the cabinet in

1756. His influence was powerful in colonial affairs many years after his retirement from the Board in 1761.

A group of rising young men received important political training as members of the Board under Halifax. Among these were James Grenville, Charles Townshend and Andrew Stone, the tutor of George III. Townshend was even president of the Board for a short time in 1763, to be followed by Lord Shelburne. He in turn was succeeded by Hillsborough, who became a full secretary of state for the colonies and was directly responsible for many of the unfortunate policies between 1764 and 1772 that ultimately led to the Revolution. His most offensive colonial activities were connected with his attempt to force Massachusetts to rescind its famous Circular Letter*qv* and his use of troops in Boston, culminating in the Boston Massacre*qv*.

The permanent secretaries of the Board were among the best-informed men on colonial affairs in England. At the head of these were the Popples, William, William, Jr. and Alured, all related, who occupied the office from 1696 to 1737, and John Pownall, 1758–61. Another important officer was a solicitor and clerk of reports whose duties were to prepare all formal reports, to assemble information for use of the Board and to represent it before other departments of the government. The most famous of these was John Pownall, who served from 1745 to 1758 and personally prepared the reports associated with the work of Halifax. Another important officer was an attorney to whom all colonial laws were sent for examination and report as soon as they arrived from America. These reports on colonial laws subjected every American statute to a constitutional test. Three men, Richard West, Francis Fane and Matthew Lamb, filled this important position from 1718 to the end of the active work of the Board.

[O. M. Dickerson, *American Colonial Government, A Study of the British Board of Trade in Its Relation to the American Colonies.*]

O. M. DICKERSON

Boards of Trade. *See* Chambers of Commerce.

"Body of Liberties" (1641). *See* Massachusetts Body of Liberties.

Bog Iron Mining. Bog ore is a brown hematite deposited in pond and bog bottoms and was found by the early American settlers in the coastal lowlands from Massachusetts to Delaware. Since it was near water transportation and easily dug or raked from pond bottoms or picked up on marsh meadows it was the first important source of native iron supply, although superior but less accessible and tractable rock ores were also known to exist in America. These hematites were employed in the earliest New England works at Lynn and Braintree where they were smelted with charcoal in small furnaces which cast, directly from the ore, kettles and other hollow ware, as well as pig for refining into bars for nails and implements. American bog ore castings, such as kettles, were preferred in colonial households as tougher and lighter than imported ironware. Bog ores had been largely displaced by rock ores by the time of the Revolution and virtually ceased to be used toward the middle of the following century. The latest furnaces employing them extensively were built in Ohio on the south shore of Lake Erie about 1825 and shipped pig via the newly opened Erie Canal to Albany for casting stove plates.

[James M. Swank, *History of the Manufacture of Iron.*]

VICTOR S. CLARK

Boisé, Fort, was a fur trading post of the Hudson's Bay Company*qv* in Idaho. First built in 1834 on the Boisé River about seven miles above its mouth, it was relocated in 1838 near the confluence of the Boisé and Snake rivers. It was a small adobe-walled fort, famous as a stopping point on the Oregon Trail*qv*. Partially destroyed by flood waters in 1853, it was finally abandoned after the Indian War of 1855.

[C. J. Brosnan, *History of the State of Idaho.*]

CORNELIUS JAMES BROSNAN

Boll Weevil, a maggot which eats the buds and young bolls of cotton*qv*, may have existed in Mexico and Central America for centuries. About 1892–93 it crossed into Texas, somewhere near Brownsville, and in 1894 was found in cotton fields 125 to 175 miles to the northward. Thereafter it advanced north and east at the rate of about 100 miles per year, until by 1923 it had reached the Atlantic coast. In 1930 it was said that 90% of the cotton-growing area was infested, though the fight upon it had decreased its ravages in the worst spots, and 1921 is called the peak year of the pest. During the ten previous years it was estimated to have destroyed an average of more than 2,200,000 bales annually. The cotton growers' woes were increased in 1916 by the appearance of the pink bollworm, another probable immigrant from Mexico.

[*An Annotated Bibliography of the Mexican Cotton Boll Weevil,* United States Entomology Bureau, Circular 140.]

ALVIN F. HARLOW

Bollman Case. In *ex parte* Bollman and Swartwout (1807) the Supreme Court upheld its power to issue a writ of habeas corpus[qv] to review a commitment by an inferior Federal court, and upon hearing ordered the release of two petitioners held on charges of treason as participants in the Burr conspiracy[qv]. Justus Erich Bollman and Samuel Swartwout, by separate routes, had carried copies of a letter in cipher from Burr to Gen. Wilkinson at New Orleans. Wilkinson arrested them and sent them to Washington, where they were committed for trial by the Circuit Court for the District of Columbia. While the case was pending in the Circuit Court President Jefferson attempted, unsuccessfully, to induce Congress to suspend the privilege of the writ of habeas corpus. In holding that the evidence had been insufficient to support a charge of treason, Chief Justice Marshall said for the Supreme Court that "there must be an actual assembling of men for the treasonable purpose, to constitute a levying of war." But, he added, if that be proved, then a conspirator, however remote from the scene of action, would be guilty. This dictum proved embarrassing when, a few months later, Marshall presided at the trial of Aaron Burr.

[A. J. Beveridge, *The Life of John Marshall;* Charles Warren, *The Supreme Court in United States History.*]

CHARLES FAIRMAN

Bolters are party members who do not support the regular nominee of their party. The "bolt" may occur at the convention as in 1912 when Theodore Roosevelt and his followers withdrew from the Republican party (*see* Progressive party) or it may occur after the convention or primary has been held.

[C. W. McKenzie, *Party Government in the United States.*]

C. H. HAMLIN

Bonanza Kings, THE, John W. Mackay, James G. Fair, James C. Flood and William S. O'Brien, organized the Consolidated Virginia Silver Mine near Virginia City, Nev., from a number of smaller claims on the Comstock lode[qv], in 1871. Later they added the near-by California mine. For three years after large ore bodies were uncovered in 1874 the two mines produced $3,000,000 per month. In 1876, for exhibition purposes, $6,000,000 was taken in one month from both mines. Production began to fall off in 1879 but in twenty-two years of operation the two mines yielded $150,000,000 in silver and gold, and paid $78,148,800 in dividends. The term bonanza was applied to the large ore body which lay in a vertical rift of the hanging wall of the Comstock lode.

[T. A. Rickard, *History of American Mining.*]

CARL L. CANNON

Bonanza Wheat Farming in the Red River Valley of the North during the period 1875–90 was an important factor in the settlement and development of the spring wheat region. The Cass-Cheney farm, first and most widely known of the bonanzas, was established in 1875 when George W. Cass, president of the Northern Pacific Railroad[qv] and E. P. Cheney, a director of the road, exchanged almost worthless Northern Pacific bonds for land held by the railroad in the Red River Valley. Cass took ten sections, Cheney eight and an experienced wheat farmer contracted to handle operations. Yields for the next decade were uniformly high. Capital was attracted to the region, and many Northern Pacific bondholders followed the example set by Cass and Cheney. By 1890 over 300 farms in the valley exceeded 1000 acres; a half dozen or more exceeded 15,000 acres. Some of the farms were individually owned; others were corporations. Few bonanzas were established after 1890 and most of the older farms were broken up within the next quarter century.

[H. E. Briggs, Early Bonanza Farming in the Red River Valley of the North, *Agricultural History,* VI, No. 1, January, 1932.]

ROBERT H. BAHMER

Bonds, Government. *See* Debt, Public; Liberty Bonds.

***Bonhomme Richard* and *Serapis*, Engagement between the** (Sept. 23, 1779), was one of the most notable of American naval victories. John Paul Jones' flagship the *Bonhomme Richard,* originally an Indian merchantman renamed in honor of Benjamin Franklin, was proceeding with Jones' tiny fleet up the east coast of England in quest of English cargoes. Although worn out and unseaworthy, she carried forty-two guns. About noon, Jones sighted two enemy ships of war, the *Serapis* and the *Countess of Scarborough,* convoying ships loaded with naval stores. He maneuvered his ship close to the *Serapis* and both opened broadside fire. Jones had placed some of his guns below, and two of the larger ones on his lower deck burst, killing and wounding several men. This catastrophe necessitated using only the lighter guns and musketry. The slaughter on both sides was terrible and the American ship was leaking badly. After an hour's fighting, Jones answered the British challenge to surrender: "I have not yet begun to fight." The two vessels became locked together and the battle raged for more than two hours longer. Jones was hampered by treachery of a captain in his own fleet, but finally by using British prisoners to man the pumps, he stayed afloat and wore down the enemy to the point of exhaustion and surrender.

[E. S. Maclay, *History of the United States Navy.*]

ARTHUR R. BLESSING

Bonito and the Chaco. A large prehistoric pueblo[qv] ruin known as Bonito stands in Chaco Canyon, N. Mex., northeast of Gallup. The shallow canyon contains eleven main ruins, part of them contemporary and all belonging to the prehistoric period known as Pueblo III, or the Grand period in pueblo culture. Bonito, as determined by the tree-ring[qv] method, was occupied during the interval 919–1130 A.D. It was originally four stories high, contained about 500 rooms, the architecture resembling that of modern Indian villages near Santa Fé. The ruin was partially excavated in 1896–99 by the Hyde Expedition, and in 1921–23 by the National Geographic Society.

[*National Geographic Magazine*, Vols. XXXIX, 1921, XLI, 1922, XLIV, 1923.]

CLARK WISSLER

Bonneville Dam, in the Columbia River forty-two miles from Portland, Ore., is one of numerous projects undertaken by the Public Works Administration under the National Recovery Act of 1933[qqv], with the fourfold purpose of improving navigation, controlling floods, reclaiming arid lands, and generating electric power. The Bonneville project includes a dam sixty-five feet high, a ship canal around the dam, an electric power plant, and a "fish-ladder" to enable salmon to make their annual run up the Columbia to spawn. The cost of the entire project is estimated at about $30,000,000.

[Reports of Chief Engineers, United States Army, 1934-1937.]

P. ORMAN RAY

Bonneville Expedition. Capt. B. L. E. Bonneville, U. S. Army, headed a party of trappers and traders in the Far West which started from Fort Osage, May 1, 1832. The well-known Platte-South Pass[qv] route was followed to Green River. Here, a few miles above the mouth of Horse Creek in a region favored by the mountain men[qv] as a place of annual rendezvous, Fort Bonneville was built. Abandoned shortly after completion, it was frequently called "Fort Nonsense." Bonneville moved to the headwaters of the Salmon, then continued to move during the most of the time that he was in the mountains. So thoroughly did he cover the Rocky Mountains and the Columbia drainage basin, and so good was his map making that he may be credited with having been the first to gain true geographic knowledge of the Far West. A branch expedition organized by Bonneville left Green River, July, 1833, under Joseph Reddeford Walker[qv], crossed Salt Lake Desert, descended Humboldt River, crossed the Sierras north of Yosemite Valley and spent the winter at Monterey. In the spring, it returned through the Sierras via Walker's Pass, across the Great Basin[qv], and up Bear River, joining Bonneville June 1, 1834.

Irving made of Bonneville's manuscript a compelling story, which ranks at the top of the literary contributions of the fur traders.

[Washington Irving, *The Adventures of Captain Bonneville.*]

CARL P. RUSSELL

"Bonnie Blue Flag, THE," was the title of a popular Confederate ballad that was sung throughout the South during the period of secession. Authorities disagree as to the author, as to where it was first sung and as to the meaning of bonnie blue flag. It was, however, sung often by Harry McCarthy; it was sung in New Orleans and in Richmond theaters in 1861; and the blue flag on the authority of Mrs. S. G. Stoney of South Carolina was the blue field of the United States flag bearing first a single star for South Carolina, which later, according to the song, "grew to be eleven," and was used before the adoption of an official flag.

[Mrs. S. G. Stoney, in Charleston, S. C., *News*, Oct. 16, 1904.]

CARL L. CANNON

Bonus. The policy of granting a bonus, a bounty, or a gratuity to ex-soldiers has undergone several changes within past centuries. There was a time when wars were looked upon merely as a business, however dangerous, in which the successful aggressor added to his personal possessions, and increased his power over his people. If the conquering general realized any gains or booty, they were divided among the soldiers. But in more recent times, with the rise of autonomous governments, the ex-soldiers discovered that they could, merely by their ballots, demand a share of their nation's riches. The idea that soldiers are entitled to some personal compensation over and above their monthly pay for fighting wars appeared early in this country. In 1778, the Continental Congress[qv] voted that all commissioned officers should, at the conclusion of the war, be given one half of their present pay for seven years, provided they lived that long. Noncommissioned officers were promised $80 flat bonus. Later in the war, additional demands and promises were made. The Continental Congress soon realized, however, that it could not meet all these demands. So a compromise was finally reached, whereby officers were given five years' full pay, and noncommissioned officers and privates a flat bonus. The ex-soldiers of the War of 1812, the Mexican War[qqv] and the various Indian wars were not treated so generously. At the close of the Civil War[qv] a bounty of $100 was granted to those who had served three years, and a lesser amount to those who had served shorter terms. Then in 1875 Congress passed an act to "equalize the bounty" of all ex-Union soldiers. It amounted in fact to an outright bonus. But President Grant vetoed the bill, and no later attempts were made to secure bonus payments for the Civil War soldiers (*see* Grand Army of the Republic). Neither did the ex-soldiers and sailors of the Spanish-American War[qv] receive special bonus payments. The practice of paying a bonus, or a bounty, or adjusted compensation, whatever the term may be called, had been completely abandoned, when, suddenly after the World War[qv], it was revived. The bonus, it should be emphasized, is something entirely different from a pension[qv]. The pension represents a regular payment, at stated periods, to a disabled person or dependents. The bonus represents the payment of a fixed, lump sum, and, in case of war veterans, is paid to *all* ex-soldiers, whether able-bodied or disabled.

The demands for a bonus payment to the veterans of the World War came early. It was first suggested in the St. Louis caucus of the American Legion[qv] in May, 1919, but was promptly voted down. It came up again at the fall convention of the Legion, 1919, at Minneapolis. Here, a new point of view, a "new terminology," was advanced. The point was made that the soldiers of the World War had not received sufficient compensation during the months they were in service. Had they remained at home, it was pointed out, they would have made more money. This difference in pay should be recognized, hence, they were entitled to "adjusted compensation." The Government should make up the back pay. At the same time, it was noted that certain members of Congress were eagerly soliciting the support of the ex-soldiers, and numerous bills had already been introduced aimed at giving the soldiers extra compensation for their services. A fourfold adjusted compensation bill which, among other things, provided for the payment of adjusted compensation, was passed in 1922. President Harding vetoed it. The measure was revived in 1923, and again passed both House and Senate, only to meet a second veto, this time at the hands of President Coolidge. However, both House and Senate repassed the bill over the President's veto, May 19, 1924. According to the bill, actual payment of the bonus (adjusted compensation) was deferred until 1945. Each veteran was awarded a dollar a day for each day's service in the United States, and a dollar and twenty-five cents for each day served abroad. With the exception of those whose credits fell below $50, the veterans were not given cash, but were awarded paid-up twenty-year endowment insurance policies, or Adjusted Compensation Certificates. Over 3,500,000 such certificates were issued. The face value of each certificate was equal to the amount of endowment insurance, procurable from a commercial insurance company for a net premium payment equal to the veteran's bonus credit plus 25%. The certificates bore interest at 4% compounded annually. The aggregate face values amounted to $3,500,000,000. This act was hailed as a real victory by the World War veterans. Many believed it would be the last demand made upon Congress. But not for long. In January, 1931, the American Legion led a movement asking for immediate payment of the certificates. As a result of these demands, a compromise measure was agreed upon. While the veterans were not permitted to cash their certificates in full, yet the Government would now lend each veteran 50% of the face value of his certificate, at 4½% interest. A bill, carrying these provisions, passed both House and Senate early in 1931. It, however, received an executive veto, this time from President Hoover. But it was repassed over his veto. Almost immediately the veterans made another demand, this time it was for the immediate and full payment of all certificates. The demand was attended by many spectacular events. Chief of these was the so-called "Bonus Army"[qv] that assembled in Washington in the spring and summer of 1932. A bill known as the Patman Bill, which provided for the printing of fiat money, and the immediate payment of $2,500,000,000 to the holders of Adjusted Compensation Certificates, passed the House in June, 1932. The Senate rejected it. The "Bonus Army" that had assembled in Washington, numbering from 12,000 to 15,000 men, caused some alarm and local authorities requested President Hoover to preserve order. Troops from the War Department and the local police ordered the Bonus marchers out of the city. Rioting developed and several were injured. Congress voted $100,000 to send the Bonus marchers back to their homes, and after a few days the men dispersed.

Following the inauguration of President Franklin D. Roosevelt in 1933, and the vast expenditures attending the New Deal[qv] program, a change in attitude was noted toward the immediate payment in full of soldier certificates. Many who had heretofore opposed the movement now agreed that the veterans had as valid a claim as any group in asking for the immediate payment of their bonus. In January, 1936, another bill providing for the immediate cash payment of their certificates passed the House by vote of 358 to 59. On Jan. 20 it passed the Senate by vote of 74 to 16. Four days later President Roosevelt vetoed it. But within an hour it was repassed by the House, the vote being 324 to 61, and three days later the Senate overrode the veto by a vote of 76 to 19. The result was that after some seventeen years of agitation the demands of the ex-soldiers that they be paid a special bonus, over and above their monthly pay for services rendered in the World War, were granted.

[Knowlton Durham, *Billions for Veterans;* Roger Burlingame, *Peace Veterans;* Marcus Duffield, *King Legion;* and official reports, leaflets, pamphlets compiled by the American Legion; *Congressional Record* of 73rd and 74th Congresses.]

JOHN W. OLIVER

Bonus Army, The. A spontaneous gathering of unemployed World War veterans who, late in May, 1932, began marching and hitch-hiking to Washington in small groups from all over the United States until about 15,000 were assembled there. The needy veterans, seeking some economic relief from Congress, eventually united in petitioning for immediate payment of the Adjusted Compensation, or "Bonus,"*qv* Certificates.

The problems of food, shelter and sanitation for the impoverished veterans embarrassed Washington, and there was latent danger of disorder. But the leader, Walter W. Waters, maintained almost military discipline and expelled communistic agitators, while patriotism permeated the ranks. Though the chief of police, Gen. Glassford, tried to provide quarters, most of the men built wretched hovels in which they lived.

In mid-June Congress, by a narrow margin, defeated the bonus bill, but the disappointed "Bonus Expeditionary Force" stayed on, haunting the Capitol grounds. Late in July Glassford ordered the veterans to evacuate. They failed to do so and on July 28, by instructions from the President, United States troops drove them forcibly from their quarters in public buildings and from their camps.

[Walter W. Waters, *B. E. F., The Whole Story of the Bonus Army;* E. Francis Brown, The Bonus Army Marches to Defeat, *Current History,* September, 1932.]

JOSEPH MILLS HANSON

Bonus Bill, Calhoun's. On Dec. 16, 1816, John C. Calhoun recommended that the House of Representatives appoint a committee to inquire into the expediency of creating a fund for internal improvements*qv* from the profits derived from the second National Bank*qv*. With the appointment of the committee, Calhoun, as chairman, introduced a bill on Dec. 23, 1816, to set apart as a permanent fund for internal improvements the $1,500,000 bonus exacted from the bank as a price of the charter and the profits from the $7,000,000 of the bank stock owned by the United States. Although the bill was passed, President Madison vetoed it, March 3, 1817, on the ground that it was unconstitutional, but suggested an amendment to the Constitution that would remove all doubts upon the subject.

[*Annals of Congress,* 14 Cong., 2 sess., 296, 361.]

GEORGE D. HARMON

Boodle (Boodler). A barroom or street term for money or booty applied by sensational newspapers (1884–86) to members of the New York Board of Aldermen who were charged with accepting bribes in connection with the granting of a franchise for a street railroad on Broadway. Thereafter, the term came into common use to signify bribery in general and particularly in municipal governments.

[M. Ostrogorski, *Democracy and the Organization of Political Parties.*]

P. ORMAN RAY

Book Auctions. The first recorded auction occurred in Boston (1713) and has been followed by 10,000 of which there are printed sales catalogues surviving. Earliest surviving catalogue is that of the Pemberton sale, Boston, 1717. Eighteenth-century auctions were conducted largely by booksellers, of whom Robert Bell of Philadelphia was most noteworthy. In the 19th century regular auction houses began. (Dates are those of the life of the house.) Cunningham in Boston (1824–41) was followed by Leonard (1842–78). C. F. Libbies continued in Boston, 1878 down to 1919. Royal Gurley was one of New York's earliest book auctioneers (1831–48) and closely paralleled by Cooley's which survived to 1856. Lemuel Bangs' name survived as Bangs, Platt & Co. and Bangs-Merwin, in New York (1838–1903). Bangs finally sold out to John Anderson whose name still survives in the merger of the Anderson Galleries with the American Art Association in 1929. George A. Leavitt's name spans the years 1855–92. Thomas E. Kirby began in New York in 1882 and founded the American Art Association which merged with the Anderson Galleries in 1929. But the story of New York cannot omit the name of Joseph Sabin, whose auctioneering led him to begin the compilation of his *Dictionary of Books Relating to America,* which was seventy years in being published (1867–1937). In Philadelphia Moses Thomas began the still surviving Samuel H. Freeman & Co. Stan V. Henkels' Philadelphia firm endured from 1882 to 1926.

[C. S. Brigham's introduction to G. L. McKay's *American Auction Catalogues, 1713-1934.*]

RANDOLPH G. ADAMS

Book Collecting and Book Collections. The systematic gathering of books in America must be associated with the names of great collectors. These may be divided into two groups, those whose collections went to found or to supplement institutional libraries, and those whose collections were broken up in an auction sale. The former added definitely to the cultural riches of the country. The latter did great service in preserving books until such time as a given book finally reached a great repository library.

In colonial times Increase Mather (1639–1723) and Cotton Mather (1663–1728) of Boston were noteworthy, and most of the surviving books which belonged to them are now at the American Antiquarian Society. Thomas Prince (1687–1758) built up his "American Library" with a view to writing his history of New England. The survivors of his collection are at the Public Library of the City of Boston. William Byrd (1674–1744) of Westover made one of the great libraries in Virginia, but it was scattered. The books collected by Benjamin Franklin (1706–90) were disposed of by sale, but they have been subjected to a good deal of study by George S. Eddy, and many can actually be located today in various institutional libraries. Possibly the most systematic of the colonial book collectors was Thomas Jefferson (1743–1826), whose library was sold to the United States and became the foundation of the Library of Congress[qv]. Almost as important was the library of James Logan (1674–1751) which is now, for the most part, at the Philadelphia Library Company.

The 19th century produced a host of collectors: Samuel G. Drake (1798–1875) of Boston; George Brinley of Hartford; Henry C. Murphy (1810–82) of Brooklyn; James Carson Brevoort (1818–87) of New York; William Menzies, of New York; Brayton Ives (1840–1914) of New York, and many more whose libraries ended on the auction block to the enrichment of others. The Brinley sale of 1876–93 was in many respects the "greatest Americana sale" ever held. But as these men were building up and breaking up their libraries another force was making itself apparent in the book-collecting world in America.

The Brown family of Providence, R. I., had collected since colonial times, but John Carter Brown (1797–1874) definitely forged to the front as one of the more significant. Under his guidance and that of his son, John Nicholas Brown (1861–1900), the John Carter Brown Library attained pre-eminence and was finally given to Brown University, where it is today. Paralleling the career of John Carter Brown was that of James Lenox (1800–1880) of New York, whose collection of Bibles, Americana and English literature is a foundation stone of what is now the New York Public Library. In the main, however, the 19th-century collectors were working for their own edification, and with but little idea of putting their work at the service of scholarship.

With the turn of the 20th century there came a new motive in American book collecting based on the ideas of Lenox and Carter Brown. That was the collecting of books to form permanent public or semi-public institutions. J. Pierpont Morgan (1837–1913) of New York led the field in the first decade of the century and his life work may be seen in the Pierpont Morgan Library, New York, today. Just before the death of the elder Morgan, Henry E. Huntington (1850–1927) of California forged to the front and during the remainder of his life could well be called the greatest American book collector. He collected not merely individual items but whole libraries. The Huntington Library at San Marino is his monument. At the same time Henry Clay Folger (1857–1930) of New York was collecting Shakespeare, and today the Folger Shakespeare Memorial in Washington, D. C., can count seventy-nine copies of the First Folio alone. From about 1900 to his death in 1934 William L. Clements (1862–1934) of Bay City, Mich., built up his collection of Americana which in 1923 was officially given to his alma mater, the University of Michigan. Edward Everett Ayer (1841–1927) of Chicago collected Americana, with special reference to the Southwest, and his collection is now at the Newberry Library, Chicago. William Smith Mason (1866–) of the same city specialized in collecting Benjamin Franklin. His collection is at Yale University. The Robert B. Adam library of Johnsoniana went to Rochester University. John H. Wrenn's collection of English literature, which was partly the work of the English bibliographer, Thomas J. Wise, is at the University of Texas. Hubert Howe Bancroft (1832–1918) collected the Pacific Coast, and after his death his library went to the University of California. Robert Cowan's collection of California is now at the University of California at Los Angeles.

At the same time, the work of important collectors was constantly being broken up by auctions. Among these were the Robert Hoe sale of 1911–12; the Levi Leiter sale of 1933; the Roderick Terry sales of 1934; the Ogden Goelet sale of 1935; the John B. Stetson sale of 1935. Bibliomania raged in the United States during the "hilarious decade" 1919–29, and the prices fetched were higher than ever before. Notable among the high points was the sale of the Americana of William C. Braislin of Brooklyn in 1927, and the English literature of Jerome Kern in 1929.

It has sometimes been said that a great scholar seldom forms a great library. Yet in America four historians have done so. The books of Jared Sparks (1789–1866) are at Cornell University; those of Peter Force (1790–1868) are at the Library of Congress; and the library of George Bancroft (1800–1891) is at the New York Public Library. Wilberforce Eames (1855–1937) made up and disposed of several great libraries.

[No general American treatise on this subject. See files of *Proceedings of the American Antiquarian Society; Bulletin* of the New York Public Library; *Publisher's Weekly;* A. E. Newton, *Amenities of Book Collecting;* A. S. W. Rosenbach, *Books and Bidders;* R. G. Adams, *Three Americanists.*]

RANDOLPH G. ADAMS

Book Publishing. Publishing, as it is now practised with the whole financial responsibility for the production and distribution of a printed work resting upon a firm or an individual other than the author, arose after the Revolution. From the establishment in 1638 of Stephen Daye's press at Cambridge, Mass., books were printed at the author's expense, the first being *The Bay Psalm Book*[qv] (1640). Hezekiah Usher in 1647 in Boston first imported books and took some risks in republishing successful British works. Partly because of state control of printing, few presses were set up. That at Cambridge had a monopoly for fifty years; printing was forbidden in Virginia until 1730. "After great Charge and Trouble I have brought the great Art and Mystery of printing into this part of America," wrote William Bradford, but he left Philadelphia in 1693 because of arrest and imprisonment; for thirty years he was the sole printer in New York. In 1712 Andrew Bradford went to Philadelphia; sixteen years later Benjamin Franklin opened his own shop. As towns developed throughout the colonies, printing offices with weekly newspapers were founded. Near Philadelphia in 1743 Christopher Sower began publishing German works from the first non-English press. From these presses came occasional books, the majority of which were religious in character and foreign in origin.

The successful War for Independence led to a call for native authorship and American books. Isaiah Thomas of Worcester, Mass., Mathew Carey of Philadelphia and Hudson and Goodwin of Hartford, Conn., issued nationalistic schoolbooks like Noah Webster's *Blue-Backed Speller*[qv]. Native poetry by the Hartford Wits[qv] and native fiction by Charles Brockden Brown failed to sell profitably. In 1801 Carey organized the American Company of Booksellers to foster book fairs and to stimulate American authorship. Yet, especially with the vogue of the novel after Scott's success in 1814 with *Waverley,* British books crowded American shelves, and publishers vied in securing first sheets and flooding the market with the writings of Scott, Bulwer-Lytton, Dickens, Thackeray and others. Until foreign publications were affected by the copyright[qv] law of 1891, they tended to dominate the market. Certain houses, like Carey's, Harper's and Putnam's, printed editions almost overnight to forestall competition. Only James Fenimore Cooper's and Harriet Beecher Stowe's novels competed successfully with oversea books.

Notable publishing changes were effected about 1815 by the employment of the stereotype process, which cheapened production and made possible a uniformity of editions of textbooks printed in different states. Railroad transportation, after 1840, tended to end the practice of leasing plates to printers and to centralize in one office the publication of a book. The vogue of annuals and gift books, with their beautiful "embellishments," gave rise to the arts of wood and steel engraving and lithography. By 1870 America led the world in the perfection of wood engraving[qv], but the development of photography[qv] and photo-engraving, an inexpensive process of reproducing pictures on metal, soon substituted mechanical for manual artistry. Since 1900, and especially since 1920, American publishers have paid great attention to the arts of design in manufacturing books, on the theory that beauty improves sales.

Attempts to provide good books at low prices to the masses were made by Harper's as early as 1830, but success first crowned the venture of Park Benjamin, the poet, who in the 1840's issued paper-bound quartos at prices below twenty-five cents a volume. Competitors with handier size and larger type soon ended the poet's experiment. From 1870 to 1891 a vast number of books, reprints and translations of foreign works as well as first editions of American writers flooded the market at prices ranging from twenty-five to fifty cents a copy. "The lesson of the year," declared the *American Booksellers' Guide* in 1873, "is that Americans want cheap books." Simultaneously dime novel series[qv], then never referred to as books, enjoyed enormous sales. Newspapers and magazines gave books as subscription inducements; the New York *Tribune* thus distributed thousands of copies of *Webster's Dictionary*[qv]. Door-to-door sale of religious, historical and encyclopedic books became profitable. Mark Twain, beguiled by the profits of publishing, lost a fortune in an ill-starred venture. Post-World War attempts to circulate books once a month through book clubs were resisted unsuccessfully by trade publishers. An extension of the publication of reprint editions of standard works at popular prices took place in the 1920's, when chain drug stores opened book counters and with their "dollar-ature" gave booksellers unexpected paralyzing competition.

In 1789 the Methodist Book Concern was established, the first church publishing house. Since then every sect and several interdenominational organizations have produced thousands of books to the extent of millions of copies. The American Tract Society[qv], for example, has published in 179 languages, dialects and characters. The American Bible Society[qv] has distributed millions of Bibles in many languages. Correspondence schools, like the International Correspondence School, have produced notable textbooks. To foster the printing of scientific writings, some twenty American universities have subsidized publishing houses. Other learned and professional societies similarly have created divisions for issuing writings of specialized interest. The Federal Government and state and territorial governments, as well as county and municipal divisions, issue books concerning their activities. Thus the production of books in the United States is large, that of trade publishers being probably less than half the total.

[H. W. Boynton, *Annals of American Bookselling, 1638-1850;* C. M. Depew, *One Hundred Years of American Commerce;* R. H. Shove, *Cheap Book Production in the United States, 1870 to 1891.*]

HARRY R. WARFEL

Bookshops, Old. In every large city there is at least one old bookshop with roots nourished by the literary tradition. Most notable is Boston's "Old Corner Book Store" with a sentimental history reaching back to 1812. Here Samuel G. Goodrich ("Peter Parley"[qv]) began his literary enterprises; here James T. Fields, later the publisher of the New England galaxy of writers, learned the book business as a clerk; here authors frequently congregated on their way to and from the dinners of the famous Saturday Club. In Charles Wiley's bookshop in New York City James Fenimore Cooper held court in a style becoming America's most popular novelist of the 1820's; Fitz-Greene Halleck, Joseph Rodman Drake, William Cullen Bryant and other celebrities joined the novelist. In New Haven, Hezekiah Howe, printer of Noah Webster's *American Dictionary*[qv] (1828), had an extensive collection of old books. His store became the rendezvous of Yale professors and scholars traveling overland between Boston and New York. These book dealers underwrote the publication of editions of desirable technical, professional and religious works; thus they frequently were publishers as well as booksellers. Many publishers maintained bookshops. Scribners and Putnams, among others, still conduct stores selling old and new books, although the tendency toward specialization in one department of the book business long ago set in.

Among the more notable dealers in old books in New York was William Gowans, who set up shop in 1829. At his death in 1871 his stock totaled 300,000 volumes. His customers included the noted literati of his generation. Until the middle of the 19th century old books came chiefly from England. Occasional shipments of folios and quartos and rare Americana stimulated a few dealers to specialize in rare, expensive works. In the 1850's interest grew in Americana, because Parkman, Bancroft, Cooper and Irving called attention to the pleasures of amassing collections relating to our country. Joseph Sabin, between 1864 and 1874, sold more than a million dollars' worth of such books. Sabin prepared *A Dictionary of Books Relating to America, from Its Discovery to the Present Time* (14 vols., 1868–84), a painstaking compilation, but permeated with a malevolent and saturnine spirit and marred with unscholarly remarks. In Philadelphia William Brotherhead capitalized the interest in Americana. He published several patriotic works, such as facsimiles of the signers of the Declaration of Independence.

Now that vast municipal and institutional libraries have replaced the scholar's personal library as a workshop, the antiquarian bookshop has lost some of its charm and much of its profit. The seller of old books has had to speed his pace by employing modern sales devices since the great personal libraries, like those of Lenox, Astor, Folger, Morgan and Huntington, have passed into the possession of institutions.

[H. W. Boynton, *Annals of American Bookselling, 1638-*

1850; William Brotherhead, *Forty Years among the Old Booksellers of Philadelphia;* W. L. Andrews, *The Old Booksellers of New York.*]

HARRY R. WARFEL

Boom Towns, those which sprang up like mushrooms as the result of some mineral or industrial development, were numerous in the 19th century. Rochester, N. Y., was one of the earliest notable examples, its growth after 1825 as the result of the building of the Erie Canal[qv] and the development of the Genesee water power being phenomenal for the period. There were a few boom towns in the Middle West, but the finest specimens began to be seen only with the discoveries of gold and silver[qqv] in the Far West. San Francisco itself in 1849–51 was a remarkable example. Simultaneously, in the gold regions, before there were any sawmills, villages of tents, with an occasional log hut, sprang up, and quickly formed city governments. By the time lumber began to be sawed, county governments were being organized and the crudest of small frame shacks became courthouses. Virginia City and other Nevada towns were mushroom growths from silver ore; meanwhile, in the 1860's, gold was producing many others in Idaho, Montana and Colorado, mostly ephemeral, though Helena, Mont., and Denver[qv], Colo., proved to be permanent. Gold brought Deadwood, S. Dak., into being in 1876. Two cities built on silver evolved swiftly in 1878, Tombstone, Ariz., a new foundation, and Leadville, Colo., long a somnolent hamlet, but whose population leaped from 300 to 35,000 in two years. Oil City, Pa., in 1859 was the first of a long series of petroleum boom towns, later continued in Ohio, Indiana, Oklahoma and Texas. The opening of a portion of the Indian Territory[qv] to colonization in 1889 created Guthrie and Oklahoma City almost overnight. Immediately afterward, new gold discoveries in Colorado did the same for Cripple Creek[qv] and Creede. Hopewell, Va., was a typical creation of World War munition plants, and other precocious towns arose in Florida during the land-speculation excitement of the 1920's.

[Alvin F. Harlow, *Old Waybills;* John M. Clampitt, *Echoes from the Rocky Mountains.*]

ALVIN F. HARLOW

Boomer Movement, The, is a term applied to attempts of settlers to occupy an area in Indian Territory[qv] during the period from 1879 to 1885. The Five Civilized Tribes[qv] of Indians formerly owned all of the present state of Oklahoma except the Panhandle (*see* Cimarron, Proposed Territory of). In 1866 as a punishment for having participated in the Civil War on the side of the South (*see* Indian in the Civil War), they were compelled to cede to the United States as a home for other Indians the western half of their domain. During the next ten years several tribes of Indians were given reservations on these lands but a fertile region of some 2,000,000 acres near the center of Indian Territory was not assigned to any tribe and came to be known as the "Unassigned Lands" or "Old Oklahoma."

Early in 1879 E. C. Boudinot, a railway attorney of Cherokee blood, published a newspaper article stating that this was public land, and so open to homestead entry. Widely reprinted, this article created great excitement. Later in the same year a colony of homeseekers under the leadership of C. C. Carpenter sought to enter the Indian Territory and occupy this area but was prevented by troops under Gen. Pope.

In 1880 David L. Payne became the leader of these so-called "Boomers." Payne organized the movement, charging a small fee for membership in his "Oklahoma Colony." During the next four years he and his followers made eight attempts to settle the region but in every case were ejected by soldiers. Upon his death at Wellington, Kans., in 1884 his lieutenant, W. L. Couch, led an expedition to the forbidden area, but was promptly removed by the military. The struggle was then transferred to the national capital and on April 22, 1889, the Unassigned Lands were opened to settlement under the provisions of an act of Congress.

[E. E. Dale and J. L. Rader, *Readings in Oklahoma History.*]

EDWARD EVERETT DALE

Boondoggling. On April 3, 1935, Robert C. Marshall, a witness before the Aldermanic Committee to Investigate the Relief Administration in New York City, testified that he taught various crafts, including "boondoggling," to workers on relief[qv], and described "boondoggles" as "gadgets" or useful articles made out of scrap material. The term boondoggling was thereafter rather loosely used by critics of the New Deal[qv] throughout the country to ridicule so-called useless made-work and unproductive educational, recreational and research projects of relief workers.

[L. P. Stryker, *Report to . . . the Aldermanic Committee to Investigate the Relief Administration in the City of New York; The Christian Science Monitor,* Weekly Magazine Section, Aug. 19, 1936; *The Literary Digest,* June 1, 1935, The Lexicographer's Easy Chair; *Scouting,* March, 1930, Vol. 18.]

STANLEY R. PILLSBURY

Boone, Jemima, and Callaway Girls Episode. The settlement of Boonesborough on the Kentucky River had been left in peace by the Indians until Sunday, July 14, 1776, when three girls were captured as they were floating in a canoe on the river. They were Jemima, daughter of Daniel Boone, and Elizabeth and Frances, daughters of Col. Richard Callaway. The settlement was thrown into a turmoil and a rescue party was organized by Boone. Meanwhile the girls were hurried north by their captors toward the Shawnee^qv towns across the Ohio. They attempted to mark their trail until threatened by the Indians.

The third morning, as the Indians were building a fire for breakfast, the rescuers came up. "That's Daddy's gun," cried Jemima, as one Indian was toppled into the fire. The others ran off leaving their plunder, which the whites took. The girls were escorted home in triumph. Jemima soon married one of the rescuing party, Flanders Callaway. Elizabeth Callaway married Samuel Henderson and Frances, John Holder. The episode served to put the settlers in the Kentucky wilderness on guard and prevented straying beyond the fort.

[George W. Ranck, *Boonesborough;* R. G. Thwaites, *Daniel Boone;* John Bakeless, *Life of Daniel Boone.*]

LOUISE PHELPS KELLOGG

Boone's Station was the stockaded home of Daniel Boone from 1780 to 1786. The place, which had been settled by Daniel's brother, Israel, in 1776, was on Boone's Creek in Fayette County, Ky., near the present village of Athens. Here John Filson interviewed Daniel Boone in 1784 for his *The Adventures of Colonel Daniel Boone.*

[G. W. Ranck, *Boonesborough.*]

JONATHAN T. DORRIS

Boone's Wilderness Road. *See* Wilderness Road, The.

Boonesborough, on the south side of the Kentucky River, in the present county of Madison, was founded April 2, 1775, by Daniel Boone. Despatched from the Watauga treaty ground by members of the Transylvania Company^qv to mark out a roadway to lands purchased from the Cherokees^qv, Boone and his companions blazed a trail across Cumberland Gap^qv and thence through the wilderness to the mouth of Otter Creek on the Kentucky. There they erected a stout stockaded fort which served as a rallying-point of defense for the harassed settlers throughout the Revolution. At Boonesborough, May 23–27, 1775, was held the convention called by the Transylvania proprietors to consider the needs of the colony. The novel proceedings and enactments were devoid of effective sanction, but they were timely and savored of the soil.

On July 14, 1776, three young girls, one a daughter of Boone, were captured near the fort by skulking savages, but within a day or two were rescued unharmed (*see* Boone, Jemima, and Callaway Girls Episode). On April 15, 1777, Boonesborough was subjected to a savage Indian attack, and on July 4 of the same year the assault was renewed on a larger scale. The fiercest siege and assault of all, however, occurred Sept. 7–20, 1778. The Shawnee^qv chiefs, Black Fish and Moluntha, together with the French-Canadian, Lt. Antoine Dagneaux de Quindre, were in command of a formidable body of Indians supported by a few British militiamen from Detroit and this combined force assailed the little fortress with all the arts of bravado and cunning. But neither force nor guile could bring about its downfall, and, finding their efforts futile, the invaders finally desisted and withdrew.

[George W. Ranck, *Boonesborough;* Lucille Gulliver, *Life of Boone.*]

SAMUEL M. WILSON

Boonton Iron Works, THE, were founded about 1770 by Samuel Ogden who, with others in his family, purchased a six-acre tract along the Rockaway River, near Boonton, Morris County, N. J. Here rolling and slitting mills were erected that engaged in the manufacture of nail rods and bar iron. With the building of the Morris Canal^qv in 1830 the New Jersey Iron Company was organized. This company built a new plant costing $283,000 and imported skilled mechanics from England. Under Fuller & Lord (1852–76) the enterprise tended to become an integrated industry with ore and timber reserves, canal boats, furnaces, mills and auxiliary plants. After 1881 the business slowly declined. The plant closed in 1911.

[C. S. Boyer, *Early Forges and Furnaces in New Jersey.*]

C. A. TITUS

Boonville, Mo., Battle of (June 17, 1861). In the first engagement of the Civil War in Missouri, troops of the Missouri state guard (pro-Southern) under Col. John S. Marmaduke were defeated by Brig. Gen. Lyon at Boonville, a strategic point on the Missouri River. The engagement began about five miles below Boonville. Union forces occupied Boonville and gained control of the river, and Confederate strength in Missouri was weakened.

[Walter Williams and Floyd C. Shoemaker, *Missouri, Mother of the West,* Vol. II.]

FLOYD C. SHOEMAKER

Booth v. U. S. (Feb. 5, 1934). In 1919 Congress passed an act permitting certain Federal judges to retire with full pay, at the age of seventy. On June 16, 1933, new legislation reduced their pay 15%. Retired Judge Wilbur F. Booth thereupon sued the Government. The Supreme Court unanimously ruled in his favor, holding that a retired judge did not "relinquish his office" and so, under Art. III, Sec. 1 of the Constitution, his pay could not be reduced.

[291 U. S. 339.]

ERIK McKINLEY ERIKSSON

Bootlegging is a term, derived from the early Indian traders'^qv custom of carrying a bottle of liquor^qv in the boot, especially applied to illicit deliveries of alcoholic beverages. The bootlegger is a peddler whose name differentiates his activities from those of the merchant who unlawfully purveys from a shop known variously as a "blind tiger," "blind pig" or "speakeasy"^qv. The manufacture of illicit hard liquor is termed "moonshining"^qv and the product, variously known, is perhaps most euphemistically described as "mountain dew."

Since the activity is illicit, no reliable estimates can be given as to the scope. In some sections of the country sentiment favors bootlegging as being a proper resistance to tyranny, in others it is regarded as completely reprehensible, all licensed retail liquor dealers holding the latter opinion quite determinedly. In those times and places in which alcoholic beverages can be obtained lawfully at reasonable prices the popular estimation of the bootlegger's business rapidly depreciates; but heavy taxation or legal efforts to prevent the traffic speedily render the purveyor a more respected member of society.

The profits derived from bootlegging depend somewhat upon the source of the beverage and somewhat upon the methods of retailing. To supply thirsty citizens in the days of the Eighteenth Amendment^qv liquor was smuggled across the borders, alcohol lawfully possessed for manufacturing purposes was sold for beverages and a relatively small amount was distilled without license, the annual consumption from all sources averaging perhaps 100,000,000 gallons of hard liquor (1920 to 1932). In the larger cities powerful organizations arose to cater to the bibulous. These gangs, headed by an unusually astute or intelligent man, corrupted the agencies of law enforcement, arranged for a steady supply and set up a complete system of retailing both through luxurious speakeasies, known as "night clubs,"^qv which furnished a variety of entertainment as well as food and illicit drink, and through the private calls of bootleggers upon regular customers. They tried to create a monopoly and were as ready to take a rival "for a ride" as they were thus to entertain a spy or a traitor. The unlucky recipient of this attention was likely to be found along an unfrequented road, filled with slugs from a machine gun; the methods of disposal were all quite final, however various. The St. Valentine's Day massacre of 1929 in a populous section of the Chicago North Side, within a few blocks of the great Newberry Library, was the slaughter of seven unarmed rivals by one of these bootlegging gangs. (*See also* Rum Row.)

To meet the rising tide of crime several steps were taken. An amendment to the National Prohibition Act was passed in February, 1929, raising the maximum penalty for bootlegging to a fine of $10,000 plus five years in prison, but this carried a rider stipulating that it was the intent of Congress to apply this drastic punishment to major offenders only. A year later, a Federal grand jury sitting at Chicago uncovered what was termed the largest liquor ring since the advent of prohibition^qv. The indictment of 31 corporations and 158 individuals cited violations in New York, Chicago, Detroit, Cleveland, Philadelphia, St. Louis, Minneapolis, St. Paul, Los Angeles and North Bergen, N. J. This group was charged with the diversion of more than 7,000,000 gallons of alcohol in the seven years preceding indictment and were alleged to have done a total business in excess of $50,000,000. The State of Michigan went so far as to declare bootlegging a felony and to provide that on a third conviction for felony the convict might be sentenced to imprisonment for life.

Before the end of 1930 more than 200 persons had been killed in the process of enforcement of the Volstead Act^qv and moderates were beginning to question if, after all, the game was worth the candle. The public revealed this attitude in a *Literary Digest* poll, May 24, 1930, by returning 30.5% of their votes in favor of continuance and strict enforcement of the prohibition amendment, 29.1% in favor of modification to permit light wines and beer and 40.4% for repeal.

A limited number of bootleggers has always operated and probably will continue, but since the quality of their merchandise and public support are both uncertain, their sales volume doubtless will remain relatively small.

[*Annals of American Association for the Promotion of Social Science*, Vols. XXXII, CIX, CLXIII.]

ROBERT G. RAYMER

Boots and Shoes. Boot and shoe making began in colonial America in the shops of village artisans working to order, in plantation shops employing slaves and with itinerant craftsmen who traveled from household to household to make the family footwear. Very early, however, coarse brogans were manufactured commercially in the northern colonies to ship to southern plantations. By the middle of the 18th century skilled craftsmen at Lynn, Mass., and other colonial centers were making finer footwear, especially ladies' shoes, for the general market. Little change occurred in the hand process of making shoes until about the time of the Civil War. For several decades before this, however, the industry had been developing a new organization to serve a larger commercial demand, especially in the West. Even before the Revolution, army contractors and wholesalers purchased shoes from makers working singly or in teams in "ten-footer" shops scattered through the more thickly settled parts of New England. Gradually, however, a system developed where shoes were produced in quantities by manufacturers, also principally in New England, who had warehouse-factories for cutting but who employed home workers served by wagon distributors and collectors to fit and sew uppers and to last and sole complete boots and shoes. During the 1870's and 1880's automatic machines for pegging and nailing soles, for shaping leather and for lasting were perfected. More important than this, the sewing machine was adapted to sewing uppers, welts and soles. These mechanical improvements, which were American inventions[qv], and the application of power to shoemaking machinery, caused all operations to be concentrated in factories many of which were grouped in shoe towns like Lynn, Brockton and Haverhill in Massachusetts and in larger cities. The new methods of manufacture encouraged styling and quantity production and, accompanied by improved tanning processes and a wider variety of leathers, enabled American footwear to conquer foreign markets. This development went hand in hand with the use of trade brands, extensive advertising and the practice of selling standard makes at fixed prices through chains of retail stores controlled by the manufacturer. From colonial times the principal shoemaking state of America has been Massachusetts, which still accounts for about one fourth of the billion dollars' worth of footwear made in the country. New York and Missouri, where St. Louis is a great shoemaking center, rank next to Massachusetts in this industry.

[Blanche Evans Hazard, *The Organization of the Boot and Shoe Industry in Massachusetts before 1875;* U. S. Census Reports.]

VICTOR S. CLARK

Borax. Until recently the principal source of borax in the United States was Death Valley[qv] and the adjacent mines in the Funeral Range. But the boring of a deep well near Kramer, Calif., revealed a richer deposit and the Death Valley properties were closed down.

The discovery of borax in Death Valley is credited to Aaron Winters, who sold out to William T. Coleman. He used Chinese to scrape up the "cotton-ball" borax, which he hauled 165 miles to the railroad at Daggett, Calif. The property was later taken over by F. M. Smith, the Borax King, who made the Twenty Mule Teams famous on the long haul to Mojave, Calif. Two of these huge wagons hooked together would haul 45,000 lbs. of borax, the capacity of an ordinary freight car.

[Dane Coolidge, *Death Valley Prospectors.*]

DANE COOLIDGE

Border Forts, The Evacuation of (1796). By the French and Indian War[qv] Great Britain conquered the western country, and by the Proclamation of 1763[qv] constituted it a permanent Indian preserve. This policy was reversed by the Quebec Act[qv] (1774) which annexed the entire Northwest to Quebec Province. Thereby the older colonies, which had fought to obtain the West, found themselves excluded from all share in it. During the Revolution they again renewed the struggle for the West, and at its close obtained it, with the Mississippi and the line through the middle of the Great Lakes-St. Lawrence system as the western and northern boundaries of the new nation (*see* Definitive Treaty of Peace, 1783).

Elsewhere in the treaty Great Britain agreed to evacuate all places held by her armies within the United States "with all convenient speed." These included Carleton Island (Fort Haldimand), Oswego (Fort Ontario), Niagara, Detroit and Michilimackinac, guarding the fur trade route between Montreal and the far Northwest, and serving as natural centers of control of the interior Indian tribes, allies of Great Britain in the late war. Both Gov. Haldimand and the Montreal traders were appalled by the boundary provisions of the treaty, the governor fearing the surrender of the posts would precipitate a general Indian uprising, the merchants foreseeing their own financial ruin. The early American overtures for the transfer were evaded, therefore, while their later appeals at London were met by the excuse that the Americans had not complied with the treaty in the matter of collection of debts owed to British merchants (*see*

British Debts, The), and the treatment accorded the Loyalists[qv].

For a decade Great Britain pursued a policy of opportunism, meanwhile retaining the posts and exercising *de facto* control over the Northwest. In 1793, however, she entered the continental revolutionary wars, while in America President Washington was prosecuting the conquest of the Northwestern Indian Confederacy (*see* Wayne Campaign). Faced with a war in Europe, the British Ministry had no stomach for another in America. By the Jay Treaty[qv] (ratified in 1795) the evacuation of the Western posts by June 1, 1796, was promised. The Americans proved less ready to receive than the British were to deliver them; Detroit was taken over July 11; Oswego on July 15; Niagara on Aug. 10; and Michilimackinac, Sept. 1. With the transfer American rule over the country adjacent to the Great Lakes was first established; west of Lake Michigan and on Lake Superior, however, British authority continued dominant until after the War of 1812.

[Alfred L. Burt, *The Old Province of Quebec;* Louise P. Kellogg, *The British Régime in Wisconsin and the Northwest;* A. C. McLaughlin, The Western Posts and the British Debts, in American Historical Association *Annual Report* for 1894.]

M. M. QUAIFE

Border Ruffians were citizens of western Missouri who endeavored to establish slavery in Kansas Territory. The term originated in 1855 with B. F. Stringfellow's assault upon Gov. A. H. Reeder, and was first used by the New York *Tribune*. Missourians readily adopted the name, and border ruffian stores, hotels and river boats capitalized upon it. Antislavery presses and orators soon expanded the term to include all proslavery Southerners in Kansas. Some of the "ruffians" were of the carousing type, but indiscriminate usage included such respectable leaders as Sen. D. R. Atchison. "Border ruffians" voted illegally in Kansas elections, raided Lawrence[qv] and other towns, stole horses, and in general molested free-state families (*see* Kansas Struggle, The). Much of their overzealous work was inspired by similar depredations committed by antislavery Kansans upon Missourians, and once such practices had begun a spirit of lawlessness prompted both groups to use extreme measures. (*See also* Border War.)

[W. E. Connelley, *A Standard History of Kansas and Kansans.*]

WENDELL H. STEPHENSON

Border Slave State Convention, THE (1861), also called the Peace Convention or Conference, met in Washington, D. C., Feb. 4–27, 1861, on call by the Virginia legislature, in an attempt to satisfy the states of the far South on the slavery issue. Twenty-one states were represented, with the border states[qv] most active. The seven states which had already seceded did not send delegates, nor did Arkansas, Wisconsin, Minnesota, California, Oregon. Ex-President Tyler of Virginia, chosen president of the Convention, stated its purpose—"to bring back the cotton states and thereby restore the Constitution and the Union of the States." The Crittenden Compromise[qv] plan, which formed the basis of discussion, was so modified by further compromise in the course of the deliberations that the final recommendations of the Convention satisfied no one. The recommendations, submitted to Congress on Feb. 27, 1861, constituted the last attempt at conciliation on the slavery question in the territories.

[J. G. Randall, *The Civil War and Reconstruction.*]

C. MILDRED THOMPSON

Border State Representation in the Confederacy. *See* Confederacy, Border State Representation in.

Border States, THE, was a designation applied to the tier of slave states bordering on the North, consisting of Delaware, Maryland, Virginia, Kentucky and Missouri. They were largely Southern in sentiment, though many of their economic ties were with the North. They owe their chief significance to their reaction toward secession and the Civil War[qqv]. None seceded except Virginia, from which West Virginia separated. Kentucky set up and maintained for a few months in 1861 the unique policy of neutrality, and all except Delaware sent considerable numbers of soldiers to the Confederacy. Kentucky and Delaware were the only states to cling to slavery until the Thirteenth Amendment[qv] abolished it.

[E. C. Smith, *The Borderland in the Civil War.*]

E. MERTON COULTER

Border War (1854–59), on the Kansas frontier, resulted from the opening of the territory to slavery, promoted emigration from the Northeast (*see* Emigrant Aid Movement, The), the arrival of squatters and speculators and the presence of an adventurous element recruited from both North and South. While claim jumping[qv] provoked dissension, the slavery issue was controlling. Recurring personal altercations led disputants to organize regulating associations and guerrilla bands. It is impossible to determine which side committed greater excesses in lynching, horse stealing, pillaging and pitched battles. The first eighteen months witnessed killings and robberies, but moderation and self-control prevented serious discord until the murder of a free-state settler, following a quarrel over a land claim, precipitated the bloodless Wakarusa War[qv], December, 1855. "Bleeding Kansas" soon became a grim reality. The "sack" of Lawrence[qv], May 21, 1856, by a posse of "border ruffians,"[qv] and John Brown's massacre of five proslavery men at Potawatomie[qv] three days later started a four months' reign of terror. Free-state men won victories at Black Jack, Franklin, Forts Saunders and Titus, Slough Creek and Hickory Point; their opponents pillaged and later burned Osawatomie[qv] but were prevented from destroying Lawrence by official intervention. A semblance of order restored by Gov. J. W. Geary in the fall was of brief duration. The Marais des Cygnes[qv] massacre of nine free-state men, May 19, 1858, was the last wholesale slaughter. In the same year disturbances in Linn and Bourbon counties reached critical proportions. Cessation of these early in 1859 terminated major conflict, albeit sporadic disorders continued until the Civil War inaugurated a new chapter in Kansas-Missouri relations. Anticipating a congressional appropriation which did not materialize, territorial commissioners approved claims for losses resulting from border trouble totaling over $400,000, which, though greatly exaggerated, give some notion of the extent of property damage.

[F. W. Blackmar, *The Life of Charles Robinson;* D. W. Wilder, *Annals of Kansas.*]

WENDELL H. STEPHENSON

Border War, The Religious Phase of (1857–59). Border conflicts were frequent after 1844–45 wherever the antislavery and proslavery wings of the churches met, as in Missouri, Kentucky and western Virginia. With the opening of Kansas, this conflict was extended there, and both Northern and Southern churches tried to occupy the territory. Church people were largely responsible for the formation and support of the New England Emigrant Aid Company[qv]. Thus the settlement of Kansas became for many a Christian crusade and the crusaders came singing Whittier's hymn:

We cross the prairies as of old
  The Pilgrims crossed the sea,
To make the west as they the east,
  The homestead of the free.

Such pious cant on the part of the antislavery party helps explain the fury with which the proslavery element resisted their control.

[W. W. Sweet, Some Religious Aspects of the Kansas Struggle, in *The Journal of Religion*, Vol. VII.]

WILLIAM W. SWEET

Borglum's Colossal Sculptures. The idea of carving a colossal head of Robert E. Lee on Stone Mountain, Ga., was first conceived, in 1915, by the Daughters of the Confederacy[qv], inspired by Mr. Borglum's colossal marble head of Lincoln in the Rotunda at the Capitol, Washington.

On visiting the mountain, in 1915, the sculptor refused to undertake the single head in dimensions insignificant for the mountain, and offered a design of the mobilization of the Confederate forces under their leaders, Lee, Jackson, Jefferson Davis and field officers, developing a wholly new treatment regarding memorials by departing from the conventional figure or grouping, and composing the subject into mass movement, stressing the importance of mass action relating to human events.

His conception involved the creation in the granite of Stone Mountain groupings in scale with the mountain itself. The composition contained infantry en masse marching in review before their commander, and some forty mounted general officers, supported by cavalry, and field guns. The horse and rider were approximately 160 feet in height, the length of the carving approximately 720 feet. All rough stone to a point within two feet of the finished surface was removed with dynamite and actual carving carried on with air drills and hand tools.

Stone Mountain developed a school of colossal sculpture and was progressing with great success when, in 1924, a sharp difference arose between Mr. Borglum and two members of the committee as to the degree of perfection and finish of the work, resulting in Mr. Borglum's abandoning the work and destroying his own models.

In 1930 at the call of the governor of the state, the sculptor went to Atlanta and agreed in public meeting to return as soon as the work on Mount Rushmore could spare him. The new plans for Stone Mountain will be doubled in dimensions, and in higher relief, following the highly successful carvings at Mount Rushmore.

The Mount Rushmore Memorial, begun in 1927, is located in the Black Hills of South Dakota. It is being carved on the apex of a great granite uplift. The figures, grouped in the form of a horseshoe, are scaled to the proportions of men 465 feet high, the sculptures fading into the precipice at the waistline. The first figure at the right is George Washington, commemorating the founding of the Republic. Next comes Jefferson, commemorating the development of our territorial greatness. In the center of the horseshoe is the figure of Theodore Roosevelt, commemorating the cutting of the Panama Canal. And on the left side of the horseshoe, opposite Jefferson, is the figure of Lincoln, commemorating the preservation of the Union. The horseshoe in which the figures are carved is cut back approximately 100 feet into the solid granite of the mountain and the distance between Jefferson and Lincoln is approximately 75 feet. The mountain itself is a great dyke, the front forming a vast amphitheater upon the west walls of which Borglum proposes to incise the Declaration of Independence and other national documents. The figures face southeast. The Memorial, first suggested by Doane Robinson, was sponsored by a group of patriotic individuals who had been impressed by Borglum's work on Stone Mountain. It is now entirely under the supervision of the Government of the United States.

GUTZON BORGLUM

Borgne, Lake, Battle of (Dec. 14, 1814), was the naval engagement preceding the Battle of New Orleans*qv*. The British, with a force of light barges commanded by Capt. Lockyer, captured the five American gunboats commanded by Lt. Thomas ap Catesby Jones guarding Malhereux Island Passage. This cleared the eastern approach to the city and avoided the fortifications along the river. The defeated Americans inflicted such heavy losses upon their captors as to contribute to the many delays which made it possible for the lately arrived Gen. Jackson to organize the defense of the city.

[A. T. Mahan, *The War of 1812 in Its Relations to Sea Power.*]

U. T. BRADLEY

Borough. Numerous colonial towns were patterned after the English borough, which was a trading community or town that had obtained some degree of corporate organization and certain rights of self-government. The colonial boroughs received their charters from the governors and were governed by a mayor and recorder, appointed by the governor, and aldermen elected by the freemen*qv*. Sitting as a common council, these officials passed bylaws regulating trade, industry and labor, binding out orphans, supervising poor relief, fixing the assize of bread and admitting the freemen, who in early days possessed a monopoly of retail trade, although in later times such regulations were generally relaxed. Sitting as a mayor's or sessions court, these same officials handled both civil and criminal business. After the Revolution borough charters were granted by the state legislatures. The suffrage was widened and the mayor came to be elected by popular vote and gained increasing authority in borough management.

[R. B. Morris, *Select Cases of the Mayor's Court of New York City;* A. E. Peterson and G. W. Edwards, *New York as an Eighteenth Century Municipality.*]

RICHARD B. MORRIS

Bosque Redondo, THE, was a reservation forty miles square on Pecos River, central New Mexico, to which 8000 Navajos*qv* were removed in 1863. Those who survived five years of disgraceful mismanagement were permitted by the Federal Government (1868) to return to their old habitat. Never since have the Navajos given any serious trouble.

[R. E. Twitchell, *Leading Facts of New Mexican History.*]

LANSING B. BLOOM

Boss, Political. Although not confined to the United States, the political boss has probably played a somewhat larger role in its political history, particularly since 1850, than in that of any other country. The boss has dominated city, county and state governments.

Cartoonists portray the boss as a coarse-featured, profane giant of a man who wears checked clothes and gaudy jewelry and constantly has a well-chewed cigar in his mouth. Actually there is wide variation in the physical, mental, moral and political characteristics of bosses. Usually a boss must start in precinct politics and through a process of survival of the fittest clamber to the top. He is more often than not a hard worker, courageous, a good judge of men, loyal to friends and generous to unfortunates. He may or may not be corrupt, harsh and indifferent to the public weal. As a rule he holds public office at some time, enjoys intimate relations with business and desires for himself great power or much money or both.

Tweed, Croker, Murphy, McManes, the Vares, Cox, Lundin, Prendergast and Ruef rank among notorious city bosses. Quay, Penrose, Platt, Taggart and Long are outstanding examples of state bosses.

[W. B. Munro, *Personality in Politics;* S. P. Orth, *The Boss and the Machine;* J. T. Salter, *Boss Rule;* Harold Zink, *City Bosses in the United States;* H. F. Gosnell, *Boss Platt and His New York Machine.*]

HAROLD ZINK

Boston. Capt. John Smith explored and mapped the vicinity of Boston in 1614. In 1621 a party from Plymouth visited the site of Boston, the peninsula called Shawmut by the Indians and other landmarks. Individual settlers in the next few years located there and across the Charles River. Following the Great Migration*qv* of 1630 John Winthrop's group first settled at Charlestown*qv*, but soon moved over to the Shawmut peninsula. On Sept. 7 of that year it was ordained by the Court of Assistants, sitting at Charlestown, that the new town be named Boston. In 1632 it was made the capital of Massachusetts Bay Colony[q.v.] and that year the first meetinghouse was erected. The first post office was opened in 1639; in 1652 a mint began work and in 1686 the first bank in Boston as well as the first in the colonies was established. A printing press was set up in 1674 (though there had been one in Cambridge[q.v.], across the Charles, since 1638) and in 1704 the *Boston News-Letter*[q.v.] appeared. By this time Boston was becoming the largest and most important town in America. Its population in the middle 18th century was about 15,000. It was one of the earliest and chief centers of rebellion against the government of England and the first armed conflicts of the Revolutionary War (*see* Bunker Hill; Lexington and Concord) took place in its environs. But Washington forced the British to evacuate it in March, 1776, and thereafter its peace was undisturbed during the war.

In government it was merely a town administered by selectmen until 1822, when it received a city charter. During the 19th century it became the cultural center of the continent and took pride in its nicknames, "the Hub" and "the Athens of America." The names of Agassiz, Alcott, Aldrich, Dana, Eliot, Emerson, Hawthorne, Holmes, Howells, Longfellow, Lowell, Motley, Parkman, Prescott, Thoreau, Ticknor, Whittier and others which almost concurrently graced its golden age, its institutions of learning, its numerous literary, historical, scientific and musical societies, clubs and coteries, its Beacon Hill crowded with the homes of old, aristocratic families, its numerous colonial landmarks, all these gave it an unique distinction and atmosphere. It was the nation's leading port until well into the 19th century, when it lost the supremacy to New York[q.v.] because of its lack of water communication to the westward—though it still retained a considerable foreign commerce. The city suffered numerous disastrous fires in the 17th and 18th centuries, but the worst in its history was that of 1872, when sixty acres in the business portion were swept, with a loss of $60,000,000. By the filling in of tidal marshes and inlets, the original area of 783 acres was by 1930 expanded to 1800 acres. Gradual absorption of suburbs brought the city's area by that date to 47.3 square miles and its population to 781,188.

[Justin Winsor, *The Memorial History of Boston;* Van Wyck Brooks, *The Flowering of New England.*]

ALVIN F. HARLOW

Boston, Siege of (1775–76). On the day after the battle of Lexington[q.v.] (April 19, 1775) the Massachusetts Committee of Safety[q.v.] called out the militia. On April 22 the Massachusetts Provincial Congress[q.v.] resolved that an army of 30,000 men should be raised, Massachusetts to furnish about half, the other New England colonies the rest. Progress was slow; the old militia regiments could not be held together and new ones had to be raised. On June 17 was fought the battle of Bunker Hill[q.v.], which, while technically a British success, had the moral effect of an American victory.

On July 3 Washington, chosen as commander-in-chief by the Continental Congress[q.v.], assumed command. He found the British holding Bunker Hill and Boston Neck; the Americans faced them, their left in Somerville, their right in Roxbury and their center in Cambridge. It was evident that the makeshift force could not be relied upon; so in the face of the enemy a beginning was made upon organizing a Continental Army in place of the colonial contingents (*see* Washington's Eight Months Army).

During the winter no serious operations were undertaken. The Americans needed all their energies for organization; moreover, they were practically without artillery and ammunition. On the British side, the commanders could see no advantage in starting a campaign which they could not press to a finish.

In January, 1776, the guns captured at Ticonderoga[q.v.] (May 10, 1775) reached Cambridge. On March 4 Washington seized Dorchester Heights, from which his guns commanded the city and harbor. The British forces were now in an untenable position and on the 17th they embarked for Halifax. The Americans immediately occupied Boston.

[Richard Frothingham, *The Siege of Boston.*]

OLIVER LYMAN SPAULDING

***Boston-Berceau* Action** (Oct. 12, 1800). Off Guadeloupe during naval hostilities with France, the U. S. frigate *Boston* (thirty-six guns), Capt. George Little, captured the French corvette *Berceau* after a twelve-hour chase and a stubborn engagement extending intermittently from 4:30 till after 10 P.M. Though almost completely dismantled, the *Berceau* was towed into Boston as a prize.

[G. W. Allen, *Our Naval War with France.*]

ALLAN WESTCOTT

Boston Committee of Correspondence. A revolutionary body of propaganda and administration which became an important factor in promoting American unity and made possible the first Continental Congress[q.v.] through the spread of committees elsewhere. The parent body was appointed by Boston town meeting, Nov. 2, 1772, upon motion of Samuel Adams. It formulated public opinion, played a role in the early conduct of hostilities and facilitated the transition of Massachusetts from royal government to independent statehood.

[William V. Wells, *The Life and Public Services of Samuel Adams.*]
LLOYD C. M. HARE

Boston Common, bought by the city in 1634 as a pasture and parade ground, occupies forty-eight rolling acres between Beacon and Tremont streets, just below the State House. This beautiful park is the city's chief pride. Where the British troops were entrenched in 1775 her citizens now walk under the trees while their children ride in the swan boats on the Frog Pond. From the Common, her soldiers have marched away to all the wars; here famous preachers and orators have spoken; and here, in the Central Burying Ground, lies many a citizen as well as the British soldiers killed at the battle of Bunker Hill[qv]. Monuments to her famous citizens, including the St. Gaudens memorial to Col. Robert Gould Shaw, border the paths; and here band concerts and an open-air library give pleasure to the people.

[M. A. DeWolfe Howe, *Boston Common;* S. G. Drake, *Old Landmarks and Historic Personages of Boston.*]
R. W. G. VAIL

Boston Manufacturing Company was organized during the War of 1812 by Boston merchants previously engaged in the India trade. It built at Waltham the first complete textile factory in America, combining power spinning and weaving, on looms invented by one of the proprietors. This proved a pilot plant for the larger factories later built at Lowell.
VICTOR S. CLARK

Boston Massacre (March 5, 1770). Irritated by the presence of British troops in the city and emboldened by the weakness of the royal governor, an irresponsible mob of some sixty rioters set upon a squad of ten soldiers, under the command of Capt. Thomas Preston, which had gone to the rescue of a sentry attacked by the mob. While defending themselves, some of the soldiers, without orders, fired into the mob, killing three and wounding eight, two of whom later died. Public feeling ran high. To prevent further trouble, the two regiments of royal troops were withdrawn from the city. Capt. Preston and his squad were tried; the captain and six soldiers acquitted; two found guilty of manslaughter were branded in the hand and discharged. Public feeling, already aroused, was fanned to flame by such patriots as Samuel Adams and John Hancock. Biased propaganda, including the famous but historically inaccurate picture of the "massacre" issued by Paul Revere, was widely distributed. This minor outbreak, in which the rioters were largely at fault, was the first powerful influence in forming an outspoken anti-British public opinion and a demand for American independence.

[Justin Winsor, *Memorial History of Boston;* Randolph G. Adams, New Light on the Boston Massacre, in American Antiquarian Society *Proceedings,* Oct., 1937.]
R. W. G. VAIL

"Boston Men," a term derived from the hailing place of the first Yankee ships trading along the northwest coast of America, acquired universal use there to designate Americans, as distinguished from other white men or "Kling Chautsh" men (Englishmen and Canadians). The expression was so incorporated and used in the Chinook jargon[qv].

[G. Gibbs, *Dictionary of the Chinook Jargon.*]
WILLIAM S. LEWIS

Boston News-Letter, THE, was the first newspaper published without interruption during the colonial period. Number 1 included the week April 17 to 24, 1704. The original publisher was John Campbell, postmaster, and the first printer was Bartholomew Green. In 1727 Green became the owner and changed its name to *The Weekly News-Letter.* In 1763 the title was changed to *The Boston Weekly News-Letter and New England Chronicle* and there were later changes of title. Publication ceased in 1776 with the evacuation of Boston by the British troops. No complete file is known but the New York Historical and Massachusetts Historical Societies both have comparatively good files.

[James Melvin Lee, *History of American Journalism.*]
CARL L. CANNON

Boston Police Strike. About three quarters of the Boston police force went on strike, Sept. 9, 1919, when the police commissioner refused to recognize their right to affiliate with the American Federation of Labor[qv]. Mayor Andrew J. Peters and a citizens' committee headed by James J. Storrow made compromise proposals relating to pay and working conditions in order to prevent the strike, but the police commissioner rejected them. The strike thus precipitated left Boston almost unprotected and riots, disorders and robberies occurred.

The Boston police commissioner is appointed,

not by the mayor of the city, but by the governor of the state. Before the strike occurred Calvin Coolidge, then governor, was urged by the mayor and the Storrow Committee to intervene, but refused to act. When the rioting occurred Mayor Peters called out the Boston companies of the militia, restored order and broke the strike. With the city already under control, Gov. Coolidge ordered the police commissioner again to take charge of the police and called out the entire Massachusetts militia, declaring: "There is no right to strike against the public safety by anybody, anywhere, any time." This action gave Mr. Coolidge a reputation as a courageous defender of law and order, which led to his nomination for Vice-President (1920) and his eventual succession to the Presidency.

[*Report of the Storrow Committee*, Oct. 3, 1919, manuscript copy in University of Illinois Library; William Allen White, *A Puritan in Babylon: The Story of Calvin Coolidge; The Autobiography of Calvin Coolidge.*]

CLARENCE A. BERDAHL

Boston Port Act, THE (one of the Coercion Acts[qv]), was passed by Parliament on March 31, 1774. To punish Boston for the Tea Party[qv], the act ordered the port of Boston closed on June 1, 1774, until the townspeople paid for the tea destroyed on Dec. 16, 1773, and proved to the crown's satisfaction they were peaceable subjects. Because Boston alone was punished, Lord North believed the colonies would not "take fire." It was a costly mistake: the cry was raised in America that the Port Act was merely a prelude to a "Massacre of American Liberty"; the colonies rallied to Boston's aid; and the Continental Congress[qv] was called to concert opposition to the mother country.

[J. T. Adams, *Revolutionary New England;* C. H. Van Tyne, *The Causes of the War of Independence.*]

JOHN C. MILLER

Boston Resolutions, THE, were an expression of the longing of many Massachusetts patriots to restore puritanic simplicity in New England and strengthen patriotism by barring the importation of British luxuries. In 1767, when New England's declining prosperity made economy essential and the Townshend duties[qv] threatened fresh British oppression, Sam Adams secured the passage in the Boston town meeting of resolutions pledging the citizens to abstain from the use of many British manufactures, chiefly articles of luxury. Outside of New England, however, the movement had little success and it was soon merged with the nonimportation agreement[qv].

[C. H. Van Tyne, *The Causes of the War of Independence.*]

JOHN C. MILLER

Boston Resolutions, THE, of Feb. 9, 1810, were a forecast of New England separatism in the approaching War of 1812[qv]. In them the Massachusetts legislature condemned the severity of President Madison toward Francis James Jackson, the notorious British minister, exculpated Jackson and endeavored to compel renewed diplomatic intercourse with Great Britain.

[Henry Adams, *History of the United States, 1801-1817*, V.]

LOUIS MARTIN SEARS

Boston Tea Party, THE, took place on the night of Dec. 16, 1773, when 342 chests of tea belonging to the East India Company[qv] were thrown into Boston harbor by the patriots. This audacious destruction of British property was caused by the Boston Whigs' fear that if the tea were landed, its cheapness would prove an "invincible temptation" to the people. This, it was believed, would give the East India Company a monopoly of the American tea trade and establish the right of Parliament to raise a colonial revenue by means of port duties. Therefore, when it was learned at the town meeting of Dec. 16 that Gov. Hutchinson was determined to refuse the patriots' demand that the tea ships be permitted to return to England without paying the duty required by law, Sam Adams exclaimed that the meeting could do nothing more to save the country. His words were the signal for a war whoop from the "Indians"—Sons of Liberty[qv] disguised with blankets and dusky complexions—waiting outside the meetinghouse. With the cry of "Boston harbor a tea-pot this night," the braves streamed down to the waterfront, where, surrounded by an immense crowd of spectators, they made short work of the tea.

The Tea Party was "the boldest stroke which had yet been struck in America." It marked the beginning of violence in the dispute, hitherto waged chiefly with constitutional arguments, between mother country and colonies, and it put the most radical patriots in command throughout America. The efforts of the British government to single out Massachusetts for punishment, instead of isolating the Bay colony, served only to unite the colonies and hasten them into war with the mother country.

[C. H. Van Tyne, *The Causes of the War of Independence;* John C. Miller, *Sam Adams, Pioneer in Propaganda.*]

JOHN C. MILLER

Boston Ten Townships (N. Y.), THE, was a tract of 230,400 acres north of the Susquehanna River, including parts of Broome, Tioga and Cortland counties, claimed by both New York and Massachusetts until, by the Treaty of Hartford[qv] in 1786, a compromise was effected whereby New York was granted sovereignty and Massachusetts right of pre-emption of the soil. Subsequently, in 1787, right of purchase from the Indians was granted by Massachusetts to Samuel Brown and ten associates. (*See* Phelps-Gorham Purchase.)

[R. L. Higgins, *Expansion in New York.*]

A. C. FLICK

"Bostonnais," also "Bastonais." A term once applied by French-Canadians to Americans. It dates back to the invasion of Canada^{qv} under Montgomery in 1775, and possibly to that of Sir William Phips in 1690. Meaning "People of Boston," it was given to all English colonists on the Atlantic seaboard and finally to all Americans.

LAWRENCE J. BURPEE

Botanists, Early. The earliest American botanists were field workers, who collected specimens of seeds and plants and transmitted them to European scientists, receiving many European specimens in return. Among those who carried on such a correspondence were Cotton Mather, Cadwallader Colden and John Bartram. Bartram's association with the English naturalist, Peter Collinson, is the most famous of such scientific partnerships. Other 18th-century botanists were Alexander Garden of South Carolina; John Mitchell of Virginia; Jane Colden, daughter of Cadwallader Colden of New York; Humphry Marshall of Pennsylvania; and John Bartram's son William, whose *Travels,* published in 1791, is the chief literary work of the early botanists, just as his father's garden, now in Philadelphia's park system, is their most important relic.

[William Darlington, *Memorials of John Bartram and Humphry Marshall;* R. Higgston Fox, *Dr. John Fothergill and His Friends.*]

RALPH FOSTER WELD

Bouchard Expedition, THE (1818), was an effort on the part of the Buenos Aires revolutionary authorities to bring into the anti-Spanish liberal cause the inhabitants of California. Hippolyte de Bouchard, with the *Argentina* and *Santa Rosa,* came to California by way of the Hawaiian Islands, and Nov. 20, 1818, captured Monterey. Other landings at Santa Barbara and Capistrano showed that the Californians were not anxious for freedom. Accordingly, Bouchard sailed for Chile, and California remained in the Spanish empire until April 11, 1822, when a special junta declared it dependent upon Iturbide's Mexican empire.

[C. E. Chapman, *A History of California: the Spanish Period.*]

OSGOOD HARDY

Boulder (Hoover) Dam, located in Black Canyon on the Colorado River between Arizona and Nevada, 422 miles above the mouth of the Colorado River, was authorized by the Boulder Canyon Project Act in 1928, for flood control, navigation improvement, irrigation, storage and power, subject to the Colorado River Compact; dedicated as Hoover Dam by Secretary of the Interior Ray Lyman Wilbur at the start of construction in 1930; and completed in 1936 by Six Companies, Inc., contractors for the United States Bureau of Reclamation. It rises 727 feet from bedrock, elevates the water surface 584 feet, creates a reservoir (Lake Mead) with a capacity of 30,500,000 acre feet and will generate 1,835,000 horse power of electric energy. The cost was approximately $130,000,000. In advance of construction, Secretary Wilbur secured power contracts disposing of 4,330,000,000 kilowatt hours annually, adequate to liquidate the Government's investment within fifty years, with large excess revenues. The City of Los Angeles and the Southern California Edison Company, lessees of the power plant, which was placed in regular operation June 1, 1937, will generate for ten allottees of energy, including the states of Arizona and Nevada and the Colorado River Aqueduct^{qv}.

[Wilbur and Ely, *The Hoover Dam Contracts;* Reports of the Secretary of the Interior, 1930-32 inclusive.]

NORTHCUTT ELY

Boundary Disputes, International. *See* Northeast Boundary, 1783–1842; Northwest Boundary Controversy; Mexican Boundary, The; Florida Boundary, The; Alaska Boundary Question, The; Haro Channel Dispute.

Boundary Disputes between the States. Disputes concerning more than one fourth of the present 109 interstate boundaries in the United States (including District of Columbia-Maryland and District of Columbia-Virginia in the total) have been submitted to the U. S. Supreme Court or to Congress—a few only for confirmation of an agreement already reached by the states themselves. At the time of the adoption of the Constitution controversies were pending between eleven of the thirteen states respecting their boundaries (37 U. S. 657, 723–24).

Most of the disputes have arisen concerning boundaries established by colonial grants and charters, or by treaties (1783–1848), which have become boundaries between the states. Disputes relating to boundaries established by Congress in the creation of new states (where portions of former treaty lines were not utilized) have been few; of these boundaries nearly all have been meridians or other straight lines, or parallels of latitude, which, though they disregard physiographic and human use factors, have occasioned relatively little difficulty as boundaries of states between which there are no tariff and migration barriers.

Some of the disputes concerning boundaries of colonial origin persisted more than a century. Those that have been decided by the U. S. Supreme Court include Virginia v. Tennessee (part of Virginia-North Carolina boundary until 1790), 1893; Maryland v. West Virginia (part of Virginia until 1863), 1910; Georgia v. South Carolina, 1922; Vermont v. New Hampshire, 1933; and New Jersey v. Delaware, 1934. The Massachusetts-Rhode Island boundary controversy, which originated in the Plymouth colony grant of 1630 and the Rhode Island charter of 1663, was not definitely settled until the two states agreed in 1860–61 upon a conventional line, confirmed by Supreme Court decree in 1861, part of which the states replaced in 1899 by a line which could be more readily marked. The Connecticut-New York boundary dispute, which began before 1650, was settled by the two states in 1880 and the agreement was approved by Congress in 1881. The North Carolina-South Carolina colonial dispute of 1729–87 was ended by the survey of 1815, extending the 1772 line to the Georgia corner. Similarly, the Massachusetts-New Hampshire boundary controversy, which originated in the Massachusetts charter of 1629, was finally settled by the adoption of the Mitchell-Hazzen line essentially as then monumented, in 1889–90 and 1895.

It may seem surprising that many state boundaries owe their origin to international treaties. The Mississippi River was established as a boundary by treaty between France, Spain and England, in 1763, "and this line, established by the only sovereign powers at the time interested in the subject, has remained ever since as they settled it" (Missouri v. Kentucky, 78 U. S. 395, 401). By the Definitive Treaty of Peace of 1783[qv] with Great Britain, the Mississippi River became the western boundary of the United States; it now constitutes nine interstate boundaries, two of them only in part. The northern boundary of Florida, and the Chattahoochee River as part of the Alabama-Georgia boundary, also owe their origin to the Treaty of 1783. The Oklahoma-Texas boundary (except the Panhandle portion) originated in the 1819 treaty with Spain (*see* Adams-Onís Treaty)—as did also the southern boundaries of Oregon and Idaho, concerning which there have been no outstanding disputes. The Rio Grande portion of the New Mexico-Texas boundary, decided by the Supreme Court in 1927, constituted part of the United States-Mexico boundary from the time of the Treaty of Guadalupe Hidalgo[qv], 1848, until the Gadsden Purchase[qv], 1853.

Boundaries between states of the Union are to be determined according to principles of international law (Wisconsin v. Michigan, 295 U. S. 455, 461). In rivers and bays the Supreme Court has held that the doctrine of the *thalweg,* or main channel of navigation, is applicable between states of the Union, where the boundary has not been fixed in some other way—as by agreement, practical location, prescription; and it applies even as between states that existed before the doctrine became fully established in international law (New Jersey v. Delaware, 291 U. S. 361, 383).

Water boundaries, in rivers and bays, have given rise to many more disputes than land boundaries. Disputes concerning river boundaries have been the most numerous and the most complicated. The 1783 treaty boundary in the Mississippi River was the middle of the river. The Supreme Court has held, however, that the middle of the principal navigable channel, or *thalweg,* and not the line equidistant from the two banks, constitutes the boundary (Arkansas v. Mississippi, 250 U. S. 39). Mississippi River boundary cases decided by the Supreme Court include: Missouri v. Kentucky, 1871; Iowa v. Illinois, 1893; Arkansas v. Mississippi, 1919; Louisiana v. Mississippi, 1931. Boundaries in the Missouri River which have been in dispute include: Nebraska v. Iowa, 1892, and Missouri-Nebraska, 1904, both relating to river changes by avulsion. The boundary in the Ohio River was decided in 1890 to constitute the north or right bank at low water, based upon the cession by Virginia to the United States of territory "to the northwest of the river Ohio." In the construction of this grant it was held that Virginia (territory now comprising Kentucky and West Virginia) must have intended to retain the river (Indiana v. Kentucky, 136 U. S. 479). The boundary in the Chattahoochee River is the west or right bank at average or mean stage during the entire year (Alabama v. Georgia, 64 U. S. 505). In the Connecticut River the boundary is on the right bank at low-water mark (Vermont v. New Hampshire, 289 U. S. 593). In the Potomac River the Maryland-Virginia and Maryland-West Virginia boundaries are on the south or right bank at low water; the grant to Lord Baltimore embraced the Potomac River to high-water mark on the Virginia shore, but "the evidence is sufficient to show that Virginia, from the earliest period of her history, used the South bank of the Potomac as if the soil to low water mark had been her own" (Maryland v. West Virginia, 217 U. S. 577, 579–80). The Georgia-South Carolina boundary is on the water midway between the main banks of the three boundary rivers, but the islands belong to Georgia (257 U. S. 516). The boundary in the St. Louis River, emptying into Lake Superior, was decided by the Supreme Court in 1920 (Minnesota v. Wisconsin, 252 U. S. 273).

Boundaries in waters other than rivers have been subject to dispute, and in several instances an economic factor was involved. Oyster beds have been at least partly the cause of disputes decided by the Supreme Court: Louisiana v. Mississippi, 1906 (from mouth of Pearl River to the high sea); and New Jersey v. Delaware, 1934 (Delaware River and Bay). Oyster beds were also involved in the Massachusetts-Rhode Island dispute, Rhode Island taking action to protect the oysters in 1844; and in the Maryland-Virginia dispute in Chesapeake Bay just before the Civil War. The Michigan-Wisconsin boundary in Green Bay and Lake Michigan constitutes a portion of another boundary which has been in dispute (Supreme Court decisions in 1926 and 1935), where fishing rights were among the questions involved.

Disputes which have been settled by Congress have related chiefly to boundaries originally established between territories by act of Congress; it has been intended that pending disputes be settled before the second of the two states ultimately concerned was admitted to the Union. The Ohio-Michigan dispute[qv] was notable. It was finally settled by an act of Congress in 1836 "to establish the northern boundary of the state of Ohio, and to provide for the admission of the state of Michigan into the Union"; as recompense for its loss of the disputed territory Michigan was given the upper peninsula of that state. The Illinois-Wisconsin dispute was also protracted, ending with the admission of Wisconsin into the Union in 1846. Congress has confirmed several boundary agreements reached by states, and has authorized certain states on the Mississippi River to modify their boundaries by direct agreement where tracts of territory become separated from the main body of land by sudden changes in the course of the river.

The Oklahoma-Texas boundary has given rise to the most numerous and complicated boundary questions ever submitted to the Supreme Court. Three separate problems, relating to the Red River and the 100th meridian, have presented themselves. In 1896 the Supreme Court decided the so-called Greer County[qv] question. In three decisions in 1921, 1922 and 1923 the boundary in the Red River was established on the south "cut bank"; oil wells in the bed of the stream made precise boundary location very important. In 1926 the Court decreed the true 100th meridian to be part of the Oklahoma-Texas boundary, instead of the line which had been erroneously marked.

In a number of instances two states concerned have submitted to the Supreme Court separate disputes concerning different parts of their boundary and sometimes two or more disputes concerning the same portion of boundary. There may be cited the Wisconsin-Michigan Supreme Court boundary decisions of 1926 and 1935; the Illinois-Iowa boundary decisions of 1893 and 1906; and the Oklahoma-Texas boundary questions already mentioned.

A case concerning the Arkansas-Tennessee boundary is still pending in the Supreme Court (1938). The District of Columbia-Virginia boundary, presumably at high-water mark on the south bank of the Potomac, is still in dispute. Other disputes may be anticipated, chiefly regarding boundaries in rivers and other waters.

Disputes have been somewhat heated in a few instances. When Georgia organized Walton County in 1803, the area being also claimed by North Carolina, there were riots and dissensions concerning conflicting jurisdiction. The Ohio-Michigan dispute, 1818–36, mentioned above, was one of the bitterest. The Federal Government tried unsuccessfully in 1838 to settle the Iowa-Missouri dispute; in 1839 both ordered out the militia, and hostilities were narrowly averted. But in 1846 Iowa was admitted to the Union and in 1847 the two states agreed to settle their controversy by means of an amicable suit in the Supreme Court, the decision being rendered in 1849. In general, boundary questions between states of the United States, as distinct from regional disputes, have never had a disrupting effect. (*See also* Pennsylvania-Connecticut Boundary Dispute; Pennsylvania-Maryland Boundary Dispute; Pennsylvania-Virginia Boundary Dispute; Texas Cession of 1850.)

[Paullin, *Atlas of the Historical Geography of the United States*, pp. 72-87; U. S. Geological Survey, Bulletin 817; U. S. Supreme Court Reports; James Brown Scott, *Judicial Settlement of Controversies between States of the American Union.*]

S. WHITTEMORE BOGGS

Bounties, Commercial, have played an important role in American economic development. In the colonial period Great Britain paid bounties on the export from the American colonies of hemp, flax, tar, potash, indigo and a number of other commodities in an effort to stimulate their production and to diminish her previous dependence for them on foreign nations. North and South Carolina profited the most from these bounties, and the production of naval stores and indigo became, with rice cultivation[qqv], their chief occupation. After the Revolution the loss of these bounties brought disaster to those engaged in the production of naval stores and indigo.

The colonial governments also offered bounties to encourage the manufacture of such goods as linen, woolens, iron, glass, brick and salt, and after 1775 they redoubled their efforts to build up domestic manufactures by combining cash bounties, financial subsidies and tariff protection.

In the national era bounties have been offered for various commercial purposes, the most important of which has been to encourage the production of beet sugar[qv]. In 1890 the United States offered a bounty of two cents a pound on sugar produced within the country and numerous states have likewise given bounties to the beet-sugar industry. Such bounties, coupled with high tariff protection[qv] and large expenditures in the Far West for reclamation[qv] projects on which one of the chief crops is sugar beets, have been responsible for the growth of the beet-sugar industry in the United States.

The Southern states which felt that up to 1860 bounties, tariff protection and subsidies to internal improvements[qv] had chiefly benefited other sections, incorporated a provision in the Confederate constitution which forbade them.

[G. L. Beer, *British Colonial Policy, 1754-1763;* H. L. Osgood, *American Colonies in the Eighteenth Century;* F. W. Taussig, *Some Aspects of the Tariff Question.*]

PAUL WALLACE GATES

Bounties, Fishing. *See* Fishing Bounties.

Bounties, Land. *See* Land Bounties.

Bounties, Military. When war forces were raised by volunteering instead of by conscription or militia obligations[qqv], bounties stimulated recruiting. For Indian and French campaigns, colonies offered cash inducements, sometimes solely to induce enlistments[qv], sometimes for bringing clothing or weapons into service. The practice was adopted during the Revolution by both Congress and the states. In January, 1776, $6⅔ was offered to fill the Canada expedition; in June $10 for three-year enlistments or re-enlistments; in September $20 and 100 acres for enrollments "for the war." To fill militia quotas, states offered their own bounties, so that states and Congress bid against one another and sums mounted until Congress was offering $200 and New Jersey $1000. Bounty-jumping and re-enlisting were prevalent.

With the peace, bounties shrunk to $6 in 1791 for Indian campaigns, but climbed after the Whisky Rebellion[qv] to $16, three months' pay and 160 acres. During the War of 1812 cash offers increased to $124 and 320 acres. They were abolished in 1833 but were resumed in 1847 to raise and re-enlist men for the Mexican War. Civil War bounties[qv] repeated Revolutionary history. Disappearing after Appomattox[qv], recruiting bounties were expressly forbidden by the Selective Service Act[qv] of 1917. (*See also* Land Bounties.)

[E. Upton, *Military Policy of the United States;* W. A. Ganoe, *History of the United States Army;* T. Cross, *Military Laws of the United States;* War Department, *Military Laws of the United States.*]

ELBRIDGE COLBY

Bounties, Military, in the Civil War. The earlier system of land grants was not followed except for the favored position of service men under the Homestead Act[qv], but from the start in 1861 states and localities stimulated recruiting by grants of money. This practice reached large proportions during the militia draft of 1862 when even the Federal Government offered $25 for nine-month and $50 for twelve-month volunteers. Since July, 1861, Congress had allowed $100 for three-year men and the latter bounty was offered during the draft[qv], even to conscripts who would volunteer for the longer term.

The climax was reached after the Enrollment Act of March 3, 1863, which legalized the earlier practice of giving $100 to conscripts and substitutes. Also, since those able to do so could avoid the draft on payment of $300, for several months an equivalent sum was given to all three-year and $400 to all five-year volunteers. But, since these bounties were divided over the term of service and were included in the monthly pay, they merely served as an addition to the legal wages. A worse system prevailed for state bounties. It was considered a disgrace for any congressional district to have to submit to a draft, so funds were raised to the utmost limit to fill the quotas before the wheel was set in motion. In consequence, the richer districts by offering $1000 or more could entice volunteers from poorer localities and fill their quotas with ease, whereas the low-bounty regions were badly depleted of man power by the exodus and then had to give an additional quota by draft. Furthermore, a loathsome profession of bounty brokers arose, who not only recruited men and then robbed them of much of their bonus, but also resorted to bribery to secure the muster of broken-down derelicts who had to be discharged later. The problem of the bounty-jumper[qv] was greatly aggravated by these practices.

In four years' time the Federal Government paid over $300,000,000 in bounties, and in the last two years alone the states and localities paid about the same amount. The total mercenary fees for the war, including local bounties in the first two years and substitute fees, amounted to about three quarters of a billion dollars.

[F. A. Shannon, *Organization and Administration of the Union Army.*]

FRED A. SHANNON

Bounty-Jumper, THE, was a product of the system of military bounties[qv] in the Civil War. Aided and abetted by bounty brokers, men would enlist, collect bounties, desert and then re-enlist elsewhere, repeating the process until finally caught. One deserter was sentenced to four years' imprisonment after confessing to jumping bounties thirty-two times. The large initial bounty payments was one of the major causes of the more than 268,000 desertions from the ranks of the Union Army.

[F. A. Shannon, *Organization and Administration of the Union Army.*]

FRED A. SHANNON

Bouquet's Expedition (1763–65). At the outbreak of Pontiac's War[qv] Col. Henry Bouquet was sent with 500 regulars to relieve Fort Pitt[qv]. Leaving Carlisle, he marched westward, and after defeating the Indians at the battle of Bushy Run[qv] he relieved the beleaguered fort. Bouquet's force was too small to march against the Delaware and Shawnee[qqv] in the Ohio country, but in 1765 the Pennsylvania Assembly voted an adequate force for the expedition. Desertions from the militia, however, forced Bouquet to call for Virginia volunteers to meet him at Fort Pitt. After many delays he collected some 1500 men and in October, 1765, marched unopposed to the Muskingum River, near the mouth of the Tuscarawas. There he was met by chiefs bringing in eighteen white prisoners and suing for peace. Bouquet demanded the return of all the captives; and, taking the principal chiefs as hostages, he moved south to the forks of the Muskingum in the heart of the Indian country. Here he waited until some 200 prisoners had been surrendered to him.

He then made peace with the Indians, directed them to go to Sir William Johnson to make treaties (*see* Indian Policy, Colonial) and took hostages for the performance of this obligation and for the delivery of about 100 prisoners still in the hands of the Shawnee. He returned to Fort Pitt, and the Indians subsequently kept their promises and delivered there the remaining captives. Bouquet's expedition overawed the Indians and ended the reign of terror on the border. (*See also* Bradstreet's Expedition to Lake Erie.)

[Francis Parkman, *The Conspiracy of Pontiac.*]

SOLON J. BUCK

Bourbon County was established by Georgia in 1785, on the Mississippi River, lying north of the 31st parallel and extending to the mouth of the Yazoo River, above Natchez[qv]. Being largely a land speculation, it was to be governed by fourteen men mentioned in the act; and when a land office should be opened, the price per acre should not be more than twenty-five cents. As Spain had not yet evacuated this territory and as the United States disputed Georgia's claim to these western lands, the act was repealed three years later.

[A. P. Whitaker, *Spanish-American Frontier;* E. C. Burnett, Papers relating to Bourbon County, Georgia, 1785-1786, in *American Historical Review,* XV.]

E. MERTON COULTER

Bourgeois. The term was one used in the fur trade[qv], especially in the Northwest, and was applied to the leader of a unit. The bourgeois was governor of the pack train, master of the canoe brigade and despot of the trading post. His word was law and his orders were implicitly obeyed. His was the responsibility for the well-being of the men and the success of the trade venture. When the great companies were organized the bourgeois were the wintering partners. A collection of their diaries was published at Quebec in 1889 under the title *Les Bourgeois de la Compagnie du Nord-Ouest,* by L. E. Masson.

[Grace Lee Nute, *The Voyageur.*]

LOUISE PHELPS KELLOGG

Bourgmont's Explorations (1706–24). Etienne Veniard de Bourgmont, first French scientific explorer of the Missouri River, commanded Fort Detroit[qv] in 1706. By 1712 he was exploring the lower Missouri Valley. His "Route to follow to mount the Missouri River" (*ca.* 1714), dryly topographic, and "Exact Description of Louisiana" (*ca.* 1717), show he reached the Platte River. Search for a route to the fabulous silver mines of New Mexico and activities of the Spanish made imperative a French post in Missouri. Authorized by Louis XV, in 1723 Bourgmont led an expedition up the Mississippi from New Orleans and with the help of friendly Missouri Indians built Fort d'Orleans[qv] on the north bank of the Missouri River in Carroll County, probably two miles above the Wakenda, opposite Waverly, Mo. In 1724 he conducted an overland trip to the village of the Kansas Indians[qv] near present Doniphan, Kans., effecting peace with them and, further to the southwest, with the Padoucas.

[G. J. Garraghan, *Chapters in Frontier History.*]

DOROTHY PENN

Bouweries. When the Dutch West India Company[qv] took over Manhattan Island[qv] in 1626 (*see* New Netherland), it divided a large tract of land in what is now New York City's lower East Side into six bouweries or farms, placed buildings on them and leased them to tenants. One large farm, "the Company's Bouwerie," just west of these, was retained and operated to aid in providing for the company's officers and servants. Other tracts of forest land were granted to individuals, who cleared them and created their own bouweries.

[J. H. Innes, *New Amsterdam and Its People.*]

ALVIN F. HARLOW

Bowditch's *American Practical Navigator* was published in 1802 and has remained the textbook of American seamen. It has played the important part of guiding the navigator in every American adventure on the sea.

One edition followed another bringing up-to-date methods to the mariner. In 1866 the copyright and plates were bought by the Hydrographic Office of the Navy. It is not only a notable book but is one of our nautical institutions.

GERSHOM BRADFORD

Bowery, The, in New York City. First known in the 17th century as the Bowery Lane or Bowery Road, because it led from New Amsterdam[qv] out to the bouwerie[qv] or farm of Gov. Stuyvesant. Later it was the beginning of the road to Boston, and the first mail between New York and Boston started over it in 1673. By 1800 the slums[qv] growing up around it determined its future character. Some famous theaters were located on it; but it eventually attained world-wide notoriety because of the swindling, political chicanery, prostitution, crime and gang warfare carried on in its vicinity. It is now an ordinary business street.

[Alvin F. Harlow, *Old Bowery Days.*]

ALVIN F. HARLOW

Bowie Knife. Perhaps devised by Rezin P. Bowie, perhaps by his brother James, who died in the Alamo[qv], the knife both in origin and use has been the subject of a cycle of heroic folk tales. It achieved fame in the Sandbar Duel[qv] in 1827. Although supplanted largely by the six-shooter[qv], it was for four decades a part of the regular equipment of frontiersmen and backwoodsmen from Florida to California. The Mountain Men[qv] used a modified form of it. The Texas Rangers[qv] rode with it. The "pirates" of the Mississippi disemboweled their victims with it. Its steel of superb temper, the blade well guarded, handle and blade so balanced that it could be thrown as well as wielded, it was both economical and practical for skinning, cutting up meat, eating, fighting duels, stabbing enemies, hammering and performing other services.

J. FRANK DOBIE

Bowles' Filibustering Expeditions. William Augustus Bowles, after an adventurous life among the Creek Indians[qv], turned up in the Bahamas where he became acquainted with Lord Dunmore, governor of the islands, and with the trading house of Miller (Millar), Bonnamy (Bonamy) & Co. Here was the mainspring of his subsequent activities, for he became the agent of this commercial house, re-enforced with the benevolent and probable financial interest of Lord Dunmore, and in this capacity he sought the trade of the Creeks, which at this time was rather securely held by another English firm, Panton, Leslie & Co.,[qv] who had secured their concessions from Spain and from Alexander McGillivray, the half-breed Creek chief.

In pursuance of his aims, Bowles appeared on the west coast of Florida in 1788 with a cargo of goods which he liberally distributed among the Indians, without arousing the suspicion of McGillivray, but suspected of evil designs by the Spaniards. It was probably Bowles' purpose to attack the Spaniards through Indian allies, but the desertion of some of his men caused him to leave. In 1791, the year after McGillivray[qv] had made the Treaty of New York with the United States, Bowles returned to Florida with the idea of supplanting him in Creek leadership, being aided by the unpopularity of that agreement. Cunningly he plundered the storehouse of Panton, Leslie & Co., at St. Marks, but fell a prey to Spanish duplicity when he agreed to go to New Orleans to treat with the authorities there. For the next few years he was held prisoner in Havana, Madrid, Cadiz and in the Philippines. Escaping he returned to Nassau, in 1799, and soon put out for Florida on his third and last filibustering expedition. The next year he attacked the Spanish fort at St. Marks, successfully seized it, and held it for a few months. Being forced out he escaped into the hinterland, where for the next few years he was a menace to the Spaniards. At the suggestion of the United States, the Spaniards offered a reward of $4500 for him and in May, 1803, he was seized on American soil through a ruse connived in by American authorities, Spain and Great Britain. He died two years later in Morro Castle, Havana. Bowles' whole career in Florida had been directed assiduously against the Spanish power and in the interest of Great Britain generally, but more specifically to promote the commercial ambitions of Miller, Bonnamy & Co. (*See also* Spanish-Indian Relations.)

[A. P. Whitaker, *The Mississippi Question, 1795-1803;* J. W. Caughey, *McGillivray of the Creeks;* G. White, *Historical Collections of Georgia;* A. Stephens, ed., *The Life of General W. A. Bowles.*]

E. MERTON COULTER

Bowling Green in New York was originally a small open space before the fort at the foot of Broadway, sometimes called The Parade. It was leased for a bowling green in 1733. The leaden statute of George III was erected there in 1770, and destroyed by the populace at the outbreak of the Revolution in 1775.

[I. N. Phelps Stokes, *The Iconography of Manhattan Island.*]

ALVIN F. HARLOW

Bowyer, Fort, Attack upon (Sept. 15, 1814). From this fort, commanding the entrance to Mobile Bay, Maj. William Lawrence, with 130 troops, inflicted a mortifying defeat upon a British combined land and sea force of 6 vessels and 1300 men, under Capt. Henry Percy, killing 162 and wounding 70 British while losing only 8 Americans killed and wounded.

[Oliver L. Spaulding, *The United States Army in War and Peace;* William A. Ganoe, *The History of the United States Army.*]

ROBERT S. THOMAS

Boxer Rebellion, THE, was an antiforeign uprising in China beginning in May, 1900. A total of 231 foreigners and many Christian Chinese were murdered. On June 17 began the siege of the legations in Peking. The United States concerted with Great Britain, Russia, Germany, France and Japan to conduct a military expedition for the relief of the legations, sending 5000 troops for this purpose. The international relief expedition marched from Taku to Tientsin and thence to Peking, raising the siege of the legation on Aug. 4. The United States, however, did not join in the punitive expedition under the German Commander in Chief Count von Waldersee. In July Secretary of State John Hay issued a circular note to "preserve Chinese territorial and administrative entity," and during the Peking Congress*qv* (Feb. 5–Sept. 7, 1901) the United States opposed the demand for a punitive indemnity which might lead to the dismemberment of China. The Boxer Protocol finally fixed the indemnity at $332,000,000, provided for the punishment of guilty Chinese officials, and permitted the Powers to maintain legation guards at Peking and between the capital and the sea.

[H. B. Morse, *The International Relations of the Chinese Empire;* Tyler Dennett, *Americans in Eastern Asia.*]

KENNETH COLEGROVE

Boxing. *See* Prize Fights.

Boy Scouts of America, THE, was incorporated Feb. 8, 1910, and granted a Federal charter from Congress in 1916. It was based on the English principles modified to meet the needs of American youth. The membership, Dec. 31, 1938, was as follows: total men, 261,396; total boys, 957,-217; total membership, 1,271,900, including 33,-174 members of the Philippine Islands.

The purpose is to develop character and to train for citizenship. The organization consists of a younger boys' program for boys from nine to eleven, who are known as Cubs; boys from twelve years upward are Scouts, and boys fifteen years of age and upward, Senior Scouts.

It supplements the work of the home, church and school, provides a constructive program of leisure-time activities, very appealing to boys. It aims, through outdoor projects, such as camping, hiking, signaling, cooking in the open and nature study, to teach boys to be self-reliant and resourceful and, through knowledge of first aid, life saving, swimming, etc., to enable them to be of service to others.

Volunteer leadership is a fundamental element in the Boy Scout scheme. Scouts are organized in Patrols, under a boy leader, and Troops, under a volunteer leader known as a Scoutmaster. The boy enters scouting as a Tenderfoot. As he advances in skill he advances in rank, receiving recognition. The official scout uniform is protected by Congress.

Since the beginning of the organization 8,411,-949 persons have been connected with the movement. The world scout membership is 2,774,323 (Jan. 1, 1937), divided among some seventy-three different lands.

[*The History of the Boy Scouts of America,* published by the National Council of the Boy Scouts of America; The Twenty-ninth Annual Report of the Boy Scouts of America.]

E. S. MARTIN

Boycotting. A boycott is a collective refusal to purchase commodities or services from a manufacturer or merchant whose employment or trade practices are regarded as unfair. Occasionally the economic boycott has been used by consumers against aggressor nations. Its chief use is by organized workers to secure better conditions of employment. Means for effecting a boycott include the distribution of cards, handbills, fair lists, unfair lists and picketing[qv].

In the United States the courts have made a distinction between "primary" and "secondary" boycotts. The former involves refusal of patronage by employees directly concerned in an industrial dispute; the latter involves attempts to persuade or coerce third parties to boycott an employer.

Considerable uncertainty and confusion characterize the law of boycotts in the United States, but a few general principles are fairly well established. In most jurisdictions it is not unlawful for an association of aggrieved workers to withhold patronage. Moreover, it does not appear to be unlawful in the several states for such workers to ask or persuade others to assist in their cause. It is illegal, however, to use physical violence, coercion or intimidation. The behavior of pickets must be peaceful and customers must be accorded complete freedom in entering and leaving the boycotted establishment.

The pivotal point in the law of boycotts is the use of pressure against third parties. Because most manufacturers do not distribute their goods directly but through wholesalers and retailers, organized labor can make a boycott effective only by bringing pressure upon such dealers. This is in essence a secondary boycott, which is regarded as unlawful in most jurisdictions. In Arizona, California and Oklahoma, however, all peacefully conducted boycotts have been held legal, and some of the lower courts of New York have sustained them. In Missouri and Montana the printing and distributing of circulars for purposes of boycott may not be directly enjoined by the courts.

The boycott was held unlawful in the United States as early as 1886. In 1908 the United States Supreme Court in the Danbury hatters case[qv] decided that the secondary boycott constitutes a conspiracy in restraint of trade under the provisions of the Sherman Antitrust Law[qv] (1890). The Court held that treble damages might be recovered for losses sustained by the manufacturer through the interstate boycott. In the Buck Stove and Range Company case[qv] (1911), the same tribunal decided that all means employed to make effective an unlawful boycott are illegal, even though in themselves such means are innocent. Disregard of an injunction in this case by certain officials of the American Federation of Labor[qv] resulted in citation for contempt and jail sentence for one year. Although the sentence was subsequently set aside, the decision greatly discouraged the use of the boycott in labor disputes.

An attempt to escape from the restrictions of the Sherman Act was made through Section 20 of the Clayton Antitrust Act[qv] (1914), which prohibits the use of the injunction[qv] to restrain employees from picketing, boycotting and advising others to withhold patronage from an employer when such activities are carried on by peaceful and lawful means. In the Duplex Printing Press Company case (1921), however, the United States Supreme Court ruled that all methods employed to make effective interstate boycotts involving third parties are unlawful.

[Francis B. Sayre, *Cases on Labor Law.*]

GORDON S. WATKINS

Boydton Plank Road (also known as Hatcher's Run, Va.), ENGAGEMENTS AT (Oct. 27–28, 1864). While moving Union troops on the Boydton Plank Road where it crossed Hatcher's Run, a gap opened between Hancock's Second Corps and Warren's Fifth Corps. Confederates pushed into this opening and attacked Hancock's right and rear, provoking a bloody battle.

[*Battles and Leaders of the Civil War;* War of the Rebellion, *Official Records of the Union and Confederate Armies,* Series, I, Vol. XLII and Vol. LI.]

ROBERT S. THOMAS

Bozeman Trail, THE, was traced by John M. Bozeman, 1863–65, as the shortest and easiest route for emigrants to the Virginia City[qv] gold fields. The trail continued the route from the South Platte at Julesburg (Fort Sedgwick), past Fort Laramie, where it crossed the Oregon Trail, to the Powder River Crossing at Fort Connor[qqv]. Thence it passed eastward of the Big Horn Mountains to the Yellowstone River and westward to Virginia City.

The first caravan used the trail in the summer following the Powder River Campaign[qv] (*see* Indian Commissions, The). Notwithstanding the Treaty of Laramie[qv] in 1851 the Sioux Indians resented the invasion and when Forts Reno, Phil Kearny and C. F. Smith[qqv] were established for emigrant protection they went on the warpath. Red Cloud's War[qv] followed. By 1868 all posts along the trail had been abandoned (*see* Laramie, Fort, Treaty of, 1868).

Following suppression of the Sioux in 1877 (*see* Sioux Wars) the Bozeman Trail became an important route for cattle moving north from

Texas into Wyoming and Montana (*see* Cattle Drives).

[Brininstool and Hebard, *The Bozeman Trail.*]

PAUL I. WELLMAN

Bracito, Skirmish at. *See* Brazito Battle, Mexican War.

Braddock's Expedition (1755). After the battle of Great Meadows[qv] England and France prepared for war. Gen. Edward Braddock, appointed commander of all the British forces in America, was dispatched with two regiments for a campaign the first objective of which was Fort Duquesne[qv]. The regulars and the colonial forces rendezvoused at Fort Cumberland[qv], to start for Fort Duquesne by the route later called Braddock's Road[qv]. Wagons and horses were secured from Pennsylvania with Franklin's aid; Indian allies came from Aughwick[qv], but most of them deserted when Braddock ordered their families home.

The army, 2200 strong, started west June 7, but had advanced only to Little Meadows (near Grantsville, Md.) by June 16. Then, on the advice of Washington, his aide-de-camp, Braddock pushed on rapidly with some 1200 men and a minimum of artillery, leaving a command under Col. Dunbar to bring up the heavier goods. On July 9 the expedition crossed and recrossed the Monongahela near Turtle Creek. Up to this point every precaution had been taken against surprise, but apparently the officers now grew overconfident. A hill commanding the route was left unoccupied and the troops marched in an order too close for safety.

From Fort Duquesne Capt. Beaujeu led some 250 French and 600 Indians to oppose Braddock. He had not laid his ambush when the two parties unexpectedly met. The British opened fire, putting most of the French to flight and killing Beaujeu. His subordinate Dumas, however, rallied the Indians to seize the hill that Braddock had neglected and to surround the British line. The van of the English, falling back, became entangled with the main body so that order was lost and maneuvering was impossible. For three hours the British stood under a galling fire; then Braddock ordered a retreat. The general was mortally wounded; many of the officers were killed; the retreat became a rout. Washington, sent to Dunbar by Braddock, reported the defeat and dispatched wagons for the wounded.

Dunbar, now in command, ordered quantities of stores destroyed, and retreated rapidly to Fort Cumberland. Refusing the request of Virginia and Pennsylvania that he build a fort at Raystown (Bedford, Pa.) and defend the frontier, he marched to Philadelphia in August and left the border to suffer Indian raids. Though Braddock's expedition failed, it demonstrated that an army could be marched over the Alleghenies, it taught the troops something of Indian fighting and its very mistakes contributed to the success of the Forbes Expedition[qv].

[Francis Parkman, *Montcalm and Wolfe*, Vol. 1; Stanley Pargellis, Braddock's Defeat, in *American Historical Review*, January, 1936.]

SOLON J. BUCK

Braddock's Road ran from the Potomac at Will's Creek (Cumberland, Md.) to the Monongahela at Turtle Creek. The section from Will's Creek to the upper Youghiogheny River was opened by the Ohio Company[qv], probably in 1752. In 1754 Washington improved the road to Great Meadows[qv] and extended it to Gist's plantation (six miles northeast of the present Uniontown, Pa.). In 1755 Braddock's Expedition[qv] used the road and extended it almost to Fort Duquesne[qv]. After Braddock's defeat the road facilitated Indian raids; still later it became a highway for western emigration and part of it was incorporated in the National Road[qv]. (*See also* Cumberland Road.)

[A. B. Hulbert, *Historic Highways of America*, Vols. 3 and 4; J. K. Lacock, Braddock Road, in *Pennsylvania Magazine of History and Biography*, 1914.]

SOLON J. BUCK

Bradford Oil Field (Pa.), THE, is the most important of the Appalachian oil fields. Though not far from where the first well drilled for the purpose of producing petroleum was sunk in 1859, the early wells in this pool were not drilled deep enough to reach the producing sand and it was not until after 1874 that effective production began. By 1881 it was producing four fifths of the total production of Pennsylvania, nearly 25,000,000 barrels yearly, but thereafter steadily declined, until in the early 1900's its output was only about 5% of the peak. Experiments with flooding the sands with water to drive out more oil (a new technique) proved so successful that thirty years later it was again one of the most active of the eastern fields.

T. T. READ

Bradstreet's Expedition against Fort Frontenac (1758). After the disaster at Ticonderoga[qv] in July, 1758, Lt. Col. John Bradstreet led a successful raid which went far to restore American morale.

Taking command in early August of 2600 men secretly mobilized in the Mohawk Valley, Bradstreet moved swiftly forward along the waterways. He reached Oswego on the 24th and, crossing Lake Ontario, effected a surprise which enabled him to capture the fort at Cataraqui (present Kingston) on the 27th. Both the post and the French shipping were put to the torch. This bold campaign broke the French hold of the water routes by which the western posts were supplied, contributing to the evacuation of Fort Duquesne^qv^ later in the same year and to the surrender of Fort Niagara^qv^ in 1759.

[*Documents Relative to Colonial History, State of New York; Papers of Sir William Johnson;* George W. Schuyler, *Colonial New York,* Vol. II.]

ARTHUR POUND

Bradstreet's Expedition to Lake Erie (1764). Col. John Bradstreet emerged from two wars with high credit, first as Sir William Pepperell's capable assistant at the capture of Louisburg^qv^ in 1748, and later as the conqueror of Fort Frontenac in 1758 (*see* Bradstreet's Expedition against Fort Frontenac). Unfortunately, his record suffered from his next assignment, command of the expedition of 1764 to the Great Lakes area to place Indian relations on a peace footing following the uprising under Pontiac^qv^.

On the shores of Lake Erie, Bradstreet revealed ignorance of Indian affairs by concluding improper treaties with unimportant delegations of Delawares and Shawnees^qqv^. In this he went beyond his instructions; worse yet, he did not recover possession of all prisoners held by the former foes. To Col. Bouquet^qv^, advancing from the Forks of the Ohio^qv^, fell the duty of pushing far into Ohio to restore white prestige.

Bradstreet proceeded to Detroit, where he was only partially successful. While returning, he failed to carry out instructions to move on mutinous Scioto villages, a dangerous situation in that quarter being saved by Bouquet's steadiness. Delaying too long on the Sandusky shore, Bradstreet's forces, near to mutiny, encountered severe hardships. His reputation as a popular hero did not survive.

[*Johnson Papers; Documents Relative to Colonial History, State of New York;* A. Pound, *Native Stock.*]

ARTHUR POUND

Brady Photographs, THE. A collection of over 7000 photographs (two negatives, in most cases) taken by M. B. Brady and his associates during the Civil War at an expenditure of over $100,000. They included portraits of officers and soldiers and scenes at the front and in the rear, along the battle lines from Washington to New Orleans.

After the fighting ceased one set passed into the Government's possession; the other, after many adventures, was largely included in the collection printed in the ten-volume *Photographic History of the Civil War.*

[F. T. Miller, *The Photographic History of the Civil War.*]

THOMAS ROBSON HAY

"Brain Trust." Prior to his nomination as the Democratic candidate for the Presidency in 1932 (*see* Campaign of 1932), Franklin D. Roosevelt had brought together three close advisers, Raymond Moley, Rexford G. Tugwell and Adolph A. Berle, Jr., all professors in Columbia University. These three continued to aid Mr. Roosevelt during his campaign for election and, after his inauguration on March 4, 1933, they became prominent in the councils of the chief executive. To keep them in Washington they were given salaried offices, Mr. Moley in the Department of State, Mr. Tugwell in the Department of Agriculture and Mr. Berle in the Reconstruction Finance Corporation. They and all professors or "intellectuals" who subsequently joined the administration were indiscriminately dubbed the "Brain Trust," whether or not they were close to the President. The impression was created that they were responsible for everything that was done, so the expression "Brain Trust" became a symbol for all New Deal^qv^ experimentation.

[Ernest K. Lindley, *The Roosevelt Revolution;* Unofficial Observer, *The New Dealers.*]

ERIK McKINLEY ERIKSSON

Brands, Private and National. From the beginning of American commerce, much merchandise offered for sale has been identified by marks of origin, ownership or sponsorship. On casks, boxes, etc., they were literally "brands," but the term was loosely used to cover other kinds of craftsmen's or merchants' marks. Only recently have the trade-marks^qv^ of merchants or other distributors been set apart as a class called "private brands" to distinguish them from the trademarks of manufacturers. The manufacturer's trade-marked merchandise may be distributed and advertised nationally; the private-branded merchandise usually has only sectional distribution.

The rivalry between the two classes originated in the latter part of the 19th century, but did not become clearly evident until the 20th. The earliest manufacturers of trade-marked products who used national advertising^qv^ to stimulate consumer demand met little opposition from wholesalers and dealers. Their articles were usually of a new type or manifestly superior to unidentified bulk goods. But gradually, nationally advertised brands entered commodity fields where the dealer's influence had been dominant. Here he already had his own "private brand," or an unadvertised brand that allowed a larger margin of profit. The manufacturer's brands, procurable through other channels, weakened his hold on his customers.

For this reason and others, the large department stores, mail-order houses and chains[qqv] promoted the sale of private brands they controlled and established new ones. Some of these private brands were made by manufacturers who marketed their own nationally advertised brands. Often the only important difference was that one was sponsored by a manufacturer and bore a craftsman's mark, the other by a distributor and bore a merchant's mark.

[Maynard, Weidler and Beckman, *Principles of Marketing.*]

G. B. HOTCHKISS

Brandy Station, Battle of (June 9, 1863). Ordered by Hooker (U.) to ascertain whether Lee's army was moving northward, Pleasonton threw the Federal cavalry, 7981 strong, with 3000 infantry, across the Rappahannock. At Beverly Ford, Buford's division drove part of Stuart's (C.) 10,292 cavalry toward Fleetwood Hill and Brandy Station. Gregg's and Duffie's divisions, crossing below, attacked Stuart's rear at Fleetwood. Stuart hurried troops thither, precipitating the greatest cavalry conflict of the war. The Confederates retained the field, but Pleasonton learned that Lee was marching toward Maryland.

[John W. Thomason, Jr., *Jeb Stuart; Official Records, Union and Confederate Armies*, Vol. XXVII, Parts 1, 2.]

JOSEPH MILLS HANSON

Brandywine, Battle of the (Sept. 11, 1777), was fought near Brandywine Creek, Chester County, Pa. The British and Hessian[qv] troops commanded by Howe, Cornwallis and Knyphausen composed a force of 18,000. The American Army under Washingon numbered 11,000, of whom a large number were militia. Following a feint attack by the Hessians upon the Americans at Chad's Ford, the British crossed the East Brandywine at Jefferis' Ford, continued southward and suddenly attacked Sullivan's troops near Birmingham Meetinghouse. The Americans, though outnumbered, fought gallantly, but were compelled to retire. Washington had received faulty news concerning the approach of the British. At night Washington withdrew his army without demoralization to Chester, Pa.

[C. W. Heathcote, *History of Chester County.*]

CHARLES W. HEATHCOTE

Brattleboro. *See* Dummer, Fort.

Brazil, Confederate Expatriates to. Perhaps nearly half of the eight or ten thousand Southerners who emigrated to foreign lands after the Civil War went to Brazil. The expatriates formed associations and sent agents to the southern empire to make arrangements and to select lands for homes. Coming from every Southern state and some Northern states, they represented every social class and profession. Many had been leaders in the Old South. At first the chief embarkation point was New Orleans; later it became New York. Rio de Janeiro received nearly all the immigrants, though the colonists settling on the Amazon went via Pará.

The greater number settled in colonies located in the wilderness of the provinces of Paraná, São Paulo, Rio de Janeiro, Espirito Santo, and Pará. Most of them tried agriculture and stock raising. They were comparatively successful at Villa Americana, in the hinterland of São Paulo, which at its peak was a thriving community of several hundred families. The experiments as a rule were not successful and broke up after a few months' or at most a few years' endurance, the colonists going to São Paulo, or, more often, returning to the United States. The failures were due to lack of access to markets; unsatisfactory labor supply (the Brazilian Negro could not be kept in isolated interior communities); climatic conditions, tropical insects and disease; lack of capital and the ordinary social institutions; and homesickness for friends and relatives. Yet many traces still remain of these Southern expatriates in Brazil.

[Lawrence F. Hill, The Confederate Exodus to Latin America, *Southwestern Historical Quarterly*, October, 1935, January and April, 1936.]

LAWRENCE F. HILL

Brazito Battle, Mexican War (Dec. 25, 1846). Reaching the Rio Grande east bank by midafternoon, Doniphan, with 500 Missouri volunteers, received Ponce de León's messenger, under a black flag, demanding surrender. In the ensuing thirty-minute fight, the Americans' superior fire and tactics triumphed. Ponce fled in disorder, losing a hundred killed and wounded to the American loss of seven slightly wounded.

[Justin Smith, *The War with Mexico.*]

ROBERT S. THOMAS

Breda, Treaty of, signed July 21/31, 1667, by England and France after the naval war between England and Holland in which France joined the latter, provided in Article 10 for the restoration of Acadia to France. King Charles II's order (1668) for its return was delayed by the claims of Thomas Temple to part of the region, based on a grant from Cromwell (1656). Restoration took place in 1670, France returning to England at the same time part of the island of St. Christopher.

[F. G. Davenport, ed., *European Treaties Bearing on the History of the United States*, Vol. II.]

ROBERT E. MOODY

Breed's Hill. *See* Bunker Hill.

Brewing. There is evidence of brewing by Europeans in America almost immediately after their first harvest of grains. Members of Sir Walter Raleigh's "Lost Colony"[qv] brewed beer from Indian corn as early as 1587 in Virginia. One of the first commercial breweries of record operated in 1623 in New Amsterdam[qv]. An early New England brewery was operated by Capt. Sedgwick in Massachusetts Bay Colony[qv] in 1637. A brewery was established in 1638 as a community enterprise of Roger Williams' colonists in what is now Portsmouth, R. I.

The Swedes arrived on the Delaware[qv] in 1638 and although no date has been fixed for the establishment of their first brewery, the records of the colony allude to beer as one of its commodities and articles of commerce. William Penn was the first English brewer of that region. He erected his brewery in 1683 in Pennsbury, Bucks County, Pa.

When Gen. James Oglethorpe colonized Georgia, he introduced brewing to further moderation in drinking. Many other colonizers and leaders encouraged beer and ale as temperance beverages either by setting up their own breweries or advocating lower taxes to foster production. Samuel Adams, George Washington and Gen. Israel Putnam were among the famous colonial leaders proud of their brews. Most of the colonial manors maintained private breweries, for beer was not only a daily article of diet but also an ingredient in many tasty dishes.

The middle of the 19th century found brewing assuming new industrial importance, as brewers developed scientific control of their product to give it greater uniformity and stability. Lager brewing was introduced to America about 1840 permitting the better storage of American beers. In 1876, Louis Pasteur announced the epochal results of his studies on fermentation of French beer and his findings quickly became basic for American beer. Modern air-conditioning[qv] grew from a brewery installation in Alexandria, Va., in 1880, providing pure air and even temperature, so vital in the fermentation and aging process.

American beer and ale reached a record consumption of 66,000,000 barrels—21 gallons per capita—in 1914. National prohibition[qv] in 1920 suspended beer brewing for thirteen years and cereal or near-beer was produced in this period. On April 7, 1933, beer was relegalized, gaining in consumption with each passing year, due chiefly to its growing favor as a home beverage. Consumption for the first five years has totaled 223,000,000 barrels, with a retail value of about $7,000,000,000.

[The Research Library, United Brewers Industrial Foundation, New York, N. Y.]

HUGH HARLEY

Briand-Kellogg Pact, THE, was signed in Paris by fifteen nations on Aug. 27, 1928. Eventually forty-eight other governments adhered to the treaty. It grew out of negotiations which were begun between the United States and France. Article I provides that the parties renounce war as an instrument of national policy in their relations with one another. Article II provides that the settlement of disputes between the parties shall never be sought except by pacific means. Connected with the text of the pact are certain interpretations of Secretary of State Kellogg which were included as a part of the negotiations and which made clear that the treaty did not prevent wars of self-defense, that it was not inconsistent with the Covenant of the League of Nations[qv] and that it did not interfere with the rendering of aid under the Locarno treaties[qv] and the so-called treaties of neutrality.

[J. T. Shotwell, *War as an Instrument of National Policy and Its Renunciation in the Pact of Paris;* D. H. Miller, *The Peace Pact of Paris, a Study of the Briand-Kellogg Treaty.*]

BENJAMIN H. WILLIAMS

Briar Creek, Ga., Battle of (March 4, 1779). Gen. Augustine Prevost, British commander, trapped and routed a force of about 1200 Southern militia and regular Continentals under Col. John Ashe at Briar Creek, in Severn County. American loss was 150 killed and wounded; 189 captured. The British lost but 16, killed and wounded.

[Charles Stedman, *History of the American War.*]

ROBERT S. THOMAS

Bricks were made in Virginia as early as 1612. The first brick kiln of which we have any record in New England began work in Salem, Mass., in 1629. Up to that time, most dwelling-house chimneys had been built of wood, coated with clay. In that year, 1629, 10,000 bricks were imported from England to Massachusetts, where they were used principally for chimneys and fireplaces. The first brick house in Boston was built in 1638. Brick making was begun by the Dutch settlers near Albany in 1656. But in that century and the next, quantities of bricks continued to be imported from England and Holland, builders of fine residences believing, whether rightly or not, that a better quality of brick was made abroad than in America. As late as 1790, about as many bricks were being imported as were made in this country. Importation was curbed, however, in 1794 by the imposition of a 15% duty. Meanwhile, exportation had begun; in 1791 we shipped 743,000 bricks, mostly to the West Indies. The first patent on a brick-making machine was taken out in 1800, but not until 1829 did successful manufacture by machine begin, this in New York.

[J. Leander Bishop, *A History of American Manufactures.*]

ALVIN F. HARLOW

Bridge, then called Bridge Whist, was first played in America, in its original Russian form, with no bidding, before 1900. In 1907 Auction Bridge was introduced, coming from England, and by 1909 magazine articles deploring the craze were appearing. The first American code for Auction was drawn up in 1910. In 1925, on a coastwise steamer, Contract Bridge was first played, Harold S. Vanderbilt, capitalist, being given credit for its invention. After this innovation, the bridge fad assumed enormous proportions. Bridge discussions by radio were introduced in 1925. Expert players became wealthy from teaching and writing on the subject. No other indoor game in history was ever so popular.

[R. F. Foster, *Foster's Complete Hoyle.*]

ALVIN F. HARLOW

Bridger, Fort, was a frontier trading post and later a fort of the United States Army, located on Black's Fork, Uinta County, Wyo. It was named after James (Jim) Bridger, trapper and scout, who with his partner, Louis Vasquez, built it in 1843 and operated it for a number of years.

Although trading in pelts was carried on, Bridger's post is best known as a way station and supply point for emigrants bound for Oregon, Utah and California (*see* Oregon Trail). Its establishment marks the beginning of caravan travel to the Pacific Coast. The post was taken over by Mormon[qv] colonists from Utah about 1855; was burned by the Mormons on the approach of United States troops in the Mormon War[qv] of 1857; was rebuilt as a military post by the United States Army in 1858; and was finally abandoned in 1890. For many years it was famous as a mail, express and telegraph station.

[Cecil B. Alter, *James Bridger.*]

RUPERT N. RICHARDSON

Bridges. The earlier bridges in America were all of wood, many of them—when they crossed marshy streams or inlets—being supported by wooden piles or cribs of logs. Farther inland, stone piers were frequently built, and in the latter 17th century small stone arches began to appear. Spans were short and bridges were all open to the air until shortly after 1800, when trusses began to be devised, making longer and higher spans possible; and then the covered, completely boxed-in bridge appeared. The covering had two uses: it protected the trusses from the weather and consequent decay, and it prevented horses from being frightened if the bridge was high above the stream. Palmer, Town, Wernwag, Burr and Howe, inventor of the Howe Truss, were noted builders in wood. They became so adept that some covered truss spans of 200 and 250 feet length were built. Many of these bridges were private toll[qv] monopolies and very remunerative. The early traveler on rare occasions encountered a floating bridge—just thick planks fastened together by wooden stringers and floating on the water surface, sinking slightly as horse and vehicle passed over them. Wooden bridges and viaducts—those across deep gorges containing hundreds or thousands of heavy timbers—were used by railroads through a considerable portion of the 19th century; new ones were built in the West and South even after 1870. Serious wrecks, sometimes with great loss of life, were caused by the occasional burning of such bridges.

Wrought-iron bridges began to be built about 1800, chain suspension[qv] spans (the first one built in 1796) being the earliest type using iron. A little later came iron arches and trusses, mostly cast. The first iron truss bridge, a mixture of wrought and cast metal, was erected over the Erie Canal[qv] at Frankfort, N. Y., in 1840. Squire Whipple was the first real exponent and developer of the iron truss in America, though Fink (designer of the mile-long iron railroad bridge over the Ohio Falls at Louisville, built 1867–70), Bollman, Pratt, McCollum, Post, Warren and others designed trusses of great utility. In the 20th century bridge building became an exact science, and through the genius of such engineers as Gustav Lindenthal, Ralph Modjeski, O. H. Ammann and Joseph B. Strauss, bridges rapidly became more gigantic in capacity and span. With the crossing of the Hudson at New York in 1931, the James near Norfolk in 1928 and the Mississippi at New Orleans in 1935, the last of the streams once considered unbridgable was conquered. The crossing of San Francisco Bay[qv] (1936) and of the Golden Gate[qv] (1937) were still more colossal achievements.

Reinforced concrete began to be used cautiously in bridge building before 1900, but did not come into wide use until the second decade of the present century. Thereafter, some long and often very beautiful bridges and viaducts were built of this material.

[Wilbur J. Watson, *Bridge Architecture;* Henry Grattan Tyrrell, *History of Bridge Engineering.*]

ALVIN F. HARLOW

Bridges, Steel. James B. Eads[qv] first used steel in American bridge building when (1868–74) he designed and erected the great arched structure crossing the Mississippi at St. Louis. The supporting ribs of its three 500-foot arches are steel tubes, 18 inches in diameter, fabricated by a company headed by Andrew Carnegie, who had just introduced the Bessemer process into America. When rolled steel began to be produced in quantity in the early 1880's, it rapidly came into favor for all types of bridges. The cantilever railroad bridge across the Niagara River, with its 975-foot span, built during that decade, used the new material. The Washington Bridge across the Harlem River, completed 1889, with two beautiful 508-foot arches, was a fine product of the period. Another arch, this one of 840 feet, was thrown across the Niagara gorge in 1898 and was the wonder of the period. But the steel arch was still growing. Gustav Lindenthal's Hell Gate Bridge at New York, completed 1916, with a 1000-foot span, was overshadowed in 1932 by the Kill Van Kull Bridge at Bayonne, N. J., with a 1675-foot arch. A notable American example of the cantilever type was the Queensboro Bridge over the East River at New York, completed in 1909, whose longest span measures 1182 feet. The Southern Pacific Railroad over the Pecos River, 320 feet high, completed in the early 1890's, was built with the aid of a traveling crane which thrust out one half of the great central span as far as it could go and was then dismantled and shipped by rail over a 1200-mile detour so that it might build the other end of the bridge. The less spectacular steel truss was being greatly developed during those decades, one of its most remarkable manifestations being Lindenthal's bridge over the Ohio at Sciotoville, with one continuous truss, 1550 feet long, supported on three piers. (*See also* Bridges, Suspension.)

[Archibald Black, *The Story of Bridges.*]

ALVIN F. HARLOW

Bridges, Suspension. James Finley, an attorney, designed the first suspension bridge in America in 1801, a seventy-foot span across Jacob's Creek in western Pennsylvania. He took out a patent, and several bridges were erected under it. His bridges were suspended by "chains" of iron eye-bars from three to eight feet in length. The first wire suspension bridge was swung across the Schuylkill River near Philadelphia in 1816 —a footbridge supported by six 3/8-inch wires. Charles Ellet, Jr. and John A. Roebling, a German immigrant, did much to develop the cable suspension bridge in America. Ellet built bridges across the Schuylkill (1842), the Niagara (1847), and the Ohio at Wheeling (1849). Roebling built the second bridge across the Niagara (1855), bridged the Ohio at Cincinnati (1867) and then designed the Brooklyn Bridge[qv] (1869), the greatest of his achievements. This was followed by Lindenthal's Williamsburg (1903) and Manhattan (1909) bridges across the East River at New York. Twenty years later vastly greater spans were appearing. The George Washington Bridge across the Hudson at New York (1927–32) with a main span of 3500 feet was soon surpassed by the Golden Gate Bridge[qv] at San Francisco, with a 4200-foot span and 740-foot towers, built with amazing speed in less than four years, 1933–36. In almost the same time San Francisco Bay was bridged to Oakland with five miles of steel structures, including a 1400-foot cantilever, 19 truss spans and a double suspension bridge with 2 spans of 2310 feet each.

ALVIN F. HARLOW

Bridgewater, Battle of. *See* Lundy's Lane, Battle at.

Briscoe v. Bank of the Commonwealth of Kentucky, 1837 (11 Peters 257). The Bank of Kentucky was entirely owned by the state and its officers and directors were appointed by the state legislature. The question was whether notes issued by such a bank constituted a subterfuge by which the state in effect was emitting bills of credit[qv] in the sense forbidden by the Constitution. The court found the notes to be backed by the resources of the bank and not the credit of the state and the bank to be a separate entity suable on its own account; therefore, such notes were not bills of credit in the prohibited sense. This case "completely repudiated" the decision in Craig v. Missouri[qv].

[A. J. Beveridge, *John Marshall.*]

HARVEY PINNEY

Bristoe Campaign (Oct. 9–22, 1863). Lee (C.) crossed the Rapidan, Oct. 9, turning Meade's

(U.) right flank, and advanced toward Washington. Using parallel roads Meade marched rapidly to cover the capital. He reached Centreville first, his rear guard, under Warren (U.), severely repulsing A. P. Hill's (C.) corps at Bristoe Station, Oct. 14. A battle under favorable conditions proving impossible, Lee returned to the Rappahannock.

[Douglas S. Freeman, *R. E. Lee*, Vol. III; *Official Records, Union and Confederate Armies*, Vol. XXIX.]

JOSEPH MILLS HANSON

Bristol Trade. During the early 16th century Bristol found its location in southwestern England a great advantage in capturing trade with America; by the 17th century it had become the foremost English port. Throughout the 16th century Bristol merchants showed a steady willingness to support overseas expansion, alike in the realms of trade, fisheries and exploration. Hakluyt the geographer, Ferdinando Gorges[qqv] and a Newfoundland fishery syndicate, not to mention other important elements in American development, had Bristol contacts. Moreover, prevailing winds and ocean currents enabled the city's traders to share in the profitable Caribbean commerce. In the later 17th century Bristol became the port of departure for many American colonists. Although the city lost its commercial priority in the 18th century, it still shared heavily in western enterprises, especially through the slave trade and the fisheries[qqv]. On the eve of the American Revolution it was the second city in Britain, and its merchants greatly influenced British colonial policy[qv].

[*Cambridge History of the British Empire*, Vol. I; C. P. Lucas, *The Beginnings of English Overseas Enterprise.*]

CHARLES F. MULLETT

British Campaign of 1777. As the year 1776 ended, the British ministry came to think of the problem in America as one of reconquest, rather than of policing. A reasoned procedure was evolved in consultation with Gen. Sir John Burgoyne, lately returned to London from Canada. The plan decided on provided for an expedition to proceed from Montreal southward along the familiar Champlain-Hudson route. A large army moving up the Hudson from New York would meet Burgoyne at Albany, after which a subsidiary force might proceed eastward down the Connecticut River. As Burgoyne moved from Montreal, an auxiliary force would go up the St. Lawrence River to Oswego and, with Indian aid, would strike into the Mohawk Valley. It was also proposed that a force of Southern Indians, Negroes and British regulars be used "to awe the Southern provinces." A "numerous fleet" would "sweep the whole coast." It was believed that the plan, properly concerted and carried out, "might possibly do the business [of ending the colonial revolt] in one campaign."

To carry out this plan, the British force in the colonies would be re-enforced from England. American auxiliaries of every description—Tories[qv], Canadians and Indians—would be recruited and foreign regular troops would be hired for service in America (*see* Hessians, The). An unusual complement of guns was to be taken, as it was expected some of the numerous forts along the proposed route of invasion would need to be besieged and reduced by gunfire.

Because the active theater of war was comprised in a long narrow band along the North Atlantic seaboard, bisected from north to south by the Champlain-Hudson route, it was clear that if this route could be occupied and held, the revolt would soon come to an end. In fact, such occupation was "the indispensable first step in reconquering the colonies."

The reasoning was correct, but the plan failed because of the shortcomings of the commanding general, because of the physical barriers of river, forest and terrain, which impeded transport and troop movements, and the difficulty of securing adequate supplies of food and munitions. Final important causes were the uncertain allegiance of Canada and of the American Tories, and the overrating of Indian co-operation. The American opposition, at opportune moments, capitalized on these handicaps and was finally able to win a decisive victory. (*See* Burgoyne's Invasion; Highlands, The; Oriskany, Battle of; Bennington, Battle of.)

[Hoffman Nickerson, *The Turning Point of the Revolution.*]

THOMAS ROBSON HAY

British Debts, The, were the debts owed by the American colonial merchants and planters to British merchants before the Revolution and which, obviously remaining unpaid during the war, continued a subject of dispute between the United States and England till 1802. The debts were a natural consequence of the economic system prevalent in the colonies. The merchants of the Northern colonies and the planters of the Southern colonies bought practically all of their manufactured articles from English merchants. The merchants of the northern colonies depended on their trade and the planters upon their prospective crops to pay the balances due in England. The result, from 1763 to 1775, was a rather constant indebtedness of some £3,000,000—most of which was owed by the Southern planters.

Stoppage of payment on these debts was frequently resorted to by the colonies in their fight against the colonial legislation of Parliament in the period, 1763–75. And the possibility of wiping out the indebtedness by war was one of the contributing causes of the Revolution.

During the Revolution all of the states enacted laws affecting these debts. In the states north of Maryland most of the debts were due to Loyalists^qv^, while in the Southern states most of the debts belonged to the British merchants. Some of the laws confiscated Loyalist estates, including debts (England later claimed that debts due to Loyalists should be included with those due to British merchants); some laws sequestered the debts due to British merchants; others confiscated such debts; while still others banished or restricted the activities of the agents of the British merchants; other laws, such as paper money legislation, just as effectively abolished or barred the collection of the debts. In Maryland £144,536 of debts due to British merchants were paid into the state treasury; in Virginia about £287,000; and in North Carolina over £50,000.

These debts were an important problem in the negotiation of the Definitive Treaty of Peace in 1782–83^qv^. At one time the British ministers were ready to make peace without any guarantee for the Loyalists and merchants. However, John Adams, more interested in the fisheries^qv^ than in the debts of the planters and having "no notion of cheating anybody," was responsible for the provision (Article IV) that the debts due before the war were to be paid in sterling. Article V required that Congress should recommend to the several states the restoration of the confiscated estates of the Loyalists. Article IV met with determined opposition in the Southern states and Article V in all of the states. Practically all of the states either delayed or refused compliance. British merchants and their agents were denied admission to some states; courts were frequently closed to the debt cases; installment laws were passed; wartime interest was disallowed; and in some cases the debts were declared to have been terminated by the war and the wartime legislation of the states. On the other hand, American Negro slaves were carried off by the British troops; American posts along the Canadian border were occupied by the British (*see* Border Forts, The Evacuation of); and Indians were incited to attack the frontier.

With the adoption of the Constitution, opposed by many of the debtors, a new chapter in the debts controversy opened. The Federal courts facilitated the collection of many of the debts; and the new administration was able to negotiate more effectively with England relative to the infractions of the treaty of peace. After Gouverneur Morris' mission to London an English minister, George Hammond, was sent to the United States. However, the Jefferson-Hammond negotiations failed to settle the debt question. Nothing more was done till the strained relations of 1792–93 led to the mission of John Jay and the famous Jay's Treaty^qv^. By Article VI of this treaty the United States accepted liability for such of the debts as could not at that date be recovered due to legal impediments imposed by the states. A five-man commission, to adjudicate the claims, sat at Philadelphia from May 29, 1797, till July 31, 1799. Claims to the amount of £5,638,629 8s. 1d. were received. The commissioners, however, were unable to agree on such important matters as: the jurisdiction of the commission; the nature of legal impediments; the question of the solvency of debtors; wartime interest, etc. The entire matter, therefore, fell again into the regular diplomatic channels. A final settlement was negotiated by Rufus King and the Addington Ministry on Jan. 8, 1802. By the terms of this settlement the United States was to pay, in lieu of its liability under Article VI of Jay's Treaty, the lump sum of £600,000. An English commission sat till 1811 adjusting the claims. It found only about 20–25% of the claims good, but even so was able to pay, with the £600,000, only about 45% of the approved claims.

[J. B. Moore, *International Adjudications*, Vol. III; unpublished work by the writer on *The Debts Owed by Americans to British Merchants, 1763-1802*, to be found at Indiana University.]

BEN R. BALDWIN

British Florida (1763–83). *See* Florida, British.

British Plan of Campaign in the West (1780). British authorities, during the spring of 1780, were prepared to carry out a comprehensive plan for the recapture of the Illinois country^qv^ and to attack St. Louis, New Orleans and other Spanish posts on the Mississippi. Spain, allied with France, was then the enemy of Great Britain. Four simultaneous movements were begun. Col. Henry Bird with a force from Detroit was directed to "amuse" George Rogers Clark at the Falls of the Ohio^qv^. Gen. John Campbell, from Pensacola^qv^, after taking New Orleans was to proceed up the Mississippi to Natchez^qv^ where he was to be joined by a force which was to have captured St. Louis. Capt. Charles de Langlade was to advance down the Illinois River while another party was ordered to watch Vincennes^qv^.

No part of the plan proved successful. Col.

Bird^qv^, after taking two small posts in Kentucky, retreated. Gen. Campbell, frightened at the display of strength by Gov. Bernardo de Galvez at New Orleans, remained at Pensacola. A force of British and Indians from Michilimackinac^qv^, after their first repulse at St. Louis^qv^, withdrew. Capt. Langlade retreated precipitately upon learning of the approach of Illinois cavalry.

[James A. James, *The Life of George Rogers Clark.*]

JAMES A. JAMES

British Travelers in the United States, Early. Precisely because the British and American peoples have so much in common, British travelers were quick to note points of difference. Few failed to mention with disapproval the great use of ice and iced drinks, the sallow unhealthy look, the lack of recreation, the addiction to boarding houses and the omnipresent rocking-chair habit. American men bore additional charges of constant tobacco chewing, indiscriminate, though admittedly accurate, spitting, and sprawling with feet on chairs and tables. Of our abstract social traits, we were credited with hospitality, good nature and high sexual morality, but condemned for low political and business ethics, dollar chasing, hurrying, social equality, inquisitiveness, bragging and hypersensitiveness to British criticism.

Wansey (1794) and especially Melish (1806–11) made valuable observations concerning economic life in the East and South. Birkbeck (1818) and Flower (1818–21) viewed the Western frontier realistically but with confidence in its future development. The actor, Bernard (1797–1811), excelled in genial anecdotal description. The irrepressible journalist, Cobbett (1792–99; 1817–18), was no more critical of us than of his own native country. Fearon (1817–18), a trustworthy and penetrating observer, who covered 5000 miles, concluded that the United States was the poor man's land of opportunity. On the other hand, Weld (1795–97) and Ashe (1806) were neither favorable nor always reliable; Janson (1807) was often mendacious; Faux (1815) was a deliberately abusive faultfinder.

After 1825 professional commentators began to replace the earlier incidental observers. British condescension toward Jacksonian democracy^qv^ became evident. Mrs. Frances Trollope (1827–31) was ill-tempered in tone and her generalizations concerning particulars which she disliked led her many European readers to unfair conclusions and infuriated Americans. Hall (1827–28) wrote with an aristocratic political bias and even a capable observer like Marryat (1837–39) could not approve our "mob government." Harriet Martineau (1834–37) commended our good points and condemned our shortcomings with excellent judgment. In common with nearly all British travelers she wrote scathingly of slavery. Dickens (1841–42), our most famous visitor, made justifiable criticisms, but Americans overlooked the fact that he had not spared his own country and resented it that he should criticize us at all. With the coming of such impartial observers as Buckingham (1837–40), the geologist Lyell (1841; 1845–46) and Mackay (1846–47), the pendulum of opinion swung back in our favor. America must have had its attractions to change Isabella Bird (1855) from antagonism to admiration and induce Beste (1852) to travel for pleasure by canal, river, rail and wagon with a wife and eleven children. (*See also* French Travelers in the United States.)

[Allan Nevins, *American Social History as Recorded by British Travelers;* H. T. Tuckerman, *America and Her Commentators;* Jane L. Mesick, *The English Traveler in America, 1785-1835.*]

HARVEY L. CARTER

Broad Seal War. Following the closely contested election of 1838 two groups sought admission to Congress from New Jersey. Both held commissions bearing the great (broad) seal of the state; only the Whig^qv^ commissions, however, were legally executed and signed by the governor. Charging their opponents with fraud and facing loss of control of the House, the Democratic^qv^ majority refused to seat all but one Whig. When it was proved that the county clerks in Cumberland and Middlesex counties had suppressed the returns in certain townships that would have given the Democrats a majority, the House, on Feb. 28, 1840, seated the five Democratic claimants.

[I. S. Kull, ed., *New Jersey, A History.*]

C. A. TITUS

Broadsides. A name given to sheets printed on one side only. In 17th-century America broadsides were used for poetical effusions, news items and political propaganda. In the Revolution they were used for political purposes, often reprinted in the printer's newspaper. Later they were used in political, antislavery and temperance campaigns; also for song sheets, especially during the Civil War. Parodies often resulted. Broadsides were also used for memorials, obituaries, accounts of trials, executions, sometimes in crude poetry. Newspaper carriers used them for New Year's offerings. They have also been used for official proclamations and posters. Broadsides are ephemeral, become scarce and increase in value. Good collections are in a few libraries. Recently newspapers and radio^qqv^ have superseded broadsides, but they were used in the World War.

AUGUSTUS H. SHEARER

Broadway. Most of the lower course of Broadway is said to follow the routes of old Indian trails. In New Amsterdam*qv* its first quarter mile of existence was called the Heerewegh or Heere Straat. The name was anglicized to Broadway about 1668. Two public wells were dug in the middle of it in 1677 and abolished in 1806. The first paving, a ten-foot strip of cobblestones on each side of an earthen center, was done in 1707. The first sidewalks, four blocks on both sides, were laid in 1790. Washington for a time during his Presidency lived at 39 Broadway. In 1852 a franchise was granted for a cable car line on Broadway, then the city's chief residential street. The line, which was fought in the courts for more than thirty years, was finally built in 1885, but long before that time the street had ceased to be residential and had become the main business thoroughfare of the city. As it progressed northward, it followed in general the line of the Bloomingdale Road to 207th Street. Beyond the Harlem River it becomes a part of the road to Albany. The first subway line under it was begun in 1900. In the latter 19th century theaters congregated along it, first below and then above Longacre (now Times) Square, until its name became a symbol for the American theater. The first "arc" electric street lights in New York were placed on Broadway in 1880 and the brilliant lighting in the early 20th century brought it the nickname of "The Great White Way."

[Stephen Jenkins, *The Longest Street in the World.*]

ALVIN F. HARLOW

Brodhead's Allegheny Campaign (1779). Col. Daniel Brodhead set out from Fort Pitt*qv*, Aug. 11, 1779, with 600 regulars, volunteers and a few Delaware*qv* warriors against the Seneca*qv* on the upper Allegheny. A party of Indians coming downstream was defeated, but warned the villages, and the inhabitants fled. After destroying their houses and corn, Brodhead returned to Pittsburgh. The spell of the Iroquois*qv* had been broken and provisional treaties were made with the Wyandotte*qv* and a branch of the Shawnee*qv* which for a short time saved the frontier from invasion. (*See also* Sullivan-Clinton Campaign.)

[Louise P. Kellogg, *Frontier Advance on the Upper Ohio*, and *Frontier Retreat on the Upper Ohio.*]

JAMES A. JAMES

Bronco, a Spanish word, was early used in America to characterize hostile savages as opposed to *Indios mansos*—gentle Indians. In time the Spaniards applied the adjective to wild horses, a usage peculiar to America. Frontiersmen borrowed the adjective and converted it into a noun, often misspelled *bronk* or *broncho.* The mustang*qv* is not synonymous with the bronco until caught and more or less broken. Loosely, a bronco is a range horse, a cow horse; more specifically and accurately, a range horse that pitches or bucks. Through Wild West shows, Rodeos, Cowboy Reunions, Frontier Days celebrations, the Calgary Stampede, etc., he is familiar to the American public; he is found in the *remuda*qv of every sizable ranch. The range horse is basically of Spanish (Andalusian and Arabian) stock, but in the Americas he developed a buck virtually unknown in Europe or Asia. There horses are traditionally "gentled"; but by Indians, cowboys*qv*, vaqueros and gauchos they are "broken," usually a rough process hardly conducive to gentleness.

[William H. Carter, *The Horses of the World;* William R. Leigh, *The Western Pony.*]

J. FRANK DOBIE

Bronson v. Rodes, 1868 (7 Wall. 229), was an action on a New York executor's bond of 1851 to repay a loan "in gold or silver coin." In 1865 the obligor tendered payment in United States notes, which Congress had declared "lawful money and a legal tender*qv* in payment of debts." The tender was refused and the obligor sued to cancel a mortgage securing the bond. Decrees in his favor by two state courts were reversed by the United States Supreme Court, which held "that express contracts to pay coined dollars are not debts which may be satisfied by the tender of U. S. Notes."

[Carson, Great Dissenting Opinions, *Albany Law Journal*, L, 140.]

C. SUMNER LOBINGIER

Brook Farm Institute of Agriculture and Education, THE, grew out of the realistic social criticism of the day, touched by German Transcendentalism. George Ripley was the indefatigable and brave center of the group which moved to a farm of 200 acres in West Roxbury, Mass., in April, 1841. The members undertook to build a co-operative community in which manual and intellectual labor might be united and men and women live in a simple but cultivated society. They worked hard, erected new buildings and did their best with the poor soil.

Ripley came to believe more organization was necessary and an adaptation of the Fourier*qv* phalanx was adopted in 1845, with the primary departments of agricultural, domestic and mechanic arts. Since communal living and centralized efficiency were basic to their new doctrine, they built a large phalanstery. Fire destroyed it in 1846 while the members were celebrating its completion. Money was depleted, they could not pay the promised 5% on investments, and the experiment had to end, but not in great debt.

Though not a financial success, Brook Farm was a great social success. Gaiety, entertainment, music, spirited talk, a successful progressive educational program with outside pupils and a generous economic democracy were there. Although the great Transcendentalists[qv] had too little faith in external reform to join the group, Hawthorne, Charles A. Dana and John S. Dwight were members and the famous of Boston and Concord came often to talk or lecture. Their interest has kept the farm in memory.

[Lindsay Swift, *Brook Farm;* J. R. Codman, *Brook Farm.*]

ALLAN MACDONALD

Brooklyn, N. Y. The first settlements within the present boundaries of Brooklyn were made at Gowanus and the Wallabout in 1636 and 1637. In 1642 a ferry was established connecting Long Island with New Amsterdam[qv], and within four years a hamlet called Breuckelen, after a village in Holland, was laid out about a mile from the ferry slip. This community, with its neighboring settlements, was organized as the town of Breuckelen in 1646. The name finally became Brooklyn, although for a century there were variant spellings. The district near the slip, called "the Ferry," became a market for Long Island agricultural products. After the Revolution there was an influx of non-Dutch settlers. In 1801 Brooklyn Navy Yard[qv] was established at the Wallabout. A district covering a square mile, with the Ferry as its nucleus, having a population of about 4000, was chartered as Brooklyn village in 1816. Growth was now very rapid. In 1834 Brooklyn township, numbering 24,000, was chartered as a city. During the quarter century before the Civil War Brooklyn's population multiplied more than eleven times. In 1854 the city of Williamsburgh was annexed. A residential suburb of New York—the "city of homes and churches"—it was also a great manufacturing, shipping and commercial center. By 1896 Brooklyn had expanded to take in the entire county of Kings, and on Jan. 1, 1898, as the borough of Brooklyn, it became part of the city of New York[qv]. It is now the largest borough of the city, with an estimated population (1939) of 2,792,-600. Ferry lines, subway tunnels and three great suspension bridges connect Brooklyn with Manhattan.

[Henry R. Stiles, *A History of the City of Brooklyn;* Ralph Foster Weld, *Brooklyn Village, 1816-1834.*]

RALPH FOSTER WELD

Brooklyn Bridge was the first bridge built across the East River between New York and Brooklyn, and at the time the longest of all suspension bridges[qv]. There had been talk of bridging the river as early as 1840. The corporation to build the structure was organized in 1867, the city of Brooklyn subscribing for $3,000,000 stock and New York for $1,500,000. John A. Roebling was chosen chief engineer, but he died in 1869, and his son Washington completed the task. The bridge was thirteen years in building, and cost $15,500,000. It was opened on May 24, 1883.

[E. F. Farrington, *History of the Building of the Great Bridge.*]

ALVIN F. HARLOW

Brooklyn Heights, Battle of. *See* Long Island, Battle of.

Brooklyn Navy Yard, THE (officially the New York Navy Yard), is situated on Wallabout Bay, East River. Here were moored the *Old Jersey* and other prison ships during the Revolutionary War[qv]. Many deceased American prisoners of war were buried on the adjacent shore. In 1801 Jackson's shipyard comprising about thirty acres was purchased by the Federal Government for a Navy Yard, and Lt. Thorne appointed commandant. Additional land was acquired subsequently. Extensive improvements were begun in 1806. During the War of 1812[qv] over 100 vessels were fitted out. The ship-of-the-line *Ohio* was launched in 1820. The first granite dry dock was completed in 1851. During the Civil War[qv] over 400 vessels were fitted out and 14 built; the employees increasing from 1650 to over 6000. In later years the yard has been constantly expanded to keep pace with the growth of the Navy and to become the largest naval industrial establishment. It now has very extensive facilities for fitting out, repairing, docking and building all classes of warships, including battleships of the maximum size. Since 1895 ten battleships and many smaller vessels have been constructed. During the World War[qv] about 17,500 men were employed.

[*Long Island Historical Society Proceedings*, 1877.]

DUDLEY W. KNOX

Brooks-Baxter War, THE, was a dispute between Elisha Baxter, Arkansas governor (1873–74), and his political opponent, the Rev. Joseph Brooks, who, refusing to accept the election returns marched with followers on the State House and took possession. The State Supreme Court decided in favor of Brooks, but President Grant ruled that decision rested with the state legislature which supported Baxter's claims, May 11, 1874.

CHARLES J. FINGER

Brooks-Sumner Affair (May 22, 1856). Sen. Charles Sumner, in the course of his famous speech, "The Crime Against Kansas," ridiculed Sen. Andrew P. Butler of South Carolina for his devotion to "the harlot, Slavery." Three days after these remarks, during Butler's absence from Washington, his nephew, Preston S. Brooks, a member of Congress from South Carolina, sought out the Massachusetts senator at his desk and, rebuking him for his insult, struck him over the head repeatedly with a cane. When the attack ended Sumner sank to the floor with injuries that incapacitated him for some years. This demonstration, and the investigation ordered by the House, heightened the tension of the sectional controversy. Brooks, who was saved from expulsion by the two-thirds rule, was praised in the South and rewarded with re-election.

[Rhodes, *History of the United States*, II.]

ARTHUR C. COLE

Brotherhood of Locomotive Engineers. *See* Railroad Brotherhoods.

Brown, Fort, at Brownsville, Texas, was established in 1846 by Gen. Zachary Taylor and named for Maj. Jacob Brown, who was killed later in that year in its defense against a Mexican attack. It was captured and held for a short time in 1859 by the Mexican brigand Juan Cortina, and in the last year of the Civil War was taken from the Confederates by Federal troops. Since 1865 its 288 acres have been occupied by a United States garrison.

L. W. NEWTON

Brown University, founded in 1764 as Rhode Island College, and located at Warren, R. I., is the seventh oldest institution of higher learning in the United States. Brown was established under the fostering care of the Baptists but with the aid of other Christian denominations admitted to a share in the corporate control. The charter was most liberal—the embodiment of a spiritual heritage from Roger Williams—declaring that "all the Members hereof shall forever enjoy full free absolute and uninterrupted Liberty of Conscience."

The first president, James Manning, was elected and the first students were admitted in 1765. The first class was graduated in 1769. In 1770 the college was moved to Providence.

The college was closely associated with the struggle for independence. It was closed from 1776 to 1782 and University Hall was occupied as hospital and barracks by American and French troops.

In 1804 the college was named Brown University in honor of Nicholas Brown, a generous benefactor.

Brown has developed from a small English colonial college into a collegiate university consisting of three major subdivisions: The College, an undergraduate college for men; Pembroke College, an undergraduate college for women; and the Graduate School, for men and women.

[W. C. Bronson, *The History of Brown University, 1764-1914.*]

JAMES P. ADAMS

Brown v. Maryland, 1827 (12 Wheaton 419), which related to the right of a state to control the sale of imported merchandise, afforded Marshall an opportunity to supplement his first opinion on the meaning of the commerce clause[qv] of the Constitution as originally stated in Gibbons v. Ogden[qv].

Affirmed by the Court of Appeals, the case came to the Supreme Court on a writ of error. Marshall's opinion reversed the affirmation on the ground that the Constitution prohibits a state from levying imposts or duties on imports or exports, except what may be "absolutely necessary for executing its inspection laws." The principles stated have been upheld by nearly all courts that have dealt with the subject of commerce.

[A. J. Beveridge, *John Marshall*, Vol. 4.]

THOMAS ROBSON HAY

Brownists, a term applied to groups in England (*ca.* 1580–1660) which openly separated from the established church, was derived from Robert Browne, author of *Reformation without tarrying for anie*, 1583. Browne advocated an essentially Congregational[qv] polity, a church made up only of the visible elect who were to choose and install their own officers. Later Separatists[qv], including the Pilgrims[qv] at Plymouth, probably owed much to Browne, as also did the settlers of Massachusetts Bay[qv], although the latter always insisted that they had never "separated" from the Church of England.

[Henry Martyn Dexter, *Congregationalism of the Last Three Hundred Years;* Perry Miller, *Orthodoxy in Massachusetts.*]

PERRY MILLER

Brown's, John, Raid. *See* Harpers Ferry Raid, The.

Brownstown and Detroit Treaties (1807–8). At Detroit, Nov. 17, 1807, Gov. William Hull negotiated the cession of the Indian title to the southeast quarter of Michigan plus the portion of Ohio lying north of the Maumee. Between this tract and the settled portion of the United States lay an extensive area still in Indian possession.

Accordingly, at Brownstown, Nov. 25, 1808, Hull negotiated a second treaty whereby title to a roadway 120 feet wide, running from Maumee Rapids to Lower Sandusky (modern Fremont) and thence southward to the Greenville Treaty^qv^ line, was secured. The object of the Brownstown Treaty was to make possible travel by land to Detroit, without trespassing upon the Indian domain.

[*See* U. S. Statutes at Large, VII, for the treaties; C. C. Royce, *Indian Land Cessions*, House Docs., 56 Cong., 1 Sess., Vol. 118, for analysis of treaties and maps of cessions made.]

M. M. QUAIFE

Brownstown and Monguagon Battles (Aug. 5, 9, 1812). Gen. Hull invaded Canada from Detroit in July, 1812. The British, operating from Fort Malden^qv^, cut his line of communications with Ohio, which ran along the Detroit River. Two successive efforts to reopen it failed. In the first, Maj. Van Horne's 200 dragoons were routed by Tecumseh (Brownstown, Aug. 5). In the second, Col. Miller's force of 600 men won a victory (Monguagon, Aug. 9) but were unable to follow it up. The road remained closed, compelling Hull to withdraw from Canada a few days later.

[M. M. Quaife, The Story of Brownstown, in *Burton Historical Collection Leaflet*, IV, 65-80.]

M. M. QUAIFE

Brownsville Affair. About midnight of Aug. 13, 1906, unidentified Negro soldiers of Companies B, C and D, 25th U. S. Infantry at Fort Brown, Brownsville, Texas, angered at slights from white civilians, marched into town and shot into houses and at citizens indiscriminately, killing one man and wounding a policeman. Their officers investigated next morning but learned nothing. President Roosevelt ordered a thorough investigation which resulted in proof that the guilty men were from these companies but failed to identify them because no soldier would give evidence against his comrades. On Nov. 5 the President ordered 159 privates and non-commissioned officers from these companies and eight others "discharged without honor from the Army" and "forever debarred from the Army or Navy" because of their "conspiracy of silence." Sen. J. B. Foraker championed the cause of the discharged men; but after the Senate Committee on Military Affairs had conducted a lengthy investigation the majority sustained the President.

[U. S. Documents 5252-6; 5888-9.]

CHARLES W. RAMSDELL

Brussels Monetary Conference, THE (Nov. 22–Dec. 17, 1892), authorized by the Sherman Silver Purchase Act^qv^, failed because Great Britain rejected American proposals for increasing silver coinage; the Americans rejected the British plan for small European silver purchases. This, with other circumstances, caused the repeal of the Sherman Act.

[International Monetary Conference, *Report and Journal.*]

W. C. MALLALIEU

Bryan-Chamorro Treaty, THE, between the United States and Nicaragua was signed Aug. 5, 1914. It granted to the United States in perpetuity the exclusive right to build an interoceanic canal in Nicaragua^qv^, subject to a subsequent agreement regarding details of construction and operation; and also a ninety-nine-year lease of Great and Little Corn Islands and a right to establish a naval base in the Gulf of Fonseca. Nicaragua received $3,000,000.

Costa Rica and El Salvador protested against the treaty. Costa Rica claimed that an arbitral award by President Cleveland in 1888 had bound Nicaragua not to make grants for canal purposes without consulting her, because of her interest in the San Juan River. El Salvador asserted that the waters of the Gulf of Fonseca belonged jointly to El Salvador, Nicaragua and Honduras. Both appealed to the Central American Court^qv^ which decided that Nicaragua had violated her neighbors' rights and should take steps to restore the legal status existing before the treaty. It did not declare the treaty itself invalid, because it had no jurisdiction over the United States. Nicaragua refused to accept the decision and the treaty remained in force. The proposed naval base has not been established and the Corn Islands remain under Nicaraguan jurisdiction, except for a small area occupied by the United States for a lighthouse.

[I. J. Cox, *Nicaragua and the United States, 1909-1927.*]

DANA G. MUNRO

Bryan Treaty Model ("Cooling-Off"), THE, was used in the treaties for the Advancement of Peace negotiated by William J. Bryan, Secretary of State (1913–15). By separate negotiations, thirty treaties were signed in which the essential features are, (1) submission of all controversies to investigation before proceeding to arbitration or satisfaction of honor, (2) a permanent international commission to make the investigation, (3) one year to be allowed for investigation and no hostilities to occur before report is made and (4) reservation by each nation of the right to decide, after the report, what action it should take. Ratifications of twenty-two treaties were exchanged, and commissions were appointed; however, no questions have been submitted under the terms of these treaties.

[Carnegie Endowment for International Peace, *Treaties for the Advancement of Peace.*]

ROSCOE R. HILL

Bryan's Station, Ky., was established in 1779 by four Bryan brothers from North Carolina. The occupants of this parallelogram of some forty cabins withstood several Indian attacks, the most important of which occurred in August, 1782, when they were besieged by about 300 Indians and Canadians under Capt. William Caldwell and Simon Girty. The battle of Blue Licks*qv* occurred about sixty miles northeast three days later.

[Reuben T. Durrett, *Bryan's Station,* Filson Club Publication, No. 12.]

JONATHAN T. DORRIS

Buccaneers, or Freebooters, called by the Dutch *Vlijbooters,* are terms commonly applied to the adventurers who infested the West Indies in the 16th, 17th and 18th centuries. Among themselves they were known as "Brethren of the Coast." It seems probable that a group of Normans early settled on an island, perhaps Tortuga, and organized themselves into a small band, living off wild animals and preying upon the neighboring Spanish colonies. They formed a picturesque lot, traveling in pairs, living in the open, dyeing their clothes in blood and going about armed to the teeth. The Spaniards early began to attack these groups and to destroy the wild cattle and swine which were their principal source of food. Driven to self-defense and finally to open warfare with Spain, they took to the sea and began a career of piracy*qv*, plunder, murder and rapine, attacking Spanish commerce and colonial towns. This life appealed to many individuals of various nationalities and the number of buccaneers increased rapidly. But about 1670 a partial stop was put to this piracy in the Caribbean and some of the buccaneers went to the Pacific to continue their profession. Finally by the Treaty of Ryswick*qv* in 1697 buccaneering was practically suppressed. Among the picturesque leaders of the buccaneers were Pierre La Grand, François l'Olonnais, Henry Morgan, Van Horn, Jacques Cassard, Edward Teach (Blackbeard), Bartholomew Roberts, François Thurot, Jean d'Albarade and Montbars "The Exterminator."

[Maurice Besson, *The Scourge of the Indies;* Alfred Sternbeck, *Filibusters and Buccaneers.*]

A. CURTIS WILGUS

Buck Stove and Range Case. In 1906 the metal polishers in the Buck Stove and Range Company, St. Louis, struck for a nine-hour day. The American Federation of Labor*qv* put the company on their "unfair list," whereupon the company obtained a sweeping injunction forbidding this boycott*qv*. For refusal to obey, Samuel Gompers, John Mitchell and Frank Morrison were sentenced to prison for contempt, but did not serve. The case was outlawed in 1914 by the Supreme Court under the statute of limitations (*see* Clayton Act).

[H. W. Laidler, *Boycotts and the Labor Struggle.*]

H. U. FAULKNER

Buckboards. Originally designed for personal transportation in mountain regions, these distinctively American four-wheeled vehicles, with one seat resting upon elastic boards fastened directly to the axles, were widely used in newly settled sections.

[Buckboards may be seen in many museums and institutes.]

HARVEY L. CARTER

Buckland Races. Near Buckland Mills, on Broad Run, J. E. B. Stuart (C.), with Wade Hampton's cavalry division, covering Lee's retirement from Bristoe to the Rappahannock*qqv*, on Oct. 19, 1863, turned on Kilpatrick's pursuing Federal cavalry, while Fitzhugh Lee's division charged the Federal flank. Kilpatrick was routed, fleeing five miles to Haymarket and Gainesville. The Confederates derisively called the affair "Buckland Races."

[J. W. Thomason, Jr., *Jeb Stuart; Official Records, Union and Confederate Armies,* Vol. XXIX.]

JOSEPH MILLS HANSON

Buckshot War (1838). As a result of the state election of 1838, both parties claimed control of the Pennsylvania House of Representatives. Two speakers were elected. A mob, largely from Philadelphia, assembled in Harrisburg, threatened violence and forced Thaddeus Stevens, Charles B. Penrose and Thomas H. Burrowes to escape from the Senate chamber through a window. Gov. Ritner called for United States troops which the President refused, whereupon the governor called out the Philadelphia militia, requisitioning among other equipment thirteen rounds of buckshot cartridges, whence the name "The Buckshot War." Three Whigs voted with the Democrats enabling them to organize the House, whereupon order was restored.

[Mueller, *The Whig Party in Pennsylvania.*]

H. H. SHENK

Bucktails, THE (1818–26), were a New York State party opposed to the canal policy of Gov.

DeWitt Clinton; named from a Tammany insignia, a deer's tail worn in the hat.

[J. D. Hammond, *Political History of the State of New York.*]

MILTON W. HAMILTON

Budget, Director of the, is an official created by the Budget and Accounting Act[qv] passed by Congress in 1921. The Director, who is the head of the Bureau of the Budget, is appointed by the President alone and for an indefinite term. Although nominally attached to the Treasury Department[qv], the Director enjoys complete freedom from control either by Congress or by any of the executive departments, being responsible to the President alone, as his personal agent. Annually, the Bureau of the Budget obtains from the various branches of the Government their respective estimates of funds needed for the ensuing fiscal period. These estimates the Director and his staff examine carefully in consultation with the agencies concerned. The revised estimates are then gone over by the President and Director, and may undergo further and drastic revision. When in final form, they become the basis for the annual budget submitted to Congress each January.

[W. F. Willoughby, *The National Budget System;* C. G. Dawes, *The First Year of the Budget in the United States.*]

P. ORMAN RAY

Budget and Accounting Act of 1921. Several states began experimenting with budgetary procedures around 1910, and President Taft's Commission on Economy and Efficiency recommended them for the Federal Government in 1911. After much discussion, Congress passed a bill in 1919, but it was vetoed, for technical reasons, by President Wilson. The adoption of such legislation was made a campaign issue by the Republicans in 1920; a budget bill was enacted in 1921 and signed by President Harding. Drafted by W. F. Willoughby and other experts in fiscal procedure, the act has two main parts : (1) that providing for the Bureau of the Budget, under a Director[qv], appointed by the President for an indefinite term and responsible to him; (2) that providing for the General Accounting Office, under a Controller General, appointed by the President for a term of fifteen years and intended to be entirely independent.

[Daniel T. Selko, *The Administration of Federal Finances;* W. F. Willoughby, *The National Budget System with Suggestions for Its Improvement.*]

W. BROOKE GRAVES

Buena Vista, Battle of (Feb. 22–23, 1847). During the Mexican War[qv] Gen. Zachary Taylor had advanced his army of 4700 men from Monterrey[qv] to a mountain pass south of Saltillo. Near the hacienda of Buena Vista he encountered a Mexican force under Santa Anna three times the size of his own. Though the Americans lost ground the first day, they won a brilliant victory on the second and the Mexicans withdrew. Taylor gained a reputation which made him President, but the further conquest of Mexico was entrusted to Gen. Scott.

[N. W. Stephenson, *Texas and the Mexican War.*]

L. W. NEWTON

Buenaventura River Myth was based on erroneous early Spanish and American maps which showed a river flowing from the Rockies into Great Salt Lake and emptying into the Pacific Ocean. Some overland emigrant parties even expected to reach California in boats. As late as 1844 Frémont was searching for this fabulous river.

[Allan Nevins, *Frémont, the West's Greatest Adventurer.*]

JEANNE ELIZABETH WIER

Buffalo, N. Y., was named for Buffalo Creek, which in the French occupation was known as Rivière aux Chevaux. There are many theories to account for the "translation" from Chevaux to Buffalo; none have been fully substantiated, but it is reasonably certain that the native habitat of the buffalo was never so far east. When in 1799 Dutch land speculators (the Holland Land Company[qv]) bought most of the Phelps-Gorham Purchase[qv], consisting of a million acres west of the Genesee River, they commissioned Joseph Ellicott to survey and offer for sale lots in a village on Buffalo Creek, to be called New Amsterdam. The Dutch name, however, never was generally used and when the village became the county seat in 1807 it officially took the new name. The town was completely destroyed by the British and Indians in December, 1813, but was rapidly rebuilt, became the terminus of the Erie Canal[qv] in 1825 and was a city by 1832.

[F. H. Severance, *An Old Frontier of France;* R. W. Bingham, *The Cradle of the Queen City.*]

JULIAN PARK

Buffalo, The, or more properly the American bison, at the time of the discovery occupied about one third of the continent from 63° N. Lat. in Canada to about 25° N. Lat. in Mexico, and from the Blue Mountains of Oregon to the western portions of New York, Pennsylvania, Virginia and the Carolinas. The chief habitat was, however, the plains between the Missouri River and the Rocky Mountains. Fossil remains date to the mid-Pleistocene period.

Easily hunted and of large size—the males reaching 2000 pounds—the buffalo were everywhere a favorite source of food for the Indians and frontier whites. As civilization advanced westward the animals were exterminated and by 1850 few if any remained east of the Mississippi. The dry plains, however, still contained numbers so vast as to be almost impossible of computation. Gen. Phil H. Sheridan, in 1866, estimated 100,000,000 buffalo in the region between Camp Supply, I. T., and Fort Dodge, Kans., and this was only part of the western buffalo.

Plains Indians based their civilization and religion to a large extent on the buffalo, as those farther east based theirs on the maize. Methods of killing included stalking, stampeding herds over cliffs, and driving them into *cul de sacs*. When horses were introduced in the plains, the methods of pursuit and the surround were added. Every part of the buffalo was useful to the Indians, who depended on the bison for food, shelter, weapons and clothing. Natural increase, however, kept pace with the slaughter until the advent of the white man.

Building of the Union Pacific and Kansas Pacific railroads[qqv], the early trains of which were sometimes stopped by herds crossing the tracks, led to the disappearance of the animals in the central plains and by 1875 there were two distinct groups, the northern and southern. The railroads furnished transportation outlets and in the 1870's hide and meat hunters began a systematic and wholesale destruction, shipping robes and meat to the East. By 1878 the southern herd was practically extinct, although the four last survivors were not killed until 1889. Similarly the northern herd was exterminated by 1884, except for a few individuals. Buffalo bones, gathered by settlers, later were important in commerce.

Dr. William T. Hornaday, of the National Museum, first called the nation's attention to the virtual disappearance of the buffalo in 1886. He made a census in 1889 which showed a total of only 1091 American bison existing throughout the world. This was the low ebb. Many individuals became interested and in 1905 the American Bison Society was organized. Through its efforts public consciousness was aroused and today the danger of complete extinction seems ended.

In 1903 a census revealed in the United States 41 herds in 24 states, with 969 animals, and a total in the world of 1644. The 1933 census showed 121 herds in 41 states, with 4404 animals, while Canada contained 17,043 and the world total was 21,701.

[Martin S. Garretson, *The American Bison;* E. Douglas Branch, *The Hunting of the Buffalo.*]

PAUL I. WELLMAN

Buffalo Chips was the dried excrement of the American bison. It was widely used for fuel by the first white men on the Great Plains.

EVERETT DICK

Buffalo Hunters' War (1877). Comanche[qv] malcontents led by Black Horse (Tu-ukumah) left the Indian Territory[qv], December, 1876, for the Staked Plains[qv] of Texas. Feb. 22, 1877, they attacked buffalo hunters' camps in the Red River country of the Texas Panhandle, killing or wounding several. Forty-five hunters left Rath's trading post on Double Mountain Creek a few days later, and trailed the Indians, whose camp was attacked near Thompson's Canyon, Texas, March 18. The hunters were repulsed and the Indians escaped. One white man was killed and several were wounded; the Indian loss is not known. The inconclusive battle ended Comanche attacks.

[John R. Cook, *The Border and the Buffalo;* Paul I. Wellman, *Death on the Prairie.*]

PAUL I. WELLMAN

Buffalo Trails. The first thoroughfares of this continent, save for the time-obliterated paths of mastodon, musk-ox and Moundbuilder, were the traces made by buffalo and deer in seasonal migration and in quest of—or between—feeding-grounds and salt licks[qv]. Many of these routes, hammered by countless hoofs instinctively following watersheds and the crests of ridges in avoidance of lower places' summer muck and winter snowdrifts, were followed by the Indians as courses to hunting grounds and as warriors' paths; were invaluable to explorers and adopted by pioneers. Buffalo traces were characteristically north and south; yet their major east-west trails —through Cumberland Gap[qv]; along the New York watershed; from the Potomac through the Allegheny divide to the Ohio headwaters; through the Blue Ridge Mountains to upper Kentucky—anticipated the courses of trunk railways. And in Sen. Thomas Benton's phrase saluting these sagacious pathmakers, the buffalo blazed the way for the railroads to the Pacific.

[A. B. Hulbert, *Historic Highways of America*, I.]

E. DOUGLAS BRANCH

Buffer State. *See* Indian Barrier State (Proposed).

Buffington Island Skirmish, THE (July 19, 1863), in Meigs County, Ohio, contributed to the capture of the Confederate raider, Gen. John Morgan, who was seeking to escape across the Ohio River at a ford opposite Buffington Island (*see* Morgan's Raids, The). Delayed overnight, he was almost surrounded by Federal cavalry next day and the battle ended in a rout. Morgan and some 1200 men escaped but the raid finally ended in his capture at Salineville on July 26.

[Whitelaw Reid, *Ohio in the War*, Vol. I.]

EUGENE H. ROSEBOOM

Buford Expedition (1856). As a part of the effort to make Kansas a slave state (*see* Border War; Kansas Struggle), Col. Jefferson Buford of Eufaula, Ala., in April organized and equipped for settlement, mainly at his own expense, 400 men largely from Alabama, Georgia and South Carolina. In Kansas, Buford's men participated in many of the conflicts between the free and slave state factions.

[W. L. Fleming, The Buford Expedition to Kansas, *American Historical Review*, VI, 38-48.]

HENRY T. SHANKS

Building and Loan Associations, started in Frankford, Pa., in 1831, are the most successful form of co-operative credit in the United States. There have been various forms: (1) the terminating, ending when the given group all have their homes; (2) the serial, which start new groups at intervals; (3) the permanent, where one may start any time; (4) the Dayton, Ohio, plan started in 1870, where the payments do not have to be made regularly. At their best they permit doing business at low cost, making use of the knowledge of the members and what amounts to an amortization plan in paying back the loans. In the 1890's national associations failed and after 1931 there were more failures. The Reconstruction Finance Corporation[qv] has aided associations by lending them money. The Federal Home Loan Bank Act of June 13, 1933, permits them to get Federal charters and become Federal Savings and Loan Associations[qv].

[R. L. Garis, *Principles of Money Credit and Banking.*]

JAMES D. MAGEE

Building Materials. The first settlers in America naturally had to depend upon timber for a quick building material, and thatched, clay-chinked log cabins[qv], with greased-paper windows if any at all, were the first houses. Hand-split shingles (clapboards or shakes) soon began to be riven from four-foot blocks of wood with mallet and frow. Such roofs, usually of white oak, may still be seen upon a few houses in our Southern hill region. The first chimneys were of rough stone, sometimes topped with wood and clay. In later years pioneer cabins where stone was scarce often had the fireplace only of stone, the chimney from there upward being a pen of hand-split, two-inch oaken sticks, laid log-cabin fashion, chinked and lined with clay. A few such chimneys still survive.

The next type of house was of lumber, often hand-sawn. When sawmills were brought from Europe we could turn out our own plain lumber, but for many decades we continued to import for the finer houses columns, pilasters, molding, newel posts, balustrades, panelling, etc., not to mention glass and brass door hardware. Laths were split by hand until about 1825.

The Dutch and German settlers showed a liking for stone, with the result that eastern and southern New York, New Jersey and eastern Pennsylvania are still dotted with sturdy dwellings, barns and water mills of rough stone. On Long Island, where stone was scarce, most Dutch houses had all-shingled exteriors, like some on the New England coast. The Dutch stone houses often had weatherboarded gables. Many an old house, rebuilt or enlarged, shows a commingling of materials—this outer wall of stone, that one of brick, perhaps another one weatherboarded. The first brick[qv] were imported from England and Holland. Careful New England builders immersed their brick in boiling oil to make them damp-proof. Hollow wooden columns were sometimes filled with rock salt to guard against moisture and worms.

Although there was a short-lived attempt at glass making at Salem, Mass., about 1640, and though glass making was more soundly established at New Amsterdam in 1645, many American communities saw no glass windows until 1700 or afterward. The industry grew rapidly in the 18th century. Until after 1800 such glass as was used in the Ohio Valley crossed the Alleghenies on pack horses. Hand-wrought nails were a very early product in America. By 1790, machine-made nails were beginning to appear, coming first from England; but wrought nails were still being used long after 1800. By the middle of the 19th century we were producing our own brick, nails, glass, millwork, iron door hardware, and fire irons.

No buildings of American marble were erected until the latter half of the 19th century. Marble mantels were imported from Italy for the finer houses as long as the wood fireplace prevailed. The hob grate for burning coal was introduced about 1750, and as a finish around it, pictorial glazed tiles were brought from Holland. Wallpapers, highly pictorial, began to be imported from Europe about 1735. Pennsylvania's slate quarries were producing in the 18th century and roofing many of the better houses of that region. Metal roofing appeared in the 19th century—first, sheet copper, then tin, then—toward the close of the century—galvanized iron, accompanied by tarred paper and gravel. Composition shingles containing asbestos and other elements are 20th-century devices. Tile roofs were rare in America until this century.

The adobe[qv] house of the dry Southwest, usually built of huge, sun-dried earthen bricks—though sometimes with one-piece, molded walls—was an early feature of the landscape which has been returning to favor in that area since 1900. Protected on the outside with stucco, it makes a durable and comfortable house.

Brick and stone were laid in lime mortar until after 1818, when cement-making rock was discovered in central New York and soon afterwards in other places. A house of reinforced concrete beams and slabs was built in 1875 and in the latter 1880's and 1890's some small poured concrete or monolithic buildings were erected, reinforced with hoop iron and wire rope. Concrete blocks began to be manufactured about the same time.

Some wrought-iron beams and girders were brought to this country from Europe about 1840 and mixed with timber in building construction. Cooper Institute in New York, built 1854–59 by Peter Cooper, who manufactured bridge iron, was probably the first building in America with floors resting entirely upon iron frames. Even in the 1870's and 1880's buildings eight and ten stories in height were being supported entirely on masonry walls, which of course must be inconveniently thick near the ground. The production of steel beams, begun in 1885, brought about the birth of the skyscraper[qv] about five years later. With it came metal lath and the hollow terra-cotta wall. Quartz glass, which admits the ultra-violet rays of the sun, glass bricks, which make translucent walls possible, and the all-steel frame house, cut for assembly on the site of the proposed house, are among the most important products of the third and fourth decades of the 20th century.

[J. Leander Bishop, *A History of American Manufactures.*]

ALVIN F. HARLOW

Buildings. *See* Architecture, American.

Bull Boats. When Hudson's Bay Company[qv] traders first visited the Mandan Indians[qv] in 1790 they found that tribe possessed of tublike boats with framework of willow poles, covered with raw buffalo hides. Later, frontiersmen who ascended the Missouri noted this light, convenient craft. From 1810 to 1830, American fur traders on the tributaries of the Missouri regularly built boats eighteen to thirty feet long, using the methods of construction employed by the Indians in making their circular boats. These elongated bull boats were capable of transporting two tons of fur down the shallow waters of the Platte.

[Phil E. Chappell, *A History of the Missouri River.*]

CARL P. RUSSELL

Bull Garrison House, THE (Dec. 15, 1675), was located on Tower Hill, South Kingstown, R. I. During King Philip's War[qv] it was attacked and burned by the Narragansett Indians[qv], fifteen of its defenders losing their lives.

[*Rhode Island Historical Society Collection,* January, 1918, and July, 1925.]

HOWARD M. CHAPIN

"Bull Moose" Party, THE, was a popular nickname given to the Progressive party[qv] of 1912–16 which nominated Theodore Roosevelt for the Presidency at a national convention in Chicago, Ill., in August, 1912. The Progressives seceded from the Republican party[qv] following the renomination of President William H. Taft. The name itself was a tribute to Mr. Roosevelt who often used the term "bull moose" to describe the strength and vigor of a person.

Thus he wrote, following his nomination for the Vice-Presidency on the Republican ticket in 1900, in a letter to Sen. M. A. Hanna, "I am as strong as a bull moose and you can use me to the limit." Also, when shot by a would-be assassin in Milwaukee, Wis., on the evening of Oct. 14, 1912, he insisted on immediately filling an engagement to speak, saying to the audience, "It takes more than that to kill a Bull Moose."

The party was in large part reunited with and reabsorbed into the Republican party during the campaign of 1916[qv], after the nomination of Charles E. Hughes, who was acceptable to Mr. Roosevelt and the leading Progressives.

[J. B. Bishop, *Theodore Roosevelt and His Time.*]

WILLIAM STARR MYERS

Bull Run, First Battle of (July 21, 1861). This, the first major engagement, has been described as "the best planned and worst fought battle" of the Civil War. The principal Union army, under Gen. Irvin McDowell, was mobilized about Washington. Gen. Robert Patterson (U.), with a smaller army, was sent to "retain" Gen.

Joseph E. Johnston (C.) in the Shenandoah Valley. Gen. P. G. T. Beauregard (C.) occupied the line of Bull Run Creek, which lies across the main highways from Washington southward. His advanced force under Gen. M. L. Bonham was based on Fairfax Courthouse to watch McDowell's army. McDowell had available about 30,000 men and 49 guns; Beauregard, about 24,000 and 35 guns; Johnston, about 9000 to Patterson's 12,000. None of these armies was thoroughly organized or disciplined.

Public opinion compelled President Lincoln to order McDowell to move forward. The Federal advance guard drove in Bonham's pickets on July 17. In accordance with previous orders, Bonham withdrew to Centreville, waited until dark, then retired behind Bull Run where the road from Washington to Richmond crossed at Mitchell's Ford and where Beauregard expected the main attack. The Confederates were disposed as follows: Ewell held the right at Union Mills Ford below the Orange and Alexandria Railroad; D. R. Jones protected McLean's Ford two miles upstream; Longstreet held Blackburn's Ford a mile above; Bonham was a mile and a half farther; Cocke guarded Ball's and Lewis' fords, one and one half and two and a half miles above Mitchell's; a mile farther Evans held the Stone Bridge where the Warrenton Turnpike crossed Bull Run. Thus the Confederate line extended about eight miles behind a shallow, meandering creek. Ewell was supported by Holmes' brigade, while Early was behind Jones and Longstreet. Tyler (U.), commanding McDowell's advanced force, on his own initiative, made a reconnoissance in force on July 18, but was sharply repulsed by Longstreet and Bonham aided by Early (*see* Blackburn's Ford, Battle at).

Eluding Patterson, Johnston and part of his army reached Bull Run on Saturday, July 20. Though the ranking officer, Johnston did not assume personal direction of the Confederate operations till the middle of the ensuing battle, meanwhile stationing his troops on the slope behind Beauregard's line. McDowell and Beauregard planned to turn each other's left flank. Ewell, on the Confederate right, was to cross Bull Run at daylight of July 21, the other brigades to follow. Beauregard's order did not reach Ewell. Longstreet, after crossing, waited in vain for word of his attack. By 7 A.M., when Jones received his orders, Sherman (U.) and Schenck (U.) were attacking the Confederate left at the Stone Bridge, Burnside (U.), at the same time, attempting to flank this end of the Confederate line. Evans, at the Stone Bridge, promptly deployed his scant half brigade to meet these movements. Johnston sent Jackson (C.) and Imboden (C.) to support Evans and soon Bee (C.) and Hampton (C.) followed. Fierce fighting raged from Bull Run to the Henry House plateau, to which the Confederates were driven. Here Bee lost his life and Jackson won his name of "Stonewall." The arrival of another portion of Johnston's army turned the tide in favor of the Confederates. The Federals were driven across Bull Run in disorder, pursued along the Warrenton Pike. No fighting of any consequence had taken place on the Confederate right.

When the break took place on the Federal right, Johnston ordered Bonham and Longstreet to move in pursuit. The Federal withdrawal turned into a rout as the troops streamed back in the direction of Washington. The Confederate pursuit started from Mitchell's Ford in the direction of Centreville at which point it was halted, the Confederates later returning to Bull Run. Bitter controversy afterwards ensued between Davis and Johnston and Beauregard as to the responsibility for not pursuing the defeated Federals into Washington. Military critics think this was not feasible. The staff work and courier service on both sides was miserable and a heavy rainstorm added to the confusion and uncertainty. From some 13,000 men actually engaged, the Federals lost about 500 killed, 1000 wounded and 1200 missing; the Confederates, with about 11,000 engaged, lost about 400 killed, 1600 wounded and 13 missing. They captured 25 guns and much other material. But it was a Pyrrhic victory. The South was made overconfident, while the North was spurred to earnest effort.

[R. M. Johnston, *Bull Run: Its Strategy and Tactics.*]

MILLEDGE L. BONHAM, JR.

Bull Run, The Second Battle of, was initiated by the decision of Gen. R. E. Lee, Aug. 24, 1862, at Jeffersonton, Va., to send the 23,000 troops of Lt. Gen. T. J. ("Stonewall") Jackson to break the communications of Maj. Gen. John Pope's Army of Virginia^{qv}, which was unassailably placed on the upper stretches of the Rappahannock River, Virginia. Jackson started before daylight, Aug. 25, passed Thoroughfare Gap and, on the evening of the 26th, reached Bristoe Station. The next day Jackson plundered Pope's base at Manassas Junction and proceeded to Groveton Heights, five miles N.W. of Manassas. There, on the 28th, he attacked King's division. On Aug. 29 Pope in turn attacked Jackson, who with difficulty beat off repeated assaults. Lee, meantime, had brought up the remainder of his army, 32,000 men, and had formed them on Jackson's right. By nightfall of the 29th Lee's line formed an obtuse angle from N. to S. (Longstreet) and thence S.W. to N.E. (Jackson). Pope, re-enforced by a large part of the Army of the Potomac[qv], renewed the attack on Jackson on the 30th, but failed to confront Longstreet with sufficient force. Lee accordingly ordered a general attack which swept Pope from his positions. Heavy rain on Aug. 31 delayed pursuit and made possible the retreat by Pope within the Washington defenses. Pope blamed his defeat on FitzJohn Porter[qv], who was cashiered and was not vindicated until 1886, but Pope himself was not again trusted with field command. His losses, Aug. 16–Sept. 2, were 14,462; those of Lee were 9112.

[J. C. Ropes, *The Army under Pope;* D. S. Freeman, *R. E. Lee*, Vol. 2.] DOUGLAS SOUTHALL FREEMAN

Bull-Whacker. *See* Mule Skinner.

Bulldoze. During the Reconstruction[qv] period a Federal marshal was investigating an attempt to assassinate a registrar of voters in East Feliciana Parish, La. (1875). The natives refused him all information, and as the marshal stood pondering he was approached by a half-witted German who shouted, "Bull dooza mit der hooza!" The expletive had no meaning whatsoever, but to the frightened marshal it sounded like a threat from the Ku Klux Klan and he fled, which result was so satisfactory that the term "Bulldoze" came into general use throughout the South, with the generic meaning to intimidate in a bullying manner.

[T. Jones Cross, The True Etymology of Bulldoze, *Proceedings of the Historical Society of East and West Baton Rouge*, 1918.] MILLEDGE L. BONHAM, JR.

Bullion. Although both silver and gold were standards of value from 1792 to 1834, bimetallism[qv] did not prevail in practice, the circulating medium continuing to be a mixture of foreign and domestic coins and notes. The mint ratio overvalued silver, which would theoretically have caused silver imports and gold exports. Lack of gold and other factors prevented this, and in the years prior to 1806 silver dollars were exported as rapidly as minted until their coinage was discontinued.

Congress changed the mint ratio to approximately 16 to 1 in 1834, but this overvalued gold. Silver dollars, however, were slow to disappear, and from 1834 to 1844—the only such period in our history—silver and gold circulated interchangeably.

After 1844 silver dollars disappeared from circulation, and in 1851 silver was made a subordinate monetary metal, which it has ever since remained. From 1862 to 1879 the actual standard was paper. In 1873 Congress dropped the long unfamiliar "standard silver dollar" and provided for a "silver trade dollar" for export purposes, a gesture to mining interests. The increasing output of American silver mines, however, demonetization in Europe and the consequent declining market price of silver soon made free coinage of silver a national political issue. The "Crime of '73"[qv] was discovered. Free coinage of silver was demanded.

A compromise, the Bland-Allison Act[qv] (Feb. 28, 1878), resulted in the purchase and coinage during twelve years of 291,000,000 oz. of silver at a cost of $308,000,000. However, the price of silver was not thereby stabilized. On June 17, 1890, Congress passed the Sherman Silver Purchase Act[qv], increasing the monthly purchases to 4,500,000 oz.; but the act was repealed Nov. 1, 1893, after 169,000,000 oz., costing about $156,000,000, had been bought. Depression fostered further inflation sentiment. Silver featured the 1896 election campaign, but such factors as transition to world-power status, returning prosperity and discovery of new gold fields, discouraged bimetallism and the act of March 14, 1900, specifically fixed the gold dollar as "the standard unit of value."

During the World War the gold standard was temporarily suspended through an export embargo. The sale of up to 350,000,000 oz. of silver coin to Great Britain and its subsequent replacement was authorized by the Pittman Act of 1918[qv]. March 6, 1933, gold payments and exports were again suspended; on April 5 gold circulation was discontinued and the metal nationalized. The "Thomas Amendment"[qv] of May 12, 1933, granted the President important currency powers. On June 5, 1933, all forms of United States currency[qv] were made unlimited legal tender[qv]. At London in July a silver agreement providing *inter alia* for United States Treasury purchases of silver was reached between eight countries, and on Dec. 21, 1933, President Roosevelt, by proclamation, opened the mints to the full American mine production of silver for four years on a basis yielding the domestic producer 64.64¢ an oz., or a substantial premium over the market price. This proclamation was several times amended, and extended through June, 1939. By congressional action completed July 5, 1939, domestic-mined silver was given a Treasury market at 71.11¢ an oz. on a permanent basis.

On Jan. 30, 1934, the Gold Reserve Act[qv] temporarily authorized the President to fix the dollar at from 60% to 50% of its former gold content. The President thereupon proclaimed its content at 15 5/21 grains of gold 9/10ths fine. The official price of gold was thus fixed at $35 an ounce and the dollar was externally linked to gold, although left internally inconvertible. The Gold Reserve Act created a $2,000,000,000 Stabilization Fund. It also continued to vest in the Secretary of the Treasury broad, permanent powers to buy and sell gold without price or other restriction.

The Silver Purchase Act of 1934[qv], approved June 19, called for indefinite purchases of silver until one fourth of the total national stock of gold and silver at their monetary values shall consist of silver, unless the price of silver should previously reach its monetary value ($1.29 + an ounce). Under this act over 1,673,100,000 oz. of silver had been acquired through May 31, 1939, and under the proclamation of Dec. 21, 1933, as amended, 277,100,000 oz.

[Neil Carothers, *Fractional Money;* Charles J. Bullock, *Monetary History of the United States.*]

HERBERT M. BRATTER

Bummers. A nickname applied to foragers of Sherman's army during its March to the Sea[qv] and north through the Carolinas[qv].

[*Battles and Leaders of the Civil War*, Vol. IV; B. H. Liddell Hart, *Sherman; Soldier, Realist, American.*]

JOSEPH MILLS HANSON

Buncombe is a term which, by 1828, had come into general use in political Washington to mean speechmaking designed for show or public applause. It is reputed to have originated a few years earlier in connection with a speech which Felix Walker made in Congress to please Buncombe County, N. C., in his congressional district.

[*Niles' Weekly Register*, XXXV, 1828, p. 66; J. H. Wheeler, *Historical Sketches of North Carolina, from 1584 to 1851*, II.]

E. MERTON COULTER

Bundling, a mode of courtship in colonial days where the parties instead of sitting up together went to bed together, with their clothes on. This custom, inherited from Europe, apparently originated as a matter of convenience and necessity where space and heat were lacking. It was confined largely to the poorer classes. Its prevalence seems to have ended in the late 18th century with the general improvement of living conditions.

[Henry Reed Stiles, *Bundling; Its Origin, Progress and Decline in America.*]

HUGH T. LEFLER

Bunker Hill (June 17, 1775). To force the British from Boston, on the night of the 16th of June the American militia besieging the town sent 1200 men to seize Bunker Hill, on the peninsula of Charlestown. Instead, the detachment built a small redoubt on Breed's Hill, nearer Boston[qv] but easily flanked. Working silently, they were not discovered until daybreak, when British warships, anchored below, opened an ineffective fire. Col. William Prescott, commanding in the redoubt, strengthened his left flank, toward the Mystic River, by a breastwork, a rail fence stuffed with hay, and a slight defense of stones on the beach. The defenders of these were joined by perhaps 2000 men, and were commanded by Maj. Gen. Israel Putnam, while in the redoubt Brig. Gen. Joseph Warren served as a volunteer. Meanwhile, under the command of Maj. Gen. Sir William Howe, 2000 British infantry, with a few field guns, landed below the redoubt.

Dividing his men into two wings, early in the afternoon Howe attacked both the redoubt and the rail fence, expecting first to turn the fence by a column along the beach, which would make it easily possible to storm in front. The attack was bloodily repulsed by the provincials, chiefly New Hampshire men under John Stark, and the remainder of the British withdrew after being but briefly in touch with the Americans. At the second attack the British advanced on both wings with great courage; but the provincials, as before holding their fire until the regulars were close, cut them to pieces and forced their withdrawal. Still trusting to the desperate frontal attack, in the final attempt Howe merely feinted against the fence, and for the first time attacked the redoubt with the bayonet. For the first time, also, his fieldpieces got within effective range and drove the defenders from the breastwork. What would have happened had the Americans had enough powder cannot be known; but Prescott's men were out of ammunition and, after a first severe fire, on his order, quitted the redoubt. In this assault fell Maj. Pitcairn, British commander at Lexington, and Joseph Warren. The defenders of the fence covered the American retreat. After an engagement lasting less than two hours, the British were masters of the peninsula, but with heavy casualties of 1054, while the Americans lost, in killed, wounded and prisoners, but 441. At first regarded by the Americans as a defeat, Bunker Hill, because of the way in which militia resisted regulars, came to be regarded as a moral victory, leading to a dangerous overconfidence in unpreparedness.

[*Historical Magazine*, June, 1868; S. A. Drake, *Bunker*

Hill; Richard Frothingham, *Siege of Boston;* Allen French, *First Year of the American Revolution.*]

ALLEN FRENCH

Bunker Hill Monument, commemorating the Revolutionary battle, its cornerstone laid by Lafayette in 1825, was dedicated in 1843, Daniel Webster being chief orator.

ALVIN F. HARLOW

Burchard Incident, THE, arose when Rev. S. D. Burchard, speaking from the same political platform as the Republican candidate, James G. Blaine, Oct. 30, 1884, described the Democracy as the party of "rum, Romanism and rebellion." Blaine's failure to offset the diatribe cost him Irish support and the election.

[David S. Muzzey, *James G. Blaine.*]

JEANNETTE P. NICHOLS

Bureaucracy. The term bureaucracy is used in both a narrow and a broad sense. Used narrowly, it means a system of conducting government through special bureaus each headed by a chief. Thus, in the national Treasury Department is the Bureau of Engraving and Printing, in the Department of Justice is the Bureau of Prisons, in the Navy Department is the Bureau of Navigation, in the Department of the Interior is the Bureau of Mines, in the Department of Agriculture is the Bureau of Animal Husbandry, in the Department of Commerce is the Bureau of the Census, while in the Department of Labor is the Children's Bureau, to mention only a few.

As generally used, however, the term has a much broader meaning, embracing within its scope all government officials. In this broad sense, bureaucracy in the United States includes not only the officials of the Federal Government but also those who conduct the affairs of the state and local governments.

From small beginnings, American bureaucracy has developed until it has attained gigantic proportions. The thirteen original states, each with simple machinery of government, have expanded to forty-eight, each with a complex governmental setup, requiring the services of about 250,000 persons. Within these states, over 175,000 local units of government have been developed, each having the powers to borrow money and to tax and each having a set of officials to carry on the functions of its particular unit. Altogether more than 900,000 persons are employed by these local governmental agencies. This figure does not include those engaged in public education, of whom there are over 1,000,000.

Likewise, the Federal Government has developed from a simple organization in 1789 to the complex establishment of today. From a mere handful of employees at first, the Federal civil service increased to about 3000 in 1800 and then grew until it reached 841,664 on June 30, 1937. This last figure was the highest in American history with the exception of the World War period.

Congress took the first steps to create a Federal bureaucracy in 1789 when it created the departments of State, Treasury and War, together with the office of Attorney General. By 1938 the Federal administrative machinery included approximately 140 different agencies. Among these were ten departments; a number of executive agencies under the President, but not connected with any of the regular departments, such as the Civil Service[qv] Commission which was created in 1883; and a group of about a dozen independent regulatory organizations, the first of which was the Interstate Commerce Commission[qv], created in 1887.

During the World War and again during the New Deal[qv], the Federal organization was complicated by agencies, known as councils, commissions, boards, administrations and governmental corporations[qv], which were set up for special purposes. Most of these were placed under the direction of the President in the executive branch of the government.

As the various governments, local, state and national, have assumed new functions, adding new officials to perform each function, the evils associated with bureaucracy have tended to become more pronounced. The more complex an organization is, the more likely it is to be involved in red tape. Action is impeded by a multitude of rules and regulations drawn up by the agency itself. Traditions, precedents and paper work become all important. Again there is a tendency to avoid responsibility. Each official is afraid to act without the approval of his superior. "Buck passing" is a common characteristic of bureaucrats.

In a bureaucracy the tendency is for officials to forget that they are in office to serve the people rather than to be served. They tend to become arrogant and arbitrary in their official conduct. Concerned with self-perpetuation in office they too often ignore the public welfare and become mere "time servers." Usually the public is too apathetic or indifferent to make any attempt to remedy the condition.

To prevent these evils the theory of rotation in office[qv] was early developed. Under this theory, officeholders were to be replaced before they developed an attitude of proprietorship toward their offices. Unfortunately, in practice, rotation in office degenerated into the spoils system[qv] and resulted in "amateurism" in government.

Experts in administration now are generally agreed that the evils of bureaucracy can be avoided by the establishment of a real career service in government. Admission to the service would be on the basis of ability, special training would be provided and promotions would be made in accordance with the manner in which the duties of office were performed. The chief policy determination, instead of being delegated to administrative officials, would properly be left to the legislative body while secondary discretion in carrying out policies would be exercised by a comparatively small group of elected officials.

[James M. Beck, *Our Wonderland of Bureaucracy; Better Government Personnel Report* of the Commission of Inquiry on Public Service Personnel.]

ERIK McKINLEY ERIKSSON

Burgesses, House of. *See* Colonial Assemblies.

Burghers were those citizens of an incorporated city who, under the Dutch (1657), enjoyed great or small burgher rights, and under the English were entitled by birth or admission by the magistrates to the designation of freemen[qv]. In New York and Albany only freemen, who had paid the required fees, could do business or ply a trade.

[A. C. Flick, ed., *History of the State of New York.*]

A. C. FLICK

Burgoyne's Invasion. In late spring, 1777, Gen. Burgoyne prepared to invade New York from Canada by the Lake Champlain-Hudson River route (*see* British Campaign of 1777). Lt. Col. St. Leger was given command of a small expedition which was to ascend the St. Lawrence, cross Lake Ontario and advance on Albany by the Mohawk Valley. Both commanders were instructed that their principal objective was junction with Sir William Howe. An order was prepared, but, through a mischance, never sent from England, commanding Howe to proceed up the Hudson. In spite of this fateful blunder, Howe knew the British plans, for he had received a copy of Burgoyne's instructions.

Burgoyne's army was made up of 3700 British regulars, 3000 German troops, 250 Canadians and Tories and 400 Indians. With his well equipped force he proceeded up Lake Champlain in late June and on July 1 was within four miles of Ticonderoga[qv], which, with Mt. Independence east of the lake, was garrisoned by about 2300 Continentals under Gen. St. Clair. In spite of militia reinforcements St. Clair wisely abandoned the fortress the night of July 5–6. Engagements with pursuing British at Hubbardton[qv], Skenesborough (now Whitehall) and Fort Ann did not prevent St. Clair from saving his army to form the nucleus of later resistance. The taking of Ticonderoga increased the confidence of the British and was at first a severe shock to the patriots; later, it proved a stimulus to resistance.

Burgoyne's progress now became very deliberate. He was retarded by his extensive baggage and by the fact that the transportation of his artillery up Lake George required all available boats, while his army proceeded overland. To oppose him there were 2000 Americans under Gen. Schuyler at Fort Edward; but Schuyler was reinforced July 12 by about 1700 from St. Clair's command and 600 Continentals from Peekskill. Retreating before Burgoyne's slow advance, Schuyler felled trees across the roads and encouraged the country people to burn their standing crops and drive off their cattle. His steadiness was of the utmost value to the American cause.

Meanwhile Howe, evidently believing the rebellion nearly crushed and that Burgoyne did not require his active co-operation, left Clinton at New York to make a sortie up the Hudson with such troops as could be spared from the garrison and went to Philadelphia.

Fortune now began to turn against Burgoyne. A raiding force despatched to secure patriot stores at Bennington[qv] was overwhelmed, Aug. 16, by Stark's New Hampshire militia and Warner's small force. St. Leger, besieging Fort Stanwix[qv], managed, at Oriskany[qv], to repulse a relieving body of militia under Herkimer, but his Indian allies fled in panic at news of the approach of a patriot force under Benedict Arnold and he abandoned his campaign.

Gen. Gates, now in command of the American army near the mouth of the Mohawk, had about 6000 effective troops. Reinforced by Morgan's Virginia riflemen, he moved northward and entrenched at Bemis Heights, about eight miles south of the hamlet of Saratoga[qv], now Schuylerville. Burgoyne, whose Indian scouts had fled, was close upon the American army before he realized its presence. The first battle of Freeman's Farm[qv] was fought Sept. 19. Both armies remained in position and Burgoyne waited, hoping for news of Clinton's expected advance up the Hudson. Clinton got no farther than the Highlands[qv], however. Meanwhile Gates' numbers were increasing, bodies of New England militia were gathering in Burgoyne's rear and the British supplies were running dangerously low. It was necessary to fight or to retreat. By Oct. 7 Burgoyne's effective troops numbered about 5000, while the Americans in front of him were nearly 8000. A reconnaissance in force to examine the American left was repulsed, the British were driven back into their lines and a determined attack led by Gen. Arnold threatened their whole position (*see* Freeman's Farm, Second Battle of). Burgoyne now had no alternative and fell back toward Saratoga (Schuylerville). His movement was so deliberate that the Americans were able to surround him, and on Oct. 17, finding himself opposed by over 17,000 regulars and militia, with less than 3500 infantry ready for duty, he surrendered his army to Gates. (*See also* Convention Army; Franco-American Alliance of 1778.)

[Hoffman Nickerson, *The Turning Point of the Revolution.*]

RALPH FOSTER WELD

Burke Act, THE (1906), was designed to correct certain defects in the Dawes Act[qv] of 1887, under which the land in the Indian tribal reservations was to be broken up and distributed in severalty to the individual Indians. Because of the unpreparedness of most Indians for citizenship it provided that citizenship be granted on the final validation of their trust patents at the end of the probationary period of twenty-five years instead of on the receipt of the trust patents as stated in the Dawes Act. Thus the Government, when advisable, could continue paternalistic control as a safeguard against exploitation and debauchery.

[Robert E. Riegel, *America Moves West.*]

ASA E. MARTIN

Burlingame Treaty, THE (July 28, 1868), consisted of articles added to the Reed Treaty of 1858[qv] between the United States and China. These acknowledged Chinese territorial jurisdiction in China, left trade privileges in China to the discretion of the Chinese government and established free immigration between the countries (*see* Chinese Exclusion Acts). It placed China on the "most favored nation"[qv] plane with regard to treatment of consuls, immunity and privileges in travel, residence and education of Chinese subjects in the United States. It guaranteed nonintervention by the United States in Chinese domestic administration. It was signed in Washington by William H. Seward, Secretary of State, Anson Burlingame, acting as "Envoy Extraordinary and Minister Plenipotentiary" of the Emperor of China, and two Chinese envoys.

[Frederick Wells Williams, *Anson Burlingame and the First Chinese Mission to Foreign Powers.*]

ROGER BURLINGAME

Burlington Company, THE, was a group of eight investors of Burlington, N. J., which absorbed various mortgages of George Croghan between 1768 and 1770. The mortgages, issued to Gov. William Franklin and assigned by him to the company, included one for £3000 on 40,000 acres of Croghan's Otsego[qv], N. Y., purchase. Franklin, besides personal loans to Croghan, had purchased a 50% stock interest in the company for £1500 (1772). The remaining original shareholders sold their stock and rights, including Franklin's mortgages, to Andrew Craig and William Cooper who, without notifying Franklin, instituted sheriff's sale proceedings under a judgment of 1773 and, by questionable methods, purchased the Otsego tract for £2700 (January, 1786). Efforts of Franklin and Croghan's heirs to contest title proved fruitless.

[A. T. Volwiler, *George Croghan and the Westward Movement, 1741-1782.*]

C. A. TITUS

Burlington Route. *See* Chicago, Burlington & Quincy Railroad, The.

Burlington Strike, THE. On Feb. 27, 1888, locomotive engine men of the Burlington Railway, members of the Brotherhood of Locomotive Engineers[qv], struck for higher wages and abandonment of the system of classification. The strike was supported by the Knights of Labor[qv]. As it dragged on, violence flamed, trains were wrecked, men were shot and property was burned or otherwise destroyed. The Brotherhood finally gave in, but the railway damage was enormous. Since this time no serious railway strikes have been permitted. By Feb. 1, 1889, train operations were normal.

[John R. Commons, *History of Labor in the United States*, Vol. II.]

THOMAS ROBSON HAY

Burning Spring, THE, was located in present Kanawha County, W. Va., at or near Malden and was referred to by pioneers as "one of the wonders of the world." It is not known when this "boiling pot," which could be ignited and extinguished at will, was first seen by white persons, but in 1755 Mrs. Mary Ingles, a captive, assisted Indians in making salt there. The 250-acre tract on which the spring was located was patented by Generals George Washington and Andrew Lewis, but Washington never saw it. It was his intention to give the spring site to the "public forever," but instead it went to his nephew, Lawrence Augustine Washington who, in turn, sold it to Dickinson and Shrewsberry, who incorporated it in their salt plant.

[West Virginia Geological Survey, *Kanawha County,*

Wheeling, 1914, pp. 296-298; John P. Hale, *Trans-Allegheny Pioneers.*]

CHARLES H. AMBLER

Burns Fugitive Slave Case (1854) was one of three famous fugitive slave cases arising in Boston, Mass., after the enactment of the Fugitive Slave Law of 1850[qv]. Part of the Vigilance Committee (1850–61) planned to rescue Anthony Burns, an escaped slave, from an upper room of the courthouse. They battered in a door of the building at night, May 26, entered and one of them shot and killed Marshal Batchelder. Despite the committee's efforts, United States Commissioner Edward G. Loring remanded Burns to his owner, Suttle, of Alexandria, Va. On June 2 throngs witnessed the slave's departure. Several rich citizens paid $1300 and got him back early in 1855.

[C. E. Stevens, *Anthony Burns;* T. W. Higginson in *Atlantic Monthly,* March, 1897; W. H. Siebert, *The Underground Railroad in Massachusetts.*]

WILBUR H. SIEBERT

Burnt Corn, The Battle of, was an encounter between the Creek Indians[qv] and the Alabama frontiersmen, July 27, 1813, on Burnt Corn Creek in Conecuh County, Ala. On their return from Pensacola[qv] where aid had been received from the British, a party of Creeks led by Peter McQueen were attacked by three companies of frontiersmen under command of Col. James Caller and aides. The Indians, having at first been dispersed, later rallied and defeated the Alabamians who had busied themselves seizing Indian pack horses and plunder. Two frontiersmen were killed and fifteen wounded, Capt. Sam Dale being among the latter.

[W. G. Brown, *History of Alabama;* J. C. DuBose, *Alabama History;* A. J. Pickett, *History of Alabama.*]

JOHN B. CLARK

Burnt District, The. On Oct. 3, 1864, when Gen. Philip H. Sheridan's army was encamped around Harrisonburg and Dayton, Rockingham County, Va., Maj. John Rodgers Meigs was killed in a fight with Confederate scouts. Sheridan, told that Meigs had been shot by bushwhackers[qv], ordered all buildings burned within a radius of five miles. This order was countermanded before it was fully carried out.

[John W. Wayland, *Virginia Valley Records.*]

JOHN W. WAYLAND

Burr Conspiracy, The, is one of the most involved and mysterious episodes in early American history. Because it climaxed the dramatic struggle for power between Jefferson, the President, and Aaron Burr, a discredited political adventurer, it bulks large in the history of the period. Essentially it was a compound of personal and political rivalry, discredited ambition and land hunger.

Burr's exact intentions probably cannot ever be known. Following his duel with Hamilton (*see* below) he became a creature of circumstances, always hoping and scheming to regain at least something of his one-time popularity and power. To accomplish this he chose what he considered the most likely road to wealth and power—land conquest or seizure in Spanish territory west of the Mississippi.

Burr's first act was an attempt to attach England to his cause. Failing in this, he served out his term as Vice-President, meantime intriguing with those who might be of help, yet never disclosing his exact intentions. He went to the West, down the Mississippi to New Orleans and back overland, seeking friendly help and necessary funds. Returned to the East he sought successively to draw France and then Spain into his web of intrigue, but to no avail. Without the hope of foreign help, he was ready to accept funds from whatever source. Blennerhassett[qv], a trusting, visionary Irishman, who lived on an island in the Ohio River, was only one, though the most bizarre and reputedly the heaviest of the contributors to this weird venture.

Before leaving Philadelphia in the summer of 1806, Burr wrote his friend Gen. James Wilkinson, who commanded the American army on the Mississippi, that the expedition would start for New Orleans before the end of the year. But Wilkinson, thoughtful for his own safety and uncertain as to Burr, declined to be involved. Instead, when Burr's advance flotilla reached the lower Mississippi, Wilkinson ordered its members arrested. As Burr came down he, too, was seized and then paroled. He attempted to escape to Spanish territory, but was again captured and taken East for trial (*see* below). Burr was acquitted, but the "conspiracy" had already collapsed.

[W. F. McCaleb, *The Aaron Burr Conspiracy.*]

THOMAS ROBSON HAY

Burr-Hamilton Duel, The, was the culminating point in the early partisan struggles of New York. It grew out of aspersions by Hamilton upon his rival's character. Burr, some weeks after his defeat, in 1804, for the governorship of New York, asked for an explanation and when Hamilton sought to evade the issue, Burr peremptorily challenged. Hamilton, in principle opposed to duelling[qv], averred that "peculiar necessity" forced him to accept the challenge. He wished to be useful, he explained, in those future crises which might affect the public weal. This enigmatical expression may be interpreted as a wish to break up plans to disrupt the Union. By facing Burr he may have thought to prevent his opponent from becoming a leader of disaffected New England Federalists[qv]. An alternative explanation was the prospect of war with Spain, which would carry with it leadership in the emancipation of Mexico (*see* Burr Conspiracy; Miranda's Intrigues). Both Hamilton and Burr wished to achieve this honor, and it seems to present a more compelling motive for the challenge and its acceptance.

The outcome of the duel at Weehawken, N. J., July 11, 1804, was fatal to both. Each fired once although Hamilton's friends claim that his shot was intentionally discharged in the air. Burr's reached its mark and his victim, mortally wounded, died the next day. Bankrupt in fortune and reputation and under indictment in New York and New Jersey, Burr thenceforth became a political outcast.

[Wandell and Minnigerode, *Aaron Burr.*]

ISAAC J. COX

Burr Trial, The Constitutional Aspects of the, have to do largely with the interpretation of the constitutional provision concerning treason[qv]. Aaron Burr was indicted for treason in 1807 (*see* Burr Conspiracy) and brought to trial in the United States Circuit Court at Richmond, Va., before Chief Justice John Marshall sitting as a circuit judge. The political passions of the times and the friction between President Jefferson and Chief Justice Marshall carried over into the trial and render appraisal difficult. An early incident of the trial was the Marshall opinion that a Federal court might issue a subpœna *duces tecum* to the President of the United States. In guiding the jury as to the law of treason the Chief Justice gave an interpretation so restricting the meaning of the words "levying war" that in the case at hand only the assemblage at Blennerhassett's Island[qv] could come within it. Burr, however much he may have counseled, advised or planned that assemblage, was not present. Under the Marshall interpretation his absentee connection was not sufficient to render him guilty of treason. Marshall held that the broader definition asked by counsel for the prosecution would include the English doctrine of constructive treason, which the phrasing of the constitutional provision was intended to exclude. This statement of the law resulted in a verdict of acquittal. The Chief Justice was sharply criticised for inconsistency and bias, in that in a dictum in an earlier case in the Supreme Court involving two of Burr's messengers (*see* Bollman Case) he had stated the law in a way which seemingly should have linked Burr with the treasonable assemblage.

[*Reports of the Trials of Colonel Aaron Burr for Treason and for a Misdemeanor;* Albert J. Beveridge, *The Life of John Marshall.*]

CARL BRENT SWISHER

Bushwackers. This term, originally used as far back as Washington Irving's day to describe a backwoodsman, came during the Civil War to be applied by Federal soldiers to Confederate guerrilla[qv] fighters, with a distinct implication of private plunder. Used in Missouri as synonymous with "Border Ruffians,"[qv] it was more commonly applied in the mountain sections of Virginia and Kentucky.

JAMES ELLIOTT WALMSLEY

Bushy Run, Battle of (Aug. 5, 6, 1763). Bouquet's expedition[qv] was attacked by Indians near Bushy Run, twenty-five miles east of Pittsburgh. After indecisive fighting until nightfall, the men rested on their arms, suffering greatly from thirst. In the morning Bouquet, feigning retreat, drew the Indians forward to receive a flanking fire from companies ambushed for the purpose. The Indians, completely routed, fled. Though the British loss of over a hundred officers and men probably exceeded that of the Indians, the victory relieved Fort Pitt[qv] and heartened the colonists.

[Francis Parkman, *Conspiracy of Pontiac.*]

SOLON J. BUCK

Business. *See* Trade, Domestic; Trade, Foreign.

Business, Big. The term "Big Business" first came into use in a symbolic sense subsequent to the Civil War, particularly after 1880, in connection with the combination movement that began in American business at that time (*see* Corporations; Trusts). Although the term has become common, there has never been general agreement as to what constituted "bigness." The large consolidated railroad and public utility systems have commonly been considered "big" because of the size of their fixed investments and their gross incomes. Industrial companies have been considered "big" both because of the absolute size of their assets and because of the size of their assets relative to the assets of other firms, especially competitors. The term has also been used in connection with the volume of sales of a particular business, especially when the sales of one concern were a substantial portion of the industry's sales. In a more sophisticated sense "bigness" has had reference to the extent to which an individual company, either by virtue of its size or for other reasons, was able to influence substantially the ruling prices in the trade. Certain banking houses have generally been acknowledged to be "big" not so much because of the size of their resources as because of the influence their members could exert on many companies and in many fields of activity.

The social consequences of the concentration of economic power in the hands of those persons controlling "Big Business" has been a constant concern both of economists and of politicians since the end of the 19th century. Various attempts have been made to investigate the effects of "bigness" upon labor, consumers and investors, as well as upon prices and competition. "Big Business" has been accused of a wide variety of misdeeds that range from the exploitation of the working man to the corruption of politicians and the fomenting of war. At the same time it has been generally admitted that much of the technological progress since 1850 has been dependent on and fostered by the growth in size and the increase in financial strength of individual business units. The long series of statutes and legal decisions designed to control or to regulate business, that begin with the Interstate Commerce Act and the Sherman Antitrust Act[qqv] and which have not yet come to an end, are in effect an attempt by society to mitigate the evils of "Big Business" while preserving its benefits.

[A. A. Berle and G. C. Means, *The Modern Corporation and Private Property;* Louis D. Brandeis, *The Curse of Bigness;* Eliot Jones, *The Trust Problem in the United States;* Henry R. Seager and Charles A. Gulick, *Trust and Corporation Problems.*]

CHARLES C. ABBOTT

Business, Mechanical Devices Used in. The first really important step toward the use of mechanical devices for business came in 1873 when the first commercial typewriter[qv] was manufactured by Remington. While this was a distinctly elementary machine, working like a sewing machine with foot pedal, and typewriting only capital letters, it started the forward development of machinery for office use.

From that point on, the history of the use of mechanical devices in business offices has progressed at a very rapid pace. The production of card-indexing methods and filing systems followed in the period from 1880 to 1885. In 1893 at the World's Fair in Chicago the first filing cabinet was on display. These two factors in office equipment development set the pace for further developments in the creation of office devices.

The adding machine in its early stages and even today follows the principle of registering and printing characters through ribbon just as they are printed on a typewriter. The first bookkeeping machines were merely extensions of the carriages on typewriters. Many of that type still remain.

Practical duplicating machines and devices made their appearance during the period from 1910 to 1920. The principles upon which duplicating machines were developed resulted in the perfection of addressing machines and other devices which reproduce both drawings and type matter.

The more complicated requirements of business called for more complicated machinery for accounting and bookkeeping problems. The most modern device for accounting procedure is the punch card accounting and tabulating machine. This was developed between 1900 and 1910, and was first used by the United States Government in census work. Subsequently it was applied to all the complicated business of accounting. These machines operate through the use of punched cards whereon the holes indicate specific information relating to inventory, prices, payments, debts, etc.

Dictating machines are a direct result of the invention of the phonograph[qv] and are coming into more frequent use as timesavers.

The development of radio and wireless telegraphy has made possible interoffice communication by voice through the mere turning of a switch. Large offices are now equipped with devices whereby voices of executives can reach all parts of large factories from offices, or all parts of large offices themselves.

Another development is the photographing machine for offices where photographic copies of records are required speedily in quantity. The photostat machine, the dexigraph and other photographic record machinery are now available to and used by many hundreds of large organizations. These devices apply the principles of photography to the use of business, and have now been developed to the point where photographs are made on strips of film like the films used in motion pictures. These are projected frame by frame on a screen.

Retail business utilizes the adding machine principle in the form of the cash register. Other devices now used in business are numbering and dating machines, stapling machines, stenotype machines, devices for sealing, stamping and folding letters, machines for wrapping packages quickly, cash and change-making devices, etc.

LOUIS M. COTTIN

Business, Public Control of. In mediæval England many trades and professions were classed as public callings, and persons engaged in them were required to serve all who applied for service. The surgeon was thus classed, because of the importance of his services and the scarcity of surgeons. Likewise the smith, for if a horse cast a shoe, the rider was at the mercy of the nearest farrier. For similar reasons were classed the innkeeper, the victualer, the baker, the miller, the common carrier, ferryman and wharfinger. This was the common law. But Parliament also took a hand and regulated wages and the price of wool and food. Such statutes were in force in England when America was settled and the colonists brought to America with them the idea of legislative supervision of trades and professions. Hence, the prices of board and staple commodities like tobacco, bread and corn were regulated by most of the colonial assemblies[qv].

When the Federal Constitution and the various state constitutions were adopted, it was in accordance with "due process of law" for legislatures to regulate those businesses which had been regulated at common law[qqv]. But the types of business classed as common callings changed with economic conditions. The tailor, surgeon and smith, for example, soon ceased to be so classed, but the ferryman, wharfinger, innkeeper and common carrier continued in the category, with the addition in the 19th century of proprietors of turnpikes, bridges and canals[qqv]. But the popularity of *laissez-faire*[qv] economics during the first half of the 19th century caused governmental regulation to reach its lowest ebb during that period.

About the middle of the 19th century the business corporation[qv] began to emerge and for a time the view seemed likely to prevail that unless the state, in granting a charter of incorporation to a business, had imposed upon it a duty of public service, or granted it a special or monopolistic franchise, the corporation was free to conduct its business as it liked, though it partook of the nature of a public calling. But with the growth of business corporations controlling products or services upon which people greatly depended, the pendulum began to swing the other way, and, in a series of decisions beginning with the historic case of Munn v. Illinois[qv] in 1874, the United States Supreme Court developed the doctrine that all businesses, regardless of their franchise or charter powers, were liable to legislative regulation, if they were "affected with a public interest."

Statutes regulating the sale of foods and drugs, stock-yard transactions, insurance rates, insurance agents' commissions and rents were passed and held valid. In 1890 the Sherman Antitrust Act[qv], making monopolies illegal, was enacted by Congress and its validity upheld. The distinction between a public utility[qv] and a private business seemed to be breaking down in favor of a rule that any business is subject to regulation to the degree required by the public need. To the objection raised in each case that the "due process" clause of the Constitution was being infringed, the courts replied that the "due process" clause must yield to the police power[qv], when regulatory legislation seemed reasonably calculated to correct recognized economic or social evils. There were occasional setbacks, but the march of state regulation was relentless. Recent illustrations of the trend are statutes regulating the price of milk and of handling and selling leaf tobacco (Nebbia v. New York[qv], 291 U. S. 502, 1934; Townsend v. Yeomans, 57 Sup. Ct. 842, 1937).

With the creation of the Interstate Commerce Commission[qv] in 1887, with power to regulate the rates and conditions of railroad service (and since 1935 interstate motor carrier service), there was inaugurated the policy of administrative regulation of public utilities. Since then, most states have created public utility commissions, charged with the duty of determining reasonable rates and conditions of service of light, heat, power, water and telephone companies, and have set up administrative officers to regulate insurance, banking, mining, etc. In 1920 Congress created the Federal Power Commission[qv], at first composed of the Secretaries of War, Interior and Agriculture, but since 1930, of five commissioners appointed by the President. The commission has power to regulate the licensing of water-power rights on public lands, and since 1935, "the transmission of electric energy in interstate commerce." Congress has also created the Federal Communications Commission[qv] (acts of 1927 and 1934) with wide regulatory powers over radio broadcasting and other agencies of communication. Usually such commissions have power to find the facts, but their acts are subject to judicial review[qv] on matters of law.

The Federal Trade Commission and the Clayton Acts, passed in 1914, and the Robinson-Patman Act[qqv], passed in 1936, extended the principle of administrative regulation to businesses usually classed as private, i.e., not public utilities. These acts, re-enforcing and extending the Sherman Antitrust Act, made monopolies illegal, and prohibited interlocking directorates, price discrimination, "tying" contracts and other methods of "unfair" competition calculated to promote monopolistic control. Into this class of legislation also falls the National Labor Relations Act[qv] passed in 1935 (declared valid in National Labor Relations Board v. Jones and Laughlin[qv]), which prohibits employers from resorting to unfair labor practices and sets up a board for administering the law; and also the Securities Exchange Act of 1934 which created the Securities Exchange Commission[qv] with power to regulate security sales on stock exchanges and, since 1935, all securities issued or dealt in by public utility holding companies.

An act of Congress may be invalid not only because it infringes the "due process" clause of the Constitution, but because it is not among the powers expressly delegated to Congress. Since power to regulate business has not been expressly granted to Congress, regulatory acts of this nature are valid only if they come within some other congressional power, such as that to regulate commerce among the states or to tax for the general welfare. This is illustrated by the abortive attempt of Congress in 1932 to set up the National Recovery Administration[qv] with power to impose upon business codes of fair competition, minimum wages and maximum hours for employees. The act was held invalid (Schechter Poultry Corp. v. United States[qv]) not because of violation of the "due process" clause, but because its subject matter did not come within the power of Congress over interstate commerce, or any other congressional power. Similarly the Agricultural Adjustment Act[qv] of 1933, designed to regulate agricultural production, fell because it involved an improper exercise of the taxing power (United States v. Butler[qv]).

Many other Federal and state acts have been passed regulating various aspects of business, and proprietors have complained that much of the Government's intervention has been unjustifiable and oppressive and has operated to discourage and curtail individual initiative and enterprise. Whether or not governmental regulation has extended too far for the common weal, it has been one of the most significant political and economic developments of the last half century.

[Bruce Wyman, *Public Service Corporations*, Vol. I; National Industrial Conference Board, *Competitive Regulation of Competitive Practices.*]

GEORGE W. GOBLE

Business Clubs, such as Kiwanis, Lions and Rotarians[qv], were first organized on an international scale during the second decade of the 20th century. Rotary was the pioneer, dating its international beginning back to November, 1910. Kiwanis followed in 1916, and Lions in 1917.

These leaders among the business clubs have similar aims and purposes. Typical among them are civic improvement and beautification of various kinds, aid to underprivileged children, cultivation of high ideals of civic life, the promotion of a friendly spirit among business competitors and, in general, the making of one's home town a better place in which to live. Rotary advertises a motto, "Service above Self"; Kiwanis insist that "We Build"; and the Lions are named from the initial letters of "Liberty, Intelligence, Our Nation's Safety." These and similar organizations have international officers and conventions.

Rotary has the best claim to the adjective international and is the largest as well as the oldest of the groups. On March 1, 1938, there were approximately 4500 Rotary clubs including 187,000 individual members in "70 or more countries and geographical regions." There were more than 2800 Lions clubs numbering slightly less than 100,000 members in eight countries. The 1900-odd Kiwanis clubs of 95,000 members were confined to the United States and Canada. The club magazine for each group is sent to every active member and keeps the individual alive to the activities, aims and achievements of his organization.

In addition to the three larger fraternities there are many others of the same nature. Among these should be mentioned: Altrurians; American Business Club; Association of 20–30 Clubs; Civitan; Coöperative Club; Gyro; National Exchange; National Monarch; Optimist; Round Table; and National Metro Clubs.

[Charles F. Marden, *Rotary and Its Brothers.*]

S. S. MCKAY

Business Cycles, i.e., recurring phases of depression, revival, prosperity and crisis or recession, have characterized the annals of American business since the beginnings of the country. Although the different phases of the business cycle have usually followed each other in the order noted, their intensity and duration have varied in marked fashion from cycle to cycle. At times, moreover, the revival or prosperity phases have been interrupted by minor recessions or depressions in business, while crises, which usually mark the termination of a speculative boom, have occasionally occurred in a period of depression.

The first major depression in this country occurred in the half-decade 1784–89 as a result of dislocations attributable to the Revolutionary War*qv*. A period of prosperity, interrupted by a minor depression in 1807–10, ensued and lasted until after the War of 1812*qv* when a severe depression, lasting from 1815 to 1821, set in (*see* Panic of 1819). This was followed, after a few years of moderate prosperity, by another depression of mild character which ran from 1825 to 1829. Prosperity followed, culminating in the Panic of 1837*qv* and a long depression which continued to 1843. The next major depression took place in 1857–58 (*see* Panic of 1857), shortly before the Civil War*qv*.

Extended wars always breed depression and the Civil War was no exception. A depression in industry occurred in 1865–66, according to some authorities, or in 1866–67, according to others. This was followed by recovery and prosperity which finally ended with a Panic in 1873*qv*. The long depression of the 1870's, lasting until 1879, ensued. The subsequent recovery was interrupted by the depression of 1883–85, which began as a minor recession but was prolonged and intensified by the crisis of 1884. By 1887 prosperity had returned and continued until 1893 with the exception of a short depression in 1890–91. The Panic of 1893*qv* ushered in a severe depression which lasted, with the exception of a few months of prosperous conditions in 1895, until 1897, when business again turned upward. The prosperity which followed was broken briefly by a very mild recession in 1900 and, later, by the "Rich Man's Panic" of 1903–4. The latter was a financial rather than an industrial depression. The Panic of 1907*qv* was the forerunner of a comparatively short but severe depression which ran into the following year. Recovery from this depression carried business through until 1913, although there was an extremely mild recession in 1910–11.

The depression beginning in 1913 started out to be a comparatively mild one, but the outbreak of hostilities in Europe intensified it considerably. By 1915, however, war demands had induced renewed prosperity which continued, with the exception of a slight readjustment in 1919, until the late spring of 1920 when a crisis occurred followed by a rapid recession in business (*see* Panic of 1920).

The depression of 1920–22 was severe, although not unduly extended. Recovery brought a long stretch of prosperity to the country, broken by minor depressions in 1924 and 1927, which ended with the stock-market crash in the fall of 1929 (*see* Panic of 1929). There followed a long and severe depression from which recovery did not set in until after the Banking Crisis of 1933*qv*. The ensuing recovery was not regular but was interrupted by recessions in 1933, 1934 and 1935, followed by a fairly severe depression in 1937–38 (*see* Recession of 1937).

[E. C. Bratt, *Business Cycles and Forecasting;* C. Snyder, *Business Cycles and Business Measurements.*]

FREDERICK A. BRADFORD

Business Forecasting, as it is known today, would not be possible without the collection and dissemination of business statistics by government and trade agencies. Since the beginning of the 20th century, numerous services have come into existence for the sole purpose of forecasting business but all of them have, at one time or another, been found wanting. More recently, almost all attempts have been futile and must continue so as long as international markets are unsettled and government attempts to control or direct economic movements.

The earliest attempts to forecast business were, perforce, based upon the scanty basic statistics of interest rates, bond yields and such reports of current production as were available, mainly pig iron. For some years, the number of iron furnaces in blast had a vogue because orders for pig iron were a certain reflection of demand. This "index" failed to function after the World War because the erection of very large blast furnaces in place of many smaller units destroyed its flexibility.

The current vogue in business forecasting is concerned with the delineation of past business cycles as a measure of present-day movements. Graphical comparisons are frequently resorted to in the attempt to fit current cycles to some bygone cycle in order to establish some basis to forecast completion of the current cycle. Most of the statistics are thrown into the form of index or relative numbers and the various series are then combined into a single index number of business.

The oldest regularly published annual business forecast is only thirty years old. Many of the better known forecasts are published in connection with advisory services with which business forecasts are incidental. All, or nearly all, large corporations attempt to forecast business for short intervals.

Never before has so much factual data been available nor have we been so well and so promptly informed of what is going on. Formerly, the behavior of various indices could perhaps be the basis for forecasting business but now that developments may be determined by the direct influence of persons in power, business predictions are futile.

WILLIAM WREN HAY

"Busy Bees of Deseret," THE, were the Mormon settlers (1848) in what became Utah; Deseret is the "land of the honeybee" of the Book of Mormon.

WHEELER PRESTON

Bute, Fort, or Manchac Post, named for the British Prime Minister, was established in 1763 at the junction of Iberville River (Bayou Manchac) with the Mississippi, and remained an important British military and trading post in West Florida[qv] until captured by Spanish forces under Bernardo Galvez of Louisiana on Sept. 7, 1779.

[Alcée Fortier, *History of Louisiana*, II.]

WALTER PRICHARD

Butler's General Order No. 28. Gen. B. F. Butler established himself as military commander in New Orleans, May 1, 1862. The marked hostility of the inhabitants of the city to the Federal Government was exhibited in insults to which Federal officers and men were subjected by the women. Accordingly on May 15 Butler issued an order to the effect that any female insulting or showing contempt for any officer or soldier of the United States should be treated as a woman of the town plying her avocation. The order evoked a storm of protest at home and abroad, and was a cause of Butler's removal from command of New Orleans, Dec. 16, 1862.

[James Ford Rhodes, *History of the United States*, Vol. IV.]

JAMES E. WINSTON

Butler's Rangers (1777–84) was a regiment of Loyalists[qv], recruited by Col. John Butler with the consent of Sir Guy Carleton to serve with the Indians against the colonists. Eight companies were recruited. Their uniforms consisted of a green coat and waistcoat faced with red, buff breeches, white leggings and a hat of the Foot Regiment pattern. From their headquarters at Fort Niagara[qv], the Rangers embarked on forays which spread terror throughout New York and Pennsylvania. They perpetrated the Wyoming massacre[qv] in July, 1778, and took part in Johnson's raid on the Mohawk settlements in 1780. The regiment was disbanded in June, 1784.

[E. Cruikshank, *The Story of Butler's Rangers.*]

ROBERT W. BINGHAM

Butte des Morts Council (1827). Lewis Cass, governor of Michigan Territory, and Thomas L. McKenney, United States Indian commissioner, held a council with the Chippewa, Menominee and Winnebago Indians[qqv] at Little Butte des Morts, north of Lake Winnebago, near where the Fox River flows out. A treaty was signed there Aug. 11, 1827, adjusting boundaries and the relations of these tribes with the Indians migrating to Wisconsin from New York.

[Kappler, *Indian Treaties of the United States.*]

LOUISE PHELPS KELLOGG

Butter. *See* Dairy Industry.

Butterfield Claims (1854–90). The name is derived from the firm that handled the negotiations. In 1854 two ships, loaded with war materials, cleared at New York for St. Thomas. Suspicion arose that they were destined for Venezuelan rebels. Because of lack of evidence they were cleared in a libel suit. When they arrived at St. Thomas, Danish West Indies, trouble arose again because of their suspicious character. The owners presented a large claim for damages because the vessels were detained by the Danish government. Thirty-four years of negotiations ended in a Danish-American arbitration treaty (1888), as a result of which the claim was disallowed on the ground that the Danish government had observed strictly the neutrality laws involved.

[S. J. M. P. Fogdall, *Danish-American Diplomacy, 1776-1920.*]

S. P. FOGDALL

Butterfield Overland Dispatch. Because of much travel to Colorado after the discovery of gold there, D. A. Butterfield, backed by New York capital, organized a joint-stock express and passenger carrying service between the Missouri River and Denver. In July, 1865, the route via the Smoky Hill River was surveyed and soon thereafter coaches were in operation. Ben Holladay, acting for a competing organization, bought the Butterfield Overland Dispatch in March, 1866, when Eastern express companies threatened to take it over and establish a service between the Missouri River and Sacramento, Calif.

[LeRoy Hafen, *The Overland Mail.*]

C. C. RISTER

Butterfield Overland Mail. *See* Southern Overland Mail.

Byrd's Polar Flights. On April 5, 1926, Commander Byrd sailed on the S.S. *Chantier* for Kings Bay, Spitzbergen, which he intended using as the base for a flight to the North Pole. The vessel arrived in the bay on April 29. The only pier in the harbor was occupied by a Norwegian gunboat; therefore, it was necessary to ferry the big trimotored Fokker airplane, *Josephine Ford,* ashore through the drifting ice, which choked the bay, on a raft constructed from four ship's boats. This operation was successfully accomplished, and preparations for the flight commenced. After being held up by defects in the skis for some days, Byrd and his pilot, Floyd Bennett, eventually took off for the Pole shortly after midnight on May 9. The flight proceeded uneventfully until the airplane was one hour's flight short of the Pole, at which time a leak was discovered in an oil tank. In spite of this they continued onward. At 9:02 A.M., Greenwich Civil Time, the Pole was reached. After circling around it, the coarse was set for Spitzbergen. The return flight was uneventful, and the motors continued to function in spite of the oil leak.

Early in the Antarctic spring of 1929 Byrd made a flight from his base at Little America to the foot of the Queen Maud Mountains and laid down a gasoline base. On Nov. 29, 1929, at 3:29 P.M., the polar flight party took off in the Ford airplane, *Floyd Bennett,* for the Pole. At 9:15 they started up the Liv Glacier Pass for the Polar Plateau. The plane was so heavily loaded that she could not gain enough altitude to clear the head of the glacier. It was necessary to dump several hundred pounds of emergency food to lighten the plane enough to clear the "Hump." Once over the plateau the plane made good time. At 1:14, Greenwich Civil Time, the Pole was reached. A few minutes later the course was changed to head back to the mountains. This part of the flight developed into a race against clouds moving in from the east. The party just managed to get down Axel Heiberg Glacier before it was enshrouded. After a short flight to the eastward the plane was landed at the fuel base. At six o'clock the return journey to Little America began. Shortly after ten the party landed at the camp.

R. E. BYRD

Cabanne's Trading Post, located ten miles above Omaha on the west side of the Missouri River, was established between 1822 and 1826 for the American Fur Company[qv] by John Pierre Cabanne. Between 1833 and 1840 the post was moved to Bellevue, Nebr., and placed under the management of Peter A. Sarpy.

[Hiram Chittenden, *The American Fur Trade of the Far West.*]

EVERETT DICK

Cabeza de Vaca, Alvar Núñez, Travels of. In 1527, at about the age of thirty-seven, Cabeza de Vaca went to America as treasurer of the expedition led by Pánfilo de Narváez[qv], which landed near the present city of Tampa, Fla., in April, 1528. After a brief and disastrous exploration of the country the colonists built five horsehide boats and sailed for Cuba. A hurricane sank all but the one commanded by Cabeza de Vaca, and soon it was wrecked on the Texas coast. From the fall of 1528 to the spring of 1536 Cabeza de Vaca and his companions endured untold hardships in a 6000-mile journey through the American Southwest and northern Mexico. Finally safe in New Spain, Cabeza de Vaca returned to Old Spain to request of Charles V the governorship of "La Florida." Instead he was given the governorship of Paraguay. His account of his travels was printed in 1555 at Valladolid, Spain, under the title *Relación y Comentarios.*

[Morris Bishop, *The Odyssey of Cabeza de Vaca.*]

A. CURTIS WILGUS

Cabildo, THE, was the Spanish governmental organization for the province of Louisiana. It was established by O'Reilly in 1769, superseding the French Superior Council, and was abolished by Laussat when France regained possession of the province in 1803. Besides the governor, who presided, it consisted of two ordinary *alcaldes* (judges in New Orleans), *alferez real* (royal standard-bearer), provincial *alcalde* (judge outside New Orleans), *alguacil mayor* (high sheriff), depositary-general (treasurer and storekeeper), receiver of fines (collector), attorney-general-syndic (public prosecutor), *mayordomo-de-propios* (municipal treasurer of New Orleans) and *escribano* (clerk). It met in the Government House (*Casa Capitular* or *Principal*), commonly known today as the "Cabildo."

[J. S. Kendall, *History of New Orleans,* I.]

WALTER PRICHARD

Cabin Rights. At an early period in the settlement of the West, pioneers asserted their claims to parts of wild lands by blazing trees around the desired boundary, and later comers customarily recognized the claims: tomahawk rights[qv], they were called. Building a cabin and raising a crop, however small, of grain of any kind, led to "cabin rights," which were recognized not only customarily but by law. The laws of the colonies and states varied in their requirements of the settler. In Virginia the occupant was entitled to 400 acres of land and to a preemption[qv] right to 1000 acres more adjoining, to be secured in either case by a land-office warrant, the basis of a later patent or grant from colonial or state authorities.

SAMUEL C. WILLIAMS

Cabinet, THE, of the President[qv] is the result of custom and was created neither by the Constitution[qv] nor by statute law (*see* Revolutionary

Committees). The Constitution says (Article II, Section II) that the President "may require the Opinion, in writing, of the principal Officer in each of the executive Departments, upon any Subject relating to the Duties of their respective Offices." These offices were created by act of Congress at various times and their holders were considered to be the personal assistants of the President in the work of administration. Washington tried to carry out the intentions of the makers of the Constitution that the Senate[qv] should serve as a privy council on the British model, but he dropped the method of personal attendance and conference with the Senate when he found that this was creating friction with certain members of that body. Also in 1793 he tried to secure the advice of the United States Supreme Court[qv] at a time of crisis in our relations with France. He submitted to the Court a number of questions with regard to the interpretation of our treaties with France, but the justices refused to answer these questions on the ground that they lay outside their duties. Washington then turned to his three secretaries or department heads of State, War and Navy, and called them, along with the attorney general into a council of four. This conference in time was recognized by the public as the official council or cabinet of the President.

The name "cabinet" was first used about the year 1793. Congressional debates show that the term was used in Congress in 1798 and again in 1802, but it was only some twenty years after the establishment of the national government that the idea and name of a cabinet council was understood and accepted by the people. The name "cabinet" was not recognized in Federal statute law until the act of Feb. 26, 1907, which provided for an increase in the salary of those "heads of the Executive Departments who are members of the President's Cabinet." Thus it may be repeated that the name and establishment of the President's cabinet originated in custom as in England and in process of time became an accepted part of the National Government. Washington, at first, undertook to conduct his administration on a nonpartisan basis and his first cabinet was chosen equally between the two wings of his supporters—those who were of strong nationalist[qv] and those who were of states' rights[qv] tendencies. Finding that the emergence of vital issues of policy made necessary united support of his department heads or cabinet, he changed its membership so that it became united in support of his views.

At the time of the death of President William Henry Harrison his cabinet resigned and his successor, Vice-President Tyler, reconstructed his administration according to his own views. It has now become the understanding that the members of the cabinet are the personal appointees and advisers of the President, and Congress[qv] usually confirms a presidential nomination to one of these offices. Furthermore, while certain cabinet members, as the head of the Treasury Department or of the Department of Commerce, usually are business men especially fitted for the work of that department, yet in general cabinet positions are given upon a basis of geographical or political influence in order to consolidate party support behind the administration of a President. The actual influence of a cabinet depends in large part upon the desires and intentions of the President himself. In certain cases the cabinet may be a collection of political leaders, at another time of executive administrators. Also the personality of a specific cabinet member and his personal influence with the President may count for much. In recent years the creation of numerous departments or independent commissions has weakened cabinet influence. In addition, the private unofficial advisers of a President may have more influence than the cabinet as a united body. The so-called Brain Trust[qv] of Franklin D. Roosevelt is an illustration of this situation.

At the present time there are ten members of the cabinet, each one of whom presides over his respective department. These departments are State (foreign affairs), Treasury, War, Navy, Post Office, Interior, Justice, Agriculture, Commerce and Labor[qqv]. Each department has one or more "under secretaries" or "assistant secretaries" who act as assistants to or under the direction of the cabinet member. They may attend cabinet meetings in the absence of the head of the department or upon special occasions, but generally are not considered part of the "Ministry" as would be the case in Great Britain. The salary of each member of the cabinet is $15,000 a year. The term of office is four years or at the pleasure and discretion of the President.

At various times there has been discussion of the advisability of the President inviting the Vice-President[qv] to attend cabinet meetings. But this seems to have been the custom only in the administration of President Harding who in 1921 invited the regular attendance of Vice-President Calvin Coolidge, otherwise the attendance of the Vice-President has been merely personal and for some special purpose.

[H. B. Learned, *The President's Cabinet;* M. L. Hinsdale, *A History of the President's Cabinet.*]

WILLIAM STARR MYERS

Cables, Transatlantic. The submarine cable was scarce invented (1844), and its first successful experiment concluded across the English Channel (1850), when Atlantic cables[qv] were projected. Success came in 1866. Since that time, transatlantic cables have been taken as a matter of course, as a matter of necessity, completely demonstrated when storms and quakes disturb the depths and break the wires, as in 1929.

The conformation of the Atlantic sea bottom makes cable laying more possible, cable maintenance more practical than is true in other oceans. A "telegraph plateau," broad, level, relatively shallow, lies convenient where cables can rest—perhaps the "lost continent"—but in any event facilitating communication between Europe and America, in business, in diplomacy, in amity. It carries more than a score of cables, directly to North Europe, by "ports of call" in the Azores to South Europe.

The United States, which had been eager for cables, became absorbed after the Civil War in the lands of the West and in land telegraph[qv]. Germany and France and later Italy entered the field; but from the lack of imperial necessity, lack of capital and through the effects of the Great War, the majority of transatlantic cables are British-owned, the majority American-leased.

American government control operates through the granting of landing licenses, with anti-monopoly provisions, an executive function exercised by all Presidents since Grant, but under law only since 1921. To this extent only does the Government assume any authority over international submarine cables. It is a signatory to the international convention of 1884.

[Keith Clark, *International Communications;* George A. Schreiner, *Cables and Wireless;* Eugene W. Sharp, *International News Communications.*]

KEITH CLARK

Cabot Voyages (1497–99). Early in 1496 a petition was placed before Henry VII in the name of John Cabot and his three sons, Sebastian, Lewes and Sancto, for the privilege of making explorations in the New World. Letters patent dated March 5, 1496, were granted to the Cabots, and in the spring of 1497 they sailed west. Coasting southward they discovered Cape Breton Island and Nova Scotia. The following year (1498) letters patent were granted to John Cabot alone, authorizing him to make further explorations along the eastern coast of North America. The discoveries made on this voyage were supposedly recorded on a map and globe made by the explorer. Both are now lost. Because there is no firsthand data concerning the Cabot voyages, Sebastian Cabot has been called the "Sphynx of North American history." His identity is often confused with that of his father, John. Important contributions to geographical knowledge were made by the Cabots, though "the descriptions of the regions they explored apply to no portion of the United States."

[C. H. Coote in *Dictionary of National Biography;* Justin Winsor, *Narrative and Critical History of North America.*]

LLOYD A. BROWN

Cabrillo Expedition, THE (June 27, 1542–April 14, 1543). In the hope of finding a direct route from Spain to the East Indies through Spanish waters, Juan Rodríguez Cabrillo and Bartolomé Ferrelo sailed from Navidad, Mexico, and, Sept. 28, 1542, reached a port, "closed and very good, which they named San Miguel." They were in fact at San Diego and thus were the discoverers of California[qv]. After getting as far north as Drake's Bay they were forced back to the Santa Barbara Islands where Rodríguez died. Ferrelo carried on and is believed to have reached the vicinity of the Rogue River in Oregon.

[H. E. Bolton, *Spanish Explorations in the Southwest, 1542-1706.*]

OSGOOD HARDY

Cabusto, Battle of (November, 1540). Cabusto, an Indian (Chickasaw?) town situated, apparently, on the Black Warrior River near old Erie (Ala.), was the scene of one of DeSoto's[qv] conflicts with the Indians. A series of engagements were fought round about the old town in which it is claimed that about 8000 Indians participated. With Cabusto as a base, DeSoto broke through the palisaded defenses of the Indians north of the river and advanced up the Tombigbee valley.

[A. B. Meek, *Romantic Passages in Southwestern History.*]

A. B. MOORE

Cahaba Old Towns was a cluster of villages along the Cahaba River, some six miles northeast of Marion, Perry County, Ala. From Fort Claiborne in Monroe, Col. Gilbert Russell in the spring of 1814 was sent northward to Cahaba Old Towns in a futile effort to provide defense against the hostile Creek Indians[qv].

[W. G. Brown, *History of Alabama;* A. J. Pickett, *History of Alabama.*]

JOHN B. CLARK

Cahokia, the first permanent white settlement of consequence in Illinois, was founded in March, 1699, when priests of the Seminary of Quebec established there the Mission of the Holy Family. Their chapel, which became the nucleus of the village, was located near the left bank of the

Mississippi a short distance south of the present city of East St. Louis. Cahokia took its name from the adjacent Indian village, which in 1699 contained about 2000 Tamaroa and Cahokia.

The mission at Cahokia quickly attracted French settlers, principally from Canada, occasionally from Louisiana. Their number, however, was never large. A census in 1723 enumerated only twelve white residents, while at Kaskaskia and Fort de Chartres^qqv^, the other principal settlements, 196 and 126 were counted. In 1767, after many French had removed to St. Louis^qv^ because of the cession of the Illinois country^qv^ to Great Britain, Cahokia contained 300 whites and 80 Negroes—about half the population of Kaskaskia. By 1800, however, its population had increased to 719, while that of Kaskaskia had dropped to 467.

Throughout the 18th century Cahokia exemplified several of the features of a typical French village. There was a common pasture land and a large common field divided into strips for cultivation. The church was the center of village life and the priest the most influential resident. Although a few families were distinguished by education and cultivated manners, most of the inhabitants were *coureurs de bois, voyageurs*^qqv^ and traders who mingled freely with the Indians. English and American travelers usually criticized their squalor and lack of enterprise, but they noted also a carefree gaiety impervious to the hardships and uncertainties of their way of life.

Although Cahokia became the seat of St. Clair County, the first county organized in Illinois, its growth was not commensurate with that of the territory. With the removal of the county seat in 1814, decline commenced. By 1900 all vestiges of village life had disappeared.

[Gilbert J. Garraghan, New Light on Old Cahokia, *Illinois Catholic Historical Review*, Oct., 1928; C. W. Alvord, *Cahokia Records, 1778-1790; History of St. Clair County, Illinois.*]

PAUL M. ANGLE

Cahokia Mounds is a group of eighty-five prehistoric Indian mounds^qv^ four miles northeast of East St. Louis, Ill. This group is the nucleus of a larger group, which is believed to have numbered originally between 200 and 300. Monks' Mound, 100 feet high with a rectangular base 1000 feet by 700 feet, is not only the largest mound in the group, but also the largest prehistoric monument in the United States. The Cahokia Mounds are believed to have been built between 1200 and 1500 A.D., perhaps much earlier.

[Warren K. Moorehead, et al., The Cahokia Mounds, University of Illinois *Bulletin*, Vol. XXVI, No. 4.]

PAUL M. ANGLE

Cahuenga Capitulation, THE (Jan. 13, 1847), ended California's part in the Mexican War^qv^. After preliminary negotiations, at the old Cahuenga ranch house, John C. Frémont and Andrés Pico signed a document, the liberal terms of which were in complete accord with Polk's conciliatory policy.

[R. G. Cleland, *A History of California: the American Period.*]

OSGOOD HARDY

Cairo, Ill., the "Eden" of Dickens' *Martin Chuzzlewit,* was founded in 1837 by the Cairo City and Canal Company, after an earlier effort (1818) had failed. For fifteen years the town grew slowly, but the sale of lots, which commenced in 1853, and the completion of the Illinois Central Railroad^qv^ attracted settlers, with the result that by 1860 the population exceeded 2000. During the Civil War Cairo was of great strategic importance and for several months both Grant and Foote had headquarters there (*see* Belmont, Battle of). Because of its low elevation, its existence depends upon extensive levees, but even these have failed to prevent several severe inundations.

[John M. Lansden, *A History of the City of Cairo, Illinois.*]

PAUL M. ANGLE

Cajans. A local term applied in southeast Mississippi and southwest Alabama to designate a people of mixed bloods whose racial integrity is not determined. Physical aspects indicate a conglomeration of Gulf Coast Creole blood of the better type with Indian, African and Central American Negro and pure white. Socially they are not accepted by the better whites and refuse to be classed as Negroes. It has now become necessary for the educational systems of the states to provide school facilities and classify them other than White or Colored. The term is hardly more than forty years old, adopted to differentiate the group from a large colored Creole population. These people should not be confused with ones of Teche Louisiana called Acadians^qv^.

PETER A. BRANNON

Cajon Pass, THE, the best route from the Mojave Desert to southern California, was probably first known to white men when, March, 1776, it was traversed by Father Francisco Garcés. The first American to discover it was Jedediah Smith^qv^ (November, 1826). Shortly afterwards it became a part of the route between California and Santa Fé.

OSGOOD HARDY

Calamity Howler, a slang phrase contemptuously hurled by political opponents of the discontented Populists^qv and agrarians during the late 1880's and 1890's, signifies a noisy pessimist, particularly one who disagrees with the measures and policies of the ruling political party and who foretells the economic ruin of a section or the nation. The term first appeared in print, it is thought, in the *Congressional Record,* March 2, 1892, page 1654, column 1. Representative Jeremiah Simpson of Kansas, in speaking to a bill appropriating funds for charitable institutions in Washington, D. C., said, "If the destitution is so great here in the capital of the country, what must it be in the other portions of our Union? It seems to me time that we had some 'calamity howlers' here in Washington as well as in Kansas."

HARRY R. WARFEL

Calaveras Skull, THE, was allegedly found, in 1886, in auriferous gravels which would imply a very great antiquity. Unfortunately the circumstances attending the discovery, in Calaveras County, Calif., are not entirely satisfactory notwithstanding the claim made that the skull was found in the gravels of Bald Mountain at a depth of approximately 130 feet. Even if in comparatively recent years there has accumulated evidence to demonstrate that man in America existed in late Pleistocene times, nothing has been found approaching the antiquity postulated for the Calaveras skull. The skull, which is now in the Peabody Museum, is patently of Indian type not differing essentially from modern Indians of California. This in itself is a telling argument against hoary antiquity.

[Calaveras Man, in *Bulletin 30*, Bureau of American Ethnology; Skeletal Remains Suggesting or Attributed to Early Man in North America, *Bulletin 33*, Bureau of American Ethnology, Chap. IX, pp. 21-28.]

TRUMAN MICHELSON

Calder v. Bull, 1798 (3 Dallas 386). The *locus classicus* wherein the Supreme Court defined an *ex post facto* law: one which makes criminal an act not punishable when committed; or retrospectively increases the punishment; or alters the rules of evidence in order to convict the offender. Thus it was not unconstitutional for the Connecticut legislature to grant a retrial in a civil case.

CHARLES FAIRMAN

Calendar, THE. In 1582 Pope Gregory III, to correct the errors of the Julian calendar (established by Julius Cæsar), which made the year about eleven minutes too long, gave Europe (except Russia, Greece and the Near East) the Gregorian calendar which we still use, often referred to as New Style to distinguish it from the Julian calendar or Old Style. To correct the error, which by that time had amounted to ten days, the Pope ordained that the year 1582 should have the days between Oct. 4 and 15 stricken from the calendar. By providing bissextile or leap year, he further corrected the calendar so that three days are saved in every 400 years, leaving only an error of one day in 5200 years. This New Style of reckoning was not officially adopted (though frequently used) in Great Britain and her colonies until Sept. 3, Old Style, or 14, New Style, 1752, by which time the correction had increased by another day. According to the New Style, the year 1700 had only 365 days, while according to the Old Style it had 366 days. This discrepancy of one day has caused many errors in reducing Old Style to New, for it has not always been understood that events before 1700 require a correction of only ten days, while those from 1700 to 1752 require eleven days. For example, the Pilgrims landed at Plymouth on Dec. 11, 1620 O. S. (Old Style) or Dec. 21, N. S. (New Style) but at the time of the first local celebration of that event, the day was erroneously reckoned as Dec. 22, N. S., since the mistake was made of adopting the correction of eleven days, in use after 1700, not realizing that the event took place in the previous century when only ten days' correction was required. Many dates in American colonial history and biography have been recorded incorrectly in similar fashion.

From the 12th century until the adoption of New Style in 1752, the Civil, Ecclesiastical and Legal Year began in Great Britain and her colonies on March 25, while from 1582 the Historical Year was often unofficially figured from Jan. 1, as provided in the Gregorian calendar. Both styles of reckoning were in use at the same time and so it became customary to annex the date of the Historical to that of the Legal Year when referring to any date between the 1st of January and the 25th of March. When double-dating occurs, the upper or first figure indicates the Legal and the lower or last figure the Historical Year, as $162\frac{1}{2}$ or 1621/2. In the Julian calendar the months were numbered, beginning with March (a practice followed by the Quakers who preferred not to use the pagan names of the months), so we frequently find a date written thus: "10th: 11th mo.; 1621," that is, the 10th day in the 11th month in the Civil Year 1621, which corresponds with Jan. 10 of the Historical Year 1622. Double-dating was always used in referring to time between the last day of February and March 25, when the year commenced on the latter date, since it would not otherwise be possible to tell to what year the date referred.

[N. B. Shurtleff, *A Perpetual Calendar for Old and New Style.*]

R. W. G. VAIL

Calhoun's *Disquisition on Government* represents John C. Calhoun's reasoned views on government as seen from the point of view of the permanent minority. Begun in 1843, finished to Calhoun's own satisfaction in five years' time, it elaborates the doctrine of his *Exposition*[qv]. Its keynote is the idea of a concurrent majority. Simple majority government always results in despotism over the minority unless some way is devised to secure the assent of all classes, sections and interests.

The argument is close-knit and convincing if one accepts the belief of Calhoun that the states retain absolute sovereignty over the Constitution and can do with it as they wish. This doctrine could be made effective by nullification[qv]. But Calhoun believed that the clear recognition of rights on the part of the states (*see* States' Rights) on the one hand and of the national majority on the other would prevent matters ever coming to a crisis. South Carolina and other Southern states, in the three decades preceding the Civil War, had provided legislatures in which the vested interests of land and slaves dominated in the upper houses, while the popular will of the numerical majority prevailed in the lower houses. This was done in conscious acceptance of the doctrine of the *Disquisition*.

[Richard K. Cralle, ed., *Works of John C. Calhoun*, Vol. I.]

JAMES ELLIOTT WALMSLEY

Calhoun's *Exposition* (1828). After the passage of the "Tariff of Abominations"[qv] the South Carolina legislature resolved that it was "expedient to protest against the unconstitutionality and oppressive operation of the system of protective duties" and appointed a committee to report thereon. At the request of William C. Preston of the committee, John C. Calhoun prepared his *Exposition* in which he declared the tariff of 1828 "unconstitutional, unequal and oppressive; and calculated to corrupt public virtue and destroy the liberty of the country." Drawing on the "Resolutions of 1798" (*see* Virginia and Kentucky Resolutions), Calhoun proposed nullification[qv] as the constitutional remedy. South Carolina should call a convention which should interpose the state's veto, to be binding upon its citizens and the general government unless three fourths of the states should amend the Constitution. Amended and published, although not adopted, by the legislature, Calhoun's *Exposition* was applied four years later in the nullification of the tariff acts of 1828 and 1832.

[Frederic Bancroft, *Calhoun and the South Carolina Nullification Movement;* John C. Calhoun, *Works*, Vol. VI; D. F. Houston, *A Critical Study of Nullification in South Carolina;* Gaillard Hunt, *John C. Calhoun;* W. M. Meigs, *Life of John Caldwell Calhoun.*]

FLETCHER M. GREEN

Calico Railroad, THE, was the derisive name applied to the Lyons, Iowa, Central Railroad which was to have been built across Iowa from Lyons, Iowa, to Council Bluffs. The company was organized in 1853. Iowa residents purchased stock and Iowa counties voted bonds to help build the road. Early in 1854 work on the track between Lyons and Iowa City was begun and progressed rapidly. The funds, however, were inadequate and some were misappropriated. As a result, work was stopped in June and engineers, contractors and laborers, involving some 2000 persons in all, were left without their pay and without work. The Iowa counties, however, were compelled to redeem their bonds. The railroad company had a store at Lyons and the goods (including a supply of calico) were distributed in partial payment to the workers; hence the name.

[Ruth Irish Preston, The Lyons and Iowa Central Railroad in the *Annals of Iowa*, Third Series, Vol. IX.]

RUTH A. GALLAHER

California, American Immigration to (1826–48). The few Americans in California before 1826 were deserters from New England trading ships. Overland immigration began with the arrival of Jedediah Smith[qv] in 1826. During the next fifteen years, about thirty different groups came to California. The majority of these were trappers from the Hudson's Bay Company[qv] post in Oregon, or traders from New Mexico. Probably about 300 Americans had established themselves in California by 1841, the year that home seekers began their trek across the plains.

During the winter and spring of 1840–41 numerous small groups along the frontier, particularly in Missouri and Arkansas, discussed the advisability of a move to California. As a result, in May, 1841, small parties assembled at Sapling Grove, a few miles west of the present site of Kansas City, and organized under the leadership of John Bartleson and John Bidwell. These pioneers crossed the Sierras in the vicinity of the headwaters of the Stanislaus River and reached various destinations in California by Nov. 1. Meanwhile another company, the Workman-Rowland, traveling over the Gila-Colorado route, arrived in Los Angeles.

Apparently there was no organized overland

expedition from the East to California in 1842, but the following year the movement was resumed. The Chiles-Walker party of 1843; the Stevens-Murphy Company of 1844 (the first immigrants to bring wagons into the settled part of California, and probably the first to enter California by way of the Truckee River route); the McMahon-Clyman, the Swasey-Todd, the Grigsby-Ide, the Hastings-Semple, the Sublette and probably other companies of 1845; various expeditions bringing approximately 500 people in 1846, including the ill-fated Donner party[qv], can only be mentioned here. In the latter half of 1846, following the outbreak of the Mexican War[qv], many immigrants to California were sailors or soldiers. The treaty of Guadalupe Hidalgo[qv], ending the war, was concluded Feb. 2, 1848, and California became a part of the United States. After that the account of immigration to California merges into that of the gold rush[qv] period.

[R. G. Cleland, *A History of California: The American Period;* Cardinal Goodwin, *The Trans-Mississippi West, 1803-1853.*]

CARDINAL GOODWIN

California, Russians in. It was fear of Russia which caused Spain to occupy California in 1769. Eventually the fear was justified. By the end of the 18th century Russian fur-trading posts were extended down the Alaska[qv] coast, a new Russian American Fur Company[qv] was established with Count Rezánof at its head and Baránof as chief factor at Sitka, the new capital. Shortage of supplies being a vital problem, Rezánof visited California (1806) with a view to opening trade in foodstuffs, but his success was only partial. His diplomacy included betrothal to Doña Concepción Arguello, daughter of the commander at San Francisco. This romance has been popularized by Bret Harte in a poem and by Gertrude Atherton in an historical novel. Rezánof died on his way back to St. Petersburg, but Russian interest in California continued. Without Spain's permission Kushkof in 1811 established north of San Francisco Bay the post called Fort Ross, which became the center of an agricultural colony and a base for an extensive sea-otter trade[qv] all down the California coast. A smaller settlement was founded on Bodega Bay. As a defensive move, first Spain, then Mexico, established settlements north of San Francisco Bay (San Rafael, 1817, and San Francisco Solano, or Sonoma, 1823). In 1824 Russia yielded all territorial claims south of 54° 40′ (*see* Oregon Question). By this time profits in the sea-otter trade had dwindled and Mexico's liberal trade policy enabled Russia to purchase supplies in California, thus lessening the agricultural importance of Fort Ross. As a result, in 1841 the establishment was sold to Sutter[qv] of New Helvetia (Sacramento) and Russia withdrew. Considerable ruins of Fort Ross are still to be seen.

[H. H. Bancroft, *History of California;* C. E. Chapman, *California: the Spanish Period;* H. Chevigny, *Lost Empire;* E. O. Essig, A. Ogden and C. J. DuFour, *The Russians in California;* Gertrude Atherton, *Rezánof,* a novel.]

HERBERT E. BOLTON

California, Spanish Exploration of. The discovery and early exploration of California were the work of the conqueror Cortés and his agents. Jiménez, one of his mariners, discovered the Peninsula in 1533. Two years later Cortés himself led a colony to the Bay of La Paz. In 1539 Juan de Ulloa, also sent by Cortés, rounded the Peninsula from the head of the Gulf to Cabo del Engaño, near N. Lat. 30°. Three years later Juan Rodríguez Cabrillo[qv] explored the entire outer coast of the Peninsula, discovered San Diego Bay (calling it San Miguel), the Channel Islands, Monterey Bay and perhaps Point Reyes, then returned to the Channel Islands, on one of which he died. The voyage was continued by Ferrelo (Ferrer), Cabrillo's second in command, who reached the vicinity of the Oregon border, returning thence to Mexico.

Because of English ravages on the Pacific (Drake[qv] and Cavendish) and the heavy toll of scurvy on the Manila galleons, Spain conceived the idea of founding a settlement on the Alta California[qv] coast to serve for defense and a port of call. California would be a cabbage patch for the support of the Manila trade. On this errand Sebastián Vizcaíno sailed from Mexico in 1602. He retraced the route of Cabrillo, changed the name of San Miguel Bay to San Diego[qv], explored and overpraised Monterey Bay and continued north to the vicinity of the Oregon border, about where the Cabrillo expedition had turned back. Plans to colonize Monterey Bay failed to mature and for nearly 170 years the California coast was seen by Spaniards only on the merchant galleons returning (southbound) from Manila. Under Spain (1769–1822) the interior of Alta California was extensively explored north from San Diego to Upper Sacramento valley and east to the Sierra Nevada.

[C. E. Chapman, *California: the Spanish Period;* H. E. Bolton, *Spanish Exploration in the Southwest;* H. R. Wagner, *Spanish Voyages to the Northwest Coast of America.*]

HERBERT E. BOLTON

California, The Conquest of (1846–7), is divided into two distinct phases. The first is characterized by considerable scurrying of men, by frequent raising of flags and by an absence of fighting. Frémont took over the command of the men at Sonoma on July 5, 1846, and ten days later led them through the streets of Monterey. Commodore Sloat raised the American flag at Monterey on July 7; it was unfurled at San Francisco and at Sonoma July 9 and two days later at Sacramento. On July 29 Frémont landed with his company at San Diego and Commodore Stockton succeeded Sloat as commander of the Pacific squadron and issued an offensive proclamation. On Aug. 4 and 6 Stockton raised flags over Santa Barbara and San Pedro respectively. On the 13th he met Frémont in Los Angeles (*see* California Battalion), raised the flag and four days later issued another proclamation. The first phase of the conquest was over.

In the second phase there was fighting and bloodshed. It began in the early morning of Sept. 23, with an attack by Californians (Mexicans) on the American garrison stationed at Los Angeles under the command of Capt. Gillespie. Capt. Mervine, sent by Stockton from Monterey with 350 troops, joined Gillespie's defeated forces at San Pedro and attempted a march on Los Angeles, but was driven back following an engagement with Capt. Flores' Californians. Both Santa Barbara and San Diego were quickly retaken by the Californians. Annoying guerrilla warfare in the north culminated in the battle of Natividad, Nov. 16, between Californians and a band of American frontiersmen on their way to join Frémont. The Californians retreated and the Americans moved south with Frémont to aid in recapturing Los Angeles.

Out of the inhospitable desert on Dec. 2 came Gen. Stephen W. Kearny to Warner's ranch with about 100 exhausted United States soldiers (*see* Kearny's March to California). On Dec. 5 he was joined by thirty-five men sent from San Diego by Stockton. On the following day Kearny fought the battle of San Pascual[qv]—the most stubborn engagement of the period. The Americans were left in possession of the field, but their loss was about a score killed and an equal number wounded. Among the latter was Gen. Kearny. Additional troops sent by Stockton arrived Dec. 10 and relieved the Americans. Two days later Kearny joined Stockton in San Diego. The united forces moved north and after two minor engagements (*see* San Gabriel, Battle of) again raised the American flag over Los Angeles. Three days later, Jan. 13, 1847, papers were signed at Cahuenga Rancho by Gen. Andrés Pico and Col. Frémont. This concluded the second and final phase of the conquest just seven months, lacking one day, after the occupation of Sonoma.

[R. G. Cleland, *A History of California: The American Period;* Cardinal Goodwin, *John Charles Frémont, an Explanation of His Career.*]

CARDINAL GOODWIN

California Alien Land Law. To check the increasing competition of Japanese immigrant farmers, the California legislature passed the Alien Land Law of 1913. The act was amended and extended by popular initiative in 1920, and by the legislature in 1923 and 1927. These laws expressly permit aliens who are eligible to American citizenship to acquire, enjoy and transfer real property in the state to the same extent as citizens of the United States. On the other hand, individual aliens who are not eligible to citizenship and corporations in which a majority of members are such aliens, or in which a majority of the capital stock is owned by them, are permitted to hold real property only as may be stipulated in existing treaties between the United States and their respective countries.

[*Statutes of California* . . . 1913, Chap. 113; *ibid.*, 1921, lxxxiii; *ibid.*, 1923, Chap. 441; *ibid.*, 1927, Chap. 528; *So. Calif. Law Rev.*, III, 423-428, June, 1930; *Calif. Law Rev.*, XIX, 295-303, March, 1931; Porterfield v. Webb, 263 U. S. 225, 1923; People v. Cockrill, 268 U. S. 258, 1925; Tashiro v. Jordan, 256 Pacific, 545, 1927.]

P. ORMAN RAY

California Bank Notes. In 1822 began the hide and tallow[qv] trade through which California became well known to the New England states. Californians depended on "Boston Ships" for all goods of foreign manufacture and generally paid for them with hides, commonly known as "California bank notes," and averaging $1.50 to $2.00 in value.

[R. H. Dana, *Two Years Before the Mast.*]

OSGOOD HARDY

California Battalion, The. On July 5, 1846, at Sonoma, Capt. John C. Frémont absorbed into his command most of the American settlers and adventurers who had begun the Bear Flag Revolt[qv] on June 14. The total of 234 men was, at Monterey on July 23, enlisted by Commodore Robert F. Stockton, U. S. N., as the "Navy Battalion of Mounted Riflemen." Augmented to some 400 volunteers, the California Battalion served through the remainder of the American campaign against the Spanish Californians, participating under Frémont in Stockton's first capture of Los Angeles[qv], Aug. 13, and later receiving the final surrender of Gen. Andrés Pico's Californians to Frémont at Rancho Cahuenga on Jan. 13, 1847. It was mustered out of service, unpaid, April 1–19, 1847. The question of merging the Battalion with the regular United States forces under Gen. Stephen W. Kearny was an important part of the Kearny-Frémont controversy[qv] which led to Frémont's later arrest and court-martial.

[H. H. Bancroft, *History of California*, Vol. V; J. C. Frémont, *Memoirs of My Life;* Allan Nevins, *Frémont, the West's Greatest Adventurer.*]

RUFUS KAY WYLLYS

California Gold Rush. Gold was discovered by James W. Marshall at Coloma on the south fork of the American River on Jan. 24, 1848 (*see* Sutter's Fort). Further discoveries were made in the surrounding country during the month of February. The earliest reports to reach the communities along the coast were received dubiously, but by the end of May all uncertainty was removed. By the middle of June people were deserting homes and towns for the gold fields. Already, on June 1, United States Consul Larkin had forwarded official news of the discovery and his information reached Washington by the middle of September. Further dispatches, carried by Lt. Beale and dated a month later, were also received in the national capital. On June 12 Gov. R. B. Mason left Monterey to inspect the mines. About the middle of August he sent his report to the adjutant general, accompanied by a sample of gold. From $30,000 to $50,000, "if not more," he estimated were taken daily from the mines, and "there is more gold in the country drained by the Sacramento and San Joaquin rivers than will pay the cost of the present war with Mexico a hundred times over." A pick, a shovel and a tin pan were all that was required to obtain it. Mason's report, with its sensational observations, was included with the President's message to Congress on Dec. 5, 1848, and was published in the principal newspapers throughout the country.

The effect was immediate. By Jan. 18, 1849, sixty-one vessels, each carrying an average of fifty passengers, left Boston, Salem, New York, Philadelphia, Baltimore and Norfolk for the Pacific coast. Other ships carrying an unknown number of gold seekers sailed from Charleston and New Orleans during the same period. In February sixty ships were booked to leave New York and seventy from Boston and Philadelphia. The demand for accommodations to California had become so great that vessels were diverted from various services to provide passage for eager emigrants.

Both in Europe and in Asia populations were aroused by sensational reports from the gold fields. Five California trading and mining companies were organized in London at a cost of more than £1,250,000. Notices regarding the departure of vessels from the principal ports of Great Britain and from ports in France, Spain, Holland and Germany were published in foreign newspapers and magazines. Among the Asiatic peoples those most affected by the gold malady were the Chinese. The *Alta Californian* for May 10, 1852, estimates the number of Chinese in the territory Feb. 1, 1849, at fifty-four. By Dec. 31 of the same year there were 791. A year later there were more than 4000. The Japanese apparently heard of the discovery with stolid indifference. But in Australia the excitement was given free play. Shipmasters circulated reports and streets of the principal cities were placarded with announcements of "Gold! Gold!" in California, and soon it became difficult to secure passage on departing vessels. Even the inhabitants of the Marquesas Islands were affected. Members of the French colony who were free departed immediately and were quickly followed by the soldiers, leaving the governor alone to represent the government.

The spring of 1849 brought overland migration from Mexico and from the United States. "The mania that pervades the whole country, our own camp included," wrote an army officer regarding Mexico, "is beyond all description or credulity. The whole state of Sonora is on the move. . . ." Four thousand left for the gold fields before the beginning of summer, while in various rendezvous along the Missouri River numerous parties had gathered by the first of April. Bancroft estimates the number at 20,000. Bayard Taylor thought 30,000 crossed the plains and reached the gold fields before the beginning of winter. Throughout the summer of 1849, he says, the rich meadows of the Platte "were settled for the time, and a single traveler could have journeyed for the space of a thousand miles, as certain of his lodging and regular meals as if he were riding through the old agricultural districts of the middle states." Peter H. Burnett, later to be elected the first governor of the State of California, thought that at least "two thirds of the population of Oregon capable of bearing arms" migrated to the gold fields.

Probably more than 80,000 people came to California during 1848 and 1849. The Federal census for 1850 gives the total population, excluding Indians, as 92,597, but these figures do not include returns from San Francisco, Contra Costa and Santa Clara counties. The returns from the first were destroyed by fire and those of the last two were lost. Whatever the number, it was sufficient to create more intricate social, economic and political problems than had confronted any former frontier settlements in the history of the United States.

[Hubert Howe Bancroft, *The Works of*, Vol. XXIII; R. G. Cleland, *A History of California: The American Period;* Owen Cochran Coy, *The Great Trek.*]

CARDINAL GOODWIN

California Missions. California has no "old" missions and never had any. California was the very last province occupied, at the end of three centuries of mission founding, all the way from Buenos Aires to San Francisco and Jamestown. The missions founded by the Jesuits[qv] in Lower (Baja) California in the 17th and 18th centuries were taken over by the Franciscans[qv] in 1768. Next year the Franciscans advanced into Upper (Alta) California and three years later withdrew entirely from the southern district, yielding it to the Dominicans[qv]. The California Franciscans were members of the College of San Fernando in Mexico City, by which they were governed. The founder and moving spirit of the California missions was Father Junípero Serra. San Carlos Borromeo (Carmel) was his capital. Nine missions were founded in his presidency (1769–84) and nine under Lasuén (1785–1803), three more being added by 1823. They were established in the following order: San Diego, 1769; San Carlos, 1770; San Antonio, 1771; San Gabriel, 1771; San Luís Obispo, 1772; San Francisco de Asís, 1776; San Juan Capistrano, 1776; Santa Clara, 1777; San Buenaventura, 1782; Santa Bárbara, 1786; La Purísima Concepción, 1787; Santa Cruz, 1791; Soledad, 1791; San José, 1797; San Juan Bautista, 1797; San Miguel, 1797; San Fernando, 1797; San Luís Rey, 1798; Santa Inés, 1804; San Rafael, 1817; San Francisco Solano (Sonoma), 1823 (under Mexico).

The missions were both Christian seminaries and training schools in the rudiments of European civilization. The native Californians, except the Yumas, had no agriculture whatsoever and few of them had fixed abodes. Under the missionaries they became skilled in raising grain and fruits, tending cattle, horses and other stock; in building, spinning, weaving, tanning, leather work, blacksmithing, soap-making and many other crafts. Under the direction of the missionaries they built a score of beautiful missions. A complete mission plant comprised church, living quarters for the friars, the Indian village, shops, irrigation works, tallow vats, orchards, fields and vast pastures for flocks and herds. At each mission there were usually two priests and a small soldier guard.

At their height in 1821 the missions had in residence over 21,000 neophytes. By 1846 the total number of baptisms had reached 98,000. Under Mexico the California missions fared badly. Laws providing for secularization brought on a struggle which ended in the dispersion of the neophytes and the passing of most of the mission property into the hands of secular owners. The buildings fell into decay. Most of the churches are still (or again) used for religious purposes, but the rest of the buildings have largely disappeared. At some sites extensive restorations have been made or are in progress.

[Fr. Zephyrin Engelhardt, O.F.M., *Missions and Missionaries of California;* Nellie V. Sánchez, *Spanish Arcadia;* H. H. Bancroft, *History of California;* Helen Hunt Jackson, *Ramona*, a novel.]

HERBERT E. BOLTON

California since 1848. With the signing of the Treaty of Guadalupe Hidalgo[qv], Feb. 2, 1848, California, along with other lands wrested from Mexico by war (*see* Mexican War), was formally annexed to the United States. Thus was climaxed a half century of United States commercial and diplomatic interest in the region. The hide, tallow and fur trade[qqv] had brought Americans to California during the Spanish and Mexican periods[qqv]; organized American migrations had begun in the 1840's; Presidents Jackson, Tyler and Polk had futilely attempted the territory's purchase; annexation was the logical and inevitable outcome.

Two weeks before California formally became a part of the United States, gold was discovered in the Sierra Nevadas and soon pastoral California was invaded by a host of adventurers, among whom the vicious element was inevitably large (*see* California Gold Rush). By 1852 the population had jumped from 10,000 in 1846 (including 4000 Americans) to 250,000, centered mostly in San Francisco and the gold fields. This turbulent influx and the resultant clash between native Californian and Anglo-American custom rendered inadequate the military government set up during the Mexican War. The establishment of effective civil authority was imperative. Yet Congress, harassed by the question of slavery in the Mexican Cession, for two years remained deaf to California's plea for territorial government. At length, exasperated Californians took the initiative, devising a state constitution, ratified Nov. 13, 1849. This emergency document outlawed slavery[qv], wherefore Southern congressmen blocked Federal recognition of California's act for nearly a year. At last, on Sept. 9, 1850, President Fillmore signed the bill admitting California as a free state, as part of the Compromise of 1850[qv].

During the hectic decade which followed, California struggled to adjust herself to rapidly changing conditions. Crime was rife, leading several times to vigilante[qv] action. Anglo-American antipathy toward Spanish-Americans, whose numbers increased sharply during the gold rush, and toward the small but growing Chinese element led to frequent race riots. A further complication was added by the lack of homogeneity between the mining and commercial north and the pastoral south. Politics was corrupt and left by public indifference in the hands of a few. Concerned mainly with problems peculiar to herself, the state was for years but little affected by national issues. In 1860, however, the nationwide rift in the Democratic party[qv] extended to California, resulting in a Republican electoral victory. During the Civil War[qv], an active minority of Southern sympathizers endeavored to aid the Confederacy[qv], but sentiment predominantly favored the Union, to which were contributed both money and men.

One of California's most vital needs was communication with the East. In the absence of a transcontinental railway, long delayed by sectional differences and disagreement as to route, the Overland Mail[qv] was established in 1857 and the Pony Express[qv] in 1860. Construction of the railroad was at length undertaken during the Civil War and when the Central Pacific[qv], the California enterprise, met the Union Pacific[qv] near Ogden, Utah, May 10, 1869, a new era for California had begun.

Meanwhile economic and social changes were going on apace. The mining population dwindled, cities grew and the cattle industry declined sharply after the severe drought of 1864, thus paving the way for agricultural growth.

During the 1870's California was swept by a wave of popular discontent, in keeping with similar developments in other parts of the West (*see* Greenback Party; Granger Movement), but with causes which were in some respects peculiarly Californian. The presence of numerous Chinese antagonized white labor, leading to bloody anti-Chinese riots and, eventually, to the Federal Chinese Exclusion Act[qv] of 1882. Large agricultural estates, as well as confused land titles, produced especially by the survival of Spanish and Mexican land grants[qv], caused further dissatisfaction. More particularly, however, popular grievances turned upon the Central Pacific's monopoly of railroad transportation, its huge land investments and its political dictation. To remedy these and other evils, a new constitution was adopted in 1879, one of whose significant features was the extension of public control over the railroads, especially by the provision for a state Board of Railroad Commissioners.

Nearly thirty years elapsed before the state experienced another major political upheaval. Meanwhile, many of the conditions which prompted the agitation of the 1870's had disappeared. Government remained corrupt, however, and the railroads and other large corporations continued to incur public odium because of their political activities, real or alleged. By 1910 a popular reform movement, gaining impetus from a clean-up of municipal government in San Francisco and Los Angeles, had won control of state politics as well. Then followed various measures to render government more responsible to public will and to curb the political influence of the railroads.

Striking 20th-century developments were the rapid population increase of Los Angeles and southern California and the growth of a highly diversified agriculture, involving the reclamation[qv] of desert areas. By the second decade of the century, California, long absorbed in her own unique problems, had definitely entered the current of national affairs.

[R. G. Cleland, *A History of California: The American Period.*]

CHARLES EDWARD CHAPMAN AND ROBERT HALE SHIELDS

California Trail. A term applied to various through trails to California, the earliest ones being up the peninsula (1769) and northwest from Sonora (1774). From Santa Fé[qv] the Old Spanish Trail, made known (1776) by the Escalante expedition[qv], followed the Chama River, crossed Colorado into Utah and later was extended southwest to Los Angeles. Early traders and trappers also went west through Zuñi; then southwest by Salt River and west by the Gila[qv]; or (later) from Zuñi west to the Mohave country. Still others followed the Rio Grande south, then struck west to the headwaters of the Gila. In the 1840's gold-seekers converged in the Salt Lake Valley via the Platte River, Pueblo-Fort Bridger[qv], and Frémont trails[qv]; then continued west into northern California.

[R. P. Bieber, The Southwestern Trails to California in 1849, in *Mississippi Valley Historical Review*, XII, 1925.]

LANSING B. BLOOM

California under Mexico. For a quarter century, after 1822, California was a province of the Republic of Mexico. Outside of the missions this was a period of rapid and promising material development, whose direction was changed by the American conquest and the discovery of gold.

Of nearly 1000 so-called "Spanish" land grants, all but about a score were made under Mexico. Mexican colonists entered the province in considerable numbers, obtained vast ranches, built substantial country homes, raised great herds of cattle, horses and other stock, sold hides and tallow[qv], engaged in sea-otter[qv] hunting, enriched themselves by obtaining the property of the secularized missions and led a carefree pastoral life.

During this period California was invaded by foreign intruders on all sides. Sailors deserted their ships and remained in the province; Hudson's Bay[qv] trappers (Scotch, French and half-breeds) came yearly from the north. Stockton, for example, was founded by them as French Camp. American hunters and rovers came overland, without asking leave; English and American hide and tallow traders visited the California ports and set up the large establishments described by Dana in *Two Years Before the Mast*. Many of these foreigners settled in the country, married señoritas, acquired ranches, engaged in business or mechanical pursuits. Some of them became citizens of substance and influence. In 1841, contemporaneously with the movement of the covered wagon[qv] into Oregon, American immigrants began to come to California in caravans[qv], no less than fifteen of which arrived before the Gold Rush[qv]. Thus the forty-niners were by no means the pioneer Americans in California.

Politics were turbulent in these years. Mexico was disturbed and exercised little authority in the distant province. Governors sent from Mexico were generally unpopular and sometimes were ousted by local patriots. But native governors fared little better, because of the sectional rivalries between north and south California. Prominent in the politics of the period was the question of the secularization of the missions and the division of the plunder (*see* California Missions). The outstanding native Californian of this era was Gen. Mariano Vallejo, lord of the Sonoma March. Immigrants entered politics and became involved in the disturbances. After 1840 Sutter's vast estate, called New Helvetia (*see* Sutter's Fort), became the center of a quasi-independent community of Anglo-American immigrants, who had come with or without permission. Thus the way was being prepared for the Bear Flag Revolt[qv] and conquest by the United States.

[R. G. Cleland, *California: The American Period;* Nellie V. Sánchez, *Spanish Arcadia;* H. H. Bancroft, *California Pastoral;* R. H. Dana, *Two Years Before the Mast.*]

HERBERT E. BOLTON

California under Spain. In the 17th century Baja (Lower[qv]) California and Pimería Alta (now southern Arizona) were colonized by Spain, largely through the work of the Jesuit[qv] missionaries. After the expulsion of the Jesuits in 1767 their work was taken over by the Franciscans[qv]. There had been frequent talk of extending the settlements from these two bases northward into Alta (Upper) California[qv], but the step was not taken until foreign danger threatened. As a result of Bering's explorations in the North Pacific (1728–41), Russian fur traders established posts on the Aleutian Islands and began their southward march down the Alaska coast (*see* California, Russians in). Fearing the loss of Alta California, Spain now decided to occupy the province. The plan was carried out under the vigorous direction of José de Gálvez, Inspector-General of New Spain. He made use of men and means at hand. Gaspar de Portolá, governor of (Lower) California, was put at the head of a colony and Father Junípero Serra, president of the (Lower) California missions[qv], accompanied him with missionaries. Part of the colony went by sea, part overland up the peninsula. They met at San Diego Bay, and there founded the mission and presidio of San Diego[qv]. Continuing up the coast by land, over what is essentially the main railroad route, Portolá reconnoitered Monterey Bay and discovered San Francisco Bay, which all earlier explorers seem to have missed. Next year (June 3, 1770), Portolá and Serra founded the presidio and mission of San Carlos (Monterey), which became respectively the military and missionary capitals of the province. Within two years the missions of San Antonio, San Gabriel and San Luis Obispo were founded at intermediate points between San Diego and Monterey.

Two important problems were now solved by Juan Bautista de Anza, captain of the presidio of Tubac, in Pimería Alta (now southern Arizona). With twenty soldiers, Indian guides, cattle for food and Fathers Garcés and Díaz as diarists, in 1774 Anza[qv] explored a land route from the Mexican mainland over the mountains to San Gabriel. Next year he raised in Mexico a colony of settlers for San Francisco Bay, and led them over the same trail to California. His leadership was superb. Starting with 240 persons, he arrived at Monterey with 242, one death on the way being more than offset by the birth of three children. With this colony San Francisco[qv] was begun in June, 1776. Next year Felipe de Neve became the first governor of Alta California, which hitherto had been nominally ruled from Loreto, in Baja California.

When fully developed California under Spain was divided into four military districts (San Diego, Santa Barbara, Monterey and San Francisco). There were twenty missions, extending from San Diego to San Rafael (on the north shore of San Francisco Bay). Another, San Francisco Solano, was added in the rule of Mexico. Most of these mission colonies have become towns or cities. Three municipalities were founded, San José 1777, Los Angeles 1781 and Branciforte, now Santa Cruz, 1798. The chief industries of the province were agriculture, stock raising, and trade in sea-otter[qv] skins, the greater part of which was carried on by the missions. Spain's rule in California came to an end in 1822, independence being officially celebrated at Monterey on April 11.

[C. E. Chapman, *California: the Spanish Period;* Nellie V. Sánchez, *Spanish Arcadia;* H. E. Bolton, *Outpost of Empire.*]

HERBERT E. BOLTON

California v. Central Pacific R. R. Co. (1888). The Supreme Court held that, under the commerce and other clauses, Congress has power to construct interstate means of transportation directly or by charter through corporations; and that California could not tax the franchise thus granted by the United States.

[Charles Warren, *The Supreme Court in U. S. History.*]

JAMES D. MAGEE

Callabee Creek, Battle of (Jan. 27, 1814). In Macon County, Ala., fifty miles west of Fort Mitchell, Gen. Floyd, with 1200 Georgia volunteers, a company of cavalry and 400 friendly Indians, repulsed a night attack of the Red Stick Indians[qv] on his camp. Floyd lost so many in this hostile country that he immediately withdrew to the Chattahoochee.

[Benson J. Lossing, *Pictorial Field Book of the War of 1812.*]

ROBERT S. THOMAS

Calomel (monochloride of mercury) was throughout the 19th century a popular medication, especially for malarial fevers. Although known in colonial days, calomel first came to be widely used as a result of its administration by Benjamin Rush in the Philadelphia yellow-fever[qv] epidemic of 1793. Rush, believing the fever due to gas from decaying vegetation, attempted to remove the poison by bleeding and strong purgatives (calomel, rhubarb and jalap), a practice borrowed from John Mitchell of Virginia (1741). One of Rush's pupils, John Esten Cooke, extending the theory to practically all diseases, gave wide currency to the practice through his lectures and writings at Transylvania University (1827–37). He advised repeated and strong doses, even a dram in extreme cases. At the Louisville Medical Institute (1837–44) Cooke found complaints against his teaching, which finally caused his resignation. A milder dosage known as "Cooke's pills" (1–2 grams of calomel with aloes, rhubarb and soap) was popular for many years. In the army it was customary to take a pint of blood from each new recruit and give him Rush's "ten and ten." While W. A. Hammond was surgeon general (1862–64), calomel and tartar emetic were banned from the supply list, but later restored. Calomel is still used in acute malarial fevers as a preliminary purgative.

[F. R. Packard, *History of Medicine in the United States;* Robert Peter, *History of the Medical Department of Transylvania University.*]

W. C. MALLALIEU

Calumet, The. *See* Pipe, Indian.

Calumet and Hecla Mine, THE. A copper mine in the Keweenaw Peninsula of Lake Superior in northwest Michigan. For some years previous to its discovery by Edwin J. Hulbert in 1859 copper exploration and mining had been taking place in the region. Hulbert uncovered the conglomerate lode in 1864. The geological deductions which led to this result were based upon the discovery of masses of breccia scattered upon the ground, which suggested to Hulbert a search for the mother lode. The Calumet and the Hecla mines opened as separate undertakings under Hulbert's management, but soon afterwards Alexander Agassiz was sent out from Boston to superintend the initial stages of development. The problem of separating the conglomerate copper from its rock matrix was solved with great difficulty. The country was then very remote and wild, having only water transportation in the summer and none in the winter. In spite of difficulties the two original mines paid dividends in 1869 and 1870, and were consolidated into the Calumet and Hecla Mining Company in 1871. Other mining companies were opened in the vicinity, at first under distinct corporations, but by 1923 most of them had consolidated with the Calumet and Hecla Company.

Several shafts reached a depth of over a mile on the vertical and considerably over that on the vein or incline. Early milling methods did not recover all the copper from the rock, and the old tailings have been reworked with modern methods with remarkable results. By 1933 the aggregate tonnage of ore mined and treated had been 165,000,000. The various mines of the Calumet and Hecla have produced 4,808,000,000 pounds of copper metal, which sold for $771,000,000.

[T. A. Richard, *A History of American Mining.*]

LEW A. CHASE

Calvinism in its broadest sense is the entire body of conceptions arising from the teachings of John Calvin. Its fundamental principle is the conception of God as absolutely sovereign. The statement of Calvinism most influential in America was the Westminster Confession[qv] (1647). Its doctrinal portion was accepted by the New England Congregationalists[qv] and embodied in their Cambridge Platform[qv] (1648). American Presbyterians[qv] coming from Scotland and North Ireland were sternly Calvinistic. The Synod of Philadelphia, the oldest general Presbyterian body in America, passed the Adopting Act in 1729, which required all ministers and licentiates to subscribe to the Westminster Confession. Other Calvinistic bodies in America are the two Reformed Churches, the Dutch and the German, and all other Presbyterian bodies.

[W. W. Sweet, *Story of Religions in America.*]

WILLIAM W. SWEET

Calvo Doctrine, THE, enunciated in 1885 by C. Calvo, the Argentinian international jurist, held that the use of neither force nor diplomatic pressure is justifiable in the prosecution of claims or indemnities with respect to either public or private debts or losses, resulting from civil war or other causes. The Calvo Doctrine is to be distinguished from the Drago Doctrine[qv] given validity by the Hague Convention[qv] of 1907 prohibiting the use of force in the collection of public debts.

[A. S. Hershey, The Calvo and Drago Doctrines, *American Journal of International Law*, 1907, 1926.]

PHILLIPS BRADLEY

Cambridge, Mass., was settled in 1631. Originally intended as the seat of government of the Massachusetts Bay Colony[qv], the town was early abandoned by Gov. John Winthrop and others in favor of Boston[qv], leaving Deputy Gov. Thomas Dudley and Simon Bradstreet as the principal founders of the "newe towne," as it was first called. For a time Rev. Thomas Hooker's company settled there (1632–36) before removing to Connecticut[qv]. Their places were taken by the company of Rev. Thomas Shepard, who became the first permanent minister of the town. The name of Newtown was changed to Cambridge when Harvard College[qv] was founded there in 1638. The following year the college set up the first printing press in North America with Stephen Day as printer.

[L. R. Paige, *History of Cambridge;* S. A. Drake, *History of Middlesex County;* Hannah Winthrop Chapter, D. A. R., *Historic Guide to Cambridge.*]

R. W. G. VAIL

Cambridge Agreement, THE (1629), was the decision made and signed by Puritan[qv] members of the Massachusetts Bay Company[qv] that if the charter and company could be legally transferred to New England, they would migrate thither with their families. By accepting the agreement and overcoming the legal obstacle concerning removal, the company, originally organized for purposes of trade, shifted its emphasis of interest from commerce to religion. Although the joint stock remained under the direction of English business men for some time afterward, henceforth the control of the plantation was in the hands of Puritans, who, dissatisfied with the prospect of religious and political reform at home, looked to the Massachusetts project as an opportunity to establish a Calvinistic utopia. The sequel to the Cambridge Agreement was the Great Migration[qv] of March, 1630, when more than 1000 Puritans transferred families and effects to New England for the purpose of building a colony based on their ideas of close union of church and state.

[C. M. Andrews, *The Colonial Period of American History,* I.]

VIOLA F. BARNES

Cambridge Platform, THE, was drawn up by a synod of ministers from Massachusetts and Connecticut (August, 1648), which met pursuant to a request of the Massachusetts General Court[qv]. The New England authorities desired a formal statement of polity and a confession of faith because of the current Presbyterian ascendancy in England and the activities of local Presbyterians[qv] such as Dr. Robert Child. The declaration endorsed the Westminster Confession[qv] and for ecclesiastical organization upheld the existing Congregational[qv] practice. The Cambridge Platform remained the standard formulation in Massachusetts through the 18th century and in Connecticut until the Saybrook Platform[qv] of 1708.

[Williston Walker, *The Creeds and Platforms of Congregationalism;* Perry Miller, *Orthodoxy in Massachusetts.*]

PERRY MILLER

Camden, Battle of (Aug. 16, 1780). Following Lincoln's disaster at Charleston[qv], Gates was given command of the Southern army consisting of 1400 regulars under DeKalb and 2052 militia. Marching southward from Hillsborough, Gates occupied Rugelys Mill, a strong position about thirteen miles northeast of Camden which had been occupied by the British under Lord Rawden. Gates unwisely sent 400 regulars to aid Sumter cut the British lines of communication far to the southeast (*see* Hanging Rock, S. C., Action at). Then failing to attack promptly, he allowed Cornwallis time to arrive with reinforcements. The two generals decided to suprise each other. Cornwallis, with 2000 veterans, marched northward and met Gates marching southward early in the morning of Aug. 16. The Americans were exhausted from long marches, many helpless with dysentery, and more than half were militia who had never been under fire. At the first attack the militia fled. The regulars, standing their ground, were surrounded and almost annihilated. DeKalb was captured, mortally wounded. The Americans lost 2000 killed, wounded and captured, seven cannon, 2000 muskets and their transport. The British loss was 324. Gates fled to Hillsborough and vainly attempted to rally his demoralized army and call out more militia, but his day was over. Dec. 2 he was replaced by Greene. Many Americans fled to the swamps and mountains and carried on guerrilla warfare (*see* Southern Campaigns, 1780–81).

[John W. Fortescue, *History of the British Army*, III; Edward McCrady, *The History of South Carolina in the Revolution.*]

NELSON VANCE RUSSELL

Camden-Yorke Opinion. A written opinion, professional and not judicial in character, was given in 1769 by Lord Camden, who was at the time Lord Chancellor of Great Britain, and Charles Yorke, who was later to be raised to the same eminent position. It related to the rights of private persons who had taken conveyances of lands from native tribes of India, and supported such titles, grants from the king not being necessary. It was held that the king only had sovereignty over the inhabitants as English subjects. The opinion was seized on by certain western land companies in America as applicable to any purchases they might make from the aborigines as proprietors of the soil. Many public men and lawyers in America concurred in the soundness of the opinion, Patrick Henry among them. However, when the matter came to judicial test in this country after the Revolution, the contrary view prevailed: titles to lands acquired from the Indian tribes were void when the state had not given consent; the real title was held to be in the state as sovereign.

[C. W. Alvord, *Mississippi Valley in British Politics.*]

SAMUEL C. WILLIAMS

Camels in the West. At the close of the Mexican War the United States added 529,189 square miles to its area. This territory contained no railroads and the difficulties of transportation were so great that an effort was made to establish across this new country fast express routes by using camels. Congress (1855) appropriated $30,000 to purchase camels in Egypt and Asia. Seventy-six camels were brought to Texas. Twenty-eight of them were taken to California (1857) to be used on mail and express routes through the desert country, but after a few trips their use was discontinued. They were later (1864) sold at auction, most of them being taken to Nevada and used to carry freight to and from the mines. Those remaining in Texas were sold to circuses and zoölogical gardens. The only other importation of camels was in 1860–62. Forty-five animals were brought from Siberia to San Francisco by Otto Esche, a German merchant, who planned to use them on eastbound express routes. He never started this service, but sold most of the camels to a mining company in British Columbia. Years later wild camels were occasionally seen in the Northwest, in Nevada, and especially in Arizona. All are now (1939) extinct.

[Lewis B. Lesley, Uncle Sam's Camels, *California Historical Society Quarterly*, December, 1930.]

A. A. GRAY

Camino del Diablo (the Devil's Highway), an old and difficult trail connecting a series of desert water-holes northwestward from the Rio de Sonóita to the Gila River near its confluence with the Colorado. Apparently it was first traced by white men when the Jesuit[qv] missionary, Padre Eusebio Francisco Kino, traversed it in February, 1699. The trail crossed the present international boundary some forty miles northwest of the border town of Sonóita, and thence crossed the Tule Desert westward to the southeastern end of the Gila Range, following the latter's eastern slope to the Gila River. As a shortcut from the settled portion of Sonora through the lands of the Pápago Indians to the Colorado and thence into California, it was frequently used by travelers, including Juan Bautista de Anza's[qv] exploring party of 1774 to California.

[H. E. Bolton, *Rim of Christendom*, and *Outpost of Empire;* K. Bryan, *Guide to Desert Watering Places.*]

RUFUS KAY WYLLYS

Camp Butler (1861–66), concentration camp for Illinois volunteers, was established in August, 1861, and used until June, 1866. It was located six miles east of Springfield. Here nearly a third of the Illinois regiments were mustered into the

Federal service and later discharged. After the capture of Fort Donelson^qv^, Camp Butler was used also as a prison camp^qv^, housing at one time as many as 3600 captured Confederates.

[Helen E. Sheppley, Camp Butler in the Civil War Days, *Journal of the Illinois State Historical Society*, January, 1933.]

PAUL M. ANGLE

Camp Chase, located just west of Columbus, Ohio, served the dual purpose of training camp and military prison during the Civil War. As the war continued, its importance as a prison camp^qv^ increased and Confederate prisoners continued to be received in large numbers until the cessation of hostilities. The high tide of prison population was reached in 1863 when some 8000 Confederate soldiers were confined there. In 1864 a Confederate plan to release the prisoners at Johnson's Island^qv^ in Lake Erie, seize Sandusky and release the prisoners at Camp Chase, miscarried.

[William H. Knauss, *The Story of Camp Chase.*]

FRANCIS R. AUMANN

Camp Douglas (1861–65) was established in September, 1861, for the concentration and training of Illinois volunteers. It covered sixty acres near the then southern limit of Chicago. After the fall of Fort Donelson^qv^, Camp Douglas served also as a prison camp^qv^, 30,000 Confederates being confined there at one time or another. It was dismantled in November, 1865.

[A. T. Andreas, *History of Chicago.*]

PAUL M. ANGLE

Camp Followers. There were various types of camp followers in our early wars—peddlers, sutlers, gamblers, Indians, Negroes; but most surely present of all were the women—sometimes wives of officers and soldiers, but more often not. The *Memoirs* of Baroness Riedesel tell how she and her children followed her husband with Burgoyne's army to Saratoga^qv^, and war diaries and army orders tell of quite another type of woman, often the lowest imaginable. They became a problem in the French and Indian War^qv^ though it is humorously noted that if an army settled down in a far northern camp for the winter, most of the women disappeared before December. Washington's orders in that war permitted a limited number, finally fixed at six to every hundred men, in camp and on the march, and even to draw rations, on condition that they behaved themselves well and did washing for the soldiers. Later, cooking was added to their duties. They were omnipresent in the Revolutionary War, the British army having more than the American because of its better pay and rations. The American army before Boston in February, 1776, sternly drummed two women out of camp (David How's *Diary*), but later relaxed its attitude. Several times, however, Washington had to issue orders against their being permitted to ride on the wagons when the army was on the march. When the army passed through Philadelphia, Aug. 23, 1777, Washington ordered that "Not a Woman belonging to the Army is to be seen with the troops on their march through the City." The women were therefore herded through alleys and back streets. A few women even participated in Arnold's dreadful march to Quebec^qv^, including a squaw, the mistress of Aaron Burr. Some Indian men became hangers-on in the French and Indian War, drawing rations but giving little or no service in return. One finds sutlers and peddlers frequently whipped during that war for selling liquor to the soldiers. In the Carolinas during the Revolution, Negroes forsook the plantations by hundreds to follow Cornwallis' army, apparently regarding the British as their deliverers from slavery, but incidentally drawing free rations and having an adventure without work. The War of 1812 presents a somewhat similar picture, though Indians figure in it more largely. Just before the Battle of Lake Erie^qv^, the British commissaries were feeding 14,000 Indians, men, women and children, of whom not even all the men could be depended upon to give service when it was desired.

[George Washington, *Writings;* Journal of Capt. Samuel Jenks, *Massachusetts Historical Society Proceedings*, March, 1890.]

ALVIN F. HARLOW

Camp Grant Massacre (April 30, 1871). An attack on Aravaipa Apaches^qv^ at Camp Grant, Arizona Territory, by a party of Mexicans, Americans and Papago Indians from Tucson and San Xavier, who attributed to the Camp Grant Indians a series of murders and outrages, particularly a raid on San Xavier in which horses and mules were stolen. Twenty-seven bodies were found, nearly all women and children, and twenty-eight children were carried off, seven of whom were recovered. The leaders were acquitted in a jury trial.

[Frank C. Lockwood, *The Apache Indians.*]

DON RUSSELL

Camp Jackson Affair (May 3–10, 1861). Capt. Nathaniel Lyon, in command of United States Arsenal in St. Louis, imbued with the idea that Missouri authorities were planning to capture the arsenal, collected and armed a number of politico-military organizations as Home Guards. With over 8000 of these, mostly Germans and other foreigners, Capt. Lyon seized, on his own initiative and without resistance, the 669 militiamen encamped at Camp Jackson, St. Louis. While being marched away several miles to prison, these men were fired upon, three of them killed, about twenty-eight civilians killed and many men, women and children wounded. Many of the militiamen were opponents of secession and all were subsequently released on parole, subject to exchange as prisoners of war. (*See* Confederacy, Border State Representation in.)

[*War of the Rebellion: Official Records of the Union and Confederate Armies*, Ser. II, Vol. I; *Missouri Republican*, May 11-14, 1861.]

STELLA M. DRUMM

Camp Meetings. Outdoor religious meetings were a feature of the evangelical revival^qv in both England and America in the 18th century. Baptists^qv held meetings similar to the later camp meetings during the American Revolution. The meeting conducted jointly by Presbyterian and Methodist^qqv ministers in Logan County, Ky., in July, 1800, is generally accepted as the first regular camp meeting. Held in a wood, near a supply of water, the encampments usually lasted four days or longer. There were several services each day and sometimes four or five ministers spoke at the same time from different parts of the camp ground. The animated evening services of the frontier assemblies, accentuated by pine knots flickering in the dense darkness, were usually tense with excitement and frequently marked by emotional irregularities such as jerking, falling, barking, rolling and dancing.

Camp meetings were not confined to the frontier, but extended throughout the United States during the early 19th century. Steamboats carried many hundreds of people at excursion rates from Eastern cities to near-by camp meetings. In many cases cottages replaced tents and permanent auditoriums were erected. During the late 19th century popular educational movements, such as Chautauqua^qv, and summer resort communities, such as Ocean Grove, N. J., developed from camp-meeting beginnings. Many summer assemblies still function as outgrowths of the camp meeting.

[Catherine C. Cleveland, *The Great Revival in the West, 1797-1805*.]

W. B. POSEY

Camp Supply. *See* Supply, Camp.

Camp Wild-Cat was a natural fortification in the Rockcastle Hills of Laurel County, Ky., where Union troops, under Col. T. T. Garrard, decisively repulsed Gen. Zollicoffer on Oct. 21, 1861.

[*War of the Rebellion: Official Records of the Union and Confederate Armies*, Ser. I, Vol. IV.]

JONATHAN T. DORRIS

Campaign Literature is the term used to cover all varieties of material circulated during a political campaign to influence the voter. This includes campaign textbooks, which contain a miscellaneous collection of information, statistical tables, documents and arguments particularly for the use of the party worker; biographies of the candidates; special pamphlets on the issues of the campaign; news stories and press releases; pictures, lithographs and cartoons; campaign songs and slogans; letters and postcards; posters, windshield stickers and other similar material, all of which has increased enormously with the growth of the electorate. In 1896 about 100,000,000 pieces were shipped from the Chicago headquarters of the Republican National Committee, while in 1936 at least 370,000,000 pieces were issued from the same headquarters and probably almost as much from the Democratic headquarters.

[Robert C. Brooks, *Political Parties and Electoral Problems*, 3rd edition; Ralph D. Casey, Party Campaign Propaganda, *Annals of the American Academy of Political and Social Science*, Vol. CLXXIX; Burton Bigelow, The Machinery behind Political Pamphleteering, *Journalism Quarterly*, Vol. XIV.]

CLARENCE A. BERDAHL

Campaign of 1788 and of 1792, THE, had no formal nominations, only one presidential candidate, and little opposition to the second choice. The Constitution ratified, the Continental Congress^qv delayed three months before fixing the first Wednesday in January, 1789, for choosing electors, the first Wednesday in February for their voting and the first Wednesday in March for starting the new government. Pennsylvania, Maryland and Virginia elected electors; Massachusetts' legislature chose hers from elected electors; New Hampshire's election failed and her legislature, as did those of the remaining states, appointed electors. Thirteen states could cast ninety-one votes; but two states had not ratified and one (New York) failed to elect or appoint; four electors failed to vote. Washington received the entire sixty-nine votes cast. John Adams received thirty-four as second choice and the other thirty-five were scattered among ten different candidates. In 1792 fifteen states could cast 132 electoral votes, when Hamilton's financial measures and the consolidation of national power (*see* Federalist Party) roused an opposition (Jeffersonian antifederalists) which centered its efforts on the defeat of Adams by the antifederalist[qv] George Clinton, as to defeat Washington was seen to be futile. The attempt failed. Washington's vote was again unanimous, and Adams defeated Clinton by seventy-seven to fifty.

[Edward A. Stanwood, *A History of the Presidency.*]

JOHN C. FITZPATRICK

Campaign of 1796, THE, was the first national election in American history to be contested by political parties. The French Revolution, Genêt and the Jay Treaty[qv] resulted in bitter partisanship. Without the modern machinery of nomination the Federalists[qv] informally agreed upon John Adams as Washington's successor; with him they chose Thomas Pinckney. With more enthusiasm the Republicans (*see* Republican Party, Jeffersonian) chose their leaders, Thomas Jefferson and Aaron Burr. Electors were chosen in sixteen states—in six by popular vote, in ten by the legislature. Of the total electoral votes Adams secured seventy-one, Jefferson sixty-eight, Pinckney fifty-nine, Burr thirty and the remaining forty-eight were divided among nine others, several of whom were distinctly not candidates.

[Edward A. Stanwood, *A History of the Presidency.*]

FRANK MONAGHAN

Campaign of 1800 and of 1804, THE. The election of 1800 forms a turning point in American political history. Its preliminaries were expressed in the famous Virginia and Kentucky Resolutions[qv], proffered by Jefferson and Madison as a party platform. Its party machinery, still more essential to success, was directed by Aaron Burr with supplemental support in Pennsylvania and South Carolina.

Burr had already established the nucleus of a political machine[qv] that was later to develop into Tammany Hall[qv]. With this organization he swept the City of New York with an outstanding legislative ticket, gained control of the state assembly and secured the electoral votes of New York for the Republicans (*see* Republican Party, Jeffersonian). He had already secured a pledge from the Republican (Jeffersonian) members of Congress to support him equally with Jefferson. Hence the tie vote which gave him a dubious chance for the Presidency.

Publicly disclaiming any intent to secure that office, Burr was, nevertheless, put forward by the Federalists[qv] in order to defeat Jefferson and bring about another election (*see* Jefferson-Burr Election Dispute). A slight majority in the House of Representatives enabled them to rally six states to Burr and divide the vote of two others, thus neutralizing the vote of the eight states that supported Jefferson. The contest was prolonged through thirty-five fruitless ballotings; on the thirty-sixth, by prearrangement, a sufficient number of Federalists cast blank ballots to give Jefferson ten states and the Presidency.

This narrow escape from frustrating the popular will led the incoming administration to pass the Twelfth Amendment[qv] to the Constitution. Jefferson covertly helped eliminate Burr in New York, and the party caucus brought George Clinton forward as candidate for the Vice-Presidency. Burr, already divining his political ostracism, attempted to recover ground as an independent candidate for governor of New York. Representative Federalists of New England sought his support in their plans for disunion, but he refused to commit himself to such a program. Jefferson, pre-eminently successful in the more important measures of his administration, was triumphantly re-elected in 1804 as President with George Clinton as Vice-President, the first to be elected as such under the new amendment.

[Edward A. Stanwood, *A History of the Presidency.*]

ISAAC J. COX

Campaign of 1808 and of 1812, THE. Candidates for the Republican (Jeffersonian)[qv] nomination in 1808 were James Madison, the choice of Jefferson; James Monroe, somewhat tainted by affiliation with John Randolph and the "Quids"[qv], who were anathema to the outgoing administration; and George Clinton, a New Yorker not favored by the "Virginia Dynasty."[qv] Jefferson's own refusal to consider a third term confirmed the two-term tradition for a President. At the party caucus[qv] Madison received eighty-three votes; his rivals three each.

The Federalist[qv] opposition was led by Charles Cotesworth Pinckney and Rufus King, but the chief obstacle to the Madison slate came from his own party, notably in Virginia and Pennsylvania, where William Duane, a powerful journalist, was unreconcilable. The malcontents finally voted the party ticket, however, and in the electoral college Madison obtained 122 out of 176 votes. Clinton ran behind the ticket by 9 votes to be Vice-President. Defeated for the Presidency, the Federalists nevertheless made serious inroads upon the Republican majority in the House of Representatives.

In 1812 Madison secured his renomination by a tacit rather than a formal yielding to the demands of Henry Clay and the "War Hawks."[qv] The vice-presidential nomination, tendered first to John Langdon of New Hampshire, went to

Elbridge Gerry of Massachusetts. Opposition to the party slate was led by DeWitt Clinton of New York, who finally accepted nomination from the Federalists, with Jared Ingersoll of Pennsylvania as his running mate. The electoral college gave Madison 128 votes, as against 89 for Clinton. Vermont and Pennsylvania stood by Madison, but New York was led by Martin Van Buren into the Clinton column. Gerry and the ticket could not carry the candidate's own state of Massachusetts, notwithstanding his recent election as governor. Thus, on the eve of the War of 1812[qv], the Republican party was seriously divided.

[Edward Channing, *The Jeffersonian System;* K. C. Babcock, *The Rise of American Nationality.*]

LOUIS MARTIN SEARS

Campaign of 1816 and of 1820, THE. There was no campaign by parties in 1816 worth the name, none at all in 1820. President Madison's choice was James Monroe, old Jeffersonian protégé, Secretary of State and War. Some Republicans (Jeffersonian)[qv] favored Gov. Tompkins of New York. Younger Republicans, interested in nationalist measures following the War of 1812, including a bank, protective tariffs and internal improvements[qqv] to speed the development of the West, preferred Crawford, Secretary of the Treasury, a citizen of Georgia. They gave him 54 votes in the congressional caucus[qv] to 65 for Monroe. Here was the election of 1816, for in the electoral college Monroe overwhelmed Rufus King, signer of the Constitution and statesman of note, but a Federalist[qv] whose party now was thoroughly discredited by the Hartford Convention[qv]. Monroe was given 183 votes to 34 for King. Newer sectional conflicts and rivalry among the younger leaders embittered the "Era of Good Feeling,"[qv] but President Monroe was secure. He was re-elected in 1820, with only one dissenting electoral vote. Federalists saw a greater menace to their propertied interests rising with the democracy of the West; it was to dethrone "King Caucus" and the "Virginia Dynasty"[qv] in the free-for-all campaign of 1824.

[Edward A. Stanwood, *A History of the Presidency.*]

ARTHUR B. DARLING

Campaign of 1824, THE, preparations for which began with the second inauguration of Monroe, marked the beginning of the transition from federalism to democracy with resulting voter realignment under new party emblems. The five candidates were prominent in national affairs and represented sections or factions rather than parties. In general, the politicians supported Crawford; John Quincy Adams represented business; Calhoun, the South and the rising slavocracy[qv]; Clay, the expanding West; Jackson, the people everywhere. The first three were Cabinet members, Clay was Speaker of the House and Jackson was the country's most popular military figure.

Crawford was virtually eliminated by sickness; Jackson was brought in late by his friends; Clay's support was never impressive; Calhoun withdrew and became candidate for Vice-President on both the Adams and Jackson tickets. No candidate received a majority electoral vote. Jackson secured the greatest number, 99; Adams, 84; Crawford, 41; and Clay, 37. Selection was made by the House. Adams was chosen. Jackson's supporters could only charge a "Corrupt Bargain"[qv] and bide their time. (*See* Campaign of 1828.)

[Bennett Champ Clark, *John Quincy Adams;* Marquis James, *Andrew Jackson: Portrait of a President.*]

THOMAS ROBSON HAY

Campaign of 1828 and of 1832, THE. In 1828 President John Quincy Adams stood for re-election and Andrew Jackson of Tennessee made his second campaign for the Presidency. Designated the people's candidate by the action of friends in the legislature of his own State of Tennessee, Jackson won and held the necessary support of influential leaders in New York, Pennsylvania and South Carolina. The campaign was waged throughout the administration of Adams. It was not marked by any clear-cut declaration of political principle or program and Jackson came to think of it as a personal vindication. Of the twenty-four states, Delaware and South Carolina still expressed their choice by vote of the legislature. In twenty-two states the elections were held in the period from late October to early December. There was a great increase in the popular vote cast and both candidates shared in the increase; 643,000 being cast for Jackson and 507,000 for Adams. The electoral vote stood 178 for Jackson to 83 for Adams. John C. Calhoun of South Carolina was again elected Vice-President. In many parts of the nation there was evidence of a more effective organization of the vote than in any previous contest, yet, over and above all considerations in this election was the appeal that the frontier hero made to an increasing body of democratically minded voters. Jackson, himself, was the cause of an alignment of public opinion in the years that followed (*see* Jacksonian Democracy). Jackson men controlled the Congress, and platforms and programs were supported by leaders and sections and groups, but not by clearly defined political parties^qv^. Naturally Jackson stood for re-election although he had spoken in favor of a single term, and the campaign to renominate him began at once. After December of 1831, when Henry Clay returned to the Senate, he, rather than Adams, received the support of most of those who were opposed to Jackson. This did not include Calhoun, who in 1830 had broken with Jackson. Clay was formally presented by a national convention that met in December of 1831. He was endorsed by a national convention of young men which prepared a platform in a meeting held in May of 1832. In that month a national convention of Jackson supporters nominated Martin Van Buren of New York for the Vice-Presidency. In this election the recently gathered Anti-Masonic party^qv^ supported William Wirt of Maryland. The campaign not only witnessed the general use of the national party convention^qv^ but platforms^qv^ were presented and cartoons^qv^ freely used, and there was concentration of popular attention upon the pageantry of parades^qv^. Aside from the personal contest between Jackson and Clay the issue between the two centered upon Jackson's attack upon the United States Bank^qv^ and particularly upon his veto of the bill for the recharter of the bank, a bill which had the backing of the supporters of Clay in both Houses of Congress. Twenty-four states participated in this election and all except South Carolina provided a popular vote. The electorate endorsed the administration of Jackson, for the distribution of the vote in twenty-three states gave Jackson 707,000, Clay 329,000 and Wirt 255,000. In the electoral college the vote stood Jackson 219, Clay 49, Wirt 7, with 11 votes representing the vote of South Carolina cast for John Floyd of Virginia. Jackson had a greater proportion of the popular vote in 1832 than he had had in 1828.

[S. R. Gammon, *The Presidential Campaign of 1832;* Claude G. Bowers, *Party Battles of the Jackson Period.*]

EDGAR EUGENE ROBINSON

Campaign of 1836, The. Made up chiefly of Anti-Masons^qv^, National Republicans^qv^ and anti-Jackson Democrats, the Whig party^qv^, formed in 1834, naturally lacked unity. Because of this, the Whig leaders decided to put forward several sectional candidates in the 1836 presidential campaign. Accordingly, Judge Hugh L. White was entered in the race through nomination by legislative caucuses in Tennessee and Alabama, held in January, 1835. At about the same time, Judge John McLean was nominated by a legislative caucus in Ohio, but he withdrew from the race in the following August. Sen. Daniel Webster was nominated by a Massachusetts legislative caucus, also in January, 1835. Still another candidate of the Whigs was Gen. William H. Harrison, who was formally nominated by both Anti-Masonic and Whig state conventions in Pennsylvania in December, 1835.

Meanwhile at a national convention held in Baltimore on May 21–22, 1835, Martin Van Buren, who was President Jackson's personal choice, had been unanimously nominated for the Presidency by the Democrats^qv^. No platform was adopted by the convention, but a committee was authorized to draw up an address. Published in the party organ, the Washington *Globe,* on Aug. 26, 1835, this address presented Van Buren as one who would, if elected, continue "that wise course of national policy pursued by Gen. Jackson." For all practical purposes, this address may be regarded as the first platform^qv^ ever issued by the Democratic party.

When the election returns were finally in, it was found that Van Buren had won the Presidency with 170 electoral votes and a popular vote of 761,549 to 736,656 for his opponents. White received 26 electoral votes, Webster 14, and Harrison 73, while South Carolina bestowed its 11 votes on W. P. Mangum. No candidate for the Vice-Presidency received a majority of the electoral vote, so on Feb. 8, 1837, the Senate chose the Democratic candidate, Richard M. Johnson, over his leading rival, Francis Granger.

[Edward A. Stanwood, *A History of the Presidency.*]

ERIK McKINLEY ERIKSSON

Campaign of 1840, The. Distinctive in American history as the first national victory of the Whig party^qv^, the campaign of 1840 was unique for its popular and emotional appeal, organized on an unprecedented scale. To the Whigs belongs the credit of introducing into a presidential battle every political device calculated to sway the "common man."

The Whig convention, assembled at Harrisburg, Dec. 2, 1839, nominated Gen. William Henry Harrison of Indiana for President, and John Tyler of Virginia for Vice-President. No attempt was made to frame a platform^qv^; indeed, the only bond uniting the various groups under the Whig banner was a determination to defeat the Democrats^qv^. The Democratic convention held at Baltimore, May 5, 1840, was united on Martin Van Buren for President, but left to the state electors the choice of a Vice-President. A platform on strict construction^qv^ lines was adopted.

The Whigs conducted their campaign at a rollicking pitch. Harrison was adroitly celebrated as the "Hard Cider and Log Cabin" candidate, a phrase which the Democrats had used in contempt. Popular meetings, "log cabin raisin's," oratory, invective against Van Buren the aristocrat, songs and slogans ("Tippecanoe and Tyler Too"[qv]) swamped the country. In the election Harrison polled an electoral vote of 234, a popular vote of 1,275,016; Van Buren received 60 electoral votes and 1,129,102 popular votes. A minor feature in the campaign was the appearance of an abolition (the Liberty[qv]) party, whose candidate, James G. Birney, received 7059 votes. Although the causes for Van Buren's defeat should be traced back to opposition to Jackson, the Panic of 1837[qv] and the unpopular Seminole War[qv], the campaign methods employed by the Whigs contributed largely to Harrison's success.

[Edward A. Stanwood, *A History of the Presidency;* D. B. Goebel, *William Henry Harrison.*]

DOROTHY BURNE GOEBEL

Campaign of 1844, THE. No outstanding Democratic[qv] candidate could muster the necessary two-thirds vote[qv] in the convention, so James K. Polk of Tennessee, the first "dark horse,"[qv] was nominated, with George M. Dallas of Pennsylvania as running mate, on a platform demanding "the re-annexation of Texas and the re-occupation of Oregon" and in favor of tariff reform. The Whigs[qv] nominated Henry Clay of Kentucky and Theodore Frelinghuysen of New Jersey, on a platform favoring protective tariff and a national bank but quibbling on the Texan annexation issue, which alienated some of the Whigs. Polk carried New York by a small popular majority and was elected, with 170 electoral votes to 105 for Clay. The popular vote was: Polk, 1,337,243; Clay, 1,299,062.

[Edward A. Stanwood, *A History of the Presidency.*]

WALTER PRICHARD

Campaign of 1848, THE, resulted in the election of the Whig[qv] nominee, Zachary Taylor, who side-stepped the burning issue of slavery[qv] extension and coasted to victory on his military reputation. His Democratic[qv] opponent, Lewis Cass, straddled the slavery extension question by advocating state sovereignty[qv]. The new Free Soil party[qv], specifically opposed to extension and headed by Martin Van Buren, split the Democratic vote in New York and thus contributed materially to Taylor's triumph. Taylor carried half the states, eight in the South and seven in the North. The popular vote was: Taylor, 1,360,099; Cass, 1,220,544; Van Buren, 291,263. The electoral vote was: Taylor, 163; Cass, 127.

[Edward A. Stanwood, *A History of the Presidency.*]

HOLMAN HAMILTON

Campaign of 1852, THE. The Whig party[qv] was apathetic and demoralized, so Democratic[qv] victory seemed almost certain. The question of greatest interest was who would be the Democratic candidate. After many ballots, the leading Democrats, Cass, Buchanan and Douglas, were eliminated and a "dark horse,"[qv] Franklin Pierce of New Hampshire, was nominated with William R. King of Alabama. The Whigs nominated Gen. Winfield Scott; and the Free-Soilers[qv], John P. Hale. Both major parties endorsed the Compromise of 1850[qv], so there were no issues and little contest. Pierce carried all states save Massachusetts, Vermont, Kentucky and Tennessee, though in the popular vote he received scarcely 30,000 majority. The popular vote was: Pierce, 1,601,274; Scott, 1,386,580; Hale, 155,825. The electoral vote was: Pierce, 254; Scott, 42.

[R. F. Nichols, *Franklin Pierce.*]

ROY F. NICHOLS

Campaign of 1856, THE. The Republican party[qv] in this, its first presidential campaign, nominated John C. Frémont. Its platform opposed slavery expansion and condemned slavery and Mormonism[qqv] as twin relics of barbarism. The American, or Know-Nothing, party[qv] nominated ex-President Millard Fillmore. The Democrats[qv] nominated James Buchanan. Their conservative platform stressed States' Rights[qv], opposed sectionalism[qv] and favored a somewhat ambiguous plank, giving Popular Sovereignty[qv] to the territories. The electoral vote was Buchanan, 174; Frémont, 114; Fillmore, 8. The popular vote was Buchanan, 1,838,169; Frémont, 1,341,264; Fillmore, 874,534. The Republicans rejoiced in their showing, while the Democrats congratulated themselves upon having saved the Union.

[A. K. McClure, *Our Presidents and How We Make Them.*]

PHILIP G. AUCHAMPAUGH

Campaign of 1860, THE. The Democratic[qv] national convention met amid great excitement and bitterness at Charleston, S. C., April 23, 1860. The delegates from the eight states of the far South demanded the inclusion of a plank in the platform providing that Congress should guarantee slave property in the territories. This was refused, and after several days of useless wrangling and failure to unite the convention upon a candidate an adjournment was taken to Baltimore on June 18 following. At this meeting the convention nominated Stephen A. Douglas of Illinois for President, and later the national committee nominated Herschel V. Johnson of Georgia for Vice-President. The platform pledged the party to stand by the Dred Scott decision^qv^ or any future Supreme Court decision that dealt with the rights of property in the various states and territories. Seceding Democratic delegates met at Baltimore on June 28 and nominated John C. Breckinridge of Kentucky for President and Joseph Lane of Oregon for Vice-President. The platform reaffirmed the extreme Southern view with regard to slavery^qv^. Meanwhile, the remains of the "old-line" Whigs and American ("Know-Nothing") parties^qqv^ had met in a convention at Baltimore on May 9 and adopted the name of the Constitutional Union party^qv^, also the platform of "the Constitution of the Country, the Union of the states and the enforcement of the laws." They nominated John Bell of Tennessee for President and Edward Everett of Massachusetts for Vice-President and attempted to ignore the slavery and other sectional issues, with a plea for the preservation of the Union.

Also, the Republican^qv^ national convention had met in Chicago on May 16. By means of the platform issues of nonextension of slavery and of a Homestead law^qv^ and by advocacy of a protective tariff^qv^, the agricultural elements of the northern and western parts of the country and the industrial elements of Pennsylvania, New England and other northern and eastern sections of the country were united. At first it seemed that the convention would nominate either William H. Seward of New York or Salmon P. Chase of Ohio, but a deadlock between their respective supporters being threatened the convention nominated Abraham Lincoln on the third ballot. Hannibal Hamlin of Maine was nominated for Vice-President on the second ballot.

The split in the Democratic party made possible the election of Lincoln. He received 180 electoral votes as against 72 for Breckinridge who carried the extreme southern states, and 39 for Bell who carried the border states^qv^. Douglas received but 12 (9 from Missouri and 3 of the 7 from New Jersey). The popular vote was far otherwise since it totaled 1,857,610 for Lincoln, 1,291,574 for Douglas, 850,082 for Breckinridge and 646,124 for Bell. The combined opponents thus received 930,170 over Lincoln who was a minority President during his first administration.

[Edward A. Stanwood, *A History of the Presidency;* W. S. Myers, *The Republican Party, a History.*]

WILLIAM STARR MYERS

Campaign of 1864, THE. A national convention was called in the name of "the executive committee created by the national convention held in Chicago on the sixteenth day of May 1860." The use of the name Republican^qv^ was carefully avoided. The convention met in Baltimore on June 7, 1864, and named itself the Union National Convention. The Republican leaders desired to appeal to Union sentiment and do away as far as possible with partisan influence. The platform, which was unanimously adopted, was a statement of "unconditional Union" principles and pledged the convention to put down rebellion by force of arms. Abraham Lincoln was nominated for a second term by the vote of every delegate except those from Missouri who had been instructed to vote for Gen. Grant. The nomination then was made unanimous. Andrew Johnson of Tennessee, a leading Southern Democrat who had been staunch in his loyalty to the Union, was nominated for Vice-President.

The Democratic party^qv^ met in convention on Aug. 29, at Chicago. Its platform declared the war a failure and advocated the immediate cessation of hostilities and the restoration of the Union by peaceable means. The convention nominated Gen. George B. McClellan for President and George H. Pendleton for Vice-President. McClellan accepted the nomination but at the same time virtually repudiated the platform, for he was thoroughly loyal to the cause of the Union.

At first it appeared that the Democrats might defeat Lincoln, but the victories of the Union Army in the field proved that the war was not a failure and rallied the people to the support of Lincoln and Johnson and the Union cause. The election took place on Nov. 8. For the first time in our history certain states, those of the South, deliberately declined to choose electors for the choice of President. Lincoln carried every state that took part in the election but New Jersey, Delaware and Kentucky. He received 212 electoral votes. McClellan received 21. Lincoln was given a popular majority of only 494,567 in a total of 4,166,537. This election was one of the most vital in the history of the country since upon its result might depend the perpetuation of the national Union.

[W. S. Myers, *General George B. McClellan;* Edward A. Stanwood, *A History of the Presidency.*]

WILLIAM STARR MYERS

Campaign of 1868 and of 1872, THE. The issues in 1868 were Southern reconstruction^qv^ and the "Ohio Idea."^qv^ Horatio Seymour of New

York and Frank Blair of Missouri, the Democratic[qv] nominees, ran on a platform calling for a restoration of the rights of the Southern states and payment of the war bonds in greenbacks[qv]. Alarmed by Democratic victories in 1867, the Republicans[qv] nominated the war hero, Grant, and Schuyler Colfax of Indiana. Their platform acclaimed the success of reconstruction and denounced as repudiation the payment of the bonds in greenbacks.

Personal attacks on the candidates and Republican "waving the bloody shirt"[qv] featured the campaign. An effort to replace the Democratic nominees in October failed but foreshadowed defeat. Grant received 214 electoral votes to Seymour's 80, and nearly 53% of the popular vote, receiving 3,012,833 votes to 2,709,249 for Seymour. Seymour carried eight states. The result was a personal victory for Grant rather than for Republican policies.

Dissatisfaction with the reconstruction policy and a desire for reform led to a Liberal Republican[qv] organization, supported by tariff and civil-service reformers, independent editors and disgruntled politicians. The new party nominated Horace Greeley, with B. Gratz Brown of Missouri, to oppose Grant's re-election in 1872. Its platform demanded civil-service reform[qv], universal amnesty and specie payment[qv]. The tariff[qv] issue was straddled to please Greeley, a protectionist. The Democrats accepted the Liberal Republican platform and nominees. The Greeley campaign lacked enthusiasm, and he was mercilessly lampooned. Grant received 286 electoral votes to Greeley's 66, and over 55% of the popular vote, receiving 3,597,132 votes to 2,834,125 for Greeley.

[C. H. Coleman, *The Election of 1868;* E. D. Ross, *The Liberal Republican Movement.*]

CHARLES H. COLEMAN

Campaign of 1876, THE, is memorable because it resulted in the famous disputed presidential election. The leading aspirant for the Republican[qv] nomination was James G. Blaine of Maine. His name was presented to the national convention at Cincinnati by Robert G. Ingersoll in a striking speech in which he dubbed Blaine "the Plumed Knight." Among the other candidates were Benjamin H. Bristow of Kentucky, Roscoe Conkling of New York, Oliver P. Morton of Indiana and Rutherford B. Hayes of Ohio. For six ballots Blaine led the field, but on the seventh a stampede to Rutherford B. Hayes resulted in his nomination. William A. Wheeler was named as his running mate. The platform indorsed the Resumption Act[qv] and eulogized the Republican party for its work during the Civil War and Reconstruction[qqv].

Thomas F. Bayard of Delaware, Allen G. Thurman of Ohio, Winfield Scott Hancock of Pennsylvania and Thomas A. Hendricks of Indiana sought the Democratic[qv] nomination, but the logical contender was Gov. Samuel J. Tilden of New York, who was named on the first ballot. Hendricks was then nominated for the Vice-Presidency. The scandals of the Grant administration were denounced in unsparing terms (*see* Crédit Mobilier; Whisky Ring; Sanborn Contracts) and "Reform" was declared to be the paramount issue. Repeal of the clause of the act of 1875 providing for the resumption of specie payments[qv] was advocated, but Mr. Tilden personally was known to be a sound-money man rather than a Greenbacker[qv]. The platform also declared in favor of civil-service reform[qv].

In the campaign the Democratic speakers dwelt heavily upon the scandals under Republican rule and contended that only through a change of men and parties could there be any real reform. Republican orators resorted to "bloody shirt"[qv] tactics—that is, revived the Civil War issues—questioned Tilden's loyalty during that conflict and praised Hayes' military record: four honorable wounds and a brevet major generalcy. In the North the campaign was a quiet one, but in some of the Southern states attempts to intimidate Negro voters produced violent disorders and considerable bloodshed.

Early returns on election night indicated the election of Tilden, but presently it appeared that the result would be in doubt. When the electoral colleges met and voted, Tilden received 184 unquestioned votes, Hayes 165; with 4 votes of Florida, the 8 votes of Louisiana, the 7 votes of South Carolina and 1 vote of Oregon claimed by both parties. After a protracted, bitter dispute, Congress created an Electoral Commission of five Senators, five Representatives and five judges of the Supreme Court to help decide the result. Of the Senators, three were to be Republicans and two Democrats; of the Representatives three were to be Democrats and two Republicans; four of the judges, two Republicans and two Democrats, were designated by their districts and they were to choose the fifth judge. It was expected that the fifth judge would be David Davis, but his election to the Senate by the Democrats in the Illinois legislature gave him an excuse to decline the thankless task. The choice then fell upon Joseph P. Bradley, who had been appointed to the bench as a Republican, but some of whose decisions made him acceptable, temporarily, to the Democrats

In case the two Houses of Congress voting separately refused to accept any return the dispute was to be referred to the Commission, whose decision was to be final unless it was rejected by both Houses. The two Houses, voting separately on strict party lines, did disagree. Decision, therefore, rested with the Commission, which, in all cases, by a vote of 8 to 7 (Bradley voting with the majority), refused to go behind the election results as certified by the state authorities (in the case of Oregon by the Secretary of State) and declared in favor of the Republican contenders. In each case the Senate accepted this decision, the House rejected it. All the disputed votes were therefore counted for Hayes and Wheeler and they were declared elected.

[P. L. Haworth, *The Hayes-Tilden Election;* J. H. Dougherty, *The Electoral System of the United States.*]

PAUL L. HAWORTH

Campaign of 1880, THE, took place during a business revival and with no definite issue before the country. It was routine politics. The Republicans[qv] overcame a serious split between groups headed by James G. Blaine and Roscoe Conkling respectively, by nominating James A. Garfield, a member of neither faction, over President Grant, supported by the Conkling wing for a third term. Against Garfield the Democrats[qv] nominated Winfield Scott Hancock, a nonpolitical Civil War general; but their party had no positive program, was discredited by its factious opposition to the Hayes administration and was defeated by a close vote. The Republicans carried the "doubtful states" and regained control over Congress. The popular vote was: Garfield, 4,454,416; Hancock, 4,444,952. The electoral vote was: Garfield, 214; Hancock, 155.

[E. E. Oberholtzer, *United States Since the Civil War,* Vol. IV; T. C. Smith, *Life of James A. Garfield.*]

THEODORE CLARKE SMITH

Campaign of 1884, THE, fought primarily between James G. Blaine and Grover Cleveland as Republican and Democratic[qqv] candidates respectively, was one of the most vituperative in American history. There were several reasons why it became relentlessly personal in character. From the moment of Blaine's nomination at Chicago on June 6 he came under heavy fire from the reform element of all parties. He was believed to be allied with the spoils element in Republican politics; he had an unhappy record for baiting the South; he favored certain big business interests; and his railroad transactions had raised a suspicion that he had used his official position for personal profit. To divert attention from these attacks certain Republicans published evidence that Cleveland, nominated on July 10 at Chicago, was the father of an illegitimate son born in Buffalo some ten years earlier. Of serious issues between the two parties there were virtually none; both had good reason not to meddle seriously with the currency question or tariff[qv], and international affairs attracted little attention. One leading feature of the campaign was the secession of a large body of Republicans who could not stomach Blaine and who became Cleveland Democrats or Mugwumps[qv]. Another feature was the open enmity of Tammany Hall[qv], under Boss John Kelly, for Cleveland, and the success of it and other malcontents in carrying many Irish voters over to Blaine or to the new Anti-Monopoly party[qv] headed by Benjamin F. Butler. After exchanges which one observer compared to the billingsgate of quarreling tenement dwellers, the two parties approached election day running neck and neck. Democratic victory was finally decided by the vote of New York state, in which the Rev. Dr. Burchard's[qv] "Rum, Romanism and Rebellion" speech at a reception to Blaine, the "Belshazzar's Feast" of Republican millionaires and politicians at Delmonico's just before election and Roscoe Conkling's knifing of Blaine all played a part. Cleveland obtained a popular vote of 4,874,986 against Blaine's 4,851,981, and an electoral vote of 219 against Blaine's 182. Butler's popular vote was just over 175,000, and that of John P. St. John, Prohibition[qv] candidate, was just over 150,000.

[Allan Nevins, *Grover Cleveland—A Study in Courage.*]

ALLAN NEVINS

Campaign of 1888, THE, turned chiefly on the tariff[qv] issue, and resulted in the election of Benjamin Harrison over Grover Cleveland by a majority of the electoral college[qv] but not of the popular vote. The Republicans[qv] had approached the election with scant hope of victory, for Cleveland had proved an admirable President, when his annual message of 1887, devoted entirely to arguments for tariff reform, gave them new heart. The issue was one on which they could rally nearly all manufacturers, most general business and perhaps a majority of workingmen. Benjamin Harrison, who represented extreme high-tariff demands, was nominated by the Republicans at Chicago on June 25, after Blaine had withdrawn for reasons of health, and John Sherman and Walter Q. Gresham, whose tariff views were moderate, had failed to gain strength. Levi P. Morton was named for Vice-

President. Harrison, supported by Blaine, by manufacturing interests who were induced by the Republican Chairman, Matthew S. Quay, to subscribe large campaign funds and by Civil War veterans hungry for pension[qv] legislation, waged an aggressive campaign. His speech-making abilities made a deep impression on the country. Cleveland, who was renominated by the Democrats[qv] at St. Louis early in June, felt that his presidential office made it improper for him to do active campaigning; his running-mate, Allen G. Thurman of Ohio, was too old and infirm to be anything but a liability to the party; and campaign funds were slender. Worst of all for the Democrats, their national chairman, Sen. Calvin S. Brice of Ohio, held high-tariff convictions, was allied with big business and refused to put his heart into the battle. Two weeks before election day the Republicans published an indiscreet letter by Lord Sackville, the British minister, hinting to a supposed British subject that Cleveland would probably be more friendly to England than Harrison; and though Cleveland at once had Sackville recalled, the incident cost him many Irish votes (*see* Sackville-West Incident). Cleveland received 5,540,329 popular votes, Harrison but 5,439,853; but Cleveland had only 168 electors against Harrison's 233. Charles B. Fisk of New Jersey, Prohibition[qv] candidate, polled 249,506 votes; Alson J. Streeter of Illinois, Union Labor nominee, 146,935.

[Edward A. Stanwood, *A History of the Presidency.*]

ALLAN NEVINS

Campaign of 1892, THE, brought the re-election of Grover Cleveland over Benjamin Harrison by a majority the size of which surprised observers of both parties. Cleveland had been named on the first ballot at the Democratic[qv] convention in Chicago, although David B. Hill of New York had made a demagogic attempt to displace him. Harrison, who had estranged the professional politicians of his party, who had quarreled with its most popular figure, Blaine, and who had impressed the country as cold and unlikable, was reluctantly accepted by the Republicans[qv] at Minneapolis on June 10. It was impossible to repudiate his administration. However, the McKinley Tariff[qv] of 1890 had excited widespread discontent, the Sherman Silver-Purchase Act[qv] of the same year had angered the conservative East and heavy Federal expenditures had caused general uneasiness. Cleveland's firm stand on behalf of the gold standard and low tariffs[qqv] and his known strength of character commended him to large numbers of independent voters. One factor adverse to the Republicans was the great strength manifested by the Populists[qv], who polled 1,040,000 votes for James B. Weaver of Iowa and James G. Field of Virginia; most of this coming from old Republican strongholds in the Middle West. Another factor was the labor war at Homestead[qv], Pa., which showed that the highly protected steel industry did not properly pass on its tariff benefits to the worker. Cleveland, with a popular vote of 5,556,543, had 277 electors; Harrison, with a popular vote of 5,175,582, had 145; while Weaver won 22 electoral votes.

[Allan Nevins, *Grover Cleveland—A Study in Courage.*]

ALLAN NEVINS

Campaign of 1896, THE, ended a twenty-two-year period in which neither major party had been able to control the National Government for more than the life of a single Congress; it ushered in a period of Republican[qv] domination which lasted until 1911.

Favored by Mark Hanna's cannily managed campaign, William McKinley of Ohio was named on the first ballot by the Republican convention meeting at St. Louis. The traditional party platform was adopted with the exception of a declaration for the gold standard[qv] until bimetallism[qv] could be secured by international agreement. A bloc of Western delegates bolted and organized the Silver Republican party[qv].

There was no dominant candidate for the Democratic[qv] nomination. The important contest was over the platform. As presented to the delegates, it was an anti-administration document favoring free silver[qv] at the sixteen-to-one ratio, criticizing the use of injunctions[qv] in labor disputes and denouncing the overthrow of the Federal income tax[qv]. In its support William Jennings Bryan delivered his "Cross of Gold"[qv] oration and endeared himself to the silver delegates by his effective answers to the criticisms of the administration orators.

The enthusiasm growing out of that speech gave impetus to Bryan's candidacy for the presidential nomination. Back of this was also the long campaign he had waged by personal conferences, speeches and correspondence with the inflationist delegates from the South and West. Another factor was the bolting Republicans and the Populists[qv], who saw themselves being forced to support the Democratic nominee and demanded some one not too closely identified with the regular Democracy. Bryan appealed to the delegates as the Democrat who could unite the silver and agrarian factions.

The Populists, Silver Republicans and National Silver party members joined the Democrats in support of Bryan. The administration Democrats placed a National Democratic ticket in the field to hold conservative Democratic votes away from him.

The campaign was highly spectacular. The Democrats exploited Bryan's oratory by sending him on speaking tours back and forth across the country during which enormous crowds came out to hear him. In sharp contrast, the Republican management kept McKinley at his home in Canton, Ohio, where carefully selected delegations made formal calls and listened to "front porch" speeches by the candidate. More important were the flood of advertising, the funds for building local organizations and the large group of speakers on the hustings, which were maintained by Hanna's organization. The metropolitan press, like the other business groups—except the silver miners—was essentially a unit in opposing Bryan. The results showed a sharp city-versus-rural division, with Bryan carrying the Solid South[qv] and most of the trans-Missouri states. The remainder, including California, Oregon, North Dakota, Kentucky and Maryland, went to McKinley. With him were elected a Republican House and a Senate in which various minor party members held a nominal balance of power. The popular vote was unusually large, each candidate receiving larger totals than any previous candidate of his party, McKinley's vote being 7,098,474 and Bryan's 6,379,830. Their electoral vote was 271 and 176 respectively.

[E. E. Robinson, *The Evolution of American Political Parties;* Marian Silveus, *The Antecedents of the Campaign of 1896*, unpublished thesis, University of Wisconsin, 1933.]

ELMER ELLIS

Campaign of 1900, THE, carried over the presidential candidates and most of the issues of 1896. With the trend of prices upward, the pressure for inflation[qv] had declined, and the expansion of American control over new territories had created the issue of imperialism[qv].

At the Republican[qv] convention in Philadelphia a combination of circumstances forced Hanna and McKinley to accept Theodore Roosevelt as the vice-presidential candidate. The party's position on the new territories was defined as American retention with "the largest measure of self-government consistent with their welfare and our duties."

When the Democrats[qv] met at Kansas City, they were unwilling to accept the conservatives' proposal to forget the last platform and make anti-imperialism the only issue. The 1896 platform was reindorsed, an antitrust plank added and imperialism designated the "paramount issue." The campaign lacked the fire of 1896. The Republicans emphasized the "full dinner pail"[qv] and the danger threatening it from the Democratic platform; the Democrats stressed the growth of monopolies[qv] under the McKinley administration and the danger of imperialistic government. The result was a more emphatic Republican victory than in 1896, one generally interpreted as an endorsement of both McKinley's domestic and foreign policies. The popular vote was: McKinley, 7,218,491; Bryan, 6,356,-734. McKinley obtained 292 electoral votes to 155 for Bryan. This election made Roosevelt's elevation to the Presidency automatic upon McKinley's death in 1901.

[E. E. Robinson, *The Evolution of American Political Parties;* Edward A. Stanwood, *A History of the Presidency.*]

ELMER ELLIS

Campaign of 1904, THE. Theodore Roosevelt, who succeeded to the Presidency on the death of McKinley in 1901 (*see* Assassinations, Political), ardently hoped to be nominated and elected "in his own right." The death of Marcus A. Hanna of Ohio, whom the "big business"[qv] interests of the country would have preferred, made possible the President's nomination by acclamation when the Republican[qv] convention met in Chicago, June 21. Charles W. Fairbanks of Indiana was chosen for second place.

The Democrats[qv], meeting at St. Louis, July 6, pointedly turned their backs upon "Bryanism" by omitting from their platform all reference to the money question (*see* Free Silver) and by nominating for President, Alton B. Parker, a conservative New York judge, who at once pledged himself to maintain the gold standard[qv], and for Vice-President, Henry Gassaway Davis, a wealthy West Virginia octogenarian. Business leaders, however, more afraid of the Democratic party than of Roosevelt, contributed so heavily to the Republican campaign chest that Parker rashly charged "blackmail." Corporations, he said, were being forced to contribute in return for the suppression of evidence that the Government had against them. Roosevelt, indignantly denying the charge, won by a landslide that reclaimed Missouri from the Solid South[qv], gave him 336 electoral votes to Parker's 140 and a popular plurality of 2,540,067. Prohibitionist, Populist, Socialist and Socialist-Labor[qqv] candidates received only negligible support.

[Edward A. Stanwood, *A History of the Presidency.*]

JOHN D. HICKS

Campaign of 1908, THE. Theodore Roosevelt, though at the height of his popularity, refused to be a third-term candidate in 1908, but swung his support in the Republican[qv] convention to William Howard Taft, who was nominated.

The Democratic[qv] convention was as completely dominated by William Jennings Bryan, who became its nominee. Party differences were not significant. After an apathetic campaign Bryan carried only the Solid South[qv], Kansas, Colorado and Nevada, though he received 43% of the popular vote, securing 6,409,106 to Taft's 7,679,006. Taft's electoral vote was 321; Bryan's 162. The Republicans won the Presidency and both Houses of Congress.

[Samuel Eliot Morison and Henry Steele Commager, *The Growth of the American Republic.*]

CHESTER LLOYD JONES

Campaign of 1912, The, marked the culmination of the progressive movement[qv] in national politics and resulted in the return of the Democrats[qv] after sixteen years of Republican[qv] Presidents.

The struggle for the Republican nomination became a sanguinary battle between the progressive and conservative wings, aided in each case by personal followings and some division of support from large interests. In the beginning it was the progressive, LaFollette, against the incumbent, Taft. But former President Theodore Roosevelt, who had been largely responsible for Taft's nomination in 1908, entered the race to rally behind him Republicans who believed Taft had been too friendly with the conservative Old Guard. The influence in Taft's hands was sufficient to return delegates pledged to him in most cases where they were named by conventions, but Roosevelt or LaFollette were successful in all states save one where presidential primaries[qv] were held. The conservative controlled National Committee placed Taft delegates on the temporary roll in all contests and the small majority resulting gave Taft the nomination. Roosevelt was later nominated by the newly organized Progressive party[qv], consisting largely of Republican bolters.

The contest for the Democratic nomination was also hard fought with both of the leading candidates accepted as progressives. Champ Clark led from the beginning and had an actual majority in the convention for a time, but when Bryan transferred his support to the second progressive, Woodrow Wilson, a shift began which resulted in the latter's nomination. All three party platforms[qv] were unusually favorable to progressive policies. Wilson, backed by a united party, won easily and Roosevelt was second. There was an unusual amount of shifting of party loyalties, although most Democrats voted for Wilson and most Republicans for Roosevelt or Taft. Wilson's popular vote was 6,296,547, Roosevelt's was 4,126,020 and Taft's was 3,486,720. Their electoral vote was, respectively, 435, 88 and 8. The Democrats won majorities in both branches of Congress. In spite of the three-way contest, a fourth candidate, Eugene V. Debs, Socialist, secured approximately 900,000 votes, the highest percentage of the total vote his party ever received.

[Edward A. Stanwood, *A History of the Presidency;* E. E. Robinson, *Evolution of American Political Parties.*]

ELMER ELLIS

Campaign of 1916, The, reunited the Republican party[qv] and determined that American foreign policy should be left in Wilson's hands. The Republicans reunited when, after the nomination of Charles Evans Hughes, Theodore Roosevelt, already nominated by the rapidly declining Progressive party[qv], announced support of the ticket.

There was no opposition to Wilson's renomination. The Democrats[qv] defended the policies of the administration, especially the Underwood Tariff[qv] and the measures for the regulation of business. They also praised the foreign policy[qv] as one which had kept us out of war and preserved national honor.

The Republicans attacked the policies of the administration, promised a "stronger" foreign policy and were supported by the more extreme partisans of both alliances in the European war.

The results were in doubt for several days because of the close vote in several states. Wilson won the Presidency, carrying Ohio, New Hampshire, the South and most of the border and trans-Missouri states, including California, with an electoral vote of 277, against 254 for Hughes. The popular vote was: Wilson, 9,127,695; Hughes, 8,533,507. Congress remained Democratic only because independent members of the House were friendly.

[E. E. Robinson, *Evolution of American Political Parties.*]

ELMER ELLIS

Campaign of 1920, The. The debate on the League of Nations[qv] determined the alignment of political forces in the spring of 1920. The Republicans[qv] were confident; the wounds of the intraparty strife of 1912 had been healed; the mistaken strategy of 1916 admitted; and the conservative mood of the country was easily interpreted. They met in convention in Chicago, could not agree upon any one of the leading pre-convention candidates, Frank O. Lowden, Hiram

Johnson or Leonard Wood, and nominated Warren G. Harding, Senator from Ohio, on the tenth ballot. Calvin Coolidge, Governor of Massachusetts, was nominated for the Vice-Presidency.

The Democrats^qv met in San Francisco. None of the discussed candidates, William G. McAdoo, Alfred E. Smith, John W. Davis, A. Mitchell Palmer or James M. Cox, commanded a great following. The last-named was nominated on the forty-fourth ballot, with Franklin D. Roosevelt as vice-presidential nominee.

Neither platform was unexpected or significant on domestic issues. The Republicans attacked the President and opposed American entrance into the League.

The Socialist party^qv, meeting in May, nominated Eugene Debs for the fifth time. A Farmer-Labor^qv ticket appeared also. The Democratic national committee supported Wilson's appeal for a "solemn referendum" on the covenant of the League; Cox waged a persistent and vigorous campaign; Harding, remaining at his home for the most part, contented himself with vague generalizations. Neither candidate had been nationally known at the outset of the contest, and no clear-cut issue developed and no real contest transpired. The total vote cast was 26,748,224. The Nineteenth Amendment^qv had been proclaimed in August and in every state women were entitled to vote. Harding had 60.35% of the total vote cast. Cox won the electoral vote in only eleven states, receiving 127 electoral votes to Harding's 404. The Socialist vote was 902,310, but the strength of all the third parties totaled only 5.52%.

[E. E. Robinson, *The Presidential Vote, 1896-1932.*]

EDGAR EUGENE ROBINSON

Campaign of 1924, THE. As in 1920, so in 1924, the candidates were new in a presidential canvass. The Republican^qv convention meeting in Cleveland, with a few scattering votes in dissent, nominated Calvin Coolidge, who as Vice-President had succeeded to the Presidency in the summer of 1923. The vice-presidential nomination, refused by several, was accepted by Charles G. Dawes. The platform was marked by extreme conservatism.

The Democrats^qv met in New York and were in almost continuous session for two and a half weeks. Not only was there serious division upon the matter of American adherence to the League of Nations^qv and upon the proposed denunciation of the Ku Klux Klan^qv, but also upon the choice of the nominee. Each of the two leading candidates, Alfred E. Smith and William G. McAdoo, was sufficiently powerful to prevent the nomination of the other, and finally on the 103rd ballot the nomination went to John W. Davis. Charles W. Bryan of Nebraska was nominated for Vice-President. The platform called for a popular referendum on the League of Nations.

A Conference for Progressive Political Action brought about a series of meetings and eventually a widespread support of Sen. Robert M. LaFollette^qv in his independent candidacy, with Burton K. Wheeler as his running mate. LaFollette's platform, in which appeared most of the progressive^qv proposals of the previous twenty years, was endorsed by the Socialist party^qv and the officers of the American Federation of Labor^qv. So real did the threat of the third party candidacy appear to be that much of the attack of the Republicans was upon LaFollette, who waged an aggressive campaign.

The total vote cast exceeded that of 1920 by two and a third million, but because of the vote cast for LaFollette (nearly 5,000,000) that cast for Republican and for Democratic tickets was less than four years earlier, Coolidge securing 15,718,211 votes, and Davis, 8,385,283. LaFollette carried Wisconsin. Coolidge topped the poll in thirty-five states, receiving 382 electoral votes, leaving the electoral vote for Davis in only twelve states, or 136 votes.

[E. E. Robinson, *The Presidential Vote, 1896-1932.*]

EDGAR EUGENE ROBINSON

Campaign of 1928, THE. On Aug. 2, 1927, President Calvin Coolidge announced that he "did not choose to run" for President in 1928. The majority of the leaders of the Republican party^qv were undecided with regard to the candidate they should support. A popular movement having its strength in the rank and file of the voters forced the nomination of Herbert Hoover on the first ballot at the Republican National Convention which met at Kansas City, Mo., on June 12, 1928. The platform contained strong support of the usual Republican policies such as a protective tariff^qv and sound business administration. It advocated the observance and rigorous enforcement of the Eighteenth Amendment^qv. Charles Curtis was nominated for Vice-President.

The Democrats^qv met at Houston, Texas, and on June 28 nominated Alfred E. Smith for President. They then nominated Joseph T. Robinson for Vice-President. The platform did not differ strikingly from that of the Republicans. The contest became one between rival personalities. Gov. Smith, an avowed "wet," took a stand in favor of a change in the Prohibition Amendment, and advocated that the question of prohibition and its enforcement be left to the determination of the individual states.

At the election on Nov. 6 Mr. Hoover was overwhelmingly successful. He carried forty states, including five from the old South, with a total of 444 electoral votes. Gov. Smith carried eight states with an electoral vote of 87. The popular plurality of Mr. Hoover over Gov. Smith was 6,375,747 in a total vote of 36,879,414.

[W. S. Myers, *The Republican Party.*]

WILLIAM STARR MYERS

Campaign of 1932 and of 1936, The. The presidential campaign of 1932 began in earnest with the holding of the Republican National Convention at Chicago on June 14–16. President Herbert Hoover and Vice-President Charles Curtis were renominated on the first ballot. The platform praised the Hoover record including his program for combatting the depression*qv*. After a long debate a "wet-dry" plank on prohibition*qv* was adopted which favored giving the people an opportunity to pass on a repeal amendment.

The Democratic National Convention was also held at Chicago, June 27–July 2, 1932. On the fourth ballot, Gov. Franklin Delano Roosevelt of New York was nominated for the Presidency, defeating Alfred E. Smith and ten other candidates. The platform pledged economy, a sound currency, unemployment relief, old-age and unemployment insurance under state laws, the "restoration of agriculture" and repeal of the Eighteenth Amendment together with immediate legalization of beer*qqv*.

After a campaign featured by Mr. Roosevelt's promise of "a new deal,"*qv* the elections were held on Nov. 5. The popular vote for each party was as follows: Democratic, 22,821,857; Republican, 15,761,841; Socialist, 884,781; Socialist-Labor, 33,276; Communist, 102,991; Prohibition, 81,869; Liberty, 53,425; and Farm-Labor, 7309. The electoral vote was 472 for the Democrats and 59 for the Republicans.

In 1936 the Republican National Convention was held at Cleveland beginning on June 9. Gov. Alfred M. Landon of Kansas and Frank Knox, Chicago publisher, were nominated for the Presidency and Vice-Presidency, respectively. The platform strongly denounced the "New Deal administration," from both constitutional and economic viewpoints. It pledged the Republicans "To maintain the American system of constitutional and local self-government" and "To preserve the American system of free enterprise."

The Democratic National Convention assembled at Philadelphia on June 25 for what proved to be a ratification meeting for the New Deal. President Roosevelt and Vice-President Garner were renominated without opposition. The platform vigorously defended the New Deal and pledged its continuance.

When the election was held on Nov. 3, the Democrats again won an overwhelming victory, carrying every state except Maine and Vermont. The popular vote for each party was as follows: Democratic, 27,476,673; Republican, 16,679,583; Union, 882,479; Socialist, 187,720; Communist, 80,159; Prohibition, 37,847; and Socialist-Labor, 12,777. The Democrats received 523 electoral votes while the Republicans received only 8. The popular vote was the largest ever polled in an election in the United States.

[*American Year Book*, 1933, 1936; *World Almanac*, 1933, 1934, 1937, 1938.]

ERIK McKINLEY ERIKSSON

Campaign Pledges. Campaigns of the modern type are usually dated from that of 1840*qv*, when the famous slogan, "Tippecanoe and Tyler Too," inaugurated the era of political fanfare and mass appeal. Prior to the election of Jackson, nomination of presidential candidates had been by congressional caucuses*qv*, which had issued addresses to the people, the forerunners of the later party platforms. When the national nominating conventions*qv* began to develop after 1831, the custom became general of stating the party program in specific statements of the parties' objectives if returned to power. Today the platform*qv* has become an important element in campaign strategy. Platform pledges are generally of two kinds. On the more noncontroversial issues, parties tend to be precise in their advocacy of, or opposition to, particular proposals. On questions on which there is widespread popular disagreement, the platform pledges frequently become vague and noncommittal. Sectional*qv* issues, whether geographical, racial or economic (if these can be distinguished), are likely to fall in the latter group. Questions of a political nature, on which national opinion has crystallized, are likely to be treated with fervor and directness. The influence of the minor parties, and of many pressure groups*qv*, in advocating specific reforms and so educating public opinion on them, has been important in developing party policy on many questions, such as regulation of public utilities or woman suffrage.

Beside the general campaign pledges enunciated in party platforms, candidates for office often make specific campaign pledges implementing the platforms or recognizing and accepting responsibility for national or local demands. Presidential candidates rarely go beyond the frontiers of their party's pledges in defining their position, but on controversial questions sometimes clarify their personal position. Congressional candidates not infrequently have to state their attitude toward specific planks in order to conciliate local interests. It is significant to note that a specific campaign pledge is one of the two exemptions allowed Congressmen in failing to uphold a caucus decision on the floor of the House of Representatives.

PHILLIPS BRADLEY

Campaign Resources and Uses. Prior to 1888 little attention was paid to the matter of conducting political campaigns. In that year, with the tariff[T] as the chief issue, the era of large campaign funds began. During the 1892 campaign the Republicans spent about $1,500,000; while in 1896, during the free-silver campaign, they raised $3,500,000. During the same campaign the Democrats raised a fund estimated at from $650,000 to $1,700,000. These amounts were not exceeded until 1916. The year 1920 saw campaign funds rise to a new high peak. In 1921 there was published a report on this campaign compiled by the Senate Committee on Privileges and Elections of which William S. Kenyon was chairman. This report showed that the two major parties spent a total of $10,338,509 during the campaign. Of this amount, the Republicans spent $8,100,739 and the Democrats, $2,237,770. The report included the expenditures of the national, senatorial, congressional and state committees but did not include the amounts spent by district, county and city committees or the sums collected and spent by non-party committees, such as the League to Enforce Peace.

In dealing with the subject of campaign expenditures, one must give consideration to the uses made of the money. While these expenditures have increased much faster than the size of the electorate, the costs of campaigning have also multiplied. Generally speaking, more money is spent for publicity than for any other purpose, whether the election is national, state or local. Enormous sums are required for newspaper and magazine advertisements, billboard posters, pamphlets, buttons, banners and placards. Another important item of expense is the maintenance of headquarters for party organizations ranging from the national committee down to the city or even precinct committees. Money raised by the national committee must be apportioned, in part, to the state committees. Beginning especially with the campaign of 1924, radio[T] has become an indispensable part of political campaigns, and large sums are required to purchase time. Furthermore, speakers must be secured for meetings in all parts of the country. In addition, heavy expenditures are required for field workers, for election-day expenses and for miscellaneous items such as the preparation of registration lists and traveling expenses.

Because of the general belief that corruption and large campaign funds go hand in hand, both the state and Federal governments have passed regulative laws, usually referred to as "corrupt practices acts." Beginning with New York in 1890 all the states except Illinois, Mississippi, Rhode Island and Tennessee had, by 1926, enacted some sort of legislation to deal with campaign funds. While they differ considerably, all the laws have provisions dealing with bribery. Only thirty-three states have laws which may be described as fairly comprehensive. These usually require publicity regarding receipts and expenditures; limit the expenditures by candidates; prohibit expenditures for any purpose except those enumerated in the laws; prohibit contributions to campaign funds by corporations; and define persons and committees who may receive and spend money in political campaigns. As a whole the state corrupt practices acts are defective in that they lack adequate publicity and enforcement provisions. Nevertheless, the legislation has raised "the moral tone" of elections.

Except for a provision in the Civil Service Act of 1883 (*see* Pendleton Act, The) which prohibited contributions for political purposes by civilian employees of the United States, the Federal Government enacted no corrupt practices legislation until 1907. Then a law was passed prohibiting national banks and corporations from making contributions to the campaign fund of any candidate for a national office. In 1910 the first law was passed by Congress to require publicity for the campaign funds of Congressmen. This Campaign Expense Act was amended in 1911 by extending its provisions to Senators; by limiting the amount that could be spent; and by extending Federal regulation to nominations as well as elections. This last provision was invalidated, however, by the Supreme Court, which in 1921, in the case of Newberry v. U. S.[T], ruled that a primary is not an election and therefore not subject to regulation by Federal legislation. In 1925 Congress enacted the "Federal Corrupt Practices Act" which applies exclusively to elections. It is largely a consolidation of previous Federal legislation. Periodic reports of expenditures are required, not only from party committees but also from non-party committees. The total expenditures by candidates for the United

States Senate or House in general may not exceed the maximum fixed by state laws.

Unquestionably, the Federal corrupt practices legislation, together with the state legislation, has eliminated many evils previously connected with political campaigns. Like the state laws, the Federal legislation is defective in its publicity and enforcement provisions. The legislation has not proved adequate to prevent all political contributions by governmental employees, especially through such devices as party dinners for which a price of $5 to as high as $100 is charged. Nor has the legislation prevented campaign books containing the President's autograph from being sold at high prices to corporations. The extension of governmental activity after 1929 created new campaign resources not always to be measured in terms of dollars. The party in power, by liberal Federal "benefits" to farmers, by relief to the unemployed through the Works Progress Administration and other agencies, by grants for public works through the Public Works Administration[qqv], as well as other devices, created groups whose self-interest would dictate political support for that party. In 1934 and 1936 these new "vested interests" unquestionably were an important source of strength to the party controlling the Federal Government. Because of repeated protests, particularly against playing politics with relief workers, the Senate, in 1938, created a Campaign Investigating Committee headed by Sen. Morris Sheppard of Texas. Prior to the elections on Nov. 8, 1938, the committee received about 1000 complaints of improper political activity. It carried on investigations in sixteen states. Most of the complaints were discarded as groundless but 300 charges involving 183 cases were retained on the committee's docket. As a result, Congress, in February, 1939, prohibited political activity on the part of the officials of the Works Progress Administration. (*See also* Hatch Bill.)

[James K. Pollock, *Party Campaign Funds;* Edward M. Sait, *American Parties and Elections.*]

ERIK McKINLEY ERIKSSON

Campaign Songs are partisan ditties used in American political canvasses and more especially in presidential contests. The words were commonly set to established melodies like "Yankee Doodle," "Hail, Columbia," "Rosin the Bow," "Hail to the Chief," "John Brown's Body," "Dixie" and "O Tannenbaum" ("Maryland, My Maryland"); or to tunes widely popular at the time, such as "Few Days," "Champagne Charlie," "The Wearing of the Green" from "Arrah-na-Pogue" or "Down in a Coal Mine," which served for "Up in the White House." Perhaps the best known of them was "Tippecanoe and Tyler Too,"[qv] in which words by Alexander C. Ross (1812–83) were adapted to the folk tune, "Little Pigs." First heard at Zanesville, Ohio, this spread rapidly over the country, furnishing a party slogan. It has been said: "What the Marseilles Hymn was to Frenchmen, 'Tippecanoe and Tyler Too' was to the Whigs of 1840." In 1872 an attempt was made to revive the air for "Greeley Is the Real True Blue."

The words, sometimes with music, of campaign songs were distributed in paper-covered song books or "songsters." Among these were the *Log Cabin Song Book* of 1840 and *Hutchinson's Republican Songster for the Campaign of 1860*, compiled by J. W. Hutchinson. For many years national campaigns included itinerant stump-speakers[qv], live animals, fife-and-drum corps, red fire, floats, transparencies and rousing mass meetings in courthouses and town halls. Glee clubs were organized to introduce campaign songs and to lead audiences and marchers in singing them. The songs were real factors in holding the interest of crowds, emphasizing issues, developing enthusiasm and satirizing opponents. With changes in the methods of campaigning, the campaign song declined as a popular expression.

[S. L. Cook, *Torchlight Parade.*]

G. S. BRYAN

Campaigns, Political. A political campaign is a drive for votes made by parties, their various auxiliary organizations and candidates, the aim being to achieve the election of the latter by a majority or plurality as required by constitutional or other legal provisions. Campaigns are also waged for nominations in conventions or direct primary[qqv] elections, and for or against initiative and referendum[qqv] projects. In the last-mentioned case they are seldom hotly contested since the element of party or personal rivalry is absent.

So far as the areas involved are concerned political campaigns in the United States range all the way from the quadrennial national contests to small township or borough affairs. Since the beginning of our national history the number of voters who must be reached has increased enormously, partly of course as a result of the growth of population, but also because of the extension of the right of suffrage[qv] to poorer white males prior to 1850, to Negroes[qv] following the Civil War, and finally to women culminating with the adoption of the Nineteenth Amendment[qv] to the Constitution in 1920. Estimates of the proportion of the total population qualified to vote are as follows: in 1789, 4%; at present from 40 to 45%.

With expansion on so gigantic a scale confronting them, party organizations in the United States developed *pari passu* until they have become by far the largest and most complicated in any democratic country. As the active agent in campaigns they parallel the structure of our constitutional government from the National Committees which act for the Democratic and Republican parties in Federal contests to the Executive Committees which take charge in each of the forty-eight states, and so on down to innumerable district, county, city and precinct committees. More or less dormant at other times, these committees collect large funds (*see* Campaign Resources and Uses), call into being many auxiliary bodies and develop tremendous activity during the course of campaigns and particularly just before elections.

Coincident with the above organizational development, elaborate techniques have been worked out, often aided by new inventions such as the motion picture and the radio[qqv], which enable party workers to reach the masses of voters. Appeals are made to individual voters—canvassing, "buttonholing," "door-bell ringing"; also and more largely to voters in the mass by public meetings of every description. Partisan newspapers are called into the service; "campaign literature,"[qv] optimistically so-called, involving every combination of emotional and rational exhortation and ranging in format from fat official textbooks to small pamphlets and dodgers, is distributed in enormous quantities. Every propagandist device is employed to present in the most favorable light to each element of the electorate: first, the traditions and record of the party, especially during the recent past; second, the principles and policies of the party particularly as expounded in its current platform[qv]; and, finally, the life and character of the candidates. In close contests much depends upon party strategy, i.e., the choice of a paramount issue, the distribution of funds and orators in various sections of the country, and the like. Third parties enter into the fray to the limit of their straitened resources. Knowing their candidates foredoomed to defeat, they are more interested than the major parties in preaching party doctrines.

Practical politicians are accustomed to say that the next campaign begins the day after an election has been held. However, the general public takes little interest in their "fence-building" until the pre-primary contest starts, namely, prior to early February of a presidential election year. Following the pre-primary campaign the preconvention campaign continues until nominations are made at the national conventions in late June or early July. Thereafter the presidential campaign[qv] proper gets off to a slow start in dog-days but gathers speed up to the climactic finish on "the first Tuesday after the first Monday in November."

[Charles A. Beard, *The American Party Battle.*]

ROBERT C. BROOKS

Campaigns, Presidential, have occurred in the United States every fourth year, beginning in 1788, and will so continue as long as the present constitutional provisions remain in force. Each campaign has been ushered in since the 1830's by the holding of national party conventions[qv] to select presidential and vice-presidential candidates and to draw up platforms[qv]. The method of selecting delegates to these conventions was for a long time wholly extra-legal, and determined by local party traditions, but in many states presidential primaries are now held, by means of which the voters may register their preference for the supporters of a particular candidate. Each convention represents the various political units of the nation approximately according to population.

Sometimes, as in the case of a popular President desiring renomination, there is no contest in the convention, but often the nomination is awarded only after long balloting and much excitement. State delegations rally around their "favorite sons," and win or yield votes in accordance with backstage deals and promises. Doubtful states, that is, states that may vote either way in the election, have a decided advantage over the rest; New York and Ohio, for example, have furnished a disproportionate share of the presidential nominees. If the contest is not decided on an early ballot, a "dark-horse" candidate, one not previously regarded as a serious contender for the place, sometimes wins out. Until 1936 Democratic conventions required a two-thirds majority[qv] to nominate, but at that time the Democrats adopted the rule long current in Republican conventions that a simple majority would be sufficient. While military heroes, Congressmen, cabinet members and judges have all been accorded presidential nominations, in general the governor of an important close state has an advantage over all other contenders.

After the nominations are made the Chairman of the National Committee, an officer personally selected by the presidential candidate, takes command of the party forces. Under his direction the campaign treasurer raises and expends huge sums of money to send "stump speakers," campaign literature and funds for less circumspect purposes into the doubtful states (*see* Campaign Resources and Uses). In earlier times presidential candidates either stood aloof from the campaign, or made only dignified and sedate appearances, such as were a part of McKinley's "front-porch" campaign of 1896. Of late, however, presidential candidates have become themselves the chief campaigners. Frequent "swings around the circle" take them to every part of the country and the radio[qv] reports their every utterance to millions of listeners. Indeed, "radio appeal" has become one of the most important assets a candidate can have.

Campaign speeches and documents are usually formulated with a view to pleasing the maximum number of voters and real issues are often sidetracked in favor of blind appeals to partisanship. Thus "waving the bloody shirt"[qv] was the chief reliance of Republican orators for a long time after the Civil War, while the desire to maintain white supremacy[qv] outweighed all other considerations in the "Solid South."[qv] On the other hand, Bryan's battle for "free silver" and his attack on "imperialism," Wilson's advocacy of the "New Freedom" and Franklin D. Roosevelt's defense of the "New Deal"[qqv] are instances in which important policies were set before the electorate for acceptance or rejection.

[Edward A. Stanwood, *A History of the Presidency.*]

JOHN D. HICKS

Campbellites. *See* Disciples of Christ.

Campo Bello Fiasco, THE (April 9–28, 1866), was an attempt by the O'Mahony Fenians to seize the island of Campo Bello, New Brunswick, for Ireland. The British, aware of the plan, sent a vessel to Eastport, Maine, and increased their garrisons. Three United States vessels and troops under Gen. Meade successfully intercepted shipments of Fenian[qv] arms and prevented violations of our neutrality laws. Disheartened, the Fenians returned home to plan anew.

[J. Stephens, *Fenian Brotherhood.*]

EZRA H. PIEPER

Camps and Cantonments, World War. To build the camps and cantonments required for housing and training of our World War National Guard and National Army[qqv] divisions, the Construction Division of the army was created in May, 1917. This unit, later known as the "Cantonment Division," was first commanded by Brig. Gen. Isaac W. Littell—later by Brig. Gen. R. C. Marshall, Jr., under whose administration it became a part of the office of the Chief of Staff.

The Secretary of War (Hon. Newton D. Baker) ordered the building of sixteen cantonments with wooden barracks for the new National Army and, in addition, sixteen National Guard camps where troops would be quartered in tents with wood floors, with wooden buildings for kitchens and mess halls. Projected dates for calling conscripted men to the colors forced construction work to be crowded practically within a ninety-day period.

Each National Army cantonment contained, in addition to the barracks, quarters and administration buildings, a hospital, warehouses, railroad tracks, permanent highways, water supply, electricity, sewerage, refrigeration, welfare buildings, sewage-disposal plant, remount depot, target range and, in many cases, a power station. Each cantonment could accommodate a "Pershing" division, approximately 28,000 men.

The National Guard camps, in addition to tent facilities above described, included the principal installations of the National Army cantonments, but on a limited scale.

With the exception of two donated parcels, land for cantonments was purchased; sites for National Guard camps were all loaned gratis or rented.

By Sept. 1, 1917, the thirty-two construction projects were housing troops and a month later all tent camps were substantially complete. On Nov. 15 the same was true of the cantonments.

Physical work of building was done by civilian labor (reaching a peak of 200,000 men), employed by contractors working on a "cost plus"[qv] emergency contract. The average cost of construction per cantonment was $11,600,000, exclusive of land; for the National Guard tent camps, the average was $2,400,000.

National Army cantonments built were: Custer, Battle Creek, Mich.; Devens, Ayer, Mass.; Dodge, Des Moines, Iowa; Dix, Wrightstown, N. J.; Funston, Fort Riley, Kans.; Gordon, Atlanta, Ga.; Grant, Rockford, Ill.; Jackson, Columbia, S. C.; Lee, Petersburg, Va.; Lewis, American Lake, Wash.; Meade, Admiral, Md.; Pike, Little Rock, Ark.; Sherman, Chillicothe, Ohio; Taylor, Louisville, Ky.; Travis, San Antonio, Tex.; and Upton, Yaphank, Long Island, N. Y.

National Guard camps built were: Beauregard, Alexandria, La.; Bowie, Fort Worth, Tex.; Cody, Deming, N. Mex.; Doniphan, Fort Sill, Okla.; Frémont, Palo Alto, Calif.; Greene, Charlotte, N. C.; Hancock, Augusta, Ga.; Kearney, Linda Vista, Calif.; Logan, Houston, Tex.; MacArthur, Waco, Tex.; McClellan, Anniston, Ala.; Sevier, Greenville, S. C.; Shelby, Hattiesburg, Miss.; Sheridan, Montgomery, Ala.; Wadsworth, Spartanburg, S. C.; Wheeler, Macon, Ga.

Total capacity in men for the National Army cantonments was 654,786; for the National Guard camps, 438,042.

In addition to the above, three embarkation camps were built: Merritt, Tenafly, N. J.; Stewart and Hill, Newport News, Va. Two Quartermaster camps were constructed: Ordway, Washington, D. C.; and J. E. Johnston, Jacksonville, Fla.

After cessation of hostilities, the Government salvaged a vast quantity of material and disposed of all remaining installations either at auction or by sales preceded by advertising for sealed bids.

[Annual Reports of the War Department, Chief of Construction Division, 1918 and 1919.]

ROBERT S. THOMAS

Canada, American Invasion of, 1775–76. In attempting the conquest of Canada, the Continental Congress[qv] wished not only to effect a diversion favorable to the colonial operations around Boston (*see* Boston, Siege of; Bunker Hill), but, still more, to deprive Britain of a base for attack upon the revolutionary colonies. The idea was encouraged by the capture of Ticonderoga and Crown Point[qqv], which secured the route northward. Hopes of success were increased by the knowledge that there were few regular troops in Canada, and the plausible expectation of a rising of the French Canadians. After some hesitation, Congress authorized Gen. Schuyler (June 27, 1775) to undertake the invasion if he found it practicable. Active direction of the expedition fell to Brig. Gen. Richard Montgomery.

A first hasty enterprise against Montreal resulted only in the capture of Ethan Allen by the British (Sept. 25, 1775). The real gateway of Canada, St. Johns[qv] on the Richelieu, held by a large proportion of Canada's regular garrison, fell after a siege lasting from Sept. 17 to Nov. 2, during which the invaders were strengthened by ammunition and provisions obtained by the capture of Fort Chambly[qv]. Montreal was occupied Nov. 13, 1775.

Gen. Guy Carleton, governor of the province, fled to Quebec, which was already threatened by the force which Arnold had brought up by the tremendously difficult Kennebec route (*see* Arnold's March to Quebec); but even after Arnold's junction (Dec. 2) with Montgomery's depleted army, the colonial troops available for the siege of Quebec numbered only about 1000. The one assault which was attempted (Dec. 31) failed completely, Montgomery being killed; and in spite of considerable reinforcements toward spring the siege ended abruptly with the opening of navigation, when the first of 10,000 regulars arrived from England (May 5, 1776). On May 16 a British force from the west captured 400 Americans at Cedars, above Montreal; on June 7 part of the American main force, strengthened by a brigade under Gen. John Sullivan, who assumed command, met disaster at Three Rivers[qv]. On June 15 Montreal was evacuated. Sullivan's force and the small body under Arnold from Montreal were reunited at St. Johns. On June 18 the last Americans left that fortress. Carleton's pursuit was delayed while he built a fleet, which destroyed Arnold's (*see* Valcour Island, Battle of), but it was too late in the season for further operations, and invasion of the colonies was postponed until 1777 (*see* Burgoyne's Invasion).

The failure of the American invasion was due to inadequate military measures, to British sea power, and to the generally neutral attitude of the French-Canadians. It has been argued that the campaign was advantageous to the revolutionary cause in the end by forcing the British to divert the reinforcements of 1776 to the St. Lawrence, thus causing a dispersion of the royal forces which led to the decisive success at Saratoga[qv] in the following year.

[Justin H. Smith, *Our Struggle for the Fourteenth Colony;* G. M. Wrong, *Canada and the American Revolution.*]

C. P. STACEY

Canada, Attempts to Win, to American Revolution. For strategic reasons, if for no others, it seemed to the revolutionists essential to win Canada to their cause. On Oct. 24, 1774, accordingly, the Continental Congress[qv] despatched a letter appealing to the Canadians, dwelling upon their supposed grievances against the British government and inviting them to send delegates to the next Congress; it added that if they refused to be friends they would be treated as foes. Massachusetts made similar overtures on her own account, appointing a committee to correspond with the Canadians and early in 1775 sending John Brown to Canada to advance the cause. In the absence of any actual rising in the province, Congress later in the year decided to seize it by force (*see* Canada, American Invasion of, 1775–76); and in 1776 it supplemented its military effort by sending to Montreal a mission composed of Benjamin Franklin, Samuel Chase and Charles Carroll, and equipped with a printing press to assist in spreading revolutionary propaganda. The mission made little impression upon Canadian opinion and retired from Canada at the end of May, after the siege of Quebec had been raised by troops from England. The failure to win the French-Canadians to the American cause was due in great part to traditional animosities, largely based on religion, which were reinforced by resentment aroused by the exactions of the American Army; while even the English-speaking merchants, bound by close commercial ties to London, were unfavorable to actual secession from the Empire. Various proposals for enterprises toward Canada made later in the war were thwarted by the mutual jealousy of the French and Americans; neither party wished its ally to gain control of the colony.

[A. L. Burt, *The Old Province of Quebec;* Justin H. Smith, *Our Struggle for the Fourteenth Colony.*]

C. P. STACEY

Canada, Confederate Activities in, directed against Northern prison camps[qv] were reported as early as November, 1863, but had little basis until after arrival in Canada of Confederate commissioners Jacob Thompson, J. P. Holcombe and C. C. Clay in May, 1864.

A peace movement[qv] in July and a "Northwest Conspiracy"[qv] in August having failed, an effort was made to seize Federal ships on Lake Erie in Beall's raid[qv] in September and an attack was made on St. Albans[qv], Vt., in October, 1864. About this time plans to release Confederate prisoners in Northern prison camps uniformly failed.

Plots to burn Northern cities, including New York[qv] and Cincinnati, followed. In New York eleven hotels and Barnum's Museum[qv] were fired on Nov. 25, 1864, but the blazes were quickly extinguished. A train-wrecking effort near Buffalo in December, to release captured Confederate generals, failed and one plotter was executed.

Confederates in Canada supplied cash for buying gold, shipping it to England and selling it in order to depress Federal currency values. Two million dollars were thus shipped with no permanent result. About $300,000 was spent by Confederates in Canada in promoting these various futile schemes.

[John W. Headley, *Confederate Operations in Canada and New York.*]

CHARLES H. COLEMAN

Canada, Immigration to and Emigration from. Acadians[qv], expelled from Nova Scotia in 1755, went in some hundreds to southern Louisiana. Replacing the Acadians, emigrants from New England, New Jersey and Pennsylvania moved into Nova Scotia. The American Revolution caused a second considerable wave of northeastward migration when "Loyalists"[qv] fled to the Maritime Provinces. Many "Loyalists" also crossed the upper St. Lawrence and the Niagara frontier. A post-Loyalist movement, chiefly into Upper Canada, essentially part of the trans-Appalachian westward movement, gained momentum till the War of 1812, slackening thereafter in face of stimulated British immigration and diminished Canadian hospitality. By the 1840's Upper Canadians were overflowing to United States frontiers of settlement beyond Detroit and after 1880 French-Canadians emigrated to New England mill towns. Gold discoveries in British Columbia in 1858 attracted American miners; and the Canadian prairies, after American wheat lands were occupied, drew at the turn of the century heavy American immigration, partly of Canadian ancestry. Emigration from older parts of the Dominion to American cities persisted for nearly a century though recently restricted. By censuses of 1930–31 there were 344,374 American-born in Canada, 3.3% of the population, rather evenly distributed, and 1,278,421 Canadian-born in the United States, mostly concentrated in Northern states. Perhaps a third of all persons of Canadian ancestry are in the United States.

[M. L. Hansen, R. H. Coats, et al., Movements of Population, in R. G. Trotter, A. B. Corey, W. W. McLaren, eds., *Proceedings of Conference on Canadian-American Affairs, June, 1937.*]

REGINALD G. TROTTER

Canada, Invasion of, 1812–14. Since the destruction of British power in Canada was a primary object of those responsible for bringing on the War of 1812 (*see* War Hawks) it was inevitable that the United States in the course of the struggle should attempt the conquest of the colony. In 1812 an attempted invasion on the Detroit frontier resulted in disaster (*see* Detroit, Surrender of) and an enterprise on the Niagara met the same fate (*see* Queenston Heights, Battle of). The next year brought more success; Perry's victory (*see* Erie, Lake, Battle of) permitted a successful invasion of western Upper Canada (*see* Thames, Battle of the) and the Detroit frontier region remained in American hands until the end of the war. Farther east, the Americans successfully raided York[qv], but initial successes on the Niagara (*see* George, Fort) were followed by a check at Stoney Creek[qv] and no permanent foothold was gained; while the campaign against Montreal was a total failure (*see* Chrysler's Field and Chateaugay). In 1814 invasion was again attempted on the Niagara, but though the American troops now gave a better account of themselves (*see* Chippewa; Lundy's Lane; and Erie, Fort) no conquest of territory resulted.

Among the causes of the American failures, the military unpreparedness of the United States and the large degree of skill with which the defense was conducted by the British regular troops in Canada are important. The determined resistance of the Canadian population was contrary to American expectations and was also a powerful factor. Finally, the American strategic plans were in general decidedly unsound, in that they wasted the country's military resources in ill-conceived enterprises against Canada's western settlements, instead of concentrating them in an effective offensive movement against the essential British line of communication in the St. Lawrence Valley.

[Sir C. P. Lucas, *The Canadian War of 1812;* A. T. Mahan, *Sea Power in its Relations to the War of 1812;* Julius W. Pratt, *Expansionists of 1812.*]

C. P. STACEY

Canada, Proposed Expedition against (1778). The opposition to Washington did not subside with the exposure of the Conway Cabal[qv]. In the hope of achieving control, Gates and his friends fixed on an invasion of Canada. Lafayette's interest and support were enlisted; he was to be leader of this fantastic "irruption into Canada" in the dead of winter. In February, 1778, he went to Albany. Nothing had been done. Lafayette was enraged and humiliated. By April he was back with Washington. Gates and his friends had blundered again. Six months later they attempted, unsuccessfully, to revive the plan.

[Justin H. Smith, *Our Struggle for the Fourteenth Colony.*]

THOMAS ROBSON HAY

Canadian-American International Joint Commission. *See* International Joint Commission.

Canadian-American Reciprocity. In order to help offset annexation sentiment and relieve economic distress in Canada Lord Elgin[qv], the Governor-General, negotiated a reciprocity[qv] agreement with the United States in 1854. There was no formal treaty, but it was agreed that certain agricultural, forest and mineral products, as well as those of the fisheries, should be imported from one country to the other on a reciprocal basis. The agreement did not apply to manufactures. American vessels were also permitted to navigate the St. Lawrence in return for a like privilege for Canadian vessels on Lake Michigan. The agreement was to operate for ten years and might then be terminated by one year's notice by either party. It was so terminated by the United States in 1866, largely as a result of diplomatic friction on issues growing out of the American Civil War (*see* Fisheries Dispute, Arbitration of).

Canadian statesmen of both political parties tried at different times to obtain another reciprocity arrangement with the United States. Such an agreement was made in 1911, but the Laurier government in Canada, which negotiated the agreement, was overthrown in a general election and the proposal was thereby rejected by Canada.

[Haynes, *The Reciprocity Treaty with Canada of 1854;* Allin and Jones, *Annexation, Preferential Trade and Reciprocity.*]

WILSON PORTER SHORTRIDGE

Canadian-American Relations. The present relationship of mutual confidence between the United States and Canada is of comparatively recent growth. In their earlier history issues arising between the republic and the British Empire produced not only an era of armed conflict (ending in 1815) but a long period of mistrust and difficulty thereafter.

Canadian-American relations in their earliest phase took the form of the chronic hostility, fanned by four intercolonial wars, which existed between the French Catholic settlers of New France and the English Protestant inhabitants of the thirteen colonies. Though the last of these wars (*see* French and Indian War) brought Canada under the British flag, the traditional animosities survived, and in the American Revolution[qv] which followed they undoubtedly tended to restrain the French-Canadians from active co-operation with the Americans (*see* Canada, American Invasion of, 1775–76; Canada, Attempts to Win, to American Revolution). The Definitive Treaty of Peace, 1783[qv], partitioned the continent between the new republic and a group of continuing British colonies in the north; and the arrival in those colonies of perhaps 40,000 Loyalists[qv] expelled from the States, who founded the provinces of New Brunswick and Upper Canada (now Ontario), went far to render the division permanent, for the views of these men, inevitably strongly anti-American, colored the political life of their communities for generations.

Relations between republic and colonies were stormy from the beginning. The allied questions of the western posts on American soil which the British persisted in retaining, despite the treaty, until 1796 (*see* Border Forts, Evacuation of), and of the alliances which, as part of the Canadian defense system, they kept up with Indian tribes within the United States (*see* Defiance, Fort; Fallen Timbers, Battle of; Wayne Campaign), rendered British rule in Canada obnoxious to the American frontiersman; and the latter factor was probably more instrumental than the problems of impressment[qv] and neutral rights at sea in producing the American declaration of war in 1812. The repeated unsuccessful invasions of Canada that followed (*see* Canada, Invasion of, 1812–14) only strengthened anti-American prejudices in the provinces. Memories of this war contributed materially to the growth of Canadian nationalism; for just as American national feeling was largely founded on antipathy to England, that of Canada was nurtured on antipathy to the United States. Though the Treaty of Ghent[qv] in general merely restored the *status quo,* the provision of Jay's Treaty[qv] which had permitted British intercourse with American Indians was not renewed and one historic cause of Anglo-American friction was thus greatly weakened. The Rush-Bagot Agreement[qv] of 1817 prevented a perpetuation of the wartime naval rivalry on the Lakes, but no limitation was imposed on land armaments, nor has any such limitation ever been negotiated.

Increasingly pacific relations were abruptly interrupted in 1837 when rebellions in Canada inaugurated another period of strain. The activity of American "sympathizers" and filibusters (*see* Hunters' Lodges) produced serious border incidents, notably that of the *Caroline*[qv], and these difficulties were soon reinforced by those over the Maine boundary (*see* Northeast Boundary), which led in 1839 to troop movements and apprehension of war (*see* Aroostook War). These matters were resolved by the Webster-Ashburton Treaty[qv], but the Oregon question[qv] prolonged the troubles to 1846. The next fifteen years, on the whole peaceful, were marked by the large development of commercial intercourse fostered by the Elgin-Marcy Reciprocity Treaty[qv] of 1854. The Senate's acceptance of this treaty has been attributed to Southern politicians' desire to avert the increase of free-soil territory by the annexation of Canada, which was represented as inevitable unless commercial concessions were made. An annexation movement which temporary commercial distress had produced in Montreal in 1849 gave color to this argument.

With the Civil War there commenced a decade of extreme danger in Anglo-American relations[qv]. The *Trent* Affair[qv] of 1861 caused the most serious threat of war since 1815 and the state of the border thereafter was one of armed and precarious peace. The *Alabama* Affair[qv] and similar incidents inflamed Northern opinion, and there was talk of annexing Canada in revenge. In 1864 the Confederates made attempts at using Canada as a base of operations against the North (*see* Canada, Confederate Activities in) and fortification projects undertaken on both sides of the border in this and the following year reflected the increasing tension. At the end of the war the recrudescence of filibustering in the form of the Fenian Raids[qv] maintained this dangerous atmosphere, and the abrogation of the Reciprocity Treaty by the United States in 1866 embittered it. Fear of American attack lent impetus to the movement for federation of the several British provinces, which bore fruit in the organization of the Dominion of Canada (July 1, 1867). The British government was more than willing to transfer its own responsibilities in America to the new government at Ottawa, which henceforth played an increasingly important role in negotiations with Washington.

The year 1871 is an important turning point. In that year the Treaty of Washington[qv], by providing for arbitration of the *Alabama* claims, ended ten years of tension, and simultaneously the withdrawal of British troops from central Canada encouraged the growth of a less military atmosphere along the border. The fundamental territorial controversies between the two communities had now been settled; furthermore, the abolition of slavery in the United States and the attainment of responsible government in Canada had removed domestic problems which had invited foreign interference. As memories of old conflicts faded, the influence of common racial and political traditions was freer to assert itself and to open the way for more peaceful relations; and from 1871 it is possible to speak with some truth of the Canadian border as an "unguarded" frontier, for no fortifications have since been built. The worst difficulties of the next period were the chronic Atlantic Fisheries dispute[qv] and the Bering Sea fur-seal question[qv], both ultimately decided by arbitration; but the repeated refusal of the United States (now committed to high protection[qv]) to consider a renewal of reciprocity caused constant irritation and influenced Canada's own decision to turn to protection (1878) and the subsequent maintenance of this policy. In 1895 the Venezuela Boundary crisis[qv] aroused fears of war, and President Theodore Roosevelt's handling of the Alaska Boundary question[qv] (1903) further revived old animosities. In 1911 these helped to defeat President Taft's project of a new reciprocity treaty; traditional Canadian patriotism, fearing American penetration, now combined with the influence of new business interests which had grown up behind the Canadian tariff to bring about the rejection of Sir Wilfrid Laurier's government in a general election on this issue (*see* Reciprocity). In these same years, however, there was created (1909) the International Joint Commission[qv] on boundary waters, which ever since has done unostentatious but valuable work in settling disputes arising along the border.

American neutrality in the early stages of the World War[qv] did not increase the popularity of the United States with Canadians; but the improvement in Anglo-American relations, produced by this conflict in the end, prepared the way for a new era in Canadian-American relations also. In the post-war years, the complete and obvious abandonment by the United States of any expansionist ideas combined with growing national self-confidence in Canada to create a more frank and generous atmosphere. The gradual growth of Canada's international status culminated in 1927 in the inauguration of direct diplomatic intercourse between Ottawa and Washington by an exchange of ministers; since that year all Canadian-American issues have been dealt with through these channels. The most unpleasant incident so treated has been that of the sinking of the *I'm Alone*[qv] (1929), and the mutually satisfactory manner in which it was disposed of by arbitration (1935) is evidence of the existing state of relations. Commercial friction, it is true, continued, and the American Hawley-Smoot tariff[qv] and the Canadian emergency tariff of 1930 amounted to an exchange of economic blows. Such episodes, however, did not prevent an increasing assimilation of the economic systems of the two nations.

[J. M. Callahan, *American Foreign Policy in Canadian Relations;* H. L. Keenleyside, *Canada and the United States.*]

C. P. STACEY

Canadian-American Waterways. The use by white men, as means of transportation, of the system of waterways that extends from the Gulf of St. Lawrence into the heart of North America, began with the second voyage of Jacques Cartier in 1535. In that year he not only discovered the St. Lawrence River, but, first in a small sailing ship, and finally in longboats, made his way upstream to the island of Montreal. His successors—explorers, missionaries, fur-traders, soldiers and settlers, by canoe, boat or sailing ship—finally traveled to every corner of the Great Lakes. The first sailing vessels on the Lakes, the *Frontenac* and the *Griffon*[qv], were built by La Salle, the former at Fort Frontenac[qv], now Kingston, Ontario, in 1678, and the latter near the present Buffalo in 1679. About 1737 LaRonde built a small sailing ship at Sault Ste. Marie and used her on Lake Superior in a search for copper mines. It was not until 1816 that the *Frontenac,* the first steam-driven craft on the Lakes, was launched near Kingston, on Lake Ontario. Two years later the *Walk-in-the-Water*[qv], the first steamboat on the upper lakes, was launched not far from the place where LaSalle had built the *Griffon.* When the need arose to carry large quantities of ore and grain down the Lakes from Superior and equally immense cargoes of coal from Erie ports up to Duluth and Superior, special types of lake vessels were designed of unprecedented capacity and the traffic up and down the Detroit River grew by leaps and bounds until it exceeded 100,000,000 tons annually of a value of more than $1,000,000,000. A suggestion of the growth of transportation facilities on these waters may be got by comparing LaSalle's 10-ton *Frontenac* with the *Lemoyne,* built at Midland, Ontario, in 1926, 613 feet long, and carrying a cargo of 570,000 bushels of wheat.

Navigation between Lake Superior and the sea was, in a state of nature, limited by waterfalls, rapids or shallows in the connecting streams and in the upper St. Lawrence. Since 1783, when the first canals were opened for navigation on the Canadian side of the St. Lawrence, the United States and Canadian governments have spent several hundred millions of dollars in improvements to navigation between Duluth, Fort William or Chicago and the sea, notably in building the American and Canadian canals at Sault Ste. Marie and the Welland ship canal[qv] connecting Lakes Erie and Ontario. Since the opening of the latter in 1930 the largest freighters can travel from the head of Lake Superior to the foot of Lake Ontario. From there to the sea the Canadian canals are only fourteen feet in draft.

To determine the practicability of deepening this remaining section of the waterway from the upper lakes to the Gulf, the International Joint Commission[qv] carried out an investigation and reported favorably in 1921. Subsequently the engineering side of the problem was reviewed by a board of American and Canadian government engineers and the economic aspects by American and Canadian committees, all of which reported favorably. A treaty to carry out the project, which also involved the development of water power on the upper St. Lawrence[qv], was signed at Washington in 1932, but failed to win the approval of the United States Senate. In 1938 a revised treaty, dealing also with works designed to improve the scenic beauty of Niagara Falls and to govern diversions at Chicago, was submitted by the United States Government to Canada. In 1936 the International Joint Commission investigated the feasibility of a deep waterway from the St. Lawrence by way of Lake Champlain to the Hudson and reported adversely.

[Geo. A. Cuthbertson, *Freshwater;* Moulton, Morgan and Lee, *The St. Lawrence Navigation and Power Project;* G. W. Stephens, *The St. Lawrence Waterway Project.*]

LAWRENCE J. BURPEE

Canadian and United States Boundary Disputes. *See* Northeast Boundary; Northwest Boundary Controversy; Alaska Boundary Question.

Canadian Annexation Movement, THE (1849), was sponsored by urban and commercial interests, primarily in Montreal, to offset the serious decline in trade, prices and property values in Canada which resulted from the capture of western trade by the Erie Canal route[qv], granting of bonding privileges by the United States, repeal of the Corn Laws and imperial preference, and failure of the United States to satisfy the Canadian demand for reciprocity[qv] in natural products in 1848 and 1849. An annexation manifesto, issued on Oct. 10, 1849, received over 1000 signatures among which were some of the most prominent political and financial leaders of Montreal. Widespread opposition, counter manifestoes and return of prosperity ended the movement within six months.

[C. D. Allin and G. M. Jones, *Annexation, Preferential Trade and Reciprocity.*]

ALBERT B. COREY

Canadian Boundary, Disarmament of. *See* Canadian-American Relations; Great Lakes, Agreement for Disarmament on the.

Canadian River, THE, is a part of the Arkansas River[qv] system. Early French traders and explorers followed its course west into the Spanish territory. The name Canadian possibly was given to the river by early French hunters and traders who came from Canada. The upper part was called by the Spanish, Rio Colorado. By the Treaty of Doak's Stand[qv] in 1820, Canadian River was made the northern boundary of the Choctaw[qv] nation. Early emigrants to California followed the south bank of the Canadian on to Santa Fé.[qv]

[Thoburn and Wright, *History of Oklahoma;* Grant Foreman, *Pioneer Days in the Early Southwest.*]

ANNA LEWIS

Canal Boats, THE. On the early American canals[qv], the blunt, horse-drawn boats were of three general types—freight boats carrying from 25 to 100 tons each of various commodities; passenger "packets"; and so-called line boats, which carried both freight and passengers, the latter getting poorer accommodations than on the packets. On the passenger boats the traveler both dined and slept in a central "saloon," a species of narrow canvas hammocks being affixed to the walls in tiers at night for berths.

[Alvin F. Harlow, *Old Towpaths.*]

ALVIN F. HARLOW

Canal Building was an early phase of the struggle to provide transportation facilities adequate to develop and to unite the country. The first problem was to get around the falls of the rivers flowing into the Atlantic (*see* Fall Line, The). To accomplish this, some canals were completed by private companies between 1789 and 1802. The second problem was to connect the coast with the Ohio and Mississippi River valleys and the rivers with the Great Lakes[qqv]. During this second phase, the mania for canal building by the states (with some Federal aid) can be understood only in the light of the success of the Erie Canal[qv] and the widespread speculation and wildcat banking[qv] which characterized frontier enthusiasm for the development of the resources of the West.

The Erie Canal, started in 1817 by New York state, and completed in 1825, gave the first low-cost transportation from the coast to the interior of the country. Following the lowest crossing of the Appalachians along the course of an old Indian trail, it was a great success. It carried a vast traffic, it was largely responsible for the development of New York City and the towns along its course and it paid for itself in a brief time.

Other states believed that the same success would crown their efforts. Canal building seemed essential both to those who wished to exploit the resources of the country and to those primarily interested in speculation. Wildcat bankers took long chances and viewed hopefully projects which now seem fantastic. Foreign investors carelessly assumed that state credit was as good as that of the Federal Government, which was practically out of debt in the 1830's. Thus the sound position of the Federal Government played a strange role, encouraging foreigners to buy state bond issues, the proceeds of which went into canal construction. In 1825 Ohio, with a population of about 700,000, undertook canal projects estimated to cost approximately $5,800,000, one tenth of its taxable wealth. In the end they cost more. By 1838 the debts of twelve states for canal construction amounted to over $60,-

000,000. The actual construction appears all the more remarkable when we remember that the builders had only human and horse power to remove soil, only black powder[qv] for blasting and that holes for blasting had to be drilled in the rock with hand drills.

The canals, together with the natural waterways, aided greatly in the development of the country. In fact, the superiority of the railroad[qv] over the canal was not clearly evident until the late 1860's. The peak load on the Erie Canal was in the late 1880's. The financial results, however, were not so favorable. Unlike the Erie, few of the canals were profitable, and there were defaults by states on canal debts as follows: Indiana, 1841–47; Maryland, 1841–48; Pennsylvania, 1842–45; and Illinois, 1842–47 (*see* Repudiation of State Debts).

The Federal Government has played a large role in more recent canal building. The St. Mary's River Canal[qv] between Lake Superior and the other Great Lakes, built by Michigan in 1853–55, was improved by the United States in 1870–71. In 1880 the Federal Government took over the whole project. The Cape Cod Canal makes traffic to and from Boston possible without going around the Cape. The building of the Panama Canal[qv], completed by the Federal Government in 1914, was marked by the utilization of modern machinery in moving vast quantities of earth and in the triumph of medical science over tropical diseases (*see* Yellow Fever).

The greatest state project in recent years (1903–18) is that of New York in rebuilding the Barge Canal system.

[Alvin F. Harlow, *Old Towpaths.*]

JAMES D. MAGEE

Canal Lands. Congress granted 4,424,073.06 acres of the public domain[qv] to the states for canals between 1824 and 1874, as follows:

Indiana	1,457,366.06 acres	
Ohio	1,100,361.00 acres	
Illinois	290,915.00 acres,	plus 210,132.00 (1841) for general internal improvements, used for canal purposes
Wisconsin	325,431.00 acres	
Michigan	1,250,000.00 acres	

These canal lands were about 8% of the total of 52,251,937.19 acres granted during the same period for all internal improvements[qv].

Canal lands in Ohio were sold quickly (except the right of way and terminal grounds). Within twenty years (1848) 908,003 acres had been sold for $1,408,812.73. Ultimately Ohio received $2,257,487, about one seventh of the building cost. Indiana records are inadequate, but the total receipts from land sales and canal tolls were $5,477,238. Illinois received (to 1871) $5,858,547.47 or five sixths of the total construction cost. Speculation in canal lands contributed to the land speculation preceding the panic of 1837[qv]. Eighty acres of canal land in the heart of Chicago sold for $1.55 per acre in 1830. Six years later 375 canal lots brought $1,355,755. Ohio, Indiana and Illinois still have a small income from the canal rights of way.

[T. C. Donaldson, *Public Domain;* A. F. Harlow, *Old Towpaths.*]

HAROLD E. DAVIS

Canal Ring, THE. A group of corrupt contractors and politicians who conspired shortly after the Civil War to defraud the State of New York by overcharging for repairs and improvement of the state's canal system. It defied an "investigation" in 1868 and for years was powerful enough to prevent interference and to defeat unfriendly candidates for office.

[D. S. Alexander, *Political History of the State of New York.*]

ALVIN F. HARLOW

Canary Islands, THE, served as a way station for Spain's New World voyages, besides supplying wine for Spanish America and skilled workers for West Indian sugar plantations. New England early began a profitable intercourse with the Canaries, together with Portugal's Madeiras and Azores, involving mainly the exchange of lumber and fish for wine. Although illegal according to English interpretation of the Navigation Act[qv] of 1663, trade with the Canaries continued until the 1770's, causing much friction between New England and royal authorities.

[G. L. Beer, *The Old Colonial System, 1660-1754;* W. B. Weeden, *Economic and Social History of New England, 1620-1789.*]

CHARLES EDWARD CHAPMAN AND ROBERT HALE SHIELDS

Candles lighted most American homes, public buildings and streets until kerosene lamps and gas replaced them. The housewives made many kinds, namely—bear grease, deer suet, bayberry, beeswax (expensive, for state occasions largely), tallow dip (commonest), from well-rendered mutton fat, and spermaceti (the waxy solid from the head of whales). Every autumn the housekeepers filled their leather or tin candle boxes to last through the winter. It was a long, hard task to dip or mold several hundred candles by hand. First, women prepared wicks from rough hemp, milkweed or cotton spun in large quantity. The homemaker was the only manufacturer until the 1700's when an itinerant candle-maker could be hired. Later, professional chandlers prospered in the cities. Although factories were numerous after 1750, the home-dipping was continued as late as 1880. There was a large market for sperm candles in the West Indies. In 1768 they bought over 500,000 lbs. of sperm and tallow candles from the colonies. The total production from both factories and homes reached an estimated $8,000,000 in 1810. The New England factories, which produced most, imported supplies of fat from Russia. There were large plants, also, in New Orleans, St. Louis, and Hudson, N. Y. South Carolina and Georgia produced quantities of seeds and capsules from tallow trees used extensively for candle-making in the South. Allied industries grew rapidly for making metal and pottery candle holders.

[Marion Nicholl Rawson, *Candle Days;* Alice Morse Earle, *Home Life in Colonial Days,* and *Customs and Fashions in Old New England;* Arthur H. Hayward, *Colonial Lighting;* Victor S. Clark, *History of Manufactures in the United States.*]

LENA G. FITZ HUGH

Cane Ridge Revival, THE, was the culmination of a great spiritual awakening in Kentucky, which began at the close of the 18th century (*see* Great Revival). This special manifestation of religious fervor occurred in August, 1801, at a camp meeting[qv] near the Cane Ridge Meeting House in Bourbon County. The number attending has been estimated at 20,000. Those under conviction exhibited peculiar physical and vocal exercises that indicated an abnormal religious experience. The Disciples[qv], or Christians, developed from the intellectual quickening of the movement.

[James R. Rogers, *The Cane Ridge Meeting House;* Alonzo Willard Fortune, *The Disciples in Kentucky.*]

JONATHAN T. DORRIS

Canning Industry, THE, has expanded in America due to simultaneous advances in the technic of manufacturing cans, agricultural research, the invention of automatic machinery and the art of canning. These have progressed rapidly during the past 140 years and the United States is in the forefront of canning nations, leading in volume and variety of canned products. Some 300 food products are canned and the enterprise has become one of the billion-dollar industries.

Pioneers of American canning were Thomas Kensett, Sr., and Ezra Daggett of New York, 1819, and William Underwood at Boston, 1821. They used the Appert process (sealing in airtight containers and immersing in boiling water) on oysters, meats, fruits, berries and vegetables, packing in glass. The tin can[qv], its name derived from the original English canister, was introduced here by Peter Durand in 1818. Underwood and Kensett changed from glass to tin in 1839. Canning sprang up rapidly thereafter in Maryland, Maine, New Brunswick, New York and Delaware, with new products added. Methods of obtaining higher temperatures were evolved, the cooking time thus shortened and pack volume rose.

The Civil War produced the first "boom" and canneries sprang up in the Midwest, to supply the armies. From about 5,000,000 annual cans, the national pack increased sixfold. Canning was introduced in California, now a leading producing state, in 1862. Two years later George W. Hume and A. S. Hapgood, Maine salmon canners, transferred their activities to the Pacific Coast. David S. Page, Dixon, Ill., made the first condensed milk can in Switzerland in 1865, paving the way for a major expansion in that product, carried forward later by Gail Borden and others (*see* Dairy Industry).

In the following decades machinery inventions and development led the way, while can-making refinements continued. Andrew K. Shriver, Baltimore, patented the first closed steam-pressure kettle in 1875. R. P. Scott of Ohio and Messrs. C. P. and J. A. Chisholm of Ontario evolved an automatic pea podder in 1885. William H. Sells, in 1892, built the first automatic corn husker, deriving his idea from the principle of the clothes wringer. Other revolutionary improvements in machinery were made.

Early in this century the can itself was radically improved. Solid food particles had been forced into the can through a hole in the top, over which a metal disc was soldered. Mutilation of food was common. An open-top can was developed by Charles M. Ams, W. Y. Bogle and George W. Cobb, Sr., which, known as the "sanitary can," has become the standard, modern tin container for food. Soon after this, scientific research laboratories sprang up throughout the industry, launching programs of investigation as to causes of spoilage and contamination. Nutritive values were analyzed and proved. Raw products research led to refinements in planting, growing and harvesting canning crops. Popular prejudices against canned foods waned and public acceptance grew, as the results of this work became trade practice. At the present time, in a normal year, between eight and nine billion cans of food are produced in the United States.

[J. H. Collins, *The Story of Canned Foods;* E. C. May, *The Canning Clan.*]

NELSON H. BUDD

Cannonism, a term common during Joseph G. Cannon's tenure of the Speakership of the House (1903–11) when the great powers of that office were used in the interest of the ultraconservative elements.

[D. S. Alexander, *History and Procedure of the House of Representatives.*]

W. A. ROBINSON

Canoe, THE. When one mentions the canoe in American and Canadian history, it is usually with the understanding that a craft made of the rind of the white birch tree is meant. On occasions other materials were used for canoes, but never, apparently, if birch-bark could be secured.

The Algonquian Indians[qv] had learned both the secret of making and of guiding canoes expertly before white men reached North America. The latter adopted the canoe immediately. Until railroads became common–about 1850–the canoe was the chief vehicle for reaching much of northern North America. Thus it became the usual craft in the transportation of furs and is always associated with the great explorers and the fur traders[qv]. It was admirably adapted to the waterways of the continent, being light enough to be portaged easily, responsive enough to be guided with precision through rapids and over low waterfalls, and so built as to be capable of repair at almost any place on the route from materials to be found along that route. Besides bark these materials were cedar for the frame and paddles, wattape (tree-root fibers) for sewing pieces of bark together and for lashing the bark to the gunwales, and resin for gumming the seams. No metal was used in its construction.

There were several kinds of canoes: the Montreal canoe, or *canot du maître,* from thirty to forty feet long, manned by ten to fourteen men; the *canot du nord,* or North canoe, from twenty to twenty-five feet in length, manned by four to eight men; a half canoe, somewhat smaller; and Indian canoes, still smaller. A light canoe was usually an express canoe without freight aboard. The Montreal canoes weighed about 300 lbs. and carried about five tons' weight of men and freight. They were used primarily on the St. Lawrence and the Great Lakes[qv]. The North canoes were used beyond the Great Lakes, in smaller rivers and on lesser lakes.

[Grace Lee Nute, *The Voyageur.*]

GRACE LEE NUTE

Cantigny, Americans Attack at. The American 1st Division (Bullard) on April 25, 1918, joined the French First Army. It occupied the sector facing Cantigny, held by the German XVIII Army. To test the Americans' offensive ability in their first active sector, the French command ordered the new division to capture Cantigny. After careful preparations the 28th Infantry attacked at 6.45 A.M., May 28. The assailants, assisted by French tanks, took all objectives, with 250 prisoners, in forty-five minutes. Thereafter the Americans repulsed several violent German counterattacks, losing 1067 killed and wounded, but maintaining their position.

[C. R. Howland, *A Military History of the World War;* J. M. Hanson, History of the American Combat Divisions, *The Stars and Stripes.*]

JOSEPH MILLS HANSON

Canton, The Fur Trade with, developed from the search for some staple, other than specie, which American merchants could exchange for the teas and silks of China. Furs met with a ready sale; the cargo of the first American vessel to Canton, Feb. 22, 1784, included furs. But only such rare furs as otter, seal, beaver and fox were acceptable. Boston merchants decided to seek sea-otter[qv] skins on the Northwest coast. The *Columbia* (Sept. 30, 1787–Aug. 9, 1790) returned with a cargo of teas–product of sea-otter skins bartered from the natives. Others hastened to follow. By 1796 American vessels were engaged in contraband fur trade with the Californians and by 1804 were borrowing Aleutian sea-otter hunters, on shares, from the Russian governor at Novarkhangelsk. In 1783, in the Southern Pacific, had begun the mass slaughter of the fur seal. When, after the War of 1812[qv], the fur trade with Canton was renewed, the growing scarcity of the sea otter, increased competition and a consequent decline in profits reduced the American vessels engaged from thirteen in 1821 to two in 1830. Trading in furs with Canton became merely one aspect of a more general "Pacific trade." ". . . by 1837 the old Northwest fur trade . . . was a thing of the past."

[F. R. Dulles, *The Old China Trade;* K. W. Porter, *John Jacob Astor;* Samuel Eliot Morison, *Maritime History of Massachusetts, 1783-1860.*]

KENNETH WIGGINS PORTER

Cantonments. *See* Camps and Cantonments, World War.

Canvass. The word is used to describe two political processes. First it means to ascertain by direct personal approach how citizens intend to vote at a coming election. During earlier decades such canvasses were often made ninety, sixty and fifteen days before the election. The practice is somewhat less common now partly because of the expense involved, partly because of the increasing tendency of voters to refuse information and finally because of the polls made locally by newspapers and nationally by magazines of wide circulation. Second, in a somewhat looser sense, to canvass means to make a campaign for the support of a given candidate or ticket.

ROBERT C. BROOKS

Cape Ann, Mass., was known in 1605 to Champlain as Le Cap aux Isles, and the next year he entered the cape's harbor. Capt. John Smith in 1614 called it Cape Tragabigzanda, after a Turkish lady, but it was renamed Cape Ann for the wife of James I. In 1623 the Dorchester Company[qv] of merchants in England established a fishing station at the cape, to which came disaffected settlers from Plymouth and Nantucket. Among these Roger Conant was a leader. In 1624 he quieted friction over fishing rights asserted for Plymouth by Myles Standish. For ships of that time the fishing grounds were too distant and the soil was poor, so that the enterprise failed in 1626. For twenty years the settlement languished, till Rev. Richard Blynman came in 1642. Then, under the name Gloucester, it began to grow as a deep-sea fishing port, absorbed Portuguese and Italian crews, and has never lost its eminence.

A moorland section of the cape, called Dogtown, was abandoned after the 18th century and its odd settlers became figures of rather sordid romance. Other sections, Annisquam and Pigeon Cove, are now given over to artists. Their works, together with Kipling's *Captains Courageous* and J. B. Connolly's *Out of Gloucester,* have kept Cape Ann in the public eye. Off the shore of West Gloucester is the reef of Norman's Woe, scene of Longfellow's "Wreck of the Hesperus."

[Charles B. Hawes, *Gloucester by Land and Sea.*]

CHARLES KNOWLES BOLTON

Cape Breton Expedition. *See* Louisburg Expedition, The (1745).

Cape Cod was a landmark for early explorers, possibly the "Promontory of Vinland"[qv] of the Norse voyagers (985–1025). Verrazano in 1524 approached it from the south, and Gomez the next year called it Cape St. James. Gosnold in 1602 gave it the name that survives. Champlain charted its sand-silted harbors in 1606 and Henry Hudson landed there in 1609. Capt. John Smith noted it on his map of 1614 and at last the Pilgrims[qv] entered the "Cape Harbor" on Nov. 11, 1620. Aside from Barnstable and Sandwich (1638) and Yarmouth (1639) the cape's fifteen towns developed slowly. Provincetown was a group of huts until the 18th century. A channel from Massachusetts Bay to Buzzards Bay is shown on Southack's map of 1717, but the present canal had a troubled development (*see* Cape Cod Canal) from 1870 to 1914. The Federal Government purchased it in 1928.

Whaling and cod fishing[qqv] arose in the 18th century and lost out to New Bedford and Gloucester, but oysters and clams still bring wealth to Wellfleet. Salt[qv] by evaporation of sea water became an industry before 1800. Cranberry growing started about 1816 at North Dennis. At Falmouth and elsewhere shipbuilding flourished before and after the Revolution. Sandwich was famous from 1825 to 1888 for its glass works. Whaling started migration of Portuguese from Lisbon, from the Azores and the Cape Verde Islands (*Bravas*). The cape has a long chronicle of shipwrecks, to which the ancient gravestones bear testimony. Ribs of the *Sparrow-Hawk* (1626) are at Pilgrim Hall. The United States submarine "S4" sank off Wood End, Dec. 17, 1927, when her crew of forty slowly died of suffocation, while sending out messages by the Morse code.

[Jeremiah Digges, *The Cape Cod Pilot;* Henry C. Kittredge, *Cape Cod: Its People and Their History.*]

CHARLES KNOWLES BOLTON

Cape Cod Canal, The, connects Buzzards Bay and Cape Cod Bay and saves going around the cape. After many proposals and many failures, the eight-mile-long canal was built (1909 to 1914) by the Boston, Cape Cod and New York Canal Co. The Federal Government now operates it without tolls, having bought it in 1928. It forms part of the intracoastal waterway system.

[Henry C. Kittredge, *Cape Cod: Its People and Their History.*]

JAMES D. MAGEE

Cape Fear, Action at, 1865. *See* Fisher, Fort, Capture of, 1864–65.

Cape Fear River Settlements (N. C.). In 1664 and 1665 several hundred Barbadians planted a colony on the lower Cape Fear, which was abandoned in 1667. Little interest was shown in this region until after the removal of the Indian and pirate menace during the second decade of the next century. About 1723 settlers from South Carolina and from Albemarle[qv] began to move in, and in 1725 the town of Brunswick was laid out on the west bank of the river, about fourteen miles from the sea. Eight years later Wilmington was begun and became the colony's chief port. From 1735 to 1775 thousands of Scotch Highlanders settled on the upper Cape Fear. Naval stores and rice*qv* became the most important products of the region.

[R. D. W. Connor, *North Carolina: Rebuilding an Ancient Commonwealth,* I.]

HUGH T. LEFLER

Cape Girardeau. As early as 1765, a bend in the Mississippi River about sixty miles south of the French village of Ste. Genevieve*qv* had been referred to as Cape Girardot or Girardeau. The settlement there dates from 1793 when the Spanish government, which had secured Louisiana in 1762, granted Louis Lorimier, a French-Canadian, the right of establishing a trading post. His grant gave him extensive trading privileges and a large tract of land surrounding his post. Lorimier was made commandant of the district and prospered from the returns of his land sales and trade with the Indians.

[Louis Houck, *History of Missouri.*]

W. J. HAMILTON

Cape Horn, southernmost point of the American continent, lies practically due south of Eastport, Maine, easternmost point of the United States. Traditionally the most dreaded of ocean headlands both because of the almost ceaseless storms for which it is noted and the fact that it lies within the southern ice line, Cape Horn was first sighted by the Dutch navigators le Maire and Schouten when on a voyage toward the East Indies in 1616. These were the first to enter the Pacific Ocean by way of Cape Horn, previous navigators having used the Straits of Magellan. William Schouten named the point Cape Hoorn after the town of Hoorn in Holland where he was born. The difficulty of making the west-bound passage of Cape Horn in sailing ships played a part in retarding the growth of California, but the discovery of gold*qv* on Sutter's*qv* ranch near Sacramento in the latter part of 1848 stimulated both the passage of the cape and the growth of the American mercantile marine. Because of the necessity always to contend with the rigors of Cape Horn when making a coast-to-coast voyage, American shipbuilders were compelled to produce fast, weatherly and immensely strong vessels. The stimulus given by the rapid growth of the trade to California went far to put American square-rigged ships in the forefront of the world. Famous Cape Horn ships of this period include the *Flying Cloud, Andrew Jackson* (which shared the record of eighty-nine days, New York to San Francisco), *Sea Witch, Great Republic, John Gilpin, Flying Fish, James Baines* (which logged the fastest speed ever recorded under sail, twenty-one knots). The rigors of the Horn passage, the growth of intercontinental trade, the greater development of the American Navy, the difficulty of adequately protecting the Pacific and the Atlantic coasts turned the attention of the United States to the building of the Panama Canal*qv*. From that time the importance of the route around Cape Horn, used long previously only by freight ships, most of them steamers, rapidly declined. The last American sailing ship to beat round Cape Horn is probably the schooner *Wanderbird,* in 1936. The last American Cape Horner in existence is the wooden ship *Benjamin Packard,* now in an amusement park at Rye, N. Y.

ALAN VILLIERS

Capital, National, The Location of, played an important part in Hamilton's successful establishment of the national credit. Immediately after the Continental Congress*qv* hastily adjourned (1783) from Philadelphia to New York, because of Pennsylvania's failure to protect it from the insults of mutinous soldiery (*see* Mutiny of Pennsylvania Troops), agitation was begun in Congress for establishing a permanent seat of government. Nearly every one of the Eastern and Middle Atlantic states offered a location, or urged a claim. The struggle continued for five years and carried over into the Congress under the Constitution. In 1790 Hamilton, cleverly using the desire of the Southern states to obtain the capital, traded, through Jefferson, Pennsylvania support for the Potomac River location, in return for Virginia support for his plan of the assumption*qv* of the states' Revolutionary War debts. The location act was approved July 16, 1790, and Virginia fulfilled her bargain by voting for the act (approved Aug. 4) making provision for the public debt.

[Claude G. Bowers, *Jefferson and Hamilton.*]

JOHN C. FITZPATRICK

Capital Gains Tax, 1936 and 1938. In the taxation of personal incomes one troublesome problem has been how satisfactorily to handle capital gains, that is, the gain from the sale of capital assets. Changes have been made in many of the revenue acts but a satisfactory method seems difficult to find. In the 1936 law gains and losses from sales of capital assets were to be taken into account in the calculation of taxable income. If the asset had been owned one year or less before sale, then the entire gain was to be included; ownership between one year and two years, 80% of the gain or loss was to be included; between two and five years, 60%; between five and ten years, 40%; and if ownership were more than ten years, only 30% of the gain was included. Realized losses were deductible in an amount equal to the capital gains and might be allowed beyond this to an amount of $2000. Any capital gains of corporations were taxed in full while losses were allowed only to the extent of gains plus $2000.

With an attempt better to differentiate between what might be considered investment and speculative gains, changes were made in the 1938 act. Profits from the sale of assets which have been owned for one and one-half years or less are to be taxed in their entirety, but if the ownership has been between one and one-half and two years only two thirds of the gains are taxable while ownership for more than two years makes but one half of the gain subject to taxation. Losses within the one-and-one-half-year period may be deducted from the gains and, if greater than the gains may, under certain restrictions, be carried forward to the next period. Losses in the longer period may also be deducted from gains, but no carry-over of losses is permitted. The provision for corporate gains and losses remains the same as in the 1936 act.

[R. H. Montgomery, *Income Tax Procedure.*]

MERLIN H. HUNTER

Capital Punishment. Prior to the Revolutionary War, most felonies were punishable by death. Popular thought held that a criminal deliberately chose to be wicked and was, therefore, entitled to no mercy. In harmony with this general attitude, executions were public exhibitions, and conducted as such, to deter others from crime.

Gradually, however, the states began to limit the number of capital offenses. In 1788 Ohio effected the first substantial reform by making murder the only crime punishable by death. Although this modification in severity was not as extensive in other jurisdictions, there was a definite tendency toward leniency after Ohio set the example. Today, murder is subject to the death penalty in all states applying capital punishment; rape in some Southern states; and burglary, robbery and arson in a few jurisdictions.

Compatible with the more humane instincts and, possibly, because some concluded that the death sentence was not a powerful deterrent, executions commenced to be held privately. New York abolished public hangings in 1835 and since then other states have followed suit. However, in a few Southern jurisdictions, those guilty of rape are still publicly executed.

During the middle of the 19th century the humanitarian spirit impelled many to seek the abolition of capital punishment. Michigan was the first to wipe out the death penalty in 1847. Other states followed although in a few instances the death penalty was re-established. Those jurisdictions without it today are Maine, Michigan, Minnesota, North Dakota, South Dakota, Rhode Island and Wisconsin.

A great number of other states allow the judge or jury to recommend life imprisonment instead of execution. However, there are still a great many who contend that capital punishment is the most effective measure as a safeguard against crime.

LEWIS E. LAWES

Capitalism is an economic system in which the ownership and control of land, capital and natural resources, the production and marketing of goods, the employment of labor and the organization and operation of the system as a whole are entrusted to private enterprise working under competitive conditions. Private property, contract, freedom of enterprise and profit making are basic rules; acquisition of consumption goods (food, clothing, etc.) is the goal; and accumulation, control and use of capital, as the essential instrument, is the way the goal is most quickly reached.

Most economists think of capital as "produced goods intended for further production." Tools, machines, coal, oil, lumber, unfinished or unsold goods, supplies are all examples. Cash and bank deposits are sometimes called "liquid capital" because they may be directed to any use the possessor wishes, but they are really only titles to capital. Capital is man-made and can be created only through some one's saving. Interest is the rental price for the use of capital. Throughout history the capitalistic or indirect process of production—creating capital to make consumption goods, such as making a net to catch fish—has been found more efficient than the direct method, involving no capital, such as catching fish by hand. Generous use of capital is the secret of the economies of mass production*qv*, and the nations with the most capital per person have the highest standards of living.

Virginia and Plymouth were handicapped at the outset by lack of capital, lack of artisans and lack of the profit motive. The Pilgrims did not bring a horse, cow or plow, and their fishhooks and nets were too large for cod. When the meager supplies soon gave out there was a period of "starving" because there was little incentive in either colony for the individual to work hard to build up a surplus since the settlers were expected to put all their produce into a common fund from which all would be supported and out of which the companies financing the expeditions would receive repayment and profit, a system bordering on communism so far as the settlers were concerned. John Smith remarked "When our people were fed out of the common store and laboured jointly together . . . the most honest among them would hardly take so much true paines in a weeke, as now for themselves they will doe in a day: . . ."

When the settlers were permitted greater freedom of enterprise and allowed to accumulate private property, colonies grew and prospered. Although the English urged Virginia to produce wheat and naval stores, tobacco was far more profitable, so the Virginians grew it. All along the eastern seaboard capital was created when land was cleared, fenced and otherwise improved, sawmills, tobacco warehouses, corn cribs, indigo vats, blast furnaces, rope walks and ships were built; or when men fashioned countless household tools in the leisure moments of the evening. Usually the profits from their occupations were plowed back into the business, and since people were "skimming the cream" off the resources of a virgin continent, the profits were frequently sizable.

An outstanding factor in our economic development until the 20th century was the plentifulness of land and the scarcity of labor and capital, the reverse of conditions in Europe. Since most men preferred to work for themselves, even if only on a log-cabin farm, labor for hire was scarce and there were thousands of small capitalists. The problem of the dearth of labor was met by the indentured servant system and by Negro slavery[qqv]. The lack of capital was not so well handled. Many confused capital with money and, presuming that the interest rates were high owing to a scarcity of money, urged the Government to provide more money somehow. Whether the consequent inflation[qv] in the colonies greatly retarded the inflow of capital, or whether it put to quicker use savings that would otherwise have been uselessly hoarded is still disputed. The absence of banks of deposit and discount to pool and distribute the community's savings made the flow of "liquid" capital sluggish when its efficient use was highly desirable.

British interference with the operation of our capitalistic system was a major cause of the Revolution. Parliamentary taxation took private property without our leave; enforcement of trade and navigation acts, especially the Sugar Act of 1764 which threatened a profitable triangular trade[qqv], restricted our freedom of enterprise; and the laws forbidding legal-tender paper money seemed to dry up the supply of capital.

When our weakly confederated Government broke down, propertied men were largely instrumental in drawing up and securing the adoption of the Constitution which restored some sanctity to contract, put an end to legal-tender paper money and gave increased protection to private property.

Numerous factors affected the growth of capital in the next few decades. European wars augmented the demand for our agricultural products and led to a tripling of our foreign merchant marine between 1790 and 1807. After the embargo[qv] and other decrees reduced the supply of foreign manufactures the North diverted its savings to manufacturing and after the war higher tariffs were imposed to protect this new capital. Meanwhile the invention of the cotton gin and the power loom[qqv] at the close of the 18th century stimulated the demand for the South's cotton and revived slavery. Southerners grew cotton[qv] to buy more land and slaves to grow more cotton to buy more land and slaves, etc. By the middle of the century the supply of new cotton land had been greatly reduced, much land had been exhausted and little capital invested in its restoration, the output of the slave had not increased much, for that form of capital is not easily improved, and the South had little mechanical capital to show for its efforts, a fact that lost it the Civil War.

This demand for food and cotton was a chief cause of the westward movement[qv]. Thomas Jefferson had estimated in 1800 that it would take 1000 years to fill up the region east of the Mississippi but thanks to improvements in transportation the period was much shortened. Turnpikes, canals and then railroads[qqv] enabled people to market their goods more cheaply and brought about regional specialization. Growing knowledge of how to make iron and steel, the use of coke and the standardization of parts made possible larger-sized machines, which the small capitalist or artisan could not afford, and helped cause the shift from the domestic to the factory system. Yet without the corporation[qv] with its distinguishing features of limited liability and perpetual life, capital for railroads and factories could hardly have been obtained. Now that laborer and capitalist were no longer one, or working close together, their interests diverged. Skilled labor gradually organized to deal with organized capital. Reaction to the discipline of more specialized jobs stimulated interest in the 1840's in communistic experiments like the Brook Farm[qv].

Capitalism

The period following the Civil War was one of tremendous business expansion. A good index of capital increase is the amount of power used in industry which grew from 2,300,000 horsepower in 1870 to 22,300,000 in 1914. The number of iron and steel establishments increased about 63% between 1860 and 1910, their output 14,730% and the number of their wage earners 1296%, indicating the greater average size of the plants and the extent to which capital had enabled labor to accomplish more in a day. Profits were large: because regulations were few; many resources were being exploited for the first time; high tariffs[qv] kept foreign competition out of the great free-trade area within the nation; and our patent system and the relative scarceness of labor stimulated invention. Most of the capital for this expansion was drawn from within the nation. Jay Cooke[qv] set the precedent by selling government bonds to the general public during the Civil War and stocks later, and thus did much to arouse the interest of people of moderate means in securities. In 1886 New York stock exchange[qv] transactions first exceeded a million shares a day.

This get-rich-quick era produced giant railroad companies and industrial combinations known as "trusts,"[qv] which frequently used unfair methods of competition against rivals, exploited the people and corrupted governments. Both the Interstate Commerce Act, appointing a commission to regulate the railroads, and the Sherman Antitrust Act[qqv], to break up the "trusts" and make the members compete, were at first rendered ineffective by court decisions. According to the census of 1900 there were 185 "trusts" comprising a half of 1% of all establishments in the country but owning 15% of the capital and turning out 14% of the products. Public reaction, under the leadership of Theodore Roosevelt, produced a "trust busting" and reform era. The trusts fought state laws to regulate them and to give labor and the public some measure of protection by citing the clause in the Fourteenth Amendment providing that a person may not be deprived of his property without due process[qv] of law. Attempts to establish by law the ten-hour day in bakeries (Lochner case[qv]) or set a minimum wage for women (Adkins case[qv]) were deemed by the courts to interfere with freedom of contract[qv]. Yet in the end human rights received greater recognition without capitalists suffering seriously. An increasing number and variety of businesses were declared "affected with a public interest" and put under commission supervision. The income-tax[qv] amendment and laws made inroads on former rights of private property. It is noteworthy that the Socialist presidential candidate in 1912 polled nearly a million votes, a sixteenth of the total cast in an election where there were two liberal candidates.

War is hard on capitalism, for it results in the destruction of capital and necessitates the curtailment of individual rights of private property, freedom of enterprise and contract if the economic forces of the nation are to be organized for victory. Men were drafted into the army, a war industries board[qv] set prices and restricted non-war production and the railroads were run by the Government. With peace the nation attempted to return to "normalcy," however.

The decade following the war was one of great prosperity and at such times capital accumulates rapidly. The sale of Liberty bonds[qv] had made the public security-minded and now corporation stocks came to be more widely held. Between 1919–29 the number of common stockholders of the American Telephone and Telegraph Company[qv] increased from 116,721 to 458,135 and private corporations issued $64,000,000,000 of new capital securities and reinvested about $20,000,000,000 of savings. The horsepower of the average manufacturing industry increased 49% and the number of wage earners declined about 7%. Many economists believe that overinvestment in plant and equipment was largely responsible for the depression beginning in 1929 but this theory also has many critics.

During a depression savings are drawn upon heavily. The 1934 income-tax report shows that over the four years, 1931–34, industrial corporations as a whole operated at a loss of above $11,000,000,000. Between 1931–36 private corporations acquired only $10,000,000,000 of new capital from the securities markets. After 1933 the F. D. Roosevelt administration made some radical experiments. Adopting the policy advocated by the English economist, J. M. Keynes, it tried to spend the country out of depression and in six years doubled the national debt. Under the short-lived National Industrial Recovery Act[qv] minimum wages and maximum hours were set, and trade associations were told to draw up codes of fair practice and permitted to control prices and determine production. Utilities were faced with government competition; laborers were encouraged to believe that they had a property right in their jobs; and corporate saving was discouraged by the corporations undistributed profits tax, the avowed policy of price raising and abrogation of the gold clause[qv] in debt contracts. Most of these new developments represent a departure from the conditions under which the $120,000,000,000 of capital of the country has been built up, under which, for example, Henry Ford made his great and useful fortune, and under which real wages were quadrupled between 1791 and 1933.

[B. M. Anderson, Eating the Seed Corn, *Chase Econ. Bull. XVI*, 2; C. A. Beard, *An Economic Interpretation of the Constitution of the U. S.;* E. L. Bogart, *Economic History of the American People;* V. Clark, *History of Manufactures in the U. S.;* A. M. Earle, *Home Life in Colonial Days;* H. G. Moulton, *The Formation of Capital;* C. Nettels, *The Roots of American Civilization;* E. G. Nourse, *America's Capacity to Produce; Statistical Abstract of the U. S.;* A. C. Pigou, *Capitalism versus Socialism;* B. Wootton, *Plan or No Plan;* S. S. Kuznets, *National Income and Capital Formation, 1919-35;* E. A. Keller, *A Study of the Physical Assets, Sometimes Called Wealth, of the United States, 1922-33;* C. F. Ware and G. C. Means, *The Modern Economy in Action.*]

DONALD L. KEMMERER

Capitation Taxes. The Federal Government is forbidden by Article I, Section 9, of the Constitution from levying a capitation or other direct tax, "unless in Proportion to the Census of Enumeration" laid down in Section 2. Section 9, however, in accord with colonial practices of placing taxes on the importation of convicts and Negro slaves, permits a tax or duty to be imposed on persons entering the United States, "not exceeding ten dollars for each person." The poll-tax restriction does not apply to the states. Following colonial precedents, the states have employed this tax, generally placed on all males above twenty-one, sometimes sixteen, regardless of income or property. In Southern states the poll tax has often been made a prerequisite to the exercise of the suffrage, thus disqualifying the Negro or controlling his vote.

[H. Walker, The Poll Tax in the United States, National Tax Association, *Bulletin*, Vol. IX.]

RICHARD B. MORRIS

Capitol at Washington, The. In a disappointing public competition in 1791 of amateur and professional plans, Stephen Hallet's, though not satisfactory, was judged the best. Dr. William Thornton, by permission, submitted a more artistic design and Hallet was employed to make working drawings of it, and to superintend the erection. Accused of substituting his own plan for Thornton's, he was dismissed in 1794 and George Hadfield, an English architect, succeeded him. The cornerstone was laid with Masonic ceremonies by President Washington, Sept. 18, 1793; but the center portion had not been erected when the British burned the public buildings in 1814 (*see* Washington Burned). Rebuilding commenced in 1815, under Benjamin H. Latrobe, and the center portion of Acquia freestone with a low dome, designed by Charles Bulfinch, was finished in 1827. The present north and south wings of Massachusetts marble (the fluted pillars are from Maryland) were begun in 1851, from designs of Thomas Ustick Walter, and finished in 1857–59. The present dome of cast iron, an adaptation of Michelangelo's St. Peter's (Rome) and Sir Christopher Wren's St. Paul's (London), was begun in 1856 and finished in 1865. It is surmounted by Crawford's heroic bronze of Freedom, 19½ feet high. The dome is, roughly, 300 feet in height.

[W. B. Bryan, *History of the National Capitol.*]

JOHN C. FITZPATRICK

Capper-Volstead Act, The (Feb. 18, 1922). As a consequence of the depression of agricultural prices subsequent to the World War, farm organizations intensified their drive for government aid and managed to get a farm bloc established in Congress. Sen. Capper was a member of this bloc and the Capper-Volstead Act was a part of the farm legislative program. The act authorized various kinds of agricultural producers to form voluntary co-operative associations for purposes of producing, handling and marketing farm products—that is, it exempted such associations from the application of the antitrust laws. The Secretary of Agriculture was given power, on his own motion, to prevent such associations from achieving and maintaining monopolies. He could hold hearings, determine facts and issue orders ultimately subject to review by Federal district courts. The act is an example of legislative aid to agricultural co-operatives and of the delegation of adjudicative power to an administrative agency[qv].

HARVEY PINNEY

Capron Trail, The, one of the important east and west trails of Florida, was probably first run about 1850, the date of the establishment of Fort Capron (St. Lucie in St. Lucie County). It passed from Fort Capron through Fort Vinton, Fort Drum, Fort Kissimee, Fort Clinch, Fort Meade to Fort Brooke (Tampa). Fort Capron and the Capron Trail commemorated the valor of Capt. Erastus A. Capron who was killed Aug. 20, 1847, at the battle of Churubusco[qv], Mexico.

[Frederick W. Dau, *Florida Old and New.*]

KATHRYN T. ABBEY

Capuchins, The, a branch of Franciscan[qv] Friars Minor, came to America when Richelieu assigned them missions in New England (1630) and Acadia (1632). In 1722 the order was given ecclesiastical jurisdiction over Louisiana. They built (1728) St. Louis Church, the first permanent church building in Louisiana, and established the first school in the Mississippi Valley (1725). When the Jesuits[qv] came (1726) a controversy over jurisdiction began, involving the civil authorities; it continued until the Jesuits were expelled (1763). The Capuchins have been inactive in Louisiana for a century, but their work continues elsewhere in America.

[Claude L. Vogel, *The Capuchins in French Louisiana, 1722-1766;* Otto Jeron, The Capuchins in America, *Historical Records and Studies,* V.] MACK SWEARINGEN

Caracas, Mixed Commissions at, were established subsequent to the 1902 crisis in the Venezuelan debt controversy[qv]. After negotiations at Washington in which the United States played a decisive part, protocols were signed in February and March, 1903, between Venezuela and ten creditor powers (Great Britain, Germany, Italy, France, Belgium, The Netherlands, Norway-Sweden, Mexico, Spain and the United States), providing for settlement of claims by commissions consisting of one member appointed by each party and a neutral umpire. Venezuela allotted 30% of customs revenues at La Guayra and Puerto Cabello for payments awarded. The commissions sat at Caracas (June–December, 1903) and awarded sums ranging from over 10,000,000 bolivars (francs) to Belgium to 174,000 bolivars to Norway-Sweden. The United States received about 2,250,000 bolivars. All claims were drastically cut down except for those of Belgium and Mexico. Great Britain, Germany and Italy (the blockading powers) were given priority in payment by an arbitration tribunal at The Hague[qv].

[U. S. Department of State, *Papers Relating to the Foreign Relations of the United States, 1903, 1904.*]

CHARLES C. GRIFFIN

Caravan Traffic of the Great Plains existed from approximately 1825 to 1875 and reached its maximum development during the first few years after the Civil War. During this period both immigrant and trade caravans were employed, particularly after the beginning of the Oregon movement (1842), the Mormon migration (1847) and the discovery of gold in California (1848)[qqv].

The first important caravan traffic across the Great Plains[qv] was via the Santa Fé Trail[qv]. William Becknell drove the first wagon from western Missouri to Santa Fé in 1822. This was eight years before Jedediah Smith[qv], David E. Jackson and William Sublette took a party of eighty-one men and ten large wagons (drawn by five mules each) from St. Louis to the trappers' rendezvous[qv] on the Wind River; and it was ten years before Capt. B. L. E. Bonneville[qv] conducted still another wagon train across South Pass[qv]. Caravans of twenty-five wagons or more were used largely to transport trade goods over the Santa Fé Trail to the value of $35,000 in 1824, $90,000 in 1826 and $150,000 in 1828. The distance traveled from Franklin, Mo., to Santa Fé was 870 miles. After the first few years, Lexington, some 60 miles farther west, was the point of departure; and still later, Independence[qv], 100 miles farther west, was the starting point.

Caravan movements over the Oregon Trail[qv] were equally significant, although perhaps not so important commercially. Elm Grove, about twelve miles southwest of Independence, was a favorite starting point; and later West Port. At the former place, beginning in 1842, immigrants came in covered wagons[qv] each spring, elected their captains, guides and other officers and began the long trek westward via the Oregon Trail. The caravan of 1842, organized by Dr. Elijah White, traveled as far as Fort Hall[qv] before the wagons were abandoned. From here the immigrants traveled on foot, horseback or by raft down the Snake and Columbia rivers[qqv]. The following year upward of 1000 immigrants moved over the same route in many wagons, some of which reached the banks of the Columbia.

During the 1850's, caravans, large and small, were thronging all roads across the Great Plains. Randolph B. Marcy conducted a caravan of 100 wagons from Fort Smith[qv] to New Mexico via the Canadian River[qv] in 1849, on the first leg of its journey to California; and agent William Bent (for the Comanches and Kiowas[qqv]) estimated 60,000 immigrants to have crossed the plains along the Arkansas route[qv] in 1859. Heavy freight caravans plied the routes between San Antonio and Chihuahua, between Santa Fé and Chihuahua; and from points in Nebraska, Kansas and Colorado to the far West by 1860. From Council Bluff to the Great Salt Lake via Fort Bridger[qv] was a well-known road over which thousands of Mormon[qv] pilgrims traveled from 1847 to 1860.

The Army Appropriation Bill of 1853 made available $150,000 to be spent by the Secretary of War, Jefferson Davis, to survey routes for western railways, and soon thereafter four surveys were made. This promised a new era that was formally initiated by the first Union Pacific[qv] Act of 1862. Seven years later the first transcontinental line was completed. But caravan trade and travel were to remain for a decade yet until railroads could offer adequate facilities.

[Josiah Gregg, *Commerce of the Prairies;* Alexander

Majors, *Seventy Years on the Frontier;* Col. Henry Inman and Col. William F. Cody, *The Great Salt Lake Trail;* F. L. Paxson, *History of the American Frontier;* W. J. Ghent, *The Early Far West, A Narrative Outline, 1540-1850.*]

C. C. RISTER

Caravans, Outfitting of. A visitor to the West in 1860 estimated that 20,000 wagons were in use transporting immigrants and supplies, requiring around 100,000 oxen and 40,000 mules to pull them. Western towns such as St. Louis, Fort Smith, Little Rock, San Antonio, Denver and Salt Lake City[qqv] did a thriving business in consequence. At one of these (or others equally active), immigrants bound for the far West had a last opportunity to purchase necessities. Food (such as meal, flour, sugar, coffee and bacon), clothing, blankets, guns and ammunition, farm implements (such as an ax, hoe, shovel or an occasional plow) were a few of the purchases. In addition, immigrant wagons were generally burdened with certain household goods (a bedstead, a framed picture of grandfather or grandmother, a favorite chair and perhaps one or more heirlooms), and other sundry things considered as necessities. Many an immigrant traveling the Oregon Trail[qv] to the Columbia or the Platte route to California discarded much of his impedimenta before he arrived at his destination. In consequence many intermediate towns and communities profited. Settlers at Salt Lake City and in the Great Basin[qv] did a thriving exchange trade with the Forty-niners[qv], buying worn-out horses and cattle, or exchanging potatoes and flour for their excess burdens. Likewise Denver was to profit as a supply center during Colorado's gold-rush days, 1858–65 (*see* Pikes Peak Gold Rush).

The great rush for western lands following the enactment of the Federal homestead law[qv] of 1862 greatly increased caravan traffic[qv]; and in every town of considerable size along the frontier was one or more well-known supply firms. Guns and ammunition were generally bought. During the period of the destruction of the bison (*see* Buffalo, The) from the southern plains, a general supply store at Fort Griffin[qv], Texas, during a one-day period (1877), sold goods to the value of better than $4000, of which $2500 represented guns and ammunition. Other supplies were plows, farm tools, staple groceries, wagons, kerosene, dry goods, seed and feed for livestock. Such quantities of supplies were required that numerous freighting firms were organized and long trains of wagons were on every well-traveled road.

[Alexander Majors, *Seventy Years on the Frontier;* F. L. Paxson, *History of the American Frontier.*]

C. C. RISTER

Cardiff Giant, THE. A human figure weighing 2966 lbs. cut from Iowa gypsum in Chicago for George Hull, transported to Cardiff, N. Y., and secretly buried on the Newell farm. In 1869 it was "discovered" and exhibited as a petrified prehistoric giant, creating much excitement and deceiving many people until the hoax was revealed.

[*Autobiography of Andrew Dickson White.*]

DEXTER S. KIMBALL

Carey Desert Land Grant Act, THE (Aug. 18, 1894), authorized the President to grant to each public land state[qv] not exceeding 1,000,000 acres of desert lands in the public domain[qv] within its boundaries for sale to settlers, and for irrigation, reclamation, cultivation and occupancy, in tracts not exceeding 160 acres each, of which 20 acres in each tract must be cultivated on penalty of reversion of the tract to the public domain. Surplus derived by states from such land sales, in excess of cost of reclamation, was to be held as a trust fund for reclamation of other desert land in the state.

[William H. and Richard Olney Mason, *Mason's United States Code, Annotated.*]

FRED A. EMERY

Caribbean Policy. The special interest of the United States in the Caribbean, manifest from the earliest days of the Republic, greatly increased after the Spanish-American War[qv]. Puerto Rico[qv] had become an American colony and Cuba[qv] under the Platt Amendment[qv], a quasi-protectorate. The construction of the Panama Canal[qv], begun soon afterward, greatly increased the strategic importance of the lands which controlled its approaches. At the same time, political disorder and the resulting inability to meet obligations to foreigners exposed the smaller Central American and West Indian republics to increasingly frequent foreign intervention. This situation led President Theodore Roosevelt in 1905 to enunciate his so-called corollary to the Monroe Doctrine[qv]: that the United States could not prevent European intervention in the weaker American republics unless it took steps itself to correct conditions which invited such intervention.

The policy of Roosevelt and his immediate successors appears to have been based on this principle. Roosevelt himself occasionally interfered in the affairs of the Caribbean countries when serious crises occurred, as in the adjustment of the debts of the Dominican Republic[qv], the second intervention in Cuba and the Central-American disturbances of 1906–7. The Taft administration intervened forcibly in Nicaragua[qv], and in other countries adopted the so-called preventive policy, giving advice or exerting diplomatic pressure to prevent the development of situations which might make intervention necessary. The Wilson administration went farther, seeking to persuade several of the more disorderly countries to agree to the reorganization of their military forces under American instructors and the control of their expenditures as well as their revenues by American fiscal experts. The failure of these efforts was followed by the actual military occupation of Haiti^qv^ and the Dominican Republic. The United States continued during this period to exercise much influence in the internal politics of Nicaragua, Panama and Cuba.

Under Presidents Harding and Coolidge, the general trend was toward less interference. Crowder's special mission in Cuba terminated, and the military government was withdrawn from the Dominican Republic. On the other hand, the United States made more definite its policy of refusing to recognize revolutionary governments in Central America and the withdrawal of the American marines from Nicaragua in 1925 was followed by the second intervention there. This latter event caused a strong reaction against "imperialism"^qv^ both in the United States and in Latin America. Influenced by this sentiment, the Hoover administration adopted a definite policy of nonintervention. American forces were withdrawn from Nicaragua and American control in Haiti was greatly restricted.

President Franklin Roosevelt announced in December, 1933, that "the definite policy of the United States from now on is one opposed to armed intervention." In pursuance of the "Good Neighbor Policy"^qv^ new treaties have been signed superseding those authorizing American intervention in Cuba and Panama, and the American marines have been withdrawn from Haiti. The policy of not recognizing revolutionary governments appears to have been largely abandoned. A measure of financial control, for the protection of bondholders, still exists in Haiti and in the Dominican Republic.

[Council on Foreign Relations, *Survey of American Foreign Relations, 1929;* Chester Lloyd Jones, *The Caribbean Since 1900.*]

DANA G. MUNRO

Carillion, Fort. *See* Ticonderoga, Fort.

Carlisle, Pa., founded 1751, became the center of the Scotch-Irish^qv^ settlement in the Cumberland Valley. At the crossroads of important Indian trails, and the site of Fort Louther, it was a refuge and trading center for pioneers.

[C. P. Wing, *History Cumberland County, Pa.*]

MULFORD STOUGH

Carlisle Commission. *See* Peace Commission of 1778 (British).

Carlisle (Pa.) Indian School was established in 1879 by Capt. R. H. Pratt, under whose twenty-five-year direction it grew from 136 to 1000 pupils (boys and girls), the equipment expanding accordingly. Instruction included practical training in farming, horticulture, dressmaking, cooking, laundering, housekeeping and twenty trades. A distinctive feature was the "Outing System." Pupils were urged to spend a year working on farms, in homes or industries of the neighborhood. The school was closed in 1918.

[Elaine Goodale Eastman, *Pratt, The Red Man's Moses.*]

MULFORD STOUGH

Carlotta, Confederate Colony of. In 1865 many ex-Confederates left their native land for Mexico. Emperor Maximilian encouraged this exodus by appointing Commodore M. F. Maury Imperial Commissioner of Immigration. Military and civil colonies were to be established along the railway between Vera Cruz and Mexico City. The best-known colony, comprising 500,000 acres, was Carlotta, in the Cordova Valley, named in honor of the Empress. Among reasons for failure were a hostile American press; lack of funds; improper colonization methods; forcible land seizure and occupation; disturbed political condition in Mexico; local hostility; and opposition of the United States Government.

[George D. Harmon, Confederate Migration to Mexico, *Hispanic American Historical Review,* November, 1937, pp. 458-88.]

C. C. RISTER

Carlsbad Caverns, southeastern New Mexico, discovered by Jim White, Texas cowboy, in 1901, became a national monument in 1923 and a national park in 1930. The caverns occupy a tract of 720 acres. Largest of the explored part of the caverns is the "Big Room," more than three quarters of a mile long, 625 feet wide and 350 feet high.

[Ford Sibley, *My Trip Through Carlsbad Caverns.*]

S. S. MCKAY

Carmelites, THE, were one of the Roman Catholic monastic orders which came to Louisiana in the early days of French settlement. When the province was divided into three ecclesiastical districts on May 16, 1722, they were given charge of all the region east of the Mississippi, from the Gulf of Mexico to the Wabash River, with headquarters at Mobile. Their administration was short-lived, for their jurisdiction was added to that of the Capuchins[qv] on Dec. 19, 1722, and they returned to France.

[A. Fortier, *History of Louisiana.*]

WALTER PRICHARD

Carmelo River, The, which enters the Pacific Ocean from the southeast about five miles southwest of Monterey[qv], Calif., was discovered in 1602 by Sebastián Vizcaíno who exaggerated it to the proportions of a mighty river. It was long sought by subsequent explorers.

OSGOOD HARDY

Carnegie Corporation of New York, established by Andrew Carnegie in 1911, is for the advancement and diffusion of knowledge and understanding among the people of the United States and the British Dominions and colonies. Its endowment consists of two funds totaling $135,000,000, of which $10,000,000 is applicable in the British Dominions and colonies. The income only is subject to the disposal of the trustees.

For the first eight years of the Corporation's history, and until the time of his death, Mr. Carnegie was the president of the governing board of trustees and the administration of the Corporation was, in those years, chiefly under his personal direction and authority. Shortly after his death the trustees provided for a president who should give his whole time to the service of the board and should be its executive officer.

Before creating the Carnegie Corporation Mr. Carnegie had founded and endowed separately five other agencies in the United States: Carnegie Institute of Pittsburgh, Carnegie Institution of Washington[qv], Carnegie Hero Fund Commission[qv], Carnegie Foundation for the Advancement of Teaching[qv] and the Carnegie Endowment for International Peace.

The present program of the Corporation includes the support of educational and scientific research, publications of professional and scholarly societies and associations, fine arts education through educational institutions and national organizations, adult education, library service and training, and support of various related projects which give promise of providing new knowledge through (1) research, (2) studies which, through examination of existing conditions, may point to better conditions in the future, or (3) demonstrations, local or regional, of how new knowledge may most effectively be applied.

[Frederick Paul Keppel, *The Foundation; Its Place in American Life;* Robert M. Lester, *The Corporation; A Digest of Its Financial Record, 1911-1936.*]

ROBERT M. LESTER

Carnegie Foundation for the Advancement of Teaching, The, established in 1905 by Andrew Carnegie, was incorporated by act of Congress approved March 10, 1906, "to provide retiring pensions for the teachers of Universities, Colleges, and Technical Schools in our Country, Canada, and Newfoundland" and "in general to do and perform all things necessary to uphold and dignify the profession of the teacher and the cause of higher education." Initial endowment of $10,000,000 from Mr. Carnegie was increased in 1908 to $15,000,000 to include publicly controlled higher institutions of education. Other gifts have come from Carnegie Corporation of New York[qv]. The self-perpetuating board of trustees consists of twenty-five members. Retiring allowances are provided only within a list of specified persons. The Foundation has disbursed (1938) more than $33,000,000 for allowances and widows' pensions in 168 institutions for 2755 individuals comprising 1855 retired college teachers and administrative officers and 900 widows.

In 1913 an endowment of $1,250,000 for its Division of Educational Enquiry was accepted from Mr. Carnegie. Studies made in or for the Division have dealt with medical, legal, engineering and dental education, college athletics, teacher training and the relation of colleges and secondary schools in Pennsylvania, etc. Results have been issued in twenty-nine bulletins, thirty-two annual reports and thirty-seven miscellaneous publications. Resources (1938) are $28,052,-465. The Foundation offers no fellowships or scholarships of any kind.

[Annual Reports, 1906-37.]

HOWARD J. SAVAGE

Carnegie Hero Fund Commission, The, was created in 1904 for the purpose of making annual awards from a trust income of $5,000,000, given by Andrew Carnegie, to recognize acts of heroism in the United States, Canada and Newfoundland. The Commission awards medals to heroes and gives out of this trust fund financial assistance when needed by those it recognizes for heroic acts, and for education, purchase of homes, liquidation of debts and pensions for dependents, according to merits of each case.

FRED A. EMERY

Carnegie Institution of Washington, The, was founded in 1902 by Andrew Carnegie "to encourage in the broadest and most liberal manner investigation, research, and discovery, and the application of knowledge to the improvement of mankind."

The Institution attempts to advance fundamental research in fields not normally covered by the activities of other agencies and to concentrate its attention upon specific problems, with the idea of shifting attack from time to time to meet the more pressing needs of research as they develop with increase of knowledge. Constant efforts are made to facilitate interpretation and application of results of research activities of the Institution.

JOHN C. MERRIAM

Carnegie Steel Company. *See* United States Steel Corporation.

Carnifex Ferry, Battles at (1861). An Ohio regiment posted at this river-crossing in West Virginia was routed on Aug. 26 by a Confederate brigade under Gen. John B. Floyd, who thereupon entrenched and remained there until attacked on Sept. 10 by Rosecrans' small army. After a sharp action, Floyd, slightly wounded, retreated with his command during the night.

[*Battles and Leaders of the Civil War.*]

ALVIN F. HARLOW

"Carolana" was a colony projected by Daniel Coxe, a British physician and land speculator, who by 1698 had acquired title to the Sir Robert Heath grant[qv] of 1629, under which he claimed the region in the rear of the Carolina settlements and including the lower Mississippi Valley. The expedition sent out to plant the colony landed at Charleston (S. C.), but one ship sailed up the Mississippi River for 100 miles, turning back when Bienville informed the captain, on Sept. 15, 1699, that the French already occupied the region (*see* Louisiana, as a French and Spanish Colony). Coxe reasserted his claim to the territory, but his colony never materialized.

[Edward McCrady, *The History of South Carolina under the Proprietary Government, 1670-1719;* Samuel A. Ashe, *History of North Carolina;* R. G. Thwaites, *France in America, 1497-1763;* Grace King, *Jean Baptiste LeMoyne, Sieur de Bienville;* Alcée Fortier, *History of Louisiana;* Charles Gayarré, *History of Louisiana.*]

WALTER PRICHARD

Carolina, The Fundamental Constitutions of, the most pretentious of the attempts to establish a feudal aristocracy in English America, were drawn up in 1669 by John Locke under the direction of his employer and patron the Earl of Shaftesbury. Between that date and 1698 four revisions were issued by the Lords Proprietors. Outstanding features were the provisions for a provincial nobility of proprietors, landgraves and caziques[qqv] having permanent ownership of two fifths of the land; for a Grand Council made up of proprietors and their councilors which should have the executive and judicial authority, and—through its control of the initiative—should likewise control legislation; for an established Anglican Church and religious toleration; and for serfdom and slavery.

Shelving the top-heavy system for a time at the beginning of settlement, the proprietors set up revised Grand Councils in North and in South Carolina, but in the former the Fundamental Constitutions had little weight. In South Carolina they greatly strengthened the tendency toward a dominant landed aristocracy, and to them may be traced the ballot and certain land ownership requirements for voting and officeholding. The attempts of the proprietors to force the complete system upon the assembly came to a climax and failure about 1690.

[Edward McCrady, *The History of South Carolina under the Proprietary Government;* S. A. Ashe, *History of North Carolina.*]

R. L. MERIWETHER

Carolina Proprietors. The first Carolina patent was granted by Charles I to Sir Robert Heath[qv] in 1629. By its terms the province extended from ocean to ocean between the 31st and 36th parallels. This patent was declared forfeited on the ground of nonuse by Charles II, who in 1663 issued a charter with the same bounds to eight joint proprietors: Edward Hyde, Earl of Clarendon; George Monk, Duke of Albemarle; William, Lord Craven; John, Lord Berkeley; Anthony Ashley Cooper, Lord Ashley (later Earl of Shaftesbury); Sir George Carteret; Sir John Colleton; and Sir William Berkeley. In 1665 the boundaries were extended to include the territory from 29° to 36° 30′ N. Lat. "Declarations and Proposals," the first organic law, issued by the proprietors in 1663, promised land to settlers who should emigrate within five years, representation of freeholders in a provincial assembly and liberty of conscience. The Fundamental Constitutions of Carolina[qv], formulated by John Locke in 1669, never went into effect in the colony.

The enterprise resulting in loss, proprietary neglect became chronic. Great discontent was caused by the indifference of the proprietors during the war with the Tuscaroras (1711–12), and the Yamasee War (1715–16)[qqv] and by their lack of support when the province was threatened from the West Indies by the French and the Spanish (1706, 1719) and when it was attacked by pirates (1718). Proprietary orders destructive of provincial interests brought about a revolutionary movement in South Carolina[qv] (1719), which the crown thereupon took over as a royal colony, leaving North Carolina^qv^ to the proprietors until purchase of the proprietorship of both provinces for the crown (1729). Lord Carteret retained his interest in the form of a strip of land lying south of Virginia and estimated at an eighth of the original grant (*see* Granville Grant).

[S. A. Ashe, *History of North Carolina;* R. D. W. Connor, *History of North Carolina;* Edward McCrady, *The History of South Carolina under the Proprietary Government;* D. D. Wallace, *History of South Carolina.*]

D. D. WALLACE

Carolina Road. *See* Virginia Path, The.

Carolinas, Sherman's March through the. In February, 1865, Sherman's (U.) army left Savannah^qv^ on its way northward "to make South Carolina feel the severities of war" and to unite with Grant (U.) in Virginia. By Feb. 17 it was at Columbia^qv^, S. C., which was burned. None in Sherman's army ever admitted responsibility for this act. On March 10 the army was at Fayetteville, N. C. As Sherman advanced, opposition became stronger. At Bentonville^qv^ on March 19 the advance was delayed several days, but by the 25th Sherman was at Goldsboro. On April 13 he had reached Raleigh.

The news of Lee's surrender^qv^ caused Gen. J. E. Johnston (C.) to negotiate for the surrender of the Confederate Army. A conditional agreement was signed, April 18, but was repudiated because of too liberal terms. On the 26th Johnston surrendered on the same terms Lee had received.

Sherman marched nearly 500 miles in about eight weeks, impeded as much by the multitude of slaves and their families who mingled with the marching troops as by the weak and unorganized Confederate opposition.

[*Battles and Leaders of the Civil War.*]

THOMAS ROBSON HAY

Caroline, Fort. *See* Florida, French in.

***Caroline* Affair.** In November, 1837, William Lyon McKenzie launched a rebellion in Upper Canada. Defeated by the government forces, McKenzie and his followers fled to Navy Island in the Niagara River. Sympathizers on the American side of the river supplied them with food, arms and recruits. In this service the steamer *Caroline* was employed. On the night of Dec. 29 a body of Canadian troops crossed to the American side and seized the *Caroline,* killing Amos Durfee, an American, in the struggle. The steamer was towed into midstream, set afire and turned adrift. President Van Buren caused the State Department to protest vigorously to the British minister at Washington and to lodge a protest at London, all of which was ignored. For a time feeling ran high on both sides of the border and steps were taken to forestall invasion from Canada and to prevent Americans from violating the frontier. However, the case dragged on for some years and meanwhile became complicated by the arrest, in New York, of Alexander McLeod^qv^ for the murder of Durfee. As an adjunct of the Webster-Ashburton Treaty^qv^ the affair was settled in 1842 by an expression of regret on the part of England that there had not been an immediate explanation and apology for the occurrence.

[*Canadian Historical Review,* June, 1931; *New York History,* April, 1937; J. B. McMaster, *History of the People of the United States,* VI.]

MILLEDGE L. BONHAM, JR.

Carondelet, THE, was a Mississippi River steamboat with a sloping iron casemate and thirteen guns, built at St. Louis by Eads, which fought at Fort Henry and Fort Donelson^qqv^. In April, 1862, under Commander Henry Walke it forced the evacuation of Island Number Ten^qv^ by running past the batteries at night to safeguard Union troops crossing below.

[*Battles and Leaders of the Civil War.*]

WALTER B. NORRIS

Carondelet Canal, THE, named for the Spanish governor who sponsored it in 1794 as a navigation and drainage project, extended a mile and a half from New Orleans to Bayou St. John, thus opening water communication between the city and Lake Pontchartrain and eliminating the necessity of the long Mississippi River voyage.

[J. S. Kendall, *History of New Orleans.*]

WALTER PRICHARD

Carondelet Intrigue. Hector, Baron de Carondelet, was one of the governors of Spanish Louisiana who intrigued with western communities of the United States, notably Kentucky, for the purpose of detaching them from the Union. His purpose was to thwart the policy of the United States to secure unchallenged access to the Mississippi River^qv^, a tendency which made Spanish colonial officials fear for the safety of Louisiana and New Spain. The movement came to an end with the ratification (1795) of Pinckney's Treaty^qv^.

[Arthur Preston Whitaker, *The Spanish American Frontier, 1783-1795;* Samuel Flagg Bemis, *Pinckney's Treaty.*]

SAMUEL FLAGG BEMIS

Carpenters' Hall, Philadelphia, on Chestnut Street between Third and Fourth streets, was built by the Carpenters' Guild in 1770 as a meeting place for its members. It was here the first Continental Congress[qv] convened, on Sept. 5, 1774.

[Minutes Carpenters' Company, 1873; J. T. Schraft, *History of Philadelphia.*]

CHARLES W. HEATHCOTE

Carpet Manufacture. Carpetings first appeared in American homes around 1700. For over a century the meager domestic supply was a product of households, itinerant handicraftsmen, or small shops operated under a putting-out system. Aided by favorable tariff rates, transition to the factory organization began in 1791 when William P. Sprague set up a plant in Philadelphia. The linking of the Jacquard[qv] apparatus to the hand looms in 1828 gave a further impetus to this movement; and by 1835 the industry was dominated by sizeable mills located chiefly in the eastern coastal states. At this early date practically all varieties of modern floor coverings were being produced. Inventions by Erastus B. Bigelow and Halcyon Skinner between 1840 and 1875 made power weaving possible and by the latter date production was organized along modern lines in large plants, employing in some instances over 1000 workers. Lowered production costs and increasing national wealth combined to make the use of carpetings almost commonplace after 1870.

[A. H. Cole and H. F. Williamson, *The American Carpet and Rug Industry.*]

HAROLD FRANCIS WILLIAMSON

Carpetbaggers were persons from the North who went to the South after the Civil War[qv] and who, through affiliation with the Republican party[qv], became exploiters of the South, sometimes as financial adventurers, but more often as officeholders. Carpetbagger was an epithet of opprobrium applied by Southerners of the antebellum dominant class to these newcomers who were presumably settlers so transitory and propertyless that their entire goods could be carried in carpetbags, the characteristic hand luggage of the period. The term was used primarily of the Reconstruction[qv] period, 1865–77, but especially after the Reconstruction Acts of 1867 brought the states of the former Confederacy under radical control.

Many of the carpetbaggers were young men who had served in the Union Army during the war or in the Treasury Department and who, at the close of the war, became agents of the Freedmen's Bureau[qv]. Some were missionaries sent from the North to minister to the needs of the Negroes. Others went South not in any official capacity, but in search of their fortunes. All groups found their chance for political activity when the Reconstruction Acts of 1867 demanded a thoroughgoing reorganization of all the former Confederate states, except Tennessee. Because the old officeholding class was disqualified and because the new electorate was not experienced in holding office, there was opportunity for leadership which the newcomers avidly seized. Even before 1867 some of these newcomers in each state had become experienced in political activity as organizers of the Loyal Leagues[qv], which attempted to bring the Negroes and the former white unionists together in loyalty to the Republican party.

In the constitutional conventions elected in 1867–68 in the South, carpetbaggers were strongly represented and took active part in shaping the new state constitutions. In the seven states which were restored to the Union in 1868, four of the governors were carpetbaggers. In Congress there were many carpetbaggers in the delegations from the newly reconstructed states, twenty out of thirty-five members in 1868 in the House of Representatives and ten of the fourteen members of the United States Senate. Among the newcomers from the North there were a few Negroes who rose to conspicuous position as leaders of their race. Such were Hiram R. Revels, a colored preacher who succeeded Jefferson Davis as Senator from Mississippi, and Robert Elliott, who rose to power in state politics in South Carolina. Within the states, as in Congress, carpetbaggers generally supported the various schemes of fraudulent bond issues and other extravagant and corrupt financial programs which helped to bring the radical reconstruction governments into ill repute. After the political machinery of radical reconstruction in the South collapsed in 1876 or earlier, many carpetbaggers returned to the North; others who remained in the South ceased to live by public office and were absorbed in the ordinary class of work-a-day citizens. With the restoration of home rule in the South carpetbaggers as a class disappeared.

[E. P. Oberholtzer, *History of the United States since the Civil War*, Vol. II.]

C. MILDRED THOMPSON

Carriage Making. Horse-drawn vehicles were made in the colonies from their settlement. Prior to the Revolution, however, pleasure vehicles were rare and confined to towns. Most country travel was on horseback on account of poor roads.

Extensive road building and a rapid increase of horse-drawn vehicles began with the birth of the Republic, testifying to the territorial expansion of the country, the greater mobility of its population and the democratization of travel. Famous builders of wagons and stagecoaches established themselves at strategic points like Troy, N. Y., and Concord, N. H. (*see* Concord Coach).

After carriages for the well-to-do, such as the fifty-nine owned in New York in 1770, ceased to measure the demand for personal wheeled transportation, private conveyances developed along popular lines typical of American manufactures. The first example of this was the "one-horse shay," a light vehicle with two high wheels adapted to the rough roads and numerous fords of the still undeveloped country. For fifty years these were so popular that proprietors of carriage shops were usually known as chaise-makers.

By the middle of the last century the chaise was superseded by the four-wheel buggy, the most typical American vehicle prior to the cheap motor car. It was simpler, lighter, stronger and cheaper than other corresponding conveyances and culminated the 100-year era of horse-drawn transportation in the United States.

Carriage making, long since a factory industry, reached the height of its development in 1904. Since then it has declined rapidly. The number of horse-drawn vehicles of all kinds made annually in this country is less than 50,000, compared with 1,700,000 thirty years ago, and the number of wage earners engaged in making such vehicles has fallen to less than 5% of the number at the opening of the century.

[Ezra M. Stratton, *The World on Wheels;* Chauncey M. Depew, *One Hundred Years of American Commerce;* Victor S. Clark, *History of Manufactures in the United States.*]

VICTOR S. CLARK

Carriage Tax, Constitutionality of. In the case of Hylton v. U. S. (3 Dallas 171, 1796) the question of whether a tax on carriages imposed by an act of Congress (June 5, 1794) was a direct tax, and therefore subject to the rule of apportionment, was decided in the negative. Three justices, Chase, Paterson and Iredell, sitting without their colleagues, decided unanimously that the tax was an excise or duty and not a direct tax[qv]. The case is chiefly interesting as the first in which the constitutionality of an act of Congress was directly reviewed by the Court.

[Charles Warren, *History of the Supreme Court of the United States.*]

PHILLIPS BRADLEY

Carrion Crow Bayou (Bayou Carencro), Battle of, was fought on Oct. 14–15, 1863, when the Confederates attempted to turn back a Federal raid up the Teche from Berwick Bay (Brashear City) to Opelousas and Washington, La. Other skirmishes occurred there on Nov. 3, 11, 18, 1863, during the return of the Federal raiders to New Iberia.

[*War of the Rebellion Records*, Series 1, XXVI, Part I, 332-395; C. A. Evans, ed., *Confederate Military History*, X, 105-106.]

WALTER PRICHARD

Carrizal, Skirmish of (June 21, 1916). Two troops of the 10th Cavalry, on a reconnaissance mission, attempted to force passage through the town of Carrizal, Chihuahua, Mexico (*see* Mexico, Punitive Expedition into). Four hundred Carranzistas, representatives of the Mexican government, resisted. In the skirmish that followed the American troops were defeated and forced to withdraw, leaving two officers and forty-three enlisted men killed, wounded or taken prisoner. This incident resulted in an exchange of sharp notes between the two governments and the massing of troops for quick action. However, further conflict was avoided by the appointment of a joint commission and the eventual withdrawal of American troops from Mexico.

[Frank Tompkins, *Chasing Villa.*]

C. A. WILLOUGHBY

Carrying Trade. *See* Shipping, Ocean; Freight; Motor Truck Transport.

Cartagena Expedition, The, organized in England and composed of 30 ships of the line, some 90 other vessels, 15,000 sailors and 12,000 land troops, was designed to capture the great Spanish stronghold of the Caribbean region (*see* King George's War). At Jamaica the expedition was re-enforced by 3600 troops from the colonies, consisting of 5 companies from Massachusetts, 2 from Rhode Island, 2 from Connecticut, 5 from New York, 3 from New Jersey, 8 from Pennsylvania, 3 from Maryland, 4 from Virginia and 4 from North Carolina. The attacks on Cartagena, from March 9 to April 11, 1741, failed, and about two thirds of the land force was lost from illness and in battle.

[H. L. Osgood, *The American Colonies in the 18th Century.*]

PERCY SCOTT FLIPPIN

Carter v. Carter Coal Company, 1936 (298 U. S. 238). In this case the Guffey Coal Act[qv] regulating wages, hours, conditions of work and prices in the coal industry was declared unconstitutional on grounds that the production of coal is not within the interstate commerce power and that the act also made an unconstitutional delegation of legislative power. The price-fixing provisions were not passed upon. Seven states presented briefs on behalf of the act, arguing that the problems of the coal industry could not be solved by independent state action.

HARVEY PINNEY

Carter's Valley Settlement. John Carter, later leader in the Watauga settlement[qv], located a trading house on the west side of the Holston River below Long Island and south of the Virginia line in 1770, and that section of the Holston Valley has ever since borne the name of Carter's Valley. Carter sold supplies to emigrants who came to Long Island to begin the water journey to the Natchez district, and also to the Cherokee Indians[qv] out on hunts. The Indian chiefs objected to this trading post and in 1772 it was robbed by the Indians and abandoned by Carter, who removed to the Watauga. In the early part of 1776 another settlement of the valley was attempted only to be broken up in the summer of that year. Settlements by the hardier of the pioneers were renewed in 1777, and they thereafter held the fertile region in fair security.

[S. C. Williams, *Dawn of Tennessee Valley and Tennessee History.*]

SAMUEL C. WILLIAMS

Carthage (Mo.), Battle of (July 5, 1861). Defeated at Boonville[qv] by Gen. Nathaniel Lyon, the secessionists under Gov. Jackson and Gen. Sterling Price retreated into southwest Missouri (*see* Price in Missouri), hoping for reinforcements from Arkansas. Anticipating this, Lyon sent Col. Franz Sigel to Springfield. Sigel advanced to check the retreating enemy until Lyon arrived. Near Carthage on July 5, although greatly outnumbered, he attacked Jackson. Defeated, Sigel retreated to Springfield. Impeded by high waters, Lyon arrived a week later. Encouraged by victory and reinforcements, the secessionists prepared to advance on Springfield.

[E. M. Violette, *A History of Missouri.*]

GLENN H. BENTON

Cartoons, Political. Early cartoons were woodcuts or engravings. Benjamin Franklin printed his "Join or Die" snake cartoon in the *Pennsylvania Gazette*[qv], May 9, 1754; and it was widely copied in the colonial period. Paul Revere and other artists depicted the effects of the Stamp Act, the Boston Massacre[qqv], etc., in separately issued engravings. The ratification of the Constitution[qv] was celebrated by Benjamin Russell with the rising columns of the "Federal Edifice" cartoon in the *Massachusetts Centinel* (1788); but woodcut cartoons were used sparingly in newspapers. From the Jackson period through the Civil War many poster cartoons, wood engravings and lithographs were produced. These often contained portraits of political figures, with lettering issuing from their mouths. Civil War cartoons appeared in periodicals such as *Harper's Weekly* and *Vanity Fair.* The modern cartoon, a pen drawing with effective caricatures, was the creation of Thomas Nast[qv] of *Harper's Weekly* in the post-war period. He popularized such symbols as the Republican elephant and the Tammany tiger. The first newspaper editorial cartoons were those of Walt McDougall used by the New York *World* in 1884; and were followed by those of Homer Davenport and Frederick Opper, creators of the dollar-marked suit and bloated "trust" figures in the *Journal.*

[William Murrell, *A History of American Graphic Humor, 1747-1938*, 2 vols.]

MILTON W. HAMILTON

Carver Claim, The, grew out of the assertion that at St. Paul on May 1, 1767, the Sioux[qv] nation granted to Jonathan Carver an extensive tract embracing approximately the northwestern one fourth of modern Wisconsin. The American Government rejected the claim over a century ago, but until recent decades credulous individuals have continued to press land titles based upon it.

[M. M. Quaife, Jonathan Carver and the Carver Grant, in *Mississippi Valley Historical Review*, VII, 3-25.]

M. M. QUAIFE

Carver's Travels (1766–68). The first Englishman to visit and publicly describe the region of the upper Great Lakes and the upper Mississippi was Capt. Jonathan Carver of Massachusetts. His tour, performed in 1766–68, was described in his *Travels,* first published in London in 1778. The book proved immensely popular, and many editions, in several different languages, were issued. In recent decades the reliability of the narrative has been keenly debated by scholars; examination of Carver's manuscript journal establishes that it differs in important respects from the published version. More recent research points to the conclusion that while Carver actually made the tour he describes, he suppressed the fact that he performed it as a hired agent of Maj. Robert Rogers, who was intent on finding the Northwest Passage[qv] to the Pacific Ocean, rather than on his own responsibility.

[Louise P. Kellogg, *British Régime in Wisconsin and the Northwest*, 49-75.]

M. M. QUAIFE

Cary's Rebellion, an uprising in colonial North Carolina occasioned by the disfranchisement of the Quakers[qv], a numerous sect in that province. In 1707 Thomas Cary, deputy governor, was deposed at the solicitation of the Quakers, but for two years refused to abandon his office. When the proprietors sent Edward Hyde as governor, Cary revolted, though he had promised to support Hyde. With Virginia aid, Cary was defeated, captured and sent to England on a treason charge, but was never tried.

[R. D. W. Connor, *North Carolina.*]

HUGH T. LEFLER

Cascades of the Columbia, The, are falls or rapids in the Columbia River near where the Bonneville Dam[qv] now stands. They were a cause of great difficulty to the explorers and fur traders, and were especially dreaded by the settlers, who often preferred the toil and hardships of crossing mountain passes to the dangers to life and property encountered in descending these cascades.

[Lewis A. McArthur, *Oregon Geographic Names.*]

DAN E. CLARK

Casco, Treaty of (1678), brought to a close the war between the eastern Indians and the English settlers of Massachusetts Bay[qv] and sought to re-establish the friendly relations between the Indians and English that had characterized the northern settlements previous to the outbreak of King Philip's War[qv] in 1675. By the terms of this treaty all captives were to be surrendered without ransom. The treaty also stipulated that the English should give the Indians one peck of corn annually for each family settled on Indian lands, with the exception of Maj. Phillips of Saco, a great proprietor, who was required to give a bushel.

[Francis Parkman, *A Half-Century of Conflict,* Vol. I.]

ELIZABETH RING

Casco, Treaty of (1703), was an unsuccessful attempt made by Gov. Dudley of Massachusetts Bay[qv] to prevent further Indian hostilities from breaking out along the northern frontier. War was already going on in Europe between England and France (*see* Queen Anne's War) and the eastern Indians from whom trouble was expected were under the influence of French Jesuits[qv]. Accordingly, Gov. Dudley appointed a meeting of the several chiefs and their tribes to confer with him and his councilors to reconcile whatever differences had arisen since the last treaty. They met in Casco, Maine, June 20, 1703. The Indians made the customary professions of peace, disavowing any conspiracy with the French to exterminate the English. They then presented the governor with a belt of wampum[qv] and ended the ceremony with an exchange of volleys. The Indians undoubtedly intended to make the white leaders their victims on the spot, but the white and Indian leaders were so placed that one group could not be destroyed without the other. Within two months the eastern Indians were again on the warpath and the people of New England prepared for another period of surprise attacks from Indian enemies.

[J. G. Palfrey, *History of New England,* Vol. III.]

ELIZABETH RING

Casimir, Fort. *See* New Castle.

Casket Girls were women imported into Louisiana by the *Compagnie des Indes* as wives for settlers. Their name derives from the small chests (*cassettes*) in which they carried their clothes. They were conspicuous by reason of their virtue. Normally women were supplied to the colonists by raking the streets of Paris for undesirables, or by emptying the houses of correction. The Casket Girls, however, were recruited from church charitable institutions and, although poor, were practically guaranteed to be virtuous. For this reason, says Gayarré, it later became a matter of pride in Louisiana to show descent from them rather than from the more numerous prostitutes. Aside from providing respectable ancestry for some Creoles, the Casket Girls are not important. The first consignment reached Biloxi[qv] in 1719; and New Orleans[qv] in 1727–28. They inspired Victor Herbert's *Naughty Marietta.*

[Charles Gayarré, *History of Louisiana;* Dunbar Rowland, *Mississippi, the Heart of the South.*]

MACK SWEARINGEN

Castine, a town on the east side of Penobscot Bay, incorporated 1796, occupies a peninsula called by the French Pentegoet[qv] and by the English Majorbagwaduce. Strategically located in respect to the Penobscot Indians and their trade and within the area in dispute between the English and the French, the place was a center of international rivalry from the earliest days. The trading post established in 1630 by Edward Ashley and the Plymouth colonists in the right of the Beauchamp and Leverett patent passed into the control of the French in 1635 by the Treaty of St. Germain[qv]. English again by conquest in 1654, it was returned to the French in 1670 by the Treaty of Breda[qv], the trade being dominated by the Baron de St. Castin[qv] until his return to France in 1701. From the beginning of the Indian wars in 1688 until 1759, the Indians, instigated by the French, prevented settlement by the English. Soon after 1763 the first English settlers took possession.

[George A. Wheeler, *History of Castine, Penobscot and Brooksville.*]

ROBERT E. MOODY

Castle Thunder was a tobacco warehouse in Richmond, Va., used (1861–65) by the Confederates to confine political prisoners and occasional spies and criminals who were charged with treason. Similar in general purposes to the "Old Capitol" prison in Washington, it enjoyed an unsavory reputation and its officers were accused of unnecessary brutality toward their charges. Upon the fall of Richmond^qv^ the prison was used by the Federal authorities to house Confederates charged with crimes under international law.

W. B. HESSELTINE

Castorland Company, The, was organized in Paris in 1792 as the *Compagnie de New Yorck* to colonize French aristocrats and others dissatisfied with conditions following the French Revolution. Land in Lewis County, N. Y., part of the Macomb Purchase^qv^, was bought from William Constable. Settlers arrived in 1796; within four years the colony had failed. The transplanted French people, unfitted for the vigorous open life and hard work of the frontier, preferred more civilized communities.

[A. M. Sakolski, *The Great American Land Bubble.*]

THOMAS ROBSON HAY

Casualties during Wars are often sketchily recorded, in so far as the major conflicts of the United States are concerned. During the Revolutionary War 231,721 Continental army enlistments were noted and about 145,000 for the militia; but, as many served several enlistments, it is probable that these figures represent not more than 250,000 individuals. The Adjutant General's Office has accounted for only 4044 killed and 6004 wounded, considerably below the real numbers. No disease deaths are recorded.

Multiple enlistments enlarge the figures for those engaged in the War of 1812 to 527,654, of whom 1877 were killed in action and 4000 wounded. The number of deaths resulting from disease is not known.

For the War with Mexico, a figure of 115,847 enlistments may be reduced to about 111,300 individuals, of whom 1192 were killed in action, 529 died of wounds, 11,155 of disease and 361 of other causes, giving a total of 13,237 deaths from all causes. The number of wounded who did not die is not available.

Union enlistments during the Civil War totaled 2,865,028, a figure which may have represented 2,250,000 individuals. Sixty-seven thousand and fifty-eight were killed in action, 43,012 died of wounds, 224,586 of disease and 24,872 of other causes, a total of 359,528 deaths. Because of the loss and destruction of records, Confederate statistics are far from complete. Probably 800,000 to 900,000 men served the Confederacy, of whom the Adjutant General's Office records 52,954 killed in action, 21,570 died of wounds and 59,297 of disease, giving a total of recorded deaths of 133,821. These figures are incomplete, that for disease deaths being far below actual losses from this cause. Total actual deaths in the Confederate service would probably be about twice as large as those given.

During the War with Spain, 280,564 men wore the uniform and 45,590 of these served abroad, of whom 498 were killed in action, 202 died of wounds, 5423 of disease and 349 of other causes, a total of 6472. Wounds, not mortal, amounted to 2974.

For army service in the World War, the United States uniformed 4,000,000 men and sent 2,086,000 to France, of whom 1,390,000 were engaged. Of these, 37,568 were killed in action and 12,942 died of wounds, a total of 50,510 killed in battle. Disease caused 62,670 deaths on both sides of the Atlantic and 6776 died from other causes. Men to the number of 182,674 suffered 193,663 wounds. Total casualties were 119,956 dead and 182,674 wounded.

[The Adjutant General's Office, Department of War; Francis B. Heitman, *Historical Register and Dictionary of the United States Army;* Leonard P. Ayres, *The War with Germany.*]

GEORGE FREDERICK ASHWORTH

Cat Nation, The, or the Erie (cat or panther), was an Indian tribe of Iroquoian stock, but not a member of the confederacy. During the 17th century they lived south of Lake Erie, from the Genesee and Allegheny valleys to about the present western boundary of Ohio. Their two principal towns were Gentaienton (meadows lying together) and Riqué (place of panthers) near the present Erie, Pa. The Iroquois Confederacy^qv^ annihilated them between 1653 and 1655. Remnants of the tribe were absorbed into the Senecas.

[Francis Parkman, *Jesuits in North America.*]

HAROLD E. DAVIS

Catalina Island, Santa, located about twenty-five miles southeast of Los Angeles harbor, was discovered Oct. 7, 1542, by Juan Rodríguez Cabrillo^qv^. The chief bay, Avalon, during the Spanish and Mexican period was one of the most frequented ports of refuge for smugglers, sea-otter and seal hunters, and hide and tallow traders^qqv^.

[J. N. Stewart, *Catalina's Yesterdays;* C. F. Holder, *The Channel Islands of California.*]

OSGOOD HARDY

Catawba, THE, from the first contact with Europeans have had their village or villages on the river of that name just below the North-South Carolina boundary. Wasted by rum, disease and their feud with the Iroquois, which latter was a plague to those colonies through which the war trail led, they had by 1760 declined to less than 100 fighting men. Save for their defection in the Yamasee War[qv] of 1715 they were the steadfast friends of South Carolina. Since 1840 they have resided on a square mile of their original lands and have subsisted largely on the bounty of the state.

[James Mooney, *Siouan Tribes of the East; Reports and Resolutions of the General Assembly of South Carolina.*]

R. L. MERIWETHER

Catholic Parochial School System. The Jesuits[qv] who attended the small Maryland and Pennsylvania missions assumed teaching soon after their arrival but it is impossible to give the date of the beginning of the first parish school. The school in connection with St. Mary's Church, built in Philadelphia in 1763, became the prototype of later parochial schools. Its history can be definitely traced from 1782 when a new schoolhouse was completed. In 1810 Mother Elizabeth Seton and her companions began the first free parochial school for boys and girls taught by Religious: St. Joseph's School, Emmitsburg, Md. Parochial schools became more numerous with the increase in Catholic population that began about 1848, and by 1870 this type of school was recognized as the accepted means of providing early education for Catholic children. The Third Plenary Council of Baltimore (1884) made the founding of a school obligatory on every parish, and to this school all children of the parish were to be sent; exceptions to the rule might be granted by the various bishops. Toward the close of the 19th century parish schools began to expand to include secondary schoolwork. In 1930 there were 7923 Catholic elementary (mostly parish) schools with an enrollment of 2,222,598 pupils.

[J. A. Burns and Bernard J. Kohlbrenner, *A History of Catholic Education in the United States.*]

BERNARD J. KOHLBRENNER

Catholicism in the United States. Organized Catholic life in the new Republic dates from the appointment of Father John Carroll as Prefect-Apostolic of the American Church in 1784. Six years later (Aug. 15, 1790) Carroll was consecrated first Bishop of Baltimore with spiritual jurisdiction over all Catholics in the nation; probably 40,000. The growth of the Church warranted (1808) a division of Bishop Carroll's labors, and suffragan Sees were erected at Boston, New York, Philadelphia and Bardstown, Ky. Since that time the Church in the United States has developed to an extent without parallel in the history of any other nation. From one ecclesiastical unit in 1808, there are today eighteen such provinces presided over by as many archbishops; from one diocese in 1789, there are today ninety-one; from twoscore priests in Carroll's day, there are now about 32,000; from an organization of 40,000 members a century and a half ago, the latest (1938) official figures give a total of about 21,000,000. The peaks of this growth came in the decades: 1840–50 (increase of one million); 1850–60 (increase of two millions); 1870–80 (increase of three millions); and 1900–1910 (increase of five millions).

Such tremendous vitality, due mainly to natural increase and to immigration, in one single religious group was bound to create rivalries, if not antagonisms; and the impact of such a powerful organization as the Catholic Church on the social, economic and political life of what is still popularly believed to be a Protestant nation may justly be recognized in the various attempts to curb both the religious and political freedom of American Catholics. From the founding of the first of these anti-Catholic societies, the American Protestant Association in New York in 1830, down to the recent activities of the Ku Klux Klan[qv], scarcely a decade has passed without a revival of various charges, chief of which is the alleged incompatibility of Catholic principles with American democratic ideals. This was the main theme of those public debates in the 1830's between Hughes and Breckinridge and between Purcell and Campbell. It was the principal weapon of attack by the strongly entrenched Protestant religious press of the country. It was during the same period that the Catholic Church made one of its most important contributions to the stability of the American nation—that of assimilating the millions of Catholic immigrants from other lands to a proper understanding of American social and political ideals and to American standards of living. No religious organization ever faced a problem more fraught with the possibility of failure; for, sharp difference of language, customs, traditions and racial characteristics threatened to retard for generations the Americanization of the newcomers. Fortunately, the American Church possessed all through this critical period leaders of uncommon courage and sagacity. Even in the midst of violent antagonism, bishops, priests and laity went quietly on with their work of making loyal Americans out of these millions of Catholics from abroad.

Although formal education is not a primary part of the Church's work in the world, nevertheless, it has been her policy in the United States, since the first legislative act of the Synod of 1791, to build up a school system exclusively Catholic. This has been accomplished at great odds. Generally speaking, Catholics have been of the poorer class; and with only a few and very minor exceptions (and then only for a short time in a few cities), they have carried the double tax burden of their own and of the public schools (*see* Catholic Parochial School System). The official statistics for 1938 reveal a total attendance in the Catholic elementary schools of 2,170,065; a total of 1984 Catholic high schools, 105 Catholic colleges for women and 56 for men, with a total student body of 288,684. There are 23 Catholic universities. The Catholic University of America, Washington, D. C., the principal link in this chain of educational institutions, was founded in 1889.

The very rapidity of the development of the Church in the United States during the past 150 years has necessitated a strict observance by the episcopate over the uniformity of Church discipline. Consequently, meetings of bishops with their priests in diocesan synods, meetings of bishops with the archbishop of a single province in provincial councils and meetings of the entire hierarchy in national or plenary councils have been held for the purpose of enacting canonical legislation on many aspects of Catholic life. During the years when the entire country was within the single province of Baltimore (1808–49), there were seven provincial councils (1829, 1833, 1837, 1840, 1843, 1846, 1849), the legislation of which was made known to the clergy and laity by joint Pastoral Letters. On three occasions (1852, 1866, 1884) the entire episcopate has held plenary councils in Baltimore and the legislation passed in these assemblies governed the Church in the United States, until the revised Code of Canon Law was issued by the Holy See in 1918 for the universal Church.

A striking fact in the recent history of the Church in the United States is the continuance of the War Council, created by the bishops and archbishops under the chairmanship of Cardinal Gibbons in 1917 to centralize all Catholic forces during America's participation in the World War, as the National Catholic Welfare Conference, located in Washington, D. C. Apart from societies of Catholic men and women which have become national in scope, legislation for the entire body of Catholics can only be enacted in a national or plenary council in which all the members of the hierarchy participate. Such a council can only be held with the permission of the Holy See, and is presided over by an Apostolic Delegate appointed by the Pope. The National Catholic Welfare Conference, the N. C. W. C. as it is popularly called, is not a legislative body, but is purely informational and administrative. It has at present six departments: education, the Catholic press, social action, legislation, i.e., the safeguarding of Catholic interests in state or Federal legislation, Catholic lay action and information. Each of these has a chairman, a member of the episcopate, and once a year, in November, the hierarchy meets at the Catholic University of America to hear reports from these episcopal officials. The National Catholic Welfare Conference News Service to the press (Catholic and secular) has become a powerful influence for the dissemination of truth on all mooted Catholic questions. The death of Pius XI and the election of Pius XII (Cardinal Pacelli, who visited the United States in 1936) accentuated the attention of the nation to the papacy and to the Church as stabilizing agencies for world peace.

[There is no complete guide to the sources for American Catholic history. The four volumes of the *History of the Catholic Church in the United States*, by John Gilmary Shea, is authoritative, though its value ceases with 1866. Partial catalogues of archival and printed material will be found in Guilday, *John Carroll* (to 1815), *John England* (to 1842), *John Gilmary Shea* (to 1892), and Recent Studies in American Catholic History: 1892-1930, *Ecclesiastical Review*, May, 1931. Selected bibliographies will be found in the series, *Studies in American Church History* (28 vols. to date) issued by the Department of History in the Catholic University of America, Washington, D. C. A short account of Church legislation will be found in Guilday, *History of the Councils of Baltimore*.]

PETER GUILDAY

Catlin's Indian Paintings. From 1830 to 1838 George Catlin, a young, self-taught artist, roamed the trans-Mississippi wilderness, sketching and painting some 600 Indian portraits, scenes of native life and landscapes. His expedition up the Missouri by the steamboat *Yellowstone*[qv] and downstream by canoe in the summer of 1832 with a long stay at Fort Clark produced a splendid Mandan[qv] ethnological series of portraits and ceremonies. In 1834 he accompanied the First Dragoons into Texas and the Comanche[qv] country, and spent the following two seasons on the upper Mississippi and Minnesota rivers among the Sioux[qv] and other northern tribes. Catlin exhibited his collection in Europe for years after 1838 and added the 603 items of the so-called Catlin Cartoon Collection. The original collection was presented to the Smithsonian in 1879 by Mrs. Joseph Harrison, Jr. While not a great artist, Catlin faithfully depicted the primitive Indians, their lives and surroundings.

[George Catlin, *Letters and Notes of the Manners, Customs, and Condition of the North American Indians;* Washington Matthews, *The Catlin Collection of Indian Paintings*, Smithsonian Institution, 1892.]

WILLOUGHBY M. BABCOCK

Catskill Mountains, N. Y., THE, took their name from the many wildcats roaming their hemlock-wooded slopes during the early days of New Netherland[qv]. The Dutch thought the mountains haunted. Rip Van Winkle's[qv] long sleep, after his tipsy encounter with the crew of the *Half Moon*[qv], as told by Washington Irving, is supposed to have occurred in Schneider's Hollow.

[H. A. Haring, *Our Catskill Mountains.*]

A. C. FLICK

Cattle Associations is a term applied principally to organizations of cattlemen after 1865 on the Western ranges. In scope these were local, district, sectional and national and, like miners' associations and squatter claim clubs[qqv], functioned on the frontiers. The Colorado Cattle Growers' Association was formed as early as 1867. The Southwestern Cattle Growers' Association of Kansas and the Montana Stock Growers' Association began in 1884. The Wyoming Stock Growers' Association, organized in 1873, had memberships of 400 in 1886 from nineteen states. Its 2,000,000 cattle, real estate, plants and horses were valued in 1885 at $100,000,000. In 1884 the National Cattle and Horse Growers' Association was organized at St. Louis.

A president, secretary, treasurer and executive committee were the usual officials to administer an association's affairs and to make reports at the annual or semiannual meetings. In the Wyoming Stock Growers' Association brand inspectors supervised the sale and transportation of 1,000,000 cattle in 1885. Roundup districts were laid out, rules for strays or mavericks adopted and thousands of brands recorded. Associations co-operated with local and state officials and were alert to urge favorable legislation by Congress.

[Louis Pelzer, *The Cattlemen's Frontier;* Ora B. Peake, *The Colorado Range Cattle Industry.*]

LOUIS PELZER

Cattle Brands, although traceable back to Egypt before Christ, are peculiarly associated with ranching. The institution of ranching[qv] as taken over from Mexico by Texas and California included brands. They are burned on range horses also. Attempted substitutions for fire-branding have proved impracticable. After all, suffering from the process is brief and not intense. The brand is a mark of ownership. If names and addresses were not so long, they would be branded on stock. Every legitimate brand is recorded by either state or county, thus preventing duplication within a given territory. Identification of range stock is necessary among honest people as well as against thieves, in fenced pastures as well as on open range[qv].

In form, brands are made up of (1) letters, (2) figures and (3) geometric designs, symbols, or representations of objects. Combinations are endless. Because brands reduce the value of hides and also induce screw worms, they are now generally smaller and simpler than they were when cattle were less valuable. They may or may not signify something peculiar to the originator; usually they have a significance. A seaman turned rancher gave the Anchor brand; a cowman who won a big game of poker on a hand of four sixes adopted 6666 as his brand; a rancher honored his wife Ella with "E Bar." Brands are the heraldry of the range. Reading and calling them is an art known only to range men. A straight line burned on the side of a cow may be a "Dash," a "Bar," a "Rail." The letter H set upright cannot be misread; lying on its side, however, it is "Lazy H"; in an oblique position, "Tumbling H"; joined to a segment of circle under it, "Rocking H"; separated from the segment, "H Half-Circle," etc. Happily, the art of running out, or blotting, brands—burning one device into another—is obsolescent.

[J. Frank Dobie, *On the Open Range.*]

J. FRANK DOBIE

Cattle Drives. Contrary to popular conception, long-distance cattle driving was traditional not only in Texas but elsewhere in America long before the Chisholm Trail[qv] was dreamed of. The Spaniards, always to be remembered as establishers of the ranching industry, drove herds northward from Mexico as far back as 1540. In the 18th century and on into the 19th the Spanish settlements in Texas derived most of their meager revenue from horses and cattle driven into Louisiana, though such trade was usually contraband (*see* Natchitoches). Meantime in the United States herds were sometimes driven long distances. In 1790 the boy David Crockett helped drive "a large stock of cattle" 400 miles from Tennessee into Virginia; twenty years later he took a drove of horses from the Tennessee River into southern North Carolina. In 1815 Timothy Flint "encountered a drove of more than 1000 cattle and swine" being driven from the interior of Ohio to Philadelphia. The stock in the states was gentle, often managed on foot. The history of trail driving[qv] involves horses as well as cattle.

Notwithstanding antecedent examples, Texans established trail driving as a regular occupation. Before they revolted from Mexico in 1836, they had a "Beef Trail" to New Orleans. In the 1840's they extended their markets northward into Missouri—Sedalia, Baxter Springs, Springfield and St. Louis becoming the principal markets. During the 1850's emigration and freighting from the Missouri River westward demanded great numbers of oxen, the firm of Russell, Majors and Waddell[qv] in 1858 utilizing 40,000 oxen[qv]. Texas longhorn[qv] steers by the thousands were broken for work oxen. Herds of longhorns were driven to Chicago; one herd at least to New York.

Under Spanish-Mexican ownership, California as well as Texas developed ranching and during the 1830's and 1840's a limited number of cattle were trailed thence to Oregon. But the discovery of gold in California[qv] arrested for a while all development there of cattle industry and created a high demand for outside beef. During the 1850's cattle were occasionally driven to California from Missouri, Arkansas and perhaps other states; the big drives, however, were from Texas. Steers worth $15 in Texas were selling in San Francisco for as high as $150. One Texas rancher in 1854 hired for $1500 a famous Indian fighter to captain his herd of 1000 steers to California; thirty-five armed men accompanied it. These drives were fraught with great danger from both Indians and desert thirst.

During the Civil War Texas drove beeves here and there for the Confederate forces. At the close of the war she had probably 5,000,000 cattle—and no market. Late in 1865 a few cowmen tried to find a market. In 1866 there were many drives northward without a definite destination and without much financial success; also to the old but limited New Orleans market, following mostly well-established trails to the wharves of Shreveport and Jefferson (Texas). In 1867 Joseph G. McCoy opened a regular market at Abilene[qv], Kans. The great cattle trails, moving successively westward, were established and trail driving boomed. In 1867 also the Goodnight-Loving Trail[qv] opened up New Mexico and Colorado to Texas cattle. By the tens of thousands they were soon driven into Arizona. In Texas itself cattle raising was expanding like wildfire. Caldwell, Dodge City, Ogallala, Cheyenne[qqv] and other towns became famous on account of trail-driver patronage.

During the 1870's the buffaloes[qv] were virtually exterminated and the Indians of the Plains and Rockies were at the same time subjugated, penned up and put on beef rations. An empire was left vacant. It was first occupied by Texas longhorns, driven by Texas cowboys. The course of empire in America has been west, but over much of Oklahoma, Kansas, Nebraska, the Dakotas, Wyoming, Montana and parts of Nevada and Idaho the precursors of this movement were trail men from the South. The Long Trail extended into Canada. In the 1890's herds were still driven from the Panhandle of Texas to Montana, but trail driving virtually closed in 1895. Barbed wire, railroads and "nesters"[qqv] closed it. During three swift decades it had moved over 10,000,000 cattle and 1,000,000 range horses, stamped the entire West with its character, given economic and personality prestige to Texas, made the longhorn the most historic brute in bovine history, glorified the cowboy[qv] over the globe and endowed America with its most romantic tradition relating to any occupation—a peer to England's tradition of the sea.

[Andy Adams, *The Log of a Cowboy;* J. H. Cook, *Fifty Years on the Old Frontier;* E. E. Dale, *The Range Cattle Industry;* J. Evetts Haley, *Charles Goodnight;* J. M. Hunter, *The Trail Drivers of Texas;* E. S. Osgood, *The Day of the Cattleman;* W. M. Raine and Will C. Barnes, *Cattle;* Walter P. Webb, *The Great Plains.*]

J. FRANK DOBIE

Cattle Industry, The, was introduced into what is now the United States about 1600 by Spanish colonists from Mexico. During the next two centuries Spain's liberal land grants to settlers (*see* Empresario System) caused the industry to expand rapidly northward and by 1821, at the close of the Spanish regime in North America, large numbers of the lean, long-horned[qv] Spanish type of cattle were reared in California, Arizona, New Mexico and Texas.

In the meantime the early English colonists along the Atlantic seaboard brought over cattle of the breeds common to northern Europe. As English settlement advanced westward cattle growers tended to occupy lands along the frontier where pasturage was readily available. Once the Appalachians had been crossed the industry grew rapidly, since farm products could not be transported profitably across the mountains. Accordingly, the Westerners fed their surplus grain and hay to cattle which, when fully grown and fat, could be driven to market. By 1860 the cattle industry was very important in Kentucky and the states of the Old Northwest and had extended across the Mississippi into Missouri, Iowa, Arkansas, Indian Territory and eastern Kansas.

In the Southwest the Republic of Mexico, as well as the Texas Republic, had continued the liberal land policy of Spain. Texas, when annexed to the United States in 1845, retained possession of its own unoccupied lands and often sold large tracts to cattle raisers. By 1860 Texas had more than 3,500,000 head of cattle.

During the Civil War the number of cattle in most states was reduced from 30 to 50%. Texas, little touched by the war, however, was at the close of that struggle overflowing with cattle. In 1866 Texas ranchmen began to drive large herds north to railway points in Kansas and Nebraska known as "cow towns."*qv* Here, the fat, mature animals were shipped to market for slaughter while young cattle were sold to stock new ranges on the Central and Northern plains. By 1885 some 5,500,000 cattle had been driven north from Texas and the so-called range area had come to cover a vast region reaching from Mexico to Canada and extending from eastern Kansas far beyond the Rocky Mountains.

Shipments of dressed beef to Europe, which began in 1875 and grew to over 17,000,000 lbs. in 1884, gave impetus to the industry and helped to bring much European capital into the business. By 1885 the cattle industry in the United States had grown to gigantic proportions. The range area supplied the corn-growing states with enormous numbers of cattle to be fattened for market and received from these states many registered or high-grade breeding animals to improve its own herds. Great packing plants and stockyards*qqv* were built at the important market centers, as Chicago, Kansas City and Fort Worth. Cattle brokerage companies and banks specializing in cattle loans were established to finance the industry and railways provided specially equipped cars for the shipment of cattle and meat products.

After 1885 the character of the industry began to change. Much of the range area was occupied by settlers, necessitating smaller scale operation. The Department of Agriculture through its Bureaus of Animal Industry and of Agricultural Economics, did much to promote better breeding, care and feeding of cattle, and the same is true of the various agricultural colleges. The cattle industry is still very important, but the great ranches*qv* have with few exceptions given place to smaller ones, or livestock farms, producing by scientific methods cattle of high quality that can be marketed for slaughter at a far earlier age than was formerly done.

[E. E. Dale, *The Range Cattle Industry.*]

EDWARD EVERETT DALE

Cattle Rustlers, or cattle thieves, have been a problem wherever cattle have been run on the range upon an extensive scale. They drove off cattle in herds when Texas was a republic; they carry them off in trucks in Montana, today. Their methods have varied from open and forceful taking of cattle in pitched battles, to that of sneaking away with "dogie" or motherless calves. The former method, never prevalent, passed with the open range*qv*; the latter is still a favorite resort.

Cattle are branded to distinguish their ownership, but rustlers sometimes changed the old brand by tracing over it with a hot iron to alter the design into their own brand—a practice known as "burning brands" (*see* Cattle Brands). The taking of large and unbranded calves from the cows and then placing them in the rustler's brand was and is a favorite method. But the principal loss by rustlers today is through their use of automobiles and trucks. They kill cattle on the range and haul away the beef, and they load calves in their trucks of a night and are hundreds of miles from the scene by morning.

Laws for the recording of brands for the protection of livestock owners have long been rigid. But when the laws proved insufficient, cowmen came together in posses, in vigilance committees and finally in local and state associations to protect their herds (*see* Cattle Associations). The greatest deterrent in the early days (decade of the 1880's) was the fencing of the land with wire. That retarded the mobility of the rustler, but the automobile and the opening of roads greatly accelerated it and plenty of rustlers are still on the range.

J. EVETTS HALEY

Cattle Tick, THE, was the worst plague of the Western range during the trail-driving*qv* days (1865–95). It caused widespread outbreaks of what was variously known as Spanish, Texas and tick fever and pleuro-pneumonia, though for years the cause was unknown. Many states established quarantines against the Texas longhorns*qv*. The tick has now been virtually eradicated by dipping.

J. EVETTS HALEY

Caucus, Congressional (1796–1824), was the earliest method of nominating presidential candidates. No nominations were made for the first two presidential elections, since Washington was the choice of all. His retirement having been announced, the Federalist*qv* members of Congress met in secret conference in 1796 and agreed to support John Adams and Thomas Pinckney for President and Vice-President. Shortly afterwards the Jeffersonian Republican*qv* members agreed on Jefferson and Burr. In 1800 the respective party members met again for the same purpose.

After that date the congressional caucus was no longer secret, but an open meeting. Since the Federalist party was almost wiped out by the election of 1800, there was no Federalist caucus after that year, the Republican caucus nominations becoming practically nominations by Congress itself.

The system became increasingly unpopular. Many thought it contrary to the spirit of the Constitution for members of Congress thus virtually to select the President. The friends of Andrew Jackson were particularly bitter against the caucus and it was denounced by mass meetings throughout the country. In 1824 only about a fourth of the members of Congress attended, nominating William H. Crawford, who stood third in the electoral vote (*see* Campaign of 1824). The caucus never met again, being succeeded in the next decade by the national convention[qv] system.

[Edward A. Stanwood, *A History of the Presidency;* Frederick W. Dallinger, *Nominations for Elective Office in the United States.*]

CLARENCE A. BERDAHL

Caucus, Party, in Congress, is a meeting of the respective party members in either House for the purpose of determining their attitude toward legislation and other matters. The Federalists[qv] in the House certainly caucused as early as 1796; the membership of Senate committees was thus arranged by secret party conferences in 1797; and the Jeffersonian Republicans[qv] in the House used this method to nominate John Rutledge for Speaker in 1799. The caucus was probably used even earlier and was firmly established by 1825.

In general the caucus has these purposes or functions: (1) to nominate candidates for Speaker and other House or Senate offices; (2) to elect or provide for the selection of the party officers and committees, such as the Floor Leader, Whips, Committee on Committees and Steering Committee; (3) to decide what action is to be taken with respect to legislation, either in broad terms or in detail. Caucus decisions are generally accepted by the respective party members, since bolting is likely to bring punishment in the form of poorer committee assignments, loss of patronage and the like; and hence the caucus has become a most important, although extraconstitutional, device in legislative organization and procedure.

[W. F. Willoughby, *Principles of Legislative Organization and Administration;* W. G. Haines, The Congressional Caucus Today, *American Political Science Review,* Vol. IX, pp. 696-706.]

CLARENCE A. BERDAHL

Caucus, Primary, is a general meeting of the party members in a local community, for the purpose of nominating candidates for local office, or for electing delegates to county or state conventions. Such a caucus is ordinarily open to all voters in the community who consider themselves members of the particular party involved, and it constitutes the first formal step in the nominating procedure. The caucus was used in the colonies at least as early as 1725 and particularly in Boston, where several clubs, attended largely by ship mechanics or caulkers, endorsed candidates for office before the regular election and which came to be known as "caucus clubs." The gentry also organized their "parlor caucuses" and this method of nomination soon became the regular practice within the political parties. It was entirely unregulated by law until 1866, became subject to considerable abuse and during the early 1900's was subjected to more drastic regulation by the state. Now the caucus has in many cases been completely supplanted by the direct primary[qv].

[F. W. Dallinger, *Nominations for Elective Office in the United States;* Harold R. Bruce, *American Parties and Politics,* 3rd edition.]

CLARENCE A. BERDAHL

Cavaliers is a term applied to adherents of the Stuart kings of England, who fled to Virginia[qv] after the fall of Charles I (1647–49). They introduced luxury and greater refinement into the colony, set the tone of its society, in sharp contrast to that of New England, gave a stimulus to the slave trade[qv] and founded a sort of aristocratic oligarchy.

[George Bancroft, *History of the United States.*]

ALVIN F. HARLOW

Cavalry, Horse, a branch of the United States Army[qv], has figured prominently in American history. During the American Revolution it was usually employed as a raiding weapon, only occasionally being used in a pitched battle. Cavalry, particularly on the Plains and in the Southwest, escorted settlers, punished Indian marauders and did police duty along the frontier. As the settlers continued westward into Indian hunting grounds, Indian opposition increased and both the demand and the need for protection became more urgent. In 1855 the cavalry was substantially increased and for the next forty years it was engaged constantly in Indian warfare.

The development of horse cavalry, in the modern sense, first appeared in the Southern forces during the Civil War. The great efficiency of the Southern cavalry, able to make sustained, rapid marches across country, expert in scouting and equally prepared to fight mounted or dismounted in battle, soon was realized by the Northern leaders who, by the end of the Civil War, utilized masses of horse cavalry with destructive effect. In the succeeding years of continuous fighting with the Indians in the West (*see* Sioux Wars) and in guarding our Southwestern frontier, the characteristics of mobility, fire power and shock, as well as the adaptability to all types of fighting, were further developed. Because of combat conditions during the World War[qv] only four American cavalry regiments were sent to France. (*See* Cavalry, Mechanized.)

[O. L. Spaulding, *The United States Army.*]

FENTON S. JACOBS

Cavalry, Mechanized, a branch of the United States Army[qv], consists of manned fighting vehicles, constructed with a view to securing a combination of maximum mobility, fire power and shock, *together with protection,* for employment in the execution of *cavalry* objectives. It is a post-World War development. Its role is essentially that of horse cavalry[qv], making combined action of horse and mechanized cavalry possible and desirable. To obtain the maximum efficiency and effect, however, each must be used in conjunction with the other. Motor-wheeled vehicles (motorization) have a limited cross-country mobility, but a high road mobility; whereas, tracklaying vehicles (mechanization) have a comparatively high cross-country mobility. These terms should not be confused. Fighting vehicles intended to close with the enemy are tracklaying. Fighting vehicles (armored cars and scout cars) intended primarily for reconnaissance, and only secondarily or incidentally for combat, are of the wheeled type. Armored fighting vehicles can derive only partial protection from the armor carried, for the use of armor must result in a compromise between the opposing factors of protection and mobility.

American mechanized cavalry units, based upon tracklaying vehicles, and with the necessary complement of wheeled vehicles, have a high tactical as well as strategical mobility. Such vehicles have many obvious limitations, however, because of the development of antitank weapons, portable mines and antitank auxiliaries. Nevertheless, the light fast tank and its cavalry counterpart, the combat car, are among the most redoubtable weapons of modern armies. They are tactically self-contained and capable of independent employment as well as operating in conjunction with horse cavalry or infantry.

[U. S. Cavalry Association, *Cavalry Combat.*]

FENTON S. JACOBS

Cave-in-Rock is a cave in Hardin County, Ill., on the Ohio River, about thirty miles below the mouth of the Wabash. In pioneer times it was used as an inn patronized by flatboatmen[qv]. It often served as a rendezvous for outlaws who robbed flatboats going down the river. Among its early occupants were Sam Mason[qv] and his gang of river pirates and highwaymen and the bloodthirsty Harpe[qv] brothers.

[Otto A. Rothert, *The Outlaws of Cave-in-Rock.*]

OTTO A. ROTHERT

Cayuse, THE, inhabited the Blue Mountain region in northeastern Oregon. They were a powerful, warlike tribe, allied to the Umatillas and Walla Wallas with whom they participated in the Whitman massacre[qv] and the early Indian wars of Oregon and Washington. They were noted for their wealth in horses. The tribal name has entered American dictionaries as denoting the sturdy type of Indian pony. The tribe now resides on the Umatilla reservation.

[H. H. Bancroft, *History of Oregon.*]

WILLIAM S. LEWIS

Cayuse War, THE (1847–50). Following the Whitman massacre[qv] (Nov. 29, 1847) volunteer troops were equipped to the extent of the meager resources of a pioneer settlement that war might be waged against the Cayuse Indians[qv] responsible for the massacre. The declared objective was to punish the guilty tribe and to force the surrender of the murderers. After enduring a severe winter the troops pursued the Cayuse during the spring and summer without having any decisive engagements. The discouraging and indecisive struggle dragged on until the spring of 1850 when it was ended by the voluntary surrender of five confessed murderers who thus made the close of the war possible. These Indians were later tried and hanged at Oregon City.

[George W. Fuller, *A History of the Pacific Northwest.*]

ROBERT MOULTON GATKE

Cazique **(*Cacique*)** was the Indian title for chieftains of the petty tribes on the Carolina coast. It was adopted by the Lords Proprietors for the third rank of their proposed provincial nobility and was conferred upon a dozen individuals.

[A. S. Salley, *Narratives of Early Carolina;* E. McCrady, *South Carolina under the Proprietary Government.*]

R. L. MERIWETHER

Cedar Creek, Battle of (Oct. 19, 1864). Following the battle of Fisher's Hill[qv], the Union and Confederate armies marched up and down the Shenandoah Valley (*see* Shenandoah Campaign), the former destroying property and crops as it went. Sheridan (U.) finally halted his army across Cedar Creek, east of Fisher's Hill. Shortly afterward he went to Washington. The Confederate Army unexpectedly attacked and after defeating the Union troops halted unnecessarily. The delay was fatal. Returning from Washington, Sheridan rode (*see* Sheridan's Ride) from "Winchester, twenty miles away," rallied his men and led them back into battle. The Confederates were defeated, suffering heavy losses. A Confederate victory was turned into a rout. Thereafter, both armies were transferred to Richmond.

[*Battles and Leaders of the Civil War;* John B. Gordon, *Reminiscences of the Civil War.*]

THOMAS ROBSON HAY

Cedar Mountain, Battle of (Aug. 9, 1862), the first encounter in the Second Bull Run campaign^qv^. Pope's (U.) advance under Banks (U.) at Cedar Run, near Culpeper, Va., was opposed by Jackson's (C.) troops, under Ewell (C.) and Winder (C.). Though outnumbered, Banks advanced, but, after bitter fighting, his troops were repulsed everywhere. Following a brief pursuit Jackson withdrew to join Lee's (C.) army. The Confederates, numbering over 20,000, lost about 1300; the Federals, numbering about 8000, lost nearly 2400.

[*Battles and Leaders of the Civil War.*]

THOMAS ROBSON HAY

Céloron's Lead Plates (1749) mark one step in the French-English rivalry over the Ohio Valley. By 1749 the English were pressing across the Alleghenies into the rich valley beyond the mountains. Unable to make reply in kind, the governor of New France sent an army, led by Pierre Joseph Céloron, to enforce its authority on the Ohio. He descended the river as far as the Great Miami, where he turned northward toward Detroit. En route, in frequent councils, he urged the natives to cease all intercourse with the English and warned the latter to leave the country. At strategic points along the Ohio, lead plates were planted, bearing an inscription reciting the French monarch's title to the country. One of them was found prior to 1821 at Marietta, Ohio, and is now owned by the American Antiquarian Society (Worcester, Mass.). Another plate was found at Point Pleasant, W. Va., and since 1849 has belonged to the Virginia Historical Society at Richmond. Both the English and the Indians ignored the admonitions of Céloron; the ownership of the Ohio Valley remained to be determined by the French and Indian War^qv^.

[M. M. Quaife, Pierre Joseph Céloron, in *Burton Historical Collection* Leaflet, VII, 33-48; Margry, *Découvertes et Etablissements des Français dans L'Amérique Septentrionale,* VI, 666-726; Information supplied by Librarian of American Antiquarian Society and by Corresponding Secretary of Virginia Historical Society.]

M. M. QUAIFE

Cement. In newly discovered lands adventurers seek gold; colonists seek limestone to make cement. American colonists made their first dwellings of logs, with log fireplaces and chimneys plastered inside, caulked outside, with mud or clay. To replace these the first brick^qv^ were imported. Brick masonry requires mortar; mortar requires cement, which was first made of lime burned from oyster shells. In 1662 limestone was found at Providence, R. I., and manufacture of "stone" lime began. Some limes made better cement than others, but not until 1791 did John Smeaton, English engineer, establish the fact that argillaceous (silica and alumina) impurity gave lime improved cementing value. Burning such limestones made hydraulic lime—a cement that hardens under water. Some of the colonial limes unwittingly may have been hydraulic, but it was after the beginning of the country's first major public works, the Erie Canal^qv^, 1817, that American engineers learned to make and use a true hydraulic cement (one that had to be pulverized after burning to slake or react with water). The first masonry on the Erie Canal was contracted to be done with common quick lime; when it failed to slake a local experimenter pulverized some and discovered a "natural" cement, that is, one made from natural rock. Canvass White, subsequently chief engineer of the Erie Canal, pursued investigations, perfected manufacture and use, obtained a patent and is credited with being the father of the American cement industry. During the canal and later railway building era, demand rapidly increased and suitable cement rocks were discovered in many localities: 1818, Fayetteville, N. Y.; 1828, Rosendale, N. Y.; 1829, Louisville, Ky.; 1836, Cumberland, Md.; 1838, Utica, Ill.; 1850, Siegfried's Bridge (Coplay), Pa.; 1875, Milwaukee, Wis.; 1883, Mankato, Minn., to mention a few. Cement made at Rosendale, N. Y., was the most famous, that at Coplay, Pa., the most significant, because it became the first American Portland cement. The name Portland cement was given by an English bricklayer, Joseph Aspdin, in 1824, to a cement made by burning and pulverizing briquets of an artificial mixture of limestone (chalk) and clay, because the hardened cement resembled a well-known building stone from the Isle of Portland. Manufacture of Portland cement developed abroad at the same time the manufacture of natural cements was spreading in America. Soon after the Civil War, Portland cements, because of their more dependable qualities, began to be imported. Manufacture was started at Coplay, Pa., about 1870, by David O. Saylor, by selecting from his natural cement rock such as was approximately of the same composition as the Portland cement artificial mixture. The Lehigh Valley around Coplay contained many similar deposits, and until 1907 this locality produced annually half (at first much more) of all the cement made in this country. By 1900 the practice of grinding together ordinary limestone and clay, burning or calcining the mixture in rotary kilns and pulverizing the burned clinker, had become so well known that the Portland cement industry spread rapidly to all parts of the country and by 1935 there were 165 plants in thirty-five states. Production increased from 350,000 bbls. in 1890 to 176,000,000 bbls. in 1928, the year of peak demand. At first cement was used only for mortar in brick and stone masonry. Gradually mixtures of cement, sand, stone or gravel (aggregates) and water, known as concrete, poured into temporary forms where it hardened into a kind of conglomerate rock, came to be substituted for brick and stone, particularly for massive work like bridge abutments and piers, dams, foundations, etc. Today it is hardly possible to conceive of constructing subways, waterworks, power plants, pavements, bridges and other public utilities without cement.

[Robert W. Leslie, *History of the Portland Cement Industry in the United States.*]

NATHAN C. ROCKWOOD

Cemeteries, National. Soldiers, sailors, marines and officers and men of the Coast Guard dying in the service of the United States, or dying in a destitute condition after having been honorably discharged from the service may be buried in any national cemetery free of cost. With the consent of the Secretary of War, any citizen of the United States who served in the army or navy of any government at war with Germany or Austria during the World War and who died while in such service or after honorable discharge therefrom also may be so buried (act of July 17, 1862; April 15, 1920). Provision for the acquisition of lands for national cemetery purposes was made in an act of Feb. 22, 1867. Ninety-one cemeteries have been established in twenty-nine states and the District of Columbia. Interments in these Federal burying grounds in 1935 totaled 436,189, of which some 10,700 were those of Confederates. Eighteen national cemeteries are found in the State of Virginia; the largest and most notable is the Arlington[qv] Cemetery. In the permanent American cemeteries in Europe, 30,895 veterans of the World War are buried. At Mexico City, Mexico, the remains of 1563 officers, soldiers and citizens of the United States who fell in battle or died in and around that city rest in an American cemetery established in 1873.

In 1933 the following national cemeteries were transferred from the War Department to the National Park Service of the Interior Department: Antietam, Md.; Battleground, District of Columbia; Chattanooga, Tenn.; Fort Donelson, Tenn.; Fredericksburg, Va.; Gettysburg, Pa.; Poplar Grove, Va.; Shiloh, Tenn.; Stones River, Tenn.; Vicksburg, Miss.; and Yorktown, Va.

[The Code of the Laws of the United States of America, Washington, 1935, pp. 1-3026. See pp. 47, 49, 991-994.]

CARL P. RUSSELL

Censorship. There is no record of censorship in the armies of the United States prior to the Civil War. Even during the first year of the Civil War censorship was not effective; this oversight enabled the Confederates to know the strength and disposition of the Union Army simply by reading the Northern newspapers. Original efforts to correct this evil were undertaken by the State Department. The War Department became equally interested as a result of an article appearing in the New York *Tribune* concerning the advance on Manassas[qv]. This article appeared the very morning the movement was to take place. Gen. Scott, Assistant Secretary of War, realized the seriousness of this situation and ordered that the telegraph convey no messages concerning military operations except those authorized by himself. The State Department also issued instructions which would not permit newspapers to publish military matters before being censored by them. When Edwin M. Stanton became Secretary of War he demanded that this function be under complete military control; he obtained this authority and from then on censorship was vigorously enforced and offenders were severely punished.

During the World War censorship was rigidly enforced within the army. Regulations issued to our army in France were based on those used by the British and contained implicit instructions as to letter writing, addressing envelopes, method of censoring outgoing letters and restrictions on photographs and telegraphic communications. Soldiers were forbidden to carry on their person any documents or written matter which would in any way aid the enemy, including letters received from home. While on leave, officers and soldiers were not permitted to discuss military matters of any nature. In order to reduce the task of censoring all letters written in the field, a green envelope was authorized in which letters could be forwarded for mailing; this green envelope bore a certificate which had to be signed by the sender; letters placed in this unsealed green envelope were ordinarily not censored at the base but were sealed, stamped and forwarded.

The army was especially sensitive on the subject of newspaper publicity; press articles were censored before leaving the theater of operations and were subject to further censoring before final publication.

[A. H. Meneely, *The War Department, 1861;* Censorship Orders for Troops in the Field, American Expeditionary Force.]

C. A. WILLOUGHBY

Censures of the President by Congress. Congress had vested in the Secretary of the Treasury discretion as to the deposit of government funds in the Bank of the United States[qv]. In order to compel removal of such deposits[qv] from the bank, President Jackson dismissed one Secretary of the Treasury and appointed another (1833), whereupon the Senate passed a resolution censuring him for assuming "authority and power not conferred by the Constitution and laws and in derogation of both." The Senate refused to receive the President's "Protest," but four years later expunged the censure from its journal. After President Tyler's veto of a tariff measure (1842) a select committee of the House of Representatives reported a resolution censuring the President for strangling legislation by misuse of the veto power and refused to receive his protest. A censure of President Cleveland was implied in a Senate resolution (1885) expressing "condemnation of the refusal of the Attorney-General under whatever influence, to send to the Senate copies of the papers sent for. . . ."

[W. E. Binkley, *Powers of the President.*]

W. E. BINKLEY

Census. Article I of the Federal Constitution, which provides that Representatives "be apportioned among the several States . . . according to their respective numbers," provides also for a decennial census to furnish the necessary basis for such apportionment. It was only as an incident to the establishment of its democratic political machinery that the United States in 1789 became the first nation in the world to provide by law for a periodic enumeration of its people.

The first two censuses, those of 1790 and 1800, gathered little more than the necessary population figures, distinguishing colored from white and slave from free because slaves were to count as three fifths the same number of free persons in apportioning representation (*see* Compromises of the Federal Constitution). The census of 1810 was the first in which an effort was made to collect statistics on matters other than population, notably manufactures, but the results were uneven and incomplete. In 1840 an attempt, perhaps overambitious, was made to collect information on mines, agriculture, commerce, manufactures, occupations, schools, illiteracy, insane and idiots, pensioners and other subjects. The accuracy of the census figures for many of these subjects has been questioned, although the information gathered is of great value to the historian. In 1850 there was still further expansion of the categories to include, among others, newspapers and periodicals, libraries, religious bodies, criminals and mortality figures. The censuses of 1860 and 1870 were taken under the same law as that for 1850. Because of the difficulties of Reconstruction[qv] in the South, the results of the 1870 census for that region are somewhat under suspicion.

All censuses prior to that of 1880 were taken under the supervision of United States marshals who hired assistants of their own to do the actual work of enumeration. Very little control from Washington was possible over these temporary political appointees and the results became less reliable as the schedules grew more complicated. The act providing for the 1880 census substituted a field force of supervisors and enumerators directly under the control of the Superintendent of the Census. The census of 1880 was vastly larger in scope, its results being published in twenty-four volumes, whereas five volumes had sufficed for any previous census. The census of 1890 was still larger. It was the first in which use was made of punch cards and electric tabulating machines, inventions which made possible tabulations of many combinations which were previously impracticable.

After long agitation, a permanent Census Office was established by act of March 6, 1902. Previously, every ten years since 1830, when the returns were first checked in Washington, a temporary organization had been called into existence to compile, edit and publish the results. This temporary Office, after 1849, was always set up in the Interior Department, and the permanent Office was placed there too, only to be transferred in 1903 to the newly established Department of Commerce and Labor, where it gradually came to be known as the Bureau of the Census. From 1913 it has been in the Department of Commerce.

Since it has become a permanent organization,

the Bureau has endeavored to restrict the scope of the decennial census by shifting some of its special inquiries to the in-between years. A census of manufacturers is now taken every two years and a census of agriculture every five years. A recent innovation of importance is a census of the distributive industries. The Bureau also regularly collects and publishes statistics on crime, births and deaths, finances of states, cities and local governments and on a large number of special industries and commodities. The permanently preserved Census records are of inestimable value to historians and social scientists since they constitute a practically complete record of the population of the nation for the 150 years of its existence and of that population's social and economic life.

[W. Stull Holt, *The Bureau of the Census*, 1929.]

OLIVER W. HOLMES

Cent, First American Use of. Our cent came from the adoption of the dollar[qv] as the unit and its division decimally. Colonial accounts were kept in pounds, shillings and pence but the circulation was mostly Spanish dollars. A privately issued coin dated 1783 (called the Washington cent) had the word cent on it. Vermont and Connecticut in 1785 coined cents, but Massachusetts, in 1787, was the first state to have the word on its coin. The "Fugio"[qv] cent in 1787 was the first cent issued under the authority of the United States. Cents were minted regularly by the Federal Government starting with 1793.

[Neil Carothers, *Fractional Money.*]

JAMES D. MAGEE

Centennial Exposition, Philadelphia (1876), celebrating the one hundredth anniversary of the Declaration of Independence, was the first great international exposition held in America. It was ten years in the planning and building; it covered more than 450 acres in Fairmount Park; its total cost was more than $11,000,000. Thirty-seven foreign nations constructed pavilions, many in their native architectural styles. The 167 buildings of the exposition housed more than 30,000 exhibitors from 50 nations. The gates were opened on May 10 and during the 159 days that followed there were 8,004,274 cash admissions. There were seven principal divisions in the exposition: mining and metallurgy, manufactured products, science and education, fine arts, machinery, agriculture and horticulture. The Woman's Building, an innovation in expositions, demonstrated the relative emancipation of women in America.

There was no midway or similar amusement, for nothing could have competed with the intense public interest in the working models of many new machines and processes. The architecture was confused, but impressive. The influence of various foreign exhibits evoked a new interest in interior decoration in America. In this exposition the world, for the first time, saw industrial America on display. Americans realized that the Machine Age had arrived and that their country was, in many ways, at last coming of age. The Centennial was honest, homely and revealing; it provided an immense stimulus to the growing æsthetic, social and industrial consciousness of America.

[J. S. Ingram, *Complete History of the Centennial Exposition;* James D. McCabe, *History of the Centennial Exposition.*]

FRANK MONAGHAN

Centinel of the North-Western Territory, The, published in Cincinnati by William Maxwell, was the first newspaper in the Northwest Territory[qv]. It appeared Nov. 9, 1793, and weekly thereafter until June, 1796, when it was merged with *Freeman's Journal.* Subscription was "250 cents" per annum, and 7 cents a single copy. The motto of the *Centinel:* "Open to all Parties —but influenced by none," expressed the publisher's aims: to afford an isolated community a medium to make known its varied wants and to record local happenings, as well as those of the outside world. A complete file is in the library of the Historical and Philosophical Society of Ohio in Cincinnati.

[*Proceedings*, American Antiquarian Society, New Series, Vol. XXIX, p. 141.]

BEVERLEY W. BOND, JR.

Central American Court of Justice, The, was a tribunal established by the five Central American republics in accordance with a treaty signed at the Central American Peace Conference held in Washington in 1907 under the sponsorship of the United States and Mexico. It consisted of five judges, one selected by each signatory state. It was given jurisdiction over all controversies arising among the signatories regarding which a diplomatic understanding could not be reached. The court was also authorized to hear cases of an international character brought by a citizen of one of the five republics against one of the other governments. The court was installed at Cartago, Costa Rica, on May 25, 1908. In 1916 and 1917 suits were brought in the court by Costa Rica and Salvador to prevent Nicaragua from carrying out the terms of the Bryan-Chamorro Treaty[qv] of 1914 between the United States and Nicaragua regarding a canal route.

The court decided both cases against Nicaragua. Since Nicaragua refused to accept the decision and since the United States failed to support the court, the tribunal was in a futile position. When the period of ten years for which the court was established expired in 1918 nothing was done to renew it and the court was dissolved.

[M. O. Hudson, *The Permanent Court of International Justice.*]

BENJAMIN H. WILLIAMS

Central Overland, California and Pikes Peak Express, The, was chartered by the Kansas legislature in February, 1860. It absorbed the stage lines running from Missouri to Denver and to Salt Lake City. Through its president, William H. Russell (*see* Russell, Majors and Waddell), it launched the famous Pony Express[qv]. In May, 1860, it succeeded to the Chorpenning contract for mail service from Utah to California. Maintenance of frequent stage service and heavy losses from the Pony Express brought embarrassment to the C. O. C. & P. P. Express. Employees dubbed it "Clean Out of Cash and Poor Pay." On March 21, 1862, Ben Holladay purchased the holdings at public sale for $100,000.

[L. R. Hafen, *The Overland Mail.*]

LeROY R. HAFEN

Central Pacific Race with the Union Pacific. This was a construction contest between the two companies bidding for government subsidies, land grants[qv] and public favor. The original Pacific Railway Act, 1862, authorized the Central Pacific to build east to the California line and the Union Pacific[qv] to build west to the western Nevada boundary. This legislation was unpopular with the railroad companies and they planned to build beyond the designated boundaries. Their attitude led to amendments to the Pacific Railway Act, 1865–66, and the roads were authorized to continue construction until they met. The amendments precipitated the now historic race, 1867–69, because the company building the most track would receive the larger subsidy.

The competing companies projected their lines 300 miles in advance of actual construction, which was technically within the law. But when surveys crossed and recrossed the railroad officials got into legal battles and the crews into personal ones. When the two roads were about 100 miles apart, Congress passed a law compelling the companies to join their tracks at Promontory Point[qv], Utah, some fifty miles from the end of each completed line. The final, and most spectacular, lap of the race was made toward this point in the winter and the spring of 1869, the tracks being joined on May 10. Nobody won the race because there was no definite goal on Promontory Point that had to be reached. The race was a dead heat if anything because both tracks reached the immediate vicinity about the same time.

[Gen. G. M. Dodge, *The Dodge Records.*]

J. R. PERKINS

Central Route, The, is a term frequently applied to the overland route used most extensively during the twenty years following 1848, by immigrants bound for California. There were many deviations. From Independence[qv] or other points on the Missouri the immigrants followed the Platte, went through South Pass[qv] in Wyoming, went around to the north of Great Salt Lake[qv], followed the Humboldt to the sinks and proceeded to California by different passes through the Sierras. Beginning with 1851, mail service was maintained over this route.

[Cardinal Goodwin, *The Trans-Mississippi West;* LeRoy Hafen, *The Overland Mail.*]

RUPERT N. RICHARDSON

Centralization. In national affairs, this term usually refers to the growing concentration of authority in the Federal Government over fields which formerly were occupied only in part, or not at all, by the state governments. Centralizing tendencies have been most conspicuous since the adoption of the Fourteenth Amendment[qv], which gave a veto upon state legislative acts to the Federal courts and thus placed in their hands the protection of fundamental property rights. But centralization has been stimulated mainly through congressional legislation regulating and protecting interstate commerce[qv], particularly through investigative and regulatory agencies centering in Washington (*see* Interstate Commerce Commission; Federal Trade Commission). More clearly has centralization been accelerated through Federal appropriations of money for a great variety of state enterprises or needs, called grants-in-aid[qv]. For example, Congress may not require a state to construct and maintain a system of highways of specified length, width and materials, or to maintain a state highway department. Yet, through its power to appropriate money and to prescribe conditions with which a state must comply if it wishes to share in the Federal funds, the National Government, through the Bureau of Public Roads in the Department of Agriculture, is able to do indirectly what it cannot do directly.

Centralization is viewed with alarm by some, who fear the ultimate reduction of the states to mere administrative areas of the National Government, like the French *départements.* By others, centralization is viewed as inevitable once national unity has been attained and social and economic interests have developed to a point where they overlap state boundaries.

In state affairs, centralization refers to the expanding activities of state governments, whereby they have assumed supervision, direct control, or actual performance of activities previously carried on inadequately, if at all, by counties, cities or other local governments. Such centralization has appeared notably in connection with the support of schools, highway construction and maintenance, charities and corrections and public health protection.

[F. A. Ogg and P. O. Ray, *Introduction to American Government*, 6th edition; A. F. Macdonald, *Federal Aid*, and *American State Government and Administration;* W. B. Graves, The Future of the American States, *American Political Science Review*, XXX, 24-51, February, 1936; L. W. Lancaster, *Government in Rural America.*]

P. ORMAN RAY

Centralized Purchasing. The rise of large-scale business, which early found central purchasing advantageous, brought the practice to the attention of governments. By the close of the World War most of the states and large cities had set up central purchasing offices staffed by expert buyers. The executive departments and independent offices of the National Government continued independent buying, with some coordination in the purchase of items needed by a number of agencies, until June 10, 1933. Then the President, by executive order, set up a procurement division in the Treasury Department[qv]. This division now buys all articles needed by two or more departments in the District of Columbia except the War Department, the Navy Department[qqv] and the District government. The division is gradually extending its jurisdiction in the field services and to items required by only one agency. By 1937 centralized purchasing was in use in 36 states and more than 200 cities in the United States.

[Russell Forbes, *Governmental Purchasing.*]

HARVEY WALKER

Century Dictionary of the English Language, THE, was completed in eight volumes between 1889 and 1891 under the editorship of William Dwight Whitney. Its 450,000 entries define all the ordinary words and phrases of the English language, including those generally omitted from such works as obsolete, dialectal, provincial or technical. The distinguishing merit of the work lies in its encyclopedic method; in addition to the definitions and purely philological matter, there is much technical, historical and practical information. The same method was applied to proper names—names of persons, places, characters in fiction, books—in *The Century Dictionary of Names* (1894). In 1897 an Atlas formed the tenth volume. In 1909 a two-volume supplement to the dictionary appeared, and the whole work was reissued in twelve volumes. In 1927 an abridged, condensed and popular rendering of the great work was published, in two volumes, as *The New Century Dictionary.*

[M. M. Mathews, *A Survey of English Dictionaries.*]

HARRY R. WARFEL

Century of Progress International Exposition, Chicago (1933–34), was the greatest financial success in the recent history of world fairs. It was planned during a period of prosperity and successfully held in the midst of a great depression. It was designed to celebrate the one hundredth anniversary of the founding of the City of Chicago[qv] and to demonstrate a century's progress in many fields. The original plans were frequently scaled down to meet the exigencies of shrinking budgets. During the 170 days beginning May 27, 1933, there were 22,565,859 paid admissions; during the 163 days beginning May 26, 1934, there were 16,486,377; a total of 39,052,236. Official foreign participation was extremely limited. The schematic pattern of the fair was vague and confusing. The modernistic architecture of the exposition has exerted much influence and the color effects have made themselves clearly evident in commercial design.

FRANK MONAGHAN

Cerro Gordo, Battle of (April 18, 1847). Advancing to the interior after taking Vera Cruz[qv], Gen. Scott found a Mexican army under Santa Anna entrenched on the National Road, eighteen miles below Jalapa. Twiggs' division stormed two fortified hills after a turning movement suggested and guided by Capt. R. E. Lee. Shields' brigade gained the rear of the position and the Mexicans fled. Santa Anna escaped, leaving 3000 prisoners, guns, baggage and $11,000 in specie. The American loss was 431.

[Justin H. Smith, *The War with Mexico.*]

CHARLES WINSLOW ELLIOTT

Chad's Ford. *See* Brandywine, Battle of the.

Chain Gangs were occasionally used by Southern sheriffs in ante-bellum days, much as they had been used by the wardens of debtor prisons in the North and in England during the latter part of the 18th century. But the wide and systematic use of this form of convict labor did not appear until it was employed by the lessees who took full control over most of the convicts in the Southern states during the first decades following the Civil War. In place of the old ball-and-chain, the lessees substituted shackles fastened to both ankles of each convict and joined by a chain that permitted only short steps; a long chain was then strung through one of the links of each short chain, thus binding scores of convicts together. Compelled to work, eat and sleep together, the basest sort of conditions were maintained.

In the late 1880's protests against the convict leases (*see* Convict Labor Systems) led to their gradual abandonment in favor of penal plantations which usually dispensed with the chains. But it was not long before an increasing demand for good roads prompted the county sheriffs to hold a larger portion of the convicts for labor on the local roads, reviving the chain-gang system for this purpose. By the late 1890's the major portion of the convicts of Georgia, Florida, North Carolina, South Carolina and other Southern states were coupled together in road gangs. Humanitarian protests gradually led to state inspection of the county road gangs in several states and to state operation of the system in Georgia. The introduction of road-making machinery antiquated the chain gang and enabled the reformers to carry their opposition to the system to partial success in most of the states, but chain gangs still persist in many counties throughout a large section of the South.

[Blake McKelvey, *American Prisons;* J. F. Steiner and R. M. Brown, *The North Carolina Chain Gangs.*]

BLAKE McKELVEY

Chain Stores. This term may be applied to any organization made up of two or more stores in the same general business. The United States Bureau of the Census, however, in defining chains, excludes all organizations having less than four stores and also specifies that chain operation normally includes central buying and warehousing. Organizations of department stores[qv], although centrally owned, are rarely operated under central buying and warehousing and are consequently termed "ownership groups." Leased departments of stores, operated by utility companies, retailing household appliances to increase the use of gas and electricity, are considered as chains.

Chain stores are usually classified as "local" if their units are located in and around one city; "sectional" if located in two or more cities within a limited geographical area; and "national" if located in more than one section of the country.

The growth of chain-store systems has occurred chiefly within the past half century. The Great Atlantic and Pacific Tea Company[qv], largest chain in the United States, began as a single store in 1859. The F. W. Woolworth Company, oldest and largest of the variety chains, made its first unit beginning in 1879. Many of the other well-known chains made their beginnings, often in obscure little shops, in the 1890's and early 1900's. Chain stores introduced many improvements in retailing, including greater emphasis on light, fresh air and cleanliness, better and fresher stocks of merchandise and lower costs of operation.

The most rapid progress in chain-store development took place in the decade following the World War. This was a period of rapid retail trade expansion for the country as a whole. Total retail sales gained by at least 50%. All channels of distribution benefited, and while chains probably gained more than other types of retailers, it is probable that most of their growth was due to the general increase in business. The rising importance of the chains, however, aroused their competitors to serious efforts to protect their position. Independent retailers, dependent for their supplies of goods upon wholesalers, have had to meet chain-store competition in a number of constructive ways, such as in improvement of their stores in appearance, cleanliness, merchandise displays, lighting, advertising, accounting, personal salesmanship, closer study of consumer demand, better selection of merchandise and purchasing goods in quantities in co-operation with other retailers handling the same line of goods.

In recent years independent retailers have sought to remove chain-store competition by placing legal handicaps upon the chains, thus raising their costs of operation artificially. Such legislation has generally taken the form of discriminatory taxes, graduated according (a) to the total gross sales of the chain, or (b) to the number of store units operated in the state. The Indiana antichain-store tax law (1929), basing its discrimination against chains on the latter principle, was the first law of this nature to withstand the test of the courts (State Board of Tax Commissioners of Indiana v. Jackson, 283 U. S. 527). Later a Kentucky law assessing a graduated discriminatory tax based on volume of gross receipts, was declared unconstitutional (Steward Dry Goods Co. v. Lewis, 294 U. S. 550). The Louisiana act of 1934 established a new principle in that the tax was graduated according to the number of chain-store units operated regardless of location. This principle was approved by the United States Supreme Court in 1937 (Great

Atlantic & Pacific Tea Co. v. Grosjean, 301 U. S. 412) and has since been widely advocated by the enemies of chain stores.

The Patman bill, introduced in Congress in 1938, and again in 1939, sought to carry anti-chain taxation into Federal law and with such severity as to wipe out of existence all chains having stores in more than one state. Any remaining chain systems doing business solely on an intrastate basis could then be dealt with in any manner seen fit by the states. (*See also* Super-Market.)

[J. P. Nichols, *Chain Store Manual;* P. H. Nystrom, *Economics of Retailing;* J. P. Nichols et al., *Retailers' Manual of Taxes and Regulation;* Commerce Clearing House, *Tax Systems of the World.*]

PAUL H. NYSTROM

Chair Making. Among the numerous woodworking industries in the American colonies furniture making soon reached a point where it supplied articles for export to the South and to the Caribbean. The most common product was chairs, which are often recorded in coastal and sugar island cargoes. Their manufacture, which was already specialized before the Revolution, was recognized as a distinct branch of furniture making in the census of 1810. Rockers, said to be an American invention, were popular in Spanish America. Vessels leaving Baltimore for points around the Horn (*see* Cape Horn) in a single day of 1827 carried 12,000 chairs.

An expanding commercial market early invited quantity production and the use of mechanical aids in manufacture. Philadelphia chair shops had steam-driven machinery before 1825. About 1850 a Fitchburg factory producing principally for export had a capacity of sixty-five dozen chairs a day, and employed special machines to shape interchangeable parts[qv] which were boxed separately for shipment and assembled at their destination. Until after 1890 Massachusetts made more chairs than any other state. Towns like Ashburnham, Gardner and Westminster were centers for their production.

Chair design has accommodated itself to period fashions. Nevertheless popular types like the Windsor chair have remained in general use since introduced at Philadelphia about 1700, where they were known at first as Philadelphia chairs. Windsors were advertised during the 18th century by cabinetmakers who specialized in them.

Chairs are not as large a fraction of furniture[qv] output today as they were when household equipment was less elaborate. Modern statistics record them by groups like household, office, public building, wood, wicker and metal chairs. Today New York manufactures far more chairs than any other state and an increasing but still modest share of the annual output is made of metal.

[Thomas H. Ormsbee, *The Story of American Furniture;* Victor S. Clark, *History of Manufactures in the United States; United States Census of Manufactures.*]

VICTOR S. CLARK

Chalmette Plantation. Four or five miles below New Orleans[qv], on the east bank of the Mississippi, is the imposing Chalmette Monument which marks the site of Jackson's battle of 1815. The extensive sugar plantation was the property of Ignace de Lino de Chalmette, a wellborn French Creole. For Jackson's military convenience, Chalmette and his wife abandoned their plantation home. After the battle, only the charred ruins of their dwelling remained and many of the fine oaks with their drooping Spanish moss were missing. Chalmette died three weeks later.

[Grace King, *Creole Families of New Orleans.*]

L. W. NEWTON

Chambers of Commerce may be described as voluntary associations of businessmen approaching the problems of the community from the business angle. The Chamber of Commerce of the State of New York is the oldest such organization in this country, its original charter having come from King George III in 1768.

In general, American chambers of commerce follow the British, rather than the Continental, types and usually are broader in the scope of their activities than even the British prototype.

Although in many American cities the chambers of commerce were started as such, in most of the older cities they were derived from either one of two types of previous organizations. The first of these was the Board of Trade, established originally for the purpose of regulating or supervising trading activities. In Boston, Baltimore, Minneapolis, Milwaukee, St. Louis and Cincinnati as well as in other cities the present Chamber of Commerce has, as at least one of its component parts, a former trading body and some even continue this activity.

In the chambers growing out of trading bodies the growth usually has been effected by merger with other types of organization, the basis of combination being a common concern with civic affairs.

The second type of older American chamber is the organization characterized by having been originally a group of tax-paying businessmen—a Tax-Payers' League or a Civic Association, etc.

—united for defense, or to foster some civic interest.

The most common activities engaged in by American chambers of commerce include industrial and commercial development and expansion, and dealing with problems connected with agriculture, transportation, publicity, charity solicitation (community chests), regulation and promotion of trade and commercial arbitration*qqv*.

The Chamber of Commerce of the United States (which was established in 1912) is a federation of local chambers and other business organizations and individuals to apply similar principles to national affairs. One of its principal activities is the conducting of referenda on legislative matters and other public questions.

[Wm. George Bruce, *Commercial Organizations.*]

PAUL T. CHERINGTON

Chambersburg, Pa., Burning of (July 30, 1864). Gen. Hunter (U.), defeated by Early (C.), in the course of his retreat up the Shenandoah Valley*qv* wantonly burned crops, homes and villages. In retaliation, Early dispatched a cavalry force under Gen. John McCausland to Chambersburg, in adjacent Union territory, to demand a ransom of $100,000 in gold or $500,000 in greenbacks*qv*, failing the delivery of which, he was ordered to burn the town. McCausland went as directed. No ransom of the amount demanded could be paid. The town was burned.

[R. H. Early, ed., *Gen. Jubal A. Early: Autobiographical Sketch and Narrative.*]

THOMAS ROBSON HAY

Chambly, Fort, at the foot of the Richelieu River rapids, was built by the British, 1775, on the site of Fort St. Louis (erected 1764). Captured Oct. 20, 1775 (*see* Canada, American Invasion of, 1775–76), it was held until the spring of 1776 when it was evacuated and burned, as the Americans retreated southward to Ticonderoga*qv*.

[J. H. Smith, *Our Struggle for the Fourteenth Colony.*]

ROBERT S. THOMAS

Champ d'Asile, The. In 1817 a group of Napoleonic exiles under the leadership of Generals Lallemand and Rigaud made a fortified camp in Texas on the Trinity River, about thirty leagues from the coast, calling it Champ d'Asile. It was charged that they hoped to take Mexico and rescue Napoleon from St. Helena. Scarcely were the forts and dwellings completed when the Spanish, who claimed the territory, forced the colonists to withdraw to Galveston Island. There they remained for weeks, the victims of hunger, sickness and tropical storms. At last, aided by Lafitte the Pirate, they made their way to the French settlements in Louisiana.

[Jesse R. Reeves, *The Napoleonic Exiles in America, 1815-1819;* Anne Boreman Lyon, The Bonapartists in Alabama, in *The Gulf States Historical Magazine*, March, 1903.]

FANNIE RATCHFORD

Champagne-Marne Operation (July 15–18, 1918). This German offensive had several objectives. One was to correct their faulty supply in the Marne salient; another was to draw reserves to assure success in the offensive planned against the British in Flanders. The attack was made by three armies of the German Crown Prince Group. The plan was for the 7th Army (Boehn) to cross the Marne east of Château-Thierry and advance up the valley to Epernay. The 1st Army (Mudra) and 3rd Army (Einem) were to attack east of Reims in the direction of Epernay, swing south of the forest of Reims and capture Epernay and Chalons. The attack was definitely halted east of Reims on the first day by the efficient defense plans of the 4th French Army (Gouraud). West of Reims some fourteen divisions crossed the Marne but, unaided by the attack east of Reims and without artillery support, this attack soon bogged down. Orders were given on the 17th for their withdrawal, preparatory to a general withdrawal, from the Marne salient. The 3rd, 42nd and part of the 28th American Divisions participated. The approximate number of Americans engaged was 85,000. The 38th Infantry Regiment (3rd Division) here won the sobriquet, "Rock of the Marne" (*see* Aisne-Marne Operation, The).

[Girard L. McEntee, *The Military History of the World War.*]

GIRARD L. McENTEE

Champaign County Rescue Cases, The, arising from an attempt to enforce the Fugitive Slave Act*qv*, involved the conflict of state and Federal authorities. In April, 1857, Udney Hyde harbored, on his farm near Mechanicsburg, Champaign County, Ohio, a fugitive slave from Kentucky. The owner sent three United States deputy marshals and five Kentuckians for the chattel on May 21. The Negro nearly shot a marshal. Friends summoned by Hyde from Mechanicsburg scared the posse away, but it returned six days later and carried off four citizens. At South Charleston it assaulted an Ohio sheriff for trying to serve a writ of habeas corpus*qv*, but next morning was overtaken by officers and a crowd and bound over to the Common Pleas Court of Clark County. Proslavery sympathizers appealed to Judge Humphrey H. Leavitt of the United

States District Court at Cincinnati, who assumed jurisdiction and released the defendants as having rightfully performed their duties and not being amenable to the state's laws. The payment of $950 by Hyde's neighbors for the slave's manumission terminated Federal suits against leading obstructors.

[*Ohio Archæological and Historical Publications*, XVI, 293-309; *Ohio Archæological and Historical Quarterly*, XLIII, No. 3.]

WILBUR H. SIEBERT

Champion's Hill, Battle of (May 16, 1863). When Pemberton (C.) at Edward's Station learned that Grant's (U.) army was about to move westward from the vicinity of Jackson toward Vicksburg[qqv], he decided to attack. He must defeat Grant to prevent being shut up in Vicksburg. By the morning of May 16, 1863, the Confederates had moved eastward to Champion's Hill. While Grant concentrated his army, Pemberton, uncertain as to what to do, halted his troops to await the expected attack. Grant handled his troops with energy and decision. The Union attack was successful. After several hours of battle, Pemberton's army was driven from the field toward Vicksburg.

[F. V. Greene, *The Mississippi.*]

THOMAS ROBSON HAY

Champlain, Lake. *See* Lake Champlain.

Champlain Fires a Shot. In 1608 Champlain made an alliance with the Indians of the St. Lawrence and with the Hurons[qv] from the interior; in 1609 their chiefs called upon him to assist them in a campaign against their enemies, the Iroquois[qv]. Champlain, with a small contingent of Frenchmen, accompanied the Indian war party up Richelieu River, and through Lake Champlain. At its southern end in a battle, July 29, three chiefs were killed by bullets from Champlain's arquebus. The Iroquois, astonished at the firearms, broke and fled.

It has been asserted by many early historians of Canada that the Iroquois thenceforth became the enemies of the French colony, and that by this act Champlain endangered his life work. This view attributes too much influence to a single battle, although Champlain in 1610 and again in 1615 attacked the Iroquois enemies with his Algonquian[qv] and Huron allies. The strategic position of the Iroquois and their ability to obtain firearms from the Dutch at Albany created a situation that made the Iroquois the natural enemies of New France. Champlain could not have foreseen that the Dutch would settle on the Hudson River and his obligation to help his allies created the situation. Had he not kept his promise to them, he could not have maintained his position at Quebec.

[H. P. Biggar, ed., *Champlain's Works*, Vol. II, 96-101, 134; L. P. Kellogg, *French Régime in Wisconsin and the Northwest.*]

LOUISE PHELPS KELLOGG

Champlain's Voyages. A sojourn of two years in Mexico and the West Indies (1599) prepared Samuel de Champlain for his first Canadian voyage (1603) when he served as geographer for the DeChastes expedition, authorized by Henry IV of France to make a general survey and fix settlements. Champlain justified his appointment by vigorously prosecuting a cartographic survey of the St. Lawrence region including the gulf, Gaspé and Isle Percé and the Saguenay River, resulting in a report prolific in valuable information. In 1604 under DeMonts, he explored Nova Scotia. A year later he explored the New England coast, mapping 1000 miles of coast line. Returning to France several times with his reports, he repeatedly voyaged to Canada, after 1607 being Lieutenant Governor. Other voyages of 1610, 1611, 1613 made him the acknowledged master of all that related to New France. A final voyage in 1633 ended in his effort to win the friendship of the Iroquois, whom he had previously attacked (*see* Champlain Fires a Shot).

[Edmund F. Slafter, in Winsor's *Narrative and Critical History of America.*]

ARTHUR C. PARKER

Champoeg Convention. On May 2, 1843, Oregon settlers met at Champoeg in the Willamette Valley to create a civil government which was to continue until either Great Britain or the United States established control (*see* Oregon Question, The). The plan was contested by the British settlers who looked upon it as pro-American. This provisional government was the only one in the Pacific Northwest until the Oregon territorial government was established by the United States on March 3, 1849.

[Charles H. Carey, *A General History of Oregon Prior to 1861.*]

ROBERT MOULTON GATKE

Chancellorsville, Battle of (May 2–4, 1863). In April Hooker (U.), with almost 130,000 men, lay across the Rappahannock River from Fredericksburg, Va. Intrenched behind Fredericksburg Lee (C.) awaited another attack such as that of Burnside (U.) in the previous December. In the absence of Longstreet's (C.) divisions in southeastern Virginia, Lee had approximately 60,000 men.

Beginning April 27, Hooker in rapid movements got four army corps across the Rappahannock on Lee's left flank, while maintaining his old lines and sending an army corps of 20,000 men under Sedgwick across the river below Lee's right flank. On May 1, with the forces on Lee's left, Hooker advanced across the river beyond Chancellorsville, only to retire behind Chancellorsville on the approach of the enemy. Lee, threatened by Hooker's movements, ran the risk of having his communication with Richmond cut and of being caught in an encircling trap. The greatest danger being on his left, Lee, leaving a force of about 10,000 men at Fredericksburg under Early, marched with the remainder of his troops toward Chancellorsville. The opposing armies, late in the day of May 1, took position for battle on lines nearly perpendicular to the Rappahannock. At night Lee and Stonewall Jackson (C.), conferring upon their dangerous situation, decided on a daring measure, that of dividing their forces and having Jackson with about 30,000 men march the next day around Hooker's right flank, while Lee with less than 20,000 men held the line in front of Hooker. Accordingly on May 2, while Lee deployed his men in skirmishes against Hooker, Jackson moved rapidly around Hooker's right flank.

In spite of adequate information of Jackson's movement, the army corps on Hooker's extreme right were unprepared when Jackson, late on May 2, fell upon them with irresistible fury. Howard's (U.) corps was routed and another corps badly demoralized. In the confusion and darkness greater disaster might have happened had not Jackson been dangerously wounded by the fire of his own troops and carried from the battlefield. In the renewed conflict of May 3 a cannon ball struck a column against which Hooker was leaning. Dazed by the effect and in doubt about the security of his army, Hooker withdrew his troops to the banks of the river, where they remained throughout May 4 in disorder and uncertainty.

Lee, meanwhile, turned back to deal with Sedgwick's corps, which had routed the Confederate force under Early and was rapidly approaching Chancellorsville. Under the fierce attack of Lee's veterans, Sedgwick likewise retired to the Rappahannock, which he crossed during the night of May 4. When, on May 5, Lee advanced again beyond Chancellorsville, Hooker withdrew the Union forces north of the river. In the battle Hooker lost 17,287 men and Lee 12,423. But Lee suffered the irreparable loss of Jackson, who after days of intense suffering died of his wounds.

[*War of the Rebellion, A Compilation of the Official Records of the Union and Confederate Armies*, Vol. XXV; John Bigelow, *The Campaign of Chancellorsville.*]

ALFRED P. JAMES

Change, Social, in America has been influenced chiefly by economic circumstances. The middle-class Englishmen who settled Massachusetts Bay organized their towns for purposes of good neighborhood and protection against the Indians. The self-contained communities which centered about the New England churches fostered an intense provincialism. By way of contrast, the first settlements in Virginia were early abandoned as the plantations drew people away from the towns. Agriculture on a broad scale, cultivated by slave labor, left few people in the towns, except those who were engaged either in the government of the colony or in its external commerce. The New England clergy strove to keep the people within the tidewater[qv] towns without success. The frontier[qv] beckoned with its allurements of free lands and less burdensome taxation. People refused to remain within the seaboard towns where they might be nonproprietors or at most proprietors of a tiny acreage, when by moving westward they could become proprietors of unlimited soil.

At the close of the Revolution the frontier had already become an important factor in social change. The Northwest Territory[qv] was thrown open to settlement as a part of the public domain[qv]. A joint-stock company had been formed by two enterprising citizens of Massachusetts to promote the settlement of the unoccupied lands (*see* Ohio Company of Associates); eager, impoverished veterans of the war were ready to go and take possession. In the Convention of 1787[qv] the propertied and commercial classes were anxious lest the tidewater sections be outvoted in the new government by the men of the interior. Elbridge Gerry, who feared the influx of Scotch-Irish, French Huguenots and Germans[qqv] along the frontier, pleaded that those who remained on the Atlantic seaboard might not "be at the mercy of the emigrants." Gouverneur Morris insisted that "the busy haunts of men, not the remote wilderness, was the proper school of political talents. If the western people get the power into their hands they will ruin the Atlantic interests."

Profound changes followed the expansion of the frontier (*see* Westward Movement). The growth of democracy[qv] in the United States was accompanied by an intensive cultivation of the principle of individualism. The abundance of free land, the extent and richness of the natural resources, the enterprise and optimism of the people and the scope for individual initiative combined to give the country an era of unparalleled prosperity. In such a society there was little place for aristocratic pretensions. The South with its slave economy stood apart from this democratizing influence, despite the efforts of Southern statesmen to link their section with the growing West. The Civil War, because it destroyed slavery[qv], ended the isolation of the South, but it was not until the present century that this section recovered from the ravages of the war sufficiently to partake of the national prosperity.

The end of the Civil War found the United States well on its way to becoming a great industrial nation. New social classes arose embracing those persons who worked for wages (*see* Labor). Free land[qv] disappeared and there was no further opportunity for the enterprising to seek independence by moving westward. Cities grew rapidly until more than 50% of the population dwelt in urban communities. Large aggregations of capital engaged in the exploitation of the natural resources and in transportation and commerce drove small competitors out of business to become employees of great corporations. When the economic collapse of 1929 came, the United States had passed through three centuries of development and had justified the fears of Thomas Jefferson when he warned of the dangers which would follow if agriculture gave place to industry.

[J. B. McMaster, *History of the People of the United States.*]

WILLIAM S. CARPENTER

Chantier in the fur trade signified the place near the larger posts where lumber was made up, boats and canoes built and other craftsmanship necessary for the post performed. The word comes from the French meaning shipyard.

[H. M. Chittenden, *History of the American Fur Trade of the Far West.*]

CARL L. CANNON

Chantilly, Battle of (Sept. 1, 1862), occurred during Pope's (U.) withdrawal to Fairfax Courthouse (Va.) after his defeat at the second battle of Bull Run[qv]. Jackson (C.), seeking to command the road on which Pope was retreating, encountered Federal troops protecting the line of retreat. A sharp engagement followed, accompanied by a terrific thunderstorm. Losses were heavy, Generals Isaac I. Stevens (U.) and Philip Kearny (U.) being killed. Jackson could not interrupt Pope's retreat, the Federals reaching Fairfax Courthouse without further disaster.

[*Battles and Leaders of the Civil War*, II.]

W. N. C. CARLTON

Chaparral, from Spanish *chaparro,* as used by Mexicans, who gave the word to the Southwest, generally means any kind of thick or thorny brush, but never timber. In California, chaparral is specifically the manzanita oak; in parts of Texas, the black chaparral. Chaparral peculiar to arid and semi-arid regions of the Southwest includes juajillo, granjeno, mesquite, all-thorn and huisache, the bushes often interspersed with various kinds of cacti, agaves and yuccas. Only dogs, horses and men used to the chaparral can run in it, and the "brush popper," armored in leather and ducking, is a distinctly different type from the plains cowpuncher. The leaves of chaparral growth are as slender as the thorns are sharp, preventing evaporation. Some varieties afford good browsing; others are as bitter as gall. Before the era of overgrazing, a solid turf and frequent grass fires kept the brush down. Now it usurps millions of acres once prairie. Cattle ranging in it tend to become wild. It hides rattlesnakes, coyotes and other "varments."

[J. Frank Dobie, *A Vaquero of the Brush Country.*]

J. FRANK DOBIE

Chapbooks were cheap popular pamphlets, generally printed on a single sheet and folded to form twenty-four pages or less, often crudely illustrated with woodcuts, sold by chapmen (Anglo-Saxon *céap* [trade] *men*) or peddlers. Published by tens of thousands in America to about 1850, they were most numerous from about 1800 to 1825. Famous authors and peddlers of American chapbooks were Rev. Mason Locke Weems of Virginia (author of the Washington cherry-tree story), Josiah Priest of New York state and Chapman Whitcomb of Massachusetts. Prominent among the publishers were Andrew Steuart of Philadelphia, Isaiah Thomas of Worcester, Fowle and Draper and Nathaniel Coverly of Boston, Samuel Wood & Sons and Mahlon Day of New York. The beginning of popular literature in the United States, with emphasis on the wonderful, the sad and the humorous, they were for over 100 years the only literature available in the average home except the Bible, the almanac and the newspaper[qqv]. They included fairy tales, lives of heroes and rascals, riddles, jests, poems, songs, hymns, speeches, shipwrecks, Indian captivities, highwaymen, deathbed scenes, executions, romances, astrology, palmistry, etiquette books, letter-writers, valentine-writers, moral and (sometimes) immoral tales.

[H. B. Weiss, *Catalogue of the Chapbooks in the New York Public Library;* same, *American Chapbooks; Catalogue of English and American Chapbooks in Harvard College Library;* W. W. Watt, *Shilling Shockers of the Gothic School.*]

R. W. G. VAIL

Chaplin Hills, Battle of. *See* Perryville, Battle at.

Chapultepec, Battle of (Sept. 13, 1847). The western approaches to Mexico City were commanded by Chapultepec, a rocky eminence, 200 feet high, crowned with stone buildings. After vigorous bombardment, Scott launched Pillow's division against the southern slopes. The garrison resisted desperately, but the Americans mounted the walls on scaling ladders and carried the *Castillo*. Quitman's and Worth's divisions then attacked the Belén and San Cosme gates, and the city surrendered the next morning. The American loss (for the day) was 138 killed, 673 wounded. Mexican casualties are unknown, but 760 were captured.

[Justin H. Smith, *The War with Mexico*, II.]

CHARLES WINSLOW ELLIOTT

Charity Organization Movement, THE. Private and secular charity organizations existed in America as far back as the Scots Charitable Society of Boston (1657). After the American Revolution such societies appeared in the principal cities, but the New York Society for the Prevention of Pauperism (1817) was the first to propose a general attack upon the problem of destitution. A movement led by Joseph Tuckerman, under the influence of William Ellery Channing's Unitarianism[qv], culminated (1832–34) in the organization of the Association of Delegates from the Benevolent Societies of Boston. Handicapped by their sectarianism, these societies declined into almsgiving agencies.

Rapid industrialization following the Civil War accelerated the growth of cities and increased pauperism, especially among immigrants crowded in slums[qqv]. This brought a large increase in organizations attacking special aspects of the problem, and, eventually, a movement to coordinate them which was influenced by the work of Frederic Ozanam in Paris, Dr. Thomas Chalmers in Edinburgh, Count Rumford in Bavaria and Edward Dennison and Octavia Hill in London, as well as by the municipal plans of Elberfeld and Hamburg in Germany.

The charity organization movement prided itself on its "scientific" character. It planned to eliminate poverty and crime by the reconstruction and rehabilitation of individuals and families and the suppression of mendicity. All the resources of organized private philanthropy were to be focused upon the problem through the Charity Organization Society. The first city-wide society thus organized was in Buffalo (1877). From there the movement spread within five years to all the principal cities, and by 1904 there were 150 societies, leaving only 45 cities with population over 25,000 unorganized. In many cities, United Charities buildings were erected. The movement produced notable periodicals, such as the Philadelphia Society's *Monthly Register* (1880); Alexander Johnson's *Reporter of Organized Charity,* Chicago, 1888–89; and the *Charities Review,* started in 1891 in New York.

Beginning in the late 1880's this program of individual and family rehabilitation was supplemented by settlement work[qv] inspired by Toynbee Hall, in London. Organized charity had much in common with the contemporary development of state boards of charity and it also stimulated the development of such welfare agencies as wayfarers' lodges, penny provident funds and fuel societies.

The movement assumed national proportions in the National Association of Societies for Organizing Charities (1888) and the National Council of Charity Officers, both in connection with the National Conference of Charities and Corrections, founded 1873. Working relations were established with such organizations as Hebrew Charities, the Society of St. Vincent de Paul, the Red Cross[qv] and the Salvation Army[qv].

In the early years of the 20th century social workers gradually lost faith in the elimination of poverty by organized charity. Professionalization, beginning with the New York School of Philanthropy (1904), set more practical limits to social work. The American Association for Organizing Family Work took the place of the American Association for Organizing Charities, and child welfare agencies and courts of domestic relations[qv] assumed many of the functions of family work.

Post-war disillusionment brought doubt whether organized charity was not aggravating the situation by its "relief from above." On the other hand, welfare agencies increased in numbers and activity, particularly those supported from public funds. When organized charity proved inadequate to deal with relief in the early 1930's government agencies of direct relief, work relief and social security[qv] took over much of the burden. Although organized private charity has continued, it remains to be seen how much its basic structure will be changed by the new developments. (*See* Relief.)

[F. D. Watson, *Charity Organization Movement in the United States;* A. Johnson, *Adventures in Social Welfare.*]

HAROLD E. DAVIS

Charity Schools. In the early days, free education generally meant instruction for the poor and underprivileged children. Numerous schools were established in the American colonies and many were found also in the American states that were organized and supported by benevolent persons and societies, a practice which served to fasten on the idea of free education an odium that was difficult to remove. The pauper-school conception came directly from England and persisted far into the 19th century. Infant-school societies, Sunday-school[qv] societies and other organizations engaged in such work. Schools were sometimes supported also in part by rate bills, charges levied upon parents according to the number of their children in school. Declaration of poverty exempted parents from the payment of rate bills, which also often put the element of charity in certain educational practices. In the history of education in the United States philanthropy and charity have played important parts, on the theory that the level of life among the masses could thus be raised and their moral, religious and economic conditions be improved. As a result many kinds of charity schools were established in this country, and in some instances the children were not only instructed but provided with food, clothes and lodgings. Generally the curriculum was of the most elementary character.

[Frank P. Graves, *A Student's History of Education;* Edgar W. Knight, *Education in the United States.*]

EDGAR W. KNIGHT

Charivari. A French word of unknown origin meaning rough music. Corrupted into *shivaree* in America it designates an old custom, particularly in the Middle West, of serenading newly wedded couples with every type of noise-making device, the object being to exact a "treat." Refusal to serve the serenaders with refreshments resulted in some form of hazing, the groom often being compelled to "ride a rail." The *shivaree* was a manifestation of mob instinct, and like the barn dance was a popular form of rural entertainment. In New England the custom took the name of *serenade* or *callathump.*

[*American Speech,* April, 1933, Vol. VIII.]

W. J. BURKE

Charles River Bridge Case, 1837 (11 Peters 420). In 1785 the Massachusetts legislature incorporated the Proprietors of the Charles River Bridge, for the purpose of erecting a toll bridge between Boston and Charlestown. In 1828, long before the expiration of the charter, the legislature incorporated the Warren Bridge Company to build another bridge a few rods from the first. The new bridge was to become free to the public within six years. Was the second charter unconstitutional as impairing the obligation of the first? (*See* Contract Clause.)

The case was carried from the highest court in Massachusetts (6 Pick. 376, 7 Pick. 344) to the Supreme Court of the United States, where it was first argued in 1831. Chief Justice Marshall would have held the second grant invalid; but because of absences and disagreement it was impossible to reach a decision until 1837. By that time new appointments had worked a transformation in the Court, which now upheld the constitutionality of the second charter with only two dissenting votes. In an opinion which marked that leaning against monopolistic power which characterized Jacksonian political philosophy (*see* Jacksonian Democracy), Taney, the new Chief Justice, developed the rule that corporate charters are to be construed strictly in favor of the public.

[C. B. Swisher, *Roger B. Taney;* Charles Warren, *The Supreme Court in United States History.*]

CHARLES FAIRMAN

Charleston, Capture of (May 12, 1780). In March, 1780, the British, under Gen. Clinton and Admiral Arbuthnot, besieged Charleston by land and sea. The Americans, commanded by Gen. Benjamin Lincoln, made little use of the bar at the entrance of the harbor and the adjacent sea islands, the natural defenses of the town. The fall of Charleston, after a brave but futile resistance, for a time paralyzed the American cause in the Carolinas. (*See also* Southern Campaigns, 1780–81.)

[E. McCrady, *South Carolina in the Revolution, 1775-1780.*]

R. L. MERIWETHER

Charleston, S. C. In 1670 an English expedition under Gov. William Sayle founded a settlement—the first permanent one in the Carolinas[qv]—on the Ashley River, three miles from the present center of Charleston, and named it Charles Towne, in honor of King Charles II. Other immigrants settled on the present city site, and in 1680 the public offices were removed thither. This soon became the largest and wealthiest town south of Philadelphia. A definitely French tinge was imparted to its population by the coming of Huguenot[qv] refugees from France in 1685–86, of 1200 Acadian[qv] exiles in 1755 and 500 French Revolutionary refugees from Santo Domingo in 1793. In 1706 the city withstood an attack by a combined Spanish and French fleet. In February, 1776, the Provincial Congress met here and adopted the first state constitution. The city was unsuccessfully attacked by the British in 1776 and 1779, but fell into their hands in 1780 (*see* Charleston, Capture of) and so remained until 1782. Until it received a city charter in 1783 it was governed by ordinances of the legislature, which were administered in part by provincial officials, in part by the churchwardens. It continued as the state capital until 1790. It was the center of the nullification[q.v.] agitation of 1832–33, and of the secession[q.v.] spirit of 1860. The first fighting of the Civil War[q.v.] took place in its harbor (*see* Sumter, Fort). In the decades following the war, its beautiful old homes and churches, its aristocratic pride, its serenity and mellow atmosphere of the past gave it a charm all its own. It has suffered many calamities—not only sieges and bombardments, but hurricanes in 1699, 1752 and 1854, epidemics in 1699 and 1854, fire in 1740 and, on Aug. 31, 1886, the great earthquake which damaged nine tenths of its buildings. The foreign commerce of its port increased greatly after the World War.

[Mrs. St. Julien Ravenel, *Charleston, the Place and the People;* William A. Courtenay, *Charleston, S. C., the Centennial of Incorporation.*]

ALVIN F. HARLOW

Charleston, Siege of (1861–65). This popular term is a misnomer, for Charleston was never besieged, nor was any serious effort made either to fortify it or to invest it on the land side. The operations consisted in a blockade begun in May, 1861, with land and sea attacks upon the harbor fortifications. The harbor was well fortified and great ingenuity was displayed by the defenders in constructing an ironclad flotilla, a system of torpedo defense and even submarine boats. The wooden blockading fleet could not close in and even when Federal monitors arrived they could accomplish little against the land works. In 1863 Fort Sumter[q.v.] was bombarded and almost destroyed, but the ruins could not be taken. Battery Wagner[q.v.] was taken by formal siege operations, but no further progress could be made. It was in the course of these operations that the famous "Swamp Angel," an eight-inch 200-pounder Parrott rifle, was emplaced on a platform floated on deep mud, and fired five miles into the city, but burst on the thirty-sixth round. The city held out until February, 1865, and was finally evacuated on account of Gen. Sherman's advance northward from Savannah after his March to the Sea[q.v.] (*see* Carolinas, Sherman's March through the).

[John Johnson, *The Defense of Charleston Harbor; Battles and Leaders of the Civil War,* IV.]

OLIVER LYMAN SPAULDING

Charleston, Spanish Expedition against. *See* South Carolina, Spanish Expeditions against.

Charleston, W. Va., took its name from Charles Clendenin, whose son George acquired lands at the junction of the Elk and Kanawha rivers in the year 1787. Here was located Fort Lee, a refuge for wilderness settlers for a generation following the French and Indian War. Here Gen. Andrew Lewis halted his army in his march from Lewisburg to Point Pleasant[q.v.] in Dunmore's War[q.v.]. In 1791 Daniel Boone lived in a cabin in the suburbs of the present city and represented the county in the Virginia Assembly.

Charleston was a pivotal point in the early part of the Civil War and changed hands between the Confederates and Union forces a half-dozen times.

[Phil M. Conley, *West Virginia Encyclopedia;* Roy Bird Cook, *The Annals of Fort Lee.*]

MORRIS P. SHAWKEY

Charleston and Hamburg Railroad. *See* South Carolina Railroad, The.

Charleston Gardens. The Revolutionary and Civil wars took heavy toll of the 18th- and 19th-century gardens of Charleston and the neighboring parishes. Middleton Place has the only surviving colonial garden, laid out about 1740 by Henry Middleton. Its formal terraces rise from the west bank of the Ashley River and the camellias and evergreens planted by the botanist Michaux are its special pride. Magnolia Gardens, on the Ashley, were created during the 1840's by the Rev. John Grimke Drayton. Informal in style, their charm lies in the brilliance of massed azaleas, considered the finest in the world. Cypress Gardens, near Summerville, is the outstanding 20th-century garden achievement. The winding waterways of the old Dean rice plantation are utilized as its setting.

MARGARET B. MERIWETHER

Charleston Harbor, Defense of (1776). On June 1, 1776, a British squadron, led by Sir Henry Clinton and Peter Parker, anchored off Sullivan's Island, at the entrance to Charleston Harbor, S. C. The city was held by 6000 militia, while a much smaller force, led by Col. William Moultrie, was stationed on the island. On June 28 the British tried to batter down the island fort, only to find that their shots buried themselves in the green palmetto logs of the crude fortification. After the loss of one ship, the British retired and soon sailed for New York. Thus the Carolinas averted the threatened British invasion of the South.

[Edward McCrady, *South Carolina in the Revolution.*]

HUGH T. LEFLER

Charleston Indian Trade. As the only considerable English town on the southern coast, Charleston was from the beginning in position to reap a golden harvest from the trade to the Indians in English woolens, tools, weapons and trinkets. These goods, cheaper and better than those of the Spanish and French, soon became indispensable to the Indians and made the trade not only the first road to wealth in the colony but likewise the chief means by which the Carolinians drove back the Spanish and, after 1700, competed with the French for control of the region from the Tennessee River to the Gulf.

At first the proprietors and planters contended for the trade, but by 1700 it was the Charleston merchant who financed the traders and received the profits. After the French and Indian War[qv] the growth of Savannah and the acquisition by the British of Pensacola caused the center of the Southern Indian trade to shift westward.

[V. W. Crane, *The Southern Frontier.*]

R. L. MERIWETHER

Charleston (Ill.) Riot, The, on March 28, 1864, between soldiers on leave and Copperheads[qv], resulted in nine killed and twelve wounded. Fifteen Copperheads were held for military trial but on Lincoln's order were released to the civil authorities. Two were indicted, tried and acquitted. Others involved escaped arrest.

CHARLES H. COLEMAN

Charlestown, Mass., was founded July 4, 1629, by Thomas Graves, Rev. Francis Bright, Ralph, Richard and William Sprague and about 100 others, who preceded the Great Migration[qv]. John Winthrop's company stopped here for some time in 1630, before deciding to settle across the Charles River at Boston.[qv]

[Richard Frothingham, *History of Charlestown;* J. F. Hunnewell, *A Century of Town Life: A History of Charlestown, 1775-1887;* Justin Winsor, *Memorial History of Boston.*]

R. W. G. VAIL

Charlevoix's Journey (1721) to America was an attempt on the part of the French authorities to discover a route to the Western Sea, through the continent of North America. The regent of France, not wishing to have his purpose known, disguised the journey as a tour of inspection of the posts and missions of interior America. Charlevoix left France in July, 1720, arrived at Quebec in September, too late to join the flotillas that ascended to the "Upper Country." In May, 1721, he went around the Great Lakes, arriving in Mackinac[qv] in time to accompany the new commandant at La Baye[qv] to his post. There he conversed with Sioux Indians[qv] on their knowledge of the Western Sea. Finding it too late for an excursion into Lake Superior, Charlevoix decided to visit Louisiana[qv]. He entered Illinois[qv] by the St. Joseph-Kankakee route, and at Kaskaskia[qv] spent the winter interviewing traders from the Missouri. Thence he went down the river to New Orleans[qv] where he spent fifteen days, and continued to Biloxi[qv] where in February, 1722, he fell ill. Not being able to remount the Mississippi as he had planned, he returned to France, where he arrived in December, 1722. His recommendations to the regent resulted in a post among the Sioux, established in 1727. His experiences in America he wrote in *Journal Historique* which was published in 1744, first translated into English in 1761 and republished and edited for the Caxton Club, Chicago, 1923, by the author of this sketch.

[Louise Phelps Kellogg, *French Régime in Wisconsin and the Northwest.*]

LOUISE PHELPS KELLOGG

"Charlotina" was the name proposed for a colony, the establishment of which was suggested in a pamphlet appearing in Edinburgh in 1763, entitled *The Expediency of Securing our American Colonies by Settling the Country Adjoining the River Missisippi, and the Country upon the Ohio, Considered.* Had such a colony been erected it would have included the region lying between the Maumee, Wabash and Ohio rivers, the upper Mississippi and the Great Lakes.

[C. W. Alvord and C. E. Carter, *The Critical Period, 1763-1765.*]

WAYNE E. STEVENS

Charlotte, Fort, was the name given to the French Fort Condé at Mobile[qv] when the English took over the town at the close of the French and Indian War[qv] in 1763. Fort Charlotte was captured by the Spaniards in March, 1780, and was held by them until United States troops under Gen. Wilkinson took possession in April, 1813 (*see* Mobile Seized). After the purchase of Florida by the United States in 1819 (*see* Adams-Onís Treaty), Fort Charlotte was of no further importance and was gradually demolished.

[P. J. Hamilton, *Colonial Mobile.*]

R. S. COTTERILL

Charlotte, The Treaty of Camp (October, 1774), ended Dunmore's War[qv] with the Shawnee[qv]. The site was on Pickaway plains, Pickaway County, Ohio; Dunmore marked the name with red chalk on a peeled oak. Here Chief Cornstalk, defeated by Col. Andrew Lewis at Point Pleasant[qv], made a treaty, agreeing that the tribe would give up all prisoners, would not hunt south of the Ohio, and would obey trade regulations of the British government.

[Ohio Archeological and Historical Society *Publications*, XXXVII, 1928.]

LOUISE PHELPS KELLOGG

Charter Colonies were promoted through private enterprise under charters from the crown. They were founded by trading companies, by lords proprietors and by squatters later incorporated. Colonies of the first type for the most part either disappeared or changed their status early. The Virginia Company[qv] lost its charter in 1624, the New England Council[qv] surrendered its patent in 1635, the Providence Island colony[qv] was conquered by Spain in 1641 and the Massachusetts Bay Company[qv] became a theocracy, leaving the Bermuda Company as the only one of its kind in control of a colony through the greater part of the 17th century. Connecticut and Rhode Island[qqv], founded as squatter colonies by dissenters from Puritan Massachusetts, received charters of incorporation early in the Restoration Period. The predominating type throughout the 17th century was the proprietary colony. Of this sort was Carlisle's Caribbean grant, Maryland and Maine, in the early part of the century, and after 1660 the Carolinas, New York, the Jerseys, the Bahamas and Pennsylvania.

Similar institutions of government developed in all of the charter colonies. All ultimately had governor, council and house of representatives, the two former chosen by company or lord proprietor, and in the corporation colonies, indirectly by the people. The house of representatives, first the voluntary concession of the trading company, as in Virginia and Bermuda, later became a generally accepted institution in all chartered colonies except New York. Government in the corporation colonies was the freest from outside control. Perhaps because they were settled without the mediation of trading company or proprietor, the inhabitants of those colonies from the beginning cherished a conception of government based on sovereignty of the people.

When the restoration English government turned its attention to the building of a colonial policy, it found charters obstacles in the path. Several colonies were royalized, and, with the view of ultimate consolidation of all colonial possessions into a few large units, the Dominion of New England[qv] was established. Its failure brought temporary reaction in favor of charter colonies, but throughout the 18th century the process of royalization went on until by 1776 only two proprieties, Maryland and Pennsylvania, and two corporation colonies, Connecticut and Rhode Island, remained. Except in the corporation colonies the people seem to have preferred royal rule.

[C. M. Andrews, *Colonial Period of American History.*]

VIOLA F. BARNES

Charter Oak, THE. *See* Connecticut: Charter of 1662.

Charter of Liberties (1683), drafted by New York's first assembly, was approved by James Duke of York as an instrument of government for his province. Recalling the rights of Englishmen and the principles of the great liberty documents, this charter described the framework of government, the functions of governor, council and a legislative assembly representative of the qualified freeholders, and guaranteed the freedom of the assembly, which was to meet at least once in three years, trial by jury, due course of law in all proceedings, protection of the property of women, freedom from feudal exactions, exemption from quartering of soldiers and especially religious toleration for all Christians.

[J. R. Brodhead, *History of the State of New York.*]

RICHARD J. PURCELL

Charter of Privileges, granted by William Penn to Pennsylvania, Oct. 28, 1701, guaranteed freedom of worship to all who professed faith in "*One* almighty God." All who believed in Jesus Christ were eligible to office. A unicameral legislature was established and the Council ceased to be a representative body.

[W. R. Shepherd, *History of Proprietary Government in Pennsylvania;* J. Paul Selsam, *The Pennsylvania Constitution of 1776.*]

J. PAUL SELSAM

Chartered Companies played an important part in colonization in the New World, though they did not originate for that purpose. The joint-stock company was already in existence in many countries in the 16th century as an effective means of carrying on foreign trade and when the New World attracted the interest of merchants, companies were formed for purposes of trade in that direction. Since production of certain desired articles required the transportation of laborers, colonization became a by-product of the trading company[qv]. The first English company to undertake successful colonization was the Virginia Company[qv], first chartered in 1606 and, through two sub-companies, authorized to operate on the Atlantic coast between 34° and 45° N. Lat. By later charters in 1609 and 1612 to the London branch of the Virginia Company, and in 1620 to the Council for New England[qv], the successor to the Plymouth branch, the original project was somewhat enlarged and developed more in detail. Down to the Puritan Revolution this method of sponsoring colonization predominated. The Newfoundland Company of 1610, the Bermuda Company of 1615, an enlargement of an earlier project under the auspices of the Virginia Company, the Massachusetts Bay Company*qv* of 1629 and the Providence Island Company*qv* of 1630 represent the most important attempts at trade and colonization. After the Puritan Revolution, the Lord Proprietor superseded the trading company as preferred sponsor of colonization, both king and colonists becoming increasingly distrustful of corporations. Massachusetts and Bermuda, the last of the companies in control of colonization, lost their charters in 1684, but the former had long since ceased to be commercial in character.

[C. M. Andrews, *The Colonial Period of American History*, I; H. L. Osgood, *The American Colonies in the Seventeenth Century.*]

VIOLA F. BARNES

Charters, Municipal, are legal constitutions which incorporate communities, set up organs of government, distribute powers, create rights and obligations. American city charters reflect theories prevalent in four distinct historical periods—namely the Colonial, Post-Revolution, Post-Civil War and Twentieth-Century eras.

Early American charters followed their English prototype. Prior to 1688 borough charters were granted by the king through the royal governors and proprietors. Between 1688 and 1776, the British Parliament and the colonial assemblies*qv* gained the power of amendment at the expense of the king.

Immediately after the Revolution, American municipal charters began to depart from their English pattern. State legislatures replaced the king as the charter-granting agency. Thus to this day American cities are creatures of their respective states. Checks and balances, separation of powers*qv* became the theory of municipal as well as of state and Federal governments. Post-Revolution charters were characterized by elected mayors, bicameral councils, popularly elected judiciaries, extended franchise, short terms, rotation in office and low salaries.

Following the Civil War, municipal charters reached their lowest point of efficiency. Responsibility was divided among numerous unco-ordinated administrative heads. Powers of mayors were curtailed while powers of councils were unduly inflated.

Reaction resulted in fundamental reforms in 20th-century charters. Home Rule*qv* which had been granted by Missouri to its cities as early as 1875 was taken up by other states. Civil Service*qv* became an integral part of the administrative structure. Executive powers again expanded. Councilmanic power decreased. Bicameral councils gave way to unicameral bodies. Centralization of power and responsibility became the accepted theory. Longer terms and better salaries were provided. The initiative, referendum and recall*qqv* were added.

Contemporary municipal charters are divided into mayor-council, commission*qv* and city-manager*qv* types. The majority of American cities are still operating under the old mayor-council system, while approximately 400 cities have commission charters and 450 have city-manager charters.

[National Municipal League, *A Model City Charter;* Joseph D. McGoldrick, *The Law and Practice of Municipal Home Rule, 1916-1930.*]

FRANCES L. REINHOLD

Chartres, Fort de (1719–72), seat of civil and military government in the Illinois country*qv* for more than half a century, stood near the present village of Prairie du Rocher in Randolph County, Ill. Named in honor of the son of the Regent of France, it was commenced in 1719 and completed the following year. Built of wood, and exposed to the flood waters of the Mississippi, the fort quickly fell into disrepair. In 1727 it was rebuilt, but by 1732 it was so dilapidated that St. Ange, the commandant, built a new fort with the same name at some distance from the river. By 1747, when a general Indian uprising seemed imminent, this too had fallen into such bad condition that repair was considered impossible and the garrison was withdrawn to Kaskaskia*qv*.

In 1751 the French government decided to build a new fort at Kaskaskia, but the engineer in charge, Jean Baptiste Saucier, decided on a location near the old fort. Foundations were laid in 1753; three years later the structure was substantially finished. Costing 200,000 livres, the new Fort de Chartres was an irregular quadrangle with sides 490 ft. long and stone walls 2 ft. 2 in. thick. Ten years after its completion a competent English officer described it as "the most commodious and best built fort in North America." It was capable of housing 400 men, although its garrison rarely exceeded half that number.

Fort de Chartres, transferred to the British on Oct. 10, 1765, was the last French post in North America to be surrendered under the Treaty of Paris*qv*. Renamed Fort Cavendish, it was the seat of British rule in the Illinois country until 1772 when it was abandoned and destroyed.

[C. W. Alvord, *The Illinois Country, 1673-1818.*]

PAUL M. ANGLE

Chartres, Fort de, Treaty (1766), is the name given to an agreement made by George Croghan, deputy superintendent of Indian affairs, with the Western Indians, by which the Indians acknowledged the authority of the king of England, and agreed to return prisoners and stolen horses and to permit the establishment of trading posts. The conference was held at Fort de Chartres^qv^, beginning on Aug. 25, 1766. Twenty-two tribes, including the Kaskaskia, Piankashaw, Kickapoo, Miami, Sacs and Foxes^qqv^, were present; later three other tribes adhered to the pact. The peace established at this conference lasted for the duration of British rule in the Illinois country.

[A. T. Volwiler, *Croghan and the Westward Movement.*]

PAUL M. ANGLE

Chase Impeachment Trial, THE (June 2–March 1, 1805), was generally considered as part of a concerted Republican (Jeffersonian)^qv^ effort to curb the power of the Federal bench. Justice Chase, an arbitrary personage with an abusive tongue and an unswerving confidence in the righteousness of the Federalist party^qv^ which had elevated him to the bench was charged in the articles of impeachment with unbecoming conduct and disregard of law. The outcome of the trial before the Senate hinged largely on the question whether his conduct, admittedly objectionable, constituted "a high crime or misdemeanor." His acquittal, March 1, 1805, was probably a distinct gain for judicial independence.

[Charles Warren, *The Supreme Court in United States History.*]

W. A. ROBINSON

Château-Thierry Bridge, Americans at. Having broken the French front on the Aisne^qv^, the Germans entered Château-Thierry on May 31, 1918. Gen. Foch, rushing troops to stop them, sent the American 3rd Division (Dickman) to the region of Château-Thierry, where, aided by French Colonials, the Americans prevented the enemy from crossing on May 31 and June 1. The German attacks then ceased.

[De Chambrun and De Marenches, *The American Army in the European Conflict;* J. M. Hanson, History of the American Combat Divisions, in *The Stars and Stripes.*]

JOSEPH MILLS HANSON

Chateaugay (Canada), Battle of (Oct. 25, 1813). During the autumn of 1813, Maj. Gen. Wade Hampton advanced along the Chateaugay River into Canada with over 4000 troops. On Oct. 22 he halted about fifteen miles from the St. Lawrence. Here, three days later, he attempted to dislodge 800 hostile troops barring his farther progress. In this engagement the British suffered only twenty-five casualties, the Americans double this number. Hampton retired to United States territory.

[Henry Adams, *History of the United States,* Vol. VII.]

JAMES RIPLEY JACOBS

Chattanooga Campaign (Oct.–Nov., 1863). Before the battle of Chickamauga^qv^ the Union troops under Grant, released by the capture of Vicksburg^qv^, had begun to move eastward. Bragg (C.) had failed to follow through after Chickamauga. All he could do was to "besiege" Rosecrans' (U.) army in Chattanooga. Grant, placed in general command of all Union forces in the West, replaced Rosecrans by Thomas and instructed him to hold Chattanooga "at all hazards." Food was running short and supply lines were constantly interrupted. Grant's first act was to open a new and protected line of supply, via Brown's Ferry^qv^. Re-enforcements arrived. Vigorous action turned the tables on Bragg, whose only act was to weaken himself unnecessarily by detaching Longstreet (C.) on a fruitless expedition to capture Knoxville^qv^. Bragg then awaited Grant's next move. President Davis (C.) visited the army and tried, unsuccessfully, to restore confidence.

On Nov. 24, 1863, Hooker (U.) captured Lookout Mountain^qv^ on the left of Bragg's line. The next day Grant attacked all along the line. The Confederate center on Missionary Ridge^qv^ gave way; the left had retreated; only the right held firm and covered the retreat southward into northern Georgia. A brilliant rear-guard stand at Ringgold Gap^qv^ halted Grant's pursuit. The Union troops returned to Chattanooga; the Confederate Army went into winter quarters at Dalton, Ga.

[*Battles and Leaders of the Civil War,* Vol. III.]

THOMAS ROBSON HAY

Chautauqua Movement, THE, had its beginning in an assembly held at Chautauqua, on the shore of Lake Chautauqua, N. Y., Aug. 4–18, 1874. Here John H. Vincent, a Methodist clergyman of New York, later Bishop, and Lewis Miller of Akron, Ohio, who were interested in developing Sunday schools^qv^, planned a course of meetings to give instruction in Sunday-school organization, management and teaching, and study of the Bible. They also arranged to include some recreation and a few lectures not actually relating to Sunday schools. The visitors were at first housed in a sort of camp, which rapidly grew into a permanent summer colony. In 1876 the session was lengthened to three weeks and later, with the introduction of new subjects, it extended to two months. In 1878 the Literary and Scientific Circle (home-study courses) was launched, and 7000 persons took this work in the first year. At times in after years as many as 25,000 were enrolled at once. At the assembly grounds in 1879 a school for teachers in secular subjects was opened, also a school of languages, later known as the College of Liberal Arts. Other developments, year after year, were Schools of Mathematics and Sciences, of Library Training, Domestic Science, Music, Arts and Crafts, Expression, Physical Education, Practical Arts and —in co-operation with Cornell University in 1912—Agriculture. The growth of the institution was rapid. Although founded by Methodists, many churches were represented at the first gathering and there was never any disposition to make the teaching of religious subjects denominational. One after another there came to be built on the grounds lecture halls with seating capacities of from 200 to 5000, a theater, clubhouses, gymnasiums, a memorial church, memorial library, a colonial market place, etc. Between 1924 and 1932 (when the attendance fell off considerably because of the industrial depression) about 45,000 persons attended the general assembly each season. A magazine, the *Chautauquan,* was published from 1880 to 1914.

Hundreds of local assemblies appeared within two or three decades in the United States and Canada, imitating in a limited degree the Chautauqua plan and often calling themselves "Chautauquas." At least two of these, the Catholic Summer School at Lake Champlain and the Jewish Chautauqua Society at Atlantic City, N. J., have been permanent and extensive in their programs. Shortly after 1900 the traveling Chautauqua appeared—promoted by a lecture bureau, moving from town to town, giving a week or more of lectures, concerts and recitals, from two to three programs a day, usually in a large tent. This had a considerable popularity for more than a decade.

[John H. Vincent, *The Chautauqua Movement;* J. L. Hurlburt, *The Story of Chautauqua;* J. S. Noffsinger, *Correspondence Schools, Lyceums, Chautauquas.*]

ALVIN F. HARLOW

Check Currency is the term applied to bank deposits subject to check. Although checks were used in making payments in New York and other large cities for years before the Civil War, extending back as far as the beginning of the 19th century, it is only since the Civil War that the widespread use of check currency in all parts of the United States has had its major development. Various estimates indicate that since 1900 from 85% to 90% of all payments in the United States are made by check.

[D. Kinley, *The Use of Credit Instruments in Payments in the United States.*]

FREDERICK A. BRADFORD

Checkoff, THE, is a system under which the employer by agreement with a union deducts union dues and assessments from the pay of union members. Funds thus collected are turned over to union officials. Coal mining provided the background of the checkoff. Deductions from the pay of the miner for advances by the employer of powder, tools, supplies, etc., were a regular feature of the industry from the outset. Such a practice readily lent itself to the union insistence on the checkoff. The practice had undoubtedly appeared earlier, but the United Mine Workers^qv^ organized in 1890 sponsored the checkoff on a nationwide basis. In the unionized bituminous^qv^ areas the demand was generally gained. The anthracite^qv^ industry resisted the checkoff successfully until the 1937 agreement with the United Mine Workers. The checkoff has appeared in other industries, notably among the hosiery workers, but on nothing like so extensive a scale as in mining. The checkoff is frequently coupled with a demand for the closed shop^qv^. Its advantages to the union are the automatic collection of dues from the members and the enforcement of the closed-shop policy. Employers have usually resisted the demand for the checkoff. Fragmentary evidence would indicate further extension of the checkoff system since 1933.

[*Monthly Labor Review,* January, 1930; A. Haring, *The Checkoff in the American Coal Industry,* an unpublished dissertation available at the Yale University Library.]

HERBERT MAYNARD DIAMOND

Checks and Balances is the term used to denote the "separation of powers"^qv^ of government that was the underlying principle upon which the Government of the United States was created by the Convention of 1787^qv^. This theory became popular in America in large part due to the writings of Montesquieu and William Blackstone. It consists in setting off legislative and executive departments from each other and the courts against both. Each department of government is supposed to operate as far as possible within a separate sphere of administration, but the co-operation of all three is necessary for the conduct of the government.

The makers of our Constitution were aware of the weakness of the Continental government under the Articles of Confederation^qv^. This consisted in the complete conduct of the government by the Continental Congress^qv^ with practically no executive or judicial departments. For this reason the office of President of the United States was created and largely modeled upon the kingship of Great Britain. In order to prevent executive aggression, such as had caused the misgovernment of George III, the system of checks and balances was introduced and also provision was made for a Federal judiciary^qv^. Furthermore it was provided that the Senate and House of Representatives should act as checks upon each other in the national Congress^qv^.

[W. Wilson, *Constitutional Government in the United States.*]

WILLIAM STARR MYERS

Chemical Warfare. Before the World War, suffocating gases were used but these were nonlethal. On April 22, 1915, where the French and British lines joined in the Ypres salient, the Germans, waiting until wind conditions were favorable, launched a chlorine gas attack which inflicted fearful casualties. Dec. 19, 1915, they attacked again, this time with phosgene. These offensives were made by lining up cylinders on the battle front and releasing therefrom gas to be carried by the wind to the enemy. Should the wind change, the attacker suffered from his own weapon. In 1916 this form of gas attack gave way to the use of artillery shell filled with gas agents. In 1917 and 1918 British methods still further modified gas warfare by the introduction of the Livens projector and the Stokes mortar.

Aug. 17, 1917, Gen. Pershing requested authority to make Lt. Col. Amos A. Fries Chief of Gas Service in the American Expeditionary Forces^qv^. This was done five days later and Fries began the work which later became our Chemical Warfare Service abroad. The duties of this service were chemical research, development and manufacture; filling of shell and other containers with poisonous gases, smoke and incendiary materials; purchase and development of gas masks and other protective materials; supply of chemical agents in the field; training army personnel in chemical warfare duties, offensive and defensive; organizing, equipping and operating special gas troops. Schools were established in France at Langres and at Hanlon.

In America a Chemical Service Station was authorized Oct. 16, 1917. By May 11, 1918, the date when Maj. Gen. William L. Sibert was appointed Director of Chemical Warfare Service, with Fries in charge overseas, a condition had arisen wherein the Medical Corps directed gas defense production; the Ordnance Department, certain other defense functions; the Signal Corps controlled alarm devices; the Engineers had the "Gas and Flame" regiment; and the Bureau of Mines directed the Research Section. Sibert's appointment coalesced and co-ordinated activities at home and abroad and the 30th Engineers, a six-company regiment, became our First Gas Regiment. Edgewood Arsenal, originally known as Gunpowder Neck, Maryland, became the center of our chemical warfare production at home, and continues today as the center of such production, training and experimentation.

Abroad, the First Gas Regiment, which took part in every big battle from the second Marne to the Armistice^qv^, was subsequently expanded into an 18-company organization; and two additional, similarly constituted, chemical warfare regiments were authorized to be formed. The signing of the Armistice precluded this action.

[Official Cablegrams exchanged between War Department and the American Expeditionary Forces; General Orders of the War Department and of the A. E. F.; Brig. Gen. Amos A. Fries, *Gas in Attack and Gas in Defense;* Brig. Gen. Amos A. Fries and Maj. Clarence J. West, *Chemical Warfare;* Col. Harry L. Gilchrist, *A Comparative Study of World War Casualties from Gas and other Weapons;* James T. Addison, *The Story of the First Gas Regiment; A History of DuPont Company's Relations with the United States Government* prepared by that company; Maj. S. J. M. Auld, *Gas and Flame.*]

ROBERT S. THOMAS

Chemistry, Industrial. The manufacture of tar, potash and glass was attempted in Virginia in 1608 and leather, salt and iron were made there on a small scale in 1620. All these enterprises were wiped out in the Great Massacre of 1622^qv^. Salt^qv^ making began in the Plymouth colony the next year; but the projects of John Winthrop, Jr., in Massachusetts, beginning in 1633, are generally regarded as the initiation of industrial chemistry in America. It has kept pace with the growth of the nation and has utilized a vast store of natural resources. The production of sugar, fertilizers, iron, paints, the vulcanization of rubber and many other important advances mark its course. The history of American manufactures throughout the 19th century is closely related to this development.

The inorganic chemical industry had become well established before 1900 and developed rapidly thereafter. The 20th century witnessed the beginning of the synthetic organic chemical industry in this country. Both phases of chemical development have grown to great proportions, assuming world leadership in many specialties. In 1900 came the contact process for sulfuric acid and the production of carbon disulfide by an electric process. The commercial expansion of chlorine began in 1901, since when this basic chemical has enjoyed a great ascendancy with the development of chlorinated products and its wider use in bleaching and in public health. The first patent for synthetic resins, Bakelite, was issued in 1907. The industry has expanded enormously and developed hundreds of new types from a great range of raw materials. Carbon black, an important substance in tire compounding, was introduced in 1915; accelerators for vulcanization in 1906; and rubber[qv] antioxidants in 1925. The direct use of rubber latex began in 1921, electrodeposition of rubber in 1927 and the use of rayon[qv] cord in tire construction in 1937. In 1922 ethylene glycol came on the market and America began to synthesize ammonia by the fixation of atmospheric nitrogen, to be followed later by synthetic sodium nitrate[qv] capable of competing with Chilean nitrate in the world market. Nineteen nineteen was marked by the production of butanol and acetone by fermentation, leading later to the development of the first of the lacquers of the Duco type and producing something of a revolution in the protective coating industry. Chromium plating and solid carbon dioxide, introduced under the name of "dry ice," came in 1925 (*see* Refrigeration); the development of a quick freezing process for the preservation of foods in 1926; safety glass in 1927 and synthetic phenol and aniline in 1928. The hydrogenation of petroleum was begun in 1929; the polymerization of refinery gases to produce high antiknock gasolines in 1936; isooctane fuel, especially for aviation[qv], became commercial in 1934; solvent refining of lubricating oil in 1933; the Dowell process for increasing the production of old oil wells by the use of corrosion-inhibited acid in 1932; and tetraethyl lead, the well-known antiknock reagent, in 1922.

Dichlorodifluoro methane, a nontoxic, nonflammable refrigerant, was made in 1930. Alphacellulose of high purity was produced from wood pulp[qv] in 1927; camphor was synthesized from turpentine in 1933; bromine was separated from sea water on a commercial scale in 1934; and kodachrome for amateur motion pictures[qv] was introduced in 1935. Vitamin B_1 was synthesized in 1936. Other vitamins have been crystallized by American workers and hormones have been synthesized. The outstanding industrial development of 1938 was Nylon, the first truly synthetic fiber. First used commercially in bristles for tooth brushes, it promises to become of the utmost importance in the textile[qv] field, since it surpasses natural silk in important characteristics.

The chemical industry has served agriculture by supplying fertilizers[qv], insecticides and fungicides, methods of food processing and industrial outlets for such products as starch, cellulose and building boards such as Celotex. Manufacturing has been aided by such things as alloys, dyes, acids, alkalies and many specialties. Chemistry has supplied to buildings an unending variety of new materials, colors and shapes. Public health has benefited by disinfectants, germicides and bactericides, as well as by pharmacy and medicinal chemistry.

[E. E. Slosson, *Creative Chemistry;* H. E. Howe, ed., *Chemistry in Industry;* H. E. Howe, *Chemistry in the World's Work.*]

H. E. HOWE

Chequamegon Bay, on the southern coast of Lake Superior, is noted as the site of the first dwelling occupied by white men in what is now Wisconsin. The French traders, Groseilliers and Radisson[qv], built a hut somewhere on the west shore of the bay, probably in 1658. Other traders dwelt on this bay 1660–63 and were visited in the spring of 1661 by Father Ménard, first missionary to the Northwest. In 1665 Father Claude Allouez built a mission house near the southwest end of the bay. There his successor, Father Jacques Marquette[qv], came in 1669 and remained for two years.

In 1693 the largest island, now known as Madeline, at the mouth of the bay, was occupied by a fort built by Pierre LeSueur. This was abandoned before the close of the century. In 1718 a French fort was built on the island, where Louis Denis de la Ronde had an establishment for fur trading and exploration for copper mines. The post was called La Pointe, and a French garrison was maintained there until 1759. The first English trader to reach this distant post was Alexander Henry, whose French partner, Jean Baptiste Cadotte, founded a permanent trading post at this place. In 1818 two Massachusetts traders, Lyman and Truman Warren, came thither, married daughters of Michel Cadotte and became the leading fur traders of the region. Truman Warren died early; Lyman maintained his home at La Pointe until his death in 1847. A village of retired *voyageurs* and fur traders grew up here during the early 19th century and the American Fur Company[qv] had a post here for many years. The first Protestant mission was begun here in 1831.

[L. P. Kellogg, *French Régime in Wisconsin and the Northwest;* R. G. Thwaites, The Story of Chequamegon Bay, in *Wisconsin Historical Collections*, VIII.]

LOUISE PHELPS KELLOGG

Cherokee, THE, at the beginning of the 18th century, occupied or claimed all that region south of the Ohio and west of the Great Kanawha rivers, extending as far as the northern parts of South Carolina, Georgia and Alabama. DeSoto's[qv] march in 1540 gave them their first contact with white men. During the last quarter of the 17th century, first the Virginians and then the South Carolinians established commercial relations with them, and by 1700 French traders had come in. In 1730 Sir Alexander Cuming allied them to the British in a treaty and sealed it by taking a group of chiefs on a visit to England. In 1757 the British built for the Cherokees Fort Loudoun[qv] on the Tennessee River. During the French and Indian War[qv] the Cherokees remained true to their alliance, until near the end when trouble broke out which resulted in a fierce war lasting for two years (1760–61), in which the Cherokees captured Fort Loudoun and massacred many of the prisoners. During the Revolution they took up hostilities against the Americans, and for some years thereafter bloody encounters continued (*see* Cherokee Wars).

Beginning in 1721 the whites gradually whittled away by treaties the Cherokee country until, by 1819, the Indians were reduced to a small fragment of their former domain, most of which now lay in Georgia, but with small areas in North Carolina, Tennessee and Alabama. The Cherokees now determined to stand on their treaty rights and cede no more land. Under the tutelage of missionaries from New England and by the aid of the Federal Government they had already begun to take on much of the civilization of the white man, and in 1827 they organized a government with a written constitution. With an alphabet which Sequoyah[qv] devised, they published a newspaper, the *Cherokee Phoenix*, and issued from their printing press at New Echota many pamphlets. Unable to tolerate the organization of a nation within her borders, Georgia demanded the Cherokee country and the removal of the Indians to the reservations beyond the Mississippi. A bitter legal fight took place between Georgia and the Cherokees aided by the United States Supreme Court in two decisions, Cherokee Nation v. Georgia and Worcester v. Georgia[qqv], both of which the state ignored. With President Andrew Jackson sympathizing with Georgia, a treaty of cession was made in 1835 (*see* New Echota, Treaty of) and within the next three years all the Cherokees with the exception of a few in North Carolina were removed to the Indian Territory[qv].

[C. C. Royce, The Cherokee Nation of Indians, in *Fifth Annual Report of the Bureau of Ethnology to the Secretary of the Smithsonian Institution, 1883-84;* J. P. Brown, *Old Frontiers;* V. W. Crane, *The Southern Frontier, 1670-1732;* G. Foreman, *Indian Removal;* U. B. Phillips, *Georgia and State Rights.*]

E. MERTON COULTER

Cherokee Nation v. Georgia (5 Peters 1). In 1791 the Cherokee[qv] made a treaty of cession with the United States (*see* Holston Treaty) wherein they were guaranteed the remainder of their territory. When Georgia, in 1802, ceded her western lands to the Federal Government (*see* Georgia Compact, The) she received the promise that all Indians should be removed from her limits as soon as it could be done peaceably and on reasonable terms. Embittered by the failure of the Government to effect removal and by the organization of an independent Cherokee government within her borders, Georgia in 1828 and 1829 extended her laws over the Indians and began to occupy their territory. The Cherokees could get no protection from President Jackson (*see* Indian Removals) and therefore appealed to the Supreme Court, filing an original bill (Dec. 12, 1830) for an injunction restraining Georgia from interfering with the Cherokees or enforcing her laws within the Cherokee Nation. Georgia refused to defend the suit. The sympathies of the Court were with the Cherokees, but the majority opinion was that since the Cherokees were not citizens of the United States, nor, as contended by them, a foreign nation, they were not competent to appear as a party to a suit in the Supreme Court. (*See also* Worcester v. Georgia.)

[U. B. Phillips, *Georgia and State Rights;* Charles Warren, *The Supreme Court in the United States.*]

E. MERTON COULTER

Cherokee River, THE, was the early name for the Tennessee, so called because it ran through the Cherokee Indian[qv] country.

[James Adair, *History of the American Indians.*]

E. MERTON COULTER

Cherokee Strip, THE, is a term improperly applied to an area officially designated as "a perpetual outlet, West." Both the terms "Strip" and "Outlet" are used. Guaranteed to the Cherokee Indians[qv] by treaties of 1828 and 1833 as an outlet, it was not to be occupied for homes.

The area comprises about 12,000 square miles, and lies between 96° and 100° W. Long., and 36° and 37° N. Lat. The Treaty of 1866 compelled the Cherokee Nation to sell portions to friendly Indians.

The Strip was leased by the Cherokee Nation in 1883 to the Cherokee Strip Livestock Association for five years at $100,000 a year; the lease was renewed, but was terminated before expiration by the United States. In 1891 the United States purchased the Cherokee Strip for $8,595,736.12. Opened by a "run" on Sept. 16, 1893, it became part of the Territory of Oklahoma[qv].

[George Rainey, *The Cherokee Strip.*]

M. L. WARDELL

Cherokee Trail, THE, sometimes called the "Trappers' Trail," was laid out and marked in the summer of 1848 by Lt. Abraham Buford in command of Company H of the First Dragoons, though it had previously been followed by trappers en route to the Rocky Mountains. It extended from the vicinity of Fort Gibson[qv] up the Arkansas River to the mouth of the Cimarron and up the latter stream to a point in the northwestern part of what is now Oklahoma. From here it ran west to the Santa Fé Trail[qv], which it joined at Middle Cimarron Spring. It was followed by numerous Cherokees[qv] and many whites from northeastern Arkansas on their way to the gold fields of California[qv].

[Ralph P. Bieber, ed., *Southern Trails to California,* Southwest Historical Series, Vol. V.]

EDWARD EVERETT DALE

Cherokee Wars, THE (1776–81). In April, 1776, commissioners of the Continental Congress[qv] held a conference with the Cherokee[qv] at Fort Charlotte with the purpose of conciliating the tribe, restless because of continued encroachment on its lands. Notwithstanding this, the Cherokee, disregarding the advice of the British agents among them, and yielding to the incitement of Shawnee[qv] and other northern Indians, attacked the frontiers of Georgia and the Carolinas. Their most ambitious attacks–against Watauga and the upper Holston settlements[qqv]–were beaten off, and in return, South Carolina, aided by Congress, arranged for retaliatory expeditions converging from Georgia, the Carolinas and Virginia. Against these the Cherokee, dispirited because of the refusal of the Creeks[qv] to aid them, offered little resistance; practically all their towns were destroyed, several hundred of them forced to find refuge in Florida, and the tribe purchased peace from the four states in treaties of June and July, 1777, only by extensive land cessions in the two Carolinas.

From 1776 to 1781 Cherokee affairs were under the supervision of North Carolina and Virginia, each of which appointed a Cherokee agent. James Robertson, the Carolina agent, resided at Echota[qv], the Cherokee "capital," and exerted sufficient influence to keep the Cherokee at peace, except a disgruntled element which had built new towns down the Tennessee on Chickamauga Creek where the British agents established their headquarters. The Chickamauga[qv], aided by some of the Creek towns, constantly raided the frontiers and in 1779 entered into an alliance with the northern Indians to aid Lt. Gov. Henry Hamilton in his campaign against George Rogers Clark. At Clark's suggestion a company of Virginia militia moving down the Tennessee to Illinois stopped off at Chickamauga Creek and, with the aid of Watauga forces, destroyed the Indian towns and carried off great quantities of supplies gathered there by the British. The towns were rebuilt and the Indian attacks continued, with the result that in the fall of 1779 another joint expedition from Virginia and North Carolina repeated the destruction of the preceding spring.

In the fall of 1779 Robertson left Echota for the new settlement Henderson was establishing on the Cumberland[qv] and, with his influence withdrawn, the Overhill Cherokee relapsed into hostility, joining the Chickamauga and the Creeks in co-operating with Gen. Cornwallis and Maj. Patrick Ferguson by attacking the frontier. Joseph Martin, the Virginia agent, was unable to keep the Indians quiet, and again Virginia and North Carolina had recourse to a joint expedition, following the battle of King's Mountain[qv]. The devastation this time was as complete as in 1776. In the spring of 1781 Gen. Greene, now Federal Indian superintendent in the South, appointed commissioners to make peace with the Cherokee, which was done in April. This treaty, confirming the land cessions made at the treaties of DeWitt's Corner and Long Island in 1777, was thereafter steadily adhered to by all the Cherokee except the Chickamauga. Against the latter John Sevier led constant expeditions in 1781 and 1782 with the result that they moved farther down the Tennessee, where they built their Five Lower Towns and continued their hostility.

[A. V. Goodpasture, Indian Wars and Warriors of the Old Southwest, in the *Tennessee Historical Magazine*, Vol. IV, March, 1918; W. H. Mohr, *Federal Indian Relations, 1774-1788;* H. L. Shaw, *British Administration of the Southern Indians, 1756-1783.*]

R. S. COTTERILL

Cherry Valley Massacre, THE (Nov. 11, 1778), in which Butler's Rangers[qv], with Indians under Brant, attacked this important outpost in the upper Susquehanna Valley, was marked by special Indian savagery in retaliation for their losses at Oriskany[qv]. Whole families were surprised in their homes. A few escaped, thirty were killed, while seventy-one, taken prisoners, were mostly released next day. All the buildings were burned and cattle taken. Sixteen soldiers were killed but the remainder held the fort and cared for the returning refugees.

This massacre directly determined the Sullivan expedition[qv] against the Iroquois (1779).

[F. W. Halsey, *The Old New York Frontier;* Howard Swiggett, *War out of Niagara.*] FRANCES DORRANCE

Chesapeake and Delaware Canal. As early as 1764 a survey was made for a canal route between Chesapeake and Delaware bays. A company was organized in 1803, but languished and was not revived until 1822. The canal, 13⅝ miles long, with three locks, was finally built 1825–29. It had cost $165,000 per mile, making it the most expensive waterway of its time. A cut ninety feet deep through earth and stone was the heaviest engineering project yet undertaken in America. In 1919 the Government purchased it and made it into a sea-level ship canal.

[Alvin F. Harlow, *Old Towpaths.*]

ALVIN F. HARLOW

Chesapeake and Ohio Canal, THE, popularly known as "the Old Ditch," was a joint project of the United States, Maryland and Virginia. It was the legal successor of the Potomac Company[qv] in the attempt to connect the Chesapeake Bay with the Ohio River by a system of water transportation. The plan was to construct a series of locks and canals around the rapids and falls of the Potomac from Georgetown to Cumberland. From there the Ohio was to be reached at one of its tributaries, the Youghiogheny. Ground was first broken on July 4, 1828, and the canal was completed to Cumberland by 1850. Funds were contributed principally by Maryland, the terminal cities and the United States. The fifty shares of stock in the Potomac Company which George Washington had donated to a proposed National University[qv] were also invested and lost, for the corporation was not successful in reaching the Ohio. It failed on account of the inherent difficulty of the task, and because of competition from the Baltimore and Ohio Railroad[qv], which reached Wheeling about 1852. Continuing as a local enterprise on the Potomac River, it was placed (1889) in the hands of receivers, who, in 1938, sold the property to the United States.

[George W. Ward, *The Early Development of the Chesapeake and Ohio Canal Project.*]

LEONARD C. HELDERMAN

Chesapeake Capes, Battle of (1781). A naval engagement, Sept. 5–9, which led to the surrender of Cornwallis at Yorktown[qv]. When a British fleet of nineteen ships arrived at the entrance of the Chesapeake with reinforcements for Cornwallis, it found a French fleet of twenty-four ships, under DeGrasse, already there. The battle was fought on an easterly course in converging lines. The British lost one ship and had several badly damaged; as a result they could not attack again and Barras' French squadron of eight ships, transporting siege guns from Newport for the attack on Yorktown, was enabled to enter the Capes. The British fleet returned to New York and Cornwallis was trapped.

[A. T. Mahan, *Major Operations of the Navies in the War of American Independence.*]

WALTER B. NORRIS

Chesapeake* Captured by *Shannon. On June 1, 1813, the United States frigate *Chesapeake,* 38 guns, Capt. James Lawrence, with an untrained crew sailed out of Boston on a cruise. At 5:45 P.M. she met H. B. M. frigate *Shannon,* 38 guns, 330 highly trained men, Capt. Philip Vere Broke commanding. In the opening maneuvers, Lawrence lost an opportunity to rake his enemy and exposed his own ship to a terrible bombardment at pistol range. By 5:55 all the American officers were killed or wounded and the crew was in a panic. Lawrence, dying, gave his last order "Don't give up the ship."[qv] Leading his crew personally Broke boarded, and at 6:05 had taken the *Chesapeake.*

[Theodore Roosevelt, *Naval War of 1812.*]

MARION V. BREWINGTON

***Chesapeake–Leopard* Incident** (1807). On June 22, off Hampton Roads, the American frigate *Chesapeake* was stopped by the British ship *Leopard,* whose commander demanded the surrender of four seamen, claiming them to be deserters from the British ships *Melampus* and *Halifax* (*see* Impressment of Seamen). Upon the refusal of the American commander, Capt. James Barron, to give up the men, the *Leopard* opened fire. The American vessel, having just begun a long voyage to the Mediterranean, was unprepared for battle, and to the repeated broadsides from the British replied with only one gun which was discharged with a live coal from the galley. After the *Chesapeake's* hull had been struck with fourteen round shot, her mainmast and mizzenmast had been "irreparably injured" (Decatur's letter to Secretary of Navy, July 4, 1807), her rigging had been greatly damaged and her crew had lost "three men killed and twenty wounded" (Log of *Chesapeake*), Barron surrendered his vessel.

The British boarding party recovered only one deserter, the others having left the *Chesapeake* before she sailed; but three American seamen were also removed by force. The British captain refused to accept the *Chesapeake* as a prize, but forced her to creep back into port in her crippled condition. Barron was court-martialed, found guilty of "neglecting, on the probability of an engagement, to clear his ship for action" (*Proceedings . . . Court-Martial . . . Barron*), and suspended from the navy for five years without pay. England's offer to make reparations enabled President Jefferson to avert war, in spite of the widespread anger throughout the United States. Negotiations were prolonged by Great Britain until 1811 when she formally disavowed the act and returned two of the men, one having meanwhile died and another having been hanged as a deserter.

[Charles Lee Lewis, *The Romantic Decatur.*]

CHARLES LEE LEWIS

Cheyenne, THE. An important tribe of Algonquian^qv Indians, their name being a corruption of the Dakota *Shahiyena,* "people of alien speech." Originally living in Minnesota, from where they visited LaSalle's Illinois River fort in 1680, they were pushed out on the plains by the Sioux^qv, being reported by Lewis and Clark^qv in 1804 as living west of the Black Hills^qv.

They early confederated with the Arapahoes^qv, but fought constantly with the Sioux, Crows^qv and Hidatsas. In 1835 William Bent, who married a Cheyenne woman, induced about half the tribe, including part of the Arapahoes, to move south to the Arkansas River^qv and hunt and trade near Bent's Fort^qv. This artificial division between "Northern" and "Southern" Cheyennes still continues.

After Gen. W. S. Harney's Ash Hollow^qv campaign of 1855, the Cheyennes joined the Sioux in hostility and from 1860 to 1878 were the most implacable foes of the whites, losing, according to James Mooney, more lives in fighting them than any other plains tribe, in proportion to their numbers.

They participated in the destruction of the commands of Capt. William J. Fetterman^qv, Dec. 21, 1866, and Gen. George A. Custer, June 26, 1876 (*see* Little Big Horn Battle). They were terrifically punished when their villages were destroyed by troops at Sand Creek, Nov. 29, 1864; Washita River^qqv, Nov. 27, 1868; Sappa Creek, April 23, 1875 and Crazy Woman Creek, Nov. 25, 1876. Other notable actions included Beecher Island^qv, Sept. 17, 1868; Adobe Walls^qv, June 27, 1874; Rosebud River, June 17, 1876, and the entire Dull Knife campaign^qv of September, 1878, to January, 1879.

Throughout their wars the Cheyennes were characterized by desperate valor and they did perhaps more than any other tribes, save the Sioux and Apaches^qv, to hold back settlement of the West.

[George Bird Grinnell, *The Fighting Cheyennes;* George W. Manypenny, *Our Indian Wards.*]

PAUL I. WELLMAN

Cheyenne, Wyo., was established in 1867 by the advancing Union Pacific Railroad^qv. After a brief boom as "Hell on Wheels"^qv it became the chief outfitting point for the hordes of gold seekers flocking into the mining booms in the Sweetwater region and the Black Hills^qv, and, as home of the Wyoming Stock Growers' Association, "the administrative and social metropolis of the immensely larger cattlemen's range" of the Northern Plains. The collapse of the cattle boom of the 1880's ended its great days of glamour and romance.

[Louis Pelzer, *The Cattlemen's Frontier.*]

LAURA A. WHITE

Chicaca, Indian Town. A principal village of the Chickasaw Indian in north Mississippi, where, in March, 1541, Hernando DeSoto^qv fought a disastrous battle with southern Indians. He lost over forty of his men, about fifty horses and the greater part of his herd of swine. Some historians place the village on the Yalobusha River.

[*Spanish Explorers in the Southern United States,* in Original Narratives of Early American History Series.]

SAMUEL C. WILLIAMS

Chicago, Burlington & Quincy Railroad, THE, sprang from the urgent need of prairie settlers for transportation. Between 1849 and 1855 four small ambitious pioneer lines in Illinois—Peoria & Oquawka, Northern Cross (from Quincy), Central Military Tract (Galesburg) and Aurora Branch—were joined in one system centering at Galesburg. The Oquawka terminal was shifted to Burlington and the railroad assumed its present title in 1855, popularly known as the "Burlington Route." Eventually it was extended west of the Mississippi, by construction and by the purchase of 203 small roads. Giving access to eastern markets, it played a major role in the development of the prairie states.

[Albert J. Perry, *History of Knox County, Ill.;* H. G. Greenleaf, *John Murray Forbes.*]

EARNEST ELMO CALKINS

Chicago, Ill. The name, an Indian word variously spelled and defined, was first associated with the portage (*see* Chicago Portage) between the Des Plaines River and the shallow prairie stream flowing into Lake Michigan at this point, thus linking the Great Lakes with the Mississippi. The portage was a trail center and the principal objective of early travelers. The first white man of record to sojourn on the site of the present city was Father Marquette who, overcome by illness, spent four months, December, 1674, to March, 1675, on the bank of the little river. By the Treaty of Greenville[qv], 1795, the United States acquired a tract six miles square at the river mouth on which Fort Dearborn[qv] was built in 1803. Evacuation of the fort at the opening of the War of 1812[qv] led to an attack by a band of Potawatomis[qv] on the retreating garrison in which thirty-eight of the sixty-seven soldiers, besides two women and twelve children, were killed, and a number taken captive, Aug. 15, 1812. The first white settler was John Kinzie, the "father of Chicago," a Canadian trader who came in 1804. After the Black Hawk War[qv] and the subsequent extinction of Indian titles, settlers began to arrive in numbers. On Aug. 4, 1830, the first official date in Chicago annals, the Illinois and Michigan Canal[qv] Commissioners published a plat for the "Town of Chicago" on part of the easternmost of the sections of land granted by the United States to the State of Illinois in aid of the canal. This was the first use of the name as a topographical designation. Organization of a village was voted Aug. 4, 1833, with an electorate of 28 and a population of 150, and on March 4, 1837, Chicago was incorporated as a city with a population of 4071. The canal, first suggested by Jolliet in 1673, was not completed until 1848, when it was quickly superseded by the railroads, the first of which, the Galena and Chicago Union, opened a ten-mile section westward, Oct. 28, 1848. Eastern roads built into Chicago in 1851, and by 1857 eight railways had entered the city. An era of expansion followed, population rising from 29,963 in 1850 to 300,000 in 1870. On Oct. 9–10, 1871, more than half the city was destroyed by a great fire which burned over 2200 acres, consumed 15,768 buildings and caused the loss of $188,000,000 and 300 lives (*see* Chicago Fire). Recovery was rapid and Chicago was rebuilt in stone and steel in place of the jerry-built pioneer town that had met a long-foreseen fate. Expansion was resumed on a wider scale and firmer foundation. Commerce and industry flourished, accompanied by labor disputes and social unrest issuing in several serious conflicts, among them the railroad strike of 1877, the Haymarket riot, May 4, 1886, and the Pullman strike of 1894[qqv]. Annexation of surrounding suburbs, especially between 1880 and 1890, increased the city's area from the original fraction of one section to 205 square miles. In the same decade the population was doubled, from 503,185 to 1,099,850. The World's Columbian Exposition[qv] brought Chicago to international attention as more than a commercial metropolis and incidentally exerted lasting influence upon its own development. The Chicago Plan Commission, engaged in a continuous program of city planning, is the direct issue and heir of the Exposition and, in general, the period since the "World's Fair" has been characterized by an awakened public spirit manifested in numerous organizations and activities concerned with the promotion of civic progress. The Century of Progress Exposition[qv], 1933, marked the centennial of the organization of the village of Chicago.

[A. T. Andreas, *History of Chicago;* B. L. Pierce, *History of Chicago.*]

C. B. RODEN

Chicago, Milwaukee & St. Paul Railway Co. v. Minnesota, 1890 (134 U. S. 418). An act of the Minnesota legislature, in 1887, established the Minnesota Railroad and Warehouse Commission and defined its duties in relation to common carriers. The supreme court of the state held that rates recommended and published by the Commission should be final as to what were equitable and reasonable charges; that there could be no judicial inquiry as to the reasonableness of such rates; and that a railroad company, contending that such rates were unreasonable, was not entitled to submit testimony on the question.

The United States Supreme Court declared the act unconstitutional because it deprived a railroad of property without due process of law and deprived it of equal protection of the law, substituting therefor the action of a commission without judicial functions or the machinery of a court of justice. The findings of the state court were therefore reversed.

JULIUS H. PARMELEE

Chicago, Milwaukee, St. Paul & Pacific Railroad, THE, operates 11,097 miles of road in twelve states between the Great Lakes and the Pacific Northwest. Its original predecessor company, the Milwaukee & Waukesha Railroad, chartered in 1847, was the first road in Wisconsin, and the first to operate through trains between Chicago and the Twin Cities (1867). It was extended to Omaha, 1882; Kansas City, 1887; Black Hills, 1907; Seattle-Tacoma, 1909. The Chicago, Terre Haute & Southeastern Railway was leased, July 1, 1921. Six hundred and fifty-six miles of main line in Montana and Washington are electrified. Its traffic, in order of volume, comprises mine products, manufactures, agricultural, forest and animal products.

[F. H. Johnson, *The Milwaukee Road, 1847-1935.*]

F. H. JOHNSON

Chicago and North Western Railway was organized on June 6, 1859. Its actual beginning reverts to 1836 when the Illinois legislature incorporated the Galena and Chicago Union, the first railroad built west of Chicago and Lake Michigan. By 1855 the G. and C. U. tapped the Mississippi at Dunleith and Fulton. When it merged with the North Western on June 2, 1864, the consolidated line comprised 860 miles of track. The North Western was completed to Council Bluffs early in 1867, the first railroad connection with the Union Pacific[qv]. By 1910 a maze of 118 corporations and 144 proprietary companies formed the gigantic cyclops substantially as it existed in 1939.

[W. J. Petersen, The North Western Comes, in *The Palimpsest,* Vol. XIV; *Yesterday and To-day: A History of the Chicago & North Western Railway System.*]

WILLIAM J. PETERSEN

Chicago and Rock Island Railroad, the first railroad constructed to the Mississippi, was incorporated by the Illinois legislature in 1847 as the Rock Island and LaSalle Railroad Company. The name was changed to Chicago and Rock Island in 1851. Completed to the Mississippi on Feb. 22, 1854, it linked the Atlantic with the Mississippi by its connection with the Michigan Southern and Northern Indiana Railroad. The first bridge across the Mississippi was completed in 1856. The Missouri was reached at Council Bluffs, Iowa, in 1869, and opposite Atchison, Kans., in 1871. Further consolidation led to the assumption, in 1880, of the present title, The Chicago, Rock Island and Pacific Railway Company. By 1922 the Rock Island network approximated 8000 miles.

[W. J. Petersen, The Rock Island Comes, in *The Palimpsest,* Vol. XIV.]

WILLIAM J. PETERSEN

Chicago Board of Trade. *See* Pit, The.

Chicago Crime Commission, The, is an Illinois corporation organized in 1919 by the Chicago Association of Commerce and supported by private subscriptions. Its purpose is to promote the efficiency and activity of all state and local officers charged with the enforcement of criminal laws.

[*Bulletins of the Chicago Crime Commission,* 1919- .]

P. ORMAN RAY

Chicago Drainage Canal, The. The geography of Chicago is such that the problems of water supply and drainage have always been extremely difficult. In 1886 the city council created a special commission, whose investigations ultimately resulted in the construction (1893–1900) of the Drainage Canal from Chicago to Lockport, whereby the flow of the Chicago River was reversed and the city sewage, diluted with water from Lake Michigan, was sent down the Illinois. The canal answered the city's needs for many years, but the diversion of the lake water provoked the increasing opposition of adjoining states and Canada, finally inducing the Federal Government to compel the city to provide other means of sewage disposal. (*See also* Chicago Sanitary District Case.)

[Curry, *Chicago: Its History and Its Builders,* III.]

M. M. QUAIFE

Chicago Fire, The (Oct. 8–9, 1871). Modern Chicago began its growth in 1833; by 1871 it had a population of 300,000. Across the broad plain which skirts the river's mouth buildings by the thousand extended, constructed with no thought of resistance to fire. Even the sidewalks were built of resinous pine and the single pumping station which supplied the mains with water was covered with a wooden roof! The season was one of excessive dryness. Up from the plains of the far Southwest blew week after week a scorching wind which withered the growing crops and made the structures of pine-built Chicago dry as tinder. A conflagration of appalling proportions awaited only the starting spark.

It began on Sunday evening, Oct. 8. Where it started is clear; how it started no man knows. Living in a hovel at the corner of Jefferson and DeKoven streets was a poor Irish family by the name of O'Leary. The traditional story is that Mrs. O'Leary[qv] went out to the barn with a lamp to milk her cow; the lamp was upset and cow, stable and Chicago were engulfed in one common ruin. But Mrs. O'Leary testified under oath that she was safe abed and knew nothing about the fire until she was called by a friend of the family.

Once started, the fire moved onward resistlessly to the north and east until there was nothing more to burn. Between nine o'clock on Sunday evening and ten-thirty the following night an area of three and one half square miles, including the business center of the city, was burned, over 17,000 buildings were destroyed, and 100,000 people were rendered homeless. From Taylor Street to Lincoln Park, from the river to the lake, the city lay in ruins. The direct property loss was about $200,000,000. The loss of human lives, while never known, is commonly estimated at about 300. The mass of misery and the indirect material losses entailed by the fire were never measured; but the cost of the lesson Chicago learned on that October night and day was exceedingly high.

[Sheahan and Upton, *The Great Conflagration.*]

M. M. QUAIFE

Chicago Portage, THE. The Des Plaines River runs close to the head of the Chicago River and over the intervening portage the traveler could transport his boat from the Great Lakes–St. Lawrence to the Mississippi River system. The development of Chicago is primarily due to her strategic location at the head of Lake Michigan and on this natural thoroughfare to and from the Mississippi.

The length of the Chicago Portage varied greatly with the seasons. During a spring flood boats might sometimes pass between Lake Michigan and the Illinois River without any land carriage, while in dry seasons a portage of 100 miles, to LaSalle, was often necessary. The importance of this route was recognized by Jolliet*qv*, who in 1673 pointed out the need of a canal across the Chicago Portage, but not until 1848 was the Illinois and Michigan Canal*qv* completed. With the advent of the canal and the railroad, the importance of the Chicago Portage ceased; already, however, it had determined the location of America's second metropolis.

[M. M. Quaife, *Chicago and the Old Northwest;* Robert Knight and Lucius H. Zeuch, *The Location of the Chicago Portage Route of the Seventeenth Century.*]

M. M. QUAIFE

Chicago Road, THE, is the ancient highway from Detroit to Chicago. For uncounted generations it was an important Indian trail, the explorer LaSalle in 1680 being probably the first white man to travel it. The disasters suffered in the War of 1812 taught the Government the bitter lesson that it could not defend the western country without highways over which to move its armies. In 1824 Congress appropriated money for the survey of roads of national importance (*see* Survey Act of 1824, The General), and the President allocated one third the entire sum to surveying a military highway connecting Detroit with Fort Dearborn*qv* at Chicago. From about 1830 on, an ever-increasing flood of settlers poured into the Northwest and thousands of them traveled the new highway leading to Chicago, which has ever since been called the Chicago Road. Its route is approximately represented today by United States Highway 112.

[M. M. Quaife, *Chicago's Highways Old and New,* 29-50.]

M. M. QUAIFE

Chicago Sanitary District Case, THE (Wisconsin v. Illinois, 289 U. S. 395, 710) involved the question of whether the equitable power of the United States can be utilized to impose positive action on one of the states in a situation in which nonaction would result in damage to the interests of other states. The immediate problem was the increasing diversion of Great Lakes waters by the city of Chicago to carry off sewage through the long-established drainage canal (*see* Chicago Drainage Canal). It was claimed that the increasing amounts of water diverted, made necessary by the growth of the city, was lowering lake levels, thus impairing the transportation facilities of the bordering states. After exhaustive hearings, the Supreme Court had fixed (281 U. S. 696) maximum diversion at a point below that necessary to continued utilization of the drainage canal system alone, thus requiring the construction of sewage disposal works, but the city and state procrastinated. The opinion of the Court settled finally the question of the authority of the United States to intervene to enforce action by a state in such a situation. "In deciding the controversy between States, the authority of the Court to enjoin the continued perpetration of the wrong inflicted on the complainants, necessarily embraces the authority to require measures to be taken to end the conditions, within the control of the defendant state, which may stand in the way of the execution of the decree."

PHILLIPS BRADLEY

Chicago Treaties, THE (1821, 1833). In August, 1821, 3000 Indians assembled at Chicago to confer with Lewis Cass and Solomon Sibley, spokesmen of the United States Government, which desired to procure from the Potawatomi and allied tribes the southwestern part of Michigan, extending from Grand River to the south end of Lake Michigan. The Indians proved amenable and their title to this portion of Michigan was surrendered.

Twelve years later, a second and more imposing council was convened at Chicago. This time the Government wished to acquire from the Potawatomi and their allies several million acres of land lying between Lake Michigan and Rock River in northeastern Illinois and southeastern Wisconsin and to remove these Indians to new homes west of the Mississippi. Several thousand Indians attended the council and the picturesque conferences were extended many days. Eventually, everything was arranged and the Indians bade their native land a sad farewell; the future of Chicago belonged to the white race.

[M. M. Quaife, *Chicago and the Old Northwest.*]

M. M. QUAIFE

Chickamauga, Battle of (Sept. 19–20, 1863). The Army of the Cumberland^{qv}, under Gen. W. S. Rosecrans (U.), maneuvered an inferior Confederate force under Gen. Braxton Bragg out of Chattanooga, an important railway center, by threatening it from the west while sending two flanking columns far to the south. On finding that Bragg had evacuated the city and was retreating, Rosecrans pushed his forces eastward in a "general pursuit" until he found that the main Confederate Army had halted directly in his front. In order to unite his scattered corps he moved northward to concentrate in front of Chattanooga. Bragg attacked on the morning of Sept. 19 in the valley of Chickamauga Creek, about ten miles from Chattanooga. The effective strength was: Confederate, 66,000; Union, 58,000.

The fighting began with a series of poorly coordinated attacks in *echelon* by Confederate divisions which were met by Union counterattacks. From the start it was the concern of Rosecrans to keep open his communications with Chattanooga and this made him constantly anxious for the situation on his left wing. On the second day the battle was resumed by the Confederate right in such a way as to make Rosecrans fear a turning movement. A needless transfer of troops to the Union left, plus a blundering order which opened a gap in the center, so weakened the right that it was swept from the field by Longstreet's attack. Rosecrans and his staff were carried along by the routed soldiers. Thomas (U.), commanding the Federal left, with the aid of troops under Granger, held the army together and after nightfall withdrew into Chattanooga. Both commanding generals lost heavily in reputation, Rosecrans because of his ill-considered orders and his flight from the battlefield, Bragg because of his failure to follow up his subordinates' success and his subjecting his troops to needless slaughter. Rosecrans was presently superseded by Grant, but President Davis sustained Bragg, against his corps commanders' protests until after his defeat by Grant at Chattanooga^{qv}.

[*Battles and Leaders of the Civil War*, Vol. III.]

THEODORE CLARKE SMITH

Chickamauga, The, was a lawless tribe of Indians, composed in largest part of Overhill Cherokees^{qv}, who seceded in 1777 under Chief Dragging Canoe, removed from the towns of the Little Tennessee River and settled on Chickamauga Creek near the site of the present Chattanooga. Later the seceders were joined by discontented or outlawed Creeks^{qv}. Their villages were at and near the Suck of the Tennessee. In this natural stronghold they gave much trouble to emigrants going down the Tennessee, and to the Cumberland settlements^{qv}, as well as the whites in east Tennessee.

[J. P. Brown, *Old Frontiers.*]

SAMUEL C. WILLIAMS

Chickasaw, The. An important Muskhogean tribe closely related to the Choctaw^{qv} in language and custom, though formerly these tribes were mutually hostile. From their earliest history their habitat was northern Mississippi. They were noted from remote times for bravery, independence and warlike disposition toward surrounding tribes (*see* Chickasaw-Creek War; *also* Chickasaw-French War). Early in the 19th century they began sending their youth to Eastern schools, and mission schools in their nation, and in time became a literate people. As the result of white intrusion in their country, these Indians in 1832 entered into a treaty ceding their country to the United States (*see* Pontotoc, Treaty of). In 1837 they purchased from the Choctaw the western half of their domain in the Indian Territory^{qv} and in that year the 6000 members of the tribe began emigration to the West. They first settled among the Choctaw and shared in a common government until 1855. The Chickasaw, considerably intermarried with the whites, possessed a constitutional government, a school system and became known as one of the Five Civilized Tribes^{qv}. Early in the present century their communal land holdings were allotted in severalty to the individual members and tribal government was dissolved (*see* Burke Act). Their citizens and land are now included in the State of Oklahoma.

[F. W. Hodge, *Handbook of American Indians.*]

GRANT FOREMAN

Chickasaw Bluffs. The high bank of the Mississippi at the mouth of the Wolf River, where LaSalle built Fort Prudhomme^{qv} (1682) and Bienville built Fort Assumption (1739). Much intrigue with the Chickasaws^{qv} centered around this post, especially during the Spanish occupation of Louisiana. Gayoso built Fort Ferdinand there in 1797; later that year the United States successfully claimed it and built Fort Pickering, near which John Overton settled the town of Memphis^{qv} in 1820.

[John W. Monette, *History of the Discovery and Settlement of the Valley of the Mississippi.*]

MACK SWEARINGEN

Chickasaw Bluffs, Battle of (Dec. 29, 1862). Sherman's (U.) attack from the Chickasaw Bayou, off the Yazoo River, was part of a threefold Federal plan to reduce and capture Vicksburg^qv^. Porter's (U.) co-operating gunboats could not be brought within range; and Grant (U.), instead of keeping Pemberton (C.) in check near Granada, was compelled to fall back on Memphis when Van Dorn (C.) captured his depot at Holly Springs^qv^. The repulse of Sherman's troops at Chickasaw Bluffs demonstrated the futility of any attack against Vicksburg from the Yazoo.

[Richard S. West, Jr., *The Second Admiral, a Life of David Dixon Porter.*] RICHARD S. WEST, JR.

Chickasaw Council House, The Treaty of (Sept. 20, 1816), was negotiated by Andrew Jackson and other commissioners. By its terms the United States promised annuity to Chickasaw Nation, money and land to chiefs and warriors; engaged to exclude pedlars from their country. Chickasaw Nation ceded to United States land on both sides of Tennessee River.

[Charles J. Kappler, *Indian Affairs, Laws and Treaties.*] GRANT FOREMAN

Chickasaw-Creek War, THE (1793). On Feb. 13, 1793, a Chickasaw^qv^ national council declared war against the Creek^qv^, to avenge the murder of two Chickasaw hunters; on Feb. 14 Chief Tatholah and forty warriors started on the warpath. Chief Piomingo, attributing the murders to Creek resentment at the Chickasaw refusal to join an alliance against the Anglo-Americans, sought American aid. Gov. Blount, of the Southwest Territory^qv^, favored such aid, to divert the Creek from attacks upon the Cumberland settlement^qv^; Indian Agent Seagrove, in Georgia, promised the Creek American support in return for "peace and friendship with us." The Federal Government, however, committed from motives of idealism and economy to a moderate Indian policy, using force only as a last resort, refused armed intervention; though Blount was allowed to give the Chickasaw part of the Federal treaty annuity supplies.

Much talk, little fighting ensued; Spanish officials of Louisiana and West Florida^qqv^, following their Indian-solidarity and Indian-buffer policy, held intertribal hostilities to a minimum, and on Oct. 28 engineered at Nogales^qv^ a treaty of alliance of the Chickasaw, Creek and other Southern tribes with one another and with Spain. Outstanding points in this incident are: (1) Indian anti-American confederation; (2) difficulties of Federal Indian policy.

[*American State Papers, Indian Affairs,* I; Serrano y Sanz, *España y los Indios Cherokis y Chactas en la Segunda Mitad del Siglo XVIII.*] ELIZABETH HOWARD WEST

Chickasaw-French War (1736–40). Prominent among the great events which the 18th century witnessed was the contest between England and France for the control of the Mississippi Valley^qv^. By 1725 an ultimate French victory seemed certain. One of the few obstacles to their policy of uniting their St. Lawrence settlements with those on the Gulf of Mexico by a series of forts throughout the intervening valley was the hostility of the Chickasaws^qv^, smallest but most warlike of the Southern Indian tribes and one which had an undying hatred for the French.

Incensed by several decades of irritating and effective opposition from this valiant tribe, which was entrenched along the eastern bank of the Mississippi south of the Ohio, Bienville, governor of Louisiana^qv^, at length decided that its extermination was imperative. The Chickasaw-French War which followed (1736–40) consisted of two unsuccessful military efforts. The first resulted in the wiping out of D'Artaguette's^qv^ expedition from Illinois and Bienville's defeat at the battle of Ackia^qv^ (1736) on the upper Tombigbee (present northeastern Mississippi). The second consisted in the assembling of 3600 soldiers during the winter of 1739 at Fort Assumption on the lower Chickasaw Bluff^qv^. For some strange reason no attack was attempted and with this ignominious fiasco Bienville's "war" against the Chickasaws ended.

[F. X. Martin, *History of Louisiana;* S. C. Williams, *Beginnings of West Tennessee.*] GERALD M. CAPERS, JR.

Chickasaw Old Fields were located on the north bank of the Tennessee River, four miles below the mouth of the Flint River, in the present Madison County, Ala. At this place the Chickasaw, according to their traditions, fixed their easternmost villages when they migrated east of the Mississippi although their chief towns were in northern Mississippi. The Chickasaw defended their claim to the adjacent land by driving out the Shawnee^qv^ in 1714 and by overwhelming the Cherokee^qv^ in 1769. The villages in Madison County seem to have been occupied until the American Revolution, and then abandoned, due to pressure from the Cherokee, who were extending their towns down the Tennessee. The Old Fields were claimed by the Chickasaw until 1805, when they were included in a land cession to the United States.

[F. W. Hodge, *Handbook of American Indians;* J. R. Swanton, Early History of the Creek Indians, Bulletin 73, *Bureau of American Ethnology.*] R. S. COTTERILL

Chickasaw Treaty, The (1783), was negotiated by Virginia's commissioners with the Chickasaws^ℱ, under the great Piomingo and other chiefs, at Nashborough (Nashville). This treaty removed the claim of that tribe to the territory between Cumberland River and the ridge that divided the waters of that stream from those of the Tennessee, to the south of Nashborough. The primary purpose of the Virginia government was to obtain a cession of western Kentucky, between the Tennessee and the Mississippi. That failed, and the remarkable result was that, at Virginia's expense, her commissioners, treating on North Carolina soil, cleared for North Carolinians the Indian title from one of the most fertile stretches of land in the West. Another result was the cementing of a firm friendship between the Cumberland settlers^ℱ and the Chickasaws, a tribe ever noted for its fidelity.

[T. P. Abernethy, *Western Lands and the American Revolution.*]

SAMUEL C. WILLIAMS

Chicora was a portion of northern Spanish "La Florida," located in the present-day Carolinas, thought to have been inhabited in the 16th century by Indians of great wealth but of queer form, some having tails, others having feet so large they could be used for umbrellas, and some having an eye in the middle of their chests. In 1523 Lucas Vásquez de Ayllón^ℱ obtained from Charles V a grant to the region to search for a giant king.

[Herbert E. Bolton, *The Spanish Borderlands.*]

A. CURTIS WILGUS

Chief Joseph's Campaign. *See* Nez Percé War (1877).

Chihuahua Trail, The. In the late 16th century Spanish exploration and colonization had advanced from Mexico City northward by the great central plateau to its ultimate goal in Santa Fé^ℱ. Until Mexican independence (1821) all intercourse of New Mexico with the outer world was restricted to this 1500-mile trail. Over it came ox carts and mule trains, missionaries and governors, soldiers and colonists. When the Santa Fé Trail^ℱ sprang up, traders from the United States extended their operations southward over the Chihuahua Trail and beyond to Durango and Zacatecas. Superseded by railroads, the ancient Mexico City–Santa Fé highway has recently been revived as a great automobile highway of Mexico. The part in New Mexico, State Highway 85, pioneered by Franciscan missionaries in 1581 (*see* Rodríguez-Chamuscado Expedition), may claim to be the oldest highway in the United States.

[L. B. Bloom, The Chihuahua Highway, in *New Mexico Historical Review,* July, 1937.]

LANSING B. BLOOM

Child Labor statistics were not available prior to 1870. Knowledge of the extent of juvenile employment at earlier periods is fragmentary. The seed of the child labor system may first have appeared in the spinning schools established early in the colonies. Textile^ℱ mills founded after the Revolution promptly utilized the labor of children. Contemporary opinion did not disfavor such employment, and undoubtedly in early years no acute problem existed. Yet hours were excessively long. As the 19th century advanced child labor became prevalent. Two fifths of the factory workers in New England were alleged to be children in a report in 1832. Agitation for compulsory school attendance had appeared in the previous decade. In the 1840's laws of Connecticut, Massachusetts and Pennsylvania limited the hours of child habor in textile factories.

Hence by the time of the census of 1870, which reported the employment of three quarters of a million children between ten and fifteen years of age, the problem had grown to the point of national significance. From 1870 to 1910 the number of children reported as gainfully employed steadily increased as did also their percentage of the total number of children in the population. Aroused to action, the Knights of Labor^ℱ projected a campaign in the 1870's and 1880's for child labor legislation and many states enacted laws. Conditions in canneries, the glass industry, anthracite mining and other industries began to attract attention in the closing years of the century.

Very early in the 20th century aggressive campaigns for the enactment of restrictive legislation developed. Conditions in the South, where the number of child laborers had multiplied threefold in the decade ending in 1900, aroused public sentiment for child labor laws. In the North, insistence upon improved standards of legislation and adequate enforcement of child labor laws led to the organization of the National Child Labor Committee in 1904. This committee investigated conditions in various states and in various industries. Child labor legislation was pushed in the various state legislatures. Conspicuous success attended its efforts. The results of this activity appeared in the absolute and relative declines in child labor reported by the 1920 and 1930 census enumerations. This trend probably also continued in the 1930's.

However, the backwardness of certain states, the lack of uniformity of state laws and the competitive difficulties arising therefrom led to demands for Federal regulation of child labor after 1910. Endeavors at congressional regulation were set aside by the United States Supreme Court in 1918 and 1922 (*see* Hammer v. Dagenhart; Bailey v. Drexel Furniture Co.). Undaunted by this failure, efforts were now made by child-labor reformists for a Child Labor Amendment[qv]. In 1924 the Amendment was submitted to the states for ratification, which has not yet been achieved. However, the Fair Labor Standards Act[qv] of 1938 prohibited child labor in the industries affected by its provisions and will materially affect factory employment of children. Problems remaining in the field of child labor, however, include the employment of children in agriculture, street trading, industrial homework and other areas in which effective regulatory measures are not yet universal or applicable.

[U. S. Bureau of Labor Statistics, *Bulletin* No. 604; *History of Wages in the United States from Colonial Times to 1928;* Commons and associates, *History of Labor in the United States*, Vols. I and IV; Millis and Montgomery, *Labor's Progress and Problems*, Vol. I.]

HERBERT MAYNARD DIAMOND

Child Labor Amendment, THE, submitted to the states for ratification in June, 1924, followed two unsuccessful attempts to achieve uniformity of child labor standards throughout the nation: the Child Labor Act of 1916, which invoked the interstate commerce power of the Federal Government, and the law of 1919, based upon the taxing power. Both were held unconstitutional, as improper exercise of the power invoked. (*See* Child Labor Cases.) The apparent impossibility of circumventing judicial hindrances to Federal legislation brought about the submission of a Constitutional amendment which would give Congress power "to limit, regulate and prohibit the labor of persons under 18 years of age." The use of the word "labor" instead of "employment," which was designed to permit whatever child labor legislation Congress might see fit to enact, and the coverage of persons between sixteen and eighteen years of age, were responsible for much of the opposition aroused. By the end of 1938 twenty-eight states had ratified, eight less than the number necessary to make the amendment part of the Federal Constitution.

ROYAL E. MONTGOMERY

Child Labor Cases. The United States Child Labor Law was enacted in 1916 to become effective Sept. 1, 1917. The act prohibited shipment in foreign and interstate commerce of goods produced in factories and canneries which within thirty days preceding removal of such goods had employed children under fourteen years of age, or children between the ages of fourteen and sixteen for more than eight hours a day or six days a week, or after 7 P.M. and before 6 A.M. The same restrictions were imposed on articles produced in mines and quarries employing children under sixteen years of age.

Upholding the decision of the Western District Court of North Carolina (1917), the United States Supreme Court on June 3, 1918, declared the law unconstitutional as an invalid use of the commerce power of the Federal Congress to infringe freedom of contract and prevent child labor within the respective states (*see* Hammer v. Dagenhart).

The revenue act of 1919 included almost the identical provisions of the 1916 Child Labor Law, except that a 10% tax on the net profits of employers violating the provisions was imposed. In May, 1922, the United States Supreme Court again upheld the decision of the same district court in declaring the measure an unconstitutional use of the Federal taxing power in regulation of something entirely within the police power of the several states (*see* Bailey v. Drexel Furniture Company).

[J. R. Commons and J. B. Andrews, *Principles of Labor Legislation.*]

GORDON S. WATKINS

Child Life and Welfare. In the writings of 18th-century philosophers of democracy came the first modern expression of the importance of child life in its influence upon society. There followed a succession of thinkers whose recognition of the worth of the child has had lasting influence in this country. With the advent of industrialization the desire to improve the environment of children adversely affected by factory, slum and sweatshop conditions gave rise to a mass of remedial legislation. In recent years health measures (*see* Hygiene) have lowered the infant death rate as well as the proportion of deaths from tuberculosis and diphtheria, and nutrition work and behavior clinics have lessened the hazards of childhood in other regards. The value of recreational programs has been recognized, and improved nursery school, kindergarten and experimental school methods have been developed to give the child his full chance.

The White House Conferences of 1909 and 1919 on the care of dependent children exercised a wide influence on subsequent legislation. In 1913 Ohio enacted a unified children's code, and has been followed by twenty-nine other states. Today many governmental and private organizations are engaged in child welfare activities, including churches, neighborhood houses, homes for wayward girls, health conferences for mothers and children, public health nurseries, children's hospitals, dental clinics, child guidance clinics, fresh air camps, traveling health conferences and public schools. The Child Welfare League of America, the Child Study Association, the National Child Welfare Association, the American Child Health Association, the National Congress of Parents and Teachers and hundreds of other organizations carry on various phases of child welfare work. The Federal Children's Bureau and many state departments of child welfare engage in research and education. The state agencies, sometimes supplemented by county boards, supervise the administration of institutions for delinquent and handicapped children and the care of dependent children, and administer child labor and illegitimacy laws.

[Sophonisba Breckenridge, American Sociological Society, *Papers and Proceedings*, Vol. XII; Paul H. Furfey, *Social Problems of Childhood;* M. V. O'Shea, ed., *The Child, His Nature and Needs;* Janet E. Lane Claypon, *The Child Welfare Movement;* George H. Payne, *The Child in Human Progress;* Philip Van Ingen, The History of Child Welfare Work in the United States in American Public Health Association, *A Half Century of Public Health*, ed. by M. P. Ravenel, pp. 290-332; James A. Tobey, *The Children's Bureau;* Grace Abbot, *Federal Aid for the Protection of Maternity and Infancy; Standards of Child Welfare*, Publication No. 60, Children's Bureau, Washington, 1919; *An International Handbook of Child Care and Protection*, compiled by Edward Fuller.]

FRANCIS R. AUMANN

Children's Books, American. The earliest American children's books were aids to piety, such as John Cotton's *Spiritual Milk for Boston Babes* (1684) and *The New-England Primer*[qv]. In the later 18th century Isaiah Thomas reprinted attractive British books, such as *The History of Margery Two Shoes* and *Babes in the Wood.* Mother Goose and tales of giants and of monsters became popular, and epitomes of British novels circulated widely. The exploitation of American scenes and character began with Irving's *Rip Van Winkle*[qv], while Cooper romanticized Indians, trappers and seamen. More popular than frontier tales were travel stories by "Peter Parley"[qv] and Jacob Abbott (1803–79), whose Rollo series was begun in 1834. Nathaniel Hawthorne's *Grandfather's Chair* (1841), *A Wonder-Book* (1852) and *Tanglewood Tales* (1853) demonstrate the truth that the best children's books are written by famous authors.

Mary Mapes Dodge's *Hans Brinker* (1865) was followed by Louisa M. Alcott's *Little Women* (1867), Thomas Bailey Aldrich's *The Story of a Bad Boy* (1870), Mark Twain's *Tom Sawyer* (1876) and *Huckleberry Finn* (1884) and John Bennett's stories of American home life and pioneer adventure. After 1880 the books of Horatio Alger vied with dime novels[qv] of adventure, detection and military exploit. The most memorable combination of picture and prose was attained by the artist Howard Pyle, in stories based upon old tales and romances of chivalry. Supreme among dialect stories were the Uncle Remus books of Joel Chandler Harris.

[A. W. S. Rosenbach, *Early American Children's Books, 1682-1840.*]

HARRY R. WARFEL

Children's Courts. *See* Juvenile Courts.

Children's Magazines, American. The first American periodical for juveniles was *The Children's Magazine* (Hartford, 1789), a work designed to supplement schoolwork between the ages of seven and twelve and to lead children "from the easy language of the spelling books up to the more difficult style of the best writers." The rising Sunday-school[qv] movement produced *The Youth's Friend and Scholar's Magazine* (Philadelphia, 1823–64), the first of hundreds of such papers, some interdenominational and some denominational, devoted to the inculcation of religious truth in fiction, verse and essay. Samuel G. Goodrich ("Peter Parley"[qv]) founded *Parley's Magazine* in 1833; eleven years later it was merged with *Merry's Museum for Boys and Girls* (1841–72), edited in 1867 by Louisa M. Alcott and attractively illustrated with woodcuts. Most famous of all children's magazines was *The Youth's Companion* (1827–1929), founded by Nathaniel Willis, a conservative Congregationalist anxious with an old man's extreme piety to exert a positive religious influence. Beyond all compare the most notable monthly children's publication was *St. Nicholas, An Illustrated Magazine for Young Folks,* founded in 1873 and edited for over thirty years by Mary Mapes Dodge. To it Kipling contributed his Jungle Stories. Other contributors included Mark Twain, Tennyson, Bryant, Longfellow, Bret Harte, Robert Louis Stevenson, Joel Chandler Harris, Jack London, Edna St. Vincent Millay, William Faulkner, Elinor Wylie and, to close the list, Ringgold Lardner. *The Little Corporal* (Chicago, 1865–74), under the editorship of Edward Eggleston and Emily H. Miller, attained an extraordinary popularity; its career ended in a merger with *St. Nicholas.* Other popular 19th-century magazines were *Harper's Young People* (1879–95) and the *Golden Argosy* (1882–88).

Among the most successful periodicals of the 20th century is *The American Boy* (1899–), devoted chiefly to fiction, whose editor declared: "The American boy is a boy of action. . . . He wants the literature of achievement." This point of view, emphasizing the contemporary scene, characterizes such juvenile magazines as the official scouting papers, *Boys' Life* (1911–) and the *American Girl* (1917–). Best among the younger children's magazines was *John Martin's Book* (1912–33), a colorful, cheery monthly edited by Morgan Shepard, who also compiled the several issues of *John Martin's Annual. Scholastic* (1920–), sturdiest of classroom aids, is a semimonthly embracing all high-school interests.

The life of nearly every independent children's magazine, in comparison with that of the adult journal, has been short, due to the fact that the audience grows up.

[F. L. Mott, *A History of American Magazines.*]

HARRY R. WARFEL

Chillicothe was the name of one of the four tribal divisions of the Shawnee^qv^, but it was also used for the chief town of the tribe. Since the Shawnee in Ohio changed their location, several "Chillicothes" existed, a cause for confusion and controversy among local historians. Some half a dozen places bore this designation. Three were located in the lower Scioto Valley in present Pickaway and Ross counties as follows: one on the west side of the river about four miles south of present Circleville; a second three miles north of the city of Chillicothe; the third on the present site of the village of Frankfort. The first of these is the Chillicothe of Dunmore's War^qv^. Better known was the "Old Chillicothe" on the Little Miami, three miles north of present Xenia. It was attacked by Bowman in 1779 and destroyed by the Indians themselves on Clark's approach in 1780. Boone, Kenton and others were captives here. Another Chillicothe, located on the Great Miami at Piqua^qv^, was destroyed by Clark in 1782.

[F. W. Hodge, ed., *Handbook of American Indians;* articles in *Ohio Archæological and Historical Society Publications,* especially Vols. XI and XII.]

EUGENE H. ROSEBOOM

Chillicothe Junto, The, was a term applied to a group of Chillicothe (Ohio) Jeffersonian Republican^qv^ politicians who brought about the admission of Ohio as a state (1803) and largely controlled its politics for some years thereafter. The best known were Thomas Worthington, Edward Tiffin and Nathaniel Massie.

[E. H. Roseboom and F. P. Weisenburger, *A History of Ohio.*]

EUGENE H. ROSEBOOM

Chimney Rock. A landmark visible at forty miles from any direction in western Nebraska east of the point where the River Platte cuts a way into the highlands and to the plains, listed by Johnson and Hunter in their *Guide Book to Emigrants,* 1847, as being 595 miles from Independence, Mo., and "where the trail leaves the river."

CHARLES J. FINGER

China, American Attitude toward. American contact with China began (1784) with trade. Its second chapter opened (1811) with the sending from the United States to China of missionaries. From the outset there were involved special problems of regulation, including safeguarding of life and mimimizing of friction between peoples of different backgrounds and different temperaments. The American Government in 1843 enjoined upon American nationals respect for the rights and susceptibilities of the Chinese; and it asked for and obtained from the Chinese government in its first treaty with China (1844) equality of treatment for American nationals and the right of extraterritorial^qv^ jurisdiction.

The people and the Government of the United States have consistently been well disposed toward China. From this country there have gone to China a large number of missionaries and a large investment in cultural and philanthropic institutions. To this country there have come from China and from it there have returned to China large numbers of students. During recent years, in the foreign trade of China, this country has ranked first both in imports and in exports.

In 1899 Secretary of State John Hay gave expression to the doctrine of equality of commercial opportunity in the so-called "Open Door"^qv^ notes; and in 1900 this Government suggested that the powers all pledge themselves to respect China's territorial and administrative integrity. In 1922 the American Government led the way in the elaboration, at the Washington Conference^qv^, of a group of treaties and agreements whereby the principal powers undertook to respect China's sovereignty, to refrain from interference in China's internal affairs, to foster the principle of equal commercial opportunity in China and to refrain from action in China prejudicial to each other's rights and interests.

In 1932, in identical notes to the Chinese and the Japanese governments, Secretary of State Henry Stimson gave renewed and clear utterance to the principle of "nonrecognition"^qv^ as enunciated by Secretary of State William Jennings Bryan in 1915, in regard to treaties, agreements or situations brought about in violation of existing rights in international law or under the treaty provisions.

In relations with China, the American Government has consistently been guided by the attitude and wishes of the American people as indicated in the national support of the positions taken as outlined above.

[Tyler Dennett, *Americans in Eastern Asia;* Stanley K. Hornbeck, Has the United States a Chinese Policy? *Foreign Affairs,* July, 1927; Stanley K. Hornbeck, *China Today: Political;* H. B. Morse, *The International Relations of the Chinese Empire;* W. W. Willoughby, *Foreign Rights and Interests in China.*]

STANLEY K. HORNBECK

China Clipper, THE, was the first hydroplane in the San Francisco–Manila transpacific service. This airliner, with Capt. Edwin C. Musick at the controls and a crew of seven, took off from Alameda, near San Francisco, for the first transpacific mail flight on Nov. 22, 1935, and reached Manila seven days later, having touched at Honolulu, Midway Island, Wake Island and Guam on the way. On Oct. 7, 1936, the same ship inaugurated the first passenger service to Manila, and in April, 1937, a fortnightly service to Hong Kong.

[*New York Times,* Nov. 30, 1935.]

KENNETH COLEGROVE

***China* Incident,** THE, was a World War analogue of the *Trent* Affair^qv^. A British cruiser (February, 1916) removed thirty-eight enemy aliens, including fifteen reservists, from the American ship *China* in the Yellow Sea. The prisoners were released on American demand, but the British assertion that enemy reservists were legally liable to seizure from neutral vessels remained untested.

[T. A. Bailey, World War Analogues of the Trent Affair, *American Historical Review,* XXXVIII.]

RICHARD W. VAN ALSTYNE

China Trade. Cut off from the West Indian Trade^qv^, important in the colonial period, American merchants in the years following the Revolution sought new opportunities. Such were discovered in the China trade, which grew rapidly after the *Empress of China* returned to New York in 1785 from a successful voyage. Although New York sent the first vessel, the merchants of Philadelphia, Boston, Baltimore, Providence, Salem and lesser ports were quick to grasp the new possibilities. In the early years the routes generally followed were from the Atlantic ports, around the Cape of Good Hope, across the Indian Ocean and by way of the Dutch East Indies to China. Until after the Treaty of Nanking (1842) the only Chinese port open to foreign trade was Canton.

The early cargoes carried to China comprised chiefly silver dollars and ginseng^qv^, a plant erroneously believed by the Chinese to have curative properties. When in 1787 Capts. John Kendrick in the *Columbia* and Robert Gray in the *Lady Washington* sailed from Boston for the northwest coast of America, and Gray with a load of sea-otter^qv^ peltries continued to Canton where his furs found a ready sale, the problem of a salable commodity for the Chinese market was solved (*see* Canton, The Fur Trade with). For the next two decades Americans exchanged clothing, hardware and various knickknacks in the Northwest for sea otter and other furs, thus developing a three-cornered trade route. As sea otters gradually disappeared traders shifted to seals, found in large numbers on the southern coast of Chile and the islands of the south Pacific. Sandalwood, obtained in Hawaii and other Pacific islands, also became early an important item of trade. In return American sea-captains brought back tea, china, enameled ware, nankeens and silks. The China trade was characterized by long voyages and frequently by great personal danger in trading with Indians and South Sea islanders. Success rested largely on the business capacity of the ship's captain. The profits, however, were usually large. At its height in 1818–19 the old China trade (combined imports and exports) reached about $19,000,000.

After the Opium War (1840–42) between Great Britain and China, the latter nation was forced to open four additional ports to British trade. Similar rights for Americans were demanded by Commodore Lawrence Kearney and, shortly after, by the Treaty of Wanghia (1844) (*see* Cushing's Treaty), such privileges were obtained.

[F. R. Dulles, *The Old China Trade.*]

H. U. FAULKNER

Chinch Bugs rank with Hessian flies, gypsy moths, boll weevils and grasshoppers as "economic enemies." Discovered in North Carolina in 1785, chinch bugs were first described in 1831 by Thomas Say. In 1871 they caused $30,000,000 crop damages and $79,000,000 in 1887. One sixth of an inch long, black with white markings, they develop on Ohio, Mississippi and Missouri valley grasses—wheat, oats, rye; but not on legumes —clover, alfalfa, garden crops. They are attacked by spraying, burning, dusting and raising crops not eaten by them.

[W. P. Flint, The Chinch Bug and How to Fight It, *Farmers' Bulletin,* 1498, United States Department of Agriculture, June, 1926.]

LOUIS PELZER

Chinese Exclusion Acts. After the discovery of gold in California^qv^ in 1848 workers were scarce, and the immigration of Chinese laborers was welcomed. The Burlingame Treaty of 1868[q.v.] facilitated this immigration. But the completion of the transcontinental railways brought more white laborers to the West, who now complained of Oriental competition. In 1871 in a San Francisco riot twenty-one Chinese were killed. The agitation for exclusion came to be led by Dennis Kearney, president of the Workingman's party. In 1877 a committee of the United States Senate reported in favor of modification of the Burlingame Treaty and in 1879 Congress passed an act restricting Chinese immigration, which was vetoed by President Hayes as a violation of the treaty. Two years later, the Angell Commission negotiated a treaty with China permitting restrictions upon the immigration of laborers, but exempting teachers, students, merchants and travelers. This was followed by the Exclusion Act of 1882. Subsequent acts of 1888 and 1892 contained flagrant violations of the treaty of 1880, partly induced by the failure of China to ratify the Bayard Treaty of 1888, sanctioning a prohibition of immigration of laborers for twenty years. A new treaty with China, in 1894, permitted for ten years the absolute prohibition of the entrance of Chinese laborers into the United States. The act of 1894 enforced this severe prohibition. In the following years, many Chinese laborers entered the United States (and after 1898 the Philippines) on fraudulent certificates issued by Chinese officials. In 1904 the Chinese government refused to renew the treaty of 1894, while harsh enforcement of the immigration laws in the United States led in 1905 to a boycott of American goods in China. Nevertheless, the laws excluding Chinese laborers remained on the statute book. Chinese resentment of this treatment was more than offset by the good will resulting from American friendly relations in the events following the Boxer Rebellion[q.v.] in 1900 and the establishment of the republic in 1911, and friction over the exclusion policy soon disappeared. In the meanwhile the number of Chinese in the United States declined from 107,488 in 1890 to 71,531 in 1910.

[M. R. Coolidge, *Chinese Immigration;* E. T. Williams, *China: Yesterday and To-day;* J. B. Moore, *Digest of International Law.*]

KENNETH COLEGROVE

Chinese Immigration and Labor. Beset by wars and famine at home and attracted by the story of gold in California[q.v.], Chinese began to come to America in large numbers in the middle of the 19th century. The first recorded Chinese immigrants reached San Francisco in 1848, though the first really significant immigration occurred in 1852, when some 18,000 Chinese arrived in San Francisco, which then had fewer than 37,000 inhabitants. The need for unskilled labor, created by the Civil War and the construction of the Union Pacific Railroad[q.v.], paved the way for the Burlingame Treaty[q.v.] of 1868 which, among other things, recognized the reciprocal rights of Chinese and Americans to immigrate at will. Until 1882, when coolie immigration was shut off, the yearly average of Chinese arrivals was around 16,000. Approximately 375,000 had entered the United States by that year (*see* Chinese Exclusion Acts).

Barred from staking claims or working virgin properties in California, the majority turned to other fields. At one time, of the 25,000 mechanics and laborers employed by the Central Pacific Railroad Company[q.v.], 15,000 were Chinese. In the 1870's and 1880's many turned to the land for a living. In 1870, 90% of the agricultural labor in California was Chinese; in 1880, 75%; in 1930, less than 1%. The second generation moved from the land and by 1920 there were but 57 Chinese-owned farms in the United States. In lumbering camps and mills Chinese were cutters, scalers and road builders. Today they have almost disappeared from the industry. They were once important in Pacific coast fisheries, as late as 1890 constituting one half of the 2000 permanent employees of canneries and 7000 to 9000 of the seasonal labor. Today less than 1000 Chinese work in fisheries and canneries. Chinese entered manufacturing and commerce: woolen mills, shoe and cigar factories, underwear factories, pork-packing and fish-drying industries, banking, wholesaling and retailing, exporting and importing. In coastal states approximately 100 important Chinese firms are now engaged in importation and sale of Oriental goods and wares.

With the completion of the Union Pacific Railroad thousands of Chinese were left without employment and so many white settlers had come to California that in 1871 there were said to be three men for every job. In the 1870's Chinese competition at low wages with white labor caused anti-Chinese feeling, expressed by boycotts[q.v.], "que" and laundry ordinances, antialien land laws, police taxes, etc. Typical of the times was the agitation led by Dennis Kearney in 1877 (*see* Kearneyites; Chinese Riots).

In 1880 the Burlingame Treaty was modified and China recognized the right of the United States to "regulate, limit or suspend . . . but . . . not absolutely prohibit" immigration of Chinese laborers. The way was now paved for the Exclusion Law of 1882, marking the beginning of the policy of Chinese exclusion from the

United States, which was extended to Hawaii and the Philippines in 1900 and 1902. Chinese are also subject to the general immigration[qv] laws of 1917 and 1924. Under the latter act all aliens not eligible to citizenship are excluded from the country. This applies to Chinese, as the courts have ruled that aliens of Asiatic race are ineligible for American citizenship. Allowances are made for students, business executives and visitors. American-born Orientals possess all the legal rights of citizenship.

Since the 20th century the Chinese in the United States have concentrated in large cities and are chiefly engaged in the laundry and restaurant businesses. They generally live in "Chinatown," an area where they maintain their own system of internal government and observe Oriental customs and holidays. A few enter the professions and many find employment in domestic service, retail shops, cafés, unorganized trades and establishments in Chinatown. The 1930 census records 74,954 Chinese, including 30,868 American-born, in the country. Of the 44,086 foreign-born, 38,377 live in urban centers, and men outnumber women 39,109 to 4977.

[Ira B. Cross, *A History of the Labor Movement in California;* Eliot G. Mears, *Resident Orientals on the Pacific Coast;* California's Attitude Towards the Oriental, *The Annals*, Vol. CXXII; G. T. Renner, Chinese Influence in the Development of the Western United States, *ibid.*, Vol. CLII; G. M. Stephenson, *A History of American Immigration;* W. C. Van Vleck, *The Administrative Control of Aliens.*]

LUTHER GULICK

Chinese Indemnity. *See* Boxer Rebellion, The.

Chinese Riots. Ill feeling against the Chinese began in California as early as 1852, when they were sometimes ejected from mining towns. In 1871 there was a serious riot in Los Angeles, when fifteen Chinese were hung and six shot to death. Hard times and the labor troubles of 1877 brought anti-Chinese feeling to the fore again in San Francisco, where it was fomented by the Kearneyites[qv], and in July, 1877, several laundries in San Francisco were wrecked and a number of Chinese killed. Upon the publication of the Morey Letter[qv] a mob attacked the Chinese quarter in Denver, Oct. 31, 1880, and did much damage before it was dispersed with fire hose.

[E. Benjamin Andrews, *History of the Last Quarter-Century in the United States.*]

ALVIN F. HARLOW

Chinook Jargon, The, is a medium of communication composed of a combination of about 300 Indian, French and English words. It was employed generally by Indian traders, missionaries and miners and known to Indian interpreters along the Pacific coast from northern California to Alaska. Several Chinook-English dictionaries and religious tracts have been published.

[G. C. Shaw, *The Chinook Jargon.*]

WILLIAM S. LEWIS

Chinook Winds, peculiar to the Pacific Northwest, took their name from the Chinook Indian tribe. Blowing west and southwest from the Pacific during winter and early spring, they penetrate far into the interior and even to the eastern slope of the Rocky Mountains, melting and evaporating ice and snow and bringing sudden relief from the most severe winter weather.

[H. J. Winser, *The Great Northwest.*]

WILLIAM S. LEWIS

Chippewa, Battle of (July 5, 1814). On the north bank of Chippewa Creek, Gen. Riall had under his command a British force numbering about 2000. Gen. Jacob Brown with 4000 Americans was encamped near by. Riall began his attack at 4 P.M. Simultaneously, Brown ordered an advance of his left. The Americans were repulsed. Winfield Scott's brigade and the artillery were moved forward and engaged the British on the plain south of Chippewa Creek. Superior maneuvering and the effectiveness of the American artillery soon compelled the British to retire in confusion.

[Louis L. Babcock, *The War of 1812 on the Niagara Frontier.*]

ROBERT W. BINGHAM

Chippewa, The. This tribe, the name a corruption of Ojibwa, meaning "to pucker up," of Algonquian linguistic stock was living, about 1640, in the Sault Ste. Marie area of Michigan. During the first half of the 18th century, gradually moving westward along both shores of Lake Superior, they decisively defeated the Fox and the Sioux[qqv] of northern Wisconsin and Minnesota and seized their lands. Meanwhile certain groups, such as the Ottawa and Potawatomi[qqv], split off to occupy the Lake Michigan area.

Typical forest culture Indians, using the dome-shaped bark and matting wigwam[qv] and the birchbark canoe[qv], the Chippewa eventually controlled splendid hunting, fishing and wild-rice areas. Although wars with the Sioux continued sporadically until 1858, no further territorial advances beyond the compromise Prairie du Chien Treaty[qv] line of 1825 were made. Successive treaties with the United States Government in 1837, 1854, 1855 and 1863 gradually transferred most of the Chippewa lands to the whites and restricted these Indians to relatively small reservations in Minnesota, Wisconsin and Michigan, where they now live to the number of several thousands. They still receive small government annuities from early timberland sales.

[W. W. Warren, *History of the Ojibway Nation;* F. W. Hodge, ed., *Handbook of American Indians;* Frances Densmore, *Chippewa Customs.*]

WILLOUGHBY M. BABCOCK

Chisholm Trail, THE, was a cattle trail leading north from Texas, across Oklahoma to Abilene[qv], Kans. Much controversy has existed as to the origin of its name and even as to its exact location. It was apparently named for Jesse Chisholm, a mixed blood Cherokee, who followed a part of this route in freighting supplies and may have guided a detachment of soldiers over it soon after the close of the Civil War. The southern extension of the Chisholm Trail originated near San Antonio, Tex., though there is considerable doubt as to whether or not the Texas portion of it was ever known by that name. From here it ran north and a little east to the Red River which it crossed a few miles from the site of the present town of Ringgold, Tex. It continued north across Oklahoma, passing near the sites of the present towns of Waurika, Duncan, Marlow, Chickasha, El Reno and Enid to Caldwell, Kans. It therefore ran not far from the line of the 98th meridian. From Caldwell it ran north and a little east past the site of Wichita to Abilene, Kans. At the close of the Civil War the low price of cattle in Texas and the much higher prices in the North and East caused many Texas ranchmen to drive large herds north to market (*see* Cattle Drives). The establishment of a cattle depot and shipping point at Abilene, Kans., in 1867 brought many herds to that point to be shipped to market over the southern branch of the Union Pacific Railway[qv]. Many of these were driven over the Chisholm Trail which in a few years became the most popular route for driving cattle from Texas to the North.

The Chisholm Trail decreased in importance after 1871 when Abilene lost its pre-eminence as a shipping point for Texas cattle, due to the westward advance of settlement. Dodge City[qv] became the chief shipping point and another trail farther west, crossing the Red River near Doan's Store, Tex., became of paramount importance. The extension of the Atchison, Topeka and Santa Fé Railway[qv] to Caldwell, Kans., in 1880, however, again made the Chisholm Trail a most important route for driving Texas cattle to the North, and this position it retained until the building of additional trunk lines of railway south into Texas caused rail shipments to take the place of the former trail driving[qv] of Texas cattle north to market.

[Sam P. Ridings, *The Chisholm Trail;* Evan G. Barnard, *A Rider of the Cherokee Strip;* E. E. Dale, *The Range Cattle Industry.*]

EDWARD EVERETT DALE

Chisholm v. Georgia, 1793 (2 Dallas, 419). The heirs of Alexander Chisholm, citizens of South Carolina, sued the State of Georgia to enforce payment of claims against that state. Georgia refused to defend the suit and the Supreme Court, upholding the right of citizens of one state to sue another state, under Art. III, Sec. 2 of the Federal Constitution, ordered judgment by default against Georgia. No writ of execution was attempted because of threats by the lower house of the Georgia legislature. The Eleventh Amendment[qv] ended such actions. (*See also* States' Rights.)

[U. B. Phillips, *Georgia and State Rights;* Charles Warren, *The Supreme Court in United States History.*]

E. MERTON COULTER

Chiswell's Mines in the present Wythe County, Va., were known from the first discovery of that region, when the mines were operated by their owner, Col. John Chiswell. A fort built in 1758 was named Fort Chiswell and in 1772 it became the seat of the newly erected county of Fincastle[qv]. In 1776 the State of Virginia took over the mines. During the revolt in 1779 and 1780 of the loyalists in southwestern Virginia, a plot was formed to seize the mines, but it was thwarted by the patriots, who seized the plotters and confined them in the mines. From their treatment by Col. Lynch is derived the term "lynch law."[qv] The mines continued to produce throughout the Revolutionary War.

[Eckenrode, *Virginia in the Revolution.*]

LOUISE PHELPS KELLOGG

Chivington's Massacre. *See* Sand Creek Massacre or Battle, The.

Choctaw, THE, were one of the Five Civilized Tribes[qv] of the southern United States, formerly in southeastern Mississippi and southwestern Alabama. They were encountered in 1540 by DeSoto[qv]. After 1699, when Louisiana was founded, they became allied with the French although an English faction existed which brought on civil war between 1748 and 1750. After the French surrendered their territories in 1763 (*see* Paris, The Treaty of) Choctaws began to cross into Louisiana where a few of them still remain. Relations with the United States were uniformly friendly and, thanks to this fact and the personal eloquence of the great Choctaw chief Pushmataha, they refused in 1811 to join Tecumseh's℣ coalition against the whites. In 1830, by the Treaty of Dancing Rabbit Creek℣, they ceded their lands to the United States and accepted in exchange a large area in the southeastern part of the present Oklahoma to which the greater part of them migrated between 1831 and 1833 (*see* Indian Removals). Here they gradually evolved a government patterned somewhat after that of the United States which lasted until 1907 when their territory became an organic part of the new State of Oklahoma.

[Angie Debo, *The Rise and Fall of the Choctaw Republic.*]

J. R. SWANTON

Choctaw Land Frauds. After ceding their lands to the United States by the Treaty of Dancing Rabbit Creek℣, Sept. 28, 1830, most of the Choctaws removed west of the Mississippi (*see* Indian Removals), those remaining behind being promised lands in Mississippi. Unscrupulous speculators acquired this Indian land script, on which they claimed title to $6,000,000 worth of government land. The fraud was exposed and the intended looting of the Federal treasury blocked. After dragging out from 1835 to 1846, the controversy was finally settled.

[Franklin L. Riley, Choctaw Land Claims, in *Publications of the Mississippi Historical Society*, VIII, 1904; J. F. H. Claiborne, *Mississippi, as a Province, Territory and State.*]

WALTER PRICHARD

Choctaw Trading House, Treaty of (Oct. 24, 1816), signed at St. Stephens℣, Ala., provided for the purchase by the United States, for $10,000 in goods and a 20-year annuity of $6000, of the Choctaw℣ lands, mostly in Alabama, east of the Tombigbee, south of the Tennessee and north of the line established by the Treaty of Mount Dexter (1805).

[American State Papers, *Indian Affairs*, Vol. II.]

MACK SWEARINGEN

Choctaw Trail designates any of several Indian paths through Choctaw country—central and southern Mississippi and western Alabama. Most important was a trail from the Natchez country (Mississippi River) to the Mobile area; another apparently ran roughly parallel but farther north. These met the Creek trails to Carolina called the "Great Trading Path."℣ They were used by British traders and emigrants headed for Natchez℣. The French while occupying Mobile℣ used a trail running northwestward. Another ran northeastward from the Natchez area to the Chickasaw country; this became part of the Natchez Trace℣.

MACK SWEARINGEN

Cholera Epidemics. True cholera, whose endemic home is the delta of the Ganges, waited until the 19th century before crossing the Atlantic (1832). The devastation was terrible, the first assault of Asiatic cholera on Bellevue Hospital in New York being one of the main horrors of American medicine. It traveled along the waterways, for two years desolating a wide path from Canada to Yucatan. When cholera again came to this country (1848) it was quarantined at New York, but, escaping at New Orleans, invaded the Mississippi Valley, and was carried across the continent by the California gold-seekers (1849). For the third time, immigrant ships brought the epidemic to America, finding the door open in a less vigilant New York (1854). The fourth (1866) and fifth (1867) epidemics were less serious, and the sixth (1873), which again gained entrance through the portal of New Orleans, was the last.

[A Bibliography of Cholera, in John Shaw Billings' *The Cholera Epidemic in the United States.*]

VICTOR ROBINSON

Chouteau (P. Jr.) and Company was the successor to Pratte, Chouteau and Company. The latter was the Western Department of the American Fur Company℣, which was sold out by John Jacob Astor to Bartholomew Berthold, Bernard Pratte, Pierre Chouteau, Jr., and Jean Pierre Cabanne in 1834. The company previously had been operated on a basis of an equal division of profits and losses with the parent company on returns from all posts on the Missouri River and its tributaries; those of the Mississippi below Prairie du Chien; posts in the Osage country in present Oklahoma; and in southwest Missouri. Some of the important forts controlled by this company were: Forts Pierre, Clark, Mackenzie, Union, Benton, Sarpy and John. Most of their business was on the Missouri River and its dependencies. The name of the company was changed in 1838 to Pierre Chouteau, Jr. and Company, with name Pierre being commonly abbreviated. The company carried on business until about 1866. P. Chouteau, Jr. and Company made a practice of distributing shares of the company among its most capable agents. (*See also* Fur Trade on the Upper Mississippi and Missouri Rivers.)

[Hiram Chittenden, *American Fur Trade of the Far West;* Chouteau mss. in Mo. Hist. Soc., St. Louis.]

STELLA M. DRUMM

Chouteau's Trading Posts. The Chouteau family had more extensive interests in the fur trade℣ than the several posts established by them directly would indicate. Pierre Chouteau spent most of his time among the Indians. His brother Auguste attended to the purchasing of goods used by them in their trade and to the sale of the furs gathered therefrom. Trading largely among the Big and Little Osage[qv], the Chouteaus, in 1794, erected a post called Fort Carondelet, of considerable size and well fortified, in what is now Bates County, Mo. The Chouteau brothers were given, by the Spanish government, the exclusive right to trade with these Indians for a period of six years. At the expiration of this time Pierre Chouteau persuaded the Osage to move to the Arkansas River, where a fur-trading rendezvous was established, about 1802, at the junction of the Verdigris and Grand rivers in the present State of Oklahoma. In 1809, Pierre and his son, A. P. Chouteau, became stockholders in the St. Louis Missouri Fur Company[qv] and were restrained by agreement from trading on their private account. Auguste Chouteau continued to send out trappers on his individual account. By 1820 the elder Chouteaus had retired from active participation in the trade.

In 1822 Col. A. P. Chouteau occupied the trading post called "La Saline," where Salina, Okla., now stands. The following years he enlarged his operations and established a trading house just below the falls of the Verdigris. In 1836 he built a stockade fort, near the present town of Purcell, Okla., where extensive trade was carried on with the Comanche, Kiowa, Wichita[qqv] and allied tribes, until his death in 1838. These posts bore the name of Chouteau.

The only other trading post bearing the name was established by François G. Chouteau on an island three miles below the mouth of Kansas River. This was washed into the river in 1826 and another built about ten miles up the Kansas.

[Grant Foreman, *Pioneer Days in Early Southwest*, and *Advancing Frontier;* Hiram M. Chittenden, *American Fur Trade of the Far West.*]

STELLA M. DRUMM

Christian Commission, UNITED STATES, was formed in New York in 1861 to provide comforts and supplies to the armies and navies not furnished by the Federal Government. It received its support primarily from the churches. During the four years of the Civil War it collected more than $2,500,000 in cash, besides immense quantities of stores and clothing. (*See also* Sanitary Commission, United States.)

[Lemuial Moss, *Annals of the United States Christian Commission.*]

WILLIAM W. SWEET

Christian Endeavor, Young People's Society of, a Christian organization for young people of evangelical Protestant churches. The first society was founded Feb. 2, 1881, at the Williston Congregational Church, Portland, Maine, by Rev. Francis E. Clark. Its principles include open commitment to Christ, training in Christian service, loyalty to the Church and widespread Christian fellowship. It is interdenominational, international and interracial, and (1938) numbers 80,000 societies and 4,000,000 members, in more than 100 nations.

[Bert H. Davis, *Leadership through Christian Endeavor;* Amos R. Wells and Stanley B. Vandersall, *Christian Endeavor Essentials.*]

STANLEY B. VANDERSALL

Christian Science is the religion founded by Mary Baker Eddy (1821–1910) and represented by the Church of Christ, Scientist. The Christian Science denomination was founded by Mrs. Eddy at Boston in 1879, following her discovery of this religion and science in 1866 and her issuing of its textbook, *Science and Health with Key to the Scriptures,* in 1875. It consists of the Mother Church, the First Church of Christ, Scientist, in Boston, Mass., and branch churches or societies composed of local congregations.

Branch Churches of Christ, Scientist, and Christian Science Societies began to be organized in the 1880's. At the end of 1938 they numbered 2825, of which 2167 are in the United States. There are also sixty-five Christian Science organizations at universities or colleges.

Christian Science Sunday services consist mainly of a Lesson-Sermon, prepared readings from the Bible and the Christian Science textbook. Wednesday evening meetings include selected passages from the Bible and from the Christian Science textbook, and testimonies of healing from persons in the audience. Christian Science churches are also notable for the size of their Sunday schools.

The Christian Science buildings in Boston form an imposing group. They include the Original Church, erected in 1894, its large connected Extension, 1906, the Administration Building, 1908, and the monumental Publishing House, completed in 1933.

Mrs. Eddy's most important book, *Science and Health with Key to the Scriptures,* is published in English, French and German; also, in Braille. Some of her less important writings are published in ten languages; also, in Braille and Moon types. The Christian Science periodicals consist of the *Quarterly,* containing citations for Lesson-Sermons; the *Journal,* monthly in English, including directories of churches, reading rooms and practitioners; the *Sentinel,* weekly in English; the *Herald,* monthly or quarterly in different languages; and *The Christian Science Monitor,* an international daily newspaper issued in several editions.

[Lyman P. Powell, *Mary Baker Eddy, A Life Size Portrait;* E. Mary Ramsay, *Christian Science and Its Discoverer;* Sibyl Wilbur, *The Life of Mary Baker Eddy.*]

CLIFFORD P. SMITH

Christiana (Pa.) Fugitive Affair (1851). When an attempt was made to recover runaway slaves, a Maryland slave owner, Edward Gorsuch, was killed. Later, because he refused to assist in recovering the fugitives, Casper Hanway, a Quaker, was tried for treason, but acquitted.

[W. U. Hensel, *The Christiana Riot,* and *Treason Trials of 1851.*]

H. H. SHENK

Christina, Fort, was established by Peter Minuit and the Swedes who landed with him at "The Rocks" on March 29, 1638. It was the capital of New Sweden^qv^ until 1643 and was made the seat of authority again in 1654. The following year it was surrendered to the Dutch (*see* New Netherland) who in turn surrendered it to the English in 1664. The town that grew around the fort was not only the first permanent white settlement in Delaware and the whole Delaware River valley, but was also the antecedent of the present city of Wilmington.

[Amandus Johnson, *The Swedish Settlements on the Delaware 1638-1664;* Anna T. Lincoln, *Three Centuries under Four Flags.*]

LEON DE VALINGER, JR.

Christmas, Puritan Attitude toward. The Puritans^qv^ objected to the observance of Christmas on two counts: first on the ground of its pagan origin; second, they disliked even more the excesses which had grown up about its celebration. A law forbidding its observance was passed by the General Court of Massachusetts Bay (May 11, 1659) which stated that, "Whosoever shall be found observing any such days as Christmas or the like, either by forbearing labor, feasting, or any other way . . . shall pay for every such offense five shillings."

[W. W. Sweet, Christmas in American History, *The Chicago Theological Seminary Register,* January, 1934.]

WILLIAM W. SWEET

Christmas Seals. Adopting an idea applied in Denmark in 1904, Miss Emily P. Bissell, Delaware Red Cross secretary, sponsored a $3000 sale of stamplike seals at the 1907 Christmas season to support a cottage for indigent tuberculosis sufferers in Wilmington. The American Red Cross^qv^ extended the sale nationally in 1908, and from 1920 it was an activity of the National Tuberculosis Association.

[Elizabeth Cole, *The Story of the Christmas Seal.*]

IRVING DILLIARD

Chrysler's Field (Canada), Battle of (Nov. 11, 1813). On Nov. 10, 1813, the American Army bent on capturing Montreal^qv^ halted a mile east of Chrysler's farm on the north bank, overlooking the St. Lawrence River. Next morning Gen. James Wilkinson, commanding, delayed starting until sure that his front was clear. At about 11 A.M. the British gunboats began firing upon the American rear, 800 regulars, militia and Indians co-operating on land. Wilkinson directed Gen. John P. Boyd to drive the enemy back, employing about 2500 troops. They were poorly organized and ineptly led. Toward the end of the day, the Americans, after heavy casualties, retreated to their boats, leaving behind their dead and badly wounded. In proportion to their numbers the British had also suffered heavily, and made no efforts to pursue.

[James Ripley Jacobs, *Tarnished Warrior.*]

JAMES RIPLEY JACOBS

Church and State, Separation of. Nine of the thirteen American colonies had established churches. In Massachusetts, Connecticut and New Hampshire the Congregational Church^qv^ was established by law; in Maryland, Virginia, North Carolina, South Carolina and Georgia, and in New York City and three neighboring counties, the Anglican Church^qv^ was established.

With the formation of new state governments following the Declaration of Independence, separation of church and state came about more or less as a matter of course where establishment had been more a matter of theory than of fact. Such was the case in all the Anglican states except Virginia. Here the church had been strongly intrenched and a bitter struggle ensued. Baptists, Presbyterians, Methodists and Lutherans^qqv^, assisted by such liberal statesmen as Jefferson and Madison, combined to fight establishment. Petitions flooded the Virginia Assembly from 1776 to 1779 and in the latter year a bill was passed cutting off state support. In this year also Jefferson's "Bill for establishing religious freedom" was introduced and after six years of bitter debate finally passed (Dec. 17, 1785).

In the New England states disestablishment was much longer delayed. The unpopularity of the Anglican Church, due to its large Tory^qv^ membership, aided in its disestablishment. In New England, on the other hand, the Congregational Church was the church of the patriots.

The Revolution, nevertheless, brought with it a strong movement to separate church and state in New England, led by the Baptists. Though unsuccessful at the time, the agitation was continued, and with the growth of Methodism and Episcopalianism in New England after 1790, the nonconforming bodies united with a growing liberal element in Congregationalism to bring about separation. This was accomplished in 1818 in Connecticut, in 1819 in New Hampshire, but not until 1833 in Massachusetts.

[S. H. Cobb, *Rise of Religious Liberty in America;* J. C. Meyer, *Church and State in Massachusetts from 1740 to 1833;* W. T. Thom, *The Struggle for Religious Freedom in Virginia.*]

WILLIAM W. SWEET

Church Membership. Although the religious motive was strongly present in the establishment of a majority of the thirteen colonies, yet the economic motive was far more powerful in bringing individual colonists. This fact, together with the barriers placed in the way of the average person becoming a church member in a new country, meant that only a relatively small proportion of the colonial population was actually churched. At the close of the colonial period there were, according to careful investigation, 3105 congregations of all kinds in the English colonies. Of these 658 were Congregational, 543 Presbyterian, 498 Baptist, 480 Anglican, 298 Quaker, 251 Dutch and German Reformed, 151 Lutheran and 50 Catholic[qqv]. The German sectaries are not included, but their number was relatively small. New England was the best-churched section, though even here the proportion of church members to the total population was about one to eight. In the Middle colonies, where the German and Scotch-Irish[qqv] element was large and widely scattered and had come largely without ministers, the proportion was much smaller, probably not more than one to fifteen. In the Southern colonies the proportion was still less.

With the opening of the national period the churches which formerly had Old World connections achieved national organizations and began to think in terms of national need. This was particularly true of the Presbyterian, Methodist and Baptist bodies, and these were the groups most successful in following population westward, resulting in rapid growth. Thus the Methodists[qv] with but 15,000 members at the time of their organization into a separate church (1784) had grown to 740,459 by 1840. The Baptists numbered 740,026 in 1844. The Presbyterians at the time of their great division (1837) had more than 200,000. The Congregational and Episcopalian bodies, the two churches which had been established in nine of the colonies and for that reason had the largest colonial prestige, failed to develop any adequate method of following population westward and as a result lagged far behind. The great German and Irish immigration[qv] brought the Catholic membership to 600,000 by 1830; by 1860 it had increased to 4,500,000. The Protestant group to profit most from immigration was the Lutheran. In 1821 they numbered 41,201; by 1861 they had increased to 246,788, and by 1901 to 1,625,185, the latter figure showing the result of the large Scandinavian influx following the Civil War. In more recent years the Jews[qv] also have grown tremendously and now rank as one of the major religious bodies in America.

According to the last Federal religious census (1926) there were 44,382,189 adult church members in the United States in 213 denominations. The largest bodies are the Roman Catholics with 13,826,800 (18,605,003 including baptized children); Baptists 7,859,626; Methodists 7,237,449; members of Jewish congregations 2,930,332; Lutherans 2,826,658; Presbyterians 2,482,498; Protestant Episcopalians 1,366,262; Disciples of Christ 1,275,617; Congregationalists 859,911; Reformed (Dutch and German) 577,427; Latter Day Saints (Mormons) 474,973; Churches of Christ 433,714; United Brethren 358,824; Evangelical Synod (now united with the German Reformed) 314,518; Church of Christ Scientist 202,098. More recent statistics (estimates, 1933) place the total church membership in the United States at 60,812,874, a gain of 15.8% over a period of seven years.

[W. W. Sweet, *The Story of Religions in America;* C. Luther Fry, *The United States Looks at Its Churches; Census of Religious Bodies.*]

WILLIAM W. SWEET

Church Membership Suffrage was the means used by New England Puritans[qv] to control their theocracies against dissent. When the Puritans in the trading company of Massachusetts Bay[qv] retreated to America with their charter they established a theocracy[qv], but without disturbing the outer shell of the trading company[qv] structure. They could maintain this theocracy successfully only so long as they could control the General Court of freemen[qv] or stockholders, which necessitated limiting freemanship to those who approved of the theocracy. This they could do by refusing to admit new freemen, but when pressure from dissatisfied non-freemen became too great, they decided to accept a limited number on condition of orthodox church membership. After the restoration the king demanded of

Massachusetts that the church membership qualification be removed, but although the colony made a gesture of complying, the requirement was not essentially altered. Through the influence of Massachusetts the colony of New Haven[qv] also adopted the principle of church membership suffrage. Among the other New England colonies it did not exist by specific regulation, although voters had to be in good standing in Connecticut and Plymouth[qqv]. By the fusion of Connecticut and New Haven in the charter of 1662 the narrow suffrage ended in the latter colony, as it did in Massachusetts when the charter was annulled in 1684.

[H. L. Osgood, *American Colonies in the Seventeenth Century*, I; I. M. Calder, *The New Haven Colony.*]

VIOLA F. BARNES

Church of England in the Colonies, THE. The first successful English settlement in America was made by members of the established church at Jamestown in 1607. The church was provided for in the earliest plans for Virginia, and as soon as the colony was strong enough, it was legally established. All the other Southern colonies, except Maryland, were founded under the leadership of churchmen, and, in time, the Church of England was established in all of them, though this did not occur in North Carolina until 1765. Maryland was founded by a Roman Catholic proprietor, but the Protestant settlers there obtained control in the Revolution of 1689 and by 1702 had secured the establishment of the Church of England. In New York the church was established in the four leading counties, but not elsewhere. In the other Northern colonies it enjoyed no establishment and depended for support largely upon the English Society for the Propagation of the Gospel[qv] in Foreign Parts, founded in 1701.

During the 18th century the Church of England advanced in the colonies where it was not established and lost ground in those where it was—a phenomenon which corresponded with the general breakdown of colonial religious barriers that marked that century. The American Revolution deprived the church of its establishments in the South and of the aid of the S. P. G. in the North, exposed it to some popular opposition and confronted it with the problem of forming a national organization and obtaining a native episcopate.

[W. S. Perry, *History of the American Episcopal Church; Historical Collections Relating to the American Colonial Church;* W. W. Manross, *History of the American Episcopal Church.*]

W. W. MANROSS

Church of Jesus Christ of Latter Day Saints. *See* Mormons.

Church Trials. *See* Heresy Trials.

Church Union Movements. As early as 1648 the Cambridge Platform[qv] recognized the ideal unity of the church. Colonial governments attempted, in varying degrees, to enforce conformity to established churches or to penalize dissent. The establishment of legal equality for all sects by the Federal Constitution[qv] and the gradual disappearance of restrictive laws in the states put church union, like religion itself, on a purely voluntary basis.

The Plan of Union (1801) uniting the missionary work of Congregational and Presbyterian[qqv] churches was operative until 1837. Many interdenominational societies were formed for the promotion of missions, education, temperance and emancipation[qqv]. Co-operation for religious causes, often with the explicit approval of denominational authorities, produced the American Bible Society, Evangelical Alliance, Young Men's Christian Association, Young Women's Christian Association, Woman's Christian Temperance Union, International Sunday School Association, Young People's Society of Christian Endeavor and similar organizations of individuals[qqv]. Denominational boards formed co-operative councils in many fields. Certain denominations, especially the Episcopalians and Disciples of Christ[qqv], have constantly stressed union. Some of the divisions within the Lutheran, Presbyterian and Baptist[qqv] groups have been healed. Three Methodist[qv] bodies reunited in 1938. The Federal Council of Churches of Christ in America[qv] (1908) has been the most comprehensive agency of the American churches for united action.

[H. P. Douglass, *Church Unity Movements in the United States.*]

WINFRED ERNEST GARRISON

Churches, Attitude of, toward War. The colonial churches inevitably transplanted from Europe the current theories of war. Nonresistance and the incompatibility of war with Christianity were proclaimed by the Friends and some of the small German sects. The remainder accepted the Catholic and humanist view which discriminated between just and unjust war. The civil magistrate was primarily responsible for determining the justice of a war; the church attempted to soften its barbarities; the citizen did the fighting.

The Revolutionary cause was fervently championed by the Congregationalists and, to a lesser degree, by the Presbyterians, the Dutch and German Reformed clergy and the Roman Catholics. The Anglicans were torn by a clash of loyalties. The majority of the Friends and Mennonites, and some of the Methodists refused to support either side. The War of 1812 encountered the widespread opposition of the Congregationalists echoing the sentiment of New England. The Mexican War was sanctioned by the Methodists, Roman Catholics, and the Baptists and Presbyterians in the South. Clean-cut opposition came from the Friends, Congregationalists and the newly organized Unitarians. So zealously did the churches support both sides in the Civil War that most of them were disrupted (*see* Churches, Split of, by the Slavery Issue). Even the ranks of the nonresistant sects suffered some defections. The Spanish-American War was very popular. Almost the only attempts to stem the pro-war current in the churches were made by the Friends and the Unitarians. Preliminary surveys of the World War show that prominent clergy were overwhelmingly in favor of it. Of the mere handful of outspoken ministerial pacifists, over half came from the Unitarians, Congregationalists and Universalists. Since the World War, church opinion has swung far toward a pacifism[qv] at once idealistic and realistic.

[W. W. Sweet, *The Story of Religions in America;* W. W. Van Kirk, *Religion Renounces War.*]

CLAYTON S. ELLSWORTH

Churches, Established. *See* Church and State, Separation of.

Churches, Split of, by the Slavery Issue. At the opening of the Civil War three of the great American churches had already divided into Northern and Southern branches. A Presbyterian schism had occurred in 1837–38, dividing that body into Old School and New School, the New School being confined largely to the North. Though slavery had not been the principal issue, nevertheless it had played an important part in the division. In 1844–45 both Baptist and Methodist churches had divided squarely over the slavery issue and when the Civil War began each adhered to their own section in the struggle. Up to 1861 the Old School Presbyterians were still an intersectional church, and had excluded slavery as a subject for discussion in their General Assemblies. The New School had not done so, and as a result they were divided over slavery in 1857. The secession of the Southern states, however, brought division both to the Old School Presbyterians and to the Protestant Episcopalians, each forming independent denominations in the Confederate states. The slavery issue had been avoided by the Protestant Episcopalians in the General Conventions, and as a result there was an absence of bitterness on both sides. This fact made reunion relatively easy, following the end of hostilities.

The Roman Catholics experienced no divisions and very little controversy as a result of either slavery or the Civil War. This was due to the fact that the principal Catholic authority lay outside the nation and also to the fact that each Catholic diocese was largely independent. Other churches, like the Congregational, avoided splits because they were confined almost entirely to the North, while such bodies as the Quakers and some other small denominations had solved the slavery issue previous to the Civil War by excluding slave owners. The Disciples, though a religious body confined mostly to the border, experienced no real division, due to the looseness of their organization and the neutral position taken by their great leader, Alexander Campbell.

[Vander Velde, *The Presbyterian Churches and the Federal Union;* J. H. Norwood, *The Schism in the Methodist Episcopal Church, 1844.*]

WILLIAM W. SWEET

Churches and the World War. The beginning of the war found two Presbyterian elders with strong pacifist tendencies at the head of the American Government, Woodrow Wilson and William Jennings Bryan. Pacifist idealism also was strong among the American churches, their support of the war being secured by proclaiming that it was a "war to end war." With few exceptions church leaders supported every war policy of the Government. Each of the important churches formed wartime commissions, and a general War Time Commission was created by the Federal Council of Churches[qv], representing not less than thirty-five denominations. The Catholics also had a National War Council. Ministers from their pulpits urged enlistments; opened their churches for the work of war organizations; helped gather contributions for the numerous special war funds; preached propaganda sermons from outlines furnished by the Government; went to training camps and into the army and navy as chaplains and gave full support to the war work of the Y. M. C. A.[qv] and numerous other interchurch war agencies.

[Charles S. MacFarland, *The Churches of Christ in Time of War;* Gaius Glenn Atkins, *Religion in Our Times;* Ray H. Abrams, *Preachers Present Arms.*]

WILLIAM W. SWEET

Churubusco, Battle of (Mexican War, Aug. 20, 1847). Victorious at Contreras[qv], Scott the same day encountered Santa Anna's principal army at Churubusco, four miles below Mexico City. Mexican engineers had prepared scientifically constructed works of great strength covering the bridge over the Churubusco River and fortified a massive convent near by. These Scott assaulted simultaneously. The defenders resisted stubbornly, but after losing 6000 killed, wounded and prisoners, were routed and retreated to the capital. Scott reported 133 killed, 905 wounded and missing. Eighty American deserters, enlisted in a Mexican "Foreign Legion," were captured.

[Justin H. Smith, *The War with Mexico*, II.]
CHARLES WINSLOW ELLIOTT

Cíbola, a native name for the Zuñi[qv] country, first heard by Fray Marcos de Niza in 1539. His report (garbled and exaggerated in Mexico City) of "seven very great cities" in the North resulted in the Coronado expedition[qv]. As exploration advanced, the name Cíbola came to mean the entire Pueblo[qv] Indian country, and was extended to the Great Plains which, until late Spanish times, were called *los llanos de Cíbola.* As an administrative term, Cíbola was soon changed to New Mexico, but in one way the older name survived. The strange "cows" found on the plains were first called *vacas de Cíbola;* later this was shortened to *cíbolos* (buffalo).

[Bloom and Donnelly, *New Mexico History and Civics.*]
LANSING B. BLOOM

Cimarron, Proposed Territory of, known as the Public Land Strip, or No Man's Land, extended in longitude from 100° to 103°, in latitude from 36° 30' to 37°.

Settled by squatters[qv] and cattlemen, the territory had no law, so to protect the squatter claims a movement was started to organize the country into Cimarron Territory. In March, 1887, territorial representatives drew up resolutions assuming authority for the territory. The proposal was referred to the Committee on Territories in Congress. There it remained. The area now constitutes the panhandle of Oklahoma.

[Rainey, *No Man's Land;* Thoburn, *History of Oklahoma.*]
ANNA LEWIS

Cincinnati was located opposite the mouth of the Licking River in the Symmes Purchase[qv] by three proprietors, Matthias Denman, Robert Patterson and John Filson. Israel Ludlow replaced Filson, who mysteriously disappeared in the fall of 1788. The first houses were built in the winter of 1788–89. The original name of Losantiville (*L* for Licking, *os* for mouth, *anti* for opposite, *ville* for city) was changed to Cincinnati (after the society of that name) by Gov. Arthur St. Clair, who made it the capital of the Northwest Territory[qv], 1790–1800. Fort Washington[qv] added to the importance of the little town, which had 2540 people by 1800. It was incorporated as a town in 1802 and as a city in 1819.

The early inhabitants were chiefly of New Jersey and Pennsylvania origin, but the population became more cosmopolitan as the city grew. By 1860 Cincinnati had 161,044 inhabitants, 45% of whom were foreign-born. The large German element, arriving in the decades 1830–60, played a particularly important part in the city's history.

The importance of Southern trade, and prejudice against the many illiterate free Negroes, made Cincinnati hostile to abolitionists[qv], a mob on one occasion destroying the press of Birney's *Philanthropist*[qv]. Know-Nothingism[qv], directed against the Germans and Irish, flared up in the 1850's, but soon subsided. In the Civil War Cincinnati, though losing its Southern trade, was loyal to the Union. In 1862, when threatened by Confederate advances, its citizens quickly organized to defend it, but the danger soon passed. Morgan's raid[qv] of 1863 went around the city.

Well located on the Ohio River to command Western and Southern markets, for many years Cincinnati rightly claimed the titles of "Queen City of the West" and "Porkopolis." In manufacturing it ranked third among American cities by 1860. But iron ore and coal were too remote, meat packing moved westward to the newer farming states, trunk-line railroads reduced the importance of the Ohio River and Cincinnati's leadership passed away.

[E. O. Randall and D. J. Ryan, *History of Ohio;* Charles T. Greve, *Centennial History of Cincinnati and Representative Citizens.*]
EUGENE H. ROSEBOOM

Cincinnati, Society of the. In June, 1783, shortly before the disbanding of the Continental Army[qv], an organization of its officers who had formed lasting friendships through service together was suggested by Gen. Henry Knox. At the headquarters of Baron von Steuben near Fishkill, N. Y., the organization was consummated, with Washington as the first president, and was named in honor of Cincinnatus, the Roman dictator, in allusion to the approaching return of the officers to civil pursuits. Its first object was to raise a fund for the widows and children of those slain in the Revolutionary War and it also hoped to promote a closer union among the states. Its membership consisted of the army officers and their eldest male descendants, or if direct descent failed, collateral descendants were eligible. It was divided into state societies, and there was a branch in France, which was destroyed by the Revolution in 1792. The Society aroused antagonism at first among ultra-republicans who believed that it was setting itself up as an aristocracy. Alexander Hamilton was the second president. Hamilton Fish (1808–93), son of Nicholas Fish, one of the founders, was president from 1854 until his death. Through failure of heirs, most of the state societies had disintegrated by 1900, but a revival of the general organization was effected in 1902.

[Francis Apthorp Foster, *Institution of the Society of the Cincinnati, Together with Resolutions, etc., of the General Society of the Cincinnati, 1783-1920.*]

ALVIN F. HARLOW

Cincinnati Riots (1884). The criminal courts had become corrupt in Cincinnati early in 1884, and when one Berners, a self-confessed and atrocious murderer, was convicted only of manslaughter, a mob attacked the jail on Friday evening, March 28, and burst open the main door with a huge timber; but Berners had been spirited out by a rear way. A company of militia hurried to the scene and drove off the rioters. On Saturday night mobs gathered again, broke into gun stores and armed themselves, attacked the jail and set fire to the courthouse, which was almost destroyed. Again troops drove the rioters away after a bloody battle. Sunday was disorderly, and that night mobs looted stores and shops. Troops with artillery were rushed from all parts of the state and threw up street barricades, where some hard fighting ensued. Not until the sixth day were the barricades removed and street-car service resumed. At least 45 persons had been killed and 138 injured.

[Lewis Alexander Leonard, *Greater Cincinnati and Its People.*]

ALVIN F. HARLOW

"Cipher Dispatches," THE, were code telegrams relative to the possible use of money to insure the votes of Florida and South Carolina for Tilden in the presidential campaign of 1876[qv]. Their publication in 1878 helped to nullify the political effect of the reputedly questionable proceedings of the Republicans in winning the electoral votes of Louisiana, Florida and South Carolina.

[C. R. Williams, *Life of Rutherford B. Hayes.*]

ASA E. MARTIN

Circuit Courts. *See* Judiciary, The.

Circuit Riders (Ministerial). Circuit riding was devised by John Wesley for carrying on his religious movement in England. A circuit consisted of numerous preaching places scattered over a relatively large district served by one or more lay preachers. The original American circuit riders introduced Methodism into the colonies. Robert Strawbridge, who came to America about 1764, was the first in the long line. John Wesley sent eight official lay missionaries to America (1769–76), and several came on their own responsibility. By the end of the American Revolution there were about 100 circuit riders in the United States, none of whom was ordained. With the formation of the Methodist Episcopal Church[qv] (1784), Francis Asbury was chosen bishop, several of the circuit riders were ordained and the system was widely extended wherever settlements were springing up. It was found peculiarly adaptable to frontier conditions, since one man, equipped with horse and saddlebags, served a great many communities, a circuit often having as many as twenty-five or thirty preaching places. In this way the riders kept pace with the frontier, bringing the influence of religion to new and raw communities. The salary of the preachers was at first uniform, $64 a year, which by 1800 had become $100. Marriage was discouraged, for it usually caused withdrawal from the work. Peter Cartwright is the best known of the frontier preachers. His active career covered the first half of the 19th century, the scene of his labors being Kentucky, Tennessee, Ohio, Indiana and Illinois. The circuit system largely accounts for the even distribution of Methodism throughout the United States. Other religious bodies partially adopted it, particularly the Cumberland Presbyterians[qv].

[*Autobiography of Peter Cartwright the Backwoods Preacher*, edited by W. P. Strickland; W. W. Sweet, *The Rise of Methodism in the West.*]

WILLIAM W. SWEET

Circuits, Judicial, and Circuit Riding. When the Federal judicial system, under the Constitution, was established, the country was divided into three circuits (Eastern, Middle and Southern) to each of which two of the justices of the Supreme Court were assigned. They were required to hold the courts twice a year, sitting with district judges. During the first three years of its existence, the Supreme Court had practically no business to transact and the Chief Justice and his associates found employment in riding the circuits and trying cases at *nisi prius*. The roads and accommodations were bad and the duty proved to be onerous. The opening of the first courts in the spring of 1790 found, for example, Justice Iredell, of North Carolina, presiding in Boston. The justices complained, and President Washington wrote in August, 1791, that he hoped Congress would give "relief from these disagreeable tours" to hold twenty-seven courts from New Hampshire to Georgia. Some relief was granted in 1793 in a change by which only one justice was required to sit with a district judge; and thereafter the justices rode the circuits in turn, instead of being confined to fixed circuits. The development of the West added another and another circuit which meant yet more magnificent distances between court sites. The system was changed in 1869. Then circuit judges were appointed, most of whom traveled over several states. The bar, generally speaking, did not ride circuit with the Supreme Court justices or Federal circuit judges.

In the states, from the outset, circuit courts existed, and in the early days the judge, accompanied by many lawyers, rode large circuits. The system tended to develop lawyers of initiative, originality and resourcefulness. The "case lawyer" was a later product.

[Charles Warren, *The Supreme Court in United States History.*]

SAMUEL C. WILLIAMS

Circus, THE, is a development of the old Roman and mediæval types of amusement to fit American conditions. Before the Revolutionary War Jacob Bates displayed feats of horsemanship. During the 18th century circuses were more or less stationary, performing for some time in a semipermanent enclosure. Between horsemanship acts, clowns and jugglers performed and brilliant fireworks were shown. Rural conditions gave rise to the nomadic institution peculiar to America. So-called rolling shows made their appearance about 1800. By 1820 there were thirty or more of these primitive shows on the road. By 1828 Buckley and Weeks boasted 8 wagons, 35 horses and a canvas tent with a capacity of 800 people. The wagon show of the middle of the 19th century consisted of trapeze performances, horsemanship, clowns, tricks and animal acts. A trick mule, with a prize to any one who could ride him, climaxed the acting. Spaulding and Rogers operated the first rail circus in 1858.

Puritan feeling antagonistic to the circus led showmen to use Bible texts and terms. The lion cage was a den, and Solomon and the Queen of Sheba were impersonated. Cages were ornamented with Bible scenes. The menagerie accompaniment grew gradually in an attempt to get newer attractions as the result of competition. The two-ring circus came in 1869. Phineas T. Barnum and James A. Bailey during the last quarter of the century operated a three-ring circus called the "Greatest Show on Earth." In the 20th century a five-ring circus has developed.

About 1890 William F. Cody instituted the Wild West show rivaling the larger circus in interest and profit. Western cowboys performed, Indians danced and frontier scenes were re-enacted. With the advent of the aeroplane came the flying circus, consisting of a group of aeroplanes presenting a program of stunt flying.

[I. J. Greenwood, *The Circus.*]

EVERETT DICK

Cities, Colonial. Over 90% of the colonial people lived rural lives. The exploitation of rich natural resources called them to farms and plantations, to the forest and sea. The demands of commerce drew a few to urban centers. Five "cities," favorably located by geography, became the chief marts and ports of commerce, centers of culture and fashion, political and financial capitals. At the head of the list stood Boston[qv], for many years the largest town, rising from 7000 people in 1690 to 17,000 in 1740. After mid-century, Philadelphia[qv] forged far ahead with a count of about 40,000 in 1774, while Boston census at the same time was 20,000. Next to Philadelphia came New York City[qv] with 30,000 in 1774. In that year Newport, the chief port of commerce for the region of Rhode Island, numbered about 12,000. After 1750 rich planters from Carolina and wealthy merchants of Philadelphia summered at Newport[qv]. The only "city" in the South was Charleston[qv], a thriving port and town of a dominant political and social aristocracy. In Charleston, planters from the country had their town houses. Urban communities of less than 12,000 inhabitants included Salem, Providence and New Haven in New England and after mid-century Baltimore, Richmond, Wilmington (N. C.) and Savannah in the South.

[C. P. Nettels, *The Roots of American Civilization.*]

WINFRED T. ROOT

Cities, Growth of. In America during the colonial era there was relatively little urban growth. On the eve of the Revolutionary War there were only five communities with more than 8000 inhabitants and their combined strength was little more than 100,000 or only 3% of the total population. Nor was there much increase in the rapidity of city growth during the half century which followed the winning of independence. In 1820 there were only thirteen municipalities with over 8000 inhabitants, but a few of these were now attaining considerable size. New York, for example, had passed the 150,000 mark.

It was not until well into the twenties and thirties of the 19th century that the growth of American cities began to exceed that of the country as a whole. Immigrants began to flock in from Europe and many of them settled in the seaboard communities. The building of turnpikes and canals[qqv] stimulated internal trade. Forty-four cities were able to show more than 8000 population in 1840, and the largest ones were now becoming comparable with the great urban centers of Europe. Steamboat[qv] navigation on the Great Lakes and the larger navigable rivers gave added momentum to the development of the inland cities, and the railroads[qv], when they came, served to accelerate the pace.

The Civil War, while it lasted, placed a damper on city growth, but the setback was only for the moment. The march of agriculture, industry and trade across the face of the continent was resumed after the war, and city populations expanded in keeping with this progress. This growth kept up to the end of the century and beyond. In 1900 the percentage of the national population living in communities of over 8000 was 33%, in 1910 it was 38%, in 1920 it had risen to 44% and in 1930 it was slightly above 49%. The figures for 1940 will undoubtedly disclose that well over half the population of the United States has become urbanized.

The great urbanizing forces are still at work with undiminished vigor. The continued development of large-scale production, the greater facilities which the large city gives to industry in the way of a flexible labor supply, and the advantages derivable from a sizable labor market close at hand—these and the various social allurements of the city are still contributing to its growth. The increased productivity of agriculture is releasing men from the soil and it is to the cities that they go. This steadily strengthening urbanism is not an American phenomenon. It has its counterpart in nearly all other countries as well.

[J. G. Thompson, *Urbanization.*]

WILLIAM B. MUNRO

"Citizens' Alliances" were formed first in Kansas, and then in the neighboring states of Iowa and Nebraska, by townsmen who sympathized with the Farmers' Alliances[qv]. When the Supreme Council of the "Southern" Alliance met at Ocala, Fla., in December, 1890, it recognized the value of such support and assisted in the organization of these groups into the National Citizens' Alliance as a kind of auxiliary. Even more eager than the farmers for third-party action, members of the Citizens' Alliance were prominent in the several conventions that led to the formation of the People's party[qv], into which their order was speedily absorbed.

[H. R. Chamberlain, *The Farmers' Alliance.*]

JOHN D. HICKS

Citizens' Military Training Camps. Initiated in the summer of 1913 at Gettysburg, Pa., and Monterey, Calif., for 244 college undergraduates attending at their own expense, continued on the same basis in 1914 at Burlington, Vt., Asheville, N. C., Ludington, Mich., and Monterey for 667 students, the Citizens' Military Training Camp was widely publicized in 1915 when fostered at Plattsburg, N. Y., by Gen. Leonard Wood for business and professional men. It became part of the "preparedness" movement[qv]. In 1916 there were 12,200 enrolled at Plattsburg, Fort Oglethorpe, Fort Terry and Fort Wadsworth, and many who attended were the following winter commissioned in the embryo Officers' Reserve Corps[qv]. Re-established by the act of 1920 with transportation, rations and equipment furnished by the Government, these camps have enrolled more than 30,000 students annually, many of whom have earned commissions in the Officers' Reserve Corps.

[W. A. Ganoe, *History of the United States Army;* R. B. Perry, *The Plattsburg Movement.*]

ELBRIDGE COLBY

Citizenship may be defined as membership in a political community. During the colonial period, the American people were accustomed to calling themselves "subjects" of the English king, the term subject having a connotation appropriate to a monarchy. The English law, feudal in origin, made each person born within the colonies, save minor exceptions, a subject of the king. Through acts of Parliament and of the colonial assemblies, provisions were made whereby other persons, except certain classes disqualified on grounds of religious faith, could be naturalized as British subjects. With the signing of the Definitive Treaty of Peace of 1783[qv], and especially with the adoption of the Constitution[qv], the term "citizen" gained in favor as more descriptive of membership in a republican political community.

The Constitution recognizes a dual American citizenship, that of the United States and that of the state. It was not at first clear which carried the primary obligation. The earlier opinion, as expressed by Justice Story, was that "every citizen of a State is *ipso facto* a citizen of the United States." This view, that the state claim is antecedent, found acceptance in the Dred Scott Case[qv] of 1857. After the Civil War, however, the determination of the North to settle once and for all the status of the Negro led to the enactment of the Fourteenth Amendment[qv], which provided that "All persons born or naturalized in the United States, and subject to the jurisdiction thereof, are citizens of the United States and of the State wherein they reside." Thus, United States citizenship is now primary, that of the state derivative.

The Fourteenth Amendment embodies the English principle of *jus soli,* which fixes citizenship according to the place of birth. As interpreted by the American courts, not only are Negroes, born in this country, citizens of the United States, but so also are Orientals (U. S. v. Wong Kim Ark, 1898[qv]). The Indians, living in tribal relations, were not at first deemed to be "under the jurisdiction" of the United States in the sense of the Fourteenth Amendment (Elk v. Williams, 1884), but in 1924 Congress conferred citizenship upon all non-citizen Indians born within the territorial limits of the United States. The principle of *jus sanguinis,* which bases citizenship upon parentage, and which is widely accepted on the continent of Europe, has had some influence upon American policy. By Federal statutes, children born of American parents resident in foreign countries are presumed to be American citizens, though, by the act of 1907, such presumption will lapse unless on attaining the age of eighteen they record at an American consulate their intention to become residents of the United States and to retain their citizenship.

The Constitution, moreover, authorizes Congress to establish "an uniform rule of naturalization." Our Government has from the beginning been friendly to the idea of "acquired" citizenship. An early Federal pronouncement dignifies expatriation as "a natural and inherent right of all people." Hence, laws have been passed making provisions for naturalization[qv] of individuals, and special acts have conferred collective American citizenship (with certain exceptions) upon the inhabitants of Hawaii (1900), Puerto Rico (1917) and the Virgin Islands (1927)[qqv].

[F. A. Cleveland, *American Citizenship as Distinguished from Alien Status;* L. Gettys, *The Law of Citizenship in the United States;* Government Printing Office, *Naturalization, Citizenship, and Expatriation Laws;* C. H. Maxson, *Citizenship.*]

ROBERT PHILLIPS

Citrus Industry, THE, including production, packing and marketing of oranges, grapefruit and lemons, got its start in China (*Citrus sinensis*). From 16th-century Spain came a bittersweet orange to Florida, where it spread as a wild fruit. The first orange trees in California grew at Mission San Gabriel (1804). In 1863 the Federal Government began a collection of citrus with the purchase of three varieties of oranges, a Maltese oval, a St. Michael and a Mandarin. The Bahia navel was imported in 1868, and the collection was augmented in 1871 by additional European specimens.

California now leads the industry, with its production of Valencia and navel oranges, lemons and grapefruit. The sweet, round orange is the most important citrus fruit in Florida; next in importance is the grapefruit; the tangerine and the Satsuma orange rank next; limes are grown in the extreme southern part of Florida. An extensive citrus culture, largely grapefruit, has developed since 1920 in Texas. Satsuma oranges are grown along the Gulf, in Alabama, Mississippi, Louisiana and Texas. There is also a growing citrus industry in Arizona.

By 1890 production of American citrus fruit had reached 4000 carloads. Since then the trend has been steadily upward. In 1936–37 the production of boxes of oranges by states was as follows: California, 29,827,000; Florida, 22,500,000; Texas, 2,000,000; Arizona, 220,000; other states, 391,000; a total of 54,938,000 boxes, an increase of 30,155,000 over the 1919–20 season. Grapefruit production by boxes was as follows in 1937–38: Florida, 14,600,000; Texas, 11,800,000; Arizona, 2,750,000; California, 1,728,000; a total for four states of 30,878,000 boxes, an increase of 24,585,000 over the 1919–20 season. Lemon production by California amounted to 7,597,000 boxes in 1936–37, an increase of 3,277,000 boxes over the 1921–22 season. During the 1930's the grapefruit canning industry has grown rapidly, the number of boxes used for canning in 1937–38 being, by states: Florida, 6,000,000; Texas, 5,200,000; Arizona, 625,000; California, 400,000; a total for four states of 12,225,000, an increase of 12,075,000 over the 1922–23 season.

Co-operative marketing prevails widely in California and Florida. The California Fruit Growers Exchange packs about 75% of the California crop. The general officials of the co-operatives look to the advertising and marketing; local packing houses pick the fruit, haul it to packing shed, wash, wax, sort, wrap and pack. Low-grade fruit is made into marmalade, jelly, peel, vinegar, citric acid, calcium citrate, oil of orange and lemon, etc.

Irrigation is practised to a limited extent in Florida and is necessary for moisture control in southern California. Groves in frosty sections have various types of heaters. Insect pests are checked by spray gun and fumigation tent, and are prevented from importation by inspection at state borders. Trees are fed with phosphates and nitrates. Owners of all but the largest tracts do much of the labor themselves; other laborers vary with the sections, being largely mestizos in California.

[R. G. Cleland and Osgood Hardy, *March of Industry; Bulletins* of the U. S. Dept. of Agriculture.]

ROBERT G. RAYMER

City Government. *See* Municipal Government.

City Manager Plan, THE, is a simplified form of municipal government which originated in Staunton, Va. (1908), but did not attract much attention until after its adoption in Dayton, Ohio, six years later. Then it spread rapidly, particularly in states which have the home-rule charter system (*see* Charters, City), until eventually it gained acceptance in several hundred cities, large and small. Its chief vogue, however, is in the smaller municipalities.

The essential features of the city manager plan are, first, a small council elected by the voters of the city on a nonpartisan ballot; and, second, the appointment by this council of a chief administrative officer known as the city manager who assumes full responsibility for the entire work of municipal administration. The manager is chosen for his administrative capacity; he holds office during the pleasure of the council, and is the most highly paid officer of the city government. In some cases a member of the council serves as titular mayor, but without any important administrative duties.

The city manager attends all meetings of the council, prepares the budget for the council's consideration and appoints all the administrative officials, with a few exceptions such as the city clerk and the members of the public library board. The city charter usually forbids all interference by members of the city council in the manager's routine work, but the council retains the power to enact the ordinances and to decide all questions of general policy. City managers may be chosen from outside the city and in many instances this policy has been pursued.

On the whole the city manager plan has operated successfully, but its success has been most uniform in the smaller municipalities. In the larger cities it has proved a more difficult problem to find competent managers and to keep the managerial office out of politics.

[T. H. Reed, *Municipal Government in the United States.*]

WILLIAM B. MUNRO

City Planning in the United States had its beginnings a long time ago. In 1692 William Penn devised a complete plan for his new city of Philadelphia, a plan which covered an area of about two square miles. A number of open spaces were reserved for public buildings and for parks while the rest of the tract was laid out with pencil and ruler in checkerboard fashion. Arterial highways and cross streets intersected one another at uniform intervals and at right angles.

More than a century later Maj. L'Enfant was brought over from Paris to plan the new national capital on the banks of the Potomac. This was a much larger enterprise with an area of about forty square miles. The French engineer varied the checkerboard plan by superimposing upon it a number of great diagonal avenues. Then came the upper portion of New York City, which was planned by a special commission in 1807. This commission merely cut up the area into 2000 city blocks, each exactly 200 feet wide, with serial numbers to designate all the newly planned avenues and streets. Other cities followed New York's unimaginative example until nearly all of them presented the same dull, drab symmetry.

About the beginning of the 20th century, however, city planning began to undergo a transformation both in scope and in technique. The public authorities commenced to realize that effective planning must take into account many things besides street layout: for example, the location of public buildings, transportation facilities, zoning, height of buildings and the facilitation of motor traffic. More weight must also be given to æsthetic considerations. Consequently in all the larger cities, and in most of the smaller ones, the local authorities were empowered to enact city planning ordinances and to establish planning boards with regulatory functions. The direction and nature of growth in virtually all American cities is now being guided by these boards. (*See also* Detroit, Woodward Plan of.)

[N. P. Lewis, *The Planning of the Modern City;* K. B. Lohman, *Principles of City Planning.*]

WILLIAM B. MUNRO

Civil Aeronautics Act (1938). The Civilian Aviation Act of 1926 established a Bureau of Commercial Aviation in the Department of Commerce, to map airways[qv], improve landing facilities and establish beacons and it also provided regulations for civilian flyers and for the operation of civilian air routes. The Post Office Department and the Interstate Commerce Commission[qqv] both exercised certain measures of control over air lines which carried mail, passengers and freight, as they did over railroads. The Lea-

McCarren Civil Aeronautics Act, which became law in June, 1938, created a Civil Aeronautics Authority of five members—to be appointed by the President—whose jurisdiction over aviation combines the authority formerly exercised by the Bureau of Commercial Aviation created in 1926, the Post Office and the Interstate Commerce Commission. A Safety Board of five members within the Authority's governance is also appointed by the President. The Authority regulates passenger, freight and mail rates and schedules, promulgates safety regulations, supervises the financial arrangements of air-line companies, passes upon all mergers and agreements between companies and may even designate and establish new airways. Existing air-mail[qv] contracts were terminated by the act, and the Post Office Department had the right to place mail upon any air line at rates approved by the Authority.

ALVIN F. HARLOW

Civil Liberties is a term generally used in the United States to indicate not only the idea of civil rights, privileges, prerogatives, franchises and freedom in general but also the concept of immunity or protection of individuals or groups from undue interference by the Government.

In England the idea of liberty was formulated particularly in the Magna Carta in 1215; in the Petition of Right in 1628; in the Habeas Corpus Act in 1679 and in the Bill of Rights signed in 1689. The concept was transferred to America by the Virginia charter of 1606 and by the charters of later colonies.

Subsequently, in the period from 1763 to 1775, when England undertook to increase its control over the American colonists, the latter objected strenuously. In the Declarations of Rights issued by the Stamp Act Congress in 1765 and the First Continental Congress in 1774, it was insisted that the colonists were entitled to all the rights and liberties of Englishmen[qqv]. In 1776 the Declaration of Independence[qv] held that "life, liberty, and the pursuit of happiness" were "inalienable rights" of men.

Meanwhile, the idea of civil liberties in America had been strengthened by legislative guarantees in at least eleven colonies. Six of the first state constitutions, drawn up during the Revolutionary War, contained elaborate bills of rights (*see* Bills of Rights, State). The national Constitution of 1787 included six guarantees of liberty but did not include a comprehensive bill of rights. As a result of popular demand, ten amendments, commonly called the Bill of Rights[qv], were added to the fundamental law in 1791.

The liberties guaranteed by the Bill of Rights and by the original Constitution include the prohibition of a state church; freedom of religion, speech and the press; the right of petition; liberty to assemble peaceably; the right to bear arms; protection against the quartering of troops; the right to a jury trial; immunity from unreasonable search and seizure, self-incrimination, double jeopardy, cruel and unusual punishments and excessive bail; the guarantee of just compensation for property taken by the Government by eminent domain; the guarantee that Congress will not deprive a person "of life, liberty, or property, without due process of law"; the privilege of the writ of habeas corpus; and the prohibitions of bills of attainder, ex post facto laws, grants of titles of nobility, religious tests for officeholders and convictions for treason except as defined in the Constitution.

The constitutional history of the United States abounds with illustrations of the different executive, legislative, judicial and popular interpretations of civil liberties at various times. Congress in 1798 and again in the World War period curbed freedom of speech and of the press by sedition laws. In the post-Civil War period the Ku Klux Klan Act[qv] sought to protect the civil liberties of Negroes. During the Civil War, President Lincoln suspended the writ of habeas corpus outside the war zone. The Civil Rights Cases and the Scottsboro Case[qqv] are examples of Supreme Court interpretations of the civil liberties of Negroes.

[T. M. Cooley, *Constitutional Limitations;* J. M. Mathews, *The American Constitutional System.*]

ERIK McKINLEY ERIKSSON

Civil Rights Act, THE (April 9, 1866), was the first Federal statute to define citizenship and to safeguard civil rights within states. "All persons born in the United States and not subject to any foreign power, excluding Indians not taxed," were declared to be citizens of the United States. Such persons, "of every race and color," should have rights equal with white citizens for the security of person and property, in any state or territory. Jurisdiction over enforcement was given to Federal courts. The purpose of the act was to nullify the Black Codes[qv] of various Southern states. Since there was some doubt in Congress as to the constitutionality of the act, the Civil Rights section was later incorporated in the resolution framing the Fourteenth Amendment[qv]. After President Johnson vetoed the act (March 27, 1866) the opponents of the President won a two-thirds majority in Congress to override the veto, and thereafter Congress was in full command of Reconstruction^qv legislation (*see* Civil Rights Cases; Force Acts).

[E. P. Oberholtzer, *A History of the United States since the Civil War*, Vol. I.]

C. MILDRED THOMPSON

Civil Rights Cases, 1883 (109 U. S. 3). Individuals are protected from violations of their civil rights on the part of the Federal authorities by the Bill of Rights^qv in the Federal Constitution. They are protected from such violations on the part of state authorities by the Fourteenth Amendment^qv and by the bills of rights in their respective state constitutions. The Civil Rights Cases clearly establish the fact that individuals have no constitutional protection—Federal or state—from violations of their civil rights on the part of other individuals. They may secure redress, but by court action, and under statutory rather than constitutional authorization. Furthermore, the statute must be a state, and may not be a Federal, one.

During the period of Reconstruction^qv, Congress adopted a series of acts known as the Force Acts^qv, of which the Civil Rights Act was one. For years Sen. Charles Sumner of Massachusetts had urged the adoption of such a measure; upon his death his erstwhile colleagues waived their doubts as to the measure's constitutionality, in their anxiety to pay tribute to a departed friend. This act (March 1, 1875), which was the last to be adopted in the group of Force Acts, sought to guarantee to all citizens of the United States full and equal enjoyment of the privileges of inns, theaters, restaurants, public conveyances, etc., and stipulated that such enjoyment should not be subject to any conditions applicable only to citizens of a particular race or color, or who had been in a previous condition of servitude. Suit was brought against certain proprietors—Stanley, Ryan, Nichols, Singleton and the Memphis and Charleston Railroad Company—for violation of the law.

The Court sustained the arguments of the defendants, who alleged that the act was unconstitutional. It was held that the denial of such privileges is not an indication of slavery or involuntary servitude; that the Fourteenth Amendment applies to states, not to individuals; that no law had been made by a state abridging rights or denying equal privileges to citizens of the United States, and that the acts complained of were committed by individuals, hence the cases did not come within the meaning of the Fourteenth Amendment. The decision, like that in the Slaughter House Cases^qv ten years earlier, is one of permanent significance. If the Court had accepted the opposite view, the whole nature of the American constitutional system would have been changed in a manner and to an extent never contemplated by the Congress which proposed or by the states which ratified the War Amendments.

[Charles K. Burdick, *The Law of the American Constitution;* William A. Dunning, *Reconstruction, Political and Economic;* Andrew C. McLaughlin, *A Constitutional History of the United States;* J. G. Randall, *The Civil War and Reconstruction;* Charles Warren, *The Supreme Court in United States History;* W. W. Willoughby, *Constitutional Law of the United States.*]

W. BROOKE GRAVES

Civil Service, as distinct from military, naval and foreign service, is the term applied to those public employees who provide an administrative liaison between the state and the individual. All governmental units are thus operated by a civil service, with classified and unclassified divisions, expansion of which keeps pace with an increase in governmental functions. The classified service is characterized by appointment through competitive examination, salary standardization, permanent tenure, merit promotion and pension compensation; the unclassified service, on the other hand, is characterized by political appointment and rapid turnover in positions.

Corruption of civil service in the United States dates from 1789, but it was not until the Jacksonian era that political rotation of governmental posts became a widespread abuse which ultimately reached unprecedented proportions immediately after the Civil War. Then it was that reform organizations launched a campaign to make "civil service" synonymous with the "merit system"^qv—a campaign which has been continued for more than fifty years. Civil service reform has been undertaken during four major periods in United States history—namely, the post-Civil War era, the post-Spanish-American War era, the post-World War era and the post-Depression era. Three major pressure groups^qv—namely, the National Civil Service Reform League, the Civil Service Assembly of the United States and Canada, and the League of Women Voters^qv—have concentrated their efforts on drafting better civil service laws, on improving relations between public employees and legislators, and latterly on improving relations between civil servants and citizens whom they serve.

Significant landmarks in Federal civil service reform have been the laws of 1853, 1855, 1871, 1883 and 1919. In 1853 and again in 1855 a simple system of "pass examinations" was inaugurated by Congress for Federal civil servants. In 1871 Congress gave the President power to determine a general system of personnel selection.

However, it was not until 1883, by the Pendleton Act^qv^, which received the support of President Arthur, that a Civil Service Act of any moment was passed. This is still the basic statute. It has been supplemented by a major set of Civil Service Rules and Orders promulgated by President Theodore Roosevelt in 1903, which have been amended from time to time; and by the Classification Act of 1923. In 1919 war veterans were granted special preference. Congressional bills for complete reorganization of the existing civil service and for the extension of the merit system to first-, second- and third-class postmasters are pending as of 1938.

In 1883 New York adopted the first state Civil Service Act, the statute of which was later (1894) incorporated in the state constitution. Massachusetts followed in 1884; Wisconsin and Illinois in 1905 (the latter's statute amended in 1911); Colorado in 1907 (statute incorporated in the constitution, 1919); New Jersey in 1908; Ohio in 1912 (constitutional amendment; supplemented by a statute in 1913); California in 1913 (statute amended in 1929; incorporated in state constitution in 1934); Connecticut in 1913 (repealed in 1921; re-enacted in 1937); Kansas in 1915 (now defunct since 1920 for lack of funds); Maryland in 1920; Kentucky in 1936; Arkansas, Tennessee and Maine in 1937.

The same periods that have witnessed reform in Federal and state civil services have also seen similar reforms in municipalities. Approximately 450 cities (of the 960 having a population greater than 10,000) now use the merit principle for selection of personnel, though many of these confine merit appointments to police and fire services. Most cities operate their own statutes, but state commissions in Massachusetts and New Jersey directly control local civil services, while state commissions in New York and Ohio have partial local jurisdiction. About 40 of the 3056 counties have adopted the merit system to date (1939).

[Leonard D. White, *Trends in Public Administration.*]

FRANCES L. REINHOLD

Civil War, Economic Consequences of (North). Destructive as it was of material as well as of human values, the Civil War proved to be a great stimulus to the economic life of the North. Government contracts, paper-money inflation and a new protective tariff system^qqv^ brought a rapid expansion of capital and a new prosperity to Northern industry, with large-scale industry increasingly common. Cotton manufacturing declined because of a shortage of raw material, but woolen manufacturing and the munitions and war supplies industries in general experienced sharp gains. The young petroleum^qv^ industry was given an important place in the rapid growth of American capitalism. The telegraphs and railways^qqv^ led the way to a new era of corporate consolidation. The later years of the war brought a new national banking system^qv^ which promised a check upon the paper issues of the existing state banks. Out of these developments and, in addition, a frenzied stock-market speculation, came new fortunes that were often summed up as constituting a "shoddy" aristocracy.

To the common man this prosperity was not an unmixed boon. Agriculture experienced new gains with an expanded area and an increased use of farm machinery^qv^; this was often, however, at the price of overexpansion and debt. With wages lagging far behind a price rise that more than doubled the cost of living, labor found even less in which to rejoice; it therefore turned new energies toward organizing its forces in national craft unions. The burden of taxation was borne with little complaint. Excise taxes were levied upon as many articles as possible; tariff schedules reached in 1864 an average rate of 47%, partly offset by the internal revenue levies; income taxes came to be assessed upon all incomes in excess of $600 a year, with, however, less than a half-million persons affected. Thus was secured one fifth of the wartime needs of the Government. The rest was borrowed directly or indirectly; the war ended with a Federal debt of over $2,600,000,000. Yet the national wealth had been greatly increased and a new era of American capitalism was ahead.

[Fite, *Social and Industrial Conditions in the North during the Civil War.*]

ARTHUR C. COLE

Civil War, Economic Consequences of (South). The Civil War brought economic suffering, devastation and ruin to the South. As a result of the blockade^qv^, the interruption of intercourse with the North and the strain of supporting the armed forces, the people were subjected to extreme privation. Large land areas were laid waste by military operations. Accumulated capital resources were dissipated. Railroads were either destroyed or allowed to deteriorate to the point of worthlessness. Live stock was reduced by almost two thirds. Slave property valued at about $2,000,000,000 was wiped out. Approximately one fourth of the productive white male population was killed or incapacitated. Land values were undermined; agricultural production was greatly retarded; trade was disrupted; banks and mercantile houses were forced into bankruptcy; the credit system was disorganized; and commercial ties with foreign nations were broken. (*See also* Reconstruction.)

The war also brought sweeping changes in the economy of the South. The destruction of slavery[qv] together with the devastation wrought by the conflict forced the plantation system to give way to a sharecropper, tenancy and small farm system. A central feature of this transition was the rise of the crop lien which tended to make necessary continued concentration on cotton cultivation. With the breakup of the plantations[qv] there occurred a great increase in the number and economic importance of the small towns and their inhabitants—merchants, bankers, lawyers and doctors.

The war also brought a diminution in the part the South has played in the determination of national economic policies. During the period since the war, tariff, monetary, railroad, banking and other such matters have generally been decided without any consideration for the wishes and needs of the South. The result has been what amounts to economic exploitation of the South by other sections of the nation.

[J. A. C. Chandler, ed., and others, *The South in the Building of the Nation*, especially Vols. V and VI; W. L. Fleming, *Documentary History of Reconstruction.*]

HAYWOOD J. PEARCE, JR.

Civil War, Financing Problems of the (Federal). When Salmon P. Chase reluctantly resigned from the Senate to become Secretary of the Treasury in March, 1861, the state of the Federal finances was not encouraging, especially in view of the impending war. During the preceding four years of the Buchanan administration the treasury had financed deficits annually through the flotation of government obligations, a factor which had shaken the confidence of investors in these securities. Chase, himself, at first, could only float additional loans to meet the essential expenditures of government.

Shortly, faced with the problem of financing the war, Secretary Chase decided on a tax program to cover the regular expenses of government, while the extraordinary expenses resulting from the war were to be financed by the sale of bonds and notes. During the fiscal year 1861, 64.3% of total net receipts came from taxes and only 35.7% from loans.

The situation changed radically in the next fiscal year. The customs law which had been enacted on Chase's recommendation did not yield sufficient revenue to cover even the ordinary expenses, and war expenditures, of course, increased rapidly. Moreover, the sale of government securities was not easy as it was usually required by law that such securities could not be put on the market below par, while the interest authorized was not sufficient to attract investors at par or above.

It was under these circumstances that Mr. Stevens and Mr. Spaulding of the House Ways and Means Committee were able to secure the passage of the first legal tender act[qv] (authorizing the issuance of $150,000,000 of greenbacks[qv]) on Feb. 25, 1862. Passage of this act was procured under the plea of dire necessity, although the opposition showed that by selling government obligations on the market for what they would bring the issuance of greenbacks could have been avoided.

In the fiscal year 1862 only 10.7% of total net receipts were obtained from taxes, whereas, of the remaining 89.3%, over one third came from non-interest-bearing obligations, mainly United States notes (greenbacks).

A second legal tender act was passed on July 11, 1862, and a third on March 3, 1863, each authorizing $150,000,000 of greenbacks. Further issues were avoided as a result of increased revenues from taxation with a concurrent and consequent improvement in the Government's credit. Thus, in the fiscal years 1863–66 the proportion of net receipts coming from taxes increased successively from 15.8% to 25.9% to 26.9% to 83% in the order given.

The reasons for the failure to tax more heavily in the earlier years of the war are easily explained. Secretary Chase was not experienced in finance and also contemplated a relatively short struggle. The Republican party[qv] was new and lacked solidarity. Internal taxes had not been levied for many years and the Republicans did not dare to risk the unpopularity that a heavy internal tax would probably have called forth. Accordingly, although heavier taxes early in the war would have been sounder financially, they were obviously not politically feasible until a later period.

[D. R. Dewey, *Financial History of the United States;* W. C. Mitchell, *A History of the Greenbacks.*]

FREDERICK A. BRADFORD

Civil War: General Orders No. 100 was a code comprising 157 articles "for the government of armies in the field" according to the "laws and usages of war." By order of Secretary Stanton, it was drawn up by Francis Lieber and a special board, and utilized by Union officers. The first code of its kind, it later formed the basis for many codes of military field law and for the conventions of the Hague Conferences[qv] of 1899 and 1907.

[Elihu Root, *Addresses on International Subjects.*]

FRANK FREIDEL

Civil War: Propaganda and Undercover Activities. The Abolition[qv] crusade and the proslavery reaction laid the psychological bases for the war. Upon the outbreak of the conflict, press and pulpit, North and South, further stirred the emotions of the people. In the South, propagandists devoted their efforts to asserting the right to secede and to proving that the aggressive North was invading Southern territory. In the North, the preservation of the Union, patriotism and the crusade against slavery were the major *motifs* in propaganda. On both sides, atrocity[qv] stories—largely concerned with the brutal treatment of the wounded, of military prisoners and of political dissenters—abounded. Southern efforts in propaganda lacked co-ordination, but in the North the radical Committee on the Conduct of the War[qv] gave official direction to the gathering and dissemination of atrocity stories which professed to reveal rebel depravity and to show the felonious and savage nature of the Southerners. The Sanitary Commission and the Union Leagues[qqv] were the chief unofficial agencies in this work. Both sides attempted to influence European opinion and Lincoln sent journalists and ecclesiastics to England and the Continent to create favorable sentiment.

Despite these efforts, many on both sides remained unconvinced. The Knights of the Golden Circle[qv] in the North were paralleled by numerous secret "peace societies" in the South. These organizations encouraged desertion; aided fugitive slaves, refugees and escaping prisoners; and occasionally attempted direct sabotage.

[W. B. Hesseltine, *Civil War Prisons;* G. Tatum, *Disloyalty in the Confederacy;* J. T. Adams, *America's Tragedy.*]

W. B. HESSELTINE

Civil War: Surrender of the Confederate Armies. The most important surrender after Appomattox[qv] was that of Joseph E. Johnston (C.) to William T. Sherman (U.) at the Bennett house near Durham Station, N. C., April 26, 1865. Parole was granted to 37,047 prisoners on the same terms Grant (U.) had given Lee (C.). Previously Sherman had joined Schofield (U.) at Goldsboro, N. C., on March 23, their combined force being about 80,000. Johnston, stationed before the town of Raleigh, had about 33,000 effective troops. On April 10, two days before the news of Appomattox arrived, Sherman advanced to Raleigh and Johnston retreated toward Greensboro, where he convinced President Jefferson Davis that further resistance, though possible, would merely entail prolonged suffering with ultimate subjection. The result was a conference between Sherman and Johnston on April 17–18, resulting in a memorandum to be submitted to Davis and the Government at Washington. The proposed surrender included President Lincoln's principles of reconstruction[qv] which, though far more reasonable than the ultimate congressional plan, were outside Sherman's authority to offer. The refusal of Secretary of War Stanton to accept these terms led Johnston, from motives of humanity, to agree to unconditional surrender. Not content with this outcome, Stanton published an embellished account of Sherman's action, made unjust accusations and created a national scandal.

The capitulation of the rest of the Confederate forces followed as a matter of course. On May 4 Richard Taylor (C.) surrendered to E. R. S. Canby (U.) at Citronelle, Ala., thus ending Confederate forces east of the Mississippi. Six days later Jefferson Davis was captured by James H. Wilson's (U.) cavalry near Irwinville, Ga., and was imprisoned at Fortress Monroe[qv]. The final act was the surrender of Kirby Smith (C.) and the trans-Mississippi troops to Canby at New Orleans on May 26. The total number surrendered and paroled from April 9 to May 26 was 174,223.

[J. F. Rhodes, *History of the United States.*]

FRED A. SHANNON

Civil War, THE. The causes and preliminaries of the American Civil War (1861–65) are treated elsewhere in this work (*see* South, Civilization of the Old; Abolition Movement; Nashville Convention; Slavery; Missouri Compromise; Kansas–Nebraska Act; Republican Party; Campaign of 1860; Secession; Fort Sumter; The Confederate States of America). In understanding the background of the struggle it is essential to distinguish such broad factors as Southernism in terms of culture types, economic and political motives of the planter aristocracy, Southern defense reaction to Northern criticism, the whipping up of excitement by agitators on both sides, economic sectionalism (agrarian v. industrial tendencies), Northern thought-patterns as to democracy and slavery, Republican party strategy and the highly overemphasized issue of slavery in the territories. Sectional tension grew ominously in the 1850's and a major Southern crisis, accompanied by intense popular excitement, followed the election of Lincoln in November, 1860. By early February, 1861, the seven states of the Lower South had withdrawn from the Union and had begun the erection of the Southern Confederacy. After a period of inaction, the sending of an expedition by President Lincoln to relieve the Federal garrison at Fort Sumter in Charleston Harbor precipitated a Southern attack upon that fort, which was surrendered on April 13. This specifically was the opening of the war. Each side claimed that the other began it. Southerners argued that Lincoln's expedition was an invasion of a sovereign state; the Washington Government maintained that it meant no aggression in "holding" its own fort and that the "first shot" had been fired by the South.

Lincoln's inaugural address of March 4, 1861, had been conciliatory in tone; nevertheless his decision to retain Sumter, which necessitated sending food to the garrison, placed the opening "incident" in precisely that area where peace was most unstable and where emotion had been roused to greatest sensitivity. Fort Pickens[qv] in Florida, though similar in status to Sumter, presented no such menace of emotional outbreak. Lincoln's Sumter policy involved two main points: the sending of the provisioning expedition, and, after the fort had been fired upon, the call for 75,000 militia to be furnished by the states. This policy, while it produced a united North, served equally to unite the South; it was not until after Lincoln's call for militia that the four important states of the Upper South (Virginia, Arkansas, Tennessee and North Carolina) withdrew from the Union and joined the Confederacy. In this sense Lincoln's April policy, interpreted in the South as coercion, played into the hands of the secessionists while Buchanan's avoidance of an outbreak had supplied the setting for compromise efforts.

On the side of the Union there were twenty-three states with 22,000,000 people as against eleven states and 9,000,000 (including 3,500,000 slaves) within the Confederacy. In wealth and population as well as in industrial, commercial and financial strength the Union was definitely superior to the Confederacy. On the other hand the South had the advantage of bold leadership, gallant tradition, martial spirit, unopposed seizure of many Federal forts and arsenals, interior military lines and unusual ability among its generals. Its military problem was that of defense, which required far less men than offensive campaigns and widely extended hostile occupation. Between the two sections was a populous middle region (the Union slave states of Delaware, Maryland, Kentucky and Missouri; the area that became West Virginia; and the southern portions of Ohio, Indiana and Illinois) within which the choice of the people was for the Union while on the other hand there was cultural sympathy for the South and spirited opposition to the Lincoln administration (*see* Border States).

Legally the war began with Lincoln's proclamations: the proclamation of April 15, 1861, which summoned the militia to suppress "combinations" in the seven states of the Lower South, and the proclamations of April 19 and April 27, 1861, which launched a blockade[qv] of Southern ports. Internationally the Confederacy achieved recognition of belligerency, as in the British queen's proclamation of neutrality (May 13, 1861), but never achieved full standing in the sense of a recognition of independence by any foreign power. Nor did any foreign nation intervene in the struggle, though the British government seemed at times to be seriously contemplating it and the government of Napoleon III did offer mediation which was indignantly rejected by the United States (February–March, 1863).

Before Lincoln's first Congress met in July, 1861, the President had taken those measures which gave to Union war policy its controlling character. Besides proclaiming an insurrection, declaring a blockade and summoning the militia (definite war measures), he had suspended the habeas corpus[qv] privilege, expanded the regular army, directed emergency expenditures and in general had assumed executive functions beyond existing law. A tardy ratification of his acts was passed by Congress on Aug. 6, 1861 (U. S. *Statutes at Large,* XII, 326) and in 1863 these strongly contested executive measures were given sanction by the Supreme Court in a five-to-four decision sustained chiefly by Lincoln's own judicial appointees (*see* Prize Cases). In general, Lincoln's method of meeting the emergency and suppressing disloyal tendencies was not to proceed within the pattern of regular statutes, but to grasp arbitrary power by executive orders or proclamations, as in the Emancipation Proclamation[qv] (in which the President exercised a power which he insisted Congress did not have even in time of war), and his extensive program of arbitrary arrests[qv] wherein thousands of citizens were thrust into prison on suspicion of disloyal or dangerous activity. These arrests were quite irregular. Prisoners were given no trial (usually not even military trial); they were deprived of civil guarantees and were subjected to no regular accusations under the law. Such measures led to severe and widespread opposition to the Lincoln administration. In their denial of the habeas corpus privilege they were denounced as unconstitutional in a hearing before Chief Justice Taney (*ex parte* Merryman[qv], May, 1861), but in the Vallandigham case[qv] the Supreme Court, to which the Merryman case had not been brought, declined to interpose any obstacle to arbitrary arrest, thus in a negative way sustaining the President. (In 1866, however, the Court did overrule a wartime military commission in the Milligan case[qv].) Yet it cannot be said that Lincoln became in the 20th-century sense a "dictator." He allowed freedom of speech and of the press[qqv], contrary examples being exceptional, not typical. He tolerated widespread newspaper criticism of himself and of the Government, interposed no party uniformity, permitted free assembly, avoided partisan violence, recognized opponents in appointments and above all submitted himself, even during war, to the test of popular election. This testing resulted in marked Republican loss in the congressional election of 1862, while in 1864, though the situation looked very dark for the Republicans in August, the election in November brought in a considerable electoral majority.

In the military sense both sides were unprepared; had any conceivable policy of prewar preparedness been promoted (under the Southern secretaries of war of the 1850's) it could hardly have given the Union side that advantage which military writers often assume. The battle of Bull Run[qv] (July 21) was the only large-scale engagement in 1861. Though a Union defeat, it was, like most of the battles, an indecisive struggle. Except during the generalship of McClellan (U.), Meade (U.) and Grant (U.) the Southerners had the undoubted advantage of military leadership on the main eastern front; Lee's (C.) notable, though indecisive, victories of Second Bull Run, Fredericksburg and Chancellorsville[qqv] were won against Pope, Burnside and Hooker. At Antietam[qv], however, McClellan stopped Lee's Northern invasion of September, 1862, while the ambitious Confederate offensive of 1863 was checked at Gettysburg[qv]. In the West most of the operations were favorable to the Union side. This was especially true of the "river war" (resulting in the capture of Columbus, Forts Henry and Donelson, Nashville, Corinth and Memphis), the Federal half-victory of Shiloh; and more especially the important Union victories of 1863 at Vicksburg and in the Chattanooga area[qqv]. Later campaigns involved J. E. Johnston's (C.) unsuccessful operations against Sherman (U.) in upper Georgia, Sherman's capture of Atlanta and his famous raid through Georgia and the Carolinas, Sheridan's (U.) devastating operations in the Valley of Virginia, the Grant-Meade operations against Lee in Virginia (involving the costly battles of the Wilderness, Spotsylvania and Cold Harbor), the Hood-Thomas campaign in Tennessee and final operations in the Petersburg and Appomattox areas, which culminated in the fall of Richmond and the close of the war[qqv]. In the naval aspects Union superiority was impressively shown in the blockade of Southern ports which were eventually closed to the Confederacy's own warships, the capture and occupation of coastal positions, the co-operation of western flotillas with the armies, the seizure of New Orleans in April, 1862, the complete control of the Mississippi River after the fall of Vicksburg and Port Hudson in July, 1863, and the defeat and sinking of the Confederacy's proudest ship, the *Alabama,* by the *Kearsarge* (June 19, 1864)[qqv]. On the other hand Confederate cruisers and privateers did considerable damage to Union commerce (*see Alabama* Claims), the Union Navy failed in the operations against Richmond, and several ports (Wilmington, Charleston, Mobile) remained in Southern hands till late in the war. Galveston did not yield till after the war was over, June, 1865. Privateering was authorized by both sides but practised only by the Confederacy, and that chiefly in the first year of the war. The military decision in favor of the United States was registered in the surrender of Lee to Grant at Appomattox, April 9, 1865, and the surrender of J. E. Johnston to Sherman near Durham, N. C., on April 26. (For conditions within the Confederacy, *see* Confederate States of America.)

Methods of military recruiting and administration were amateurish, haphazard and inefficient. Conscription[qv] was used on both sides but by neither side with real effectiveness. Such factors as commutation money, bounties, bargaining in substitutes, draft riots[qqv], irregular popular recruiting, undue multiplication of military units, lack of a general staff and inadequate use of the very small regular army, marred the Union system of army administration. Somewhat similar difficulties existed also in the South. Guerrilla warfare[qv], though never a decisive factor nor a part of major strategy, was extensively practised. The administration of the War Department under Secretary Cameron (to January, 1862) was marred by fraud and corruption; under Secretary Stanton the system was improved, but profiteering and military blundering existed to a marked degree throughout the war. In addition, the Union cause was weakened by state control of national military processes, congressional interference (*see* Committee on the Conduct of the War), anti-McClellanism (involving the unwise abandonment of McClellan's peninsular campaign[qv] in the summer of 1862), confusion and circumlocution among divers army boards, councils and advisers, undue control of army matters by such men as Halleck and Stanton, extensive desertion[qv] and atrocious inadequacy in the care of hundreds of thousands of prisoners, the last-named abuse being chiefly due to utter breakdown in the exchange or cartel system. Negro troops[qv] were extensively used in the Union armies. The Confederate Government, late in the war, authorized their enrollment, but this was never put into practice.

What happened behind the lines would constitute a very elaborate story. Civilian relief was supplied by the United States Sanitary Commission[qv] (similar to the later Red Cross[qv]); war propaganda was spread by the Union League[qv] and the Loyal Publication Society; antiadministration effort was promoted by the Sons of Liberty and Knights of the Golden Circle[qqv]. Financial instability and monetary abnormality carried prices to fantastic heights in the South; in the North the disturbance was far less, but specie payments[qv] were suspended and treasury notes ("greenbacks"[qv]) depreciated to such an extent that the paper price of gold reached $2.84 in July, 1864. Taxation was heavy, yet a Federal debt of approximately three billions was accumulated. Federal bonds were marketed by the semiofficial efforts of Jay Cooke and Company[qv]. Currency and banking regulations were drastically modified by the establishment of the national banking system[qv]. Labor obtained from the war far less advantage than business entrepreneurs. Immigration[qv] was encouraged and the wartime increase of wages was not commensurate with the depreciation of the money system. Greed was widespread, stock speculation was rife, lobbying was rampant, contractors cheated the Government (*see* Civil War Contracts) and large numbers of men became unjustifiably rich. High wartime tariff[qv] laws gave ample protection[qv] to manufacturers. Various reforms and progressive schemes were delayed or wrecked by the war, but laws were passed for assigning free homesteads to settlers (*see* Homestead Movement, The), for encouraging Western railroad building (*see* Land Grants to Railways) and for Federal aid in the establishment of land-grant colleges[qv]. To a people once united but split asunder by the tragedy of war there came the inevitable horrors of war psychosis; this took manifold forms including un-Christian sputterings of hatred in the churches. One of the most savage of the wartime fanatics was "Parson" (W. G.) Brownlow of Tennessee. Yet Quakers[qv] and other honest religious objectors to war were given, by administrative procedure and later by law, the alternative of noncombatant service when drafted. Efforts of peace groups to end the war in 1864 received notable support from Horace Greeley (*see* Peace Movement in 1864), but, being associated with partisan politics, they met failure in every case; even the official efforts of high-placed statesmen met a like failure in the Hampton Roads Conference[qv] of February, 1865. War aims changed as the conflict progressed; the declaration of Congress on July 22, 1861, that the war was waged merely for the restoration of the Union was belied by the Radical Republicans[qv] who by 1864 had determined in the event of victory to treat the South as a subordinate section upon which drastic modifications would be imposed. One of the striking examples of wartime Radical policy was seen in the second confiscation act[qv] (July 17, 1862) which, against Lincoln's better judgment, decreed the forfeiture to the United States of the property of all adherents to the "rebellion." The relation of the war to the slavery question appeared in various emancipating measures passed by Congress, in Lincoln's Emancipation Proclamation as well as his abortive compensated emancipation scheme, in state measures of abolition, and finally in the antislavery amendment to the Constitution (*see* Thirteenth Amendment). (For international aspects of the struggle *see Trent* Affair; *Alabama* Claims; Civil War Diplomacy; Confederate States, Blockade of; Mexico, French in.) The distinction of Lincoln was discernible not in the enactment of laws through his advocacy, nor in the adoption of his ideals as a continuing postwar policy, nor even in the persuasion of his own party to follow his lead. Rather, the qualities which marked him as leader were personal tact (shown notably in a Cabinet crisis of December, 1862), fairness toward opponents, popular appeal, dignity and effectiveness in state papers, absence of vindictiveness and withal a personality which was remembered for its own uniqueness while it was almost canonized as a symbol of the Union cause. Military success, though long delayed, and the dramatic martyrdom of his assassination[qv] must also be reckoned as factors in the emancipator's fame. On the other side Southern memory of a cherished lost cause has been equally identified with the lofty perfection of Lee's personality.

To measure the war in terms of man power and casualties is a highly controversial task made doubly difficult by sectional pride, popular tradition, amateur history writing and inadequate statistics. Gen. Marcus J. Wright, a Confederate officer, after the war attached to the War Department, estimated Confederate man power at 600,000 to 700,000 men. Others, including T. L. Livermore and J. F. Rhodes, have put it much higher. Col. W. F. Fox, a careful military statistician, considered that the Union forces did not exceed 2,000,000 separate individuals. Comprehensive records are especially lacking on the Confederate side, while the better statistics on the Union side are in terms of enlistments and have been only conjecturally corrected to allow for numerous cases of reenlistment. Comparable units of military measurement have been hard to obtain in determining the totals involved in particular campaigns or battles, and inadequate attention has been given to the precise meaning of such terms as "effectives," men "present for duty," forces "actually engaged," etc. Grand totals include men in home guards, thousands who were missing and many other thousands who enlisted in the final weeks or were otherwise distant from fighting areas. On the Federal side in April, 1865, there were approximately a million men in the field, with two millions of the "national forces" not yet called out. The number of those subject to military call at the North was actually greater at the end of the war than at the beginning. Confederate dead have been estimated at 258,000, Union dead at 360,000. The stupendous economic and material loss has never been more than roughly estimated.

Aside from the obvious consequences of slaughter and destruction, the results of the war (or concomitants of the war and postwar period) involved suppression of the "heresy" of secession, legal fixation of an "indestructible" Union, national abolition of slavery, overthrow of the Southern planter class, rise of middle-class power in the South, decline of the merchant marine[qv], ascendancy of the Republican party, inauguration of a continuing high-tariff policy, far-reaching developments in terms of capitalistic growth associated with centralization[qv] of government functions and adoption of the Fourteenth Amendment[qv] (intended to consolidate party control by the protection of Negro civil rights but later applied as a shield to corporations). But with the mention of these factors the enumeration of long-time results is only begun. A full enumeration, impossible in these pages, would also include postwar intolerance, partisanship associated with the "bloody shirt" tradition, immense pension claims with their many abuses, a deplorable complex of "reconstruction" evils and excesses, carpetbag and scalawag corruption and, as the continuing result of all this, the "solid South."[qqv] Another way of viewing the whole subject is to consider what would have happened if no war had been fought, but such an inquiry is beyond historical testing. As of about 1900 it could be said that the wounds had been so far healed as to allow for a contented South within a reunited nation, but the antilynching filibuster of 1938 illustrated the persistence of sectionalism[qv] and the tendency of old intolerances to flare up more than seven decades after Appomattox.

[James Truslow Adams, *America's Tragedy;* Arthur C. Cole, *The Irrepressible Conflict, 1850-1865;* Edward Channing, *History of the United States,* VI; C. R. Fish, *The American Civil War;* D. S. Freeman, *R. E. Lee;* J. G. Randall, *Civil War and Reconstruction.*]

J. G. RANDALL

Civil War, The Navy in. On account of divided personnel, scattered forces and inadequate appropriations, the United States Navy was near to demoralization at the outbreak of the war. But the new Secretary, Gideon Welles, and the Assistant Secretary, Gustavus V. Fox, approached their task with intelligence and force.

The year 1861 was marked by a great disaster and two victories. The disaster, eight days after Fort Sumter was fired on, was the abandoning of the Norfolk Navy Yard[qqv]. The Federal Government not only lost eleven ships including the steam frigate *Merrimack,* but 3000 pieces of ordnance, 300 of them Dahlgren guns of the latest type. On the other hand, Admiral Stringham's squadron in August easily took the forts at the entrance to Hatteras Inlet, and DuPont's fleet in November captured two forts defending Port Royal, S. C.[qqv].

The year 1862 began with successful military and naval operations on the Tennessee and Cumberland rivers as Grant and Foote took Fort Henry and Fort Donelson[qqv], breaking the Confederate line of defense in the West, and saving Kentucky for the Union. On the Mississippi Foote's squadron co-operated with the army under Pope in taking Island No. 10[qv] and later advanced as far as Vicksburg. Farragut, at about the same time, coming from the Gulf with a strong seagoing fleet, succeeded in passing the strong forts of Jackson and St. Philip[qv] (April 24) and overpowering the Confederate Defense Squadron. New Orleans[qv] surrendered and the forts soon capitulated. This brilliant campaign prevented intervention on the part of France and possibly of England. On the Atlantic coast, the Confederate ironclad *Merrimack,* coming from Norfolk into Hampton Roads, destroyed the *Cumberland* and the *Congress* and threatened to break the Union blockade (March 8). But the *Monitor*[qv], arriving most opportunely, engaged the champion on the following morning and effectually checked her career.

In 1863, the Union ironclads increasing in numbers, naval attacks on Charleston[qv] became more determined. But even the *New Ironsides,* probably the strongest ship afloat, was unequal to the task. However, the blockade[qv] of South Carolina and other parts of the Southern coast was now highly effective. Of the first importance was the service rendered by Porter commanding the Mississippi Squadron[qv]. By his aid Grant, campaigning against Vicksburg, was able to cross the Mississippi and attack the city from the south and east. When he captured it (July 4) the Union controlled the entire Mississippi basin and split the Confederacy in two.

In 1864 the *Alabama*[qv] was sunk by the *Kearsarge* off Cherbourg, France (June 11). The *Alabama, Florida* and *Shenandoah*[qqv] were highly successful in their depredations on Northern commerce, and because all three had been built in British shipyards the United States claimed a heavy indemnity from England after the war (*see* Alabama Claims). On the 5th of August Farragut won his second decisive victory. With a fleet of wooden ships and ironclads he forced his way past Fort Morgan at the entrance to Mobile Bay[qv]. Later in the same morning he fought the Confederate ironclad *Tennessee* and compelled its surrender. Soon Mobile was barred from all approaches to the sea.

In 1865, on the 15th of January, the South's one remaining access to the sea was closed when the fleet commanded by Porter and the military forces by Terry took Fort Fisher[qv], the key to Wilmington, N. C. With the capture of Fort Fisher, a termination of the war favorable to the North was assured.

The service of the navy consisted in establishing an effective blockade; in carrying on joint operations with the army to capture strategic positions on the coast and to gain control of the Mississippi; and in pursuing and capturing the cruisers that preyed on Northern commerce. It was essential for the preservation of the Union.

[*Official Records of the Union and Confederate Navies.*]

CARROLL S. ALDEN

Civil War, Trade in Cotton during the. At the beginning of the Civil War the United States Government decided to permit a restricted trade in cotton in the districts held by the Union forces. This was done partly because of the foreign demand for cotton and partly to supply destitute Southerners with necessities. The trade was authorized by acts of Congress passed July 13, 1861, and July 2, 1864. In accordance with these laws, regulations were issued at various times, notably on Sept. 11, 1863, and on July 29, 1864, to control the trade. By them the commerce was restricted to treasury agents; private individuals and members of the military and naval forces were not allowed to participate in the traffic and there was to be no commercial intercourse with the Confederates. These rules covered the subject thoroughly, but owing to the profits involved they could not be enforced. Cotton at Boston was worth ten times as much as at the front and consequently Memphis and New Orleans, the principal trade centers, were infested with unscrupulous cotton buyers who proffered bribes for connivance in their illicit trade. Traders were thus allowed to purchase cotton from the Confederates in exchange for military supplies and to engage in private trade with them. Military expeditions, even, were sent out to get cotton for the traders: the Confederates would be warned of impending raids—in which they parted with cotton and in return received supplies that enabled them to maintain their forces.

The trade, legal and illegal, attained immense size. In the spring and summer of 1864 enough cotton went North to supply the factories, while each week $500,000 worth of goods was going South through Memphis. The results of the trade were harmful to the Union cause. According to Gen. Grant and other officers it prolonged the war at least a year.

[E. Channing, *History of the United States,* Vol. VI; J. F. Rhodes, *History of the United States from 1850 to 1877,* Vol. V; A. S. Roberts, Federal Government and Confederate Cotton, *American Historical Review,* Vol. XXXII, No. 2.]

A. SELLEW ROBERTS

Civil War and the Freedom of the Seas. During the American Civil War the United States "set on foot" a blockade[qv] of the Confederacy which was far from satisfying the most stringent requirements of international law set down in the Declaration of Paris[qv] (not ratified by the United States) and of previous diplomatic practice of the United States (*see* Foreign Policy). Further, the Supreme Court on appeal from prize courts developed the doctrine of continuous voyage[qv] one step beyond British practice during the Napoleonic Wars: it applied the doctrine to confiscate neutral property, contraband or no contraband, in transit between

Great Britain and British West Indian islands, when that property was ultimately destined, by a subsequent maritime leg of an essentially continuous voyage, to a blockaded Confederate port (*see Bermuda* Admiralty Case; *Springbok* Admiralty Case). When the property was ultimately destined by a subsequent terrestrial journey (via the neutral port of Matamoras, as in the case of the *Peterhoff*[qv]) continuously to the Confederacy, the Court did not construe the blockade to exist on land between the neutral country (Mexico) and the Confederacy, but it did confiscate the absolute contraband found on board.

Great Britain cheerfully acquiesced in the loose blockade and in the new interpretation of the doctrine of continuous voyage, which later gave her a valuable precedent with which to enforce, as against the United States, 1914–17, an imperfect blockade of Germany.

In the *Trent* case[qv] the United States acknowledged the force, if not the justice, of a British protest, accompanied by an ultimatum, against forcibly taking rebellious American citizens off a British merchant ship on the high seas, an act analogous to British impressment of disobedient subjects (some of them naturalized American citizens) from American neutral vessels on the high seas during the Napoleonic Wars.

[James P. Baxter, 3rd, The British Government and Neutral Rights, 1861-1865, *American Historical Review*, XXXIV, 1928; Samuel Flagg Bemis, *A Diplomatic History of the United States;* F. L. Owsley, *King Cotton Diplomacy;* J. W. Pratt, British Blockade and American Precedent, *U. S. Naval Institute Proceedings*, XLVI, November, 1920.]

SAMUEL FLAGG BEMIS

Civil War Contracts. In the first year of the Civil War the Federal Government and a score of states were bidding against each other for war supplies, with disgraceful consequences. Too often the rule was to let the contract to the highest bidder, that is, to the one who would give the biggest cut to the officials and inspectors. Simon Cameron himself, as Secretary of War, apparently was not guiltless. It is a notorious fact that several of the great fortunes of the modern day had their origin in Civil War contracts. Colt's revolvers[qv], which sold at $14.50 on the market, brought $25 by army contracts, or $35 when bought by Frémont. Furthermore, goods of inferior quality often found readier sales than first-class products. Shoddy for clothing, sand for sugar, parched grain for coffee, brown paper for sole leather and worthless foreign guns for weapons were among the things foisted on the soldiers. After a year of this sort of orgy the War Department began serious efforts at reform, but the contract business remained slightly malodorous till the end of the war. The situation seems to have been not much better in the Confederacy. At any rate, there was much grumbling against contractors and blockade runners[qv].

[F. A. Shannon, *Organization and Administration of the Union Army.*]

FRED A. SHANNON

Civil War Diplomacy. The basic diplomatic policy of the United States during the Civil War was twofold: to prevent foreign intervention in behalf of the Southern Confederacy; and to gain the acquiescence of the great maritime powers, England and France, in the vast extension of maritime belligerent rights which was considered necessary in order to crush the South. The chief diplomatic figures in Northern diplomacy were Secretary of State William H. Seward, supported and advised by President Lincoln, Charles Francis Adams, minister to England, William Dayton, minister to France, John Bigelow, consul general in France and, after Dayton's death in 1864, minister in his stead, and Thomas Corwin, minister to the Juarez government of Mexico. The United States, of course, had its diplomatic representatives in all the other principal civilized nations. But since France and England were great maritime powers and none too friendly toward the United States at the time, they seemed to offer the only serious danger of foreign intervention, and at the same time they were the nations which had to be appeased because of aggression against their commerce in prosecution of the war against Confederate trade. So Federal diplomacy was largely concerned with these two nations as far as it related to the Civil War.

In the very beginning, Seward deliberately created the impression upon the British government that he was willing if not anxious for the United States to fight Great Britain should that country show undue sympathy for the Confederacy. The recognition of Confederate belligerency[qv] before war had really begun—except the firing on Fort Sumter[qv]—gave Seward and Charles Francis Adams a tangible and even bitter grievance against both England and France. It resulted in Seward's issuing an ultimatum to England, threatening to break off diplomatic relations should England receive, even unofficially, the Confederate diplomatic agents. This grievance was constantly held up by Adams and Seward; and the launching of the Confederate cruisers (*see Alabama,* The; *Florida,* The; *Shenandoah,* The) and the building of the Confederate rams[qv] in England—and France—gave other even stronger grounds upon which the American diplomats could complain. The sale of munitions and the colossal blockade-running[qv] business carried on with the Confederacy furnished further and constant complaints, particularly against England. French intervention in Mexico[qv] was an added score against France. The piling up of grievances by the United States against France and England, particularly the latter, cannot be overlooked as a powerful factor in making these two Western European powers extremely cautious with reference to even friendly intervention in the Civil War. It helped create the very definite belief that intervention meant a declaration of war by the United States. As for war, neither France nor England cared to pay such a price to see the United States permanently divided. These grievances of the United States were used to counteract the grievances of England and France in the blockade of their West Indian ports and the seizure of their merchant vessels, under the doctrine of "ultimate destination,"[qv] hundreds of miles from the Confederate coast when apparently destined to neutral ports. England, of course, was glad to see the re-establishing of the paper blockade[qv] and the doctrine of ultimate destination; but the methods employed in the seizure and search of scores of vessels, including the *Trent*[qv], created deep resentment in England, and Adams and Seward cleverly used the *Alabama* claims[qv] and other similar grievances as counterirritants.

The objective of Confederate diplomacy was to obtain foreign assistance in gaining independence. The Confederate government based its plans upon European dependence upon Southern cotton, at first; and finally upon the well-known desire of England to see a powerful commercial rival weakened, and of Napoleon III to see the champion of the Monroe Doctrine[qv] rendered impotent to frustrate his attempted annexation of Mexico. The Confederacy first sent William L. Yancey, Pierre A. Rost and A. Dudley Mann as joint commissioners to obtain European aid and recognition. Later Yancey resigned, the commission was dissolved, Mann was sent to Belgium as permanent commissioner and Rost to Spain. James M. Mason and John Slidell—taken prisoner by Wilkes and later released by the Federal Government on the demand of Great Britain—were sent to Great Britain and France respectively as Confederate diplomatic agents. The Confederacy sent John T. Pickett to the Juarez government in Mexico and Juan Quintero to the government of Santiago Vadaurri, governor-dictator of Nuevo Leon and virtual ruler of several of the neighboring border states of Mexico. The Confederate diplomats were ably supported by propagandist agents in both England and France. Edwin DeLeon and Henry Hotze were the chief propagandist agents. The Confederate diplomatic agents were informally received in May, 1861, in England; but after that Lord Russell refused even that much recognition under the pressure of Seward's ultimatum. However, the British government did continue to deal with the Confederate agents by means of correspondence. In Belgium, Spain, France, Mexico and even at the Vatican, Confederate diplomatic agents were received informally but freely. In fact, Slidell in France was on such good terms with Napoleon that the latter made a practice of intercepting messages to United States Minister Dayton for him.

The causes for the failure of the Confederacy to obtain foreign intervention were that the things to be gained by war on the part of England and France would not offset war losses. Europe had a surplus of cotton during the first year of the war; and after this surplus gave out, war profits, particularly in England, from cotton speculation, linen and woolen industries, munitions, blockade running and the destruction or transfer of the American merchant marine[qv] to British registry, dwarfed the losses among the cotton-mill operatives and removed the chief economic motives for intervention. It is also contended that the wheat famine in England made that country dependent upon the United States for its bread supply, and that this operated as an important factor in preserving the neutrality of the British.

[E. D. Adams, *Great Britain and the American Civil War;* E. M. Callahan, *Diplomatic History of the Southern Confederacy;* F. L. Owsley, *King Cotton Diplomacy.*]

FRANK L. OWSLEY

Civil War Munitions. The standard equipment of the Union Army was muzzle-loading Springfield or Enfield rifles and the type of cannon now so often found cluttering up courthouse lawns. Many early regiments, however, went to the front with nondescript arms of their own procuring. Other hundreds of thousands of rifles were furnished by contractors who took all the antiquated, castoff weapons which European governments could drag from the junk heaps of their armies. A large proportion of these, sold to the War Department at extravagant prices, had to be scrapped immediately. Others, which were issued to the soldiers, proved more dangerous to the man behind the breech than to the enemy before the muzzle. Before 1861 various American companies were making breech-loading repeating rifles which, by repeated testimony of experts, would fire fifteen times as rapidly as the best of muzzle-loaders, with equal accuracy and force, and with greater ease of manipulation. But the traditional backwardness of the War Department and its staff prevented the use of such improved weapons. All sorts of excuses, none of them valid, were conjured up against them. In the closing months of the war a new Chief of Ordnance, Alexander B. Dyer, equipped a few companies in the Southwest with repeating rifles, and with these weapons in their hands the men proved invincible. When the war was over the same arms were adopted for the regular army.

Throughout the war those persons responsible for its conduct preferred to set up huge armies with inferior guns to form a larger target for the enemy, rather than equip a smaller and more compact force with weapons of multiple effectiveness. Even Gatling guns[qv], firing 250 shots a minute with frightful precision, were dismissed in cavalier fashion. A dozen of them were supplied to Gen. B. F. Butler, whose men proved their merits. But again, the weapon was not adopted for general use till after the war. Following a few initial blunders there was not much difficulty in procuring a plentiful supply of good muzzle-loading guns, or of powder and shot.

The munitions of the Confederacy were inferior to those of the North. Battlefield captures, raiding expeditions, imports from Europe and an increasing production from Southern munitions plants kept the troops armed. Largely cut off by the blockade[qv] from European supplies, and with little industrial development, manufacturing plants had to be built and manned, and materials had to be obtained and prepared. While saltpeter and sulphur in the raw state were plentiful in the Confederacy, machinery and labor for conversion were generally lacking. Yet, in 1864, lead-smelting works, bronze foundries, a cannon foundry, rifle, carbine and pistol factories were operating (*see* Tredegar Iron Works). The big problem of supply was the lack of adequate transportation.

[F. A. Shannon, *Organization and Administration of the Union Army.*]

FRED A. SHANNON

Civil Works Administration, THE, was created by executive order in the winter of 1933–34 as a branch of the Federal Emergency Relief Administration[qv], in order to launch an emergency program of public works projects, for the purpose of re-employing some 4,000,000 persons at regular wages until they could be absorbed by the Public Works Administration[qv] or by private industry. This "civil works program" of local improvements required an abundance of labor and a minimum of materials, and included a wide variety of projects such as the maintenance and landscaping of roads and highways, repair of buildings and equipment of schools and universities, improvement of public parks and playgrounds, erosion control, pest control and the improvement of municipally owned water, gas and electric utilities. Public administrators, engineers and accountants handled the projects instead of private contractors, and the pay rolls were disbursed directly by the Federal Government. While critics occasionally questioned the social urgency of some of the projects, this experiment in public welfare temporarily boosted both the morale and the purchasing power of a large segment of population. About $900,000,000 was spent on this work, which was liquidated in the spring of 1934.

[F.E.R.A., *Monthly Reports,* December, 1933-July, 1934.]

MARTIN P. CLAUSSEN

Civilian Conservation Corps, UNITED STATES, is an organization created by acts of Congress March 31, 1933, and June 28, 1937, for the purpose of providing employment, particularly to young men, ages seventeen to twenty-three, who are unemployed and in need of employment, on projects which increase, preserve and restore the natural resources of the United States. The men enrolled in the Corps receive a basic cash allowance of $30 per month ($36 for assistant leaders and $45 for leaders), plus food, clothing, shelter, transportation, medical attention and education. They live in camps, each housing approximately 200 enrollees.

Approximately 200 major types of work are prosecuted on forest, park, agricultural and other types of lands. Indicative of the magnitude of the work is the fact that through March 31, 1939, approximately 8,500,000 man-days had been used in forest fire suppression and presuppression, more than 1,575,400,000 forest trees had been planted and 140,000 miles of roads and trails had been completed and maintained. Through March 31, 1939, approximately 2,180,000 men had served in the Civilian Conservation Corps (plus an additional 40,000 Indians and 20,000 territorials). Enrollment is for a period of six months, with a maximum service for young men of two years permissible.

[Annual Reports of the Civilian Conservation Corps.]

ROBERT FECHNER

Civilized Tribes, The Five. *See* Five Civilized Tribes.

Claiborne Settlement. Acting upon a trading license, William Claiborne established in 1631 a plantation upon Kent Island in the upper reaches of the Chesapeake Bay. The settlement was recognized as an outpost of Virginia and was represented in its General Assembly. This claim to prior occupation tended to invalidate Lord Baltimore's title according to the terms of the Maryland charter which passed the royal seal in 1632. In 1638 Gov. Calvert seized Kent Island, although during the civil war in England Claiborne temporarily regained control.

[M. P. Andrews, *Virginia, the Old Dominion;* J. H. Claiborne, *William Claiborne of Virginia.*]

MATTHEW PAGE ANDREWS

Claim Associations were frontier institutions designed to provide a quasi-legal land system in areas where no land law existed. Settlers who preceded the government surveyor into a new area and established their homes therein or who located on public land[qv] not yet offered at public auction sale made their improvements with no certainty of continued ownership. Before 1841 settlement in advance of survey and sale was contrary to law. Settlers had no protection against speculators buying their lands at the public auction; they had no protection against the "claim jumper"[qv] who sought to oust them and steal their improvements; nor had they means for registering, transferring or mortgaging their claims. Where squatters[qv] were fairly numerous it was natural that they should organize to protect their common interests. Claim associations or claim clubs appeared early in the 19th century and were found in practically every part of the public land area which received settlers before 1870. The squatters would come together, adopt a more or less stereotyped constitution or bylaws guaranteeing mutual protection to each claimant of 160 or 320 acres who met the simple requirements for improvements. Claim jumpers were dealt with in summary fashion by these associations. A "register" was selected who kept a record of all claims and their transfers, and a bidder was chosen to represent the group at the public auction sale.

The most important event in the life of the frontier was the government land auction and to it flocked the squatters, well armed and determined to defend their claims against any speculators who contemplated outbidding them. When the sale began, the bidder, flanked by the motley crowd of squatters, took a prominent position near the auctioneer, and as the squatters' sections were offered bid the government minimum price and no more. If higher bids were made, drastic action was at once taken, the offending speculator being treated as roughly as the claim jumper.

The claim associations' registry made it possible to buy and sell claims without the government patent and there frequently developed a large claim business, much of which was speculative. Early state and territorial law gave legal sanction to many of the practices of the associations, including the registering and transferring of claims. After the public auction and the establishment of state or territorial transfer laws the associations disappeared.

The Pre-emption Law of 1841[qv] legalized squatting upon surveyed lands and gave the settler the right of pre-empting his claim before the public sale, thereby protecting him against competitive bidding, but only if he could raise the funds to pay for the land. Claim associations were still necessary to give community sanction and force to the quasi land regulations in areas where no legal system existed. The heyday of the associations was in the 1840's and 1850's in Iowa, Kansas and Nebraska, where practically every township had its protective organization.

[B. H. Hibbard, *History of the Public Land Policies.*]

PAUL WALLACE GATES

Claim Jumper, The, was one who drove a squatter[qv] from his claim or, in his absence, seized it. Next to the horse thief he was the most detested person on the frontier. The squatter's only recourse was to appeal to the local claim association[qv], which undertook to rid the community of such undesirable characters.

[B. H. Hibbard, *History of the Public Land Policies.*]

PAUL WALLACE GATES

Claims, The Federal Court of, was created by Congress (1855) under its power to appropriate money to pay the debts of the United States. The court investigates contractual claims against the United States brought before the court by private parties, or referred to it by an executive department or by Congress. In some cases the decisions of the court are final, subject to appeal to the Supreme Court; in others, the court merely reports its findings to Congress or to the department concerned.

[F. W. Booth, The Court of Claims, *United States Daily,* Dec. 1, 3, 4, 5, 1928.]

P. ORMAN RAY

Clark, Fort (1813–19), was a frontier post erected, September, 1813, where Peoria, Ill., now stands. A wooden stockade mounting cannon, it was named in honor of George Rogers Clark. Although the force which built it withdrew before the end of 1813, it was garrisoned for at least considerable periods in 1814 and 1815. It was the scene of no serious conflicts, but it was an effective restraint upon hostile Indians during the War of 1812. Unoccupied, it was destroyed by Indians, partly in 1818, completely in 1819.

[E. E. East in *Peoria Journal-Transcript*, March 6, 1936, July 23, 1937.]

PAUL M. ANGLE

Clark, Fort (Mo.). *See* Osage, Fort.

Clark's Northwest Campaign (1778–79). During the early years of the Revolution the British exercised undisputed control over the country northwest of the Ohio River. Their most important center of influence was Detroit[qv], the headquarters of the posts and the key to the control of the fur trade and the Indian tribes. From Detroit emanated the influences which dominated the savages of the entire Northwest, and instigated the dispatching of uncounted war parties against the frontier settlements south of the Ohio. So terribly were the settlers of infant Kentucky harassed that they were considering abandoning the country altogether, when George Rogers Clark stepped forward as their leader and protector.

Clark perceived that Kentucky could best be defended by the conquest of Detroit, the center whence the raids were instigated. Too weak to make a frontal attack upon Detroit, or even upon Vincennes, he directed his first blow against the towns of the French in Illinois. Kaskaskia[qv] was occupied, July 4, 1778, and the remaining Illinois towns, and even Vincennes[qv], were easily persuaded to join the rebel standard. Upon learning of these developments, Lt. Gov. Hamilton of Detroit prepared to effect a counterstroke. Under great difficulties he marched upon Vincennes, which was retaken, Dec. 17; but instead of pushing on against Kaskaskia, Hamilton now dismissed his Indian allies and settled down for the winter.

The situation was thus placed in the balance and victory would favor the leader who struck first. Instantly perceiving this, Clark led his little army eastward across Illinois to tempt his fate at Vincennes. An untimely thaw flooded the prairies and drowned the river bottoms and the story of the difficulties encountered and vanquished surpasses many a flight of fiction. Even Clark himself said the recital of them would be too incredible for belief by any one not well acquainted with him.

A bullet through the breast of a British soldier apprised Hamilton of Clark's arrival. After an investment of thirty-six hours, Hamilton yielded his fort and garrison to the rebel leader, Feb. 24, 1779. Although Detroit, Clark's ultimate goal, was never attained, he retained his grip upon the southern end of the Northwest[qv] until the close of the war, and this possession proved an important factor in obtaining the Northwest for the United States in the Definitive Treaty of Peace of 1783.[qv]

[J. A. James, *Life of George Rogers Clark;* M. M. Quaife, *Capture of Old Vincennes.*]

M. M. QUAIFE

Class Struggle. The phrase "class struggle" refers to an alleged conflict between capitalist and wage-earning classes. The doctrine is identified with Karl Marx, founder of modern "scientific" socialism, who, with Friedrich Engels, first formally stated the concept in the *Communist Manifesto,* written in 1848 for the League of Communists. Marx contended that the determining factors of social evolution are economic, that the nature and functioning of social institutions—legal, political, religious, moral and literary—are in every epoch determined by the prevailing modes of production, exchange and distribution of wealth.

In this materialistically determined historical development, subsequent to the primitive community landownership, there has been a series of relentless class wars. Always the exploited, dispossessed class has rebelled against the possessing, exploiting class which is constantly fashioning new forms of production that are irreconcilable with existing forms. Thus feudalism was destroyed by the bourgeoisie and capitalism is expected to be overthrown by the revolutionary proletariat. The historical struggle is to culminate in a society freed from exploitation, oppression, class distinctions and class struggles.

The theory of the class struggle has been a dynamic influence in radical movements in every country. In the United States such organizations as the Socialist Labor party (1877), Social Democracy of America (1897), the Socialist party of America (1901), the Industrial Workers of the World (1905), the Communist party (1919), and the Communist Labor party[qqv] (1919) have been constructed around this theory. The national socialist movements of various countries have organized international workingmen's associations, including the First International (London, 1864); the Second International (Paris, 1889); and the Third International (Moscow, 1919).

[Karl Marx and Friedrich Engels, *Communist Manifesto;* H. W. Laidler, *The History of Socialist Thought.*]

GORDON S. WATKINS

Clayton Act of 1914, THE, was the result of a growing conviction that the Sherman Antitrust Law[qv] of 1890 did not reach some important evils of big business. The Sherman law was leveled mainly at the evils of monopoly and restraint of trade, and at the time it was passed the dominant method of combination was the business trust, where properties were transferred to trustees, a legal form different from the corporation[qqv]. In the years after the Sherman law, combinations began to organize as holding companies, interlocking directorates[qqv], under trade agreements of various kinds, and eventually as aggregations of nonrelated industries. A new situation had developed which the Clayton Act and the Federal Trade Commission Act[qv], passed the same year, were designed to cover. The Clayton law provided mainly prohibitions against practices which "substantially tended to lessen competition," or "substantially" tended to create monopoly, such as discrimination in prices among different producers, acquisition of stock by one company in another, the use of interlocking directorates where restraint was involved, and under certain conditions, a similar provision relative to banks. Another clause placed restrictions on the relation of common carriers to construction and supply companies. In some respects the rigors of the Sherman law were relaxed with respect to labor and agricultural organizations. In regard to labor, in some jurisdictions certain customary activities of unions were interpreted as restraints of trade. It was provided in the Clayton Act that nothing in the Federal antitrust statutes was to be construed to prohibit the existence of "labor, agricultural, or horticultural organizations, instituted for the purposes of mutual help . . . or to forbid or restrain individual members . . . from lawfully carrying out the legitimate objects thereof." Section 20 of the law prohibited the use of restraining orders or injunctions[qv] "unless necessary to prevent irreparable injury to property, or to a property right, of the party making the application, for which injury there is no adequate remedy at law."

[J. M. Clark, *Social Control of Business;* E. W. Crecraft, *Government and Business;* L. H. Haney, *Business Organization and Combination.*]

ISAAC LIPPINCOTT

Clayton-Bulwer Treaty, THE (1850), was a compromise arrangement resulting from the conflicting interests of Great Britain and the United States in Central America. In the late 1840's Great Britain, on the basis of claims dating from the 18th century, was occupying the Bay Islands, which belonged to Honduras, and also the eastern coast of Central America, as "protector" of the pseudo-kingdom of the Mosquito Indians (*see* Mosquito Question). After war broke out between the United States and Mexico the British government quickly saw that the assured American victory would stimulate American interest in a ship canal across the isthmus (*see* Squier Treaty). Therefore, on Jan. 1, 1848, British authorities, acting for the Mosquito king, seized the mouth of the San Juan River, the logical eastern terminus of any future canal in the region.

Strained relations at once developed between the two governments, though each assured the other that it had no selfish designs on the transit route. Negotiations in England having failed to end the dispute, Sir Henry Bulwer was sent to Washington, where, with Secretary of State John M. Clayton, he negotiated the treaty which bears their names. This provided that the two countries should jointly control and protect the canal which it was expected would soon be built somewhere on the isthmus. The introductory article, drafted by Clayton with the aim of ousting the British from Central America, pledged the two countries not to "occupy, or fortify, or colonize, or assume or exercise any dominion over Nicaragua, Costa Rica, the Mosquito Coast, or any part of Central America." The agreement was ratified July 4, 1850.

Almost immediately, however, the interpretation of the self-denying clause just mentioned became the subject of a bitter dispute between the two governments. The United States held that the pledge not to "occupy" required that Great Britain withdraw. The British replied that if the agreement had been intended to be retroactive this fact would have been definitely stated; and they failed to get out of the Bay Islands and the Mosquito territory. War again threatened, but Great Britain, valuing her cotton trade with the United States more than she did her claims in Central America, finally acquiesced in the American interpretation and withdrew in 1858–60.

The Clayton-Bulwer Treaty had become very unpopular in the United States, however, and when, after several decades, the canal was still unbuilt, popular demand grew for abrogation of the agreement, to make possible construction of an American-controlled canal. Finally, in 1902, the Hay-Pauncefote Treaty[qv] superseded the Clayton-Bulwer arrangement.

Critics have correctly charged that the latter, by taking Great Britain into American partnership in controlling the proposed canal, violated the spirit of the Monroe Doctrine[qv]. But it should be noted that the United States, by insisting upon a retroactive interpretation of the treaty, forced the British to give up long-existing territorial claims, which was a unique triumph for the Doctrine.

[M. W. Williams, *Anglo-American Isthmian Diplomacy, 1815-1915;* same, John Middleton Clayton, in *The American Secretaries of State and Their Diplomacy*, S. F. Bemis, ed., Vol. VI.]

MARY WILHELMINE WILLIAMS

Clayton Compromise, THE (1848), was the name given the plan drawn up by a bipartisan Senate committee headed by John M. Clayton for organizing Oregon and the Southwest. It excluded slavery from Oregon, prohibited the territorial legislatures of New Mexico and California from acting on slavery, and provided for appeal of all slavery cases from the territorial courts to the Supreme Court of the United States. It passed the Senate July 27, 1848, but was tabled in the House.

[G. P. Garrison, *Westward Extension, 1841-1850.*]

MARY WILHELMINE WILLIAMS

Clearing Houses. The first formal provision for a clearing-house association in the United States, that of New York City, was adopted on Sept. 13, 1853, by thirty-eight New York banks, and the first clearing of checks took place on Oct. 11. Clearing houses were subsequently established by the banks of Boston (1856), Philadelphia (1858), Chicago (1865) and St. Louis (1868). From the latter date on, growth in the number of clearing houses was rapid, with the result that associations of this character were soon to be found in all of the larger and a considerable number of smaller cities. At the time of reopening the banks, following the banking crisis of 1933[qv], there were more than 250 clearing-house cities in the United States.

Although the ostensible reason for the organization of clearing houses has been the clearing of checks, many of these associations have performed valuable collateral functions. Among the latter may be noted: (1) rendering assistance to weaker members in times of stress, (2) fixing uniform rates of interest and uniform collection charges, (3) examining members of the association and publishing statements of condition and volume of clearings, (4) gathering credit data for members and (5) issuing clearing-house loan certificates in times of strain.

A number of these functions were of more significance prior to the establishment of the Federal Reserve system[qv] than they have been since. In the fifty years prior to the World War, it is safe to say that the clearing-house associations of the United States were among the most efficient and valuable agencies connected with the conduct of American banking. Since 1914, various banking reforms have somewhat diminished the importance of their collateral functions. Nevertheless, clearing-house associations still continue to play an indispensable part in the operation of the American banking system.

[J. G. Cannon, *Clearing Houses;* W. E. Spahr, *The Clearing and Collection of Checks.*]

FREDERICK A. BRADFORD

Clearwater River, Battle on (July 11–13, 1877). During the Joseph campaign the hostile Nez Percé[qv] Indians under Joseph, White Bird and Toohulhulsote withdrew from Craig's Mountain and established camp on the Clearwater River, west of Kamiah, Idaho. Gen. O. O. Howard attacked with infantry, cavalry and artillery. The latter was ineffective. The battle was marked by charges and countercharges and established Joseph's position as head war chief. The Indian barricades were eventually carried and the Indians driven in retreat past Kamiah to the Lolo trail leading into Montana.

[H. H. Bancroft, *History of Washington, Idaho and Montana.*]

WILLIAM S. LEWIS

Clermont, THE (1807). *See* "Fulton's Folly."

Cleveland, Ohio. A trading post was located at the mouth of the Cuyahoga River as early as 1786; in the same year an Indian village named Pilgerruh was founded by three Moravian[qv] missionaries on a site ten or twelve miles upstream. In 1796 Moses Cleaveland, agent of the Connecticut Land Company[qv], which had acquired from Connecticut a large part of the Western Reserve[qv], laid out a town which was given his name. Granted a township government in 1800, made the seat of the new county of Cuyahoga in 1810, incorporated as a village in 1814, Cleveland in 1836 began its history as an incorporated city with a population of about 4000. Originally important commercially only as a post on the route from Pittsburgh to Detroit, with the opening of the Ohio Canal[qv]—to Akron in 1827 and to the Ohio River in 1832—it became an increasingly important outlet for products of the interior of the state, and for the Pennsylvania, West Virginia and Ohio coal that was soon brought in quantity to smelt the iron ore shipped from the Lake Superior mines. A railroad development, ambitiously planned in the 1830's but not realized until the 1850's, made additional contributions to the important iron industry of the Civil War period, since which time Cleveland has had the history of a rapidly expanding industrial city.

ARTHUR C. COLE

Cleveland Democrats, THE, were those Democrats who in Cleveland's second administration continued to support him after silverites, high-tariff men and other dissident elements had broken from his leadership. His insistence upon repeal of the Sherman Silver Purchase Act[qv] in 1893 and veto of the bill to coin the silver seigniorage on May 27, 1894, aroused an anger among the free-silver Democrats of the West and South which his successive bond issues to preserve the gold standard[qv] (1894–95) increased; his fight with a senatorial group over the Wilson Tariff Bill[qv], ending in an outspoken denunciation of their "perfidy," estranged protectionist Democrats; and he had the abiding ill will of Tammany[qv] members and David B. Hill's followers. In the Democratic National Convention of 1896 the Cleveland Democrats, led by William C. Whitney and William E. Russell, were decisively defeated (*see* Campaign of 1896); their refusal to accept the result brought about the formation of the National Democratic ("Gold Democratic"[qv]) party.

[Allan Nevins, *Grover Cleveland, A Study in Courage.*]

ALLAN NEVINS

Cliff Dwellers, THE, were a prehistoric race of Indians who built their dwellings under overhanging cliffs in rocky canyon walls. Most of the cliff dwellings are found within a hundred miles radius of the point where the boundaries of Colorado, Utah, New Mexico and Arizona meet. However, some have been reported as far north as Lodore Canyon, Colorado, and as far south as Sierra Madre, Mexico. The most important groups of these ruins are being preserved at Mesa Verde National Park. Other groups have been declared national monuments, e.g., Canyon de Chelly, Hovenweep, Montezuma Castle, Walnut Canyon and Navajo.

The cliff dwellers were an agricultural people raising corn, beans, melons and turkeys. Cisterns, ollas or water jars and irrigation systems give evidence of their struggle against an arid climate. The attacks of roving Indian enemies, disease, superstition and an increased aridity in the region caused the complete abandonment of these dwellings before the white man discovered America. Some of the present-day Pueblo Indians[qv] may be their descendants.

The cliff dwellings vary from single isolated rooms to large communal villages built solid to the roof of the cave. Several are three and four stories containing over 100 rooms. They are built of stone, much of it quarried and hewn with stone hammers, and adobe mortar and plaster. Many of the lower chambers are circular ceremonial rooms called kivas. Ceilings are timbered and these timbers enabled Dr. Douglass with his tree ring[qv] calendar definitely to date these ruins between 919 and 1273 A.D.

The dwellings are hundreds of feet above the floor of the canyon. Their inaccessibility made them safer from attack by enemies. Further protection was furnished by tall watchtowers built on the top of the mesas overlooking the canyons.

[F. H. Chapin, *The Land of the Cliff Dwellers;* National Park Service, *Mesa Verde National Park.*]

PERCY S. FRITZ

Climate. The influence of climate upon American history has been both economic and biological. Economic effects, such as variations in crops, are widely recognized as important historical factors. Biological effects, such as regional differences in human health and activity, have received little recognition. One of the obvious economic effects of climate has arisen through disasters, such as the floods[qv] of the Mississippi (1927) and Ohio (1936), the hurricanes[qv] that wrecked Galveston (1900) and Miami (1926) and the "Big Freeze" that put an end to orange growing in northern Florida (1894–95). Far more important, though less spectacular, is the way in which drought[qv] has repeatedly plunged thousands of families into poverty in the dry western plains, and has led to migration on a large scale. The great droughts of 1933–36 actually led California temporarily to flout the Constitution by excluding American citizens who came from the ruined "Dust Bowl"[qv] farther east. During the 19th century each major drought was followed by a major financial depression. Crop failures strained an imperfect financial structure to the breaking point. They have also been a powerful incentive to political agitation, as in the Populist Movement[qv] for free silver (1896). In fact, repeated droughts have tended to make the drier parts of the Great Plains[qv] a political hotbed, especially in North Dakota and Alberta, where unseasonable frosts combine with droughts to make the crops unreliable.

The effect of climate upon the health of man is even more important than its effect on the health of crops. Both effects depend upon the biological law that every living creature has an *optimum* climate, and cannot be at its best in any other. The best climate for human progress, however, depends upon the optimum not only for (1) health, but for (2) the suppression of dangerous parasitic organisms of all sorts, (3) the production of abundant crops with no danger of shortage, (4) the growth of plants supplying a wholesome diet for man and beast, as well as valuable raw materials and (5) freedom from disasters due to drought, flood, storm, etc. In the long run the first of these criteria, health, appears to be the most important. Where climate has the best direct effect upon health, however, it also ranks high in the other criteria. Putting all these conditions together we find the best American climates in three strips; namely, (1) the Atlantic coast from Maine to Maryland; (2) the southern Great Lakes region; (3) the Pacific coast from Puget Sound to southern California. The Pacific strip maintains its distinctive character for scarcely a hundred miles inland. The two eastern strips merge into a large peripheral area of good, but slightly less perfect climate. The strips and the peripheral area together extend from the Maritime Provinces, New England and New Jersey westward to the Mississippi and beyond. The best part of South America, in central Argentina, Uruguay and central Chile, is comparable to the edges of this peripheral area.

Historically, this distribution of climate has been of primary importance. It appears to be a main determinant of the general distribution of intensive agriculture, manufacturing, cities and the development of literature, education and science. Among the forty largest cities of America, eighteen (averaging 1,200,000 in population) lie directly in the narrow strips defined above, fourteen (700,000) in the eastern peripheral region and the corresponding part of South America, and only eight (700,000) in the remaining 95% of the two continents. Coal, waterways and land routes have influenced the situation of the cities, but climate is the main factor in their general location. The areas of favorable climate carry on practically all the more complex manufacturing industries. Only such relatively simple occupations as the making of cotton cloth and the preparation of raw materials for market, or such purely local industries as railroad yards, garages, printing establishments and bakeries are greatly developed outside the limits of the climates which closely approach the human optimum. For this reason the northeastern quarter of the United States, with an adjacent bit of Canada, forms a conspicuous historical unit which has often been politically at odds with other climatic areas, as in the case of its desire for a protective tariff[qv].

The northern parts of New England, New York, Michigan and Wisconsin, with adjacent parts of Canada, form another distinct climatic province. There the relatively conservative agricultural and commercial life is different from the hurry and bustle of the manufacturing zone. The fact that Maine and Vermont were the only Republican states in 1936 and that Quebec is the most conservative part of Canada illustrates the matter. Other factors of course play a large part in this, but the long, snowy and comparatively idle winters, the cool, short and very busy summers, the limited variety of crops and the difficulties imposed by cold weather upon machinery and transportation all combine to prevent such restless activity as is found in New York. Many people, to be sure, ascribe this difference to purely cultural causes. The geographer, however, finds that all over the world human society tends strongly to be organized in harmony with the physical environment. Cultural tendencies which are in harmony with the climate tend to persist, whereas tendencies which are at variance with the climate are sloughed off.

The Southern states illustrate this same point in a third climatic region. The development there of a small colonial aristocracy among a far larger number of poor white farmers was absolutely in harmony with the climate and with the plants which grow best in that climate. So, too, were the development of slavery[qv], the Civil War and the present contrast between North and South. Just as the long, cold winters act as a damper upon human activity in Quebec, so the long, hot summers act as a damper in the South. The heat does not make it impossible for white men to carry on manual labor in the South as many people suppose. The health of white men there, and in even warmer climates, is actually improved by working out of doors. Nevertheless, prolonged heat creates a strong disinclination to work. Therefore, the person who can refrain from work and enjoy the fruits of others' labor is envied. Hence the prevalent ideal has been to have some one else do the work, whereas in the most favored zone the social system is built around the physical fact that during most of the year the climate makes people feel like working.

Add now to this the influence of crops which thrive in the South but not in the North. In colonial days rice and especially tobacco, and in later times cotton[qqv], were crops of this kind that could be very profitably exported. They demand a far greater amount of monotonous labor in the hot sun than do corn, wheat and oats. Therefore, the urge to use indentured labor or slaves was far greater than in the North. At the same time, the warm climate made it possible to keep such labor at work most of the year, and to support it at relatively small expense.

Thus in the South the biological effect of climate upon man and plants encouraged slavery and a social system which sharply distinguished between aristocratic slave-holding land owners and poor men with little land and no slaves. It would not be correct to say that the Civil War was caused by the climatic difference between North and South, but the conditions which caused the war could not have developed as they did if the climatic influences, both economic and biological, had been different. Although slavery is now gone, the disinclination to work engendered by prolonged heat still makes it more difficult in the South than in the North to become a skilled mechanic, or inventor, or to make progress in education, literature, science, industry and social organization. Thus, to the climatologist it appears inevitable that the historic development of the two sections will continue to be different.

West of these three eastern climatic regions lies the widely extended belt of grassy plains where deficiency of moisture prevents the growth of trees. There the extremes of heat and cold, moisture and drought are very great. Hence, not only are the crops unreliable, but the density of population is small and the market for manufactured goods is both small and unreliable. Moreover, the people often feel that they may move on at any time, and there is constant talk of political and economic change. These conditions create a social and economic atmosphere unfavorable to manufacturing. Thus, from far north in Canada to the borders of Mexico we have a long climatic province dependent mainly upon grain and cattle[qv]. Its problems are bound to be very different from those of either the East or the Far West.

Still farther westward the Rocky Mountain region is characterized not only by mining, but by dry climatic conditions which find expression in irrigation[qv] and in the raising of cattle or sheep. Hence, a very scanty population is either grouped in small and isolated units, or widely scattered on ranches. One historical effect of this has been to permit the Mormons[qv] to develop a unique social system almost unhampered by their neighbors. Another has been to separate the narrow strip of unusual climate along the Pacific coast from the rest of the country. Dryness has done more than mountains to preserve this separation. The rapid development of wealth, industry, science, education and new social movements on the Pacific coast could scarcely have followed its actual course without the help of the stimulating coastal climate and the isolation arising from the dryness of the Rocky Mountain area and the western plains.

North and south of the regions thus far described lie other huge climatic provinces. One of these, embracing most of Canada and Alaska, has had relatively little effect on history. Another, on the south, has been extremely important. When Columbus set sail from Spain the steady trade winds led him to hold a somewhat southerly course. For a hundred years thereafter most of the ships coming to America were similarly influenced by this climatic feature. Hence, Europe established contact with America in low latitudes, and in the part of the continent where the climate most favored the development of a relatively high primitive culture. On the plateaus of Mexico and Peru the dominant climatic elements are a warm, but not hot, summer with abundant rain, and a mild winter so dry that neither forests nor turfy grass will thrive. Hence the land is naturally free from forests without the help of the axe. Moreover, it is easy to cultivate. Not only are the grasses of a bunchy type which can easily be pulled up by hand, but summer floods from small mountain streams provide natural irrigation. In such a region agriculture is practicable even with no tools except a pointed stick and a clamshell or shoulder blade of a deer. More important still, this particular kind of climate was especially favorable to corn[qv], which is the outstanding native food plant of America. Then, too, the Mexican and Peruvian highlands, although depressingly monotonous, are so high and cool that they are fairly healthful and conducive to work. The enervating climate of the neighboring lowlands, either directly or through diet and disease, apparently had much to do with the decay of the Maya civilization after its brilliant intrusion from the highlands. In the highlands, the climate made it permanently possible for agriculture to become the foundation for a genuine civilization, with well established towns, regular trade routes, and many features of an advanced culture.

The presence of these relatively civilized people had an almost immeasurable effect on the early history of America. It determined the regions where the Spaniards could profitably search for gold and where they finally settled. It made it easy for them to master the Indians and make slaves of them. In climates where prolonged heat or monotony has an enervating effect people tend to alternate strongly between activity and careless indifference. In the best climates, on the contrary, people tend to be steadily active without great ups and downs. This is one of the most important climatic effects. Even in the highlands the tendency of the tropical Indians to relax after a brief effort assisted the Spaniards not only in conquering them, but in enslaving them. The enslavement resulted in extermination, or more often, in intermarriage. Thus there arose a new racial type, which has had a large share in determining the later history of Latin America.

One of the most interesting illustrations of the effect of climate upon history is found in the contrast between the relatively submissive Indians of tropical America and the warlike Indians farther north. The most virile of the latter may be represented by the Iroquois[qv] of New York who lived in the most stimulating climate of America. In harmony with this they were characterized by intense and constant activity, alertness and persistence. Such qualities, to be sure, depend on inheritance and training, but they are intensified by a climate where strong, but not undue contrasts of weather from day to day and season to season engender a state of nervous tension and at the same time promote physical health. In our own day, as we have seen, the climate from New England and New Jersey westward makes people always want to "do something," even if they have not fully thought out a plan. Indian wars and raids were an expression of a similar feeling, and in this respect were parallel to the feverish rush of modern New York and Chicago.

The quality thus expressed was an important element in delaying the settlement of the best part of North America and later in keeping the French out of what is now the United States. It also found expression in a surprisingly advanced form of political organization. It could not express itself in what is commonly called civilization because the climate which is best for human efficiency renders a fully sedentary, agricultural life impossible so long as iron tools are unknown. Without such tools extensive clearings cannot be made among the hardwood trees which are here dominant, and even a small field quickly becomes useless because choked with grass. Although the persistent energy of the Iroquois was thus denied expression along the lines of material culture, it was free politically. The Iroquois League with its representative form of organization was the highest expression of political capacity ever reached by the Indians. It enjoyed an extraordinary duration of two centuries (approximately 1570–1780). It is very doubtful whether it could have flourished so well in a less favorable climate, just as it is doubtful whether Harvard and Yale would hold their present prestige if they had always been located in an unstimulating climate.

This brings us to a final generalization as to the relation between climate and American history. Although many other factors introduce modifications, the degree of political stability varies as a rule in close harmony with the climate. The most stable portions of North America are the Northern states and southern Canada. The Southern states have staged one great uprising against the general government. Farther south we find Mexico repeatedly in the throes of revolution, and the governments of Central America, Colombia and Venezuela are still more unstable—not that revolutions necessarily occur in all tropical climates, but a tropical climate, even when fairly cool by reason of altitude, tends to break down people's self control, and make their activity spasmodic. When excited, they act too hastily, and then, becoming quickly exhausted, they submit to misgovernment without making persistent and effective efforts to correct it. Another historical effect of climate that must be noted is the remarkable contrast between the British who settled in southern New England from 1630 to 1643 and the larger number who settled at practically the same time in the West Indies. The first group, in a stimulating healthful climate, has progressed and increased. The other, in an unfavorable climate, has diminished not only in numbers, but in influence.

[Ellsworth Huntington, *Civilization and Climate; The Red Man's Continent*, in The Chronicles of America; and *World Power and Evolution;* Edward J. Payne, *History of the New World*, Vols. I and II; A. Grenfell Price, *White Settlers in the Tropics.*]

ELLSWORTH HUNTINGTON

Clinton and Montgomery, Forts, Capture of. *See* Highlands, The, 1777–81.

Clinton Riot, The, Sept. 4, 1875, was one of the worst disturbances during Reconstruction[qv] in Mississippi. Four whites and an undetermined number of Negroes were killed. It is important because President Grant refused to send the Army, thus allowing the whites to discard Radical Reconstruction.

[Charles Hillman Brough, The Clinton Riot, *Publications of the Mississippi Historical Society*, Vol. VI.]

MACK SWEARINGEN

Clipper Ships were long and narrow wooden sailing vessels, with lofty canvas. Their era lasted for a quarter of a century, from about 1843 to 1868, and gave to the world the greatest development of the sailing ship in speed and beauty. The word "clipper" has its origin, perhaps, in the verb "clip," meaning to run swiftly. The clipper ships were designed to do just that thing.

Tea from China quickly lost its flavor in the hold of a ship, and about 1843 the clippers began quicker delivery of that product. The discovery of gold in California[qv] induced many in the decade from 1849 to 1859 to take the voyage around Cape Horn[qv] in fast clipper ships. After carrying their cargoes of men and merchandise to California, the ships would either return to Atlantic ports for another such cargo, or would cross the Pacific to China in ballast, and load there with tea, silk and spices (*see* China Trade). The discovery of gold in Australia in 1851 also gave a great impetus to the building of clipper ships.

They were much more dependable than the old-type sailing vessel. In a heavy sea they strained less and were thus able to take better care of their cargoes; and they crossed belts of calm better than the low-rigged ships. The swift brigs and schooners built at Baltimore during the War of 1812 were known as Baltimore clippers[qv]; but the first real clipper was the *Ann McKim,* built there in 1832. Beginning about 1850 the California clippers increased rapidly in size, ranging from 1500 to 2000 tons register. Of this type the *Stag-Hound,* built in Boston in 1850, was the pioneer. Six of the clipper ships established speed records that have never been broken. Practically all of them were faster than the steamships of their day, and it was more than a quarter of a century before the steamship was able to break the record of the fastest clippers. Their great speed is attested by the fact that eighteen ships made passages from New York or Boston to San Francisco in less than 100 days. The four best passages were made by the *Flying Cloud*[qv], built in Boston in 1851, in 89, 89, 105 and 108 days, an average of 97¾ days. Then came the *Andrew Jackson,* built at Mystic, Conn., in 1855, in 89, 100, 102 and 103 days, an average of 98½ days. Those records were followed by the *Flying Fish,* built in Boston in 1851, in 92, 98, 105 and 106 days, an average of 100¼ days.

By 1855 the "extreme" clippers were succeeded by the "medium" clippers, vessels that did not carry so much canvas, but that could be handled by a smaller crew. Shortly after the close of the Civil War, American shipbuilding for oversea carrying trade declined. Although some clipper ships were built, the steamships[qv] gradually displaced them.

[A. H. Clark, *The Clipper Ship Era;* O. T. Howe and F. C. Matthews, *American Clipper Ships, 1835-1858;* Helen La Grange, *Clipper Ships of America and Great Britain, 1833-1869.*]

CHARLES GARRETT VANNEST

Clockmaking. Clocks were brought to America by the early settlers, and contemporary colonial artisans repaired them and probably made new ones. By the 18th century, at least, both household timepieces and belfry clocks were made to order. Fine examples of these are still cherished by collectors. Connecticut, whose population was outgrowing its agricultural resources before the Revolution, early developed several mechanical industries, including clockmaking. Its craftsmen received their skill from Holland, through New York, as well as from Great Britain. Finer timepieces had metal works, but wooden clocks were made in America soon after 1700. Being cheaper, they were in more demand and until the middle 1830's dominated the market. Itinerant vendors, like "Sam Slick,"[qv] peddled them, with tinware, through the country. Works were often sold separately from cases, and the more democratic shelf clocks supplanted the tall eight-day clocks of our grandfathers in the homes of the people. Even these, however, were long a luxury, the cheapest models costing fifteen dollars.

In the Connecticut Valley the use of interchangeable parts[qv] soon suggested itself to clockmakers, and early in the last century power machinery assembled in factories was used to shape wheels and other parts. Then quantity production began. The fact that Connecticut was already a brassworking center facilitated the transition to that metal. As a result American clocks, which could not be exported as long as they had wooden works affected by atmospheric changes, were soon sold throughout the world at prices incredibly low to foreigners. A long step toward this was the invention, about 1837, of one-day brass clocks, which could be manufactured for six dollars; in 1855 they were made to sell for seventy-five cents.

Notable pioneers who invented improvements which simplified and cheapened the American product were Ely Terry, who began making wooden clocks at Waterbury in 1793 and built up an extensive business at Thomaston, where the Seth Thomas clocks were subsequently manufactured; and Chauncey Jerome, once employed by Terry, who became the first large exporter and whose works developed into the New Haven Clock Company. Even earlier a family named Willard built up a business at Roxbury, Mass., which sold tall striking clocks and public timepieces in all parts of the country.

Steamboats and railroads made timepieces more necessary, foretelling the modern multiplication of time signaling and recording devices. It was not until the beginning of the present century, however, that electric clocks appeared prominently in manufacturing statistics.

Today about 10,000,000 clocks are made annually in the United States as compared with 10,000 in the first decade of the last century. More than 2,000,000 are electric clocks and nearly 7,000,000 alarm clocks. Connecticut still leads in this manufacture, followed by Illinois, Massachusetts and New York. Exports no longer play as important a part as formerly, though a half million or more alarm clocks are sold annually to foreigners.

[Chauncey Jerome, *History of American Clock Business;* Henry Terry, *American Clock Making;* William G. Lathrop, *The Brass Industry in the United States.*]

VICTOR S. CLARK

Closed Shop, THE. Demands that employers hire only union members arose at an early date. Such union rules appeared as early as 1799. Closed-shop demands in 1836 were attacked in the courts as conspiracies. Although in Commonwealth v. Hunt[qv] (1842), which legalized unions, the Massachusetts court upheld a closed-shop strike, even in 1939 a Federal court questioned the validity of such a strike. The National Labor Relations Act[qv] (1935) permits such agreements between employers and unions.

Campaigns for the closed shop were carried on by many unions after 1870. As union organization proceeded several types of arrangement relative to the employment of union men developed, among which were the open–union shop in which both union and nonunion men are employed, but the union is recognized and dealt with, as with the Congress of Industrial Organizations[qv] unions in the steel and automobile industries after 1937. The chief type of closed shop has been the closed shop with the open union. Here nonunion workers may be hired, but all subsequently must join the union. This policy, found among garment trades unions and the United Mine Workers[qv], characterizes unions in seasonal and competitive industries. The closed shop with the closed union, which permits the employer to hire only union men, has characterized the building and other trades in which skilled workers control and limit their supply.

Employers have usually resisted recognition of unions and the closed-shop demands. So-called open-shop drives, embarked upon by American employers, appeared about the beginning of the 20th century. After 1886 gains of many unions had forced employers to deal with labor organizations. About 1900 strong employer associations undertook an open-shop drive, or an antiunion campaign to restrain further union growth and throw off union control. Again, subsequent to the World War, during which organized labor made great headway, a nationwide campaign for the so-called American Plan, actually a drive for the open shop, began. This was prosecuted to the New Deal[qv] period.

[Commons and associates, *History of Labor in the United States;* C. R. Daugherty, *Labor Problems in American Industry;* L. Lorwin, *The American Federation of Labor.*]

HERBERT MAYNARD DIAMOND

Closure is a technical term in legislative procedure, applied to rules for the limitation of debate. The House of Representatives, because of its large membership, has found it necessary to curtail speeches by resorting to the five-minute rule with permission for a member to extend his remarks in the *Congressional Record*[qv], as a substitute for free debate. In 1917 the Senate adopted a mild closure rule which provided a one-hour limit for speeches when, upon petition signed by sixteen senators, the rule was invoked by a two-thirds vote. Since this rule did not prevent a filibuster near the end of the session nor "unrestrained garrulity" at other times, Vice-President Dawes in 1925 vigorously advocated reform; but nothing has yet (1939) been done to strengthen the 1917 rule. The only form of closure generally in use in state legislatures arises from motions for special orders, or for the previous question.

[Robert Luce, *Legislative Procedure;* W. F. Willoughby, *Principles of Legislative Organization and Administration.*]

W. BROOKE GRAVES

Coahuila and Texas, State of. On May 7, 1824, the Mexican Congress which established the federal system in Mexico united the former Spanish provinces of Coahuila and Texas, declaring that Texas might become a state when it acquired the necessary population and resources. The state was governed by a governor, a lieutenant governor, and a unicameral legislature of twelve members, in which Texas had first one member and ultimately three. The state constitution, effective in 1827, permitted a considerable degree of local political independence, but in state legislation and administration Texans were at a disadvantage. The union was ended by the Texas revolution[qv].

[G. P. Garrison, *Texas.*]

E. C. BARKER

Coal. *See* Anthracite; Bituminous.

Coal Mining and Organized Labor. One of the first coal miners' labor organizations in this highly seasonal industry, was a local unit formed in 1849. The American Miners' Association was formed in St. Louis in 1861, succeeded by the Miners' National Association founded at Youngstown, Ohio, in 1873, which was, in turn, succeeded by the National Federation of Miners in 1885. This latter organization, affiliated with the Knights of Labor[qv] in 1890, became one of the constituent elements of the United Mine Workers[qv].

The growth of the mine union movement was coincident with the growth of business and manufacturing. Labor was beginning to become articulate and to demand a larger share of the profits of industry. A strike in 1894 nearly destroyed the new miners' union, but one in 1897 in the bituminous coal[qv] field was successful and one in the anthracite[qv] field in 1902 gave the union bargaining power. By means of joint agreements with coal operators, wages, hours and working conditions were gradually improved and standardized. Union recognition and the check-off[qv] followed. Strikes, particularly in the bituminous field, were more frequent and increasingly bitter (*see* Colorado Coal Strikes; Herrin Massacre). As a result of concessions due to World War demands, the union had been able greatly to strengthen its bargaining power. The depression of 1920–21, with accompanying reduction in wages, produced a wave of strikes, particularly in West Virginia and in Indiana, Illinois, Kentucky and Kansas. In the prosperous years that followed, as wages were increased, hours shortened and working conditions improved, production costs increased. This was accompanied by an increase in captive (steel- and railroad-owned) mines, by consolidations with consequent elimination of small operators, and by increasing substitution of gas, oil and electricity for coal.

The World War had caused much more coal land to be opened for production than was needed to meet peace-time requirements. As in agriculture, the supply far exceeded the demand; there were too many mines and too many miners; increasing substitution of other fuels aggravated an already bad condition. Each time coal production costs increased, consumer substitution, likewise, increased. And so demand and supply fluctuated up and down with voluntary or forced adjustments, either by worker or operator or both. The New Deal[qv], in response particularly to the demands of the United Mine Workers, sought to stabilize and control the coal industry, first through the National Recovery Act and then by the Guffey Coal Acts[qqv], but this legislation neither increased the total volume of coal consumed nor the number of miners employed. Because of the conditions prevailing in the industry, which are so difficult to control or to anticipate, the miners have striven to secure an agreement guaranteeing an annual wage, but, as yet (1939), nothing in this direction has been agreed on.

[C. Evans, *History of the United Mine Workers.*]

THOMAS ROBSON HAY

Coast and Geodetic Survey, THE UNITED STATES (formerly designated as Survey of the Coast, and United States Coast Survey). When first proposed by President Jefferson and authorized by Congress on Feb. 10, 1807, the Survey of the Coast had as its mission the supplying to mariners of scientific data to aid navigation along the Atlantic coast. The Survey was placed under the Treasury Department, with Prof. Ferdinand Rudolph Hassler, an eminent Swiss scientist who had submitted the most acceptable plans, as its first superintendent.

Despite the clarity and simplicity of his plans, it was no easy matter for Hassler to execute them. His purchases of scientific instruments in England were delayed by the War of 1812. When finally he began his survey of primary base lines on Long Island and the New Jersey coasts in 1816, he was compelled by the amphibious nature of his task to employ army officers, naval officers and civilians as assistants. Personnel difficulties resulted in the temporary transfer of the Coast Survey from the Treasury to the Navy Department. In various years Congress failed to provide adequate funds. Delay in furnishing practical navigation charts led shipowners to precipitate congressional investigations.

From its initial handicaps, however, the Survey was freed in 1843 when Congress formally approved Hassler's scientific methods and adopted the "permanent plan of organization." Since 1843 the expansion of the United States across the continent and the accession of island dependencies have brought the total coast line under the Survey to approximately 100,000 miles. When land questions incident to the opening of the West imperatively demanded extensive inland surveys, Congress (June 20, 1878) enlarged the work of the Coast Survey to cover inland operations and the designation of the organization was changed to "Coast and Geodetic Survey." Since July 1, 1903, when the organization came under the Department of Commerce and Labor (now Department of Commerce), its duties have increased along with the growing interest of the Federal Government in problems of a social and economic nature. In 1925 it undertook seismological observations and investi-

gations, to supply data on designing structures to reduce earthquake hazard; and under the air commerce act of 1926 it has issued aeronautical charts.

Thus today the activities of the Coast and Geodetic Survey are sixfold: (1) to survey and keep up to date charts of nearly 100,000 miles of coast line; (2) to determine geographical positions inland, connecting the coastal surveys and providing the framework for mapping and other engineering work; (3) to study tides and currents, furnishing datum planes to engineers and current tables to mariners; (4) to compile and furnish magnetic information essential to mariner, aviator, land surveyor, radio engineer; (5) to supply seismological data; and (6) to compile aeronautical charts for pilots of aircraft. The results of field investigations and surveys are analyzed in Washington and published as nautical and aeronautical charts, annual tables of predicted tides and currents, charts showing magnetic declination, annual lists of United States earthquakes, publications of geographical positions, "Coast Pilots," "Notices to Mariners" and manuals prescribing correct methods for its various classes of surveying. (*See also* Hydrographic Survey.)

[Florian Cajori, *The Chequered Career of Ferdinand Rudolph Hassler;* G. A. Webber, *The Coast and Geodetic Survey; The United States Coast and Geodetic Survey: Its Work, Methods and Organization,* Special Publication No. 23, Government Printing Office.]

RICHARD S. WEST, JR.

Coast Defense is a term applied to measures to defend coastal cities and important anchorages by guns, searchlights, submarine mines and obstacles to navigation against attack by aircraft and surface and submarine vessels. At the beginning of the Revolution, Boston was the only port in the revolting colonies provided with coast defenses. When the British evacuated it, March 17, 1776, they attempted to destroy the forts. The Americans recovered 250 cannon and rebuilt the defenses. Thanks to these defenses, Boston was the only important American port not taken or burnt during the remainder of the war. Fort Moultrie[qv], a new work at Charleston[qv], repulsed a British fleet, June 28, 1776. A system of coast defenses was begun in 1794. In the War of 1812 the successful defense of Fort McHenry[qv] at Baltimore, Sept. 14, 1814, furnished the theme of America's national anthem. On the following day, Fort Bowyer[qv] (now Fort Morgan) at the mouth of Mobile Bay defeated four British vessels and destroyed one of them.

New and more complete fortifications were begun in 1816–17. Most of the Southern forts were seized by the Confederates in 1861, and many of them became objectives of Federal military and naval expeditions. Admiral Farragut ran by Forts St. Philip and Jackson[qv] below New Orleans, April 24, 1862, and Forts Gaines[qv] and Morgan, Aug. 5, 1864; but the defenses of Charleston repulsed a Federal ironclad fleet, April 7, 1863. No American coast defense was attacked in the Mexican, Spanish-American, and World wars, and none in the Northern states in the Civil War. The present coast defense system was planned by the Endicott Board of 1885–86. It was revised by the Taft Board of 1905–6, and extended to naval bases, the Canal Zone, Hawaii and the Philippine Islands. A single unit is called a "harbor defense."

[Robert Arthur, *History of Fort Monroe.*]

S. C. VESTAL

Coast Guard, THE. Its duties, which cover a wide range, include the enforcement of the navigation and other maritime laws of the United States, the rendering of assistance to vessels in distress, the saving of life and property, the destruction of derelicts, and the removal of obstructions and menaces to navigation. It also maintains the International Ice Patrol in the North Atlantic and the Bering Sea Patrol, and gives medical aid to deep-sea fishermen and the natives of Alaska.

Replacing two older organizations, the Revenue Cutter Service, and the Life Saving Service, the United States Coast Guard was established under a law approved by President Wilson on Jan. 28, 1915. On Aug. 4, 1790, Congress authorized a Revenue Cutter Service, to provide customs collectors with the aid of a sea-going military organization in discharging their duties. In 1871 Congress created the Life Saving Service. This was administered by the Revenue Cutter Service until 1878, when Congress established in the Treasury an independent bureau of the Life Saving Service. The United States Coast Guard, on its establishment in 1915, took over the duties of the two older services.

In peace time, it operates under the Treasury Department. In war time, it becomes part of the Navy, subject to the orders of the Secretary of the Navy. The Coast Guard has a present strength of about 10,000 and its floating equipment includes about 225 ships, ranging in size from large sea-going cutters to small harbor patrol craft.

[Darrel H. Smith and Fred Wilbur Powell, *The United States Coast Guard.*]

OLIVER MCKEE, JR.

Coasting Trade. From the beginning of British settlement in North America until after 1850, shipping along the coasts offered the principal means of transportation and communication between sections of the area. In the colonial period it served to distribute European imports as well as to exchange local products. With the growing diversity of sectional production, and the expansion of intersectional trade, coastwise shipping grew from 68,607 tons in 1789 to 516,979 tons in 1830 and 2,644,867 tons in 1860. Manufactured goods of the Northeast were exchanged for the cotton and tobacco of the South, while the surplus agricultural products of the Mississippi Valley came to the Atlantic coast by way of New Orleans. Following the completion of railroad trunk lines along the coast and across the Appalachians after 1850, passengers, merchandise and commodities of value went increasingly by rail, while such bulk cargoes as coal, lumber, ice, iron, steel and oil were shipped by sea. After 1865 the tonnage engaged in coastwise shipping continued to increase (4,286,516 tons in 1900, 10,049,000 tons in 1935), but not with the rapidity shown by rail and motor transportation. The years following 1870 witnessed bitter struggles between ship and railroad operators, characterized by rate wars, followed by agreements and growing control of coastwise trade by the railroads.

Coasting trade was reserved to British and colonial vessels by the Navigation Acts[qv] of 1651 and 1660; and with the formation of the Federal Union, the policy was continued, a prohibitive tax being placed on foreign built and owned ships in 1789, followed by their complete exclusion from coastwise competition under the Navigation Act of 1817[qv], which remains in force.

From 1800 until the Civil War, the schooner was the typical American coasting vessel, but after 1865 steamers and barges towed by steamers were used increasingly, until by 1920 the sailing vessel had largely disappeared.

[E. R. Johnson, T. W. Van Metre, G. G. Huebner, D. S. Hanchett, *History of Domestic and Foreign Commerce of the United States.*]

JOHN HASKELL KEMBLE

Coastwise Steamship Lines. American steamers made coastwise voyages as early as 1809, but the first regular lines were placed in operation in the sheltered waters of Long Island Sound and between Boston and the coast of Maine about 1825. Local services were established in the Gulf of Mexico by Charles Morgan in 1835, while the United States Mail Steamship Company opened a regular line from New York to Charleston, S. C., Havana, New Orleans and the Isthmus of Panama in 1848. In 1849 the Pacific Mail Steamship Company pioneered the route from Panama to San Francisco and Oregon. Prior to 1860 the railroads served chiefly as feeders for the steamship lines, but after the Civil War they offered serious competition. Although the coastwise lines remained active, they were forced to consolidate (Eastern Steamship Co., Atlantic, Gulf and West Indies Steamship Co.), and in some cases the railroads gained control of the steamships, as when the Southern Pacific Railroad acquired the Morgan line (1885). Increasing competition from railroads, motor busses and trucks, mounting operating costs and labor difficulties resulted in the withdrawal of a considerable part of the coastwise steamship service on the Atlantic and virtually all from the Pacific coast south of Alaska by 1937.

[Fred Erving Dayton, *Steamboat Days.*]

JOHN HASKELL KEMBLE

Cobb, Fort, was established by Maj. W. H. Emory, Oct. 1, 1859, on the Washita River, Indian territory. The Confederates occupied it for a time during the Civil War, but later abandoned it and the post fell into disrepair. Reoccupied by troops under Col. W. B. Hazen in November, 1868, to protect the nearby Indian agency (*see* Washita, Sheridan's Operations on), it was once more abandoned the following year in favor of Fort Sill[qv].

[W. S. Nye, *Carbine and Lance.*]

PAUL I. WELLMAN

Cochise Incident. *See* Apache Pass Expedition (Feb. 4–23, 1861).

Cod Fisheries, The, of North America lie off the coasts of New England, Newfoundland and Labrador. The earliest explorers to the northeastern coast of North America noted the presence of the codfish. Cabot spoke of it, and in 1602 Gosnold gave Cape Cod its name because of the abundance of the fish in its waters. The earliest fishermen came from Spain and France, attracted by the lure of the bank fisheries off Newfoundland. In the 16th century Englishmen made frequent fishing voyages to the "banks."

Capt. John Smith's successful fishing venture in 1614 off the New England coast helped to establish the popularity of that region. Within a few years fishing colonies were established in Massachusetts (Cape Ann) and Maine (Monhegan Island and Pemaquid[qqv]). Massachusetts Bay[qv] early engaged in the codfishery. Within less than forty years after its settlement Boston was a busy trade center for fish.

England often exasperated the colonies by failing in treaties with France to accord a proper interest to the fisheries. In treaties from St. Germain (1632) to Ryswick*qqv* (1697), the French fisheries benefited. British colonists were particularly bitter in 1697 when Acadia was returned to France. The Treaty of Utrecht*qv* (1713) awarded Newfoundland and Nova Scotia (Acadia) to England, but France retained the island of Cape Breton and some fishing privileges.

The final defeat of France in the great colonial struggle with England, concluded by the Treaty of Paris*qv* (1763), left France only the fishing islands of St. Pierre and Miquelon and restricted fishing privileges. The New England cod fisheries expected to benefit by the triumph, but new discontent appeared when Parliament passed the Sugar Act*qv* of 1764. Its enforcement threatened to ruin the profitable trade with the French West Indies that was based on the exchange of the poorer grade of cod for sugar and molasses, which were manufactured into rum. Like the earlier Molasses Act of 1733*qv* this, too, was ineffective, largely because of smuggling*qv*.

Codfishing suffered severely from the Revolutionary War, but expectations were held for its revival when the United States secured extensive fishing privileges from England in the Definitive Treaty of Peace*qv* (1783). This revival was delayed not only by the contraction of the market in Catholic Europe, but also by the immediate exclusion of Americans from trade with the British West Indies. Fishing bounties*qv* began to be paid in 1789, but did not become a real aid to the fisheries until considerably later.

The Peace of Ghent*qv* (1814) did not provide for the continuance of the fishing privileges which Americans had been enjoying in British colonial waters. The Convention of 1818*qv* attempted to settle the fisheries*qv* question, but it continued to be a sore spot in British-American relations until the award of the Hague Tribunal of Arbitration in 1910.

After the War of 1812 the cod and mackerel*qv* fisheries entered on a long period of expansion. The European market for salt codfish declined, but the domestic market more than offset this loss. The Erie Canal*qv* provided access to the Mississippi Valley, and introduction of the use of ice for preservation opened a wide domestic market for fresh fish (*see* Refrigeration). Tariffs from 1816 to 1846 on imported fish greatly helped New England fishermen to control the home market.

After the Civil War the cod lost the distinction of being the principal food fish of the American seas. From about 1885 the cod fisheries began not only to decline in relation to other American fisheries, but also in the amount of tonnage employed. Such cities as Boston and Gloucester in Massachusetts, and Portland in Maine, however, still serve as centers for an industry whose importance in American history is symbolized by Massachusetts' use of the "sacred codfish" as its emblem.

[Raymond McFarland, *A History of the New England Fisheries;* C. B. Judah, Jr., *The North American Fisheries and British Policy to 1713;* S. E. Morison, *Maritime History of Massachusetts, 1783-1860.*]

F. HARDEE ALLEN

Code Napoléon. One important reform resulting from the French Revolution was the unification and simplification of the French laws, prepared under Napoleon Bonaparte's direction and promulgated in 1804 as the "Code Civil," commonly called the "Code Napoléon." It served as the model for the "Digest of the Civil Laws" of Orleans Territory*qv*, promulgated in 1808 and commonly called the "Old Louisiana Code," which, revised and amended in 1825 and 1870 as the "Civil Code of Louisiana," remains today the basic law of the State of Louisiana.

[Alcée Fortier, ed., *Louisiana;* Charles Gayarré, *History of Louisiana;* François Xavier Martin, *History of Louisiana;* Alcée Fortier, *History of Louisiana.*]

WALTER PRICHARD

Code Noir (Black Code) is the name commonly applied to the "Edict Concerning the Negro Slaves in Louisiana," issued by Louis XV in March, 1724, and promulgated in the colony by Gov. Bienville on Sept. 10, 1724. A large number of Negro slaves had been brought to the colony during the administrations of Antoine Crozat and John Law, and a definition of their legal status had become desirable. The "Code," consisting of fifty-four articles, fixes the legal status of Negro slaves and imposes certain specific obligations and prohibitions upon their masters. Regulations as to holidays, marriage, religious instruction, burial, clothing and subsistence, punishment and manumission of Negro slaves are prescribed in detail. The legal position and proper conduct of freed or free Negroes in the colony are defined. Article I of the "Code," rather curiously, decreed expulsion of Jews from the colony. Article III prohibited the exercise of any religious creed than the Roman Catholic and Article IV decreed confiscation for Negro slaves placed under the direction or supervision of any person not a Catholic. The essential provisions of the "Code" remained in force in Louisiana until 1803 and many of them were embodied in later American "Black Codes."*qv*

[C. Gayarré, *History of Louisiana;* A. Fortier, ed., *Louisiana.*]

WALTER PRICHARD

Code of the Laws of the United States, THE (1934), is the official compilation, in a single volume of 3026 pages, of all acts of Congress in force on Jan. 3, 1935, arranged under fifty "Titles" or heads, such as aliens and citizenship, agriculture, banks and banking, commerce and trade, criminal code and procedure, internal revenue, public lands and railroads. It supplants not only the codification contained in the Revised Statutes of 1874 and 1878 but also the original Code of 1925 and seven volumes of "Supplements" published in 1926–34. The Code was prepared under the direction of the House of Representatives committee on the revision of the laws. No new law was enacted, and no old law repealed, by the Code; and its contents are declared to be "prima facie the law." The Code is usually cited as "U. S. C."

[Preface to *Code of the Laws of the United States*, 1925, 1934.]

P. ORMAN RAY

Codes of Fair Competition. This phrase technically, though not literally, describes the agreements negotiated under the authority of the National Industrial Recovery Act*qv* (N.R.A.) of June 16, 1933. Although not known as "codes," the rules of fair trade practice promulgated, after conferences with businessmen, by the Federal Trade Commission*qv* during the preceding decade were taken more seriously than previous codes of business ethics. But the sanctions supporting them were inadequate to assure their full effectiveness. On the other hand, violation of any provision of N.R.A. code was made a misdemeanor. This, and the penalty of being deprived of the blue-eagle*qv* symbol, encouraged general compliance. Although there were many qualifications in practice, the N.R.A. codes represented, in theory, agreements among members of particular branches of trade upon the rules or standards they would observe in the conduct of business, such agreements being subject to the approval of the President.

[L. S. Lyon and associates, *The National Recovery Administration;* J. M. Clark and others, The National Recovery Administration, Report of the Committee of Industrial Analysis, *House Doc. 158, 75 Cong., I Sess.*, Washington, 1937.]

MYRON W. WATKINS

Coeducation. During the colonial period girls were generally excluded from charity schools, free schools*qqv* and tax-supported town schools. However, there were certain communities which admitted them for instruction out of the regular school hours. Late in the colonial period and in the early national period they were generally admitted to the modified elementary schools, dame schools*qv* and tax-supported public free schools, as they had been earlier to many private charity schools. During the early national period many of the academies*qv* were coeducational in character because they were dependent upon tuition fees. When the academies were gradually replaced by public high schools*qv* girls were commonly admitted because high schools were tax-supported and equal educational privileges were taken for granted.

Coeducation in higher education first appeared in the Middle West, and before 1860 numerous colleges and state universities*qv* were open to women on terms of equality with men. It was firmly established by 1872, when the University of Michigan admitted women, and thereafter it became quite general. By this time the coeducational high school and the free-school system prevailed throughout the country.

[Thomas Woody, *A History of the Education of Women in the United States;* Paul Monroe, *The Founding of the American Public School System.*]

PAUL MONROE

Coercion Acts, THE, also known as the Restraining Acts and, in part, as the Intolerable Acts*qv*, were a series of four measures passed by the English Parliament in the spring and summer of 1774, partly in retaliation for such incidents as the *Gaspee* affair and the Boston Tea Party*qqv*, but also partly as the enunciation of a more vigorous colonial policy. The Boston Port Act*qv*, designed as a direct reply to the Tea Party, closed the harbor to all shipping until the town had indemnified the East India Company for the destruction of its tea and assured the king of its future loyalty, pending which Marblehead was made the port of entry. The Massachusetts Government Act*qv* deprived Massachusetts of its charter and the right to choose its own magistrates, reducing it to the status of a crown colony. An Act for the Impartial Administration of Justice*qv* provided that judges, soldiers and revenue officers indicted for murder in Massachusetts should be taken to England for trial, and lastly, the Quartering Act*qv* removed all obstacles to the billeting of troops in any town in Massachusetts.

[C. H. Van Tyne, *The Causes of the War of Independence;* G. E. Howard, *The Preliminaries of the Revolution.*]

FRANK J. KLINGBERG

***Coetus-Conferentie* Controversy,** THE, was a conflict in the 18th century between the progressive and the conservative parties in the Dutch Reformed churches, now the Reformed Church in America*qv*. The issue was American independence especially as related to the education and ordination of ministers and the power of discipline. Beginning in 1628 the churches had been under authority of the church in Holland, ministers generally being sent over by the classis (ecclesiastical jurisdiction) of Amsterdam. A century later positive movement for freedom began. An assembly known as a *coetus,* or informal classis, assuming some power, was formed in 1737. Its opponents gradually grouped themselves in a so-called *conferentie.* The controversy divided the ministers and the congregations. In 1771 a plan of union brought from Holland by the Rev. John H. Livingston reconciled the two parties and established virtually complete independence of the church in America.

[*Ecclesiastical Records of the State of New York.*]

W. H. S. DEMAREST

Cœur d'Alene Mission, THE, was a Roman Catholic Indian mission established, 1842, near the town of Cataldo, Idaho, by Father Nicholas Point and Brother Charles Huet, sent by Father Peter J. DeSmet. In 1877 the mission was removed to the vicinity of the town of Desmet, in the present Benewah County. The church gradually fell into decay, but was restored in 1929. The present church, a landmark, is Idaho's oldest structure reared by the hands of white men.

[Edward Cody, *History of the Cœur d'Alene Mission of the Sacred Heart;* Cornelius James Brosnan, *History of the State of Idaho.*]

CORNELIUS JAMES BROSNAN

Cœur d'Alene Riots, THE, in the lead and silver mines of northern Idaho, resulted from a strike of union miners in 1892. The mine owners protected nonunion labor with armed guards, and obtained injunctions against the unions. On July 11, 1892, armed union miners expelled nonunion men from the district, a mill was dynamited, and a pitched battle was fought. State and Federal troops took charge and martial law was proclaimed. In 1893 the local miners' unions were affiliated with the Western Federation of Miners^qv^. There were strikes in 1894 and 1899, when Federal troops suppressed violence. The Cœur d'Alene labor trouble gained national attention when Idaho's former governor, Frank Steunenberg, was killed, Dec. 30, 1905. The murderer, Harry Orchard, a former miner, claimed that the crime was instigated by officers of the Federation. He was chief witness for the state in the trial of "Big Bill" Haywood, secretary of the Federation, held in Boise in May, 1907. In 1908 Orchard was sentenced to be hanged, a punishment later commuted to life imprisonment. Haywood was acquitted, as was George A. Pettibone, the Federation's president, and the prosecution against Charles H. Moyer, member of the Federation's official board, was dropped.

[C. J. Brosnan, *History of the State of Idaho.*]

CORNELIUS JAMES BROSNAN

Coffee's Trading Posts were maintained by Holland Coffee and others under the name of Coffee, Calville and Company. In 1834 they located a post on the north bank of Red River, near the 99th meridian. Shortly thereafter they established another post on the same stream above the mouth of Walnut Bayou, in the present Love County, Oklahoma. As late as 1836 trading operations were carried on at both places, although the latter post was considered headquarters. During the late 1830's Coffee and his traders exercised a strong influence over the Indians and ransomed numbers of white captives brought from Texas.

[Grant Foreman, *Pioneer Days in the Early Southwest.*]

RUPERT N. RICHARDSON

Cohens v. Virginia, 1821 (6 Wheaton 264). The Supreme Court upheld its jurisdiction to review the judgment of a state court where, in a criminal case, it was alleged that the conviction violated some right under the Federal Constitution or laws (*see also* McCulloch v. Maryland; Osborn et al. v. U. S. Bank). This was one of Marshall's greatest opinions establishing national authority over the states.

[A. J. Beveridge, *The Life of John Marshall;* Charles Warren, *The Supreme Court in United States History.*]

CHARLES FAIRMAN

Coinage. The colonists never achieved a satisfactory coin currency. Spanish coins, the chief currency, were inadequate. In 1691 William Penn urged immigrants to bring one third of their property in coins. The scarcity was most acute in small change, the colonists being forced to "carrying Sugar and Tobacco upon their backs to barter for little Common Necessarys."

The efforts of the colonists to obtain coin from England and to find relief in such substitutes as wampum^qv^ and beaver skins testify to the need, as well as their determined efforts to set up mints in the face of a shortsighted policy of suppression by the mother country. Virginia, Maryland and New York passed futile statutes for the establishment of mints. Only Massachusetts succeeded. In the latter part of the 17th century coins from her mint were widely popular. In an effort to keep them at home the colony gave them an excess legal value in British terms (*see* Pine Tree Shilling).

Release from English control in the Revolutionary period gave the colonies opportunity for state coinage. The Articles of Confederation^{qv} actually sanctioned such coinage. From 1776 to 1789 state patents of coinage to private persons or direct minting by the states was widely prevalent. New Hampshire was attempting its own coinage in 1776. None of these projects got beyond coinage of a few copper pieces, although Massachusetts in 1786 provided for gold and silver as well as copper. One of the pieces from this mint was a "cent," 1/100 of the Spanish dollar^{qv}. It was the first official coin on a decimal basis in history.

The national coinage system established in 1792 had unique features. It created *de novo* a coinage system for a nation, with new units, new principles of legal tender^{qv} and a decimal system. The arts of coinage were unfamiliar, and the mint^{qv}, established in Philadelphia, made small progress. The costs of coinage were heavy. The ratio change in 1834 encouraged gold^{qv} coinage, and a new mint, with horsepower, set up in 1836, initiated an era of coinage on a large scale. The subsidiary coinage laws^{qv} of 1851 and 1853 and the new copper-nickel cent provision of 1857 called forth a tremendous volume of coinage.

For the first seventy years of the mint's existence counterfeiting^{qv} was a national evil. Private coinage was not prohibited before the Civil War, and privately minted gold coins from Georgia, Colorado and California were widely used. The Civil War period was marked by the rivalry of copper, nickel and silver interests for preference in coinage materials, and the history of our coinage in the years after the war was marked by ugly political intrigue (*see* Silver Legislation).

The period since the Civil War has been marked by a continuous improvement in the efficiency of the mint, while the denominations, materials and physical qualities of the coins have been steadily improved, until the mint establishment has become one of the finest in the world, with the quality of its product unsurpassed.

[S. S. Crosby, *Early Coins of America;* D. K. Watson, *History of American Coinage;* Neil Carothers, *Fractional Money.*]

NEIL CAROTHERS

Coinage, Subsidiary. The establishment of subsidiary coinage in the United States has an importance far beyond its retail currency significance. At the time Alexander Hamilton devised the American coinage system, in 1792, the principles of subsidiary coinage were unknown. Since small silver coins were a necessity, silver had to be a standard. Since the world had been for 500 years slowly turning to gold as the major medium, gold had to be a standard. The double standard was Hamilton's only choice, although he himself and subsequent historians failed to realize it. This is the only explanation of a system which makes a five-cent "half-disme" a full legal tender piece with unlimited coinage.

The system was a failure. There could be no material coinage of gold at the fifteen-to-one ratio. The only source of silver bullion was from recoinage of the Mexican pieces in universal circulation, but they were so worn that recoinage meant a heavy loss. In 1834 a new ratio of sixteen to one was adopted, with a slight alteration in 1837. This ratio was designed to favor gold coinage. Its inevitable result would be a complete cessation of silver coinage. Certain temporary conditions actually encouraged small silver coinage for a time, but after 1840 the ratio gradually choked off silver coinage. When adverse conditions in Mexico reduced the flow of coins to this country, the rapidly expanding economic life of the United States faced a small-change famine. For ten years the country's retail currency was a dwindling mass of foreign coins worn beyond recognition.

In 1851 Congress created a three-cent piece of mixed silver and copper, to be made by the Treasury and sold to the public. England had stumbled accidentally and extra-legally into a single gold standard with subsidiary silver in 1816. Some understanding of its operation had reached America. This three-cent piece, devised for postage purposes, was a genuine subsidiary coin, although its creators only vaguely understood it.

By 1852 retail trade was paralyzed by the scarcity of small change. The business of hotels, ferries, railways and retail shops of all kinds was demoralized. The three-cent pieces poured into the gap. After two years of needless delay Congress passed in 1853 a subsidiary coinage law. It created five-cent, ten-cent, twenty-five-cent and fifty-cent silver coins, "debased" below their face values, to be made and sold for gold by the Treasury. It was the second subsidiary coinage system in history and the first system officially recognized as such.

A flood of the new coins poured into circulation, the mint running day and night. By 1857 the country had an abundant small change, after 250 years of scarcity. The British accounting and the Spanish currency disappeared.

[Neil Carothers, *Fractional Money.*]

NEIL CAROTHERS

Coinage Names. The nomenclature of colonial and United States coins[qv] constitutes an interesting chapter in our history. The Spanish *reale,* the commonest coin of the colonies, one eighth of the Spanish dollar[qv], was equivalent to the six-penny "bit." In the 17th century it came to be known as the "bit." More than a century later the term was transferred to the new American coinage, and one quarter-dollar became "two bits." Historically "two bits" or "four bits" is the oldest monetary term in America. In Pennsylvania the *reale* was valued at 11 pence, the half-*reale* at 5½ and the two coins came to be known as a "levy" and a "fip." These terms were also transferred to the American coinage, and for many years a dime was a "levy," a half-dime a "fip." The smallest silver coin in the Louisiana territory was the *picaillon,* and our five-cent piece eventually became a "picayune." The word survives in our language.

A national coinage on a decimal basis resulted in an entirely new nomenclature. The term "dollar" was old when Shakespeare was making puns on it. The word came from Germany as "thaler," from the Joachimsthal silver mines. The English applied it to the Spanish *peso,* corrupting it to "dollar." But the terms "eagle," "disme," "cent" and "mille" were new. Historians have credited Gouverneur Morris with the invention of "cent" and possibly of "mille" and "disme," but the term "cent" was known earlier and he never used "mille" or "disme" in his writings on money. Only one other new term has appeared since 1792, the word "nickel" being used for years as the name of the "flying-eagle cent" and then being transferred to our five-cent piece.

[Neil Carothers, *Fractional Money.*]

NEIL CAROTHERS

Coins. In the 300 years of their history the American people have used as common currency an astonishing diversity of coins and paper money. During the entire colonial period there was a scarcity of coins, and the colonists used coins from any source. Small quantities of coins were brought by immigrants. The English brought shillings, sixpences, threepences, copper pence and halfpence. The Dutch brought *guilders* and *stivers,* the French *crowns, livres* and *picaillons,* the Swedes *dalers* and *skillings.* Pirates left in the ports coins from all the world, gold pieces from Spain, Portugal and Arabia, silver from Spain and Germany.

From the early 17th century the predominant coin was the Spanish dollar[qv] and its parts, the half, quarter, eighth and sixteenth. They poured into the country from 1650 until after 1850. For 200 years the commonest coin in America was the *reale,* the eighth of the Spanish dollar or "bit."[qv]

The scarcity of coins below the *reale* or sixpence was acute. There never was enough small change from 1607 to 1857. Massachusetts set up her own mint before 1700. Connecticut tried to coin her own copper pieces in 1738. In 1681 New Jersey legalized "Patrick's pence," copper pieces made by an Irish adventurer, and in 1722 England granted to William Wood the right to coin private copper pieces for the colonies. In the period of the Confederation a hodgepodge of private and state coins of copper were in circulation.

The currency confusion of the colonial period beggars description. Each colony legalized such coins as it chose and at such values in shillings and pence as it preferred. South Carolina in 1701 made legal tender thirteen varieties of coins. A traveler from Boston to Norfolk in 1750 might have had in his pouch paper notes, an English shilling and a sixpence or so, four or five Spanish *reales* and sixteenths, and a few copper Spanish *maravedis* and English halfpence. This assortment he had to revalue three times en route.

The establishment of a national coinage[qv] in 1792 added gold coins of $10, $5, and $2.50, a silver dollar, half-dollar, quarter-dollar, *disme* and half-*disme,* and two clumsy cent and half-cent pieces of pure copper. All the gold and silver pieces were unlimited legal tender. But Spanish coins remained the ordinary currency of everyday life.

After 1834 there was an abundant currency of gold[qv]. In 1849 a gold dollar was added, and this inconvenient piece enjoyed wide circulation. In 1851 a three-cent silver piece was added. In the three years of acute coin scarcity from 1851 to 1854 one-dollar gold coins, three-cent pieces and Spanish pieces worn beyond identification were the only small change (*see* Coinage, Subsidiary). The scarcity of small coins and the unpleasant physical qualities of Hamilton's pure copper pieces had created a universal prejudice against coins below sixpence.

All these adverse conditions were removed by two measures. An excellent subsidiary coinage of silver[qv] was created in 1853, with a half-dollar, quarter-dollar, dime and half-dime, and in 1857 the cent and half-cent of 1792 were replaced by a new one-cent piece of mixed nickel and copper, the "flying-eagle cent." With these measures the Spanish currency at last disappeared, and with it the two-centuries-old practice of keeping accounts in shillings and pence.

During the long Civil War period in which the people used fractional paper notes for small change the mint experimented with nickel, aluminum and bronze small coins (*see* Fractional Currency). The result was the creation of a five-cent nickel-copper coin, a three-cent nickel-copper coin, a two-cent bronze coin, and a one-cent bronze coin. The first and last of these are our present-day coins. These coins were the first to bear the inscription "In God We Trust."*qv* In the 1870's the people used as small change an assortment of three-, five-, ten-, fifteen- and twenty-five-cent notes; three-, five-, ten- and twenty-five-cent silver pieces; three- and five-cent nickel coins, and one- and two-cent bronze coins.

After 1875 coins gradually displaced the paper fractions. In that year Congress undertook to introduce a twenty-cent silver piece, a coin originally recommended by Jefferson in 1792. Also in this period the two-cent bronze coin, the three-cent nickel coin and the five-cent silver piece were abolished, while two unwise statutes forced into limited circulation an over-size silver "trade dollar"*qv* and the old and forgotten "standard" silver dollar*qv*.

Since 1880 the common coin currency has been adequate and satisfactory. Various efforts to force the coinage of six-, three-, two-and-one-half and half-cent pieces have been unsuccessful.

[A. B. Hepburn, *History of the Currency;* C. J. Bullock, *Essays on Monetary History of the United States;* D. K. Watson, *History of American Coinage;* Neil Carothers, *Fractional Money.*]

NEIL CAROTHERS

Coin's Financial School was written by W. H. ("Coin") Harvey to convert to bimetallism*qv*, at sixteen to one, people suffering from the hard times prevailing in 1894 (*see* Panic of 1893). It represented prominent bankers, editors and other gold monometallists as asking and taking instruction from "Coin, the smooth little financier." By graphic illustrations, homely allusions, glib arguments and the use of prominent names, the book obtained wide credence as a narrative of actual occurrences. Printed in cheap paper editions, it circulated very widely among farmers, debtors and other distressed classes, preparing many minds to receive Bryan's arguments.

[Allan Nevins, *Grover Cleveland, A Study in Courage.*]

JEANNETTE P. NICHOLS

Colbert's Gang was a band of whites, half-breeds and Chickasaw*qv* led by James Colbert. The band assisted the British in the defense of Mobile and Pensacola against the Spaniards in the Revolution; and later, by harrying the Spaniards from Chickasaw Bluffs, saved the east bank of the Mississippi for Great Britain and ultimately for the United States.

[D. C. Corbitt, James Colbert and the Spanish Claims to the East Bank of the Mississippi, *The Mississippi Valley Historical Review,* XXIV.]

R. S. COTTERILL

Cold Harbor (June 3, 1864). Following failures to smash and outflank Lee (C.) at Spotsylvania*qv*, Grant (U.) on May 20 directed the Army of the Potomac*qv* southeast on a turning movement. Lee retired behind the North Anna*qv*. Grant recognized this position's strength and continued "side-slipping toward Richmond" by successive marches and deployments until the Confederates stood on a six-mile front without reserves, their right on the Chickahominy, their center at Cold Harbor. Estimating Confederate morale low and Lee's center weak, Grant ordered a direct drive, 60,000 men on 4000 yards frontage. The assault at 4:30 P.M., June 3, against well-entrenched lines cost 5600 casualties and failed completely. Grant dug in, held Lee in position until June 12, then resumed "side-slipping" and, crossing the James, threatened Richmond through Petersburg*qv*.

[A. A. Humphreys, *The Virginia Campaigns of 1864 and 1865;* D. S. Freeman, *R. E. Lee.*]

ELBRIDGE COLBY

Cold Storage. *See* Refrigeration.

Collective Bargaining is the joint determination of the terms of employment by an organization of workers and an employer or association of employers through their duly authorized representatives. From joint conferences there issue trade agreements which cover such matters as wage rates, time and method of payment, physical conditions of work, the hiring and dismissal of employees and interpretation and enforcement. Under the common-law*qv* doctrine, inherited by the United States from England, combinations of workers to increase wages and reduce hours of labor were, until the middle of the 19th century, held to be illegal conspiracies against the public welfare. Attempts to make collective bargaining effective through the boycott and picketing have been greatly restricted under the Sherman Antitrust Act (1890) and the Clayton Antitrust Law (1914)*qqv*.

From 1792 to 1850 collective bargaining was local in character because unions, such as the Typographical Society of New York (1794) and the Society of Journeymen Cordwainers of Philadelphia (1794), were local organizations. Subsequent to 1850, when the Typographical Union and other associations of skilled artisans organized into national unions, collective arrangements have generally been on a national basis. Collective bargaining is frequently industry-wide, covering most employers and workers in a given industry, as in coal mining in which joint negotiations are held between the United Mine Workers[qv] (1890), an industrial union, and the coal operators.

[J. R. Commons and J. B. Andrews, *Principles of Labor Legislation;* F. B. Sayre, *Cases on Labor Law.*]

GORDON S. WATKINS

Collector v. Day. Probate Judge Day of Barnstable County, Mass., having paid the Civil War income tax[qv] upon his salary under protest, brought suit to recover it and obtained judgment. The tax collector then sued out a writ of error. The United States Supreme Court in 1870 decided that it was not competent for Congress to levy a tax upon the salary of a judicial officer; the judgment obtained by Day was affirmed. (*See also* Taxation, Reciprocal Immunity from.)

[Lawrence B. Evans, *Cases on Constitutional Law.*]

ALVIN F. HARLOW

Colleges, Denominational, have been a distinctive feature in the development of higher education in the United States. Of the colonial colleges, all, with the possible exception of the College of Philadelphia, now the University of Pennsylvania[qv], were established by churches, primarily for the training of ministers. The period from the Revolution to the Civil War was by far the most fruitful in the founding of church colleges. During these years the churches dominated higher education in America, even the first state universities, with the exception of the University of Virginia[qv], being largely under the control of ministers. Between 1780 and 1829 forty permanent colleges were established, thirteen by Presbyterians, five by Congregationalists, six by Episcopalians, one by Catholics, three by Baptists[qqv], one by German Reformed and eleven by the states. In these early years Presbyterians and Congregationalists were the most influential in higher education, but beginning in 1830 the Baptists and Methodists entered upon an unprecedented era of college founding. By 1860 the Baptists had twenty-five colleges in nineteen states and the Methodists had established thirty-four permanent institutions.

Since the Civil War college founding by the churches has been much less rapid, but the movement has by no means disappeared. In more recent years the stronger denominational colleges have tended to become undenominational, though many still retain some relationship to the founding bodies.

[D. G. Tewksbury, *The Founding of American Colleges and Universities before the Civil War.*]

WILLIAM W. SWEET

Colleges and Universities, The, of the United States, grew from about a dozen small colonial collegiate institutions, with only a few students, to several hundred colleges, with about 53,000 students, by 1860. Today approximately 1400 institutions of higher learning, with more than 2,000,000 students and almost numberless alumni, exist in this country.

There are three definite periods in the history of higher education in the United States: from the establishment of Harvard[qv] in 1636 to about 1860; from 1860 to the World War; and since the World War. The first of these periods was marked by the domination of the classics in a fixed collegiate curriculum. These subjects were standard in most of the American colleges for nearly two centuries; and their completion was required because of their alleged cultural values and the dignity which they were supposed to bestow upon college students. The second period may be said to have begun about 1869, when Charles W. Eliot became president of Harvard and introduced the elective system. During this period the classics began to yield to sciences and other subjects which were slowly given places in the curriculum. The third period roughly covers the past two decades, which have been marked by a tendency away from freedom of election to a measure of prescription.

The administration of higher education has, meantime, shown considerable change. Prior to 1860 most of the college presidents and trustees were clergymen or energetic members of denominational groups. It is significant that at least 40% of American college presidents prior to 1860 were born in New England, and that religion or denominationalism was one of the most potent influences in the movement to provide higher education.

Most of the early colleges were founded upon evangelical zeal and became agencies of denominational expansion. Also, it should be noted, the early colleges were frontier institutions, established to meet frontier needs. This purpose caused the American college to depart from its antecedents in Europe and to acquire features quite different from foreign institutions.

Higher educational institutions increased very rapidly down to 1860, legislatures granting charters to countless private ventures. But their mortality rate was very high due to financial difficulties, denominational competition, internal religious and political dissensions, unfavorable locations and natural disasters.

After the Civil War, when great fortunes were being amassed, business leaders were importuned for support and endowments, and gradually the change from ecclesiastical to lay control was made. This led to a change in collegiate curricula. The old classical tradition which had come down from the theologians and had so long prevailed began to give way and the religious purposes of higher education lost ground. This change was also hastened by the growth of the natural sciences as subjects of instruction, and the curriculum began to point towards business and the secular professions.

After the Revolution attempts were made to change some of the colonial colleges into state universities, but all such efforts failed. The most prominent instance was in 1816, in connection with Dartmouth College, which led to Daniel Webster's famous plea before the Supreme Court in 1819 (*see* Dartmouth College v. Woodward). The decision, which held that a charter is a contract which cannot be impaired by legislation, guaranteed the perpetuity of educational endowments. As a result, an energetic period of private and denominational higher educational effort followed. Another influence of the decision was to encourage the establishment of state universities[qv].

Interest in agricultural education began to grow before the middle of the 19th century. In the 1840's memorials were presented to Congress asking for the establishment of technical institutions for the training of students in agriculture, mechanics, architecture and road building. In 1862 Sen. Justin S. Morrill, of Vermont, was able to get through Congress a bill which appropriated public lands[qv] to the various states for the purpose of providing institutions that have come to be known as the land-grant colleges[qv]. The states and territories now receive Federal aid for the purpose of carrying on work in agriculture, mechanical arts, engineering and allied subjects (*see* Morrill Act).

Since about 1914 questions have been raised concerning the elective system, many of whose promises were found to be unfulfilled. There was a growing belief also that college students needed acquaintance with "a common intellectual world," and opportunities to develop more social intelligence. This tendency has taken the form of numerous experiments with required or elective orientation, general, overview or survey courses in the social and the natural sciences and, recently, even in the humanities. There has also been an increasing effort to guide students without hampering their initiative and to adjust the work of the college to their needs. This change has been due in part to the changed student personnel, to the necessity brought about by an increasingly complex world and to the recognition of individual differences. These modifications do not necessarily mean that the elective system has been abandoned, but rather that the principle of election has been adapted to changed conditions.

Higher education in the United States today includes institutions for men only, institutions for women only and coeducational institutions, professional and technical schools, teacher education institutions and junior colleges. The development of graduate work may be said to have begun with the opening of Johns Hopkins University in 1876. Graduate work is carried on in numerous colleges, but the Association of American Universities, largely an organization of graduate schools, now numbers only thirty-two institutions.

Enrollment in higher educational institutions has greatly increased since the World War. There are today approximately seven college students for every one in 1890, although the population of the United States has little more than doubled. In 1890 about half of the graduates of secondary schools went to college. With the number of high-school graduates so greatly increased in recent years, probably not more than one fifth of them now enter college.

[E. P. Cubberley, *Public Education in the United States;* Edgar W. Knight, *Education in the United States;* E. V. Wills, *The Growth of American Higher Education.*]

EDGAR W. KNIGHT

Collot's Journey (1796). Gen. Victor Collot came to Philadelphia after the British took possession of Guadeloupe, West Indies, where he had been governor. When litigation prevented his departure for France, he undertook a boat journey into the western country. He left McKeesport, Pa., June 6, 1796, visited the Ohio River settlements, made an excursion into the Illinois country[qv] and then turned back down the Mississippi to New Orleans[qv]. His journal illustrates the enlightened appreciation of the potentialities of the American West displayed by many of his countrymen of the period.

[Victor Collot, *Voyage dans l'Amerique Septentrionale.*]

EDGAR B. NIXON

Colombia, Canal Controversy with. The Hay-Herran Treaty[qv], signed between the United States and Colombia January, 1903, authorized the building of a canal across Panama under American auspices; but the Colombian Senate failed to ratify the agreement. The province of Panama, resentful over this failure, revolted in November, 1903, and, aided by the United States, established its independence (*see* Panama Revolution). The United States at once made a canal treaty with the infant republic (*see* Hay–Bunau-Varilla Treaty, The). Colombia, deeply hostile towards the United States for its part in the proceedings, repeatedly demanded amends. Finally, by an agreement made in 1921, the United States paid Colombia $25,000,000 for the loss of Panama.

[M. W. Williams, *The People and Politics of Latin America.*]

MARY WILHELMINE WILLIAMS

Colonial Agent, THE, was the representative sent to England by the colonies in America during the 17th and 18th centuries. Since the practice of maintaining an agent grew out of the exigencies of the times when communication was slow and uncertain, a representative formed an indispensable link between the mother country and her far-flung empire.

In the 17th century an agent went to England only on special missions. For instance, John Clarke was sent by Rhode Island to secure a charter for that community from the Restoration government. As soon as he had accomplished his arduous task, which took two years, he returned home. In the 18th century, however, when the business of colonial administration had greatly increased in volume and complexity, the agent, like the diplomat of today, remained at his post year after year. Benjamin Franklin was in England from 1757 to 1762 as agent of the Pennsylvania assembly.

The agent was not necessarily always a colonist; not infrequently an Englishman, especially interested in the American colonies, was appointed as, for example, the brilliant lawyer, Richard Jackson, who represented Connecticut during the Revolutionary period.

Though the agent was never an official member of the loose-jointed imperial machinery, yet his importance can hardly be overestimated. He served as a clearing house of information at a time when ignorance of colonial conditions was widespread; he attended hearings on various matters held by the Board of Trade and the Privy Council[qqv]; he prepared petitions embodying specific claims or requests; he worked on the perennial Indian problems; and he wrestled with boundary disputes which, because of prodigal land grants, caused endless difficulties.

It can be seen that many of these tasks were of a routine nature requiring only industry and an understanding of colonial aspirations. At times, however, emergencies arose which made unlimited demands on the resourcefulness and indeed the strength of the representative. After 1660 the home government tried repeatedly to revise or revoke altogether the colonial charters in the interest of more centralized government. As this would mean a serious curtailment of precious liberties, the agent was always instructed to fight such action as forcibly as possible. In 1730 a bill establishing a monopoly in West Indian rum, sugar and molasses was introduced into Parliament. This obviously favored the West Indian sugar planters at the expense of the New England merchants (*see* **Trade**, Triangular). The struggle over this measure, the famous Molasses Act[qv], lasted three years and absorbed the New England agents and their West Indian rivals almost to the exclusion of everything else.

Nothing throws more light on the management of the British colonies in its early years than a study of the colonial agent. In and out of the offices of the Board of Trade he passed, conferring with an army of clerks, committee members and minor officials, attending hearings, talking with influential members of Parliament, chatting with friends and colleagues. Faithful, alert, friendly, an ambassador of frontier philosophy to the Old World, he did much to facilitate the administration of the first British empire.

[E. P. Tanner, Colonial Agencies in England, *Science Quarterly*, XVI, 1901; M. Appleton, Richard Partridge —Colonial Agent, *New England Quarterly*, V, No. 2, 1932.]

MARGUERITE APPLETON

Colonial Assemblies had their beginnings in the Virginia House of Burgesses called by Gov. Yeardley in 1619. The first Virginia assembly was an outcome of a new policy inaugurated after the Sandys-Southampton group gained control of the Virginia Company[qv]. It was unicameral[qv] in organization and was composed of the governor, his council and two burgesses elected for each of the towns, plantations and hundreds. Subsequently the units of representation were certain privileged towns or cities and the counties. Not until the latter part of the 17th century did the elected element separate from the parent assembly, resulting in a bicameral[qv] legislative body. From the beginning the Virginia assembly claimed and exercised the right to initiate legislation, and under Gov. Harvey vindicated the right to control taxation. After the withdrawal of

Colonial Assemblies

Gov. Berkeley from public life in 1652 the House of Burgesses exercised great authority scarcely checked by any outside interference except that embodied in the Navigation Act of 1651[qv], which placed certain limitations upon commercial intercourse. When Berkeley returned to power he failed to call elections, and retained the old assembly for many years prior to Bacon's Rebellion[qv] in 1676. Popular resentment of this means of attempting to control the legislative branch by the executive had the effect of restoring the representative character of the assembly.

Plymouth[qv] colony set up a popular assembly consisting of all qualified freemen[qv]. With the growth of out-settlements this evolved into a representative bicameral body. In Massachusetts Bay[qv] an effort was made by Gov. Winthrop and his supporters to concentrate legislative authority in the Court of Assistants[qv], with the Great and General Court limited to the activities of a court of election. This failed in face of the demand by deputies of the towns that the provisions of the royal charter should be fully observed. After experimenting with a primary assembly of all freemen of the company and with proxy voting, a representative bicameral system was evolved there as in Plymouth.

In Rhode Island[qv], after the federation of Providence, Portsmouth, Newport and Warwick, the towns were empowered to initiate legislation which was thereupon referred to the assembly; or, on the other hand, the assembly would refer measures to the towns for their approval or disapproval. The system was ineffective, and the charter of 1663 gave the assembly a dominating role in all matters of government.

Connecticut under its Fundamental Orders[qv] of 1639 had a General Court which was both a representative body and, upon sitting as a court of election, a primary assembly. The latter feature continued under the charter of 1662, although in the middle of the 18th century it disappeared in favor of local election of colonial officials. As in Rhode Island, the assembly was the real center of governmental authority and throughout the colonial period enjoyed great freedom from outside interference in the making of laws.

On coming into possession of his Maryland[qv] proprietary, Cecil Calvert, Lord Baltimore, called an assembly of freemen. However, he attempted to establish the principle that the proprietor alone might initiate legislation, and sent over drafts of a series of measures. The assembly rejected them, claiming sole powers of initiation, and passed a number of bills framed by its own members. Although these were rejected by Baltimore as in violation of his rights, he finally admitted the competence of the assembly to initiate laws, but insisted that all measures be submitted to him for acceptance or rejection.

During the 17th century law-making processes in Carolina[qv] were confused by the divergent aims of the eight proprietors and the settlers. The latter were determined to uphold the binding nature of the so-called Concessions and Agreement[qv] of 1665, which provided for a popularly elected assembly of freeholders. In opposition to this the proprietors attempted to enforce the feudal Fundamental Constitutions[qv] with its extraordinarily complicated law-making machinery, designed to guarantee proprietarial control of legislation.

Contemporaneously, New York under the Duke of York[qv] was ruled for many years without the aid of any popularly elected body, much to the dissatisfaction of the English-speaking population. However, with the retirement of Gov. Edmund Andros to England in 1680, the settlers refused to pay imposts, which made it necessary for the Duke either to send an army to subdue the people, or to grant an assembly. He chose the latter course in sending out Gov. Dongan; but the laws passed by the deputies were never ratified; and when James became king future assemblies were forbidden.

From the time of its founding Pennsylvania[qv] was provided with a popularly elected assembly. After the withdrawal of the charter of Massachusetts Bay in 1684, a process of consolidation took place in New England. With the establishment of the Dominion of New England[qv], the assemblies were suppressed and law-making powers were centered in the appointed Dominion council. New York, East New Jersey and West New Jersey[qqv], the two last with popularly elected assemblies, were also embodied in the Dominion before it collapsed in 1689.

During the 18th century the assemblies frequently came into collision with the governors (*see* Colonial Governors, The). In Massachusetts Bay such issues arose as those involving appropriations for a permanent establishment and for the building of forts and the control of the office of speaker of the house of representatives. In New York and in New Jersey, as the result of the maladministration of Cornbury, joint-governor of those provinces, the assemblies gained new powers over financial disbursements and administration generally. In Pennsylvania, with the beginning of the French and Indian War[qv] a controversy developed over the force of proprietorial instructions to the governor, as well as over the issue of paper money[qv], and the determination of the assembly, a unicameral body, to tax proprietorial lands. When Parliament threatened to compel all officeholders in Pennsylvania to take the required oaths rather than to affirm, in 1756 the Quaker majority in the assembly disappeared through resignations, with the result that for a short period harmony was restored between executive and legislature. Conflicts with the governors, as a rule, left the assemblies in a strongly entrenched position, in spite of the continued control of colonial legislation on the part of the Privy Council[qv].

With the approach of the Revolution, breaches took place between the assemblies and their governors in all of the colonies except the two corporate colonies (Connecticut and Rhode Island), although the degree of friction varied from the violent manifestations in Massachusetts Bay to the not unsympathetic relations that subsisted between Gov. John Penn and the Pennsylvania assembly.

[H. L. Osgood, *The American Colonies in the Seventeenth Century*, and *The American Colonies in the Eighteenth Century.*]

LAWRENCE HENRY GIPSON

Colonial Charters. Royal charters represented the king's authorization of colonization under private enterprise and his definition of the relationship of the projected colony to the mother country. They were at the outset issued to two chief types of promoters, the trading company and the lords proprietors[qqv], the former interested chiefly in trade, the latter in land as a source of profit. In the Restoration period, charters of incorporation which very closely resembled those previously given to trading companies were granted also to two already well-established squatter colonies, Rhode Island and Connecticut[qqv].

Charters to trading companies vested powers of government in the company in England. That body could determine what officers, laws and ordinances were necessary for the colony, subject only to the condition that the laws must conform to those of England. In the proprietary charters[qv] the authority to govern was granted to the lord proprietor, who could determine the form of government, choose the officers and make the laws, subject to the advice and consent of the freemen[qv]. According to the corporation charters of Connecticut and Rhode Island, government was to be administered by governor, council and house of representatives; the latter chosen directly, the former indirectly by the people. In all types of charter the settlers who might go to the colonies were promised the rights and privileges of Englishmen[qv], a phrase which, because of its vagueness, was to give considerable trouble later.

Toward the end of the 17th century the king began to find charters obstacles in the path of colonial control and tried to substitute the royal province[qv] for corporation and proprietary governments. In course of time he was almost completely successful, for by 1776 there remained only two proprietary provinces, Maryland and Pennsylvania[qqv], and two corporation colonies, Connecticut and Rhode Island. Massachusetts[qv], though operating under a charter, was governed in the 18th century as a royal province.

[H. L. Osgood, *American Colonies in the Seventeenth Century;* C. M. Andrews, *The Colonial Period in American History.*]

VIOLA F. BARNES

Colonial Commerce took various forms. There was the two-way commerce: that between a colony and the mother country, as was the case with respect to the tobacco trade; or that between two colonies or between a colony and a British or a foreign West India port, such as characterized the provision trade of Pennsylvania and the limited commercial relations of Connecticut. However, a triangular trade[qv] was a common, if not the most common, form that colonial commerce took. This might involve a colony, the African coasts and the West Indies, typified by Rhode Island's trade in rum, slaves and molasses; or involve a colony, a European country, such as Spain or Portugal, and Great Britain, as in the case of the trade of Massachusetts Bay in prime fish, in wines and British commodities; or a colony, Newfoundland and the West Indies, as was characterized by the trade of the same colony in merchandise, including rum, prize fish and molasses; or a Northern colony, a Southern colony and Great Britain, involving provisions, tobacco or rice from the Carolinas and British and European merchandise.

This commerce was carried on, as a rule, in American-built ships. When ships themselves were articles of commerce they were generally built in New England, loaded in a Southern port and then sent to their destination in England. The two greatest colonial commercial centers before the American Revolution were Boston and Philadelphia, each exercising a dominating influence over an extended region. However, New York controlled the business of that province and of western Connecticut and east New Jersey; Newport that of Rhode Island and of southern Massachusetts Bay; and Charleston that of South Carolina, Georgia and southern North Carolina. This commerce involved not only barter, specie transactions in Spanish or Portuguese coins and bills of exchange, but credit extensions on a great scale. For example, as the result of credit extensions to Virginia planters by British merchants before the outbreak of the Revolutionary War, the former were in many instances hopelessly involved in debt (*see* British Debts, The).

The commercial relations of the colonies with the outside world were subject to some restrictions from the beginning as the result of the comprehension of the plantations within the English realm, such, for example, as the prohibition of the export of English specie. However, the development of restrictions with particular reference to the colonies, outside of early restrictions by the crown on the sale of tobacco, is associated with the body of legislation known as the trade and navigation acts[qv], including the Woolen, the Molasses[qv], the Hat, the Iron[qv] and the Sugar Acts[qv]. Under these, certain colonial products, such as American woolens or beaver hats, could not enter into commerce; other products, placed on the enumerated list[qv], such as sugar, molasses, tobacco, dyewoods, indigo, cotton, rice, furs, ginger, copper, potash, hides, raw silk, ship-timber, naval stores and iron, could be carried directly only to the mother country or to another colony, with certain relaxations ultimately provided for the marketing in Europe of sugar and rice. Ships engaged in colonial commerce were confined, with certain exceptions in favor of prizes captured, to vessels of English, later British, or colonial construction and manned chiefly by those owing allegiance to the crown. All such vessels were required to have a British or colonial registry, to be commanded by British or colonial officers and to sail under British colors. Also it was incumbent upon colonial merchants who desired to import European commodities to do so through a British port, with the exception of a few specified articles such as salt for the New England and Newfoundland fisheries[qv], Madeira and Azores wines, and servants, provisions and horses from Ireland and Scotland.

[L. H. Gipson, *The British Empire before the American Revolution;* G. L. Beer, *Commercial Policy of England toward the American Colonies.*]

LAWRENCE HENRY GIPSON

Colonial Councils existed in all the colonies. In general they represented the same control as did the governor. In the royal provinces[qv] they were appointed directly by the crown, usually on recommendation of the Board of Trade[qv]. In the proprietary colonies[qv] they were appointed by the Proprietor, and in Massachusetts, Rhode Island and Connecticut the councils were elective. In the royal and proprietary provinces the members of the council served during good behavior. The governor could suspend members for cause, but they could be removed only by action of the crown or the proprietors.

Councils varied in size, although the standard practice tended to a uniform council of twelve in the royal provinces. Rhode Island had ten, Pennsylvania a council of eighteen and Massachusetts one of twenty-eight. Colonial councils acted as the upper house of the legislature and when so acting the governor was directed (1736) not to be present. The council together with the governor formed a supreme court of appeals in civil cases. Finally the council was an executive and administrative body for the governor, and many of his acts could be carried out only with the approval of the council. The duties of the council were specified in charters or in instructions to the royal governor, although custom gradually changed practices.

[Leonard Woods Labaree, *Royal Government in America.*]

O. M. DICKERSON

Colonial Currency. *See* Currency, Colonial.

Colonial Dames of America, THE. Women are eligible for membership who are descended from some ancestor who came to reside in America prior to 1750, and who served his country in the founding of a town which has survived and developed, or who held an important position, or who contributed to the achievement of American independence. The society, organized in 1890, has as its objects the collection of relics and mementoes for preservation, the creation of interest in American history and the promotion of social fellowship.

FRANCES PARKINSON KEYES

Colonial Governors, THE, were the chief civil officers in the American colonies before the Revolution. Some were appointed by the king as, for instance, the governor of the royal colony[qv] of Virginia; others were nominated by a proprietor (*see* Proprietary Provinces), such as William Penn, and were approved by the crown; and a few, those of the chartered colonies[qv], were elected by deputies of the freemen[qv] of the community.

Their duties were the usual ones of an administrative officer: defense, preservation of law and order, promotion of the general welfare. To these were added enforcement of the Navigation Acts[qv] and supervision of the collection of customs duties. And so necessary did those last-named functions seem to the home government, believing in the principles of mercantilism^{qv}, that even the governors of the chartered colonies were required to give oath and bond that they would execute the commercial laws.

The tasks of the executive of the chartered colonies were relatively simple. Chosen by his own people and linked by only nebulous bonds to the mother country, he suffered under no conflict of loyalties, and consideration of local interests easily took precedence over imperial policies.

The position of the governor of the royal or proprietary colonies, however, was always uncertain and often unpleasant. Saddled with definite instructions, he faced provincially minded and stubborn assemblies (*see* Colonial Assemblies). Therefore, he was forced to decide between either constant bickering and possible loss of salary—for the assembly controlled the purse strings—or jettisoning most of his instructions.

After the Restoration England attempted to reorganize her loose-jointed empire in order to establish uniform government in the colonies, but this was never accomplished. Consequently the colonial assemblies, overshadowing the governors, became the real executives and soon learned the art of self-government.

[G. L. Beer, *British Colonial Policy, 1754-1765;* O. M. Dickerson, *American Colonial Government.*]

MARGUERITE APPLETON

Colonial Governors – Instructions. Instructions were issued in the king's name by the Privy Council^{qv} to every royal governor of a province. They elaborated and explained the general powers set forth in the governor's commission. They touched upon nearly every subject involved in colonial government—the council and assembly^{qqv} and the governor's relations thereto, legislation, finance, justice, military and naval matters, as well as many other subjects such as religion and morals, Indian affairs, land distribution, alien groups and trade and commerce. Due to opposition on the part of the colonists or ignorance of colonial conditions on the part of the ministry, such instructions were often unenforced and unenforceable. But, as expressions of British authority, they definitely controlled the free development of colonial policies.

[L. W. Labaree, *Royal Instructions to British Colonial Governors, 1670-1776.*]

JULIAN P. BOYD

Colonial Judiciary, THE, was created in each colony by act of the assembly^{qv} and followed the general pattern of English procedure. Each colony had a system of local courts to try petty offenses. There was a county court in most of the colonies to try major civil and criminal cases, which was presided over by one of the superior judges who travelled on circuit^{qv}. There was a superior court made up of the superior court judges sitting *en banc* and presided over by a chief justice. Each colony had an attorney general.

In the royal provinces^{qv} the chief justice and the judges of the superior court were at first appointed directly by the Crown. Every effort was made to secure competent men. In some cases well-trained lawyers were induced to emigrate to America to fill such vacancies, as was the case when William Atwood was appointed chief justice of New York (1701). Apparently, the first commissions were at the will of the crown, as were those of other important colonial officers. There were, however, no actual removals. The Act of Settlement had made English judges independent of the crown, with commissions during good behavior. Governors were authorized by instructions to fill vacancies when they occurred. Their instructions were not very clear on this point, except they were not to impose "any limitation of time" in any commissions they might issue. By the middle of the 18th century many judges had received commissions during good behavior. Gov. Clinton's appointment of William DeLancey as chief justice of New York attracted the attention of the Board of Trade^{qv} to the obscurity of the instruction and in 1754, it instructed every governor that in future all judicial officers should be appointed "during pleasure only." In Pennsylvania the assembly enacted a law providing that judges could only be removed on address of the assembly (1759). This act was promptly disallowed in England (*see* Royal Disallowance).

The death of George II in 1760 terminated all judicial commissions, many of which had been granted by the governors during good behavior. The Board of Trade insisted that all renewals should be "at the pleasure of the Crown." This precipitated a controversy with the assemblies, which refused to pay judges unless their commissions read as formerly "during good behavior." Gov. Hardy of New Jersey had already renewed commissions under the former terms (1761). These commissions were held void by the Privy Council^{qv} in England and funds were found to pay the judges so as to make them entirely independent of the local assemblies. This enforced solution of the question rankled with the Americans, as it deprived Englishmen in America of rights guaranteed to Englishmen in

England, and is one of the specific acts of tyranny charged against George III in the Declaration of Independence^qv^.

[O. M. Dickerson, *American Colonial Government, 1696-1765.*]

O. M. DICKERSON

Colonial Newspaper, THE. The first newspaper in the American colonies, entitled *Publick Occurrences*^qv^, was published in Boston, Sept. 25, 1690, but, after a single issue, was suppressed by the authorities. The first regularly published newspaper was *The Boston News-Letter*^qv^, established in Boston, April 24, 1704. This was followed by other papers in Boston, then in Philadelphia, New York, Annapolis, Charleston, Newport and Williamsburg, all before 1750. By April, 1775, there were thirty-seven newspapers in eleven of the colonies on the Atlantic seaboard. The colonial newspaper was a small folio weekly, almost invariably of four pages, including foreign news on the first page, domestic news on the second, local news on the third and advertisements on the fourth. Political news and the proceedings of legislative bodies aroused a lively interest, and important documents and letters were often quoted at length, providing a means of disseminating information throughout the colonies, which more than any one cause welded the people together in their resistance to the mother country. Local news was negligible, and in fact the greatest amount of local information comes from the advertisements. Yet the history of no town could be written without access to its file of newspapers. Essays and poetry filled a considerable portion of the papers, especially the *Pennsylvania Gazette*^qv^, published by Benjamin Franklin in Philadelphia. Because of the scarcity of all but theological books, secular literature was almost unread in the colonies except through the newspapers. Outside of the Bible and the Almanac^qqv^, the newspaper was the only printed matter found in most colonial families.

[Isaiah Thomas, *History of Printing in America;* Check-list of files in *Proceedings* of American Antiquarian Society, 1913-27.]

C. S. BRIGHAM

Colonial Plans of Union (1643–1754). The separate founding of the colonies, coupled with difficulties of travel, prevented effective union until the Revolution. However, many proposals for union grew out of the common problems faced by the colonies. The most continuous problem was that of frontier defense against Indian attack. Rivalry with the Dutch and French aggravated this problem. Trade and boundary disputes emphasized the need of a common arbitrator. A common culture and allegiance suggested the reasonableness of unity. Moreover, the English home government, desiring to make the colonies an effective unit for imperial trade and defense, in some cases encouraged a union. The chief plans, which varied widely in origin and the number of colonies to be included, were: 1. The United Colonies of New England, 1643–1684^qv^. Massachusetts Bay, Plymouth, Connecticut and New Haven, united in a league largely for frontier defense. 2. Dominion of New England, 1688^qv^. The British crown made Sir Edmund Andros governor-general of all the New England colonies, New York, East and West Jersey. 3. Intercolonial Congress, 1689–91. New York, Massachusetts, Plymouth and Connecticut entered a temporary military league for frontier defense. 4. William Penn's "Briefe and Plaine Scheam" for Union, 1697. Penn's proposal for a loose confederation grew out of the conditions prevailing during King William's War^qv^. 5. Union under the Earl of Bellomont, 1698–1701, who was commissioned governor of New York, Massachusetts and New Hampshire, and commander of the military forces of Connecticut, Rhode Island and the Jerseys. This step was taken by the crown because of colonial failure to co-operate in defense. 6. Hamilton's Plan, 1699, for frontier defense and production of naval supplies for the Royal Navy proposed by the deputy-governor of Pennsylvania. An intercolonial assembly was to levy a poll tax to finance the work which was to be done by British regulars. 7. A Virginian's Plan of Union, 1701, was an anonymous publication issued in London which advocated abolishing all the proprietary governments and uniting the colonies under an intercolonial congress and governor-general. 8. Robert Livingston's Plan, 1701. In a letter to the Lords of Trade^qv^ Livingston proposed that the colonies be grouped into three units, which would be co-ordinated by the Council of Trade for frontier defense. 9. Earl of Stair's Plan, 1721, submitted by the Earl of Stair to the Board of Trade^qv^, was to include all the continental colonies and the British West Indies. There was to be a governor-in-chief appointed by the crown. An advisory council of two members from each colony was to assist this official. The governor and his council could levy assessments against the colonies for defense purposes. The scheme was to be established by action of Parliament. 10. The Lords of Trade Plan, 1721, was contained in a report given the king. It was essentially a brief outline of the Stair plan. 11. Daniel Coxe's Plan, 1722, appeared in a book of travel published in London.

It proposed a union of all the continental colonies under one governor, represented by a lieutenant in each colony. A great council composed of two delegates from each colony was to advise the governor and make the allotments of money and men needed for colonial defense. 12. The Kennedy-Franklin Plan, 1751, was published by Archibald Kennedy, receiver-general of New York, in a pamphlet dealing with Indian trade and frontier defense. These were to be directed by a superintendent to be assigned to the colonies by commissioners representing the colonial assemblies. Benjamin Franklin added some details which closely resembled his later Albany Plan. 13. The Albany Plan, 1754[qv]. This best known of all the colonial plans was largely the work of Franklin. It called for an intercolonial council with membership apportioned according to wealth and population. The president-general was to be appointed by the crown. Control of Indian affairs and frontier defense was to be under control of this royal officer and his council. The colonial legislatures rejected the plan and it was not pressed by the home government.

[Herbert L. Osgood, *The American Colonies in the Seventeenth Century* and *The American Colonies in the Eighteenth Century.*]

ROBERT MOULTON GATKE

Colonial Policy, The British, is technically that policy that was laid down or was evolved after the union of England and Scotland in 1707. This policy was based largely upon the earlier English policy, which envisaged the promotion of domestic industry, foreign trade, the fisheries and shipping, and the planting of crown lands in the New World with the establishment of colonial settlements, or the exploitation of the resources of America through such commercial companies as the Hudson's Bay Company[qv] and the South Sea Company. It also included the policy of encouraging the utilization of the vast labor resources of Africa in the establishment and maintenance of plantations for the production of so-called colonial staples (*see* Slavery).

The earliest manifestations of English colonial policy are embodied in the 16th-century patents to Gilbert and Raleigh[qv]; then in 1606 came those to the London and Plymouth companies[qqv] of Virginia in connection with which a settlement policy was laid down which, among other features, embodied the idea of direct crown control; but in 1609 this was modified in the charter of that year issued in favor of the Virginia Company substituting indirect for direct control and providing for a definite and extensive grant of land; this new policy also found expression in the creation of the Council for New England[qv] in 1620. Direct control, however, made its reappearance in 1624 when with the withdrawal of the political powers of the Virginia Company, Virginia took its place as the first of the so-called royal colonies under a system of government that permitted the survival of the colonial assembly[qv]. Nevertheless, this new policy was not to become basic until the beginning of the new century, for the year 1629 saw the appearance of the corporate colony of Massachusetts Bay[qv] with a charter that was sufficiently broad to permit the transfer of the government of the company to the New World, and 1632 that of the proprietaryship of Maryland with the granting to the Baltimore family of very wide powers. Thus three types of colonial government appeared as the result of the formulation of colonial policy—or perhaps one might suggest more accurately as the result of the failure of the Government to formulate a policy—royal, proprietary and charter[qqv].

Up to the Interregnum, colonial policy emanated from the crown and was directed by it. Then with the outbreak of the English Civil War the Long Parliament assumed control, acting mainly through a special commission or council provided for by the Ordinance of 1643, which gave to its president, the Earl of Warwick, the title of Governor-in-Chief and Lord High Admiral of all the English colonies in America (*see* Warwick Commission). Moreover, between the years 1645 and 1651 Parliament laid down various regulations which looked to a strict control of colonial commerce in favor of English shipping and manufactures. Nor did this parliamentary interference with the colonies cease with the Restoration, which not only gave validity to these restrictions but added to them in a series of measures beginning with the so-called First Navigation Act of 1660 and culminating in the very comprehensive Act of 1696 (*see* Navigation Acts). During the Commonwealth period Cromwell introduced a striking but temporary departure in colonial policy in 1654 with his ambitious plan known as the Western Design[qv] which had a twofold purpose: the acquisition of the Spanish empire in the New World and in this connection the removal of Northern English colonists to the warmer climes.

The growth in importance of the colonies led, moreover, to various experiments in their supervision such as the Laud Commission (*see* High Commission, Court of) appointed by Charles I, and the various councils of Charles II ending with the transference in 1675 of this function to the Lords of Trade[qv], a committee of the Privy Council[qv], which continued to function after a manner until in 1696 William III brought into existence the Lords Commissioners for Trade and Plantations, a body which survived until after the American Revolution and which in the main fully justified its existence.

Colonial policy in the 18th century was characterized not only by efforts to reduce the colonies to a uniform type—that of the royal colony—which met with considerable success, but also by increased restrictions upon colonial enterprise with such acts as the Woolen Act of 1699, the White Pine Acts, the Hat Act of 1731, the Sugar Acts[qv] of 1733 and 1764 and the Iron Act[qv] of 1750. With the middle of the 18th century an important modification of policy may be noted with the growing menace of French competition. Side by side with mercantilism[qv] (with the emphasis upon immediate economic gain), modern imperialism (with the emphasis upon power politics, territorial aggrandizement, centralization of authority and a unified Indian policy) made its appearance. With the collapse of French empire in North America (*see* Paris, The Treaty of) Parliament also turned its attention to securing a direct revenue from the colonies, passing for this purpose the Stamp Act of 1765 and the Townshend Acts of 1767[qqv]. Reliance upon these new policies helped to bring on a crisis in colonial affairs that led to the Revolution.

[*Cambridge History of the British Empire*, I; L. H. Gipson, *The British Empire before the American Revolution.*]

LAWRENCE HENRY GIPSON

Colonial Policy of United States. *See* Insular Possessions.

Colonial Settlements. Various little colonies were planted along the coastal ribbon of the Atlantic for different reasons. Government encouraged them to serve the economic needs of the nation, capitalists hoped for profit and people sought better opportunities. Tragedy stalked the efforts to colonize. Ships, abundant capital, many people were demanded to found a prosperous colony. The loss of life and money was tragic. Some ventures were stillborn, others were nursed through a puling infancy to maturity, a few grew lustily from birth.

Humphrey Gilbert landed with his company on Newfoundland's shores in 1584. A few months saw them sail away. Walter Raleigh[qv] in 1585 settled a few colonists on Roanoke Island (Carolina coast), but sustained effort failed to keep the venture alive. The time was not ripe and the cost was too heavy for private purses. The close of the war with Spain in 1604 freed England to turn to America. Joint-stock companies (*see* Trading Companies), combining capital and credit, entered into colonization. In 1607 the Plymouth Company[qv] tried a settlement on the Kennebec River (Maine), the London Company[qv] on the James River (Virginia). A rigorous winter and the death of the chief promoter sent the Kennebec settlers soon away (*see* Popham Colony, The). The Council for New England[qv] (1620) proved to be only a land company whose subgrants resulted in a few fishing, trading, lumbering camps on New England's shores. Against heavy odds the London Company persisted. During its existence about 5500 emigrants left England for Virginia[qv]; in 1625 a few over a thousand were living in the colony. The distress on a long voyage, disease, starvation and Indians in the colony took a deadly toll. Virginia lived to be the first permanent English colony, with a population of 5000 in 1634, rising to 50,000 in 1690.

England was not the only mother of colonies. In 1624 the Dutch West India Company sent over thirty families which founded New Amsterdam and Fort Orange (Albany)[qqv]. Forty years of effort showed a population of only about 8000. The Dutch were not a migrating people, and a grasping company attracted few settlers. In 1638 the New Sweden Company began Fort Christina on the Delaware with a few people, but New Sweden[qqv] never contained over a few hundred Swedes and Finns. Sweden's wars in Europe left her inadequate sources for colonial ventures. New Sweden ceased to be when captured by the Dutch in 1655.

The economic motive was not the only factor in colonial enterprise. Abundant land meant little without people. At first no urgent expulsive forces drove people away. Settlers were hard to secure until intolerable conditions sent them to the new land. This stream began in 1620 when the Pilgrims found their weary way to plant the colony of Plymouth[qv]. Villagers from northern England, denied freedom of worship, went to Holland for refuge, but finding Dutch life uncomfortable, they came to New England. The stream widened with the exodus of over 16,000 to New England during 1630–40 (*see* Great Migration, The). Various motives explain the migration, but primary was the purpose to establish in Massachusetts a city of God on Puritan lines (*see* Massachusetts Bay Company). Unable to reform the Anglican Church, visited with harsh royal authority, the Puritan leaders found the answer in Massachusetts. Villagers from Massachusetts Bay, in 1635, founded the colony of Connecticut[qv], where better land was available and a milder brand of Puritanism was practised. A small band of devoted Puritans began the colony of New Haven[qv] in 1638. In 1662 New Haven was merged with Connecticut and thirty years later the greater colony numbered about 18,000 people. Intolerable conditions in Massachusetts peopled Rhode Island[qv]. The Bay colony dealt severely with dissent. The radical views of Roger Williams drove him to find refuge in the settlement of Providence in 1636. The strange ideas of Mrs. Hutchinson and her followers brought exile, some settling at Portsmouth, others at Newport (*see* Antinomian Controversy, The). Rhode Island contained about 4000 souls by 1690. Massachusetts added Maine[qv] by purchase and secured Plymouth colony by merger and before 1700 the Bay province had over 50,000 people. New Hampshire[qv] was a slender little colony which harbored a few people under the proprietorship of Capt. John Mason. Maryland[qv] owed its genesis to Lord Baltimore, who under a royal charter in 1632 desired to find a refuge for Catholics and to build up a great landed estate. From small beginnings its population rose to 30,000 within sixty years.

After 1660 colonial expansion took on a renewed life. Again promoters sought profit and people better opportunities. The circle of English colonies was completed by the conquest of New Netherland[qv] in 1664, renamed New York[qv] and granted to the Duke of York. He subgranted New Jersey[qv] to Sir George Carteret and Lord John Berkeley. Carolina, granted to eight men by charter in 1663, divided into two colonies, North Carolina peopled from Virginia and South Carolina[qqv] settled by discontented planters from Barbados and persecuted Protestants from France and England. After thirty years of effort neither colony had over 3000 people. Quakerism, with its democratic and mystical principles, came into tragic collision with orthodoxy in both Old and New England. The Quakers[qv] found a welcome in Rhode Island and established their own colonies on the Delaware. In 1674 Berkeley sold West Jersey[qv], which finally came into the hands of the Quakers who settled along the Delaware at Burlington and other places. East Jersey[qv], purchased from the Carteret estate in 1680, soon fell under the control of a large board in which the Quakers were prominent. Before the century closed East Jersey counted less than 10,000, West Jersey about 4000. In 1681 William Penn received a charter for Pennsylvania[qv] where he tried a "Holy Experiment"[qv] in Quaker principles. The province became a haven of refuge for the persecuted, welcoming English, Welsh and Irish Quakers, and Germans. It grew lustily, having a population, inclusive of Delaware[qv], of over 12,000 within a decade. Delaware, granted to William Penn by the Duke of York, governed at first as part of Pennsylvania, in 1704 became a province with Penn as proprietor. Thus ends the founding of the original colonies except for Georgia[qv], which came into existence in 1732, in response to humanitarian motives. Georgia harbored debtors from English jails, and Lutheran exiles from Germany.

[C. M. Andrews, *Colonial Period of American History*, Vols. I-III.]

WINFRED T. ROOT

Colonial Ships, THE, were very small. Sir Humphrey Gilbert's vessel, on which he lost his life, was one of ten tons. Newport's three ships, in which the first Virginians came to America, were of 100, 40 and 20 tons, respectively. The *Mayflower's*[qv] tonnage was 180, her keel length 64 feet, beam width 26 feet and depth from beam to keel 11 feet, while the full length was 90 feet. The *Dove*, and the *Ark*[qv], which carried Baltimore's company to Maryland, were of 50 and 400 tons, respectively.

On these vessels, passengers were weeks crossing the Atlantic. One ship made the journey in four weeks but the Pilgrims were ten weeks, the first Virginians and Calvert's party were four months and some Germans six months. Because of this delay, food and water were soon wretched. Biscuits and cereals were full of maggots and weevils. Water was covered with slime and became so nauseous that one had to hold his nose to drink it. Scurvy generally incapacitated one tenth of those on board. It was only when lemons and oranges were found to be specifics for scurvy that this condition was changed. Overcrowding, smallpox, seasickness, fevers, dysentery, cancer and mouth-rot added their quota to the misery and suffering of the transatlantic voyage.

Small vessels were soon being made in the colonies, often in the forests whence they were rolled on tree trunks to the water's edge. By 1676, 730 ships had been built in Massachusetts alone, and hundreds more in other New England colonies. It cost from six to ten pounds sterling for the voyage across the Atlantic and from forty to fifty dollars to go by ship from South Carolina to New York.

[James Lind, *Treatise on Scurvy;* C. B. Swaney, The Transatlantic Voyage in the Age of Sails, *Social Science,* Fall Number, 1937.]

CHARLES B. SWANEY

Colonial Society. The genius and temper of colonial society lay largely in the breed of the people who settled America. In the beginning New England and the South were settled by the English. A few Dutch and Walloons lived along the Hudson, a fewer Swedes[qv] along the Delaware. In general English institutions modified by American conditions formed the basis of the various colonial structures. England was not the only mother of colonies. The 18th century saw a great influx of foreigners. A population of about a quarter of a million in 1700 became over two million by 1775, of whom about a sixth were foreign born. In large numbers came the Scotsmen from Ulster in Ireland (*see* Scotch-Irish, The) and the Germans from the Rhine country. In smaller numbers came the Swiss, the French Huguenots[qv], the Scotch Highlanders and a few Celtic Irish. The African reservoir was tapped to supply the colonies with servile labor, especially the South (*see* Slave Trade).

Nor was Europe a kindly mother. Intolerable conditions in Europe peopled the colonies. Not the privileged classes, but the poor, the distressed, the opponents of arbitrary authority migrated to the colonies. Devastating wars, bitter religious persecution, economic disabilities, the exactions of arbitrary princes, harsh legal codes were the forces of expulsion. America beckoned because it offered the opportunity for self-expression and human betterment. Abundant land provided room for all groups to fashion life in response to needs and desires and a broad and hostile ocean protected them from undue pressure from Europe.

English America became a laboratory of social experimentation. Religion played a large role in the unfolding of colonial society. In fact, colonization was a phase of the Protestant Reformation. The great secession from Rome broke Christianity into many factions. Unable to realize their religious principles at home, they took refuge in America. Their varying religious creeds were of an even greater variety than the racial stocks. England supplied the Puritans, Quakers, Baptists, Anglicans and others; Germany sent Lutherans, German Reformed and the Pietists (Mennonites, Dunkers, Moravians); Ulster the Scotch Presbyterians; France the Huguenots; Holland the Dutch Reformed[qqv]. Each group found room to give practical application to its peculiar beliefs. Massachusetts and Connecticut experimented in Puritan conceptions of life, Pennsylvania in Quaker principles, Georgia in humanitarian ideas, to mention only the major ventures. Ideals played a large part in the making of not one, but many societies.

In America there was at first no society prepared to receive the settlers, no institutions to lean upon. Here was plenty of land and raw nature. The colonists were forced to build social structures from the bottom. Nature knew no favorites and men were forced to be self-reliant and courageous. In time the frontier was overcome, a primitive society grew into an established order entrenched in institutions. In the 18th century there emerged in each colony a controlling aristocracy, in the North the rich merchants, in the South the wealthy planters. In Puritan New England they attended the Congregational Church, in the South the Anglican Church, both established by law. In Pennsylvania the Quakers dominated the colony. Each little colonial aristocracy was knit together by marriage ties. They enjoyed the wealth and leisure for refined living, for books and education. And they controlled politics.

America provided plenty of land, Europe plenty of people seeking refuge. With the growth of little aristocracies along the coast, there developed a democratic society composed of laborers, artisans, little shop-keepers in the port towns and villages, but more particularly of the farmers who pushed into the vacant lands of the interior. Beyond the coastal plain people lived under a maximum of labor and debt and a minimum of leisure. Here then were two societies in each colony, an aristocratic minority and a democratic majority, which touched each other at many points and the contacts produced friction. These conflicts were a major force in shaping society. The dissenting religious groups opposed the established churches in New England and the South and they resented Quaker domination in Pennsylvania. The Great Awakening[qv], a burning religious revival which swept across the colonies in mid-century, split the Congregational and Presbyterian churches apart. These divisions were the evidence of conflicts between democratic and aristocratic tendencies.

Social cleavages showed themselves in various ways. The democracy of the interior protested against unfair representation in the controlling legislatures. They were angry because they received inadequate protection against the Indians. Frequent were the quarrels between the settlers and the absentee landlords and land speculators. Bitter were the contests between the creditor East and the democratic West over questions of currency and taxation. These antagonisms came to a dramatic conclusion in some colonies on the eve of the American Revolution. The Revolution itself not only emancipated America from Europe, but it also brought the democratic transformation of colonial society and politics.

[James Truslow Adams, *Provincial Society;* Curtis P. Nettels, *The Roots of American Civilization.*]

WINFRED T. ROOT

Colonial Wars. Although English, French and Spanish colonies in North America were repeatedly plunged into war by the outbreak of hostilities in Europe involving their parent states, the colonial wars, from the outset, were much more than mere New World phases of Old World conflicts. America's natural resources and the supposed advantages of owning American markets led Europeans to seek vast holdings here, and economic rivalries among the colonials themselves were intensified by racial and religious antagonisms. Louis XIV, concentrating on aggressions in Europe, gave little practical support to offensives in America; thus Frontenac, in King William's War[qv] (1689–97), resorted to the employment of Indian allies in ruthless border raids. Similar raids were utilized, chiefly by the French, in the subsequent conflicts: Queen Anne's War (1702–13), King George's War (1744–48) and the French and Indian War (1754–63)[qqv].

At the outset of hostilities, and in 1711, English colonials and English regulars tried, futilely, to capture Quebec[qv], the ultimate conquest of which by Wolfe, in 1759, is the best known of many dramatic episodes of these wars. English forces, chiefly colonial, captured Port Royal[qv] in 1690 and again in 1710, although not until the Treaty of Utrecht[qv] (1713) was Acadia[qv] confirmed to the English, becoming then their outpost, Nova Scotia. At Utrecht the French also yielded Newfoundland and their claims to the Hudson Bay territory. During "the long peace" following 1713 (actually marred by hostilities in America and the West Indies) France established Louisbourg[qv] on Cape Breton Island, a base of operations against English participation in North Atlantic fisheries and trade routes. The restoration of Louisbourg to France (1748) after its capture by New Englanders (1745) embittered many colonials, already indignant at England's tragic mismanagement of colonial volunteers in an expedition against Cartagena[qv] (1740). Other friction between England and her colonies was caused by the former's attempts to dominate military operations and the latter's failure to meet, fully or promptly, English requisitions for men, money and supplies, as well as by the colonies' persistence in trading with the enemy. Spain entered the conflict in the second war, exchanging blows with the English in Florida and South Carolina. When King George's War began Spain and England already were engaged in the War of Jenkin's Ear[qv]. Spain, a late entrant in the last colonial war, lost Florida to England. This conflict, the French and Indian War, was precipitated by English expansion westward and French advances into the Ohio Valley, the link between New France (Canada) and French Illinois and Louisiana[qqv]. Braddock's defeat[qv] (1755) near Fort Duquesne was followed by English disappointments and defeats at Crown Point, Niagara, Oswego, Ticonderoga[qqv] and elsewhere, until the turning of the tide in 1758, usually accredited to England's new war minister, William Pitt. By the Treaty of Paris[qv] (1763) France retained most of her West Indian Islands and some fishing bases off Canada; her other North American possessions east of the Mississippi, except the neighborhood of New Orleans, she ceded to England.

[G. M. Wrong, *The Conquest of New France;* W. Wood and R. H. Gabriel, *The Winning of Freedom;* S. M. Pargellis, ed., *Military Affairs in North America, 1748-1765;* S. M. Pargellis, *Lord Loudoun in North America;* F. Parkman, *A Half-Century of Conflict*, and *Montcalm and Wolfe;* T. C. Pease, *Anglo-French Boundary Disputes in the West, 1749-1763.*]

LOUISE B. DUNBAR

Colonies, Manufacturing in the. *See* Industries, Colonial.

Colonies, Vindication of the British, one of several tracts by James Otis, defending the colonies against British policy, appeared in 1765 when Otis engaged in a controversy with the Tory, Martin Howard. Specifically repudiating any thought of independence on the part of the colonists, Otis in this thirty-page tract insisted on their possession of the rights of Englishmen[qv], particularly that of self-taxation.

[C. F. Mullett, ed., *Some Political Writings of James Otis.*]

CHARLES F. MULLETT

Colorado was first visited by white men under the banner of Spain. Coronado[qv], seeking fabled wealth, penetrated the American Southwest. Returning, disillusioned, he probably touched the southeast corner of Colorado in 1541. New Mexico[qv], settled about 1600, then included the Colorado region. Spanish slave-catching and prospecting expeditions reached this country during the 17th century. In 1706 Ulibarri crossed the upper Arkansas, took formal possession for Spain and called the region Santo Domingo.

Frenchmen, from the Great Lakes region,

pushed toward the Rockies. The alarmed Spaniards countered. In 1719 and 1720 Valverde and Villasur[qv] led unsuccessful expeditions against the intruders. The Mallet[qv] brothers, in 1739, crossed Colorado territory and reached Santa Fé. With France eliminated in 1763 (*see* Paris, The Treaty of), Spain was again in undisputed possession of the Colorado region.

Through the Louisiana Purchase[qv], 1803, the eastern part of Colorado became American. Z. M. Pike[qv], first official explorer, led a small party up the Arkansas in 1806. Failing to climb the peak that bears his name, he turned south and built a log fort on the Conejos River. From here he was taken, as a prisoner, to Santa Fé[qv] and was finally released on the Louisiana border. His *Journal,* published in American, English, French, Dutch and German editions within four years, is an important historical sourcebook. The western boundary of the Louisiana Purchase was fixed in 1819 (*see* Adams-Onís Treaty). Through Colorado, it followed the Arkansas to its source and thence north to the 42nd parallel. S. H. Long, 1820, Frémont on his five expeditions, 1842–53, Gunnison, 1853, were official explorers who gave enlightening reports on the Colorado country[qqv].

Unofficial explorers, trappers and fur traders thoroughly examined the region from 1800 to 1840. These almost unknown Mountain Men[qv] are perhaps the most picturesque characters in Colorado history. They came in search of beaver skins and their annual summer rendezvous was at once a trade fair and a fiesta (*see* Trappers' Rendezvous). Pursuit of furs made them pathfinders. Depletion of beaver and invention of the silk hat ruined their trapping. They turned to buffalo robes. Barter with Indians created Bent's Fort[qv] and other trading posts in the region. This trade augmented the overland commerce to New Mexico that made the Santa Fé Trail[qv], which cut the southeast section of Colorado. The Mexican War brought Kearny's army over this trail and added the rest of Colorado Territory to the United States in 1848 (*see* Guadalupe Hidalgo, Treaty of).

Settlements in Colorado, established in the 1850's by New Mexicans, were typical Spanish towns, with dirt-roofed adobe houses[qv] enclosing a plaza. Irrigated agriculture and grazing were their economic bases. Need for Indian protection caused the establishment, in 1852, of Fort Massachusetts[qv], first United States military fort in Colorado.

Anglo-American settlement resulted from gold discoveries. News of finds at Cherry Creek, in 1858, caused the Pikes Peak Gold Rush[qv] of 1859. As a result of the reports, and of the panic of 1857[qv], some hundred thousand persons set out for the new Eldorado. Many turned back, disgusted at the meager prospects. Fortunately, real discoveries saved the movement from collapse. J. H. Gregory found lode gold near present Central City, May 6, 1859. Other discoveries followed. Mining camps and towns sprang up in the mountains, and outfitting towns at their eastern base. The influx of population brought need for government. Jefferson Territory[qv], locally organized in 1859, maintained some authority until replaced by Colorado Territory, created by Congress Feb. 28, 1861. Colorado troops sustained the Union in the Civil War, giving decisive aid in the battle of Glorieta[qv].

Refractory ores and Indian wars retarded growth in the 1860's. With the close of the Civil War, expulsion of the Plains Indians and the coming of the railroad, conditions improved. Founding of "colony" towns and opening of new mines increased population and helped bring statehood, Aug. 1, 1876. Development of the range cattle industry[qv], opening of the Ute reservation, and the discovery of great silver lodes at Leadville and Aspen furthered prosperity. Colorado's population of 39,864 in 1870 increased to 413,249 by 1890. Demonetization of silver and the Panic of 1893[qqv] brought distress. Abrupt reduction in silver output was offset by the rise of the great gold camp of Cripple Creek[qv]. Metal production reached its peak of $50,000,000 in 1900. Since then mining has rapidly declined. Farming became the leading industry. Canals and reservoirs increased irrigated acreage, with dry farming[qv] on the plains. Manufacturing and the tourist business added wealth.

[L. R. Hafen, *Colorado, the Story of a Western Commonwealth.*]

LEROY R. HAFEN

Colorado, Narrow-Gauge Railroads of. Beginning in the late 1860's Colorado became the center of the construction of narrow-gauge (three feet) railroads. In 1873 over half of the narrow-gauge mileage in this country was in Colorado. The Denver and Rio Grande[qv] was the pioneer, longest and best known narrow-gauge railway in the United States. Close study of the Festiniog Railway in Wales had convinced Gen. W. J. Palmer, first president of the Denver and Rio Grande, that a gauge of three feet was practicable in mountainous regions. Advantages cited for narrow-gauge construction were: lower costs of construction, operation and maintenance; greater curvature and higher gradients; larger pay loads in proportion to weight of rolling stock, and ability to penetrate areas closed to broad-gauge lines. Although many lines have been abandoned or broad gauged since the early 1890's, a considerable number are still in operation.

[J. H. Baker and L. R. Hafen, *History of Colorado.*]

GEORGE L. ANDERSON

Colorado Coal Strikes, THE, of 1903–4 and 1913–14, were produced by essentially the same causes: refusal of the operators to recognize the right of unionization and demands by the workers for higher pay and more healthful working conditions, as well as for the right to board, trade and seek medical attention wherever they pleased. The last demand grew out of the maintenance of "closed" camps and towns by the Colorado Fuel and Iron Company, the Gould-Rockefeller controlled operating companies, where none but company stores were permitted and into which only company-approved persons might enter.

The earlier strike, involving 10,000 workers, began on Nov. 9, 1903, following the refusal of the operators to confer with representatives of the United Mine Workers[qv]. Those in the northern field returned to work on Nov. 27, but the remainder continued on strike. After some loss of life and property the militia was sent to Trinidad and order was restored. In June, 1904, the troops were withdrawn, after which the strikers returned to work without having won any material advantages.

The strike of 1913–14 began on Sept. 23, 1913, following the refusal of the worker demands drawn up a week earlier. It involved a mixed reign of terror and civil war of several months' duration in the area between Walsenburg and Trinidad. The Ludlow massacre of April 20, 1914, in which many men, women and children were killed, was the most tragic event of the strike. Federal troops were sent into the area in May, 1914, order was gradually restored, strikers returned to work under more satisfactory working conditions, the state enacted legislation to prevent similar occurrences in the future and the Colorado Fuel and Iron Company adopted a more constructive labor policy.

[W. F. Stone, *History of Colorado.*]

GEORGE L. ANDERSON

Colorado River, Exploration of. In 1539 the Spaniard Ulloa reached the mouth of the Colorado, without knowing of the river's existence. Wrote he: "... we perceived the sea to run with so great a rage into the land that it was a thing to be marvelled at; and with the like fury it returned back again with the ebb . . . some great river might be the cause thereof." The actual discovery was made in August, 1540, by Alarcón, who, conquering the fierce tidal bore of the river's mouth, anchored and proceeded upstream in boats drawn by tow ropes. He reached a point near Lighthouse Rock, but did not make a junction with the overland expedition under Coronado[qv]. Two of Coronado's officers, Diaz and Cárdenas, reached the Colorado, and Cárdenas discovered the Grand Canyon[qv]. In the next two centuries exploration of the river was in the hands of the padres, who were more interested in souls than geography. Outstanding among the padres were the Franciscans, Garcés and Escalante, in the 1770's. It was Garcés who first made regular use of the name Colorado, doing so because, draining a red country, the stream was tinged with red during the spring melting of the snows.

In the early 19th century exploration was mostly by American trappers and fur traders. Gen. William Henry Ashley[qv], fur trader, descended the canyons of the Green River by "bullboat"[qv] in 1825 and supplied the first authentic information concerning the upper Colorado. At Ashley Falls he painted "Ashley, 1825" on a huge overhanging rock; the black lettering was still partly visible in 1911. In 1826 a British naval officer, Lt. R. W. H. Hardy, explored the lower Colorado and wrote the first dependable description of the country near the mouth. Most important of the trappers was James O. Pattie, whose narrative was vitiated and mutilated by the editor. Each pioneer contributed to the gradual accumulation of knowledge, in spite of the contradictions in their narratives.

With the establishment of a military post at the mouth of the Gila for the protection of California-bound gold seekers, the United States Government became interested in scientific exploration of the Colorado. The topographical engineers of the War Department sent several expeditions: Lt. G. H. Derby, 1850–51; Lt. J. C. Ives, 1857–58; Lt. G. M. Wheeler, 1871; and towering over all, the two expeditions of Maj. J. W. Powell, 1869 and 1871–72. Powell's work of blueprinting the stream has since been completed by the Geological Survey. A civilian, George A. Johnson, first ascended the river to the head of navigation, above the Black Canyon, in his steamer, the *General Jessup,* in 1858.

Most of the world's rivers are attractive routes for interior exploration and highways of settlement and commerce. Through most of its history the Colorado has been none of these things. It has been "a veritable dragon, loud in its dangerous lair . . . a formidable host of snarling waters." It has been anything but a friend and ally of man, and it is precisely this feature that has restrained man's interest and distributed exploration over three centuries. It is only in recent decades that man has utilized the waters of the Colorado for irrigation and other purposes.

[F. S. Dellenbaugh, *The Romance of the Colorado River;* L. R. Freeman, *The Colorado River.*]

FRANK EDWARD ROSS

Colorado River Aqueduct, The, 242 miles long, estimated to cost $212,000,000, and scheduled for completion in 1939, was the first project initiated under the Hoover self-liquidating public works program. It will carry 1500 cubic feet of water per second for domestic use from the Colorado River to Los Angeles and other cities comprising the Metropolitan Water District. Boulder (Hoover) Dam[qv] power is used to lift the water about 1600 feet over the intervening mountains.

[Wilbur and Ely, *The Hoover Dam Contracts;* Reports of the Secretary of the Interior, 1930-32.]

NORTHCUTT ELY

Colorado River Projects. The Colorado River Compact, executed in 1922, under the chairmanship of Herbert Hoover, representing the United States, apportioned waters of the Colorado between the "Lower Basin" (Arizona, California and Nevada) and the "Upper Basin" (Colorado, Utah, New Mexico and Wyoming). It was the forty-seventh interstate compact[qv] authorized or ratified by Congress, and the first to apportion interstate waters.

Ratified by all parties except Arizona, it was approved by Congress as a six-state agreement in the Boulder Canyon Project Act (1928), which impressed the compact upon all projects built thereafter on the Colorado River system, and authorized construction of Boulder (Hoover) Dam[qv], the All American Canal[qv] and other Lower Basin projects. In 1930 Secretary of the Interior Ray Lyman Wilbur initiated a co-ordinated Lower Basin power and water program, which included an agreement settling water controversies in Arizona; contracts controlling use of Boulder (Hoover) Dam power in California and reserving waters for Arizona; power contracts for all Boulder (Hoover) Dam power, but reserving a "drawback privilege" on 36% of the energy for future use in Arizona and Nevada; and a repayment contract assuring construction of the All American Canal. Under that project, Boulder (Hoover) Dam has been constructed, and Parker Dam, the Colorado River Aqueduct[qv], Imperial Dam and the All American Canal are scheduled for completion before 1939. Other reclamation projects under construction (1939) are the Parker-Gila (Arizona), Bartlett Dam (Verde River, Arizona) and transmountain diversion (Colorado).

[Wilbur and Ely, *The Hoover Dam Contracts;* Reports of the Secretary of the Interior, 1930-32 inclusive.]

NORTHCUTT ELY

Colt Six Shooter, The, the invention of Samuel Colt, was the first practical arm of its kind. With the rifle, it had its place in revolutionizing methods of warfare, and was an important link in the development of arms from the muzzle-loading musket to the magazine rifles and machine-guns of today.

Its manufacture began at Paterson, N. J., in 1836. Colt's patent, secured Feb. 25, 1836, covered the revolution and locking of the cylinder firmly in place, so that the chambers of the cylinder came in line with the barrel by simply pulling the hammer back to full cock. From the first, all the barrels were expertly rifled to give the greatest possible accuracy to the bullet. Although various models were produced at Paterson, the arms did not at first receive the endorsement of government officials, and the company failed in 1842.

A few Colt arms, used by army officers in the Seminole War and by Texas Rangers[qqv] during the border troubles, proved the worth of the "revolving pistol," and a supply was ordered by the Government in 1847. As Colt had no factory at that time, the first 2000 or 3000 were made for him at the plant of Eli Whitney in New Haven, Conn. These were heavy revolvers of .44 caliber and soon became the standard of the United States Army and the Texas Rangers. Colt resumed the manufacture of revolvers at Hartford, Conn., in 1848. From 1856 to 1865 there were 554,283 of the powder and ball revolvers manufactured at the Hartford factory. Large quantities of these arms were used during the Civil War by both Union and Confederate troops. All Colt revolvers, up to the early 1870's, were made to shoot loose powder and lead bullets, the powder being ignited by a percussion cap. From that period, envelope cartridges, enclosing powder and bullet, were used until the advent of metallic ammunition.

Colt six shooters played a prominent part in the development of the West. When first used in Indian fighting the six shooter was a surprise weapon, as the savages did not look for more than one shot and when opposed by a single-shot arm it was their custom to draw fire and then rush the settler while he was reloading.

The six shooter won its popularity in the West because it was easily carried, accurate and of high capacity. Sheriffs, cowboys[qv] and plainsmen quickly became expert marksmen. It was an ideal weapon for mounted rangers and cattlemen, and was used for hunting as well as for defense. The extinction of the buffalo[qv] can be laid, in part, to the efficiency of the six shooter in the hands of hunting horsemen.

SAMUEL M. STONE

Columbia, Burning of. Sherman's army reached Columbia, S. C., Feb. 17, 1865, on its famous march through the Carolinas[qv]. The fact that Columbia was the capital city of the state which was held peculiarly responsible for the war, and the desire of the Union soldiers for vengeance, probably account for the burning of the city, which occurred that night. Sherman's assertion that the fire spread from bales of cotton ignited by evacuating Confederates under Gen. Wade Hampton is not acceptable, for the cotton appears to have been drenched by fire engines long before the fires of the night of Feb. 17 gained headway. The house fires, reported to have been started by Union soldiers, originated on the windward side of the long-extinguished cotton in the middle of a very wide street and swept over that street and eastward across the city. It is probable that only by confining his men to camp could Gen. Sherman have prevented the conflagration. He later asserted that he would not have done that to save the city. In his memoirs Sherman wrote: "Having utterly ruined Columbia, the right wing began its march northward."

[D. D. Wallace, *History of South Carolina*, III.]

D. D. WALLACE

Columbia College, established by royal charter on Oct. 31, 1754, as the College of the Province of New-York, was known from the beginning as King's College. The first president, Rev. Samuel Johnson, D.D., began instruction with a class of eight students in the schoolhouse in the rear of Trinity Church. In 1760 the college moved into a new building on what is now Park Place, New York City. Rev. Myles Cooper of Oxford, who succeeded Johnson as president in 1763, developed the college and conformed it as much as possible to English patterns, adding a medical school in 1767. Upon the occupation of New York by the American army at the outbreak of the Revolution, the building was taken over for use as a military hospital, all teaching ceased, and the students were dispersed. The corporation maintained its existence, however, and was rechartered, in 1784, as Columbia College under the Regents of the University of the State of New York. This form of government proving unsatisfactory, in 1787 an act was passed confirming the royal charter of 1754, and vesting the property and franchises of King's College in the trustees of Columbia College in the city of New York, under which charter it has continued to operate. The medical faculty was revived in 1785, but discontinued in 1813, its work being carried on by the College of Physicians and Surgeons, which was again incorporated in the college in 1860. During the first half of the 19th century the enrollment remained at about 100 annually, with a small faculty and a traditional curriculum. The administration of Charles King (1849–64) saw the establishment of the Law School (1858), the Medical School (1860), the School of Mines (1864), the enlargement of the faculty and curriculum and the awakening of the university idea. During King's administration the college was moved (1857) from its original site to Madison Avenue and 49th Street. Under Pres. Frederick A. P. Barnard (1864–89), Columbia achieved university status, which was confirmed by the revised corporation statutes of 1891; the first graduate school, that of Political Science, was established in 1880; women were permitted to study for Columbia degrees (1883) and the library began to grow in size and usefulness. Under Seth Low, president from 1889 to 1901, Columbia was moved (1897) to its present site on Morningside Heights, and the graduate faculties of Philosophy (1890) and Pure Science (1892) established. Columbia University now (1939) includes, in addition to the schools above mentioned, Barnard College (1889), Teachers College (1898); Schools of Architecture (1881), Pharmacy (1904), Journalism (1912), Business (1916), Dental and Oral Surgery (1916) and Library Service (1926); Bard College (1928) and the New York Post-Graduate Medical School (1931). Barnard College, Teachers College, College of Pharmacy and Bard College are financially independent but affiliated corporations.

[*A History of Columbia University.*]

MILTON HALSEY THOMAS

Columbia Fur Company, THE, founded about 1822 and operating in the countries of the Sioux and Omaha, had, by 1827, gained a place of such strength as to become a serious competitor of the western branch of John Jacob Astor's American Fur Company[qv]. Accordingly, negotiations were completed, during the summer of that year, which made the smaller company a part of the Astor firm. The former Columbia Fur Company thereafter transacted business under the name of the "Upper Missouri Outfit" and confined its operations to the territory above the mouth of the Big Sioux.

[H. M. Chittenden, *The American Fur Trade.*]

CARL P. RUSSELL

Columbia River, Exploration and Settlement. The estuary of the Columbia was first seen, described and mapped in 1775 by Capt. Bruno Hezeta, who named it Bahia de la Asumpcion, though Spanish maps showed it as Ensenada de Hezeta. In 1792 Capt. Robert Gray of Boston sailed ten miles up the river proper and six miles up Gray's Bay, naming it Columbia's River after his ship. The same year W. R. Broughton of Vancouver's[qv] party surveyed and charted to Cottonwood Point, 119 statute miles from the ocean.

In 1800 Lagasse and LeBlanc reached the upper river from the Rocky Mountains. Lewis and Clark[qv], in 1805, explored from the mouth of the Yakima to Cottonwood Point, 214 miles. In 1807 David Thompson explored for 111 miles, from the mouth of Blaeberry Creek to the Columbia River's source in Columbia Lake; and in 1811 Finan McDonald navigated from Kettle Falls to Death Rapids, 255 miles. In the same year Thompson navigated the entire river.

Prior to the great wagon train of 1843, settlements had been started along the river in over forty localities. The posts of the fur traders included those of the North West Company, the Astorian posts[qqv] and those of independent traders. Among the earliest were Fort Clatsop (1805) and Chouteau's post (1807). Other settlements were Fort Colville (1825); Willamette Valley, an agricultural settlement (1829); Bonneville's cantonment (1832); Whitman Mission (1836); and Cœur d'Alene (1842)[qqv]. After 1843 the wagon train rapidly opened the country, and subsequently the steamboat, railroads and highways have transformed the wilderness into a prosperous and populous region.

[H. H. Bancroft, *History of the North West Coast*, and *History of Oregon.*]

J. NEILSON BARRY

Comanche, THE, were a tribe, or a group of tribes more or less closely related, belonging to the Shoshonean stock. There were once twelve divisions of the Comanches, the most important being the Yamparika, Kotsoteka, Nokini, Kwahadi and Penateka.

The Comanches appeared in New Mexico early in the 18th century. Soon they drove the Apaches[qv] out of the South Plains country. By the middle of the century they were causing the Spaniards at San Antonio considerable annoyance, and thereafter, for a century and a quarter they harried the frontier settlements of Texas. By 1840, when they had reached the limit of their southward migration, the Comanche country was the South Plains from the Arkansas River to the San Saba River in Texas. At peace with the Comanches lived the Kiowas[qv] in the northern part, and the Wichitas and other Caddoan peoples in the southeastern part, of the vast domain the Comanches claimed. War parties of Comanches frequently raided settlements as far north as the Platte River and as far south as Durango. They were not a numerous people; 20,000 souls, in 1800, and 10,000, in 1850, represent liberal estimates.

A reservation for Comanches, maintained in Texas from 1855 to 1859, did not lessen their marauding operations (*see* Washita, Sheridan's Operations on). A larger reservation assigned to them in southwestern Oklahoma, in 1867 (*see* Medicine Lodge, Treaty of), was not occupied by the more warlike divisions until they were driven in by troops eight years later (*see* Red River Indian War).

Superb horsemen, nomadic and warlike, the Comanches constituted the greatest human factor in retarding the settlement of the South Plains.

[Rupert N. Richardson, *The Comanche Barrier to South Plains Settlement.*]

RUPERT N. RICHARDSON

Combine, THE, is a farm machine that makes harvesting and threshing a single process. It was developed by 1828, but not perfected until the 1870's. Between 1870 and 1873 the United States Patent Office recorded the invention of six harvester-threshers; and by 1880 the combine was commercially established.

Until 1920 this machine was used primarily on the west coast, because fair weather and dry grain were considered essential to its operation. High grain prices and the popularity of labor-saving devices after the World War brought the combine to the states of the Middle West where large-scale farming was being practised. About this same time a desire for efficiency in the harvesting of soybeans brought the harvester-thresher into extensive use.

Early in the 1930's a small or baby combine was perfected. Weighing about two tons, selling for less than $500, and covering twenty acres per day, these machines have brought increased efficiency to small farms. Great numbers of farmers are now able to own and operate combines with a resulting saving of labor. Consequently the substitution of machine-power for man-power has reduced labor requirements and increased the effectiveness of each laboring unit.

[W. M. Hurst and W. R. Humphries, Harvesting with Combines, United States Department of Agriculture *Farmers Bulletin*, 1761.]

BENJAMIN F. SHAMBAUGH

Comic Strips and Funny Papers were a natural extension of the robust humor of the 1870's and 1880's, abetted by an expanding newspaperdom, bent on circulation and experimenting with color printing. James Swinnerton drew comic bear pictures for the San Francisco *Examiner* in 1892, and the New York *Daily News* printed an isolated comic strip as early as 1884, but the forerunner of the colored "funny paper" was R. F. Outcault's "Origin of a New Species," which appeared, Sunday, Nov. 18, 1894, in the New York *World*. In 1896 Hearst lured Outcault, who meanwhile devised the "Yellow Kid," highly popular bad-boy character, to the New York *Journal*. The ensuing battle, with both newspapers printing Sunday "Yellow Kid" pages, and attendant sensationalism, provoked the term, "yellow journalism."*qv*

Early comic characters, such as Happy Hooligan, Buster Brown, Foxy Grandpa, Little Jimmy, Hans and Fritz and Nemo, if not elevating, were relatively harmless; yet critics soon denounced the funny paper's influence, and in 1907 the International Kindergarten Union asked parents to bar it from their homes. Power over circulation, however, was manifest when strips set styles, and on the fortieth anniversary of Outcault's first page, the New York *Times* alone among important newspapers still resisted them. Brisbane rated comic strips second to news in the elements of "a successful newspaper," surveys showed a majority of readers had favorites, while the dispute of two Washington newspapers over rights to Andy Gump was carried to the United States Supreme Court.

Syndicates grew around leading strips and bought them away from one another as a fortune-making business developed from Mutt and Jeff, Jiggs, Toonerville Folks and others. As many as 2500 newspapers used some 250 strips and single panels from 75 agencies. At its peak, Hearst's *Comic Weekly: Puck*, distributed by 17 newspapers with a circulation reaching 5,500,000, alone ran 50 comics in its 32 pages. One syndicate claimed a circulation of more than 50,000,000. Comic section advertising skyrocketed from a $360,000 business in 1931 to more than $16,500,000 in 1937, cost per page reaching $17,000.

Meantime the strips generally changed from comics to serial picture stories, presenting everything from domestic affairs and Negro life to high adventure and crime. Many found them more degrading than ever, but syndicates employed linguists to prepare the strips for increasing demand over the world; when Orphan Annie's dog was lost, Henry Ford telegraphed her creator to do all he could to find it. If juvenile delinquency could be traced to some, Briggs' "Days of Real Sport" was a genuine contribution to humor. Perspective reveals the comics as a machine age's folk tales with Popeye supplanting Paul Bunyan and the popular characters literally being handed down from one drawing board to another.

[A. M. Lee, *The Daily Newspaper in America;* W. G. Bleyer, *Main Currents in the History of American Journalism;* Frank Weitenkampf, *Bookman*, July, 1925; *News Week*, Dec. 1, 1934; Rube Goldberg, *Saturday Evening Post*, Dec. 15, 1928; D. F. McCord, *American Mercury*, July, 1935; J. K. Ryan, *Forum*, May, 1936; B. Price, *World's Work*, August, 1931; *Fortune*, April, 1937; S. M. Smith, *Pictorial Review*, January, 1935; R. L. Neuberger, *New Republic*, July 11, 1934; *Literary Digest*, Dec. 12, 1936, also April 7, 1934; L. Thompson, *Saturday Review of Literature*, Nov. 13, 1937; *Editor & Publisher*, July 21, 1934; William Murrell, *A History of American Graphic Humor*, 1865-1938.]

IRVING DILLIARD

Commander in Chief. The Constitution makes the President the commander in chief of the Army and Navy of the United States, and of the state militia when called into the service of the United States. The powers that the President may actually exercise in this capacity are not, however, explicitly defined, and the Supreme Court has held, in Ex parte Milligan*qv*, that their extent must be determined "by their nature and by the principles of our institutions." This means, in general, that although Congress may decide the general military policy and must provide for the armed forces, the President has almost complete control of such forces as are provided, and may exercise this control in such a way as to formulate important domestic and foreign policies. President Polk thus used his power as commander in chief virtually to force a war with Mexico, President Cleveland to break a railway strike in Chicago (*see* Pullman Strike of 1894), President Coolidge to supervise elections in Nicaragua, and there are numerous other instances that demonstrate how broad this power has become in practice and to what extent its exercise depends upon the President's own interpretation of his responsibility under the Constitution.

[Clarence A. Berdahl, *War Powers of the Executive in the United States;* The Powers of the President as Commander in Chief, *Foreign Policy Association Information Service*, Vol. IV, no. 10, July 10, 1928; C. C. Tansill, War Powers of the President of the United States with Special Reference to the Beginning of Hostilities, *Political Science Quarterly*, Vol. XLV, pp. 1-55, March, 1930.]

CLARENCE A. BERDAHL

Commander in Chief of the British Forces in North America was a position of highest importance in the last half of the 18th century, held by Horatio Sharpe (1754), Braddock (1755), Shirley (1755–56), Loudoun (1756–57), Abercromby (1758), Amherst (1758–63) and Gage (1763–75); and, with more limited control, Howe (1775–78), Clinton (1778–82), Carleton (1783 f.), etc. Responsible to the crown and appointed by the crown, these commanders were supervised directly by the ministry. Supreme in American military supervision and significant in financial expenditures, the duties of the position involved an astonishing scope of responsibility and power, touching many aspects of American life.

[Stanley Pargellis, *Lord Loudoun in America;* Clarence Carter, ed., *The Correspondence of General Thomas Gage.*]

ALFRED P. JAMES

Commerce. *See* Trade, Domestic; Trade, Foreign.

Commerce, Court of. This court, created by act of Congress, June 18, 1910, was intended to provide a specialized tribunal for a constantly growing and increasingly complex volume of litigation, and to expedite the course of justice. It consisted of five judges appointed by the President for five-year terms, on the expiration of which, new members were to be assigned by the Chief Justice of the United States from among the circuit judges. In broad terms, its jurisdiction covered all civil suits arising under the Interstate Commerce Act, the Elkins Act, the orders of the Interstate Commerce Commission*qqv*, etc. Its early decisions created a popular impression that the court was unduly solicitous for railroad interests and inclined to hamper effective regulation by the Interstate Commerce Commission. A strong congressional minority had opposed its creation in 1910 and there was a growing demand two years later for its abolition. When one of its members, Judge Robert W. Archbald, was impeached, convicted of corruption and removed from the bench Jan. 13, 1913, the demand became so imperative that Congress dissolved the court, Oct. 22, 1913.

[I. L. Sharfmann, *The Interstate Commerce Commission.*]

W. A. ROBINSON

Commerce, Department of, was created, by an act of Congress, Feb. 14, 1903, "to foster, promote, and develop the foreign and domestic commerce, the mining, manufacturing, shipping, and fishery industries, the labor interests, and the transportation facilities of the United States." This law was modified by an act of March 4, 1913, establishing the Department of Labor*qv*. The Department of Commerce in the narrower sense came into being at the latter date. But many of the functions of the department are as old as the Federal Government and many of its agencies, under various names, were organized early in our history.

After the formation of the Department of Labor in 1913, the Department of Commerce retained the Bureaus of the Census*qv*, Corporations, Fisheries, Foreign and Domestic Commerce, Lighthouses, Navigation, and Standards*qv*, and the United States Coast and Geodetic Survey*qv* and Steamboat Inspection Service. Lighthouse service*qv* and aids to navigation were authorized by law as early as 1789. The first census was taken in 1790. Coast and geodetic surveys, vital to shipping and defense, were authorized in 1807. The statistical work of the Bureau of Foreign and Domestic Commerce has been traced to an office established in the Treasury Department*qv* in 1820. The beginnings of the varied research and experimental work of the Bureau of Standards were authorized as early as 1830. A Commissioner of Fish and Fisheries was appointed in 1871. The Bureau of Navigation was established in 1884.

Under Mr. Hoover, as Secretary of Commerce and later as President, the department acquired jurisdiction over the Patent Office and the Bureau of Mines (1925), greatly expanded the work of many of its agencies (notably the Bureau of Standards and the Bureau of Foreign and Domestic Commerce) and added new services such as the Aeronautics Division (later the Bureau of Air Commerce), the Radio Division and the Federal Employment Stabilization Board.

Many services falling under the broad statutory definition of the department's functions remained in other departments or under independent agencies such as the Interstate Commerce Commission*qv*. On the other hand, some of the agencies under the jurisdiction of the Department of Commerce, such as the Bureau of the Census, performed general functions equally relevant to the work of other departments. During the presidency of Franklin D. Roosevelt, the historic problems of differentiation and co-ordination were accentuated by the increasingly varied and vital responsibilities of Government. Changes affecting the Department of Commerce included the transfer, in 1938, of the work of the Bureau of Air Commerce to the newly organized Civil Aeronautics Authority.

[U. S. Department of Commerce and Labor, *Organization and Law of the Department of Commerce and Labor*, Washington, 1904; U. S. Department of Commerce, *The Department of Commerce: Condensed History, Duties, . . .*, Washington, 1913.]

WITT BOWDEN

Commerce Clause, THE JUDICIAL HISTORY OF THE, properly begins with the famous case of Gibbons v. Ogden[qv] (1824) in which Chief Justice Marshall defined commerce as intercourse. On the basis of this definition, the Supreme Court has held that Congress' power to regulate commerce among the states is the power to govern commercial intercourse among them. This power of Congress Marshall considered to be plenary and unaffected by the states and their powers.

When Roger B. Taney became Chief Justice, the Court assumed a view more congenial to states' rights[qv], and the rule was laid down that there is a field of jurisdiction which is exclusively reserved to the states (*see* License Cases, 1847). However, the supremacy of Federal power was asserted again four years later when the Court maintained that where the subject matter is local in character the states may act, but only until Congress chooses to legislate. Whatever subjects of commerce are in their nature national, or admit only of uniform regulation, must be left to the exclusive control of Congress (Cooley v. Bd. of Wardens[qv], 1852).

Until the Civil War most interstate commerce was by water, and few questions of jurisdiction arose between the Federal and state governments. But the construction of railroads[qv] throughout the United States created new problems. Illinois undertook to regulate that part of an interstate journey which was entirely within the state. This exercise of state power the Supreme Court held unconstitutional (Wabash St. L. and P. Ry. Co. v. Illinois[qv], 1886). In order that the railroads might not be wholly unregulated, Congress in 1887 established the Interstate Commerce Commission[qv].

The growth of the regulatory power of Congress in the field of commerce after 1887 was rapid. The Sherman Antitrust Act[qv] in 1890 extended the power of Congress to prohibit combinations in restraint of trade[qv] among the states. This act was early given a judicial interpretation which greatly restricted its scope (U. S. v. E. C. Knight Co.[qv], 1895), but in subsequent decisions came to represent an important exercise of the Federal regulatory power. The act was applied to combinations of labor as well as capital (Loewe v. Lawlor[qv], 1908), a step which aroused the opposition of the trade unions[qv] and led in 1914 to the passage of the Clayton Act[qv]. At the same time Congress established the Federal Trade Commission[qv].

The field of transportation was gradually confided by Congress to the supervision of the Interstate Commerce Commission. Beginning with the Elkins Act[qv] in 1903, a series of measures strengthened the powers of the commission and enabled it to assume jurisdiction of steamship and railroad companies, express and sleeping-car companies, motor bus and motor truck concerns, power transmission lines, telephone and telegraph lines and oil pipe line companies when engaged in interstate commerce. The Supreme Court in the late 1890's ruled that the commission could forbid discriminatory and unreasonable rates but did not admit the right to impose any definite rate or schedules on a railroad. The rule was laid down that a common carrier was entitled to a fair return upon the value of the property dedicated to the public use (Smyth v. Ames[qv], 1898). When Congress in 1906 authorized the commission to fix rates for the future (*see* Hepburn Act), the courts had to determine a basis upon which the value of the property of a common carrier was to be ascertained. In other words, the judges were obliged to delve into the realm of economic theory to discover a rate basis[qv] which could be applied.

Meanwhile, conflicts arose between the commerce power and the reserved powers[qv] of the states. Within the legitimate exercise of the police power[qv], the states might forbid the running of freight trains on Sunday, prohibit the importation within their borders of diseased cattle, and enact many other laws designed to promote the health, safety, and moral welfare of citizens. But in 1918 a majority of the justices of the Supreme Court refused their assent to an act of Congress prohibiting the transportation in interstate commerce of goods the product of child labor[qv]. The field of production was therefore to be considered as falling within the reserved powers of the states (Hammer v. Dagenhart[qv]). However, the Supreme Court had already admitted a large sphere of police power to Congress. The Mann White Slave Act[qv] and the act forbidding the distribution of lottery tickets through interstate commerce were police regulations.

The Transportation Act of 1920[qv] assumed the judicial rulings already laid down in behalf of the power of Congress. Among these was the rule that "wherever the interstate and intrastate transactions of the carriers are so related that the government of the one involves the control of the other," Congress is entitled to regulate both classes of transactions (Shreveport Case[qv], 1914). The extension of Federal power to the regulation of the business of the commission men and of the livestock dealers in the great stockyards of the country was upheld by the Supreme Court (Stafford v. Wallace[qv], 1922). In this case the Court held that stockyards are not a place of rest or final destination but a throat through which the current of commerce flows. While the Supreme Court clung to its decision in the child-labor case, it upheld an act of Congress forbidding the transportation in interstate commerce of goods made by convict labor[qv] into any state where the goods are to be sold or used in violation of its laws. This decision assumed that where state policy condemned a practice the power of Congress might be put forth to prevent interstate commerce from frustrating the policy (Kentucky Whip and Collar Co., v. Illinois Central R. R. Co., 1937).

While the Supreme Court was permitting these extensions of Federal power, it was confronted with a case involving the validity of the National Industrial Recovery Act[qv], in which Congress sought to delegate to the President control over the entire field of production where it affected interstate commerce. The N.I.R.A. was overturned not only as an unconstitutional delegation of power to the President but also as an invasion of the reserved powers of the states (Schechter Poultry Corp. v. U. S.[qv], 1935). Two years later the Court receded markedly from the position it had taken not only in the latter portion of this decision but also from its position in the child-labor case. In upholding the validity of the National Labor Relations Act[qv], a majority of the justices agreed that manufacturing, although carried out wholly within a state, may affect interstate commerce in such a way that it comes within the scope of Federal power (N.L.R.B. v. Jones and Laughlin Steel Corp.[qv], 1937).

The judicial interpretation of the commerce clause has taken many bypaths since the decision of John Marshall more than a century ago. Most of these have been pointed out by states' rights, and it is only as the philosophy of particularism has succumbed to the nationalizing tendencies of the last two generations that the Supreme Court has been able to return to the fundamental principles of the decision in Gibbons v. Ogden.

[E. S. Corwin, *The Constitution and What It Means Today*, 6th ed.]

WILLIAM S. CARPENTER

Commerce Commission. *See* Interstate Commerce Commission, The.

Commercial Cable Company, The, founded in 1883 by John W. Mackay and James Gordon Bennett, was the principal competitor of the Western Union[qv] in the field of communications. In 1884 it laid two transatlantic cables to compete with those leased by the latter from the American Telegraph & Cable Co., and its land lines were operated in conjunction with the Postal Telegraph[qv], most of whose stock it controlled.

[I. M. Tarbell, *The Nationalizing of Business.*]

WHEELER PRESTON

Commercial Committee (Revolutionary), The, was one of the principal standing committees of the Continental Congress[qv]. Originating as the "Secret Committee," appointed (Sept. 19, 1775) to make purchase of powder, its functions were little by little enlarged until it became the chief agency of Congress in the extensive business of exchanging American products for arms and ammunition abroad, having its own agents both in America and in Europe. It was reconstituted July 5, 1777, with the name Committee of Commerce (although oftener called the Commercial Committee), and again Dec. 14, 1778. During its career the committee was more than once under the fire of severe criticism. Its chief figure was Robert Morris, who, as Superintendent of Finance (1781), took over most of its functions. (*See also* Revolutionary Committees.)

[Jennings B. Sanders, *Evolution of Executive Departments of the Continental Congress, 1774-1789.*]

EDMUND C. BURNETT

Commission Government is a system of municipal government in which all executive and legislative powers are concentrated in the hands of a small elective board, usually of five members. The plan, in its present form, was originated by Galveston, Tex., during an emergency caused by the tidal flood which partially destroyed that city in 1900 (*see* Galveston Storm, The). It was not intended to be a permanent scheme of city government, but having proved successful it was retained after the emergency had passed. Attracting attention in other parts of the country, the commission plan spread northward and in due course was adopted by several hundred cities, most of them small communities. During more recent years, however, it has lost ground. Many cities have abandoned the commission plan in favor of city manager government[qv] or have restored the older mayor-and-council type of government.

The essence of the plan is its simplicity. The voters elect a commission, usually of five members, on a nonpartisan ballot. One of the commissioners serves as chairman and may bear the title of mayor but he has no independent executive powers. All questions of general policy are decided by the commissioners as a group. They enact the ordinances, determine the tax rate, vote the appropriations, and so on. But each individual commissioner takes immediate charge of an administrative department and for this purpose all the administrative work of the city is consolidated into five departments.

The commission plan has demonstrated the value of simplification in city government; on the other hand it has disclosed some organic defects. Chief among these is the absence of unified executive authority. It provides a five-headed mayoralty which often becomes divided within itself. So far as large cities are concerned, moreover, a legislative body of only five members is not deemed to be adequately representative.

[W. B. Munro, *The Government of American Cities.*]

WILLIAM B. MUNRO

Commission Merchants and Factors. The factor or commission merchant was one of the significant figures in the early commercial life of the country. Legally "a factor is an agent employed to purchase or sell goods on commission in his own name, or in the name of his principal," and is distinguished from a broker in that he "is entrusted with the possession, management, control and disposal of the goods to be bought or sold."

The factorage system was introduced into the colonies soon after the dissolution of the Virginia Company[qv] (1624); developed through the colonial and early national periods; and probably was of most importance from 1815 to 1860. During these years the great staple crops of cotton, tobacco, sugar and rice[qqv] were produced in the South for distant markets in the Northeast and Europe, from whence were received manufactured goods and supplies. Commission merchants, either possessed of large capital or able to procure it from the banks, advanced money during the period of production to planters and manufacturers, in return for which the products of farm and factory were consigned to them for sale. The planter and manufacturer were thus freed from the expense and trouble of selling and could devote their time, capital and energy to the production of goods.

The chief disadvantages of the system were: 1, that the merchant might be more interested in a quick rather than a profitable sale; and 2, that frequently the proceeds of the sales did not equal the sum advanced by the merchant, leaving the planter or manufacturer in debt. Southern planters had the added grievance that since most goods were imported by Northern merchants and a substantial portion of the produce handled by the same agents, the profits of their trade were going to a rival section. Consequently there were numerous attempts by Southerners to build up direct trade connections between Europe and the Southern ports, and from 1850 to 1860 an attempt by Southern planters to deal directly with the European manufacturer without any intermediary at all, thus eliminating the Southern and European as well as the Northern merchant. All of these attempts failed, and it was only the development of the commodity exchanges, the tremendous increase of industrial capital and the improved methods of transportation and communication, that ended the dominant position of the commission merchant in American economy.

[L. C. Gray, *History of Agriculture in the Southern United States to 1860;* N. S. Buck, *The Development of the Organization of Anglo-American Trade.*]

T. P. GOVAN

Committee for Industrial Organization. *See* Congress of Industrial Organizations.

Committee Form of Government during the American Revolution. *See* Revolutionary Committees.

Committee of the States, The. The Articles of Confederation[qv] empowered Congress to appoint a committee consisting of one delegate from each state, "to be denominated 'A Committee of the States,'" to sit in the recess of Congress and to exercise such powers as Congress, "by the consent of nine states, shall from time to time think expedient to vest them with"; with the one proviso, that the committee should not be authorized to do any act requiring the voice of nine states.

Once only, in June, 1784, was the Committee of the States called into existence. Early in August certain members, who had opposed the appointment of the committee, withdrew, leaving the committee without a quorum (nine), and the committee was not thereafter able to reassemble.

[Edmund C. Burnett, The Committee of the States, in American Historical Association, *Annual Report*, 1913, Vol. I.]

EDMUND C. BURNETT

Committee of the Whole, THE, consists of all the members of a legislative chamber, but organized as a committee and thus enabled to operate under less rigid procedures than if sitting formally as a house. A smaller number is required for a quorum, there is more freedom of debate, there is usually no roll call or other record vote, and in other ways it is easier to do business in Committee of the Whole. Although now discontinued by the United States Senate and by several state legislatures, it is regularly used by the national House of Representatives.

[D. S. Alexander, *History and Procedure of the House of Representatives;* W. F. Willoughby, *Principles of Legislative Organization and Administration.*]

CLARENCE A. BERDAHL

Committee of Thirteen, THE (1850), was a select committee of the Senate agreed to on April 18 upon motion of Sen. Henry S. Foote of Mississippi, to which were to be sent the compromise resolutions of Senators Henry Clay of Kentucky and John Bell of Tennessee. The original provision that the committee should mature a scheme of compromise for the adjustment of all the pending issues of slavery was dropped out as unnecessary. Chosen by ballot on April 19, the committee, with Clay as chairman, included six Democrats and seven Whigs; three of the former and four of the latter were from the slave states. On May 8 the committee reported, offering two bills: an omnibus bill[qv] providing for the admission of California and for the territorial organization, without the Wilmot Proviso[qv], of Utah and New Mexico, together with a settlement of the disputed Texas boundary, and a bill to terminate the slave trade[qv] in the District of Columbia. A lengthy amendment to the fugitive slave law[qv] was also submitted. (*See also* Compromise of 1850.)

[J. B. McMaster, *History of the People of the United States*, VII.]

ARTHUR C. COLE

Committee of Thirteen, THE, of the United States Senate was constituted Dec. 18, 1860, under resolution of Sen. Powell of Kentucky, to consider the compromise proposals of Sen. Crittenden[qv]. It included leaders of different groups —Seward and Wade, Republicans; Davis and Toombs, Secessionists; Crittenden, Powell and Hunter, for the Border States[qv]. The Committee rejected by a vote of 7 to 6 the test compromise proposal concerning slavery in the territories, and made no recommendation to the Senate. (*See also* Committee of Thirty-three.)

[James Ford Rhodes, *History of the United States, 1850-1877*, Vol. III.]

C. MILDRED THOMPSON

Committee of Thirty-three, THE, of the United States House of Representatives, was constituted Dec. 6, 1860, one member from each state, on motion of Mr. Boteler of Virginia. This committee to consider Crittenden's compromise[qv] measures operated at the same time as the Senate Committee of Thirteen[qv], but independently of it. No decision was reached, and no report made.

[James Ford Rhodes, *History of the United States, 1850-1877*, Vol. III.]

C. MILDRED THOMPSON

Committee on Public Information, THE, was set up by executive order of President Wilson, April 14, 1917. Formally it was the Secretaries of State, War and Navy with Mr. George Creel as civilian chairman. Actually it was the latter and a far-flung organization abroad and at home presenting the war issues by pamphlets, films, cables, posters, speakers (Four-Minute Men[qv]). Its function was informational, not censorship. The first year's budget was supplied by the President ($1,600,000); the second year by an appropriation of $1,250,000.

[G. Creel, *How We Advertised America;* G. S. Ford, *On and Off the Campus.*]

GUY STANTON FORD

Committee on the Conduct of the War, THE, was a joint committee of Congress to inquire into the management of the Civil War. It was organized on Dec. 20, 1861, and continued until ninety days after the close of the Thirty-eighth Congress, i.e., June, 1865. Sen. Wade of Ohio was chairman. The other members were: for the Senate, Chandler (Michigan) and Andrew Johnson (Tennessee); for the House, Gooch (Massachusetts), Covode (Pennsylvania), Julian (Indiana) and Odell (New York). Most of the members belonged to the radical wing of the Republican party[qv], and grew more out of sympathy with the Lincoln administration as the war progressed. In 1864 the functions of the committee were extended to include investigation into contracts and expenditures, as well as military affairs. The eight published volumes of the committee, including reports, testimony and papers, deal chiefly with military campaigns and the competency of commanding officers. Of the generals who commanded the Army of the Potomac[qv] all except Grant were investigated by this committee.

[W. W. Pierson, Jr., The Committee on the Conduct of the Civil War, in *American Historical Review*, XXIII.]

C. MILDRED THOMPSON

Committees of Correspondence, organized as part of the transitional Revolutionary machinery to facilitate the spread of propaganda and coordinate the patriot party, were of three general types. Samuel Adams was the promoter of the first local committees on Nov. 2, 1772, and within three months Gov. Hutchinson reported that there were more than eighty such committees in Massachusetts. On March 12, 1773, Virginia organized the second type, the colony committees which were in reality standing committees of the legislature. The third type and the most important was the county committee which was chosen by the local units and acted as the agent of the central colonial committees. The importance of these committees as channels for the creation and direction of public opinion during the preliminaries of the Revolution can hardly be overemphasized. They exercised at times judicial, legislative and executive functions and, containing the germ of government, gave rise to the later committee system.

[E. D. Collins, Committees of Correspondence in the American Revolution, *Annual Report*, American Historical Association, 1901, Vol. I; H. M. Flick, The Rise of the Revolutionary Committee System, *History of the State of New York*, Vol. III.]

A. C. FLICK

Committees of Safety carried on and extended the work of the Revolutionary Committees of Correspondence[qv], and with the breakdown of constitutional modes of government, anarchy might have prevailed had not these extralegal committees developed to guide and stabilize the Revolutionary movement. The Second Continental Congress[qv] on July 18, 1775, recommended the establishment of such committees in the various colonies to carry on the all-important functions of government. Many of these committees had been active since 1774 and with the sanction of Congress they rapidly developed into a unified system which supplied the armies with men and equipment, apprehended Tories[qv] and carried on other exacting and unceasing duties of government. With the adoption of state constitutions[qv] the committees were largely replaced by constitutional agencies, New Hampshire and Connecticut alone continuing their committees throughout the war. So useful, however, had the committees proved themselves to be that many of them continued unofficially throughout the greater part of the war.

[Agnes Hunt, *The Provincial Committees of Safety of the American Revolution.*]

A. C. FLICK

Commodities as Money were found in use chiefly in the colonial period where there was a scarcity of coin or other suitable currency. By 1700 the use of commodity currencies was giving way to coin payments in the towns and cities, although remaining common for some years in the rural districts.

Commodities which were used as money consisted of wool, cattle and corn in New England, tobacco in Maryland and Virginia, lumber and tobacco in New York, beaver skins in Pennsylvania, New York and New England, and rice, pitch and corn in the Carolinas. In several cases colonial legislatures declared certain commodities legal tender[qv] in the payment of debts. Trade with the Indians led to the use of wampum[qv]—under a variety of local names—as currency in practically all of the colonies.

[N. Carothers, *Fractional Money;* J. L. Laughlin, *The Principles of Money.*]

FREDERICK A. BRADFORD

Commodities Exchange Act, THE (1936), was passed by Congress to prevent and remove obstructions and burdens upon interstate commerce resulting from market manipulation and excessive speculation upon exchanges dealing in agricultural commodities. (*See also* Securities and Exchange Commission.)

[Public-No.675—74th Congress; *United States News*, July 20, 1936, p. 14, Oct. 5, 1936, p. 3.]

P. ORMAN RAY

Commodity Exchanges. The enormous expansion of markets after 1850 required the formation of organizations which could handle exchanges of commodities on a large scale. The buyers and sellers of commodities in every city and market of large commercial importance formed these boards of trade or chambers of commerce[qv] as they are sometimes called. The Chicago Board of Trade was organized in 1848. The New York Produce Exchange was formed in 1850. The Merchants Exchange of St. Louis had the characteristics of a modern exchange about 1854. The New York Cotton Exchange was organized in 1870 and the New York Coffee Exchange in 1882.

[American Produce Exchange Markets, *The Annals of the American Academy of Political and Social Science*, Vol. XXXVIII, No. 2.]

FRED M. JONES

Commodity Prices. As revealed by indices of wholesale prices, commodities in the United

States have experienced three major price swings during which they reached their highest levels in 1814–15, 1864–65 and 1919–20. In these periods they were about 65% (1814) to 150% (1864 and 1920) above the levels prevailing a few years prior to the peaks.

The rapid upward movement of prices must be largely attributed to currency disturbances. The expansion and depreciation of state bank issues following the expiration of the charter of the First United States Bank (1811), the issuance of Treasury notes to aid in financing the War of 1812, and the suspension of specie payments[qqv] in 1814 combined to cause the first peak. The depreciation of the greenbacks[qv] issued in financing the Civil War accounts for the height of the peak in the 1860's and the credit expansion which accompanied the World War largely explains the high point in 1919–20.

Decades of irregularly declining prices followed each period of inflation. Not until 1848 was the turning point from such a decline reached after the early 19th-century inflation. Following the high prices of the 1860's the decline continued until about 1896, when a gradual increase began, became greatly accelerated in 1915, and finally culminated in the peak prices of 1919–20. The turning point in the decline of prices following the World War is not yet (1939) clearly established.

Over shorter periods of time, commodity prices have for the most part followed the so-called cycle of general business activity, constituting symptomatic indicators of the speculative excesses which characterize periods of prosperity. There are, however, important exceptions to this rule. In the decade of the 1920's commodity prices did not share in the upward movement which typified security prices.

As the prices of commodities have fluctuated between higher and lower levels inequalities in price movements have appeared. Prices of agriculture products have been notably sensitive, exhibiting a more rapid and violent movement than the general average of commodity prices or than the prices of industrial products. The unequal pressure or benefit of price movements upon debtors and creditors, agriculture and industry has occasioned much political activity as evidenced by the organized opposition to the First and Second United States Banks, the post Civil War free-silver controversy, which came to focus with the organization of the People's party in 1892, and the reaction to the post World War deflation, which culminated in the devaluation of the dollar (1934) and large-scale silver purchases under the Silver Purchase Act of 1934[qqv].

[Warren, Pearson and Stoker, *Wholesale Prices for 213 Years*, Cornell University Agricultural Experiment Station.]

WILLIAM A. NEISWANGER, JR.

Commodore. A naval title applied to captains commanding, or having commanded, squadrons. They were authorized to fly a broad pennant distinctive of that rank, although until 1862 the rank itself did not legally exist in the United States Navy. The rank is next above captain and corresponded to that of a brigadier general of the army. With minor exceptions the rank was abolished in 1899.

DUDLEY W. KNOX

Common Lands in early New England towns were either lands held in common by the proprietors in which the individual owners had fractional rights and carried on farming in accordance with open field practices, or, more generally, undivided and unallotted land on the outskirts of the New England settlements, used for pasturage and woodland. In the latter part of the 17th century newcomers insisted on sharing these undivided lands with the proprietors, but the rights of the "noncommoners," as the newcomers were called, were seldom recognized. Statutes in the 18th century and court decisions upheld the town proprietors.

[A. Maclear, *Early New England Town;* R. H. Akagi, *Town Proprietors of the New England Colonies.*]

RICHARD B. MORRIS

Common Law, originally custom and usage, became the law "common" to all the people of England by judicial enforcement. Thus it originated in England, but has come to consist in great part in the principles which have been declared and developed in the decisions of the courts when adjudicating upon the private law in countries of Anglo-Saxon origins. It is usually not incorporated in the constitution or written statutes of a country but is the term generally used to describe that system of fundamental law which is in force among English-speaking peoples as contrasted with Roman Law and derivative systems based on an enacted code. The early settlers of the United States claimed, and were in fact supposed, to have brought with them to America their inherent common-law rights of person and property. It is the English common law which thus is recognized throughout the United States as the common law of the country and is the fundamental basis of our institutions of government.

The common law is enforced primarily by the governments of each of the states and territories. It has been influenced to some extent by the Code Napoleon[qv] in its development in the State of Louisiana due to the original French settlement there. It is, of course, subject to repeal or amendment by statute, but primarily the common law has been developed and extended by the state and Federal courts, past and present.

In those states where the common law has been codified, these codes consist in large part of a restatement of common-law doctrines and their later development up to the time of codification. In addition, the common-law rights of the individual, as generally accepted, have been stated to a greater or lesser extent at various times in American history. Among these statements is that in the Declaration of Independence[qv] which says that all men "are endowed by their Creator with certain unalienable rights, that among these are life, liberty, and the pursuit of happiness." Also the Bill of Rights[qv] or the first ten Amendments to the United States Constitution and the bills of rights in the various state constitutions[qv] are in whole or in large part made up of statements of common-law rights and of methods of protecting these rights which are inborn, inherent and inalienable, and not granted by any government, according to Anglo-Saxon and American theory. Thus, the American governments, national and state, are merely the added protection to the common-law rights which the citizens already possess.

[T. E. Holland, *Jurisprudence;* W. W. Willoughby and L. Rogers, *An Introduction to the Problem of Government;* R. Pound, *Spirit of the Common Law.*]

WILLIAM STARR MYERS

Common Sense, a tract by Thomas Paine, was published in Philadelphia, January, 1776. In contrast to writers who denounced British tyranny but insisted on colonial loyalty, Paine described reconciliation as only "an agreeable dream." He maintained that, being of age, the colonies were qualified for independence and that their future interest demanded it. While many men had similar beliefs, none had so graphically stated the case. With its circulation of 120,000 in the first three months, the tract greatly fertilized the independence spirit which flowered so brilliantly in July, 1776.

[M. D. Conway, ed., *The Writings of Thomas Paine.*]

CHARLES F. MULLETT

Commonwealth v. Hunt. This case, decided by the Supreme Court of Massachusetts in 1842, held the Boston Journeymen Bootmakers Society, defendant, to be a lawful organization. Previously, associations of workers had been judged unlawful conspiracies (*see* Philadelphia Cordwainers' Case). The doctrine of conspiracy rests upon the assumption that an act which is innocent and legal when performed by an individual becomes dangerous and illegal when performed by a group. The historical significance of the case lies in the fact that it marks the legal recognition of labor unions as lawful institutions, provided the methods of attaining their ends are "honorable and peaceful."

[Francis B. Sayre, *Cases in Labor Law.*]

GORDON S. WATKINS

Communications, International. Save for some cross-border roads and trails, the United States, prior to 1850, depended on waterways for communication with other countries (*see* Waterways, Inland; Shipping, Ocean). Even today, though much trade and travel with Canada and Mexico are via rail and highway, the steamship is still our chief international carrier, despite promising developments in aircraft.

Our first international rail connection (1851) linked Montreal and Boston via Rouse's Point, N. Y.; in 1853 the Montreal–Portland route was completed; and by 1879 the Grand Trunk controlled tracks to Chicago via Toronto. By 1910 the Canadian Pacific, Canadian Northern (now Canadian National), Northern Pacific and Great Northern had border crossings between the "Soo" and Vancouver, and rails crossed into Mexico at three places. Motor bus routes, largely postwar, in 1935 entered Canada at thirteen points. In 1919 commercial air flights began across Puget Sound, and the Navy's flying boat NC–4[qv] made the first Atlantic crossing, followed in the same year by the British dirigible R–34. In 1928 the *Graf Zeppelin* made the first *commercial* flight of lighter-than-air craft to the United States. Meanwhile the Kelly Act (1925) had provided for air-mail contracts (subsidies), and by 1926 services had been started; by 1930 they had been extended to Canada and most of Latin America. In 1937 transpacific air service was inaugurated (*see* China Clipper, The), and in 1939 transatlantic air service began. On the Canadian and Latin-American routes 154,091 passengers were carried, 1936–37.

For international transmission of news and messages, the United States depended on private and public postal services which, with the development of packet lines after 1800, were fairly regular. By 1850 New York–Halifax telegraph[qv] service was opened, and was extended via cable[qv] to Europe temporarily in 1858 and permanently in 1866. There are now (1939) twenty-one cables across the Atlantic alone. Telephone[qv] service began with Canada before 1900. Speech was transmitted experimentally by radio telephone to Paris in 1915; in 1921 telephone cable was laid to Cuba and in 1927 telephone service was opened with London and Mexico. By 1938, 93% of the world's telephones were interconnected. Supplementing telephone, telegraph and cable communication is international short-wave radio for transmission of messages and broadcasting of radio programs; and since 1929 American long-wave programs have been sent by private wire to Montreal and Toronto for rebroadcast.

FRANK A. SOUTHARD, JR.

Communism is a social system in which wealth and the agencies for producing, distributing and exchanging wealth are owned in common. Movements seeking communal ownership have included the numerous utopian schemes beginning with Plato's *Republic* and reappearing periodically to the middle of the 19th century (*see* Communities), and the modern socialistic schools which had their inception with the publication of the *Communist Manifesto* by Karl Marx and Friedrich Engels in 1848 (*see* Class Struggle). At the present time the term communism generally indicates the Marxian revolutionary movement that seeks the overthrow of capitalism. This phase of communism stems from the Bolshevik Revolution in Russia in 1917.

Contemporary communism in the United States derives its inspiration and ideology from Marxism, which believes in the class struggle, the economic interpretation of history, the inevitable realization of communism, the disappearance of the state and world revolution. The communist movement was formally organized in 1919, when the Communist party of America and the Communist Labor party were formed from certain dissident left-wing elements of the Socialist party[qv] of America. Driven under ground for a time, the movement reappeared in 1921 as the Workers (Communist) party, which assumed political leadership of revolutionary forces. In industry the Trade Union Unity League, affiliated with the Red (Moscow) International of Labor Unions, was organized. Likewise, the Young Communist League was formed.

The movement has been hopelessly divided from the beginning. The Communist party and the Communist Labor party could not agree on unity. In 1928 the Communist League of America, consisting of Trotsky sympathizers opposed to Stalin, was created; and in 1929 there was organized the Communist party of the United States of America, comprising those who believed the methods urged by Moscow were unsuited to American conditions. Recently all communist groups have sought to capture the American labor movement by boring from within or forming centers of influence in the American Federation of Labor and the Congress of Industrial Organization[qqv]. The communist movement has never gained significant numerical strength in this country, due partly to a lack of unity but primarily to the fact that its ideology finds little fertile soil here.

[Max Eastman, *Marx, Lenin and the Science of Revolution;* Karl Kautsky, *The Ecomonic Doctrines of Karl Marx;* H. J. Laski, *Communism.*]

GORDON S. WATKINS

Communities. Among the earliest settlements that were deliberate communistic experiments were the shortlived community founded by Plockhoy, a Dutch Mennonite, on Delaware Bay in 1662; the Labadist[qv] Community of Protestant Mystics, founded in northern Maryland in 1680; the Mennonite Community at Germantown, Pa., founded in 1683; and the community of "The Women in the Wilderness" in Pennsylvania, in 1694. After the disappearance of the latter, Conrad Beissel, who had expected to join it, adopted the Dunker[qv] religion and founded, in 1732, the Ephrata Community[qv].

The first of the Shaker Communities[qv], which now (1939) number twenty-seven and are scattered over seven states, was the Jerusalem Community, founded in 1786 by Jemima Wilkinson at Gates County, N. Y. The main branch of Shakers were followers of Ann Lee; their first permanent community was established in 1787 at Mt. Lebanon, N. Y. Other important Shaker societies are at Watervliet, N. Y., Union Village, Ohio, and East Canterbury, N. Y.

Two communities, the Harmony Community and the Zoar Community[qqv], were founded by groups of Separatists from Württemberg, Germany, led by George Rapp and Joseph Blaumiler, respectively. The Harmony Society was originally, in 1805, in Butler County, Pa.; in 1814 the Harmonists removed to Indiana; and in 1825 they located at Economy, Pa. Zoar was founded in Ohio in 1817 and maintained its community organization until 1898.

Other religious communities were those of Perfectionists, led by Noyes at Oneida, N. Y., Brooklyn, N. Y., and Wallingford, Conn.; the Hopedale Community, Massachusetts (1842–57); the Amana Community in New York, and later in Iowa (1842–); the Bishop Hill Colony in Illinois (1848–62)[qqv]; the Mormon Community at Orderville, Utah (1874–84), and the communities of the Huterian Brethren.

The nonreligious communities in America

have been experiments in some economic or social philosophy. An example of the former was Robert Owen's unsuccessful communistic experiment at New Harmony,[qv] Ind., which he purchased from the Rappists in 1825.

In 1841 a group of Boston intellectuals established a literary community known as West Rexburg Community. In 1842, when the entire community was converted to Fourierism[qv], they transformed their society into a Fourierist "phalanx," which was called the Brook Farm Association[qv]. Other Fourierist communities were the Wisconsin Phalanx (1844–50) and the North American Phalanx, New Jersey (1843–56).

Other settlements founded on social or economic communism were at Teutonia, Pa. (1843), Icania, Iowa (1848–98), Equity, Ohio (1830–32), Eutopia, Ohio (1847–51), Modern Times, Long Island, N. Y. (1851–60), Steelton, N. J. (1915–), the Ruskin Commonwealth, Tennessee, and later Georgia (1894–1901), New Llano, Calif., and later Louisiana (1914–), and Fairhope, Ala.

[Wm. Alfred Hinds, *American Communities.*]

H. H. SHENK

Community Chests, a system for raising and apportioning funds for social welfare through a single annual campaign, started in Ohio in 1913. The system has spread widely, 419 cities conducting such campaigns in 1937. Of these, 317 raised $63,927,265.

[Elwood Street, *Social Work Administration;* Association of Community Chests and Councils, New York, *Community Chest Campaigns.*]

FRED A. EMERY

Commutation Bill, THE (1783). Delegates from nine states in the Continental Congress[qv] concurred, March 22, 1783, in a resolution commuting the half-pay promised officers of the army on disbandment into a lump sum equal to five years' full pay, to be discharged by certificates bearing 6% interest. New Hampshire and New Jersey voted negatively. (*See also* Newburgh Addresses.)

[George Bancroft, *History of the United States;* Richard Hildreth, *History of the United States.*]

CHARLES WINSLOW ELLIOTT

Compact Theory, THE, involves the idea that the basis of government is in the agreement of the people. Its appearance in America coincides with the first settlements and it is implicit in the Mayflower Compact[qv]. Church covenants and trading company charters[qqv] gave support to the compact philosophy. Thomas Hooker in his *Survey of the Summe of Church Discipline* (1648) declared that the foundation of authority in both church and state is in the consent of the people. The idea of compact is therefore equally valid as the basis of ecclesiastical and civil government. But the 17th century theologians found no means of interpreting the compact, except by divine revelation. It was left for John Locke[qv] to find in natural law a means of interpretation. Following Pufendorf, the guide of Locke, an Ipswich clergyman named John Wise in 1717 developed the compact theory in the light of the newer currents of thought. It was not long before the New England clergy were appealing to natural law and the social compact to dismiss absolutism on both sides of the Atlantic. Their homilies undoubtedly paved the way for the adoption of the compact idea in the revolutionary philosophy. Jefferson as he compiled the Declaration of Independence[qv] could with truth declare that the ideas it contained were hackneyed. The theory as it existed in 1776 in America was distinctly more individualistic than the English prototype. Locke envisaged the reversion of power upon the dissolution of the compact to the whole community but many Americans were not satisfied unless the individual, from whom the rights were originally granted, regained possession upon the exercise of the right of revolution.

[W. S. Carpenter, *The Development of American Political Thought.*]

WILLIAM S. CARPENTER

Compagnie de L'Occident (Western Company), also known as the "Mississippi Company" or "Mississippi Bubble,"[qv] was organized by John Law in 1717 for exploiting the resources of Louisiana. The scope of its activities was expanded, and in 1719 it became the Compagnie des Indes (Company of the Indies), which retained control of Louisiana until 1731.

[A. Fortier, *Louisiana,* Cyclopedic, II.]

WALTER PRICHARD

Companionate Marriage. M. M. Knight first used the term "companionate" in 1924, to mean a marriage entered for the sake of companionship rather than children. Judge Benjamin Lindsey then (1927) proposed legal recognition of "companionate marriage" by permitting divorce by mutual consent to childless couples, while retaining the usual divorce procedures for others. No American state has yet carried out this proposal. Strictly used, the term implies no change in the marriage laws, nor any license to cohabitation without marriage.

[B. B. Lindsey and W. Evans, *The Companionate Marriage.*]

JOSEPH K. FOLSOM

Company of One Hundred Associates, THE (less frequently called the Company of New France), was a privileged commercial company established by Richelieu in 1627 for the colonization of New France or Canada. Its charter required the company to send colonists to Canada for the next fifteen years; to provide for them for three years; and thereafter to furnish them enough cleared land for their support. In return the company was given political power over the colony, seigneurial control of the land and monopoly of trade excepting the whale and cod fisheries. Since the company was more interested in trade than in colonization the colony failed to prosper and the charter was revoked in 1663.

[H. P. Biggar, *The Early Trading Companies of New France.*]

SISTER MARY BORGIAS PALM, S.N.D.

Compromise Movement of 1860, THE, was an attempt, following the election of Lincoln (*see* Campaign of 1860), to check the movement towards secession[qv] and to avert war, by meeting the grievances of the South in regard to slavery. It emanated from the Border States[qv] and took form first in the Crittenden Resolutions[qv] for amendment to the United States Constitution. When Congress rejected the Crittenden Compromise[qv] the movement continued in the Border Slave State Convention[qv] of February, 1861. No agreement was reached upon the chief demand of the South, the recognition of property rights in slavery in the territories.

[James Ford Rhodes, *History of the United States, 1850-1877.*]

C. MILDRED THOMPSON

Compromise of 1850, THE, a designation commonly given to five statutes enacted in September, 1850, following a bitter controversy between the representatives of the North and of the South. The controversy reached a fever heat during the weeks following the assembling of Congress in December, 1849, while the election of a speaker under the customary majority rule was prevented by the unwillingness of the Free Soil[qv] members, who held the balance of power, to be drawn into an arrangement with either of the two major parties. In the course of the prolonged balloting criminations and recriminations passed between the hotheaded spokesmen of the two sections. Pointing to indications that the principle of the Wilmot Proviso[qv] might be enacted into law and receive the signature of President Taylor, Southerners insisted as a matter of right upon the recognition of the Calhoun[qv] doctrine that under the Constitution all the territories should be deemed open to slavery. There was talk of secession[qv] unless this principle was recognized in fact or as a basis for some adjustment. Plans were under way for the discussion of a satisfactory Southern program at a Southern convention called to meet at Nashville[qv] in June.

In the face of increasing sectional strife Henry Clay returned to the United States Senate and on Jan. 29, 1850, suggested a series of resolutions intended to provide the basis for the prompt adjustment of the main questions at issue between the two sections. His resolutions were shortly referred to a select committee of thirteen[qv] of which he was made chairman. Its report (May 8), which covered the ground of Clay's resolutions, recommended an "omnibus bill" providing for the admission of California under its free state constitution, for territorial governments for Utah and New Mexico[qqv], silent on slavery, and for the settlement of the boundary dispute between Texas and the United States (*see* Texas Cession of 1850). It also recommended a bill for the abolition of the slave trade in the District of Columbia and an amendment to the fugitive slave law[qqv].

The hope of compromise was tied up with the fate of the omnibus bill. Clay rallied to his support the outstanding Union men, including Daniel Webster, Lewis Cass, Henry S. Foote and Stephen A. Douglas; the latter became the active force in the promotion of the necessary legislation. President Taylor wanted the admission of California but no action on New Mexico and Utah until they should be ready to become states; he was, therefore, a formidable obstacle to the plans of the compromisers until his death on July 9. Even the active support of his successor, however, did not offset the fact that the idea of compromise "united the opponents instead of securing the friends" of each proposition.

Compromise as such had clearly failed; the ground which it had contemplated was covered in five statutes each formerly included as sections of the proposed omnibus bill. The act establishing a territorial government for Utah (Sept. 9) contained the important "popular sovereignty"[qv] clause providing that any state or states formed out of this territory should be admitted with or without slavery as their constitutions should prescribe. An identical clause was appended to the New Mexico territorial act (Sept. 9), which also resolved the conflict between Texas and the Federal Government over the Santa Fé region by a cession, with compensation to Texas, to the newly created territory. On the same date the act admitting California under its constitution prohibiting slavery in the new state was approved. The Fugitive Slave Act of Sept. 18, 1850[qv], which amended the original statute of Feb. 12, 1793, provided for the appointment of special commissioners to supplement the regular courts empowered after a summary hearing to issue a certificate of arrest of a fugitive "from labor," which authorized the claimant to seize and return the fugitive (with a fee of $10 when the certificate was issued and of only $5 when denied); in no trial or hearing was the testimony of the alleged fugitive to be admitted as evidence nor was a fugitive claiming to be a freeman to have the right of trial by jury; Federal marshals and deputy marshals were to execute the warrants under a heavy fine for refusing and were made liable for the full value of fugitives who escaped their custody; these officials were empowered to call to their aid when necessary any bystanders or *posse comitatus;* finally, any person wilfully hindering the arrest of a fugitive or aiding in his rescue or escape was subject to heavy fine and imprisonment, as well as to heavy civil damages.

These statutes were shortly presented to the country as a series of compromise measures. They did not, however, magically calm the sectional storm. In the North there was widespread denunciation of the "iniquitous" features of the Fugitive Slave Act and deliberate declaration that its enforcement would never be tolerated. At the same time the conservative forces organized a series of Union meetings and pleaded the obligations of the North to pacify the South. In the latter section the other four enactments precipitated the most serious disunion crisis that the country had ever faced. In the states of Georgia, Mississippi and South Carolina the "Southern Rights," or secession, forces were checkmated only by the most strenuous efforts of the Union or Constitutional Union elements. Both sides foreswore old party labels and fought under their new banners to win control over the official state conventions that were ordered. The Southern Rights forces lost in the first test fight in Georgia (*see* Georgia Platform) and had to carry this moral handicap in the remaining contests. It was not until 1852 that the country at large made clear its acquiescence in what at length became known by the oversimple label, "The Compromise of 1850."

[J. B. McMaster, *History of the People of the United States*, Vol. VIII; J. F. Rhodes, *History of the United States since the Compromise of 1850*, Vol. I.]

ARTHUR C. COLE

Compromise Tariff of 1833, THE, ended the dangerous national crisis produced by South Carolina's nullification[qv] of the high tariff acts of 1828 and 1832 (*see* Calhoun's *Exposition*). Sponsored by Henry Clay, this measure provided for systematic reduction of duties until July 1, 1842, when a uniform rate of 20% would be established. Patriotism, Northern fears of drastic tariff reductions, and states' rights[qv] perturbations in regard to the Force Bill[qv] helped to ensure the passage of the Compromise. The bill mollified South Carolina and started a lower tariff trend that was not definitely reversed until after the outbreak of the Civil War.

[C. G. Bowers, *The Party Battles of the Jackson Period;* G. G. Van Deusen, *The Life of Henry Clay.*]

GLYNDON G. VAN DEUSEN

Compromises of the Federal Constitution, THE. To a great extent the whole work of the Convention of 1787[qv] was a compromise among the views, more or less local or sectional, of the populations of the thirteen different states which recently had been colonies of Great Britain. In fact, at the close of the Revolution the National Government consisted of little more than a league of thirteen independent and autonomous nations. It was the question of strengthening this league or creating an entirely new national government that caused most of the debate in the convention.

On May 29, 1787, Edmund Randolph of Virginia submitted the so-called Virginia Plan which aimed to create an entirely new national government that should operate upon the citizens as individuals and, in large part, disregard the autonomy of the separate states. This alarmed the states' rights people and on June 15 William Paterson of New Jersey laid before the convention the so-called New Jersey Plan. This provided for a revision of the Articles of Confederation[qv] and an increase in the powers of the National Government of that day. But that Government was to operate upon the states as such, and not upon individual citizens. Of course, both sides of the question were immediately involved in the determination of the form of the national legislative body and the representation therein. At the suggestion of delegates from Connecticut the compromise was agreed upon that the national legislative body, or Congress[qv], should consist of two Houses, in one of which (the Senate) the states should have equal representation and in the other (the House of Representatives) the representation should be based upon population.

This at once brought up the question of the representation of the slave population of the states. The Northern states claimed that the

Negroes were property, hence should not be counted among the inhabitants for the purposes of apportionment. The Southern states claimed that they were individuals, hence should be included. These arguments on both sides, which were inconsistent with the usual convictions of the respective sections, were compromised by the provision that representatives should be apportioned among the states "according to their respective numbers" which shall be determined by adding to the whole numbers of free persons "including those bound to service for a term of years and excluding Indians not taxed, three-fifths of all other persons" (Constitution, Art. I, Sec. 2, Par. 3).

The third of these most important compromises was concerned with the slave trade^{qv}. It was desired by the Northern states that this trade be prohibited, but that Congress be empowered to pass navigation acts and otherwise regulate commerce. South Carolina and Georgia wished a continuation of the slave trade but feared the national control of navigation acts and commerce. This in turn was compromised by granting to Congress the power to pass navigation acts and otherwise regulate commerce, but that it should be prohibited from taxing exports. On the other hand, the Northern states consented to a continuance of the slave trade for twenty years, or until 1808. As a further concession it was recommended that until that year a tariff of ten dollars a head be levied upon all Negroes imported, while a clause was added to insure the recovery of fugitive slaves[qv]. This compromise secured absolute free trade between the states with the entire control of commerce in the hands of the Federal Government. The price to be paid was a postponement for twenty years of the abolition of the foreign slave trade.

[John Fiske, *Critical Period of American History;* Max Farrand, *The Records of the Federal Constitution of 1787.*]

WILLIAM STARR MYERS

Comptroller General of the United States, The, is head of the general accounting office created by the Budget and Accounting Act of 1921[qv]. He is appointed by the President and Senate for a fifteen-year term, and is removable only by Congress. His office is charged with performance of the auditing functions previously performed by sundry other officials, with the task of devising and installing an up-to-date system of accounting for all government offices, and with the duty of reviewing all financial transactions of administrative officers and agencies, which he must disallow if found not to be in accord with law.

[W. F. Willoughby, *The Legal Status and Functions of the General Accounting Office.*]

P. ORMAN RAY

Comptroller of the Currency. This office was created by the act of Feb. 25, 1863, providing for the organization of national banks[qv] and was retained in the revised law of June 3, 1864. The law provided that the Comptroller of the Currency be appointed by the President, upon recommendation of the Secretary of the Treasury, for a term of five years. His duties were to take charge of plates and dies used in printing national bank notes, to examine national banks, and to make an annual report to Congress. From Aug. 10, 1914, to Feb. 1, 1936, the Comptroller also served as an ex-officio member of the Federal Reserve Board, and he acts as a director in the Federal Deposit Insurance Corporation[qqv].

[F. A. Bradford, *Money and Banking.*]

FREDERICK A. BRADFORD

Comstock Lode, The, Virginia City, Nev., from its discovery in 1859 to its decline in 1879, held the spotlight of the world. During this period more than $500,000,000 in silver and gold were taken from these mines.

To mine this ore great hoisting machines, giant pumps, heavy stamps, drills, cables and hundreds of other things were manufactured. To drain hot water from underground reservoirs, Adolph Sutro[qv] completed a five-mile tunnel from the floor of the Carson River to the Comstock mines in 1878. To extract the silver from the rock, the old Mexican patio method was first used; later, the amalgamating process was employed for the reduction of the ore.

Water, for the 40,000 inhabitants of Virginia City and vicinity, was brought from Marlette, an artificial lake, thirty miles away in the Sierra Nevada Mountains, through pipes, tunnels, flumes and a large inverted siphon. The pipe and siphon were made, piece by piece, in San Francisco, to fit around mountains, to cross Washoe Valley and to extend up the Virginia Mountains.

The discovery of the Big Bonanza[qv] in the California Consolidated Mine, 1873, made multimillionaires of John W. Mackay, James G. Fair, James C. Flood, William S. O'Brien, William Sharon and William C. Ralston.

San Francisco was the residuary legatee of the Comstock wealth. With this money palatial homes were built; banks, the San Francisco Stock Exchange, and dozens of other businesses were established.

[Eliot Lord, *Comstock Mining and Miners.*]

EFFIE MONA MACK

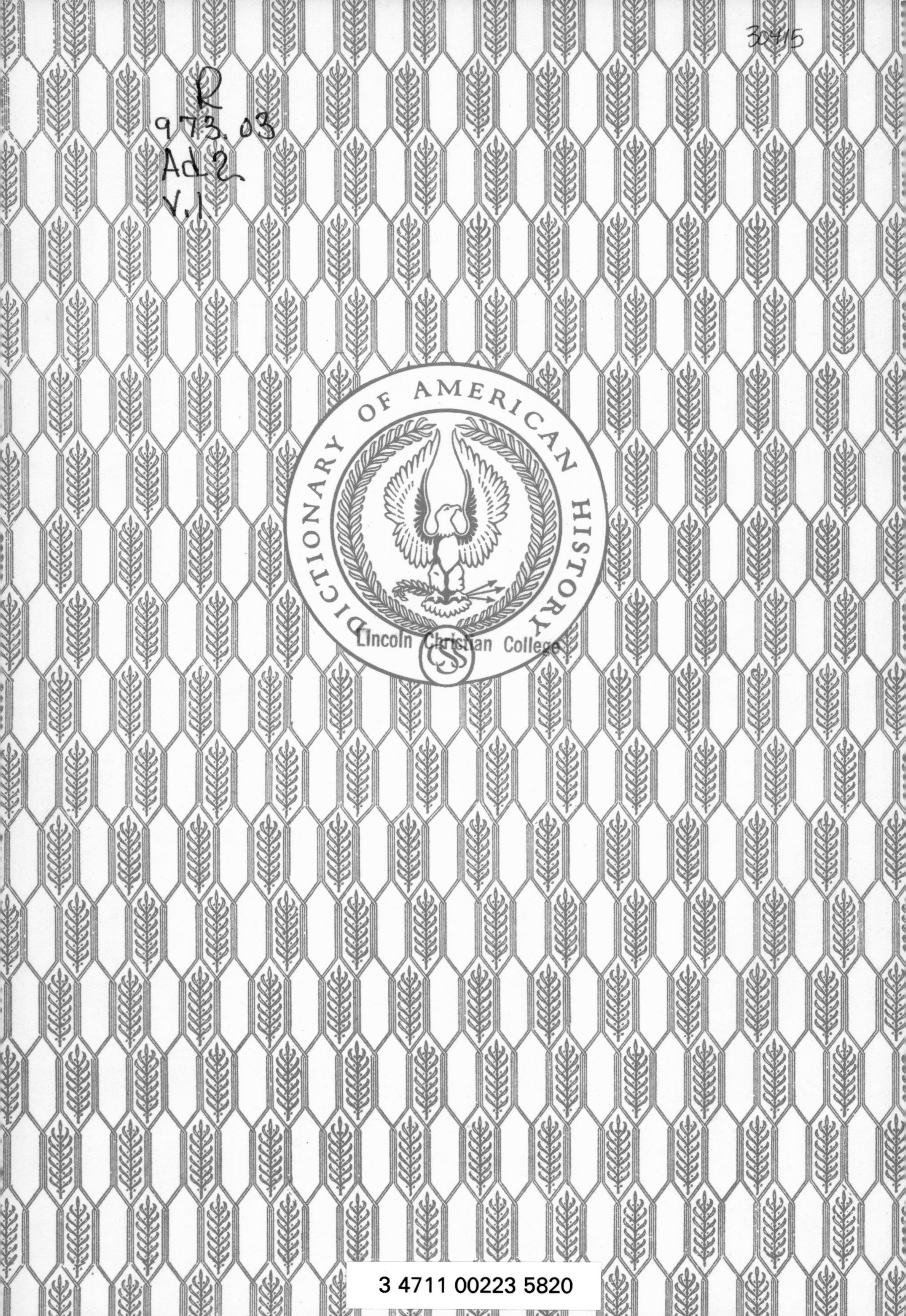
DICTIONARY OF AMERICAN HISTORY